D1403802

A MORMON BIBLIOGRAPHY
1830 – 1930

BOOK

OF

COMMANDMENTS,

FOR THE GOVERNMENT OF THE

Church of Christ,

ORGANIZED ACCORDING TO LAW, ON THE

6th of April, 1830.

ZION:

PUBLISHED BY W. W. PHELPS & CO.

1833.

A MORMON BIBLIOGRAPHY
1830 – 1930

Books, Pamphlets, Periodicals, and Broadsides
Relating to the First Century of Mormonism

Edited by
CHAD J. FLAKE

Introduction by
DALE L. MORGAN

UNIVERSITY OF UTAH PRESS
SALT LAKE CITY
1978

Salt Lake City, Utah 84112
Printed in the United States of America

L. C. Catalog Card Number 74-22639
University of Utah Press ISBN 0-87480-016-1
Utah State Historical Society ISBN 0-913738-13-1

xxxii, 828[84] pp.

In publishing *A Mormon Bibliography*, the following institutions provided funds and professional services: Brigham Young University, University of Utah, Utah State University, Utah State Historical Society, and Church of Jesus Christ of Latter-day Saints Historical Department.

FRONTISPIECE
Item 2854. The uncompleted first printing of Joseph Smith's revelations, salvaged from the wreckage of the Mormon press at Independence, Missouri. This copy is without a border on the title. From the University of Utah collection.

To

DALE L. MORGAN

who first began a methodical compilation of sources for the study of Mormonism, and whose years of dedication paved the way for others to build upon his pioneering efforts and complete this work.

ADVISORY COMMITTEE ON MORMON BIBLIOGRAPHY

Contents

Editor's Preface

Probably no one approached the *Mormon Bibliography, 1830–1930* more naively than I did. Though I had been working in the Special Collections at Brigham Young University for ten years, I had spent only a portion of that time on Mormonism. As with most small rare-book collections, my time was divided between building collections in early European history, Biblical literature, English and American literature, Americana, Western Americana, ad infinitum. There were always such chores as book selection, personnel, cataloging, teaching, in fact, everything except a concentrated effort in Mormon bibliography. Nevertheless, when I was asked in 1965 to edit the then-named "Union Catalog on Mormonism," it seemed to be a great challenge, for I saw the bibliography as a needed tool for my own library as well as others.

The Union Catalog cards were reproduced for the project and students were hired to search the major western bibliographies, such as Sabin's *Dictionary of Books Relating to America*, Howe's *U.S.iana* and others. The task presented to me that winter was to take these cards and edit them as needed. After working with the entries during the spring, it became apparent that a great deal more work needed to be done in the Mormon collections around the country. With the aid of a sabbatical leave from Brigham Young University and a research grant from the University of Utah, this was begun. Due to both limited time and money, it was decided that I would visit only those libraries that were known to have sizeable collections. During the winter I examined all the cards, dividing them into three categories:

1. Books completely on Mormonism.
2. Books with some Mormon material already identified as such on the cards.
3. Books included in the Union Catalog but with no indication as to why they were included.

The first two libraries I visited, H. H. Bancroft Library and Henry E. Huntington Library, convinced me that the program would have to be expanded due to the many new imprints discovered, problems in bibliographic descriptions on the cards, discrepancies between the cards and the library holdings, and discrepancies between the library cards and the actual book.

During the summer of 1965 I visited the following libraries: Yale University, Boston Public Library, New York Public Library, the Library of Congress, Newberry Library, Wisconsin Historical Society, and Kansas City Public Library. Upon my return to Utah that fall I worked at the University of Utah, Salt Lake Public Library, Brigham Young University, and the L.D.S. Church Historian's Library. For the first time the uncataloged material of the Church Historian's Library was made available, which added hundreds of entries to the Union Catalog.

At the end of the winter of 1966 in anticipation of another summer in the Eastern libraries, I had a short-title catalog made for the entries which seemed complete, and a full entry for those still needing examination. Throughout that summer I revisited libraries already mentioned and in addition went to Harvard University, the Chicago Historical Society, Wheaton College Library, and the Reorganized Church of Jesus Christ of Latter Day Saints. The total result of the two years' bibliographic search was to add approximately a third more titles to the existing Union Catalog. Upon my return to Provo that fall, the first rough draft of the bibliography was typed and one could see the various problems still unresolved. The basic problems were the result of various workers through the years bringing varying competency and different styles into the bibliography and the fact that few catalogers of the various libraries had real knowledge of Mormonism.

The next two years were spent in trying to standardize the entries and in searching the literature of Mormonism to add further to the bibliography. Finally, a second compilation was sent to Dale Morgan for his expert perusal. His own notes and remarkable memory were tapped once more for the bibliography. His help at this stage was of great value.

Early in the project certain limitations were placed on the bibliography. It was decided that in the present work the scope would be restricted to books, periodicals, Mormon newspapers or predominantly Mormon newspapers (that is, excluding the newspapers that have only a few Mormon items), pamphlets, and broadsides pertaining to the first century of Mormonism. This would, therefore, exclude newspaper articles, periodical articles, manuscripts, maps, and prints.

It was also agreed that the purpose of the bibliography was not to provide a complete union catalog of Mormonism but to include adequate locations where an item could be found. In cases of relatively common books held by many libraries, locations would be given within geographical areas to aid the scholar to find a copy in a collection in a particular area. Although this has not been adhered to in all cases, many locations were deliberately eliminated where the duplication factor was great.

It is in the nature of a cooperative project that it demonstrates both strength and weakness: strength in that several persons working fairly independently will uncover much more material than one person is able to do; weakness in that each person brings into the project his own ideas as to form, inclusion, exclusion, etc. This is particularly acute in this bibliography as no standard form was adopted until late in the project. Although there has been an attempt to eliminate inconsistencies, with over 10,000 entries it has not been altogether possible. A second problem of form relates particularly to the dating of pamphlets by the various workers, libraries, and sources. In case of important imprints, care has been taken to substantiate all variant printings, but for pamphlets of lesser importance, this care has not always been feasible. In some cases several printings with insignificant changes have appeared during the same year, sometimes without imprint date; in these cases only a note has been given to show these variants. If a new date or edition note is given on the printing, a separate entry is made even though the text is basically the same. Thus, in imprints such as Orson Pratt's series of pamphlets published between 1849–1852, variants are shown in only one entry rather than establishing a separate entry for each state, showing the minor variations.

Generally the establishment of entries has followed the American Library Association rules for author entry, with cross references for titles or authors which are used in previous bibliographies. Thus, the *Book of Mormon*, for instance, follows the rule for religious classics rather than being placed under Joseph Smith where it is usually found in both bibliographies and libraries. Where an author has tentatively been established, this entry is used unless the authorship seems dubious. Pseudonyms have also been used for main entries in cases where real names cannot be found or where the pseudonym has particular significance. Such indefinite authorship as "the Lord's Servant" or "A Mormon" has not been used, and the item is entered under title. In the case of imprints in which only a calculated guess has been made as to authorship, the item is also placed under title.

Corporate headings have been used only when it seems definite that a particular body is the actual author of a given work. For example, missionary tracts have been placed under individual authors or titles rather than the church or the mission that published them. A few synthetic entries, such as UTAH (TERRITORY) CITIZENS, have been made in order to incorporate similar material into a general group. In the case of most publications released by printing companies, a title entry has been used except for companies that are well known by potential users of the bibliographies.

In the case of non-Roman alphabets, the title has been transliterated in accordance with generally practiced rules for romanization of foreign languages and the title translated in the note.

The inclusion of a given work in the bibliography has depended on the value of the section of the particular book to a study of Mormonism, rather than whether it contains an arbitrary number of pages on the subject. Therefore, occasionally only a paragraph is needed to secure its inclusion; however, in a few cases the exclusion of material on Mormonism is as significant as if it had been included. This has been true to a limited extent of periodicals as well as books and pamphlets.

There has been no attempt to include books which may have background material relative to Mormonism. Therefore, books on the New York revival movement, the general westward movement, or on American church history have not been included unless they relate specifically to Mormonism. One of the most difficult areas in which to differentiate has been early Utah imprints. The editor has tried to include imprints that have a direct bearing on the church and to eliminate material dealing with early Utah — realizing, of course, that these should not really be separated. This problem can be more nearly resolved by an imprints catalog for Utah Territory.

The form decided upon was a natural form in regard to capitalization: in English, only words that are normally capitalized; in other languages, in accordance with the rules of the language. With rare imprints the whole title has been reproduced, while common items with lengthy titles have been abbreviated slightly for convenience. The arrangement of items has also been standardized as much as possible: title, subtitle, edition note, editor, translator, illustrator, etc., place of publication, publisher, and date of publication. In most cases street addresses have been eliminated unless they determine a specific edition, state, or show the approximate time of publication. Edition notes are given either as they appear on the title page or are abbreviated by standard means.

References are given to a minimum of printed source books. Library codes are given in standard form. Except for a few items where an original has not been located, the codes refer to the actual physical volume. Those that are not original are identified as reproductions. Unlocated material has not been included except when it appears in one of the reference sources with enough proof that the item actually exists.

One of the peculiar problems of many Mormon entries is that certain printers use a variety of imprints. For example, the Deseret News Press is listed as "The Deseret News," "Deseret News," "Deseret News Publishing Company," or "Deseret News Publishing and Printing Company." It has not always been easy to determine whether an item is standardized or published under a peculiar imprint.

Finally, the problem of completeness was aggravated by the fact that when the Reorganized Church of Jesus Christ of Latter Day Saints Library was surveyed, it was in the process of being recataloged so that it was impossible to see the complete holdings. The same was true of the Church of Jesus Christ of Latter-day Saints Historical Department. In an effort to make the bibliography as complete as possible, the staff of the Historian's Library has cooperated on material as it is cataloged. However, as the project is not yet complete, items may turn up in the collection not previously noted. It is contemplated by the editors that supplemental volumes be published as new material is located and their pertinence ascertained.

Chad J. Flake

Harold B. Lee Library
Brigham Young University

Acknowledgments

The Committee on Mormon Bibliography expresses its thanks to the many libraries and individuals who have contributed money and time toward the completion of this initial volume in the Mormon bibliography series. Without the superb cooperation of these individuals and libraries it would have been impossible to bring together a bibliography of the first century of Mormonism.

Libraries that have been particularly helpful are: Harvard University, Yale University, New York Public Library, Library of Congress, Princeton University, Chicago Historical Society, Newberry Library, Wisconsin Historical Society, Reorganized Church of Jesus Christ of Latter Day Saints History Department, University of Utah, Utah State University, Brigham Young University, Salt Lake City Public Library, Church of Jesus Christ of Latter-day Saints Historical Department, Bancroft Library, and the Henry E. Huntington Library.

Individuals who have helped the Committee in particular ways include: Archibald Hanna, Curator, Western History Collection, Yale University; Alfred L. Bush, Curator, Rollins Collection, Princeton University; Colton Storm, Newberry Library; Andrew J. Simmonds, Special Collections Librarian, Utah State University; Ruth Yeaman, University of Utah Marriott Libraries; Earl E. Olson, Paul Foulger, and Janet Jenson, of the Church of Jesus Christ of Latter-day Saints Historical Department. Acknowledgments are also made to Peter Crawley, Brigham Young University, and D. Leon Storrs, who proofread some entries for the bibliography; to Carlo Mustonen who proofread the Scandinavian entries; to Ernst Correll who proofread the German entries; and to Earl E. Olson who arranged to have the Polynesian, Welsh, and Icelandic entries verified. Special acknowledgment should be made to Keith Eddington, who designed the book; to Donald M. Henriksen, who performed the monumental task of setting the type; and to Norma B. Mikkelsen, Director of the University of Utah Press, who served valiantly and well as manuscript editor, and who saw the project through to its completion.

The following institutions have contributed financial assistance: Utah State Historical Society, which has maintained the Union Catalog for many years; University of Utah, which provided a study grant to survey Mormon Collections; Church of Jesus Christ of Latter-day Saints Historical Department and Utah State University, both of which provided publication grants; and Brigham Young University, which provided a sabbatical leave for the editor and secretarial assistants for the project.

Finally, to Dale L. Morgan, who began the project and did most of the preliminary work and who read the manuscript and made copious changes, corrections, and additions, a great debt is owed.

Introduction

No large bibliography materializes suddenly out of nowhere, like a weed in your backyard; bibliography-making has more in common with dahlia culture. So I have been asked to scratch my memory in public, to recall just how it happened that the massive work now at hand ever got started, and with the understanding that this must amount to a chapter of autobiography — not a short chapter, either.

Well, then: I entered the world of history more than thirty years ago, in a capacity sometimes called historian, sometimes historical editor, of the Utah Historical Records Survey, one of the units of the U.S. Works Progress Administration (later Work Projects Administration). My particular responsibility was the preparation of historical sketches of the various Utah counties, to accompany inventories of the records of those counties. At the same time a former University of Utah classmate, John D. Thornley, as "church editor," was addressing himself to historical sketches of the various religious denominations in Utah, for an inventory of church records was also a task that had been taken on by the HRS. Still another nationwide activity of the Historical Records Survey was the American Imprints Inventory, inspired by that indefatigable bibliographer, Douglas C. McMurtrie; project workers were laboring in various Utah libraries, as elsewhere, to record titles published before certain cutoff dates. These dates varied for different states, according to how early printing had begun in each; for Utah (and, I think, most of the other mountain states) the cutoff date was 1890.

The American Imprints Inventory made a significant contribution in the assemblage of information about the existence of titles, located all over the nation, but was not at all concerned with their content. Moreover, in Utah the imprints work was being done primarily out of Salt Lake City, then a sub-office of the Historical Records Survey. The state headquarters at this time was maintained in Ogden, where Jack Thornley and I labored under the general direction of Hugh F. O'Neil, the state editor. Spurred by our special needs, Jack and I inaugurated bibliographical researches, begun in the Carnegie Free Library in Ogden, but extended to Salt Lake City institutions as our needs and our historical sophistication grew. Some of this research we did personally, but more of it was performed by workers under our direction. The chief published fruits of this labor took the form of a *History and Bibliography of Religion in Utah*, completed by Thornley in 1940 as a foundation volume for the inventory of the Church Archives of Utah, and individual county bibliographies published with the inventories of the County Archives of Utah from 1939 to 1942. The bibliographical sheets prepared by our WPA people are doubtless still among the survey remains deposited in the Utah State Historical Society when World War II terminated HRS early in 1943.

In the summer of 1939, both Thornley and I were transferred to Salt Lake City, which had library resources more commensurate to our needs. It was there, early in 1940, that I was drafted to help complete the volume published the next year by the Utah Writers' Project, *Utah: A Guide to the State.* For the next five months my mornings were reserved for the Historical Records Survey, my afternoons for the Writers' Project. One of the minor problems that vexed the latter was how to handle the bibliography that must appear in the *Guide*, for we were aware that the Church of Jesus Christ of Latter-day Saints Historian's Office had long classified books relating to Mormonism in two simple categories, pro-Mormon and anti-Mormon (an elementary approach to bibliographical classification since abandoned, through the agency of the Church Librarian, Earl Olson. Actually, I had no trouble at all with the bibliography for the *Utah Guide*; in the subsection that chiefly mattered I herded together a selection of sheep and goats under the heading, "Mormons and Anti-Mormons," and to this day no one has ever complained to me about that solution to the problem of "recommended reading."

The point is, my labors first with the Historical Records Survey and then with the Utah Writers' Project, of which I was named supervisor in July, 1940, gave me a liberal education in bibliography as a finding and reporting tool in Utah and Mormon history. They also made me painfully conscious of the limitations under which any Utah student must operate.

The truth is that Utah, just prior to our entrance into the Second World War, was a sadly impoverished area, bibliographically speaking. The student used what he could find in the local libraries or hopefully visited libraries farther afield on exploratory tours. (The depression was still very much with us, and money was always a critical factor for students and libraries alike.) If Mormon history was the primary preoccupation of any student, he understood that two outside institutions principally existed to serve him, the New York Public Library on one coast, and the Bancroft Library on the other. No doctoral programs in history were in being at any Utah university, and it is questionable whether library resources then sufficed to support doctoral studies, outside the archives of the L.D.S. Church. The Utah scene was, in fact, bibliographically naïve. The student might never have heard of standard bibliographical tools like Joseph Sabin's multivolume *Bibliotheca Americana*, commenced in 1868 and carried to a conclusion in 1936, by Wilberforce Eames and R. W. G. Vail. Moreover, unless there was a set at the University of Utah, I don't think Sabin was to be found in any Utah institution as of 1940; and as another example, neither did any Utah library have a copy of that valuable finding medium, the *Union List of Newspapers*, which was published in 1937; copies were acquired in my native state only after I moved to Washington and began to report back to Salt Lake what was going on in the world. (Things were done pretty much by ear, and in just this way in the Utah of that time.)

It further displays the bibliographical situation that few Utah students or libraries even knew of the existence of the New York Public Library's 1909 *Bulletin* listing works pertaining to Mormonism that had come to that institution mainly through a benefaction by Miss Helen M. Gould. Still fewer knew of more imaginatively constructed bibliographies like Henry R. Wagner's

INTRODUCTION

The Plains and the Rockies (a bibliography of travel narratives published between 1800 and 1865), although an enlarged edition prepared by Charles L. Camp had appeared in 1937. A little better known, perhaps, was Douglas McMurtrie's monograph of 1931, *The Beginnings of Printing in Utah, 1849–1860*, (the foundation work for studies of Utah imprints). The only generally available or widely known bibliographical tool was the frustratingly imperfect list of "Authorities Consulted" prefixed to H. H. Bancroft's 1889 *History of Utah*.

What I am saying is that the resources of the wide world of scholarship were essentially unavailable to the Utah student of 1940. There was a fairly "well-lighted room" for work in the Church Historian's Office (if one had entrée there), or the Salt Lake City Free Public Library; and Brigham Young University was showing signs of bibliographical enlightenment, thanks mainly to the efforts of M. Wilford Poulson. Major growth of the Mormon collections at the University of Utah waited upon the postwar Widtsoe and Auerbach accessions, however; and other Utah institutions had only scattered items of real interest. It was at this time almost impossible to write definitively on any topic relating to Utah or the Mormons, solely by reference to materials accessible within the state. If one knew that relevant titles existed, or once had existed, in the outside world, blind search after them was the only real expedient. As for tapping distant repositories by microfilm, if you did succeed in locating an item and could have it filmed, I don't think there was a viewer within a thousand miles of Salt Lake City other than that in the L.D.S. Genealogical Society; and photostating entire books (or pamphlets, even) very quickly ran into real money.

With such a background, I left Utah for Washington, D.C., in October, 1942, to engage in war work for the federal government. The loss of my hearing through meningitis thirteen years earlier had effectively foreclosed the possibility that I might enter the ranks as a drafted buck private and, in fulfillment of the American dream, rise to the dignity of four-star general. Instead, for the duration of the war, I labored as an information specialist in the Office of Price Administration. I had by this time become aware, especially through the first-hand experiences of such good friends as Maurice L. Howe and Nels Anderson, that Washington was a true Mecca for any scholar concerned with Mormon or Western history, what with the staggering and largely unplumbed manuscript resources of the still-new National Archives and the imposing book, manuscript, newspaper, and map collections of the Library of Congress (to name just two of Washington's cultural monuments). Research presented problems; it had to be done on evenings and Sundays (Saturday was a federal work-day for the duration); and it also soon developed that many rarities had been shipped out of Washington to be safe in case of German air raids. (This happened again at the time of the Korean War, by which time the far greater possibilities of devastation implicit in the A-bomb had aroused ancient fears in scholars, librarians, and archivists.)

One scholarly resource always at hand, though, was the card catalog of the Library of Congress. Quite soon I began to search this catalog for titles that were new to me and warranted examination; and by now I had seen Maurice Howe's copy of *The Plains and the Rockies*, as well as a group of highly educational booksellers' catalogs, opening up fresh possibilities in the "peripheral" Mormon field. After looking at some books and making notes on others, I began to feel the need of a more systematic approach, if any permanent benefit was to come of this work. Accordingly I began to copy on bibliographical cards all the titles segregated by the Library of Congress under the subject headings "Utah," "Mormons and Mormonism," "Church of Jesus Christ of Latter-day Saints," and "Reorganized Church of Jesus Christ of Latter Day Saints." The following summer I made the first of a series of visits to the New York Public Library, where I addressed myself to the chore of similarly copying everything relevantly cataloged by that institution. This was an immense job, and with my limited opportunities, required several years to complete. After that, I had the beginnings of a respectable bibliography on Mormonism, keyed to the holdings of two major institutions.

The next forward step came after the John Simon Guggenheim Memorial Foundation granted me in 1945 a post-service fellowship for studies in the early history of Mormonism, a fellowship activated when I left the Office of Price Administration in the spring of 1947. Very soon after I embarked upon the transcontinental researches I had envisioned, from Vermont and Massachusetts to California, I realized the imperative importance of two cognate bibliographical investigations. One would undertake to locate and describe all the publications, of whatever date and wherever found, relating to the lesser churches of Mormonism, the viewpoint of which on Mormon phenomena had been given inadequate attention by scholars. The other would deal as comprehensively with Mormonism, but only for the foundational years (reasonable limits had to be set, after all, to what could be aimed at within the space of one year). At first I thought to make the inclusive years 1830–1844, Joseph Smith's period in Mormonism, but it soon became evident that I should add another five years, as that would provide a full epilogue to the Prophet's life and death, cover the evacuation from Nauvoo, and extend to the beginnings of printing in Utah and the substantial diminution (for a time) of Mormon publication elsewhere in the world.

Accordingly, as I traveled about the country in 1947–1948, I made the most minute notes, on the basis of personal examination, of individual titles published prior to 1850 which included even a glancing reference to Mormons or Mormonism. A good many of these titles — and I ended up with more than 700 just for the first two decades of Mormon history — would never have occurred to a subject cataloger to set apart as Mormon, but I had my reasons, as will presently appear. I also introduced the refinement, applicable to both of these bibliographical searches, of listing titles I knew to have been published (usually through a contemporary reference in manuscript or in other published work), but which could not be located anywhere.

All this work was essentially completed when I surveyed the holdings of the Church Historian's Office, the Salt Lake City Free Public Library, the University of Utah, the Utah State Agricultural College (as then known), and Brigham Young University in the spring of 1948. I compiled checklists of my discoveries and sent these to various interested booksellers and librarians, as also to the collectors Everett D. Graff and Thomas W. Streeter, who had become my cordial correspondents.

My intention had been to publish the bibliography for 1830–1849 in the year 1949, and I had some discussions with the University of Utah Press on the matter. The Press, however, was in a transitional condition about that time, and it became evident that we could have no reasonable assurance the large bibliography (further swelled in size by voluminous notes on content) could be published very soon. Since I, for my part, was having to scratch for a living just then, I was in no position to make an extensive investment of time on a project that might have to wait indefinitely for publication. Instead, I agreed with Harold Bentley and William Mulder that I would embark upon a series of bibliographies of the lesser Mormon churches, to be published at intervals in the *Western Humanities Review.*

Over the next several years, three such studies were published in the *Review* and reprinted with altered pagination for my use in an eventual small limited edition when I should have completed the series. The methodology employed was the same as that contemplated for the large bibliography, 1830–1849 — the individual works were described, their history given when recoverable, something said about content, and if copies were known to exist, a census provided. This series has not been completed yet, what with the pressure of other responsibilities; most imperatively it requires a study of the literature of the Church of Christ (Temple Lot) and its many modern offshoots.

Meanwhile, the problem remained of the basic bibliography I had commenced in the Library of Congress. I should rather say, "problems," for they were definitely multiple and largely different in kind from those of the bibliographies with more limited objectives. It became obvious to me that the basic bibliography should be "institutionalized." Accordingly, in 1951 I proposed to A. R. Mortensen, the new director of the Utah State Historical Society, a way in which this might be done under the Society's auspices. By this time I was again living in the Washington area, with full access to the immense resources of the Library of Congress. What I proposed was that I should expand the basic bibliography by looking in every conceivable place for Mormon titles, including the bibliographies of Sabin and others, booksellers' catalogs, the auction catalogs of the Auerbach sales of 1947 and 1948, and the Eberstadt catalogs of the great Coe Collection which had now been given to Yale and was accessible to scholars there. This expanded list of authors (or titles, where authorship was not known) I would check in detail against the huge Union Catalogue maintained in the Library of Congress, to which libraries all over the nation have been reporting holdings for many years. This would provide a census for each title insofar as that title had been reported to the Union Catalogue. (I should point out that the Union Catalogue in the Library of Congress is an author rather than a subject catalogue; therefore it was useful only on a spot-research basis, looking up individual authors or titles.)

I further proposed that when I had done all this preliminary labor in the Library of Congress I would send all my cards to the Society in Salt Lake City. There, a further check would be made for the holdings of Utah institutions, and after all this work had been done, the cards would be typed up in triplicate or quadruplicate so that we might have three or four different means of access to Mormon literature. We desired to have an author catalog; a title catalog; a chronological catalog, filed according to imprint date; and for good measure a foreign-language catalog, segregating works published in languages other than English. The Society would also try to conclude an arrangement by which the Library of Congress and four or five other libraries with significant Mormon collections would send copies of all new Mormon catalog cards to the Society in an effort to keep the whole project reasonably up-to-date.

As I had proposed, so was it done, though the backup work done by the Society in Salt Lake City required a great deal of labor over a considerable period of time. What had now come into existence we all referred to as the "Union Catalogue of Works on Mormonism." A first principle of the reporting of titles was that any given title had to exist in some library, preferably an institutional library, to be eligible for inclusion. In this principle, the Union Catalogue differed from the bibliography of 1830–1849. It was not possible to analyze the titles to any significant extent or evaluate them; that would have to wait for secondary bibliographies that I or others might tackle, dealing with particular periods or topics. Quite simply, we had created in the Utah State Historical Society a fundamental bibliographical tool for the study of Mormonism in all its aspects.

Still, it was hard to rest content with that. Could not this Union Catalogue be published? An author list was the main desideratum, for we had started up another hare while loosing the hounds on the Union Catalogue. The Society had inherited the American Imprints Inventory slips recorded for Utah imprints, 1849–1890 — that is, the carbon copies retained by the Historical Records Survey in Utah — and I had located the master file prepared in the Washington offices of the Historical Records Survey, turned over to the Library of Congress in 1942. Photocopies of these latter were made for the Society by the Library of Congress, and thus we had at hand in Salt Lake City the raw material for another major bibliography, this time of Utah imprints to 1890. The chronological card file prepared for the Union Catalogue proper also presented possibilities as a major contributor of information. Although it would cost a scholar immense pains and labor to build on this foundation an adequate study of Utah imprints — perhaps extended to the close of 1895, to coincide exactly with the close of the Utah Territorial period — such a job had become feasible. In fact, Alfred L. Bush of the Princeton University Library, of Mormon extraction and therefore possessed of a strong personal interest in Utah bibliography, fell heir to the imprints study, and has for some time now been preoccupied with it.

(Perhaps I should observe that another essential bibliographical enterprise waiting to be done is the preparation of a checklist of state documents, from 1896 on. A study of territorial documents, 1851–1895, or of the predecessor Provisional State of Deseret documents, 1849–1851, seems less urgent, for the time-span of the imprints volume presumably would cover the ground, and I am not at the moment aware of any official territorial documents printed outside Utah.)

Since the imprints volume would address itself only to titles actually printed in Utah, the coverage would not be quite the same as the chronological card index for the whole range of Mormon literature; but again, this gap should be closed when my bibliography for the years 1830–1849 and any similar works for later periods fill out the general record.

Here we are again, back at the nagging question of publication. One proposal made was that a mimeographed reduction of the Union Catalogue be prepared from the card catalog in the Utah State Historical Society library. The idea had some merit; but Gresham's Law operates in bibliography as elsewhere, and I, for one, was opposed to expedients which the perspective of time might reveal to have been shoddy, meanwhile setting up roadblocks to a truly fitting mode of publication. Still more imperatively, perhaps, some backbreaking editorial work would have to be done before *any* kind of publication was feasible. The bibliographical descriptions we had gathered had come from dozens, if not scores, of sources. There were all sorts of inconsistencies in the descriptions (in some degree reflecting the circumstance that a portion of the cards dated back seventy years or so) — differing standards of measurement, differing approaches to pagination, lack of attention to illustrations, and so forth. There were also problems bequeathed by earlier catalogers who had dealt, without sufficient understanding, with subtle points of difference in text or edition. And with all the rest, we could be well assured that still with us was that old and horrendous problem, human error.

By this time the care and feeding of the Union Catalogue of Works on Mormonism had devolved upon Everett L. Cooley, who in September, 1961, succeeded to the directorship of the Utah State Historical Society, a responsibility that was his until he became Curator of Western Americana in the University of Utah Marriott Libraries in January, 1969. Everett has given me this interesting account of the developments which have culminated in the publication of the bibliography in this fitting form, after so many years:

> In 1952 John James became librarian of the Utah State Historical Society, and soon began work on the Mormon bibliography. As he could find time from his other duties, he worked with Dale Morgan in developing and expanding the bibliography. He directed the activities of a staff member who checked the holdings of the Salt Lake Public Library, the L.D.S. Church Historian's Library, the Brigham Young University Library, and the University of Utah Library. All the while the typing of Dale's handwritten cards proceeded as staff time would allow. Then in 1958, Dr. S. Lyman Tyler, Director of the B.Y.U. Library, saw the value of the Mormon bibliography to his own acquisitions program for B.Y.U., so he employed a typist to copy all Dale's cards at the Historical Society plus those added by the Society staff. In addition, the typist completed the typing of Dale's cards, which were returned to him.
>
> And here is where the project rested when I came into the picture in 1961. After some discussion among librarians and scholars interested in

seeing the bibliography published, an Advisory Committee was organized with me as chairman and Lyman Tyler as editor of the project.

It was considered advisable that all three of Utah's universities be represented on the committee as well as the Utah State Historical Society and the L.D.S. Church Historian's Library. The Society was represented by John James, who had continued work on the bibliography since 1952 and outside of Dale Morgan knew most about the project. Earl E. Olson, assistant Church Historian and head of the L.D.S. Church Library, was selected to represent that interest; Ray L. Canning, Professor of Sociology and scholar of Mormonism, was chosen to represent the University of Utah; and S. George Ellsworth, Professor of History and Mormon scholar, was chosen from Utah State University.

All of the Historical Society bibliography cards were Xeroxed by the L.D.S. Historian's Office and sent to the Brigham Young University. These served as work copies from which Lyman Tyler had his staff begin preparations of a publishable manuscript. At this point Lyman left Brigham Young University for the University of Utah, so Chad Flake, Special Collections Librarian at the B.Y.U., took over the position of editor. Lyman agreed to continue to serve on the committee.

Chad's willingness to take on the tremendous task of editing the bibliography was greeted with great enthusiasm by the committee, for he was a man of considerable background and persistence. Chad advised the committee that a visit to the leading Mormon collections was an imperative if the bibliography was to be reliable on each library's present holdings. Funds were not immediately available, but Dr. Ray Canning found a solution to the committee's dilemma by persuading the University of Utah Research Council to make a grant to him to assist in the project. So with details of financial management left in Ray's capable hands, Chad, during his sabbatical leave from the Brigham Young University, visited libraries on the East and West coasts, as well as in the Mid-West.

Throughout the project, Chad kept in touch with John James and Dale Morgan to assure a continuity in the project. As Chad's work neared completion, the committee consulted with Richard Y. Thurman, director of the University of Utah Press, on publication of the bibliography. The Press agreed to accept the manuscript for publication. And Utah State University agreed to support the printing with a grant of funds in order to assure a quality publishing venture.

Meanwhile, the committee sensing the limitations of the projected bibliography, proposed that the scope of the project be broadened. Since government documents, periodical literature, newspapers, and manuscripts are not treated in this bibliography, the committee conceived the idea that a series be inaugurated with this volume; the second in the series to carry the bibliography of Mormonism from 1930 to a more recent cutoff date, and that subsequent individual bibliographies be more specialized in scope. And so it was that Dale Morgan was persuaded to serve as overall editor of such a series. Individuals were approached to commit themselves to editing the separate volumes being contemplated. Several gave their consent. Hopefully this volume will be but the first in a series of bibliographies on Utah and the Mormons.

The energy, devotion, and applied intelligence of Chad Flake at the operative point, and of Everett Cooley, Lyman Tyler, and their associates at the management level, have now brought to final fruition, in publication, what might otherwise have remained a card catalog in the library of the Utah State

INTRODUCTION

Historical Society. Too much cannot be said of Chad's labors; he married this bibliography, and is now committed to living with it the rest of his life, by turns elated and depressed by the new finds and the disclosure of obvious omissions that time will bring. Chad himself relates elsewhere in this volume some of the problems he confronted and how he dealt with them, what criteria he adopted governing inclusion and exclusion. We have demanded that he also relate something of his travels in search of the bibliographical Holy Grail and his adventures along the way.

After he had completed his preliminary editing, Chad sent me a Xerox copy of the manuscript for criticism. I went over it with care, giving it the critical attention it deserved, and impressed by new titles that had been found. After some conferences with Chad in Salt Lake, I was able to arrange with the Bancroft Library (where I have hung my hat since 1954) to have a student under my supervision check the entire bibliography against the card catalog of the University of California Libraries. Besides improving the census, this turned up still other titles and variant editions meriting inclusion. Meanwhile, Brigham Young University and other institutions were acquiring rarities from the great Streeter auction and other sources, bibliographical novelties of greater or lesser importance demanding attention . . . and this sort of thing can go on forever.

There comes a time, though, when a book, like a baby, must be born. That time has now arrived for our foundation work in Mormon bibliography. At this moment of birth, it seems a good idea to ask just what we have wrought, what is the real significance of such a book, apart from the toil and infinite pains that have gone into the making of it.

Well, a bibliography is in itself, if properly designed and constructed in depth, an index to a culture. Anyone who leafs through this volume, even in idle curiosity, is going to acquire a new and paroramic view of, a fresh insight into, Mormonism as a phenomenon in American and world history. The titles and authorship of the various books speak eloquently not only of Mormonism but also of the general culture exemplified by Mormonism as religion, society, and personal experience. Throughout, the human animal is very much in evidence, never more cross-grained.

Below this overview, the bibliography is an index to the literature of Mormonism itself. To take two names at random, what did Parley P. Pratt or George J. Adams publish during their varyingly long and stormy association with Mormonism? Here is the bibliographical record, insofar as we have been able to recover it. Here is the total known inventory of books, pamphlets, broadsheets, and broadsides — and for good measure, information on where copies may be found. It would be useful just to be able to see the whole dimensions of the literature, but the bibliography is a means of access to that literature. In effect, it places spigots on the originals, so that their content may be tapped. Amazing advances that have come in the technology of photo-duplication and xerography mean that one need only know where a copy of a work is preserved to obtain a reproduction; few are the libraries that cannot now provide inexpensive copy service, and still fewer are those that will not sanction the reproduction of their treasures. (More have scruples about manuscripts than about printed works; it is true that manuscripts do present special problems.) Through persistent microfilming by interested institutions and dedicated individuals, numerous printed works that were beyond the grasp of Utah scholars thirty years ago may now quite comfortably be studied "at home" — that is to say, thoughtfully and at leisure. Such a development is by no means important to scholars in Utah alone, but its local significance is beyond estimation — as is the fact that a cooperative effort of Utah's major institutions of higher learning has directed itself toward the breaking-down of the kind of scholarly parochialism that has long plagued the local scene. I think it not too much to say that bibliography is the cutting edge of historianship of the future, and here, with a Mormon bibliography, we can test the sharpness of the blade.

I do not want to claim too much for the present bibliography, however. From here on it is going to be a basic tool, but other tools must join it in the chest before Mormon scholarship can be considered adequately equipped for its job. We badly need a bibliography of articles pertaining to Mormonism published in general American periodicals from earliest times. Let no one underestimate the difficulty of compiling such a work, for despite modern printed guides to periodical literature, very little primary labor has been done, digging out the necessary information. The Church Historian's Office, the New York Public Library, and other institutions have catalogued particular items that have come along, but always on an ad hoc basis, not by systematic examination of the literature. Similarly, we very much need a bibliography of articles pertaining to Mormonism in the religious press of the nineteenth and twentieth centuries; until this buried information is brought forth, no one can realistically study the impact of Mormonism on contemporary religion. Even the preliminary digging has not been done for such a job as this; e.g., what denominations were publishing what periodicals in 1835? The *Union List of Serials* will help to locate files, once a scholar really knows what he is doing, but consider the mass of material that must be examined almost page by page, and in how many depositories!

Yet another bibliographical inquiry would properly have fallen within the purview of the present work, had there been any feasible way of going about it within the practical limitations that hedged us in. That is, what of references to Mormonism, and even more to individual Mormons, or men who spent time among the Mormons, anywhere on the continent, in all the county histories that have been published over the past hundred-odd years? Thousands of counties exist in the United States, and I think there must be at least a thousand county histories. Those which have been urgently involved with Mormon history — the histories for areas in New York, Pennsylvania, Ohio, Missouri, Illinois, and Iowa, for example — have sometimes been recognized by catalogers as forming a part of Mormon literature, and many such titles are incorporated into the present work. Still others have been added from time to time by Chad Flake and myself as we have stumbled upon them while pursuing other researches. The need here, however, is for systematic examination of the literature, preferably beginning in some institution like the Library of Congress, which has a national rather than a regional orientation. The search would have to be the laborious page-by-page kind. Since I am proposing that such a labor can and must eventually be undertaken, I will at the same time propose that whatever person or group tackles the job shall simultaneously survey these county histories for information relative to the Far West in general — men who traveled in the West, to Oregon or California or New Mexico, as well as to Utah, men active in the fur or cattle trade, etc., who afterwards settled down in some town or upon some farm to leave a printed record of their experiences only in the biography prepared for their local county history. I have made just enough accidental discoveries myself to realize the potential in the national treasure trove of county histories.

Should the happy day arrive when the above bibliographies have been brought into existence, all the necessary jobs even yet will not have been done. Sooner or later, on a sufficiently broad and systematic basis, all the American newspapers from about 1820 to (name your own terminal date) must be examined to extract material pertaining to the early history of Mormonism. Whether the result may properly be called a bibliography is questionable. Whatever the name put upon it, the job must be done; the integrity of Mormon historianship demands it. After that, what of Mormonism on other continents and in other languages? What of Mormonism as reflected in the public documents of the United States government? What of Mormonism in the literature of travel?

We are now coming full circle back to our basic bibliography, which attempts after a fashion to cope with the last of these questions, but the indicated limitations of our bibliography serve to define its scale. It should be regarded not as an exterminator of Mormon bibliographies but as a progenitor of them. I am gestating some of the progeny myself, as we have seen, but there is no lack of room for others.

I should like to express a few final ideas in connection with this bibliography. The work embraces two general approaches to the literature of Mormonism, for it is minutely particularistic, yet exceptionally broad in its coverage, or vision, ranging from acrid disputes in local congregations to the policy of nations.

It would have greatly simplified the construction of the bibliography had it been focused more narrowly upon publications primarily concerned with Mormons and Mormonism, John Corrill's *Brief History* of 1839, for example. But making life simpler for the bibliographers is not the raison d'être of bibliography-making. On such principles, we should at once lose *The Life of David Marks,* published as early as 1831, with remarks on Mormons at Fayette, New York, a few weeks before the church was even founded. Again, no professional cataloger in his right mind would outfit *The Diary of James K. Polk During his Presidency, 1845 to 1849* with a subject entry for Mormons and Mormonism, but students can ill spare Polk's diary entries relative to the Mormons during the period of the evacuation from Nauvoo and the conquest of New Mexico and California.

A MORMON BIBLIOGRAPHY

Draw the dividing line where you will, it cannot suffice in all circumstances. In the final analysis total inclusiveness, with all its burdens and liabilities to error, seems to be the only satisfactory answer. If you are concerned with the Mormons in a total cultural sense, their measurable impact upon society throughout their history, even a glancing reference has significance for you, and a bibliographer must reckon with your necessities.

Chad Flake and I came independently to this conclusion quite early in our labors, and in the long run it has materially influenced the final form of the bibliography. When we found a reference to the Mormons in some book, that qualified the book for description in the bibliography. (It has not been possible, regretfully, to provide specific page references for all such items, but this has been done in many instances.) Neither of us, nor twenty like us working together, could have turned up all passing allusions to the Mormons, but it seemed to us that a beginning had to be made, a foundation laid upon which others might build. And not others only. As long as we are still sound of mind and body, we will go on expanding this bibliography. The thing is, it will be easier from now on, and every new title found we will be able to see in definable relationship to the whole literature.

DALE L. MORGAN
Bancroft Library
1970

The death of a productive, vigorous person is always untimely. This is certainly the case with Dale L. Morgan whose life ended on March 30, 1971, while he was in the midst of several scholarly undertakings. And so while Dale was not permitted to see the publication of the *Mormon Bibliography* upon which he labored for so many years, we are certain he would rejoice at its completion.

Board of Editors
1976

Key to Symbols

ArU	University of Arkansas, Fayetteville, Ark.
AzU	University of Arizona, Tucson, Ariz.
C	California State Library, Sacramento, Calif.
CaTU	University of Toronto, Canada
CDU	University of California, Davis, Calif.
CHi	California Historical Society, San Francisco, Calif.
CL	Rufus B. von KleinSmid Central Library, Los Angeles, Calif.
CLSU	University of Southern California, Los Angeles, Calif.
CLU	University of California at Los Angeles, Calif.
CMC	Mills College, Oakland, Calif.
CoD	Denver Public Library, Denver, Colo.
CSmH	Henry E. Huntington Library, San Marino, Calif.
CSt	Stanford University Libraries, Stanford, Calif.
CtHT-W	Trinity College, Hartford, Conn.
CtU	University of Connecticut, Storrs, Conn.
CtY	Yale University, New Haven, Conn.
CU	University of California, Berkeley, Calif.
CU-B	University of California, Bancroft Library, Berkeley, Calif.
DA	U.S. Department of Agriculture Library, Washington, D.C.
DE	U.S. Office of Education, Washington, D.C.
DHU	Howard University, Washington, D.C.
DI-GS	U.S. Geological Survey Library, Washington, D.C.
DLC	U.S. Library of Congress, Washington, D.C.
DN	U.S. Department of the Navy Library, Washington, D.C.
DNA	National Archives, Washington, D.C.
DNR	U.S. Office of Naval Records and Library, Washington, D.C.
DSG	U.S. Surgeon General's Office Library, Washington, D.C.
DSI	Smithsonian Institution Library, Washington, D.C.
DW	U.S. Army War College Library (Ft. McNair) Washington, D.C.
FOA	Albertson Public Library, Orlando, Fla.
GEU	Emory University, Atlanta, Ga.
GGS	Georgia Southern, Collegeboro, Ga.
I	Illinois State Library, Springfield, Ill.
Ia	Iowa State Traveling Library, Des Moines, Iowa
IaCb	Council Bluffs Free Public Library, Council Bluffs, Iowa

IaCrM	Iowa Masonic Library, Cedar Rapids, Iowa
IaHa	Iowa State Department of History and Archives, Des Moines, Iowa
IaHi	State Historical Society of Iowa, Iowa City, Iowa
IaLG	Graceland College, Lamoni, Iowa
IaU	University of Iowa, Iowa City, Iowa
IC	Chicago Public Library, Chicago, Ill.
ICHi	Chicago Historical Society, Chicago, Ill.
ICJ	John Crerar Library, Chicago, Ill.
ICN	Newberry Library, Chicago, Ill.
ICU	University of Chicago, Chicago, Ill.
IdB	Boise Public Library, Boise, Idaho
IdIf	Idaho Falls Public Library, Idaho Falls, Idaho
IGK	Knox College, Galesburg, Idaho
IHi	Illinois State Historical Library, Springfield, Ill.
IMunS	Saint Mary of the Lake Seminary, Mundelein, Ill.
InU	Indiana University, Bloomington, Ind.
IU	University of Illinois, Urbana, Ill.
IWW	Wheaton College Library, Wheaton, Ill.
KHi	Kansas State Historical Society, Topeka, Kans.
KU	University of Kansas, Lawrence, Kans.
M	Massachusetts State Library, Boston, Mass.
MB	Boston Public Library, Boston, Mass.
MBAt	Boston Athenaeum, Boston, Mass.
MBBC	Boston College, Chestnut Hill, Mass.
MBFM	Massachusetts Grand Lodge, F. & A. M., Boston, Mass.
MBrZ	Zion Research Library, Brookline, Mass.
MChi	Chicopee Public Library, Chicopee, Mass.
MdBP	Peabody Institute, Baltimore, Md.
MH	Harvard University, Cambridge, Mass.
MH-A	Harvard University, Arnold Arboretum, Cambridge, Mass.
MH-L	Harvard University, Law School Library, Cambridge, Mass.
MiD	Detroit Public Library, Detroit, Mich.
MiD-B	Detroit Public Library, Burton Historical Collection, Detroit, Mich.
MiHi	Michigan Historical Society, Lansing, Mich.
MiMtpT	Central Michigan College, Mount Pleasant, Mich.
MiU	University of Michigan, Ann Arbor, Mich.
MiU-C	University of Michigan, William L. Clements Library, Ann Arbor, Mich.
MiU-H	University of Michigan, Michigan Historical Collection, Ann Arbor, Mich.
MiU-L	University of Michigan, Law Library, Ann Arbor, Mich.
MnHi	Minnesota Historical Society, St. Paul, Minn.
MnU	University of Minnesota, Minneapolis, Minn.
MoHi	Missouri State Historical Society, Columbia, Mo.
MoInRC	Reorganized Church of Jesus Christ of Latter Day Saints, Independence, Mo.
MoInRC-CE	Reorganized Church of Jesus Christ of Latter Day Saints, Department of Continuing Education, Independence, Mo.
MoK	Kansas City Public Library, Kansas City, Mo.
MoKU	University of Missouri at Kansas City, Kansas City, Mo.
MoS	St. Louis Public Library, St. Louis, Mo.

KEY TO SYMBOLS

MoSHi	Missouri Historical Society, St. Louis, Mo.
MoSM	Mercantile Library Association, St. Louis, Mo.
MoU	University of Missouri, Columbia, Mo.
MSaE	Essex Institute, Salem, Mass.
MWA	American Antiquarian Society, Worcester, Mass.
MWH	College of the Holy Cross, Worcester, Mass.
NAuT	Auburn Theological Seminary, Auburn, N.Y.
NBG	Brooklyn Botanic Garden, Brooklyn, N.Y.
NBuG	Grosvenor Reference Division, Buffalo and Erie County Public Library, Buffalo, N.Y.
NcD	Duke University, Durham, N.C.
NH	Hamilton Public Library, Hamilton, N.Y.
NIC	Cornell University, Ithaca, N.Y.
NjMD	Drew University, Madison, N.J.
NjN	Newark Public Library, Newark, N.J.
NjP	Princeton University, Princeton, N.J.
NjPT	Princeton Theological Seminary, Princeton, N.J.
NjR	Rutgers, The State University, New Brunswick, N.J.
NN	New York Public Library, New York, N.Y.
NNC	Columbia University, New York, N.Y.
NNH	Hispanic Society of America, New York, N.Y.
NNHi	New York Historical Society, New York, N.Y.
NNUN	United Nations Library, New York, N.Y.
NNUT	Union Theological Seminary, New York, N.Y.
NNU–W	New York University, Washington Square Library, New York, N.Y.
NP	Adriance Memorial Library, Poughkeepsie, N.Y.
NRU	University of Rochester, Rochester, N.Y.
NvHi	Nevada State Historical Society, Reno, Nev.
NY	Yonkers Public Library, Yonkers, N.Y.
OC	Public Library of Cincinnati and Hamilton County, Cincinnati, Ohio
OCHP	Historical and Philosophical Society of Ohio, Cincinnati, Ohio
OCl	Cleveland Public Library, Cleveland, Ohio
OClFC	Fenn College, Cleveland, Ohio
OClh	Cleveland Heights Public Library, Cleveland, Ohio
OClW	Western Reserve University, Cleveland, Ohio
OClWHi	Western Reserve Historical Society, Cleveland, Ohio
OCU	University of Cincinnati, Cincinnati, Ohio
ODa	Dayton and Montgomery County Library, Dayton, Ohio
ODW	Ohio Wesleyan University, Delaware, Ohio
OEac	East Cleveland Public Library, Cleveland, Ohio
OFH	Rutherford B. Hayes Library, Fremont, Ohio (Formerly Hayes Memorial Library)
OkStA	Oklahoma State University, Stillwater, Oklahoma
OLaK	Lakewood Public Library, Lakewood, Ohio
OO	Oberlin College, Oberlin, Ohio
OOxM	Miami University, Oxford, Ohio
OrHi	Oregon Historical Society, Portland, Oreg.
OrP	Library Association of Portland, Portland, Oreg.
OrU	University of Oregon, Eugene, Oreg.
OU	Ohio State University, Columbus, Ohio

P	Pennsylvania State Library, Harrisburg, Pa.
PBa	Academy of the New Church, Bryn Athyn, Pa.
PBM	Moravian College and Theological Seminary, Bethlehem, Pa.
PCA	American Baptist Historical Society, Chester, Pa.
PCC	Crozer Theological Seminary, Chester, Pa.
PH	Haverford Public Library, Haverford, Pa.
PHC	Haverford College, Haverford, Pa.
PHi	Historical Society of Pennsylvania, Philadelphia, Pa.
PLL	Lincoln University Library, Lincoln University, Lincoln, Pa.
PMA	Allegheny College, Meadville, Pa.
PMonC	Church of Jesus Christ, Monongahela, Pa.
PNt	Newtown Library Company, Newtown, Pa.
PP	Free Library of Philadelphia, Philadelphia, Pa.
PPA	Athenaeum of Philadelphia, Philadelphia, Pa.
PPAmP	American Philosophical Society, Philadelphia, Pa.
PPC	College of Physicians of Philadelphia, Philadelphia, Pa.
PPCC	Carpenters' Company, Philadelphia, Pa.
PPCS	National Carl Schurz Memorial Foundation, Philadelphia, Pa.
PPD	Drexel Institute of Technology, Philadelphia, Pa.
PPeSchw	Schwenckfelder Historical Library, Pennsburg, Pa.
PPF	Franklin Institute, Philadelphia, Pa.
PPFr	Friends' Free Library of Germantown, Philadelphia, Pa.
PPG	German Society of Pennsylvania, Philadelphia, Pa.
PPGeo	Geographical Society of Philadelphia, Philadelphia, Pa.
PPiU	University of Pittsburgh, Pittsburgh, Pa.
PPL	Library Company of Philadelphia, Philadelphia, Pa.
PPL-R	Library Company of Philadelphia, Ridgeway Branch, Philadelphia, Pa.
PPLT	Lutheran Theological Seminary, Krauth Memorial Library, Philadelphia, Pa.
PPM	Mercantile Library, Philadelphia, Pa.
PPPrHi	Presbyterian Historical Society, Philadelphia, Pa.
PPRCl	Rittenhouse Club, Philadelphia, Pa.
PPTU	Temple University, Philadelphia, Pa.
PPWe	Westminister Theological Seminary, Philadelphia, Pa.
PSC	Swarthmore College, Swarthmore, Pa.
PU	University of Pennsylvania, Philadelphia, Pa.
RP	Providence Public Library, Providence, R.I.
RPB	Brown University, Providence, R.I.
RWoU	L'Union St.-Jean-Baptiste d'Amerique, Woonsocket, R.I.
TU	University of Tennessee, Knoxville, Tenn.
TKL	Knoxville Public Library System, Knoxville, Tenn.
TxH	Houston Public Library, Houston, Tex.
TxU	University of Texas, Austin, Tex.
UHi	Utah State Historical Society, Salt Lake City, Utah
ULA	Utah State University, Logan, Utah
UOg	Ogden Public Library, Ogden, Utah
UOgW	Weber State College, Ogden, Utah

KEY TO SYMBOLS

UPB	Brigham Young University, Provo, Utah
USl	Salt Lake City Public Library, Salt Lake City, Utah
USlC	Church Historical Department, Church of Jesus Christ of Latter-day Saints, Salt Lake City, Utah
USlD	Daughters of Utah Pioneers Museum Library, Salt Lake City, Utah
UU	University of Utah, Salt Lake City, Utah
Vi	Virginia State Library, Richmond, Va.
ViU	University of Virginia, Charlottesville, Va.
ViU-L	University of Virginia, Law Library, Charlottesville, Va.
Vt	Vermont State Library, Montpelier, Vt.
Wa	Washington State Library, Olympia, Wash.
WaA	Aberdeen Public Library, Aberdeen, Wash.
WaPS	Washington State University, Pullman, Wash.
WaS	Seattle Public Library, Seattle, Wash.
WaSp	Spokane Public Library, Spokane, Wash.
WaT	Tacoma Public Library, Tacoma, Wash.
WaU	University of Washington, Seattle, Wash.
WaV	Fort Vancouver Regional Library, Vancouver, Wash.
WaW	Walla Walla Public Library, Walla Walla, Wash.
WaWW	Whitman College, Walla Walla, Wash.
WBuC	Church of Jesus Christ of Latter Day Saints [Strangite], Burlington, Wis.
WHi	State Historical Society of Wisconsin, Madison, Wis.
WShe	Mead Public Library, Sheboygan, Wis.

A FEW

PLAIN FACTS,

SHEWING THE

FOLLY, WICKEDNESS, AND IMPOSITION

OF THE

REV. TIMOTHY R. MATTHEWS;

ALSO A SHORT SKETCH OF THE

RISE, FAITH, AND DOCTRINE

OF THE CHURCH OF JESUS CHRIST OF

LATTER DAY SAINTS.

BY GEORGE J. ADAMS,

MINISTER OF THE GOSPEL, BEDFORD, ENGLAND.

"Should thy lies make men hold their peace? and when thou mockest, shall no man make thee ashamed." Job 5 ch. 11 v.

BEDFORD:

PRINTED BY C. B. MERRY.

1841.

Item 16. The first tract by George J. Adams, who, in the 1860s, led the ill-fated colony to Jerusalem that was later immortalized in Mark Twain's *Innocents Abroad*. From the LDS church collection.

A., W.

1. **A., W.** Which is the Church? Jesus Christ established but one visible Church. [Lamoni, Ia., Herald Publishing House, n.d.]
8p. 18 cm. (No. 32)
Deals with the problem of succession in the RLDS Church.
Signed: W. A.
CU–B, MoInRC

2. ———. (same) [Lamoni, Ia., Herald Publishing House, n.d.]
4p. 23 cm. (No. 32)
A variant of the above.
MoInRC

Aaronic Herald. *See Melchisedek and Aaronic Herald.*

3. **Abbey, James.** California: a trip across the plains in the spring of 1850, being a daily record of incidents of the trip over the plains, the desert, and the mountains, sketches of the country, distances from camp to camp. New Albany, Ind., Kent & Norman and J. R. Nunmacher, 1850.
64p. 17½cm.
Passed through Salt Lake City in 1850, were happy for the Sabbath, but stayed at their wagons due to the fact that the people were "votaries of a strange faith."
Howes A5, W–C 178
CU–B, DLC, NjP

4. **Abbott, Ernest Hamblin.** Religious life in America; a record of personal observation by Ernest Hamblin Abbott. [New York, The Outlook Company, 1902]
xii [2] 3–370p. 21½cm.
The RLDS Church briefly described. "I had a glimpse of the seamy side of irresponsible religious Caesarism."
Another edition: 1903. CU–B, NjP, UPB
DLC, NN

5. **Abbott, John Stevens Cabot.** The history of the State of Ohio: from the discovery of the great valley, to the present time, including narratives of early exploration . . . by John S. C. Abbott . . . Detroit, Northwestern Publishing Company, 1875.
2p.l. [xi]–xivp. [1]l. [17]–876 p. illus., ports. 22½cm.
A brief description of the Mormon era, p. 694–717.
DLC, MnH, NN, NjP, OCl, UHi, USIC

6. **Abdy, Edward Strutt.** Journal of a residence and tour in the United States of North America, from April, 1833, to October, 1834. By E. S. Abdy . . . London, J. Murray, 1835.
3v. 19½cm.
Describes Mormonism in New York and Ohio.
Howes A8, Sabin 45
CtY, DLC, ICN, NjP, NN, UHi, USIC, WHi

7. **Abert, J. W.** Report of the Secretary of War, communicating, in answer to a resolution of the Senate, a report and map of the examination of New Mexico, made by Lieutenant J. W. Abert, of the Topographical Corps. Washington, 1848.
132p. 23cm. (U.S. 30 Cong. 1st Sess. Senate. Executive Doc. No.23)
Tells of his encounter with Mormon Battalion during the expedition.
Howes A11, Sabin 57, W–C 143
CtY, DLC, NjP, USIC

8. **Der Abfall vom ursprünglichen Evangelium und dessen Wiederherstellung.** Zürich, Herausgegeben von Hugh J. Cannon und Levi Edgar Young [ca. 1901]
15 [1]p. 18cm. (Tractat. Nr. I)
Articles of faith on the back cover.
Title in English: The apostasy from the true church and its restoration.
USIC

9. ———. (same) Berlin, Herausgegeben von Hugh J. Cannon, 1902.
15 [1]p. 18cm. (Tractat. Nr. I)
USIC

10. ———. (same) Zurich, Schweiz, Herausgegeben von Serge F. Ballif, 1906.
16p. 18cm. (Traktat. Nr. 1)
UPB

The abominations of the Latter-day Saints. *See The gates of the Mormon Hell opened.*

11. **The Academic Review.** A Journal of the Polysophical Society of the Brigham Young University. Provo, Utah, October 1884–May 1885.
1v #1–8. 22cm.
Published by the students of Brigham Young Academy.
NjP, UPB

Achilles [*pseud.*] *See Sirrine, Samuel D.*

12. **Ackley, Mary E.** Crossing the plains and early days in California. Memories of girlhood days in California's golden age. San Francisco, Privately printed for the author, 1928.
68p. mounted illus. 24cm.
Brief mention of Salt Lake City. She was there during July 24, heard of a celebration, but didn't know what it was.
Howes A33
CU–B, DLC

13. **The Acorn.** Ogden, Utah, Published by the students of Weber Stake Academy, 1903?–1905?
2v. 23cm.
#6 (May, 1905) is an octogon shaped publication, 24 × 24cm.

Souvenir (annual) 1906, 1908, 1909, 1920, 1921, 1922, 1923, 1924, 1925, 1926, 1927, 1928, 1930.
USIC
USIC V. 1 #1, 3, 4, 5; V. 2 #1, 2, 3, 5, 6

14. Adams, Charles A. Collection of sacred hymns for the Church of Jesus Christ of Latter-day Saints. Selected and published by Charles A. Adams. Bellows Falls, Printed by S. M. Blake, 1845.
iv [5]–160p. 11cm.
An unofficial publication of the hymns of the Church.
CtY, MH, RPB

15. Adams, Frank David. Ancestors and descendants of Elias Adams: the pioneer, 600–1930, compiled and edited by Frank D. Adams . . . Kaysville, Utah, Inland Printing Company [1930]
3p.l., 260 [8]p. illus., plates, ports. 23½cm.
Biography and genealogy of a Mormon pioneer which includes historical material on Kaysville and Utah.
CSmH, CtY, DLC, NjP, NN, UHi, ULA, USIC, UU

16. Adams, George J. A few plain facts, shewing [sic] the folly, wickedness, and imposition of the Rev. Timothy R. Matthews; also, a short sketch of the rise, faith, and doctrine of the Church of Jesus Christ of Latter-day Saints. By George J. Adams, Minister of the gospel, Bedford, England. Bedford, Printed by C. B. Merry, 1841.
iv [5]–16p. 17½cm.
The author was later associated with James J. Strang.
CtY, MH, MoInRC, NN, USI, USIC

17. ———. A lecture on the authenticity and scriptural character of the Book of Mormon. By G. J. Adams, Minister of the gospel. Delivered at the town hall, Charlestown, Mass[.] on Sunday evening, February 4th, and Wednesday evening, February 7th. Reported and published by his friend C. P. B. [Curtis P. Bolton?] Boston, Printed by J. E. Farwell . . . 1844.
24p. 19½cm.
Howes A48
CtY, MH, MoInRC, UPB, USIC

18. ———. Lecture on the destiny and mission of America, and the true origin of the Indians. By G. J. Adams, Minister of the gospel. Kingston, New York, Romeyn's Power Presses, 1860.
16p. 19½cm.
The author's first known work after his break with James J. Strang. He then founded the Church of the Messiah.
Morgan
NN

19. ———. A lecture on the doctrine of baptism for the dead: and preaching to spirits in prison by Elder G. J. Adams, missionary to Russia, as originally delivered by him in the City of New York on the 7th of January, 1844. Reported and published by his friend David Rogers. New York, Printed by C. A. Calhoun, 1844.
12p. 21cm.
CtY, MH, MoInRC, NN, USIC

20. ———. A letter to his excellency John Tyler, President of the United States, touching the signs of the times, and the political destiny of the world; by G. J. Adams, Minister of the gospel. New York, Printed by C. A. Calhoun . . . 1844.
16p. 17cm.
Cover-title.
MoInRC, USIC, WHi

21. ———. A true history of the rise of the Church of Jesus Christ of Latter Day Saints — of the restoration of the holy priesthood. And of the late discovery of ancient American records collected from the most authentic sources ever published to the world, which unfold the history of this continent from the earliest ages after the flood, to the beginning of the fifth century of the Christian era. With a sketch of the faith and doctrine of the Church of Jesus Christ of Latter Day Saints. Also a brief outline of the persecution, and martyrdom of their Prophet, Joseph Smith, and the appointment of his successor James J. Strang. By G. J. Adams, Minister of the gospel . . . Baltimore, Hoffman, Printer . . . [1849?]
44p. 15½cm.
Primarily the pamphlet is an adaptation of Orson Pratt's *An interesting account of several Remarkable Visions, and of the Late Discovery of Ancient American Records.*
The text with few variations was also published the same year at Geneva, N.Y., showing Thomas Horton as author. See below.
USIC lacks wrapper.
Morgan
USIC, WHi

22. ———. (same) By T. Horton, Minister of the Gospel. Geneva, N.Y.: Gazette Print. [1849?]
47p. 15cm.
A reset edition of the George J. Adams pamphlet with a few notes added by Horton.
Morgan
CtY, NN

23. Adams, John Quincy. The birth of Mormonism, by John Quincy Adams, D. D. Boston, The Gorham Press; Toronto, The Copp Clark Co., Limited [1916]
3p.l., 9–106p. 19½cm.
On cover: Library of religious thought.
CtY, DLC, NN, UHi, UPB, USI, USIC, UU

24. Adams, William L. A melodrama entitled "Treason, strategems, and spoils," in five acts. By Breakspear [*pseud.*] . . . Portland, Printed by Thos. J. Dryer, "Oregonian" Office, 1852.

32p. 3 plates. 17½ × 26½cm.
"Political satire lampooning the leading Oregon Democrats, employing in part Mormon vocabulary, imagery, and theology as literary devices."
Published in at least four editions. An edition of 38p. is at Oregon Historical Society. It is listed as "De Lux" and dated — Salem, 1899. This copy has no title page, dedication, or illustrations.
CtY

An Address by a minister of the Church of Jesus Christ. *See Pratt, Parley Parker.*

25. Adeler, Max. Snurrige historier fra en afkrog af verden. Ved Ingeborg Raunkjaer . . . Kobenhavn, 1890.
188p.
Title in English: Unusual stories from remote places of the Earth.
Schmidt

Adeler, Max [*pseud.*] *See Clark, Charles Heber.*

26. The Adventure. Edited by D. L. Shinn. Clarksburg, West Virginia, June–October, 1875.
lv. (5 nos. in 72p.) 23½cm.
Edited by a member of the Bickerton group.
Morgan
MoK #2, p. 9–24

27. The Advocate.
lv. monthly. 23cm.
Begun January, 1873. A publication for the branches in Northern England (RLDS)
Double columns.
MoInRC (inc.), MoK V.1 #2, p. [9]–24

28. Agee, Alfred W. Reflections. Ogden, Utah, 1926.
[12]l. 21½cm.
Cover-title.
Mormon poetry.
UPB

29. Ahmanson, John. Vor tids Muhamed. En historisk og kritisk Fremstilling af Mormonismens Fremkomst og Udbredelse, samt Skildringer af Utahs hemmelige Historie. af John Ahmanson. Omaha, "Den Danske Pioneer's Tykkeri," 1876.
170p. 24cm.
Title in English: Today's Mohammed.
DLC, NjP, USIC

30. Aiken, Albert W. Eagle plume, the white avenger. A tale of the Mormon trail by Albert W. Aiken. New York, Beadle and Company, Publishers [1870]
2p. l. [9]–98p. front. 16½cm. (Beadle's Dime Novels, No. 196, February 1, 1870)
Fiction. Dakotah Indians, Danites, and Mormons along the North Fork of the Green River and at Salt Lake at the time of the first Mormon settlements in Utah.
UHi

31. ———. Gold Dan, or Dick Talbot in Utah. New York, Beadle and Adams, Publishers, 1898.
29p. 30cm. (The Dime Library, No. 1003. V. LXXVII)
Fiction dealing with the Danites of Utah.
USIC

32. ———. Gold Dan; or, the white savage of the Great Salt Lake. A terrible tale of the Danites of Mormon land. VIII, No. 400, Nov. 10, 1877, to VIII, No. 411, Jan. 26, 1878.
Saturday Journal #400
The sixth Dick Talbot story.
Also published in the Dime library.
SJ–400, DL–41, 1003.
No copy located

33. ———. Iron dagger; or, the high horse in silverland. A tale of strange adventures in the Mogollon country. III. No. 139, July 11, 1885 to III, No. 150, Sept. 26, 1885.
Beadle Weekly #193. 32cm.
Southwestern New Mexico, mining, Mormons, and murder.
DLC

34. ———. Old Lynx, the Mormon detective; or, Saved from a terrible fate! By the author of "The Scotland Yard Detective," "Gold Dan," "The California Detective," "Old Pink West," etc. New York, Norman L. Munroe, 1884.
8, 8p. illus. 52cm. (The family story paper. V.12, No. 583)
Fiction concerning Mormonism.
DLC

35. Aikman, Duncan. The taming of the frontier . . . by ten authors, edited by Duncan Aikman. New York, Minton, Balch & company, 1925.
xv, 319p. plates. 21½cm.
Includes, "Ogden the underwriters of salvation," by B. DeVoto.
Mormons and Mormon doctrine.
CU–B, DLC, NjP, NN, UHi, UPB, USIC, UU

36. Aitken, W. A journey up the Mississippi River, from its mouth to Nauvoo, the City of the Latter-day Saints. By W. Aitken, of Ashton-Under-Lyne . . . Ashton-under-Lyne, Printed by John Williamson [1845?]
56p. 21½cm.
Preface dated February 8, 1845.
Howes A92
CtY, IHi

37. ———. (same) [Second edition] Ashton-under-Lyne, Printed by W. B. Micklethwaite . . . [1845?]
2p.l. [5]–58p. 21½cm.
Howes A92
CtY, ICN

38. Ajax, Ivor. Our Utah pioneers. Words and music by Ivor Ajax. [Salt Lake City] Deseret News Press, c1930.
[2]l. 30cm.
Mormon music.
UHi

39. Te akatu-akaou-anga i te Ekalesia a Iesu mesia ra i te Tuatau openga nei. Papiete, Imprimerie G. Coulon, Rue de, L'est. [n.d.]
4p. 23 cm.
Title in English: The establishment of the Church.
UPB

Albach, James R. *See Perkins, James Handasyd.*

40. Alberta. A complete and comprehensive description of the agricultural stock raising and mineral resources of Southern Alberta, Canada. Also statistics in regard to its climate. Compiled from the latest reports. Salt Lake City, The Deseret News Printers, 1899.
26[6]p. 19cm.
Information for the benefit of Mormons interested in migrating to Canada.
UPB, USlC

The Albertype Company. *See Salt Lake City in photo-gravure; Souvenir of Salt Lake City.*

41. Albright, Horace Marden. "Oh, Ranger." A book about the national parks. By H. M. Albright and Frank J. Taylor. Illustrated by Ruth Taylor White. Stanford, Calif., Stanford University Press, 1929.
xii, 178p. illus., plates, port. 23cm.
The Mountain Meadows massacre blamed on the Paiute Indians.
NjP, UPB, USlC

Album of Salt Lake City. *See Dwyer, James.*

42. Alcock, P. Latter-day Saints. A letter from the Reverend P. Alcock, Baptist minister, Berwick St. John's Dorsetshire, to his nephew, E. H. Webb, Elder in the Church of the Latter-day Saints, Bristol, late of Cheltenham . . . Bristol, Printed by William Taylor, 39, Temple Street, 1842.
8p. 21cm.
Includes P. Alcock's plea for his nephew to reject Mormonism and E. H. Webb's reply, p. 4–8.
USlC

43. Alder, Lydia D. Mormon Tabernacle Choir in California. A story in verse by Lydia D. Alder. Dedicated to Prof. Evan Stephens. [Salt Lake City? 1898]
[16]p. 21cm.
Signed: "California Excursion, April 13, 1898."
MH, USlC

44. Aldrich, Lewis Cass, *compiler.* History of Ontario County, New York, with illustrations and family skeletons of some of the prominent men and families; ed. by George S. Conover, Comp. by Lewis Cass Aldrich. Syracuse, N.Y., D. Mason & Co., 1888.
1p.l. [5]–713p. ports. 26½cm.
Early Mormon history in New York.
DLC

45. Alexander, Charles Wesley. Brigham Young's daughter. A most thrilling narrative of her escape from Utah, with her intended husband, their pursuit by the Mormon Danites or avenging angels. Together with an account of the adventures and perils of the fugitives . . . To which is added a full exposure of the schemes of the Mormon leaders to defy and defeat the U.S. Government in its attempts to suppress the horrible practice of polygamy in Utah. Philadelphia, C. W. Alexander [c1870]
1p.l.,19–78p. port. 23cm.
Introduction signed: Wesley Bradshaw [*pseud.*]
CtY, NN

46. ———. (same) Croydon [Eng.] M. Mowbray [187–?]
1p.l. [19]–78p. illus. 23cm.
CtY

47. Alexander, Louis C. The wife sealers. By L. C. Alexander. London, Grant Richards, 1903.
3p.l. [7]–346p. 19½cm.
A semi-fictional work on Mormonism.
MH, USlC

48. Alf. [*pseud.*] The history of Mormonism from its commencement to the present time; and revelations of their secrets and mysteries. By Alf. London, Published by T. Owen . . . [n.d.]
46p. 16½cm.
MH

49. Algermissen, Konrad. Die Mormonen oder die heiligen der letzten Tage . . . Hannover, Joseph Giesel, 1928.
3p.l., 7–76p. 16cm.
A sketch of Mormon history, and an attempt to disprove the Book of Mormon, by an Episcopalian minister.
Title in English: The Mormonism of the Latter-day Saints.
ULA, UPB

50. Allen, Edith (Hedden). Mormonism, a present day peril. New York, Published by the Women's Board of Domestic Missions, Reform Church in America, [n.d.]
Broadside. fold. in 6p. 15cm.
Received Nov. 14, 1917 by Princeton Genealogical Library.
NjPT

ALLEN, W. B.

51. Allen, William Barret. A history of Kentucky, embracing gleanings, reminiscences, antiquities, natural curiosities, statistics and biological sketches of pioneers, soldiers, jurists, lawyers, statesmen, divines, mechanics, farmers, merchants, and other leading men of all occupations and pursuits. Louisville, Ky., Bradley & Gilbert, 1872.
xiv [17]–449p. port. 23cm.
"Lorin Farr preaches Mormon doctrine," p. 14, 229–30.
DLC

52. Allen's living topics cyclopedia, supplementing all other cyclopedias. A record of recent events and of the Worlds' progress in all departments of knowledge. New York, Henry G. Allen & Co. [c1897]
2v. 21cm.
"Mormons" and "Utah" in V.2.
USIC

53. Allison, J. Trans-continental letter, written in [sic] vacations. By Rev. J. Allison . . . Milwaukee, Godfrey and Crandall's Steam Printing House, 1871.
67p. 18½cm.
Letter #1, 2, from Salt Lake City. Description of the Mormon trail, Ogden, Salt Lake City, etc. Analyses the Godbeite movement and why it will succeed.
Howes A174
CtY

54. Alston, Hood. Wasatch echoes. Modern saints and other poems by Hood Alston . . . [Salt Lake City] For sale by Alston and Brewer [1874?]
4p.l. [9]–104p. 13½cm.
Preface signed 1874.
"Printed at the Herald office"
Mormon poetry.
CtY, MH, USIC

55. Alter, J. Cecil. James Bridger, trapper, frontiersman, scout and guide: a historical narrative . . . by J. Cecil Alter. With which is incorporated a verbatim copy, annotated, of James Bridger, a biographical sketch . . . by Maj. Gen. Grenville M. Dodge. Salt Lake City, Shepard Book Company [c1925]
xvii, 546p. illus., plates, ports., map. 24½cm.
"Edition limited to one thousand copies."
"The Mormon pioneers," p. 223–230, and other Mormon references.
Howes A191
CU–B, DLC, NjP, NN, UHi, ULA, UPB, USl, USIC, UU

56. ———. Through the heart of the scenic West, by J. Cecil Alter . . . with 65 illustrations. Salt Lake City, Shepard Book Company, 1927.
xiv, 220p. illus., plates, map. 20½cm.
"Limited, special edition of one thousand copies."
Descriptions of Utah with many Mormon references.
DLC, NjP, UHi, ULA, UPB, USl, USIC, UU

57. Ålund, O. W. Amerika. Dess Uppstäckt, eröfring och fyrahundra åriga utveckling af O.W. Ålund. Med 35 Porträtt, 31 scenir och ŏyer smt 10 kartor. Stockholm, Albert Bonniers, forlag [1892]
5p.l., 373 p. illus., ports., maps. 21cm.
Mormonism, p. 306–7, with portrait of Joseph Smith, p. 305.
Title in English: America, its conquest and four hundred year development.
USIC

58. The Amateur. Ogden, Utah, Office of Ogden Junction. November, 1877–July 15, 1879?
2v. weekly, semi-monthly. 41cm.
Official organ of the Mutual Improvement Association of Weber County. Predecessor of the *Contributor*.
USIC (all but v.2 #2, 3)

59. The American Almanac and repository of useful knowledge . . . Boston, 1838–1861.
32v. tables. 19cm.
Mormonites listed in 1838 as a religious body with 12,000 members and dropped in 1843. Mention of the death of Joseph Smith in 1844. Later notes on Utah and the Mormons.
1838 CtY, CU–B, UPB, UU, WHi
1839 CU–B, IaH, UPB, UU, WHi
1840 CU–B, IaH, UPB, UU, WHi
1841 UPB
1842 UPB, UU
1844 CtY, CU–B, UPB, UU, WHi

60. The American Anti-Mormon Association.
Appeal [for money. Grayson, Kentucky, R. B. Neal, n.d.]
[1]p. 21cm.
An appeal for money to continue the activities of the association.
MH

61. American Association of University Professors. Committee of Inquiry on conditions at the University of Utah. . . . Report of the Committee of inquiry on conditions at the University of Utah. July, 1915. [New York? 1915]
2p.l., 3–82p. 23cm.
The committee was formed to investigate discrimination in hiring Mormons as faculty members for a state university.
CU–B, DLC, NjJ, UHi

62. American Baptist Home Mission Society. Utah's need of the Gospel. By one who knows. Chicago [n.d.]
6p. 16cm.
The need of protestant missionary work in Utah.
USIC

63. The American Christian record: containing the history, confession of faith, and statistics of each religious denomination in the United States and Europe. . . New York, W. R. C. Clark & Meeker, 1860.

2p.l. [5]–696p. 19cm.
Includes a section on the Mormons or Latter-day Saints.
Sabin 1070
NjP, UPB

64. American Geographical Society of New York. Memorial volume of the transcontinental excursion of 1912 of the American Geographical Society of New York. New York, The society, 1915.
xi, 407p. illus., plates (part fold.) ports., maps (1 fold) diagrs. 26cm.
Lucien Ballois "Quelques notes sur l'Utah," p. 329–342.
CU–B, DLC, NjP, UHi, UPB, USlC

65. American Party. Utah. The American Party's best campaign document. [Salt Lake City, Allied Printing, 1905?]
[3]p. 22cm.
A tract designed to disprove a circular called "The Fusion ticket." Church and politics during the period of the Reed Smoot investigations.
MH

66. ———. Glaring Interference in spite of denials. The church commands its way. Candidates seeking political preferment told to first obtain consent of priesthood — Severance of church and state decreed by the church itself .The rule in the Thatcher Case. [Salt Lake City, Issued by the State Committee of the American Party. Willard F. Snyder, chairman, 1905?]
[10]l. 21cm.
"Our position defined." leaf #3.
MH

67. ———. Our position defined. Here is an opportunity for every man and woman in Utah to know what the American Party stands for. No fight up on members of any church. [Salt Lake City, 1905?]
[16]p. 21½cm. (No.1)
ULA, USlC

68. The American Scrapbook; The year's golden harvest of thought and achievement. New York, Wm. H. Wise & Co. [c1928]
3v. plates (1 col.) ports. (1 col.) 27½cm.
"Salt Lake City," v.1, p.95–96. The dual nature of Salt Lake City: ½ Mormon, ½ jack Mormon and gentile.
DLC, NjP, USlC

69. American Sight-seeing Car and Coach Company. "Seeing Salt Lake City" being an illustrated description of a tour through Salt Lake City on the observation cars of The American Sight-seeing Car and Coach Company. [n.p., 1905?]
[34]l. illus., ports., plates (fold. col.) 22cm.
"Mormonism, its birth, growth and purpose."
USlC

70. Ampère, Jean Jacques Antoine. Promenade en Amérique; États-Unis — Cuba — Mexique, par J. J. Ampère. Paris, Michel Lévy frères, 1855.
2v. 22cm.
Visit to Utah and a discussion of Mormonism.
Title in English: Stroll in America.
Other edition: 1856. DLC; 1860. DLC; 1867. DLC; 1874. DLC
Howes A222, Sabin 1347
CU–B, DLC, NjP, UU

71. Andersen, Niels Chr. Hvem har sendt os Mormonspraedikanterne? Et spørgsmaal samtiden anbefalet. Gjennemtaenkt af N. C. A. Hjerring, 1882.
16p.
Schmidt
Title in English: Who has sent us Mormon preachers.

72. Andersen, Peter. Var Joseph Smith en sand Guds Profet? Udgivet af den gjenorganixerede Jesu Kristi Kirke. Ved Peter Andersen, og Mads Sörensen missionaerer. [Aalborg, Trykt hos Oluf Olufsen, n.d.]
15 [1]p. 21cm.
"En Indbydelse til Guds Rige," p. 13–15.
"Christi Laerdom," p. 16.
No title-page.
Title in English: Was Joseph Smith a true prophet of God?
NN

73. Anderson, A. A. Tjugu År i vilda Västern; erfarenheter och Iakttagelser som missionär och församlingslärare. Minneapolis, Minnesota, Missionstidningens Tryckeri, 1910.
180p. illus. 19½cm.
Includes missionary work in Utah among the Mormons.
Title in English: Twenty years in the wild west.
UHi

74. Anderson, Audentia. *See Anderson, Mary Audentia.*

Anderson, C. A. *See Andersson, C. A.*

75. Anderson, C. C., *compiler.* The boy prophet's wonderful sermon at the funeral of King Follett, Nauvoo, Illinois, 1844. Also, a war prophecy, or the story of the white horse, and the marvelous visions of George Washington, Newman Bulkley, S. M. Farnsworth, C. D. Evans. Compiled by C. C. Anderson. Salt Lake City [1906?]
47p. 15½cm.
CtY, USlC

76. ———. (same) Salt Lake City [n.d.]
47p. 15cm.
Variant edition.
"War prophecy" covered with paper, crossed out in pencil on title page.
USlC

ANDERSON, C. E.

77. Anderson, C. E. Bulletin, No. 1. Written by C. E. Anderson. [n.p., n.d.]
4p. 22cm.
The author was Bishop's agent for Galland Grove District, RLDS Church.
MoInRC

78. Anderson, Edward Henry. The apostles of Jesus Christ; a brief account of their lives and acts; and of the rise and expansion of the Christian church up to A.D. 68, written for the Deseret Sunday School Union, by Edward H. Anderson. Salt Lake City, Deseret Sunday School Union, 1917.
XII, 284p. plates, maps. 19cm.
Includes references to Mormons; Mormon interpretations of Christian history.
DLC, UHi, UPB, USIC, UU

79. ———. (same) 4th ed. Salt Lake City, Published by the Deseret Book Company, 1924.
xii, 284p. 19cm.
NjP, USIC

80. ———. The Book of Mormon, a book divine; Address delivered over Radio Station KSL, Sunday Evening, June 5, 1927. [Salt Lake City] 1927.
Broadside. 45½ × 25cm.
Reprinted from the *Deseret News*.
UPB

81. ———. A brief history of the Church of Jesus Christ of Later-day Saints from the birth of the Prophet Joseph Smith to the present time. By the author of the "Life of Brigham Young." Salt Lake City, George Q. Cannon & Sons Co., 1893.
viii [9]–173p. 20cm.
CSmH, CtY, CU–B, DLC, NjP, NN, UHi, ULA, UPB, USIC

82. ———. (same) Salt Lake City, George Q. Cannon and Sons Co. [1896]
viii [9]–173p. 19cm.
Cover date: 1896. The text is the same as the 1893 edition.
USIC

83. ———. (same) Salt Lake City, George Q. Cannon & Sons Co., 1893 [1899]
vii [9]–173p. 19cm.
Cover date: 1899. The text is the same as the 1893 edition.
MH, USIC

84. ———. (same) . . . Ten-cent edition. Second edition. Chicago, Published by Missions of the Church of Jesus Christ of Latter-day Saints [c1902]
1p.l., v [3]–264p. 13cm.
NN, UHi, USIC

85. ———. (same) Ten cent edition . . . Independence Mo., Published by the Missions of the Church of Jesus Christ of Latter-day Saints [Zions Printing and Publishing Co., 1902?]
143p. 18cm.
Preface signed: 1902.
OO

86. ———. (same) Second edition . . . Salt Lake City, The Deseret News, 1902.
vii [9]–192p. 19cm.
CU–B, DLC, MoInRC, NN, UHi, ULA, USIC, WHi

87. ———. (same) Third Edition. Salt Lake City, The Deseret News, 1905.
viii [9]–192p. 20cm.
CU–B, ICN, MH, MoKu, ULA, USIC

88. ———. (same) . . . Independence, Mo., Published by the Missions of the Church of Jesus Christ of Latter-day Saints in the United States [Zion's Printing and Publishing Company, 1920]
182p. 19cm.
CU–B, MH, NN, UHi, UPB, USIC

89. ———. (same) . . . Independence, Mo., Zion's Printing and Publishing Company [1925]
3p.l. [7]–245p. 19cm.
Fourth edition.
UPB, USIC

90. ———. (same) [Fourth revised edition] Independence, Mo., Press of Zions' Printing and Publishing Company [c1926]
3p.l. [7]–245p. 17½cm.
Includes preface to the fourth edition, 1925. Copyright by Heber J. Grant.
CU–B, NJP, UHi, USIC, UU

91. ———. (same) . . . Independence, Mo., Press of Zion's Printing and Publishing Company, 1928 [c1926]
3p.l. [7]–245p. illus., ports. 18½cm.
Includes preface to fourth edition, 1926.
"Edition of 1928."
DLC, NN, UHi, USI, USIC, UU

92. ———. (same, in Dutch) Eene korte geschiedenis der Kerk van Jezus Christus van de Heiligen der Laatste Dagen van de geboorte von den Profeet Joseph Smith tot op den tegenwoordigen tijd. Door Edward H. Anderson [Rotterdam?] Vertaald door Willard T. Cannon, 1904.
viii, 228 [1]p. front. 19½cm.
UHi, USIC

93. ———. (same, in Japanese) Matsu Jitsu Seito Iesu Kirisuto Kyokai Ryaku Shi; Choro John W. Stocker Honyayu; Morumon Kyokei to Ippu Ta Sai. Tokyo, Nihon Dendobu, 1907.
300p. illus., maps, plates, ports. 19½cm.
UPB, USIC

———. Come into his fold. *See Clive, William C.*

94. ———. The life of Brigham Young by Edward H. Anderson . . . Salt Lake City, Geo. Q. Cannon & Sons Co., 1893.
viii, 173p. 21cm.
CtY, CU-B, ICN, MH, NN, UHi, USl, USlC, UU

95. ———. (same) . . . Salt Lake City, Bureau of Information, 1915.
2p.l. [vii]-viii [9]-176p. illus. 20cm.
MDBP, NjP, UHi, UPB

96. ———. (same, in Danish) Brigham Young levnedslöb. Af Edward H. Anderson. Oversat fra Engelsk af John S. Hansen. Med Tilladelse fra "Deseret News Book Store." [Salt Lake City] "Bikuben's Bibliotek," 1918.
241p. 18½cm.
The L.D.S. church historian's office has galley proofs, only.
NjP, USlC

97. ———, *compiler.* Local chronology and church directory;brief memoranda of the leading events of 1898 and a church directory of the Weber Stake of Zion, 1899. Ogden [1899]
92p. 22½cm.
USlC

98. ———. Local chronology and church directory, 1899. Brief memoranda of the leading local events in Ogden City and Weber County for the year 1899. [Ogden? 1899]
78p. 22½cm.
"Local church directory of the Church of Jesus Christ of Latter-day Saints of the Weber Stake of Zion," 1900, p. 63-72. Also, "missionaries (on missions and those who returned) in 1899," p. 73-78.
UPB, USlC, UU

99. ———. The Lord's law of health. The word of wisdom. Compiled and written by E. H. Anderson of the presidency of the Granite Stake for the use of ward teachers and for the weekly home evenings. [Salt Lake City, n.d.]
[7]p. 16½cm.
UPB, USlC

100. ———. (same) [Salt Lake City, Church of Jesus Christ of Latter-day Saints, 193-]
[8]p. 16½cm.
"Section 99 of the *Doctrine and Covenants.*"
USlC, UU

———. Y.M.M.I.A. handbook. *See Church of Jesus Christ of Latter-day Saints. Young Men's Mutual Improvement Association. Y.M.M.I.A. handbook.*

101. Anderson, George Edward. A key to the floral record of the Savior, the Prophet Joseph, the Patriarch Hyrum, First Presidency, Apostles and Temples of the Church of Jesus Christ of Latter-day Saints. By G. E. Anderson, Temple Bazar, Manti. Manti, Home Sentinel Print [n.d.]
14p. 15cm.
An index to an amalgamate photograph. Includes short biographies.
UPB, WHi

102. Anderson, Galusha. Condition of Mormon children in Utah. Chicago, Ill. [Published by the Womens' Baptist Home Mission Society, n.d.]
10p. 16cm.
A work demonstrating the poor condition of the family group in Utah.
NN

103. Anderson, George Wood. Modern misbeliefs by George Wood Anderson. [A sermon. New York, c1914]
2p.l. [5]-31p. port. 18cm.
According to the author, "Mormonism, Christian Science, and Russellism" are the three most dangerous and outstanding misbeliefs.
MoInRC, USlC

104. ———. (same) [Scranton, Pennsylvania, W. C. Turnstal, c1914]
2p.l. [5]-31p. 20cm.
MoInRC

105. Anderson, James A. *probable author.* The Story of Alice. Morgan, Utah, Chimes Press, 1925.
36p. 20½cm.
A doctrinal poem with references to pioneer life.
USlC

106. Anderson, James Henry. Book of Mormon promises and prophecies. [Salt Lake City, 1929]
[18]l. 28cm.
Caption-title.
Signed at end: James H. Anderson.
CU-B, USlC

107. ———. The Church of Jesus Christ of Latter-day Saints, its religion, history, condition, and destiny. By J. H. Anderson. Liverpool, Millennial Star Office [1892]
1p.l. [3]-64p. 14cm.
MH, UPB, USlC

108. ———. (same) An Address delivered before the Ethical Society, at South Place Institute, London by James H. Anderson. Salt Lake City, Deseret News Publishing Co., 1892.
1p.l. [3]-64p. 15cm.
CU-B, MH, SHi, USlC

109. ———. (same) Liverpool, Millennial Star Office, 1898.
64p. 13cm.
NN, USlC

110. ———. (same) Salt Lake City, Bureau of Information and Church Literature, 1902.
64p. 14cm.
IU, MiU, MoInRC, USlC

111. ———. (same) Liverpool, Millennial Star Office, 1905.
64p. 13½cm.
USl

112. ———. (same, in Dutch) De kerk van Jezus Christus van de heiligen der Laatste-Dagen. Hare Godsdienst, Geschiedenis, Toestand en Bastemming. Eene predikatie, hehouden voor de Ethical Society in het South Place Institute to London, door James H. Anderson . . . [Rotterdam? n.d.]
64[1]p. 13cm.
UPB, USlC

113. ———. (same, in Maori) Ko te Hahi o Ihu Karaiti o te Hunga Tapu o nga Ra o Muri Nei. Ko tona karakia, tona kaerenga, tona ahua me tona tutukitanga. He mea tuhituhi na tetahi kaumatua o te hahi na Hemi H. Aneishana (James H. Anderson.) Na etahi o nga kaumatua o te hui Maori o Hiona te whakamaoritanga. Salt Lake City, Star Printing Co., 1897.
2p.l. [3]–75p. front. 14cm.
UPB, USlC

114. ———. Notable mothers of scripture. [Salt Lake City, Y.L.M.I.A., 1929]
47p. 21cm.
A manual for instruction.
See also Church of Jesus Christ of Latter-day Saints. Young Women's Mutual Improvement Association. Courses of study . . . 1929–30.
USlC

115. ———. Present time and prophecy. [By] Elder James H. Anderson. An address given before the General Board of the Relief, and the combined Salt Lake City Relief Society officers, December 15, 1917. [Salt Lake City? 1917?]
19p. 22cm.
USlC

116. ———. The present time, and prophecy. "The testimony of Jesus is the spirit of prophecy," as a Bible Test, applied to Joseph Smith, relative to events in Palestine and and the war of 1914–18 and ensuing effects. [Salt Lake City?] 1917.
26p. 28cm.
Mimeographed copy.
UPB

117. ———. Significance of the M.I.A. slogan; address delivered over Radio Station KSL, Sunday Evening, January 30, 1927. [Salt Lake City] 1927.
Broadside. 51cm. × 25cm.
Reprinted from the *Deseret News.*
UPB

118. ———. Story of the Gospel of Christ as told in the New Testament . . . [Salt Lake City, 1929]
18p. 28cm.
Caption-title.
Signed at end: James H. Anderson.
CU–B, USlC

119. ———. (same) Salt Lake City [Deseret Book Company] 1930.
18p. illus. 23cm.
"Series No. 1."
UHi, USlC

120. ———. Ten women of the olden days who have influenced history to the end of time. Gods' story in mothers from Eden's garden till warring nations sink to rise no more. Dedicated to those noble women in Israel whose blissful sway in the Young Ladies' M.I.A. extends to every land and clime. By James H. Anderson. Salt Lake City, 1929.
3p.l., 3–122 numb. l. 23½cm.
Mimeographed text. Printed title page in black and red.
DLC, NN, UHi, UPB, USl, UU

121. Anderson, Martha [*pseud.*] The other house, a true story of the modern Mormon polygamy, by Martha Anderson and Harvey J. O'Higgins. Boston, Mass., The C. M. Clark Publishing Company [c1912]
3p.l., 93p. 19cm.
O'Higgins worked with Frank J. Cannon on his *Under the Prophet in Utah.*
According to the *Salt Lake Herald Republican,* August 8, 1911, Martha Anderson is a pseudonym for Frank J. Cannon.
DLC, MH, USlC, WHi

122. Anderson, Mary Audentia (Smith). Ancestry and posterity of Joseph Smith and Emma Hale, with little sketches of their immigrant ancestors, all of whom came to America between the years 1620 and 1865, and settled in the states of Massachusetts and Connecticut, compiled and written by Mary Audentia Smith Anderson. Independence, Mo. [Herald Printing House] 1929.
2p.l. [51]–720p. illus., ports., fold. geneal. tables. 24cm.
"Limited edition."
CU–B, DLC, ICN, MH, NjP, UHi, USlC

123. ———. Objectives and essential points in the program of the Women's Department by Audentia Anderson. Independence, Mo., Women's Department of the Reorganized Church of Jesus Christ of Latter Day Saints [n.d.]
9p. 18cm.
USlC

124. Anderson, Nephi. Added upon. A story. By Nephi Anderson . . . Salt Lake City, Deseret News Publishing Company, 1898.
2p.l. [5]–140p. 19½cm.
Mormon fiction.
DLC, MH, NjP, UPB, USlC, WHi

ANDERSON, N.

125. ———. (same) Salt Lake City, The Deseret News, 1902.
133p. 19cm.
NN

126. ———. (same) [3d ed.] Salt Lake City, The Deseret News, 1904.
3p.l. [5]–133p. 19cm.
UPB, UU

127. ———. (same) . . . 4th ed. Salt Lake City, The Deseret News, 1907.
3p.l. [7]–135p. 19cm.
UU

128. ———. (same) . . . 5th and enlarged ed. Salt Lake City, The Deseret News, 1912.
4p.l. [7]–228p. 20cm.
DLC, RPB, ULA, USIC

129. ———. (same) 6th ed. Independence, Mo., Zion's Printing and Publishing Co. [c1912]
2p.l. [7]–228p. 19cm.
MoInRC, UPB

130. ———. (same) . . . 7th ed. Independence, Mo., Zion's Printing and Publishing Co. [c1912]
4p.l. [7]–228p. 19cm.
UHi, UPB, UU

131. ———. (same) 8th ed. Salt Lake City, The Deseret News Press [c1912]
4p.l. [7]–228p. 19cm.
UPB

132. ———. (same) 10th ed. Salt Lake City, The Deseret News Press [c1912]
3p.l. [7]–228p. 19cm.
UHi, UU

133. ———. (same) 11th ed. Salt Lake City, The Deseret News Press [c1912]
4p.l. [7]–228p. 19cm.
UHi, UU

134. ———. (same) 12th ed. Salt Lake City, The Deseret News Press [c1912]
3p.l. [7]–228p. 19cm.
UU

135. ———. (same, in Danish) Fortaelling af Nephi Anderson. Oversatt af John S. Hansen. Salt Lake City, "Bikubens" Bibliotek, 1916.
1p.l. [3]–254p. 18cm.
Schmidt lists an 1898 edition which is probably an error and refers to this edition.
UPB, USIC, UU

136. ———. (same, in Swedish) Krönta med större härlighet av Nephi Anderson. Översattning fran Engelskan av Clara Lundberb . . . Salt Lake City, De Associerade Tidningarnas Tryckeri, 1928.
368p. 15cm.
UPB, USIC

137. ———. The Boys of Springtown, with special reference to William Wallace Jones and Ned Fisher. By Nephi Anderson . . . drawings by C. E. Tillotson. Independence, Mo., Zion's Printing and Publishing Company, 1920.
3p.l. [7]–160p. illus. 18½cm.
Mormon fiction.
DLC, NjP, UHi, UPB, USIC, UU

138. ———. The Castle Builder [a story] by Nephi Anderson . . . Salt Lake City, The Improvement Era, 1902.
viii [9]–188p. 21cm.
Mormon fiction.
DLC, MH, USIC

139. ———. (same) Salt Lake City, The Deseret News, 1909.
2p.l. [v]–viii [9]–239p. 19½cm.
UHi, ULA, UPB, USIC, UU

140. ———. A Daughter of the North, by Nephi Anderson . . . with five drawings by C. E. Tillotson. [Salt Lake City, Printed by De Utah-Nederlander Pub. Co.] c1915.
2p.l. [5]–256p. illus. 19½cm.
Mormon fiction.
DLC, NjP, UHi, UPB, USIC, UU

141. ———. The Dimmed vision. By Nephi Anderson, author of "Added upon." [n.p., n.d]
18p. 15½cm.
A genealogical story. The second printing of a revised edition dated 1935.
UPB, USIC

142. ———. Dorian, by Nephi Anderson . . . Salt Lake City [Printed by the Bikuben Publishing Company] 1921.
1p.l. [3]–223p. 19½cm.
Mormon fiction.
DLC, NjP, UHi, UPB, USIC, UU

143. ———. A gospel outline; a few of the most important references bearing on the gospel of Jesus Christ, arranged in logical order, and designed to give to missionaries — and all other students of the gospel — a working knowledge of such scriptural quotations as may be required from the first. By Elder Nephi Anderson . . . Independence, Mo., Central States Mission, Church of Jesus Christ of Latter-day Saints, 1910.
19p. 16cm.
MH

ANDERSON, N.

144. ———. John St. John; a story of Missouri and Illinois. By Nephi Anderson . . . [Independence, Mo., Zion's Printing and Publishing Company] 1917.
2p.l. [5]–227p. 19cm.
Mormon fiction.
DLC, NjP, UHi, UPB, USlC

145. ———. Marcus King, Mormon. Salt Lake City, George Q. Cannon & Sons, 1900.
2p.l. [5]–211p. 15cm.
Mormon fiction.
CU–B, UPB, USlC

146. ———. (same) Salt Lake City, The Deseret News Publishers, 1908.
1p.l. [3]–133p. 19½cm.
MH, ULA, UPB, UU

147. ———. (same) Salt Lake City, The Deseret News, 1916.
1p.l. [3]–133p. 19cm.
UHi, UPB

148. ———. Piney Ridge cottage; the love story of a "Mormon" country girl, by Nephi Anderson . . . Salt Lake City, The Deseret News, 1912.
1p.l. [3]–237p. 20cm.
Mormon fiction.
CSmH, MH, NjP, UHi, UPB, USlC, UU

149. ———. Place of genealogy in the plan of salvation. A paper read by Nephi Anderson at the quarterly meeting of the Genealogical Society of Utah, in the Assembly Hall, Salt Lake City, October 6, 1911. [Salt Lake City] Skelton Publishing Co. [1911?]
16p. 19½cm.
MoInRC, UPB, USlC

150. ———. Romance of a missionary; a story of English life and missionary experiences. By Nephi Anderson . . . Independence, Mo., Zion's Printing and Publishing Company, 1919.
3p.l. [7]–190p. 18½cm.
Mormon fiction.
DLC, NjP, UHi, UPB, USlC, WHi

151. ———. Story of Chester Lawrence; being the completed account of one who played an important part in "Piney Ridge cottage," by Nephi Anderson . . . Salt Lake City, The Deseret News, 1913.
1p.l. [3]–237p. 20cm.
Mormon fiction.
DLC, NjP, UHi, UPB, USlC, UU

152. ———. Tru fethranna. [Reykjavík, Útgefandi: Loftur Bjarnasen 1905]
4p. 19½cm.
Tract in Icelandic.
Title in English: Faith of our fathers.
USlC

153. ———. A young folks' history of the Church of Jesus Christ of Latter-day Saints. With maps and illustrations. Salt Lake City, George Q. Cannon & Sons Co., 1900.
viii [9]–198p. illus., ports., maps. 19cm.
CU–B, DLC, UHi, UPB, USlC

154. ———. (same) New and revised ed. Salt Lake City, The Deseret News, 1906.
1p.l. viii [9]–182p. illus., ports., maps. 19½cm.
NN, ULA, UPB, USlC, UU

155. ———. (same) Salt Lake City, Deseret Sunday School Union, 1916.
1p.l. viii [9]–183p. illus., ports., maps. 20cm.
USlC

156. ———. (same) Salt Lake City, Deseret Sunday School Union, 1917.
1p.l., viii [9]–184p. illus., ports., maps. 19½cm.
DLC, MoInRC, NN, USl, USlC

157. ———. (same) Salt Lake City, Deseret Sunday School Union, 1919.
viii [9]–187p. illus., ports., maps. 19½cm.
UHi, UPB

158. ———. (same) Salt Lake City, Deseret Book Company, 1923.
viii [9]–187p. illus., ports., maps. 19½cm.
UHi, UPB

159. Anderson, Rasmus Björn. The first chapter of Norwegian immigration (1821–1840) its causes and results. With an introduction on the services rendered by the Scandinavians to the world and to America. Madison, Wisconsin, The author, 1895.
xvi, 476p. ports., plates. 23½cm.
Includes a chapter entitled: "Mormon immigrants to Utah."
Another edition: 1896. UPB
DLC, UPB

160. Anderson, Rufus. The Hawaiian Islands: their progress and condition under missionary labors . . . Boston, Gould and Lincoln, 1864.
xii, 23–450p. illus., plates, ports., fold. map. 21cm.
Reference to Mormon missionary work in Hawaii.
Other editions: [2d ed.] 1864. Sabin 1419. CU–B; [3d ed.] 1865. CU–B, NjB, USlC
DLC, UPB, USlC

161. Andersson, C. A. Vapen mot Mormonismen. Samt en Kort Skildring om Dess uppkomst, organization, lära och utveckling af C. A. A. F. D. Mormon -Missionär. Stockholm, C. A. Anderssons förlag, 1886.
32p. 15½cm.
Title in English: Weapons against Mormonism.
USlC

162. Andreas, Alfred Theodore. An illustrated historical atlas of Hancock County, Illinois. Map work of townships and plats made by Gen. Chas. A. Gilchrist. Chicago, Ill., A. T. Andreas, 1874.
137p. illus., maps. 46cm.
Includes a history of Mormonism in Illinois.
USIC

163. Andree, Karl Theodor. Geographische wanderungen; von Karl Andree . . . Dresden, R. Kuntze, 1859.
2v. in 1. 20cm.
A brief mention of his visit among the Mormons in Nauvoo.
Title in English: Geographical wanderings.
Howes A246, Sabin 1463
CtY, DLC

164. ———. Nord-Amerika in geographischen und geschichtlichen umrissen mit besonderer Berücksichtigung der eingeborenen und der Indianischen Alterthümer, der Einwanderung, und der Ansiedelunger, des Ackerbaues, der Gewerbe, der Schiffahrt und des Handels. Von dr. Karl Andree. Braunschweig, George Westermann, 1851.
810p. illus. 25cm.
A description of Utah, Mormonism, and its origin.
Title in English: North America in geographical and historical sketches.
Another edition: 2. aufl. verm. mit einem kartenwerke von achtzehn blättern. Braunschweig, George Westermann, 1854. CU, DLC.
Howes A-248, Sabin 1461
CU-B, DLC

165. Andrews, Elisha Benjamin. The history of the last quarter-century in the United States, by E. Benjamin Andrews . . . With more than three hundred and fifty illustrations. New York, Charles Scribners' Sons, 1896.
2v. illus., ports., plates. 24½cm.
"Mormonism," v.2, p.210–214. The legal moves against polygamy.
NjP, ULA, USIC

166. Andrews, J. C. Baptism for the dead by Rev. J. C. Andrews, Provo City, Utah. Provo, Utah [n.d.]
[10]p. fold. 14cm. (Tract. No. 5)
A polemic on the Mormon doctrine of salvation for the dead.
UPB

167. ———. The Everlasting gospel, by Rev. J. C. Andrews, Provo City, Utah. [Provo, n.d.]
[7]p. 13½cm. (Tract. No. 4)
USIC

168. ———. Fallacies of the Mormon priesthood. By Reverend J. C. Andrews. Provo City, Utah [Provo, McEwen & Field, n.d.]
20p. 12½cm. (Tract. No. 3)
MH, USIC

169. ———. False prophecies of Joseph Smith. Elijah made into two prophets. Priesthood built on a false foundation. By Rev. J. C. Andrews. Provo City, Utah. [Provo? n.d.]
8p. 12cm. (Tract. No. 2)
MH

170. ———. Polygamy as taught by Latter-day Saints. By Rev. J. C. Andrews, Provo, Utah. [Provo, 189–?]
4p. 13½cm. (Tract. No. 1)
Cover-title.
USIC

171. ———. (same, under title) Mormon polygamy. By Reverend J. C. Andrews, Provo City, Utah. [Provo, 1892?]
8p. 14cm. (Tract. No. 1)
Revised edition of *Polygamy as taught by Latter-day Saints.*
USIC

172. Anderson, T. J. No Mormon should be allowed to vote! [Salt Lake City, 1889?]
[2]p. 9×15cm.
Mormons and politics.
UPB, USIC

173. Andrews, Thomas J. The fullness of the everlasting Gospel; or, Only way to be saved. [San Francisco, Turnbull, & Smith, 1861?]
28p. 22cm.
Signed by Thos. J. Andrews. Includes an appendix.
NN, UPB

174. Andrus, Milo. Milo Andrus Genealogy. [n.p., ca. 1917]
13p. 23cm.
"Autobiographical sketch," p.1–6.
USIC

175. Angel, Myron, *editor.* History of Nevada. With illustrations and biographical sketches of its prominent men and pioneers. Oakland, California, Thompson & West, 1881.
xiv [15]–680p. illus., plates (part double) ports. 30½cm.
Includes Mormon colonization in Nevada.
CSmH, CtY, CU-B, DLC, NN, UHi, UPB

Anquetil, Georges. *See Georges-Anquetil.*

176. Anthony, R. J. Crooked paths. By Elders R. J. Anthony and P. Anderson. [Lamoni, Ia., Herald Publishing House, 189–?]
15[1]p. 23cm. ([Tract] No. 44)
A work against Utah L.D.S. church. On back: No. 4. Epitome of the faith and doctrines of the Reorganized Church of Jesus Christ of Latter Day Saints.
CU-B, MH, MoInRC, NN, UPB, USl, USIC

177. ———. (same) [Lamoni, Ia., Printed by the Reorganized Church of Jesus Christ of Latter Day Saints, n.d.]
15p. 23cm. ([Tract] No. 44)
USlC

178. The Antidote to Mormonism and infidel error. Edited by John Brindley. Birmingham, London, June 27–Nov. 21, 1857.
22 nos. weekly. 24½cm.
USlC

179. Anti-Mormon Almanac, for 1842. Containing, besides the usual astronomical calculations, a variety of interesting and important facts, showing the treasonable tendency, and the wicked imposture of that great delusion, advocated by a sect, lately risen up in the United States, calling themselves Mormons, or Latter Day Saints; with quotations from their writings and from public document no. 189, published by order of Congress, February 15, 1841, showing that Mormonism authorizes the crimes of theft, robbery, treason, and murder; together with the number of the sect, their views, character of their leaders &c., &c. New York, Sold wholesale and retail, at the Health Book Store, 126 Fulton Street [1841]
[24]p. 19cm.
CtY, CU-B, DLC inc., USlC

180. Anti-Mormon slanders denied. By the Commercial Club, Salt Lake City. By the ministers of Christian Churches. By prominent business men and officials in Utah. And in the United States Senate, Washington D.C. [Liverpool? 1919]
8p. 22cm.
UPB

181. Anti-polygamy standard. Salt Lake City, April, 1880–March, 1883.
3v. illus. monthly. 61cm.
Issued in the interest of the Ladies Anti-polygamy Society of Utah. From April to August, 1880. Organ of the Woman's National Anti-polygamy Society from September, 1880 to March, 1883.
NjP V. 3 # 10, NN, USl, USlC

182. Appollinaire, Guillaume. . . . La Femme assise. 2. ed. . . . Paris, Editions de la Nouvelle revue Francaise, 1920.
2p.l., 7–268p., [1]l. 19½cm.
Novel concerning Mormonism.
Title in English: The seated woman.
DLC, OCl

183. ———. (same) 5th ed. Paris, 1920.
CtY, NN

184. ———. (same) 9th ed. Paris, Gallimard [1928?]
ICU

185. L'apostasie du véritable evangile et sa restauration. Liège, Ernest C. Rossiter [n.d.]
15 [1]p. 16cm.
At the head of title: L'eternelle vérité.
Title in English: Apostacy and restoration of the true church.
UPB

185a. Appalling disclosures! Mormon revelations, being the history of fourteen females, Emma Hale. Mrs. Hatfield. Lucy Murray. Alice Foster. Mrs. Williams. Lizzie Monroe. Marian Gage. Adeline Young. Mrs. Jones. Lady Bula. Marg. Guildford. Maud Hatfield. Rose Hatfield, Mrs. Richards. Victims of Mormon spiritual marriages! Wives, mothers, daughters, and sisters Lured away from their Homes, and United to the same Husbands! The tragic Deaths of Mrs. Hatfield and her Husband, Through the Double Marriages of their Eldest and Youngest Daughters to Richards, the Mormon Missionary; and the Awful Murder of Maud Hatfield By the first Mrs. Richards, who became a Maniac through Jealousy and the Desertion of her Two Babes; Including the Sufferings of other once happy Women, entrapped by the Prophets and Elders of the Latter Day Saints; with their Lives an [sic] Crimes, from the rise of Joseph Smith, the Founder of their Profliga[te] Church, to the dark deeds of Brigham Young, and his Disciples, now carried on in their Pandemonium at Utah. London: Printed and Published by H. Elliot, 475 New Oxford Street. [1856?]
1p. l., [3]–16p. 21cm.
Caption-title: The history of fourteen females, victims of Mormonism.
Published after the departure of Judges Brandenbury and Brocchus (1851), the Wintering of Col. Steptoe in California (1854) and the Utah expedition (1857)
UPB

186. An appeal to the American Congress. The Bible law of marriage against Mormonism. [By one of the people, author of opinions concerning the Bible law of marriage] [Philadelphia, 1873?]
16p. 18cm.
Cover-title.
DLC, MH, NN, UU

An appeal to the American people; being an account on the persecutions of the Church. . . . *See Rigdon, Sydney.*

187. An appeal to the Latter Day Saints. Philadelphia, Newton, Richards, and Stanley, 1863.
72p. 17cm.
Rigdonite tract.
MoInRC

188. Appleby, William I. A dissertation on Nebuchadnezzar's dream: showing that the kingdom spoken of by Daniel the Prophet was not set up in the days of the Apostles; and the order of the kingdom set up then explained. Also: The rise and faith of the

most notable orthodox societies of the present day, together with a synopsis of the origin and faith of the Church of "Latter-day Saints" comparing their faith with the faith of other societies. By W. I. Appleby, Minister of the Gospel "Pro Bono Publico". Philadelphia, Printed by Brown, Bicking & Guilbert, 1844.
24p. 18cm.
DLC, MH, USIC, WHi

189. ———. A few important questions for the reverend clergy to answer, being a scale to weigh priestcraft and sectarianism in. By William I. Appleby, Elder in the Church of "Latter-day Saints." Philadelphia, Brown, Bicking & Guilbert, Printers, 1843.
12p. 16½cm.
CtY, MH, MoInRC, ULA

190. ———. Lines suggested and composed on the present state of the world . . . [Philadelphia] Bicking & Guilbert [1848?]
Broadside. 33×23cm.
Mormon poem.
Signed: Philadelphia, May 1, 1848.
USIC

191. ———. Mormonism consistent! Truth vindicated, and falsehood exposed and refuted: being a reply to A. H. Wickersham. By W. I. Appleby, Elder in the Church of "Latter-day Saints." Wilmington, Del., Porter & Neff, 1843.
24p. 21cm.
NN

Apples of Sodom; a story of Mormon life.
See Gilchrist, Rosetta Luce.

192. Appletons' hand-book of American travel. Western tour. Embracing eighteen through routes to the West and Far West, tours of the Great Lakes and rivers, and all local routes of the states of Ohio, Indiana, Illinois, Iowa, Michigan, Wisconsin, Minnesota, Missouri, Kansas, Nebraska, Colorado, Nevada, California, and Oregon, and territories of Dakota, Wyoming, Montana, Idaho, Utah, Washington, and Alaska . . . Rev. for autumn of 1872. New York, D. Appleton and Company, 1872.
317p. illus., fold. maps, fold. plans. 19½cm.
A brief but thorough treatment of Mormonism and the Utah story. Yearly from 1855.
DLC, UPB

193. Arceneaux, J. Early. Mormonism, a system of infidelity. Austin, Texas, Firm Foundation Publishing House [n.d.]
59p. 14cm.
Cover-title.
Discussion of the *Book of Mormon*, the inspired Bible, and doctrines of the Church.
UPB, USIC

194. ———. (same) Austin, Texas, Firm Foundation Publishing House [n.d.]
32p. 22cm.
MoInRC

195. Archbold, Ann. A book for the married and single, the grave and the gay: and especially designed for steamboat passengers. By Miss Ann Archbold . . . East Plainfield, O., Printed at the office of the "Practical preacher," N. A. Baker, Printer, 1850.
xiv [15]–192p. 14½cm.
Tells of the execution of two Mormons in Iowa, with a description of their trial; other Mormon depredations.
Howes A299
CSmH, CtY, DLC, ICHi, ICN, NN

196. Argyle, Annie. Cupids' album. By Archie Argyle [*pseud.*] New York, M. Doolady, 1866.
2p.l. vi [7]–322p. 19cm.
In the novel, he visits Salt Lake City, converses with an apostle.
Author's name identified in Howes, 1962 edition.
Howes A306
CU–B, DLC, NjP, UPB

197. The Arimat. Lincoln, Nebraska. June, 1919–July, 1920.
2v. monthly. 23cm.
RLDS Southern Nebraska District.
Ends with v.2 #2.
MoInRC

198. Armbrust, J. L. Reformation or restoration, or which is the Church? Jesus Christ established but one visible church. [Armbrust, Pa.?] 1929.
4p. 21½cm.
Signed at end: August 15, 1929.
A tract of the Bickerton group.
D. L. Morgan

199. ———. A statement issued by the Re-Organized Church of Jesus Christ. Youngwood, 1908.
6p. 16cm.
Signed: Youngwood, Penn., July 4, 1908.
A tract of the Bickerton group.
MoInRC

200. Arms, Mary L. Day. The world as I have found it. Sequel to incidents in the life of a blind girl. By Mary L. Day Arms. With an introduction by Rev. Charles F. Deems, Ll.D. Baltimore, J. Young, 1878.
1p.l. [3]–312p. illus., port. 18½cm.
Visit to Salt Lake City, p. 183–44. She left Salt Lake City with the "highest respect and gratitude for its citizens."
Another edition: 3d ed. Baltimore [1878?] USIC
CU–B, DLC, USIC

201. Armstrong, C. *probable author.* "He that readeth let him understand" . . . [London, Printed by W. Aubrey, n.d.]

[4]p. 18½cm.
Includes "The faith and doctrines of the Latter-day Saints, with scriptural proof [signed] Joseph Smith." The fourteen articles of faith with scriptural references as they appear in *Zion's Watchman* in 1854.
USIC

202. **Armstrong, Edward Ambler.** The Sinaites; a chronicle of happy days. Princeton, N. J., 1922.
188p. 23cm.
About the Mormons, p. 36–47.
NjP, USIC

203. **Arnesen, Erik.** Mormonismen. Fra "Et Blik paa vor Ted." Kobenhavn, 1913.
18p.
Title in English: Mormonism, from "a look at our times."
Schmidt.

204. **Arnold, W. S.** An important address. [Salt Lake City, n.d.]
24p. 13×18½cm.
A judge, but also an officer in the LDS Church. The address was used for missionary work.
UPB, USIC

205. **Arrowsmith, Albert.** The Dark ages, a brief historical sketch of ecclesiastical history, from the first to the twentieth century, inclusive, together with a chapter on the dream of King Nebuchadnezzar . . . [Chattanooga, Tenn., 1900]
1p.l. [3]–128p. 14cm.
History of the apostasy and the church's restoration by Joseph Smith.
MH, UPB, USIC

Art Publishing Company. *See Ogden City, Utah . . . ; Salt Lake City, Utah. . . .*

206. **Art work of Utah.** Published in twelve parts. Chicago, W. H. Parish Publishing Co., 1896.
12 pts. in 1. photos, plates. 35½cm.
A brief history of the Mormons and plates of Mormon buildings.
CU-B, MH, NN, UHi, ULA, UPB, USIC, UU

207. **Artemus Ward's Mormon entertainment.** Opinions of the New York Press. New York, 1865.
24p.
Eberstadt — *Utah and the Mormons.*

208. **Asbury, Henry.** Reminiscences of Quincy, Illinois, containing historical events, anecdotes, matters concerning old settlers and old times, etc., by Henry Asbury. Quincy, Ill., D. Wilcox & Sons, Printers, 1882.
224p. front. 23½cm.
Cover-title: History of Quincy, old times and old stories.
Sympathetic feeling of local people on the death of Joseph Smith.
CtY, DLC, MB, NjP, UHi, UPB, USIC

209. **Ashley, Francis Busteed.** Mormonism: an exposure of the impositions adopted by the sect called "The Latter-day Saints," by the Rev. F. B. Ashley . . . London, John Hatchard, 1851.
36p. 21cm.
Cover-title.
CtY, MoK, UHi

210. ———. (same) Revised and with editions. London, John Hatchard; Wycombe; W. Butler, 1851.
36p. 21cm.
Cover-title
"Second thousand"
NjP

211. ———. (same) Revised and with additions. London, J. Hatchard . . . 1851.
32p. 21cm.
"Third thousand"
Howes A357, Sabin 2188
CtY, NN

212. **Ashworth, Mary Elizabeth (Shepherd).** History in verse. A family sketch written for the fifty-fifth wedding anniversary of the marriage of William and Mary E. Shepherd Ashworth, May 26, 1928, Provo, Utah. [Provo, 1928]
18p. 19cm.
Includes her religious poem "Shepherds at the front."
Mormon poetry.
UPB, USIC

213. **Assar, Assar Olsson.** Mormonernas Zion; studier och iakttagelser fran Saltsjöstaden, af A. O. Assar. Stockholm, Bohlin & Co. [1911]
60p. illus., ports. 22½cm.
Title in English: Mormon Zion.
DLC, MN, NN

214. **Association of Veteran Artillerymen of the Nauvoo Legion.** Association of Veteran Artillerymen of the Nauvoo Legion. Organized, Salt Lake City, Utah, Sept. 14th, 1897. [Salt Lake City, 1897]
[3]p. 21½cm.
Purpose of the organization, and application for membership.
USIC

215. ———. Muster of old comrades. [Salt Lake City, 1900?]
Broadside. 21½×14cm.
Social gathering for Nauvoo Legion veterans.
USIC

216. **Attwood, R. H.** The Mountain of the Lord's House. [Plano, Ill., True Latter Day Saints' Herald, 1865]
8p. 24cm.
First edition.
MoInRC

217. ———. (same) Rev. ed. [Plano, Ill., before 1876]
8p. 23cm. (No. 1)
Sabin 51190
MoInRC, UPB

218. ———. (same) [Plano, Ill.] Published by the Reorganized Church of Jesus Christ of Latter Day Saints [before 1881]
4p. 23cm. (No. 26)
A reduction of the revised edition, and published without author.
MoInRC, USIC

219. ———. (same) [Plano, Ill.?] Published by the Reorganized Church of Jesus Christ of Latter Day Saints [n.d.]
4p. 23cm. (No. 26)
Variant printing.
USIC

220. ———. (same) Rev. ed. Lamoni, Ia., Reorganized Church of Jesus Christ of Latter Day Saints. [n.d.]
8p. 22cm. (No. 29)
CtY, MoInRC

221. ———. Persecution in Salt Lake City. [Aberdar, Jones a'i Fab., 1865]
4p. 16cm.
Signed: R. H. Attwood.
In English and Welsh. An RLDS Church publication concerning the Utah church.
NN

222. Auchampaugh, Philip Gerald. James Buchanan and his cabinet on the eve of secession. . . . [Lancaster, Pa., The author] 1926.
ix, 224p. 22½cm.
Includes material on the Utah expedition.
DLC, NjP, UHi, ULA, UPB

223. Audouard, Olympe de Jouval. A travers l'Amérique; le Far-West, par Mme. Olympe Audouard. Paris, E. Dentu, 1869.
2p.l., 370p., [1]l. 18cm.
A long discussion of Mormonism.
Title in English: Through America.
Another edition: 1871. DLC
Howes A 384
CtY, CU-B, DLC, UPB

224. Auerbach, Herbert Samuel. Have faith, ye saints. New York, Published by Lyric Music Corporation [c1923]
[3]p. music. 27cm. (Zion Series of Sacred Songs)
Lyric by Bert Auerbach. Music by A. C. Lund and Bert Auerbach.
"Dedicated to President Heber J. Grant."
USIC

225. Auerbach Company, Salt Lake City. An exhibition of the furniture and relics of the Prophet Joseph Smith is being displayed from April 5th to 12th, 1930, at the Auerbach Co., Broadway at State, Salt Lake City, Utah. The Auerbach Company, one of the pioneer institutions of Utah, is exhibiting this unique collection on the occasion of the centenary anniversary of the Church of Jesus Christ of Latter-day Saints. [Salt Lake City, 1930]
[8]p. illus. 23½cm.
CSmH, CU-B, DLC, MH, UHi, UPB

226. ———. Relic collection holds great interest. Pieces from Joseph Smith's home exemplify beauty and simplicity of earlier days. The Herbert S. Auerbach furniture collection . . . [Salt Lake City, n.d.]
Broadside. 56×40½cm.
Text by Levi Edgar Young.
MH

227. ———. A Remarkable exhibition of relics of the Prophet Joseph Smith; on display for a limited time in a reproduction of a room from the Nauvoo Mansion, Nauvoo, Ill., at Auerbach Co. . . . Salt Lake City [n.d.]
[3]p. 17½cm.
Cover-title.
UHi, UPB

228. ———. A Remarkable exhibition of relics of the Prophet Joseph Smith on display from 9 a.m. to 6 p.m. Thursday, Friday and Saturday, October 3, 4, and 5, 1929. Salt Lake City, 1929.
[4]p. 19cm.
USIC

229. Aukema, J. De Verderfelijke leerstellingen der Mormonen en mijn bevinding in Utah. Groningen, Uitgave van: J. Aukema [1924]
15 [1]p. 21cm.
Title in English: The teachings of the Mormons.
USIC

230. The Auricle. Idaho Falls, Idaho, Latter-day Saints Hospital Training School, 1927–
4 v. 28cm.
Yearbook of student nurses of the Latter-day Saints Hospital.
USIC 1927, 1929, 1930.

231. Austin, Emily M. Mormonism; or, Life among the Mormons . . . being an autobiographical sketch, including experience of fourteen years of Mormon life. Madison, Wis., M. J. Cantwell, Book and Job Printers, 1882.
[3]–253p. 17cm.
The early experiences of the Mormons, including the New York period.
Notes and correspondence relating to the author of the work are on deposit in the Manuscripts Division of the Wisconsin State Historical Society.
CSmH, CU-B, MH, NN, UHi, UPB, USIC, WHi

AUSTRAL STAR

232. The Austral Star. Sydney, Australia, Published by the Australian Mission of the Church of Jesus Christ of Latter-day Saints. August 20, 1929–

3 v. monthly. 24cm.

Edited by the missionaries of the Australian Mission.

UPB v. 1–3 inc., USIC comp.

233. An Authentic history of remarkable persons, who have attracted public attention, in various parts of the World; including a full exposure of the iniquities of the pretended Prophet, Joe Smith, and of the seven degrees of the Mormon Temple; also an account of the frauds practised by Matthias the Prophet, and other religious imposters. New York, Wilson and Company, 1849.

[3] 4–64p. ports., plates. 21½cm.

Howes A411, Sabin 50728

CSmH, CtY, UHi, UPB

234. Authenticity of the Book of Mormon. Address delivered over Radio Station KSL Sunday Eveni[ ]ng, October 23, 1927. By Elder James H. Moyle. [Salt Lake City] 1927.

Broadside. 56½×36½cm.

Reprint from The *Deseret News* on Saturday, October 29th.

A correction appears on the reprint of the same speech given by James H. Moyle, Nov. 20, 1927. "Due to lack of information, the Radio Sermon entitled "Authenticity of the Book of Mormon," published Saturday, Oct. 29, was erroneously attributed to Elder James H. Moyle. We are still without information and would kindly ask the writer of this article to send in his name that proper credit may be given him."

USIC

235. L'autorité divine; ordonnaces nulles quand elles sont administrées sans autorité divine. [n.p., n.d.]

16p. 16cm.

Title page missing.

Title in English: Divine authority.

UPB

236. Autumn Leaves, Published for the youth of the Reorganized Church of Jesus Christ of Latter Day Saints. Lamoni, Iowa, Herald Publishing House, January, 1888–December, 1929.

41v. monthly. 28cm.

Title varies: *Autumn leaves*, 1888–1928; *Vision*, a magazine for youth, 1929.

Merged with *Saints' Herald* in 1933.

Chief editor: Marietta Walker.

MoInRC comp.; UPB 1, 5, 6, 7, 36–38; USIC 1, 4, 9, 11–12, 26–28, 30, 32–43; WHi 1–14

237. Awful disclosures of Mormonism and its mysteries. [London?] Printed for the Booksellers [186?]

viii [9]–192p. illus. 17½cm.

Purports to be the experiences of an Englishwoman among the Mormons at Salt Lake City.

A penny dreadful.

CtY, MH, NN, USIC, UU, WHi

238. Ayer, I. Winslow. Life in the wilds of America and wonders of the west, in and beyond the bounds of civilization. Illustrated . . . by I. Winslow Ayer. Grand Rapids, Mich., Published by the Central Publishing Company, 1880.

2p.l. [5]–528p. front. 22cm.

Chap. XIV. A description of Utah and the Mormons, 1877, p. 240–250.

NjP, UPB

THE

BOOK OF MORMON:

AN ACCOUNT WRITTEN BY THE HAND OF MORMON, UPON PLATES TAKEN FROM THE PLATES OF NEPHI.

Wherefore it is an abridgment of the Record of the People of Nephi; and also of the Lamanites; written to the Lamanites, which are a remnant of the House of Israel; and also to Jew and Gentile; written by way of commandment, and also by the spirit of Prophesy and of Revelation. Written, and sealed up, and hid up unto the LORD, that they might not be destroyed; to come forth by the gift and power of GOD unto the interpretation thereof; sealed by the hand of Moroni, and hid up unto the LORD, to come forth in due time by the way of Gentile; the interpretation thereof by the gift of GOD; an abridgment taken from the Book of Ether.

Also, which is a Record of the People of Jared, which were scattered at the time the LORD confounded the language of the people when they were building a tower to get to Heaven: which is to shew unto the remnant of the House of Israel how great things the LORD hath done for their fathers; and that they may know the covenants of the LORD, that they are not cast off forever; and also to the convincing of the Jew and Gentile that JESUS is the CHRIST, the ETERNAL GOD, manifesting Himself unto all nations. And now if there be fault, it be the mistake of men; wherefore condemn not the things of GOD, that ye may be found spotless at the judgment seat of CHRIST.

BY JOSEPH SMITH, JUNIOR,

AUTHOR AND PROPRIETOR.

PALMYRA:

PRINTED BY E. B. GRANDIN, FOR THE AUTHOR.

1830.

Item 595. The foundation of the Mormon religion, published by the editor of the Palmyra *Wayne Sentinel* between August 1829 and March 1830. From the University of Utah collection.

239. B., H. Diary during a tour round the world: Written and posted for my wife during absence: By H. B. Torquay, Printed at the "Directory" Office [1874?]
4p.l. [11]–205p. fold. maps. 22cm.
Preface dated: Fontainebleau, Torquay.
A brief statement concerning Mormonism. He visits a meeting in Salt Lake City and listens to Mr. Pratt preach "to a congregation of as ignorant, untaught looking vacant starers as any lunatic asylum."
USIC

240. Babbitt, Almon W. To the citizens of Pottawotamie County, Iowa. [St. Louis? 1850]
Broadside. 26½×21cm.
Concerning a libelous letter over the signature of Daniel F. Miller printed in the *Frontier Guardian*. Signed: St. Louis. August 24th, 1850.
USIC

241. Babbitt, Charles Henry. Early days at Council Bluffs, by Charles H. Babbitt . . . Washington, D.C., Press of B. S. Adams, 1916.
1p.l. [3]–96p. illus., maps. 24cm.
The Mormon era, p. 77–96.
Howes B4
CSmH, CtY, CU, DLC, NjP, UHi, UPB, USIC, UU

242. Bacheler, Origen. Mormonism exposed, internally and externally. By Origen Bacheler. New York, 1838.
3–48p. 1 plate. 17cm.
A work against the Book of Mormon written to combat the missionary work of Parley P. Pratt.
Howes B13, Sabin 2598
CtY, DLC, MH, MoK, NN, USIC, UU, WHi

Backenstos, Jacob B. Proclamations. *See Hancock Co., Ill. Sheriff.*

243. Badger, Joseph E. Sweet William the trapper detective; or, the chief of the crimson clan. New York, Beadle & Adams, 1882.
29p. 21½cm. [Beadle's Dime Library. January 25, 1882. V. 14, #170)
The Prophet, Joseph Smith, in Misouri, and a hooded vigilance committee.
NN

244. Bailey, Florence Augusta (Merriam). My Summer in a Mormon village. Boston and New York, Houghton, Mifflin and Company, 1894.
2p.l., 171p. front. 18cm.
Visited Utah after 1890.
CSmH, CtY, CU–B, DLC, MH, NjP, NN, UHi, UPB, USl, UU, WHi

245. ———. (same) Boston and New York, Houghton, Mifflin and Company, 1899 [c1894]
2p.l., 171p. front. 18cm.
USIC, UU

246. Bailey, Melville Knox. The Right Reverend Daniel Sylvester Tuttle, Missionary Bishop of Montana, Idaho, and Utah, Missionary Bishop of Utah, Bishop of Missouri, and presiding Bishop of the American Church. Hartford, Conn., Church Missions Publ. Co., 1923.
39p., illus., plates. 23cm. ("Soldier and Servant series," publication No. 133, Nov. 1923)
Brief statement concerning his missionary efforts among the Mormons. Civilly treated by Brigham Young and aided in missionary work.
NN, UU

247. Bailey, Washington. A trip to California in 1853 by Washington Bailey. Recollections of a gold seeking trip by ox train across the plains and mountains by an old Illinois pioneer. [Leroy, Ill.] Leroy Journal Printing Co., 1915.
1p.l., 50 p. port. 23cm.
He takes the upper route to avoid being killed by Danites and Brigham Young.
Reference to Mormons at Cainsville, p. 7.
Howes B35
CU–B, DLC, ICN, NjP, UPB

248. Bailey, William Francis. The story of the first trans-continental railroad; its projectors, construction and history . . . Compiled . . . by W. F. Bailey. [Fair Oaks, Cal.] W. F. Bailey [c1906]
164p. 20cm.
Material on the Mormons under "Utah Railroad."
CSmH, CU, DLC, ICJ, UHi

249. Bair, Fred. Visits among the Mormons. Gerard, Kan., Haldeman — Julius Publications [c1928]
32p. 13cm. (Little blue books, 1270)
Contains: Visits among the Mormons, by Fred Bair; Ebenezer Hansen, Polygamist and patriarch, by Don Lewis; An intellectual Christian, by Gaylord DuBois.
USIC, WHi

250. Baird, Gertrude Luck. Genealogisches Ausgebenbuch und die Deutschen Familiennamen. Aus dem Englischen üebersetzt von Mrs. Gertrude L. Baird. [n.p., 1917?]
92p. 21cm.
Translated for the German Mission.
Title in English: Geneological handbook and German family names.
USIC

251. Baird, Robert. Religion in the United States of America. Or, an account of the origin, progress, relations to the state, and present condition of the evangelical churches in the United States. With notices of unevangelical denominations. By the Rev. Robert Baird . . . Glasgow and Edinburgh, Blackie and Son; [etc., etc.] 1844.
xix [1] 736p. 2 maps (incl. front.) 24cm.
Section on Mormons, or Latter-day Saints, p. 647–649.

Translated under title: Kerkelijke geschiedenis, kerkelijke statistiek en godsdienstig le ven der Vereenigde Staten van Noord-America. Schoonhoven, S. E. van Nooten, 1846–49. CU–B, DLC
Sabin 2792.
CtY, DLC, NN, USlC, UU

252. ———. (same, under title) Religion in America; or, an account of the origin, progress, relation to the state, and present condition of the evangelical churches in the United States. With notices of the unevangelical denominations by Robert Baird. New York, Published by Harper & Brothers, No. 82 Cliff-street, 1845.
xii [9]–343p. 24cm.
Mormons, p. 285–6.
Other editions: 1856. CtY, CU–B, DLC, NN, NjP, ULA; 1861. USlC
UPB, USl

253. ———. State and prospects of religion in America; being a report made at the conference of the evangelical alliance, in Paris, August 25th, 1855. New-York, Robert Carter & Brothers, 1856.
58p. 21cm.
Mormonism a desperate wickedness, p. 41–42.
NjP, USlC

254. Baker, Amenzo White. The Baker genealogy and collateral branches. By Amenzo White Baker of Mendon, Utah. Revised and published by Merlin J. Stone. Ogden, Utah, A. T. Hestmark Printer [1910?]
3p.l., 9–226p. 26cm.
Biographies of many Utah families, with a great deal of historical material.
USlC

255. Baker, Harry Edgar. The word of the Lord to his church in the wilderness; and to all the nations of the gentiles; being the words of Jesus Christ, the Son of God, to the sheep of Israel, who are not in the fold; and to all the present generation of the earth. Chicago, R. C. Baker, Publisher [1917]
4p.l. [9]–62p. 19½cm.
Publication of his revelations in 1916.
Revelations for the Church of Christ.
DLC, UPB, USlC

256. ———. The Word of the Lord to his church of the latter-days and to all the nations of the gentiles; being the words of Jesus Christ, the Son of God to the scattered sheep of the Houes of Israel in all the world. Chicago, R. C. Baker [c1918]
3p.l., 9–68p. 19½cm.
On cover: "The word of the Lord, second message."
UPB, USlC

257. Baker, Hozial H. Overland journey to Carson Valley, Utah; through Kansas, Nebraska and Utah; also, return trip from San Francisco to Seneca Falls, via the Isthmus. Seneca Falls, N.Y., Published by F. M. Baker, 1861.
[3]–38p. illus., port. 20½cm.
Added engraved title page.
Traveled via Great Salt Lake City in 1859.
Howes B49, W–C 367a
CtY, ICN

258. Baker, James L. Men and things; or, Short essays on various subjects, including free trade. By James L. Baker. Boston, Crosby, Nichols and Company, 1858.
3p.l. [7]–287p. 20cm.
"The Mormons," p. 131–134. Mormonism is no more strange than Shakerism, nor is it hardly more disgusting."
USlC, UU

259. Baldwin, Nathaniel. Law of tithing; the law of consecration; a discussion with scriptural references. [Salt Lake City? 1921?]
52p. 15cm.
IWW, UHi, USlC, UU

260. ———. Spirit of God, the Holy Ghost. A discussion with scriptural references. [n.p. n.d.]
42p. 16½cm.
USlC

261. ———. Times of the Gentiles; fulness of the Gentiles; a discussion with scriptural references by Nathaniel Baldwin. Salt Lake City, Paragon Printing Co. [1917?]
42p. 15cm.
"Written about May, 1917."
UHi, USlC, UU

262. Baldwin, Thomas. . . . A new and complete gazatteer of the United States; giving a full and comprehensive review of the present condition, industry, and resources of the American confederacy, embracing also, important topographical, statistical, and historical information, from recent and original sources; together with the results of the census of 1850, and population and statistics in many cases to 1853 by Thomas Baldwin and J. Thomas. Philadelphia, Lippincott, Grambo & Co., 1854.
1344p. map. 22½cm.
Brief material on the Mormons.
CU, UHi, ULA

263. Ball, Nicholas. The pioneers of '49. A history of the excursion of the Society of California Pioneers of New England from Boston to the leading cities of the Golden States, April 10–May 7, 1890. With reminiscences and descriptions by Nicholas Ball. . . . Illustrated with over one hundred fine engravings. Boston, Lee and Shepard, 1891.
xv [1]–288p. illus., plates, ports. 24cm.
Description of Salt Lake City with historical notes and a resumé of Mormon doctrine.
Howes B67
CU–B, DLC, NjP, ULA, UPB

BALLANTINE, W.

264. Ballantine, William. The old world and the new, by Mr. Serjeant Ballantine, being a continuation of his "Experiences." London, R. Bentley & Son, 1884.
xvi, 259p. port. 22½cm.
Utah and the Mormons, p. 134–168.
CtY, CU–B, DLC, MH, NN, USIC, UU

265. Ballantyne, Richard. Dialogue between A. and B. on polygamy. By Elder R. Ballantyne. [Madras, Hindostan, Printed at the Oriental Press, 1854]
8p. 21cm.
UPB, USIC

266. ———. A reply to a tract written by the Rev. J. Richards, M. A., giving a more correct answer to the question "What is Mormonism?" — Purporting to be answered by him. By Richard Ballantyne, Elder in the Church of Jesus Christ of Latter-day Saints. [Madras, S. Bowie, Printer, 1854?]
8p. 21cm.
UPB, USIC

267. ———. A Reply to the second tract written by the Rev. J. Richards, giving a more correct answer to the question "What is Mormonism?" purporting to be answered by him, by Richard Ballantyne, Elder in the Church of Jesus Christ of Latter-day Saints. Containing also, Three lectures, on the character, attributes, and perfections of the Diety. Madras, Printed by S. Bowie [1854]
18p. 21cm.
UPB, USIC

268. Ballard, Frank. Why not Mormonism. By Frank Ballard. London, Epworth Press [1922]
57p. 19cm.
Cover: Why not Mormonism. The origin of Mormonism. The development of Mormonism. Present position and attitude of Mormonism. Present-day social and Christian attitude.
MH, NN, USIC, UU

269. Ballard, Mattie J. The trail and trails of the Mormon pioneers. A senaria [sic] by Mattie J. Ballard and Florinda Gardner. [n.p.] c1923.
21p. 22cm.
Cover-title.
Copyright by Florinda Gardner.
DLC

270. Ballard, Melvin Joseph. Bulletin describing relationship of Relief Society organization to women's activities throughout the regions and stakes in connection with the Church Security Program, by Melvin J. Ballard and Louise Y. Robison. [Salt Lake City, ca. 1930]
3p. 28cm.
USIC

271. ———. "Temple work in connection with church security program." [Salt Lake City, Church of Jesus Christ of Latter-day Saints, 193–]
[4]p. 19cm.
Caption-title.
USIC

272. ———. Three degrees of glory; a discourse delivered in the Ogden Tabernacle, September 22, 1922. [Independence, Mo., Published by the Missions of the Church of Jesus Christ of Latter-day Saints, 1922]
32p. 17½cm.
At head of title: Discourse.
Discourse delivered September 22, 1922.
NN, ULA, UPB, USIC

273. ———. (same) Salt Lake City, Deseret Book Co. [n.d.]
31 [1]p. 18cm.
UPB

274. ———. (same) [Salt Lake City, Magazine Printing, n.d.]
42p. 15½cm.
UHi

275. ———. (same) [Ogden?] 1922.
45 [1]p. 15½cm.
"Published under the direction of Mount Ogden State Genealogical Committee."
CU–B, USI, UU

276. ———. (same) [n.d., c1926]
45 [1]p. 15½cm.
Distributed by Neuteboom Printing Co., Ogden, Utah.
UPB

277. ———. (same) [Ogden, Neuteboom Printing, c1926]
48p. 15cm.
Cover-title.
USIC

278. Ballou, Maturin Murray. Due west, or round the world in ten months, by Maturin Murray Ballou . . . Boston, Houghton, Mifflin and Co., 1884.
2p.l., vii–xii, 387p. 20cm.
Visited Salt Lake in 1882; remarks on " 'celestial marriage' humbug," p. 5–7.
Other editions: 6th ed. 1888. USIC, UPB; 7th ed. 1890. UU; 11th ed. 1895. USIC
CU–B, DLC

279. ———. Foot-prints of travel; or, Journeyings in many lands . . . Boston, Ginn & Company, 1889.
x, 391p. illus., port. 19cm.
Brief notes on visit to Salt Lake, with reference to Mormons.
Another edition: 1896. UPB
CU–B, UHi

BANCROFT, H. H.

280. Balmer, Edwin. Resurrection rock by Edwin Balmer, with frontispiece by Anton Otto Fischer. Boston, Little, Brown, and Company, 1920.
3p.l., 383p. plate. 19½cm.
Fiction; a section concerns a girl whose father belonged to the Strang group, p. 354–363.
USlC

280a. Bancroft, Hubert Howe. Bancroft's guide for travelers by railway, stage, and steam navigation in the Pacific States . . . San Francisco, H. H. Bancroft & Co., 1869.
144p. illus. 17cm.
Salt Lake City and Mormons, p. 26, 71, 109, 113.
USlC

281. ———. Chronicles of the builders of the commonwealth; historical character study. By Hubert Howe Bancroft . . . San Francisco, The History Company, 1891–92.
7v. fronts., ports. 23cm.
Includes references to Utah, Salt Lake City, Mormons and Mormonism, the Mormon Battalion, Mormon Station in Nevada, Brigham Young, Parley P. Pratt, and Sam Brannan. It also includes William T. Coleman's impressions of Salt Lake City in 1849, v. 1, p. 312–313.
CU–B

282. ———. . . . History of Arizona and New Mexico, 1530–1888. San Francisco, The History Company, 1889.
xxxviii, 820p. illus., maps. 24cm. (The Works of Hubert Howe Bancroft, V. 17)
Mormon battalion and Mormon colonization in Arizona and New Mexico.
Another edition: 1890. DLC.
Bancroft library has a facsimile of an 1889 edition published coincident to 50th anniversary of New Mexico and Arizona.
CU–B, NjP, UHi, ULA, UPB

283. ———. History of California, 1552–[1890] San Francisco, The History Co., 1884–1890.
7v. illus., maps. (The Works of Hubert Howe Bancroft. V. 18–24) 23½cm.
Includes a history of Mormonism in California.
CSmH, CU–B, DLC, NjP, NN, UHi, ULA, UPB, USlC

284. ———. History of Nevada, Colorado, and Wyoming, 1540–1888. San Francisco, The History Company, 1890.
xxxii, 828p. illus., maps. 23½cm. (The Works of Hubert Howe Bancroft. V. 25)
Mormon colonization in Nevada.
Another edition: Published separately. DLC
CU, DLC, NjP, ULA, UPB

285. ———. *History of Utah.* [San Francisco, The History Company, 1889]
22p. 21cm.
Review of the *History of Utah* by Hubert H. Bancroft from the *New York Tribune,* November 3, 1889.
NjP, USlC

286. ———. . . . History of Utah. 1540–1886. San Francisco, The History Company, 1889.
xlvii, 808p. illus., maps. 23½cm. (The Works of Hubert Howe Bancroft. V. 26)
According to C. A. Morris in v. 4 of the *Oregon Historical Society Quarterly,* most of this was written by Alfred Bates.
Another edition: Variant title page. UHi
CU, CU–B, DLC, MoInRC, NjP, NN, UHi, UPB, USl, USlC

287. ———. History of Utah, by Hubert Howe Bancroft. 1540–1887. San Francisco, The History Company, Publishers, 1890.
1p.l., xlvii, 808p. plates (some col.) ports, maps. 24cm.
Added engraved title-page.
Some copies issued without plates, or added t.p. Other variants, such as a list of Bancroft's works, etc.
CSmH, CU–B, DLC, MH, NN, ULA, UPB, USlC, UU

288. ———. (same) San Francisco, The History Company, Publishers, 1891.
xlvii, 808p. illus., ports., plates. 24cm.
MH, NN, UHi

289. ———. . . . History of Washington, Idaho and Montana, 1845–1889. San Francisco, The History Company, 1890.
xxvi, 836p. illus., maps. 23½cm. (The Works of Hubert Howe Bancroft. V. 31)
Written by Mrs. Frances Fuller Victor, according to W. A. Morris. Cf. *Quarterly of the Oregon Historical Society,* V. 4, p. 324–331.
Mormons in Idaho, 402–03, 548–49; legislation against the Mormons in Idaho, p. 585–87.
CU–B, DLC, UPB, USlC

290. ———. . . . Literary industries. San Francisco, The History Company, 1890.
vii, 808p. port. 23½cm. (The Works of Hubert Howe Bancroft. V. 39)
Published also as v.34 of his *History of the Pacific states of North America.*
Describes his collection of material for his *History of Utah.* Quotes many letters between H. H. Bancroft and church officials, p. 631–40, 759–61.
Other editions: 1891. CU–B, NN, UU; New York, Harper & Bros., 1891. CU–B, UU
CSmH, CU–B, DLC, NjP, UHi, UPB

291. ———. The Native races of the Pacific states of North America. By Hubert Howe Bancroft . . . New York, D. Appleton and Company, 1874–75.
5v. illus., fold. maps, fold. tab. 24cm.
According to W. A. Morris, this work was written by H. L. Oak, T. A. Harcourt, Albert Goldschmidt, W. M. Fisher and William Nemos. Cf. *Oregon Historical Society Quarterly,* V. 4, p. 301–310
Also published in the Works of Hubert Howe Bancroft. V. 1–5. DLC, UPB, USlC
"Origin of the Americans [Indians]" according to Mormon doctrine, V. 5, p. 96–102.
CU–B, UPB

292. ———. . . . Popular tribunals . . . San Francisco, The History Company, 1887.
2v. illus., facsims., fold. plan. 24cm. (The Works of Hubert Howe Bancroft. V. 36–37)
Brief mention of early Mormon justice.
CU–B, DLC, UPB, USIC

293. ———. Retrospection, political and personal. New York, The Bancroft Company, 1912.
x, 562p. 20½cm.
Chapter on Utopian dreams. Tells of the early persecutions of the Mormons: "Like the Chinese, they were temperate, kept to themselves, worked hard, and were thrifty and honest, and so were hated by the lazy and licentious. This was the real cause of their offending, as it was with the Chinese."
CU–B, NjP, UU

294. The Banyan. Provo [Published by the Associated Students at Brigham Young University, 1909–1930.
20v. yearly. 24×16–28cm.
None published in 1910. Published in 1913 under title BYUtah.
UPB, USIC

Baptism for remission of sins. *See Bliss, Charles H.*

295. Baptism, how and by whom administered. [Liverpool, Printed at the Millennial Star Office, 189–?]
[2]p. 21cm.
Caption-title.
CU–B, UPB, USIC

296. ———. (same) [Independence, Mo., Published by the Missions of the Church of Jesus Christ of Latter-day Saints. Press of Zions' Printing and Publishing Co., n.d.]
4p. 16cm.
Published with and without pagination.
NN, UPB, USIC

297. Baptist Congress. Fourth annual Session of the Baptist Congress for the discussion of current questions held at Calvary Baptist Church, New York City, November 10, 11, and 12, 1885. New-York, The Century Co., 1886.
1p.l., 15–22p. 21½cm.
The Mormon questions, p. 15–22p.
USIC

298. Barber, John Warner. All the western states and territories, from the Alleghanies to the Pacific, and from the lakes to the gulf, containing their history from the earliest times . . . the whole being illustrated by 240 engravings . . . principally from drawings taken on the spot by the authors. By John W. Barber . . . and Henry Howe . . . Cincinnati, O., Howe's Subscription Book Concern, 1867.
6, vii–xi [1] [13]–704p. illus., port., map. 22½cm.
A reissue, with some changes, of a portion of their earlier work, *Our whole country.*
A sketch on Mormonism by John Cradlebaugh.
Another edition: 1868. NjP
CU–B, DLC, NN, UHi, UPB, WHi

299. ———. Historical collections of the State of New York; containing a general collection of the most interesting facts, traditions, biographical sketches, anecdotes, &c. relating to its history and antiquities, with geographical descriptions of every township in the state. Illustrated by 230 engravings. By John W. Barber . . . and Henry Howe . . . New York, Published for the authors by S. Tuttle, 1841.
[1–3]4–608p. illus., map. 24cm.
The founding of Mormonism in the History of Wayne Co., p. 396–398.
Other editions: 1842. CtY, DLC, IaH, ULA; 1845. UHi; 1846. DLC, PHi; New York, Clark, Austin & Co., 1851. DLC, NjP
CU, DLC, UHi, ULA, UPB, USIC

299a. ———. The loyal west in the times of the rebellion; also, before and since: being an encyclopedia and panorama of the western states, pacific states and territories of the Union. Historical, geographical, and pictorial. Illustrated by more than two hundred engravings, . . . principally from drawings taken on the spot by the author. By John W. Barber, . . . and Henry Howe, . . . Cincinnati, Published by F. A. Howe, successor of Henry Howe, 1865.
764p. 22½cm.
Utah Territory p. [727]–736.
NjP

300. ———. Our whole country; or, The past and present of the United States, historical and descriptive. In two volumes, containing the general and local histories and descriptions of each of the states, territories, cities, and towns of the Union; also biographical sketches of distinguished persons . . . Illustrated by six hundred engravings . . . almost wholly from drawings taken on the spot by the authors, the entire work being on their part the result of over 16,000 miles of travel and four years of labor. By John Warner Barber . . . and Henry Howe . . . Cincinnati, H. Howe, 1861.
2v. illus., ports., maps, facsim. 24cm.
Description of Utah which includes John Cradlebaugh's sketch of the Mormons.
CU, DLC, UHi

301. Barclay, James W. Mormonism exposed. The other side. An English view of the case. By James W. Barclay, esq. . . . [Salt Lake City?] 1884.
[1–5] 6–30p. 21½cm.
Originally published in "Nineteenth century," a magazine published in London, England, V.15 under title: A new view of Mormonism.
CSmH, CU–B, ICN, MH, NN, UHi, ULA, USI, USIC, UU, WHi

301a. Bard, Richard. Mormonism pulled down: the Kingdom of Christ set up: and the Pope dethroned; by Richard Bard, M.C.C., Author of "An Exegetical Work on Prophecy." Omaha, Nebraska, Omaha Herald Steam Printing Establishment, 1870.
24p. 15cm.
UPB

302. Barfoot, Joseph L. Handbook guide to the Salt Lake Museum (established 1869) opposite the Tabernacle gates, No. 1242 South Temple Street, Salt Lake City, Utah. [Salt Lake City] Juvenile Instructor Print. [1881]
8p. 14cm.
Relics of Mormonism.
CU–B, UPB

303. Barkman, Antony. To the public, I was arrested by the Sheriff of Hancock . . . Nauvoo, 1845.
Broadside. 25×10cm.
Signed: Sept. 26, 1845.
Humane treatment by the law in Nauvoo.
UPB, USIC

304. Barnard, Helen M. The Chorpenning claim. [n.p., M'Intosh, Printer, n.d.]
22p. 23cm.
Cover-title.
Mail contracts to Utah, 1851–1857.
CU–B

305. Barneby, William Henry. Life and labour in the far, far west being notes of a tour in the western states, British Columbia, Manitoba, and the Northwest Territory. By W. Henry Barneby . . . London, New York [etc.] Cassell & Company, 1884.
xvi, 432p. 21½cm.
"Through Mormonland to San Francisco," p. 30–35.
Another edition: 2d ed., London, 1884. USIC
CU–B, DLC, NjP, NN, UHi, USIC, UU

306. Barnes, Charles J. The library of Charles J. Barnes . . . New York, The Anderson Galleries, 1920.
v. facsims. 23cm.
Pt.1. sale no. 1519. Sold Oct. 13–14, 1920.
Contents: Pt. 1. Americana. Section on Mormonism, p. 37–46. Sale prices.
CU–B

307. Barnes, Demas. From the Atlantic to the Pacific, overland. A series of letters by Demas Barnes, describing a trip from New York . . . to San Francisco, thence home, by Acapulco, and the Isthmus of Panama. New York, D. Van Nostrand, 1866.
[1–5] 6–136. port. 19½cm.
Polygamy and Brigham Young.
Howes B153
CSmH, DLC, ICN, NjP, NN, UHi, ULA, USIC, UU

308. Barnes, Lorenzo D. The bold pilgrim; written mostly on board the ship "Southerner," by Lorenzo D. Barnes, Elder of the Church of Jesus Christ of Latter-day Saints: While on his voyage from New York to England, on a mission. January, 1842. [Liverpool? 1842?]
Broadside. 37×25cm.
Mormon poetry.
USIC

309. ———. A key to the bible. [n.p. 1841?]
12p. 15 cm.
Another edition of this work was revised by Daniel Shearer and published under his name as author ca. 1844.
CU–B

310. ———. (same, under title) References; to prove the gospel in its fulness; the ushering in the dispensation of the fulness of times and the latter-day glory. [n.p., 1841]
8p. 12½ cm.
Caption-title.
Byrd 603
CtY, CU–B, MH, USI

311. ———. (same, under title) Very important references, to prove the religion and principles of the Latter-day Saints to be true. By Lorenzo D. Barnes. Bradford, Yorkshire: Printed by B. Walker, Westgate, 1842.
8p. 11cm.
CtY

312. ———. (same) Norwich, Printed by A. Charlwood, 1848.
8p. 12cm.
CU–B

313. Barnes, Rhoda Caroline Rice. Leonard G. Rice [n.p., n.d.]
41p. 26cm.
Mormon biography.
USIC

314. Barney, Elvira (Stevens). The Stevens genealogy; embracing branches of the family descended from Puritan ancestry, New England families not traceable to Puritan ancestry . . . from 1650 to the present time of the author, Dr. Elvira Stevens Barney. Salt Lake City, Skelton Publishing Co., 1907.
xiii [14]–319p. illus., plates, ports. 24cm.
Stevens family in Utah and church history in detail.
UHi, UPB, USIC, UU

315. Barns, Chancy Rufus, *editor.* The commonwealth of Missouri; a centennial record . . . Ed. by C. R. Barns. St. Louis, Bryan, Brand & Co., 1877.
xxiv, 936p. illus., plates, 48 ports. 25½cm.
Chapter 21 entitled: "The Mormons in Missouri."
DLC, NjP, NN, UHi, USIC

BARR, W. A.

316. Barr, William A. A Book entitled, Who holds the key or secret to the Church of Jesus Christ and how the mark or sign of circumcision is developed in the flesh and a name which no man knoweth except they who receive it in effect. [Quincy, Ill.? 1907?]
20p. 18½cm.
A strange work on a Mormon doctrinal subject.
USIC

317. ———. Luke 12th chapter and 2nd verse. [Quincy, Ill., 1911]
Broadside. 21½×13cm.
A letter to Joseph F. Smith.
USIC

318. Barrows, John Henry. Christian education for the Mormons. [Colorado Springs? 1878?]
[4]p. illus., map. 26cm.
Caption-title.
At head of title: Colorado College.
"From a Prelude to the 118th Lecture in the Monday Lectureship, Boston Advertiser Report, December 25, 1878."
CU–B, UPB

319. Barrows, Walter Manning. How shall the Mormon question be settled? [Chicago, 1881]
[8]p. 23cm.
"From an address at the Home Missionary Anniversary in Chicago, June 8, 1881."
CtY, CU–B, ICN, MH, NN, USl

320. ———. The Mormon problem. Boston, Home Missionary, 1878.
[1–7] 8–16. illus., map. 23½cm.
At head of title: The New West.
"Reprint from the *Home Missionary* of December, 1878."
CSmH, CtY, USIC, WHi

321. Barrows, William. An appeal to the Christian women in America. In behalf of the Mormon and the Mexican woman, and their children. [n.p., 1879]
4p. 23cm.
CSmH, MH

Bartlett, A. Jennie. Elder Northfields' home.
See Switzer, Jennie (Bartlett)

322. Bartlett, Daniel Henry Charles. The Mormons or Latter-day Saints, their genesis, teachings, and present activities. By Rev. Daniel H. C. Bartlett . . . London, Chas. J. Thynne . . . [1911?]
vi [7]–32p. 17½cm. (Church of England manuals. No. 21)
MH, USl, USIC

323. ———. The Mormons; or, Latter-day Saints. Whence came they? With appendices on Mormon doctrines, claims, contentions, and finance, forming suggestions to Christian workers as to the refutation of plausible Mormon tracts, and an introduction by the Right Rev. the Lord Bishop of Liverpool. London, James Nisbet & Co., Ltd., 1911.
xi, 90p. 20cm.
MH, NjP, NN, UHi, ULA, UPB, USl, USIC, UU

324. Bartlett, Ichabod S. *editor.* History of Wyoming. I. S. Bartlett, ed. . . . Chicago, The S. J. Clarke Publishing Company, 1918.
3v. illus., ports., col. front. 27½cm.
V. 1, Chapter 4 "Mormons & Argonauts," p. 124–131, 277, 311, 326. Mormon church history, particularly the trek across Wyoming.
CU–B, DLC, ICJ, NjP, UPB, WaU

325. Bartlett, John Russell. Personal narrative of explorations and incidents in Texas, New Mexico, California, Sonora, and Chihuahua, connected with the United States and Mexican Boundary Commission, during the years 1850, '51, '52, and '53. By John Russell Bartlett . . . New York, D. Appleton & Co., 1854.
2v. fold. fronts., illus., plates. 23cm.
Visited Lyman Wight's colony at Zodiac, Texas, Oct. 14, 1850, v. 1, p. 58–59; survivors of Oatman massacre, v. 1, p. 202–204; San Bernardino, v. 2, p. 118–119; other Mormons (Brewsterites) at Tubac, v. 2, p. 304–305.
W–C 234.
CU–B, DLC

326. Bartlett, S. C. Historical sketch of Hawaiian Mission, and the missions to Micronesia and the Marquesas Islands. By Prof. S. C. Bartlett, D. D. Boston, American Board of Commissioners for Foreign Missions, 1869.
1p.l. [3]–32p. map on end paper. 17cm.
"The Mormons," p. 21. Paragraph on Mormon activities, 1859–69.
Another edition: 1871. NjPT
NN, USIC

327. Bashford, Herbert. A man unafraid; the story of John Charles Frémont, by Herbert Bashford and Harr Wagner. San Francisco, Calif., Harr Wagner Publishing Company [c1927]
5p.l., 406p. front., col. mounted illus., plates, ports. 24cm.
References on the Mormons, p. 153, 355–358.
CU–B, DLC, USIC

328. Baskin, Robert Newton. Argument against the admission of Utah. By R. N. Baskin. And the recent message of Governor West to the Utah legislature. Washington, Judd & Detweiler, 1888.
22p. 22cm.
Caption-title: Utah statehood.
The author was chief justice of the Supreme Court of Utah.
ICN, MH, NN, USl, USIC

329. ———. House of Representatives. Forty-fourth Congress. First session. Committee on Elections. Papers in the case of Baskin v. Cannon. Contest for the seat as delegate from Utah Territory. Papers for the contestant. Robert N. Baskin . . . Washington, R. O. Polkinhorn, Printer [1877]
19p. 23½cm.
Cover-title.
DLC, NN, ULA, UPB

330. ———. Reminiscences of early Utah, by R. N. Baskin . . . [Salt Lake City, Tribune-reporter Printer Co.] c1914.
3p.l., 5–252p. illus., ports. 23½cm.
Howes B226
CSmH, CtY, CU–B, DLC, ICN, NjP, UHi, USIC, UU, WHi

331. ———. Reply by R. N. Baskin to certain statements, by O. F. Whitney in his history of Utah, published in 1916. [Salt Lake City, Lakeside Ptg. Co., 1916?]
29p. 3 ports. 23cm.
Cover-title.
CSmH, DLC, MH, NN, UHi, USI, USIC

332. Bateman, Newton, *editor.* Historical encyclopedia of Illinois, edited by Newton Bateman, Ll.D., Paul Selby, A.M., and History of Jo Daviess County, edited by Hon. William Spensby. Illustrated. Chicago, Munsell Publishing Company, Publishers, 1904.
2p.l., 705p. illus., ports., plates, maps (part col.) 27cm.
Mormon items under Illinois, Mormons, Joseph Smith, and Brigham Young.
USIC

333. ———. Historical encyclopedia of Illinois. Edited by Newton Bateman, Ll.D., Paul Selby, A.M., J. Seymour Currey, and history of Hancock County, edited by Charles J. Scofield. Chicago, Munsell Publishing Company, 1921.
2v. (1437p.) 28½cm.
Vol. 2. Capt. X. "Mormon history in Hancock County," based on Thomas Gregg's *Prophet of Palmyra.*
NjP, UHi, UL, USIC

Bates, Alfred. *See Bancroft, Hubert Howe. History of Utah.*

334. Bates, Emily Katharine. A year in the great republic, by E. Catherine Bates . . . London, Ward & Downey, 1887.
2v. 19cm.
Includes a description of Salt Lake City; interviews with Mormons and a description of Mormonism.
DLC, MiU, NjP, NN, UHi, USIC

335. Bates, J. H. Notes of a tour in Mexico and California by J. H. Bates. Printed for private distribution. New York, Burr Printing House, 1887.
viii, 167p. 17½cm.
Salt Lake City and the Mormons, p. 141–158.
UHi

336. Bauditz, Sophus. Udvalgte noveller . . . Kobenhavn, 1898.
317p.
Title in English: Selected short stories. Includes a story on Mormonism.
Schmidt.

337. Baumann, F. Mormonernes Fâerd i Tanderup sogn. Fremstillet af F. Baumen Stedets praest. Odense, Forlagt af den Hempelske Boghandel, 1854.
1p.l., 24p. 19cm.
Title in English: Mormon travels in the Tanderup Parish.
CtY, NN, UPB, USIC

338. Bayard, Samuel John. The life of George Dashiell Bayard, late captain U.S.A., and brigadier-general of volunteers, killed in the battle of Fredericksburg, December, 1862. By Samuel J. Bayard. New York, G. P. Putman's Sons, 1874.
iv [11]–337p. illus., plates, port., fold. map. 19cm.
Biography of an army officer who was with the Utah expedition.
Howes B258
CSmH, DLC, NjP

339. Bays, Davis H. The doctrines and dogmas of Mormonism examined and refuted, by Elder Davis H. Bays. St. Louis, Christian Publishing Company, 1897.
[8]–459p. illus., ports., facsim. 20cm.
CSmH, CU–B, DLC, MH, NjP, NN, UHi, UPB, USIC, UU, WHi

340. ———. (same) St. Louis, Christian Publishing Company [c1897]
[8]–459p. illus., ports, facsim. 20cm.
Variant printing with no date on title page.
ULA, USIC

341. Bays, Joseph. The "Blood of Christ," or the Mormon Baptist water; by Joseph Bays, Chatteris, Isle of Ely . . . Chatteris: J. Southwell, Printer, &c., 1849.
11p. 17cm.
Caption-title: Mormonism. February 24th, 1849. "The present state of the Latter-day Saints."
USIC

342. The Beacon. Snowflake, Arizona, Published by Snowflake Seminary, 1925?–
1v. 21cm.
USIC No. 11. May 21, 1926.

BEADLE, J. H.

343. **Beadle, John Hanson.** The history of Mormonism; its rise, progress, present condition and mysteries: being an exposé of the secret rites and ceremonies of the Latter-day Saints; with a full and authentic account of polygamy and the Mormon sect from its origin to the present time. Toronto, Ont., A. H. Hovey, 1873.
xviii, 415p. illus. 20½cm.
UHi

344. ———. Life in Utah; or, The mysteries and crimes of Mormonism. Being an exposé of the secret rites and ceremonies of the Latter-day Saints, with a full and authentic history of polygamy and the Mormon sect from its origin to the present time. By J. H. Beadle . . . Philadelphia, Pa., Chicago, Ill.; Cincinnati, Ohio; St. Louis, Mo.; Atlanta, Ga., National Publishing Company [1870]
540p. illus., plates, ports., facsims., fold. map. 22½cm.
CtY, CU–B, DLC, ICN, MH, NjP, NN, ULA, UPB, USI

345. ———. (same) Philadelphia, Pa. [etc.] National Publishing Company [1870]
540p. illus., plates, ports., facsims., fold. map. 22½cm.
Publisher's address differs as follows: Boston, Massachusetts added.
MH

346. ———. (same) Philadelphia, Pa [etc.] National Publishing Company [1870]
608p. illus., plates, ports., fold. map., facsim. 22cm.
CSmH, CU–B, DLC, ICN, UHi, ULA, WHi

347. ———. (same) Toronto, James Spencer, 1872.
xviii, 415p. illus. 21½cm.
Cover-title: The mysteries and crimes of Mormonism.
CU–B, MoInRC, NN, UHi

348. ———. (same) Toronto, A. H. Hovey, 1872.
xviii, 415p. illus. 22cm.
USlC

349. ———. (same, under title) Life in Utah and on the plains; being an account of the settlement of the Great West, and embracing the history of the rise and progress of Mormonism, and the occupation of Utah by that people . . . Toronto, Dominion Publishing Co., 1876.
xviii [21]–415p. illus., ports. 20cm.
Cover-title: The mysteries and crimes of Mormorism.
UHi

350. ———. (same, under title) Polygamy; or, The mysteries and crimes of Mormonism, being a full and authentic history of polygamy and the Mormon sect from its origin to the present time. With a complete analysis of Mormon society and theocracy, and an expose of the secret rites and ceremonies of the Latter-day Saints, by J. H. Beadle . . . Assisted by Hon. O. J. Hollister . . . Philadelphia, The National Publishing Co. [c1882]
2p.l., 3–572p. illus., ports. 22½cm.
Copyright date mutilated on many copies, making it seem to be 1880.
CSmH, CU–B, MH, MoInRC, NN, UHi, UPB, USlC

351. ———. (same) Boston, Mass., B. B. Russell [c1882]
572p. illus. 22½cm.
MH, UHi, USlC

352. ———. (same) Auckland, N. Z., A. F. Porter & Sons [c1882]
572p. illus., plates. 22½cm.
USlC

353. ———. (same) Cincinnati, O. W. E. Dibble & Co. [c1882]
2p.l. [3]–572p. 2 fronts., illus. 22½cm.
CtY

354. ———. (same) Philadelphia, National Publishing Co. [c1904]
1p.l., xvi, 648p. illus., plates. 24cm.
CSmH, CtY, CU–B, DLC, ICN, IWW, MH, MoInRC, NAUT, NjP, NN, OClFC, UHi, USlC, UU

355. ———. (same) Philadelphia, World Bible House [c1904]
604p. illus. 23cm.
USlC

356. ———. Polygamy; or, the mysteries and crimes of Mormonism. [n.p., c1904]
xvi, 648p. illus. 23½cm.
Some copies lack Chapter 29 "New testimony proving the Mormons violated the laws and defied the government."
CSmH, USlC (both)

357. ———. (same, in German) Das Leben in Utah; oder, Die Mysterien und Verbrechen des Mörmonenthums. Enthaltend eine Enthüllung der Geheimenritualien und Ceremonien der Heiligen vom Jüngsten Gericht . . . Aus dem englischen übertragen von Carl Theodor Eben. Philadelphia, National Publications, 1870.
544p. illus., fold. map. 22½cm.
MBuG, MH, NjP, PPeSchu, UHi

358. ———. (same, in Russian) Zhizn' Mormonov v Uta; ili Tainstva i prestupleniia Mormonizma; izlozhenie tainikh obriadov i tseremonii sviatikh posldnikh dnei. Sanktpeterburg, Tip. M. Khana, 1872.
415p. 25cm.
DLC

359. ———. The underdeveloped West; or, Five years in the territories: being a complete history of that vast region between the Mississippi and the Pacific, its resources, climate, inhabitants, natural curiosities, etc., etc. Life and adventure on prairies, mountains, and the Pacific coast. With two hundred and forty illustrations from original sketches and photographic views of the scenery . . . of the great West. By J. H. Beadle . . . Philadelphia, National Publishing Company [c1873]
1p.l., 15–823p. illus., plates, double map. 22cm.
Lived in Utah, Sept. 1868 to Sept. 1869.
Several chapters on Mormonism. Orson Pratt described as the only man of learning in the Church, and Brigham Young not at all a talented man. His power largely a result of immense potency.
Howes B269
CSmH, CU–B, DLC, ICN, MB, NjP, NN, UHi, ULA, UPB, USIC

360. ———. Western wilds, and the men who redeem them. An authentic narrative, embracing an account of seven years travel and adventure in the far West; wild life in Arizona; perils of the plains; life in the canon and death on the desert . . . adventures among the red and white savages of the West . . . the Mountain Meadow massacre; the Custer defeat; life and death of Brigham Young, etc. By J. H. Beadle . . . Cincinnati, Chicago [etc.] Jones Brothers & Company, 1878.
xci, 17–624. illus., fold. map. 24cm.
Expanded edition of the above.
Other editions: Cincinnati, Jones Brothers Publ. Co. [c1879] CSmH, USIC; 1880. UHi; 1881. DLC, ULA, UPB
CtY, CU–B, DLC, ICN, UPB, USIC

361. Bean, Charley. A boys' life in the West, by Charley Bean. [Rexburg? Id., c1911]
3p.l. [9]–125 [1]p. plates. 17cm.
Chapter on his "Life with the Mormons." Meets Mormon missionaries in Liverpool, baptized in Richmond, Utah. No mention of Mormonism after leaving Utah.
CtY, DLC

362. Bean, Orestes U. Corianton, an Aztec romance. A romantic spectacular drama, in four acts. By Orestes U. Bean . . . [n.p., 1902?]
[1–3] 4–60p. 19cm.
"Place, South America; 75 years B.C." A Book of Mormon drama.
CU–B, MH, UHi, UPB, USIC, UU

363. Bean, Willard W. Gospel conversations by Willard W. Bean . . . [Independence, Mo., Press of Zion's Printing and Publishing Co., 1925?]
[1–3] 4–123p. 17cm.
ULA, UPB, USIC, UU

364. Bear Lake and River Water Works and Irrigation Company. A description of the location, works and business of the Bear Lake and River Water Works and Irrigation Co. [Kansas City, Mo., Hudson-Kimberly Publishing Co., 1889?]
92[1]p. fold. map. 22½cm.
Reefrence to Mormons, p. 10–12.
DLC, USIC

Bear Lake Stake Academy. *See Fielding Academy.*

365. Beaugrand, Honoré. Six mois dans les Montagnes-Rocheuses. Colorado — Utah — Nouveau-Mexique; . . . Avec une préface de Louis Fréchette. Montréal, Granger Frères, 1890.
2p.l. [8]–323p., [1]l. illus., plates, fold. map. 23cm.
Includes a summary of the history of Mormonism and its beliefs.
Title in English: Six months in the Rocky Mountains.
CSmH, CU–B, DLC, UPB, USIC

Beaver Stake Academy. *See Murdock Academy.*

366. Bechdolt, Frederick Ritchie. Giants of the old West, by Frederick R. Bechdolt . . . New York, London, The Century Co. [c1930]
7p.l., 3–245p. illus., plates, ports., maps. 19½cm.
Includes a chapter on Brigham Young.
DLC, NN, UHi, UPB, USI, USIC, UU

367. Beck, T. J. Mormonism exposed, by Reverend T. Beck. Westport, Ind., Brengle & Dickens [189–?]
15p. 19cm.
Cover-title.
CtY

Beckstead, G. W. *See Stevenson, Edward S.*

368. Beckwith, Edward Griffin. Report of exploration of a route for the Pacific railroad [Part I] near the 38th and 39th parallels of latitude, from the mouth of the Kansas to Sevier River, in the Great Basin. [Part 2] On the line of the forty-first parallel of north latitude. By Lt. E. G. Beckwith, third artillery. 1854. [Washington, 1855]
2v. 23½cm. (U.S. 33rd Cong., 1st Sess. House. Ex. Doc. No. 129)
Includes a section on Utah and Mormonism. He assumed command after Capt. J. W. Gunnison was killed in 1853.
Also a Senate edition published.
(U.S. Cong. 33rd Sess. Senate Ex. Doc. No. 78) CU–B.
CtY, DLC, MH, NjP, ULA

369. Bedford-Jones, Henry James O'Brien. Mormon Valley, by H. Bedford-Jones. Garden City, Garden City Publ. Co., 1923.
5p.l., 120p. 20cm.
First edition [c1918, Street & Smith Corporation] An adventure story with a locale in a valley on the Nevada-California boundary. No relevance to Mormonism.
Colored paper wrapper.
CU–B

BEE YEE

370. Bee Yee. [Provo, Utah] May, 1921.
1v. illus. 27cm.
Published by Students of Brigham Young University. Probably only one issue published.
UPB

371. Beecher, Henry Ward. A circuit of the continent: account of a tour through the West and South. By Henry Ward Beecher. <With portrait> Being his Thanksgiving day discourse at Plymouth church, Brooklyn, Nov. 29th, 1883, describing his trip through thirty states and territories . . . New York, Fords, Howard, & Hulbert, 1884.
17p. port. 20½cm.
Includes a trip to Salt Lake City for a lecture. He was shown around town by John Taylor. A description of Mormonism and what must be done about it.
CSmH, CtY, DLC, MH

372. Beecher, Jacob F. Notes of travel: a summer trip across the continent. What we saw and how we saw it, and our impressions of persons, places and things, as taken from our diary, memory, conversations, railway guides, etc. By J. F. Beecher. New Holland, Pa., Clarion Steam Job Printing House, 1885.
3p.l., 52p. 23½cm.
Cover-title.
Description of Salt Lake City, p. 25–32, with a discussion of Mormon doctrine and a little history of the settlement of Salt Lake City.
DLC, PPL

373. Beeley, Arthur Lawton. Being a summary statement of the investigation made by the British government of the "Mormon" question in England. By Elder Arthur L. Beeley. Liverpool, Millennial Star Office [1914?]
15p. 17 cm.
MH, NN, UPB, USIC

374. ———. The Mormon way of life. Address delivered over Radio Station KSL, Sunday, October 30, 1927. [Salt Lake City, 1927]
Broadside. 46×25cm.
Reprint from the *Deseret News* of Saturday, November 5th.
UPB

———. Society and personality. *See Church of Jesus Christ of Latter-day Saints. Young Women's Mutual Improvement Association. Courses of study . . . 1929–1930.*

375. Beers, Robert Welsted. The Mormon puzzle, and how to solve it. Chicago, New York, Funk & Wagnall, Publishers, 1887.
xiv [2] [17]–195p. 19½cm.
CSmH, CtY, CU-B, DLC, ICN, MH, NjP, NjPT, NN, UHi, ULA, USl, USIC, UU, WHi

376. Beesley, Clarissa A. Believing and doing. By Clarissa A. Beesley. Salt Lake City, Published by the General Board of the Young Ladies' Mutual Improvement Association, 1930.
111p. 21cm. (Course of Study for the Junior Department of the Y.L.M.I.A. 1930–31)
USIC

377. Beesley, Ebenezer, *compiler.* A collection of hymns and anthems set to music by home composers. Compiled by E. Beesley for the use of the Salt Lake City Tabernacle Choir. Salt Lake City, Printed at the Juvenile Instructor Office, 1883.
45p. 16×20½cm.
USIC

378. ———. The Improvement Association song book. A collection of original and selected songs and hymns set to music, prepared especially for the use of Mutual Improvement and other association choirs. Arranged by E. Beesley . . . Salt Lake City, Juvenile Instructor Office, 1887.
[1–5] 6–78 [2]p. 16×21cm.
NN, UHi, UPB, USIC, UU

379. Behold! The Bridegroom cometh! [n.p., n.d.]
[4]p. 22cm.
Leaflet of the Church of Christ, Temple Lot.
MoInRC

380. Beijer, J. De Mormonen in Zuid-Afrika. Eene waarschuwing aan allen, die de waarheid, in Christus Jezus, liefhebben . . . Door J. Beijer . . . Groningen, P. Beijer, 1863.
2p.l. [5]–48p. 22cm.
Title in English: Mormonism in South Africa.
MH, NN, USl

381. Belcher, Joseph. The religious denominations in the United States; their history, doctrine, government and statistics. With a preliminary sketch of Judaism, paganism, and Mohammedanism. Philadelphia, Published by J. E. Potter, 1854.
xii, 13–1024p. illus., plates. 24cm.
Section on "Latter Day Saints, or Mormons."
Other editions: 1857. NjP; 1859. UPB; New and rev. ed., 1864. USIC, UU
Sabin 4402
DLC, ULA, UPB

382. Belisle, Orvilla S. Mormonism unveiled; or, A history of Mormonism from its rise to the present time. London, Charles Clarke [1855]
2p.l. [ix]–xiv [15]–235p. 17cm.
Preface signed: 1855.
Fiction concerning Mormonism.
Sabin 50758
CSmH, CtY, MH, USIC, WHi

383. ———. (same, under title) The prophets; or, Mormonism unveiled. With illustrations. Philadelphia, Published by William White Smith . . . London, Trubner & Co., 1855.
2p.l., 5–6, xi–xvi [17]–412p. 19cm.
On verso of title page: Entered according to act of Congress . . . by Orvilla S. Belisle.
Sabin 66011, Howes B321
CSmH, CtY, DLC, ICN, MH, NjP, NN, UHi, ULA, UPB, USIC, UU

384. ———. (same, under title) In the grip of the Mormons, by an escaped wife of a Mormon elder. London, Henry Hardingham [c1919]
1p.l. [5]–151 [1]p. 18cm.
CU–B, MH, NN, USIC

385. Bell, Alfreda Eva. Boadicea; the Mormon wife. Life scenes in Utah. Beautifully illustrated. Edited by Alfreda Eva Bell. Baltimore [etc.] Arthur R. Orton [c1855]
102p. illus. 23cm.
98–101 advertisements.
Fiction concerning Mormonism.
Issued in variant wrappers CSmH
CSmH, CtY, CU–B, ICN, USIC, UU

386. Bell, Edward John. Latter-day delusions, or, The inconsistencies of Mormonism. By the Rev. Edward John Bell . . . Norwich: Thomas Priest . . . London: Wertheim and Macintosh, 1853.
2p.l. [5]–34p. 18cm.
Book against Mormon doctrines such as materiality of the deity, polygamy, miracles, etc.
Peter Crawley, USI

387. Bell, Horace. On the old West coast: being further reminiscences of a ranger, Major Horace Bell. Ed. by Lanier Bartlett. New York, William Morrow, 1930.
xiv [1]l., 336p. illus. 24cm.
Includes a section on Mormonism and its importance to California history.
CSmH, CU–B, DLC, NjP, UHi, UPB

388. ———. Reminiscences of a ranger; or, Early times in Southern California . . . Los Angeles, Yarnell, Caystile & Mathes, 1881.
3p.l. [9]–457p. 23½cm.
Scattered references to Mormons in California.
Another edition: Santa Barbara, Wallace Hebbard, 1927. DLC, NjP
DLC, UHi, UPB

389. Bell, J. F. A reply to the bare-faced falsehoods and misrepresentations of Mr. John Theobald. [Liverpool, F. D. Richards, 1851?]
8p. 21½cm.
Caption-title.
ICN, UHi, UPB, USIC

390. Bell, James. A letter to the Rev. Mr. Osborne, Minister of Darlington Street chapel, Wolverhampton. By James Bell, an Elder in the Church of Jesus Christ of Latter Day Saints. [Wolverhampton] Hinde, Printer [1849]
4p. 19cm.
Dated: Wolverhampton, June, 1849.
Published in the *Millennial Star*, Dec. 15, 1849.
MH

391. ———. A reply to the objections of the Rev. Mr. Osborne, Minister of Darlington Street Chapel, Wolverhampton. By J. Bell, An Elder of the Church of Jesus Christ of Latter Day Saints. Being the substance of a sermon delivered in the Saints' Room, St. James's Square. [Wolverhampton, Hinde, Printer, 1849]
8p. 20½cm.
Published in the *Millennial Star*, Oct. 15, 1849.
MH, USIC

392. Bell, John C. The pilgrim and the pioneer; the social and material developments in the Rocky Mountains by John C. Bell . . . Lincoln, Printed by the International Publishing Ass'n [c1906]
xii [13]–531p. plates. 20½cm.
Claims that polygamy really stopped when the girls saw how the gentiles had only one wife and was queen of the show, and sold it to the boys.
CU–B, NjP, ULA, USIC

393. Bell, William Abraham. New tracks in North America. A journal of travel and adventure whilst engaged in the survey for a southern railroad to the Pacific Ocean during 1867–8. By William A. Bell . . . With contributions by General W. J. Palmer, Major A. R. Calhoun, C. C. Parry . . . and Captain W. F. Colton . . . London, Chapman and Hall; New York, Scribner, Welford & Co., 1869.
2v. illus., plates (part. col.) fold. map. 22½cm.
Mormons and polygamy.
Other editions: 2d ed. 1870. DLC, USIC; 2d ed. New York, G. P. Putnam & Sons, 1871. DW, PPA
Howes B330
CSmH, CtY, CU–B, DLC, ICN, MH, NjP, NN, ULA, USIC

394. Bell, William Morrison. Other countries. By Major William Morrison Bell. With maps and illustrations . . . London, Chapman and Hall, 1872.
2v. illus., maps. 23cm.
A stop in Utah with an account on Mormonism.
DLC, UPB, USIC

395. Benjamin, Israel Joseph. Drei Jahre in Amerika 1859–1862. Von J. J. Benjamin II . . . Hannover, Selbstverlag des Verfassers. Druck von Wilh. Reimschneider, 1862.
3 pts. in 2 v. port. 22cm.
The last part of the book entitled "Zweiter Theil, Desert und Deseret oder Wüste und Mormonen," has a considerable description of Utah and the Mormons whom he visited eastbound from San Francisco in 1861. It has recently been translated into English.
Title in English: Three Years in America
Howes B351, W–C 380
CtY, CU–B, DLC, NjP, NN, CU–B

BENNET, J. A.

Bennet, James Arlington. Correspondence between Joseph Smith. *See Smith, Joseph, 1805–1844.*

396. ———. Hell demolished, heaven gained; science triumphant; Moses, the old Jew, on his back and the almighty vindicated against the pretentions and falsehoods of men . . . Thomas Chalmers . . . against J. Arlington Bennet . . . New York, Printed for the author, 1855.
vii [9]–188p. port. 18½cm.
Published also under title: A new revelation of mankind, drawn from axioms, or self-evident truths in nature, mathematically demonstrated.
Brief references to Mormons and Joe Smith as a prophet and Brigham Young as a Moses.
DLC

397. Bennett, Fred E. Fred Bennett the Mormon detective, or, adventures in the wild west by Fred E. Bennett . . . Mormonism unmasked. Chicago, Laird & Lee [c1887]
1p.l. [13]–283p. port., plates. 19cm.
On cover: Columbia series.
Fiction concerning Mormonism.
CtY, CU–B, NN, USIC

398. ———. (same) Chicago, Laird & Lee, Publishers [1888]
3p.l. [13]–283p. 18cm. (The Pinkerton detective series. No. 15)
Cover: The Pinkerton detective series. No. 15, May, 1888. Copyright on title page: c1887. Title page varies from the c1887 printing.
USIC

399. ———. (same, under title) A detective's experience among the Mormons; or, Polygamist Mormons, how they live and the land they live in, by F. E. Bennett, Deputy U.S. Marshall. Mormonism unmasked . . . Chicago, Laird & Lee, c1887.
[1]l., 13–294p. 3 plates, 1 port. 19½cm.
CSmH, CtY, DLC, ICN, MH, NN, UHi, USI, USIC, UPB, UU, WHi

400. ———. (same, under title) The Mormon detective, or adventures in the west. By Fred E. Bennett, deputy U.S. Marshal. Mormonism unmasked. New York, J. S. Ogilvie Publishing Co., 1887.
2p.l., 16–283p. 19cm.
NN, UHi, UPB, USIC

401. ———. (same) New York, J. S. Ogilvie Publishing Co. [1889?]
2p.l., 16–283p. 19cm.
USIC

402. Bennett, John Cook. Hear the testimony — then Judge ye Mormonism! [Alton? 1843]
Broadside. 39×28cm.
Announcement for a lecture. Jan 13, 1843 at Alton, Illinois.
USIC

403. ———. The history of the Saints; or, an exposé of Joe Smith and Mormonism. By John C. Bennett. Boston: Leland & Whiting, 71 Washington St. New York: Bradbury, Soden, & Co., 127 Nassau Street. Cincinnati: E. S. Norris & Co., 247 Main Street, 1842.
ii, 344p. plates, 2 ports., plan. 19cm.
CSmH, CtY, DLC, ICN, NjP, NN, UHi, UPB, USIC, UU, WHi

404. ———. (same) 3d ed. Boston, Leland & Whiting; New York, Bradbury, Soden, & Co. [etc., etc.] 1842.
1p.l., ii [3]–344p. plates, 2 ports., plan. 18cm.
Cover-title: Mormonism exposed.
Howes B358, Sabin 4733
CSmH, CtY, CU–B, DLC, ICN, MH, NjPT, NN, UHi, ULA, UPB, USIC

405. Bennett, Risden Tyler. . . . Speeches of Hon. Risden T. Bennett of North Carolina, in the House of Representatives, Wednesday, January 12, and Thursday, February 17, 1887, against the Edmunds-Tucker Anti-Mormon bill. Washington, 1887.
18p. 21cm.
CSmH, CU–B, ULA, USIC, UU

406. Bennett, Samuel. A few remarks by way of reply to an anonymous scribbler, calling himself A Philanthropist, disabusing the Church of Jesus Christ of Latter-day Saints of the slanders and falsehoods which he has attempted to fasten upon it. By S. Bennett. Philadelphia, Brown, Bicking & Guilbert, Printers, 1840.
16p. 20½cm.
CtY, CU–B, DLC, MH, USIC

407. Bennett, William P. The first baby in camp. A full account of the scenes of adventures during the pioneer days of '49. George Francis Train. — Staging in early days. — A mad, wild ride. — The pony express. — Some of the old time drivers. By Wm. P. Bennett . . . (Picture 22×28 accompanies this book) Salt Lake City, The Rancher Publishing Co., 1893.
68p. fold. plate. 18½cm.
The father of the first baby was a Mormon.
CU–B, DLC, NjP, UHi, UPB, USIC

408. ———. The sky-sifter, the great chieftainess and "medicine woman" of the Mohawks. Remarkable adventures and experiences of her white foster son as related by himself . . . By William P. Bennett. [Oakland, Cal., Pacific Press Publishing Co., c1892]
302p. plates. 18½cm.
A fictional account of his aunt being captured by Mormons p. 269–286.
CU–B, DLC, NjP, UHi, UPB, USIC

409. Bennion, Adam Samuel. A brief summary of the historical background, the present status, and the possible future development of the Latter-day Saint educational system. [Salt Lake City? 1928?]
8p. 28cm.
USIC

BENNION, H.

410. ———. Fundamental problems in teaching religion. Designed for quorum instruction and auxiliary class teachers of the Church of Jesus Christ of Latter-day Saints. [Salt Lake City] General Boards of the Auxiliary Organizations of the Church, 1921.
4p.l., 175 p. 20cm. (Teacher training outline, 1921)
UPB, USIC, UU

411. ———. Gleaning. A course of study for the Gleaner Department of the Y.L.M.I.A., 1930–31. Salt Lake City, Published by the General Board of the Young Ladies Mutual Improvement Association, 1930.
4p.l. [9]–136p. 22cm.
UPB

412. ———. Latter-day Saint seminaries and American education . . . [Salt Lake City? 1928?]
Broadside. 56½×26cm.
UHi

413. ———. Principles of teaching by Adam S. Bennion, Superintendent of Church Schools. Designed for Quorum Instructors and Auxiliary Class Teachers of the Church of Jesus Christ of Latter-day Saints. [Salt Lake City] Published by the General Board of the Auxiliary Organizations of the Church, 1921.
3p.l., 173p. 20cm.
USIC

414. ———. (same) Salt Lake City, Deseret Sunday School Union Board, c1928.
59p. 23½cm.
Reprinted from *The Juvenile Instructor.*
Religious teaching from an L.D.S. point of view.
UPB

415. ———. Shall I believe? Address delivered over Radio Station KSL, Sunday Evening, May 27, 1928 [Salt Lake City] 1928.
Broadside. 56×25cm.
Reprinted from the *Deseret News*, Saturday, June 2nd, 1928.
UPB

416. ———. What it means to be a Mormon, written for the Deseret Sunday School Union, by Adam S. Bennion. Salt Lake City, The Deseret Sunday School Union, 1917.
vi [7]–176p. 19cm.
CU–B, DLC, MH, NjP, NN, ULA, UPB, USI, USIC, UU, WHi

417. ———. (same) Salt Lake City, The Deseret Sunday School Union, 1925.
vi [7]–176p. 19cm.
Printed by the Press of Zion's Printing and Publishing Co.
MoInRC, USIC

418. ———. (same) Revised by the author for the Junior Seminaries, 1929. Salt Lake City, Published by the Deseret Book Company, 1930.
168p. 18½cm.
USIC

419. ———. (same, in German) Was es heisst, ein Mormone zu sein. Für die Deseret Sunday School Union geschrieben von Adam S. Bennion. Aus dem Englishchen übersetzt von Jean Wanderlich. Bassel (Schweiz) Herausgegeben von Fred Tadje, 1925.
3p.l. [7]–137p. 19½cm.
UPB, USI, USIC

420. ———. Why have a religion? An address delivered over Radio Station KSL, Sunday evening, Sept. 8, 1929 [Salt Lake City] Church of Jesus Christ of Latter-day Saints, 1929.
7[1]p. 23cm.
USIC

421. Bennion, Heber. A crazy world. Government price-fixing versus incorporated price-fixing. What's the matter with our economic system? [Salt Lake City, 1923?]
11p. 21½cm.
An ex-Mormon discusses the problems of government using Mormon sources.
CU–B, USIC

422. ———. A Devine [sic] ultimatum to gentiles, Jews, saints and sinners . . . Compliments of Heber Bennion. [n.p., n.d.]
[11]p. 32cm.
A tract on the United Order.
UPB

423. ———. A divine ultimatum to gentiles, Jews, saints and sinners. Compliments of Heber Bennion. [n.p., n.d.]
[11]p. 32cm.
A printing with the correction of the spelling of divine.
USIC

424. ———. The ethics of the New Testament in outline. [Salt Lake City] University of Utah. 1926.
29p. 27½cm.
USIC

425. ———. Free press? Free speech? Free trade? Free love? [Salt Lake City, n.d.]
[10]p. 23cm.
USIC

426. ———. Gospel problems . . . [Salt Lake City? 1920?]
72p. 19cm.
At head of title: Signs of the times.
"The authors' name is withheld."
UPB, USIC, UU

427. ———. Supplement to gospel problems . . . [Salt Lake City? The Theatre Book Shop, 1922?]
112p. 19cm.
CtY, UPB, USl, USIC, UU

428. ———. Humanity vs. the dollar. By Heber Bennion. [Salt Lake City, Paragon Printing Co.] 1923.
[6]p. 20cm.
USIC

429. ———. An Open letter. Salt Lake City, American Printery [1920?]
14p. 20cm.
Cover-title.
A letter from an ex-Mormon, dated: May 2, 1920.
UPB, USIC

430. ———. Problems of the age as signs of the times . . . Compliments of Heber Bennion. [Salt Lake City, ca. 1925]
[14]p. 22½×9½cm.
A commentary on the value of the United Order, and the problems of the capitalistic order, by an ex-Mormon.
UPB, USIC

431. ———. A word of warning. . . . Compliments of Heber Bennion. [Salt Lake City, n.d.]
[8]p. 23cm.
A doctrinal tract to disprove the League of Nations, etc.
USIC

432. ———. (same) [Salt Lake City, n.d.]
[7]p. 23½cm.
USIC

433. ———. World paralysis . . . Compliments of Heber Bennion. [Salt Lake City? n.d.]
[14]p. 23×10cm.
Mormon materials to disprove the current economic system.
UPB, USIC

434. ———. World problems in brief. [Salt Lake City, n.d.]
[15]p. 23cm.
Uses Mormon sources to demonstrate world problems.
USIC

435. Bennion, Milton. The Ethics of the New Testament in outline. By Milton Bennion. [Salt Lake City] 1926.
[30]l. 27½cm.
USIC

436. ———. Moral teachings of the New Testament. A source book with commentaries. By Milton Bennion. Salt Lake City, Published by the Deseret Book Company, 1928.
239p. 19½cm.
Moral teachings from a Mormon point of view.
A mimeographed version was published in 1927. USIC
UPB, USIC

437. Benoit, Pierre. . . . Le lac salé, roman . . . Paris, A. Michel [c1921]
3p.l. [9]–317p. [1]l. 19cm.
Fiction concerning Mormonism.
Title in English: The Salt Lake.
DLC, NjP, NN, ULA, USIC, UU

438. ———. (same, in Danish) Salt søen; roman. [autoriseret oversaettelse for Danmark og Norge af Pierre Benoit: Le Lac Sales ved Eva de Mautort] København, H. Hagerups, 1928.
2p.l. [5]–204p. 20cm.
NN, UPB, UU

439. ———. (same, in English) Salt Lake; a novel by Pierre Benoit, tr. from the French by Florence and Victor Llona . . . New York, A. A. Knopf, 1922.
377p. 19½cm.
CU–B, DLC, NjP, NN, UHi, USl, USIC, UU

439a. ———. (same, in German). Mormonenliebe [Le Lac Salé] von Pierre Benoit. Berlin-Schöneberg, Delta-Verlag [1929]
286p. 18cm.
Title in English: Mormon life. A variant edition of his *Le Lac Sale.*
USIC

440. Bernhisel, John Milton. To the authors, editors and publishers of the United States. [New York, 1850.]
Broadside. 25×20cm.
On blue foolscap. Signed: Nov. 1850.
An appeal for books for the Utah Territorial Library.
USIC

440a. ———. (same) . . . [New York, 1850]
Broadside. 25×19½cm.
On white paper.
In double columns.
USIC

441. Berrian, William. Catalogue of books, early newspapers and pamphlets, on Mormonism. Collected by the late William Berrian. New York: V. H. Everson, Print., 1898.
48p. 20½cm.
The collection is now located at the New York Public library.
Reprinted later in the *Bulletin of the New York Public Library.* V. XIII, No. 3. March, 1909.
CSmH, DLC, ICN, NjP, NN, WHi

442. Berry, James H. Speech of Hon. James H. Berry, of Arkansas, in the Senate of the United States, on the question of excluding Hon. Reed Smoot, of Utah, from the United States Senate, Monday, February 11, 1907. Washington, 1907.
23p. 21½cm.
UPB

443. Berry, John. Plain facts against the Latter-day Saints, proving their doctrines contrary to the doctrines of the Bible, also the lecture which was delivered at the Carpenter Hall in the discussion, proving the Book of Mormon to be untrue, and also that water baptism by immersion not essential to salvation. By John Berry, Altringham, Cheshire. Altringham, T. Balshaw, 1841.
11p. 18cm.
NN, USIC

444. Berry, Orville F. "The Mormon Settlement in Illinois." Address delivered by Senator O. F. Berry before the Illinois State Historical Society, Springfield, Illinois, January 24th, 1906. [Springfield? 1906?]
17p. plates. 25cm.
Also published in their *Transactions* for 1906.
USIC

445. Berthold, Victor Maximilian. The story of Mormon island . . . [New York, c1929]
[4]l. illus., facsims., maps. 26cm.
Cover-title. Reprinted from *Collectors Club Philatelist* V. 8, No. 3, July 1929.
Material on the Mormon Battalion.
MH, NN

446. Bertrand, Louis Alphonso. Autorité divine; ou, Résponse a cette question: Joseph Smith était-il envoyé de Dieu? Suivie du credo do l'Eglise de Jésus-Christ des Saints-des-Dernier-jours, par l'Elder L. A. Bertrand . . . [Paris, Imp. de Marc Ducloux et comp., 1852]
2p.l., 32p. 22cm.
Also published at Lausanne, chez M.T.B.H. Stenhouse-Cité derriére, No. 1.
The author was president of the French Mission from 1859 to 1864.
Title in English: Divine Authority.
Sabin 5027
CU-B, ICN, USIC

447. ———. Mémoires d'un Mormon, par L. A. Bertrand. Paris, Collection Hetzel, E. Jung-Treuttel [1862]
2p.l., 323p. 18cm.
Imprint date from British Museum.
Title in English: Writings of a Mormon.
Sabin 5029
DLC, ICN, NN, UPB, USIC

448. ———. (same) Paris, Collection Hetzel, E. Dentu [1862?]
2p.l. 323p. 19cm.
CSmH, CtY, CU-B, ICN, NjP, UPB, USIC

449. Beveridge, Albert J. The Reed Smoot case. Speech of Hon. Albert J. Beveridge, of Indiana, in the Senate of the United States, in support of the minority report on the resolution that Reed Smoot is not entitled to a seat in the Senate as a senator from Utah. February 20, 1907. Washington. 1907.
15p. 23cm.
In favor of seating Mr. Smoot.
MH

450. Beyer, Alfred. Et Forsvar for den i Danmark bestaaende Kirkes Daab, og navnlig for Barnedaaben uden Tro, med stadigt Hensyn til Angreb Paa den, isaer fra mormonerne. Kjøbenhavn, Forlagt af Unnersitetsboghandler, Anor. Fred. Høst, 1858.
30p. 17cm.
Title in English: A defense of baptism.
NN, USIC

Beware of Mormonism. *See National Anti-Mormon Literature and Information Bureau.*

451. Biancour, Felix Fernand de. Quatre mille lieues aux États-Unis par F. De Biancour . . . Paris, Paul Ollendorff, Éditeur. 1888.
3p.l., 408p. 18cm.
Chapter LI deals with his visit to Salt Lake City. An account of Mormonism, with emphasis on polygamy.
Title in English: Four thousand miles through the United States.
MH

452. Bibelsprängd. [Salt Lake City, Korrespondenten, 1893?]
8p. 13½cm.
A missionary tract in Swedish.
Title in English: The one who knew the Bible too well.
UPB

453. Bible. English. 1867. Inspired Version. The Holy Scriptures, translated and corrected by the spirit of revelation, by Joseph Smith, jr., the Seer. Published by the Church of Jesus Christ of Latter-Day Saints. Plano, Ill., J. Smith, I. L. Rogers, E. Robinson, Publishing Committee, 1867.
917, 286p. 17½cm.
The New Testament under title: "The Holy Scriptures of the New Testament, translated and corrected by the spirit of revelation, by Joseph Smith, jr., the Seer" has special title-page. It is also printed separately.
CSmH, CtY, CU-B, DLC, NN, UPB, USIC, UU, WHi

454. ———. 1867. (same) [Plano, Ill.] 1867.
917, 286p. 17½cm.
Variant printing without Plano, Ill. included on the title page.
ULA, USIC

455. ———. **1901.** (same) 12th ed. Lamoni, Ia., Published by the Reorganized Church of Jesus Christ of Latter Day Saints, 1901.
917, 286p. 19cm.
Unsigned preface. Revelation given to Joseph Smith precedes the Old Testament.
No indication as to the numbering of earlier editions.
MoInRC, USIC

456. ———. **1903.** (same) 13th ed. Lamoni, Ia., Published by the Reorganized Church of Jesus Christ of Latter Day Saints, 1903.
917, 286p. 18½cm.
Sabin 83248
MoInRC, USIC

457. ———. **1906.** (same) 14th ed. Lamoni, Ia., Published by the Reorganized Church of Jesus Christ of Latter Day Saints, 1906.
917, 286p. 18cm.
MoInRC, UPB

458. ———. **1909.** (same) 16th edition. Lamoni, Ia., Published by the Reorganized Church of Jesus Christ of Latter Day Saints, 1909.
917, 286p. 19cm.
CU–B, MoInRC, UPB

459. ———. **1915.** (same) 18th ed. Lamoni, Ia., Published by the Reorganized Church of Jesus Christ of Latter Day Saints, 1915.
917, 286p. 19cm.
MoInRC

460. ———. **1916.** (same) 19th ed. Lamoni, Ia., Published by the Reorganized Church of Jesus Christ of Latter Day Saints, 1916.
917, 286p. 18½cm.
UPB

461. ———. **1920.** (same) 20th ed. Lamoni, Ia., Reorganized Church of Jesus Christ of Latter Day Saints, 1920.
917, 286p. 19cm.
IWW, MoInRC, UPB

462. ———. **1925.** (same) 22nd ed. Independence, Mo., Reorganized Church of Jesus Christ of Latter Day Saints, 1925.
917, 286p. 19cm.
Sabin 83249
NN, UPB

463. ———. **1927.** (same) 23rd ed. Independence, Mo., Reorganized Church of Jesus Christ of Latter Day Saints, 1927.
917, 286p. 19cm.
MoInRC, UPB, USIC

464. Bible. N.T. English. 1867. Inspired Version. The Holy Scriptures of the New Testament translated and corrected by the spirit of Revelation by Joseph Smith Jr., the Seer, Published by the Church of Jesus Christ of Latter-Day Saints. Plano, Ill., Joseph Smith, I. L. Rogers, E. Robinson, Publishing Committee, 1867.
286p. 18cm.
Same edition as that printed in the *Holy Scriptures.*
MoInRC

465. ———. **1867.** (same) Plano, Ill., 1867.
286p. 18cm.
Plano, Ill. not included on the title page.
MoInRC

466. ———. **1892.** (same) Lamoni, Ia., Published by the Reorganized Church of Jesus Christ of Latter Day Saints, 1892.
374p. 26cm.
Cover-title: The Two records.
With this is bound Book of Mormon. English. 1905.
MoInRC Copy bound with a concordance to the later placed between the two books.
MoInRC, UPB

467. ———. **1912.** (same) 17th ed. Lamoni, Ia., Published by the Reorganized Church of Jesus Christ of Latter Day Saints, 1912.
286p. 20cm.
MoInRC, UHi

468. Bible. N.T. Matthew XXIV. English. 1836? Inspired Version. Extract from the new translation of the Bible, It being the 24th chapter of Matthew; but in order to show the connection we will commence with the last verse of the 23rd chapter, viz: . . . Published for the benefit of the Saints. [Kirtland, 1836?]
Broadside. 30×20cm.
Enclosed in ornamental border.
The two copies located have different borders but are printed from the same type.
Possibly published as early as 1836 as it is reprinted in present form in John Corrill's *History of the church* published in 1893. Or possibly published as late as 1843 to combat the Millerite excitement.
Type similar to the type of the *Messenger and Advocate* and the *Elder's Journal.*
CtY, UPB

469. Bible. Selections. Danish. Bibelske henviisninger betraessende Laerdomme om det evige Evangelium og Praestedømme, den nye og evige pagt og Guds Forsamling i de Sidste Dage med meget mere. [Kjøbenhavn? Udgivne af J. H. Christensen . . . Trykt hos Behrends Ente. n.d.]
[2]p. 21×23cm.
A biblical ready-reference for Danish missionaries.
USIC

470. ———. **1854.** Bibelske henviisninger i Overeensstemmelse med de Sioste Dags helliges Laere. [Kjøbenhavn, Udgivet af J. Van Cott. Trykt hos F. E. Bording, ca. 1854]
4p. 22cm.
USIC

471. ———. **1855.** (same) [Kjøbenhavn, Udgivet af Hector C. Haight. Trykt hos F. E. Bording, ca. 1855]
4p. 22cm.
USIC

472. ———. **1857.** (same) [Kjøbenhavn, Udgivet og forlagt af Hector C. Haight. Trykt hos F. E. Bording, 1857]
8p. 21½cm.
USIC, UU

473. ———. **1865.** (same) [Kjøbenhavn, C. Widerborn, 1865]
8p. 20cm.
CtY, USIC

474. ———. **1873.** (same) [Kjøbenhavn, K. Peterson, Trykt hos F. E. Bording, 1873]
8p. 22cm.
Caption-title.
CDU, CtY, UHi, UPB, USIC

475. ———. **1880.** Bibelske Henvisninger, i Overensstemmelse med De Sidste Dages helliges Tro og Laerdomme. Fjerde Tusinde. Kjøbenhavn, Udgivet og forlagt af N. Wilhelmsen, Trykt hos F. E. Bording, 1880.
1p.l., 61p. 17cm.
NN, USIC

476. ———. **1881.** (same) Kjøbenhavn, Udgivet og forlagt af Andrew Jenson. Trykt hos F. E. Bording, 1881.
64p. 16cm.
"Tredie Oplag"
UHi

477. ———. **1890.** Haandbog for Bibelforskere. En samling af skrifsteder og historiske citater ordnede i kapitler framstillende evangeliet eller frelsningsplanens grundsaetninger i overensstemmelse med de Sideste Dages Helliges tro og laerdomme. Kjøbenhavn, Udgivet og forlagt af C.D. Fjelsted. Trykt hos F. E. Bording, 1890.
4p.l., 112p. 17½cm.
"Forste oplag"
USIC

478. ———. **1900.** Bibel-citater, en samling af skriftsteder of Historiske citater, Ordnede i Kapitler, fiemstillende Evangeliet eller Freslens Grundsaetninger i Oversstemmelse med de oprindelige Kristnes og de Sidste Dages Helliges, tro og Laerdomme. Tredie Oplag. København, Udgivet og forlagt af Andreas Peterson, 1900.
120p. 16cm.
Articles of faith and short chronology of events on 2p.l.
UHi, UPB, USIC, UU

479. ———. **1912.** Citater og Henvisninger en samling af citater fra Bibelen samt henvisninger til Mormons bog, Pagtens bog, den Kostelige Perle og kirkelhistoriske Vaerker fremstillende Jesu Kristi Evangelium i overensstemmelse med de oprindelige Kristnes og de Sidste-dages Helliges tro og laerdomme udabejdet af Andrew Jenson. Kjøbenhavn, Udgivet af forlagt af Andrew Jensen, 1912.
xii, 153p. 14½cm.
UPB, USIC

480. Bible. Selections. Dutch. 1906. Leerstellingen van de Kerk van Jezus Christus van der Laatste Dagen. Verwijzingen naar de boeken der kerk. Aanbevolen bij het Bestudeeren en het Evangelie, en bij de studiën der Theolgische Afdeelingen in de Zondagscholen. Rotterdam, Uitgegeven door Jacob H. Trayner, 1906.
35p. 17cm.
USIC

481. Bible. Selections. English. 1884. Ready references. A compilation of scripture texts, arranged in subjective order, with numerous annotations from eminent writers, Designed especially for the use of missionaries and scripture students. Liverpool, Millennial Star Office, 1884.
140p. 16cm.
MH, UHi, UPB, USIC

482. ———. **1886.** (same) Salt Lake City, The Deseret News, 1886.
2p.l., [5]–168p. 13½cm.
USIC

483. ———. **1887.** (same) 2d edition. Salt Lake City, The Deseret News Co., 1887.
2p.l. [5]–168p. 16cm.
DLC, NN, UPB, USIC, UU

484. ———. **1891.** (same) Salt Lake City, George Q. Cannon & Sons Company, 1891.
2p.l. [5]–168p. 15½cm.
NjP, UHi

485. ———. **1892.** (same) Salt Lake City, The Deseret News Publishing Company, 1892.
2p.l. [5]–168p. 16cm.
DLC, IWW, NjP, NN, UHi

486. ———. **1895.** (same) Liverpool, Printed and for sale at the Millennial Star Office, 1895.
140p. 16½cm.
USIC

487. ———. 1899. (same) Salt Lake City, George Q. Cannon and Sons Co., 1899.
2p.l. [5]–168p. 15½cm.
NN, USlC

488. ———. 1900. (same) Liverpool, Printed and Published at the Millennial Star Office [1900]
4p.l. [9]–105p. 15cm.
Preface signed 1900.
UU

489. ———. 1900. (same) Liverpool, Printed and for sale at the Millennial Star Office, 1900.
4p.l. [9]–118p. 14cm.
USlC

490. ———. 1917. (same) [Salt Lake City] The Church of Jesus Christ of Latter-day Saints, 1917.
112p. 17½cm.
On cover: Bible ready references.
DLC, UHi, UPB, USlC, UU

491. ———. 1918. (same) [Salt Lake City] The Church of Jesus Christ of Latter-day Saints, 1918.
112p. 18cm.
UHi

492. ———. 1920. (same) [Salt Lake City] Church of Jesus Christ of Latter-day Saints, 1920.
2p.l., 5–112p. 13cm.
USlC

493. **Bible. Selections. English. 1891.** Bible selections. 1891. Simple Bible stories. Adapted to the capacity of young children, and designed for use in Sabbath Schools, Primary Associations, and for home reading. Salt Lake City, 1891.
2v. 22cm.
V. 2 lists publishers as George Q. Cannon and Sons, Company.
USlC

494. **Bible. Selections. German. 1891.** Biblische Hinweisungen. Eine Zussamenstellung von Schriftstellen. In subjectiver Reihenfolge, mit zahlreichen Anführungen von hervorragenden Schriftstellern. Besonders geeignet für den Gebrauch der Missionare und solcher, welche die heiligen Schriften studiren. Aus dem Englischen von Theodore Brändli. Herausgegeben von der schweizerischen und deutschen Mission der Kirche Jesu Christi der Heiligen der Letzten Tage. Bern, Druck von Guter & Lierow, 1891.
2p.l. [5]–179p. 17½cm.
USlC

495. ———. 1901. Biblische Hinweisungen; Eine Zusammenstellung von Schriftstellen, in thematischer Reihenfolge, mit zahlreichen Ausführungen von geschichtlichen Quellen. Besonders geeignet für den Gebrauch der Missionare und solcher, welche die heiligen Schriften studieren. Aus dem Englischen von Theodor Brändli. Frei bearbeitet von A. H. Schulthess. Herausgegeben von der deutschen Mission der Kirche Jesu Christi der Heiligen der Letzten Tage. Berlin, H. Dusedann, 1901.
3p.l. [7]–163p. 16½cm.
UHi, USlC, UU

496. **Bible. Selections. Hawaiian. 1894.** Papa haawina no na Hui Opio me Kula Sabati iloko o ka Ekalesia o Jesu Karisto o ka Poe Hoano o na La Hope nei, ma ko Hawaii nei Paeina. Hoomakaukau ia e Makaio Noala, a hooponoponoia e kekahi Komite i kohoia ma Laie ma ka hui o Aperila, M. H., 1894.
1p.l. [3]–73p. 15cm.
UPB

497. **Bible. Selections. Icelandic. 1895.** Biblíu tílvisanir. [Rvik, Útgefandi, Thórarinn Bjarnason, 1895]
8p. 19½cm.
USlC

498. ———. 1902. (same) [Kaupmannahöfn, Utgefandi, Anthon L. Skanchy, Pretath hjá S. L. Möller, 1902]
8p. 18cm.
UPB, USlC

499. **Bible. Selections. Maori.** He Whakaaturanga Tere. He huihuinga no nga rarangi karaipiture, he mea ata whakatokoto ki tona wahi ki tona wahi kia rite ki tona tikanga ki tona tikanga. He mea ata whakarite ma nga kai kauwhau me nga kai-ako karaipiture. Akarana, He mea ta na Henare Perete, i Hotereni-tiriti [1893?]
vii, 174p. 16cm.
"He Korero whakaata" at forward. Signed Na W. T. Tuati, 1893.
UPB, USlC

500. **Bible. Selections. Samoan. 1920.** O le Tusi Mau. Ua Faasamoaina e Misi Kuinise. 1920. Ua Faatatauina Mo le Au Faifeau ma le Au Paia a le Ekalesia a Ieus Keriso o le Au Paia o Aso e Gata Ai. [Salt Lake City?] 1920.
24p. 16cm.
Variant printing. USlC
USlC

501. ———. 1928. (same) A le Tusi mau ua Faatatauina mo le Au Faifeau ma le Au Paia a le Ekalesia a Iesu Keriso a le Au Paia a Aso e Gata Ai. [Salt Lake City, The Deseret News, 1928]
24p. 16cm.
USlC

502. **Bible. Selections. Swedish. 1886.** Bibliska anvisningar, i öfverensstämmelse med de sista dagarnas heliges tro och lärdomar . . . Fjerde upplagan. Köpenhamn, Utgifven och förlagd af N. C. Flygare. Tryckt hos F. E. Bording, 1886.
2p.l. [5]–72p. 16½cm.
USlC

BIGAMY AND POLYGAMY

503. ———. 1890. (same) Handbok för bebleforskare. En samling af skriftspråk och historiska citat ordnade i kapitel framställande evangeliet eller frälsningsplanens grundsatser öfverensstämmande med de Sista Dagars Heliges tro och Lärdomar. Första upplagan. Köpenhamn, Utgifven och förlagd af C. D. Fjeldsted. Trykt hos F. E. Bording (V. Petersen) 1890.
4p.l., [11]l. 18cm.
USIC

504. ———. 1892. (same) Andra upplagan. Köpenhamn, Utgifven och förlagd af Edw. H. Anderson. Tryckt hos F. E. Bording (V. Petersen) 1892.
4p.l., [11]l. 17cm.
USIC

505. ———. 1900. (same) Handbok för bibelforskare. En samling af skriftspråk och historiska citat ordnade i kapitel framställande evangeliets eller frälsningsplanens frandsatser. Tredje upplagan. Köpenhamn, Utgifven och förlagd af Andreas Peterson. Tryckt hos J. D. Ovist & Komp. (A. Larsen) 1900.
2pl., 120 [8]p. 14½cm.
USIC

506. ———. 1908. (same) Fjärde upplagan. Stockholm, Utgifven och förlagd af P. Sundwall, 1908.
2p.l., 120 [8]p. 14cm.
UPB, USIC

507. Bible. Selections. Tahitian. 1919. Te mau irava parau iritihia no roto mai i te Biblia, te Buka a Mormona, te Buka fafau e te Buka Poe Tao's Rahi. Papeete, Tahiti, Ekalesia a Iesú Mesia i te Feia mo'a i te mau Mahana Hopea nei, 1919.
8p.l. 330p. 17½cm.
USIC

Bibliu tilvisaner. *See Bjarnason, Thorarinn.*

508. Bickersteth, Edward. The divine warning to the Church, at this time, of our present enemies, dangers, and duties, and as to our future prospects. A sermon [on Rev. xvi. 12] etc. With notes and an appendix, containing information respecting the present diffusion of infidelity, lawlessness and popery . . . Fifth thousand. London, Protestant Association, 1842.
50p. 8°
Answered briefly in the *Millennial Star*, May, 1843. V. IV, p. 14.
Other editions: Sixth thousand, enlarged. London, Protestant Association, 1843. Fourth edition, much enlarged. London, Seeley, Burnside & Seeley, 1846.
Brit. Mus.

509. Bicknell, Edmond, *compiler.* Ralphs' scrapbook illustrated by his own camera and collection of photographs, and compiled by his father Edmond Bicknell. Published in Laurence, Mass., Privately printed, 1905.
452 [1]p. Illus., col. plate, port. 14½×19½cm.
DLC, NjP

Bidamon, Emma (Hale) Smith. *See Church of Jesus Christ of Latter-day Saints. Hymnal. English. 1835.*

510. Biddle, George Washington. Writ of error to the Supreme Court of the Territory of Utah. George Reynolds, Plaintiff in error, vs. the U.S., Defendant in error. October session, 1876, No. 180. [n.p., 1876]
63p. 21½cm.
At head of title: In the Supreme Court of the United States.
The test case to determine the constitutionality of the anti-polygamy laws.
CU–B, UPB, USIC

Bidwell, John. *See Hazen, M.B.*

511. Bierbower, V. Speech of V. Bierbower, assistant United States District Attorney in the case of the United States vs. Lorenzo Snow. [n.p., 1882?]
11p. 23cm.
The polygamy trial of Lorenzo Snow.
MH

512. Bierderwolf, William Edward. Mormonism under the searchlight. Chicago, Published by the Glad Tidings Publishing Co. [1910?]
1p.l., 5–69p. 18cm.
CSmH, MH, USIC

513. Biery, George. The answer to what is wrong with the Church of Jesus Christ of Latter-day Saints. Northville [Michigan, n.d.]
16p. 16½cm.
Apostasy of the L.D.S Church, a little during Brigham Young's time and more later.
USIC

514. ———. A Mormons' judgment. Excerpts taken from a tract titled: Facts for thinkers. A Mormon publication. Northville [Michigan? n.d.]
[1]p. 13½cm.
Caption-title.
USIC

515. Big Horn Stake Academy, Cowley, Wyoming. Big Horn Academy. Circular. 1909–
10v. 19½cm.
USIC 1910 (No. 2), 1912–13, 1913–14, 1914–15, 1915–16, 1916–17, 1917–18, 1918–19.

Bigamy and Polygamy. *See Reed, Henry.*

BIGELOW, M. E.

516. Bigelow, M. E. Zions' bondage and redemption, By M. E. Bigelow . . . Salt Lake City, Published by the author, 1927.
48p. 18cm.
An L.D.S. member using many quotations from Latter-day Saint scriptures.
USlC

517. Bikuben. Salt Lake City, Anders W. Winberg, August 1, 1876–October 3, 1935.
15v. bi-weekly, weekly. 40×60cm.
Founded to oppose the *Utah Skandinav*, an anti-Mormon publication.
Editors: John A. Bruun, Andrew Jenson and Peter O. Thomassen.
Title in English: The beehive.
CU–B few issues, MnHi 1918, USlC

518. ———. Centennial Jubilee number, April 6, 1830. Salt Lake City, 1930.
64p. illus. (part col.) 40cm.
UHi, UPB, USlC

519. Bingel, J. P. D. Et lille Schrift til Adversel og Formaning imod Mormonismen, grundlagt paa den hellige Skrift, Guds sande Ord. Dertil en Formaning og Alvarsel imod Oprør i social henseende begrundet efter den hellige Skrift og de 10 Bud. 24 gudelige Sange, forfattede efter nogle gamle, kjendte Melodier fro Psalmebogen. Dertil en lille Eftertale og fluttes med Bon. Forfattet og foelges alene af J. P. D. Bingel fra Aarhus. Aalborg, Trykt i det Bechske Bogtrykkeri [n.d.]
52p. 16½cm.
Music with words only.
Title in English: A little tract against Mormonism.
USlC

520. Binder, Christian. Et maerkvaerdigt Brev fra en Mand, der som medlem af Mormonkirken laerte at kjende og indse Mormonernes skraekkelige Bedragerier og beretter endeel om deres Skjaendselsgjerninger. Oversat af Tydsk. Kjobenhavn, E. G. Iversons Forlag, 1855.
22 [2]p. 18cm.
Title in English: A remarkable letter from a man who was a member of the Mormon church who learned to know and understand the terrible deception and related a portion of their scandalous works.
Sabin: Maerkvaerdigt Brev om Mormonernes Skjaendigheder. Kiobenhavn: Gondrup, 1854. 5427.
UPB

521. Bingham, John Armor. Increase of the army. Speech of Hon. John A. Bingham, of Ohio, in the House of Representatives, March 17, 1858. [Washington, Printed at the Congressional Globe Office, 1858]
7p. 24½cm.
Caption-title.
Related particularly to the raising of troops for use in Utah.
DLC, OClWHi

522. Binheim, Max, *editor.* Women of the West; a series of biographical sketches of living eminent women in the eleven western states of the United States of America. 1928 ed. Compiled and edited by Max Binheim, editor in chief, Charles A. Elvin, associate editor . . . Los Angeles, Calif., Publishers Press [c1928]
6p.l., 223p. ports. 23½cm.
"Pioneer Women of Utah," by Amy Brown Lyman; "Art in Utah in Pioneer Days," by Alice L. Reynolds; List of biographies of Utah women, p. 167–180.
CU–B, UPB

523. Biographical record of Salt Lake City and vicinity, containing biographes of well known citizens of the past and present. Chicago, National Historical Record Co., 1902.
3p.l. [11]–654 [4]p. plates, ports. 29×23½cm.
Includes many Mormon biographies.
CU–B, DLC, NjP, NN, UHi, ULA, UPB, USl, USlC, UU

524. Biographical sketches of Brigham Young and his twenty-nine wives. Beautifully illustrated. Philadelphia, S. C. Upham, 1873.
[6]l. illus., ports. 25½cm.
Advertising matter on verso of leaves.
DLC, USlC

525. Biography of Myron Tanner, by authority of the family. Salt Lake City, The Deseret News, 1907.
35p. 23½cm.
A biography of a Mormon pioneer.
UHi, UPB, USl, USlC

526. Bird, George Robert. Tenderfoot days in territorial Utah, by George Robert Bird . . . Boston, The Gorham Press, 1918.
6p., [2]l., 9–221p. plates. 19½cm.
Includes a great deal of Mormon history.
CSmH, CtY, CU–B, DLC, NjB, NN, UHi, USl, USlC, UU, WHi

527. Bird, Harriet Goble. Sketch of the life of Harriet Goble Bird. Nephi, Utah, Record Publishing Co. [1904?]
14p. 15½cm.
A Mormon biography.
UPB

528. Birge, Julius Charles. The Awakening of the deseret, by Julius C. Birge; with illustrations. Boston, R. G. Badger [c1912]
429p. 22 plates, 3 port. 19½cm.
Chapter XVI "The Mormon Trail," p. 196–210.
Chapters XXIV–XXVI on Mormon history, social life and customers.
Another edition: London, Heath, Cranton & Ouseley Ltd., 1913. DLC.
Howes B463
DLC, ICN, MB, NjP, NN, OO, UHi, UPB, USlC, UU

529. Birney, Hoffman. Roads to roam, by Hoffman Birney; drawings by Charles Hargens. Philadelphia, The Penn Publishing Company [c1930]
4p.l., 7–305p. illus., plates, port. 21cm.
Illustrated lining-papers.
He was impressed by a religion which produces such happiness and contented people.
Another edition: New York, A. L. Burt Co. [c1930] NN, UHi
DLC, MB, NjP, OEac, OLak, PP, PPM, UHi, USl, USIC

530. Birthday reception held in the Salt Lake Temple, Friday, December 11th, 1904. In honor of President John R. Winder on the eighty-second anniversary of his birth. [Salt Lake City, 1904]
2p.l. [5]–46p. port. 17cm.
Includes biographical information.
USIC

531. Bishop, Francis Gladden. An address to the Sons and Daughters of Zion, scattered abroad, through all the earth. [Kirtland, O.?, 1851]
50p. 16½cm.
Written after his dissociation from the body of the church.
Morgan
USIC

532. ———. A brief history of the Church of Jesus Christ of Latter Day Saints, from their rise until the present time, containing an account of, and showing the cause of their sufferings in the state of Missouri, in the years 1833–38. And likewise a summary view of their religious faith. By Francis G. Bishop, a Minister of the order. Salem [Mass.] Printed by Blum & Son, 1839.
14p. 17cm.
DLC

533. ———. The Ensign light of Zion, shepherd of Israel! And "Book of Remembrance." . . . [By Francis Gladden Bishop] Kanesville, Ia., 1852.
42p. 16cm.
Morgan
ULA, USIC

533a. ———. A proclamation from the Lord to His people, scattered throughout all the earth. 1851, Apr. 6, Kirtland [Ohio] [Kirtland? 1851?]
Broadsheet. 61×23cm.
Included is a description of the golden plates and a revelation from the "Book of Life."
USIC

534. ———. A voice of warning and proclamation to all. Voree, Ricine County, Wisconsin Territory, North America, May 20th, 1848. Voree, Wis., 1848.
4p. 19cm.
A prophecy proclaiming James J. Strang as well as Joseph Smith, fallen prophets.
IWW

535. Bishop George Romney. In memoriam. Salt Lake City [1920?]
2p.l. [5]–38p. plates, ports. 21cm.
Includes biographical information.
UPB, USIC, UU

536. Bishop, Isabella Lucy (Bird). A lady's life in the Rocky Mountains. London, J. Murray, 1879.
xii, 296p. 19½cm.
She passed through Utah; some remarks about Mormon women, p. 27; sees Mormon men and wives from the train.
Other editions: New York, Putnams, 1879. UHi, UPB; 5th ed. London, 1885. USIC; New York, Putnam's, 1890. ULA; New York, Scribners, 1901. NN, UHi
CU–B, DLC, NjP, UPB

537. O bit o tauk between two berry chaps, abeawt th' Latter-Day Saints un th' Christion Magozeen, Exhibition th' Church us it awt to be, un so on. Bury: Printed by Dennis Barker, Union Street . . . 1848.
8p. 18cm.
Dialogue rebutting the Spaulding theory.
USIC

538. Bitner, Irma Felt. The birth and growth of Mormonism; a pageant for boys and girls of the Primary Associations. Written and arranged by Irma Felt Bitner. Salt Lake City, General Board of the Primary Association [n.d.]
16p. 18cm.
UPB

539. Bjarnasen, Loftur. His almenna trúarfráfall. [Prentsmithjan Gutenberg, 1905]
8p. 19½cm.
Signed: Loftur Bjarnasen, Jón J. Thortharson.
Title in English: The universal apostacy.
USIC

540. ———. Vinsamleg umraetha um truarefni. [Prentsm. Porv. Porvsonar. 1903?]
31 [1]p. 18cm.
Signed: Loftur Bjarnasen, Jon J. Thortharson. Dec. 11, 1903.
Title in English: A friendly discussion on faith.
USIC

541. Bjarnason, Thórarinn. Biblíu tilvísanir. [Kaupmannahöfn, Utgefandi: Anthon L. Skanchy, Prentath hjá S. L. Möller, 1902]
8p. 18cm.
UPB, USIC

542. Black, Alexander. The story of Ohio, by Alexander Black. Illustrations by L. J. Bridgman. Boston, D. Lathrop Company [c1888]
5p.l. [13]–326p. illus., plates. 21½cm.
At head of title: The Story of the states.
Claims that the Spalding story came into the possession of Joe Smith and he began Mormonism. Christian churches more elevating, p. 176–181.
USIC

BLACK, B.

543. Black, Bynum. Sixty-four loaded bomb-shells in the Mormon ranks . . . By Bynum Black, Williford, Arkansas, Batesville, Arkansas, Christian Pilot Pub. Co. [1910]
40p. 20½cm.
A critical work on Mormonism.
UHi, MoInRC

544. Black, Jeremiah Sullivan. Federal jurisdiction in the territories. Right of local self-government. Judge Black's argument for Utah before the Judiciary Committee of the House of Representatives, February 1, 1883. Salt Lake City, Utah, Deseret News Company, 1883.
28p. 22cm.
Cover-title.
CSmH, DLC, MH, MiU, NN, UHi, UPB, USl, USlC, UU

545. ———. (same) Washignton, D.C., Gibson Brothers, Printers, 1883.
31p. 22cm.
CtY, DLC, MH, USlC, NN, UHi

546. ———. (same, in Danish) Dommer Black's Forsvar for Utah. Central Regeringens Ret til at regere Territorierne. Ret til total Selvregering. Dommer Jeromiah [sic] S. Black's Tale in Underhusets Retskomite, den lste Februar, 1883. Salt Lake City, Trykt i "Bikuben's" Tryklert, 1883.
31p. 18½cm.
USlC

547. Blackman, Emily C. History of Susquehanna County, Pennsylvania. From a period preceding its settlement to recent times, including the annals and geography of each township . . . Also, a sketch of woman's work in the county for the United States sanitary commission, and a list of the soldiers of the national army furnished by many of the townships. By Emily C. Blackman. Philadelphia, Claxton, Remsen & Haffelfinger, 1873.
xp., [1]l., 640p. illus., plates (1 fold.) ports., fold. maps. 23cm.
Mormonism p. 517–582.
Another edition: 1900. DLC
CSmH, DLC, NN, UHi, UPB, USlC

548. Blackman, Louisa. Louisa Blackman's escape from the Mormons. Written by herself. Friends, have you not something to give to the unfortunate one who had her feet frozen off one year ago last winter while trying to escape from Salt Lake City to the States? My mother and two sisters died from starvation on the plains in making their escape. I am left destitute and alone, at the mercy of strangers. I am now trying to raise money to get me a pair of artificial feet. Indianapolis, Ben Franklin Steam Printing House, 1867.
23p. 20½cm.
An improbable account by an improbable lady.
DLC

549. Blaikie, William Garden. Summer suns in the far West; a holiday trip to the Pacific slope, by W. G. Blaikie . . . London, New York [etc.] T. Nelson and Sons, 1890.
3p.l. [9]–160p. front. 18½cm.
A glimpse of Mormon history and the question of its survival. He doesn't believe it will survive.
CU–B, NjP, UHi, USlC

550. Blair, D. H. Polygamy and the Bible. A statement and refutation of arguments, used by Mormons in support of polygamy. By Rev. D. H. Blair . . . [College Springs, Ia.] The author [1893]
vi, 22p. 18½cm.
DLC

551. Blair, George E., *editor.* The mountain empire Utah; a brief and reasonably authentic presentation of the material conditions of a state that lies in the heart of the mountains of the West . . . Ed. and pub. by Geo. E. Blair & R. W. Sloan, Salt Lake City, Utah. [Chicago, Press of W. P. Dunn Co.] c1904.
142 [2]p. illus., ports. 24cm.
Cover-title: The mountain empire Utah. Bulletin of the plains.
A brief history of the Mormon pioneers.
CSmH, CU–B, DLC, MH, NjP, NN, UHi, ULA, UPB, USl, USlC

552. Blair, James G. Polygamous marriages in Utah. Speech of Hon. James G. Blair, of Missouri, in the House of Representatives, February 17, 1872. [Washington, Printed at the Congressional Globe Office, 1872]
7p. 23½cm.
Caption-title.
DLC, MH, OO, USlC

553. Blair, Walter Acheson. A raft pilot's log; a history of the great rafting industry on the Upper Mississippi, 1840–1915. Cleveland, The Arthur H. Clark Company, 1930.
328p. illus., plates, ports., fold. map. 24½cm.
Includes the use of rafts on Black River, Wis. for buildings in Nauvoo.
CU, DLC, NjP, NN, ULA, UPB

554. Blair, William Wallace. The future state. Sermon by Pres. W. W. Blair, delivered at the General Church Reunion, Logan, Iowa, October 16, 1892. Reported for the Herald by Belle B. Robinson. [Lamoni, Ia., 1892]
[49]–56p. 25½cm.
Also published as part of the Sermon series.
NN, USlC

555. ———. Joseph the seer; his prophetic mission vindicated, and the divine origin of the Book of Mormon defended and maintained; being a reply by Elder William W. Blair . . . to Elder William Sheldon . . . Plano, Ill., Printed and Published by the Board

of Publication of the Reorganized Church of Jesus Christ of Latter Day Saints, 1877.
iv [5]–200p. 17½cm.
CSmH, CtY, CU–B, DLC, NjPT, NN, USl, USlC

556. ———. (same) Lamoni, Ia., Printed and Published by the Reorganized Church of Jesus Christ of Later Day Saints, 1877.
iv [5]–200p. 17½cm.
Possibility also an 1887 edition.
NN

557. ———. (same) Lamoni, Ia., Published by the Reorganized Church of Jesus Christ of Latter Day Saints, 1889.
iv [5]–208p. 19cm.
CtY, MoKU, USlC, WHi

558. ———. The memoirs of President W. W. Blair. Compiled by Elder Frederick B. Blair, from Saints' Herald with a preface by President Joseph Smith, an obituary by Elder Mark H. Forscutt, and a statement by Elder Frederick B. Blair . . . Lamoni, Ia., Herald Publishing House, 1908.
4p.l. [5]–204p. port. 20cm.
MoInRC, UHi, ULA

559. Blake, Mary Elizabeth (McGrath). On the wing. Rambling notes of a trip to the Pacific. By Mary E. Blake . . . Boston, Lee and Shepard, 1883.
4p.l., 235p. 16½cm.
Chapter XV "In the City of Zion," p. 185–198. Authors' visit to Salt Lake City and her comments on Mormonism.
Author's visit to Salt Lake City and her comments on
Other editions: 2d ed. CU–B, USl, WAU; 3rd ed. CU–B, ICN, UPB; 4th ed. UHi
CSmH, DLC, MH, NjP, NN, ULA, USlC, UU

560. Blakeley, Albert. For a Good work we are stoned. [n.p., 1906?]
4p. 23cm.
Church of the Firstborn. Vindication of the character of Albert and Jennie Blakeley.
MoInRC

561. ———. Thus saith the Lord. [Chicago, Illinois? 1906?]
3 [1]p. 22½cm.
[1]p. a Hymn.
Prophecies of a member of the Church of the Firstborn. Signed: August, 1906.
MoInRC

562. ———. (same) [n.p., 1906]
4p. 22½cm.
"Divine certificate and Table of Covenant of the kingdom of Heaven, Church of the First-born," p. 3.
MoInRC

562a. Blanchard, Rufus. History of Illinois, to accompany an historical map of the state. Chicago, National School Furnishing Co., 1883.
128p. fold. map. 23cm.
Mormons mentioned, p. 69.
USlC

563. Bleeker, Sylvester. Gen. Tom Thumb's three years' tour around the world, accompanied by his wife — Lovinia Warren Stratton, Commodore Nutt, Miss Minnie Warren and party. New York, Booth, 1872.
144p. illus., plates. 18cm.
Includes a visit to Salt Lake City with substantial material on his impressions of Mormonism.
CtY, CU, DLC, ICN, MH, NjP, NN, UHi, WHi

564. Bliss, Charles H. Baptism for the remission of sins. By C. H. Bliss, an Elder of the Church of Jesus Christ of Latter-day Saints. [Salt Lake City] Juvenile Instructor Office [1882?]
4p. 19½cm.
CU–B, NN, USlC, UU

565. ———. (same) [Salt Lake City, Printed and for sale at Deseret News Office, n.d.]
4p. 19cm.
UPB, USlC

566. ———. (same) [Liverpool? Printed at the Millennial Star Office? 1907?]
[2]p. 22cm.
Caption-title.
UPB

567. ———. (same) [Liverpool Church of Jesus Christ of Latter-day Saints. British Mission, 1911?]
[2]p. 21cm.
Caption-title.
UHi, UPB

568. ———. (same) [n.p., n.d.]
2]p. 21½cm.
A missionary tract. Published in many variants, with and without printing information.
UHi, UPB, USlC

569. ———. Beauty, courtship, marriage. By C. H. Bliss. Salt Lake City, 1883.
2p.l. [5]–55p. 16½cm.
Uses Mormon illustrations.
USlC

570. ———. Happiness; and its fundamental principles. By C. H. Bliss, Editor of "Our life and home." . . . Salt Lake City, Published by Egan & Bliss, 1884.
3p.l., 39p. 22cm.
MH, USlC

BLISS, C. H.

571. ———. Is baptism essential to salvation? [Independence, Mo., Published by the Missions of the Church of Jesus Christ of Latter-day Saints, Press of Zion's Printing and Publishing Co., 1882?]
[4]p. 16cm.
A missionary tract.
NN, DLC

572. ———. (same) [Liverpool? Millennial Star Office? 1908?]
[2]p. 22cm.
Caption-title.
UPB

573. ———. (same) [Liverpool? Church of Jesus Christ of Latter-day Saints. British Mission, 1911?]
[2]p. 21cm.
Caption-title.
Variant printing.
UHi

574. ———. (same) [Salt Lake City, The Deseret News, n.d.]
[4]p. 17cm.
MH, MoInRC

575. ———. (same) [Salt Lake City, Printed and for sale at the Juvenile Instructor Office, n.d.]
4p. 19cm.
Caption-title.
Several variant editions. None dated.
CU-B, DLC, NN, UHi, UPB, USlC, UU

576. ———. (same, in Spanish) Es El Bautismo Esencial á la Salvación? Traducido del Inglés por el Elder Rey L. Pratt Y El Bautismo á Quien y Como Debe Ser Administrado por el Elder Helaman Pratt. El Paso, Publicado por la Misión Mexicana de la Iglesia de Jesu Cristo de los Santos de los Ultimos Dias [n.d.]
16p. 18cm.
USlC

577. **Bliss, Charles R.** The New West Education Commission. A paper presented to the triennial council of congregational churches by Rev. Charles R. Bliss, Worchester, Mass. October 1889. [Chicago, 1889]
22p. 21cm.
Activities of the Commission in regard to Mormonism.
MH

Blood Atonement. *See Mills, William G.; Old Residenter [pseud.]*

578. **Blunt, John Henry.** Dictionary of sects, heresies, ecclesiastical parties, and schools of religious thought, edited by the Rev. John Henry Blunt . . . Philadelphia, J. B. Lippincott & Co.: London, Rivingtons, 1874.
viii, 647 [1]p. 27cm.
"Mormons," p. 344–354.
NjPT, UPB

579. **Boddam-Whetham, John Whetham.** Western wanderings: a record of travel in the evening land, by J. W. Boddam-Whetham . . . London, R. Bentley and Son, 1874.
xiip., [1]l., 364p. 12 plates. 23cm.
Visit to Salt Lake City and a description of the Mormons.
CSmH, CtY, CU-B, DLC, NjP, NN, UHi, ULA, UPB, USlC, UU

580. **Bodenstedt, Frederich Martin von.** Vom Atlantischen zum Stillen Ocean. Leipzig, F. A. Brockhaus, 1882.
xi, 426p. 22cm.
His travel through America with a chapter on the Mormons.
Title in English: From the Atlantic to the Pacific.
CU-B, DLC, NjP, UHi, UPB

581. **Bogard, Benjamin M.** El Mormonismo. Estudio en doce capitulos escrito por el Señor Benjamin M. Bogard para combatir tan perniciosa secta. Mexico, Casa Metodista de Publicaciones, 1910.
70p. 16cm.
Title in English: Mormonism.
USlC

582. **Boller, Henry A.** Among the Indians. Eight years in the far West: 1858–1866. Embracing sketches of Montana and Salt Lake. By Henry A. Boller . . . Philadelphia, T. Ellwood Zell, 1868.
xvi [17]–428p. front., 1 fold. map. 19½cm.
Three chapters devoted to Mormonism and Salt Lake City. Praise for accomplishments of the Mormons in Salt Lake City; coarseness of Mormon sermons; tirades against gentiles and apostates; feels women's votes will kill polygamy. No one can take Brigham Young's place so it will end with him.
Sabin B6221
CSmH, CtY, CU-B, DLC, ICN, NjP, NN

583. **Bollman, Calvin P.** Religious liberty and the Mormon question. Oakland, Calif., Published by the International Religious Liberty Association, 1893.
17p. 19cm. (The religious liberty library. No. 10, June, 1893)
UPB

584. **Bond, M. H.** If Christ came to Chicago. [n.p., n.d.]
8p. 14cm.
A RLDS tract showing which church Christ would recognize.
MoInRC

585. ———. Polygamy. Independence, Mo., Ensign Publishing House, 1903.
14p. 16cm. (The Gospel Banner. V. 11, No. 4. Extra A)
A pamphlet concerning the Utah doctrine of polygamy.
MoInRC

———. The Seer of Palmyra. See below.

586. ———. Spiritual gifts and the seer of Palmyra. A sequel to spiritual gifts and spirit manifestations. By M. H. Bond . . . Providence, R. I. [E. A. Johnson & Co., Printers, 1891?]
103, 58p. 19cm.
Part 2 has special t.-p.: The seer of Palmyra, or the three witnesses. A sequel to *Spiritual Gifts.* 58p.
USIC, WHi

587. Bond, William. The early history of Mormonism; and the true source where the aborigines of the continent came from. By Wm. Bond. Portland, Schwab Bros., Printing and Lithographing Co., 1890.
24p. 23cm.
A work concerning the claims of the Book of Mormon.
NN, USIC

588. Bonner, Geraldine. The Emigrant trail. New York, Grosset & Dunlap [1910]
496p. col. front. 20cm.
A western novel with many references to the Mormons.
CU–B, UPB

589. ———. Tomorrow's tangle, by Geraldine Bonner; illustrations by Arthur I. Kellar. Indianapolis, The Bobbs-Merrill Company [1903]
5p.l., 458p. front., 4 plates. 20cm.
Fiction, with Mormon background.
DLC, USIC

590. Bonney, Edward. The banditti of the prairies, or, The murderer's doom!! A tale of the Mississippi valley, by Edward Bonney. Chicago, E. Bonney, 1850.
2p.l. [9]–196p. plates, port. 22cm.
For the other side of Bonney's story, see Heman C. Smith's articles in the *Lamoni Patriot,* March 10, 17, 24, 1910.
Includes the Mormon's unlawful activities in Nauvoo.
Other editions: Chicago, W. W. Danenhower, 1853. CtY; Chicago, D. B. Cooke & Co., 1856. DLC; also published in numerous editions 1857–1893
Howes B 606
DLC, ICN, USIC, WaA, WHi

591. Bonsal, Stephen. Edward Fitzgerald Beale, a pioneer in the path of empire, 1882–1903. By Stephen Bonsal. With 17 illustrations. New York and London, G. P. Putnam's Sons . . . 1912.
xii p., [1]l., 312p. plates, 2 ports. 23cm.
Reference to the Mormons in route across southern Utah, 1853, largely based upon journal of Gwynn Harris Heap, p. 99, 133–34, 136, 138–49, 152, 157, 164, 172.
CU–B

592. Bonsall, Marian. The tragedy of the Mormon woman. By Marian Bonsall . . . Minneapolis, Minn., The Housekeeper Corporation, 1908.
3p.l. [5]–96p. plates, ports. 22cm.
"Originally published in the *Housekeeper,* July 1905 to February 1906, inclusive," — Introd.
Fiction concerning Mormonism.
DLC, ICJ, NN, UHi, USIC, WHi

593. Bonwick, James. The Mormons and the silver mines. By James Bonwick . . . London, Hodder and Stoughton, 1872.
vi p. 1l., 425p. 19cm.
Mormonism in Nevada.
CSmH, CtY, ICJ, ICN, MoInRC, NjP, NN, UHi, ULA, UPB, USIC, UU, WHi

594. ———. An octogenarian's reminiscences. London, James Nichols, 1902.
xiv, 367 [4]p. illus. 18½cm.
UHi

Book of Commandments. *See Doctrine and Covenants.*

595. Book of Mormon. English. 1830. The Book of Mormon: an account written by the hand of Mormon, upon plates taken from the plates of Nephi . . . By Joseph Smith, Junior. Palmyra, Printed by E. B. Grandin, for the author, 1830.
iv [5]–588 [2]p. 19cm.
First edition issued with several variants: p. iv is listed as vi; p. 97 is poorly printed in some copies; p. 207, seven lines from the bottom exceeding reads exceding; p. 207, seven lines from the bottom, great reads grert; p. 201, the l is raised on many copies; p. 212 is printed as p. 122; p. 487 reads 48 on some copies; on p. 575, Elder or priest reads Elder priest. No order of printing has been determined at the present time. Many copies have the iv p. index inserted.
This is a later printing.
Sabin 83038
CSmH, CtY, CU–B, DLC, ICN, IHi, MB, MH, MU, MoInRC, MWA, NjP, NjPS, NjPT, NN, OC, PP, PU, UHi, ULA, UPB, USIC, UU

596. ———. **1837.** The Book of Mormon: an account written by the hand of Mormon, upon plates taken from the plates of Nephi . . . Translated by Joseph Smith, Jr. Kirtland, Ohio, Printed by O. Cowdery and Co., for P. P. Pratt and J. Goodson, 1837.
[v]–iv [7]–619 [2]p. 15cm.
Second edition. Corrected by Joseph Smith and Oliver Cowdery. With a new preface by Parley P. Pratt.
Sabin 83039
CSmH, CtY, CU–B, DLC, ICN, MH, NN, UHi, UPB, USIC

597. ———. **1840.** The Book of Mormon. Translated by Joseph Smith, Jr. Third Edition, carefully revised by the translator. Nauvoo, Ill.,

Printed by Robinson and Smith. Stereotyped by Shepard and Stearns, Cincinnati, Ohio, 1840.
2p.l., 7–571 [2]p. 15cm.
Published by Ebenezer Robinson and Don Carlos Smith, younger brother of Joseph Smith. In some editions, an index of vii pages has been added, not part of the original printing.
Sabin 83040
CSmH, CtY, CU–B, DLC, ICN, MoInRC, NjP, NN, UHi, UPB, USIC, WHi

598. ———. **1841.** The Book of Mormon: an account written by the hand of Mormon upon the plates taken from the plates of Nephi . . . Translated by Joseph Smith, Jr. First European Edition, from the Second American Edition. Liverpool, Printed by J. Tompkins for B. Young, H. C. Kimball and P. P. Pratt, 1841.
2p.l., 643p. 14cm.
Published under the guidance of Brigham Young, who did not seem to be aware of the American 1840 edition.
Sabin 83041
CtY, CU–B, DLC, ICN, MH, NjP, NN, UPB, USIC, UU

599. ———. **1842.** The Book of Mormon: Translated by Joseph Smith. Fourth American and Second Stereotype Edition, carefully revised by the Translator. Nauvoo, Illinois, Printed by Joseph Smith, 1842.
[4] 7–571 [2]p. 15cm.
The only edition in which the jr. or jun. is dropped from Joseph Smith. His father died in September, 1840.
Sabin 83042
CtY, CU–B, DLC, ICN, NjP, NN, OC, DLC, UPB, USIC, UU, WHi

600. ———. **1849.** The Book of Mormon: an Account written by the Hand of Mormon, upon Plates taken from the Plates of Nephi . . . Translated by Joseph Smith, Jun. Second European Edition. Liverpool, Published by Orson Pratt . . . 1849.
[iv]–xii, 563p. 16cm.
Index transferred to the front of the work.
Sabin 83043
CU–B, ICHi, MH, MoInRC, NN, UPB, USIC

601. ———. **1852.** (same) Third European Edition, Liverpool, Published by F. D. Richards . . . 1852.
2p.l. [iv]–xii, 563 [1]p. 15½cm.
Stereotyped edition.
Sabin 83044
CU–B, DLC, MH, MiU–C, NjP, NN, UHi, UPB, USIC, UU

602. ———. **1854.** (same) Fourth European Edition. Liverpool, Published for Orson Pratt by S. W. Richards, 1854.
xii, 563p. 16cm.
Sabin 83045
CtY, CU, CU–B, MH, MoInRC, MoK, NjP, NN, UHi, UU

603. ———. **1854.** (same) Fifth European Edition. Stereotyped. Liverpool, Published by F. D. Richards, 1854.
xii, 563p. 16cm.
Sabin 83046
MB, MH, MoInRC, NN, UPB, USIC, UU

604. ———. **1858.** The Book of Mormon. Translated by Joseph Smith, Jr. Reprinted from the Third American Edition, carefully revised by the translator. New York, Jas. O. Wright & Company [1858]
xix, 380p. 20cm.
Known as the "Wright edition." Published before 1862. This is the first unauthorized edition, published as a business venture.
Morgan, Sabin S3047
CtY, DLC, IWW, MH, MoInRC, NjP, NjPT, NN, UPB, ViU

605. ———. **1858.** (same) New York, J. O. Wright and Co. [1858]
v–x [xiii]–xix, 380p. 20cm.
An unauthorized edition which was published by Zadoc Brooks from the Wright edition with his introduction.
CU–B, DLC, MH, MoInRC, NN, UHi, UPB, USIC, UU

606. ———. **1866.** (same as 5th European edition) Sixth European Edition. Stereotyped. Liverpool, Published by Brigham Young . . . 1866.
xii, 563p. 16cm.
NN, MoInRC, UHI UPB, USI, USIC, UU

607. ———. **1869.** Deseret Alphabet. The Book of Mormon: an account written by the hand of Mormon upon plates taken from the plates of Nephi . . . Translated by Joseph Smith, jun. New York, Published for the Deseret University, by Russell Bros., 1869.
3p.l. [v]–xi, 443p. 23cm.
Title and text printed in the Deseret alphabet.
Title transliterated.
Sabin 83050
CSmH, CtY, CU–B, DLC, ICN, MH, NjP, NN, UHi, ULA, UPB, USIC, UU

608. ———. **1869.** Deseret Alphabet. The Book of Mormon, upon plates taken from the plates of Nephi . . . Translated by Joseph Smith, jun. Part I. New York, Published for the Deseret University by Russell Bros., 1869.
116p. 23cm.
Includes the first section of the Book of Mormon (above).
Title transliterated.
CU–B, DLC, NjP, NN, UHi, ULA, UPB, USIC, UU

BOOK OF MORMON. ENGLISH. 1888

609. ———. **1871.** (same as 1866 edition) Salt Lake City . . . Published by George Q. Cannon, 1871.
xii, 563p. 16cm.
Sabin 83051
DLC, ICN, MH, MoInRC, NjP, NN, UPB, USlC

610. ———. **1874.** (same) Salt Lake City, . . . Published by David O. Calder, 1874.
xii, 563p. 16cm.
Sabin 83052
CtY, DLC, ICHi, ICN, UHi, UPB, USlC

611. ———. **1874.** The Book of Mormon. Translated by Joseph Smith, Jun. Reprinted from the Third American Edition. Plano, Ill., Published by the Reorganized Church of Jesus Christ of Latter Day Saints, 1874.
xii, 545p. 16cm.
The first edition published by the Reorganized Church of Jesus Christ of Latter Day Saints. It is not a reprint from the third American edition as the title indicates, but follows the Liverpool stereotyped edition of 1852.
Sabin 83053
CtY, ICN, MH, MoInRC, NjP, NN, UPB, USlC

612. ———. **1874.** (same) Lamoni, Ia., Published by the Reorganized Church of Jesus Christ of Latter Day Saints, 1874.
xii, 545p. 16cm.
Sabin 83054
CtY, DLC, IWW, MH, MoInRC, MoK, NjP, NN, UHi

613. ———. **1876.** (same as 1874, Salt Lake City edition) Salt Lake City, Published by David O. Calder, 1876.
[v]–xii, 563p. 16cm.
MH, NjPT, NN, UPB, USl, USlC, UU

614. ———. **1877.** (same) Salt Lake City, Published by Cannon and Young, 1877.
xii, 563p. 16cm.
Sabin 83055
MoInRC, NN, UPB, USlC, UU

615. ———. **1879.** (same) Division into chapters & verses, with references, by Orson Pratt, Sen. Electrotype Edition. Liverpool, Printed and Published by William Budge . . . 1879.
xii, 623p. 16cm.
Sabin 83056
CSmH, MoInRC, UHi, UPB, USlC

616. ———. **1879.** (same) Salt Lake City, Deseret News Printing and Publishing Establishment, 1879.
xii, 623p. 19cm.
Sabin 83057
CtY, CU–B, DLC, MoInRC, NjP, UU, ViU

617. ———. **1881.** (same) Second Electrotype Edition. Liverpool, A. Carrington, 1881.
xii, 623p. 16cm.
Sabin 83058
DLC, NjP, NN, UPB, UU

618. ———. **1881.** (same) Salt Lake City, Deseret News Printing and Publishing Establishment, 1881.
xii, 623p. 18cm.
Sabin 83059
DLC, MoInRC, NN, USlC

619. ———. **1882.** (same) Salt Lake City, Deseret News Co., Printers and Publishers, 1882.
xii, 623p. 19cm.
Sabin 83060
CU–B, ICHi, MH, MoInRC, NjP, NN, UPB, USlC

620. ———. **1883.** (same) Salt Lake City, Deseret News Company, Printers and Publishers, 1883.
xii, 623p. 19cm.
Sabin 83062
MB, MoInRC, PPD, USlC

621. ———. **1883.** (same) Third Electrotype Edition. Liverpool, Printed & Published by John Henry Smith, 1883.
xii, 623p. 16cm.
Sabin 83061
DLC, MoInRC, UPB, USlC

622. ———. **1885.** (same) Salt Lake City, Deseret News Co., Printers and Publishers, 1885.
xii, 623p. 25½cm.
Sabin 83063
MoInRC, UPB, USl, USlC, UU

623. ———. **1888.** (same) Fourth Electrotype Edition. Liverpool, Printed and Published by George Teasdale, 1888.
xii, 623p. 16cm.
Sabin 83064
MoInRC, UPB

624. ———. **1888.** (same) Salt Lake City, Deseret News Co., Printers and Publishers, 1888.
xii, 623p. 16cm.
Sabin 83065
MoInRC, NjP, NN, USlC

625. ———. **1888.** (same) Salt Lake City, Juvenile Instructor Office, 1888.
xii, 623p. 25½cm.
A large type edition.
Sabin 83066
DLC, IWW, MH, MoInRC, NjP, UHi, ULA, UPB

BOOK OF MORMON. ENGLISH. 1889

626. ———. 1889. (same) Fifth Electrotype Edition. Liverpool, Printed and Published by George Teasdale, 1889.
xii, 623p. 16cm.
Sabin 83067
MoInRC, UPB

627. ———. 1891. (same) Third Electrotype Edition. Salt Lake City, George Q. Cannon and Sons., Co., 1891.
xii, 623p. 17cm.
Sabin 83068.
CSmH, CU-B, DLC, MH, MoInRC, NN, UHi, UPB, USI, USIC, ViU

628. ———. 1892. The Book of Mormon. An Account written by the Hand of Mormon upon Plates taken from the Plates of Nephi . . . Translated by Joseph Smith, Jun. Lamoni, Published by the Reorganized Church of Jesus Christ of Latter Day Saints, 1892.
xi, 485p. 25½cm.
Large type edition of the RLDS Church. Published with the New Testament of the Inspired Version under binder's title "Two records"
Sabin 83069
MH, MoInRC, MoK, UPB, USIC

629. ———. 1893. (same as 1891 edition) Salt Lake City, Deseret News Co., 1893.
xii, 623p. 17cm.
UU

630. ———. 1898. (same) Sixth Electrotype Edition. Liverpool, Printed and Published by Rulon S. Wells, 1898.
xii, 623p. 16cm.
Sabin 83070
UPB, USIC, UU

631. ———. 1899. The Nephite records. An account written by the hand of Mormon upon plates taken from the plates of Nephi . . . Translated by Joseph Smith, Jun. [Independence, Mo.] Published by the Church of Christ, Printed from the Palmyra edition (1830) which edition was printed from the original manuscript, 1899.
xiii, 721p. 16½cm.
Published by the Church of Christ (Whitmer). Sabin lists this edition as published in Kansas City, Mo. There is some question as to actual publication location.
Sabin 83071
IWW, MoInRC, UPB, USIC

632. ———. 1900. (same as 1874, Lamoni edition) Twenty-second Edition. Lamoni, Ia., Published by the Reorganized Church of Jesus Christ of Latter Day Saints, 1900.
xii, 545p. 16cm.
This is the first Reorganized Church edition to bear an edition number. The earlier editions and printings were probably used for unnumbered editions.
Sabin 83074
MoInRC, NjPT

633. ———. 1900. (same as 1898 edition) Seventh Electrotype Edition. Liverpool, Printed and Published by Platte D. Lyman, 1900.
xii, 623p. 16cm.
Sabin 83072
USIC

634. ———. 1900. (same) Salt Lake City, The Deseret News, Printers and Publishers, 1900.
xii, 623p. 17cm.
Sabin 83073
MoInRC, UPB, USIC

635. ———. 1901. (same as 1900, Lamoni edition) Twenty-fifth Edition. Lamoni, Published by the Reorganized Church of Jesus Christ of Latter Day Saints, 1901.
xii, 545p. 16cm.
The word "Junior" after Smith is spelled in full.
Sabin 83075
MoInRC, USIC

636. ———. 1902. (same) Twenty-sixth Edition. Lamoni, Ia., Published by the Reorganized Church of Jesus Christ of Latter Day Saints, 1902.
xii, 545p. 17cm.
Sabin 83076
MoInRC, UPB

637. ———. 1902. (same as 1892 edition) Eighth Edition. Lamoni, Ia., Published by the Reorganized Church of Jesus Christ of Latter Day Saints, 1902.
xi, 485p. 27cm.
The Reorganized Church had two series of Book of Mormons running at the same time. The earlier series began with the 1874 edition. The second began with the 1892 edition.
MoInRC

638. ———. 1902. (same as 1900, Salt Lake City edition) Fourth Electrotype Edition. Kansas City, Mo., Southwestern States Mission, Publishers, 1902.
[4]-12, 623p. 17cm.
Sabin 83077
ICHi, MoInRC, UHi, UPB, USIC, UU

639. ———. 1903. (same) Eighth Electrotype Edition. Liverpool, Printed & Published by Francis M. Lyman, 1903.
xii, 623p. 16cm.
Also published as a triple combination: Book of Mormon, Doctrine and Covenants, and Pearl of Great Price.
Sabin 83078
USIC

640. ———. 1903. (same) Salt Lake City, The Deseret News, Printers and Publishers, 1903.
[4] vii-xii, 623p. 17cm.
Sabin 83079
CU-B, UPB, USIC, UU

641. ———. **1903.** (same as 1902, Lamoni, Twenty-sixth edition) Twenty-eighth Edition. Lamoni, Ia., Published by the Reorganized Church of Jesus Christ of Latter Day Saints, 1903.
545p. 17cm.
From the 1874 edition.
MoInRC

642. ———. **1903.** (same as the 1902, Lamoni, large type Edition) Tenth Edition. Lamoni, Ia., Reorganized Church of Jesus Christ of Latter Day Saints, 1903.
xi, 485p. 26cm.
CU-B

643. ———. **1904.** (same as 1903, Salt Lake City edition) Salt Lake City, The Deseret News, Printers & Publishers, 1904.
[4] [vii]-xii [2] 623p. 17cm.
Printed from new plates. Also published as a triple combination.
Sabin 83080
MH, MoInRC, NN, UPB, ULA, USIC

644. ———. **1904.** (same as 1903, Lamoni. Twenty-eighth Edition) Twenty-ninth Edition. Lamoni, Ia., Published by the Reorganized Church of Jesus Christ of Latter Day Saints, 1904.
xii, 545p. 17cm.
Sabin 83081
MoInRC, OCl

645. ———. **1905.** (same) Thirtieth Edition. Lamoni, Ia., Published by the Reorganized Church of Jesus Christ of Latter Day Saints, 1905.
xii, 545p. 16cm.
Sabin 83082
MoInRC

646. ———. **1905.** (same as 1903, Lamoni, large type edition) Eleventh Edition. Lamoni, Ia., Published by the Reorganized Church of Jesus Christ of Latter Day Saints, 1905.
5, vi-xi, 485, 14p. 26cm.
MoInRC, UPB

647. ———. **1905.** (same as 1904, Salt Lake City edition) Salt Lake City, Church of Jesus Christ of Latter-day Saints, Deseret Sunday School Union, 1905.
xiv, 654p. 10cm.
Vest pocket edition.
Sabin 83083
USIC

648. ———. **1905.** (same) Chicago, Northern States Mission, Church of Jesus Christ of Latter-day Saints, Publishers [Press of H. C. Etten] 1905.
[8] vii-xii, 623p. 16cm.
Sabin 83084
MH, MoInRC, NN, USIC, UU ViU, WHi

649. ———. **1905.** (same) Chattanooga, Tenn., Southern States Mission, Church of Jesus Christ of Latter-day Saints, Publisher [Press of H. C. Etten] 1905.
xii, 623p. 16cm.
USIC

650. ———. **1905.** (same) Kansas City, Mo., Central States Mission, Church of Jesus Christ of Latter-day Saints, 1905.
xii [2] 623p. 16cm.
Printed from the plates of the Chicago edition.
Sabin 83085
MoInRC, USIC

651. ———. **1905.** (same) Denver, Col., Western States Mission, Church of Jesus Christ of Latter-day Saints, 1905.
xii, 623p. 17cm.
Printed from the plates of the Chicago, 1905 edition.
ViU

652. ———. **1905.** (same) Salt Lake City, Bureau of Information, Church of Jesus Christ of Latter-day Saints, 1905.
xii, 623p. 17cm.
PHC, UU

653. ———. **1906.** (same) Salt Lake City, The Deseret News, Printers and Publishers, 1906.
[4] vii-xii [2] 623p. 25½cm.
From the 1888 large type edition.
Sabin 83087
NjP, NN, USIC, UPB, UU

654. ———. **1906.** (same) Ninth Electrotype Edition. Liverpool, Printed and Published by Heber J. Grant, 1906.
xii, 623p. 18cm.
Also published in a triple combination.
MoInRC, USIC, UU

655. ———. **1906.** (same) Chicago, Northern States Mission of the Church of Jesus Christ of Latter-day Saints, Publishers, 1906.
[8] vii-xii, 623p. 17cm.
On page facing half title: Second Chicago Edition. Press of Henry C. Etten & Co., Chicago. 12,000 copies printed.
Sabin 83088.
USIC

656. ———. **1906.** (Same as 1905, Lamoni, thirtieth edition) Thirty-first Edition. Lamoni, Ia., Published by the Reorganized Church of Jesus Christ of Latter Day Saints, 1906.
xii, 545p. 16cm.
Sabin 83089
MoInRC

BOOK OF MORMON. ENGLISH. 1907

657. ———. **1907.** (same) Thirty-third Edition. Lamoni, Ia., Published by the Reorganized Church of Jesus Christ of Latter Day Saints, 1907.
xii, 545, 12p. 17cm.
The plates were discarded after this edition.
Sabin 83090
MoInRC

658. ———. **1907.** (same as 1906, Chicago edition) Chicago, Northern States Mission, Church of Jesus Christ of Latter-day Saints, 1907.
[8] vii–xii, 623p. 17cm.
On page facing half title: Third Chicago Edition, Press of Henry C. Etten & Co., 27,000 copies printed.
Sabin 83091
MH, NjP, NN, UPB, USIC, ViU

659. ———. **1907.** (same) Salt Lake City, The Deseret News, Printers and Publishers, 1907.
[4] vii–xii [2] 623p. 17cm.
Also published as a triple combination.
Sabin 83092
MoInRC, UPB, USIC

660. ———. **1907.** (same) Salt Lake City, Published by the Deseret Sunday School Union, 1907.
xiv, 654p. 12cm.
Vest pocket edition.
Sabin 83093
MH, UPB, USIC, UU

661. ———. **1907.** (same) Independence, Mo., Central States Mission, Church of Jesus Christ of Latter-day Saints, 1907.
xii, 623p. 17cm.
"Third Chicago Edition. Press of Henry C. Etten & Co., Chicago."
MH, UPB

662. ———. **1908.** (same) Salt Lake City, Bureau of Information, Church of Jesus Christ of Latter-day Saints, 1908.
xii, 623p. 17cm.
UU

663. ———. **1908.** (same as 1905, Lamoni, large type edition) Twelfth Edition. Lamoni, Ia., Published by the Reorganized Church of Jesus Christ of Latter Day Saints, 1908.
xi, 485, 14p. 27cm.
From the 1892 plates.
MoInRC, UHi, UPB

664. ———. **1908.** (same as 1907, Salt Lake City, Deseret Sunday School edition) Salt Lake City, Published by the Deseret Sunday School School, 1908.
xiv, 654p. 12cm.
Vest pocket edition.
Sabin 83094
USIC

665. ———. **1908.** (same) Compared with the original manuscript and the Kirtland Edition of 1837, which was carfeully re-examined and compared with the original manuscript by Joseph Smith and Oliver Cowdrey. Authorized Edition. Lamoni, Ia., Board of Publication of the Reorganized Church of Jesus Christ of Latter Day Saints, 1908.
viii, 822p. 19cm.
First edition "authorized" by the General Conference of the Reorganized Church, 1906. Compared extensively with the manuscript, 1830 and 1837 editions.
Sabin 83095
MoInRC, UU

666. ———. **1908.** (same as 1907, Chicago third edition) Chicago, Northern States Mission, Church of Jesus Christ of Latter Day Saints, 1908.
4p.l. [vii]–xii, 623p. 17cm.
On page facing half title: Fourth Chicago Edition. Press of Henry C. Etten, Chicago.
Sabin 83097
CU–B, DLC, NN, UHi, UPB, USIC, UU

667. ———. **1908.** (same) Denver, Col., Western States Mission, Church of Jesus Christ of Latter Day Saints, 1908.
xii, 623p. 16cm.
UPB

668. ———. **1908.** (same) New York, Eastern States Mission, Church of Jesus Christ of Latter-day Saints, Publishers, 1908.
xii, 623p. 16cm.
MB, MH, NN copy imperfect, PBa, PP, PU

669. ———. **1908.** (same) Independence, Mo., Central States Mission. Church of Jesus Christ of Latter-day Saints, 1908.
xii, 623p. 17cm.
"Fourth Chicago edition"
Press of Henry C. Etten & Co., Chicago.
USIC

670. ———. **1909.** (same) Ninth Electrotype Edition. Liverpool, Printed and Published by Charles W. Penrose, 1909.
xii, 623p. 16cm.
Also published as a triple combination.
Sabin 83098
NN, UPB, USIC

671. ———. **1911.** (same as 1908, Lamoni, "authorized edition") Lamoni, Ia., [Reorganized Church of Jesus Christ of Latter Day Saints] 1911.
viii, 822p. 19cm.
Sabin 83099
MoInRC, NN

672. ———. **1911?** (same as 1909, Liverpool, ninth electrotype edition) [Chicago] Missions of the Church of Jesus Christ of Latter Day Saints [1911].
xii, 623 [1]p. 17cm.
UPB, USIC

673. ———. **1911?** (same) Chicago, Ill., Church of Jesus Christ of Latter-day Saints [1911].
xii, 623 [1]p. 22cm.
Large type edition.
Sabin 83100
NN, UPB, USIC

674. ———. **1912.** (same as 1911, Chicago edition) Third Electrotype Edition. Liverpool, Printed and Published by Rudgar Clawson, 1912.
xii, 623p. 16cm.
Also published as triple combination.
Sabin 83101
USIC

675. ———. **1912?** (same as 1908, fourth Chicago edition) Chicago, Mission of the Church of Jesus Christ of Latter-day Saints [1912]
xii, 623p. 17cm.
On page facing title: Fifth Chicago Edition. Press of Henry C. Etten and Co., Chicago.
Sabin 83102
MoInRC, UHi, UPB, USI, USIC

676. ———. **1913.** (same as 1908, Salt Lake City, Deseret Sunday School edition) Salt Lake City, Deseret Sunday School Union, 1913.
xiv, 654p. 12cm.
Vest pocket edition.
Sabin 83103
USIC

677. ———. **1913.** (same as 1911, Lamoni, "authorized" edition) Lamoni, Ia. [The Reorganized Church of Jesus Christ of Latter Day Saints] 1913.
viii, 822p. 19cm.
Sabin 83104
IWW, MoInRC, OO, USI, USIC

678. ———. **1913.** (same as the 1912, fifth Chicago edition) First Independence Edition. [Independence] Published by the Mission of the Church of Jesus Christ of Latter-day Saints, 1913.
xii, 623p. 17cm.
This is the first Independence edition, of 5,000 copies. Editions 1–8 published from 1913–1918. Press of Zions Printing and Publishing Co.
Sabin 83105
MoInRC, NN, PU, UPB, USIC

679. ———. **1913.** (same) [Independence, n.d.]
xii, 623p. 17cm.
"Second Independence Edition."
MoInRC, UPB, USIC

680. ———. **1913.** (same) [Independence, n.d.]
xii, 623p. 17½cm.
"Third Independence Edition."
MoK, UHi, UPB, USIC, WHi

681. ———. **1913.** (same) [Independence, n.d.]
xii, 623p. 17cm.
"Fourth Independence Edition."
MoInRC, UPB

682. ———. **1913.** (same) [Independence, n.d.]
xii, 623p. 18cm.
"Fifth Independence Edition."
IU, NBUG, NN, UPB

683. ———. **1913.** (same) [Independence, n.d.]
xii, 623p. 17cm.
"Sixth Independence Edition."
MH, MoInRC, NN, UPB, USIC

684. ———. **1913.** (same) [Independence, n.d.]
xii, 623p. 17½cm.
"Seventh Independence Edition."
MoInRC, UPB, USIC

685. ———. **1913.** (same) [Independence, n.d.]
xii, 623p. 17cm.
"Eighth Independence Edition."
MoInRC, UPB, USIC

686. ———. **1914.** (same) Salt Lake City, Deseret News, 1914.
[4] vii–xii [2] 623p. 17cm.
Sabin 83106
MoInRC, UHi, UPB, USIC

687. ———. **1916.** (same as 1908, Salt Lake City, Deseret Sunday School edition) Salt Lake City, Deseret Sunday School Union, 1916.
654p. 12cm.
Vest pocket edition.
Sabin 83107
MoInRC, USIC

688. ———. **1916.** (same as 1908, Lamoni, twelfth edition) Thirteenth Edition. Lamoni, Ia. [Reorganized Church of Jesus Christ of Latter Day Saints] 1916.
xi, 485p. 27cm.
This is the large type edition from the 1892 plates.
Sabin 83108
MoInRC, NN, USIC

689. ———. **1917.** (same as 1914 edition) Third Electrotype Edition. Liverpool, Printed and Published by George F. Richards, 1917.
[v]–xii, 623p. 17c.
UPB

690. ———. **1917.** (same as 1913, Lamoni edition) Lamoni, Ia. [The Reorganized Church of Jesus Christ of Latter-day Saints] 1917.
viii, 822p. 19cm.
Sabin 83109
MoInRC, NjPT, USIC

691. **———. 1918.** (same as 1917, Salt Lake City edition) Salt Lake City, The Deseret News, 1918.
[4] vii–xii [2] 623p. 17cm.
Sabin 83110
MH, ULA, UPB, USIC

692. **———. 1919.** (same as 1917, Lamoni edition) Lamoni, Ia. [Reorganized Church of Jesus Christ of Latter Day Saints] 1919.
vii, 822p. 19cm.
MiD, MoInRC

693. **———. 1920.** (same as 1918 edition) Salt Lake City, Published by the Church of Jesus Christ of Latter-day Saints, 1920.
4p.l., 568p. 20cm.
This is the first edition issued in double-column pages, with chapter headings, chronological data, revised footnote references, pronouncing vocabulary and index. Some issues have "cannot" on p. 298 spelled "connot." Revised by James E. Talmage.
Sabin 83112
CSmH, CU–B, DLC, MH, MiU–C, NjP, NN, ULA, UPB, UU

694. **———. 1920.** (same as 1917, Liverpool edition) Third Electrotype Edition. Liverpool, George Albert Smith, 1920.
vii, 623p. 17cm.
Also published as a triple combination.
Sabin 83111
USIC, UU

695. **———. 1921.** (same as 1920, Salt Lake City edition) Salt Lake City, Published by the Church of Jesus Christ of Latter-day Saints, 1921.
4p.l., 568p. 20cm.
Also published as a triple combination.
CtY, CU, DLC, ICN, IWW, NjPT, NN, ULA, UPB, USIC, UU, ViU

696. **———. 1921.** (same) Salt Lake City, Church of Jesus Christ of Latter-day Saints, 1921.
1921 Primary Edition. Triple combination.
Lambert.
No copy located

697. **———. 1921.** (same as 1917, Lamoni edition) Independence, Mo., Published by the Reorganized Church of Jesus Christ of Latter-day Saints, 1921.
viii, 822p. 18cm.
Sabin 83113
MoInRC

698. **———. 1923.** (same as 1920, Salt Lake City edition) Salt Lake City, Published by the Church of Jesus Christ of Latter-day Saints, 1923.
4p.l. 568p. 20cm.
Also published as a triple combination.
NN, UPB, USIC

699. **———. 1923.** (same as 1921, Independence edition) Lamoni, Ia. [Reorganized Church of Jesus Christ of Latter Day Saints] 1923.
viii, 822p. 19cm.
OCl, OClWHi

700. **———. 1924.** (same as 1923, Salt Lake City edition) Salt Lake City, Published by the Church of Jesus Christ of Latter-day Saints, 1924.
4p.l., 568p. 20cm.
OO, UPB, UU

701. **———. 1926.** (same) Salt Lake City, Published by the Church of Jesus Christ of Latter-day Saints, 1926.
4p.l., 568p. 20cm.
Also published as a triple combination.
USI, USIC

702. **———. 1926.** (same as 1923, Lamoni edition) Independence, Mo., Published by the Reorganized Church of Jesus Christ of Latter Day Saints, 1926.
viii, 822p. 19cm.
MoInRC, USIC

703. **———. 1927.** (same as 1926, Salt Lake City edition) Salt Lake City, Published by the Church of Jesus Christ of Latter-day Saints [1927]
4p.l., 568p. 20cm.
MH, OCl, UPB, USIC

704. **———. 1928.** (same) Salt Lake City, Published by the Church of Jesus Christ of Latter-day Saints, 1928.
4p.l., 568p. 20cm.
Also published as a triple combination.
USIC

705. **Book of Mormon. Danish. 1851.** Mormons Bog. En Beretning, skreven ved Mormons Haand paa Tavler, efter Nephis Tavler . . . Oversat paa Engelsk fra Grundtexten af Joseph Smith den Yngre. Kjöbenhavn, Udgivet og forlagt af Erastus Snow. Trykt i F. E. Bordings Bogtrykkeri, 1851.
4p.l., 568p. 16cm.
The first edition of the Book of Mormon in a foreign language.
Sabin 83115
CSmH, MH, NjP, NN, UPB, USIC

706. **———. 1858.** (same) [Andet Oplag] Kjöbenhavn, Udgivet og forlagt af Hector C. Haight. Trykt i F. E. Bordings, Bogtrykkeri, 1858.
4p.l., 568, 12p. 16cm.
Sabin 83116
CtY, DLC, MoInRC, UPB, USIC, UU

707. **———. 1881.** Mormons Bog, en Beretning, skreven ved Mormons Haand paa Plader efter Nephis Plader . . . Oversat paa Engelsk fra

Grundtexten af Joseph Smith, Jun. Inddelt i Kapitler og Vers med Henvisninger af Orson Pratt, sen. Tredje. Danske oplag. Kjöbenhavn, N. Wilhelmsen, 1881.
[6] 758p. 19cm.
Sabin 83117
MH, NjP, UHi, USIC, UU

708. ———. 1902. (same) Fjerde Danske Udgave. Kjöbenhavn, Udgivet og forlagt af Anthon L. Skanchy, 1902.
[8] 644p. 20½cm.
Sabin 83118
NjP, NN, UHi, UPB, USIC

709. ———. 1903. Mormons Bog. En Beretning skreven ved Mormons Haand paa Plader efter Nephis Plader . . . Oversat paa Engelsk fra Grundteksten af Josef Smith, jun. [Porsgrund] Udgivet af Jesu Kristi gjenorganiserede Kirke af Sidste Dages Hellige [1903]
2p.l., 5–512p. 21cm.
First RLDS edition in Danish.
Sabin 83119
MoInRC, USIC, UU

710. ———. 1911. (same as 1902, Kjobenhavn edition) Femte Danske Udgave. Kjöbenhavn, Andrew Jenson, 1911.
648p. 16½cm.
UHi, UPB, USIC, UU

711. Book of Mormon. Dutch. 1890. Het Boek van Mormon. Een verslag geschreven door de Hand van Mormon. Op Platen genomen van de Platen van Nephi . . . Vertaald door Jozef Smith Jr. Verdeeld in Hoofdstukken en verzen met aanhalingen, door Orson Pratt, Sen. Uit het Engelsch vertaald door J. W. F. Volker. Eerste Nederlandsche Uitgave. Amsterdam, Door Francis A. Brown, Gedrukt bij I. Bremer, 1890.
xvi, 650p. 16½cm.
Sabin 83120
MoInRC, NN, UPB, USIC

712. ———. 1909. (same) Tweede Nederlandsche Uitgave. Rotterdam, Uitgegeven door Sylvester Q. Cannon, 1909.
4p.l., 632p. 17½cm.
Sabin 83121
MiU, NjP, NN, UHi, UPB, USIC

713. ———. 1924. (same) Derde Nederlandsche Uitgave. Rotterdam, Uitgegeven door Chas. S. Hyde, 1924.
6p.l., 688p. 18½cm.
UHi, UPB, USIC

714. Book of Mormon. French. 1852. Le livre de Mormon, Récit Écrit de la main de Mormon sur des plaques prises des plaques de Néphi . . . Traduit en anglais par Joseph Smith, junior. Traduit de L'anglais par John Taylor et Curtis E. Bolton. Publiëe par John Taylor. Paris, Rue de Tournon, 7, 1852.
xv, 519p. 16½cm.
"Edition stereotype."
ULA, USIC

715. ———. 1852. (same) Paris, Publiee par John Taylor, Rue de Paradis-Poissonnière, 37, 1852.
xv, 519p. 16½cm.
DLC, NjP, NN

716. ———. 1852. (same) Paris, Impriemerie de Marc Ducloux, et compagnie, rue Saint-Benoit, 7, 1852.
xv, 519p. 16½cm.
Deuxieme edition.
Sabin 83122
CSmH, CtY, DLC, MiU, NN, UPB, USIC

717. ———. 1907. (same) Zurich, Serge F. Ballif, 1907.
39, 623p. 17cm.
Deuxieme edition.
CU–B, LU, MH, NjP, NNUT, UHi, USIC

718. Book of Mormon. German. 1852. Das Buch Mormon: ein Bericht geschrieben von der Hand Mormon's auf Tafeln. Nephi's Tafeln entnommen . . . In das Englische, übersetzt von Joseph Smith, jun. Aus dem Englischen von John Taylor und G. Parker Dykes. Stereotyp-ausgabe herausgegeben von John Taylor. Hamburg, Gedruckt bei F. H. Nestler und Melle, 1852.
xii, 519p. 18cm.
Translated by George P. Dykes. In Orange printed wrapper.
Sabin 83124
DLC, MH, NjP, OclWHi, ULA, USIC, UU

719. ———. 1871. (same) Zweite Auflage. Hamburg, F. H. Nestler und Melle, 1852. [Bern, 1871]
xii, 519p. 18cm.
DLC, MH, NN

720. ———. 1873. (**same**) Dritte Auflage . . . Bern, Stereotypendruck von Lang, Blau & Cie, 1873.
xii, 519p. 18½cm.
MoInRC, UPB, USIC

721. ———. 1886. (same) Vierte Auflage . . . Hamburg, Gedruckt bei F. H. Nestler & Melle, 1852. [Bern, 1886]
xii, 519p. 18cm.
Sabin 83126

722. ———. 1893. (same) Fünfte Auflage. In Kapitel und Verse eingetheilt und mit Randerläuterungen versehen, im Einklange mit der Englischen Ausgabe, von Fried. W. Schönfield. Zu

beziehen In Bern, von der Schweizerischen und Deutschen Mission . . . Stereotyp-Ausgabe. Salt Lake City, Deseret News Publishing Company, 1893.
xii, 623p. 18cm.
Sabin 83128
MiD, NjP, NN, UHi, ULA, UPB, USlC, UU

723. ———. 1902. (same) Sechste Auflage . . . Berlin, Herausgegeben von Hugh J. Cannon, 1902.
[6] 35, 623p. 17cm.
Sabin 83128
NjP, NN, PP, UHi, ULA, UPB, USlC, UU

724. ———. 1911. Das Buch Mormon. Übersetzt von Joseph Smith, jr. Verglichen mit dem Original-Manuskript und der Kirtland-Ausgabe von 1837, welche sorgfältig, nachgeprüft und verglichen wurde mit dem Or[i]ginal-Manuskript von Joseph Smith jr. und Oliver Cowdery. Autorisierte Ausgabe. Aus dem Englischen übersetzt von Alexander Kippe, Gross-Lichterfelde. Lamoni, Ia., Veröffentlicht vom Ausschuss der Reorganisierten Kirche Jesu Christi der Heiligen der letzten Tage im Jahre 1908. Gedruckte von J. F. Starcke, Berlin . . . [1911]
[4] 834, lii [1]p. 18cm.
This edition was printed in 1911. The 1908 date appears as an indication from which American edition it was taken. First RLDS edition in German.
Sabin 83129
MoInRC

725. ———. 1920. (same as 1902, Berlin edition) Siebente Auflage . . . Basel, Herausgegeben von der Schweizerisch-Deutschen Mission, 1920.
[8]–623p. 17½cm.
UPB

726. ———. 1924. (same) Achte Deutsche Auflage. Basel, Fred Tadje, 1924.
[4] iii–x, 585p. 18½cm.
Also published in a triple combination.
Sabin 83130
NN, UHi, USlC

727. ———. 1928. (same) Neunte Auflage. Dresden, Herausgegeben von Hugh J. Cannon . . . und Hyrum W. Valentine . . . , 1928.
x, 585p. 18cm.
Also published as a triple combination.
UPB, USlC, UU

728. Book of Mormon. Hawaiian. 1855. Ka Buke a Moramona: He mooolelo i kakauia e ka lima o Moramona, maluna iho o na Papa i laweia mailoko mai o na Papa o Nepai . . . I unuhiia ma ka Olelo Beritania e Josepa Samika, Opio. Na Geogi Q. Pukuniahi i unuhi ma ka olelo Hawaii. San Francisco, Paiia e Geogi Q. Pukuniahi, 1855.
xii, 520p. 22½cm.
A press was sent to Hawaii to print the Book of Mormon, but it was never printed there, and was subsequently printed by George Q. Cannon in San Francisco.
Sabin 83131
CtY, CU–B, DLC, MH, NN, ULA, UPB, USlC, ViU

729. ———. 1898. Ka Buke a Moramona. Unuhiia e Ioseph Kamaka opio. Unuhiia a hoolahaia ma ka olelo Hawaii malalo o ke Kauoha a Gilbert J. Waller, ka lunakahika peresidena o ka Misiona Hawaii o ka Ekalesia i Hoonohonoho Hou ia o Iesu Karisto no na Poe Hoano o na La Hope. Honolulu, Paiia a ka Hawaiian Gazette Co., 1898.
xix, 722p. 23cm.
The first RLDS Book of Mormon in Hawaiian.
Sabin 83132
MoInRC, NjP, NN, USlC

730. ———. 1905. Ka Buke a Moramona He Mooolelo I Kakauia ma ka Limo o Moramona Maluna iho o na Papa i Laweia Mailoko mai o na Papa o Nepai . . . Ua Unuhiia ma ka Olelo Beritania e Josepa Samika, Opio . . . Salt Lake City, The Deseret News, 1905.
8p.l., 675, xxiv p. 24cm.
Sabin 83133
CU–B, NjP, NN, UHi, UPB, USlC

731. Book of Mormon. Italian. 1852. Il libro di Mormon: ragguaglio scritto per mano di Mormon, sopra tavole prese fra le tavole de Neft . . . Tradotto in lingua inglese da Giuseppe Smith il giovane, tradotto e pubblicato, dall' inglese in lingua italiana d'ordine &c., di Lorenzo Snow. Londra [London] Stamperia di Guflielmo Bowden, 1852.
viii, 580p. 15cm.
Sabin 83134
CtY, MB, MiU–C, NN, UHi, USlC, UU

732. ———. 1929. Il libro di Mormon sommario scritto per mano di Mormon sulle tavolette preso dalle Tavolette di Nefi . . . Tradotto in lingua Inglese da Giuseppe Smith, il Giovane. Publicato dalla Chiesa di Gesu Christo. W. H. Cadman, Presidente. [Monongahela, Pa., Stampato dalla Frediani Printing Co.] 1929.
[8] 638p. 19cm.
An Italian translation of the Book of Mormon published by the Church of Jesus Christ (Bickerton)
Morgan
MiD, PMoNS, USlC

733. Book of Mormon. Japanese. 1909. Mormon Kei. Elyadusha Josefu Sumisu nidai wayaku shuninsha Aruma O. Teira. Nihon, Matsu Jitsu Seito Iesu Kirisuto Kyokai [1909]
[922]p. 19cm.
Title transliterated.
Sabin 83135
MH, MoInRC, NN, UHi, UPB, USlC

734. Book of Mormon. Maori. 1889. Ko to Pukapuka a Moromona: he tuhituhinga i tuhituiha e te ringa o Moromona, i runga i nga papa i tangohia i nga papa a niwhai . . . He mea whakamaori mai ki te reo Ingarihi e Hohepa Mete, tamaiti. Auckland, New Zealand, Niu Tireni: He mea ta e Henare Perete, Akarana, 1889.
xii, 748p. 18½cm.
This translation into the Maori language was made by Ezra F. Richards and Sandra Sanders.
Sabin 83136
UPB, USIC

735. ———. 1918. (same) Arkarana, Arkarana Printing Works, 1918.
[8] vii–xiv, 736p. 18cm.
Sabin 83137
NjP, USIC

736. Book of Mormon. Samoan. 1903. O le Tusi a Momona. O le tala na tusia i le lima o Mamona i papatusi ua Siitia mai mai papatusi a Nifae . . . Ua faaliliuina e Iosefa Samita . . . Salt Lake City, Deseret News Company, 1903.
[6] 632, vii [1]p. 23cm.
Translated into the Samoan language by Elders William G. Sears, Frank E. Lewis, Edwin Smart and G. C. Pillsbury. 5,000 copies printed.
Sabin 83138
CU–B, NjP, NN, UHi, UPB, USIC

737. Book of Mormon. Spanish. 1886. Libro de Mormon: Relacion escrita por la mano de Mormon, sobre planchas tomadas de las planchas de Nefi . . . Traducido por Joseph Smith, Junior. Traducido al Español bajo la direccion del Apóstol Moisés Thatcher, por Meliton G. Trejo y Jáime Z. Stewart. Salt Lake City, Impreso y publicado por la Compañía de Deseret News, 1886.
xiv, 626p. 16½cm.
Sabin 83140
CtY, DLC, NN, UPB, USIC

738. ———. 1920. Libro de Mormón, relación escrita por la mano de Mormón, sobre planchas tomadas de las planchas de Nefi . . . Traducido por José Smith, hijo. Dividido en capítulos y versículos, con referencias por Orson Pratt. Traducido al español bajo la dirección del apóstol Moisés Thatcher, por Melitón G. Trejo y Jáime Z. Stewart. Diligentemente comparado con anteriores ediciones y rev.; y las referencias traducidas al español y agregadas por Rey L. Pratt. [Independence, Mo.] Publicado por la Misión Mexicana de la Iglesia de Jesu Cristo de los Santos de los Ultimos Días. [Independence, Imprenta de Zion's Printing and Publishing Company] 1920.
xiv, 631p. 17cm.
Sabin 83141
DLC, MH, NN, UHi, UPB, USIC

739. ———. 1929. (same) Independence, Mo., Published by the Mexican Mission, Church of Jesus Christ of Latter-day Saints, 1929.
528p. 17cm.
OkStA, UPB, USIC

740. ———. Selections. Spanish. 1875. Trozos selectos del Libro de Mormon; que es una narracion escrita por la mano de Mormon, sobra placas tomada de las placas de Nephi . . . Traducido al Español por Meliton G. Trejo y Daniel W. Jones. Salt Lake City, Impreso para Daniel W. Jones en imprenta del Deseret News, 1875.
iv [5]–96p. 18cm.
Contents: First Book of Nephi, Second Book of Nephi, Book of Omni, Book of Nephi, Book of Mormon.
CU–B, NN, USIC, UU

741. ———. 1875. Trozos selectos del libro de Mormon; que es la Historia Sacrada de los antiquos habitantes de America. Salt Lake City, Impreso en la imprente del Deseret News, 1875.
iv [3] 8–96p. 18cm.
USIC

742. Book of Mormon. Swedish. 1878. Mormons Bok. En berättelse, skrifven med Mormons hand på plåtar efter Nephi plåtar . . . Üfversatt från Engelskan. Köpenhamn, Utgifven af N. C. Flygare. Tryckt hos F. E. Bording, 1878.
676 [8]p. 19½cm.
Sabin 83142
MoInRC, NjP, NN, UPB, USIC

743. ———. 1907. Mormons Bok. En Berättelse Skrifven med Mormons Hand på plåtar efter Nephis plåtar . . . Öfversatt från grundtexten till engelska språket af Joseph Smith, Juor. Indelad i kapitel och vers med hänvisningar af Orson Pratt. Andra Svenska Upplagan. Stockholm, Utgifven och förlagd af P. Matson, 1907.
[iv] 643p. 21cm.
Sabin 83143
UHi, UPB, USIC

744. Book of Mormon. Tahitian. 1904. Te Buka a Moromona: Te parau i papaihia e te rima o Moromona, i nia i te mau api i iritihia no nia mai i te mau Api a Nephi . . . Iritihia ei re'o Beritani e Iosepha Semita. I neneihia i te re'o Tahiti, i roto miti, i Utah. Salt Lake City, The Deseret News, 1904.
691, xxvp. 23½cm.
Translated by Frank Cutler, Eugene M. Cannon, Daniel T. Miller, and David Neff.
Sabin 83144
NjP, UHi, UPB, USIC

745. ———. 1905. (same) Salt Lake City, Church of Jesus Christ of Latter-day Saints, 1905.
675p. 23½cm.
USIC

746. Book of Mormon. Turkish. 1906. Mormonen qutbabe . . . H. K. Jefahr re A. M. Boil moulavinethi ile F. F. Hintze tarafghntan terjeme oloinaoish ter . . . [Boston] 1906.
[8] 699p. 21cm.
Translated into Turkish by H. K. Jefahr and A. M. Boil.
Sabin 83145
DLC, UPB, USlC, UU

747. Book of Mormon. Welsh. 1852. Llyfr Mormon; sef, hanes wedi ei ysgrifenu gan law Mormon, ar lafnau a gymmerwyd o lafnau Nephi . . . A gyfieithwyd i'r saesneg gan Joseph Smith, icu.; ac a gyfieithwyd o'r ail argraffiad saesneg ewropaidd gan John Davis. Merthyr-Tydfil, J. Davis, 1852.
xii, 483p. 17½cm.
Translated by John Davis.
Sabin 83146
MH, NjP, NN, UPB, USlC

747a. The Book of Mormon. [n.p., n.d.]
Broadside. 20½×13cm.
Text within ornamental border.
NjP, USlC

Book of Mormon; its history, and an analysis of its contents. *See Clay, Edmund.*

748. Book of Mormon picture charts. Part I. 1 January, 1892. The life of Nephi (the son of Lehi) Salt Lake City, Deseret Sunday School Union, 1892.
1 map, 12 plates. 32cm.
NN

The Book of Mormon proved to be a blasphemous and impudent forgery. *See Clay, Edmund.*

Book of Mormon stories. . . . *See Cannon (George Q.) and Sons.*

749. Booker, Alma. True position of the Reorganized Church of Jesus Christ of Latter Day Saints. [n.p., 191–]
22p. 23cm.
MoInRC

750. Booth, H. E. Address of Hon. H. E. Booth to the gentiles of Salt Lake City, upon the "American Party." Delivered at the Twentieth Ward Amusement Hall, on Thursday Evening, November 3rd, 1904. [Salt Lake City, 1904]
[4]p. 21cm.
A non-Mormon discusses the Mormon dominance of politics.
MH

751. Booth, Joseph W. Come listen to a prophet's voice. Aleppo, Syria, Mission Armenienne de L' Eglise de Jesus Christ des Saints du dernier jour, 1925.
24 [2]p. 19cm.
Cover-title.
Miscellaneous material written and compiled by J. W. Booth.
USlC

752. Boquist, Mrs. Laura (Brewster). Crossing the plains with ox teams in 1862. [Los Angeles, c1930]
1p.l., 5–32p. 24½cm.
Mormon material, p. 16–22. Mormons cause a murder (a man named Scott). "None of the emigrants had much use for Mormons." Spies in Salt Lake City so they couldn't talk freely or they would be murdered.
DLC

753. Borlace, William Copeland. Sunways, a record of rambles in many lands. Plymouth, W. Brendon and Son, 1878.
viii [3] 2–484p. 22cm.
Preface signed: W. C. B.
In a few pages he dismisses Mormons as amiable fanatics and the Book of Mormon as a travesty on the Bible. His trip to Salt Lake City was in 1875.
UHi, UU

754. Bosqui, Edward. Memoirs. [San Francisco, 1904]
821p. 24½cm.
Privately printed in an edition of 50 copies.
Remarks on Sam Brannan and the Mormons, p. 78–81.
CSfU, CSmH, CU–B

755. Bosson, Charles P., *editor.* Prospectus of the Independent Inquirer, and Journal of the Times. Charles P. Bosson, Editor, George J. Adams, Proprietor, H. L. Southworth, Publisher. Boston, Mass., November 20th, 1846.
Broadside. 25×21cm.
By a follower of James J. Strang.
CtY

756. Bostwick, F. E. As I found it; Life and experiences in Utah among the Mormons. Doctrines and practices of the Mormon church, polygamy, endoument [sic] secrets, destroying angels, Mountain Meadows massacre, present physical and political condition. [St. Louis, Mo., 1894?]
148p. plates, ports., map. 19½cm.
Cover-title.
Binders title: "Mormonism, as I found it."
CtY, MH, MoSM

757. Botten-Hansen, Paul. Mormonismens historie tilligemed en kirt ovesigt over sektens trosslaerdomme og kirke-ordning . . . Christiania, 1853.
[6] 52p.
Title in English: History of Mormonism.
Howes B637, Sabin 6824

758. Bourke, John Gregory. The snake-dance of the Moquis of Arizona; being a narrative of a journey from Santa Fe, New Mexico, to the villages of the Moqui Indians of Arizona . . . New York, Charles Scribner's Sons, 1884.
xvi, 371p. illus., xxxi plates (part col. 1 fold.) 23½cm.
Last chapter discusses Mormons in Sunset, Arizona.
CU-B, DLC, NjP

759. Bourkersson, N. Tre år i Mormonlandet. Berättelser efter egna iakttagelser af N. Bourkersson. På författarens förlag. Malmö, Tryckt hos B. Cronholm, 1867.
196p. 18½cm.
Title in English: Three years in the land of the Mormons.
Sabin 1868 #6908
CtY, CU-B, DLC, MH, MnU, NN

760. Boutwell, George S. Proposed legislation for Utah. Arguments against the new Edmunds Bill, being Senate Bill No. 10: A bill to amend an act entitled "An act to amend section 5356 of the revised statutes of the United States in reference to bigamy and for other purposes, approved March 22, 1882, made by Hon. George S. Boutwell, Jeff. Chandler, F. S. Richards, A. M. Gibson, Esq., Joseph A. Vest, and John T. Caine. Made before the Committee on the Judiciary of the United States House of Representatives, 1st Sess., 49th Cong. Washington, Govt. Print. Off., 1886.
1p.l., [17]-255, iv p. 21cm.
CSmH, CU-B, UU

761. Bowen, James Charles. A plea for liberty, being an open letter to President Lorenzo Snow, and members of the Church of Jesus Christ of Latter-day Saints. By the deposed Mormon teacher, J. C. Bowen. [Salt Lake City] c1899.
31p. 15cm.
Church and politics.
CSmH, MH, NN, USIC

762. Bowen, Sybil Spande. Through the Gate. A one act play by Sybil Spande Bowen. [Salt Lake City] Published by the General M.I.A. Board, 1928.
6p. 20cm.
After a dream the heroine decides to go to Mutual instead of a road-house.
USIC

763. Bowes, John. Mormonism exposed, in its swindling and licentious abominations, refuted in its principles, and in the claims of its head, the modern Mohammed Joseph Smith, who is proved to have been a deceiver, and no prophet of God. London, E. Ward . . . [1850?]
71 [1]p. 18cm.
CtY, OClWHi, MiU, NN, USIC

764. ———. (same) London, E. Ward [1851]
71[1]p. 18cm.
2d edition.
NN, USI

765. ———. (same) London, R. Bulman [1854]
84p. 18cm.
MH, NN, OClWHi

766. ———. The spiritual wife doctrine of the Mormons. *See Brandebury, Lemuel G.*

767. Bowles, Samuel. Across the continent: a summer's journey to the Rocky Mountains, the Mormons, and the Pacific states, with Speaker Colfax. By Samuel Bowles . . . Springfield, Mass., S. Bowles & Company; New York, Hurd & Houghton, 1865.
xx [21]-452p. illus., map. 23cm.
Contains a detailed discussion of Mormonism. Party left Atchison, Kansas, May 21, 1865; reached San Francisco, July, 1865.
Other editions: Springfield, Mass., S. Bowles and Co., 1866. CU-B, DLC, UPB; 1868. DLC, NN; 1869. DLC, UHi, CU; abridged in German under title: Von Ocean zu Ocean. Leipzig, B. Schlicke, 1869. MiU
W-C 410
CSmH, CtY, CU, CU-B, DLC, MH, NjP, NN, UHi, ULA, UPB, USI, WHi

768. ———. Our new West. Records of travel between the Mississippi River and the Pacific Ocean. Over the plains — over the mountains — through the great interior basin — over the Sierra Nevadas — to and up and down the Pacific Coast. With details of the wonderful natural scenery, agriculture, mines, business, social life, progress, and prospects . . . including a full description of the Pacific railroad; and of the life of the Mormons, Indians, and Chinese. With map, portraits, and twelve full page illustrations. By Samuel Bowles. Hartford, Ct., Hartford Publishing Co.; New York, J. D. Dennison; etc., etc., 1869.
xx [21]-524p. plates, map, ports. 23cm.
Devotes several chapters to Mormonism.
Other editions: 1869. USIC; 1870. OCU
Sabin 7079
CSmH, CtY, CU-B, DLC, ICN, NjP, NN, UPB, USI, WHi

769. ———. The Pacific railroad — open. How to go: what to see. Guide for travel to and through western America. By Samuel Bowles . . . Boston, Fields, Osgood & Co., 1869.
122p. 17cm.
Includes a chapter entitled: "The Mountain and the Mormons."
CSmH, CU-B, DLC, NjP, NN, UHi, UPB, USIC

770. Boyd, James Penny. Building and ruling the republic. Philadelphia, Bradley, Garretson & Co. . . . 1884.
784, 67p. illus. 23cm.
"Polygamy," p. 645-60.
USIC

771. ———. The political history of the United States; or, Popular sovereignty and citizenship . . . Philadelphia, Chicago, P. W. Ziegler, 1888.
628, 112p. illus., ports., map, facsim. 22cm.
Polygamy listed under "Present political questions."
DLC, UHi, UPB, UU

772. ———. Recent Indian wars, under the lead of Sitting Bull, and other chiefs; with a full account of the Messiah craze, and ghost dances. [n.p.] Publishers Union, 1891.
320p. 19½cm.
"The affair at Mountain Meadow," p. 73–78.
Reprinted under title: Red Men on the War Path. [c. 1895] DLC, USIC
CU–B, NjP, UHi

773. **Boyd, R. P.** Biblical Priesthood, By R. P. Boyd, of Paris, Idaho . . . [Paris?] 1894.
16p. 15cm.
Study of Mormon priesthood by a protestant minister.
UPB, USIC

774. ———. (same) [Paris? 1900]
16p. 14cm.
MH

775. ———. False apostles; or, A scriptural examination of the claims of Mormon apostles. By R. P. Boyd, Paris, Idaho. [Philadelphia, American Printing House, 1905?]
16p. 16cm.
MH, USIC

776. ———. The Mormon God is not the God of the Bible. By R. P. Boyd, Presbyterian Minister at Paris, Idaho. Philadelphia, Presbyterian Board of Publication and Sabbath-School Work [1890]
63p. 15cm. (No. 225)
MoInRC, UPB

777. ———. (same) Philadelphia, Presbyterian Board of Publication and Sabbath School work, 1900.
63p. 15cm.
USIC

778. ———. (same) Philadelphia, Presbyterian Board of Publication and Sabbath School Work, 1916 [c1890]
1p.l. [3]–46p. 16½cm.
MoInRC, USIC

779. ———. A open reply to Jesse R. S. Budge, esq., of Salt Lake City, Utah, regarding the Mormon tithing system. [Paris, Idaho? 1906?]
44p. 14½cm.
Cover-title.
USIC, WHi

780. ———. The Pre-existence of Spirits (a Mormon doctrine) Refuted by the Bible. Philadelphia, Presbyterian Board of Publication [190–?]
31p. 15cm.
USIC

781. ———. Some facts presented for the consideration of the people of Bear Lake Co., Idaho. By one deeply interested in their welfare. Philadelphia, American Printing House [190–?]
31 [1]p. 15½cm.
Mormonism in Idaho.
USIC

782. ———. Some fatal objections to the Mormon tithing system. [Paris, Idaho? 190–?]
24p. 17½cm.
USIC

Boyer, Claire Stewart. *See Church of Jesus Christ of Latter-day Saints. Relief Society. Semi-centennial review . . .*

783. **Boyer, Lanson.** From the Orient to the Occident, or L. Boyer's trip across the Rocky Mountains, in April 1877. New York, E. W. Sackett & Bro., Printers, 1878.
2p.l. [7]–145p. port. 24cm.
Material on Salt Lake City and the Mormons, p. 53–65. Five Odd Fellow lectures with part of #2 devoted to Mormonism and Utah.
CSmH, CtY, CU–B, ICN, MnU, NjP, NN, USIC

784. **Bozarth, C. E.** Reply to Bishop Clark of Des Moines, Iowa, of the Reorganized Church of Latter Day Saints, in his attack on Elder Macgregor and Church of Christ. [Independence, Mo.? c1918]
14p. 22½cm.
A defense of the Church of Christ (Temple Lot) Also includes material on supreme direction control in the RLDS church.
USIC

785. ———. (same) [Independence, Mo.?, ca. 1926]
15p. 22½cm.
MoInRC, USIC

786. ———. (same) [Milwaukee, Wis., 1927?]
15p. 17½cm.
MoInRC, NN, UU

787. **Brackett, Albert Gallatin.** History of the United States Cavalry, from the formation of the Federal Government to the 1st of June, 1863 . . . By Albert G. Brackett . . . [New York] Harper & Bros., 1865.
xii [13]–337p. front., 1 plate, maps. 19½cm.
Includes an account of the Utah Expedition.
Howes B692, Sabin 7195, W–C 411
CU–B, DLC, MH, NjP, NN, UHi, UU

788. Braden, Clark. The Braden-Kelley debate on Mormonism, held in Kirtland, Lake Co., Ohio, beginning Tuesday night, Feb. 12, 1884 and closing Friday night, March 7, 1884. [St. Louis, Christian Publishing Company, 1884?]
4p. 21cm.
Caption-title.
Signed: Clark Braden.
A summary of the debate and an advertisement for books including the debate and supplementary material.
CtY

789. ———. Christianity vs. Mormonism; an acceptance of the challenges of Josephite Mormonism. Endorsements of Clark Braden by church papers, church boards, churches, colleges, and preachers. Salem, Ill., C. D. Merritt, Printer, 1900.
8p. 23½cm.
CtY, MoInRC, USlC

790. ———. Lectures against Mormonism! Clark Braden, who has had three debates with champions of Mormonism, and who has for four years backed out its champions, will lecture at Plum Hollow, Sunday, June 9 . . . [n.p., n.d.]
Broadside. 29×14cm.
MoInRC

Bradlaugh, W. R. Mormon infidelity and Polygamy. *See Presbytery of Utah.*

791. Bradley, Glenn Danford. The story of the pony express; an account of the most remarkable mail service ever in existence, and its place in history. Chicago, A. C. McClurg & Co., 1913.
7p.l., 175p. plates. 17cm.
Scattered references to early mail service in Utah. Mention of Johnston's army.
Another edition: 1920. UHi
CU-B, UHi, ULA

792. Bradley, Walter H. Why I am not a Mormon, by Walter H. Bradley. [Mountain View, Calif., Pacific Press Publishing Assn., n.d.]
8p. 18cm. (Bible truth series. No. 49)
MoInRC, NN, USlC

Bradshaw, Wesley. *See Alexander, Charles Wesley.*

793. Brady, Cyrus Townsend. Recollections of a missionary in the great West, by the Rev. Cyrus Townsend Brady . . . New York, C. Scribner's Sons, 1900.
6p.l., 200p. port. 19cm.
Includes his reasons why the Mormons failed in Utah.
Another edition: 1901.
CU, CU-B, DLC, NjP, NN, OCL, PHC, PPL, PPM, PPTU

794. Bramwell, Enoch Ernest. Notable religious teachers . . . written for the general board of education by E. Ernest Bramwell. [Salt Lake City] Deseret Book Co. [1925]
160p. 19cm. (Teacher Training Lesson Book, 1925–26)
Also a variant edition of 161p. USlC
UHi, USlC, UU

795. ———. Why do I believe? by E. Ernest Bramwell . . . Salt Lake City, The Deseret News Press, 1926.
238 [2]p. illus. 20cm.
DLC, NjP, UPB, USlC, UU

796. ———. (same) 2d ed. Salt Lake City, Deseret News Press, 1929.
245 [i.e. 247]p. 19½cm.
MH, UHi, USlC, UU

797. Branch, Edward Douglas. Westward; the romance of the American frontier, by E. Douglas Branch. Woodcuts by Lucina Smith Wakefield. New York and London, D. Appleton and Company, 1930.
ix [1]p., [2]l., 3–626 [1]p. illus., maps (1 double). 22½cm.
Chapter 23 "Garden in the Deseret." Early Mormon history and settlement of Salt Lake Valley.
DLC, NjP, UHi, ULA, USlC

798. Brand, E. C. The word of wisdom. [With extracts from the Inspired translation of the Bible. San Francisco, 1865]
8p. 20cm.
MoInRC, NN

799. Brandebury, Lemuel G. Polygamy revived in the West. Report by the judges of Utah Territory to the President of the United States, on the conduct of the Mormonites. Liverpool, Printed by T. Brakell, 1852.
12p. 17cm.
"Report . . . taken from the *New York Herald*, of Jan. the 10th, 1852 . . . By order of the Committee of Instruction appointed by the Liverpool Church of England Scripture Readers' Society."
Signed: Lemuel G. Brandeburg [sic] Chief Justice of the Supreme Court of the United States for the Territory of Utah, Perry A. Brocchus, Associate Justice of the Supreme Court of the United States for the Territory of Utah, B. D. Harris, Secretary of the Territory of Utah.
CU-B

800. ———. (same, under title) The spiritual wife doctrine of the Mormons proved from the Report of the Judges of Utah Territory to the President of the United States. Given entire from the New York Herald, of January the 10th, 1852. [Cheltenham, Eng., R. Edwards, Printer, 1852?]
12p. 18cm.
CtY, USlC

BRANDLEY, E. T.

Brandley, Elsie Talmage. An ode to youth. *See Cornwall, J. Spencer.*

801. **Brändli, Theodor.** Die Gründung und Lehren der Kirche Jesu Christi der Heiligen der Letzten Tage. In Kürze dargestellt vom Aeltesten Theodor Brändli. [Bern, Druck von Suter & Lierom, n.d.]
24p. 22½cm.
Title in English: Principles and teachings of the Church of Jesus Christ of Latter-day Saints.
USIC

802. **Brann, William Cowper.** Brann, the Iconoclast. A collection of the writings of W. C. Brann with biography by J. D. Shaw . . . Waco, Texas, Press of Knight Printing Co., 1898–1905.
2v. 23½cm.
"The Mormons in Mexico," V.1, p. 355–360.
CU, DLC, ULA, USIC

803. **Brannan, Samuel.** Religious notice [of Mormon lectures Elder S. Brannan of New-York City. At the American Republican Hall, Broadway & Grand Streets, New York, Aug.–Oct. 5, 1845] New York, 1845.
Broadside. 17½×19½cm.
NN

804. **Breitner, Burghard. . . .** Mormonen und Medizinmänner. Zurich, Amalthea-Verlag [c1930]
3p.l., 7–169p. 20cm.
Travel through America, with a brief visit to Salt Lake City, June 23–4, 1915, p. 72–85.
Title in English: Mormons and medicine men.
NN, UHi, UPB, UU

805. **Brent, John.** The Empire of the West. (A compilation) By John Brent. Omaha, Nebraska, Issued by Passenger Department, Union Pacific Railroad Company [c1910]
2p.l., 5–503 [3]p. illus., maps. 18cm.
"Salt Lake City and Its Temple," p. 91–109.
CU-B, UPB

Breakspear [*pseud.*] *See Adams, William L.*

806. **Brett, Edwin J.** Ned Nimble amongst the Mormons: or, the cruise of the "Rattler." London [c1890]
1p.l. [3]–251p. illus. 25cm.
Fiction concerning the Mormons.
USIC

807. **Brev fra en Mormonerinde.** Efterretninger om den skraekkelige tilstand hvori Mormonerne leve i Saltso-staden. Bidrag til Mormonernes charakteristik. Dansk Kirke-tidende offentliggor et brev fra Saltso-staden fra en qvinde, som var falden i den Mormonske vildfarelse og reiste derover fra Egnen ved Cambridge. Kobenhavn, 1855.
10p.
Title in English: A letter from a lady Mormon.
Schmidt.

808. **Brewer, Charles.** Retribution at last. A Mormon tragedy of the Rockies. By Chas. Brewer, M.D. Cincinnati, The Editor Publishing Company, 1899.
2p.l., v, 101p. 17½cm.
Fiction concerning the Mountain Meadows massacre.
CSmH, CtY, DLC, NjP

809. **Brewster, James Colin.** An address to the Church of Christ, and Latter Day Saints. By James Colin Brewster. Springfield, 1848.
24p. 22½cm.
Caption-title.
Signed: Springfield, Ill., March 22, 1848.
J. C. Brewster had left the body of Mormonism and was gathering his own congregation.
Byrd 1297, Morgan
CtY, PPPrHi, USIC

810. **———.** Very important! To the Mormon money-diggers. Why do the Mormons rage, and the people imagine a vain thing? By James Colin Brewster. [Springfield, Ill., March 20, 1843]
12p. 19½cm.
Caption-title.
Byrd 763, Morgan
USIC

811. **———.** A warning to the Latter Day Saints, generally called Mormons. An abridgement of the ninth book of Esdras, by James Colin Brewster. [Springfield, Ill.: 1845]
16p. 21½cm.
Caption-title.
Revelations concerning the path the Mormons should take.
Byrd 938, Morgan
CtY, USIC

812. **———.** The words of righteousness to all men, written from one of the Books of Esdras which was written by the five ready writers, in the forty days, which was spoken of by Esdras in his second book, fourteenth chapter of the Apocrypha, being one of the books which was lost and has now come forth, by the gift of God, in the last days. By James C. Brewster. Springfield, Illinois, Ballard & Roberts, Printer, 1842.
48p. 20cm.
Morgan
CtY, USIC

813. **Bridges, F. D.** Journal of a lady's travels round the world, by F. D. Bridges . . . With illustrations from sketches by the author. London, John Murray, 1883.
xi [1]l., 413p. illus., plates. 21cm.
A visit to Salt Lake City in 1880. Chapter XXVI. Decline in polygamy and other distinctive features of Mormonism due to a new generation.
USIC, UU

Bridwell, John T. "Was Joseph Smith Jr., a Prophet?" *See Coombs, James V.*

A brief account of the discovery of the Brass plates . . . *See Times and Seasons.*

A brief account of the life and character of Joseph Smith, the "prophet" of Mormonism. *See Clay, Edmund. Tracts on Mormonism. Number I.*

814. Brigadier General Richard W. Young. Biographical sketch, funeral ceremonies. Resolutions of respect. Salt Lake City, 1920.
2p.l. [7]–30p. 21½cm.
Cover-title: Richard W. Young: In Memoriam.
"Issued with the compliments of Heber J. Grant & Co., Utah-Idaho Sugar Co., Beneficial Life Insurance Co., Utah State National Bank."
UHi, UPB, USlC, UU

815. Briggs, Edmund C. Address to the Saints in Utah. Polygamy proven an abomination by Holy Writ. Is Brigham Young president of the Church of Jesus Christ, or is he not? San Francisco, Turnbull & Smith, 1864.
48p. 18cm.
Signed: Great Salt Lake City, June 21, 1864. Truth conquers.
An early RLDS pamphlet on polygamy.
"The testimony." Poem by David H. Smith, p. 48.
CSmH, MoInRC

816. ———. (same) London, Nichols and Sons, Printers, 1866.
15p. 18cm.
Signed: Truth Conquers, Great Salt Lake City, June 21st, 1864.
NN, USlC

817. ———. (same, under title) Address to the Saints in Utah and California. Polygamy proven an abomination by holy writ. Is Brigham Young president of the Church of Jesus Christ, or is he not? Written by E. C. Briggs and R. M. Atwood. Revised by Joseph Smith and Wm. W. Blair. Plano, Ill., Published by the Church of J.C. of L.D. Saints, 1869.
48p. 16cm.
Cover-title. USlC has variant cover.
CtY, CU, CU–B, MH, MoInRC, NN, ULA, UPB, USlC, WHi

818. ———. Polygamy not of God. [n.p., 1899?]
4p. 23cm.
Reprinted from *Zions' Ensign* of April 13, 1899.
MoInRC

819. ———. A retrospective view of the Reorganization. Independence, Mo., Ensign Publishing House, 1897.
36p. 16cm. (The Gospel Banner, Vol. 4, No. 2, Extra B)
MoInRC

820. ———. Who is afraid to have the light turned on? Correspondence between Elder E. C. Briggs of the Reorganized Church of Jesus Christ of Latter Day Saints and Joseph F. Smith, Jr., of the Utah Church, also claiming to be the Church of Jesus Christ of Latter Day Saints. Independence, Mo., Ensign Publishing House [1907?]
16p. 17cm.
Cover-title.
MoInRC, UHi, USlC

821. Briggs, Hugh L. A lecture on the moral, social and political condition of Utah Territory, by Hugh L. Briggs, Esq. [n.p.] 1857.
18p. 22cm.
Sabin H–7949
CSmH, DLC, MH

822. Briggs, Jason W. . . . The basis of Brighamite polygamy: a criticism upon the (so called) revelation of July 12th, 1843. By Elder Jason W. Briggs. Lamoni, Ia., Reorganized Church of Christ [1875]
8p. 21½cm. (No. 28)
Caption-title.
Dated at end: Salt Lake City, Utah, July, 1875.
MoInRC, USlC

823. ———. (same) Plano, Ill., Published by the Reorganized Church of Latter Day Saints [after 1875]
8p. 25cm.
USlC

824. ———. (same) Lamoni, Ia., Reorganized Church of Christ [1881?]
8p. 25cm. (No. 47)
A reprint of the 1875 edition.
CSmH, CtY, MH, MoInRC, MoK, ULA, UPB

825. ———. (same) Lamoni, Ia., Reorganized Church of Jesus Christ of Latter Day Saints [n.d.]
8p. 23cm. (No. 48)
CSmH, CU–B

826. ———. (same) Lamoni, Ia., Published by the Herald Publishing House [n.d.]
31p. 18cm.
CU–B, MoInRC, UHi, USlC

———. Trial of the witnesses to the resurrection of Jesus. *See Reorganized Church of Jesus Christ of Latter Day Saints.*

827. ———. A word of consolation to the scattered Saints. The law of succession in the First Presidency of the Church of Jesus Christ of Latter-day Saints. The duty of the Saints and the redemption of Zion. [Janesville, Wis., D. W. Scott and Co's. Job Office, 1853]
24p. 21½cm.
Caption-title.
Signed: J. W. Briggs, Z. H. Gurley, J. Harrington; Committee.
Howes B772
CtY, MoInRC, NN

828. ———. A word of consolation to the Saints scattered abroad in the British Isles. A defence of the law of succession. Joseph, the son of Joseph the martyr, the only successor in the First Presidency of the Church of Jesus Christ of Latter Day Saints. The doctrine of polygamy proved false by the testimony of the Bible, Book of Mormon and Doctrine and Covenants. The renewal of the work and the redemption of Zion, the gathering, etc., etc. By Elder J. W. Briggs. [West Bromwich, England, 1863?]
16p. 22cm.
Dated at end: June 5th, 1863.
CU–B, MoInRC, NN

829. Briggs, Riley W. Consciousness after death, by Riley W. Briggs. [Plano, Ill., Reorganized Church of Jesus Christ of Latter Day Saints, n.d.]
4p. 23cm. (True Latter Day Saints Herald. Tract. No. 2)
Caption-title.
Includes a "Letter from Lizzie Redmon," and reply by Isaac Sheen.
MoInRC, UHi

Brigham Young Academy, Provo, Utah. *See Brigham Young University.*

830. Brigham Young College, Logan, Utah. Brigham Young College bulletin series. Alumni number. Logan, Utah, 1903–1918.
16v. 21cm.
USIC 1903, 1904, 1906, 1910, 1911, 1912, 1913, 1914, 1915, 1916, 1917, 1918

831. ———. Catalog. 1884–
30v. 21cm.
Includes: Commencement, 1926; The place of the junior college in our educational system, 1926; Views, 1907, 1909, 1911, 1914; Student directory 1910–1919; Alumni directory, 1910–1918.
CU 1897
UPB 1892–3, 1895–6, 1897–8, 1899–1900, 1900–01, 1901–02, 1903–04, 1920–21, 1921–22, 1922–23, 1923–24, 1924–25
USIC 1884–85 (prospectus) 1885–86, 1888–89, 1889–90, 1890–91, 1891–92, 1893–94, 1894–95, 1895–96, 1896–97, 1897–98, 1898–99, 1899–1900, 1900–01, 1901–02, 1902–03, 1903–04, 1904–05, 1905–06, 1906–07, 1907–08, 1908–09, 1909–10, 1910–11, 1911–12, 1912–13, 1913–14, 1914–15

832. ———. The College record. Logan, Utah, 1892–May 26, 1893.
1v. #1–12. 28cm.
USIC

833 ———. Memorial services. Logan, 1926.
12p. illus. 21½cm.
Brief chronology of Brigham Young College, and its influence on the community.
UPB

834. Brigham Young College. Society of American Archeology. Book of Mormon geography. Society report. Logan, Published by Brigham Young College, 1904.
19p. 23cm. (Brigham Young College. Bulletin V.3, No. 2)
UPB, USIC

835. Brigham Young, or, Perhaps she's on the Railway. [n.p., n.d.]
Broadside. 24½×18½cm.
Text of a song concerning Brigham Young.
UPB

836. The "Brigham Young" songster. Containing without any exception, the best collection of stunning, bang-up rip roaring comic songs of the day ever published . . . New York, Robert M. DeWitt, Publisher, c1871.
64p. 16cm.
"Brigham Young by J. B. Geoghegan," p. 12–13. Words and music.
DLC, MH, NN

837. Brigham Young University. Articles of incorporation of the Brigham Young University [Brigham Young Academy] with amendments. [Provo, 1905]
16p. 22cm.
Blue printed wrapper.
UHi, UPB, USIC

838. ———. Catalog. Provo, 1877–
54v. 19cm.
Begun under title: Circular of the Brigham Young Academy. Name changed to Catalogue and announcements. Merged as part of the Quarterly series, 1905.
NjP inc., UPB, USIC inc.

839. ———. Messenger. May, 1926–
v. monthly. various sizes.
A miscellaneous series published by the University. Series ranges from publicity releases to Christmas cards.
UPB

840. ———. Principal's annual report to the Board of Trustees . . . Provo, Utah, 1891–
v. 21cm.
USIC 1891–92

841. ———. Prospectus of the Brigham Young Academy, Provo. [Provo, Utah, 1876]
[4]p. 22cm.
USIC

842. ———. Quarterly. Provo, Utah, May 1, 1905–
v. quarterly. various sizes.
Includes catalogs, announcements and other publications. Some of special interest are: V.1 #4, Dr. Karl G. Maeser memorial; V.6 #2, Pictorial

number; V.12 #4, Spiritual training indispensable; V.15 #4, Sketches commemorating the century of the Prophet Joseph Smith's first vision; V.28 #1, In the service of the Church.
UPB

843. ———. Sketches commemorating the centenary of the Prophet Joseph Smith's First Vision. Illustrated, including an Art Pageant . . . Provo, Brigham Young University, 1920.
16l. illus., ports., plates. 22cm. (Brigham Young University Quarterly, V. xv, No. 4)
UPB, USIC

844. ———. Souvenir album of the Brigham Young University . . . Provo, Utah, 1904.
[36]l. illus., ports., plates. 11×18cm.
Pictorial views of the University.
UPB

845. ———. Theology papers. Provo, Brigham Young University, 1921.
Various pagings. 28cm.
A series of short papers on theological problems.
UPB

845a. Brigham Young's daughter. Terrible excitement in Utah among the Mormons. A bloody struggle coming. [n.p., n.d.]
Broadside. 28×22cm.
Describes a book that is on sale about Brigham Young's daughter and her husband escaping from Utah, the Mrs. McLean affair, the Mountain Meadow Massacre, and the Danites.
USIC

Brigham Young's will. *See Young, Brigham.*

846. Brigham Young's will & Fraud on the will. [n.p., n.d.]
24p. 21½cm.
Without title page.
In two sections with separate caption-titles.
WHi

847. ———. (same) [n.p., n.d.]
28p. 21cm.
USIC

848. Brighouse, James. The voice of the seventh angel, proclaiming the end of time! The resurrection of the dead! The day of final judgment! and The rule of righteousness and peace. South Cottonwood, Utah, 1887–92.
5v. in 1. 25cm.
In five parts with separate title pages and imprints for each part.
Preface and pt. 5 signed: James Brighouse; pt. [1]–4 signed: James Brighouse, Henry I. Doremus.
An unorthodox doctrinal work on the last days.
CSmH, CU-B, DLC, MH, NN, RPB, UPB, UU, WHi

849. Brimhall, George Henry. The ethics of the Doctrine and Covenants. [Salt Lake City, Young Ladies' Mutual Improvement Association, 1930]
30p. 22cm. (Courses of study, Adult Women's Department of the Y.L.M.I.A., Pt. 1)
With this are four music programs and Elsie Talmage Brandley's *Indian Love.*
UPB

850. ———. The scope of forgiveness; address delivered over Radio Station KSL, Sunday evening, March 27, 1927. Salt Lake City, 1927.
[1]p. 35½×25cm.
Reprinted from the *Deseret News.*
UPB

851. ———. Tithing, By Elder George H. Brimhall. [Independence, Mo., Press of Zion's Printing and Publishing Co., 1909]
8p. 17½cm.
"Printed in the '*Improvement Era,*' February, 1909."
MH, NN, UHi, USI, USIC

852. ———. Tithing — a divine doctrine; address delivered over Radio Station KSL, Sunday Evening, December 18, 1927. [Salt Lake City] 1927.
[1]p. 32cm.×25cm.
Reprinted from the *Deseret News,* Saturday, December 24, 1927.
UPB

853. ———. Vertiending door George H. Brimhall, President van de Brigham Young University. Uit het Engelsch vertaald door Frank I. Kooyman. Rotterdam, Uitgegeven door Chas. S. Hyde [n.d.]
15p. 17½cm.
Title in English: Defense by George H. Brimhall.
USIC

854. Brimhall, George Washington. The workers of Utah. Provo City, Utah, Printed by the Enquirer Co., 1889.
95p. 18cm.
Mormon autobiography.
DLC, USIC

Brindley, John. *See Antidote to Mormonism.*

855. Britannic Association refutes anti-Mormon slanders. [Salt Lake City, n.d.]
[1]p. 22cm.
UPB

856. The British and American Commercial Joint Stock Company. The British and American Commercial Joint Stock Company. [n.p., 1846?]
Broadside. 25×20cm.
A forerunner of the Perpetual Emigrating Company, but along more commercial lines.
USIC

BRITISH AND AMERICAN

857. ———. Deed of settlement of the British and American Commercial Joint Stock Company established for the purpose of trading between the United Kingdom of Great Britain and Ireland and North and South America. Liverpool, Printed by R. James, 1846.
2p.l. [5]–31p. 21 cm.
Incorporated to secure money partially to aid immigration.
MH

858. The British Anti-Mormon League. The British Anti-Mormon league. [Supporters and objectives] London [n.d.]
[1]p. 23½cm.
Handbill.
On verso: Plan of campaign.
UPB, USIC

859. Britton, Alexander Thompson. Anti-polygamy bill. [Opinion] In re bill recommended by the committees of Conference on the disagreeing votes of the two houses of Congress. [Alexander Thompson] Britton and [H. T.] Gray. March, 1882. [n.p., 1882]
7p. 21cm.
DLC, NN, UPB, USIC

860. Britton, Rollin J. Early Days on Grand River and the Mormon War, by Rollin J. Britton. Columbia, Mo., The State Historical Society of Missouri, 1920.
1p.l., 111p. 23cm.
Includes Mormonism in Missouri.
CtY, CU-B, ICN, ICU, MoInRC, MoK, NN, UPB, WHi

861. ———. Gen. Alexander W. Doniphan, address of Rollin J. Britton at the eighth annual banquet of the Gallatin Commercial Club, February 20th, 1914. [Gallatin, Mo., 1914]
16p. 15½cm.
Prefaces his remarks by an account of showing the location of Adam-ondi-Ahmon to 17 Mormon missionaries and the results of this action. Brief information on the Mormon war in Missouri.
CtY

862. Broadbent, Joseph Leslie. Celestial marriage? J. L. Broadbent, comp. [Salt Lake City, 1927]
24p. 19cm.
NN, USIC

863. ——— (same) 2d ed. [Salt Lake City, 1928]
28p. 19cm.
Cover-title.
UHi, USIC

864. ———. (same) 3d ed. [Salt Lake City, 1929?]
30p. 19cm.
Cover title.
CU–B, NN

———. In the case of Church of Jesus Christ of Latter Day Saint svs. Joseph Leslie Broadbent. *See Church of Jesus Christ of Latter-day Saints.*

865. Broadhead, James Overton. In the Supreme Court of the Territory of Utah, No. __ of __ term. In Equity. The United States of America, plaintiff vs. The Perpetual Emigrating Fund Company, Albert Carrington [etc.] [Salt Lake City, 1888?]
[2]p. 22cm.
Signed: James O. Broadhead, J. E. McDonald, Franklin S. Richards, Legrand Young.
Litigation caused by the Edmunds-Tucker Act.
USIC

866. ———. In the Supreme Court of the Territory of Utah, No. __ of __ term. In Equity. The United States of America, plaintiff vs. The Late Church of Jesus Christ of Latter-day Saints and John Taylor [etc.] [Salt Lake City? 1889]
[4]p. 22cm.
Signed: James O. Broadhead, J. E. McDonald, Franklin S. Richards, Legrand Young.
USIC

867. ———. The Late Corporation of the Church of Jesus Christ of Latter-day Saints et al., Appellants v. The United States, Appellees. No. 1,423. Appeal from Supreme Court of the Territory of Utah. [Washington? 1887]
11p. 21cm.
At head of title: Supreme Court of the United States, October Term, 1888.
Signed: James O. Broadhead, Joseph E. McDonald, John M. Butler, Franklin S. Richards, Solicitors for the appellants.
USIC

868. ———. The Late Corporation of the Church of Jesus Christ of Latter-day Saints, et al., Appellees, v. The United States. No. 1423. George Romney, Henry Dinwoodey, James Watson, and John Clark, Appellants. v. The United States. No. 1457. Appeals from the Supreme Court of Utah Territory. Brief and argument for Appellants. [Washington, 1888]
120p. 21cm.
At head of title: In the Supreme Court of the United States, October Term, 1888.
Signed: James O. Broadhead, Franklin S. Richards, for Appellants. Joseph E. McDonald, John M. Butler, of Counsel.
USIC

869. ———. . . . The late corporation of the Church of Jesus Christ of latter-day Saints et al., appellants, vs. the United States. Argument of Hon. James O. Broadhead, for the Appellants. Delivered January 16 and 17, 1889. Washington, Gibson Bros., Printers, 1889.
80p. 23cm.
Cover-title.
At head of title: Supreme court of the United States.

BROOKBANK, T. W.

"This suit was instituted in the Supreme court of the Territory of Utah, and final judgment rendered by that court, escheating all the personal property belonging to this corporation at the time of the institution of the suit, to the United States, and turning over the real property to the District Court of the Third Judicial District of Utah, for the purpose of instituting proceedings to forfeit that property, under the provisions of the acts of July 1, 1862." — p. 7.
DLC, MH, UHi, USlC

870. ———. Mormon Church property. Argument of Hon. James O. Broadhead, of St. Louis, on Senate bill No. 4047, proposing to dispose of the confiscated personal property of the Mormon Church for the use and benefit of the public schools in the Territory of Utah, before the House Committee on the Judiciary, Saturday, July 19, 1890. Washington, Govt. Print. Off., 1890.
1p.l., 16p. 22cm.
USlC

871. Brocchus, Perry E. Letter of Judge Brocchus, of Alabama, to the public, upon the difficulties in the territory of Utah. Washington, Printed by L. Towers, 1852.
30p. 22cm.
Sabin H8151
DLC, MH, NN, PPL

872. ———. (same) Washington, H. Polkinhorn, 1859.
32p. 23cm.
Includes: Letter to Hon. Daniel Webster, dated 1852, p. 15–32.
NN

873. Brockett, Linus Pierpont. Handbook of the United States of America, and guide to emigration; giving the latest and most complete statistics of the government, army, navy . . . etc. furnishing all the necessary information concerning the country for the settler, the businessman, the merchant, the farmer, the importer & the professional man. Comp. by L. P. Brockett . . . New York, G. Watson, 1879.
vi [7]–176p. front. 23½cm.
A mention of Utah and the Mormons indicating that the country is very satisfactory, but the Mormons hold very strange and crude views.
DLC

874. ———. Our western empire; or, the new West beyond the Mississippi; the latest and most comprehensive work on the states and territories west of the Mississippi. Containing . . . description . . . of the geography, geology . . . the climate, soil, agriculture, the mineral and mining products . . . To which is added the various routes, and prices of passage and transportation . . . with full information concerning Manitoba, British Columbia . . . Philadelphia, Bradley, Garretson and Co., 1881.
1312p. plates, maps (part double). 24½cm.
Chapter 19 includes the history of Mormon colonization.
Another edition: 1882. DLC, CSmH, UPB
CU–B, DLC, NjP, NN, UHi, ULA, USl, USlC, WaU

875. Brodie, MacLean. Round the world with a loop thrown in. Glasgow, Blackie & Son, 1892.
140 [8]p. 19½cm.
Visit to Salt Lake City, with substantial remarks on Mormonism.
UHi, UPB

876. Bromfield, Edward T. *editor.* Picturesque journeys in America of the Junior United Tourist Club. Ed. by the Rev. Edward T. Bromfield . . . New York, R. Worthington, 1883.
vi, 200p. illus. 24½×19cm.
Cover-title: Picturesque journeys in America.
Chapter entitled: Salt Lake and the Mormons.
Another editor under title: The land we live in, or America illustrated. New York: Worthington Co., 1891.
DLC, MB, MiD, MiU, NN, NjP

877. ———. Picturesque tours in America, The Junior United Tourist Club, including vivid description of the most wonderful scenery in the United States. Edited by the Rev. Edward T. Bromfield . . . New York, R. Worthington, 1885.
vi, 216p. illus. 25cm.
Chapter on Mormonism.
MB

878. Brook, Zadoc. Introduction to the Book of Mormon. Written by Z. Brook. [n.p., 1923]
[4]p. 20½×10cm.
Reprinted by Church of Jesus Christ (Bickerton group) Originally published as an introduction in the New York, Brooks-Hundley, printing of the Book of Mormon in 1858.
Morgan
NN, PMoNC

879. Brookbank, Thomas W. Are the lost tribes found? Salt Lake City, Salt Lake City Efficiency Printing Co., 1929.
27p. 23cm.
An attempt to locate the lost tribes of Israel.
USlC

880. ———. Concerning the Brass Plates. By Thomas W. Brookbank. Liverpool, Printed and Published at the Millennial Star Office [ca. 1924]
27p. 21½cm.
Defense of the *Book of Mormon* story of brass plates.
USlC

881. ———. Is geloof alleen voedoende? [Amsterdam? n.d.]
[4]p. 21½cm.
Title in English: Is belief alone sufficient?
USlC

882. ———. A study in Hebrew and Indian languages. Salt Lake City, Salt Lake Efficiency Printing Co., 1926.
26p. 23cm.
An attempt to show the similarity of Hebrew and some Indian languages in defense of the *Book of Mormon.*
USIC

883. Brookes, Joshua. Fads and fallacies by Joshua Brookes. With chapters by Antony Ludovici and Ellis Barker. New York, London, Paris, Brentano's [1929]
3p.l., 7–253p. 22cm.
"Mormonism," p. 44–72. "Of the many follies that have emanated from America not one has been more ridiculous or more gross than the religion of the Mormons."
USIC

884. Brooks, James. A seven months' run, up, down, and around the world, by James Brooks. (Written in letters to the N.Y. Evening Express) New York, D. Appleton & Company, 1872.
xiv, 375p. map. 19cm.
Mormons, p. 9–17.
CU–B, DLC, UHi, UPB, USIC

Brooks, Juanita. History of Sarah Sturdevant Leavitt. *See Leavitt, Sarah Sturdevant.*

885. Brooks, Keith L. The Mormon creed examined. Los Angeles, California, American Prophetic League [n.d.]
8p. 16cm.
MoInRC, UPB

886. ———. Truth and error. [n.p., 1928?]
Folded chart to [16]l. 11½cm. (W. S. M. U. Series. No. 10)
A comparison of beliefs of various Christian churches. Includes Mormonism. Published before May, 1928.
UPB

887. Brooks, Noah. The boy emigrants, with illustrations by Thomas Moran and W. S. Sheppard. New York, Scribner, Armstrong & Co., 1877 [c1876]
viii [1]l., 309p. illus. 19cm.
Novel with a chapter entitled "In Mormondom."
Other editions: 1891. UPB; 1894. CU–B; 1903. DLC; illustrated by H. T. Dunn. New York, Scribners, 1914. DLC, ULA, USIC; 1925. NjP, UHi
CU–B, UPB, USIC

888. Broom, W. W. Is the Mormon a man? By W. W. Broom. Salisbury, Published at 31, Catherine Street [1857?]
12p. 19cm.
Cover-title.
USIC

889. Brosnan, Cornelius James. History of the state of Idaho. New York, Chicago, Boston, Charles Scribner's Sons, 1918.
2p.l., vii–xiii, 237p. illus., maps. 20cm.
Includes Mormon colonization in Idaho; Fort Lemhi, p. 80–82.
Another edition: c1926. DLC, ULA
DLC, UHi, UPB, USIC

890. Brotherton, Edward. Mormonism: its rise and progress, and the prophet Joseph Smith. By Edward Brotherton, Manchester, Printed and Published by J. & S. Smith [1845?]
36p. 22½cm.
Emphasis on Kirtland Safety Society scandal, the trouble caused by the Mormons in both Missouri and Illinois. A discussion of the Book of Mormon. He predicts that if they go west only half will survive the trip. Printed between Sept. 1845 and a time when the departure would have been public information in Manchester.
ICN, MH, NN, USIC

891. Brough, Charles Hillman. Irrigation in Utah. Baltimore, The Johns Hopkins Press, 1898.
xv, 212p. 4 plates. 24cm.
Includes Mormon participation in irrigation projects.
CSmH, CU, DLC, NjP, UHi, UPB, ULA, USIC, UU

892. Brown, Benjamin. Testimonies for the truth: A record of manifestations of the power or God, miraculous and providential, witnessed in the travels and experience of Benjamin Brown, High Priest in the Church of Jesus Christ of Latter-day Saints, Liverpool, Published by S. W. Richards; London, L.D. Saints' Book and Millennial Star Depot, 1853.
32p. 21½cm.
Howes B828
CSmH, CtY, ICN, MH, NjP, NN, UPB, USIC, UU

893. Brown, Clarence T. In the matter of Brigham H. Roberts, Member-elect from the State of Utah. Protest and Petition of C. T. Brown, Wm. Paden and T. C. Iliff. [Salt Lake City? 1899]
18p. 22cm.
Signed: Salt Lake City, Utah, January 6th, 1899.
At head of title: House of Representatives, Fifty-sixth Congress.
OO

894. Brown, David. Dairy [sic] of a voyage from Liverpool to New Orleans on board the ship International commanded by Capt. David Brown. *See Diary [spelled Dairy] of a Voyage.*

895. Brown, Francis Almond. A heroic and eloquent plea. F. A. Brown states his motives and aspirations, bears a powerful testimony, and asks the court some pointed questions. Salt Lake City, Utah, Deseret News Company, 1885.
4p. 21cm.
Polygamy trial.
CSmH, MH, USIC

896. Brown, Henry. The history of Illinois, from its first discovery and settlement to the present time. By Henry Brown . . . New York, J. Winchester, 1844.
x, 492p. fold. map. 22½cm.
History of the Mormons in Illinois, p. 386–403, 487–492.
Howes B839, Sabin 8484
CSmH, DLC, ICN, NjP, UHi, USIC, UU

897. Brown, Hugh B. Practical religion; an address delivered over Radio Station KSL Sunday evening, Sept. 29th, 1929. By Elder Hugh B. Brown. [Salt Lake City, Church of Jesus Christ of Latter-day Saints, 1929]
7p. 22cm.
USIC

898. Brown, J. Robert. A journal of a trip across the plains of the U.S., from Missouri to California, in the year 1856: Giving a correct view of the country, anecdotes, Indian stories, mountaineers' tales, etc., by J. Robert Brown. Columbus [O.] The author, 1860.
119p. 22½cm.
Encounters Mormons, particularly one who is fleeing from the wrath of Brigham Young.
W-C 352
CtY, DLC, NjP

899. Brown, James Stephens. California gold; an authentic history of the first find, with the names of those interested in the discovery. Pub. by the author, James S. Brown . . . Oakland, Cal., Pacific Press Publishing Company, 1894.
1p.l., 5–20p. port. 18cm.
Tells of the Mormon part in the gold discovery.
Howes B848
CU-B, DLC, ICN, MH, USIC

900. ———. Life of a pioneer; being the autobiography of James S. Brown. Salt Lake City, George Q. Cannon & Sons, Co., 1900.
xix [9]–520p. illus., port. 22cm.
Howes B849
CSmH, CtY, CU-B, DLC, NjP, NN, UHi, ULA, USI, USIC

901. ———. Route to Arizona Territory per Elder James S. Brown. [Salt Lake City? 1876?]
4p. 18cm.
Travel guide to Arizona. Probably used by Mormon colonizers and visitors to the settlements.
USIC

902. Brown, John. History of San Bernardino and Riverside County; by John Brown, jr., editor for San Bernardino County and James Boyd, editor for Riverside County; with selected biography of actors and witnesses of the period of growth and achievement . . . [Madison, Wis.] The Western Historical Association, 1922.
3v. illus., plates, ports. 26½cm.
"During Mormon occupation," V.1, chapter 3, p. 37–49 and other scattered references.
CU-B, DLC, UPB

903. Brown, John. Mediumistic experiences of John Brown, the Medium of the Rockies. San Francisco, Office of the Philosophical Journal, 1897.
viii [9]–192p. 20½cm.
In paper wrapper with port.
References by a former mountain man and subsequent Spiritualist to the Mormons at San Bernardino, p. 54, 71–72, 76–78, 103–105, 169–70.
First printed: Des Moines, M. Hull & Co., 1887.
CU-B, UPB

904. Brown, John, 1843– *editor.* Twenty-five years a parson in the wild West; being the experience of Parson Ralph Riley, by Rev. John Brown . . . Fall River, Mass., Printed for the Author, 1896.
215p. port. 18½cm.
Chapter xiv. The Mormons.
DLC, NjP, UHi

905. Brown, John Elward. "In the cult kingdom" Mormonism, Eddyism, Russellism, by John Elward Brown . . . Chicago, Siloam Springs, Ark. [etc.,] International Federation Publishing Company [1918]
124p. 19cm.
CU-B, DLC, NjP, NN, USIC

906. Brown, John Newton, *editor.* Encyclopedia of religious knowledge, or, dictionary of the Bible, theology, religious biography, all religions, ecclesiastical history, and missions . . . To which is added a missionary gazetteer . . . by Rev. B. B. Edwards . . . Edited by Rev. J. Newton Brown . . . Brattleboro, Vt., Brattleboro Typographic Co., 1834.
1275, vip. illus., plates, ports., maps. 27½cm.
Entry under "Mormonites."
In various editions from 1834 to 1876.
ScCot

907. Brown, Joseph Emerson. The Mormon question. Speech of Hon. Joseph E. Brown, of Georgia, in the Senate of the United States, Friday, January 11, 1884. [Washington, Govt. Print. Off., 1884]
24p. 22cm.
Caption-title.
Speech in opposition to the Edmunds Act.
CSmH, CtY, CU-B, DLC, MH, NN, UHi, USIC

908. ———. Polygamy in Utah and New England contrasted. Speech of Hon. Joseph E. Brown, of Georgia, delivered in the Senate of the United States, Tuesday, May 27, 1884 . . . Washington [Govt. Print. off.] 1884.
32p. 22cm.
States that all men who marry after divorce are polygamists.
CtY, CU-B, DLC, UPB, USIC, UU

909. ———. Speech . . . on the Mormon question, delivered in the Senate of the United States, on the 16th day of February, 1882. Washington, 1882.
15p. 21cm.
CtY

BROWN, M. W.

910. Brown, Maria Ward. The life of Dan Rice. Long Branch, N.J., Published by the author [c1901]
ix, 501p. port., plates. 24cm.
A fictional story of Mormons in Nauvoo, where, he sees Joseph Smith fail to fake a miracle. Escapes from Nauvoo.
NjP, USlC

Brown, Paula [*pseud.*] *See Dykes, Pauline Browning (Higgins)*

911. Brown, S. C. Latter-day Saints reformation. Eternal punishment and salvation through the atonement of Jesus Christ. By S. C. Brown. Richfield, Utah, Reaper Job Print., 1901.
42p. 23cm.
Cover-title.
Unorthodox treatise on Mormon doctrine.
USlC

912. Brown, Thomas D. and Son. Utah! Its silver mines, ores, minerals, produce, and other resources. [Great Salt Lake, n.d.]
13p. 21½cm.
Caption-title.
Information concerning people of Utah as well as ore discoveries. A benevolent picture for prospective investors. "They are strange but good."
CU, CU-B

913. ———. (same) Great Salt Lake City, 1865.
15p. 23cm.
CSmH

914. Brown, Thomas Dunlop. Letter to W. Cunningham, Esq. T. D. Brown's Letter to W. Cunningham, Esq., of Lainshaw, Ayrshire . . . [Liverpool, R. James, Printer . . . 1848]
16p. 21cm.
Caption-title.
Dated at end: 1848.
Defense of Mormonism in answer to a letter against the church.
USlC

915. Brown, W. P. Defense of the Church of Christ, and exposure of the errors of Mormonism. By W. P. Brown. Newton, Kansas, Democrat Publishing House [1887]
[2] 30p. 22½cm.
Cover-title.
Champions of the David Whitmer group. The Church of Christ in Zion.
Morgan
MH, MoInRC, NN, ULA, USlC

916. ———. Exposure of the errors of Mormonism, and defense of the Church of Christ. [Newton, Kansas, Republican Printing House] 1887.
52p. 22cm. (Pamphlet, No. 2)
Morgan
MH, MoInRC, NN, USlC, WHi

917. ———. (same) Newton, Kansas, Reynolds, Bros. Printing House, 1888.
1p.l., 103p. 21cm. (Pamphlet, No. 3)
Morgan
MoInRC, NN, USlC

918. Brown, W. Towers. Notes of travel. Extracts from home letters written during a two years' tour round the world, 1879–1881. By W. Towers Brown . . . [London] Printed for private circulation, 1882.
xiv [1]l., 372p. fold. maps. 19½cm.
He traveled to Salt Lake City in 1879, attended a church meeting, and talked to several residents.
USlC

919. Browne, Charles Farrar. Artemus Ward, his book, with many comic illustrations. New-York, Carleton, Publisher, [Late Rudd & Carleton] MDCCCLXII [1862]
6p.l. [17]–262 [2]p. plates. 19cm.
First edition.
"A visit to Brigham Young," p. 103.
CU, DLC, UPB

920. ———. (same) New York, Carleton, 1863.
262p. plates. 18½cm.
UHi

921. ———. (same) New York, Carleton, 1864.
262 [2]p. plates. 19cm.
DLC, NjP

922. ———. (same) New York, Carleton, 1865.
xp., [3]l. [17]–262 [2]p. plates. 19cm.
CSmH, CU-B, NjP

923. ———. (same) With notes and a preface by the editor of the Biglow papers. London, J. C. Hotten, 1865.
3p.l., 167p. 19cm.
CtY, CU-B, NjP, UPB, UU

924. ———. (same) New York, Carleton, 1867.
vi [2] [9]–224p. illus., plates. 19cm.
DLC, NjPT

925. ———. Artemus Ward (his travels) among the Mormons. Part I. –On the rampage. Part II. –Porlite litteratoor. Ed. by E. P. Hingston . . . London, John Camden Hotten, 1865.
xxx, 192p. front. 18cm.
Part I chiefly devoted to Mormons. Also, one section in part II.
Sabin 8645
CU-B, NjP, ULA, UPB

925a. ———. (same) Part I. Miscellaneous. Part II. Among the Mormons . . . New York, Carleton, Publisher; London, S. Low, Son & Co., MDCCCLXV (1865)
231p. 12cm.
CtY, NN

BROWNE, C. F.

926. ———. (same) With comic illustrations by Mullen. New York, Carleton [etc., etc.] 1865.
231p. plates. 19cm.
Added title page.
Part II. Among the Mormons.
CSmH, CU, NjP, UPB

927. ———. (same) New York, Carleton [etc., etc.] 1866.
231p. plates. 19cm.
DLC

928. ———. (same) New York, Carleton [etc., etc.] 1867.
231p. plates. 19cm.
CSmH, UPB

929. ———. (same) Part I. Miscellaneous. Part II. Among the Mormons. With comic illustrations by Mullen. Reprinted from the American copyright edition. Montreal, C. R. Chisholm Railway and Steamboat News Agent [n.d.]
3p.l. [9]–94p. 24cm.
Cover-title.
USl

930. ———. (same) With an introduction by George Augustus Sala. Reprinted from the original. London, G. Routledge & Sons [186–?]
121p. 18½cm.
CSmH

931. ———. Artemus Ward's lecture (as delivered at the Egyptian Hall, London) Edited by his executors, T. W. Robertson & E. P. Hingston . . . London, J. C. Hotten; New York, G. W. Carleton & Co., 1869.
vii [8]–213 [1]p. plates, port. 19cm.
New York edition has title: Artemus Ward's panorama. Includes some of his 18 lectures on Mormonism.
CU–B, NjP

932. ———. (same) Artemus Ward's lecture on the Mormons, ed. with a prefatory note, by Edward P. Hingston; with thirty-two illustrations. London, Chatto and Windus, 1882.
64p. plates. 18½cm.
CU–B, DLC, NjP

933. ———. (same under title) Artemus Ward's panorama. (As exhibited at the Egyptian Hall, London) Edited by his executors, T. W. Robertson, & E. P. Hingston . . . New York, G. W. Carlton, Publisher; London, J. C. Hotten, 1869.
213p. illus. 19cm.
London edition has title: Artemus Wards' lecture. A reprint of his travels among the Mormons.
CU–B, DLC, NjP, UPB

934. ———. (same) London, John Camden Hotten [n.d.]
196, 11p. 19cm.
UPB

935. ———. The Complete work of Charles F. Browne, better known as "Artemus Ward." London, Chatto and Windus [1869?]
xi p. 21 [27]–518p. 19cm.
Includes his section on travel among the Mormons.
CSmH

936. ———. (same) With portrait by Geflowski the sculptor, facsimile of handwriting, &c. London, John Camden Hotten [1871?]
xi [2] [27]-518p. port., facsim. 19cm.
"A Visit to Brigham Young" and also his travels among the Mormons.
CSmH, CU–B

937. ———. (same) With a biographical sketch (by Melville D. Landon, "Eli Perkins") New York, G. W. Carleton & Co.; London, Chatto & Wendus, 1879.
ix [10]–347 [1]p. illus., port., plates. 19cm.
CSmH

938. ———. (same) A new edition, with a portrait by Geflowski, facsimile of handwriting &c. London, Chatto and Wendus, 1884.
xi [2] [27]–518. port., facsim. 20cm.
CU–B

939. ———. (same) New York, G. W. Dillingham, 1887.
347p. 20cm.
NjP., UHi

940. ———. (same) London, Chatto & Wendus, 1890.
ix [25]–518p. 15½cm.
DLC

941. ———. (same) New York, A. L. Burt Co., 1898.
449p. illus. 19cm.
UPB

942. ———. (same) With a biographical sketch (By Melville D. Landon "Eli Perkins") and many humerous illustration. Revised Edition. New York, G. W. Dillingham Co., Publisher [c1898]
x, 11–449p. 19cm.
Contains much of his Mormon material.
CU–B, NjP, USlC

943. ———. Sandwiches, by Artemus Ward. New York, Carleton, Publisher [c1870]
31p. illus. 27cm.
Cover-title.
Includes "A visit to Brigham Young."
CU–B

944. ———. To California and back. [n.p., after 1865]
92p. 13cm. (Pocket series)
Caption-title.
From Artemus Ward (his travels) among the Mormons.
"Salt Lake City and Brigham Young."
Another edition: 95p. (Ten Cent Pocket Series. No. 368) USlC
CU–B

945. Browne, John Ross. . . . Indian war in Oregon and Washington territories. Letter from the Secretary of the Interior, transmitting, in compliance with the resolution of the House of the 15th instant, the report of J. Ross Browne, on the subject of the Indian war in Oregon and Washington Territories. Washington, 1858.
62p. 23cm. (U.S. 35th Cong., 1st Sess. House Ex. doc. 38)
On page 12: Allegations of Mormon interference.
CU, CU–B, DLC, NN, ULA

Browne, Valentine Charles. *See Church of Jesus Christ of Latter-day Saints. Missions. European.*

946. Brownell, Henry Howard. The pioneer heroes of the New World. From the earliest period (982) to the present time. By Henry Howard Brownell . . . Cincinnati, O., M. R. Barnitz, 1857.
2p.l. [3]–639, 720–736p., col. plates, ports. 22½cm.
The Mormon settlement, p. 613–625.
DLC, UHi, USlC

947. Bryant, Edwin. What I saw in California: being the journal of a tour, by the emigrant route and South pass of the Rocky Mountains, across the continent of North America, the great desert basin, and through California, in the years 1846, 1847 . . . By Edwin Bryant . . . New York, D. Appleton & Company; Philadelphia, G. S. Appleton, 1848.
455p. 19cm.
Visited Utah in 1846. Brief description of Salt Lake City area as well as encounters with Mormons on the trail.
Published in several editions between 1848–1849. Howes, B903, Sabin C. H. 8804, W–C 146
CSmH, CTY, CU–B, DLC, MBwT, MH, NjP, UHi, USl, UU

948. ———. (same, under title) Rocky Mountain adventures, bristling with animated details of fearful fights of American hunters with savage Indians, Mexican rancheros, and beasts of prey . . . By Edwin Bryant. To which is added a full account of the Bear conquest of California, by a handful of American adventurers, who levelled the way for the triumphs of Stockmon [sic] and Fremont, and the glorious and glittering days of '48 and '49. [Arlington ed.] New York, Hurst & Co., c1885.
452p. front. 19cm.
CLU, CU, NjP, NN, OClWHi

949. Bryas, Madeleine de, *comtesse.* A Frenchwoman's impressions of America, by Comtesse Medeleine de Bryas and Jacqueline de Bryas. New York, The Century Co., 1920.
xivp., [2]l., 3–268p. 19cm.
A visit to Utah about 1918 with interviews.
DLC, MB, NN, UHi, USl

Das Buck der Welt. *See Gr. Th.*

950. Das buch Mormon. Frankfurt [n.d.]
[4]p. 21cm.
Title in English: The Book of Mormon.
UPB

951. Buchanan, C. O. Mormons and the Bible, a warning. Cheadle, Cheshire, Cheadle Parish Bookroom [n.d.]
5p. 21cm.
A tract on the Book of Mormon.
MoInRC

952. Buchanan, James. The administration on the eve of the rebellion. A history of four years before the war. By James Buchanan. London, S. Low, Son and Marston, 1865.
x [9]–296p. 25cm.
Tells of the Utah Expedition. Explains President Buchanan's part in the Utah Expedition.
Another edition: New York, Appleton and Co., 1866. CU, CSmH, DLC, USlC
Sabin
CSmH, CtY, DLC, MiU–C, PPM

953. ———. The works of James Buchanan, comprising his speeches, state papers and private correspondence, Collected and edited by John Bassett Moore. Philadelphia and London, J. B. Lippincott and Co., 1908–11.
12v. 25cm.
Includes messages, correspondence, and proclamations of President Buchanan on the Mormon uprising and the Utah Expedition.
CSmH, CU, DLC, NjP, UPB

954. Buchanan, Robert Williams. Saint Abe and his seven wives, a tale of Salt Lake City. New York, G. Routledge and Sons, 1872.
ix, 169p. 19cm.
Poetry concerning Mormonism.
CU–B, DLC, IU, MB, MH, MoInRC, NjP, NN, ULA, WHi

955. ———. (same) Toronto, Adam, Stevenson & Co., 1872.
4p.l. [3]–169p. 17½cm.
CaTU, MiD

956. ———. (same) London, Strahan & Co., 1872.
ix, 169p. 19½cm.
CSmH, CU–B, DLC, MB, NN, USl, USlC, UU

957. ———. (same) 3d ed. London, Strahan & Co., 1872.
ix, 169p. 19½cm.
CSmH

958. ———. (same) A tale of Salt Lake City, by the author of "White Rose and Red," with a frontispiece by A. B. Houghton. New York, Chatto, Piccadilly, 1882.
ix, 1l. [3]–169p. 18½cm.
USlC

959. ———. (same) London, Strahan & Co., 1882.
169p. 19cm.
USlC

960. ———. (same) London, Chatto & Windus, 1882.
ix, 169p. 19½cm.
USlC

961. ———. (same) [in verse] With a bibliographical note. By Robert Buchanan. First cheap edition. London, Robert Buchanan, 1896.
ix [1] 169 [2]p. plate. 19cm.
Copies include eight papers of criticism after text.
CtY, MB, MH, MiU, PU

Buck, Dudley. Deseret. *See Croffut, William Augustus.*

962. **Buckingham, James Silk.** The Eastern and Western States of America, by J. S. Buckingham. London, Paris, Fisher, Sons & Co., 1842.
3v. fold. plates. 23cm.
V.3, Chapter XI: "Village of the Mormons," p. 190–194. Mormons at Keokuck, Iowa. Deceit of the Mormons.
NjP, USlC

963. **Buckley, James Monroe.** Faith-healing Christian Science and kindred phenomena. London, 1892.
2p.l., 7–11, 308. 20cm.
Faith-healing by Mormons, p. 35–37, 45.
Other editions: New York, Century Co., 1892. DLC, NjP, NjPT, UPB; 1906. DLC
USlC

964. **Buckley, W. P.** A brief history of the Church of Christ (Temple Lot) Headquarters: Independence, Mo. Compiled by W. P. Buckley, General Church Recorder. 1929. [Independence, Mo.? 1929?]
70p. 21cm.
Inside front cover is p. [1]. Page 34–70 devoted to "Visits of the Messenger to Otto Fetting." (first 12 visitations)
MoInRC

965. **Budd, George Henry,** *compiler.* The history of the Taylor Stake as presented in this volume has been compiled from records kept in the various wards, quorums and organizations . . . Compiled and published by George H. Budd, Stake Recorder. Raymond, The Chronicle Print, 1906.
72p. port. 19cm.
USlC

966. **Budge, Jesse Robert Stratford.** The life of William Budge, by his son Jesse R. S. Budge. Salt Lake City, The Deseret News, 1915.
vi, 241p. port. 23cm.
CSmH, CtY, NjP, UHi, UPB, USlC, UU

967. ———. A review of a tract written by the Rev. R. P. Boyd, entitled "Fatal objections to the Mormon tithing system," by J. R. S. Budge, Paris, Idaho, February, 1906. Salt Lake City, The Deseret News, 1906.
20p. 18½cm.
A defense of tithing.
USlC

968. **Budge, William.** The gospel message. Being a discourse, giving an explanation of some of the prominent doctrines of the Church of Jesus Christ of Latter-day Saints, delivered by Elder William Budge, at Chesterfield, August 10th, 1879. [Liverpool, Printed and Published by William Budge, 1879]
12p. 21cm.
Caption-title.
Reported by Joseph May.
CSmH, DLC, ICN, MH, NN, UPB, USl, USlC, UU

969. ———. (same) (Phonetically reported) [Liverpool, Printed and Published by Albert Carrington, at the Latter-day Saint Print., Publishing and Emigration office, 188?]
12p. 21cm.
NN, UHi, UPB

970. ———. Life's probation after death. A Discourse delivered by President William Budge before the Elders' quorum, at Paris, Idaho, Reported by Elder James H. Wallis. March 23, 1896, Paris, Idaho, 1896.
[6]p. 22cm.
USlC

971. ———. The marriage institution. A discourse, giving an explanation of some of the views of the Latter-day Saints on the marital relation, delivered at a conference held in Goswell Hall, Goswell Road, London, November 9th, 1879, by William Budge an Elder of the Church of Jesus Christ of Latter-day Saints . . . (Reported by Joseph May of Sheffield) [Liverpool, Printed and Published by W. Budge at the Latter-day Saint Printing, Publishing & Emigration Office. 1879?]
16p. 22½cm.
Caption-title.
Variant printings.
CSmH, DLC, ICN, MH, NN, UPB, USl, USlC, UU

BUDGE, W.

972. ———. (same, in Danish) De Sidste-Dages Helliges Anskuelser om Aegteskab. En Tale, holdt af Praesident Wm. Budge ved en Konference, alholdt i Goswell hall, Goswell Road, London, den 9de November 1879. Kjøbenhavn, Udgivet og forlagt af R. Wilhelmsen, Trykt hos F. E. Bording, 1880.
 1p.l., 15 [1]p. 21½cm.
 UPB

973. ———. (same) Kjøbenhavn, Udgivet og forlagt af C. D. Fjeldsted. Trykt hos F. E. Bording, 1882.
 15 [1]p. 21cm.
 USIC

974. ———. (same, in Icelandic) Hinn eini sanni nátharbothskapur etha trú hinna fyrstu kristnu. Eftir William Budge . . . [Reykjavik, Utgefandi, Loftur Bjarnasen, 1905]
 16p. 17½cm.
 USIC

975. ———. (same, in Swedish) De Sista Dagars Heliges åsigter om äktenskap. Framsatta i ett föredrag af President William Budge i en konferens i London, den 9 Nov. 1879. Köpenhamn, Utgifven och förlagd af N. Wilhelmsen, 1880.
 16p. 21½cm.
 Cover-title.
 CtY, UHi, USIC

976. ———. (same) De sista dagarnes heliges Asigter om Äktenskap Föredrag af William Budge i London den 9 November 1879. Tredje upplagan. [Köpenhamn, Utgifven och förlagd af N. C. Flygare. Tryckt hos F. E. Bording, 1887]
 16p. 23½cm.
 USIC

977. ———. The only true gospel, or the primitive Christian faith, by William Budge. [Liverpool, Printed and Published by William Budge, at the Latter-day Saints' Printing, Publishing, and Emigration Office, 1878?]
 4p. 22½cm.
 Signed: November 15th, 1878.
 UPB, USIC

978. ———. (same) [Liverpool, Printed and Published by William Budge, 1879]
 4p. 21½cm.
 Binder title: "Gospel tracts."
 CSmH, CtY, ICN, MH, NN, USl, USIC

979. ———. (same) [Liverpool, Printed and Published by Albert Carrington, Millennial Star Office? ca. 1881]
 4p. 22cm.
 Caption-title.
 UHi, USIC, UU

980. ———. (same) [Liverpool, Printed and Published by John Henry Smith at the Latter-day Saints' Printing, Publishing, and Emigration Office, ca. 1884]
 4p. 21cm.
 USIC

981. ———. (same) [Liverpool, Printed and Published by Daniel H. Wells at the Latter-Day Saints' Printing, Publishing, and Emigration Office, ca. 1886]
 4p. 23cm.
 NN

982. ———. (same) [Liverpool, Printed and Published by the European Missions of the Church of Jesus Christ of Latter-day Saints, ca. 1910]
 4p. 21cm.
 UPB, USIC

983. ———. (same) By William Budge . . . [Salt Lake City, Printed by the Deseret News Co., n.d.]
 6p. 16½×10½cm.
 Caption-title.
 CU, ICN, MH, MoInRC, USIC, WHi

984. ———. (same, in Danish) Det eneste sande Evangelium eller de første Kristnes Tro. Af William Budge. [Kjøbenhavn, Udgivet og forlagt af Andreas Peterson . . . Trykt hos E. E. Bording . . . 1899]
 [4]p. 22cm.
 USIC

985. ———. (same) [Kjøbenhavn, Udgivet og forlagt af Andreas Peterson . . . Trykt hos Emil Petersen . . . 1900]
 [4]p. 22cm.
 USIC

986. ———. (same) [Kobenhavn, Udgivet og forlagt af A. L. Skancky . . . Trykt hos L. A. Nielsen, 1901]
 [4]p. 23cm.
 USIC

987. ———. (same) [Kobenhavn, Udgivet og forlagt af A. L. Skancky . . . Trykt hos L. A. Nielsen . . . 1902]
 [4]p. 22cm.
 USIC

988. ———. (same) [Kjobenhavn, Udgivet og forlagt af A. L. Skancky. L. A. Nielsens Trykt, 1903?]
 [4]p. 24cm.
 USIC

989. ———. (same) [Kjøbenhavn, Udgivet og forlagt af A. L. Skancky . . . Trykt hos P. S. Christiansen . . . 1904]
 [4]p. 22cm.
 USIC

990. ———. (same in French) Le seul vrai evangile, ou la foi des premiers chrétiens, par William Budge. [St.-Hélier, Publié par Joseph A. A. Bunot, 1883]
4p. 22cm.
USlC

991. ———. (same) [Berne, Publie par Geo. C. Naegle, 1895?]
4p. 24cm.
USlC

992. ———. (same, in Swedish) Det sanna evangeliet eller de första kristnas tro. Af William Budge . . . [Malmö, Tryckt å Landby & Lundgrens Boktryckeri, 1905]
[4]p. 22cm.
UPB, USlC

993. ———. (same) [Stockholm, Exp. av Nordstjärnan . . . Bröderna olofssons Trckeri, 1926]
[4]p. 22cm.
USlC

994. ———. Pre-existence of spirits. Discourse delivered by President William Budge, before the Elders' Quorum, December 19, 1895. [Salt Lake City? 1895?]
[4]p. 24cm.
UPB, USlC

995. ———. Pres. Wm. Budge sounds a note of warning to the people in regard to the coming election. Advises the people against voting for a political combination whose leaders threaten the safety of our government. [Paris, Idaho, The Post, 1900]
[8]p. 22cm.
Church and politics.
UPB, USlC

996. ———. A reply to "The Mormon purgatory" (a tract written by S. E. Wishard) [Salt Lake City, Juvenile Instructor Office, 1890?]
16p. 18½×11½cm.
Caption-title.
Signed: March 15, 1890.
MH, MoInRC, USlC, WHi

997. **Buechler, August F.** History of Hall County, Nebraska, a narrative of the past, with special emphasis upon the pioneer period of the country's history, and chronological presentation of its social, commercial, educational, religious, and civic development from the early days to the present time, and special analysis of its military and civil participation in the late world war, by A. F. Buechler and R. J. Barr, Editors-in-chief, Dale P. Stough, Associate compiling editor, . . . Lincoln, Nebraska, Western Publishing and Engraving Company, 1920.
xii, [1]l., 965p. illus., ports. 26cm.
Mormonism, p. 63–64.
UPB

998. **Buel, James William.** America's wonderlands. A pictorial and descriptive history of our country's scenic marvels, magnificent photographic views . . . Interspersed with history, legend, adventure, and natural wonders embraced within our vast domain, from Alaskas frigid clime to Florida's summerlands. Denver, World Publishing Company [1893]
503p. illus., plates. 24×31.
Chap. IV, "Marvels of the Great Deseret," has many references to Mormon settlements and historic areas.
Another edition: Boston, Mass., E. Gately & Co. [c1893] USlC
CU-B, NjP, UPB

999. ———. Glimpses of America; a pictorial and descriptive history of our country's scenic marvels, delineated by pen and camera. Philadelphia, Historical Publishing Co. [1894]
5p.l., 11–502p. illus., plates. 29×36½cm. (Historical Fine Art Series)
Detailed description of the area, with mention of history, cities, etc.
DLC

1000. ———. Metropolitan life unveiled; or, The mysteries and miseries of America's great cities, embracing New York, Washington City, San Francisco, Salt Lake City, and New Orleans, by J. W. Buel . . . St. Louis, Mo., Historical Publishing Co., 1882.
2p.l., 606p. illus. 21cm.
Added ornamental t.-p.
Includes "Salt Lake City — Polygamy"
Also issued in 1883 under title: Mysteries and miseries of America's great cities. San Francisco, 1883. CU-B, NN
Other editions: 1883. DLC, NN
CSmH, CU-B, DLC, MH, UHi, USlC

1001. ———. Sunlight and shadow of America's great cities. By the author of "heroes of the plains," etc. Illustrated with numerous engravings. Philadelphia, West Philadelphia Publishing Co., c1889.
1p.l., 606p. illus. 23cm.
Prologue signed: J.W.B.
Cover-title: Metropolitan life unveiled. America's great cities. "Salt Lake City — Polygamy," p. 345–495.
ICU, NN, ULA, USl, UU

1002. **Buford, L. M.** Mormons. July, 1896. (In Consular reports. July, 1896. V.51 #190. Washington, Govt. Print. Off., 1896. xv, 369–599p.)
ULA, UU

1003. **Bukki** [*pseud.*] A supplement to Mormon, containing the Book of Anak. Cooperstown, Y.Y. [sic] Printed for the publisher, by J. I. Hendryx, 1851.
Satire on the Book of Mormon.
18p. 19cm.
WHi

BULKLEY, N.

1004. **Bulkley, Newman.** A vision as seen by Newman Bulkley. In Springville, Utah, January 8, 1886. Bloomington, Utah, Printed at the Union Office, 1886.
8p. 13½cm.
Cover-title.
A revelation concerning the state of the nation and how it will be saved by the Mormon Elders.
NjP, UPB

1005. **Bullock, Alonzo Mansfield.** Mormonism and the Mormons. An epitome. By Rev. A. M. Bullock . . . Menasha, Wis., The Breeze Printing Company, 1898.
48p. 21½cm.
Bibliography: p. 48.
CU–B, DLC, ICHi, MiU, NN, UHi, USlC

1006. **Bundy, L. A.** Mormonism exposed; a faithful expose of the secrets and evils of the Mormon country, by one who possessed the sixteenth part of a husband. L. A. Bundy. New York, Ornum & Co. [1872?]
64p. ports. 24cm.
CtY lists 185–? but material seems later.
CtY, CU–B, MH, NN

1007. **Bunner, A. A.** The Bunner — Rich debate. A public discussion between Mr. A. A. Bunner . . . and Elder Ben E. Rich . . . held March 4th, 5th, 6th, 7th, and 8th, 1912. [Chicago, Henry C. Etten & Co.] 1912.
163p. 17½cm.
Published for the Missions of the Church of Jesus Christ of Latter-day Saints.
IWW, NjP, UHi, ULA, UPB, USlC

1008. **Bunting, Jabez.** Mormonism; its origin and character. Reprinted from the *Eclectic Review*. With an introduction by Jabez Bunting. Second Edition. Sydney, Printed by W. Lambert [1853?]
iv [5]–16p. 21cm.
USlC

1009. **Burbidge, George William.** A new grammar of the Tahitian dialect of the Polynesian language and combined with a vocabulary of English, French, Tahitian. Second edition. Arranged and Published by Geo. W. Burbidge for the Church of Jesus Christ of Latter-day Saints. [n.p.] 1930.
334p. 20cm.
USlC

1010. **Burder, William.** A history of all religions; with accounts of the ceremonies and customs, or the forms of worship practiced by the several nations of the known world, from the earliest records to the year 1872, with a full account, historical, doctrinal, and statistical, of all the religious denominations. Philadelphia, William W. Harding [c1872?]
ix, 7–807p. 22cm.
Mormonism, p. 587–601. A very inaccurate account of Mormonism. He claims that Smith was a Methodist on probation who fell away and considers the Book of Mormon to be a pirating of Spaulding's *Manuscript Found*. Admission to membership "includes a stripping" and "there is no such crime as incest" in Mormonism.
MoInRC, NN, UU

1011. **Burdette, Mary G.** Twenty-two years' work among Mormons. Compiled by Mary G. Burdette, Corresponding Secretary. Chicago, Women's Baptist Home Mission Society [1905]
116p. illus., ports. 19½cm.
Compiled by the corresponding secretary of the Women's Baptist Home Mission Society.
First chapter is an explanation of Mormon doctrine.
MH, USlC, UU

1012. **Burge, C. O.** Adventures of a civil engineer. Fifty years on five continents by C. O. Burge . . . London, Alston Rivers, Ltd. . . . 1909.
xiv [1]l., 319 [1]p. illus. 22cm.
He visits Salt Lake City on Sunday in order to attend service, where the Mormons attempt to convert him.
CU, USlC

1013. **Burgess, Alice Chase.** The centennial pageant, fulfillment, a panorama of the Christian cycle. Independence, Mo., Reorganized Church of Jesus Christ of Latter Day Saints [1930?]
15p. 21cm.
Centennial program.
MoInRC

1014. ———. The Temple builders book, a manual of instructions and suggestions for Temple builders. [Lamoni, Ia.] Reorganized Church of Jesus Christ of Latter Day Saints. Woman's Department, Young Woman's Bureau [1920?]
67p. 27cm.
Dated: June, 1920.
MoInRC

1015. **Burgess, J. M.** The Book of Mormon contradictory to common sense, reason and revelation; or, The Mormon hierarchy founded upon a fiction. Liverpool, J. Blevin, 1850.
1p.l., 30p. 18cm.
MH, NN, USlC

1016. **Burgess, Samuel A.** The early history of Nauvoo, together with a sketch of the people who built this beautiful city and whose leaders suffered persecution and martyrdom for their religion's sake. Independence, Mo., Reorganized Church of Jesus Christ of Latter Day Saints [192–?]
16p. illus. 19½cm.
Cover-title.
ICHi, MoInRC, UHi, UPB

1017. ———. Nauvoo, a midwestern experiment in Christian community life, by S. A. Burgess . . . [Independence, Mo., Reorganized church of Jesus Christ of Latter Day Saints, 19 - -?]
15p. illus., ports. 20cm.
CU–B

1018. Burke, William S. An outline history of Council Bluffs and its railroads; showing the commercial advances. Chicago, Horton & Leonard, Steam Book and Job Printers, 1867.
31p. 21cm.
First two pages are on the Mormon period in Council Bluffs or "Cainsville."
Howes B987
CSmH

1019. Burleson, Hugh Latimer. The conquest of the continent. New York, Domestic and Foreign Missionary Society [c1911]
212p. plates, ports., maps. 19½cm.
Many references to Mormonism.
DLC, ULA, UPB, USlC

1020. Burnett, Peter Hardeman. Recollections and opinions of an old pioneer. New York, D. Appleton & Company, 1880.
xiii, 448. 20½cm.
References to Mormons in Missouri under such headings as Danites, Capt. Bogard, etc.
Howes B1000
CSmH, CU-B, DLC, NjP, NN, UHi, UPB, UU

1021. Burns, Dawson. Mormonism, explained and exposed. By Dawson Burns, Baptist Minister, Sacford. London, Houlston & Stoneman, 1853.
56p. 13½cm.
CtY, NN, USlC, UU

1022. Burrows, John McDowell. Fifty years in Iowa; being the personal reminiscences of J. M. D. Burrows, concerning the men and events, social life, industrial interests, physical development, and commercial progress of Davenport and Scott County, during the period from 1838 to 1888. Davenport, Ia., Glass & Company, 1888.
xi, 182p. illus. 18½cm.
History of the Mormons in Nauvoo and the martyrdom of Joseph Smith.
Howes B1023
CSmH, CtY, DLC, ICHi, ICN, NjP, UHi, UPB, USlC

1023. Burrows, Julius Caeser. The Burrows and Dubois speeches, the difference between the Reorganized Church of Jesus Christ of Latter Day Saints and the Brighamite Mormon Church clearly stated in speeches delivered in the United States Senate by two distinguished statesmen. [n.p., 1906?]
4p. 31cm.
The question of succession as raised during the Reed Smoot hearings.
MoInRC

1024. ———. In support of the resolution reported from the committee on privileges and elections "That Reed Smoot is not entitled to a seat as a senator of the United States from the state of Utah." Speech of Hon. Julius C. Burrows, of Michigan, in the Senate of the United States, Tuesday, December 11, 1906. Washington, 1906.
44p. 22cm.
Cover-title.
CU-B, MoInRC, UPB

1025. ———. Senator from Utah. The scope of the power of the Senate, under the Constitution, to "judge of the elections, returns, and qualifications of its own members," and the grounds upon which Reed Smoot is disqualified. Speech of Hon. Julius C. Burrows, of Michigan, Senate of the United States, Wednesday, February 20, 1907. Washington, 1907.
31p. 23cm.
Cover-title.
CU-B, MH, UHi, UU

1026. Burton, Emma Beatrice (Witherspoon) Beatrice Witherspoon; autobiography of Emma Beatrice Burton, written during her first mission to the South Sea Islands, from the year 1896 to the year 1900. Rev. and completed in 1914. Lamoni, Ia., Herald Publishing House, 1915.
8p.l. [9]–383p. illus. 20½cm.
First published in the *Autumn Leaves.*
MoInRC, UHi, UPB

1027. Burton, *Sir* Richard Francis. The City of the saints, and across the Rocky Mountains to California, by Richard F. Burton . . . London, Longman, Green, Longman, and Roberts, 1861.
x [2] 707 [1]p. illus., plates, fold. map, fold. plan. 22cm.
Howes B1033, Sabin 9497, W-C 370
CSmH, CtY, CU-B, DLC, MH, NjP, UHi, ULA, UPB, UU, VU

1028. ———. (same) 2d ed. London, Longman, Green, Longman and Roberts, 1862.
x [2] 707 [1]p. illus., plates, fold. map, fold. plan. 21½cm.
USlC

1029. ———. (same) New York, Harper & Brothers, 1862.
2p.l. [ix]–xiip., [2]l., 574p. illus., plates, fold. map, fold. plan. 24½cm.
Howes B1033, Sabin 9497
CSmH, CU-B, DLC, ICN, MoInRC, NjP, NN, UHi, USlC, UU

1030. ———. (same, in Italian) I mormoni e la citta dei santi; viaggio del capitano Riccardo Burton . . . Milano, Fratelli Trevis, Editori, 1875.
2p.l., 161 [3]p. illus., ports., facsim., map. 21½cm. (Bibliotecce de viaggi. xxi)
Reduced edition
CU-B, UPB, USlC

BURTON, R. F.

1031. ———. Voyages de capitaine Burton à La Mecque aux grands lacs d'Afrique et chez les Mormons, abregés par J. Belin-de Launay d'après les texte original et les traductions de Mme. H. Loreau. Paris, Librairie Hachette & Cie, 1870.
xvi, 336p. maps. 19cm.
Title in English: Travels of Captain Burton.
NN

1032. ———. (same) Deuxième ed. Paris, Librairie Hachette et Cie, 1874.
xvi, 336p. maps. 19cm.
On cover: Bibliothéque Rose Illustrée.
CU–B

1033. ———. Wanderings in three continents. By the Late Captain Sir Richard Francis Burton, K.C.M.G. Edited, with a preface, by W. H. Wilkins . . . With a photogravure portrait and with illustrations by A. D. McCormick. With illustrations. London, Hutchinson & Co., 1901.
xiii, 313p. port., plates. 21cm.
"The City of the Mormons, 1860," p. 147–195.
NjP, USIC

1034. Burton, William Walton. Verses written by William Walton Burton assembled on the occasion of his eightieth anniversary March twenty-third, nineteen hundred thirteen. Presented at a gathering held Monday, March twenty-Fourth . . . Ogden, Utah [1913]
50p. port. 23½cm.
Mormon poetry.
USIC

1035. Busch, Moritz. Geschichte der Mormonen, nebst einer Darstellung ihres glaubens und ihrer gegenwärtigen socialen und politischen Verhältnisse, von dr. Mortiz Busch. Leipzig, Verlag von Ambrosius Abel [1869]
viii, 444 [4]p. 21cm.
"Vorwart" Signed: 1869.
Title in English: History of Mormonism.
Sabin 1859 9519[a]
CSmH, CtY, CU–B, DLC, ICN, IU, MB, MH, NjPT, NN, UHi, UU, WHi

1036. ———. De Mormonen. Een overzigt van het onstaan, de inrigting en geloofsleer dezer sekte Door Dr. Moritz Busch. Uit het Hoogduitsch. Amsterdam, H. W. Mooij, 1856.
viii, 185p. 24cm.
Title in English: The Mormons.
Sabin 1855 9519
CSmH, MH, NN, UHi, USIC, WHi

1037. ———. Die Mormonen, Ihr Prophet, ihr Staat und ihr Glaube. Leipzig, Verlag von Carl B. Lorck, 1855.
2p.l., 158p. 17cm. (Conversations und Reisebibliothek)
Title in English: The Mormons, their prophet, their state, and their religion.
Sabin C9518
CSmH, CtY, CU–B, DLC, ICN, MH, MiU, NjP, NN, UHi, USIC

1038. ———. (same) 2d issue. Leipzig, Verlag von Carl B. Lorck, 1855.
2p.l., 158p. 17cm. (Lorcks' Eisenbahnbucher)
UPB

1039. ———. (same, in Danish) Mormonerne. Deres prophet, deres stat og deres religion, oversat fra det tydske. Odense, Forlagt af den Miloske Boghandel. [n.p.] Trykt i Joh. Milos, 1857.
138p. 21cm.
USIC

1040. ———. Mormonernes fleerkoneri. Et bidrag til Mormonernes saedelaere, efter "Die Mormonen." Kobenhavn, 1855.
32p.
Title in English: Mormon Polygamy.
Schmidt

1041. ———. Wanderungen zwischen Hudson und Mississippi, 1851 und 1852, von Moritz Busch . . . Stuttgart und Tubíngen, J. G. Cotta, 1854.
2v. in 1. 22½cm.
First section of V. 2 on the development of the church.
Title in English: Journeys between the Hudson and the Mississippi.
Howes B1138, Sabin 9520
CtY, DLC, ICHi, MB, NjP, NN, UHi

1042. Buschlen, George. Is baptism in water essential to salvation. [n.p., n.d.]
36p. 15cm.
An RLDS doctrinal tract.
MoInRC

1043. ———. Where is the Church of Jesus Christ? [n.p., n.d.]
38p. 15cm.
The RLDS Church the one true Church.
MoInRC

1044. Buschlen, John Preston. Peter Bosten. Lamoni, Ia., Herald Publishing House, 1915.
4p.l., 9–352p. 19½cm.
A story about realities. RLDS fiction.
MoInRC, UU

1045. Bush, B. N. From within one heart. [7th ed.] New York, Literature Department of the Women's Board of Home Missions of the Presbyterian Church [1905]
11p. 14cm. (No. 177)
Missionary work in Utah and success against Mormonism.
USIC

BY THE WAY

1046. Bush, C. S. Plain facts shewing [sic] The falsehood and folly of the Mormonites, or Latter-day Saints; being an exposition of the imposture, and a proof of the wickedness and impiety of following or hearing them; because they have not God's word as the only standard of their faith, but mix it up with a foolish and inconsistent romance, written by Solomon Spaulding of the United States of America. Macclesfield, Printed by J. Swinnerton . . . 1840.
15p. 17cm.
USlC

1047. Bushnell, Horace. Barbarism the first danger. A discourse for home missions. By Horace Bushnell . . . New York, Printed for the American Home Missionary Society, 1847.
32p. 22½cm.
Effects of Mormon and Romanish migrations to the West, p. 23–25.
DLC

1048. The Business Journal. Provo, October 26, 1891 — April 29, 1892.
lv. (#1–10) monthly. 27cm.
Published by the students of Brigham Young University.
UPB

1049. Buss, Henry. Eighty years' experience of life. By H. Buss. London, Thomas Danks & Sons [1893?]
2p.l., 379p. 22cm.
Visit to Salt Lake City in 1870; favorably impressed with Mormons except for polygamy.
USlC

1050. Butler, John M. The late Corporation of the Church of Jesus Christ of Latter-day Saints, et al., Appellants vs. The United States. No. 1423. Brief of Joseph E. McDonald and John M. Butler in Behalf of Appellants. By James M. Butler. Indianapolis, Frank H. Smith, 1888.
109p. 22cm.
Cover-title.
At head of title: Supreme Court of the United States, October Term, 1888.
USlC

1051. Butterworth, Hezekiah. Zigzag journeys in the Occident; the Atlantic to the Pacific, a summer trip of the zigzag club from Boston to the Golden Gate . . . Boston, Estes and Lauriat, 1883.
viii [9]–320p. illus., map on inside covers. 21cm.
Chapter VII entitled "The Story of Mormonism."
Another edition: 1885. USlC
CU–B, UHi, UPB

1052. By the way. Sidelights on points of interest which President Harding's party will see on the trip to Zion National Park. [Salt Lake City, Deseret News Press, 192?]
14p. 24cm.
Mormon settlement of Southern Utah.
UHi

DELUSIONS.

AN ANALYSIS

OF THE

BOOK OF MORMON;

WITH AN

EXAMINATION OF ITS INTERNAL AND EXTERNAL EVIDENCES, AND A REFUTATION OF ITS PRETENCES TO DIVINE AUTHORITY.

BY ALEXANDER CAMPBELL.

WITH

PREFATORY REMARKS,

BY JOSHUA V. HIMES.

BOSTON:
BENJAMIN H. GREENE.
1832.

Item 1107. The first anti-Mormon book, reprinting Alexander Campbell's article first published in the *Millennial Harbinger*. From the Brigham Young University collection.

CABALLERIA Y COLLEL, J.

1053. Caballeria y Collel, Juan. History of San Bernardino Valley from the padres to the pioneers, 1810–1851. By Reverend Father Juan Caballeria; illustrated by Constance Farris. [San Bernardino, California, Times-index Press, 1902]
4p.l., 17–130p. illus., port. 20½cm.
Relates the Mormon contribution to the colonization of San Bernardino.
Howes C–1
CU–B, DLC, UHi, UPB, USlC

1054. Caccia, Antonio. Europa ed America; scene della vita dal 1848 al 1850, del Dr. Antonio Caccia. Monaco, Presso Georgio Franz, 1850.
2p.l., 500p. 17½cm.
Brief history of Mormonism and its dispersion after the death of Joseph Smith; the Mormon trek.
Title in English: Europe and America.
Sabin 9820
CtY, CU–B, DLC

1055. Cadman, Sadie B. Scriptural lessons. Composed by Sadie B. Cadman. Published by the Ladies' Uplift Circle, A.D. 1927. Uniontown, Pa., Herald-Genius, 1927.
56p. 19½cm.
Bickertonite publication.
Morgan
PMonC, UHi

1056. Cadman, William. Daniel's Little Horn, by Wm. Cadman. West Elizabeth, Pa., U.S.A. [Pittsburgh, Pa.? 1894]
16p. 25cm.
Cover-title.
A doctrinal treatise by a member of the Church of Jesus Christ (Bickerton)
Morgan
DLC, MoInRC, NN, PMonC, UHi, USlC

1057. ———. Faith and doctrines of the Church of Jesus Christ, published by order of the church in 1897. Committee: Wm. Cadman, J. L. Armbrust, W. D. Wright, West Elizabeth, Pa. [Pittsburgh, Pa.? 1897]
24p. 23½cm.
Morgan
MoInRC, PMonC, UHi, UPB, USlC

1058. ———. Faith and doctrines of the Church of Jesus Christ. Series No. 2. Published by order of the church in 1902. By Wm. Cadman, West Elizabeth, Pa. Roscoe, Pa., Roscoe Ledger Print [1902]
20p. 23cm.
Cover-title.
Morgan
MoInRC, PMonC, UHi, USlC

1059. ———. Religious experiences and expectations, by Wm. Cadman, West Elizabeth, Pa. U.S.A. Pittsburgh, Devin & Co., Printers, 1899.
23p. 19½cm.
Morgan
MoInRC, NN, PMonC, UHi, UPB, USlC

1060. Cadman, William H. Retrogression of the primitive church. Published by The Ladies' Uplift Circle of the Church of Jesus Christ. [Signed] Wm. H. Cadman, Jr., President of the Church . . . [n.p., 1923]
7p. 20½cm.
Morgan
PMonC, UHi, USlC

1061. ———. The way of salvation, by W. H. Cadman, Charles Ashton, Committee. Published by the Ladies' Uplift Circle of the Church of Jesus Christ. Monongahela, Printed by Zimmer Printing, 1920.
7p . 20½cm.
Morgan
PMonC, UHi

1062. ———. (same) Monongahela, Printed by Harry Lorber, 1930.
7p. 15½cm.
Second series.
Morgan
PMonC, UHi

1063. ———. (same, in Italian) La Via della "Salvazione," Publicata del Circolo Sollevare delle Donne della Chiesa di Gesu Cristo. [Monongahela, Printed by Zimmer Printing, 1921]
8p. 20cm.
Morgan
PMonC, UHi

1064. ———. What is the Indian mission? By W. H. Cadman. [n.p.] 1924.
4p. 22cm.
Signed: January 5th, 1924.
Morgan
PMonC, UHi

1065. Caffall, James. Apostasy or perpetuity, which? By Elder James Caffall. Lamoni, Ia., Herald Publishing House [189–?]
20p. 22cm. (Tract No. 28)
NN

1066. ———. Does Christ's Church exist to-day. [Chesterfield and Clay Cross, Bales & Wilde, Printers, n.d.]
[4]p. 17cm.
At head of title: No. 2 . "Come let us reason."
RLDS pamphlet.
USlC

1067. Cain, Joseph. Mormon way-bill, to the gold mines, from the Pacific Springs by the northern and southern routes, viz: — Fort Hall, Salt Lake and Los Angelos [sic] including Sublets, Hudspeths and the various cutoffs; — Also from Los Angeles to San Francisco by the coast route, with distances to the different rivers in Cal. Together with important

information to emigrants. By Joseph Cain and Arieh C. Brower. G. S. L. City, Deseret, W. Richards, Printer, 1851.
40p., [1]l. 14½cm.
Both the CU–B copy and the USlC copy have 32 pages, which omits the section on "Oregon Route, from Pacific Springs to Oregon City" which seem to indicate that this is an earlier printing of the guide book. This is substantiated by the lack of the Oregon portion of the guide book mentioned on the title page.
Howes C–18, W–C 196
CtY, CU–B, ICN, USlC

1068. Caine, Frederick Augustus. Mormon Kei to wa nanzo ya? Tokyō, Nihon, Matsu Jitsu Seito Iesu Kirisuto Kyōkai Nihon Dendobu [1909]
93p. 19cm.
Title in English: What is the Book of Mormon?
USlC

1069. Caine, John T. Admission of Idaho. Disfranchisement of Mormons. Argument of Hon. John T. Caine . . . April 23, 1890. Washington, 1890.
14p. 22cm.
Includes a proclamation of Dec. 12, 1889 by the L.D.S. church authorities.
USlC

1070. ———. Admission of Idaho. Disfranchisement of Mormons because of their Church membership. Speech of Hon. John T. Caine of Utah, in the House of Representatives, Thursday, April 3, 1890, on the bill (H. R. 4562) to provide for the admission of the state of Idaho into the Union. Washigton, 1890.
15p. 21cm.
UPB, USlC

1071. ———. Admission of Utah. Argument of Hon. John T. Caine of Utah, in favor of the admission of Utah as a state, made before the House Committee on Territories. Second Session, Fiftieth Congress, January 16–17, 1889. Washington, Govt. Print. Off., 1889.
29p. 22cm.
UPB, USlC

1072. ———. A bill for the local government of Utah Territory, and to provide for the election of certain officers in said Territory. Washington, 1892.
16p. 32cm. (H. R. 524)
Eberstadt. *Utah and the Mormons*

1073. ———. A bill for the local government of the Territory of Utah, and to provide for the election of certain officers in said Territory. Washington, 1892.
16p. 32cm. (H. R. 7590)
Eberstadt. *Utah and the Mormons*

1074. ———. A bill to enable the people of Utah to form a constitution and State government, and to be admitted into the Union on an equal footing with the original States. Washington, 1892.
15p. 32cm. (H. R. 9689)
Eberstadt. *Utah and the Mormons*

1075. ———. Deligate [sic] Caine's letter of acceptance. Salt Lake City, 1890.
4p. 23cm.
Acceptance of the nomination as candidate of the People's Party.
Signed: October 18th, 1890.
USlC

1076. ———. The legislative commission scheme. Address of Hon. John T. Caine, delivered at the people's mass meeting, held in the theatre, Salt Lake City, Utah, Monday, November 3d, 1884 . . . Salt Lake City, Herald Printing & Publishing Co., 1884.
12p. 22½cm.
CSmH, UHi, USlC, UU

1077. ———. Mormon facts vs. anti-Mormon fictions . . . Speech of Hon. John T. Caine, of Utah, in the House of Representatives, Thursday, October 4, 1888, on aid to Industrial Christian Home of Utah. Washington, 1888.
30p. 22½cm.
USlC

1078. ———. The Mormon problem. Speech of Hon. John T. Caine, of Utah, in the House of Representatives, Wednesday, January 12, 1887, in opposition to the so-called Edmunds-Tucker anti-polygamy bill . . . Washington [Govt. Print. Off.] 1887.
31p. 23cm.
CSmH, CtY, CU–B, DLC, ICN, NN, UHi, ULA, UPB, USlC, UU

1079. ———. Polygamy in Utah — a dead issue. Speech of Hon. J. T. Caine of Utah in the House of Representatives, August 25, 1888. Washington, 1888.
16p. 22½cm.
Cover-title.
CU–B, DLC, ICN, MH, UHi, USl, USlC, UU

1080. ———. Report. To the Latter-day Saints in the several stakes of Zion, Greeting . . . [Washington? 1885]
3p. 21½cm.
Caption-title.
Signed at end: John T. Caine, John W. Taylor, John Q. Cannon.
State of polygamy legislation, etc.
UHi

1081. Cake, Lu B. Peepstone Joe and the Peck manuscript, by Lu B. Cake . . . New York City, Published and sold by L. B. Cake [1899]
144p. illus. 17½cm.
Cover-title: Old Mormon manuscript found. Peepstone Joe exposed.
"Reminiscences of the Mormons in Missouri," by Reed Peck.
CtY, CU–B, DLC, ICN, MoInRC, NN, UHi, UPB, USl, USlC, WHi

CALDWELL, E. L. N.

1082. Caldwell, Estelle Love Neff. Andrew Love, 1808–1890, Utah pioneer of 1847. [Vernal, Utah, Vernal Express Printing, n.d.]
18p. ports. 19½cm.
CU–B, UPB

1083. Calhoun, Arthur Wallace. A social history of the American family from colonial times to the present, by Arthur W. Calhoun . . . Cleveland, The Arthur H. Clark Company, 1917–19.
3v. 24½cm.
A section on Mormonism and polygamy.
Howes C–27
DLC, NjP, NN, UHi, ULA, USl, ViU

Califf, John A. *See Roberts, B. H.*

1084. California gold regions, with a full account of their mineral resources; how to get there, and what to take; with expenses, the time, and the various routes. With sketches of California; an account of the life, manners, and customs of the inhabitants, its history, climate, soil, productions, &c. A cheap edition for the people . . . New York, F. M. Pratt, Publisher, W. H. Graham, Agent for supplying the trade [1849?]
48p. 23cm.
Incorporates Col. Mason's letter of August 17, 1848, with its references to the Mormons, p. 6, 8, 11–12; and refers on p. 4 to Sam Brannan, "well known in N.Y."
CtY, CU–B, DLC, WHi

1085. California; its past history; its present position; its future prospects: containing a history of the country from its colonization by the Spaniards to the present time; a sketch of its geographical and physical features and a minute and authentic account of the discovery of the gold region, and the subsequent important proceedings. Including a history of the rise, progress, and present condition of the Mormon settlements. With an appendix, containing the official reports made to the government of the United States. London, The proprietors . . . 1850.
viii, 270p. plates, map. 23cm.
Added t.–p. illus. in color.
Written when Utah was considered part of California.
Attributed by Howe to G. A. Fleming.
Other editions: Without date on title page. CU–B
Howes F178, Sabin 9973
CSmH, CtY, CU–B, DLC, ICN, MH, NjP, NN, USl, USlC, WHi

1086. California. Legislature. Assembly. Journal of the proceedings of the House of Assembly of the State of California; at its first session begun and held at Puebla de San José, on the fifteenth day of December, 1949. San José, J. Winchester, State Printer, 1850.
[571]–1347p. 23cm.
Includes letter from John Wilson and Amasa Lyman, San Francisco, January 8, 1850, proposing a united effort toward statehood by those living in California east and west of the Sierra Nevada. Message, and letter from the Deseret delegates, incorporated in the proceedings. Proposal rejected by the assembly, p. 756–772.
CU–B

1087. California. Legislature. Senate. Journal of the Senate of the State of California; at their first session begun and held at Puebla de San José, on the fifteenth day of December, 1849. San Jose, J. Winchester, State Printer, 1850.
1333p. 23cm.
Proceedings in the Senate, February 2, 1850, when Governor Peter H. Burnett's message concerning the Deseret memorial, the letter to Burnett by the Deseret agents, John Wilson and Amasa Lyman, San Francisco, January 8, 1850, and a copy of the Constitution of Deseret were received and tabled, the documents being published as appendices J., K., and L., p. 129, 429–451.
CU–B

1088. California Star. Yerba Buena [San Francisco] California, Samuel Brannan, Publisher, January 1847–December 23, 1848.
2v. weekly. 35×48cm.
First editor, E. P. Jones.
Superseded by *The California Star* and *Californian* after the publication of an unnumbered broadside for June 14.
Printed on the press formerly used by the *New York* Messenger. Early issues have Mormon news notes.
CSmH 1947–June 1848, exc. v.2, 9, 10; CU–B 1847–June 1848; DLC 1847–Dec. 1848; ULA Jan. 30, 1847–May 22, 1847, June 26, 1847, Nov. 20, 1847–Dec. 18, 1847; USlC V.1 #3–9, 12–14, V.2 #1–17, 19, 21–22.

1089. California Star. California Star extra. To the Saints in England and America. Yerba Buena, January 1, 1847.
Broadside.
Concerning emigration. This extra is known only through a reprint in the *Millennial Star* of October 15, 1847.

The Californian Crusoe. *See Richards, Robert.*

1090. Call, Lamoni. The anti-Mormon. Points out fallacies in the arguments used by the Mormon Church. Quotes especially what the church considers authentic publications. Designed for the use of those who may need to contend with Mormon missionaries. By Lamoni Call. Bountiful, Utah, 1899.
1v. #1–3 [80]p. 21cm.
V.1 #1.
V.1 #2: [5]–44 and #3: 45–80.
NN V.1 #2; ULA V.1 #2; USlC V.1 #1–3

1091. ———. A few pages of "Mormon inspiration." Salt Lake City [192–?]
[8]l. 12cm.
Caption-title.
NN, UPB

1092. ———. The gospel in a nut shell. Containing scriptural quotations, with a few suggestive words to start the beginner on the thread of argument. Comp. and Printed by Lamoni Call. Bountiful, Utah [1895?]
108p. 9½cm.
Published while still a member of the church.
MH, OClWHi, USlC, WHi

1093. ———. (same) Bountiful, Utah, Lamoni Call, 1897.
108p. 10½cm.
Second edition.
USlC

1094. ———. Mormon Inspiration. Salt Lake City, The author, 1928.
96p. 13cm. (Vest pocket Mormonism . . . Evidence not slander — Vol. 2)
CU-B, IWW, MH, MoInRC, NjP, NN, UPB, USl, USlC

1095. ———. Science and Mormonism. Salt Lake City, The author, 1926.
80 [2]p. (Vest pocket Mormonism. V. 1)
V. 1 of "Evidence, not slander."
CU-B, IWW, MH, MoInRC, NjP, NN, UPB, USl, USlC

1096. ———. Sunday School manual. Published at the suggestion of the six missionaries from Davis Stake . . . Contains the methods of teaching and the principal diagrams given their missionaries . . . Bountiful, Utah [n.d.]
1p.l., 30p. 16½cm.
How to teach Sunday School for stake missionaries.
USlC

1097. ———. 2000 changes in the Book of Mormon, containing the way the book is claimed to have been translated, the amendments which have been made in the book, what an inspired translation should have been, and the reasons given by the church for making the many grammatical changes. Showing that the claims are inconsistent and untrue. . . . Bountiful, Utah, The author, 1898.
4p.l., 17–128p. 16cm.
Sabin 83114
CU-B, ICN, IWW, MH, MoInRC, NjP, NN, OO, UPB, USl, USlC, UU, WHi

———. Vest pocket Mormonism; *See his Mormon inspiration; Science and Mormonism.*

1098. Call, Wilkinson. On the amendment to the bill to suppress polygamy in Utah. Speech of Hon. Wilkinson Call, of Florida, in the Senate of the United States, February 18, 1887. Washington, 1887.
13p. 22cm.
Cover-title.
A speech in opposition to the bill.
UHi

1099. Callahan, D. A. A catalogue of new and second hand books . . . chiefly books on Mormonism . . . Salt Lake City [189–?]
30p. 20cm.
Some description of the books but chiefly a list of those offered for sale.
NN, USl

1100. ———. A catalogue of new and second hand books . . . chiefly books on Mormonism. [Salt Lake City] 1899.
32p. 21cm.
NN

1101. ———. Catalogue of new old rare books including a fine collection of rare books on Mormonism and a miscellaneous lot of scarce literary odds and ends . . . Salt Lake City [1902?]
[32]p. 21cm.
Date of most recent book in stock: 1902.
UPB

1102. Callis, Charles A. Fast day and fast offerings. [Independence, Press of Zion's Printing and Publishing Company, n.d.]
4p. 15cm.
USlC

1103. ———. The Lord's Day by Elder Charles A. Callis. [Independence, Press of Zion's Printing and Publishing Co., n.d.]
7p. 16cm.
NN

1104. ———. Old-time Southern States missionary songs, composed by missionaries. Also popular Southern songs. Compiled by Elder Chas. A. Callis. [Atlanta, Georgia, 1921]
32p. 16cm.
Cover-title.
UHi

1105. ———. Take heed, by Elder Charles A. Callis. [Independence, Mo., Zion's Printing and Publishing Company, 193–?]
7 [1]p. 15½cm.
Caption-title.
UHi, UPB

1106. The Cambridge History of American Literature. Edited by William Peterfield Trent [and others] New York, G. P. Putnam's Sons; Cambridge, England, University Press, 1917–1921.
4v. 25cm.
"The Book of Mormon," V. 3, p. 517–522, in a section on "Popular Bibles . . ."
NjP, ULA, UPB, USlC

1107. Campbell, Alexander. Delusions. An analysis of the Book of Mormon; with an examination of its internal and external evidences and a refutation

of its pretences to divine authority. By Alexander Campbell. With prefatory remarks by Joshua V. Himes. Boston, Benjamin H. Greene, 1832.
16p. 22½cm.
CU–B, CtY, DLC, ICN, MA, MH, MoK, NN, PU, USl, USlC, UU, WHi

1108. ———. (same) Boston, B. H. Greene, 1832. [Repr. Salt Lake City, Morgan-Bruce book Co., 1925]
16p. 21cm.
CU–B, MH, MnU, NjPT, UHi, USlC, UPB

1109. ———. (same, under title) Alexander Campbell on the Book of Mormon . . . Omaha, Neb., Reprinted by W. T. Hilton [n.d.]
32p. 13½cm.
Cover-title.
Original dated: February 10, 1831.
MoInRC

1110. ———. (same, under title) Mormonism weighed in the balances and found wanting: being an analysis of the internal and external evidences of the Book of Mormon, by Alexander Campbell, President of Bethany College, U.S. . . . London, Arthur Hall, Virtue, & Co., . . . Edinburgh, A. Muirhead . . . [Nottingham, H. Hudston, Printer, 1850?]
23 [1]p. 18cm.
Howes C–87
USlC

1111. ———. (same) [Nottingham, H. Hudston, Printer, 1850]
23 [1]p. 17cm.
At head of title: "Second edition." This copy was sold in the Auerbach sale, 1947; the last page bore an 1850 post office stamp.

———. Memoirs of Alexander Campbell. *See Richardson, Robert.*

———. What is Mormonism? *See Richardson, Robert.*

1112. Campbell, Allen G. Polygamy and the Mormon question. Letter . . . to President Garfield. [Washington, 1881]
6p. 23cm.
A work on polygamy.
DLC

1113. ———. The Utah contest for delegate to Congress. George Q. Cannon, Contestant, vs. Allen G. Campbell, Contestee. The case stated in behalf of Mr. Campbell, including the evidence taken by the parties, and other facts bearing on the case. Salt Lake City, Tribune Printing and Publishing Company, 1881.
27, lviii p. 23½cm.
Cover-title.
ICN, NN

1114. ———. The Utah contest. Which of the claimants is entitled to be sworn as delegate? Respectfully submitted to the 47th Congress of the United States. [Washington] National Republican Print. [1880?]
9p. 23cm.
NN

———. *See also The delegate from Utah.*

1115. Campbell, Isabella W. Our Master's will. With love for the gospel of Jesus Christ, and in honor of the pioneers. Salt Lake City, 1915.
[2]p. 19½cm.
Poem in honor of the Mormon pioneers.
UPB

1116. Campbell, John Francis. My circular notes. Extracts from journals, letters sent home, geological and other notes, written while travelling westwards round the World from July 6, 1874, to July 6, 1875. By J. F. Campbell. London, MacMillan and Co., 1876.
2v. illus., plates. 20½cm.
"Salt Water and seedy Saints." Letter of August 24th, 1874. V.1, p. 48–50.
USlC

1117. Campbell, J. L. Idaho: Six months in the new gold diggings; the emigrants guide overland. Itinerary of the routes, features of the country, journal of residence, etc., etc. By J. L. Campbell. New York, J. L. Campbell, 1864.
52p. illus., map. 21½cm.
Cover has imprint: Chicago, J. R. Walsh 1864.
Encounters followers of Joseph Morris.
Another edition: Chicago, J. R. Walsh, 1864.
Cover has imprint: New York S. Tousey, 1864. DLC
CtY, DLC, UPB

Campbell, James, [*pseud.*] *See Jencks, E. N.*

1118. Campbell, Marius Robinson. . . . Guidebook of the western United States. Part E. The Denver & Rio Grande Western route, by Marius R. Campbell. Washington, Govt. Print. Off., 1922.
xi, 266p. illus., xcvi plates, 10 fold. maps, tables, diagrs. 23cm. (U.S. Geological survey. Bulletin 707)
Continuation of U.S. Geological survey. Bulletins 611–614.
Detailed geological information on Utah with some historical information.
CSmH, CU, DLC, ICj, PP, PPM, OO, UHi, ULA, UPB, UU

1119. Campbell, Robert. Church of Christ (Temple Lot) — Danger. [n.p., ca. 192–]
[4]p. 33cm.
Necessity of adhering to Church of Christ doctrines and not allowing them to be dropped.
USlC

1120. ———. Light — in the darkness. John the Baptist has come as he did in the days of Christ to prepare for the coming of Christ. Warn the nations of destruction. Preach repentance and baptism. Re-establish the church. [n.p., 192–?]
19p. double cols. 23cm.
Signed: Robert Campbell, p. 2.
MoInRC, UPB

1121. ———. (same) [Independence, Mo., n.d.]
12p. 11cm.
MoInRC, USlC

1122. ———. Notice. Mr. Robert Campbell, a Latter-day Saint Missionary, From Eastern Upper California, North America, will deliver a course of lectures on the fulness of the gospel of Jesus Christ . . . in the Loudoun Hall, Boat Vennel, . . . Ayr, 25th Nov., 1850. Ayr, Printed by Thomas M. Gemmell, at the Ayr Advertiser Office [1850]
Broadside. 28×22cm.
USlC

1123. Campbell, Robert Allen. Campbell's gazetteer of Missouri, from articles contributed by prominent gentlemen in each country of the state, and information collected and collated from official and other authentic sources, by a corps of experienced canvassers, under the personal supervision of the editor, R. A. Campbell, . . . Illustrated with maps and engravings. St. Louis, R. A. Campbell, Publisher, 1874.
2p.l. [7]–807p. illus., plates, maps (mostly double) 25½cm.
Mormons in Missouri, p. 151–2, 266–7.
Another edition: 1875. CU
UPB, USlC

1124. Campbell, William R. How a daughter of Brigham Young teaches polygamy, and defends her polygymous people. [New York City, The Willet Press, The Interdenominational Council for Christian and Patriotic Service, 1902?]
IIp. 14cm.
Reprinted interviews with Mrs. Susa Young Gates, defending the Mormons; interspersed with anti-Mormon propaganda.
NN

1125. ———. Methods of Mormon missionaries, by Wm. R. Campbell. New York, League for Social Service, 1899.
14p. 15cm. (Social Service. Series D. Anti-Mormon)
WHi

1126. ———. Methods of Mormon missionaries by Rev. William R. Campbell. New York City, League for Social Service [1899]
14 [2]p. 15cm. (Social service. Series D. Anti-Mormon)
MiU, MoInRC, NjPT, NN, UPB, USl, USlC

1127. ———. Mormon promises repudiated. Shown by documentary evidence. Signed statement of Mr. Roberts. Elected to make a test case to ascertain whether Congress will hold the Mormon people to their pledges. [Salt Lake City, 1899]
[8]p. 27cm. (Circular No. 4)
Mormons and politics.
USlC

1128. ———. Questions and answers on Mormonism. New York, Published by the Women's Board of Home Missions of the Presbyterian Church in the U.S.A. [n.d.]
[16]p. 15cm. (No. 390)
USlC

1129. ———. (same) 3d ed. New York, Published by the Women's Board of Home Missions of the Presbyterian Church in the U.S.A. [1903]
15 [1]p. 15cm. (No. 204)
NN, USlC

1130. Canadian Messenger. Stratford, Ontario, January, 1903–December? 1908.
v. monthly. 28cm.
Canadian Mission of RLDS Church.
Succeeded by *The Canadian Mirror.*
MoInRC inc.

1131. The Canadian Mirror. London, Ontario, Canadian Mission of the Reorganized Church of Jesus Christ of Latter Day Saints, April 1909–August, 1911.
v. monthly. 28cm.
Succeeded the *Canadian Messenger.* In 1911 merged with the *Saint's Herald.*
MoInRC inc.

1132. Candland, David. The fireside visitor; or, plain reasoner. [Liverpool, Printed for the author by R. James, 1846]
3 nos. (4 [5]–8 [9]–16p.) 20½cm.
Signed: David C. Kimball [i.e. David Candland]
No. 1. On the necessity of baptism as a means of salvation.
No. 2. On the departure from the true order of the kingdom foretold.
No. 3. The restoration of the kingdom.
CtY, MH, #1, 2; UPB, USl #1, 3; USlC #1, 2; WHi

1133. Canney, Maurice A. An encyclopedia of religions. London, G. Routledge & Sons, Ltd., 1921.
ix, 397p. 25½cm.
Entries under Book of Mormon; Mormons.
CU, DLC, USlC

1134. Canning, Josiah Dean. Poems, by Josiah D. Canning. Greenfield [Mass.] Phelps & Ingersoll, Printers, 1838.
VIII [9]–205p. 15cm.
Poem: "The review," deals with Joseph Smith, p. 107.
DLC, NjP, USlC

CANNON, A. H.

1135. **Cannon, Abraham Hoagland.** A hand-book of reference to the history, chronology, religion and country of the Latter-day Saints, including the revelation on celestial marriage, for the use of saints and strangers. Salt Lake City, Juvenile Instructor Office, 1884.
1p.l., 157 [1]p. 19cm.
CSmH, CtY, DLC, ICN, MH, NjP, NN, OO, UHi, UU, ViU

1136. ———. Questions and answers on the Book of Mormon. Designed and prepared especially for the use of the Sunday schools in Zion, by A. H. Cannon. Salt Lake City, Juvenile Instructor Office, 1886.
vii [9]–62p. 19cm.
DLC, MH, NN, NjP, UHi, ULA, UPB, USl, USlC, UU

1137. ———. (same, in Samoan) A fesili ma tali i le tusi a Mamona. Na tusia e A. H. Cannon, I le Tausaga e 1886, Mo Ekalesia a Iesu Keriso o le Au Paia o Aso e Gata ai. Ua Faa-Samoaina e misi alapeti (Elder G. A. Goates), Tutuila, Samoa, Iulai, aso e 25, 1904. Ua Faasa'oina ma Faalomia e Misi Matina (Elder Martin F. Sanders) Provo, Na lomia e siliva ma falani i le Fale lomi tusi o siliva. 1905.
72p. 19½cm.
USlC

1138. **Cannon, Angus Jenne.** A latter-day prophet, by Angus J. Cannon. [Independence, Mo., Zion's Printing and Publishing Co., 19–?]
15 [1]p. illus., port. 18½cm.
CSmH, MH, NN, UPB, USlC

1139. **Cannon, Angus Munn,** *defendant.* The Edmunds law. "Unlawful cohabitation," as defined by Chief Justice Chas. S. Zane, of the Territory of Utah, in the trial of Angus M. Cannon, esq., in the Third District Court, Salt Lake City, April 27, 28, 29, 1885. Full report of the arguments as to the term "cohabitation" in the above law. Reported by John Irvine. Salt Lake City, Juvenile Instructor Office, 1885.
iv [5]–118p. 17½cm.
"Appendix. The Musser case," p. 107–118.
CSmH, CU–B, DLC, MH, MH–L, NN, UHi, USl, USlC

Cannon, Elizabeth Rachel. *See Porter, Elizabeth Rachel (Cannon)*

1140. **Cannon, Frank Jenne.** Brigham Young and his Mormon empire [by] Frank J. Cannon and George L. Knapp . . . New York, Chicago [etc.] Fleming H. Revell Company [c1913]
398p. plates, ports. 21cm.
Written after his excommunication from the church.
CSmH, CUB, DLC, ICN, MoInRC, NjP, NN, UHi, ULA, UPB, USl, USlC, UU

———. Directory of Ogden City. *See Haefeli, Leo.*

1141. ———. Excommunication of Frank J. Cannon from the Mormon Church. [Salt Lake City, 1905]
11p. 22½cm.
Cover-title.
Caption-title: . . . fell under the juggernaut! Free speech in Utah! Hierarchy on the throne!
Reprinted from *Salt Lake Tribune,* March 7, 1905.
ICN, MoInRC, UHi, ULA, USl, USlC

1142. ———. (same, under title) Fell under the Juggernaut! Free Speech in Utah! Hierarchy on the Throne! [Salt Lake City, 1905]
8p. 23cm.
Salt Lake Tribune, March 7, 1905.
Includes the proceedings of the Bishops court against Frank J. Cannon, some of his correspondence, and other material.
USlC

1143. ———. Ex-Senator Frank J. Cannon's opinion of the Mormon Prophet Joseph F. Smith. [Independence, Mo.?] Missions of the Church of Jesus Christ of Latter-day Saints [1902?]
[4]p. 15½cm.
Shows his high opinion of President Smith even after being excommunicated from the church.
USlC

———. The other house. *See Anderson, Martha.*

1144. ———. Under the prophet in Utah; the national menace of a political priestcraft, by Frank J. Cannon . . . and Harvey J. O'Higgins . . . Boston, Mass., The C. M. Clark Publishing Co., 1911.
402p. port. 19½cm.
First published in *Everybody's Magazine.*
CSmH, CtY, CU–B, DLC, ICN, NjP, NN, UHi, ULA, UPB, USl, USlC, UU

1145. ———. Under the prophet in Utah. The treasons and crimes of the Mormon kingdom. Boston, The C. M. Clark Publishing Co. [1911]
[4]p. 28cm.
A publicity release for his book of the same title.
USlC

1146. **Cannon, George Quayle.** An address to the members of the Church of Jesus Christ of Latter-day Saints. [Salt Lake City, 1882]
6p. 20cm.
Caption-title.
Signed: August 29th, 1882.
USlC

1147. ———. Argument of Hon. George Q. Cannon, delegate from Utah, before the Committee on Territories of the House of Representatives, March 21, 1876, in favor of H. B. 178, a bill to enable the people of Utah to form a constitution and state government and for the admission of the said state

into the Union on an equal footing with the original states. Philadelphia, J. B. Lippincott & Co. [1876]
20p. 21½cm.
At head of title: [House Bill No. 178]
DLC, NN, USlC

1148. ———. Before Territorial canvassers, Utah Territory, Allen G. Campbell vs. George Q. Cannon. Reply of George Q. Cannon to protest filed by Allen G. Campbell. Washington, Thomas McGill & Co., Printers [1881]
18p. 21cm.
Signed: Dec. 20, 1880.
DLC, NjP, USlC

1149. ———. Deacons' book of questions for instructors only, Third year. The Latter-day prophet. Prepared and issued under the direction of the General Authorities of the Church. Salt Lake City, 1912.
48p. 23cm.
USlC

———. The Delegate from Utah. *See The Delegate from Utah.*

1150. ———. Dedicatory prayer at the dedication of the Brigham City Tabernacle. Offered by President George Q. Cannon. [n.p., 1914?]
8p. 18cm.
Stenographic report by Henry Sieger.
MH

1151. ———. Exhibit of extracts from newspapers relating to proclamation of President Woodruff and conference of Mormon Church, transmitted to Secretary by Governor Thomas . . . Remarks by President George Q. Cannon. [n.p., 1890]
151–154p. 22½cm. (U.S. 51st Cong. 2d Sess. House. Ex. Doc. No. 1, pt. 5)
In Department of Interior. Messages and Documents. 1890. Appendix D.
DLC, ULA, UPB

1152. ———. He olelo hoolaha. I no Hoahanau o ka Ekalesia o Iesu Kristo o ka poe Hoano o na La Hope nei, ma ko Hawaii pae aina; a i na kanaka a pau ia aloha i ka oiaio. [San Francisco, 1855?]
8p. 23cm.
Signed: San Francisco, Deke. 27, 1855.
Printed on the press of the *Western Standard.*
Title in English: A word of instruction to all Hawaiians who love the truth.
UPB

1153. ———. The history of the Mormons, their persecutions and travels. By President George Q. Cannon. Also a manifesto of the Presidency of the Church of Jesus Christ of Latter-day Saints and members of the Council of the Apostles. Salt Lake City, Juvneile Instructor Office, 1890.
19 [1]p. 20cm.
Cover-title.
CSmH, MH, NjP, NN, UHi, ULA, UPB, USlC

1154. ———. (same) [n.p., n.d.]
19 [1]p. 20cm.
Variant edition.
MH, MoInRC, USlC

1155. ———. (same) Salt Lake City, George Q. Cannon & Sons Co., 1891.
19 [1]p. 24½cm.
Cover-title.
CtY, DLC, ICN, MH, MoInRC, UHi, UPB, USlC

1156. ———. The latter day prophet. History of Joseph Smith written for young people by George Q. Cannon. Illustrated. Salt Lake City, Juvenile Instructor Office, 1900.
viii [9]–216p. illus., ports., maps. 17½cm.
MH, MoInRC, NjP, UHi, ULA, UPB, USlC, UU

1157. ———. The latter-day prophet. Young people's history of Joseph Smith. Salt Lake City, The Deseret News, 1912 [c1900]
192p. illus., ports. 17½cm.
UPB, USlC

1158. ———. (same) [Salt Lake City, George Q. Cannon & Sons] 1912 [c1900]
2p.l. [5]–192p. illus., ports., map. 18cm.
Deacon's Quorum edition, issued under the direction of the General Authorities of the Church.
UHi, USlC

1159. ———. (same) Salt Lake City, The Deseret News, 1914.
192p. illus., ports., maps. 17½cm.
OClWhi

1160. ———. (same) Salt Lake City, The Deseret News, 1918.
192p. illus., ports., maps. 17cm.
UPB, USlC

1161. ———. The life of Joseph Smith, the prophet. By George Q. Cannon. Salt Lake City, Juvenile Instructor Office, 1888.
xxviip., [1]l. [31]–512p. 2 port. 22½cm.
CSmH, CtY, DLC, MH, MoInRC, NjP, NN, UHi, ULA, UPB, USlC, UU, WHi

1162. ———. (same) 2d ed. Salt Lake City, The Deseret News, 1907.
xxviip., [1]l., 550p. 22½cm.
CtY, UPB, USl, USlC, UU

1163. ———. (same, in Tahitian) E parau Tuatapapa No Te Peropheta O Iosepha Semita. Papaihia e George Q. Cannon, Aposelolo, Iritihia ei reo Tahiti e O. B. Peterson (ole) Peresident . . . Papeete, Tahiti, 1925.
2p.l. [5]–236 [6]p. 21½cm.
"1st ed."
USlC

CANNON, G. Q.

1164. ———. The life of Nephi, the son of Lehi, who emigrated from Jerusalem, in Judea, to the land which is now known as South America, about six centuries before the coming of the Savior . . . By George Q. Cannon . . . Salt Lake City, Juvenile Instructor Office, 1883.
x [11]–108p. 19cm. (Faith-promoting series. Book 9)
CSmH, CtY, CU, DLC, ICN, MH, NjP, NN, UHi, ULA, UPB, USl, USlC

1165. ———. (same) Salt Lake City, The Contributor Co., 1888.
[2] xi [13]–147p. 17cm.
CDU, CtY, ICU, IU, MH, UHi, UPB, USlC, UU

1166. ———. . . . My first mission. By George Q. Cannon. Salt Lake City, Juvenile Instructor Office, 1879.
3p.l., 66p. 18cm. (Faith promoting series. Book 1)
Author's account of his mission to the Sandwich Islands, 1850.
CSmH, CtY, CU–B, DLC, ICN, NjP, NN, UHi, ULA, UPB, UU, WHi

1167. ———. (same) The first book of the faith promoting series. By George Q. Cannon. Designed for the instruction and encouragement of young latter-day saints. 2d ed. Salt Lake City, Juvenile Instructor Office, 1882.
75p. 18cm. (Faith promoting series. Book 1)
CSmH, CtY, CU, CU–B, DLC, ICN, MH, MoInRC, NN, UHi, ULA, UPB, USlC, UU

1168. ———. Reply to A. G. Campbell's letter to President Garfield. Salt Lake City, 1881.
Broadside. 70½×27cm.
From the *Deseret Evening News* of April 13, 1881.
USlC

1169. ———. A review of the decision of the Supreme Court of the United States, in the case of Geo. Reynolds vs. the United States. By George Q. Cannon. Salt Lake City, Deseret News Printing and Publishing Establishment, 1879.
v., 57p. 24cm.
CSmH, CtY, CU–B, DLC, ICN, MH, NjP, NN, UHi, ULA, UPB, USl, USlC

1170. Cannon, George Quayle, *editor.* A string of pearls. Second book of the faith-promoting series. Designed for the instruction and encouragement of young Latter-day Saints. Salt Lake City, Juvenile Instructor Office, 1880.
4p.l., 88p. 18cm. (Faith Promoting Series. Book 2)
"1st ed."
Partial contents: T. B. Lewis, Anecdotes of Elder Grant. John Taylor, Journey across the plains.
CU–B, ICN, NN, UHi, UPB, ULA, USlC

1171. ———. (same) 2d ed. Salt Lake City, Juvenile Instructor, 1882.
viii [9]–96p. 18cm. (Faith Promoting Series. Book 2)
CSmH, CtY, CU–B, DLC, ICN, MH, NjP, NN, UHi, USl, USlC, UU, WHi

1172. ———. To the readers of the testimony of George Q. Cannon & Joseph Smith. Which do you believe and uphold with your faith, prayers, and uplifted hands before God? [n.p., ca. 1892)
4p. 22½cm.
Speech of George Q. Cannon of Nov. 20, 1892 contrasted with a clipping of Joseph Smith, Sept. 26, 1833.
USlC

1173. ———. Utah contested-election case. Speech of George Q. Cannon, of Utah, in the House of Representatives, Wednesday, April 19, 1882. Washington, 1882.
15p. 21cm.
Cover-title.
CU–B, USlC

1174. ———. Writings from the "Western standard," published in San Francisco, California. By Elder George Quayle Cannon. Liverpool, G. Q. Cannon, 1864.
xv [1] 512p. 22cm.
Howes C 115
CSmH, CtY, DLC, ICN, NjP, UHi, ULA, UPB, USl, USlC, UU, WHi

———. *See also Pratt, Orson, Great discussion! Pratt, Orson; Discourses on celestial Marriage.*

1175. Cannon, George Q., and Sons Company. Book of Mormon stories. No. 1 [Salt Lake City] George Q. Cannon & Sons Co., 1892.
55p. 22cm.
MH, NjP, NN, UPB, USl, USlC, WHi

1176. ———. Book of Mormon stories. No. 2. Illus. Adapted to the capacity of young children, and designed for use in Sabbath Schools, Primary Assns., and for home reading. Salt Lake City, George Q. Cannon & Sons, 1899.
3p.l. [7]–53p. 22cm.
NN, UPB, USl, USlC, WHi

1177. ———. Catalogue & price list of church publications, school books, miscellaneous books, etc. etc. Salt Lake City, Geo. Q. Cannon & Sons Company, 1898.
40p. 15cm.
Signed: September 1, 1898.
USlC

1178. ———. Catalogue of books and stationary . . . March, 1895. Salt Lake City, Geo. Q. Cannon & Sons Co.; Ogden, Utah, A. H. Cannon [1895]
34p. 13cm.
Cover-title: Catalogue and price list.
CtY

1179. Cannon, Hugh J. Is "Mormonism" carrying on? Address delivered over Radio Station KSL, Sunday evening, July 8, 1928. [Salt Lake City] 1928.
Broadside. 61×25cm.
Reprinted from the *Deseret News*, Saturday, July 4th, 1928.
UPB

1180. ———. Liebe Brüder, was soll ich tun, dass ich selig werde? (Apostelgeschichte 16, 30) Eine kurze Erklärung der für jeden Menschen zur Seligkeit notwendigen Grundsätze des Evangeliums Jesu Christi vom Ältesten Hugh J. Cannon. Traktat nr. II. Zurich, Herausgegeben von Serge F. Ballif, 1906.
15p. 18cm.
Cover-title.
Articles of faith on back cover.
Title in English: Dear brother; What must I do to be saved? Missionary tract.
UPB

1181. ———. (same, under title) Was soll ich tun, dass ich selig werde? Eine kurze Erklärung der Grundsätze des Evangeliums Jesu Christi, die für jeden Menschen zur Seligkeit notwendig sind. Vom Ältesten Hugh J. Cannon. Basel, Herausgegeben von der Schweizerisch-Deutschen Mission, 1917.
16p. 16½cm.
USIC

1182. ———. (same) Vom Ältesten Hugh J. Cannon herausgegeben von George F. Ballif. Basel, Schweizerischen und Deutschen Mission, 1922.
16p. 18cm.
Articles of faith on back cover.
UPB, USIC

1183. ———. Why is it? Pertinent questions regarding "Mormonism." [n.p., n.d.]
4p. 21½cm.
Missionary tract.
UPB

1184. Cannon, John Quayle. George Cannon, the immigrant, Isle of Man, 1794-St. Louis, U.S.A., 1844. His ancestry, his life, his native land, his posterity. By John Q. Cannon eldest son of his eldest son. Salt Lake City [The Deseret News Press] 1927.
211p., [1]l. illus., ports., map, fold. general. tab. 19½cm.
DLC, NjP, UHi, UPB, USIC, UU

1185. Cannon, Ramona Stevenson (Wilcox). Biographical sketch of Samuel Whitney Richards. [Bountiful, Utah, Carr Printing Co., 192–?]
3p.l., 24p. 23cm.
UHi, UPB, USIC

1186. Carbutt, Mary (Rhodes) *Lady.* Five months' fine weather. In Canada, Western United States, and Mexico. London, Sampson Low, Marston, Searle & Rivington (etc.) 1889.
1p.l., 243p. 19cm.
Visit to Salt Lake City in 1888, p. 130–141. No strong impression, just assumes that what she has heard is true. Rumor of extreme immorality "Even Amelia, the Prophets favourite wife, having sunk to the lowest depth."
CU–B, USIC, UU

1186a. Card, Charles Ora. 200 men with teams wanted. [Alberta, Canada, n.d.]
Broadside. 30×21cm.
Encouraging Latter-day Saints to settle in Southern Alberta, Canada. It describes the major city, Cardston; the climate; the land; and the industries.
USIC

1187. Cardon, Joseph Emanuel, *compiler.* Testimonies of the divinity of the church of Jesus Christ of Latter-day Saints by its leaders. Compiled by Joseph E. Cardon and Samuel O. Bennion. [Independence, Mo., Press of Zions Printing and Publishing Co., c1930]
311p. illus., ports., 1 plate. 22½cm.
NjP, UHi, UPB, USI, USIC, UU

1188. Carleton, James Henry. . . . Mountain Meadow massacre . . . Special report of the Mountain Meadow massacre, by J. H. Carleton, Brevet Major, United States Army, Captain, First Dragoons. [Washington, Govt. Print. Off., 1902]
17p. 23cm. (U.S. 57th Cong. 1st Sess. House Doc. No. 605)
Dated: Camp at Mountain Meadows, Utah Territory, May 25, 1859, and addressed to the Assistant Adjutant-general, U.S.A., San Francisco, Cal.
Reprinted from U.S. 40th Cong. 2d session, Report No. 79, p. 26–40. See U.S. Congress. House. Committee on Elections. McGrorty vs. Hooper.
CSmH, CU–B, DLC, NjP, NN, UHi, ULA, UPB, USIC

1189. ———. Report on the subject of the massacre at the Mountain Meadows, in Utah Territory in September, 1857, of one hundred and twenty men, women and children, who were from Arkansas. By Brevet Major James Henry Carleton, U.S. Army, and report of the Hon. William C. Mitchell, relative to the seventeen surviving children who were brought back by the authorities of the U.S. after their parents and others with whom they were emigrating had been murdered. Little Rock, True Democrat Steam Press Printing, 1860.
32p. 23½cm.
Addressed to the Governor of Arkansas.
W–C 354
CtY, ICN, NjP

CARLETON, J. H.

1190. ———. Report on the subject of the massacre at the Mountain Meadows, in Utah Territory in September, 1857 . . . Little Rock, ohnson [sic] & Yerkes, State Printers, 1860.
32p. 22cm.
At head of title: Senate Document.
Howes C–147
ARU, KU

1191. Carlier, Auguste. Le mariage aux Etats-Unis, par Auguste Carlier. Paris, L. Hachette et Cie, 1860.
3p.l. [3]–264p. 18½cm.
Brief section on Mormon temple marriage. Also an appendix on polygamy among the Mormons.
CU–B, DLC

1192. ———. (same, in English) Marriage in the United States, by Auguste Carlier . . . Translated from the French by B. Joy Jeffries . . . Boston, De Vries, Ibarra & Co.; New York, Leypoldt and Holt, 1867.
xv, 179p. 18cm.
Another edition. 3d ed. 1867. DLC
CU–B, DLC, NjP, UHi, USIC, ViU

1193. Carlton, Ambrose B. The wonderlands of the wild West, with sketches of the Mormons. By A. B. Carlton . . . [n.p.] 1891.
1p.l. [v]–vii [9]–346 [2]p. plates, ports. 23cm.
In Utah in 1882–1890 as a member of the Utah Commission.
CSmH, DLC, ICN, NjP, NN, UHi, ULA, UPB, USl, USIC, UU, WHi

1194. Carlton, I. W. Letter no. 2. A series of communications written by I. W. Carlton. [San Francisco? 1887?]
[6]p. 21½cm.
Letter dated: Weber, August 15th, 1887.
A follower of Joseph Morris, and a member of the Church of the Firstborn.
USIC

1195. ———. Precious jewels [written by Bro I. W. Carlton] Circular and Advertisement for "The Spirit Prevails," a book unto all the scattered Israel, and whosoever will. Accepted by the Church of the Firstborn. San Francisco, 1886.
6 [2]p. 23cm. (Tract No. 1)
At head of title: Take one free. Tract No. 1.
CtY, MH, USIC

1196. ———. A series of communications written by I. W. Caryton [sic] showing some proof, history and principles of the Church of the Firstborn. [San Francisco? 1876?]
4p. 23cm.
MH

1197. Carman, William Cooper. Rattling, roaring rhymes on Mormon Utah and her institutions. Life among the Rocky Mountain Saints, the land of many wives and much silver; or, The follies and crimes of Bigamy Young and his po-lig. divines. By "Will Cooper" [*pseud.*] Chicago, Union Publishing Company, 1874.
iv, 7–140p. 19½cm.
Poetry concerning Mormons.
DLC

1198. Carmichael, Albert. Church finance, its relation to the gathering. Independence, Mo., Reorganized Church of Jesus Christ of Latter Day Saints, 1929.
29p. 20cm.
Stewardship in the RLDS church.
MoInRC, UHi

1199. ———. The elements of stewardship and our social program. By Bishop Albert Carmichael. 3d ed. [Independence, Mo., Herald Publishing House, 19 - -]
104p. diagrs. 19cm.
MoInRC, NN

1200. ———. The gathering. [Independence, Mo., Published and Distributed by Herald Publishing House, n.d.]
16p. 19½cm.
MoInRC, NN

1201. ———. The Order of Enoch. Independence, Mo., Herald Publishing House [n.d.]
22p. 20cm.
An attempt at a cooperative organization.
MoInRC

1202. ———. (same) "Enl. ed." Independence, Mo., Herald Publishing House [n.d.]
39p. 20cm.
MoInRC, NN

1203. Carpenter, Frank George. Carpenter's geographical reader; North America. New York, Cincinnati [etc.] American Book Company [1898]
352p. illus., maps. 19cm.
Chapter XXXIV. Across the rockies to Salt Lake. Description of Salt Lake City.
Other editions: c1910. ULA, UPB; c1915. CU
UPB

1204. Carpenter, George E. Salt Lake City fire and police departments. [Salt Lake City, The Deseret News, 1901]
4p.l. [1] 7–105p. illus., plates, ports. 31cm.
Cover-title.
"Compiled by A. G. Conklin."
History of the Fire Department and also a brief history of the city.
CSmH, UHi, ULA, UU

1205. Carpenter, William Henry, *editor.* The history of Illinois, from its earliest settlement to the present time. Ed. by W. H. Carpenter and T. S. Arthur. Philadelphia, Lippincott, Grambo & Company, 1854.
255p. port. 16cm.
Chap. XIII: The Mormons or Latter-day Saints. Biography of Joseph Smith and history through the

expulsion from Illinois. "The second race, according to this silly fiction."
Another edition: Philadelphia, J. B. Lippincott and Co., 1857 [c1854]
Sabin 11008
NN, USIC

1206. ———. The history of Ohio, from its earliest settlement to the present time. Ed. by W. H. Carpenter and T. S. Arthur. Philadelphia, Lippincott, Grambo & Co., 1853.
3p.l., 5–277p. port. 16cm. (Half-title: Lippincott's cabinet histories of the states . . .)
History of Mormonism in Ohio.
Other editions: 1854. DLC, PHi, UHi; 1856. PPL; 1857. CtY, USIC; 1858. MNH, PPTU; 1865. DLC; 1869. ICJ; 1872. MWH
PHi

1207. Carr, Clark Ezra. My day and generation, by Clark E. Carr . . . with sixty-three illustrations. Chicago, A. C. McClurg & Co., 1908.
6p.l., 15–452p. plates, ports., fold. facsim. 23½cm.
Salt Lake City, p. 22–36. A view of Mormonism and a visit with Brigham Young.
CSmH, CU–B, DLC, NjP, NN, UHi, USl, USIC, UPB

1208. Carr, John. Pioneer days in California: by John Carr. Historical and personal sketches. Eureka, Calif., Times Publishing Co., Book and Job Printers, 1891.
2p.l. [11]–452p. port. 22½cm.
Chap. II. "To Salt Lake City." Description of Salt Lake City in 1850, an interview with Brigham Young; Mormon achievements.
Howes C 167
CtY, CU–B, ICN, NjJ

1209. Carr, Lucien. . . . Missouri, a bone of contention; by Lucien Carr. Boston and New York, Houghton, Mifflin & Company, 1888.
x, 377p. fold. map. 18cm. (Half-title: American commonwealths. Ed. by H. E. Scudder)
Series title also at head of t.–p.
Material on Mormons in Missouri, p. 179–185.
Other editions: 1892. DLC, PP, PPD; 1894. ODW; 1896. PHi; 1899. PP–W, WaU; c1916. OEac
CU–B, DLC, MH, NjP, NN, UHi, ULA, UPB, USIC, UU

1210. Carrier's address, to the patrons of the Hancock Jeffersonian, January 1st, 1858. [n.p., n.d.]
[2]p. 20cm.
Text printed in blue within embossed border.
Poem about Brigham Young and the Utah War.
USIC

1211. Carrington, Janette. Worship God (and other poems) [n.p., n.d.]
[4]p. 21cm.
Final poem signed by Janette Carrington.
Poems: Worship God, The Prophet Joseph Smith, Zion's Leaders, An Apostrophe to Zion.
MH

1212. Carroll, A. Carroll-Lloyd exposé. Rev. A. Carroll, of Independence, Missouri, attacks the divine authenticity of the Book of Mormon and the Mission of Joseph Smith. [n.p., 189–?]
20p. facsim. 22cm.
Caption-title.
A letter from A. Carroll and a reply by T. E. Lloyd.
CtY, MoInRC

1213. Carroll, Elsie Chamberlain. Latter-day Saint ideals of home and home life (second year) [Salt Lake City, Young Ladies Mutual Improvement Association, 1929]
48p. 21cm.
"Course of study for the Gleaner Dept. of the Young Ladies' Mutual Improvement Association."
"Lessons I–XVI of this series are published in the Young Woman's Journal, July, August, September, October, 1929."
UPB, USIC

1214. ———. "Success" a play in three acts by Elsie C. Carroll with Elsie T. Brandley and W. O. Robinson. [Salt Lake City] Published by General Boards of the M.I.A., 1929.
39p. 18cm.
Mormon drama.
USIC

1215. Carroll, Mary Teresa Austin, *Mother.* Essays educational and historic; or, X-rays on some important episodes, by a member of the Order of Mercy. New York, O'Shea and Co., 1899.
4p.l., 9–408p. 18½cm.
"Forty years in the American Wilderness," "When Brigham Young was king," "About the Utah Saints," "A glance at the Latter-Day Saints," p. 142–266.
A long account of Mormonism.
UPB

1216. Carson Valley (Nevada) Citizens. . . . Message from the President of the United States, transmitting a memorial of citizens of Carson's Valley, asking for the establishment of a territorial government over them. [Washington, James B. Steedman] 1858.
3p. (U.S. 35th Cong. 1st Sess. House Ex. Doc. No. 102) 23½cm.
Some mention of the Mormons and their system of government as well as the atrocities committed by them.
CU, CU–B, NjP, UU

1217. Carter, Charles W. The exodus of 1847; being a full and interesting account of the Latter-day Saints journey, etc. Salt Lake City, Lithographing Co., 1897.
14p. 17cm.
ICN, MH, USIC

1218. ———. Organization of the church of Jesus Christ of Latter-day Saints and their belief: Also the life and history of their Prophet Seer and Revelator,

Joseph Smith, during his brief life of 38½ years. By Charles W. Carter. Salt Lake City, The Utah Lithographing Co., 1897.
v. [7]–41p. 17×13cm.
CU–B, MH, USl

1219. ———. The life and history of the late president Brigham Young. [Salt Lake City, 1898?]
1p.l., 34p. 18½cm.
Cover-title.
MH, USl

1220. **Carter, James.** In the wake of the setting sun by James Carter . . . Illustrated. London, Hurst and Blackett, Ltd., 1908.
xii, 456p. illus., plates. 23cm.
A visit to Salt Lake City in 1907. "Mormonism as an issue has outlived its usefulness."
CU–B, USlC

1221. **Carter, Mary Leland.** An instrument in His hands, by Mary Leland Carter . . . [Lamoni, Ia., Herald Publishing House] 1913.
80p. illus. 19cm.
Under title: The two story book along with "The Minister who was different," by Elbert A. Smith.
A story of conversion to the RLDS Church. Published with and without publishing date.
CU–B, UPB, USlC

———. The two story book. *See Carter, Mary Leland. An instrument in his hands. Smith, Elbert A. The Minister who was different.*

1222. **Carthage, Illinois. Convention, 1845.** The proceedings of a convention, held at Carthage, Ill., on Tuesday and Wednesday, October 1st–2nd, 1845. Published by order of the convention, under the superintendence of the military committee of Quincy, Illinois. [Quincy, Illinois, Printed at the Quincy Whig Book and Job Office, 1845]
9p. 23cm.
Caption-title and colophon.
Discussion of a permanent solution to the Mormon problem during a respite. Committee to investigate Mormon depredations. Resolutions adopted dismissing Mormon allegations and substituting the anti-Mormon ones. Affidavit at end.
Byrd 942
CtY, ICHi, MH, MoKU, NN

1223. **Cartwright, Peter.** Autobiography of Peter Cartwright, the backwoods preacher. Edited by W. P. Strickland. New York, Carlton and Porter [c1856]
525p. port. 19cm.
Chapter XXII, "Mormonism," p. 341–346. His exposé of meetings with Joseph Smith.
Other editions: 8th thousand, 1857. USlC; 9th thousand, 1857. USlC; 15th thousand, 1857. UPB; 23d thousand, 1857, 1859
Howes 208a, Sabin C11160
CU, NjP, ULA, USlC

1224. **Carvalho, Solomon Nunes.** Incidents of travel and adventure in the far West; with Col. Fremont's last expedition across the Rocky Mountains: including three months residence in Utah, and a perilous trip across the great American desert to the Pacific. By S. N. Carvalho, artist to the expedition. New York, Derby & Jackson, 1856.
xv [17]–380p. front. 19½cm.
Last section contains sermons, discourses, addresses, etc. by various Mormons with running title: Mormonism. He was with Fremont in Utah in 1853–1854.
Other editions: London, 1856. CSmH; 1857. DLC, USlC; 1858. UHi; 1859. CU–B, NN
W–C 273
ICJ

1225. **Case, Hubert.** The church the Indians have long looked for; the Reorganized Church of Jesus Christ of Latter Day Saints. [Lamoni, Ia., Reorganized Church of Jesus Christ of Latter Day Saints, n.d.]
11p. 19cm. (No. 1899)
CSmH, CU–B, MoInRC

1226. ———. Te hoe pae no te hoe paraparau raa ahiahi. Papeete, Tahiti, Etaretia faaapi Hia no Jetu Metia i te Mau Mahana Hopea Nei, 1898.
8p. 24½cm. (No. 2)
Title in English: Selections from an afternoon discussion.
USlC

1227. **Casler, Melyer.** A journal, giving the incidents of a journey to California in the summer of 1859, by the overland route. By Mell Casler, Toledo, Commercial Steam Book and Job Office, 1863.
iv [5]–48p. 5½cm.
Via Great Salt Lake City.
Howes C220, W–C 385a
CtY

1228. **Cassia Stake Academy. Oakley, Idaho.** Cassia Stake Academy, Oakley, Idaho (Announcement) 1911–
7v. 19cm.
USlC 1911–12, 1912–13, 1913–14, 1914–15, 1915–16, 1916–17, 1917–18.

1229. ———. School songs and cheers. [Oakley, Idaho, n.d.]
[8]p. 14cm.
USlC

1230. **Casteel, F. L.** Appeal. To the President and Conference of the Church of the Latter Day Saints. [n.p., 1868?]
16p. 21cm.
Signed: Sacramento, Cal. January 16, 1868.
In the same group as G. P. Dykes. Against the RLDS church.
MoInRC

Castlerose, Viscount. *See Browne, Valentine Charles.*

1231. Caswall, Henry. America and the American church, by the Rev. Henry Caswall. London, Printed for J. G. & F. Rivington, 1839.
xviii p. [1]l., 368 p. 3 plates, fold. map. 20cm.
Section entitled "Joseph Smith and the Mormons," p. 322–323.
Visited Nauvoo April 17–19, 1842.
Other editions: 2d ed. 1851. NjP, NN; 1851. CU–B, ICN, USlC, WHi
Howes C233, Sabin 11473
CSmH, CtY, CU–B, DLC, ICN, NjP, USlC

1232. ———. The city of the Mormons; or three days at Nauvoo in 1842 by the Rev. Henry Caswall, M. A. . . . London, Printed for J. G. F. & J. Rivington and sold by W. Grapel, 1842.
2p.l., 82 [1]p. front. 17cm.
Character of the Mormons.
Howes C234
CtY, CU–B, ICHi, ICN, MH, MoK, NjP, NN, Ocl, PPL–R, UPB, USlC, UU

1233. ———. (same) 2d ed., rev. and enl. London, Printed for J. G. F. & J. Rivington, 1843.
2p.l., 87 [1]p. front. 16cm.
Howes C234, Sabin 11476
CSmH, CtY, DLC, ICN, NN, USlC

1234. ———. Mormonism and its author; or, A statement of the doctrines of the "Latter-day Saints." By the Rev. Henry Caswall . . . London, Printed for the Society for Promoting Christian Knowledge, 1851.
16p. 17½cm.
IHi, MH, USlC

1235. ———. (same) London, Printed for the Society for Promoting Christian Knowledge, 1852.
16p. 17cm. (No. 866)
CtY, MH, NN, USlC

1236. ———. (same) London, Printed for the Society for Promoting Christian Knowledge, 1856.
22p. 17cm.
MH

1237. ———. The prophet of the nineteenth century; or, The rise, progress, and present state of the Mormons, or Latter-day saints: to which is appended, an analysis of the Book of Mormon. By the Rev. Henry Caswall . . . London, Printed for J. G. F. & J. Rivington, 1843.
xx, 277 [1]p. front. 21½cm.
Cover-title: History of the Mormons or Latter-day Saints.
Howes C235, Sabin 11478
CSmH, CtY, CU–B, DLC, ICN, MH, NjP, NjPT, NN, UHi, ULA, UPB, USl, USlC, UU

1238. ———. The western world revisited. By the Rev. Henry Caswall . . . Oxford & London, John Henry Parker, 1854.
xvl, 351p. 16½cm.
Story of an almost destroyed box "supposed to house plates." The exposé of Joseph Smith as an impostor and of the deluded being converted to Mormonism.
Howes C236, Sabin 11479
CtY, DLC, ICU, NN, PU

Catalogue of the Relics. *See Utah. Semi-Centennial Commission.*

1239. Cather, W. C. An investigation of truth and error, or the path of right and where found, carefully examined and compiled. Atchison, Kansas, W. C. Cather, Publisher [n.d.]
82p. 20cm.
Cover-title: The Salt Land Heresies.
MoInRC

1240. Caurdisto, Sols. A cardston manifestation. [Salt Lake City, E. Hollings, ca. 1925]
[6]p. 22cm.
Introduction by Edward J. Wood.
Tract on the last days.
USlC

1241. ———. (same) [S. L. City, Zion's Book Store, ca. 1925]
[6]p. 22cm.
USlC

1242. Cavling, Henrik. Fra Amerika. Kobenhavn, 1897.
2v.
Includes a section on Mormonism.
Title in English: From America.
Schmidt

1242a. Celebration of the fifteenth anniversary of the arrival of the pioneers in G.S.L. Valley. [Great Salt Lake City, 1862]
4p. 19½cm.
USlC

1243. ———. (same) [Great Salt Lake City, 1862?] **arrival of the pioneers in G. S. L. Valley.** [Great Salt Lake City, 1862?]
4p. 19cm.
UPB photocopy from original in private hands.

1244. Centennial jubilee number April 6, 1830–April 6, 1930. Salt Lake City Beobachter. [Bikuben. Utah-posten. De Utahnederlander] Salt Lake City [1930]
64, 64, 64, 60p. illus. (part. col., incl. ports.) 39cm.
Cover-title.
"Festnummer zur hundertjahrfeier der Kirche Jesu Christi der heiligen der letzten tage."
The four newspapers contain the same material in Danish, Dutch, German, and Swedish.
DLC, UPB, USl, USlC, UU

1245. Cestre, Charles. Les États-Unis, par Charles Cestre . . . 593 reproductions photographiques. 4 plans en noir. 5 cartes hors texte en couleurs. 12 hors-texte monochromes dont 4 en héliogravure. 4 héliogravures en couleurs. Paris, Librairie Larousse [c1927]

3p.l., 343 [1]p. illus., ports., plates (part col.) maps (1 double) 32cm.

Description of Utah and notes on Mormonism, p. 6, 268–272.

Title in English: The United States.

DLC, NjP, UPB

1246. Chalmer, E. Boteler. Mormonism a delusion. A lecture, delivered in the Tintwistle church school on Thursday, August 26, 1852. London, Wertheim and Macintosh, 1852.

47p. 16½cm.

CtY, MH, USlC

1247. Chamberlain, Leander Trowbridge. Mormonism and polygamy; an address delivered in the Broadway church, Norwich, Conn., Feb. 19, 1882. [Norwich? 1882]

21p. 23½cm.

Cover-title.

CtY, ICN, MH, MiD, NN, UHi, ULA, UPB, USl, USlC

1248. ———. (same) [Chicago, New West Education Commission, 1887?]

21p. 22cm.

CSmH, WHi

1249. Chamberlin, Ralph Vary. Life and philosophy of W. H. Chamberlin, by Ralph V. Chamberlin . . . Salt Lake City, The Deseret News Press, 1925.

2p.l. [7]–384p. 20cm.

Mormon biography.

CU–B, DLC, NjP, UHi, UPB, USlC, UU

1250. Chamberlin, William Henry. The Life of Man; an introduction to philosophy. By W. H. Chamaerlin [sic] Logan, Utah, 1920.

22p. 22½cm.

Philosophy of the purpose of life by a professor of Brigham Young College.

USlC

1251. Chambers, Robert. History of the Mormons. [Edinburgh, Printed by W. and R. Chambers, 1853]

31 [1]p. illus. 18½cm. (Chamber's Repository. Vol. VII, no. 53)

Caption-title.

Reprinted from *Chambers' Miscellany.* V. 3, no. 46.

CtY, CU–B, DLC, MH, NN, ULA, USl, UU

1252. Chandless, William. A visit to Salt Lake; being a journey across the plains and a residence in the Mormon settlements at Utah. London, Smith, Elder and Co., 1857.

xii, 346p. front. (fold. map) 19½cm.

A description of Mormonism in 1855 during his trip through Utah.

He arrived at Salt Lake City about November 1, 1855. He left January, 1856 for California.

Advertisements dated April, 1857 [ICN] or, more common, Dec., 1858.

Howes C286, Sabin C–11889, W–C 287

CLSU, CSmH, CtY, DLC, ICN, NjP, NN, UHi, ULA, USl, USlC, UU

1253. ———. (same, in Danish) Ved Saltsøen; et besog hos Mormonerne i Utah. Oversat fra Engelsk af Ferd. G. Serensen. Kjøbenhavn, Forlagtaf F. Wøldife, 1858.

6p.l., 322p. 17cm.

UU

1254. Chapman, Arthur. John Crews. Boston-New York, Houghton Mifflin Co., Riverside Press, Cambridge, 1926.

4p.l. [3]–303p. 19½cm.

Novel with references to Mormons.

CU, DLC, NjP, UPB, USlC

1255. Chapman, C. H. The Mormon elder or the triumph of virtue; a farce. Portland, Ore., The Futurists, 1912.

41p. 19cm.

Poem about Mormonism.

UPB

1256. Chapman, Frederick William. The Pratt family: or, The descendants of Lieut. William Pratt, one of the first settlers of Hartford and Say-Brook, with genealogical notes of John Pratt, of Hartford; Peter Pratt, of Lyme; John Pratt (Taylor) of Say-Brook. By Rev. F. W. Chapman . . . Hartford, Printed by Case, Lockwood and Company, 1864.

420p. [1]l. front. (coat of arms) ports. 23½cm.

Biographies of Orson Pratt, P. P. Pratt, and other Mormon Pratts.

Sabin #11980. 1865

DLC, MnH, MWA, NN, PHi, PPL, PPPrHi

Character of the Latter-day Saints. . . . *See Church of Jesus Christ of Latter-day Saints. Missions. British.*

1257. Charles F. Middleton, February 24th, 1834–August 3rd, 1915. [Ogden, Scoville Press, 1915]

27 [1]p. port. 24cm.

Mormon biography.

USlC

1258. Chase, A. M. The Bondsman's awakening. Lamoni, Ia., Herald Publishing House [1906?]

[2]p. 18½cm.

Signed: Escalante, Utah, November 22, 1902. An allegorical piece about his leaving the Utah Mormons and going to the RLDS church.

MH

1259. ———. "The sin against the Holy Ghost;" betraying the revelations of God. [Lamoni, Ia., Herald Publishing House, n.d.]

8p. 18cm.

Signed: Salt Lake City.

MH, UPB, USl, USlC

1259a. Chase, Joseph Smeaton. California desert trails. Boston and New York, Houghton Mifflin, 1919.
xvi, 387p. illus. 22½cm.
Mormon Battalion mentioned, p. 245, 249, 275.
USIC

1260. Chase, Philander. A pastoral letter of Bishop Chase, to the clergy of his diocese of Illinois. [Peoria? 1843]
8p. 19½cm.
Contains a letter to Chase dated Dec. 24, 1842 and Chase's reply, of Jan. 3, 1843, in which he comments on Joseph Smith and Mormonism.
Byrd 769
IHi

1261. Chasles, Philarète. Anglo-America literature and manners: From the French of Philarète Chasles. New York: Charles Scribner, 1852.
xii, 312p. 19½cm.
In a discussion of American autobiographies, he quotes from the "Memoirs of Jonathan Sharp" concerning his conversion to Mormonism.
NjP, UPB

1262. Cherry, Alexander. Article on "Book of Mormon and latter day work," begun by Brother Alex. Cherry (now deceased and continued by brother Charles Ashton) [n.p., 1924]
6p. 21½cm.
The author belonged to the Bickerton group.
Morgan
PMonC, UHi

1263. Chesterton, Gilbert K. The uses of diversity, a book of essays by G. K. Chesterton. New York, Dodd, Mead & Company, 1921.
4p.l., 289p. 19½cm.
"Mormonism," p. 182–189. The basic beliefs of Mormonism, a primitive cult.
CU, USIC

1264. Chetlain, Augustus Louis. Recollections of seventy years. Galena [Ill.] The Gazette Publishing Company, 1899.
2p.l. [5]–304p. front. 22cm.
He was U.S. Assessor of Internal Revenue, Salt Lake City, 1867–9. Includes a discussion on Mormonism.
CtY, DLC, NjP, UHi, ULA, UPB, USIC

1264a. Chicago Museum. A complete guide to the Chicago Museum, including a description of the wonderful antediluvian monster, the great zeuglodon, catalogue of birds, quadrupeds, fishes . . . mummies, models and curiosities. [Chicago] Evening Journal Book and Job Print, 1868.
46p. 19cm.
Cover title: A guide to the Chicago Museum now open every day and evening . . . Joseph Smith and the Egyptian Papyri, p. 42.
USIC photostat

1265. The Children's Friend. Salt Lake City, January, 1902–
v. monthly. 23–30cm.
Organ of the Primary Association of the Church of Jesus Christ of Latter-day Saints.
ULA v.2–22; UPB v.1 inc., 2–22, 23 inc., 24–; USIC comp.

1266. Children's Magazine. Salt Lake City, Published by William A. Morton. January, 1896–
v. bi-monthly. 26cm.
Magazine designed primarily for L.D.S. children.
USIC June 22, Dec. 7, 1896. V. 1 #8, 22.

1267. Chiniquy, Père. The priest, the woman, and the confessional, by Père Chiniquy. London, W. T. Gibson, 1874.
iv, 192p. 19½cm.
America does not allow its great love of liberty to stand in the way of crushing Mormonism to free enslaved women, p. 187–88.
Other editions: 5th ed. London, 1878; 36th ed., Chicago, 1890.
USIC

1268. Chittenden, Hiram Martin. History of early steamboat navigation on the Missouri river; life and adventures of Joseph La Barge . . . by Hiram Martin Chittenden . . . New York, F. P. Harper, 1903.
2v. plates, ports., map. 23½cm. (Half-title: American explorers series, IV)
V.1 contains brief material on Mormonism in Missouri and Illinois.
CSmH, CU, DLC, NjP, NN, UHi, USIC, UU, WaS, WaU

1269. Chorpenning, George, *claimant.* The case of George Chorpenning vs. the United States. A brief history of the facts by the claimant. Washington, D. C. May 1, 1874. Washington, M'Gill & Wintherow, 1874.
56p. 23½cm.
Cover-title.
Concerning his mail contracting between Utah and California, 1851–1857.
CU–B

1270. ———. Statement and appendix of the claim of George Chorpenning against the United States. [Washington? 1889?]
iii, iii, 103. fold. map. 23cm.
Cover-title.
Mail contracts, 1851–1857.
CU–B

1271. Christ or Barabbas? A word on Mormonism . . . Weston-super-Mare, J. Whereat, Gazette Office, London, Wertheim and Macintosh, Paternoster Row [n.d.]
16p. 13½cm.
USIC

CHRIST, P.

1272. Christ, Potter. Revelations of Potter Christ, the Messenger of the New Covenant. Given by inspiration of God for the salvation of the whole world, containing a portrait of the author. Second edition of one thousand copies. Council Bluffs, Evening Bugle News, Books, and Job Printing House, 1870.
16p. 14cm.
On his way to Australia on a Mormon mission, he receives revelations and ministrations of angels and is called to preach the celestial law, not found in the *Book of Mormon, Doctrine and Covenants, Bible,* or anywhere else. Mormonism had apostatized after Joseph Smith.
MH, MoK, NN

1273. Christensen, Carl Christian Anton. Eeen blik de geestenwereld [uit het Engelset. Millennial Star. n.p. Gedruckt op last van A. L. Farrell, n.d.]
[2]p. 22cm.
Missionary tract.
Title in English: A look into the spirit world.
USIC

1274. ———. Poetiske Arbejder Artikler og Afhandlinger tilligemed hans Levnedsløb. Samlede og redigerde af John S. Hansen. Mindeudgave. Salt Lake City "Bikubens" Bibliotek, 1921.
3p.l. [7]–381 [5]p. port. 19½cm. (Bikubens Bibliotek. No. 10)
Cover-title: Digte og Afhandlinger.
Mormon poetry and essays.
Title in English: Poetical worker's articles and essays as well as his life story.
UHi, UPB, USIC, UU

1275. Christensen, James Miller. Lommebog til vejledning for aeldsterne i den Skandinaviske Mission. Udgivet og forlagt af J. M. Christensen. København, 1907.
22 [2]p. 15½cm.
Cover-title.
Title in English: A pocket guide for Elders in the Scandinavian Mission.
USIC

1276. Christian Convention, Salt Lake City, Utah. Christian progress in Utah. The discussions of the Christian convention held in Salt Lake City, April 3rd, 4th and 5th, 1888. Salt Lake City, Frank H. Nelden & Co., 1888.
130p. 21cm.
On cover: The situation in Utah. The discussions of the Christian convention . . . Salt Lake City, Parsons, Kendall & Co., 1888.
CSmH, ICN, MH, MWA, NN, USIC, UU

Christian fellowship. *See Presbytery of Utah. Ten reasons . . .*

1277. Christiani, Carl Emil Anton. Christelige oplysninger om de sidste Dage, til Brug for Laegfolk af Christiani, praest. Randers, L. Jacobsens forlag, 1857.
36p. 18cm.
Title in English: Christian-like enlightenment concerning the last days.
CNU, CtY, NN

1278. ———. En liden modgift mod Mormonernes falske laerdomme, til brug for menigmand. Randers, L. Jacobsens Forlag, 1857.
28p. 17½cm.
Title in English: A little antidote against false Mormon teachings.
CDU, CtY, NN

1279. ———. (same) 2 oplag. Randers, L. Jacobsens Forlag [1857]
30p. 16cm.
NN

1280. ———. (same) 3 oplag. Randers, L. Jacobsens Forlag, 1857.
24p. 16cm.
NN

1281. Christiansen, Hans J. Adlyd Loverne! (af Missions praesident Hans J. Christiansen) [Kjobenhavn? n.d.]
[4]p. 23cm.
Title in English: Keep the covenants.
USIC

1281a. Christiansen, Jens. Correspondence. [San Francisco? J. A. Dove & Co.? ca1890]
10p. 21½cm.
Letters in English and Danish concerning the Church of the Firstborn (Morrisites)
USIC

1282. Christiansen, N. Wolle (Jengang han wa mae a tog) Af N. C., laerer i Svingelbjerg. Kobenhavn, 1906.
24p.
Schmidt

1283. Christopher [*pseud.*] Remarkable adventures of the Mormon prophet in search of the "better land." By Christopher. [n.p., n.d.]
4, 4p.
Sabin 69375

1284. The Church Directory Calendar. Salt Lake City, April 24, 1897.
1v. semi-monthly. 26½cm.
Edited by P. Elliot.
"In the interests of all the organizations in all the Ecclesiastical Wards throughout the Stakes of Zion.
Probably the only one issued.
USIC

1285. Church of Christ (Fetting). A warning to all people of the second coming of Christ. Twelfth message. [Independence, Mo., Church of Christ, 1929?]
[4]p. 21cm.
UU

CHURCH OF JESUS CHRIST (BICKERTON)

1286. Church of Christ (Temple Lot). An account of a conference held by five brethren in Salt Lake City, Utah, May 8th, 1921, to consider receiving the work which the Lord started in 1829. [n.p., 1921?]
17p. 24cm.
MoInRC, USlC

1287. ———. Articles of faith and practice of the Church of Christ. [Independence, Mo.? n.d.]
Broadside. 28×21cm.
MoInRC

1288. ———. Brief history of the Church of Christ and the Articles of faith and practice. Independence, Mo., The Church of Christ (Temple Lot) c1930.
[5]p. 22cm.
USlC

———. Fourteen revelations reprinted from the Book of Commandments. *See Doctrine and Covenants. English. Selections. 1921.*

1289. ———. Fulfillment of prophecy. [Independence, Mo.] Board of Publication, Church of Christ (Temple Lot) [n.d.]
[3] folded pages. 20cm.
UPB

1290. ———. History of the Church of Christ. [Englewood, Mo., Published by Zion's Advocate, 192–]
Broadside. 26×19½cm.
In double columns.
Largely reprinted from *The Searchlight*, March 2, 1896, relative to authority of the Church of Christ.
MoInRC

1291. ———. Program for the breaking of the ground for the Temple. Church of Christ. [Independence, Mo.? 1929]
3p. 18½cm.
Ceremony held April 6, 1929.
MoInRC

1292. Church of Christ (Whitmer). Church of Christ. [n.p., n.d.]
22p. 16cm.
USlC

1293. Church of Christ (Zahnd). Report of the General Conference of the Church of Christ in Conference at Kansas City, Missouri, September 7th, 1920. [Kansas City, John Zahnd, 1920?]
[2]p. 21cm.
USlC

1294. Church of England in Canada. Council for Social Service. Mormonism. Toronto, 1921.
Mormonism. Toronto, 1921.
38p. 22½cm. (Bulletin 48)
UPB

1295. Church of Jesus Christ (Bickerton). Constitution and by-laws of the missionary and benevolent association of the Church of Jesus Christ. Roscoe, Pa., Roscoe Ledger Print., 1906.
8p. 12½cm.
Morgan
PMonC, UHi

1296. ———. The Ensign: or a light to lighten the gentiles, in which the doctrine of the Church of Jesus Christ of Latter-day Saints, is set forth, and scripture evidence adduced to establish it. Also a brief treatise upon the most important prophecies recorded in the Old and New Testaments, which relate to the great work of God of the latter days. Published by Church of Jesus Christ of Latter-day Saints. William Bickerton, [etc.] Publishing committee. Pittsburgh, Ferguson & Co., 1863.
26p. 21½cm.
Morgan
PMonC, UHi

1297. ———. The Ensign: or a light to lighten the gentiles, in which the doctrine of the Church of Jesus Christ of Latter-day Saints, is set forth, and scripture evidence adduced to establish it . . . Published by the authority of the Church of Jesus Christ of Latter-day Saints, West Elizabeth, Pa. Pittsburgh, Ferguson & Co., 1864.
[27]–52p. 21½cm.
Note: Paging continues from 1863 publication, includes journal of William Cadman, etc.
Morgan
MoInRC, PMonC

1298. ———. Hymns and spiritual songs, original and selected for the use of the Church of Jesus Christ of Latter-day Saints. Revised and compiled by W. Bickerton, T. Bickerton, and J. Stranger. Elders of the Church in West Elizabeth, Pa. Pittsburgh, Printed by J. T. Shryock Book and Job Printer, 1855.
314p. 9cm.
Words only.
Morgan
PMonC

1299. ———. (same) Revised and compiled by the Elders of the Church in West Elizabeth, Pa., U. S. Pittsburgh, Printed by Ferguson, 84 Fifth street, 1864.
378p. 11cm.
Words only.
Morgan
CU–B, PMonC

1300. ———. Hmyns [sic] and spiritual songs, original and selected for the use of the Church of Christ, L.D.S. Revised and compiled by the Elders of the Church. Pittsburgh, Wisener & Sippy, Print. 55 Virgin Alley, 1875.
2p.l., 378p. 11½cm.
390 hymns in 367p. 10p. of index.
USlC

CHURCH OF JESUS CHRIST (BICKERTON)

1301. ———. Hymns and spiritual songs, original and selected for use in the Church of Jesus Christ. Compiled by the Elders of the Church at West Elizabeth, Pa., U.S.A. Revised edition. Greensburg, Pa., Printed by "Press of Greensburg Press Co.," [189–?]
407 [11]p. 11½cm.
Morgan
PMonC, UHi

1302. ———. The last witness dead. [n.p., 1929]
7p. 15½cm.
The death of David Whitmer
Morgan
PMonC, UHi

1303. ———. Law and order of the Church of Jesus Christ, organized July 7, 1862. [Roscoe, Pa.] Roscoe Ledger Print., 1905.
12p. 17½cm.
Morgan
MoInRC, PMonC, UHi, UPB

1304. ———. Law and order of the Church of Jesus Christ, . . . organized July 7, 1862, and incorporated June 10, 1865. Published 1925. Uniontown, Pa., Herald-Genius, 1925.
29p. 19½cm.
Morgan
PMonC, UHi

1305. ———. The Saints' hymnal. Monongahela, Pa., Printed by Geo. Ashworth [1919]
165p. 18cm.
Morgan
PMonC, UHi

1306. ———. Saints hymnal of the Church of Jesus Christ. Monesson, Pa., Printed by Goodloe Thomas, 1923.
120p. 20cm.
Morgan
PMonC, UHi

1307. Church of Jesus Christ of Latter-day Saints. Aaronic Priesthood. The preparation, ordination and training of young men. Prepared and Issued under the direction of the General Authorities of the Church. Salt Lake City, 1922.
15p. 15½cm.
UPB, USIC

1308. ———. (same) Salt Lake City, 1925.
16p. 18cm.
UHi, UPB, USIC

1309. ———. Aaronic priesthood — Stake comparisons [n.p.] 1929.
v. charts. 29cm.
Mimeographed.
UPB September 30, 1928, March 31, June 30, 1929

1310. ———. An address; the Church of Jesus Christ of Latter-day Saints to the world. "Let facts be submitted to a candid world." Salt Lake City, Church of Jesus Christ of Latter-day Saints, April, 1907.
20p. 23cm.
"Extract from report of General Conference, April, 1904," p. 19–20.
Signed: Joseph F. Smith, John R. Winder, Anthon H. Lund.
CSmH, NN, UHi, UPB, USIC, UU

1310a. ———. (same, in Danish) En officiel erklaering af det første praesident-skab over Jesu Kristi Kirke af Sidste-Dages Hellige enstemmigt vedtaget i General Konferencen in Salt Lake City, den 5te April 1907. [Kobenhavn? ca1907]
20p.? 20½cm.
Copy defective, lacks p. 11 to end.
USIC

1311. ———. An address: The Church of Jesus Christ of Latter-day Saints to the world. Salt Lake City, 1907.
19, 26, 56p. 22½cm.
With this is bound Ministerial Association's Review of Mormon address to the world (26p.) and answer to Ministerial Association Review by B. H. Roberts (56p.)
Text signed: Joseph F. Smith, John R. Winder, Anthon H. Lund.
"In behalf of the Church of Jesus Christ of Latter-day Saints, March 26, 1907. Adopted by vote of the Church, in General Conference, April 5, 1907."
Also bound with cover title: Recent discussion of Mormon affairs. UPB, USIC. *See also Roberts, Brigham Henry.*
CSmH (Imperfect), CtY, CU–B, MH, UPB, USIC, WHi

1312. ———. Affidavits and certificates disproving the statements and affidavits contained in John C. Bennett's letters. Nauvoo, Ill., August 31, 1842.
2p. 39cm.
Bennett's letters had been published mostly in the *Sangamo Journal.* They became the basis of his *History of the Saints.*
Byrd 702
USIC

1313. ———. The Alberta Temple. Cardston, Alberta, Cardston News Print. [1923?]
8p. 14½cm.
USIC

1314. ———. Alberta Temple, Cardston, Canada. Dedication Ceremonies. Aug. 26, 1923. [Cardston, Cardston Review Print. 1923]
[4]p. 18cm.
UHi, USIC

1315. ———. . . . The Apostolic Age. Prepared and issued under the direction of the General Authorities of the Church. Salt Lake City, 1912.
[3]–40p. 23cm. (Course of study for the Quorums of the Priesthood. Church of Jesus Christ of Latter-day Saints. Teachers. Third Year)
UPB, USIC

CHURCH OF JESUS CHRIST OF LATTER-DAY SAINTS

1316. ———. (same) Salt Lake City, 1916.
103p. 19cm. (Course of study for the Priesthood of the Church of Jesus Christ of Latter-day Saints. Teachers. 1916)
Issued previously in 1911–1912.
UPB, USIC

1317. ———. Articles of association. [Salt Lake City, 187–]
32p. 18cm.
Form for United Order incorporations.
First printed in a 19p. edition. UPB. Pages added to 32p.
USIC

1318. ———. (same) [Salt Lake City, 1874]
40p. 18cm.
"Extracts from a letter from St. George, August 2nd, 1874."
CN, CtY, NjP, UPB, USIC

1319. ———. (same) United order — Articles of Association. Form used for articles of Association of various United Orders and by-laws and rules to be observed by members. Salt Lake City, 1874.
40p. 18cm.
Variant printing.
USIC

1320. ———. The Articles of faith applied. Prepared and issued under the direction of the General Authorities of the Church. Salt Lake City, 1912.
72p. 22cm. (Course of study for the Quorums of the Priesthood, Church of Jesus Christ of Latter-day Saints. Elders.)
UPB, USIC

1321. ———. . . . Book of Mormon. Prepared and issued under the direction of the General Authorities of the Church. Salt Lake City, 1910.
[3]–103p. 21½cm. (Course of study for the Quorums of the Priesthood, Church of Jesus Christ of Latter-day Saints. Deacons. Second Year.)
UPB, USIC

1322. ———. Brigham Young, Trustee in Trust of the Church of Jesus Christ of Latter-day Saints, Plaintiff in error, vs. William S. Godbe. In error to the Supreme Court of the Territory of Utah. [Washington? 1870?]
17p. 22cm.
Civil suit brought again Brigham Young as Trustee in Trust.
USIC

1323. ———. [Broadside in double columns, under date Nauvoo, September 24, 1845, reply to the Quincy Committee by the "council of the authorities of the Church of Jesus Christ of Latter Day Saints, at Nauvoo.] Text begins: Whereas a council of the Church of Jesus Christ of Latter Day Saints. . . . [Nauvoo, 1845]
Broadside. 30×13½cm.
CtY, ICHi

1324. ———. Bulletin compiled from reports of the year 1920. [Salt Lake City, 1920]
21p. 21cm.
Statistics of 1918–1920.
USIC

1325. ———. By-laws of the corporation of the members of the Church of Jesus Christ of Latter-day Saints . . . [Salt Lake City, 188–?]
4p. 15½cm.
Caption-title.
NjP, USIC

1326. ———. A Call to the women of the church. [Salt Lake City, 1916]
[2]p. 25½cm.
Includes letter from the First presidency, dated September 22, 1916, and signed by Joseph F. Smith, Anthony H. Lund, Charles W. Penrose. Circular signed by Committee on the General Boards of the Relief Society, Young Ladies' Mutual Improvement Association, Primary Association.
USIC

1327. ———. Catalogue of publications of the Church of Jesus Christ of Latter-day Saints for sale at the Deseret News Office. Salt Lake City, 1883.
[4]l. 16½cm.
UPB, USIC

1328. ———. (same) Salt Lake City, 1884.
[8]p. 20cm.
Cover-title.
CU–B, NjP, NN

1329. ———. (same) Salt Lake City, 1887.
[8]p. 16cm.
USIC, WHi

1330. ———. (same) Salt Lake City, 1889.
[12]p. 15½cm.
Cover-title.
NjP, UHi

1331. ———. (same) [Liverpool, Printed at the "Millennial Star" Office, 1890?]
[2]p. 22cm.
"Articles of faith" on verso.
USIC

1332. ———. Catalogue of works published by the Church of Jesus Christ of Latter-day Saints, and for sale by F. D. Richards, at their General Repository, and "Millennial Star" Office . . . [Liverpool, Printed by J. Sadler] June, 1855.
4p. 22cm.
USIC

1333. ———. (same) [Liverpool, Printed by R. James, 1856]
4p. 22½cm.
USIC

CHURCH OF JESUS CHRIST OF LATTER-DAY SAINTS

1334. ———. (same) [Liverpool, Printed by R. James, 1857]
4p. 22cm.
Only copy found in possession of Peter Crawley.

1335. ———. [Catechisms. Salt Lake City, Juvenile Instructor Print., 189–?]
6 cards. 16–18½cm.
Each card is a catechism on a particular subject. i.e. The Church, Book of Mormon, prayer, angels, etc.
CtY, NjP

1336. ———. Centennial conference announcement . . . April 1930. Salt Lake City [1930]
32p. 19½cm.
UPB

1337. ———. Church organization and history. Prepared and issued under the direction of the General Authorities of the Church. Salt Lake City, 1909.
[3]–114p. 18½cm. (Course of study for the quorums of the Priesthood . . . High Priests. First Year)
UHi, UPB, USlC

1337a. ———. Circular of instructions. Settlement of tithes for the year 1890. To the presidents of stakes, bishops of wards and stake tithing clerks in Zion: Brethren. — We forward you blanks for the rendering of your annual statements of the tithes . . . Salt Lake City, 1890.
4p. 22cm.
Signed: Wilford Woodruff, Geo. Q. Cannon, Jos. F. Smith, First Presidency, and the Presiding Bishopric.
Dated: December 10, 1890.
USlC

1337b. ———. Circular of instructions. Settlement of tithes for the year 1891. To the presidents of stakes, bishops of wards and stake tithing clerks in Zion: Brethren. — We forward you blanks for the rendering of your annual statements of the tithes . . . Salt Lake City, 1891.
4p. 21½cm.
Signed: Wilford Woodruff, Geo. Q. Cannon, Jos. F. Smith, First Presidency, and the Presiding Bishopric.
Dated: December, 1891.
USlC

1338. ———. A circular, of the High council. To the members of the Church of Jesus Christ of Latter-day Saints, and to all whom it may concern: Greeting. [Nauvoo, 1846]
Broadside. 30×24cm.
Signed by Samuel Bent, James Allred [and 10 others]
In ornamental border.
Dated: Jan. 20, 1846.
A call for members to leave for the Rocky Mountains; grievances against the residents of Illinois.
CtY, UPB, USlC

1339. ———. Circular to the whole Church of Jesus Christ of Latter Day Saints. [Nauvoo, 1845]
Broadside. 42×29cm.
In four columns.
First meeting in the Temple, October 5, 1845 and extract from the minutes of a general conference . . . Oct. 6th, 7th, & 8th, 1845. Minutes signed by Brigham Young.
Also includes lists of men in charge of companies leaving Nauvoo in the Spring.
Byrd 945
ICHi, USlC

1340. ———. Communication on dress. [Salt Lake City, 1917?]
[3]p. 18cm.
UPB

1341. ———. Comparative report — Elders quorums. [Salt Lake City, n.d.]
v. charts. 29cm.
Mimeographed.
UPB 1927, 1928

1342. ———. A complete answer to the false charges of the Utah Commission. There is no union of Church and State. [Salt Lake City, Star Print. 1892?]
12p. 20cm.
Official statements of Church leaders to refute the Utah Commission.
USlC

1343. ———. Conference-convention song folder, 1923. Compliments of the General Boards of the Auxiliary Organizations of the Church of Jesus Christ of Latter-day Saints. [Salt Lake City, 1923]
8p. 19½cm.
USlC

1344. ———. Conference [report] of the Church of Jesus Christ of Latter-day Saints. Salt Lake City, 1880, 1897–
v. annual; semi-annual. 22cm.
The 1880 report under title "The Year of Jubilee." Semi-annual from 1897.
CSmH, NjP, UHi, ULA, UPB, USlC

1345. ———. A copy of this should be given to each family, or individual having temple work to do . . . [Salt Lake City, 1921?]
[4]p. 24cm.
UHi

1346. ———. Course of study. [Salt Lake City, 1909?]
15p. 19½cm.
Outlines of study for each quorum of the priesthood.
USlC

CHURCH OF JESUS CHRIST OF LATTER-DAY SAINTS

1347. ———. Deacons. [Biography — Old Testament] Prepared and issued under the direction of the General Authorities of the Church. Salt Lake City, 1909.
71p. 19cm. (Course of study for the Quorums of the Priesthood, Church of Jesus Christ of Latter-day Saints. Deacons)
UPB, USIC

1348. ———. (same) Salt Lake City, 1923.
60p. 18cm. (Course of study for the quorums of the Priesthood. Church of Jesus Christ of Latter-day Saints. Deacons)
UPB

1349. ———. Deacons [manual] Prepared and issued under the direction of the General Authorities of the Church. Salt Lake City, 1924.
73p. 18cm. (Course of study for the Quorums of the Priesthood, Church of Jesus Christ of Latter-day Saints. Deacons)
Deacons' duties and lives of Biblical characters.
USIC, UPB

———. Deseret News Extra containing a revelation on Celestial Marriage. *See Church of Jesus Christ of Latter-day Saints. Minutes of conference . . .*

1350. ———. Divine authenticity of the Book of Mormon. Duties of Elders. Prepared and issued under the direction of the General Authorities of the Church. Salt Lake City, 1909.
124p. 19cm. (Course of study for the Quorums of the Priesthood of the Church of Jesus Christ of Latter-day Saints. Elders)
UPB, USIC

1351. ———. . . . Divine Mission of the Savior. Prepared and issued under the direction of the General Authorities of the Church. Salt Lake City, 1910.
[3]–91p. 21½cm. (Course of study for the Quorums of the Priesthood. Church of Jesus Christ of Latter-day Saints. Priests. Second year)
UPB, USIC

1352. ———. Duties and principles from the Doctrine and Covenants and modern revelation. Prepared and issued under the direction of the General Authorities of the Church. Salt Lake City, 1910.
100p. 21cm. (Course of study for the Quorums of the Priesthood, Church of Jesus Christ of Latter-day Saints. Elders)
UPB, USIC

1353. ———. Duty stories from the Book of Mormon. Prepared and issued under the direction of the General Authorities of the Church. Salt Lake City, 1922.
[3]–45p. 19cm. (Course of study for the Deacons Quorums of the Church of Jesus Christ of Latter-day Saints)
UPB, USIC

1354. ———. The educational system of the Church of Jesus Christ of latter day saints. [n.p., 1913?]
32p. illus., ports. 19½cm.
Cover-title.
CSmH, DLC, ICJ, UHi, USIC

1355. ———. Experiences in the lives of early Church leaders and members. Prepared and issued under the direction of the General Authorities of the Church. Salt Lake City, 1913.
130p. 22cm. (Course of study for the Quorums of the Priesthood of the Church of Jesus Christ of Latter-day Saints. Deacons. 4th year)
UPB, USIC

1356. ———. (same, under title) Experiences of early church leaders and members. Prepared and issued under the direction of the General Authorities of the Church. Salt Lake City, 1916.
124 [1]p. 19cm. (Course of study for the Quorums of the Priesthood of the Church of Jesus Christ of Latter-day Saints. Deacons. 1916)
UPB, USIC

1357. ———. Fathers and sons annual outing. Summer, 1923. [Salt Lake City] 1923.
[8]p. illus. 23cm.
UPB

1358. ———. Fiftieth birthday anniversary, General Boards of Women's Organizations of the Church of Jesus Christ of Latter-day Saints. June 19, 1880 — June 19, 1930. [Salt Lake City] 1930.
[4]p. 25cm.
UHi

1359. ———. The first hundred years; a century of progress of the Church of Jesus Christ of Latter-day Saints. [Salt Lake City, Deseret News Press, 1930?]
31 [1]p. illus. 19cm.
Cover-title.
NjP, UHi, UPB, USIC

1360. ———. First principles of the true gospel of Christ. [Liverpool? 189–?]
4p. 21cm.
CU–B

1361. ———. For family or individual, having Temple work to do. Salt Lake City [n.d.]
[4]p. 22½cm.
Instruction for temple genealogy.
UPB

———. General Conference of the Church of Jesus Christ of Latter-day Saints. *See Church of Jesus Christ of Latter-day Saints. Conference [report]*

1362. ———. Gospel teachings illustrated by biographical incidents. Prepared and issued under the General Authorities of the Church. Salt Lake City, 1919.
[3]–96p. 19cm. (Course of study for the Quorums of the Priesthood of the Church of Jesus Christ of Latter-day Saints. Deacons. 1919)
UPB, USIC

1363. ———. Grand jubilee-[in the]-new Tabernacle, Salt Lake City, on the Twenty-fourth of July, 1877. Celebrating the entrance of the Pioneers into this Territory . . . [Salt Lake City, J. C. Graham & Co., Printers, 1877]
[4]p. 22cm.
Caption-title.
Programme.
MH

———. Guide for conference visitors. *See Church of Jesus Christ of Latter-day Saints. Bureau of Information.*

1364. ———. A guide for quorums of the Melchizedek Priesthood . . . First Edition. Salt Lake City, Published under authority of the Council of the Twelve Apostles of the Church of Jesus Christ of Latter-day Saints by the Deseret Book Company, 1928.
91p. 19cm.
For general use of the priesthood for the year.
UHi, USIC

1365. ———. (same) 3d ed. Salt Lake City, Deseret Book Company, Reprinted 1930.
91p. 18cm.
UPB, USIC

———. Handbook of instructions for stake presidents. *See Church of Jesus Christ of Latter-day Saints. Instructions to presidents* [*etc.*]

1366. ———. "He that readeth, let him understand." [Cripplegate, Printed by Bt [sic] Briscoe, n.d.]
[4]p. 19cm.
"The faith and doctrines of the Latter-day Saints, with scriptural proofs." The 14 articles of faith (signed) Joseph Smith.
"To be had of Edmund C. Brand, at the Office, 35, Jewin Street, City [sic]
CSmH

———. History of the Church of Jesus Christ of Latter-day Saints. *See Smith, Joseph, 1832–1914.*

1367. ———. History of the gospel. Prepared and issued under direction of the General Authorities of the Church. Salt Lake City, 1910.
4p.l. [9]–96p. 21cm. (Course of study for the Quorums of the Priesthood, Church of Jesus Christ of Latter-day Saints. High Priests)
UPB, USIC

1368. ———. House of the Lord. Historical and descriptive sketch of the Salt Lake Temple from April 6, 1853, to April, 1893. Complete guide to the interior, and explanatory notes — Other temples of the Saints. Also the dedicatory prayer. Salt Lake City, Deseret News Publishing Co., 1893.
36p. illus., ports., plates. 21cm.
MH, NN, ULA, USIC

1369. ———. (same) Salt Lake City, G. Q. Cannon & Sons Co., 1897.
36p. port. 20½cm.
MiU, NN

1370. ———. "In Consequence of the sickness . . ." [Salt Lake City, 1887?]
Broadside. 36×28cm.
Report of meetings due to sickness of Brigham Young and other meetings up to 1887.
USIC

1371. ———. In the case of the Church of Jesus Christ of Latter-day Saints vs. Joseph Leslie Broadbent. [Salt Lake City, 1929?]
30p. 19cm.
A polygamy excommunication trial.
MoInRC, NN, UHi, USIC, UU

1372. ———. In the realm of quorum activity. Suggestions for Quorums of the Melchizedek Priesthood. Published under authority of the Council of the Twelve Apostles. Independence, Mo., Zion's Printing and Publishing Company, 1929.
109p. 18cm.
UPB, USIC

1373. ———. (same) 3d ed. Independence, Mo., Zion's Printing and Publishing Company, 1930.
109p. 19cm.
USIC

1374. ———. Incidents from the lives of our Church leaders. Prepared and issued under the direction of the General Authorities of the Church. Salt Lake City, 1914.
136p. 23cm. (Course of study for the Quorums of the Priesthood, Church of Jesus Christ of Latter-day Saints. Deacons. 1914)
UPB, USIC

1375. ———. (same) Salt Lake City, 1917.
[3]–115p. 19cm. (Course of study for the Quorums of the Priesthood of the Church of Jesus Christ of Latter-day Saints. Deacons. 1917)
UPB, USIC

1376. ———. (same) Salt Lake City, 1920.
116p. 19cm. (Course of study for the Quorums of the Priesthood of the Church of Jesus Christ of Latter-day Saints. Deacons. 1920)
UPB

CHURCH OF JESUS CHRIST OF LATTER-DAY SAINTS

1377. ———. (same) Salt Lake City, 1927.
116p. 19cm. (Course of study for the Quorums of the Priesthood of the Church of Jesus Christ of Latter-day Saints. Deacons. 1927)
Reissue of the 1920 edition.
UPB, USIC

1378. ———. Instructions on social work. [Issued by the General Boards of Relief Society, Deseret Sunday School Union, Young Men's Mutual Improvement Associations, Young Ladies' Mutual Improvement Association, Primary Associations, Religion classes. Approved by the First Presidency of the Church of Jesus Christ of Latter-day Saints] Salt Lake City, 1917.
16p. illus. 15½cm.
UPB, USIC

1379. ———. Instructions to Presidents of Stakes, Bishops of Wards, and Stake Tithing Clerks. Salt Lake City, 1899 [–1928]
14v. (No. 1–14) 16–17cm.
Cover-title #1–11.
Title varies: #2. Instructions to Presidents of Stakes, Bishops and Clerks, 1900. #3. Instructions to Presidents of Stakes and Counselors, Bishops and Counselors and Stake Tithing Clerk, 1901. #4. Annual Instructions to Presidents of Stakes and Counselors, Presidents of missions, High Councilors, Bishops and Counselors, and Stake Tithing Clerks in Zion. #5 (misnumbered #4) Annual Instructions to Presidents of Missions, Presidents of Conferences, Presidents of Branches, Clerks and Elders from Zion, 1903–4. #6 (misnumbered #5) Annual Instructions to Presidents of Stakes, and Counselors, High Counselors, Bishops and Counselors, and Stake Tithing Clerks in Zion, 1903–4. #7 (misnumbered #6) Annual Instructions to Presidents of Stakes and Counselors, High Counselors, Bishops and Counselors, and Stake Tithing Clerks in Zion, 1904. #8 (misnumbered #7) Annual Instructions to Presidents of Stakes, and Counselors, High Counselors, Bishops, and Counselors and Stake Tithing Clerks in Zion, 1905. #9 (misnumbered #8) Annual instructions to Presidents to Stake, and counselors, Bishops and Counselors, Stake Tithing Clerks and General Authorities in Zion, 1906. #10. Annual Instructions to Presidents of Stakes, and Counselors, Presidents of Missions, Bishops and Counselors, Stake, Mission and Ward Clerks and all church authorities, (circular #10) 1909. #11 (misnumbered #12) Circular of Instructions to Presidents of Stakes and counselors, Presidents of Missions, Bishops and counselors, Stake, Mission, and Ward Clerks and all Church Authorities, 1913. #12 (misnumbered #13) Instructions to Bishops and counselors, Stake and ward clerks, 1921. #13. Instructions to Bishops and Counselors, Stake and ward clerks. 2d ed. 1923. #14. Handbook of Instructions for Bishops and Counselors, Stake and Ward Clerks of the Church of Jesus Christ of Latter-day Saints. 1928.
UPB, USIC

1380. ———. Instructions to stake and ward committees on recreation. [Salt Lake City, n.d.]
[3]p. 20cm.
UPB

1381. ———. Instructions of the Bishops. [G. S. L. City, U. T., 1859]
7p. 19½cm.
Signed: Brigham Young. Trustee in Trust for the C. of J. C. of L. D. S. General Tithing Office. G. S. L. City, U. T. November 23, 1859.
Instruction on transaction of tithing business.
USIC

1382. ———. Jesu Kristi Kirke av de siste Dages Hellige. 100 Ars Jubileum. [Oslo, Braute & Søns, 1930]
13 [2]p. illus., plates, ports. 15½×21cm.
The centennial of the founding of the Church.
Title in English: Church of Jesus Christ of Latter day Saints. 100 year jubilee.
UU

1383. ———. July twenty-fourth. Pioneer day, also, Our year of Jubilee. Grand historical celebration. Salt Lake City, Deseret News Print. 1880.
[4]p. 21cm.
Orders of march and programs.
CU-B, MH

1384. ———. The Latter-day prophet. Book of questions for instructors only. Prepared and issued under the direction of the General Authorities of the Church. Salt Lake City, 1912.
48p. 22cm. (Course of study for the Quorums of the Priesthood, Church of Jesus Christ of Latter-day Saints. Deacons)
UPB, USIC

1385. ———. The Latter-day prophet. Prepared and issued under the direction of the Central [sic] Authorities of the Church. Salt Lake City, 1918.
3–64p. 19½cm. (Course of study for the Quorums of the Priesthood of the Church of Jesus Christ of Latter-day Saints. Deacons. 1918)
UPB

1386. ———. Latter-day Saints seminaries and American education. [Salt Lake City, 1928?]
Broadside. 56×45cm.
Historical development and list of seminaries, 1927–28.
USIC

1387. ———. The Latter-day Saints church office building . . . [Salt Lake City, Deseret Book Company, 192 ?]
[8]p. illus.
UHi, USIC

1388. ———. L.D.S. program for ward teaching. [n.p., n.d.]
[4]p. 18½cm.
USIC

CHURCH OF JESUS CHRIST OF LATTER-DAY SAINTS

1389. ———. Latter-day Saint temples. [Salt Lake City, Deseret News Press, n.d.]
[16]p. illus. 23cm.
CU-B, UPB

1390. ———. Lesson outlines for the Melchizedek Priesthood classes for the year 1925, to be used with "A study of the Articles of Faith" by James E. Talmage. Salt Lake City, Deseret Book Company, 1925.
14p. 17cm.
Cover-title.
UPB, USlC

1391. ———. [Letter to citizens of Quincy, Ill. relating the intention of the Mormons to emigrate the next spring, dated Nauvoo, Sept. 24, 1845. Nauvoo, Ill., 1845]
Broadside. 28×13cm.
Signed: Brigham Young, Pres. Willard Richards, Clerk.
CtY, USlC

1392. ———. Life of Christ. Prepared and issued under the direction of the General Authorities of the Church. Salt Lake City, 1910.
90p. 21cm. (Course of study for the Quorums of the Priesthood, Church of Jesus Christ of Latter-day Saints. Teachers.)
UPB, USlC

1393. ———. (same) Salt Lake City, 1914.
90p. 23cm. (Course of study for the Quorums of the Priesthood, Church of Jesus Christ of Latter-day Saints. Teachers. 1914)
Reissue of the 1910 edition.
UPB

1394. ———. (same) Salt Lake City, 1915.
96p. 16cm. (Course of study for the Quorums of the Priesthood, Church of Jesus Christ of Latter-day Saints. Teachers. 1915)
USlC

1395. ———. (same) Salt Lake City, 1917.
96p. 17cm. (Course of study for the Quorums of the Priesthood, Church of Jesus Christ of Latter-day Saints. Teachers. 1917)
Reissue of the 1915 edition.
USlC

1396. ———. (same) Salt Lake City, 1922.
96p. 19cm. (Course of study for the Quorums of the Priesthood, Church of Jesus Christ of Latter-day Saints. Teachers. 1922)
Reissue of the 1915 edition.
UPB

1397. ———. (same) Salt Lake City, 1925.
96p. 18cm. (Course of study for the Quorums of the Priesthood, Church of Jesus Christ of Latter-day Saints. Teachers. 1925)
Reissue of the 1915 edition.
UPB, USlC

1398. ———. "The Lord's law of health." [Salt Lake City, 193?]
[8]p. 11½cm.
UHi

1399. ———. Manifesto of the presidency and apostles, issued December 12, 1889. Also, the official declaration or manifesto, by President Wilford Woodruff, prohibiting further plural marriages, and its adoption by the General Conference, October 6, 1890. Salt Lake City, The Deseret News [1890?]
4p. 20cm.
Cover title.
Manifesto also published in 1889 under tittle: Official declaration.
CSmH, CtY

1400. ———. The message of the ages; a sacred pageant commemorating the one hundredth anniversary of the organization of the Church of Jesus Christ of Latter-day Saints . . . [Salt Lake City, Deseret News Press, c1930]
48p. illus., ports. 25cm.
DLC, NjP, ULA, UPB, USlC

1401. ———. Minutes of conference. A special conference of the elders of the Church of Jesus Christ of Latter-day Saints, assembled in the Tabernacle, Great Salt Lake City, August 28th, 1852, 10 o'clock a.m., pursuant to public notice . . . Great Salt Lake City, U.T., September 14, 1852.
48p. 13×21½cm.
At head of title: Deseret news — Extra. Great Salt Lake City, U.T., September 14, 1852.
Contains addresses by Brigham Young, Orson Pratt, H. C. Kimball, John Taylor, and others; includes the official announcement of the doctrine of plural marriage.
CtY, ICN, MH, NjP, NN, UHi, USlC

1401a. ———. (same, under title) A special conference of the Elders of the Church of Jesus Christ of Latter-Day-Saints, assembled in the Tabernacle, Great Salt Lake City, August 28, 1852 . . . [Great Salt Lake City, 1852]
48p. 20½cm.
Deseret News Extra, Sept. 14, 1852.
Variant printing.
USlC

1402. ———. (same, under title) Deseret News extra containing a revelation on Celestial marriage, a remarkable vision, two discoveries, delivered by President Brigham Young. One discourse by Elder Orson Pratt; remarks by Elders H. C. Kimball, John Taylor and others. St. Louis, Mo., Reprinted for H. S. Eldredge [1852?]
48p. 21cm.
Cover-title.
MH

1403. ———. (same) Liverpool, Edited by S. W. Richards . . . 1853.
64p. 22½cm.
Printed as a supplement to the *Millennial Star*, V. 15.
MH, UPB

1404. ———. Minutes of the General Conference held at Great Salt Lake City, April 6, 1850. [Salt Lake, Print., 1850]
9–20p. 19cm.
Signed: Thomas Bullock, Clerk of Conference.
Possibly printed to be published with the Third General Epistle, printed April 12. p. 1–8.
NjP, USIC

1405. ———. Minutes of the semi-annual meeting of Ward Bishoprics, Ward clerks and supervisors of Aaronic Priesthood quorums. Held in the Assembly Hall. Salt Lake City, 1928–1929.
2v. 21cm.
UPB

1406. ———. Names of the presidency and bishops of the Church of Jesus Christ of Latter-day Saints and organized stakes of Zion. John Taylor, President and Trustee-in-trust . Edward Hunter, Presiding Bishop, Leonard W. Hardy and Robert T. Burton, Counselors. [Salt Lake City? 1881?]
Broadside. 63×50cm.
Imprint date inferred from textual information.
CSmH

1407. ———. The New Testament. Issued under direction of the Council of the Twelve Apostles. [Salt Lake City] 1924.
178p. 19cm. (Manual for the Melchizedek Priesthood classes. 1924)
UPB, USIC

1408. ———. Notice. A public meeting will be held at the Seventies Hall tomorrow (Saturday) at 2:00 P.M., for the purpose of selecting suitable persons as candidates . . . Friday, July 26, 1844. [Nauvoo, 1844]
Broadside. 32×24cm.
Meeting to choose suitable candidates for the Mormon people in the upcoming elections.
Byrd 888
USIC

1409. ———. Office building of the Church of Jesus Christ of Latter-day Saints, Salt Lake City, Utah. [Salt Lake City, 192?]
[10]p. col. plates. 12cm.
UHi

1410. ———. Official declaration. [Salt Lake City, 1889]
3p. 21½cm.
Caption-title.
A denial of the stock charges against the Church and declaration on polygamy.
Signed: Wilford Woodruff and others . . . Presidency . . . Members of the Councils of the Apostles . . . [and] Counselors [of the Church of Jesus Christ of Latter-day Saints]
CtY, CU-B, ICN, MH, NjP, UHi, UPB, USIC

1411. ———. (same) [Salt Lake City, 1890]
[2]p. 11cm.
Signed: Wilford Woodruff.
USIC

1412. ———. Official program. Pioneer Day celebration, July 24th, 1912. Liberty Park, Salt Lake City. This pamphlet contains valuable historic information furnished by Prof. Levi Edgar Young, of the University of Utah. [Salt Lake City, 1912]
8p. 19cm.
MH

1413. ———. Official souvenir program and directory. Grant pioneer day celebration. Monday, July 15th, 1904. All day at Liberty Park. [Salt Lake City] Deseret News, 1904.
30p. 14½cm.
Cover title.
Itinerary of events, list of Pioneers of 1847 still living.
MH

1414. ———. Old Testament history. Prepared and issued under the direction of the General Authorities of the Church. Salt Lake City, 1913.
92p. 22cm. (Course of study for the Quorums of the Priesthood of the Church of Jesus Christ of Latter-day Saints. Teachers. 4th year)
Issued again in 1915.
USIC, UPB

1415. ———. (same) Salt Lake City, 1920.
104p. 19cm.
UPB, USIC

1416. ———. Organ recitals in the tabernacle, Salt Lake City, Utah. Given under the direction of the First Presidency of the Church of Jesus Christ of Latter-day Saints. Salt Lake City, 1915–
v. 18cm.
Programs.
USIC inc.

1417. ———. An outline study of the principles of the gospel. Designed for Quorum instructors and auxiliary class teachers of the Church of Jesus Christ of Latter-day Saints. Salt Lake City, Published by the General Boards of the Auxiliary Organizations of the Church, 1922.
4p.l., 12–100p. 19cm.
CU-B, USIC

1418. ———. Pertinent facts on Utah's loyalty and war record. Salt Lake City, 1918.
24p. 18cm.
UHi

CHURCH OF JESUS CHRIST OF LATTER-DAY SAINTS

1419. ———. The pioneer home. [Salt Lake City, 192?]
Broadside. 21×15cm.
Caption-title.
UHi

1420. ———. Preamble and resolutions unanimously adopted at semi-annual conference of the Mormon Church held at Salt Lake City, Utah, October 6, 1891. Washington, 1891.
clxxi p. [1]l. 22½cm.
From Messages and documents. 1891. Report of the Secretary of the Interior. Appendix H.
ULA, UPB

1421. ———. The Priesthood: Old testament history. Prepared and issued under the direction of the General Authorities of the Church. Salt Lake City, 1909.
116p. 19cm. (Course of study for the Quorums of the Priesthood, Church of Jesus Christ of Latter-day Saints. Teachers)
UPB, USIC

1422. ———. (same) Salt Lake City, 1923.
112p. 17½cm. (Course of study for the Quorums of the Priesthood, Church of Jesus Christ of Latter-day Saints. Teachers. 1923)
UPB

1423. ———. [Priesthood conventions and Priesthood conferences] 1923–
v. 30cm.
Title varies.
USIC has 1923, 1925–1930.

1424. ———. Principles of the Gospel. Prepared and issued under the direction of the General Authorities of the Church. Salt Lake City, 1911.
108p. 22cm. (Course of study for the Quorums of the Priesthood, Church of Jesus Christ of Latter-day Saints. High Priests. Third year)
UPB, USIC

1425. ———. (same) 2d ed. Salt Lake City, 1912.
108p. 22cm.
USIC

1426. ———. Proclamation. To Col. Levi Williams . . . Nauvoo, 1845.
Broadside. 16×8cm.
Signed by Brigham Young and others. Concerning the Mormons' decision to leave Nauvoo. Dated: Sept. 16, 1845.
USIC

1427. ———. Program. Auxiliary group conventions; program held in connection with regular quarterly conferences. [Salt Lake City] 1921–1930.
10v. 19½cm.
UPB 1923; USIC inc.; UU 1921–1930

1428. ———. Program of one-day conventions of the Y.M. and Y.L.M.I.A. and Religion Classes for 1921 . . . [Salt Lake City] 1921.
[4]p. 20cm.
USIC

1429. ———. Program of the dedicatory services of the Arizona Temple of the Church of Jesus Christ of Latter-day Saints. Held in Mesa, Arizona, October 23rd to October 26th, 1927. [Mesa, Arizona, 1927]
16p. illus., plates. 23cm.
UHi, UPB, UU

1430. ———. Programme of exercises, rendered by a solemn assembly on Pioneer Day in the large tabernacle commemorating the entrance of the Pioneers into the Great Salt Lake Valley, July 24, 1847. Salt Lake City, Deseret News Co., 1886.
8p. 17½cm.
Cover-title.
At head of title: July 24, 1847–July 24, 1886.
Brief description of pioneers, Articles of faith, etc.
CU-B, MH, USIC, UU

1431. ———. Programme of the singing exercises for the dedication of the Manti Temple. Monday, May 21st, 1888. [n.p., 1888]
[4]p. 17½cm.
Cover-title.
MH

1432. ———. Questions to be asked the Latter Day Saints. [Salt Lake City, 1856?]
Broadside. 40×37cm.
Issued in connection with the reformation begun in the fall of 1856.
UHi, ULA, UPB, USIC

1432a. ———. Record Keeping. To presidents of stakes and missions, bishops of wards, and other presiding authorities. Dear Brethren: At a meeting of the First Presidency and Twelve Apostles . . . Salt Lake City, 1902.
4p. 23½cm.
Signed: Anthon H. Lund, Rudger Clawson, Andrew Jenson, Committee on Records.
The establishing of a Record Day in the church.
Dated: February 1, 1902.
UPB, USIC

1433. ———. [Reply to the Quincy Committee by the council of the authorities of the Church of Jesus Christ of Latter Day Saints, at Nauvoo] [Nauvoo, 1845]
Broadside. 30×13½cm.
Signed: September 24, 1845.
CtY, ICHi

1434. ———. [Restoration of the gospel and church history. Duties of Priests] Prepared and issued under

the direction of the General Authorities of the Church. Salt Lake City, 1909.
ix [10]–147p. 19cm. (Course of study for the Quorums of the Priesthood, Church of Jesus Christ of Latter-day Saints. Priests)
UPB, USIC

1435. ———. Rules that should be observed by members of the United Order. Salt Lake City, Printed at the Deseret News Printing Establishment [187–?]
Broadside. 50×30cm.
Fourteen rules.
USIC

1436. ———. The sacredness of parenthood. [Salt Lake City? 192?]
16p. 19cm.
Cover-title.
Includes articles and poetry by John Taylor, Rosetta Wallace Bennett, Ruth May Fox, and others.
UHi

1437. ———. De sande vidners liv og Laerdomme i Jesu Christi Kirke af Sidste Dages Hellige. [Kjøbenhavn, Udgivet af Sidste Dages Hellige i Jesu Kristi Kirke. Trykt hos F. E. Bording, ca. 1904]
8p. 18cm.
Title in English: The life of the true witnesses.
USIC

1438. ———. Scandinavian jubilee album. Issued in commemoration of the fifteenth anniversary of the introduction of the gospel to the three Scandinavian countries by Elder Erastus Snow and fellow laborers. [Salt Lake City, Press of the Deseret News, 1900]
3p.l., 239p. illus., ports. 16½×26cm.
Preface signed by Anthon H. Lund, Andrew Jerson, J. M. Sjodahl, C. A. F. Orlob.
NjP, NN, UHi, ULA, UPB, USIC, UU

1439. ———. Un Siècle de l'Evangile quelques événnements et quelques doctrines que sont époque. Traduit de l'Anglais par Anna Arthaud et Oscar Frieden. Cours d'études pour l'Association d'Amélioration des Jeunes Gens dans la Mission Francaise de l'Eglíse de Jésus-Christ des Saints des Derniers Jours. Pour l'Annèe 1929–1930. Liège, Publié par l'Eglise de Jésus-Christ des Saints des Derniers Jours, 1930.
94p. 20cm.
Title in English: A century of the gospel.
USIC

———. A special Conference of the Elders of the Church. *See Minutes of Conference.*

1440. ———. Study for the Melchizedek Priesthood and Priests. Church of Jesus Christ of Latter-day Saints. 1916. "Jesus the Christ" By Elder James E. Talmage of the Quorum of the Twelve. Prepared and Issued Under the Direction of the General Authorities of the Church. Salt Lake City, 1916.
[3]–56p. 20cm.
A study guide only.
NjP, UPB

1441. ———. (same) Salt Lake City, 1916.
[3]–56p. 20cm.
Variant printing.
UPB, USIC

1442. ———. Suggested program for ward celebrations of the one-hundredth anniversary of the message of Moroni to the Prophet Joseph Smith. [Salt Lake City, 1923]
[8]p. 23cm.
UPB

1443. ———. Suggestions for quorums of Priesthood and M.I.A. Salt Lake City, Published by the General Authorities of the Church of Jesus Christ of Latter-day Saints, 1928.
42p. 18cm.
UPB, USIC

1444. ———. Suggestive lines of activity and principles and conduct for quorums of priesthood. June–July–August, 1928. Salt Lake City, 1928.
16p. 19cm.
UPB, USIC

1445. ———. Temple ordinances essential. [n.p., n.d.]
[4]p. 23cm.
"Publication authorized by the President of the Church."
UPB

———. The testimony of the "great prophet of the nineteenth century." *See Smith, Joseph, 1805–1844.*

1446. ———. Thirtieth anniversary; Grand jubilee in the new tabernacle, Salt Lake City, on the Twenty-fourth of July, 1877, celebrating the entrance of the pioneers into this Territory . . . [Salt Lake City, J. C. Graham & Co., 1877]
[4]p. 19½cm.
Caption-title.
UHi

1447. ———. To the bishops and members of the Church of Jesus Christ of Latter-day Saints, residing in the various settlements throughout these mountains. [Salt Lake City, 1876]
2p. 35½cm.
Caption-title.
Signed and dated at end: Brigham Young, John W. Young, Daniel H. Wells, [and others] Salt Lake City, U. T. 25th October, 1876.
USIC

CHURCH OF JESUS CHRIST OF LATTER-DAY SAINTS

1447a. ———. To the presidency and bishopric of —— stake. Dear Brethren: We enclose you herewith an order covering your requisition on account of Charity "Contingent Fund" . . . Salt Lake City, 1891.
3p. 28cm.
Signed: Wilford Woodruff, George Q. Cannon, Joseph F. Smith, and the Presiding Bishopric.
Concerning the payment of fast offerings.
Dated: June 1st, 1891.
USIC

1448. ———. To the Presidents, Bishop's agents and bishops of the several stakes and wards of Zion . . . Salt Lake City, 1883.
4p. 20½cm.
Signed: John Taylor, Leonard W. Hardy, and Robert T. Burton. December 10, 1883.
USIC

1448a. ———. To the presidents, bishop's agents and bishops of the several stakes and wards of Zion: Dear Brethren. In making the annual settlement of the tithes and offering of the people, . . . Salt Lake City, 1887.
4p. 21cm.
Signed: Wilford Woodruff, Wm. B. Preston.
Concerning the annual settlement of tithes and offerings.
Dated: December 13th, 1887.
USIC

1448b. ———. Trustee-in-trust's and presiding bishop's office, To the presidents, bishop's agents and bishops of the several stakes and wards of Zion: Brethren: The immense amount of labor involved . . . Salt Lake City, 1884.
4p. 23cm.
Signed: John Taylor, Trustee-in-Trust, and Wm. B. Preston, Presiding Bishop.
Concerning more condensed methods in keeping and reporting tithing settlement accounts.
Dated: December 10th, 1884.
USIC

1449. ———. The truth about the "Mormons." [Independence, Mo., Press of Zion's Printing and Publishing Co., 1922]
[4]p. 16cm.
NN, UHi, UPB

1450. ———. The Twelve Apostles . . . The Seven Presidents of the Seventy Elders . . . [Kirtland? 1836?]
Broadside. 31×20cm.
Printed between the organization of the Twelve Apostles in 1835 and the apostasy of John F. Boynton in 1837.
List of members.
USIC

———. United States Government Officials commend colonization work of Mormon Church . . . *See United States Government Officials . . .*

———. Vision and faith of the Latter-day Saints. Addresses delivered . . . *See United States Government Officials. . . .*

1451. ———. Ward teaching program of the Church. [n.p., n.d.]
25p. 28cm.
USIC

1452. ———. What the priest should know and do. Prepared and issued under the direction of the General Authorities of the Church. Salt Lake City, Deseret News, 1913.
44p. 22cm. (Course of study for the Quorums of the Priesthood, Church of Jesus Christ of Latter-day Saints. Priests. 4th year)
UPB, USIC

1453. ———. (same) Salt Lake City, Deseret News, 1915.
84p. 19cm. (Course of study for the Quorums of the Priesthood. Priests. 1915)
UPB

1454. ———. . . . Whereas a council of the authorities of the Church of Jesus Christ of Latter-day Saints . . . "communicate in writing our disposition and intention at this time, particularly with regard to moving . . ." . . . [Nauvoo, 1845]
Broadside. 28½×13½cm.
Signed: By order of the Council. Brigham Young, prest. Willard Richards, clerk. The Mormons' plans to leave the city would be more successful if harassment stopped.
Dated: Nauvoo, September 24, 1845.
Byrd 946
CtY, ICHi, USIC

1455. ———. The year of jubilee. A full report of the proceedings of the Fiftieth Annual Conference of the Church of Jesus Christ of Latter-day Saints, held in the large tabernacle, Salt Lake City, Utah, April 6th, 7th, and 8th, A.D. 1880. Also, a report of the exercises in the Salt Lake Assembly Hall, on the Sunday and Monday just preceding the conference. Reported by George F. Gibbs and John Irvine. Salt Lake City, Deseret News Printing and Publishing Establishment, 1880.
2p.l. [5]–110p. 21½cm.
CSmH, CtY, CU-B, ICN, MH, NN, UHi, UPB, USIC, UU

1456. Church of Jesus Christ of Latter Day Saints, *Appellant.* The Late Corporation of the Church of Jesus Christ of Latter-day Saints, et. al., Appellants, v. The United States. No. 1423. George Romney, Henry Dinwoody, James Watson and John Clark, Appellants v. The United States. No. 1457. Appeals from the Supreme Court of Utah Territory. Brief and argument for appellants . . . [Washington, 1888?]
120p. 22½cm.
At head of title: In the Supreme Court of the United States. October Term. 1888.
UPB

CHURCH . . . . BUREAU OF INFORMATION

1457. ———. The Late Corporation of the Church of Jesus Christ of Latter-day Saints; No. 1031. George Romney et. al. vs. the United States. No. 1054. [Washington? 1889]
80p. 22cm.
At head of title: In the Senate of the United States. October term. 1889.
USIC

1458. Church of Jesus Christ of Latter-day Saints. Bureau of Information. Salt Lake City. The following quotations are inscribed on the balcony panels of the Church of Jesus Christ of Latter-day Saints Museum, on Temple Square . . . [Salt Lake City, 192?]
Broadside. 17½×11cm.
Caption-title.
UHi

1459. ———. Illustrated souvenir. Salt Lake City, Utah. Salt Lake City [n.d.]
2p.l. plates, ports. 17½×23cm.
Tourist information with plates and some church history.
USIC

1460. ———. In honor of the pioneers. A monument unveiled at Pioneer View, July 25th, 1921. Proceedings, speeches and oration at the spot where Brigham Young stopped to view the valley, and where he exclaimed, "This is the place." Salt Lake City, Bureau of Information, 1921.
26p. illus. 17cm.
UHi, UPB, USIC

1461. ———. Information for tourists. [Salt Lake City, Magazine Printing Co., 1902]
8p. fold. illus. 15cm.
CSmH, USIC

1462. ———. The Latter-day Saints' Museum at Salt Lake City . . . [Salt Lake City, 192?]
Broadside 17½×11cm.
Caption-title.
UHi

1463. ———. Official conference guide. Salt Lake City, 1909–1930.
v. illus. 20cm.
Earlier editions under title: Guide for conference visitors.
UHi 1923; UPB 1927; USIC 1909, 1911, 1920–30; UU 1921–26.

1464. ———. A parting word; "trip around temple block." Salt Lake City, Bureau of Information [190?]
24p. illus., port. 17cm.
MoInRC, NN, UPB, USIC

———. Truths for truth seekers on Utah and the Mormons. *See Goddard, Benjamin.*

1465. ———. Utah and her people; information for tourists. Salt Lake City [1903]
[32]p. illus. 11×15cm.
A tourist brochure given out at Temple Square, Salt Lake City.
CSmH, DLC, NjP, UPB, USIC

1466. ———. Utah; its people, attractions, resources and institutions. Compiled from authentic information and latest reports. [Chicago, Printed at the Press of H.C. Ellen and Co., 1905]
63 [1]p. 17cm.
UPB, USIC

1467. ———. (same) Salt Lake City [1907]
2p.l., 5–61 [3]p. illus. 17cm.
UHi, UPB, USIC

1468. ———. (same) Salt Lake City [1908]
62p. illus. 17cm.
UHi

1469. ———. (same) Salt Lake City [1909]
94p. illus. 17cm.
USIC

1470. ———. (same) Salt Lake City [1910]
2p.l. [5]–94 [2]p. illus. 17cm.
Printer's device: Wheat design.
UPB

1471. ———. (same) Salt Lake City [1911]
2p.l. [5]–93 [3]p. illus. 17cm.
Printer's device: Wheat design.
UPB, USIC

1472. ———. (same) Salt Lake City [1912]
2p.l. [5]–94 [2]p. illus. 17cm.
Printers' device: Oak tree design.
Cover-title: Utah
UHi, UPB, USIC

1473. ———. (same) Salt Lake City [1913]
2p.l. [5]–96p. illus. 17cm.
Printer's device: Laurel wreath design.
UHi, UPB, USIC, UU

1474. ———. (same) Salt Lake City [1914]
2p.l. [5]–77 [3]p. illus. 17cm.
Printer's device: Sego lily bouquet photograph.
UPB, USIC

1475. ———. (same) Salt Lake City [1915]
1p.l. [5]–79p. illus. 18cm.
Printer's device: Sego lily bouquet photograph.
UHi, UPB, USIC, UU, WHi

1476. ———. (same) Salt Lake City [1916]
93 [1]p. illus. 17cm.
UPB, USIC

CHURCH. . . . BUREAU OF INFORMATION

1477. ———. (same) Salt Lake City [1917?]
91p. illus. 18½cm.
USlC

1478. ———. (same) Salt Lake City [1918]
1p.l. [5]–91 [3]p. illus. 18cm.
Inset of great seal of Utah on title-page.
CSmH, UPB, USlC

1479. ———. (same) Salt Lake City [1919]
95 [1]p. illus. 18cm.
CSmH, UHi, USlC

1480. ———. (same) Salt Lake City [1920]
2p.l. [3]–95 [1]p. illus. 17cm.
Inset of Great Seal of Utah on title page.
UHi, UPB, USlC

1481. ———. (same) Salt Lake City [1921]
95 [1]p. illus. 18cm.
USlC

1482. ———. (same) Salt Lake City [1923]
1p.l. [5]–95 [1]p. illus. 18cm.
Inset of Great Seal of Utah on title-page.
Text and illustration printed in green.
UHi, UPB, UU

1483. ———. (same) Salt Lake City [1925]
99 [1]p. illus. 18cm.
UPB, USlC

1484. ———. (same) Salt Lake City [1926]
98 [2]p. illus. 18cm.
UHi, USlC

1485. ———. (same) Salt Lake City [1927]
91 [1]p. illus. 18cm.
UPB

1486. ———. (same) Salt Lake City [1929?]
98 [2]p. illus. 18½cm.
USlC

1487. ———. (same) Salt Lake City [1930]
2p.l. [5]–98 [2]p. illus. (part. col.) 18cm.
Cover-title: Utah; the tourists guide.
UPB, USlC

1488. ———. (same) Salt Lake City [n.d.]
90 [6]p. illus. 17cm.
USlC

1489. ———. (same) Salt Lake City [n.d.]
78 [2]p. illus. 18cm.
USlC

1490. ———. (same) Salt Lake City [n.d.]
93 [1]p. illus. 18cm.
USlC

1491. ———. (same) Salt Lake City [n.d.]
97p. illus. 18cm.
USlC

1492. Church of Jesus Christ of Latter-day Saints. Centennial Celebration Committee. The Mormon century book. The romantic story of one hundred year's achievement. [Salt Lake City] The Pioneer Centennial Publishing Committee, 1930.
50p. 30½cm.
UPB

1493. ———. One hundred years, 1830–1930; centennial celebration of the organization of the Church of Jesus Christ of Latter-day Saints, beginning April 6, 1930. [Salt Lake City] H. J. Grant, c1930.
115p. illus., ports. 30½cm.
CSmH, CU–B, MoInRC, NjP, NN, UHi, ULA, UPB, USlC, UU

1494. Church of Jesus Christ of Latter-day Saints. Church Music Committee. Choristers' manual; a brief course of instruction in the art of choral conducting. Prepared by the Church Music Committee for the use of the choristers of the Church of Jesus Christ of Latter-day Saints. Salt Lake City, Deseret Book Company, 1927.
3p.l. [7]–82p. 23cm.
Joseph Smith on "Worship music," p. 73.
USlC, UU

1495. ———. Deseret Anthems. Salt Lake City, Deseret Book company [T.A. Hooper, 1926?]
3v. words and music. 26½cm.
V. 1. Six anthems selected from the publications of Novello and Company . . .
V. 2. Ten original anthems by L.D.S. composers.
V. 3. Reprints of favorite anthems by L.D.S. composers.
ULA, USlC

1496. ———. (same) No. 2. Sixteen original anthems by Latter-day Saint composers. Salt Lake City, T. A. Hooper, c1926.
1v. 27cm.
Variant printing of V. 2 of above.
USlC

1497. ———. Latter-day Saints Music Bulletin. July, 1921–April, 1929.
12 nos. irregularly. 21½cm.
No. 11–12 combined.
No. 1 has title *L.D.S. Music Bulletin.*
USlC

1498. Church of Jesus Christ of Latter-day Saints. Committee on Personal Welfare. Suggestions for Melchizedek Quorum Committees. [Salt Lake City] 1929.
5p. 19cm.
USlC

CHURCH. . . . COUNCIL OF THE TWELVE APOSTLES

1499. Church of Jesus Christ of Latter-day Saints. Correlation Committee. Teacher-training. A guide to the proceeding of each auxiliary organization, giving the nature of the work in each of the four monthly meetings. [Salt Lake City] Published by the Correlation Committee of the Church, 1920.
12 [2]p. 23cm.
UPB

1500. Church of Jesus Christ of Latter-day Saints. Council of the Twelve Apostles. Circular from the Twelve Apostles: To the presidents of stakes and bishops of the several wards. April 16, 1880. Salt Lake City, 1880.
4p. 24cm.
Caption-title.
Signed: John Taylor, in behalf of the Council of Apostles.
CU–B, UPB, USlC

1501. ———. Circular of the Twelve, and Trustees in Trust. An epistle of the Twelve of the Church of Jesus Christ of Latter-day Saints in all the world. Greeting . . . Nauvoo, January 22, 1845.
Broadside. 50×30cm. (Times and Seasons. Extra. January 14, 1845)
Need for renewed vigor to build the temple, etc.
USlC

1501a. ———. (same).
Broadside. 38×31cm.
Times & Seasons — Extra. Nauvoo, January 22, 1845.
Signed: Brigham Young Pres't, Willard Richards Clerk.
Includes: To whom it may concern, from the Trustees in Trust . . .
In four columns.
UPB, USlC

1502. ———. An epistle of the Council of the Twelve Apostles of the Church of Jesus Christ of Latter-day Saints, read Oct. 10, 1887, at the general semi-annual conference, held in Salt Lake City. [Salt Lake City] The Deseret News Co., Printers [1887]
16p. 21½cm.
Cover-title.
Signed: Wilford Woodruff in behalf of the Twelve Apostles. General epistle.
CSmH, CtY, CU–B, DLC, NjP, UHi, UPB, USlC

1503. ———. An Epistle of the Twelve, to the Church of Jesus Christ of Latter-day Saints, in its various branches and conferences in Europe, Greeting: [Nauvoo, 1842]
Broadside. 47×30cm.
Need to have the offerings sent to Nauvoo.
Signed: March 20, 1842.
USlC

1504. ———. Epistle of the Twelve Apostles and counselors of the Church of Jesus Christ of Latter-day Saints in all the world. [Salt Lake City, 1877]
4p. 23cm.
Concerning the death of Brigham Young and the presidency of the Church. General epistle.
CSmH, CtY, DLC, NjP, USlC

1505. ———. Epistle of the Twelve Apostles and counselors to the Church of Jesus Christ of Latter-day Saints in all the world. [Salt Lake City, 1878]
4p. 23cm.
Caption-title. General epistle.
CU–B, DLC, MH, NjP, NN, USlC

1506. ———. An Epistle to the members of the Church of Jesus Christ of Latter-day Saints. [Salt Lake City, 1888]
16p. 21cm.
Signed: Wilford Woodruff.
After death of John Taylor it was difficult getting the Quorum together to choose a new president.
USlC

1507. ———. General epistle from the Council of the Twelve Apostles, to the Church of Jesus Christ of Latter-day Saints abroad, dispersed through the early, greeting. [St. Louis, 1848]
8p. 21½cm.
Caption-title.
At foot of p. 8: Written at Winter Quarters, Omaha nation, west bank of Missouri River, near Council Bluffs, North America, and signed December 23d, 1847, in behalf of the Quorum of the Twelve Apostles. Brigham Young, president. Willard Richards, clerk.
Sent to St. Louis & printed in mid January, according to letter of Brigham Young, cf. Streeter, T. W. *Americana-beginnings.*
W–C 160
CSmH, CtY, CU–B, DLC, ICN, MH, UPB, USlC

1508. ———. (same) [Liverpool, Printed by R. James, 1848]
8p. 22½cm.
Caption-title.
CtY, CU–B, NjP, UHi, UPB, USlC

1509. ———. (same, in Welsh) Annerchiad y deuddeg apostol, yn eglwys Iesu Grist; Saint y dyddiau diweddaf. At holl frenhinoedd y ddaear, at Raglaw, ac at Llwiawdwyr unol daleithiau yr Amerig, ac at Lywyddion, a holl bobl y byd. Rhydybont, Cyfieithwyd a Chyhoeddwyd Gan Capt. Jones, Argraffwyd gan John Jones [1845]
12p. 18cm.
Signed: Rhagfyr las, 1845. D. J.
CSmH, USlC

1510. ———. The "Great proclamation"; or, "Trumpet message," of the authority of God. Liverpool, L.D.S. Printing, Publishing and Emigrating Co., J. F. Smith [188–?]
4p. 21cm.
Caption-title.
Signed: N.
CSmH, DLC, UPB, USlC

CHURCH. . . . COUNCIL OF THE TWELVE APOSTLES

1511. ———. Proclamation of the Twelve Apostles of the Church of Jesus Christ of Latter-day Saints. To all the kings of the world; to the President of the United States of America; to the governors of the several states and to the rulers and peoples of all nations . . . [New York, Prophet Office, 1845?]
16p. 23cm.
Caption-title.
Dated at end: New York, April 6, 1845.
Written by Parley P. Pratt.
CU–B, MBAt, MH, MoInRC, NN, USlC

1512. ———. (same) [Liverpool, Published by Wilford Woodruff, James and Woodburn, 1845]
16p. 20½cm.
Caption-title.
CSmH, CtY, CU–B, ICN, MH, MoInRC, N, NjP, NN, UHi, UPB, USlC

1513. ———. Suggestions for Melchizedek Quorum Committees. Committee on class instruction. [Salt Lake City] 1929.
4v. 19cm.
UPB

1514. Church of Jesus Christ of Latter-day Saints. Department of Education. Advantages of Church School Education. [Salt Lake City, n.d.]
[4]p. 23cm.
USlC

1515. ———. Circular of the General Board of Education, Church of Jesus Christ of Latter-day Saints. Salt Lake City, From the press [of] G. Q. Cannon & Sons Co., 1889–1897.
4–9 nos. 20–22cm.
No indication as to the nature of the first three circulars.
CSmH 4, 6, 8; MH 6–9; NjP 8; UPB 4–8; UU 4, 6–8

1516. ———. Circular of instructions of the General Board of Education of the Church of Jesus Christ of Latter-day Saints. Salt Lake City, 1911.
1p.l., 29 [1]p. 19cm.
USlC

1517. ———. (same) Salt Lake City, 1915.
39 [1]p. 19cm.
UHi, USlC

1518. ———. A handbook for the officers and teachers in the religion classes of the Church of Jesus Christ of Latter-day Saints. Salt Lake City, Published for the General Board of Education by the Deseret Book Co., 1924.
60p. 18cm.
USlC

1519. ———. A handbook for the officers and teachers in the religion classes of the Church of Jesus Christ of Latter-day Saints. 1–8 grades. [Salt Lake City, The General Board of Education, Deseret Book Company, 1925]
118p. 18cm.
Binder's title.
UHi, UPB

1520. ———. How we learn. [Salt Lake City, General Church Board of Education, 1923]
3p.l. [7]–108p . 19cm. (Teacher-training outline, 1923)
CU–B, USlC

1521. ———. Introduction to a study of the Book of Mormon. Prepared especially for use in the schools of the Church of Jesus Christ of Latter-day Saints. Salt Lake City, Published by the authority of the General Church Board of Education, 1914.
62 [1]p. 18cm.
UPB

1522. ———. (same) [Salt Lake City] General Church Board of Education, 1917.
62 [1]p. 19cm.
USlC

1523. ———. (same) [Salt Lake City] General Church Board of Education, 1920.
62 [1]p. 19cm.
USlC

1524. ———. Department of Education. Outlines in Religious Education . . . [Salt Lake City] Published by Authority of the General Board of Education, 1907–1930.
v. 18cm.
Contents: First year: The Nephite Dispensation; 1907, 38p. (UPB); 1916, 64p. (UPB); 1917, 64p. (IWW, USlC); 1920, 62 [1]p. (USlC)
Second year: The New Testament Dispensation; 1907, 54p. (UPB); 1918, 54p. (USlC); 1921, 129p. (UPB); 1922, 248p. (USlC); 1923, 248p. (IWW, UHi, USlC); 1924, 262p. (USlC); 1925, 229p. (UPB); 1926, 229p. (UPB); 1927, 229p. (UPB).
Third year: The Old Testament Dispensation; 1907, 52p. (UPB); 1918, 52p. (IWW, UPB, USlC, UU); 1921, 162p. (USlC); 1922, 262p. (UPB); 1924, 262p. (USlC); 1925, 284p. (UPB); 1926, 284p. (USlC); Reprinted 1927, 284p. (UHi); 1928, 308p. (UPB); 1929, 308p. (UPB)
Fourth year: The Dispensation of the Fullness of time; 1907, 52p. (UPB, USlC); 1907, 64p. (USlC)
Church history and doctrine: 1921, 152p. (UPB); 1922, 238p. (UPB); 1922, 32p. (UPB, USlC); 1926, 211p. (UHi, USlC); Reprinted 1927, 211p. (UPB); Reprinted 1928, 211p. (UPB); Reprinted 1929, 211p. (USlC)
Title varies: Outlines in theology . . .

CHURCH. . . . DESERET SUNDAY SCHOOL UNION

1525. ———. An outline study of the principles of the Gospel. Salt Lake City, Deseret Book Co., 1922.
100p. 19cm. (Teaching training. 1922)
CU-B, UHi, USIC

1526. ———. Purpose and organization of the Religion Classes of the Church of Jesus Christ of Latter-day Saints. [Salt Lake City, 1922]
4p. 21cm.
USIC

1527. ———. (same) Salt Lake City [1924]
[8]p. 21½cm.
USIC

1528. ———. The purpose, plan and procedure of seminary work. [Salt Lake City, 1926]
[8]p. 19½cm.
USIC

1529. ———. Readings in method; teacher training text, 1926–27, for use in the Teacher Training Classes of the church . . . [Salt Lake City] Deseret Book Co. [1926?]
vii [9]–159p. 18cm. (Teacher training text. 1926–27)
UPB, USIC

1530. ———. Souvenir of the L.D.S. Schools. [Salt Lake City] The Deseret News [n.d.]
[16]l. plates. 14cm.
"Compliments of Horace H. Cummings, Gen. Supt. L.D.S. Schools."
MH, USIC

1531. ———. Supplementary lessons in Teacher Training. 1923–24. Salt Lake City, Published by the General Church Board of Education of the Church of Jesus Christ of Latter-day Saints, 1923.
16p. 19½cm.
UPB, USIC

1532. ———. Teacher training in the Church of Jesus Christ of Latter-day Saints. [Salt Lake City, 1923]
[4]p. 15cm.
USIC

1533. Church of Jesus Christ of Latter-day Saints. Deseret Sunday School Union. Bible and church history stories for the Primary Department of the Sunday School. Salt Lake City, 1922.
190, 164, 113p. illus., ports., facsims. 19½cm.
DLC, UPB

1534. ———. (same) 2d ed. Salt Lake City, 1925.
195p., 162p., 115p. 19½cm.
UPB

1535. ———. (same) 3d ed. Salt Lake City, 1927.
5p.l. [11]–195, 162, 115. illus. 19½cm.
UHi, USIC

1536. ———. Birth of Mormonism in picture; scenes and incidents in early church history from photographs by George E. Anderson . . . Narrative and notes by Prof. John Henry Evans. Salt Lake City [c1909]
62 [2]p. illus., ports., plates. 18×22cm.
NjP, UPB

1537. ———. Catalogue of books. [Salt Lake City] Deseret News [n.d.]
[12]p. 19cm.
USIC

1538. ———. A catalogue of books for Sunday School libraries, selected by the Committee appointed by The Deseret Sunday School Union. Salt Lake City, Deseret News [1873]
22p. 20cm.
UU

1539. ———. (same) Salt Lake City [n.d.]
12p. 19cm.
UPB, USIC

1540. ———. Concert recitations for use in the Sunday Schools of the Church of Jesus Christ of Latter-day Saints. Salt Lake City. [n.d.]
18 [1]p. 16cm.
USIC

1541. ———. Conference of the Deseret Sunday School Union. Salt Lake City, 1917–
v. 23cm.
Title varies. Program of a convention . . . also of the annual conference of the Deseret Sunday School Union, 1907; Semi-annual conference, 1922–1924; Program, annual conference, 1928.
USIC Ap. 1907, Oct. 1922, Ap. 1924, Ap. 1928.

1542. ———. Deseret Sunday School reader. First book for our little friends. Salt Lake City, Printed at the Juvenile Instructor Office, 1879.
2p.l., 44p. illus. 18½cm.
MH, USIC

1543. ———. (same) 2d ed. Salt Lake City, Juvenile Instructor Office, 1881.
2p.l., 44p. illus. 19cm.
CU-B, UHi

1544. ———. 3d ed. Salt Lake City, Juvenile Instructor Office, 1881.
2p.l., 44p. 14½cm.
CU-B

1545. ———. (same) 3d ed. Salt Lake City, Juvenile Instructor Office, 1884.
2p.l., 44p. illus. 19cm.
USIC

CHURCH. . . . DESERET SUNDAY SCHOOL UNION

1546. ———. (same) 4th ed. Salt Lake City, Juvenile Instructor Office, 1886.
2p.l., 44p. illus. 18cm.
CSmH, MH, NjP, UHi, USlC

1547. ———. Deseret Sunday School reader. Second book for our little friends. Salt Lake City, Printed at the Juvenile Instructor Office, 1880.
2p.l., 116p. illus. 19cm.
MH, NjP, USlC, UU

1548. ———. (same) 2d ed. Salt Lake City, Printed at the Juvenile Instructor Office, 1883.
2p.l., 116p. illus. 19cm.
CSmH, CU-B, UHi, USlC

1549. ———. (same) Salt Lake City, G. Q. Cannon and Sons, Co., Printers, 1892.
2p.l., 116p. illus. 18cm.
CSmH, MH, NjP, UHi, USlC, UU

1550. ———. Deseret Sunday School Union leaflets. Topical arrangement. Second Division: Life of Christ. Numbers 1 to 31. Salt Lake City [1889]
[64]p. 25cm.
UPB

1551. ———. Deseret Sunday School Union leaflets. Lessons 1 to 56 inclusive. Salt Lake City, Geo. Q. Cannon & Sons Co., 1897.
[116]p. 25cm.
NjP, UHi, UPB, USlC, WHi

1552. ———. Deseret Sunday School Union leaflets. Lessons 1 to 136 inclusive. Salt Lake City, Geo. Q. Cannon & Sons Co., 1898.
[276]p. 25cm.
UPB

1553. ———. Deseret Sunday School leaflets. Lesson No. 57 to No. 212. [Salt Lake City, Published by the Deseret Sunday School Union and by George Q. Cannon & Sons Co., 1896–1900]
lv (unnumbered leaflets) 26cm.
UPB, USlC

1554. ———. Deseret Sunday School Union leaflets. Topical Arrangement. Fifth Division: Numbers 173 to 212. Salt Lake City, Published and Issued by the Deseret Sunday School Union [1900]
80p. 24½cm.
UPB

1555. ———. Deseret Sunday School Union leaflets. Lessons 1 to 212, inclusive, with index to leaflet notes and chapter of subjects, etc. Salt Lake City, Deseret Sunday School Union, 1901.
212 leaflets. 25cm.
UHi, ULA

1556. ———. Grosse Männer der Bibel und des Buches Mormon; Ein Unterrichtsplan für die Sonntagschulen. [n.d.] Herausgegeben vom Hauptvorstand des Sonntagschulwerkes [n.d.]
2p.l., 5–32p. 18½cm.
Title in English: Great men of the Bible and the Book of Mormon.
See also under: Wunderlich, Jean.
UPB

1557. ———. Guide for the officers and teachers of Sunday Schools in the various stakes of Zion. Salt Lake City, Published by the Deseret Sunday School Union, Printed by Merchants Printing Co., 1893.
24p. 16½cm.
MH, NN, USlC

1558. ———. The intermediate Sunday School reader for the use of our little friend . . . Salt Lake City, Juvenile Instructor Office, 1888.
vii [9]–144p. illus. 18½cm.
NjP, UHi, UU

1559. ———. Jubilee history of Latter-day Saints Sunday Schools. 1849–1899 . . . illustrated. Salt Lake City, 1900.
viii [9]–546 [16]p. front., plates, ports. 23cm.
Prepared by a committee of the Deseret Sunday School Union Board.
Sixteen pages at end blank for "Sunday school and personal history memoranda."
"Edwin F. Parry has been our editor." cf. p. vi.
Report of the committee (p. [iv]–vi) signed by Joseph W. Summerhays, Thomas C. Griggs, Levi W. Richards, John M. Mills, George D. Pyper, and Horace S. Ensign.
CSmH, CU-B, DLC, NjP, NN, UHi, ULA, UPB, USlC, UU, WHi

1560. ———. The Jubilee Songster, containing original music prepared for a grand jubilee of Sunday School children, of the Salt Lake Stake. To be held in the large tabernacle, Salt Lake City, July 24th, 1885. Salt Lake City, Printed at The Juvenile Instructor Office [1885]
[14]p. 15×19½cm.
USlC

1561. ———. (same) Salt Lake City, Published by Daynes & Coalter, 1885.
[12]p. 15×19cm.
USlC

1562. ———. July Twenty-fourth celebration of Pioneer Day; also pioneer Sunday School, in the large tabernacle, commencing at 10 A.M., July 24th, 1888. [Salt Lake City] Juvenile Instructor Print., 1888.
8p. 15½cm.
At head of title: 1847–1888.
UHi, USlC

1563. ———. Latter-day Saints' Sunday School treatise. Salt Lake City, Deseret Sunday School, J. H. Parry, Printer, 1896.
124p. 19cm.
CSmH, DLC, NjP, UHi, UPB

1564. ———. (same) 2d ed. Salt Lake City, Geo. Q. Cannon & Sons Co., 1898.
vi [9]–127p. 19cm.
UHi, ULA, UPB, UU, WHi

1565. ———. Deseret Sunday School Union. Das leben Jesu für die Primarklassen. Aus dem Englischen Übersetzt von Jean Wunderlich. Basel, Herausgegeben von Fred Tadje, Präsident der Schweizerischen und Deutschen Mission der Kirche Jesu Christi der Heiligen der Letzten Tage, 1924.
68p. 21cm.
Sunday School Manual.
Title in English: The life of Christ for primary children.
USIC

1566. ———. Manner of conducting and grading of Sunday Schools. Annual statistical and financial report of Sunday Schools in various stakes of Zion, and various missions, for the year ending December 31st, 1894. And minutes of the annual Sunday School Conference, held April 8th, 1894. [Salt Lake City, 1894]
[11]p. tables. 26½cm.
UPB, USIC

1567. ———. Original songs & music, specially prepared for a grand jubilee of Sunday School children, held in the New Tabernacle, Salt Lake City, July 24th, 1874, being the 27th anniversary of the entrance of the Pioneers into Salt Lake Valley. Salt Lake City, 1874.
[11]p. 29cm.
USIC

1568. ———. Parent and child. A series of essays and lessons for use in the Parents' Department of the Latter-day Saints Sunday Schools. Appropriate also for home study. Salt Lake City [1908–1916]
3v. (224, 288, 191p.) 18cm.
Contents: V. 1. 1908. Child development, as affected by ancestors. Child development as affected by home and family. Child development as affected by self participation. V. 2. 1909. The social or pleasure side of community life. Our educational system. V. 3. 1916. Child study and training by Mosiah Hall.
CSmH, DLC v.1, NN, UHi, ULA, UPB, USIC, UU

1569. ———. (same) V. 2. Second edition. Eleventh thousand. Salt Lake City [c1909]
288p. 17cm.
Variants: Thirteenth thousand; Fourteenth thousand; Eighteenth thousand; Nineteenth thousand.
CSmH, UPB
CSmH, UPB, USIC

1570. ———. Primary Department, Bible stories; issued by the Deseret Sunday School Union, January 13, 1907–December 30, 1907. [Salt Lake City, 1907]
36 nos. 17cm.
USIC

1571. ———. Proceedings of the first Sunday School Convention of the Church of Jesus Christ of Latter-day Saints, held in the assembly hall, Salt Lake City, Monday, Nov. 28th and Tuesday 29th, 1898. Reported by Arthur Winter and Leo Hunsaker. Salt Lake City, 1899.
108p. 21½cm.
MH, UHi, ULA, USIC

1572. ———. Program of general and local jubilee celebration commemorating the establishment of the Sunday Schools of the Latter-day Saints in the Rocky Mountains . . . [Salt Lake City, 1899]
[8]p. illus. 16cm.
UPB

1573. ———. Programme District Sunday School Convention to be held in Ogden Tabernacle March 25 and 26, 1905. Weber, Box Elder, Summit and Morgan Stakes. Saturday Evening at 7:30 o'clock. . . . [Ogden? 1905]
[9]p. 23cm.
UPB

1574. ———. Questions and answers on the life and mission of the Prophet Joseph Smith. Published by the Deseret Sunday School Union. Salt Lake City, Juvenile Instructor Office, 1882.
vi, [9]–52p. 18cm. (Deseret Sunday School Catechism. No. 1)
CU–B, NjP, UPB, USIC

1575. ———. (same) Salt Lake City, George Q. Cannon and Sons Co., Publishers, 1891.
Catechism. No. 2)
MoInRC, UPB, USIC

1576. ———. . . . Recreation and play; containing extracts from magazine articles, addresses, text books, government bulletins, etc., bearing upon the subject of the recreation, play and amusements of children and young people. Compiled by the Parents' Department of the Deseret Sunday School Union. Salt Lake City [1914]
47p. 23cm. (Parents' bulletin. No. 1)
"Compiled . . . by Dr. E. G. Gowans." — Pref.
DLC, UPB

1577. ———. Report of the Sunday School Stake Board to the Stake Presidency through the Sunday School Representative on the High Council. [Salt Lake City] 1930.
Foldout pamphlet [5]p. 15cm.
UPB, USIC

CHURCH. . . . DESERET SUNDAY SCHOOL UNION

1578. ———. Restoration of the gospel. Salt Lake City, 1878.
One Card. [2]p. 18cm.
Card with questions and answers on the restoration.
NN, USlC

1579. ———. (same) Salt Lake City, 1878.
One Card [2]p. 18cm.
Variant printing.
USlC

1580. ———. Songs to be sung by the congregation at the semi-annual conference of the Deseret Sunday School Union . . . Salt Lake City, October 8th, 1906. [Salt Lake City, 1906]
[4]p. music. 22½cm.
USlC

1581. ———. Stories from the life of Christ for the Primary Department of the Sunday School. Salt Lake City, 1916.
131p. plates. 20cm.
"A compilation of outlines and suggestions to teachers, heretofore published in the *Juvenile instructor*." — Pref.
DLC, USlC

1582. ———. Stories from the Life of Christ for the Primary Department of the Sunday School. Salt Lake City, 1919.
1p.l. [2]–153p. 19cm.
UPB

1583. ———. Stories from the Old Testament for the Primary Department of the Sunday School. Salt Lake City, 1917.
232p. illus. 20cm.
USlC

1584. ———. Suggestions for topics and department work, Sunday School conventions and conferences. Salt Lake City, Arrow Press, 1917.
23p. 15½cm.
UPB

1585. ———. Sunday morning in the kindergarten. Illustrated lessons for the Kindergarten Department of the Sunday School. [Salt Lake City 1916.
3p.l., 157p. plates. 19cm.
USlC

1586. ———. Sunday morning in the kindergarten. Lessons for the Kindergarten Department of the Sunday School. First and second years. Salt Lake City, 1920.
[3]–233p., [1]l. 20cm.
"The A. L. Scoville Press, lithographers — printers, Ogden & Salt Lake."
UPB

1587. ———. (same) Salt Lake City, Published by the Deseret Book Co., 1923.
[3]–233p. 20cm.
UHi, UPB

1588. ———. (same) Salt Lake City, Published by the Deseret Book Co., 1927 [c1920]
[3]–233p. 20cm.
UHi

1589. ———. Sunday School conventions and conferences. [Salt Lake City] 1915.
v. 23cm.
NjP 1920, UPB 1915

1590. ———. Sunday School dialogues and recitations. (Number one) Designed for public and private entertainments. Salt Lake City, Printed at the Juvenile Instructor Office, 1884.
3p.l. [7]–98p. 18½cm. (No. 1)
NN, UHi, ULA USlC

1591. ———. The Sunday School handbook. [Salt Lake City, 1924?]
122p. 19cm.
UPB, USlC

1592. ———. Sunday school lessons. Vol. 1 . . . [Salt Lake City, 1928]
1v. (various pagings) 24cm.
Contents: Church History Department. Book of Mormon Department. Course A. Old Testament Department. Course B. New Testament Department. Course C. The teachings of Christ applied. Missionary Department. Department of Gospel Doctrine. Divine authority–History of the Priesthood.
UPB, USlC

1593. ———. Sunday School lessons for the Church of Jesus Christ of Latter-day Saints. Vol. 2. Salt Lake City, 1929.
lv. (various pagings) 23½cm.
Issued in unnumbered leaflets for each week's lesson.
Contents: Primary Dept. Stories from the Old Testament. Church history [From the first vision to date] New Testament "A." The life of Christ. Book of Mormon. Gospel teachings in Book of Mormon. Old Testament Dept. Prophets and prophecies of the Old Testament. Missionary Dept. Gospel Doctrine Dept. Divine authority: History of the Priesthood (continued)
UPB

1594. ———. Sunday School lessons for the Church of Jesus Christ of Latter-day Saints. Vol. 3. Salt Lake City, 1930.
1v. (various pagings) 24cm.
Issued in unnumbered leaflets for each week's lesson.
Contents: Primary Dept. Church History Dept. New Testament Dept. (Paul's journeys) Book of Mormon Dept. The divinity of the Book of Mormon.

Old Testament Dept. Missionary Dept. Gospel Doctrine Dept. The Gospel applied to daily life.
UPB

1595. ———. The Sunday School officers and teachers handbook. Salt Lake City [1928?]
3p.l. [7]–84p. 19cm.
USlC, UU

1596. ———. Sunday school outlines, Series A. Nos. 1–5. Salt Lake City [1903]
5 nos. (42, 56, 30, 33, 38p.) 19½cm.
Contents: No. 1. Kindergarten and primary departments. No. 2. First and second intermediate departments. No. 3. Theological department, 1st and 2nd years.
UPB, WHi

1597. ———. (same) [Salt Lake City, 1905?]
5 nos. (43, 56, 31, 33, 38p.) 19cm.
Revised edition.
UPB, USlC

1598. ———. Sunday School outlines . . . Series B. Nos. 1–5. Salt Lake City [1903]
5 nos. (42, 56, 30, 33, 38p.) 19½cm.
The same lessons as in Series A.
UPB, USlC

1599. ———. (same) [Salt Lake City, 1907]
10 nos. (35, 35, 40, 42, 44, 42, 42, 38, 42, 52p.) 20cm.
MH, UPB

1599a. ———. A tribute of respect to the memory of Elder L. John Nuttall. Adopted by the Deseret Sunday School Union Board, April 4, 1905. [Salt Lake City, 1905]
[9]l. port. 15×20cm.
USlC

1600. ———. Words of the songs to be sung at the grand jubilee of Sunday School children, held in the new tabernacle, Salt Lake City, July 24th, 1875, being the twenty-eighth anniversary of the entrance of the pioneers into Salt Lake Valley. [Salt Lake City, 1875?]
12p. 16cm.
MH, USlC, UU

1601. Church of Jesus Christ of Latter-day Saints. Deseret Sunday School Union. Hymnal. Danish.
Sange til brug for de sidste-dages helliges søndagsskoler. København, Udgivet og forlagt af C. H. Lund. Trykt hos F. E. Bording, 1898.
38 [2]p. 18cm.
112p. 10cm.
USlC

1602. ———. (same) København, Udgivet og forlagt af Andreas Peterson, 1900.
112p. 10cm.
USlC

1603. ———. (same) København, Udgivet og forlagt af J. Christiansen, 1916.
2p.l. [5]–116 [3] 32p. 12½cm.
UPB, USlC, UU

1604. ———. (same) København, Udgivet og forlagt af J. Christiansen, 1916.
2p.l. [5]–116 [3]p. 12½cm.
Variant printing without the final "Tillaeg" 32p.
USlC

1605. ———. **Deseret Sunday School Union. Hymnal. Dutch.** Zondagsschool-liederen voor de Kerk van Jezus Christus van de Heiligen der Laatste Dagen in de Nederlandsche Zending. Vierde druk. Rotterdam, Uitgegeven door John P. Lillywhite, 1922.
71p. 12cm.
USlC

1606. ———. **Deseret Sunday School Union. Hymnal. English.** Children's hymn book. For use in the Sunday Schools of the Church of Jesus Christ of Latter-day Saints. Salt Lake City, 1896.
2p.l. [5]–221 [7]p. 12½cm.
Without music.
MH, MoInRC, NN, UPB

1607. ———. (same) 2d ed. Salt Lake City, 1897.
222p. 12½cm.
NN, ULA, USlC

1608. ———. (same) 3d ed. Salt Lake City, 1899.
2p.l. [5]–226 [14]p. 12½cm.
Without music.
NN, RPB, UPB, USlC

1609. ———. Deseret Sunday School music book. Containing a large collection of choice pieces for the use of Sunday Schools. Salt Lake City, 1884.
2p.l. [100]p. music. 16½×21cm.
CU-B, MH, NN, ULA, UPB, USlC

1610. ———. Deseret Sunday School Union music book, containing a large collection of choice pieces for the use of Sunday Schools. 2d ed. Salt Lake City, 1884.
2p.l., 100p. 16½×21cm.
IWW, MH, NjP, NN, RPB, USlC, UU

1611. ———. (same) 3d ed. Salt Lake City, Juvenile Instructor Office, 1888.
2p.l., 100p. 16½×20½cm.
Words and music.
CSmH, NjP, UHi, USlC

1612. ———. Deseret Sunday School song book. A collection of choice pieces for the use of Sunday Schools and suitable for other occasions. Salt Lake City, 1892.
viii [9]–200p. music. 14×17cm.
With the music.
UHi, UPB, USlC, UU

1613. ———. (same) Salt Lake City, Printed by G. Q. Cannon and Sons Co., 1894.
viii [9]–200p. music. 14×17cm.
MH, USIC

1614. ———. (same) Salt Lake City, 1899.
viii [1] 10–216p. music. 14×18cm.
"3d edition"
NN, WHi

1615. ———. (same) Salt Lake City, 1901.
4p.l. [9]–216p. music. 13×17cm.
"4th edition."
UPB, USIC, UU

1616. ———. (same) Salt Lake City, 1901.
5p.l. [9]–216p. 13×17cm.
"5th edition"
USIC

1617. ———. (same) [6th edition] Salt Lake City, 1903.
8p.l. [9]–220p. music. 13×17cm.
UPB, USIC, UU

1618. ———. (same) [7th edition] Salt Lake City, 1904.
8p.l. [9]–220p. music. 12½×17cm.
USIC, UU

1619. ———. (same) [8th edition] Salt Lake City, 1905.
8p.l. [9]–220p. music. 13×17cm.
With music.
UHi, USIC, UU

1620. ———. (same) Salt Lake City, 1905.
8p.l. [9]–220p. music. 13×17cm.
Preface to 6th ed dated January 1, 1905.
USIC

1621. ———. (same) [9th edition] Salt Lake City, 1906.
8p.l. [9]–220p. music. 13×17cm.
UPB, USIC

1622. ———. (same) 10th edition. Salt Lake City, 1908.
8p.l. [7]–220p. music. 13×17cm.
UPB, USIC

1623. ———. Deseret Sunday School songs. For the use of Sunday Schools and suitable for Primary Associations, Religion Classes, Quorum meetings, social gatherings and the home. Independence, Mo., Zions' Printing and Publishing Co., c1909.
295 nos. 20½cm.
Issued in several printings.
IWW, MB, MH, MoInRC, RPB, USIC, UU, WHi

1624. ———. (same) 2d ed. Independence, Mo., Zion's Printing and Publishing Co., c1909.
296 nos. [5]p. 21cm.
No. 296 added to an earlier edition.
USIC

1625. ———. (same) Salt Lake City, Published by Deseret Book Company [c1909]
32p. 20½cm.
Several printings with minor variations.
UPB, USIC

1626. ———. Hymns and sacred songs, designed for the use of the children of the Latter-day Saints. Salt Lake City, 1888.
2p.l. [5]–254 [2]p. 12½cm.
Without music.
IWW, MH, UPB, USIC

1627. ———. Latter-day Saints' Sunday School hymn book; the word companion of the Deseret Sunday School song book . . . 4th edition. Salt Lake City, 1901.
226 [14]p. 12cm.
Words only.
PPAMS, USIC, UU, WHi

1628. ———. (same) 5th edition. Salt Lake City, 1903.
230 [14]p. 12cm.
USIC

1629. ———. (same) 6th edition. Salt Lake City, 1906.
231 [14]p. 12cm.
Words only.
USIC

1630. ———. (same) 7th edition. Salt Lake City, 1908.
2p.l. [5]–231 [14]p. 12cm.
USIC

1631. ———. **Deseret Sunday School Union. Hymnal. German.** Der Zions-Sänger. Eine Sammlung von Sonntagsschulliedern für Heiligen der letzten Tage der Deutschen und der Schweizerischen Mission, sowie aller Länder, wo die deutsche Sprache gebraucht wird. Gesammelt und frei bearbeitet vom Aeltesten Richard T. Haag. Herausgegeben von der "Stern." Berlin, 1900.
100p. 19cm.
Without music.
UPB

1632. ———. (same) Zurich, 1904.
100p. 19cm.
Without music.
UPB

1633. ———. Deseret Sonntagschullieder für die Heiligen der letzten Tage. Fünfte vergrösserte Auflage. Basel, Herausgegeben von Hyrum W. Valentine, 1912.
vii [8]–128p. 13½cm.
Words only.
USlC

1634. ———. (same, under title) Deseret Sonntagschulliederbuch für die Schweiberische U. Deutsche Mission der Kirche Jesu-Christe der Heiligen der letzten Tage. Zweite Auflage mit Noten. Schweizerische U. Deutsche mission. Basel, 1921.
3p.l., 106 nos. 17cm.
USlC

1635. ———. (same) Dritte Auflage mit Noten. Basel, Herausgegeben von Fred Tadje, Präsident der Schweizerischen und Deutschen Mission, 1923.
viii, 178p. 17cm.
UPB, USlC, UU

1636. ———. (same) Vierte Auflage mit Noten. Basel, Herausgegeben von Fred Tadje, Präsdent der Schweizerischen und Deutschen Mission, 1925.
viii, 178p. 17cm.
UPB, USlC, UU

1637. ———. (same) Fünfte Auflage mit Noten. Dresden, Herausgegeben von der Deutsch-Österrechischen Mission, und Basel, Der Schweizerisch-Deutschen Mission, 1930.
viii, 178p. 17cm.
UPB

1638. ———. **Deseret Sunday School Union. Hymnal. Swedish.** Sånger till bruk för de sista dagars heliges söndagsskolor. Första upplagan. Köpenhamn, Udgifven och förlagd af Andrea Peterson, 1899.
103 [3]p. 10½cm.
Words only.
USlC

1639. ———. (same) Andra upplagan. Köpenhamn, Utgifven och Förlagd af Andreas Peterson, 1900.
104 [3]p. 11cm.
Words only.
UHi, USlC

1640. ———. (same) Tredje upplagan. Stockholm, Utgiven och förlagd av Gideon N. Hulterström, 1923.
137 [4]p. 10½cm.
Words only.
USlC

1641. Church of Jesus Christ of Latter-day Saints. First Council of the Seventy. An epistle. Salt Lake City, Jan. 25th, 1888.
4p. 21cm.
Signed: H. S. Eldredge, In behalf of the First Seven Presidents of the Seventies. General epistle.
USlC

1642. ———. An epistle of the First Seven Presidents of the Seventies to the Presidents and members of the respective quorums in Zion and throughout the world. [Salt Lake City? 1886?]
4p. 16½cm.
MH, UHi, UPB

1643. ———. An epistle to the seventies. Salt Lake City, 1888.
4p. 21cm.
Signed: July 25th, 1888, by H. S. Eldredge.
UHi, USlC

1644. ———. Instructions to the presidents of quorums of Seventies . . . Salt Lake City, 1857.
Broadside. 27½×20cm.
Signed: Joseph Young [and others] dated March, 1857, by Robert Campbell, General Clerk.
Missionary work.
UHi

1645. ———. Seventies' hand book of instructions. [Salt Lake City] Issued by the First Council of the Seventy, 1904.
2p.l. [5]–32p. 16cm.
UHi, USlC, UU

1646. ———. To the Presidents and members of Seventies. Salt Lake City, December 1, 1880.
4p. 21cm.
Answers to questions on gospel subjects.
USlC

1647. ———. To the Presidents of the ——— Quorum of Seventies. Salt Lake City, March, 1891.
4p. 21½cm.
At head of title: Seventies' Council Rooms . . .
General epistle. The need for new seventies, missionary work, etc.
USlC

1648. ———. To the Presidents of the ——— Quorum of Seventies. Salt Lake City, September, 1892.
4p. 21½cm.
At head of title: Seventies' Council Rooms . . .
General epistle.
USlC

1649. ———. To the presidents of the Quorum of Seventy, Dear Brethern: . . . Salt Lake City, 1907.
4p. 27½cm.
A letter to the seventies quorums in relation to creating better working conditions in the quorums.
Signed: Seymour B. Young. July 12, 1907.
NjP, UPB

CHURCH. . . . FIRST PRESIDENCY

1650. Church of Jesus Christ of Latter-day Saints. First Presidency. An address to the Latter-day Saints in the Rocky Mountain region, and throughout the world. [Salt Lake City, 1885]
4p. 21cm.
Dated: July 24, 1885.
Signed: John Taylor, George Q. Cannon.
CU–B, UPB, USIC

1651. ———. An address to the members of the Church of Jesus Christ of Latter-day Saints. [Salt Lake City, 1882]
6p. 20½cm.
Caption-title.
Concerning the Edmunds law.
Signed: John Taylor, Geo. Q. Cannon, Jos. F. Smith, August 29, 1882.
CU–B, NjP, UPB, USIC

1652. ———. An address to the officers and members of the Church of Jesus Christ of Latter-day Saints. [Salt Lake City, ca. 1893]
[2]p. 29cm.
In anticipation of the dedication of the temple.
UPB

1653. ———. Bishop Hunter, Dear Brother . . . Salt Lake City, 1868.
Broadside. 25×19cm.
Letter addressed to Bishop Hunter concerning the sending of teams to meet the saints immigrating from Europe at the terminus of the Union Pacific Railroad. Dated March 10, 1868, signed by Brigham Young, Heber C. Kimball, Daniel H. Wells.
USIC

1654. ———. Ett budskap från det Första Presidentskapet i Jesu Kristi kyrka av de Sista Dagars Heliga. Stockholm, Svenska Missionen, 1930.
xiv [1]p. 22cm.
At head of title: 1830 Etthundraårs jubileum 1930.
Title in English: An official declaration from the First Presidency . . .
UPB, USIC

1655. ———. A call to the women of the Church. Salt Lake City, 1916.
[2]p. 25½cm.
Request for more work through the auxiliaries to cut down indecency of attire, etc.
USIC

1655a. ———. Circular from the First Presidency in relation to religion classes in public school buildings. To the presidents of stakes, bishops of wards and superintendents of religion classes: In answer to inquiries . . . [Salt Lake City, 190–?]
[2]p. 24½cm.
Signed: Joseph F. Smith, John R. Winder, Anthon H. Lund, First Presidency.
In relation to the holding of religion classes in public school buildings.
USIC

1656. ———. Circular. To Bishop Edward Hunter, and the Bishops throughout the territory. [Salt Lake City, n.d.]
7p. 19½cm.
Outfitting church wagon trains.
USIC

1657. ———. Circular. To the presidents, bishops, and their counselors, and all the brethren in the various branches of the Church in the Valleys of the Mountains. [Salt Lake City, 1854?]
Broadside. 31½×20cm.
Published between April 6, 1854 (Calling of J. M. Grant as counselor on death of Willard Richards) and Dec. 1, 1856 (death of Jedediah M. Grant)
It was probably printed before Ebenezer Hanks gave financial assistance to the San Bernardino project in 1855.
Aid for the San Bernardino colonization.
UPB, USIC, USID

1658. ———. Circular of the First Presidency of the Church of Jesus Christ of Latter-day Saints to the presidency of the various stakes of Zion, to the bishops of the different wards, and to all the officers and members of the Church: greeting. [Salt Lake City, 1877]
10p. 23cm.
Dated: Salt Lake City, July 11, 1877.
Church organization, school, etc.
CSmH, CtY, CU–B, DLC, MH, NN, UHi, UPB, USIC, UU

1658a. ———. Dear Brother: Owing to some confusion that has existed in the past in relation to recommending young men . . . Salt Lake City, 1903.
Broadside. 28×21½cm.
Signed: Jos. F. Smith, John R. Winder, Anthon H. Lund.
Dated: Aug. 10, 1903.
Concerning careful selection of missionaries.
USIC

1658b. ———. Dear Brethren: We have been pained quite frequently of late, when perusing . . . Salt Lake City, 1897.
3p. 82cm.
Signed: Wilford Woodruff, Geo. Q. Cannon, Jos. F. Smith.
Dated: Salt Lake City, Utah, Nov. 20, 1897.
Concerning the honorability of men sent to the mission fields.
UPB

1659. ———. Dedicatory services, Bishops Building. January 27, 1910. [Salt Lake City, 1910]
[10]p. illus. 15cm.
USIC

1660. ———. Declaration and defense. The Church of Jesus Christ of Latter-day Saints to the World. Greeting. [Salt Lake City, 1907?]
51p. 30½cm.

CHURCH. . . FIRST PRESIDENCY

Begins the same as "An address. The Church of Jesus Christ of Latter-day Saints to the World."
Probably a working copy.
USIC

1661. ———. An epistle of the First Presidency to the Church of Jesus Christ of Latter-day Saints in general confreence assembled [March, 1886] [Salt Lake City, 1886?]
19p. 21cm.
Caption-title.
Signed: John Taylor, George Q. Cannon.
Epistle concerning polygamy.
CSmH, CU-B, ICHi, ICN, UPB, USIC

1662. ———. An epistle of the First Presidency, to the Church of Jesus Christ of Latter-day Saints, in General Conference assembled. Read April 6th, 1886 at the Fifty-sixth General Annual Conference, held at Provo, Utah. Salt Lake City, Deseret News Company, 1886.
19p. 22½cm.
Polygamy and other subjects.
NjP, NN, UPB, USIC

1663. ———. An epistle of the First Presidency to the Church of Jesus Christ of Latter-day Saints. Read at the Semi-annual Conference, held at Coalville, Summit County, Utah, October, 1886. [Salt Lake City, 1886]
14p. 21cm.
Caption-title.
Signed at end: John Taylor, George A. Cannon. October 6, 1886.
Polygamy and other subjects.
CSmH, CU-B, MH, NN, UHi, UPB, USIC

1664. ———. An epistle of the First Presidency to the Church of Jesus Christ of Latter-day Saints, in General Conference assembled. Read April 8, 1887 at the 57th general annual conference, held at Provo, Utah. Salt Lake City, Deseret News Co., Printers, 1887.
15p. 22cm.
Caption-title.
Current problems of the Church membership.
CtY, DLC, ICN, MH, UHi, UPB, USIC, UU

1665. ———. An epistle to the presidents of stakes, high councils, bishops and other authorities of the Church. Salt Lake City, 1882.
IIp. 21cm.
Signed: May 1, 1882.
Regarding financial affairs including trading with gentiles.
USIC

1666. ———. Yr epistol cyffredinol cyntaf oddiwrth brif lywyddiaeth Eglwys Iesu Grist o Saint y dyddiau diweddaf, o ddyffryn y llyn halen fawr, at y Saint Gwasgaredig ar hyd y ddaear, yn anerch. [Merthyr-Tydfil, 1849]
12p. 16½cm.
Cyfieithwyd o'r New York Herald, am Fehef 2, 1849, gan J. Davis.
Title in English: The first general epistle of the First Presidency.
UPB

1667. ———. The Father and the son; a doctrinal exposition by the First Presidency and the Twelve. [Salt Lake City, 1916]
8p. 23cm.
Caption-title.
Doctrine of the Godhead.
NjP, UHi, UPB, USIC, UU

1668. ———. General instructions for missionaries. Missionaries should report at the Historian's Office. . . . Salt Lake City [189–?]
Broadside. 28×21½cm.
Signed: Joseph F. Smith, Franklin D. Richards, Missionary Committee of the Apostles.
USIC

1669. ———. Greeting from the First Presidency. [Salt Lake City, 1924?]
[4]p. 17cm.
Cover-title.
Signed at end: Heber J. Grant, Anthony W. Ivins, Charles W. Nibley.
CU-B, UHi, UPB

1669a. ———. Harmony between presiding authorities in the priesthood and in auxiliary organizations. [Salt Lake City, 190–?]
[2]p. 27cm.
Signed: Joseph F. Smith.
USIC

1670. ———. Important to the people of the British Isles. [Liverpool? Millennial Star Office? 1911?]
4p. 21cm.
Caption-title.
A letter to the *London Evening Times.*
Signed: February 6, 1911.
False nature of polygamy and other charges.
UHi

1671. ———. Instructions on social work. Salt Lake City, 1917.
16p. illus. 15cm.
USIC

1672. ———. De kerk van Jezus Christus van de Heiligen der Laatste Dagen aan de Wereld. Een officieele Verklaring door het Eerste Presedentschap. Salt Lake City, 1907.
16p. 20½cm.
Title in English: The Church of Jesus Christ of Latter-day Saints and the world.
USIC

CHURCH. . . . FIRST PRESIDENCY

1673. ———. [Letter] To Elder——— [Concerning the prompt and honest reporting of tithing] Salt Lake City [n.d.]
[1]p. 28cm.
USIC

1674. ———. . . . A Message from the . . . First Presidency of the Church of Jesus Christ of Latter-day Saints. Salt Lake City, 1930.
[16]p. 23cm.
At head of title: This address is not to be released before Sunday, April 6, 1930.
Signed: Heber J. Grant, Anthony W. Ivins, Charles W. Nibley, the First Presidency.
Centennial message.
Variant printings.
CU-B, NjP, NN, UPB, USIC

1674a. ———. Official announcement. To the officers and members of the Church of Jesus Christ of Latter-day Saints: Dear Brethren and Sisters: For several years past, . . . Salt Lake City, 1894.
[4]p. 21½cm.
Signed: Wilford Woodruff, Geo. Q. Cannon, Jos. F. Smith.
Concerning the establishment of a Church University in Salt Lake City.
Dated: August 18, 1894.
UPB, USIC

1675. ———. En officiel Erklaering af det Første Praesidentskab over Jesu Cristi Kirke af Sidste-Dages Hellige, enstemmigt vedtaget i General Konferencen i Salt Lake City, den 5te April 1907. [København, Udgivet og forlagt af J. M. Christensen. Trykt hos P. S. Christiansen, 1907]
12p. 20½cm.
Title in English: An official declaration of the First Presidency . . .
USIC

1676. ———. (same) København, Udgivet og forlagt af Andrew Jenson, 1911.
12p. 20½cm.
USIC

1677. ———. Second general epistle of the presidency of the Church of Jesus Christ of Latter-day Saints from the Great Salt Lake Valley to the saints scattered throughout the earth. Greeting: beloved brethren: . . . Great Salt Lake City, Brigham H. Young, Printer, Oct. 20th, 1849.
10p. 15×25cm.
Caption-title.
"Minutes of the General Conference held in Great Salt Lake City, Deseret, October 6, 1849."
W-C 177
CtY, NjP, USIC

1678. ———. Statement by the Presidency of the Church of Jesus Christ of Latter-day Saints. In reference to magazine slanders. The following address was read at the General Conference of the Church at Salt Lake City, April 9th, 1911. Salt Lake City, 1911.
8p. 22½cm.
NjP, UPB

1679. ———. Third general epistle of the presidency of the Church of Jesus Christ of Latter-day Saints from the Great Salt Lake Valley to the saints scattered throughout the earth, Greeting: Beloved Brethren: . . . [Great Salt Lake City, Deseret, N.A., April 12, 1850]
8p. 14½×23cm.
Caption-title.
CtY, USIC

1680. ———. To Bishop ———: [Salt Lake City] August 18, 1870.
Broadside. 27×20½cm.
A circular letter announcing the visit of a committee to solicit support for sale of bonds of Utah Central Railroad.
ULA

1680a. ———. To bishoprics of wards, Dear Brethren: At the stake clerks' meeting, . . . [Salt Lake City] 1916.
Broadside. 21½×14cm.
Signed: Joseph F. Smith, Anthon H. Lund, Charles W. Penrose, First Presidency.
Dated: June 19th, 1916.
Concerning confessions of transgressions of young people in church meetings.
USIC

1681. ———. To Elder [Letter to Elders in the Missions concerning the use and keeping of tithing collected] Salt Lake City [n.d.]
[1]p. 28cm.
Signed: Brigham Young, Jno. W. Young, Daniel H. Wells.
USIC

1682. ———. To the Bishop and the Board of the United Order in your ward. Salt Lake City, 1874.
Broadside. 27×21½cm.
Letter dated August, 1874 and signed by Brigham Young, George A. Smith, and Daniel H. Wells.
USIC

1683. ———. To the bishops and presiding elders of the various wards and settlements of Utah Territory, from St. Charles, Richland County, in the South: November 1, 1865. [Salt Lake City] 1865.
Broadside. 27×19cm.
Letter announcing plans for the Deseret Telegraph and calling for support for it from local authorities.
ULA

1683a. ———. To the bishops, seventies, high priests and elders. Dear Brethren: It is expected, in accordance with a circular issued some time ago,

CHURCH. . . . FIRST PRESIDENCY

"That the labor upon the Temple . . ." [Salt Lake City, 1876?]
Broadside. 28×21½cm.
Signed: John W. Young, Daniel H. Wells, of the First Presidency, and John Taylor, in behalf of the Twelve Apostles.
Concerning the work on the temple.
USIC

1684. ———. To the First Council of the Seventy. Salt Lake City, 1907.
Broadside. 27½×21cm.
Need for regular meetings to increase missionary efficiency.
UPB

1684a. ———. To the Maori saints. Dear Brethren and Sisters. We sincerely hope that at your approaching annual Conference in Wairarapa . . . Salt Lake City, 1897.
4p. 23½cm.
Signed: Wilford Woodruff, George Q. Cannon, Joseph F. Smith.
Exhorting the Maori saints to continue in their righteousness.
Dated: February 17, 1897.
The letter first written in English and then in Maori.
USIC

1685. ———. To the officers and members of the Church of Jesus Christ of Latter-day Saints . . . Salt Lake City, 1891.
Broadside. 24×18cm.
Signed: Wilford Woodruff, Geo. Q. Cannon and Jos. F. Smith.
A letter advising the church members to subscribe to the *Deseret News*.
USIC

1686. ———. To the presidents of stakes and bishops of wards. Dear Brethren — Acting on our advice . . . [Salt Lake City, 1891]
[4]p. 20½cm.
Signed: Your brethren of the gospel of Christ: Wilford Woodruff, George Q. Cannon, Joseph F. Smith, First presidency of the church.
NjP

1686a. ———. To the presidents of stakes and bishops of wards. Dear Brethren: In December, 1891, acting under our advice and direction, . . . Salt Lake City, 1894.
[2]p. 28cm.
Signed: Wilford Woodruff, George Q. Cannon, Joseph F. Smith.
Dated: November 22, 1894.
Concerning the raising of funds for the erecting of a monument to the pioneers of Utah and President Brigham Young.
UPB, USIC

1686b. ———. To the presidents of stakes and bishops of wards: Dear Brethren: It has been decided that it is no longer necessary . . . [Salt Lake City] 1891.
Broadside. 21½×13½cm.
Signed: Wilford Woodruff, Geo. Q. Cannon, Jos. F. Smith.
Dated: November 6th, 1891.
It is no longer necessary for temple recommends to be signed by President Woodruff, except for Second Anointings, which will require his approval.
USIC

1686c. ———. To the presidents of stakes and bishops of wards: Dear Brethren: Owing to the peculiar circumstances . . . [Salt Lake City] 1886.
Broadside. 21½×14cm.
Signed: John Taylor.
Dated: July 31, 1886.
Concerning the procuration of recommends to the temple before going to the temple.
USIC

1687. ———. To the presidents of stakes and bishops of wards. The question of conducting Sunday Schools without interruption . . . [Salt Lake City, 189–?]
[2]p. 19cm.
Signed: Wilford Woodruff, George Q. Cannon, Joseph F. Smith, First Presidency.
USIC

1687a. ———. To the presidents of stakes and bishops throughout Zion: Dear Brethren: It has been decided by the First Presidency that the missionary classes . . . Salt Lake City, 1904.
Broadside. 28×21½cm.
Signed: Jos. F. Smith, John R. Winder, Anthon H. Lund.
Dated: August 5th, 1904.
Concerning careful selection of missionaries.
USIC

1687b. ———. To the presidents of stakes and missions, bishops of wards and other presiding authorities. Salt Lake City, 1902.
4p. 21cm.
Signed: Anthon H. Lund, Rudgar Clawson, Andrew Jensen, Committee on records.
Record keeping in the church.
NjP

1688. ———. To the presidents of stakes and their counselors, the bishops and their counselors, and the Latter-day Saints generally. [Salt Lake City, 1885]
3p. 28cm.
Signed: John Taylor, George Q. Cannon, May 26, 1885.
A communication suggesting that preparations be made for the defense of the practice of plural marriages against attacks by U. S. Federal Government.
CSmH, DLC, USIC

CHURCH. . . . FIRST PRESIDENCY

1688a. ———. To the presidents of stakes and their counselors: Dear Brethren: There never was a time . . . Salt Lake City, 1889.
3p. 27cm.
Signed: Wilford Woodruff, Geo. Q. Cannon, Jos. F. Smith.
Dated: Dec. 2, 1889.
The setting aside of the anniversary of Joseph Smith's birthday as a day of fasting and prayer.
USIC

1689. ———. To the presidents of stakes, bishops and all whom it may concern: Salt Lake City, 1890.
[2]p. 27½cm.
Move to establish church schools.
NjP, UPB

1690. ———. To the presidents of stakes, bishops and parents in Zion. [Salt Lake City, 1915]
[3]p. 17½cm.
Signed: Heber J. Grant, Anthony W. Ivins, Charles Nibley.
USIC, UU

1691. ———. To the presidents of stakes, bishops and parents in Zion. Salt Lake City, 1916.
[3]p. 18cm.
A statement on family life.
USIC, UPB

1692. ———. To the presidents of stakes, bishops of wards, and stake tithing clerks in Zion. Salt Lake City, 1889.
4p. 20½cm.
Signed by the First Presidency and Presiding Bishopric.
Concerning account records.
Dated 1888 on p. 1.
UPB, USIC

1693. ———. To the presiding elders and saints of the places where there are, or where they wish to have, telegraph stations and operators. [Salt Lake City, 1867]
Broadside. 25½×19½cm.
Letter of April 20, 1867, signed by Brigham Young.
USIC

1694. ———. To the seventies, the following instructions were presented at a meeting of the First Presidency of the Church and the Council of the Twelve Apostles and the first Seven Presidents of the Seventies. Salt Lake City, 1883.
4p. 20½cm.
CU–B, NjP, UPB, USIC

1695. ———. To whom it may concern. Salt Lake City, 1891.
[1]p. 21½cm.
A message of the First Presidency to accompany a circular on the lectures of Mr. Charles Ellis.
USIC

1696. ———. United Order — articles of association. *See Church of Jesus Christ of Latter-day Saints. Articles of association.*

1697. Church of Jesus Christ of Latter-day Saints. Genealogical Society of Utah. Articles of association and by-laws of the Genealogical Society of Utah. [Salt Lake City] Deseret News [1894]
24p. 15½cm.
UPB, USIC, UU

1698. ———. (same) [Salt Lake City] Deseret News [1908?]
23p. 15½cm.
USIC

1699. ———. (same) [Salt Lake City, Deseret News, 1908?]
23p. 15cm.
Variant printing.
USIC

1700. ———. (same) Salt Lake City] Deseret News [1908?]
24p. 15½cm.
USIC

1701. ———. (same) [Salt Lake City, Deseret News, 1908?]
24p. 15½cm.
Variant printing.
UHi

1702. ———. Catalogue-index of family histories in the Library of the Genealogical Society of Utah. [Salt Lake City] 1918.
55p. 23½cm.
USIC

1703. ———. The Church genealogical archive . . . [Salt Lake City, 1922?]
Folder, 6p. 21½cm.
UHi

1704. ———. Circular of the Genealogical Society of Utah. Historian's Office. [Salt Lake City, 1907?]
8p. 20cm.
USIC, UU

1705. ———. Deposit your pedigree in the church genealogical archive . . . [Salt Lake City, 1921?]
[4]p. 15cm.
UHi

1706. ———. For family or individual, having temple work to do. [Salt Lake City, n.d.]
[4]p. chart. 24cm.
Caption-title: Sample forms for compiling records for temple work.
Variant printings.
USIC

CHURCH. . . . GENEALOGICAL SOCIETY OF UTAH

1707. ———. Genealogical archive service and the making of index cards. [Salt Lake City, n.d.]
6p. illus. 21½cm.
USIC

1708. ———. Genealogical information for missionary and convert . . . [Salt Lake City, 1921?]
[8]p. 19½cm.
UHi

1709. ———. (same) [Salt Lake City, 1922?]
[7]p. 20cm.
UHi

1710. ———. A guide for leaders in temple work and genealogy. [Salt Lake City] Published by the Genalogical Society of Utah, 1929.
48p. 18cm.
CU-B, UHi, UPB, USIC

1711. ———. Handbook of genealogy and temple work. Salt Lake City, Published by the Genealogical Society of Utah, 1924.
336p. illus. 19½cm.
DLC, ICN, UHi, UPB, USI, USIC, UU

1712. ———. How the Genealogical Society can help you . . . [Salt Lake City, 1921?]
[4]p. 19cm.
UHi

1713. ———. How to place an order and submit pedigrees . . . [Salt Lake City, 1921?]
4p. 15cm.
UHi

1714. ———. How we can help you. [Salt Lake City, n.d.]
[4]p. 18cm.
Instructions for teaching genealogy.
Variant printings.
UPB

1715. ———. Instructions for stake & ward genealogical workers. Salt Lake City, Genealogical Society of Utah, 1922.
[11]p. 15cm.
UHi

1716. ———. Instructions to stake and ward genealogical committees . . . [Salt Lake City, 1921?]
Broadside. 20×12½cm.
UHi

1717. ———. Lessons in genealogy. Salt Lake City, Published by the Genealogical Society of Utah, 1912.
32, 16, 45p. 19cm.
Includes: Salvation universal, by J. F. Smith Jr.; The place of genealogy in the plan of salvation, by Nephi Anderson; Lessons in Genealogy, by Susa Young Gates.
UHi

1718. ———. Lessons in genealogy. Salt Lake City, Published by the Genalogical Society of Utah, 1913.
1p.l. [3]–64p. 19cm.
UPB, USIC

1719. ———. (same) 3d ed. Salt Lake City, Published by the Genealogical Society, 1915.
1p.l. [3]–72p. 19½cm.
UHi, UPB, USIC

1720. ———. (same) 4th ed. Salt Lake City, Published by the Genealogical Society, 1919.
71p. 20cm.
UHi, USIC

1721. ———. (same) 5th ed. Salt Lake City, Published by the Genealogical Society of Utah, 1921.
71p. 18cm.
UHi, UPB

1722. ———. Lessons on salvation for the dead, genealogy and temple work. For use in the Missions of the Church of Jesus Christ of Latter-day Saints. Salt Lake City, Genealogical Society of Utah, 1927.
1p.l. [3]–76p. 19cm.
UHi, UPB, USIC, UU

1723. ———. Mission temple work. [Salt Lake City, n.d.]
4p. 22½cm.
UPB

1724. ———. New home of the Genealogical Society of Utah. [Salt Lake City, 1917]
[3]p. 18cm.
Purpose of the society in relation to the church.
Variant printings.
USIC

1725. ———. Outlines of studies and activities for the Genealogical Society for the season of 1918; prepared and issued by the Genealogical Society of Utah. [Salt Lake City, 1917?]
7 [1]p. 17cm.
UHi

1726. ———. (same) [Salt Lake City, 1919?]
6 [1]p. 23cm.
UHi

1727. ———. Seeking after our dead, our greatest responsibility; a course of lessons for study in classes in genealogy. [Salt Lake City] Genealogical Society of Utah, 1928.
2p.l. [5]–288p. 19½cm.
Includes the Mormon doctrine of salvation for the dead.
UHi, ULA, UPB, USIC, WHi

1728. ———. Suggested program for ward celebrations of the one-hundredth anniversary of the message of Moroni to the Prophet Joseph Smith; to be given September 23, 1923. [Salt Lake City? 1923]
8p. 22½cm.
UHi

1729. ———. To the Latter-day Saints. [Salt Lake City, 1894?]
[4]p. 23cm.
Organized in 1894. Membership drive.
UHi, USIC

1730. ———. (same) [Salt Lake City, 1894?]
[4]p. 15cm.
Variant printing.
USIC

1731. ———. Year book of the Woman's Committee of the Genealogical Society, 1911– [Salt Lake City, 1912]
v. 15cm.
UHi 1912–13, USIC 1911–12

1732. ———. . . . Year book of the Woman's Committee of the Genealogical Society, 1913–1914 . . . [Salt Lake City, 1913]
[6]p. 17½cm.
UHi

———. Genealogical Society. Polynesian.
See Church of Jesus Christ of Latter-day Saints. Polynesian Genealogical Society.

1733. Church of Jesus Christ of Latter-day Saints. General Priesthood Committee. Address to the priesthood. [Salt Lake City, n.d.]
7p. 22cm.
David O. McKay, Chairman.
MH

1734. ———. Report of the Committee on Priesthood Outlines to the general priesthood; read at the annual conference priesthood meeting, April, 1913. Salt Lake City, Presiding Bishops Office, 1913.
14p. 17cm.
USIC

1734a. Church of Jesus Christ of Latter-day Saints. General Tithing Office. Instructions to the bishops. [Salt Lake City, 1859]
7p. 19½cm.
USIC

1735. ———. List of tithing prices, weights and measures. Salt Lake City, 1883.
Broadside. 25×19½cm.
Signed: August 6, 1883.
USIC

1736. ———. (same) Salt Lake City, 1884.
Broadside. 32×19½cm
USIC

1737. Church of Jesus Christ of Latter-day Saints. Hymnal. Danish. 1851. En samling af hellige lovsange og hymner, til brug i Jesu Christi kirke af Sidste Dages hellige. Kjobenhavn, Udgivet og forlagt af S. Snow. Trykt hos F. E. Bording, 1851.
2p.l. [5]–110 [2]p. 11cm.
Second edition.
USIC

1738. ———. **1852.** (same) Tredie Udgave. Kjobenhavn, Udgivet og forlagt af P. O. Hansen og Medhjaelper. Trykt hos F. E. Bording, 1852.
2p.l. [5]–125 [3]p. 11cm.
USIC

1739. ———. **1853.** (same) Psalmer og aandelige Sange til brug for Jesu Christi kirke af Sidste dages hellige i Scankinavien. Fierde Udgave. Kjobenhavn, Udgivet og forlagt af J. Van Cott. Trykt hos F. E. Bording, 1853.
361 [1]p. 9½cm.
USIC

1740. ———. **1856.** (same) Kjobenhavn, H. C. Haight, 1856.
2p.l. [1] 4–5 [i]–vi–xii, 368p. 12cm.
5te Udgave.
NN, USIC

1741. ———. **1861.** (same) Psalmer til Brug for Jesu Christi Kirke af Sidste-Dages Hellige. 6 Udgave. Kobenhavn, Udgivet og forlagt af John Van Cott. 1861.
xxiii, 392p. 12cm.
CSmH, USIC, UU

1742. ———. **1862.** (same) 7de Udgave. Kjobenhavn, Udgivet of forlagt af John Van Cott. Trykt hos F. E. Bording, 1862.
xxiii, 424p. 11½cm.
USIC

1743. ———. **1867.** (same) Kjøbenhavn, Utgivet forlagt C. Widerborg. Trykt hos F. E. Bording, 1867.
xxiii, 389p. 12½cm.
8de Udgave.
NN, UPB, USIC

1744. ———. **1871.** (same) Niende Udgave. Kjobenhavn, Udgivet og forlagt af W. W. Cluff. Trykt hos F. E. Bording, 1871.
xxix, 424p. 12½cm.
MH, USIC

1745. ———. **1875.** (same) Tiende Udgave. Kjøbenhavn, Udgivet og forlagt af C. G. Larsen. Trykt hos F. E. Bording, 1875.
xxiv, 424p. 11½cm.
USIC

1746. ———. **1879.** (same) Ellevte Udgave. Kjobenhavn, Udgivet og forlagt af N. C. Flygare. Trykt hos F. E. Bording, 1879.
3p.l. [7]–430, xvi p. 12cm.
NN, UPB, USlC

1747. ———. **1885.** (same) Tolvte Udgave. Kjøbenhavn, Udgivet og forlagt af Anthon H. Lund. Trykt hos F. E. Bording, 1885.
2p.l., 496p. xix. 10½cm.
UHi, USlC

1748. ———. **1900.** (same) Salmer og aandelige Sange for Jesu Kriste Kirke af Sidste-Dages Hellige. Fjortende udgave. Kjobenhavn, Udgivet og forlagt af Andreas Peterson, 1900.
2p.l., 496, xix p. 11cm.
USlC, UU

1749. ———. **1906.** (same) Femtende Udgave. Revideret under tilsyn af Anthon H. Lund. Kjøbenhavn, Udgivet og Forlagt af J. M. Christensen. Trykt hos F. E. Bording (V. Petersen) 1906.
2p.l., 386, x p. 11½cm.
UPB, USlC, UU

1750. ———. **1881.** Udvalg af Psalmer til Brug for Jesu Christi Kirke af Sidste-Dages Hellige af den Neu-Zealandske Mission. Napier, Udgivet og forlagt af John P. Sorenson. Trykt hos F. E. Bording. 1881.
48p. 12½cm.
Cover-title.
A Danish hymnal published in New Zealand for the Danish colonists there.
USlC

1751. ———. **1888.** Salmer til Brug for Jesu Kristi Kirke af Sidste-Dages Hellige. Forste Amerikanske Udgave. Salt Lake City, Udgivet og Forlagt af A. A. Widerg. Trykt i Bikubens trykkeri, 1888.
2p.l., xix, 496p. 11cm.
First American edition.
UPB, USlC, UU

1752. ———. **1910.** Zions sange en Samling af Udbalgte sange for de Sidste-Dages Helliges møder, søndagsskoler, Mission aerforeninger og hjemmet. Salt Lake City, Udgivet og Forlagt af Jesu Kriste Kirke af de Siste-dages Hellige, 1910.
211 nos. [3]p. 20cm.
ULA, USlC, UU

1753. ———. **Hymnal. Dutch. 1884.** Heilige lofzangen en Geestelijke Liederen voor de Kerk van Jezus Christus van de Heiligen der laatste Dagen in Nederland. Amsterdam, 1884.
64p. 14cm.
Words only.
USlC

1754. ———. **1892.** (same) Luik, Drukkerij von A. Faust, Soeurs-de-Hasque Straat, 7, 1892.
55p. 17cm.
USlC

1755. ———. **1895.** (same) [Rotterdam, Asa W. Judd, 1895]
iv, 206p. 15½cm.
Date from preface. Signed: Asa W. Judd.
USlC

1756. ———. **1899.** (same, under title) Heilige Lofzangen en geestdijke liederen voor De Kerk van Jezus Christus van de Heiligen der laatste Dagen in de Nederlandish-Belgisch Zending Dordrecht, J. de Zeeuw, 1899. Rotterdam, Holland, Netherlands Mission, 1899.
iv, 384p. 18cm.
USlC

1757. ———. **1904.** (same) Zending, Amsterdam, W. Kesselaaer, 1904.
2p.l., 188 [14]p. 10½cm.
Words only.
Index.
USlC

1758. ———. **1907.** (same, under title) Heilige Lofzangen en Geestelijka Liederen voor de Kirk van Jezus Christus van de Heiligen der Laatste Dagen. Rotterdam, Uitgegeven door de Nederlandsch-Belgishe Zending, 1907.
3p.l., 416 [10]p. 17cm.
USlC

1759. ———. **1920.** (same) Rotterdam, Uitgegeven door de Nederlandsch-Belgische Zending . . . [1920, c1907]
[4]p.l., 416 [5]p. 16½cm.
USlC

1760. ———. **Hymnal. English. 1835.** A collection of sacred hymns for the church of the Latter day Saints, selected by Emma Smith. Kirtland, Ohio, Printed by F. G. Williams & Co., 1835.
iv [5]–121, v p. 11cm.
Sabin lists an 1832 edition which is inaccurate. Probably due to the fact that it had been authorized in a conference in 1832.
CSmH, CtY, MoInRC, UPB, USlC

1761. ———. **1841.** (same) A collection of sacred hymns, for the Church of Jesus Christ of Latter day Saints. Selected by Emma Smith. Nauvoo, Ill., Printed by E. Robinson, 1841.
iv, 5–351p.
New York Public Library listed an item under "Mormon hymns." New York, 1845. Eight hymns on a broadside sheet. It was reported lost in 1947.
Byrd 661
CtY, DLC, ICN, MoInRC, MWA, NN, NNUT, PHi, PPHi, UPB, USlC

CHURCH. . . . HYMNAL. ENGLISH

1762. ———. **1840.** A collection of sacred hymns, for the Church of Jesus Christ of Latter-day Saints in Europe, selected by Brigham Young, Parley P. Pratt, and John Taylor. Published by order of a general conference, and for sale at 124, Oldham Road, Manchester, and by Agents throughout England. Manchester, Printed by W. R. Thomas . . . 1840.
2p.l. 5–336p. 10½cm.
2d ed. published in Manchester, 1841. *Times and Seasons*, v.4: 162–5.
3d ed. mentioned in *Millennial Star*, v. 13: 249. No copies located of this, or previous edition. Both could be reprints of the 1840 edition.
Words only.
MB, MH, MoInRC, USIC

1763. ———. **1844.** (same) Liverpool, Published and sold by R. Hedlock and R. Ward, 1844.
2p.l. [5]–336p. 13cm.
Fourth edition.
USIC

1764. ———. **1847.** (same) 5th edition. Liverpool: Published and sold by Orson Spencer . . . and by the agents throughout England, 1847.
352p. 10cm.
Preface to the 5th edition signed by Orson Spencer and Franklin D. Richards. It contains 16 additional pages of hymns.
USI

1765. ———. **1848.** (same) 6th edition. Liverpool, Published by Orson Spencer, 1848.
352p. 11cm.
7th ed. of the same year noted in *Millennial Star*, v. 13: 249.
MoInRC, USIC

1766. ———. **1849.** (same) Sacred hymns and spiritual songs . . . 8th European edition. Liverpool, 1849.
352p. 12cm.
Preface signed: Orson Pratt. Liverpool, July 30, 1849.
USIC has no t.p.

1767. ———. **1851.** (same) Sacred hymns and spiritual songs, for the Church of Jesus Christ of Latter-day Saints, in Europe. 9th edition, revised and enlarged. Liverpool & London, Published and sold by F. D. Richards [etc., etc.] 1851.
vii [5]–379 [1]p. 11½cm.
296 hymns. 11cm.
Preface to the first edition signed: Brigham Young, Parley Parker Pratt, John Taylor: Preface to 9th edition signed Franklin D. Richards.
CtY, CU-B, MH, MoInRC, NNUT, UHi, USIC, UU

1768. ———. **1854.** (same) 10th European edition. Liverpool, Published for Orson Pratt, 1854.
379p. 11½cm.
MH, NjPT, PPLT, USIC

1769. ———. **1856.** (same) 11th edition, revised and enlarged. Liverpool, F. D. Richards, 36, Islington. London, Latter-Day Saints' Book Depot, 35, Jewin Street, City, 1856.
2p.l. [5]–415 [1]p. 11½cm.
MoInRC, NN, ULA, UPB, USIC

1770. ———. **1863.** (same) 12th edition, revised and corrected. Liverpool, George Q. Cannon, 1863.
2p.l. [5]–415 [1]p. 12½cm.
UHi, UPB, USIC

1771. ———. **1869.** (same) 13th edition. Liverpool, Albert Carrington, 1869.
415p. 21cm.
NN, USIC

1772. ———. **1871.** (same) 14th edition. Salt Lake City, Published by George Q. Cannon, 1871.
2p.l. [5]–432p. 12½cm.
On spine: L.D.S. Hymns.
First of this series printed by America.
Apparently the Salt Lake City 14th–16th editions were the only ones so designated. Thereafter both series were numbered as one series.
CU, DLC, ICN, MH, NN, NNUT, PU, UHi, UPB, USIC, UU

1773. ———. **1871.** (same) 15th edition. Liverpool, Albert Carrington; London, Latter Day Saints' Book, 1871.
2p.l. [5]–432p. 12cm.
MoInRC, UPB, USIC, UU

1774. ———. **1877.** (same) 16th edition. Liverpool, A. Carrington; London, L.D. Saints' Book Depot, 1877.
432p. 21cm.
ICHi, MoInRC, NjPT, USIC, UU

1775. ———. **1881.** (same) 17th edition. Liverpool, Printed and Published by Albert Carrington, 42 Islington, 1881.
2p.l. [5]–432p. 12cm.
USIC

1776. ———. **1883.** (same) 15th edition. Salt Lake City, Deseret News Co. Printers and Publishers, 1883.
432p. 12cm.
Series continues from 14th ed., which was numbered with the English editions, but continued as a Salt Lake series.
ICN, USIC

1777. ———. **1884.** (same) 18th edition [sic] Liverpool, Printed and Published by John Henry Smith, 1884.
2p.l. [5]–432p. 12cm.
CtY, DLC, NjP, NN, Ocl, UHi, UPB, USIC, UU

CHURCH. . . . HYMNAL. ENGLISH

1778. ———. **1887.** (same) 16th edition. Salt Lake City, Deseret News Co., 1887.
2p.l. [5]–432p. 13cm.
The final edition of this series. Afterwards the editions continue from the English editions.
MoInRC, UPB, USIC

1779. ———. **1889.** (same) 19th edition. Liverpool, Printed and Published by George Teasdale, 42, Islington, 1889.
445p. 12cm.
ULA, USIC

1780. ———. **1890.** (same) 20th edition. Liverpool, Printed and Published by George Teasdale, 42, Islington, 1890.
448p. 13½cm.
ULA, USIC

1781. ———. **1891.** (same) 20th edition. Salt Lake City, Deseret News Co., 1891.
2p.l. [5]–464p. 12cm.
CtY, NjP, NjPT, NN, UH, UHi, UPB, USIC

1782. ———. **1894.** (same) 21st edition. Salt Lake City, G. Q. Cannon and Sons, 1894.
2p.l. [5]–464p. 21cm.
MH, ULA, USIC

1783. ———. **1897.** (same) 22nd edition. Salt Lake City, Geo. Q. Cannon and Sons Co., 1897.
2p.l. [5]–464p. 12cm.
UPB, USIC, UU

1784. ———. **1899.** (same) 23rd edition. Salt Lake City, Geo. Q. Cannon and Sons Co., 1899.
464p. 12cm.
NBUG, USIC, WHi

1785. ———. **1905.** (same) 24th edition. Salt Lake City, Deseret News Co., 1905.
2p.l. [5]–480p. 12½cm.
NjP, UHi, ULA, UPB, USIC, UU

1786. ———. **1912.** (same) 25th edition. Salt Lake City, The Deseret News Company, 1912.
2p.l. [5]–486p. 12½cm.
DLC, NN, UHi, ULA, UPB, USIC, UU

1787. ———. **1889.** The Latter-day Saints' psalmody. A collection of original tunes composed and compiled by the following committee: G. Careless, E. Beesley, J. J. Daynes, E. Stephens, T. C. Griggs, also embracing compositions of other well known composers, together with a number of old and familiar tunes specially arranged for the work, providing music for every hymn in the L.D.S. hymn book, gotten up under the approval of the late President John Taylor, and accepted by President Wilford Woodruff and Council, for the use of the members of the Church of Jesus Christ of Latter-day Saints. Salt Lake City, Deseret News Co., 1889.
2p.l., 333 no. [6]p. music. 26cm.
CSmH, MH, NN, UHi, UPB, USIC

1788. ———. **1896.** (same) 2d ed., rev. & enl. Salt Lake City, Deseret News Co., 1896.
2p.l., 353 nos. [6]p. music. 25cm.
IWW, NN, UHi, UPB, USI, USIC

1789. ———. **1902.** (same) 2d ed., rev. and enl. Salt Lake City, Deseret News, 1902.
2p.l., 353 nos. [6]p. music. 24½cm.
UPB, USIC

1790. ———. **1906.** (same) 3d ed., rev. and enl. Salt Lake City, Published by the Deseret News, 1906.
2p.l., 367 nos. music. 21cm.
NjP, UHi, ULA, UPB, UU

1791. ———. **1908.** (same) 4th ed. [rev. and enl.] Salt Lake City, Deseret News, 1908.
2p.l., 366 nos. [5]p. music. 21cm.
RPB, UHi, ULA, UPB, USIC

1792. ———. **1912.** (same) 5th ed. rev. and enl. Salt Lake City, Pub. by Deseret News, 1912.
2p.l., 364 nos. [3]p. music. 21cm.
CSmH, UPB, UU

1793. ———. **1915.** (same) 6th ed [rev. and enl.] Salt Lake City, Deseret News, 1915.
2p.l., 367 nos. [5]p. music. 21cm.
USIC

1794. ———. **1920.** (same) 7th ed. [rev. and enl.] Salt Lake City, Deseret Book Co., 1920.
2p.l., 367 nos. [5]p. music. 21cm.
USIC

1795. ———. **1897.** The Latter Day Saints anthem book by local composers . . . Vol. 1. Salt Lake City, Published Daynes and Coalter, c1897.
101p. music. 28½cm.
USIC

1796. ———. **1899.** Missionary song book for use of elders of the Church of Jesus Christ of Latter Day Saints, in the missionary field, being a choice selection of the most popular songs in the Southern States Mission, comprising all of Prof. E. Stephens' Y.M.M.I.A. and Missionary Selections; Songs from the Sunday School Book, Some choice hymns from the Hymnal; also a few of Mr. Ira D. Sankey's favorite songs. Chattanooga, Tenn., Published by the Southern States Mission [1899]
2p.l., 232p. 12cm.
Words only.
MoInRC, UPB, USIC, UU

CHURCH. . . . HYMNAL. ENGLISH

1797. ———. **1901.** (same) Chattanooga, Tenn., Southern States Mission [ca. 1901]
226p. 12cm.
USIC

1798. ———. **1908.** The Songs of Zion; a collection of choice songs especially selected and arranged for the home and for all meetings, Sunday schools and gatherings of elders and saints in the mission field. Chicago [etc.] Published by Missions of the Church of Jesus Christ of Latter-day Saints, c1908.
1p.l., 246 nos. [4]p. music. 19½cm.
MH, NjP, NNUT, RPB, UHi, UPB, USIC

1799. ———. **1909.** (same) Chicago [etc.] Published by the Missions of the Church of Jesus Christ of Latter-day Saints, c1908. [1909]
1p.l., 246 nos. [4]p. music. 19cm.
USIC

1800. ———. **1910.** (same) Chicago [etc.] Published by Missions of the Church of Jesus Christ of Latter-day Saints, c1908. [1910]
1p.l., 246 nos. [4]p. music. 19½cm.
USIC

1801. ———. **1912.** (same) [Chicago] Published for the Missions of the Church of Jesus Christ of Latter-day Saints [1912, c1908]
1p.l., 269 nos. [4]p. music. 19½cm.
"Press of Zion's Printing and Publishing Co., Independence, Mo."
Copyright by J. F. Smith.
RPB, UPB, USIC

1802. ———. **1915.** (same) [Chicago] Published for the Missions of the Church of Jesus Christ of Latter-day Saints [ca. 1915]
1p.l., 269 nos. [4]p. music. 20cm.
USIC

1803. ———. **1918.** (same) [Chicago] Published by the Missions of the Church of Jesus Christ of Latter-day Saints, c1918.
1p.l., 269 nos. [4]p. music. 20cm.
NjP, UHi, UPB, USIC

1804. ———. **1919.** (same) [Independence, Mo.] Missions of the Church of Jesus Christ of Latter-day Saints, c1918 [1919]
269 nos. [4]p. music. 19cm.
"Press of Zion's Printing and Publishing Co."
USIC

1805. ———. **1920.** The songs of Zion. A collection of choice songs especially selected and arranged for the home and for all meetings, Sunday Schools and gatherings of Elders and Saints in the Mission Field. [Independence, Mo.] Published by the Missions of the Church of Jesus Christ of Latter-day Saints. c1918. [ca. 1920)
1p.l., 269 nos. [4]p. music. 19½cm.
Date approximated by addresses of mission homes.
USIC

1806. ———. **1921.** (same) [Independence, Mo.] Published by the Missions of the Church of Jesus Christ of Latter-day Saints [ca. 1921]
1p.l., 269 nos. music. 19½cm.
USIC

1807. ———. **1925.** (same) [Independence, Mo.] Published by the Missions of the Church of Jesus Christ of Latter-day Saints [ca. 1925]
1p.l., 269 nos. music. 20cm.
USIC

1808. ———. **1919.** Latter-day Saints congregational hymns. Arranged and published by Prof. Henry E. Giles, chorister, Ensign State. 1st edition. Independence, Mo., Press of Zion's Printing and Publishing, 1919.
367 nos. [5]p. music. 20cm.
Vol. 1 only published.
UPB

1809. ———. **1919.** (same) Independence, Mo., Press of Zion's Printing and Publishing Co., 1919.
73 [1] nos. music. 19½cm.
USIC

1810. ———. **1927.** Latter-day Saint hymns; a collection of hymns and spiritual songs, containing words and music, for use of choirs and congregations of the Church of Jesus Christ of Latter-day Saints. Salt Lake City, Deseret Book Company [1927]
2p.l., 421 nos., xxvii p. music. 20cm.
Edition of Nov., 1927.
Index xxvii p.
CtY, UHi, ULA, UPB, USIC, UU

1811. ———. **1928.** (same) Salt Lake City, Deseret Book Company [c1927, 1928]
421 nos. xxviii p. music. 20cm.
UPB, USIC

1812. ———. **Hymnal. English. Selections. 1908.** A selection of seventeen songs made from the Songs of Zion . . . Chicago, Northern States mission [1908]
[20]p. music. 19cm.
UPB, USIC

1813. ———. **1908.** (same) New York City, Eastern States Mission [1908?]
[20]p. music. 19cm.
UPB, USIC

1814. ———. **1908.** (same) Independence, Mo., Central States Mission [1908]
[20]p. music. 19cm.
UPB, USIC, UU

1815. ———. **1924.** (same) Independence, Mo., Printing and Publishing Company [ca. 1924]
32p. music. 19½cm.
USIC

1816. ———. **n.d.** A selection from the songs of Zion. Independence, Mo., Zion's Printing and Publishing Company [n.d.]
[33]p. music. 15½cm.
UPB

1817. ———. **n.d.** (same) Independence, Mo., Zion's Printing and Publishing Company [n.d.]
35p. music. 16cm.
USIC

1818. ———. **n.d.** (same) Independence, Mo., Zion's Printing and Publishing Company [n.d.]
35p. music. 16cm.
Variant printing.
USIC

1819. ———. **n.d.** (same) Independence, Mo., Published by the Missions of the Church of Jesus Christ of Latter-day Saints. Zion's Printing and Publishing Company, [n.d.]
[36]p. music. 15cm.
UHi

1820. ———. **n.d.** (same) Independence, Mo., Zion's Printing and Publishing Company [n.d.]
48p. music. 19½cm.
Cover-title.
UPB, USIC

1821. ———. **1930.** Latter-day Saint hymns for use during the centennial celebration of the organization of the Church of Jesus Christ of Latter-day Saints, to be held at the tabernacle, Salt Lake City, Utah, beginning April 6, 1930. [Salt Lake City, 1930]
[24]p. music. 19½cm.
Cover-title.
Hymns extracted from the regular hymnal.
UHi, UPB, USIC, UU

1822. ———. Hymns used by the Latter-day Saints. [n.p., n.d.]
16p. music. 10½cm.
Cover missing.
UU

1823. Church of Jesus Christ of Latter-day Saints. Hymnal. French. 1857. Recueil de Cantiques a l'usage des Saints-des-Derniers-jours. Publié par Jno. L. Smith. Genève Imprimerie C. L. Sabot [sic] Rue de Rive, 18, 1857.
iv [5]–56p. 13½cm.
Words only.
USIC

1824. ———. **1886.** Chants évangéliques . . . Deuxième édition. Lausanne, Bureau de l'Appel, 1886.
2p.l., 309p. music. 16½cm.
USIC

1825. ———. **1899.** Hymnes l'usage des brances francaises de l'Eglise de Jésus-Christ des Saints de derniers jours. Traduits et recueillis par D. B. Richards et N. C. Giauque. Berne, Bureau de la Mission Suisse, 1899.
4p.l., 160p. music. 19½cm.
NN, UPB, USIC, UU

1826. ———. **1907.** Hymnes de l'Eglise de Jésus-Christ des Saints des derniers Jours pour les Conferences francaises des Mission Suisse-Allemande et Néerlando-Belge. Rotterdam, La Mission Néerlando-Belge [1907]
2p.l., 272 [7]p. and table. 17cm.
Preface signed 1907.
UPB, USIC, UU

1827. ———. **1930.** Cantiques de l'Eglise de Jésus-Christ des Saints des Derniers Jours . . . Edition Centenaire . . . Liége, Bureau de District Belge, 1930.
61 [2]p. 18½cm.
Copy includes 14 mimeographed songs added.
USIC

1828. ———. **Hymnal. German. 1861.** Liederbuch für die kirche Jesu Christi der Heiligen der letzten Tage. Herausgegeben von Jabez Woodard, Druck von J. H. Tillmann. Zürich, 1861.
iv, 175 [1]p. 14cm.
Words only.
ULA, USIC

1829. ———. **1869.** Liederbuch für de deutsche und Schweizer-mission der Kirche Jesu Christi der Heiligen der letzten Tage . . . Zürich, J. Schabelitz, 1869.
xii, 176p. 14cm.
2. Auflage.
Words only.
NN, USIC

1830. ———. **1875.** Gesangbuch für de Schweizerische und Deutsche Mission der Kirche Jesu Christi der Heiligen der letzten Tage. Dritte Auflage. Bern, Druck von Lang & Comp., 1875.
xii, 197p. 12½cm.
UHi, USIC

1831. ———. **1881.** (same) Vierte verbesserte Auflage. Bern, Druck von Lang & Company, 1881.
2p.l., vii–xp. [1]l., 208p. music. 16cm.
Partly without music.
ULA, UPB, USIC

1832. ———. **1890.** (same) Fünfte verbesserte und vergrösserte Auflage. Bern, Druck von Suter & Lierow, 1890.
xi, 299p. music. 16cm.
UHi, UPB, USIC, UU

1833. ———. **1901.** (same) Gesangbuch der Hieligen der letzten Tage. Sechste Auflage. Berlin, Verlag: Die Deutsche Mission Kirche Jesu Christi der Heiligen der letzten Tage, 1901.
vii, 324p. music. 17cm.
MH, ULa, UPB, USIC, UU

1834. ———. **1922.** (same) Sechste Auflage. Basel, Herausgegeben von Serge F. Ballif, Präsident der Schweizerischen und Deutschen Mission der Kirche Jesu der Heiligen der letzten Tage, 1922.
viii, 324p. music. 17cm.
UPB

1835. ———. **1924.** (same) Achte Auflage. Basel, Herausgegeben von Fred Tadje, Präsident der Schweizerischen und Deutschen Mission der Kirche Jesu der Heiligen der letzten Tage, 1924.
vii, 324p. music. 17cm.
UPB, USIC

1836. ———. **1927.** (same) Basel, Herausgegeben von Fred Tadje . . . , 1927.
vii, 324p. music. 17cm.
USIC

1837. ———. **1928.** (same) Neunte Auflage. Basel, Herausgegeben von der Kirche Jesu Christi der Heiligen der letzten Tage. Deutsch-Österreichische Mission . . . Schweizerisch-Deutsche Mission, 1928.
vii, 324p. music. 16½cm.
USIC

1838. ———. **1925.** Chorliederbuch für die Chore der Schweizerisch-Deutschen und der Deutsch-Österriechischen Mission der Kirche Jesu-Christi der Heiligen der letzten Tage. Für die Herausgabe verantwortlich H. W. Valentine. Basel, Leimenstrasse Udressen der Missionen, 1925.
4p.l., 202p. 27cm.
UPB, USIC

1839. ———. **1923.** (same) Nihon, Matsuzitsu Seito Jesu Kirisuto, 1915 [ca. 1923]
22, 393, xp. music. 18½cm.
Title page and index in English at end. English preface follows Japanese title page.
English title: The songs of Zion . . . Tokyo, Japan Mission, c1915.
Edited by Vinal G. Mauss.
USIC

1840. ———. **1927.** (same) Basel, Leimenstrasse Udressen der Missionen, 1927.
4p.l., 202p. 27cm.
UPB

1841. ———. **Hymnal. Hawaiian. 1885.** Na halelu Hoano. He mau himeni no na kula sabati ame na Halawai cae. Hoakoakoaia la Frederika Bikale [Frederick Beesley] Paiia ma ka Juvenile Instructor Office, Lokopaakai, Uta [ca. 1885]
31 [1]p. 12cm.
USIC

1842. ———. **1909.** Na Mele O Ziona. He Mau Himeni No Ka Home, Ke Kula Sabati, Ame Na Halawai e ae. Hoakoakoaia e Frederika Bikale. No ka Misiona o ka Ekalesia o Iesu Kristo. O ka Poe Hoano o No La Hope Nei. Ma Ka Hawaii Pae Aina. Chicago, Ill., Paiia e Henry C. Etten & Co. [1909]
1p.l. [18] [2]p. 19cm.
USIC

1843. ———. **1924.** Na Mele o Ziona. Published by the L.D.S. Hawaiian Mission . . . [Salt Lake City] Printed in the United States of America, The Deseret News Press, c1924.
222 nos. [10]p. music. 20cm.
UPB

1844. ———. **Hymnal. Icelandic. 1903.** Sálmar Theirra sídustu daga heilögu. Á Íslandi, Fyrsta Hefti. Reykjavík, Prentsmidja Thjódólfs, 1903.
56p. 12cm.
Words only.
UPB, USIC

1845. ———. **Hymnal. Japanese. 1905.** Matsu Jitsu Seito Sanbika. Tokyo, Nihon, Matsu Jitsu Seito Iesu Kirisuto Kyōkai Nihon Dendobu [1905]
66 nos. [4]p. 21½cm.
English title page at end: Psalmody of the Japan Mission of the Church of Jesus Christ of Latter-day Saints. Compiled by Elders Horace S. Ensign and Frederich A. Caine. First edition.
CSmH, UPB, USIC

1846. ———. **1915.** (same) Tokyo, Japan, Matsu Jitsu Seito Jesu Kirisuto Kyōkai Nihon Dendobu, 1915.
xxii, 393, xp. [1]l. music. 19cm.
Added title-page: Song titles in English. The Songs of Zion . . .
UPB, USIC

1847. ———. **1915.** (same) Tokyo, Japan, Matsu itsu Seito Jesu Kirisuto Kyōkai Nihon Dendobu, 1915.
xxii, 393, xp. [1]l. music. 19cm.
Variant printing.
USIC

1848. ———. **1916.** (same) Joseph H. Stimpson, heng sang. [Tokyo, Japan Mission of the Church of Jesus Christ of Latter-day Saints, c1916]
xxxix, 256, xvp., [1]l. 19cm.

Added title-page in English: The Latter-day Saints' hymn book. Containing words to the hymns in the "Song of Zion."
Without music.
UPB, USIC

1848a. ———. **1923.** (same) Nihon, Matsu Jitsu Seito Jesu Kirisuto, 1915 [ca. 1923]
22, 393, xp. music. 18½cm.
Title page and index in English at end. English preface follows Japanese title page.
English title: The songs of Zion . . . Tokyo, Japan Mission, c1915.
Edited by Vinal G. Mauss.
USIC

1849. ———. **Hymnal. Norwegian. 1878.** Salmer og snage paa veiene til himmelen. Udgivne efter Beflutning af conferentsen i Bergen, 1877. Bergen, N. Nilssen, 1878.
4p.l., 535, xv p. 12½cm.
Words only.
USIC

1850. ———. **Hymnal. Samoan. 1908.** O Pese O Siona Mo Le Ekalesia a Iesu Keriso o le Au Paia o Aso e Gata ai. Na lomia i le Fale Lomi Tusi a le Ekalesia. Salt Lake City, The Deseret News, Printers and Publishers, 1908.
224p. 12½cm.
Words only.
UHi, USIC

1851. ———. **1918.** (same) Honolulu, Paradise of the Pacific Print, 1918.
[2]p.l., 269 nos. [4]l. 21½cm.
Words and music.
USIC

1852. ———. **Hymnal. Spanish. 1907.** Himnario Mormon . . . Mexico, Talleres Tipográficos de Müller Hnos., 1907.
91 [3]p. 16½cm.
Without music.
UPB

1853. ———. **1911.** Canciones de Sion o'del Culto Mormon . . . Salt Lake City, Skelton Publishing Co., 1911.
4p.l., 197p. 19cm.
Words only.
UHi, UPB, USIC

1854. ———. **1912.** Himnos de Sion de la Iglesia de Jesucristo de los Santos de los Ultimos Días. México, Publicado por Rey L. Pratt, 1912.
88 [4]p. 17cm.
Imprenta y litografia de Muller Hnos.
USIC

1855. ———. **1912.** (same) Independence, Mo. Zion's Printing and Publishing Co., 1912.
106 [4]p. 17cm.
Words only.
"Publicato por la Mision Mexicana."
CSmH, UPB, USIC

1856. ———. **1927.** (same) Independence, Mo., Impr. de Zion's Printing and Publishing Company, 1927.
156 [5]p. 17cm.
DLC, UHi, UPB

1857. ———. **Hymnal. Swedish. 1860.** Andeliga Sånger till bruk för Jesu Christi Kyrkas Sista Dagars helige, Öfwersatta af Jonas Engberg. Första Upplagan. København, Utgifwen och förlaggd af John Van Cott. Tryckt hos F. E. Bording, 1860.
viii, 230p. 10½cm.
Words only.
USIC

1858. ———. **1863.** (same) Öfwersatta och bearbetade af Jonas Engberg. Andra Upplagan. Kopenhamn, Utgifvna och förlaggda af Jesse N. Smith. Tryckta hos F. E. Bording, 1863.
463p. 11½cm.
MH, USIC

1859. ———. **1873.** (same) Tredje Upplagan. Kopenhamn, Utgifvna och förlaggda af R. Peterson. Tryckta hos F. E. Bording, 1873.
3p.l., vii–xvi, 463p. 11cm.
Without music.
UPB, USIC

1860. ———. **1881.** (same) Fjerde Upplagan. Kopenhamn, Utgifna och förlaggda af N. Wilhelmsen, 1881.
2p.l., 488p. 11cm.
Without music.
UPB, USIC

1861. ———. **1889.** (same) Femte Upplagan, Genomsedd. Kopenhamn, C. D. Fjeldsteds Forlag, 1889.
3p.l., 488p. 11cm.
Without music.
UPB, USIC

1862. ———. **1900.** (same) Sjette Genomsedda Upplagan. Köpenhamn, Andreas Petersons förlag, 1900.
3p.l., 488p. 12½cm.
USIC

1863. ———. **1910.** (same) Sjunde Genomsedda Upplagan. Stockholm, Peter Sundwalls Förlag, 1910.
4p.l. [9]–496p. 10½cm.
Words only.
UHi, USIC

1864. ———. **1895.** De Skandinaviska Sista Dagarnes Heligas koralbok; unnehållande harmoniserade melodier till alla i den senaste upplagan af både svenska och danska sångboken förekommande sånger. Utgifven och förlagd af Olof Nilson. Salt Lake City, Trykt a Deseret News, Tryckeri, 1895.
[34]l. 22cm.
Songs with music.
UU

1865. ———. **1910.** Zions sanger; en samling af utvalda sånger för de Sista dagars heliges Möten, söndagsskolor, missionärsföreningar, och hemmet Utgifven och förlagd af Jesu Kristi kyrka af sista dagars helige. [Chicago] 1910.
1p.l., 112l. 19cm.
Close score compiled by Hugo D. F. Peterson.
Printed by Henry C. Etten.
NN, UHi, USIC, UU

1866. ———. **1910.** (same) Salt Lake City, Utgifven och förlagd af Jesu Kristi Kyrka af Sista Dagars Helige, 1910.
1p.l., 209 nos. [3]p. 20cm.
UU

1867. ———. **Hymnal. Tahitian. 1913.** E buka himene evanelia, i Faaauhia ei Haamaitairaa i te Atua. Papeete, Tahiti, I Neia i te piha neneiraa a te Ekalesia a Iesu Mesia i te Feia Mo'a i te Mau Mahana Hopea Nei, 1913.
[116]p. 15½cm.
Without music.
UPB, USIC

1868. ———. **1918.** (same) Papeete, Tahiti, Neneihia e Eraneta Rositera, 1918.
[156]p. 151 nos. [8]p. 12½cm.
"I neia i te piha neneiraa a te Ekalesia a Iesu Mesia i te Feia Mo'a i te Mau Mahana Hopea Nei."
Without music.
UPB

1869. ———. **1921.** (same) [Papeete] Neneihia e L. H. Kennard [ca. 1921]
[154]p. 151 nos. [7]p. 15½cm.
"I neia i te Feia Mo'a i te Mau Mahana Hopea Nei."
UPB

1870. ———. **Hymnal. Tongan. 1912.** Koe ga'ahi Himo O Saione. Koe ma'obo 'obo oe ga' ahi himi ki he abi Ki he Lau Tohi Fakasabata Moe ga'abi lotu kehekehe . . . Chicago, Buluji e Henry E. Etten [1912]
1p.l., 35 nos. [2]p. 19cm.
USIC

1871. ———. **Hymnal. Welsh. 1849.** Casgliad o hymnau newyddion ynghyd ag odlau ysbrydol, at Wasanaeth Saint y dyddiau diweddaf. Merthyr-Tydfil: Argraffwyd ac ar Werth gan J. Davis, yn Georgetown, 1849.
194 nos. 11cm.
UPB

1872. ———. **1851.** (same) Hymnau, wedi eu Cyfansoddi a'u Casglu, yn Fwyaf Neillduol, at wasanaeth Saint Y Dyddiau Diweddaf. Ail argraffiad. Merthyr-Tydfil, Argraffwyd ac ar Werth Gan J. Davis, Georgetown, 1851.
viii, 56p. 10½cm.
133 hymns; words only.
UHi

1873. ———. **1852.** (same) Casgliad o hymnau, caniadau, ac Odlau Ysbrydol at wasanaeth Saint Y Dyddiau Diweddaf yn Nghymru. Methry-Tyfil, Cyhoeddwyd ac ar Werth Gan J. Davis yn Georgetown, 1852.
xxxii [5]–355 [1]p. 577 nos. 12cm.
Without music.
NjP, UPB, USIC, UU

1874. Church of Jesus Christ of Latter-day Saints. L.D.S. Missionary Correspondence School. L.D.S. Missionary Correspondence School. [Salt Lake City, ca. 1917]
8p. 23cm.
USIC

1875. Church of Jesus Christ of Latter-day Saints. Missions. The elders' manual. Published by the Missions of the Church of Jesus Christ of Latter day Saints in the United States. [Independence, Mo., Zion's Printing & Publishing Company, 1919]
3p.l., 7–64 p. 18cm.
IWW, NjP, UHi, UPB, USIC, UU

1876. ———. (same) [Independence, Mo., Zion's Printing & Publishing Company, 1921]
3p.l., 7–64p. 18cm.
USIC

1877. ———. (same) [Independence, Mo., Zion's Printing & Publishing Company, 1926?]
3p.l., 7–64p. 18cm.
USIC

1878. ———. (same) [Independence, Mo., Zion's Printing & Publishing Company, 1927?]
3p.l., 7–64 p. 18cm.
USIC

1879. ———. The elders' reference. [Chattanooga, Tenn.] Southern States Mission, 1906.
32p. 18½cm.
Bulk of material by Ben E. Rich, with some material by other mission presidents.
UPB, USIC

1880. ———. (same) New York, Eastern States Mission, 1913.
2p.l., 3–64p. 15½cm.
CSmH, USIC

CHURCH. . . MISSIONS. BRITISH

1881. ———. Home Sunday service for members and friends of the Church of Jesus Christ of Latter-day Saints. Part I. Independence, Published for the Missions of the Church by the Deseret Sunday School Union Board [n.d.]
31p. 23cm.
UPB

1882. ———. Invitation . . . "Parallel scripture references to prove the Latter Day Saint's faith and doctrines." [n.p., n.d.]
[3]p. 18½cm.
Scriptures concerning the fourteen Articles of faith.
UU

1882a. ———. (same) [Liverpool, 1851]
3 [1]p. 19½cm.
Dated from list of works on [1]p.
UPB

1883. ———. Invitation . . . [Liverpool, Printed by J. Sadler, 188–?]
4p. 18cm.
Includes, invitation to attend meeting, articles of faith (L.D.S.' faith) Scriptural references & available literature.
USIC

1884. ———. **Missions. Australasian.** Australasian mission of the Church of Jesus Christ of Latter-day Saints. Selection of hymns for special services. Auckland, H. Brett, 1894.
14p. 17cm.
Cover-title within border.
Words only.
USIC

———. **Missions. British.** Articles of faith. *See Joseph Smith, 1805–1844.*

1885. ———. Catalogue and price list of church publications, Bibles, church records, missionary tracts, etc. [Liverpool, The Millennial Star Office, n.d.]
1p.l., 8p. 12cm.
NN, UHi

1886. ———. Catalogue of works published by the Church of Jesus Christ of Latter-day Saints, and for sale by Orson Pratt, at their general repository, and "Millennial Star" Office, 42, Islington, Liverpool. Liverpool, Church of Jesus Christ of Latter-day Saints. Printed by R. James [1856?]
4p. 24cm.
NN, UHi

1887. ———. . . . Character of the Latter-day Saints, opinions of prominent individuals who have lived with them. [Liverpool? Millennial Star Office? 1898?]
4p. 22cm.
Caption-title.
Variant texts.
CU–B, UHi, UPB, USIC

1888. ———. The Church of Jesus Christ of Latter-day Saints. [London] J. B. Franklin [1850]
[1]p. 21cm.
Statistics of London Conference and other facts.
MH

1889. ———. Dear Friend, are you looking for more truth for the gospel of Jesus Christ in its primitive purity and power, and a church with Apostles and prophets? . . . [Liverpool? Millennial Star Office? 1911?]
[2]p. 21cm.
Caption-title.
On verso: Articles of faith.
UHi

1889a. ———. Everybody should read the Book of Mormon. [Mar. 1889, England]
Broadside. 15×27cm.
Explaining the contents of the Book of Mormon. Also gives the price for a copy.
USIC

1890. ———. The gospel and health; a study course for the Mutual Improvement Associations in the British Mission of the Church of Jesus Christ of Latter-day Saints. Y.M.M.I.A. Manual, No. 25, Revised. Liverpool, Published by John A. Widtsoe, 1928.
52p. 21cm.
UHi, USIC

———. A gospel century. Some epoch-making events and doctrine. *See Church of Jesus Christ of Latter-day Saints. Missions. European.*

1891. ———. Handbook for the Mutual Improvement Associations of the British Mission. Liverpool, Published by the British Mission . . . [1926]
37 [1]p. 18½cm.
USIC

———. Invitation. *See Church of Jesus Christ of Latter-day Saints. Missions.*

———. Jarman and the Mormons. *See Jarman and the Mormons.*

1892. ———. The Latter-day Saints' belief. [Liverpool, Millennial Star Office, n.d.]
[1]p. 20½×12cm.
Missionary tract.
USIC

1893. ———. (same) [Hull, Oliver's Printing Establishment, n.d.]
[1]p. 20½cm.
USIC

CHURCH. . . . MISSIONS. BRITISH

1893a ———. The Latter-day Saints meet for public worship . . . Liverpool [n.d.]
Broadside. 22×14cm.
Announcement of meetings, address of the mission headquarters and a copy of the Articles of Faith.
USIC

1894. ———. Modern revelation as contained in the Book of Doctrine and Covenants. A study course for the Mutual Improvement Associations in the British Mission of the Church of Jesus Christ of Latter-day Saints. For the year 1930–31. Liverpool, Birmingham, Published by the Latter-day Saints, 1930.
64p. 21½cm.
UHi, UPB, USIC

1895. ———. My brother, read, and, then judge. [Manchester? n.d.]
Broadside. 19×11cm.
Truth of Joseph Smith by fulfillment of his Civil War prophecy.
MH

1896. ———. A new volume of scriptures! The revelations of God to the ancient Americans. [London? n.d.]
2 [1]p. 23cm.
Missionary tract.
USIC

1897. ———. Programme of a grand soiree and festival to be held in the Baths Lecture Hall, Nelson Street, Woolwich, on Whit-Monday, May 31st, 1852. Woolwich, Eng., M. Cherry, 1852.
[1]–4p. 21½cm.
UPB

1898. ———. Spiritual growth; a study course for the Mutual Improvement Associations in the British Mission of the Church of Jesus Christ of Latter-day Saints. Y.M.M.I.A. Manual, No. 24, Revised. Liverpool, Published by the Latter-day Saints, 1928.
55p. 21cm.
UHi, USIC

1899. ———. Statement. To the british public and press protesting against the circulation of slanders, lies, sensational stories, etc., levelled against the Church of Jesus Christ of Latter-day Saints (commonly known as the "Mormon's Church") [n.p., 1921]
[5]p. 24½cm.
Statement and signatures.
USIC

1900. ———. (same) [n.p., n.d.]
[13]p. 24cm.
Includes also statements from various newspapers.
USIC

1901. ———. Tract no. ——— of the Latter-day Saints' Circulating Tract Society, of the London Conference. [London, J. Somerfield, Printer, 1849 or 50]
4p. 21½cm.
Enclosed in border; printed on yellow paper.
Introduction to Mormon pamphlets and missionary tracts.
p. 3–4: List of publications.
CtY

1902. ———. The value of life here and hereafter. A study course for the Relief Societies in the British and South African Missions. Birmingham, British Mission, Church of Jesus Christ of Latter-day Saints [n.d.]
2p.l. [5]–111p. 21½cm.
UPB

1903. ———. The Word of Wisdom. [Birmingham, n.d.]
[4]p. 21½cm.
A missionary tract.
USIC

1904. ———. **Missions. British. Birmingham Conference.** Invitation. Birmingham [n.d.]
Broadside. 17½×8½cm.
Missionary leaflet.
UPB

1905. ———. **Missions. British. Bradford Conference.** Report of the Bradford Quarterly Conference of the Church of Jesus Christ of Latter Day Saints, held in Bradford, March 9, 1851. Bradford, Printed by J. M. Jowett, Tyrrel Street, 1851.
8p. 21cm.
UPB, USIC

1906. ———. Second report of the Bradford Conference of the Church of Jesus Christ of Latter-day Saints, held at Bradford, June 7 and 8, 1851 . . . Bradford, Printed by J. M. Jowett . . . 1851.
8p. 21½cm.
Robert O. Menzies, President. Jonathan Midgley, William Burton, Conference Secs.
USIC

1907. ———. Third report of the Bradford Quarterly Conference of the Church of Jesus Christ of Latter-day Saints, held at the meeting room South Market, Leeds, Nov. 8th and 9th, 1851. Bradford, J. Drake, Printer & Bookbinder, Northgate [1851]
8p. 21cm.
USIC

1908. ———. Fourth report of the Bradford Quarterly Conference, of the Church of Jesus Christ of Latter-day Saints held at the meeting room Sun

Bridge, Bradford, January 24th & 25th, 1852. Bradford, John Drake, Printer & Bookbinder, Northgate [1852]
8p. 21cm.
USIC

1909. ———. Fifth report of the Bradford Quarterly Conference, of the Church of Jesus Christ of Latter Day Saints held at the Odd Fellows Hall, Thornton Road, Bradford, May 8th & 9th, 1852. Bradford, A. O'Leary, Printer . . . [1852]
10p. 21cm.
USIC

1910. ———. Sixth report of the Bradford Quarterly Conference, of the Church of Jesus Christ of Latter Day Saints, held at the meeting room Sun Bridge, Bradford, August 7th & 8th, 1852. Bradford, A. O'Leary, Printer . . . [1852]
8p. 21cm.
USIC

1911. ———. Report of a conference held in Bradford, Sunday, August 10, 1862. [Bradford? 1862]
16p. 21cm.
Reported by E. L. Sloan.
MH, USIC

1912. ———. **Missions. British. Dundee Conference.** Report of the Dundee Conference, from November 30, 1851, to May 30, 1852, held in Watt Institution Hall. [Dundee? 1852]
8p. 21cm.
James M. Naughton, Pres. James Mair, Secretary.
OClWHi, UPB, USIC

1913. ———. Report of the Dundee Conference of the Church of Jesus Christ of Latter-day Saints, held in the Royal Arms lecture-room Lindsay Street, on Sabbath, 18th December, 1853 . . . Dundee, Printed by J. Pellow, New Inn Entry, 1854.
8p. 21½cm.
Andrew Ferguson, President. James Mair, Clerk.
USIC

1914. ———. **Missions. British. Edinburgh Conference.** Latter Day Saints. The Edinburgh Branch of this Society now meet, for public worship, in Mr. M'Pherson's large hall . . . Edinburgh, 1847.
Broadside. 21×29cm.
Printed to publicize meetings in order to refute Dr. Lee, who at the meeting of the Edinburgh Presbytery, "assert that we taught principles so absurd, that even a Hottentot would not believe them . . ."
Signed: Edinburgh, May, 1847.
USIC

1915. ———. Report of the Edinburgh Conference. From January 6th, 1850 to June 9th, 1850, held in the Whitefield Chapel, High Street. [Edinburgh, 1850?]
6 [2]p. 21cm.
Crandall Dunn, president.
USIC

1916. ———. Report of the Edinburgh Conference. From June 9th to December 8th, 1850, held in Whitefield Chapel, High Street. Edinburgh, 1850.
3 [1]p. 21cm.
Crandall Dunn, President. G. G. Waugh, Clerk.
USIC

1917. ———. The quarterly report of the Edinburgh Conference of the Church of Jesus Christ of Latter-day Saints, held in Whitefield chapel . . . Edinburgh, September 5, 1852. [Edinburgh?] 1852.
8p. 21cm.
MH, OClWHi, UPB, USIC

1918. ———. **Missions. British. Glasgow Conference.** Report of the Glasgow Quarterly Conference, held in the Mechanics' Institution, Canning Street, Calton, Glasgow, March 24 and 25, 1849. [Glasgow? 1849]
8p. 21cm.
"Eli B. Kelsey, President. Walter Thompson, Clerk"
MH, UHi, UPB, USIC

1919. ———. Report of the Glasgow Quarterly Conference, held in the Merchants' Hall, Hutchison Street, Glasgow, June 24th, 1849. [Liverpool, R. James] 1849.
8p. 20cm.
President, Eli B. Kelsey. Clerk, Walter Thompson.
UHi, USIC

1920. ———. Report of the Glasgow Quarterly Conference held in the Mechanics' Institution, Canning St. Calton, 1st January, 1850. [Liverpool? 1850?]
8p. 21cm.
President, Harrison Burgess. Clerk, Walter Thompson.
MH, UPB, USIC

1921. ———. Report of the Glasgow Quarterly Conference held in the Mechanics' Institution Hall, Canning St., Calton, Glasgow, June 15th and 16th, 1850. [Glasgow? 1850?]
8p. 21cm.
Joseph Clements, President. Walter Thompson, Clerk.
MH, UPB, USIC

1922. ———. Report of the Glasgow Quarterly Conference held in the Mechanic's hall, Canning Street, Calton, Glasgow, on 1st Jan. 1851. Glasgow, Printed by J. and J. Taylor [1851]
8p. 21cm.
MH

1923. ———. Report of the Glasgow Quarterly Conference, June 1, 1851. Liverpool, 1851.
24p. 21cm.
USIC

CHURCH. . . . MISSIONS. BRITISH. GLASGOW

1924. ———. Glasgow Quarterly Conference report . . . December 6, 7, 1851. Liverpool, 1851.
16p. 21cm.
USIC

1925. ———. Report of the Glasgow Conference of the Church of Jesus Christ of Latter-day Saints held in the Mechanic's Institution Hall, Canning Street, Calton, Glasgow, 1st Jan. 1852. Glasgow, Printed by E. Malcolm, 1852.
14 [1]p. 20½cm.
Robert Campbell, President.
MH, UPB

1926. ———. Report of the Glasgow Conference of the Church of Jesus Christ of Latter-day Saints for the half-year ending 27th June, 1852, held in the Mechanics' Hall, Canning Street, Calton, Glasgow, June 27th, 1852. Dundee, Printed by J. Pellew, 1852.
4p. 21cm.
John Lyon, President.
MH, OClWHi

1927. ———. Report of the Glasgow Conference of the Church of Jesus Christ of Latter-day Saints, held in the Mechanics' Institution Hall, Canning Street, Calton, Glasgow, 3d July, 1853. Glasgow, William Gilchrist, 1853.
16p. 21cm.
Cover-title.
Edward Martin, President. Patrick Lynch, Secretary.
MH, UHi

1928. ———. **Missions. British. Hull Conference.** Minutes of a council of the priesthood, of Hull Conference of the Church of Jesus Christ of Latter-day Saints, held in the Wilberforce Room, St. John-street, Hull, June 12, 13th, 14th, 1852. [Hull? 1852]
10p. 21cm.
UPB, USIC

1929. ———. Programme of the Latter Day Saints' festival, to be held in the Temperance Hall, Paragon-Street, Hull, on Good Friday, April the 9th, 1852. President of the Conference, Elder J. T. Hardy. President of the Branch. Elder W. L. N. Allen. [Hull, Aliver's Printing Establishment, 1852]
4p. 21cm.
USIC

1930. ———. **Missions. British. Liverpool Conference.** Programme of the Latter-day Saints' soirée to be held in the music hall, Bond Street on Wednesday, July 9th, 1851. President of the Conference, Elder G. Rodger. President of the Branch, Elder J. Clements. [Liverpool, Printed by J. Sadler, 1851]
4 [1]p. 20cm.
Includes the songs to be sung.
USIC

1931. ———. **Missions. British. London Conference.** Circular to the presidents of branches, priesthood, and saints generally, of the London Conference, of the Church of Jesus Christ of Latter-day Saints. [London, 1851?]
4p. 21cm.
Caption-title.
Signed: Eli B. Kelsey, President.
MH, USIC

1932. ———. Minutes of the London Conference held at Aldenham Street and Theobald's Road, on the 22nd and 23rd of December, 1849, and the 1st and 2nd of June, 1850. London, Printed by W. Bowden, 1850.
16p. 20½cm.
MH, NN, OCl, UPB, USIC

1933. ———. Half-yearly report of the London Conference of the Church of Jesus Christ of Latter-day Saints, held in the City of London, Saturday and Sunday, Nov. 30th and Dec. 1st, 1850. Also, a report of the proceedings of a meeting of the priesthood of the London Conference, held in the hall of the Whitechapel Branch, London, Sabbath, the 5th day of January, 1851. [London, J. Teulon, 1851]
20p. 21cm.
MH, UPB

1934. ———. Report of the London Conference of the Church of Jesus Christ of Latter-day Saints, held in the city of London, Saturday and Sunday, May 31st, and June 1st, 1851. London, Printed by W. Aubrey [1851?]
24p. 22cm.
Elder Eli B. Kelsey, President.
MH, OCl, UHi, USIC

1935. ———. Half-yearly report of the London Conference of Latter-day Saints, held in the City of London, Saturday and Sunday, May 31st, and June 1st, 1851. London, Printed by W. Aubrey, 1851.
24p. 21cm.
MH, UPB, USIC

1936. ———. The programme of the London Conference festival to be held in the Freemason's Hall, Great Queen Street, on Monday, June 2nd, 1851. [London? Printed by J. B. Franklin, 1851?]
8p. 21cm.
CSmH, MH, UPB, USIC

1937. ———. The semi-half-yearly circular of the President of the London Conference of the Church of Jesus Christ of Latter-day Saints to the presidents of branches and priesthood generally. London, Printed by W. Aubrey, 1851.
8p. 20½cm.
UPB

1938. ———. Half-yearly report of the London Conference of the Church of Jesus Christ of Latter-day Saints, held in the city of London, Saturday & Sunday, December 6th and 7th, 1851. London, Printed by J. B. Franklin [1852]
16p. 21cm.
MH, USlC

1939. ———. Half-yearly report of the London Conference of the Church of Jesus Christ of Latter-day Saints, held in the City of London, June 5th and 6th, 1852. [London, Printed by J. B. Franklin, 1852?]
7 [3]p. 21cm.
MH, UPB, USlC

1940. ———. Report of the Pastoral Conference of the Church of Jesus Christ of Latter-day Saints held in the Freemasons' Hall, Great Queen Street, Long acre, on Saturday and Sunday, December 25th and 26th, 1852. Also, a brief half-yearly report of the London Conference, held in the eastern lecture hall, Whitechapel, Saturday, Dec. 5th, 1852. [London, Printed by J. B. Franklin, 1853?]
12 [4]p. 21cm.
Testimonial to Elder Jacob Gates . . . , report, p.[4]
[4]p. 21cm.
MH

1940a. ———. Half yearly report of the London Conference of the Church of Jesus Christ of Latter-day Saints, held on Saturday & Sunday, 2nd & 3rd July, 1853. [London] 1853.
[4]p. 21cm.
Variant printing without date.
USlC

———. Testimonial presented to Elder Jacob Gates. *See the Report of the Pastoral Conference. 1853.*

1941. ———. Minutes of the London Conference of the Church of Jesus Christ of Latter-day Saints held in the Eastern Lecture Hall, on the evening of the 24th, and in the Linwood gallery, Leicester Square, on the 25th, of June, 1854. [London? 1854?]
[4]p. 21cm.
MH

1942. ———. Minutes of the London Conference of the Church of Jesus Christ of Latter-day Saints, held in the Eastern Lecture Hall, on the evening of the 29th, and in the Linwood Gallery, Leicester Square, on December the 30th, 1855. [London? 1855?]
4 [4]p. 20½cm.
USlC

1943. ———. **Missions. British. Newcastle Conference.** Half-yearly report of the Newcastle-upon-Tyne Conference of the Church of Jesus Christ of Latter-day Saints. Held at Sunderland on Saturday and Sunday, May 14th and 15th, 1853. London, Printed for W. Bowden [1853]
14p. 20½cm.
Elder Thomas Squires, President. Elder Ebenezer Gillies, Secretary.
USlC

1944. ———. Selected hymns for semi-annual conference of the Church of Jesus Christ of Latter-day Saints. Newcastle District. May 27th, 1928. [Newcastle? 1928]
10p. 18cm.
USlC

1945. ———. **Missions. British. Norwich Conference.** The Programme of the Norwich Conference Festival to be held in Saint Andrew's Hall, Monday, the 28th Day of July, 1851. [Norwich, P. Otty, Printer] 1851.
5p. 21cm.
Conference and Pioneer Day celebration.
USlC

1945a. ———. **Missions. British. Nottinghamshire Conference.** . . . A conference of the Church of Jesus Christ of Latter-day Saints in the Nottingham Conference District will be held in the Gladstone Lecture Hall, Lamartine Street, Nottingham, on Sunday, March 14, 1897. [n.p., 1897]
[2]p. 21½cm.
On verso are the Articles of Faith.
USlC

1945b. ———. . . . Dear friends: you are kindly invited to attend a district meeting to be held by elders of the Church of Jesus Christ of Latter-day Saints in Room 3, Temperance Hall, Curzon Street, Derby, on Sunday February 28, 1897. [n.p., 1897]
[2]p. 21½cm.
On verso are the Articles of Faith.
USlC

1945c. ———. Mormonism! Come and hear its principles expounded at a conference of the Latter-day Saints, in the Nottingham District, which will be held in the Temperance Hall, St. Ann's Street, Nottingham, on Sunday, October 25, 1896. [n.p., 1896]
[2]p. 21½cm.
On verso are the Articles of Faith.
USlC

1946. ———. Nottinghamshire conference [second quarterly] report of the Church of Jesus Christ of Latter-day Saints held in St. Ann's chapel, Nottingham, on the twenty-ninth day of June, 1852. [Nottinghamshire?] 1852.
8p. 21½cm.
Henry Savage, President.
MH, USlC

1947. ———. Report of the first quarterly meeting of the Nottinghamshire Conference of the Church of Jesus Christ of Latter-day Saints held in St. Ann's chapel, St. Ann's Street, Nottingham, on the twenty-eighth day of March, 1852. [n.p., 1852]
4p. 21½cm.
Caption-title.
MH, UPB

1948. ———. Report of the Nottinghamshire Conference of the Church of Jesus Christ of Latter-day Saints held in St. Ann's chapel, St. Anns; Nottingham, on the 26th day of Dec. 1852. [n.p.] 1853.
13p. 21cm.
MH

1948a. ———. To the citizens of Loughborough. Latter-day Saint elders from America will hold a district meeting in your town on Sunday, Dec. 20, at 2:30 & 6:30 P.M. in the Co-operative Hall, Woodgate. [n.p., n.d.]
[2]p. 21½cm.
On verso are the Articles of Faith.
USIC

1949. ———. **Missions. British. Sheffield Conference.** Report of the Sheffield Quarterly Conference held in the Hall of Science, Rockingham Street, Sheffield, December 23d, 1849. [Sheffield, T. Potter, Printer, 1849?]
8p. 21cm.
President, Crandell Dunn. Clerks, Walter Savage & S. J. Lees
CtY, ICN, USIC

1950. ———. Report of the Sheffield Conference of the Church of Jesus Christ of Latter-day Saints, held in the Hall of Science, Rockingham Street, Sheffield, May 19, 1850. [Sheffield, T. Potter, Printer, 1850?]
8p. 21cm.
President, J. W. Cummings. Secretaries, W. S. Savage and S. J. Lees.
ICN, MH, USIC

1951. ———. Report of the Sheffield Conference of the Church of Jesus Christ of Latter-day Saints, held in the Hall of Science, Rockingham Street, Sheffield, November 24th, 1850. Sheffield, Stephen New, Printer, 1850.
12p. 21cm.
President J. W. Cummings. Secretaries, H. J. Hudson, S. J. Lees.
ICN, MH, UPB, USIC

1952. ———. Report of the Sheffield Conference of the Church of Jesus Christ of Latter-day Saints, held in the Hall of Science, Rockingham Street, Sheffield, on the eighth day of June, 1851. J. V. Long, reporter. [Sheffield, Stephen New, Printer, 1851?]
12p. 21cm.
Lewis Robbins, President. W. S. Myers, Secretary.
ICN, UPB, USIC

1953. ———. **Missions. British. South Conference.** A report of meetings of the South Conference of the Church of Jesus Christ of Latter-day Saints, held in the large room, no. 34, Thomas Street, Bristol, Saturday and Sunday, 6th & 7th of December, 1851. Bristol, Printed by Bonner & Strickland [1851?]
9 [3]p. 21cm.
MH, USIC

1954. ———. **Missions. British. Southampton Conference.** Programme of the Southampton Conference festival, to be held at the Yorke Rooms, Southsea, Portsmouth, On Monday December 13th, 1852. [n.p., 1852]
[4]p. 21cm.
MH

1955. ———. Programme of the Southampton Conference festival . . . June 28th, 1852. [Southampton, 1852]
1852. [n.p., 1852]
[4]p. 21cm.
MH

1956. ———. **Missions. British. Warwickshire Conference.** Report of the Warwickshire Conference, held in the Latter Day Saints' Hall, Guy Street, Leamington Spa, Sunday, September 1, 1850. [Leamington, J. W. Brierly, 1850]
10p. 21cm.
USIC

1957. ———. **Missions. Central States.** Outlines of the doctrines of the Church of Jesus Christ of Latter-day Saints. Kansas City, Mo., Central States Mission, Church of Jesus Christ of Latter-day Saints [n.d.]
27p. 17cm.
UU

1958. ———. **Missions. Czechoslovakia.** Sto let Mormonismu. Stručné dějiny a náslin učení Cirkve Ježíše Krista Svatých poslednich Dnů (Mormonů) Vydáno, Církve Ježíše Krista svatých poslednich dnů v Praze Tiskli Stursa, Kraut a spol. v. Brne [1930?]
103 [1]p. 22½cm.
USIC, UU

1959. ———. **Missions. Danish.** Er de Sidste-Dages Hellige Kristne? [Kobenhavn, Udgivet og forlagt af John S. Hansen . . . 1925]
4p. 21cm.
Title in English: Are the Latter-day Saints Christians?
USIC

1960. ———. Et venligt ord. [København, Udgivet og forlagt af Joseph L. Peterson . . . Trykt i "Aka" . . . 1927]
4p. 23cm.
Title in English: A friendly voice.
USIC

CHURCH. . . MISSIONS. EUROPEAN

1961. ———. Mormonerne, skildret af Ikke-Mormoner. [Kjøbenhavn, Udgivet og forlagt af N. C. Flygare . . . Trykt hos F. E. Bording (B. Peterson) n.d.]
16p. 22cm.
Title in English: Non-Mormons describe the Mormons.
CSmH

———. Nogle Anerkendende ord. *See Nogle Anerkendende ord.*

1962. ———. Polygamie og hvid Slavehandel. Sandheden om Mormonerne. [Kjobenhavn, Udgivet og forlagt af H. J. Christiansen. Trykt hos F. E. Bording, 1914]
4p. 21cm.
Title in English: Polygamy and white slavery.
USIC

1963. ———. Profetiske Vidnesbyrd. [København, Udgivet og forlagt af John S. Hansen . . . 1925]
4p. 21cm.
Title in English: Prophetic testimony.
USIC

1964. ———. Et Tidernes Tegn. [København, Udgivet og forlagt af John S. Hansen . . . 1925]
4p. 21cm.
Title in English: A sign of the times.
USIC

1965. ———. **Missions. Eastern States.** Annual conference of conference presidents of the Eastern States Mission of the Church of Jesus Christ of Latter-day Saints, held March 2nd to 7th, 1910, at New York City. [New York City, 1910]
66p. 19cm.
UPB, USIC

1966. ———. Program of the first general conference of the Eastern States Mission of the Church of Jesus Christ of L.D.S., held at the Hill Cumorah. Celebrating the one hundredth anniversary of the revealed existence of the Book of Mormon, September 21–22, 1923. [Brooklyn, 1923]
[8]p. 18cm.
Cover-title.
UPB

1967. ———. A statement from Josiah Quincy . . . concerning an interview had in 1844 with Joseph Smith . . . Some of the sayings and predictions made by the Prophet Joseph Smith. A letter to Mr. Wentworth from the prophet in answer to a request from him for a statement of belief, to be published in the Chicago Democrat. New York, Eastern States Mission [188 ?]
32p. 14cm.
Cover-title.
CtY, MH, NN, UPB, UU

1968. ———. (same) New York, Eastern States Mission [ca. 1915]
32p. 14cm.
Variant edition.
USIC

1969. ———. **Missions. European.** Centennial lessons for the Relief Society in the European Missions of the Church of Jesus Christ of Latter-day Saints. British Mission manual for the year 1930. Liverpool, Published by the Latter-day Saints, 1930.
3p.l., 9–112p. map. 22cm.
Compiled by Leah D. Widtsoe.
USIC

1970. ———. 1830. Centennial year. 1930 (Materials to be used for pageants during the year) Liverpool, 1930.
2 pts. (16, 82p.) 21cm.
Pt. 1. Womanhood by Elder C. Lowell Lees, and The light of Truth by Elder Kemmie Bagley. Pt. 2. A sheaf of home-made pageants and plays. . . .
UHi, UPB, USIC

1971. ———. A gospel century; some epoch-making events and doctrine; a study course for the Mutual Improvement Associations in the British Mission of the Church of Jesus Christ of Latter-day Saints. Liverpool, British Mission, 1930.
77p. 21½cm.
UHi, USIC

1972. ———. Instructions for district supervision. European Mission, Church of Jesus Christ of Latter-day Saints. Liverpool, European Mission, 1929.
48p. 18cm.
UHi, UPB, USIC

1973. ———. . . . Misrepresentation decried . . . [Liverpool, Printed and Published by the European Missions of the Church of Jesus Christ of Latter-day Saints, 1926]
[4]p. 22cm.
Caption-title.
At head of title: From *Millennial Star*, Feb. 25, 1926.
Prepared by James E. Talmage.
"Fair play for the Mormons" by Viscount Castlerose.
UHi, UPB, USIC

———. A sheaf of home-made pageants and plays for use in the European Missions, Liverpool, 1930. *See Church of Jesus Christ of Latter-day Saints. Missions. European. 1830. Centennial year. 1930.*

1974. ———. Studies in priesthood for the use of the priesthood classes of the European Missions of the Church of Jesus Christ of Latter-day Saints. Liverpool, European Mission, 1930.
3p.l., 7–92p. 18½cm.
UHi, UPB

CHURCH. . . . MISSIONS. EUROPEAN

1975. ———. (same, in French) Etudes de prétrise; à l'usage des prétrises de la Mission Européenne de l'Eglise de Jésus-Christ des Saints des Derniers Jours. Traduit de l'anglais par A. Horbach. Ville d'Avray (Seine-et-Oise) Publié par la Mission Francaise [1930]
3p.l. [7]–63p. 21½cm.
UPB, USIC

1976. ———. (same) Paris, Chambery [n.d.]
72p. 20cm.
USIC

1977. ———. The Word of wisdom. [Dresden, n.d.]
[6]p. 11½cm.
UPB

1978. ———. **Missions. French.** Cours d'Etudes. Revelation moderne. Ville d' Avray, France [1930]
118p. 21½cm. (Societe d'Amélioration Mutuelle. Programmes des activites et concours, 1930–1931)
Title in English: Course of study. Modern revelation.
UPB, USIC

1979. ———. Epitre du président de la mission Francaise à l' Eglise des Saints des Derniers-jours in France et dans les Isles de la Manche. [Saint-Helier, Jersey, 1854]
11p. 22cm.
Signed: Andre L. Lamoreaux, Jacques H. Hart, Louis A. Bertrand, Gullaume Taylor.
Title in English: Letter of the president of the French Mission.
ICN, NN, USIC

1980. ———. l'Eternelle Vérité. Explications sur les Doctrines de l'Eglise de Jésus-Christ des Saints des Derniers Jours. Apostasie et Restauration de Véritable Evangile. Liége [ca. 1907]
15 [1]p. 17cm.
USIC

1981. ———. Exposition des premiers principes de la doctrine de l'Eglise de Jésus-Christ des Saints des derniers jours. Rotterdam, Publieé par Willard T. Cannon, 1904.
16p. 18cm.
Title in English: Exposition of the first principles of the gospel.
USIC

1982. ———. L'Evangile que Christ enseignait et son etablissement aux Derniers Jours. Rotterdam, Publieé par Willard T. Cannon, 1904.
16 [1]p. 17½cm.
Title in English: The Church that Christ established.
USIC

1983. ———. Le sabbat du Seigneur. Pourquoi l'Eglise de Jésus-Christ des Saints des Derniers Jours admet, comme jour particulier de service spécial et déclaration du Seigneur ce'qu on appelle generalé-le Sabbat Chretien. Liege, Publié par Ernest C. Rossiter [n.d.]
14 [1]p. 16cm.
Title in English: The Lords' day.
UPB, USIC

1984. ———. Un Siècle de l'Evangile quelques événements et quelques doctrines qui font époque traduit de l'anglais par Anna Arthaud et Oscar Frieden. Liège, Publie par l'Eglise de Jesus-Christ des Saints des Derniers Jours, 1930.
3p.l., 7–94p. 21½cm.
Cours d'etudes pour l'Association d'Amélioration des Jeunes Gens dans la mission francaise de l'eglise de Jesus-Christ des Saints des Derniers Jours.
Title in English: A century of the gospel.
UPB, USIC

1985. ———. **Missions. German.** Missionen d. Kirche Jesu Christi der Heiligen der letzten Tage (Mormonen) . . . [Dresden, Drueger & Horn, 1930?]
Broadside. 21×15cm.
UHi

1986. ———. Der Mormonismus. Seine einsetzung und ersten Grundsätze. Bern [Buch Druckerei von C. Gutknecht] 1872.
1p.l., 46p. 21cm.
Signed: Eduard Schönfeld, Johannes Huber, Karl H. Wilcken.
Title in English: Mormonism.
MH, USIC

1987. ———. **Missions. German-Austrian.** G. F. V. Handbuch. Dresden, Deutsch, Österreichischen Mission der Kirche Jesu Christi der Heiligen der letzten Tage, 1928.
109p. 19cm.
Title in English: M.I.A. handbook.
UPB

1988. ———. Dem Priesterschafts jubiläum gewidmet. [Dresden, Germany, 1929]
11p. 22½cm.
Title in English: Celebration of the priesthood.
USIC

1989. ———. **Missions. Hawaiian.** I Na Hoahanau o ka Ekalesia o Iesu Kristo o ka Poe Hoano o na La Hope nei, ma ka Misiona o Hawaii. [Honolulu, 1919?]
4p. 24cm.
Title in English: Ecclesiastical letter to the missionaries and to the brethren in the church.
UPB, USIC

CHURCH . . . MISSIONS. NETHERLANDS

1990. ———. Ke alakai oia hoi he mau haawina e hoakaka mai ana i na kumu manaoio. Ka Ekalesia o Iesu Kristo o ka Poe Hoano o no la Hope nei. L.D.S. Hawaiian Mission. Honolulu, Hoopukaia e ka Misiona Hawaii, 1924.
60 [2]p. 19cm.
Title in English: A lesson guide to make clear our faith.
UPB, USIC

1991. ———. Na Kau o Ka Euanelio. He Mau Haawina i Hoomakaukau Ia No Na Halawai O Ka Oihanakahuna A Me Ka Hui Manawalea No Ka Ekalesia o Iesu Kristo O Ka Poe Hoano O Na La Hope Nei Ma Ka Misiona o Hawaii. [Honolulu, ca. 1928]
40p. 23cm.
Lesson book for the priesthood and for the Relief Society.
Title in English: A leader's guide.
UPB, USIC

1992. ———. Souvenir. 1850–1900. [Honolulu, The Mercantile Ptg. Co., Ltd., 1900]
26p. 14½cm.
In Hawaiian and English.
USIC

1993. ———. **Missions. Icelandic.** Skilabod fra hinmum. [n.d., Prentsmithjan Gutenberg, n.d.]
8p. 17½cm.
Title in English: A message from heaven.
UPB, USIC

1994. ———. **Missions. Netherlands.** Beproeft alle dingen; behoudt het goede . . . [Rotterdam] 1904.
4p. 23cm.
"April, 1904. 140ste Duesendtal"
Title in English: Search all things, hold the good.
USIC

1995. ———. Enkele getuigenissen aangaande de Kerk van Jezuz Christus van de Heiligen der laatste Dagen, den Profeet Joseph Smith, en het "Mormoniche" volk. [Rotterdam, n.d.]
[4]p. 22cm.
Title in English: Angelic testimony of the Church of Jesus Christ of Latter-day Saints.
USIC

1996. ———. L'Evangile que Christ enseignait et son établissement aux Derniers Jours . . . Rotterdam, Publiée par Willard T. Cannon, 1904.
16p. 18cm.
Title in English: The Church which Christ taught.
USIC

1997. ———. Het evangelie. Wat is het? Waarom is het noodig in ons leven. [Rotterdam, Uidgave van de Nederlandsch-Belgische Zending, 1913]
8 [1]p. 18cm. (Boekje. No. 1)
Title in English: The gospel, what is it?
USIC

1998. ———. Geloof, bekeering en de Wedergeboorte. Als gepredikt door Jezus en Zijne Apostelen. [Rotterdam, Uitgave van de Nederlandsch-Belgische Zending, 1913]
12p. 18cm. (Boekje. No. 2)
Title in English: Faith, conversion and the new birth.
USIC

1999. ———. Goddelijke beloegdheid in de krek van Christus. Rotterdam, Uitgave van Roscoe W. Eardley [1913]
8 [1]p. 18cm. (Boekje. No. 3)
Title in English: Divine authority in the Church of Christ.
USIC

2000. ———. De Herstelling van het Evangélie van Jezus Christus in de 19e eeuw. [Rotterdam, Uitgave van de Nederlandsch-Belgische, 1913]
12 [1]p. 18cm. (Boekje. No. 4)
Title in English: The restoration of the gospel of Jesus Christ.
USIC

2001. ———. Een vriendschappelijk onderhoud over Belangrijke Godsdienst-Waarheden. Rotterdam . . . Kerk van Jezus Christus van de Heiligen der laatste Dagen [1913]
19 [1]p. 17½cm.
Title in English: A friendly conversation.
USIC

———. De Zaligheid door Genade. *See Parry, Edwin F.*

2002. ———. Zondagsschool-Liederen voor de Kerk van Jezus Christus van de Heiligen der laatste Dagen in de Nederlandsche Zending. Vierde druk. Rotterdam, Uitgegeven door John P. Lillywhite, 1922.
71p. 12cm.
Title in English: Sunday School hymnal of the Church of Jesus Christ of Latter-day Saints.
USIC

2003. ———. Zondagsschool-schetsen. De artikelen des Geloofs. Rotterdam, Uitgegeven door de Nederlandsch-Belgische Zending [ca. 1907]
12p. 21cm.
Title in English: The Articles of faith.
USIC

2004. ———. Zondagsschool-schetsen. Jezus, de Christus. Rotterdam, Uitgegeven door de Nederlandsch-Belgische Zending [ca. 1907]
12p. 21cm.
Title in English: Jesus, the Christ.
USIC

2005. ———. Zondagsschool-schetsen. Jongens en en meisjes uit den Bijbel. — Het leven der Apostelen. Rotterdam, Uitgegeven door de Nederlandsch-Belgische Zending [ca. 1907]
8p. 21cm.
Title in English: Boys and girls of the Bible — The lives of the Apostles.
USIC

2006. ———. Zondagsschool-schetsen. Ouder en kind. Rotterdam, Uitgegeven door de Nederlandsch-Belgische Zending [ca. 1907]
27p. 19½cm.
Title in English: Parent and child.
USIC

2007. ———. Zondagschool-Schetsen. Ten dienste der Zondagscholen in de Nederlandsch-Belgische Zending van de Heiligen der Laatste Dagen. Voor 1907. . . . Rotterdam, Uitgegeven door: Alex Nibley [1907]
15p. 16cm.
Title in English: Sunday school service in the mission . . .
USIC

2008. ———. **Missions. Northern States.** Corner stones of "Reorganization"; a few facts concerning its founders, compiled from early church history. [Chicago, Northern States Mission, 1909]
16p. 19cm.
MoInRC, UPB, USI, USIC, UU

2009. ———. (same, in Swedish) Den omorganiserade kyrkans Hörnstenar. Historiska Sammandrag. Öfversättning från Engelskan. Stockholm, Utgifven och förlagd af Andreas Petersen . . . Tryckt hos Smedbergs, 1911.
24p. 18cm.
UPB, USIC

2010. ———. Gospel reference, concise and logical. [Chicago, n.d.]
31p. 16cm.
UPB, USIC

2011. ———. Reorganization weighed, presidency-permanency. [Chicago, Northern States Mission, 1910]
16p. 18½cm.
MoInRC, UPB, USIC, UU

2012. ———. **Missions. Northwestern States.** In commemoration of the opening of new chapel, Church of Jesus Christ of Latter-day Saints, February 15, 16, 17, 1929. Portland, Oregon. [Portland, 1929?]
39p. plates, ports. 27½cm.
Historical information concerning the L.D.S. Church in the Northwest.
USIC, UU

2013. ———. **Missions. Norwegian.** Jesu Cristi Kirke av de siste Dages Hellige. 100 års jubileum. [Oslo, Braute & Sons. Bok. og Aksidenstrykkeri, 1930]
13 [2]p. 16½×26cm.
Title in English: Church of Jesus Christ of Latter-day Saints.
USIC

2014. ———. **Missions. Samoan.** E i ai i lenei tusi nai tusi itiiti e igoa. "Ole taitai," "O le ala," "O le faitotoa," "Ole malo l le atua," atoa ma "O le pogai." ia fai ia tusi ma tulaga o le Apefai o le Evagelia Moni, Ina ia Maua ai le Tonu i e Savavali i ai. Na Tusia e Ed. J. Laau. Salt Lake City, The Deseret News, 1910.
186p. 16½cm.
Each part has separate title page.
Contents: The leader. The Road-way. The Door. The Kingdom of God. The origin.
Title in English: A collection of small writings.
NjP, UPB, USIC

2015. ———. O le molimau fou le galuega moni a le atua, ma le faamatalaga o le tusi a mamona. O le tupuga o tagata eena o nei atunuu. Mo Le Ekalesia a Iesu Keriso o le au paia o Aso e Gata ai . . . Na Tusia e misi Alaaeti (Elder G. A. Goates) . . . Ua Faatonuina ma Faalomia e misi Matina (Elder Martin F. Sanders), ma Ua Fesoasoani foi Faatonuina e misi Samati (Elder E. H. Smart). Na lomia e siliva ma falani i le fale lomi Tusi o siliva. Provo, Utah, 1905.
77p. 21½cm.
Title in English: A testimony of the true Church of God.
UPB, USIC

2016. ———. **Missions. Southern States.** The elders' manual. [Chattanooga, Tenn., 1914?]
3p.l., 7–93p. 15½cm.
Later revised and published by the Missions of the Church of Jesus Christ of Latter-day Saints.
USIC

2017. ———. Report of the St. Louis Conference of the Church of Jesus Christ of Latter Day Saints held in Concert Hall, St. Louis, Mo., Printed by Moritz Neidner, 1852.
6p. 21½cm.
USIC defective copy

2018. ———. The resurrection of children. Atlanta, Georgia [n.d.]
[4]p. 16cm.
USIC

———. **Missions. Swedish.** Et gladt budskap. *See Ett gladt budskap.*

———. Vittnesbörd af framstående män af "Mormonerna." *See Peterson, Andreas.*

2019. ———. **Missions. Swiss-German.** Der Abfall des ursprunglischen Evangeliums und dessen Wiederherstellung. Zurich, Herausgegeben von Hugh J. Cannon and Levi Edgar Young [ca. 1901]
15 [1]p. 18cm. (Tractat Nr. I)
Title in English: Apostasy of the original church . . .
USIC

2020. ———. (same) Berlin, Herausgegeben von Hugh J. Cannon, 1902.
15 [1]p. 18cm. (Tractat Nr. I)
USIC

2021. ———. L'Authorite diviné; Ordonnances nulles quand elles sont administrées sans autorité divine. Zurich, Thos. E. McKay, 1909.
12p. 18cm.
Title in English: Divine authority.
USIC

2022. ———. Erlösung für die Toten. Präerestenz und herkunft des Menschen. Taufe für die toten. Herausgegeben von der Redaktion des "Stern." Berlin, H. Dusedann . . . 1901.
15 [1]p. 18m.
Cover-title.
In blue printed wrapper.
Title in English: Redemption of the dead.
USIC

2023. ———. (same) Basel, Herausgegeben von Serge F. Ballif, Präsident der Schweizerischen und Deutschen Mission der Kirche Jesu Christi der heiligen der Letzten Tage, 1922.
16p. 15cm.
USIC

2024. ———. L'Eternelle Vérité. Explications sur les Doctrines de l'Église de Jésus-Christ des Saints des Derniers Jours. Apostasie et Restauration de Véritable Évangile. Berne, Publié par la Redáction de "Stern" [1898]
16p. 18cm.
Cover dated 1898.
Title in English: Eternal truths.
USIC

2025. ———. (same) Berne, Publié par le Bureau de la Mission Suisse [ca 1900]
16p. 18cm. (Traité No. 1)
USIC

2026. ———. (same) Liége, Publié par Jacob H. Trayner. Implimerie industrielle, 1905.
16p. 17½cm.
USIC

2027. ———. Friede sei in diesem hause! Zürich, Herausgegeben von Hugh J. Cannon [n.d.]
[4]p. 22cm.
Glaubensartikel der kirche Jesu Christi, der heiligen der letzten Tage, p. [4]
Title in English: May peace be in your home.
USIC

2028. ———. (same, in Hungarian) Békesség legyen e házban! [Zurich, Thomas E. McKay, n.d.]
[4]p. 22cm.
Jézus Kristus templomának hitcikkelyei, a szenteknek utolsó napjai, p. [4]
USIC

2029. ———. Eine kurze Darstellung der hauptsächlichsten Lehren des Evangeliums Jesu Christi. Herausgegeben durch die Mission der Kirche in der Schwiez und Deutschland. Bern [Buchdruckerei von G. Gutkrecht] 1872.
46p. 23½cm.
Title in English: A short presentation of the main teachings of the gospel of Jesus Christ.
MH

2030. ———. Das los des Evangeliums. Eine kurzgefasste Erklärung über den Abfall und die Wiederherstellung des Evangeliums Jesu Christi. Basel, Herausgegeben von Serge F. Ballif, Präsident der Schweizerischen und Deutschen Mission der Kirche Jesu Christ der heiligen der Letzten Tage, 1922.
16p. 16½cm.
Title in English: The destiny of the gospel.
USIC

2031. ———. Les Principes fondamentaux de l'Evangile de Jésus-Christ comme ils furent Etablis par luimême . . . Zürich, Serge F. Ballif [n.d.]
12p. 20cm.
Title in English: Fundamental principles of the Church . . .
USIC

2032. ———. (same) Traité No. 2. Foi, Repentance, Baptême, Don du St-Exprit Autorité Révélation. Berne, Publié par la Rédaction du "Stern." [n.d.]
16p. 20cm.
Title in English: Faith, repentance, baptism . . .
USIC

2033. ———. La restauration de l'Evangile. Zürich, Serge F. Ballif, 1907.
16p. 15cm.
Title in English: The restoration of the church.
USIC

2034. ———. Richtlinien für die Arbeit des Fortbildungsvereins im Jahre 1925–26. [Basel] Herausgegeben von der Deutsch-Österreichischen

und Schweizerisch Deutschen Mission der Kirche Jesu Christi der heiligen der Letzten Tage [1925]
10 [1]p. 21cm.
Title in English: Instruction for the work of the Mutual Improvement Association.
USIC

2035. ———. Offenbarungen der Neuzeit. Geschichte und Botschaft der "Lehre und Bündnisse." Aus dem Englischen "Manual for the Young Men's Mutual Improvement Associations" übersetzt. Basel, Herausgegeben von der Schweizerisch-Deutschen Mission der Kirche Jesu Christi der heiligen der Letzten Tage, 1920.
144p. 18cm.
"Zweite Auflage."
Title in English: Revelations of our time.
USIC

2036. ———. (same) Basel, Herausgegeben von Fred Tadje, Präsident der Schweizerischen und Deutschen Mission Der Kirche Jesu Christi der heiligen der Letzten Tage. 1925.
140p. 20cm.
"Ersten Auflage."
USIC

2037. ———. Eine Unterredung. Ein Berichterstatter informiert sich über die Kirche Jesu Christi der heiligen der Letzten Tage. Basel, Herausgegeben von der Schweizerisch-Deutschen Mission, 1917.
16p. 16½cm.
Title in English: A conversation.
USIC

2038. ———. Unterrichtspläne fur 1922 für die Sonntagsschulen in der Schweiberischen und Deutschen Mission der kirche Jesu Christi der heiligen der Letzten Tage. Nach Englischen Quellen bearbeitet von Ältester Max Zimmer. Basel, Herausgegeben von Serge F. Ballif . . . 1922.
2p.l., 171p. 21. 22cm.
Title in English: Lesson plans for 1922 for the Sunday School . . .
USIC

2039. ———. Die Wiederherstellung des ursprünglichen Evangeliums. Eine kurze Abhandlung über die Lehre der Kirche Jesu Christi der heiligen der Letzten Tage. Bern, Herausgegeben von J. S. Horne, 1877.
32p. 20½cm.
Cover-title.
Title in English: The Restoration of the primitive church.
MH, USIC

———. *See also Hoyer, Margaret; Stoof, Reinhold, Wunderlich, Jean.*

2040. ———. **Missions. Tahitian.** Te mau ira va parau iritihia no roto mai i te Biblia, te Buka a Mormona, te Buka Fafau e te Buka Poe Tao'a Rahi. Neneihia e Eraneta A. Rositera. Tahiti, Neia te piha neneiraa a te Ekalesia a Iesu Mesia i te Feia Mo'a it te Mau mahana Hopea nei . . . 1919.
7p.l., 330p. 17½cm.
Title in English: The great promise in the four standard words.
USIC

2041. ———. Na Pomaret Orometua. [Papeete, Tahiti, Ekalesia a Iesu Mesia . . . n.d.]
[4]p. 21cm.
Title in English: Talk on confirmation by laying on of hands.
USIC

2042. ———. E Parau Tuatapapa. No te peresideniraa e te pupu ahuru ma piti aposetolo e te toroa patereareha. No te Ekalesia a Iesu Mesia i te Feia Mo'a i te Mau Mahana Hopea Nei. Tahaiti, Papaihia e Viliamu Setemila [n.d.]
13p. 18½cm.
Title in English: A history of the First Presidency.
USIC

2043. Church of Jesus Christ of Latter-day Saints. Mutual Improvement Association. Annual Convention. Salt Lake City, Published by the General Boards of the M.I.A., 1896–
v. annual. 20cm.
USIC 1903–09, 1922, 1924–25, 1927, 1929–30.

2044. ———. Captains of industry. Salt Lake City, Published by the General Boards, Y.M. and Y.L.M.I.A., 1928.
3p.l. [7]–108p. 21½cm. (The Adult Department. M.I.A. manual . . . No. 3)
UPB, USIC

2045. ———. A century of progress . . . Salt Lake City, Published by the General Boards Y.M. and Y.L.M.I.A., 1929.
4p.l. [9]–213p. illus. 21cm. (Manual for the Adult Department of the M.I.A. 1929–30)
UPB, USIC, UU

2046. ———. Champions of liberty. Salt Lake City, Published by the General Boards of Y.M. and Y.L.M.I.A., 1927.
146p. 22cm. (Joint Advanced Senior class. M.I.A. Manual. No. 2)
UPB, USIC

2047. ———. Conference hymns and community songs. Twenty-sixth general annual conference of the Y.M. and Y.L.M.I.A. June 10, 11, and 12, 1921. Salt Lake City, 1921.
13p. 19½cm.
USIC

CHURCH. . . . MUTUAL IMPROVEMENT ASSOCIATION

2048. ———. Handbook of the Young Men's and Young Ladies' Mutual Improvement Associations. Official guide for the leisure-time and recreational program of the Church of Jesus Christ of Latter-day Saints. [Salt Lake City] Published by the General Boards of M.I.A., 1928.
2p.l., 5–464p. illus. 19cm.
This handbook combines the Young Men's and Young Ladies' handbooks and the official recreation guide.
NjP, NN, UHi, UPB

2049. ———. Heroes of Science. No. 1. Salt Lake City, Published by the General Board of the Y.M. and Y.L.M.I.A., 1926.
2p.l. [5]–70p. 21cm. (M.I.A. Advanced Senior Department Manual for the Joint Advanced Senior Classes. 1926–1927
UPB

2050. ———. The Improvement Association song book. A collection of original and selected songs and hymns set to music, prepared especially for the use of Mutual Improvement and other Association Choirs. Arranged by E. Beesley, Director of the Salt Lake City Tabernacle Choir. Salt Lake City, Juvenile Instructor Off., 1887.
2p.l. [5]–78p. 15½×21cm.
Words and music.
UPB, USIC, UU

2051. ———. In commemoration of the divine ushering in of the dispensation of the fulness of times through Joseph Smith, the prophet in the spring of 1820 . . . [Salt Lake City] Issued by the General Boards of the Mutual Improvement Association of the Church of Jesus Christ of Latter-day Saints, 1920.
[4]p. illus., port. 16½cm.
UPB

2052. ———. A mission as a factor in education . . . [Salt Lake City, Improvement Era, 1919]
[12]–14p., 1[l]. 21cm.
UPB

2053. ———. M.I.A. annual conference song folder. June, 1927. [Salt Lake City, 1927]
16p. 15cm.
Words only.
USIC

2054. ———. The M.I.A. Book of plays. Six one-act plays. Salt Lake City, Published by the General Boards of M.I.A., 1929.
124p. 18cm.
Mormon drama.
USIC

2055. ———. The M.I.A. Book of plays. Volume II. Six one-act plays. Salt Lake City, Published by The General Boards of M.I.A., 1930.
88p. 18cm.
Mormon drama.
USIC

2056. ———. M.I.A. conference. Salt Lake City, 1888–
v. 23cm.
Published by the Y.M.M.I.A. through 1895.
Title varies: Programme of exercises of the Y.M.M.I.A. General Conference, 1888–89; General Conference of the Y.M. and Y.L.M.I.A., 1891–1907; General annual conference of the Y.M. and Y.L.M.I.A., 1908–1927; Annual conference . . . 1928–1930.
NjP 1891; USIC 1896, 1898, 1901–04, 1906–12, 1914–24, 1926–30

2057. ———. M.I.A. monthly special programs including joint Sunday evening programs and studieis for associations meeting weekly during summer months, 1923–24. [Salt Lake City, 1923]
[32]p. 19cm.
USIC

2058. ———. M.I.A. monthly special programs, including joint Sunday evening programs and lesson outlines for associations meeting weekly during summer months. 1924–1925. [Salt Lake City, General Boards of the M.I.A.] 1924.
14p. 19cm.
UPB

2059. ———. Mutual Improvement Associations recreation bulletin No. 5. A compilation of all former M.I.A. publications on recreation with additional new material. A reference book for presiding officers; and for Stake and Ward M.I.A. Committees on Recreation, and other recreation leaders. Salt Lake City, Published by the General Boards of M.I.A., 1925.
2p.l. [5]–156p. 18½cm.
UPB

2060. ———. M.I.A. song folder. Salt Lake City, 1928.
[96]p. illus. 17½cm.
UPB, USIC

2061. ———. M.I.A. song folder. Devotional, M.I.A., and recreational songs. Salt Lake City, YM's and YLMIA, 1924.
32p. 18½cm.
USIC, UU

2062. ———. M.I.A. song folder. M.I.A. Songs — Social and fun songs, old-time songs — semi-popular songs. Patriotic and semi-patriotic songs. Christmas

carols — Religious songs — Hymns. Salt Lake City, Published by Mutual Improvement Association, 1926.
64p. 14cm.
Without music.
UPB, USIC, UU

2063. ———. (same) Salt Lake City, Published by the General Boards of the Mutual Improvement Associations, 1927.
64p. 15cm.
UPB

2064. ———. M.I.A. song folder. Sacred, M.I.A., popular and community. June Conference. Young Men's and Young Ladies' Mutual Improvement Association. Latter-day Saints Church. Salt Lake City [General Boards of the M.I.A.] 1922.
1p.l. [3]–28p. 18½cm.
UPB

2065. ———. M.I.A. songs and sociability songs. Salt Lake City, General Boards of Y.M. and Y.L.M.I.A. [c1928]
112p. 22cm.
USIC

2066. ———. M.I.A. songs. Songs for everybody. New revised edition. Salt Lake City, General Boards of M.I.A. [1927 or 8?]
112 [1]p. 22cm.
Words and music.
USIC

2067. ———. M.I.A. songs and sociability songs. Salt Lake City, Young Men's and Young Ladies' Mutual Improvement Association [1929?]
64 [32] 65–128p. music. 22cm.
The M.I.A. songs are added to the middle of Rodenheaver's Sociability Songs. c1928. With new cover.
Cover-title.
USIC

2068. ———. (same) 2d ed. [Salt Lake City, Young Men's and Young Ladies' Mutual Improvement Association, 1929?]
64 [32] 65–128. music. 22cm.
USIC

2069. ———. M.I.A. special activities, 1920–22. [Salt Lake City, 1920]
16p. 22cm.
USIC 1920–21, 1921–22 inc.

2070. ———. M.I.A. Year-Round program including recreation bulletin No. 7. 1927–1928. [Salt Lake City] 1927.
38p. 18cm.
USIC, UU

2071. ———. M.I.A. year-round program of recreation, 1925–26. [Salt Lake City, 1925]
15p. 19cm.
UPB

2072. ———. M.I.A. year-round recreation program & contests, 1926–7. Salt Lake City, Published by the General Boards, M.I.A. [1926]
27 [1]p. 19cm.
USIC

2073. ———. Outline of the M.I.A. Program for 1928–1929. [Salt Lake City] Published by the General Boards M.I.A. [1928]
24p. 17cm.
USIC

2074. ———. Prophecies and promises of the Lord as recorded in the Book of Doctrine and Covenants . . . [Salt Lake City, Improvement Era, 1919]
11p. 21cm.
Caption-title.
"Study course for Joint Advanced Senior M.I.A. Classes, 1919–20."
UPB

2075. ———. Recreation. Bulletin No. 1. Suggested program for recreation, including assignment of responsibility, organization, objectives, methods, standards and helpful suggestions. [Salt Lake City] Issued by the General Boards of M.I.A., 1923.
[13]p. 18½cm.
UPB

2076. ———. Recreation Bulletin No. 3. Salt Lake City, Published By General Boards of M.I.A., 1924.
3–99p. 18½cm.
UPB, UU

2077. ———. Recreation. Bulletin No. 4. A bulletin for committees on recreation containing a discussion of the stages of development and classification of recreational activities. Salt Lake City, Published by the General Board of the M.I.A. 1924.
[13]p. 22½cm.
UPB, UU

2078. ———. Recreation Bulletin No. 6. How to study local recreation problems. Salt Lake City, Publised by General Boards of M.I.A., 1926.
[1]–27p. 18½cm.
UPB

2079. ———. Recreation in the home, prepared by the Community Activity Committee of the General Boards of M.I.A. For use in the leisure-time program of the Church. [Salt Lake City] Published by the General Boards of M.I.A., 1930.
24p. 21½cm.
NN, UPB, UU

2080. ———. Recreation. Organization and leadership. Official recreation guide. Salt Lake City, Published by the General Boards of M.I.A., 1926.
2p.l. [5]–180p. 18½cm.
UPB

2080a. ———. Rules for the regulation and government of the Y.M. & Y.L.M.I.A. Library of the Seventeenth Ward. [Salt Lake City, n.d.]
Broadside. 24×13cm.
Lists twelve rules for the regulation of the library. Text within ornamental border.
USIC

2081. ———. Souvenir program M.I.A. jubilee. Celebrating the fiftieth anniversary of the organization of the Y.M.M.I.A. Salt Lake City, 1925.
[42]p. 21cm.
UHi, UPB, USIC

2082. ———. Special M.I.A. song folder. Annual June Conference, 1930. [Salt Lake City, 1930]
10p. 19cm.
Words only.
USIC

2083. ———. Summer work. Mutual Improvement Association. Session of 1919. Salt Lake City, Issued by the General Boards of the Young Ladies' and Young Men's Mutual Improvement Associations, 1919.
6p. 22cm.
USIC

2084. ———. (same) Salt Lake City, Issued by the General Boards of the Young Ladies' and Young Men's Mutual Improvement Association, 1920.
6p. 22cm.
USIC

2085. ———. (same) Salt Lake City, Issued by the General Boards of the Young Ladies' and Young Men's Mutual Improvement Associations, 1922.
8p. 21½cm.
USIC

2086. ———. Supplement to the M.I.A. handbook program 1929–30. [Salt Lake City] General Boards of M.I.A., 1929.
50p. 19cm.
UHi, USIC

———. *See also Church of Jesus Christ of Latter-day Saints. Young Men's Mutual Improvement Association. Young Women's Mutual Improvement Association.*

2086a. Church of Jesus Christ of Latter-day Saints. Old Folks Committee. Annual Old Folk's excursion, 1891. [Salt Lake City, 1891]
Broadside. 23×15½cm.
NjP

2087. ———. A fraternal greeting from the Old Folks' Central Committee. [Salt Lake City, Deseret News, 1905]
[3]p. 23cm.
MH, UHi, ULA, UPB

2088. ———. Reception and banquet tendered to the old folks of Utah irrespective of race, creed or color. Tabernacle grounds, Salt Lake City, Tuesday, June 27, 1916. [Salt Lake City] 1916.
[4]p. 19cm.
USIC

2088a. ———. Year of Jubilee. Old Folks will come to Salt Lake Lake [sic] next week. Warm hospitality is assured. Visitors will go to Fort Douglas and the Lake — generous offer by the railroads. [Salt Lake City, 1897?]
Broadside. 28×17cm.
NjP

2089. Church of Jesus Christ of Latter-day Saints. Perpetual Emigrating Fund Company. Circular to presidents and bishops of the Church of Jesus Christ of Latter-day Saints, throughout the Territory of Utah. [Salt Lake City, 1855]
Broadside. 62×33cm.
List of money owed to the Perpetual Emigrating Fund and a letter signed by Brigham Young telling of need for payment.
USIC

2090. ———. Instructions to Bishops. [Salt Lake City, n.d.]
Broadside. 31×20½cm.
Signed by Brigham Young.
Liquidation of indebtedness urged by Brigham Young.
USIC

2091. ———. Names of persons and sureties indebted to the Perpetual Emigrating Fund Company from 1850 to 1877 inclusive. Salt Lake City, Printed at the Star Book and Job Printing Office, 1877.
1p.l., 194p. 23½cm.
UPB, USIC

2092. ———. Office of Perpetual Emigrating Fund Co., Salt Lake City, Utah, ——— 18—. Dear Brother: [Salt Lake City, n.d.]
[3]p. 21cm.
Signed by John Taylor, Trustee in Trust of the Church of Jesus Christ of Latter-day Saints: Albert Carrington, President of the Company. Letter to accompany list of 19,000 debtors to the fund.
MH, USIC

2093. Church of Jesus Christ of Latter-day Saints. Polynesian Genealogical Society. He mau haawina mookuauhau. Honolulu, Oahu, Polynesian Genealogical Society, 1922.
24p. 23½cm.
A genealogical textbook.
USIC

2094. ———. (same) Honolulu, Oahu, Polynesian Genealogical Society, 1922.
30 [1]p. illus. 22½cm.
UHi

2095. Church of Jesus Christ of Latter-day Saints. Presiding Bishopric. Aaronic priesthood and branch teaching in the missions. [Salt Lake City, 1930]
12p. 19cm.
Instructions concerning meetings, ordinations, and suggestions for teaching.
UPB, USIC

2096. ———. Aaronic priesthood — organization, duties and standards. [n.p., n.d.]
19p. charts. 19cm.
UPB

2097. ———. Bulletins. [Salt Lake City] 1916–1930.
No. 1–171. 27½cm.
Attendance records.
USIC, UU

2098. ———. Circular. To Bishop . . . [Salt Lake City, 185?]
Broadside. 25×20cm.
Need to obtain tithing.
USIC

2099. ———. Course of study for the Deacons' Quorums, Church of Jesus Christ of Latter-day Saints. No. 1. Salt Lake City [1928]
176p. 19cm.
A revised edition of the 1924 Deacons' manual.
UPB

2100. ———. Guide for stake and ward leaders of adult members of Aaronic Priesthood. Let's go Back and get them. Salt Lake City, The Presiding Bishopric [n.d.]
19p. 17cm.
USIC

2101. ———. How to teach. Salt Lake City [n.d.]
8p. 17½cm.
UPB, USIC

2102. ———. . . . Incidents from the lives of our Church leaders. Salt Lake City [Deseret News Press] 1927.
133 [1]p. (Lesson book for the Deacons. No. 3)
UPB

2103. ———. . . . (same) Salt Lake City [Deseret News Press, 1930]
149p. 18cm. (Lesson book for the Deacons. No. 3)
Revised edition of 1927 Deacons' manual.
UPB

2104. ———. Instructions relative to weekly ward meetings of acting ward teachers and all members of Aaronic priesthood. [Salt Lake City] 1928.
38p. 18cm.
UHi, UPB, USIC, UU

2105. ———. Lesson book for the Deacons. No. 2. Salt Lake City, 1926.
143p. 19cm.
UPB

2106. ———. Lesson book for the Deacons. Salt Lake City [Deseret News Press] 1929.
144p. 19cm.
A revised edition of the 1926 deacons' manual.
UPB

2107. ———. Lesson Book for the ordained teachers. Prepared under the direction of the Presiding Bishopric of the Church of Jesus Christ of Latter-day Saints. Salt Lake City [1926?]
[3]–126p. 19cm.
UPB

2108. ———. Lesson book for the ordained teachers. Salt Lake City [Deseret News Press] 1929.
155p. 19cm.
Revised edition of the 1926 Teachers' manual.
UPB

2109. ———. List of recommends received at the Presiding Bishop's Office up to and including December 31st, 1909. Remaining unclaimed June 30, 1910. [Salt Lake City, 1910]
40p. 22cm.
List of members who cannot be located.
UPB, USIC

2110. ———. Minutes of the semi-annual meeting of ward bishoprics, ward clerks and supervisors of aaronic priesthood quorums held in the Assembly Hall, Friday, October 8th 1927. [Salt Lake City, 1927]
[9]p. 27cm.
Mimeographed.
UPB

2111. ———. Names of Presidency and Bishops of the organized stakes of Zion. Wm. B. Preston, Presiding Bishop; Robert T. Burton and John R. Winder, Counselors. [Salt Lake City? 1888?]
Broadside. 45½×35½cm.
Imprint date from textual information.
CSmH

2112. ———. Report of the Committee on Priesthood outlines to the general Priesthood. Read at the annual Conference Priesthood Meeting. April, 1913. Salt Lake City, 1913.
14p. 17cm.
USIC

2113. ———. Suggestions on ward teaching. Salt Lake City [1912?]
10 [1]p. 17½cm.
Reprinted from the *Improvement Era*, Nov., 1912.
UPB, USIC

2114. ———. The Teacher's responsibilities. Prepared under the direction of the Presiding Bishopric of the Church of Jesus Christ of Latter-day Saints. Salt Lake City [1928?]
[3]–222p. 19cm. (Lesson Book for the Ordained Teachers No. 2)
UPB

2115. ———. To the Saints scattered abroad, the Bishop and his counselors of Kirtland send greeting . . . Kirtland, Ohio, September 18th, 1837.
Broadside. 52×32cm.
Signed: N. K. Whitney, R. Cahoon, V. Knight.
Need of support to build Zion.
UPB, USIC

2116. ———. Ward charity; details of administration, prepared by the Presiding Bishopric. [Salt Lake City? 1930]
6p. 19cm.
UHi, UPB

2117. Church of Jesus Christ of Latter-day Saints. Primary Association. Annual Convention. Salt Lake City, 1902?–
v. 20cm.
USIC 10 (1902), 14 (1916), 21, 22, 24 (1926), 27 (1929)

2118. ———. A handbook for the officers and teachers in the Primary Association (Religion class) of the Church of Jesus Christ of Latter-day Saints. [Salt Lake City] The General Board of Primary Associations, 1930.
5p.l. [11]–195p. illus. 18½cm.
UHi, UPB, USIC, UU

2119. ———. Hymns and songs; selected from various authors for the primary association . . . *See Smith, Eliza Roxey Snow.*

2120. ———. Primary Association song book. Including marches and voluntaries. Salt Lake City, General Board of Primary Associations [n.d.]
1p.l., 7–242, iv p. 19cm.
Words and music.
USIC

2121. ———. Primary song book including marches and voluntaries. [Independence, Mo., Zion's Printing and Publishing Co., 1905?]
170 nos., vii p. 19cm.
Advertisement for an edition. *Children's Friend.* V.4, p. 328, Nov. 1905.
USIC

2122. ———. (same) 2d ed. Salt Lake City, Published by the General Board of the Primary Association, 1907.
[124]p. 20cm.
UPB, UU

2123. ———. (same) Salt Lake City, Published by the General Boards of Primary Associations of the Church of Jesus Christ of Latter-day Saints, 1909.
3p.l., 93 songs. 19cm.
UHi, UU

2124. ———. (same) Salt Lake City, Published by the General Board of the Primary Association [ca. 1920]
7–242, ivp. music. 19cm.
USIC

2125. ———. (same) Salt Lake City, Published by the General Board of the Primary Association [ca. 1925]
154 nos., vip. music. 19cm.
Printed at Zions' Printing and Publishing Co., Independence, Mo.
USIC

2126. ———. (same) Salt Lake City, Published by the General Board of the Primary Association [ca. 1927]
170 nos., viip. music. 19cm.
Printed at Zion's Printing and Publishing Co., Independence, Mo.
USIC

2127. ———. Souvenir program; Children's jubilee, celebrating the fiftieth anniversary of the organization of the Primary Association. To be held at Salt Lake City, Utah, June 8, 9, 10, 1928. [Salt Lake City, 1928]
[52]p. 25½cm.
UPB

2128. ———. Stake conventions of Primary Associations. Program for the year 1912. [Salt Lake City, 1912]
2p. 19½cm.
UPB

2129. Church of Jesus Christ of Latter-day Saints. Relief Society. Annual report of the Relief Society of the Church of Jesus Christ of Latter-day Saints for the year ending 1916 . . . Salt Lake City 1917–
v. annual. 21½cm.
UHi 1917, 1918, 1920, 1921, 1922, 1923, 1924, 1925, 1926, 1927, 1928; USIC 1916, 1917, 1918, 1920.

2130. ———. A brief history of the grain storing by the women of Zion. Prepared by a committee of the General Board appointed by the general president, Sister Bathsheba W. Smith. [Salt Lake City, 1906?]
7p. 23cm.
Caption-title.

CHURCH. . . . RELIEF SOCIETY

Signed: Annie Wells Cannon [and others] Committee.
Relief Society work in food storage.
CU–B, MH, UPB

2131. ———. Circular of instructions for the use of officers and members of the Relief Society. . . . [Salt Lake City] Published by the General Board, 1915.
31 [1]p. 23cm.
UHi, USIC

2132. ———. Conference of the General Relief Society of the Church of Jesus Christ of Latter-day Saints . . . Salt Lake City, 1916–
v. 23cm.
Title varies: Semi-annual conference of the Women's Relief Society, 1916–17; Conference of the General Relief Society, 1929–
UHi 1930; USIC Oct. 1916, Apr. 1917, Apr. 1929, Apr. 1930

2133. ———. The General Relief Society. Officers, objects and status. Minutes of first organization. Biographical sketch of President Bathsheba W. Smith. General instructions. . . . Salt Lake City, Published by the general officers, 1902.
2p.l. [5]–97p. 18½cm.
Page 97 added later as a note.
UPB, USIC

2134. ———. A historical sketch of the first organization of the Female Relief Society of the Church of Jesus Christ of Latter-day Saints. At Nauvoo, Ill. March 17th 1842. [Springville, Printed by J. M. Westwood for the Relief Society of Springville, Utah, 1900?]
14p. 13½cm.
Cover-title.
CtY

2135. ———. . . . Names of stake and branch presidents of the Relief Society of Latter-day Saints in the valleys of the mountains. [Salt Lake City? 188 ?]
Broadside. 42×29cm.
CU–B

2136. ———. A pageant presented on the 50th anniversary of the stake Relief Societies of Weber Co., 1927. Ogden, Chimes Press, 1927.
11p. illus., port. 22½cm.
UPB

2137. ———. Plan and program for the study of child culture and the Book of Mormon. Second Edition. Salt Lake City, 1903.
22p. 18cm.
UPB

2138. ———. Program for Relief Society genealogical convention, April 7th, 8th, 9th, 1914 . . . Salt Lake City, 1914.
[4]p. 22½cm.
UHi

2139. ———. The Relief Society. Organization of the L.D.S. Relief Society and instructions given by President Joseph Smith. [n.p., Printed by Grant Ward Relief Society, 18– ?]
[5]p. 21cm.
Cover-title.
CU–B

2140. ———. Relief Society by-laws. [Salt Lake City, n.d.]
8p. 12½cm.
With blanks for the names of each ward to be added.
USIC

2141. ———. (same) [Salt Lake City, n.d.]
8p. 12½cm.
Variant edition.
USIC

2142. ———. Relief Society guide. 1914. [Salt Lake City] 1914.
31p. 23cm.
USIC

2143. ———. Relief Society song book; a collection of selected hymns and songs especially arranged for the use of the Relief Societies of the Church of Jesus Christ of Latter-day Saints. Salt Lake City, General Board of Relief Society, 1919.
157 nos. [9]p. 23½cm.
Index.
"Music arranged and compiled by Brigham Cecil Gates."
CU–B, UPB, USIC

2144. ———. (same) 2d ed. Music arranged and compiled by Brigham Cecil Gates. Salt Lake City, General Board of Relief Society, 1923.
1p.l., 157 nos. [9]p. 23½cm.
ULA, UPB, USIC

2145. ———. (same) 3d ed. [Salt Lake City. General Boards of the Relief Society, 1927 c1923]
157 nos. [9]p. 23cm.
UHi, USIC

2146. ———. (same) 4th ed. [Salt Lake City, General Boards of the Relief Society, 1930?]
157 nos. [9]p. music. 23cm.
USIC

2147. ———. Relief Society stake conferences for 1917– [Salt Lake City, 1917–]
v. 23½cm.
USIC has 1917, 1918, 1919

2148. ———. Semi-centennial review of the Relief Societies of Salt Lake County. Salt Lake Tabernacle . . . March the Sixteenth, 1928. [Salt Lake City, 1928]
[14]p. 25½cm.
Written by Claire Stewart Boyer.
UHi, USIC

2149. ———. To the officers of the Relief Society organizations. [Salt Lake City, n.d.]
[3]p. 22cm.
Instructions.
USIC

2150. ———. Woman's Relief Society of the Church of Jesus Christ of Latter-day Saints. [Salt Lake City? 1910?]
[3]p. 21½cm.
UPB, USIC

2151. Church of Jesus Christ of Latter-day Saints. Religion Classes. A handbook for the officers and teachers in the Religion Classes of the Church of Jesus Christ of Latter-day Saints. Salt Lake City, Published for the General Board of Education, 1924.
60p. 19cm.
USIC

2152. ———. Lesson book for the Religion Classes in the Church of Jesus Christ of Latter-day Saints. [Salt Lake City, General Board of Religion Classes, 1910–25]
v. 19cm.
1910, Primary Department — First Year.
62p. 19cm.
UPB, USIC
1910, First Intermediate, Second Intermediate and Advanced Department.
92p. 19cm.
UPB
1911, Primary and First Intermediate Departments.
84p. 19cm.
UPB
1911, Second Intermediate & Advanced Departments.
76p. 19cm.
USIC
1912, First Intermediate Department.
77p. 19cm.
UPB
1912, Second Intermediate Department.
69p. 19cm.
USIC
1912, Advanced Department.
44p. 19cm.
USIC
1913, First and Second Grades.
56p. 19cm.
USIC
1913, Third and Fourth Grades.
60p. 19cm.
USIC
1913, Fifth and Sixth Grades.
64p. 19cm.
UPB, USIC
1913, Seventh and Eighth Grades.
72p. 19cm.
USIC
1914, Fifth and Second Grades.
80p. 19cm.
UPB, USIC
1914, Third and Fourth Grades.
60p. 19cm.
UPB, USIC
1914, Fifth and Sixth Grades.
64p. 19cm.
UPB, USIC
1914, Seventh and Eighth Grades.
72p. 19cm.
UPB, USIC
1915, First and Second Grades.
76p. 19cm.
UPB, USIC
1915, Third and Fourth Grades.
82p. 19cm.
UPB, USIC
1915, Fifth and Sixth Grades.
86p. 19cm.
UPB, USIC
1915, Seventh and Eighth Grades.
116p. 19cm.
UPB, USIC
1916, First and Second Grades.
85p. 19cm.
UPB, USIC
1916, Third and Fourth Grades.
90p. 19cm.
UPB, USIC
1916, Fifth and Sixth Grades.
38p. 19cm.
UPB, USIC
1916, Seventh and Eighth Grades.
99p. 19cm.
UPB, USIC
1917, First and Second Grades.
88p. 19cm.
UPB, USIC
1917, Third and Fourth Grades.
86p. 19cm.
UPB, USIC
1917, Fifth and Sixth Grades.
91p. 19cm.
UPB, USIC
1917, Seventh and Eighth Grades.
95p. 19cm.
UPB, USIC
1918, First and Second Grades.
83p. 19cm.
UPB, USIC
1918, Third and Fourth Grades.
90p. 19cm.
UPB, USIC
1918, Fifth and Sixth Grades.
54p. 19cm.
UPB, USIC
1918, Seventh and Eighth Grades.
120p. 19cm.
UPB, USIC
1920–21, First and Second Grades.
96p. 19cm.
USIC
1920–21, Third and Fourth Grades.
104p. 19cm.
USIC
1920–21, Fifth and Sixth Grades.
94p. 19cm.
USIC
1920–21, Seventh and Eighth Grades.
132p. 19cm.
USIC
1921–22, First and Second Grades.
97p. 19cm.
USIC

CHURCH. . . . RELIGION CLASSES

1921–22, Third and Fourth Grades.
82p. 19cm.
USIC
1921–22, Fifth and Sixth Grades.
135p. 19cm.
UPB, USIC
1921–22, Seventh and Eighth Grades.
117p. 19cm.
USIC
1922–23.
118p. 19cm.
USIC
1924–25, First Grade.
USIC

2153. ———. Outlines of Religion Class work 1896 [–1910] [Salt Lake City] General Board of Religion Classes, 1896–1910.
v. 23cm.
UPB 1901, 1903–04, 1904–05, 1906–07; USIC 1896, 1899, 1900, 1901, 1903–04, 1904–05, 1905–06, 1906–07, 1907–08, 1908–09, 1909–10.

2154. ———. Program of Lund Day Exercises in Religion Classes. [Salt Lake City] 1912.
[4]p. 20cm.
In honor of President Anthon H. Lund. Includes a biography.
UPB, USIC

2155. Church of Jesus Christ of Latter-day Saints. Social Advisory Committee. The case against tobacco. Salt Lake City, Church of Jesus Christ of Latter-day Saints, Social Advisory Board, 1921.
16p. 21½cm. (Pamphlet No. 8)
CSmH, UPB, USIC

2156. ———. Report of the Correlation–Social Advisory Committee to the First Presidency and the Council of Twelve on the definition and assignment of auxiliary functions and organizations. [Salt Lake City] 1921.
27p. fold. chart. 35½cm.
USIC

2157. ———. Social dancing, a course in dancing and dance problems. Salt Lake City [n.d.]
[8]p. 21½cm. (Pamphlet No. 4)
Program and recommendations.
UPB

2158. ———. Syllabus for stake institutes, in teacher training, social and recreational leadership, charities and relief work. Manual for stake and ward social committees. Salt Lake City, 1920.
93p. 21cm.
UPB, USIC

2159. Church of Jesus Christ of Latter-day Saints. Stakes. Alberta. Greeting from the Presidency of the Alberta Stake of Zion. Cardston, Alberta, 1928.
32p. 18cm.
Book of Mormon poetry.
USIC

2160. ———. **Stakes. Alpine.** Ward teachers' manual. Alpine Stake, 1916–17. [Lehi] Lehi Sun Print [1916?]
31p. 21cm.
USIC

2161. ———. **Stakes. Bannock.** History of the Stake and Wards of Bannock. [n.p., n.d.]
35p. 19cm.
USIC also has a [127]–162 copy from an unidentified source.
USIC

2162. ———. **Stakes. Bingham.** Instructions and outline of work for stake and ward genealogical committees. Idaho Falls, Post Perfection Printing, 1922.
[15]l. 18cm.
Published for regional use after it was read at the first Inter-Stake Genealogical convention.
USIC

2163. ———. Program. Prepared by the Stake Committee. Appointed by the Stake Presidency and High Council for home missionaries and ward teachers of Bingham Stake, 1925. [n.p., 1925]
14p. 22cm.
USIC

2164. ———. **Stakes. Boise.** Annual calendar [and directory] 1924. Boise, Idaho, 1924.
[1]l., 28 cm. folded to [6]p. 21½×9½cm.
USIC

2165. ———. Ward teachers manual. Boise, 1927.
8p. 17½cm.
UU

2166. ———. **Stakes. Cache.** Outlines for Religion Class work. Published by order of the Stake Board of Religion Classes. Logan, Utah, Smith, Cumming & Co., 1901.
16p. 22cm.
USIC

2167. ———. **Stakes. Cassia.** Honoring Cassia Stake Presidency, Oakley, Idaho, May 14, 1926. [Independence, Mo., Press of Zion's Printing and Publishing Company, 1926]
[12]l. ports. 19½cm.
UPB, USIC

2168. ———. **Stakes. Ensign.** The Ensign Speedometer. January 31, 1914–June, 1927.
14v. weekly. 38cm.
Young Men's Mutual Improvement Association bulletin.
USIC V. 1 #17; V. 14 # 1.

2169. ———. Ensign Stake. History of stake and directory of stake and ward officers. [Salt Lake City, J. Frank Pickering, c1904]
[35] l. 16½cm.
1905 date given in the introduction.
USIC

2170. ———. **Stakes. Granite.** Bishops' convention. Papers read at a convention of the Stake Presidency, High Council, Bishops, Counselors and Ward Clerks of the Granite Stake of Zion. Held in the Granite Stake Tabernacle. September 13th, 14th, 15th, 16th and 20th, 1914. Salt Lake City, 1915.
76p. 21cm.
UPB

2171. ———. An expression of appreciation to Pres. Frank Y. Young. Granite Stake Tabernacle, Thursday, October 4th, 1928, at 8:00 P.M. [Salt Lake City, 1928]
[4]l., port. 23cm.
Mormon biography.
USIC

2172. ———. First principles of Relief Society work. Outlines for the Granite Stake Relief Societies for 1912. . . . [Salt Lake City] 1912.
16p. 18½cm.
UPB

2173. ———. Granite giant "Gubilee" [sic]. Granite Stake Tabernacle . . . October 26–27–28–29, 1920. [Salt Lake City, 1920]
[12]p. 23cm.
USIC

2174. ———. Granite Stake. History of stake and directory of stake and ward officers. [Salt Lake City, J. Frank Pickering, c1904]
[47]l. 16½cm.
1905 date given in the introduction.
USIC

2175. ———. Home Evening, with suggested exercises and explanations. Also a sermon on family government by President Joseph F. Smith, and a special message from the First Presidency of Granite Stake. [Salt Lake City] Granite Stake of Zion, 1927.
62p. 18½cm.
UPB, USIC

2176. ———. Home evening with suggestive exercises and explanations, also a sermon on family government, by Pres. Joseph F. Smith. [Salt Lake City? 1909]
51 [1]p. 16cm.
USIC, UU

2177. ———. Outlines of lessons for the lesser priesthood quorums of the Granite Stake of Zion. Issued under the direction of the Stake Presidency and High Council. Salt Lake City, 1908.
31p. 18½cm.
UHi, UPB, USIC

2178. ———. Reports of Stake High Council Committee on ward teaching and home evening. [Salt Lake City] 1924.
16p. 22½cm.
USIC

2179. ———. Reports of Stake High Council Committee on ward teaching and home evening. [n.p., 1924]
[24]p. 22cm.
UPB, USIC

2180. ———. Silver anniversary of Granite Stake. 1900–1925. [Salt Lake City, 1925]
[16]p. 22cm.
USIC

2181. ———. Suggestive outlines for a family and surname Organization. By Granite Stake Genealogical Board. [Salt Lake City, n.d.]
[20]p. 19cm.
USIC

2181a. ———. Ward Teachers outline . . . Granite Stake. [Salt Lake City, 1930]
v. 23cm.
UPB Nov. 1930, Dec. 1930; USIC Nov. 1930, Dec. 1930

2181b. ———. **Stakes. Grant.** 1929 June outline for Ward Teaching and home night. Grant Stake. [Salt Lake City, 1929]
[4]p. 16×8cm.
UPB, USIC

2182. ———. **Stakes. Hollywood.** Dedication, Hollywood Stake Tabernacle, April, 1929. [Hollywood, California, 1929]
31p. illus. 27½cm. (Hollywood Stake Herald. Vol. 1, No. 16)
UHi, UPB, USIC

2183. ———. Hollywood Stake Herald. Los Angeles, Chimes Press, November, 1927?–
v. monthly. 28cm.
USIC V. 1 #9, 12, 15

2184. ———. **Stakes. Hyrum.** M.I.A. outlines for summer work, 1908. Young Men's and Young Ladies' Mutual Improvement Association. Logan, J. P. Smith, 1908.
12p. 15cm.
Cover-title.
USIC

2184a. ———. **Stakes. Idaho Falls.** Idaho Falls Stake of Zion Ward Teachers' outline, July 1930. The majesty of law. [Idaho Falls? 1930]
[4]p. 15½cm.
UPB, USIC

2184b. ———. **Stakes. Jordan.** Jordan Junior and Senior Seminary leaflet, July, 1930. [Salt Lake City, 1930]
1 card. 16cm.
UPB, USIC

2185. ———. Jordan Stake. History of stake and directory of stake and ward officers. [Salt Lake City, J. Frank Pickering, c1904]
[42]l. 17cm.
1905 given as year in the introduction.
UPB, USIC

2186. ———. Outlines, Lesser Priesthood, Jordan Stake. [September 11, 1905–August 13, 1906] [Salt Lake City, 1905]
20p. 19cm.
USIC

2187. ———. Prophecies of Joseph Smith and their fulfillment. Lesser priesthood Jordan Stake. [Salt Lake City? n.d.]
24p. 18cm.
UPB, USIC

2187a. ———. Ward Teachers' topic for East and West Jordan Stakes, July, 1929. The L.D.S. Seminary. [Salt Lake City, 1929]
1 card. 16cm.
UPB, USIC

2188. ———. **Stakes. Lehi.** Dedicatory services, Lehi Tabernacle, May 15, 1910. [Lehi, Utah] 1910.
[4]p. 21cm.
USIC

2189. ———. **Stakes. Lethbridge.** Lethbridge Stake directory. [Lethbridge] 1924–1928.
3v. 14cm.
USIC 1924, 1925, 1928.

2190. ———. **Stakes. Liberty.** For use of ward teachers in Liberty Stake of Zion during June, 1922. Prepared under the direction of the Stake Presidency and Stake Bishoprics. [Salt Lake City? 1922]
[4]p. 22cm. (Leaflet No. 15, Series B)
Signed [p. 3] Hugh J. Cannon, B. S. Hinckley, P. M. Michelsen, Stake Presidency.
Imperfect: p. [3–4] mutilated with loss of text.
CU–B

2190a. ———. For use of Ward Teachers in Liberty Stake of Zion during August, 1925. Prepared under the direction of the Stake Presidency and Ward Bishoprics. [Salt Lake City, 1925]
[4]p. 21½×13½cm. (Leafllet No. 47, Series B)
Signed at end: Bryant S. Hinckley, Fred M. Michelsen, Wilson McCarthy.
UPB, USIC

2191. ———. Leaflet No. 1 [–12] for use of block teachers in Liberty Stake of Zion during 1920. Salt Lake City [1920?]
12 pamphlets. 21½cm.
Subjects and suggestions for teachers.
UPB No. 1, 2, 4, 5, 8, 10; USIC

2192. ———. Liberty Stake. History of stake and directory of stake and ward officers. [Salt Lake City, J. Frank Pickering, c. 1904]
[35]l. 17cm.
1905 given as the date in the introduction.
USIC

2193. ———. To the Latter-day Saints of Liberty Stake, June 15, 1911. [Salt Lake City, 1911]
[4]p. 21cm.
Signed: Hugh J. Cannon, A. H. Schulthess, B. S. Hinckley.
Pastoral epistle.
USIC

2194. ———. Ward teachers' manual. Subjects for study and discussion. [Salt Lake City] 1918.
31p. 19½cm.
USIC

2194a. ———. **Stakes. Logan.** Logan Stake Ward teaching outline for 1929. [Logan? 1929]
[4]p. 14cm.
UPB, USIC

2195. ———. **Stakes. Los Angeles.** Dedication souvenir; Los Angeles Stake Tabernacle, Huntington Park, California, June 2, 1929. [Los Angeles, Everett L. Sanders, 1929]
[10]l. ports., plates. 28cm.
Articles by various people on the stake.
USIC, UU

2196. ———. Official directory. Los Angeles Stake of the Church of Jesus Christ of Latter-day Saints. 1925. [Los Angeles, 1925]
87p. 23cm.
USIC

2197. ———. **Stakes. Maricopa.** Ward teachers' manual. Maricopa Stake of Zion, Church of Jesus Christ of Latter-day Saints. [Mesa, Ariz.?] 1918.
32 [1]p. 17cm.
USIC

2198. ———. **Stakes. Mesa.** Directory. Mesa First Ward. Church of Jesus Christ of Latter-day Saints. 1923–1924. Phoenix, Watkins Printing Co., 1923.
[18]l. 22½cm.
Cover-title.
USIC

2199. ———. **Stakes. Millard.** Plan for the Millard Stake Relief Society. For the year 1911. To be followed as closely as possible at every meeting by all members . . . [Salt Lake City?] 1911.
[3]p. 17½cm.
UPB

2200. ———. **Stakes. Minidoka. . . .** Minidoka Stake year book, 1927–1929. [Rupert, Idaho], 1927 [–1928]
3v. 16½cm.
UPB, USIC

2201. ———. **Stakes. Mount Ogden.** Ward teacher's manual. The hymns of the Latter-day Saints. Mount Ogden Stake for the year of 1923. Ogden, 1923.
20p. 20cm.
USIC

2201a. ———. **Stakes. North Davis.** North Davis Stake Ward teaching . . . A right spirit. [Salt Lake City, 1928?–]
v. 13½cm.
UPB July 1928, Aug. 1930; USIC July 1928, Aug. 1930

2201b. ———. **Stakes. North Weber.** Handling of transgression cases [and other instructions in the form of letters from the First Presidency. Ogden, Utah, ca1920]
9 letters. 17½cm.
USIC copy starts with #2.

2202. ———. Ward teacher's manual. North Weber Stake. "Back to first principles." Prepared by the Committee of the High Council under the direction of the Stake Presidency, North Weber Stake of Zion. Ogden, Utah, 1920, 1928–1929.
3v. (22, 24p.) 19½cm.
"Studies from the *Doctrine and Covenants.*" "Present day revelation."
UPB 1928, USIC 1929

2203. ———. **Stakes. Ogden.** Ward teachers year book. Doctrinal topics . . . Ogden, Utah, 1922–1929.
5v. 19½cm.
USIC 1921, 1922, 1923, 1925, 1929

2204. ———. **Stakes. Oneida.** Community songs. Oneida Stake M.I.A. [n.d., n.d.]
12p. 15½cm.
USIC

2205. ———. The Oneida Stake of Zion's Sunday School song book. Ogden, T. A. Smith, 1887.
iv [5]–100p. 13cm.
Without music.
USIC

2206. ———. Suggestive outlines for the Religion Classes of the Oneida Stake of Zion. [Preston, Idaho? n.d.]
[8]p. 23cm.
USIC

2207. ———. **Stakes. Pioneer.** Outlines of lectures for Pioneer Stake Relief Society. [Salt Lake City, 1907]
[3]p. 22cm.
USIC

2208. ———. Pioneer Stake. History of stake and directory of stake and ward officers . . . Salt Lake City, Published by J. Frank Pickering [c1904]
[48]l. 17cm.
Cover-title.
USIC

2209. ———. Pioneer Stake Silver anniversary jubilee and homecoming, March 24, 25, 1924. [Salt Lake City, 1924]
[8]p. ports. 23½cm.
Historical information of Pioneer Stake.
USIC

2210. ———. Souvenir program of the 20th anniversary reunion of Pioneer Stake. Monday evening, March 24th, 1924. Salt Lake City, The Deseret News Press, 1924.
[7]l. 23cm.
Biographical information.
USIC

2210a. ———. Teachers' outline, Pioneer Stake, June, 1930. Parental responsibility. [Salt Lake City, 1930]
Broadside. 18×11cm.
UPB, USIC

2211. ———. **Stakes. St. George.** Report of the convention on prices of labor, products and manufactures for St. George Stake of Zion. [St. George? 1874]
[8]p. 17½cm.
Report of the Stake Board of Directors of the United Order, September 15th, 1874.
USIC

2212. ———. Rules which should be observed in dancing parties in St. George Stake of Zion. [St. George, Utah, 1887]
Broadside. 20½×14cm.
CSmH

CHURCH. . . . STAKES. ST. JOSEPH

2213. ———. **Stakes. St. Joseph.** Directory of the St. Joseph Stake of the Church of Jesus Christ of Latter-day Saints and teacher's subjects for 1922. Thatcher, Arizona, 1922.
28p. 15cm.
USIC

2214. ———. Outlines for religion class work. Published by order of the Stake Board of Religion Classes. Safford, Ariz., Guardian Print., 1902.
13p. 19½cm.
USIC

2215. ———. **Stakes. Salt Lake.** Anniversary celebration of the Salt Lake Stake of Zion honoring early church leaders who have resided within the stake, in picture, song and story. [Salt Lake City, Printed by Stevens and Wallis] 1926.
[8]p. illus. 23cm.
Program in the Salt Lake Tabernacle.
Pictures and biographies of prominent men.
UHi, USIC

2216. ———. Annual circular of the Central Seminary, of the Salt Lake Stake of Zion. Located at Mill Creek, Utah. [Salt Lake City] 1890–93.
v. 21½cm.
UPB 1890–1891; USIC 1891–92, 1892–93

2217. ———. Course of study for Salt Lake Stake Relief Societies, 1911–12. [Salt Lake City, 1911]
31p. 19cm.
Subjects: Hygiene and domestic science and life of Christ.
USIC

2218. ———. June festival. Salt Lake Stake Sunday Schools. Theme: The Word of wisdom. A day of flowers and song 10:00 A.M. Tabernacle, June 25, 1911. [Salt Lake City, 1911]
4p. 22cm.
Program.
MH

2219. ———. Guide for the officers and teachers of Sunday School in the Salt Lake Stake of Zion. Salt Lake City, Merchants Printing Co., 1892.
24p. 17cm.
USIC

2220. ———. Outlines for mother's work in the Salt Lake Stake Relief Societies arranged by Georgiana Fox Young, Nettie D. Bradford, Ida D. Rees, Harriet C. Jensen . . . Approved by the Stake Presidency and General Board of Relief Society. [Salt Lake City, 1904]
18p. 17½cm.
USIC

2221. ———. (same) [Salt Lake City, n.d.]
8p. 18cm.
USIC

2222. ———. Salt Lake Stake. History of stake and directory of stake and ward officers. [Salt Lake City, J. Frank Pickering, c1904]
[47]l. 17cm.
1905 given as the date in the introduction.
USIC

2223. ———. Salt Lake Stake Mutual Improvement activity guide, 1917–1918 [1919–1920, 1922–23] Salt Lake City, Published by Stake Board of Young Mens Mutual Improvement Association; Stake Board of Young Ladies Mutual Improvement Association, 1917 [–1923]
3v. 15cm.
USIC

2224. ———. Young Ladies' National Mutual Improvement Association of the Salt Lake Stake. Directory of General Board, Stake Board and Ward Officers, 1903. [Salt Lake City] 1903.
16p. 15cm.
USIC

2225. ———. **Stakes. San Francisco.** Directory. San Francisco Stake of Zion. [San Francisco, 1929]
[4]p. 18cm.
USIC

2226. ———. **Stakes. Sevier.** By-laws of the Church Association of Sevier Stake of Zion. Richfield, Utah, 1887.
4p. 18cm.
USIC

2227. ———. **Stakes. Shelley.** Ward Teachers leaflet for April, 1929. Shelley Stake. The home. [n.p., 1929]
Broadside. 16½×8½cm.
Quotation from Joseph F. Smith's *Gospel doctrine.*
USIC

2228. ———. **Stakes. South Sanpete.** South Sanpete Stake ward teachers' bulletin for March, 1930. [n.p.] 1930.
[2]p. 22½cm.
UPB

2229. ———. **Stakes. Star Valley.** Book of the words, M.I.A. historical pageant of Star Valley, Wyoming . . . Compiled and directed by Adelbert Wilde, Maud Burton, Josephine Burton. Presented in Afton, August 28th, 1915. [Afton? Wyo.] Star Valley Independent, 1915.
20p. 23cm.
Includes a historical sketch and the pageant.
CtY, USIC, UU

2230. ———. **Stakes. Teton.** Season's Greeting. Stake officers, Teton Stake to fellow workers, stake and ward officers. Driggs, Idaho. 1923.
14p. 20cm.
USIC

2231. ———. Teton stake quarter-centennial jubilee, 1926. Driggs, Idaho, Teton Valley News [1926]
[28]p. illus., ports., maps. 26½cm.
UPB, USIC, UU

2232. ———. **Stakes. Tooele.** Ward Teachers manual for Tooele Stake. [Tooele, Press of the Bulletin] 1917.
27p. 19½cm.
UPB

2233. ———. **Stakes. Union.** Ward Teacher's manual. 1926. Le Grande, Oregon, 1926.
10 [1]p. 20½cm.
USIC

2234. ———. **Stakes. Utah.** Suggestive outlines for applied religion and science in the home; a five-year course for use in the Relief Society, Utah Stake of Zion. [n.p.] 1907.
viii, 119p. 18½cm. (Third series)
UPB, USIC

2235. ———. Temple souvenir of Utah Stake chorus. Containing the words of inspired writers to be sung and chanted at the dedicatory services of the great Salt Lake Temple on Friday, April 14, 1893. [Provo? 1893]
4p. 15cm.
Cover-title.
UHi

2236. ———. **Stakes. Weber.** Directory of Weber Stake. Ogden, Utah, 1910–1930.
v. 15cm.
USIC 1910, 1920, 1921, 1923, 1925, 1926, 1930

2237. ———. . . . One third of a century of service: Weber Stake of Zion, Ogden, Utah, U.S.A. [Ogden, Designed, Written and Printed in the A. L. Scoville Press] 1916.
11 [1]p. port. 33cm.
In honor of Lewis W. Shurtliff.
CSmH, UPB, USIC, UU

2238. ———. Outlines for religion class work for the Weber Stake of Zion. Published by order of the Stake Board of Religion Class. [Ogden, Utah, A. T. Hestmark] 1901.
21p. 22cm.
USIC

2239. ———. Rules for the government of the Sunday School in the Weber Stake of Zion revised and adopted by the stake board, May 20th, 1908. [Ogden] 1908.
14p. 18cm.
USIC

2240. ———. Thoughts issued under auspices of the Religion Class workers of Weber and Ogden Stakes, Ogden, Utah [The A. L. Scoville Press] 1912.
[38]l. 22cm.
Collection of thoughts, not necessarily Mormon.
USIC

2241. ———. **Stakes. West Jordan.** Ward Teachers' topic. West Jordan Stake, April, 1929. The purpose of life. [Ogden? 1929]
[4]p. 14½cm.
USIC

2242. Church of Jesus Christ of Latter-day Saints. Tabernacle Choir. The Mormon Church choir special to the World's Fair, 1893. [Salt Lake City] 1893.
[4]p. 19cm.
USIC

2243. ———. The Mormons and their great choir. Views and descriptive matter of this great organization including views of the great Mormon Temple, tabernacle, etc. Salt Lake City, Liberty Advertising Co., 1911.
27p. illus., plates, ports. 23cm.
Cover-title.
CU–B, MH, UHi, UPB

Church of Jesus Christ of Latter-day Saints. United Order of Enoch. *See Church of Jesus Christ of Latter-day Saints. Articles of association.*

2244. Church of Jesus Christ of Latter-day Saints. Wards. Brooklyn. Program. Dedicatory services. Brooklyn Chapel of the Church of Jesus Christ of Latter-day Saints. February sixteenth, nineteen nineteen. [n.p., 1919]
[4]l. illus. 26½cm.
Includes songs, etc.
USIC

2245. ———. **Wards. Burton.** The Burton Banner. March 27, 1915 — August 15, 1916.
2v. monthly. 22½cm.
USIC V. 1 #1, 3, 5–9; V. 2 #9.

2246. ———. **Wards. Eighth.** Dedication week program. November 24th to 30th, 1924. Dedication services, Sunday, November 30th, 6:30 P.M. [Salt Lake City] 1924.
[2]l. illus. 22½cm.
UPB, USIC

2247. ———. History of the Eighth Ward [Liberty Stake, 1847–1921] In commemoration of laying cornerstone of the new chapel . . . March twenty-sixth, nineteen hundred twenty-one. [Salt Lake City? 1921]
[26]p. illus., ports. 21cm.
Pagination includes advertising.

"Compiled March, 1921, by Robert W. Smith from data in the Historian's Office and from information furnished by pioneers of the ward."
CU-B, ULA

2248. ———. **Wards. Eleventh.** The budget. [Salt Lake City, 1897?]
v. 26½cm.
Ward bulletin. Edward B. Phippen, ed.
USIC V. 3 #1 May, 1899.

2249. ———. Constitution and by-laws of the Eleventh Ward Literary Association. Organized, November 16, 1874 in Salt Lake City. Salt Lake City, Printed at the Deseret News Steam Printing Establishment [1874]
8p. 14cm.
USIC

2250. ———. **Wards. Fifteenth.** History of the Fifteenth Ward Sunday School. Fifteenth Ward, Salt Lake City, Utah, 1886. [Salt Lake City] Printed at the Juvenile Instructor Office, 1886.
14p. 18cm.
In green printed wrapper.
USIC

2251. ———. **Wards. Grant.** The Relief Society. Organization of the L.D.S. Relief Society and instructions given by President Joseph Smith. [Salt Lake City? American Eagle Print, 1901]
[5]p. 21cm.
Variant printing: Without printer and variant plates USIC.
USIC

2252. ———. **Wards. Highland Park.** Souvenir album — Highland Park Ward, June 28–29–30, 1918. [Salt Lake City] 1918.
[32]p. illus. 27cm.
Dedication of the Highland Park Ward chapel.
USIC

2253. ———. Souvenir Album Highland Park Chapel. [Salt Lake City, 1925]
[32]p. illus. 26½cm.
USIC

2254. ——— **Wards. Huntsville.** Huntsville Ward forty-eighth anniversary and missionary reunion. Huntsville, Utah, 1925.
47 [1]p. 24cm.
UHi, USIC

2255. ———. **Wards. Lincoln.** Over the top! Lincoln Ward [and] Granite Stake. [Salt Lake City, 1929?]
42p. illus. 30cm.
USIC

2256. ———. **Wards. Mar Vista.** Dedication. Mar Vista, California, 1928.
43 [1]p. illus., ports. 20cm.
UPB, USIC

2257. ———. **Wards. North Manti Ward.** Dedicatory services of the North Ward Chapel, held Sunday, November 5, 1911. Bishop N. R. Peterson of the North Ward of Manti presiding. Manti, Utah, 1911.
9p. 28cm.
Mimeographed.
UPB

2258. ———. **Wards. Phoenix.** Directory, Phoenix Ward, Church of Jesus Christ of Latter-day Saints, 1923–1924. Phoenix, Watkins Printing Co., 1923.
[36]p. illus. 23cm.
UPB, USIC

2259. ———. **Wards. Richmond South.** Dedicatory Services. Richmond South Ward Chapel. Sunday, February 4th, 1923. [n.p., 1923]
[2]l. illus. 21½cm.
USIC

2260. ———. **Wards. Seventeenth.** Constitution and by-laws of the Young Men's Mutual Improvement Association of the 17th Ward, Salt Lake City. 1879. [Salt Lake City] Printed at the Deseret News Office, 1879.
6p. 13cm.
USIC

2261. ———. Seventeenth Ward M.I.A. song book. Everybody sing. [Salt Lake City] 1923.
119 [4]p. 19½cm.
Without music.
USIC

2262. ———. **Wards. Twenty-first.** Memories 1926; t'was a "Welcome au-revoir" to the old Twenty-first Ward meeting house, March 17, 1926. [Salt Lake City] 1926.
[4]p. 23cm.
USIC

2263. ———. **Wards. Vernal.** Souvenir program. Dedication of Vernal First Ward chapel. Uintah Stake. [Vernal, Vernal Express Print.] 1921.
[4]p. illus. 24cm.
USIC

2264. ———. **Wards. Wasatch.** Wasatch Ward broadcaster. [Salt Lake City, January, 1925]
[8]p. 19cm.
UPB

2265. ———. **Wards. Wilford.** Annual conference. Monday, November 15, to Tuesday, November 23, inclusive. [Salt Lake City, 1926]
[4]p. 18cm.
USIC

CHURCH . . . Y. M. M. I. A.

Church of Jesus Christ of Latter-day Saints. Young Ladies' Mutual Improvement Association. *See Church of Jesus Christ of Latter-day Saints. Young Women's Mutual Improvement Association.*

2266. Church of Jesus Christ of Latter-day Saints. Young Men's Mutual Improvement Association. The Acts of the Apostles. [Salt Lake City] Published by the General Board of Y.M.M.I.A. [1902]
59 [1]p. 21cm. (Young Men's Mutual Improvement Associations. Manual for Junior Classes. 1902–1903)
UPB, USIC

2267. ———. (same) [Salt Lake City] Published by the General Board of Y.M.M.I.A. 1907.
59 [1]p. 21cm. (Young Men's Mutual Improvement Associations. Manual for Junior classes. 1907–8)
UPB

2268. ———. The Ancient prophets. [Salt Lake City] Published by The General Board of the Y.M.M.I.A., c1903.
108p. 22cm. (Young Men's Mutual Improvement Associations. Manual for Junior Classes. 1903–1904)
USIC

2269. ———. (same) [Salt Lake City] Published by The General Board of the Y.M.M.I.A. [1903]
108p. 22cm. (Young Men's Mutual Improvement Associations. Manual for Junior Classes. 1903–1904)
Variant edition: No copyright information on title page.
USIC

2270. ———. The Ancient prophets (continued) [Salt Lake City] Published by the General Board of Y.M.M.I.A., 1904.
120p. 22cm. (Young Men's Mutual Improvement Associations. Manual for Junior Classes. 1904–1905)
USIC

2271. ———. The apostolic age. Published by the General Board. [Salt Lake City, n.d.]
94p. col. double map, fold. chart. 22cm. (Young Men's Mutual Improvement Associations. Manual. 1898–99)
Folded chart between p. 88 and 89. Analysis of the Book of Revelation, by B. H. Roberts.
UPB

2272. ———. Campfire stories, of conditions, incidents and adventures connected with crossing the plains in early days. Salt Lake City, Published by the General Board of Y.M.M.I.A., 1920.
88p. illus. 22cm. (Young Men's Mutual Improvement Associations. Manual for the Junior Department, 1920–21)
UPB

2273. ———. Characters from ancient history. [Salt Lake City] The Deseret News, 1905.
118p. 23cm. (Young Men's Mutual Improvement Associations. Manual for Junior classes, 1905–1906)
UPB, USIC

2274. ———. . . . Choosing an occupation. [Salt Lake City] Published by the General Board of Y.M.M.I.A., 1930.
5p.l. [11]–149p. 22cm. (Course of study and M Men-Gleaner program for 1930–31)
UPB, USIC

2275. ———. The church as an organization for social service. Salt Lake City, Published by the General Board, Y.M.M.I.A., 1916.
103 [1]p. 23cm. (Young Men's Mutual Improvement Associations. Manual for Senior Classes, No. 20)
UHi, UPB, USIC

2276. ———. Conditions of success. Salt Lake City, Published by the General Board of Y.M.M.I.A., 1915.
80p. 23cm. (Young Men's Mutual Improvement Associations. Manual for Senior Classes, 1915–1916. No. 19)
UPB, USIC

2277. ———. The Development of character. Salt Lake City, Published by the General Board of the Y.M.M.I.A. [1910–1914]
3v. 22½cm. (Young Men's Mutual Improvement Associations. Manual for Junior Classes, 1910–1911–1914)
I. Lessons on Conduct.
II. Lessons on Success.
III. Lessons on Courage.
ULA, UPB, USIC

2278. ———. (same) Salt Lake City, Published by the General Board of Y.M.M.I.A., 1914–1916.
3v. 22cm. (Young Men's Mutual Improvement Associations. Manuals for Junior classes, 1914–15, 1915–16, 1916–17)
Second edition.
UPB, USIC

2279. ———. (same) Salt Lake City, Published by the General Board of Y.M.M.I.A., 1917–1919.
2v. 18cm. (Young Men's Mutual Improvement Association. Manual for Junior Classes, 1917–18, 1918–19)
1918–19 has size of 22cm.
Reprinted with new plates of Nos. II and III.
UPB, USIC

2280. ———. Digest of instructions. Young Men's Mutual Improvement Associations, the Church of Jesus Christ of Latter-day Saints for guidance of stake and ward officers. [Salt Lake City] Deseret News, 1904.
24p. 18cm.
UHi, UPB, USIC

CHURCH. . . . Y. M. M. I. A.

2281. ———. Dispensation of the fullness of times. Published by the General Board of the Y.M.M.I.A. [Salt Lake City] The Deseret News, 1899–1900.
2v. 22cm.
Contents: Part I. 1805–1839. Part II. 1838–1846.
UPB, USIC

2282. ———. Father and sons' annual outing. [Salt Lake City, 1926–1930]
7v. illus. 19–19½cm.
1924 14[1]p. 15cm.
1925 15p. 19cm.
1926 22[1]p. 19cm.
1927 22p. 19½cm.
1928 22p. 19cm.
1929 16p. 16cm.
1930 16p. 19½cm.
UPB, USIC

2283. ———. The gospel and health. A study course for the Mutual Improvement Associations in the British Mission of the Church of Jesus Christ of Latter-day Saints. Y.M.M.I.A. Manual, No. 25, Rev. Liverpool, Published by John A. Widtsoe, 1928.
52p. 20½cm.
USIC

2284. ———. Health and achievement . . . Salt Lake City, Published by the General Board of Y.M.M.I.A., 1922.
108p. 22cm. (Achievement series, No. 1)
Young Men's Mutual Improvement Association. Senior manual, 1922–23. No. 25.
UPB, USIC

2285. ———. How science contributes to religion. Salt Lake City, Published by the General Board of Y.M.M.I.A., 1927.
3p.l. [7]–94p. 22cm. (Achievement series, No. 6)
Young Men's Mutual Improvement Association. Senior manual . . . No. 30.
UPB, USIC

2286. ———. The individual and society. Salt Lake City, Published by the General Board of Y.M.M.I.A., 1912.
100, xvi p. 22½cm. (Young Men's Mutual Improvement Associations. 1912–1913. Manual No. 16)
UPB, USIC

2287. ———. L.D.S. Young Men's Mutual Improvement Associations. Manual. Part one. 1891–92. Salt Lake City, 1891.
60 [2]p. 21cm.
USIC

2288. ———. (same) 2d ed., with additional review questions. Salt Lake City, 1891.
89 [2]p. 21cm.
USIC

2289. ———. (same) 3d ed. of 5,000. 1892–1893. Salt Lake City, 1893.
89 [2]p. 21cm.
USIC

2290. ———. (same) 4th ed. of 5,000. 1894–1895. Published by authority. Salt Lake City, Printed and for sale by the Contributor Co., 1894.
85 [3]p. 24cm.
NN

2291. ———. Latter-day Saints' Young Men's Mutual Improvement Associations. The first twelve lessons, of manual, part two. 1894–1895. Published by authority. Salt Lake City, Printed and for sale by the Contributor Co., 1895.
51p. 24cm.
NN

2292. ———. Lessons in church history (stated in biographical sketches) Salt Lake City, Published by the General Board of the Y.M.M.I.A., 1908–1909.
2v. 22cm. (Young Men's Mutual Improvement Associations. Manual for Junior classes, 1908–1909, 1909–1910)
UPB, USIC

2293. ———. Life and work under spiritual guidance. Salt Lake City, Published by the General Board of Y.M.M.I.A., 1917.
2p.l. [5]–51 [1]p. 21cm. (Young Men's Mutual Improvement Associations. Manual for Senior Classes, No. 21)
UPB, USIC

2294. ———. The Life of Jesus. Salt Lake City, Magazine Printing Company, 1897.
xxii [2] 73p. col. map. 22cm. (Young Men's Mutual Improvement Association manual, 1897–8)
USIC

2295. ———. (same) Salt Lake City, Published by the General Board, Geo. Q. Cannon and Sons, Co.,
[3]–74p. col. map. 22½cm. (Young Men's Mutual Improvement Associations. Manual, 1897–98)
UPB, USIC

2296. ———. (same) Salt Lake City, Magazine Printing Company, 1902.
77p. col. map. 22cm. (Young Men's Mutual Improvement Associations. Manual, 1897–8)
USIC

2297. ———. (same) 5th ed. [Salt Lake City] Published by the General Board. [1906]
78p. 22cm. (Young Men's Mutual Improvement Associations. Manual for junior classes, 1906–7)
Issued previously as the senior manual.
UPB, USIC

CHURCH. . . . Y. M. M. I. A.

2298. ———. M Men guide and course of study for 1929–30. "Men who have made good" [Salt Lake City] Published by General Board of Y.M.M.I.A., 1929.
4p.l. [11]–174p. 18cm.
Course of study is an edited and retitled version of *Captains of industry* used by the Adult Dept. in 1928.
UPB, USIC

2299. ———. The making of a citizen . . . Salt Lake City, Published by the General Board of Y.M.M.I.A. 1910–1911.
2v. 22cm. (Young Men's Mutual Improvement Associations. Manual No. 14–15)
Contents: I. Lessons in economics. [II] Problems in economics — agriculture and public finance.
ULA, UPA, USIC

2300. ———. The making of the man. Salt Lake City, Published by the General Board of Y.M.M.I.A., 1909.
128p. 22cm. (Young Men's Mutual Improvement Associations. Manual, No. 13)
UPB, USIC

2301. ———. Man in relation to his work. Salt Lake City, Published by the General Board of Y.M.M.I.A., 1913.
2p.l. [5]–92p. 22cm. (Young Men's Mutual Improvement Associations. Manual for senior classes, 1913–1914, No. 17)
UPB, USIC

———. A Mission as a factor in education . . . A study for the advanced Junior Y.M.M.I.A. Classes, 1919–20. *See Improvement Era.*

2302. ———. Missionary stories. Part One. Stories of missionary experiences in the early years of the Church. Salt Lake City, Published by the General Board of Y.M.M.I.A., 1922.
2p.l. [5]–80p. 22cm. (Young Men's Mutual Improvement Associations. Manual for the Junior Department, 1922–1923)
UPB, USIC

2303. ———. Modern revelation, the history and message of the Doctrine and Covenants. Salt Lake City, Published by the General Board of the Y.M.M.I.A., Skelton Publishing Co., Printers [1906]
3p.l. [11]–138p. 22cm. (Young Men's Mutual Improvement Associations. Manual, No. 10)
Advertisements in front and back of Manual.
UPB, USIC

2304. ———. Pioneer stories; portraying the faith, zeal and adventures of some of the pioneers who established themselves in the Great American Desert. Salt Lake City, Published by the General Board of Y.M.M.I.A., 1921.
2p.l. [5]–80p. illus., ports. 22cm. (Young Men's Mutual Improvement Associations. Manual for the Junior Department, 1921–22)
UPB, USIC

2305. ———. (same) Salt Lake City, Published by the General Board of Y.M.M.I.A., 1925.
87p. illus., ports. 22 cm. (Story series, No. 2)
Young Men's Mutual Improvement Associations. Manual for the Junior classes, 1925–26.
UPB, USIC

2306. ———. Practical religion. Salt Lake City, Published by the General Board of Y.M.M.I.A., 1921.
109 [3]p. 22cm. (Young Men's Mutual Improvement Associations. Manual for the Senior Department, 1921–22)
UPB, USIC

2307. ———. . . . Principles of the Gospel. [Salt Lake City] Published by the General Board of the Y.M.M.I.A., The Deseret News, 1901–2.
2v. 22cm. (Young Men's Mutual Improvement Associations. Manual, 1901–1902, 1902–1903)
UPB, USIC

2308. ———. Sketches of eminent characters. Salt Lake City, Published by the General Board of Y.M.M.I.A. 1925.
3p.l. [7]–68p. 21cm. (Character-building series, No. 2)
Young Men's Mutual Improvement Associations. Manual for Advanced Junior Classes, 1925–1926.
UPB, USIC

2309. ———. Social achievement. The young man and his social world. (Book II–Achievement Series) Salt Lake City, Published by the General Board of the Y.M.M.I.A., 1923.
2p.l. [5]–128p. 20½cm. (Young Men's Mutual Improvement Associations. Senior Manual, 1923–1924)
UPB, USIC

2310. ———. Some epoch-making events in church history . . . Salt Lake City, Published by the General Board of Y.M.M.I.A., 1918.
102 [2]p. 22cm. (Young Men's Mutual Improvement Associations. Manual for Senior Classes . . . No. 22)
UPB, USIC

2311. ———. . . . Some essentials of character. Salt Lake City, Published by the General Board of Y.M.M.I.A., 1924.
3p.l. [7]–72p. 22½cm. (Character building series. No. 1)
Young Men's Mutual Improvement Associations. Manual for Advanced Junior classes, 1924–25.
UPB, USIC

2312. ———. Spiritual growth; lessons on practical religion. Salt Lake City, Published by the General Board of the Y.M.M.I.A., 1907.
4 p.l. [9]–114p. 22cm. (Young Men's Mutual Improvement Associations. Manual, No. 11)
UPB, USIC

CHURCH. . . . Y. M. M. I. A.

2313. ———. Stories of courage and devotion. Taken from experiences of modern missionaries of the Church. Salt Lake City, Published by the General Board of the Y.M.M.I.A., 1926.
2p.l. [4]–91[1]p. 21cm. (Story Series. Book III)
Young Men's Mutual Improvement Association. Junior Department. Manual for Junior classes, 1926–1927.
UPB, USIC

2314. ———. Stories of faith and courage, taken from experiences of modern missionaries of the Church. Salt Lake City, Published by the General Board of Y.M.M.I.A., 1923.
2p.l. [5]–80p. 20½cm. (Young Men's Mutual Improvement Association. Manual for the Junior Department, 1923–1924)
UPB, USIC

2315. ———. Stories of the plains. Salt Lake City, Published by the General Board of the Y.M.M.I.A., 1924.
96p. illus. 22½cm. (Story series. No. 1)
Young Men's Mutual Improvement Associations. Junior Department. Manual for the Junior classes, 1924–1925.
UPB, USIC

2316. ———. (same) Salt Lake City, Published by the General Board of Y.M.M.I.A., 1927.
2p.l. [5]–96p. illus. 22cm. (Story series. No. 1)
Young Men's Mutual Improvement Associations. Manual for the Junior Classes, 1927–28.
UPB, USIC

2317. ———. Supplement to the M.I.A. hand book program, 1929–30. Special Y.M.M.I.A. Executive Officers edition. [Salt Lake City] Published by the General Board of Y.M.M.I.A., 1929.
[3]–116p. 19cm.
Cover-title.
UHi, UPB, USIC

2318. ———. Supplement to the M.I.A. hand book, Program 1930–31. [Salt Lake City] Published by the General Board of Y.M.M.I.A., 1930.
46 [2]p. 18cm.
UHi, UPB, USIC

2319. ———. A tribute of respect to the memory of Francis Marion Lyman a member of the General Board of the Y.M.M.I.A. Salt Lake City [1916?]
[1]p. 21½cm.
On verso: A tribute from President Heber J. Grant.
UPB

2320. ———. Vanguard–Scout guide; prepared under the supervision of the Vanguard — Scout committees of the M.I.A. General Board and the Utah Scout executives, by William B. Hawkins . . . [Salt Lake City, Published by the General Board of the Y.M.M.I.A. of the Church of Jesus Christ of Latter-day Saints, 1929]
47p. 19cm.
UHi

2321. ———. Vanguard–Scout guide. Prepared under the supervision of the Executive Secretary and the Vanguard — Scout Committees of the Y.M.M.I.A. General Board. [Salt Lake City, Published by the General Board of Young Men's Mutual Improvement Association, 1930]
77p. 19cm.
Revised edition of 1929 manual by William B. Hawkins.
UPB

2322. ———. The vocations of man. Salt Lake City, Published by the General Board of Y.M.M.I.A., 1914.
80p. 22cm. (Young Men's Mutual Improvement Associations. Manual for senior classes, No. 18. 1914–1915)
UHi, UPB, USIC, UU

2323. ———. The Young man and religion. Book V-Achievement series. No. 29. Salt Lake City, Published by the General Board, Y.M.M.I.A., 1926.
3p.l. [7]–100p. 21cm. (Young Men's Mutual Improvement Association. Senior Manual, 1926–1927)
UPB, USIC

2324. ———. The Young man and the economic world. (Book III-Achievement Series) No. 27. Salt Lake City, Published by the General Board of the Y.M.M.I.A., 1924.
3p.l. [7]–108p. 22½cm. (Young Men's Mutual Improvement Association. Senior Manual, 1924–1925)
UPB, USIC

———. Y.M.M.I.A. and missionary hymn and tune book. *See Stephens, Evan.*

2325. ———. Y.M.M.I.A. Boy Scout bulletin. Salt Lake City, 1921.
2p.l. [5]–45p. 19½cm.
USIC, UU

2326. ———. Y.M.M.I.A. handbook. Published by the General Board as a guide for the stake and ward officers of the Young Men's Mutual Improvement Associations of the Church of Jesus Christ of Latter-day Saints. Salt Lake City, 1914.
2p.l. [5]–72p. 19cm.
UPB, USIC

2327. ———. (same) 2d ed., rev. and enl. [Salt Lake City] Published by the General Board, 1915.
116p. 19cm.
UPB

2328. ———. (same) 3d ed., rev. and enl. [Salt Lake City] Published by the General Board, 1917.
2p.l. [5]–126p. 18cm.
UPB

CHURCH. . . . Y. W. M. I. A.

2329. ———. (same) 4th ed. rev. and enl. [Salt Lake City, Published by the General Board] 1921.
120p. 18cm.
USIC

2330. ———. (same) 5th ed., rev. and enl. [Salt Lake City] Published by the General Board, 1923.
[3]–192p. 18½cm.
UHi, UPB

2331. ———. (same) 6th ed., rev. Ed. by Edward H. Anderson. [Salt Lake City] Published by the General Board, 1924.
199p. illus. 19cm.
UPB

2332. ———. (same) 7th ed., rev. Ed. by Edward H. Anderson. [Salt Lake City] Published by the General Board, 1925.
208p. illus. 18½cm.
UPB, UU

2333. Church of Jesus Christ of Latter-day Saints. Young Women's Mutual Improvement Association. The Bee-keepers' book. Bee-hive girls. 1921 edition. Salt Lake City, Published by the General Board of the Young Ladies' Mutual Improvement Association, 1921.
1p.l. [3]–192p. 22½cm.
UPB

2334. ———. (same) 1925 edition . . . Martha H. Tingey, President; Ruth May Fox, First Counselor; Lucy Grant Cannon, Second Counselor. Salt Lake City, Published by the Young Ladies Mutual Improvement Association, 1925.
224p. 24cm.
NN, USIC

2335. ———. Courses of study. Adult Women's Department of the Young Ladies' Mutual Improvement Association, 1929–1930. [Salt Lake City, 1929]
80p. 21cm.
Contents: Notable mothers of scripture, by James H. Anderson. Abundant life for the adult woman. Society and personality, by Arthur L. Beeley.
UPB, USIC

2336. ———. Four music programs. [Salt Lake City, Young Ladies' Mutual Improvement Association, 1930]
[31]–45p. illus. 22cm. (Courses of study, Adult Women's Department of the Y.L.M.I.A., Pt. 2)
Contents: Music appreciation by Evangeline T. Beesley. Home songs, by Ethel S. Anderson. Stephen Collins Foster, by Evangeline T. Beesley. Indian music, by Frank W. Asper.
UPB

2337. ———. . . . Guide for the junior department of the Young Ladies Mutual Improvement Associations, 1903–04. [Salt Lake City] Published by the General Board, 1903.
28p. 23cm.
UHi

2338. ———. Guide to the first year's course of study in the Young Ladies' Mutual Improvement Association. Prepared by the General Board of the Young Ladies' Mutual Improvement Association, and issued as sanctioned by the First Presidency of the Church. Salt Lake City, George Q. Cannon & Sons Co. [188?]
41p. 21½cm.
Guide prepared by Susa Young Gates.
NN, UHi, USIC

2339. ———. Guide to the first year's course of study in the Young Ladies' Mutual Improvement Association. Prepared by the General Board of the Young Ladies' Mutual Improvement Association, and issued as sanctioned by the First Presidency of the Church. Salt Lake City, George Q. Cannon & Sons Co., Printers [n.d.]
49p. 20½cm.
USIC

2340. ———. Guide to the second year's course of study in the Young Ladies' Mutual Improvement Association. Prepared by the General Board of the Young Ladies' Mutual Improvement Association, and issued as sanctioned by the First Presidency. Salt Lake City, George Q. Cannon and Sons Company [1896?]
83p. 24cm.
NjP, NN, UHi

2341. ———. (same) Guide [second half year's course] for the Junior Department of the Young Ladies' National Mutual Improvement Association, 1903–1904, [Salt Lake City] 1904.
32p. 21½cm.
USIC

2342. ———. Hand book for the Bee-hive girls of the Y.L.M.I.A. 1st ed. Salt Lake City, Published by the General Board of the Young Ladies' Mutual Improvement Association. c1915.
36p. illus. 22cm.
UPB, USIC

2343. ———. (same) 2d ed. Salt Lake City, Published by the General Board of the Young Ladies' Mutual Improvement Association, 1916.
48p. illus. 22cm.
With music.
UPB, USIC

2344. ———. (same) 3d ed., war emergency. 1918. Salt Lake City, Published by the General Board of the Young Ladies' Mutual Improvement Association, 1918 [c1916]
3p.l. [9]–52 [8]p. illus. 21cm.
With music.
UPB, USIC

2345. ———. (same) 4th ed. Salt Lake City, General Board of the Young Ladies' Mutual Improvement Association, 1919 [c1916]
52p. 23cm.
USIC

2346. ———. (same) 5th ed. 1920. Salt Lake City, Published by the General Board of the Young Ladies' Mutual Improvement Association, 1920 [c1916]
8p.l. [9]–52p. [4]l. 22½cm.
UPB, USIC

2347. ———. (same) 6th ed. Salt Lake City, Published by the General Board of the Young Ladies' Mutual Improvement Association, 1921.
64p. 23cm.
UHi, USIC

2348. ———. (same) 7th ed. Salt Lake City, Published by the General Board of the Young Ladies' Mutual Improvement Association, 1923 [c1916]
4p.l. [9]–88 [8]p. illus. 21cm.
With music.
UPB

2349. ———. (same) 9th ed. Salt Lake City, Published by the General Board of the Young Ladies' Mutual Improvement Association, 1927.
96p. music. 22cm.
USIC

2350. ———. (same) 10th ed. Salt Lake City, Published by the General Board of the Young Ladies' Mutual Improvement Association, 1928.
4p.l. [9]–80[8]p. illus. 21cm.
UPB

2351. ———. Instructions to Bee-keepers of the Bee-hive girls . . . Salt Lake City, Published by the General Board of the Young Ladies' Mutual Improvement Associations, 1919.
32p. 23cm.
UPB, UHi

2352. ———. Instructions to Y.L.N.M.I.A. officers. Improvement our motto; perfection our aim. 1914. [Salt Lake City, 1914]
15p. 19½cm.
Cover-title.
The "National" appeared for a year or two but was not a part of the official name.
USIC, UU

2353. ———. Latter-day Saint ideals of home and home life. (Second Year) Course of study for the Gleaner Department of the Young Ladies Mutual Improvement Association. 1929–1930. [Salt Lake City, General Board of the Y.L.M.I.A., 1929?]
[3]–48p. 21cm.
NN, UPB

2354. ———. Lion House Social Center for girls and women. [Salt Lake City, n.d.]
[4]p. 19cm.
USIC

2355. ———. An Outline of courses of study for Intermediate Classes of the Young Ladies' Mutual Improvement Association. For the use of class leaders. [Salt Lake City] Published by the General Board of the Y.L.M.I.A., 1921.
31p. 23cm.
UPB, USIC

2356. ———. (same) Number three. For the use of class leaders. [Salt Lake City] Published by the General Board of the Y.L.M.I.A., 1924.
35p. 22½cm.
UPB

2357. ———. Selections from writings of pioneer poets. Y.L.M.I.A. literary course for 1909–10. [Salt Lake City] The Deseret News, 1909.
15p. 14½cm.
Cover-title.
Includes poetry by Eliza R. Snow, Emily H. Woodmansee, and Emmeline B. Wells.
UHi, UPB, USIC

2358. ———. Y.L.M.I.A. annual conventions. Salt Lake City, Utah, July 31st, 1903. To stake presidents, counselors, and all stake officers of the Young Ladies' Mutual Improvement Association: Dear sisters: Salt Lake City, 1903.
8p. 21cm.
UPB

2359. ———. Y.L.M.I.A. hand book. A guide for stake and ward officers of the Young Ladies' Mutual Improvement Associations of the Church of Jesus Christ of Latter-day Saints. [Salt Lake City] Published by the General Board, 1923.
3p.l. [7]–102 [2]p. illus. 17cm.
UPB, USIC

2360. ———. (same) 2d ed. [Salt Lake City] Published by the General Board, 1924.
3p.l. [7]–109p. 18½cm.
UPB, USIC

2361. ———. (same) 3d ed. [Salt Lake City] Published by the General Board, 1926.
144p. 18½cm.
USIC, UU

CITY OF SALT LAKE

2362. ———. Y.L.M.I.A. songbook. Volume 1. [Salt Lake City, Young Ladies' Mutual Improvement Association, c1916]
2p.l. [5]–64p. music. 27cm.
USIC

2363. ———. Y.L.M.I.A. summer camp bulletin. Salt Lake City, Published by the General Board of the Young Ladies Mutual Improvement Association, 1930.
64p. 17cm.
NN, USIC

2364. Church of Jesus Christ of Latter Day Saints (Strang). A collection of sacred hymns; adapted to the faith and views of the Church of Jesus Christ of Latter Day Saints. Voree [Wis.] Gospel Press, 1849.
172p. 10½cm.
Morgan
CtY, DLC, NNHi

2365. ———. A collection of sacred hymns; adapted to the faith and views of the Church of Jesus Christ of Latter Day Saints. Voree [Wis.] Gospel Press, 1850.
172p. 11cm.
2d edition.
An 1852 3d ed. and an 1856 4th ed. might have been printed.
Morgan, Sabin 92682
NNUT, WHi

2366. ———. Facts for thinkers. [Pueblo, Colo.? 1930?]
Broadside. 23×13cm.
Morgan
MoInRC, USIC

2367. ———. Memorial. To the President and Congress of the United States, and to all the people of the nation — we, James J. Strang, George J. Adams, and William Marks, presidents of the Church of the Saints, Apostles of the Lord Jesus Christ, and Witnesses of His name unto all nations, and others, our fellow servants, send greeting: — [Voree, Wis., Gospel Press, 1850]
4p. 32½cm.
Caption-title.
Signed: Buffalo. April 6, 1850.
Final issue of the *Gospel Herald*, June 6, 1850.
Presented to the U.S. Senate June 15, 1850, and referred to the Committee on Public Lands over the objection of the chairman. On September 21, 1850, the Committee asked to be discharged from further consideration of the Memorial. See *Congressional Globe*, Vol. 19, p. 1221, 1907.
Reprinted in Milo M. Quaife *The Kingdom of St. James*, p. 249–255 and *Prophetic Controversy* No. 14.
Morgan
CtY

2368. Church of the Firstborn. Articles of faith. Published by committee of the Church of the Firstborn, organized in San Francisco, California, July 2nd, 1876 . . . San Francisco, 1887.
16p. 15cm. (Tract No. 3)
Followers of Joseph Morris.
USIC

2369. ———. For missionary work. [San Francisco? ca. 1887]
[2]p. 21½cm.
USIC

2370. ———. Millenial [sic] hymns. [San Francisco] D. Bruce Print. [after 1864]
18p. 16cm.
Without music.
Published after the death of Joseph Morris, who is mentioned in the 10th hymn.
Cover-title.
CU–B

2371. Church University, Salt Lake City. Announcement of the Church University. Salt Lake City, 1893–
v. 24½cm.
USIC 1893–4

2372. ———. **Theology Class.** The articles of faith. Salt Lake City, 1893–
v. 20½cm.
USIC No. 9

2373. Churchill, Caroline M. (Nichols). Over the purple hills: or, Sketches of travel in California of important points usually visited by tourists. Chicago, Hazlitt & Reed, 1877 [c1876]
256p. plates. 15½cm.
A trip through Salt Lake City. The tabernacle is an oblong plum pudding; "gift" of healing causes many to go through life warped physically as well as mentally.
Other editions: 1878. UPB, USIC; Denver, Mrs. C. M. Churchill, 1881. DLC; Denver, Mrs. C. M. Churchill, 1884. CU–B, DLC, UPB, USIC
CU, UPB, USIC

2374. Circular. Joseph's politics. [n.p., n.d.]
[2]l. 30×26cm.
Copy may be defective. A description of Joseph Smith's political views.
USIC

2375. The City of Salt Lake! Her relations as a centre of trade; manufacturing establishments, and business houses. Salt Lake City, Sylvanus, Stone & Shaw, 1890.
2p.l. [5]–128p. illus., plates. 22cm.
Historical, descriptive and statistical information.
MH

CITY OF THE SAINTS

2376. The City of the Saints. Containing views and descriptions of principal points of interest in Salt Lake City and vicinity. Also brief sketches of the history and religions of the Latter-day Saints. Salt Lake City, Geo. Q. Cannon and Sons Co. [189–]
66p. plates, ports. 13×18cm.
CSmH, CtY, DLC, NM, OCl, UHi, UPB, USIC, UU

2377. ———. (same) Salt Lake City, Geo. Q. Cannon & Sons, Co. [1897?]
67 [2]p. illus., plates, ports. 13cm.
NjP, USIC

2378. The city of the Saints, in picture and story; the great pilgrimage of the pioneers. How they blazed a pathway to the promised land. Building of their home by the mysterious inland sea . . . Salt Lake City, The Deseret News, 1906.
2p.l., 5–64p. illus., ports., tables. 29½cm.
CtY, MoInRC, NM, UHi, UPB, USIC, UU

2379. Clagett, William H. Speech of Hon. William H. Clagett of Montana in the House of Representatives, January 28 and 29, 1873. [Washington, Congressional Globe Office, 1873]
[9]–16p. 23cm.
Caption-title.
At head of title: Colorado Territory.
Speech concerning Utah and its religious situation.
UU

2380. Claiborne, D. J. The story of a Mormon convert. How he was lured into Mormonism, and how he found the light again; as told by himself. [Cleveland, O., Utah Gospel Mission, 1904]
8p. 16cm.
Caption-title.
Signed: D. J. Claiborne.
MH, MoInRC, NjPT, NN, OClWHi

2381. ———. (same) [Cleveland, O., Utah Gospel Mission, 1922]
7 [1]p. 16½cm.
Caption-title.
Edited by John D. Nutting.
Letter signed: New York, January 1903.
UHi, NN, UU

Claims of Mormonism. *See Gentile Bureau of Information.*

2382. Clampitt, John Wesley. Echoes from the Rocky Mountains; reminiscences and thrilling incidents of the romantic and golden age of the great West, with a graphic account of its discovery, settlement and grand development. Chicago, National Book Concern [c1888]
xvi [19]–671p. illus., ports., plates. 25cm.
Profuse with material concerning Mormonism, Gentile-Mormon relations, Brigham Young, etc.
Other editions: London, 1888; Chicago, Belford Clarke & Co., 1889. ICN, NjP, NN, PP, USIC; Chicago, American Mutual Literary Assoc., 1890. UHi
MH, MiU, MoK, OCU, PSC, USIC, ViU

2383. Clark, Braden. A challenge to E. L. Kelley. [n.p., 1891?]
2p. 21cm.
Written at Stratton, Nebraska, 1891.
Challenge for a debate on Mormonism.
MoInRC

2383a. Clark, Charles Heber. Out of the Hurly-Burly; or, life in an odd corner. By Max Adeler [*pseud.*] With nearly four hundred illustrations, By Arthur B. Frost, Fred B. Schell, Wm. L. Sheppard and Ed. B. Bensell. Philadelphia, New York, Boston, Cincinnati and Chicago, George Maclean & Co., 1874.
3p.l. [5]–398p. illus. 19½cm.
"Bishop Potts." p. 245–254. A story of Mormon polygamy.
CtY, DLC, KU, TU, UPB

2384. ———. The tragedy of Thompson Dunbar. A tale of Salt Lake City, by Max Adeler [*pseud.*] Philadelphia, J. M. Stoddart and Co., 1879.
2p.l. [9]–56p. illus. 18cm.
Fiction concerning Mormonism.
CU–B, USIC

2385. Clark, Charles M. A trip to Pike's Peak and notes by the way, with numerous illustrations: Being descriptive of incidents and accidents that attended the pilgrimage; of the country through Kansas and Nebraska; Rocky Mountains; Mining regions, mining operations, etc., etc. By C. M. Clark, M. D. . . . Chicago, S. P. Round's Steam Book and Job Printing House . . . 1861.
2p.l. [vi]–viip., 1[l.], 134p., 1[l.]. 18 plates. 21½cm.
Utes called "Tools of the Mormons," p. 97; encounter with young man who had gone to Utah with Johnston's Army, p. 120.
W–C 372
CU–B, DLC, ICN

2386. Clark, E. O. An Open letter to Daniel MacGregor, also an article from the pen of Daniel MacGregor, in defense of the Reorganization from an attack, and a challenge of its president to a debate, by R. C. Evans. [n.p., 1917?]
10 [1]p. 23cm.
Signed: St. Thomas, Ontario, April 4, 1917.
Includes a letter from Clark to MacGregor, and Daniel MacGregor's response to a statement by R. C. Evans.
MoInRC, NM

2387. Clark, Frank H. Over blazed trails and country highways; the story of a midsummer journey. Lisle, New York, 1919.
4p.l., 9–146p. 20cm.
"The Seventh Day at Nauvoo," "Joseph & Moroni," "Brigham Young," p. 79–85.
NjP, UHi

2388. Clark, John Alonzo. Gleanings by the way, by Reverend John A. Clark. Philadelphia, W. J. & J. K. Simon; New York, R. Carter, 1842.
v, [7]–352p. 19½cm.
Several chapters on Mormonism under such headings as "The origin of the Mormon's delusion," "Mormon Jesuitism," p. 216–352.
Howe C440
CSmH, CtY, CU–B, DLC, ICN, NM, UHi, ULA, USlC, UU, WHi

2389. Clark, John Tanner. The last records to come forth. The Lord's strange act. The Manifesto, a covenent with death and an agreement with hell. [Salt Lake City, 1905?]
52p. 20cm.
Against the polygamy manifesto.
UPB, USlC, UU

2390. ———. The one mighty and strong. As "Thus saith men." Published in the Deseret News in 1905 & in the Improvement Era in 1907 by the LDS Church authorities; & "The one mighty and strong" as "Thus saith the Lord" taken from Holy Writ, etc. [Salt Lake City, 1922?]
vi, 165p. 20½cm.
Fundamentalist viewpoint of Mormon history.
CU–B, NM, UHi, UPB, UU

2391. ———. (same) [Salt Lake City, 1930]
xiv, 200p. 21cm.
Caption-title.
NN, USlC

2392. Clark, Joseph B. Leavening the nation. The story of American home missions. New York, The Baker & Taylor Co. [1903]
3p.l., v–vii [14]p., 1[l.], 11–362p. plates, ports., map. 19½cm.
Chapter 15. Mormonism and Utah history.
DLC, USlC

2393. Clark, Joshua Reuben. Concerning the personality of God; address delivered over Radio Station KSL, Sunday Evening, June 26, 1927. [Salt Lake City] 1927.
Broadside. 56×25cm.
Reprinted from the *Deseret News.*
UPB

2394. ———. Personality of God from Biblical standpoint; address delivered over Radio Station KSL Sunday Evening, July 10, 1927. [Salt Lake City] 1927.
Broadside. 58½×25cm.
Reprinted from the *Deseret News.*
UPB

2395. Clark, Orson. A temple in Hawaii. Words by Ruth May Fox. Music by Orson Clark. [n.p., 1919?]
[2]p. 23cm.
USlC

2396. Clark, Rena. The New West Education Commission. A glimpse of life in Utah, by a teacher. Chicago, Brown, Pettibone & Co., 1886.
11p. 14cm.
The work of the New West Education Commission.
USlC

2397. Clark, Sterling Benjamin Franklin. How many miles from St. Jo? The log of Sterling B. F. Clark, forty-niner. With comments by Ella Sterling Mighels together with a brief autobiography of James Phelan, 1819 [i.e. 1820]–1892, pioneer merchant. San Francisco, Privately printed, 1929.
xii, 56p., 1[l.]. ports., facsim. 20½cm.
Via Salt Lake in 1849; reference to the Mormons, p. 19–20, 27–28, 30; Mormon Island, p. 26, 30, 32.
CU–B, DLC

2398. Clark, Susie Champney. The round trip from the hub to the Golden Gate. Boston, Lee and Shepard, 1890.
2p.l. [5]–193p. 19cm.
A visit to Utah after "polygamy was dead." She attends a meeting at the Mormon tabernacle.
CU–B, DLC, NjP, UHi

2399. Clarke, Charles H. Mormonism unveiled; or, A history of Mormonism from its rise to the present time. London, Charles H. Clarke [1855?]
xiv [15]–235p. 17cm.
Preface signed: 1855.
An exposé of Mormonism, with no footnotes or references.
USl, USlC

2400. Clarke, Charles Russell. Clarke's new school geography; forming the third part of Bancroft's geographical and historical series. San Francisco, H. H. Bancroft and Company, 1866.
108p. illus., maps. 33cm.
Cover-title: Descriptive atlas of the Pacific states.
Utah map, p. 24–25. "Utah, its valleys" with Mormon references, p. 44–46.
CU–B, USlC

2401. Clarke, R. Mormonism unmasked; or, the Latter-day Saints in a fix, by R. Clarke, one of the apologists of the every day saints. [London, Houlston & Stoneman, 1849?]
20p. 22½cm.
Caption-title.
CtY, CU–B, MH, NN, OClWHi, USl, USlC

2402. ———. (same) [London, G., J. & R. Banks, Printers, 1849]
32p. 17cm.
"Second Edition."
Caption-title.
ULA, USlC

2403. ———. (same) [London, G., J. & R. Banks, Printers, 1850?]
32p. 17½cm.
"Third Edition."
CtY, CU–B, ICN, MH, NN, OClWHi, ULA, USl, USlC

2404. Clarke, S. J. History of McDonough County, Illinois, its cities, towns, and villages, with early reminiscences, personal incidents and anecdotes, and a complete business directory of the county . . . Springfield, Ill., D. W. Tusk, State Printer, 1878.
692 (i.e. 688)p. illus., plates. 24cm.
Doctrines of the Mormons and its history in Illinois, with particular emphasis on the Mormon vote.
Another edition: Staunton, Va. 1882.
CSmH, CU, DLC, InU, MB, MnH, NjP, NN, UHi

2405. Clawson, Hiram B. Yankee story, by H. B. Clawson. [Salt Lake City, 1857]
7p. 19cm.
Cover-title.
A satire on the Utah expedition.
USlC

2406. Clawson, Rudger. The anti-"Mormon" moving pictures and play. [Liverpool? Millennial Star Office? 1911?]
4p. 21cm.
Caption-title.
Results of Anti-Mormon plays in England.
UHi, USlC

2407. ———. Important to the people of the British Isles. [Liverpool, n.d.]
[4]p. 22½cm.
Caption-title.
Missionary tract.
UPB

2408. ———. "Mormonism" versus fiction — a rejected letter. [Liverpool? Millennial Star Office? 1912?]
4p. 21cm.
Caption-title.
Contains correspondence with the *London Tid-Bits.* Discussion of Anti-Mormon literature.
UHi

2409. ———. The Mountain Meadows massacre. [Liverpool, British Mission Headquarters, 1912?]
[2]p. 22½cm.
Caption-title.
UHi, UPB

2410. ———. "The People's" attack on the Mormons — a rejected letter. The unfairness of the British press in general towards the Latter-day Saints is strongly emphasized by the action of *The People*, a London weekly publication, in rejecting a respectful letter addressed to the editor by the undersigned. The full text of said letter is as follows . . . [Liverpool, British Mission Headquarters, 1912?]
4p. 22cm.
Caption-title.
UHi, UPB, USlC

2411. ———. The Question of the hour. [Liverpool? Millennial Star Office? 1911?]
4p. 21cm.
Caption-title.
Problem of poor newspaper reporting of Mormonism.
UHi, UPB

2412. Clay, Edmund. The doctrines and practices of "The Mormons" and the immoral character of their prophet Joseph Smith, delineated from authentic sources. London, Wertheim and Macintosh [etc. etc.] 1853.
1p.l., 70p. 18cm.
Four tracts originally issued [1851–52] with general title "Tracts on Mormonism."
CtY, MH, NN, USlC, WHi

2413. ———. Tracts on Mormonism. London, Wertheim and Macintosh, 1851–52.
4 nos. 16½cm.
Each tract has also special caption title. Published (1853) under title: The doctrines and practices of "The Mormons," each tract having caption-title only.
CSmH, CtY, NN, USlC

2414. ———. Tracts on Mormonism. Number 1. A brief account of the life and character of Joseph Smith, the "prophet" of Mormonism. J. Glover printer, No. 1, Victoria Terrace, Leamington, Third Thousand. London, Wertheim and Macintosh, 1850.
17p. 17cm.
MH, NN

2415. ———. (same) 2d ed. London, Wertheim and Macintosh, 1850.
17p. 17cm.
CSmH, USlC

2416. ———. (same) 6th thousand. London, Wertheim and Macintosh, 1851.
18p. 17cm.
CtY, USlC

2417. ———. Tracts on Mormonism. No. 2. The Book of Mormon; its history, and an analysis of its contents. [London] Wertheim and Macintosh, J. Glover, 1850.
18p. 21cm.
CtY, USlC

2418. ———. (same) 3d thousand. London, Wertheim and Macintosh; Leamington, J. Glover, 1851.
18p. 17cm.
CtY

2419. ———. (same) 5th thousand. London, Wertheim and Macintosh, 1851.
20p. 20cm.
CSmH, NN

2420. ———. Tracts on Mormonism. No. 3. The Book of Mormon proved to be a blasphemous and impudent forgery. London, Wertheim and Macintosh, 1850.
16p. 21cm.
USlC

2421. ———. (same) London, Wertheim and Macintosh, 1851.
16p. 20cm.
CSmH

2422. ———. (same) London, Wertheim and Macintosh; Leamington, J. Glover, 1852.
16p. 17cm.
7th thousand.
CtY

2423. ———. Tracts on Mormonism. No. 4. The Book of Doctrine and Covenants of the "Church of Jesus Christ of Latter-day Saints: selected from "The Revelations of God," by "Joseph Smith," President. "Second European Edition. Liverpool: Orson Pratt, 15, Wilton Street. 1849." London, Wertheim and
20p. 17cm.
Macintosh; Leamington, J. Glover, 1852.
USlC

2424. Clayton, William. The Latter-day Saints' emigrants' guide; being a table of distances, showing all the springs, creeks, rivers, hills, mountains, camping places, and all other notable places, from Council Bluffs, to the valley of the Great Salt Lake. Also, the latitude, longitude, and altitudes of the prominent points on the route. Together with remarks on the nature of the land, timber, grass, &c. The whole route having been carefully measured by a roadometer, and the distance from point to point, in English miles, accurately shown. By W. Clayton. St. Louis, Mo., Republican Steam Power Press — Chambers & Knapp, 1848.
24p. 18cm.
Howes C475, Sabin 13580, W-C 147
CSmH, CtY, DLC, ICN, MoInRC, UPB, USlC

2425. ———. (same) St. Louis, Mo., Republican Steam Power Press, Chambers & Knapp, 1848. [Reprinted, 1897]
24p. 18cm.
Reprinted from the Brigham Young copy.
DLC, MH, NN

2426. ———. (same) Salt Lake City [1921]
24p. 20cm.
Reprinted in connection with Brigham H. Robert's *Comprehensive History of the church.*
CU-B, NjP, ULA, UPB, USlC

2427. ———. William Clayton's journal; a daily record of the journey of the original company of "Mormon" pioneers from Nauvoo, Illinois, to the valley of the Great Salt Lake. Published by the Clayton Family Association. Salt Lake City, The Deseret News, 1921.
[viii] 376p. port. 19½cm.
Howes C474
CSmH, CtY, CU-B, DLC, ICN, NjP, UHi, ULA, UPB, USlC, UU

2428. Cleaveland, Nehemiah. An address delivered at Topsfield, Mass., August 28, 1850: The two hundred and fiftieth anniversary of the incorporation of the town. By Nehemiah Cleaveland. New York, Pudney & Russell, Printers, 1851.
74, xxxix p. ports. 22½cm.
Appendix, note XVII gives short biographies of the Smiths with notes on how to handle the Mormon problem.
Sabin 13604
CSmH, DLC, MBaT, MnH, NH, NN

2429. Clegg, William. A galaxy of gems. Salt Lake City, 1900.
iv [5]-96p. port. 20cm.
"The Springville poet."
Mormon poetry.
NjP, UHi, UPB, USlC

2430. ———. A plea for the slighted ones, an original poem by William Clegg . . . Provo City, Utah, Sleater & McEwan . . . [1876]
15p. 19½cm.
Mormon poetry.
USlC

2431. Clemens, Samuel Langhorne. Roughing it by Mark Twain [*pseud.*] Hartford, Conn., American Publishing Co., 1872.
xviii [19]-591p. 22½cm.
Visit to Utah with a description of places and events.
Republished in various editions.
Howes C481
CU-B, DLC, NjP, UPB, USlC

2432. Clemenson, N. E. The great debate from *The Kinsman.* Salt Lake City, Kinsman Publishing Co. [1899?]
9 [1]p. 12cm.
Cover-title.
Debate between the Utah and the RLDS Church.
UHi

2433. ———. Plural Marriage essential to the integrity of Mormonism. By Rev. N. E. Clemenson. Logan, Utah. [Logan? 1905?]
12p. 14cm.
The two cannot be divided without showing the first false.
UPB, USlC

CLEMENTS, F. W.

2434. Clements, Frank W. A poem written, January, 1928. Bountiful [1928?]
[2]p. 15½cm.
Mormon poetry.
USlC

2435. Clive, William C. Come into His fold: Music by Wm. C. Clive. Words by Edward H. Anderson. Salt Lake City, Published and for sale by W. C. Clive, c1909.
8p. 22cm.
Mormon music.
USl

2436. ———. The pioneers . . . 2d ed. Words by Edward H. Anderson. Music by Wm. C. Clive. Salt Lake City [n.d.]
[2]l. music. 22½cm.
USlC

2437. Cluff, Benjamin. Myths and traditions of the Hawaiians. An address by Prof. Benq. Cluff, jr., Professor of the Brigham Young University, Provo, at the fourth annual reunion of Polynesian missionaries held at Lagoon, Davis Co., Utah, July 24, 1899. Salt Lake City, Published by the General Committee, 1899.
8p. 22cm.
UPB, USlC

2438. The Cluff family journal. [Salt Lake City?] June 20, 1899–September 20, 1904.
1v. #1–20 [2p.l., 394p.] ports. quarterly. 23cm.
Publication suspended June 3, 1903–March, 1904. Biographical information on the Cluff family in the Mormon Church and Utah. Published by the Cluff family reunion.
CtY; UPB vi, #19–20; USlC

2439. Clyman, James. James Clyman, American frontiersman, 1792–1881; the adventures of a trapper and covered wagon emigrant as told in his own reminiscences and diaries, edited by Charles L. Camp. San Francisco, California Historical Society, 1928.
2p.l. [9]–247 [4]p. illus., 2 ports., maps. 26½cm. (Special publication. No. 3)
Encounter with the Mississippi Saints in 1846. Material on the Mormon Battalion.
Howes C–81
CU–B, DLC, ICN, IdIf, MH, NjP, NN, OCl, UHi, ULA, UU

2440. Cobb, Benjamin F. Jack Henderson out west, by Benj. F. Cobb. Illustrations by Marshall D. Smith. New York, Hurst & Co. [c1905]
2p.l. [5]–126p. front. 16½cm.
Contains a long chapter entitled "Among the Mormons" dated, Salt Lake City, July, 190–. Letter to "Dear Billy." An earthy monologue patterned after the tale-spinners. "It seems that a wise guy by the name of Joe Smith started this gospel camp [etc.]"
DLC, USlC

2441. Cobb, Irvin Shrewsbury. Roughing it de luxe. By Irvin S. Cobb . . . Illustrated by John T. McCutcheon. New York, George H. Doran Co. [c1914]
6p.l. [15]–219p. 21cm.
A delightful description of his visit to Salt Lake City.
CU–B, NjP, USlC

2442. Codman, John. The Mormon country. A summer with the "Latter-day Saints." By John Codman. New York, United States Publishing Co., 1874.
2p.l., 225p. plates, map. 19cm.
CSmH, CtY, CU–B, DLC, ICN, MH, MoInRC, NjP, UHi, ULA, UPB, USl, USlC, UU

2443. ———. The round trip by way of Panama through California, Oregon, Nevada, Utah, Idaho and Colorado; with notes on railroads, commerce, agriculture, mining, scenery and people. New York, G. P. Putnam's Sons, 1879.
xiii, 331p. 20cm.
Trip through Utah with his impressions of Mormonism in 1874.
Other editions: 1881. MNH, UPB; 1882. I
CSmH, CU–B, NjP, NN, UHi, UPB, USl, USlC

2444. ———. . . . A solution of the Mormon problem, by John Codman . . . New York & London, G. P. Putnam's sons, The Knickerbocker Press, 1885.
2p.l., 25p. 20cm. (Questions of the day — xxi)
CSmH, CtY, CU–B, DLC, ICN, MH, NjP, NN, UPB, USl, USlC

2445. ———. Through Utah. By John Codman. (From The Galaxy for September–December 1875) New York, 1875.
1p.l., 313–[324], [487]–496, 613–626, 789–799p. 22½cm.
Pages from *The Galaxy*, with new title page and cover. Trip to Utah in 1874 with a great deal of material on Mormonism.
DLC, USlC

2446. Cody, William Frederick. Life and adventures of "Buffalo Bill" Colonel William F. Cody. This thrilling autobiography tells in Colonel Cody's own graphic language the wonderful story of his long, eventful and heroic career and is supplemented with a chapter by a loving, life-long friend covering his last days, death and burial . . . Chicago, Charles C. Thompson Company [c1917]
xiii, 15–352p. 21½cm.
Another edition: New York, Willey Book Co., 1927. CU–B
Captured by the Danites. The rail destroyed by the Mormons, p. 50–53. A great deal of fiction in his "autobiography."
NjP, UPB, USlC

2447. Coffee, Frank, *compiler.* Forty years on the Pacific, the lure of the great ocean; a book of reference for the traveler and pleasure for the stay-at-home. Compiled by Frank Coffee. Second edition. San Francisco, Oceanic Publishing Company, [c1925]
xvii, 403p. plates, ports., maps (part fold.) diagr. 23½cm.
"Mormon missionaries," p. 203.
UPB

2448. Coffin, Charles Carleton. Our new way round the world. Boston, J. R. Osgood & Co. [1859]
xix, 524p. 22½cm.
Brigham Young combines "police systems of Fouche, of the first empire of Ignatius Loyola and the Order of the Jesuits to keep law and order in Utah, a theocratic state." Chapter LXI "Salt Lake City."
Other editions: Boston, Fields, Osgood, & Co., 1869. DLC, USlC; London, Sampson Low, Son, & Marston, 1869. CU–B; New York, Lovell, 1879. USlC; Boston, Estes and Lauriat, c1880. DLC, OO; Boston, Estes & Lauriat, 1881. Sabin 14169, DLC, USlC, UU; London, F. Warne & Co., 1883. CU–B
DLC

2449. Coke, Henry John. A ride over the Rocky Mountains to Oregon and California. With a glance at some of the tropical islands, including the West Indies and the Sandwich Isles. London, R. Bentley, 1852.
x, 388 [2]p. port. 22cm.
Brief encounter with Mormon emigrants going to Salt Lake City in 1850.
Sabin 14240, Howes C548, W–C 211
CU–B, DLC, ICN, NjP, UPB

2450. Colborn, Edward Fenton. A glimpse of Utah, its resources, attractions and natural wonders, by Edward Fenton Colborn. [Denver, The Carson-Harper Co.] 1906.
56p. illus. 26cm.
"Issued by the Passenger department of the Denver and Rio Grande railroad."
"Early settlement of Utah," "The Mormon and gentiles"; deals mostly with description and travel, but has sketchy information on early history and a two page section "about the Mormons and gentiles" showing that all can live peaceably in Utah.
Other editions: Denver, Carson-Harper Co., 1908. DLC, UPB; 1909. DLC, USlC; 1910. CU–B, UHi, USlC
CU–B, UHi, USlC

———. An open letter to the world. *See An open letter to the world.*

2451. ———. A vision of the Great Salt Lake, the City and surroundings, as seen from the dining hall of the Hotel Templeton. [Salt Lake City, 189–?]
[20]p. illus., post. 13×20cm.
Cover-title.
Salt Lake City. The tabernacle, Brigham Young's residences and a brief sketch of Brigham Young. Issued as an advertisement for the Hotel Templeton.
MH

2452. Cole, Cornelius. Memoirs of Cornelius Cole, Ex-senator of the United States from California. New York, McLoughlin Brothers, 1908.
x, 354p. port. 24½cm.
Brief mention of Brigham Young and Salt Lake City in 1849.
Howes C 565
CU–B, DLC, NjP, NN, UPB

2453. Cole, William L. California, its scenery, climate, productions and inhabitants. Notes of an overland trip to the Pacific Coast, by Major William L. Cole. New York, Irish-American Office, 1871.
103p. 23cm.
He learned the background of the Church from Mormons en route. Description of Salt Lake City and its inhabitants.
Cover-title is dated 1872.
Howes C 569
CMC, CtY, CU–B, MWA

2454. Coleman, Alice Blanchard. The menace of Mormonism [by] Mrs. Geo. W. Coleman . . . Chicago, Womans' American Baptist Home Mission Society [1912]
11p. 16cm.
NN

2455. Coleman, Mrs. George W. Mormonism to-day. New York City, Woman's board of Home Mission [n.d.]
12p. 14cm.
NN

2456. Colfax, Schuyler. The Mormon question. Being a speech of Vice-president Schuyler Colfax, at Salt Lake City. A reply thereto by Elder John Taylor; and a letter of Vice-president Colfax published in the "New York Independent," with Elder Taylor's reply. Salt Lake City, Deseret News Office, 1870.
25p. 22cm.
Sabin 50749
CSmH, CtY, CU–B, DLC, ICN, MH, NN, UHi, USlC, UU

2457. College Free Press Bureau. Mormons sure of victory; claim that America will always be the land of the free . . . [Chicago, 1917]
Broadside. 45×15cm.
World war, 1914–18, in the light of Mormon revelation.
USlC

2458. Collins, Joseph. The doctor looks at biography; psychological studies of life and letters, by Joseph Collins . . . New York, George H. Doran Company [c1925]
x p. [2]l., 15–344p. mounted ports. 22½cm.
Brief biography of Brigham Young in the section entitled statesmen.
CU, DLC, UPB, USlC

COLMAN, R. J.

2459. Colman, Russell J. Trifles from a tourist. In letters from abroad. Norwich, Eng. [1886]
247p. fold-out map. 22cm.
Mormons mentioned on p. 36–37. He attended a meeting at the tabernacle; admitted that the Mormons were good citizens, though coming from the lower class. Includes general information and impressions of Salt Lake City.
Signed: December, 1886.
USIC

2460. Colorado State Historical Society. History of Colorado, prepared under the supervision of the State Historical and Natural History Society of Colorado: James H. Baker, editor . . . Le Roy R. Hafen, Ph.D., Associate editor . . . Denver, Linderman Co. Inc., 1927.
5v. plates, ports., maps. 23½cm.
Vols. I–III paged continuously (1320p.)
Vols. IV–V contains biographical material written and edited by the publishers.
Reference to Mormons, p. 323, 340, 349, 456, 577, 1195, 1219–1220.
CU–B, DLC, UPB

2461. Colton, Walter. Three years in California, by Rev. Walter Colton, U.S.N.; Cincinnati, H. W. Derby & Co., 1850.
456p. plates, ports., map, fold. facsim. 18½cm.
Encounter with the emigrants from the Ship "Brooklyn."
Reprinted 1850, 1851, 1852, 1854, 1856, 1859. Another edition under the title, "The land of Gold." 1860.
CU–B, DLC, UPB, USI

2462. Coman, Katharine. Economic beginnings of the far West; how we won the land beyond the Mississippi, by Katharine Coman . . . New York, The Macmillan Company, 1912.
2v. illus., plates, maps (1 fold.) 21cm.
Volume II, Chapter II, entitled, "The Mormon migration," p. 167–206. There are other scattered references to Mormons in California.
Other editions: New York, Macmillan Co., 1925. DLC, UU; Reprinted: 1930. MH, ViU
CSmH, CU, CU–B, DLC, MoK, NjP, NN, USIC

2463. Combs, George Hamilton. Some latter-day religions. Chicago, Fleming H. Revell Company, 1899.
261p. 19½cm.
"Mormonism," p. 205–222. A superficial account of Mormonism.
MoK, UPB

2464. Comettant, Jean Pierre Oscar. . . . Les civilisations inconnues. Paris, Pagnerre, 1863.
2p.l., 401p. 18½cm.
First chapter entitled "l'Utah." Summary of history of Mormonism in America; Mormon church in France.
Title in English: The unknown civilizations.
CU–B, MH, MiU, PPD, PU

2465. ———. (same, in Spanish) . . . Las civilizaciones deconocidas, por Oscar Comettant. Mexico, I Cumplido, 1874.
232p. 19cm.
At head of title: Edicion del "Siglo xix."
Deals with the Mormons under title "Utah." It is devoted mostly to Joseph Smith and Mormon doctrine, p. 1–60.
MH, NN

2465a. ———. Trois ans aux États-Unis étude des moeurs et coutumes Amèricainès par M. Jean Pierre Oscar Comettant. Paris, Pagnerre, Libraire-Editeur, 1857.
2p.l., 364p. 18½cm.
Includes a description of Belinda Pratt's defence of polygamy.
NjP, UPB

2466. Commercial Club of Chicago. A history of the pilgrimage of the Chicago Commercial Club to centers of Western commerce. Chicago, R. R. Donnelley & Sons Co., 1901.
2p.l., 9–146p. 18cm.
Trip to Salt Lake City in 1901, with comments on Mormonism.
USIC

2467. A complete answer to the false charges of the Utah Commission. There is no union of church and state . . . "Falsehood in politics and falsehood in faith," Declarations of the Church Authorities," "Times interview with the First Presidency," Editorials from the "Deseret News." [Salt Lake City, Star Print, 1892?]
12p. 20cm.
MH

2468. Comstock, William. Hur book of goaks with a full akkownt of the coartship and maridge to a 4 said Artemus, and Mister Ward's cutting-up with the Mormon fare secks. With pikturs drawed by Mrs. B. Jane Ward . . . New York, James O'Kane, Publisher [c1866]
vii [9]–321p. plates. 19cm.
Called humorous chiefly because of its spelling; satire on the Mormons.
CSmH, CtY, UPB

2469. Conard, Howard Louis, *editor.* Encyclopedia of the history of Missouri, a compendium of history and biography for ready reference. New York, Louisville, St. Louis, The Southern History Co., 1901.
6v. ports. 27cm.
"Mormonism" by Daniel M. Grissom, V. 4, p. 481–487.
DLC, MoInRC, UPB

2470. ———. "Uncle Dick" Wootten, the pioneer frontiersman of the Rocky Mountain region; an account of the adventures and thrilling experiences of the most noted American hunter, trapper, guide,

scout, and Indian fighter now living; by Howard Louis Conard, with an introduction by Maj. Joseph Kirkland. Chicago, W. E. Dibble & Co., 1890.
viii [9]–473p. illus., 17 plates, 12 ports. 23½cm.
Includes his encounter with the Mormons.
CU–B, DLC

2471. Concordance and reference guide to the book of Doctrine and Covenants, Published by the Reorganized Church of Jesus Christ of Latter Day Saints. Lamoni, Ia., Published by the Reorganized Church of Jesus Christ [1864?]
32p. 16½cm.
Bound with a *Doctrine and Covenants* for 1864.
USIC

2472. ———. (same) [Lamoni, Ia.] Herald Publishing House, 1893.
30p. 17cm.
Sabin lists a Plano, 1870 ed. 23p.
MoInRC

2473. Conely, Edwin F. In the matter of the appointment of Orlando W. Powers as associate justice of the Supreme Court of the Territory of Utah. Supplemental proofs. Edwin F. Conely, Attorney for objectors. [Salt Lake City? 1885?]
90p. 18½cm.
Among other things, the author tries to prove that Powers was not employed by the Mormons.
MH

2473a. Conference Grand Concert, Monday evening, October 5, 1891, in the Tabernacle Salt Lake City. For benefit of the Deseret Sunday School Union, 700 voices, 40 instruments, 11 soloists. The whole under the direction of E. Stephens. [Salt Lake City] Cannon Publishing House [1891]
[4]p. 16cm.
NjP

2474. Conference on the History of the Trans-Mississippi West, *University of Colorado,* 1929. The trans-Mississippi West; papers read at a conference held at the University of Colorado, June 18–June 21, 1929. Edited by James F. Willard and Colin B. Goodykoontz. Boulder, University of Colorado, 1930.
xi, 366p. 20cm.
CU–B, DLC

2475. Conger, O. T. Autobiography of a pioneer, or, The nativity, experience, travels, and labors of Rev. Samuel Peckard, The "Converted Quaker," containing stirring incidents and practical thoughts, with sermons by the author, and some account of the labors of Elder Jacob Knapp . . . Edited by O. T. Conger. Illustrated. Chicago, Church & Goodman, Publishers, 1866.
xii [13]–403p. 19cm.
He taught school for Mormons near Nauvoo. The difficulties of teaching children of "hateful scamps."
USIC

2476. Connelley, William Elsey. Quantrill and the border wars, by William Elsey Connelley . . . Cedar Rapids, Ia., The Torch Press, 1910.
542p. illus., ports., facsim., fold. map. 24½cm.
Material on the Utah Expedition.
Howes C 689
CU, DLC, NjP, UPB

Conover, George S. *See Aldrich, Lewis Cass.*

2477. The Conquest of Santa Fe and subjugation of New Mexico, by the military forces of the United States. With a history of Colonel Doniphan's campaign in Chihuahua. By A Captain of Volunteers. Philadelphia, H. Packer & Co., Publishers . . . 1847.
48p. 22cm.
Brief references to the Mormon Battalion, p. 13, 25–26.
CSmH, CtY, CU–B, WHi

Constitutional and governmental rights of the Mormons. *See Parry, Joseph Hyrum.*

2478. The Continental, Salt Lake City. Victory, Salt Lake City carried by the gentiles at the August election. What it means! Salt Lake City [1889]
[2]p. 27½×21cm.
Results of the non-Mormon vote after the Edmunds-Tucker Act. Editorials from local and regional papers.
USIC

2479. The Contributor. Salt Lake City, The Contributor Company, 1879–1896.
17v. monthly. 25cm.
Successor to *The Amateur*; predecessor of *The Improvement Era.*
Editor: Junius F. Wells.
CtY, CU–B, MH, NjP, UHi, ULA, UPB, USI, USIC, UU

2480. Conversations on Mormonism. The route of the Mormon Elder. [London, The Religious Tract Society, n.d.]
20p. 18cm. (No. 272)
MH

2481. Conway, Cornelius. The Utah expedition; containing a general account of the Mormon campaign . . . from its commencement to the present time. By a wagon master of the expedition. Cincinnati, "Safety Fund Reporter," Office Print., 1858.
48p. illus. 23cm.
Howes C721, Sabin C16214, W–C 298
CtY, DLC, ViU

2482. Conybeare, William John. Essays, ecclesiastical and social. Reprinted, with additions, from the Edinburgh review . . . London, Longman, 1855.

xi, 440p. 23cm.
Reprinted with revisions from the *Edinburgh Review*.
Mormonism, p. 280–376.
CSmH, CU–B, DLC, ICN, NN, USIC, UU

2483. ———. Mormonism; reprinted from The Edinburgh Review. No. CCII, for April, 1854. London, Longman, Brown, Green and Longmans, 1854.
1p.l. [3]–112p. 18cm. (The Traveler's library. V. 67)
Sabin 50754
CU–B, ICN, MB, MH, NN, UHi, ULA, USI, USIC, UU

2484. ———. (same) No. 202. April, 1854. Printed by subscription. Cuttack [Indiana] Printed at the Orissa Mission Press, W. Brooks, 1855.
2p.l. [5]–68p. 20½cm.
USIC

2485. ———. (same) London, Longman, Brown, Green and Longmans, 1863.
2p.l., 112p. 17½cm. (The Traveler's Library. V. 25)
MH, UHi

2486. ———. (same, in Danish) Mormon-staten ved Saltsoen. I Danske Maanedsskrift 1855 (efter Edinburg Review nr. 202, April 1854) Kobenhavn, 1855.
40p.
Schmidt

2487. ———. (same, in French) Le Mormonisme; histoire et doctrines des Mormons. Extrait et treduction libre d'un article de la Revue d' Edinbourg (Avril, 1854) Paris, Borrani et Droz, Lausaane, D. Martignier; Genève, J. Cherbuliez, 1855.
2p.l. [5]–91p. 21½cm.
CSmH, CtY, DLC, MH, NN, USI, USIC, WaU

2488. ———. Perversion: or, the causes and consequences of infidelity. A tale for the times . . . By Rev. W. J. Conybeare, M. A., . . . New York, Wiley & Halstead, 1856.
vi [7]–495p. 20cm.
Mormonism, p. 114–131.
Fiction concerning Mormonism.
Another edition: 2d ed. London, Smith, Elder & Co. [1856]. USIC
USIC

2489. Conyers, Josiah B. A brief history of the leading causes of the Hancock mob, in the year 1846. By Josiah B. Conyers, M.D., Quincy, Illinois. Saint Louis, Printed for the author by Cathcart & Prescott, 1846.
1p.l. [3]–83 [1]p. 19cm.
History from the death of Joseph Smith and Hyrum until the expulsion of the Mormons from the state. He was against the mob and the actions that illegally uprooted the Mormons.
Howes C725, Sabin 16227
ICN, MB, MH, MWA, PH, USIC

2490. Cook, Joseph. Six questions on the Mormon problem. With replies by the Reverend Dr. McNiece, Judge Boreman, Judge Rosborough, Colonel Nelson, Attorney Royle, and Professor Coyner of Salt Lake City. [Salt Lake City? 1884]
8p. 22½cm.
CSmH, CU–B, ICN, ULA

2491. Cook, Mrs. Joseph. Face to face with Mormonism. A paper read at the semi-annual meeting of the Woman's Home Missionary Association, March 27, 1884, and printed by permission. By Mrs. Joseph Cook. Boston, Frank Wood, 1884.
16p. 14cm.
At head of title: Woman's Home Missionary Association.
NN

2492. Cook, M. E. A free thinker's warning. To the pilgrim fathers of Salt Lake City of 1887 . . . Also, the lost Eden is found in the restoration of the Kingdom of God by the cleansing of the sanctuary. Philomath [1887]
60p. 171m.
Cover-title.
A doctrinal pamphlet on the last days.
CtY, UPB

2493. Cook, Thomas Lathrop. Palmyra and vicinity, written by Thomas L. Cook. [Palmyra, New York, Press of the Palmyra Courier-journal, 1930]
1p.l., 310p., [1]l., 20p. illus., plates, ports. 27cm.
Mormons at Palmyra, p. 64–65, 219–222, 238.
MH, NN, NRU, UHi, UPB, USIC

2494. Cook, William. A friendly warning to the Latter-day Saints; or Mormons, in which the true character of the Mormon misionaries is plainly set forth, by one who was of that community, and a resident in Salt Lake. London, Wertheim, Macintosh and Hunt, 1860.
iv, 61p. 16cm.
MH, NN, USIC

2495. ———. The Mormons, the dream and the reality; or, Leaves from the sketch book of experience of one who left England to join the Mormons in the City of Zion, and awoke to a consciousness of its heinous wickedness and abominations. Edited by a clergyman. [William B. Fowler] London, J. Masters [etc., etc.] 1857.
viii, 92p. 16½cm.
"Editor's preface" signed: W.B.F. (i.e. William B. Fowler)
Sabin 50762
CtY, CU–B, MH, NN, WHi

2496. ———. (same, under title) The "Fowler's snare," as craftily laid to catch unwary souls, now fully unmasked and exposed to view, by one who has broken the snare and escaped. London, J. Masters, 1858.
1p.l., viii, 92p. 17cm.
CtY, MH, NN, USlC

2497. Cooke, Lucy Rutledge. Crossing the plains in 1852. Narrative of a trip from Iowa to "the land of gold," as told in letters written during the journey. Modesto, California, 1923.
94p. ports. 19cm.
Letters #6 and #7 concern her 9-month stay in Salt Lake City during the winter of 1852–53.
Howes E 737

2498. Cooke, Nicholas Francis. Satan in society. By a physician . . . Cincinnati and New York, C. F. Vent . . . 1871.
312p. 20cm.
Polygamy and Mormonism in 1870.
Other editions: Cincinnati and San Francisco, E. F. Hovey, 1880. CU; Cincinnati and San Francisco, Edward F. Hover, 1882. USlC
UPB, USlC

2499. Cooke, Philip St. George. The conquest of New Mexico and California; and historical and personal narrative. By P. St. Geo. Cooke . . . New York, G. P. Putnam's Sons, 1878.
iv p., [1]l., 307p. fold. map. 19cm.
Commander of the Mormon Battalion.
Howes C 738
CSmH, CU–B, DLC, ICN, MH, NjP, NN, UHi, ULA, UPB, USlC

2500. ———. . . . Report from the Secretary of War, communicating, in compliance with a resolution of the Senate, of the 21st February, 1849, a copy of the official journal of Lieutenant Colonel Philip St. George Cooke, from Santa Fe to San Diego, etc. . . . [Washington, Govt. Print. Off., 1849]
85p. 22cm. (U.S. 31st Cong. Special Session. Senate. Doc. No. 2)
The march of the Mormon Battalion.
Howes C 739, W–C 165
CSmH, CtY, CU, DLC, ICN, MiU, NjP, UHi, ULA, UPB, WHi

2501. Cooke, Mrs. S. A. Dear madam: The ladies' anti-polygamy society. [Salt Lake City, 1880?]
[3]p. 19cm.
Address by Mrs. S. A. Cooke, President, February, 1880.
NN

2502. Coolidge, Richard H. . . . Statistical report on the sickness and morality in the Army of the United States, compiled from the records of the Surgeon General's Office; embracing a period of five years, from January 1, 1855, to January, 1860 . . . Washington, George W. Bowman, 1860.
525p. map, tables. 29½cm. (U.S. 36th Cong. 1st Sess. Senate. Ex. Doc. No. 52)
Sanitation and disease among the troops in Utah. Chastises the Mormons and their belief in faith healing.
DLC, UHi

2503. Coombs, James Vincent. Religious delusions. Studies of the false faiths today by J. V. Coombs. Cincinnati, Ohio, The Standard Publishing Co., c1904.
vii, 208p. 20cm.
Material on "Mormonism," taken from the tract *Was Joseph Smith jr., a prophet,* by John T. Bridwell.
Another edition: Cincinnati, The Standard Publishing Company [c1904]
DLC, USl, USlC, UU

2504. Coombs, Leo Mark. A temple Anthem. Words by Ruth May Fox; Music by Leo M. Coombs . . . Lethbridge, Canada, Published by Leo M. Coombs [c1919]
5p. music. 26cm.
"Written expressly for the Cardston Temple."
USlC

2505. Cooper, Charles. Signes of the Day. No. 7. Polygamy. [Salt Lake City, n.d.]
[4]p. 17½cm.
Mormon poetry.
MH

2506. Cooper, Charles. Signes of the Day. No. 10. [Salt Lake City, n.d.]
10p. 12½cm.
Mormon poetry.
MH

2507. Cooper, Ethel. Echoes from Zion's hill tops. [Salt Lake City, 1927?]
39p. 19cm.
First edition.
Poems dedicated to Samuel Eastman.
UPB, USlC

2508. Cooper, F. M. The law of life. Independence, Mo., Ensign Publishing House, 1899.
38p. 16cm. (The Gospel Banner. V. 6, No. 4)
Theological law and sermons of F. M. Cooper.
MoInRC

2509. ———. Teachings in contrast. Lamoni, Ia., Board of Publications of the Reorganized Church of Jesus Christ of Latter Day Saints [n.d.]
17 [1]p. 18cm. (No. 208)
RLDS doctrines.
CtY, MoInRC, UPB

2510. Cooper, I. N. W. The gathering, or, The plans and principles that should govern Latter Day Saints generally in organizing settlements in the "Regions round about the land of Zion." Being also the

initiatory step toward organizing the "Common Sense Mutual Agricultural Association" According to the received doctrines of the Church of Jesus Christ of Latter-Day Saints. Plano, Ill., Herald Office, 1877.
20p. 13cm.
CSmH, MoInRC

2511. Cooper, R. T. The Moral-code. A Compilation of church law touching violations of the seventh commandment and divorce. Sources of the law and usage. Bible, Book of Mormon, Doctrine and Covenants, General Conferences resolutions, Church history. [Plano? Ill.] Reorganized Church of Jesus Christ of Latter Day Saints [n.d.]
20p. 19½cm.
MoInRC

2512. Cooper, Thomas V. American politics (non-partisan) from the beginning to date, embodying a history of all the political parties, with their views and records on all important questions. Great speeches on all great issues, the text of all existing political laws, a complete tabulated history of American politics. Seventh and revised ed. Philadelphia, Fireside Publishing Company, 1884.
7 bks. in lv. 24cm.
"Supressing Mormonism," p. 264–269.
USIC

2513. Cooper, W. H. The Book of Mormon proved to be a fraud, and Latter-day Saints shown to be building upon a false foundation. Milverton, Canada, The Sun Print. [n.d.]
16p. 23cm.
MoInRC

Cooper, Will (*pseud.*) *See Carman, William Cooper.*

2514. Cope, Cyprian. Arabesques; a perspective. London, Leonard Smithers and Co., 1899.
352p. 26½cm.
Includes: "A Mormon record." Deals with polygamy.
NjP, UHi, USIC, UU

2515. Corinne Citizens. Memorial of Citizens of Corinne, Utah, asking for a grant of lands to aid in constructing a canal for irrigating Bear River Valley. Washington, Chronicle Publishing Co., 1871.
7, 5p. 21cm.
Need for irrigation due to the fact that Corinne is the only place in Utah not under the tyranny of the Mormon hierarchy. How to get irrigation from Mormon control. Appendix concerns granting of lands to Mormon leaders.
MnHi

2516. Cornaby, Hannah (Last). Autobiography and poems, by Hannah Cornaby . . . Salt Lake City, J. C. Graham and Co., 1881.
158p. 18½cm.
Mormon poetry and autobiography.
CSmH, CtY, CU-B, NBuG, NjP, NN, RPB, UHi, USl, USIC, UU

2517. Cornish, John J. Cornish to Evans. An open letter to R. C. Evans, by J. J. Cornish. [Lamoni, Ia., Printed by The Herald Publishing House, 1919?]
16p. 19cm.
Defense against statements of R. C. Evans concerning his apostasy.
CU-B, DLC, MoInRC, NN, UPB, USIC

2518. ———. He is just the same to-day. Miraculous manifestations of the power of God in connection with the ministry of the author. Together with scripture texts and arguments showing that the signs still follow the believers. Grand Rapids, Mich., Glad Tidings Tract and Book Society, 1900.
46p. 19cm.
MoInRC

2519. ———. Into the Latter Day light, an autobiography by John J. Cornish; a lifetime missionary for the Latter Day Saints. Independence, Mo., Herald Publishing House, 1929.
2p.l., 186p. 20cm.
MoInRC

2520. ———. The resurrection. Independence, 1893.
40p. (Bospel Banner. V. 2, No. 1)
MoInRC

2521. ———. A synopsis of the Holy Bible, by Elder John J. Cornish. With some notes, comments, a remarkable vision, and testimonies of healing, etc. Also a portrait of the author. [Reed City, Mich.] 1886.
2p.l., 5–564p. 16cm.
An RLDS publication, with scriptural proofs of their doctrines, and some miraculous healings.
MoInRC

2522. Cornwall, J. Spencer. An ode to youth; mixed voices, with choruses for male and female voices. Optional solos for baritone and contralto. Text by Elsie Talmage Brandley. Music by J. Spencer Cornwall. Salt Lake City, Mutual Improvement Association [n.d.]
24p. music. 22cm.
UU

2523. Corrill, John. A brief history of the Church of Christ of Latter Day Saints, (commonly called Mormons;) including an account of their doctrine and discipline; with the reasons of the author for leaving the church. By John Corrill. St. Louis, Printed for the author, 1839.

2p.l. [7]–50p. 22cm.
Howes C789
CtY, MoInRC, MoK, MoS, MWA, NN, USIC, WHi

Cory, Matilda Winifred Muriel (Graham). *See Cory, Winifred (Graham)*

2524. Cory, Vivian. Daughters of Heaven, by Victoria Cross [*pseud.*] New York, Brentano's [c1920]
229p. 19cm.
Fiction concerning Mormonism.
DLC

2525. ———. (same) New York, The Macaulay Company [c1921]
6p.l., 11–299p. 19cm.
DLC

2526. Cory, Winifred (Graham). Eve and the elders, by Winifred Graham . . . Third Edition. London, Hutchinson & Co. Paternoster Row [ca. 1910]
2p.l., 7–286p. 18cm.
Fiction concerning the Mormons.
USIC

2527. ———. Ezra the Mormon, by Winifred Graham. London, Everett and Co., 1907.
vi [7]–320p. 18½cm.
Fiction concerning Mormonism.
UU

2528. ———. (same) London, George Newnes, Limited [1907?]
3p.l. [9]–128p. 21½cm. (Newnes' sixpenny copyright novels. No. 240)
NN, USIC

2529. ———. (same) London, Everett and Co., 1908.
3p.l. [7]–320p. 19cm.
Third impression.
MH

2530. ———. (same) London, Everett and Co., 1908.
2p.l. [7]–320p. 19cm.
Fourth impression.
MH, NN, PPL, USIC

2531. ———. The love story of a Mormon, by Winifred Graham. With a preface by the Right Rev. Bishop Welldon . . . London, Mills & Boon, Limited [1911]
viii, 310p. 19½cm.
Fiction concerning Mormonism.
DLC, USIC

2532. ———. Mormonism absurd and dangerous: report of World Commission on Mormonism, read at the Third World's Christian Citizenship Conference, Pittsburg, Pa., U.S.A., November 12, 1919, by Mrs. Theodore Cory (Winifred Graham) Chairman. Pittsburg, Published by the National Reform Association, 1919.
12p. 23½cm.
Cover-title.
UHi

2533. ———. The Mormons. A popular history from earliest times to the present day, by Winifred Graham . . . London, Hurst and Blackett, Ltd., 1913.
3p.l., 309 [1]p. 20cm.
CU, DLC, MH, NjP, NN, UHi, ULA, UPB, USIC, UU, WHi

2534. ———. Sealed women, by Winifred Graham . . . London, Hutchinson & Co., Paternoster Row [ca. 1910]
2p.l. [5]–288p. 18cm.
Fiction concerning Mormonism.
USIC

2535. ———. The sin of Utah, by Winifred Graham. London, Everett and Co., Ltd. [ca. 1910]
2p.l. [5]–240p. 18½cm.
Fiction concerning Mormonism.
USIC, UU

2536. Cosgrave, Luke. A review. By Luke Cosgrave. Illustrated by LeConte Stewart. [Salt Lake City, The F. W. Gardiner Co. Press] c1917.
[13]p. 12×15½cm.
Poem about the Mormon pioneers.
USIC

2537. Couch, Edward T. The everlasting covenant or prophets of God teach alike. By Edward T. Couch of the Church of Jesus Christ of Latter-day Saints. Boyne City, Charlexoix Co., Mich., July, 1906.
56p. 18½cm.
By a member of the Strang group.
Morgan
CtY, MoInRC, UHi, USIC, WBuC

2538. ———. Evidences of inspiration by Edward T. Couch. Bay Springs, Mich., Feb. 1890 . . . [Boyne, Mich?] 1890.
38p. 21½cm.
Morgan
CtY, WBuC

2539. ———. The prophetic office. By Edward T. Couch of the Church of Jesus Christ of Latter-day Saints. Boyne City, Charlevoix Co., Mich., September, 1908.
67p. 18cm.
A description of the claims of Joseph Smith III and James J. Strang.
Morgan
CtY, CU–B, MoInRC, UHi, UPB, USIC

COUCH, E. T.

2540. ———. The Sabbath and the restitution. By Edward T. Couch, Bay Springs, Charlevoix County, Michigan, March, 1891. [Boyne City, Mich? 1891]
51p. 21½cm.
Morgan
MH, MoInRC, UHi, USlC

2541. ———. The teachings of Jesus. By Edward T. Couch of the Church of Jesus Christ of Latter-day Saints. Boyne City, Charlevoix County, Michigan, May, 1913. [Boyne City? 1913]
44p. 22cm.
Morgan
CtY, MoInRC, UHi, USlC

2542. ———. The two Bibles or scholarship and inspiration compared. By Edward T. Couch. Boyne City, Charlevoix Co., Mich., April, 1907. [Boyne City? 1907?]
71p. 22cm.
King James version of the Bible compared to the inspired version.
Morgan
CSmH, CtY, CU-B, MH, UHi, USlC

Couch, Enos. Victoria assembly rooms. The inhabitants of Southampton are respectfully informed that a public discussion on the doctrines taught by the Latter-day Saints will take place between the Rev. Enos Couch, and Elder T. B. H. Stenhouse . . . *See Stenhouse, T. B. H.*

2543. **Coutant, Charles Griffin.** The history of Wyoming from the earliest known discoveries. In 3 vols. Vol. 1. Laramie, Chaplin, Spafford & Mathison, 1899.
712p. illus., ports., map. 23cm.
Carries the history to the year 1869. Only the first volume was published.
Mormons in Wyoming; Mormon trail; Mormon colonization.
Howes C810
CU-B, DLC, ICN, NjP, ULA

Cowdery, A. E. The life of Oliver Cowdery. *See Mehling, Mary Bryant.*

2544. **Cowdery, Oliver.** Defence in a rehearsal of my grounds for separating myself from the Latter-Day Saints. [Norton, Ohio, Pressley's Job Office, 1839]
[8]p. 17½cm.
All copies are photostat. The photostat of the title page is from the R. B. Neal publication; *Oliver Cowdery's defence and renunciation.* Whether the pamphlet ever existed is doubtful.
CtY, UHi, ULA, UPB

2545. ———. (same, under title) "Second Elder" Oliver Cowdery's renunciation of Mormonism and his "defence" for so doing. Striking statements by Joseph Smith, Oliver Cowdery and David Whitmer . . . Cleveland, Ohio., The Utah Gospel Mission, 1927.
16p. 17cm.
MH, NN, USlC

2546. ———. Letters by Oliver Cowdery to W. W. Phelps on the origin of the Book of Mormon and the rise of the Church of Jesus Christ of Latter-day Saints. Liverpool, Thomas Ward and John Cairns, 1844.
2p.l. [5]–48p. 17½cm.
Eight letters discussing the restoration of the Gospel from the *Messenger and Advocate*, 1834–1835. Changes in text from the *Messenger and Advocate.*
Howes C814
CSmH, CtY, CU-B, DLC, UPB, USlC

2547. ———. (same, under title) The epistles of Oliver Cowdery, on the bringing in of a new dispensation. St. James [Beaver Island, Mich.] Cooper and Chidester, 1854.
iv [5]–56p. 21cm.
Preface signed: James J. Strang.
Morgan
CtY, MH

2548. ———. (same, under title) Cowdery's letters on the bringing in of the new dispensation. Milwaukee, Wisc., Macrorie and Pitcher, 1880.
1p.l., 33p. 19½cm.
Morgan
CtY, NN, WHi

2549. ———. (same) Burlington, Wis., Free Press Print., 1899.
iv, 31p. 19½cm.
Morgan
CSmH, MH, UHi, USlC, WBuC

2550. ———. (same, under title) Letters of Oliver Cowdery. [Lamoni, Ia., Reorganized Church of Jesus Christ of Latter Day Saints, n.d.?]
40p. 21½cm. (No. 43)
Added to the letters is an article entitled "The Records of the Nephites."
CSmH, MoInRC, USlC

2551. ———. (same) Lamoni, Ia., Published by the Reorganized Church of Jesus Christ of Latter Day Saints [n.d.]
40p. 21½cm. (No. 43)
Variant edition.
CSmH, CtY, IWW, UHi, UPB, WHi

2552. ———. (same) [Independence, Mo.? Reorganized Church of Jesus Christ of Latter Day Saints, 190 ?]
40p. 22cm. (No. 1244)
Caption-title.
At head of title: No. 1244.
CSmH, IU, MH, UHi, ULA

———. "Second Elder" Oliver Cowdery's renunciation of Mormonism and his "defence" for so doing. *See his Defence.*

———. Supplement to J. Seixas' Manual Hebrew Grammar. *See Seixas, Joshua.*

2553. Cowles, George Washington. Landmarks of Wayne County, New York . . . edited by Hon. George W. Cowles . . . assisted by H. P. Smith and others. Syracuse, N.Y., D. Mason & Company, 1895.
viii, 437, 41, 343p. illus., ports., fold. map. 25cm.
Includes a history of the origin of Mormonism.
DLC, MWA, OCl, OClWHi, PHi, USlC

2554. Cowley, Matthew. The gospel of repentance; address delivered over Radio Station KSL, Sunday Evening, July 31, 1927. [Salt Lake City] 1927.
Broadside. 57½×20½cm.
Reprint from the *Deseret News.*
UPB

2555. Cowley, Matthias Foss. The blood of the prophets; biographical sketches by Apostle Matthias F. Cowley, selected from his work entitled "Prophets and Patriarchs." Chattanooga, Tenn., Ben E. Rich [1902]
3p.l. [7]–87p. ports. 20cm.
Mormon biographies.
UU

2556. ———. Cowley's talks on doctrine. Chattanooga, Tenn., Published by Ben E. Rich, 1902.
187p., [1]l. 17cm.
CU–B, IWW, NN, UHi, ULA, UPB, USl, USlC, UU

2557. ———. (same) Atlanta, Ga., Published by Ben E. Rich, 1904.
261p. 13cm.
DLC, ICN, UHi, UPB

2558. ———. (same) Chattanooga, Tenn., Published by Ben E. Rich, 1905.
262p. port. 14cm.
CU–B

2559. ———. (same) Independence, Mo., Central States Mission [1905]
2p.l., 7–287p. 13cm.
USlC

2560. ———. (same) Chicago, Ill., Published by Missions of the Church of Jesus Christ of Latter-day Saints [1905?]
2p.l., 7–287 [1]p. 13cm.
DLC, ICN, MH, NN, ULA, UPB, USlC

2561. ———. (same) [Independence, Mo.] Published by the Missions of the Church of Jesus Christ of Latter-day Saints [1915?]
113p. 18½cm.
Printed at the Press of "Zion's Printing & Publishing Co."
UPB

2562. ———. Prophets and patriarchs of the Church of Jesus Christ of Latter-day Saints. Chattanooga, Tenn., Published by Ben E. Rich [1902]
2p.l. [5]–318 [1]p. ports. 17½cm.
Biographical sketches of 39 deceased and then-living leaders of the church.
NN, UHi, USlC, WHi

2563. ———. (same) Chattanooga, Tenn., Published by Ben E. Rich, 1902.
iv [5]–505p. ports. 20cm.
CU–B, ICU, NN, UHi, UPB, USlC, UU

———. Wilford, Woodruff . . . *See Woodruff, Wilford.*

2564. Cox, James. My native land; the United States: its wonders, its beauties, and its people; with descriptive notes, character sketches, folk lore, traditions, legends and history . . . St. Louis, Mo., Blair Publishing Co., 1895.
400p. plates. 23cm.
Chapter 5. "The Mormons and their wives." A pilgrimage across the bad lands of Utah.
Another edition: Philadelphia, Blair Publishing Co., 1903. NjP, UHi, UPB
CU–B, DLC, NjP, UHi, UPB, USlC, UU

2565. Cox, Samuel Hanson. Interviews: Memorable and useful; from diary and memory reproduced. By Samuel Hanson Cox, D. D. Pastor of the First Presbyterian Church, Brooklyn, New York . . . New York . . . New York, Harper & Brothers, Publishers, 1853.
2p.l. [5]–325p. 20cm.
Chapter entitled "Visit extraordinary" and "Two Pseudo-apostles" concerns Mormonism. Meets 2 Mormon missionaries and records the interview with "those squalid beauties."
Another edition: 1855. CU–B
UPB, USlC

2566. Coy, Owen Cochran. Gold days; by Owen Cochran Coy . . . San Francisco, Powell Publishing Company [c1929]
8p.l., 381p. illus., plates, index. 24cm.
Mormons involved in the gold discovery.
CU–B, DLC, NjP, UHi, UPB

2567. Coyner, John McCutchen. Hand-book on Mormonism . . . Salt Lake City, Hand-book Publishing Co., 1882.
95 [1]p. illus., plans. 22cm.
Cover-title.

COYNER, J. M.

Some 25 articles, ranging from an exposé of endowment ceremony and polygamy, a defense of gentiles in Utah, and an account of mission work in the territory.
CSmH, CtY, DLC, NjP, NjPT, NN, UHi, ULA, USl, USlC, UU, WHi

2568. ———. Letters on Mormonism by J. M. Coyner, Ph.D. Salt Lake City, Tribune Printing and Publishing Co., 1879.
24p. 22cm.
Double columns.
Bancroft library has "Letters" numbered I, II, III, III, IV, VI, all single column in broadside form varying from 29 to 46 cm., the last dated Jan. 1879. These seem to be galley proof and were reprinted from the *National Journal of Education*, Boston, Mass.
CSmH, CtY, NN, USlC, USl, UU

2569. ———. Women parading for polygamy. [Salt Lake City? 1879?]
[2]p. 33×14cm.
Printed in double columns.
Signed: Salt Lake City, February, 1879.
CU–B

2570. ———. The Utah problem, an address before the National Educational Association, July 15, 1884, at Madison, Wis., by J. M. Coyner, Ph.D. Salt Lake City, C. H. Parsons & Co., 1884.
16p. 23cm.
NN, UHi

2571. Cradlebaugh, John. Mormonism. A doctrine that embraces polygamy, adultery, incest, perjury, blasphemy, robbery and murder. Speech of Judge Cradlebaugh in the House of Representatives. [Salt Lake City? 1877?]
18p. 22cm.
Reprinted from *Salt Lake Daily Tribune*, Apr. 8, 1877.
ICN, NN, USl

2572. ———. Utah and the Mormons. Speech of Hon. John Cradlebaugh, of Nevada, on the admission of Utah as a state. Delivered in the House of Representatives, February 7, 1863. [Washington, L. Towers & Co., 1863?]
67p. 26cm.
Appendix: Massacre at the Mountain Meadows. Murder of the parishes and Potter. Murder of the Aiken party. Murder of Jones and his mother. Murder of Forbes.
The speech was not given due to a shortage of time, but Mr. Cradlebaugh was allowed to print it.
Howes C840, Sabin 17331
CSmH, CtY, CU–B, DLC, MH, NN, UHi, ULA, USlC, WHi

2573. Crafts, Eliza Persis (Russell) Robbins. Pioneer days in the San Bernardino Valley, by Mrs. E. P. R. Crafts, assisted by Mrs. Fannie P. McGehee. Redlands, Calif. [Kingsley, Moles & Collins Co.] 1906.
3p.l. [4]–214p. illus. 19½cm.
Mormon colonization at San Bernardino.
DLC, NjP, UHi, UPB

2574. Cragin, Aaron Harrison. Execution of laws in Utah. Speech of Hon. Aaron H. Cragin, of New Hampshire, delivered in the Senate of the United States, May 18, 1870. Washington, F. & J. Rives & G. A. Bailey, Printers, 1870.
23p. 24cm.
Political situation in Utah.
Sabin 17354
CU–B, DLC, ICN, MB, MH, MoK, NN, UHi

2575. Crane, Richard Teller. The utility of all kinds of higher schooling. An investigation by R. T. Crane. Chicago, 1909.
331p. 20½cm.
"The Mormon Temple" (i.e. Tabernacle) p. 178–79.
USlC

2576. Crary, Christopher G. Pioneer and personal reminiscences. Marshalltown, Ia., Marshall Printing Company, 1893.
1p.l. [4]–105p. 22½cm.
Mormon activities in Kirtland, Ohio.
CSmH, CtY, DLC, MoK, NN, USlC

2577. Crawford, Lewis Ferandus. Rekindling camp fires, the exploits of Ben Arnold (Connor) (Wa-si-cu Tam-a-he-ca) an authentic narrative of sixty years in the old West as Indian fighter, gold miner, cowboy, hunter and army scout; map, illustrations, bibliography, index, and notes, by Lewis F. Crawford . . . Bismarck, N.D., Capital Book Co. [c1926]
4p.l., 7–324p. port., plates, map. 22½cm.
Brief references to Mormon immigrants coming to Utah. Tithing, p. 34–35; coming of the Danites, p. 72–87.
Howes C 872
CU, DLC, NjP, UHi, USlC

2578. Crawford, Robert P. An index, or reference to the second and third editions of the Book of Mormon, alphabetically arranged. By Robert P. Crawford. Philadelphia, Brown, Bicking, & Guilbert, Printers, 1842.
21p. 15cm.
CtY, PHi, UPB incomplete

2579. Cream from the Journals [*sic*] of Discourses and writings of the Apostles. Ogden, Utah, June 1, 1887.
v. 1 #1 [4]p. 22cm.
A prospectus for a 36p. monthly pamphlet to be published for $2.00 a year. No record of actual publication.
USlC

CROFFUT, W. A.

2580. Creel, George. Sons of the eagle; soaring figures from America's past, by George Creel, illustrated by Herbert Morton Stoops. Indianapolis, The Bobbs-Merrill Company [c1927]
5p.l., 321 [1]p. plates. 22cm.
Chapter XVIII. "The promised land," p. 212–224. Brigham Young and the Mormons.
CU–B, NjP, UPB, USlC

2581. Creer, Leland Hargrave. . . . Utah and the nation, by Leland Hargrave Creer. Seattle, Wash., University of Washington Press, 1929.
2p.l., vii–x p., [1]l., 275p. illus., maps. 26cm. (University of Washington publications on the social sciences. V. 7)
CSmH, CtY, CU–B, DLC, NjP, NN, UHi, ULA, UPB, USl, USlC, UU

2582. Creuzbaur, Robert. Route from the Gulf of Mexico, and the lower Mississippi Valley to California and the Pacific Ocean, illustrated by a general map and sectional maps; with directions to travelers. Compiled by R. Creuzbar, 1849 . . . New York, Published by H. Long & Brother, Austin, Texas, 1849.
40 [1]p. 5 maps in pocket. 18cm.
Includes Mormon Battalion route.
Howes C881, Sabin 17492, W–C 166
CSmH, CtY, DLC, ICN, MBaT, NjP, NN, TxU

2583. Crimes and treason of the Mormon Church exposed. [Chicago, c1910]
30p. [1]l. 20½cm.
"Reprinted from the *Chicago Daily Journal.*"
Controversy involving Senator Reed Smoot.
CtY, USlC

2584. The crimes of the Latter-day Saints in Utah. By a Mormon of 1831. A demand for a Legislative Commission. A book of horrors. San Francisco, A. J. Leary, 1884.
1p.l., iii, 82p. 17cm.
Cover-title: A Book of Horrors! Chairman of Committee, A. Lowry.
Possible author: Sarah E. Goforth.
A bloody history of Mormon crimes of murder, sex, child neglect, etc. There is a bibliographic notation for a Cincinnati, 1899 edition of 101p. It is late for this title.
CSmH, CtY, CU–B, DLC, MH, NN, USlC

2585. The Crimson. Logan, Utah, Brigham Young College, Dec. 17, 1903–
v. monthly. 21–23½cm.
Annual (yearbook) various sizes. ULA, UPB v.3 #5, v. 13–14, USlC has misc. numbers of 12 volumes; 1913, 1914, 1915, 1916, 1921, 1924

Criticus [*pseud.*] *See Goodwin, Charles Carroll.*

2586. Crocheron, Augusta (Joyce). The children's book, a collection of short stories and poems. A Mormon book for Mormon children. Bountiful, Utah, Published for the author, 1890.
x [11]–292p. illus. 18½cm.
CSmH, MH, NjP, UHi, UPB, USlC, UU

2587. ———. Representative women of Deseret, a book of biographical sketches, to accompany the picture bearing the same title. Comp. and written by Augusta Joyce Crocheron, and dedicated to the originals of this picture and book, their co-laborers in the Church and every true heart that will receive their testimonies. Salt Lake City, Printed by J. C. Graham & Co., 1884.
4p.l., 131p. 18cm.
CtY, CU–B, DLC, ICN, MH, MoInRC, NjP, NN, UHi, ULA, UPB, USl, USlC, UU, WHi

2588. ———. Wild flowers of Deseret, a collection of efforts in verse, by Augusta Joyce Crocheron . . . Salt Lake City, Printed at the Juvenile Instructor Office, 1881.
viii, 240p. 18½cm.
Mormon poetry.
CU–B, DLC, MH, NjP, UHi, ULA, USlC, UU

2589. Crockwell, James H. Ogden City, Utah. In photo-gravure from recent negatives by Jas. H. Crockwell, . . . Salt Lake City, c1893.
[36]l. of pictures, [1]l. of text. 18½cm.
Printed in New York by the Albertype Company.
Scenes in Ogden.
NjP, UHi, USlC

2590. ———. Pictures and biographies of Brigham Young and his wives. Being a true and correct statement of the birth, life, and death of President Brigham Young, second president of the Church of Jesus Christ of Latter-day Saints, and brief biographies of his twenty-six wives, and names and number of children born to them . . . Salt Lake City, J. H. Crockwell, Press of George Q. Cannon & Sons [1887?]
40p. ports., plates. 13½×17½cm.
CSmH, CtY, CU–B, DLC, MH, MiU, NjP, UHi, UPB, USl, USlC, WHi

2591.———. (same) 2d ed. Salt Lake City, c1896.
40p. illus., ports. 13×17½cm.
CSmH, MoInRC, NN, UHi, ULA, UPB, USlC

2592. Croffut, William Augustus. Deseret; or, A saint's afflictions. An American opera. In three acts. Libretto by W. A. Croffut. Music by Dudley Buck . . . New York, 1880.
16p. 18cm.
Cover-title.
Mormon drama.
ICN, ICU, MB, NN, RPB, ULA, USlC

CROFUTT, G. A.

2593. Crofutt, George Andrews. Crofutt's new overland tourist and Pacific coast guide . . . over the Union, Central and Southern Pacific Railroads, their branches and connections, by rail, water and stage. By Geo. A. Crofutt. Vol. 1. 1878–9. Chicago, Overland Publishing Company, 1878.
3p.l. [25]–322p. illus., double plates. 20½cm.
Paging irregular: 1–25, 257–299 omitted.
Description of Utah and Mormonism.
Vol. 2. Chicago, c1879. A revision of V. 1. DLC
1889 2v. under title *overland tours.*
Republished several times 1879–1883.
DLC, NjP, NN, OCl, OO, OrP, PPFr, PPM, UHi, WaS, WaU

2594. ———. Crofutt's overland guide, consisting of over six thousand miles of main tours, and three thousand miles of side tours. Also six thousand miles by stage and water . . . Chicago, Rand McNally. 1890.
283p. illus., plates (part double) 21cm.
On cover: No. 1. Crofutt's overland tours.
Tourist information and material on Mormonism.
Another edition: St. Louis, C. E. Ware, 1892. MH
CtY, MH, OCl, OrHi, UU, WaU, WHi

2595. ———. Crofutt's overland tours, consisting of nearly five thousand miles of main tours, and three thousand miles of side tours. Also two thousand miles by stage and water . . . By Geo. A. Crofutt. Chicago. A. H. Day & Co., 1888.
254p. illus., ports., 6 double plates, map. 23½cm.
Tourist information and brief information on Mormonism.
Republished in 1889. NjP
DLC, IU, MB, NN, UHi

2596. ———. Great trans-continental railroad guide. A description of over five hundred cities, stations, government forts . . . summer resorts; where to look for and hunt the buffalo, antelope, deer, trout fishing. In fact to tell you what is worth seeing, where to see it, where to go, how to go, and whom to stop with while passing. By Bill Dodd, the Scribe [*pseud.*] Chicago, G. A. Crofutt & Co., 1869.
244p. illus., plates, port., fold. tab. 17½cm.
Tourist information with historical sketches at several points such as Fort Bridger, Echo Canyon, settlement of territory, sketch of Brigham Young.
Other editions: 1st rev. ed., New York, 1870. CtY, DLC, UPB; 2d temporary rev. ed., 1870. DLC; 3d ed. to 7th ed. c1871–1876. Under title *Great transcontinental tourist's guide.* UHi
Howes C901, Sabin 17587
DLC, MoKU, NjP

2597. Cromer, Evelyn Baring, *1st earl of.* Political and literature essays. 2d series. By the Earl of Cromer. London, Macmillan and Co., Ltd., 1914.
viii, 362p. 23cm.
Chap. XXXVIII, "The Spectator," April 11, 1914. Relates the Spaulding theory. Quotes from Frank J. Cannon's *Brigham Young and his Mormon empire.* Polygamy still practiced and he is astonished why the government doesn't do something about it.
DLC

2598. Cross, Osborne. A report, in the form of a journal, to the Quartermaster General, of the march of the regiment of mounted riflemen to Oregon, from May 18 to October 5, 1849, by Major O. Cross, Quartermaster, United States Army. (In: War Department. Report, 1849/50. Washington, Printed for the Senate, 1850)
126–244p. 36 plates. 23cm. (U.S. 31st Cong. 2d Sess. Senate. Doc. No. 1, Pt. II)
Reference to Mormon ferry at North Platte, p. 165, 168, 170; at Green River, p. 177; [Isaac] Brown's [Mormon] trading house on Bear River, p. 183.
CU–B, DLC, NjP

Cross, Victoria [*pseud.*] *See Cory, Vivian.*

Crossing the divide. *See Miller, "Walk In."* [*pseud.*]

2599. Crouch, William. The story of the house of Israel. By Wm. Crouch. Salt Lake City, 1885–86.
2 v. [40, 79]p. 17cm.
Mormon point of view on Israel.
MH, USl, USlC, UU

2600. Crowe, W. L. The Mormon Waterloo, being a condensed and classified array of testimony and arguments against the false prophet, Joseph Smith, his works, and his church system and doctrines, based upon standard history, science, the Bible, and Smith against himself, by Elder W. L. Crowe . . . [St. Paul, Neb., 1902?]
2p.l., 5–160p. 19½cm.
CtY, CU–B, DLC, ICN, MH, MoInRC, USl, USlC, WHi

2601. Crumpacker, Edgar Dean. Case of Brigham H. Roberts, of Utah. Speech of Hon. Edgar D. Crumpacker of Indiana in the House of Representatives, January 24, 1900. Washington [Govt. Print. Off.] 1900.
16p. 23cm.
DLC

2602. Crumrine, Boyd. History of Washington County, Pennsylvania, with biographical sketches of pioneers and prominent men. Ed. by Boyd Crumrine. Illustrated. Phil., L. H. Everets & Co., 1882.
6 [13]–1002p. illus., ports., col. map. 28cm.
Chap. 35. "Solomon Spaulding and the Book of Mormon." Explains how Rigdon received the Spaulding manuscript and his connection with the writing of the Book of Mormon.
Howes C938
DLC

2603. Cullom, Shelby Moore. Enforcement of laws in Utah. Speech of Hon. Shelby M. Cullom, of Illinois, . . . delivered in the House of Representatives, Feb. 17, 1870. [Washington, 1870]
15p. 23½cm.
DLC, UPB

2604. ———. Fifty years of public service; personal recollections of Shelby M. Cullom, senior United States Senator from Illinois. Chicago, A. C. McClurg & Co., 1911.
xi, 467p. ports. 21½cm.
Brief account of his work in getting the anti-polygamy legislation passed.
CU, DLC, NjP, NN, UHi, UPB, UU

2605. ———. The Mormon problem. Address of Hon. Shelby M. Cullom, in support of his bill to reorganize the legislative power of the Territory of Utah. Delivered in the United States Senate, Friday, January 11, 1884. Washington, Govt. Print. Off., 1884.
11p. 22cm.
DLC

2606. ———. Senator Cullom's anti-Mormon bill. [n.p., n.d.]
5p. 22cm.
UPB, USIC

2607. Culmer, Frederick. The inner world. A new theory, based on scientific and theological facts, showing that the earth is a hollow sphere containing an internal inhabited region. By Frederick Culmer, Sr. Salt Lake City, 1886.
41p. 23cm.
Uses Mormon sources for part of his proof.
USIC

2608. Culmer, Henry L. A. *compiler.* The resources and attractions of Utah as they exist today. Set forth for the inquiring public, especially for the mid-winter fair. California, 1894. Comp. by H. L. A. Culmer for the mid-winter fair committee and the Salt Lake Chamber of Commerce. Salt Lake City, George Q. Cannon, 1894.
97p. illus. 23cm.
Pioneer settlements, music, etc.
ICU, MH, MWA, NjP, NN, UHi, USIC

2609. Culmer, Horace Cummings. Conspiracy of Nauvoo (from The Contributor). Salt Lake City, Magazine Printing Co. [1884?]
15p. 20cm.
Reprint of an article originally appearing in *The Contributor.*
USIC

2610. Cumorah Monthly Bulletin. South African Mission of the Church of Jesus Christ of Latter Day Saints. Mowbray, June 15, 1927–
3v. (v. 1, #1 — V. 3, #6) monthly. 26½cm.
V. 3, #7 July, 1929 title changed to *Cumorah's Southern Cross.* USIC comp.

2611. Cumorah's Southern Cross. Mowbray, South Africa, Published by the South African Mission of the Church of Jesus Christ of Latter-day Saints. July, 1929–
v. monthly. 23cm.
Originally *Cumorah Monthly Bulletin,* June 15, 1927–June, 1929. UPB V.4–, USIC comp.

2612. Curtis, Benjamin Robbins. Dottings round the circle. By Benjamin Robbins Curtis. Boston, J. R. Osgood and Company, 1876.
x, 329p. front., plates. 21cm.
Trip through Salt Lake City in 1875. Interview with Brigham Young and an attendance at a church service.
DLC, UHi, UPB, USIC

2613. Curtis, George Ticknor. Admission of Utah. Limitation of state sovereignty by compact with the United States. An opinion given by George Ticknor Curtis. New York, Printed for the author by Hart & Von Arx, 1887.
22p. 23½cm.
DLC, ICN, MH, NN, UPB, USIC, UU

2614. ———. Ex parte: In the matter of Lorenzo Snow, petitioner, appellant. Appeal from order of Third District Court of Utah Territory, refusing application for writ of Habeas Corpus. Brief for Appellant. George Ticknor Curtis, Franklin S. Richards for Petitioner. [Washington, Gibson Bros. . . . 1887]
34p. 21cm.
At head of title: Supreme Court of the United States. October term. No. 1282.
USIC

2615. ———. A letter to the N.Y. Evening Post on the admission of Utah as a state, with editorial comments thereon and a reply, by Geo. Ticknor Curtis. [Washington? 188–]
13p. 23cm.
Polygamy and the admission of Utah as a state.
NjP, USIC

2616. ———. Letter to the Secretary of the Interior on the affairs of Utah. Polygamy, "cohabitation," etc. Washington, printed for the author by Gibson Bros., 1886.
1p.l., 32p. 23cm.
Cover-title.
CSmH, CU–B, DLC, ICN, MH, NjP, UHi, USIC, WHi

2617. ———. Lorenzo Snow, Plaintiff in Error v. the United States, Defendant in Error No. 1,278. Lorenzo Snow, Plaintiff in Error v. The United States, Defendant in Error No. 1,277. Brief for Plaintiff in Error. [Washington, Gibson Bros., Printers and Bookbinders, 1886]
39p. 22cm.
Signed: George Ticknor Curtis, Franklin S. Richards.
At head of title: Supreme Court of the United States. October term, 1885.
USIC

2618. ———. A plea for religious liberty and the rights of conscience. An argument delivered in the Supreme Court of the United States, April 28, 1886, in three cases of Lorenzo Snow, Plaintiff in error, v. The United States, on writs of error to the Supreme Court of Utah Territory. Washington, D.C., Printed for the author by Gibson Brothers, Printers and Bookbinders, 1886.
80p. 23½cm.
Plea for religious liberty (title page) p. 1–42.
An argument delivered in the Supreme Court of the United States, by Franklin S. Richards, p. 43–80.
Cover-title. Pleas for religious liberty and the rights of conscience. Arguments delivered in the Supreme Court of the United States, April 28, 1886, in three cases of Lorenzo Snow, Plaintiff in Error, v. the United States on writs of Error to the Supreme Court of Utah territory by George Tichnor Curtis and Franklin S. Richards.
CSmH, CtY, DLC, MH, NjP, NN, ULA, UPB

2619. ———. (same) Washington, D.C., Printed for the author by Gibson Brothers, Printers and Bookbinders, 1886.
64p. 23cm.
Second section has title: Extract from an argument delivered in the Supreme Court of the United States, April 28, 1886 . . .
In green paper wrappers.
CU–B

2620. Curtis, J. T. An Instrument in my hands. By J. T. Curtis. [Independence, Mo., 1930?]
28p. 18½cm.
Purpose of the book is to acquaint the unbelievers with the Latter-day work, divinity of the Book of Mormon, etc.
MoInRC

2621. Curtis, James F. Our beliefs defended; an examination of the claims for the Book of Doctrine and Covenants, the Quorum of First Presidency, the Office of High Priest, the High Council of the Church; also a brief glance at the inconsistencies of the Church of Christ, whose first president was Granville Hedrick, by Apostle J. F. Curtis. Independence, Mo., Herald Publishing House, 1928.
2p.l., 5–146 [14]p. 19½cm.
RLDS doctrinal publications.
MoInRC, UHi

2622. ———. The temple of the Lord; who shall build it. [n.p., n.d.]
62p. 20cm.
MoInRC

2623. ———. (same) Independence, Mo., Herald Publishing House, 1929.
63p. 19½cm.
MoInRC

2624. Curtis, Samuel Ryan. The Mormon rebellion and the bill to raise volunteers. Speech of Hon. Samuel R. Curtis, of Iowa. Delivered in the U. S. House of Representatives, March 10, 1858. [Washington, 1858]
16p. 23½cm.
Caption-title.
Sabin 18065
CU–B, DLC, MH, UPB, USI

2625. Curtis, Theodore Edward. In the temples of the great outdoors, by Theodore Edward Curtis. [Salt Lake City] c1927.
46p. 1 double plate. 18cm.
Mormon poetry.
USIC

2626. ———. Mother — heart of Gold. Salt Lake City [1927–1930]
4v. 16cm.
Book 1, Mother. c1927. Book 2, 4th ed. c1928. Book 3, c1929. Book 4, c1930.
Mormon poetry.
USIC

2627. ———. Sunbeams of truth. Volume I. [Salt Lake City, Press of Hooper Printing Co.] c1916.
29 [2]p. port. 18cm.
Mormon poetry.
USIC

2628. Curtis, Theodore W. The Mormon problem the nation's dilemma. New data, new method, involving leading questions of the day. By Theodore W. Curtis. New Haven, Hoggson & Robinson Printers, 1885.
vii, 62p. 22½cm.
CSmH, CtY, CU–B, DLC, ICN, MH, NN, USI, USIC

2629. Curtis, William A. History of creeds and confessions of faith. In Christendom and beyond. With historical tables by William A. Curtis . . . Edinburgh, T & T Clark, 1911.
xix, 502p. 23cm.
"Church of Jesus Christ of Latter-day Saints," p. 394–99.
USIC

2630. Curwood, James Oliver. The courage of Captain Plum, by James Oliver Curwood; with illustrations by Frank E. Schoonover. Indianapolis, The Bobbs-Merrill company [1908]
3p.l., 319 [1]p. plates. 19½cm.
A novel concerned with the Strangite Mormons on Lake Michigan.
DLC, NjP, NN, OCl, OO, USIC

2631. Custer, George Armstrong. Wild life on the plains and horrors of Indian warfare, by General G. A. Custer, U. S. A. with a graphic account of his

last fight on the Little Big Horn, as told by his wily foe Sitting Bill. Also sketches and anecdotes of the most renowned guides, scouts and plainsmen of the West. General Crook and the Apaches. Profusely illustrated. St. Louis, Mo., Sun Publishing Co., 1886.
2 p.l. [5]–528p. plates. 23½cm.
Includes material on the Mountain Meadows massacre, p. 498–528. plate.
Another edition: St. Louis, Published by Royal Publishing Co. [c1891] DLC, USIC
UPB

2632. Cutler, Frank. Haapiiraa evaneria no te Ekalesia a Iesu mesia in te Fera mo'a i te mau Mahana Hopea nei. [Papeete, Nenei raa Vea L. Brault, 1895–6]
22 nos. 22cm.
First publication of the church in Tahitian.
Title in English: Prepare.
USIC 1–8, 12–17, 22

2633. ———. Te Hoe Parau iti, El Faaitoitoraa i te Taata'toa e imi i te Basileia o te Atua, E e titau hoi i ta Te Varua Ra. Tahiti, Papaiha e Farani Tuterera, 1895.
34p. 18cm.
Title in English: A brief talk to encourage all who seek the kingdom of God.
USIC

2634. ———. Te monoraa I te Toroa peresideni No to Ekalesia a Iesu Mesia i te Feia Mo'a i te Mau Mahana Hopea Nei. XX E Te Tumu No te Ekalesia i Faaapihia Ra . . . Papaihia e Farani Tuterera raua o Butera. Papeete, Tahiti, Ekalesia a Iesu Mesia, 1908.
33p. 20cm.
Title in English: The succession to the Presidency.
USIC

2635. ———. Na te Feia Atoa e Hiaai i te Ite. Papeete, Tahiti [Ekalesia a Iesu Mesia . . . n.d.]
[2]p. 21cm.
Title in English: For all those who seek knowledge.
USIC

2636. Cutten, George Barton. Speaking with tongues, historically and psychologically considered, by George Barton Cutten . . . New Haven, Yale University Press; London, H. Milford, Oxford University Press, 1927.
xii, 193p. 21cm.
Mormon "gift of tongues" discussed, p. 70–76, 168, 182.
CU, DLC, NjP, NjPT, UHi, UPB, USl

2637. Cutts, James Madison. The conquest of California and New Mexico, by the forces of the United States, in the years 1846 & 1847. By James Madison Cutts. With engravings, plans of battle, etc. Philadelphia, Published by Carey & Hart, 1847.
1p.l., 264p. port., maps, plans. 18½cm.
Mormon Battalion and background information, p. 69–70, 212, 215.
Howes C989, Sabin 18209, W-C 131
CtY, CU, DLC, MB, MBaT, NjP, WHi

2638. Cyipz Herald and IABBA's Evangel. Philadelphia. [ca. May, 1888]
Notation of this in the *History of the* [Reorganized] *Church of Jesus Christ of Latter Day Saints*, Vol. 4, p. 604.
Morgan
Publication of Charles Blancher Thompson.
No copy located.

CORRECT ACCOUNT

OF THE

Murder of Generals Joseph and Hyrum Smith,

AT CARTHAGE,

ON THE 27TH DAY OF JUNE, 1844;

BY WM. M. DANIELS, AN EYE WITNESS.

PUBLISHED BY JOHN TAYLOR,
FOR THE PROPRIETOR;
NAUVOO, ILL.;
1845.

Item 2658. The account of Joseph Smith's assassination, actually written by Lyman O. Littlefield, that helped make a farce of the murderers' trial. From the LDS church collection.

D., T.

2639. D., T. The Kingdom of Christ. [Plano, Ill., True Latter Day Saints Herald, 1865]
4p. 23cm. (Tract. No. 9)
Signed: T. D.
Cty, MoInRC, NjP, NN, UPB

2640. Daab, der skinner i mørket. [Kjøbenhavn, n.d.]
4p. 22cm.
A missionary leaflet.
Title in English: Baptism.
USIC

2641. Dabadie, F. . . . Recits et types Américains . . . Paris, F. Sartories, 1860.
384p. 18½cm.
The last chapter is entitled, "Le premier Mormon." Material on Mormonism; Brigham Young and polygamy; Joseph Smith and early history, etc.
Title in English: About typical Americans.
Sabin 18242
CU, DLC, MH, NN, PPL

2642. Dahl, J. Joseph Smiths Levnet. 3die oplag. Kjøbenhavn, Af Foreningen til gudelige Smaaskrifters Udbredilse, 1888.
80p. 17cm. (No. 78)
Cover-title.
Signed by: J. Dahl and D. Rothe on verso of cover.
Title in English: The life of Joseph Smith.
USIC

2643. ———. Mormonernes laerdomme ifolge deres egne skrifter og betragtede i Christendommens lys, udgivet ved J. Dahl, Cappellan p.p. i Jetsmark. [Aalborg, Trykt hos O. Olufsen, 1857]
4 pts. (16p.) 21cm.
Title in English: Mormon doctrine according to their own scriptures.
USIC No. 3–4 (p. [9]–16)

2643a. ———. (same) [Aalborg, Trykt hos Oluf Olufsen, ca. 1862]
4 pts. (16p.) 21cm.
No. 1–2 are 2det oplag.
USIC

2643b. ———. (same) Kjøbenhavn, udgivet af Foreningen til gudelige Smaaskrifters Udbredelse. Trykt i Graebes Bogtrykkeri, 1877.
28p. 17cm. (No. 249)
Cover-title.
USIC

2644. Daily Northern Islander. St. James, Lake Michigan, Cooper & Chidester, April 1, 1856–June 20, 1856.
lv. (33 nos.) daily. 32–37cm.
A daily added to the *Weekly Northern Islander.*
Suspended due to the assault on James J. Strang resulting in his death.
Morgan
CtY Ap 1, Je 20, 1856; MoInRC My 5, 1856.

2645. Daines, Franklin David. . . . Separatism in Utah, 1847–1870. By Franklin D. Daines . . . (In American Historical Association. Annual report . . . for the year 1917. Washington, 1920. P. 331–343)
CtY, CU, DLC, NjP, ULA, UPB

2646. Daines, Lyman Luther. Community health and hygiene; a study-course for adult education groups. Prepared by Lyman Luther Daines and Arthur Lawton Beeley for the Adult Department, Young Men's and Young Ladies' Mutual Improvement Associations, Church of Jesus Christ of Latter-day Saints. Salt Lake City [General Boards, M.I.A.] 1930.
248p. 22cm.
On cover: A study course for the Adult Department of the M.I.A. 1930–31.
DLC, OSG, UHi, UU

2647. Dake, Sarah Almira. The story of Joseph Lawrence Kahler. Illustrated by George F. Weston. Independence, Mo., 1922.
2p.l. [7]–131p. illus., port. 17cm.
Biography told in 1st person.
MoInRC, NjP, UPB

2648. Dalby, Ezra Christiansen. Land and leaders of Israel; lessons in the Old Testament, by Ezra C. Dalby . . . Salt Lake City, Published by the Deseret Book Company for the Dept. of Education [1930]
xiii [1] 534p. illus., 2 maps. 22½cm.
DLC, NjP, UPB, USIC

2649. Dale, Harrison Clifford. The Ashley-Smith explorations and the discovery of a central route to the Pacific, 1822–1829, with the original journals, ed. by Harrison Clifford Dale . . . Cleveland, The Arthur H. Clark Company, 1918.
352p. front., 3 plates, map. 25cm.
Reference to Mormons, p. 144, 185.
CU-B, DLC, UPB

2650. Daley, Pearl Simira. Jerd Cless, by Myra Daley. New York, Cochrane Publishing Co., 1909.
484p. 19½cm.
Novel with a Mormon family concerned, and references to Mormonism.
DLC, USl, USIC

2651. ———. (same) New York, Cochrane Publishing Co., 1910.
484p. 19½cm.
DLC

2652. Dall, Caroline Wells Healey. My first holiday; or letters home from Colorado, Utah and California, by Caroline H. Dall . . . Boston, Roberts Brothers, 1881.
2p.l. [3]–430p. 19cm.
Mormons, p. 76–109. She passed through Salt Lake City in 1880.
CSmH, CU, NjP, NN, UHi, USIC

2653. Dallin, William. True Mormonism; or, the horrors of polygamy, from the pen of an ex-Mormon Elder, who was ordained to that office at the age of fourteen, and resided in Utah for many years. Chicago, W. P. Dunn and Co., 1885.
46p. 19½cm.
Cover imprint: Chicago, Wm. Dallin & Co., 1885.
CtY, DLC, ICHi, MH, MoInRC, NN, UHi, WHi

2654. Dalton, Matthew William. The period of God's work on this planet; or, How science agrees with the revelations of our beloved redeemer; a key to this earth. [Willard, Utah] 1906.
88p. fold. chart. 15cm.
Representation of the terrestrial scheme attributed to Joseph Smith.
MH, UHi, UPB, USlC, UU, WHi

2655. Dana, C. W. The garden of the world; or, The great West; its history, its wealth, its natural advantages, and its future. Also comprising a complete guide to emigrants, with a full description of the different routes westward. By an old settler. With statistics and facts, from Hon. Thomas H. Benton, Hon. Sam Houston, Col. John C. Fremont, and other "old settlers." Boston, Westworth and Company, 1856.
7 [13]–396p. illus. 18½cm.
Includes a chapter on Utah (p. 269–276) which gives general information and a few remarks concerning Mormonism.
Sabin 18398
CSmH, DLC, ICN, NjP, UHi, UPB, ViU, WA

2656. ———. (same, under title) The great West; or, the garden of the world; its history, its wealth, its natural advantages, and its future. Also comprising a complete guide to emigrants, with a full description of the different routes westward. By C. W. Dana . . . With statistics and facts, from Hon. Thomas H. Benton, Gen. Sam Houston and Col. John Fremont. Boston, Wentworth and Company, 1857 [c1856]
7 [13]–396p. illus., fold. map. 20cm.
Another edition: 1861. CU–B
DGS, ICU, MiU–C, PPM, UHi, UPB, USlC, Wa, WaS, WaSp, WaU

2657. Dana, Charles A. The United States illustrated; in views of city and country; with descriptive and historical articles . . . New York, Meyer, 1854.
2v. plates. 29cm.
V.1, pt. 3 has a section on Nauvoo, with emphasis on the Mormon era.
Another edition [1855?] NjP
Howes D45
NN

2658. Daniels, William M. *supposed author.* A correct account of the murder of generals, Joseph and Hyrum Smith, at Carthage, on the 27th day of June, 1844. By William M. Daniels an eye witness. Nauvoo, Ill., J. Taylor, 1845.
24p. illus., plates. 22½cm.
"The Martyrs," a poem by L. O. Littlefield, p. 24.
There is a second issue, with some typographic corrections and with the following notation above the title: Entered according to the act of Congress in the year 1845, by Wm. M. Daniels in the Clerk's Office of the District Court of Illinois.
According to the Court records of Hancock Co., Daniels admits that the publication was written by a man named L. O. Littlefield and only published by Daniels. In Littlefield's *The Martyrs*, he states that the account was given by Wm. M. Daniels and written carefully by Littlefield, p. 71.
Byrd 948
CSmH, CtY, CU–B, DLC, ICN, IHi, MoInRC, MoSHi, NN, UPB, USlC, UU

2659. ———. (same) [Independence, Mo., 1917]
24[2]p. illus. 24½cm.
Reprinted by the Church of Christ, Independence, Missouri, 1917.
cf. p. [2]
CSmH, CtY, MoInRC, UHi, USlC

2660. Danielsen, Vernon J. Mormonism exposed; or the crimes and treasons of the Mormon kingdom. By Vernon J. Danielsen. Ex-High Priest and formerly Secretary of European Missions. Independence, Missouri, 1917.
63 [1]p. port. 15cm.
Mormon politics; polygamy still the cornerstone of the church. Includes a description of the temple ceremony.
CSmH, USlC

2661. Danielson, Marie, *compiler.* The trail blazer. History of the development of southeastern Idaho. Compiled by Marie Danielson. [n.p.] 1930.
126p. illus. 21cm.
110–126 are advertisement.
Mormon colonization of Idaho.
NjP, UHi, USlC, UU

Dansk Luthersk Mission in Utah. *See Fremodt-Moller, H. O.*

2661a. Danske i Amerika. Minneapolis og Chicago, C. Rasmussen Publishing Co., 1908.
368, xvip. illus. 26cm.
Mormons, p. 202–205, 237–239.
USlC

2662. Darby, John Fletcher. Personal recollections of many prominent people whom I have known, and of events, especially of those relating to the history of St. Louis—during the first half of the present century. By John F. Darby. Pub. by subscription. St. Louis, G. I. Jones and Company, 1880.
2p.l., 480p. port. 21½cm.
A brief statement on Mormons in Missouri and Illinois and why the attitude changed in regard to them.
DLC, NN, USlC

2663. Darke, Sidney W., and Co. Salt Lake City illustrated . . . Salt Lake City, Published by S. W. Darke Co., c1887.
[104] p. illus., plates, ports., large folded drawing of Salt Lake City. 30 cm.
Cover-title.
Tourist guide to Salt Lake City, with lavish illustrations and a history of Mormons in Utah.
CtY, DLC, NjP, UHi, USlC, UU

2664. ———. (same) Salt Lake City, Published by S. W. Darke Co., 1888.
[104]p. illus., plates, ports. 29cm.
USlC

2665. Der Darsteller der Heiligen der letzten Tage. . . . Geneva, Switzerland. May, 1855–Feb. 1861.
4v. monthly. 20cm.
Official organ of the L.D.S. Swiss-German mission. Editors: 1855–1857. John L. Smith; 1857–1861. Jabez Woodard.
V.4 printed at Zurich in 7 nos. (692p.)
Title in English: The representative of the Latter-day Saints.
MH V.1, 2, 3 #1–6; UPB V.2, 3; USlC comp.

2666. Darter, Francis Michael. The gathering of Israel. From a scriptural standpoint. The coming of John the revelator, the Elias and forerunner of the second coming of Jesus Christ, who, as it is written, must first come and restore all things and gather the twelve tribes of Israel. Long Beach, 1915.
123p. 17cm.
Written while still a member of the L.D.S. Church.
MoInRC, UPB, USlC

2667. ———. The Lord's strange work. The return of John, the Revelator. A voice of warning, the approaching end. Long Beach, Cal., 1917.
185 [1]p., [1]l. 16½cm.
CtY, CU-B, NjP, NN, UHi, UPB, USl, USlC, UU

2668. ———. Minutes of excommunication of Francis M. Darter. Salt Lake City [Shepard Book Co., 1918]
8p. 16½cm.
Caption-title.
Includes a letter from Darter to the First Presidency, and their reply.
UHi, UPB, USl, UU

2669. ———. On what day was Christ crucified? Salt Lake City, Francis M. Darter [n.d]
14p. 20cm.
UHi, UPB

2670. ———. "The time of the end." Daniel identifies Latter day temples and Jesus as the Christ. The voice of God. The mysteries of Daniel unveiled. God sets a date for the restoration of the gospel of Jesus Christ, including His holy Latter day sanctuary — the temple. The approaching end. By Francis M. Darter. Los Angeles, Calif. [Printed by Wetzel Publishing Company] 1928.
6p.l. [13]–295p. fold. plate. 21cm.
An unorthodox doctrinal work on the last days.
DLC, MH, NjP, NN, UHi, ULA, USlC, UU

2671. ———. Why say to the law and testimony? [Long Beach, 1918]
[4]p. 15½cm.
Incident concerning brutality of a local bishop.
USlC

2672. Daughters of Utah Pioneers. Constitution and by-laws. Salt Lake City [1901?]
16p. 15cm.
Cover-title.
Organized April 11, 1901.
USlC

2673. ———. Do you know what the Daughters of Utah Pioneers are doing? . . . This brief sketch will give you an idea. [Salt Lake City] 1927.
[4]p. 22cm.
UPB

2674. ———. Historical sketch of the Daughters of the Pioneers and president's report. Salt Lake City, The Deseret News [n.d.]
14p. 14cm.
UU

2675. ———. **Weber County Company.** Souvenir program of the dedication of Pioneer Hall by the Daughters of Utah Pioneers, Weber County. Ogden, 1929.
[19]p. illus., plates, ports. 22cm.
Cover-title.
UHi, UPB, USlC

2676. Davenport, Frederick Morgan. Primitive traits in religious revivals; a study in mental and social evolution, by Frederick Morgan Davenport . . . New York, The Macmillan Company; London, Macmillan & Co., Ltd., 1905.
xii, p., [1]l., 323p. 20cm.
References to Mormons speaking in tongues; casting out evil spirits; polygamy.
Another edition: 1910. CU
CU, DLC, MWA, NjP, NjPT, NN, PCA, PPM, PPWe, UPB

2677. Davenport, Montague. Under the gridiron. A summer in the United States and the far West, including a run through Canada by M. Davenport. Illustrated. London, Tinsley Brothers, 1876.
xi [1] 143p. illus. 16½cm.
Chapter 8 deals with the trip through Salt Lake City in 1875.
Tells of the loss of power by Brigham Young.
CU-B, NjP, UHi, USlC

2678. David Whitmer, Sr., tested and sustained. He denounces polygamy and so-called Mormonism. Omaha, Neb., Published by Gibson, Miller and Richardson [n.d.]
3p. 21cm.
ICHi

2679. Davidson, Alexander. A complete history of Illinois, from 1673 to 1873; embracing the physical features of the country; its early explorations; aboriginal inhabitants; French and British occupation; conquest by Virginia; territorial condition. And the subsequent civil, military and political events of the State. By Alexander Davidson and Bernard Stuve. Springfield, Illinois, Journal Co., 1874.
x, 944p. 23½cm.
Includes Mormon history in Illinois.
Other editions: Springfield, 1876, 1877. IDBP; 2d ed., Springfield, H. W. Rokker, 1884. CU, DLC; Springfield, 1877. USl
Howes D87
CSmH, CtY, DLC, NjP, NN, UHi, USl

2680. Davidson, Matilda. Folly and falsehood of the golden Book of Mormon . . . Hexham, E. Pruddah [1839]
4p. 12cm.
The author was the wife of Solomon Spaulding.
Reprinted from the *Lunenburgh Colonial Churchman*, January [June?] 25, 1839.
NN

2681. Davies, Charles Maurice. Heterodox London; or, phases of free thought in the metropolis. London, Tinsley Brothers, 1874.
2v. 21cm.
"Interviewing a Mormon Elder," V. 1. p. 241–273.
Includes *The Prophet Joseph Smith tells his own story* and *Revelation on Celestial Marriage*, 1852.
NjPT, UPB

2682. Davies, Richard. Mormonism unmasked; being a statement of facts relating to the self-styled "Latter-day Saints" and the Book of Mormon: Compiled from well authenticated records. Burnley, J. Clegg [1841]
16p. 19cm.
NN

2683. Davis, David R. What the "Latter-day Saints" teach and practice in Salt Lake City, Utah, U.S.A. Startling exposures of Mormonism, By David R. Davis. Watford, A. Warner [ca. 1887]
Broadside. 22×14cm.
Advance agent for William Jarman.
USlC

2684. Davis, Ellis A. Davis' commercial encyclopedia, Nevada, Utah, and Arizona. The Pacific Southwest. Edited and published by Ellis A. Davis. Berkeley, Cal., c1910.
6–196 (i.e. 198)p. illus., col. maps. 38cm.
Brief historical sketch of Utah and Utah towns.
Other editions: Davis' Commercial encyclopedia of the Pacific Southwest. Berkeley, Calif., c1911. CU–B; Berkeley, c1914. CU–B; Oakland, Calif., c1915. NjP, UPB
CU–B, DLC

2685. Davis, Emerson. The half century; or, A history of the changes that have taken place, and events that have transpired, chiefly in the United States, between 1800 and 1850. With an introduction by Mark Hopkins, D. D. By Emerson Davis, D. D. Boston, Tappan & Whittemore, 1851.
xxiii, 444p. 20½cm.
Brief section on Mormonism.
CU, DLC, NjP, NN, UPB, USlC

2686. Davis, Evan V. Souvenir of Independence, Mo. Brooklyn, N.Y., The Albertype Co., c1908.
[22]l. plates. 13½×18½cm.
Photography by Evan V. Davis.
Brief history of Mormonism in Independence and the litigation for the Temple block.
USlC

2687. Davis, Franklin Saville. Lesson book for the Religion Classes in the Church of Jesus Christ of Latter-day Saints. Eighth grade. Truths we live by. Written for the General Board of Education by Franklin S. Davis. [Salt Lake City] Published by the Deseret Book Company, 1925.
129p. 19cm.
USlC

2688. ———. (same) [Salt Lake City] Published by the Deseret Book Company, 1925.
112p. 19½cm.
Variant printing.
UPB

2689. ——— (same) [Salt Lake City] Deseret Book, 1927.
141p. 19cm.
USlC

2690. Davis, George Turnbull Moore. An authentic account of the massacre of Joseph Smith, the Mormon prophet, and Hyrum Smith, his brother. Together with a brief history of the rise and progress of Mormonism, and all the circumstances which led to their death. By Geo. T. M. Davis of Alton, Ills. St. Louis, Printed by Chambers and Knapp, 1844.
47p. 23cm.
Howes D–112, Sabin 18824
CSmH, CtY, ICHi, IHi, NN, PHi, UPB, USlC

2691. ———. Autobiography of the late Col. Geo. T. M. Davis, Captain and aid-de-camp Scott's army of invasion (Mexico). From post-humous papers. Pub. by his legal representatives. New York [Press of Jenkins and McCowan] 1891.

2p.l. [7]–395p. 20cm.
Chapters VIII and IX deal with the Mormons in Illinois.
Howes D–113
CtY, DLC, ICHi, ICN, UHi, UPB

2692. Davis, John. Adolygiad ar draethawd W. Jones, Bethesda, yr hwn a elwir "Egwyddorion Saint y dyddiau diweddaf yn cael eu pwyso yn nghlorianau rhesymau ac ysgrythrau." Gan John Davis, Merthyr, Golygydd "Udgorn Seion." [Merthyr-Tydfil, J. Davis, Argraffydd. 1850?]
16p. 18cm.
Title in English: Reply to Anti-Mormon lectures.
USlC

2693. ———. Athrawiaeth Iachus. [Merthyr-Tydfil, John Davis, Argraffydd, 1850?]
4p. 18cm.
Signed at end: John Davis, Argraffydd.
Title in English: Sound doctrine.
CU–B, MH, NjP, USlC

2694. ———. Bedydd. [Merthyr-Tydfil, Argraffydd J. Davis, 1850?]
12p. 18cm.
Signed: J. Davis.
Title in English: Baptism.
CU–B, MH, NjP, USlC

2695. ———. Can pregethwr. Gan awdwr yr "ymddyddan rhwng y parchedig a'r bachgenyn." Wrth lyncu peleni, Gofaled pob un na fyddo, yn fyrbwyll, yn llyncu ei hun. [Merthyr-Tydfil, J. Davis, 1850?]
[1]l. 18cm.
Title in English: A minister's songbook.
USlC

2696. ———. Y casgl; neu grynhoad o draethodau, caniadau, a llythyron, perthynol i Saint y dyddiau diweddaf . . . Gan Jan Davis . . . Merthyr-Tydfil, Argraffwyd ac ar Werth gan J. Davis, Georgetown . . . 1851.
[2]p. 18cm.
An introduction to a collection of Welsh pamphlets.
MH

2697. ———. (same) Georgetown, 1851.
[2]p. 19cm.
Variant printing.
USlC

2698. ———. Corff Crist, Neu yr eglwys. [Merthyr-Tydfil, John Davis, Argraffydd, 1850?]
12p. 18cm.
Signed: Merthyr, Mai 10, 1850. J. Davis.
Title in English: The body or Church of Christ.
CU–B, MH, NjP, USlC

2699. ———. Crefydd a Grym [and other poems] [Merthyr-Tydfil, Argraffwyd gan John Davis, Georgetown, 1850?]
[2]p. 18cm.
Mormon poetry.
Also includes: Seion [by] J. D. Llawenydd y Saint [by] T. H.
Title in English: A collection of poems.
NjP, USlC

2700. ———. Dyddiau Noah gan J. Davis, Merthyr. [Merthyr-Tydfil, John Davis, Argraffydd, 1850?]
4p. 18cm.
Signed: Mehefin 28, 1850.
Title in English: The days of Noah.
CU–B, MH, NjP, USlC

2701. ———. Ewch, a dysgwch. [Merthyr-Tydfil, Argraffwyd gan J. Davis, 1850?]
2p. 18cm.
Signed: J. Davis.
Title in English: Go and teach.
MH, NjP, USlC

2702. ———. Ffordd y bywyd tragywyddol, a ddarlunie yn yr ysgrythyrau Santaidd . . . Gan John Davis. Merthyr-Tydfil, Argraffwyd, ac ar werth gan J. Davis . . . 1850.
12p. 18cm.
Title in English: The way of Eternal life.
MH, NjP, USlC

2703. ———. Pregethu i'r ysbrydion yn ngharchar, a bedyddio dros y meirw . . . Gan John Davis . . . Merthyr-Tydfil, Argaffwyd ac ar Werth gan J. Davis . . . 1851.
8p. 18cm.
Title in English: Preaching to the spirits in prison.
MH, NjP, USlC

2704. ———. Profwch Bob Peth. "Athrawiaeth bedyddiaudau." [Merthyr-Tydfil, J. Davis, Argraffydd, 1850?]
4p. 18cm.
P.2 signed J.D.; p.3 signed R. Evans; p.4 signed J.D.
Title in English: Prove all things.
MH, NjP, USlC

2705. ———. Sylwadau ar Bregeth ynghylch "Saint y dyddiau diweddaf a Doniau gwyrthiol." [Merthyr-Tydfil, Argraffwyd gan J. Davis, 1850?]
8p. 18cm.
Signed at end: J. Davis.
Title in English: The Latter-day Saints and the miraculous gifts.
CU–B, MH, NjP, USlC

2706. ———. Sylwadau ar yr Hyn sydd o ran, a'r Hyn sydd berffaith . . . Gan J. Davis, Merthyr-Tydfil, Argraffydd, cyhoeddwyd, ac ar werth gan J. Davis, . . . 1850.
16p. 18cm.
Title in English: That which is in part.
CU–B, NjP, UPB, USlC

DAVIS, J. E.

2707. ———. (same) [Merthyr-Tydfil, J. Davis, Argraffydd, 1850]
12p. 18cm.
Variant edition.
MH

2708. ———. Traethawd ar Wyrthiau yn Darlunio pa beth ydynt, eu dyben, y pryd eu cyflawnir, a'r safonolrwydd i brofi dwyfoldeb crefydd . . . Gan John Davis. Merthyr-Tydfil, Argraffwyd ac ar werth gan J. Davis . . . 1850.
12p. 18cm.
Title in English: Treatise on miracles.
MH, UPB, USIC

2709. ———. (same) Gan John Davis, Merthyr. Merthyr-Tydfil, Argraffwyd ac ar werth gan J. Davis, Georgetown . . . 1851.
12p. 18cm.
Signed at end: J. Davis, Merthyr, Mai 5, 1851.
MH, USIC

2710. ———. Traethodau ar wyrthiau, yn cynnwys adolygiad ar ddarlithiau y Parch. J. Jones Llangollen, a llyfryn y Parch. J. Davies, Llanelli, ar yr un pwnc. Mewn chwech o draethodau . . . Gan John Davis. Merthyr-Tydfil, Argraffwyd, Cyhoeddwyd, ac ar werth gan J. Davis, 1852.
6 nos. in 70p. 18cm.
6 pamphlets of answers to anti-Mormon lectures of J. Jones and J. Davies.
Signed: Merthyr, Gorph 15, 1852.
Title in English: Treatise on miracles.
CU–B, UPB, USIC

2711. ———. Tystiolaeth y sant. [Merthyr Tydfil, J. Davis, Argraffydd. 1850?]
[1]p. 18cm.
Mormon poem.
Dated: Merthyr, Mehefin 28, 1850.
Title in English: The Saint's testimony.
CU–B, USIC

2712. ———. A welcome Hymn; sung in a conference, at Merthyr-Tydfil, held on the 9th of June, 1850, while the Apostle John Taylor was present, who was about leaving, on his mission, for France. Merthyr-Tydfil, J. Davis, Printer [1850?]
[1]p. 18cm.
Signed: J.D.
MH, NjP, USIC

2713. ———. Welcome song. Composed on the occasion of Elder Lorenzo Snow, one of Twelve Apostles, visiting the saints in Wales. [Merthyr-Tydfil, 1851?]
[1]p. 18cm.
Signed: Merthyr, Nov. 3, 1851.
USIC

2714. ———. Ymddyddan rhwng y parchedig a'r bachgenyn . . . [Merthyr Tydfil, John Davis, Argraffydd, 1850?]
[1]l., 18cm.
A Mormon boy refutes a minister.
Title in English: Dialogue between the Reverend and the boy.
CU–B, MH, NjP, USIC

2715. ———. (same, in English) A dialogue between the Reverend and the Boy; a translation. [Merthyr-Tydfil, Printed by John Davis, 1852?]
[1]l. 18cm.
Signed: May 28, 1852.
On back: Tom's escape, by J. Davis. Signed: April 27, 1848.
USIC

2716. ———. Ymddyddanion. Buddioldeb beilblau pr pagahiaid. [Merthyr-Tydfil, Argraffwyd gan J. Davis, 1850?]
4p. 18cm.
"Allan o *Udgorn Seion.*"
Title in English: Dialogue in Welsh and English.
CU–B, MH, NjP, USIC

2717. Davis, John (*Australian*). Mormonism; or, the doctrines of the self-styled Latter-day Saints compared with itself and the Bible and found wanting, by John Davis. Sydney, Australia, Published by John S. Sheriff, . . . 1857.
x, 85 [1]p. 17cm.
MH, USIC

2718. Davis, John E. Mormonism unveiled; or, peep into the principles and practices of the Latter-day Saints, by John E. Davis . . . a deluded brother of the sect, who has had the happiness of recovering from his infatuation by discovering the iniquitous proceedings of the leaders, during nine months' residence among them . . . A warning to the credulous. Bristol, England, Printed by C. T. Jefferies, 1856.
24p. 20½cm.
USIC

2719. ———. (same) Second Edition, Revised and Enlarged. To which is added a dissertation on "Polygamy and the Bible" [Bristol, England, Printed by C. T. Jefferies . . . 1856]
2p.l. [5]–48p. 20cm.
Howes D–124, W–C 253
USIC

2720. ———. (same) 3d ed., revised and enlarged. Cardiff, Printed by J. C. Paterson, 1858.
48 [2]p. 18cm.
Text on rear cover.
Cover-title reads: "Mormon imposture exposed."
A dissertation on "Polygamy and the Bible" is added to the original text.
Howes D–124, W–C 253
CtY, CU–B, MH

DAVIS, J. P.

2721. Davis, John Patterson. The Union Pacific Railway; a study in railway politics, history, and economics, by John P. Davis . . . Chicago, S. C. Griggs and Company, 1894.
1p.l., 5–247p. 2 fold. maps. 22cm.
Brief reference to Mormons in connection with route of railroad, p. 152. Other scattered references. to Salt Lake City.
DLC, NjP, UHi

2721a. Davis, John Sylvanus. Acrostic, to my wife. Great Salt Lake City, 1867.
Broadside. 16×12cm.
Dated: Jan. 17, 1867.
A poem about his wife, Elizabeth Davis.
USIC

2722. ———. The bee-hive songster, being a selection of original songs . . . composed by "Ieuan" [*pseud.*] . . . Salt Lake City, Printed at the Daily Telegraph, 1868.
30 [2]p. 13cm.
Mormon songs. Words only.
CtY, MH, NjP, NN, RPB, UHi, UPB, USIC

2722a. ———. Come, heavenly dove. Great Salt Lake City, 1858.
Broadside. 13×10cm.
Dated: Jan. 7, 1858.
A poem about the Holy Ghost that was translated from the Welsh Hymn Book.
USIC

2722b. ———. The Great Salt Lake [Great Salt Lake City?, n.d.]
Broadside. 5×14 cm.
A poem about the Great Salt Lake.
USIC

2722c. ———. The kingdom of God or nothing. Great Salt Lake City, 1858.
Broadside. 14×10cm.
Dated: Jan. 18, 1858.
A poem composed for the Welsh 'Eisteddvod' held in Salt Lake City, Utah.
USIC

2722d. ———. A song for Deseret. [Great Salt Lake City?, 1859]
Broadside. 14×7cm.
Dated: Oct. 23
A poem about the future of the Church in Deseret. This poem was published later in "The Bee-Hive Songster" page 25.
USIC

2722e. ———. Zion's future. Great Salt Lake City, 1862.
Broadside. 21×10cm.
Dated: Feb. 2, 1862.
A poem that recounts the events of the last days. It was published later in "The Bee-Hive Songster" page 23.
USIC

Davis, May Belle Thurman. *See Utah. Mormon Battalion Monument Commission.*

2723. Davis, Oscar Franklyn. A world-wide survey of present day Mormonism as made by a national commission under the direction of the National Reform Association and presented to the second World's Christian Citizenship Conference, Portland, Oregon, July 3d, 1913. Pittsburg, The National Reform Association [1913]
15 [1]p. 19cm.
Cover-title: Latest word on Mormonism; a survey of "the Mormon Kingdom."
MoInRC, NN, UHi, USIC, WHi

2724. Davis, S. J. S. Origin of the Book of Mormon together with an account of the rise and progress of the Mormon Church. By Rev. S. J. S. Davis. Louisville, Ky., Pentecostal Publishing Co., 1899.
4p.l., 144p. 17cm.
MoInRC

2725. ———. (same) Louisville, Ky., Pentecostal Publishing Co., 1899.
3p.l., 7–130p. 17½cm.
DLC, USIC, UU, UPB

2726. Davis, Sam P. The history of Nevada; edited by Sam P. Davis. Reno, The Elms Publishing Co., 1913.
2v. illus. 24½cm.
Includes a section on Mormon colonization in Nevada. Vol. 1, p. 273, Vol. 2, p. 807, 809, 1019.
USIC

2727. Davis, Walter Bickford. An illustrated history of Missouri; comprising its early record and civil, political and military history from the first exploration to the present time . . . and biographical sketches of prominent citizens by Walter Bickford Davis and Daniel S. Durrie . . . St. Louis, A. J. Hall, 1876.
xx, 639p. plates, ports. 24cm.
The Mormon troubles briefly related in chap. 11.
CU-B, DLC, UPB, USIC, UU

2728. Davy, Robert Harry. Some of the principles of the Latter-day Saints discussed. In the form of a dialogue between an elder of the Latter-day Saints and an inquirer and his friend. Cheltenham, 1852.
24p. 18cm.
USIC

2729. ———. (same) London, Ward & Co. [1853?]
24p. 18½cm.
CtY

2730. ———. Pioneer tales of the Oregon Trail and of Jefferson County. By Charles Dawson. Topeka, Crane & Company, 1912.
xv, 488p. 23½cm.
"The Mormons," p. 61. "The Mormon trail," p. 63–68.
USIC

2731. Dawson, Charles. Pioneer tales of the Oregon Trail and of Jefferson County [Nebraska] Topeka, Crane & Company, 1912.
488p. 23cm.
Material on the Mormons and the Mormon Trail.
ICN

2732. Dawson, Thomas Fulton. The Ute war; a history of the White River massacre and the privations and hardships of the captive white women among the hostiles of Grant River, Illustrated. Written and compiled by Thomas F. Dawson and F. J. V. Skiff, of the Denver Tribune. Denver, Printed by the Denver Tribune Publishing House, 1879.
2p.l. [5]–192p. illus. 21cm.
p. 185–192 advertisements.
Death of "The Jew" (Isaac Goldstein) as known to all, who had spent years in the West trying to locate his sister who he believed had survived the Mountain Meadows massacre.
Chief Douglas, principal villain, was also supposed to have been at Mountain Meadows.
Howes
CtY, NjP, NN, UPB

2733. Day, Charles. The Latter-day Saints, or Mormonites: Who and what are they? By the Reverend Charles Day. London, Wertheim and Macintosh [1854?]
30p. 16cm.
CSmH, CtY, NN

2734. Day, Samuel Phillips. Life and society in America. By Samuel Phillips Day . . . London, Newman and Co., 1880.
2v. 23cm.
"Camp of Zion," Salt Lake City. V. 1, p. 235–252.
CU, DLC, MiU, NN, PSC, UPB

2735. Deam, W. H. Our missionaries in Bible lands. Profusely illustrated. Compiled and arranged by W. H. Deam. Photos by Elder and Mrs. F. G. Pitt. Independence, Mo., Published at Ensign Publishing House [n.d.]
2p.l., (5)–127p. illus., ports, plates. 23cm.
RLDS missionary activities in Palestine.
MoInRC, UPB

2736. Dean, James. Mormonism not Christianity, as proved in a discussion between a Mormon Elder and a defender of evangelical christianity; containing also an account of the death of Joseph Smith, and the casting out of 319 devils, by a Mormon elder. [Norwich, Otty (Late Charlwood) Printer, Orford Hill, 1847?]
16p. 18cm.
Caption-title.
MH

Dean, Joseph H. Ka elele Euanelio. *See Morgan, John. Na Kumu Manaoio.*

2737. ———. O le ala moni e Ola ai ma ona faamatalaga i le Ekalisia Moni a Jesu Keriso. Sa Toe faaalia mai mai le lagi i ona po nei o i tatou . . . na tusia e Iosefa H. Dina. Salt Lake City, The Deseret News Company, 1890.
70p. 21½cm.
Title in English: The true way of life.
UPB, USIC

2738. ———. He leo kahea [Honolulu, ca. 1888]
[3]p. 21cm.
Missionary tract.
USIC

2739. DeArmond, David Albaugh. Case of Brigham H. Roberts of Utah. Speech of Hon. David A. DeArmond, of Missouri, in the House of Representatives . . . January 25, 1900. Washington [Govt. Print. Off., 1900]
16p. 23cm.
CU–B, DLC

2740. Death of President Brigham Young. Brief sketch of his life and labors. Funeral ceremonies, with a full report of the addresses, resolution of respect, etc. Salt Lake City, Printed at the Deseret News Steam Printing Establishment, 1877.
35p. 24cm.
Reprinted from *Deseret Evening News*, August 19–31, September 1–4, 1877.
Cover-title.
CSmH, CtY, DLC, MH, NjP, UHi, UPB, USI, USIC

2740a. The Death of the prophets. [n.p., n.d.]
Broadside. 26×19cm.
Printed in two columns. The second column is "Written while crossing the Atlantic, by W. Clayton." Also printed in R. B. Tompson's *Journal of Heber C. Kimball.*
USIC

2741. Deatherage, Charles P. Early history of greater Kansas City, Missouri and Kansas, the prophetic city at the mouth of the Kaw. Diamond Jubilee ed. 1928 . . . early history from October 12, 1492 to 1870 . . . Kansas City, Mo., The author, 1927.
3p.l. [9]–701p. illus., maps. 26cm.
Vol. I all published.
Chapter 13: "The Mormon invasion."
MoInRC, NjP, UHi

2742. ———. Steamboating on the Missouri river in the 'sixties . . . [Kansas City, Mo., Alexander Printing Company, 1924]
39p. illus. 22cm.
A compilation of a series of articles . . . published in June and July in *The Kansas City News-Press.*
"The Mormon war in Missouri," p. 20–21.
NjP, UHi, USIC

2743. De Barthe, Joseph. The life and adventures of Frank Grouard, Chief of scouts, U.S.A. by Joe De Barthe . . . St. Joseph, Mo., Combe Printing Company [c1894]
545p. illus., ports. 23cm.
Born in Tahiti, 1850, reared in Beaver, Utah by Addison Pratt family, p. 22, 31–32, 58–59; site of Mountain Meadow massacre, 1865; encounter with "Old Brigham Young," p. 59. Principally concerned with the Sioux campaigns of the 1870's.
CU–B

2744. De Bary, Richard. The land of promise, an account of the material and spiritual unity of America. London, Longmans, Green, and Co., 1908.
xv [1] 311p. 20cm.
"Mountain and Desert Empire." An ideal place for a theocratic form of society.
USlC

Deborah; the advanced woman. By M. I. T.
See Todd, Mary Van Lennup (Ives)

2745. De Brij, William James. Leer en leven der Mormonen. Door Wm. J. De Brij, Geillustreerd. Rotterdam, Uitgegeven door J. H. Walker [1909?]
16p. 21cm.
Title in English: Teachings and life of the Mormons.
USlC

2746. ———. Vanwaar en Waarheen. [Rotterdam?, n.d.]
4p. 22½cm.
Title in English: From whence to where.
USlC

2747. Declaration of grievances and protest. [Salt Lake City, 1885]
[1]8 numb. l. 35cm.
Signed: May 2d, 1885. John T. Caine, Chairman. Heber M. Wells, Secretary.
Series of protests against the Edmunds Act drawn up by a committee appointed after the general conference of the Church of Jesus Christ of Latter-day Saints, held in Logan, Utah, April 6, 1885.
UPB, USlC

2748. The Dee Crier. Ogden, Utah, Dee School of Nursing, 1927.
40p. illus., plates, ports. 28cm.
Published by the student nurses. The nursing school had been taken over by the Church.
USlC

Defense of plural marriage. *See Utah County. Women.*

2749. Defense of the constitutional and religious rights of the people of Utah. Speeches of Senators Vest, Morgan, Call, Brown, Pendleton and Lamar. [Salt Lake City? 1882]
40p. 22cm.
Cover-title: The defense of the constitutional and religious rights . . .
CtY, MH, UPB, USlC

2750. DeGroot, Henry. Sketches of the Washoe Silver Mines, with a description of the soil, climate and mineral resources, of the country east of the Sierra by Henry DeGroot. San Francisco, Hutchins & Rosenfield, 1860.
24p. 23cm.
DeGroot gives a first-hand description of a wide region in what was until 1861 Western Utah, mentioning the Mormon settlements, Carson City, and the first mines.
Howes D–220, W–C 354a
CtY

2751. Deland, Margaret Wade (Campbell). R. J.'s mother, and some other people . . . New York and London, Harper Brothers, Publishers, 1908.
3p.l., 3–312 [1]p. plates. 20cm.
Contents: R. J.'s mother. The Mormon. Many waters. The house of Rimmon. A black drop. The white feather.
Fiction concerning Mormonism.
DLC, NjP, UPB, UU

2752. Delano, Alonzo. Life on the plains and among the diggings; being scenes and adventures of an overland journey to California; with particular incidents of the route, mistakes and sufferings of the emigrants, the Indian tribes, the present and the future of the great West. By A. Delano. Auburn and Buffalo, Miller, Orton & Mulligan, 1854.
384p. front., plates. 20cm.
References to the Mormon ferry on the North Platte, p. 88, 94, 124; to "Mormon City," which Delano bypassed, p. 124, 150.
Other editions: 1854. CU–B; 1857. CU–B
W–C 238
CU–B

2753. The delegate from Utah; The position of George Q. Cannon, to whom the seat was awarded. A reply to a pamphlet issued in behalf of A. G. Campbell. Salt Lake City, Deseret News Company, 1881.
24, lviip. 20½cm.
Caption-title.
"Declaration of result of election by and certificate of Governor Murray." p. lvii.
CtY, CU–B, MH, NjP, NN, UPB

2754. The delegate from Utah. Speeches in the House of Representatives of the United States for the admission of Hon. Geo. Q. Cannon to the seat in Congress to which he had been elected by a vote of 18,568, against 1,357. Salt Lake City, Deseret News Company, 1882.
59p. 21½cm.
CtY, CU–B, MH, NjP, NN, UHi, UPB, USlC

2755. De Leon, Edwin. Thirty years of my life on three continents, by Edwin De Leon . . . with a Chapter on the life of women in the East, by Mrs. De Leon . . . London, Ward and Downey, 1890.
2v. 23cm.
An account of a "visit to Joseph Smith at Nauvoo." V. 1 p. 37–73.
CtY, CU–B, DLC, MB, NN, USl, USlC

2756. Dellen, I. Van. Det Mormonisme. Door Rev. I. Van Dellen met een inleidend woord van Prof. Dr. H. Bouwman. Kampen, J. H. Kok, 1911.
viii [9]–248p. 10 plates, 3 ports., 3 facsims. 20cm.
Title in English: Mormonism.
MH, NN, USlC

2757. Dellenbaugh, Frederick Samuel. Breaking the wilderness. The story of the conquest of the Far West, from the wanderings of Cabeza de Vaca to the first descent of the Colorado by Powell . . . New York and London, G. P. Putnam's Sons [c1905]
xxiii, 360p. illus., maps, photos. 23½cm.
Much of Chapter XVI is devoted to the history of the Mormons including Fremont's report, Mormon trek, *Book of Mormon*, Joseph Smith and Brigham Young, Mountain Meadow massacre, Jacob Hamblin, and St. George.
In Utah 1871–1872.
Another edition: 1908. CU
CU–B, DLC, NjP, ULA, UPB

2758. ———. A canyon voyage; the narrative of the second Powell expedition down the Green-Colorado river from Wyoming, and the explorations on land in the years 1871 and 1872, by Frederick S. Dellenbaugh, artist, and assistant topographer of the expedition . . . with fifty illustrations. New York and London, G. P. Putnam's Sons, 1908.
xx [2] 277p. illus., 47 plates (1 col.) port., 5 maps (4 fold) 23½cm.
Scattered, general references to Mormons, their settlements, and Jacob Hamblin.
Another edition: 2d ed. New Haven, Yale University Press, 1926. DLC
CU–B, DLC, NjP, NN, UHi, ULA, USlC

2759. ———. Fremont and '49. The story of a remarkable career and its relation to the exploration and development of our western territory, especially of California. With maps and fifty illustrations. New York, London, G. P. Putnam's Sons, 1914.
xxiii, 547p. plates, fold-out maps. 23cm.
Numerous, but scattered references to Mormon settlements in Utah, Brigham Young, Mormon battalion, etc.
CSmH, CU–B, DLC, NjP, UHi, UPB

2760. ———. The romance of the Colorado River; the story of its discovery in 1540, with an account of later explorations, and with special reference to the voyages of Powell through the line of the great canyons. New York and London, G. P. Putnam's Sons, 1902.
xxv, 399p. col. front., illus., ports., map. 23cm.
Mormon references, p. 138, 147, 272, 200, 304.
The author was in Utah in 1871, 1872, 1873, 1874, 1876, 1885, 1899.
Other editions: 1906. DLC, UPB; 1909. DLC, NjP, UPB, USlC
DLC

2761. Demetrius, Jr., [*pseud.*] An epistle of Demetrius junior, the silversmith, to the workmen of like occupation and all others whom it may concern, — Greeting: Showing the best way to preserve our craft and to put down the Latter-day Saints. Manchester [England] W. Shackleton and Son [1842?]
Broadside. 36×25cm.
A satire on sectarianism. Might have been written by Parley P. Pratt.
Sabin (Pittsburgh [1842?]) 50756
NN, USlC, WHi

2762. Democratic party, Utah (Territory) The facts of the Utah case. Salt Lake City, Tribune Job Printing Co., 1892.
23p. 22cm.
Signed: O. W. Powers, Fred J. Kiesel.
Memorial to the Democratic National Convention, 1892, from the delegates and alternates representing Utah Territory.
UHi, UU

2763. The demoralizing doctrines and disloyal teachings of the Mormon hierarchy. The conditions of woman in polygamy. New York, 1866.
18p. 23cm.
Sabin 50733
CSmH, DLC, ICN, IHi, MH, NN, UPB, USlC

2764. Denchfield, L. J. Mormonism. A sermon . . . delivered at the Baptist chapel, Rangoon, 12th October 1884, on the origin, history and teaching of Mormonism . . . [Rangoon] Rangoon Central Press, 1885.
8p. 23cm.
Cover-title.
"Reprinted from the *Anglo-Burman Advocate*."
CtY

2765. Dennett, John. John Dennett's first volume on the horrible enormities of Mormonism: Mysteries of singing in long and short metre unveiled: A dash at the spiritual wife system. Also, an exposure of unparalleled wrongs and sufferings while a member of that peculiar sect. Together with an answer to the following conundrum richly applied: Why is it that the inhabitants of Boston are so much like South Boston and Neponset bridges? Boston, Published by John Dennett, 1846.
36p. 25cm.
In green printed wrapper.
CSmH

2766. Dennis, Jesse Herbert. . . . The work of the church among the Mormons, by the Reverend Jesse Herbert Dennis. Preached in St. Barnabas' church in the city of Chicago, on the fourth Sunday after Easter, April 24, 1921. Together with appendices. Milwaukee, Wis., Pub. for the Western Theological Seminary; Chicago, by Morehouse Publishing Co. [1921]
41p. illus. 22cm. (The Hale memorial sermon. No. 12)
CtY, DLC, ICN, MH, NjP, NjPT, NN, USl, USlC, ViU

2767. Dent, George J. The gospel of Christ. [Liverpool, Printed & Published by Daniel H. Wells, 1885?]
4p. 21½cm.
Originally published in the *Millennial Star* V. 47, p. 737.
UU

2768. ———. (same, in Dutch) Het Evangelle van Christus. [n.p., after 1885]
4p. 26cm.
Title in English: The gospel of Christ.
USlC

2769. Denton, William. What is right? A discourse. By William Denton. Boston, Published by William Denton . . . 1872.
31p. 17cm.
Mormonism, p. 17–23.
CU, MH

Denver and Rio Grande Railway. *See Rio Grande Western Railway Company.*

De Quille, Dan [*pseud.*] *See Wright, William.*

2770. De Radius, J. S. C. Historical account of every sect of the Christian Religion: its origin, progress, rites and ceremonies, with a brief description of Judaism and Mahometanism, compiled from the latest authorities. By J. S. C. De Radius . . . 2d ed. (revised) London [Printed by T. Blower] 1864.
vi [9]–173, 8p. 16½cm.
An account of Mormonism p. 111–120.
"Whether by insanity or sheer hypocrisy the lad professed . . . to have a miraculous vision."
USlC

2771. Derby, Elias Hasket. The overland route to the Pacific. A report on the condition, capacity and resources of the Union Pacific and Central Pacific railways. By E. H. Derby . . . October, 1869. Boston, Lee & Shepard, 1869.
97p. 23cm.
Visit to Salt Lake City with a few notes concerning the Mormons. He attended a meeting in the tabernacle; visited with church leaders.
Howes D–266, Sabin 19661.
CU–B, DLC, ICJ, MiU

2772. Derge, A. R., and Company. Catalogue of publications of the Church of Jesus Christ of Latter-day Saints. Salt Lake City, 1884.
[4]l. [2 lists inserted] 16cm.
NN

2772a. De Roo, P. History of America before Columbus according to documents and Approved authors. Philadelphia, J. B. Lippincott, 1900.
2v. illus. 22½cm.
Book of Mormon, V. 1, p. 204–205.
UPB, USlC

2773. Derry, Charles. A manual of the priesthood; or, God's ministry as revealed in these last days, from the Doctrine and Covenants and church history, by Charles Derry. Lamoni, Ia., Printed at Herald Publishing House [189–?]
iv [5]–132p. 18cm.
MoInRC, NN, OClWHi, UPB, USlC

2774. ———. The gospel of the kingdom of God. [Plano, Ill., True Latter Day Saints Herald, 1866?]
8p. 23cm.
CtY, NN

2775. ———. The voice of the good shepherd. [Plano, Ill., Reorganized Church of Jesus Christ of Latter Day Saints, 1865]
4p. 22cm. (Tract No. 3)
CtY, MoInRC, NN, USlC

2776. ———. (same) [Plano, Ill., Reorganized Church of Jesus Christ of Latter Day Saints, before 1876]
4p. 22cm. (Tract No. 3)
Variant printing; no author listed.
NN, UPB

2777. ———. (same) [Plano, Ill., True Latter Day Saints Herald, n.d.]
4p. 23cm.
Variant printings.
MoInRC, UPB

2778. ———. (same, in Swedish) Den gode Herdens Röst, utgifvet af den återupprättade Jesu Kristi kyrka af de Sista Dagars Heliga. [Lamoni, Ia., 1901?]
6p. 21½cm.
MoInRC, NN

2779. De Rupert, A. E. D. Californians and Mormons, by A. E. D. De Rupert. New York, J. W. Lovell, 1881.
2p.l. [5]–166p. 19½cm.
CSmH, CU–B, ICHi, ICN, DLC, NjP, NN, ULA, UPB, USlC, UU

DESERET (STATE) GOVERNOR

2780. Deseret Agricultural and Manufacturing Society. Catalogue of premiums of the Deseret Agricultural and Manufacturing Society, for the year 1869. Salt Lake City, Printed at the Deseret News Office, 1869.
9p. 22cm.
A church sponsored institution.
Republished in 1872. UPB
USIC

2780a. The Deseret Alphabet. [Great Salt Lake City? 1854?]
[2]l. 20cm.
Seems to be dated in 1854, after the committee was organized and before Brigham Young announced that the alphabet should be taught in every school.
UPB

2781. Deseret (State) Citizens. To the General Assembly of the State of Deseret . . . Your petitioners beg leave to say that they feel . . . the many difficulties they are daily called to encounter . . . for the want of a good education . . . and . . . earnestly solicit the immediate attention of your honorable body to the important subject of education . . . Great Salt Lake City, 1850.
4p. 22½cm.
Caption-title.
Dated: Great Salt Lake City, Feb. 8, 1850.
CtY, NjP, UPB, USIC

2782. ———. Constitution. Constitution of the State of Deseret, with the journal of the convention which formed it, and the proceedings of the legislature consequent thereon. Kanesville, Published by Orson Hyde, 1849.
16p. 22cm.
Howes M 813, Sabin 98219
CU-B, CtY, DLC, ICN, KU, MH, ULA, USIC

2783. ———. Constitution of the State of Deseret. [Great Salt Lake City, 1850?]
34p. 18½cm.
Howes M813
DLC, MH, USIC

2784. ———. . . . Constitution of the State of Deseret, with the journal of the convention which formed it, and the proceedings of the legislature consequent thereon. [Washington, Wm. M. Belt] 1850.
12p. 23½cm. (U.S. 31st Cong. 1st Sess. House. Misc. Doc. No. 18)
At head of title: Deseret.
For Senate version, *see Memorial . . .*
C, CU, ULA, UPB

2785. ———. Constitution of the State of Deseret . . . [Washington, William A. Harris, 1858.]
10p. 23½cm. (U.S. 35th Cong. 1st Sess. Senate. Misc. Doc. No. 240)
UPB

2786. ———. Constitution of the State of Deseret. Memorials of the legislature and Constitutional Convention of Utah Territory, praying the admission into the Union as the State of Deseret. [Washington, Govt. Print. Off.] 1862.
11p. 23cm. (U.S. 37th Cong. 2d Sess. House. Misc. Doc. No. 78)
UHi, UPB, UU

2787. ———. Constitution of the State of Deseret, with accompanying memorial to Congress. Adopted March 2, 1872. Salt Lake City: Printed at the Deseret News Book and Job Establishment, 1872.
21p. 23cm.
In printed wrapper.
CSmH, CtY, UPB, USIC

2788. ———. . . . Memorial of the convention to frame a constitution for the admission of Utah into the Union as a state, convened at Salt Lake City, February 19, 1872, ratified by vote of the people, March 18, 1872. [Washington, Govt. Print. Off.] 1872.
21p. 23½cm. (U.S. 42nd Cong. 2d Sess. House. Misc. Doc. No. 165)
Praying to be admitted as a State under the name of Deseret.
ULA, UPB

2789. ———. Memorial of the members of the legislative council of the provisional government of Deseret, praying for admission into the Union as a State, or for a Territorial Government. Dec. 27, 1849. [Washington, Wm. M. Belt, 1850]
14p. 23½cm. (U.S. 31st Cong. 1st Sess. Senate. Misc. Doc. No. 10)
Includes the Constitution of the proposed State of Deseret.
DLC, ICN, UHi, ULA, UPB

2790. ———. Proposed State of Deseret. Memorial of the Legislative Assembly of the proposed State, for the admission of the State of Deseret into the Union, and accompanying papers. March 20, 1867. [Washington, Govt. Print. Off., 1868]
8p. 23½cm. (U.S. 40th Cong. 1st Sess. House. Misc. Doc. No. 26)
Request to be admitted into the Union as the State of Deseret.
CtY, CU-B, DLC, ULA, UPB

2791. ———. Governor. Governor's message; Deseret, December 2, 1850. To the Senators and Representatives of the State of Deseret. [Great Salt Lake City, 1850]
3p. 20½cm.
Signed: Brigham Young.
Chiefly a governmental address. The pattern of settlement, etc.
UPB, USIC

2792. ———. Governor's message to the first general assembly of the State of Deseret. [Great Salt Lake City, 1862]

3p. 19cm.
Caption-title.
Printed in double columns.
Signed and dated: Brigham Young, Great Salt Lake City, April 14, 1862.
The ghost legislature which met after the regular session of the Territorial Legislature.
CSmH, NjP, NN, UPB, USlC

2793. ———. Message of the Governor of the State of Deseret. [Great Salt Lake City, January 19, 1863]
2p. 19½cm.
USlC

2794. ———. Governor's Message to the General Assembly of the State of Deseret. [Great Salt Lake City, 1865]
3p. 18½cm.
Congress had not deemed it proper to admit Deseret as a state.
UPB, USlC

2795. ———. Ordinances, passed by the Legislative Council of Great Salt Lake City, and ordered to be printed. [Great Salt Lake City, 1850?]
4p., [1]l. 18½cm.
Caption-title.
Ordinances passed between February 24 and December 29, 1849.
DLC, MH, USlC

2795a. ———. Ordinances passed by the General Assembly of the State of Deseret. [Great Salt Lake City, 1851]
80p. 17½cm.
USlC

2796. Deseret deserted; or, The last days of Brigham Young. Being a strictly business transaction in four acts and several deeds, involving both prophet and loss. By the [Moon] club. As performed at Wallack's Theatre. New York, S. French [c1858]
DLC, IaU, MG, NBuG, NN, NRU, OCl

2797. Deseret Evening News. Salt Lake City, 1867–
v. daily. 55cm.
Begun in 1867 after the completion of the Deseret Telegraph.
Both the weekly and semi-weekly papers continued to be printed and were printed until the *Deseret Weekly* was discontinued in 1898.
USlC

2798. ———. Description of the Salt Lake Temple. Salt Lake City [Deseret Evening News] 1892.
8p. 22½cm.
CU–B, USlC

2799. Deseret Gymnasium. The Deseret Gymnasium where the road to health begins. Salt Lake City [1920?]
32p. illus. 10cm.
Religion and health.
USlC

2800. Deseret Musical Association. Songs, duets and glees to be sung at the concert of the Deseret Musical Association to be given at the theatre, G.S.L. City, On Wednesday Eve., Oct. 1, 1863. Conductor, D. O. Calder. G.S.L. City. Deseret News Print., 1863.
16p. 14½cm.
USlC

Deseret News. *See Deseret Weekly; Deseret Evening News.*

———. Death of President Brigham Young. *See Death of President Brigham Young.*

———. Deseret News Extra containing a revelation on Celestial marriage, . . . *See Church of Jesus Christ of Latter-day Saints. Minutes of conference.*

2801. ———. Deseret News Extra. Great Salt Lake City, U.T., Jan. 31. [1852]
Broadside. 36×16½cm.
Concerning the Civil War and its effect upon Utah Territory.
Quotes from New York Tribune concerning Governor Young's squandering of money appropriated by Congress.
UPB, USlC

2802. ———. Deseret News Extra. Great Salt Lake City, Thursday morning, August 25, 1853.
Broadside. 33½×21cm.
Proclamation of Governor Young on Indian problems, etc.
USlC

2803. ———. Deseret News Extra. Great Salt Lake City, April 2, 1859.
Broadside. 41×27½cm.
Activity of Judge Cradlebaugh and his court.
USlC

2804. ———. Deseret News Extra. Great Salt Lake City, U.T., August 25, 1863.
Broadside. 35½×21cm.
Includes the proclamation by Brigham Young concerning Indian wars.
USlC

2805. ———. The Deseret News white book, automobile maps and logs . . . Salt Lake City, Deseret News, 1922.
48p. illus., maps. 21½cm.
"The old Mormon trail to . . . Los Angeles" F.D.B. Gay, manager.
A description of each city and the Mormon trail.
UHi

2806. ———. New Year's issue, Salt Lake City, 1893.
48p. illus., ports. 30cm.
Special issue with historical importance.
CSmH, NNU–W, UHi

DESERET WEEKLY

2807. ———. . . . The sources of Utah's greatness . . . Salt Lake City, 1903.
88p. illus., ports., maps. 58½cm.
Cover-title.
"Christmas, 1903."
Includes historical information.
DLC

2808. ———. Utah, the inland empire, illustrated. The story of the pioneers, resources and industries of the state, attractions of Salt Lake City, leading men of the community. Salt Lake City, Deseret News, 1902.
110p. illus., plates, ports. 28cm.
CSmH, UHi, ULA, UPB, USIC, UU

2809. Deseret News Book Store. Catalogue and price list of church publications, Bibles, etc. Authorized church records of all kinds. April 1, 1905. Salt Lake City, For sale by Deseret News Book Store, 1905.
62p. 15cm.
USIC

2809a. ———. (same) Salt Lake City, Deseret News Book Store, 1908.
47p. 15cm.
NjP, UPB

2810. ———. Catalogue and price list of church publications, Bibles, etc., etc. Authorized church records, certificates and blanks. Salt Lake City, Deseret News Bookstore, 1916.
56p. 14cm.
USIC

2811. Deseret News Office. Catalogue of publications of the Church of Jesus Christ of Latter-day Saints. For sale at the Deseret News Office [Salt Lake City] 1881.
[4]p. 17½cm.
USIC

2812. The Deseret primer: containing lessons for juveniles. Great Salt Lake City, Elias Smith, Publisher, 1863.
24p. 18cm.
CSmH

2813. Deseret Silk Association of Utah Territory. Treatise on silk raising, by the Deseret Silk Association of Utah Territory, 1877. [Salt Lake City? 1877]
9p. 23cm.
Successful part of home industry.
UPB, USIC

2814. Deseret Silk Association. Utah County Branch. Constitution of the Utah County Branch of the Deseret Silk Association. [n.p., about 1877?]
[2]p. 22cm.
Organized within the confines of the church.
UPB

2815. Deseret Summer Institute; a school for teachers and other qualified applicants. . . . Conducted under the auspices of the Latter-day Saints' Church School System and the special supervision of the general Board of Examiners for church schools. [Salt Lake City, The Deseret News, 1904–]
v. annual. 14cm.
USIC 1904; 1905, # 1, 2

2816. Deseret. University. Annual of the University of Deseret. Salt Lake City, 1868–1892.
v. 21cm.
Title varies: Annual catalogue of the officers and students in the University of Deseret . . . 1868–1871; University of Deseret circular, 1876–1878; Circular of the academic department . . . 1880–1882; Annual of the University of Deseret, 1882–1892.
USIC, UU

2817. ———. The Deseret furst bok by th Regents of th Yionivursiti. [Salt Lake City, Deseret University] 1868.
36p. 19cm.
Title transliterated. The Deseret Alphabet was also printed on cards. None located.
CSmH, CtY, CU-B, NjP, UHi, ULA, UPB, UU

2818. ———. The Deseret Second bok by th Regents of th Deseret Yionivursiti. [Salt Lake City, Deseret University] 1868.
72p. 19cm.
CSmH, CtY, CU-B, NjP, UHi, ULA, UPB, USIC, UU

2819. ———. Report of Chancellor and Board of Regents of the Deseret University . . . [Salt Lake City, 1872–]
v. 21cm.
USIC 1872, 1892

2820. ———. Supplementary catalogue of books in the library of the University of Deseret. Salt Lake City, 1876.
16p. 22½cm.
Alphabetically arranged.
USIC

2821. ———. To the honorable, the County Court . . . [Salt Lake City, 1875]
Broadside. 24×21cm.
Dated: May 25, 1875.
Educational aspects of the Mormon Church.
USIC

2822. The Deseret Weekly. Salt Lake City, Deseret News Company, 1850–1898.
57v. weekly (except various periods when trouble curtailed it.) 21–42cm.
Title varies: Deseret News, Deseret News Weekly, Deseret Weekly.

The first newspaper in Utah. Continued weekly after a semi-weekly and daily were added, as a combination of newspaper and magazine.
V. 1 #1 reprinted twice. UPB, USlC
A good description of the first volumes in the Eberstadt: *Utah and the Mormons.*
CtY V. 1–14, 17–26, 31–32, 38–50; CU–B V. 38–39, 41–43, 56–66; MH V. 1–13; NjP V. 38–44, 46–55; ULA V. 2, 38–57; UPB V. 1–12, 19–23, 25–26, 38–57; USlC comp.; WHi V. 2–16, 38–55

De Smet, Pierre Jean. *See Smet, Pierre Jean de.*

2823. Desmons, Frederic. . . . Essai historique et critique der Mormonisme . . . Strasbourg, Imprimeric de veuve, Berger-Levrault, 1856.
2p.l., 97p. 21cm.
At head of title: Universite' de France Faculte' de Theologie Protestante de Strasbourg.
Title in English: Historical and critical essay on Mormonism.
MH, MnU

2824. Devens, Richard Miller. The national memorial volume. Being a popular descriptive portraiture of the great events of our past century. Including also delineations of all our great historic characters in the most striking phases of their career. By R. M. Devens . . . Tecumseh, Mich., Published by C. A. Nichols & Co. . . . 1880.
1p.l. [7]–706p. illus., plates, ports. 28cm.
Chapter 26 "Rise and progress of the Mormons of 'Latter-day Saints' under Joseph Smith, the 'Prophet of the Lord.' " 1830.
Also published under title: American progress. Chicago, Published by Hugh Heron, 1881. USlC
UPB, USlC

2825. ———. Our first century, being a popular descriptive portraiture of the one hundred great and memorable events . . . in the history of our country, political, military, mechanical, social, scientific, and commercial: embracing also delineations of all the great historic characters celebrated in the annals of the republic; . . . by R. M. Devens . . . Springfield, Mass., C. A. Nichols & Co.; Easton, Pa., J W. Lyon, 1876.
3p.l. [7]–1004p. front., illus., ports., facsims. 28cm.
"Rise and progress of the Mormons . . ."
Other editions: 1878. DLC; 1879, 1882. CU; 1880. NjP; 1885. UPB
DLC

2826. Devos, Julius E. The three ages of progress. With preface by the Lord Bishop of Ogdensburg. By Julius E. Devos. Wisconsin, M. H. Wiltzius, 1899.
xvi, 352, xxxvi p. 23cm.
Mormonism one of the "Two monster evils" that threatened the U.S.
USlC

De Vries, Hugo. *See Vries, Hugo de.*

2827. De Wolff, J. H. Pawnee Bill (Major Gordon W. Lillie), his experience and adventures on the western plains; or, From the saddle of a "cowboy and ranger" to the chair of a "bank president." [n.p.] Pawnee Bill's Historic Wild West Co., 1902.
3p.l., 7–108p. illus., plates, ports. 24cm.
Chapter on the Mountain Meadows massacre, p. 76–81.
Howes D–311
DLC, NjP, UHi, UPB

Dialogue between a Latter-day Saint and an enquirer after truth. *See Pratt, Parley P.*

Dialogue between Joseph Smith and the Devil. *See Pratt, Parley P.*

2828. The diamond jubilee of the coming of the Utah Pioneers, July 22–23–24–1922. Salt Lake City, Published by the Committees. [Salt Lake City, The Deseret News Press, c1923]
[49]p. illus., ports. 24×30cm.
CSmH, DLC, ICN, UHi, ULA, UPB, UU

Diary during a tour round the world. *See B., H.*

The Diary of a Utah girl. *See McLaughlin, Mrs. W. J.*

2829. Dibble, Roy Floyd. Strenuous Americans [by] R. F. Dibble . . . New York, Boni and Liveright [c1923]
9p., [3]l., 15–370p. ports. 22½cm.
Includes a biography of Brigham Young.
Another edition: London, G. Routledge, 1925. UPB
CU–B, DLC, NjP, NN, UHi, ULA, USlC, WHi

2830. Dickens, Charles. The uncommercial traveller, by Charles Dickens. London, Chapman and Hall, 1866 [1865]
204p. front. 19cm.
His reactions at seeing Mormon emigrants sailing from England.
First printed in *All the Year Round.* July 4, 1863. p. 444–449.
Reprinted in many editions.
MH, NjP

2831. Dickin, J. P. The Mormon miracle, at Rochdale, tested and exposed; being a compilation of articles from various authentic sources . . . Rochdale [Eng] J. Phillips, Printer; Published by A. Heywood, Manchester, 1854.
16p. 17cm.
Relates to the supposed healing of Alston Marsden, at the hands of Mormon elders.
CtY

2832. Dickinson, Ellen E. New light on Mormonism, by Mrs. Ellen E. Dickinson, with introduction by Thurlow Weed. New York, Funk & Wagnalls, 1885.

4p., [2]l. [11]–272p. 19½cm.
CSmH, CtY, DLC, ICN, NjPT, NN, UHi, ULA, USl, USlC, UU, WHi

2832a. Dickinson Family. Reunion of the Dickinson Family, at Amherst, Mass., August 8th and 9th, 1883. With appendix. [Binghamton, N. Y.] Binghamton Publishing Co., 1884.
vii, 206p. illus. 22cm.
Daniel H. Wells and Mormons, p. 116–119.
USlC

2833. Dickson, Albert Jerome. Covered wagon days; a journey across the plains in the sixties, and pioneer days in the Northwest; from the private journals of Albert Jerome Dickson, edited by Arthur Jerome Dickson. Cleveland, The Arthur H. Clark Company, 1929.
287p. plates, ports., fold. map. 24½cm.
Brief reference to Mormons and Mormon immigration.
CU–B, DLC, ICN, MH, NjP, ULA, USlC, UU

2834. Dickson, William Howard. In the matter of the charges preferred by A. A. Law against Alfred W. McCune. March 1, 1899. Argument of W. H. Dickson for Alfred W. McCune. [Salt Lake City, Star Printing Co., 1899]
41p. 8cm.
Contested Utah election of 1899.
NN, USl

2835. ———. Solid facts from a loyal man. Speech of U. S. Attorney William H. Dickson, at G. A. R. meeting Thurs. Eve. July 27, [1886?] Salt Lake City, Salt Lake Tribune printing [1886?]
4p. 24cm.
Caption-title.
Disloyalty of the Mormons.
CSmH, MH, NN, UHi, USl

2836. ———. United States of America vs. The late Corporation of the Church of Jesus Christ of Latter-Day Saints, et al. Brief of W. H. Dickson, of Counsel for Defendants. [Salt Lake City] Star Print. [1887?]
28p. 22cm.
Concerning the dissolution of property ownership during the polygamy period.
USlC, UU

2837. Didriksson, Thordur. Athvörunar og sannleiksraust um höfurthatrithi trúar "Jesú Kristi Kirju af sithustu daga heilögum." Samin af Thórdi Didrikssyni. Kaupmannahöfn, Utgefin af N. Vilhelmsen, Prentuth hja F. E. Bording, 1879.
2p.l. [3]–165 [1]p. 16½cm.
Concerning the chief beliefs of the faith of the Mormon church.
Title in English: Warning and voice of Truth.
UPB, USlC

2838. Dietrichson, Johannes Wilhelm Christian. Reise blandt de norske emigranter i "De Forenede nordamerikanske Fristater," af J. W. C. Dietrichson . . . Stavanger, L. C. Kielland, 1846.
128p. 19cm.
P. 95–112 contain an account of the Mormons in Illinois.
Title in English: Journeys among the Norwegian emigrants . . .
CtY

2839. Dilke, Charles Wentworth. Greater Britain: A record of travel in English-speaking countries during 1866 and 1867. By Charles Wentworth Dilke. In two volumes . . . with maps and illustrations. London: Macmillan and Co., 1868.
2v. illus., plates, maps. 21cm.
Visit to Utah. A sympathetic treatment of Mormonism, comparing it to Kansas.
He tells of perfect freedom to leave Utah (despite Danite stories) and a prediction of the future of Mormonism.
Other editions: New York, Harper & brothers, 1869. NjPT; London, Macmillan, 1869. USlC; London, Macmillan, 1870. USlC
CU–B, NN, PP, PU, ULA, UPB, UU

2840. Dillingham, William P. The Senator from Utah. Speech of Hon. Wm. P. Dillingham, of Vermont, in the Senate of the United States, Tuesday, February 19, 1907. Washington, 1907.
34p. 22cm.
Reed Smoot hearings.
CU–B, UPB, USlC

Dina, Joseph H. *See Dean, Joseph Henry.*

———. *See also Church of Jesus Christ of Latter-day Saints. Missions. Hawaiian.*

2841. Dinsmore, Hugh Anderson. The Roberts case. Speech of Hon. Hugh A. Dinsmore, of Arkansas, in the House of Representatives, December 5, 1899. Washington [Govt. Print. Off.] 1899.
7p. 23cm.
DLC, NjP

2842. Disturnell, John. The emigrant's guide to New Mexico, California, and Oregon; giving the different overland and sea routes. Compiled from reliable authorities . . . New York, J. Disturnell, 1849.
46p. fold. map. 20cm.
Cover title: Disturnell's map of California, New-Mexico, &c.
Comprehensive gathering of guides including Kearny and Cooke. Reference of Mormons p. 12, 16–18.
Another edition: 1850. CtY, DLC
Howes D352
CSmH, CtY, CU–B, DLC, MH, NjP

DIVINE AUTHORITY

2843. Divine authority. . . . [Liverpool? 19 - - ?]
4p. 21cm.
A missionary tract.
USlC

Dix, John Ross [*pseud.*] *See Phillips, George Spencer.*

2844. Dixie College, St. George, Utah. Announcements. St. George Utah, 1888–1930.
v. 19½–22cm.
Name changes: St. George Stake Academy, Dixie Normal College.
UPB 1888–89, 1922–31; USlC 1915–16, 1920–21, 1921–22, 1928–29, 1929–30, 1930–31

2845. ———. The Dixie (yearbook) 1888–
v. 27cm.
Name change. "D" 1915.
USlC 1888–89, 1915–16, 1922–23, 1923–24, 1924–25, 1925–26, 1926–27, 1927–28, 1928–29, 1929–30, 1930–31

2846. ———. To the Latter-day Saints in St. George Stake of Zion. [St. George, 1907]
[4]p. 16cm.
Signed: St. George, Nov. 8th, 1907. On establishing of an academy, by the Board of Trustees.
USlC

2847. Dixon, William Hepworth. New America. By William Hepworth Dixon . . . London, Hurst and Blackett, 1867.
2v. plates, ports. 22½cm.
Section on Utah and Mormonism with particular emphasis on Mormon marriage customs, polygamy, etc., V. 1, p. 175–359.
Published in many editions in English, as well as in French and German.
Sabin 20373
CSmH, CtY, DLC, NjP, NN, UHi, ULA, UPB, USlC, UU

2848. ———. Spiritual wives. By William Hepworth Dixon . . . Leipzig, B. Tauchnity, 1868.
2v. in 1. 15½cm.
Copyright edition.
Vol. 1. Chap. viii includes a discussion of spiritual wives among the Mormons.
Other editions: 2d ed. Philadelphia, J. B. Lippincott & Co., 1868. CtY, DLC, USlC, UU; London, Hurst & Blackett, 1868. CtY, UHi, ULA; 2d edition. London, Hurst, 1868. MH, NN; 4th edition, with a new preface, 1868. CU–B, MB, NN
Sabin 20378
MB, NjP, NjPT, UPB

2849. ———. White conquest. By William Hepworth Dixon. London, Chatto and Windus, 1876.
2v. 22cm.
Mormon doctrine. V. 1, p. 182–238. Mormons and Indians compared.
Other editions: Copyright ed. Leipzig, 1876. DLC, UHi; French: La conquete blance. tr. . . . par Hipp. Vattemare. Paris, Hachette et cie, 1877. DLC, UHi
CU–B, DLC, NjP, NN, UHi, USlC, Vi

2850. Dixon, Winifred Hawkridge. Westward hoboes; ups and downs of frontier motoring, by Winifred Hawkridge Dixon; photographs by Katherine Thaxter and Rollin Lester Dixon. New York, C. Scribner's Sons, 1921.
ix, 377p. plates. 22½cm.
Brief mention made of the Mormon country and some references to the foresight of the Mormons, p. 317–318. As the Mesa Temple was to be dedicated, "Gentile" visitors could visit the temple, p. 353–355 (plus plate)
Other editions: New York, Charles Scribner's Sons, 1922. NjP; 1930. USlC
CU–B, DLC, UHi, USlC

2851. Do the Latter Day Saint teachings agree with the Book of Mormon. Independence, Mo. [n.d.]
10 [1]p. 15cm.
Signed at end: Bible and Book of Mormon class . . . Independence, Mo. Church of Christ publication.
UPB

2852. Dr. Bassett's Free European Gallery of Anatomy, Science, Art & Nature. Salt Lake Mormons . . . The most prominent of these people have been accurately reproduced in wax . . . Chicago [after 1877]
[2]p. 30½×11cm.
A brochure for a wax museum featuring a section on Mormonism. A descriptive catalogue was also included, but has not been located.
USlC

2853. Dr. Bassett's Museum of Anatomy. Catalogue. Dr. Bassett's Museum of Anatomy, 187 and 189 South Clark St., Chicago, Ills. [Chicago, 1879]
13, 56 [1]p. port. of Brigham Young on back cover. 20cm.
Final section entitled "The Salt Lake Mormons, life-like figures in wax, representing Brigham Young surrounded by his harem of twenty wives.
"John D. Lee, The leader of the Mountain Meadows murderers, as he appeared on the day of his execution."
"The celebrated Danite chiefs, in full costume, such as worn by them at Salt Lake City."
CtY

2854. Doctrine and Covenants. English. 1833. A Book of Commandments, for the government of the Church of Christ. Organized according to law, on the 6th of April, 1830. Zion [Independence, Mo.] Published by W. W. Phelps and Co., 1833.
160p. 11½cm.
Five signatures that were saved at the destruction of *The Evening and the Morning Star* Press.
Found in three states, with and without a border on title page.
Sabin 83147
CSmH, CtY, CU–B, DLC, ICN, MoInRC, NN, UPB, USlC

DOCTRINE AND COVENANTS. ENGLISH. 1866

2855. ———. 1833 (1884) (same) Reprinted verbatim. [Salt Lake City] Salt Lake Tribune, 1884.
93p. 15cm.
Sabin 83148
CtY, MH, NjP, NN, ULA, UPB, USlC

2856. ———. 1833 (1903) (same) Reprinted verbatim. [Salt Lake City, Tribune Printing Co.] 1903.
93p. 15cm.
Sabin 83149
IWW, UHi, USlC

2857. ———. 1833 (1903) (same) [Reprinted verbatim, by C. A. Wickes, Lamoni, Ia., 1903]
133p. 16cm.
Morgan, Sabin 83150
MH, MoInRC, USlC

2858. ———. 1833 (1926) (same) [Reprinted verbatim, Independence, Mo., by Charles F. Putnam and Daniel Macgregor, 1926]
127p. 16cm.
Sabin 83151
UHi, USlC, UU

2859. ———. 1833 (1930?) (same) [Reprinted by the Board of Publications of Church of Christ, Temple Lot, Independence, Missouri, 1930?]
127p. 17cm.
NjP, UHi, UPB

2860. ———. 1835. Doctrine and Covenants of the Church of the Latter-day Saints: carefully selected from the Revelations of God, and compiled by Joseph Smith, Junior, Oliver Cowdery, Sidney Rigdon, Frederick G. Williams [presiding elders of said church] Proprietors. Kirtland, Ohio, Printed by F. G. Williams & Co. for the proprietors, 1835.
iv [5]–257, xxv p. 15½cm.
First edition under title *Doctrine and Covenants.* First to include the Lectures on Faith, and many new revelations.
Although no authorship has clearly been established for the Lectures on Faith, and it might have been a composite of various persons, most of the doctrinal contents seems to be by Joseph Smith. cf. John A. Widtsoe. N. B. Lundwall's *A compilation containing the Lectures on Faith.*
Sabin 83152
CSmH, CtY, CU–B, DLC, ICN, MH, NjP, NjPT, NN, UPB, USl, USlC, UU, WHi

2861. ———. 1844. The Doctrine and Covenants of the Church of Jesus Christ of Latter Day Saints. Carefully selected from the Revelations of God. By Joseph Smith, President of said Church. Second edition. Nauvoo, Ill., Printed by John Taylor, 1844.
1p.l. [1] 6–448p. 14½cm.
Byrd 896
CtY, ICN, MH, MoInRC, NN, OClWhi, UPB, USlC, WHi

2862. ———. 1845. (same) Third edition. Nauvoo, Ill., Printed by John Taylor, 1845.
[2]l. [5]–448p. 14½cm.
Reprinted from the stereotype plates of the second edition.
Byrd 997, Sabin 83154
CtY, CU–B, DLC, ICHi, MoInRC, NN, OCl, USlC, UU, WHi

2863. ———. 1845. The Book of Doctrine & Covenants, of the Church of Jesus Christ of Latter-day Saints; selected from the Revelations of God. By Joseph Smith, President. First European edition. Liverpool, Wilford Woodruff, Stanley Buildings, Bath Street [1845]
2p.l., [iv]–xxiii, 336p. 18cm.
Preface by Thomas Ward dated June 14th, 1845. Printed by James and Woodburn, Printers, Liverpool.
Sabin 83155
CSmH, CtY, DLC, MH, MoInRC, NN, UHi, USl, USlC

2864. ———. 1846. (same) Fourth American edition. Nauvoo, Ill., Printed by John Taylor, 1846.
1p. [5]–448p. 14½cm.
Byrd 1117, Sabin 83156
CtY, DLC, ICN, MH, MoInRC, NjP, UHi, UU, WHi

2865. ———. 1849. (same) Second European edition. Liverpool, Orson Pratt, 15 Wilton Street, Pr. by R. James, 1849.
2p.l., [iv]–xxiii, 336p. 15cm.
Sabin 83157
DLC, IChi, MoInRC, NN, USlC, UU

2866. ———. 1852. (same) Third European edition. Stereotyped. Liverpool, Published by S. W. Richards . . . London: Sold at the L. D. Saints' Book Depot, 1852.
[4] vii–xxiii, 336p. 15cm.
Sabin 83158
CU–B, ICN, IWW, MH, UHi, UPB, USlC, UU

2867. ———. 1854. (same) Fourth European edition. Stereotyped. Liverpool, Published for Orson Pratt, by S. W. Richards, 1854.
2p.l., [iv]–xxiii, 336p. 15½cm.
Sabin 83159
CtY, CU, IHi, IWW, MoInRC, MWA, NN, UHi, ULA, UPB, USlC, UU

2868. ———. 1866. (same) Fifth European edition. Stereotyped. Liverpool, Published by Brigham Young, Jun., 42, Islington, London. Sold at the L. D. Saints' Book Depot . . . 1866.
2p.l., [iv]–xxiii, 336p. 16cm.
Sabin 83161
MoInRC, USlC

DOCTRINE AND COVENANTS. ENGLISH. 1869

2869. ———. **1869.** (same) Sixth European edition. Stereotyped. Liverpool, Published by Albert Carrington . . . London, Sold at the L. D. Saints' Book Depot . . . 1869.
2p.l., [iv]–xxiii, 336p. 16cm.
Sabin 83162
UHi, USIC, UU

2870. ———. **1876.** The Doctrine and Covenants of the Church of Jesus Christ of Latter-day Saints, containing the revelations given to Joseph Smith, jun, the Prophet, for the Building up of the Kingdom of God in the Last Days. Salt Lake City, Published at the Deseret News Office, 1876.
xxxix, 448p. 18½cm.
First Salt Lake City edition, and first edition with 136 sections including "The Word and will of the Lord," given through President Brigham Young [concerning the Camp of Israel in their journeys to the West] January 14th, 1847. Revised throughout and arranged in chronological order by Orson Pratt.
Sabin 83163
CSmH, CU–B, DLC, NN, RPB, UHi, USIC, UU

2871. ———. **1879.** (same) Divided into verses, with references, by Orson Pratt Sen. Electrotype edition. Liverpool, Printed and Published by William Budge, 1879.
4p.l., 503p. 19cm.
Reprint of the revised edition of 1876.
Sabin 83164
CSmH, NN, UHi, UPB, UU

2872. ———. **1880.** (same) Salt Lake City, Deseret News Company, Printers and Publishers, 1880.
2p.l., 503p. 17cm.
Sabin 83165
CU, DLC, MH, NjP, OClW, OClWHi, MoInRC, USIC, UU

2873. ———. **1882.** (same) Second Electrotype edition. Liverpool, Printed and Published by Albert Carrington, 1882.
2p.l., 503p. 19cm.
Sabin 83168
DLC, ULA, UPB, USIC, UU

2874. ———. **1883.** (same) Salt Lake City, Deseret News Company, Printers and Publishers, 1883.
2p.l., 503p. 17½cm.
Sabin 83169
ICN, MH, MiU, NN, UHi, USIC, UU

2875. ———. **1884.** (same) Third Electrotype edition. Liverpool, Printed and Published by John Henry Smith, 1884.
2p.l., 503p. 17cm.
Sabin 83170
CtY, DLC, MH, NN, OCl, OO, PU, UHi, UPB, USIC, UU

2876. ———. **1886.** (same) Salt Lake City, Deseret News Company, Publishers and Printers, 1886.
2p.l., 503p. 17cm.
Sabin 83171
CU, ICN, MoInRC, UPB, USIC, UU

2877. ———. **1890.** (same) Salt Lake City, Deseret News Company, Publishers and Printers, 1890.
2p.l., 503p. 17cm.
Sabin 83172
CtY, DLC, IWW, MB, MoInRC, NH, NjP, OClWHi, UHi, USIC, UU

2878. ———. **1891.** (same) Salt Lake City, George Q. Cannon & Sons Co., Printers and Publishers, 1891.
2p.l., 503p. 25½cm.
Large octavo edition.
Sabin 83174
CtY, MH, MoInRC, NN, UHi, USIC, UU, WHi

2879. ———. **1891.** (same) Third Electrotype edition. Liverpool, Printed and Published by Brigham Young, Jun., 1891.
2p.l., 503 p. 16½cm.
Sabin 83173
CtY, MH, MiU, OClWHi, UHi, ULA, UPB, USIC, UU

2880. ———. **1898.** (same) Salt Lake City, Geo. Q. Cannon & Sons Co., 1898.
2p.l., 503p. 16½cm.
USIC

2881. ———. **1898.** (same) Fourth Electrotype edition. Liverpool, Printed and Published by Rulon S. Wells, 1898.
2p.l., 503p. 17½cm.
First edition on India Paper.
Sabin 83177
USIC

2882. ———. **1900?** (same) Salt Lake City, Deseret Sunday School Union [19 - - ?]
2p.l., 503p. 12cm.
CU–B

2883. ———. **1901.** (same) Salt Lake City, The Deseret News, Printers and Publishers, 1901.
2p.l., 503p. 17cm.
Sabin 83178
CU–B, UPB, USIC, UU, ViU

2884. ———. **1902.** (same) Salt Lake City, The Deseret News, Printers and Publishers, 1902.
2p.l., 503p. 17cm.
Sabin 83181
MoInRC, UPB

2885. ———. **1903.** (same) Salt Lake City, The Deseret News, Printers and Publishers, 1903.
2p.l., 503p. 17cm.
Sabin 83183
MoInRC, USIC

2886. ———. **1903.** (same) Fifth Electrotype edition. Liverpool, Printed and Published by Francis M. Lyman. 1903.
2p.l., 503p. 17cm.
Also included as part of a triple combination.
Sabin 83182
NjP, USlC

2887. ———. **1904.** (same) Salt Lake City, The Deseret News, Printers and Publishers [1904]
2p.l., 503p. 17½cm.
Printed as part of a triple combination.
USlC

2888. ———. **1904.** (same) Salt Lake City, Published by the Deseret Sunday School Union, 1904.
2p.l., 503p. 11cm.
Printed on India paper from plates made in Philadelphia.
Vest pocket edition.
Sabin 83185
MoInRC, USlC

2889. ———. **1905.** (same) Salt Lake City, Deseret Sunday School Union, 1905.
2p.l., 503p. 11cm.
Vest pocket edition.
Sabin 83186
USlC

2890. ———. **1906.** (same) Sixth Electrotype edition. Liverpool, Printed and Published by Heber J. Grant, 1906.
2p.l., 503p. 17½cm.
Also published in a triple combination on India paper.
Sabin SLC 83188
UU

2891. ———. **1906.** (same) Salt Lake City, The Deseret News, Printers and Publishers, 1906.
2p.l., 503p. 18cm.
Sabin 83189
MoInRC

2892. ———. **1907.** (same) [Salt Lake City, Published by the Deseret Sunday School Union] 1907.
2p.l., 503p. 11cm.
Vest pocket edition.
Sabin 83192
USlC

2893. ———. **1908.** (same) Salt Lake City, Deseret Sunday School Union, 1908.
2p.l., 503p. 11cm.
Vest pocket edition and published in a triple combination.
Sabin 83193
MH, USlC

2894. ———. **1908.** (same) Salt Lake City, The Deseret News, Printers and Publishers, 1908.
2p.l., 544p. 17½cm.
Includes a concordance, p. 504–42 and the manifesto of Wilford Woodruff, p. 543–44.
UHi, ULA

2895. ———. **1909.** (same) Third Electrotype edition. Liverpool, Printed and Published by Charles W. Penrose, 1909.
2p.l., 503p. 18½cm.
Also part of a triple combination issued in 1909.
Sabin 83196
USlC

2896. ———. **1910.** (same) Salt Lake City, Published by the Deseret Sunday School Union, 1910.
2p.l., 503p. 11cm.
Vest pocket edition.
Sabin 83197
IWW, MoInRC

2897. ———. **1911.** (same) Salt Lake City, The Deseret News, Printers and Publishers, 1911.
542p. 18cm.
Concordance, p. 504–542
Sabin 83198
IWW, MoInRC, UPB, USlC, UU

2898. ———. **1912.** (same) Third Electrotype edition. Liverpool, Printed and Published by Rudger Clawson, 295 Edge Lane, 1912.
2p.l., 503p. 17cm.
Also published as part of a triple combination the same year.
USlC

2899. ———. **1913.** (same) Salt Lake City, Deseret Sunday School Union, 1913.
2p.l., 503p. 12cm.
Vest pocket edition. Double combination: *Doctrine and Covenants*, and *Pearl of Great Price*.
Sabin 83201
USlC

2900. ———. **1914.** (same) Salt Lake City, The Deseret News, Printers and Publishers, 1914.
542p. 17½cm.
Error in pagination p. [493]–494 used twice.
Declaration (manifesto of Wilford Woodruff) is added with an error in pagination.
USlC

2900a. ———. **1916.** The Doctrine and Covenants, containing revelations given to Joseph Smith, Jun, the Prophet, with an introduction by Joseph F. Smith, . . . and historical and exegetical notes by Hyrum M. Smith . . . Liverpool, Printed and published by Hyrum M. Smith, 1916.
1100p. 18cm.
Includes title-page and preface; pasted introduction from *Millennial Star*, Vol. 78, p. 369–74, 385–91, June 15, 22, 1916; and Sections 1, 23, and 37.
USlC

DOCTRINE AND COVENANTS. ENGLISH. 1917

2900b. ———. 1917. (same) [Liverpool, 1917?]
1100p. 19½cm.
Loose signatures without title page. Lacks p. 817–832, 865–1042, 1055–1088.
USlC

2900c. ———. 1917. (same) Third electrotype edition. Printed and Published by George F. Richards . . . 1917.
2p.l., 503p.
UPB

2901. ———. 1918. (same) Salt Lake City, The Deseret News, Printers and Publishers, 1918.
549p. 18cm.
Same duplication of p. [493]–494.
Also a new and revised concordance by Joseph B. Keeler, p. [493]–549.
MH, UHi

2902. ———. 1919. The Doctrine and Covenants, containing revelations given to Joseph Smith with an introduction and historical and exegetical notes by Hyrum M. Smith of the Council of the Twelve Apostles. Divided into verses by Orson Pratt, Sen. Liverpool, Printed and Published by George F. Richards, 1919.
vii, 1100p. 19cm.
UHi, USlC

2903. ———. 1920. (same as 1912) Third Electrotype edition. Liverpool, Printed and Published by George Albert Smith, 1920.
2p.l., 503p. 16cm.
A reprint on smaller paper of the triple combination of 1912.
Leaf between p. 492 and the index contains the Official Declaration of 1890.
Sabin 83207
USlC

2904. ———. 1921. The Doctrine and Covenants of the Church of Jesus Christ of Latter-day Saints; containing revelations given to Joseph Smith, the prophet, with some additions by his successors in the presidency of the church. Salt Lake City, The Church of Jesus Christ of Latter-day Saints, 1921.
ix, 312p. 19cm.
"First published in double-column pages, with present chapter headings, revised foot-note references, and index, in 1921."
Printed by W. B. Conkey Co., Hammond, Ind. Also printed as part of a triple combination and a double combination.
Sabin 83208
CSmH, CU, DLC, USlC, UU, ViU

2905. ———. 1922. (same) Salt Lake City, Church of Jesus Christ of Latter-day Saints, 1922.
ix, 312p. 13×19cm.
A re-issue of the 1921 edition.
Sabin 83209
USlC

2906. ———. 1923. (same) Salt Lake City, The Church of Jesus Christ of Latter-day Saints, 1923.
ix, 312p. 20cm.
Also issued as part of the triple combination in limp leather.
Sabin 83211
CSmH, NjP, NN, OO, ULA, USlC

2907. ———. 1923. (same as 1919, under title) The Doctrine and Covenants containing revelations given to Joseph Smith, Jr., the Prophet. With an introduction and exegetical notes, by Hyrum M. Smith of the Council of the Twelve Apostles and Janne M. Sjodahl. Salt Lake City, Deseret Book Co., 1923.
vii [3]–1100p. 19½cm.
Cover-title: Doctrine and Covenants commentary.
UHi, USlC

2908. ———. 1925. (same as 1921) Salt Lake City, The Church of Jesus Christ of Latter-day Saints, 1925.
ix, 312p. 17cm.
USlC has copies of this edition, bound with and without the *Pearl of Great Price*.
Sabin 83213
NN, UPB, USlC

2909. ———. 1926. (same) Salt Lake City, The Church of Jesus Christ of Latter-day Saints, 1926.
ix, 312p. 16cm.
Published in a triple combination.
USlC

2910. ———. 1927. (same as 1919) Salt Lake City, The Deseret News, 1927.
1100p. 19½cm.
UU

2911. ———. 1928. (same as 1921) Salt Lake City, The Church of Jesus Christ of Latter-day Saints, 1926.
ix, 312p. 16cm.
Published in a triple combination.
USlC

2912. ———. 1929. (same) Salt Lake City, Church of Jesus Christ of Latter-day Saints, 1929.
ix, 312p. 18cm.
A re-issue of the 1921 primary edition, double combination.
Lambert

2913. Doctrine and Covenants. English. Selections. 1841. Revelations. [Nauvoo, Ill.? 1841?]
10p. 22cm.
Includes Doctrine and Covenants, Section 103 (formerly 101) and material from *Lectures on Faith.*
USlC

2913a. ———. 1921. Fourteen revelations reprinted from the Book of Commandments; being the only ones in that book which came through the Urim and

Thummim, by which the Nephite Record was translated. Salt Lake City, Pub. by the Church of Christ, 1921.
43p. 15cm.
Cover-title.
UHi

2914. ———. 1930. Latter-day revelation; selections from the book of Doctrine and Covenants of the Church of Jesus Christ of Latter-day Saints, containing revelations given through Joseph Smith, the Prophet. Salt Lake City, The Church of Jesus Christ of Latter-day Saints, 1930.
vii, 176p. 17½cm.
Preface explains why only fourteen revelations were used.
DLC, NN, UHi, USl, USlC, UU

2914a. ———. Section 59. English. Behold, blessed saith the Lord, are they who have come up unto this land with an eye single to my glory, according to my commandments: . . . [Kirtland, 1834?]
Broadside. 24½×18cm.
USlC

2915. ———. Section 76. English. A vision. [Plano, Ill., Printed and Published by the Reorganized Church of Jesus Christ of Latter Day Saints, n.d.]
4p. 22cm. (No. 29)
USlC

2916. ———. (same) [Lamoni, Ia., Reorganized Church of Jesus Christ of Latter Day Saints, 189–?]
[4]p. 22cm. (No. 29)
Caption-title.
MoInRC, NN, UPB, USlC, WHi

2916a. ———. Section 88. English. 1834. Verily, thus saith the Lord unto you, who have assembled yourselves together to receive his will concerning you. . . . [Kirtland, 1834?]
[2]p. 32cm.
Printed in Kirtland before the publication of the 1835 *Doctrine & Covenants.*
Includes Section 89 on p. 2.
In double columns.
UPB

2917. ———. Section 89. English. 1833. Word of wisdom. Revelation given through Joseph, the Seer, at Kirtland, Geauga County, Ohio, February 27th, 1833. (Doctrine and Covenants. Section 89) [Salt Lake City, Deseret Sunday School Union, n.d.]
[1]l. 17½×11½cm.
MoInRC, WHi

2918. ———. 1928. The Word of wisdom. Revelation to Joseph Smith, the Prophet, given February 27, 1833 . . . [n.p., after 1928]
folded card. 10cm.
Includes the revelation and some statistics taken from the *League of Nations International Yearbook* for 1928, included to show the beneficial effects of the Word of wisdom.
USlC

2919. ———. 1930. The Word of wisdom. [Dresden, Missions of the Church of Jesus Christ of Latter-day Saints (Mormon) Kruegar & Horn, 1930?]
Folder. 11½cm.
UHi

2920. ———. (same, in German) Das wort der Wersheit [Dresden, Missionen der Kirche Jesu Christi der Heiligen der Letzten Tage (Mormonen) Kruegar & Horn, 1930?]
Folder. 11½cm.
UHi

2920a. ———. Section 101. English. 1834. Verily, I say unto you, concerning your brethren who have been afflicted, and persecuted, and cast out from the land of their inheritance. . . . [Kirtland, 1834?]
[2]p. 32cm.
Printed in Kirtland before the publication of the 1835 *Doctrine & Covenants.*
In double columns.
UPB

2921. ———. Section 109. English. 1836. Prayer, at the dedication of the Lord's House in Kirtland, Ohio, March 27, 1836, — By Joseph Smith, jr. President of the Church of the Latter Day Saints. [Kirtland, 1836]
Broadside. 31×20cm.
MoInRC, USlC

2922. Doctrine and Covenants. Danish. 1852. Laerdommens og pagtens bog for Jesu Christi Kirke af Sidste Dages Hellige. Samlet udaf guds aabenbaringer af Joseph Smith, Praesident. Oversat fra anden engelske udgave. Kjöbenhavn, Udgivet og forlagt af Erastus Snow. Trykt hos G. Trier, 1852.
[6] 318p. 16cm.
First Danish edition. Translated by Miss Matheisen and checked by E.S. and Peter O. Hansen.
Sabin 83215
MH, NjP, USlC

2923. ———. 1854. (same) Andet Oplag. Kjöbenhavn, Udgivet og Forlagt af J. Van Cott. Trykt hos F. E. Bording, 1854.
[6] 318p. 17cm.
Sabin 83216
USlC

2924. ———. 1856. (same) Tredie Oplag. Kjöbenhavn, Udgivet og forlagt af H. C. Haight. Trykt hos F. E. Bording, 1856.
LXXXI [1]l., 242p. (i.e. 342p.) 15½cm.
p. 327–342 numbered 227–242.
USlC, UPB

2925. ———. 1864. (same) Fjerde Oplag. Kjöbenhavn, Udgivet og Forlagt af C. Widerborg. Trykt hos F. E. Bording, 1864.
LXXXI [2] 318 [2] 321–344p. 16cm.
"Index" p. 321–44. Same error in numbering as above.
Lectures on faith added to this edition.
Sabin 83217
NjP, UHi, UPB, USIC

2926. ———. 1873. (same) Femte Oplag. Kjöbenhavn, Udgivet og Forlagt af C. G. Larsen. Trykt hos F. E. Bording, 1873.
LXXXI [2] 348p. 16cm.
Sabin 83218
MH, UHi, UPB, USIC, UU

2927. ———. 1900. Laerdommens og pagtens bog for Jesu Kristi Kirke af Sidste Dages Hellige; indeholdende Guds Aabenbaringer til profeten Joseph Smith, for Guds Riges Opbyggelse i de Sidste Dage. Indelt i vers med henvisninger af Orson Pratt. Revideret og tildels oversat af Anthon H. Lund. Salt Lake City, Forlagt af Deseret News, 1900.
2p.l., 528p. 17½cm.
Sabin 83219
NjP, UHi, ULA, USIC, UU

2928. Doctrine and Covenants. Dutch. 1908. Het Boek der Leer en Verbonden van de Kerk van Jezus Christus van de Heiligen der Laatste Dagen, Bevattende de openbaringen aan den profeet Joseph Smith, Jr., voor de oplouwing van het koninkrijk Gods in de Laatste Dagen. Uit het Engelsch vertaald door H. De Brij Fz. met medewerking van Sylvester Q. Cannon. Eerste Nederlandsche Uitgave. Uitgegeven door Sylvester Q. Cannon, Rotterdam, 1908.
2p.l., 547 [3]p. 17cm.
Sabin 83220
NjP, UHi, UPB, USIC

2929. ———. 1929. (same)
Lambert lists copies of the 1929 edition with pages 177–192 (1 signature) re-translated. No indication if there was a new title page.
No copy located

2930. Doctrine and Covenants. French. Selections. 1908. Les doctrines et alliances de l'Église de Jésus-Christ des Saints des Derniers Jours, contenant les révélations données a Joseph Smith Fils, le Prophète pour l'Édification du royaume de Dieu aux derniers jours. Traduit de l'anglais par A.-A. Ramseyer. Zurick, Serge F. Ballif, Editeur, 1908.
1p.l., 166p. 14½cm.
Sabin 83221
UHi, UPB, USIC, UU

2931. Doctrine and Covenants. German. 1876. Das Buch der Lehre und Bündnisse der Kirche Jesu Christi der Heiligen der letzten Tage, Zusammengestellt aus den Offenbarungen Gottes von Präsident Joseph Smith. Aus dem Englischen übersetzt von Heinrich Eyring. Herausgegeben von J. U. Stucki, Bern, 1876.
XXII [1]l. 370p. 15½cm.
Sabin 83222
UHi, UPB, USIC

2932. ———. 1893. Das Buch der Lehre und Bündnisse der Kirche Jesu Christi der Heiligen der letzten Tage, welches die Offenbarungen enthält dem Propheten Joseph Smith, jun., gegeben nebst einem Anhange von Offenbarungen der Präsidentschaft der Kirche Jesu Christi, ertheilt. Aus dem Englischen übersetzt von Heinrich Eyring. . . . Stereotype-Ausgebe der Deseret News Publishing Company, Salt Lake City, 1893.
2p.l., 516p. 18½cm.
Sabin 83223
NjP, NN, UHi, ULA, UPB, USI, USIC, UU

2933. ———. 1903. (same) Dritte Auflage. Herausgegeben von Hugh J. Cannon, Berlin, 1903.
2p.l., 516p. 18½cm.
Sabin 83223
A reprint of this edition was printed in 1920. Published at Basel by Henry Eyring.
UHi, UPB, USI, USIC

2934. ———. 1923. Lehre und Bündnisse der Kirche Jesu Christi der Heiligen der letzten Tage. Enthält Offenbarungen, die dem Profeten Joseph Smith gegeben wurden nebst einigen Zusätzen seiner Nachfolger in der Präsidentschaft der Kirche. Vierte deutsche Auflage. Herausgegeben von Fred Tadje . . . Basel, 1923.
VIII [1] 359p. 18½cm.
Sabin 83225
DLC, UPB, USIC

2935. ———. 1929. (same) Fünfte Deutsche Auflage. Basel, Dresden, Schweizerisch-Deutschen und Deutsch-Österreichischen Mission, 1929.
VIII[1] 359p. 18cm.
UU

2936. Doctrine and Covenants. Hawaiian. 1893. Ka Buke o na Berita a me na Kauoha a ka Ekalesia o Iesu Karisto no na Poe Hoano a na La Hope. Wae Akaheleia mai na olelo Hoike mai a ke Akua a Hoonohoia ma na Manawa o ko Lakou Haawiia ana. Honolulu, Hawaiian Gazette Electric Press, 1893.
422p. 18½cm.
Sabin 83226
MoInRC, UHi, UPB

2937. ———. 1914. Na Berita a me na Kauoha o ka Ekalesia o Iesu Kristo o ka Poe Hoano o na La Hope nei, i haawi ia ia Iosepa Kamika, Opio, ke Kaula, no ke Kukulu ana i ke Aupuni o ke Akua ma na La Hope Nei. Unuhi ia mai ka olelo Beritania a i ka olelo Hawaii a hoopuka ia e ka Misiona Hawaii o ka Ekalesia o Iesu Kristo o ka Poe Hoano o na La Hope

nei. Honolulu, T. H. Paiia ma ka hale pai Hawaiian Gazette Co., Ltd., 1914.
1p.l., 533p. 16½cm.
Sabin 83227
UHi, UPB, USlC

2938. Doctrine and Covenants. Maori. 1919. Ko nga Akoranga me nga Kawenata o te Hahi o Ihu Karaiti o te Hunga Tapu o nga Ra o Muri nei me nga whakakitenga i homai ki a Hohepa Mete, Tamaiti, te Poropiti, mo te Hanganga o te Kingitanga o te Atua i nga ra Whakamutunga. He mea panui na Hemi Nitama Ramapata mo te Hahi o Ihu Karaiti o te Hunga Tapu o nga Ra o Muri nei. Akarana, Niu Tereni, 1919.
1p.l. [3]–444p. 19cm.
Sabin 83228
UHi, UPB, USlC

2939. Doctrine and Covenants. Spanish. Selections. 1887. Extractos del libro Doctrina y Convenios de la Iglesia de Jesu-Cristo de los Santos de los Ultimos Dias; el cual libro contene las revelaciones dadas a Joseph Smith Jun., El Profeta. Traducidos del Ingles por los Elders Horacio Cummings y Fernando A. Lara. Mexico, 1887.
33p. 18cm.
USlC

2940. Doctrine and Covenants. Swedish. 1888. Lärdomens och Förbundets Bok. Innehållande Uppenbarelser, gifna åt Jesu Kristi Kyrka af Sista Dagarnas Heliga genom Profeten Joseph Smith D. Y. För uppbyggandet af Guds rike i de yttersta dagarna. Indelad i vers af Orson Pratt D. Ä. Öfversaat på Svenska af J. M. Sjödahl. Salt Lake City, Förlagt af "Deseret News" Co., 1888.
vii, 487 [1]p. 18cm.
Contains revelations of 1882, 1883 by John Taylor.
Sabin 83229
NjP, NN, UHi, ULA, UPB, USl, USlC

2941. ———. 1928. (same) Andra Genomsedda Upplagan. Stockholm, Utgiven och förlagd av Gideon N. Hulterström, 1928.
xix, 310p. 20cm.
NjP, UHi, UPB, USlC, UU

2942. Doctrine and Covenants. Welsh. 1851. Llyfr athrawiaeth a chyfammodau perthynol i eglwys Iesu Grist o Saint y Dyddiau Diweddaf; a gasglwyd o ddadguddiadau duw. Gan Joseph Smith, Llywydd. Wedi ei gyfieithu o'r ail argraffaid Ewropaidd gan John Davis. Merthyr-Tydfil, Cyhoeddwyd ac ar Werth gan J. Davis, Georgetown; ar werth hefyd Gan y Saint yn gyffredinol, a llawer o Lyfrwerthwyr, trwy y Deau a'r Gogledd. 1851.
xvi, 304p. 13cm.
Sabin 83231
MiU, MH, NjP, UPB, USl, USlC, UU

2943. Doctrine and Covenants (Reorganized Church) English. 1864. Book of Doctrine and Covenants of the Church of Jesus Christ of Latter-Day Saints. Carefully selected from the revelations of God, and given in the order of their dates. Cincinnati, Printed by the Publishing Committee of the Reorganized Church of Jesus Christ of Latter-Day Saints, 1864.
vi, 335p. 16cm.
First edition of the *Doctrine and Covenants* published by the RLDS church. It was recommended by the General Conference, October 6–9, 1863. Includes revelations from 1828 to 1842.
Sabin 83160
DLC, MH, MoInRC, NN, OClWHi, OFH, UPB, USlC, UU, WHi

2944. ———. 1880. (same) Lamoni, Ia., Printed by the Board of Publication of the Reorganized Church of Latter Day Saints, 1880.
vi, 341p. 15½cm.
A reprint of the 1864 edition, with a new title page, and revelations since the Reorganization.
Sabin 83166
MH, MoInRC, UU

2945. ———. 1880 (1882?) (same) Lamoni, Ia., Printed by the Board of Publication of the Reorganized Church of Jesus Christ of Latter Day Saints, 1880 [1882?]
vi, 352p. 16cm.
Revelations included in the 1880 edition plus a revelation of September 28, 1882, numbered as section 118. Other copies include section 119–121.
Sabin 83168
MoInRC, UPB, USlC, UU

2946. ———. 1894. (same) Lamoni, Ia., Published by the Reorganized Church of Jesus Christ of Latter Day Saints, 1894.
vi, 359p. 17cm.
Addition of Sections 122, 123.
Sabin 83175
MoInRC

2947. ———. 1896. (same) Lamoni, Ia., Published by the Reorganized Church of Jesus Christ of Latter Day Saints, 1896.
vi, 359p. 16cm.
MoInRC

2948. ———. 1897. (same) Lamoni, Ia., Printed by the Board of Publication, of the Reorganized Church of Jesus Christ of Latter Day Saints, 1897.
6, 385, 32p. 18½cm.
Concordance and reference guide to the "Book of Doctrine and Covenants" 32p. at end.
Addition of Section 124.
Sabin 83176
DLC, IWW, MoInRC, UHi

DOCTRINE AND COVENANTS (RLDS) ENGLISH. 1900

2949. ———. **1900.** (same) Twenty fifth edition. Lamoni, Ia. [Herald Publishing House] 1900.
6, 394, 32p. 16cm.
First numbered edition. Numbering seems to continue from earlier pre-Reorganization editions and printings of the earlier RLDS editions.
UHi

2950. ———. **1901.** (same) Twenty sixth edition. Lamoni, Ia., Printed by the Board of Publication of the Reorganized Church of Jesus Christ of Latter Day Saints, 1901.
6, 391p. 16cm.
Addition of Section 125, printed separately as a supplement and included in the printing.
MoInRC

2951. ———. **1902.** (same) Twenty seventh edition. Lamoni, Ia., Printed by the Board of Publication of the Reorganized Church of Jesus Christ of Latter Day Saints, 1902.
6, 394, 32p. 16cm.
Addition of Section 126, printed separately as well as added to this printing.
MoInRC, UPB

2952. ———. **1903.** (same) Twenty eighth edition. Lamoni, Ia., Printed by the Board of Publication of the Reorganized Church of Jesus Christ of Latter Day Saints, 1903.
6, 394p. 16cm.
MoInRC

2953. ———. **1904.** (same) Twenty ninth edition. Lamoni, Ia., Printed by the Board of Publication of the Reorganized Church of Jesus Christ of Latter Day Saints, 1904.
2, 394, 32p. 17cm.
CSmH, MoInRC, OCl, USlC

2954. ———. **1904.** (same) Thirtieth edition. Lamoni, Ia., Printed by the Board of Publication of the Reorganized Church of Jesus Christ of Latter Day Saints, 1904.
6, 394, 32p. 17cm.
MoInRC

2955. ———. **1905.** (same) Thirty first edition. Lamoni, Ia., Printed by the Board of Publication of the Reorganized Church of Jesus Christ of Latter Day Saints, 1905.
6, 397, 32p. 16cm.
Addition of Section 127.
Sabin 83187
MoInRC

2956. ———. **1906.** (same) Thirty second edition. Lamoni, Ia., Printed by the Board of Publication of the Reorganized Church of Jesus Christ of Latter Day Saints, 1906.
6, 397, 32p. 16½cm.
Sabin 83190
MoInRC, ULA

2957. ———. **1907.** (same) Lamoni, Ia., Printed by the Board of Publication of the Reorganized Church of Jesus Christ of Latter Day Saints [1907?]
6, 397, 32p. 17cm.
Edition not dated, but includes the additions of 1906. Printed in 1907 or 1908.
Sabin 83191
MoInRC, ULA

2958. ———. **1909.** (same) Lamoni, Ia., Printed by the Board of Publication of the Reorganized Church of Jesus Christ of Latter Day Saints [1909?]
6, 404, 32p. 17½cm.
Addition of p. 397–404. Sections 128–129. Probably the last edition from the 1897 plates with additions.
Sabin 83195
MoInRC, UHi

2959. ———. **1911.** (same) Lamoni, Ia., Printed by the Board of Publication of the Reorganized Church of Jesus Christ of Later Day Saints, 1911.
294, 60p. 18cm.
Concordance at end of text.
Printed from new electrotype plates, including revelations through 1909.
Supplementary leaves of Sections 130–133 were printed in 1913, 1914, 1916, 1920 and laid into the MoInRC copy.
Sabin 83199
MoInRC, NN

2960. ———. **1913.** (same) Lamoni, Ia., Printed by the Board of Publication of the Reorganized Church of Jesus Christ of Latter Day Saints, 1913.
296, 60p. 19cm.
A reissue from the 1911 plates, with addition of Section 130.
Sabin 83202
IWW, MoInRC, MoK, OCl, USlC

2961. ———. **1917.** (same) Lamoni, Ia., Printed by the Board of Publication of the Reorganized Church of Jesus Christ of Latter Day Saints, 1917.
299, 60p. 18cm.
Reissue from the 1911 plates with addition of Section 130, 131, 132.
MoInRC

2962. ———. **1919.** (same) Lamoni, Ia., Printed by the Board of Publication of the Reorganized Church of Jesus Christ of Latter Day Saints, 1919.
299, 60p. 18cm.
Addition of Section 132.
Sabin 83206
MoInRC

2963. ———. **1922.** (same) [Lamoni, Ia.?] Printed by the Board of Publication of the Reorganized Church of Jesus Christ of Latter Day Saints, 1922.
299, 60p. 18cm.
Addition of Sections 132–133.
MoInRC

2964. ———. **1922.** (same) [Lamoni, Ia.?] Printed by the Board of Publication of the Reorganized Church of Jesus Christ of Latter Day Saints, 1922.
300, [4] 60p. 17cm.
Addition of Section 134.
MoInRC

2965. ———. **1923.** (same) Independence, Mo., Printed by the Board of Publication of the Reorganized Church of Jesus Christ of Latter Day Saints, 1923.
300, [4] 60p. 18½cm.
UPB

2966. ———. **1925.** (same) Independence, Mo., Printed by the Board of Publication of the Reorganized Church of Jesus Christ of Latter Day Saints, 1925.
301, [4]p. 17cm.
Addition of Section 135.
Sabin 83212
OClW

2967. ———. **1927.** (same) Independence Mo., Board of Publication of the Reorganized Church of Jesus Christ of Latter Day Saints, 1927.
301, 30p. 18cm.
MoInRC, UU

2968. Doctrine and Covenants (Reorganized Church) Tahitian. 1904. Buka no te Parau Haapii e te mau parau Fafau. I maiti-maite-hia na roto mai i te mau hereuraa a te Atua e ua faaaforahia i roto i teienei buka, mai te au i te mahana i fariihia mai ai. Na te Etaretia a Iesu Mesia no te Feia Mo'a i faaapihia, no te mau Mahana Hopea nei. I iritihia teienei buka ei parau Tahiti e Isaac S. Henry, mai roto mai i te buka o tei neneihia i Lamoni, Iowa, i te Matahiti 1897. Papeete, Tahiti, I neneihi e C. Brault. I te fare neneiraa no teienei anotau api, 1904.
vii, 368p. 16½cm.
UPB

2969. The Doctrine and Covenants. [n.p., n.d.]
Broadside. 20½×12½cm.
Text within ornamental border.
NjP, UPB, USlC

Doctrines of Mormonism. *See Religious Tract Society.*

2970. The doctrines of the Latter-day Saints, or Mormonites. [Hereford, England, R. Elliot, Printer, 1847?]
8p. 17½cm.
Might have been written by R. Elliot.
USlC

2971. Dodds, Peter Fabian. Mormonism, a serio-comic poem, by Peter F. Dodds. Mt. Pleasant, Mich., Northwestern Tribune, 1890.
[15]p. 20½cm.
A satiric poem.
DLC

2972. Dodge, Grenville Mellen. Biographical sketch of James Bridger; mountaineer, trapper and guide, by Major Gen'l Grenville M. Dodge. [Kansas City, R. M. Rigby Printing Co., 1904?]
[18]p., [1]l., plate, port. 23cm.
Cover-title.
Tells of Bridger's association with the Mormons.
Another edition: New York, Unz and Co., 1905.
NjP, USlC, UPB
Howes D-392 [1905]
DLC, NjP, OClWHi, OFH

2973. Domenech, Emmanuel Henri Dieudonné. Seven years residence in the great deserts of North America, by the Abbe Emmanuel Domenech . . . Illustrated with fifty-eight woodcuts by A. Jobet, three plates of ancient Indian music, and a map showing the actual situation of the Indian tribes and the country described by the author. London, Longman, Green, Longman and Roberts, 1860.
2v. fronts., col. plates, fold. map. 22cm.
Includes an analysis of Mormonism.
Other editions: 2d ed., London, 1869. USlC; French: Voyage pittoresque dans les grands deserts du nouveau monde. Paris, Libraire Classique et d'education [1860?] UHi, UPB; Paris, Morizot, Libraire-Editeur, 1862. UHi
Howes D 410, Sabin 20554, W-C 356a
CtY, CU-B, DLC, ICN, NjP, NN, UHi, ULA, USlC, UU

Donaghe, M. Virginia. Pictorial reflex of Salt Lake City. *See Savage, Charles R.*

2974. Donan, Patrick. Utah; a peep into a mountain walled treasury of the gods. By P. Donan. Rhymes by Cy. Warman . . . [Buffalo, N. Y., Matthews, Northrup Co., c1891]
96p. illus., ports., maps. 24cm.
Includes Mormon history.
Published in connection with the Rio Grande Western Railway.
CSmH, CU-B, DLC, MH, NN, UHi, ULA, UPB, USl, USlC, UU

2975. ———. (same) Buffalo, N.Y., Matthews, Northrup Co., c1895.
96p. illus., ports., maps. 24cm.
NjP, USlC

2976. ———. (same) [Buffalo, N.Y., Matthews, Northrup Co., 1900]
96p. illus. 22½cm.
CU, DLC, NjP, UPB

2977. Done, Willard. Distinctiveness of the true Church; address delivered over Radio Station KSL, Sunday evening, April 29, 1928. [Salt Lake City] 1928.
Broadside. 61×25cm.
Reprinted from the *Deseret News*, Saturday, May 5, 1928.
UPB

2978. ———. The Sacrament of the Lord's supper; address delivered over Radio Station KSL, Sunday Evening, August 28, 1927. [Salt Lake City] 1927.
Broadside. 57×25cm.
Reprinted from the *Deseret News*.
UPB

2979. ———. Women of the Bible. A series of story and character sketches of the great women who have aided in making Bible history. Salt Lake City, 1900.
224p. illus. 20cm.
ULA, USlC, WHi

2980. Y Doniau ysbrydol ym mrawdlys y gelyn; yn cynnwys sylwadau ar ysgrifau "sylwedydd o'r gogledd," yn seren gomer (1 Hydref, 1848) hyd chwefror 1849, ynghylch y "Doniau ysbrydol." Gan olygydd "Udgorn Seion." Merthyr-Tydfil, Argraffwyd ac ar Werth Gan. J. Davis, Georgetown . . . 1849.
24p. 18cm.
Title in English: The Spiritual gifts before their enemies' tribunal.
MH, NjP, USlC

2981. Doty, Lockwood R. History of the Genesee country (Western New York) comprising the counties of Allegany, Cattaraugus, Chautauqua, Chemung, Er Genesee, Livingston, Monroe, Niagara, Onta Orleans, Schuyler, Steuben, Wayne, Wyoming and Yates. Chicago, S.J. Clarke, 1925.
2v. illus. 28cm.
Wayne County and Palmyra, p. 1311–1339.
Mormons, p. 449, 561–63.
USlC

2982. Dougall, Lily. The Mormon prophet, by Lily Dougall . . . New York, D. Appleton and Company, 1899.
x, 427p. 19cm.
A novel dealing with Joseph Smith and Mormonism.
CSmH, CU-B, DLC, ICN, MH, MoInRC, NjP, NN, UHi, ULA, UPB, USl, USlC, UU

2983. ———. (same) London, Adam and Charles Black, 1899.
viii, 444p. 20cm.
OClWHi, UHi, USlC

2984. Douglas, Stephen Arnold. Kansas-Utah-Dred Scott decision. Speech of Hon. S. A. Douglas, delivered at Springfield, Illinois, June 12, 1856. Springfield [Ill.] Lanphier and Walker Printers, 1857.
14p. 21½cm.
Speech against polygamy as well as slavery.
CSmH, IHi, MH, PHi

2985. ———. Remarks of the Hon. Stephen A. Douglas on Kansas, Utah and the Dred Scott decision. Delivered at Springfield, Ill., June 12th, 1857. Chicago, Printed at the Daily Times Book and Job Office, 1857.
15p. 24cm.
CtY, DLC, MnH, OClWHi, ViU-L

2986. Dove, George S. Roll of membership. Names of persons baptized into the fulness of the gospel. [San Francisco?] Published by Geo. S. Dove and Co., 1886.
8p. 18cm.
Publication of the Church of the Firstborn.
MoInRC

2987. ———. A voice from the West to the scattered people of Weber and all the seed of Abraham. San Francisco, Jos. A. Dove, 1879.
40 [2]p. 21½cm.
Signed: George S. Dove, James Dove, Elizabeth Hughes, Scribe.
CU-B, NN, USlC

2988. Dove, James. Articles of faith: Published by Committee of the Church of the First-born. Organized in San Francisco, California, July 2nd, 1876 . . . San Francisco, 1887.
16p. 15cm. (Tract No. 3)
USlC

2989. ———. A few items in the history of the Morrisites . [San Francisco, Published by the order of the Committee of the Church of the Firstborn, 1890?]
20p. 15cm.
USlC

2990. ———. Joseph Morris' crowns . . . [San Francisco, James Dove & Co., 1879?]
Broadside. 21½×14½cm.
A book mark, printed in gold, red & blue with various crowns of men in the church.
Advertisement for "A voice from the West."
CtY

2991. ———. The man of sin in the old and new church. By James Dove. [San Francisco, Don & Taylor, Printers, 1893]
51p. 15cm.
USlC

2992. ———. Present knowledge and past revealments combined. San Francisco, Published by James Dove, 1884.
38 [2]p. 14½cm.
MoInRC, USlC

2993. ———. The resurrection by regeneration compared with a resurrection from the grave. Published by James Dove, San Francisco, J. A. Dove, Printer, 1891.
44p. 16½cm.
NN

2994. ———. A treatise on the priesthood by spiritual birthright; reprobation and election. Published by James Dove, San Francisco, J. A. Dove and Co., Printers, 1891.
58 [1]p. 17cm.
Poem "Toiling On" by Eliza A. Pittsinger on recto of back cover.
NN

2995. ———. A treatise on re-incarnation or re-embodiment. Published by James Dove, San Francisco, Dove & Taylor, Printers, 1892.
46p. 17½cm.
Re-incarnation or The Song of Eve., by Eliza A. Pittsinger, p. 41.
CLU, NN

2996. The downfall of the Mormonites and Brigham Young. [n.p., 185?]
Broadside. 24½×6½cm.
A poem cut in two sections from a larger piece, pasted together to form a narrow strip.
CtY

2997. Doyle, Arthur Conan. Our second American adventure, by Sir Arthur Conan Doyle . . . London, Hodder and Stroughton Ltd. [1924]
3p.l., 250p. plates, 2 ports. 22cm.
Lecture in Salt Lake City; visits meetings; impressions of Mormonism. A long account on the Book of Mormon story.
Another edition: Boston, Little, Brown, and Co. 1924. DLC
NN, OC

2998. ———. A study in scarlet. London, Ward, Lock & Co., 1888.
169p. 22cm.
First published in *Beeton's Christmas annual.* Twenty-Eighth season, 1887.
A Mormon Danite story. First Sherlock Holmes adventure.
Reprinted in many editions.
DLC

2999. Doyle, Sherman Hoadley. Presbyterian home missions; an account of the home missions of the Presbyterian church in the U.S.A., by Sherman H. Doyle . . . Philadelphia, Presbyterian board of Publication and Sabbath-school Work, 1902.
xiv, 318p. plates, maps. 20cm.
Chap. V, p. 137–165. Account of the history and doctrines of Mormonism and the need for missionary work in Utah.
Other editions: 1904. NjP; 1905. DLC, UPB
DLC, NjPT, UPB

3000. Drake, Francis W. [A letter written by the author to a friend at Blue Earth, Minn., concerning Salt Lake City and the Mormons, published in the Blue Earth Post] [Blue Earth, Minn.? Blue Earth Post? 1917?]
[12]p. 22½cm.
Title supplied. Copy begins with the letter and followed by columns from the paper.
USlC

3001. Drake, Samuel Adams. The making of the great West; 1512–1833, by Samuel Adams Drake. New York, C. Scribner's Sons, 1887.
xii p., [1]l., 339p. illus. 19½cm. (His Stories of American history for young readers)
"The Mormons in Utah," with other references.
Other editions: London, 1887. USlC; London, Gibbings & Company, Ltd., 1894. DLC; New York, Charles Scribner's Sons, 1894, NjP
UPB

3002. Drannan, William F. Thirty-one years on the plains and in the mountains; or, The last voice from the plains. An authentic record of a life time of hunting, trapping, scouting and Indian fighting in the far West, by Capt. William F. Drannan . . . Copiously illustrated by H. S. De Lay . . . Chicago, Rhodes & McClure Publishing Company [1900]
1 p.l. [7]–586p. illus., plates, ports. 20cm.
Reference to Mormons slaughtering Indians, p. 362–364. "Spies among the Mormons," p. 364–370.
Other editions: Chicago, Thos. W. Jackson Publishing Co. [c1900] NjP, USlC; Chicago, Rhodes & McClure, 1910. CU–B, ULA
DLC, UHi, UU

3003. Draper, Elias Johnson. An autobiography of Elias J. Draper, a pioneer of California; containing some thrilling incidents relative to crossing the plains by ox team, and some very interesting particulars of life in California in the early days. Fresno, Evening Democrat Print. 1904.
1p.l., 7–76p. port. 21cm.
Overland journey via Salt Lake in 1853, 1858, with other references to Mormons and Brigham Young in 1858.
Howes D 484
CU–B

3004. Draper, John S. Shams; or, Uncle Ben's experience with hypocrites. A story of simple country life giving a humorous and entertaining picture of every day life and incidents in the rural districts, with Uncle Ben's trip to the city of Chicago and to California, and his experience with the shams and sharpers of the Metropolitan World, by John S. Draper, otherwise, Uncle Ben Morgan, of Morganville, N.Y. Chicago, National Book and Picture Co. [c1887]
xv [11]–412p. illus. 21½cm.
Ten days in Salt Lake City, p. 297–312. He was impressed with the Tabernacle but was told that people in the middle seats couldn't hear a word. He was convinced that money was the mainspring of the

church; that leaders never intended to finish the Temple but keep building and getting money from the faithful forever.

Other editions: Philadelphia, John E. Potter & Co., Ltd. [c1887] NjP; Chicago, Thompson & Thomas [c1899] USlC; Chicago, C. C. Thompson Co. [c1899] USlC

CU–B, USlC, UU

3005. Draper, John William. Thoughts on the future civil policy of America, by John William Draper. New York, Harper & Brothers, Publishers, 1865.

vii [9]–317p. 21cm.

"Detestation" of the practice of polygamy despite its temptations. It might spread in America.

Another edition: 1875. CU–B

NjP, USlC

3006. Dreiser, Theodore. A gallery of women. New York, Horace Liveright, 1929.

2v. 19½cm.

Fiction. Includes "Olive Brand," Story of a Mormon girl.

CU, DLC, NjP, UPB

3007. Dresser, Norman B. Millard County ballads and other verse by Norman B. Dresser. Illustrated. Printed by the author. Salt Lake City, 1914.

[38]l. port., plates. 22cm.

Mormon poetry: Millard County, and other historical and religious poems.

USlC

3008. Drew, John. My years on the stage, by John Drew: with a foreword by Booth Tarkington. New York, E. P. Dutton & Company [c1922]

xii p., [1]l., 242p. illus., plates, ports., facsims. 23cm.

An unprofitable visit with Brigham Young; he was too old and feeble to get material as Artemus Ward did.

CU, DLC, NjP, USlC

3009. The Drift of the times. Sound the alarm. Mormonism! A political, social, and religious ulcer. Kansas City, Mo. [Gospel Union Publishing Company, n.d.]

8p. 13cm. (G.M.U. No. 543)

USlC

3010. Driggs, Benjamin Woodbury. History of Teton Valley, Idaho, by B. W. Driggs. Caldwell, Id., The Caxton Printers, Ltd., 1926.

227p. plates. 24cm.

Mormon colonies near Teton Creek, p. 145–148, 161–164.

CU, MH, NjP, NN, UHi, UPB, USlC, UU

3011. Driggs, Howard Roscoe. Art of teaching; a teachers training course, designed for quorum instructors and auxiliary class of teachers of church of Latter-day Saints. Salt Lake City, General Board of Auxiliary Organizations of the Church, 1919.

121p. 20½cm.

CU–B, NjP, ULA, UPB, USl, USlC, UU

3012. ———. Wild roses; a tale of the Rockies, by Howard R. Driggs. Chicago and Lincoln, University Publishing Company [c1916]

4p.l., 248p., [1]l. front. 20cm.

History of the Mormons made into fiction.

DLC, NjP, UHi, UPB, USlC, UU

3013. Driggs, Jean Russell, *compiler*. The Palestine of America. [Salt Lake City, 1925]

[8]p. 2 maps. unfolded to 23×42 cm.

"Maps compiled and drawn by Jean Russell Driggs."

Book of Mormon geography.

UHi, UPB, USlC

3014. Drummond, Peter. Mormons "Only way to be saved" not the way to be saved; or, The plausible logic of Mormonism refuted. A reply to Lorensow [sic] Snow's "Only way to be saved." London, the author [1850?]

8p. 17cm. (Stirling Tracts No. 340)

A pamphlet on the L.D.S. doctrines of baptism, revelation, etc.

Partly answered in *Millennial Star*. V. 20, p. 203, 285, 342, 420.

USlC

3015. ———. (same) [Glasgow: W. G. Blackie & Co., 1854?]

8p. 17½cm. (Stirling Tracts No. 340)

NN, USlC

3016. ———. Mormonism, an imposture . . . London [185?]

For answers to some of his accusations, see *Millennial Star*, V. 19, p. 385, 476, 551, 730.

No copy located

3017 Dubois, Fred Thomas. Senator from Utah . . . Speech of Hon. Fred T. Dubois, of Idaho, in the Senate of the United States, Thursday, December 13, 1906. Washington, 1906.

57p. 22cm.

Concerning the Reed Smoot hearings.

MoInRC, UPB

3018. ———. Senator from Utah . . . Speech of Hon. Fred T. Dubois, of Idaho, in the Senate of the United States, Wednesday, February 20, 1907. Washington, 1907.

13p. 22cm.

Mormon domination and priestly rule.

CU–B, UPB

3019. Dubois, Louise. Hilton Hall; or, A thorn in the flesh . . . Salt Lake City, George Q. Cannon & Sons Co., Printers, 1898.

2p.l., [vi] vii, [9]–304p. 18½cm.

Mormon fiction.

DLC, MH, UPB, UU

3020. Dudley, Mary Elizabeth. Tangled threads; a tale of Mormonism, by M. E. Dudley. Boston, R. G. Badger, 1905.
48p. plates. 20cm.
Poetry concerning Mormonism.
CU-B, DLC, MH, NN, PPM, ULA, USIC

3021. Du Faÿ, Hortense G. Coup d'oeil sur le prophete du xix° siecle, et autres socialistes modernes; precede d'une notice sur le genie de la poesie Anglaise ... Deuxieme edition ... Paris, Chez L'Auteur, 1866.
308p. 21½cm.
Title in English: A glance at the prophet of the 19th century.
UHi

3022. ———. Le prophète du xix° siècle; ou, Vie des Saints des derniers jours (Mormons) prédédé d'un apercu sur d'autres socialistes unitaires et sur le génie de la poésie anglaise; par M*me* Hortense D. Du Faÿ ... Paris, Dentu, 1863.
215 [1]p. 22½cm.
"Extraits, par traductions littérales, des plus grand poëtes anglais, comparés aux productions des imitateurs francais ... Cette notice sur les poëtes conduit à un aperçu historique des socialistes unitaires, notamment des Mormons et de leur religion comparée à celle du vrai Christ. Le tout terminé par la profession de foi de Napoléon I." p. [2]
Title in English: The prophet of the 19th century.
CtY, CU-B, DLC, MH, NN

3023. Duff, J. G. The martyrs of Jesus, safely lodged behind the vale. Manchester, Jacques, Printer [ca. 1845]
Broadside. 25×20cm.
Text within border.
Mormon poem.
USIC

3024. Duffin, James G. The Mormon people, their true character. [Compiled and written by Elder James G. Duffin] [Kansas City, Printed for the Central States Mission of the Church of Jesus Christ of Latter-day Saints, 1903]
32p. 15cm.
Cover-title.
MoInRC, UPB

3025. ———. (same) [Kansas City, Mo., Southwestern States Mission, 1903]
32p. 15cm.
Imprint from cover.
Variant printing.
UPB, USIC

3026. ———. (same) Salt Lake City, 1905.
32p. 14cm.
USIC, UPB

3027. Duffus, Robert Luther. The Santa Fe trail, by R. L. Duffus. London, New York [etc.] Longmans, Green and Co., 1930.
xip., [1]l., 283p. plates, ports., map. 24cm.
Reference to Mormon Battalion, p. 204–212.
CU-B, DLC, NjP, UHi, ULA

3028. Duke, Thomas S. Celebrated criminal cases of America ... San Francisco, The James H. Barry Company, 1910.
xii, 657p. illus. 23½cm.
Includes the murder of Joseph Smith; Mountain Meadows massacre.
CtY, CU-B, UHi

3029. Dunbar, Edward Ely. The romance of the age; or, The discovery of gold in California. By Edward E. Dunbar. New York, D. Appleton and Company, 1867.
134p. port., 2 plates. 19cm.
The Mormons in California, p. 42–46.
CU-B, DLC, NjP, NN, PPL, PU, UHi, ULA, UPB, USIC

3030. Dunbar, Seymour. A history of travel in America, being an outline of the development in modes of travel from archaic vehicles of colonial times to the completion of the first transcontinental railroad: the influence of the Indians on the free movement and territorial unity of the white race: the part played by travel methods in the economic conquest of the continent: and those related human experiences, changing social conditions and governmental attitudes which accompanied the growth of a national travel system, by Seymour Dunbar; with two maps, twelve colored plates and four hundred illustrations. Indianapolis, Bobbs, Merrill Company [c1915]
4v. illus., col. plates, maps (2 double) facsims. 23cm.
Chapter LIII entitled "The Mormon overland pilgrimage of 1846–48 ..." p. 1237–1269, including plates.
Howes D-557
CU, NjP, NN, OCl, OClW, OCU, OU, UHi, ULA, UU, ViU

3031. Duncan Charles R. The Latter-Day Saints, who are they? [n.p., n.d.]
4p. 16cm.
RLDS missionary tract.
MoInRC, ULA

3032. Duncan, George. Mormon murders! An expose by Rev. George Duncan, D. D. [London, James Shailer, n.d.]
8p. 19cm.
USI, USIC

3033. Dundas, J. H. The better way to serve the Lord. [Auburn, Nebr., Republican Print., 1917?]

43p. 20½cm.
Sympathetic view of Mormonism.
USlC

3034. Dundass, Samuel Rutherford. Journal of Samuel Rutherford Dundass, formerly auditor of Jefferson County, Ohio, including his entire route to California as a member of the Steubenville Company bound for San Francisco, in the year 1849. Steubenville, Ohio, Printed at Conn's Job Office, 1857.
60p. 19cm.
Includes mention of the Mormon Ferry on North Platte, p. 30; a stop in Salt Lake City and an attendance at a service in the "Mormon Temple," p. 39–42; Capt. Brown's settlement, p. 42.
Howes D566, W–C 290
CU–B, NjP

3035. Die Dunkelheit gewichen. [Dresden, Deutsche-Österreische Mission, n.d.]
[4]p. 19½cm.
Title in English: The darkness is overcome.
UPB

3036. Dunlop, John I. Joseph Smith, an impostor. The substance of a lecture, delivered on Monday Evening, June 25, 1851, By John I. Dunlop. [London] Published by J. Paul, 1851.
[189]–196p. 22cm. (The Penny Pulpit. No. 1, 758)
USlC

3037. Dunn, Ballard S. How to solve the Mormon problem. Three letters by Reverend Ballard S. Dunn. New York, American News Company, 1877.
30p. 22½cm.
Cover-title.
In the form of letters "To the Editor of the Tribune" written from Salt Lake City.
DLC, ICN, MH, NN, USl, USlC, WHi

3038. ———. (same) New York, American News Company, 1877.
30p. 22½cm.
Includes a broadside supplement, 1880.
NN

3039. ———. [Letter to the New York Evening Post, on the subject of the Anti-Mormon bill, which has passed the Senate and is now before the House of Representatives. n.p., 1882]
[3]p. 23cm.
Title supplied.
NN

3040. ———. The twin monsters: and how national legislation may help to solve the Mormon problem, and restore to society, somewhat of the sacramental character of the rite of Holy Matrimony. New York [1884]
31p. 23½cm.
Sponsored by the American Institute of Christian Philosophy.
CtY, NN, UHi, UPB

3041. ———. (same) 2d ed. New York, James Pott [1884?]
31p. 21½cm.
Cover-title.
CtY, DLC, ICN, MH, ULA, WHi

3042. ———. (same) [3d ed.] New York, James Pott & Co. [1886]
31p. 23cm.
Cover-title.
CtY, DLC, OClWHi, UHi, WHi

3043. Dunn, Charles W. Exiles, pilgrims and pioneers in three parts. The messenger of truth, by Charles W. Dunn. Logan, Utah, 1925.
32p. 20½cm.
Mormon poetry.
CU–B, USlC

3044. ———. The master's other sheep; an epic of ancient America and other poems. Logan, Utah [J. P. Smith & Son] c1929.
103p. port. 20½cm.
Mormon poetry.
UU

3045. Dunn, Crandell. To seekers of the kingdom of God. [Edinburgh, 1850?]
4p. 20cm.
Caption-title.
Signed: Edinburgh, June, 1850.
A missionary tract.
USlC

3046. Dunn, Jacob Piatt. Massacres of the mountains; a history of the Indian wars of the far West, by J. P. Dunn, jr. . . . New York, Harper & Brothers, 1886.
[iii]–ix, 784p. illus., plates, ports., maps (part fold.) plans. 21½cm.
Includes the Mountain Meadows massacre.
Other editions: London, S. Low, Marston, Searle and Rivington, 1886. USlC
Howes D575
CSmH, CU–B, DLC, ICN, MH, UPB

3047. Dunn, James. Janet Dixon, the plural wife. A true story of Mormon polygamy by James Dunn. [Tooele, Utah?] 1896.
61p. 18cm.
Mormon fiction.
MH, UPB, USlC

3048. Duplessis, Paul. Les Mormons. Paris, A. Cadot, 1859.
3v. 18cm.
1858 edition listed in Bibl. Nat. Not located.
Sabin 21372
Bibl. Nat.

3049. ———. (same) Paris, Alexandré Cadot, éditeur [1859?]
5v. 21cm.
V. 3 has end of 2d part and of 3d volume, showing it was probably a reprint of 1858 edition.
Sabin 21372
MH, MOKU

3050. ———. (same) Suite der Batteur d'estrade . . . New York, C. Lassale, 1859.
319p. 25cm.
At head of title: Semaine litteraire du courrier des États-Unis.
Sabin 21372
ICN, PPL-R, PPM

3051. ———. (same) Deuxiéme édition . . . Paris, Alexandré Cadot, éditeur [1860?]
2v. in 1. 18cm.
NN, USIC

3052. ———. (same) Paris, Degorce-Cadot [186?]
220p. 29cm.
UHi

3053. Duret, Victor. L'Icarie en Amérique, d'après des documents inédits . . . Neuchatel [etc.] C. Leidecker, 1856.
31p. 20cm.
Cover-title.
The attempt to found a Icarian colony at Nauvoo, Ill., and the purchase of the remains of the Mormon temple there, p. [1]–4.
Title in English: Icarians in American.
CtY

3054. Dusenberry, Ida Smoot. Lesson book for the Religion Classes in the Church of Jesus Christ of Latter-day Saints. First grade. Written for the General Church Board of Education by Ida Smoot Dusenberry. [Salt Lake City] Published by the Deseret Book Company, 1924–25.
130p. 19cm.
UPB, USIC

3055. Duvegier de Hauranne, Ernest (i.e., Louis Prosper Ernest) Huit mois en Amérique; lettres et notes de voyage, 1864–65. Par Ernest Duvegier de Hauranne . . . Paris, Lacroix, Verboeckhouen et Cie, 1866.
2v. 18½cm.
Trip down the Mississippi from St. Paul to St. Louis. He passes Nauvoo and makes brief comment on it and the Mormons who have gone, v.1, p. 247–48.
Title in English: Eight months in America.
Howes D 604, Sabin 21489
DLC, ICHi

3056. Dwinell, M. Common sense views of foreign lands. A series of letters from the East and the West, by M. Dwinell. Rome, Georgia, Printed at the Office of The Courier, 1878.
iv [5]–402p. 20cm.
"The substance of most of the following letters was originally published in the Rome, Ga. Courier." — Pref.
Utah and the Mormons, p. 329–344.
DLC, UHi

3057. Dwyer, James. Album of Salt Lake City, Utah. [Salt Lake City, James Dwyer, 1890?]
11p. 15 plates. 9×13cm.
Cover-title.
Plates on one side of strip attached to inside front cover to form 16 leaves.
Pictures with text concerning basic history and major buildings of Salt Lake City.
CU-B, NN, UHi, UPB, USIC

3058. Dykes, George Parker. A catechism for the children of the Church of Jesus Christ of Latter-day Saints in California. San Francisco, Printed by Turnbull and Smith, 1864.
2p.l. [5]–83p. 15cm.
Written before his quarrel with the RLDS church.
MH

3059. ———. "The Choice Seer." [San Francisco? 1866?]
16p. 22cm.
Signed: Anderson Hall, August 7th, 1866.
The mission of Joseph Smith.
MoInRC

3060. ———. The city of refuge. [San Francisco, 186–]
7p. 20cm.
Caption-title.
Why Jackson County, Mo. couldn't have been the gathering place, or Mount Zion. Proved by the *Bible, Book of Mormon*, and *Doctrine and Covenants*.
MH, MoInRC

3061. ———. The closing scenes. [Sacramento? 186–]
16p. 22cm.
Dated October 7th, 1871.
His controversy with the RLDS Church.
MoInRC

3062. ———. The enquirer. By G. Parker Dykes. [Sacramento? 1867?]
4p. 21cm.
Signed: October 25, 1867.
Demand to be heard by the RLDS Church members.
MoInRC

3063. ———. The Examiner. [Letter to Bros. Alexander and David Smith, W. W. Blair's successors as missionaries in Calif. San Francisco, 186–]
8p. 21cm.
Renewal of offer to debate the issues, refused by W. W. Blair.
MoInRC (defective)

DYKES, G. P.

3064. ———. The expositor. [Sacramento? 1868?]
16p. 21cm.
Signed: Sacramento, Cal., August 17, 1868.
The error of the RLDS church.
MoInRC

3065. ———. Glaubens-Artikel in der Kirche Jesu Christi der Heiligen der letsten Tage. [n.p., ca. 1851]
[4]p. 22cm.
Caption-title.
Title in English: Articles of faith.
UPB, USIC

3066. ———. Hireling preachers. [n.p., n.d.]
16p. 21cm.
Validity of the actions of RLDS ministers who defected.
MoInRC

3067. ———. Memorabilia. [Vallejo? 1868?]
23p. 21cm.
Signed: "Vallejo, December 22, 1868."
The error of the Reorganization and Utah Mormonism.
MoInRC

3068 ———. Mineblad efter Aeldste George Parker Dykes til Jesu Christi Kirke af Sidste Dages Hellige i Aalborg. [Aalborg, 1851]
[4]p. 20cm.
Signed: 24th April, 1851.
Title in English: Memorial writings concerning Elder George Parker Dykes.
USIC

3069. ———. The Molliental [sic] Harbinger. [Sacramento? 1867?]
8p. 21cm.
Signed: Sacramento, December 31, 1867.
The apostasy of the church.
MoInRC

3070. ———. Observanda. Sacramento, Cal. [1869]
4p. 21cm.
Signed: October 20, 1869.
Letter to W. W. Blair.
Dispute with the RLDS church because W. W. Blair wouldn't debate with him.
MoInRC

3071. ———. Ordinations. [Sacramento? 1867?]
8p. 21cm.
Signed: Volcano, Amador Co., Cal. November 12th, 1867.
Answer to letter on ordinations, contrary to the RLDS church.
MoInRC

3072. ———. The paracletes. [Valley Home, Calif.? 1868?]
16p. 21cm.
Signed: Valley Home, Calif. July 20, 1868.
Against RLDS priesthood.
MoInRC

3073. ———. The penalties of adultery, backbiting, talebearing, slandering, tatling, evil speaking and idle words. By G. Parker Dykes. [San Francisco, 186–]
7 [1]p. 21cm.
Philosophy of life with *Book of Mormon* quotes.
Also, an untitled poem after text.
MoInRC

3074. ———. The Priesthood. [Vallejo? 1868]
15p. 21cm.
Signed: Vallejo, Cal. April 12, 1868.
Error of the Reorganization.
MoInRC

3075. ———. The rejoinder. No. 1–2. [Sacramento? 1868]
2v. (27, 20p.) 21cm.
Signed: Walltown, Cal. Jan. 12, 1867 and Sacramento, Jan. 16, 1868.
Continuance of the quarrel between Dykes and the RLDS Church.
MoInRC

3076. ———. "Show my people their transgressions." [Sacramento, 1867?]
4p. 21cm.
Signed: October 25, 1867.
Demand to be heard by the RLDS church.
MoInRC

3077. ———. To the Saints on the Pacific coast. [San Francisco, 1863]
16p. 23½cm.
Caption-title.
Signed: December 21, 1863.
An RLDS publication concerning the condition of Utah church.
NN, USIC

3077a. ———. To the Saints on the Pacific Coast. San Francisco, February 12th, 1864. [San Francisco? 1864]
8p. 20½cm.
Caption-title.
"A word of advice to those that look for me to be the prophet [a poem]." Question of succession.
UPB, USIC

3078. ———. Troes-artikler i Jesu Christi Kirke af Sidste Dages Hellige i Danmark. Aalborg, 1851.
4p.
Title in English: The articles of faith . . .
Schmidt

3079. ———. (same) [Kjøbenhavn, Trykt hos F. E. Bording, n.d.]
[4]p. 18cm.
Signed: 25th, Feb. 1851.
USIC

3080. ———. Truth vindicated. [Sacramento? 1867?]
27p. 22cm.
Signed: Folsom Cal., June 1, 1866.
"Form of a trial in the Church of L.D.S. By G. Parker Dykes," p. [22]–27.
Both sects (Utah and RLDS) apostate and their priestcraft exposed.
MoInRC

3081. ———. Ultimatum (To W. W. Blair and E. Banta) [San Francisco? 1868?]
24p. 21½cm.
Signed: Sacramento, July 8, 1868.
A poem "Sunny side," p. 24.
MoInRC

3082. ———. [Ultimatum] Appendix to the Ultimatum: Concerning the validity of actions of RLDS ministers. [San Francisco? 1869?]
16p. 21cm.
Signed: May 2, 1869
MoInRC

3083. Dykes, Pauline Browning (Higgins) The Mormon girl, by Paula Brown [*pseud.*] Lamoni, Ia., Herald Publishing House, 1912.
4p.l., 11–205p. plates. 20cm.
RLDS church fiction.
DLC, NjP, NN, MoInRC, UU

3084. Dyrholm, Jens Sorensen. En Røst i wor bevaegede Tid Mod Baptismen, Mormonismen og Andre religiose forverringer, af huusmand Jens Sørensen Dyrholm. Odense, Trykt i Joh. Milos Officin, 1852.
257p. [1]l. 17½cm.
Title in English: A voice in our troublesome days against baptism by immersion.
NN

3085. ———. Oplysning om Mormonerne; eller, Som de kalde sig self: "Jesu Christi Kirke af de sidste Dages Hellige." Odense, J. Milo, 1852.
63p. 18cm.
Title in English: Enlightenment concerning the Mormons.
NN, USIC

The Evening and the Morning Star Extra.

JULY 16, 1833.

Having learned with regret, that an article entitled **FREE PEOPLE OF COLOR**, in the last number of the Star, has been misunderstood, we feel in duty bound to state, in this Extra, that our intention was not only to stop free people of color from emigrating to this state, but to prevent them from being admitted as members of the church. In the first column of the 111th page of the same paper, may be found this paragraph: "Our brethren will find an extract of the law of this state, relative to free people of color, on another page of this paper. Great care should be taken on this point. The saints must shun every appearance of evil. As to slaves we have nothing to say. In connexion with the wonderful events of this age, much is doing towards abolishing slavery, and colonizing the blacks in Africa."

We often lament the situation of our sister states in the south, and we fear, lest, as has been the case, the blacks should rise and spill innocent blood: for they are ignorant, and a little may lead them to disturb the peace of society. To be short, we are opposed to have free people of color admitted into the state; and we say, that none will be admitted into the church, for we are determined to obey the laws and constitutions of our country, that we may have that protection which the sons of liberty inherit from the legacy of Washington, through the favorable auspices of a Jefferson, and Jackson.

Item 3272a. The *Star* extra rushed off the press in an unsuccessful attempt to dispel the wrath of local Missourians over W. W. Phelps's article "Free People of Color." From the LDS church collection.

E., B. E.

3085a. E., B. E. Wanderings in distant lands. A brief account of our ten months' tour dedicated, with much affection, to all my old friends. England, 1884.
187p. 19cm.
Mormons, p. 18–21.
USlC

3086. Eades, Jacob Allen. The sword of the spirit. Salt Lake City, Skelton Publ. Co. [c1908]
2p.l., 5–133 [3]p. 18cm.
Agains the claims of the RLDS church.
DLC, NjP, USlC

3087. Eardley, J. R. Gems of inspiration. A collection of sublime thoughts by modern prophets. Compiled by J. R. Eardley, San Francisco, Calif., Joseph A. Dove, Printer, 1899.
2p.l. [3]–98p. 21cm.
A short history of the Church of the Firstborn, keys of the priesthood, etc.
MoInRC, USlC

3088. Earle, George. An argument of the legal effect of the award and repealing resolution in the Chorpenning case. By George Earle, Attorney for George Chorpenning. [Washington, 1871?]
20p. 23cm.
Cover-title.
Mail contracts from Utah to California, 1851–1857.
CU–B

3089. Earle, William E. A brief on report of Judiciary Committee on the House of Representatives. No. 1637. Senate Bill 905, for relief of J. and R. H. Porter. Wm. E. Earle, Attorney for Claimant. [Leavenworth] H. I. Rothrock [1865]
22p. 22½cm.
To obtain money for wagons destroyed during the Utah Expedition.
USlC

3090. Early scenes in church history. Designed for the instruction and encouragement of young Latter-day Saints. Salt Lake City, Juvenile Instructor Office, 1882.
viii, 9–96p. 18cm. (Faith promoting series. Book 8)
Contents: B. F. Johnson. Show us a sign; H. G. B. Contest with evil spirits; A. O. Smoot. Early experience; Scenes in the British mission; Remarkable healings; Philo Dibble. Narrative.
CSmH, CU–B, DLC, MH, NjP, NN, UHi, ULA, UPB, USl, USlC, UU, WHi

3091. Eastman, Samuel. . . . Addresses delivered by Samuel Eastman. Designed to give a brief historical sketch of the circumstances under which the message of the establishment of God's Kingdom was announced to the Mormon People, With a commentary on how the priesthood should be exercised. Salt Lake City, Published by the author, 1927.
36p. 17cm.
On the establishment of the Eastman faction.
CU–B, UPB, USlC

3092. ———. Das Aktive Königreich Gottes [Aus dem Englischen ins Deutsche übersetzt von: Eduard Janoschek, Joseph G. Fueger, Else Wever. Breslau, Th. Schatzky, 1910?]
30p. 20cm.
Title in English: The real kingdom of God.
Translations of his Pamphlets without title.
USlC

3093. ———. Brief memoir in honor of my seventieth birthday. By Samuel Eastman, Salt Lake City, May 24, 1930. [Salt Lake City, 1930]
20p. 21cm.
At head of title: To all of my bitter religious antagonists and assailants. I have always reminded them "The Lord will surely judge between thee and me."
Includes his own revelations and calling.
CU–B, USlC

3094. ———. Discourses of great importance to be given concerning the whole house of Israel. [Salt Lake City, 1926]
[2]p. 14cm.
Announcement of his sermons on Israel and the New Jerusalem.
USlC

3095. ———. Fundamental articles of our faith. [Salt Lake City, 1915]
12p. 20cm.
UPB, USl, USlC, UU

3095a. ———. The olive branch; an epitome of my religious faith . . . [Salt Lake City, 1925]
[8]p. 16½cm.
"Written from a pure Israelitish standpoint. By one who is of the tribe of Judah and of Ephraim."
USlC

3096. ———. [Pamphlets without title, sent as letters to members of the church] Salt Lake City, 1909–1910.
2 pamp. (8, 8p.) 22cm.
March 10, 1909.
June 29, 1910
Both reprinted under title *Pamphlets Nos. 1, 2, 3.*
USlC

3097. ———. Pamphlets Nos. 1, 2, 3, treating upon the prophecies now to be fulfilled, relating to the great latter-day work and setting up of the actual kingdom of God. [Salt Lake City, 1913?]
49p. 20cm.
MoInRC, UPB, USl, USlC

3098. ———. Reminiscences of my life . . . [Salt Lake City, The Liberty Press, 1914?]
61p. 20cm.
CSmH, MoInRC, NjP, ULA, USl, USlC

3099. ———. Ten years of my mission. [Salt Lake City] The Liberty Press [1914?]
193p. 20cm.
Preface signed: Salt Lake City, August 1, 1914.
MoInRC, UHi, ULA, USIC

3100. ———. . . . "A voice in the wilderness? . . . [Salt Lake City] 1927.
34p. 17cm.
Signed: Salt Lake City, February, 1927.
Doctrinal work explaining the reasons for his divergence from the Church.
UPB, USI, USIC, UU

3101. Easy roads to Hell. [North Carolina] Printed by the Pilgrim Tract Society [n.d.]
[4]p. 17½cm.
Caption-title.
Mormonism one of the easy roads along with Russellism, Spiritualists, Unitarians, etc.
USIC

Eaton, Anna R. Handbook on Mormonism. *See Coyner, John McCutchen.*

3102. Eaton, Anna Ruth (Webster). Mormonism. [New York? Woman's Executive Committee of Home Missions, 1882?]
4p. 26cm.
NN

3103. ———. The origin of Mormonism. By Mrs. Dr. Horace Eaton, of Palmyra, N.Y. [New York, Woman's Executive Committee of Home Missions, 1881]
[4]p. 22cm.
Caption-title.
"Read . . . at the Union Home Missionary Meeting . . . Buffalo, N.Y., May 27th, 1881."
NN, WHi

3104. Eaton, Horace. The early history of Palmyra: a Thanksgiving sermon, delivered at Palmyra, N.Y., November 26, 1857, by Horace Eaton . . . Published by request of the descendants of the first settler. Rochester, Press of A. Strong &c., 1858.
26p. 22½cm.
Mention in passing: "The hill, where Joe Smith dug for golden plates — the printer — the old press that struck off his Bible, and the proof sheets, are still with us, but of the Mormons . . . we know not a single follower."
Sabin 21722
DLC, NBuG

Eaton, Mrs. Horace. *See Eaton, Anna Ruth (Webster)*

3105. Eaton, John. The Mormons of today, a series of articles from "The Christian Herald." Prepared by Gen. John Eaton, Ll. D. Ex.–U.S. Commissioner of Education. [Washington, 1897]
1p.l. [3]–34p. 20½cm.
DLC, NjPS, USIC, UU

3106. ———. (same) [Washington, 1898?]
40p. 20½cm.
"Second Edition."
DLC, NH, NN, UPB, USIC

Ebeling, F. J. Debate held at the Pennsville Ohio, Church of Christ. *See McVey, A. M.*

3107. ———. The Ebeling-Riggle discussion on the Kingdom of God, universal salvation of the human family, the Church of God, and the practices and teachings of the Reorganized Church of Jesus Christ of Latter Day Saints. By Eld. F. J. Ebeling, representing the Reorganized Church of Jesus Christ of Latter Day Saints, and Eld. H. M. Riggle, representing the Church of God. [n.p., n.d.]
1p.l., 5–494p. 20cm.
MoInRC, NjP, USIC

3108. Eckfeldt, Jacob Reese. New varieties of gold and silver coins, counterfeit coins, and bullion; with mint values. By Jacob R. Eckfeldt, and William E. Du Bois . . . Philadelphia, The authors, 1850.
60p., [1]l. illus., plates. 18cm.
Mention of Mormon gold pieces with pictures in black and white and color.
Other editions: 2d ed. Inclusive. New York, G. P. Putnam, 1881. DLC; 3d ed. 1852. CU
CU–B, DLC, MBAt, MWA, NN, PP, PPL–R, PU

3109. Edler, Lars. To breven om Mormonerne i Utah fra Lars Edler . . . Kjøbenhavn, I. Commission hos Boghandler Eibe, 1868.
24p. 16½cm.
Title in English: Two letters about Mormons in Utah.
UPB, USIC

3110. ———. To Breve om Mormonerne i Utah fra Lars Edler . . . Odense, 1868.
24p. 16½cm.
USIC

3111. Edmunds, George Franklin. . . . The Reorganized Church of Jesus Christ of Latter Day Saints, Complainant, vs. The Church of Christ, at Independence, Missouri, Richard Hill, *et al.*, Defendants. Brief and argument by G. Edmunds, on behalf of Complainant, one of its solicitors. Lamoni, Ia., Herald Publishing House and Bindery, 1893.
19p. 26cm.
Cover-title.
At head of title: In the circuit court of the United States for the Western District of Missouri.
CtY, USIC

EDMUNDS-TUCKER LAW

3112. Edmunds-Tucker law, as agreed upon by Conference Committee, and adopted by the Senate and House of Representatives, and which became a law by lapse of time after being referred to the president. [n.p., 1887?]
8p. 20½cm.
Caption-title.
MH, NjP, ULA USlC

3113. Edward Irving and the Catholic Apostolic Church. [London, Bosworth and Harrison, Publishers, 1856]
8p. 17cm.
Denial of William John Conybeare's statement of their sympathy to Mormonism.
USlC

3114. Edwards, F. Henry. The background of Church history, a topical study of the history of the Church of Jesus Christ of Latter Day Saints from 1805 to 1920. Independence, Mo., Herald Publishing House, 1929.
37p. 20cm.
RLDS church history.
MoInRC, NjP, ULA

3115. ———. The place and meaning of personal evangelism. Independence, Mo., Herald Publishing House, 1929.
29p. 19½cm.
MoInRC, UPB

3116. ———. Sermon outlines for our stewardship at Graceland. Arranged by F. Henry Edwards. [n.p., n.d.]
21p. 19cm.
Introduction by Frederick M. Smith.
NN

3117. Edwards, Frank S. A Campaign in New Mexico with Colonel Doniphan. By Frank S. Edwards, a volunteer. With a map of the route, and a table of the distances traversed. Philadelphia, Carey and Hart, 1847.
xvi [17]–184p. 18½cm.
Mention of Mormon Battalion, p. 70.
W-C 132
CtY, DLC

3118. Edwards, Sir Henry. A two months tour in Canada and the United States. By Sir Henry Edwards. London, 1889.
2p.l., 62p. 20cm.
Trip through Salt Lake City in 1889; he attended conference and discussed the fact that Mormonism was declining due to polygamy having been reduced to a common crime.
USlC

3119. Edwards Brothers, Philadelphia. An illustrated historical atlas of Caldwell County, Missouri. Compiled, drawn and published from personal examinations and surveys by Edwards Brothers, of Missouri . . . Philadelphia, Pa. 1876.
2p.l., 5–52p. illus., plates, ports., maps (part col., part fold.) 45cm.
Brief history of Mormonism in Caldwell County.
UPB

3120. ———. An illustrated historical atlas of Ray County, Missouri. Compiled, drawn and published from personal examinations and surveys by Edwards Brothers of Missouri . . . Philadelphia, Pa., 1877.
50p. illus., maps. 44½cm.
"Mormon war" p. 9, David Whitmer reference, p. 13, sketch of Alexander W. Doniphan, p. 31, sketch of David Whitmer, p. 45.
USlC

3121. Egan, Howard. Pioneering the West, 1846 to 1878; Major Howard Egan's diary, also thrilling experiences of pre-frontier life among Indians, their traits, civil and savage, and part of autobiography, inter-related to his father's by Howard R. Egan. Edited, compiled, and connected in nearly chronological order, by Wm. M. Egan . . . Richmond, Utah, Howard R. Egan Estate, 1917.
302p. illus., ports., plate. 19½cm.
CSmH, CtY, DLC, ICN, NjP, NN, UHi, ULA, UPB, USl, USlC, UU, WHi

3122. ———, *defendant.* "Mormonism"! Indictment for the murder of James Monroe, referred to in the report of the returned judges from the Territory of Utah. October term, 1851. Before the Hon. Z. Snow, Judge of the First Judicial District Court of the United States for the Territory of Utah. United States versus Howard Egan . . . [Liverpool, R. James, 1852?]
8p. 21½cm.
Caption-title.
George A. Smith's plea in favor of Egan and Judge Snow's charge to the jury.
CtY, UHi

3122a. Eickemeyer, Carl. The giant killer. New York, 1909.
30p. port. 16cm.
A polemic against the Mormon church.
USlC

3123. Eighty-fourth anniversary of American Independence. July 4, 1860. Programme. Great Salt Lake City, July 3rd, 1860.
Broadside. 28×14½cm.
Signed: Robert T. Burton, Andrew Cunningham, William C. Staines, John T. Caine, John Sharp; Committee of Arrangements.
USlC

3124. Elder Abraham H. Cannon: Funeral July 26, 1896. Salt Lake City, 1896.
[2]p. 21cm.
USIC

3125. The Elders' Journal. Atlanta, Georgia [Chattanooga, Tenn.] August 1903–June, 1907.
4v. monthly, semi-monthly. 25cm.
Publisher and editor: Ben E. Rich.
Combined with *Liahona*, beginning June 22, 1907 to form *Liahona, The Elders' Journal.* Voluming continues from *The Elders' Journal.*
V. 4 has 18 nos. only.
CSmH 2–3, MH, MoInRC, NjP, NN 2–4, ULA, UPB, USIC

3126. Elders' Journal of the Church of Latter Day Saints. Kirtland, Ohio [Far West, Missouri] October, 1837–August, 1838.
1v. (4 nos. in 64p.) 25cm.
First editor: Joseph Smith jr.
Follows the *L.D.S. Messenger and Advocate.*
Suspended December 1837–June 1838.
Final issues (3, 4) printed in Far West, Mo.
CtY, CU-B, MH, MoInRC, NN, UPB, USIC, WHi, #1–3

3127. ———. Prospectus for the Elders' Journal, Of the Church of Jesus Christ, of Latter Day Saints. [Far West, 1838]
Broadside. 26×40½cm.
USIC

3128. Eldredge, Fred E. Seven questions . . . Marysvale, Utah, c1922.
2p.l., 70, 144p. 21cm.
"The notes" on questions follow as p. 1–144.
Seven questions: 1. Is it true that the finer the object or the substance to be seen, the stronger is the light required for it to be seen? 2. Is a spirit an individual being, of a substance finer than organized matter? 3. Is it true that there has been special supernatural light? 4. What is God? 5. What is "the gospel" of the Mormons? 6. Is it a part of that gospel, that deception is right, when the motive for it is good? 7. Do you believe that the prophet Joseph Smith Jun. did cohabit with other women besides his lawful wife?
Believes Joseph Smith's first vision, but not the *Book of Mormon.*
DLC

3129. Eldredge, Jane Jennings. The Leavitts of America; a compilation of five branches and gleanings, from New England to California and Canada . . . Salt Lake City, 1924.
8p.l., 254p. 23½cm.
Many of this family were born in Utah.
UPB

3130. Eldredge, Zoeth Skinner. History of California. New York, The Century History Co. [c1915]
5v. plates, ports., maps (part fold.) 25cm.
The "Mormons," V.5, p. 163–196, by Orson F. Whitney.
Mormon history in California.
CU-B, DLC, NjP, UPB

Eleanor [*pseud.*] *See Kearney, Eleanor.*

3131. Ka Elele Oiaio. Honolulu, Hawaii, November 1, 1908–October, 1911.
3v. (72 nos.) bi-monthly. 25cm.
Publication of the LDS Hawaiian Mission.
Title in English: A voice of warning.
UPB V.1 inc., V.2, V.3 inc.; USIC comp.

3132. Elísabet: saga frá Utah. Reykjavík, Prentsmidja D. Östlunds, 1913.
2p.l. [7]–112p. 18cm.
Icelandic novel concerning Mormonism.
Title in English: Elizabet, a story from Utah.
NIC, NN

3133. Eliza [*pseud.*] Truth made manifest; a dialogue on the first principles of the oracles of God, by Eliza [*pseud.*] [Plano, Ill., Reorganized Church of Jesus Christ of Latter Day Saints, 1864?]
12p. 21½cm.
Listed as out of print in the *True Latter Day Saints' Herald*, Jan. 1, 1865.
MoInRC, UPB, USIC

3134. ———. (same) [Plano, Ill., Reorganized Church of Jesus Christ of Latter Day Saints, n.d.]
12p. 21½cm.
Variant printings without date.
MH, NN, USIC

3135. ———. (same) Lamoni, Ia., Reorganized Church of Jesus Christ of Latter Day Saints [187–]
12p. 21cm. (No. 2)
CtY, MH

Elkholk, Carl F. *See Eltzholtz, Carl F.*

3136. Ellinwood, Frank F. Mormonism. A new religion of the nineteenth century by Frank F. Ellinwood, D.D., LL.D., senior secretary of the Presbyterian Board of Foreign Missions, New York City, New York. New York, Published by the Women's Board of Home Missions of the Presbyterian Church in the U.S.A. [1903]
1p.l., 324–329p. 22½cm.
From the *Homiletic Review*, November, 1903.
New title-page. Variant printings.
Uses a murder in New York by William Hooper Young as a proof of Mormon depravity.
USIC

3137. Elliot, Richard Smith. Notes taken in sixty years . . . by Richard Smith Elliott. St. Louis, R. P. Studley & Co., 1883.
2p.l., 336p. 22½cm.
Account of Mormonism in Illinois.
NjP, NN, UPB, USIC

3138. Elliott, P. F. Mormonism exposed; Joseph Smith a false prophet. [n.p., n.d.]
10p. 14cm.
Exposé of Mormonism, particularly the *Pearl of Great Price.*
MoInRC

3139. Ellis, Alvin R. The Divinity of the Book of Mormon. Grand Rapids, Mich., The Evans Printing Co. [n.d.]
23p. 21½cm.
RLDS defense of the Book of Mormon.
MoInRC

3140. ———. "Where there is no vision the people perish." Grand Rapids, Michigan, Glad Tidings [n.d.]
17p. 15cm.
RLDS doctrinal tract.
MoInRC

3141. Ellis, Charles. The cat on the roof; or, Utah republicanism, by Charles Ellis, non-Mormon . . . [Salt Lake City, The Deseret News, c1900]
[3]–22 [1]p. 19cm.
Cover-title.
p. 17 numbered p. 7.
Concerns Mormon political activities.
MH, MoKU, NN, ULA, USlC

3142. ———. "Christian" and "Mormon" doctrines of God — origin and destiny of man — future life — eternal torments — endless progress — all damned — all saved. [By] Charles Ellis. Salt Lake City, the author, 1902.
38 [1]p. 19½cm.
MoInRC, NjP, NN, UPB, USl

3143. ———. Church and state. A lecture delivered in the Salt Lake Theatre, Jan. 24, 1892. Salt Lake City, 1892.
16p. 20cm.
Mormon application of church and state.
CSmH, DLC, MoInRC, UHi, ULA, UPB, USlC

3144. ———. Monogamy imperiled. [Salt Lake City, 1897]
Broadside. 21×18cm.
Reprinted from the *Salt Lake Herald.*
Signed: A gentile.
USlC

3145. ———. Mormons and Mormonism, why they have been opposed, maligned and persecuted — inside history of the present anti-Mormon crusade. By a non-Mormon. Salt Lake City [Magazine Printing Co.] 1899.
23p. 20cm.
CtY, CU-B, MB, MH, NjP, NN, UHi, UPB, USlC, WHi

3146. ———. (same, under title) Mormons and Mormonism. Why maligned — the people — industry — education — morals — polygamy — the religion. Rev. ed. [Salt Lake City, Deseret News, c1899]
24p. 18½cm.
UPB, USlC

3147. ———. (same) Lecture by . . . a non-Mormon. [Salt Lake City, 19 - -]
27p. 16½cm.
CSmH, USlC

3148. ———. (same, in Danish) Mormoner og Mormonismen. Mormon-folket, deres industri, opdragelse og moraler, hvad meningen er om dette folk af en ikke-Mormon, som for mange aar har opholdt sig iblandt dem. Et foredrag af Charles Ellis . . . Oversat fra Engelsk af Lars Frederickson. Februar, 1921. [Hjøring, Bogtrykkeriet, 1921?]
20p. 21½cm.
Caption-title.
USlC

3149. ———. Our country as it is. A lecture delivered in the Salt Lake Theatre, February 21st, 1892, by Charles Ellis. Salt Lake City, 1892.
16p. 22½cm.
Cover-title.
Social conditions of the U.S. compared to those in Utah under Mormonism.
DLC, NjP, UHi, UPB, USlC

3150. ———. Our country as it should be. A lecture delivered in the Salt Lake Theatre, February 28th, 1892, by Charles Ellis. Salt Lake City, 1892.
15p. 22½cm.
Bound in brown paper printed wrapper.
UPB, USlC

3151. ———. Statehood. A lecture delivered in the Salt Lake Theatre, February 7th, 1892, by Charles Ellis. Salt Lake City, 1892.
15p. 22½cm.
DLC, MoInRC, UHi, USlC

3152. ———. Utah, 1847 to 1870. By Charles Ellis (non-Mormon) 1st ed. of five thousand. Salt Lake City, 1891.
32p. 23½cm.
CSmH, CtY, CU-B, DLC, ICN, MH, MoInRC, NjP, NN, UHi, USl, USlC, UU

3153. ———. (same) 2d ed. of 5000. Salt Lake City, 1891.
32p. 23½cm.
UU

3154. ———. (same) 3d ed. of 5000. Salt Lake City, 1891.
32p. 23½cm.
NjP, NN

3154a. Ellis, Edith M. O. (Lees) James Hinton, a sketch. By Mrs. Havelock Ellis . . . London, Stanley Paul & Co. [1918]
xxviii, 283p. illus. 22½cm.
Mormon polygamy mentioned, p. 168–169.
USlC

3155. Ellis, Edward Sylvester. Ellis's history of the United States; from the discovery of America to the present time . . . Including a comprehensive historical introduction, copious annotations, a list of authorities and references, etc. . . . Philadelphia, Syndicate Publishing Company [c1899]
6v. illus., plates, ports., maps, facsims. 26cm.
Utah expedition, V. 3, p. 841–842.
DLC, UPB

3156. Ellison, Nina E. Nadine, a romance of two lives. Nashville, Gospel Advocate Pub. Co., 1897.
343p. illus., plates, ports. 19½cm.
Has a partial setting in Salt Lake City with a discussion of Mormonism and its beliefs in a letter to "Cousin M——."
CSmH, DLC, UU

3157. Ells, Josiah. Prophetic truth confirmed in the appearing of the Book of Mormon. An Israelitish record of a fallen people. Being the subject of an evening's conversation respecting its origin. Its divinity proved by the scriptures and collateral evidence. Prefaced with a brief sketch of the life of the Prophet, showing the way and manner of his becoming possessed of the record, By Elder Josiah Ells, of the Reorganized Church of Jesus Christ of Latter Day Saints. [Pittsburgh, 1881]
ix, 58p. 21cm.
MoInRC, NjP, NN, OClWHi, OO, USlC

3158. Ellwood, Charles Abram. Sociology and modern social problems. Rev. & enl. ed. New York, American Book Co., c1910.
331p. 19cm.
Mormonism and polygamy.
Other editions: Rev.-enl. ed. [1913] CU, NjPT; 1919. CU
DLC, UHi, UPB, USlC

3159. Elsbree, George M. Polygamy, a sermon by Rev. George M. Elsbree. Mr. Harvey O'Higgins, the author of the play, was present and prefaced the sermon with a brief story of the writing of the play. New York, The Kumbak Printery, 1915.
8p. 17cm.
NN

3160. Elsworth, Benjamin C., *compiler.* A collection of sacred hymns for the Church of Christ of the Latter-day Saints, selected and published by Benjamin C. Elsworth. [n.p.] 1839.
iv [5]–152, viip. 11cm.
Words only.
CtY, USlC

3160a. Eltzholtz, Carl F. Et Vaaben mod Mormonismen. Af Carl F. Eltzholtz. Kjøbenhavn, J. Kommission hos Andr. Fred høst & Søn [n.d.]
14p. 18½cm.
Title in English: A weapon against Mormonism.
USlC

3160b. ———. (same) Med et Forord af Provst R. S. Deichmann, Dallerup pr. Laven. Kjøbenhavn J. Komm, hos Andr. Fred. høst & Søn. [1883]
2p.l., 62 [3]p. 18½cm.
USlC

3161. Emanuel, Victor Rousseau. The messiah of the cylinder, by Victor Rousseau [*pseud.*] Illustrated by Joseph Clement Coll. Chicago, A. C. McClurg & Co., 1917.
5p.l., 319p. plates (part double) 19½cm.
First published in *Everybody's Magazine.*
A novel of the future in which Mormonism figures as the menace.
DLC

3162. Emery Stake Academy, Castle Dale, Utah. Emery Stake Academy. Announcement. 1908–
v. 21½cm.
USlC 1908–19.

3163. Emmons, S. B. The spirit land by S. B. Emmons. Philadelphia, John E. Potter and Company, 1857.
2p.l. [5]–288p. front. 17½cm.
Chapter 8. Mormon superstition; an account of the first vision and other Mormon delusions exposed by the Van Dusens.
USlC

3164. Emory, William Hemsley. . . . Notes of a military reconnaissance from Fort Leavenworth, in Missouri to San Diego, in California, including part of the Arkansas, Del Norte, and Gila Rivers. By Lieut. Col. W. H. Emory. Made in 1846–7, with the advanced guard of the "Army of the West" . . . Washington, Wendell and Van Benthuysen, Printers, 1848.
416p., plates, 3 fold. maps. 23cm. (U.S. 30 Cong. 1st Sess. Senate. Ex. Doc. No. 7)
Includes material on the Mormon Battalion.
Other editions: New York, H. Long & Bro., 1848. CSmH, DLC
Howes E145, Sabin 22536, W-C 148
CU-B, DLC, ICN, NjP, UHi, ULA, UPB, USlC, UU

3165. ———. (same) Washington: Wendell and Van Benthuysen, Printers, 1848.
3p.l. [7]–614p. plates, maps, part fold. 23cm. (U.S. Cong. 1st Sess. House. Ex. Doc. No. 41)
Also includes the report of Lieut. J. W. Abert, on his examination of New Mexico, 1846–'47; Report of Lieut. Col. P. St. George Cooke on his march from Santa Fe, New Mexico to San Diego; and Journal of Captain A. R. Johnston, First Dragoons.
CU, MB, MH, UPB, USlC

ENANDER, J. A.

3166. Enander, Johan Alfred. Mormonismens historia från sektens uppkomst till närwarande tid. Af Joh. A. Edr. [*pseud.*] Wenersborg, Bagge och Petterson, 1865.
51p. 17½cm.
According to NN card "Johan Anders Enander" is the pseudonym for Johan Alfred Enander.
Title in English: A history of Mormonism . . .
DLC, NN

3167. Engelstoft, Christian Thorning. Om Mormonerne af Bishop Dr. Christian T. Engelstoft. Odense, Trygt hos, M. C. Hempel, 1855.
2p.l., 16p. 15½cm.
Reprinted from: *Fyens Stiftstedende*, No. 47, og 48.
Title in English: About the Mormons.
CtY, NN, UHi

3168. English, Thomas Dunn. The Mormons; or, Life at Salt Lake City. A drama in three acts by Thomas Dunn English, M.D., as performed at Burton's Theatre, March 1858. New York, Samuel French [c1858]
43p. 20cm. (French's standard drama, acting edition. No. 205)
Mormon drama.
Sabin 22605
CSmH, CtY, DLC, ICN, MH, UHi, UPB, USl, USlC

3169. Enoch's Advocate; A temporary journal devoted to the interests of the United Order of Wooden Shoes. Salt Lake City, 1874.
v.1 #1–6. illus. 32cm.
Satirical magazine against the church and the Order of Enoch.
NjP, USlC

3170. Enos, A. A., *editor*. Across the plains. in 1850. [Stanton, Neb., ca. 1905]
[58]p. 29cm.
Cover-title.
Letter #8 concerning Salt Lake visit; a description of the valley, and of Mormonism with which he is not impressed; agreeable visit with Brigham Young.
Howes E–160
CU–B, ICN

3171. The Ensign. Buffalo, Scott County (I.T.) July 15, 1844–June 1845.
1v. (12 nos. in 192p.) monthly. 34cm.
Published by George M. Hinkle and William E. McLellin, and "devoted to the dissemination of the religious principles and views of 'The Church of Jesus Christ, the Bride, the Lamb's Wife."
Morgan
MoInRC July, August, 1844; January, March–June, 1945.

3172. The Ensign of Liberty, of the Church of Christ. Kirtland, Lake Co., March, 1847–August, 1849.
V. 1 (7 nos. in 112p.) published irregularly. 24cm.
Editor: Wm. W. McLellin.
William McLellin's attempt to nurture the cause of David Whitmer (Church of Christ)
Morgan, Sabin 50736
CtY comp.; OCHP comp.; UPB March, 1847–March, 1848; USlC comp.

3173. Ensign to the Nations. To gather Israel. Kirtland, Ohio. April 1851–
v. 1 #1. 21cm.
Published by Moses R. Norris for the "Scattered lambs of Christ's flock."
Apparently the only issue published.
Morgan
NN

3174. An entertainment will be given in the 12th Ward schoolhouse . . . [Salt Lake City] Printed by the Deseret News Co., 1884.
Broadside. 35×18cm.
Dated: Jan. 4, 1884.
Announcement of entertainment for the benefit of the Sunday School including the program with list of performers. Mr. H. M. Wells gave a reading.
USlC

3175. The Envoy. Birmingham, England, Reorganized Church of Jesus Christ of Latter Day Saints. February 1, 1926–July 1, 1927.
v. monthly. 21cm.
Official RLDS periodical for the British Mission.
MoInRC V.1, #1,2

3176. Equality. Independence, Published by the United Order of Equality, 1909–
v. 28cm.
Magazine of the Order of Enoch.
USlC V.1, #2,4

3177. Er Daab en Belingelse for frelse? [Kjøbenhavn, n.d.]
[2]p. 23cm.
Title in English: Is baptism necessary for salvation?
USlC

3178. Er de Sidste-Dages hellige Kristne? . . . [Kjøbenhavn, Udgivet og Forlagt af John S. Hansen . . . 1925]
4p. 22½cm.
Title in English: Are the Latter-day Saints Christians?
USlC

3179. Er Tro alene tilstraekkelig til frelse? [Köbenhavn, Udgivet og forlagt af A. L. Skancky . . . Trykt hos L. A. Nielsen . . . 1901]
[4]p. 22cm.
Title in English: Is faith alone enough for salvation?
USlC

3180. Ericksen, Ephraim Edward. The psychological and ethical aspects of Mormon group life, by Ephraim Edward Ericksen . . . Chicago, Ill., The University of Chicago Press [1922]
101p. 25cm.
Published also as thesis (Ph.D.) University of Chicago, 1918.
CSmH, CtY, CU–B, DLC, MoInRC, NjP, NjPT, NN, UHi, ULA, USlC, UU

Erlösung Für die Toten. *See Church of Jesus Christ of Latter-day Saints. Missions. Swiss-German.*

3181. ¿Es el bautismo esencial á la salvación? Traducido del Ingles por el Elder Rey L. Pratt; y El buatismo á quien y como debe ser administrado pro el Elder Helaman Pratt. El Paso, Publicado por la Misión Mexicano [n.d.]
16p. 18cm.
Title in English: Is baptism essential to salvation? and The baptism, by whom and how it is to be administered.
UPB

3182. Esshom, Frank Ellwood. Pioneers and prominent men of Utah, comprising photographs, genealogies, biographies . . . the early history of the Church of Jesus Christ of Latter-day Saints . . . by Frank Esshom . . . [Ed. de luxe] Salt Lake City, Utah Pioneers Book Publishing Company, 1913.
4p.l., 1319p. ports. 31cm.
"There were forty-five hundred copies of this volume printed."
CSmH, CtY, CU–B, DLC, ICN, NjP, NN, UHi, ULA, UPB, USl, USlC, UU, WHi

3183. Estournelles de Constant, Paul Henri Benjamin, *baron* **d'.** America and her problems, by Paul H. B. d'Estournelles de Constant . . . New York, The Macmillan Company, 1915.
xxii, 545p. port. 20½cm.
Comments on polygamy and its purpose and the fact that it was still around.
Another edition: 1918.
CU, DLC, NjP, ULA

3184. Etheridge, Emerson. Speech of Emerson Etheridge, of Tennessee, delivered in the House of Representatives, April 2, 1860. [Washington] Printed by L. Towers [1860]
16p. 24cm.
Caption-title.
On the bill for prohibiting and punishing polygamy in the territories.
CU–B, DLC, OClWHi

3185. Étoile de Déseret; organe de l'Eglise de Jésus-Christ des Saints-des-Derniers-jours. [Paris, Imp. de M. Ducloux et comp.] Mai, 1851–Avril, 1852.
1v. (12 nos. in 191 [1]p.) monthly. 23½cm.
Edited and published by John Taylor.
Succeeded in 1853 by *Le Reflecteur.*
Title in English: Star of Deseret.
CSmH #2–12; CtY; DLC; UPB #1–11; USlC, WHi

3186. l'Etoile de la Mission Francaise de l'Église de Jésus-Christ des Saints des Derniers Jours. Jan. 1927–
v. monthly. 20½cm.
Publication of the LDS French Mission.
Title in English: Star of the French Mission.
UPB V. 3 #3–12; USlC comp.

3187. Étourneau, M. Les Mormons par M. Étourneau. Préface par Pierre Vicard avec un portrait de Joseph Smith et une vue de Nauvoo. Paris, Bestel et Cie . . . A. Pelit-Pierre . . . 1856.
2p.l., xi, 282 [1]p. 16½cm.
Title in English: The Mormons.
CSmH, CtY, CU–B, DLC, ICN, MH, NN, UHi, USl, USlC

3188. Etzenhouser, Mrs. M. A. Economics of Zion, lecture at the Stone Church, Independence, Mo., Oct. 12, 1922. [Independence, Mo., Herald Publishing House, 1922?]
13p. 19½cm.
RLDS doctrine of Zion.
MoInRC, NjP

3189. ———. Social service, lecture at the Stone Church, Independence, Missouri, October 5, 1922. [Independence, Herald Publishing House, 1922?]
14p. 20cm.
RLDS doctrine.
MoInRC

3190. Etzenhouser, Rudolph. The Book of Mormon and its translator. Independence, Mo., Ensign Publishing House [1899]
61p. 21cm.
IWW, MoInRC, UPB

3191. ———. (same) Independence, Mo., Ensign Publishing House, 1899.
27p. 22cm.
MoInRC

3192. ———. The book unsealed; an exposition of prophecy and American antiquities. The claims of the Book of Mormon examined and sustained. Independence, Mo., Ensign Print., 1892.
2p.l., 85p. 17cm.
CtY, MoInRC, OClWHi, UHi, MoInRC, USlC

3193. ———. The books and Utah Mormonism in contrast, prepared by Elder R. Etzenhouser, the books were law and governed till the death of Joseph and Hyrum Smith in 1844. Strong denials of polygamy up to and on Nov. 26, 1853. Independence, Mo., Ensign Publishing House, 1894.
25p. 18cm.
MoInRC

3194. ———. The books and Utah Mormonism in contrast by Elder R. Etzenhouser, of the

Reorganized Church of Jesus Christ of Latter Day Saints, prepared while Laboring in Utah in 1893. Independence, Mo., Ensign Publishing House, 1897.
52p. 21cm.
"Revised, 1897."
CSmH, MoInRC, PHi, UPB, USl

3195. ———. (same) Independence, Mo., Ensign Publishing House, 1901.
2p.l. [5]–77p. 22cm.
"Revised, 1897."
MoInRC, USIC

3196. ———. (same) Independence, Mo., Ensign Publishing House, 1908.
52p. 22cm.
"Revised, 1897."
MoInRC

3197. ———. A creed or catechism examined; involving fatal errors of all creeds. Independence, Mo., Ensign Publishing House [n.d.]
20p. 22cm.
Errors of other creeds prove the truthfulness of the RLDS claim.
MoInRC

3198. ——— . (same) Independence, Mo., Ensign Publishing House, 1896.
2p.l. [5]–23p. 21½cm.
Cover-title: The creeds laid bare.
MoInRC, UHi, USIC

3199. ———. From Palmyra, New York, 1830 to Independence, Mo., 1894 . . . By Elder R. Etzenhouser of the Reorganized Church of Jesus Christ of Latter Day Saints. Independence, Mo., Ensign Publishing House, 1894.
2p.l., 444 [1]p. 19½cm.
Contains: "The Book Unsealed, rev. and enl."
Howes E–210
CtY, Ia, ICN, ICU, MoInRC, MoK, NjP, NN, UHi, USl, USIC

3200. ———. The Three Bibles, scholarship and inspiration compared, an arrangement in parallel columns of prominent passages from the King James' and Revised Versions of the Bible as well as the Holy Scriptures, translated by inspiration through Joseph Smith. Independence, Mo. Ensign Publishing House, 1894.
59p. 22cm.
Variant edition without date on title page. NjP
MoInRC, MoK, NjP

3201. ———. (same) Independence, Mo., Ensign Publishing House, 1895.
59p. 22cm.
MoInRC

3202. ———. (same) 3d ed. Independence, Mo., Ensign Publishing House, 1898.
59p. 22cm.
MoInRC

3203. ———. (same) Independence, Mo., Ensign Publishing House [1899]
ii [3]–61p. 22½cm.
Text signed: July 5, 1899.
Preface signed: 1894.
NjPT, USIC

3204. ———. (same) [Lamoni, Ia.? The Herald Publishing House [1899]
ii [3]–61p. 22cm.
MoInRC

3205. ———. (same) [Lamoni, Ia., Herald Publishing House, 1899]
ii [3]–61p. 21½cm.
Variant printing.
MoInRC, UHi, UPB

3206. ———. (same) 4th ed. Independence, Mo., Ensign Publishing House, 1903.
ii [3]–61p. 22cm.
MoInRC, UHi, UU

3207. ———. The whole gospel briefly set forth. Lamoni, Ia., Reorganized Church of Jesus Christ of Latter Day Saints, 1908.
28p. 19cm. (No. 306)
IWW, MoInRC, USIC

3207a. Evan Stephens song fest. Salt Lake Tabernacle, Friday, April 2, 1926 . . . [sponsored by Granite Stake Primary Association] Salt Lake City [The Seagull Press, 1926]
[7]p. illus. 22cm.
USIC

3208. Evangelio Restaurado. El Paso, Texas [Los Angeles] March 1, 1927 — September, 1930.
4v. monthly. 20cm.
Published to V. 4 #6.
Publication of the Mexican Mission of the L.D.S. church.
V. 3-V. 4 #6 published in Los Angeles.
Title in English: The restored gospel.
UPB, USIC V. 1 # 1, V. 4 #6

3209. L'Evangile. [Merthyr-Tydfil, Wales, Printed by John Davis, Georgetown, 1850?]
2p. 18cm.
Title in English: The gospel.
USIC

3210. Evans, Benjamin Ifor. Encounters with all sorts of people including myself, by B. Ifor Evans. Boston, New York, Houghton Mifflin Company [1926?]
3p.l., 7–256p. 23cm.
Chapter 28. "With the Mormons at Salt Lake City."
CU, USIC

3211. Evans, John. History of all Christian sects and denominations; their origin, peculiar tenents, and present condition. With an introduction account of Atheists, Deists, Jews, Mohametans, Pagans, &c. By John Evans, LL.D. From the fifteenth London edition. Revised and enlarged, with the addition of the most recent statistics relating to religious sects in the United States. By the American editor. New York, Burgess and Stringer, 1844.
x [11]–288p. 18cm.
Mormonism first included in the 1844 edition.
Published in many editions.
NH, NN, OO, RPB

3212. Evans, John Henry. Birth of Mormonism in picture; scenes and incidents in early church history from photographs by George E. Anderson of Springville, Utah, narrative and notes by Prof. John Henry Evans. Salt Lake City, Deseret Sunday School Union [c1909]
62 [2]p. illus. 19×23½cm.
Presented by Evans to the Deseret Sunday School Union.
CSmH, DLC, NjP, NN, UHi, UPB, USl, USlC, UU

3213. ———. Black Gipsy and other stories, written at the request of the General Board of Religion Classes of the Church of Jesus Christ of Latter-day Saints for the Primary Dept. Salt Lake City, The Deseret News, 1907.
xi, 152p. 17cm.
Mormon fiction.
USlC, UU

3214. ———. Children of the promise; stories from the Old Testament, prepared for the Deseret Sunday School Union by John Henry Evans . . . Salt Lake City, The Deseret Book Company, 1926.
3p.l. [v]–viii [9]–218p. 20cm.
Mormon stories.
DLC, NjP, USl, USlC, UU

3215. ———. The heart of Mormonism . . . [written for the senior seminaries] of the Church of Jesus Christ of Latter-day Saints. Salt Lake City, Published for the Department of Education, by the Deseret Book Company, 1930.
xii, 529p. illus., ports. 22½cm.
DLC, NjP, NN, USl, USlC, UU

3216. ———. How to teach religion, by John Henry Evans . . . and P. Joseph Jensen . . . Salt Lake City, The Deseret News, 1912.
160p. 18½cm.
DLC, UHi, UPB, USlC, UU

3217. ———. Joseph Smith, a spiritual expert; address delivered over Radio Station KSL, Sunday Evening, February 5, 1928. [Salt Lake City] 1928.
Broadside. 56×23½cm.
Reprinted from the *Deseret News*, Saturday, February 11, 1928.
UPB

3218. ———. Marks of the true spiritual expert. Address delivered over Radio Station KSL, Sunday evening, January 29, 1928. [Salt Lake City] 1928.
Broadside. 47×23½cm.
Reprinted from the *Deseret News*, Saturday, February 5, 1928.
UPB

3219. ———. Message & characters of the Book of Mormon, written in commemoration of the one hundredth anniversary of the publication of the Nephite record by John Henry Evans . . . drawings illustrating ancient American culture and civilization made by John Henry Evans, jr. [Salt Lake City] 1929.
392p. illus., plates, ports., facsim. 25cm.
DLC, NjP, USl, USlC, UU

3220. ———. The New Testament in literature and history, being two reasons for studying that volume, by John Henry Evans of the Latter-day Saints University, 1912. [Salt Lake City] 1912.
14p. 21½cm.
"From the *Improvement Era*."
New Testament study as demonstrated to a Mormon audience.
UU

3221. ———. One hundred years of Mormonism, a history of the Church of Jesus Christ of Latter-day Saints from 1805 to 1905, by John Henry Evans . . . Salt Lake City, The Deseret News, 1905.
xxxviii, 528p. 20½cm.
DLC, MB, NN, OClW, ULA, USl, USlC, WHi

3222. ———. (same) 2d ed. Rev. by the author. Salt Lake City, Deseret Sunday School Union, 1909.
viii, 536p. 20cm.
CSmH, ICN, IWW, MoInRC, NN, USlC, UU

3223. ———. (same) 3d ed. Salt Lake City, Deseret Sunday School Union, 1909.
viii, 536p. 20cm.
CU–B, ICN, IU, NjP, NjPT, NN, OCl, OClWHi, UHi, UPB, USlC, UU

3224. ———. Our church and people, written for the Deseret Sunday School Union, by John Henry Evans . . . Salt Lake City, The Deseret Book Company, 1924.
298p. plates, ports. 20cm.
DLC, NjPT, NN, PCC, UHi, USl, USlC, UU, WHi

3225. ———. (same) 2d ed., 1927. Salt Lake City, The Deseret Book Company, 1927.
298p. illus., ports. 20cm.
1924 in imprint.
NjP, UPB, USlC

3226. ———. Personal and institutional religion; address delivered over Radio Station KSL, Sunday, January 22, 1928. [Salt Lake City] 1928.

Broadside. 50½×23½cm.
Reprinted from the *Deseret News*, Saturday, January 28, 1928.
UPB

3227. ———. Sources of spiritual knowledge; address delivered over Radio Station KSL, Sunday evening, January 15, 1928. [Salt Lake City] 1928.
Broadside. 47×23½cm.
Reprinted from the *Deseret News*, Saturday, January 21, 1928.
UPB

3228. ———. The spiritual expert; address delivered over Radio Station KSL, Sunday Evening, November 6, 1927. [Salt Lake City] 1927.
Broadside. 55½×26cm.
Reprinted from the *Deseret News*, Saturday, November 12, 1927.
UPB

3229. ———. The spoken word; a manual of story-telling and public speaking, including debating . . . Salt Lake City, The Deseret News, 1916.
176p. 18cm.
Public speaking in the church.
DLC, UHi, UPB, USlC

3230. Evans, Richard C. Autobiography of Elder R. C. Evans, one of the First Presidency of the Reorganized Church of Jesus Christ of Latter Day Saints. London, Ont., Advertiser Print., 1907.
xxii, 358p. 20½cm.
MoInRC

3231. ———. Autobiography of Bishop R. C. Evans of the Reorganized Church of Jesus Christ of Latter Day Saints. Lamoni, Ia., Herald Publishing House, 1909.
284p., ports. 20cm.
CtY, MoInRC, NjP, UHi, UPB, USlC

3232. ———. Baptism is immersion. Clifford, Ontario [Printed by R. C. Evans, General Book and Job Printer] 1890.
65p. 15cm.
RLDS doctrine.
MoInRC

3233. ———. Bishop Richard C. Evans makes reply. [Toronto? 19- -]
Broadside. 36×22cm.
Challenge to Frederick M. Smith for a debate.
CU-B, MoInRC, UPB

3234. ———. The Bishop's letter to the public, August 26, 1920. [Toronto] 1920.
[2]p. 27½cm.
At head of title: The Church of the Christian Brotherhood. Office of Presiding Bishopric.
CU-B, IWW, UPB, USlC

3235. ———. The Book of Mormon; evidences of its divinity. Independence, Mo., Ensign Publishing House [n.d.]
31p. 15cm.
MoInRC, USlC

3235a. ———. (same) Independence, Mo., Ensign Publishing House [n.d.]
16p. 19cm.
USlC

3236. ———. (same) Independence, Mo., Ensign Publishing House, 1896.
48p. 16cm. (The Gospel Banner. Vol. 3, No. 1)
MoInRC, USlC

3237. ———. Church unity and how to obtain it; Sermon by R. C. Evans. Toronto, Canada [n.d.]
8p. 26cm.
MoInRC

3238. ———. Controversy between Bishop R. C. Evans of the Reorganized Church of Jesus Christ of Latter Day Saints, Toronto, Ontario, and the Reverend J. A. McKenzie of the Presbyterian Church, Ontario . . . Canada. [Ontario, 1917]
26p. 18cm.
Defense of the RLDS Church.
MoInCR

3239. ———. An examination of Campbellism. Lamoni, Ia., Herald Publishing House, 1908.
41p. 19cm. (No. 305)
RLDS examination of the Disciples of Christ, with many references to their own belief.
MoInRC

3240. ———. (same) Lamoni, Ia., Herald Publishing House, 1915.
41p. 19cm. (No. 1138)
IWW, MoInRC

3241. ———. Faulty creeds. Prominent ministers confirm the Angel's message, by Elder R. C. Evans. Independence, Mo., Ensign Publishing House, 1898.
2p.l., 70p. front. 21cm.
RLDS treatise against Christianity.
MoInRC, UHi

3242. ———. Forty years in the Mormon church, why I left it! By Bishop R. C. Evans. Toronto, Canada [1920?]
173p., [1]l. port. 21cm.
Preface signed: 1920.
His apostasy from the RLDS Church.
CU-B, IWW, MoInRC, NjP, NjPT, RPB, UHi, ULA, UPB, USlC, UU

3243. ———. Future punishment. Independence, Mo., Ensign Publishing House [n.d.]
20p. 16cm.
RLDS doctrine.
MoInRC

EVANS, R. C.

3244. ———. (same) Independence, Mo., Ensign Publishing House [n.d.]
16p. 19cm.
MoInRC, USIC

3245. ———. Future punishment, as described by some of the leading clergymen. Independence, Mo., Ensign Publ. Co., 1906.
24p. 15cm. (The Gospel Banner. V. 14, No. 1)
MoInRC

3246. ———. History of the law suit between Bishop McGuire of the [Reorganized] Latter Day Saint Church and Bishop R. C. Evans of the Church of the Christian Brotherhood. [Toronto, The author, 1921]
[4] p. 21cm.
Caption-title.
Signed: R. C. Evans.
CU-B, UPB, USIC

3247. ———. How can a man be born again. [n.p., n.d.]
8p. 24cm.
RLDS doctrine.
MoInRC

3248. ———. Jesus from the cradle to the grave. Independence, Mo., Ensign Publishing House, 1896.
36p. 15cm. (The Gospel Banner. V. 3, No. 4)
RLDS doctrine.
MoInRC

3249. ———. Joseph Smith: Was he a prophet of God? Independence, Mo., Ensign Publishing House [n.d.]
20p. 20cm.
MoInRC

3250. ———. (same) Independence, Mo., Ensign Publishing House [n.d.]
32p. 16cm.
MoInRC

3251. ———. (same) Independence, Mo., Ensign Publishing House, 1894.
48p. 16cm. (The Gospel Banner. V. 1, No. 3)
MoInRC

3252. ———. (same) Independence, Mo., Ensign Publishing House [191?]
40p. 16cm.
IWW, MoInRC

3253. ———. Latter-day polygamy; its origin. [n.p., n.d.]
16p. 24cm.
MoInRC

3254. ———. (same) Independence, Mo., Ensign Publishing House [n.d.]
21p. 16cm.
MoInRC

3255. ———. (same) Independence, Mo., Ensign Publishing House [ca. 1900]
31p. 15cm.
USIC

3256. ———. Latter-day polygamy, its origin. Independence, Mo., Ensign Publishing House, 1905.
31p. 17cm. (The Gospel Banner. V. 13, No. 1)
MoInRC

3257. ———. Mormonism or Latter-day Saintism by Bishop R. C. Evans. [Toronto, The author, 191–]
[8]p. 27cm.
IWW, UPB

3258. ———. Mormonism unmasked. By Bishop R. C. Evans. [Toronto, The author, 1919]
16p. 26cm.
An attack on Mormonism after he left the Church.
CU-B, MoInRC, UPB, USIC

3259. ———. Purported angelic visitation to R. C. Evans (Recited by R. C. Evans at Broadway Hall, Toronto, Sunday Morning, June 9, 1918, purported to have been received by him, June 3, 1918. Reported by Blanche Allen Needham) [Toronto? 1918?]
8p. 19cm.
MoInRC

3260. ———. The restitution. Independence, Mo., Ensign Publishing House, 1896.
32p. 15cm. (The Gospel Banner series)
RLDS doctrine of salvation.
MoInRC, UPB

3261. ———. The resurrection, sermon by Bishop R. C. Evans. [Toronto, Ontario, n.d.]
8p. 26cm.
RLDS doctrine of the resurrection.
MoInRC

3262. ———. Sermons. By Bishop R. C. Evans. London, Ont., Advertiser Job Print., 1912.
3p.l. [9]–420p. 1 port. 26½cm.
MH, MoInRC, NN, UPB

3263. ———. (same) London, Canada, The London Advertiser, 1913.
56p. 26cm.
UHi

3264. ———. Songs, poems, notes and correspondence of Bishop R. C. Evans and some addresses presented to him from many parts of the world. [London, Ontario, Canada, Advertiser Job Print., 1918]
6p.l., 208p. 23½cm.
MoInRC

EVANS, R. C.

3265. ———. The unchangeability of God. [Toronto? 191?]
6p. 23cm.
A sermon.
IWW, MoInRC

3266. ———. Was Joseph Smith a polygamist? [Toronto, Ontario, 1919]
[16]p. 26cm.
Caption-title.
Signed: R. C. Evans.
CU–B, IWW, MoHi, MoInRC, USlC

3267. ———. Was the thief on the cross a baptized believer? A sermon by Bishop R. C. Evans. [n.p., n.d.]
8p. 26cm.
RLDS doctrine of baptism.
MoInRC

3268. ———. Where is the heathen? Does death end all? Sermon by Bishop Richard C. Evans, Toronto, Canada. [Toronto, 19 - -]
8p. 26cm.
Mention of preaching in spirit prison.
CU–B

3269. ———. Why I left the Latter Day Saint church. [n.p., 1918]
64p. 26cm.
Cover-title.
An early version of his "Forty years in the Mormon church and why I left it."
USl, USlC

3270. Evans, Robley Dunglison. A sailor's log; recollections of forty years of naval life, by Robley D. Evans . . . New York, D. Appleton and Company, 1901.
1p.l., ix, 467p. ports., plates. 21½cm.
Chapter III. "In the Mormon Country," p. 25–34, has some general views of a visit to Salt Lake City and Brigham Young.
Other editions: New York, D. Appleton, 1902. UHi; New York, D. Appleton, 1911. CU
DLC, NjP, ULA, USlC

3271. Evans, William Davies. Dros Gyfanfor a Chyfandir: sef Hanes Taith o gymru at lanau y mor tawelog ac yn ol, Trwy brif Dalaethau a Thiriogaethau yr Undeb Americanaidd. Gan William Davies Evans. Aberystwyth: Argraffwyd gan J. Gibson, swyddfa'r "Cambrian News." [1883]
252p. 21½cm.
Mormons, p. 217–227.
Title in English: Over ocean and continent.
NjP

3272. The Evening and the Morning Star. Independence, Mo. [Kirtland, Ohio] June 1832–September 1834.
2v. (24 nos.) monthly. 30cm.
V. 1, #1–12 not paged continuously.
V. 1, #1–V. 2, #14 (numbering continues through volumes) June, 1832–July, 1833 published at Independence, Mo.; edited by W. W. Phelps.
V. 2 #15–V. 2 #24, December, 1833–September, 1834, published at Kirtland, Ohio; edited by Oliver Cowdery.
None published between July and December, 1833
Followed by *Latter-day Saints' Messenger and Advocate*
CSmH, MoInRC #1–14, USlC

3272a. ———. The Evening and the Morning Star Extra.—July 16, 1833. [Independence, Mo.] 1833.
Broadside. 21½×16cm.
W. W. Phelp's retraction of the article "Free people of color" on p. 111 of issue #14.
USlC

3272b. ———. The Evening and the Morning Star Extra. Kirtland, Ohio, February, 1834.
Broadsheet. 33×21½cm.
"From Missouri" and "The Mormons" so called. Signed by Parley Pratt, Newel Knight, John Carrill December 12, 1833. Sections later published in Pratt's *History of the Late Persecutions . . .*
USlC

3272c. ———. The Evening and the Morning Star Extra. Kirtland, Ohio, August, 1834.
Broadsheet. 33×22cm.
"An appeal" signed by W. W. Phelps, David Whitmer, John Whitmer and others. Concerning Missouri persecutions.
USlC

3273. Evening and Morning Star. Kirtland, Ohio, 1832–34. [i.e. 1835–36]
2v. (24 nos.) monthly. 20cm.
A reprint with changes published at Kirtland, Ohio, from January, 1835 to October, 1836; # 1–11 were published by F. G. Williams & Co., # 12–24 by O. Cowdery.
The numbers have dates and place of publication of original issue (# 1–14. Independence, Mo.; nos. 15–24, Kirtland, Ohio)
Date and plate of reprint is given at end of each number.
CSmH, CtY, CU–B, UPB, USlC

3274. The Evening and Morning Star; issued monthly in the interests of the Church of Christ. Independence, Mo., Printed and Published at the Church of Christ Publishing House on the Temple Lot, May 15, 1900–August 1916.
18v. monthly. 35cm.
Official organ of the Church of Christ (Temple Lot)
John Haldeman, Editor. Followed by Geo. P. Frisby and Abraham L. Hartley.
Includes a reprint of the Independence issues of the *Evening and Morning Star* 1832–1833, V. 12–15.
Published in double columns V. 1, # 1–V. 2, # 5; V. 3, # 1 in triple columns; V. 17, # 7 in double columns.
CU–B V. 12 #2–V. 15 #3; MH V. 1–11 #13; MoInRC inc.; UPB V. 12–15; USlC V. 1–15 #3.

3275. Eventful narratives. . . . Designed for the instruction and encouragement of young Latter-day Saints. Salt Lake City, Juvenile Instructor Office, 1887.
vii [9]–98p. 19cm. (Faith promoting series. 13th book)
Contents: Leaving home, by Robert Aveson. A boy's love; a man's devotion. A trip to Carson Valley, by O. B. Huntington.
CSmH, CU–B, DLC, ICN, MH, NjP, NN, UHi, UPB, UU

3276. Everhart, John R. By boat and rail by John R. Everhart. New York, G. P. Putnam's Sons, 1892.
x, 233p. port. 19cm.
Two trips to Salt Lake City. Some arithmetic shows how the Church gets 3/10 for tithing.
CU–B, USlC

3277. Everitt, Nicholas. Round the world in strange company, America, British Columbia and the West. By Nicholas Everitt . . . Illustrated. London, T. Werner Laurie, Ltd. [n.d.]
xv, 283p. 21½cm.
Describes Salt Lake City and the Temple block; states that the belief is essentially good.
USlC

3278. The Everlasting Gospel of Jesus Christ our Lord. . . . Written by Joseph the Prophet, of the last part of the day. [n.p., n.d.]
42p. 17½cm.
Baptized into the church in 1886, the author has visions, revelations, etc.
USlC

3279. Ewing, Hugh Boyle. The blacklist. A tale of early California. By General Hugh Ewing. New York, P. F. Collier, 1893.
288p. 18cm.
On cover: Once a week. Semi-monthly library.
Deals partially with Mormon vigilantes in San Francisco. Fiction.
CU, ULA, USlC

3280. Ewing, Leon R. A rejected manuscript. The other side. [n.p., n.d.]
15p. 20½cm.
Defense of Mormonism "rejected" by eastern papers.
MH, USlC

3281. The Ex Luminus. Salt Lake City, L. D. S. Hospital. School of Nursing, 1929–
v. illus., plates, ports. 23½cm.
USlC 1929

3282. The Excelsior Star. Ephraim, Utah, Published by the Students of the Sanpete Stake Academy, February, 1898–
v. irregular. 26cm.
Published by the student body.
USlC #1, 1898; #6, March, 1899.

3283. The Expositor. Oakland, Calif., Pacific Coast Mission, January, 1885–December, 1888.
4v. monthly. 35½×26cm.
Editor: H. P. Brown.
Published through V. 4 # 11.
RLDS church periodical.
MoInRC

3284. An exposure of Mormonism. [Exeter? 1891]
Broadside. 12½×6cm.
A quote from the *Gentleman's Journal* reviewing W. Jarman's lectures.
MH

Extracts from pioneer G. O.'s journal. *See Osborne, George.*

3285. Eyring Henry. Ein Wort der Verteidigung oder Antworten auf Fragen in Betreff der Lehren der Kirche Jesu Christi der Heiligen der letzten Tage, von Heinrich Eyring. Bern, Herausgegeben von J. U. Stucki, 1875.
16p. 21½cm.
Cover-title.
Title in English: A word of defense or answers to questions about the beliefs and teachings of the Church . . .
NjPT, USlC, UU

3286. Eytinge, Rose. The memories of Rose Eytinge; being recollections and observations of men, women, and events, during half a century, by Rose Eytinge. New York, F. A. Stokes Company [1905]
xiip., [2]l., 3–311p. 8 port. 19½cm.
Chapter 34. Visit to Salt Lake City as a guest of Brigham Young.
DLC, MB, NjP, NN, PP, PPM, PU, USlC, UU, ViU

3287. Ezzell, Levi H. Is polygamy ordained of the Lord. [Independence? 1897?]
24p. 16cm.
Signed: Independence, Mo., Aug. 1897.
MoInRC

3288. ———. Parable of Zenos. Independence, Mo. [1915?]
38p. 18cm.
Signed: March 18, 1915.
Parable portraying the rise and fall of the Jews and the restoration of the gospel, with its various off-shoots.
MoInRC

"THE MORMONS"

OR

"LATTER-DAY SAINTS"

REPLY

BY

HUGH FINDLAY

Elder of the Church of Jesus Christ of Latter-Day Saints.

TO A TRACT BEARING THE ABOVE TITLE BY J. G. DECK AND REPRINTED AT THE BOMBAY "TIMES PRESS."

"*He that judgeth a matter before he heareth it, is not wise*"

BOMBAY

Duftur Ashkara Press.

1853.

Item 3352. One of the earliest Mormon tracts published in India, symbolic of the spread of Mormonism beyond the United States and western Europe in the 1850s. From the LDS church collection.

F., H.

3289. F., H. The first principles of the gospel, by H. F. [Plano, Ill., True Latter-day Saints' Herald, 1866?]
4p. 23cm. [True Latter Day Saints' Herald. Tract No. 5]
Signed: H. F.
CtY, MoInRC, NN, UPB

3290. Fac-Simile of the Brass Plates recently taken from a mound in the vicinity of Kinderhook, Pike County, Illinois. [Liverpool, 1850?]
Broadside. 41×25cm.
Twelve plates with background material, including certifications of authenticity.
CSmH, UPB

3291. Facts and queries for Mr. Jarman. [Liverpool, Church of Jesus Christ of Latter-day Saints, n.d.]
[2]p. 18cm.
Refutation of some of W. Jarman's anti-Mormon lectures.
USIC

Facts for the times. *See Pratt, Parley Parker.*

3292. The facts of the Utah case. Salt Lake City, Tribune Job Printing Company, 1892.
23p. 22cm.
Caption-title: "The situation in Utah."
"To the delegates to the Democratic National Convention."
MH

Fagerstjerna, P. W. P. *See The Light of Messiah.*

3292a. Fairbanks, Edward Taylor. The town of St. Johnsbury Vt.; a review of one hundred twenty-five years to the anniversary pageant 1912. St. Johnsbury, The Cowles Press, 1914.
592p. ports. 23½cm.
Mormons, p. 217–219.
USIC

3293. Fairchild, James Harris. . . . Manuscript of Solomon Spaulding and the Book of Mormon, a paper read before the Northern Ohio and Western Reserve Historical Society, March 23, 1886. [Cleveland, 1892?]
1p.l. [187]–200p. 24½cm. (Western Reserve Historical Society. Tract No. 77)
Cover-title.
Printed with a new title page.
CU–B, DLC, ICN, MH, NN, UPB

3294. Fairfield, Asa Merrill. Fairfield's pioneer history of Lassen County, California, containing everything that can be learned about it from the beginning of the world to the year of our Lord 1870 . . . showing the efforts of the settlers to obtain freedom from Mormon rule . . . San Francisco, H. S. Crocker Co. [c1916]
xxii, 506p. fold. map. 22½cm.
Mormons, p. 50–53, 70–76.
USIC

3295. Fairfield, Edmund B. The early history of Joseph Smith. [Oberlin, Ohio? 1902?]
8p. 15cm.
USIC

3296. Faithfull, Emily. Three visits to America, by Emily Faithfull . . . Edinburgh, D. Douglas, 1884.
xv, 377p. 21½cm.
Chapter XI deals with polygamy; exposé of the endowment ceremony, p. 150–178. Chapter XII deals with the Book of Mormon, etc., p. 179–199.
Another edition: New York, Fowler & Wells c1884. DLC
CSmH, CtY, CU–B, DLC, MH, NjP, NN, ULA, UPB, USl, USIC, UU

3297. Falck, Lilliebell. "Lest we forget"; our World War heroes. Ogden, Utah, 1927.
47p. illus. 24cm.
Cover-title.
Biographies of Utah men killed in World War I.
DLC, UHi, UPB, USIC

Falconer, M. A. *See Walker, Marietta.*

3298. Falding, Frederick J. Notes of a journey round the world; made in 1875, by Thomas Coote, esq., jun. and Dr. Falding. [By] F. J. Falding. Sheffield, Leader and Sons Printers, 1876.
2p.l., 208p. 18½cm.
"Notes . . . printed almost exactly as they first appeared in the columns of *The Independent*."
"A Sunday amongst the Mormons at Salt Lake City" 1875, p. 192–204.
NN, OClW, OO, PSC, UHi

3299. Falk, Alfred. Trans-Pacific sketches; a tour through the United States and Canada, by Alfred Falk. Melbourne, George Robertson, 1877.
xv, 313p. 18½cm.
Travels through Salt Lake City in 1876.
Description of the city and notes on Mormonism with a little on its political and social aspects. The whole thing a "gigantic" fraud.
UHi, USIC, UU

3300. Fallows, Samuel. Hot shot fired at fashion's follies and society's abominations. Portrayed by eminent thinkers and writers. Introduction by Rt. Rev. Samuel Fallows . . . Illustrated. Chicago, Standard Publishing Co., 1889.
xxxi, 9–569p. plates. 22cm.
"Mormon Question," [by] The Rev. J. P. Newman, p. 99–113.
How to offset Mormonism.
USIC

3301. ———. The Mormon menace, by Rt. Rev. Samuel Fallows . . . and Helen M. Fallows, A. M. Chicago, Woman's Temperance Publishing Association, 1903.
122p., [1]l. 19½cm.
CSmH, CtY, DLC, NN, UPB, USlC, WHi

3302. Faris, John Thomson. On the trail of the pioneers; romance, tragedy and triumph of the path of empire, by John T. Faris . . . New York, George H. Doran Company [c1920]
xii, 15–319p. col. front., plates, port., maps. 21cm.
Tells of 5000 Mormons crossing the Kansas River in 1846, marching with 10 brass-pieces, every man having rifle, brace of pistols & bowie knife.
Notes the fear of emigrants on the Santa Fe Trail concerning these Mormons.
CU–B, DLC, NjP, NN, UHi, UPB, USlC, UU

3303. ———. Roaming the Rockies; through national parks and national forests of the Rocky Mountain wonderland. With an introductory note by Horace M. Albright. New York, Farrar & Rinehart, 1930.
xiv, 333p. illus., plates, map. 21cm.
Maps on inside covers.
Chap. V. "Through Utah's forests." References made to the Mormon settlement of the Salt Lake Valley.
CU–B, NjP, UPB

3304. ———. The romance of forgotten towns. New York, Harper & Brothers, 1924.
xiv, 335p. illus. 22½cm.
Chap. 29. Six stirring years at Nauvoo, Ill.
Chap. 30. The Kingdom of Beaver Island.
CU, NjP, UHi, USlC

3304a. ———. Seeing the Far West. Philadelphia & London, J. B. Lippincott Co., 1920.
303[1]p. illus. 22½cm.
Mormons, p. 85–86, 92–104, 190–191.
USlC

3305. Farish, Thomas Edwin. History of Arizona, by Thomas Edwin Farish, Arizona historian . . . Phoenix, Ariz. [San Francisco, The Filmer Brothers Electrotype Company] 1915–18.
8v. plates, ports., maps. 21½cm.
Mormon colonization in Arizona; Mormon battalion.
Howes F37
CU–B, DLC, NjP, UHi, UPB

3306. Farnham, Thomas Jefferson. Travels in the great western prairies, the Anahuac and Rocky Mountains and in the Oregon Territory. By Thomas J. Farnham. Poughkeepsie, Killey and Lossing, Printers, 1841.
197p. 19cm.
Mormons driven from Missouri; Spaulding manuscript; other references.
Other editions: London, R. Bentley, 1843. DLC, ICJ, MH; Poughkeepsie, Killey and Lossing; New York and London, Wiley & Putnam, 1843. CSmH, CtY; New York, Greeley and McElrath, 1843. CtY, CU–B, DLC, MA
Also in Reuben G. Thwaites' *Early Western Travels*. V. 28–29.
Published in German under title: Wanderungen über die Felsenbirge in das Oregongebiet . . . Leipzig, Mayer, 1846. OrP, OrU, WaU
Howes F 50, Sabin 23872, W–C 85
CtY, CU–B, DLC, NjP, NN, NP, ULA

3307. Farnsworth, Moses Franklin. Farnsworth memorial. Being a record of Matthias Farnsworth and his descendants in America. Gathered from authentic sources and comp. by Moses Franklin Farnsworth . . . Manti, Utah, L. A. Lauber, 1897.
514p. ports. 23cm.
Includes biographies and genealogies of several Mormons.
CSmH, DLC

3308. Farnsworth, Stephen M. Farnsworth's vision . . . [Salt Lake City? n.d.]
8p. 11½cm.
Written on first page: William Jex, 1854.
Cover missing.
Printed in many forms, but never given official sanction.
USlC

3309. ———. A vision, as seen by Stephen M. Farnsworth in Nauvoo, Ill., early in the Spring of 1844. As related by himself . . . Bloomington, Utah, Printed at the Union Office, 1886.
8p. 13cm.
USlC

3310. ———. (same) Springville, Utah, Printed by J. M. Westwood [n.d.]
4p. 14½cm.
Cover-title.
UPB

3311. ———. Washington's vision. The Wars of 1812 and 1861 revealed to him. Mother Shipton's prophecy, and S. M. Farnsworth's vision. Salt Lake City, 1877.
8p. 16½cm.
Cover-title.
UHi

Farr, Julia [*pseud.*] *See Mosehauer, Julia Abbey (Trumpler)*

Faulconer, M. A. *See Walker, Marietta.*

FAULKNER, C. J.

3312. Faulkner, Charles James. A bill for the local government of Utah Territory and to provide for the election of certain officers in said Territory. Washington, 1892.
16p. 33cm. (S. 1306)
Eberstadt: *Utah and the Mormons*

3313. ———. A bill to enable the people of Utah to form a constitution and state government, and to be admitted into the Union on an equal footing with the original states. Washington, 1893.
16p. 32cm. (S. 3766)
Eberstadt: *Utah and the Mormons*

3314. ———. Speech of the Hon. Charles J. Faulkner of Virginia in favor of an increase of the army and in opposition to the employment of volunteers in Utah. Delivered in the House of Representatives, March 9, 1858. Washington, 1858.
18p. 21cm.
A speech against the church situation after the expedition; his opinion that hiring volunteers would be folly.
Vi, ViU

3315. Favez, Louis. Fragments sur les Mormons. Lausanne, Switzerland, Delafontaine et cie [et] Mme. Duret-Corbaz, 1854–56.
2v. [84, 82p.] 19cm.
I. Joseph Smith et les Mormons, ou examen de leurs prétentions relativement a leur Bible, a leur prophetè et a leur église.
II. Le Mormonisme jugé d'après ses doctrines: exposé succinct des notions Mormonnes, et de leur valeur relativement a la Sainte Ecriture.
Title in English: Fragments on the Mormons.
CtY, CU–B V. I, MH V. I, WaU V. II, WHi

3316. ———. Lettre sur les Mormons de la Californie. Vevey, Impr. de E. Buvelot, 1851.
46p. 18½cm.
Signed: L. Favez.
An essay on Mormon theology.
Title in English: Letter on the Mormons of California.
CtY

3317. Featherstone, Joseph F. Iesu Kirisuto no Ryakuden oyobi Shimei. Toykō, Nihon, Matsu Jitsu Seito Iesu Kirisuto Kyōkai Nihon Dendōbu [1907]
62p. 15½cm.
Title in English: The brief life of Christ and His mission.
USIC

3318. ———. (same) [Tokyō, Nihon, Matsu Jitsu Seito Iesu Kirisuto Kyōkai Nihon Dendōbu] [1909]
62p. 15cm.
"2d edition"
USIC

3319. Feil, Paul. A solemn appeal unto all Israel (Ephraim and Manasse) [Salt Lake City, 1929?]
Broadside. 28×21cm.
Pres. Grant's refusal to read a divine message through Feil in conference.
Signed: Paul Feil, "The Messenger the Lord's Servant."
USIC, UPB, UU

3320. Felt, Charles Brigham. Teaching in the home. Salt Lake City, Presiding Bishop's Office [n.d.]
12p. 17½cm.
Instructions for ward teaching.
USIC

3321. ———. (same) [n.p., n.d.]
12p. 15cm.
Variant edition.
UPB

3322. ———. (same) [n.p., n.d.]
15p. 17cm.
USIC

3323. ———. What the restored gospel of Jesus Christ means to me; address delivered over Radio Station KSL, Sunday, Nov. 13, 1927. [Salt Lake City] 1927.
Broadside. 51×20½cm.
Reprinted from the *Deseret News*, Saturday, Nov. 19th, 1927.
UPB

3324. Ferguson, Charles D. The experiences of a Forty-niner during thirty-four years' residence in California and Australia; by Charles D. Ferguson, edited by Frederick T. Wallace. Cleveland, Ohio, The Williams Publishing Co., 1888.
xviii, 9–507p. illus., plates, port. 22½cm.
Cover-title: A third of a century in the gold fields.
Trip through Utah in 1850 with a discussion of Mormonism.
Another edition: Chico, Calif., M. A. Carson, 1924. CU–B, UHi
CU–B, DLC, ICN, NjP, UPB, USIC

3325. Ferguson, Charles Wright. Confusion of tongues. A review of modern isms. A biography of sects. Garden City, New York, Doubleday, Doran & Co., 1928.
7p.l., 464p. 21cm.
Mormonism among the isms.
"A religion may flourish without any historical truth of any sort beneath it."
Another edition under title: The new books of revelations. 1929. NjP, USIC
DLC, NjPT, UPB, USIC

3326. Fernhagel, D. T. Die Wahrheit über das Mormonenthum. Blätter aus Utah. Zürich, Verlags-Magazine, 1889.
iv, 111p. 22cm.

Chapters on Utah territory: the founding of the Church of Jesus Christ of Latter-day Saints, the Book of Mormon, history of the Mormons, Salt Lake City, Brigham Young and polygamy.
Title in English: The truth about Mormondom.
ICN, MH, NN, UPB

3327. Ferril, Thomas Hornsby. High passage [by] Thomas Hornsby Ferril. New Haven, Yale University Press; London, H. Milford, Oxford University Press, 1926.
50p. 19½cm. (On cover: The Yale series of younger poets)
Poem: The hands of Joseph Smith, p. 35–6.
CU, DLC, NjP, UHi

3328. Ferris, Benjamin G. Utah and the Mormons. The history, government, doctrines, customs and prospects of the Latter-day Saints. From personal observation during a six months' residence at Great Salt Lake City, by Benjamin G. Ferris. New York, Harper and Brothers, 1854.
xii [13]–347p. illus., ports., plates. 20cm.
In Utah, October, 1852–May, 1853.
Howes F98, Sabin 24184, W–C 238a
CSmH, CtY, CU–B, MoInRC, MoK, NjP, NjPT, ULA, UPB, USl, WHi

3329. ———. (same) New York, Harper & Brothers, 1856.
xii [13]–377p. illus., port., plates. 20cm.
CSmH, NjP, NN, OO, UHi, UPB

3330. Ferris, Cornelia (Woodcock). The Mormons at home; with some incidents of travel from Missouri to California, 1852–3. In a series of letters. By Mrs. B. G. Ferris . . . New York, Dix & Edwards; [etc., etc.] 1856.
viii, 299p. 19cm.
Appeared first in a series of letters in *Putnam's Monthly* under title "Female life among the Mormons." They arrived in Salt Lake City before October 30, 1852 and left for California via Carson Valley May 5, 1853.
Howes F 99, Sabin 24186, W–C 274
CSmH, CtY, CU–B, DLC, ICN, MoInRC, NjP, UHi, ULA, USl, USlC, UU, WHi

3331. Ferris, George Titus. Our native land: or, Glances at American scenery and places, with sketches of life and adventure, with three hundred and thirty-six illustrations. New York, D. Appleton and Company [c1882]
xv, 615p. illus. 27cm.
Description of area through Utah.
"The Mormons despite their abominable faults . . . their bigotry, and the crimes of murder and spoilation; are thrifty and hard working."
Another edition: 1886. UHi
USlC

3332. Ferry, Jeannette Hollister. The Industrial Christian Home Association of Utah. Salt Lake City, Utah Territory. Salt Lake City, Salt Lake Lithographing Co., 1893.
90p. 22cm.
Compilation of the various reports & statements concerning the Industrial Christian Home, created to aid polygamist women.
UHi, USlC, UU

3333. Fetting, Otto. Eleventh visitation of the messenger. Port Huron, Mich. [192–]
3p. 21cm.
Church of Christ (Fetting)
MoInRC

3334. ———. Ninth visitation of the messenger to Elder Otto Fetting, Port Huron, Mich. [1929?]
[2]l. 21½cm.
"Supplement to Revelation on building the Temple."
UPB, USlC

3335. ———. Revelation on building of the Temple. Given to Apostle Otto Fetting, Port Huron, Michigan, March the 22nd, 1928. Port Huron, Mich., 1928.
Broadside. 27½×21½cm.
The 5th message.
UPB

3336. ———. Revelation to build the Temple. The time is at hand. The Lord has spoken and revealed His purpose by the mouth of His Servant "John" . . . Port Huron, Mich., Zions Advocate, Printed by Elder H. L. MacPherson [1928?]
16p. 22cm.
MoInRC, UPB, USlC

3337. ———. (same) [Printed by Elder H. L. MacPherson, Port Huron, Mich., 1929?]
20p. 22cm.
UPB, USlC

3338. ———. Revelations on the building of the Temple. The time is at hand. The Lord has spoken and revealed His purpose, by the mouth of his Servant "John." Port Huron, Mich. [Printed by H. L. MacPherson, 1929?]
14p. 22½cm.
In double columns.
Contains first 12 messages.
MoInRC

3338a. ———. Supplement revelation on the building of the temple and instruction to the Church of Christ. Twentieth visit of the messenger to Elder Otto Fetting, April 8, 1930. [Independence, Mo.? 1930?]
[2]p. 22cm.
USlC

FETTING, O.

3338b. ———. Supplement revelations on the building of the temple and instruction to the Church of Christ. Twenty-first visitation. [Port Huron, Michigan, Mrs. Otto Fetting, Box 212, 1930?]
[2]p. 22cm.
USIC

3338c. ———. Tenth visitation of the messenger to Elder Otto Fetting, Port Huron, Mich. Supplement to revelation on building the temple. Port Huron, Michigan, Mrs. Otto Fetting, Box 212 [Printed by Elder H. L. MacPherson, Port Huron, Michigan, 1929?]
[3]p. 21½cm.
USIC

3339. ———. A Warning to all people of the second coming of Christ. Revelations on the building of the temple and instruction to the Church of Christ . . . The time is at hand. The Lord has spoken and revealed His purpose by the mouth of His servant "John" (The Baptist) [Port Huron? 1930?]
20p. 22×21½cm.
Last message (19th) dated February 28th, 1930.
MoInRC, USIC

3340. ———. A warning to all people of the second coming of Christ. Twelfth message. [Independence, Mo., Church of Christ, 1929?]
[4]p. 21cm.
UU

3341. Few choice examples of Mormon practices and sermons. [n.p., 1886?]
[73]p. 22cm.
Contents: Mysteries of the Endowment House; Brigham Young's will; Fraud on the will; Mormon expositor; Mountain Meadows massacre; Mormon absurdities; Saintly falsity; David Whitmer talks.
CSmH, CtY, CU–B, DLC, MH, NjP, UPB, USI

3342. A few historical facts concerning the murderous assault at Pine River. Also the life, ministry, ancestry and childhood of James J. Strang. Lansing, Mich., Reprinted by Charles J. Strang, 1892.
7p. 21cm.
Reprint of the *Northern Islander Extra* of July 14, 1853 and a sketch of the "Ancestry and Childhood of James J. Strang written by himself, 1855."
WBuC

3343. ———. (same) [Kansas City, Mo.? 1902?]
9p. 23cm.
Contents: Northern Islander extra, Sant [sic] James, Thursday, July 14, 1853. Ancestry and childhood of James J. Strang written by himself, 1855. . . . Faithful account of the murder of James J. Strang.
CtY, CU–B, MH, MoInRC, WBuC

3344. A few plain words about Mormonism, showing that Latter-day Saints are no saints at all proved by extracts from their writings. By the author of a few plain words about Popery and the Pope, Pope or Queen, &c. Bristol [For the author by Wright Steam Press, 185–]
16p. 16½cm.
CtY, CU–B, NN, USIC

3345. A few thoughts suggested by the term "Latter-day Saint." Ledbury, Printed and Sold by J. Gibbs, jun. [ca. 1840]
Broadside. 22½×14cm.
Possible author. W. J. Morrish.
UPB

3346. A few words about the Mormons. [n.p., n.d.]
2v. 21cm. (Nos. 1–2)
Cover-title.
USIC

3347. Fidelity Picture Plays Syndicate. . . . "The Power of the Mormons . . ." Cleveland [1919?]
6p. illus. 26cm.
A promotional pamphlet for a projected movie.
USIC

3348. Field, Homer Howard. History of Pottawattamie County, Iowa, from the earliest historic times to 1907. By Homer H. Field and Hon. Joseph R. Reed, also biographical sketches of some prominent citizens of the county. Chicago, The S. J. Clarke Publishing Co., 1907.
2v. plates, ports. 27cm.
Mormons in Pottawattamie County, V.1, p.7–17.
DLC, NN, USIC

3349. Fielding Academy, Paris, Idaho. Fielding Academy. Announcements. 1899–
v. 20cm.
Previously called Bear Lake Stake Academy.
USIC 1899–1900, 1902–19

3350. Fields, James Thomas, *ed.* Good company for every day in the year. . . . Boston, Ticknor and Fields, 1866.
iv, 326p. illus., plates, ports. 19cm.
Rose Terry: The Mormon's Wife, p. 89–108.
DLC

3350a. Fike, Veva Jeanette Walton. Jealous of God. By Rose B. Blossom [*pseud.*] Du Quoin, Ill., Bierman Printing Service, 1929.
166p. illus. 22cm.
Mormon biography.
USIC

3351. Findlay, Allen M. Prove all things; hold fast that which is Good. — Paul. Secunderabad [India] Advertiser Press [1855]
Broadside. 20×12½cm.
An advertisement of a series of 12 lectures by Elder Allen M. Findlay of the East Indian Mission on Mormonism.
USIC

3352. Findlay, Hugh. Mormons or "Latter-day Saints," a reply by Hugh Findlay, Elder of the Church of Jesus Christ of Latter-day Saints. To a tract bearing the above title of Jesus Christ of Latter-day Saints. To a tract bearing the above title by J. G. Deck and reprinted at the Bombay "Times Press." Bombay, Dustur Ashkara Press, 1853.
2p.l., 20 [1]p. 21cm.
USIC

3353. ———. The overthrow of infidel Mormonism: Being a report of the Louth discussion, which took place in the Guild Hall, Louth, Lincolnshire, August 28, 29, 30 and September 2, 3, & 6, 1850; between Mr. Hugh Findlay, Mormon Elder, from Scotland; and Mr. John Theobald . . . London, Published by W. Horsell [1850]
143p. 18cm.
USIC

3354. ———. (same) To which is added account of the discussion which took place at Spondon on the 26th of May, 1848, between Mr. Theobald and Mr. George Henry, Mormon delegate . . . London [Published by] W. Horsell, 1850.
175 [1]p . 16cm.
P. 145–175 [1] The Report of a public discussion on Mormonism between Mr. George Henry . . . and Mr. John Theobald.
Has separate title-page and the date of the debate is given as May 26th, 1849.
"Second Edition."
UU

3355. ———. To the Marattas of Hindoostan. A treatise on the true and living God and His religion. By H. Findlay, Elder of the Church of Jesus Christ of Latter-day Saints . . . Translated by Chintamon Bulall Josee. Bombay, Printed at Gunput Crushnagee's Press, 1855.
1p.l., 16 [1]p. 21cm.
Enclosed in border.
Title repeated in Hindustani. Text in Hindustani.
USIC

3356. Finks, Delos Edwin. An illustrated lecture on Mormonism. A despotism within a republic. Prepared for the Home Mission Boards by Rev. Delos Edwin Finks, for use in the churches . . . New York, Literature Department, Home Missions of the Presbyterian Church [n.d.]
32p. 18cm.
USIC

3357. Fireside sketches of scenery and travel. . . . Battle Creek, Mich., The Central Manufacturing Co., 1890.
1p.l., 5–192p. illus., ports., plates. 29½cm.
"Salt Lake City," by Rev. J. H. Waggoner, p. 39–44.
Mostly tourist information, some information on Mormonism.
Another edition: Nashville, Tenn., Nashville Illustrating Co., 1904. UHi
USIC

The Fireside Visitor; or, plain reasoner. *See Candland, David.*

3358. Firkins, O. W. The reticent convict; a one-act play. [Salt Lake City] General Boards of M.I.A., 1929.
16p. 19cm.
USIC

3359. First century of national existence; the United States as they were and are. . . . by an eminent corps of scientific and literary men. Hartford, Conn., Published by L. Stebbins, 1872.
xiv [2] [17]–585p. illus., plates, maps. 25cm.
Brief, inaccurate section on Mormons.
Other editions: 1873. DLC; 1874. DLC; 1876. CSmH
CSmH, DLC, UU

The First principles of the gospel. *See F., H.*

3360. First principles of the true gospel of Christ. [Liverpool, Millennial Star Office? 1908?]
4p. 21½cm.
Caption-title.
Probable author: Joshua Hughes Paul.
UHi, UPB, USIC

3361. ———. (same) [Liverpool, n.d.]
4p. 21cm.
Variant printing.
UPB, USIC

3362. Fisher, George J. Scouting in Utah. [In a personal letter to Oscar A. Kirkham, Executive Director of the Y.M.M.I.A.] February 2, 1924. New York, 1924.
[1]p. 28cm.
Multilithed.
UPB

3363. Fisher, Hugh Dunn. The gun and the gospel; early Kansas and Chaplain Fisher, by Rev. H. D. Fisher . . . Chicago, Medical Century Company, 1896.
xi [10]–344p. plates, ports. 21cm.
Chap. xxxi "Pastoral experiences in Salt Lake City." "Bible work among the Mormons."
Other editions: 2d ed. 1897. DLC, UPB; 3d ed. 1899. UPB, UU; Chicago, Kenwood press, 1896. DLC, UPB
USIC

3364. Fisher, Margaret May (Merrill). Utah and the civil war, being the story of the part played by the people of Utah in that great conflict, with special reference to the Lot Smith expedition and the Robert T. Burton expedition; compiled and edited by Margaret M. Fisher, and assisted by C. N. Lund

and Judge Nephi Jensen, under direction of the J. Q. Knowlton post of the G. A. R. . . . [Salt Lake City, The Deseret Book Company, c1929]
173p. illus., plates, ports. 22½cm.
CU–B, DLC, NjP, NN, UHi, ULA, UPB, USl, USlC, UU

3365. Fisher, Sidney George. The law of the territories. Philadelphia, Printed by C. Sherman & Son, 1859.
xxiv [25]–127p. 19cm.
Signed: Cecil.
Brief mention of the problems in Utah as they reflect the whole territorial problem.
CU, USlC

3366. Fisher, Vardis. Toilers of the hills. Boston and New York, Houghton Mifflin Company, 1928.
3p.l., 361p. 21cm.
Fiction with Mormon setting.
UPB

3367. Fisher, W. R. Poems. Caldwell, Idaho, 1910.
39p. 33cm.
Mormon poetry.
USlC

3368. Fishwick, J. F. The false prophet tested; or Mormonism refuted by J. F. Fishwick. London, Wertheim and Macintosh, 1853.
16p. 13cm.
NN

3369. Fitch, Thomas. Argument of Hon. Thomas Fitch. Addressed to the House Judiciary Committee in reply to the memorial of the Salt Lake Bar, and in opposition to House bill, 3791, February 10, 1873. Washington, Gibson Brothers, Printers, 1873.
34p. 22cm.
The evils of the anti-polygamy bill as contrasted with the belief that the peculiarities of Utah would rapidly disappear.
DLC, MH, MnH, NN, PHi, UHi

3370. ———. United States of America; Plaintiff vs. Ammon M. Tenney, Defendant. Brief by Thos. Fitch, of Counsel for Appellant. Phoenix, Herald Print., 1885.
8p. 25cm.
Polygamy trial.
USlC

3371. ———. The Utah bill. Speeches of Hon. Thos. Fitch, of Nevada, and Hon. A. A. Sargent, of California. Delivered in the House of Representatives, Feb. 23, 1870. [Washington? Cunningham and McIntosh Printers] 1870.
8p. 24cm.
Caption-title.
Against the practice of polygamy.
CU–B, DLC, UPB

3372. ———. The Utah problem. Review of the course of Judge James B. McKean, and an appeal for the surrender of polygamy. Speech of Hon. Thomas Fitch, in the Constitutional Convention of Utah, February 20, 1872. [Salt Lake City] Printed at the Salt Lake Herald Office, 1872.
20p. 21½cm.
Sabin 24590
CtY, DLC, ICN, MnH, NN, USlC

3373. Flagg, Edmund. The far West: or, A tour beyond the mountains. Embracing outlines of western life and scenery; sketches of the prairies, rivers, ancient mounds, early settlements of the French, etc. . . . New York, Harper & Brothers, 1838.
2v. 18½cm.
Early history of Mormons in Ohio and Illinois. Mormons listed on the chart as heretics.
Reprinted in Reuben G. Thwaites, *Early Western Travels.*
Howes F–169, Sabin 24651 London
CSmH, CtY, DLC, IHi, MB, MH, NjP, NN, OCl, OClW, UHi, UPB, USlC

3374. Flanigan, J. H. Mormonism triumphant! Truth vindicated, lies refuted, the Devil mad, and priestcraft in danger!!! By J. H. Flanigan, Elder in the Church of Jesus Christ of Latter-day Saints. Being a reply to Palmer's internal evidence against the Book of Mormon . . . Liverpool, Printed by R. James, 1849.
32p. 21½cm.
Cover-title.
Also one of the first printings of the fourteen articles of faith.
Howes F–171, Sabin 24674
CSmH, CtY, CU–B, ICN, MH, MnH, MoInRC, NjP, NN, ULA, UPB, USl, USlC, UU

3375. ———. Reply to a sheet entitled "The result of two meetings between the L. D. Saints and Primitive Methodists," at Gravely, Cambridgeshire. By James H. Flanigan, L.D.S. [Liverpool? 1849?]
8p. 21cm.
Signed: Bedford, March 1, 1849.
Caption-title.
MH

Fleming, G. A. *See California; its past history.*

3376. Fletcher, C. H. B. Utah's industries, resources, enterprises. Descriptive, statistical, comparative. Salt Lake City, c1888.
64p. 12½cm.
NN, UPB

3377 Fletcher, Fred Nathaniel. Early Nevada. The period of exploration, 1776–1848. By F. N. Fletcher. [Reno, Nevada, Printed by A. Carlisle & Co. of Nevada, 1929]
1p.l. [i] iii, 183p. front., mounted fold. map. 19cm.
References to the Mormons in Nevada, p. 169, 171, 176, 180–183.
CU–B, DLC

FOLLOWING

3378. Flint, Thomas. Diary of Dr. Thomas Flint, California to Maine and return, 1851–1855. [Los Angeles, 1924]
78p. 3 port. on 1 plate, fold. map. 22½cm.
Cover-title.
Trip through Utah, 1853.
Reprinted from the *Evening Lance*, Hollister, California. Also reprinted from the *Annual of the Historical Society of California*.
Another edition: 2d ed. Hollister, Cal., Commercial Print. Co., 1927. MH
DLC, ICN, NjP, NN, UHi, USlC, UU

3379. Florence, William Jermyn. Florence fables, by William J. Florence (comedian). New York [etc.] Belford, Clarke & Co. [1888]
4p.l. [9]–246p. 2 ports. 19½cm.
Includes "Teelie's Grave." A Mormon story.
DLC, UHi, UPB, USlC

3379a. Flint, Wilson. Report of Mr. Flint, of the Select Committee, to Whom was referred the resolutions of Miner's Convention at Shasta County. Submitted March 28, 1855. [Sacramento, B. B. Redding, State Printer, 1855]
13p. 22½cm. (Calif. Senate. Session 1855. Doc. No. 19)
Mormons mentioned, p. 4–5.
USlC

3380. Flory, Joseph. Watchman what of the night? or, Where do we stand? Hanford, Calif., 1914.
2p.l., 65p. 20½cm.
Cover-title.
Written for members of the RLDS Church showing the undesirable condition of the church.
MoInRC, UHi

3381. Flygare, N. C. Mormonerne skildret af Ikke-Mormoner. Kobenhavn, 1888.
16p.
Title in English: Mormons described by non-Mormons.
Schmidt

3382. Fog, Carl. Mormonerne; en historisk skildring. [n.p.] Nyt Theologiske Tidsskrift, 1851.
Title in English: The Mormons; a historical sketch.
Mulder

3383. Fohlin, Ernest Victor. Handbok för Skandivanier i Utah, innehållande beskrifvning öfver Salt Lake City, och des omgifningar, jemte laganvisningar, formulärer och pristabeller, för allmänt bruk, samt andra nyttiga och intressants ämmen . . . Utgifven af E. V. Fohlin. [Salt Lake City, J. D. Graham & Co., 1882]
2p.l., 47p. 15cm.
Title in English: A handbook of Utah for Scandinavians.
DLC

3384. ———. Salt Lake City, past and present; a narrative of its history and romance, its people and cultures, its industry and commerce . . . E. V. Fohlin, author. Salt Lake City, E. V. Fohlin [c1908]
208p. illus., ports. 24½cm.
CSmH, CU–B, DLC, MB, NjP, NN, OCl, UHi, ULA, USl, USlC, UU

3385. ———. (same) Salt Lake City, 1909 [c1908]
208p. illus., ports. 24½cm.
UPB

3386. Foley, Samantha T. (Brimhall) Conciones de Sion ó del culto Mormon, por la Señora {Samona / Samantha} T. Brimhall de Foley. [Salt Lake City, Skelton Pub. Co., c1911]
v. [3] 197p. 19cm.
Title in English: Songs of Zion.
CU–B, DLC, UHi, USl, UU

3387. Folk, Edgar Estes. The Mormon monster; or, the story of Mormonism, embracing the history of Mormonism, Mormonism as a religious system, Mormonism as a social system, Mormonism as a political system; with a full discussion of the subject of polygamy, by Edgar E. Folk . . . with an introduction by George A. Lofton . . . Chicago, New York [etc.] Fleming H. Revell Company, 1900.
6p.l., 5–372p. plates, ports. 21½cm.
DLC, MB, MoInRC, NjP, NjPT, NN, PCC, PU, UHi, ULA, UPB, USl, USlC, WHi

3388. Follett, Frederick. History of the press of western New York; prepared at the request of a committee, by Frederick Follett of Batavia. Together with the proceedings of the Printers' Festival held on the 141st anniversary of the birth-day of Franklin in the City of Rochester, on Monday, January 18, 1847. Rochester, Printed by Jerome and Brother, Daily American Office, 1847.
1p.l., 76p. 22½cm.
Short sketch of W. W. Phelps and his anti-Masonic paper in Ontario County, p.44, and of E. B. Grandin, printer of the *Book of Mormon* in Wayne County, p.65.
Another edition: New York, Reprinted for C. F. Heartman, 1920. NjP
Howes F–223
CSmH, ICN, MH, NN, PLL

3389. The following are some quotations from the teachings of Jesus Christ in the New Testament and from the teachings of the Christ of the Doctrine and Covenants, arranged alternately to facilitate comparison: . . . [Tooele City, Utah, 1894]
[3]p. 21½cm.
Comparison of the teachings of the New Testament and the Doctrine and Covenants.
No author or title.
USlC

3390. Fonnesbeck, Christian. Svar paa Sognespraesten A. Bulows angreb paa Mormonerne. [Copenhagen, I Holstebro avis "og" Holstebro "Dagblad" for 10 November, 1903]
8p. 21cm.
Title in English: An answer to a parish priest.
USlC

3391. ———. (same) [Copenhagen, I holstebro avis "og" holstebro "Dagblad" for 10 November 1903 og folgende dage, 1903?]
16p. 21½cm.
USlC

3392. Foote, Edward Bliss. Plain home talk about the human system — the habits of men and women — the causes and prevention of disease — our sexual relations and social natures. Embracing medical common sense applied to causes, prevention, and cure of chronic diseases — the natural relations of men and women to each other — society — love — marriage — parentage — etc., etc. By Edward B. Foote . . . New York, Murray Hill Publishing Company [etc., etc.] 1874.
xxiv [25]–924p. illus. 20cm.
Mormon polygamy, p. 647–659; Joseph Smith, p. 739; Brigham Young, p. 743–48.
Another edition: New York, Murray Hill Publishing Company, 1899. UHi
UPB

3393. Foraker, Joseph B. Senator from Utah. Remarks of Hon. Joseph B. Foraker, of Ohio, in the Senate of the United States, February 20, 1907. Washington, 1907.
8p. 23cm.
Cover-title.
The seating of Reed Smoot.
UHi

3394. Forbes, Edward. Literary papers by the late Professor Edward Forbes, F.R.S. Selected from his writings in "The Literary Gazette." London, L. Reeve, 1855.
xvi, 300p. 18cm.
Chapter 10. The Salt Lake and the Mormonites, p. 263–277. Social conditions.
CU, DGS, DLC, MH, NN, NjP, USlC

3395. Ford, David. The Mormon lion; chapters from the secret memoirs of David Ford. London, J. Long, Limited [1915?]
320p. 19½cm.
"First pub. in 1915."
Fiction concerning Mormonism.
CSmH, UPB, UU

3396. Ford, Maria B. Who is Mr. Jarman? Letter from his first wife. Extract from the "Barnsley Independent," September 17, 1887. [n.p., 1887?]
Broadside. 27×13½cm.
Refutation of William Jarman's lectures on Mormonism.
USlC

3397. Ford, Thomas. A history of Illinois from its commencement as a state in 1818, to 1847. Containing a full account of the Black Hawk War, the rise, progress, and fall of Mormonism, the Alton and Lovejoy riots, and other important and interesting events. By the late Gov. Thomas Ford. Chicago, Published by S. C. Griggs & Co.; New York, Ivison & Phinney, 1854.
1p.l. [v]–xvii, [19]–447p. 20½cm.
Variant edition copyrighted in New York with printer note: Printed by John F. Trow, 49 Ann St. Date on title page reads: Commencement as a state in 1814 to 1847.
Another edition: Chicago, S. C. Griggs & Co.; New York, Ivison & Phinney, 1859. CtY
Howes F–254, Sabin 25070
CSmH, CtY, CU, DLC, ICN, NjP, NN, UHi, ULA, USl, USlC, UU, WHi

———. *See also Illinois. Governor, 1842–1846 (Ford).*

3398. Fordham, K. E. Sego Lily. Words and music by K. E. Fordham. [Chicago, Rayner, Dalheim & Co., Music Printers, c1918]
2p. music. 29½cm.
Mormon music.
UHi, UPB

3399. Forepaugh's Great All-Feature Show. The progress of civilization; thrilling incidents in actual border life in the wild West, the great drama enacted by frontier heroes. [Philadelphia, Morrell Brothers, ca. 1890]
[32]p. illus. 26cm.
Includes: "The atrocious Mountain Meadow massacre; the realistic portrayal of the perils of early Western emigration." Circus promotion.
UHi

3400. The Forerunner. Independence, Jackson County, Missouri, Zion's Printing and Publishing Company, June, 1908–
v. monthly. 28cm.
Editor: B. F. Cummings.
Vol. 1 #1. All published.
USlC

3401. Forgeron, Kenelm D. Treason in Utah; a true account of the insults perpetrated by rebellious Mormons against the government on July 4th, 1885 . . . By Kenelm D. Forgeron. Brattleboro, Vt., F. E. Housh, 1885.
18p. 20cm.
CtY, DLC, MH, USlC

FOURTH OF JULY

3402. Förlofnings-ringen. [Salt Lake City, Korrespondenten, 1893?]
24p. 14cm.
Title in English: The engagement ring.
A doctrinal work in Danish.
UPB

3403. Formation of a division for parade purposes. [Great Salt Lake City, ca. 1860]
Broadside. 26×11cm.
Formations for 4th and 24th parades.
USlC

Forscutt, Mark H. *See Shinn, John L.*

3404. Forster, Arthur Haire. Four modern religious movements, by Arthur Haire Forster. Boston, R. G. Badger [c1919]
95p. 19½cm. (On cover: Library of religious thought)
Includes Mormonism. Lacks references.
DLC, MB, NjPT, NN, UHi, USl, USlC

3405. Forsyth, Goerge Alexander. The story of the soldier, by Brevet Brigadier-General Goerge A. Forsyth . . . Illustrated by R. F. Zogbaum. New York, D. Appleton and Company, c1900.
xv, 389p. front., plate. 19cm. (Half-title: The story of the West)
The Mormon battalion, Mountain Meadows massacre, Utah Expedition.
Howes F 270
DLC, ICN, UHi, ULA, UPB, USlC

3406. Foster, George G. The gold regions of California; being a succinct description of the geography history, topography, and general features of California: including a carefully prepared account of the gold regions of that fortunate country. Prepared from official documents and other authentic sources. Edited by G. G. Foster. New York, Dewitt and Davenport, 1848.
vii [9]–80p. map. 23cm.
A reproduction of the author's, "The gold mines of California." cf. Sabin.
Mormons would not leave for Salt Lake City from gold diggings unless gold was found there. Informed by an intelligent Mormon that it had been found near Great Salt Lake.
Other editions: 2d ed. New York, Dewitt and Davenport, 1848. CU, OU; 3d ed. New York, 1848. CtY, DLC, NN
Howes F287, Sabin 25225
CSmH, CtY, CU–B, DLC, ICN, PHi, PMA, PPL, PU

3407. Foster, Roxana (Cheney). The Foster family. California pioneers of 1849. [San Jose? Calif., 1889]
46 numb. l., ports. 20×16½cm.
Diary of a trip to Salt Lake City in 1849 to trade with the Mormons. Description of Brigham Young and harem; attendance at a July 4th celebration.
DLC

3408. ———. The Foster family, California pioneer's first overland trip, 1849; second overland trip (via Panama) 1857. [Santa Barbara, The Schauer Printing Studio, c1925]
285p. illus., ports. 20cm.
Enlarged edition of the 1889 book.
Howes F 292
CU–B

3409. Foster, Stephen C. Republican land policy—homes for the million. Give the public lands to the people, and you settle the slavery question, obliterate the frontiers, dispense with a standing army and extinguish Mormonism. Speech of Hon. Stephen C. Foster, of Maine, delivered in the House of Representatives, April 27, 1860. Washington, Buell & Blanchard, Printers, 1860.
8p. 21½cm.
Caption-title.
UHi

3410. Fotsch, Wilhelm. Denkwürdigkeiten aus der Neuen Welt. Ein Beitrag zum 400 jähringen Jubiläum der Entdeckung Amerikas. Von W. Fotsch . . . Im selbstverlag des Verfassers. In Kommission: Cranston und Stowe, Cincinnati, O. [etc., Druck vom] Verlag des Traktathauses, Bremen [1890–91]
2v. in 1. 21½cm.
"II bd. Zur Kenntoris der Mormonen."
Title in English: Remarkable things of the new world.
CtY, DLC, MH, NN

3411. Foulke, William Dudley. Random record of travel during fifty years, by William Dudley Foulke . . . New York, Oxford University Press, 1925.
vii, 241p. plates. 21½cm.
"The Mormon orator," p. 27–30. Attends the theatre and a service in the tabernacle. His reactions to the service.
CU, NjP, USlC

3412. Fountain, Paul. The eleven eaglets of the West. London, J. Murray, 1906.
x, [1]l., 362. 23cm.
Includes a description of Utah with commentary on Mormonism.
CU–B, DLC, NjP, UHi, ULA, UPB, USlC, UU

3413. Fourth of July celebration at Great Salt Lake City, 1865. Order of Exercises. [Great Salt Lake City] Daily Telegraph Print., 1865.
Broadside. 27×20cm.
Signed: G. S. L. City, July 1, 1865.
USlC

3414. Fourth of July, 1869. Celebration on the 4th. [Salt Lake City] News Print., 1869.
Broadside. 40×13½cm.
Text in ornamental border.
Signed: R. T. Burton, H. W. Lawrence, S. W. Richards, Wm. Jennings, Heber P. Kimball, Committee of Arrangements.
USlC

3415. Fowler, Leonard. In the shadow of Moroni. Being a compendium of the various advantages to be derived by living in the Rome of America (Salt Lake City). A complete and revised history of the city by the sea, from the time of the old Spanish explorers, and a full description of its many advantages for the home-seeker, speculator, health-seeker, and investor. [Salt Lake City] Souvenir Guide Co. [c1895]
127p. illus., ports. 23cm.
CU–B, DLC, MH, UHi, ULA, USl, USlC

Fowler, William B. *See Cook, William. The Mormons.*

3416. Fox, Jesse Williams. General courses and distance from G.S.L. City to Fort Limhi and gold diggings on Salmon River. By Jesse W. Fox, Territorial Surveyor-General. Great Salt Lake City, Deseret News Print., 1862.
8p. 19½cm.
On brown paper.
Adv. on verso of title, and on page 8.
The route traveled by Brigham Young in 1857 while visiting the Salmon River Mission.
W–C 381
CSmH, CtY, ICN

3417. Fox, Ruth (May). May blossoms. [Salt Lake City, General Board of the Young Ladies' Mutual Improvement Association] 1923.
3p.l., 115p. front. 19cm.
Mormon poetry.
UHi, USlC

———. A temple anthem. *See Coombs, Leo Mark.*

3418. Fragments of experience. Designed for the instruction and encouragement of young Latter-day Saints. Salt Lake City, Juvenile Instructor Office, 1882.
viii [9]–96p. 19cm. (Faith promoting series. 6th book)
Partial contents: Anson Call. Disobedience to counsel. Lorenzo Dow Young. Narrative. William Budge. An instance of divine interposition. William W. Cluff. My last mission to the Sandwich Islands. B. F. Johnson. A prophecy fulfilled; an incident of missionary experience.
CtY, CU–B, ICN, MH, MoInRC, NN, UHi, UPB, USl, USlC, WHi

3419. Frame, Nathan T. Reminiscences of Nathan T. Frame and Esther G. Frame. [Cleveland, The Britton Printing Co.] 1907.
2p.l., vip., [1]l., 9–673p. plates, ports. 24cm.
Material on Salt Lake City and Mormons in 1901, p. 573–8.
DLC, NjP, USl, UU

3420. France, George W. The struggles for life and home in the North-west. By a pioneer homebuilder. Life, 1865–1889. [By] Geo. W. France. New York, I. Goldmann, Printer, 1890.
607 [1]p. illus., port., facsims. 25cm.
"All about the Mormons," p. 44–61.
CSmH, CU–B, DLC, ICN, NjP, NN, UHi, USlC, WaS, WaU, WaWW

Frances [*pseud.*] *See Walker, Marietta.*

3420a. Frank Merriwell among the Mormons; or, The lost tribe of Israel. By the author of "Frank Merriwell." New York, Street and Smith, 1897.
32p. 26cm. (Tip Top Weekly. June 19, 1897. Vol. 1. No. 62)
Bound in original colored pictorial wrappers.
UPB

3421. Frankau, Gilbert. My unsentimental journey. 1st ed. London, Hutchinson & Co. Ltd. [1926?]
6p.l. [17]–285p. 19½cm.
Half-title: Gilbert Frankau's unsentimental journey.
"The home of the Mormons — A visit to Salt Lake City. 1926."
CU–B, DLC, UU

3422. Franklin, John Benjamin. A cheap trip to the Great Salt Lake City. An annotated lecture delivered before the President of America and representatives; th Mayors of Liverpool & Manchester, by J. Benjamin Franklin, LL.D., (Late Manager of the Mormon Printing Office, Great Salt Lake City.) . . . 3rd Edition. Ipswich, Printed and Published by J. Scoggins, Orwell Place [1864]
33p. 20½cm.
Cover-title.
Howes F335
CSmH, CtY, MnU, NN, UHi, UPB, WHi

3423. ———. (same) Ipswich, J. Scoggins [1864]
31 [1]p. 19½cm.
"Fourth edition."
Cover-title.
CSmH, CtY, CU–B, DLC, NjP, NN, UHi, USlC, WHi

3424. ———. The horrors of Mormonism; being a lecture delivered by John Benjamin Franklin (late manager of the Mormon printing office at Great Salt Lake City) in several places in England &c. [London, J. Appold, 1858]
16p. 18cm.
ICN, NN

3425. ———. (same, under title) The mysteries and the crimes of Mormonism; or, a voice from the Utah pandemonium, by J. B. Franklin . . . 2d edition, revised. London, Published by C. Elliot [186–]
16p. illus. 18½cm.
"Second edition, price one penny. Revised by the author, with additions."
MH, USlC

3426. ———. One year at the Great Salt Lake City; or, A voice from the Utah pandemonium. Manchester, England, John Heywood, etc. etc. [18 - -]
48p. 16cm.
MH, NN

3427. Franson, F. Forsörelsens Kunstgreb afslørede; eller 70 af Mormonernes misforstaaede Bibelsprog betragede i Skriftens Lys ved F. Franson. Ifaerdeleshed tilegnet Skandinaverne i Utah, samt Alle med Mormonismen bekjendte i Norge, Sverige og Danmark saavelsom andre Lande. Chicago, "Skandinavens" Bogtrykkeri [1880]
213 [4]p. 15cm.
USIC

3428. ———. (same, in English) Wiles or error unveiled, or 70 Bible passages misunderstood by the Mormons considered in the light of the scriptures. By Rev. F. Franson . . . Chicago, Distributed by John Martenson [n.d.]
239 [1]p. 17cm.
IWW, USIC

3429. Fraser, John Foster. Round the world on a wheel; being the narrative of a bicycle ride . . . through seventeen counties and across three continents by John Foster Fraser, S. Edward Lunn, and F. H. Lowe. Written by John Foster Fraser. London, New York [etc. pref. 1849]
vi [9] [17]–558p. plates, port. 16cm.
Visit to Salt Lake City; spends an afternoon in the Tabernacle.
Other editions: New York, Thomas Nelson & Sons, 1899? UPB, USIC; London, Methuen & Co., 1899. DLC
CU–B

3430. ———. (same, in Swedish) Verlden rundt på cycle. Thugufem månders ridt på bicykel genom Europa Asien och Amerika, Utförd af John Foster Fraser, S. Edvard Lunn och F. H. Lowe. Skildrad af John Foster Fraser. Med 245 illustrationer. Stockholm, C. L. Gullbergs Förlag [1900]
3p.l., 437p. illus., ports. 26½cm.
"Till Utah och Klipphergen." The Utah portion of the trip, with reactions to Mormonism, p. 395–400.
USIC

3431. Fraud on the will [of Brigham Young]. Over a million dollars stolen by Taylor and Co. Suit of the heirs to recover the money. Full exposure of the robbery, trickery and collusion . . . In the District Court of the Third Judicial District of Utah Territory. Emeline A. Young, on behalf of herself and the heirs . . . and beneficiaries under the last will and testament of Brigham Young, Executors . . . and John Taylor, John Sharp, Edward Hunter [and others] Defendants. [Salt Lake City, 1879]
9–27p. 25cm.
Caption-title.
CtY, CU–B, NN, UHi

Fraud on the Will. *See Brigham Young's will and fraud on the will; Young, Brigham.*

3432. Frazee, W. D. San Bernardino County, its climate and resources. By W. D. Frazee, esq. . . . San Bernardino California, San Bernardino, Daily and weekly Argus Office, 1876.
2p.l. [ii]–iv [5]–101, xviip. 25cm.
Includes Mormon settlement of San Bernardino.
DLC

3433. Frazier, Esther Yates. Pearl; an ocean waif by Esther Yates Frazier. Denver, The Reed Publishing Company, 1903.
237p. 20½cm.
A sentimental love story with a Mormon setting.
DLC

3434. Frazier, Mrs. R. Reminiscences of travel from 1855 to 1867. By a lady. Also, a graphic and accurate account of the seven day's battle before Richmond, and a history of Mormon life. San Francisco, 1868.
2p.l., 156p. 19cm.
Other editions: San Francisco, 1869. MH, USIC; 1871. USIC (1869 ed. printed with a 1871 cover)
Cty, CU–B

3435. Freece, Blanche K. Stewart. How Mormons recruit abroad [by] Blanche K. Stewart-Freece and Hans P. Freece. [New York, 1911]
1p.l. [1] 6–34p., [1]l. 22½cm.
Abridged report of investigations . . . for "the Interdenominational Council of Women for Christian and Patriotic Service."
NN, USIC

3436. Freece, Hans P. Hans P. Freece; popular lectures. Des Moines, Midland Chautauqua Circuit [c1909]
[21]p. 30cm.
Subject: Mormonism in four lectures.
USIC

3437. ———. How a young girl became a Mormon. New York City, Spectator Print, Columbia University [n.d.]
10p. fold. 17cm.
USIC

3438. ———. The letters of an apostate Mormon to his son, by Hans P. Freece; illustrated by Verona P. Turini. [New York, The Wolfer press, c1908]
2p.l., 73p. illus., port. 21cm.
CSmH, CU–B, DLC, ICN, MoInRC, NjPT, NN, UHi, USI, USIC, WHi

3439. ———. (same) 2d ed. [Elmira, New York, c1908]
2p.l., 73p. illus., ports. 21cm.
CtY, NN

3440. ———. (same) 3d ed. [New York? c1908]
2p.l., 73p. illus., ports. 20cm.
MH, MoKu, NjPT

3441. ———. (same) [New York, c1908]
2p.l., 7–73p. illus., port. 20cm.
"Fifth edition."
MH, NN, OClWHi, PCC

3442. ———. (same) [New York, c1908]
60p. illus., port. 21cm.
"Sixth edition."
NN, ULA, UPB

3443. ———. (same) [New York, c1908]
68 [1]p. 21cm.
"Seventh edition."
CSmH, NN, UHi, UPB

———. Mormon chief confesses. *See Smith, Joseph Fielding, 1838–1918.*

3444. ———. The Mormon peril. Salt Lake City [1909?]
[2]p. 22cm.
Extracts from *Salt Lake Tribune* and advertisement for his *The letters of an apostate Mormon to his son.*
UPB

3445. ———. The truth about the recent Anti-Mormon riots in England. [New York City, 1911?]
34 [1]p. 21cm.
Preface signed: Blanche K. Stewart-Freece and Hans P. Freece.
Caption-title.
UPB

3446. Freeman, Lewis Ransome. Down the Grand Canyon. New York, Dodd, Mead and Co., 1924.
6p.l., 3–371p. plates. 23cm.
Mormons, p. 77, 84, 87, 91–93, 179, 180, 192–95, 307, 309–10, 317.
DLC, UHi, UPB, USlC

3447. Freemasons. Illinois, Grand Lodge. Proceedings of the Grand Lodge of Illinois in the town of Jacksonville. Jacksonville, Ill., 1842–1844.
3v. 22cm.
Nauvoo lodge first mentioned in the proceedings for 1842, in which a resolution is put forward to suspend labors of Nauvoo lodge until a committee has inquired into irregularities. [Mormonism not mentioned]
In 1844 proceedings it was resolved expedient to abandon the lodge in Nauvoo.
Reprinted in 1 V. (p. 34–45, 45–46, 58, 59, 73) Freeport, Ill., Journal Print., 1892. DLC
DLC, IHi, MBFM, NNFM

3447a. M.·. W.·. Grand Lodge (Nevada) Proceedings of the M.·. W.·. Grand Lodge of Free and accepted Masons of the state of Nevada, at its second annual grand communication, held at Masonic Hall, in the City of Virginia, September 18, 19, 20, and 21, A.L. 5866. San Francisco, Frank Eastman, 1866.
iii [117]–205p. 21½cm.
Mormons and Mount Moriah Lodge in Salt Lake City, p. 120–121, 166, 169.
USlC

3448. Freer, Romeo Hoyt. The Roberts case . . . Speech of Hon. R. H. Freer, of West Virginia, in the House of Representatives . . . January 25, 1900. Washington [Govt. Print. Off.] 1900.
8p. 23cm.
DLC

3448a. Fremodt-Moller, H. O. Luk Døren for Mormonerne! Adversel! [Salt Lake City?] Udgivet af Udvalget for Dansk Luthersk Mission i Utah, 1907.
[4]p. 20cm.
Title in English: Close the door to the Mormons.
USlC

3448b. (same) [Salt Lake City?] Udgivet af Ulvalget for Dansk Luthersk Mission i Utah, 1911.
[4]p. 21cm.
USlC

3449. Frémont, Elizabeth Benton. Recollections of Elizabeth Benton Frémont, daughter of the pathfinder General John C. Frémont and Jessie Benton Frémont, his wife. Compiled by I. T. Martin. New York, Frederick H. Hitchcock, MCMXII [1912]
184p. plates, ports. 19½cm.
Reference to the Mormons, p. 72–73.
CU–B, DLC

3450. Frémont, Jessie (Benton). Far-West sketches. Boston, D. Lathrop Company [c1890]
1p.l., 9–206p. 18½cm.
John C. Frémont stopped in Parowan in 1854 and sent material to Washington by Almon W. Babbitt.
DLC, UHi, ULA, UPB

3451. Frémont, John Charles. Geographical memoir upon upper California, in illustration of his map of Oregon and California, by John Charles Frémont: Addressed to the Senate of the United States. Washington, Wendell and Van Benthuysen, Printers, 1848.
67p. 23cm. (U.S. 30th Cong. 1st Sess. Senate. Misc. No. 148)
Mention of Mormons, p. 7–8. The map drawn by Charles Preuss, was the first published map to reflect the Mormon settlement of the Utah region.
CSmH, CtY, CU, CU–B, DLC, IaH, WHi

3452. ———. (same) Washington, Printed by Tippin & Streeper, 1849.
40p. 23cm. (U.S. 30th Cong. 2d Sess. House. Misc. No. 5)
CtY, CU, CU–B, DLC, WHi

3453. ———. (same, under title) Geographical memoir upon upper California. By John Charles Frémont. Addressed to the Senate of the United States in 1848. To which are now added, extracts from Hakluyt's collection of voyages, La Peyrouse's voyage, Venega's history of California, Harris's collection of voyages, von Langdorff's travels, Alcedo's geographical and historical dictionary, Hastings's guide to Oregon and California, Farnham's life and adventures in California. The President's Message to Congress, December 6, 1848, Col. Mason's report to the Secretary at [sic] War, Letter of the Rev. Walter Colton, August 29, 1848, Certificate of the Mint, Letter of Thomas O. Larkin, Late Consul at Monterey, Letter from Com. Jones to the Secretary of the Navy, Oct. 25, 1848, Editor of the Oregon Spectator — His account of Oregon. By William McCarty. Philadelphia, Published by William McCarty, and for sale by Booksellers generally, 1849.
80p. 24½cm.
Frémont's references to the Mormons, p. 7–8; Col. Mason's mention of the Mormons in the gold fields, p. 69, 71–72.
CtY, CU–B, WHi

3454. ———. Letter of J. C. Frémont to the editors of the National Intelligencer, communicating some general results of a recent winter expedition across the Rocky Mountains, for the survey of a route for a railroad to the Pacific. June 15, 1854. Referred to the Select Committee on the Pacific Railroad and ordered to be printed. [Washington, 1854]
7p. 22½cm.
Describes his winter journey of 1853–54, with an account of the Mormon settlements of Parowan and Cedar City, and mention of Mormon explorations of the Virgin River, p. 4–6.
C, CU, CU–B, DLC

3455. ———. . . . Message of the U.S. communicating the proceedings of the Court Martial in the trial of Lt. Col. Frémont, Apr. 7, 1848. Washington, 1848.
447p. 22½cm.
At head of title: (U.S. 30th Cong. 1st Sess. Senate. Executive No. 33)
Caption-title.
References to the Mormons, p. 29, 33, 42, 80, 99, 122, 137, 140–143, 150, 165–166, 171, 203, 233–234, 242–243, 259–263, 271, 273–275.
CSmH, CtY, CU, CU–B, DLC, WHi

3456. ———. Memoirs of my life by John Charles Frémont. Including in the narrative five journeys of western exploration, during the years 1842, 1843–44, 1845–6–7, 1848–9, 1853–4. Together with a sketch of the life of Senator Benton, in connection with western expansion. By Jessie Benton Frémont. A retrospect of fifty years covering the most eventful periods of modern American history . . . With maps and colored plates. Vol. 1. Chicago and New York, Belford, Clarke & Company, 1887.
vii [iii]–iv [xv]–xix, 655p. illus., plates, ports., maps (part. fold.) 28cm.
Includes a section: "Why the Mormons chose Salt Lake," and his association with the Mormons during his exploration expedition.
CU–B, DLC, MH, NjP, OCl, UHi, ULA, USl, USlC, UU

3457. ———. Notes of travel in California; comprising the prominent geographical, agricultural, geological and mineralogical features of the country; also, the route from Fort Leavenworth, in Missouri, to San Diego, in California, including parts of the Arkansas, Del Norte, and Gila Rivers. From the official reports of Col. Frémont and Maj. Emory. New-York, D. Appleton & Company; Philadelphia, G. A. Appelton [sic] 1849.
29, 3–83p. map. 22½×13½cm.
Brief mention of Mormonism in the Frémont report.
Other editions: London, McGlashon, 1849. Sabin; Dublin, Published by James M'Glashan, 1849. NjP
Sabin 25846
CU–B, DLC, MH, NN, UU, WHi

3458. Fremont Stake Academy. First annual report of the Fremont Stake Academy Tabernacle Building for the year ending December 31st, 1900. Rexburg, Idaho, Press of the Fremont Journal, 1901.
[17]l. illus. 17½cm.
USlC

3459. French, A. B. Gleanings from the rostrum, by A. B. French. Columbus, Ohio, Hann & Adair, 1892.
299p. front. 18½cm.
"Joseph Smith and the Book of Mormon," delivered at Cassadaga, N.Y., p. 108–138.
UHi

French, Augustus C. *See Illinois. Governor, 1846–53 (French)*

3460. French, Hiram Taylor. History of Idaho; a narrative account of its historical progress, its people and its principle interests. Chicago, The Lewis Publishing Company, 1914.
3v. illus. 27cm.
Mormon colonization and activities in Idaho.
CU–B, DLC, NjP, UHi, ULA, UPB

3461. French, John Homer, *editor.* Gazetteer of the state of New York; embracing a comprehensive view of the geography, geology, and general history of the state, and a complete history of the state, and a complete history and description of every county, city,

town, village and locality with full tables of statistics. By J. H. French . . . 8th ed. [Syracuse, R. P. Smith] 1860.
2p.l., 3–739p. illus., plates. 25½cm.
Mormons at Palmyra, p. 693.
Another edition: 1861. USlC has a defective earlier edition without title page.
Sabin 25862
CU, DLC

3462. French, R. H. Mormonism; a reply to the doctrine of polygamy; sketches of the prophets, Smith and Young, and the origin of their systems. By R. H. French. Newport, Printed by J. C. Patterson, 1858.
vi, 71 [1]p. 17cm.
Reply to P.P. Pratt's *Marriage and morals in Utah.*
ICHi, MH

3463. Frere, John. A short history of the Mormonites; or, Latter-day Saints. With an account of the real origin of the Book of Mormon. Compiled from various sources. By the Reverend John Frere. London, J. Masters, 1850.
24p. 18½cm.
Howes F–378, Sabin 25907
CSmH, CtY, MH, NN, UU

3464. Fridriksson, Fridrik. Mormona-villan. Stutt yfirlit yfir trú og kinninger "hinna sidousta daga heilögu." Eptir Fr. Fridriksson. [Reykjavík, a Kostnad höfundarins, 1901]
18p. 18cm.
Caption-title.
Title in English: The false beliefs of Mormonism.
NN, USlC

3465. Die Friedensbotschaft. Bamberg, Germany. April 1, 1926–October, 1939.
v. monthly. 18cm.
RLDS publication in German.
Title in English: Message of peace.
MoInRC Vol. 1 inc., 2–5, 6 inc., 7, 8–14 inc.

3466. Friendly warnings on the subject of Mormonism; addressed to his parishioners, by a country clergyman. London, Francis and John Rivington, 1850.
35p. 17½cm.
MH, OClWHi

3467. A Friendly warning to the Latter-day Saints, or Mormons; in which the true character of the Mormon missionaries is plainly set forth by one who was of that community, and a resident in Salt Lake. . . . London, Wertheim, Macintosh, & Hunt, 1860.
61p. 18cm.
NN

3468. Fries, Louis J. One hundred and fifty years of Catholicity in Utah, by the Rev. Louis J. Fries, S.T.B. with a foreword by His Eminence Patrick Cardinal Hayes, Archbishop of New York. Souvenir volume of the installation of the Right Reverend John J. Mitty, D. D., as the Third Bishop of Salt Lake on October 7th, 1926. Salt Lake City, Intermountain Catholic Press, 1926.
143p. illus., ports. 28½cm.
Includes Mormon treatment of Catholicism and Catholic missionary work.
NjP, ULA, USlC

3469. Frimodt-Moller, H. O. Luk doren for Mormonerne. Advarsel! Udgivet af udvalget for Danske Luthersk Mission i Utah. [Kobenhavn, 1907]
[4]p. 20cm.
Title in English: Lock your doors because of the Mormons.
USlC

3470. Frizzell, Lodisa. Across the plains to California in 1852. Journal of Mrs. Lodisa Frizzell. Edited from the original manuscript in the New York Public Library by Victor Hugo Paltsits . . . New York, the New York Public Library, 1915.
30p. 3 plates, 3 maps on 1 plate. 25½cm.
Reprinted from the *Bulletin of the New York Public Library*, April, 1915, p. 335–362.
Remarks on the wreck of the steamer Saluda on which many Mormon emigrants were lost, p. 8; encounter with Mormon emigrants, p. 22.
DLC

3471. Froiseth, Jennie Anderson. The women of Mormonism; or, The story of polygamy as told by the victims themselves. Edited by Jennie Anderson Froiseth . . . with an introduction by Miss Frances E. Willard, and supplementary papers by Rev. Leonard Bacon . . . Hon. P. T. Van Zile, and others . . . Illustrated. Detroit, Mich., C. G. G. Paine, 1882.
xviii, 19–416p. illus., plates, ports. 20cm.
CSmH, CtY, CU-B, DLC, ICN, MH, MoInRC, NjP, NjPT, NN, UHi, USl, USlC, WHi

3472. ———. (same) Detroit, Mich., C. G. G. Paine, W. H. Thompson & Co., Boston, Mass.; A. G. Nettleton & Co., Chicago, Ill.; [etc., etc.] 1882.
xviii, 19–416p. illus. 20cm.
USlC

3473. ———. (same) Detroit, Mich., C.G.G. Paine, 1884.
xviii, 19–416p. illus., plates, ports. 20cm.
CtY

3474. ———. (same) Detroit, Mich., C.G.G. Paine, 1886.
xviii, 19–416p. illus., plates, ports. 20cm.
UPB, WHi

3475. ———. (same) Detroit, Mich., C.G.G. Paine, 1887.
xviii, 19–416p. illus., plates, ports. 20cm.
DLC, UHi, USlC, UU

3475a. ———. (same, in Swedish) Mormonismens qvinnor eller manggiftets historia, berattad af offren sjelfva. Ofversttning från engelskan af K. A. J. Stockholm, Litteraturforeningens forlag [1883]
xii, 142p. 17cm.
USlC

3476. From England to California: Life among the Mormons and Indians. . . . Sacramento, J. A. Wilson, Publisher [1868]
146p. 18½cm.
"The most thrilling account of murders in Utah."
Copyright by F. Merryweather.
C, CSmH, CU–B, ICN

3477. Frontier Guardian. Kanesville, Iowa. Published by Orson Hyde, Feb. 7, 1849–Feb. 20, 1852. [As Frontier guardian and Iowa sentinel] March 4–July 2, 1852.
4v. (80 nos. Frontier guardian and Iowa sentinel. V. 4 #3–20) weekly, semi-monthly. 22cm.
Publisher and editor: Orson Hyde.
Frontier Guardian and Iowa Sentinel edited by Jacob Dawson.
CtY. CU–B Jl 16–Ag 13, 1852 #22–26. DLC My 29, Je 12, 1850; Je 13, O 3, 1851; F 6, Mr–Je 1852. ICN Ap 18, My 16, 30. MH. USlC V.1–V.5 #13

3478. Frost, W. Dialogue between a Latter-day Saint and a Methodist, in which some of the errors of that strange people are exposed, as the dialogue has actually taken place in substance, the facts here stated may be relied on, and can be proved from their printed works. By W. Frost. Aylshem [England] Printed by C. Clements [1849?]
10p. 17cm.
Dated at end: Banningham, April, 1849.
USlC

3479. Froude, James Anthony. Oceana; or, England and her colonies. By James Anthony Froude. New York, C. Scribners and Sons, 1886.
ixp., [1]l., 396p. plates. 22cm.
Evaluation of the durability of Mormonism after Brigham Young's death.
Other editions: London, Longmans, Green, 1886. CSmH, CU, CU–B, NjP; Copyright ed. Leipzig, B. T. Auchmitz, 1887. CU; New York, Scribners, 1887. DLC; London, Longmans, Green, 1888. ICJ; New York, Scribners, 1888. CSmH; (same) 1897. NN; London, Longmans, Green & Co., 1894. CU
CSmH, DLC, MH, NN, PU, USlC, ViU

3480. Fry, Charles. Reasons why I believe the Book of Mormon. [n.p., n.d.]
31p. 19cm.
MoInRC

3481. ———. Twelve reasons why I believe the Book of Mormon. Independence, Mo., Published by Ensign Publishing House [n.d.]
31p. 16cm.
MoInRC, UPB

3482. ———. (same) Independence, Mo., Published by Ensign Publishing House [n.d.]
22p. 17½cm.
MoInRC, NjP

3483. ———. (same) Independence, Mo., Ensign Publishing House, 1906.
31p. 15½cm. (The Gospel Banner. V. 15, No. 1)
MoInRC

3484. Fry, Frederick. Fry's traveler's guide and descriptive journal of the great north-western territories of the United States of America; comprising the territories of Idaho, Washington, Montana, and the state of Oregon, with sketches of Colorado, Utah, Nebraska and British America. The grain, pastural [sic] and gold regions defined, with a sketch of Utah, with a history of its settlements, some new views of their future greatness. Cincinnati, Published for the author, Applegate and Co., 1865.
vi, 7–264p. 19cm.
"A sketch of Utah — Its early history, Mormon settlements, etc."
Howes F 398, Sabin 26093, W-C 416
CU–B, DGS, DLC, ICN, MiU–C, OCl, OOxM, OrP, WaU, WaWW

3485. Fulfillment of prophecy. The Lord has spoken and his work is sure . . . [Independence, Mo., Board of Publication of the Church of Christ, n.d.]
[4]p. 20cm.
MoInRC

3486. Fulk, R. L. The Fulfillment of latter-day prophecy. Independence, Mo., Reorganized Church of Jesus Christ of Latter Day Saints, 1923–4.
2 pamp. [19, 19p] 20cm.
Part 1: The scattering. Part 2: The regathering.
CU–B, MoInRC, USl, USlC

3487. Fuller, Frank. A state government for Utah. Speech of Hon. Frank Fuller, (member of Congress-elect from the State of Deseret) Before the Committee of Territories of the House of Representatives, Tuesday, April 23, 1872. Washington [1872]
15p. 24cm.
The fallacy of the reasoning that the Mormon influence in Utah should restrict statehood.
CtY

3487a. Fuller, George N. Historic Michigan, land of the Great lakes; its life, resources, industries, people, politics, government, wars, institutions, achievements, the press, schools and churches, legendary and

prehistoric lore, edited by George N. Fuller . . . [Dayton, Ohio] National Historical Association, Inc. [1924?]
3v. plates, ports. 26cm.
Vol. 1, chap. XXXI: "The Beaver Island Mormons, a Michigan Monarchy. Sketch of James J. Strang and the Mormon Kingdom of Beaver Island."
USlC

Fuller, Metta Victoria. *See Victor, Metta Victoria (Fuller)*

3488. Fullmer, John S. Assassination of Joseph and Hyrum Smith, the prophet and the patriarch of the Church of Jesus Christ of Latter-day saints. Also a condensed history of the expulsion of the saints from Nauvoo. By Elder John S. Fullmer . . . Liverpool, F. D. Richards; London, L.D.S. Book Depot, 1855.
40p. 21cm.
[17]–40 "Expulsion of the Saints from Nauvoo."
Howes F409
CMC, CSmH, CtY, CU–B, DLC, IHi, MoInRC, NjP, UHi, USl, USlC

3489. Fullness of times. Written at the request of President Heber J. Grant and Bishop Charles W. Nibley, December 20th, 1919, to January 8th, 1920, at "Pine Lodge," Salt Lake City, Utah. Salt Lake City [Church of Jesus Christ of Latter-day Saints] 1920.
46p. 27½cm.
Restoration of the true church.
UPB, USlC

3490. Fullom, Stephen Watson. The great highway; a story of the world's struggles. By S. W. Fullom . . . with illustrations on steel by John Leech . . . 3d ed. London, New York, G. Routledge & Co., 1854.
vi p., [1]l., 428p. port., 3 plates. 18cm.
Mormons, p. 224–271.
Sabin 26191
CU, DLC, USlC

3491. Funeral of Wilford Woodruff, President of the Church of Jesus Christ of Latter-day Saints, September 8th, 1898. Salt Lake City, 1898.
[4]p. port. 20½cm.
Cover-title.
UHi

3492. Funeral services for Junius Free Wells. Held in the Assembly Hall, Salt Lake City, Easter Sunday, 20th April, 1930. [Salt Lake City, 1930]
2p.l., 7–39p. port. 22cm.
NjP, UHi, USlC

3493. Funeral services held in the Salt Lake Assembly Hall over the remains of Elder W. C. Staines, Friday, August 5, 1881. Reported by John Irvine. Salt Lake City, Published for Mrs. Priscilla M. Staines at Juvenile Instructor Office, 1881.
18p. 17½cm.
Cover-title.
NjP, USlC

3494. Funeral services in honor of Elias Conway Ashton held in the Assembly Hall. Salt Lake City, Utah, October 17th, 1919. [Salt Lake City] 1920.
44 [1]p. 22cm.
USlC

3494a. Funeral services, Pres. John Henry Smith, Tabernacle, Salt Lake City, October 17, 1911 . . . [Salt Lake City, 1911]
[4]p. port. 18cm.
USlC

3495. Fyrando, M. Efterfolgeren i det prophetiske embede og Praesidentskab for Kirken, af M. Fyrando og H. N. Hansen. Kobenhavn, Den Reorganiserede Kirke, 1875.
16p.
Title in English: Succession of the office of the Prophet and First Presidency of the church.
Schmidt

3496. ———. Kirkens forkastelse, offentliggjort of den Reorganiserede Jesu Christi Kirke af Sidste Dages Hellige i Plano, Kendall County i Staten Illinois, af M. Fyrando og H. N. Hansen. Kobenhavn, 1875.
8p.
Title in English: The rejection of the Church announced by the Reorganized church . . .
Schmidt

3497. ———. Saliggorelsens plan. Med "Indholdet af troen og laerdommen" . . . af M. Fyrando og H. N. Hansen. Kobenhavn, 1875.
20p.
Title in English: The plan of salvation.
Schmidt

J. M. GRANT'S
RIGDON.

NUMBER ONE.

BROWN, BICKING & GUILBERT, PRINTERS,
NO. 56 NORTH THIRD STREET.
1844.

☞ *One sheet Periodical.* POSTAGE—*Under* 100 *miles,* 1½ *cts.; over* 200 *miles,* 2½ *cts.*

Item 3683. The printed wrapper of J. M. Grant's attack upon the disaffected Sidney Rigdon. From the Brigham Young University collection.

GABE

3498. Die Gabe des Heiligen Geistes. Basel, Serge J. Ballif [n.d.]
4p. 23cm.
Title in English: The gift of the Holy Ghost.
UPB

3499. Galbreath, Charles Burleigh. History of Ohio by Charles B. Galbreath. Chicago and New York, The American Historical Society, 1925.
5v. illus., plates, ports., maps. 27½cm.
Vol. I includes an account of Mormonism in Ohio, p. 452–453.
Another edition: 1928. NjP
DLC, NN, UPB

3500. Galland, Isaac. Doctor Isaac Galland's reply to various falsehoods, misstatements, misrepresentations concerning the Latter-day Saints, reproachfully called Mormons . . . [Philadelphia, 1841]
7p. 20½cm.
Isaac Galland was an Iowa land speculator, and did a great deal of business with the Mormons.
Caption-title.
Dated at end: Philadelphia, July 13th, 1841.
USlC

3501. ———. Villainy exposed! Being a minority report of the Board of Trustees of the Desmoines Land Association, alias the New York Company. [Keokuk, 1849]
74p. 8vo.
Offered by Eberstadt catalogue 140, 1957. Previously known only from D. W. Kilbourne's reply of 1850.
Mormons and land dealings.

3502. Gallichan, Walter M. Women under polygamy, by Walter M. Gallichan, with 15 illustrations. London, Holden & Hardingham, 1914.
ix, 11–335 [5]p. plates. 23cm.
Bibliography: p. 333–[336]
Includes Mormon polygamy.
Another edition: New York, Dodd, Mead and company, 1915. DLC, NN
CU, DLC, DSG, NN, OCl

3503. Gannett, Henry. . . . A gazetteer of Utah, by Henry Gannett. Washington, Govt. Print. Off., 1900.
43, xip., [1]l. fold. map. 23cm.
(Geological survey. Bulletin. No. 166)
Includes historical information.
CSmH, CU–B, DLC, NN, UHi, ULA

3504. Garde, Christian Benedict. Om de Mormonske vildfarelser. Til mine menigheder. Holbek, Friis's Boghandling, Chr. Dechs Bogtrykkeri, 1854.
99 [1]p. 17½cm.
Title in English: About the Mormon's erring ways to my churches.
CtY, UPB

3505. ———. (same) Holbek, Friis's Boghandling, Chr. Dech Bogtrykkeri, 1854.
92p. 17½cm.
Variant edition.
CtY, NN

3506. Gardner, Andrew. A voice of warning; or, The Mormonite imposture analized [sic] and exposed in the light of the Scriptures. By A. Gardner, late Mormonite Elder. Rochdale [Eng.] Printed by Jesse Hall, 1842.
12p. 17½cm.

3507. Gardner, Hamilton. History of Lehi, including a biographical section . . . Published by the Lehi Pioneer Committee; written by Hamilton Gardner. Salt Lake City, The Deseret News, 1913.
xvi, 463p. illus., ports., col. plate. 20cm.
CSmH, CU–B, DLC, NjP, UHi, ULA, UPB, USl, USlC, UU

3508. Gardner, James, *compiler.* The faiths of the world; an account of all religions and religious sects, their doctrines, rites, ceremonies and customs. Compiled from the latest and best authorities by James Gardner. Edinburgh, A. Fullarton [1858–1860?]
2v. illus., plates, ports. 27½cm.
Added title-page.
Gives the Joseph Smith story and a brief history and doctrinal exposition.
UU, NjPT, NN

Garland, A. H. *See U.S. Attorney General. The late Corporation . . .*

3508a. Garner, Henry. Songs and verses composed by Henry Garner, Notting Hill, London, W. April, 1884. [London, England? 1884?]
12p. 21½cm.
Mormon poetry.
USlC

3509. Garrard, Lewis Hector. Wah-to-yah, and the Taos trail, or, Prairie travel and scalp dances, with a look at los rancheros from muleback and the Rocky Mountain camp-fire. By Lewis H. Garrard. Cincinnati, H. W. Derby & Co.; New York, A. S. Barnes & Co., 1850.
vip., [1]l. 349p. 19½cm.
Encounters "Captain Thompson, U.S. Dragoons and Lieutenant Colonel of the Mormon Battalion" on Arkansas River, Oct. 30, 1846, p. 10.
W–C 182
CU–B, DLC

3509a. Garstin, Crosbie. The dragon and the lotus. New York, Frederick A. Stokes Col, 1927.
vii, 343p. illus. 21½cm.
Mormons, p. 21–23.
USlC

3510. Gash, Abram Dale. The false star; a tale of the occident, by A. D. Gash . . . Chicago, W. B. Conkey Co., 1899.
3p.l., 7–578p. front. 20cm.
Fiction concerning Mormonism.
DLC, MoInRC, NjP, OCl, UHi, UPB, USlC, UU, WHi

3511. Gates, Brigham Cecil. Birthday of the Lion House and of Susa Young Gates. Master of Ceremonies Jacob F. Gates. Informal Program Directed by Brigham Cecil Gates. [Salt Lake City, 1926]
[4]p. 21cm.
NjP

3512. ———. Concert and oratorio "Salvation for the Dead." Composed by Brigham Cecil Gates. Scriptural text prepared by Elder John A. Widtsoe . . . Salt Lake City, 1923.
[4]l. 30cm.
At head of title: Salt Lake Tabernacle, Saturday Oct. 6, 1923.
USlC

3513. ———. Gates' modern anthems. Series No. 1. Salt Lake City, Modern Music Publishing Co. [c1919]
48p. music. 25½cm.
Mormon church music.
USlC

3514. ———. The restoration. An oratorio for chorus and soli. With orchestra accompaniment. The words by Mrs. Susa Young Gates; the music by Brigham Cecil Gates . . . Salt Lake City, Published under the auspices of the Church of Jesus Christ of Latter-day Saints [c1917]
vi[1]63p. port., music. 27cm.
Words and music.
MoInRC, UHi

3515. Gates, Susa (Young). Brigham Young, patriot, pioneer, prophet. Address delivered over KSL, Saturday, June 1, 1929, by his daughter, Susa Young Gates. [Salt Lake City, 1929]
36p. illus., ports. 23cm.
UPB, USlC

———. Guide to the first year's course of study in the Young Ladies' Mutual Improvement Association. *See Church of Jesus Christ of Latter-day Saints. Young Women's Mutual Improvement Association.*

3516. ———. History of the Young Ladies' Mutual Improvement Association of the Church of Jesus Christ of Latter-day Saints, from November 1869 to June 1910 by Susa Young Gates. Rev. and Pub. by the General Board of Y.L.M.I.A. Salt Lake City, The Deseret News, 1911.
viii, 488p. illus., ports. 20½cm.
Contains biographical sketches.
CU–B, DLC, NjP, NN, UHi, ULA, USl, USlC, UU, WHi

3517. ———. John Stevens' courtship. A story of the Echo Canyon War. By Susa Young Gates. Salt Lake City, The Deseret News, 1909.
viii, 377p. front. 18½cm.
Mormon fiction.
CU–B, DLC, MoInRC, NjP, UHi, ULA, UPB, USl, USlC, UU

3518. ———. The life story of Brigham Young, by Susa Young Gates (one of his daughters) in collaboration with Leah D. Widtsoe, with a foreword by Reed Smoot. New York, The Macmillan Company, 1930.
xviiip. [1]l., 388p. plates, ports. 24½cm.
CSmH, CtY, CU–B, DLC, MH, MoInRC, NjP, NN, UHi, ULA, UPB, USlC, UU, WHi

3519. ———. (same, under title) The life story of Brigham Young, Mormon leader, founder of Salt Lake City, and builder of an empire in the uncharted wastes of western America, by Susa Young Gates (one of his daughters) . . . in collaboration with Leah D. Widtsoe. London, Jarrolds Limited [1930]
287p. illus., plates, ports., map. 24cm.
CU–B, DLC, MH, NN, ICN, UHi, USlC

3520. ———. Lydia Knight's history. By "Homespun" [*pseud.*] Salt Lake City, Juvenile Instructor Office, 1883.
102p. 20cm. (Noble Women's Lives series. V.1)
NjP, UHi, UPB, USlC, UU, WHi

3521. ———. Memorial to Elizabeth Claridge McCune, missionary, philanthropist, architect. By Susa Young Gates. Salt Lake City, 1924.
117p. [1]l. illus., ports. 25cm.
Mormon biography.
DLC, ICN, MB, MWA, NjP, NN, UHi, ULA, USlC, UU

3522. ———. Polygamy? Probable! American marriage ideals to be shattered by war. Brigham Young's daughter makes startling prophecy. San Francisco, Pacific Bureau Service, 1917.
Broadside. 53×35cm. (Article I)
"Polygamy more romantic."
USlC

———. The restoration. *See Gates, Brigham Cecil.*

3523. ———. Right polygamy cure for social evil and double moral standard. San Francisco, Pacific Bureau Service, 1917.
Broadside. 53×35cm. (Article II)
USlC

3524. ———. Says plural marriage will never prevail on economic ground alone . . . San Francisco, Pacific Bureau Service, 1917.
Broadside. 35½×23cm. (Article III)
USlC

3525. ———. Surname book and racial history. A compilation and arrangement of genealogical and historical data for use by the students and members of the Relief Society of the Church of Jesus Christ of Latter-day Saints. Prepared and pub. under the auspices of the General Board of the Relief Society with the approval of the Board of the Genealogical Society of Utah. Susa Young Gates, Ed. and Comp. Salt Lake City, 1918.
viii [2] 576p. illus., maps. 23½cm.
Chiefly names but with some Mormon doctrine.
CSmH, DLC, MB, MWA, NN, PHi, UHi, USlC, UU

3526. ———. Why I believe the Gospel of Jesus Christ. By Susa Young Gates, a daughter of Brigham Young . . . [Independence, Mo., Zions' Printing and Publishing Company, 1930?]
29p. illus. 19cm.
NjP, NN, USl, USlC

3527. ———. (same) [Salt Lake City, The Deseret News Press, 1930?]
34 [2]p. illus., plates on inside covers. 19cm.
Cover-title.
UHi, USlC

3528. ———. Women of the "Mormon" church, by Susa Young Gates and Leah D. Widtsoe . . . Salt Lake City, The Deseret News Press, 1926.
34p. illus., ports. 23cm.
Cover-title.
CU–B, DLC, MH, NjP, NN, UHi, UPB, USl, USlC, WHi

3529. ———. (same) Independence, Mo., Zion's Printing and Publishing Co., 1928.
34p. illus. 23½cm.
Cover-title.
UHi, USlC

3530. ———. (same, in French) Femmes de l'Eglise Mormone, par Susa Young Gates et Leah D. Widtsoe . . . [Salt Lake City? 1929?]
41p. illus. 23cm.
Cover-title.
UHi, UPB, USlC

3531. The gates of the Mormon Hell opened, exhibiting the licentious abominations and revellings of the high priest of the Latter-day-Saints Rev. Brigham Young and his 90 wives; and the vile scenes enacted by the elders and apostles with their many spiritual concubines in the secret chambers of the harem, or institution of cloistered Saints, privately attached to the Temple. . . . London, Hewitt, Wych Street Strand [n.d.]
8p. 21cm.
Cover-title.
At head of title: Price one penny. The most complete authentic exposure ever published of the spiritual courtship and marriages of the Mormons.
USlC

3532. The gates of the Mormon hell opened. Or the licentious revellings of the Rev. Brigham Young, and the elders, apostles, & priests of the Church of Latter-day-Saints, with their many spiritual wives and concubines; and all the other abominations of Mormonism denounced. London, Printed and Published by James Gilbert, Printer [n.d.]
12p. 20½cm.
USlC

3533. Gatlin, William. Women of Clerkenwill. Attend the Mormon conference in Sadler's Wells Theatre, Sunday evening, April 22, at 6:30 . . . [London? 1876?]
Broadside. 12½×18½cm.
Signed: William Gatlin.
Urges attendance to demonstrate against Mormonism.
CtY

3534. Gavitt, Elnathan Corrington. Crumbs from my saddle bags; or, Reminiscences of pioneer life and biographical sketches . . . by the Rev. Elnathan Corrington Gavitt. Toledo, Ohio, Blade Printing and Paper Co., 1884.
xi [3] 208p. port. 20½cm.
Mention of Charles Elliot and wives; and the murder of Mr. Miller by Hodge Brothers with Mormon involvement.
NN

3535. Gay, F. D. B. *publisher.* The old Mormon trail, Salt Lake City to Los Angeles . . . [Provo, Utah, F. D. B. Gay, Publisher, 1920]
48p . illus., map. 21cm. (The White book)
Cover-title.
The Mormon corridor.
UHi

3536. Geddes, Joseph Arch. The United Order among the Mormons (Missouri phase) an unfinished experiment in economic organization. By Joseph A. Geddes . . . [Salt Lake City, The Deseret News Press 1924]
172p. 23cm.
Thesis (Ph.D.) — Columbia University, 1924.
CSmH, CU, DLC, ICN, MiU, MoInRC, NcD, NN, PU, UHi, ULA

3537. ———. (same) Salt Lake City, The Deseret News Press, 1924.
172p. 23½cm.
Published without thesis note.
CSmH, CU–B, DLC, MiU, NN, ULA, UPB, USl, USlC, UU

The Geese of Ganderica. *See Meears, George A.*

3538. Gems for the young folks. Salt Lake City. Juvenile Instructor Office, 1881.
4p.l., 88p. 18cm. (Faith promoting series, 4th book)
Partial contents: Abraham A. Kimball. Finding a father; John Nicholson. Saved by providence; Benjamin Brown. Testimonies for the truth.
CU, DLC, MH, NN, RPB, UHi, ULA, UPB, USIC, UU, WHi

Genealogical Society of Utah. *See Church of Jesus Christ of Latter-day Saints. Genealogical Society of Utah.*

3539. Genealogical and Historical Magazine of Arizona Temple District. Mesa, Arizona, Published by Frank T. Pomeroy, January, 1924–January, 1947.
24v. (100 issues) quarterly. 22–24cm.
Publisher and editor: Frank T. Pomeroy.
Organ of the Genealogical Society of Maricopa Stake and the Arizona Temple District.
UPB, USIC

3540. Gentile Bureau of Information. Salt Lake City. Claims of Mormonism to be considered seriously. Salt Lake City, Published by the Gentile Bureau of Information [1903]
10p. 15½cm.
"Facts" the people should know concerning politics, etc. An anti-Mormon organization.
MH

3541. ———. No parallel in history. Nothing like Deseret News on earth. Dishonest, unjust, impure, and infamous in everything. It is a perfect ideal of consummate and universal depravity. [Salt Lake City, 1905]
7p. 22cm.
Cover-title.
Chiefly quotes from the *Salt Lake Tribune*.
MH, USIC

3542. ———. Temple Mormonism. [Salt Lake City, 190–]
7p. 23cm.
Caption-title.
Expose of the Temple ceremony.
MoInRC, WHi

3543. ———. (same) [Salt Lake City, 190–]
8p. 18cm.
USIC

3544. George Sheffer Clark. ... [Provo, Utah, Press of the Skelton Publishing Co., after 1891]
[10]p. 15×22½cm.
Mormon biography.
USIC

3545. Georges-Anquetil. La maitresse légitime. Essai sur le mariage polygamique De Demain. Paris, Les éditions Georges-Anquetil, 5 Rue Boudreau, 5 Paris (ix) 1923 [c1922]
7p.l. [15]–443p. front. 19cm.
Chap. V. "La polygamie chez les Mormons (d'après Raymond Duquet et Jules Remy) p. 143–165. Its religious and social implications.
Title in English: The legitimate mistress.
DLC, MH, UHi, USIC

3546. Gerhard, Frederick. Illinois as it is; its history, geography, statistics, constitution, laws, government ... etc. By Frederick Gerhard. With a prairie and wood map, a geological map, a population map, and other illustrations. Chicago, Keen and Lee, Philadelphia, C. Desilver, 1857.
451p. illus., 2 plates, fold. maps. 20cm.
Material on the Mormons in Illinois, p. 95–122.
Sabin 27133
DLC, ICHi, NjP, NN, UHi, USIC, UU

3547. Gerould, Katharine (Fullerton). The aristocratic West, by Katharine Fullerton Gerould ... New York and London, Harper & Brothers, 1925.
5p.l., 220p. plates. 22½cm.
Chap. II, p. 34–68. Salt Lake; the city of the saints.
A modern view of Mormonism.
CtY, CU-B, DLC, ICN, NjP, NN, USl, USIC, UU, WHi

3548. Ghent, William James. The road to Oregon, a chronicle of the great emigrant trail, by W. J. Ghent; with 32 illustrations and a map. London, New York [etc.] Longmans, Green and Co., 1929.
xvi p., [1]l., 274p. plates, ports., map. 24cm.
Mormon movement to Utah; Mountain Meadows massacre, Johnston's Army.
DLC, NjP, OU, UHi, USl, ViU, WaU

3548a. Gibbons, James, *Cardinal.* Our Christian heritage. Baltimore, John Murphy & Co., 1889.
viii, 523p. port. 19½cm.
Mormons, p. 485–486.
USIC

3549. Gibbs, Josiah Francis. Episode in the life of A. Milton Musser as narrated by an esteemed friend. [Marysvale, Utah, 1903]
4p. 21cm.
Cover-title.
CSmH, UHi, USIC

3550. ———. The essence of Mormonism. Quotations from Mormon sermons and writings and a few paragraphs of friendly criticism, also a brief sketch of the Mountain Meadows massacre (illustrated) [by] J. F. Gibbs. [Salt Lake City, J. F. Gibbs, 1909]
17p. 23cm.
Cover-title.
UHi

GIBBS, J. F.

3551. ———. Kawich's gold mine; an historical narrative of mining in the Grand Canyon of the Colorado, and of love and adventure among the polygamous Mormons of southern Utah. (Author's edition) . . . Salt Lake City, Century Printing Company, 1913.
228p. illus. 22½cm.
Fiction with a Mormon setting.
CSmH, CtY, CU–B, DLC, NjP, NN, UHi, ULA, UPB, USlC, UU

3552. ———. Lights and shadows of Mormonism. [By] J. F. Gibbs. [Salt Lake City, Salt Lake Tribune Publishing Co., c1909]
535p. illus., ports. 21cm.
CSmH, CU–B, DLC, ICN, MoInRC, NjP, NjPT, NN, UHi, ULA, UPB, USl, USlC, UU, WHi

3553. ———. The Mountain Meadows massacre, by Josiah F. Gibbs. Illustrated by nine full-page and five half-page engravings from photographs taken on the ground. [Salt Lake City] Salt Lake Tribune Publishing Co., 1910.
56p. illus., ports. 23cm.
CSmH, CU–B, ICN, MoInRC, NN, ULA, USl, WHi

3554. ———. (same) 2d ed. [Salt Lake City] Salt Lake Tribune Publishing Co., c1910.
59p. illus., plates, ports. 22½cm.
CSmH, DLC, MH, NjP, UHi, USl, USlC, UU, WHi

3555. ———. An open letter to Latter-day Saints who think for themselves. By J. F. Gibbs. [Salt Lake City, 1907?]
19 [1]p. 22½cm.
Signed: Salt Lake City, November 25, 1907.
Concerning the Reed Smoot case and Joseph F. Smith's testimony.
MoInRC

3556. Gibson, Albert M. Brief in re Senate bill No. 10. A bill to amend an act entitled "An act to amend section fifty-three hundred and fifty-two of the revised statutes of the United States in reference to bigamy and for other purposes," approved March 22, 1882. [n.p., 1886?]
87p. 23cm.
Cover-title.
CSmH, ICN, NN

3557. ———. (same, under title) Have Mormons any rights? The new Edmunds bill. Brief in re Senate bill No. 10. A bill to amend an act entitled "An Act to amend section fifty-three hundred and fifty-two of the Revised statutes of the United States in reference to bigamy, and for other purposes" approved March 22, 1882. [Salt Lake City? 1886?]
87p. 21cm.
Cover-title.
Variant cover of the above.
CSmH, CtY, CU–B, DLC, ICN, MH, NjP, NN, UHi, UPB, USl, USlC

3557a. ———. The rights of citizenship. Brief in Re H. R. Bills Nos. 1478, 6153, and the petition of the citizens of Bear Lake County, Idaho Territory. [n.p., 1885?]
27p. 23cm.
USlC

3558. Gibson, J. Watt. Recollections of a pioneer, by J. W. (Watt) Gibson. [St. Joseph, Mo., Press of Nelson-Hanne Printing Co., 1912]
216p. port. 20cm.
Overland journey through Salt Lake City.
CU–B

3559. Gibson, Walter Murray. The Prison of Weltervreden; and a glance at the East Indian Archipelago. By Walter M. Gibson. Illustrated from original sketches. New York: J. C. Riker, 129 Fulton Street, 1855.
xiv, 495p. illus. 20cm.
Includes biographical information of his early life.
CDU

3560. ———. The shepherd saint of Lanai. Rich "Primacy" revelations, gathered from various sources and produced in historical form for the first time in the "Saturday Press," Dec. 24, 1881 to Jan. 21, 1882. Honolulu, Thos. G. Thrum, Publisher, 1882.
47p. 22cm.
Cover-title.
Extracts of writings by Gibson; letters from Gibson; statements of contributions and miscellaneous material about Gibson.
CtY, CU–B, DLC, MH, NN, UHi, USlC

3561. Gibson, William. Report of three nights' public discussion in Bolton, between William Gibson, H.P., presiding elder of the Manchester Conference of the Church of Jesus Christ of Latter-day Saints, and the Rev. Woodville Woodman . . . Reported by G. D. Watt. Liverpool, Published by Franklin D. Richards, 1851.
1p.l., 46 p. fold. pl. 21cm.
Subjects of discussion: First night. What is God? . . . Second night. The Godhead: are the Father and Son two distinct and separate persons . . . Third night. The true nature of the signs promised to follow faith . . .
Some copies with port. of George D. Watt.
Printed from variant plates.
CSmH, CtY, DLC, NjP, NN, ULA, UPB, USl, USlC

3562. Gide, Charles. Communist and co-operative colonies. By Charles Gide . . . Translated by Ernest F. Row. New York, Thomas Y. Crowell Company [1930?]
222p., [1]l. 21cm.
Includes the Mormon attempts at the United Order in Utah, p. 108–111.
Another edition: London [etc.] G. G. Harrop & Co., Ltd. [1930] DLC
CU, NjP, UPB

Gideon [*pseud.*] *See LeBaron, Alonzo H.*

3563. Gifford, Moses E. A collection of songs, poems and tributes. Reminiscent of pioneer days in Utah's Dixie. Springdale, Utah, M. E. Gifford, c1930.
[57]p. illus. 18½cm.
A second volume was published in 1932.
CSmH, DLC, UHi

3564. Gila Academy. Thatcher, Arizona. The Gila Academy. Announcement. Thatcher, 1901–1931.
v. 19cm.
Formerly St. Joseph Stake Academy.
UPB 1912–1916, 1917–1921, 1922–23, 1925–1931; USlC 1901–02, 1917–18, 1918–19, 1919–20, 1922–23, 1924–25

3565. Gilchrist, Rosetta Luce. Apples of Sodom; a story of Mormon life. Cleveland, W. W. Williams, 1883.
322p. 19cm.
Fiction concerning Mormonism.
CSmH, CU–B, DLC, MH, NN, UPB, USl, USlC

3566. Giles, Alfred E. Marriage, monogamy and polygamy on the basis of divine law of natural law and constitutional law. An open letter to the Massachusetts members of Congress by one of their constituents, with observations on the opinion of the Supreme Court in Reynolds vs. United States, 98 U.S. Supreme Court reports. By a citizen of Massachusetts . . . Boston, James Campbell, 1882.
4p.l. [9]–76p. 23½cm.
Cover-title: The Mormon problem.
Authorship attributed variously to Alfred E. Giles and James T. Hart.
CSmH, CU–B, DLC, ICHi, ICN, MB, MH, MiU, MWA, NjP, NN, UPB, USl, USlC, UU, WHi

3567. Giles, Barnet Moses. The Jews in Jerusalem and the Jews in Utah. [n.p., n.d.]
5p. 20½cm.
Unorthodox doctrinal exposition of Israel.
MH

3568. ———. The pure testimony to the Church of Jesus Christ of Latter-day Saints, and unto all nations of the world. By Barnet Moses Giles, a literal descendant of Israel. Salt Lake City, 1875.
45p. 20½cm.
CSmH, MoInRC, NN, USl, USlC, UU

3569. ———. The Pyramid. The Pyramid again, which is in Upper Egypt. By Barnet Moses Giles, The Israelite prophet of the tribe of Ephraim. [Salt Lake City, 1879]
7p. 20cm.
Unorthodox prophetic exposition.
MH

3570. ———. A voice from our Father and God in Heaven. A call from his son, our Lord and Saviour, Jesus Christ, of Nazareth, and a small, calm and sweet whisper of the Holy Ghost, the inspirer. To the Church of Jesus Christ of Latter-day Saints . . . [Salt Lake City, 187–]
Broadside. 52×35cm.
Announcement of lectures of Latter-day Saints by Barnet Moses Giles, prophet and revelator.
USlC

3571. ———. Voice of warning to the Church of Jesus Christ of Latter-day Saints, composed by Barnet Moses Giles, a literal descendant of the House of Israel. Salt Lake City, 1874.
37 [1]p. 20½cm.
MH, USlC

3572. Giles, Henry Evans. Anthem. The truth has spoken from the dust . . . Written for the one hundredth anniversary celebration of the delivery of the plates from which the Book of Mormon was translated to the Prophet Joseph Smith . . . [Salt Lake City] 1927.
[4]p. music. 26cm.
Cover-title within border.
UPB, USlC

3573. ———. "How will the Saints rejoice" recitative. Arranged from Doctrine and Covenants, by H. E. Giles. [Salt Lake City, n.d.]
[4]p. music. 22cm.
Includes hymn: "How beauteous are their feet." Arranged by H. E. Giles [p. 4]
UPB, USlC

3574. ———. In sacred song service "The plan of salvation," by H. E. Giles. [Salt Lake City, n.d.]
6 pamphlets. 24cm.
A series of anthems by H. E. Giles under above series title.
Partial contents: No. 18. Comfort ye, my people. No. 22. Glory to God in the Highest. No. 28. Christ is Risen from the Tomb. No. 43. And it shall come to pass. Jehovah's praise. The plan of Salvation. (Final two without number)
USlC

3575. ———, *compiler.* Latter-day Saints congregational hymns. Published by Professor Henry E. Giles, chorister, Ensign Stake. Volume I. First edition, 1919. Independence, Mo., Zion's Printing and Publishing Co., 1919.
2p.l. [75]p. 19cm.
Vol. I only published.
ULA, UPB, USl, USlC, UU

3576. ———. The new song; anthem. Arranged from Sec. 84, Doctrine and Covenants by H. E. Giles. [Salt Lake City, n.d.]
[4]p. music. 26cm.
UPB, USIC

3577. ———. Recitative (The Seer) [Salt Lake City, n.d.]
[4]p. 22½cm.
A prophecy related by Lehi in the Book of Mormon.
USIC

3578. ———. Sunday School music album. A collection of marches, also sacramental and funeral selections suitable for Sunday Schools and Church Services. Composed, selected and arranged by H. E. Giles. Salt Lake City, Published by John D. Giles [n.d.]
22p. 15×22½cm.
UPB

3579. ———. Youth of Zion. Ensign Stake Choir series. Words by J. L. Townsend. Welsh Melody. Arr. H. E. Giles. [n.p., n.d.]
[2]p. music. 22½cm.
USIC

3580. Giles, John Davis, *compiler.* A picture story of Mormonism; a picture history of the Church of Jesus Christ of Latter-day Saints, designed for the use of missionaries in presenting to the world the story of the origin, growth and progress of the Church. [Salt Lake City, Church of Jesus Christ of Latter-day Saints, 1930?]
[57]l. illus., plates (part col.) 28½cm.
UPB

3581. Gillen, James A. Quotations on Church government. [n.p., n.d.]
16p. 21cm.
RLDS church government.
MoInRC

3582. Gillilan, James David. Trail tales, by James David Gillilan. New York, The Abingdon Press [1915]
4p.l., 9–182p. illus. 19½cm.
Includes chapters: "Mormondom" and "Great Salt Lake," p. 123–247.
DLC, NjP, UHi, USIC

3583. ———. Thomas Corwin Iliff, apostle of home missions in the Rocky Mountains, by James David Gillilan. New York, Cincinnati, The Methodist Book Concern [c1919]
193p. plates, ports., facsim. 19cm.
Chap. VII. "Mormonism, a menace to the nation."
A description of Mormonism after 1911 with emphasis on polygamy.
Appendix I. Mormonism and anti-polygamy work.
DLC, ICU, NjPT, UHi, USIC

3584. Gillogly, Mrs. L. L. A sketch of the women of Utah, read before the Anti-Rust Literary Club, Macon, Mo., April 20, 1891, by Mrs. L. L. Gillogly . . . Macon, Mo., Republican Print. [1891?]
16p. 23cm.
"Very few Mormons are not happy that polygamy has been abandoned."
UHi

3584a. Gilson, S. H. $800 reward! To be paid for the arrest of John Taylor and George Q. Cannon. 1887. Jan. 31, Salt Lake City.
Broadside. 36×22cm.
Offered for information that will lead to the arrest of John Taylor and George Q. Cannon.
Alfred L. Bush Collection.

3585. Gilstrap, W. H. Dynamite. This is a double-header. Here it comes. A dynamite in the Brighamite camp. Their claims proven false by their own books as written by undeniable evidences gathered and compiled by W. H. Gilstrap. Seneca, South Carolina [n.d.]
32p. 24cm.
MoInRC, USIC

3586. ———. Priesthood authority and the Gathering of Zion, Her people and place. Seneca, South Carolina, Compiled by W. H. Gilstrap [n.p., 1930?]
16p. 15cm.
Purpose of the Reorganization.
USIC

3587. The Glad Tidings. Clifford, Ontario, 1891–92.
2v. monthly. 28cm.
An unofficial publication for RLDS members.
USIC V. 1, # 9–23; V. 2, # 1–8

3588. The Glad Tidings. Peoria, Ill., Published by the Glad Tidings Co. November 1, 1897?–
v. 28cm.
"Published in the interests of the Restored Gospel."
Official organ of the Southern Michigan and Northern Indiana District.
E. K. Evans, editor.
The editor also published a *Glad Tidings* at Grand Rapids, Michigan.
USIC May 15, 1901.

Glad tidings of great joy. *See Teasdale, George.*

3589. Ett gladt budskap; inbjudning till guds rike. . . . Tredje Svenska upplagan. Köpenhamn, Utgifven och förlagd af Andreas Peterson, 1899.
12p. 18½cm.
Articles of faith on outside cover.
Title in English: The glad message.
UPB

3590. ———. (same) Åttonde svenska upplagan. Stockholm, Utgiven och forlagd av Gideon N. Hulterström, 1930.
12p. 17½cm.
UPB

3591. ———. (same) Nionde svenska upplagan. Stockholm, Utgiven och forlagd av Gideon N. Hulterström, 1930.
12p. 18cm.
USlC

3591a. Glaedelige tidender! En indbydelse til Guds Rige. [Kjøbenhavn, Udgivet og forlagt af C. D. Fjeldsted. Trykt hos F. E. Bording (V. Petersen) 1889]
8p. 23½cm.
Missionary tract.
Title in English: The glad message.
USlC

3592. ———. (same) [Kjøbenhavn, Udgivet og forlagt af Edward H. Anderson . . . Trykt hos F. E. Bording (V. Petersen) 1891]
8p. 21cm.
CSmH

3593. ———. (same) [Kjøbenhavn, Udgivet og forlagt af Peter Sundwall . . . 1895]
8p. 21cm.
USlC

3593a. ———. (same) [Kjøbenhavn, Udgivet og forlagt af Andreas Peterson. Trykt hos F. E. Bording (V. Petersen) 1898]
8p. 24cm.
USlC

3594. ———. (same) [Kjøbenhavn, Udgivet og forlagt af Andreas Peterson . . . Trykt hos F. E. Bording . . . 1899]
8p. 23cm.
USlC

3594a. ———. (same) [Kjøbenhavn, Udgivet og forlagt af Anthon L. Skanchy. Trykt hos L. A. Nielsen, 1902]
8p. 23½cm.
USlC

3594b. ———. (same) [Kjøbenhavn, Udgivet og forlagt af Soren Rasmusen. Trykt hos P. S. Christiansen, 1908]
8p. 21cm.
USlC

3595. Glass, Chester. The world: Round it and over it, by Chester Glass . . . Being letters written by the author from England, Ireland . . . California, Nevada, Utah and New York. Together with ninety-six illustrations engraved on wood . . . Toronto, Rose-Belford Publishing Company, 1881.
viii, 528p. illus., plates. 18½cm.
His viewpoint on polygamy and his visit with John Taylor in 1880.
USlC

3596. Glazier, Willard. Down the great river; embracing an account of the discovery of the true source of the Mississippi, together with views, descriptive and pictorial, of the cities, towns, villages and scenery on the banks of the River . . . Philadelphia, Hubbard Brothers, 1888.
xxvi, 29–443, lxiiip. illus., ports., plates, map (1 fold) 19½cm.
"Sixty-ninth day" Trip includes Nauvoo, with resume of the history of the Mormons in Illinois.
Other editions: 1889. CU, DLC, UPB; 1892. NjP, UHi, USlC; Chicago and New York, Rand, McNally & Co., 1893. DLC
DLC

3597. ———. Ocean to ocean on horseback; being the story of a tour in the saddle from the Atlantic to the Pacific, with special reference to the early history and development of cities and towns along the route, and regions traversed beyond the Mississippi, together with incidents, anecdotes and adventures of the journey. Philadelphia, P. W. Ziegler, 1895.
xx [21]–544p. plates. 19½cm.
Includes a visit to Salt Lake City.
Other editions: Philadelphia, Hubbard Publ. Co., 1896. DLC, UPB; 1898. USlC
CU–B, NjP, UU

3598. ———. Peculiarities of American cities. Philadelphia, Hubbard, 1883.
xv, 25–558p. port., plates. 19cm.
Chapter 32: Salt Lake City. Emphasis on the Mormons and their dominance of the city.
Republished 1884. UHi, USlC, UU; 1886. UPB; 1889. NjP
DLC

3599. Glenn, Allen. History of Cass County, Missouri. Topeka, Cleveland, Historical Publishing Co., 1917.
[23] 34–837p. illus. 27½cm.
Address of Judge Noah M. Given, 1879; remarks on the Mormon difficulties of 1833–1838, especially affairs of June, 1834, when Cass was part of Jackson County, p. 234–237.
CU–B

3600. Glyn, Elizabeth (Sutherland). Elizabeth visits America. New York, Duffield & Co., 1909.
349 [1]p. port. 19½cm.
Mormons, p. 233, 248–250.
USlC

Goates, George Albert. O le moliman fou le galuega moni a le atua. *See Church of Jesus Christ of Latter-day Saints. Missions. Samoan.*

GODBE, W. S.

3601. Godbe, William S. Manifesto from W. S. Godbe and E. L. T. Harrison . . . [Salt Lake City, Godbe & Harrison, 1869]
4p. 29cm.
Caption-title.
"From the *Utah Magazine*, Nov. 27, 1869."
Proposes reform of the church because of its rising power against the individual.
CtY, MH, USIC

3602. ———. Polygamy; its solution in Utah — a question of the hour. An address delivered in Liberal institute. Sunday, July 30, 1871. By William S. Godbe. [Salt Lake City] Printed at the office of the Salt Lake Tribune, 1871.
16p. 23cm.
CLU, CtY, MH, NjP, UPB, USIC

3603. ———. To the Public, and especially the Mormon portion of it. Highly Important Communication from W. S. Godbe. Salt Lake City [Salt Lake] Tribune, 1872.
[2]p. 35cm.
At head of title: Tribune Supplement. Salt Lake City, U. T., Monday, February 19, 1872.
The church and local politics.
USIC

3604. Goddard, Benjamin, *compiler.* Pertinent facts on Utah's loyalty and war record. [Salt Lake City, Bureau of Information] 1918.
24p. 18½cm.
Cover-title: Relates to the European war.
MB, MoInRC, NN, UHi, ULA, UPB, USIC

3605. ———. (same) 2d ed. [Salt Lake City, Bureau of Information] 1918.
24p. 18½cm.
USIC

3606. ———. Truths for truth-seekers on Utah and the Mormons. By non-Mormons. [Salt Lake City, Bureau of Information, 1913?]
32p. 18cm.
MH, NN, USIC, UU

3607. ———. (same) Salt Lake City, Bureau of Information [1919]
32p. illus. 18cm.
Article on p. 10 dated 1919.
MB, MoInRC, NN, UW

3608. Goddard, Frederick Bartlett. Where to emigrate and why. Homes and fortunes in the boundless West and the sunny South . . . with a complete history and description of the Pacific Railroad. By Frederick B. Goddard . . . Philadelphia, Cincinnati [etc.] The Peoples Publishing Company, 1869.
2p.l. [iii]–xvi, 9–591p. plates, maps (part fold.) 23cm.
Added t.–p. illus.
New York edition of the same year.
Section on Utah includes general information on Utah as well as Mormonism, p. 148–159.
Sabin 27633
CU–B, DLC, NjP, UHi, USIC, UU

Goforth, Sarah E. *See The Crimes of Latter-day Saints in Utah.*

3609. The Gold and Blue. Salt Lake City, L.D.S. College, 1900–
v. 29cm.
USIC V. 1, # 1–12; V. 2, # 3, 4, 6, 8, 9, 10, 14–16; V. 3, # 1–4, 6–12, 21–22; V. 4, # 13–14; V. 5, # 1, 15; V. 6, # 4; V. 10, # 1

3610. Golder, Frank Alfred. The march of the Mormon Battalion from Council Bluffs to California; taken from the journal of Henry Standage, by Frank Alfred Golder in collaboration with Thomas A. Bailey and J. Lyman Smith. New York, London, The Century Co. [c1928]
xiii, 295p. illus., plates, ports., map. 21cm.
Maps on lining-papers.
Foreword by Reed Smoot.
CSmH, CU, DLC, MoInRC, NjP, NN, UHi, UPB, USl, USIC, UU, WHi

3611. Goldsmith, Oliver. Overland in forty nine. The recollections of a Wolverine ranger after a lapse of forty-seven years. Exclusively for my family and friends . . . Detroit, Mich., The author, 1896.
148p. port., plates. 20cm.
Pegleg Smith and the Mormons, p. 52–53; Mormons met on the trail, p. 54–55, 84. They by-passed Utah.
CtY, DLC

3612. Gooch, Daniel Wheelwright. Polygamy in Utah. Speech of Hon. Daniel W. Gooch, of Mass., delivered in the House of Representatives, April 4, 1860. [Washington, 1860]
8p. 24½cm.
Caption-title.
Sabin 27828
CSmH, CtY, CU–B, DLC, ICN, MH, UHi, ULA

3613. Gooch, John, *compiler.* Death of the prophets Joseph and Hyrum Smith, who were murdered while in prison at Carthage, Ill., on the 27th day of June, A.D., 1844. Compiled, and printed for our venerable brother in Christ, Freeman Nickerson . . . Boston, Printed by J. Gooch, 1844.
12p. 22cm.
Preface signed: J. G.
Usually listed under Freeman Nickerson.
CtY, MH, USIC

3614. Good company for every day of the year. Boston, Ticknor and Field, 1865.
326p. 19cm.
A story by Rose Terry entitled "The Mormon's Wife," p. 89–108.
DLC

3615. Goodkind, Ben. A poor American in Ireland and Scotland, By Windy Bill [*pseud.*] San Francisco, W. S. Van Cott & Company [c1913]
2p.l. [5]–286p. 18cm.
A trip through Utah with some comments on Mormonism.
CU, USlC

3616. Goodrich, E. S. Mormonism unveiled. The other side. From an American standpoint. By E. S. Goodrich, esq. Copied from the Chicago "Times." [Salt Lake City?] 1884.
12p. 22cm. (No. 2)
In tan wrapper.
Dated: Salt Lake City, Jan. 24, 1884.
CSmH, CU–B, NjP, NjPT, ULA

3617. ———. (same) [Salt Lake City? 1884]
1p.l. [33]–42p. 21½cm.
Pt. 2 of a series of 5 pamphlets continuously paged, the first being James W. Barclay's Mormonism exposed. For list of pamphlets, *see Barclay, James W.*
CSmH, ICHi, NN, UHi, UPB, USlC, UU

3617a. Goodrich, Samuel Griswold. Les États-Unis d'Amérique, aperçu statistique, historique, géographique industriel et social a l'usage de ceux qui recherchent des renseignements précis sur cette partee du Nouveau-Monde . . . Paris, Guillaumin et Cie Libraires-Éditeurs . . . 1852.
2 p.l., [v]–xvi, 376p. map. 19½cm.
Includes a section on Mormonism.
Title in English: The United States of America.
DLC, NjP

3618. Goodwin, Cardinal Leonidas. The trans-Mississippi West (1803–1853) a history of its acquisition and settlement, by Cardinal Goodwin . . . New York, London, D. Appleton and Company, 1922.
xp., [2]l., 528p. maps (part fold.) 22cm.
The settlement of the Great Salt Lake basin . . . p. 392–422. History up to the first settlement by the Mormons.
Howes G247
CSmH, DLC, NjP, NN, UHi, USlC, UU

3618a. Goodwin, Charles Carroll. The Goodwin platform. [Salt Lake City] 1890.
Broadside. 41×29cm.
Dated: Nov. 2, 1890.
Sample statements of his position on disfranchisement of the Mormons, confiscation of Church property and Utah becoming a state.
USlC

———. History of the bench and bar of Utah.
See History of the bench and bar in Utah.

3619. ———. Mormon absurdities. More Tabernacle babbling and preposterous rant. Elder John Morgan's "Loyalty" . . . [Salt Lake City, 1886]
12p. 22½cm.
Caption-title.
A reply to a sermon preached by Elder Morgan in the Mormon Tabernacle.
Signed: Criticus, Salt Lake City, Aug. 31, 1886.
Also included in "A few choice examples."
CSmH, CtY, MH

3620. ———. . . . Steel rails on the old trails in the western Pacific country. By C. C. Goodwin. [San Francisco, Taylor, Nash and Taylor, c1913]
31p. map and illus. on cover. 23cm.
"Issued by the Passenger Department of the Western Pacific Railway Company."
Brief history of the church and material concerning the sea gulls. In literary style.
MH

3621. ———. That brief. [Washington, 1886]
22p. 22½cm.
Cover-title.
Signed: C. C. Goodwin.
Related to A. M. Gibson's "Brief in re Senate Bill no. 10," or his "Have the Mormons any rights?"
CtY, ICN, NN, WHi

3622. Goodwin, Samuel Henry. Additional studies in Mormonism and masonry. By S. H. Goodwin . . . Salt Lake City, 1927.
38p. 22cm.
CSmH, MoInRC, NjP, ULA, USl

3623. ———. Freemasonry in Utah. Issued by the Committee on Masonic Education and Instruction. Grand Lodge of Utah F. & A.M. [Salt Lake City, 1927]
1p.l., 16p. illus. 22cm.
The Mormon domination of Utah and the work of the masons.
USlC

3624. ———. Freemasonry in Utah. Issued by the Committee on Masonic Education and instruction. Grand lodge of Utah F. & A.M. Wasatch lodge no. 1 [Salt Lake City, 1925]
16p. 22½cm. (Educational Bulletin. No. 3)
Gentile-Mormon relations in Utah.
UHi, UPB, USlC

3625. ———. (same) Grand lodge of Utah F. & A.M. . . . [Salt Lake City] 1925.
19p. 22½cm. (Educational Bulletin. No. 4)
Plan of the Mormons to take over the Masonic lodges in Utah.
UHi

GOODWIN, S. H.

3626. ———. (same) Grand lodge of Utah F. & A.M. [Salt Lake City] 1926.
38p. illus. 22½cm. ([Educational] bulletin. No. 5)
Information concerning Brigham Young and his desire for isolationism.
UHi, USIC

3627. ———. (same) Grand lodge of Utah F. & A.M. [Salt Lake City] 1926.
30p. 22½cm. (Educational bulletin. No. 6)
Barriers between Mormons and gentiles.
UHi

3628. ———. (same) [Salt Lake City] 1928.
32p. illus. 22½cm. (Educational bulletin. No. 7)
Mormon colonization.
UHi

3629. ———. (same) The masonic public library 1877–1897. With notes on movements to establish public libraries in Utah prior to 1877. By S. H. Goodwin, grand secretary, grand historian. Salt Lake City, 1929.
59p. illus. 22½cm.
Early Mormon and other attempts to start libraries.
UHi

3630. ———. (same) Thirty years of Mt. Moriah Lodge No. 2, F. & A.M. 1866–1896. By S. H. Goodwin P.G.M., grand secretary. Salt Lake City, 1930.
57p. illus., plates. 22½cm.
Mormon discouragement of gentiles in Utah.
CSmH, UHi

3631. ———. Mormonism and masonry; a Utah point of view by S. H. Goodwin P.G.M. Salt Lake City, 1921.
35p. 24cm.
CSmH, MH, UPB, USIC

3632. ———. (same) Salt Lake City [Sugar House Press] 1921.
45p. 23cm.
Special edition, printed for the National Masonic Research Society, Anamosa, Iowa.
CSmH, CtY, CU–B, MH, NN, USIC, UU

3633. ———. (same) [Third impression] Salt Lake City, 1921.
35p. 24cm.
CSmH, UU

3634. ———. (same) [Third impression] Salt Lake City, 1922.
45p. 24cm.
USIC

3635. ———. (same) Washington, D.C., The Masonic Service Association of the United States [c1924]
x, 106p. 16cm. (Little masonic library. No. 8)
CtY, DLC, NjP, NN, USI

3636. ———. (same) Salt Lake City, Grand Lodge F. & A.M. of Utah, 1925.
59p. 23cm.
CSmH, MH, MoInRC, UHi, ULA, USIC

3637. ———. (same) Salt Lake City, Grand Lodge F. & A.M. of Utah, 1927.
59p. 23cm.
USIC

3638. Gorrie, P. Douglass. The churches and sects of the United States: containing a brief account of the origin, history, doctrines, church government, mode of worship, usages, and statistics of each religious denomination, so far as known. New York, Published by Lewis Colby, 1850.
xii [13]–240p. 19cm.
Article XLVI. Latter day Saints (Mormons)
Sabin 28034
NjP, UPB

3639. Gospel Dollar League. The Mormon-Christian war; R. B. Neal, Grayson, Ky, a unique place in Evangelism. [Grayson, Ky, Gospel Dollar League, n.d.]
[4]p. port. 21½cm.
P. [1]–[2] an editorial from the Herald-Dispatch, Huntington, West Virginia.
R. B. Neal's anti-Mormon activity.
MoInRC

3640. ———. (same, under title) A unique place in Evangelism. [n.p., n.d.]
[4]p. 21½cm.
MoInRC

3641. Gospel herald . . . for the Church of Jesus Christ of Latter-day Saints. . . . Voree, Wisconsin, 1846–50.
5v. weekly. 28–30cm.
Official organ of the Church of Jesus Christ of Latter Day Saints (Strang)
Title varies: V. I Voree herald, V. II # 1–26 Zion's reveille, V. II # 27– Gospel herald.
Editor James J. Strang and others.
Morgan
CtY My 1846; Je 29, 1848; Jl 26, 1849. MoInRC Mr, Je*, Jl, Ag*, S*, O*, 1846; F 11*, 18, Mr 4–18, 25*, Ap 22–Jl 15, 22*, 29, Ag 5*, 12*, 19–O 7, 14*, 21–D 30, 1847; Ja 6–27, F 3*, 10–17, Mr 23–30, Ap 13–D 28, 1848; Ja 4–D 27, 1849; Ja 3–Je 6, 1850. [Imperfect numbers are indicated with an asterisk.] NN Ap, S 1846; Ja 14–21, F 11, Mr 11, Ag 26–S 2, 16–23, O 28, N 25–D 9, 1847; Ja 6, F 3, 17–24, Mr 9–30, Ap 13–27, My 25–Je 8, Ag 17, O 5, 19, D 14, 1848; Ja 18–25, F 8–Mr 23, My 31–Je 28, Ag 16, S 6, O 11, N 1, D 6–13, 1849; Ja 17–24, F 7–14, Ap 11, 25, My 16, 1850. ULA misc. #. USIC F–S 1846; D 16, 1847. WBuC F–My, Jl–N 1846; Ja 14, 28–N 25, D 23–30, 1847; Ja 6–F 3, 17–Mr 9, Ap 6–20, My 11–D 28, 1848; Ja 4–Mr 1, 15–Jl 26, Ag 16–23, S 27–O 11, 25–N 8, 22–D 27, 1849; Ja 3, 17, 31–F 21,

Mr 7–Ap 11, 25–My 23, Je 6, 1850. [This file was formerly Wingfield Watson's. Missing numbers have been supplied in photostat so as to complete it except for V. I, # 1, 6, 12; V. II, # 47, 52; V. III, # 7; and V. V, # 11.] WHi F, Ag–O 1846; Ja 14, Je 1, S 2, 23–O 7, N 18–25, D 16–23, 1847; Ag 24–D 28, 1848; Ja 4–Mr 15, 29–D 27, 1849; Ja 3–F 28, Mr 14, 28–My 9, 1850. [Missing numbers in this file have been supplied in photostat, principally from Wingfield Watson's file, so as to complete it except for those numbers listed as lacking in the WBuC file above.]

3642. The Gospel light. Edited and Published by John E. Page. Pittsburgh, June, 1843–May, 1844.
lv. (3 nos. in 24p.) 25cm.
"Devoted to the promulgation and defense of the doctrines advocated by The Church of Jesus Christ of Latter day Saints."
USlC V.1, # 1–3, June, 1843, February, May, 1844

3643. The Gospel Messenger. Perth, Western Australia, July 9–October 22, 1907.
V.1, #1–8. bi-weekly. 22cm.
RLDS church publication.
MoInRC

3644. The Gospel Monitor. Hannibal, Mo., 1880–
3v. monthly. 31½cm.
Editor: J. J. Cranmer, Elder in the Church of Christ.
Morgan
CtY 1880 V. 1, #11; V. 2, #6–7; V. 3, #9

3645. Gospel Quarterly. Published by the General Sunday School Association of the Reorganized Church of Jesus Christ of Latter Day Saints. Lamoni, Ia., 1891–
v. quarterly. 24cm.
MoInRC–CE Beginner 1913–29; Intermediate and Primary Combines 1894–95; Primary 1896–1929; Junior 1913–29; Intermediate 1896–1928; Senior 1929; Senior (17, 18 and adult) 1893–1928; Young People 1929; Young Adult 1928–29; Adult 1926–29. NN Primary V.2: 2–18 (called Second Primary Grade); Intermediate Grade V.1: 2–18 (1904–28); 17: 1–2, 18–22 (Jan.–June, Oct. 1929–March 1934); Junior Grade V.7–8: 1–2, 4, 9–22 (1919–34); Beginner Grade V.14–29: 2 (1919–34); Senior Grade V.1, 2: 2–4, 3: 3–4, 5: 4, 6: 1–2, 7: 1, 8: 4, 9: 1, 12–41 1892–1934. UPB Beginner Grade 1925–26, 1930; Primary 1930; Intermediate 1927–30; Senior 1916, 1922, 1926, 1928–30; Adult Grade 1927–30. USlC Intermediate Grade V.5: 4 (1897)

3646. The Gospel Reflector. Roscoe, Pa. Edited by Alexander Cherry. August, 1905–August, 1910.
3v. (24 issues per volume) monthly. 33cm.
The only known file, at Monongahela, ends with the issue for August, 1910, (V.3, #13)
Church of Jesus Christ (Bickerton)
Morgan
PMonC

3647. The Gospel Reflector, in which the doctrine of the Church of Jesus Christ of Latter-day Saints is set forth, and scripture evidence adduced to establish it . . . Philadelphia, Brown, Bicking and Guilbert, Printers, January 1, to June 15, 1841.
12 nos. (316p) semi-monthly. 19cm.
Edited by Benjamin Winchester, Presiding Elder of the Church of Jesus Christ of Latter-day Saints, in Philadelphia.
Complete with title-page and table of contents.
CSmH, CU–B, DLC, ICN, MH, NN, ULA, UPB, USlC, WHi

3648. The Gospel Standard. Rozelle [Victoria] New South Wales. January 18, 1902–October, 1933.
v. monthly. 31cm.
Changed to the *Standard* after 1933.
Published at Rozelle, 1902–04; Victoria, 1904–06; Rozelle, 1906–33.
MoInRC V. 1–5, 9, inc., 10, 13 #3, 16 #12, 19 #2–5, 20 inc., 28 inc., 31 inc., 32 inc., 33–34, 35 inc., 36 inc., 37 inc., 38 inc., 39–60 #3

Gospel Witness. *See Spencer, Orson.*

3649. Gottfredson, Peter, *editor.* History of Indian depredations in Utah . . . Comp. and ed. by Peter Gottfredson. [Salt Lake City, Press of Skelton Publishing Co., c1919]
352p. plates, ports. 19½cm.
Mormon-Indian relations.
Includes a 16p. supplement. USlC
DLC, ICN, MB, NjP, UHi, ULA, USlC, UU

3650. Gougar, Helen Mar (Jackson). Matthew Peters. A foreign immigrant. The true story of a life by Helen M. Gougar. Pen sketches by F. A. Carter. Lafayette, Indiana, Published by Helen M. Gougar [1898?]
6p.l. [9]–133p. illus. 16cm.
Anise Sharp Roberts joins the Mormon church and moves to Nauvoo, but does not go west or join a faction.
USlC

3651. Gourd, Alphonse. Les Mormons, Conference faite a la Societé d'économie politique de Lyon dans sa séance du 22 mars, 1889. Lyon, A. Bonnaviat, 1889.
61p. 22cm.
Author's inscription on title-page of CU–B copy.
Title in English: The Mormons.
CU–B, MiU

3652. Gove, Jesse Augustus. The Utah expedition, 1857–1858; letters of Capt. Jesse A. Gove, 10th inf., U.S.A. . . . to Mrs. Gove, and special correspondence of the New York Herald . . . edited by Otis G. Hammond . . . Concord, H. H., New Hampshire Historical Society, 1928.
442p. illus., plates, port., facsim. 23½cm. (New Hampshire Historical Society. Collections. V. 12)
CSmH, CU–B, DLC, ICN, MH, MoInRC, NjP, ULA, UPB, WHi

GOWELL, M. F.

3653. Gowell, M. F. An appeal to Latter Day Saints of the Utah Church, and state of what we believe. [Provo? n.d.]
[4]p. 23cm.
RLDS doctrine of succession with scriptural proofs chiefly from the *Doctrine and Covenants.*
MoInRC

3654. Gower, Ronald. My reminiscences. By Lord Ronald Gower. New edition. London, Kegan Paul, Trench, Trubner & Co., Ltd., 1895.
x, 517p. port. 20cm.
A brief stay in Salt Lake City in 1878. Brigham Young a thief, a murderer, and a fanatic.
USlC

3655. Gr., Th. Ein Ritt nach Californien. [In:] "Das Buch der Welt, . . ." Stuttgart. Hoffman'sche Verlags-Buchhandlung, 1859.
34–40, 44–48, 52–57, 61–64p. illus. 21½cm.
They encounter a party of Mexican traders returning from Southern Utah and describe the Mormons in Southern Utah towns.
Title in English: A ride to California.
W–C 326b
C

3656. Graceland College Bulletin. Lamoni, Iowa, June, 1904[?]–
v. quarterly. 26cm.
Graceland College holdings not surveyed.
IaLG comp.; USlC V.6 #5 (1910), V.7 #2

3657. Graham, J. C. & Company. The Utah directory, for 1883–84. Published by J. C. Graham and Co., containing the name and occupation of every resident in Salt Lake City and a complete business directory of every city and town in Utah together with a compendium of general information. Salt Lake City, J. C. Graham & Co., 1883.
xvi, 17–278p. 18cm.
Description of Salt Lake City and other Mormon settlements in the guide book section.
CU–B, DLC, UPB

3658. Graham, Martha Morgan. The polygamist's victim; or, The life experiences of the author during a six years' residence among the Mormon Saints, being a description of the massacres, struggles, dangers, toils and vicissitudes of border-life, with miraculous preservations in many dangers by the intervention of mysterious powers. San Francisco, Women's Union Printing Office, 1872.
72p. 19½cm.
Mrs. Graham was deserted by her first husband so married Jesse Morgan and emigrated to Salt Lake City in 1849. In 1850 continued to California where Mr. Morgan died. She was forced to keep herself and wrote her "horrible" story of crossing the plains and of Mormonism, which she peddled door to door.
Howes G289
CU, CU–B, ICN, MH

3659. ———. (same, under title) An interesting life history of Mrs. Martha Stout Morgan Graham from early childhood until the present Day . . . San Francisco, Women's Co-operative Printing Union, 1875.
2p.l. [5]–67p. 21cm.
Caption-title: The polygamist's victim.
MH

———. A trip across the plains in the year 1849. *See Morgan, Jesse.*

3660. Graham, Stephen. Tramping with a poet in the Rockies. With thirty-eight emblems by Vernon Hill. New York, D. Appleton and Co., 1922.
xp. [1]l., 279p. illus. 21cm.
Includes material of Utah and the Mormons.
CU, DLC, NjP, UHi, USlC, UU

3661. Graham, Thomas. My travels east and west by Thomas Graham. [n.p., n.d.]
1p.l. [3]–96p. illus., plates. 23cm.
A trip to Salt Lake City. All traffic through Salt Lake had to go through the Eagle Gate and pay a toll.
Articles of faith included.
USlC

Graham, Winifred. The Mormons. *See Cory, Winifred Graham.*

3662. Grainger, John. Reincarnation. A message to Latter Day Saints. [n.p., n.d.]
11p. 21cm.
Lecture given in the Hall of Theosophy, Kansas City, Missouri.
MoInRC

3663. Granson, *directeur des Postes.* Des Mormons par M. Granson, Directeur des Postes . . . Havre, Impr. Lepelletier, 1863.
24p. 24cm.
UPB has the same, excerpted from an unknown source, p. 401–422.
CU–B

Grant, Carter E. *See Kimball, Crozier.*

3664. Grant, Heber Jeddy. An address delivered by invitation before the Chamber of Commerce, Kansas City, Missouri, Wednesday, December 10, 1924. Independence, Mo., Press of Zion's Printing and Publishing Co. [1924]
16p. 23cm.
MoInRC, USlC

3665. ———. An announcement concerning the Church of Jesus Christ of Latter-day Saints. [Tokyo? n.d.]

7p. 15cm.
Missionary tract. Includes the Articles of faith with references.
USlC

3666. ———. Birthday is Mother's Day. [Salt Lake City, n.d.]
[4]p. 21cm.
Sentiment of President Heber J. Grant.
USlC

3667. ———. Commandments and promises. A message to the Latter-day Saints. By President Heber J. Grant. [Salt Lake City, n.d.]
[8]p. 19cm.
USlC

3668. ———. How I learned to sing in the native American. By Heber J. Grant. [Mesa? 1925?]
5p. 25cm.
Mention of use of hymns for learning the language.
USlC

3669. ———. Matsu Jitsu Seito Iesu Kirisuto Kyōkai ni kansuru Kinkyū Rinkoku. Tokyō, Nihon, Matsu Jitsu Seito Iesu Kirisuto Kyōkai Nihon Dendobu [1903]
14p. 15½cm.
Title in English: The Church of Jesus Christ of Latter-day Saints. An urgent message.
USlC

3670. ———. (same) Tokyō, Nihon, Matsu Jitsu Seito Iesu Kirisuto Kyōkai Nihon Dendobu [1903]
13p. 15cm.
USlC

3671. ———. (same) Tokyō, Nihon, Matsu Jitsu Seito Iesu Kirisuto Kyōkai Nihon Dendobu [1904]
14p. 16cm.
USlC

3672. ———. (same) Tokyō, Nihon, Matsu Jitsu Seito Iesu Kirisuto Kyōkai Nihon Dendobu [1905]
14p. 15cm.
USlC

3673. ———. (same) Tokyō, Nihon, Matsu Jitsu Seito Iesu Kirisuto Kyōkai Nihon Dendobu [n.d.]
13p. 15cm.
USlC

3674. ———. Nineteenth annual conference themes. An opening address of the annual conference of the Church of Jesus Christ of Latter-day Saints, delivered Sunday morning April 4, 1920, in the Salt Lake Tabernacle. [Salt Lake City, 1920]
17p. 52½cm.
Cover-title.
"Reprinted from the *Improvement Era*."
UHi, USlC

3675. ———. Prohibition. Address on M.I.A. Slogan by Superintendent Heber J. Grant. Delivered at Joint M.I.A. officer's meeting, June 9, 1916. [Salt Lake City] 1916.
4p. 24cm.
NjP, UPB

3676. ———. Report by President Heber J. Grant at the annual conference of the Church of Jesus Christ of Latter-day Saints, April, 1922–April, 1924. [Salt Lake City, 1922–1924]
3 nos. 19cm.
Financial and statistical reports.
USlC

3677. ———. Strength of the "Mormon" church. An address delivered by invitation at the banquet of the Knife and Fork Club, Kansas City, Missouri. December 16, 1920. Salt Lake City, Bureau of Information, 1921.
32p. 17½cm.
"Published in the March 1921 issue of the *Coast Banker*, San Francisco and Los Angeles."
CU-B, MH, NGUB, UHi, USlC

3678. ———. (same, in German) Die Stärke der Mormonenkirche. Ein Blick auf ihre Geschichte, Prüfungen, Reinsen, ihren Glauben, ihre Leistungen, ihren Plan für die Zukunft. Ansprache gehalten auf Einladung des "Knife and Fork Clubs" in Kansas City, Missouri am 16. Dezember, 1920. [Basel, Schweizerishchen und Deutschen Mission, 1921]
23p. 22cm.
Articles of faith on back cover.
Translated by Mark Zimmer.
USlC

———. A tribute of respect to the memory of Francis Marion Lyman. *See Church of Jesus Christ of Latter-day Saints. Young Men's Mutual Improvement Association. A tribute of respect.*

3679. ———. Tribute to Erastus Snow. [Salt Lake City, 1911]
[4]p. 20cm.
USlC

3680. ———. Upholding of the constituted law and order. Address delivered in the Tabernacle, Sunday February 12, 1928. [Salt Lake City, 1928]
10p. port. 23½cm.
USlC

3681. ———. When great sorrows are our portion. By Heber J. Grant . . . [Salt Lake City 1918]
[4]p. 21½cm.
USlC

3681a. ———. (same) [Salt Lake City] Improvement Era [1920]
[8]p. 21½cm.
UHi, USlC

3682. Grant, Jay Smith. Pictorial ancient America. Los Angeles, Pub. by Jay S. Grant [c1927]
4p.l. [9]–152p. plates. 19½cm.
Book of Mormon evidences.
NjP, USlC

3683. Grant, Jedediah Morgan. A collection of facts, relative to the course taken by Elder Sidney Rigdon, in the states of Ohio, Missouri, Illinois and Pennsylvania. By Jedediah M. Grant, one of the Quorum of Seventies. Philadelphia, Brown, Bicking and Guilbert, Printers, 1844.
2p.l. [5]–48p. 19cm.
Cover-title: J. M. Grant's Rigdon. Number One. No more published.
Howes G310
CtY, USlC

3684. ———. Three letters to the New York Herald from J. M. Grant, of Utah. [New York, 1852]
64p. 24cm.
Reprinted, New York Herald, March 9, 1852.
Title on cover: The truth for the Mormons.
A series of letters explaining Mormon doctrine and telling of the crimes committed against them.
An answer to the *Report of Messrs. Brandebury, Brocchus, and Harris, to the President of the United States* on political conditions in Utah.
It is understood to have been written by Thomas L. Kane for J. M. Grant.
Sabin BH28305
CtY, CU–B, DLC, MoInRC, NN, USl, USlC

———. The truth for the Mormons. *See Grant, Jedediah M. Three letters . . .*

3685. Grant, Robert E. An appeal to all Latter Day Saints in which the church is warned of judgments fast coming upon it. [Grand Rapids, Mich., 1911]
8p. 21cm.
Cover-title.
Signed: Grand Rapids, Mich., December 1, 1911. An excommunicated member of the RLDS church.
MoInRC, UPB, USlC

3686. ———. The Book of Commandments. It was printed and finished. [Grand Rapids, Mich., n.d.]
[4]p. 17cm.
USlC

3687. ———. An open letter written to Joseph R. Lambert of Lamoni, Iowa. [Grand Rapids, Mich., 1909?]
16p. 21cm.
Signed: Grand Rapids, Mich., Sept. 25, 1909.
Critical of the RLDS church.
MoInRC, USlC

3688. ———. Open letter No. 2, written to Joseph R. Lambert of Lamoni, Iowa. [Grand Rapids, 1910?]
8p. 20½cm.
Excommunicated RLDS church member against Joseph Smith as a prophet.
Dated: Grand Rapids, March 31st, 1910.
MoInRC, USlC

3689. ———. Open letter No. 3 to Joseph Lambert and the Reorganized Church. [Grand Rapids, Mich., 1911?]
8p. 21½cm.
Caption-title.
Pertaining to the false and changed revelations received in the *Doctrine and Covenants.*
Signed: Grand Rapids, Mich., Jan. 1st, 1911.
MoInRC, USlC

3690. ———. Questions and answers. By Elder R. E. Grant. Lamoni, Ia., Published by the Herald House [187–]
2p. 21cm.
Variant printings.
RLDS doctrine.
MoInRC

3691. Grass, Eric T. Thoughts of reality; a challenge to the churches and to the Mormons in particular . . . By Eric T. Grass. Salt Lake City, the author [n.d.]
32p. port. 16cm.
Claims the Mormons are pantheists and have no real basis for claim to authority as a true church. Demands "a decent answer to how they got divine power."
UU

3692. Gratten, Thomas Colley. Civilized America. By Thomas Colley Gratten. London, Bradbury & Evans, London, 1859.
2v. 2 maps (1 fold.) 22cm.
"Second edition"
Mormonism mentioned among fanatical religions.
Howes G319, Sabin 28339
CU–B, DLC, NjP, USlC

3693. Graul, K. De forskjellige christelige troesbekjendelser i deres indbyrdes afvigelser i laeren, belyste af Guds Ord samt efterviisning af den rene laeres hoie betydning for de christelige liv og et afrids af de giftigste falske religiose retninger. Kobenhavn, 1857.
174p.
Title in English: Diverse Christian confessions of faith . . .
Schmidt

3694. Graves, H. A. Andrew Jackson Potter. The fighting parson of the Texan frontier. Nashville, Tenn., Southern Methodist Publishing House, 1881.
2p.l. [5]–471p. port. 19cm.
In 1851 Potter accompanied the "Olive Branch Division" of the Mormons, to the Colorado River. Their prophet was James Colin Brewster.
USlC

3695. Gray, Albert Frederick. The menace of Mormonism, by A. F. Gray. Anderson, Ind., Gospel Trumpet Company [c1926]
128p. illus., plates, port., map. 19cm.
DLC, IWW, MoInRC, NN, UPB, UU, WHi

3696. Gray, J. H. Plurality of wives among the Mormons. London, Wertheim & Macintosh, 1853.
Broadside. 16×20cm.
USlC

3697. ———. Principles and practices of Mormons, tested in two lectures: delivered before the Religious and Useful Knowledge Society of Douglas, on November 24th, and December 1st, 1852 . . . (2d ed., considerably enl.) By the Rev. J. H. Gray . . . Douglas, M. P. Backwell; [etc., etc.] 1853.
78p. 17½cm.
CSmH, CtY, CU-B, DLC, NN, USlC

3698. ———. The substance of two lectures on Mormonism delivered in Sutton, Bonnington, and Muskham, Notts., by the Rev. J. H. Gray . . . London, James Nesbit and Co., 1852.
32p. 16½cm.
UU

3698a. Great Britain. Census Office. Census of Great Britain, 1851. Religious worship. England and Wales. Report and tables. Presented to both Houses of Parliament by Command of Her Majesty. London, Printed by George E. Eyre and William Spottiswoode . . . 1853.
ccc, 134p. tables. 24½cm.
"The Latter Day Saints; or Mormons," p. cvi–cxii. Other miscellaneous references.
USlC

The "Great proclamation"; or "Trump message," of the authority of God. *See Church of Jesus Christ of Latter-day Saints. Council of the Twelve Apostles.*

Great Salt Lake City. *See Salt Lake City.*

3698b. The Great Mormon Remedy Company. The Mormons. Come out and hear all about these strange people! Their queer practices! And learn more about their peculiar religion, especial revelations, manner of living, temples, tabernacles, the Great Salt Lake, etc. . . . [St. Paul, Minn.? 1892?]
[4]p. 30½cm.
Advertisement for an anti-Mormon lecture.
USlC

3698c. ———. Read this! Then hand it to a friend. The "Mormons" . . . [St. Paul? ca. 1892]
[4]p. 28cm.
USlC

3699. The great West, its attractions and resources, containing a popular description of the marvelous scenery, physical geography, fossils and glaciers of this wonderful region, and the recent explorations in the Yellowstone Park, "The Wonderland of America" by Prof. F. V. Hayden. Also, valuable information to travellers and settlers concerning climate, health, money, husbandry, education, the Indians, Mormonism, the Chinese . . . Bloomington, Ill., C. R. Brodix, 1880.
1p.l., 5–528p. ports., plates, maps. 25cm.
A discussion on Mormonism explaining that the best ones had apostatized, p. 312–339.
CU-B, DLC, MiU, NjP, NN, UHi, ULA, UPB, UU

3700. Greeley, Horace. An overland journey, from New York to San Francisco, in the summer of 1859. By Horace Greeley. New York, C. N. Saxton, Barker and Co.; San Francisco, H. H. Bancroft and Co., 1860.
386p. 19½cm.
Several chapters on Mormonism. His visit to Brigham Young, impressions of the Mormon meetings, etc. He was in Salt Lake City July 11–21, 1859.
Howes G355, Sabin 28490, W-C 359
CSmH, DLC, ICN, NjP, UHi, UPB, USl, USlC

3701. ———. Recollections of a busy life: including reminiscences of American politics and politicians, from the opening of the Missouri contest to the downfall of slavery; to which are added miscellanies . . . also, a discussion with Robert Dale Owen of the law of divorce. By Horace Greeley. New York, J. B. Ford & Co.; Boston, H. A. Brown & Co.; [etc., etc.] 1868.
2p.l. [vii]–xv [17]–624p. illus., plates, port., facsim. 22½cm.
Visited Salt Lake City in 1859; liked Mormon industry, p. 373, 374–375.
Other editions: New York, 1868. DLC; 1869. DLC; New York, Tribune Association Pub., 1873. CU
Sabin 28491
DLC, NjP, UHi

3702. Greely, Adolphus Washington. Reminiscences of adventure and service; a record of sixty-five years, by Major-General A. W. Greely . . . New York, London, C. Scribner's Sons, 1927.
xi p.[1]l., 356p. illus., plates, ports., facsims. 22cm.
Stationed at Fort Douglas. "Brigham Young and Salt Lake City in the sixties."
CU, DLC, ICHi, NjP, UHi, UPB

3702a. Green, Lucy May (Hilton). The opened door. Cantata for ladies voices by Lucy May Green and Ida Horne White. Story by Louise Y. Robison. Salt Lake City, Granite State [sic] Relief Society, c1917.
31p. 26½cm.
Music.
USlC

GREEN, N. W.

3703. Green, Nelson Winch. Fifteen years among the Mormons: being the narrative of Mrs. Mary Ettie V. Smith, late of Great Salt Lake City; a sister of one of the Mormon high priests, she having been personally acquainted with most of the Mormon leaders, and long in the confidence of the "Prophet" Brigham Young. By Nelson Winch Green. New York, C. Scribner, 1858.
xvi, 17–388p. port. 20cm.
Mrs. Smith's narrative is in the first person, but authorship is claimed by Green in the introduction.
Sabin 38553, W–C 300
CSmH, CtY, DLC, ICN, NN, UHi, ULA, UU

3704. ———. (same) New York, H. Dayton, 1858.
xvi, 17–408p. 18½cm.
CSmH, UHi, UPB

3705. ———. (same) New York, H. Dayton; Indianapolis, Ind., Asher & Company, 1859.
xvi, 17–408p. 19cm.
Variant printing. USlC
DLC, MWA, NjP, OClWHi, OOxM, PPTU, USlC, UU

3706. ———. (same) New York, H. Dayton, 1860 [c1857]
xvi, 17–408p. 19cm.
CSmH, CU–B, MH, OClWHi, PPPrHi, UHi, UPB

3707. ———. (same, under title) Fifteen years' residence with the Mormons. With startling disclosures of the mysteries of polygamy. By a sister of one of the high priests. Chicago, Phoenix Publishing Co., 1876.
xvi [17]–472p. plates. 18½cm.
W–C 300
CU, ICN, NN, OCl, OCU, UHi, UPB, USlC, UU

3708. ———. (same, under title) Mormonism; its rise, progress and present condition. Embracing the narrative of Mrs. Ettie V. Smith, of her residence and experience of fifteen years with the Mormons; containing a full and authentic account of their social condition — their religious doctrines and political government . . . with other startling facts and statements, being a full disclosure of the rites, ceremonies and mysteries of polygamy. Together with the speech recently delivered before the "Elders" in Utah by Vice President Schuyler Colfax, and the answer of John Taylor. By N. W. Green. Hartford, Belknap and Bliss, 1870.
xvi [17]–472p. ports., plates. 20cm.
Sabin 28554
Cover title: Expose of Mormons and Mormonism.
CSmH, CtY, CU–B, DLC, ICN, MH, MoInRC, NjP, NjPT, NN, UHi, ULA, USlC, UU, WHi

3709. ———. (same) Hartford, Belknap & Bliss, 1872.
488p. plates. 19cm.
CSmH, NN, OCl

Greene, Evarts Boutell, *editor*. Governors' letter-books, 1840–1853. *See Illinois. Governor.*

3710. Greene, John Portineus. Facts relative to the expulsion of the Mormons, or Latter-day Saints from the State of Missouri, under the "exterminating order." By John P. Greene, an authorised representative of the Mormons. Cincinnati, Printed by R. P. Brooks, 1839.
iv [5]–43p. 22cm.
The author, a cousin of Brigham Young, was present during these events.
Variant printing. Without "or Latter-day Saints" in title. Signatures vary. CU–B, UPB
Howes G382, Sabin 28606
CSmH, CtY, DLC, ICHi, ICN, MB, MH, MoHi, MoK, NN, USlC, WHi

3711. Greene, Mary. Life, three sermons, and some of the miscellaneous writings of Rev. Jesse Greene, a presiding Elder in the St. Louis Conference — long a devoted minister in the M. E. Church South, by his surviving companion, Mary Greene . . . Lexington, Mo., Patterson & Julian — Express Machine Press, 1852.
3p.l. [5]–280p. port. 19cm.
Includes a letter from Jesse Greene on Dec. 11, 1838 concerning the Mormon problem in Missouri, p. 82–83.
USlC

3712. Greene, Max. The Kansas region: forest, prairie, desert, mountain, vale, and river. Descriptions of scenery, climate, wild productions, capabilities of soil, and commercial resources; interspersed with incidents of travel, and anecdotes, illustrative of the character of the traders and red man; to which are added directions as to routes, out-fit for the pioneer, and sketches of desirable localities for present settlement. By Max Greene. New York, Fowler and Wells, Publishers, 1856.
viii [9]–192 (i.e. 190) p. map. 19½cm.
Material on Mormons in Utah and their doctrines.
Howes G383, Sabin 28607, W–C 276
CU–B, DLC, NjP

3713. Greenlagh, James. Narrative of James Greenhalgh [sic.], cotton spinner, Egerton, near Bolton-le-Moors, . . . [Preston, England, Printed and Published by J. Livesey, . . . 1842?]
4p. map. 24½cm. (The Struggle, No. 36)
A map of the United States of America on cover. The title and text starting on page 2.
USlC

3713a. ———. Narrative of James Greenlagh, cotton-spinner, Egerton, Bolton-Le Moors. Earnestly recommended to the consideration of any who may have attended the Mormonite meetings, in Concert Street. Showing the occurrences and difficulties that himself, wife, and four children (the youngest one, and the eldest, seven years old) endured during an absence of twenty three weeks from England; having

sailed from Liverpool to New Orleans, and from thence traversing the course of the Mississippi to St. Louis, thence to Nauvoo, the Mormonites' settlement in the State of Ill., from thence back to St. Louis and Pittsburgh. Philadelphia and New York, thence to Liverpool. [Liverpool, Richard Scragg, Printer, 1843?]
12p. 17cm.
Caption-title.
Signed: July 19, 1842.
USlC

3714. Greenman, Mrs. C. M. A Revelation. Published for the enlightenment of a deluded people by Mrs. C. M. Greenman A.D. 1914. [Westerly, R.I., 1914]
24p. 10cm.
The Mormons are the deluded people.
NN, OO

3715. ———. Solomon Spauldings "Manuscript found," 1805–1830 A.D. Now unsealed, 1914. [Westerly, R.I., 1914]
[2]l. 21cm.
Caption-title.
No title page.
NN

Greenwood, Grace. *See Lippincott, Sara.*

3715a. Greg, Percy. History of the United States from the foundation of Virginia to the reconstruction of the Union. London, W. H. Allen & Co., 1887.
2v. 22½cm.
"The Mormons," Vol. 2, p. 159–176.
USlC

3716. Gregg, Josiah. Commerce of the prairies: or, The journal of a Santa Fe trader, during eight expeditions across the great western prairies, and a residence of nearly nine years in northern Mexico . . . By Josiah Gregg . . . New York, H. G. Langley, 1844.
2v. illus., plates, 2 maps (1 fold.) 19cm.
Includes Mormons in Independence, Far West, and Nauvoo.
Many editions in various languages, from 1845.
Howes G401, Sabin 28712, W-C 108
CSmH, CtY, DLC, ICN, IHi, MiU, MWA, NjP, NN, OCU

3717. Gregg, Thomas. A descriptive, statistical and historical chart of the county of Hancock. Prepared and published by Th. Gregg — Warsaw, Illinois, Feb. 1, 1846. [Second edition-revised and corrected by the author] [Brackets in source] [Warsaw, 1846]
Broadside. 59×77cm.
One column devoted to "Mormon History."
IHi

3718. ———. History of Hancock County, Illinois, together with an outline history of the state, and a digest of state laws. By Thomas Gregg. Chicago, Chas. C. Chapman & Co., 1880.
3p.l. [17]–1036p. illus., plates, ports., double map. 25½cm.
"The Mormon war. The Mormon period," p. 104–109, 242, 328.
Howes G403
CU–B, DLC, ICN, MoK, MWA, NjP, NN, UPB, USlC

3719. ———. The prophet of Palmyra; Mormonism reviewed and examined in the life, character, and career of its founder, from "Cumorah Hill" to Carthage Jail and the desert, together with a complete history of the Mormon era in Illinois, and an exhaustive investigation of the "Spalding [sic] manuscript" theory of the origin of the Book of Mormon, by Thomas Gregg. New York, John B. Alden, 1890.
xiv p., [1]l., 552p. plates, ports. 19½cm.
Howes G404
CSmH, DLC, NjP, NjPT, NN, UHi, ULA, UPB, USl, USlC, UU, WHi

3720. Gregory, Frederick. Which is the right church. [n.p., n.d.]
52p. 16cm.
RLDS publication.
MoInRC

3721. Gresty, John T. The course of time; a dramatic oratorio. . . . to be sung at the centennial celebration of the founding of the Reorganized Church of Jesus Christ of Latter Day Saints, April 6, 1930, Independence, Missouri. [Chicago, Reorganized Church of Jesus Christ of Latter Day Saints, c1929]
263p. illus. with music. 26½cm.
First edition.
At head of title: "Centennial souvenir edition."
UPB

3722. Grey, Zane. The heritage of the desert; a novel, by Zane Grey. New York and London, Harper & Brothers, 1910.
3p.l., 297 [1]p. front. 19½cm.
Western novel with partial Mormon setting.
Other editions: New York, Grosset and Dunlap, c1910. UHi; 1920. DLC
DLC, MB, NjP, ULA, UU

3723. ———. The rainbow trail; a romance, by Zane Grey . . . New York and London, Harper & Brothers [1915]
4p.l. 372 [1]p. col. front. 19½cm.
"Appeared serially in a different form in one of the monthly magazines under the title of 'The desert crucible.' " — Foreword
Novel with Mormon background.
Sequel to *Riders of the purple sage.*
Republished in many editions.
DLC, MiU, NjP, NN, OO, PNt, PP, PPM, PU, ULA, USlC

3724. ———. Riders of the purple sage; a novel . . . New York, Harper & Brothers Publishers [c1912]
4p.l., 334 [1]p. plates. 19cm.
Novel with Mormon background.
Other editions: New York, London, Grosset & Dunlap publishers [c1912]; London, 1912. USIC
In German under title: Das gesetz der Mormonen. Berlin Verlag von Th. Knaur Nachf [n.d.] USIC
USIC, DLC, NjP, ULA, UPB

3725. Griffith, William. History of Kansas City illustrated in three decades. Being a chronicle wherein is set forth the true account of the founding, rise, and present position occupied by Kansas City in municipal America. By William Griffith. Kansas City, Mo., Hudson-Kimberly Publishing Co., 1900.
141p. plates. 21cm.
Chapter IV includes "Mormon difficulties in Jackson County."
DLC, NjP, UHi, UPB

3726. Griffiths, D., Jr. Two years' residence in the new settlements of Ohio, North America: with directions to emigrants. By D. Griffiths, Jun. London, Westley and Davis; Jackson and Walford; Toller, Kettering; Abel and Wheeler [etc.] 1835.
vii [9]–197p. port. 19cm.
Chapter 6 contains some history and a description of the Mormons, 1832–33.
Howes G427, Sabin C28833
CtY, DLC, ICN, NN, USIC

3727. Griffiths, Gomer T. An exegesis of the priesthood, by Gomer T. Griffiths . . . [Cleveland, Savage Press, 1902?]
viii, 154p. illus. 18cm.
RLDS doctrine.
MoInRC, UHi

3728. ———, *compiler.* The Instructor, a synopsis of the faith and doctrine of the Reorganized Church of Jesus Christ of Latter Day Saints. Together with historical and general evidences from the works of eminent theological writers past and present. Compiled and arranged by Elder G. T. Griffiths. To which is added memorable events and items of interest connected with the history of the church. Lamoni, Ia., Herald Publishing House, 1893.
iv, 231p. 20cm.
IWW, MoInRC, NN, UHi, USIC

3729. ———. Interpreter, by Gomer T. Griffiths. Sydney, Australia, The Standard Publishing House, 1915.
152p. port. 20½cm.
Doctrines of the RLDS church.
MoInRC, UPB

3730. ———. The True Church of Jesus Christ of Latter Day Saints and the Kirtland Temple . . . [n.p., n.d.]
15p. 19½cm.
Question of succession from the RLDS viewpoint.
USIC

3731. ———. (same) By Gomer T. Griffiths. [n.p., n.d.]
13p. 19cm.
USIC

3732. Griffiths, Willard. Mormon doings. When freemen rise and shed their ink. The heads of petty tyrants shrink. [Elkhorn, Wis.? 1846]
Broadside. 48×27cm.
Protest meeting against the tyranny of James J. Strang. Signed by Willard Griffiths, Collins Pemberton, Isaac Scott, Allen Waite.
Morgan
USIC

3733. Grimshaw, Jonathan. The journal of Jonathan Grimshaw. [n.p., n.d.]
[19]l. 27½cm.
December 5, 1850 to June 22, 1851.
Describes his conversation to Mormonism and detailed description of the sea voyage. Ends at Winter Quarters.
NN

3733a. Gripenberg, Alexandra, *friherrinna,* **1857–1913.** Ett halfår i Nya Verlden. Strödda resebilder från Firenta Staterna, af Alexandra Gripenberg. Helsing fors, G. W. Edlund, 1889.
2p.l., 290p. [1]l. 18½cm.
An inaccurate description of Mormonism from her trip to Utah in 1888.
Also published in Finnish under title: Uudesta Maarlmasta; Hajanarsia matkakuvia Ameriikasta. Published into English in 1854.
Title in English: A half year in the new world.
DLC

3734. Grube, August Wilhelm. Skildringer ur Folkens seliga och religiösa lif . . . öfversättning af Oscar B. Grafström. Stockholm, Tryckt hos. P. G. Berg, 1863.
4p.l., 260p. col. plates. 21cm.
"Mormonerna," p. 38–48.
Title in English: Sketches of the folk customs and religious life.
CtY

3735. Grünwald-Zerkovitz, Sidonie. Die lieder der Mormonin. Leipzig, Verlag von Hermann Durselen, 1888. 3. auflage.
123p. 16cm.
Title in English: The songs of a Mormon woman.
USIC

3735a. ———. (same) Leipzig. 5. auflage. Berlin, 1889.
A cycle of poems depicting the sad lot of a polygamous Mormon woman. D. L. Ashliman, "Mormonism and the Germans." *BYU Studies.* Autumn, 1967.

3736. Grund, Francis Joseph. Handbuch und Wegweiser für Auswanderer nach den Vereinigten Staaten von Nordamerika, und Texas . . . Von Francis J. Grund. Stuttgart, J. G. Cotta, 1843.
iv, 251p. tables. 21cm.
Section on Mormonism.
Republished in 1846. CtY, DLC
Title in English: Handbook and guide for immigrants to the United States . . .
MH, NN

3737. Gue, Benjamin F. History of Iowa from the earliest times to the beginning of the twentieth century . . . by Benjamin F. Gue; illustrated with photographic views of the natural scenery of the state, public buildings, pioneer life, etc., with portraits and biographies of notable men and women of Iowa . . . New York, The Century History Company [1903]
4v. illus., plates, ports., maps, facsims. 24cm.
Sections on Mormon church under: Elections, Mormon Battalion, Mormons in Iowa.
DLC, NjP, UPB

3738. Guernsey, Alice M. Under our flag; A study of national conditions from the standpoint of Women's home missionary work by Alice M. Guernsey . . . New York, [etc.] Fleming H. Revell Company [c1903]
1p.l., 5–193p. 20cm.
"Mormonism and the Mormons," p. 132–160. A group of quotes (mostly undocumented) to prove what Mormonism was. Heavy emphasis on polygamy.
CU–B, USlC

3739. Guers, Emile. Irvingism and Mormonism tested by scripture. By the Rev. Emilius Guers. With prefatory note by James Bridges. London, J. Nisbet and Co., 1854.
xxiv, 94p. 18½cm.
MH, NN, UPB, USl, USlC, UU

3740. ———. (same, in French) L'Irvingisme et le Mormonisme jugis par la Parole de Dieu . . . Génève, E. Beroud, (etc., etc.) 1853.
vii, 128p. 21cm.
CLU, MH, NN, ULA, USlC

3740a. ———. El Mormonisme polygame. Réponse a la brocure de M. Stenhouse intitulée Le Mormons et leurs ennemis. Par E. Guers . . . Extrait du Journal l'Avenir. Genève, Librairie d'Émile Beroud, 1855.
2p.l., [5]–40p. 18½cm.
"Imprimerie de F. Ramboz & Cie."
Title in English: Mormon polygamy.
UPB

3741. Guest, Theodora (Grosvenor). A round trip in North America, by Lady Theodora Guest. London, Edward Stanford, 1895.
4p.l., 270p. xvi plates. 22cm.
"Utah, the Salt Lake City." Brief description of area, with casual reference to Mormons.
CU–B, DLC, UHi, UPB, USlC

3742. Guide to Salt Lake City, Ogden, and the Utah Central Railroad. Salt Lake City, Printed at the Deseret News Office [1870].
[5]–30p. 14cm.
Tourist information concerning the Salt Lake area and Ogden. More information on places in Salt Lake City, such as the temple, the tabernacle, etc., with several colored pages of advertisement at front and rear. ZCMI advertisement in text.
CSmH

Guide to the route map of the Mormon pioneers. *See Millroy & Hayes.*

3743. Guillemard, Arthur G. Over land and sea; a log of travel round the world in 1873–1874. London, Tinsley Bros., 1875.
1p.l., xv, 355p. illus. 23cm.
Visit to Salt Lake and a discussion of Mormonism, p. 275–288.
CU–B, DLC, NjP, UPB, UU

3744. Guinn, James Miller. A history of California and extended history of its southern coast counties, also containing biographies of well-known citizens of the past and present . . . Los Angeles, Historic Record Co., 1907.
2v. plates, ports. 30cm.
Mormon Battalion, San Bernardino settlement, etc. V. 1, p. 437–443.
Another edition: 1915. NjP
CU–B, DLC, UPB

3745. Guldmann, G. P. Kaere forvildede soskende blandt Mormonerne. Kobenhavn, 1915.
8p.
Title in English: Dear strayed brethren and sisters among the Mormons.
Schmidt.

3746. Gunnison, John Williams. The Mormons, or, Latter-day saints, in the valley of the Great Salt Lake: a history of the rise and progress, peculiar doctrines, present condition, and prospects, derived from personal observation, during a residence among them. By Lieut. J. W. Gunnison . . . Philadelphia, Lippincott, Grambo & Co., 1852.
vi [1] vii–ix, 13–168p. illus. 18½cm.
"More than a year's residence among them" 1850–51.
Howes G463
CSmH, CU–B, DLC, MH, NjPT, NN, UHi, ULA, USl, USlC, UU, ViU, WHi

3747. ———. (same) London, Sampson Low, 1852.
ix, 13–168p. 18cm.
CSmH

3748. ———. (same) Philadelphia, Lippincott, Grambo & Co., 1853.
ix, 13–168p. front. 19½cm.
Howes G463, Sabin 29285
CSmH, CU, DLC, ICN, IHi, MWA, NjP, PPLT, UHi, USIC

3749. ———. (same) Toronto, T. Maclear, 1853.
100p. 21½cm.
CSmH, CtY, MH

3750. ———. (same) Philadelphia, J. B. Lippincott & Co., 1856.
ix, 13–168p. illus. 19cm.
Howes G463
CSmH, CtY, DLC, NjP, NN, OO, PP, PPC, UHi, ULA, USIC, WaU, WHi

3751. ———. (same) Philadelphia, J. B. Lippincott and Co., 1857 [c1852]
ix, 13–168p. illus. 19cm.
CtY, CU-B, MH, NN

3752. ———. (same) Philadelphia, J. B. Lippincott and Co., 1860.
xvii [13]–168p. illus. 19cm.
Includes a narrative of the death of Capt. Gunnison by W. W. Drummond, p. vii–xiv.
CU-B, MH, MiU, MWA, NjP, NN, UHi, UPB

3753. ———. (same) Philadelphia, J. B. Lippincott and Co., 1862.
xvii [13]–168p. illus. 18cm.
PU

3754. ———. (same) New York, J. W. Lovell Co. [1884]
xvii, 13–168p. illus. 18½cm. (Lovell's library. V.8, No. 440)
CSmH, CtY, DLC, ICN, NN, ULA, USIC, UU

3755. ———. (same) New York, G. Munro, 1890.
xvii, 13–168p. 18cm. (Seaside library. No. 1610)
NN, UHi, USIC

3756. ———. (same, in German) Die Mormonen im Thale des grossen Salzsee's nach persönlicher Beobachtung geschildert von J. W. Gunnison. Deutsch von M. R. Lindau. Hamburg und Leipsig, Verlag von Rudolf Kuntze, 1855.
vii [2] 247 [1]p. illus. 18cm.
Howes G463
CU-B, ICU, MH, OCl

3757. Gunsaulus, Frank Wakely. Addresses at the annual meeting of the New West Educational Commission. Oct. 14, 1890, in the First Congregational Church, Chicago. By F. W. Gunsaulus . . . H. E. Gordon . . . W. F. Slocum. Chicago, 1890.
27p. 21cm.
Cover-title: Mormonism and Jesuitism.
CU, NN, WHi

3758. Gunter, Archibald Clavering. Miss Dividends. A novel by Archibald Clavering Gunter. New York, Hurst & Company, 1892.
1p.l. [5]–276p. 18½cm.
Novel with Mormon background.
Chapter VIII. The City of the Saints. Chapter IX. The Ball in Salt Lake.
Published in Danish under title: Miss Dividends eller damen med millionerne. Roman oversat af B. M. Kristiania, 1900. Schmidt.
226p.
CU, USIC

3759. Gurley, Zenos Hovey. Evidences that Joseph Smith, the martyr, was a prophet of God, by Zenos H. Gurley and Isaac Sheen. [Plano, Ill., True Latter-day Saints' Herald, 1864?]
8p. 24cm. (No. 47)
CtY, MoInRC, NN, WHi

3760. ———. (same) [Plano, Ill., True Latter-day Saints' Herald, n.d.]
8p. 24cm.
Variant printing.
USIC, WHi

3761. ———. History of the Reorganization. [n.p., 1886?]
[4]p. 20cm.
Caption-title.
Signed: Pleasanton, Iowa, May 12, 1886.
MH, MoInRC

3762. ———. The legal succession of Joseph Smith, son of Joseph Smith the Martyr. Sermon . . . reported by Edwin Stafford. [Plano, Ill., True Latter-day Saints' Herald, 1866?]
8p. 23cm.
Listed for sale by *The True Latter-Day Saints' Herald*, Jan 1, 1866.
Published in the *Saints' Herald* in two parts: Dec. 15, 1865, Jan. 1, 1866.
MoInRC, NN, USl, USIC

3763. ———. The polygamic revelations. Fraud! Fraud! Fraud! Revelation on the eternity of the marriage covenant, including plurality of wives, presented by Brigham Young to the church in Utah, August 29th, 1852. [Lamoni, Ia., Printed at the True Latter Day Saints' Herald Office, 1882]

8p. 26cm.
At head of title: Supplement to *Saints' Herald.*
Variant edition without notation: Supplement to *Saints Herald.*
Sabin 83285
CtY, DLC, USlC

3764. ———. Polygamy a crime — Not a Religion. 1. By the textbooks of the Mormon Church and laws of the land. 2. By the purported polygamic revelation itself. Washington, 1882.
16p. 21½cm.
Signed: Z. H. Gurley and E. L. Kelley. Washington, February 14, 1882.
USlC

3765. ———. The Utah problem and the solution . . . Washington [Printed by J. M. Burnett, 1882]
5p. 27cm.
USlC

3766. Gurney, Alfred. A ramble through the United States: a lecture delivered (in part) in S. Barnadas' School, February 3, 1886, by Alfred Gurney. [London, Printed by William Clowes & Sons, 1886]
4p.l., 63p. 22cm.
A short, but disparaging section of Mormonism, p. 14–17.
CU–B, DLC, NjP, UHi, UPB, USlC

3767. Guthrie, Edwin. Lee County anti-Mormon meeting. [Minutes of meeting in Fort Madison, Iowa, October 18, 1845, signed by Edwin Guthrie, president of the meeting] [n.p., 1845]
Broadside. 57×37cm.
Includes: Address to the voters and tax-payers of Lee County, Iowa, signed by John Burns and others.
NN

B. S. Youngs

MORMONISM UNVAILED:

OR,

A FAITHFUL ACCOUNT OF THAT SINGULAR IMPOSITION AND

DELUSION,

FROM ITS RISE TO THE PRESENT TIME.

WITH SKETCHES OF THE CHARACTERS OF ITS PROPAGATORS,

AND A FULL DETAIL OF THE MANNER IN WHICH THE FAMOUS

GOLDEN BIBLE

WAS BROUGHT BEFORE THE WORLD.

TO WHICH ARE ADDED,

INQUIRIES INTO THE PROBABILITY THAT THE HISTORICAL PART

OF THE SAID BIBLE WAS WRITTEN BY ONE

SOLOMON SPALDING,

MORE THAN TWENTY YEARS AGO, AND BY HIM INTENDED TO HAVE

BEEN PUBLISHED AS A ROMANCE.

BY E. D. HOWE.

PAINESVILLE:

PRINTED AND PUBLISHED BY THE AUTHOR.

1834.

Item 4104. The foundation of anti-Mormon writing. From the Brigham Young University collection.

H., M.

3767a. H., M. Mormonismen og Saltsøstaden. Kjøbenhavn, Karl Schønbergs forlag. Trykt hos Nielsen & Lydiche, 1893.
76p. 21cm. (Smaaskrifter til oplysning for kristne udgivne af Prof. Dr. Fredrik Nielsen, viii, 4)
Signed: M.H.
Title in English: Mormonism of Salt Lake City.
NN, USlC

3768. Haandsräekningfor Menigmand i Kampen mod Mormonerne. Kjobenhavn, G. E. C. Gad, 1857.
15p. 18cm. (No. 18)
Title in English: A helping hand for people in the fight against the Mormons.
NN, USlC

3769. Hadley, Albert Whipple. Hadley's Mormon rhymes. Ogden, A. L. Scoville Press, 1921.
24p. illus. 20½cm.
Mormon poetry by a "non-Mormon."
UHi, USlC

3770. Hadley, Charles Whipple. Evolution vs. Genesis . . . Kaysville, Utah, Inland Printing Company [c1927]
47 [1]p. 18cm.
Unorthodox views.
CSmH

3771. Haefeli, Leo. As you like it. Things and thoughts . . . Ogden, Utah, Union Printing and Publishing Co., 1889–1891.
3v. 21cm.
Literary miscellany. A few items have Mormon interest.
DLC V. 2, MH, USlC, UU

3772. ———. Directory of Ogden City and Weber County, 1883. Compiled and Published by Leo Haefeli and Frank J. Cannon. Ogden City, Utah, Ogden Herald Publishing Company, Printers, 1883.
214p. 21cm.
Historical background information.
UHi, UOg

———. One day in Utah. *See Haussonville, Gabriel Paul Othenin.*

3773. Hafen, Arthur K. A biographical sketch of John G. Hafen, by Arthur K. Hafen. St. George, 1929.
2p.l., 5–46p. plates. 18cm.
USlC

3774. Hafen, LeRoy Reuben. Hand cart migration across the plains. Reprint. 1930. [Cleveland? 1930]
103–121p. 19½cm.
Reprinted from "Conference on the History of the Trans-Mississippi West, University of Colorado, 1929."
At head of title: The Trans-Mississippi West . . . Boulder, 1930.
CSmH, MH, NjP, NN, USl, USlC

3775. ———. The overland mail 1849–1869; promoter of settlement, precursor of railroads, by LeRoy R. Hafen . . . Cleveland, The A. H. Clark Company, 1926.
361p. plates, ports., fold. map, facsims. 24½cm.
Mormons mentioned in several places.
Howes H11
CSmH, CU, DLC, NjP, OU, UHi, USlC, ViU, WaU

3776. Hagar, George Jotham. What the world believes, the false and the true, embracing the people of all races and nations, their peculiar teachings, rites, ceremonies, traditions, and customs, public and private; with a full account of the origin, rise and progress of their various sects, historical, doctrinal, statistical, and biographical, from the earliest pagan times to the present . . . New York, Gay Brothers, 1886.
v, 647, 85p. illus. 23cm.
Chapter XLVI entitled "Church of Jesus Christ of Latter Day Saints," p. 586–614. Includes plates.
Another edition: New York, Gay brothers and Co., c1888. USlC
UHi, USlC

3777. Hagberg, Carl M. Den norske misjons historie nogle historske skildringer samlet og utarbeidt av Carl M. Hagberg. Oslo, Universal-trykkeriet, 1928.
2p.l., 5–56p. illus., plates. 23½cm.
Norwegian mission history.
Title in English: The history of the Norwegian Mission.
UU

3778. Hague, James Duncan. Mining Industry, by James D. Hague; with geological contributions, by Clarence King . . . Washington, Govt. Print. Off., 1870.
xiip., [2]l., 447p. front., xxvii plates (part fold.) incl. map. 30cm. And Atlas of 14 plates (part fold., part col., incl. maps) 49½×64cm.
(United States Geological Exploration of the fortieth parallel [Report . . . Vol. III])
Half-title: Professional papers of the Engineer Department, U.S. Army. No. 18.
Report on "The Green River Coal Basin" by Clarence King includes remarks on the deposits near Coalville mined by the Mormons, with comment on complications in ownership introduced by the "arbitrary and peculiar" land policy of the Mormon church, p. 455–458, 467–469.
CU-B, DL-GS, UPB

3779. Hail to our Elders. [n.p.] Dept. A. Edward B. Phippen Advertising Agent [1888?]
Broadside. 20½×6cm.
Mormon song. MH copy has autograph: Mary Freeze.
MH

3780. Hailey, John. The history of Idaho. Boise, Idaho, Syms-York Company, 1910.
5p.l., 395 [5]p. port. 23½cm.
Includes Mormon history in Idaho.
Howes H16
DLC, NjP, ULA, UPB

3781. Haining, Samuel. Mormonism weighed in the balances, of the sanctuary, and found wanting; the substance of four lectures. By Samuel Haining. Douglas [Isle of Man] Printed for the author by Robert Fargher, 1840.
66p. 17½cm.
CtY, CU-B, MH, MoK, NN, UPB, USIC

3782. Haldeman, John R. Origin of polygamy among the Latter-day Saints. Independence, Mo., Church of Christ Publishing House, 1904.
48p. 13cm.
"Belief in purity of 1830." Admits Joseph Smith practiced polygamy but doesn't condone it.
MH, MoInRC, UPB, USIC, UU

3783. ———. The unauthorized use of consecrated oil. Independence, Mo., Church of Christ Publishing House, 1901.
8p. 20cm. (Tract No. 2)
MoInRC

3784. Hale, Annie Riley. Bull moose trails: supplement to "Rooseveltian fact and fable," by Mrs. Annie Riley Hale . . . New York, the author [c1912]
3p.l., 123p. 19½cm.
Includes "Roosevelt's pact with the Mormons." Chapter III on polygamy.
CU, DLC, NjP, UPB

3785. Hale, Eugene. Polygamy. The work of the Industrial Christian Home Association of Utah Territory. Speech of Hon. Eugene Hale . . . in the Senate of the United States, October 2, 1888. Washington, 1888.
16p. 23cm.
CtY, MH, NjP

3786. Hale, Heber Q. "Mormonism" — a defense. Caldwell, Idaho, 1914.
40p. 18cm.
Reprint from *State Rural* for July, 1914.
MoInRC, USIC

3787. Hale, Richard Walden. Sir Richard F. Burton; a foot-note to history. Being an account of his trip from St. Joseph, August 7, 1860, to Salt Lake City, with sartorial particulars of his call on Brigham Young. Boston, Printed for Richard Walden Hale, by A. C. Gretchell & Son, 1930.
11p. port. 24cm.
"Found in a diary by Mr. Hale's great aunt [Mrs. Dana] who rode in the stage with Mr. Burton from St. Joseph to Salt Lake City."
MH, NjP, UHi

3788. Hale, Wilfred Silvester. Mormon doctrines analyzed and their errors demonstrated in the light of the Holy Scriptures, by Wilfred S. Hale . . . Albany, N.Y. [The Argus Co., 1904]
2p.l., 18p. port. 17×13cm.
DLC, MH, NN, OO, PCC, USIC, WHi

3789. Hales, Alfred Greenwood. McGlusky the Mormon. London, John Long, Limited [1929]
3p.l., xi, 13–288p. 19cm.
Fiction concerning Mormonism.
UHi, USIC

3790. Haley, T. P. Historical and biographical sketches of the early churches and pioneer preachers of the Christian Church in Missouri. By T. P. Haley. St. Louis, Christian Publishing Co., 1888.
5p.l., 11–589p. port. 20cm.
Chapter I includes the Mormon War and other Mormon problems.
MoInRC

3791. Half hours in the wide West, over mountains, rivers and prairies. With numerous illustrations. London, William Isbister Limited, 1877.
xii, 345p. 17½cm. (The half hour library of travel . . .)
Trip to Salt Lake City, p. [279]–293.
Other editions: 1880. CU-B; 1883. USIC; 1884. CU-B; London, C. Burnet & Co., 1887. CU-B; London, J. Naisbet & Co., 1900. CU-B
USIC

3792. Halils frieri. [Salt Lake City, Korrespondenten, 1893?]
16p. 14cm.
Missionary tract in Swedish.
Title in English: Halil's proposal.
USIC

3793. Hall, Edward Hepple. The Great West; emigrants', settlers' and travellers' guide and hand-book to the states of California and Oregon, and the territories of Nebraska, Utah, Colorado, Idaho, Montana, Nevada, and Washington. With a full and accurate account of their climate, soil, resources, and products, accompanied by a map showing the several routes to the gold fields, and a complete table of distances. By Edward H. Hall . . . New York, Published and for sale at the Tribune Office, 1864.
iv [5]–89p. fold. map. 18½cm.
History of the Territory of Utah. Mormonism deliberately played down to make the area seem desirable.
Other editions: New York, Appleton & Co., 1865. ICN; [n.d.] ICN
Howes H55, Sabin 29761, W-C 400
DLC, ICJ, ICN, MB, MWA, NN, ULA, WaU

HALL, E. T.

3794. Hall, Enos T. The Mormon bible; a fabrication and a stupendous fraud; its condemnation of polygamy. Columbus, Ohio, Fred J. Heer, Printer, 1899.
55p. 17cm.
USIC, WHi

3795. Hall, Henry. Interview with President Smith. Respected church leader makes plain statement of facts concerning Smoot Case. . . . Church not in politics. Chicago, Northern States Mission [1903]
16p. 13½cm.
Henry Hall special correspondent of the Pittsburgh, Pa., *Times*, interviews the head of the Mormon church.
NjP, USIC

3796. ———. (same) Pittsburgh Times. Salt Lake City, Bureau of Information and Church Literature [1905]
15p. 14cm.
USIC, WHi

3797. ———. (same, under title) President Joseph F. Smith denies charges . . . Chattanooga, Tenn., Published by the Southern States Mission, 1905.
16p. 14cm.
USIC

3798. Hall, James E. "The voice of the people is the voice of God." A statement by James E. Hall to the members of the Church of Jesus Christ of Latter-day Saints in the Utah Stakes. Springville, Utah, Nov., 1914.
31p. 23cm.
Excommunicated from the church due to faith healing and ensuing problems.
USIC, UPB

3798a. Hall, Marshall R. Storm of the old frontier. Philadelphia, Henry Altemus Company, 1927.
302p. 17cm.
Mentions Mormons on a trip through Salt Lake City, p. 143–147.
UPB

Hall, Mosiah. Child study and training. *See Church of Jesus Christ of Latter-day Saints. Deseret Sunday School Union. Parent and child.*

3799. ———. Talks to parents on home and life problems. Prepared for Deseret Sunday School Union by Mosiah Hall. Salt Lake City, Deseret Book Co. [n.d.]
3p.l., 7–77p. 18½cm.
UPB

3800. Hall, Thomas Cuming. The religious background of American culture, by Thomas Cuming Hall. Boston, Little, Brown, and Company, 1930.
xiv, 348p. 23cm.
A cultural look at Mormonism, p. 304–309.
CU, DLC, NjP, UPB

3801. Hall, William. The abominations of Mormonism exposed. Containing many facts and doctrines concerning that singular people, during seven years' membership with them, from 1840 to 1847. By William Hall. Cincinnati, Published for the author by I. Hart & Co., 1852.
iv, 5–155 [1]p. 18½cm.
Howes H89, Sabin 29858
CU-B, DLC, NN, OFH, USIC, WHi

3802. Halls, William. Selections from the writings of William Halls; with an autobiographical sketch of the author. Edited by Edward H. Anderson. Salt Lake City, Deseret News, 1911.
3p.l., 149p. port. 19cm.
On spine: Select writings.
Mormon inspirational writings.
UHi, UPB, USI

3803. ———. (same) 2d ed. Salt Lake City, Deseret News, 1912.
3p.l., 149p. port. 19½cm.
NjP, UHi, UPB, UU

3804. Halsey, Francis W., *editor.* Great epochs in American history described by famous writers from Columbus to Roosevelt; edited, with introduction and explanatory notes by Francis W. Halsey . . . Patrons' ed. New York, Funk & Wagnalls Company [1912]
10v. illus. 15½cm.
Vol. 7 contains: The Mormon Migration to Utah (1846–1848) by William A. Linn.
Another edition: New York, Current literature Publ. Co. 1916. DLC
CU, DLC, UHi, UPB

3805. Ham, George H. Reminiscences of a raconteur. Between the '40s and the '20s by George H. Ham. Toronto, The Mission Book Company Limited [c1921]
xvi, 330p. illus., plates, ports. 20½cm.
Encounter with Mormons in Alberta in 1904, p. 155–158. Though the Mormons were probably bad earlier, they had improved.
USIC

Hamblin, Jacob. *See Little, James A.*

3806. Hamburger traktat-verein. Der Mormonismus. [Hamburg, Druck von Ackermann und Wulff, 1855?]
32p. 17cm.
"Herausgegeben von dem Hamburger Traktat-verein," p. 32.
Title in English: Mormonism.
CU-B

HANCOCK EAGLE

3807. Hamilton, Henry S. Reminiscences of a veteran, by Henry S. Hamilton. Concord, N.H., Republican Press Association, 1897.
2p.l., 180p. front., ports. 18½cm.
Account of the Utah Expedition, p. 68–118.
Howes H128
CtY, CU–B, DLC, MB, MWA, Nh, NjP, NN, UHi

3808. Hammerich, Frederik. Kort udsigt over Mormonernes Historie og Laerdomme. Kjøbenhavn, N. D. Ditlewsen, 1852.
16p. 18cm.
Title in English: A glimpse of Mormon history and doctrine.
NN

3809. Hammond, T. C. Mormonism its founder and his creed; a lecture delivered in the City of Dublin Young Men's Christian Association, April, 1907. Dublin, Irish Union of Young Men's Christian Associations [1907?]
30p. 16cm.
MoInRC

3810. Hancock, Charles S. The Hancock and Adams families. By Charles S. Hancock, Sen. [n.p., n.d.]
68p. 17cm.
Includes Mormon genealogy.
USlC

3811. Hancock, G. Harris. Beware of the Mormons! Otherwise known as Latter Day Saints . . . Ipswich, England [185–]
[1]p. 21×15cm.
UHi, ULA, UU

3812. Hancock, Golman Bluford. Mormonism exposed, Joseph Smith an imposter and the Book of Mormon a fraud. By Elder G. B. Hancock. Marionville, Mo., A. Doggett, Printer, 1902.
3p.l. [5]–151p. plates, port. 20½cm.
CtY, CU–B, DLC, MoInRC, NjP, UPB, USlC

3813. Hancock County, Illinois. [Broadside showing Democratic, Whig, and anti-Mormon ballots, Hancock County election, 1846] [n.p., 1846?]
Broadside. 30½×14cm.
In double columns.
ICHi

3814. ———. Citizens. Memorial. To the honorable, The Senate and the House of Representatives of the state of Illinois . . . [Warsaw? 1845]
Broadside. 20×25cm.
Refers to Governor Ford's message to the General Assembly of Dec., 1844, concerning the disturbances in Hancock County.
Byrd 1063
ICHi

3815. ———. Sheriff. Proclamation to the citizens of Hancock County. [Green Plains, Ill., 1845]
Broadside. 28½×32cm.
Signed: J. B. Backenstos, Sheriff, and dated Green Plains, Sept. 13, 1845.
Mormon troubles.
CtY, USlC

3816. ———. Proclamation No. 2. To the citizens of Hancock County, Ill., and the surrounding country. It is truly painful that my first proclamation did not have the desired effect of quelling the mob in Hancock county . . . [Nauvoo, 1845]
Broadside. 38×28cm.
Caption and beginning of text used as title.
Signed and dated: J. B. Backenstos, Sheriff, Hancock County, Ill. Sept. 16, 1845.
Byrd 911
CtY, ICHi, USlC

3816a. ———. Proclamation No. 3. Hancock County, Illinois, 1845.
Broadside. 31×28cm.
Dated: Sept. 17, 1845.
Informing the citizens of the activities of the mob including the persecution of his and other officials' families.
USlC

3817. ———. Proclamation No. 4. To the Citizens of Hancock County, Ill., and the surrounding country. [Nauvoo? 1845]
Broadside. 40×28cm.
Dated: Sept. 20, 1845.
Defense of his position in defending Mormons.
USlC

3818. ———. Proclamation no. 5. To the Citizens of Hancock County, and the surrounding Country. [Nauvoo?] 1845.
Broadside. 46×30cm.
Dated: Sept. 25, 1845.
Defense of Mormons in the anti-mob actions.
Byrd 912
ICHi, USlC

3819. ———. Tax notice. To the tax payers of Hancock County, Illinois. [Carthage? 1846]
Broadside. 30×19½cm.
Signed: Carthage, Jan. 3, 1846.
J. B. Backenstos, sheriff and ex-officio collector.
ICHi

3820. Hancock Eagle. Nauvoo, Ill., April 3, 1846–August 28, 1846?
v. 40cm.
Edited by William E. Matlack.
Succeeded by Nauvoo New Citizen (weekly)
ICHi F 24, Mr 10, 1847; NN D 23, 1846
NN V.1 #1–2, 9–12, 14–16, 19–21; USlC V.1 #1–21, April 3, 1846–August 28, 1846 and supplement 2 for April 3, 1846

HANCOCK EAGLE

3821. ———. Prospectus of the Hancock Eagle a weekly newspaper, devoted to literature, news, politics — the arts and sciences, commerce and agriculture; to be published at Nauvoo, Hancock, Illinois . . . [Nauvoo, 1846]

Broadside. 26×37½cm.

The editor was a gentile, who started operations in the vacuum of the Mormon expulsion.

Signed: February 23, 1846.

USIC

3822. ———. Hancock Eagle — Extra. Thursday, June 11, 1846. Resumption of hostilities in Hancock. Lynch law in the ascendant! [Nauvoo, 1846]

Broadside. 27×41cm.

Contains rumors of the invasion of Nauvoo by non- or anti-Mormon forces. Invasion was said to be aimed at the prosperity of the city rather than at the Mormons themselves.

Byrd 1064

ICHi

3823. ———. Hancock Eagle — Extra. The War in Hancock. Saturday night 12 o'clock, June 13, 1846. [Nauvoo, Ill., 1846]

Broadside. 33×20½cm.

The war in Hancock.

NN, USIC

3824. ———. Hancock Eagle — Extra. Nauvoo, Saturday night, July 11, 1846. The mob again in the field, more lynching, 8 men brutally mangled by the regulators . . . [Nauvoo, 1846]

Broadside. 27×41cm.

Eight men were flayed by a mob, until almost dead.

Byrd 1065

USIC

3825. ———. Hancock Eagle — Extra. Nauvoo, Monday night, July 13, 1846. Progress of the insurrection in Hancock . . . [Nauvoo, 1846]

Broadside. 17×52cm.

Vicious action of the anti-Mormon mobs; plea made to all to retire to Nauvoo for the defense of the city. Mention of the Mormon battalion being mustered into U.S. service under Stephen W. Kearny.

Byrd 1066

ICHi, USIC

3826. ———. Hancock Eagle — Extra. Nauvoo, Illinois, August 18, 1846. Mob law in Hancock . . . [Nauvoo, 1846]

Broadside. 15×61cm.

Arrest of three men and their subsequent murder, and a protest of the illegality of what had happened.

Byrd 1067

ICHi, USIC

3827. ———. Hancock Eagle — Extra. Nauvoo, Illinois, August 20, 1846. Proclamation! To the citizens of Hancock County . . . Nauvoo, 1846.

Broadside. 27×40cm.

Indication of the attempt to take legal action against the anti-Mormons who had participated in the mob action.

Byrd 1068

ICHi, USIC

3828. ———. Hancock Eagle — Extra. Nauvoo, Hancock County, October 5, 1846. [Nauvoo, 1846]

Broadside. 30×35½cm.

A publication of the terms by which peace in Hancock can be gained. Expulsion of Mormons within 10 days was part of the bargain, along with Mormon surrender of arms. Damage to the temple by the mobs mentioned.

Byrd 1069

USIC

3829. Handbook of reference to the history, chronology, religion and country of the Latter-day Saints, including the revelation on celestial marriage. Salt Lake City, Juvenile Instructor Office, 1884.

1p.l., 157 [1]p. 19cm.

Contents: History of the Latter-day Saints. Chronology of church history. Religion of the Latter-day Saints. Utah: past and present. Appendix.

Copyrighted by A. H. Cannon.

CSmH, ICN, MoInRC, NjP, ULA, USIC, UU, WHi

3830. Hanes Saint y Dyddiau Diweddaf, o'u Sefydliad yn y flwyddyn 1823, hyd yr amser yr alltudiwyd tri chan mil o honynt o'r America oherwydd eu crefydd, yn y flwyddyn 1846. Merthyr-Tydvil, Capt. Jones [n.d.]

2p.l. [3]–102p. 17cm.

Title in English: History of the Latter-day Saints, 1823–46.

UPB, USIC

3831. Hanks, Lucile. Stanzas to Brigham Young. [n.p., n.d.]

Broadside. 15½×10cm.

Mormon poetry.

UPB

3832. Hanks, Nymphus Coridon. Up from the hills. His story. 1st ed. [Pittsburg, Byron J. King, Printer, c1921]

31p. 19cm.

Biography of a Mormon blinded and maimed by an explosion.

UHi, USIC

3833. ———. (same) Chicago, W. B. Conkey Co., 1921.

32p. 17cm.

CU-B, UHi

3834. ———. (same) [Chicago, Hammond Press, c1921]

32p. 15cm.

Cover-title: Autobiography.

UPB

3835. ———. (same) [Salt Lake City, Deseret News, c1921)
32p. 15cm.
NjP, USlC

3836. ———. (same) Salt Lake City, The Deseret News Press, 1921.
31p. 18cm.
USlC

3837. ———. (same) [Salt Lake City, Deseret News, 1923]
32p. 18cm.
CU-B

3838. Hannett, Arthur Thomas. In the days of Brigham Young, by Arthur Thomas [*pseud.*] New York, Broadway Publishing Co. [c1914]
2p.l., 109p. 20cm.
Fiction concerning Mormonism.
CU-B, DLC, MH, MoInRC, NjP, UHi, UPB, USlC, UU

3839. Hansen, John S. Søndagsskole-Haandbog indeholdende lektier og korlaesninger til brug for den Skandinaviske missions søndagsskoler og Bibelklasser, sanlede og arrangerede af John S. Hansen. Kjøbenhavn, Udgivet og forlagt af Martin Christophersen, 1913.
73 [1]p. 18cm.
Title in English: Sunday School handbook.
UPB

3839a. Hansen, Niels. Hvad tykkes eder om Christo? Et vidnesbyrd imod Mormonerne. Praediken paa 18de Sondag efter Trinitatis 1854. Aalborg, Forfatterens Forlag, Trykt hos Carl Bech, 1854.
17p. 18cm.
An anti-Mormon polemic.
Title in English: What think ye of Christ.
USlC

3840. Hanson, Paul M. The apostolic office . . . Lamoni, Ia., Published by Herald Publishing House [1908]
24p. 18½cm. (No. 303)
MoInRC, MoK

3841. ———. Baptism in water. Lamoni, Ia., Published by the Herald House . . . [n.d.]
[47]-64p. 19½cm.
Chapter 5. The Angel Message tracts.
MoInRC

3842. ———. The Church of England in the crucible and challenged. Sydney, Australia, The Standard Publishing House [n.d.]
17p. 18cm.
The Church of England disproved and the RLDS church defended.
MoInRC

3843. ———. A glimpse at the government of God. By Elder Paul M. Hanson. Independence, Mo., Ensign Publishing House [190-]
19p. 18cm.
Cover-title.
Government in the RLDS church.
MoInRC

3844. ———. (same) Views of the Kingdom as seen through the eyes of a Latter Day Saint [n.p., n.d.]
19p. 19cm.
MoInRC

3845. ———. (same) Independence, Mo., Ensign Publishing House [n.d.]
29p. 15½cm.
MoInRC

3846. ———. (same) Independence, Mo., Ensign Publishing House, 1904.
32p. 16cm. (The Gospel Banner. V.12 #1)
MoInRC

3847. ———. (same, under title) The Government of God. Independence, Mo., Ensign Publishing House [n.d.]
19p. 19cm.
MoInRC

3848. ———. The Great apostasy in Utah. [n.p., n.d.]
4p. 20cm.
MoInRC

3849. ———. A reply to modern misbeliefs; an impeachment of Rev. George Wood Anderson and a challenge to the Methodist Episcopal Church. [n.p., n.d.]
16p. 20cm.
Reply to G. W. Anderson's tract "Modern misbeliefs" with a section on Mormonism.
MoInRC

3849a. ———. The true church. By Paul M. Hanson. [Sydney] Published by the Reorganized Church of Jesus Christ of Latter Day Saints [ca. 1918]
24p. 20½cm.
Printed by the Standard Publishing House.
NjP

3850. Hanson, Samuel. Interviews: Memorable and useful; from diary and memory reproduced. By Samuel Hanson . . . New York, Harper & Brothers . . . 1853.
2p.l. [5]-325p. 20cm.
"Two-pseudo-apostles." Section on Mormonism.
USlC

3851. Harbaugh, Thomas Chalmers. Silver Steve, the branded sport; or, the man-mystery of Moonstone. By Captain Howard Holmes [*pseud.*] New York, Beadle & Adams [c1892]
30p. 31cm. (Beadle's Dime library, March 30, 1892. V. 54, No. 701)
"Moonstone," a mining town in the San Juan Mountains. A Mormon is a principal character.
UPB

3852. Hardin, John J. Citizens of Hancock: By order of the Governor, an armed force has again been marched into your County. Acts of disobedience of the laws, and open violence by mobs, have been frequent in your county for two years past . . . Such flagrant violation of law be they committed by whom they may, must be stopped. [Warsaw, 1845]
Broadside. 29½×20½cm.
Dated: Sept. 27, 1845 in manuscript.
Signed: J. J. Hardin, Commanding Detachment, Illinois Volunteers.
The purpose of the armed force in Hancock County.
Byrd 957
CtY, USlC

———. To the anti-Mormon citizens of Hancock and the surrounding countries. *See To the Anti Mormon Citizens . . .*

3853. Harding, Martin. 1st October, 1853. Grand Mormon temperance celebration at the City of Council Bluffs. Kanesville [Printed at the Office of the Western Trumpeter] Sept., 1853.
Broadside. 46×32cm.
Signed: Martin Harding, esq.
Satire on Mormons and temperance, etc.
USlC

3854. Harding, Samuel Bannister. Life of George R. Smith, founder of Sedalia, Mo., in its relations to the political, economic, and social life of Southwestern Missouri, before and during the civil war, by Samuel Bannister Harding, Ph.D., . . . Sedalia, Mo. [The Hollenbeck Press, Indianapolis] 1904.
xiv p., [1]l., 398p. plates, 4 ports., fold. map. 21cm.
"Mormon war . . ." p. 58–61.
CU, NjP, UPB

3855. Hardy, Iza Duffus. Between two oceans: or sketches of American travel. By Iza Duffus Hardy . . . London, Hurst and Blackett, 1884.
4p.l., 355p. 23cm.
"In the City of the Saints," p. 117–135.
CtY, CU–B, DLC, NjP, PP, PPL, PSC, UHi, UPB

3856. Hardy, John, *compiler.* A collection of sacred hymns, adapted to the faith and views of the Church of Jesus Christ of Latter Day Saints. Compiled by John Hardy. Boston, Dow & Jackson's Press, 1840.
2p.l. [5]–160p. 12cm.
USlC

3857. ———. (same) Boston, Dow & Jackson's Press, 1843.
2p.l., 160p. 12cm.
MB, MH, MoInRC, USlC

3858. ———. Hypocrisy exposed, or J. V. Himes weighed in the balances of truth, honesty and common sense, and found wanting; being a reply to a pamphlet put forth by him, entitled, Mormon delusions and monstrosities. By John Hardy. Boston, Printed by Albert Morgan, 1842.
16p. 19½×13cm.
DLC, MH

3859. ———. Startling developments of crim. con.! [sic] or two Mormon apostles exposed, in practising the spiritual wife system in Boston; consisting of the trials of Elder John Hardy, who was excommunicated from the Mormon church worshiping in Suffolk Hall, for exposing the base and licentious "Teachings and practices" of Elders G. J. Adams and William Smith, the particulars of which are here made public. Boston, Conway and Company, 1844.
12p. 22cm.
Cover-title.
Caption-title: History of the trials of Elder John Hardy.
Sabin 30355
CtY, ICN, MH, NN

3860. Hardy, Mary (McDowell) Duffus, *Lady.* Through cities and prairie lands. Sketches of an American tour. By Lady Duffus Hardy. New York, R. Worthington, 1881.
xii, 338p. 21½cm.
"The city of the Saints," and "Among the Mormons."
She spent several days in Ogden and Salt Lake City in 1880.
Other editions: London, Chapman and Hall, 1881. ICN; Chicago, Belford, Clarke & Co., 1882. ULA, UU; New York, Worthington, 1890. UPB
CSmH, CU–B, DLC, NjP, NN, OO, PHC, PSC, PU, UHi, USlC

3861. Harlan, Edgar Rubey. The location and name of the Mormon trail by Edgar Harlan . . . An address delivered at Keokuk, Iowa, Oct. 22, 1912. Knoxville, Ia., The Knoxville Express, 1914.
[4]l. illus., map. 25½cm.
Conditions of Mormons in Iowa in 1846, and the use of the Mormon trail. A description of its course through Iowa.
DLC

3862. Harlan, Jacob Wright. California '46 to '88. By Jacob Wright Harlan . . . San Francisco, The Bancroft Company, 1888.
2p.l. 7–242p. port. 22cm.
Encounters Mormons near Nauvoo and San Francisco. Brief.
AzU

3863. Harpending, Asbury. The great diamond hoax and other stirring incidents in the life of Asbury Harpending. Edited by James H. Wilkins . . . San Francisco, The James H. Barry Co. [c1913]
4p.l., 11–283p., [1]l. ports. 21cm.
Includes material on Sam Brannan and his relations with Mormon officials.
CU–B, DLC, UHi, USIC

3864. Harris, Franklin Stewart. The fruits of Mormonism, by Franklin Stewart Harris . . . and Newbern Isaac Butt . . . New York, The Macmillan Company, 1925.
ixp., [2]l., 146p. diagrs. 20cm.
CSmH, CtY, CU–B, DLC, ICN, MH, NjP, NjPT, NN, UPB, USIC, UU, WHi

3865. ———. The young man and his vocation . . . Salt Lake City, Published by the General Board of Y.M.M.I.A., 1925.
3p.l. [7]–100p. 22cm. (Achievement series. No. 4)
Young Men's Mutual Improvement Association. Senior manual . . . No. 28.
UPB, USIC

3866. Harris, Martin. A proclamation. And a warning voice unto all people, first to all Kings, Governors and rulers in authority, and unto every kindred tongue and people under the whole heavens, to who this word shall come. Cleveland, May 13, 1855. [Cleveland? 1855?]
8p. 17½×11½cm.
Signed: Moses, Elias, Elijah and John.
The copy of this tract at the Utah Church historian's office has written in pen the following: "May 13/55. Proclamation. Martin Harris to all people." The writing is old and seems to have been written soon after the tract was printed.
Authorship given in a letter to Brigham Young from Martin Harris dated Kirtland, Ohio, August 13, 1855.
USIC

3867. Harris, Sarah Hollister. An unwritten chapter of Salt Lake City, 1851–1901. By Sarah Hollister Harris. New York, Printed privately, 1901.
88 [1]p. 18½cm.
Wife of the first Secretary of Utah Territory.
Howes H231
CSmH, CtY, CU–B, DLC, ICN, MH, NjP, NN, OClWHi, USIC

3868. Harris, William. Mormonism portrayed; its errors and absurdities exposed, and the spirit and designs of its authors made manifest: by William Harris, with emendations by a citinen [sic] To which is added an appendix, containing the testimony of the most prominent witnesses as taken at the trial of Joe Smith, jr., and others for high treason against the state of Missouri, before Judge King, of the Fifth judicial district. Warsaw, Ill., Sharp & Gamble, 1841.
64p. 21½cm.
Ghost-written by Thomas C. Sharp.
Byrd 628, Howes H237
CSmH, ICHi, ICN, IHi, NN, MoSM, NN, USIC

3869. Harris, William Richard. The Catholic church in Utah, including an exposition of Catholic faith by Bishop Scanlan. A review of Spanish and missionary explorations. Tribal divisions, names and regional habitats of the pre-European tribes. The journal of the Franciscan explorers and discoverers of Utah lake. The trailing of the priests from Santa Fe, N.M., with map of route, illustrations and delimitations of the Great basin. By Very Reverend W. R. Harris . . . Salt Lake City, Intermountain Catholic Press [c1909]
4p.l., iii, iii, 350p. illus., plates (1 double) ports., double map. 25cm.
Early contacts and treatment of Catholics by the Mormons.
CSmH, CU, CU–B, DLC, ICN, ICU, NjP, NN, OCl, UHi, ULA, UPB, USIC

3870. Harrison, Paul. Mormonism triumphant. [by Paul Harrison] [Bury, D. Barker, Printer, 1850?]
4p. 17cm.
Paul Harrison "Late an Elder in the Mormon Church."
MH

———. *See also Jacob, Udney Hay.*

3871. Hart, Fred H. The Sazerac lying club; a Nevada book. 2d ed. San Francisco, Henry Keller & Co., 1878.
240p. 23cm.
Mormons, p. 59–62, 90, 113–118, 131–136, 187.
USIC

3872. Hart, James H. An interview with David Whitmer in August, 1883 by James H. Hart. [n.p., 1883]
9p. 11cm.
USIC

3873. ———. An interview with David Whitmer in August, 1883. [n.p., 1883]
Broadside. 28×20cm.
USIC

Hart, James T. Marriage, monogamy and polygamy. *See Giles, Alfred E.*

3874. Hartzell, J. C., *compiler.* Christian educators in council. Sixty addresses by American educators; with historical notes upon the National Education assembly, held at Ocean Grove, N.J., August 9–12, 1883. Also, illiteracy and education tables from census of 1880. Compiled and edited by Rev. J. C. Hartzell, D.D. New York, Phillip & Hunt, 1883.

1p.l. [3]–266p. front. 24½cm.
Section VII on Mormonism. 1. The Utah Problem by A. J. Kynett. 2. Mormonism, by Henry Kendall. 3. Disloyalty of Mormons by John M. Coyner. 4. Sources of Mormon strength by Robert G. M'Niece. 5. Polygamy Woman's Creed by Angie N. Newman. 6. Doctrines of Mormonism by Theophilus B. Hilton.
USlC

3875. Harvey, R. A. N. . . . Around the world in twelve years. Salt Lake City, J. C. Graham & Co., 1885.
172p. 17½cm.
At head of title: Life's real romance; a picture from life from 1838 to 1883. Vol. II.
Cover-title: Twelve year's travel around the world. R.A.N.H.
"Incidents in the life of Jonathan E. Howard, as recorded by his son, Arthur N. Howard."
His impression of Salt Lake City and a church meeting, 1870.
NjP, UHi, UPB, USlC

3876. Hasbrouck, Eva. Key to pictorial chart illustrating the organization of the Church of Jesus Christ of Latter-day Saints, showing the introduction of the fulness of the gospel into the different nations of the earth. By Mrs. Eva Hasbrouck. Salt Lake City, The Deseret News Publishing Co., 1893.
1p.l. [3]–25p. 17½cm.
Cover-title.
USlC

3877. Haskell, Dudley Chase. Mormonism: An address at the national anniversary of the American Home Missionary Society in Chicago, June 8, 1881. New York, The American Home Missionary Society, 1881.
26p. 23cm.
CSmH, CtY, CU–B, DLC, ICN, NN, OClWHi, PPPrHi, WHi

3878. ———. (same, under title) Mormonism and polygamy: an address delivered by D. C. Haskell . . . at Central Music Hall, Chicago, June 8th, 1881, before the National Convention of the American Home Missionary Society. Lawrence, Kan., Republican Journal Printing Establishment, 1881.
43p. 22½cm.
DLC, ICN, KHi

3879. Haslam, James Holt. Supplement to the lecture on the Mountain Meadows massacre [by Charles W. Penrose] Important additional testimony recently received. Salt Lake City, Published at the Juvenile Instructor Office, 1885.
[81]–104p. 17½cm.
CSmH, CU–B, MH, NjP

3880. Hass, L. D. Mormonernes Laerdomme, Oprindelse og Fremgang. Kjøbenhavn, F. H. Eibes, 1851.
32p. 19½cm.
Title in English: The teaching of Mormonism.
CtY, NN, USlC

3880a. Hastings, H. L. Will the old book stand? Boston, H. L. Hastings, Publisher, 1890.
23p. 18cm. (The Anti-Infidel Library, Five-cent series. No. 1, Jan. '90)
Running title: The inspiration of the Bible. Book of Mormon mentioned, p. 4.
USlC

3881. Hatch Genealogical Society. Genealogy & history of the Hatch family. Descendants of Thomas & Grace Hatch . . . Salt Lake City, Compiled by the Hatch Genealogical Society [1925?] — 1931.
7pts. (778p.) 22½cm.
Includes biographies and genealogies of Mormons.
NjP, USlC

3882. Hathaway, Thomas T. Speech of Honorable T. T. Hathaway, delivered in the Missouri Senate on the joint and concurrent resolution, instructing our senators and requesting our representatives in Congress to use their influence to procure the withdrawal of the army from the territories, for the admission of the territories into the union, and for the enfranchisement of the Indians and Mormons. March, 1883. Jefferson City, Tribune Printing Co., 1883.
12p. 23½cm.
Cover-title.
NN

3883. Hatton, W. A. Mormonism versus Mormonism and the Bible. The witnesses to the Book of Mormon examined and their testimony ruled out of court . . . Farmington, Ia., Farmington Herald Print., 1899.
106p. 19½cm.
An essay concerning the testimony of the witnesses for the *Book of Mormon.*
CSmH, MoInRC

3884. ———. The origin of the Book of Mormon, the character of its authors examined and weighed in the balance and found wanting; the revelation on polygamy and the doctrines of the Latter Day Saints in Conflict with the Bible. [Farmington, Ia., 1898]
162, 6p. 19cm.
Includes supplement: Book inspired by a debate held in Farmington, September, 1892, involving Mormon and Baptist beliefs, 6p.
CSmH, MoInRC

3885. Haussonville, Gabriel Paul Othenin de Cleron, *comte d'.* One day in Utah. A literary French nobleman's views on the Mormon question from "A travers les etats unis," of the Vicomte d' Haussonville. Translated and published by Leo Haefeli. Ogden, printed by the Ogden Herald Publishing Co., 1883.
2p.l. [5]–41p. 19cm.
CSmH, MH, NN, UHi, UPB, USlC

3886. ———. (same) 2d ed. Ogden, Utah, 1883.
41p. 20cm.
NN

3887. ———. (same) 2d ed. Salt Lake City, Deseret News Company [1883?]
2p.l. [7]–41p. 19cm.
CU–B, NjP, NN, USlC

3888. ———. A travers les Etats Unis, notes et impressions, par le Vicomte D'Haussonville. Paris, Calmann Levy, 1883.
2p.l., 440p. 19cm.
Spends a day in Utah; description of Salt Lake City, Mormonism. Chapters: "La Famille d'un Mormon." "Salt Lake City." "Joseph Smith."
Title in English: Through the United States.
Another edition: 1888. DLC, NN
CSmH, MiU–C, NN, NNC, PP, PPEx, PRB

3889. Havard, Aline. Where the trail divides by Aline Havard author of "Fighting Westward," with illustrations. New York, Charles Scribner's Sons, 1924.
5p.l., 299p. plate. 19½cm.
At head of title: The young pioneers.
Chapter four: Trading with the Mormons.
UPB

3890. Have you read the Book of Mormon? [London, Partridge and Oakey, Publishers, n.d.]
4p. 17cm.
USlC

3891. Haven, Jesse. Celestial marriage and the plurality of wives! By Jesse Haven one of the presidents of the Seventies of the Church of Jesus Christ of Latter-day Saints and President of the Mission at the Cape of Good Hope. [Cape Town, Printed by W. Foelscher, ca.1854]
8p. 20cm.
Caption-title.
Cover on MH copy: Tract n.— of the Latter-day Saints' Circulating Tract Society, of the Land's End Conference. 1p. signed by W. G. Mills.
First Mormon imprint in South Africa.
MH, USlC

3892. ———. Some doctrines and principles of the Church of Jesus Christ of Latter-day Saints. By Jesse Haven, one of the Presidents of the Seventies of said Church and President of the Mission at the Cape of Good Hope. Cape Town [ca.1854]
8p. 21½cm.
"Stanza on the presentation of the *Book of Mormon* to Queen Victoria by Miss Eliza R. Snow," p. 7–8.
USlC

Havington, Alonzo LeBaron [*pseud.*]
See LeBaron, Alonzo H.

3893. Hawaiian Missionary Society. Constitution of the Hawaiian Missionary Society. [n.p. 1903]
[4]p. 15cm.
To develop a fraternal spirit among L.D.S. missionaries and members.
UPB

3894. Hawaiian "Mormon" Temple nearing completion. [n.p., 1919?]
[2]p. 36cm.
USlC

3895. Haweis, Hugh Reginald. Travel and talk, 1885–93–95. My hundred thousand miles of travel through America, Australia, Tasmania, Canada, New Zealand, Ceylon, and the paradises of the Pacific. By the Reverend H. R. Haweis. London, Chatto and Windus; New York, Dodd Mead and Co., 1896.
2v. ports. 19½cm.
Section entitled "Mormon land." Vol. 1, p. 247–308. Such headings as: Rise of Joseph Smith, Book of Mormon, Nauvoo the beautiful, Death of the prophet Joseph Smith, Estimate of Joseph Smith, Exodus, etc., through death of Brigham Young.
Another edition: 1897. USlC
CSmH, CU, DLC, MB, NjP, NN, PPA, PPL, PPM, USlC, WHi

3896. Hawkins, Nehemiah. The Mormon of the Little Maitou Island; an historical romance, by the Knight of Chillon of Switzerland and associates. New York [etc.] Uplift Company [1916]
5p.l., 526p. plates, ports., map. 19½cm.
A leaf giving title of Book II (The Mormon king) inserted between p. 394 and 395.
Fiction concerning Strangite Mormons.
CU–B, DLC, MoInRC, NN, UHi, USlC

3897. Hawkins, Thomas Samuel. Some recollections of a busy life. San Francisco, Privately printed for the author by Paul Elder and Company [1913]
v, 160p. illus., ports. 22cm.
300 copies printed.
Includes overland journey via Salt Lake City, 1860, p. 99–104.
CU–B

3898. Hawkins, William B. Vanguard-Scout guide. Prepared under the supervision of the Vanguard-Scout Committees of the M.I.A. General Board and the Utah Scout Executives of the M.I.A. General Board and Utah Scout executives by William B. Hawkins . . . [Salt Lake City, Published by the General Boards of Young Men's Mutual Improvement Associations, 1929]
1p.l., 5–47p. 19cm.
UPB, USlC

Hawley, Cyrus M. *See U.S. District Court. Utah. (Third District).*

3899. ———. Supreme Court of Utah Territory. Opinion of Justice C. M. Hawley on the original jurisdiction of the Supreme Court. Salt Lake City . . . [n.d.]
8p. 21cm.
DLC

3900. Hawley, Henry W. The life story of Henry W. Hawley. Together with such genealogical and historical data as the author thought might be of interest to future generations of this rapidly increasing branch of the Hawley Family. [n.p., n.d.]
xi, 101p. port. 20cm.
Mormon biography.
USlC

3901. Hawley, James H. History of Idaho, the gem of the mountains. James H. Hawley, ed. Chicago, The S. L. J. Clarke Publishing Company, 1920.
3v. illus. 28cm.
Includes material on Mormons in Idaho.
CU–B, NjP, UHi, UPB

3902. Haworth, Walter J. The Book of Mormon on trial. Wallsend, Australia, Published by the Wallsend Branch of the Reorganized Church of Jesus Christ of Latter Day Saints in aid of the Wallsend Chapel building fund, 1900.
61p. 21cm. (Two Sermon Lectures)
MoInRC, NjP

3903. ———. The fall of Babylon and the triumph of the Kingdom of God. By W. J. Haworth. Illustrated by Elder A. J. Corbett. Rozelle, N. S. W. The Standard Publishing House, 1910.
xv, 382p. 18½cm.
USlC

3903a. ———. (same) Lamoni, Ia., Herald Publishing House, 1911.
2 p.l., [1] 8–407p. illus., port. 22cm.
MoInRC, NN

3903b. ———. John three sixteen. By W. J. Haworth. Sydney, The Standard Publishing House [ca. 1918]
14p. 19cm.
NjP

3904. ———. Man here and hereafter; a study of the nature and destiny of man. Sydney, N.S.W., Australia, Standard Publishing House [n.d.]
xvi, 462p. 19½cm.
RLDS doctrine.
USlC

3905. ———. The many Gods of Mormonism versus the one true God. Rozelle, Australia, Standard Publishing House, 1913.
39p. 15cm.
MoInRC

3906. ———. The Mormons. By Elder W. J. Haworth. Published by the Australasian Board of Publication of the Re-organized Church of Jesus Christ of Latter Day Saints, 65 Nelson Street, Rozelle, N.S.W. Newcastle: Federal Printing Works, Bolton and King Streets, 1903.
12p. 18½cm. (The gospel standard library. No. 4)
Cover-title.
Bound in pink printed wrapper.
UPB

3907. ———. A Royal priesthood, by W. J. Haworth. Sydney, Australia, The Standard Publishing House [n.d.]
vii, 175p. 21½cm.
The Restoration of the priesthood, and its current role in the RLDS church.
MoInRC

3907a. ———. The second coming of Christ. By W. J. Haworth. [Sydney, The Standard Publishing House, 1918]
18p. 18cm. (The Gospel Standard. Reprint No. 1. November 1, 1918)
NjP

3908. ———. The spirit filled life. [Rozelle, Australia, Reorganized Church of Jesus Christ of Latter Day Saints, ca. 1920]
8p. 18cm. (The Angel message series. No. 28)
USlC

3909. ———. Valid Christian baptism. New Castle, Australia, Published by the Board of Publication of the Australian Mission of the Reorganized Church of Jesus Christ of Latter Day Saints, 1902.
47p. 21cm.
MoInRC

3910. ———. (same) Rozelle, N. S. W., Australia, The Standard Publishing House, 1922.
68p. 21cm.
USlC

3911. ———. Ye must be born again. [Rozelle, N. S. Australia, Reorganized Church of Jesus Christ of Latter Day Saints, ca. 1920]
15p. 18cm.
USlC

3912. Haws, Albert. Sabbatarian theories; a delusion. Independence, Mo., Ensign Publishing House, c1899.
94p. 18½cm.
Doctrinal work of the RLDS church.
MoInRC

3913. The Hawthorne bulletin. [Salt Lake City] Hawthorne Ward, Granite Stake, October 24, 1925–June 12, 1926.
1v. (#1–32) weekly. 25×31cm.
V.1 #1 has title: The Hawthorne Ward Times-Bulletin.
USlC

3914. Hawthorne Ward Review. Salt Lake City 1919–[1925?]
v. 31cm.
Later called the *Hawthorne Bulletin*, 1925.
USIC October, December, 1919

3915. Hawthornthwaithe, Samuel. Mr. Hawthornthwaithe's adventures among the Mormons as an elder during eight years. Manchester, England, The author, 1857.
132p. 21cm.
Howes H334
CSmH, CU–B, MH, NjPT, NN, OClWHi, USl, USIC, WHi

3916. Hay, James. Notes of a trip from Chicago to Victoria, Vancouver's Island and return. Printed for private circulation. Chicago, Rand, McNally & Co., Printers and Engravers, 1885.
2p.l., 5–77p. illus., plates. 20½cm.
Goes through Utah. Describes Mormon cooperatives, Salt Lake City, a church service, and Mormonism in general.
USIC

3917. Hayden, Amos Sutton. Early history of the Disciples in the Western Reserve, Ohio: with biographical sketches of the principal agents in their religious movement. By A. S. Hayden. Cincinnati, Chase and Hall, 1875.
xiii, 14–475p. 20cm.
Reference to Sidney Rigdon in chapter, "The advent of Mormonism." Also other references.
Another edition: 1876. DLC, UPB
DLC, NjPT, OCl, OClWHi, OFH

3918. Hayden, F. L. Mormonism. A sermon by Rev. F. L. Hayden, D.D. North Yakima, Wash. Delivered Sunday Evening, June 17, 1906, and printed in this form at the unanimous request of the congregation. [North Yakima, Wash.? 1906]
15p. 21½cm.
Caption-title.
UPB

Hayden, Ferdinand Vandeveer. The Great West. *See The Great West.*

3919. ———. North America. Edited and enlarged by Professor F. V. Hayden . . . and Professor A. R. C. Selwyn . . . Maps and illustrations. London, Edward Stanford, 1883.
xvi, 652p. illus., maps (part col.) 21cm.
"Mormonism," p. 252–260. Includes sections on Joseph Smith, Nauvoo, Brigham Young, polygamy, etc.
CU, NjP, NjPT, UPB

3920. ———. Sun pictures of Rocky Mountain scenery, with a description of the geographical and geological features, and some account of the resources of the great West; containing thirty photographic views along the line of the Pacific railroad, from Omaha to Sacramento, by F. B. Hayden . . . New York, J. Bien, 1870.
viii, 150p., [1]l. xxx mounted photos. 32×24½cm.
Description of Utah. Very little on Mormons.
Howes H337, Sabin 31007
CU–B, DLC, GGS, MiH, NjP, NN, OO, PPD, UHi, UPB

3921. Hayes, Benjamin Ignatius. Pioneer notes from the diaries of Judge Benjamin Hayes, 1849–1875. Los Angeles, 1929.
xi, 13–307p. plates, ports., map, facsims. 23½cm.
"Edited and published by Marjorie Tisdale Wolcott."
References to Mormons in Salt Lake City and San Bernardino.
CU–B, DLC, NjP, UHi, UPB

3922. Haynes, John. The Book of Mormon examined; and its claims to be a revelation from God, proved to be false by John Haynes. Brighton, Edward Verrall . . . London, Seeley & Co. . . . 1853.
20p. 18cm.
OClWHi, USIC

3923. ———. A Refutation of the Mormon doctrines of I. The Gospel. II. Baptism. III. The Apostolate. IV. The Priesthood. V. The Deity. VI. Faith. Especially addressed to Latter-day Saints; being the substance of a lecture delivered in the Town Hall, Brighton, on Tuesday, October the 5th 1852. By John Haynes. Brighton and London, Edward Verrall [etc., etc.] 1853.
1p.l. [5]–33p. 17cm.
USIC

3924. Hayward, Ira N. The invisible hand. The M.I.A. contest play 1928–29. [Salt Lake City] Published by General Boards of M.I.A., 1928.
23p. 16½cm.
Mormon drama.
USIC

3925. Hayward, John. The book of religions; comprising the views, creeds, sentiments, or opinions, of all the principal religious sects in the world, particularly of all Christian denominations in Europe and America, to which are added church and missionary statistics, together with biographical sketches. By John Hayward . . . Boston, John Howard, 1842.
432p. 20cm.
Includes "Mormonites, or Church of the Latter-day Saints."
Various editions to 1873 have this section.
Sabin 31065
DLC, MWA, MoInRC, NN

3926. ———. The religious creeds and statistics of every Christian denomination in the United States and British provinces. With some account of the religious sentiments of the Jews, American Indians, Deists, Mahometans, &c., alphabetically arranged. By John Hayward. Boston, Published by John Hayward, 1836.
156p. 18½cm.
An account of Mormonism, p. 130–142.
CSmH, CtY, CU–B, DLC, MB, MH, MiU, MWA, UHi, USlC

3927. Hayward, Silvanus. History of the town of Gilsum, New Hampshire, from 1752 to 1879 . . . By Silvanus Hayward . . . Manchester, N.H., Printed for the author, by J. B. Clarke, 1881.
468p. plates, ports., 3 maps (2 fold.) 26cm.
Mormons, or Latter Day Saints, p. 123.
Mormon activity in Gilsum from 1836, when Joseph Smith senior visited relatives, to 1857. Also biographies of relatives of Joseph Smith.
DLC, MnH, MWA, PHi, USlC

3928. Haywood, William Dudley. Bill Haywood's book; the autobiography of William D. Haywood. New York, International Publishers [c1929]
368p. port. 21cm.
"Boyhood among the Mormons."
DLC, NjP, UHi, UPB, USlC

3929. Hazelton, George Cochrane. Speech of G. C. Hazelton, of Wisconsin, against permitting polygamy to be represented in . . . Congress. Delivered in the House, April 18, 1882. Washington, 1882.
15p. 23cm.
NN

3930. Hazen, M. B. Utah Territory. Resolution of Hon. John Bidwell, relative to affairs in Utah Territory. [Washington, Govt. Print. Off.] 1867.
5p. 23cm. (U.S. 39th Cong. 2d Sess. House. Misc. Doc. No. 75)
Instructing the Committee on Territories to inquire into the necessity of having larger force of troops to protect the people from Indian hostilities and to preserve order to Utah Territory, with a report of Bvt. Maj. Gen. H. B. Hazen on the condition of affairs in said Territory.
CU–B, NN, UPB

He that readeth let him understand. *See Armstrong, C.*

He that hath ears to hear. *See Hyde, Orson.*

3931. Head, Franklin H. Untrodden fields in history and literature and other essays by Franklin H. Head. Edited by George Brooks Shepard. Cleveland, The Rowfant Club, 1923.
2v. 20½cm.
V. 2. Miscellanea III. Salt Lake City, p. 137–168.
A panning of the miraculous portion of the founding of Salt Lake City, and a general downgrading of the Mormon problem. His solution: leave it alone and it will be gone.
ICN, UPB, UHi

3932. Heading, C. N. The law of lineage. [Centralia, Washington, Church of Christ, n.d.]
35p. 21cm.
Succession in the Presidency.
MoInRC

3933. ———. The Temple lot. Centralia, Washington, Church of Christ [n.d.]
8p. 21cm.
Who owns the Temple Lot in Independence, Mo.?
MoInRC

3934. Heap, Gwynn Harris. Central route to the Pacific, from the valley of the Mississippi to California. Journal of the expedition of E. F. Beale, Superintendent of Indian affairs in California, and Gwynn Harris Heap, from Missouri to California, in 1853, by Gwynn Harris Heap. Philadelphia, Lippincott, Grambo & Company, 1854.
2p.l. [4]–136p. xiii plates, fold. map. 23cm.
Witnesses the evacuation of Paragonah as ordered by Brigham Young during the Walker War; visits Parowan; description of it and Little Salt Lake; Mormon custom of securing Indian babies; Mormon-Indian relations; polygamy.
Howes H 378, Sabin 31175, W–C 235
CSmH, CtY, DLC, ICN, NjP, NN, ULA, UPB

3935. Heap o'pep. Salt Lake City, March 1922–
v. monthly. 29cm.
"Published every month by the senior clubs of Y.M. & Y.L.M.I.A. of Granite Stake.
USlC March, 1922. V. 1 # 2

Heavington, Alonzo LeBaron [*pseud.*] *See LeBaron, Alonzo H.*

3936. Hebard, Grace Raymond. The Bozeman trail; historical accounts of the blazing of the overland routes into the Northwest, and the fights with Red Cloud's warriors, by Grace Raymond Hebard and E. A. Brininstool, with introduction by General Charles King . . . Cleveland, The Arthur H. Clark Company, 1922.
2v. plates, ports., maps (1 fold.) plans. 24½cm.
Scattered references to Mormons; Mormon Trail.
Howes H 382
CU–B, DLC, MB, MiU, NjP, PPL, ULA, USlC, UU, ViU, WaU

3937. ———. The pathbreakers from river to ocean; the story of the great West from the time of Coronado to the present [by] Grace Raymond Hebard . . . four maps and numerous illustrations. Chicago, The Lakeside Press, 1911.

xp., [1]l., 263p. illus., ports., 4 maps. 19½cm.
"The Mormons in Utah." Other references.
Other editions: Chicago, 1912. USIC; 3d ed. Chicago, 1913. CU, USIC; Lincoln, University Publ. Co., 1923. MB
CSmH, DLC, IdB, IdIf, NN, UHi, USIC, UU, WaS, WaSp, WaU

3938. ———. Washakie; an account of Indian resistance of the covered wagon and Union Pacific Railroad invasions of their territory, by Grace Raymond Hebard . . . Cleveland, The Arthur H. Clark Company, 1930.
337p. plates, ports., maps (part fold.) 24½cm.
Chief Washakie and Brigham Young, p. 75–91. Howes H384
CU–B, DLC, MB, NjP, OO, OU, UHi, USIC, UU, ViU, WaU

3939. Hedges, Sanford Wells. Kitō no hitsuyoo. Sandofuorudo W. Hedges Cho, Matsu Jitsu Seito Iesu Kirisuto Kyokai senkyoshi. [Tōkyō] Matsu Jitsu Seito Iesu Kirisuto Kyōkai Nihon Dendo-bu [1906?]
26p. 15cm.
Title in English: The necessity of prayer.
USIC

3940. ———. Matsu Jitsu Seito. Tōkyō, Nihon, Matsu Jitsu Seito Iesu Kirisuto Kyōkai Nihon Dendobu [1905]
16p. 15½cm.
Title in English: Latter-day Saints.
USIC

3940a. ———. (same) [Tōkyō] Matsu Jitsu Seito Iesu Kirisuto Kyōkai Nihon Dendobu [1911]
18[3]p. illus. 14cm.
7th Edition.
USIC

3941. Hedrick, Granville. The spiritual wife system. True order of Church discipline. By G. Hedrick. Bloomington, Ill., 1856.
118p. 13cm.
Publication antedating the Church of Christ. Byrd 2455
MoInRC inc., USIC

3942. Hedrick, James A. A correction. [Independence, Mo.? 1913?]
[2]p. 32cm.
Caption-title. In triple columns.
Printed on inner pages of a folded sheet. Reply to some remarks in the *Evening and Morning Star*, September, 1913, relative to a suit for possession of Temple lot.
MoInRC, PH

3943. Heiberg, I. A. En rejse i Amerika. Odense, 1892.
36p.
A section on Mormonism.
Title in English: A trip to America.
Schmidt

3944. Hein, F. C. Den evangelisk lutherske laeres sammenligning med Mormonismen, Katholicismen og Judaismen, fremstillet i breve. Kobenhavn, 1854.
106p.
Title in English: The likeness of Evangelic Lutheran doctrine with Mormonism . . .
Schmidt

3945. Heiner, Daniel. A short sketch written by my own hand in my own language. Dedicated to my descendants with best wishes. Morgan, Utah, 1929.
2p.l., 71p. port. 19½cm.
Portrait on title-page.
Mormon biography.
UHi, UPB

3946. Heitman, Francis Bernard. Historical register and dictionary of the United States Army, From its organization September 29, 1789 to March 2, 1903. Washington, Govt. Print. Off., 1903.
2v. 26½cm. (U.S. 57th Cong. 2d Sess. House. Doc. No. 466)
Lists the officers of the Mormon battalion.
CU, CU–B, DLC, NjP

3947. Helms, Ludvig Verner. Pioneering in the East, and journeys to California in 1849 and to the White Sea in 1878. London, W. H. Allen & Co., 1882.
vi [2] 408p. plates, maps (1 fold.) 22½cm.
Visit with Brigham Young in route east in 1872, p. 327–328.
CU-B

3948. Helmick, Daniel M. Claims of the Book of Mormon critically examined from evidence found in the book itself. By the Rev. Daniel M. Helmick. [Salt Lake City, 1906]
24p. 14½cm.
MH, MoInRC, UPB, USI, USIC

3949. The Helper. Morehead, Ky. 1902?–
v. 30cm.
An anti-Mormon periodical. R. B. Neal, editor.
USIC V.3 #7–8, April–May, 1905.

3950. Helpful visions. The fourteenth book of the faith promoting series. . . . Designed for the instruction and encouragement of young Latter-day Saints. Salt Lake City, Juvenile Instructor Office, 1887.
3p.l. [9]–95p. 18cm. (Fourteenth book of the Faith promoting series)
Contents: A terrible ordeal, by O. F. Whitney. Briant S. Stevens, by Kennon [*pseud.*] Finding comfort, by Thomas A. Shreeve. Traitors, by Ben E. Rich.
CSmH, CtY, CU–B, DLC, MH, NjP, NN, UHi, ULA, UPB, USIC, WHi

3951. Hemans, Lawton T. History of Michigan. 1st ed. Lansing, Michigan, Hammond Publishing Co., 1906.

1p.l. [5]–278p. illus. 19cm.
Colony of Mormons and James J. Strang, p. 173–174.
DLC, UPB, USlC

3952. Hemenway, Charles W. Memoirs of my day. In and out of Mormondom. By Charles W. Hemenway, a journalist. Written in prison while the author was undergoing sentence for alleged libel. Salt Lake City [Printed by the Deseret News Company] 1887.
ix, 265p. port. 19cm.
Several chapters on his stay in Salt Lake City and his impressions of Mormonism and the Utah situation.
CSmH, CU–B, DLC, MN, NjP, NN, UHi, ULA, UPB, USl, USlC, UU, WHi

3953. Hemingray, J. C. Mormonism. Argument of Hon. J. C. Hemingray, delegate of the Liberal Party of Utah, before the House Sub-committee on Territories, on the bill "to regulate elections and elective franchise in the Territory of Utah," January 22, 1878. Washington, W. H. Moore, Printer, 1878.
30p. 21½cm.
CSmH, CtY, DLC, ICHi, OClWHi, NN, ULA

3954. Henderson, W. W. The real purpose of life; address delivered over Radio Station KSL, Sunday Evening, February 13, 1927. Salt Lake City, 1927.
Broadside. 29×24cm.
Reprinted from the *Deseret News.*
UPB

3955. Hendrix, Eugene Russell. Around the world, by the Rev. E. R. Hendrix with an introduction by the Rev. Bishop Marvin. Nashville, Tennessee, A. H. Redford, 1878.
2p.l. [5]–598p. 18½cm.
First published in the form of letters to the *St. Louis Christian Advocate.*
Chapter II "Among the Mormons," in 1876.
Another edition: 2d ed. 1878. USlC
UHi

3956. Henningsen, L. Mormonismen eller den nyere tids hedenskab. En kort levnedtegning af stifteren, Josef Smith, og uddrag af samfundets laere og liv til advarsel for paene folk. Aarhus, 1911.
Title in English: Mormonism or the Modern Paganism.
Schmidt.

3957. Henry, Alfred Hylas. By order of the prophet; a tale of Utah, by Alfred H. Henry . . . Chicago, New York [etc.] Fleming H. Revell Company, 1902.
3p.l., 5–402p. plates. 20½cm.
Fiction concerning Mormonism.
CSmH, DLC, MH, MoInRC, NHi, NjP, ULA, UPB, USl, USlC, UU, ViU

3958. Hensel, Rudolph. Amerika aus Tagebuchblättern einer Reise, von Rudolph Hensel. Berlin, Presse, Dr. Selle-Eipler, 1928.
277 [1]p. front., map. 23cm.
Chapter "Bei den Mormonen." His stay in Salt Lake City; his comments on Mormonism and Utah.
Title in English: The diary of a trip to America.
Another edition: Druck und Verlag, von Jacob Hegner in Hellerau dei Dresden [c1929] UU
DLC

3959. Hepburn, Andrew Balfour. The doctrines, rites and ceremonies of Latter Day Saints, or Mormons, exposed; showing from their own books, &c, that they are, without exception, the most depraved, immoral, blasphemous, and ridiculous sect that ever polluted this earth. The extracts furnished by Mr. A. B. Hepburn, anti-Mormon lecturer. London, Partridge and Oakey . . . and the Anti-Mormon Tract Depot [ca. 1853]
8p. 21cm.
USlC

3960. ———. An exposition of the blasphemous doctrines and delusions of the so-called Latter-day Saints, or Mormons, containing an authentic account of the impositions, spiritual wife doctrine, and the other abominable practices of Joseph Smith, the American Mahomet, and his Twelve Apostles, elders, and followers to the present time. By A. B. Hepburn . . . Sheffield, M. Thomas & Son, 1852.
2p.l., 68p. 18cm.
CU–B

3961. ———. Mormonism exploded or the religion of the Latter-day Saints. Proved to be a system of imposture, blasphemy, and immorality; with the autobiography and portrait of the author. In two parts. Pt. I. By A. B. Hepburn. Anti-Mormon lecturer. Edited by Rev. Charles Short, A. M. London & Swansea, Simpkin, Marshall and Co., 1855.
48p. 17½cm.
Only part I found.
CU–B, USlC (defective)

3962. Te herauraa api. . . . Papeete, Tahiti, Atopa, 1907–
v. monthly. 21cm.
Official organ of the Tahitian Mission of the LDS church.
UPB V. 1, 3, 4, 9, 11–13, 14 inc., 15 inc.; USlC V. 1, 2, 4, 5, 6, 9, 10 inc., 15, 17–24

3963. Herndon, Sarah (Raymond). Days on the road; crossing the plains in 1865. New York, Burr Printing House, 1902.
xvi, 270p. 18cm.
Encounters "sad and sorrowful." Mormon women in towns in Idaho; other comments.
Howes H 439
CU–B, DLC, ICN, NjP

3964. Heroines of "Mormondom." Salt Lake City, Juvenile Instructor Office, 1884.
1p.l. [9]–96p. 19cm. (Noble Women's Lives series. V.2)
CtY, CU–B, DLC, ICN, MH, NjP, NN, UHi, UPB, USl, USlC, UU

3965. Herrick, Samuel. Herrick's public land and mining decisions. [Washington, 1918?]
[8]p. 23cm.
"Third signature of Volume VI" reprint.
Material on Mormons and the Indians.
USlC

3966. Herringshaw, Thomas William. The biographical review of prominent men and women of the day; with biographical sketches and reminiscences. To which is added a birdseye view of the history of our republic . . . Chicago, Donohue & Hennebery [1888]
576p. illus. 23cm.
Biographical sketch of George Q. Cannon (The Mormon Monster)
Also published in Swedish.
UHi

3967. ———. Local and national poets of America; with interesting biographical sketches and choice selections . . . Chicago, American Publishers' Association, 1890.
iv, x [33]–1036p. illus. 25cm.
Biographies of several Mormon poets such as Amelia C. Bigler, Augusta Joyce Crocheron, Hannah Cornaby, and Edwin F. Parry.
Another edition: 1892. CU
DLC, UHi, UPB

3968. Hershey, Scott F. Mormonism unscriptural, pagan and immoral. Boston, J. R. Rivier & Company, Printers, 1900.
21p. 21½cm.
MH, ULA

3968a. Herstine, Mrs. C. M. Nature of the apostasy. [Davis City, Iowa, 1896]
8p. 20cm.
Publication of the Church of Christ (Whitmer)
Morgan
USlC

3969. Hertwig, John George. Polygamy in the United States. [By John George Hertwig. Washington, 1884]
4p. 20cm.
Reprinted from *Salamanca Freethinkers' Magazine*, May, 1884.
NN

3970. Hesse-Wartegg, Ernst von. Nord-Amerika, seine Städte und Naturwunder, sein Land und seine Leute . . . Leipzig, Gustav Weigel, 1880.
4v. illus. 26cm.
"Salt Lake City und die Mormonen," V. 3, p. 57–63.
Title in English: North America, its cities and natural wonders . . .
UHi

Hete, Joseph. *See Kennard, Leonidas Hamlin.*

3971. Hewitson, Anthony. History (from A.D. 705 to 1883) of Preston, in the County of Lancaster. By Anthony Hewitson. Preston, England, "Chronicle" Office, 1883.
2p.l., 566, xi [2]p. illus., plates, maps (party fold.) 19½cm.
"The Mormons," p. 538. Mormon activities in Preston, England.
USlC, UU

3972. Hewitt, Randall Henry. Notes by the way. Memoranda of a journey West in 1862. Olympia, Printed at the Office of the Washington Standard, 1863.
58p. 22cm.
Meets Mormon wagon trains, passes north of Salt Lake "the kingdom of the 'Latter-day Saints' or sinners."
Howes H457, W–C 391
CtY, NjP

3973. ———. (same, under title) Across the plains and over the divide. New York, Broadway Publishing Co. [c1906]
521p. 21½cm.
CU–B, DLC, NN

3974. Hewitt, William. Exposition of the errors and fallacies of the self-named "Latter-day Saints." In which the author exposes the fallacies of the L.D.S. by publishing his sentiments. Lane-End, England, 1840.
11p. 18cm.
USlC

3975. Hewlett, Alfred. One wife, or many wives. By the Rev. Alfred Hewlett . . . Manchester, The author; London, Wertheim and MacIntosh [n.d.]
12p. 17cm. (The District Visitor. No. 13)
USlC

3976. Heys, Robert. Address to the members of the Wesleyan Societies and Congregations in Douglas and its vicinity on the subject of Mormonism. [Douglas, Isle of Man? 1840]
Circular replied to by John Taylor's *An answer.*
no copy located

HICKENLOOPER, F.

3977. Hickenlooper, Frank. An illustrated history of Monroe County, Iowa; a complete civil, political, and military history of the county, from its earliest period of organization down to 1896 . . . Albia, Ia. [The author] 1896.
2p.l., 7–360p. illus., map. 20cm.
The Mormons and the election of 1848, p. 33–36.
NjP, UHi, USlC

3978. Hickey, Lorenzo Dow. A card to the kind and brave people of Utah. By Apostle L. D. Hickey. [Monte Vista, Colo.? 1896?]
8p. 17½cm.
Caption-title.
A pro-Strang tract. Includes the supposed letter from Joseph Smith, 1844, and revelations of James J. Strang.
Morgan
MH, USlC

3979. ———. A card to the public defending Hon. James J. Strang. [By L. D. Hickey and D. B. Alvord. Monte Vista, Colo.?, 1896?]
[4]p. 19×15cm.
In double columns.
Signed: L. D. Hickey, D. B. Albert. (i.e. Alvord)
Morgan
CtY, MoInRC, UHi

3980. ———. Rejection of the Church from Nauvoo. By Eld. L. D. Hickey. [Coldwater, Mich., 1892]
8p. 19cm.
Signed: Coldwater, Mich., April 6, 1892. L. D. Hickey, D. B. Alvord, F. A. Wake, J. C. Hambleton. An affirmation of the claims of James J. Strang.
Not in Morgan.
USlC

3981. ———. Who was the successor of Joseph Smith? [Coldwater, Mich.?, 1891]
5p. 23½×16cm.
Signed: L. D. Hickey, Coldwater, Mich., June 15, 1891.
Morgan
CtY, DLC, WBuC

3982. ———. (same) [Monte Vista, Colo.? 1896?]
6p. 19×15cm.
Signed: L. D. Hickey.
In double columns.
p. 1 being on the verso of the title.
Morgan
CtY

3983. Hickman, Edward B. Mormonism sifted; or the question, was Joseph Smith sent by God? Examined; being the substance of a lecture delivered in the Independent Chapel, Boxford, Friday Evening, March 8th, 1850, by Edward B. Hickman. Published by request. [Norwich, England, Printed by Jarrold & Sons, 1850?]
27p. 17cm.
CU–B

3984. ———. (same) 2d ed. London, Brandon, Jarrold and Sons; Brandon, J. Clarke; Norwich, J. Clarke [1850?]
27p. 17½cm.
Caption-title.
USlC

3985. ———. (same) 3d ed. London, Norwich and Brandon, Jarrold and Sons, 1850.
27p. 18cm.
CU–B, NN, USlC

3986. Hickman, Josiah Edwin. The greatest seer of the ages; address delivered over Radio Station KSL, Sunday Evening, April 15, 1928. [Salt Lake City] 1928.
Broadside. 48×19cm.
Reprinted from the *Deseret News*, Saturday, April 12th, 1928.
UPB

3987. ———. The Offspring of the Mormon people. J. E. Hickman. [Logan, Utah, 1924?]
55–68p. 25cm.
Reprinted, without change of pagination from the *Journal of Heredity*. Vol. xv, No. 2. February 1924, with separate title page.
UPB

3988. ———. A story of the banishment of the Mormon people. An address delivered over Radio Station, KSL, Sunday Evening, Sept. 15th, 1929. By Professor J. E. Hickman . . . [Salt Lake City, Church of Jesus Christ of Latter-day Saints, 1929]
7p. 22cm.
USlC

3989. Hickman, W. Z. History of Jackson County, Missouri, illustrated. Topeka, Cleveland, Historical Publishing Company, 1920.
10p.l. [65]–832p. illus., ports. 27½cm.
"The Mormons" in Jackson County, by Orson F. Whitney, p. 191–194. "Reorganized Church of Jesus Christ of Latter Day Saints," by Walter W. Smith, p. 194–198.
MoInRC, USlC

3990. Hickman, William A. Brigham's destroying angel: being the life, confession, and startling disclosures of the notorious Bill Hickman, the Danite chief of Utah. Written by himself, with explanatory notes by J. H. Beadle esq., of Salt Lake City. New York, Geo. A. Crofutt, Publisher, 1872.
vii [1] [9]–219p. illus. 18cm.
Variant editions. Address of publisher varies. USlC
Howes H465
CSmH, CtY, CU–B, DLC, ICN, MoInRC, NjP, NN, UHi, UPB, USl, USlC, UU, WHi

3991. ———. (same) Salt Lake City, Shepard Book Company, 1904.
vii [2] 10–221p. illus., port. 17½cm.
Introduction by Richard B. Shepard.
CtY. CU–B, DLC, MoInRC, NjPT, NN, UHi, ULA, USlC, WHi

3992. Higbee, Elias. An address by Judge Higbee and Parley P. Pratt, ministers of the gospel of the Church of Jesus Christ of "Latter-day Saints," to the citizens of Washington, and to the public in general. [Washington, 1840?]
4p. 21cm.
Signed: Washington, Feb. 9, 1840.
Caption-title.
CtY, NN, PPL

3993. ———. "Latter-Day Saints," alias Mormons. The petition of the Latter-Day Saints, commonly known as Mormons, stating that they have purchased lands of the General Government, lying in the State of Missouri, from which they have been driven with force by the constituted authorities of the State, and prevented from occupying the same; and have suffered other wrongs, for which they pray Congress to provide a remedy. [Washington, 1840]
13p. 23cm. (U.S. 26th Cong. 2d Sess. House. Doc. No. 22)
Signed: Elias Higbee, Robert B. Thompson.
C, CSmH, CtY, CU, CU–B, DLC, NN, UHi, UPB

3994. Higbie, Alfred. Polygamy versus christianity; a discourse against polygamy, and baptism for the dead, delivered at Watsonville, June 14th, 1857. By Reverend Alfred Higbie, of Santa Cruz, Cal. San Francisco, Printed by B. F. Sterett, 1857.
29p. 22½cm.
CSmH, CtY, CU–B

3995. Higgins, Charles A. To California and back, a book of practical information for travelers to the Pacific, by C. A. Higgins; with some notes on Southern California by Charles Keeler. New York, Doubleday, Page & Company, 1903.
x, 317p. illus., 25 plates, map. 19½cm.
Chap. VII, Nevada and Utah. Account of the Mormon settlement of Utah; description of the principal cities.
Other editions: Chicago, Passenger Department, Santa Fe Route, 1897. USlC; 1907. NjP
NjP, ULA, UPB, USlC

3996. Hill, H. J., *compiler.* Pocket directory of business houses of the Latter-day Saints, including trades and provisions. Salt Lake City [1886]
80p. illus. 20×9cm.
Cover-title.
Text on p. [2–3] of cover.
Compiler, H. J. Hill. cf. verso of cover.
CU–B

3997. Hill, John Alexander. Stories of the railroad, by John A. Hill. New York, Doubleday & McClure Co., 1899.
297p. 7 plates. 19cm.
Includes: Mormon Joe, the robber, p. 193–225. A short story about a railroad man who had formerly been an engineer in Utah and may have been a Mormon.
Another edition: 1900. UHi, UPB
DLC, NjP

3998. Hill, John Wesley. Mormonism vs. Americanism; a series of lectures by Rev. J. Wesley Hill, delivered in the M.E. Church at Ogden City, Utah, December 9th, 16th, and 23rd, 1888. Salt Lake City, Tribune Printing and Publishing Company, 1889.
2p.l. [5]–29p. port. 20½cm.
Mormonism a caricature of religion.
CSmH, MH, USl, USlC

3999. Hill, Thomas E. Hill's album of biography and art: Containing portraits and pen-sketches of many persons who have been and are prominent as religionists, military heroes, inventors, financiers [etc.] . . . Together with chapters relating to history, science, and important work in which prominent people have been engaged at various periods of time. By Thos. E. Hill. Chicago, Hill Standard Book Company, 1888.
3p.l. [5]–589p. illus., ports. 27cm.
"Joseph Smith, sketch of the rise and progress of Mormonism," p. 32–33.
USlC

4000. Hill, William Nicholas. The book of life by W. N. Hill . . . [n.p., c1920]
92p. 18½cm.
Questions and answers pertaining to Mormonism.
USlC

4001. Hills, Louis Edward. Friendly discussion of the Book of Mormon geography by L. E. Hills and F. F. Wipper at the Stone Church, Independence, Mo., May 20 to May 30, 1924. [Independence] 1924.
32p. 19½cm.
Sponsored by Zion's Religious Literary Society.
MoInRC

4002. ———. Geography of Mexico and Central America from 2234 B.C. to 421 A.D. Independence, Mo. [c1917]
42p. fold. map. 22cm.
Book of Mormon geography. References to the RLDS version of the *Book of Mormon.*
USlC

4003. ———. Historical data from ancient records and ruins of Mexico and Central America. Independence, Mo., 1919.
48p. 18cm.
CU–B, MoInRC

4004. ———. New light on American archaeology, by L. E. Hills. Independence, Mo., Lambert Moon Printers and Stationers [1924]
323p. illus. 18½cm.
MoInRC, UHi

4005. ———. (same) Independence, Mo., Lambert Moon Printers and Stationers [1924]
198p. 19cm.
DLC

4006. ———. A short work on the geography of Mexico and Central America, from 2234 B.C. to 421 A.D., by L. E. Hills. Independence, Mo. [c1917]
46p. fold. map. 22½cm.
Evidences to establish the credibility of the *Book of Mormon*, cf. pref.
DLC, MoInRC, NN, UHi

4007. ———. A short work on the Popol vuh and the traditional history of the ancient Americans, by Ist-lil-xochitl. By L. E. Hills. [Kansas City, Mo., Franklin Hudson Publ. Co. [c1918]
30p. plates, port., maps (part. fold.) 22½cm.
Evidences for the credibility of the *Book of Mormon*.
DLC, MoInRC, NN, UHi

4008. ———. A Study of the geography of the Book of Mormon. [n.p., n.d.]
4p. 22cm.
MoInRC

4009. ———. Traditional history of ancient Americans in Mexico and Central America. Independence, Mo. [c1918]
30p. port., fold. map. 22cm.
Book of Mormon geography from the RLDS *Book of Mormon*.
USlC

4010. Himes, Joshua Vaughan. Mormon delusions and monstrosities. A review of the Book of Mormon and an illustration of Mormon principles and practices. Compiled and edited by Joshua V. Himes. Boston, Published by Joshua V. Himes, 1842.
vi [7]–90p. 17cm.
Incorporates Alexander Campbell's *Delusions*, p. 7–32.
Howes H498, Sabin 31922
CtY, MB, MBAt, MH–A, MoK, USlC, WHi

4011. Hinckley, Bryant Stringham. Religion a vital factor in character building. Book III. Character-building series. Prepared for the General Board of the Y.M.M.I.A. by B. S. Hinckley under the direction of the Junior Committee. Salt Lake City, Published by the General Board of the Y.M.M.I.A., 1926.
3p.l. [7]–80p. 21cm. (Young Men's Mutual Improvement Association. Advanced Junior Manual)
UPB

4012. ———. Some essentials of character. Salt Lake City, Published by the General Board of Y.M.M.I.A., 1927.
3p.l. [7]–72p. illus., ports. 21cm. (Character-building series. No. 1)
First edition written by a committee in 1924.
USlC

4013. Hindle, Eugene. The Latter-day Saints or "Mormons." A criticism by an outsider. Nelson, Lancashire, England [n.d.]
15p. 21½cm.
UPB, USlC

4014. Hingston, Edward P. The genial showman. Being reminiscences of the life of Artemus Ward and pictures of a showman's career in the western world. Popular ed. London, John Camden Hotten [1870?]
363, 395p. illus. 19½cm.
"Complete in one volume."
Includes his lectures on Mormonism.
Other editions: New illustrated ed. 1871. CU–B, DLC; 3d ed. London, Chattoe and Windus, 187–. UHi; New York, Harper & Brothers, 1871. UPB
Sabin 31959
NjP, UHi

4015. Hinte, J. van. Nederlanders in Amerika, een studie over landverhuizers en volkpalnters in de 19[e] en 20[ste] eeuw in de Vereenigde Staten van Amerika. Groningen, P. Noordhoof, 1928.
2v. 25½cm.
"De Mormonen," V.2.
Title in English: Dutchmen in America.
DLC

4016. Hintze, Ferdinand Fritz. An invitation to the kingdom of God; written for the Turkish Mission. [Salt Lake City, Printed by George Q. Cannon and Sons Co., 1895]
20p. 23cm.
Signed: Constantinople, 1888.
"Part first partially translated from the Danish."
MH, ULA, USlC

4017. ———. (same, in Armenian) Melekhivith voullahen pesharetineda'ir pir izahat. [Nasheri, F. F. Hintze Istanbul v. minassian matpasa, 1899]
36p. 18cm.
UPB, USlC

4018. ———. (same, in Greek) Melekout oullachen pezaretine tair pir izachat. Nazeri F. F. Hintze. Istanbul, v. minassian matpasa, 1899]
36p. 18cm.
Caption-title.
UPB, USlC

4019. ———. Rviovhlaren iklh mevjwooditzete ve emvaten khelase. [Nasheri F. F. Hintze. Istanbul, v. minassian matapasa, 1899]

16p. 18cm.
Title in English: Pre-existence of spirits and salvation for the dead.
UPB, USlC

4020. ———. (same, in Greek) Rouchlaren ilk mevtzoutiget ve emvaten chelase. [Naseri F. F. Hintze. Istanbul, v. misassian matpasa, 1899]
16p. 18cm.
Caption-title.
UPB, USlC

Historical and descriptive sketch of the Salt Lake Temple from April 6, 1853, to April 6, 1893. *See House of the Lord.*

Historical encyclopedia of Illinois. *See Bateman, Newton.*

4021. Historical, pictorial and biographical record of Chariton County, Missouri. Salisbury, Pictorial and Biographical Pub., 1896.
3p.l. [7]–91, 248p. illus., ports. 23½cm.
Includes material on Mormon activities in Chariton Co., Missouri.
UPB

Historical Record. *See Jenson, Andrew.*

4022. Historical Society of Geauga County, Ohio. Pioneer and general history of Geauga County, with sketches of some of the pioneers and prominent men. [Burton? Ohio, n.d.]
7 p.l. [9]–822p. 24½cm.
At head of title: 1798.
References to the Mormons, p. 447, 581–582, 751.
UPB

Historicus. Blood Atonement. *See Mills, William G.*

4023. The history of Adams County, Illinois. Containing a history of the county — its cities . . . a biographical directory . . . war record . . . statistics . . . etc., etc. . . . Chicago, Murray, Williamson and Phelps, 1879.
vii [7]–971p. illus., plates, ports., double map. 24cm.
Includes Mormonism in Illinois.
DLC, ICN, MB, NN, OCl, OClWHi

4024. History of all the religious denominations in the U.S.: containing authentic accounts of the rise and progress, faith and practice, localities and statistics, of the different persuasions: written expressly for the work, by fifty-three eminent authors, belonging to the respective denominations. Second improved and portrait edition. Harrisburg, Pa., John Winebrenner, 1849.
viii, 598p. ports. 24½cm.
"History of the Latter-day Saints, by Joseph Smith, Nauvoo, Illinois:" p. 344–349.
The first edition was edited by Isr Daniel Rupp and listed under him.
Other editions: 1857? DLC; 1859. DLC
MH, NN, OClWHi, OO, UPB, USlC, ViU

4025. History of Benton, Washington, Carroll, Madison, Crawford, Franklin and Sebastian Counties, Arkansas. From the earliest time to the present, including a department devoted to the preservation of sundry personal, business, professional and private records; besides a valuable fund of notes, original observations, etc., etc. Illustrated. Chicago, The Goodspeed Publishing Co., 1889.
5p.l., viii–x [1]14–1382p. illus., plates. 28cm.
An account of the Mountain Meadows massacre, p. 346–350.
UPB

4026. History of Caldwell and Livingston counties, Missouri . . . including a history of their townships, towns, and villages, together with a condensed history of Missouri . . . biographical sketches of prominent citizens; general and local statistics . . . incidents and reminiscences. St. Louis, National Historical Company, 1886.
xiv, 1227p. illus. 26cm.
"The Mormon occupation; The Mormon War; The massacre at Haun's Mill," etc.
CU–B, DLC, NN, UHi, UPB

4027. History of Cass County, Iowa. Together with sketches of its towns, villages and townships; educational, civil, military and political history; portraits of prominent persons, and biographies of old settlers and representative citizens. [Also] History of Iowa embracing accounts of the pre-historic races and a brief review of its civil, political and military history. Springfield, Ill., Continental Historical Co., 1884.
x [13]–910p. illus. 25½cm.
Mormons in Cass County, Iowa, p. 241–244.
USlC

4028. History of Clay and Platte Counties, Missouri, written and compiled from the most authentic official private sources, including a history of their townships, towns and villages, together with a condensed history of Missouri. A reliable and detailed history of Clay and Platte counties, their pioneer record resources, biographical sketches of prominent citizens, general and local statistics of great value; incidents and reminiscences. St. Louis, National Historical Co., 1885.
1121p. 25cm.
"Mormon difficulties. The Mormon war. Salt Lake and Indian trade," p. 54–57, 132–135, 594–596, 608–610.
ICN, ICU, MoInRC, NN

4029. The history of Daviess County, Missouri. An encyclopedia of useful information, and a compendium of actual facts . . . Kansas City, Mo., Birdsall and Dean, 1882.

9 [9]–868p. illus., ports., fold. map. 27cm.

Material on the "Mormon War," p. 184–206.

CtY, ICN, ICU, NN

4030. History of Franklin County, Pennsylvania. Containing a history of the county, its townships, towns, villages, schools, churches, industries . . . biographies; history of Pennsylvania, statistical and miscellaneous matter, etc. . . . Chicago, Warner, Beers and Co., 1887.

viip. [1]l. [15]–968p. illus., ports., double map. 25½cm.

Mormonism. On p. 259 a reference to Ebenezer Robinson's *Conococheague Herald,* begun in August 1848 and sold after a year to Charles Martin. On p. 316 a cross-reference to Mormonism in Antrim Township. On p. 563–564: Account of Mormonism in Antrim largely based on I. H. M'Cauley's *Historical sketch of Franklin County.*

DLC, NN

4031. . . . History of Geauga and Lake counties, Ohio, with illustrations and biographical sketches of its pioneers and most prominent men. Philadelphia, Williams Brothers, 1878.

259p., illus., plates, ports., map. 36½cm.

Chapter VIII: Mormonism, fugitive slave incidents, etc. Terse statement of short Mormon sojourn in Kirtland; Geauga County people don't put up with such nonsense.

CtY, DLC, MH, MWA, NN, OO, OOxM

4032. History of Howard and Cooper Counties, Missouri, written and compiled from the most authentic official and private sources, including a history of its townships, towns, and villages. Together with a condensed history of Missouri . . . detailed history of Howard and Cooper Counties — its pioneer record, resources, biographical sketches of prominent citizens . . . St. Louis, National Historical Company, 1883.

ix, 1167p., [3]l. 26½cm.

"The Mormons," p. 54–57, 753–754.

CU–B, DLC, NN, OClWHi

4033. The history of Jackson County, Missouri, containing a history of the county, its cities, towns, etc., biographical sketches of its citizens, Jackson County in the late war . . . history of Missouri, map of Jackson County. Kansas City, Mo., Union Historical Company, 1881.

iv, vii–x[1] [9]–1006p. illus., ports., fold. map. 25½cm.

Chapter XII. Mormons in Jackson County. The Mormon War.

CU–B, DLC, MoInRC, OClWHi, USlC, UU

4034. History of LaSalle County, Illinois, together with sketches of its cities, villages and towns, educational, religious, civil, military, and political history, portraits of prominent persons, and biographies of representative citizens. . . . Also a condensed history of Illinois embodying accounts of prehistoric races, aborigines, Winnebago and Black Hawk Wars and brief review of its civil and political history. Chicago, Inter-State Publishing Company, 1886.

2v. ports. 26½cm.

"The Mormon War," V.1, p. 104–118.

DLC, NjP

4035. The history of Lee County, Iowa, containing a history of the county, its cities, towns, &c., a biographical directory of citizens, war record of its volunteers in the late rebellion, general and local statistics, portraits of early settlers and prominent men, history of the Northwest, history of Iowa, map of Lee County. . . . Chicago, Western Historical Company, 1879.

4p.l., 19–887p. illus., ports., double map. 24cm.

Mormonism and Mormon outrages, p. 465–483.

Another edition: Chicago, H. H. Hill and Co., 1881. DLC

DLC, IaHi, NjP, NN

4036. History of Logan County, Illinois, together with sketches of its cities, villages and towns, educational, religious, civil, military, and political history, portraits of prominent persons, and biographies of representative citizens. Also a condensed history of Illinois . . . Chicago, Inter-state Publishing Co., 1886.

6p.l. [17]–909p. illus., ports., plates. 25½cm.

Mormon war, p. 104–118.

UPB

4037. The history of Marshall County, Iowa, containing a history of the county, its cities, towns, &c., a biographical directory of citizens, war record of its volunteers . . . general and local statistics . . . history of the Northwest, history of Iowa, map of Marshall County, Constitution of the United States. . . . Chicago, Western Historical Company, 1878.

3p.l., 19–666p., [1]l., 667–696 (i.e. 690)p. illus., ports., double map. 24½cm.

A short history of the Mormon Church from foundation to founding of Utah. Little Iowa material except 1846 flight from Nauvoo and the passage of the Emmett Company through Marshall County, p. 318–326.

Mention of two "honorable" Mormons; local residents not believing in polygamy.

DLC, MiU

The history of Mormonism from its commencement to the present time. *See Alf.* [*pseud.*]

4037a. History of Nevada with illustrations and biographical sketches of its prominent men and pioneers. Oakland, Calif., Thompson & West, 1881.
680p. illus. 30cm.
Mormons, p. 42–48, 192, 476–92, 653.
USlC

4038. History of Pike County, Illinois; together with sketches of its cities, villages and townships, educational, religious, civil, military, and political history; portraits of prominent persons and biographies of representative citizens. History of Illinois, embracing accounts of the pre-historic races, aborigines, French, English and American conquests and a general review of its civil, political and military history. Digest of state laws. Illustrated. Chicago, Chas. C. Chapman & Co., 1880.
5p.l. [17]–966p. illus., plates, ports., maps. 24cm.
"Mormon war," p. 104–118.
UPB

4039. History of Pottawattamie County, Iowa. Containing a history from the earliest settlement to the present time . . . biographical sketches; portraits of some early settlers, prominent men, etc. . . . Chicago, O. L. Baskin & Co., 1883.
vii, 11–364, 277p. plates, ports. 25½×21cm.
History of Council Bluffs by J. H. Keatley.
He tells of the residence of the Mormons in that city, formerly Kanesville, p. 69–239.
Various other references to Mormons in Iowa.
DLC, IaHi, NN, ULA

4040. History of Ray County, Mo., carefully written and compiled from the most authentic official and private sources, including a history of its townships, city, towns and villages, together with a condensed history of Missouri; the constitution of the United States, and state of Missouri; a military record of its volunteers in either army of the great civil war; general and local statistics; miscellany . . . biographical sketches of prominent men . . . identified with . . . the county. . . . St. Louis, Missouri Historical Company, 1881.
1p.l., 2–160, 160A–160E [2] 161–818p. illus., plates, ports. 24½cm.
Section entitled: "The sole surviving witness of the authenticity of the Book of Mormon" –David Whitmer.
DLC, ICU, NN, UPB, USlC

4041. History of San Bernardino County, California. Including biographical sketches. San Francisco, Cal., W. W. Elliot and Co., 1883.
2p.l. [17]–204 (i.e. 299)p. illus., plates (part double) ports., maps. 35cm.
"Mormon settlers of San Bernardino." Mormon doctrine and some material on the RLDS church.
CSmH, CU-B, DLC

4042. History of Sanpete and Emery Counties, Utah, with sketches of cities, towns and villages, chronology of important events, records of Indian wars, portraits of prominent persons and biographies of representative citizens. Ogden, W. H. Lever, 1898.
681 [2]p. plates, ports. 24½cm.
Howes L303
CSmH, DLC, ICU, NjP, UHi, UPB, USlC, UU

4043. . . . History of Seneca Co., New York, with illustrations descriptive of its scenery, palatial residences, public buildings . . . and important manufactories from original sketches by artists of the highest ability. . . . Philadelphia, Everts, Ensign & Everts, 1876.
iv [3]–170p. illus., plates (part double), ports., map. 37×30cm.
At head of title: 1786.
Under Fayette Township: "The Mormon prophet — First baptism" includes personal recollections of Joseph Smith by Hon. D. S. Kendig. First baptism according to this source was at Thomas Creek.
Tells of Joseph Smith translating by looking into a hat.
DLC, MB, MiU, OClWHi

4044. History of Tazewell County, Illinois. Together with sketches of its cities, villages and townships; educational, religious, civil, military, and political history; portraits of prominent persons and biographies of representative citizens. History of Illinois . . . Digest of laws. Chicago, Chas. C. Chapman & Co., 1879.
3p.l. [17]–794p. illus., col. map. 24cm.
"The Mormon War," p. 104–118.
USlC

4045. History of the bench and bar of Utah. Salt Lake City, Interstate Press Association, 1913.
221p. illus., ports. 26½cm.
Edited by Charles Carroll Goodwin.
Biography of Brigham Young and others; some famous Utah legal cases including the Reynolds case.
CU, DLC, MiU-L, NjP, UHi, UPB

4046. History of the First Presidency. Lamoni, Ia., Reorganized Church of Jesus Christ of Latter Day Saints [n.d.]
6p. ports. 21cm. (F.S. No. 2)
MoInRC

History of the Mormons . . . *See Chambers, Robert.*

4047. History of the Mormons, or, Latter-day Saints, with an account of their persecutions in Missouri and Illinois, from an authentic source. Whitehaven [Eng.] Printed and Sold by W. Wilson, 1844.
8p. 17½cm.
CtY

History of the Mountain Meadows massacre . . . *See Pacific Art Company, San Francisco.*

4048. A history of the pilgrimage of the Chicago Commercial Club to centers of western commerce. Chicago, R. R. Donnelley & Sons Co., 1901.
3p.l., 9–146p. 18cm.
Excuse concerning non-healing by Brigham Young.
USIC

4049. History of Walworth County, Wisconsin, containing an account of its settlement, growth, development and resources . . . its war record, biographical sketches, portraits of prominent men and early settlers; the whole preceded by a history of Wisconsin . . . and an abstract of its laws and constitution. . . . Chicago, Western Historical Company, 1882.
vii, [19]–967p. illus., plates, ports., maps. 25½×21½cm.
"The Mormon [Strang] church in Spring Prairie," p. 902–903.
DLC, OClWHi

4050. History of Wayne county, New York, with illustrations descriptive of its scenery, palatial residences, public buildings, fine blocks, and important manufactories, from original sketches by artists of the highest ability. Philadelphia, Everts, Ensign and Everts [1877]
216p. illus., plates, ports. 32cm.
Includes material on Mormonism in Wayne County.
UPB

4051. Hittell, John Shertzer. Bancroft's Pacific coast guidebook, by John S. Hittell. San Francisco, A. L. Bancroft and Co., 1882.
270p. illus., fold. maps. 22cm.
Salt Lake City, p. 21–25. Brief mention of Mormonism in Salt Lake City and other Utah towns.
CU–B, DLC, USIC

4052. ———. (same, under title) Hittell's hand-book of Pacific Coast travel. By John S. Hittell. San Francisco, A. L. Bancroft and Co., 1885.
263p. illus., 2 fold. maps. 17½cm.
First published in 1882 as Bancroft's Pacific coast guide book.
Information on Salt Lake City and Mormons with emphasis on a strange religion.
Another edition: 1887. NN
CU–B, USl, WaS

4053. ———. The commerce and industries of the Pacific coast of North America; comprising the rise, progress, products, present condition, and prospects of the useful arts on the western side of our continent, and some account of its resources, with elaborate treatment of manufactures, briefer consideration of commerce, transportation, agriculture, and mining; and mention of leading establishments and prominent men in various departments of business. By John S. Hittell.
819p. illus., plates, 2 double maps. 29½cm.
General information on Utah and Salt Lake City.
Another edition: 2d ed. 1882. CU–B
DLC, NN, OrU, PPL, Wa, WaS, WaT, WaU

4054. Hobart, Chauncey. Recollections of my life; fifty years of itinerancy in the Northwest . . . Red Wing, Minnesota, Red Wing Printing Co., 1885.
409p. port. 20cm.
Lectures against Mormonism in Missouri; some historical notes.
Howes H548
CU–B, DLC, NjP, NN

4055. Hobbs, James. Wild Life in the Far West; personal adventures of a border mountain man. Comprising hunting and trapping adventures with Kit Carson and others; captivity and life among the Comanches; services under Doniphan in the war with Mexico, and in the Mexican War against the French; desperate combats with Apaches, grizzly bears, etc., etc. By Captain James Hobbs, of California. Illustrated with numerous engravings. Published by subscription only. Hartford, Conn., Wiley, Waterman & Eaton; St. Louis, Mo., and Chicago, Ill., F. A. Hitchingson & Company, 1873.
488p. plates, fold. map. 21½cm.
The lynching of nine Mormon mule stealers in retribution to the "Green Meadow massacre," p. 331–333.
UPB, USIC

4056. Hogan, Tilly. With prejudice. By Tilly Hogan. [Rhodesia? 1930?]
[3]–92 [2]p. 24cm.
A garbled, anti-Mormon diatribe.
IWW

4056a. Hodges, Ellen G. E.G.H. Surprise land. A girl's letters from the west. Boston, Cupples, Upham & Co. The Old Corner Bookstore, 1887.
2 p.l., 121 [3]p. 18½cm.
Letter XV tells of her visit to the tabernacle for meeting and impression of Mormonism.
UPB

4056b. Hoge, E. D. . . . John Miles, Plaintiff in error vs. United States, Defendant in error. Error to Supreme Court of Utah. Brief for Plaintiff in error. E. D. Hoge, W. N. Dusenberry, Arthur Brown, for Plaintiff in error. [Washington, D.C.? ca. 1880]
18p. 26½cm.
At head of title: Supreme Court of the United States . . .
A polygamy trial.
USIC

4056c. Holdaway, Lucinda (Haws). Biographical sketch of Lucinda Haws Holdaway. [Provo, ca. 1910]
42p. 14cm.
Poetry, p. 21–36.
USIC

4057. Holland, Rupert Sargent. Historic adventures. Tales from American history. By Rupert S. Holland. Philadelphia, George W. Jacobs and Company, Publishers [c1913]
4p.l. [9]–288p. plates. 22cm.
Chapter VII. "How the Mormons came to settle Utah."
CU–B, USlC

4058. De Hollander. Salt Lake City, Published by Peter and Claus Dee, September 4–October 26, 1907.
7 nos. weekly. 46cm.
Editor: Frank I. Kooyman.
Newspaper for the Dutch members of the church in Salt Lake City.
No copies located.

4059. Hollenbeck, Benjamin W. Zion. A drama . . . By B. W. Hollenbeck . . . O. Clyde, A. D. Ames, 1886.
38p. 19cm. (Ames series of standard and minor drama. No. 192)
A Mormon drama.
NN

4060. Holley, Marietta. The lament of the Mormon wife. A poem by Marietta Holley . . . Hartford, Conn., American Publishing Co., 1880.
[13]l. illus., 3 plates. 25cm.
Poetry concerning the Mormons.
DLC, NjP, NN, UHi, USlC

4061. ———. My wayward pardner; or My trials with Josiah, America, The Widow Bump, and etcetery. by Josiah Allen's wife (Marietta Holley) . . . Illustrations by True W. Williams. Hartford, Conn., American Publishing Company, 1880.
xvi, 490p. illus., plates. 20½cm.
Partially a satire on Mormonism, particularly on polygamy.
Other editions: 1884. NjP, USlC; 1888. NjP
CU, DLC

4062. Hollings, Ernest, *compiler.* Christ vs. Anti-Christ . . . Salt Lake City [193–]
96p. 21cm.
Cover-title.
An anti-semitic appeal to Mormons. Includes some of the *Remarkable visions,* by Orson Pratt.
UU

4063. Hollingsworth, John McHenry. The journal of Lieutenant John McHenry Hollingsworth of the first New York volunteers [Stevenson's regiment] September 1845–August 1849. Being a rental of the voyage of the Susan Drew to California; the arrival of the regiment in 1847; its military movements and adventures during 1847–1848–1849; incidents of daily life, and adventures of the author in the gold mines. San Francisco, California Historical Society, 1923.
vii, [1]l., 61p. front. 26cm.
Reprinted from the *California Historical Society Quarterly,* January, 1923.
Mormons in California, p. 40, 42–43.
CU–B, DLC

4064. Hollister, Ovando James. The boycotters squeal; food results from organizing the Loyal League. Boycotting and other boycotting. A glimpse of the Mormon past — biting the hand that fed them — cruel wrongs and mockery of the gentiles. [Salt Lake City, 1886]
[4]p. 22cm.
Caption-title.
Addressed to "Editor, *Tribune.*"
With this is bound a mounted newspaper clipping, letter to the *Salt Lake Tribune* from O. J. Hollister entitled "The Utah loyal league," dated Jan. 15, 1887.
CU–B

4065. ———. The life of Schuyler Colfax. By O. J. Hollister. New York [etc.] Funk and Wagnall, 1886.
535p. plates, 2 ports., facsim. 22½cm.
Includes his trip to Salt Lake in 1870 and notes on his speech.
CSmH, CU–B, NjP, UHi, USlC, UU

4066. ———. The resources and attractions of the Territory of Utah. Prepared by the Utah Board of Trade. [Omaha, Neb.] Printed at the Omaha Republican Publishing House, 1879.
74p. plates. 23½cm.
"Submitted by the Secretary O. J. Hollister . . . and 15,000 copies ordered printed." — Intro. note.
Mormonism ignored except on final page, under political. An explanation is given that with polygamy legislation in force, a gentile or monogamist legislature would end Mormonism.
CSmH, DLC, MiU, NjP, UHi, USlC, UU

4067. ———. (same) Salt Lake City, Tribune Printing and Publishing Co., 1882.
93p. 23½cm.
CU–B, DLC, MiU, NjP, OO, USl, USlC

———. Supreme Court decision in the Reynolds case. *See Taylor, John.*

4068. ———. To the Committee on Credentials of the National Republican Convention. [Salt Lake City, 1872]
3p. 21½cm.
Protest concerning Mormon representation to the National Convention.
USlC

4069. ———. Words and deeds; the Mormons and temperance — how the lamb roils the stream for the wolf. [Salt Lake City? 1884?]
2p. 21×11cm.
Caption-title.
Reprint of a letter to the *Salt Lake Tribune.*
MH, NN, UHi, UPB, WHi

HOLLY-ROAD

4070. The Holly-road boomerang. Liverpool, 1906.
v. 26cm.
Bulletin issued from 10 Holly-road for local members of the church. Dittoed paper with photographs pasted into the newspaper.
USIC March, 1906, V. 1 #2

4071. Hollywood Stake herald. November, 1927–January, 1929.
V. 1 (#1–15) illus., ports. 28cm.
Organ of the Church of Jesus Christ of Latter-day Saints. Hollywood Stake.
CU–B #12, 14–15; USIC #9–15

4072. Holm, Jak. Hvad er aarsagen til at saa mange Danske gaa over til Mormonismen? Med en kort fremstilling af denne sekts historie og falske laerdomme . . . Aalborg, M. A. Schultz, 1882.
1p.l., 29p. 18½cm.
Title in English: What is the reason why so many Danes go over to Mormonism?
CtY

4073. Holmes, Reed M. Church, school and evangelism. On teaching and educating the converts so as to keep them in the church. Independence, Mo., Reorganized Church of Jesus Christ of Latter Day Saints [n.d.]
15p. 21cm.
USIC

4074. Homans, J. E. The case against Mormonism; a plain discussion and analysis of the stock allegations and arguments against the Church of Jesus Christ of Latter-day saints and its founder, Joseph Smith, with the intention of determining their evidential value, also their actual significance to the claims made for the system of teaching and practice, popularly known as "Mormonism." By Robert C. Webb [*pseud.*] non"Mormon" . . . New York, L. L. Walton, 1915.
1p.l., 157p. illus. 21½cm.
A criticism of: A Fourfold test of Mormonism, by H. C. Sheldon.
A defense of Mormonism by a non-Mormon.
DLC, ICN, MH, NjP, NN, ULA, UPB, USl, USIC, UU, WHi

4075. ———. The real Mormonism; a candid analysis of an interesting but much misunderstood subject in history, life and thought, by Robert C. Webb [*pseud.*] . . . New York, Sturgis and Walton Company, 1916.
2p.l., iii–xii, 463p. 21½cm.
CU, DLC, MoInRC, NjP, NN, UHi, UPB, USl, USIC, UU, WHi

4076. The Home Circle; a monthly magazine devoted to home improvement. Provo, Published by the Home Circle Company, November, 1887–June, 1888.
1v. (6 nos. in 130p.) monthly. 24cm.
Caption-title: The home circle. Love one another.
Mormon articles; Mormon oriented.
CtY

Homespun [*pseud.*] *See Gates, Susa Young.*

4077. Hood, Edmund Lyman. The New West Education Commission 1880–1893 [by] Rev. E. Lyman Hood . . . Jacksonville, Fla., The H. & W.B. Drew Company, 1905.
151p. port. 20½cm.
The commission and its anti-Mormon activities.
CU, DLC, NN

4078. Hood, Edwin Paxton. The lamps of the temple. Crayon sketches of the men of the modern pulpit. Third ed., rev. and greatly enl. London, John Snow, 1856.
iv [2]l., 597p. 19½cm.
"The lamps of the Temple of Mudfog." A satirical history of the Mormon church. The allegory is soon dropped and the rest is very anti-Mormon.
USIC

4079. Hook, R. Through dust and foam; or, Travels, sight-seeing, and adventure by land and sea in the far West and far East, By R. and G. D. Hook. Hartford, Conn. Columbian Book Company, 1876.
xvi, 456p. illus. 22½cm.
Chapter V. A visit to Salt Lake City and the tabernacle, V.5, p. 70–72.
CU–B, DLC, NjP, UHi, UPB

4080. Hooper, William Henry. Extension of boundaries. Speech of Hon. William H. Hooper, of Utah, delivered in the House of Representatives, February 25, 1869. Washington, F. & J. Rives & G. A. Bailey, Printers, 1869.
14p. 23cm.
Utah statehood.
CSmH, CtY, CU–B, DHU, DLC, MH, MoInRC, NN, PHi, USl, USIC

4081. ———. Speech of Hon. W. H. Hooper, of Utah, Delivered in the House of Representatives, February 25, 1869. [Salt Lake City] 1869.
4p. 40cm.
At head of title: The Deseret News.
The speech appears to have been included in the April 7, 1869 issue of the *Deseret News.*
UPB, USIC

4082. ———. The Utah bill. Plea for religious liberty. Speech of Hon. W. H. Hooper of Utah, delivered in the House of Representatives, March 23, 1870. Washington, Gibson Brothers, Printers, 1870.
31p. 21½cm.
Defense of the right to practice polygamy.
CtY, DHU, DLC, MH, ULA, USIC, WHi

4083. ———. (same) Washington, Gibson Brothers, Printers, 1870.
32p. 22cm.
Variant printings.
UPB, USIC

4084. ———. (same) Delivered in the House of Representatives, March 23, 1870, together with the remonstrance of the citizens of Salt Lake City, in mass meeting, held March 31, 1870, to the Senate of the United States. Washington, Gibson brothers, Printers, 1870.
40p. 22½cm.
Sabin 32880
CSmH, CtY, CU-B, DLC, NjP, NN, UHi, USl, USlC, WHi

4085. ———. Vindication of the people of Utah. Remarks of Hon. William H. Hooper of Utah in the House of Representatives, January 29, 1873, in reply to the charges of Hon. W. H. Clagett of Montana, on the 28th and 29th of January, 1873. [Washington, Printed at the Congressional Globe Office, 1873?]
16p. 23cm.
A plea for understanding.
CU-B, ICN, UU

4086. ———. (same) Remarks of Hon. W. H. Hooper of Utah in reply to the charges of Hon. W. H. Clagett, of Montana, on the 28th and 29th of January, 1873, which are printed herewith; delivered in the House of Representatives, January 29, 1873. Washington, F. and J. Rives, 1873.
16p. 23cm.
Cover-title.
CSmH, ICN, NN, PPL, USlC

4087. Hopkins, Albert J. Senator Reed Smoot and the Mormon Church. Speech of Hon. Albert J. Hopkins, of Illinois, in the Senate of the United States, Friday, January 11, 1907. Washington, 1907.
36p. 23cm.
Cover-title.
CU-B, NjP, UHi, USlC

4088. Hopkins, John Castell. Canada: an encyclopedia of the country; the Canadian Dominion considered in its historic relations, its natural resources, its material progress and its national development, by a corps of eminent writers and specialists . . . Ed. by J. Castell Hopkins . . . Toronto, Linscott Pub. Co. [1898–1900]
6v. illus., plates, ports., maps. 28½cm.
Includes material on Mormonism in Canada, V.4.
CU, DLC, UPB

4089. Horne, Alice Merrill. Devotees and their shrines; a hand book of Utah art, by Alice Merrill Horne. Salt Lake City, The Deseret News, 1914.
3p.l., 9–158 [2]p. illus., plates. 24½cm.
Mormon art and architecture.
DLC, NjP, UHi, ULA, UPB, USl, USlC, UU

4090. Horsley, Ernest S. Fifty years ago this week at and around Price. [Price, Utah? 1929]
[8]p. illus., plates. 22½cm.
Brief history of Price and biographies of some of its founders.
UPB

4091. Horton, Emily (McCowen). Our family, with a glimpse of their pioneer life. [n.p.] 1922.
46p. 18cm.
Trip through Utah on the way to California. Briefly mentions the Mountain Meadows massacre.
ICN

Horton, Thomas. A true history of the rise of the Church . . . *See Adams, George J.*

4092. Hoskins, Nathan. Notes upon the western country. Contained within the states of Ohio, Indiana, Illinois, and the Territory of Michigan: taken on a tour through that country in the summer of 1832. By Nathan Hoskins, jr. . . . Greenfield [Mass.] Printed by J. P. Fogg, 1833.
108p. 20cm.
Brief account of Mormonism in Ohio.
Howes H656, Sabin 33097
DLC, NN

4093. Hougard, A. Dedicatory services of the North Ward Chapel, held Sunday, November 5, 1911. Bishop N. R. Peterson of the North Ward of Manti presiding. Manti, Utah [n.d.]
9p. 28cm.
Mimeographed.
UPB

4094. Hough, Emerson. The covered wagon. New York, D. Appleton and Co., 1922.
378[1]p. front. 19½cm.
Fiction with mention of Mormons on p. 26, 31, 35, 108, 127, 132–133, 137, 146, 150, 185, 188, 190, 280, 298, 355.
DLC, USlC

4095. ———. The Way to the West and the lives of three early Americans. Boone-Crockett-Carson. By Emerson Hough . . . With illustrations by Frederic Remington. Indianapolis, The Bobbs-Merrill Company, Publishers [c1903]
4p.l., 446p. illus. 19cm.
The Mormons, p. 296–298. Fort Bridger and the Mormon war.
USlC

4096. House, John Ford. Utah contested election case — Cannon vs. Campbell; speech of Hon. John F. House, of Tennessee, in the House of Representatives, April 18, 1882. Washington, 1882.
15p. 23cm.
Cover-title.
CSmH, CU-B, UHi, USlC

4097. House of the Lord. Historical and descriptive sketch of the Salt Lake Temple. From April 6, 1853, to April 6, 1893. — Complete guide to interior, and explanatory notes. Other temples of the Saints. Also the Dedicatory Prayer. Salt Lake City, Geo. G. Cannon & Sons Co., 1893.
36p. illus. 22cm.
NN, UPB, USlC

HOUSE

4098. ———. (same) Salt Lake City, Geo. Q. Cannon & Sons Co., 1897.
36p. illus. 22cm.
USlC has variant without title page.
NN, UPB

4099. Houston, Edwin James. The jaws of death; or, In and around the cañons of the Colorado, by Prof. Edwin J. Houston . . . Illustrated by H. Weston Taylor. Philadelphia, Boston [etc.] The Griffith and Rowland Press [1911]
395p. illus., plates, map. 20cm.
Story of the release of father and grandfather from clutches of the Mormons and Joseph Smith in Utah.
DLC, USl

4100. Hoving, Lucie. The x-rays turned on Mormonism. By Lucie Hoving. Logan, 1901.
1p.l., ii, 83p. 19cm.
Printed by Vredevoogd & Co., Groningen, Holland.
DLC, ICN, MH, USlC, WHi

4101. How Polygamy is Dying. Salt Lake City, Tribune Print, 1884.
Broadside. 19×10cm.
A reprint from the *Salt Lake Tribune*, October 17, 1887.
Undated edition at NjP.
USlC

Howard, Jonathan E. Life's real romance. *See Harvey, R. A. N.*

Howard, Mary J. Sketch of the life and experiences . . . *See Spencer, Hiram Theron.*

4102. Howard *of Glossop,* **Winefred Mary (De Lisle)** *baroness.* Journal of a tour in the United States, Canada and Mexico by Winefred, Lady Howard of Glossop. London, Sampson Low, Marston, and Co., Ltd., 1897.
xii, 355p. illus., plates. 19½cm.
Trip in 1895. A few pages describe Utah; mention of polygamy, secret temple rites and unprepared speakers, p. 47–53.
DLC, UHi, USlC, UU

4103. Howe, Eber D. Autobiography and recollections of a pioneer printer. By Eber D. Howe. Painesville, Ohio, Telegraph Steam Printing House, 1878.
59p. 22½cm.
Cover-title.
Printed in double columns.
Recollections of Mormons. Claims that his book was the basis of all anti-Mormon literature for 40 years. Mormons in Geauga County; history of the movement.
Howes H716
ICN, NN, OClWhi, OO

4104. ———. Mormonism unvailed: or, A faithful account of that singular imposition and delusion, from its rise to the present time. With sketches of the characters of its propagators, and a full detail of the manner in which the famous Golden Bible was brought before the world. To which are added, inquiries into the probability that the historical part of the said Bible was written by one Solomon Spalding [sic], more than twenty years ago, and by him intended to have been published as a romance. By E. D. Howe. Painesville [O.] Printed and Published by the author, 1834.
ix [11]–290 (i.e. 292)p. front. 18½cm.
P. 175–176 appears twice in the numbering.
Howes H717, Sabin 33290
CSmH, CtY, CU–B, DLC, ICN, NjP, UHi, UPB, USlC, WHi

4105. ———. (same, under title) History of Mormonism; or, a faithful account of that singular imposition and delusion, with sketches of the characters of its propagators, to which are added inquiries into the probability that the historical part of the Golden Bible was written by one Solomon Spalding [sic] . . . Painesville [O.] The author, 1840.
ix [11]–290 (i.e. 292)p. front. 18½cm.
Howes H717
CtY, CU–B, NN, OClWhi, UHi, ULA UPB, USl, USlC, ViU

4106. ———. (same) Painesville [O.] The author, 1840.
ix [11] 291 (i.e. 293)p. front. 18½cm.
Last leaf replaced of the text above, and printed on p. 289, 290, 291 with different type and paper.
CU–B

4107. Howe, Edgar Watson. Plain people. New York, Dodd, Mead & Co., 1929.
3p.l., 317p. port. 22cm.
While in Salt Lake City, heard Mormons preach polygamy, etc. Found nothing unusual about Mormons except polygamy. Worked on *Deseret News*, and met Brigham Young there.
DLC, NjP, UPB, USlC

Howe, Henry. All the western states. *See Barber, J. W.*

4108. ———. The great West: containing narratives of the most important and interesting events in western history — remarkable individual adventures — sketches of frontier life — descriptions of natural curiosities: to which is appended historical and descriptive sketches of Oregon, New Mexico, Texas, Minnesota, Utah, California, Washington, Nebraska, Kansas, etc., etc., etc. By Henry Howe . . . Enlarged ed. New York, Published by Geo. F. Tuttle; Cincinnati, Published by Henry Howe, 1858.
xi, 15–576p. illus., col. plates, maps. 22½cm.
"Utah," p. 460–487 contains an account of the Mormon beliefs, and is sympathetic on the hardships of the pioneers.
UPB

4109. ———. Historical collections of Ohio; containing a collection of the most interesting facts, traditions, biographical sketches, anecdotes, etc., relating to its general and local history: with descriptions of its counties, principal towns and villages. Illustrated by 177 engravings . . . By Henry Howe. Cincinnati, Derby, Bradley & Co., 1847.
581 [1]p. illus., plates, fold. map. 23cm.
The Mormons in Lake County, Ohio, p. 282–288.
Various editions: 1848–1908.
Howes H720, Sabin B 33299
DLC, ULA, UPB, USlC

4110. ———. Historical collections of the great West: containing narratives of the most important and interesting events in western history . . . to which is appended historical and descriptive sketches of Oregon, New Mexico, Texas, Minnesota, Utah and California. By Henry Howe . . . Cincinnati, Published by H. Howe, 1851.
2v. in 1. 32 plates, maps. 24cm.
Sketch of Utah, V.2.
Various editions: 1851–1873.
Howes H721, Sabin BA. 33300
DLC, MB, NjP, OCl, OClWHi, OFH, WaU

4110a. How polygamy is dying. Salt Lake City, Tribune Print, 1884.
Broadside. 24cm.
NjP

4111. Howe, Mark Anthony De Wolfe. The Life and labors of Bishop Hare, Apostle to the Sioux by M. A. De Wolfe. New York, Sturgis & Walton Company, 1911.
6p.l., 3–417p. plates, ports. 22½cm.
Anglican bishop's impression of Mormonism.
Other editions: New York, 1912. CU, NjPT; New York, 1913. USlC; New York, 1914. UPB
CtY, NN, USlC

4112. Howell, J. M., *editor.* History of Decatur County, Iowa, and its people; Prof. J. M. Howell and Heman C. Smith, supervising editors . . . Chicago, The S. J. Clarke Publishing Company, 1915.
2v. plates, ports. 27cm.
Much Mormon and RLDS church material; Lamoni being in this county.
CSmH, DLC, IaHa, IaHi, MoInRC, MWA, NN

4113. Howlett, W. J. Life of the Right Reverend Joseph P. Marchebeuf, D. D. Pioneer priest of Ohio, Pioneer priest of New Mexico, Pioneer priest of Colorado, Vicar Apostolic of Colorado and Utah, and first Bishop of Denver. By the Rev. W. J. Howlett. Pueblo, Colorado [The Franklin Press] 1908.
419p. ports. 23½cm.
Brief account of the late entry of the Catholics into Utah due to Mormon influence.
USlC

4114. Hoyer, Margaret, *trans.* Begebenheiten aus der Kirchengeschichte. Für die erste Mittelklasse. Aus dem Englischen übersetzt von M. Hoyer. Basel, Herausgegeben von Fred Tadje, Präsident der Schweizerischen und Deutschen Mission der Kirche Jesu Christi der Heiligen der Letzten Tage, 1924.
2p.l. [7]–63p. 21cm.
Outlines for the study of "Essentials in Church History," by J. F. Smith.
Title in English: Events in Church history.
USlC

4115. ———. Die göttliche Mission des Heilandes. Aus dem Englischen übersetzt von Mar. Hoyer. Basel, Herausgegeben von Fred Tadje. Präsident der Schweizerischen und Deutschen Mission der Kirche Jesu Christi der Heiligen der Letzten Tage [1924?]
64p. 20½cm.
Title in English: The divine mission of the Savior.
USlC

4116. ———. Über weibliche Tugenden und Fähigkeiten. Basel, Schweizerisch-Deutschen Mission der Kirche Jesu Christi der Heiligen der Letzten Tage, 1924.
77p. 20cm.
Title in English: About womanly virtues and abilities.
UPB

4117. ———. Vorbildliche Frauen der Bibel, Der Welt- und Literaturgeschichte und der Kirche. Basel, Herausgegeben von der Deutsch-Österreichischen . . . [1926]
122 [1]p. 20½cm.
Title in English: Representative Women of the Bible.
UU

4118. ———. Weibliche Berufe und die Grundlagen zu deren Erfolg. Bearbeitet von Marg. Hoyer. Basel, Herausgegeben von der Deutsch-Oesterreichischen und Schweizerrisch-Deutschen Mission der Kirche Jesu Christi der Heiligen der Letzten Tage. [1926?]
1p.l., 111 [1]p. 20½cm.
Title in English: Vocations for women and the principles of their success.
USlC

4119. Hubbard, Elbert. A little journey to Utah and investment opportunities I found there. By Elbert Hubbard. New York. The Roycrofters [c1915]
32p. plates. 20½cm.
Descriptions of Salt Lake and Ogden with many Mormon references.
USlC

4120. Hübner, Joseph Alexander *graf* **von.** Promenade autour du monde, 1871, par m. le baron de Hübner . . . 2. éd. Paris, Hachette et Cie, 1873.
Description of Salt Lake City and the Mormons during trip.

Title in English: A ramble round the world.
Various editions in several languages.
DLC, NjP

4121. ———. (same, in English) A ramble round the world, 1871, By le baron de Hübner, translated by Lady Herbert. London, Macmillan and Co., 1874.
2v. 22½cm.
"Salt Lake City." He gives his impressions of the Mormons and the gentiles. Talks with Brigham Young, and with anti-Mormons.
NjP, NN, UHi, USlC

4122. Hudgens, J. W. The Reorganization. What is it? From whence did it come? [Hiawatha, Kansas, The Harrington Printing Co., 1901]
47p. 23cm.
A work to disprove the claims of the Reorganization.
UPB

4123. Hudson, Mary Worrell (Smith) "*Mrs.* J. K. Hudson." Esther the gentile, by Mrs. Mary W. Hudson. Topeka, Kan., G. W. Crane & Co., Printers, 1888.
2p.l., 167p. 22½cm.
Fiction concerning Mormonism.
CU-B, DLC, NN, UHi, USl, USlC, WHi

4124. Hudson, T. S. A scamper through America; or, Fifteen thousand miles of ocean and continent in sixty days. By T. S. Hudson. London, Griffith and Farran, New York, E. P. Dutton and Co., 1882.
xxii, 289 [1]p. map. 19½cm.
A trip through the United States with stopover in Salt Lake City; description of Mormons and their leaders.
CU-B, DLC, NN, PSC, UPB, USlC, UU

4125. Hughes, J. Vaughan. Seventy years of life in the Victorian Era, embracing a travelling record in Australia, New Zealand and America, &c. By a physician. London, T. Fisher Unwin, 1893.
2p.l., 283p. port. 19½cm.
Trip to Salt Lake City, p. 233–238.
Chiefly tourist information.
USlC

4126. Hughes, John Taylor. Doniphan's expedition; containing an account of the conquest of New Mexico; General Kearney's overland expedition to California; Doniphan's campaign against the Navajos; his unparalleled march upon Chihuahua and Durango; and the operations of General Price at Santa Fe: with a sketch of the life of Col. Doniphan ... By John T. Hughes ... Cincinnati, U. P. James [1847]
viii, 9–144p. illus., plans. 23½cm.
Material on the Mormon Battalion.
Other editions: Cincinnati, J. A. & U. P. James, 1848. NjP; (same) 1849, 1850. DLC; Topeka, Kan., 1907. DLC, UPB; Washington, Govt. Print. Off., 1914. DLC
W-C 134
CtY, CU-B, DLC, ICN, NjP, NN, USlC, ViU, WHi

4127. Hughes, Marion. Oklahoma Charley. By Marion Hughes. St. Louis, Mo., John P. Wagner & Co. [c1910]
2p.l., 5–159p. 18½cm.
Fiction. Mormon wives flee drunken husbands, and one spends the winter with "Charley" before he boots her out.
USlC

4128. Hughes, T. W. The Mormons as I have found them. Liverpool, Mission Headquarters [n.d.]
4p. 22cm.
Missionary tract.
UPB, USlC

4129. Huhl, Charles W. The way of peace, by Chas. W. Huhl. Salt Lake City, Liberty Press [c1915]
32p. 17cm.
Mormon tract on salvation.
USlC

4130. De Huisvriend. Ogden, Utah [Salt Lake City] 1905–[1914?]
v. irregular.
Editor: William James DeBray.
Title in English: The house friend.
"No copies extant; even DeBray lost his."—Mulder.

4131. Huling, Franklin G. What is the difference between Mormonism and Biblical Christianity? A kindly word of distinction, by Franklin G. Huling, M.A. New York, The Christian Alliance Publishing Company [c1927]
38p. 19cm.
Bibliography, p. 37–38.
DLC, IWW, WHi

4132. Humason, William Lawrence. From the Atlantic surf to the Golden Gate. First trip on the great Pacific Railroad. Two days and nights among the Mormons, with scenes and incidents. By W. L. Humason. Hartford, Press of Wm. C. Hutchings, 1869.
56p. 25cm.
Howes H 785, Sabin 33685
CMC, CSmH, CtY, CU-B, DLC, ICN, NjP, NN, UHi, ULA, UPB, USlC, WHi

4133. Hume, Hugo. The superior American religions. Los Angeles, The Libertarian Pub. Co., 1928.
2p.l., 5–170p. 20cm.
Includes a satirical account of the birth of Mormonism.
NjP, UU

4134. Humphrey, Grace. Illinois, the story of the prairie state, by Grace Humphrey, illustrated with photographs. Indianapolis, The Bobbs-Merrill Company [c1917]
5p.l., 267p. plates, ports. 19½cm.

Chapter XVII entitled "Religion mixed with politics," deals with Mormons in Illinois from 1839 until their expulsion, p. 134–144, and other brief notes. References to Icarians taking over the Nauvoo Temple and using it as a dining hall, p. 232.
DLC, MoInRC, UHi, UPB

4135. Hunt, Charles Joseph. The Book of Mormon. Its divine origin — peopling of America centuries before Columbus — Origin of the American Indian — Organization of the Church of Christ in 1830. By Elder C. J. Hunt, Deloit, Iowa. [Lamoni, Ia., Herald Publishing House, n.d.]
[4]p. 20½cm.
CtY

4136. ———. Chronicles by Saint Charles, Bishop of the Gallands Grove, Iowa District of the Reorganized Church of Jesus Christ of Latter Day Saints. Dow City, Ia., Enterprise Print., 1910.
8p. 20cm.
The RLDS principle of stewardship.
MoInRC

4137. ———. Holiday greetings to the members of the Holden Stake by the Stake Bishopric. [n.p., n.d.]
[3]p. illus. 21cm. (Bulletin. No. 5)
MoInRC

4138. ———. The opinions of sixty-five leading ministers and bible commentators on Isaiah 29:11–24 and Ezekiel 37:15–20. Lamoni, Ia., Published by the Reorganized Church of Jesus Christ of Latter Day Saints, 1900.
56p. 19cm.
Book of Mormon references.
MoInRC, UPB, USIC

4139. ———. Our topical booklet, ten essays on temporalities by ten church workers for the Dept. of the Bishopric of the Gallands Grove, Iowa District. [Dow City, Ia., Dow City Enterprise Print., 1911]
22p. 21cm.
RLDS church doctrine of stewardship.
MoInRC

4140. ———. Two world wide important truths only half told by Utah Mormon dignitaries. [n.p., n.d.]
[1]p. 35cm.
Mimeographed.
Truth of the RLDS church.
MoInRC

4141. Hunt, D. G. The right relation of Church and state, by the Right Reverend D. G. Hunt and Anthony W. Ivins. Independence, Mo., Press of Zion's Printing and Publishing Co., 1926.
21p. 20cm.
Speech of D. G. Hunt and a reply by Anthony W. Ivins.
UPB, USIC

4142. Hunt, James Henry. Mormonism; embracing the origin, rise and progress of the sect, with an examination of the Book of Mormon, also their troubles in Missouri, and final expulsion from the state . . . With an appendix, giving an account of the late disturbances in Illinois which resulted in the death of Joseph and Hyrum Smith, by G. W. Westbrook. St. Louis, Printed by Ustick and Davies, 1844.
v. [5]–304 [3]–36 [1]p. 19cm.
Howes H 805, Sabin 50755
CSmH, CtY, CU-B, ICN, IHi, MH, MoInRC, MoK, NN, UPB, USl, UU

4143. ———. (same, under title) A history of the Mormon War: with a prefix embracing the rise, progress, and peculiar tenets of Mormon doctrine; with an examination of the Book of Mormon. Also the trial of the prophet Joe Smith and his brethren for high treason, murder, &c., with the motions of the counsel and decisions of the court in each case, together with an account of the attempted assassination of ex-governor Boggs. St. Louis, Printed by Ustick & Davies, 1844.
304 [1]p. 19cm.
Includes leaf of errata.
Howes H805
CSmH, CtY, CU, ICHi, IHi, MoHi, NN, UHi, UPB

4143a. Hunt, Mark. A book of references to prove the gospel in its fullness, the ushering in of the dispensation of the fullness of times, and the latter-day glory. Ogden, Utah, Printed at the Herald Book and Job Office, 1881.
16p. 15cm.
USIC

4144. Hunter, George. Reminiscences of an old timer: a recital of the actual events, incidents, trails, hardships, vicissitudes, adventures, perils & escapes of a pioneer, hunter, miner, and scout of the Pacific northwest . . . by Colonel George Hunter. San Francisco, H. S. Crocker and Company, 1887.
1p.l., xxv, 454p. port., plates. 20½cm.
Recuperates at a Mormon home during illness. Impressions of Mormonism.
Another edition: 4th ed. Battle Creek Mich., Review & Herald, 1888. CtY
Howes H811
CtY, CU-B, DLC, NjP

4145. Huntingdon, P. P. A few words to a Latter Day Saint. By P. P. Huntingdon, Printed and Sold by R. Edis [1851?]
12p. 18cm.
A rebuttal to Lorenzo Snow's *Only Way to be saved.*
MH

4146. Huntington, Dimick Baker. Vocabulary of the Utah and Sho-sho-ne or Snake dialects, with Indian legends and traditions. Including a brief account of the life and death of Wah-ker, the Indian land pirate.

By D. B. Huntington, Indian interpreter.
Third edition — revised and enlarged. Salt Lake City, Printed at the Salt Lake Herald Office, 1872.
32p. 15½cm.
"The tradition of the Utah Indians in relation to the creation of the world" is an attempt to show Christian background of Indians in order to prove the claim of the *Book of Mormon*, p. 24–26.
First published in 1854. No copies located.
CSmH, CtY, ICN, MWA, NjP, UHi, UPB, USlC

4146a. Huntington, S. G. Mormonism and the Lord's day. Elder Brigham H. Roberts makes a confession. Sabbatarians have the advantage. No Bible authority for sanctification of Sunday. Mormons must flee for refuge behind modern prophet. Other churches embarrassed. A review by Pastor S. G. Huntington. Salt Lake City, Utah Tract and Bible Society [n.d.]
16p. 17½cm.
USlC

4147. Hunton & Chandler, *law firm.* In the matter of Senate bill 10, Report No. 2735, In the House of Representatives, January 12, 1886. [Salt Lake City? 1886]
15p. 22cm.
UPB, USlC

4148. Huntsman, Orson Welcome. A brief history of Shoal Creek, Hebron and Enterprise from 1862–1922, by Orson W. Huntsman . . . St. George, Utah, Published in connection with the History Department of the Dixie College, 1929.
[26]p. 16½cm.
History of southern Utah settlements.
UHi, UPB, USlC

4149. Huret, Jules. . . . En Amerique. De San Francisco au Canada (avec un index analytique de l' ouvrage) 9. mille. Paris, Bibliothique Charpentier, 1905.
2p.l., 564p. 19cm.
"Le Lac Sale; Les Mormons." Trip to Salt Lake City, with a detailed description of the Mormons and Mormon doctrine.
Title in English: In America.
Other editions: Paris, E. Fasquelle, 1904. NJP; 1905. DLC; 1907. UPB; 1909. CU-B, NjP; 1921. UPB
DLC, WaS

Hurlbut, *Doctor* **Philastus.** Mormonism unvailed. *See Howe, Eber D.*
"D. P. Hurlbut . . . wrote a bitter assault on the Latter-day Saints in 1836, entitled "Mormonism unvailed," which was published in the name of, or by E. D. Howe, of Painesville, Ohio, c.f. pref. Spaulding, Solomon. The *Manuscript found.* Also *The Mormon point of view.* V.1 #1, p. 89–90.

4150. Hurst, John Fletcher. Short history of the church in the United States, A.D. 1492–1890. New York, Chautauqua Press, 1890.
iv, 132p. 17½cm.
Pt. II, Chap. 12. The Mormon abomination.
NjPT, UPB, USlC

4151. Hutchins, James. An earnest appeal for justice. By James Hutchins. Black River Falls, Wis., Published by the author, 1876.
62p. 20½cm.
Cover-title.
Justice for the Mormons.
Howes H843, Morgan
CSmH, CtY, NN, USlC

4152. ———. The messenger, a timely warning, to a thoughtless world. [Independence, Mo., 1879?]
23p. 20cm.
Signed: James Hutchins, Independence, Mo., 1879.
Morgan
NN, UPB, USlC

4153. ———. The path to eternal life. A desertation [sic] by James Hutchens [sic] He who would be wise in his day will carefully read these pages. Independence, Mo., 1881.
13p. 21cm.
MiMtpT, USlC

4154. ———. Outline sketch of the travels of James Hutchins, written by himself. [Black River Falls, Wis.? 1871]
123p. 20cm.
Cover-title.
A follower of J. J. Strang visited Salt Lake to "preach the gospel of life and salvation unto them and show them their error." Discusses Mormonism and refutes it. He was denied use of the tabernacle.
James Jesse Strang's claim to authority.
Howes H844, Morgan
CtY, ViU

4155. ———. Truth developed and falsehood shown. [Black River Falls, Wis.? 1881?]
16p. 21½cm.
In double columns.
Signed: James Hutchins, February 27th, 1881.
P. 6 has pasted-in overlay.
The apostasy of Mormon church and exhortations to Mormons.
Morgan
USlC

4156. Hutchins, Wells Aleck. . . . Mutual irrigation companies in Utah . . . Logan, Utah, Utah Agricultural Experiment Station, 1927.
2p.l. [5]–51p. 23cm. (Utah Experiment Station Bulletin. No. 199)
Early irrigation work by the Mormon church.
CSmH, ULA, UPB

4157. Huxley, Thomas H. Science and Christian tradition. Essays by Thomas H. Huxley. New York, D. Appleton and Co., 1898.
xxxiv, 419p. 19½cm.
"Mormons" p. [257]–259.
USlC

4158. Hvem är lyckligast? [Salt Lake City, Korrespondenten, 1893?]
4p. 14cm.
Title in English: Who are the happiest?
UPB

4159. Hvezdika. Prague, Czechoslovakia, 1929–
v. monthly. 28cm.
Official organ of the Czechoslovakian Mission. Ran for about 10 volumes.
Title in English: The Star.
UPB V. 1 inc., 4, 5 inc.; USlC V. 2–10

4159a. Hyde, A. B. The story of Methodism: tracing the rise and progress of that wonderful religious movement, which, like the Gulf stream, has given warmth to wide waters and verdure to many lands; and giving an account of its various influences and institutions of to-day. Springfield, Mass., Willey & Co., 1886 [c1887]
469p. illus. 22½cm.
Mormons, p. 224–225.
USlC

4160. Hyde, Charles S. Uiteengetting van bijbensche beginselen door Charles S. Hyde. Rotterdam, Uitgegeven door de Nederl. Zending [n.d.]
31p. 16cm.
Title in English: A collection of Biblical principles.
Variant printings.
USlC

4161. Hyde, John. Modern Christianity. A dialogue between a Baptist and an infidel. [Charlotte, Mich., J. V. Johnson and Co., 18 - -]
4p. 24cm.
Unsigned reprint of an article originally appearing in the *Millennial Star*, V. xii, p. 4–9. January 1, 1850.
Dialogue in which a Mormon explains the truth of Joseph Smith.
NN, UHi

4162. ———. (same) Charlotte, Mich., J. V. Johnson & Co. [n.d.]
8p. 21cm.
NN

4163. ———. (same) [Boyne, Mich.? 1884?]
10p. 20½cm.
Caption-title.
In double columns.
Notes and comments by Wingfield Watson.
Morgan
CtY, UHi, WBuC, WHi

4164. ———. Mormonism: its leaders and designs. By John Hyde, jun. Formerly a Mormon Elder, and resident of Salt Lake City . . . New York, W. P. Fetridge & Company, 1857.
xii [13]–355p. illus., plates, ports. 18½cm.
Sabin 34124
CSmH, CtY, CU, DLC, ICN, MH, MoInRC, NjPT, NN, UHi, ULA, UPB, USl, USlC, WHi

4165. ———. (same) 2d ed. New York, W. P. Fetridge & Company, 1857.
xii [13]–355p. illus., plates, ports. 19½cm.
Sabin 34124
CSmH, DLC, ICHi, IWW, NjP, OClWHi, PPPrHi, ViU

4165a. Hyde, Orson. Circular. Liverpool, 1846.
Broadside. 21×13cm.
Dated: Oct. 3, 1846.
Signed: Orson Hyde and John Taylor.
Tells of their appointment to regulate and set in order the Church in England and calls a conference to be held in Manchester. It also states that Parley P. Pratt is expected soon.
USlC

4166. ———. . . . "He that hath ears to hear, let him hear what the Spirit saith unto the Churches." Printed in Nauvoo, March 14, 1846.
Broadside. 26×19cm.
Caption-title.
In double columns.
A revelation against James J. Strang and in favor of westward immigration.
USlC

4167. ———. (same) [Printed in Nauvoo, March 14, 1846]
Broadside, folded to [4]p. 26×19cm.
On p. [2] is a letter from Orson Hyde to "Brother Sanger" claiming the authorship of the revelation. p. [3, 4] are blank.
Originally printed on the right hand half of one side of a sheet of paper, folded to make a four page folder.
CtY

4168. ———. A Prophetic Warning To all the Churches, of every sect and denomination, and to every Individual into whose hands it may fall. By O. Hyde, Preacher of the Gospel, and Citizen of the United States. [Dated at end: Toronto, August, 1836]
Broadside. 46½×30cm.
In three columns.
An early version of his *A timely warning.*
MoInRC

HYDE, O.

4169. ———. Ein Ruf aus der Wüste. Eine Stimme aus dem Schoose der Erde. Kurzer Ueberblick des Ursprungs und der Lehre der Kirche "Jesus Christ of Latter-day Saints," gekannt von manchen unter der Benennung "Die Mormonen" Von Orson Hyde, Priester dieser Kirche. Frankfurt, 1842.
6p.l. [13]–115p. 18cm.
First Mormon imprint in a foreign language.
Title in English: A cry out of the wilderness.
H. H. Bancroft lists a publication of this at Rotterdam, Holland, dated, June 24, 1841.
USlC

4170. ———. Speech of Elder Orson Hyde delivered before the High Priests Quorum in Nauvoo, April 27th, 1845, upon the course and conduct of Mr. Sidney Rigdon, and upon the merits of his claims to the presidency of the Church of Jesus Christ of Latter-day Saints. City of Joseph [Nauvoo] Printed by John Taylor, 1845.
36p. 17½cm.
Dated: Rotterdam, June 24, 1841.
Byrd 963
MoInRC, NN, USlC

4171. ———. (same) Liverpool, Printed by Janes and Woodburn, 1845.
36p. 19cm.
CSmH, MH, NN, USlC

4172. ———. A timely warning to the people of England of every sect and denomination, and to every individual into whose hands it may fall, by an Elder of the Church of Latter Day Saints. Manchester, Reprinted by W. R. Thomas [1840?]
Broadside. 40×37cm.
Signed: Preston, 1837; Dated May 4, 1839.
USlC

4173. ———. (same) Manchester, Reprinted by W. R. Thomas [1840]
Broadside. 40×37cm.
Signed: August 22, 1840. Different border from above.
UPB, USlC

4174. ———. (same) (Late from America) Preston, 19th August, 1837. [Oxford-hill, A. Charlwood, 1840]
8p. 20½cm.
Caption-title.
Sabin 95839
MH, USlC

4174a. ———. To the saints scattered abroad — greeting. [n.p., 1848]
Broadside. 25×21cm.
An answer to a pamphlet written by Lyman Wight concerning his claims of leadership. Included is an explanation of the Law of Consecration as taught by Joseph Smith.
USlC

4175. ———. A voice from Jerusalem, or a sketch of the travels and ministry of Elder Orson Hyde, missionary of the Church of Jesus Christ of Latter Day Saints, to Germany, Constantinople, and Jerusalem, containing a description of Mount Zion . . . and some accounts of the manners and customs of the East . . . Comp. from his late letters and documents . . . Liverpool, Published by P. P. Pratt [1842]
v [1] 7–36p. 18cm.
CSmH, CtY, CU–B, DLC, MH, NN, USlC

4176. ———. (same) Boston, Printed by Albert Morgan, 1842.
v [1] 7–36p. 18cm.
Cover-title: Published by P. P. Pratt, Liverpool, Eng. Re-published by G. J. Adams, Boston, Mass., 1842.
CSmH, CtY, CU–B, DLC, MH, NN, UPB, USlC

4177. ———. (same under title) A sketch of the travels and ministry of Elder Orson Hyde, a missionary of the Church of Jesus Christ of Latter-day Saints . . . To Germany, Constantinople and Jerusalem, containing a description of Mount Zion, the Pool of Siloam and other ancient places, and some account of the manners and customs of the east . . . Compiled from his late letters and documents, the last of which bears date at Bavaria, on the Danube, Jan. 18, 1842. Salt Lake City, Printed at the Deseret News Office, 1869.
24p. 24cm.
CSmH, CU–B, MH, NjP, UHi, UPB, USlC

ILLINOIS LEGIS. | SENATE. | 14TH ASSEM. 1ST SESSION.

Jackson

MESSAGE

OF THE

GOVERNOR OF THE STATE OF ILLINOIS,

IN RELATION

TO THE DISTURBANCES IN HANCOCK COUNTY,

DECEMBER, 23, 1844.

Laid on the table, and 2,500 copies ordered to be printed for the use of the two houses.

SPRINGFIELD:

WALTERS & WEBER, PUBLIC PRINTERS,

1844.

Item 4196. Governor Thomas Ford's explication of the events surrounding the murders of Joseph and Hyrum Smith. From the LDS church collection.

4178. I., E. J. My dear friends. [n.p., Printed by R. & B. Powle, n.d.]
4p. 12½cm.
Caption-title.
Signed: E. J. I.
At head of title: Galatians, ch. 1, v. 6, 7, 8, 9.
A tract against Mormonism.
USlC

4179. Idaho. Constitutional Convention, 1889. Proceedings and debates of the Constitutional Convention of Idaho, 1889; ed. and annotated by I. W. Hart. Caldwell, Idaho, Caxton Printers, Ltd., 1912.
2v. 23cm.
Includes material on Mormon polygamy in Idaho.
DLC, NjP, UPB

4180. Idaho. Governor, 1880–1883 (Neil) Special message of John B. Neil, Governor of Idaho, to the Eleventh Session of the Legislature of Idaho Territory. Boise City, 1881.
5p. 20cm.
Caption-title.
Proposed Idaho legislation on polygamy.
IHi, NN, ULA

4181. Idaho. Governor, 1889 (Shoup) Report of the Governor of Idaho to the Secretary of the Interior. 1889. Washington, Govt. Print. Off., 1889.
108p. illus. 22cm.
"Mormonism," p. 101–02. Its statehood implications. Reports for the years 1886, and 1888 also have a mention of Mormonism.
MH, ULA

4182. Idaho (Territory) Legislative Assembly. . . . Memorial of the Legislative Assembly of the Territory of Idaho, protesting against the admission of Utah as a state. [Washington, Govt. Print. Off., 1889]
2p. 22½cm. (U.S. 50th Cong. 2d Sess. Senate. Misc. Doc. No. 37)
Caption-title.
Protest predicated on "treasonability" of the L.D.S. church in Utah.
CtY, UPB

4183. Idaho scimitar. . . . Boise, Idaho, Scimitar Publishing Company, November 2, 1907–October 3, 1908.
lv. (49 nos. in 784p.) weekly. 55cm.
Designed to fight the menace of the Mormon organization under the presidency of Joseph F. Smith. Edited by F. T. Dubois.
DLC

4184. The Idea. . . . Salt Lake City, Latter-day Saints College, 1893–
v. monthly. 30cm.
Organ of the students of the L.D.S. College. Editor: 1893– J. H. Hubbard.
A literary journal, with reports on special lectures, etc.
CU–B inc.; USlC inc.

Ieuan [*pseud.*] *See Davis, John Sylvanus.*

Illinois annual register, and western business directory. *See Norris, James W.*

4185. Illinois. General Assembly. Reports made to the Senate and House of Representatives of the State of Illinois, at their session begun and held at Springfield, December 2, 1844. Springfield, Walters & Weber, Public Printers, 1845.
2v. 21cm.
City of Nauvoo. In Senate, Dec. 16, 1844. Read and laid on the table. (Ill. Legislature. 14th Assembly. 1st Session. Senate) Report of Mr. Dougherty from the Committee on the Judiciary, recommending the repeal of the charter of the City of Nauvoo, V.1, p. [139]–140.
Message of the Governor of the State of Illinois, in relation to the disturbances in Hancock County, December 21, 1844, V.1, p. [65]–85. Also published as a separate.
CtY, NN

4186. Illinois. General Assembly. House of Representatives. Reports made to the House of Representatives of the State of Illinois, at their session begun and held at Springfield, December 2, 1844. Springfield, Walters & Weber, Public Printers, 1845.
xii, 394p. 21cm.
In relation to the Mormon war. House of Representatives, Feb. 26, 1845. Read, and laid on the table. (Illinois. Legislature. 14th Assembly. 1st Session. House of Representatives) p. [249]–250.
IHi

4187. ———. Committee on Finance. Report of the Committee on Finance, fixing the rates of pay of officers and privates, called into service under command of Gen. Hardin and Maj. Warren, in 1845–'46. February 23, 1847. Read and laid on the table. [Springfield, George R. Weber, 1847]
3p. 21cm. (In Illinois. General Assembly. House of Representatives. Reports, 1846–47, p. 325–327)
At head of title: Illinois Legis. H.R. 15th Assem. 1st Session.
Troops used during the Mormon War.
Caption-title
CSmH, NN

4188. ———. Report of the minority of the Committee on Finance, in relation to pay of the troops under command of Gen. Hardin and Maj. Warren. February 23, 1847. Read, and laid on the table. [Springfield, George R. Weber, Public Printer, 1847]
4p. 21cm. (In Illinois. General Assembly. House of Representatives. Reports, 1846–47, p. 329–332)
At head of title: Illinois Legis. H.R. 15th Assem. 1st Session.
Caption-title.
CSmH, NN

ILLINOIS. GOVERNOR

4189. ———. Committee on the Militia. Report of the Committee on the Militia, in relation to the pay of the troops in the Mormon war, in 1846. February 25, 1847. Read and laid on the table.
[1]l. 21cm. (In Illinois. General Assembly. House of Representatives. Reports, 1846–47, p. 335)
At head of title: Illinois Legis. H.R. 15th Assem. 1st Session.
Caption-title.
CSmH, NN

4190. ———. Select Committee, relative to the Sinking Fund. Report of the Select Committee, relative to the Sinking Fund. March 1st 1846. Read and laid on the table. [Springfield, George R. Weber? 1847]
12p. 21cm. (In Illinois. General Assembly. House of Representatives. Reports, 1846–47, p. 339–350.
At head of title: Illinois Legis. H.R. 15th Assem. 1st Session.
Caption-title.
Expenditures made in connection with the prosecution of the supposed murders of J. and H. Smith, and to expenditures in connection with the Hancock difficulties in 1845 and 1846. On p. 7–12 appears Ford's reply of Feb. 25, discussing the Mormon matters.
CSmH, NN

4191. Illinois. General Assembly. Senate. Committee on Finance. Report of the Committee on Finance, Relative to certain claims against the State for services in the Hancock war. Read and laid on the table. [Springfield, Charles H. Lanphier, Public Printer, 1849]
3p. 21cm. (In Illinois. General Assembly. Senate. Reports, 1848–49, p. 101–103)
At head of title: Illinois Legis. Senate. 1st Session, 16th Assem.
Caption-title.
CSmH

4192. ———. Committee on the Judiciary. . . . City of Nauvoo . . . Springfield: 1844.
2p. 21½cm.
At head of title: Illinois. Legis. Senate. 14th Assem. 1st Session.
Caption-title.
CtY

4193. ———. Report of the Committee of the Judiciary to whom was referred the preamble and resolutions in relation to the Nauvoo City Charter, &c. December 19, 1842. Read and laid on the table. Springfield, William Walters, Public Printer, 1842.
4p. 20½cm. (In Illinois. General Assembly. 13th Assembly. 1st Session, p. 127–130)
At head of title: Illinois. Legis. Senate. 13th Assem. 1st Session.
Caption-title.
Defends the Nauvoo Charter as essentially the same as the Chicago, Springfield, and Quincy charters though all have some objectionable features.
CSmH

4194. Illinois. Governor. . . . Governors' letter-books, 1840–1853; Edited with introduction and notes by Evarts Boutell Greene [and] Charles Manfred Thompson . . . Springfield, Illinois State Historical Library, 1911.
cxviii, 469p. illus. 22½cm. (Illinois Historical Library. Collections. V. 7)
"The Mormons in Illinois," ixxviii–civ.
Also includes various letters by Governor Ford.
CU, DLC, NjP, UHi

4195. Illinois. Governor, 1842–1846 (Ford). Message of the Governor of the State of Illinois in relation to the disturbances in Hancock County, December 21, 1844. Springfield, Walters & Weber, Public Printers, 1844.
21p. 25cm. (Illinois. Legislature. Senate. 14th Assembly. 1st Session)
State of things after the 1844 Session and the death of Joseph Smith.
Also published in Journal of the Senate of the Fourteenth Assembly of the State of Illinois, at their regular session, begun and held at Springfield, December 2, 1844. Springfield, Walters & Weber, Public Printers, 1844, p. 91–110.
MoKU, NN

4196. ———. (same) Springfield, Walters & Weber, Public Printers, 1844.
[3]–21p. 22cm.
Without series note.
UHi

4197. ———. Message of the Governor of the State of Illinois transmitted to the General Assembly, December 7, 1846. Springfield, George R. Weber, Public Printers, 1846.
3p. 21½cm. (In Illinois. General Assembly. Senate. Reports, 1846–47, p. 1–3)
At head of title: Illinois Legis. Senate. 15th Assem. 1st Session.
Caption-title
In relation to the difficulties in Hancock County.
CSmH, NN

4198. ———. . . . Mormon difficulties. Report of the Governor in relation to the difficulties in Hancock county Senate, Dec. 10, 1846. Read, laid on the table and 1,500 copies ordered to be printed. [Springfield, Assembly. George R. Weber, Public Printers, 1846]
7p. 21½cm.
At head of title: Illinois. Legislature. Senate. 15th Assembly. 1st Session.
Dated: December 7, 1846.
Treatment of Mormons during 1845–1946.
Also in: Reports made to the Senate and House of Representatives of the State of Illinois at their Session begun . . . December 7, 1846. V.1, p. [5]–11.
P.137 corrects an error in the report.
CtY, ICHi, UPB

ILLINOIS. GOVERNOR

4198a. ———. A proclamation. [Springfield, Illinois] 1844.
Broadside. 23×31cm.
Dated Sept. 27, 1844.
Offering a reward of two hundred dollars for the apprehension of Levi Williams, Thomas C. Sharp, and Joseph H. Jackson.
USlC

4199. ———. A proclamation by the Governor of the State of Illinois. [Springfield? 1845?]
Broadside. 23½×31cm.
Warning to men outside the state not to attempt to come in and start a civil war over Mormonism.
Dated: Sept. 26, 1845.
USlC

4200. ———. To the people of Warsaw, in Hancock County. I am continually informed of your preparations and threats to renew the war, and exterminate the Mormons. One would suppose that you ought to rest satisfied with what you have already done . . . [Quincy? 1844]
Broadside. 23×14½cm.
An attempt by Ford to quiet threats of another Mormon war. Dated: July 25, 1844.
Byrd 860
NN

4201. Illinois. Governor, 1846–53 (French). To the citizens of Hancock. Springfield, Dec. 12, 1846.
Broadside. 16×16cm.
Withdrawal of troops from Nauvoo.
USlC

4202. Illinois. Governor's troops (Volunteers). Insult to the Governor! In publishing the following proceedings of the officers and men belonging to the detachment of volunteers now at Nauvoo, it is due to the respectable portion of the anti-Mormon party to say, that it is believed, they had nothing to do in the matter . . . All the printers in the state are respectfully invited to publish these proceedings, as a mere act of justice, to a man who has been much undeservedly persecuted, merely for the conscientious discharge of his duty. [Nauvoo? 1846?]
Broadside. 46×30cm.
Resolutions in defense of Gov. Ford. 167 lines in 3 columns.
Signed by the officers of Governor Thomas Ford's command, Nov. 7, 1846.
Ford had taken charge of the troops in Nauvoo to restore order. There he was presented with a petticoat, a symbol of cowardice and this happening plus the profession of his troops' support is the subject of this broadside.
Byrd 1079
ICHi, ICN, NjP, NN

Illinois. Infantry. Citizens of Hancock . . .
See Hardin, John J.

4203. Illinois. Laws, statutes, etc. Laws of the State of Illinois, passed by the Twelfth General Assembly, at their Session, began and held at Springfield, on the seventh of December, one thousand eight hundred and forty. Published in pursuance of law. Springfield, Wm. Walters, Public Printer, 1841.
359, xxivp. 22cm.
An act to incorporate the City of Nauvoo, p. 52–57. In force Feb. 1, 1840.
An act to incorporate the Nauvoo Agricultural and Manufacturing Association, in the County of Hancock, p. 139–141. In force, Feb. 27, 1841.
An act in relation to a road therein named, p. 223. Section 2 of this act provides that any Hancock County citizen may, by voluntary enrollment, attach himself to the Nauvoo Legion, provided for in the act to incorporate the City of Nauvoo.
IHi

4204. ———. Laws of the State of Illinois, passed by the Fourteenth General Assembly, at their regular session, began and held at Springfield, December 2nd, 1844. Springfield, Walters & Weber, Public Printers, 1845.
340, lxvp. 21½cm.
An act to repeal the act entitled "An act to incorporate the city of Nauvoo," approved December 16, 1840, p. 187–188.
IHi

4205. Illinois State Historical Society. Transactions of the Illinois Historical Society for the year 1906. Seventh annual meeting of the Society, Springfield, Ill., January 24–25, 1906. . . . Springfield, Illinois, State Journal Company, 1906.
xvii, [1]l [3]–437p. plates. 23cm. (Illinois State Historical Library. Publication No. 11)
The Mormon settlement in Illinois, p. 88–102 by Hon. Orville F. Berry. Also Mormon articles in transactions for 1905, 1926.
NjP, UPB, USlC

4206. The illustrated book of all religions from the earliest ages to the present time, including the rise, progress, doctrines and government of all Christian denominations, compiled from their own publications and viewed from their own standpoint. . . . Chicago, Star Pub. Co. [1897]
xix, 17–592p. illus. 20½cm.
Section on "Mormons, or Latter-day Saints," p. 335–340.
Another edition: Philadelphia, J. E. Potter & Co., Ltd., 1897. DLC
DLC, ULA

4207. Illustrated centennial sketches, map and directory of Union County, Iowa. Creston, Iowa, C. J. Colby, 1876.
2p.l. [5]–145p. plates, port., maps (part. fold) 31cm.
History of troubles in Nauvoo and the trek of the Mormons across Union County, p. 8–10.
UPB

4208. An illustrated historical atlas map; Jackson County, Mo. Carefully compiled from personal examinations and surveys. Philadelphia, Published by Brink, McDonough & Co. . . . , 1877.
73p. illus., maps. 45cm.
"Mormons," p. 14; Lilburn W. Boggs and General Samuel D. Lucas biographies, p. 15; map of Independence, Mo., p. 73.
USlC

An illustrated historical atlas of Caldwell County, Mo. *See Edwards Brothers.*

An illustrated historical atlas of Ray County, Mo. *See Edwards Brothers.*

4209. An illustrated history of Southern California. Embracing the counties of San Diego, San Bernardino, Los Angeles and Orange, and the peninsula of Lower California, from the earliest period of occupancy to the present time; together with glimpses of their prospects; also, full-page portraits of some of their eminent men, and biographical mention of many of their pioneers and of prominent citizens of to-day. Chicago, The Lewis Publishing Company, 1890.
viii, 9–898p. plates, ports. 30×23½cm.
Mormons in San Bernardino, p. 416–420.
CU–B, DLC, ICN, MB, NN, OClWHi, UHi

4210. Important documents bearing on political questions in Utah. Logan, Utah, Printed by the Journal Printing and Publishing Co., 1882.
26p. 23cm.
Contents: The Edmunds bill; The Hoar amendment; People's party; Declaration of principles; Liberal party platform; Judge Van Zile's letter; Reply . . . by Moses Thatcher.
CoD, CU–B, MH, NN, USlC

4211. The Imposture unmasked; or, A complete exposure of the Mormon fraud; being a critical review of the Book of Mormon, and an expose of the character of Joseph Smith, Sidney Rigdon, Martin Harris, Parley Pratt, and other leading actors in the Latter-Day Saint delusion. . . . Second Edition. Isle of Man: Reprinted from the Mona's Herald and Central Advertiser for the British Empire, by R. Fargher, . . . 1841.
32p. 17×11cm.
CtY, NN

4212. The Improvement Era. . . . Salt Lake City, 1897–
v. illus. 23–29cm. monthly.
V. 1–10. Organ of Young Men's Mutual Improvement Assoc. V.11. Organ of the Seventies and of the Y.M.M.I.A. V.12. Organ of the Priesthood and of the Y.M.M.I.A. V.16. Organ of the Priesthood quorums and the Y.M.M.I.A. and the schools of the church. V.33. Organ of the Priesthood quorums, the M.I.A. and the Dept. of Education of the Church . . . V.33. New format.
CSmH, NjP, NN, UHi, ULA, UPB, USlC, UU, WHi

4212a. Im kampfe mit Mormonen. [Berlin, Neues Verlagshaus für Volksliteratur, n.d.]
31p. 21½cm. (Texas Jack 'Der grosse Kundschafter'. Nr. 97.)
Fiction concerning Mormonism.
Title in English: At war with the Mormons.
USlC

4212b. ———. (same) [Leipzig, Gustav Kühn Verlag] 1930.
24p. 28cm. (Buffalo Bill. Bd. 66)
USlC

4213. In affectionate memoriam of Mrs. Emma G. Bull, who died in Salt Lake City, October 24, 1895. [Salt Lake City, Joseph Bull, 1895]
26p. 23cm.
Includes biographical sketch.
CSmH, USlC

4214. In loving remembrance of Hannah Cornaby, born March 17, 1822, died Sept. 1, 1905. [Spanish Fork?] 1905.
[3]p. port. 22cm.
USlC

4215. In memoriam, Anthon Henrik Lund; biographical sketch, funeral services, resolutions of respect, letters of sympathy, editorial expressions. Salt Lake City, 1921.
67p. port. 23cm.
Biographical sketch by J. M. Sjodahl.
UHi, USlC, UU

4216. In memoriam. Edward H. Callister. . . . [Salt Lake City, 1917]
[10]l. port. 25cm.
Cover-title: Funeral services for Edward H. Callister.
Mormon biography.
USlC

4217. In memoriam; Emily Sophia Tanner Richards. [Salt Lake City? 1929?]
57p. ports., plates. 23½cm.
Includes a biography.
CSmH, UPB, USlC

4218. In memoriam. Horace G. Whitney. Biographical sketch, funeral ceremonies, resolutions of respect, editorials, personal tributes. Salt Lake City, 1920.
47p. 23cm.
USlC

IN MEMORIAM, O. COWDERY

4219. In Memoriam, Oliver Cowdery. . . . Program of the dedicatory service and unveiling of the Oliver Cowdery Monument. [n.d.] 1911.
[4]p. illus. 23cm.
USIC

4220. In memoriam, Spencer Clawson, Spencer Clawson jr. [n.p., 1916]
[36]l. ports. 21½cm.
UPB, USIC

In the grip of the Mormons. *See Belisle, Orvilla.*

4221. In the matter of Reed Smoot, Senator-elect of the State of Utah. Protests of citizens of the State of Utah against the admission to the United States Senate of Reed Smoot, Apostle of the Mormon Church. Salt Lake City, 1903.
64p. 21½cm.
Cover-title.
CSmH, MH, USl, USIC

4222. Indbydelse til Guds Rige. Kjøbenhavn, H. C. Haight. Trycht hos F. E. Bording, 1857.
8p. 22cm.
Probably written by Edwin F. Parry.
Variant printing USIC
Title in English: Invitation to the kingdom of God.
NN, USIC

4223. ———. (same) Kjøbenhavn, Udgivet og redigeret af C. Widerborg, 1858.
8p. 21cm.
"3 die oplag"
UU

4224. ———. (same) [Köpenhamn, John Van Cott. Trykt hos F. E. Bording, 1860]
4p. 21½cm.
Variant printing USIC
CSmH

4225. ———. (same) [Kjøbenhavn, Udgivet og forlagt af J. Van Cott. Trykt hos F. E. Bording, 1861]
8p. 21½cm.
"5te oplag"
USIC

4226. ———. (same) Kjøbenhavn, Redegeret og udgivet af J. Van Cott. Trykt hos F. E. Bording [n.d.]
F. E. Bording [n.d.]
4p. 21cm.
USIC

4227. ———. (same) [Kjøbenhavn, Udgivet og forlagt af R. Peterson. Trykt hos F. E. Bording, 1873]
8p. 21½cm.
"10 de Oplag."
UPB, USIC

4228. ———. (same) [Kjøbenhavn, Udgivet og forlagt af N. C. Flygare, 1876]
8p. 23cm.
UPB

4229. ———. (same) [Kjøbenhavn, Udgivet og forlagt af O. N. Liljenquist. Trykt hos F. E. Bording, 1877]
8p. 20cm.
"13 de Oplag."
USIC

4230. ———. (same) [Kjøbenhavn, Udgivet og forlagt af R. Wilhelmsen. Trykt hos F. E. Bording, 1880]
8p. 21½cm.
"14 de Oplag."
UPB, USIC

4231. ———. (same) [Kjøbenhavn, Udgivet og forlagt af C. D. Fjelsted. Trykt hos F. E. Bording, 1882]
8p. 21cm.
"15 de oplag."
UPB, USIC

4232. ———. (same) Kjøbenhavn, Udgivet og forlagt af John Van Cott. Trykt hos F. E. Bording, 1896.
8p. 22cm.
"16de oplag"
USIC

4233. ———. (same, in Swedish) Inbjudning till Guds rike. [Kopenhamn, C. Widerborg, 1865]
8p. 20cm.
Caption-title.
CtY

4234. ———. (same) [Köpenhamn, Utgafven och förlagd af R. C. Flygare, 1875]
8p. 21cm.
"34e tusende"
Caption-title.
Translated by F. E. Bording.
CtY, UHi

4235. ———. (same) [Köpenhamn, Utgafven och förlagd af N. C. Flygare. Tryckt hos F. E. Bording, 1878.
8p. 21cm.
CtY, NN, USIC

4235a. ———. (same) [Köpenhamn, Utgifven och förlagd af N. Wilhelmsen. Tryckt hos F. E. Bording, 1880]
8p. 23cm.
USIC

4235b. ———. (same) [Köpenhamn, Utgifven och förlagd af C. D. Fjeldstad. Tryckt hos F. E. Bording, 1884]
8p. 22cm.
USIC

4236. ———. (same) Viktiga fragor rörånde frälsningen, besvardde med skriftens ord. Av Edwin F. Parry. [Stockholm, Svenska missionen av Jesu Kristi kyrka av Sista Dagars Helifa, 1929]
4p. 22cm.
USIC

4237. Independence Hall. The pioneers in providing for the social, educational and religious needs of the non-Mormons of Utah Territory. History of Independence Hall—A landmark in the development of Utah. [Salt Lake City? 1882?]
[4]p. 21cm.
Independence Hall belonged to the First Congregational Church.
USIC

4238. Independent Forum. Independence, Mo., Church of Christ, October, 1929–March, 1930.
1v. monthly. 29½cm.
"Published in the Interest of all factions of Mormonism." October, 1929–June, 1930. Basically for the Church of Christ (Temple Lot). Marshall T. Jamison, Publisher, owner and business manager.
Subscription list taken over by *Voice of Warning* (Niagara Falls) in July, 1931.
CU–B V.1 #1–7, MoInRC, UPB V.1 #4–5, USIC V.1 #1–7

Independent Inquirer. Prospectus. *See Bosson, Charles P.*

4239. Industrial Christian Home Association of Utah. . . . Report of the Commissioners of Registration and Elections on the Industrial Christian Home Association of Utah. Nov. 12, 1890. [Washington, Govt. Print. Off., 1891]
6p. 23cm. (U.S. 51st Cong. 2d Sess. Senate. Misc. Doc. No. 15)
Report of the Industrial Christian Home Association of Utah for 1890, including data on Utah polygamy and the polygamy manifesto.
Signed: Nov. 13, 1890.
CU–B, UPB

4240. ———. . . . Report of Utah Commission as to the management of the Industrial Christian Home Association of Utah. [Washington, Govt. Print. Off., 1890]
10p. 23cm. (U.S. 51st Cong. 1st Sess. Senate. Misc. Doc. No. 34)
Report of Industrial Christian Home Association of Utah for 1889. Mentions polygamy.
Signed: Dec. 5, 1889.
ULA, UPB

4241. ———. **Board of Control.** Message from the President of the United States, transmitting report of the Board of Control of the Industrial Home of Utah . . . [Washington, Govt. Print. Off., 1888]
4p. 23cm. (U.S. 50th Cong. 1st Sess. Senate. Ex. Doc. No. 57)
Signed: Nov. 25, 1887.
UPB

4242. Ingalls, Rufus. General Ingalls's inspection report. Letter from the Secretary of War, in answer to a resolution of the House of February 27, transmitting report of General Ingalls's inspection made in 1866 . . . Washington, 1876.
25p. 23cm. (U.S. 39th Cong. 2d Sess. House. Doc. No. 111)
Condition in Utah due to poor administration.
ULA, UU

4243. ———. Letter to Major General Thos. S. Jesup concerning expedition through Utah with Colonel E. J. Steptoe. (In Annual Report of the Secretary of War. 1855. Washington, Printed by Beverley Tucker, 1855)
156–168p. 23cm. (U.S. 34th Cong. 1st Sess. Senate Ex. Doc. No. 1, pt. 2)
Description of the Mormons, p. 166–168.
Also published in U.S. 34th Cong. House. Ex. Doc. No. 1 . CU, CU–B
C, CU, CU–B, UPB

4244. Ingemann, B. S. Landsbybeboerne, Nytids-Roman. Kobenhavn, 1852.
729p.
Title in English: The villagers; a modern novel.
Schmidt

4245. Ingeroe, Julie. Et Aar I Utah eller, Mormonismens, Hemmeligheder ved Julie Ingeroe . . . Chicago, Trykt in "Skandinavens" Office, 1867.
62p. 19cm.
Title in English: One year in Utah, or secrets of Mormonism.
DLC

4246. ———. Et Aar i Utah eller. En Dames Reise til Mormonstaten hendes ophold der og flugt derfa . . . Kjovenhaven, 1868.
44p. 19cm.
Title in English: One year in Utah.
MH

4247. Ingersoll, Ernest. The crest of the continent: a record of a summer's ramble in the Rocky Mountains and beyond. By Ernest Ingersoll. Chicago, R. R. Donnelley and Sons, 1885.
344p. illus., fold. map. 21½cm.
Account of Salt Lake City, p. 324–334. Several chapters on his visit to Utah in the 1880's.
Published in several editions between 1885–1890.
CSmH, CU–B, DLC, ICJ, MH, NjP, NN, OCU, PHi, PPA, PPL, UHi, USIC, UU

INGERSOLL, L. A.

4248. Ingersoll, Luther A. Ingersoll's century annals of San Bernardino County, 1769 to 1904, prefaced with a brief history of the state of California; supplemented with an encyclopedia of local biography and embellished with views of historic subjects and portraits of many of its representative people. Los Angeles, L. A. Ingersoll, 1904.
xxii, 887p. illus., plates, ports., plans. 26cm.
Chapter III. "The Mormon era."
DLC, MWA, OClWHi, UHi, USlC

4249. Ingraham, Prentiss. Adventures of Buffalo Bill from boyhood to manhood. By Colonel Prentiss Ingraham. New York, Published by Beadle and Adams, c1881.
15p. 29cm. (Beadle's Boy's Library of Sport, Story and Adventure. Vol. 1 #1)
A chapter deals with his brush with the Danites.
InU

4250. ———. Buffalo Bill's Danite trail; or, The waif of the plains. By Col. Prentiss Ingraham . . . New York, Street & Smith Corporation [c1908]
3p.l., [5]–312p. 18cm. (Buffalo Bill Border Stories. No. 19)
A Danite novel. Buffalo Bill triumphs over the Mormons.
USlC

4251. ———. Gentleman Jack, the man of many masks; or Buffalo Bill's peerless pard. A romance of tangled trails followed by Buffalo Bill and his buckskin heroes, surgeon Frank Powell, Wild Bill, Texas Jack, Captain Jack Crawford, Buckskin Sam, Colorado Carl and a mysterious unknown. New York, Beadle and Adams, Nov. 22, 1890 to Feb. 21, 1891.
(The Banner Weekly. Vol. IX, No. 419 to Vol. IX, No. 432) 28cm.
Mexicans, Mormons, Brigham Young, Texas, the overland trail between Salt Lake City and San Francisco.
USlC

4252. ———. The Texan's double; or, the merciless shadower. A revelation of the mystery of the "Bravo in Black," in the romance of the "Three Bills." New York, Beadle and Adams, Aug. 30, 1890– Nov. 22, 1890.
(The Banner Weekly, Vol. VIII, No. 407 to Vol. IX, No. 419) 28cm.
Texas, Mexico, Utah, Buffalo Bill, Buckskin Sam, Mormons, The prophet, Danites, etc.
NN

4253. ———. War path Will, the traitor guide; or, the boy phantom. New York, Beadle and Adams, 1884.
15p. 27cm. (Beadle half-dime library. V. XV. No. 387)
An Indian and Mormon tale of Colorado.
MU

4254. Inman, Henry. The Great Salt Lake trail, by Colonel Henry Inman . . . and Colonel William F. Cody. New York, The Macmillan and Co., Ltd., 1898.
xiii, 529p. illus., plates, ports., fold. map. 23cm.
Includes material on Mormonism and particularly the Mountain Meadows massacre.
Other editions: 1899. WAT; Topeka, Crane and Co., 1910. MH; 1914. DLC, NjP, UPB, UHi; 1913. CU–B
Howes I55
CSmH, DLC, MiU, NjN, NN, OO, UHi, ULA, USlC, UU

4255. An Inquiry into the history of the originals of King James Bible; when were they written, where were they written; who wrote them; and how they have been preserved, and handed down. New York, Eckler Printer . . . 1868.
viii, 568. 24½cm.
Mormonism and Book of Mormon under "Probable origin of the Old Testament."
USlC

4256. The Instructor; an illustrated monthly magazine designed expressly for the education and elevation of the young. Salt Lake City, Deseret Sunday School Union, Jan. 1, 1866–
v. illus., bi-weekly, monthly. 24–32cm.
Title varies: Juvenile Instructor, 1866–1929.
First editor: George Q. Cannon.
CSmH; CtY; CU–B V. 3, 5–19, 21–31, 33–45 #6; MH; NjP; UHi; ULA; UPB; USlC

The Instructor; a synopsis of the faith and doctrine. *See Griffiths, Gomer T., compiler.*

4257. Intemperance; an appeal to the youth of Zion. The folly of drunkenness and the nobility of a temperate life compared. Figures that tell a fearful story. Examples from real life. Salt Lake City, Juvenile Instructor Office, 1881.
24p. 18cm.
Cover-title.
CSmH, MH, NN, UHi, UPB, USlC

4258. Inter-denominational Council of Women. Facts about polygamy. [New York, 1901?]
1p. fold in 4. 9×16cm.
Caption-title.
WHi

4259. ———. Questions answered. [New York, 1905?]
Broadside. 20×13½cm.
Caption-title.
Concerns polygamy.
WHi

4260. The Interdenominational Council of Women for Christian and Patriotic Service. Anti-Mormon work at home and abroad. [New York? n.d.]
[2]p. 17cm.
NN

4261. ———. Extracts from proceedings before the Committee on Privileges and Elections of the United States Senate in the matter of the protests against the right of Hon. Reed Smoot, a Senator from the State of Utah, to hold his seat. Testimony taken during the months of January, February and March, 1904. [New York, n.d.]
[10]p. 16cm.
NN

4262. ———. Mormonism; a compilation of facts for sundry authorities, notably the Salt Lake Tribune, the organ of the American Party in Utah. [New York, The Willett Press, 1907?]
[8]p. 20½cm.
MoInRC, NN

4263. ———. The Peril of Mormonism. New York [ca. 1910]
[8]p. illus. 18cm.
UPB, USIC

4264. ———. A question of fact. [New York City, n.d.]
8p. 14cm.
NN

4265. The Interior. The great American despotism. [Chicago, The Interior, 1905]
[4]p. 22½cm.
Mormon despotism.
USIC

4266. Inter-Mountain Christian Advocate. Salt Lake City, 1903?–1910?
v. monthly. 25cm.
Many anti-Mormon articles.
USIC v.2 #4–10; v.3 #1–4, 6–9; v.4 #2–3, 5–7, 9–11; v.5 #2, 4, 7, 8, 11; v.6 #3–4, 6–7, 9–10; v.7 #1–3, 5, 8–10; v.8 #1–8

4267. Inter-Mountain Christian endeavor. Salt Lake City, 1897–
v. 26½cm.
An association to promulgate Christianity and suppress Mormonism.
USIC V. 1 #5

4268. Inter-Mountain directory. Listing stake and ward officials of the Los Angeles and Hollywood Stakes, Church of Jesus Christ of Latter-day Saints. [Los Angeles] W. D. Le Cheminant Company [1928]
68p. 22cm.
Cover-title.
Compiled and printed by the W.D. Le Cheminant. Company.
USIC

4269. Inter-Mountain Republican. "What shall it profit a man." A forcible appeal to true Americans. An editorial from the Inter-mountain Republican, Published in Salt Lake City, Monday, Dec. 31, 1906. Salt Lake City, Bureau of Information [1906?]
8p. 17cm.
An appeal from a non-Mormon to stop the anti-Mormon campaign. The writer is well versed in Mormonism.
MH, MoInRC, USIC

4270. International Council for Patriotic Service. Crimes and treason of the Mormon Church. New York, 1913.
[14]l. 22½cm.
Reprint: *Chicago Daily Journal.*
NN, USIC

4271. ———. Leaflets. New York, 1912–14.
9 nos. 28cm.
Formerly Interdenominational Council of Women for Christian and Patriotic Service.
NN 1, 2, 6, 8, 9; USIC; WHi inc.

International Publishing Company. *See Valentini, Zopito, editor.*

Investigation into the murder of Dr. J. K. Robinson. *See Salt Lake County, Utah. Coroner.*

Invitation. *See Church of Jesus Christ of Latter-day Saints. Missions.*

4272. Iowa. Adjutant General. Roster and record of Iowa soldiers in miscellaneous organizations of the Mexican War, Indian campaigns, War of the Rebellion and the Spanish-American and Philippine Wars; together with historical sketches of volunteer organizations. Des Moines, Published by authority of the General Assembly, State Printer, 1911.
6v. 23cm.
Vol. 6 contains "The Mormon Battalion of Iowa Volunteers," p. 825–881.
USIC

4273. Iowa Infantry. Mormon Battalion, 1846–1848. Report of the first general festival of the renowned Mormon Battalion, which came off on Tuesday and Wednesday, Feb. 6, and 7, 1855, in the Social Hall, Great Salt Lake City, Utah, Reported by J. V. Long. [Salt Lake City] Printed at the Deseret News Office, 1855.
39p. 30cm.
CU–B, MH

4274. ———. (same) St. Louis, Printed at the St. Louis Luminary office, 1855.
36p. 29cm.
Howes L442
MH, USIC

4275. Ipsen, Pastor. Et ord til overvejelse for mine medchristne. Hobro, 1862.
34p.
Title in English: A word of thought for my Christian brothers.
Schmidt

4276. Ironside, Henry Allan. The Mormon's mistake, or, what is the gospel, by H. A. Ironside. London [1920?]
14p. 16cm. (Living streams series)
Sale of book dated 1920 on verso of cover.
MoInRC, UPB

4277. ———. (same) [Cleveland, Utah Gospel Mission, 193–]
8p. 17cm.
Caption-title.
NN, UHi, UPB, USlC

4278. Irvine, T. M. The coming of our Lord . . . [Hawthorne, California, 1929?]
10p. folded. 22cm.
Caption-title.
UHi

4279. ———. The Latter-day Israel delusion. [Hawthorne, Cal.?, 1928]
4p. 22cm.
Caption-title.
Text in double columns.
Mss at end: Signed T. M. Irvine, Hawthorne, Calif.
NN, UHi

4280. ———. Latter Day Saints, attention! [Beloit, Wis., 1928]
[10]l. 30cm.
Caption-title.
Mimeographed letter, signed by Mrs. Imogene Pyne, attached.
NN

4281. Irvine, William C., *compiler.* Heresies exposed; a brief critical examination in the light of the Holy Scriptures of some of the prevailing heresies and false teachings today. Compiled by Wm. C. Irvine, Editor, The Indian Christian. Introduction by Louis T. Talbot, Pastor, Church of the Open Door. Los Angeles, Louis T. Talbot [1925]
3p.l. [3]–225p. 18cm.
"First edition as timely warning, 1917; second edition as "Modern heresies exposed," 1818; third edition as "Heresies exposed," 1921.
Mormonism, by A. McRedwood, p. 128–135.
Another edition: New York, Loizeaux Brothers [c1921] MoInRC
USlC

4282. Irving, Edward. L'Irvingisme et le Mormonisme jugés par la parole de Dieu . . . Genève, Émile Beroud, Libraire-Editeur . . . Paris, Marc Dudoux . . . 1855.
vii, 128p. 20cm.
A comparison between the two beliefs.
Title in English: Irvingism and Mormonism.
USlC

Is Baptism Essential to Salvation? *See Bliss, Charles H.*

4282a. Is belief alone sufficient? [Liverpool? Millennial Star Office? 1908?]
4p. 21cm.
Caption-title.
Variant printings.
USlC copy has ms. note giving authorship as Thomas Walter Brookbank.
USlC

4283. Is divinity of Christ rock of Mormons? [Los Angeles, Calif., International Truth Distributors, 1927?]
21p. 16cm.
UPB

4283a. Is God a Respector of Persons? [Independence?, 1920?]
8p. 20cm.
The Negro question in Utah Mormonism.
UPB, USlC

Is Mormonism true or not? *See Religious Tract Society.*

Isbister, William. *See Half hours in the wide West.*

4284. Iverson, Heber C. Salvation, the supreme object; address delivered over Radio Station KSL, Sunday Evening, March 13, 1927. [Salt Lake City] 1927.
Broadside. 48×26cm.
UPB

4285. ———. The soul's reality and resurrection; address delivered over Radio Station KSL, Sunday Evening, April 22, 1928. [Salt Lake City] 1928.
Broadside. 55½×20cm.
Reprinted from the *Deseret News*, Saturday, April 28, 1928.
UPB

4285a. Iverson, Soren. Jesus Christ the Creator and Eternal Father; the testimony of the scriptures concerning Him. [Salt Lake City, 1891]
8p. 16cm.
USlC

4286. ———. The true gospel philosophy that proves as God was, man is, as God is, man shall be. Compiled and published by Soren Iverson. Salt Lake City [1893]
14p. 15cm.
Signed: Sept. 27, 1893.
USlC

4287. Ives, Joseph Christmas. Report upon the Colorado River of the West, explored in 1857 and 1858 by Lieutenant Joseph C. Ives, Corps of Topographical Engineers, under the direction of the Office of Explorations and Surveys, A. A. Humphreys, Captain Topographical Engineers, in charge. By order of the Secretary of War. Washington, Govt. Print. Off., 1861.
131, 14, 154, 30, 6, 31[1]p. 68 illus., 32 plates (7 col., 8 fold.) maps, profile. 29cm. (U.S. 36th Cong. 1st Sess. House. Ex. Doc. No. 90)
Reference to Mormon road, p. 80, 87–89; encounter with Jacob Hamblin party, p. 88–91; Oatman Mormons, p. 75.
DLC, MH, MnH, NjP, NN, UHi, ULA, UU

4288. ———. (same) Washington, Govt. Print. Off., 1861.
131, 14, 154, 30, 6, 31 [1]p. 68 illus., 32 plates (7 col., 8 fold.) 2 fold. maps, profile. 30cm. (U.S. 36th Cong. 1st Sess. Senate. Ex. Doc.)
CU–B, UPB

4289. Ivins, Anthony Woodward. Address of Mr. Anthony W. Ivins at the dedication of the Union Pacific's Grand Canyon Lodge at the Grand Canyon of the Colorado river in Arizona, Sept. 15, 1928. [n.p.] Union Pacific System [1928]
12p. illus. 19cm.
Brief mention of early Mormons in Arizona.
UHi, USlC

4290. ———. The Book of Mormon. Address delivered over radio station KSL, Sunday evening, September 25, 1927. [Salt Lake City, 1927]
[1]p. 44½cm.
UHi, UPB

4291. ———. The Book of Mormon; an exponent of the Christ. A sermon delivered October 7, 1923, at the Semi-annual Conference of the Church of Jesus Christ of Latter-day Saints, held in Salt Lake City. [Salt Lake City? 1923?]
15p. 17cm.
UPB, UU

4292. ———. El Mormonismo. Resumen de su origen y doctrinas por Antonio W. Ivins. Mexico, Talleres Tipográficos de Carlos Lutteroth, 1904.
2p.l. [5]–66p. 18½cm.
Contents: Introduccion, Las Primeras visiones de José Smith, El establecimiento de la Iglesia. Testimonio de hombres ilustres acerca de los Mormones.
Title in English: Mormonism. Summary of its origin and doctrines.
MH, USlC

4293. ———. (same, under title) El Mormonismo; su origen y doctrinas. Introduccion, Las Primeras visiones de José Smith. El establecimiento de la iglesia. Las doctrinas de la iglesia. Testimonio de hombres ilustres acerca de los Mormones, por Antonio W. Ivins. Independence, Mo., Zion's Printing and Publishing Company, 1927.
59p. port. 18cm.
NjP, UPB, USlC

———. Right relation of church and state. *See Hunt, D. G.*

4294. Ivins, Heber Grant. A life of Christ for Japanese students by H. Grant Ivins. Tokyo, Nakata, Fakusaburo, 1914.
155, 53, 2p. 17cm.
USlC

4295. ———. (same) Tokyo, 1916.
155, 53, 2p. 19cm.
"2d ed."
USlC

4296. Ivins, Virginia (Wilcox). Pen pictures of early western days [by] Virginia Wilcox Ivins. Illustrations by Wm. S. Ivins. [n.p.] c1908.
157p. plates. 23cm.
She was a niece of Isaac Galland who accompanied her party overland via Salt Lake City in 1853, p. 99–104.
UPB

4297. ———. Yesterdays; reminiscences of long ago. [Keokuk, Iowa?, 1915?]
107p. illus. 21cm.
Chapter II "Nauvoo" and other references.
Howes 1980
UHi

Why the "LATTER DAY SAINTS" Marry a Plurality of Wives.

A GLANCE AT

SCRIPTURE AND REASON,

IN ANSWER TO

AN ATTACK THROUGH THE POLYNESIAN,

UPON

THE SAINTS FOR POLYGAMY.

BY BENJAMIN F. JOHNSON.

Reader, the world is full of Falsehood, and our cause has many enemies, Read, therefore if you would not be DECEIVED.---After reading please lend it to your Neighbor.

SAN FRANCISCO:
PRINTED AT THE EXCELSIOR PRINTING OFFICE,
151 Clay Street, 3rd door below Montgomery.
1854.

Item 4430. An early defense of Mormon polygamy, written in response to an anti-Mormon article in the Hawaiian newspaper, *Polynesian*.
From the P. Crawley collection.

J

J., H. T.

4297a. J   , H   T. The Mormon Elders and the devils: a full exposure of an account of a terrific conflict between a Mormon Elder and 319 Devils; in which the latter were totally defeated, and two saints dispossessed: with specimens of other miracles performed by the Mormonites, or Latter-day Saints. Extracted from the "Millennial Star." By H. T. J. London, Gilbert . . . 1853.
8p. 19cm. (Tracts on Mormonism. No. 1)
"Tenth thousand."
USlC

4298. J., M. Mormonerne, eller: de Sidste Dages hellige. Slesvig, 1853.
31p.
Title in English: The Mormons, or Latter-day Saints.
Sabin

4299. Jack, Ellen E. The fate of a fairy, by Ellen E. Jack. Chicago, M. A. Donohue & Co. [c1910]
213p. illus. 20cm.
A trip through Southern Utah in Chapter IX with emphasis on some polygamy episodes. Very fictional.
NjP, UHi, USlC

4300. Jackson, Helen Maria (Fiske) Hunt. Bits of travel at home, by H. H. Boston, Toverts Bros., 1878.
vi, 413p. front. 15cm.
Impressions of Salt Lake City and the Mormons.
Other editions: 1884. CSmH; 1887. USlC; 1888. CU; 1893. CU; Boston, Little, Brown & Co., 1904. DLC
CU-B, DLC, NjP, UHi, ULA, UU

4301. Jackson, John Walker. Valuable miscellaneous books including the library of Rev. J. W. Jackson . . . many scarce works on the Mormons; to be sold . . . June 4, 1902. Catalogue compiled by Stan. V. Henkels. Philadelphia, Davis and Harvey [1902]
17p. 18cm. (Catalogue No. 882)
NN (annotated copy)

4302. Jackson, Joseph H. A narrative of the adventures and experience of Joseph H. Jackson in Nauvoo, disclosing the depth of Mormon villainy. Warsaw, Illinois, August, 1844.
32p. 21cm.
Byrd 870, Howes J24, Sabin 35443
ICHi, ICN

4303. ———. (same, under title) The adventures and experience of Joseph H. Jackson, disclosing the depths of Mormon villany [sic] practiced in Nauvoo. Warsaw, Printed for the publisher, 1846.
36p. 18½×11cm.
Dated: Sept. 3, 1846.
Copyrighted 1846, by Davie M. B. Goodrich, entered from Connecticut.
Byrd 1080, Howes J24
CSmH, CtY, DLC, ICN, MWA

4304. Jackson, Samuel MacCauley, *editor.* Concise dictionary of religious knowledge, and gazetteer; edited by S. M. Jackson; associate editors: Rev. T. W. Chambers, and Rev. F. H. Foster. New York, Maynard, Merrill, & Co., 1891.
3p.l., 996, 34p. 25cm.
Section on Mormonism by William H. Whitsitt. "Its (the *Book of Mormon's*) literary form is repulsive to the last degree, its thought is low and lacking in interest."
Other editions: 2d and rev. ed. New York, The Christian Literature Co., 1891. DLC; 3d edition. New York, 1893. DLC
NN

4305. Jackson, William Henry. . . . The pioneer photographer; Rocky Mountain adventures with a camera, by William H. Jackson in collaboration with Howard R. Driggs . . . Illustrated from sketches and photographs made by the author. Yonkers-on-Hudson, N.Y., World Book Company, 1929.
xiip., [1]l., 314p. illus. 20½cm. (Pioneer Life series)
Various references to Mormons encountered on the trail and in Salt Lake City.
DLC, MH, NjP, NN, PPGeo, PPTU, UHi

4306. Jacob, Udney Hay. An extract, from a manuscript entitled The Peacemaker, or the doctrines of the millennium: being a treatise on religion and jurisprudence, Or a new system of religion and politicks. For God, my country, and my rights. By Udney Hay Jacob, and Israelite, and a shepherd of Israel. Nauvoo, Ill., J. Smith, Printer, 1842.
37 [1]p. 20½cm.
Consists of Chap. XVIII "On the law of marriage" and Chap. XIX "Several important laws of God."
Joseph Smith denounced it immediately in the *Times and Seasons* V. 4, No. 2, December 1, 1842. Some people, have felt however, that it was part of his campaign to popularize plural marriage. By the father of Norton Jacob.
CtY, ICN, USlC

4307. ———. (same) An extract of grand selections from a manuscript entitled the Peace Maker: by the great Mormon prophet, J. Smith, wherein is contained all the secrets of Mormonism in relation to the vows of Marriage, polygamy, spiritual wives, whoredom, adultery, fornication, rapes, concubinage, virginity, etc., etc. Doctrines, however strange, if true, need not be entwined with mystery; I detest — nay abhor — sly tuition which afterward requires public denunciation; if a principle be true in secret, it is equally so in public. By Paul Harrison, (late an Elder in the Mormon Church, also president of Ireland and France) Manchester, Printed for P. Harrison by J. Leach, 1850.
15p. 17×10½cm.
A partial reprint of Udney Hay Jacob, "An extract from a manuscript entitled the Peacemaker," etc., Nauvoo, 1842.
CtY

4308. Jacob Hamblin, a drama of the early days of southern Utah played in four acts. Written and Produced by (Rock Hamblin), Grandson of the Famous Old Indian Scout. Under the Direction of Helen Hamblin. [n.p., n.d.]
Broadside. 28½×14cm.
Summary of a four act drama by Rock Hamblin.
NjP

4309. Jacobsen, I. P. Tre Breve fra Amerika om Mormonerne skrivne til deres Paarørende i Vendsyssel. Tilligemed en Attest for Brevenes Aegthed. [by] I. P. Jacobsen, M. Jenson, H. C. Jensen. Hjorring, 1863.
18p.
Title in English: Three letters from America on Mormonism.
Schmidt

4310. Jacobsen, Thomas E. Questions and answers upon the Word of wisdom. [Salt Lake City, Juvenile Instructor Print., n.d.]
[2]p. 18cm.
MoInRC

4311. Jakeman, James Thomas. Album "Daughters of the Utah pioneers and their mothers." [Salt Lake City] Western Album Pub. Co. [n.d.]
40p. illus., plates, ports. 24×32cm.
Excerpts from the larger album below.
First advance sheets of the album.
ULA, UU

4312. ———. (same) [Salt Lake City] Western Album Publishing Co. [1915]
[125]l. ports. 24×32cm.
[53]l. of text, [69]l. of plates [1]l. title page.
CSmH, UHi, UPB, USl, USlC, UU

4313. ———. (same) [Salt Lake City?] Western Album Publishing Co. [1916]
55p. ports, plates. 22×32½cm.
UPB

4314. James, George Wharton. In & around the Grand Canyon; the Grand Canyon of the Colorado River in Arizona . . . Boston, Little, Brown and Company, 1900.
xxvi, 341p. illus. 22½cm.
Chapter XX John D. Lee and the Mountain Meadows massacre.
Other editions: 1908. CU; 1911. DLC, UHi; 1913. CU
DLC, NjP, UHi

4315. ———. . . . Utah, the land of blossoming valleys; the story of its desert wastes, of its huge and fantastic rock formations, and of its fertile gardens in the sheltered valleys; a survey of its rapidly developing industries; an account of the origin, development, and beliefs of the Mormon church; and chapters on the flora and fauna, and on the scenic wonders that are a heritage of all Americans . . . with a map and fifty-six plates of which eight are in color. Boston, The Page Co., 1922.
3p.l., v–xix, 371p. col. front., plates, ports., fold. map. 24½cm.
Joseph Smith and the origin of Mormonism, p. 47–106. The organization of the Mormon church, p. 329–342.
CSmH, CtY, CU–B, DLC, ICN, NjP, NN, UHi, ULA, UPB, USlC, UU, WHi

4316. James, Jason W. Memories and viewpoints . . . Roswell, New Mexico, Privately printed, 1928.
183p. 18½cm.
With the Utah Expedition, 1858.
ICN

James, Samuel. To the members of the Church of Jesus Christ of Latter-day Saints. *See To the members of the Church . . .*

4317. James, William. The varieties of religious experience; a study in human nature being the Gifford lectures on natural religion delivered at Edinburgh in 1901–1902, by William James. New York, London [etc.] Longmans, Green & Co., 1902.
xii, 534p. 22cm.
Brief discussion of Joseph Smith and his method of receiving revelation.
Other editions: New York, London [etc.] Longmans, Green & Co., 1902. DLC; (same) 1911 [c1902] CU; (same) 1912 [c1902] CU; New York, 1916 [c1902] USlC; 1916. ULA; New York, Modern Library [c1929] USlC
DLC, NjP, NjPT

4318. James J. Strang. . . . Kansas City, Mo., 1918.
Broadside. 28×21½cm.
A proclamation asserting seven reasons why James J. Strang should be considered the prophetic successor of Joseph Smith. Includes a challenge to debate any of the above seven claims. Dated at end: Kansas City, Mo., Jan. 15, 1918.
IWW

4319. Jameson, John Franklin. Dictionary of United States history. 1492–1897. Four centuries of history. Written concisely and arranged alphabetically in dictionary form. By J. Franklin Jameson . . . Illustrated with nearly 300 portraits. Boston, Puritan Publishing Co. [1897]
2p.l., 3–733p. plate, ports., facsim. 25cm.
Mormons, Mountain Meadows massacre, Joseph Smith, and Brigham Young included.
Other editions: 1894. CU, NjP; 1898 [c1900] DLC
DLC, NjP, UPB

4320. Jannet, Claudio. Les Etats-Unis contemporains ou les moeurs, les institutions et les idees, depuis la guerre de la secession, par Claudio Jannet, Ouvrage precede d'une Lettre de M. Le Play. Deuxieme edition. Paris, E. Plon Et Cie, Imprimeurs-Editeurs, 1876.
xxiii, 524p. 18cm.
Mormonism included in the chapter on extreme religions.
Title in English: Contemporary United States or its mores, its institutions and its ideas . . .
CU-B, NjP, UPB

4321. Janoschek, Edward. A friendly discussion upon religious subjects. Compiled from a work entitled "Mr. Durant of Salt Lake City," by Ben E. Rich and continued here by Edward Janoschek. [n.p., n.d.]
8p. 19cm.
USIC

4322. ———. The Latter-day Zion, its redemption and chosen instruments. An appeal to all true Latter-day Saints and believers in the doctrine of Christ. By Elder Edward Janoschek. Salt Lake City, 1914.
102p. 19cm.
MoInRC, NjP, NN, UHi, ULA, UPB, USl, USIC

4323. Jaques, John. Catechism for children, exhibiting the prominent doctrines of the Church of Jesus Christ of Latter-day Saints. Liverpool, F. D. Richards, 1854.
iv [5]–84p. 16½cm.
MH, USIC, UU

4324. ———. (same) Tenth thousand. Liverpool, Published by F. D. Richards . . . London, For sale at the Latter-day Saints Book Depot . . . 1855.
iv [5]–84p. 16cm.
MH, USIC (correction copy for the 1870 edition)

4325. ———. (same) Salt Lake City, G. Q. Cannon, 1870.
iv [5]–81p. 17cm.
"Fifteenth thousand"
Sabin 50731
CtY, DLC, MB, USl, USIC

4326. ———. (same) Salt Lake City, G. Q. Cannon, 1872.
80p. 15½cm.
ICN, MoInRC, NN, UU

4327. ———. (same) Intended for use in schools. 21st thousand. Liverpool, Published by Albert Carrington [1877]
iv [5]–81p. 16½cm.
USIC

4328. ———. (same) Salt Lake City, David O. Calder, 1877.
iv, 5–74p. 19cm.
"25th thousand"
CtY, CU-B, MH, NjP, NjPT, NN, UPB, USIC, UU

4329. ———. (same) Intended for use in school. 17th thousand. Liverpool, Printed and Published by Horace S. Eldredge . . . [ca. 1879]
iv [5]–81p. 16½cm.
USIC

4330. ———. (same) 21st thousand. Liverpool, A. Carrington, for sale at the Latter-day Saint Book Depot, 1887.
iv, 5–81p. 17cm.
CU, DLC, NN, UHi, WHi

4331. ———. (same) 22nd thousand. Liverpool, G. Teasdale, 1888.
iv, 5–81p. 16cm.
CSmH, DLC, USIC

4332. ———. (same) Salt Lake City, The Deseret News Co., 1888.
iv [5]–92p. 17½cm.
"Thirty-fifth thousand."
NjP, UPB, USIC, WHi

4333. ———. (same, in Danish) Catechismus for Børn fremstillende de vigtigste Laerdomme i Jesu Christi Kirke af Sidste-Dages Hellige . . . Oversat fra Engelsk. Kjobenhavn, J. Van Cott, 1860.
iv, 104p. 15½cm.
NN, UPB, USIC

4334. ———. (same) Katekismus for Børn, fremstillende de vigtigste laerdomme i Jesu Kristi Kirke af Sidste-Dages Hellige. Af Aeldste John Jacques. Oversat fra Engelsk. Kjobenhavn, Udgivet og forlagt af K. Peterson, 1872.
iv, 103p. 17cm.
UPB, USIC

4335. ———. (same, in Dutch) Catechismus voor kinderin behelzende de voor-naamte leerstellingen van de kirk van Jezus Christus van de Heiligen der Laatste dazen. Naar het engelsch. Amsterdam, Gedrukt by Roeloffzen and Hubner, 1877.
iv [5]–91 [1]p. 21cm.
MH, UU

4336. ———. (same) 3d ed. Uit het Engelsch. Rotterdam, F. Pieper, 1897.
v, 98 [1]p. 21½cm.
UHi, USIC

JAQUES, J.

4337. ———. (same, in German) Der Katichismus für Kinder, oder, Eine Darstellung der hervorragendsten Lehren der Kirche Jesu Christi der Heiligen der Letzten Tage. les tausend, aus dem Englischen übersetz von Johannes Huber. Bern, 1872.
48p. 20½cm.
MH, USIC

4338. ———. (same) Erste Tausend aus dem Englischen übersetzt von Johannes Huber, 1872. Zweites Tausend. Hersausgegeben von P. F. Gass . . . Bern, 1882.
iv, 72p. 19cm.
"Zweiten Auflage."
DLC, UHi, UPB, USIC

4339. ———. (same) Bern, F. F. Scharrer, 1892.
4p.l., 72p. 18½cm.
NjP, UPB, USIC, UU

4340. ———. (same, in Hawaiian) Ke Alakai; oia hoi, he buke e hoakaka mai ana i na kumu manaoio or ka Ekalesia o Iesu Kristo o ka Poe Noano o na la Hope Nei. Unuhiia e Iosepa H. Dina. Kulanakauhale o Lokopaakai [Salt Lake City] Juvenile Instructor Office, 1882.
108p. port. 18cm.
USIC

4341. ———. (same) Honolulu, Hawaii, Hawaiian Gazette Co., 1907.
114p. 17½cm.
USIC

4342. ———. (same, in Swedish) Cateches för Barn, framställande de wigtigaste lärdomarne i Jesu Christi kyrka af de yttersta dagars helige of Äldste John Jaques . . . Öfwersättning fran Danskan. Malmö, Tryckt hos C. A. Anderson & Co., 1871.
pa W. W. Cluffs förlag.
iv, 103p. 15cm.
USIC

4343. ———. (same) Köpenhamn, Utgifwet och förlaggd af C. G. Larsen. Trykt hos F. E. Bording, 1873.
iv, 103p. 15cm.
NjP, USIC, UU

4344. ———. The Church of Jesus Christ of Latter-day Saints. Its priesthood, organization, doctrines, ordinances and history. By Elder John Jaques. Salt Lake City, Deseret News Co., 1882.
32p. 16½cm.
CSmH, CU-B, DLC, NjP, NN, PHi, UHi, UPP, USl, USIC, UU, WHi

4345. ———. (same) [Salt Lake City, Deseret News Co., n.d.]
22 [2]p. 17cm.
MH, MoInRC, NjP, UPB, UU

4346. ———. Exclusive salvation. By John Jaques, Elder in the Church of Jesus Christ of Latter-day Saints. [Liverpool, Published by Franklin D. Richards, 1852]
8p. 21cm.
Caption-title.
Variant printings.
CSmH, CtY, ICN, MH, MoInRC, NN, UPB, USl, USIC

4347. ———. (same) By John Jaques, Minister in the Church of Jesus Christ of Latter-day Saints. Liverpool, Published by F. D. Richards [1852?]
8p. 20½cm.
Variant printings.
USIC

4348. ———. (same) By John Jaques, Elder in the Church of Jesus Christ of Latter-day Saints. [Thirteenth thousand.] Liverpool, Published by F. D. Richards . . . London, For sale at the L. D. Saints' Book Depot . . . Printed by R. James [1852?]
8p. 20½cm.
UPB

4349. ———. Polygamy. [n.p., 1869?]
16p. 22cm.
Caption-title.
Reprinted from the *Millennial Star.* V. 15, No. 7, 1853.
In double columns.
Signed: J.
USIC

4350. ———. . . . Salvation: a dialogue between Elder Brownson and Mr. Whitby, by John Jaques, Elder in the Church of Jesus Christ of Latter-day Saints . . . No. 1. [Liverpool, Published by S. W. Richards, 1853?]
8p. 20cm.
Caption-title.
MH, UPB, USIC

4351. ———. (same) [Liverpool, Published by Franklin D. Richards . . . Printed by R. James, 1854?]
8p. 22cm.
Caption-title.
At head of title: Second five thousand.
CSmH, UHi, USIC

4352. ———. Salvation: a dialogue between Elder Brownson and Mr. Whitby. By John Jaques . . . No. 2 [Liverpool, Published by S. W. Richards, 1853?]
8p. 21cm.
Caption-title.
CSmH, UPB, USIC

4353. ———. (same) [Liverpool, Published by Franklin D. Richards . . . 1854?]
8p. 22cm.
Caption-title.
At head of title: Second five thousand.
CSmH, USIC

JAQUES, J.

4354. ———. (same) [Liverpool, Published by Franklin D. Richards . . . Printed by R. James, 1854?]
8p. 20cm.
Caption-title.
At head of title: Second five thousand.
CSmH, UHi

4355. Jarman, William. Anti-Mormon tracts. [London, ca. 1882–4]
15 nos. [2]p. each 19cm.
MH No. 11. To the British Mormon dupes.
MH, USIC No. 12. Mormon missionaries.
Variant printings.
Eberstadt catalog lists no. 11–15.

4356. ———. Britons!! "Beware of the vile deceivers! "Certain lewd fellows of the baser sort." By W. Jarman, ex-Mormon priest, from Salt Lake City, Utah. [Exeter, W. Jarman, Printer & Publisher, 188–]
[2]p. 16½cm.
Caption-title.
Publicity for his book and lectures.
Two variant printings with slight variations. USIC
MH, MoInRC, USIC

4357. ———. Hell upon earth! Or Mormon life exposed. By Wm. Jarman. An ex-Mormon priest. [Wehoskey, Providence, R.I.? 188–]
Broadside. 25×15cm.
Publicity for his lectures.
USIC

4358. ———. Hell on earth; scenes of Mormon life. How women and girls are ensnared. Lust and murder in the name of religion (Prospectus). [n.p., 188–]
Broadside. illus. 42×26cm.
Publicity for his book.
MH, USIC

4359. ———. Hell upon earth, the doctrines and practices of the "Latter-day Saints" in Utah. Discussion between W. Jarman, ex-Mormon priest, from Salt Lake City, and Mormon missionaries, from Utah, held at Hoyland Common, Yorkshire, June 15th, 16th, and 17th, 1887. [Exeter, 1887?]
15p. 18cm.
MH, USIC

4360. ———. Jack the Ripper Mormons. The Boss Ripper, Brigham Young, preached thus: — Cut their throats, all the people said, AMEN . . . Exeter [188–]
Broadside. 26×11cm.
Publicity for his *Hell upon Earth.*
USIC

4361. ———. Mormons. £1,000 reward. [Exeter, 1887]
6p. 21×9cm.
Reprinted from *Barnsley Independent*, Saturday, July 9th, 1887. Answers to charges against him in the *Millennial Star.* Refutation of the tract £1,000 reward.
MH

4362. ———. The Mountain Meadows massacre and the confession and execution of the Mormon Bishop John D. Lee, 120 men, women, and children murdered by the Utah "Latter-day Saints" [Exeter? ca. 1881]
8p. illus. 21cm.
Illustrations from his *U.S.A. Uncle Sam's abscess.*
At head of title: Anti-Mormon works by W. Jarman.
Variant edition without illustrations. USIC
Another variant published in Leicester. USIC
MH, USIC

4363. ———. To the British public . . . I beg to draw your attention to the enclosed testimonies. [London, ca. 1881]
[2]p. 21cm.
Caption-title.
A letter concerning his Mormon life on one side and an advertisement concerning his lecture on the other.
USIC

4364. ———. U.S.A. Uncle Sam's abscess, or, Hell upon earth for U.S. Uncle Sam. By W. Jarman who suffered twelve years in the Mormon hell on earth, as one of the "Virgins without guile," and a priest after the order of Melchizedek! where polygamy, incest, and murder are taught and practised as religion under the "all seeing eye," and the sign "Holiness unto the Lord." Exeter, England, H. Leduc's Steam Printing Works, 1884.
1p.l. [5]–194 [1]p. illus. 19cm.
CSmH, CtY, CU–B, DLC, ICN, MH, MoInRC, NjP, UHi, ULA, USl, USIC, UU, WHi

4365. ———. (same) Exeter, England, H. Leduc's Steam Printing Works, 1884.
17p.l. [5]–194p. illus. 18cm.
Includes 16 preliminary leaves of plates. Also 2 variant editions in different paper covers. USIC
NjPT, UPB, USIC

4366. ———. The Utah abomination, all sorts of cruelty, treachery and murder, practiced under a cloak of religion. Its blasphemy, polygamy & incest. A few facts with regard to the Utah "Latter-day Saints," a sermon preached by the Rev. T. DeWitt Talmage in the Tabernacle, Brooklyn, U.S., on the 26th of Sept., 1880.
8p. 18cm.
At head of title: Anti-Mormon Works.
By W. Jarman, Ex Priest from Salt Lake City.
Reprint of Talmage's sermon. p. 1–7.
MH, MoInRC, ULA, USIC

4367. ———. (same) [Exeter? n.d.]
8p. illus. 18cm.
Same with the plates from *U.S.A. Uncle Sam's abscess.*
USIC

4368. ———. . . . Wm. Jarman Ex-Mormon Elder from Salt Lake City, Utah, will give his beautifully illustrated lecture on Mormonism and exhibition of Mormon life (with) sights and scenes in the Mormon Country! Boston, Job Print. [188–]
Broadsheet. 73½×17½cm.
Advertisement for lectures with publicity material on verso.
At head of title: Town Hall — Westford, Friday Eve July 22.
USlC

4369. Jarman and the Mormons. Extract from the "Times." [Exeter? ca. 1881?]
Broadside. 21×9cm.
Advertisement for his book and lectures.
USlC

4370. Jarman and the Mormons. Interviewing a Mormon from Utah. [n.p., 1888?]
[4]p. 23½cm.
Includes an interview with B. H. Roberts from the Herald of Wales, July 14th, 1888; letter from Maria B. Ford, Jarman's divorced wife, and article on Jarman as a violator of British law.
USlC

4371. ———. (same) [Liverpool, Printed at the "Millennial Star" Office, ca. 1889]
[4]p. 23½cm.
"Investigation by the United States Congress" on the moral status of Utah added to the above edition.
CU–B, UPB, USlC

4372. ———. (same) [Liverpool, Printed at the "Millennial Star" Office, 1911]
4p. 22½cm.
"Recent expressions of prominent men," added to first edition.
UHi, USlC

———. *See also Roberts, Brigham Henry.*

4373. Jarman's "murdered" son. [Liverpool? 1889?]
[1]l. 29×14cm.
Folded circular.
Affidavit to prove that Albert Edward Jarman was not murdered by the Mormons as claimed by William Jarman, Anti-Mormon lecturer in England. One affidavit is his own statement.
MH, USlC

4374. . . . Jarman's scenes of Mormon life! 600 lovely views shown . . . [London, ca. 1881]
Broadside. 21×15cm.
Advertisement for his illustrated lecture. Other advertisement on verso.
MH

4375. Jarrod, J. Criticisms on Mormon revelations of the book of Doctrine and Covenants. By J. Jarrod. Oakland, Cal., Messiah's Advocate [after 1897]
32p. 16½cm.
MoInRC

4376. Jefferies, William. The gospel pioneer, by William Jefferies. [Salt Lake City, Juvenile Instructor Office, 1890?]
16p. 16cm.
L.D.S. statements numbered A–Z.
MoInRC, USlC, UU

4377. ———. (same) [Salt Lake City, Deseret News Publishing Co., 189–]
23p. 18cm.
MH, NjP, NN, USlC, UU, WHi

4378. Jencks, E. N. A plea for polygamy . . . Paris, C. Carrington, 1898.
xxvip., [1]l., 257p., 271–280p. 22½cm.
Editor's foreword signed: Chas. Carrington.
"Excursus" (p.[195]–257) treats of polygamy among the Mormons. "R. F. Burton of polygamy" extracted from the "City of the Saints."
1. Celestial Marriage.
2. Plurality of wives from the Mormon standpoint.
3. R. F. Burton on the motives of polygamy.
4. Letter from a Mormon's wife in favor of polygamy.
Published under title: The History & Philosophy of Marriage by a Christian Philanthropist, without the Excursus on Mormon polygamy.
Another edition: New York, The Panurge Press [c1929] USlC
CtY, DLC, USl, USlC

4379. Jenkins, Paul Burrill. The book of Lake Geneva, by Paul B. Jenkins. Chicago, Ill., Published for the Chicago Historical Society by the University of Chicago Press [c1922]
xvii, 225 [1]p. plates, fold. map. 24cm.
General information of Mormonism and in particular by the Strang faction.
DLC, NjP, NN, UPB, USlC

4379a. Jenks, G. A. Convictions for polygamy in Utah and Idaho. Letter from the acting Attorney-General, In reply to the resolution of the House in relation to convictions for polygamy in Utah and Idaho. Washington, 1888.
11p. 22½cm. (U.S. 50th Cong. 1st Sess. House. Ex. Doc. No. 447)
UPB

4380. ———. Ex parte: In the matter of Hans Nielsen, Appellant. No. 1527. Appeal from the first Judicial District Court of the Territory of Utah. Brief for Respondent. [Washington? 1889?]
9p. 23cm.
Cover-title.
At head of title: In the Supreme Court of the United States. October term.
Prepared by G. A. Jenks, Solicitor General.
Polygamy case.
UPB

JENSEN, J. M.

4381. Jensen, Jens Marinus. Early history of Provo, Utah, by J. Marinus Jensen. [Provo, Utah] Pub. by the author [New Century Printing Co.] 1924.
2p.l. [5]–182p. illus. 20cm.
NjP, UHi, USlC

4382. ———. History of Provo, Utah. [Provo, Utah] Published by the author, 1924.
2p.l. [5]–414p. illus. 20cm.
Howes J102
CSmH, ICN, ICU, MH, NjP, UHi, ULA, USl, USlC

4383. Jensen, Nephi. Joseph Smith; an oration . . . Toronto, Canada, Canadian Mission [ca. 1920]
7[1]p. 21½cm.
Early history and accomplishments.
IWW, MoInRC, UPB, USlC, UU

4384. ———. (same) [n.p., n.d.]
[173]p. 12cm.
Cover-title.
UPB

4385. ———. Missionary themes. Salt Lake City, 1925–1928.
4v. 18cm. (Manual for the Priests' Quorums)
UPB, USlC

4386. ———. Missionary themes. Manual for the Priests' Quorums. Salt Lake City [Deseret News Press] 1929–1931.
3v. 19cm.
NN

4387. ———. "Mormonism" the modern marvel. [Salt Lake City] Church of Jesus Christ of Latter-day Saints, 1922.
14 [1]p. 18cm.
Variant printing. USlC
MnU, UHi, USlC

4388. ———. What the "Mormons" believe; open letter of Elder Nephi Jensen to Rev. J. H. Oke. [Toronto, ca. 1920]
16p. 15cm.
USlC

4389. Jensen, P. Joseph. Lesson Book for the Religion Classes in the Church of Jesus Christ of Latter-day Saints. Eighth Grade. Written for the General Church Board of Education By P. Joseph Jensen. [Salt Lake City] Published by the Deseret Book Company [1924?]
107p. 19cm.
UPB

4390. Jensenius, Caspar H. Kort begreb om den egentlige Mormonisme. Af Jensenius. Christiania, Trykt og Tilkjobs hos, J. Chr. Abelsted, 1855.
16p. 20cm.
Title in English: A right understanding concerning real Mormonism.
NN, UHi, USlC

4391. ———. Mormonernes Laere og de kristnes tro af C. H. Jensenius. Trykt og forlagt af J. Chr. Abelsted. Christiana, 1855.
3p.l., 44 [i.e. 86] [1]p. 21cm.
A comparative study between Christianity and Mormonism.
Christian teaching on verso and Mormonism on recto of each facing page. (double numbers)
Index in double columns.
Title in English: Mormon doctrine and Christianity.
USlC

4392. ———. (same) Andet oplag. Kristiania, Trykt og forlagt af T. Chr. Abelsted, 1856.
5p.l., 46 [i.e. 90]p.
NN, USlC

4393. Jenson, Andrew. Biographical encyclopedia, or, condensed biographical sketches of presiding officers, veterans, missionaries and other active men and women in the Salt Lake Stake of Zion, alphabetically arranged. By Andrew Jensen. Salt Lake City, 1888.
1p.l. [3]–96p. 25cm.
"Supplement to the *Historical Record.*"
MH, NN, UHi, ULA, UPB, USl, USlC

4394. ———. The Book of Mormon; a discourse delivered by Elder Andrew Jenson, Assistant Church Historian, in the Tabernacle, Salt Lake City, September 22nd, 1907. Liverpool, Millennial Star Office [1909]
24p. 21cm.
Cover-title.
Variant cover: The Book of Mormon, History of the Witnesses. USlC
UHi, UPB, USlC

4395. ———. . . . A chronology of important events of the year 1885. Comp. by Andrew Jenson. Salt Lake City, 1887.
1p.l., vi, 24p. 24½cm.
At head of title: Supplement to the *Historical record.*
CtY, DLC, ICN, UHi, ULA, UPB, UU

4396. ———. . . . A chronology of important events of the year 1886. Comp. by Andrew Jenson. Salt Lake City, 1887.
1p.l., viii, 24p. 24½cm.
At head of title: Supplement to the *Historical record.*
CtY, DLC, ICN, UHi, UPB

JENSON, A.

4397. ———. . . . A chronology of important events of the year 1887. Comp. by Andrew Jenson. Salt Lake City, 1887.
1p.l., vii, 23p. 24½cm.
At head of title: Supplement to the *Historical record.*
CtY, DLC, ICN, UHi, UPB, USlC

4398. ———. A chronology of important events of the year 1888. Comp. by Andrew Jenson. Salt Lake City, 1889.
14p. 24½cm.
At head of title: Supplement to the *Historical record.*
Chronology through 1884.
USlC

4399. ———. . . . Church Chronology: or a record of important events connected with the history of the Church of Jesus Christ of Latter-day Saints, and the Territory of Utah. Compiled by Andrew Jenson. Salt Lake City, 1886.
2p.l., xx, 112p. 24½cm.
At head of title: "Supplement to the *Historical record.*
Chronology through 1886.
CtY, ICN, IWW, DLC, NN, UHi, ULA, USlC, UU

4400. ———. (same) Church chronology. A record of important events pertaining to the history of the Church of Jesus Christ of Latter-day Saints. 2d edition, revised and enlarged. Salt Lake City, Printed at the Deseret News, 1899.
xxviii, 259p. 24cm.
Chronology through 1898.
CSmH, CtY, ICU, NjP, NN, UHi, UPB, USlC, UU, WHi

4401. ———. (same) 2d edition, revised and enlarged, with two supplements and an elaborate index. Salt Lake City, Printed at the Deseret News, 1914.
3p.l., vii–xxxvi, 259, 32, 204p. diagrs. 23½cm.
2d t.-p. has date 1899 for the main body of the book.
Chronology through 1913.
CU–B, ICN, NN, UHi, ULA, USlC

———. Church encyclopedia. *See his Historical record.*

4402. ———. The historical record; a monthly periodical devoted exclusively to historical, biographical chronological and statistical matters. Salt Lake City, 1882–1890.
9v. 24cm.
Originally published monthly as a periodical in variant paper wrappers later issued as a nine volume set. Vol. 1–4 published under title "Morgensternen" was not republished into English. Vol. 5–8 republished with a separate title-page: "Church Encyclopedia, book 1," Salt Lake City. Vol. 9 entitled "The pioneers of 1847." The supplements usually appear in the nine volumes.
CtY, CU–B, ICN, MH, NjP, UHi, ULA, UPB, USl, USlC, UU, WHi

4403. ———. [The historical record] Prospectus. Salt Lake City, 1886.
Broadside. 22½×15½cm.
Signed: Salt Lake City, June 15, 1886.
NjP

4404. ———. History of the Scandinavian Mission. By Andrew Jenson. Salt Lake City, Deseret News Press, 1927.
xvi, 570p. illus., ports. 24cm.
CU–B, DLC, ICN, NjP, NN, UHi, ULA, UPB, USl, USlC, UU

4405. ———. Infancy of the Church. An elaborate and detailed description of persons, places and incidents connected with the early rise and progress of the Church of Jesus Christ of Latter-day Saints. A series of letters written by Elders Andrew Jenson and Edward Stevenson. Salt Lake City, 1889.
2p.l., 62p. 25cm.
Supplement to the *Historical record.*
CSmH, CtY, ICN, MoInRC, NjP, NN, UHi, USl, USlC, UU

4406. ———. Jorden Rundt; en Reisebeskrivelse. Salt Lake City, 1908.
viii, 360p. illus., ports., map. 24cm.
A trip around the world with emphasis on Mormon sights particularly in Scandinavia, 1895–97.
Title in English: A trip around the world.
NjP, UHi, USlC, UU

4407. ———. Joseph Smith as a prophet, predictions uttered by him and their signal fulfillment. His prophetic power established by scriptural rule. [Salt Lake City, Printed and sold by the Deseret News Co., c1891]
15p. 21½cm.
CSmH, MH, NjP, UPB, USl, USlC

4408. ———. Joseph Smiths levnetslöb. Oversat, samlet og uddraget fra forskjellige paalidelige vaerker ved Andrew Jenson & Joh. A. Bruun. Förste Udgave . . . Salt Lake City, udgivet og forlagt af A. Jenson & J. A. Bruun. Trykt hos D. O. Calder, "News Office," 1877.
30 pts. ([6] v–xi, 435p.) port. 23cm.
Title in English: The life of Joseph Smith.
USlC

4409. ———. (same) Oversat, samlet og udgivet af A. Jenson og J. A. Bruun . . . Salt Lake City, Trykt hos Cannon & Young, "Deseret News Office," 1879.
[6] v–xi, 435p. port. 23cm.
CU–B, DLC, MH, NjP, UHi, ULA, UPB, USl, USlC

4409a. ———. (same) Kjøbenhavn, Udgivet af Foreningen til gudelige Smaaskrifters udbredelse, Graebes Bogtrykkeri, 1888.
80p. 17cm. (No. 78)
"3dte oplag."
USlC

4410. ———. (same, under title) Joseph Smith's levnetsløb, samlet og tildels oversat of Andrew Jenson. . . . Anden udgave, . . . Kjøbenhavn, Udgivet og forlagd af C. D. Fjeldsted, 1904.
xi, 372p. 22½cm.
MH, NjP, UHi, UPB, USlC, UU

4411. ———. Kirkens historie, fra profeten Josephs död, tilligemed en kirkehistorisk kronologi. Samlet, oversat og udgivet af Andrew Jenson . . . Salt Lake City, Trykt hos "Deseret news company," 1883.
vii, 252p. 22½cm.
Title in English: History of the Church from the time of the Death of the Prophet Joseph.
DLC, USl, USlC, UU

4412. ———. Kortfattet kirkehistorie af Jesu Kristi Kirke af Sidste-Dages Hellige. Salt Lake City, 1914.
18p. 24½cm.
Caption-title.
Title in English: A short history of the Church of Jesus Christ of Latter-day Saints.
UHi, USlC

4413. ———. Latter-day Saint biographical encyclopedia. A compilation of biographical sketches of prominent men and women in the Church of Jesus Christ of Latter-day Saints; by Andrew Jenson . . . Salt Lake City, A. Jenson History Company, and Printed by the Deseret News, 1901–36.
4v. port. 25cm.
V. 4 Published by the A. Jenson Memorial Association.
CSmH, CtY, CU–B, DLC, ICN, ICU, MH, MoInRC, NjP, NN, UHi, ULA, UPB, USl, USlC, UU, WHi

4413a. ———. A Missionary experience. [Salt Lake City, n.d.]
8p. 24cm.
NjP, USlC

Jepson, Ring [*pseud.*] *See Latham, Henry Jepson.*

4414. Jerslov, Jens. Skulle vi vente en anden? Et enfoldigt vidnesbyrd imod de saakaldte Mormonpraester. Aalborg, 1854.
20p.
Title in English: Should we wait for another?
Schmidt

4415. Jessen, A. Et tilbud til danske landbrugere og mejerister fra Lucerne Land and Water Company in Utah. Kobenhavn, 1895.
8p.
Title in English: An offer to Danish farmers and dairy men from Lucerne Land and Water Company in Utah.
Schmidt

Jessie, the Mormon's daughter. *See St. John, Percy Bolingbroke.*

4416. Jex, Heber C., *editor.* Eliza Goodson Jex, Spanish Fork, Utah. Biographical sketch and family history, last reunion talk, newspaper reports and interviews, sea voyage, excerpts from funeral services, Jex family organization and constitution. [Spanish Fork Press, 1921]
55p. illus., ports. 23cm.
UPB, USl

4417. Job, Thomas. John Wesley on the spiritual gifts, and Thomas Job on the captivity and redemption of Zion. Plano, Ill., The True Latter-day Saints Herald, 1866.
4p. 23cm.
MoInRC, NN, UHi, UPB

4417a. Jochumsson, Eggert. Hvad er mormonska? [n.p., Porvardssonar, ca. 1904]
8p. 17½cm.
Title in English: What are the Mormons?
USlC

4417b. ———. (same, under title) Hvath er mormónska? Eftir Eggert Jochumsson. [Reykjavik, útgefandi og ábyrgtharmathur: Jakob B. Jónsson. Prentsm. Gutenberg, 1911]
4p. 22cm.
USlC

4417c. ———. (same) [Gutenberg, Jakob B. Jonsson, 1911]
4p. 22cm.
USlC

4418. Jocknick, Sidney. Early days on the Western slope of Colorado and campfire chats with Otto Mears, the Pathfinder, from 1870 to 1883, inclusive. By Sidney Jocknick. Denver, The Carson-Harper Co., 1913.
4p.l. [9]–384p. plates, port. 20cm.
His association with the Mormons.
CU–B, DLC, NjP, USlC

4419. Jóhanneson, John (Jón Jóhannesson). Athvörunar-og sannleiksraust. [Útgefandi: Jón Jóhannesson. Rvík., Prentsmithja Pjóthólfs, 1902]
20p. 19½cm.
Title in English: Voice of warning and truth.
USlC

4420. ———. Fátt af mörgu. Hvath er hjátrú? [Reykjavik, Glasgow-prentsmithjan, 1901]
8p. 19cm.
Title in English: Little of everything.
USlC

JOHNSON, F. S.

4421. ———. Goth fagnathartithindi, sem flytjast skulu ollum thjothum. [Reykjavik? Felagsprentsmithjan, 1901]
8p. 21½cm.
Title in English: The idol, broken by the good tidings, which will remove all nations.
USIC

4422. ———. Hith mikla verk og undur i Vesturheimi. [Reykjavik, Prentsmithjan Gutenberg, 1912?]
16p. 22cm.
Title in English: The mighty work and a wonder in America.
USIC

4423. ———. Köllun til guthsrikis; stutt ágrip af trúarlaerdómum Jesú Kriste Kirkju Sithusta Daga Heilögu safnatharins, Hofündur og Útgesandi: Jón Jóhannesson. Reykjavik, Iceland, Prentsmithja pjothefs, 1902.
iv [5]–223 [1]p. 23cm.
Doctrines of the L.D.S. church.
Title in English: Call to the Kingdom of God.
USIC, UU

4424. ———. Ljósith og sannleikurinn. Ein stutt athugasemd um misskilning og villu Fr. Frithrikssonar vithvikjandi kenningum "peirra síthustu daga heilögu." [Reykjavik, Glasgow-prentsmithjan, 1901]
24p. 19½cm.
Title in English: The light and the truth.
USIC

4425. ———. Luthurhlomurinn. [Reykjavik, Prentsmithjan Gutenberg, 1913?]
3 nos. (16, 8, 8p.) 22cm.
Caption-title.
Title in English: The sounds of the common people.
USIC

4426. ———. Man's origin and destiny. A condensed gospel doctrine. Compiled and composed by John Jóhanneson. Murray, Utah, 1920.
126p. 15cm.
CU–B, USIC

4427. Johanson, Maria. Stjärnor i natten; anteckningar om Utah och mormonerna samt korta berättelser på vers och prosa, av Maria Johanson. Sandy, Utah, På eget förlag, 1927.
71 [1]p. illus. 19½cm.
Title in English: Stars in the night sky.
DLC, USIC, UU

4428. John Taylor Prayer Circle. A Token of love from the members of the John Taylor Prayer Circle to Patriarch Joseph Horne in commemoration of his long and faithful association therewith and of his retirement from the active Presidency thereof in his old age. Salt Lake City, March 15, 1895.
[11]l. ports. 26cm.
Includes a history of the prayer circle.
NjP, USIC

4429. Johnson, Benjamin Franklin. "Mormonism as an issue." [Tempe, Arizona, 1890]
15p. 17cm.
Signed: June 25th, 1890.
CSmH, MoInRC, USIC

4430. ———. Why the "Latter-day Saints" marry a plurality of wives. A glance at scripture and reason, in answer to an attack through the Polynesian, upon the saints for polygamy. San Francisco, Excelsior Print., 1854.
23p. 22½cm.
Howes J126
CSmH, CtY, UPB, USIC

4431. Johnson, C. E. Sights and scenes in Salt Lake City; a collection of vivid photographs of the more important buildings and places of interest in the Mormon metropolis, with a brief description of each . . . photographed and compiled by C. E. Johnson. Salt Lake City, Published by the Utah View Book Co. [1906?]
32p. illus. 21×26cm.
Printed by W. G. MacFarlane, Toronto, Canada.
Plates with paragraph of explanation.
UHi

4432. Johnson, Clifton. Highways and byways of the Rocky Mountains. New York, Macmillan Co., 1910.
xi, 279p. plates. 20½cm.
(American highways and byways)
"Life in a Mormon village"
Another edition: 1913. DLC
DLC, NjP, UHi, ULA, UPB, USIC

4433. Johnson, Don Carlos. A brief history of Springville, Utah, from its first settlement, Sept. 18, 1850, to the 18th day of September, 1900. Fifty years . . . compiled and written by Don Carlos Johnson. Springville, William F. Gibson, 1900.
i–vi, 124 [1]p. illus. 24cm.
Errata on [125] printed in red.
Howes J130
CSmH, CtY, CU–B, ICN, MH, NjP, NN, UHi, ULA, USI, USIC, UU

4434. Johnson, Frank S. Mormon morals, by a disillusioned convert. Cleveland, Ohio, Utah Gospel Mission [1925?]
[4]p. 17cm.
Also included in *Mormonism Proclaiming Itself a Fraud* by John D. Nutting.
NN, USIC

4435. Johnson, George Washington. Jottings by the way a collection of rustic rhyme by Geo. W. Johnson, with a brief auto-biography. Containing also, selections from the writing of other members of the family. By George W. Johnson. St. George, Utah, Printed by C. E. Johnson, 1882.
3p.l., 36, xxviiip. 13½cm.
Mostly rhymed Mormon history, but with a prose autobiography.
Includes poetry by Benjamin F. Johnson, Joseph E. Johnson, and James H. Martineau.
Howes J135
CtY, USIC

4436. ———. A suppliment [sic] to jotting's by the way; or, Scraps from my journal by G. W. Johnson. Huntington, Utah, 1884.
1p.l., 64 [3]p. 13½cm.
USIC

4437. Johnson, Henry T. Mormonism. The claims of the Book of Mormon to be a divine revelation examined, and proved to be false. Brighton [Eng.] W. Simpson [etc., etc. 185–]
12p. 16½cm.
CtY

4438. Johnson, J. E. Mormon guide! Showing the Distances and Best Camping Places over the North Platte Route from Omaha to Salt Lake City, U., thence to the Salmon River, Bannock and Virginia gold fields. [Spring Lake Villa] "Farmer's Oracle," Print. 1864.
1p.l., 7[6]p. 13½cm.
UU

4439. Johnson, Joel Hills. Hymns of praise for the young. Selected from the songs of Joel, by Joel H. Johnson . . . Salt Lake City, Deseret News Company, Printers and Publishers, 1882.
1p.l. [3]–344p. 12½cm.
360 numbered hymns.
MH, NNUT, USIC, UU

4440. ———. A portrait of the Missouri mob, a poem. [Nauvoo? Ill., 1840?]
Broadside. 25×17½cm.
Enclosed in ornamental border.
The Missouri mobs and their treatment of the Mormons.
Text also published in John E. Page's *Slander refuted.*
CtY

4441. ———. Voice from the mountains, being a testimony of the truth of the gospel of Jesus Christ as revealed by the Lord to Joseph Smith, Jr. By Joel H. Johnson. Salt Lake City, The Juvenile Instructor Office, 1881.
24p. 18½cm.
CtY, CU-B, ICN, MH, NN, UHi, USI, USIC, WHi

4442. Johnson, Joseph. The great Mormon fraud; or, The Church of Latter-day Saints proved to have had a falsehood for its origin; a record of crime for its history; and for doctrines: cruelty, absurdity, and infamy . . . By Joseph Johnson . . . Manchester, Butterworth & Nodal, Printers, 1885.
31p. 18½cm.
DLC, NN, USIC

4443. Johnson, Matthew. America pictorially described. London, James B. Knapp [1890?]
2p.l., ii [9]–144p. illus. 22cm.
Salt Lake City and Mormonism briefly described.
USIC

4444. Johnson, O. A. Mormonismen afsløret . . . af D. A. Johnson. [Kristiana "Sundhedshladets" Trykkeri, n.d.]
24p. 18cm.
Title in English: Mormonism unveiled.
UU, USIC

4444a. ———. (same) . . . Revederet og forøget udgive. Af D. A. Johnson. [Kristiana, Den Norske Bogmissions, forlag, n.d.]
36p. 18½cm.
USIC

4445. Johnsòn, Richard Z. The Idaho test oath: Argument delivered in the Supreme Court of Idaho Territory, Feb. 10, 1888, by Hon. Richard Z. Johnson in the Cases of William Heywood Appellant, vs. Henry Bolton, et al. Respondents, and James B. Innis, Appellant, vs. same Respondents. Appeals from Bear Lake County. Salt Lake City, The Deseret News Company, Printers, 1888.
45p. 23cm.
Legality of the anti-polygamy legislation as it affected Idaho.
CU-B, NjP, USIC, UU

4446. Johnson, Thomas Cary. Some modern isms, by Thos. Cary Johnson . . . Richmond, Va., Presbyterian Committee of Publication, c1919.
192p. illus. (port. group) 20cm.
"The lectures in this volume, on Mormonism, on Christian Science, and on Russellism, were delivered to the Senior class in Union Theological Seminary in Virginia, in January 1918." — Pref.
"Literature on Mormonism," p. [9]
DLC, NjPT, NN, ViU

4447. Johnson, Warren B. From the Pacific to the Atlantic, being an account of a journey overland from Eureka, Humboldt Co., California, to Webster, Worcester Co., Mass., with a horse, carriage, cow and dog. Webster, Mass., John Cort, 1887.
iii [8]–369p. illus. 20cm.
He arrived in Utah right after the Edmunds Bill was passed. His observations were not very accurate.
CU-B, DLC, NjP, UHi

4448. Johnston, Carrie Polk. History of Clinton and Caldwell Counties, Mo., Clinton County by Carrie Polk Johnston and Caldwell County by W. H. S. McGlumphy. Topeka, Kansas, Historical Publishing Company, 1923.
11p.l. [65]–836p. plates, ports. 27cm.
Includes location of Mormon settlements, preparation for the Far West Temple, and the Mormon battles of 1838, p. 193–258.
UPB, USlC

4449. Johnston, David Emmons. Representative-elect from Utah. Speech of Hon. David E. Johnston of West Virginia in the House of Representatives, January 25, 1900. Washington [Govt. Print. Off.] 1900.
7p. 23cm.
Mormons and politics.
DLC

4450. Johnston, William Graham. Experiences of a forty-niner, by Wm. G. Johnston, a member of the wagon train first to enter California in the memorable year 1849 . . . Pittsburg, 1892.
390p. plates, ports., map (fold. blue print) 23cm.
Went via Salt Lake City; observations about the Mormons.
Howes J173
CU–B, DLC, ICN, MiU–C, NjP

4451. Johnston, William Preston. The life of Gen. Albert Sidney Johnston, embracing his services in the armies of the United States, the Republic of Texas, and the Confederate States. By William Preston Johnston . . . New York, D. Appleton and Company, 1878.
xviii, 755p. illus., port., plates, maps. 23½cm.
Chap. XIII The Mormon rebellion.
Chap. XIV Utah campaign.
Chap. XV Camp Floyd.
Another edition: New York, 1880. NjP
Howes J175
DLC, UHi

4452. Jonasson, Stanley D. A Little scout shall lead by Stanley D. Jonasson. A one act play dealing with six points of the scout law. Dedicated to Oscar A. Kirkham. [Salt Lake City] Published by the General Board of Y.M.M.I.A., 1930.
14p. 19cm.
A boy scout play, written for the M.I.A. and dedicated to a church leader.
USlC

4453. Jonathan [*pseud.*] Joseph F. Smith answered. His plain talk shown to be full of errors and misstatements. Democrats have befriended Utah, while Republicans have opposed the territory. Read it carefully . . . [Salt Lake City?, 1892?]
4p. 29×19½cm.
Caption-title.
Church and politics.
UHi

4454. Jones, Charles Sheridan. The Mormons unmasked; secrets of Salt Lake City. By C. Sheridan Jones. London, Jarrold and Sons [1911]
145p. 19cm.
CtY, NN

4455. ———. The truth about the Mormons; secrets of Salt Lake City, by C. Sheridan Jones . . . London, W. Rider & Son, Ltd., 1920.
xiii, 129 [1]p. plates, 2 port. 19cm.
CU–B, DLC, ICN, MiU, MoInRC, NjP, NjPT, NN, UHi, USl, USlC, UU, WHi

4456. Jones, Dan. Adolygiad ar ddarlithoedd y parch. E. Roberts [gweinidog y bedyddwyr yn Rymni] yn erbyn Mormoniaeth . . . gan Capt. D. Jones . . . Merthyr-Tydvil, Cyhoeddwyd ac ar Werth, gan Capt. Jones [1847]
40p. 18cm.
Signed: Merthyr, Hydref 18 Fed., 1847 D. Jones —
Title in English: A look at the lectures of the Rev. E. Roberts.
USlC

4457. ———. Adolygiad ar ddarlith olaf y Parch. E. Roberts, Rymni, yn erbyn "Mormoniaeth." [Rhydybont, Argraffwyd gan John Jones, ca. 1850]
12p. 18cm.
Title in English: A review of the Rev. E. Robert's last lecture.
Caption-title.
CU–B, USlC

4458. ———. Amddiffyniad y Saint versus cyhuddiadau Thomas Jones, Merthyr, ac ereill . . . [Merthry-Tydvil? Argraffwyd gan John Jones, 1849?]
8p. 17cm.
Title in English: The defense of the Saints in the false accusations.
UHi

4459. ———. Amddiffyniad y Saint, yn ngwyneb camghyuddiadau y rhai a alwant eu hunain yn "Gwew y Don," yn y "Seren Gomer," Ionawr, 1847. [Merthyr-Tydfil, Cyhoeddwyd ac ar werth gan D. Jones, John Jones, Argraffydd, Rhydybont, ca. 1847]
12p. 18cm.
Title in English: The defense of the Saints.
USl, USlC

4460. ———. Anfyddiaeth Sectyddiaeth! [Merthyr-Tydvil, Argraffwyd a Chyhoeddwyd gan D. Jones, 14, Castle-Street, ca. 1854]
8p. 17cm.
Title in English: Skepticism of sectarianism.
UPB

JONES, D.

4461. ———. Anmhoblogrwydd "Mormon, Iaeth?" [Abertawy, Argraffwyd a Chyhoeddwyd gan D. Jones, ca. 1854]
12p. 17cm.
Title in English: Unpopularity of Mormonism.
UPB

4462. ———. Annerchiad at Offeiriaid, Parchedigion, Pregethwyr, a Holl Athrawon Crefydd Yn Nghymru. Ail Argraffiad. Yr Wythfed Fil. [Merthyr-Tydvil, D. Jones, Argraffydd, ca. 1854]
16p. 17cm.
Title in English: Proclamation to priests, ministers preachers and to all teachers of the Gospel in Wales.
UPB

———. Annerchiad y deuddeg apostol. *See Church of Jesus Christ of Latter-day Saints. Council of the Twelve Apostles. General epistle . . . (in Welsh)*

4463. ——— . Yr Arweinydd I Seion. Gan Capt. D. Jones. [n.p., ca. 1854]
16p. 17cm.
Title in English: The guide to Zion.
UPB

4464. ———. Beth ydyw yr efengyl? [Merthyr-Tydvil? Argraffwyd gan John Jones, 1849?]
12p. 17cm.
Title in English: What is the gospel?
UHi

4465. ———. Beth Yw "Gras Cadwedigol?" [Abertawy, Cyhoeddwyd ac argraffwyd gan D. Jones, ca. 1854]
8p. 17cm.
Title in English: What is saving grace?
UPB

4466. ———. Beth yw Mormoniaeth. [Merthyr-Tydfil, Chyoeddwyd ac ar Werth gan D. Jones, n.d.]
4p. 17½cm.
Caption-title.
Title in English: What is Mormonism?
USIC

4467. ———. Pa Beth Yw "Mormoniaeth?" [Abertawy, Argraffwyd a Chyoeddwyd gan D. Jones, ca. 1854]
4p. 17cm.
Title in English: What is Mormonism?
UPB

4468. ———. Yr Eurgrawn ysgruthyrol, yn yr hwn y cynnwysir crynodeb o adnodau a nodiadau, i brofi prif byncaiau Saint y dyddiau diweddaf. [Merthyr-Tydvil, Cyhoeddwyd, ac ar werth gan Capt. Jones . . . Argraffwyd gan John Jones, 1848]
iv [5]–288p. 18cm.
Title in English: Treatise on upwards of 100 gospel subjects.
CtY, MH, USIC

4469. ———. Y Farw wedi ei chyfodi yn fyw: neu'r hen Grefydd newvdd traethawd yn dangos anghyfnewidioldeb teyrnas ddwv. Gan Capt. D. Jones . . . Gwrecsam: Argraffwyd gan William Bayley, 1845.
iv [5]–48p. 17cm.
Title in English: The old religion anew.
CSmH, USIC

4470. ———. Y Farw Yn Fyw, new yr Hen Grefydd Newydd; sef Traethawd yn dangos Adferiad Teyrnas Ddwv. Gan Capt. D. Jones. Merthyr-Tydfil, Argraffwyd ac ar werth gan D. Jones, Castel-Street, 1854.
48p. 17cm.
Title in English: Old religion restored, a treatise on the restoration of the kingdom of God.
UPB

4471. ———. Gau-brophwydi. [Merthry-Tydfil, Cyhoeddwyd ac ar werth gan D. Jones. Argraffwyd, gan John Jones Thydybond, ca. 1847]
8p. 18cm.
Title in English: False prophets.
USI, USIC

4472. ———. Y glorian yn yr hon y gwelic David yn pwyso Williams, A Williams yn pwyso David; neu David Williams, o Abercanaid, yn Gwrthddweyd ei hun, wedi ei ddal yn ei dwyll, a'i Brofi yn ddeistaidd. Gan Capt. D. Jones. Merthyr-Tydfil, Cyhoeddwyd ac ar werth gan yr Awdwr, 1846.
16p. 18cm.
Title in English: David Williams of Abercanaid contradicting himself.
CSmH, USIC

4473. ———. Gwahoddiad! Abertawy, Argraffwyd, Gan D. Jones [ca. 1854]
2p. 17cm.
Title in English: An invitation.
UPB

4474. ———. "Haman" Yn hongian ar ei grogbren ei hun! Neu Daniel Jones (ddall) a'i lyfr yn profi Jwirionedd Mormoniaeth!! [Merthyr-Tydfil, Cyhoeddwydd ac ar werth gan D. Jones, John Jones, Argraffydd, Rhydybont, ca. 1850]
8p. 18cm.
Title in English: "Haman" hanging from his own gallows.
USI

4475. ———. Hanes ymfudiad y Saint i Galifornia, yn gynnwysedug. Mewn dau lythyr o New Orleans, America, un oddiwrth Capt. D. Jones, a'r llall oddiwrth Mr. Thos. Jeremy (Gynt o Lanybydder), at olygydd "Udgorn Seion." Merthyr-Tydfil, Argraffwyd ac ar werth gan J. Davis, 1849.
iv [5]–24p. 17½cm.
Title in English: History of the Saints' emigration to California.
CU–B, MH, NjP, UPB, USIC

JONES, M. E.

4476. ———. Y Lleidr Ar Y Groes." [Abertawy, Argraffwyd a chyhoeddwyd gan D. Jones, ca. 1854]
4p. 17cm.
Title in English: Thief on the cross.
UPB

4477. ———. Llorfruddiad Joseph a Hyrum Smith. [Abertawy, Argraffwyd a chyoeddwyd gan D. Jones, ca. 1854]
16p. 17cm.
Title in English: Assassination of Joseph and Hyrum Smith.
UPB

4478. ———. Llythyr oddiwrth Capt. D. Jones at Wm. Phillips, yn cynnwys newyddion seion. [Merthyr-Tydfil, John Davis, Argraffwyd, 1851]
8p. 18cm.
Title in English: A letter from Capt. D. Jones to Wm. Phillips containing news from Zion.
USIC, MH

4479. ———. Traddodir Darlithiau gan Capt. Jones, yn Neuadd Y. Saint, Heol Orange, Abertawy. [Abertawy, Argraffwyd gan D. Jones, ca. 1854]
4p. 17cm.
Title in English: Lectures by Capt. Jones.
UPB

4480. ———. Traethawd yn egluro Pwy Yw Duw Y Saint. [Merthyr-Tydfil, Argraffwyd a Chyhoeddwyd gan D. Jones, 14, Castle Street, ca. 1854]
24p. 17cm.
Title in English: Treatise on the religious subject of who is the God of the Saints.
UPB

4481. ———. Tri llythyr oddiwrth Capt. D. Jones ac un oddiwrth Mrs. Lewis (o Gydweli) o ddinas y llyn Halen. [Merthyr-Tydfil, John Davis, Argraffydd, 1850?]
8p. 18cm.
Miscellaneous letters on Mormonism by Elizabeth Lewis, John David, Daniel Jones.
Title in English: Three letters between Capt. D. Jones . . .
MH, USIC

4482. ———. Tystioliaethau Diwrthbrawf nad o'r "Spaulding Romance" y gwnaed Llyfr Mormon!! [Abertawy, Uyhoeddwyd ac argraffwyd gan D. Jones, ca. 1854]
24p. 17cm.
Title in English: Reply to the accusations concerning the Book of Mormon and the Spaulding romance.
UPB

4483. ———. Ymddyddau rhwng meistriaid traddodiad, sectariad, a Sant. A "Mene Tekel" yr olaf ar ei gyhuddwyr. [Argraffwyd, Gan John Jones, Rhydybont, n.d.]
24p. 17½cm.
Title in English: Dialogue on the Mormon church.
CSmH, USIC

4484. Jones, Daniel Webster. Forty years among the Indians. A true yet thrilling narrative of the author's experiences among the natives. By Daniel W. Jones. Salt Lake City, Juvenile Instructor Office, 1890.
[iii]–xv, [17]–400p. 23cm.
Howes J207
CSmH, CtY, DLC, ICN, NjP, NN, UHi, ULA, UPB, USI, USIC, UU, ViU, WHi

4485. Jones, George Washington. Utah contested election case. Speech of Hon. George W. Jones, of Texas, in the House of Representatives, Wednesday, April 19, 1882 . . . Washington, 1882.
16p. 20½cm.
Church and politics.
CSmH, UU

Jones, Harry. *See Jones, R. Hervey.*

4486. Jones, John Wesley. Amusing and thrilling adventures of a California artist, while daguerreotyping a continent, amid burning deserts, savages, and perpetual snows. And a poetical companion to the Pantoscope of California, Nebraska, and Kansas, Salt Lake & the Mormons. From 1500 daguerreotypes. By J. Wesley Jones, esq., detailing the startling adventures of an overland journey of 8,000 miles, written by John Ross Dix, Esq., editor Waverly Magazine, author Pen & Ink Sketches, &c. Boston, Published for the author, 1854.
92p. illus. 19cm.
Passed through Salt Lake City in 1951; descriptions of the Mormons.
Catalogued by CtY under John Dix.
In Howes under Phillips, George Spencer.
Howes P315, W–C 240
CtY, ICN

4487. Jones, Marcus Eugene. Jones' tourist guide to Salt Lake City and Utah. Salt Lake City [c1904]
85 [1]p. 2cm.
Tourist information concerning buildings, etc.
CSmH, OO

4488. ———. Salt Lake City. By Marcus E. Jones. A.M. Published by the Salt Lake Real Estate Board. [Salt Lake City, Star Printing Office, c1889]
79 [1]p. illus. 23cm.
Cover-title.
Mormonism mentioned in a brief history.
DLC, MH, MiU, NjP, UHi, USIC, UU

4489. ———. Treasury Department. Report on the internal commerce of the United States for the year 1890 . . . [Washington, Govt. Print. Off., 1891]
1174p. 23cm. (U.S. 51st Cong. 2d Sess. House. Ex. Doc. No. 6, pt. 2)
Considerable information on Utah history and Mormons, p. 841–954.
ULA, UPB, UU

4490. ———. . . . Utah, by Marcus E. Jones . . . New York, London, The Macmillan Company, 1902.
vi, 142p. illus., maps. 18½×15½cm. (Tarr and McMurray geographies. Supplementary volume)
Includes a brief history of Mormonism and the political situation in Utah.
Published with and without index.
DLC, UHi, ULA, UPB, USlC

4491. Jones, Margaret. Can newydd, o ganmoliaeth i lywyddiaeth Eglwys Iesu Grist o Saint y Dyddiau Diweddaf. Cyfansoddwyd a chyhoeddwyd, trwy ganiatad, gan Margaret Jones, Georgetown, (Sef, Eos Cymru Newydd.) [Merthyr-Tydfil, John Davis, Argraffydd, 1850?]
2p. 16½cm.
Title in English: A new poem on the good success of the Church of Jesus Christ of Latter-day Saints.
UPB

4492. Jones, Nathaniel Vary. Correspondence between Senator Reed Smoot and N. V. Jones, including a discussion of the senator's record in the United States Senate. Salt Lake City [Century Printing Company] 1914.
30p., [1]l. 23cm.
The "correspondence" of Senator Smoot is limited to a brief letter, dated Sept. 7, 1914, relative to his re-election to the United States Senate, and requesting the support of Mr. Jones. cf. p. 3–4.
DLC, MH, ULA

4493. ———. A reply to "Mormonism unveiled." . . . by Nathaniel V. Jones. Calcutta, Sanders, Printed by Sanders, Cone and Co., 1853.
120p. 21cm.
Howes J237
CtY, MH, USlC

4494. Jones, Paul. The Bible and the Book of Mormon: some suggestive points from modern Bible study. Logan, Utah [191–]
19p. 15cm.
Biblical evidence against the *Book of Mormon.*
USlC, UU

4495. ———. Points of contact. A Consideration for dissatisfied Latter-day Saints. By The Rev. Paul Jones. Salt Lake City, The Arrow Press [n.d.]
12p. 18cm.
USlC

4496. Jones, R. Hervey. To San Francisco and back. By a London parson. Published under the direction of the Committee of General Literature and Education, appointed by the Society for Promoting Christian Knowledge. London, Society for Promoting Christian Knowledge [1878]
2p.l., 223p. illus. 18½cm.
Reprinted from the *People's Magazine,* January–July, 1871.
Chapter IX. The Mormon City. Salt Lake City.
Visit to Brigham Young in 1870. Mentions ugly women, dirty Salt Lake Theatre, unsanitary ditches, etc. Largely devoted to his views on polygamy.
Another edition: [3d ed.] [1887?] CU–B
CSmH, DLC, MH, NN, OClWHi, OFH, UHi, UPB, UU

4497. Jones, Samuel Steven. Life of the Master; a poem. By S. S. Jones. Provo, Utah, 1913.
29p. 21cm.
Dedicated to "all who believe in the divine mission of our Lord and Savior, Jesus Christ, and His infinite atonement."
DLC, UPB, USlC

4498. ———. (same) Provo, Utah, c1915.
[29]p. 21½cm.
USlC

4498a. Jónsson, Halldór. Geislar hins lifandi ljoss. [Reykjavik? Prentsmithjan Gutenberg, 1910]
16p. 19½cm.
Missionary tract.
Title in English: Rays of living light.
USlC

4499. ———. Trúaratrithi i Jesú Kristí kirkju af sithustu daga heilögum. [Reykjavik, Felagsprintsmithjan, 1898]
7p. 19cm.
Title in English: Articles of faith of the Church of Jesus Christ of Latter-day Saints.
NjP, USlC

4499a. ———. (same) [n.p., ca. 1900]
8p. 20½cm.
USlC

4499b. ———. (same) Kaupmannahofn, Anthon L. Skanchy, Prentath hja S. L. Moller, 1902.
8p. 23cm.
USlC

4500. Jonveaux, Émile. L'Amérique actuelle, par Émile Jonveaux, précédé d'une introduction par Édouard Laboulaye . . . Paris, Charpentier et c^ie^, 1869.
2p.l., xvi, 339 [1]p. 18½cm.
Chapter XIII: Les Mormons.
States that the church consists of insensitivities, fanatics, etc.

Other editions: 2d ed. 1870. CtY, DLC. Also translated in Spanish under title *La América actual,* 1871; Los Estados Unidos en la América . . . 1871. NjP
Sabin 36638
Title in English: Present day Mormonism.
CU-B

4501. Jorgensen, L. Amerika og de Danskes liv herovre. Kortelig fremstillet til slaegtninges, venners og landsmaends gavn og oplysning. Efter fem aars ophold og erfaring. Kobenhaven, 1865.
24p.
Title in English: America and the life of Danes here.
Schmidt

4502. Jorgensen, Torben. Aabenbaringens Nødvendighed. Et københavnsk dagblads udtalelser om Pastor Barfoeds "Redegørelse." Af Torben Jørgensen. [København, Udgivet og forlagt af Martin Christophersen, 1912?]
[4]p. 21½cm.
Title in English: The Necessity of Revelation.
USIC

Joseph F. Smith answered. *See Jonathan [pseud.]*

4503. Joseph Smith, the prophet. [n.p., 1898?]
56p. 13cm.
A conversation concerning the divinity of Joseph Smith.
USIC

4504. The Journal of discourses. Liverpool, Printed and published by Albert Carrington [and others] November 1, 1853–May 17, 1886.
26v. weekly, semi-monthly. 22½cm.
Sermons delivered by Church authorities, principally during the period indicated.
Fragments of another volume exist consisting of 10 signatures (p. 1–241) but unlike the preceding issues, without date or place of issue. Sermons of 1897–1898. Possibly the forerunner of the Conference Reports.
UPB, USIC
CSmH; CtY; CU-B, V. 1–3, 15–20 inc., 21–26; MH; MoInRC; NjP V.1; NN inc.; ULA; UPB; USIC

4505. Journal of History. Lamoni, Iowa, Board of Publication of the Reorganized Church of Jesus Christ of Latter Day Saints, January, 1908–October, 1925.
18v. illus., quarterly. 26cm.
Edited by H. C. Smith, F. M. Smith, and D. F. Lambert. Issued quarterly from the Herald Publishing House.
V. 1–13 Published by Board of Publication.
V. 14–18 Issued by Department of History.
CtY comp.; CU comp.; DLC comp.; ICHi V.2 #1, V.3 #1; MH V.3–17; MoInRC comp.; MoK V.10–14; UPB V.1–11, 17; USIC comp.

4506. The Journal of Pedagogy. Provo, Utah, Published monthly under the auspices of the Department of Experimental Pedagogy, Brigham Young Academy, December, 1894–February, 1896.
2v. monthly. 28cm.
Published by the students of Brigham Young Academy.
UPB

4507. A journey on the Mississippi River, being a lecture delivered before the Lyceum of the Zane Street Public School of Philadelphia. By a director, April 10th, 1847. Philadelphia, Crissy & Markley, Printers, 1847.
24p. 23cm.
Saw at Montrose the Mormons who had abandoned Nauvoo; thought that they were as much sinned against as sinning.
CtY, CU-B, MH, PHi

4508. Joyce, John A. A checkered life, by Col. John A. Joyce . . . Chicago, S. P. Rounds, Jr., 1883.
2p.l. [7]–9, [3]l., 17–318p. front. 20cm.
Trip to Salt Lake City and a visit to Brigham Young, 1874, p. 216–217.
CU-B, DLC, NjP, UHi, UPB

Juab [*pseud.*] *See Schroeder, Theodore Albert.*

4509. Juarez Stake Academy, Juarez, Mexico. Juarez Stake Academy. Announcement. Juarez, 1903–
v. 19–22cm.
UPB 1908–09, 1924–25, 1925–26, 1926–27; USIC 1903–04, 1906–07, 1921–22, 1922–23, 1923–24, 1926–27, 1927–28, 1928–29, 1929–30

4510. Jubilee songs. [Nauvoo? 1843?]
Broadside. 32×33½cm.
Text within border.
"First part written at Captain Dutch's Lancaster Post Offices. Ill. . . . and sung by the party who accompanied Gen. Joseph Smith from Springfield . . . The Second part written by E. R. Snow.
Jubilation over Joseph Smith's being released.
USIC

4511. Judgment! The Word of the Lord, unto the members of the "Church of Jesus Christ of Latter Day Saints," and all those unto whom these words may come. [n.p., n.d.]
[4]p. 27cm.
A revelation concerning the way in which the church has apostatized from its true position.
USIC

4512. Just Platero [*pseud.*] The Mormons and the apparition of Christ in his body. [By Just Platero called S . . .] London, Printed by R. Herschfeld . . . 1861.
8p. 22cm.
USIC

4513. Justice, G. C. Lines written on the departure of brother Jacob Syfrit [sic] to Jackson County, Missouri; the land for the saints of the most high God, to inherit Zion forever By Brother G. C. Justice [With] revelation given November, 1850. [Philadelphia? 1850?]
[2]l., 19cm.
Caption-title.
Text within border. Second leaf contains "Revelation [to Syfritt] given Nov. 1850."
Morgan
NN

4514. Juvenile choir songs. [n.p., n.d.]
8p. 17cm.
Some of the music is by Evan Stephens.
MH

Juvenile Instructor. *See Instructor.*

4515. Juvenile Instructor Office. Catalogue of books and stationery for sale at the Juvenile Instructor Office. Salt Lake City, April, 1887.
16p. 15½cm.
USlC

4516. ———. (same) Salt Lake City, 1890.
30[1]p. 12p.
UHi

JOURNAL

Leonora Taylor

OF

HEBER C. KIMBALL,

AN ELDER OF THE CHURCH OF JESUS CHRIST OF LATTER DAY SAINTS.

GIVING AN ACCOUNT OF HIS MISSION TO GREAT BRITAIN, AND THE COMMENCEMENT OF THE WORK OF THE LORD IN THAT LAND.

ALSO

THE SUCCESS WHICH HAS ATTENDED THE LABORS OF THE ELDERS TO THE PRESENT TIME.

BY R. B. THOMPSON.

"Go ye into all the world, and preach the gospel to every creature; he that believeth and is baptized shall be saved:" etc. Mark 16: 15 16.

NAUVOO, ILL:
PRINTED BY ROBINSON AND SMITH.

1840.

Item 4614. The first *book* to issue from the Mormon press in Nauvoo, Illinois, giving Heber Kimball's account of the beginning of Mormon missionary activities in England. From the P. Crawley collection.

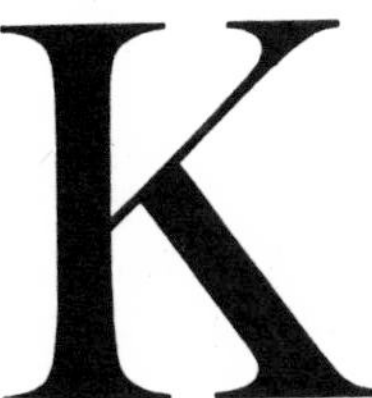

K., D.

4517. **K., D.** Mormonism self-refuted, by D. K. Camden Town, King and Company Publishers, 1851.
8p. 17cm.
Bancroft indicates a London edition.
USlC

4517a. **K., I.** Levensvragen. [n.p., n.d.]
4p. 21½cm.
Title in English: Life's questions.
USlC

4518. **Kalb, Ernst.** Kirchen und Sekten der Gegenwart. Unter Mitarbeit verschiedener evangelischer Theologen herausgegeben von Pfarrer Ernst Kalb. 2. erweiterte und verbesserte Auflage. Stuttgart, Verlag der Buchhandlung der Eveng. Gesellschaft, 1907.
xv, 655p. 22cm.
"Der Mormonismus" p. 564–590.
Title in English: Churches and sects of the present.
UPB

4519. **Kaler, John.** The one baptism. Independence, Mo., Ensign Publishing Co., 1893.
20p. 16cm. (Ensign Circulating Library. Vest Pocket ed.)
MoInRC

4520. **Kanada.** Raymond, Alberta, Canada, 1920–
v. illus., plates, ports. 28½cm.
Student yearbook of the Knight Academy.
USlC 1920, 1921

5421. **Kane, Elizabeth Dennistoun (Wood).** Twelve Mormon homes visited in succession on a journey through Utah to Arizona. Philadelphia, 1874.
2p.l., 158p. 20½cm.
Trip to southern Utah with Brigham Young in 1874 by the wife of Col. Thomas L. Kane.
Howes K6
CSmH, CtY, DLC, ICN, MH, NjP, NN, UHi, UPB, USlC

4522. **Kane, Francis Fisher.** A further report of the Indian Rights Association on the proposed removal of the Southern Utes. [By] Francis Fisher Kane [and] Frank M. Riter, Committee. [Philadelphia, Press of Wm. F. Fell & Co.] 1892.
32p. map. 23cm.
Cover-title.
Brief history of Bluff, Utah, and other San Juan County history.
NjP, UHi

4522a. **Kane, James J.** Miriam vs. Milton; or, the mystery of Everdale Lake. London, Charles Birchall; New York, American News Co., 1894.
378[2]p. 19cm.
Mormons mentioned, p. 240–242, 251, 341–342.
USlC

4523. **Kane, Thomas Leiper.** The Mormons. A discourse delivered before the Historical Society of Pennsylvania; March 26, 1850. By Thomas L. Kane . . . Philadelphia, King and Baird, Printers, 1850.
84p. 22cm.
Howes K8, W–C 185
CtY, CU–B, ICHi, ICN, MoInRC, MoK, NjP, NN, ULA, ViU, WHi

4524. ———. (same) Philadelphia, King and Baird, Printers, 1850.
92p. 23½cm.
Second edition, printed the same year.
"Postscript to the second edition," p. 85–92.
In two states. With and without a Latin inscription on the title page. The one with the Latin inscription is probably the first state.
P. 85–92 added to the plates of the 84p. edition.
Sabin 37011, W–C 185
CSmH, CtY, DLC, ICN, MH, NN, UPB, USl, USlC, UU, ViU

———. Three letters to the New York Herald. *See Grant, Jedediah Morgan.*

4525. **"Te Karere" (e tukua atu ana ia rua wiki) e te Mihana o Niu Tereni Hahi o Ihu Karaiti o te Hunga — Tapu o nga Ra a Muri nei.** Akarana Hastings, Auckland] New Zealand. 1907–
v. monthly, semi-monthly. 24cm.
Publication of the New Zealand Mission.
English and Maori interspersed in later issues.
Title in English: The Messenger.
UPB V.3–5 inc., 7, 9 inc., 10, 13, 14–17, 20–21 inc., 24 inc.; USlC V.1, 3–6 inc., 9–13 inc., 14–24

4526. **Kauffman, Ruth (Hammitt).** The Latter-day Saints; a study of the Mormons in the light of economic conditions, by Ruth Kauffman and Reginald Wright Kauffman. London, Williams & Norgate, 1912.
ix, 363p. 23½cm.
CSmH, CtY, CU–B, DLC, ICN, MH, MoInRC, NjP, NjPT, NN, PPM, UHi, ULA, USlC, USl, UU

4527. **Keairnes, Grace Baughman.** A Reasonable service. Independence, Mo., Herald Publishing House, 1922.
4p.l. [11]–197p. port. 20cm.
A story of practical Zionic ideals from an RLDS point of view.
MoInRC, UPB

4528. **Kearney, Belle.** A slaveholder's daughter. By Belle Kearney. New York, The Abbey Press [c1900]
4p.l., 269p. illus., plates, port. 20½cm.
Chapter 24 "The Latter Day Saints."
Another edition: 6th ed. St. Louis, Mo., St. Louis Christian Advocate Co. [c1900] USl
NjP, USl

4529. Kearney, Eleanor. Pattie; or, leaves from a life by Eleanor [*pseud.*] Lamoni, Ia., Herald Job Office and Book Bindery, 1892.
viii, 343p. port. 20cm.
Sentimental conversion story, written by a member of the RLDS church.
MoInRC, WHi

4530. Kearns, Thomas. Conditions in Utah. Speech of Hon. Thomas Kearns . . . Utah in the Senate of the United States. Tuesday, February 28, 1905. Washington, 1905.
14p. 24cm.
Social situation in Utah.
CSmH, CU-B, MH, MoInRC, NjP, NN, OO, PHi, UHi, USl, USIC

4531. Keatinge, Charles Wilburn. Death league of the desert, or Overland Bill's master stroke by Charles Wilburn Keatinge (Montana Charley) . . . Cleveland, Ohio, The Arthur Westbrook Publishing Company, c1927.
3p.l. [7]–191p. 18½cm.
(Early Western Life Series. No. 3.)
Fiction concerning Mormons.
CU-B, USIC

4532. Keeler, Joseph Brigham. The Bishop's court, its history and proceeding. Lecture delivered before the High Council of the Utah Stake of Zion by Joseph B. Keeler. Provo City, Utah, The Skelton Publishing Company [c1902]
22p. 15½cm.
UPB, USIC

4533. ———. First steps in church government; what church government is and what it does. A book for young members of the lesser priesthood. By Joseph B. Keeler. Salt Lake City, The Deseret News, 1906.
viii, 152p. 16cm.
DLC, IWW, NjP, NN, UHi, USl, USIC, UU

4534. ———. (same) Salt Lake City, The Deseret News, 1906.
viii, 152p. 15½cm.
Published with added title page: Course of study for the quorums of the priesthood, Church of Jesus Christ of Latter-day Saints. Priests (Third year) First steps in Church government . . . Salt Lake City, 1912.
MH, UHi, USIC

4535. ———. (same) Prepared and issued under the direction of the General Authorities of the Church. Salt Lake City, 1924.
xii [13]–116p. 18cm. (Course of study for the Quorums of the Priesthood, Church of Jesus Christ of Latter-day Saints. Teachers)
Added original title-page.
"Press of Zion's Printing and Publishing Company, Independence, Jackson County, Missouri."
USIC

4536. ———. Foundation stones of the earth, and other essays by Joseph B. Keeler. Provo, Utah, Enquirer Co. Steam Print., 1891.
31p. 20cm.
"Selected from my writings to *The Contributor* . . . V. 9, 10, and 11."
Science as taught by Joseph Smith.
CU-B, MH, UPB, USIC

4537. ———. Genealogical record of the Keeler family, 1726–1924, by Joseph Brigham Keeler . . . Provo, Utah, Post Publishing Company, 1924.
79p. 23cm.
Short Mormon biographies.
DLC, UPB

4538. ———. The law of tithing as set forth in the old scriptures and the modern revelation. [Provo, 1897?]
4p. 21cm.
Quotations from L.D.S. authorities.
UPB

4539. ———. The lesser priesthood and notes on church government, also a concordance of the Doctrine and Covenants for the use of church schools and priesthood quorums. By Joseph B. Keeler. Salt Lake City, The Deseret News [1904]
xii, 196p. 20cm.
CU-B, DLC, IWW, MoInRC, NjP, NN, UPB, USl, USIC, UU

4540. ———. (same) [2d ed.] Salt Lake City, The Deseret News [1906]
xii, 199p. 20cm.
UPB, USIC

4541. ———. The lesser priesthood and notes on church government for the use of church schools and priesthood quorums. [3d ed.] Salt Lake City, Deseret Book Company [c1929]
xii, 232p. 19cm.
CU-B, UPB, USIC, UU

4542. ———. The lesser Priesthood; program and outlines, prepared for the priesthood organizations of the Brigham Young University. Provo, Utah [1903]
43 [76]p. 20cm.
Later published under title: The lesser priesthood and notes on church government.
USIC

4543. ———. Program and outline for the lesser priesthood. [Provo?] 1902–03.
13 nos. 20½cm. (Brigham Young Academy. Lessons)
The preliminary material for his *The lesser priesthood.*
UPB, USIC

KELLEY, A. W.

4544. **Kelley, A. W.** History of the Kelley Family. By A. W. Kelley. [n.p., n.d.]
64p. 23½cm.
Their conversion and life in the RLDS church.
MoInRC

4545. **Kelley, Edmund Levi.** Antiquarian evidences concerning the Book of Mormon. Independence, Mo., Ensign Publ., 1893.
41p. 16cm. (Ensign Circulating Library. Vest Pocket edition)
MoInRC

4546. ———. (same) Independence, Mo., 1896.
40p. 15½cm. (The Gospel Banner. V.3, No. 2. June 1, 1896. Extra A)
USlC

4547. ———. Both sides . . . of the Braden-Kelley debate. [Lamoni, Ia., J. Smith; Kirtland, Ohio, E. L. Kelley, 1884]
4p. 24½cm.
An advertisement for the published account of the debate.
CtY

4548. ———. Duties, responsibilities, and faith of the Saints. [Lamoni, 1902?]
19p. 19cm.
Signed: Lamoni, Iowa, Jan. 18, 1902.
MoInRC

4549. ———. Equality, by Bishop E. L. Kelley. Lamoni, Ia., Herald Publishing House [n.d.]
16p. 18cm. (No. 309)
MH, MoInRC

4550. ———. (same) Lamoni, Ia., Herald Publishing House [n.d.]
15 [1]p. 18cm. (No. 309)
Variant printing.
MoInRC

4551. ———. Equality under the law of Christ. [Lamoni, Ia., Saints' Herald Print., 1908?]
32p. 19cm.
Sermon preached by Bishop E. L. Kelley, at Independence, Mo., on April 15, 1908.
MoInRC

4552. ———. Evidence of the authorized minister; or, Who is in the way of salvation. Independence, Mo., Ensign Publishing House [1908?]
23p. 15cm.
Sermon preached at Independence stake reunion, Aug. 9, 1908.
MoInRC

4553. ———. The law of Christ, and its fulfillment. [Lamoni, Ia., Herald Publishing House, 1912?]
122p. 20cm.
Caption-title.
Text signed: December 15, 1911.
MoInRC

4554. ———. Public discussion of the issues between the Reorganized Church of Jesus Christ of Latter Day Saints and the Church of Christ (Disciples) held in Kirtland, Ohio, beginning February 12th, and closing March 8th, 1884; between E. L. Kelley of the Reorganized Church of Jesus Christ of Latter Day Saints, and Clark Braden of the Church of Christ. St. Louis, Mo., Christian Publishing Co. [c1884]
396p. 25cm.
CtY, CU–B, DLC, MH, MoInRC, MoK, MWA, NN, UHi, USl, USlC, WHi

4555. ———. (same) St. Louis, Mo., Clark Braden [1884]
396p. 25cm.
CU–B, NjPT, NN, USlC, WHi

4556. ———. (same) Lamoni, Ia., Herald Publishing House, 1913.
400p. 25½cm.
CSmH, UHi, ULA, UPB

4557. ———. The Reply. [Independence, Mo., Ensign Publishing House, 1903?]
8p. 27cm.
Supplement to the *Saint's Herald*, January 21, 1903.
Supplement to *Zion's Ensign*, January 22, 1903.
Answer to the National Anti-Mormon Missionary Association's desire to form an association to destroy Mormonism.
MoInRC, USlC

4558. **Kelley, T. C.** The More excellent way. Independence, Mo., Ensign Publishing House, 1900.
68p. 22cm. (The Gospel Banner. V.7, No. 3)
RLDS doctrine of baptism.
MoInRC

4559. **Kelley, William H.** A Defense of monogamic marriage. Written in reply to "Race suicide, infanticide, prolicide, leprocide vs. children, letters to Messrs. Joseph Smith and Wm. H. Kelley." By A. Milton Musser, in advocacy and defense of polygamic marriage as practiced in Utah. [n.p., 1904 or later]
48p. 21cm.
CSmH, MH, MoInRC, USl, USlC

4560. ———. God is light. [Independence, Mo., Ensign Publishing House, 1897]
46p. 16cm. (The Gospel Banner. V.4, No. 3)
MoInRC

4561. ———. Presidency and priesthood. The apostasy, reformation, and restoration. Boston, Alfred Mudge and Son, Printers, 1890.
viii, 390p. 3 facsims. 19cm.
RLDS church theory of church government.
DLC, MH, MoInRC, NN, UPB, USIC

4562. ———. (same) Boston, Alfred Mudge & Son, 1891.
xx, 414p. port., facsims. 18½cm.
"Second edition."
USIC

4563. ———. (same) Lamoni, Ia., Herald Publishing House and Bookbindery, 1895.
414p. port. 19cm.
"Second edition."
OCl, OClWHi, UHi, WHi

4564. ———. (same) [Lamoni, Ia.] Herald Publishing House, 1902 [c1890]
414p. port. 19cm.
USIC

4564a. ———. (same) Lamoni, Ia., Herald Publishing House, 1908.
414p. port. 19cm.
NjP

4565. Kelly, Charles. Salt Desert trails; a history of the Hastings Cutoff and other early trails which crossed the Great Salt Desert seeking a shorter road to California [by] Charles Kelly. Salt Lake City, Western Printing Company, 1930.
5p.l. [15]–178 [3]p. illus., ports., facsim. 23½cm.
Concerned with the Hastings cut-off, but has some material on Mormon pioneers.
Howes K59
CU–B, DLC, IdIf, MH, NjP, UHi, ULA, UPB, USl, USIC, UU, WaU

4566. Kelly, J. Wells. First directory of Nevada Territory . . . San Francisco, Commercial Steam Presses, 1862.
266, xviiip. 24cm.
Includes a history of the Mormons in Nevada.
2d directory: Virginia City, Nevada, 1863.
Howes K65, Sabin 37309
C, CSmH, CU–B, DLC, NvHi

4567. Kelly, Robert L. Cooperation in education in Utah. Report on Westminster College, Salt Lake City, Utah. By Dr. Robert L. Kelly, Executive Secretary of the Council of Church Boards of Education. New York, Home Missions Council, Council of Women for Home Missions, 1922.
23p. 23cm.
The need for non-Mormon education in Utah.
UPB

4568. Kelly, William [*pseud?*] Across the Rocky Mountains, from New York to California with a visit to the celebrated Mormon colony at the Great Salt Lake, by William Kelly, esq. London, Simms and M'Intyre, 1852.
1p.l. [v]–xiv [15]–240p. 18cm.
A republication of V. 1 of his *An excursion to California.*
Howes K68, Sabin 37320, W–C 200
CSmH, CU–B, DLC, NN, UHi, USl, USIC, UU

4569. ———. An excursion to California over the prairie, Rocky Mountains, and great Sierra Nevada. With a stroll through the diggings and ranches of that country. By Wm. Kelly. London, Chapman and Hall, 1851.
2v. 20½cm.
Includes his visit to Salt Lake City in 1849.
Howes K68, Sabin 37321, W–C 200
CtY, CU–B, DLC, ICN, NN, PSC, PU, UPB, USl

4570. Kelly, William. A letter to the Christians in Guernsey, upon the pretensions of Mormonism. [Guernsey, Printed by J. F. Frost, Mont., Durant, 1848]
12p. 16½cm.
Signed: William Kelly, 8th July, 1848.
USIC

4571. Kelsch, Louis A. A practical reference arranged especially for the missionaries of the Church of Jesus Christ of Latter-day Saints. Chicago, Published by Northern States Mission, 1897.
24p. 13cm.
UPB, USIC

4572. ———. (same) Chicago, Published by the Northern States Mission, 1897 [c1899] [sic]
24p. 15cm.
Caption-title.
UHi

4573. ———. (same) [n.p., c1899]
24p. 16cm.
CU–B, UPB

4574. ———. (same) Salt Lake City, L. A. Kelsch, 1899.
24p. 16cm.
MH, UHi, UPB, USIC, UU

4575. ———. (same, in Dutch) Een practische verwijzer naar schriftuurlijke aanaligen aangaande de leerstellingen van het evangelie, door ouderling Louis A. Kelsch . . . Uit het Engelsch Door B. Tiemersma. [Rotterdam? 1915]
24p. 14cm.
USIC

KELSCH, L. A.

4575a. ———. (same) Rotterdam, Nederlandsche Zending [ca. 1930]
24p. 15cm.
USIC

4576. ———. (same, in French) References Practiques. Passages de l'ecriture concernant les doctrines de l'evangile par Louis A. Kelsch. [n.p., n.d.]
31p. 13cm.
UPB

4577. ———. (same, in Hawaiian) He mau kuhikuhi Pili Euanelio I Hooponopono ia no na Misionari o ka Ekalesia o Iesu Karisto o ka poe Hoano o no la hope nei, E. Lewis K. Kelsch, I unuhiia E. Samuel E. Woolley. [Salt Lake City, 1903?]
32p. 15½cm.
UPB, USIC

4578. ———. (same) Honolulu, Hawaii, The Printshop, 1924.
32p. 15cm.
USIC

4579. Kelson, John H. Immortality of the soul. [Letters of John H. Kelson, Mormon Elder, and Robert K. Strang] Leith, Scotland, Published by the editor of Leith Burghs Pilot, 1887.
24p. 21cm.
Defense of Mormonism.
Preface signed: Norman W. Macleod.
MH, USIC

4580. Kempe, Christopher I. A voice from prison: a letter to George C. Lambert. Salt Lake City, Deseret News Office, 1885.
[3]p. 21½cm.
Letter from a polygamist.
USIC

4581. Kenderdine, Thaddeus Stevens. California revisited, 1858–1897 . . . Newton, Pa. [Doylestown Pub. Co.] 1898.
2p.l., 310 [2]p., illus., plates. 23cm.
Trip through Salt Lake City with notes on Mormonism, p. 60–74.
Howes K77
CSmH, CU-B, DLC, NjP, UHi

4582. ———. A California tramp and later footprints; or, Life on the plains and in the Golden State thirty years ago, with miscellaneous sketches in prose and verse. Illustrated with thirty-nine wood and photo-engravings. By T. S. Kenderdine. Newton, Pa. [Philadelphia, Press of Globe Printing House] 1888.
415 [1]p. illus., plates. 22cm.
Chapters on his trip to Utah: "In the valley of the shadow," "The Saint's rest," "Among the Mormon settlements." Trip through Utah in 1858.
Howes K78
CSmH, CU-B, DLC, NjP, NN, UHi, UPB, USIC

4583. Kenley, Mac. Mormonernes blodhaevnere. Kobenhavn, 1925.
96p.
Title in English: Mormon blood vengeance.
Schmidt

4584. Kennard, Leonidas Hamlin. Te hoe aratai no te mau taata i roto i te Ekalesia a Iesu Mesia i te feia mo'a i te mau Mahana Hopea nei. Papaihia e Iosepha Hete, i Tahiti, i te Matahiti 1901, e i faaapihia e faarahihia e Viliamu Setemila i te Matahiti 1910. Neneihia e Leone A. Kenara. Papeete, Tahiti, Ekalesia a Iesu Mesia . . . 1921.
28p. 17½cm.
Written by Joseph Hete in 1901. Enlarged by William Seegmiller in 1910.
Title in English: A guide for members of the church.
USIC

4585. Kennedy, James Henry. Early days of Mormonism, Palmyra, Kirtland, and Nauvoo. By J. H. Kennedy, Editor of the Magazine of Western History. London, Reeves and Turner, 1888.
vii, 275p. 19½cm.
Author adopted the middle name of Harrison until 1915.
CSmH, CtY, CU-B, MH, MoInRC, NjP, UHi, UPB, UU

4586. ———. (same) New York, C. Scribner's Sons, 1888.
vii, 275p. illus., 2 port. plates, facsims. 19½cm.
CSmH, CtY, CU-B, ICN, MH, MiU, NjPT, NN, UHi, UPB, USI, USIC, WHi

4587. ———. The three witnesses of the Book of Mormon. [New York, 1890]
15p. 25cm.
Caption-title.
Reprinted from the *Magazine of Western History*, March, 1890.
"Address delivered before the Oneida Historical Society, Utica, N.Y., January 27, 1890."
DSI, ICHi, NjPT, NN, USIC

4588. Kenner, Scipio Africanus. The practical politician; a digest of ready information as to the fundamental differences between the great national political parties, their rise and progress, with past and present issues. Also a list of the presidents, and their cabinets, the vice-presidents, senators, congressmen, etc. With a review of the local political situation. Salt Lake City, Star Printing Co., 1892.
vi [7]–181 [1]p. 17½cm.
Includes the local Utah political situation.
MH, NjP, UHi, USIC, UU

4589. ———. Utah as it is. With a comprehensive statement of Utah as it was. Showing the founding, growth and present status of the commonwealth . . . by S. A. Kenner . . . Salt Lake City, The Deseret News, 1904.
vp., [1]l. [9]–639p. front., illus., ports. 24cm.
Section on Mormon Church, its origin and progress and what it has accomplished. Also the polygamy period cited.
CSmH, CU–B, DLC, ICU, NjP, NN, OClWHi, UHi, ULA, UPB, USl, USlC, UU

4590. Kent, Harald. Danske Mormoner, et bidrag til belysning af Mormonismens komme til Danmark, med illustrationer efter gamle traesnit. [Kobenhavn] Udgivit af Udvalget for Utahmissionen," 1913.
2p.l. [3]–42 [3]p. illus. 23cm.
Title in English: Danish Mormons.
CtY, CSmH, UHi

4591. ———. Imod Mormonismen. Oplysning om dens laere og praksis af Harald Kent . . . København, Udgivet af udvalget for Utah-Missionen, Duplex-trykkeriet, 1914.
22p. 21cm.
Cover-title.
Title in English: Against Mormonism.
UHi

4592. Kent, Henry Brainard. Graphic sketches of the West. Chicago, R. R. Donnelley & Sons, 1890.
254p. illus., port. 19½cm.
Chapter xii "In pursuit of knowledge." The difference between "indoor" and "outdoor" Mormonism.
CU–B, NjP, NN, UHi, ULA, USlC

4593. Kephart, W. H. Why I left the Baptist Church. Independence, Mo., Ensign Publishing Co., 1897.
33p. 15cm. (The Gospel Banner. V.4, No. 2)
Many references to the RLDS Church and his conversion.
MoInRC

4594. Kerr, Alfred. Yankee-Land, Eine Reise von Alfred Kerr. Berlin, Germany, Rudolf Mosse, 1925.
2p.l. [5]–205p. 22½cm.
"Die Mormonstadt," p. 151–158.
"Das Tabernakel," p. 159–166.
CU–B, NjP, USlC

4595. Kerr, Alvah Milton. Trean; or, The Mormon's daughter. A romantic story of life among the Latter-day Saints, by Alvah Milton Kerr. (Written while living in Utah) Chicago, New York, Belford, Clarke & Company [etc., etc., c1889]
184p. 19½cm. (On cover: The household library. V.4, No. 30)
Fiction concerning Mormonism.
CSmH, DLC, MH, MoInRC, NN, UHi, USlC, UU

4596. Kesler, Donnette Smith. Deseret Sunday School Union kindergarten plan book, by Donnette Smith Kesler and Rebecca Morris. Salt Lake City, Deseret Sunday School Union [1904]
208p. 26cm.
Includes music.
UHi, UPB, USlC

4597. Kester, Vaughan. Fortunes of the Landrays, by Vaughan Kester. Indianapolis, The Bobbs-Merrill Company [c1905]
4p.l. [3]–481p. 19½cm.
Chap. 24 has a description of Brigham Young. Other Mormon and Utah references.
Other editions: 1905. CU; 1912. UPB, USlC
DLC

4598. Ketone, Pepene E. Ko nga korerohari mo te haringa nui. [Auckland, E. H. Fail, Printer, n.d.]
4p. 21½cm.
Missionary tract in Maori.
Title in English: At the pleasant news concerning public rejoicing.
USlC

4599. Keyes, William. History of Quincy, Illinois. [Quincy, Ill.?] 1862.
105p.
Includes extract from *Times and Seasons* of the revelation from Joseph Smith to Isaac Galland and his part in the Mormon Church.
Howes K117, Sabin 37684
MB

4600. Keyserling, Hermann Alexander, *graf von.* The travel diary of a philosopher, by Count Hermann Keyserling, translated by J. Holroyd Reece . . . New York, Harcourt, Brace & Company [c1925]
2v. port. 23½cm.
Includes a section on Mormonism compared to oriental philosophers . . .
Salt Lake City and the Mormons . . . V.2, p. 310–318.
Other editions: 1928. DLC; London, J. Cape Ltd., 1925. BM
CU, DLC, NjP, NN, UHi, USlC

4601. Kidder, Daniel Parish. Mormonism and the Mormons: a historical view of the rise and progress of the sect self-styled Latter-day Saints. By Daniel P. Kidder . . . New-York, G. Lane & P.P. Sandford, for the Methodist Episcopal Church, 1842.
1p.l. [3]–342p. 1 illus. 14cm.
Howes K122, Sabin 37706
CSmH, CtY, DLC, ICN, MH, MWA, NN, OClWHi, OU, PU, USlC, WHi

4602. ———. (same) New York, Carlton and Lanahan [c1842]
1p.l. [3]–342p. 15cm.
Howes K122
CU–B, MoInRC, UHi, USlC

4603. ———. (same) New York, Carlton and Porter [c1842]
1p.l. [3]–342p. 15½cm.
Howes K122
CSmH, CtY, DLC, ICN, MH, OO, UU

4604. ———. (same) New York, G. Lane and C. B. Tippett, for the Methodist Episcopal Church, 1844.
1p.l. [3]–342p. 15½cm.
Howes K122
CSmH, CtY, MH, ULA, USlC

4605. ———. (same) New York, G. Lane and C. B. Tippett, for the Methodist Episcopal Church, 1845. [c1842]
1p.l. [3]–342p. 15cm.
Howes K122, Sabin 37706
MB, MH, MoKu, NjP, NN, USlC, UU, WHi

4606. ———. (same) New York, Published by Lane and Scott, 1852 [c1842]
1p.l. [3]–342p. 15½cm.
Howes K122
CU, ICHi, MB, MoInRC, NjPT

4607. ———. (same) New York, Carlton & Phillips, 1856.
1p.l. [3]–342p. 15cm.
CU–B, DLC, MWA, NN, OCl, WHi, USl

4608. Kienke, Asa Solomon. Fourteen objectives for the reading and study of the Book of Mormon. [n.p., ca.1920]
[1] 6 [1]p. 17½cm.
USlC

4609. Kierkegaard, P. Chr. Om og mod Mormonismen. Af P. Chr. Kierkegaard (Aftryk efter Dansk kirketidende) Kjøbenhavn, Forlagt af C. G. Iversen Scharlingske Bogtrykkeri, 1855.
68p. 19cm.
Reprinted from *Dansk kirketidende.* V. 1.
En leilighedstale.
Title in English: About and against Mormonism.
CtY, NN, USlC

4610. Kilbourne, David Wells. Strictures on Dr. I. Galland's pamphlet, entitled, "Villainy exposed," with some account of his transactions in lands of the Sac and Fox reservation, etc., in Lee County, Iowa. By D. W. Kilbourne. Fort Madison, Printed at the Statesman Office, 1850.
24p. 19cm.
. The Revelation of Joseph Smith for him to purchase the Nauvoo House and a letter to Joseph Smith which were published in the *Times and Seasons.*
Pamphlet against the activities of Isaac Galland.
DLC, IaCrM, IaHi, NjP, NN, UHi, UPB

4611. Kilvert, E. Mormonism. Identified with certain views maintained by T. L. Strange, esq., C. S. in his "Light of Prophecy." Madras, Printed at the Asylum Press [1853?]
13p. 15cm.
USl

4612. Kimball, Crozier. Program for the ward teachers of the Curlew Stake, by Crozier Kimball and Carter E. Grant, under the direction of the Stake Presidency. Riverton, Utah, Jordan Print Co. [1925?]
[10]p. 20cm.
UPB

Kimball, David C. *See Candland, David.*

4613. Kimball, Edward Partridge. In memoriam. [Salt Lake City, 1929?]
[15]l. port. 21½cm.
Portrait of Willard Young Kimball.
USlC

4614. Kimball, Heber Chase. Journal of Heber C. Kimball, an Elder of the Church of Jesus Christ of Latter-day Saints. Giving an account of his mission to Great Britain, and the commencement of the work of the Lord in that land. Also the success which has attended the labors of the elders to the present time. By Robert B. Thompson . . . Nauvoo, Ill.: Printed by Robinson and Smith, 1840.
viii [9]–60p. 20cm.
R. B. Thompson was secretary of Joseph Smith.
Byrd 558, Howes T202
CSmH, CtY, CU–B, DLC, ICN, MH, USl, USlC

4615. ———. President Heber C. Kimball's journal designed for the instruction and encouragement of young Latter-day Saints. Salt Lake City, Juvenile Instructor Office, 1882.
vii [9]–104p. 19cm.
(Faith promoting series. 7th book)
Contains additional text.
Howes T202
CSmH, CtY, CU–B, DLC, ICN, MH, MoInRC, NjP, NN, UHi, ULA, UPB, USl, USlC, UU, WHi

4616. ———. Prophetic sayings of Heber C. Kimball to Sister Amanda H. Wilcox. [n.p., n.d.]
8p. 14cm.
Caption-title.
Signed: Amanda H. Wilcox.
NN, UPB

4617. ———. The word of the Lord to the citizens of Bristol, of every sect and denomination; and to every individual into whose hands it may fall showing forth the plan of salvation as laid down in the New Testament: — namely, faith in our Lord Jesus Christ — repentance — baptism for the remission of sins — and the gift of the Holy Ghost by the laying on of hands. Presented by two of the elders of the Church of Jesus Christ of Latter Day Saints. Bristol, Reprinted by James John on the Weir [1840?]

8p. 16cm.
Caption-title.
Signed: Heber C. Kimbal[l], Wilford Woodruff.
CSmH

4618. ———. The word of the Lord to the citizens of London, of every sect and denomination; and to every individual into whose hands it may fall showing forth the plan of salvation as laid down in the New Testament; — namely, faith in our Lord Jesus Christ — repentance — baptism for the remission of sins — and the gift of the Holy Ghost by the laying on of hands. Presented by two of the elders of the Church of Jesus Christ of Latter Day Saints. London, Doudney and Scrymgour, City Press, Long Lane, [1840?]
8p. 16cm.
Caption-title.
Signed: Heber C. Kimball, Wilford Woodruff.
Textually the same as the above.
MH, UPB, USlC

4619. Kimball, John Calvin. . . . Mormonism exposed; the other side. A clergyman's view of the case by Rev. John C. Kimball of Hartford, Conn. [Salt Lake City?] 1884.
17p. 21cm. (No. 4)
"Copies from '*The Index*,' Boston, Mass."
At head of title: Gentile testimony to Mormon worth.
In purple printed wrapper.
Part IV (p. 67–84) of a series of pamphlets with James W. Barclay, *Mormonism exposed* as the first part.
Another edition: 1888. USlC
CSmH, CtY, MH, MnH, MoK, OClWHi, UHi, ULA, UPB, USlC, UU

4620. ———. (same) [Salt Lake City?] 1888.
17p. 21cm. (No. 4)
Reprinting ofthe 1884 edition.
In tan printed wrapper.
CU–B, UPB, USlC

4621. Kimball, Solomon Farnham. Bombshell confession! The Kearns gang under the limelight. Key to the situation regardless of politics or religion. Truths that should be known by every honest citizen of Salt Lake County. [Salt Lake City? 1908]
[4]p. 21cm.
Caption-title.
Use of the Mormon situation for political purposes.
CtY, NjP, UHi, UPB, USlC

4622. ———. Life of David P. Kimball, and other sketches. By Solomon F. Kimball. Salt Lake City, The Deseret News, 1918.
iv, 128p. illus., ports. 20cm.
CtY, CU–B, NjP, NN, UHi, ULA, UPB, USl, USlC, UU

4623. ———. Thrilling experiences, by Solomon F. Kimball. Salt Lake City, Magazine Printing Co., 1909.
157p. port. 16cm.
Pioneer life in Utah.
Howes K139
CSmH, CU–B, DLC, MH, NjP, NN, UHi, USlC, UU, WHi

4623a. King, Basil. The way home; a novel by the author of "The inner shrine" [Basil King]. New York, Harper & Brothers, 1913.
546[1]p. illus. 19½cm.
Mormons mentioned, p. 283–285.
USlC

4624. King, David. The Mormon Church, the state church, and the Christian church. Reprinted from the British Millennial Harbinger. [n.p., 1862?]
8p. 21½cm.
The substance of a discourse delivered June 1, 1862, in the Temperance Hall, Birmingham, by David King.
USlC

4625. King, Hannah Tapfield. An epic poem. A synopsis of the rise of the church of Jesus Christ of Latter-day Saints, from the birth of the prophet Joseph Smith to the arrival on the spot which the Prophet Brigham Young pronounced to be the site of the future Salt Lake City. By Hannah Tapfield King. Salt Lake City, Published at the Juvenile Instructor Office, 1884.
62p. 19cm.
Mormon poetry.
CSmH, CU–B, DLC, MH, NjP, NN, OClWHi, UHi, UPB, USlC, UU, WHi

4626. ———. Letter to a friend [in Norwich, England] [Salt Lake City? 1881]
Broadside. 27½×19½cm.
Dated: Salt Lake City, Dec. 15, 1881.
Her conversion to Mormonism and acceptance of polygamy.
MB, USlC

4627. ———. Songs of the heart. Salt Lake City, Star Book and Job Printing Office, 1879.
[6] 87 [1]p. 19½cm.
Mormon poetry.
CSmH, MH, UHi, USlC, UU

4628. ———. The women of the scriptures; to the young ladies of Utah these pages are dedicated by their affectionate Elder Sister Hannah T. King. Salt Lake City, Dernford House, 1874.
24p. 18½cm.
CU–B

4629. ———. (same) Salt Lake City, Dernford House, 1878.
24p. 18½cm.
CU–B, MH, UHi, UPB, USlC

KING, W. A.

4630. King, ***Mrs.*** **W. A.** Duncan Davidson, by Mrs. W. King. Philadelphia, Dorrance and Company [c1928]

245p. 19½cm.

Novel against polygamy. She escapes marriage to Brigham Young in an Indian disguise.

DLC, UHi, USlC

4631. King, William C. Woman, her position, influence and achievements through the civilized world. Her biography, her history, from the Garden of Eden to the twentieth century. Prepared by carefully selected writers. Designed and arranged by William C. King, illustrated. Springfield, Mass., The King-Richardson Company, 1902.

3p.l. [9]–667p. ports. 23cm.

A four-page pamphlet was prepared and tipped in for Utah buyers with portraits and biographies of Emmeline B. Wells, Zina D. H. Young, Eliza R. Snow.

USlC

The kingdom of Christ. *See D., T.*

4632. Kingsbury, John D. Mormonism, whence it came, what it is, whither it tends. By John D. Kingsbury. New York, The Congregationalist Home Missionary Society [n.d.]

16p. 15½cm.

Cover-title.

USlC

4633. Kingsley, Calvin. Round the world. A series of letters, by Calvin Kingsley. Cincinnati, Hitchcock and Walden, 1870.

2v. port. 21cm.

V. 1. Europe and America. "A visit to Salt Lake City in 1865." "Mormonism as a religion." A summary of Mormon beliefs, found "shocking."

Another edition: 1871. NjP

USlC

4634. Kinney, Bruce. Frontier missionary problems; their character and solution. By Bruce Kinney, D. D. . . . New York, Chicago, Fleming H. Revell Company . . . [c1918]

4p.l. 7–249p. illus. 19½cm.

"Mormonism, its menace," p. 83–96.

USlC

4635. ———. Mormonism and the Mormons. By Rev. Bruce Kinney. General Missionary for Utah and Wyoming. [New York, American Baptist Home Missionary Society, n.d.]

16p. 22cm.

MoInRC, NN

4636. ———. (same) Rev. ed. [New York, American Baptist Home Mission Society, n.d.]

14p. 22cm.

MoInRC

4637. ———. . . . Mormonism; the Islam of America, by Bruce Kinney . . . New York, Chicago [etc.] Flaming H. Revell Company [1912]

3p.l., 5–189p. plates. 20cm. (On verso of half-title: Interdenominational Home Mission study course 9)

At head of title: Issued under the direction of the Council of Women for Home Missions.

CtY, CU–B, DLC, ICHi, MH, NjPT, NN, OO, UHi, ULA, UPB, USl, USlC, UU, WHi

4638. ———. (same) New York, Chicago [etc.] Fleming H. Revell Company [c1912]

3p.l., 5–190p. plates, ports. 20cm.

Variant edition. Appendix on p. 190.

CU–B, MoInRC

4639. ———. (same) Revised and enlarged edition. New York, Chicago, Fleming H. Revell Company [c1916]

3p.l., 210p. plate. 21cm.

NjP, NjPT, PPC, USlC

4640. ———. (same, in Swedish) Mormonismen. Amerikas Muhammedanism, av Bruce Kinney . . . med förord av Pastor E. Lundström Bemyndigad översättning av. I. H - - d. Stockholm. P. Palmquists Aktiebolag [1914]

3p.l., 103p. 20cm.

UPB

4641. Kinney, John Fitch. Speech of Honorable John F. Kinney of Utah in reply to Honorable Fernando Wood, delivered in the House of Representatives, January 27, 1864. [Washington, H. Polkinhorn, 1864?]

8p. 21cm.

CtY, DLC, ICN, PHi

4642. ———. Speech of Hon. John F. Kinney, of Utah, upon the territories and the settlement of Utah, delivered in the House of Representatives, March 17, 1864. Washington, H. Polkinhorn, Printer, 1864.

16p. 24½cm.

Sabin 37933

CtY, CU–B, DLC, MH, NjP, PHi, UHi, USlC

Kinole, Ed. [*pseud.*] *See Olson, Edmund T.*

4643. The Kinsman. Salt Lake City, The Kinsman Company. V. 1–2, June 1897–October, 1898; n.s. V. 1–2, No. 23, November, 1898–1900.

4v. in 2. 24cm.

Anti-Mormon periodical.

USlC V.1 #9, V.2, # 16, 17, 18; WHi comp.

4644. Kipling, Rudyard. American notes. New York, International Publishing Co., 1889.
267p. 20cm.
Visit to Salt Lake City, ca. 1888, with his impressions of the Mormons. Evidently the same account as in "From sea to sea."
Other editions: New York, F. F. Lovell Co., 189–. CU-B; New York, Hurst & Co., 189–. CU-B; New York, George Munro's Sons. [c1896] NjP, UPB; London, Standard Book Co., 1930. UPB
ULA, USIC

4645. ———. From sea to sea letters of travel. New York, Doubleday & McClure, 1899.
2v. 20cm.
Vol. II. Chapter XXXII talks "Of the American Army and the City of the Saints, the Temple, the Book of Mormon and the Girl from Dorset."
An Oriental consideration of polygamy, p. 106–119.
Other editions: London, Macmillan, 1900. UPB; New York, Doubleday, Page & Co. 1907. DLC; New York, Scribners, 1907. UPB; New York, Doubleday, Page & Co., 1913. CU; (same) 1920. CU; (same) 1925. UPB; in German: Leipzig, B-Lauchnitz, 1900. DLC
NjP, ULA, USIC

4646. Kirby, George D. Salvation for the dead; address delivered over Radio Station KSL, Sunday Evening, May 20, 1928. [Salt Lake City] 1928.
Broadside. 58×20cm.
Reprinted from the *Deseret News*, Saturday, May 26, 1928.
UPB

4647. Kirby, Julia [Smith] (Duncan) . . . Biographical sketch of Joseph Duncan, fifth governor of Illinois. Read before the Historical Society of Jacksonville, Ill., May 7, 1885. By Julia Duncan Kirby . . . Chicago, Fergus Printing Company, 1888.
97p. port., 2 plates. 20cm.
(Fergus' historical series. No. 29)
Includes his relations with the Mormons.
CSmH, DLC, MB, MH, NN, OCU

4648. Kirby, William. Mormonism exposed and refuted, or, True and false religion contrasted. Forty years experience and observation among the Mormons. Nashville, Tenn., Gospel Advocate Publishing Co., 1893.
iv [5]–500p. 19cm.
CSmH, CU-B, MH, NjPT, NN, UHi, USl, USIC, WHi

4649. ———. Mormonism exposed and refuted or True and false religion contrasted. Forty years' experience and observation among the Mormons in England, Utah and Kansas. By Wm. Kirby, Doniphan, Kansas. The book contains 500 pages, good material, . . . [St. Joseph, Mo., Wm. Kirby. 1893?]
8p. folder. 14cm.
A publicity pamphlet for his book of the same title.
USIC

4650. Kirchoff, Theodor. Reisebilder und Skizzen aus Amerika. Von Theodor Kirchoff . . . Altona, C. T. Schlüter; New York, E. Steiger. 1875–76.
2v. 18½cm.
"Im Lande der Mormonen"
Title in English: Impressions of a traveler in America.
Howes K181
CU-B, DLC, ICJ

4651. Kirk, Th. J. The Mormons & Missouri: a general outline of the history of the Mormons, from their origin to the present. (Including the late disturbance in Illinois;) and a particular account of the last Mormon disturbance in Missouri, or the Mormon war; with an appendix, contaiaing [sic] an epitome of the Book of Mormon, with remarks on the nature and tendency of Mormon faith. By Th. J. Kirk. Chillicothe, Mo., J. H. Darlington, Pritner, 1844.
64p. 21cm.
ViU

4652. Kirkeberg, O. L. Mormonismen, dens historie, laerdomme og nuvaerende stilling, af O. L. Kirkeberg . . . Kjobenhavn, Lehman & Stages Forlag, 1902.
77p. 21cm.
Title in English: Mormonism: its history, teachings and now existing position.
UPB

4653. ———. Mormonismen, et klar overblik. Utgit av bestyrelsen for bokmisionen. Minneapolis, 1921.
Title in English: A clear appraisal of Mormonism.
Schmidt

4654. Kirkham, Francis Washington. He Korerotanga. Mo te Peheatanga e ora ai te Iwi Maori. He mea tuhiluhi na Te Paranihi Karakama raua Ko Wiremu Takana. Akarana, Niu Tireni, Na Hemi Nitama Ramapata, Te Kai Panui [1916]
3p.l., 3–23 [1] 15 [1] 15 [1]p. 18½cm.
Contents: He pukapuka whakaatu . . . , He kapu whai whakaaro . . . , He kapei whakamarama . . .
Title in English: A warning concerning the survival of the Maori people.
USIC

4655. ———. Lessons for beginners in the Maori Language also exercises and vocabulary. By Francis W. Kirkham, A.B., LL.B. First edition 1917. Auckland, New Zealand, Published by James N. Lambert, 1917.
x, 113p. 19cm.
A Maori lesson manual for missionaries.
USIC

4656. Kirkham, Kate Woodhouse. Daniel Stillwell Thomas, family history. Ed. by Kate Woodhouse Kirkham. [Salt Lake City] 1927.
64p. port. 15½cm.
USIC, UU

KIRTLAND

4656a. Kirtland Safety Society. Minutes of a meeting of the Stockholders of the Kirtland Safety Society Bank; held on the 2nd day of November, A.D. 1836 . . . [Kirtland, 1836]
Broadside. 32×17½cm.
The Messenger, Extra. Kirtland, Ohio, December, 1836.
Constitution of the Kirtland Safety Society, dated November, 1836.
USIC

4657. ———. Minutes of a meeting of the members of the "Kirtland Safety Society, held on the 2d day of January, 1837. [Kirtland, 1837]
Broadside. 37½×20cm.
The Messenger, Extra. March, 1837.
Constitution of the Kirtland Safety Society dated December, 1836.
USIC

Kirwan [*pseud.*] *See Murray, Nicholas.*

4658. Klemgaard, P. C. A Dream by P. C. Klemgaard . . . given in the camp of Joseph Morris, Weber, Utah, September 20, 1861, Translated from the Danish. [San Francisco, 1884?]
Broadside. 23×14cm.
Text inclosed in chain border.
No Danish edition located.
CtY

4659. Knapp, Jacob. Autobiography of a pioneer; or, The nativity, experience, travels and ministerial labors of Rev. Samuel Pickard, The "Converted Quaker," containing stirring incidents and practical thoughts; with sermons by the author, and some account of the labors of Elder Jacob Knapp . . . Edited by O. T. Conger . . . Chicago, Church & Goodman, 1866.
xii, [13]–403p. 19cm.
Rise of Mormonism, their "strange" doctrines, the Danites, polygamy in Nauvoo, etc.
USIC

4660. Knight Academy, Raymond, Alberta, Canada. Knight Academy (Announcement) 1911–
v. 20cm.
USIC 1911–12, 1912–13, 1913–14, 1914–15, 1916–17

4661. Knisley, Alvin. Dictionary of all proper names in the Book of Mormon. Independence, Mo., Published by Ensign Publishing House [1909?]
2p.l. [5]–118p. 20cm.
Tipped in is a leaf of "omissions in Book of Mormon Dictionary" and errata.
MoInRC, UPB, UU

4662. ———. Doctrinal references. Bible texts arranged under subject headings. Lamoni, Ia., Herald Publishing House, 1908.
29p. 18½cm.
MoInRC

4663. ———. Doctrinal references. Texts from the three standard books. Arranged under subject headings. Improved and enlarged edition, with index. Compiled by Alvin Knisley. Independence, Mo., Ensign Publishing House [n.d.]
48p. 15cm.
MoInRC

4663a. ———. (same) Fourth edition. Compiled by Alvin Knisley. Published by Ensign Publishing House, Independence, Mo., 1914.
71p. 15cm.
USIC

4664. ———. (same) Lamoni, Ia., Herald Publishing House [1918?]
23p. 17½cm.
MoInRC

4665. ———. Infallible proofs; a collection of spiritual communications and remarkable experiences, professedly divine, received by or through saints and testified by them from the rise of the Latter Day dispensation to the present time . . . Comp. by Alvin Knisley. Independence, Mo., Herald Publishing House, 1930.
204 [2]p. 19½cm.
MoInRC, MoK, UHi

4666. ———. Miracles, modern revelations sustained. Independence, Mo., Ensign Publishing House, 1902.
31p. 16cm. (The Gospel Banner. V.9, No. 1)
MoInRC

4667. ———. Revelations in our times; a collection of tongues, prophecies, visions, dreams and other spiritual communications, received by saints in this day and age . . . Independence, Mo., 1913.
208p. 20cm.
Compiled and published by Alvin Knisley.
MoInRC, UHi, UPB

4668. Knortz, Karl. Amerikanische Skizzen von Karl Knortz. Halle, Herman Gesenius, 1884.
3p.l., 3–311p. 17cm.
"Zur Geschichte des Mormonenthums," p. 171–205.
A discussion of Mormonism along with spiritualism and Indian legends.
Uses the Spaulding theory of the *Book of Mormon.*
Title in English: American sketches of Karl Knortz.
ICN

4669. Knox, Philander Chase. In opposition to the resolution reported from the Committee on Privileges and Elections "that Reed Smoot is not entitled to a seat as a senator of the United States from the State of Utah." Speech of Hon. Philander C. Knox, of Pennsylvania, in the Senate of the United States, Thursday, February 14, 1907. Washington [Govt. Print. Off.] 1907.
1p.l., 30p. 24cm.
DLC

4670. ———. (same) Washington [Govt. Print. Off.] 1907.
14p. 23cm.
CU–B, MH

4671. ———. (same) Washington [Govt. Print. Off.] 1907.
19p. 23cm.
USlC

4672. Knox, William Douglas. The Anti-Mormon gazette. 3d ed. March 1, 1872. [n.p., 1872]
Broadside. 26½×35½cm.
CtY

4673. Knudsen, Hans. Om navnet "Mormon." Med en afbildning af Mormon. Randers [Denmark] 1857.
8p.
Title in English: Concerning the name "Mormon."
Schmidt

4674. ———. Undervisning om Mormonerne, deres propheter og laerdomme til menige Christnes Bedste forfattet af Hans Knudsen . . . Kjobenhavn, Enidendalske Boghandling, 1863.
32p. 20cm.
Part I. "Joseph Smiths Liv og Levnet."
Title in English: Teaching concerning the Mormons.
NN, UHi

4675. ———. (same) Til menige Christnes bedste forfattet af H. K., Sognepraest til Bregninge og Bjergstedt i Sjaellands Stift. Kjobenhavn, 1863.
80p. 17½cm. (No. 78)
Part I. "Joseph Smith's Liv og Levnet."
UPB, USlC

4676. Koch, Albrecht Karl. Reise durch einen Theil der Vereinigten Staaten von Nordamerika in den Jahren 1844 bis 1846, von dr. Albert C. Koch. Nebst 2 Tafeln Abbildungen. Dresden und Leipzig, Arnold, 1847.
2p.l., 162p. col. plate. 22½cm.
Includes a short visit to Nauvoo, November 1844.
Title in English: A trip through a part of the United States in the years 1844 to 1846.
Howes K234, Sabin 38198
CtY, DLC, ICN, IHi, IU, NN, PPG, PU

4677. Koch, H. P. G. En advarsel imod de falske propheter. Aftrykt med nogle forandringer og tillaeg af Lolland-Falsters Stifstidende. Nykjobing, 1852.
19p.
Title in English: An adverse picture of the false prophet.
Schmidt

4678. Koehler, J. August. The Latter-day work, a practical religion, being an application of the principles of Christianity to present-day conditions. Independence, Mo. [Herald Publishing House] 1923.
15p. 20cm.
CU–B, MoInRC, USlC

4679. ———. Problems of industrial Zion, by Bishop J. A. Koehler. Independence, Mo. [Reorganized Church of Jesus Christ of Latter Day Saints] 1927.
163p. 19½cm.
Signed: July 20, 1927.
MoInRC, UHi, UPB

4680. Kolle, Bernard. Ole Peersens og hans Kone Dorthes rejse til Mormonerne og deres ophold der. Vise med monolog mellem versene. Kjobenhavn [1874]
[4]p. 16cm.
A street ballad about the journey to the land of the Mormons.
Title in English: A journey of Ole Peersen and his wife Dorthe to Mormon country.
UHi

4681. Kooyman, Frank I. De Heere Spreekt, door Frank I. Kooyman. Rotterdam, Ned. Zending [ca. 1930]
4 nos. (8p. each) 23cm.
Title in English: The Lord speaks.
USlC

4682. ———. (same) Rotterdam, Ned. Zending [1930]
4 nos. 23cm.
Vijfde tienduizend, Dec. 1930.
USlC

4683. ———. Joseph Smith. Door Frank I. Kooyman. Uitgegevin Door den Schrijver. Salt Lake City [1911?]
12p. port. 15cm.
Poem concerning Joseph Smith.
Variant printings.
USlC

4684. ———. Een vreemdling hier en andere versen, door Frank I. Kooyman. Tweede Boekske. Salt Lake City [1915?]
[16]p. 15½cm.
Mormon poetry.
Title in English: A stranger here and other poems.
USlC

4685. Korrespondenten. . . . Salt Lake City, November, 1890–April 15, 1915.
26v. weekly, bi-weekly. 62cm.
Organ of the Swedish Mormons in Utah.
Editors: Otto Rydman, Charles Anderson.
Title in English: The correspondent.
USlC comp.

KORT

4686. Kort omrids af Mormonernes historie. Praesto, 1862.
32p.
Title in English: Brief outlines of Mormon history.
Schmidt

4687. En kortfattet analyse af Mormons bog. [København, F. E. Bording, n.d.]
8p. 17cm.
Title in English: An abridged analysis of the Book of Mormon.
USlC

4688. Krahl, *Mrs.* David J. Social purity (No. 1) By Mrs. David J. Krahl. Independence, Mo., Women's Department of the Reorganized Church of Jesus Christ of Latter Day Saints [n.d.]
6p. 18cm.
USlC

4689. Kroupa, B. An artist's tour; gleanings and impressions of travels in North and Central America and the Sandwich islands, by B. Kroupa. With thirty-four illustrations by the author. London, Ward and Downey, 1890.
xiv p., [1]l. 339 [1]p. plates. 26cm.
Account of the Mormons, p. 13–28.
CSmH, CtY, CU-B, DLC, NN, OClW, PP, PPA, PSC

4690. Kundig, Jakob. Was haben wir von den Mormonen zu halten. Von Jakob Kundig. Zweite aufflage. Basel, Verein zur Verbreitung christlicher Schriften, 1903.
39p. 18cm.
Title in English: What can we expect from the Mormons?
UPB

4691. Kuykendall, W. L. Frontier days. [Denver?] J. M. and H. L. Kuykendall Publishers, 1917.
xi, 251p. port. 19cm.
Chapter 5. "Early recollections of the Mormons."
Recollections of Mormon pioneers and some who remained in Missouri and Iowa, 1854.
Howes K284
CU-B, ICN, NjP, UHi, UPB, USlC

4692. Kvindens liv blandt Mormonerne. Et ølevidnes beretning. Illustreret av Sverrer Knudsen. Kristiania og Trondhiem, 1912.
151p. 20cm.
Title in English: A woman's life among the Mormons.
USlC (copy defective)

THE

LATTER-DAY SAINTS MILLENNIAL STAR,

EDITED BY PARLEY P. PRATT.

No. 3, Vol. 1. JULY, 1840. Price Sixpence.

CONTENTS.

Published Monthly at Manchester, England; and for Sale by P. P. Pratt, No. 149, Oldham Road, and by Agents throughout the Kingdom.

MANCHESTER:

PRINTED BY W. R. THOMAS, 61, SPRING GARDENS.

Item 4779. The printed wrapper of the third issue of the *Millennial Star*, published continuously from May 1840 to December 1970. From the Brigham Young University collection.

L., L.

4693. L., L. Om Mormonerne. I folkekalender for Danmark, femte aargang. Kobenhavn, 1856.
53–64p.
Title in English: About the Mormons.
Schmidt

4694. Labors in the vineyard. Designed for the instruction and encouragement of young Latter-day Saints. Salt Lake City, The Juvenile Instructor Office, 1884.
viii [9]–96p. 19cm. (Faith promoting series. 12th book)
Contents: C. V. Spencer. My experience in England. William Budge. My Swiss mission. Llewellyn Harris. The faith of the Zunis. Harrison Burgess. Sketch of a well-spent life. Amasa Potter. The Lord's blessings.
CLU, DLC, ICN, NjP, NN, UHi, ULA, UPB, USl, USlC, UU, WHi

4695. Lacon [*pseud.*] The devil in America: a dramatic satire. Spirit-rapping — Mormonism; woman's rights conventions and speeches; abolitionism; Harper's Ferry raid and Black Republicanism; defeat of Satan, and final triumph of the gospel. By Lacon [*pseud.*] Philadelphia, J. B. Lippincott & Co., 1860.
1p.l., 225p. 19cm.
Satire on Mormonism, etc.
Another edition: Mobile, J. K. Randall, 1867. NjP
DLC

4696. Ladd, Horatio Oliver. History of the war with Mexico, by Horatio O. Ladd. New York, Dodd, Mead and Company, Publishers [1883]
4 [v]–xii [13]–328p. 3 fold. plates, fold. map. 19cm. (Minor wars of the United States)
References to Mormon Battalion, p. 99, 117, 121–122.
Another edition: [1911] CU–B
DLC

4697. Laden, Goldie. Dreams of youth, by Goldie Laden . . . Salt Lake City, Paragon Printing Company [c1929]
100p. illus. 18cm.
"Sixth edition."
Mormon poetry.
CSmH, DLC

4698. Ladies Anti-polygamy Society of Utah. [Circular, beginning] Salt Lake City, Utah, February 1880 . . . the . . . society has addressed a circular letter to the members of the House of Representatives, asking the expulsion of Delegate Cannon . . . [Salt Lake City, 1880?]
[2]l. 16cm.
NN

4699. Laegmand, En. Andet brev til en ven om Mormonerne. Kjobenhavn, 1854.
16p.
Title in English: Another letter to a friend about Mormons.
Schmidt

4700. ———. Et brev til en ven om Mormonerne. Kjobenhavn, 1854.
16p.
Title in English: A letter to a friend about Mormons.
Schmidt

4701. ———. Tredie brev til en ven om Mormonerne. Kjobenhavn, 1854.
16p.
Title in English: A third letter to a friend about Mormonism.
Schmidt

4702. Laing, Samuel. Modern science and modern thought, by S. Laing. Containing a supplemental chapter on Gladstone's "Dawn of creation" and "Proem of Genesis," and on Drummond's "Natural law in the spiritual world." 25th thousand. London, Chapman and Hall, 1898.
xii, 382p. illus. 23cm.
"Strange that with all the intellectual attempts to found a new sect, the only one that has met with much success is one based on the most gross and vulgar imposture — Mormonism."
USlC

4703. Lamb, Charles W. An exposition of Mormonism, and a defence of truth, being a refutation of the report that the Book of Mormon originated in Solomon Spaulding's Manuscript found." Followed by some evidence as to its real origin and the belief of the true Latter-day Saints. Grinnell, Ia., 1878.
[46]p. 17cm.
MoInRC, NN

4704. ———. Mormonism. To a leading Brighamite Mormon in Utah (by Chas. Lamb. Charlotte Lockling of the Reorganized Church of Jesus Christ) [Logan, Ia., Democrat Steam Print., 1888]
[4]p. 15cm.
Caption-title.
Signed: Magnolia.
RLDS poetry.
MH

4705. Lamb, Martin Thomas. Book of Mormon: Is it from God? Lectures delivered in the First Baptist Church, Salt Lake City, by Reverend M. T. Lamb. [Salt Lake City] Printed for the author by the Salt Lake Herald, Job Department, 1885.
2p.l. [5]–125p. 17cm.
CSmH, CtY, CU–B, ICHi, ICN, ICU, MH, MoInRC, NjP, NN, PCC, PU, UHi, ULA, USl, USlC, WHi

4706. ———. (same, under title) The golden Bible; or, The Book of Mormon. Is it from God? By Rev. M. T. Lamb. New York, Ward & Drummond, 1886.
xiv, 344p. illus., facsims. 19cm.
Enlarged edition of the above.
CSmH, CtY, DLC, ICN, IWW, MH, NjPT, NN, UHi, USlC, UU

4707. ———. (same) New York, Published by Ward & Drummond, 1887.
xiv, 344p. illus., facsims. 19cm.
CSmH, CtY, CU-B, DLC, ICN, MH, MoInRC, NjP, UHi, ULA, USl, USlC, UU, WHi

4708. ———. (same, under title) The Mormons and their Bible, by Reverend M. T. Lamb. Philadelphia, The Griffith and Rowland Press, 1901.
4p.l., 9–152p. illus., 4 ports. 19½cm.
CSmH, DLC, MoInRC, NjPT, NN, PCC, UHi, UPB

4709. ———. (same) Philadelphia, The Judson Press [c1901]
152p. illus., ports. 20cm. (Social service series)
Published by the American Baptist Republican Society.
ICN

4710. ———. (same) Philadelphia, The Judson Press [1903]
4p.l. [9]–152p. illus. 19½cm.
UHi, USlC

4711. ———. (same) Philadelphia, The Griffith & Rowland Press [1903]
4p.l. [9]–152p. plates, ports. 20cm.
USlC

Lambert, George Cannon. Early scenes in church history. *See Early scenes in church history.*

4712. ———. Gems of reminiscence. Designed for the instruction and encouragement of young Latter-day Saints. Salt Lake City, Compiled and Published by George C. Lambert, 1915.
7p.l., 15–192p. 18cm. (Faith promoting series. 17th book)
Reminiscences of James S. Brown, William J. Parkin, E. R. S. Schnelle, B. F. Cummings, Chauncey W. West, James Lawson, Wilford Woodruff, Heber J. Grant, Anson Call, J. M. Brown, T. R. Gledhill, Charles Lambert, and others.
CSmH, CtY, CU-B, NN, UHi, UPB, USlC, UU, WHi

4713. ———. Precious memories. Designed for the instruction and encouragement of young Latter-day Saints. Salt Lake City, Compiled and Published by George C. Lambert, 1914.
3p.l. [7]–96p. 17cm.
(Faith promoting series. 16th book)
CSmH, CtY, ICN, InU, NjP, UHi, UPB, USlC, UU

4714. ———. Treasures in Heaven. Designed for instruction and encouragement of young Latter-day Saints. Salt Lake City, Compiled and Published by Geo. C. Lambert, 1914.
vi [7]–96p. illus., ports. 18cm.
(Faith promoting series. 15th book)
CtY, InU, NjP, UHi, UPB, USl, USlC, UU, WHi

Lambert, J. M. Concordance to the Book of Mormon . . . *See Lampert, J. M.*

4715. Lambert, Joseph R. The nature of man. Is he possessed of immortality? by Elder J. R. Lambert. Lamoni, Ia., Reorganized Church of Jesus Christ of Latter Day Saints [189–]
22p. 19½cm.
Caption-title.
At head of title: No. 1.
MoInRC, UHi

4716. ———. (same) Lamoni, Ia., Herald publishing house [189–]
12p. 22½cm. (Reorganized Church of Jesus Christ. Tracts. No. 1)
IWW, MoInRC, NN

4717. ———. (same) Lamoni, Ia., Published by the Reorganized Church of Jesus Christ of Latter Day Saints [ca. 1910]
22p. 17½cm. (No. 1186)
USlC

4718. ———. Objections to the Book of Mormon and the Book of Doctrine and Covenants answered and refuted, By Elder J. R. Lambert. Published by the Reorganized Church of Jesus Christ of Latter Day Saints. Lamoni, Ia., Herald Publishing House, 1894.
v [3]–120p. 17cm.
Followed by a catalogue of publications, works, and tracts by Herald Publishing House.
CSmH, MoInRC

4719. ———. (same) Lamoni, Ia., Herald Publishing House [1912?]
v [3]–120p. 19cm.
CtY, MoK, NN, USlC

4720. ———. Our defense by Elder J. R. Lambert. Lamoni, Ia., Herald Publishing Co., [1912?]
49p. 19cm. (No. 6a)
NN

4721. ———. (same) Lamoni, Ia., Herald Publishing Co. [1912?]
49p. 19cm. (No. 1133)
MoInRC, NN, UHi, USlC

4722. ———. The patriarchal or evangelical order, is it essential in the Church of Jesus Christ? Calling and duties of patriarchs considered. [n.p., n.d.]
51p. 17cm.
MoInRC

LAMBERT, J. R.

4723. ———. Sermon. [Lamoni? Ia.] Lamoni Gazette, 1888.
10p. 22cm.
Sermon given in Lamoni, Ia., on Jan. 8, 1888. Supplement sheet to *Lamoni Gazette*, March 1888. RLDS church doctrine.
MoInRC

4724. ———. What is man? His nature and destiny. The spirit, or soul; is it immortal? Does it survive the death of the body in a conscious state? The views of mortal soulists examined and refuted . . . By Elder J. R. Lambert . . . Lamoni, Ia., Printed at the Patriot Office [c1891]
1p.l., iiip., [1]l. [5]–249p. 17cm.
DLC, USIC

4725. ———. (same) Lamoni, Ia., Herald Publishing House and Bookbindery, 1893 [c1891]
1p.l., iiip., [1]l. [5]–249p. 17cm.
Publishers preface dated 1893.
MH

4726. ———. (same) Lamoni, Ia., Herald Publishing House and Bookbindery, 1908.
vii [1]l. [5]–249p. 18cm.
USIC

4727. ———. (same) Lamoni, Ia., Herald Publishing House and Bookbindery, 1914.
vii, 249p. 18cm.
USIC, UU

4727a. Lambert, Louis Aloisius. Notes on Ingersoll. By Rev. L. A. Lambert, of Waterloo, N.Y. Preface by Rev. Patrick Cronin. Buffalo, N.Y., Buffalo Catholic Publication Co., 1883. 4th ed. rev. & enl.
200, iv p. 17cm.
Mormons mentioned: p. 30, 64, 67, 74, 97, 101, 166, 180.
USIC

4727b. ———. Tactics of infidels. Buffalo, Peter Paul & Brother, 1887.
iv, 357p. 17cm.
Mormons, p. 214, 219, 226, 241, 303.
USIC

4728. Lambourne, Alfred. A glimpse of Great Salt Lake, Utah. Illustrated. [Omaha] Passenger Department of the Union Pacific Railroad, 1892.
40p. plates, maps. 22cm.
Descriptive and historical material on the Great Salt Lake and its discovery.
Another edition: 1900. NjP
NjP, ULA, USIC

4729. ———. A memory of John R. Park. [Salt Lake City] The author [n.d.]
8 numb. l. port. 24cm.
USIC, UU

4730. ———. The old journey; reminiscences of pioneer days. By Alfred Lambourne. [Salt Lake City?] G. Q. Cannon and Sons Co. [c1897]
9p.l., 19–53p. plates. 21cm.
Revised from the author's larger work: *An Old Sketch Book*, 1892.
Pictures along the Mormon trail.
Howes L43
CSmH, CtY, CU–B, InU, MH, NjP, NN, UHi, ULA, USIC, UU

4731. ———. An old sketch book. Dedicated to the memory of my father. Eighteen plates on China paper with descriptive text. Boston, S. E. Cassino [c1892]
[40]l. 18 mounted plates. 41cm.
Pictures along the Mormon Trail, with narration.
Howes L43
CtY, ULA, USIC, UU

4732. ———. The pioneer trail, by Alfred Lambourne. Salt Lake City, The Deseret News, 1913.
3p.l. [7]–78p. plates, port. 24½cm.
"*An old sketch-book* and *The old journey* are now out of print, and this volume is offered in their stead."
CU–B, DLC, MoInRC, NjP, UHi, ULA, UPB, USIC

4733. ———. A play-house, being a sketch in three short letters. Reminiscences of the scene-painter's gallery; with glimpses of the pioneers and a few notables. Sidelights upon post votaries of Thălia, Clio, and Melpŏmĕne [by] Alfred Lambourne [Salt Lake City? 191–]
3p.l. [9]–64p. illus. 24½cm.
CSmH, NjP, NN, UHi, ULA, USIC

4734. Lamoreaux, Andrew L. An epistle to the Church of Jesus Christ of Latter-day Saints in France, and the Channel Islands, from the presidency of the French mission. [St. Helier's, Jersey, 1854]
10p. 20½cm.
Signed: Andres L. Lamoreaux; James H. Hart; Louis A. Bertrand, William Taylor.
CtY, USIC

4735. Lampert, J. M. Concordance to the Book of Mormon. Lamoni, Ia., Herald Publ. House, 1898.
14p. 25cm.
J. M. Lampert may be a pseudonym for Warren Peak.
MoInRC, USIC

4735a. The lamps of the temple: crayon sketches of the men of the modern pulpit. 3rd ed. rev. & enl. London, John Snow, 1856.
iv, 597p. 19½cm.
"The lamps of the temple of Mudfog," p. 466–519.
USIC

4736. Landis, Charles B. The Roberts case. Speech of Hon. C. B. Landis of Indiana, in the House of Representatives, Wednesday, January 24, 1900. Washington, 1900.
18p. 24cm.
CU–B, DLC, NN, PHi, UHi, USl, USlC, UU

4737. Landon, Melville De Lancey. . . . Kings of the platform and pulpit . . . Birmingham, Alabama, John F. Moore, 1891.
ix, 570p. illus. 23½cm.
The section on Artemus Ward concerns his Mormon lectures.
Other editions: 1890. UU; Akron, Ohio, Saalfield, Publishing Company, 1901. USlC; 1908. UPB
UHi, USlC

4738. ———. Wise, witty, eloquent kings of the platform and pulpit. Biographies, reminiscences and lectures . . . and personal reminiscences and anecdotes of noted Americans. Chicago, Werner, 1895.
570p. illus., ports., facsims. 23½cm.
Artemus Ward's Panorama, on Mormonism, p. 33–74.
CU, UPB

4739. Lang, William. History of Seneca County, from the close of the revolutionary war to July, 1880; embracing many personal sketches of pioneers, anecdotes, and faithful descriptions of events pertaining to the organization of the county and its progress. By W. Lang . . . Springfield, O., Transcript Printing Co., 1880.
691 [1] xiip. front., plates, port. 23cm.
Material on Oliver Cowdery and a brief history of the Church.
CU–B, DLC, MB, MWA, NjP, PHi, UHi, ULA, USlC, UU

4740. Lange, Henry. Atlas von Nord-Amerika, nach den neusten Materialien, mit besonderer Rücksicht auf physikalische Verhältnisse und genauer Angabe der county-Einteilung, der Eisenbahnen, Canäle, Poststrassen und Dampfschiffart, in 18 Blättern mit erläuterndem Texte, hrsg. von Henry Lange. Braunschweig, Verlag von George Westermann, 1854.
3p.l., 28p. maps. 25cm.
Atlas to accompany Andree, Karl Theodor. Nord-Amerika . . . Braunschweig, G. Westermann, 1854.
A note on the Book of Mormon and its origin.
Title in English: Atlas of North America.
Howes L76
CU–B, DLC

4741. Langford, Nathaniel Pitt. Vigilante days and ways; the pioneers of the Rockies; the makers and making of Montana, Idaho, Oregon, Washington, and Wyoming. By Nathaniel Pitt Langford . . . Boston, J. G. Cupples Co., 1890.
2v. front., ports. 19½cm.
Trip to Salt Lake City in 1864, and his impressions of Mormonism.
Other editions: New York, 1893. CU–B; Chicago, A. C. McClurg & Co., 1912. DLC, NjP, ULA, UPB
Howes L78
CU–B, DLC, NjP

4742. Langworthy, Franklin. Scenery of the plains, mountains and mines: or, A diary kept upon the overland route to California, by way of the Great Salt Lake: Travels in the cities, mines, and agricultural districts — embracing the return by the Pacific Ocean and Central America, in the years 1850, '52, and '53. By Franklin Langworthy . . . Ogdensburgh [N.Y.] Published by J. C. Sprague, Bookseller, 1855.
vi [7]–324p. 19½cm.
Mormons in "Cainsville"; Mormon speculations. Also a trip through Salt Lake City in 1850 with notes on Mormonism.
Howes L84, Sabin 38904, W–C 258
CSmH, CtY, CU–B, DLC, ICN, KU, MB, MH, MiU, NB, NjP, NN, UHi, ULA, WHi

4743. Lanier, Roy H. Mistakes of the "Latter Day Saints;" a review of the books, doctrines, and practices of "Church of Jesus Christ of Latter Day Saints," — Utah Branch. Fort Worth, Texas [193–]
59p. 15cm.
MoInRC, NN, UHi, UPB, USlC

4744. ———. (same) Fort Worth, Texas [193–]
60p. 14cm.
Variant printing. Also published at Abilene, Texas and York, Nebraska during the same period.
USlC

4745. Lanman, Charles. A summer in the wilderness; embracing a canoe voyage up the Mississippi and around Lake Superior. By Charles Lanman . . . New York, D. Appleton & Company; Philadelphia, G. S. Appleton, 1847.
2p.l. [9]–208p. 19cm.
Visit to Nauvoo after the exodus, and a discussion with a Mormon.
Another edition: "A canoe voyage up the Mississippi . . ." same collation, maps and date.
Afterwards reprinted in V.1 of his *Adventures in the wilds of the United States.*
Howes L90, Sabin 38926
CSmH, CtY, CU, DLC, ICHi, MiU, MB, MnU, NjP, PPA, PPL, NN, ULA

4746. ———. (same, under title) Adventures in the wilds of the United States and British American provinces. By Charles Lanman . . . Illustrated by the author and Oscar Bessau . . . with an appendix by Lieut. Campbell Hardy. Philadelphia, I. W. Moore, 1856.
2v. plates. 23cm.
Includes a chapter on Nauvoo with a description of the Mormon Temple after the exodus, V. 1, p. 15–18.
CU, DLC, FOA, MiU, NN, OCl, OClW, OFH, PPCC, PP

LANTERN

4747. The Lantern. Salt Lake City, Published by the students of the University of Deseret, March–June, 1891.
lv. (4 nos.) 25cm.
USlC

4748. Larimer, William Henry Harrison. Reminiscences of General William Larimer and of his son William H. H. Larimer, two of the founders of Denver City. Compiled from letters: and from notes written by the late William H. H. Larimer, of Kansas City, Missouri, by Herman S. Davis . . . Printed for private circulation under the auspices of William Larimer Mellon . . . Lancaster, Pa., The New Era Printing Company, 1918.
1p.l., 5–256 (i.e. 266)p. illus., ports., facsims., fold. geneal. table. 25cm.
Pages 194 A–B inserted between p. 194 and 195; p. 199 A–H inserted between p. 199 and 200.
Reference to Mormons, p. 28, 44, 79, 83, 93, 133, 137–138, 206–207.
CU–B

4749. Larkey, A. G. Who first acknowledged polygamy; Brighamite or Josephite? By Rev. A. G. Larkey . . . Cleveland, The Utah Gospel Mission, 1924.
16p. 17cm.
MoInRC, NN, USlC

4750. Larkin Mortuary, Salt Lake City, *compiler.* George William Larkin (and collection of appropriate sayings and verses) [n.p., n.d.]
[14]l. plates. 2½cm.
He crossed the plains with the 1863 Captain McCarthy pioneer company and settled in Salt Lake City.
Includes "appropriate" poetry.
UPB

4751. Larsen, John. Mormonismen Afsløret ved uddrag af Mormonernes egne Taler, skrifter og Historie. Af John Larsen . . . Autoiferet Udgave. Blair, Nebr., Danish Luth. Publ. House, 1910.
134p. 19½cm.
Title in English: Mormonism unveiled . . .
UHi, USlC

4752. ———. Mormonism refuted in the light of scripture and history; a testimony to the historical church, written by John Larsen . . . San Francisco, Protestant Publishing House, 1899.
2p.l. [7]–75p. [1]l. 21cm.
Two variant prints, one with price on the title page.
CtY, DLC, MH, MoInRC, USlC

4753. Larsen, Holger M. Paa deres Frugter skal I kende dam. [Udgivet og forlagt af Holger M. Larsen. København, Peder Skramsgade] 1930.
[2]p. 23cm.
A description of the general authorities of the church.
Title in English: By their fruits shall ye know them.
USlC

4754. Larsen, Thomas. Tidsbilleder fra vindsyssel (Historik samfund for Hjorring amt. En gennembrudstid. Fra de nittende Aarhundredes sidste halvdel) Hjorring, 1917.
200p.
Title in English: Picture stones from Vindsyssel.
Schmidt

4755. Larsen, Thorvald L., *editor.* Danske i Salt Lake City. Illustreret souvenir album. Udgivet af en komitee, med bistand af "Apollo" Loge, D. B. S., i anledning af Dansk Brodersamfunds Konvention i Fresno, Cal., og Dansk Søstersamfunds Knovention i Council Bluffs, Iowa. 1910. [Salt Lake City?] Udgivet af Thorvald L. Larsen. Redigeret af Axel Jørgensen. Omslag og Frise Tegnet af Jens Hvid, 1910.
36p. 27½cm.
USlC

La Rue, William Earl. Church prospectus. *See Reorganized Church of Jesus Christ of Latter Day Saints. Many sided views.*

4756. ———. The foundations of Mormonism; a study of the fundamental facts in the history and doctrines of the Mormons from original sources, by William Earl LaRue, B. D., with introduction by Alfred Williams Anthony, D. D. New York, Chicago [etc.] Fleming H. Revell Company [c1919]
243p. port. 19½cm.
On verso of t.p.: Published for the Home mission's Council, and the Council of Women for Home Missions.
CU–B, DLC, IWW, MiU, MoInRC, NjP, NjPT, UHi, ULA, USl, USlC, WHi

4757. ———. Mormonism polygamous. By William E. LaRue. [Pittsburgh, The National Reform Association, n.d.]
[4]p. 23cm.
USlC

4758. ———. Who and what we are. [Philadelphia?] Reorganized Church of Jesus Christ of Latter Day Saints [n.d.]
15p. 17cm.
Author's home was in Philadelphia where he was serving as pastor of the local RLDS church.
MoInRC

4759. Latham, Henry Jepson. Among the Mormons. How an American and an Englishman went to Salt Lake City, and married seven wives apiece. Their lively experience. A peep into the mysteries of Mormonism. By Ring Jepson [*pseud.*] San Francisco, The San Francisco News Company, 1879.
115p. 17cm.
CSmH, DLC, MH, USlC, WHi

4760. Lathrop, George. Memoirs of a pioneer; being the autobiography of George Lathrop, one of the first to help in the opening of the west. Lusk, Wyoming, The Lusk Herald [1915]
33 [1]p. 16cm.
Compiled by Luke Voorhees from notes given him by the author.
Published with additional material in 1927 under title: Some pioneer recollections.
Drove a mule team into Salt Lake City. His reaction to the Mormons, particularly their liquor.
CtY, USlC

4761. ———. Some pioneer recollections; being the autobiography of George Lathrop, one of the first to help in the opening of the West; and a statement made by John Sinclair relative to the rescue of the Donner party; also an extract from a letter written by Geo. McKinstry with reference to the rescue of the Donner Party. Philadelphia, George W. Jacobs & Co., 1927.
2 pts. (2p.l. [7]–75p.) port. 23½cm.
Mormon material in first part. Early experiences in Salt Lake City.
CU–B, DLC, NjP, NN, UHi, USlC

4762. Latimer, A. C. Why I left the Mormon church, by A. C. Latimer. Pittsburg, The National Reform Association [1916?]
19 [1]p. 15½cm.
Cover-title.
MoInRC, UHi, USlC

4763. Latta, Robert Ray. Reminiscences of pioneer life. Kansas City, Mo., Franklin, Hudson Pub. Co., 1912.
186p. illus. 19½cm.
Includes a description of a Mormon settlement in Fremont Co. Iowa and a discussion of Mormonism.
Howes L130
CU–B, DLC, NjP, NN, UHi, USlC

4764. Latter-day judgments. Liverpool, England [n.d.]
4p. 21½cm.
Missionary tract.
UPB, USlC, UU

4765. The Latter Day Precept. Kansas City, Mo., August, 1919–1920.
2v. monthly. 28cm.
Probably discontinued in 1920, due to "editorial policy" problems.
Edited by John Flanders.
A Strangite publication.
CtY V.1 #3; USlC V.1 #2, 8, V.2 #3, 4, 5

4766. The Latter-day Saints; a question of identity. . . . [n.p., n.d.]
[6]p. 20cm.
MoInRC, USlC

4767. . . . Latter-day Saints: The dupes of a foolish and wicked imposture. . . . London, John Mason [185–]
2pts. (16, 16p.) 16cm.
At head of title: pt. 1. No. 595. pt. 2. No. 596.
Variant of pt. 1 printed by the New York Tract Society. USlC
CtY, USlC

4768. ———. (same) Cape Town: Saul Solomon & Co., . . . 1853.
32p. 15½cm.
"Reprinted with slight alterations, from a tract published by John Mason, 14, City Road, London."
See Mason, John.
USlC

4769. The Latter-day Saints anthem book by local composers. . . . Salt Lake City, Published by Daynes & Coalter [c1897]
1p.l., 101 [1]p. 27cm.
USlC

4770. The Latter Day Saints (Mormons) [Independence, Mo.?] Church of Jesus Christ of Latter-day Saints [n.d.]
2 nos. (8p.) 16½cm.
A missionary tract.
USlC

4771. ———. (same) Chicago, Ill., Church of Jesus Christ of Latter-day Saints [n.d.]
8p. 16½cm.
USlC

4771a. The Latter-day Saints' belief. [Liverpool?, 1852?]
Broadside. 21×12½cm.
An expansion with scriptural passages of the 14 Articles of faith, which first appeared in 1849.
UPB

4772. L.D.S. Business College. Education is the great lifting power. Salt Lake City, 1929.
63p. 21cm.
USlC

4773. ———. A little book about the Latter-day Saints' Business College. Salt Lake City, The Deseret News, 1900.
40p. plates. 18½cm.
Cover-title.
Purpose of the school.
USlC, UU

4774. L.D.S. College. Students hand book. Salt Lake City, 1928–
v. 15cm.
USlC 1928–29, 1929–30

L. D. S. HIGH SCHOOL

4775. L.D.S. High School. L.D.S. High School and L.D.S. Business College. Official student body directory, 1930–31. [Salt Lake City, 1930]
36 [2]p. 15cm.
USIC

4776. Latter-day Saints High School and Business College. Latter-day Saints High School and business college. [Salt Lake City, n.d.]
[6]l., 16×25cm.
USIC

4777. ———. (same) [Salt Lake City, n.d.]
[6]l. 16×25cm.
Variant edition. Title in border.
USIC

4778. Latter Day Saints' Messenger and Advocate. Kirtland, Ohio, October, 1834–September, 1837.
3v. (36 nos. in 576p.) 25–28cm.
Editors: Oliver Cowdery, John Whitmer, Warren A. Cowdery.
Published by F. G. Williams & Co. October, 1834–May, 1836; Oliver Cowdery, June, 1936–January, 1837; Joseph Smith jr. & Sidney Rigdon, February–March, 1837; April, 1837–September, 1837 William Marks.
Succeeded the *Evening and Morning Star.* Superseded by the "*Elder's journal.*"
Sabin 50743
CSmH, CtY, CU–B V.1–2, MH V.1–2, NN, UPB, USIC

L.D.S. Messenger and Advocate (Pittsburg)
See Messenger and Advocate of the Church of Christ.

4779. The Latter-day Saints Millennial Star. [Manchester, Liverpool, London] The Church of Jesus Christ of Latter-day Saints in Great Britain, 1840–
v. illus. monthly, semi-monthly, weekly. 23cm.
Monthly: May, 1840–June 15, 1845.
Semi-monthly: July, 1845–April 24, 1852.
Weekly: 1852–
Published in Manchester 1840–1842, moved to Liverpool, then to London.
CSmH; CtY V. 1–21, 31–67; CU–B; MH; NjP V.1–17; ULA; UPB; USIC; WHi V.1–32, 34–65, 69–90, 93–94

4780. ———. Address to the Saints. Awful assassination. The pledged faith of the state of Illinois stained with innocent blood by a mob. [Liverpool, Supplement to the Millennial Star, August] 1844.
16p. 21½cm.
Sabin 40744
USIC

4781. ———. History of Joseph Smith. Liverpool, 1852.
88p. 23cm.
CU–B

4782. ———. Supplement to the Millennial Star, August, 1844 [death of Joseph Smith] Address to the Saints. [Liverpool] 1844.
16p. 21cm.
Caption-title.
CSmH, UPB, USIC

4783. ———. Supplement to the Millennial Star. December, 1844, Conclusion of Elder Rigdon's trial. [Liverpool] 1844.
8p. 21cm.
Caption-title.
CSmH, CU–B, MH, ULA, USIC

4784. Latter-day Saints Millennial Star and Monthly Visitor. Madras, March–November, 1854.
v.1 #1–7. monthly. 21cm.
Printed by S. Bowie at the Oriental Press.
Edited and published by R. Ballantine, April–July; Edited by R. Skelton, November, 1854.
Organ of the Church in India.
CU–B #1–4, 7; UPB #1–4; USIC comp.

4785. L.D.S. Missionary Correspondence School. L.D.S. Missionary Correspondence School. [Salt Lake City, ca. 1918]
[8]p. 23cm.
USIC

4786. ———. The restoration of the gospel. [Salt Lake City, n.d.]
16p. 19½cm.
USIC

4787. ———. A Young folks history of the Church. [Salt Lake City? n.d.]
47p. 19cm.
UPB, USIC

4788. L.D.S. Music Bulletin. Salt Lake City, 1921–1929.
12 nos. 23cm.
Nos. 11–12 issued together.
Publication of the Music Committee.
USIC comp.

4789. L.D.S. School of Music. L.D.S. School of Music. Announcement . . . Salt Lake City, 1921–
v. 19cm.
USIC 1917–18, 1919–20, 1921–22, 1922–23, 1923–24, 1924–25

4790. L.D.S. Southern Star. Chattanooga, Tenn. Southern States Mission, December 3, 1898–December 1, 1900.
2v. (840p.) weekly. 30cm.
Publisher and editor: Ben E. Rich.
Running title: The Southern Star.
CSmH, CtY, CU–B, MH, UPB, USIC, WHi

L. D. S. UNIVERSITY

4791. Latter-day Saints Tract Distribution Society. Address to the reader. [Bradford, 1851?]
[4]p. 21cm.
An explanation of missionary tracts which includes the Articles of Faith.
Signed: Robert O. Menzies, President.
MH

4792. L.D.S. University. Bi-monthly bulletin. Salt Lake City, 1906–
v. 22½cm.
Contents: V. 1 #1–V. 17 #3?
Summary of work. V. 2 #1. Courses of study.
V. 2 #2. Summary of the work of the Commercial school. (July, 1908)
Also published during the same period was the Quarterly Bulletin of the high school, in which the course of study was given.
USIC V. 1 #1, 2; V. 2 #1, 2, 3, 4; V. 3 #1, 2, 3; V. 4 #2; V. 5 #2, 4; V. 6 #4; V. 8 #2; V. 9 #4; V. 11 #2; V. 12 #4; V. 13 #1, 2; V. 17 #3

4793. ———. Commencement annual of the Latter-day Saints' College . . . June 7, 1898. Salt Lake City, 1898.
32p. illus. 18½cm.
Cover-title: Latter-day Saints' College annual, 1898.
USIC

4794. ———. Courses of study. Salt Lake City, 1886–
v. 15–25cm.
L.D.S. University started as Salt Lake Stake Academy from 1886; L.D.S. College 1889; L.D.S. University 1901; L.D.S. High School 1906; L.D.S. University 1911; L.D.S. College 1927.
L.D.S. Business College was formed in 1931 after the college was dropped and the high school discontinued on turning the system over to the state.
The Business College had been formed as a department of the University from the Salt Lake and Deseret Business Colleges.
CONTENTS: Salt Lake Stake Academy circular. 1884–85 (USI) 1886–87, 1887–88, 1888–89.
L.D.S. College. Course of study. 1888–89, 1889–90, 1890–91, 1891–92, 1892–93, 1893–94, 1894–95, 1895–96, 1896–97, 1897–98, 1898–99, 1899–1900, 1900–01, 1901–02, (later) summer 1919, 1929–30.
L.D.S. Business College. Course of Study. 1909–10. Business Dept. L.D.S. College, 1898–99. (USI)
L.D.S. High School. 1906–07, 1907–08, 1908–09, 1909–10, 1910–11, 1911–12, 1912–13, 1913–14, 1914–15, 1915–16.
L.D.S. University. Courses of study. 1901–02, 1902–03, 1903–04, 1904–05, 1913–14, 1915–16. (2d series) 1917–18, 1918–19, 1919–20 (with separate music catalog) 1920–21, 1921–22, 1922–23, 1923–24, 1925–26, 1926–27, 1927–28, 1929–30.
USIC

4795. ———. L.D.S. Business College, 80 North Main Street. Salt Lake City [n.d.]
63p. 21½cm.
USIC

4795a. ———. General regulations and daily programs for first half year, 1901–02. [Salt Lake City, 1901]
[4]p. 24½cm.
USIC

4796. ———. Latter-day Saints University. [Salt Lake City] 1922.
[16]p. illus. 15½cm.
USIC

4797. ———. Outlines and illustrations of the work given in the Latter-day Saints' University including the combined business colleges (L.D.S. and Salt Lake) Salt Lake City, 1894.
[16]l. of plates. 23×15cm.
UPB, USIC

4798. ———. The S Book [yearbook] [Salt Lake City] Published by the Students of the Latter-day Saints' University, 1913–
v. 25½–30cm.
Published in 1913 under title "The Seagull."
USIC 1913–1931.

4799. ———. S Songs and yells. Published by L.D.S.U. Oratorio Society. Salt Lake City, 1912.
[8]p. 20cm.
USIC

4800. ———. (same) Salt Lake City [c1919]
[16]p. 23cm.
USIC

4801. ———. (same) Salt Lake City [c1919]
22p. 23cm.
Variant printings.
USIC

4802. ———. (same) Also S community songs. Salt Lake City, Latter-day Saints College, 1927.
56 [2]p. 20cm.
USIC

4803. ———. Scenes; pictorial and verbal in the life of the Latter-day Saints' University. Salt Lake City, 1909]
[10]l. illus., plates. 18cm.
USIC

4804. ———. School songs for the second annual commencement of the Latter-day Saints' University, June 2, 1903. [Salt Lake City] 1903.
[4]p. illus. 21cm.
Words only.
USIC

4805. ———. Thirty-seventh anniversary of Founders' Day. Thursday, November fifteenth, 1923. [Salt Lake City, 1923]
[4]p. ports. 17cm.
Brief history of the school.
UPB, USIC

4806. ———. Sunday School. Theology class. Instructors. Elders Jas. E. Talmage and Jas. H. Anderson. Jesus, the Christ. Lectures 1–3. [Salt Lake City, n.d.]
3 pamp. [1 p. each] 20½cm.
USIC

4807. Lauder, Harry. Roamin' in the gloamin' by Sir Harry Lauder. With illustrations. Philadelphia, J. P. Lippincott Company, 1928.
2p.l., 7–200p. plates, port. 22½cm.
One of the most fascinating people he meets is Joseph [F.] Smith in Salt Lake City, p. 249–60.
NjP, USIC

4808. Laurent, Vivi. Vivis resa från saltsjostaden till Pacifikens strander. Stockholm, Wahlstrom & Widstrand [1924]
164p. illus. 20cm.
Mormons, p. 7–89.
Title in English: Vivi's journey from Salt Lake City to the Pacific shore.
USIC

4809. Laut, Agnes Christina. The overland trail; the epic path of pioneers to Oregon, by Agnes C. Laut . . . with forty-nine illustrations from photographs, two maps and two diagrams. New York, Frederick A. Stokes Company, 1929.
xx p., [1]l., 358p. illus., plates, maps. 21½cm.
Brief notes on Mormon pioneers.
CU–B, DLC, MH, NjP, NN, OO, PP, PU, UHi, UU

4810. Laveille, E. . . . Le P. de Smet (1801–1873) Introduction par G. Kurth. 2. éd. Liege, F. Dessian [etc., etc.] 1913.
2p.l. [v]–xiii, 560p. port. 22cm.
Chapter 17: "Expedition contre les Mormons."
Title in English: The Father de Smet.
Another edition: Bruxelles, A. Dewit, 1922. DLC
CU–B

4811. ———. (same, in English) The life of Father DeSmet, S. J. (1801–1873) by E. Laveille, S.J. Authorized translation by Marian Lindsay. Introd. by Charles A. Coppens. New York, P. J. Kennedy & Sons, 1915.
xxii, 400p. front. 22cm.
CU–B, DLC, NjP, UHi, USIC

4812. Lawrence, George Alfred. Silverland by the author of "Guy Livingstone," &c . . . London, Chapman & Hall, Publishers, 1873.
259p. 23cm.
Salt Lake City, Mormons, and mining, p. 46–82. In Utah, February, 1873.
CtY, CU–B, DLC, NjP, ULA, USIC

4813. Laws, Samuel Spahr. Polygamy and citizenship in church and state, by Samuel Spahr Laws . . . Washington, Judd & Detweiler, Printers, 1906.
227p. 23cm.
Many references to Mormonism.
USIC has an index [229]–240 which reads — "can be had of Woodward & Lothrop, Washington, D.C. with testimonials and index."
CSmH, CU–B, DLC, ICJ, UHi, USIC

4814. Lawson, W. B. Jesse James among the Mormons. New York, Street & Smith, 1899.
1v. (unpaged) 27cm.
At head of title: Issued weekly.
Fiction concerning Mormonism.
CSmH

4815. Layton, Christopher. Autobiography of Christopher Layton, with an account of his funeral, a personal sketch, etc., and genealogical appendix; ed. by John Q. Cannon. Salt Lake City, The Deseret News, 1911.
v p., [1]l., 317p. port. 17½cm.
Mormon biography.
CU–B, DLC, MH, UHi, UPB, USI, USIC, UU

4816. Lea, Henry Charles. Bible view of polygamy. [Philadelphia, 187–]
4p. 24cm.
Caption-title.
Introductory letter signed: Mizpah.
A description of polygamy brought about by the situation in Utah.
CtY, DLC, MH, ICHi, PHi, PPL, UPB, USI

4817. Leach, Morgan Lewis. A history of the Grand Traverse Region. By Dr. M. L. Leach. Traverse City, Michigan, Published in the Grand Traverse Herald, 1883.
59p. 28½cm.
Cover-title.
Signed: Traverse City, May 1884.
Chapter xviii: "The Mormons [Strangite] — Settlement on Beaver Island . . ."
Printed in 3 columns.
UHi, UPB

4818. League for Social Service. Anti-Mormon leaflets. New York, 1899.
7 nos. 15cm. (Social Service. Series D)
1. Methods of Mormon missionaries, by Wm. R. Campbell.
2. Present aspects of Mormonism, by R. G. McNiece.

3. Historical sketch of Mormonism, by D. J. McMillan.
4. Articles of faith of the Latter-day Saints with Mormon explanation, by J. D. Nutting.
5. Political aspects of Mormonism, by J. D. Nutting.
6. Ten reasons under Presbyterian Church why Christians cannot fellowship with the Mormon Church.
7. Reasons why Brigham H. Roberts should be expelled from the U.S. Congress.
NN #7; UPB #6–7; WHi #1–6

4819. ———. Reasons why Brigham H. Roberts should be expelled from the U.S. Congress. New York, League for Social Service [n.d.]
13p. 14½cm. (Social Service. Series D. Anti-Mormon Series)
MoInRC, NN, UPB

4820. Leaves from the book of life. [Birmingham, Published by the Reorganized Church of Jesus Christ of Latter Day Saints, n.d.]
3 nos. (4, 4, 4p.) 18cm.
Contents: Christianity; its corruption reacting. Covenant of life. The Church of Christ.
NN

4821. Leavitt, Michael Bennett. Fifty years in theatrical management. With reproductions of 500 photographs. New York, Broadway Publishing Co. [1912]
xxii [4]p., [1]l., 735 p. illus., ports., plates. 14½cm.
Salt Lake Theatre, and drama among the Mormons.
DLC, NjP, UPB, USlC

4822. Leavitt, Sarah (Sturdevant) History of Sarah Sturdevant Leavitt. Copied from her history by Juanita Leavitt Pulsipher, June, 1919. [Salt Lake City, Paragon Printing Company, 1920]
23p. 15×23½cm.
Mormon biography.
USlC

4823. LeBaron, Alonzo H. An address to every lover of truth and righteousness on the present state of affairs of Utah; and the condition in general of the people called Latter-day Saints. Also, a short treatise on the subject of The three heavens; or the three different kingdoms of glory spoken of in the scriptures; and likewise, the subject of the organization of the Church of Christ. By Alonzo H. LeBaron. Council Bluffs, Published by W. S. Burke, 1863.
2p.l., 20p. 19cm.
No confidence in Brigham Young; looking for a new leader of Mormonism.
CSmH, DLC

4823a. ———. Circular. [n.p., n.d.]
4p. 30½cm.
Proposal for a new periodical entitled *The Preparatory Restorer* and for the creation of the Preparatory Restoration Society.
Signed: Beacon, Iowa, May, 1869.
USlC

4824. ———. Circular. [On the question of Statehood for Utah] Salt Lake City, 1887.
Broadside. 21½×15cm.
Mormons in politics by an excommunicated Mormon.
USlC

4825. ———. Copy of a brief note to Elder Woodruff. Salt Lake City, 1889.
Broadside. 21½×15cm.
Signed: LeBaron Heavington. [*pseud.*]
Grievances against Bishop Miller of Provo, in 1860.
MH, USlC

4826. ———. Historical. "What the records say." LeBaron Havington [*pseud.*]
[4]p. 23cm.
A short account of Mr. LeBaron and his problems with Bishop Miller and the Mormon church.
UPB

4827. ———. The leadership of the so-called Mormon Church. "An irrepressible conflict." [Salt Lake City, 1873?]
Broadside. 24×18cm.
Written for *Zion's Deliverer.*
UHi (Mic)

4828. ———. . . . The pioneer reformer of Utah. Dr. LeBaron Havington [*pseud.*] Circular. Salt Lake City, 1884.
7, 3p. 24×18½cm.
Caption-title.
Includes *Zion's Deliverer*, Vol. 1, No. 1, November, 1873.
Zion's Deliverer, a monthly magazine. Alonzo LeBaron Havington [*pseud.*] Editor and publisher, Salt Lake City.
UHi, USlC

4829. ———. Polygamy from a new standpoint by Alonzo LeBaron Havington [*pseud.*] Salt Lake City, 1873.
Broadside. 28½×17cm.
"Written, July 7th 1871, for '*Zion's Deliverer.*' "
USlC

4830. ———. Post-office and other matters . . . Salt Lake City, 1888.
[4]p. 24cm.
Concerning his enemies in the Mormon hierarchy.
UPB

4831. ———. Rejected by the sore and tender-footed Tribune and Chronicle. Salt Lake City, 1885.
Broadside. 24½×18cm.
Caution concerning events happening with the Church. Hopes for final overthrow of "Brighamism" and polygamy.
USlC

LeBARON, A. H.

4832. ———. A short extract, containing a chapter or two from the history or journal of Elder Alonzo Le Baron . . . Leamington, Printed by J. W. Brierly, 22, Regent Street, 1851.
12p. 24cm.
USIC

4833. ———. Statement of Alonzo LeBaron Havington [*pseud.*] complainant, at a trial before the High Council of the Church of Latter-day Saints, at Provo City, Utah Territory, Nov. 17th, 1860. Bishop William Miller, defendant. [n.p., 188–]
Broadside. 35½×25½cm.
UPB

4834. ———. A strange story. (From one of Gideon's papers) [Salt Lake City? 1886?]
8p. 25½cm.
Caption-title.
Chiefly an extract from the *Carthage, Ill., Republican* of March 14, 1867.
A short biography of LeBaron Heavington [*pseud.*] and material on Mormon succession after Joseph Smith.
UHi, USIC

4835. ———. True virtue and integrity. [Beaver, Utah, 1878?]
Broadside. 22×17cm.
Intended for publication in the *Salt Lake Tribune.*
Concerning the bad treatment by the Church of LeBaron Havington [*pseud.*] and others.
Signed: Gideon. Beaver City. Nov. 1878.
MH

4836. ———. . . . "What the records say." by LeBaron Havington [*pseud.*] [Salt Lake City? 1886?]
3p. 23cm.
Caption-title.
At head of title: Historical.
A discussion of the Salt Lake City papers' coverage of the Mormon system of marriage.
UHi

4837. Lecky, William Edward Hartpole. Democracy and liberty . . . London, New York [etc.] Longmans, Green and Co., 1896.
2v. 19½cm.
The rise of Mormonism in Utah, and the crusade against polygamy, V. 1, p. 449–462.
Other editions: 2d ed. 1896. DLC; New ed. 1899. DLC, NjP; New ed. 1900. DLC
CU, CSmH, DLC, NjP, ULA

4838. Lee, Aaron. From the Atlantic to the Pacific; reminiscences of pioneer life and travels across the continent, from New England to the Pacific ocean, by an old soldier. Also a graphic account of his army experiences in the Civil War. By Aaron Lee, member of First Minnesota infantry. Seattle, Metropolitan Press, Printers [c1915]
3p.l. [7]–190p. illus., port., plate. 20cm.
Encounters the Mormons at Mt. Pisgah.
DLC, ULA, UPB, USIC

4839. Lee, Charles. Mormonism: a sketch of its rise and progress. A lecture delivered to the Derby Young Men's Christian Association. Derby, England, W. Rowbottom, 1852.
31p. 12cm.
NN

4840. Lee, E. G. The Mormons; Or, Knavery exposed. Giving an account of the discovery of the golden plates; the translation and various tricks resorted to — the proceedings at Kirtland — building a temple — establishment of a bank, a correct specimen of its notes, of which two hundred thousand dollars worth have been pawned off upon the community — the manner in which the community of Frankford, Pa., rid themselves of the Mormons — documents printed by order of the Senate of the United States. The whole being designed as a caution to the ignorant and unsuspecting against one of the most barefaced and blasphemous devices which has ever been witnessed, affording a lamentable exhibition of the credulity and weakness of human nature, in so readily allowing itself to be made the dupe of artful and designing knaves. Frankford, Pa., Published by E. G. Lee, Frankford, Pa., and George Weber and William Fenimore. Philadelphia, 1841.
24p. facsim. 22cm.
Account of Joseph Smith's career by J. A. Clark, p. 5–12; financial chicanery at Kirtland by Cyrus Smalling, p. 12–15; and discussion by E. G. Lee and others of Lee's appearance at a Mormon meeting which broke up in a riot.
Howes M815, Sabin 50761
CSmH, CtY, NN

4841. Lee, James Melvin. History of American journalism, by James Melvin Lee . . . Boston and New York, Houghton Mifflin Company, 1917.
xp., [2]l., 462p., [1]l. plates, ports., facsims. 23½cm.
Early Mormon journalism in California and Utah.
Another edition: 1923. CU, DLC
DLC, UHi, USIC

4842. Lee, John Doyle. John D. Lee's bekjendelse, samt fuldbyrdelsen af hans dom paa de blodige Mountain Meadows Marker. Andet oplag. Salt Lake City, Trykt i "Utah Skandinavs," Bogtrykkeri, 1877.
35 [1]p. illus., ports. 21cm.
Title in English: John D. Lee's confessions.
CSmH, CU–B, DLC, MH, NjP, NN, UPB, USI, USIC

4843. ———. The last dying speech and confession of the Mormon bishop, John D. Lee, who was executed for the Mountain Meadow massacre. [Exeter, 1876?]
8p. illus., plates. 19cm. (In Jarman's "Anti-Mormon works." Cover-title)
Caption-title.
MH, USI, USIC

LEE, J. D.

4844. ———. The Lee trial! An expose of the Mountain Meadows massacre, being a condensed report of the prisoner's statement, testimony of witnesses, charge of the judge, arguments of counsel, and opinions of the press upon the trial. By the Salt Lake Daily Tribune reporter. Salt Lake City, Tribune Printing Company, Publishers, 1875.
64p. 22cm.
Howes L208a
CSmH, CtY, CU–B, DLC, ICN, MB, MoK, NN, OClWHi, UU

4845. ———. The life and confession of John D. Lee, the Mormon. With a full account of the Mountain Meadows massacre and execution of Lee . . . Philadelphia, Barclay & Co. [1877]
1p.l., 19–46p. plates. 24cm.
Variant printings USlC
Howes L208a
CtY, DLC, NN, USl, USlC, WaU

4846. ———. (same) Helpless women and children butchered in cold blood by merciless Mormon assassins. Philadelphia, Barclay & Co., Publishers [1877]
1p.l. [19]–64p. 24cm.
P. 49–64 added to the 1877 edition above.
Variant printings. USlC
USlC

4847. ———. (same) Philadelphia, Barclay & Co. [c1882]
1p.l. [19]–64p. illus. 24cm.
Cover-title: The Mountain Meadows massacre, with the life, confession and execution of John D. Lee, the Mormon.
CtY, CU–B, MH

4848. ———. Life, confession and execution of Bishop John D. Lee, the Mormon fiend; his seventeen wives — startling details of his death — implication of Brigham Young — the massacre at Mountain Meadows. Also the escape of his daughter from Salt Lake City, her pursuit by the Danites for refusing to marry Orson Pratt, her exposure of the affairs of "The Lion House." Philadelphia, Old Franklin Publishing House [c1877]
78p. 24cm.
Howes L208a
UPB, USlC

4849. ———. (same, in German) Das Leben und Bekenntniss von John D. Lee, dem Mormonen. Nebst einen vollen Bericht über das Mountain Meadows Massacre und die Hinrichtung von Lee. Hilflose Frauen und Kinder kaltblütig niedergemetzelt von rachsuchtigen Mormonischen Meuchelmördern. Philadelphia, Barclay & Co., Herausgeber . . . [c1877]
1p.l., 19–46p. 22cm.
CU–B, UU

4850. ———. The Mormon menace; being the confession of John Doyle Lee, Danite, an official assassin of the Mormon church under the late Brigham Young; introduction by Alfred Henry Lewis. New York, Home Protection Publishing Co. [1905]
1p.l., xxii [23]–368p. 3 plates, port. 19½cm.
An abridgment of his *Mormonism unveiled.*
CSmH, CtY, CU–B, MoInRC, NjP, NjPT, NN, UHi, ULA, UPB, USlC, ViU, WHi

4851. ———. Mormonism unveiled; or, the life and confessions of the late Bishop, John D. Lee, embracing a history of Mormonism from its origin down to the present time, with an exposition of the secret history, signs, symbols and crimes of the Mormon Church. Also the true history of the horrible butchery known as the Mountain Meadows massacre. Illustrated. St. Louis, Byran, Brand & Co., 1877.
xiv, 390p. plates. 21cm.
First issue.
Edited by William W. Bishop, Lee's attorney.
CSmH, CU, ICN, ULA, UPB

4852. ———. (same) St. Louis, Mo., Bryan, Brand & Co., 1877.
1p.l., v–xiv, [15]–406p. plates, ports. 22cm.
Appendix, "Life of Brigham Young" p. 391–406, added to the first issue.
Howes L209
CSmH, CtY, CU–B, DLC, MH, NjP, NN, UHi, UPB, UU

4853. ———. (same) St. Louis, Bryan Brand and Co., New York, W. H. Steele & Co., 1878.
1p.l., v–xiv, [15]–406p. ports., plates. 22cm.
CSmH, MB, MoKU, MWA, UPB, USlC

4854. ———. (same) St. Louis, N. D. Thompson and Company, 1880.
1p.l., v–xiv [15]–406p. plates, ports. 22cm.
MoKU, WHi

4855. ———. (same) St. Louis, Moffat Publishing Co., 1881.
xiv [15]–413p. plates., ports. 22cm.
Addition of an appendix "Life of Brigham Young" and "a remarkable letter to the Inter-Ocean." signed J. W. R.
CSmH, DLC, USlC

4856. ———. (same) St. Louis, Scrammell and Company, 1881.
xiv [15]–413p. illus., ports., plates. 21½cm.
USlC

4857. ———. (same) Lewisburgh, Pa., S. T. Buck, Son & Co., 1882.
xiii [1] [15]–413p. plates (part col.) 22cm.
CtY

4858. ———. (same) St. Louis, Sun Publishing Company, 1882.
xiii [1] [15]–413p. illus. 22cm.
Howes L209
MH, NjP, NjPT, NN, UHi

4859. ———. (same) St. Louis, Cleveland, O., C. C. Wick and Co., 1882.
xiv [15]–413p. 22cm.
Howes L209
ODW

4860. ———. (same) Philadelphia and St. Louis, Scrammell & Co., 1882.
xiv [15]–413p. illus., plates (part col.) 22½cm.
USlC

4861. ———. (same) St. Louis, Excelsior Publishing Co., 1891.
xiv [15]–413p. 22cm.
CSmH, ICN, NN

4862. ———. (same) St. Louis, Mo., M. E. Mason, 1891.
xiii [14]–413p. col. front., plates (part col.) ports. 21½cm.
Howes L209
CSmH, DLC, ICN, MoInRC, NN, UHi, USlC, UU

4863. ———. (same) Omaha, Neb., Published by F. H. Rogers & Co., 1891.
xiii, [14]–413p. plates (part. col.) ports. 21½cm.
USlC

4864. ———. (same) St. Louis, Pease-Taylor Publishing Co., 1891.
xiv [15]–413p. plates, ports. 21½cm.
WHi

4865. ———. (same) St. Louis, Vandawalker & Co., 1892.
xiii [14]–413p. 21½cm.
Howes L209
CtY

4866. Lee, Willis Thomas. . . . Guidebook of the western United States, part B. The Overland route with a side trip to Yellowstone Park, by Willis T. Lee, Ralph W. Stone, Hoyt S. Gale, and others. Washington, Govt. Print. Off., 1915.
244p. illus., 1 plate, 25 [i.e. 29] fold. maps, diagrs. 23cm. (U.S. Geological survey. Bulletin 612)
Detailed geographic information along the line of the Union Pacific and Southern Pacific Railroads with material on cities, etc.
Another edition: Wash., Govt. Print. Off., 1916. DLC
CU–B, DL–GS, DLC, DWB, ICJ, MiU, NN, OCl, OClW, ODW, OU, UHi, UPB, UU

Lee County. Lee County anti-Mormon meeting. *See Guthrie Edwin.*

Lees, C. Lowell. *See Church of Jesus Christ of Latter-day Saints. Missions. European.*

4867. Leffler, S. Iowa contested election. Speech of Hon. S. Leffler, of Iowa, in the House of Representatives, June 27, 1850, on the Report of the Committee of Elections, in the Iowa Contested Election Case. [Washington? 1850]
8p. 22cm.
Illegality of the treatment of the Mormon vote at Kanesville in 1848.
MH

4868. Legler, Henry Eduard. Leading events of Wisconsin history. The story of the state. Milwaukee, The Sentinel Company, 1901.
viii, 322p. illus., charts, maps. 22cm.
"2d impression."
"The Strang Stake of Zion at Voree," p. 198–206.
UHi

4869. ———. A Moses of the Mormons. Strang's city of refuge and island kingdom. By Henry E. Legler. [Milwaukee, Wisc.] Printed for the Parkman Club by E. Keogh [1897]
[115]–179p. illus., port. 24½cm.
(Parkman Club publications. Nos. 15–16)
Cover-title.
"Strang's books and pamphlets," p. 174–178.
Bibliography, p. 178–179.
CSmH, CtY, DLC, MH, MiU, NjP, OCl, OO, UHi, ULA, USlC, UU

4870. ———. (same) Strang's city of refuge and island kingdom. [n.p., n.d.]
67p. port. 20cm.
Reprint of the above.
CSmH, MH, MoInRC

4871. Leib, Frank H. Guide to Salt Lake City and Articles of faith of the Mormon Church. [Salt Lake City] Curio Shop [1920?]
[3]p. 16cm.
Cover-title.
UHi

4872. Lekamlig uppståndelse. . . . [Salt Lake City, Korrespondenten Tryckeri, 1893?]
24p. 14cm.
Running-title in English: The resurrection of the body.
Cover-title missing.
USlC

4873. Leland, Lilian. Traveling alone. A woman's journey around the world. By Lilian Leland . . . New York, The American News Company, 1890.
viii, 358p. port. 20cm.
A brief description of Temple Square, 1885.
CU–B, DLC, UPB

4874. Leng, *Sir* John. America in 1876. Pencillings during a tour in the Centennial year: with a chapter on the aspects of American life. By John Leng . . . [Dundee] Dundee Advertiser Office, 1877.
3p.l. [9]–346p. 18½cm.
Visits Salt Lake City; predicts the doom of polygamy.
CU, DLC, NjP, USlC

4875. Leonard, Delavan A. Mormonism. By Rev. Delevan A. Leonard. Salt Lake City, 1885.
40p. 23cm.
Reprinted from: *Bibliotheca Sacra.* Article I.
UPB

4876. Leopard, John C. Hillman. History of Daviess and Gentry Counties, Missouri. Daviess County by John C. Hillman Leopard and Buel H. Leopard. Gentry County by R. M. McCammon and Mary McCammon Hillman. Illustrated. Topeka, Historical Publishing Company, 1922.
2p.l. [65]–1039p. plates, ports. 27cm.
"The Mormons in Daviess County."
Facts "taken largely from *Early days on Grand River and the Mormon War,* by R. J. Britton," p. 94.
ICN, ICU, NN

4877. Leslie, Miriam Florence (Folline) Squier. California. A pleasure trip from Gotham to the Golden gate. (April, May, June 1877) By Mrs. Frank Leslie . . . New York, G. W. Carleton & Co.; London, S. Low, Son & Co., 1877.
6 [vii]–xiv [17]–286p. illus., plates. 19cm.
"Salt Lake City," "Mrs. Amelia's [Young] picture," "Miss Snow, a first-class Mormon interior," "A lion that we saw and a lion that we heard," p. 72–103.
CSmH, CU–B, DLC, MB, NjP, NN, UHi, ULA, USlC, UU

4878. Lester, John Erastus. The Atlantic to the Pacific. What to see, and how to see it. By John Erastus Lester . . . Boston, Shepard and Gill, 1873.
365p. fold. map. 17cm.
Includes a stop in Salt Lake City.
Another edition: London, Longmans, Green, and Co., 1873. USlC
CSmH, CU–B, DLC, NjP, OO, UHi, ULA, USl, UU

4879. Lesueur, James Warren. Indian legends, by J. W. Lesueur . . . Independence, Mo., Zion's Printing and Publishing Company, c1928.
339p. illus., plates, ports., maps. 19½cm.
In proof of the *Book of Mormon.*
DLC, NjP, UHi, USlC

4880. Letts, John M. California illustrated, including a description of the Panama and Nicaragua routes. By a returned Californian. New York, 1852.
vii [9]–224p. plates. 23cm.
Meets Mormons at the Gold diggings in 1849.
Recounts Missouri history including the "Boggs assassination."
Another edition under title, *A Pictorial View of California.* New York, R. J. Young, 1853. NjP, RPB
Howes L300, Sabin 40722
CU–B, DLC, USlC

4881. Lewis, Alfred Henry. A word with you about the Mormon menace. Alfred Henry Lewis. [n.p., Home Protection Publishing Company, n.d.]
3p.l. [7]–11 [1]p. 13cm.
Promotion material for John D. Lee's *Mormon Menace.* Includes title-page.
MH

4882. Lewis, Carl. The blemished head. [n.p., c1919]
[1]p. 26×19cm.
Concerning the authority of the RLDS Church leaders; critical of central control.
MoInRC

4883. ———. Book of Mormon. [Lamoni, Ia., n.d.]
[2]p. 26½cm.
On back: "A righteous war . . ." a defense of the RLDS position on marriage.
MH

4884. ———. A confession. [n.p., n.d.]
[2]p. 20½cm.
RLDS doctrine of God.
MoInRC

4885. Lewis, Catherine. Narrative of some of the proceedings of the Mormons; giving an account of their iniquities, with particulars concerning the training of the Indians by them, description of the mode of endowment, plurality of wives, &c., &c. By Catherine Lewis. Lynn [Mass.] Published by the author, 1848.
iv [5]–24p. 24½cm.
Cover-title.
Howes L307, Sabin 40787
CSmH, CtY, DLC, ICN, NN, WHi

4886. ———. (same) Lynn [Mass.] The author, 1853.
16p. 24cm.
Howes L307
DLC, ICN, USlC

4887. Lewis, Charles Bertrand. Bessie Baine; or, The Mormon's victim. A tale of Utah, by Quad. M. [*pseud.*] of the Detroit Free Press. Boston, Office of Ballou's Monthly Magazine, G. W. Studley [c1876]
37p. 15cm.
Also printed with: "The Novelette. No. 4"
The Sorceress of the Campbell Island by Colonel Breuet, p. 38–66.
Cover-title.
Fiction concerning Mormonism.
CSmH, MH, OClWHi, USlC

4888. ———. (same) Chicago, M. A. Donohue and Co. [1888?]
1p.l., 97p. 17cm. (The flashlight detective series. No. 3)
NN

4889. ———. (same) Boston, G. W. Studley, 1898.
59p. illus. 24½cm. (Novelette library. No. 5)
Cover-title.
CSmH

4890. ———. (same) Chicago, M. A. Donohue and Co. [1912?]
99p. 15cm. (The flashlight detective series. No. 3)
NN (film)

4891. Lewis, Dio. Gypsies; or, Why we went gypsying in the Sierras. By Dio Lewis . . . Boston, Eastern Book Company, 1881.
2p.l. [3]–416p. plates, port. 19½cm.
Discussed polygamy with several inhabitants and found it abhorrent.
Another edition: Boston, Eastern Bk. Co., 1882. NN, OCl, OO
CU–B, DLC, MWA, NjP, NN, PPL

4892. Lewis, George. Impressions of America and the American churches: from journal of the Rev. G. Lewis. Edinburgh, W. P. Kennedy [etc., etc.] 1845.
viii, 432p. 21½cm.
P. 265–266 on Mormonism. His comments on a woman from England who was a Mormon, and on Joseph Smith.
Howes L310, Sabin 40803
NN

4893. Lewis, Henry. Das illustrierte Mississippithal, Dargestellt in 80 nach der Natur aufgenommenen Ansichten vom Wasserfalle zu St. Anthony an bis zum Gulf von Mexico . . . von H. Lewis . . . Nebst einer historischen und geographischen Beschriebung der den Fluss begränzenden Länder, mit besonderer Rücksicht auf die verschiedenen den obern Mississippi bewohnenden Indianerstämme. Düsseldorf, Arnz & Comp. [1857]
431p. col. plates. 26cm.
"Nauvoo, Ill.: die Mormon Stadt."
Originally issued in parts nos. 1–3, 1854; nos. 4–6, 1855, "Nach dem englischen original-text deutsch bearbeit von George B. Douglas," Dusseldorf, Arnz & Co.; nos. 7–20" (Deutsch und English) von George B. Douglas," Dusseldorf, Elkan, Bäumer & Co., 1857.
Published in English in 1967.
Title in English: The value of the Mississippi, illustrated.
Reprinted: Leipzig, H. Schmidt & C. Günther, 1923. NjP
Howes L312
CSmH, CU–B, DLC, UPB

4894. Lewis, Leon. The Sons of Thunder; or, The Rivals of Ruby Valley. A Romance of Nevada. New York, Beadle and Adams, 1888. (The Banner Weekly, Vol. VI, no. 261 to Vol. VI, no. 274) 28cm.
Mormon characters included.
NN

4895. Lewis, R. B. Light and truth; collected from the Bible and ancient and modern history, containing the universal history of the colored and the Indian race, from the creation of the world to the present time. By R. B. Lewis, a colored man. Boston, Published by a Committee of Colored Gentlemen, Benjamin R. Roberts, Printer, 1844.
400p. 19cm.
Mormonism, p. 34.
USlC

4896. Lewis, William A. The Church of Jesus Christ. Where is it? How shall I know it? There are many churches of men, only the one Church of Christ. [Independence, Mo.] Reorganized Church of Jesus Christ of Latter Day Saints [n.d.]
18p. 19cm.
CU–B, ULA

4897. ———. (same) [Llanelly, Wales, Guardian Offices, 1903]
24p. 18cm.
MoInRC

4898. ———. (same) [n.p.] Reorganized Church of Jesus Christ of Latter Day Saints [n.d.]
31p. 20cm.
MoInRC

4899. ———. (same) [n.p.] Reorganized Church of Jesus Christ of Latter Day Saints [n.d.]
33p. 18cm.
MoInRC

4900. ———. (same) Lamoni, Ia., Herald Publishing House [1908]
18p. 18cm. (No. 209)
In brown wrapper. Date and number from cover.
USlC

4901. ———. (same) [Lamoni, Ia.] Reorganized Church of Jesus Christ of Latter Day Saints [1911?]
18p. 17½cm.
IWW, NN, USlC

4902. ———. (same) Lamoni, Ia., Reorganized Church of Jesus Christ of Latter Day Saints, 1915.
18p. 19cm.
UPB

4903. ———. (same) [Lamoni, Ia.] Reorganized Church of Jesus Christ of Latter Day Saints [n.d.]
18p. 19cm. (No. 209)
CtY, MoInRC, UPB, USlC

4904. ———. (same) Lamoni, Ia., Board of Publication of the Reorganized Church of Jesus Christ, 1910.
18p. 18cm. (No. 209)
UPB, USIC

4905. ———. (same) Lamoni, Ia., Board of Publication of the Reorganized Church of Jesus Christ, 1915.
18p. 19cm.
MoInRC

4906. ———. Only one Church of Christ, there are many churches of Men. [n.p., n.d.]
4p. 13cm.
Author's residence: Scranton, Pa.
MoInRC

4907. ———. Some spiritual aspects of child welfare. By William A. Lewis. Independence, Mo., Women's Department of the Reorganized Church of Jesus Christ of Latter Day Saints [n.d.]
17p. 18cm.
USIC

4908. Lewis, William P. An innocent people misrepresented, their faith not understood. [n.p., 1908?]
8p. 13cm.
Author lived during this time at Cardiff, Wales. Date of the publication is likely 1908 or later.
MoInRC

4909. ———. (same) Scranton, Pa., T. E. Evans, Printer [n.d.]
8p. 19cm.
MoInRC

4910. Leyland, Ralph Watts. Round the world in 124 days. With map and illustrations. Liverpool, Gilbert G. Walmsley, 1880.
vii, [2]l., 323p. plates. 21cm.
Brief visit to Salt Lake City, with a tour of historic monuments; comments.
USIC

4911. The Liahona. Independence, Mo., April 6–June 15, 1907.
10 nos. weekly. 29cm.
Editor: B. F. Cummings.
Merged with *The Elders' Journal* into *Liahona, The Elders' Journal*, June 1, 1907.
No. 7 not issued.
MH, NN, UPB, USIC, WHi

4912. Liahona, The Elders' Journal. Chattanooga, Tenn. [Independence, Mo.] Missions of the Church of Jesus Christ of Latter-day Saints. April 6, 1907–Feb. 27, 1945.
42v. weekly, bi-weekly. 25cm.
First editor: B. F. Cummings.
Successor to *The Liahona.*
V.42 #18 the last issue.
Voluming continues from "*The Elders' Journal*, of which V. 1–4 are the *Elders' Journal.*
Weekly 1907–1919, bi-weekly 1919–
ULA; UPB; USIC; WHi V.1 #2–3, V.6 #1–V.42 #18

4913. ———. The Church of Jesus Christ of Latter-day Saints was established by our Heavenly Father to bring salvation to the Children of Men . . . Liahona, the Elders' Journal was established as a "missionary" to assist in preaching the Gospel. [Independence, Mo., Zion's Printing & Publishing Co. 1918?]
[16]p. illus. 22½cm.
The value of the *Liahona.*
USIC

4914. Liberal Party. Utah. . . . Address of the Liberal Committee, reviewing the People's Party's "Declaration of principles." Liberal war cry: Salt Lake work for Salt Lake Workmen . . . [Salt Lake City, 1889?]
15p. 21cm.
At head of title: Campaign document No. 3.
A pamphlet against the People's Party.
CSmH

4915. ———. Gentile meeting at Federal Court Room, February 10th, 1888. Proceedings and speeches. Reported by McGurrin, Official Reporter of the Third District Court. [Salt Lake City, 1888?]
47p. 20cm.
"Addresses at a meeting of the Liberal Party, held at Salt Lake City, Utah, Friday Evening, February 10, 1888."
USI

4916. ———. Memorial of the non-Mormon people of Utah. To his Excellency, the President, and the Congress of the United States . . . [Salt Lake City, Territorial Liberal Central Committee, 1882]
[4]p. 29½cm.
Caption-title.
Signed at end: J. R. McBride [and others] of the Territorial Central Committee.
Political affairs in Utah.
DLC, USIC

4917. ———. Mormon methods. Extract from the city records of Salt Lake City under Mormon control. Is it wise to give statehood or so called "home rule" to Utah territory? . . . Washington, 1892.
41p. 22cm.
MH, USIC

LIBERAL

4918. ———. Proceedings of the Territorial Liberal Convention held at Salt Lake City, February 4, 1892. Stenographically reported by Miss B. T. McMaster. Salt Lake City, Press of Tribune Job Printing Company, 1892.
65 [1]p. 23cm.
Opposition to statehood due to the fact that church and state was still an important issue.
MH, UU

4919. ———. To the Citizens of Utah. Address of the Liberal Territorial Committee. [Salt Lake City? 1882]
8p. 22cm.
Possibility of overriding the "unscrupulous theocracy" due to the Edmunds Bill.
Signed: H. W. Lawrence, M. M. Kaighn, Jno. R. McBride, L. P. Higbee. Salt Lake City, Sept. 6, 1882.
CSmH, UPB, USl

4920. Library of Universal Knowledge; being a reprint entire of the last (1879) Edinburgh and London edition of Chamber's Encyclopedia, a Dictionary of Universal Knowledge for the people. . . . New York, American Book Exchange . . . 1880.
20v. 16½cm.
"The Mormons." V.9, p. 770–777.
UPB, USIC

4921. Die Lieder der Mormonin. 3. Auflage. (1. Auflage der Buchausgabe) Leipzig, Verlag von Herman Dürselen, 1888.
123p. 15½cm.
Mormon poetry.
Title in English: Sons of a Mormon woman.
USIC

4922. Lienhard, Heinrich. Californien unmittelbar vor und nach der Entdeckung des Goldes. Bilder aus dem Leben des Heinrich Lienhard von Bilten, Kanton Glarus in Nauvoo, Nordamerika. Ein Beitrag zur Jubiläumsfeier der Goldentdeckung und zur Kulturgeschichte Californiens . . . Zürich, Fäsi & Beer, 1898.
318p. port. 22½cm.
Crossed Utah in 1846. References to Mormons at Sutter's Fort and other places.
Title in English: California after the discovery of gold.
Another edition: Zürich, E. Speidel, 1900.
CU–B, CtY, DLC, ICJ, UPB
Howes L–332
CtY, CU–B, DLC, ICN, NjP, NN, UHi, ULA

4923. The life and labors of Eliza R. Snow Smith; with a full account of her funeral services. Salt Lake City, The Juvenile Instructor Office, 1888.
2p.l. [3]–37p. 17½cm.
CU–B, DLC, NjP, UHi, ULA, UPB, USl, USIC, UU

4924. Life of a Mormon girl. [New York, Palmer & Oliver, Inc., 1911]
19p. 15cm.
Caption-title.
Reprinted from *The Independent.*
Life of a young girl in polygamy.
USIC

4925. The Life of the Emigrant: Great Salt Lake City, and Mormonism at home. By a Georgian. Milledgeville: Printed for the author, 1854.
64p. 14½cm.
In blue printed wrappers.
Trip through Utah in 1850.
OC

4926. A life sketch of Mary Alice Cannon Lambert by her children. Salt Lake City, 1908.
23p. ports. 17cm.
USIC

4927. Light from the home paper of Hans Peter Freece, The "Richfield Reaper," Thursday, May 28th, 1908. . . . [Liverpool? Millennial Star Office? 1908?]
4p. 22cm.
Caption-title.
Refutation of the falsehoods written by Freece in his *Letter of an apostate Mormon to his son.*
UHi, UPB, UU

4928. The light of Messiah. San Francisco, C. W. Gordon, 1888–91?
v. 23cm.
1v. (2p.l., ix, 380p.) 23cm.
Edited by Dr. P. W. P. Fagerstjerna.
Publication for the Church of the Firstborn.
"The Mormon priesthood at Utah has left its first inheritance and prostituted its first love." Church apostasy from truth culminating in polygamy; messages to various leaders of the church on various subjects.
CU–B, DLC, ULA, USIC, UU, WHi

4929. Light on Mormonism. . . . Cleveland, Ohio, The Utah Gospel Mission, 1922–1950.
26v. illus. 27cm.
First editor: J. D. Nutting.
Title page of first five volumes reads: The little cyclopedia of Mormonism.
CSmH V.1–10; CU–B V.1 No. 1–3, V.2 No. 3–4, V.17 No. 1–4; DLC; UHi; ULA; UPB; USIC; WHi

4930. Lillywhite, John P. [Mordersdag] Written for Mother's Day, May, 1929, by John P. Lillywhite in behalf of the missionaries of the Netherland Mission. [Rotterdam, Netherlands Mission] 1929.
[8]l. 20½cm.
In English and in Dutch.
Title from cover.
Mormon poetry.
Title in English: Mother's day.
UU

4931. ———. Een Mormoonsch antwoord. Door John P. Lillywhite. Rotterdam, Uitgegeven door de Nederlandsche zending van de Kerk van Jezus Christus van de Heiligen der Laatste Dagen [ca. 1923]
16p. 19½cm.
Title in English: An answer of a Mormon.
USIC

4932. ———. Smile posts of satisfaction, by J. P. Lillywhite. Rotterdam, Holland [1929]
1p.l. [3]–168p. 19cm.
USIC, UU

4933. ———. Wat is het Evangelie. Door John P. Lillywhite. Rotterdam, Uitgegeven door de Nederlandsche Zending [ca. 1923]
16p. 19½cm.
Title in English: What is the gospel.
USIC

4934. Lincoln, Abraham. Speech of the Hon. Abraham Lincoln, in reply to Judge Douglas, delivered in Representatives' Hall. Springfield, Illinois, June 26th, 1857. [n.p., 1857?]
7p. 23cm.
Caption-title.
Answer to Douglas' policy for Utah as proposed two weeks earlier.
Lincoln was also for legislation to ban polygamy, but assailed Douglas' position on how to accomplish it and the doctrine of self-government.
DLC

4935. Lincoln Highway Association. The complete official road guide of the Lincoln highway. Detroit, Mich., The Lincoln Highway Association, 1915.
v. 23cm.
Sections from Salt Lake City, Utah, to Gold Hill, Utah, 140 miles.
Many references to Utah history.
Another edition: 2d ed. 1916. CU–B
DLC

4936. Lindelof, O. J. S. A trip to the north pole; or, The discovery of the ten tribes as found in the Arctic Ocean. Salt Lake City, Tribune Publishing Company, 1903.
200p. 18cm.
The Mormon doctrine of the gathering.
USIC

4937. Lindencrone, Lillie DeHegermann. The sunny side of diplomatic life, 1875–1912. Illustrated with portraits, facsimiles, etc. New York, London, Harper and Brothers Publishers, 1914.
ix [1] 336 [1]p. port. 22½cm.
Visited Salt Lake City in 1875, p. 27–30.
Disappointed with treatment.
NjP, USIC

4938. Lindsay, Charles. The Big Horn Basin, by Charles Lindsay. A dissertation presented to the faculty of the Graduate College of the University of Nebraska in part fulfillment of the requirements for the degree of doctor of philosophy, Department of History. Lincoln, Neb., 1930.
4p.l., 7–274p. 23cm.
Includes Mormon settlement in the Big Horn Basin, Wyoming.
NjP, ULA, USIC

4939. Lindsay, John Shanks. The Mormons and the theatre; or, The history of theatricals in Utah; with reminiscences and comments, humorous and critical, by John S. Lindsay. Salt Lake City [Century Printing] 1905.
178p. port. 19½cm.
CSmH, CU–B, DLC, MH, MoInRC, NjP, NN, UHi, ULA, UPB, USI, USIC, UU

4940. Lineal priesthood. [Extracts from sermons delivered at Independence, Oct. 11th, 1896. Independence, Mo.? 189–]
8p. 21cm.
At head of title: Searchlight Rays! No. 1. Price 5 cents. For sale at office of "The Searchlight," Independence, Mo. . . .
Hedrickite tract.
MoInRC

4941. Lines suggested on the death of Mrs. Elizabeth P. Crombin. [Kanesville? 184–]
Broadside. 25×10cm.
Text in ornamental border.
USIC

4942. Linford, James Henry. An autobiography of James Henry Linford, Patriarch of Kaysville, Utah. [Kaysville?] Published by himself, 1919.
2p.l. [7]–87p. port. 23cm.
UHi, USIC

4943. Linforth, James. The Rev. C. W. Lawrence's, "Few words from a pastor to his people on the subject of the Latter-day Saints," replied to and refuted by James Linforth. Liverpool, Printed by J. Sadler [185–]
8p. 21cm.
Caption-title.
Variant printings.
CSmH, CtY, ICN, MH, USIC

———. *See also Piercy, Frederick.*

4944. Linn, William Alexander. The story of the Mormons, from the date of their origin to the year 1901, by William Alexander Linn. New York, The Macmillan Company; London, Macmillan & Co., Ltd., 1902.
xxv, 637p. diags., facsims. 23½cm.
Howes L366
CSmH, CtY, CU–B, DLC, ICHi, ICN, NjPT, ULA, USI, USIC, UU, WHi

4945. ———. (same) New York, The Macmillan Company; London, Macmillan and Co., Ltd., 1923.
xxv, 637p. diags., facsims. 23½cm.
Howes L366
CSmH, CtY, MoInRC, NjP, NN, OCl, OClWHi, ODW, UHi, USIC

4946. Lippincott, Sara Jane (Clarke). New life in new lands: Notes of travel. By Grace Greenwood [*pseud.*] Brooklyn, New York, D. S. Holmes [c1872]
vi, 7–413p. 20cm.
Trip to Utah; favorably impressed with Mormons, though apposed to polygamy.
Other editions: New York, J. B. Ford and Co., 1873. CSmH, CU–B, NjP; London, S. Low, Marston, Low and Searle, 1873. UU; New York, J. B. Ford and Co., 1875. PNt
CSmH, NjP, UHi

4947. Listen to the Voice of Truth. New York, Printed by S. Brannan & Co., 1844.
v. 1 no. 1 [4p.] 22½cm.
All published.
"A sketch of the faith of the Church of Jesus Christ of Latter-day Saints, particularly for those who are unacquainted with our principles."
Reprint of O. Pratt from his *Remarkable Visions. See The Prophet.* Aug., Sept., 1844.
Sabin 50745
WHi

4948. Little, Feramorz. Order of procession. Instructions and order of march for Pioneer parade. [Salt Lake City, ca. 1880]
Broadside. 26×14cm.
24th of July parade.
USIC

4949. Little, James Amasa. Biographical sketch of Feramorz Little. Salt Lake City, Juvenile Instructor Office, 1890.
vii [9]–191p. 23cm.
Howes L381
CSmH, CtY, ICN, MH, NN, UHi, UPB, USIC, UU

4950. ———. From Kirtland to Salt Lake City by James A. Little. Salt Lake City, James A. Little, Publisher. Printed at the Juvenile Instructor Office, 1890.
viii [9]–260p. illus. 23cm.
"This book may be considered an epitome of the motives and experiences of the Saints who rejoiced and suffered in the persecutions and exoduses attending the early growth of the Latter-day work." Pref.
He was converted in 1849.
CSmH, CtY, CU–B, DLC, ICN, MB, MoInRC, NjP, NjPT, UHi, ULA, UPB, USIC, UU, WHi

4951. ———. Jacob Hamblin; a narrative of his personal experience as a frontiersman, missionary to the Indians, and explorer, disclosing interpositions of Providence, severe privations, perilous situations and remarkable escapes. By James A. Little. Designed for the instruction and encouragement of young Latter-day Saints. Salt Lake City, Juvenile Instructor Office, 1881.
viii [9]–144p. 18½cm. (Faith-promoting series. 5th Book)
Catalogue of church publications p. 141–144.
Howes L383
CSmH, CtY, CU–B, DLC, MH, NjP, NN, UHi, UPB, USIC, UU, WHi

4952. ———. (same) 2d ed. Salt Lake City, The Deseret News, 1909.
viii [9]–151p. 19½cm. (Faith-promoting series. Book 5)
CSmH, CtY, DLC, UHi, ULA, UPB, USIC, WHi

4953. Little, Jesse Carter. Circular. To the Church of Jesus Christ of Latter Day Saints, scattered abroad through the eastern and middle states. Greeting: [Peterborough?, N.H., 1846?]
8p. 22cm.
Caption-title.
Signed: J. C. Little, Peterborough, N. H., April 6, 1846.
Includes emigration instructions.
CHi, UHi (Photostat)

4954. ———. Circular. Epistle to the Church of Jesus Christ of Latter Day Saints, in the Eastern States, sent greeting: [Peterborough, N.H., 1846?]
8p. 22cm.
Caption-title.
Signed: J. C. Little, President of the eastern churches. Peterborough, N. H., Nov. 12th, 1846.
Brief summary of activities of the Church in 1846 and emigration instructions.
USIC

4955. ———. Circular the second, published by Elder J. C. Little, President of the "Church of Jesus Christ of Latter Day Saints," in the Eastern States, Philadelphia, May 15th, 1846. [Philadelphia? 1846?]
8p. 21½cm.
Caption-title.
Emigration instructions.
CHi, USIC

4956. ———. A collection of sacred hymns, for the use of the Latter-day Saints. Selected and published by J. C. Little and G. B. Gardner. Bellows Falls, Printed by Blake and Bailey, 1844.
80p. 13½cm.
Words and music.
CSmH, CtY, MH, USIC, Vt

4957. The Little World. Salt Lake City, Merchant Printing Company, August 1890–
v. monthly. 25cm.
Edited by Joseph Hyrum Parry.
Doubtless designed for L.D.S. children: only one issue located.
USIC V.1 #2 Sept. 1890

4958. Littlefield, Charles Edgar. Representative-elect from Utah . . . Speech of Hon. Charles E. Littlefield of Maine, in the House of Representatives . . . January 23, 1900. Washington [Govt. Print. Off.] 1900.
52p. 23cm.
CU–B, DLC

Littlefield, Lyman Omer. A correct account of the murder of generals, Joseph and Hyrum Smith.
See Daniels, William M.

4959. ———. The martyrs; a sketch of the lives and a full account of the martyrdom of Joseph and Hyrum Smith, together with a concise review of the most prominent incidents connected with the persecutions of the saints, from the time the church was organized up to the year 1846. By Lyman O. Littlefield. Salt Lake City, Juvenile Instructor Office, 1882.
120p., 2p.l. 2 ports. 19cm.
CSmH, CtY, CU, CU–B, DLC, ICN, MH, MoInRC, NjP, NjPT, UHi, ULA, UPB, USI, USIC, UU, WHi

4959a. ———. Mrs. Fanny Murry — Dear Friend: Yours of 28th of April has been received and read over . . . [n.p., 1854?]
Broadside. 28×12½cm.
Signed: Lyman Omer Littlefield.
Dated: Council Bluffs City, Pottawatamie Co., Iowa, Sunday evening, June 18, 1854.
USIC

4959b. ———. An open letter, Addressed to President Joseph Smith, Jr., of the Re-Organized Church of Jesus Christ of Latter Day Saints, and others conspicuous at Conference recently held in the Temple at Kirtland, O. [Logan, 1883]
[4]p. 24½cm.
UPB, USIC

4960. Reminiscences of Latter-day Saints, giving an account of much individual suffering endured for religious conscience. Logan, Utah, Utah Journal Co., Printers, 1888.
viii [9]–208p. port. 22cm.
Errata slip inserted.
Reminiscences particularly of the Missouri period, with statements from other people as well as his narrative.
CSmH, CtY, CU–B, DLC, ICN, ICU, MH, MoInRC, NN, UHi, UPB, USI, USIC, ViU

4961. ———. To the Sixth Quorum of Seventies of the Church of Jesus Christ of Latter-day Saints. [n.p., n.d.]
Broadside. 41×26cm.
Written at Council Bluffs, August 13, 1854. Concerning his mission and why he remained at Council Bluffs.
USIC

4962. Lives of our leaders; character sketches of living presidents and apostles of the Church of Jesus Christ of Latter-day Saints. With portraits. Salt Lake City, Deseret News, 1901.
3p.l. [9]–264p. front., ports. 19cm.
"Character sketches contained in this volume first appeared in the *Juvenile Instructor*."
IWW, NjP, NN, UHi, UPB, USIC, UU

4963. Livesey, Richard. An exposure of Mormonism, being a statement of facts relating to the self-styled "Latter-day Saints," and the origin of the Book of Mormon, by Richard Livesey of Winchendon, Massachusetts, America, Minister of the Methodist Episcopal Church. Preston, Printed by J. Livesey, 1838.
12p. 21½cm.
NN, USIC

4964. ———. (same) Wrexham [Wales] Printed by W. Bayley, 1840.
12p. 21cm.
CtY, NN

4965. Lizzie Lester; or, The Mormon's plot. London, Published by G. Potter [n.d.]
1p.l. [3]–64p. illus. 14½cm.
(The Pocket family library. No. 48)
Cover-title: Lizzie Lorton [sic] or the Mormon's plot.
Fiction concerning Mormonism.
UU

4966. Ljusstrålar. Herren har besökt jorden. [Köpenhamn, Utgifven och förlagd af Andreas Peterson, . . . Tryckt hos F. E. Bording (V. Petersen) n.d.]
8p. 23½cm.
Title in English: Enlightenment. The Lord has visited the earth.
UPB, USIC

4967. Llewellin, Frederick G. Is Mormonism a fraud? [A revised reprint of special articles from the "Lancaster Guardian"] . . . Lancaster: E. & J. L. Milner . . . [n.d.]
16p. 22cm.
F. G. Llewellin, Curate of St. Thomas, Lancaster.
MoInRC, USIC

4968. ———. The Rise of the Joe Smith "religion" by the Rev. Frederick G. Llewellin . . . Lancaster, E. & J. L. Milner . . . [n.d.]
4p. 22cm.
At head of title: Beware of the "Latter-day Saints" or Mormon "Elders."
MoInRC

4969. ———. (same) Lancaster, England, Guardian Office [n.d.]
4p. 23cm.
MoInRC, USIC

LLOYD, T. E.

Lloyd, T. E. Carroll-Lloyd exposé. *See Carroll, A.*

4970. Lobenstine, William Christian. Extracts from the diary of William C. Lobenstine; December 31, 1851–1858. Biographical sketch by Belle W. Lobenstine. [New York] Priv. Print., 1920.
8p.l., 101p. fronts. 23cm.
Passed through Salt Lake City in 1851. Although Mormon religion has many foolish things, the social structure is very good.
Howes L410
CU–B, DLC, NjP, NN, UHi

4970a. Lockwood, Belva Anna Bennett. The Mormon question [Salt Lake City? ca. 1888]
Broadside. 43×15cm.
National women's suffrage leader. She feels that the government has been unfair towards the Mormons and that Utah should be admitted as a state. She comments on women's suffrage in Utah.
USlC

4970b. Logan Temple. Appointments, instructions and suggestions issued by The Logan Temple, January 1, 1929. For the use of presidents of stakes, bishops of wards and genealogical committees in the Logan Temple District. [Logan, Utah, 1929]
14p. 17cm.
USlC

4971. Logan temple lectures; a series of lectures delivered before the Temple School of Science during the years 1885–1886 by Moses Thatcher, Jas. A. Leishman, C. W. Nibley, Jas. Z. Steward, W. H. Apperley, John E. Carlisle. Logan, Utah, The Utah Journal Co. [1886?]
2p.l. [5]–143p. 22cm.
CSmH, MH, UHi, UPB, USlC, UU

4972. Lomax, John Avery. Cowboy songs and other frontier ballads, collected by John A. Lomax . . . with an introduction by Barrett Wendell. New York, Sturgis & Walton, 1910.
xxvi, 326p. facsim. 19½cm.
Two songs about Brigham Young: Mormon song; Mormon bishop's lament.
Other editions: New York, Sturgis & Walton, 1916. DLC; New York, The Macmillan Company, 1922. UHi, ULA, USlC; New York, 1925. NjP, UPB
DLC, NjP, UPB

4973. London, Jack. The star rover, by Jack London . . . New York, The Macmillan Company, 1915.
3p.l., 329 [1]p. col. front. 19½cm.
In the novel Darrell Standing becomes Jesse Fancher and relives the days of the Mountain Meadows massacre.
Other editions: New York, Grosset and Dunlap [1917] IU, PU; New York, Macmillan Company, 1929. DLC, MH; also, in German: *Die Zwangsjake.* Berlin, Universitas [c1930] DLC; also published under title: *The Jacket*, London, Mills and Boon [1915] UPB
CU–B, DLC, NjP, NN, PPL, PPM, ULA, UPB, USlC

4974. Long, Elmer E. The Dekalb agreement, the beginning of the end of distress and sorrow, Satan's dreadful contagion is arrested. There are brighter days ahead. Independence, Mo. [n.d.]
8p. 20cm.
A Church of Christ publication on supreme directional control.
MoInRC

4975. ———. Extracts from letters and articles written. [n.p., ca. 1925]
[1]p. 28cm.
RLDS struggle for supreme directional control.
MoInRC

4976. ———. The failures of Campbellism; or, The current reformation in contrast with truth revealed. [Lamoni, Ia., Published by the Board of Publication of the Reorganized Church of Jesus Christ of Latter Day Saints, 1914]
139p. 19cm.
MoInRC

4977. ———. Minority rights; or, In the footsteps of the fathers. The protesting saints declare themselves. Independence, Mo., The Messenger [192–]
23p. 20×10cm.
RLDS contentions.
USlC

4978. ———. (same) 2d ed. Independence, Mo., The Messenger [192–]
23 [1]p. 20cm.
MH

4979. ———. Minority rights and the Church of Christ. Rev. and enl. 3d ed. [n.p., 192–]
55p. 22cm.
Church of Christ (Temple lot) point of view on the RLDS problem of central control.
MoInRC

4980. ———. Secret mysteries; ancient and modern. By Elder E. E. Long. Lamoni, Ia., Herald Publishing House [ca. 1907]
71p. 18cm.
The problem of the individual good and evil institutions.
USlC

4981. ———. Take heed. There is danger ahead. [Douglas, Arizona? n.d.]
8p. 23cm.
Author's home: Douglas, Arizona.
Church of Christ tract on apostasy.
MoInRC

4982. Long, *Mrs.* J. "The Beautiful valley of Utah" and other poems by Mrs. J. Long. [Salt Lake City] c1924.
63p. 17cm.
Mormon poetry.
USlC

4983. Long, John Dixon. Pictures of slavery in church and state; including personal reminiscences, biographical sketches, anecdotes, etc. etc. With an appendix, containing the views of John Wesley and Richard Watson on slavery. By Rev. John Dixon Long . . . Philadelphia: The author, 1857.
1p.l., 7–410p., [1]l. 19½cm.
"Slavery and Mormonism," p. 261–264.
Another edition: 3d ed. 1857. UPB
DLC, NjP

Long, J. V. *See Iowa Infantry. Mormon Battalion, 1846–1848.*

4984. A long trail. Being the diary of a journey through North America. May–August, 1927. [n.p., n.d.]
1p.l. [3]–40p. 41½cm.
Salt Lake City, p. 21–22. Very favorably impressed with the Mormons.
USlC

4985. Longworth, Maria Theresa. Theresina in America by Therese Yelverton (*Viscountess Avonmore*) London, Richard Bentley and Son, 1875.
2v. in 1. 19cm.
Welsh girl, inspired with holy horror by polygamy and not by "poor Joe Smith, who was a mere maniac," Mormonism. Chapter III, V.2.
CU, USlC V.2, UU

4986. Loomis, Leander Vaness. A journal of the Birmingham Emigrating Co., the record of a trip from Birmingham, Iowa, to Sacramento, Cal., in 1850, together with five early itineraries covered in part by this company. Edited by Edgar M. Ledyard. Salt Lake City [Legal Printing Co.] 1928.
7p.l. 198p. plates, ports., fold. map. 23cm.
Scattered references to Mormonism.
Howes L464
CSmH, CU–B, DLC, ICN, NjP, UHi, UPB, ULA, USlC, UU

4987. Lord, Eliot. . . . Comstock mining and miners, by Eliot Lord. Washington, Govt. Print. Off., 1883.
xiv, 451p. maps. 30½×23cm. (U.S. Geological Survey. Monographs. Vol. 4)
Mormon participation in Nevada gold discoveries; their recall from Nevada.
CU–B, DLC, UHi

4988. ———. The drama of Virginia City. [Carson City, Nevada, Nevada State Print., c1925]
4p.l., 92p. 21cm.
Adapted from his *Comstock mining and miners.*
Brief mention of Mormon colonization in Nevada and gold interest.
Another edition: c1926. CU–B, UHi
UHi

4989. The Lord's harvest, or the dawn of the twelfth hour, by one of the Literal bbranches [sic] on the Root of Jesse. [Beaver, Utah? 1876]
6p. 21½cm.
Signed: Beaver, April 15, 1876.
Doctrinal dissertation on the last days.
Place of Joseph Smith and Brigham Young in the kingdom, and what is to follow.
CtY

The Lord's Servants. *See An official proclamation; see also The voice of the Lord.*

4990. Lossing, Benson John. Complete history of the United States, from the discovery of the American continent to the present time. With a valuable concordance comprising a system of cross references interwoven with foot-notes throughout the work and much important supplementary matter . . . [New York] Published for the Home educational League of America [c1902]
2v. in 1. illus., ports., facsims. 26cm.
Brief history of the Mormons, expulsion to Utah and a portrait of Joseph Smith.
USlC, UU

4991. ———. The countries of the western world. The governments and people of North, South and Central America, from the landing of Columbus to the present time . . . Prepared by Benson J. Lossing . . . and other well-known writers . . . New York, Gay Brothers & Co., 1890.
xxxip., [1]l. [53]–698 (i.e. 700)p. illus., plates, double front., port. 24½cm.
Mormonism, p. 297–303, 472, 523, 534–535.
UPB, USlC

4992. ———. A history of the United States for families and libraries. Hartford, Belknap & Bliss, 1872.
780p. illus., plates, port. 25½cm.
Mormonism, p. 499, 503–507, 537.
USlC

4993. Lotsy, Johannes Paulus. Van den Atlantischen Oceaan naar de Stille Zuidzee in 1922. Dagboek van een botanicus, die niet alleen naar planten keek door Dr. J. P. Lotsy. 's-Gravenhage — G. Naeff — 1923.
xii [1] 491p. 25cm.
Chap. XXV "In de stad en het land der Mormonen," p. [354]–365.
Title in English: From the Atlantic Ocean to the South Pacific Ocean in 1922.
DLC, USlC

4994. Loud, Grover Cleveland. Evangelized America, by Grover C. Loud. New York, L. MacVeagh, The Dial Press; Toronto, Longmans, Green & Company, 1928.
xvi p., [1]l., 373p. plates, ports. 21cm.
"The Mormon Moses." A brief history of Mormonism.
CU, DLC, MB, NjP, NjPT, NN, PSC, USl, USlC, UU, ViU

4995. Lovejoy, Mary Evelyn Wood. History of Royalton, Vermont, with family genealogies, 1769–1911, by Evelyn M. Wood Lovejoy. Published by the town and the Royalton Woman's Club. Burlington, Vt., Free Press Printing Company, 1911.
xxi, 1146p. plates, ports., 3 fold. maps, facsims. 24½cm.
Includes a history of the Joseph Smith family in Vermont, and a description of the Joseph Smith monument.
DLC, USlC

4996. Lovett, Richard. Mormonism. [London, The Religious Tract Society, n.d.]
15p. 17cm. (No. 760)
USlC

4997. ———. United States pictures drawn with pen and pencil, by Richard Lovett . . . With a map and one hundred and fifty-seven engravings. [London] The Religious Tract Society, 1891.
223 [1]p. illus., plates, fold. map, facsims. 28½cm.
A visit to Salt Lake in 1891. His account includes a brief history of Mormonism and a description of Temple Square.
DLC, UHi, UU

4998. Lowe, Josiah Beatson. "Mormonism," by the Rev. Josiah B. Lowe delivered at the Concert Hall, Liverpool, on Thursday evening, November 13th, 1851. Liverpool, W. T. Thompson [etc., etc., 185–]
1p.l. [63]–98p. 17cm. (Liverpool Church of England Institution Lectures. Second course. No. 3)
MH, USlC

4999. ———. Mormonism exposed; being a lecture on the doctrines and practices of "the Latter-day Saints" delivered in the Music Hall, Bold Street, by the Reverend J. B. Lowe . . . Liverpool, Edward Howell, 1852.
50p. 17½cm.
MH, NN, USlC

5000. ———. Reply of Rev. Josiah B. Lowe to the letter of Mr. William Collinson, addressed to him in the mail of the 28th February, 1852. [n.p.] T. Brakell, Printer, 1852.
Broadside. 22×12cm.
USlC

5001. Lowe, Percival Green. Five years a dragoon ('49 to '54) and other adventures on the great plains. Kansas City, Missouri, F. Hudson Publishing Co., 1906.
417 [1]p. illus. 20cm.
Utah Expedition, p. 299–353.
DLC, NjP, UHi, ULA

5002. Luce, Amante [*pseud.*] Distinguishing doctrines of the Utah Mormon Church examined; eternity of the marriage covenant. Lamoni, Ia., Reorganized Church of Jesus Christ of Latter-day Saints, 1908.
14p. 19cm. (No. 300)
Cover-title.
IWW, MH, MoInRC, USl, USlC

5003. ———. (same) Lamoni, Ia., Herald Publishing House [ca. 1910]
14p. 16½cm.
Cover-title: Eternity of the marriage covenant.
MH, MoInRC, USlC

5004. ———. (same) [Lamoni? Ia., Reorganized Church of Jesus Christ of Latter Day Saints? n.d.]
14p. 17cm.
CU–B, IWW, UPB

5005. ———. Errors and inconsistencies concerning the presidency of the dominant church in Utah. By Amante Luce [*pseud.*] [Lamoni, Ia., 1901?]
12p. 18cm. (No. 207)
Caption-title.
CU–B, MH, MoInRC, NN, USl, USlC

———. Eternity of the marriage covenant.
See his Distinguishing doctrines of the Utah Mormon church.

5006. ———. Joseph Smith: has he succeeded his father, the seer, in the presidency of the Church? [Lamoni, Ia., ca. 1895]
16p. 17½cm. (No. 222)
CtY, CU–B, MH, MoInRC, USl, USlC

5007. ———. Reorganization of the Church of Jesus Christ of Latter-day Saints. [Lamoni, Ia., Herald Publishing House, n.d.]
12p. 17½cm. (No. 201)
CtY, MH, MoInRC, USlC

5008. ———. (same) [Lamoni, Ia., Herald Publishing House, n.d.]
12p. 17½cm. (No. 1219)
Variant printing of the above.
USlC

5009. ———. Utah Mormons repudiate Joseph Smith, the Prophet. Independence, Mo., Ensign Publishing House, 1902.
36p. 16cm. (The Gospel Banner. V.9. Extra A)
MoInRC

5010. Lucifer's lantern. Salt Lake City, Miller Printing Co., June, 1898–May, 1900.
9 nos. (195 [1]p.) illus., port. 23½×26cm.
Editor: A. T. Schroeder.

LUFF, J.

Partial contents: #5/6 has title page: The N. Y. Times vs. Geo. Q. Cannon, being a reprint of the famous "Times" letters of 1895 with Mr. Cannon's reply in full. #8 has title: Thoughts on the Mormon problem and its solution by A. T. Schroeder of the Salt Lake City bar.
CtY #5/6, MoInRC, ULA #8, UPB #5–8, USlC #1–8, WHi comp.

5011. Lucy, *Sir* Henry William. East by west. A journey in the recess. By Henry W. Lucy . . . London, R. Bentley and Son, 1885.
2v. 20cm.
"The city of the Saints. The Mormon president [John Taylor] at home," V. 1, p. 92–116.
CtY, CU, DLC, NjP, NN, UHi, UPB, USlC, UU

5012. Ludlow, Fitz Hugh. The heart of the continent: a record of travel across the plains and in Oregon, with an examination of the Mormon principle. By Fitz Hugh Ludlow . . . New York, Hurd and Houghton; Cambridge, Riverside Press, 1870.
vi, 568p. plates. 22cm.
A lengthy description of his stay in Salt Lake City; a visit to Church leaders and his impression of Mormonism.
Another edition: New York, Hurd and Houghton, 1871. NjP, NjPT, WaS
Sabin 42648
CSmH, CtY, CU–B, DLC, ICN, NjP, NN, UHi, ULA, UPB, USl, USlC, UU, WaU, WHi

5013. Luff, Joseph. Are we orthodox? Independence, Mo., Ensign Publishing House, 1906.
31p. 16cm. (The Gospel Banner. V. 14, No. 1)
RLDS Church doctrine.
MoInRC

5014. ———. Autobiography of Elder Joseph Luff, one of the Twelve Apostles of the Reorganized Church of Jesus Christ of Latter Day Saints. Lamoni, Ia., Herald Publishing House, 1894.
ix, [1]l., 377p. ports. 20cm.
CSmH, CtY, CU–B, DLC, ICN, MH, MoInRC, UHi, UPB, USl, USlC, WHi

5015. ———. Behold, saith the Lord. [n.p., n.d.] [3]p. 20cm.
Includes a copy of "The song of admonition."
RLDS tract on prophecy.
MoInRC

5016. ———. The Book of Mormon, is it the stick of Ephraim referred to in the thirty-seventh chapter of Ezekiel, verses fifteen to nineteen? [n.p., n.d.]
8p. 18cm.
Book of Mormon apologetics.
MoInRC

5017. ———. Concerning our whereabouts; watchman, what of the night. [n.p., 1930?]
15p. 22cm.
Includes RLDS poetry.
MoInRC, NjP

5018. ———. Crucified by His friends. Independence, Mo., Ensign Publishing Company, 1897.
44p. 16cm. (The Gospel Banner. V. 1, No. 1. Extra B)
RLDS interpretation of Jesus Christ.
MoInRC

5019. ———. God is unchangeable. Independence, Mo., Ensign Publishing Company [1897]
44p. 16cm. (Ensign Circulating Library. Vest Pocket ed.)
MoInRC

5020. ———. (same) Independence, Mo., Ensign Publishing Company [1897?]
44p. 16cm. (The Gospel Banner. V. 3, No. 1. Extra B)
MoInRC

5021. ———. Gospel antiquity. Independence, Mo., Ensign Publishing Co. [n.d.]
39p. 16cm. (The Gospel Banner. V. 3, No. 2. Extra B)
RLDS doctrine.
MoInRC

5022. ———. Is water baptism essential to Salvation? Independence, Mo., Ensign Publishing House [n.d.]
14p. 19cm.
MoInRC

5023. ———. (same) Independence, Mo., Ensign Publishing House [n.d.]
12p. 19cm. (The Gospel Banner. V. 2, No. 3. Extra A)
MoInRC

5024. ———. (same) Independence, Mo., Ensign Publishing House [n.d.]
11p. 16cm.
MoInRC

5025. ———. (same) Independence, Mo., Ensign Publishing House [n.d.]
8p. 20cm.
MoInRC

5026. ———. (same) Independence, Mo., Ensign Publishing House, 1895.
11p. 12cm. (The Gospel Banner. V. 2, No. 3)
MoInRC

5027. ———. (same) Independence, Mo., Ensign Publishing House, 1901.
18p. 16cm.
MoInRC

5028. ———. (same) Independence, Mo., Ensign Publishing House, 1901.
16p. 16cm. (The Gospel Banner. V. 8, No. 1. Extra A)
MoInRC

5029. ———. (same, in Danish) Vand-daab; er den af vigtighed for vorfrelse? [Porsgrund, Brodrene Dyrings Bogtrykkeri, n.d.]
6 [1]p. 23cm.
"Kristi laere" after p.6.
USlC

5030. ———. A marvelous work and a wonder. Independence, Mo., Ensign Publishing Company, 1895.
40p. 16cm. (The Gospel Banner. V. 2, No. 2. Extra A)
Restoration and reorganization.
MoInRC

5031. ———. The name of the church; embodying the matter presented by him in a sermon on the subject delivered in the Stone Church at Independence, Mo. Independence, Mo., Reorganized Church of Jesus Christ of Latter Day Saints, 1926.
49p. 19½cm.
RLDS doctrine.
MoInRC, NjP

5032. ———. (same) With additions by himself. [Independence, Mo., Herald Publishing House, n.d.]
49p. 19½cm.
Later than the February 1926 edition.
MoInRC, NjP, UPB

5033. ———. The old Jerusalem Gospel. Twenty-nine sermons representative of the faith of the Reorganized Church of Jesus Christ of Latter Day Saints. Independence, Mo. [Ensign Publishing House] 1903.
3p.l. [7]–280p. ports. 19cm.
MoInRC, MoKU, NjP, NN, UHi, UPB, USl, USlC

5033a. ———. (same) Lamoni, Ia., Herald Publishing House, 1912.
310p. 19cm.
NjP

5034. ———. Song by the Spirit through Elder Joseph Luff. Lamoni, Ia., Herald Publishing House [n.d.]
7p. 19cm.
RLDS inspirational writings.
MoInRC

5035. ———. The true shepherd, the sheepfold, the door, the porter. [n.p., n.d.]
13p. 22cm.
RLDS interpretation of Jesus Christ.
MoInRC

5036. ———. Why I became a Latter-day Saint . . . Independence, Mo., Ensign Publishing House [189–]
13p. 19cm.
Cover-title.
CtY, MoInRC

5037. ———. (same) Independence, Mo., Ensign Publishing House, 1902.
28p. 16cm. (The Gospel Banner. V. 9, No. 5. Extra G.)
MoInRC

5038. ———. (same) Lamoni, Ia., Herald Publishing House [191–]
13p. 18½cm.
Cover-title.
UHi, MoInRC, NjP

5039. ———. (same) Independence, Mo., Ensign Publishing House [1912?]
13p. 19cm.
Cover-title.
NN, USl

5040. Luke, L. D. A journey from the Atlantic to the Pacific coast by way of Salt Lake City, returning by way of the Southern route, describing the natural and artificial scenes of both lines. Utica, N.Y., Ellis H. Roberts & Co., 1884.
79p. 23cm.
Tour of Salt Lake City and a resumé of Mormonism. A summary of one of the meetings he attended.
Howes L564
UPB

5041. Lull, De Los. Father Solon or the helper helped, by Rev. De Los Lull. New York, Wilbur K. Ketcham, 1888.
367p. 19½cm.
Fiction relating a triumph over Mormonism.
USlC

5042. Lum, Dyer Daniel. Social problems of to-day; or, The Mormon question in its economic aspects. A study of co-operation and arbitration in Mormondom, from the standpoint of a wage worker . . . By a Gentile, author of "Utah and its people." Port Jervis, New York, D. D. Lum and Co., 1886.
2p.l. [5]–91p. 23cm.
CSmH, CtY, CU–B, DLC, ICN, MH, MiU, NjP, NN, UHi, ULA, UPB, USlC, UU, WHi

5043. ———. Utah and its people. Facts and statistics bearing on the "Mormon problem" . . . By a gentile . . . New York, R. O. Ferrier & Co., 1882.
47p. 23cm.
Cover-title.
CSmH, CtY, CU–B, DLC, ICN, MH, NjPT, NN, UHi, ULA, UPB, USlC, UU, WHi

5044. Lund, A. C. Have faith, Ye Saints. [Lyric by Bert Auerbach; Music by A. C. Lund and Bert Auerbach] New York, Published by Lyric Music Corporation [1923]
[2]l. music. 27cm.
USlC

Lund, Anthon H. Scandinavian jubilee album. *See Church of Jesus Christ of Latter-day Saints. Scandinavian jubilee album.*

5045. Lusk, David W. Politics and politicians; a succinct history of the politics of Illinois from 1856 to 1884, with anecdotes and incidents, and appendix from 1809 to 1856 . . . Springfield, Ill. [H.S. Rokker, Printer] 1884 [c1883]
xiii, 526p. ports. 22cm.
Mormon war, p. 470–472.
Another edition: 2d ed. rev. & enl. 1886. USlC
DLC, NjP, UPB, USlC

5046. Lux. Official organ of the student body of the Big Horn Academy. Cowley, Wyoming, 1915–
v. illus., ports. 23cm.
UPB V.1, #4; USlC V.3, #1

5047. Lyford, C. P. Brigham Young's record of blood! or, The necessity for the famous "Bible and revolver" . . . A lecture delivered in the First M. E. Church, Salt Lake City, Jan. 23d, 1876, by Rev. C. P. Lyford . . . [Salt Lake City, Tribune Publishing Company, 1876]
15p. 20½cm.
"Published in the *Salt Lake Daily Tribune*, Jan. 25th, 1876, and *Rocky Mountain Christian Advocate*, Feb. 1st, 1876."
CtY, DLC, ICN, NN

5048. ———. The Mormon problem, an appeal to the American people. With an appendix containing four original stories of Mormon life, founded upon fact, and a graphic and thrilling account of the Mountain Meadows massacre. By Rev. C. P. Lyford . . . New York, Phillips and Hunt; Cincinnati, Cranston & Stowe, 1886.
323p. 19cm.
CSmH, CU-B, ICN, MH, MoInRC, NjP, NjPT, UHi, ULA, UPB, USl, USlC, UU, WHi

5048a. ———. Tithing. A sermon by Rev. C. P. Lyford. New York: Nelson & Phillips; Cincinnati: Hitchcock & Walden [n.d.]
32p. 14cm. (New series, No. 37)
In ornamental border.
A discussion of the Mormon doctrine of tithing.
UPB

5049. Lykke og ulykke, eller: Saltsoens mysterier. En smuk Historie om en ung pige, der blev forfort af Mormonerne til at reise til Saltsoen og hvad hun der oplevede. Men "Prospekt fra Saltsoen." Kobenhavn, 1865.
8p.
Title in English: The light shineth in darkness.
Schmidt

5050. Lykkejaeger, Hans. Luck of a wandering Dane by Hans Lykkejaeger . . . Philadelphia, Mallack & Harvey, Printers, c1885.
1p.l. [5]–130p. illus. 20cm.
Short episode in Ogden with corrupt Mormon judges.
UPB

5051. Lyman, Amy (Brown) Historical events in the Relief Society, by Mrs. Amy Brown Lyman . . . [Salt Lake City?] 1927.
8p. 21½cm.
"Address delivered at Relief Society conference, April 2, 1927."
UHi

5052. ———. National Woman's Relief Society, Church of Jesus Christ of Latter-day Saints, 1842–1925, by Mrs. Amy Brown Lyman . . . Salt Lake City, General Board Relief Society [1925]
8p. 22½cm.
Cover-title.
"Report was prepared at the request of the National Council of Women . . ."
Address delivered over Radio Station KSL, Sunday, November 29, 1925.
UHi

5053. Lyman, Chester Smith. Around the Horn to the Sandwich Islands and California 1845–1850, being a personal record kept by Chester S. Lyman sometime Professor of Astronomy and Physics in Yale University. Edited by Frederick J. Teggart, Associate Professor in the University of California. With an introduction by D. L. P. New Haven, Yale University Press, MDCCCCXXIV.
xviii, 328p. 24½cm.
Contains mention of the arrival of the ship Brooklyn at Honolulu, June 28, 1846 and other references to the Mormons in California.
CU-B, DLC, UPB

5054. Lyman, Francis Marion. Notes to be referred to daily by missionaries. Salt Lake City [1909?]
4p. 21cm.
Variant printings.
USlC

5055. Lyman, Richard Roswell. America's chief need — religion; An address in the Tabernacle at Salt Lake City, by Dr. Richard R. Lyman . . . At General Conference, Oct. 6, 1929. [Salt Lake City? 1929]
79–83p. 23cm.
"Reprint from Conference Pamphlet" with added title page.
UPB, USlC

LYMAN, R. R.

5056. ———. An appeal from "the top of the mountains" to the people of the country to come to the support of the Constitution of the United States. [Salt Lake City, 191–]
[2]p. 28cm.
Application form for people wishing law and order, especially prohibition. On verso is a argument against liquor. Signed: Richard R. Lyman, M. Am. Soc. C. E.
UPB, USIC

5057. ———. An Appreciation. By Richard R. Lyman, junior member of the Council of the Twelve. Salt Lake City, 1918.
Broadside. 30½×15½cm.
Written upon the death of, and in commemoration of President Joseph F. Smith.
UPB

5058. ———. Cigarette smoking, KSL Radio address, April 11, 1926. [Salt Lake City, Deseret Book Co., 1926]
[4]p. 23cm.
UPB

5059. ———. The cost and the consequences, by Dr. Richard R. Lyman . . . Salt Lake City, Magazine Printing Co. [193–]
[1]p. 15½×12cm.
UHi

5060. ———. Dedication of the Arizona Temple, Mesa, Arizona, October 23–26, 1927. By Dr. Richard R. Lyman . . . [Salt Lake City, Deseret Book Company, 1927]
4p. 25½cm.
"Reprint from *Improvement Era*, Dec., 1927."
USIC

5061. ———. Obedience to law, the path of safety; an address by Richard R. Lyman, in the Tabernacle at Salt Lake City, October 9, 1927. [Salt Lake City, 1927]
6p. 23cm.
"Reprint from Conference pamphlet."
USIC

5062. ———. President Grant and his family . . . [Salt Lake City, Bureau of Information, 1919]
7 [1]p. illus. 24cm.
"Reprint from the *Young Woman's Journal*, February, 1919."
NjP, UHi

5063. ———. President Joseph F. Smith. [Salt Lake City, 1919?]
4p. 23½cm.
"Reprinted from the *Young Woman's Journal*, January, 1919."
NjP, UHi, USIC

5064. ———. A tribute to John J. McClellan. By Richard R. Lyman . . . [Salt Lake City, 1925]
122–124p. 22cm.
"Reprint from Conference pamphlet."
USIC

5065. Lynch, John T. Postmaster John T. Lynch on the "Mormons." A foul and filthy libel! Young ladies vilely traduced. Atrocious slander. [Salt Lake City? 1883]
Broadside. 46½×21½cm.
Reprinted from the *Chicago Times* of May 27th, 1883.
USIC

5066. Lyne, Thomas A. A true and descriptive account of the assassination of Joseph & Hiram [sic] Smith, the Mormon Prophet and Patriarch, at Carthage, Illinois, June 27th, 1844, by an eye witness, T. A. Lyne, late of the stage, to which is annexed the speech of H. L. Reid, also, speech of James W. Woods. To which is added a brief outline of the faith and doctrine of the Latter Day Saints. New York, C. A. Calhoun, 1844.
19p. 21½cm.
Errors in pagination: CtY copy p. 18 numb. 81; MB copy verso of p. 17 is blank, p. 19 missing; NN copy pp. 14–17 scrambled.
Sabin 50740
CtY, MB, MiU–C, NN, PHi, USIC

Lyon, David R., *compiler.* *See Lyon, John.*

5067. Lyon, John. The harp of Zion, a collection of poems &c. By John Lyon, with notes and a steel portrait of the author . . . Published for the benefit of the Perpetual Emigrating Fund. Liverpool, S. W. Richards; London, T. C. Armstrong, 1853.
xi, 223 [1]p. port. 19cm.
By a Scottish Latter-day Saint who went to Utah in 1853.
Sabin 50740
CSmH, CtY, CU–B, DLC, MoInRC, NjP, NN, UHi, ULA, UPB, USIC, UU, WHi

5068. ———. Songs of a pioneer; containing writings in verse and prose by John Lyon, author of "Harp of Zion." Compiled by his son David R. Lyon. Salt Lake City, Magazine Printing Company, 1923.
viii [9]–391p. 2 ports. 20cm.
CU–B, NN, UHi, UPB, USIC

5069. Lyon, William Henry. A study of the sects . . . 5th ed. Boston, Unitarian Sunday-School Society, 1891.
v, 190p. 18½cm.
Discussion of Mormonism as a non-Christian religion with brief history and doctrine.
Other editions: Boston, Unitarian Sunday-School Society, 1894. USIC; (same) 1897. USIC
CU, DLC, UPB

LYS

5070. ———. (same, under title) A study of the Christian Sects. With an introductory chapter on the Jews. By William H. Lyon. Thirteenth Edition. Revised and enlarged by John Malick. Boston, The Beacon Press, Inc., 1926.
v, [3]–257p. 19½cm.
UPB

5071. Et Lys, der skinner i Mørket. Men mørket begriber det ikke. [Kjøbenhavn, Udgivet og Forlagt af John S. Hansen . . . 1925]
4p. 22½cm.
Missionary tract.
Title in English: A light shining in darkness.
USIC

DOCUMENT

CONTAINING THE

CORRESPONDENCE, ORDERS, &C.

IN RELATION TO THE DISTURBANCES WITH THE

MORMONS;

AND THE

EVIDENCE

GIVEN BEFORE THE HON. AUSTIN A. KING, JUDGE OF THE FIFTH JUDICIAL CIRCUIT OF THE STATE OF MISSOURI, AT THE COURT-HOUSE IN RICHMOND, IN A CRIMINAL COURT OF INQUIRY, BEGUN NOVEMBER 12, 1838, ON THE TRIAL OF JOSEPH SMITH, JR., AND OTHERS, FOR HIGH TREASON AND OTHER CRIMES AGAINST THE STATE.

PUBLISHED BY ORDER OF THE GENERAL ASSEMBLY.

Printed at the office of the Boon's Lick Democrat.

FAYETTE, MISSOURI.

1841.

Item 5427. Details of the 1838 Mormon war in northern Missouri.
From the Brigham Young University collection.

5072. M., H. Mormonismen og Saltsøstaden. Kjøbenhavn, Karl Schønbergs forlag. Trykt hos Nielsen & Lydiche, 1893.
76p. 21cm. (Smaaskrifter til oplysning for kristne udgivne af Prof. Dr. Fredrik Nielsen, viii, 4)
Title in English: Mormonism of Salt Lake City.
NN, USlC

5073. M., J. A story of Utah. Founded on fact. New York, Published by the Woman's Board of Home Missions of the Presbyterian Church in the U.S.A. [1903]
7 [1]p. 14cm.
"4th ed."
Signed: J.M.
USlC

5074. M., M. E. My first voyage around the world. Buxton, C. F. Wardley, 1889.
2p.l. [5]–55p. 18cm.
Signed: M.E. M.
Brief summary of Mormon beliefs on polygamy and a description of polygamist houses.
UHi, UPB, USlC

5075. The "M" Messenger. Official organ of the "M" Men's and Gleaner Girls' Associations of Los Angeles and Hollywood Stakes. [Los Angeles, 1926?]
v. 38cm.
USlC V.2 #4

M., Quad. [*pseud.*] *See Lewis, Charles Bertrand.*

5076. Mabie, Hamilton Wright. A topical history of the United States. Footprints of four centuries; the story of the American people, comprising the important events, episodes and incidents which make up the marvelous record from Columbus to the present time. Philadelphia, International Publishing Co., 1894.
xxvii, 21–851p. illus., ports. 26cm.
A few pages on the "Protestant cancers" which should be eliminated from the body politic. One is Mormonism.
Another edition: 1895. NjP; 1898. USlC
USlC, UU

5077. McAfee, George F. Map talk on missions among the Mormons by Geo. F. McAfee . . . New York City, The Presbyterian Church. Woman's Board of Home Missions, 1903.
20p. 15cm.
USlC

5078. ———. (same) 2d ed. New York City, The Presbyterian Church. Woman's Board of Home Missions, 1904.
20p. 14cm. (No. 243)
USlC

5078a. McAfee, Lucy H. Tim. [2d ed.] New York City, Literature Department of the Woman's Board of Home Missions of the Presbyterian Church in the U.S.A. [1903]
31[1]p. 14cm. (No. 244)
Anti-Mormon fiction
USlC

5079. McAllister, D. H. Y. Dear Friend . . . [Liverpool, 1888?]
[2]p. 22cm.
Missionary tract.
UHi

5080. McAllister, Duncan McNeil. A description of the great temple, Salt Lake City, and a statement concerning the purposes for which it has been built. Salt Lake City, Bureau of Information and Church Literature, 1904.
1p.l., 27 [1]p. illus., front. 19cm.
[1] Articles of faith.
Variant printings and covers.
CU–B, DLC, MH, NjP, NN, UPB, USl, USlC

5081. ———. (same) 2d ed. Salt Lake City, Bureau of Information, 1909.
27[1]p. illus., plate. 19cm.
[1] Articles of faith.
CU–B, MH

5082. ———. (same) Salt Lake City, Bureau of Information, 1912.
38 [2]p. illus., plates. 19½cm.
"Illustrated edition."
CSmH, DLC, MWA, NjP, UPB, USlC

5083. ———. (same) Salt Lake City, Bureau of Information and Church Literature, 1914.
38 [2]p. illus., plates. 19½cm.
"Illustrated edition."
CU–B, MoInRC

5084. ———. (same) Salt Lake City, Bureau of Information, 1922.
38 [2]p. illus., plates. 20½cm.
"Illustrated edition."
MH

5085. ———. (same) Salt Lake City, Bureau of Information, 1925.
38 [2]p. illus., plates. 19½cm.
"Illustrated edition."
UPB

5086. ———. (same) 9th ed. Salt Lake City, Bureau of Information, 1929.
38 [2]p. illus., plates. 19cm.
MiU, UPB

5086a. ———. (same) Independence, Mo., Zion's Printing and Publishing Co., 1930.
16p. 18½cm.
USlC

5087. ———. A description of the Hawaiian Temple of the Church of Jesus Christ of Latter-day Saints, erected at Laie, Oahu, Territory of Hawaii, and a statement concerning the purposes for which it has been built, by D. M. McAllister . . . Salt Lake City, The Church, 1921.
39p. illus. 18½cm.
Cover-title: The house of the Lord in Hawaii.
CU-B, DLC, NjP, NN, UHi, USlC, WHi

5088. ———. Food reform as taught by the Latter-day Saints. [Salt Lake City, 1885]
[3]p. 21cm.
Caption-title.
MH, USlC

5089. ———. How to begin temple work. Suggestions to members of the church by D. M. McAllister, Temple Recorder. [Salt Lake City] Deseret News Press, 1924.
[4]p. 22½cm.
From the *Utah Genealogical and Historical Magazine*, April 1924.
USlC

5090. ———. How to prevent sickness. [n.p., n.d.]
[4]p. 21cm.
Caption-title: Diet as shown by the Word of wisdom.
MH

5091. ———. Life's greatest questions — What am I? Why am I here? After death what? Answered from the scriptures, by Elder D. M. McAllister, Independence, Mo., Press of Zion's Printing and Publishing Company. Missions of the Church of Jesus Christ of Latter-day Saints in America [192–]
31p. 17cm.
Cover-title.
NjP, NN, USl, USlC, WaSP

5092. ———. (same) [Independence, Mo., Zion's Printing and Publishing Company, n.d.]
30 [1]p. 17½cm.
Cover-title.
Variant printings.
CU-B, UHi

5093. ———. (same) [Independence, Mo., Zion's Printing and Publishing Company, n.d.]
27 [1]p. 18cm.
UPB

5094. ———. (same) [Independence, Mo., Zion's Printing and Publishing Company, n.d.]
25 [2]p. 17cm.
UPB

5095. ———. (same) [Independence, Mo., Zion's Printing and Publishing Company, n.d.]
28p. 17½cm.
UPB

5096. ———. Temple ordinances essential by Elder D. M. McAllister. [Salt Lake City, 1916]
[4]p. 21cm.
"From *Improvement Era*, September, 1917."
UPB

5097. ———. Temples of the Church of Jesus Christ of Latter-day Saints and the sacred purposes to which they are dedicated. By D. M. McAllister, former temple recorder. [Independence, Mo.] Published by the Missions of the Church of Jesus Christ of Latter-day Saints. Press of Zion's Printing and Publishing Co., 1928.
16p. 18cm.
NN, UPB, USlC

5098. ———. (same) Independence, Mo., Press of Zion's Printing and Publishing Company, 1929.
16p. 16cm.
UPB, USlC

5099. ———. (same) Independence, Mo., Press of Zion's Printing and Publishing Co., 1930.
16p. 18½cm.
IWW, USlC

5099a. ———. (same) Independence, Mo., Zion's Printing and Publishing Co. [1930]
16p. 18½cm.
Variant printings.
USlC

5100. ———. Testimony of Duncan McNeil McAllister . . . [Salt Lake City?] 1918.
[4]p. 18cm.
Of the truthfulness of the L.D.S. church.
UHi

5101. McBride, John R. In the matter of the contested election from Utah Territory. George Q. Cannon, Contestant, vs. Allen G. Campbell, Contestee. Brief on behalf of A. G. Campbell, Contestee. Before Committee on Elections and Qualifications, House of Representatives, Washington [T. McGill & Co., 1881]
30p. 22cm.
At head of title: Forty-seventh Congress. First session.
NN, UHi

5102. McCabe, James Dabney, Jr. A comprehensive view of our country and its resources . . . Philadelphia, Hubbard, c1876.
1p.l. [5]–1241p. illus., charts. 24cm.
Section on Utah and Salt Lake City, with notes on Mormonism, p. 1106–1116.
UPB

5103. ———. An illustrated history of the great republic; being a full and complete history of the American Union, from its earliest settlement down to the present time . . . Philadelphia, William B. Evans & Co. [c1871]
1118p. illus., fold. map. 24cm.
"Utah and Mormonism," p. 1101–1109.
Another edition. [c189–] USlC
USlC

5104. ———. The life and public services of Schuyler Colfax: together with his most important speeches, by Edward Winslow Martin [*pseud.*] New York, United States Publishing Company; Chicago, P. Garret & Co; [etc., etc.] 1868.
x [11]–512p. port. 22½cm.
Speech on a resolution to expel the delegate from Utah [William H. Hooper] and background information on the speech.
DLC, UHi

5105. McCain, Joseph K. The end of the Christian dispensation and the restoration of Israel. Temple, Ga., 1885.
84p., [2]l. 21cm.
Proving Mormonism, the kingdom of God, and rightful heirs.
A Mormon exposition of dispensation, and the Mormon claim of succession of Israelite rights and a restoration.
DLC, MH, NN

5106. McCall, Ansel J. The great California trail in 1849. Wayside notes of an argonaut. By A. J. McCall, esq., Bath, New York, Reprinted from the Steuben Courier. Bath, N.Y., Steuben Courier Print., 1882.
86p. 23½cm.
"Reprinted from the *Steuben Courier*."
Traveled via Great Salt Lake City.
Sympathizes with Mormon persecutions; notes unity and harmony among the saints.
CSmH, CtY, CU–B, UHi

5107. McCarthy, John. The (Madras) "Christian instructor" versus Mormonism. [Madras, India, John McCarthy, 1856]
12p. 18cm.
CSmH

5108. McCarthy, Justin. Brigham Young. By Justin McCarthy (Excerpt from the Galaxy, Feb. 1870) [n.p., n.d.]
177–187p. 22cm.
Reprint from *The Galaxy* with new cover and title page.
USlC

5109. ———. Modern leaders. Being a series of biographical sketches, by Justin McCarthy. New York, Sheldon & Company, 1872.
3p.l. [7]–243p. 23½cm.
Brigham Young, p. 96–105.
NjP, NN, USlC

5110. ———. Reminiscences, by Justin McCarthy . . . New York and London, Harper & Brothers, 1899.
2v. ports. 21cm.
"Brigham Young and the Mormon city," p. 255–268.
DLC, NjP, UHi, UU

5111. M'Cauley, I. H. Historical sketch of Franklin County, Pennsylvania. Prepared for the centennial celebration held at Chambersburg, Penn'a, July 4th, 1876, and subsequently enlarged by I. H. M'Cauley . . . John M. Pomeroy, Publisher. To which is added a valuable appendix by J. L. Suesserott, M.D., D. M. Kennedy and others, and embellished by over one hundred lithographic illustrations, drawn by W. W. Denslow. Chambersburg, Pa., D. F. Pursel, 1878.
3p.l., [5]–322p. plates (part fold.) 23½cm.
Frontispiece and plates printed on both sides.
Account of Mormonism and the settlement of Rigdon near Greencastle, 1845–47.
Another edition: Harrisburgh, Pa., Patriot Publishing Company, 1878. DLC, MWA, OCl, PHC, PHi, PP, PU
DLC, PHi, PPL

5112. M'Chesney, James. An antidote to Mormonism; a warning to the church and nation; the purity of Christian principles defended; and truth disentangled from error and delusion. By James M'Chesney. Revised by G. J. Bennet . . . New York, Pub. by the author, at the book store of Burnett & Pollard, 1838.
iv [5]–60p. 21cm.
Howes M39, Sabin 43002
CU–B, DLC, IaCrM, ICU, MH, MoK, NN, OClWHi, USlC, WHi

5113. ———. A brief review of the proceedings of the annual conference of the Methodist Episcopal Church, her discipline and administration of government; embracing a historical sketch of the difficulties existing between Washington Street Church, Brooklyn, and some of the higher powers of this connection, by James M'Chesney. New York, Pub'd by the author at the bookstore of Barnett & Pollard, 1839.
iv [5]–44, 4p. 19½cm.
NN, USlC

5114. ———. Supplement to an antidote to Mormonism . . . [Brooklyn? 1839]
4p. 18cm.
Signed: Brooklyn, Oct. 3, 1839.
CtY, MBAt, MH, NN, USlC

5115. McClain, Josiah. The Mormon doctrine of priesthood; measured by the scriptures. Salt Lake City [n.d.]
19p. 14½cm.
USlC

5116. McClellan, J. J. O Zion, when I think of Thee. By J. J. McClellan . . . Salt Lake City, Published by Clayton Music Co. [n.d.]
[3]p. 26cm.
UPB

5117. McClellan, Rolander Guy. The golden state: a history of the region west of the Rocky Mountains; embracing California, Oregon, Nevada, Utah, Arizona, Idaho, Washington Territory, British Columbia, and Alaska, from the earliest period to the present time . . . with a history of Mormonism and the Mormons. By R. Guy McClellan . . . Philadelphia [etc.] W. Flint & company; Chicago, Union Publishing Company; [etc., etc., 1872]
1p.l., 15–685p. plates, ports., maps. 23cm.
Utah, Mormonism, and the Mormons . . . p. 549–599.
Other editions: 1874. USIC; 1876. NjP
CSmH, CU–B, DLC, ICN, MWA, NjP, NN, Nh, OO, UHi, WaU, WHi

5118. McClernand, John A. Reprint of the separate report of Hon. J. A. McClernand as a member of the Utah Commission on the Mormon question, Sept. 23, 1889. Washington, 1890.
20p. 23cm.
Cover-title.
NjP, NN, USIC, WHi

5119. McClintock, James Harvey. Arizona; prehistoric-aboriginal-pioneer-modern; the nations youngest culture. Chicago, S. J. Clarke Publishing Co., 1916.
3v. illus. 27cm.
Includes Mormonism in Arizona and the Mormon battalion.
CU–B, DLC, NjP

5120. ———. Mormon settlement in Arizona; a record of peaceful conquest of the desert, by James H. McClintock . . . Phoenix, Ariz., 1921.
xi, 307p. plates, ports., maps (1 fold.) 21½cm.
Also includes Mormon colonization in Nevada, p. 101–116.
CSmH, CtY, CU–B, DLC, ICN, NjP, NN, UHi, ULA, UPB, USI, USIC, UU, WHi

5121. McClintock, John. Cyclopedia of Biblical theological and ecclesiastical literature. Prepared by the Rev. John McClintock, D. D., and James Strong. New York, Harper and Brothers, 1867–87.
12v. illus. 25½cm.
Vol. 6, p. 618–648, contains "The Mormons; their history, sacred writings, doctrines, ordinances and practices, hierarchical organization, propagandism and literature."
Apparently printings of Vol. 6 were made in 1876, 1882, 1890, 1894.
CSmH, CtY, CU, DLC, ICU, MH, MiU, NjPT, NN, ULA, ViU

5122. McClure, Alexander Kelly. Three thousand miles through the Rocky Mountains. By A. K. McClure. Philadelphia, J. B. Lippincott and Co., 1869.
456p. plates, port. 19½cm.
Includes a trip through Utah with copious observations on Mormonism and the church system. Howes M49, Sabin 43059
CSmH, DLC, ICN, NjP, NN, PU, UHi, UPB, USIC, WaU

5123. ———. To the Pacific and Mexico. Philadelphia, London, J. B. Lippincott Company, 1901.
3p.l., 7–162p. plates, port., map. 19½cm.
A revisit to Utah with notes on earlier conclusions, p. 9–29.
DLC, UHi, USIC

5124. McClurg, Gilbert, *compiler.* The official proceedings of the Eleventh National Irrigation Congress held at Ogden, Utah, September 15–18, 1903. Officially compiled and edited by Gilbert McClurg. Ogden, Utah, Proceedings Publishing Co., 1904.
472p. illus. 23½cm.
Mormons, p. 11–19, 21, 22; Ogden, p. 35–38.
DLC, USIC

5125. McClurg, Virginia Donaghé. Picturesque Utah. Albertype illustrations from original photographs by Chas. R. Savage . . . Descriptive text by M. Virginia Donaghé. Denver, Col., F. S. Thayer, 1888.
3p.l. [7]–33p. 6 plates. 20½×28½cm.
Brief history of the Mormons and a description of Salt Lake City.
CSmH, DLC, UHi, USIC

5126. McConkie, Charles William. The Restoration of the gospel. [n.p., n.d.]
[5]p. 16½cm.
MoInRC, USIC

5126a. ———. (same) [n.p., n.d.]
[2]p. 16½cm.
Variant printing.
USIC

5127. ———. The Restoration of the gospel and how to obtain a testimony. By C. W. McConkie. [n.p., n.d.]
[6]p. 16½cm.
USIC

5128. McConnell, William John. Early history of Idaho, by W. J. McConnell, Ex.-U.S. Senator and -Governor, who was present and cognizant of the events narrated: Pub. by authority of the Idaho State Legislature. Caldwell, Idaho, The Caxton Printers, 1913.

2p.l. [7]–420p. front. 23½cm.
Establishment of the Fort Lemhi Mission, and other Mormon colonization.
Howes M62
CU–B, DLC, ICN, NjP, UHi, ULA, UPB

5129. McCosker, John. Ten millions of dollars. By Miller [*pseud.*] New York, 1870.
32p. 23cm.
"Mormonism" as a social problem, p. 10–11.
CtY

5130. McCoy, Alexander W. Pioneering on the plains, journey to Mexico in 1848, the overland trip to California. [Kaukauna, Wis., c1924]
[117]p. 2 illus., 1 port. 26cm.
Cover-title.
The Mormons found helpful on the plains despite adverse reports. Letters and diary of Alexander W., John and Samuel Finley McCoy, 1849, with letters by John A. Johnson.
Howes M66 (60p.)
CSmH, DLC, NjP

5131. M'Culloch, James Ramsey. M'Culloch's universal gazetteer. A dictionary, geographical, statistical, and historical, of the various countries, places, and principal natural objects in the world. By J. R. M'Culloch, esq. In which the articles relating to the United States have been greatly multiplied and extended, and adapted to the present condition of the country, and to the wants of its citizens. By Daniel Haskel . . . Illustrated with seven large maps. New York, Harper and Brothers, 1847–48.
2v. fold. map. 24½cm.
Vol. 2 has a short description of Nauvoo and Kirtland.
CU, UPB

5132. McCullough, R. Verne. Is there a God? Address delivered over Radio Station KSL, Sunday Evening, February 26, 1928. [Salt Lake City] 1928.
Broadside. 42½×23½cm.
Reprinted from the *Deseret News*, Saturday, March 3rd, 1928.
UPB

5133. MacDonald, Alexander Findlay. The Mexican Colonies. Description of the best routes for colonists, together with a great deal of valuable information about the climate and soil also regarding customs, duties, purchase of lands, etc. [Letter to Deseret News from A. F. McDonald and W. D. Johnson. Juarez, Mexico, September 24, 1888]
2p. 31cm.
Mormon colonization in Mexico.
NjP, UPB

5133a. ———. (same) Valuable information to intending settlers and tourists. [Salt Lake City, 1890]
[3]p. 28½cm.
"Correspondence of the *Deseret News*"
Dated: September 11th, 1890.
UPB, USIC

5134. ———. What do the Latter-day Saints believe? [Liverpool, Printed by J. Sadler, 1851]
8p. 18cm.
USIC

5135. McDonald, Angus. The future destiny of the "Mormons" will be defined to the lands of the Gentiles. [Salt Lake City, 1890?]
[1]l. 21cm.
USIC

5135a. ———. Keys for truth-seekers. A letter from Joseph Smith, Jr., to his Uncle Silas. [Salt Lake City, ca. 1885]
16p. 21½cm.
At head of title: The Mormons have stepped down and out of Celestial Government. The American Indians have stepped up and into Celestial Government.
An unorthodox author of Mormon doctrines.
Letter from Joseph Smith dated Kirtland Mills, Ohio, September 26, 1833.
USIC

5136. ———. Mormonism: the advance guard of the terrestrial kingdom of God, the work of the Father, that gathering of the seed of Joseph and scattering of the unbelieving Gentiles from this land has begun. By A. MacDonald, optical professor. [Salt Lake City? n.d.]
68p. 16½cm.
A radical tract on the gathering.
MH, USI, USIC

5137. ———. The Mormons have stepped down out of celestial government. The American Indians have stepped up into celestial government [Salt Lake City? 1892?]
4p. 21cm.
Brochure for lantern slide lectures.
MH

5138. ———. Prophetic numbers; or the rise, progress and future destiny of the "Mormons," by a free thinking optical professor, who will deliver lectures on the subject. Illustrated by stereoptican dissolving views and zodiacal map. Salt Lake City, Published by W. M. Egan, 1885.
2p.l. [4]–160p. 17cm.
Variant printing at USIC.
CU–B, DLC, MH, MoInRC, UPB, USI, USIC, UU

5139. ———. The testimony of seven witnesses. To show that the gospel dispensation given to Joseph Smith, jr., for the House of Israel by God the Father, and His Son, Jesus Christ, between the sixth of April, Eighteen hundred and twenty and the first of November, Eighteen hundred and thirty-one *is not* the gospel dispensation given to Joseph Smith for the gentiles in June o [sic] Eighteen hundred and twenty-nine, by the angels Peter, James and John. Salt Lake City [1896?]
16p. 21cm.
MH

5140. McDonald, Frank Virgil. Notes preparatory to a biography of Richard Hayes McDonald of San Francisco, California. Comp. and ed. by his eldest child, Frank V. McDonald. V.1 . . . Cambridge, University Press, 1881.
xix [1]p., [3]l. [29]–95, 119p. illus., plates, ports. 34cm.
McDonald was a "new citizen" at Nauvoo in 1846, but was ordered to leave by the "Citizens" committee. (anti-Mormon) He returned after the Mormons left.
CtY, CU-B, DLC, MH, NjP, NN, PHi, USlC, ViU

5141. McDonald, Joseph E. The Late Corporation of the Church of Jesus Christ of Latter-day Saints, Appellants, vs. The United States. Argument of Hon. Joseph E. McDonald for the Appellant. Delivered January 18, 1889. Washington, Gibson Bros., Printers and Bookbinders, 1889.
23p. 23cm.
Cover-title.
At head of title: Supreme Court of the United States.
MH, NjP, USlC

5142. ———. The Late Corporation of the Church of Jesus Christ of Latter-day Saints vs. The United States. No. 1031. George Romney et al. vs. The United States. No. 1054. Petitions for rehearing. J. E. McDonald, Attorney for Appellants. [Washington, 1889]
9p. 23cm.
Cover-title.
At head of title: In the Supreme Court of the United States, October term, 1889.
Signed Jos. E. McDonald, John C. Fay.
USlC

5143. McDonald, William. The life of Reverend John S. Inskip, President of the National Association for the Promotion of Holiness. By W. McDonald and John E. Searles. Boston, Published by McDonald & Gill, 1885.
374p. port. 19cm.
Trip to Salt Lake City in 1871 where he was assisted by Brigham Young. He attended a meeting at which an anti-Mormon sermon was preached; his reactions, p. 263–272.
UHi, USlC

5144. McDowell, Floyd M. Boy scouts and the church. Lamoni, Ia., Reorganized Church of Jesus Christ of Latter Day Saints, 1918.
16p. 16cm.
A special field representative of the boy scouts for the RLDS church.
MoInRC

5145. ———. Can we do as we please? Over Radio KLDS, December, 1925. By Pres. F. M. McDowell. [Independence, Mo., Publicity Dept., Reorganized Church of Jesus Christ of Latter Day Saints, 1925]
40p. illus., port., facsim. 20cm.
Cover-title.
Five lectures delivered over Radio KLDS, Independence, Mo., December, 1925.
MoInRC, NN

5145a. ———. Instructions and suggestions for workers in the Department of Recreation and Expression. [By] F. M. McDowell, General Superintendent. Lamoni, Iowa., Department of Recreation and Expression [ca. 1915]
16p. 19½cm.
USlC

5146. ———. An open letter to the priesthood. [Independence? Mo., Reorganized Church of Jesus Christ of Latter Day Saints, n.d.]
4p. 21cm.
RLDS tract on priesthood.
MoInRC

5147. ———. An open letter to the young people of the church. [n.p., n.d.]
4p. 22cm.
RLDS inspirational music.
MoInRC

5148. ———. The Responsibility of the adult to the adolescent. By Floyd M. McDowell. Independence, Mo., Women's Department of the Reorganized Church of Jesus Christ of Latter Day Saints [n.d.]
14p. 18cm.
USlC

5149. ———. Study outlines for stewardship; suggested by F. M. McDowell. [n.p., n.d.]
28p. 19cm.
Foreword by Frederick M. Smith.
RLDS doctrine.
MoInRC, NjP, NN

5150. ———. The way to the city. Independence, Mo. [Independence? n.d.]
16p. 19cm.
RLDS doctrine on the gathering.
MoInRC, NjP

5151. McDowell, J. F. Discipleism; or the claims of Alex. Campbell to a restored primitive christianity examined. Lamoni, Ia., [Herald Publishing House, 189–]
12p. 21cm. (Reorganized Church tracts. No. 13)
Campbellism vs. Mormonism.
CtY, MoInRC, NN

5152. ———. Songs of valor for all who love the Lord and many who ought to, by J. F. McDowell. Lamoni, Ia., Patriot Job Print., 1890.
60p. 14cm.
RLDS music.
MoInRC

McELRATH, T. P.

5153. McElrath, Thomson P. A press club outing; a trip across the continent to attend the first convention of the International League of Press Clubs, by Thomson P. McElrath, historian of the trip. New York, International League of Press Clubs, 1893.
149 [1]p. illus., ports. 29cm.
Short stopover in Salt Lake City with a brief discussion of Temple Square and Mormon meetings they attended.
CU–B, DLC, UHi, UU

5154. MacFadden, Harry Alexander. Rambles in the far West. Holidaysburg, Pa., Standard Printing House [c1906]
4p.l., 277p. illus., plates. 23½cm.
Chap. XXIX, XXX on Mormons; Salt Lake, p. 217–229.
Visit to Salt Lake City in 1905.
CU–B, NjP, UPB, USlC

5155. MacFarland, James. An address respectfully inscribed to Mrs. Little, by James MacFarland. [Salt Lake City? 189–]
[5]p. 23cm.
Mormon poetry.
UHi

5156. McGavin, Elmer Cecil. Apology for the Book of Mormon. Salt Lake City, Deseret News Press, 1930.
4p.l. [9]–182p. facsim. 19½cm.
USl, USlC, UU

5157. McGee, Joseph Hedger. Story of the Grand River country, 1821–1905. Memoirs of Major Joseph H. McGee. [Gallatin, Mo., The North Missourian Press, 1909?]
2p.l. [63]p. ports. 25cm.
Preface signed: 1909.
Relates that the Mormons saw a meteoric shower of 1833 as a sign from heaven. Includes material on the Mormon war in Missouri.
Howes M101 67p.
CtY, ICN, InU

5158. MacGowan, Alice. Trail of the little wagon, a novel for boys and girls. New York, F. A. Stokes, 1928.
vii, 341p. 19cm.
Juvenile fiction. Story of a wagon and its trip to California.
Has chapters on "The old Mormon Ferry," "Utah," "A Mormon family," and "The tithing house." They found it difficult to escape from Salt Lake City.
CtY, CU

5159. Macgregor, Daniel. Changing the revelations. By Apostle Daniel Macgregor. Milwaukee, Wis., H. B. Miner [1927]
35p. illus., port. 23½cm.
Church of Christ (Temple lot) doctrine.
MH, MoInRC, NjP, NN, UHi, UPB

5160. ———. A marvelous work and a wonder; The gospel restored. By Daniel MacGregor. [n.p., n.d.]
79p. port. 24½cm.
MoInRC, NjP

5161. ———. (same) 2d ed., 15th thousand. Lamoni, Ia., Herald Publishing House, 1911.
135p. illus., ports. 25cm.
MH, MoInRC, NjP, OClWHi

5162. ———. (same) 3d ed., 23rd thousand. Lamoni, Ia., Herald Publishing House, 1917.
168p. illus. 25½cm.
CU–B, MoInRC, NjP, UHi

5163. ———. (same) 4th ed., 33rd thousand. Independence, Mo., The Reorganized Church of Jesus Christ of Latter Day Saints, 1923.
250p. illus., ports., diagrs. 20cm.
DLC, IWW, MoInRC, NjP, OCl

5164. ———. (same, in German) Ein Wunderbares Werk und ein Wunder. Das Wiedergegebene Evangelium. Verfasser Daniel MacGregor, Siebziger. Verlag Herald Publishing House, Lamoni, Iowa, Verein. Staaten. Auch zu beziehen von der Deutschen Mission der Reorganisierten Kirche Jesu Christi der Heiligen der letzten Tage. Berlin, Druck von J. F. Starcke [n.d.]
139p. 24cm.
USlC

———. An open letter to Daniel MacGregor. *See Clark, E. O.*

5165. ———. The time of the end. By Daniel and Margaret Macgregor. [n.p., n.d.]
25p. 20cm.
Doctrine concerning the end of the world.
MoInRC

5166. ———. . . . Why? . . . [Independence, Mo., 1923?]
[4]l. port. 22½cm.
Caption-title.
The problem of Supreme directional control in the RLDS Church.
MoInRC, NN, USlC

5167. ——— (same) [np., ca. 1928]
4p. port. 20cm.
MoInRC, UPB

5168. ———. (same) Port Huron, Mich., Published by Otto Fetting [n.d.]
4p. port. 24cm.
UPB

5169. Macgregor, John. Our brothers and cousins. A summer tour in Canada and the states by John Macgregor. London, Seeley Jackson and Halliday, 1859.
xix, 156p. 16cm.
Mormonism a thing of the past in America, but continues to deceive in England.
USIC

5170. Macgregor, Maggie. Light at evening time. The gospel restored. Independence, Mo., Published under the auspices of the Board of Publication, Church of Christ [n.d.]
4p.l., 7–317p. illus., ports. 20cm.
MoInRC, UHi, UPB, USIC

5171. McGuire, Benjamin R. How much tithing do I owe? [Independence, Mo., Ensign Publishing House, n.d.]
20p. 15cm.
RLDS doctrine on tithing.
MoInRC

5172. ———. Protest against supreme directional control . . . a vigorous protest against this innovation, together with various interesting documents, is herewith published. [Independence? 1924?]
16p. 20cm.
"Reprinted from the *Saints' Herald*, Aug. 20, 1924."
Signed: B. R. McGuire, J. F. Keir, E. A. Smith [and others]
MoInRC, UPB

5173. ———. Some interesting facts relating to the General Conference Auditorium. [n.p., 1924?]
16p. 20cm.
"Reprint from *Saints' Herald*, Nov. 19, 1924."
MoInRC

5174. ———. Stewards all. [Independence Mo., 1923]
[4]p. 14cm.
Signed: Benj. R. McGuire, presiding bishop.
CU–B

5175. ———. The unbroken chain, a treatise on the law of the Lord as relating to the work of the Bishopric, written by the Presiding Bishopric. Shall the historic chain forged from the law and the testimony, extending from 1860 to 1925, continue in the Reorganization? [Independence, 1925?]
20p. 20cm.
Signed: Benj. R. McGuire, James F. Keir, and Israel A. Smith.
Against centralized control.
MoInRC, NjP

5176. McIntosh, W. H. . . . History of Wayne County, New York; with illustrations descriptive of its scenery, palatial residences, public buildings, fine blocks, and important manufactories, from original sketches by artists of the highest ability. Philadelphia, Everts, Ensign & Everts, 1877.
vi, 7–216p. illus., plates (2 double) ports., 2 maps. 36×29cm.
"Mormonism and its founder," p. 149–151.
DLC, MnHi, NBG, NN

5177. Mack, Solomon. A narraitve [sic] of the life of Solomon Mack containing an account of the many severe accidents he met with during a long series of years, together with the extraordinary manner in which he was converted to the Christian faith. To which is added, a number of hymns composed on the death of several of his relations. Windsor [Vt.] Printed at the expence of the author [1811?]
48p. 17½cm.
For imprint data, p. 18, 23.
Hymns, p. 26–42, 45–46.
Though this predates Mormonism, the relationship of the author to his grandson Joseph Smith has made it an important Mormon imprint.
Howes M116
CtY, MB, MH, NN

5178. Mackay, Charles. Life and liberty in America; or, Sketches of a tour in the United States and Canada in 1867–8. With ten illustrations. London, Smith, Elder, 1859.
2v. illus., plates. 20cm.
Chapter XVIII "The Mormons" . . p. 233–239.
A narrative of Mormonism to 1858; the Utah Expedition, and why it was necessary.
Another edition: New York, Harper & Brothers, 1859. DLC, UHi
Howes M118, Sabin 43355
CU, CU–B, DLC, NjP, NN, ULA, USIC, UU

5179. ———. The Mormons: or Latter-day Saints. With memoirs of the life and death of Joseph Smith, the "American Mahomet." Illustrated with forty engravings. London, Office of the National Illustrated Library [1851]
3p.l. [v]–x p., [1]l. [ix]–x [15]–326p. illus., ports. 20cm.
Half-title: National illustrated library.
Listed in Sabin as written by Henry Mayhew. It seems to have been edited by Charles Mackay from various sources. Published with and without half title.
Variant title pages.
Sabin 47126
CSmH, CtY, CU, CU–B, DLC, ICHi, ICN, IWW, MH, NjP, NN, UHi, ULA, UPB, USIC, UU, WHi

5180. ———. (same) 3d edition. Illustrated with forty engravings. London [Vizetelly and Co. Printers and Engravers] 1852.
viii, 10–320p. illus., ports. 19½cm.
Added engraved title page.
Sabin 47126
MH, MoInRC, MoU, NjP, NjPT, NN, UHi, ULA, USIC, UU, WHi

5181. ———. (same) A contemporary history. [Edited] by Charles Mackay . . . London, Houlston & Wright [1856?]
xiii [15]–308p. illus. 18½cm.
"Fourth edition"
CtY, CU–B, UHi, UU

5182. ———. (same) Illustrated with forty engravings. 4th ed., rev. and cor. London, Ward and Lock [1856]
2p.l. [iii]–xiii, 308p. illus., ports. 19½cm.
Sabin 47126
CU–B, DLC, MH, NN

5183. ———. (same, under title) History of the Mormons; or, Latter-day saints! With memoirs of the life and death of Joseph Smith, the "American Mahomet." Auburn [N.Y.] Derby and Miller, 1852.
viii p., [1]l. [17]–399p. plates. 20cm.
CU–B, DLC, MH, NjPT, NN, OClWHi, PMA, WHi

5184. ———. (same) Auburn [N.Y.] Derby and Miller, 1853.
vii p., [1]l. [17]–399p. plates. 20cm.
At head of title: Second thousand.
CU–B, CSmH, DLC, OO

5185. ———. (same) Auburn and Buffalo, Miller, Orton & Mulligan, 1854.
vii [1] [17]–399p. plates. 19½cm.
At head of title: Third thousand.
CU–B, DLC, ICHi, NjP, OClWHi, UHi, UPB, WHi

5186. ———. (same, under title) Life among the Mormons; or, The religious, social and political history of the Mormons from their origin to the present time; containing full statements of their doctrines, government . . . and memoirs of their founder, Joseph Smith. By Samuel M. Smucker . . . with important additions by H. L. Williams. New York, Hurst and Co., [188–]
viii [17]–466p. illus. 19cm.
"Arlington ed."
CSmH, CtY, CU–B, MoInRC, NjP, NjPT, NN, UHi, ULA, UPB

5187. ———. (same, under title) The religious, social, and political history of the Mormons, or Latter-day Saints, from their origin to the present time; containing full statements of their doctrines, government and condition, and memoirs of their founder, Joseph Smith. Edited, with important additions, by Samuel M. Smucker . . . New York and Auburn, Miller, Orton & Milligan, 1856.
viii [17]–460p. plates. 19cm.
ICN, DLC, GEU, ICU, MH, MoInRC, RPB, UHi, UPB, USlC, ViU

5188. ———. (same) New York, Miller, Orton and Co., 1857.
viii [17]–460p. plates. 19½cm.
Variant printings.
CtY, NN, UHi, UPB

5189. ———. (same) New York, C. M. Saxton, 1858.
viii [17]–460p. plates (part col.) 20cm.
CSmH, DLC, ICN, MH, NjPT, NN, UHi, WHi

5190. ———. (same) New York, C. M. Saxton, Barker & Company, 1860.
viii [17]–460p. plates (part col.) 20cm.
CU–B, UPB

5191. ———. (same) New York, Hurst & Company [c1881]
viii [17]–466p. plates. 20cm.
Variant printings. USlC
DLC, MB, MH, MWA, NN, NNC, OCl, RPB, USlC, UU, WHi

5192. ———. (same, in Swedish) Mormonerna, eller De Yttersta dagarnas heliga; ett bidrag till nutidens historia, ur engelska källor. Stockholm, Tryckt af Aftonbladets Trykheri, 1853.
3p.l., 187p. illus., ports. 19½cm.
CtY

5193. McKay, David Oman. Ancient apostles. Written for the Deseret Sunday School Union. Salt Lake City, Deseret Sunday School Union, 1918.
3p.l., 277p. illus., col. maps. 18cm.
DLC, ULA, USl, USlC, UU

5194. ———. (same) 2d ed. Salt Lake City, Published by the Deseret Sunday School Union, 1921.
vi, 248p. illus., plates, maps. 19cm.
MH, NjP, UHi, UPB, USlC

5195. ———. (same) 4th ed. Salt Lake City, Deseret Book Company, 1926.
vi, 248p. illus., maps. 20cm.
NjP, USlC

5196. ———. The reality of the resurrection; address delivered over Radio Station KSL on the evening of Easter Sunday, April 17, 1927. [Salt Lake City] 1927.
Broadside. 46×25cm.
UPB

5197. ———. The ruthlessness of war: address delivered over Radio Station KSL, Sunday Evening, January 8, 1928. [Salt Lake City] 1928.
Broadside. 45½×23½cm.
Reprinted from the *Deseret News*, Saturday, January 14th, 1928.
UPB

5198. ———. Suggestions on teaching; an address delivered by Elder David O. McKay in Tabernacle at the October Conference, 1916. [Salt Lake City, 1916]
8p. 15cm.
Teaching within the church.
UPB, USIC

5199. ———. Suggestions on Ward Teaching. Salt Lake City, Presiding Bishop's Office [1912?]
11p. 17½cm.
Reprinted from the *Improvement Era*, Nov. 1912.
UPB

5200. McKay, Emma Ray. Leitfaden für die Frauen-Hilfsvereine für das Jahr 1925. Für die Europäische Mission der Kirche Jesu Christi der Heiligen der letzten Tage bearbeitet von Emma Ray McKay. Aus dem Englischen übersetzt von Marg. Hoyer. Basel, Herausgegeben von Fred Tadje, Präsident der Schweizerischen und Deutschen Mission . . . [1925]
115p. 20cm.
Title in English: Manual for the Relief Society.
USIC

5201. McKay, Kathryn. Soul-mates; a one-act play. Salt Lake City, General Boards of M.I.A., 1929.
16p. 19cm.
Suggested by the story, "Four sides to a triangle," by Edith Bernard Delano.
USIC

5202. McKeeby, Lemuel Clarke. The memoirs of Lemuel Clarke McKeeby. The overland journey. San Francisco, California Historical Society, 1924.
75p. fold. map. 26cm.
Encounters Mormons in Salt Lake City in 1850 and along trail in Utah.
NjP, UPB

5203. McKim, B. L. An appeal. [Independence? n.d.]
13p. 21cm.
Supreme directional control in the RLDS Church.
MoInRC

5204. ———. An explanation and statement. [n.p., n.d.]
6p. 21cm.
Problem of Supreme directional control in the RLDS Church.
MoInRC

5205. ———. The first presidency. Whence comes its authority. "Is it of God or is it of men?" [n.p., n.d.]
[4]p. 28cm.
Caption-title.
Supreme directional control in the RLDS church.
CU-B, MoInRC

5206. ———. The Foundation of the Church of Jesus Christ. [Independence, Mo., n.d.]
4 pts. (4, 4, 13, 19p.) 22½cm.
Part 2 has sub-title: "The Gathering" 4p.
Part 3 has sub-title: "Revelation" 13 [1]p.
Part 4 has sub-title: "The Revelations" 19p.
MoInRC, UPB, USIC, UU

5207. ———. Has the church a prophet at its head? [n.p., n.d.]
12p. 18cm.
Signed: Ogden, Utah.
MoInRC

5208. ———. A message of hope. [n.p., n.d.]
12p. 21cm.
RLDS church doctrine.
MoInRC

5209. ———. Prepare ye the way of the Lord. [Independence, Mo., n.d.]
16p. 21cm.
RLDS doctrine of the Kingdom of God.
MoInRC

5210. ———. Succession of ministerial authority, where to be found. [n.p., n.d.]
14p. 21cm.
Signed: Independence, Mo.
MoInRC

5211. ———. What shall we do with the Book of Mormon? [Independence, Mo.? n.d.]
8p. 22½cm.
Book of Mormon apologetics.
MoInRC, UPB

5212. ———. Where does the church stand? [n.p., n.d.]
11p. 17cm.
Signed: Ogden, Utah.
Centralized authority in the RLDS church.
MoInRC

5213. McKinley, Henry J. Brigham Young; or, The prophet's last love. A play in three acts. San Francisco, Bacon and Co., 1870.
30p. 18cm.
Cover-title.
ICHi, NN, USIC

5214. Mackinnon, Lauchlan Bellingham. Atlantic and transatlantic; sketches afloat and ashore, by Captain Mackinnon, R. N. . . . New York, Harper & Brothers, 1852.
viii, 324p. 20cm.
Recounts some of the assaults against James J. Strang and discusses the seditious nature of the Utah Mormons and the foolishness of their claims.
Another edition: London, Colburn and Co., Publishers, 1852. DLC, USIC
UHi, USIC

5215. MacKnight, James Arthur. Hagar, a tale of Mormon life. By James Arthur MacKnight . . . New York, Chicago [etc.] Belford, Clarke & Co. [c1889]
321p. 19½cm.
Fiction about Mormonism.
DLC, USlC

5216. ———. (same) New York, A. L. Burt [190–]
321p. 19cm.
CSmH, WHi

5217. M'Laughlin, A. C. Mormonism measured by the gospel rule, and found deficient: being the substance of a sermon delivered at White's school house, Kenton Co., Ky. By A. C. M'Laughlin, a local preacher of the Methodist Episcopal Church. — Hold fast all things; prove that which it good. — Covington, Ky., Printed at the Office of the Licking Valley Register, 1842.
32p. 16cm.
Caption-title: Mormonism exposed.
USlC

5218. McLaughlin, *Mrs.* W. J. The diary of a Utah girl by Mrs. W. J. McLaughlin. New York, Chicago [etc.] Broadway Publishing [c1911]
2p.l., 5–159p. plates. 20cm.
A fictitious diary of a girl writing during 1902–03; a non-Mormon who has fantasies concerning Brigham Young.
DLC, UHi, USlC, WHi

5219. McLaughlin, William. Side lights on scripture; being a short treatise on various scriptural subjects — and over which there have been and still is much controversy — and an honest endeavour to place some of those controverted matters before the reader in a more intelligible light than others may have done. Sydney, S. D. Townsend & Co., Printers, 1916.
101p. 18cm.
A Biblical commentary by a RLDS member.
MoInRC, NjP

5220. MacLeod, N. W. Picturesque Cardston and environments; a story of colonization and progress in Southern Alberta. Cardston, N. W. T., and N. W. MacLeod, 1900.
116p. [20]l., plates, ports. 21½cm.
Mormon colonization in Canada.
UPB

5221. McLeod, Norman. A discourse on mobs and the mob spirit, by Rev. N. McLeod. Delivered to an immense Congregation at Independence Hall, Salt Lake City, Sunday Evening, August 4, 1872. [Salt Lake City, 1872?]
14p. 18½cm.
Castigation of Mormon leaders leading the dupes as a mob.
USlC

5222. ———. (same) [Salt Lake City, 1872?]
15p. 18cm.
USlC

5223. ———. (same) [Salt Lake City, 1872]
11p. 16cm.
USlC

5224. MacMaster, John Bach. A brief history of the United States. New York, American Book Co. [c1907]
434, xxxp. illus. 21cm.
Mormons, p. 312, 342, 410.
DLC, USlC

5224a. ———. History of the people of the U.S. from the Revolution to the Civil War . . . New York, D. Appleton and Co., 1883–1913
8v. plates, maps. (part fold.) 22½cm.
Joseph Smith and early Church history, V. 6, p. 102–107; Missouri period, V. 6, p. 249–250, 454–458; Nauvoo period, V. 7, p. 208–221.
Another edition: 1927–29. DLC
CU, DLC, NjP, NjPT, ULA, UPB

5224b. ———. A primary history of the United States. New York, American Book Co. [c1901]
254p. illus. 19cm.
Mormons, p. 188–189.
USlC

5225. McMillan, Duncan Bhann. The Bible search light thrown onto Mormonism. by D. B. McMillan . . . [n.p., 1901]
75p. port. 18cm.
DLC

5226. McMillan, Duncan James. Historical sketch of Mormonism. By Rev. D. J. McMillan. New York City, League for Social Service [189–]
14p. 15cm. (Series D — Anti-Mormon leaflets. No. 3)
At head of title: Social Science. Series D. — Anti-Mormon.
MH, MoInRC, OClWHi, UPB, USlC, USl, WHi

5227. ———. (same) Historisk Skiss öfver Mormonismen af Teol. D: R. D. J. McMillan, öfversatt af Pastor P. E. Åslev. New York City, League for Social Service [1900?]
14p. 14cm. (Serien D. — Anti-Mormon)
At head of title: Till Samhällets Tjänst.
NN

5228. ———. Mormon "Articles of faith" explained. By D. J. McMillan, D. D. [New York?] The Board of Home Missions? [189–]
8p. 22½cm. (No. 62)
Caption-title.
MoInRC, NN, OClWHi, USlC

5229. ———. (same) [New York? n.d.]
16p. 17cm.
MoInRC

5230. ———. (same) Philadelphia, The Westminster Press, 1900.
16p. 21cm.
NN

5231. McMillan, Henry G. The inside of Mormonism. A judicial examination of the endowment oaths administered in all the Mormon temples, by the United States District Court for the Third Judicial District of Utah, to determine whether membership in the Mormon church is consistent with citizenship in the United States. Salt Lake City, Published by the Utah Americans, 1903.
93p. 22½cm.
"Copyright applied for by Henry G. McMillan, Salt Lake City, Utah."
CSmH, ICN, MoInRC, NjP, NN, UHi, USlC, UU, WHi

5232. McNiece, R. G. The Christian reconstruction of Utah. Two sermons preached in the Presbyterian Church, March 23 and 30, 1879. By the Pastor, Rev. R. G. McNiece. [Salt Lake City, Tribune Office, 1879]
12p. 21½cm.
"Reprinted by the *Daily Tribune*."
NN, USlC

5233. ———. Present aspects of Mormonism. By Rev. R. G. McNiece. New York, League for Social Service, 1899.
14p. 15cm. (Social Service. Series D. Anti-Mormon)
MoInRC, NN, ULA, USl, USlC

5234. McQuarrie, John Gray. Atonement. Salt Lake City, 1906.
27p. 22cm.
Reprinted from the *Improvement Era*, February, March and April, 1906.
USlC

5235. ———. Talks to the saints by John G. McQuarrie, Pres. of the Eastern States Mission of the Church of Jesus Christ of Latter-day Saints. New York [Published by the author] 1906.
63p. 17½cm.
MH, IWW, NjP, UHi, USl, USlC, UU

5236. McRae, Joseph A. Facts for thinkers by Elder Joseph A. McRae. A tract. [Independence, Mo., Published by the Missions of the Church of Jesus Christ of Latter-day Saints, n.d.]
[4]p. 18cm.
NN, USlC

5236a. ———. (same) [Denver, Colorado, Western States Mission, 1910?]
3[1]p. 15cm.
USlC

5236b. ———. (same) [Independence, Mo., Missions of the Church of Jesus Christ of Latter-day Saints, 1918?]
3[1]p. 16½cm.
Variant printings.
USlC

5236c. ———. (same) [Independence, Mo., Missions of the Church of Jesus Christ of Latter-day Saints, 1926?]
[4]p. 17cm.
USlC

5237. ———. Story of old Carthage Jail; where an angry mob martyred Joseph and Hyrum Smith . . . Carthage, Ill. [The author, n.d.]
31p. ports. 18cm.
Half-title: Story of the old Carthage Jail and the history of the tragedy that made it world famous.
USlC, UU

McRedwood, A. Mormonism.
See Irvine, William C.

5238. McVey, A. M. Debate held at the Pennsville, Ohio, Church of Christ between A. M. McVey of the Church of Christ and F. J. Ebeling of the Reorganized Church of Christ [sic] of Latter-day Saints commencing Friday, January 5, 1906, Ending Wednesday, January 17, 1906. Cincinnati, F. L. Rowe [1906]
2p.l. [5]–200p. 22½cm.
USlC

5239. Maeser, Karl Gottfried. School and fireside, by Karl G. Maeser . . . [Provo, Utah] Skelton & Co., 1898.
1p.l., iii, 3, 358p. ports. 22cm.
Mormon education.
CU–B, DLC, NjP, UHi, UPB, USl, USlC, UU

5240. ———. Sunday School work; a series of lectures, under the auspices of the Deseret Sunday School Union, delivered in the Assembly Hall. Salt Lake City, beginning Monday evening, June 13, and closing Saturday evening, June 18, 1892. Reported by John Whitaker. Salt Lake City, Jos. Hyrum Parry, Printer [1892]
60p. 15½cm.
CLU, MH, USlC, UU

5241. Maeser, Reinhard. Karl G. Maeser, a biography by his son, Reinhard Maeser. Provo, Utah, Brigham Young University, 1928.
184p. port. 19½cm.
Biography of a Mormon educator.
CU–B, DLC, NjP, UHi, ULA, UPB, USlC, UU

5242. ———. Sketches from life and labors of Willson Gates Nowers, by Reinhard Maeser . . . Beaver, Utah, Weekly Press Print., 1914.
92p. illus., port. 22½cm.
Biography of an early Beaver pioneer.
UHi, ULA, USlC

Magazine Printing Company.
See Temple souvenir album.

5243. Magoffin, Susan (Shelby). Down the Santa Fe trail and into Mexico; the diary of Susan Shelby Magoffin, 1846–1847, edited by Stella M. Drumm . . . New Haven, Yale University Press; London, H. Milford, Oxford University Press, 1926.
xxv, 294p. plates, port., fold. map. 24cm.
Brief mention of Joseph Smith's surrender to Lucas, and Doniphan's refusal to obey the execution order, p. 121–123.
Howes M211
CU-B, DLC, NjP, UPB

5244. Mahaffey, James Ervin. Found at last! "Positive proof" that Mormonism is a fraud and the Book of Mormon a fable. Including a careful comparison of the Book of Mormon with the original Spalding [sic] MS., which shows twenty-two points of identity! By Reverend J. E. Mahaffey. Augusta, Ga., Chronicle Job Office [1902?]
70p. 22½cm.
Cover-title.
CtY, MoInRC, OO, USlC

5245. Maiben, Henry. An invitation. [Brighton, 1852]
[1]p. 19½×11cm.
Poem signed: Nov. 18, 1852.
Missionary invitation.
MH

5246. ———. A song for the "Mormons," [and other poems] [n.p., 1853?]
4p. 18½cm.
Mormon poetry.
MH

5246a. Maiben, John Bray. Dedicatory prayer offered by President John B. Maiben in the new school house at Mount Pleasant, Sanpete County, Utah, on Friday, January 15th, 1897. [n.p., 1897?]
[3]p. 26cm.
USlC

5247. Maine. Legislature. State of Maine. Resolve relating to the assassination of John King Robinson at Salt Lake City . . . [Augusta?] Stevens & Sayward, Printers to the State [1867]
2[1]p. 22cm. (Maine. 46th Legislature. House. No. 62)
Assassination by a supposed band of Mormons acting under authority.
MH, UHi

5248. Major, Gertrude (Keene). The revelation in the mountain. By Gertrude Keene Major, with an introduction by Judge C. C. Goodwin. New York, Cochrane Publishing Co., 1909.
160p. illus., ports., plates, plans. 20cm.
Chap. 1–12 short stories, 13 The oath of vengeance.
Mysteries of the endowment house and oath of vengeance of the Mormon church, as testified to by Professor Walter Wolfe, late of the B[righam] Y[oung] College at Logan, and the whole Endowment.
CSmH, DLC, MH, MoInRC, NjPT, NN, UHi, UPB, USlC, UU, WHi

5249. Majors, Alexander. Seventy years on the frontier; Alexander Majors' memoirs of a lifetime on the border; with a preface by "Buffalo Bill" (General W. F. Cody) Ed. by Colonel Prentiss Ingraham. Chicago and New York, Rand, McNally & Company, 1893.
325p. illus., plates, ports. 20½cm. (On cover: Rialto series. No. 10)
Background information concerning Mormonism with reminiscences of 10 years in Salt Lake City.
Another edition: Denver, The Western Miner and Financier, 1893? UHi, UPB
CSmH, DLC, ICN, NjP, UHi, ULA, UPB, USlC, UU

5250. Majors, John. Common sense: or, thoughts of a plain man, in regard to several things of importance written by one of the oldest settlers of Missouri Territory. [n.p.] 1878.
60p. illus. 21½cm.
"The Mormons in Missouri," p. 24–32.
The mob action in Missouri.
CtY

5251. Malad Stake Messenger. Malad, Idaho, October 1, 1921–September, 1922.
v. monthly, semi-monthly. 23–27cm.
USlC V. 1 #3–15, December 1, 1921–September, 1922

5252. Malan, Stephen. The ten tribes, discovered and identified; the four historic phases of the house of Jacob considered by Stephen Malan. [Ogden, Utah] The A. L. Scoville Press, 1912.
170p. port. 18cm.
DLC, UHi, ULA, USlC, UU

5253. Malebitis, Nikol Ath. "O kyrios e dikaisyne ymon" . . . [Athenai?] 1903.
[2]p. 23cm.
A tract distributed in No. 1 of Penrose's "Aktines zontos fotos."
Title in English: Oh God, have mercy.
USlC

5254. Malony, Richard M. Factional Mormonism. [Oklahoma City, Okla? n.d.]
37p. 20cm.
Concerning authority in the RLDS and Church of Christ (Temple Lot)
MoInRC

5255. Malortique, Edouard. Les adventures d'un Mormon; Dialogue en trois parties par Edouard Malortigue. Paris, Jules Lévy, Libraire-Editeur, 1886.
2p.l., 74p. 18½cm.
Title in English: The adventures of a Mormon.
NN

5256. Mandeville, James H. . . . Remarks of J. H. Mandeville, Counsel for plaintiff, Thomas McBride, vs. Carl Schurz, Sec. of the Interior, Supreme Court, U.S., October 12 1880. I. Are we drifting into monarchy? II. Mormon disloyalty. III. McBride's Trials in Washington. Washington, R. Beresford, Printer, 1880.
61p. 23cm.
NN

5257. Manford, Erasmus. Twenty-five years in the West. Chicago, E. Manford, 1867.
2p.l. [3]-359p. 19cm.
The autobiography of a Universalist minister. Mormonism, p. 211–212.
Reprinted several times.
Howes M250, Sabin 44246
DLC, NjP, UPB

5258. Manly, A. Stewart. Kidnapped; or, secrets of a great mystery . . . By A. Stewart Manly. Copiously illustrated by H. S. DeLay. Chicago, Rhodes & McClure Pub. Co., 1899.
xiii, 17–428p. illus., plates. 20cm.
Chap. XXX, Aunt Mandy's tour of Salt Lake City. Fiction.
USlC

5259. Manly, William Lewis. Death valley in '49. Important chapter of California pioneer history. The autobiography of a pioneer detailing his life from a humble home in the Green mountains to the gold mines of California; and particularly reciting the suffering of the band of men, women and children who gave "Death Valley" its name. By William Lewis Manly. San Jose, California, The Pacific Tree and Vine Co., 1894.
498p. plates, port. 20cm.
Distrust at traveling through Utah because of the Mormons; Chief Walker and his Mormon relations.
Other editions: Chicago, R. R. Donnelley & Sons, 1927. DLC; New York, W. Hebberd, c1929. DLC, UHi, UPB; Santa Barbara [1929] CU-B, ICN, NN
Howes M255
CU-B, DLC, ICN, MH, NjP, NN, ICN, PP, PPL, PU, USlC

5260. Manly & Litteral. Utah; Her cities, towns and resources. Together with a condensed but comprehensive account of her financial, commercial, manufacturing, mining, and agricultural enterprises. Her progress and population in the past, and possibilities for the future. Chicago, W. B. Conkey Co. Printers, 1891–1892.
viii, 224p. illus., ports. 31cm.
Mormonism mentioned as little as possible.
CSmH, CU-B, OO, UHi, ULA, UPB

5261. Mann, Horace. Census of Great Britain, 1851. Religious worship in England and Wales. Abridged from the official report made by Horace Mann, esq., to George Graham . . . London, George Routledge and Co. . . . 1854.
ix, [2]l., 142p. 21cm.
"The Latter-day Saints, or Mormons," p. 47.
History of the church with its basic doctrines and statistics of Mormonism in England.
MH, USlC

5262. ———. Sketches of the religious denominations of the present day. With the number of sects in England and Wales, and an introductory sketch of the progress of religious opinions in England till the period of the revolution of 1688 . . . and the census, comprising the number of each denomination. Abridged from the official report made by Horace Mann . . . to George Graham. 24th thousand (Rev.) London, George Routledge [n.d.]
ix, 142p. 23cm.
"The latter-day Saints, or Mormons," p. 47–52.
USlC

5263. Manning, Samuel. American pictures drawn with pen and pencil, by the Rev. Samuel Manning . . . London, The Religious Tract Society [1876?]
224p. illus., plates. 28cm.
"Amongst the Mormons," p. 61–82. Description of a stay in Salt Lake City and his impression of Mormonism.
CU-B, DLC, UHi, UPB

5263a. ———. A Travers les Etats-Unis. D'après Samuel Manning, LL.D. Avec notes et additions considérables par le traducteur du Ministère de l'Enfance. Toulouse: Société des Livres Religieux, 1880.
208p. 27½cm.
"Le Pays des Mormons," p. 47–64.
Title in English: Across the United States.
UPB

5264. Manning, William H. The Danite Chief; or, the Mormon's plot. New York, 1881.
33p. 17cm.
Fiction concerning Mormonism.
Eberstadt: *Utah and the Mormons.*

5265. ———. Gold Gauntlet, the gulch gladiator; or, Yank Yellowbird's hot campaign. By William H. Manning. New York, Beadle and Adams Publishers, 1887.
30p. 28½cm. (Beadle's Dime Library. V. XXXVI. No. 463)
Locale: Utah. Mormons, Danites, and Yank Yellowbird.
Gold Gauntlet fights against the Mormons.
NN

MANT, W. B.

5266. Mant, Walter Bishop. Mormonism a heresy, contrary to Holy Scriptures, condemned by the witness of the Catholick Church, and repugnant to common sense. A sermon, preached in the parish church of Hillsborough, on Sunday, the 30th October, 1842. With an appendix of illustrations and proofs. By the Ven. Walter B. Mant, M.A., Arch-deacon of Down. Belfast, George Phillips, Bridge-Street, W. Grapel, Liverpool, 1843.
47p. 17½cm.
CtY, CU–B

5267. Maori Agricultural College Korongata, Hasting, New Zealand. Catalogue and announcement. Korongata, Hastings, New Zealand, 1913–30.
v. 21cm.
Name changed from: Latter-day Saints Agricultural College.
USIC 1913–14, 1914, 1918, 1919, 1920, 1921, 1922, 1923, 1924, 1925, 1926, 1929, 1930

5268. Marchmont, John [*pseud.*] An appeal to the American Congress. The Bible law of marriage against Mormonism. [Philadelphia? 1873]
16p. 18cm.
Mormons and polygamy.
Reprinted in the author's *The word of God on true marriage.*
CSmH, CtY, CU–B, DLC, MH, UU

5269. ———. An appeal to the Reverend Clergymen of the United States on behalf of the primal law of God for mankind. By the author of "Opinions concerning the Bible law of marriage." Philadelphia, Claxton, Remsen and Haffelfinger, 1873.
35p. 18½cm.
A general tract against polygamy with specific reference to the "foul tenet of the Mormon doctrine."
CtY, DLC, NN

5270. ———. Opinions concerning the Bible law of marriage. By one of the people . . . Philadelphia, Claxton, Remsen & Haffelfinger, 1871.
2p.l., vii–xii, 13–239p. 19½cm.
Includes Mormonism and polygamy.
DLC, ICU, MB, NN, USIC

5271. ———. The word of God on true marriage . . . Philadelphia, Claxton, Remsen & Haffelfinger, 1877.
xii, 13–284p. 19cm.
Includes a discussion of the Mormon doctrine of plural marriage.
DLC

5272. Marcy, Randolph Barnes. The prairie traveler. A hand-book for overland expeditions. With maps, illustrations, and itineraries of the principal routes between the Mississippi and the Pacific. By Randolph B. Marcy . . . Published by authority of the War Department. New York, Harper & Brothers, 1859.
xiii [15]–340p. illus., plates, fold. map. 17½cm.
References to Mormons and the Mormon trail, p. 19–22, 31, 36, 112, 113, 143, 185, 247, 255, 256, 266, 273–277, 281–282, 287, 317–318, 323, 327–328.
Other editions: London, Sampson Low, 1860. ICN; New York, Harper & Bros., 1861. DLC, NjP; London, Trübner and Co., 1863. CtY, DLC, NjP, UPB, USIC
Howes M279, Sabin 44514, W–C 335
DLC, ICN, NjP, NN, PHi, PPA, UHi, ULA, UPB, ViU, WaU

5273. ———. Thirty years of Army life on the border. Comprising descriptions of the Indian nomads of the plains; explorations of new territory; a trip across the Rocky Mountains in the winter; descriptions of the habits of different animals found in the West, and the methods of hunting them; with incidents in the life of different frontier men, &c., &c. By Colonel R. B. Marcy . . . With numerous illustrations. New York, Harper & Brothers, 1866.
1p.l. [ix]–xvi [17]–442p. illus., plates, front. 22cm.
"Return trip to Utah," Utah expedition, etc.
Howes M280, Sabin 44516
CSmH, CU–B, DLC, MdBP, NjP, NN, OCl, OrP, OrU, OU, PU, TxH, UHi, ULA, USIC, WaS, WaU

5274. Marden, George Nathaniel. The growth and grip of Mormonism. By Professor George N. Marden. Boston, Frank Wood, Printer, 1885.
16p. illus. 14cm.
"First printed in *The Christian Union*."
CLU, ICN, MB, MH, MWA, NjP, NN, OO, USIC

5275. Marečkova, Josefina. Duchovné Prúdy v' Našej Republike. Zostavila Josefina Marečkova. II dielo: Prúdy Cerkevné. Bratislava, Nakladatel' stvo Časopisu., Bratislavská Poštä, 1926.
1p.l. [3]–424p. 31½cm.
"Mormonská cerkev u Čsl republice," p. 233–236.
Title in English: Spiritual currants in our republic.
USIC

5276. Marjoribanks, Alexander. Travels in South and North America. London, Simpkin, Marshall; New York, D. Appleton, 1853.
xiv, 480 p. col. front. 21½cm.
"The Mormonites." Under the descriptions of religious sects.
Another edition: 5th ed. 1854. CU–B, DLC
Howes M290, Sabin 44609
DLC, NjP, UPB, UU

5277. Marks, David. The life of David Marks, to the 26th year of his age. Including the particulars of his conversion, call to the ministry, and labours in itinerant preaching for nearly eleven years. Written by himself. Limerick, Me., Printed at the Office of the Morning Star, 1831.
396p. port. 18cm.
Visit with the Whitmer family in 1830; his evaluation of the *Book of Mormon* and its witnesses.
Sabin 44604
CSmH, ICN, MH, MWA, NH, NN, NNU–N, RPB, USIC

5278. ———. (same, under title) Memoirs of the life of David Marks, Minister of the gospel; edited by Mrs. Marilla Marks. Dover, N. H., Free-will Baptist Printing Establishment, 1846.
xi [13]–516p. port. 20½cm.
Another edition: 1847. CSmH
Howes M293, Sabin 44625
CSmH, CtY, CU, DLC, MWA, NH, NjP, NN, OCH, OO

5279. Marmeir, Xavier. De l'est à l'ouest; voyages et litterature . . . Paris, L. Hachette et Cie., 1867.
2p.l., 413p., [1]l., 4p. 19cm.
"Les Mormons chez eux," p. [335]–394.
Title in English: From the east to the west, voyages and literature.
CtY, ViU

Marriage, monogamy and polygamy.
See Giles, Alfred.

5280. Marryat, Frederick. Narrative of the travels and adventures of Monsieur Violet, in California, Sonora, & Western Texas. Written by Capt. Marryat, C. B. . . . London: Longmans, Brown, Green, & Longmans, Paternoster Row, 1843.
3v. fold. map. 21cm.
Also published in 1843 under the same title in Leipzig and under the title "Travels and romantic adventures" in London and in New York. Republished in many English editions and numerous translations.
Mormon material lifted verbatim from William Harris' "Mormonism portrayed," Warsaw, Ill., 1843.
W–C 97
CSmH, CtY, NjP, NN, UPB

5281. Marsden, John Buxton. Dictionary of churches and sects from the earliest ages of Christianity. By the Rev. J. B. Marsden. New ed. London, Richard Bentley, 1854.
3p.l., 954p. 22½cm.
"Mormonites or Latter-day Saints," p. 570–582.
USlC

5282. ———. (same, under title) History of Christian churches and sects, from the earliest ages of Christianity. By the Rev. J. B. Marsden . . . London, R. Bentley; [etc., etc.] 1856.
2v. 22cm.
Arranged alphabetically.
DLC

5283. Marshall, Robert. The missionary's farewell to Zion. By Robert Marshall. [n.p., 188–]
4p. 21cm.
Mormon poetry.
MH

5284. ———. Our hearts with thee, by Robert Marshall. [Suggested upon reading the cowardly attacks upon President George Q. Cannon. n.p., 188–]
4p. 21cm.
Mormon poetry.
MH

5285. Marshall, Thomas Philip. Mormonism exposed, by Thomas Philip Marshall, ex-elder of the Utah Mormon Church, with the secret workings, washings, anointings, and ceremonies performed in their temples. Together with the secret signs, grips, and their names by which they can make themselves known to one another, either in crowds, or walking along the streets of our cities. Also the horrible and barbarous punishments inflicted upon all who dare to divulge these secrets outside their temple walls. [St. Louis, Ponath — Bruewer Printing Company c1908]
4p.l. [9]–80p. 16cm.
MH, McHi, MoInRC, NjPT, UPB, USlC, WHi

5286. Marshall, Walter Gore. Through America; or, Nine months in the United States. By W. G. Marshall . . . London, S. Low, Marston, Searle and Rivington, 1881.
xx, 424p. illus., plates, port. 23cm.
Account of the Mormons Chap. VII–XI, p. 147–236. A critical discussion of Mormonism.
Published in Danish under title: Gjennem Amerika. Kjøbenhavn, O. H. Delbanco, G. E. C. Gad, F. Hegel, C. C. Lose, 1882. UPB
Published in Swedish under title: Genom Amerika. Stockholm, Albert Bonniers Förlag [1882]
NjP, NN, UPB
Another edition: London, S. Law, Marston, Searle & Rivington, 1882. CtY, MH, NjPT, USl, UU
CSmH, CtY, CU–B, DLC, IWW, MiU, NjP, NN, PPL, PSC, UHi, USlC, UU, ViU, WHi

5287. Marston, Edward. Frank's ranche; or, My holiday in the Rockies; being a contribution to the inquiry into what we are to do with our boys . . . 2d ed. London, Sampson Low, Marston, Searle and Rivington, 1886.
xvi, 214p. illus. 16½cm.
Letter no. XIV tells of polygamy and polygamist trials, p. 167–184.
Other editions: Boston, New York, Houghton-Mifflin, 1886. UPB
CU–B, NjP, ULA, USlC, UU

5288. Martens, P. Ch. Geheime Gesellschaften. Lehrbriefe zur Einführung in das Ordenwesen von P. Ch. Martens. Bad Schmiedeberg . . . und Leipzig, Verlag von F. E. Bauman [ca. 1919]
2p.l. [5]–208p. port. 17cm.
"Die Mormonen," p. [143]–144. Under a section concerning other orders.
Title in English: Secret societies.
USlC

Martin, Edward Winslow [*pseud.*]
See McCabe, James Dabney, Jr.

5289. Martin Ezra Francis. A brief history of Ezra Francis Martin; autobiography. [n.p., n.d.]
15p. 35½cm.
Mimeographed.
Mormon biography.
UPB

5290. Martin, George Washington. How the Oregon trail became a road. Salt Lake City, The Deseret News, 1906.
52p. port. 19cm.
"Published by resolution of the Presbyterian Teachers' Association, Mount Pleasant, Utah."
Mormon emigration, p. 44–46.
CU–B, DLC, UHi, UPB

5291. ———. Mormon oneness. [n.p., 1905?]
6p. 11cm.
Continuance of the political problem of Mormonism.
USIC

5292. Martin, Moses. A treatise on the fulness of the everlasting gospel, setting forth its first principles, promises, and blessings. In which some of the most prominent features that have ever characterized that system, when on the earth, are made manifest; and that it will continue to do so, so long as it can be found on the earth. By Elder Moses Martin . . . New York, J. W. Harrison, Printer, 1842.
64p. 15½cm.
Doctrinal discourse by a Mormon Elder.
Sabin 44904
CtY, DLC, NN, USI, USIC

5293. ———. (same) 2d ed. London, Printed by F. Shepard, 1846.
60p. 14½cm.
MH, UHi, UPB, USIC

5294. Martin, Samuel H. [Doctrines of the Church of Jesus Christ of Latter-day Saints. Kansas City, Kansas? 1926?]
[4]p. 23×15cm.
A Strangite tract without title, discussing divine authority, church organization, principles and doctrines of the true church, repentance, baptism, the laying on of hands, and the resurrection of the dead.
Signed at end: Elder S. H. Martin, Route 4, Kansas City, Kansas.
Morgan
UHi, WBuC

5295. ———. Important: to whom this may concern. By S. A. Martin [and others. Kansas City, Mo.? 1928?]
[1]l. 20½cm.
Strangite tract.
USIC

5295a. ———. To whom this may concern. [By] Samuel H. Martin [and others. Kansas City, Mo.? n.d.]
[1]l. 14cm.
Strangite tract.
USIC

5296. Martin, Stuart. The mystery of Mormonism [by] Stuart Martin . . . London, Odhams Press, Limited [1920]
318p. illus., plates, ports., facsim. 22cm.
CU–B, DLC, ICN, NjP, NjPT, NN, UHi, USI, USIC, UU, WHi

5297. ———. (same) New York, E. P. Dutton [1920]
318p. plates, ports. 22cm.
MoInRC, UHi, UPB

5298. Martin, T. H. Corroborative evidence of the apostasy. [n.p., 1910]
[3]p. 19cm.
Cover-title.
"The following clipping was sent in for publication in *Liahona, The Elders' Journal* by Elder Burus Cox, a missionary in the Northwestern States. It appeared in the *Anaconda Standard*, Montana, January 31, 1910, and was reproduced in *Liahona*, March 19, 1910."
Use of non-Mormon sources to prove Mormon doctrine.
Variant editions.
UHi, USIC

5299. Martin, Thomas L. Lesson book for the Religion Classes in the Church of Jesus Christ of Latter-day Saints. Fifth Grade. Written for the General Church Board of Education by Thomas L. Martin. [Salt Lake City] Published by the Deseret Book Company, 1924–25.
124p. 19cm.
UPB, USIC

5300. Martius, Moritz. Die Mormonen-karawane oder der Kampf an der Felspyramide. Eine Indianergischichte von Moritz Martius. Stereotyp-Ausgabe. Reutlingen. Druck und Verlag von Ensslin und Laiplin. [1884?]
1 p.l., [3]–62 [2]p. 16½cm.
In orange printed wrapper with series note: Neue Volksbücher Nr. 185.
Title in English: The Mormon caravan.
UPB

Mary Teresa Austin Carroll, *Mother.*
See Carroll, Mary Teresa Austin.

5301. Mason, John. The Latter-day Saints, The dupes of a foolish and wicked imposture. A reprint from a tract by John Mason of London. Cape Town, S. A., Saul Solomon and Co., 1853.
32p. 17cm.
Another tract signed J. M. entitled *Mormonism dissected* mentioned in the *Millennial Star*, V. 20, p. 380.
USIC

5302. Mason, John Yancy. The Ephraimite's vengeance, the key to Cainism, Mormonism and patriarchy. By John Yancy Mason, the Ephraimite from the wilderness of the people of Mount Vernon, Illinois. Marion, Ill., Stafford Publishing Company, 1911.
88 [2]p. 18cm.
Poetry about Mormonism.
MoInRC, UPB

5303. ———. The Horns of Joseph and key to Christian patriarchy by John Yancy Mason. [Mount Vernon, Ill.? 1909]
40p. 16cm.
First part deals with the *Book of Mormon* proofs. Second part deals with the Order of Melchizedek.
MoInRC

5304. Mather, Irwin F. The making of Illinois; historical sketches. Chicago, A. Flanagan Co. [c1911]
276p. illus., plates, ports., maps. 17½cm.
Chapter entitled "Nauvoo and the Mormons." Includes the political implications of the Nauvoo period.
Other editions: [c1913] [c1916] [c1917] 1922, 1926. DLC
DLC, UU

5305. Mathews, Amelie Veronique (Petit) Child. Plural marriage; the heart-history of Adele Hersch. By Veronique Petit. Ithaca, N.Y., E. D. Norton, Printer, 1885.
99p. 20cm.
"Pub. to aid the work of the Women's National Anti-polygamy Society."
CU-B, DLC, MH, NN

5306. ———. (same) Ithaca, E. D. Norton, 1885.
99p. 20cm.
"Second edition."
CU-B

5307. Mathews, Edward James. Crossing the plains, adventures of Edward James Mathews in '59. [n.p., privately printed, 1930?]
91p. 18cm.
Diary: April 7–September 16, 1859. Various references to Mormons; impressed by them.
DLC, MH, NN, USl

5308. Matteson, J. G. Prophecies of Jesus, or, The fulfillment of the prediction of our savior and his prophets. By J. G. Matteson. Battle Creek, Mich., International Tract Society, 1895.
566p. illus. 23cm.
Mormonism, p. 133–149, under heading: "Two false isms in the last days."
MoInRC

5309. Matthiesen, H. I. F. C. Hvad er Mormonismen? Udg. af Kirkelig Forening for den indre Mission i Danmark. København, Kirkelig forening for den Indse Mission i Danmark, 1903.
3p.l., 7–50p. 19cm.
Title in English: What about Mormonism.
CtY, NjP, UPB

5310. Mattison, Hiram. A Scriptural defence of the doctrine of the Trinity; or, A check to modern Arianism, as taught by Campbellites, Hicksites, New Lights, Universalists and Mormons; and especially by a sect calling themselves "Christians." By Rev. H. Mattison. New York, L. Colby & Co., 1846.
xii, 162p. 16cm.
Other editions: 5th ed. New York, L. Colby & Co., 1850. DLC; New York, Huntington and Savage, 1851. USIC; New York, L. Colby, 1851. DLC
DLC, USIC

5311. Maurois, Andre. La Vie de Joseph Smith. Les 49 ronins du quai malaquais . . . Paris, Edouard Champion, 1927.
59p. 20cm.
Title in English: The life of Joseph Smith.
MoU

5312. Maxwell, William Audley. Crossing the plains, days of '57; a narrative of early emigrant travel to California by the ox-team method, by Wm. Audley Maxwell. [San Francisco, Sunset Publishing House, 1915]
4p.l., 179p. front., illus., plate, ports. 18cm.
Brief mention of Mormons along the trail.
CU-B, DLC, ICN, NjP, UPB, USl

5313. Maury, Wm. A. Appeal from the district court, Territory of Utah, in the matter of Lorenzo Snow. [Washington, 1885]
12p. 21½cm.
Eberstadt: *Utah and the Mormons.*

5314. ———. Appeal from the Third Judicial District Court, Salt Lake County, Territory of Utah. Brief for the United States. [Washington, 1885]
12p. 22cm.
In blue printed wrapper.
At head of title: Supreme Court of the United States. October Term, 1886. Ex Parte: In the matter of Lorenzo Snow, Petitioner, Appellant. N. 1282.
UPB

5315. Maxwell, Archibald. A run through the United States during the autumn of 1840, by Lieut. Col. A. M. Maxwell. London, H. Colburn, 1841.
2v. front. 19½cm.
Short description of the "Mormonites."
Howes M444A, Sabin 47047
CU, NjP, NN

MAXWELL, R.

5316. Maxwell, Robert. Why the Mormon people should drop Joseph Smith as a Prophet. [Salt Lake City, 1909]
[8]p. 22cm.
From the *Salt Lake Tribune*, August 22, 1909. Politics and Mormonism.
USlC

5317. Maxwell, W. T. A statement issued by the Re-Organized Church of Jesus Christ, July 4th, 1908. J. L. Armbrust, Armbrust, Pa. [and] W. T. Maxwell, Greenburg, Pa. publishing committee. [Youngwood, Pa.?] 1908.
[6]p. 15×10cm.
Cover-title.
Signed: Elder W. T. Maxwell.
Bickertonite publication.
Morgan
MoInRC, PMonC, UHi

5318. May, Roderick. Divine Authority. [London? 1914?]
4p. 21cm.
Priesthood authority, RLDS church.
MoInRC

5319. ———. Gathering surplus, tithing and equality, by the Independence Stake Bishopric; Roderick May, A. H. Parsons, B. J. Scott. Independence, Mo., 1909.
20p. 20cm.
Tithing and stewardship in the RLDS church.
MoInRC

5320. ———. The Reorganized Church of Jesus Christ of Latter Day Saints versus the Utah Mormons, self-styled, Latter Day Saints. [n.p., n.d.]
8p. 22cm.
MoInRC

Mayhew, Henry. *See Mackay, Charles.*

5321. Mead, B. M. The history of Mormonism with particular reference to the founding of New Jerusalem in Franklin County. [Chambersburg?] 1923.
411–427p. 23½cm. (Papers read before the Kittochtinny Historical Society, Chambersburg, Pa. Vol. 9. 1923)
DLC, MiU, NN, OClWHi, PHC, PHi

5322. Meakin, John Phillips. Leaves of truth; Utah and the Mormons, by John Phillips Meakin. Papers, poems and letters. An appeal for a nobler manhood. Salt Lake City, 1909.
2p.l. [iii]–viii, 274 [2]p. plates, port. 20cm.
CU–B, DLC, MoInRC, NjP, NN, USl, UHi, ULA, UPB, USlC, UU, WHi

5323. ———. Senator Reed Smoot; the man. By John P. Meakin (not a Mormon) [n.p., n.d.]
16p. 14½cm.
USlC

5324. ———. Uplifting thoughtful articles by John P. Meakin, not a Mormon, a resident of Salt Lake City since 1869. [Salt Lake City, John P. Meakin, 1905?]
31p. 15½cm.
"John P. Meakin, not a Mormon. A Fraternalist. A resident of Salt Lake City since 1869."
NjP, WHi

5325. Meears, George A. The geese of Ganderica; their history their sense and nonsense. By a Utah goose. [Salt Lake City] Salt Lake Herald Print., c1882.
35 [1]p. 17cm.
Cover-title.
A historical satire using geese as people in the United States. Tells of Revolutional War, Civil War, and the last four pages deals with the government's effort to abolish polygamy. Geese flee from diseased geese and come to Ganderica, but will not be left alone. Written at the height of the polygamy crusade by a pro-Mormon.
DLC, MH, NN, USlC, UU, WHi

5326. Meeker, Nathan Cook. Life in the West; or, stories of the Mississippi Valley. New York, Samuel R. Wells, 1868.
vi [2] 7–360p. 20cm.
"Going to be a Mormon: or, Life on the Western Reserve," p. 252–263. Fiction.
Sabin 47378
CU–B, DLC, NjP, UPB

5327. Meeting for the relief of the Mormons. The meeting was organized on motion of the Hon. Judge Kane, who named as President, the Hon. John Swift, Mayor . . . [n.p., n.d.]
Broadside. 25×20cm.
Signed: Thomas S. Cavender, Secretary.
Including a list of officers of the meeting.
Resolving that the emigrant Mormons to Illinois receive protection as the right of every American citizen.
Printed on blue paper.
USlC

5328. Mehling, Mary Bryant. Cowdrey — Cowdery — Cowdray genealogy: William Cowdery of Lynn, Massachusetts, 1630, and his descendants. By Mary Bryant Alverson Mehling. [New York] Frank Allaben Genealogical Company [c1911]
451p. plates, ports., facsims., col. coat of arms. 23cm.
Article on the life of Oliver Cowdery, p. 172–186, by A. E. Cowdery.
DLC, MB, MoInRC, MWA, NN

5329. Meilhede, Peder. Oplysninger om Mormonsamfundet i Utah, deres løgne og Bedragerier . . . No. 1. Kjobenhavn, Petersen i Hjorring, 1863.
12 [2]p. 16cm.
Title in English: Enlightenment concerning the Mormon church in Utah.
NN, UHi

MERKLEY, C.

5330. ———. Oplysninger om Mormonsamfundet i Utah, deres løgne og Bedragerier . . . No. 2. Kjobenhaven, Petersen i Hjorring, 1864.
11 [2]p. 16cm.
NN, UHi

5331. Melchisedek & Aaronic Herald. Covington, Kentucky. February 1, 1849–April, 1850.
lv. (9 nos.) 29½cm.
Edited and published by Isaac Sheen, who parted with William Smith in May 1850, after which the paper ceased publication.
Title varies: Aaronic Herald. February 1, 1849; Melchisedec and Aaronic Herald, March, 1849 (#2); Melchisedeck and Aaronic Herald, May 1, 1849 (#3); Melchisedek & Aaronic Herald.
Morgan
MoInRC Ap. 1850; USIC Feb. 1, 1849–Sept. 1849–50; WHi Feb. 1, 1849

5332. Melish, John Howard. Franklin Spencer Spalding, man and bishop, by John Howard Melish. New York, The Macmillan Company, 1917.
vii, 297p. port. 22½cm.
Episcopal Bishop in Salt Lake City.
Includes his reactions to Mormonism and his writings to disprove it.
CU–B, DLC, NjP, NN, OCl, UHi, USIC, UU

5333. Melle, P. J. van. Het Mormonisme door P. J. Van Melle, Pred. to Nijkerk o/d Veluwe. Neerbosch, Neerbosch' Boekhandel, 1912.
16p. plates on verso of front cover; recto of back cover. 17½cm.
Cover-title.
Title in English: Mormonism.
MH

5334. Memorial addresses in honor of Dr. John R. Park, State Superintendent of Public Instruction, delivered before the joint assembly of the Legislature of the State of Utah, February 6, 1901. Salt Lake City, The Deseret News, 1901.
15p. 22½cm.
UHi, USl, USIC

5335. Memorial presented to Moses Thatcher by his friends as a testimonial in behalf of civil liberty and the American state as separate from the church. Salt Lake City, 1896.
86p. 22cm.
Cover-title: Moses Thatcher memorial presented by his friends as a testimonial in behalf of civil and religious liberty.
WHi

5335a. Memorial services and dedication of monument at the grave of Daniel H. Wells, Monday, May 29, 1905, at 4 o'clock p.m., City Cemetery, Salt Lake City, Utah. [Salt Lake City, 1905]
[8]p. illus. 21½cm.
USIC

5336. Men of affairs in the state of Utah; newspaper reference work. [Salt Lake City] Compiled by and published under the supervision of the Press Club of Salt Lake, 1914.
[394]p. ports. 32cm.
Includes biographies of many Mormons.
CSmH, NjP, UHi, ULA, UPB, USIC, UU

5337. Mendenhall, Thomas. Life and experience of Thomas Mendenhall, sen. during forty-two years in the Church of Jesus Christ of Latter-day Saints, given by himself, now over eighty years of age. Salt Lake City, 1886.
16p. 17cm.
Principal residences: Spanish Fork, Franklin, Ida.
CtY

5338. Mercy — the prize of the law abiding and obedient. Justice — the claimant of the lawless and disobedient. Judgment — The reward of lawlessness and disobedience. [San Francisco, 1884?]
[1]p. 22½cm.
Tract of the Church of the Messiah.
USIC

5339. Merewether, Henry Alworth. By sea and by land; being a trip through Egypt, India, Ceylon, Australia, New Zealand, and America, all round the world. By Henry Alworth Merewether . . . London, Macmillan and Co., 1874.
xvi, 343 [1]p. front. 19cm.
Brief stop in Salt Lake City and a discussion of polygamy.
Another edition: 1900. PPM
CtY, CU–B, DLC

5340. Mérimée, Prosper. Mélanges historiques ét littéraries, par Prosper Mérimée . . . Paris, Michel Léry frères, 1855.
2p.l., 382p., [1]l. 19cm. (On cover: Bibliotheque contemporaine, 2. serie)
First essay: Les Mormons.
Title in English: Historical and literary miscellany.
Another edition: 1876. NjP
CtY, CU, DLC, NN

5341. Merkley, Christopher. Biography of Christopher Merkley. Written by himself. Salt Lake City, J. H. Parry & Company, 1887.
46p. 18cm.
Mormon biography.
CLU, CSmH, CtY, CU–B, DLC, ICN, MH, MoInRC, NjP, NN, UHi, UPB, USIC, UU, WHi

5342. ———. A small selection of choice hymns for the Church of Jesus Christ of Latter Day Saints. By C. Merkley. [n.p.] Printed for the publisher, 1841.
32p. 11cm.
USIC

5343. Merrill, Ambrose Pond. Diagrams illustrating Latter-day Saint principles [by] A. P. Merrill. [Ogden, Utah, 1922]
[9]p. 21½×29½cm.
Cover-title.
UHi, UPB

5344. ———. (same) [n.p., 1923]
[12]p. illus. 21½×29½cm.
USIC

5345. Merrill, Amos Newlove. Balance wheels, written for junior seminary students, by Amos N. Merrill . . . Salt Lake City, Pub. by the Deseret Book Company for the Dept. of Education of the Church of Jesus Christ of Latter-day Saints [c1930]
xi, 252p. illus. 20cm. ([Church of Jesus Christ of latter-day saints. Dept. of education] Class book. No. 3)
"A book designed for the moral and ethical training of youth." — Pref.
DLC, UHi, UPB, USIC, UU

5346. ———. Lesson book for the Religion Classes in the Church of Jesus Christ of Latter-day Saints. Seventh Grade. Written for the General Church Board of Education by Amos N. Merrill. [Salt Lake City] Published by the Deseret Book Company, 1924.
162p. 19cm.
USIC

5347. ———. (same) [Salt Lake City] Published by the Deseret Book Company [c1924]
162p. 19½cm.
Variant printing.
USIC

5348. Merrill, Harrison Reuben. Bart of Kane County and other stories. Provo, Utah, Post Publishing Co. [c1925]
147p. illus. 20cm.
Story of Mormon missionaries, p. 58–72. Fiction.
UPB, USIC

5349. ———. Lesson book for the Religion Classes in the Church of Jesus Christ of Latter-day Saints. Fourth grade "In the Days of the Pioneers." Written for the General Church Board of Education by Harrison R. Merrill. [Salt Lake City] Published by the Deseret Book Company [1924]
3p.l., 7–165p. 19cm.
USIC

5350. ———. (same) [Salt Lake City] Published by the Deseret Book Company, 1925.
3p.l., 7–165p. 19cm.
Variant printing, with new title page and cover.
UPB, USIC

5351. ———. A Reader for the Religion Classes of the Church of Jesus Christ of Latter-day Saints. 1923–24. Written for the General Church Board of Education by Harrison R. Merrill of the Brigham Young University. [Salt Lake City] Published by the Deseret Book Company, 1923.
118p. 18½cm.
UHi, UPB

5352. ———. (same) [Salt Lake City] Published by the Deseret Book Company, 1925.
117p. 19cm.
USIC

5353. Merrill, Joseph Francis. The logic of the M.I.A. slogan. [Salt Lake City] 1925.
7p. 23cm.
UPB

5354. ———. Why the Mormon church? Address delivered over Radio Station KSL, Sunday Evening, May 22, 1927. [Salt Lake City] 1927.
Broadside. 48×25½cm.
Reprinted from the *Deseret News*.
UPB

5355. Merrill, Melvin C. Heroes and heroines of service and right. Written for the General Board of Education By Melvin C. and Amy Lyman Merrill. [Salt Lake City] Published by the Deseret Book Company, 1925.
167p. 19cm. (Lesson Book for the Religion Classes. Sixth Grade)
USIC

5356. ———. (same) 2d ed. of 2500. [Salt Lake City] Published by the Deseret Book Company, 1926.
167p. 19cm. (Lesson Book for the Religion Classes. Sixth Grade)
USIC, UPB

5357. Merrit, Edward A. The city of St. Anna. The story of The Man Child, written by Edward A. Merrit. [Salt Lake City, Century, c1908]
2p.l. [5]–133p. 17cm.
A novel, partially devoted to Mormonism; allegorical prose.
DLC, NN, USIC

Merryweather, F. From England to California. *See From England to California.*

5358. Messaros, Waldo. The Mormon question. Philadelphia, 1884.
18p. 18cm.
Reviews the history of the Mormons and denounces the practice of polygamy.
Noted in an Eberstadt advertisement.

5359. ———. The road to heaven, a Book for all who love the truth for truth's sake. Being a religious, philosophical, historical and scientific study of God, nature, the soul, the spiritual man, the moral man, the natural man, man as a social and immortal being, his virtues, vices, affections, hopes, aspirations, aims and destiny. And a handbook for all who seek that "city which hath foundations whose builder and maker is God . . ." Illustrated with steel engravings. Philadelphia, Globe Bible Publishing Co., 1888.
714p. 23cm.
Chap. 28. "Mormonism." Polygamy and its evils. Also includes Mormon history and a summary of its doctrine.
USlC

5360. The Messenger. The monthly organ of the Latter-day Saint Sunday School, Newcastle District. North Shields, Northumberland, England, April, 1927–[September, 1930?]
4v. monthly. 28cm.
In June, 1929, it became the organ of the district.
Last issue. V. 4, No. 9, September 1930.
USlC comp.

5361. The Messenger. Auckland, New Zealand, Published . . . by the New Zealand Mission, Church of Jesus Christ of Latter-day Saints, January, 31, 1907 — December 29, 1915.
9v. semi-monthly. 25cm.
Final issue: V. 9, No. 26.
V.1 called: *Elders' Messenger*, with last section in Maori called *Te Karere*. At first it was 8p. (5 English and 3 Maori) enlarged to 12 (7, 5) 16 (9, 7)p. V.2 issued separately.
UPB V.1 inc., 2, 3, 4 inc., 5, 6, 7 inc., 8, 9; USlC V.1, 2 inc., 3, 4, 5, 6, 7–8 inc., 9

5362. The Messenger. Independence, Mo., Published monthly in the interests of better church government in the Reorganized Church of Jesus Christ of Latter Day Saints, October 1, 1925–1932.
8v. monthly. 26–28½cm.
January 1926 sub-title reads: Published monthly in the interest of better church government (published by a group of members of the Reorganized Church)
July, 1926, Published . . . by the Church of Jesus Christ.
Editor: T. W. Williams. Merged with *Torch of Truth.*
Published by a group in opposition to the centralized control instituted by Frederick M. Smith.
DLC V.1, MoInRC, USlC

5363. Messenger and Advocate of the Church of Christ. Pittsburgh, Penn., Oct. 15, 1844–1846.
2v. semi-monthly, monthly. 22½cm.
Title varies: Oct. 15, 1845, The *Latter Day Saints Messenger and Advocate.* Apr. 15, 1845, *Messenger and Advocate of the Church of Christ.*
Editors: October 15, 1844 — February 15, 1845, Sidney Rigdon; March 1, 1845, Samuel Bennett.
Organ of the church Rigdon attempted to found after his expulsion from Nauvoo in 1844.
Morgan
CtY V. 1–2, lacking V.2 #7; DLC V.1, lacking #7; MoK V.1 #1–24; NN V.1; USlC V.1

5364. The Messenger of the Reorganized Church of Jesus Christ of Latter Day Saints. Salt Lake City, November, 1874 — February, 1877.
3v. monthly. 29cm.
RLDS publication for "the inhabitants of these valleys . . . especially the Latter-day Saints."
MoInRC, NN V.1–3 #2

5365. The Messenger of Truth. Independence, Mo., October, 1900–April 1901.
V. 1, No. 1–6. monthly. 22cm.
Published by the Church of Christ.
L. P. Hansen, ed.
Successor to *The Return*; of which the first issue calls itself "the 4th no." None published for November 1900.
USlC

5366. Messenger to the sightless. . . . Provo, Utah, Jan. 1, 1912–1953.
41v. monthly. 30cm.
Printed in braille.
Sponsored by the L.D.S. Church and the Society for the Aid of the Sightless.
Editor: Albert M. Talmage.
Abstracts of L.D.S. writers, *Deseret News* editorials, poetry, etc.
Succeeded by *The New Messenger.*
DLC inc., NN inc., UPB inc., WS inc.

5367. Metcalf, Anthony. Ten years before the mast. Shipwrecks and adventures at sea! Religious customs of the people of India and Burmah's empire. How I became a Mormon and why I became an infidel! By A. Metcalf. [Malad City, Id., 1888]
1p.l., 81p. illus. 18cm.
Howes M559 (lists date as 1880)
CtY, DLC, MH, USlC

5368. The Meteor. [Beaver] Published by the Murdock Student Body, 1917–
v. 18×26cm.
Yearbook.
USlC 1917

Methodism priestcraft exposed. *See R., W.*

5369. Methodist Episcopal Church. Mormonism a power; how and why. By a member of the Utah State S. S. Association. [New York, Woman's Home Missionary Society, Methodist Episcopal Church, n.d.]
[2]p. 16cm.
Tract against polygamy.
USlC

METHODIST EPISCOPAL CHURCH

5370. ———. Utah mission . . . General Conference exhibit of Board of Home Missions and Church Extension. Frontier Department. [n.p., 1924]
[20]p. plates. 23cm.
Views of mission scenes with both Methodist and Mormon buildings shown.
USIC

5371. ———. The world service of the Methodist Episcopal Church . . . Ralph E. Diffendorfer, ed. Chicago, 1923.
viii, [1]l., 704p. illus., maps. 25cm.
The Mormon problem, . . . p. 378–379, 382.
UPB

5372. ———. Cleveland Missionary Convention. The open door. A challenge to missionary advance. Addresses delivered before the First General Missionary Convention of the Methodist Episcopal Church, held in Cleveland, Ohio, October 21 to 24, 1902. Editors Charles H. Fabs, Stephen J. Herben, Stephen O. Benton. New York, Eaton & Mains, 1903.
viii, 404p. 23cm.
Only a short paragraph, "Mormonism spreads its loathsome cancer and befouls our republic with the putridity of polygamy."
USIC

5373. ———. Utah Mission. State of affairs in Utah. Outlook, Mormon doctrine, statistics of Christian churches, needs of Utah, ringing resolutions. Action of the Utah Mission, Methodist Episcopal Church, August 17–21, 1899 in session at Salt Lake City, Utah. Salt Lake City, Kinsman Pub. Co., 1899.
15p. 13cm.
UPB

5374. ———. Woman's Home Missionary Society. The indictment against Mormonism. New York City, Woman's Home Missionary Society, Methodist Episcopal Church [n.d.]
[2]p. 15cm.
USIC

5375. ———. Tragedies of Mormon life. New York City, Woman's Home Missionary Society, Methodist Episcopal Church [n.d.]
3p. 16cm.
USIC

5376. The Mexican Colonies. Description of the best routes of colonists, together with a great deal of valuable information about the climate and soil; also regarding customs, duties, purchase of lands, etc. [Juarez, Mexico, 1888]
Broadside. 30½×16½cm.
Letter written to "Editor Deseret News."
Signed: Sept. 24, 1888.
NjP

5377. Meyer, Eduard. Ursprung und Geschichte der Mormonen, mit Exkursen über die Anfänge des Islâms und des Christentums, von Eduard Meyer; mit fünf Abbildungen. Halle a. S. verlag von Max Niemeyer, 1912.
vi, 300p. 4 port. 23½cm.
Title in English: Origin and history of the Mormons.
Recently translated into English.
CtY, CU-B, DLC, ICN, MB, MiU, NjP, NjPT, NN, PU, USIC, UU, WHi

5378. ———. (same, in Swedish) Mormonerna deras ursprung och historia av Eduard Meyer Professor vid Berlins Universitet, Bemyndigad översättning av August Carr med ett förord av författaren. Stockholm, Hugo Gebers förlag [n.d.]
226p. 21½cm.
NjP

5379. Meynell, J. B. A few incidents of travel in England connected with the immutable principles of truth, called the gospel of Jesus Christ. By J. B. Meynell, missionary to the British Isles. Boston, Printed by John Gooch, 1845.
24p. 20½cm.
MH

Mezpah [*pseud.*] *See Lea, Henry Charles.*

5380. Michaelis, Pfarrer W. von. Die Mormonen: ein aufklärendes Wort über "Die Heiligen der letzten Tage." Chemnitz, Vert der Buchandlung des Gemeinschaftsvereins [1909]
31p. 19cm.
"3 Auflage."
Title in English: The Mormons.
NN

5380a. ———. Wer sind die Heiligen der letzten Tage? Ein aufklarendes wort uber den Mormonismus. Von P. W. Michaelis. 2. auflage. Bielefeld, Verlag von Otto Fisher [1902]
23p. 21½cm.
Title in English: Who are the Latter-day Saints?
USIC

5381. Michelsen, Christian. Fra Danmark til Saltsøen. Kobenhavn, 1885.
32p.
Title in English: From Denmark to Salt Lake City.
Mulder

5382. ———. Leventsskildring. Los Angeles, 1886.
92p.
Title in English: A biography.
Schmidt

5383. ———. Modgift mod Mormonismen eller livet ved Saltsøen . . . Odense, 1868.
62p.
Title in English: Antidote for Mormonism.
Schmidt

5384. ———. (same) Tredie oplag. Odense, J. C. Dreyer, 1872.
1p.l., 62p. 20cm.
NN, UHi

5385. ———. (same, under title) Modgift mod Mormonismen; en advarsel til mine landsmaend. Af Chr. Michelsen, Tidligere reisende Mormon-Praedikant i Danmark, derefter optaget blandt de indviede i Utah. Haderslev, "Dannevirke's" Offiein, 1872.
68p. 17cm.
CtY

5386. Michelsen, Rasmus. Perler fra Mormons Bog. Samlet og udarbejdet af Rasmus Michelsen . . . København, Udgivet og forlagt af Holger M. Larsen . . . 1929.
16p. 22½cm.
Cover-title.
Title in English: Pearls from the Book of Mormon.
USlC

5386a. Middleton, Charles Franklin. Sketch of the life of Chas. F. Middleton. [Ogden, Utah, Dee-Neuteboom Printing Co., 1914]
[16]p. port. 22cm.
Souvenir; occasion of his eightieth anniversary, 1914.
USlC

5387. Middleton, George William. After twenty years; a dissertation on the philosophy of life in narrative form, by Geo. W. Middleton, M. D. Salt Lake City, Press of the Deseret News, 1914 .
vii, 295p. 19cm.
Philosophy from a Mormon point-of-view.
CU-B, DLC, NjP, UHi, USlC, UU

5388. Midgley, Joshua Hough. Practical co-operation; a series of essays looking to the amelioration of the workingman's industrial and social condition. By J. H. Midgley. [Salt Lake City] 1922.
2p.l., 3–123p. illus., port. 20½cm.
United Order among the Mormons.
DLC, NjP, UPB, UHi, USlC

5389. ———. The United Order. A plan that will enable workers to take out more than they put in; and to have a government of, for, and by themselves. [Salt Lake City, n.d.]
5p.l. [1]–73p. 20cm.
Cover-title: The United Order, its practical accomplishments outlined.
CU-B, DLC, UPB, USlC

Mignonette [*pseud.*] *See Moore, Emily H.*

5390. Miles, Nelson Appleton. Personal recollections and observations of General Nelson A. Miles, embracing a brief view of the Civil War; or, From New England to the Golden Gate, and the story of his Indian campaigns with comments on the exploration, development and progress of our great western empire; copiously illustrated with graphic pictures by Frederic Remington and other eminent artists. Chicago, New York, The Werner Company, 1897 [c1896]
vii, 591p. illus., plates, ports. 25×21cm.
Mormons and Mormonism, p. 362–367; Salt Lake City, p. 367–370.
Another edition: 1816. DLC
Howes M595
CU-B, NjP, UPB

5391. Mill, John Stuart. On liberty. 7th ed. Boston, James R. Osgood, 1871.
223p. 18½cm.
Calls Mormonism a "product of palpable imposture." Considers Mormons and especially polygamous women as slaves to their religion, p. 176–178.
Various editions.
DLC, UPB

5392. Millard Stake Academy. Hinckley, Utah. Millard Stake Academy. Announcement. Hinckley, 1911–
v. 21cm.
USlC 1911–12, 1912–13, 1913–14, 1914–15, 1915–16, 1917–18, 1918–19

Millennial Star and supplements. *See Latter-day Saints Millennial Star.*

5393. Millennial Star Office. Catalogue and price list of Church publications and miscellaneous works. [Liverpool, Millennial Star Office, 1908?]
16p. 15cm.
Cover-title.
In brown wrapper.
For earlier catalogs *see Church of Jesus Christ of Latter-day Saints.*
USlC

Miller [*pseud.*] *See McCosker, John.*

5394. Miller, Edward. The history and doctrines of Irvingism, or of the so-called Catholic and apostolic church. By Edward Miller. London, C. K. Paul & Co., 1878.
2v. 21½cm.
Mormonism in section under title "Prophetic gifts."
DLC, USlC

MILLER, G.

5395. Miller, George. Correspondence of Bishop George Miller with the Northern Islander, from his first acquaintance with Mormonism up to near the close of his life. Written by himself in the year 1855. [Burlington, Wis.? 1916?]
50p. 21½×15cm.
Caption-title.
Originally contributed to the *Northern Islander* August 9–October 18, 1855.
Compiled by Wingfield Watson, from his file of the paper, at Burlington, Wis., probably in 1916. — cf. Dale L. Morgan, *A bibliography of the Church of Jesus Christ of Latter Day Saints.* (Strangite). [1915] p. 88–90.
Howes M605, Morgan
CtY, CU–B, ICN, MH, MiU, MoInRC, NjP, UHi, UPB, USIC, WHi

5396. ———. A Mormon bishop and his son; fragments of a diary kept by G. Miller, sr., bishop in the Mormon church, and some records of incidents in the life of G. Miller, jr., hunter and pathfinder. By Dr. H. W. Mills . . . [n.p.] 1917.
86–174p. ports. 23½cm.
Running title: "De tal palo tal astilla."
Reprinted from the Historical Society of Southern California, Publications. V. 10. Partially duplicates preceding title.
CSmH, CU–B

5397. ———. (same) [London? 192–]
91p. 23½cm.
UU

5398. Miller, H. E. History of the town of Savoy. West Commington, New York, 1875.
26p. 14½cm.
Claims that Joseph Smith founded Mormonism in Savoy, N.Y.
MWA

5399. Miller, J. W. The Cincinnati excursion to California: Its origin, progress, incidents, and results. History of a railway journey of six thousand miles; complete newspaper correspondence . . . . Cincinnati, Published for the Indianapolis, Cincinnati & Lafayette R. R., 1870.
vii, 156p. map. 18cm.
Salt Lake City and the Mormons, p. 32–38.
UHi

5400. Miller, Joaquin. The Danites: and other choice selections from the writings of Joaquin Miller, "the poet of the Sierras" . . . Ed. by A. V. D. Honeyman. New York, The American News Company, 1878.
x [2] 160p. 19½cm.
Fiction concerning the Danites.
Published in many editions.
CSmH, DLC, ICU, IU, MB, MiU, MnU, PSC, UHi

5401. ———. The Danites in the Sierras, by Joaquin Miller . . . Chicago, Jansen, McClurg & Company, 1881.
2p.l. [iii]–iv, 5–258p. 18cm.
Revised edition of his "First fam'lies of the Sierras"
Fiction concerning the Danites.
Other editions: San Francisco, 1882. NjP; Chicago, Belford-Clarde Co., 1889. CSmH; Chicago, Morrill, Higgins & Co., 1892. CSmH; San Francisco, Whitaker & Ray-Wiggin Co., 1910. CSmH, CU–B
CSmH, CU–B, DLC, ICN, MB, MoU, UHi, USl, USIC, UU

5402. ———. First fam'lies in the Sierras. By Joaquin Miller. London, G. Routledge and Sons, 1875.
4p.l., 151p. 16½cm.
Fiction concerning the Danites.
Another edition: Chicago, Jansen, McClurg & Co., 1876. CSmH, CU–B, DLC, NjP
CtY, CU–B, DLC, MH, PPL

5403. ———. Forty-nine. The gold seeker in the Sierras. New York, Funk and Wagnells, 1884.
viii [9]–148p. 19cm.
Includes mention of the Mountain Meadows massacre and the Danites.
Revised and enlarged edition of a story originally published in the *Overland Monthly.*
CU–B, DLC, NjP

5404. Miller, Marion Mills. Great debates in American history, from the debates in the British Parliament on the colonial Stamp Act (1764–1765) to the debates in Congress at the close of the Taft administration (1912–1913) ed. by Marion Mills Miller . . . [The national ed.] New York, Current Literature Publishing Company [c1913]
14v. illus., plates, ports. 24cm.
Federal recognition of polygamy, V.8, p. 401–472.
Three debates on polygamy.
CU, DLC, MoK, NjP, UHi, ULA, UPB, WHi

5405. Miller, Reuben, *compiler.* A defence of the claims of James J. Strang to the authority now usurped by the Twelve, and shewing [sic] him to be the true successor of Joseph Smith, as First President of the high priesthood. [By Reuben Miller. Keokuk, Ia., 1846]
16p. 20½cm.
Caption-title.
Morgan
CtY

5406. ———. James J. Strang, weighed in the balance of truth, and found wanting. His claims as first president of the Melchisedek priesthood refuted. By Reuben Miller, Elder of the Church of Jesus Christ of Latter-day Saints. Burlington, Wis., September, 1846.
26p. 18cm.
Cover-title.
Howes M615 24p., Morgan
CtY, USIC

5407. ———. Lecture. By Reuben Miller, delivered in Mill Creek Ward House, Feb. 11, 1877. Is plural or patriarchial marriage sanctioned by the Almighty, and does sacred history so declare it? [Salt Lake City, The Deseret News?, 1877?]
20p. 21cm.
USIC

5408. ———. Truth shall prevail; a short reply to an article published in the Voree Herald (Reveille) by J. C. Bennett; and the willful falsehoods of J. J. Strang, published in the first number of Zion's Reveille. By Reuben Miller. Burlington, W. T., 1847.
12p. 20cm.
Cover-title.
An attack on the authority of J. J. Strang.
Morgan
USIC with and without cover

5409. Miller, "Walk In" [*pseud.*] Crossing the divide. Written by the author, and read by him, with fearless candor, at a motley gathering commemorative of his first half century; the assembled guests having been first carefully searched and thoroughly disarmed. [n.p., n.d.]
11p. 20cm.
Signed: "Walk In" Miller.
Satirical poem on the Mormon pioneers.
UPB

5410. Milliken, Charles F. A history of Ontario County, New York, and its people, by Charles F. Milliken . . . New York, Lewis Historical Publishing Co., 1911.
2v. illus., ports. 27½cm.
The birth of Mormonism, p. 415–419.
DLC, MB, MWA, OClWHi

5411. Millroy & Hayes, Map Publishers, Salt Lake City. Guide to the route map of the Mormon pioneers from Nauvoo to Great Salt Lake, 1846–1847. Salt Lake City, Millroy & Hayes [1899?]
31p. illus. 23cm.
CSmH, CU-B, NjP, NN, UHi, USIC, UU

5412. Mills, Anson. My story, by Anson Mills . . . Ed. by C. H. Claudy. Washington, D.C., The author, 1918.
412p. illus. (part col.) plates, port. 21½cm.
Trip through Salt Lake City; impressed by the honesty of the Mormons and attended one of their meetings.
Another edition: 1921. NjP, USIC
CU-B, DLC, DNR, ICU, MiU, NjP, NN, OCU, OCl, OClW, USl, UHi, ViU

5413. Mills, Edward Laird. . . . Mormonism — news and views. [Portland? 1926?]
[4]p. 35½cm.
Reprinted from the *Pacific Christian Advocate*, V. 71, nos. 22, 23 (Portland, Ore., Pub. weekly by the Methodist Book Concern)
UHi

Mills, H. W. *See Miller, George. A Mormon bishop . . .*

5414. Mills, William G. Blood Atonement. Fully established as a doctrine and practice of the Mormon Church. [Salt Lake City, 1884]
8p. 26cm.
Signed: Historicus. Salt Lake City, Oct. 25, 1884.
Rebuttal to Charles W. Penrose's discourse on the same subject.
UPB

5415. Milner, Vincent L. Religious denominations of the world: comprising a general view of the origin, history, and condition, of the various sects of Christians, the Jews and Mahometans, as well as the pagan forms of religion existing in the different countries of the earth; with sketches of the founders of various religious sects. From the best authorities. By Vincent L. Milner. Philadelphia, J. W. Bradley, 1860.
xxxiii, 35–512p. front., ports. 22½cm.
A brief resume of Mormonism.
Other editions: Philadelphia, 1868. NjP; Philadelphia, W. Garretson, 1871. ULA, UPB, UU; Philadelphia, Bradley and Co., 1871. DLC; Philadelphia, Bradley and Co., 1872. CU, USIC; Philadelphia, 1873. USl; Philadelphia, Bradley Garretson & Co., 1874. DLC; 1875. CtY, UHi; Philadelphia, 1885. USIC
Also published under title: *The religions of the World*. Philadelphia, Hubbard Bros., 1888. CSmH
DLC, MnU, UU

5416. Ministerial Alliance of Utah. Appeal to the Judiciary Committee of the House of Representatives, unanimously adopted by the Ministerial Alliance of Utah. The remedy for polygamy and polygamous cohabitation. A constitutional amendment. [Salt Lake City, n.d.]
[7]l. 21cm.
Signed: S. E. Wishard.
NN, USIC

5417. Ministerial Association of Salt Lake City. Creed and conduct of the Mormon leaders, a review of the "Address to the World" issued by the General Conference of the Mormon Church, April 5, 1907. Salt Lake City, Tribune Printing, 1907.
13p. 24cm.
MoInRC, UPB

5418. ———. Report on plural marriage. Adopted by the Salt Lake Ministerial Association, February 10, 1902. [Salt Lake City, 1902]
[3]p. 23cm.
CSmH

5419. ———. Shall the American congress endorse polygamy? [Salt Lake City, 1899?]
8p. 21cm.
A paper prepared by a committee of the Salt Lake Ministerial Association.
MH

5420. Minnigerode, Meade. The fabulous forties, 1840–1850, a presentation of private life, by Meade Minnigerode . . . New York & London, G. P. Putnam's Sons, 1924.
xvi, 345p. plates. 23½cm.
References to the Mormons, p. vi, 315, 336.
CU, DLC

5421. Mintun, James F. The one faith and evils of Utah Mormonism briefly outlined. Dow City, Iowa, Enterprise, Printers [n.d.]
8p. 19cm.
MoInRC

5422. Minturn, James F. The Book of Mormon, not from Spaulding's manuscript but a Biblical necessity. Dow City, Enterprise Printers [n.d.]
8p. 20cm.
RLDS apologetics.
MoInRC

5423. ———. The "one faith" and evils of Utah Mormonism briefly outlined. Dow City, Iowa, Enterprise Printers [n.d.]
8p. 19cm.
MoInRC

5424. Minturn, William. Travels west. London, Samuel Tinsley, 1877.
x, 396p. 20½cm.
Chapters 5 and 6 relates to his stay in Salt Lake City, 1875, with his prediction of Mormonism's future.
Other editions: New ed. London, S. Tinsley, 1877. ICN; 3d ed. London, S. Tinsley, 1878. NN, UU
NjP, NN, ULA, UPB, USIC, UU

5425. Minutes of the family gathering. In memory of Alexander S. Standley's 96th birthday held May 12, 1896. At the residence of W. K. Burnham, Richmond, Cache Co., Utah. Logan, Smith, Cummings & Co. [1896]
16p. 21cm.
Mormon biography.
USIC

Misrepresentation decried.
See Church of Jesus Christ of Latter-day Saints. Missions. European.

5426. Missionary experience. . . . [n.p., n.d.]
2p. 28cm.
Duplicated edition.
From the *Deseret Semi-weekly News.* February 24, 1910.
Account of Oliver Cowdery's defense at a Minnesota Trial and his confession of faith in Iowa. The first is doubtful.
UPB

5427. Missouri. Circuit Court (5th Circuit) Document containing the correspondence, orders, &c., in relation to the disturbances with the Mormons; and the evidence given before the Hon. Austin A. King, judge of the Fifth Judicial Circuit of the State of Missouri, at the Court-house in Richmond, in a criminal court of inquiry, begun November 12, 1838, on the trail of Joseph Smith, jr., and others, for high treason and other crimes against the state. Pub. by order of the General assembly. Fayette, Mo., Printed at the Office of the Boon's Lick democrat, 1841.
2p.l., 163p. 23½cm.
Sabin 50734, 83238
CSmH, CtY, DLC, ICN, MoHi, MoK, MoSHi, MoSM, UPB, USIC

5428. ———. . . . Document showing the testimony given before the judge of the Fifth Judicial Circuit of the State of Missouri, on the trial of Joseph Smith, jr., and others, for high treason, and other crimes against that State. February 15, 1841 . . . [Washington, Blair & Rives, Printers, 1841]
47p. 22cm. (U.S. 26th Cong. 2d Sess. Senate. Doc. 189)
Caption-title.
Sabin 83239
CSmH, CtY, CU–B, NjP, NN, UHi, ULA, USIC

———. Mormonism portrayed . . .
See Harris, William.

5429. Missouri. General Assembly. House of Representatives. Journal of the House of Representatives, of the State of Missouri, at the First Session of the Tenth General Assembly, begun and held at the City of Jefferson, on Monday, the nineteenth day of November, in the year of our Lord, one thousand eight hundred and thirty-eight. [Jefferson, Printed by Calvin Gunn, 1839]
471 [1]p. 23cm.
Caption-title.
References to Mormon difficulties, p. 2, 24, 32, 56, 61, 74–75, 78–82, 90, 94, 96, 102–103, 128–129, 133, 135–136, 140, 141, 142, 157, 179, 184, 191, 203–204, 214, 235–236, 245–246, 254–255, 262, 266, 269–271, 278–279, 284, 291–292, 332–333, 367, 371–372, 385–386, 388, 395, 398, 400, 428, 431, 457, 459, 470.
CtY, MoHi, MoSHi, WHi

5430. Missouri. General Assembly. Senate. Journal of the Senate of the Eighth General Assembly of the State of Missouri, begun and held at the City of Jefferson, on Monday the seventeenth day of November, in the year of our Lord, one thousand eight hundred and thirty-four. Fayette, Printed by W. S. Napton, 1835.
412p. 23cm.
Includes Governor Daniel Dunklin's message, Nov. 18, 1834, with reference to the Mormon difficulties, p. 19.
His message is also published in the House Journal of the same year, p. 30–31.
MoSHi

5431. ———. Journal of the Senate, of the State of Missouri, at the First Session of the Tenth General Assembly, begun and held at the City of Jefferson, on Monday, the nineteenth day of November, in the year of our Lord, one thousand eight hundred and thirty-eight. City of Jefferson, Printed by Calvin Gunn, Jeffersonian Office, 1839.
308p. 23cm.
Governor's message includes reference to the Mormon difficulties, p. 13, 27. Also inquiries into Mormon difficulties, p. 47, 50, 58, 81–82, 89, 92–97, 100–104, 123–125, 141–142, 149, 160, 167–168, 172, 175, 186–188, 195, 200, 204, 267, 322, 351.
CtY, MoHi, MoSHi, WHi

5432. Missouri. Governor. 1837–41 (Boggs) Governor's message [To the Senate and House of Representatives] [Jefferson, Calvin Gunn, 1838]
Broadside. 62½×54½cm.
In 6 columns.
Signed at end: Lilburn W. Boggs. City of Jefferson, 20th Nov. 1838.
Mentions the late Mormon difficulties.
MoSHi

5433. Missouri. Laws, statutes, etc. Laws of the State of Missouri, passed at the First General Session of the Ninth General Assembly, begun and held at the City of Jefferson on Monday, the nineteenth day of November, in the year of our Lord, eighteen hundred and thirty-eight. City of Jefferson, Printed by Calvin Gunn, Jeffersonian Office, 1841.
352p. 23cm.
Mormon difficulties, p. 79–81, 314–315.
MoSHi

Missouri. State Department. Document containing the correspondence, orders, &c. *See Missouri. Circuit Court (5th Circuit)*

5434. Mitchell, Langdon Elwyn. Love in the backwoods: Two Mormons from Muddlety, Alfred's wife, by Langdon Elwyn Mitchell. Illustrated by Gilbert Gaul. New York, Harper & Brothers, 1897.
5p.l. [3]–249p. plates. 19cm.
Fiction on Mormons.
Pt. I. Two Mormons from Muddlety. Reprinted from *Harper's Magazine*.
CSmH, CU–B, DLC, ULA, UPB, USlC

5435. Mitford, Reginald Colville William Reveley. Orient and occident: a journey East from Lahore to Liverpool, by Major-General R. C. W. Reveley Mitford . . . With illustrations from sketches by the author. London, W. H. Allen & Co., 1888.
2p.l., iii, 359p. illus. (part fold.) fold. map. 18½cm.
Trip to Salt Lake City in 1884, p. 274–283.
Condemns polygamy, admits greatness of Brigham Young; not impressed otherwise.
DLC, UHi, USlC

5436. Mitton, Sarah Ellen. Keynotes of truth. By Sarah E. Mitton. Logan, Utah [J. P. Smith & Son, Printers] 1922.
28p. 23cm.
Restoration of the Church. Poetry.
USlC

Mizpah [*pseud.*] *See Lea, Henry Charles.*

5437. Mkrdouthuune eakan e phrguthean. Murri, Yetah [Murray, Utah, 1923]
6p. 16½cm.
Published by the California Mission for missionary use among the Armenians.
Title in English: Is baptism essential?
UPB, USlC

Modern Christianity. A dialogue between a Baptist and an infidel. *See Hyde, John.*

5438. Modern temples illustrated. The illustrations presented herewith, forty-six in number, are copies of plates used in the work published in October, 1912, entitled "The House of the Lord" by Dr. James E. Talmage. [n.p., 1912?]
[92]l. 46 plates. 12½cm.
Views of the interiors of the temples. Prints used in Talmage's *The House of the Lord.*
USlC

5439. Moffat, David. The Latter-day Saints' catechism; or, child's ladder . . . being a series of questions adapted for the use of the children of Latter-day Saints . . . London, T. C. Armstrong [1860?]
16p. 21cm.
CtY, USlC

5440. Møller, H. O. Frimodt. Flyveblad mod Mormonismen af H.O.F.M., Sognepraest ved St. Johannes Kirke i Aarhus. Saelges til fordel for opforelsen af en Kansk-luthersk kirke i Saltsostaden. Kirkelig forening for den indre Mission i Danmark. Kovenhavn, Kirkelig forening for den indre Mission i Danmark, 1905.
22p. 19cm.
Title in English: Flying papers [a broadside] against Mormonism.
UPB

5440a. ———. (same) [2 det oplag] Kobenhavn, Kirkelig forening for den indre Mission i Danmark, 1905.
22p. 19cm.
USlC

MÖLLHAUSEN, H. B.

5441. Möllhausen, Heinrich Balduin. Das Mormonenmädchen; eine Erzählung aus der Zeit des Kriegszuges der Vereinigten Staaten gegen die "Heiligen der letzten Tage" im Jahre 1857–1858. Jena und Leipzig, Hermann Costenoble, 1864.
544p. illus. 20cm.
Fiction.
Title in English: The Mormon girl.
W–C 401a
CU–B, USIC

5441a. ———. (same) Dresden [n.d.]
316p.
USIC

5442. ———. (same, in Danish) Mormonpigen. Roman i sex dele. Kobenhavn, 1871.
762p.
Schmidt

5443. ———. Reisen in die Felsengebirge Nord-Amerikas bis zum hoch-plateau von Neu-Mexico, unternommen als Mitglied der im Auftrage der Regierung der Vereinigten Staaten ausgesandten Colorado-expedition. Von Balduin Möllhausen. Mit 12 vom Verfasser nach der Natur aufgenommenen Landschaften und Abbildungen von Indianer-stämmen, Their- und Pflanzen-bildern in Farbendruck, nebst 1 Karte. Eingeführt durch zwei Briefe Alexander von Humboldt's in Facsimile. Leipzig, H. Gostenoble, 1861.
2v. 10 col. plates, fold. map., facsims. 22½cm.
Brief mention of Mormonism.
Title in English: Trips into the Rockies of North America.
Howes M712, Sabin 49913, W–C 362
DGS, IC, MdBP, NjP, NN, NNH, UPB

5444. ———. Tagebuch einer Reise vom Mississippi nach den Küsten der Südsee. Von Balduin Möllhausen. Eingeführt von Alexander von Humboldt. Mit 13 Illustrationen. Leipzig: Hermann Mendelssohn, 1858.
2v. (6p.l., xivp. [1]l., 494 [2]p.) col. plate, fold. map. 21cm.
Title in English: Journal of a trip from the Mississippi to the coasts of the South Sea.
W–C 305
UPB

5445. ———. (same, under title) Wanderungen durch die prairien und wüsten des westlichen Nordamerika vom Mississippi nach den küsten der Südsee, im gefolge der von der regierung der Vereinigten Staaten unter Lieutenant Whipple ausgesandten expedition, von Balduin Möllhausen. Eingeführt von Alexander von Humboldt. 2. aufl. Mit einer lithographirten karte, entworfen von dr. Henry Lange. Leipzig, H. Mendelssohn, 1860.
xvi, 492p. fold. map. 22½cm.
Title in English: Travels through the prairies and deserts of North America from Mississippi to the coasts of the South Seas.
UPB

5446. ———. (same, in Danish) Vandringer giennem det vestlige Nordamerikas prairier og udørkener, fra Mississippi til Sydhavets kyster. Af Balduin Möllhausen. Med et forard af Alexander Humboldt. Obersat af M. Novsing . . . Kjobenhavn, P. G. Philipsens forlag, 1862.
xvi, 476p. plates, fold. map. 22cm.
CU–B

5447. ———. (same, in Dutch) Reis van den Mississippi naar de kusten van den Grooten Oceaan, door B. Möllhausen. Met een voorberigt van Alexander von Humboldt. Vertaals uit het Hoogduitsch door Dr. H. C. Michaëlis . . . Zutphen, A. E. C. van Someren, 1858–1859.
2v. fold. col. plates, fold. map. 23½cm.
UPB

5448. ———. (same, in English) Diary of a journey from the Mississippi to the coasts of the Pacific with a United States government expedition. By Balduin Möllhausen . . . With an introduction by Alexander von Humboldt . . . Tr. by Mrs. Percy Sinnett . . . London, Longmans, Brown, Green, Longmans, & Roberts, 1858.
2v. illus., plates (part col.) fold. map. 22cm.
Meets traveling Mormons; stops at Salt Lake City.
Sabin 49915
CtY, DLC, ICN, MiU, MNu, MoU, NjP, NN, OCU, PPL, UPB

5448a. Mokler, Alfred James. Transition of the West. Portrayal of the Indian Problem in the West and the Trials of the Pioneers Who Reclaimed this Country from Savagery to Civilization . . . Chicago, The Lakeside Press, R. R. Donnelley & Sons Company, 1927.
ix, 228p. plates. 23½cm.
"Westward movement of the Mormons." p. 181–197.
DLC, NjP, UPB

5449. Money, C. F. S. Mormonism unmasked. By the Rev. C. F. S. Money. London, Wertheim, 1857.
17p.
Sabin

5450. Monson, I. G. The difference. A Popular guide to denominational history of doctrine. By I. G. Monson . . . St. Louis, Mo., Concordia Publishing House, 1915.
3p.l. [5]–74p. 23cm.
"The Mormons," p. 18–19.
USIC

5451. Monson, W. P. Character of anti-Mormon propaganda; letters in answer from Governors of Utah, Idaho, Wyoming, Montana, Nevada, Colorado, Washington, Oregon, Arizona, and New Mexico, comp. by Elder W. P. Monson. [Independence, Mo., Zion's Printing and Publishing Company. Published by the Missions of the Church of Jesus Christ of Latter-day Saints in the United States, 1917]
22 [2]p. 17cm.
Cover-title.
Articles of faith on back cover.
Variant printings.
CU-B, NN, UHi, USIC

5452. Monteith, James. Comprehensive geography ... New York, A. S. Barnes, 1877.
104, 7p. maps. 31cm.
On cover: Utah edition.
Geographic and historical material on Utah.
UPB

5453. Montgomery, Marcus Whitman. Admission of Utah. Statement of Rev. M. W. Montgomery, before the Committee on Territories, United States Senate, Monday, March 26, 1888. [Washington, 1888]
[163]–177p. 23cm.
Caption-title.
CtY

5454. ———. The Mormon delusion; its history, doctrines, and the outlook in Utah. Boston and Chicago, Congregational Sunday School and Publishing Society [1890]
5p.l., 11–354p. 19½cm.
CSmH, CtY, CU-B, ICN, MH, MoInRC, NjPT, OO, UHi, USIC, UU, ViU, WHi

5455. ———. Mormonismens vederstyggeligheder afslørede. En advarsel til det danske og Norske folk. Fra det Englske ven Pastor P. E. Trandberg ... Kobenhavn, 1888.
42p.
Title in English: Abominations of Mormonism unveiled.
Schmidt

5456. Moody, Dan W. The life of a rover, 1865–1926. The experiences of the author known in early Western life as Dan Moody, the Indian scout. [Chicago, Ill., 1926]
2p.l., 116p. illus., port., fold-out maps. 22cm.
Life of the Mormons in Utah, by a surveyor.
CU-B, DLC, NjP, UHi, UPB, USIC

5457. Mooney, James. The ghost-dance religion and the Sioux outbreak of 1890, by James Mooney. (In U. S. Bureau of American Ethnology. Fourteenth annual report ... 1892–93. Washington, 1896)
641–1136p. illus., plates (part col.) maps. 29cm.
Mormons, p. 703–704, 719, 790, 792–793, 818, 1108.
The author quotes "A curious pamphlet ... published anonymously at Salt Lake City" in 1892 while the Indian excitement was at its height. The pamphlet is *The Mormons have stepped down and out of Celestial Government — The American Indians have stepped up and into Celestial Government,* by Angus McDonald.
CU-B, DLC

5458. Moore, Emily H. Little gentile; a Deseret romance of captive and exile in the "New Jerusalem" By Mignonette [*pseud.*] Chicago, Printed for the author by the Religio-Philosophical Publishing House, 1879.
2p.l. [5]–94p. 18cm.
Poetry concerning Mormonism.
MH, NjP, RPB

5459. Mooso, Josiah. The life and travels of Josiah Mooso. A life on the frontier among Indians and Spaniards, not seeing the face of a white woman for fifteen years ... Winfield, Kansas, Telegram Print., 1888.
5p.l. [13]–400p. port. 20cm.
Experiences with the Mormons. Chapters on Mormon history and the Mountain Meadows massacre.
Howes M784
CU-B, NjP, ULA, USIC

5460. Moral stories for little folks; for Sunday Schools, Primary Associations and home teaching. Salt Lake City, Printed at the Juvenile Instructor Office, 1891.
vii [9]–160p. 18½cm.
Inspirational literature.
NjP, UHi, UPB, USIC, UU

5461. Morcombe, Joseph E. History of Grand Lodge of Iowa, A. F. and A. M., Volume 1, comprising the history of the Grand Lodge 1844–1865, to which is added a brief history of the Mother Grand Lodge of England and an introduction of Freemasonry into North America, together with sketches and portraits of the Grand masters for the period covered in the history by Joseph E. Morcombe, Historian ... Cedar Rapids, Grand Lodge of Iowa, 1910.
5p.l. [11]–332p. 24½cm.
Chapter V. The Mormon lodges in Iowa, p. 140–174.
Material also published in his *Story of beginning (now for the first time told); organization of Grand Lodge of Iowa, A.F. & A.M.*, 1844.
UPB

5462. ———. Masonry and Mormonism: A record and a study of events in Illinois and Iowa transpiring between the years 1840 and 1846. By Jos. E. Morcombe. [n.p., n.d.]
2 pts. in 1 (p. 445–454, 523–531) 19cm.
Reprint from the *New Age*, April, May, 1905.
ICHi

MORE ABOUT

5463. More about Mormon Roberts. More about Mormon Roberts. A description of the man and his life and some facts as to his wives. The President of the Mormon Church, although eighty-four years old, has a young helpmate and a Bab . . . [copy torn] The Priests and their power. [n.p., ca. 1900]
Broadside. 53½×20cm.
An attack upon Brigham H. Roberts, quoting extensively from the *Cleveland Leader* of Dec. 18, 1898.
IWW

5464. Morgan, D. J. The Gospel of Christ restored. [Independence, Mo., n.d.]
8p. 22cm.
RLDS doctrines.
MoInRC

5465. ———. Temples. Important facts about the building of temples by Latter-day Saints. [Independence, Mo., 1930?]
23p. 18cm.
Caption-title.
MoInRC, NN, UHi

5466. ———. Which is the Divine law? [n.p., n.d.]
4p. 15cm.
Signed: D. J. Morgan.
RLDS church stewardship; comment on changes in revelations of Joseph Smith.
MoInRC, NN

5467. Morgan, Jesse. A trip across the plains in the year 1849, with notes of a voyage to California by way of Panama. Also, some spiritual songs, &c. By Mrs. Martha M. Morgan. San Francisco, Printed at Pioneer Press, 1864.
31p. 22cm.
Journal of Jesse Morgan, published in an edition of 1000 copies by Mrs. Martha M. Morgan. They resided in Salt Lake, October 12, 1849–April 22, 1850.
W–C 402
C, ICN, MH

5468. Morgan, John. Doctrines of the Church of Jesus Christ of Latter-day Saints. [Chattanooga, Tenn., n.d.]
24p. 16cm.
MoInRC, NjP, USIC

5469. ———. Doctrines of the Church of Jesus Christ of Latter-day Saints, its faith and teachings. Liverpool, Republished by D. H. Wells, 1885.
24p. 17cm.
NN

5470. ———. (same) [Salt Lake City? Geo. Q. Cannon & Sons Co., n.d.]
23 [1]p. 17cm.
Caption-title.
At head of title: No. 1.
CSmH

5470a. ———. (same) [Salt Lake City, Geo. Q. Cannon & Co., n.d.]
24p. 17cm.
USIC

5471. ———. (same) Salt Lake City, Deseret News Co. [n.d.]
24p. 15½cm.
CSmH, UU

5472. ———. (same) [Salt Lake City, Juvenile Instructor Office, 1881]
24p. 17cm. (Tract. No. 1)
USIC has copy with wrapper which reads: Tracts on the Doctrines of the Church of Jesus Christ of Latter-day Saints. Salt Lake City, Juvenile Instructor Office, 1881. Wrapper has price lists of book on verso of title and both sides of back cover.
MH, NN, UHi, UPB, USI, USIC

5473. ———. (same) [Liverpool, Republished by George Teasdale, 1888]
24p. 18cm.
USIC

5474. ———. (same) Chicago, Ill., Northern States Mission [189–?]
23p. 16½cm.
Caption-title.
WHi

5475. ———. (same) [Liverpool, Republished by Brigham Young [Jr.] at Millennial Star Office, 1891]
24p. 17cm.
Caption-title.
At head of title: No. 1.
UHi

5476. ———. (same) [Salt Lake City [sic] Millennial Star Office, 1894]
24p. 17cm. (Tract. No. 1)
NN, USIC

5477. ———. (same) [Liverpool, Republished by Anthon H. Lund, 1894]
24p. 17½cm.
Variant printing.
CU–B, NN, USIC

5478. ———. (same) Liverpool, Printed and Published at the Millennial Star Office, 1913.
26p. 18½cm. (No. 1)
UPB, USIC

5479. ———. (same) Liverpool, George F. Richards, 1918.
26p. 18cm. (No. 1)
UHi

5480. ———. (same) [Brooklyn, New York, Eastern States Mission, n.d.]
32p. 14½cm. (No. 1)
MoInRC, UPB

MORGAN, J.

5481. ———. (same) Liverpool, 1921.
26p. 18cm. (No. 1)
NjP, UPB

5482. ———. (same) Liverpool, 1924.
26p. 19cm. (No. 1)
CU-B, UPB

5483. ———. Den Enda Sanna och Eviga Frälsningsplanen. En avhandling av äldste John Morgan . . . Utgiven och förlagd av Gideon N. Hulterström Svenska Missionens huvudkontor: Svartensgatan 3 — Stockholm. [1929]
23p. 18cm.
Title in English: The only true and eternal plan of salvation.
USIC

5484. ———. Na kumu manaoio o ka Ekalesia o Iesu Kristo o ka poe hoano o na la hope nei. Na Elder John Morgan. Unuhiia e J. H. Dina. [Honolulu: Press Publishing Company Steam Print. 1888].
54p. 17½cm.
Caption-title.
Cover-title: Ka elele euanelio. He Buke e Hoakaka Pokole ana i na Kumu Manaoio o ka Ekalesia o Iesu Kristo o ka poe hoano o na la hope nei. He kuhikuhi pauku baibala no hoi, me kekahi mau mea hoomanao e ae. Na J. H. Dina.
Title in English: The foundation of the church.
UPB, USIC

5485. ———. (same) [n.p., 1903?]
63p. 16cm.
UPB

5486. ———. . . . Opinions of the leading statesmen of the United States on the Edmunds law. Gentile opinions of the "Mormon" people. Statistics of crime and education. Refutation of the Spaulding story. Judge Sumner Howard on the Mountain Meadow massacre. By Elder John Morgan. [Salt Lake City, Juvenile Instructor Office, 1885?]
24p. 18cm.
At head of title: Tract. No. 3.
CSmH, CtY, DLC, MH, MoInRC, NjP, NN, USIC, UU, WHi

5487. ———. The Plan of salvation. Independence, Mo., Zion's Printing and Publishing Co. [n.d.]
21p. 18cm.
A brief statement of the doctrines of the Mormon church.
UPB

5488. ———. (same) Independence, Mo., Zion's Printing & Publishing Co. [n.d.]
22p. 19cm.
USIC

5489. ———. (same) Independence, Mo., Zion's Printing & Publishing Co. [n.d.]
22 [1]p. 19cm.
USIC

5490. ———. (same) Independence, Mo., Zion's Printing & Publishing Co. [n.d.]
23p. 17cm.
MoInRC

5491. ———. (same) Independence, Mo., Zion's Printing and Publishing Co. [n.d.]
24 [1]p. 18½cm.
UPB, USIC

5492. ———. (same) [Chicago, Press of A. L. Swift & Co., n.d.]
22p. 17cm.
"Tract. No. 2."
UPB

5493. ———. (same) Chattanooga, Tennessee, Published by the Southern States Mission [n.d.]
29p. 13cm.
OClWHi, USIC

5494. ———. (same) [Salt Lake City, Published and for sale, Juvenile Instructor Office, 1881]
24p. 18cm. (Tract. No. 2)
Caption-title.
USIC has copy with cover with title which reads: Tracts on the Doctrines of The Church of Jesus Christ of Latter-day Saints. Salt Lake City, Juvenile Instructor Office, 1881.
CSmH, MH, NN, UHi, USI, USIC, UU

5495. ———. (same) [Liverpool, John Henry Smith, 1883]
23p. 17½cm. (Tract. No. 2)
CtY, MH, NN, ULA, USIC

5496. ———. (same) Independence, Mo., Zions Printing and Pub. Co., [188–]
24p. 18cm.
CU-B, MoInRC, NN, OClWHi, PCC, PPRHi, UPB, USIC

5497. ———. (same) [Salt Lake City, Published by the Missions of the Church of Jesus Christ of Latter-day Saints, in America, 189–]
24p. 17cm. (Tract. No. 2)
NN, USIC

5498. ———. (same) [Liverpool, Printed at the Millennial Star Office, 1891?]
23 [1]p. 17cm. (Tract. No. 2)
Caption-title.
UHi, USIC

MORGAN, J.

5499. ———. (same) New York, Eastern States Mission [190–]
32p. 14cm.
Cover-title.
NjP, NN, USlC

5500. ———. (same) [Chicago, Northern States Mission] 1903.
32p. 14cm.
Cover-title.
UHi

5501. ———. (same) [Salt Lake City, Bureau of Information] 1905.
32p. 13cm.
USl

5502. ———. (same) [Independence, Mo., Central States Mission] 1905.
32p. 14½cm.
MH, MoInRC, UPB, WHi

5503. ———. (same) [Portland, Oregon, Northwestern States Mission] 1905.
32p. 14½cm.
Cover title.
NjP

5504. ———. (same) [Chicago, Northern States Mission] 1905.
32p. 14cm.
WHi

5505. ———. (same) [Chicago, Ill., Northern States Mission, Church of Jesus Christ of Latter-day Saints] 1908.
32p. 14cm.
MH, OClWHi, UPB, USlC

5506. ———. (same) Liverpool, Millennial Star Office, 1910.
1p.l., 26p. 18½cm.
CtY

5506a. ———. (same) [Chicago, Missions of the Church of Jesus Christ of Latter-day Saints] 1912.
32p. 14½cm.
UPB

5507. ———. (same) [Independence, Mo., Published by the Missions of the Church of Jesus Christ of Latter-day Saints] 1914.
32p. 17cm.
The articles of faith, p. 22–23. List of publications on back page.
MoInRC, NN, USlC

5508. ———. (same) Liverpool, Printed and Published at the Millennial Star Office, 1921.
1p.l., 26p. 18½cm. (No. 2)
CU–B, UPB, USlC

5508a. ———. (same, in Danish) Frelsens plan. [Kjøbenhavn, udgivet og forlagt af C. D. Fieldstad, ca. 1870]
16p. 21½cm.
2den udgave.
USlC

5509. ———. (same) [Kjøbenhavn, A. C. Flygare. Trykt hos F. G. Bording, 1887]
16p. 20½cm.
Caption-title.
UHi

5510. ———. (same) Frelsens plan. En afhandling af Aeldste John Morgan. Oversat fra Engelsk. 6te Udgave. Kjøbenhavn, Udgivet og forlagt af Andreas Peterson. Trykt hos Emil Petersen, 1901.
23p. 18½cm.
In pink printed wrapper.
USlC

5510a. ———. (same) [7de Udgave] Kjøbenhavn, Udgivet og forlagt af Anthon L. Skanchy . . . Trykt hos P. S. Christiansen i Arbejderpartiets Bogtrykkeri i Aarhus, 1903.
24p. 17cm.
USlC

5511. ———. (same, in Swedish) Frälsningsplanen. Afhandling af Aldste John Morgan. Köpenhamn, Utgifven och förlagd af P. Sundwall. Tryckt hos F. E. Bording, (V. Petersen) 1895.
23p. 17½cm.
USlC

5511a. ———. (same) Köpenhamn, Utgifven och förlagd af George Christensen. Tryckt hos F. E. Bording, 1898.
23p. 18½cm.
USlC

5511b. ———. (same) Kopenhamn [Anthon L. Skanchy] 1903.
32p. 19cm.
Includes the Articles of faith.
USlC

5511c. ———. (same) Reviderad och överflyttad till nya modererade stavsättet för svenska språket i juli 1917 av Äldste Oscar W. Söderberg. Stockholm, A. P. Anderson [1917]
36p. 18cm.
USlC

5511d. ———. (same) Stockholm, T. Tobiason [1920]
24p. 18½cm.
UPB

Morgan, Martha. *See Graham, Martha Morgan.*

MORMON ENDOWMENT

5512. Morgan, Nicholas Groesbeck, Sr. Nicholas Groesbeck. September 5, 1819–June 29, 1884. [Salt Lake City, n.d.]
20p. port. 26cm.
USlC

Morgan, *Mrs.* **Richard Cope.** *See Morgan, Wilma.*

5513. Morgan, William. Cyfarwyddiadau i'r ymfudwyr tua dinas y llyn halen, mewn llythyr oddiwrth Wm. Morgan, Kanesville, Iowa, at yr henuriaid W. Phillips, a J. Davis, Merthyr; yn yr hwn y cynnwysir Llythyr oddiwrth yr Apostolion Benson A. Smith, ynghyd a Chapt. D. Jones. Merthyr-Tydfil, Argraffwyd ac ar Werth Gan J. Davis . . . 1850.
12p. 18cm.
Title in English: Directions to emigrants to Salt Lake City.
MH, NjP, USlC

5514. Morgan, William B. Mormonism and the Bible. A contrast. By W. B. Morgan. Compiled by desire of the Committee. [London, Partride and Co., n.d.]
8p. 17cm.
USlC

5515. Morgan, Wilma, "*Mrs.* R. C. Morgan." Glimpses of four continents, being an account of the travels of Richard Cope Morgan, by Mrs. R. C. Morgan. London, Morgan & Scott, Ltd., 1911.
xi, 388p. plates, ports. 22cm.
Trip to Salt Lake City in 1897. He was offered favors by Wilford Woodruff, which he refused, p. 66–71. In particular, he mentions tithing and marriage customs.
CU, DLC, UHi, USlC

5516. Morgenstjernen. Christiania, Norway, January 1, 1922–1925.
4v. (1522p.) Semi-monthly. 23cm.
Organ of the Norwegian Mission.
Edited by President R. Peterson.
Title in English: The Morning Star.
USlC comp.

5517. Morgenstjernen et historisk-biografisk maanedsskrift. Salt Lake City, January 1882–December 1885.
4v. semi-monthly, monthly. 21cm.
The first 4 volumes of the *Historical record.*
Edited and published by Andrew Jenson. Printed in Danish and Norwegian.
Title in English: The Morning Star.
CSmH V. 1–2, ICN, UPB, USlC, UU

5518. "A Mormon." Platform of principles of the pretended reformers of Utah. [Salt Lake City, 1881]
7p. 21cm.
Editorial from the *Salt Lake Tribune* of Sunday, March 6, 1881, p. 1–4.
Answered on p. 5–7 under title "Reflections."
Signed: March 16, 1881, by "A Mormon."
CSmH, CU-B, USlC, UU

5519. The Mormon. New York City, February 17, 1855–September 19, 1857.
3v. weekly. 66cm.
Editor: John Taylor.
CtY V.1; V.2 #6–15, 26, 28–35, 40–41, 43–44, 48, 50; V.3 #8, 13–15, 17–23, 25, 27–31. NN V.1, #1–27, 29–52; V.2 #1, 7, 10. USlC comp.

Mormon absurdities. *See Goodwin, Charles Carroll.*

Mormon Bible becomes issue in League of Nations fight. See Pacific N.E.A. Bureau.

5520. The Mormon century book; the romantic story of one hundred years' achievement, 1830–1930. [Salt Lake City, The Pioneer Centennial Publishing Committee, 1930]
50p. illus., ports. 30cm.
Cover-title.
CtY, ICN, MH, USl

5520a. ———. (same) [Salt Lake City, The Pioneer Centennial Publishing Committee, 1930]
50p. illus., ports. 30cm.
Cover-title.
"Second edition."
USlC

5521. The Mormon conspiracy to establish an independent empire to be called the Kingdom of God on earth. The conspiracy exposed by the writings, sermons and legislative acts of the prophets and apostles of the Church. Salt Lake City, Printed and for sale by the Tribune Co. [1885?]
16p. 23½cm.
Cover-title.
CtY, ICN, MH, USl

5521a. Mormon Disclosures!! Polygamy!!! Twenty years experience of a Mormon wife. The inner life of polygamic households laid bare. How the elders and saints entrap young women!! . . . [n.p., 187–]
16p. 19½cm.
Cover-title.
USlC

Mormon doctrine carefully considered . . . *See Nutting, John Danforth.*

5522. Mormon doctrine of polygamy, or plurality of wives examined by the author of "plain questions for Mormonites," and prize essay, "the Church of Rome opposed to the Holy Bible and the Catholic Church." London, Wertheim and Macintosh, Pub., 1853.
16p. 17cm.
USlC

The Mormon Elders and the Devils. *See J., H. T.*

The Mormon Endowment House! . . . *See Salt Lake Tribune.*

5523. Mormon Expositor. Salt Lake City [ca. 1875]
V. 1, No. 1 [4p.] 22cm.
Only issue published.
Contains excerpts from sermons by Brigham Young, Jeter Clinton, Bishop Woolley and "The Bishop of San Pete."
"Many of the sermons of Brigham Young . . . were . . . utterly unfit for publication."
". . . We also give selections from sermons of the 'Lesser lights' which show that they have been apt scholars of a vulgar tutor." — cf. p.1. Date from final speech. Authenticity of the speeches doubtful.
A republication of *To the Clergy of the Presbyterian Church* by Josiah Welch with no introductory paragraph. Published in three printings, the first from type used to print *To the Clergy of the Presbyterian Church*, and the third bound into a pamphlet under cover-title *A Few Choice Examples of Mormon Practices and Sermons.*
CSmH, CtY, CU–B, NjP, UHi, ULA, UPB 3 variants, USlC, WHi

5524. Mormon imposture: An exposure of the fraudulent origin of the Book of Mormon. . . . London, 1851.
16p. 16½cm.
USlC

5525. ———. (same) 2d ed. London, A. Hall, Virtue, and Co. [etc., etc., 1851]
16p. 16½cm.
CtY

Mormon infidelity and polygamy.
See Presbytery of Utah.

The Mormon metropolis. *See Reynolds, George.*

5525a. Mormon morality, revelation given to Joseph Smith — Nauvoo, July 12, 1843. Orford Hill, Norwich [ca. 1853]
Broadside. 32×23cm.
Extract from the *Millennial Star* for Jan. 1, 1853 which is Joseph Smith's revelation on plural marriage, with a warning for the people to not come under the influence of the Mormons.
USlC

5526. Mormon petition. To the Honorable the Senate and House of Representatives of the United States . . . Hence your petitioners beseech your honorable body that all pending legislation regarding Utah may be at once stopped, and that our beloved polygamous delegate be at once given his seat in the House of Representatives . . . [n.p., 1882?]
Broadside. 36×22cm.
Signed: "John Taylor, Prophet, Seer and Revelator to the President of the Church of Jesus Christ of Latter-day Saints in all the world . . . [and others]"
A burlesque.
CU–B

5527. The Mormon Point of View. Provo City, Utah, N. L. Nelson, 1904.
1v. (4 nos. in 412p.) quarterly. 15cm.
A quarterly magazine, owned and edited by N. L. Nelson, Professor of English, Brigham Young University, to apply theology to daily living.
For its prospectus, *see Nelson, Nels Lars.*
CSmH, CU–B, NjP, NN, ULA, UPB, USlC, WHi #3

5528. Mormon politics and policy. Political and judicial acts of the Mormon authorities in San Bernardino Co., California. Proceedings of public meetings to counter-act the influence of Mormon doctrines as taught to the Indians. Reply to Mormon communications published in the Los Angeles Star, San Diego Herald, Bulletin, and Western Standard. An appeal to the freemen of San Bernardino City and County and the State of California. Preamble and platform of a new order established in the City and County of San Bernardino. Published pro bono publico by the order of United Independent Democrats of the County of San Bernardino. Los Angeles, Printed at the Office of El Clamor Publico, 1856.
8p.(?) 24cm.
Written by Quartus S. Sparks, W. H. Andrews, and others. The only located copy is defective, showing only 8p.
CU–B

5529. "Mormon" protest against injustice. An appeal for constitutional and religious liberty. Full report of the great mass meeting held in Salt Lake City, May 2, 1885, with the full text of the speeches and the protest and declaration of grievances. Reported by John Irvine. Salt Lake City, J. H. Parry and Co., 1885.
2p.l. [5]–48p. 20cm.
The meeting was called by the Committee on Resolutions and Protest appointed by the Church of Jesus Christ of Latter-day Saints, at general conference.
CSmH, CtY, CU–B, DLC, NjP, NN, ULA, USl, USlC, UU

5530. The Mormon Tribune; organ of the Liberal cause in Utah. Salt Lake City, January 1, 1870–June 25, 1870.
1v. (26 nos. in 208p.) weekly. 46cm.
Published by Godbe and Harrison.
Name changed to *Salt Lake Tribune,* V.2 #27; paged separately.
USlC

5531. The Mormon trip, life scenes in Utah.
[n.p., n.d.]
Sabin 50750

5532. A Mormon woman's plea. Salt Lake City, Daily Union Vedette. 1866.
[1]p. 25½cm.
Supplement. *Daily Union Vedette.*
Great Salt Lake City, February 7, 1866.
MH

MORMONISM

"Mormon" women on plural marriage . . . *See Utah (Territory) Mormon Women.*

5533. "Mormon" women's protest. An appeal for freedom and equal rights. The ladies of the Church of Jesus Christ of Latter-day Saints protest against the tyranny and indecency of Federal officials in Utah, and against their own disfranchisement without cause. Full account of proceedings at the great mass meeting held in the theatre, Salt Lake City, Saturday, March 6, 1886. [Salt Lake City] Deseret News Co. [1886]
iv [5]–91p. 23cm.
p. [79]–91: Memorial . . . prepared by the committee appointed at the mass meeting and forwarded by them to Washington. Text signed: Mrs. Sarah M. Kimball [and others]
Mass meeting called "in behalf of the committee" by Mrs. M. I. Horne, Mrs. H. M. Whitney, Mrs. E. S. Taylor [and] D. R[omania] B. Pratt.
CSmH, CU–B, DLC, ICN, MH, MWA, NjP, NN, RPB, USIC, UU, WHi

5534. Mormon Zeitung. Salt Lake City, 1882.
4 nos. 36cm.
Organ of the German Mormons.
Editor: Carl Lyn.
Title in English: Mormon Newspaper.
USIC No. 1, August, 1882

5535. La Mormona. [To J. F. Corbin, presiding elder of the El Paso district of the M. E. Church . . . South, on the Negro question. El Paso?] 1900.
8p. 23cm.
Impression of the Mormon church and its superiority. Justification of its Negro position.
Purportedly written by a Mormon woman.
Title in English: The Mormon.
NN

5536. ———. (same) [El Paso?] 1901.
1p.l., 8p. 22cm.
"To the Governor of Mississippi."
CU–B, NN

5537. . . . Die Mormonen. ["Die Heiligen der letzten Tage." Stuttgart, 1920]
4p. 23cm. (Prüfet die Geister. Nr. 5)
Caption-title.
Title in English: The Mormons.
NN

5538. Mormonens Offer; et Drama om Kaerlighed og sekterisk Fanatisme. Dette spaendende og virkningsfulde Nutids-Skuespil, som belyser den af "de Sidste Dages Hellige" . . . Aarhus [Reklametrykkeriet, Busch & Petersen, c1912]
[14]p. 22cm.
Mormon drama.
Title in English: The Mormon sacrifice.
USIC

5539. Mormonerne. Eller de sidste dages hellige. Slesvig, 1853.
31p. 12°
Title in English: Mormons, or the Latter-day Saints.
Sabin 50752

5540. Mormonerne skildret af Ikke Mormoner. [Kjøbenhavn, Udgivet og forlagt af H. E. Flygare . . . Trykt hos F. E. Bording, n.d.]
16p. 21cm.
Includes sections of John C. Kimball's *Mormonism exposed* with commentaries.
Title in English: Mormons, portrait by non-Mormons.
USIC

5541. ———. (same) For "Gentiles" existerede i saa stort antal og endnu hvor byerne er under deres (Mormonernes) bestyrelse. Aarhus, 1907.
8p.
Schmidt

5542. Mormonernes Upperstepraest Brigham Young og hans 16 koner. . . . [Kjobenhavn, gul. Strandbergs Forlag og Tryk Foals i Bohandelen, 187–]
[4]p. 16cm.
Street ballad about Brigham Young and his sixteen wives.
Title in English: Mormon High Priest, Brigham Young and his 16 wives.
UHi

5543. En Mormonhistorie. I almanak eller huuskalender for de aar efter Christi fodsel 1853, som er de forste aar efter skudaar. Kobenhaven, 1852.
1p.
Title in English: A Mormon history.
Schmidt.

5544. Mormoniad. Boston, A. Williams & Co., 1858.
100p. 18½cm.
A satiric poem on Mormonism.
Sabin 50753
CSmH, CtY, DLC, ICN, ICU, MH, NjP, NN, UHi, UPB, USIC, UU

5545. Mormonism. [New York, Derby & Jackson, 1859]
130p. 17½cm.
Sermons of prominent Mormons, along with the plural marriage revelation of Joseph Smith.

Mormonism. *See also Religious Tract Society.*

5546. Mormonism, a power, how and why. By a member of the Utah State S. S. Association. New York, Woman's Home Missionary Society, Methodist Episcopal Church [1930?]
2p. 16cm.
USIC

MORMONISM AND THE BIBLE

Mormonism and the Bible — Do they agree?
See Utah Tract Society.

5547. Mormonism and the Mormonites. [London, Wertheim and Macintosh, 185–]
8p. 16cm.
Caption-title.
CtY, NN, UPB

5548. Mormonism contrasted with the word of God. [London, Wertheim and Macintosh, etc., 1857?]
16p. 16½cm.
CtY

Mormonism dissected. *See Mason, John. The Latter-day Saints . . .*

5549. Mormonism examined: a few kind words to a Mormon. . . . Birmingham, 1855. Noted in: Bancroft, *History of Utah.*
No copy located

5550. Mormonism exposed. [By a Mormon slave wife. Chicago? n.d.]
14p. 11cm.
UPB, USlC

5551. Mormonism exposed. [A series of pamphlets continuously paged. n.p., 1884–5]
5 pts. (113p.) 21cm.
Contents: James W. Barclay. Mormonism exposed. No. 1. p. 1–30. Earle S. Goodrich. Mormonism unveiled. No. 2. 1–12p. [variant. 31–42p.] Hugh Weightman. Mormonism exposed. No. 3. [43–]–66p. John Calvin Kimball. Mormonism exposed. No. 4. 17p. [67–84] Richard W. Young. Mormonism exposed. No. 5. [85]–113p.
For holdings *see* each pamphlet under author's name.

Mormonism exposed: In which is shown the monstrous imposture, the blasphemy, and the wicked tendency of that enormous delusion.
See Sunderland, La Roy.

5552. Mormonism: its blessings and advantages. [London, John Smith & Co., Printers, 1855?]
8p. 20cm.
Caption-title.
A satirical defense of the faith by a supposed Mormon.
CtY

5553. Mormonism: its origin. [London, E. Varty, Printer, n.d.]
4p. 21cm.
Caption-title.
DLC

5554. Mormonism. Notice. The inhabitants of South Shields are respectfully informed that Elders Wm. Budge, H. W. Naisbett, and C. W. Nibley, from Salt Lake City, will deliver addresses on the above subject. . . . [n.p., 1878]
Broadside. 19½×8cm.
UPB

Mormonism, one of the delusions of Satan.
See Peck, John Mason.

5555. Mormonism or the Bible? A question for the times. By a Cambridge clergyman. [Cambridge, Eng., T. Dixon (etc.) 1852]
32p. 17cm.
Sabin 50757
NN, USlC

Mormonism: reprinted from the Edinburgh Review.
See Conybeare, William John.

5556. Mormonism revealed. Authorative [sic] information regarding the terrors and infamies of early Mormon life, upon which the play of "100 wives" is founded. Rochester, N.Y., F. M. Seaman, Theatrical Printer [1880]
8p. 11½cm.
Cover-title.
Advertisement for play "100 wives" by G. A. Pierce to be performed at the Arch St. Theatre in Philadelphia, October 18, 1880.
CtY, CU–B

Mormonism self-refuted. *See K., D.*

Mormonism sifted . . . *See Hickman, Edward B.*

5557. Mormonism traced by the Bible and condemned. Ipswich, 1855.
22p. 17cm.
NN, USlC

5557a. Mormonism unmasked, showed to be an impious imposture, and Mr. Bennett's reply answered and refuted. By A Philanthropist of Chester County. Philadelphia, T. K. & P. G. Collins, Printers, 1840.
24p. 18cm.
USlC

5558. Mormonism unveiled. A brief expose of the doctrines and practices of the so-called "Latter-day Saints" and their Prophet Joseph Smith, Jr. "Author and Proprietor of the Book of Mormon." . . . Calcutta, Printed at the Star Press, 1852.
2p.l., 57p. 21cm.
USlC

Le Mormonisme. *See Conybeare, William John.*

5559. Mormonismen. [Kjøbenhavn, Trykt hos J. Davidsen, 185–]
31p. 17cm.
Caption-title.
Title in English: Mormonism.
NN, USlC

5560. Mormonismen och Swedenborgianismen. Upsala, Wahlstrom & Co., 1854.
27p. 8°.
Title in English: Mormonism and Swedenborgianism.
Sabin 50759

Mormonismen og Saltsøstaden. *See M., H.*

5561. Mormonismen wederlagd of Den Helige Skrifts och historiens wittnesbörd. Stockholm, 1858.
68p. 8°.
Title in English: Mormonism refuted by the Holy Scriptures.
Sabin 50760

5562. Mormonismens historie tilligenmed en kort oversigt over sektens troeslaerdomme og kirkeforfatning, med 12 afbildninger. Christiania, 1853.
52p.
Title in English: History of Mormonism.
Schmidt

5563. Mormonismens laere. [Kjøbenhavn, Faaes hos F. P. Forster, 1851]
32p. 20½cm.
Mormonism's teachings.
Title in English: The Mormon doctrine.
NN, UHi, USlC

Der Mormonismus . . . *See Church of Jesus Christ of Latter-day Saints. Missions. German.*

5564. The Mormonites, or Latter-day Saints. A Country clergyman's warning to his parishioners. London, Wertheim and MacIntosh [1852]
16p. 16cm.
CtY, NN

5565. Mormonpigens Klage. [Kjøbenhavn, Trykt hos Ernst Lund, 1873?]
[4]p. 15cm.
Street ballad.
Title in English: The Mormon girl's lament.
UHi (photostat from Royal Library, Copenhagen)

Mormons and Mormonism, why they have been opposed, maligned and persecuted . . . . *See Ellis, Charles.*

The Mormons and the apparition of Christ in his body. *See Just Platero [pseud.]*

The Mormons have stepped down and out of celestial government. *See McDonald, Angus.*

5566. The Mormon's "only way to be saved," not the way to be saved; or, the plausible logic of Mormonism refuted. A reply to Lorenzo Snow's "Only way to be saved." Glasgow: W. G. Blackie & Co. [185–]
2 nos. 15cm. (Sterling tracts. No. 340, 341)
NN

The Mormons, or, Knavery exposed. *See Lee, E. G.*

5567. The Mormons; or, Life in Utah. Birmingham, England, Published by P. W. Forbes, Publishers [n.d.]
16p. 23cm.
Compiled from various sources.
USlC

The Mormons, the dream and the reality. *See Cook, William.*

5568. Morrill, Gulian Lansing. Hawaiian heathen and others. By G. L. Morrill ("Golightly") . . . Lowell L. Morrill, Photographer. [Minneapolis? c1919]
5p.l., 266 p. plates, photos. 19cm.
"A Mormon Colony," p. 206–208. " 'Hog' is a good word for the Mormon idea of money and morals." The colony is at Laie.
USlC

5569. ———. On the warpath. Minneapolis [c1918]
5p.l. [7]–258p. 20cm.
Includes a visit to Salt Lake City with short essays on various subjects.
Chapter headings: Salt Lake Saints, Free-love religion, The Mormon Bible, Old Brigham Young, Mountain Meadows massacre, etc., p. 214–231.
USlC

5570. Morrill, Justin Smith. Speech of Hon. Justin S. Morrill, of Vermont, on Utah Territory and its laws — Polygamy and its license; delivered in the House of Representatives, February 23, 1857. Washington, Office of the Congressional Globe, 1857.
14p. 24cm.
Cover-title.
CtY, CU–B, UHi, UPB, USl

5571. Morris, Bates. Joe Smith's prophecy on the rebellion examined and found wanting. By Bates Morris. Chicago, Ill. [c1927]
29p. 16cm.
Joseph Smith's prophecy on the Civil War.
CU–B, IWW, NN, ULA, UPB, USlC

5572. Morris, George Quayle. America, a land of destiny; address delivered over KSL Radio Station, Salt Lake City, Sunday, July 29. [Salt Lake City, 1927?]
Broadside. 62×21cm.
Reprinted from the *Deseret News,* Saturday, August 4th, 1927?
UPB

5573. Morris, Joseph. Advertisement for the book entitled The "Spirit prevails" containing the revelations, articles and letters written by Joseph Morris . . . . San Francisco, J. A. Dove & Co., 1886.
48p. 1 col. illus. 21cm.
At head of title: Tract number two.
CDU, CtY, CU

5574. ———. Pearls; or, Selected paragraphs from the revelations of Jesus Christ given through Joseph Morris. San Francisco, Published by George S. Dove and others, J. A. Dove & Co., Printers, 1891.
74p. [1]l., 21½cm.
CU, MH, NN, USlC

5574a. ———. [Revelations of Joseph Morris, 1857–June 15, 1862. n.p., ca. 1882]
Various pagings. 16cm.
Includes the following revelations: No. 1, 15, 22, 52, 59, 69, 105, 110, 111, 114, 150, 156, 197, 201, 219, 237, 239, 258, 259, 263, 266, 268, 269, 270, 275, 280. Numbering differs from his *The Spirit Prevails.*
UPB

5575. ———. The "Spirit prevails." Containing the revelations, articles and letters written by Joseph Morris. San Francisco, Published by Geo. S. Dove & Company, J. A. Dove & Co., Printers, 1886.
iv, 684p. 23½cm.
Scripture of the Church of the Firstborn.
Preface signed: George S. Dove.
CU–B, DLC, NjP, NN, UHi, UPB, USl, USlC

5576. Morris, Mary Lowell. A few thoughts of Mary L. Morris. Dedicated to her children. For private circulation. Salt Lake City, Magazine Printing Company, 1918.
3p.l. [7]–80p. port. 19cm.
Mormon poetry.
UPB, USlC

5577. Morris, Nephi Lowell. The "Book of Mormon," the story of its discovery — its construction — the testimony of the witnesses — the internal evidences of its truth. A lecture delivered in the Salt Lake Assembly Hall, March 24, 1897. [Salt Lake City] 1899.
28p. 16cm.
IWW, MH, MoInRC, NjP, USlC

5578. ———. Columbus and the Book of Mormon; address delivered over Radio Station KSL, Sunday evening July 1, 1928. [Salt Lake City] 1928.
Broadside. 59×20cm.
Reprinted from the *Deseret News,* Saturday, July 7, 1928.
UPB

5579. ———. Divine authority necessary; address delivered over Radio [Station] KSL, Sunday Evening, May 1, 1927. [Salt Lake City] 1927.
Broadside. 56×26½cm.
Reprinted from the *Deseret News.*
UPB

5580. ———. Equal rights to all. Is the right of self-defense to be denied the Mormon people? [Salt Lake City, 1905?]
4p. 22½cm.
Government relations with the Mormons.
NjP, USlC

5581. ———. Prophecies of Joseph Smith and their fulfillment, by Nephi Lowell Morris. Salt Lake City, Deseret Book Company, 1920.
vi [2]–198p. illus., facsims. 19cm.
CU–B, DLC, IWW, MoInRC, NjP, NN, UHi, USlC, WHi

5582. ———. (same) Salt Lake City, Deseret Book Company, 1926.
xiii [1] 329. illus., port., facsims. 19½cm.
CtY, DLC, NN, UPB, USl, UU

5583. ———. [Radio addresses given over KSL Sunday Evenings, July 7, 1929–Sept. 1, 1929. Salt Lake City, Church of Jesus Christ of Latter-day Saints, 1929]
131p. 23½cm. (Series 4)
USlC

5584. ———. The story of the discovery of the Book of Mormon. By Elder Nephi L. Morris. [Chicago? n.d.]
16p. 14½cm.
Caption-title.
CLU, CSmH, IWW, NN, UPB

Morrish, William John. A few thoughts suggested by the term "Latter-day Saint." *See A few thoughts . . .*

5585. ———. . . . The Latter-Day Saints and the Book of Mormon. A few words of warning from a minister to his flock. Ledbury, Printed by J. Gibbs, jun. [1840?]
4p. 22cm.
First issue. Not signed or dated.
UPB, USlC

5586. ———. (same) Ledbury, Printed by J. Gibbs, jun. [1840]
4p. 21cm.
Caption-title.
At head of title: <Fourth Thousand>
Signed: W. J. Morrish, September, 1840.
UPB, USlC

5587. ———. (same, in Welsh) . . . Saint y Dyddiau Diweddaf a Llyfr Mormon; cyfeiliornadau a dichellion yn cael eu dynoethi, can y parch W. J. Morrish . . . Cyfieithedig, trwy ganiatad yr awdwr gan David Roberts. Caernarfon, H. Humphreys, 1849.
4p. 17½cm.
UHi

5588. ———. The "Latter-day Saints" and the Book of Mormon. A second warning from a minister to his flock. Ledbury, England, J. Gibbs, 1840.
4p. 22cm.
Signed: October 15, 1840.
CSmH, DLC, MH, NN, USlC

5589. ———. The "Latter-day Saints" and the Book of Mormon. A second warning from a minister to his flock. Ledbury, England, J. Gibbs, 1840.
4p. 22cm.
At head of title: Fourth Thousand
Signed: October 15, 1840
DLC, USlC

5590. Morse, Elijah A. Admission of Utah as a state. Polygamy and Mormonism, the foulest blot upon American civilization. The Territory of Utah unfit for statehood and should wait until anti-Mormons are in the majority. Speech of Hon. Elijah A. Morse, . . . Of Massachusetts, in the House of Representatives, Tuesday, December 12, 1893. Washington, 1893.
13p. 23cm.
MH

5591. Mortensen, Andreas. Fra mit besøg blandt Mormonerne af Andreas Mortensen. Kristiania, P. T. Malling, Boghandels Forlag, 1887.
4p.l., 286p. illus. 19cm.
Title in English: About my visit among Mormons.
CSmH, CtY, MH, NN

5592. ———. Mormonernas hemligheter; werklighetsbilder från Utah efter egen iakttagelse tecknade af Andreas Mortensen . . . Ofwersättning från norskan med författarens tillstånd. Stockholm, C. A. V. Lundholm [1887]
214 [2]p. illus., plates, ports. 18cm.
Translation of: Fra mit besog blandt Mormonerne (in Danish)
Title in English: Secrets of the Mormons.
CSmH, DLC, MH, MnU, UHi, USlC

5593. Morton, Cyrus. Autobiography of Cyrus Morton. Omaha, Nebraska, Douglas Printing Co., 1895.
46p. port. 23cm.
Lived in Salt Lake City in 1866. Various references to Mormonism.
CU-B, UPB

5594. Morton, Julius Sterling. Illustrated history of Nebraska; a history of Nebraska from the earliest explorations of the trans-Mississippi region . . . by J. Sterling Morton, succeeded by Albert Watkins . . . [and] Dr. George L. Miller. Lincoln, Nebraska, Jacob North & Company, 1905–13.
3v. illus., maps. 27½cm.
Mormons in Nebraska, V. 2.
Revised ed.: Lincoln Neb., Western Pub. & Engraving, 1918. UHi, UPB
CU, DLC, NjP, UHi, USlC

5595. Morton, William Albert. Book of Mormon ready references. For the use of students and missionaries of the Church of Jesus Christ of Latter-day Saints. Compiled and published by Elder William A. Morton. Salt Lake City, Geo. Q. Cannon & Sons Company, Printers, 1898.
vi p., [1]l. [9]–168p. 16½cm.
IWW, MH, NjP, UHi, UPB, USlC, UU

5596. ———. (same) [New and abridged edition] Salt Lake City, Published by the author, 1903.
2p.l., 5–16p. 16cm.
UPB, USlC

5597. ———. (same) Salt Lake City, Deseret News, 1914.
170p. 14cm.
UHi, UPB

5598. ———. Character building stories for young people. Compiled by W. A. Morton. Salt Lake City, Published by Deseret Book Company [c1926]
160p. 17½cm.
USlC

5599. ———. A child's life of Brigham Young, by William A. Morton and A. Leon Taylor . . . Salt Lake City, Wm. A. Morton, Publisher [191–]
2p.l. [7]–112p. illus. 16½cm. (The Primary Helper Series. No. 5)
UHi, USlC, WHi

5600. ———. A child's life of our Savior by William A. Morton. Recommended by Deseret Sunday School Union Board as a text book for Intermediate Grades in the Sunday Schools. New and revised edition. Salt Lake City, George Q. Cannon, 1900.
122p. fold. col. map. 17cm. (The Primary helper. V. 1, No. 2)
Cover-title.
USlC, UU

MORTON, W. A.

5601. ———. (same) Suitable for Intermediate Grades in Primary Associations and Sunday Schools. [Salt Lake City] George Q. Cannon & Sons, Printers [n.d.]
2p.l. [5]–136p. fold. map. 17cm. (The Primary helper. V. 1, No. 2)
UPB

5602. ———. A collection of hymns and songs for little saints. Salt Lake City, George Q. Cannon and Sons Co. [c1900]
40p. music. 19cm. (The Primary helper series. No. 4)
Variant covers.
USIC, WHi

5603. ———. The eventide of life. Arranged by William A. Morton. [Salt Lake City, The Seagull Press, n.d.]
15p. 14½cm.
Mormon poetry.
USIC

5604. ———. . . . The Primary helper, No. 1. Written, compiled and published by William A. Morton under the direction of the General Board of Primary Associations. Salt Lake City, G. Q. Cannon & Sons Co., Printers, 1899.
96p. 17½cm.
Published quarterly.
DLC, IWW, ULA, USIC

5605. ———. From plowboy to prophet; being a short history of Joseph Smith, for children, by William A. Morton (illustrations by L. A. Ramsey). Salt Lake City, W. A. Morton, 1912.
2p.l., 130p., [1]l. plates, 2 ports. 19cm.
DLC, UPB, USIC, UU

5606. ———. (same) Salt Lake City, Deseret Book Store, 1918 [c1912]
2p.l., 131p. illus. 18½cm.
UHi, USl

5607. ———. (same) Tokyo, Japan, Published by the Church of Jesus Christ of Latter Day Saints, 1920.
2p.l. [2]–88p. 18½cm.
Title also in Japanese. Text in English only.
USIC

5608. ———. "Gems" from the Book of Mormon and Doctrine and Covenants. Compiled and published by W. A. Morton. Salt Lake City, 1925.
1p.l. [3]–64p. 15½cm.
CU-B, USl, USIC, UU

5609. ———. Good stories for boys and girls. Compiled by William A. Morton. Salt Lake City, Deseret Book Company [c1924]
2p.l. [5]–159p. 16cm.
UPB, USl, USIC

5610. ———. The gospel alphabet, by William A. Morton . . . Salt Lake City, The author, 1924.
[28]p. 15cm.
A children's book with each letter of the alphabet representing a short gospel subject.
UHi, USl, USIC

5611. ———. (same) 2d ed. Salt Lake City, The author, 1924.
[30]p. 15cm.
USIC

5612. ———. The Gospel primer. A treatise on the first principles of the Gospel. Written expressly for the young. Salt Lake City, Printed at the Juvenile Instructor Office [c1897]
3p.l. [5]–101p. 13cm.
NN, USIC

5613. ———. Helps for Religion Class teachers. Being a book of moral stories, written, selected and published by Wm. A. Morton. Recommended by the General Board for use in the Primary Department of Religion Classes. Salt Lake City [Acme Printing Co.] 1905.
2p.l., 105p. 14½cm.
USIC

5613a. ———. How the storm went 'round. Salt Lake City, 1926.
160p. 15cm.
Mormon literature.
USIC

5614. ———. In and about Salt Lake City. The Mormon paradise. Salt Lake City, W. A. Morton [n.d.]
[18]l. illus., plates (1 col.) ports. 17½×27cm.
Plates of prominent scenes in church history as well as, The articles of faith, hymn "Oh my Father," by Eliza R. Snow, and Utah and Mormonism, by O. F. Whitney.
CU-B, UHi, USIC

5615. ———. Joseph the seer in song and story (A cantata). Arranged and published by William A. Morton. Salt Lake City [c1920]
12p. 19½cm.
CU-B, NjP, UHi, USIC

5616. ———. The Latter-day Saints and the world. Liverpool, Millennial Star Office [1908?]
2p.l., 52p. 22½cm.
Cover-title.
Written in the form of a dialogue between the world, the Latter-day Saints and Biblical characters.
UHi, UPB, USIC

5617. ———. (same) 6th edition, 95,000. Liverpool, Printed at the Millennial Star Office [n.d.]
52p. 21½cm.
MH, UPB, USIC

MORTON, W. A.

5618. ———. (same) 8th edition. Liverpool, Millennial Star Office [ca. 1922]
52p. 21½cm.
USIC, CtY, UPB

5619. ———. (same) Liverpool, Millennial Star Office [1922]
52p. 21½cm.
"8th edition."
Variant printings.
CtY, UPB, USIC

5620. ———. (same, in Icelandic) Their Síthari daga heilögu fyrir rétti heimsins eftir William A. Morton. Thýtt úr Ensku. Útgefin af trúbothum Jesú Krists Kirkju Síthari Daga Heilögu. Reykjavík, Prentsmithjan Gutenberg, 1913.
60p. 18½cm.
USIC

5621. ———. Lesson book for the Religion Classes in the Church of Jesus Christ of Latter-day Saints. Second Grade. Written for the General Church Board of Education by William A. Morton. [Salt Lake City] Published by the Deseret Book Company, 1925.
127p. 19cm.
UPB, USIC

5622. ———. The life of Christ in simple language for little children. With numerous illustrations. By William A. Morton. Salt Lake City, William A. Morton, 1916.
141p. illus. 19cm.
UPB, USIC

5623. ———. Lives of the apostles. Written for young people. Salt Lake City, Deseret Sunday School Union, 1906.
68p. 18½cm.
UHi, USI, USIC

5624. ———. The making of a "Mormon," by William A. Morton. Salt Lake City, W. A. Morton [c1915]
47p. 17cm.
Mormon fiction.
DLC, USI, USIC

5625. ———. (same) 2d ed. Salt Lake City, The Deseret News, 1919.
50p. 17cm.
CU–B, IWW, UU

5626. ———. Mother O'Mine. Salt Lake City, 1925.
[24]p. 15cm.
Mormon poetry.
USIC

5627. ———. Mother stories from the Book of Mormon. Salt Lake City, W. A. Morton [c1911]
2p.l., 139p. 19½cm.
DLC, MoInRC, UPB, USIC

5628. ———. (same) Salt Lake City, Deseret Sunday School Union, 1913 [c1911]
2p.l., 135p. plates. 19cm.
DLC, UPB, UU

5629. ———. The new birth, as taught by Christ and his apostles. [Liverpool, Latter-day Saints' Headquarters, 1908?]
4p. 21cm.
Caption-title.
UHi, UPB, USIC

5630. ———. Salt Lake City through a camera. What the Mormons believe. Liverpool, Millennial Star Office [1909?]
[44]p. plates, ports. 19cm.
Text: What the Mormons believe, by Charles Penrose, is added to this picture pamphlet.
CU–B, MH, MoInRC, NjP, UHi, ULA, USIC, WHi

5631. ———. Sunday morning in the kindergarten, illustrated lessons for the Kindergarten Department of the Sunday school. Salt Lake City, Deseret Sunday School Union, 1916.
3p.l., 157p. illus., front. 20cm.
DE, DLC

5632. ———. Tributes to mothers, selected and published by William A. Morton. Salt Lake City [c1921]
14p. 15cm.
CSmH, RPB

5633. ———. . . . Utah and her people (illustrated) containing a sketch of Utah and Mormonism, the doctrine of the Mormon church and resources and attractions of the state. Compiled and published by William A. Morton. Salt Lake City, Geo. Q. Cannon & Sons, 1899.
[56]p. illus., ports. 18½×27cm.
At head of title: "By their fruits ye shall know them."
CSmH, CU–B, NjP, UPB, USI, USIC, UU

5634. ———. (same, under title) Utah and her people. Illustrated. Containing a sketch of Utah and Mormonism, the articles of faith of the Mormon church, the resources and attractions of the state, etc., etc. Compiled and published by Wm. Morton. Salt Lake City, Press of "The Deseret Evening News," 1901.
[48]p. illus., ports., col. plates. 16½×27cm.
CU–B, USIC

5635. ———. (same, in Danish) Utah og dets befolkning; en kort skildring af Utah og Mormonismen; Mormon-Kirkens laerdomme og statens hjaelpekilder og severdigheder. Oversat fra Engelsk af C. C. A. Christensen . . . Salt Lake City, Trykt hos Hayes & Morton, 1900.
51 [3]p. illus. 18½×27½cm.
Includes contributions by Orson F. Whitney, Franklin D. Richards, H. L. A. Culmer.
UHi, UPB, USlC

5636. ———. (same, in Swedish) Utah och dess Folk. (Illustrated) Innehållande. En beskrivning öfver Utah och Mormonismen, Mormon-kyrkans lärdomar Samt Statens näringskällor och sevärdheter. Öfversatt Från Engelska af äldste J. M. Sjödahl. Salt Lake City, Tryckt af Hayes & Morton, 1900.
3p.l. [7]–50 [4]p. illus., plates. 18½×27cm.
USlC

5637. ———. Why I believe the Book of Mormon to be the word of God. [Independence, Mo., Printed by Zion's Printing and Publishing Co. [c1918]
17p. 18cm.
MoInRC, UPB

5638. ———. (same) Salt Lake City [Deseret News Press, c1918]
24p. 15cm.
UPB, USlC

5639. ———. (same) [Independence, Mo., Printed by Zion's Printing and Publishing Co. [c1918]
28p. 17cm.
UPB

5640. ———. (same) [4th ed.] Salt Lake City [c1918]
23p. 16cm.
USlC

5641. ———. (same) Salt Lake City [c1918]
30[2]p. illus. 16cm.
CU–B

5642. ———. (same) [4th ed.] Salt Lake City [c1918]
23p. 16cm.
CU–B, USlC

5643. ———. (same) Independence, Mo., Printed by Zion's Printing and Publishing Co. [c1918]
30p. 16½cm.
Variant printings.
MoInRC, NN, TxU, UPB, USlC

5644. ———. (same) 5th ed. [Independence, Mo., Printed by Zion's Printing and Publishing Co. [c1918]
31p. 16½cm.
DLC, MoInRC, NjP, UPB, USlC, WHi

5645. ———. (same) Salt Lake City [c1918]
30 [2]p. illus. 16cm.
USlC

5646. Mosehauer, Julia Abbey (Trumpler). The great experience, by Julia Farr [*pseud.*] Salt Lake City, The Deseret News, 1920.
4p.l., 224p. plates. 19cm.
NN, UHi, USlC, UU

5647. ———. Venna Hastings; story of an eastern mormon convert. By Julia Farr [*pseud.*] Independence, Mo., Zion's Printing and Publishing Company, 1919.
3p.l. [7]–200p. 19cm.
Mormon fiction.
CSmH, DLC, NN, UHi, ULA, UPB, USl, USlC, UU

5648. Moses, John. Illinois, Historical statistical comprising the essential facts of its planting and growth as a province, county, territory, and state. Derived from the most authentic sources including original documents and papers, together with carefully prepared statistical tables relating to population, financial administration, industrial progress, internal growth, political and military events. . . . Chicago, Fergus Printing, 1889.
2v. illus., plates, ports., maps. 24–25cm.
Includes "The Mormon imbroglio." Mormon doctrine and history.
Another edition: 2d enl. [ed.] Chicago, 1895. DLC
Howes M856
DLC, NjP, UPB

5649. Moses, Julian. A few remarks in reply to an anonymous scribbler, styling himself "One who hates imposture," but found to be an impostor himself and ashamed to tell his name . . . By Julian Moses. Philadelphia, 1841.
15 [1]p. 22×14cm.
Against Adrian Van Brocklin Orr's *Mormonism dissected, or Knavery on two sticks exposed.*
Sabin 51057
CtY, MH, USlC

5650. The most complete and authentic exposure ever published of the spiritual courtship and marriages of the Mormons. The gates of Hell opened, exhibiting the licentious abominations and revellings of the High Priest of the Latter-day Saints, Rev. Brigham Young and his 90 wives . . . Awful fate of Martha Brotherton of Manchester. London, Hewitt . . . [1853?]
8p. 21cm.
Caption-title: The abominations of the Latter-day Saints.
CtY, USlC

5651. The most complete and authentic exposure of the spiritual courtship and marriages of the Mormons, exhibiting the licentious abominations and revellings of Brigham Young and his 90 wives; and the vile scenes enacted by the elders . . . with their many spiritual concubines in the secret chambers of the harem; the obscenity of the priesthood, and their diabolical schemes effecting the ruin of married and single females; with other acts of imposture, crime and suffering, under the guise of religion. London [c1855]
8p. 22cm.
CL, CtY

The Mountain Empire Utah . . .
See Blair, Geo. E., editor.

5652. The Mountaineer. Salt Lake City, August 27, 1859–July 20, 1861.
2v. (V.1 #1–52, V.2 #1–42) weekly. 56cm.
Editors: S. M. Blair, James Ferguson and Hosea Stout.
Supp. 1, Sept. 1, 1860; Supp. 2, Sept. 8; Supp. 3, Sept. 15; Supp. 4, Sept. 22; Supp. 5, Sept. 29. (supp. 2–5 numbered from 209–216 of V.1)
Extra: May 26, 1860. Late news.
July 2, 1860. "Late news from Baltimore, Douglas nominated."
Extra: October 13, 1860. 40×7cm.
CSmH 1859–Aug. 11, 1860; CtY Aug. 27, 1859–July 20, 1861, Supp. 1–5; USIC with extras

5653. Moyle, James H. Authenticity of the Book of Mormon. Address delivered over KSL Radio Station Sunday Evening, Nov. 20, 1927. By Elder James H. Moyle. [Salt Lake City] 1927.
Broadside. 27½×25½cm.
Reprint from The *Deseret News* on Saturday, November 26th.
Another address by the same name, given October 23, 1927, was erroneously attributed to him.
UPB

5654. Moyle, Oscar Wood. Joseph S. Richards vs. Joseph F. Smith, trustee in trust for the Church of Jesus Christ of Latter-day Saints. Respondents brief. Salt Lake City, 1907.
34p. 23cm.
At head of title: In the Supreme Court of the State of Utah.
Oscar W. Moyle was attorney for the respondent.
UPB

5655. Muir, John. Steep trails by John Muir; ed. by William Frederick Bade . . . Boston and New York, Houghton Mifflin Company, 1918.
ix [1]p., [2]l., 3–390 [2]p. front., plates. 21cm.
Chapter 6: "The City of the Saints."
CU-B, DLC, UHi, UPB, USIC

5656. Muir, Leo Joseph. Flashed from the eternal semaphore, by Leo J. Muir. Los Angeles, Calif., Everett L. Sanders Company [c1928]
3p.l., 110 [1]p. 19cm.
Mormon morals.
CU, DLC, ULA, USIC

5657. ———. (same) [2d ed.] Los Angeles, Calif., Everett L. Sanders Company [c1928]
3p.l., 112 [1]p. 29cm.
UHi

5658. ———. (same) 3d ed. Salt Lake City, Deseret News Press [c1928]
3p.l., 112p. 19cm.
MH, NjP, NN, UPB

5659. ———. (same) 4th ed. Salt Lake City, Deseret News Press [c1928]
3p.l., 112p. 19cm.
UPB

5660. ———. (same) 5th ed. Salt Lake City, Deseret News Press [c1928]
3p.l., 112p. [1]p. 20cm.
UPB

5661. ———. The upward reach, by Leo J. Muir. 1st ed. Los Angeles, Calif., Everett L. Sanders Company [1930]
4p.l., 83p. 19cm.
Inspirational writings.
DLC, UHi, USIC, UU

5662. Mulholland, James. An address to Americans. A poem in blank verse. By James Mulholland, an elder of the Church of Jesus Christ, of Latter Day Saints. Intended as a brief exposure of the cruelties and wrongs, which the church has lately experienced in the state of Missouri . . . Nauvoo, Printed by E. Robinson, 1841.
11p. 17cm.
Mormon poetry.
Published posthumously. Preface signed January 1, 1841.
Byrd 468
CSmH, ICHi, ICN, IHi, MH, MoInRC, UPB

5663. ———. (same) Batavia, Printed by D. D. Waite, 1844.
15p. 21½cm.
ICN

5664. Munday, Charles. A narrative of personal experience among the Latter Day Saints: together with some remarks on the fallacy of their peculiar doctrines. By Charles Munday. London, Partridge & Co., 1860.
iv, 32p. 12cm.
NN

MUNDSMAG

5665. En mundsmag paa Mormonismen i Utah. Udgivet af en forhenvaerende Mormonaeldste. Kobenhavn, 1863.
16p.
Title in English: An impression of Mormonism in Utah.
Schmidt

5666. Munro, Wilfred H. Among the Mormons in the days of Brigham Young, by Wilfred H. Munro. Worchester, Mass., Published by the Society, 1927.
3–19p. 25cm.
At head of title: American Antiquarian Society.
Reprinted from the *Proceedings of the American Antiquarian Society*, October, 1926, n.s. V. 36, p. 214–230.
CU–B, DLC, ICHi, MoInRC, NjP, ViU

5667. Murder by a deputy U.S. Marshal. E. M. Dalton waylaid and assassinated in cold-blood. Sworn testimony of eye witnesses. Salt Lake City, Printed and Published by the Deseret News Co., 1886.
16p. drawing. 20½cm.
Killed while resisting arrest for polygamy.
CSmH, CtY, DLC, ICN, MH, NjP, NN, UHi, USlC, UU

5668. Murdock, Orrice Abram. Succession of Joseph III. Is Joseph III the true successor of Joseph the Prophet in the Office of President of the Church of Jesus Christ of Latter-day Saints . . . Salt Lake City, The Deseret News, 1913.
3p.l., 7–72p. 15½cm.
CU–B, MoInRC, NjP, UHi, UPB, USlC, UU

5669. ———. (same, in Tahitian) E mono Mau anei o Iosepha Tamaiti. Tuaroi Parau E. mono mau anei o Iosepha Tamaiti no Iosepha metua, te peropheta, ei Peretiteni no te Ekalesia a Iesu Mesia i te Mau Mahana Hopea Nei? Iritihia no roto mai i to buko i papaihia e O. A. Muredoke. Neneihia e Eraneta A Rositera. Tahiti, Neia i te pihi neneiraa a te Ekalesia a Iesu Mesia i te Feia mo's i te mau Mahana Hopea . . . 1917.
2p.l., 64 [3]p. 16cm.
USlC

5670. Murdock Academy. Beaver, Utah. The Murdock Academy. Annual. 1909–
v. 19½–23cm.
Begun as Beaver Stake Academy; then Beaver Branch, Brigham Young University.
USlC 1903–04, 1904–05, 1905–06, 1909–10, 1910–11, 1911–12, 1912–13, 1913–14, 1916–17, 1917–18, 1918–19, 1921–22
USlC series also includes "Murdock views with sauce 'a la Shakespeare' " 1912–13. 12 [1]p. 15×20½cm. A pictorial introduction to the academy.

5671. The Murdock Lever. Beaver City, Published monthly by the Student Body of Murdock Academy 1909–
v. monthly. 22½cm.
USlC V.1 #3, January 1910

5672. Murphy, Castle Henry. History and purpose of temples. [Salt Lake City, 1930?]
16p. 17cm.
USlC

5673. Murphy, J. W. Outlaws of the Fox River country. Story of the Whiteford and Spencer tragedies, the assassination of Judge Richardson, the execution of John Baird, and the mobbing of W. J. Young. Criminal career of Frank Lane, the pseudo detective; Laura Sprouse and her lovers, and her Ohio rival; the Kansas Expedition after John B. Glenn; the raid on St. Francisville; robbery of the Luray postoffice; confessions of Brady and Marmaduke; a Clark County campaign. By J. W. Murphy. Hannibal, Mo., Hannibal Printing Company, 1882.
138p. 21cm.
Chapter 2 recounts the death of Joseph Smith and the creation of the Danite band under Bill Hickman.
Howes 907
UPB

5674. Murphy, John Mortimer. Rambles in northwestern America from the Pacific Ocean to the Rocky Mountains, being a description of the physical geography, climate, soil, productions, industrial and commercial resources, scenery, population, educational institutions, arboreal botany and game animals of Oregon, Washington Territory, Idaho, Montana, Utah, and Wyoming. London, Chapman and Hall, 1879.
xii, 364p. fold. map. 22½cm.
Chapter 16. "Among the Mormons," p. 236–265.
Tells of difficulty in convincing a Southern Utah woman that he had seen Brigham Young, as she thought him a Diety seen only by a few.
CSmH, CU-B, DLC, NjP, OCl, OrP, OrU, PPL, PSC, ULA, USlC

5675. Murphy, John R. The mineral resources of the Territory of Utah, with mining statistics and maps. By John R. Murphy. London, Trübner & Co.; San Francisco, A. L. Bancroft & Co. [etc., etc.] 1872.
2p.l., iv, 104p. fold. maps, fold. tables. 22½cm.
Extracts of the early history of the settlement of Utah. . . p. 74–104.
CSmH, CU-B, DLC, PPM, UPB

5676. Murphy, Wildman. What the Mormons teach. By Rev. Wildman Murphy. [New York, Eaton & Mains; Cincinnati, Jenning's & Pye, 189–]
16p. 13½cm. (No. 2221)
MoInRC, NN, ULA, USlC

5677. Murray, Henry Anthony. Lands of the slave and the free: or, Cuba, the United States, and Canada. By the Hon. Henry A. Murray . . . London, John W. Parker and Son, 1855.
2v. plates, maps (1 fold.) 20cm.
"Latter-day Saints and river scenes." He meets the Mormons on the Mississippi River. Resume of the Mormon beliefs.
"The Mormon Creed" Appendix A.
Another edition: 1857. NjP
Sabin 51497
CU-B, DLC, NN, ULA

5678. Murray, Nicholas. Parish and other pencilings; by Kirwan [*pseud.*] New York, Harper and Bros., 1854.
vi [7]–272p. 20cm.
"The Mormon Preacher," p. 114–120. Humorous report on the author's confrontation with a Mormon missionary.
NjP, UPB

5679. Music echoes. Salt Lake City, Published . . . by the Student body of the L.D.S. School of Music. November, 1920–
v. monthly. 20cm.
First issue under title: L.D.S. S. of M. The Bulletin.
USIC V.2 #1–8, 12, V.3 #1–7, V.4 #1–2, V.5 #1

5680. Musick, John Roy. Stories of Missouri. New York, American Book Company [1897]
1p.l., 5–288p. illus. 19cm.
"The Mormons," p. 196–207.
CU, DLC, NjP, UHi, UPB, USIC

5681. Musser, Amos Milton. . . . Brief defence of our people. Philadelphia, April, 1877. To the press of the United States. Philadelphia, 1877.
[4]p. 26cm.
Caption-title.
Signed: A. Milton Musser, "Mormon" Elder [and certified by] Henry Grow, "Mormon" Elder.
"Reprinted from the *American Issue.*"
CU–B, UHi, USIC

5682. ———. (same, under title) Malicious slanders refuted!! A few plain facts plainly spoken, in regard to the pretended "crisis," in Utah!!! [Liverpool? Millennial Star Printing, 1877?]
8p. 21cm.
CSmH, CtY, CU–B, NjP

5683. ———. The fruits of "Mormonism." By non-"Mormon" witnesses. Being for the most part brief extracts from letters, addresses, lectures, etc., by statesmen, senators, governors, judges, tourists, editors, generals, ladies, clergymen, railroad magnates, professors, doctors, and miscellaneous correspondents — all non-"Mormons" — about Utah and the "Mormons" . . . Compiled and written by Elder A. Milton Musser . . . Salt Lake City, Deseret News Steam Printing Establishment, 1878.
35p. 24cm.
CSmH, CtY, CU–B, ICN, MoInRC, NjP, NN, UHi, USl, USIC, UU, UPB, WHi

5684. ———. Mormonism exposed. [Salt Lake City, J. H. Parry & Co., The Palantic, 1888?]
4p. 21½cm. (Palantic leaflet. No. 1)
Favorable comments on the Mormons.
CSmH, NN, UHi, USIC, UU

5685. ———. Please read this free circular on "Mormonism." Then hand it to your neighbor. [By A. Milton Musser, Orson F. Whitney] Philadelphia [1877?]
8p. 22cm.
Original published in Philadelphia, 1877.
USIC

5686. ———. (same) [Philadelphia, 1878?]
8p. 24cm.
Signed: A. Milton Musser (without Orson F. Whitney)
USIC

5687. ———. "Race suicide," infanticide, prolicide, leprocide vs. children. Letters to Messrs. Joseph Smith and Wm. H. Kelley, aggressively defensive. Illustrated. By Elder A. Milton Musser. Fruits of "Mormonism" by Distinguished non-Mormons . . . [Salt Lake City? 1904]
1p.l. [3]–58p. plate, ports. 24cm.
CSmH, MH, MoInRC, NjP, UHi, USl, USIC, WHi

5688. ———. Suttee and polygamy. [Salt Lake City, n.d.]
Broadside. 29×21½cm.
Reprinted from the *Deseret News.*
UHi, UPB

5689. ———. (same) [Salt Lake City, n.d.]
[2]l. 21½cm.
Printed on second leaf: Decision of the Supreme Court of the United States in the Reynolds Case [by] Eliza R. Snow.
USIC

5690. Musser, Joseph. Mormonism from its earliest phases to the present time by Joseph Musser, ex-priest, Reorganized Church of Latter Day Saints. First edition. [n.p.] Northern Farmer and Francies Print., 1895.
[52]p. 26cm.
Cover-title.
Early church history and the RLDS Church.
OClWHi

5691. Musser, Joseph B. Walter Murray Gibson — oceanic adventurer. By Joseph B. Musser. Annapolis, U.S. Naval Institute, 1926.
[1709]–1732p. illus. 22cm.
"Reprinted from the *U. S. Naval Institute. Proceedings.* V. 52. No. 9, whole No. 283."
Brief mention of his Mormon connection.
USIC

MUTUAL

5692. Mutual Improvement League. Constitution and by-laws of the Mutual Improvement League. Salt Lake City, Utah. Organized Dec. 19, 1895. Salt Lake City, The Magazine Printing Co., 1896.
15p. 17½cm.
Cover-title: Mutual Improvement League constitution and by-laws.
A Private club with heads of the Y. M. and Y. L. M.I.A. as president and vice-president.
USIC

5693. Mutual Improvement Messenger. Salt Lake City, February, 1896[?]–October, 1931.
33v. monthly. 25cm.
Calendar of events for Salt Lake City Mutual Improvement Associations.
First volumed year 1908 [V. 12]
USIC inc.

5694. The Mutual Improvement Normal. Devoted to the interests of the Mutual Improvement Association of the Latter-day Saints . . . February 5, 1882–
1v. 22cm.
With V.1 #1–2 was issued a special number dated June 1, 1892: "Historical sketch of the Young men's Mutual Improvement Association."
CU–B

5695. Muus, Rudolf. Mormonernes Pigefangst; Fortaelling grundet paa virkelige Begivenheder, af Julius (Cand. Rudolf Muus) Kristiania, P. Omtvedts Forlag [1906]
60, iiip. 18½cm.
Title in English: Taking of girl captives by the Mormons.
UU

My diary during a foreign tour, in 1881–2. *See R., W. P.*

My first voyage round the world, by M. E. M. *See M., M. E.*

5696. Myall, William. The scenic West; a travelogue by William Myall. Boston, The Stratford Company [c1922]
3p.l., iv, 31, 231p. 23cm.
Includes a section on Salt Lake City and the Mormons.
DLC, UHi

5697. Myers, William H. Through wonderland to Alaska. By Rev. William H. Myers. Reading, Pa., Reading Times Print., 1895.
3p.l. [9]–271p. 19cm.
In Salt Lake City in 1895 for three days which made him an expert having "complete idea of their life . . ."
USIC

5698. Mynster, C. P. G. Vogt dig for Mormonerne! Venlig advarsel til gamle og unge, hoje og lave, rige og fattige, kort sagt: til alle og enhver. Fra fjende af Mormonismen. København, 1863.
35p. 18½cm.
Title in English: Beware of the Mormons.
CtY

5699. Mynster, I. P. Grundlovens bestemmelser med hensyn til de kirkelige forhold i Danmark. Kobenhavn, 1850.
23p.
Title in English: Provisions of the constitutional law regarding the position of the Church in Denmark.
Schmidt

The mysteries of Mormonism. *See Trumble, Alfred.*

5700. Mysteries of Mormonism. A history of the rise and progress of the notorious Latter-day Saints, from the time of Joe Smith . . . to that of Brigham Young . . . Southwark [Eng.] H. Wilson [1858?]
8p. 23cm.
CtY

Mysteries of the Endowment House . . . *See Salt Lake Tribune.*

THE

CITY CHARTER:

LAWS, ORDINANCES, AND ACTS

OF THE

CITY COUNCIL

OF THE

CITY OF NAUVOO.

AND ALSO, THE ORDINANCES

OF THE

NAUVOO LEGION:

FROM THE COMMENCEMENT OF THE CITY TO THIS DATE.

NAUVOO, ILL.
PUBLISHED BY ORDER OF THE CITY COUNCIL.
JOSEPH SMITH, Printer.
....
July . . . 1842.

Item 5714. First separate printing of the Nauvoo charter together with the laws passed by the city council. From the LDS church collection.

NACHASHLOGIAN

5701. The Nachashlogian. St. Louis, August, 1860.
V.1 #1. 21cm.
Periodical planned to promote the socio-religious philosophy outlined in Charles B. Thompson's Nachash Origin of the black and mixed races.
No more published?
Morgan
NNHi

5702. Naisbitt, Henry W. . . . Opening and closing hymns [for dedication of Logan Temple. Logan, Utah, May 17, 1884. Salt Lake City] Deseret News Co., Printers [1884?]
4p. 16cm.
USlC

5703. ———. Quiet chats on "Mormonism" [by H. W. Naisbitt] Salt Lake City, The Deseret News, 1902.
4p.l. [9]–174p. 1 plate. 20cm. (Home circle series. V.2)
ICN, NN, UHi, ULA, USl, USlC, WHi

5704. ———. Rhymelets in many moods . . . [Souvenir ed.] Salt Lake City, Star Printing Company, 1901.
398p. port. 19½cm. (Home circle series. V.1)
Mormon poetry.
DLC, NjP, UHi, ULA, USlC, UU

5705. ———. The Romance of history. Dedicated to the pioneers and their successors [Salt Lake City, 1900?]
Broadside. 27×21cm.
A two-column poem signed H. W. N.
Salt Lake City.
MH

5706. Naked Truths about Mormonism. Oakland, California. January–April, 1888.
1v. (#1–2) 61cm.
An anti-Mormon newspaper that ran for only two issues.
Copyright: Arthur B. Deming.
CSmH, CtY, NN, UPB, USlC

5707. Nash, Marie K. The earth renewed in paradise. [n.p., n.d.]
11p. illus. 20cm.
Cover-title.
CU–B, USlC

5708. National Anti-Mormon Literature and Information Bureau. Beware of Mormonism a word to British men and women. [Colchester, Essex, The National Anti-Mormon Literature and Information Bureau, n.d.]
[4]p. 23cm. (National Anti-Mormon Bureau. Leaflet. No. 1)
MoInRC

5709. The National cyclopaedia of American biography, being the history of the United States as illustrated in the lives of the founders, builders, and defenders of the republic, and of the men and women who are doing the work and moulding the thought of the present time, edited by distinguished biographers, selected from each state, revised and approved by the most eminent historians, scholars, and statesmen of the day. . . . New York, J. T. White, 1893–
46v. illus., ports. 28cm.
V. 16 includes biographies of George Q. Cannon, Jedediah M. Grant, Anthon H. Lund, Heber C. Kimball, Charles W. Penrose, Orson Pratt, Parley P. Pratt, Franklin D. Richards, Willard Richards, Sidney Rigdon, George Albert Smith, Hyrum Smith, John Henry Smith, Joseph Smith, Joseph F. Smith, Lorenzo Snow, James E. Talmage, John Taylor, Daniel H. Wells, John R. Winder, Wilford Woodruff, Brigham Young.
CSmH, NjP, ULA, UPB

National Education Association of the United States. Prominent educators of Utah . . . *See Prominent educators of Utah . . .*

5710. National exchanger. Kansas City, Mo. [and Louisville, Ky.] January 1, 1920–December, 1921.
2v? monthly. 28cm.
Edited by J. Zahnd.
Church of Christ advocate established as a real estate journal but took on more of a religious character.
CU–B V.2 #10; MoInRC inc.; USlC V.1 #1, Jan. 1, 1920–V.2 #12, Dec. 1921

5711. National League of Women's Organizations. Formed to protect the country against the treasonable and polygamous teachings and practices of the Mormon hierarchy, and to maintain Christian ideals of marriage. [Washington? 1904?]
Broadside. 8½×11cm.
Among other things, formed to unseat Reed Smoot.
WHi

5712. ———. To the women of America. [Philadelphia, 1904]
Broadside. 21×27cm.
"To protect the country against the treasonable and polygamous teachings and practices of the Mormon hierarchy, and to maintain Christian ideals of marriage."
WHi

5713. National Reform Association. Crusade against Mormonism. [Pittsburgh, n.d.]
[3]p. 24cm.
MoInRC

———. A world-wide survey of present day Mormonism. *See Davis, Oscar Franklyn.*

NAUVOO LEGION ASSOCIATION

5714. Nauvoo, Ill. Charters. The city charter: laws, ordinances, and acts of the City Council of the City of Nauvoo. And also the ordinances of the Nauvoo Legion from the commencement of the city to this date. Nauvoo, Published by order of the City Council, Joseph Smith, Printer, 1842.
32p. 23cm.
Byrd 725
USIC

5714a. ———. (same) Nauvoo, Published by order of the City Council, Joseph Smith, Printer, 1842.
8p. 23cm.
With the same title page as above but without the ordinances.
Byrd 725
DLC, ICN, MH, USIC

5715. Nauvoo, Ill. Citizens. Citizens of Nauvoo! Once more to arms in defense of your persons and property! . . . [Nauvoo? 1846]
Broadside. 32½×28cm.
Dated: Nauvoo, Saturday evening, July 10, 1846.
Byrd 1097
USIC

5716. ———. New Citizen doggerel; Being an account of the wonderful escape of some "respectable old citizens" from Golden's Point, June 14, 1846. [Warsaw, Printed at the "Signal" Office, 1846]
Broadside. 27½×18cm.
Poems on the departure of the Mormons.
June 14, 1846.
USIC

5717. ———. Notice. A public meeting will be held at the Seventies' Hall tomorrow . . . for the purpose of selecting suitable persons as candidates to be voted for at the ensuing August election. [Nauvoo, 1844]
Broadside. 32×25cm.
Signed: Friday, July 26, 1844.
Byrd 887
USIC

———. Proclamation. To Col. Levi Williams . . .
See Church of Jesus Christ of Latter-day Saints.

5718. ———. Public meeting, of the New Citizens of Nauvoo . . . [Nauvoo, 1846]
Broadside. 23×14cm.
Signed: J. Todd, Chairman, J. H. Dougherty, Secretary.
Repudiating inflammatory hand-bill by the other residents.
In double columns.
Byrd 1098
USIC

Nauvoo, Ill. City Council. Ordinances.
See Nauvoo, Ill. Ordinances.

5719. Nauvoo, Ill. Committee of Public Safety. Circular. Nauvoo, Hancock county, June 15, 1846. At a meeting . . . on Sunday night, June 14th a "Committee of Safety," consisting of 50 persons was appointed . . . to draft an address to the people of the state in general, and to those of the nine counties . . . represented at the Carthage Convention in October last in particular. The Committee . . . present the following address . . . [Nauvoo, 1846]
Broadside. 45½×30cm.
Abhorrence of violence during Mormon era; condemns anti-Mormon mobs.
Byrd 1096
CtY, ICHi, USIC

5720. Nauvoo Expositor. Prospectus of the Nauvoo Expositor . . . Nauvoo, May 10, 1844.
Broadside. 22×19½cm.
Signed: William Law, Wilson Law, Charles Ivins, Francis M. Higbie, Chauncey L. Higbie, Robert D. Foster, Charles A. Foster, Publishers.
Byrd 880, Morgan
USIC

5721. Nauvoo Expositor. Nauvoo, Illinois, June 7, 1844.
V.1 #1. 53½cm.
Edited by Sylvester Emmons.
Only one issue published. The press was destroyed by order of the City Council.
Purpose: To expose Joseph Smith.
Morgan
IHi, NN, USIC

5722. ———. (same) [Reprint. Independence, Mo., Published by the Church of Christ (Temple Lot) ca. 1892]
4p. 53½cm.
Reprint information given on p. 3.
NjP, UHi, UPB, USIC, USID, UU

5723. Nauvoo Legion. Rank roll of the Nauvoo Legion. [Nauvoo? 1842?]
Broadside. 38×30cm.
In double columns.
Byrd 726
ICHi, USIC

5724. ———. Revised laws of the Nauvoo Legion, from the Constitution of the United States. By authority. Nauvoo, Illinois, John Taylor, Printer, 1844.
36p. 26cm.
Byrd 881
CtY inc., MoInRC, UPB inc., USIC

5725. The Nauvoo Legion Association. Association of veteran artillerymen of the Nauvoo Legion. Organized, Salt Lake City, Utah, Sept. 14th, 1897. [Salt Lake City, 1901]
[3]p. 21½cm.
USIC

NAUVOO LEGION ASSOCIATION

5725a. ———. The Nauvoo Legion Association, organized, Salt Lake City, Utah, Sept. 14th, 1897; a benevolent society for the benefit of the members of the Church of Jesus Christ of Latter-day Saints, who are members of the above association . . . [Salt Lake City, 1905]
[4]p. illus. 21½cm.
Caption-title.
Includes application for membership.
MH, NjP, UHi, UPB, USIC

5726. Nauvoo Legion. Committee of Arrangements. Order of the day for the sixth of April, 1853, in laying the corner stones of the Temple in Great Salt Lake City, Utah Territory. [Salt Lake City, 1853].
Broadside. 40×14cm.
Signed: D. H. Wells, Amasa Lyman, Lorenzo Snow.
USIC

5727. Nauvoo Neighbor. Nauvoo, Hancock Co., Ill., May 3, 1843–October 29, 1845.
3v. weekly. 52cm.
Editor: John Taylor.
Successor to *The Wasp*.
V.1 #1–39 published by Taylor and Woodruff.
Whole numbering continues that of *The Wasp*. Nos. 3 and 5 (whole numbers 108 and 109) of V.2 omitted in numbering.
CSmH Je 24, 1844; CtY V.1 comp., V.2 #1–3, 6–52, V.3 #1–23; ICHi Je 7, 28, 1843, Ja 10, 31, Mr 27, Ap 10, Je 26, Jl 10, Ag 7, 28, O 2, 23, 30, 1844, Ja–F, Mr 26, Ap 23–30, My 14–Je 18, Jl 2, 16, Ag 13–S 3, 17–O 1845; MWA Jl 3, 1844; NN D 27, 1843, Mr 6, 27–Ap 10, 24–My 8, Je 19, Jl 17, 31, 1844, Ja 9–F 5, 19–26, Mr 12, 26–Ap 2, 30, My 21, Jl 9, S 24–O 1; USIC comp.

5728. ———. Nauvoo Neighbor, extra. Monday Morning, June 17, 1844. [Nauvoo, Ill., 1844]
Broadside. 52×44cm.
Contains proceedings of Nauvoo City Council relating to *The Expositor* and includes Joseph Smith's order to destroy *The Expositor* press.
Byrd 882
USIC

5729. ———. Nauvoo Neighbor, extra: — Friday morning (5 o'clock) June 21, 1844. [Nauvoo, Ill., 1844]
Broadside. 56½×39½cm.
"We have thought it advisable to re-publish a few of the resolves and order of the Carthagenians, Warsaw-vains, &c., for the purpose of mobbing, plundering, murdering, and utterly exterminate, the Latter day Saints."
Byrd 883
CtY, USIC

5730. ———. Nauvoo Neighbor, extra: June 29th, 1844. Proclamation . . . to the citizens of Carthage and Hancock Counties . . . [Nauvoo, Ill., June 28, 1844]
Broadside. 14×8½cm.
Concerning the situation after the martyrdom including a plea to people to stay in their houses, stating that no Mormon retaliation is imminent, and describing what was to be done with the bodies of Hyrum and Joseph. Signed: M. R. Deming, Brig. Gen., 4th Brigade and 5th Division.
Byrd 884
USIC

5731. ———. Nauvoo Neighbor, Extra: Sunday, 3 o'clock p.m., June 30th, 1844. Awful assassination [of Joseph and Hyrum Smith. Nauvoo, Ill., 1844]
Broadside. 66½×49cm.
Byrd 885
CtY, USIC

5732. ———. [Nauvoo] Neighbor — Extra. Nauvoo, Sept. 12, 1845. Mobbing again in Hancock! Friday morning, 10 o'clock. [Nauvoo, Ill., 1845]
Broadside. 27×21cm.
In double columns.
Includes "list of houses destroyed."
USIC

5733. ———. Nauvoo Neighbor, extra: Nauvoo, Nov. 19, 1845. Murder and Arson, Edmund Durfee shot — two houses burned . . . [Nauvoo, Ill., 1845]
Broadside. 30½×24cm.
The work of leaving for the west was hindered by active anti-Mormon mobs.
Byrd
ICHi

5734. ———. . . . A short chapter of interesting history. Lamoni, Ia., 1895.
11p. 24cm.
Caption-title.
A reprint of excerpts from the *Nauvoo Neighbor* of July 3, 1844, relating to the assassination of Joseph and Hyrum Smith.
Supplement to the *Saints' Herald*.
CtY, MoInRC

5735. Nauvoo, Ill. Ordinances. Ordinances of the City of Nauvoo, passed by the City Council, at different meetings, A. D. 1849. [Nauvoo? 1849?]
28p. 16cm.
Caption-title.
New ordinances, May 26–July 17, 1849, to replace those passed by the former residents.
Signed: C. Robinson, Mayor.
Byrd 1485
USIC

5736. Nead, Benjamin Mattias. Birth-place of Mormonism; the operations of Prophets Smith and Rigdon in Pennsylvania. [Chambersburg, Pa., Valley Spirit Pr., 1897?]
12p. 18cm.
Caption-title.
CtY, UHi

NEAL, R. B.

5737. ———. . . . Waynesboro; the history of a settlement in the county formerly called Cumberland but later Franklin, in the Commonwealth of Pennsylvania, in its beginnings . . . including a relation of pertinent topics of general state and county history. Harrisburg, Pub. under the auspices of the Waynesboro Centennial Association, Harrisburg Publishing Company, 1900.
428p. illus., maps. 25½cm.
A section on religious denominations (p. 299–303); discusses Mormonism after considering the orthodox sects. Mormonism is mixed up with the Millerism and Sidney Rigdon is named as the chief seer before 1844.
DLC, UHi

5738. Neal, R. B. Anti-Mormon tracts. Cincinnati, 1899–1901.
9 nos. 14½cm.
Contents: 1. Was Joe. Smith a Prophet? 16p. 2. Smithianity; or, Mormonism refuted by Mormons, 32p. 3. The Stick of Ephraim vs. The Bible of the Western Continent, or, The Manuscript Found vs. the Book of Mormon, 31p. 4. Smithianity; or Mormonism refuted by Mormons (pt. 2) 31p. 5. The Stick of Ephraim vs. the Bible of the Western Continent (pt. 2) 19p. 6. Smithianity; or, Mormonism refuted by Mormons. Booth's Bombs, 62p. 7. The Manuscript Found vs. the Book of Mormon. 8. The Manuscript Found vs. the Book of Mormon (pt. 2) 9. Oliver Cowdery's defence and renunciation, 24 [2]p.
MH #2, 4, 9; MoInRC #2–6, 9; NN #1–6; UPB #9; USIC #2; UU #1–9

5739. ———. The Book of Abraham. Greeley, Colorado, Greeley Publishing Co. [n.d.]
8p. 24cm.
MoInRC

5740. ———. Did Oliver Cowdery renounce Mormonism and join the Methodist Protestant Church at Tiffin, Ohio? Grayson, Ky., Press of Charter County News, 1915.
17 [1]p. illus. 22cm. (Gospel Dollar League pamphlets. No. 1)
MoInRC, USIC

5741. ———. Hot shots from David Whitmer for the "Brighamites" and "Josephites" [Grayson, Ky., 1909]
2p. 21cm. ("Sword of Laban" Leaflet. No. 2)
At head of title: The American Anti-Mormon Association.
Caption-title.
With this is a letter from R. B. Neal, asking for funds to fight the "False prophet of the twentieth Century." [1]p. 21cm.
MH

5742. ———. The Manuscript found vs. the Book of Mormon. Cincinnati, 1901.
2 nos. 14½cm. (Anti-Mormon tracts. Nos. 7–8)
UU

5743. ———. The Mountain Meadow massacre. Revolting crime on the plains in 1857, now an historic incident, laid at the door of the Mormon Church. By Rev. R. B. Neal. [Grayson, Ky.?] The Evangelist and Anti-Mormon Leader [n.d.]
[4]p. 16×10cm.
MoInRC, NN

5744. ———. Oliver Cowdery's defence and renunciation. [Grayson, Ky.] Ashland Independent Pub. Co. Print. 1906.
24[2]p. 15cm. (Anti-Mormon tracts. No. 9)
Chiefly Oliver Cowdery's defence, with a purported facsimile of the 1839 edition. This is the version from which all copies have been taken.
MH, UPB, USIC

5745. ———. Smithianity; or, Mormonism refuted by Mormons. Part I. [Cincinnati, O., 1898]
32p. 14½cm. (Anti-Mormon tracts. No. 2)
MH, NN

5746. ———. Smithianity; or, Mormonism refuted by Mormons. Part II. [Cincinnati, O.? 1899?]
32p. 14½cm. (Anti-Mormon tracts. No. 4)
MH, NN

5747. ———. Smithianity; or, Mormonism refuted by Mormons. By R. B. Neal, Grayson, Ky. [Cincinnati, Christian Leader Print., 1901]
2p.l. [5]–62p. 14½cm. (Anti-Mormon tracts. No. 6)
MH, NN, UPB, USIC

5748. ———. The Stick of Ephraim vs. The Bible of the western continent; or, The manuscript found, vs. the Book of Mormon. Part I. [Cincinnati, O., Christian Leader Print., 1899]
31 [1]p. 14½cm. (Anti-Mormon tracts. No. 3)
Preface by F. D. Power.
MH, NN, UPB

5749. ———. The stick of Ephraim vs. the Bible of the western continent; or, the manuscript found vs. the Book of Mormon. Part II. Grayson, Ky. [c1899]
14p. 13½cm. (Anti-Mormon tracts. No. 5)
Attacks Smith's claim as a linguist, says Hebrew would be like shorthand when compared with Egyptian, and that any one who used Egyptian as space saving should be considered a "first class candidate . . . for the weak minded institute."
UU

5750. ———. (same) [Cincinnati, c1899]
19p. 14cm. (Anti-Mormon tracts. No. 5)
NN

NEAL, R. B.

5751. ———. Sword of Laban leaflets. Pikeville, Ky. [Grayson, Ky., 1905?]
17 nos. 28cm.
Contents: 10. Was Joseph Smith, Jr. a polygamist? 11. The three Nephite apostles. 14. Joseph Smith on celestial marriage. 15. The affidavit of Joseph B. Noble. 16. Murder of General Joseph Smith, Junior. 17. Did Joseph Smith walk on water? Parts 1–9 not located.
NN #10, 11, 16–17; UPB #14; USlC #10, 11, 14, 15, 16, 17

5752. ———. "Sword of Laban" leaflets. [Second series] Grayson, Ky., American Anti-Mormon Association, 1908[–11]
16 nos. 22cm.
At head of title: The American anti-Mormon Association.
Contents: 1. Title page and preface to the original Book of Mormon. 2. Hot shots from David Whitmer for the "Brighamites" and "Josephites." 3. More hot shots from David Whitmer. 4. The Mormon a traitor to our Country, a foe to our flag. 5. The Urim and Thummim. 6. Oliver Cowdery's revelation. 7. A togo blow. 8. Saving a soul and convicting a liar. 9. "Mother Lucy's" Book. 10. That Canada Revelation. 11. Oliver Cowdery's Defense. 12. Oliver Cowdery's renunciation of Mormonism. 13. Cowdery's recantation confirmed. 14. "Gathering up Israel." 15. The picture and two opinions of the Mormon prophet. 16. From the Man who set the type on the first Book of Mormon.
MH #2–16; NN #1, 2, 5, 6, 11–16; UPB; USlC

5753. ———. Was Joe Smith a prophet? by R. B. Neal, Evangelist, Grayson, Ky. [Cincinnati, O., Christian leader Print., 1898]
16p. 15cm. (Anti-Mormon tracts. No. 1)
MH, NN, OClWHi, OO

5754. Necessity of revelation. [n.p., n.d.]
4p. 21½cm.
Caption-title.
UPB

5755. ———. (same) [Liverpool? Millennial Star Office? 1908?]
4p. 22cm.
UHi

5756. Needham, Simon B. The Lord's standard in the campaign of 1884. Waukesha, Wis., 1884.
4p.
Eberstadt *Utah and the Mormons*

5756a. Neibaur, Thomas Croft. How Private Neibaur won the Congressional medal of honor; a thrilling and wonderful war story, told in his own words. Introduction by Charles W. Nibley, Presiding Bishop of the Church. [n.p., 1920?]
8p. illus. 23½cm.
USlC

5757. Neiiendam, Machael. Frikirker og sekter. Kobenhavn, 1927.
444p.
Title in English: Free churches and sects.
Schmidt

5758. Neilsen, C. E. Autobiography of C. E. Neilsen. Period of 1839–1880. "Journal of Rasmus Neilsen, 1809–1854, from the time he left Denmark til [sic] his death; translated from the Danish by his son, C. E. Neilsen." Mona, Utah, 1902.
19p. 29cm.
Duplicated.
UPB

5759. Neilson, Clyde. The three sisters; or, faith, hope and charity. [n.p., n.d.]
8p. 18cm.
Mormon doctrinal references.
UHi

5760. Neilson, N. P. The Resurrection of life and the improvement and salvation of all mankind by N. P. Neilson. Mt. Pleasant, Utah, 1905.
[4] 2–100p. 20½cm.
USlC

5761. Nelke, D. I. Illustrated American biography containing memoirs, and engravings and etchings of representative Americans. Issued under the direction of D. I. Nelke. Chicago, The Lewis Publishing Company [c1895]
2v. ports. 40cm.
V. 2, p. 634–664 has biographies of Lorenzo Snow, Brigham Young, Joseph F. Smith, George Q. Cannon, and William B. Preston.
USlC

5762. Nelson, Bengt. An autobiography of Bengt Nelson, Sr., together with a sketch of his wife Ellen J. Nelson with a short introduction and revision by Dr. J. C. Robison. [n.p., n.d.]
[44]p. ports. 16½cm.
Mormon biography.
UPB

5763. Nelson, John Young. Fifty years on the trail; a true story of western life by Harrington O'Reilly. With over one hundred illustrations by Paul Frenzeny. New York, F. Warne & Co., 1889.
xvi, 381p. [1]l. illus. 19cm.
Printed in London.
A biography of John Y. Nelson, written by Harrington O'Reilly from facts supplied by Nelson. The narrative is in the first person, as told by Nelson.
Improbable account of his life in the West. Claims to have headed the Brigham Young train to Salt Lake City. Obviously false as is much of his Mormon narration. Later joins church for "convenience" and has to watch to keep from getting killed by the Destroying Angels.

Issued simultaneously by Chatto and Windus of London. Published in Paris the same year under title: Cinquante ans chey les Indiens. Paris, G. Chamerot, 1889. CU–B
Another edition: London, "2d ed." 1890. NjP
CSmH, CtY, DLC, NjP, OClW, PU, RP, ULA, USlC, WHi

5764. ———. Life among the American Indians; fifty years on the trail, a true story of western life, by Harrington O'Reilly. With over one-hundred illustrations by Paul Frenzeny. London, Chatto & Windus, 1891.
xvi, 381p. illus. 19½cm.
Cover-title: Fifty years on the trail; life among the Redskins, by a companion of Buffalo Bill.
Revision of his *Fifty years on the trail.*
CU–B, NN

5765. Nelson, Lowry. The Mormon settlements in Alberta . . . Toronto, Macmillan Co. [n.d.]
175–272p. illus., charts, maps. 24cm.
Reprinted from *Canadian Frontiers of Settlement,* V.7.
ULA, UPB

5766. ———. . . . The Mormon village: a study in social origins, by Lowry Nelson . . . Research Division, Brigham Young University . . . [Provo? Utah, 1930]
11–37p. illus., plans. 23cm. (Brigham Young University studies. No. 3)
Cover-title.
"Reprint from *Proceedings of the Utah Academy of Sciences.* V. 7."
CtY, DLC, MB, MiU, NjP, NN, OCl, OO, OU, UHi, UPB, USl, USlC, UU

5767. ———. . . . A social survey of Escalante, Utah, by Lowry Nelson . . . Provo, Utah, Brigham Young University, 1925.
44p. maps, diagrs. 23½cm. (Brigham Young University studies. No. 1)
Cover-title.
Research Division, Brigham Young University and Bureau of Agricultural Economics, U.S. Department of Agriculture cooperating.
DA, NjP, OCl, OO, OU, UHi, ULA, UPB

5768. ———. . . . The Utah farm village of Ephraim, by Lowry Nelson . . . Provo, Utah, Brigham Young University, 1928.
1p.l., 41p. maps, diagrs. 23cm. (Brigham Young University studies. No. 2)
Cover-title.
Research Division, Brigham Young University and Bureau of Agricultural Economics. U.S. Department of Agriculture cooperating.
DA, OO, UHi, ULA, UPB, UU

5768a. Nelson, Nels Lars. Heaven versus Nirvana: a brief examination of the rational sanction for immortality. By Prof. N. L. Nelson. [Salt Lake City? 1905?]
40p. 23cm.
Reprinted from the *Improvement Era,* V. 8, May–June 1905, p. 481, 579.
USlC

5769. ———. The Mormon point of view. A short account of Prof. Nelson's magazine. [Provo, Utah, 1904]
[4]p. 15cm.
Printed on pink paper.
A prospectus on his periodical *The Mormon Point of View.*
UPB, USlC

5770. ———. An open letter to Hon. Moses Thatcher, his position scrutinized and his utterances analyzed. By a "Mormon," who is also a democrat. Salt Lake City, Deseret News Publishing Co., 1897.
11p. 23cm.
Mormons and politics.
MH, NjP, UHi, USlC

5771. ———. Preaching and public speaking; a manual for the use of preachers of the gospel and public speakers in general. Salt Lake City, Deseret News Publishing Co., 1898.
x, 444p. 20cm.
NjP, NN, UHi, ULA, UPB, USl, USlC, UU

5772. ———. Preaching and public speaking among Latter-day Saints, a protest against abuses and a course of instructions whereby they may be overcome. 2d ed. Salt Lake City, The Deseret News, 1910 [c1898]
xi, 404p. illus. 20cm.
MH, UHi, UU

5773. ———. Scientific aspects of Mormonism: or, Religion in terms of life by Nels L. Nelson . . . New York and London, G. P. Putnam's Sons, 1904.
xi, 347p. 20½cm.
DLC, MH, MiU, NjP, NjPT, NN, UHi, ULA, UPB, USl, USlC, WHi

5774. ———. (same) Chicago, Press of Hillison & Co., 1918.
xi, 347p. 20½cm.
MH, NN, UHi, USlC

5775. Nelson, Thomas, and Sons. Great Salt Lake City, and Utah Territory. With twelve illustrations from photographs by C. R. Savage. London, Edinburgh, and New York, T. Nelson and Sons; Salt Lake City, Savage and Ottinger [187–]
24p. 16½×10cm.
Description of Salt Lake City and Mormonism in general.
UPB

NELSON, T., AND SONS

5776. ———. Salt Lake City, and the way thither. With twelve illustrations from photographs by C. R. Savage. London, Edinburgh, and New York, T. Nelson and Sons; Salt Lake City, Savage and Ottinger [1878?]
2p.l. [5]–31p. illus., col. plates. 10½×16½cm. (Nelsons' pictorial guide-books)
CtY, CU–B, UHi, UPB, USIC

5777. ———. . . . Salt Lake City, with a sketch of the route of the Central Pacific Railroad, from Omaha to Salt Lake City, and thence to San Francisco. With twelve illustrations from photographs by C. R. Savage. London, Edinburgh, New York, T. Nelson and Sons; Salt Lake City, Savage and Ottinger [1874?]
31p. illus., part fold., col. plates. 10½×17cm. (Nelson's pictorial guide-books)
Interesting notes: Johnston's bad leadership in Echo Canyon. An angel stood on a conical hill to point the place to Brigham Young. The angel, some say, was the spirit of Joseph Smith.
NjP, UPB, USIC

5778. ———. (same) . . . and from Ogden to San Francisco. With 12 illustrations from photographs by C. R. Savage. New York, T. Nelson and Sons; Salt Lake City, C. R. Savage [1878]
31p. illus., part fold., col. plates. 10½×17cm. (Nelson's pictorial guide-books)
CSmH, DLC, MH, UHi, UPB, UU

5779. ———. . . . The Union Pacific Railroad: a trip across the North American continent from Omaha to Ogden. . . . New York, T. Nelson & Sons [1871?]
2p.l. [7]–46p. illus., plates, map. 10½×16½cm. (Nelsons' pictorial guide-books)
Chap. V: A visit to Salt Lake City, p. 40–46.
CU–B, DLC, UPB

5780. Nelson, Thomas Amos Rogers. Speech of Hon. Thomas A. R. Nelson . . . on polygamy in Utah. Delivered in the House of Representatives, April 4 and 5, 1860. [Washington] Printed by L. Towers [1860]
16p. 22cm.
CU–B, DLC, MH, OClWHi, UHi, USl, USIC

5781. Nephi, Utah. Nephi's semi-centennial jubilee, 1851–1901. [Nephi, Nephi Record Print., 1901]
10 [5]p. 21cm.
Historical information as well as the program.
USIC

5782. Neslen, C. Clarence. Why religion? — why the church? Address delivered over Radio Station KSL, Sunday Evening, July 15, 1928. [Salt Lake City] 1928.
Broadside. 50½×20cm.
Reprinted from the *Deseret News*, Saturday, July 21, 1928.
UPB

5783. Nevada State Historical Society. Nevada State Historical Society Papers. Reno, Nevada, 1926.
2p.l. [ix]–xp. [5]l. [5]–505p. 18½cm.
"History of Las Vegas Mission" by Andrew Jenson, 1925–26, p. 117–284.
UPB, USIC

5784. Nevins, Allan. The emergence of modern America, 1865–78. New York, Macmillan Co., 1927.
xix, [1]l., 446. plates. 22½cm.
The social theocracy of early Utah with its advantages and drawbacks.
Another edition: 1928. DLC
CU, DLC, NjP

5785. ———. Frémont, the West's greatest adventurer; being a biography from certain hitherto unpublished sources of General John C. Frémont, together with his wife, Jessie Benton Frémont, and some account of the period of expansion which found a brilliant leader in the Pathfinder, by Allan Nevins . . . New York and London, Harper & Brothers, 1928.
2v. illus., plates, ports., maps (1 double) facsims. 24½cm.
Frémont's association with the Mormons during a winter at Parowan.
Howes N64
CU–B, DLC, NjP, UHi

5786. The New Era. Salt Lake City, August 15, 1916–November 15, 1916.
4 nos. monthly. 22½cm.
"Published every month by the Progressive Association of Latter-day Saints."
Edited by Edward Janoschek.
USIC

5787. The New Era. Salt Lake City, October, 1921–October, 1922.
v. 28cm.
"This publication is in no way connected with the Reorganized Church of Jesus Christ of Latter Day Saints, nor do the publishers believe in the claims set forth by the organization."
The first issue is a Prospectus to the publication, which is also edited by Edward Janoschek.
UPB #1–4, USIC #1–2

5788. The New Era, and Herald of Zion's Watchmen. Voree, Wis., January–February, 1847.
1v.? semi-monthly. 48cm.
Published by dissenters of the Strang group. Only two issues found.
John Gaylord, Isaac Scott and Robert Maltly (i.e. Malby?) editors.
MoInRC Jan. 1847; USIC Jan. 1847, Feb. 1847

5789. A new heresy, entitled "The Mormonites," and by themselves, "The Latter day Saints," has lately appeared. The following is believed to be a true account of its origin. [London, Wertheimer & Co., Printers, 185–]
2p. 19½cm.
USIC

5790. The new heresy! An exposure of Mormonism, showing its origin, absurdity, and impiety. A conversation between James Anxious, and his cousin Henry. 4th ed. [Dunstable, Printed and Sold by Harper Twelve-trees, 184–]

8p. 21cm.

Mormon apologetics, possibly written by Parley P. Pratt.

USIC

5791. New West Education Commission. Addresses at the annual meeting of the New West Education Commission held October 14, 1890, in the first Congregational Church, Chicago [1890?]

27p. 23cm.

Cover-title: Mormons and Jesuits; addresses by Rev. F. W. Gunsaulus and W. F. Slocum and Professor Henry E. Gordon.

CU, NN, WHi

5792. ———. Annual report. Chicago, 1881–1893.

13 nos. 22cm.

The promotion of Christian civilization in Utah and Christian education against Mormonism. Includes articles such as "Utah, will the Edmunds Law destroy polygamy," "The Law and Mormonism," "Mormonism as related to Christianity," etc.

13th report under: Congregational New West Education Commission. More emphasis on schools and less on Mormonism.

CtY comp.; DE #2–13; DLC #4, 9, 13; NN comp.; ULA #10

5793. ———. The New West Education Commission. [Chicago, 1880?]

[4]p. 22cm.

Utah in the grasp of a tyrannical priesthood.

MH

5794. ———. The New West Education Commission. [Chicago, 1885]

[6]p. 13cm.

Testimonies as to the impact of the Commission against Mormon influence in Utah.

USIC

5795. ———. The New West Education Commission. Official Statement [Chicago, ca. 1885]

[3]p. 17cm.

Brief summary of its purpose and success in Utah.

MH

5796. New York. Public library. . . . List of works in the library relating to the Mormons. New York, 1909.

57p. 26cm.

Cover-title.

"Reprinted from the *Bulletin*, March 1909, V. 13, p. 183–247."

"A large majority of the books . . . was collected by the late William Berrian, from whose estate they were bought in December, 1899, by Miss Helen Miller Gould and presented to the library."

DLC, NN, UHi, ULA, UPB, USI, USIC, UU, WHi

5797. New York Messenger. New York City, Samuel Brannan, July 5, 1845–Nov. 15, 1845.

20 issues. weekly. 34cm.

Successor to *The Prophet*, the first issue being whole no. 53 (V.2 #1) and continues to whole no. 72.

Edited by Parley P. Pratt.

CtY inc.; NN; ULA #55, 61, 67; USIC

5798. New York Messenger. . . . To emigrants . . . [New York, 1845]

Broadside. 41×28cm.

At head of title: New-York Messenger extra. Saturday, Dec. 13, 1845.

Contains particulars concerning passage and provisions for the westward voyage of Mormon emigrants.

CtY, NN, UPB

5799. New York Tribune. Tribune almanac for 1859. [New York] H. Greeley and Company [1858]

80p. 16cm.

"Utah and the Mormons," p. 37–42.

ICJ, MWA, NjP, NN

5800. Newberry, Fannie Ellsworth (Stone). A son's victory, A story of the land of the honey bee, by Fannie E. Newberrry . . . With illustrations by H. P. Barnes. Philadelphia, American Baptist Publication Society [c1897]

4p.l., 408p. plates. 18½cm.

Fiction relating to the Mormons. Triumph over Mormon beliefs.

NjP, USIC

5801. Newbigging, Anne Christena (Isaacson). A cry of the soul; a romance of 1862, by Anne C. Newbigging. Boston, Sherman, French & Company, 1917.

4p.l., 323p. 20½cm.

Fiction concerning Mormonism.

DLC, UPB, USIC

5802. Newby, R. G. Reasons why. [Independence, Mo., Church of Christ, 192–]

12p. 18cm.

Church of Christ (Temple Lot)

UPB

5803. Newman, Angelina French (Thurston). In the Senate of the U.S. Memorial of Mrs. Angie F. Newman, remonstrating against the admission of Utah Territory into the Union as a state so long as the administration of the affairs of that territory continues in the hands of the Mormon Priesthood. [Washington, Govt. Print. Off.] 1888.

16p. 23cm. (U.S. 50th Cong. 1st Sess. Senate. Misc. Doc. No. 201)

Memorial on several grounds, including polygamy and an assortment of evils perpetrated by the Mormon Church.

An answer to "the speech made in the House of Representatives, August 25, 1888, by Hon. John T. Caine of Utah."

CtY, NjP, NN, ULA, UPB, USIC

5804. ———. The scene in Salt Lake City. [Salt Lake City, 1884]
Broadside. 31×15½cm.
An account of the 2000 polygamous women gathered at the Salt Lake Theatre to protest "the execution of laws which shelter womanhood."
Eberstadt *Utah and the Mormons.*

5805. ———. Observation no. 2. Mrs. Angie Newman in Women's Home Mission, June 1884. [Salt Lake City?] 1884.
Broadside. 3½×15cm.
Experience of "a victim of this 'Mormon abomination.' "
NjP

5806. ———. . . . Woman suffrage in Utah . . . [Washington, Govt. Print. Off.] 1886.
9p. 23cm. (U.S. 49th Cong. 1st Sess. Senate. Misc. Doc. No. 122)
Petition of Mrs. Angie F. Newman relative to woman suffrage in Utah; much information on Mormonism.
UPB

5807. Newman, John Philip. A sermon by the Rev. Dr. Newman, pastor of the Metropolitan Methodist Church, on plural marriage, to which is added an answer by Elder Orson Pratt, one of the twelve apostles of the Church of Jesus Christ of Latter-day Saints. Salt Lake City, Printed at Deseret News Office, 1870.
21p. 22½cm.
Reply by Orson Pratt, p. 11–21.
CtY, DLC, ICN, MH, NN, UPB, USl, USlC, UU

5808. Newmann, R. To halvdele af udvanderlivet. Udgivet af foreningen til gudelige smaaskrifters udbredelse. Kobenhavn, 1867.
16p.
Title in English: Two sides of emigrant life.
Schmidt

5809. Newton, Joseph H. An appeal to the Latter-Day Saints. By Joseph H. Newton, William Richards, and William Stanley. Philadelphia, Printed for the authors, 1863.
iv [5]–72p. 16cm.
A renewal of the Rigdonite claim of leadership of the church.
Morgan
DLC, USlC

5810. Newyddion da o Lawenydd mawr. [Cardiff, n.d.]
4p. 21cm.
Missionary tract.
Title in English: Glad tidings of great joy.
UPB, USlC

5811. Nibley, Charles Wilson. Bishops as Presidents of priests' quorums and what priests can do in a ward. Salt Lake City, 1912.
7p. 17cm.
"From the *Improvement Era*, September, 1912."
NjP, UPB, USlC

5812. ———. Discourse by Charles W. Nibley Presiding Bishop. Delivered at the General Conference at Salt Lake City, Sunday, October 7, 1917. [Salt Lake City, 1917?]
[5]p. 20½cm.
USlC

5813. ———. (same, under title) Remarks by Charles W. Nibley, Presiding Bishop, delivered at the general conference at Salt Lake City, Sunday, October 7, 1917. [Salt Lake City, 1917]
[5]p. 20cm.
Same as his *Discourse* . . . but with new title pasted over.
USlC

5814. ———. Fast offerings care for the poor. Salt Lake City [n.d.]
[4]p. 16cm.
Variant printings. UPB, USlC
NjP, UPB, USlC

5815. ———. Tithing; a discourse by President Charles W. Nibley, given in the Salt Lake Tabernacle, Sunday, October 9, 1927. Independence, Zion's Printing and Publishing Co. [1927?]
8p. 16½cm.
Variant printings.
USl, USlC

5816. Nibley, Preston. Brigham Young, the man and leader. Address delivered at Salt Lake City, May 31, 1925 by Preston Nibley. [Independence, Mo., Zion's Printing and Publishing Company. Pub. by the Missions of the Church of Jesus Christ of Latter-day Saints, 1925]
16p. 18cm.
ICN, NjP, NN, UHi, USlC

5817. Nicaise, Auguste. . . . Une année au désert; scènes et récits du Far-West Américain. Chalons, Imprimerie de T. Martin, Place du Marché-Au-Blé, 1864.
120p. 20cm.
Chapter: Les Mormons. Left Jefferson City May 4, 1858. Visited Salt Lake City.
Title in English: A year in the desert; scenes and reports of the American Far-West.
Howes N132, W–C 404
CSmH, DLC

5818. Nichols, Reuben T. The ministerial labors of Reuben T. Nichols, in the Church of Jesus Christ of Latter-day Saints. [n.p., 1886?]
11p. 23cm.
Caption-title.
Member of the Strang faction.
Signed: Reuben T. Nichols.
Morgan
CtY, UHi, WBuC

5819. Nichols, Thomas Low. Religions of the world. An impartial history of religious creeds, forms of worship, sects, controversies, and manifestations from the earliest period to the present time. By T. L. Nichols. Cincinnati, Valentine Nicholson and Co. [c1855]
2p.l. [5]–125p. 23½cm.
"Mormonism," p. 98–103.
Quotes from the Wentworth letter, and a letter to the *Chicago Tribune*, July 24, 1854 concerning polygamy.
ICU, IMunS, IU, NN

5820. Nichols, Walter Hammond. Trust a boy! The story of four boys, showing how they were man hunters by accident on the Great Salt Lake, written by Walter H. Nichols; illustrated by Lorenz C. Braren. New York, The Macmillan Company, 1923.
xip., [1]l., 383p. plates. 19½cm.
Juvenile fiction in Mormon setting.
DLC, MiU, NjP, OCl, OClh, USl

5821. ———. The measure of a boy; the spirit in all boys as it met the challenge of tragedy, unafraid and loyal to the friendship of a man. A sequel to "Trust a boy!" by Walter H. Nichols, illustrated by Lorenzo C. Braren. New York, The Macmillan Company, 1925.
xiiip. [1]l., 270p. plates, maps. 19½cm.
Juvenile fiction in Mormon setting.
DLC, NjP, USl

5822. Nicholson, John. Comprehensive salvation: or, The Gospel to the living and the dead . . . [Liverpool, Printed and Published by A. Carrington, 1880]
16p. 19½cm.
Caption-title.
CtY, CU-B, NN, USlC

5823. ———. (same) [Liverpool, Published by the L.D.S. Printing, Publishing, & Emigrating Co., 1880]
16p. 22cm.
CU-B

5824. ———. (same) [Liverpool, Printed and Published by William Budge, 1880]
16p. 19½cm.
Caption-title.
CSmH, CU-B, ICN, MH, NjP, UHi, USl, USlC, UU

5825. ———. (same, in Welsh) Iachawdwriaeth gynwysfawr, neu Yr Efengyl i'r meirw a'r byw, gan John Nicholson, Henuriad o Eglwys Iesu Grist Saint y Dyddiau Diweddaf. (Cyt. gan yr Henuriad Evan S. Morgan.) [Liverpool, Argraffwyd a chyhoeddwyd gan Brigham Young, n.d.]
12p. 21½cm.
USlC

5826. ———. The latter-day prophet, by John Nicholson, an Elder of the Church of Jesus Christ of Latter-day Saints. [n.p., n.d.]
24p. 18cm.
Caption-title.
CU-B, UPB, USlC, UU

5827. ———. (same) [Liverpool, Printed and Published by William Budge, 1880]
16p. 21cm.
Caption-title.
CSmH, CtY, ICN, MH, NjP, NN, UHi, USlC

5828. ———. The martyrdom of Joseph Standing; or, The murder of a "Mormon" missionary. A true story. Also an appendix, giving a succint [sic] description of the Utah penitentiary and some data regarding those who had, up to date of this publication, suffered incarceration through the operations of the anti-"Mormon" crusade, begun in 1884. Written in prison, by John Nicholson . . . Salt Lake City, The Deseret News Co., Printers, 1886.
2p.l. [3]–160p. 19cm.
"The Utah penitentiary, enclosure and buildings." p. 79–160.
CSmH, CtY, CU-B, DLC, ICU, MH, NjP, NN, UHi, ULA, USl, USlC, UU, WHi

5829. ———. (same, in Swedish) Pöbelns händer eller Joseph Standings martyrdod . . . Salt Lake City, "Korrespondentens tryckeri," 1893.
107p. 14cm.
UPB

5830. ———. The means of escape; or, existing evils and their cure . . . [Liverpool, Printed and Published by Albert Carrington, 1878]
4p. 19½cm.
Caption-title.
Variant printings. USlC
CtY, USlC

5831. ———. (same) [Liverpool, Printed and Published by Wm. Budge, 1878?]
4p. 22cm.
CSmH, ICN, MH, USl, USlC, UU

5832. ———. (same) [Liverpool, Printed and Published by John Henry Smith, n.d.]
4p. 21cm.
USlC

5833. ———. (same) [Salt Lake City, Deseret News Co., n.d.]
6p. 16½cm.
MoInRC

5834. ———. The Modern prophet. Salt Lake City, The Deseret News Co., n.d.]
28p. 17cm.
Summary of church beliefs.
MH, NjP, ULA, UU

5835. ———. (same) [n.p., 1881?]
24p. 24cm.
Caption-title.
CU–B, DLC, NN, USl, USlC, WHi

5836. ———. The Preceptor. Being a simple system for enabling young men to acquire a knowledge of the doctrines of the gospel, and the ability to preach them. By Elder John Nicholson. Salt Lake City, Deseret News Co., 1883.
3p.l. [7]–60p. 16cm.
CSmH, CU–B, DLC, NjP, NN, RPB, UHi, ULA, USl, USlC, UU

5837. ———. (same) 2d ed., rev. and enl. Salt Lake City, Deseret News Co., 1885.
114p. 16cm.
CU, CU–B, IWW, DLC, MH, MoInRC, NjP, NN, OCl, UHi, UPB, USl, USlC, UU, WHi

5838. ———. Le salut pour les morts, par John Nicholson. Traduit de l'Anglais par D. J. Lang. Rotterdam, F. Pieper, 1897.
18p. 21cm.
Title in English: Salvation for the dead.
USlC

5839. ———. The Tennessee massacre and its causes; or, The Utah conspiracy, a lecture by John Nicholson, delivered in the Salt Lake Theatre, on Monday, September 22, 1884. Stenographically reported by John Irvine. Salt Lake City, Printed at Juvenile Instructor Office, 1884.
48p. 17½cm.
CSmH, CU–B, DLC, MH, NjP, NN, UHi, ULA, UPB, USl, USlC, UU

Nickerson, Freeman. *See Gooch, John.*

5840. Nielsen, Adolph. Aspect of the liquor question. Is it necessary? Does it pay? Is it scriptural? Is it legal? Is it moral? The burning issue of the day . . . American Fork, Alpine Pub. Co., Printers [n.d.]
29p. 19cm.
The Mormon point of view without Mormon statements.
CU–B

5841. Nielsen, Fr. Kort veiledning for menigmand til bedommelse af Mormonernes falske og uchristelige laerdomme, af F. N., Sognepraest for Froslev og Mollerup menigheder pass Morso. Nykjobing, 1856.
12p.
Title in English: A short guide to common people for censuring of Mormon teachings.
Schmidt

5842. Nielsen, Johan. Min Kamp med Baptister og Mormoner. Fortsaetelse of "Traek of Johan Nielsen Liv." af John Nielsen. [Middelfart] Utgivet af Kirkelig Forening for den indre Mission i Danmark, 1868.
32p. 17cm. (Missions foreningens egne Forlagsskrifter. Nr. 38)
Title in English: My argument with Baptists and Mormons.
NN, UHi, USlC

5843. ———. (same) Kobenhavn, 1894.
32p. 17cm.
Schmidt
USlC

5844. ———. Min kamp med Mormoner. Blair, Nebraska, 1902.
25p.
Title in English: My fight against the Mormons.
Mulder

5845. Nielsen, John. Keys of the Priesthood. [San Francisco, n.d.]
14p. 18cm.
A Morrisite doctrinal tract.
USlC

5846. Nielson, J. Temporary report, of printing, voluntarily paid for by J. Nielson. [San Francisco, James A. Dove? 1888]
[2]p. 21½cm.
Morrisite printing, 1882–1888.
CtY

5847. Nilson, O. Jubilee hymn. Written for the celebration by the Scandinavians in Utah of the fiftieth anniversary of the introduction of the gospel to the Scandinavian Countries. [Salt Lake City] The Deseret News [ca. 1901]
[2]l. music. 26½cm.
Title in border.
USlC

5848. Nimmo, Joseph, jr. The Mormon usurpation. An open letter addressed to the committee on the Judiciary of the House of Representatives by Joseph Nimmo, jr. Huntington L.I. N.Y., "The Long Islander" Print. [c1886]
55p. 23½cm.
Cover-title.
Mormon outrages in Utah Territory after the Edmunds Act; church domination of the territory.
CSmH, CtY, CU–B, DLC, ICN, MH, NjP, NN, UHi, ULA, UPB, UU

5849. ———. (same) N.Y., Long-Islander Print. [1899] c1886.
55p. 23½cm.
Cover-title.
Reissue of 1886 edition.
WHi

5849a. ———. The Mormon usurpation. Shall it be suppressed? [Huntington, L.I., N.Y., 1886]
3p. 23½cm.
"From *The Republic* of January 2, 1887"
USlC

No parallel in history. *See Gentile Bureau of Information. Salt Lake City.*

5850. Noailles, Amblard Marie Raymond Amédée. Souveniers d'Amérique et d'Orient. Paris, Editions Francaise de la Nouvelle Revue National [1920]
3p.l. [9]–238p., [3]l. 19½cm.
Third section: Deux jours au pays des Mormons en 1881.
Title in English: Souvenirs of America and the Orient.
USlC

5851. Noall, Matthew. Epesetola. Honolulu, Okatoba 6, 1894.
19p. 16cm.
Title in English: Epistle.
USlC

5852. ———. Papa Haawina no na Hui Opio Me Kula Sabati, iloko o ka Ekalesia o Iesu Karisto a ka Poe Hoano a na la Hope Nei, ma ko Hawaii nei Paeaina. Hoomakaukau ia e Makaio Noala, A Hooponoponoia e kekahi Komite i kohoia ma Laie ma ka hui o Aperila, M.H. 1894.
73p. 16cm.
Title in English: Lessons for Sunday School adult classes in the church.
UPB

5853. Noble, Frederick Alphonso. The Mormon iniquity, a discourse delivered before the New West Educational Commission in the First Congregational Church, Sunday evening, Nov. 2, 1884. By Rev. F. A. Noble, D.D. of the Union Park Congregational Church, Chicago, Ill. Chicago, Jameson & Morse, Printers, 1884.
20p. 22½cm.
CSmH, CtY, CU-B, ICHi, ICN, MH, NjP, NN, OO, ULA, USl, USlC

5854. ———. (same) Chicago, Clark & Longley, 1884.
20p. 22½cm.
CtY, ICHi, MH, NH, UHi, WHi

5855. ———. The need and the value of Christian schools in the present exigency of the new West. A discourse delivered in the Old South Church, Boston, Mass., May 24, 1885, by Rev. Frederick A. Noble. Chicago, Jameson & Morse, Printers, 1885.
23p. 22cm.
The need of Christian schools to draw Mormons away from the restrictive and evil Mormon Church.
ICHi, MH, NN, ULA

5856. Nødvendighed for Aabenbaring. [København, Udgivet og forlagt af Andreas Peterson . . . Trykt hos F. E. Bording . . . 1899]
[4]p. 22cm.
Title in English: The necessity of revelation.
USlC

5857. ———. (same) København, Udgivet og forlagt af Andreas Peterson . . . Trykt hos Emil Petersen . . . 1900.
[4]p. 21cm.
USlC

5858. Noell, Thomas E. Speech of Hon. Thomas E. Noell, of Missouri, on woman suffrage and reconstruction of Massachusetts; delivered in the House of Representatives, February 11 and 18, 1867 . . . Washington, Printed at the Congressional Globe Office, 1867.
16p. 21½cm.
Quotes from Artemus Ward about polygamy.
USlC

5859. Nogle anerkendende ord. En samling vidnesbyrd om De Sidste Dages Hellige som et folk, givne af fremragende maend i verden, som ikke er medlemmer af dette samfund. Udgivet i anledning af 75 Aarsdagen for Evangeliets indførelse i Norden. [København, Udgivet og forlagt af John S. Hanson . . . Trykt i "Aka," Kapelvej 1925]
8p. 21½cm.
Title in English: Some knowledgable words.
USlC

5860. Noon, Adolphus H. The last dispensation, or, an introduction to the faith, doctrines, and history of the Church of Jesus Christ of Latter-day Saints, by Elder Adolphus H. Noon, part the first. The present and future of the nations. Pietermaritzburg, P. Davis, Printer, 1862.
19p. 19½cm.
USlC

5861. Nordhoff, Charles. California: for health, pleasure, and residence. A book for travellers and settlers. By Charles Nordhoff . . . New York, Harper & Brothers, Publishers . . . 1873.
2p.l. [11]–255p. illus. 23cm.
Includes a description of Utah and the state of Mormonism; in Utah for 3 or 4 days in 1873.
Another edition: 1874. NjP
CU-B, DLC, USlC

NORDSTJÄRNAN

5862. Nordstjärnan; Sanningen, Kunskapen, Dygden och Tron äro förenade. Köpenhamn, January 8, 1877–

v. monthly. 21cm.

Publication of the Swedish Mission.

Title begins: Nordstjernan.

Title in English: The North star.

ULA 7–8; UPB 1, 4–11, 13–14, 16, 18 inc., 20–41, 42–43 inc., 44–48, 54; USIC

5863. Nordström, Esther Blenda. Amerikanskt. Som emigrant till Amerika . . . Nionde Tusendet. Stockholm, Åhlén & Åkerlunds Förlag [c1923]

3p.l. [7]–267p. 20cm.

"Mormoner," p. 199–219. Swedish emigration to Utah.

Title in English: About America.

CU, DLC, UPB, USIC

5864. The Normal. Provo, Utah, September 14, 1891–May 25, 1894.

4v. monthly. 28cm.

Published by the students of Brigham Young University.

"Commencement Annual" V.3 [2] V.4

Commencement annual for 1893 lettered V.3; the commencement annual of 1894 is the only item listed as V.4.

UPB, USIC inc.

5865. Norman, Henry Wylie. Calcutta to Liverpool by China, Japan, and America, in 1877, by H. W. N. 2d ed. Calcutta, Thacker, Spink and Co., 1881.

104p. map in front. 17cm.

Impressions of Salt Lake, p. 63–68; feels sorry for the women.

UPB

5866. Norris, James W., *compiler.* Illinois annual register, and western business directory, Norris & Gardiner, editors. Comp. by J. W. Norris and G. W. Gardiner. Chicago, 1847.

120p. 19cm.

Includes a brief description of Mormonism in Illinois.

Howes 7456

CtY, DLC, ICHi

5867. North, Marianne. Recollections of a happy life; being the autobiography of Marianne North. Edited by her sister Mrs. John Addington Symonds. 2d ed. London, New York, MacMillan and Co., 1892.

2v. illus., ports. 23cm.

Brief but descriptive account of her meeting with Brigham Young.

NjP, USIC

5868. Northern Islander. St. James, Beaver Island Cooper and Chidester, December 12, 1850– June 19, 1856.

5v. weekly. (89 nos.) 53cm.

Successor to the *Gospel Herald.*

See also *Daily Northern Islander.*

Morgan

CtY Je 24, 1852; Mr 2, S 28, 1854. USIC Ag 9, 1852. WBuC D 12, 1850; Ja 9, F 6, Ap 3, My 1–15, Je 5, Jl 24–31, Ag 14, 28, 1851; Mr 4, Ap 22, Je 17, Jl 1–Ag 19, S 2–16, 30, O 14–21, N 11, 1852; Ap 28, My 5, Je 30, 1853; F 2, Mr 2, Ap 13, Je 1–22, Jl 13, 27, Ag 17–24, S 7, 21–28, N 2, 1854; My 31, Je 14–21, Jl 5, 19, 26, Ag 9–23, S 6–20, O 11–18, N 1, D 6, 1855; Ja 24, F 14, Mr 13, Ap 3, My 1, 22, Je 5, 19, 1856. WHi My 1, 1856

5869. ———. Northern Islander. Extra! Murderous Assault — Attack on Sheriff Miller — Six men wounded. Saint James, Thurs., July 14, 1853.

Broadside. 52×23cm.

From a photostat made by M. M. Quaife. No known copy. Deals with an incident when Mackinac fishermen attacked the Mormons.

Morgan

5870. Northern light. . . . Logan, Utah, May 20– Aug. 15, 1879?

v. daily. 51cm.

Published partly in English and partly in Danish. No information as to duration.

USIC V.1 #13, August 8, 1879

5871. Northern Times. Kirtland, Ohio, Published by F. G. Williams & Co., Feb. 1835–

v. weekly. 52cm.

Editor: Oliver Cowdery, succeeded by Frederick G. Williams.

No information as to how long it was published.

CtY Oct 2, 9, 1835; USIC Dec. 2, 1835, fragment of Jan. 13, 1836

5872. Northrop, Henry Davenport. Marvelous story of one hundred years. History, achievement and progress containing great battles and conquests; the rise and fall of Nations; wonderful growth and progress of the United States; famous explorations and discoveries; amazing developments in every department of human effort . . . By Henry Davenport Northrop. Chicago, W. S. Reeve Publishing Co. [c1901]

xiv, 625p. ports., plates, fold. maps. 24½cm.

Chap. III. "Origin and Growth of Mormonism." Joseph Smith "A profligate impostor."

Published in 1900 under title: Wonderful developments of the nineteenth century. UPB

USIC

5873. Norton, Lewis Adelbert. Life and adventures of Col. L. A. Norton. Written by himself. Oakland, Cal., Pacific Press Publishing House, 1887.

vii [9]–492p. port. 20cm.

Experiences with the Mormons in Carson Valley and with Orson Hyde, 1855–1856, p. 321–333.

CU, CU-B, DLC, NjP

NUTTING, J. D.

5874. Notice. Messrs. John Wood and Wm. F. Karnes have just returned from the place where the Mormons who have left Nauvoo are encamped, and represent that they are in need of all kinds of . . . [n.p., September 23, 1846]
Broadside. 26½×17½cm.
The destitute condition of the Mormons after the battle of Nauvoo.
Byrd 1102
ICHi

5875. Nowell, Nancy. Testimony of Nancy Nowell. A copy of my journals commenced in Lapeer, Michigan. A daily account of the devotional and devout exercises of my heart, and the testimony of the truth. Salt Lake City, George Q. Cannon and Sons, Printers, 1892.
355 [1]p. 18cm.
Mormon biography.
MH, NjP, UHi, USlC

5876. Noyes, Isaac Pitman. The Latter-day Saints of Mephistopheles. [By Polaris [*pseud.*] n.p., 1905]
12p. 22cm.
Signed: Washington, D.C., January, 1905.
MH

5877. "Nuggets of truth." Hear ye the whole truth as to Joseph Smith's political views . . . [n.p., n.d.]
4p. 25½cm.
UPB

5878. Nuggets of truth and gems from the speeches and letters of the leading minds of Utah (past and present) [Salt Lake City?, 1895?]
12p. illus. 18½cm.
Republican Party pamphlet in behalf of Frank J. Cannon.
NjP, UHi

5879. Nuttall, Leonard John. Application of a basic principle; address delivered over Radio Station KSL, Sunday Evening, March 20, 1927. [Salt Lake City] 1927.
Broadside. 42½×26cm.
Reprinted from the *Deseret News.*
UPB

5880. ———. Helps in teacher-training; what psychology is and does. Written for the General Church Board of Education, by L. John Nuttall. [Salt Lake City, 1923]
4p. 23cm.
USlC

5881. Nutting, John Danforth. About the Holy Spirit and his wonderful works . . . Cleveland, Ohio, Utah Gospel Mission, 1921.
64p. illus. 17cm. (U.G.M. Series. No. 8)
Aimed at Mormonism with reference to false beliefs.
Music on cover.
MoInCR, NN

5882. ———. An Appeal to Christian young men. [Cleveland, Ohio, Utah Gospel Mission, 1911]
[4]p. 14cm.
Signed: Secretary of Utah Gospel Mission.
NN

5883. ———. Articles of faith of the "Latter-day Saints," with Mormon explanations. Compiled by Rev. J. D. Nutting [and] Rev. D. J. McMillan. N.Y., League for Social Service [1899?]
14p. 15cm. (Social service. Series D. Anti-Mormon)
MoInRC, NjPT, NN, UPB, USl, USlC

5884. ———. (same) New York, Literature Department of the Board of Home Missions and the Women's Executive Committee of the Presbyterian Church [1904]
10 [1]p. 13½cm. (No. 272)
MoInRC, USlC

5885. ———. (same) New York City, Literature Department, Woman's Board of Home Missions of the Presbyterian Church [1913]
12p. 14½cm.
USlC

5886. ———. (same) New York Literature Department. Woman's Board of Home Missions of the Presbyterian Church [1914]
12p. 16cm. (No. 272)
USlC

5887. ———. (same, in Swedish) De Sista Dagars Heligas Trosartiklar Förklarade Med deras egna skrifter. Förklaringarna samlade af Pastor J. D. Nutting och Teol. D:r. D. J. McMillan, öiversatt af Pastor P. E. Åslev. New York City, League for Social Service [1900?]
14p. 14cm.
At head of title: Till Samhellets Tjänst Serien D. –Anti Mormon.
NN

5888. ———. The Bible teachings about Christ. 2d ed., rev. Cleveland, Ohio, Utah Gospel Mission, 1915.
72p. illus. 16½cm. (U.G.M. Series. No. 6)
Cover-title.
Text and music on cover.
Sections on the errors of Mormon teachings about Christ, etc., p. 70–72.
MoInRC, NN, USlC

5889. ———. Contradictions in Mormon books and doctrines. Cleveland, Ohio, Utah Gospel Mission [n.d.]
8p. 17cm.
UPB

5890. ———. Eight reasons why no one should be a Mormon. Cleveland, Ohio [Utah Gospel Mission, n.d.]
[4]p. 16cm.
UPB

5891. ———. The fraud of the "Inspired translation" of the Bible. Purporting to have been made by Joseph Smith, 1830–3; first published in 1867 by the "Reorganized Church of Jesus Christ of Latter Day Saints," and now urged by it as the best and only correct Bible by Rev. John D. Nutting . . . Cleveland, Ohio, The Utah Gospel Mission, 1923.
24p. facsim. 17cm.
Cover-title.
CU–B, MH, MoInRC, NjPT, NN, OCl, UHi, USlC

5892. ———. The greater points of Christian truth. As held by all churches of Christ for over 1800 years, carefully considered in the light of the Holy Scriptures and other truth. By a careful student of Christianity and Mormonism. Cleveland, Ohio, The Utah Gospel Mission, 1901.
32p. 16½cm.
"The Story of John Wentworth, the Mormons," p. 27–32. How he was saved from Mormonism.
UPB, USlC

5893. ———. (same) 2d ed., rev. Cleveland, Ohio, Utah Gospel Mission, 1901.
32p. 16½cm.
Text and music on cover.
NN, UPB, USlC

5894. ———. (same) 3d ed., rev. Cleveland, Ohio, Utah Gospel Mission [1903]
32p. 17cm.
USlC

5895. ———. (same) 3d ed., rev. Cleveland, Ohio, Utah Gospel Mission, 1903.
34p. 16½cm.
Variant edition.
MoInRC

5896. ———. (same) 4th rev., ed. Cleveland, Ohio, Utah Gospel Mission, 1905.
34p. 17cm.
NjPT, USlC

5897. ———. Incidents and anecdotes illustrating Mormonism. Chiefly from letters of missionaries in the western field and reprinted from our annals 1903–1912. Edited by John D. Nutting. [Cleveland, Ohio, Utah Gospel Mission, 1912]
24p. 16cm.
Caption-title.
MH, MoInRC

5898. ———. (same) [Cleveland, O., Utah Gospel Mission, 1912]
24p. 16cm.
Variant printing.
NN, UHi

5899. ———. (same) [Cleveland, Ohio, Utah Gospel Mission, 1915?]
24p. 16½cm.
Caption-title.
"2d ed."
MH, NjPT, NN, UHi, USlC

5900. ———. John three sixteen, Noah's carpenters, wrong directions and other stories about Eternal life, for young and Old. Also "The true church" . . . Cleveland, Ohio, The Utah Gospel Missions, 1923.
32p. 18cm. (U.G.M. Series. No. 9)
Brief mention of Mormons.
MoInRC, NN

5901. ———. Josephite and Utah Mormonism essentially the same. [Cleveland, Ohio, Utah Gospel Mission, 1924]
[4]p. 17cm.
At head of title: All we have to do to see Mormonism grow is to do nothing!
A comparison of Utah and Reorganized Mormonism including statistics.
NN

5902. ———. A journey among the Mormons . . . From the Union Gospel News, Cleveland, Nov. 10, 1899. [Cleveland, Ohio, 1899?]
4p. 18cm.
OClWHi

5903. ———. The main facts regarding the growth and power of Mormonism, the Christian church and school work hitherto done among the Mormon people and the further need — Reprinted from illustrated articles by Rev. J. D. Nutting in the New York Independent and Evangelist, slightly revised with different illustrations . . . A study of the present Mormon problem. [Cleveland, Ohio, Utah Gospel Mission, 1902]
16p. 16cm.
Reprinted from *The Independent*, April 17, 1902.
NN, OClWHi, UHi

5904. ———. Money and our Utah work by Rev. J. D. Nutting, Secretary, Utah Gospel Mission of Cleveland. [Cleveland, Ohio, Utah Gospel Mission] 1913.
8p. 17cm.
Caption-title.
CU–B, NN

NUTTING, J. D.

5905. ———. Mormon doctrine carefully considered in the light of the Holy Scriptures and other truth. By a careful student of Mormonism and Christianity. By a careful student of Mormonism. Cleveland, O., The Utah Gospel Mission, 1901.
1p.l., 48p. 16cm.
Text on covers.
MH, NN, UPB

5906. ———. (same) Cleveland, O., The Utah Gospel Mission, 1901.
1p.l., 48 [2]p. 16cm.
2d rev. edition.
USlC

5907. ———. (same) Cleveland, O., Utah Gospel Mission, 1903.
1p.l., 48 [2]p. 16cm. (U.G.M. Series. No. 1)
3d rev. edition.
"A true story" by John Beaumont on verso of cover, title and both sides of rear cover.
DLC, MB, MH, NN, OClWHi, USlC

5908. ———. (same) Cleveland, O., Utah Gospel Mission, 1905.
48 [2]p. 16½cm. (U.G.M. Series. No. 1)
4th rev. ed.
Cover-title.
Text on cover.
MoInRC, NjPT, OClWHi, UHi

5909. ———. Mormonism and Christianity compared with the Bible and sound reason . . . Cleveland, O., Utah Gospel Mission, 1924.
8p. music, illus. 16cm.
UPB

5910. ———. (same) Cleveland, Ohio, Utah Gospel Mission, 1925.
8p. music, illus. 16cm.
NN

5911. ———. Mormonism proclaiming itself a fraud. [Cleveland, Ohio, Utah Gospel Mission, 1901]
21p. 16cm.
Reprinted from the *Union Gospel News*, March 7, 1901.
NN

5912. ———. (same) [Cleveland, Ohio, The Utah Gospel Mission, 1906]
16p. 16cm.
Revised.
NN

5913. ———. (same) [Cleveland, Ohio, The Utah Gospel Mission, 1913]
16p. 15cm.
NN

5913a. ———. (same) By a careful student of Mormonism, who has had over twenty years of experience with the system and a thorough knowledge of its publications. [Cleveland, Ohio, Utah Gospel Mission, 1921]
14 [2]p. 17cm.
Includes: Mormon morals by Frank S. Johnson.
USlC

5914. ———. (same) [Cleveland, Ohio, Utah Gospel Mission, 1925]
14 [2]p. 16cm.
[2] "Mormon morals, by a disillusioned convert," by Frank S. Johnson.
MH, MoInRC, NjPT, NN, USlC

5915. ———. Mormonism to-day and its remedy, by Rev. John D. Nutting. Cleveland, Ohio, Utah Gospel Mission, 1913.
20p. illus. 24½cm.
Cover-title.
Reprinted from the *Missionary Review of the World*, April, May, 1913.
CU-B, MoInRC, NjPT, NN, ULA, USlC, UU

5916. ———. (same) Rev. ed. Cleveland, Ohio, Utah Gospel Mission, 1927.
20p. illus., facsims. 23½cm.
Cover-title.
"Revised, 1927, and new matter on both Utah and Josephite Mormonism."
Reprinted (revised) with special permission of *Missionary Review of the World*, April, May, 1913.
CSmH, CU-B, MB, MH, MoInRC, NjPT, UHi, UPB, USlC

5917. ———. My field of labor — where does God call me? [Cleveland, Ohio, Utah Gospel Mission, 1910]
16p. 17cm.
His work against Mormonism. Need for more help.
NN

5918. ———. Paul's method of dealing with false religionists. [Cleveland, Ohio, Utah Gospel Mission, n.d.]
[4]p. 17cm.
Reprint from "*Light on Mormonism*, December 1927."
UPB

5919. ———. Political aspects of Mormonism. New York, League for Social Services [1899?]
14p. 15cm. (Social service. Series D. Anti-Mormon)
WHi

5920. ———. Present day Mormonism and its remedy. [Cleveland, Ohio, The Utah Gospel Mission, 1904]
19 [1]p. 16½cm.
MH, NN, MoInRC, OClWHi, UHi

5921. ———. (same) [Cleveland, Ohio, The Utah Gospel Mission, 1904]
19 [1]p. 17cm.
Variant printing.
MoInRC

5922. ———. (same) Cleveland, Ohio, Utah Gospel Mission, 1923.
19 [1]p. 17cm.
"A series of articles first published in a syndicate of religious papers early in 1904; revised and largely rewritten, 1923."
Caption-title.
CSmH, MH, MoInRC, NN, UHi, USlC

5923. ———. The private doctrines of Mormon theology by Rev. John D. Nutting. [Cleveland, Ohio, The Utah Gospel Mission, 1900]
6p. 16cm.
DLC, MB, MH, NN, OClWHi

5924. ———. (same) [Cleveland, Ohio, Utah Gospel Mission, 1912]
6p. 16cm.
Caption-title.
At head of title: Printed for private circulation only.
"4th ed."
MH, MoInRC, UHi, USlC

5925. ———. (same) [Cleveland, Ohio, Utah Gospel Mission, 1917?]
6p. 15cm.
"5th ed."
NjPT, USlC

5926. ———. The real doctrines of Mormonism, both Utah and "Reorganized" Mormonism, being the professed Articles of faith of Utah Mormonism completed and explained by other quotations, with supplement of quotations from "Reorganized" sources. Anderson, Indiana, Gospel Trumpet [n.d.]
28p. 18cm.
MoInRC

5927. ———. (same) Anderson, Indiana, Gospel Trumpet, 1899.
28p. 18cm.
"2d ed."
USl

5928. ———. (same, under title) The real doctrines of Mormonism, being the professed "Articles of faith" of the Utah Mormonism, completed and explained by other quotations, with supplement of quotations from "Reorganized" sources, by Rev. J. D. Nutting. [Cleveland, Ohio, Utah Gospel Mission, 1921]
16p. 17cm.
Caption-title.
At head of title: Both Utah and "Reorganized" Mormonism.
MoInRC, NjPT, OCl, OO, UHi, USlC

5929. ———. (same) Cleveland, Ohio, Utah Gospel Mission [1925]
16p. 17cm.
At head of title: Both Utah and "Reorganized" Mormonism.
"3d ed."
MH, NN, UHi, USlC

5930. ———. (same) 4th ed. Cleveland, Ohio, Utah Gospel Mission, 1928.
16p. 16½cm.
Cover-title.
At head of title: Both Utah and "Reorganized" Mormonism.
NjPT, UPB

5931. ———. Religious destitution in a Christian country. From the annual report of the Rev. J. D. Nutting. Cleveland, Ohio, Utah Gospel Mission, 1907.
[4]p. 16½cm.
From the *Annual Report of the Utah Gospel Mission*, 1907. Concerning Mormonism.
MH, MHi, NjPT, UPB

5932. ———. "Reorganized" or "Josephite" Mormonism, carefully considered in the light of the Bible and of good reason. Cleveland, Ohio, Utah Gospel Mission, 1917.
44p. facsims. 16½cm.
MH, MoInRC, NjPT, OO, USlC

5933. ———. (same) 2nd ed., rev. Cleveland, Ohio, Utah Gospel Mission, 1922.
44p. facsims. 16½cm.
Cover-title.
Text on covers.
NN, UHi, USlC, UU

5934. ———. The secret oaths and ceremonies of Mormonism. The secret temple work which binds Mormons together under the power of their priestly leaders. Edited by Rev. J. D. Nutting. [Cleveland, Ohio, Utah Gospel Mission, 1912]
15 [1]p. 17cm.
MH, NjPT, NN, UHi, WaPS

5935. ———. (same) [Cleveland, Ohio, Utah Gospel Mission, 1921]
15 [1]p. 16½cm.
MH, NN, USlC

5936. ———. The special difficulties of Christian work among the Mormons, and how they may be overcome. [Cleveland, Ohio, Utah Gospel Mission, 1903]
8p. 17cm.
NN, OClWHi

5937. ———. (same) Cleveland, O., Utah Gospel Mission, 1914.
8p. 16cm.
"4th ed."
NjPT, USlC

NUTTING, J. D.

5938. ———. (same) Cleveland, O., The Utah Gospel Mission, 1923.
8p. 17cm.
Caption-title.
"5th ed., revised"
MH, NN, UHi, USlC

———. The story of a Mormon convert.
See Claiborne, D. J.

5939. ———. The teachings of Mormonism and Christianity compared with the Bible and sound reason. Cleveland, O., Utah Gospel Mission, 1924.
80p. illus. 17cm. (U.G.M. Series. No. 10)
Music on p. 80 and covers.
MH

5940. ———. (same) [Cleveland, Ohio, Utah Gospel Mission, 1925]
80p. 17cm. (U.G.M. Series. No. 10)
Cover-title.
"2d edition"
MoInRC, NN, USlC

5941. ———. (same) Cleveland, Ohio, Utah Gospel Mission, 1928.
80p. 17cm. (U.G.M. Series. No. 10)
Cover-title.
"3d ed."
UHi, USlC

5942. ———. Thoughts of Heaven and how to get there. 3d ed. Cleveland, Ohio, Utah Gospel Mission, 1916.
31 [1]p. 16cm. (U.G.M. Series. No. 7)
Verso of p. 31 a hymn.
Reference to Mormonism and Mormon beliefs.
MoInRC, NN, USlC

5943. ———. Tracts and pamphlets on Mormonism. Edited by Rev. J. D. Nutting, Secretary. Cleveland, Ohio, Utah Gospel Mission, 1913–1928.
26 pamp. illus. 16½cm.
Caption-title.
Collected tracts of various dates, with collective title. Various pagings. [4]p. preliminary with index and list of publications.
MB, NN

5944. ———. "The true mormon doctrine" being the professed Mormon "Articles of faith" completed and explained by literal quotations from Mormon publications. Cleveland, Ohio, The Utah Gospel Mission, 1901.
12p. 17cm.
MB, MH, MoInRC, NN, OCl

5945. ———. (same) [Cleveland, Ohio, Utah Gospel Mission, 1913]
12p. 16½cm.
Caption-title.
NjPT, UHi

5946. ———. The truth about God according to reason and revelation, compared with the teachings of paganism, and with the later doctrines of Mormonism. 2d ed. Cleveland, Ohio, Utah Gospel Mission, 1911.
80p. illus. 17½cm.
UU

5947. ———. (same) 3d ed. Cleveland, Ohio, Utah Gospel Mission, 1912.
80p. illus. 17½cm. (U.G.M. Series. No. 5)
UPB

5948. ———. (same) 4th ed., Cleveland, Ohio, Utah Gospel Mission, 1922.
80p. illus. 17½cm. (U.G.M. Series. No. 5)
Cover-title: music on covers.
MH, MoInRC, NN, UHi, UU

5949. ———. Why care about Mormonism? Cleveland, Ohio, Utah Gospel Mission [1926]
[4]p. 15½cm.
Introduction to his bound pamphlets.
NN, USlC

5950. ———. Why I could never be a Mormon. By Rev. John D. Nutting, Formerly of Utah. Cleveland, Ohio, Utah Gospel Mission, 1911.
27p. 16½cm.
Title from cover.
NN

5951. ———. (same) 2d ed. Cleveland, Ohio, Utah Gospel Mission, 1913.
27p. illus. 17cm.
MH, NjPT, NN

5952. ———. (same) Cleveland, Ohio, Utah Gospel Mission, 1920.
27p. 16½cm.
"3d ed."
USlC

5953. ———. (same) 4th ed. Cleveland, Ohio, The Utah Gospel Mission [1922]
27p. 18½cm.
Cover-title.
NN

5954. ———. (same) 4th ed. Cleveland, Ohio, The Utah Gospel Mission [1922]
27p. illus. 18½cm.
Cover-title.
Dated on cover.
CSmH, CU-B, MH, NN, UHi, USlC

5955. ———. (same) Cleveland, Ohio, Utah Gospel Mission, 1923.
27p. 18½cm.
No edition note.
CSmH

5956. ———. (same) 5th ed. Cleveland, Ohio, Utah Gospel Mission, 1929 [c1913]
27p. 18½cm.
CSmH, UPB

5957. ———. The wonderful story of the wonderful Book . . . 3d ed. Cleveland, Ohio, Utah Gospel Mission, 1908.
103 [1]p. illus. 17½cm. (U.G.M. Series. No. 4)
Music on covers.
Concerning the Bible. Brings out why one cannot believe the Book of Mormon.
NjPT, UPB

5958. ———. (same) 5th ed. Cleveland, Ohio, Utah Gospel Mission, 1928.
103 [1]p. illus. 17½cm. (U.G.M. Series. No. 4)
MoInRC

5959. Nye, Edgar Wilson. Baled hay. A drier book than Walt Whitman's "Leaves o' grass." By Bill Nye . . . Illustrated by F. Opper, of "Puck." New York and Chicago, Belford, Clarke & Co., 1884.
320p. illus., 11 plates, port. 20cm.
Several sections on Mormonism such as "Are you a Mormon?" "A visit to the endowment house," "The revelation racket in Utah."
Other editions: Chicago, 1889. UPB; Chicago, W. B. Conkey Co., 1894. DLC
CU, DLC, NjP, USIC

5960. ———. Bill Nye and boomerang; or, the tale of a meek-eyed mule, and some other literary gems. By Bill Nye himself . . . Chicago, Belford, Clarke, & Co., 1881.
2p.l. [iii]–v [7]–286p. 18cm.
"The fragrant Mormon," p. 35–36. A description of a Mormon emigrant train. Other Mormon references, p. 232, 245–247, 282–283.
Other editions: New York, Lovell [1887] NjP; 1894. USI
USIC

5961. ———. Bill Nye's chestnuts, old and new . . . with new illustrations from original sketches, photographs, memoranda, and authentic sources, by Williams, Opper, and Hopkins. Chicago, Belford, Clarke & Co., 1888.
x, 11–286p. plates. 19½cm.
Revelation in Utah . . . p. 235–237. Satire.
Other editions: Chicago, W. B. Conkey Co., 1894. DLC; 1889. CU
DLC

5962. ———. Forty liars, and other lies. By Bill Nye . . . Illustrated by Hopkins . . . Chicago, Belford, Clarke & Co.; St. Louis, Belford & Clarke Publishing Co., 1882.
1p.l. [5]–6 [3]–5 [9]–264p. 10 plates. 19cm.
"About the Mormons," "Skowhegan Onderdonk on the Plan of Salvation," "The Mormons," "An explanation (concerning Brigham Young's grave)," "The morbidly matrimonial Mormons."
Another edition: 1893. NjP
CtY, CU, DLC, MiU, NNC, USIC

5963. ———. Remarks by Bill Nye . . . Chicago, F. T. Neely [1886]
2p.l., viii–ix, 11–504p. illus. 22½cm.
Murray and the Mormons, p. 199–200. Polygamy as a religious duty, p. 418–420.
Another edition: Chicago, A. E. Davis & Co., 1887. DLC
NjP, UPB

5964. Nye, Ephraim H. The straight and narrow way; doctrines the Savior taught. By Elder Ephraim H. Nye . . . [Independence, Mo.? Missions of the Church of Jesus Christ of Latter-day Saints, n.d.]
23p. 16cm.
MH, USIC

5965. ———. (same) Chattanooga, Tenn., The Southern States Mission [n.d.]
32p. 14cm.
UPB

5966. ———. (same) [Chattanooga, Tenn., The Southern States Mission, n.d.]
32p. 14cm.
Variant printing.
USIC

5967. ———. Which is the way to obtain eternal life? . . . A discussion between a Church of England minister and a "Mormon" Elder, Nov. 7th, 1883, at Westbourne Park, London, Nov. 7, 1883. [London, 1883]
8p. 20½cm.
Caption-title.
Signed: Ephraim H. Nye, President, London Conference.
CtY, CU–B, MH, UPB, USIC

5968. Nye-Starr, Kate. A self-sustaining woman: or, the experience of seventy-two years. Chicago, Illinois Printing and Binding Co., 1888.
161p. port. 18cm.
Overland via Salt Lake City in 1862 with a few observations.
Howes N232
CtY, CU–B

THE OLIVE BRANCH,

OR,

Herald of Peace and Truth to all Saints.

VOL. I. KIRTLAND, O., AUGUST, 1848. NO. 1.

Proclamation.

To the saints scattered abroad, in all Lands; to those that are afar off, and those that are nigh, the Church of Christ in Kirtland sendeth greeting. Grace, mercy, and peace, from God the Father and Jesus Christ our Lord, both yours and ours.

BELOVED BRETHREN, who have obtained like precious faith with us through the knowledge of our Lord Jesus Christ; Being called with an holy calling, and made partakers with us of the spirit of adoption, whereby we are enabled to say Abba Father, It seemeth good unto us to write unto you, that all saints may know (according to the revelations given unto us) the relation the church of Jesus Christ of Latter Day Saints now sustain before God the Eternal Father, and the relation in which we as saints stand, in relation to it, and to each other. And this duty devolves upon us with more imperative force, in that we have before us the writings of ancient prophets fulfilled, and present revelations given, whereby we can determine with certainty the character of the whole church, (embracing all its parts,) in the presence of the Almighty, we first proceed to show from the Book of Doctrine and Covenants, (first edition,) received by the whole Church in General Assembly convened, August 17th, 1835, as the rule of their faith and practice, that not one condition required of the church by the Lord, as a consideration in the Covenant, by which he had promised them the then designated land of Zion, had by them as a church been fulfilled. See Sections 12, page 8; 13: 8, 9, 10; 20: 8; 23: 1; 82: 3, 4, 5; 98: 1; 101: 1, 2, 3; 102: 2. The above quotations show most clearly that the church is not only without any legal claim to that land as their inheritance, but are under condemnation and a curse, as not having organized themselves under the law of Christ, even the celestial law, for the benefit of the poor. See more particularly Sections 23 and 102 on that subject.

The truth being sustained that we as a church have not kept the law given unto us, we next proceed to show that the constituted authorities of the church have fallen into darkness, having also departed from the right way. For the benefit of those who have not the law of the church, we transcribe from the 'Doctrine and Covenants' the evidence of this our position, from the revelation given through the prophet, concerning himself, Section 30, pages 1—5. "The works and designs, and the purposes of God, cannot be frustrated, neither can they come to nought, for God doth not walk in crooked paths, neither doth He turn to the right hand, nor to the left; neither doth He vary from that which He hath said: therefore his paths are straight and His course is one eternal round. Remember, remember, that it is not the work of God that is frustrated, but the work of men: for although a man may have many revelations, and have power to do many mighty works, yet if he boasts in his own strength, and sets at nought the counsels of God, and follows after the dictates of his own will, and carnal

Item 5987. Official publication of the church led by James Colin Brewster. From the Brigham Young University collection.

5969. Oaks, Lewis Weston. Medical aspects of the Latter-day Saint word of wisdom, by L. Weston Oaks, M.D. Provo, Utah, Brigham Young University [c1929]
4p.l. [7]–126p. 20½cm.
Bibliography at end of each chapter except the last.
CU–B, DLC, NjP, UHi, ULA, UPB, USl, USlC, UU

5970. ———. Science and the word of wisdom. [n.p., n.d.]
8p. 19cm.
UPB

5971. Oasis. Thatcher, Published by Associated Students, Gila College, 1929–1930.
v. plates, ports. 27½cm.
USlC 1929, 1930

5971a. Oberländer, Richard. Von Ozean zu Ozean. Kulterbilder und Naturschisderungen aus dem Fernen Westen von Amerika. Nach eigenen Beobachtungen und Reisestudien von Richard Oberländer. Mit 60 in den Text gedruckten Abbildungen sowie einem Titelbilde. Leipzig und Berlin. Verlag und Druck von Otto Spamer. 1885.
3p.l., vi–viii, 256, ivp. illus. 21cm.
Travels through Utah in 1884 and records his stay, p. 227–232.
Title in English: From Ocean to Ocean.
DLC, UPB

5972. Objections to the Cullom anti-Mormon bill. [n.p., 187–]
3p. 22cm.
CU–B, NjP, USlC

5973. O'Brien, Frederick. Atolls of the sun, with many illustrations from paintings, drawings and photographs. New York, The Century Co., 1922.
6p.l., 508p. illus. 23cm.
"Josephite Missionaries," Chap. IV, p. 67–79. "Mormon missionaries from America," Chap. VI, p. 100–113. L.D.S. missionaries in Tahiti.
CU, DLC, NjP, UHi, ULA, UPB, USlC

5973a. Ocean to ocean; tour of the Premierites told by wire and photo. [Indianapolis, Indiana, Premier Motor Mfg. Co., 1913?]
[52]p. illus. 30½cm.
Second edition.
Utah and Mormons, p. [30]–[36]
USlC

5974. O'Donovan, Jeremiah. A brief account of the author's interview with his countrymen, and of the parts of the Emerald Isle whence they emigrated, together with a direct reference to the present location in the land of their adoption, during his travels through various states of the union in 1854 and 1855. By Jeremiah O'Donovan. Pittsburgh, Pa., Published by the author, 1864.
382p. 19cm.
Includes his contact with the Mormons.
ICHi

5975. An official proclamation written to the Kings, Governors and people of the Earth. Independence, Mo., 1879.
Broadside. 53×15½cm.
Signed: "The Lord's Servants"
A call to repentance to all people.
USlC

5976. Ogden City, Utah, picturesque and descriptive. Neenah, Wisconsin, Art Publishing Co., 1889.
[53]l. 21½cm.
Published in eight parts. Views of Ogden with a brief history of its founding.
UHi, USlC

5977. Ogden Junction. Death [of Brigham Young] Junction Extra. Aug. 29, 1877. [Ogden, 1877]
Broadside. 36×15cm.
USlC

5978. O'Hanlon, John C. Life and scenery in Missouri; reminiscences of a missionary priest. Dublin, Ireland, James Duffy & Co., 1890.
xii, 292p. 15½cm.
Chap. XIX. The Mormons in Missouri. Driven out as "hypocritical and visionary" impostors.
NjP, UHi, ULA, USlC

O'Higgins, Harvey J. *See Anderson, Martha. The other house.*

5979. Ohio Church History Society. Papers of the Ohio Church History Society 1889–1901. Oberlin, 1901.
12v. 21½cm.
V.1, 1890, p. 44–60 contains: "The Mormon sojourn in Ohio, by D. L. Leonard.
DLC, ICN, MB, MH, NN

5980. Ohio. Legislature. Senate. Journal of the Senate of the State of Ohio; being the first session of the 35th General Assembly, begun and held in the City of Columbus, Monday, December 5, 1836, and in the 35th year of said state. Columbus, James B. Gardiner, Printer to the State, 1836.
856 (i.e. 836)p. 21cm.
Refusal of the Senate to pass the capitalization of the Kirtland Safety Society charter, p. 280, 360, 365.
CtY, OClWHi

5981. The Ohio railroad guide, illustrated. Cincinnati to Erie via Columbus and Cleveland. Columbus, Ohio State Journal Company, 1854.
3p.l., 135p. fold. front., plates. 19½cm.
Added illus. title-page.
"Issued by the Cincinnati, Columbus, Cleveland and Erie Railroad . . . I believe the text of his work was written by E. D. Mansfield."—Thomson, Bibl. of Ohio, 1880, p. 263.
"The Mormons at Kirtland," p. 97–100.
Howes G52, Sabin 56994
CSmH, DLC, MB, NjP, NN, PHi, PU

5982. Ólafsson, Eirík. Litith rit um Svivirthing eythileggingarinnar eda um kneykslith ethtir Brigham Young i Utah, Ethtir Eirik Olafsson adur á Brúnum. Rykjavík, Prentad í Ísafoldarprentsmidju, 1891.
63 [1]p. 16cm.
Title in English: A brief essay about the disgrace of the desertion perpetuated by Brigham Young in Utah.
USIC

5983. The Old Paths, edited by John Zahnd. New Albany, Ind. [Indianapolis, Ind.] January–November, 1922.
lv. (6 nos. in 12p.) 28cm.
Edited by John Zahnd, RLDS dissenter.
Place of publication changed to Indianapolis after No. 1.
CU–B V.1 #4, UHi, USIC V.1 #4

5984. Old Residenter [*pseud.*]. Blood Atonement. More of it in proof. [Salt Lake City, 1884]
Broadside. 25×14½cm.
Proof of blood atonement in substantiation of a pamphlet by Historicus [Wm. G. Mills] and against the speech of Charles W. Penrose on the same subject.
UPB

5985. Olden, Sarah Emilia. Little slants at Western life; a note book of travel and reflection. New York, Harold Vinal Ltd., 1927.
4p.l., 245p. 21cm.
Visit to Salt Lake City; the Mormons and their teachings.
DLC, NjP, USIC

5986. The Olive branch. San Francisco, J. Dove & Co., July 15, 1884–January, 1885.
1v. semi-monthly to Nov. 15, 1884 (#9) 35cm.
Devoted to the promulgation of the teachings of Joseph Morris.
CU–B V.1 #1–9, USIC V.1, #10

5987. The Olive branch, or Herald of Peace and truth to all Saints. Kirtland, Ohio, [Hazen Aldrich] August 1848–January 1852?
4v. monthly. 21cm.
V.1. Edited by Austin Cowles, who was succeeded by James C. Brewster.
Moved to Springfield, Ill., June, 1849.
Last issue appears to be January, 1852, V.4 #6.
Subtitle varies; Messenger of Good tidings of the week.
Morgan
CSmH V.1–4; CtY V.1,2; DLC V.1; MoInRC V.1–4 inc.; NN V.3 #10; NNHi V.1–2; OClWHi V.1; PPHi V.1–2 #1; USIC V.1,2,4 inc.; WHi V.1,2

5988. Oliver, William. Eight months in Illinois, with information to emigrants . . . Newcastle-upon-Tyne, Printed by William Mitchell and sold by E. A. T. Bruce, etc., 1843.
3p.l., iv, 141 [1]p. 20cm.
Contains a description of travel through the state with accounts of routes of travel. Brief mention of the movement of Mormons from Terre Haute toward Missouri.
Another edition: Chicago, W. M. Hill, 1924.
DLC, NjP
Howes G71, Sabin 57214
DLC

5989. Ollier, Edmund. Cassell's history of the United States. London, Paris & New York, Cassell, Petter & Galpin, 1874–77.
3v. illus., ports. 27cm.
V.3, Chap. XV–XVI on Mormonism.
CU, DLC, USIC

5990. Ollivant, Joseph Earle. A breeze from the Great Salt Lake; or, New Zealand to New York by the new mail route. By J. E. Ollivant . . . London, W. Hunt and Company, 1871.
viii [9]–176p. plates (music) fold. map. 20cm.
Material on the Mormons and appendix concerning Mormon music.
Howes G73, Sabin 57226
CtY, CU–B, DLC, IWW, NN, UHi, USl, USIC

5991. Olney, Oliver H. The absurdities of Mormonism portrayed. A brief sketch by Oliver H. Olney, Hancock Co., Illinois. March 3, 1843. [n.p., 1843?]
32p. 21cm.
Dated at end: Hancock County, Illinois. April 1, 1843.
Byrd 807, Morgan
MH, NN, USIC

5992. Olshausen, Theodor. Geschichte der Mormonen; oder, Jüngsten-Tages Heiligen in Nordamerika. Von Theodor Olshausen . . . Göttingen, Bandenhoeck und Ruprecht, 1856.
iv, 244p. 22½cm.
Title in English: History of the Mormons.
Howes G81, Sabin 57255
CSmH, CtY, CU, DLC, ICN, MH, NjP, NjPT, NN, UPB, USl, UU, WHi

5993. Olson, Edmund T. A pageantry of ghosts. Do ghosts really exist? Do angels fly through Heaven? Do spirits fill the air? Is the world to be swallowed by a kingdom of Hebrew origin? Do the gods the world worships today walk and talk with men? [Salt Lake City, c1930]
31p. 23cm.
Cover-title: A pageantry of ghosts as seen by Ed Kinole.
A satire on Mormonism among other things.
NN, UHi, USl, USIC, UU

OLSON, E. W.

5994. Olson, Ernst Wilhelm. History of the Swedes of Illinois. Edited by Ernst Olson in collaboration with Anders Schon and Martin J. Engberg. Illustrated. Chicago, The Engberg-Holmberg Publishing Company, 1908.
3 parts in 1. illus., plates, ports. 26½cm.
"The Mormons at Nauvoo," p. 47–50 in Part I. Polygamy seen as the basis of antagonism between Mormons and neighbors.
CU, DLC, NjP, USIC

5995. Olson, Leonard. The history of Smithfield. Smithfield, Utah, Published by the City of Smithfield, 1927.
2p.l. [7]–108p. illus., fold-out chart, port. 19½cm.
CSmH, NjP, UHi, ULA, UPB, USIC

5996. Om barnedaaben, svar paa Peter Jensen Lundforlunds tillaeg. [Kjobenhavn, Udgivet auf A. Aagren, 1851]
[4]p. 19cm.
Title in English: About infant baptism; an answer to Peter Jensen's remarks.
UPB

5997. Om Mormonerne. Brev fra Snedkedsvend I . . . O . . . i Amerika til hans fader, Boelm. O . . . P . . . i jetzmark sogn, hvetbo herred, Hjorring amt (dateret Juli 8de, 1856) Hjorring [Denmark] 1861.
16p. 12°.
Title in English: About Mormons.
Sabin 50751

5998. Omer [*pseud.*]. The Latter-day Saints: a poem in two cantos; by Omer [*pseud.*] author of "Eliza or the broken vow." . . . Nauvoo, Ill., Printed for the author, 1841.
iv [5]–15p. 15½cm.
Poem concerning the Missouri period of the church. The author was probably Lyman Omer Littlefield.
Byrd 650
CtY, USIC

On the false prophets of the last days.
See Ward, Thomas.

5999. Once a polygamist not always a polygamist. Salt Lake City [ca. 1882]
Broadside. 23½×13½cm.
Plural marriage.
USIC

One. [Publication of the Reorganized Church of Jesus Christ of Latter Day Saints.] *See Unity.*

6000. One hundred choice selections. No. 17. A rare collection of oratory, sentiment, eloquence and humor, public readings, winter gatherings, social entertainments, elocutionary exercises, temperance societies, exhibitions, lyceums, &c. Designed to accompany the preceding numbers. Philadelphia, P. Garrett and Company, 1887.
2p.l., 5–216p. 18cm.
Max Adeler, "The story of Bishop Potts," p. 16–20. Satire on polygamy.
USIC

6001. Oneida Stake Academy, Preston, Idaho. Office of the principal. . . . Preston, Idaho, 1908.
[4]p. 21½cm.
Letter from the principal to the students.
USIC

6001a. ———. The Oneida, published monthly by the student body. Preston, Idaho, 1914–
v. 25cm.
USIC V.3, V.7 #2

6002. ———. The Oneida Stake Academy. Catalog. 1901–
v. 19½×23cm.
USIC 1901–02, 1902–03, 1904–05, 1905–06, 1907–08, 1908–09, 1909–10, 1911–12, 1916–17

6003. An open letter to George Q. Cannon. [By Thy orthodox friend. Salt Lake City, 188–]
3p. 23cm.
Church and politics.
CU–B

6004. ———. (same) [Salt Lake City, 1897?]
4p. 17½cm. (No. 1)
Signed: Salt Lake City, May 8, 1897.
Against Mormon doctrine.
MH, UPB, USIC

6005. An open letter to the world. Salt Lake City [1893]
64p. 12×21cm.
A brochure for prospective residents. Mormonism only mentioned.
From the *Salt Lake Tribune.*
Signed on p. 7: E. F. Colborn.
MH

6006. Opinions concerning the Bible law of marriage. By one of the people . . . Philadelphia, Claxton, Remsen & Haffelfinger . . . 1871.
xiii [13]–239p. 19cm.
A book on marriage to disprove Mormonism.
UPB, USU

6006a. Order of procession and funeral services of Major General Jedediah Morgan Grant, G.S.L. City, Dec. 4, 1856. [Salt Lake City, 1856]
Broadside. 28×9cm.
USIC

6007. Order of procession at the funeral of president Brigham Young, New Tabernacle, Salt Lake City, September 2d, 1877. [Salt Lake City, 1877]
Broadside. 21½×9cm.
USIC

6007a. Order of the day. Salt Lake City, 1853.
Broadside. 40×14cm.
Dated: Apr. 6, 1853.
Procedure for the laying of the corner stones of the Salt Lake Temple. The committee of arrangements includes D. H. Wells, Amasa Lyman and Lorenzo Snow.
USIC

6008. The Order of Zion. Kansas City, October, 1918–December, 1919.
1v. (12 nos. in 89 [3]p.) monthly. 28cm.
January–March 1919 not published. Edited by John Zahnd.
CU–B, USIC

6009. Oregon Short Line Railroad Company. In and about Salt Lake, the city beautiful. Compliments of Oregon Short Line Railroad. [Salt Lake City, William A. Morton, 1898?]
[28]l. illus., ports., plates. 18×27cm.
Cover-title.
Resume of the history of the Church and its immigration to Utah as well as a summary of history since in a "sketch of Utah and Mormonism."
NN

6009a. ———. Tour of Mormon Tabernacle Choir to American Land and Irrigation Exposition, New York City, October–November 1911. By special train. [n.p.] General Passenger Departments, Oregon Short Line — Union Pacific Railroads [1911]
11p. illus. 18cm.
USIC

O'Reilly, Harrington. *See Nelson, John Young.*

Orion [*pseud.*] *See Smith, Hyrum Orion.*

6010. Te Orometua. Pepeete, Tahiti. May, 1897–
v. monthly. 27cm.
Official organ of the RLDS church in the Society Islands.
First issue, May, 1897. Last issue probably in 1926. The press was destroyed in a storm in 1906; revived in January, 1909.
Title in English: The Instructor.
USIC V.1 #1–7, V.2 #1–4

6011. Orr, Adrian Van Brocklin. Mormonism dissected, or, Knavery "on two sticks," exposed. Composed principally from notes which were taken from the arguments of Dr. Orr, in the recent debate on the a[u]thenticity of the "Book of Mormon," between him and E. H. Davis, Mormon Preacher. The whole being designed as a check to the further progress of imposition, by placing in the hands of every one the means of unmasking this "Latter Day" humbug. By one who hates imposture. Bethania, Lancaster County, Pa., Printed by Reuben Chambers, 1841.
22p. 20½×14cm.
CSmH, CtY, CU–B, UHi, USIC

6012. Orr, Charles Ebert. A religious controversy. Anderson, Ind., Gospel Trumpet Co. [n.d.]
92p. 18cm.
Concerns the nature of the Christian church, Mormonism and the Church of God.
WHi

Orr, Thomas. Life History of Thomas Orr . . . *See Taylor, Lillie Jane Orr.*

6013. Orton, Richard H. Records of California men in the War of the Rebellion, 1861–1867. Revised and compiled by Brig. Gen. Richard H. Orton . . . Sacramento, State Office, 1890.
887p. 23½cm.
Includes the correspondence of P. Edward Connor from Fort Douglas, 1862–64, with attacks on Brigham Young, etc.
CU–B, DLC, NjP, USIC

6014. The OSA Light. Preston, Published by the Oneida Stake Academy, May 24, 1907–
v. 23½cm.
Student periodical.
USIC V.1 #1

6015. Osborn, A. C. The Mormon doctrine of God and heaven. An address delivered before the Baptist ministers' conference of South Carolina, November, 1898. By Rev. A. C. Osborn . . . Nashville, Tenn., Sunday School Board, Southern Baptist Convention [1899]
63p. 17cm.
DLC, NN

6016. Osborne, George. Extracts from Pioneer G.O.'s journal. Only for saints. No man knoweth the things of God but by the Spirit of God . . . [Salt Lake City, 1905?]
39p. 17½cm.
Contains Joseph Smith's sermon on priesthood (June 2, 1839); A remarkable prophecy (White horse); Sermon of Orson Pratt (October 29, 1879); Three manifestations of God's power; and Joseph Smith's last dream.
MH, USIC

6017. Osgood, Ernest Staples. The day of the cattleman, by Ernest Staples Osgood. Minneapolis, The University of Minnesota Press, 1929.
xp., [2]l., 283p. plates, maps (part double) facsims, diagrs. 24½cm.
Tells of gentiles being driven out of Salt Lake City by the Mormons.
Howes 130
CU, DLC, NjP, UHi, ULA

6018. Osmond, Alfred. The exiles; a true and tragic story of heroic struggles and masterful achievements by Alfred Osmond . . . Salt Lake City, The Deseret News Press, 1926.
4p.l., 11–269p. illus., port. 20cm.
Mormon poetry.
CSmH, DLC, MH, NjP, NN, UHi, ULA, UPB, USl, USlC, UU

6019. ———. My philosophy of life; a popular and practical discussion of the science of life and the fine art of living, by Alfred Osmond . . . Salt Lake City, The Deseret News Press [c1927]
3p.l. [v]–vi [7]–256p. port. 19½cm.
"Miscellaneous poems," p. 231–256.
Mormon doctrine.
DLC, NjP, UHi, USlC, UU

6020. ———. The poetical works of Alfred Osmond. Arranged and published by the author . . . Salt Lake City, G. Q. Cannon & Sons Company, Printers, 1891.
viii [9]–304p. 23cm.
Mormon poetry.
CSmH, DLC, NjP, NN, UHi, USlC, UU, WHi

6021. Oswalt, Martin Luther. Pen pictures of Mormonism, by Rev. M. L. Oswalt . . . Philadelphia, American Baptist Publication Society, 1899.
95p. 19½cm.
DLC, ICN, MH, MoInRC, UHi, USlC, UU

6022. ———. (same, in Swedish) Teckningar öfver Mormonismen, af M. L. Oswalt. Översättning af E. Sandell. Philadelphia, American Baptist Publication Society, 1900.
96p. 20cm.
CU–B

Our constitutional rights and congressional privileges. *See Parry, Joseph Hyrum.*

6023. Our Deseret home. A . . . journal devoted to the industrial and productive interests and information in general. Salt Lake City, Deseret Home Co. Jan 15, 1882–Aug 1884.
3v. monthly. 23cm.
Editor: W. M. Egan.
A magazine designed for Mormon readers.
Discontinued with V.3 #8.
CtY V. 1 #7–12; V. 2; V. 3 #1–2, 4; NjP; UPB V.1, V.2, #2–7, 9–12, V.3 #1–3; USlC

6024. Our native land: or, Glances at American scenery and places, with sketches of life and adventure. New York, D. Appleton [c1882]
xvi [3]–615p. illus. 27cm.
Description of Utah with some information on Mormonism and the Danites.
CU–B, UPB, USlC

6025. Outlines of the doctrines of the Church of Jesus Christ of Latter-day Saints. [Kansas City, Central States Mission, n.d.]
27 [1]p. 16cm.
Ready reference.
UU

6026. Owen, Ephraim, Jr. Mormons. Memorial of Ephraim Owen, jr., late of Green County, Indiana, now of Davis [sic] County, Missouri, asking of Congress to afford protection to the people called Mormons, in the enjoyment of their civil rights as citizens of the United States; and complaining of loss of property, &c., December 20, 1838 . . . [Washington, Thomas Allen, Print., 1838]
5p. 22½cm. (U.S. 25th Cong. 3d Sess. House. Doc. No. 42)
Signed: December 20, 1838.
Referred to the Committee on the Judiciary, and ordered to be printed.
CSmH, CtY, CU–B, NjP, NN, UHi, UPB

6027. Owen, John. The journals and letters of Major John Owen, pioneer of the Northwest, 1850–1871, embracing his purchase of St. Mary's mission; the building of Fort Owen; his travels; his relation with the Indians; his work for the government; and his activities as a western empire builder for twenty years. Transcribed and edited from the original manuscripts in the Montana Historical Society and the collection of W. R. Coe, esq., by Seymour Dunbar: and with notes to Owen's texts by Paul C. Phillips . . . with two maps and thirty plates . . . New York, E. Eberstadt, 1927.
2v. illus., ports., xxx plates, 11 fold. maps, facsims. 24½cm.
Various references to Mormons particularly the Salmon River Mission and his visit to Salt Lake City.
Howes O163
CtY, CU–B, DLC, DN, NjP, UHi, ViU, WaU

6028. Owen, T. Grafton. Drippings from the eaves. Seattle, Press of Lowman & Hanford Company [c1911]
2p.l. [7]–172p. plates. 25cm.
Supposedly witnessed as a child the death of Joseph and Hyrum Smith; his description after 65 years.
USlC

6028a. Owen, William O. Life among the Mormons. Bristol, Printed by George Wright, Steam Printer [1863]
Broadside. 38×25cm.
Announcement of lectures by Mr. Owen concerning his experience and observation at Salt Lake City, Utah.
USlC

6029. ———. Seven years in the Great Salt Lake City. By W. O. Owen . . . 3d ed., 10th thousand. Birmingham, Printed by J. Tunnington [n.d.]
24p. 20cm.
USlC

6030. ———. (same) Bristol, Printed by J. Wright & Co. [1866?]
24p. 20cm.
Cover-title.
CSmH, CU-B, MH

6031. Owens, George, *compiler.* Salt Lake City directory, including a business directory of Provo, Springville and Ogden, Utah Territory. Compiled and Published by G. Owens. [Salt Lake City] 1867.
2–18 [6] 21–135p. 23cm.
Includes Mormon and Utah chronology.
CtY, MH

6032. Owens, John Algernon. Sword and pen; or ventures and adventures of Colonel Willard Glazier . . . in war and literature . . . by John Algernon Owens. Philadelphia, P. W. Ziegler & Co., 1881.
xvi p. [1]l., 21–436p. port., plates. 19½cm.
Chapter 47. "Among the Mormons."
Another edition: 1883. CU; 1900. USlC
DLC

6033. Oxley, William. Modern messiahs and wonder workers. A history of the various messianic claimants to special divine prerogatives, and of the sects that have arisen thereon in recent times. By William Oxley . . . London, Trübner & Co., 1889.
ivp., [1]l., 186p. plates, 7 ports. 19cm.
Section on Joseph Smith in which the success of Mormonism is determined by a strong man being able to gull a half million victims: "gulled with the blatant advertisements of theological tradesmen."
DLC, MH, NN, PPL-R, UPB

A

INTERESTING ACCOUNT

OF

SEVERAL REMARKABLE VISIONS,

AND OF

THE LATE DISCOVERY

OF

ANCIENT AMERICAN RECORDS.

BY O. PRATT,

MINISTER OF THE GOSPEL.

" For there is nothing covered, that shall not be revealed ; and hid, that shall not be known."—MATT. x. 26.

EDINBURGH :
PRINTED BY BALLANTYNE AND HUGHES,
MDCCCXL.

Item 6501. The first issue (with the incorrect article at the beginning of the title) of the earliest printed version of Joseph Smith's 1820 vision. From the LDS church collection.

6034. P., F. Berichte während einer Reise um die Erde 1877/78, von F. P. Hamburg. Verlag von Paul Jenichen [n.d.]
187p. 24½cm.
Mormonism, p. 110–117.
Title in English: Account of a voyage around the world, 1877–1878.
USIC

6035. Pacific Art Company, San Francisco. History of the Mountain Meadows massacre, or the butchery in cold blood of 134 men, women, and children by Mormons and Indians, Sept., 1857, also a full and complete account of the trial, confession and execution of John D. Lee, the leader of the murderers. Illustrated by a true likeness of John D. Lee. Published by the Pacific Art Company of San Francisco, Cal. for distribution with their celebrated picture of Mountain Meadows. [San Francisco] Spaulding and Barto, Book and Job Printers, 1877.
32p. fold. illus., port. 24cm.
Cover-title.
Howes 7217
CSmH, CtY, CU, DLC, MB

6035a. Pacific Coast Women's Press Association. La copa de oro (The cup of gold) A collection of California poems, sketches and stories by the members of the Pacific Coast Women's Press Association. Edited by Abbie E. Krebs. [Illustrated by Geo. F. Mannel. San Francisco, Geo. Spaulding & Company, 1905]
4 p.l., 7–118p. illus., plates. 28½cm.
Includes a chapter of the emigrants on the ship Brooklyn: California's first emigrant ship, by Emily S. Loud.
UPB

6036. Pacific N.E.A. Bureau. Mormon Bible becomes issue in League of Nations fight. San Francisco, [ca. 1917]
Broadside. port. 32×36cm.
Book of Mormon quoted as being against the League of Nations.
USIC

6037. Pack, Frederick James. Revelation antedating scientific discovery — an instance. [Logan, Utah? 1907]
7p. 23cm.
USIC

6037a. ———. Science and belief in God; a discussion of certain phases of science and their bearing upon belief in the Supreme Being . . . Salt Lake City, The Deseret News, 1924.
xiii, 270p. 20½cm.
UHi, ULA, USIC, UU

6038. ———. Tobacco and human efficiency, by Frederick J. Pack . . . Pub. by the Church of Jesus Christ of Latter-day Saints. Salt Lake City, The Deseret News, 1918.
xv [1] 320p. 19cm.
DLC, NjP, UHi, UPB, USIC, UU

6039. Packard, *Mrs.* **E. P. W.** An open letter, to the members of the General Assembly of the Territory of Utah — In support of the "Identity emancipation of women and woman suffrage part of the gospel." Bill to establish and protect the identity of married women. [n.p.] 1882.
4p. 21½cm.
USIC

6040. Packard, Noah. Memorial to the honorable the Governor, Senate and House of Representatives of Massachusetts, in Legislative capacity assembled. Boston, Dutton and Wentworth, Printers to the State, 1844.
12p. 25cm. (Massachusetts. General Court. House of Representatives. 1844. Doc. 64)
[Boston . . . 1844] imprint in brackets at head of title: House . . . No. 64.
A memorial pointing out the ill-treatment the Mormons have received in Ohio, Missouri and Illinois and the failure of the U.S. Government to do anything. Contained in: Documents printed by order of the House of Representatives of the Commonwealth of Massachusetts, during the session of the General Court, A. D. 1844. Boston, Dutton and Wentworth, Printers to the State, 1844.
M, MB, NN, USI

6041. ———. Political and religious detector: In which Millerism is exposed, false principles detected, and truth brought to light. By N. Packard "Minister of the Gospel." Medina, Ohio, Printed by Michael Hayes, 1843.
40p. 20cm.
"Mormonism revealed! The kingdom divided against itself cannot stand, p. 10–16.
USIC

6042. Paddock, Cornelia, "Mrs. A. G. Paddock." The fate of Madame La Tour; a tale of Great Salt Lake, by Mrs. A. G. Paddock. New York, Fords, Howard, & Hulbert, 1881.
1p.l., v–xii [13]–352p. 18cm.
Appendix. "Utah: 1870–1881," and "Utah to-day," p. 285–326.
Fiction concerning Mormonism.
CSmH, CU, DLC, ICN, MiU, NjP, OClW, PPL, UHi, ULA, UPB, USI, UU, WHi

6043. ———. (same) New York, Fords, Howard & Hulbert, 1881.
1p.l., v–xii [13]–361p. 17½cm.
CSmH, CU-B, MoInRC, MWA, NN, UPB

6044. ———. (same) New York, Fords, Howard & Hulbert, 1882.
1p.l. [v]–xii [13]–361p. 17½cm.
CSmH, DLC, ICN, MH, NjPT, PHi, UHi, USIC, ViU

PADEN, W. M.

6045. ———. (same) New York, Fords, Howard & Hulbert, 1895.
1p.l. [v]–xii [13]–352p. 18cm.
RPB

6046. ———. (same) New York, Fords, Howard & Hulbert 1900 [c1881]
1p.l. [v]–xii [13]–310p. 19cm.
"10th thousand."
CSmH, MH, NN, UU

6047. ———. (same, in Danish) Mrs. Paddock: blandt Mormoner en beretning om Madame la Tour og hendes børn oversat efter: The fate of Madame la Tour or a tale of the Great Salt Lake af C. Mønster . . . København, Forlagt af Diakonissestiftelsens Depot . . . 1902.
2p.l., 239p. 18½cm.
Reprinted in 1914.
USIC

6048. ———. In the toils; or, Martyrs of the latter days. By Mrs. A. G. Paddock. Chicago, Shepherd, Tobias, & Co., 1879.
4p.l. [7]–301p. 20cm.
Fiction concerning mormonism.
CSmH, ICN, IWW, MB, MH, NjP, NN, OClWHi, PPL, UHi, UPB, USl, USIC, UU, WHi

6049. ———. (same) Chicago, Dixon & Shepard, 1879.
4p.l. [7]–301p. 20cm.
CU–B, DLC, WHi

6050. ———. (same) New York, J. W. Lovell Company [1890]
4p.l. [7]–301p. 19cm.
On cover: American novelists' series. No. 20.
CSmH, DLC, USIC

6051. ———. (same) New York, The American News Company [c1890]
301p. 18cm.
USIC

6052. ———. (same) New York, Ogilvie Publishing Co. [c1890]
301p. 19½cm. (The Peerless series)
NN, OClWHi, UHi, UPB

6053. ———. (same) [Chicago, E. A. Weeks, 1890?]
301p. 24cm. (The Holly Library of Choice Books)
Cover has ornaments and the "work by" printed, but author and title are supplied in manuscript.
USl

6054. ———. Martyrer. En fortaelling om Mormonraedslerne. Forkortet oversaettelse. Kobenhavn, 1914.
260p.
Title in English: The Martyrs. A story of Mormon terror.
Schmidt

6055. ———. . . . Saved at last from among the Mormons. By Mrs. A. G. Paddock. [Also Mrs. Caudle's curtain lectures; by Douglas Jerrold] . . . Springfield, Ohio, Farm and Fireside Company, 1881.
1p.l., 92p. 19½cm. (On cover: Farm and fireside library. V.1, No.4)
Cover-title.
Fiction concerning Mormonism.
CSmH, CU–B, DLC, NjP, NN, USl, USIC

6056. ———. (same) Springfield, Ohio, Mast, Crowell and Kirkpatrick, 1894.
91p. 19½cm.
NjP, OClWHi, UPB

6057. Paden, William M. The churches of Utah. By William M. Paden. [New York, Woman's Board of Home Missions of the Presbyterian Church in the U.S.A., n.d.]
6p. 18cm.
UHi, UPB

6058. ———. Is Mormonism changing? By Rev. W. M. Paden. [Albany, N.Y., Press of Frank H. Evory & Co., Home Missions Council of Women for Home Missions, 1929?]
23p. 22½cm.
Cover-title.
"Reprinted by Permission of *The Biblical Review* . . . issue of July, 1929."
MoInRC, UHi, USl

6059. ———. (same) New York, Home Missions Council and Council of Women for Home Missions [1929]
23p. 23cm.
UPB

6060. ———. L. W. Moffet, esq., Humiston, Iowa [Letter] [n.p., n.d.]
[1]p. 24cm.
Answer to a query concerning the Reorganized Church and Mormonism. It states that the Mormons hate the Reorganized Church more than they do the Presbyterians. Paden was a Presbyterian minister in Salt Lake City.
MH, MoInRC

6061. ———. Missions among Mormons — Why? By Rev. Dr. Wm. M. Paden. New York, Board of Home Missions of the Presbyterian Church in the U.S.A. [1921]
8p. 16cm.
UPB

6062. ———. Questions and answers on Mormonism [by] The Reverend W. M. Paden. New York, Board of National Missions, Presbyterian Church, U.S.A. [1929?]
16p. 23cm.
MoInRC, UHi, USlC

6063. Page, Elizabeth. Wagons west; a story of the Oregon trail, by Elizabeth Page . . . New York, Farrar & Rinehart, Inc. [c1930]
xiv, 361p. plates, facsim. 24½cm.
Narrative of the overland journey of Henry Page along the Mormon trail to California in 1849, based upon his letters to his wife. It also includes a brief history of Mormonism.
CU–B, DLC, MH, NjP, NN, OCl, OO, PP, PPA, UHi, UPB, USl, USlC, UU

6064. Page, Gerome E. All secret societies, the True Church of the Devil. [n.p., n.d.]
28p. 15cm.
Uses the *Book of Mormon* as a basis for his argument.
USlC

6065. Page, John E. An address to the inhabitants and sojourners of Washington, to his excellency the President of the United States, the honorable Senators and Representatives in Congress, and all the Rev. Divines, magistrates, landlords, merchants, artists, mechanics, laborers, soldiers, marines and the world at large. [Washington? 1844?]
4p. 23cm.
Caption-title.
Dated: March 7, 1844.
A short description of L.D.S. beliefs with admonitions to call upon Mr. Page for additional information. Testimonials concerning character included.
Notice at end: Washington, March 12, 1844, signed by Jos. S. Potter, Franklin Little, clerk at the [Washington] Globe Office, F. Edmonston, Printer, with testimonial by Charles W. Fenton, Printer, L. A. Edmonston.
Sabin 58151
UPB, USlC

6066. ———. A Collection of sacred hymns for the use of Latter Day Saints. Selected and Published by John E. Page & John Cairns, Elders . . . [Pittsburgh? 1841?]
64p. 10½cm.
Caption-title.
Published prior to Emma Smith's hymn book of 1841.
MoInRC

6067. ———. Keep it constantly before the Public, that eternal life is the knowledge of God, by Direct Revelation. Published by John E. Page, Elder of the Church of Jesus Christ of Latter Day Saints, A.D. 1843. [n.p., n.d.]
Broadside.
Copy listed in Woodward: *Bibliothica Scallowagiana.* No. 115.
Sabin 50742

6068. ———. The Priesthood by John E. Page . . . Voree, W. T., Published by the Church of Jesus Christ of Latter Day Saints, 1847.
28p. 16cm. (Gospel tract. No. 3)
Caption-title.
Three chapters written by James J. Strang.
CtY, UPB defective

6069. ———. Slander refuted. By John E. Page, Elder of the Church of the Latter-day Saints. [n.p., 1842?]
16p. 22cm.
Caption-title.
"Slander refuted" p. 1–6 contains also a portrait of the Missouri mob, by Joel H. Johnson; other poems and articles.
"An address by a minister of the Church of Jesus Christ of Latter-Day Saints to the people of the United States, p.[12]–16.
Sabin 58152
MH, UPB, USlC

6070. ———. The Spaulding story concerning the origin of the Book of Mormon, duly examined and exposed to the righteous contempt of a candid public. By John E. Page, Pastor . . . in Pittsburgh, 1843. [Plano, Ill., Reorganized Church of Jesus Christ of Latter Day Saints, 1866?]
16p. 21cm.
Republished by the Reorganized Church of Jesus Christ of Latter Day Saints . . . at Plano, Illinois, Oct. 12, 1867. First edition not located.
Sabin 58153
CSmH, CtY, CU–B, MH, MoInRC, NjP, NN, OClWHi, UPB, WHi

6071. ———. Treatise on circumcision by John E. Page. [Voree, Wis., Church of Jesus Christ of Latter Day Saints, 1847]
20p. 16cm. (Gospel tract. No. 1)
Caption-title.
First published in *Zion's Reveille,* June 1, July 29, and August 5, 1847.
Morgan
CDU, CtY, UPB

6072. ———. Treatise on the spiritual covenant made with Abraham by John E. Page. [Voree, Wis., Published by the Church of Jesus Christ of Latter Day Saints [1847]
4p. 16cm. (Gospel tract. No. 2)
Originally written at Pittsburg, 1842, and published unrevised.
Caption-title.
Morgan
CDU, CtY, UPB

6073. Paine, Halbert Eleazer. Contested election. Territory of Utah. George R. Maxwell vs. George A. Cannon. Argument of Halbert E. Paine, counsel for sitting member. [Salt Lake City? 1879?]
59p. 23cm.
MH, NjP, UPB, USlC, UU

6074. ———. George Q. Cannon versus A. G. Campbell; Contested election. Argument for contestant. Salt Lake City? 1880]
62p. 23cm.
Caption-title.
Signed: H. E. Paine, Attorney for G. Q. Cannon.
CU–B

6075. Paine, Swift. Eilley Orrum: Queen of the Comstock. Indianapolis, The Bobbs-Merrill Company [c1929]
7p.l., 15–309p. 21cm.
A novel with some Mormon background.
Another edition: New York, Grosset & Dunlap [c1929] USlC
CU–B, DLC, NjP, USlC

6076. The Palantic; a monthly journal devoted to the exposition of truth and error. Salt Lake City, October, 1887–September, 1888.
1v. (12 nos., in 196p.) monthly. 27cm.
"Palantic is an abridgment of Pacific and Atlantic."
Published and edited by A. Milton Musser.
Untrimmed copy of #12 at UPB shows marginal advertisements to be cut off at binding.
Published to defend Mormonism.
CSmH, MH, NN, UPB, USlC

The Palantic Monthly. Mormonism exposed.
See Wilson, Jeremiah M.

6077. Palfrey, Louise. The divinity of the Book of Mormon proven by archaeology; a series of papers formerly published in the "Arena" Department of the Autumn Leaves. Lamoni, Ia., Published by Zion's Religio-Literary Society at the Herald Publishing House [1901]
2p.l. [5]–288p. 20cm.
MoInRC, NjP, UHi, USlC, WHi

6078. ———. (same) Lamoni, Ia., Published by Zion's Religio-Literary Society [1908]
2p.l. [5]–226p. 19½cm.
MoInRC, UHi, UPB

6079. Palmer, Annie Donovan. The Rescue; a one-act play by Annie D. Palmer. The *Improvement Era* prize play, 1926. [Salt Lake City] Published by General Board Y.M.M.I.A., 1927.
15p. 17cm.
Mormon drama. Rescue from cricket plague.
NjP, USlC

6080. Palmer, Benjamin Morgan. Mormonism. A lecture delivered before the Mercantile Library Association of Charleston, South Carolina by B. M. Palmer, D.D. January 26, 1853. Columbia, S.C., Printed by I. C. Morgan, 1853.
34p. 24cm.
Cover-title.
CU–B, MH

6081. Palmer, John W. To the Citizens of Hancock County! Nauvoo, 1846.
Broadside. 19×22cm.
Signed: John W. Palmer, Maj. Com. Anti-Mormon forces, Nauvoo, Nov. 12, 1846.
Byrd 1104
ICHi, NN

6082. Palmer, Loomis T. Gaskell's new and complete family atlas of the world. Salt Lake City, J. H. Bard & Co. [1886]
582p. illus., maps. 35cm.
Utah maps, p. 127. "Utah territory," with Mormon references, p. 320–322.
USlC

6083. Palmer, William. The bull taken by the horns; or, papal aggression calmly considered, in a letter to Lord John Russell. By W. Palmer, minister of Bethesda Chapel, Oldham Street, Manchester. Second edition, revised and enlarged, to which is added an appendix, or second letter. London, Published by Arthur Hall and Co. . . . Briscoe, Printer [1850?]
47p. 21cm.
Reference to Mormonism on p. 9 and advertisements for two of his anti-Mormon tracts at the end of the text.
NN

6084. ———. The external evidences of the Book of Mormon examined. London, Sold by Arthur Hall and Co., Briscoe, Printer [1849?]
27p. 18½cm. (No. II)
Caption-title.
At head of title: No. II.
NN, USlC

6085. ———. Mormonism briefly examined. By W. Palmer, Chatteris. [London, A. Hall & Co., 1849?]
8p. 18½cm. (No. I)
NN, USlC

6086. Palmer, William Henry. Robert Heller; his doings. Glasgow, Printed by Hay Nisbet . . . [1875?]
64p. illus. 18cm.
"Robert Heller in Great Salt Lake City, Utah." Anecdotes of his visit, his talk with Brigham Young, with quotes from Artemus Ward.
Robert Heller was the stage name of W. H. Palmer.
CtY

PALMER, W. J.

6087. Palmer, William Jackson. Report of surveys across the continent in 1867–'68, on the thirty-fifth and thirty-second parallels, for a route extending the Kansas Pacific Railway to the Pacific Ocean at San Francisco and San Diego . . . Philadelphia, W. B. Selheimer, 1869.
250p. fold. map. 22cm.
Mormonism briefly mentioned.
CU, NjP, UHi, ULA

6088. Pancoast, Charles Edward. A Quaker forty-niner, the adventures of Charles Edward Pancoast on the American frontier; edited by Anna Paschall Hannum, with a foreword by John Bach McMaster. Philadelphia, University of Pennsylvania Press; London, M. Milford, Oxford University Press, 1930.
xv, 402p. illus., plates, port., maps, facsim. 23½cm.
Maps on lining-papers.
Includes Mormons in Nauvoo, p. 52–53, and at Pueblo, p. 200.
DLC, ICN, MH, MiU, NjP, NN, PPM, UHi, USlC, ViU, WaU

Papers in the case of Baskin vs. Cannon . . .
See Baskin, Robert N. House of Representatives . . .

6089. Park, *Mrs.* **S. E.** The Mormons; their religion, and identity with the Bible. By Mrs. S. E. Park. 4th ed. San Francisco, J. Winterburn & Co., 1875.
23p. 20cm.
NN

6090. Park, Hamilton G. Address of President Hamilton G. Park. Salt Lake City [n.d.]
3p. 22cm.
Reminiscences given before the High Priests quorum, Ensign Stake.
USlC

6091. Parke, Walter. Lays of the saintly; or, the new golden legend, by Walter Parke (the London hermit) With illus. and vignette by John Leitch. London, Vizetelly [pref. 1882]
181p. illus. 19½cm.
"Originally published several years ago in the *Dublin University Magazine*," pref. p. v.
"St. Smith of Utah (a la Walt Whitman)," p. 68–74.
CU

———. Parodies of Walt Whitman.
See Saunders, Henry Scholey.

6091a. Parker, Aubrey James. Living leaves; being a selection from the writings of Aubrey Parker. Shelley, Idaho [1915]
23[1]p. 18cm.
Inspirational writings.
USlC

6091b. ———. The purple robe. Independence, Mo., Press of Zion's Printing & Publishing Co. [n.d.]
8p. 18cm.
USlC

6092. ———. A world-wide testimony. Once a Methodist preacher, — and now a "Mormon" for the past forty years . . . [n.p., n.d.]
8p. 17cm.
Testimony of the truthfulness of Mormonism.
USlC

6093. Parker, B. G. Recollections of the Mountain Meadows massacre, being an account of the awful atrocity and revealing some facts never before made public. By B. G. Parker. Plano, California, Fred W. Reed, American Printers, 1901.
31p. front. 15cm.
Howes P75
CtY, ICN

6094. Parker, James R. Circular to the citizens of Adams and the adjacent counties in this state. Nauvoo, 1846.
Broadside. 34×10cm.
Dated: August 25, 1846.
Concerning anti-Mormon activities.
USlC

6095. ———. Circular: To the citizens of Adams and the Adjacent Counties in this State. Nauvoo, 1846.
Broadside. 34×10cm.
Signed: September 5th, 1846.
No need for an armed force in the area any longer.
UPB

6096. ———. Procla[mation (copy torn)] State of Illinois. Hancock County, Whereas James R. Pa[rker (copy torn)] the 32 Regiment of the Militia of the State of Illinois have been ordered with a portion . . . [Nauvoo, 1846]
Broadside. 27×27cm.
Signed: James R. Parker, Nauvoo, Aug. 25, 1846.
Parker was sent to Nauvoo by Governor Ford to maintain peace. A plea to the citizens to maintain and aid in the keeping of the peace, during anti-Mormon troubles.
As reprinted in *Hancock Eagle,* August 28, 1846. "Proclamation. No. 1"
Byrd 1105
USlC

6097. ———. To the Public . . . Nauvoo, Ill., 1846.
Broadside. 29×27cm.
Signed: Sept. 3, 1846.
Necessity of restoring order after exodus of the Mormons.
Byrd 1106
USlC

6097a. Parker, John. Mormonism exposed and refuted. Clitheroe, December 14th, 1840.
Broadside. 21×23½cm.
UPB Xerox copy. Original in private hands.

6098. ———. Mormonism further exposed. Clitheroe, H. Whalley Printer [1841]
Broadside. 27½×22cm.
Signed: Clitheroe, February 13th, 1841.
USIC

6099. Parker, Lew. Odd people I have met. [n.p., 1910?]
120p., illus. 20½cm.
Cover-title.
"Salt Lake City and a little business deal with the famous president of the Church," p. 112–116; Salt Lake Theatre.
NjP, UHi

6100. Parker, Samuel. Journal of an exploring tour beyond the Rocky Mountains, under the direction of the A. B. C. F. M. performed in the years 1835, '36, and '37; containing a description of the geography, geology, climate, and productions and the number, manners, and customs of the natives. With a map of Oregon Territory. By Rev. Samuel Parker, A. M. Ithaca, N.Y., Published by the author, Mack, Andrus, & Woodruff, Printers, 1838.
xii [13]–371p. 19cm.
Reference to the Mormons in Missouri, 1835, p. 30.
Reprinted in many editions.
W–C 70
CSmH, CtY, CU–B, DLC, MWA

6101. Parkman, Francis. The California and Oregon trail: being sketches of prairie and Rocky Mountain life . . . By Francis Parkman, jr. New York, London, Geo. P. Putnam, 1849.
448p. front. 19cm.
Added illus. title-page.
Several encounters with Mormons on the trail, 1846, p. 49–50, 358–361, 436–437. Recounts history and notes distrust of both Mormons and gentiles.
Published later under title: *The Oregon trail.* Published in several editions.
Howes P97, Sabin 58801, W–C 170
CSmH, CtY, CU, CU–B, DLC, MH, NjP, WaU, WHi

6102. Parrish, Randall. The great plains; the romance of western American exploration, warfare, and settlement, 1527–1870, by Randall Parrish. With more than fifty illustrations. Chicago, A. C. McClurg & Co., 1907.
xivp., [1]l., 17–399p. plates, ports. 22cm.
"The Mormon Hegira; Route of the Mormons" "Mormon atrocities," etc., p. 82, 145–151, 157–159, 182–183, 231, 293–294
Other editions: 2d ed. 1907. USIC; 1915. NjP
CU–B, DLC, DW, NjP, UHi, ULA, USIC, WaT, WaU, WaW

6103. ———. Historic Illinois, a romance of the earlier days. By Randall Parrish . . . With map and fifty illustrations. Chicago, A. C. McClurg & Co., 1905.
xiv, [1]l., 15–479p. plates, ports., fold. map, facsim. 24cm.
Includes "The Mormons at Nauvoo."
Another edition: Chicago, A. C. McClurg, 1906. USIC
CU, DLC, UPB, USIC

6104. Mr. Parrott, the anti-Mormon lecturer. [Bristol, J. Wright & Co., 186–]
4p. 16cm.
An introduction to his lectures and plea for donations.
MH

6105. Parrott, William Saunders. Battle of Mormon . . . A meeting will be held in New Temperance Hall, Temple Street, on Monday & Tuesday, February 10th & 11th, 1862. [n.p., 1862]
Broadside. 38×25cm.
A challenge for Amasa M. Lyman, C. C. Rich and others to debate on Mormonism.
USIC

6106. ———. Veil uplifted; or, The religious conspirators of the Latter Day Saints exposed, who are the Mormons? And what are the Latter-day Saints about? Bristol, J. B. Taylor and Sons, 1865.
64p. 19cm.
USI, USIC

6106a. ———. The victims of Mormonism; or, a voice of warning to my countrymen. By William Saunders Parrott. 2d ed.-3d thousand. Bath: Printed by H. E. Carrington, Kingston Buildings [1857]
16p. 18½cm.
In green printed wrapper.
Owned by Peter Crawley.

6107. Parry, Edwin Francis. The beginning of the gospel of Jesus Christ. Rules that must be obeyed by all who enter Christ's Church. By Elder Edwin F. Parry. Liverpool, Millennial Star Office [1896?]
24p. 13cm. (Tract. No. 2)
NN, UHi, USI, USIC

6108. ———. (same, in Dutch) Het Begin van het Evangelie van Jezus Christus. De Verordeningen waaraan allen, die leden van de Kerk van Christus worden, moeten gahoorzamen. Door Ouderling Edwin F. Parry. Uit het Engelsch, door Paul Roelofs. Rotterdam, Gedrukt op last van Sylvester Q. Cannon [n.d.]
15p. 19½cm. (Tractaat. No. 2)
USIC

PARRY, E. F.

6109. ———. (same) Rotterdam, Gedrukt op last van Willard T. Cannon . . . 1903.
15 [2]p. 18½cm.
"Derde Druk."
USIC

6110. ———. (same) Rotterdam, Gedrukt op last van Willard T. Cannon . . . 1904.
15 [2]p. 19cm.
"Vierde druk"
USIC

6111. ———. (same) Vijfde druk. 57ste Duezendtal. Rotterdam, Gedrukt op last van Willard T. Cannon, 1905.
15p. 19cm. (Tractaat. No. 2)
USIC

6112. ———. (same) [Rotterdam, Uitgave van de Nederlandsch-Belgische Zending, 1913]
15 [2]p. 18cm. (Tractaat. No. 2)
USIC

6113. ———. (same) [Rotterdam, Uitgegeven door B. G. Thatcher, n.d.]
15 [2]p. 18½cm.
USIC

6114. ———. Marks of the Church of Christ. The outward signs by which it may be known. Liverpool, Millennial Star Office [1896]
22p. 13cm. (Tract. No. 3)
NN, USIC

6115. ———. (same, in Dutch) Kenmerken van de Kerk van Christus. De uitwendige teekenen waaraan zij kan herkend worden. Door Ouderling Edwin F. Parry. Uit het Engelsch, door Paul Roelofs. Rotterdam, Gedrukt op last van Alfred E. Farrell [n.d.]
15p. 18½cm. (Tractaat. No. 3)
USIC

6116. ———. (same) [Rotterdam, Uitgave van de Nederl.-Belg. Zending, n.d.]
16[1]p. 18cm. (Tractaat. No. 3)
USIC

6117. ———. (same) Uit het Engelsch, door Paul Roelofs. Rotterdam, Gedrukt op last van Alfred L. Farrell [n.d.]
15 [2]p. 18cm. (Tractaat. No. 3)
USIC

6118. ———. A prophet of latter days his divine mission vindicated. By Elder Edwin F. Parry. Liverpool, Millennial Star Office [1896]
108 [2]p. 13½cm. (Tract. No. 5)
MH, NN, USIC, WHi

6119. ———. A prophet of Latter Days. Liverpool, Millennial Star Office [1897?]
57p. 13½cm. (Tract. No. 5)
USIC

6120. ———. (same, in Dutch) Een profeet der Laatste Dagen. Krachtige Bewijzen voor de Ecntheid Zijner Zending. Door Edwin F. Parry. [Rotterdam, Uitgave van Sylvester Q. Cannon, n.d.]
4p [1]p. 14cm.
USIC

6121. ———. Saved by grace. [Liverpool, n.d.]
16p. 13cm. (Tract. No. 1)
USIC

6122. ———. (same, in Danish) Frelst af naade. Formedelst Lydighed. Vigtige Spørsmall besvardede, Af Aeldste Edwin F. Parry. [København, Udgivet og forlagt af Anthon L. Skanchy . . . L. A. Nielsens Trykt . . . 1902]
[4]p. 22cm.
USIC

6123. ———. (same) [Kjøbenhavn, Udgivet og forlagt af Anthon L. Skanchy . . . P. S. Christiansens Tryk., 1903]
[4]p. 23cm.
DLC, USIC

6124. ———. (same, in Dutch) De zaligheid door genade. Gewichtige vragen die betrikking hebben op de Zaligheid, brantwoord door het woord Gods. Door Edwin F. Parry. [Rotterdam, Uitgave van de Nederlansch-Belgische Zending, 1913]
8 [1]p. 18cm. (Tractaat. No. 1)
USIC

6125. ———. (same) Rotterdam, Gedrukt op last van S. Q. Cannon [n.d.]
8 [1]p. 18cm. (Tractaat. No. 1)
USIC

6126. ———. (same, in Swedish) Frälst af nåd. Viktiga frågor rörande frälsningen besvarade med Skriftens ord af Edwin F. Parry. [Köpenhamn, Utgifven och förlagd af Anthon L. Skanchy, 1904]
[4]p. 22½cm.
UPB

6127. ———. . . . Signs of Christ's second coming. What the Bible says concerning His advent. By Elder Edwin F. Parry. Liverpool, Millennial star office [1896]
16p. 13cm. (Tract. No. 4)
In green printed wrapper.
NN, UHi, USI, USIC

6128. ———. (same, in Dutch) Teekenen van de Tweede Komst van Christus. Hetgeen de Zaligmaker en Zijne Apostelen en de oude Profeten dienaangaande seegen. Door Ouderling Edwin F. Parry. Uit het Engelsch vertaald dor en gedrukt op last van Alfred L. Farrell. Rotterdam [n.d.]
12p. 18½cm. (Tractaat. No. 4)
USIC

6129. ———. (same) Tweede druk. 17de Duezendtal. Rotterdam, Gedrukt op last van Willard T. Cannon, 1904.
12p. 19cm. (Tractaat. No. 4)
USIC

6130. ———. (same) [Rotterdam, Uitgave van de Nederlansch-Belgische Zending, 1913]
12 [1]p. 18cm. (Tractaat. No. 4)
USIC

6130a. ———. (same) [Rotterdam, Nederl.-Belgische Zending, ca. 1918]
12p. 18½cm. [Traktaat. No. 4]
USIC

6131. ———. Simple Bible stories. Illustrated. Adapted to the capacity of young children, and designed for use in sabbath schools, Primary Associations, and for home reading. Salt Lake City, Published at the Juvenile Instructor Office, 1891.
3p.l. [7]–53p. illus. 21cm.
Parry given credit for the compilation in the preface of pt. 1.
UPB

6132. ———. Simple Bible stories. No. 2 . . . Adapted to the capacity of young children, and designed for use in Sabbath Schools, Primary Associations, and for home reading. Salt Lake City, George Q. Cannon & Sons Co., 1891.
3p.l. [7]–58p. illus. 21½cm.
UPB

6133. ———. Sketches of missionary life. Salt Lake City, George Q. Cannon and Sons Co., Printers, 1899.
viii [9]–144p. 16cm.
CSmH, CtY, ICN, NN, NjP, UHi, USIC, UU, WHi

6134. ———. The way of eternal life: doctrines and ordinances of Latter-day Saints. Written especially for young people by Edwin F. Parry. Salt Lake City, Deseret News Press, 1917.
vi, 156p. 16cm.
UHi, USl, USIC

6135. Parry, Joseph Hyrum. Constitutional and governmental rights of the Mormons, as defined by Congress and the Supreme Court of the United States, containing the full text of the Declaration of Independence, the Constitution of the United States, Washington's farewell address, the organic act of Utah Territory, the Anti-polygamy law of 1862, the Poland law of 1874, the Edmunds law of 1882, the Edmunds-Tucker law of 1887, the United States statute of limitations, the poor convict release act, and the Idaho test oath law. To which is appended a digest of the decisions of the Supreme court of the United States applicable to "Mormon" cases. Carefully arranged and compiled from authentic sources. Salt Lake City, 1890.
116p. 20½cm.
DLC, MH, NjP, NN, UHi, UPB, USIC, UU, WHi

6136. ———. The gospel brief. Bible references, to the leading principles of the Gospel. For students and missionaries of the Church of Jesus Christ of Latter-day Saints. Salt Lake City, 1897.
[8]p. 15cm.
Cover-title.
MH, UPB, USIC

———. Mormon metropolis. *See Reynolds, George.*

6137. ———. Our constitutional rights and congressional privileges, containing the Declaration of Independence, The Constitution of the United States, Washington's farewell address, the Anti-Polygamy Law of 1862, the Poland Law of 1874, the Edmunds Law of 1882, the Edmunds-Tucker Law of 1887, also the instructions to registrars and the test oaths formulated by the Utah Commission and the suggestions of the Central Committee of the People's Party. Salt Lake City, J. H. Parry & Co., 1887.
2p.l. [5]–92p. 18½cm.
CSmH, UHi, UPB, USIC

6138. ———. Scriptural revelations of the universal apostasy . . . [Liverpool? Millennial Star Office? 1908?]
4p. 21cm.
Caption-title.
Signed at end: J. H. P.
UHi, USIC

6139. Parry, Sydney Henry Jones-. My journey round the world . . . By Captain S. H. Jones-Parry . . . London, Hurst and Blackett, 1881.
2v. 19cm.
Two chapters on Mormons: V.2, Chaps. VII–VIII, p. 169–228.
A factual account of his observations though not impressed.
DLC, NN, OCU, PPL, UU

6140. Parsons, A. H. Parsons' text book. By A. H. Parsons. Lamoni, Ia., Herald Publishing House [c1902]
4p.l. [11]–327p. 19½cm.
RLDS doctrine of the ethics of living.
NjP, USlC

6141. Parsons, C. H. and Co. Catalogue of publications of the Church of Jesus Christ of Latter-day Saints . . . Salt Lake City, C. H. Parsons and Co., 1884.
8p. 14cm.
NN

6142. Parsons, D. A. Mormonism and the Bible. By D. A. Parsons. [London, International Tract Society, 189–]
16p. 17cm.
A summary of Mormonism written after 1890.
USlC

6143. ———. Mormonism and the Bible. The early history, prophets and doctrines of the Latter-day Saints, by D. A. Parsons. Mountain View, California, Pacific Press Publishing Association [n.d.]
32p. 18cm. (Bible Students' Library. No. 203)
IWW, UPB, USlC

6144. Parsons, Tyler. Mormon fanaticism exposed. A compendium of the Book of Mormon or Joseph Smith's golden Bible. Also, the examination of its internal and external evidences, with the argument to refute its pretences to a revelation from God: argued before the Free Discussion Society in the City of Boston, July, 1841. Between Elder Freeman Nickerson, a Mormon, and the author, Tyler Parsons. Boston, Printed for the author, 1841.
102p. [1]l. 23½cm.
Howes P108, Sabin 58916
CtY, CU–B, ICN, MH, OClWHi, NN, USl, USlC

6145. ———. (same) Boston, 1842.
104p. 22cm.
2d edition.
Sabin 58915
CSmH, CtY, DLC, ICN, MH, MWA, OClWHi, WHi

6146. Parton, James. The life of Horace Greeley, editor of the New York Tribune. By James Parton . . . Boston, Fields, Osgood & Co. . . . 1869.
xvii [19]–598p. illus., plates, facsim. 21cm.
Includes his 1859 visit to Utah, p. 455–462.
Another edition: Boston, 1872. CU, DLC
CU–B, DLC

6146a. Patten George. A short sketch of the life of George Patten. [n.p., n.d.]
[7]p. 17½cm.
USlC

6146b. Patten, Gilbert. Dick Merriwell in Utah; or, the road to "Promised Land." By Burt L. Standish, [pseud.] New York, Street & Smith, 1909.
30 [2]p. 28cm. (Tip Top Weekly. An ideal publication for the American Youth. No. 694. New York, July 31, 1909. Price five cents.)
[2] pages of advertisements.
Bound in original colored pictorial wrappers.
UPB

6147. Pattengill, C. N. Light in the valley, memorial sermon delivered at the funeral of Pomeroy Tucker, Palmyra, Wayne County, N.Y., July 3d, 1870, by Rev. C. N. Pattengill. Troy, New York, From the Times Steam Printing House, 1870.
1p.l. [3]–46p. 27½cm.
A brief statement concerning the validity of Pomeroy Tucker's *Origin, rise, and progress of Mormonism*, p. 8–9.

6148. Patterson, C. G. Business, politics and religion in Utah. The Utah-Idaho Sugar Company versus the people of Utah and Idaho. [Salt Lake City, F. W. Gardiner, c1916]
15p. 27cm.
Variant printings.
UHi, UPB, USlC

6149. ———. (same) [Third Edition. Salt Lake City, F. W. Gardiner, c1916]
23 [1] p. 27cm. (Pamphlet No. 1)
USlC

6150. Patterson, Robert. Who wrote the Book of Mormon? By Robert Patterson of Pittsburgh. Philadelphia, L. H. Everts, 1882.
16p. 28cm.
"Reprinted from the *Illustrated history of Washington County*."
Includes proofs of the use of the Spaulding story.
CSmH, CtY, DLC, ICN, NjP, MH, NN, USlC

6151. Patton, David W. Mysteries of God, as revealed to Enoch, on the Mount Mehujah, and sung in tongues by Elder D. W. Patton, of the "Church of Latter Day Saints." (who fell a martyr to the cause of Christ, in the Missouri persecution) and interpreted by Elder S. Rigdon. [n.p., n.d.]
Broadside. 26×22cm.
USlC

6152. Pattyson, W. D. C. An address to Latter Day Saints. Noblesse oblige. [n.p., n.d.]
8p. 20cm.
Subtitle: The Bishop and Zion.
An apostate RLDS member, now a member of the Church of Christ (Temple Lot)
MoInRC

6153. ———. (same) [St. Joseph, Mo., Union Printing, 1905?]
16p. 20cm.
MH, MoInRC, MoK

6154. ———. An address to the Latter Day Saints, especially to the priesthood. St. Joseph, Mo., American Printing [1908?]
24p. 16cm.
MoInRC

6155. ———. (same) St. Joseph, Mo., 1912.
24p. 16cm.
MoK, USlC

6156. ———. (same) Greeting and preparation for Zion. St. Joseph, Mo. [n.d.]
21p. 16cm.
MoInRC

6157. ———. (same) St. Joseph, Mo., 1917.
23p. 16cm.
MoInRC

6158. ———. Prophecy and redemption of Zion. St. Joseph, Mo., Combe Printing Co., 1917.
22p. 15cm.
MoInRC, USlC

6158a. Paul, Joshua Hughes. First principles of the True Gospel of Christ. [Liverpool, ca. 1908]
4p. 21cm.
Published in various editions as missionary tracts.
UPB, USlC

6158b. ———. Is belief alone sufficient? [Liverpool, "Millennial Star" Office, ca. 1908]
4p. 21cm.
Published in numerous editions as missionary tracts.
UPB, USlC

6159. ———. A marvelous doctrine — "Each for all, all for each;" address delivered over Radio Station KSL, Salt Lake City, Sunday, November 27, 1927. [Salt Lake City] 1927.
Broadside. 61×25cm.
Reprinted from the *Deseret News*, Saturday, December 3rd, 1927.
UPB

6160. ———. Scriptural revelations of the universal apostasy, foretold by the prophets and fulfilled by the present condition of the churches, creeds, and practices of men. [n.p., n.d.]
4p. 22cm.
UPB, USlC

6161. ———. Universal salvation. [Liverpool? 19 - -]
4p. 21cm.
Signed at end: J. H. Paul.
USlC

6161a. Paul Morse, in memoriam. [Wilson, Wyoming? 1906]
[8]p. 21½cm.
USlC

6162. Paxson, Frederic Logan. History of the American frontier, 1763–1893, by Frederic L. Paxson . . . Boston and New York, Houghton Mifflin Company, 1924.
xviip., [1]l., 598p. maps (2 double) 24cm.
Material on Mormonism in a chapter, "The State of Deseret."
Howes P145
CSmH, DLC, NjP, UHi, ULA, UPB, USlC

6162a. ———. The last American frontier. New York, The Macmillan Co., 1910.
xi, 402p. plates, maps. 20cm.
Chap. III entitled: "Overland with the Mormons," p. 86–103. Includes Mark Twain's appraisal of the *Book of Mormon*; the Mormon story and trek.
Another edition: 1911. UHi, UPB
CU–B, NjP, UHi, ULA, UPB

6163. Paxton, J. M. The cotter and the prisoner; or, Whisperings from the "Pen." By J. M. Paxton. Salt Lake City, 1889.
38p. 15cm.
Poetry concerning polygamy prisoners.
USlC

6164. Peaine, Mich. Township. Ordinances and by-laws of the township of Peaine, adopted in the years 1851–2. By authority. Saint James, Cooper and Chidester Printers, 1852.
1p.l., 5–18 [4]p. 18×13cm.
Cover-title: Ordinances and by-laws of the Towpship [sic] of Peaine.
Signed: James J. Strang, Chairman of the Board (and others)
Morgan
CtY

6165. Peak, W. E. Concordance and reference guide to the Book of Mormon. [Lamoni, Ia., 189–]
57p. 15½cm.
Cover-title.
MoInRC, UHi

Peak, Warren. *See Lampert, J. M.*

6166. Pearl of Great Price. English. 1851. The Pearl of Great Price; being a choice selection from the revelations, translations, and narrations of Joseph Smith, first prophet, seer, and revelator to the Church of Jesus Christ of Latter-day Saints. Liverpool, F. D. Richards, 1851.
viii, 56p. facsims. (1 fold.) 21cm.
A group of miscellaneous items published for the British Mission, some appearing in earlier sources, some unpublished.
Some bound in Orson Pratt's works have a portrait of F. D. Richards.
Howes S628, Sabin 59437
CSmH, CtY, DLC, ICN, MH, NN, UPB, USlC

PEARL OF GREAT PRICE. ENGLISH

6167. ———. **1878.** (same) Salt Lake City, Printed at the Latter-day Saints' Printing and Publishing Establishment, 1878.
2p.l., 71p. facsims. (1 fold.) 23cm.
Republished from the 1851 edition with revisions. It has been suggested that the text wasn't republished until after the death of Brigham Young due to his disapproval of it.
In addition to the material in the 1851 edition, portions of the present *Book of Moses* were added from Joseph Smith's revision of the Holy Scriptures. Also "The revelation on plural marriage" (*Doctrine and Covenants* 132) was added.
Sabin 83259
CSmH, CtY, CU-B, DLC, ICN, MH, NjP, NN, UHi, UPB, USIC

6168. ———. **1879.** (same) Liverpool, Printed and Published by William Budge . . . 1879.
1p.l. [iv]–v, 90p. facsims. (1 fold.) 22cm.
UPB, USIC, UU

6169. ———. **1882.** (same) Liverpool, Printed and Published by Albert Carrington, 1882.
1p.l. [iv]–v., 90p. facsims. (1 fold.) 22cm.
Printed from the Salt Lake City, 1878 edition.
Sabin 83260
DLC, NN, OCl, UHi, UPB, USl, USIC

6170. ———. **1888.** (same) Salt Lake City, The Deseret News Company, Printers and Publishers, 1888.
iv, 136 [1]p. facsims. (1 fold.) 18cm.
Printed from new plates in Salt Lake City.
Sabin 83261
CtY, IWW, MH, NH, NjP, OO, UHi, ULA, UPB

6171. ———. **1891.** (same) Salt Lake City, George Q. Cannon and Sons Co., Publishers, 1891.
1p.l. [iv]–v 90p. facsims. (1 fold.) 22cm.
Printed from the 1879 plates.
Sabin 83262
MH, MiU, NjP, NN, UHi, UPB, USIC

6172. ———. **1902.** The Pearl of Great Price. A selection from the revelations, translations, and narrations of Joseph Smith, first Prophet, Seer and Revelator to the Church of Jesus Christ of Latter-day Saints. Divided into chapters and verses with references, in 1902. By James E. Talmage. Salt Lake City, The Deseret News, 1902.
iv, 103p. facsims. 17½cm.
Also used as part of a triple combination. The date of the *Book of Mormon* is 1904.
James E. Talmage was appointed to "eliminate from the *Pearl of Great Price* those revelations it formerly contained which are to be found, always were, in the *Book of Doctrine and Covenants* . . ." He also made textual revisions and eliminated the poem "Oh, Say what is truth."
ICU, IWW, NjP, RPB, UHi, ULA, UPB, USIC, UU

6173. ———. **1903.** (same) Liverpool, Published and for Sale by Francis M. Lyman . . . 1903.
iv., 102p. facsims. 17cm.
New set of Liverpool plates to conform to the Salt Lake City, 1902 edition. Also published in a triple combination.
Sabin 83264
USIC

6174. ———. **1906.** (same) Liverpool, Published for sale by Heber J. Grant . . . 1906.
iv, 102p. facsims. 17cm.
Also printed as part of a triple combination.
Sabin 63265
USIC

6175. ———. **1906.** (same) Salt Lake City, Deseret Sunday School Union, 1906.
iv, 103p. facsims. 17½cm.
Sabin 83266
MoInRC, NjP, USl

6176. ———. **1907.** (same) Salt Lake City, The Deseret News, 1907.
iv, 103p. facsims. 17cm.
Also printed as part of a triple combination.
Sabin 83266
MH, NjP, OClW, UHi, ULA, UPB, USIC

6177. ———. **1909.** (same) Liverpool, Printed and Published by Charles W. Penrose, 1909.
iv, 102p. facsims. 16cm.
Sabin 83267
UHi, USIC

6178. ———. **1912.** (same) Liverpool, Printed and Published by Rudger Clawson . . . 1912.
iv, 102p. facsims. 16cm.
Also printed as part of a triple combination.
Sabin 63268
USIC

6179. ———. **1913.** (same) Salt Lake City, The Deseret News, 1913.
iv, 103p. facsims. 17cm.
UPB, USIC

6180. ———. **1917.** (same) Salt Lake City, The Deseret News, 1917.
iv, 103p. facsims. 17½cm.
MH, NjP, UHi, UPB, USIC, UU

6181. ———. **1918.** (same) Salt Lake City, Deseret Sunday School Union, 1918 [c1902]
iv, 103p. 12cm.
USIC

6182. ———. **1920.** (same) Liverpool, 1920.
iv, 102p. facsims. 16cm.
Also printed as part of the 1920 triple combination.
UPB

6183. ———. 1920. (same) Salt Lake City, The Deseret Book Company, 1920.
iv, 103p. facsims. 17cm.
Sabin 83269
MH, UPB, USIC

6184. ———. 1921. The Pearl of Great Price. A selection from the revelations, translations, and narrations of Joseph Smith, first Prophet, Seer and Revelator to the Church of Jesus Christ of Latter-day Saints. Salt Lake City, 1921.
iv, 63p. facsims. 19cm.
New plates, with no revision. Printed by the W. B. Conkey Co., Hammond, Indiana.
Also printed as part of a triple combination.
Sabin 83270
DLC

6185. ———. 1922. (same) Salt Lake City, 1922.
iv, 63p. facsims. 19cm.
Sabin 83270
USIC

6186. ———. 1923. (same) Salt Lake City, The Church of Jesus Christ of Latter-day Saints, 1923.
iv, 63p. facsims. 19cm.
Also printed as part of a triple combination.
CSmH, NjP, NN, UPB, USIC

6187. ———. 1924. (same) Salt Lake City, The Church of Jesus Christ of Latter-day Saints, 1924.
iv, 63p. facsims. 19cm.
NjP, USIC, ViU

6188. ———. 1925. (same) Salt Lake City, 1925.
iv, 63p. facsims. 19cm.
Sabin 83270
USIC

6189. ———. 1926. (same) Salt Lake City, 1926.
iv, 63p. facsims. 19cm.
Also printed as part of a triple combination.
Sabin 83270
USIC

6190. ———. 1927. The Pearl of Great Price; being a choice selection from the revelations, translations, and narrations of Joseph Smith, first Prophet, Seer, and Revelator to the Church of Jesus Christ of Latter-day Saints. Salt Lake City, 1927.
iv, 63p. facsims. 19cm.
USIC

6191. ———. 1928. (same as 1926) Salt Lake City, 1928.
iv, 63p. facsims. 19½cm.
Also printed as part of a triple combination.
UPB

6192. ———. 1929. (same) Salt Lake City, The Church of Jesus Christ of Latter-day Saints, 1929.
iv, 63p. facsims. 17cm.
MH

6193. Pearl of Great Price. Danish. 1883. Den kostelige Perle; et udvalg af profeten og seeren Joseph Smiths Aabenbaringer, Oversaettelser og Beretninger. Förste Danske udgave. Salt Lake City, Trykt hos Deseret News Company, 1883.
1p.l., 122p. facsims. (1 fold.) 15½cm.
Sabin 83271
DLC, NN, UPB, UU

6194. ———. 1909. Den Kostelige Perle et udvalg af Aabenbaringer, oversaettelset og skrivelser af Joseph Smith Forste profet, seer og aabenbarer for Jesu Kristi Kirke, af Sidste-Dages Hellige. Indelt i kapitler og forsynet med henvisninger af James E. Talmage. Oversat paa Dansk af Andrew Jenson. Kjobenhavn, Udgivet of Forlagt af Andrew Jenson, Korsgade II, 1909.
iv, 103p. facsims. 16½cm.
Sabin 83272
NjP, UPB, USIC

6195. Pearl of Great Price. Dutch. 1911. De Paarl van Groote Waarde. Eene kenze uit de openbaringen, vartalingen en varhalen van Joseph Smith de eerste profeet, siener en openbaarder tot de Kerk van Jezua Christus van de Heiligen der Laatste Dagen, Verdeeld in hoofdstukken en verzen met verwizingen, in 1902, door James E. Talmage uit het Engelisch vertaald door Wm. J. De Brij. Erste Nederlandche uitgave. Rotterdam, Uitgegeven door B. G. Thatcher, 1911.
iv, 104p. 18cm.
Sabin 83273
NjP, UPB, USIC

6196. Pearl of Great Price. German. 1882. Die köstliche Perle; Eine auskewählte Sammlung von den Offenbarungen, Uebersetzungen und Erzählungen Joseph Smiths. Erster Prophet, Seher und Offenbarer für die Kirche Jesu Christi der Heiligen der letzten Tage. Aus dem Englischen übersetzt von J. J. Walser. Bern, P. F. Gass, 1882.
vi [2]–111p. facsims. 18cm.
Sabin 83274
NjP, UHi, ULA, UPB, USIC

6197. ———. 1912. Die köstliche Perle, einige ausgewählte Offenbarungen, Übersetzungen und Erzählungen Joseph Smith's des ersten Propheten, Sehers und Offenbarers der Kirche Jesu Christi, der Heiligen der letzten Tage. Aus dem Englischen übersetzt von J. J. Walser. Eingeteilt in Kapitel und Verse und mit Erläuterungen versehen von Robert U. Stelter, in Übereinstimmung mit der von Dr. James E. Talmage bearbeiteten englischen Auflage. Zweite Auflage. Herausgegeben von Hyrum W. Valentine, Basel, 1912.
iv, 92p. facsims. 17cm.
Sabin 83275
NjP, UPB, USIC

6198. ———. 1920. (same) Dritte Auflage. Basel, Schweizerisch-Deutsche Mission . . . 1920.
4, 92p. facsims. 17cm.
UPB

6199. ———. 1924. Die köstliche Perle; eine Auswahl aus den Offenbarungen, Übersetzungen und Erzählungen Joseph Smiths . . . Vierte deutsche Auflage. Basel, 1924.
iv, 73p. facsims. 18cm.
USIC

6200. Pearl of Great Price. Hawaiian. 1914. Ka Momi Waiwai Nui: He mau mea i wae ie mailoko mai l na Hoekeana a me na Unuhina a Iosepa Kamika, ke Kaula mau, ka mea Ike a Hoano o na La Hope nei. Unuhi ia mai ka olelo Beritania a i ka olelo Hawaii a hoopuka ia e ka Misiona Hawaii a ka Ekalesia o Iesu Kristo o ka Poe Hoano o na La mai Hope nei. [Honolulu, Hawaiian Gazette Co., 1914]
1p.l., 103, 31p. 16½cm.
31p. index.
USIC

6201. Pearl of Great Price. Maori. 1919. Ko te Peara Utu Nui: He mea tongo mai i nga whakakitenga, i nga whakamaoritanga, me nga korerotanga a Hohepa Mete, te Porphiti tuatahi, te matakite, me te kaiwhakakite kie te Hahi o Ihu Karaiti o nga Ra o Muri nei. I wehewehea ki nga upoko me nga Ra o muri nei. I wehewehea ki nga upoko me nga rarangi i te tau 1902, e Hemi E. Taramete. He mea panui na Hemi Nitama Ramapata. Akarana, Nui Tireni, 1919.
iv, 84p. facsims. 19cm.
Sabin 83277
USIC

6202. Pearl of Great Price. Swedish. 1927. Den Kostliga Pärlan. Utvalda stycken ur uppenbarelser, översättningar och berättelser av Joseph Smith. Den förste profeten, siaren och uppenbararen i Jesu Kristi Kyrka av Sista Dagars Heliga. Översättning av J. M. Sjodahl. Salt Lake City, De Associerade Tidningarnas Tryckeri [1927]
84p. facsims. 20cm.
NjP, UPB, USIC

6203. ———. 1930. (same) Stockholm, 1930.
83p. facsims. 17½cm.
USIC

6204. Pearl of Great Price. Welsh. 1852. Y Perl o fawr bris; sef detholiad deiwisol allan o ddadyguddiadau cyfieithadau ac hanesion y diweddar Joseph Smith prif brophwyd, gweledydd, a dadguddiwr i Eglwys Iesu Grist o Saint y Dyddiau Diweddaf. A gyfieithwyd o'r Saesneg gan John Davis. Merthyr-Tydfil: Cyhoeddwyd, argraffwyd, ac ar werth gan John Davis, Heol John, Georgetown, 1852.
vi, 76p. facsim. 17cm.
Sabin 83278
CtY, MH, UPB, USIC

6205. The Pearl of Great Price. [n.p., n.d.]
Broadside. 20½×13cm.
Text within ornamental border.
NjP

6206. Pease, Theodore Calvin. The frontier state: 1818–1948. Springfield, Illinois Centennial Commission, 1917.
7p.l., 475p. front. 24cm. (Centennial history of Illinois. V.2)
Chapter 19. The Mormon War. A well-documented chapter on Mormonism in Nauvoo.
Other editions: Chicago, A. C. McClurg & Co., 1919. CU; (same) 1922. NjP, ULA, USIC
CU

Pebble [*pseud.*] *See Wight, Sarah Estella.*

6207. Peck, Jesse Truesdell. The history of the great republic; considered from a Christian standpoint by Jesse T. Peck, D.D. New York, Broughton and Wyman, 13 Bible house, 1868.
viii, 710p. front. 25½cm.
Mormonism, p. 499–504.
Sabin 59478
DLC, NjPT, ULA, USIC

6208. Peck, John Mason. Forty years of pioneer life. Memoir of John Mason Peck D.D. Edited from his journals and correspondence by Rufus Babcock. Philadelphia, American Baptist Publication Society [1864]
360p. plate, port. 20cm.
Mentions Peck's exposé of Mormonism, 1835, p. 259 and his encounter with Mormons in St. Clair County, Ill., 1840, p. 293.
CU, DLC

6209. ———. A gazetteer of Illinois, in three parts: containing a general view of the State; a general view of each county; and a particular description of each town, settlement, stream, prairie bottom, bluff, — Alphabetically arranged. By J. M. Peck, Author of a Guide for Emigrants, etc. Jacksonville [Ill.] Published by R. Goudy, 1834.
viii, 376p. 15×10cm.
Peck's references to the Mormons occur on p. 53 and 93.
CSmH, ICN, UHi, WHi

6210. ———. (same) Second edition, entirely revised, corrected, and enlarged. Philadelphia, Griff & Elliot, 9 North Fourth Street, 1837.
xi, 328p. 14cm.
Derisive reference to Mormonism, p. 36 and on p. 74, in section on religion, speaks of "a few Mormons, scattered through the state."
CSmH, CtY, CU, DLC, ICJ, MH, MWA, NN, OClWHi, UHi, WHi

6211. ———. Mormonism, one of the delusions of Satan, exposed. By a friend of truth. [Galena? 1835?]
4p. 20cm.
An early exposé of Mormonism, probably written by John M. Peck.
Byrd 242
MoSM

6212. Pederson, Anton, *editor.* ... Salmer med melodier til brug for Jesu Christi kirke ad Sidste dages hellige. [I. hefte] Salt Lake City, A. Pedersen, 1884.
16p. 21½cm.
Mormon hymns in Norwegian.
Title in English: Hymns with music for use in the Church of Jesus Christ of Latter-day Saints.
DLC

6213. Peebles, James Martin. Around the world; or, Travels in Polynesia, China, India, Arabia, Egypt, Syria, and other "Heathen" countries. By J. M. Peebles ... Boston, Colby and Prete, 1875 [c1874]
iv, 414p. 23cm.
Visit to Salt Lake City, 1872; short history of Mormonism and analysis of its doctrines, p. 5–16.
Another edition: 2d ed. Boston; 1876. NjPT, USlC
CU–B

6214. The Peep o' Day; a Salt Lake magazine of science, literature and art. Great Salt Lake City, U.T., Published in the Twentieth Ward, October 20, 1864 — November 25, 1864.
lv. (6 nos. in 96p.) weekly. 30cm.
Caption-title.
Edited by E. L. T. Harrison & E. W. Tullidge.
Though primarily a literary magazine, it appealed to the Mormon people, and had many Mormon articles.
CSmH, CU–B, DLC, MH, UPB, USlC

6215. Peet, Volney S. Bear River Valley, Utah. [Salt Lake City, 1904]
[4]p. 25×15cm.
Signed: V. S. Peet, August 12, 1904.
Claims that in Utah, politics and religion are not mixed. Uses 11th and 12th Articles of faith as proof.
Written by a non-Mormon.
DLC

6216. ———. One thousand dollars reward. [n.p., 1911?]
[1]p. 22cm.
Verification for his £200 reward.
Denies that girls are sent to Utah as white slaves.
USlC

6217. ———. Polygamy from a non-Mormon viewpoint. A lecture delivered in Friendship Liberal League in Philadelphia, Oct. 8th, 1806. [Philadelphia? 1906?]
16p. 18½cm.
MH, MoInRC, NjP, UHi, USlC, UU

6218. ———. (same) [Philadelphia? 1907?]
31p. 15cm.
DLC, UPB

6219. ———. $13,000 reward. Bear River Valley, Utah. How to get there; a review of the Smoot inquiry by V. S. Peet. Salt Lake City, 1905.
32p. 15cm.
Reward offered to demonstrate the question of Mormon domination of politics.
CU–B, MH, NjP, UPB, USlC

6220. ———. (same) 2d edition, enlarged. Salt Lake City, 1905.
39p. 15cm.
Mormon politics.
MH, USlC

6221. ———. £200 reward ... [Liverpool? Millennial Star Office? 1911?]
[2]p. 21cm.
Caption-title.
On verso: Utah and the Mormons.
A handbill.
To disprove the idea that girls are sent to Utah as white slaves.
NjP, UHi, UPB, USlC

6222. ———. (same) [Liverpool? Millennial Star Office? 1911?]
[2]p. 21cm.
Caption-title.
On verso: Utah.
A handbill.
UPB

6223. ———. (same, in German) 4000 mark belohnung! Zurich, G. Meyer [1911?]
[2]p. 22cm.
On verso: Was audere von den Mormonen zu sagen haben ...
USlC

———. Utah and the Mormons. Liverpool [n.d.]
See his £200 reward.

6224. "Peidiwch A'u Gwrando," Abertawy, Cyhoeddwyd ac argraffwyd gan D. Jones. [n.d., ca. 1854]
8p. 17cm.
Missionary tract.
Title in English: Don't go hear them.
UPB

6225. Peirce, E. H., *compiler.* Mormon tabernacle choir; being a collection of newspaper criticisms and cuttings from metropolitan magazines and musical journals, covering six excursions, from the World's fair trip in 1893, to the Seattle exposition in 1909; together with opinions from the professional fraternity . . . and of its capabilities for the futures. Carefully compiled, abbreviated for re-publication, in pamphlet form. . . . Salt Lake City, E. H. Peirce, 1910.
48p. 22cm.
"Compiled, abbreviated . . . and presented to Bishop Charles W. Nibley."
CtY, NjP, UPB, USlC

6226. Pender, Will S. The word "shall." How it defines the Church of Christ distinguishing it from the Utah Church and all other Churches extant. [n.p., n.d.]
32p. 16cm.
RLDS publication.
MoInRC

6227. Pennsylvania. Legislature. Senate. Journal of the Senate of the Commonwealth of Pennsylvania commenced at Harrisburg, on Tuesday, the second day of January, in the year of our Lord one thousand eight hundred and forty-four, and of the Commonwealth the sixty-eighth. Harrisburg, Isaac G. M'Kinley, State Printer, 1844.
1v. (971, 88p.) 24cm.
Includes Sidney Rigdon's memorial for redress against Missouri, asking intervention of the proper authorities of Pennsylvania, p. 208–209. Text of memorial published in *Times and Seasons,* V.5, p. 418–423.
CtY, P

6228. Penrose, Charles William. As to "the truth about Mormonism." [n.p., n.d.]
4p. 22cm.
Answer to an Englishman, supposed to have visited Salt Lake City.
UPB

6229. ———. Blood atonement, as taught by leading elders of the Church of Jesus Christ of Latter-day Saints. An address, delivered in the Twelfth Ward Assembly Hall, Salt Lake City, October 12, 1884, by Elder Charles W. Penrose. Reported by John Irvine. Salt Lake City, Printed at Juvenile Instructor Office, 1884.
54p. 17½cm.
CSmH, CtY, DLC, ICN, MH, MoInRC, NjP, NN, UHi, USl, USlC, UU

6230. ———. (same) Salt Lake City, The Deseret News, 1916.
48p. 19cm.
CSmH, CU–B, ICN, NjP, UHi, UPB

6231. ———. Divine authority. Independence, Mo., Zion's Printing and Publishing Co. [n.d.]
4p. 22cm. (Centennial series. No. 12)
Missionary tract.
Variant printings.
MoInRC, NN

6232. ———. (same) Chicago, Printed for Northern States Missions [n.d.]
4p. 21½cm.
MoInRC

———. (same) *See Widtsoe, John Andreas. Centennial Series.*

6233. ———. Is this plain enough? Some pointed answers to the question on tithing. By President Charles W. Penrose. [n.p., n.d.]
8p. 15½cm.
Variant printings.
NjP, USlC

6234. ———. (same) [Independence, Mo. Press of Zion's Printing and Publishing Co., n.d.]
8p. 16½cm.
NN

6235. ———. Lines to be sung at the funeral of Prest. Brigham Young, Sunday, September 2, 1877. Composed for the occasion by Charles W. Penrose. Music by Prof. George Careless. [Salt Lake City] 1877.
Broadside. 25×11cm.
NjP, USlC

6236. ———. "Mormon" doctrine plain and simple; or, leaves from the tree of life. By Charles W. Penrose. Salt Lake City, Juvenile Instructor Office, 1882.
viii [9]–72p. 19cm.
Advertising matter, p. 70–72.
CSmH, CU–B, ICN, MH, NjP, NN, UHi, ULA, UPB, USlC, UU, WHi, ViU

6237. ———. (same) Salt Lake City, Juvenile Instructor Office, 1888.
viii [9]–69p. 19cm.
IWW, MH, NjP, NjPT, NN, PPL, UHi, ULA, USl, USlC

6238. ———. (same) 2d ed. Salt Lake City, Geo. Q. Cannon and Sons Co., 1897.
viii [9]–87p. 17½cm.
CSmH, ICU, IWW, MH, MoInRC, NjP, OCl, ULA, USlC, WHi

6239. ———. (same) 3d ed. [Independence, Missouri, Press of Zion's Printing and Publishing Company] 1917.
3p.l. [7]–59p. 18cm.
Published by the Missions of the Church of Jesus Christ of Latter-day Saints.
CU–B, ICN, MoInRC, NjP, NN, UPB, USlC, UU

6240. ———. (same) 4th ed. [Independence, Mo., Published by the Missions of the Church of Jesus Christ of Latter-day Saints] 1921.
63p. 18cm.
MoInRC, NjP

6241. ———. (same) 5th ed. [Independence, Mo., Zion's Press and Publishing Co.] 1923.
3p.l. [7]–63p. 18½cm.
USlC

6242. ———. (same) 5th ed. [Salt Lake City?] 1923.
63p. 17cm.
Variant printing.
USlC

6243. ———. (same) 6th ed. Independence, Mo., Zion's Printing and Publishing Company [1928]
3p.l. [7]–63p. 17cm.
Imprint date from cover.
USlC

6244. ———. (same) 6th ed. Independence, Mo., Zion's Printing and Publishing Company. Published by the Missions of the Church of Jesus Christ of Latter-day Saints, 1929.
3p.l. [7]–63p. 17cm.
NN, UPB

6244a. ———. Het "Mormonisme"... [Baarn, Hollandia-Drukkerij, 1908]
52p. 20½cm. (Kerk en secte, Serie II. No. 1)
Title in English: The Mormons.
USlC

6245. ———. The Mountain Meadows massacre. Who were guilty of the crime? The subject fully discussed and important documents introduced in an address delivered in... Salt Lake City, October 26, 1884, by Elder Charles W. Penrose. Reported by John Irvine. Salt Lake City, Printed at Juvenile Instructor Office, 1884.
80p. 18½cm.
Supplement to the lecture on the Mountain Meadows massacre. *See Haslam, James Holt.*
For reply, *see Vindex [pseud.]*
Howes P214
CSmH, CU–B, DLC, MH, MiU, MoInRC, OO, UHi, ULA, USl, USlC, UU

6246. ———. (same) Salt Lake City, Geo. Q. Cannon Co., 1899.
108p. 18cm.
Howes P214
CSmH, MB, MH, NjP, NN, UHi, UU

6247. ———. (same) Salt Lake City, The Deseret News, 1906.
97p. 18cm.
CSmH, IU, UHi, ULA, USl, USlC

6248. ———. Olelo ao "Moramona." Moakada a pohihihi ole. He mau lau mai ke kumulaau mai o ke ola. Honolulu, Hoopukaia e ka Misiona Hawaii, 1923.
2p.l., 5–66p. 17cm.
Title in English: Mormon doctrine clearly stated...
UPB

6249. ———. Priesthood and presidency. Claims of the "Reorganized" Church examined and compared with reason and revelation. By C. W. P. Independence, Mo., Press of Zion's Printing and Publishing Co. [ca. 1900]
15p. 19cm.
NjP, USlC

6250. ———. (same) [Independence, Mo., Press of Zion's Printing and Publishing Co., n.d.]
16p. 18½cm.
MoInRC, NN

6251. ———. (same) Salt Lake City, G. Q. Cannon and Sons Co., 1898.
36p. 19cm.
CSmH, ICN, MH, MoInRC, NjP, NN, UHi, ULA, USl, USlC

6252. ———. (same) Liverpool, Millennial Star Office, 1909.
29p. 18cm.
MH, MoInRC, USlC

6253. ———. (same) Independence, Mo., Zion's Printing and Publishing Co. [1912?]
29p. 17½cm.
CSmH, CU–B, MoInRC, UHi, USlC

6254. ———. Rays of living light. No. 1–12. [Chicago, 1898?]
12 nos. 22½cm.
Each number separately paged.
A series of missionary tracts.
Published in various editions, separately or as a group.
Printed in Chicago for different missions as follows: Central States 100,000; Northern States, 125,000; Colorado States, 50,000; Western States, 50,000; Northwestern States, 25,000; Church Information Bureau, 25,000.
Contents: 1. Faith and works. 2. Faith. 3. Repentance and baptism. 4. The gift of the Holy Ghost. 5. Divine authority. 6. Apostasy. 7. Restoration. 8. The Book of Mormon. 9. Latter-day revelation. 10. Salvation for the dead. 11. Baptism for the dead. 12. Fruits of Mormonism.
CSmH, MH, NjP, OO, ULA, UPB, WHi

6255. ———. (same) [Liverpool? 1898]
12 nos. 18cm.
CU–B

PENROSE, C. W.

6256. ———. (same) [Independence, Mo.] Zion's Printing and Publishing Co. [n.d.]
12 nos. 18cm.
UPB

6257. ———. (same, under title) Rays of living light on the one way of salvation. [Independence, Mo., Press of Zion's Printing and Publishing Co., n.d.]
1p.l., 49p. 17½cm.
CU-B, MoInRC, UPB

6258. ———. (same, under title) Rays of living light from the doctrines of Christ. By Charles W. Penrose. Liverpool, Printed and Published at the Millennial Star Office [190–]
48p. 21½cm.
USlC

6259. ———. (same) Salt Lake City, The Deseret News, 1904.
85p. 16cm.
MiU, MoInRC, UHi, USlC

6260. ———. (same) Salt Lake City, Published by Bureau of Information, 1914.
49p. 18cm.
OClWHi, PPPrHi, UPB

6261. ———. (same) [Independence, Mo., Published by the Missions of the Church of Jesus Christ of Latter-day Saints, 1927.
89p. 18cm.
CU-B

6262. ———. (same) [Independence, Mo., Zion's Printing and Publishing Company. Published by the Missions of the Church of Jesus Christ of Latter-day Saints in the United States, 193–]
89 [2]p. 17cm.
CU-B, IWW, MoInRC, NN, UHi, UPB, USlC

6263. ———. (same, in Danish) Straaler af levende lys, Fra Kristi Laerdomme, Af Charles W. Penrose. [Kjobenhavn, Udgivet og forlagt af Andrew Jenson, 1909–1910]
12 pamphlets (4p. each) 22½cm.
UHi, USlC

6264. ———. (same, in Dutch) Stralen van Levend Licht door Charles W. Penrose. Uit het Engelsch door Paul Roelofs. [Rotterdam, Uitgave van Jacob H. Trayner and Alex. Nibley, 1906?]
12 nos. 20½cm.
USlC

6265. ———. (same) Rotterdam, Uitgave van B. G. Thatcher [1910?]
12 nos. 20½cm.
USlC

6266. ———. (same, in French) Rayons de lumière vivifiante. Rotterdam, Publié par Jacob H. Trayner [1906?]
12 nos. 22cm.
USlC

6267. ———. (same) Genève, Publié par la "Mission Francaise." [n.d.]
12 nos. 23cm.
USlC

6268. ———. (same) Liege, Publié par Ernest C. Rossiter [n.d.]
12 nos. 21½cm.
USlC

6269. ———. (same, in German) Strahlen des lebendigen Lichtes ber Lehre Christi. Zurich, Switzerland, A. Tschopp [n.d.]
12 nos. 21cm.
USlC

6270. ———. (same) Zurich, Schweiz, Thomas E. McKay, 1909.
12 nos. 47p. 18cm.
USlC

6271. ———. (same, in Finnish) Elävän valon säteitä. Helsinki, Myohempien Aikojen Phyhien Jeesuksen Kristuksen Kirko [n.d.]
48p. 23cm.
Also published as separate pamphlets.
USlC

6272. ———. (same, in Greek) Aktines Zontos Fotos . . . [Athanai, 1903]
12 nos. 24cm.
USlC #1–3

6273. ———. (same, under title) Aktines Zōntos Thōtos ek tōn Dedaska lion. Tou i Xristoi ūpo Charles W. Penrose Metaphrasis ek tou agglikou. En Athenais, Ek Tou Typographeiou paraskeya Leone, 1912.
72p. 20cm.
UU

6274. ———. (same, in Hungarian) Az élö világosság sugarai. [Budapest, Brozsa Otto, 1928?]
12 nos. 22cm.
USlC

6275. ———. (same, in Swedish) Strålar af lefvande ljus från Kristi Lärdomar. Af Charles W. Penrose. [Stockholm, Förlagd af P. Matson, 1906]
12 nos. 21cm.
Bound with cover-title.
UPB, USlC

6276. ———. (same) Tredje Svenska upplagan. [Stockholm, I. P. Thunnell, 1922]
72p. 18½cm.
USlC

6277. ———. (same) Fjärde Svenska upplagan. [Stockholm, Förlagd av John H. Anderson, 1926?]
72p. 18cm.
Cover-title.
CSmH

6278. ———. (same) Femte svenska upplagan. Stockholm, Utgiven och förlagd av Gideon N. Hulterström, 1930.
72p. 18½cm.
USlC

6279. ———. Reply to the Mormon situation. [n.p., n.d.]
5 numb. l. 20cm.
Text on one side only.
USlC, UU

6280. ———. Salvation for the living and the dead. Liberality of the "Mormon" faith. A discourse by Charles W. Penrose. Delivered in the tabernacle in Salt Lake City, Sunday afternoon, August 19, 1900. Reported by Arthur Winter. [Salt Lake City] 1900.
15p. 21½cm.
NjP, UHi, USlC

6281. ———. De sidste-Dages helliges tro. En Tale Aeldste Charles W. Penrose, holdt i Tabernaklet. Salt Lake City, Utah, Søndag den 15de Maj 1892. Kjobenhavn, Udgivet og Forlagt Af Edward H. Anderson . . . 1892.
16p. 21cm.
Title in English: The beliefs of the Latter-day Saints.
USlC

6282. ———. A spirited controversy. [Liverpool? Millennial Star Office? 1911]
51p. 21cm.
A controversy between Penrose and Rev. Daniel H. C. Bartlett, first published in the *Millennial Star*.
Caption-title.
UHi, USlC

6283. ———. Utah and statehood; objections considered; simple facts plainly told, with a brief synopsis of the State Constitution. By a resident of Utah. New York, Printed for the Author by Hart & Von Arx, 1888.
11p. 23cm.
Cover-title.
DLC, MB, MiU, NN, OCl, UHi, USlC, UU

6284. ———. What the "Mormons" believe . . . [n.p., n.d.]
[16]l. 35½cm.
USlC

6285. ———. What the "Mormons" believe. Epitome of the doctrines of the Church of Jesus Christ of Latter-day Saints. [Independence, Mo.? Published by the Missions of the Church of Jesus Christ of Latter-day Saints, n.d.]
8p. 16½cm.
Variant editions.
NN, USlC

6286. ———. (same) [Independence, Mo., Published by the Missions of the Church of Jesus Christ of Latter-day Saints, n.d.]
15 [1]p. 15cm.
UPB

6287. ———. (same) Chicago, Northern States Mission [n.d.]
16p. 14cm.
Caption-title.
WHi

6288. ———. (same) Salt Lake City, Bureau of Information [n.d.]
15p. 17cm.
UPB

6289. ———. (same) [Salt Lake City, Deseret News Press, n.d.]
16p. 16½cm.
CU-B, UPB

6290. ———. (same) [Kansas City, Mo., Central States Mission, n.d.]
16p. 14cm.
USlC

6291. ———. (same) [Chicago, Ill., Northern States Mission, 19 - -]
16p. 13½cm.
USlC

6292. ———. (same) Chattanooga, Tenn., Southern States Mission [ca. 1905]
16p. 14cm.
USlC

6293. ———. (same) Liverpool, Printed and Published at Millennial Star Office [1909]
44p. 18cm.
Portrait on the title page.
CSmH, MH

6293a. ———. (same) [Liverpool, Printed and Published at the Millennial Star Office, 1909?]
27p. 18½cm.
In printed paper wrapper.
USlC

6294. ———. (same) [n.p., n.d.]
27p. 18cm.
UHi

6295. ———. (same) [Salt Lake City, Bureau of Information, ca. 1910]
16p. 14cm.
USIC

6296. ———. (same) Salt Lake City, Bureau of Information [ca. 1920]
[15] 1p. 18½cm.
USIC

———. What Mormons believe . . . *See also Morton, William Albert. Salt Lake City through a camera . . .*

6297. ———. Why I am a "Mormon." [Independence, Mo., Press of Zion's printing and publishing Co. Pub. by the Missions of the Church of Jesus Christ of Latter-day Saints, n.d.]
13 [1]p. 18cm.–19cm.
Variant editions.
NN, UPB, USI, USIC

6298. ———. (same) [Salt Lake City, Deseret News Press, n.d.]
16p. 18cm.
CU–B, UPB

6299. ———. (same, in Swedish) Hvar for jag ar en "Mormon." [Salt Lake City, Korrespondenten, 1893]
32p. 14cm.
UPB

6300. The People's Organ. Devoted to the imvestigation [sic] of various doctrines and beliefs; religious, moral, social, and political. Pittsburgh, June 15, 1844–
v. 40cm.
The stated object is to admit all communication upon all subjects. However, it is mostly devoted to Mormonism.
Printed by A. J. Foster.
UPB June 15, 29; July 14 (#1–3)

6301. People's Party, Utah. Declaration of principles. The following declaration of principles was adopted at a Territorial Convention of the People's Porty [sic] October 13, 1882. [Salt Lake City, 1882]
3p. 21cm.
CU–B, USIC

6302. ———. Declaration of principles of The People's Party of Salt Lake City, Utah. Adopted in Municipal Convention September 18th, 1889. [Salt Lake City] The Deseret News Co., Printers [1889]
8p. 15½cm.
Cover-title.
Bound in a tan printed wrapper.
CtY, NjP, UPB, USIC

6303. ———. Delegate election. General instructions. Salt Lake City, 1890.
Broadside. 28×15cm.
General instructions for voting after Edmunds-Tucker Act.
USIC

6304. ———. (same) Salt Lake City, 1890.
3p. 23½cm.
Dated: October 13, 1890.
UPB

6305. ———. General ticket. Utah Territory. [Great Salt Lake City, 185–]
Broadside. 13×8cm.
UPB, USIC

6306. ———. Human rights . . . [Salt Lake City, n.d.]
6p. 21cm. (People's Campaign Circular. No. 1)
CU–B, USIC

6307. ———. Instructions to challengers, checkers and judges of elections. [Salt Lake City, ca. 1888]
[2]p. 21cm.
Challenging after the Edmunds-Tucker Act.
USIC

6308. ———. Platform of the People's Party. [Salt Lake City, 1890]
4p. 23½cm.
CU–B, USIC

6308a. ———. Reasons why you should not vote the "Liberal" ticket. To the respectable resident "Liberals" of Salt Lake City. [Salt Lake City, n.d.]
[4]p. 20½cm. (People's Campaign Circular)
CU–B, USIC

6309. ———. **Territorial Central Committee.** Address and instructions of the Territorial Central Committee. Salt Lake City, 1887.
13p. 16cm.
UPB, USIC

6310. The Peril of Mormonism. New York, The Interdenominational Council of Women for Christian and Patriotic Service, [n.d.]
[8]p. 18cm.
Articles and poetry against Mormonism.
USIC

6311. Perkins, Jacob Randolph. Trails, rails and war; the life of General G. M. Dodge, by J. R. Perkins . . . Indianapolis, The Bobbs-Merrill Company [c1929]
xixp., [1]l., 371p. plates, ports., facsims. 23cm.
References to the Mormons, p. 27, 35–36, 215–216, 228–230, 239.
DLC

6312. Perkins, James Handasyd. Annals of the West: embracing a concise account of principal events which have occurred in the Western States and Territories, from the discovery of the Mississippi Valley to the year eighteen hundred and forty five. Comp. from the most authentic sources. By James H. Perkins. Cincinnati, J. R. Albach, 1846.
xx, 591 [1]p. maps. 24cm.
Includes a history of Mormonism and Mormons in Illinois to 1844.
Reprinted in many editions.
Howes P231, Sabin 60954
CU–B, DLC, MB, NiC, NN, OCl, OO, RWoU, UHi, ULA

6313. Perkins, Nathan E. Events and travels of Nathan E. Perkins. From 1824–1887. Camden, Published by N. E. Perkins, 1887.
xix [17]–490p. 20cm.
1872 trip through Utah. Brief stop in Salt Lake City; dinner with Brigham Young.
USlC

Perpetual Emigrating Fund. *See The Church of Jesus Christ of Latter-day Saints. Perpetual Emigrating Fund Company.*

6314. Perrin, J. Nick. Perrin's history of Illinois. [Springfield, Ill., Printed by Illinois State Register, c1906]
2p.l., 6–231p. maps. 20½cm.
Brief history of the Mormon War, p. 175–176.
NjP, UPB, USlC

6315. Perry, C. A., & Co., *defendants.* Papers in case of C. A. Perry & Co., pending in the Treasury Department. [Washington] H. Polkinhorn & Co., Printers [1870?]
90p. 23cm.
Cover-title.
Claim of C. A. Perry & Co., for losses incurred by impressment of property under orders of Gen. Albert Sidney Johnston, commanding the Army of Utah in 1857.
DLC

6316. Perry, J. F., *compiler.* Cache County the Eden of Utah . . . Comp. by J. F. Perry. Logan, Utah, Logan Republican [1916?]
[58]p. illus. 29½cm.
Cover-title.
Settlement of Cache County and the history of Brigham Young College.
ULA, UU

6317. Perry, Rolland. Living monuments. Sea Gull Monument. Brooklyn, New York, Church of Jesus Christ of Latter-day Saints, [n.d.]
[8]p. 18cm.
A short introduction to Mormonism; a missionary tract.
CU, USlC

Persecution in Salt Lake . . . *See Attwood, R. H. . . .*

6318. Peters, George Henry. Impressions of a journey round the world including India, Burmah and Japan. London, Waterlow and Sons Limited, Printers, London Wall, 1897.
x, 373p. 23cm.
Salt Lake City and the Mormons, p. 310–317.
UHi

6319. Petersen, Joseph Lind. Vejleder for aeldsterne i den Danske Mission. Udgivet og forlagt af Joseph L. Petersen. København, Trykt i "Aka," Kapelvej, 1927.
22 [2]p. 16cm.
Title in English: A guide for the Elders in the Danish mission.
USlC

6320. Petersen, R. J. Hvad er sandhed? Kom frem med eders sag, siger herren, og fremfor eders staerke beviser, siger Jacobs Gud (Es. 41.21). Eller: en brevvexling mellem Hr. Pastor C. A. Biltzing i agri og forhenvaerende Kjobmand, R. J. Petersen i Femmoller. Kobenhavn, 1874.
16p.
Title in English: What is the truth.
Schmidt.

6321. Peterson, Andreas. Huru Kristi blod renar . . . [Stockholm, Smedbergs Boktryckeri, 1911]
4p. 23cm.
Caption-title.
Missionary tract.
Title in English: How the blood of Christ cleanses.
USlC

6322. ———. Vittnesbörd af framstående män om "Mormonerna". Hvad de Säga om polygami och Andra viktiga frågor samt en petition till sveriges konung. Stockholm, Samlade och utgifna af Andreas Peterson . . . Tryckt hos Smedbergs tr., 1911.
24p. 18cm.
Cover-title.
Title in English: What others say about Mormonism.
UPB, USlC

6323. Peterson, Ephraim. An ideal city for an ideal people, by E. Peterson. How to build an ideal city for an ideal people, where the principles of Christianity, including economic equality, domestic virtue, and temperance in all things can become practical. Independence, Mo., 1905.
2p.l. [3]–134p., [1]l. port. 19½cm.
City to be built on Joseph Smith's model as inspired by Book of Enoch. The Chapter, "Mormonism dissected," used to prove Joseph Smith a true prophet.
DLC, ICJ MoInRC, NN

6324. ———. Official plans and purposes of the United Order of Equality. A fraternal beneficial order incorporated July, 1909. Constitution and By-laws. Its colony proposition. Independence, Mo., 1910.
48p. 16cm.
United Order of Equality is a semi-official RLDS group.
MoInRC

6325. ———. Redemption, by E. Peterson. Independence, Mo., The author [1909]
3p.l. [7]–140p. 18½cm.
Cover-title.
DLC, MoInRC, NN, USlC

6326. ———. The two systems or scientific economics. The one producing an irrepressible conflict; the other universal peace and happiness. Based on the natural laws of cause and effect. Independence, Mo., 1912.
48p. 18cm.
United Order of Equality.
MoInRC

6327. Peterson, J. W. Are you interested? An article setting forth in plain facts and direct terms the history and defense of a misrepresented people. [n.p., n.d.]
15p. 19cm.
RLDS apologetics.
MoInRC

6328. ———. Broken Baptist succession. [Lamoni, Ia., Herald Publishing House, n.d.]
35p. 18cm.
The error of the Baptists and the truthfulness of the Restoration.
MoInRC

6329. ———. Joseph Smith defended, and his divine vision vindicated; an answer to the attacks of his enemies, religious and political. Lamoni, Ia., Herald Publishing House [191–]
225p. 1 port. 16cm.
MoInRC, MoK, MWA, NjP, UHi, USlC, WHi

6330. ———. Reasons why; shall we hear them? Independence, Mo., Ensign Publishing House, 1905.
14p. 16cm. (The Gospel Banner. V.13, No.2)
MoInRC

6331. ———. Reasons why; shall we hear them? Rev. ed. Independence, Mo., Ensign Publishing House [n.d.]
30p. 16cm.
MoInRC

6332. ———. Salvation by faith. Independence, Mo., Ensign Publishing House [n.d.]
16p. 16cm.
RLDS doctrine of faith.
MoInRC

6333. ———. Who was Joseph Smith? Was he a false prophet? Independence, Mo., Ensign Publishing House, 1897.
39p. 22cm.
RLDS apologetics.
MoInRC

6334. ———. (same) Independence, Mo., Ensign Publishing House [191–]
36p. 18cm.
IWW, MoInRC, UU

6335. ———. Why not a first presidency; a reply to the critics of the church organization and of the Book of Doctrine and Covenants. Independence, Mo., Herald Publishing House [n.d.]
36p. 20cm.
RLDS tract on church government.
MoInRC

6336. Peterson, L. The Choice seer and false prophets. Independence, Mo., 1887.
12p. 20cm.
RLDS apologetic work.
MoInRC

6337. ———. Mormonism unveiled. Independence, Mo., 1891.
5p. 21cm.
The need for "one mighty and strong" to reunite the church.
USlC

6337a. Peterson, Lars. The mystery of God. The hired laborers mission in the eleventh hour. The gospel which was preached by Enoch, Noah, and Jesus Christ the Son of God. All are now invited for to save themselves from this untoward Generation. Independence, Mo., 1878.
30p. 20½cm.
Cover-title.
Title within ornamental border.
Authorship from note to Joseph F. Smith included in pamphlet.
Signed: "The Mission of Baurak Ale."
USlC

6337b. ———. The voice at midnight. Independence, Mo., 1884.
[4]p. 20½cm.
Dated December 25, 1884 and signed by Lars Peterson and James Brighouse.
USlC

6337c. Peterson, Ole Bertrand. E parau tuatapapa utuafare. Faauhia e O. B. Peterson. Papeete, Tahiti, Ekalesia a Iesu Mesia i te Feia Mo'a i te Mau Mahana Hopea Nei, 1922.
[10]p. 22cm.
Title in English: A talk on genealogy.
USlC

Petit, Veronique. *See Mathews, Amelie Veronique (Petit) Child.*

6338. Petrelli, Carl Magnus Joakim. Josef Smith och Mormonismen. Öfversigt af C. M. J. Petrelli. Linköping, C. F. Ridderstad, 1858.
98p. 19cm.
Title in English: Joseph Smith and Mormonism.
DLC, NN

6339. Pettit, Edwin. Biography of Edwin Pettit, 1834–1912. Salt Lake City, Arrow Press [1912]
22p. port. 20cm.
Pioneer of 1847; California settler of 1851.
CSmH, USlC

6340. Petty, Charles B. The Albert Petty family; a genealogical and historical story of a sturdy pioneer family of the west. Salt Lake City, Deseret News Press [n.d.]
vi [2] 322p. plates, photos. 27½cm.
Albert Petty's conversion to Mormonism; trek westward; life in Utah; descendants.
UPB

6341. ———. A diagram of the church established by Jesus Christ . . . [London? British Mission Office 192–]
[2]p. 22cm.
UHi, UPB, USlC

6342. ———. Map of primitive church as established by Christ. [Liverpool? Millennial Star Office? 1908?]
2p. chart. 21cm.
Caption-title.
UHi

6343. Pfeiffer, Emily. Flying leaves from East and West by Emily Pfeiffer. London, Field and Tuer, the Leadenhall Press, E. C. Simpkin, Marshall and Co.; Hamilton Adams & Co., New York, Scribner and Welford, 1885.
2p.l., 302 p. 20cm.
Trip through Salt Lake City; description of the Mormons.
Another edition: 2d ed. USlC
CU-B, NjP, UHi, USlC

6343a. Pfeiffer, Ida. A lady's second journey round the world: from London to the Cape of Good Hope, Borneo, Java, Sumatra, Celebes, Ceram, the Moluccas, etc. California, Panama, Peru, Ecuador, and the United States . . . London: Longman, Brown, Green, and Longmans, 1885.
2v. 20½cm.
Her travels through a Strangite village, V.2, p. 324–326.
UPB

6344. Phelps, William Wines. Deseret almanac for the year of our Lord 1851, The third after leap year, and after the 6th of April the 22nd year of the Church of Jesus Christ of Latter Day Saints; and the first of the last half century of this dispensation. Compiled by W. W. Phelps. G.S.L. City, Deseret, Printed by W. Richards, 1851.
16p. port. 10×15cm.
"No. 1"
Includes a chronology of events in Church history.
USlC

6345. ———. Deseret almanac for the year of our Lord 1852: Being leap year, and after the 6th of April, the 23rd year of the Church of Jesus Christ of Latter Day Saints; and the 2nd of the last half century . . . of this dispensation. By W. W. Phelps, K.J. G.S.L. City, U.T., W. Richards, Printer, 1852.
48p. 19½cm.
"No. 2"
Includes poetry by the author, list of territorial and county officials, ordinance incorporating the University of the State of Deseret, church officers, sketch of the Melchisedek Priesthood, remarks of Elder Phelps in September Conference, 1851, on tithing. The miscellaneous events in the almanac are also L.D.S. oriented.
CtY, ULA, UPB, USlC

6346. ———. Deseret almanac for the year of our Lord 1853. Being the first after leap year, and after the sixth of April the twenty-fourth year of the Church of Jesus Christ of Latter Day Saints; and the third of the last half century of this dispensation. By W. W. Phelps. Great S.L. City, U.T., W. Richards [1852?]
32p. 19½cm.
"No. 3"
Includes poem "Mormonism is truth"; territorial information; Nauvoo Legion.
USlC

6347. ———. Deseret Almanac for the year of our Lord 1854. Being the second after leap year, and after the sixth of April, the twenty-fifth year of the Church of Jesus Christ of Latter Day Saints. And the third of the last half century of this dispensation. By W. W. Phelps . . . G.S.L. City, U.T., W. Richards, [1853]
32p. 18½cm.
"No. 4"
Poetry, Mormon miscellany, discourse on Spirits, church and state officials, etc.
CtY, UPB, USlC

6348. ———. Deseret Almanac for the year 1855; Being the third after leap year, and after the sixth of April, the twenty fifth year of the Church of Jesus Christ of Latter Day Saints: And the fifth of the last half century of this dispensation . . . By W. W. Phelps . . . Great Salt Lake City, Arieh C. Brower, Printer, 1855.

32p. 18cm.
Includes poems by W. W. Phelps, a copy of the Deseret alphabet and miscellaneous territorial information.
Almanacs between 1856–1859 have no Mormon material.
USlC

6349. ———. Almanac for the year 1860. Being leap year, and after the 6th of April, the thirty-first year of the Church of Jesus Christ of Latter Day Saints. By W. W. Phelps. Great Salt Lake City, Printed by J. McKnight, 1860.
32p. 12½cm.
Brief text with poetry and short informational paragraphs.
CtY, USlC

6350. ———. Almanac for the year 1861. Being the thirty second year of the Church of Jesus Christ of Latter-day Saints (From April 6, 1830) by W. W. Phelps. Great Salt Lake City, Utah, at 'Deseret News' Office, 1861.
32p. 13cm.
Includes "a revelation and prophecy by the Prophet, Seer, and Revelator, Joseph Smith, given December 25th, 1832 (Civil War prophecy) etc."
CtY, USlC

6351. ———. Almanac for the year 1862. Being the thirty third year of the Church of Jesus Christ of Latter-day Saints (From April 6, 1830) By W. W. Phelps. Great Salt Lake City, Printed at 'Deseret News' Office, 1861.
32p. 13cm.
Civil war prophecy repeated. Two brief articles entitled "mark this" and "(Extract from a Revelation given in December, 1832) to the children of Zion." One poem by the author.
CtY

6352. ———. Almanac for the year 1863. Being the thirty fourth year of the Church of Jesus Christ of Latter-day Saints. (From April 6, 1830) . . . By W. W. Phelps. Great Salt Lake City, Printed at 'Deseret News' Office, 1862.
32p. 13cm.
Joseph Smith's last dream, p. 27. A revelation to Joseph Smith, Jun., given, June, 1830, p. 29.
CtY, USlC

6353. ———. Almanac for the year 1864. Being the thirty fifth year of the Church of Jesus Christ of Latter-day Saints. (From April 6, 1830) By W. W. Phelps. Great Salt Lake City, Printed at 'Deseret News' Office, 1864.
32p. 13cm.
Article on Joseph Smith in Missouri, entitled "Twenty years ago." Also Civil War prophecy repeated. Several poems by W. W. Phelps.
CtY, NjP, UHi

6353a. ———. A song of Zion. By W. W. Phelps. [Nauvoo, 1844]
Broadside. 13×7cm.
USlC

6354. ———. A voice from the prophet. "Come to Me." By W. W. Phelps, Esq. [Nauvoo? 1844?]
Broadside. 13×6cm.
A poem to the tune of "Indian Hunter" on the Prophet Joseph Smith.
USlC

6355. Philadelphia. Citizens. Meeting for the relief of the Mormons. Organized on motion of the Hon. Judge Kane. [Philadelphia, 1846?]
Broadside. 25×18cm.
Signed: Thomas S. Cavender, Secretary.
CtY copy postmarked Philadelphia, December 4.
CtY, NN

Philips, John F. *See U.S. Circuit Court.*

6356. Phillips, Arthur Bernicie. The Book of Mormon verified; established by forty eminent archeologists and authors, by Elder A. B. Phillips. Lamoni, Ia., Herald Publishing House, 1908.
44p. 18½cm. (No. 231)
Cover-title.
CU–B, IWW, PHi, UHi

6357. ———. (same) Lamoni, Ia., Herald Publishing House, 1912.
44p. 18cm. (No. 231)
CU–B, MoInRC, NjP

6358. ———. De Heiligen der Laatste Dagen en wat zij geloven door A. B. Phillips . . . Rotterdam, Uitgegeven door de Gereorganiseerde Kerk van Jezus Christus van de Heiligen der Laatste Dagen, Holland [n.d.]
32p. ports. 19cm.
Title in English: The Latter Day Saints and what they believe.
UPB

6359. ———. Helps to Bible study . . . 240 illustrations . . . Compiled . . . by Arthur B. Phillips, Richard S. Salyards, John W. Peterson, and Hyrum O. Smith. Independence, Mo., Herald Publishing House, 1924.
2p.l. [7]–701 [8]p. illus., maps. 22½cm.
Bibliography, p. 575–577.
Includes material on the Inspired Version of the Bible revised by Joseph Smith.
DLC, NjP, UHi

6360. ———. The Inspired Version compared with other Bible versions, edited and arranged by A. B. Phillips. Independence, Mo., Herald Publishing House [n.d.]
64p. 23cm.
MoInRC, NjP, USlC

6361. ———. The Latter Day Saints and what they believe. By A. B. Phillips. Independence, Mo., Herald Publishing House [n.d.]
31p. 19cm. (The Angel Message Series. No. 9)
MoInRC, NcD, UHi, ULA, USlC

6362. ———. The Old Jerusalem Gospel restored. Lamoni, Ia., Reorganized Church of Jesus Christ of Latter Day Saints [n.d.]
12p. 20cm.
MoInRC

6363. ———. (same) Lamoni, Ia., Reorganized Church of Jesus Christ of Latter Day Saints [n.d.]
12p. 20p. (No. 1216)
Variant printing.
MoInRC

6364. ———. (same) Lamoni, Ia., Reorganized Church of Jesus Christ of Latter Day Saints, 1909.
12p. 19cm. (No. 35)
MoInRC, NjP

6365. ———. A remarkable church with an unusual message. Independence, Mo., Herald Publishing House [n.d.]
32p. 20cm.
MoInRC, NjP

6366. ———. The restoration movement and The Latter Day Saints; a book of ideals, pioneers, and martyrs. By Arthur B. Phillips. Independence, Mo., The Herald Publishing House, 1928.
335p. 20½cm.
CSmH, MoInRC, NjP, USlC

6367. ———. (same) Revised ed. Independence, Mo., Published by The Herald Publishing House, 1929.
2p.l. [5]–342p. 20½cm.
CU–B, MoInRC, NjP

6367a. ———. Study helps for sermon preparation and class work; man and his relationship to God, to the church, and to his fellow man. Independence, Missouri, Reorganized Church of Jesus Christ of Latter Day Saints, [n.d.]
62p. 20cm.
MoInRC

6367b. ———. (same) Independence, Missouri, The Herald Publishing House, [n.d.]
64p. 19cm.
USlC

6368. ———. Why we believe in a restored Gospel. [n.p., n.d.]
13p. 19cm.
RLDS mission tract.
MoInRC

Phillips, George Spencer. *See Jones, John Wesley.*

6369. Phillips, George Whitefield. The Mormon menace. A discourse before the New West Education Commission on its fifth anniversary at Chicago, November 15, 1885. By George Whitefield Phillips, Pastor of Plymouth Church. Worcester, Mass., 1885.
16p. 22½cm.
CSmH, CtY, CU–B, DLC, ICHi, ICN, MH, MoInRC, NjP, NN, UPB, UHi, ULA, USlC, WHi,

6370. Phillips, Morris. Abroad and at home: practical hints for tourists. New York, Brentanos [c1891]
3p.l. [1] 6–251p. 4 plates, 1 port. 19cm.
"Salt Lake City," p. 239–242. A short sketch of the author's impressions of Mormons, a meeting which he attended, and Salt Lake attractions.
Another edition: 1892 DLC
CSmH, NN, OU, PPD

6371. Phillips, Philip. Song pilgrimage around the world. Illustrated by pen and pencil, including experiences, sights, anecdotes, incidents, impressions of men and things, throughout twenty different countries, with an introduction by Rev. J. H. Vincent. Edited by Alfred H. Miles. New York, Phillips & Hunt, c1882.
xii [13]–216p. illus., port., map. 28½cm.
Stopped over in Salt Lake City in order to preach to the Mormon people.
UPB

6372. Philp, Robert Kemp. The Denominational reason why, giving the origin, history, and tenets of the Christian sects, with the reasons assigned by themselves, for their specialties of faith and forms of worship. The twelfth thousand, revised and enlarged. London, Houlston and Sons, 1890.
viii, 376p. 19cm.
"What are the leading tenets of the Mormons . . ." p. 350–352.
Another edition: 1900. First published in 1860. DLC
UPB

6373. Pichot, Amédée. Les mormons, par m. Amédée Pichot. Paris, L. Hachette et c[ie], 1854.
2p.l., iii, 292p. 18cm. (Half-title: Bibliothèque des chemins de fer. 2 ser.: Histoire et voyages)
Sabin 62612
Title in English: The Mormons.
CSmH, CtY, DLC, ICN, NN, UHi, ULA, USl, USlC, WHi

6374. Pickard, Samuel. Autobiography of a pioneer: or, The nativity, experience, travels and ministerial labors of Rev. Samuel Pickard, the "converted Quaker," containing stirring incidents and practical thoughts; with sermons by the author, and some account of the labors of Elder Jacob Knapp . . . Edited by O. T. Conger . . . Chicago, Church & Goodman, 1866.
xii [13]–403p. illus., plates. 19cm.
Pickard taught school among the Mormons at Charleston, near Nauvoo, and gives an extended account of them.
Sabin 62615
CtY, DLC, ICU, IHi, MiU, PCC, UHi, USlC

6375. Pickering, Frank J., *compiler.* Peteetneet sketches; special souvenir edition in honor of Payson's sixtieth birthday, October 20, 1910. Payson, Utah, The author, 1910.
26p. illus., ports. 25×16cm.
History of Payson and sketches of business firms.
UU

6376. Pickett, Charles Edward. Oration delivered in the Congregational Church, Sacramento, California, July 4, 1857. San Francisco, Whitton, Towne & Co's Excelsior Steam Presses, 1857.
32p. 22cm.
Mormonism is basically conservative; if a problem, let it die out.
UPB

6376a. Pickett, Oliver. Mormon service. [n.p.] 1902.
Broadside. 16×21cm.
Dated: Oct. 19, 1902.
Announcing a service in Hart's Hall. The elders conducting are Oliver Pickett and S. S. Hiatt.
USlC

6377. Picturesque Cardston and environments. A Story of colonization and progress in Southern Alberta, Cardston, N. W. Macleod, 1900.
159p. 22½cm.
Much on the Mormons, their settlement of Cardston and their place in the community.
UPB

6378. Pidgin, Charles Felton. The house of shame; a novel . . . by Charles Felton Pidgin . . . New York, The Cosmopolitan Press, 1912.
6p.l., 11–244p. 19cm.
Fiction concerning Mormonism.
DLC, NN, USlC

6379. Pieper, Frederick. Réponse des Saints des Derniers Jours aux Attaques, Calomnies et Défis contenus dans une brochure. Publiée par le pasteur Baptiste aimè cadot contre les Mormons . . . Par Frederick Pieper . . . Liége, Imp. Math, Thône, 1896.
30p. 21cm.
Title in English: Answer of the Mormons to the attacks . . . of a pamphlet.
USlC

6380. Pierce, Ray Vaughn. The people's common sense medical adviser, in plain English; or Medicine simplified by R. V. Pierce. 78th ed. Buffalo, New York, Worlds Dispensary Printing Office and Bindery, 1875.
viii, 9–885p. 20½cm.
Includes the Mormon Church and its practice of polygamy. A Mormon can have not less than 3 wives but as many more as he can support.
Published in many editions.
ULA, UPB, USlC

6381. Piercy, Frederick. Route from Liverpool to Great Salt Lake Valley illustrated with steel engravings and wood cuts from sketches made by Frederick Piercy, including views of Nauvoo and the ruins of the Temple, with a historical account of the city; views of Carthage Jail; and portraits and memoirs of Joseph and Hyrum Smith; their mother, Lucy Smith; Joseph and David Smith, sons of the Prophet Joseph; President Brigham Young; Heber C. Kimball; Willard Richards; Jedediah M. Grant; John Taylor; the late Chief Patriarch, Father John Smith; and the present Chief Patriarch, John Smith, son of Hyrum. Together with a geographical and historical description of Utah, and a map of the overland routes to that Territory, from the Missouri River. Also, an authentic history of the Latter-day Saints' emigration from Europe from the commencement up to the close of 1855, with statistics. Edited by James Linforth. Liverpool: Published by Franklin D. Richards, 36, Islington. London: Latter-day Saints' Book Depot, 35, Jewin Street, City. MDCCCLV. [1855]
viii, 120p. illus., plates, ports., fold. map. 32cm.
Howes L359, Sabin 41325, W-C 259
Folded map varies. In some copies Utah is printed in color.
Also published in parts, bound in printed green wrappers. UPB
CSmH, CtY, CU-B, DLC, ICHi, ICN, MH, NjP, NN, UHi, ULA, UPB, USlC, UU, WHi

6382. Pierrepont, Edward. Fifth avenue to Alaska. With maps by Leonard Forbes Beckwith. New York, G. P. Putnam's Sons, 1884.
vi, 329p. maps (1 fold) 20cm.
The Mormon City and the Mormons, p. 17–40 (Chap. IV) A sympathetic treatment of Mormons, though not in favor in polygamy or believing in the Book of Mormon.
CSmH, CU-B, NjP, NN, UU

6383. Pine, George W. Beyond the West; containing an account of two years' travel in the other half of our great continent far beyond the old West, on the plains, in the Rocky Mountains, and picturesque parks of Colorado. Also characteristic features of New Mexico, Arizona, Wyoming, Montana, Idaho . . . Oregon, Utah, Nevada, and . . . California, the end of the West . . . the great continental railroad together with the . . . most wonderful natural scenery in the world. Utica, New York, T. J. Griffiths, 1870.

2p.l. [iii]–xiii [13]–444p. plates. 19½cm.
"The Mormon settlements." Expresses admiration for Mormon accomplishments but a disgust for their religion.
Another edition: 2d ed. 1871. USlC; Buffalo, N.Y. Baker, Jones & Co., 1873. USlC
Howes P381, Sabin 62923
CSmH, CU–B, DLC, IdB, NjP, OrU, PU, WaS, WaU

Pioneer and general history of Geaugo County. *See Historical Society of Geauga County, Ohio.*

6384. Pioneer celebration. Salt Lake City, July 22, 23, 24, 1922. Given in honor of pioneers of 1847. [Salt Lake City? 1922?]
16p. 19½cm.
UHi, UPB, USlC

6384a. Pioneer day, also, our year of jubilee. Grand historical celebration. Salt Lake City, Deseret News Print [1880]
[4]p. 21cm.
At head of title: 1847. 1880. July twenty-fourth.
USlC

6385. Pioneer Day! Grand Musical Celebration, in the large Tabernacle, Salt Lake City, Utah, July 24th, 1883. Salt Lake City, Jos. Hyrum Parry, Printer, 1883.
[16]p. 14cm.
Caption-title.
NjP

6386. The Pioneer Home. [n.p., n.d.]
Broadside. 20½×13cm.
Text within ornamental border.
NjP

6386a. Pioneers' Day. Thirty-third anniversary. Jubilee and rejoicing. [Salt Lake City] 1880.
[2]p. 64cm.
Deseret News. Weekly-extra. Wednesday, July 28, 1880. Republished with variations under title: Utah pioneers.
UPB

6387. The pioneers of 1847; [data on the old Mormon Trail, comp. from the journals of Orson Pratt and William Clayton] (U.S. Cong. House. Committee on Roads. The old Oregon trail, p. 83–174, 1925)
22cm.
Reprinted from the *Historical Record.* V.9, 1890.
WHi

6388. De Pionier. Rotterdam, Manndblad Uitgegeven door de minuut Mannen der Nederlandschezendin van de Kerk van Jezus Christus van de heiligen der Laatste dagen. July, 1929–June, 1930.
1v. (12 nos.) monthly. 22½cm.
Title in English: Of pioneers.
USlC

6389. Pitt, George. The collected remarkable travels of George Pitt (accompanied by his wife) round and over the world . . . Glasgow, R. Smeal, 1886.
320p. 16cm.
"Originally published in *The British Friend* at occasional intervals."
"The Mormons," p. 301–303. An account of a visit about 1880; regards Mormons as religious impostors.
Another edition: 1887. USlC
CU–B

Plain facts against . . . *See Berry, John.*

6390. Plain facts for students of the Book of Mormon, with a map of the Promised Land. [n.p., n.d.]
4 [1]p. map. 25cm.
USlC

Plain facts, showing the falsehood and folly of the Rev. C. S. Bush. *See Pratt, Parley Parker.*

6391. Plain questions for Mormonites, by one who knows they are not saints. 2d ed. London, Wertheim and Macintosh, Thomas Ragg, Birmingham, 1852.
12p. 17cm.
CSmH, USlC

Platform of principles of the pretended reformers of Utah. *See "A Mormon"*

6392. Platt, Philip L. The Travelers' guide across the plains, upon the overland route to California, showing distances from point to point, accurately measured by roadometer, and describing the springs, streams of water, hills, mountains, camping-places and other notable objects along the route; with an appendix containing the routes from Council Bluffs to Fort Laramie; from Fort Leavenworth to the Big Blue River; the routes by way of Salt Lake and Ft. Hall, and a general summary of distances. By P. L. Platt and N. Slater, A. M. Chicago, Printed at the Daily Journal Office, 1852.
vi [7]–64p. map. 14½cm.
Includes a reference to the Mormon ferry on the North Platte; the northern routes through Utah (with a description of Parley P. Pratt's new "Golden Pass Road" through the Wasatch), description of Great Salt Lake City and the Mormon settlements north; mention of Mormon Station on the Carson River.
ICN, UPB

6393. Platt, Ward. The frontier [by] Ward Platt. The Baptist Movement for Missionary Education. Philadelphia, Published for the American Baptist Home Mission Society by the American Baptist Publication Society [c1908]
xii, 292p. col. fold. map. 19cm.
Mormonism on the decline due to a political revolt and the difference between what the missionaries teach and how Mormons live.
DLC, NjP, UHi, USl, USlC

6394. Player-Frowd, J. G. Six months in California. By J. G. Player-Frowd. London, Longmans, Green, and Co., 1872.
3p.l., 164p. 20cm.
"Salt Lake City," p. 36–39. A brief account of his trip through Salt Lake City. He attended a meeting and gives an unglamorous account of it.
CU–B, DI–GS, DLC, MB, OCl, PPFr, PPL, PSC, UHi, USIC

A plea for polygamy . . . *See Jencks, E. N.*

6394a. Pledges have been broken. Church dictates in politics. Compact made by Mormon leaders with country set aside. Denver News comments upon the conditions as presented by Senator Kearns. [Salt Lake City? Gentile Information Bureau? 1905?]
[2]p. 22cm.
Includes Mrs. John A. Logan's views on the Smoot inquiry.
USIC

Plural Marriage and the manifesto.
See Tanner, Nathan, Jr.

Polaris [*pseud.*] *See Noyes, Isaac Pitman.*

6395. Political history of Jackson County. Biographical sketches of men who have helped to make it. [Kansas City, Mo.] Marshall & Morrison, 1902.
247p. ports. 19cm.
History of Mormonism in Chapter III; political episodes.
USIC

6396. Polk, James Knox. The diary of James K. Polk during his presidency, 1845 to 1849, now first printed from the original manuscript in the collections of the Chicago Historical Society; ed. and annotated by Milo Milton Quaife . . . with an introduction by Andrew Cunningham McLaughlin . . . Chicago, A. C. McClurg & Co., 1910.
4v. ports., facsim. 23½cm.
"This work forms volumes VI–IX of the *Chicago Historical Society's Collections*, a special issue of 500 copies being printed for the purposes of that society."
Mention of the Mormons' emigration from Missouri to Illinois and thence to Utah, and their willingness to supply a battalion for the Mexican War.
Howes P445
CU, DLC, NjP, NN, OO, OU, TKL, UHi, ULA, USIC, UU, ViU

6397. ———. Polk; the diary of a president, 1845–1849, covering the Mexican War, the acquisition of Oregon, and the conquest of California and the Southwest, edited by Allan Nevins . . . London, New York [etc.] Longmans, Green and Co., 1929.
xxvp., [1]l., 412p. plates, ports. 24½cm.
Mention of the emigration of the Mormons from Missouri, and of their being willing to supply the battalion for the Mexican War.
CU, NjP, UHi

6398. Pollock, A. J. Mormonism a great delusion by A. J. Pollock. London [n.d.]
16p. 17½cm.
Distributed by the Central Bible Truth Depot.
USIC

6399. Polygami og hvid slavenhandel. Sandheden om "Mormonerne." Kobenhavn, 1914.
14p.
Title in English: Polygamy and white slave market.
Schmidt

6399a. Polygamy. [Liverpool? Millennial Star Office? n.d.]
16p. 25½cm.
USIC

6399b. "Polygamy" a new American play. [New York City, ca. 1915]
Broadside. 27×13cm.
Concerning a play by Harvey O'Higgins and Harriet Ford being presented in New York City about the Mormons and polygamy. Included is a list of the cast and synopsis of the acts.
USIC

6400. [Polygamy oath; pamphlet stating the oath that persons were to take concerning violation of act against polygamy. n.p., n.d.]
3p. 24cm.
USIC

Polygamy, or the veil uplifted . . .
See Sheen, John K.

6401. Pomeroy, Charles. Polygamy in Utah. Speech of Chas. Pomeroy, of Iowa, delivered in the House of Representatives, March 22, 1870. Washington, F. J. Rives and G. A. Bailey, 1870.
8p. 21cm.
Sabin 63919
CSmH, DLC, NN,

6402. Pond, James Burton. Eccentricities of Genius, memories of famous men and women of the platform and stage. By Major J. B. Pond. New York, G. W. Dillingham Company, 1900.
xxvip., [3]l., 3–564p. illus., ports. 22½cm.
Discussion of Ann Eliza Young in the introduction.
Another edition: London, Chatto & Windus, 1901. NjP
DLC, UHi, UPB, USIC

6403. Pooley, William Vipond. . . . The settlement of Illinois from 1830 to 1850, by William Vipond Pooley; a thesis submitted for the degree of Doctor of Philosophy, University of Wisconsin, 1905 . . . Madison, Wisconsin, University of Wisconsin, 1908.
309p. maps. 23cm. (Wisconsin University Bulletin. No. 220)
Mormons in Illinois, p. 508–525.
CU, NjP, UHi, UPB

6404. Popham, William Lee. Garden of the Gods romance. Describing the Pike's Peak region, Crystal Park, Cripple Creek, Pike's Peak, The Royal Gorge, The Grand Canyon of the Arkansas, the Mountain of the Holy Cross, Utah Deserts, Castle Gate, the Great Salt Lake, the Mormon Tabernacle, and the Great Organ, Etc., Etc. Description being from the author's observations. Louisville, Ky., The World Supply Company [c1911]
5p.l. [11]–110p. plates. 19cm.
With a detailed description of Temple Square.
USlC

6405. Popplewell, Thomas H. Was Joseph Smith Jr. a Polygamist? Colfax, Ia., Colfax Tribune Print., 1903.
43p. 20cm.
MoInRC

6406. Portalis, A. Édouard. Lés États-Unis: le self-government et le Césarisme par A. Édouard Portalis. Paris, Armand le Chevalier, éditeur, 1869.
280p. 19cm.
Chap. IV "Les Mormons." A trip through Salt Lake City with a description of Mormonism, p. [53]–87.
Title in English: The United States.
Sabin 64191
NjP, WHi

6407. Porter, Charles H. The Battle Axe of Jehovah, or Israel among the Nations. By Charles H. Porter . . . 1st ed. Independence, Mo., Herald Publishing House, 1928.
4p.l., 11–224p. port. 20cm.
RLDS doctrine.
MoInRC, NjP, USlC

6408. ———. Gleanings by the way . . . Beatrice, Nebr., Milburn & Scott Co., 1919.
258p. 20½cm.
RLDS inspired writings.
CSmH, MoInRC

6409. Porter, Elizabeth Rachel (Cannon). The cities of the sun; stories of ancient America founded on historical incidents in the Book of Mormon by Elizabeth Rachel Cannon, illustrated from paintings by Geo. M. Ottinger and photographs by the author. Salt Lake City, The Deseret News, 1910.
3p.l., 118 [2]p. front., illus. 19½cm.
DLC, MoInRC, ULA, UPB, USl, USlC, UU

6410. ———. (same) 2d ed. Salt Lake City, The Deseret News, 1911.
3p.l., 118 [2]p. 20cm.
NjP, UPB

6411. Porter, Jeremiah. The Earliest religious history of Chicago. Chicago, Fergus Printing Co., 1881.
[53]–164p. 21cm.
The case of Jo. Smith, the Mormon prophet, p. 134. Extracted from: *Reminiscences of the Illinois-Bar forty years ago* . . . By Isaac N. Arnold.
UPB

6412. Porter, Kirk Harold. National party platforms, compiled by Kirk H. Porter. New York, The Macmillan Co., 1924.
xvi, [1]l., 522p. 20½cm. (Political parties and politics series)
Includes anti-polygamy platforms.
CU, DLC, NjP

6413. Porter, Lavinia Honeyman. By ox team to California; a narrative of crossing the plains in 1860, by Lavinia Honeyman Porter. Oakland, Cal., Oakland Enquirer Publishing Co., 1910.
xi, 139p. 24½cm.
Via Great Salt Lake City on the Cherokee Trail; encounters Mormon emigrants on the trail; goes through Salt Lake City; takes Simpson route to California.
Howes P488
CtY, CU–B, NjP, UPB

6414. Porter, Robert Percival. The West, from the census of 1880; a history of the industrial, commercial, social and political development of the states and territories of the West from 1800 to 1880, by Robert P. Porter, Henry Gannett, and Wm. P. Jones. Chicago, Rand, McNally, 1882.
vip., [1]l. [9]–630p. charts, fold. map. 24cm.
Brief summary of church history in chapter on Utah.
CU–B, DLC, NjP, UU

6415. Porter, S. F. The origin of the Book of Mormon. Chicago, National Christian Association [187–]
16p. 19½cm.
CSmH, USlC

6416. Porter, Thomas Cunningham. Impressions of America by T. C. Porter. Illustrated with diagrams and stereoscopic views. London, 1899.
xxix, 241p. illus., plates. 22½cm.
Power of Brigham Young; polygamy.
UPB, USlC

6417. Portrait, genealogical and biographical record of the State of Utah, containing biographies of many well known citizens of the past and present. Chicago, National Historical Record Co., 1902.
3p.l. [v]–499 [3]p. ports., plates. 28½cm.
Includes Mormon biographies.
UPB, USlC

6418. Post, Marie Caroline (de Trobriand). The life and mémoirs of Comte Régis de Trobriand, major-general in the army of the United States, by his daughter, Marie Caroline Post (Mrs. Charles Alfred Post); with two portraits in photogravure. New York, E. P. Dutton & Company, 1910.
3p.l., v–ix, 539p. 20 port. 24½cm.
With the army in Utah in 1870. Contacts with Mormon leaders, etc.
CU–B, DLC, NjP, NN, UHi

6419. Post, Stephen. A treatise on the Melchisedek priesthood and the callings of God. Respectfully dedicated to a Gospel Ministry. By Stephen Post . . . Council Bluffs, Ia., Nonpareil Printing Co., 1872.
22p. 21cm.
Cover-title.
A late tract in behalf of Sidney Rigdon.
Morgan
MH

6420. ———. Zion's Messenger. Published by Stephen Post and William Hamilton, elders of the Church of Jesus Christ for the benefit of the scattered Zion. Erie, Pa., Sterrett & Gara, Printers, 1864.
16p. 22cm.
A continuation of the argument of Joseph H. Newton's *An Appeal.*
Morgan
MoInRC, USIC 8p.

6421. Post, Truman A. Truman Marcellus Post, D.D. A biography, personal and literary . . . Boston, Congregational Sunday-School and Publishing Society [c1891]
xvi, 507p. 21cm.
Observed the troubles of the Mormons both in Illinois and Iowa.
ICN

6422. Potter, Charles Francis. The story of religion, as told in the lives of its leaders. New York, [Simon and Schuster, Inc., c1929]
xx, 627p. plates. 21½cm.
Joseph Smith and the Mormons . . . p. 527–537.
Statements about Joseph Smith and the Mormons taken from anti-Mormon sources.
Other editions: Garden City, N.Y., Garden City Publishing Co. [c1929] CU–B, USIC; London, G. G. Hurrap, 1930. NjPT
DLC, UPB, USIC

6423. Poulson, Ezra J. Songs for the toilers. Boston, The Stratford Co., 1922.
3p.l., 42p. 19cm.
Mormon poetry.
DLC, UPB

6424. Poulson, Martin Wilford. Human nature in religious education readings and problems in educational psychology. Teacher training lesson book 1927–28. Compiled and written for the General Church Board of Education. Salt Lake City, Deseret Book Co. [c1927]
xii, 184p. 19cm. (Teacher training lesson book. 1927–28)
CU–B, UHi, ULA, USIC

6425. ———. An interesting old volume on health [Journal of Health]; background of Mormon word of wisdom. [Provo, Utah? 1930]
8, 2p. 18cm.
Copied from *The Scratch.* (Brigham Young University. V.2, No.2, March, 1930)
CSmH, NjP, UHi, UPB

6426. ———. Library resources for the scientific study of Mormonism. By M. Wilford Poulson. [Provo, Utah? 1930]
37–38p. 18cm.
Reprint: *Utah Academy of Sciences. Proceedings.* V.7, July 15, 1930.
Brief summary of Mormon collections in 1930.
CSmH, UHi, UPB

6427. Poulson, P. Wm. Tydsklands Politik og Skandinavien og Rusland. Betragtninger i Diplomatien Dr. med P. Wm. Poulson . . . Chicago, Trykt i "Skandinavens" Bog-og Accidents-Trykkeri, 1870.
23p. 21½cm.
A convert who sees both Buddha and Nephi giving instructions to the First Presidency of the Church.
Title in English: Germany's foreign policy with Scandinavia and Russia.
UPB (photostat)

6428. Powell, John. The latter-day Saints alphabet. (With references) By John Powell. For general use among the children of the Saints. Salt Lake City, 1905.
[9]p. 19cm.
Moralistic book.
NjP, UPB, USIC

6429. Powell, John Wesley. Exploration of the Colorado River of the west and its tributaries. Explored in 1869, 1870, 1871, and 1872, under the direction of the Secretary of the Smithsonian Institution. Washington, Govt. Print. Off., 1875.
xi, 291p. plates, maps. 30cm.
A few references to Mormons; but more important as an item of Utah exploration.
Republished in 1895 under title: Canyons of the Colorado. Meadville, Pa. Flood & Vincent, 1895. DLC
Howes P528, Sabin 64753
CU, NjP, UHi, ULA, UPB

6430. ———. First through the Grand Canyon. New York, Outing Publishing Co., 1915.
320p. 22cm.
Brief encounters with Mormons.
Other editions: 1916. UHi; New York, Macmillan Co., 1925. CU
CU–B, DLC, NjP, NN, UHi, UPB, UU

6431. ———. . . . Report on the lands of the arid region of the United States, with a more detailed account of the lands of Utah. With maps. By J. W. Powell . . . Washington, Govt. Print. Off., 1878.
xiii, 195p. 3 fold. maps. 29½cm.
(U.S. 45th Cong. 2d Sess. House. Ex. Doc. No. 73)
A description of land and water availability with material concerning location of settlements; land utilization, etc.
Another edition: 2d ed. 1879. CU, DLC, NjP, UPB
CSmH, CU–B, DLC, ULA

6432. Powell, Lyman Pierson. . . . Historic towns of the western states, ed. by Lyman P. Powell . . . New York & London, G. P. Putnam's Sons, 1901.
xxxvi p., [1]l., 702p. illus., ports. 22cm.
(American historic towns)
Salt Lake City, by James E. Talmage.
Another edition: New York, Putnam, 1904. PPF
CU–B, DLC, ICJ, MB, MiU, NjP, NN, OCl, OCU, UHi, UPB, UU, ViU, WaU

6433. Powers, H. Henry. Remarks of Hon. H. Henry Powers of Vermont, on the resolution to exclude B. H. Roberts, Member-elect from Utah, from his seat in the House of Representatives, January 24, 1900. Washington, 1900.
8p. 24cm.
Cover-title: In favor of unseating B. H. Roberts.
UHi

6434. Powers, Orlando Woodworth. Campaign document No. 3. Address of the Liberal Committee, reviewing the People's Party's "Declaration of principles." Liberal war cry: Salt Lake work for Salt Lake workman. Salt Lake City, 1889.
8p. 23cm.
MH, NjP

6435. ———. Judge O. W. Powers. Candidate for United States Senator. His position on public questions. [Salt Lake City, 1898?]
24p. 23½cm.
Mormons and politics.
USlC

6436. ———. Mormon methods. Extracted from the city records of Salt Lake City under Mormon control. [Washington, Liberal Committee, 1892]
41p. 23cm.
Cover-title.
"From a speech . . . delivered in Salt Lake City on July 26, 1890."
ICN, MH, WHi

6437. ———. Powers' answer. There was no attack whatever intended upon the First Presidency. Cannon and the trust . . . Salt Lake City, 1894.
[4]p. 19½cm.
A letter to the *Salt Lake Herald* trying to separate criticism of the First Presidency from that of a political figure.
USlC

6438. ———. "Unlawful cohabitation," under the Edmunds Act. An able and lucid opinion, delivered at Salt Lake City, February 13th, 1886, in the Supreme Court. [Salt Lake City, 1886?]
8p. 22½cm.
WHi

6439. Powers, William Penn. Some annals of the Powers Family. Compiled by W. P. Powers. Los Angeles, Cal., 1924.
304p., [1]l. illus., ports., fold. port. 21cm.
DLC

6440. Pratt, Belinda Marden. Defence of polygamy, by a lady of Utah, in a letter to her sister in New Hampshire. [Great Salt Lake City, 1854?]
9p. 21½cm.
Half title: "Polygamy exposed by a lady of Utah."
Republished in the *Millennial Star*, July 29, 1854.
CtY, CU, MH, USlC

6441. ———. (same) Salt Lake City [1854?]
11p. 18½cm.
CU–B, USlC

6442. Pratt, Milson R. America in the war. [n.p.] 1915
32p. 20cm.
What the scriptures say about World War I.
USlC

6442a. ———. (same) Tells what the scriptures say about the world-war. 2d ed. Salt Lake City [c1918]
32p. 20cm.
USlC

6443. ———. The Capture of the Kaiser, His trial and death and the death of the Crown Prince. As foretold in prophecy. By M. R. Pratt. Salt Lake City [ca. 1918]
32p. 20cm.
References to Joseph Smith and Zion in America.
NjP, UPB, USlC

6444. ———. The house of Israel; Who and where they are . . . [Salt Lake City? 1930?]
Broadside. 21×11½cm.
The Mormon doctrine of the dispersion of Israel.
UHi

PRATT, M. R.

6445. ———. Vote for M. R. Pratt.
[Salt Lake City, n.d.]
Broadside. 35½×13½.
Mormons and politics.
USlC

6446. Pratt, Orson. Absurdities of immaterialism; or, A reply to T. W. P. Taylder's pamphlet, entitled: "The materialism of the Mormons or Latter-day Saints examined and exposed." By Orson Pratt. [Liverpool, R. James, 1849]
32p. 22cm.
Caption-title.
Signed: July 31st, 1849.
Published from variant plates.
Sabin 64949
CSmH, CtY, CU–B, ICHi, ICN, MH, MoInRC, NjP, NN, ULA, UPB, USl, USlC, UU

———. The Bible & polygamy.
See his Great discussion.

6447. ———. Det celestiale Aegteskab eller den af Gud Aabenbarede Aegteskabsorden for tid og al evighed, og det Nye Jerusalem. Første danske udgave. Kjøbenhavn, Udgivet og forlagt af John Van Cott, 1855.
2p.l. [7]–228, 60p. 16½cm.
Title in English: Celestial marriage . . . and New Jerusalem. "Det Nye Jerusalem af J. N. Smith," 60p.
CU–B, MH, NjP, UU

6448. ———. (same) Anden danske udgave. Kjobenhavn, J. N. Smith, Trykt hos F. E. Bording [pref. 1855]
3p.l., 7–232, 62p. 17cm.
CU–B, MH, UPB, USlC, UU

6449. ———. Circular sobre Mormonismo. Articulos de fé de la Iglesia de Nuestro Señor Jesu Cristo de los santos del ultimo dia. De Las obras del apostol Orson Pratt. Traducido al español por L. M. Peterson . . . Salt Lake City Impreso en la imprinta [sic] del Deseret News, 1879.
11p. 18cm.
Cover-title.
Title in English: Pamphlet about Mormonism.
CLU, CtY, CU–B, NjP, UPB, USlC

6450. ———. Discourses on celestial marriage, delivered in the New Tabernacle, Salt Lake City, October 7th, 8th, and 9th, 1869, by Elder Orson Pratt, President George A. Smith, and Elder George Q. Cannon. Salt Lake City, Printed at the Deseret News Office, 1869.
24p. 19½cm.
Cover-title.
Sabin H64950
CSmH, CtY, CU–B, DLC, ICN, MH, MoK, NjP, NN, PHi, USlC, WHi

6451. ———. (same) By President George A. Smith, Elder Orson Pratt, and Elder George Q. Cannon. Salt Lake City, Printed at the Deseret News Office, 1869.
24p. 19½cm.
Cover-title.
Same as above, but with President George A. Smith's name placed first on the cover-title.
UHi

6452. ———. Divine authenticity of the Book of Mormon. Liverpool, R. James, 1850–1852.
6 pts. (96p.) 23cm.
Paging continuous.
First part has imprint, S. W. Richards, etc. Two series of printings for the 1851 and 1852 editions of his series of pamphlets.
Part 1 reprinted in 1852; part 6 printed with and without date (1851).
UPB has a copy of No. 5 enclosed in cover entitled: Tract No. 5 of the Latter Day Saints'-Loan Tract Society. Shropshire conference . . .
Sabin 64951
CtY, NjP, NN, ULA, UPB, USl, USlC, UU

6453. ———. (same, in Danish) Mormons Bogs guddommelige Travaerdighed. Af Orson Pratt . . . Oversat fra Engelsk af F. J. Hahn. [Kjobenhavn, Udgivet af W. Snow. Trykt hos F. E. Bording, n.d.]
6 pts. 21cm.
"4de oplag."
USlC

6454. ———. (same) Udgivet paa Dansk af W. Snow. (Nr. 1-2 oversat fra Engelsk af F. J. Hahn. Nr. 3-6 oversat fra Engelsk af Alexander Weihe). Kjobenhavn, Trykt hos F. E. Bording, 1853.
6 pts. 21½cm.
Variant edition. USlC
CSmH, CU–B, MH, MnU, NN, USlC

6455. ———. (same) Kjobenhavn, Udgivet og forlagt af Hector C. Haight. Trykt hos F. E. Bording, 1857.
6 pts. 21½cm.
CSmH, CtY, UHi, UPB, USl, USlC, UU

6456. ———. (same) Kjobenhavn, H. C. Haight, 1860.
6 pts. 20cm.
USlC

6457. ———. Divine authority, or the question, was Joseph Smith sent of God? By Orson Pratt, one of the Twelve Apostles of the Church of Jesus Christ of Latter-day Saints. Liverpool, R. James, 1848.
16p. 22½cm.
Caption-title.
At head of title: "No. 1"
Signed: September 3, 1848.
Sabin 64952
CSmH, CtY, MoK, NjP, NN, UHi, ULA, UPB, USl, USlC, UU

6458. ———. (same, under title) Was Joseph Smith sent of God? Written by Orson Pratt: One of the Twelve Apostles of the Church of Jesus Christ of Latter Day Saints, in Liverpool, England. 1848. [Cambridge, Mass.? 1849?]
16p. 23cm.
Caption-title. Preface by Wilford Woodruff says "thousands of copies have been circulated in the British Isles, and I have been induced to published this pamphlet in this country . . ."
At end: Letter to Pratt by John Hyde, November 13, 1848, written subsequent to publication of the tract under title *Divine authority*.
CU-B, MoInRC, USlC

6459. ———. (same) By the late Elder Orson Pratt. [Liverpool, Millennial Star Office, 1908?]
22[2]p. 21cm.
Caption-title.
UHi, USlC

6460. ———. (same, in Danish) Guddommelig Fuldmagt; eller det Spørgsmaal: var Joseph Smith sendt af Gud? af Orson Pratt . . . [Kjøbenhavn] Trykt hos F. E. Bording. Udgivet og forlagt af H. C. Haight [1857?]
24p. 19cm.
Variant printing. USlC
CSmH, NN, USlC

6461. ———. (same) Kjøbenhavn, Udgivet og forlagt af W. Snow. Trykt hos F. E. Bording [n.d.]
24p. 21cm.
USlC

6462. ———. (same) Kjøbenhavn. Udgivet og forlagt af H. C. Haight. Trykt i Kjobenhavn hos F. E. Bording [n.d.]
24p. 21cm.
"4de oplag."
NN, USlC, UU

6463. ———. (same) [Kjobenhavn, Redigeret og Udgivet af John Van Cott. Trykt hos F. E. Bording, 1860]
24p. 22cm.
CtY, MnU, USlC

6464. ———. (same) [Kjobenhavn, C. Winderborg, 1867]
24p. 20cm.
Caption-title.
"5te oplag."
CtY, NjP, UHi, USlC

6464a. ———. (same) [Kjobenhavn, Udgivet og forlagt af C. G. Larsen. Trykt hos F. E. Bording, 1873]
24p. 21cm.
USlC

6465. ———. (same) Kjobenhavn, Udgivet og forlagt af N. C. Flygare, 1875.
24p. 23cm.
CtY, UPB, USlC

6466. ———. (same) [Kjobenhavn, Udgivet og forlagt af C. D. Fjeldsted. Trykt hos F. E. Bording, 1881]
24p. 20½cm.
Caption-title.
UHi, USlC

6467. ———. (same, in Dutch) Goddelijke Roeping, of de vraag. Was Joseph Smith, den Profeet en Stichter der kerk van Jezus Christus heilige der laatste dagen, van God gezonden? door Orson Pratt, een der twaalf apostelen. Zwolle, Bockdrukkerij van W. F. Zweers, 1875.
31p. 23cm.
Cover-title.
USlC

6468. ———. (same, in Swedish) Guddomelig myndighet; eller det spörgsmål: Var Joseph Smith sendt af Gud? Översat från Aengelsk af Alexander V. Wejge . . . [Kjobenhavn, Trykt hos J. G. Salomon, 1852?]
23 [1]p. 22cm.
USlC

6469. ———. (same) [Kjobenhavn, Trykt hos J. W. Salomon, 1856?]
23p. 22cm.
MnU, USlC

6470. ———. (same) [Kjobenhavn, Forlagt af C. D. Fjeldsted. Trykt hos F. E. Bording, 1889]
16p. 23cm.
USlC

6471. ———. (same) [Kjøbenhavn, Udgivet og forlagt af Peter Sundwall . . . 1895]
16p. 21cm.
USlC

6472. ———. Evangeliets sande grundsaetninger, fremstillede af Orson Pratt oversat fra Engelsk . . . Kjobenhavn, Udgivet og forlagt af Hector C. Haight. Trykt hos F. E. Bording, 1857.
141p. 21cm.
Title in English: True principles of the gospel.
CSmH, UHi, USlC

6473. ———. (same) Kjobenhavn, Udgivet og forlagt af C. Widerborg, 1865.
1p.l., 121p. 21cm.
MH, NN, UHi, ULA, USl, USlC

6474. ———. (same) Kjobenhavn, Udgivet og forlagt af C. G. Larsen, 1874.
133p. 21½cm.
UPB, USlC

PRATT, O.

6475. ———. (same) Kjobenhavn, Udgivet og forlagt af C. D. Fjeldsted. Trykt hos F. E. Bording, 1882.
1p.l., 133p. 21cm.
UHi, UPB, USIC

6476. ———. (same) København, Udgivet og forlagt af A. L. Skanchy, 1902.
197 [1]p. 18cm.
NjP, UHi, USIC

6477. ———. (same, in Swedish) Evangelii sanna grundsatser framställda af Orson Pratt . . . en af de tolf apostlarne i Jesu Kristi Kyrka af sista dagars heliga. Öfversatt fran dansk. Köpenhamn, Utgifven och förlagd af N. C. Flygare, 1876.
3p.l., 258p. 16½cm.
UPB, USIC, UU

6478. ———. (same) Andra upplagan. Öfversatt från engelskan Köpenhamn, Utgifven och förlagd af C. D. Fjeldsted. Tryckt hos F. E. Bording, 1884.
3p.l., 269p. 16½cm.
MH, UPB

6479. ———. (same) Tredje Upplagan. Köpenhamn, Utgifven och förlagd af Peter Sundwall. Tryckt hos F. E. Bording, 1895.
285p. 16½cm.
USIC

6480. ———. (same) Andra upplagan . . . Öfversatt fran engelskan. Köpenhamn, Utgifven och förlagd af C. D. Fjeldsted. Tryckt hos Emil Petersen, 1900.
2p.l., 285p. 16½cm.
First 2 plates added to an earlier printing. Includes new title-page and preface.
USIC

6481. ———. (same) Tredje svenska upplagan . . . Öfversatt fran engelskan, Köpenhamn, Utgifven och Förlagd af Anthon L. Skanchy. Tryckt hos F. E. Bording, 1903.
3p.l., 280p. 17cm.
USIC

6482. ———. (same) Tredje svenska upplagan . . . Öfversatt fran engelskan, Köpenhamn, Utgifven och förlagt af Anthon L. Skanchy, 1903.
4p.l., 280p. 16½cm.
DLC, UHi, UPB, USI, USIC, UPB

6483. ———. (same) Fjärde Svenska upplagan . . . Översatt fran Engelskan. Stockholm, Utgifven och förlagd av Gideon N. Hulterström [Bröderna, Olofssons Tryckeri, 1923]
3p.l. [7]–288p. 16½cm.
UHi, UPB, USIC

6484. ———. . . . Great discussion! Does the Bible sanction polygamy! held in the New Tabernacle at Salt Lake City, August 12th, 1870, before assembled thousands, between Professor Orson Pratt one of the Twelve Apostles, selected by President Brigham Young to represent the Mormon faith and Rev. Dr. J. P. Newman, Chaplain of the United States Senate and Pastor of the Methodist Metropolitan Church, Washington, D.C., Cleveland, O., 1873.
64p. illus. 22cm.
Cover-title.
First edition.
NN, WHi

6485. ———. (same) 2d ed. Cleveland, Ohio, 1874.
64p. 21½cm.
Sabin 64953
CSmH, NN

6486. ———. (same) Baltimore, 1874.
64p. 21½cm.
"2d ed."
Cover-title.
DLC, NN, WHi

6487. ———. (same) [Third edition] Baltimore, 1874.
56p. 21cm.
In orange printed wrapper.
Text interspersed with advertisement.
Edition note from cover.
UPB

6488. ———. (same) Milwaukee, 1875.
58p. 21½cm.
At head of title: 5th ed.
Sabin 64953
CSmH

6489. ———. (same, under title) The Bible & polygamy. Does the Bible sanction polygamy? A discussion between Professor Orson Pratt . . . and Rev. Doctor J. P. Newman . . . in the New Tabernacle, Salt Lake City, August 12, 13, and 14, 1870. To which is added three sermons on the same subject, by Prest. George A. Smith, and Elders Orson Pratt and George Q. Cannon. Salt Lake City, Deseret News Steam Printing Establishment, 1874.
1p.l., 99p. 23½cm.
CSmH, CU-B, DLC, ICHi, MoInRC, NBuG, NjP, NN, USIC

6490. ———. (same) Salt Lake City, Deseret News Steam Print. Establishment, 1876.
105p. 22cm.
CSmH, CU-B, OCl, UHi

6491. ———. (same) Salt Lake City, Deseret News Steam Printing Establishment, 1877.
105p. 23cm.
Variant printing. USIC
CSmH, CtY, CU-B, DLC, ICN, MH, NjP, NN, OClWHi, UHi, USI, USIC, WHi

6492. ———. (same) Salt Lake City, Deseret News, 1892.
183p. 18cm.
CSmH, ICN, IWW, MH, MoInRC, NjP, UHi, UPB, USlC

6493. ———. Great first cause; or the self-moving forces of the universe. [Liverpool, R. James Printer, 1851]
16p. 21cm.
Signed: January 1, 1851.
Sabin 64954
CSmH, NjP, NN, PPM, UHi, ULA, UPB, USlC

6494. ———. (same, in Welsh) Yr achos mawr cyntaf, neu alluoedd Hunan-symudawl y bydyssawd. Wedi ei gyfieitau allan o saesneg Orson Pratt. [Merthyr-Tydfil, J. Davis Argaffydd, 1851?]
28p. 18cm.
Signed: Ion 1, 1851.
MH, USlC

6495. ———. Guds rige i de sidste dage eller forberedelserne for Kristi anden Tilkommelse. Udg. af C. N. Lund. Kobenhavn, 1897.
16p.
Title in English: God's kingdom in the last days.
Schmidt

6496. ———. (same) København, Udgivet og forlagt af Andreas Peterson. Trykt hos F. E. Bording (V. Petersen) 1899.
16p. 23cm.
USlC

6496a. ———. (same) Kobenhavn, Udgivet og forlagt af A. L. Skanchy. Trykt hos L. A. Nielsen, 1902.
23p. 18½cm.
Cover-title.
In brown printed wrapper.
UPB, USlC

6497. ———. The Holy Spirit, by Orson Pratt . . . Liverpool, Latter-day saints Book and Millennial Star Depot [185–]
[49]–64, 4p. 21cm.
Cover-title.
At head of title: Chapter IV.
Designed as part of a book but issued separately.
Some copies are found in printed wrappers.
MH, UHi, ULA, UPB, USlC

6498. ———. (same) Kobenhavn, Udgivet og forlagt af A. L. Skanchy. Trykt hos L. A. Nielsen . . . 1902.
23p. 18½cm.
USlC

6499. ———. (same) Kobenhavn, Udgivet og forlagt af A. L. Skanchy. Trykt hos L. A. Nielsen . . . 1902.
16p. 19cm.
"4th ed."
USlC

6500. ———. How to live acceptably. Salt Lake City, Nels B. Lundwall [n.d.]
16p. port. on cover. 20cm.
"Copied verbatim from the *Deseret Evening News.* V.8, No.265, October 2, 1875."
UPB

6501. ———. A interesting account of several remarkable visions, and of the late discovery of ancient American records. By O. Pratt, minister of the gospel. Edinburgh, Printed by Ballantyne and Hughes, MDCCCXL [1840]
31p. 18cm.
Variant printing: Without the A before interesting. USlC
CtY, CU-B, MoInRC, MoK, UPB, USlC

6502. ———. An interesting account of several remarkable visions, and of the late discovery of ancient American records [which unfold the history of this continent from the earliest ages after the flood, to the beginning of the fifth century of the Christian era. With a sketch of the rise, faith, and doctrine of the Church of Jesus Christ of Latter-day Saints] By O. Pratt, Minister of the gospel. (First American Edition) New York, Joseph W. Harrison, Printer, 1841.
36p. 17×11cm.
The portion of the title enclosed in brackets is taken from the cover-title.
Republished in 1848 with title: Remarkable Visions.
Sabin 64955
CSmH, ICHi, MH, MWA, NjP, NN, UPB, USlC, UU

6503. ———. (same) (Second American edition) New York, Joseph W. Harrison, 1841.
36p. 17cm.
Slight typographical variations.
NN, USlC

6504. ———. (same) Third American edition. New York, Joseph W. Harrison, Printer, 1842.
36p. 16½cm.
CSmH, CtY, CU-B, MoInRC, NN, UHi, UPB, USlC

6505. ———. (same) First Australian, from the Third American Edition. Sydney: Printed by Albert Mason . . . 1851.
36p. 18cm.
CSmH

6506. ———. Key to the universe, or a new theory of its mechanism . . . First ed. Liverpool, For Sale by William Budge, 1879.
xii [13]–118p. 22½cm.
Basically a scientific treatise, but included because many of Pratt's studies are scientific-theological.
USlC

6507. ———. Key to the universe; or, a new theory of its mechanism founded upon a I. continuous orbital propulsion, arising from the velocity of gravity and its consequent aberrations. II. resisting ethereal medium of variable density, with mathematical demonstrations and tables. 2d ed. from the first European edition. Salt Lake City [c1879]
xii, 118p. tables. 22cm.
"Published by the author."
CSmH, MH, NjP, NN, ULA, UPB, USlC

6508. ———. The kingdom of God. By Orson Pratt, one of the Twelve Apostles of the Church of Jesus Christ of Latter-day Saints. [Liverpool, R. James 1848–49]
4pts. 21cm.
At head of title: No. 2–5.
Two variants. UPB
Sabin 64956
CSmH, CtY, ICN, MH, NjP, NN, UHi, ULA, UPB, USl, USlC, UU

6509. ———. (same) Liverpool, S. W. Richards; London: For sale at the Latter-day Saints' Book and Millennial Star Depot [n.d.]
31p. 18cm.
Undated, but with same publisher.
USlC

6510. ———. Latter-day kingdom, or the preparations for the second advent. Liverpool . . . , London; L.D.S. Book and Star Depot, 1857.
[113]–128p. 21½cm.
At head of title: Chapter VIII.
Some copies are in printed wrappers.
Published as part of a projected book, but issued separately.
MH, ULA, UPB, USlC

———. Listen to the voice of truth.
See Listen to the voice of truth.

6511. ———. Necessity for miracles. Liverpool [etc.] Latter-day Saints Book & Millennial Star Depot, 1857.
81–96p. 20½cm.
Cover-title.
At head of title: Chapter VI.
CtY copy in original wrappers with catalog of Utah publications by the Church of Jesus Christ of Latter-day Saints and for sale by Orson Pratt. 4p. with *Necessity for miracles* within.
CtY, NN, UPB

6512. ———. New Jerusalem, and equality and oneness of the Saints; a forecast of events to be established by a chosen and dedicated people. Salt Lake City, Parker P. Robison [n.d.]
73p. 19cm.
On back cover: The world's answer to communism.
UPB

6513. ———. New Jerusalem; or, The fulfilment of modern prophecy. By Orson Pratt, one of the Twelve Apostles of the Church of Jesus Christ of Latter-day Saints. [Liverpool, R. James, Printer, 1849]
24p. 21cm.
At head of title: (No. 7)
Dated at end: Liverpool, October 1, 1849.
Variant printing without Printer after R. James. USlC
Sabin 64957
CSmH, CtY, ICN, MH, MoInRC, NjP, NN, UHi, ULA, UPB, USl, USlC, UU

6514. ———. Prophetic almanac for 1845, being the first after bissextile or leap year. Calculated for the Eastern, Middle and Western States and territories, the northern portions of the slave states, and British provinces. By Orson Pratt, A.M., Professor of Mathematics in the University of the City of Nauvoo. New York: Published at the Prophet Office [1844]
24p. 20cm.
At head of title: "No. 1. To be continued annually."
Announced as just published in *The Prophet*, August 3, 1844.
Also includes his "Dialogue between tradition, reason and scriptus. Missouri outrages, Illinois persecutions, and an appeal for protection, included.
Sabin 64958
CtY, DLC, NN, UPB, USlC inc., UU

6515. ———. The Prophetic almanac for 1846, being the second after bissextile or leap year. Calculated for the Eastern, Middle and Western States and territories, the northern portions of the slave states, and British provinces. By Orson Pratt, A.M. New York, Published at the "New York Messenger" Office [1845]
24p. 19½cm.
At head of title: No. 2. To be continued annually.
No more published.
Includes comparison between "Saint" and "Sectarian" beliefs as well as other Mormon material.
Announced as first published in *New York Messenger*, August 9, 1845.
Sabin 64958
CSmH, DLC, MoInRC, NN, USlC, UU

6516. ———. Remarkable visions. Visions of Joseph Smith — discovery of Gold Plates, filled with Egyptian Characters and hieroglyphics — their translation into the English language by the aid of the Urim and Thummim — the sacred history of ancient America, now clearly revealed from the earliest ages after the flood, to the beginning of the fifth century of the Christian era, — A sketch of the rise, faith, and doctrine of the Church of Jesus Christ of Latter-Day Saints. [Liverpool, R. James, 1848]
16p. 21cm. (No. 6)
Revised edition of *An interesting account.*
Variant edition. USIC
Sabin 64959
CSmH, CtY, ICN, MH, NjP, NN, OO, UHi, ULA, UPB, USIC

6517. ———. (same, in Danish) Maerkvaerdige syner . . . [Kjobenhavn, 1851]
16p. 22cm.
Defective copy.
UPB

6518. ———. (same) [Kjobenhavn, Trykt hos F. E. Bording, n.d.]
16p. 20cm.
USIC

6519. ———. (same) Af magister Orson Pratt. Kjøbenhavn. Trykt F. E. Bording, 1851.
16p. 21cm.
USIC

6519a. ———. (same) [København? Udgivet af Hector C. Haight. Trykt hos F. E. Bording, ca. 1857]
16p. 21cm.
USIC

6520. ———. (same) [Kjobenhavn] Udgivet af C. Widerborg. Trykt hos F. E. Bording [1857?]
16p. 21cm.
UU

6521. ———. (same) [Kjobenhavn?, Udgivet af R. Petersen. Trykt hos F. E. Bording, 1872]
16p. 21½cm.
Caption-title.
"Tillaeg" signed by Erastus Snow.
"21st tusende."
UHi, USIC

6521a. ———. (same) [København? Udgivet af C. G. Larsen. Trykt hos F. E. Bording, 1873]
16p. 20½cm.
24de Tusind.
USIC

6522. ———. (same) København, Udgivet af C. E. Larsen. Tryckt hos F. E. Bording, 1875.
16p. 21cm.
USIC

6523. ———. (same) [Kjøbenhavn? F. E. Bording, 1877]
16p. 23cm.
UPB

6524. ———. (same) Af Orson Pratt en af en Tolve Apostle i Jesu Kristi Kirke af Sidste-dages Hellige. [Kjøbenhavn, Udgivet og forlagt af R. Wilhalmsen. Trykt hos F. E. Bording, 1880]
16p. 21cm.
Caption-title.
"37te Tusende."
UPB, USIC

6525. ———. (same) København, Udgivet og forlagt af A. L. Skanchy. Tryckt hos Emil Petersen . . . 1901.
23 [1]p. 18½cm.
Cover-title.
UPB, USIC

6525a. ———. (same) Kjøbenhavn, Udgivet og forlagt af Anthon L. Skanchy, 1903.
24p. 18½cm.
USIC

6526. ———. (same) Kjøbenhavn, Udgivet og forlagt af Søren Rasmussen, . . . [P.S. Christiansen, Aarhus] 1907.
24p. 18½cm.
Cover-title.
Articles of Faith on back cover.
UPB, USIC

6527. ———. (same, in Dutch) Merkwaardige verschijningen aan den Profeet Joseph Smith Jr.; en Het Nieuw Jeruzalem; of De vervulling der vieuwe openbaringen door Orson Pratt . . . Uit het Engelsch. Gedrukt op last van P. J. Lammers . . . Amsterdam, Snelpersdruk van I. Bremer [n.d.]
98p. 20½cm.
Remarkable Visions and *New Jerusalem.*
UHi, USIC

6528. ———. (same, in Swedish) Märkwärdiga Syner af Orson Pratt, Köpenhamn [Udgifwet John Van Cott, 1860]
18p. 21cm.
CSmH

6529. ———. (same) Köpenhamn, C. Widerborg, 1865.
18p. 20cm.
Caption-title.
"7de upplagan."
CtY

6530. ———. (same) [Köpenhamn, Utgifwet och förlagdt af Knud Peterson. Trykt hos F. E. Bording, 1872]
16p. 21cm.
"21de Tusende."
USIC

PRATT, O.

6531. ———. (same) [Köpenhamn, Utgiven och förlagd af R. C. Flygare. Trykt hos F. E. Bording, 1876]
16p. 21cm.
Caption-title.
"24de Tusende."
UHi

6532. ———. (same) [Köpenhamn, N. C. Flygare. Tryckt hos F. E. Bording, 1878]
16p. 22cm.
Caption-title.
CDU, CSmH, CtY

6532a. ———. (same) Köpenhamn, Utgifven och förlagd af N. Wilhalmsen, 1880.
16p. 21½cm.
"37te Tusende."
UPB, USIC

6533. ———. (same) [Köpenhamn. Utgifven och förlagd af P. Sundwall. Tryckt hos F. E. Bording. 1895]
24p. 17½cm.
"Tillägg" signed Erastus Snow, p. [20]–24.
USIC

6533a. ———. (same) [Köpenhamn, ca. 1892]
19p. 17½cm.
USIC

6533b. ———. (same) [Köpenhamn, Utgifven och förlagd af Andreas Peterson, 1901]
24p. 18½cm.
USIC

6533c. ———. (same) [Köpenhamn. Tryckt hos Emil Petersen, Grønnegade 33. 1901]
24p. 18cm.
UPB, USIC

6534. ———. (same) Köpenhamn, Tryckt hos Landby & Lundgren, 1904.
23p. 19cm.
UPB

6535. ———. (same) Märkvärdiga syner av Orson Pratt. Var och en som avviker och icke förbliver i Kristi lära han har ingen Gud; den som förbliver i Läran han har både fadern och sonon. Stockholm, Hugo D. E. Peterson. Utgiven och förlagd av Gideon N. Hulterström, Svartensgatan 3, Stockholm [1914]
24p. 21cm.
USIC

6536. ———. (same) Stockholm, T. Tobiason, 1914.
23p. 18½cm.
UPB

6537. ———. Reply to a pamphlet printed at Glasgow, with the "approbation of Clergymen of different denominations," entitled "Remarks on Mormonism." By Orson Pratt . . . [Liverpool, R. James, Printer, 1849]
16p. 21cm.
Caption-title.
Variant edition. UPB, USIC
Sabin 64960
CSmH, CtY, ICN, MoK, NjP, NN, UHi, ULA, UPB, USI, USIC, UU

6538. ———. Sammanlikning emellan bewiserna för Bibeln och Mormons Bok. Tall . . . afhällt i Tabernaklet i Stora Salsjostaden den 2dra Januari 1859. [n.p., 1859?]
22p. 20cm.
Translated from the *Journal of Discourses*, V.7, p. 22–38.
Title in English: Similarity between evidences for Bible and Book of Mormon.
CtY

6539. ———. (same) Kjobenhavn, Utgivet af forlagt af J. Van Cott. Trykt hos F. E. Bording, 1860.
22p. 21½cm.
UHi, USIC

6540. ———. (same, under title) Sammanliking mellan beviserna for Bibelen och Mormons Bok. Tale of Äldste Orson Pratt. Köpenhamn, Utgifwen och förlaggd af C. Widerborg. Tryckt hos F. E. Bording, 1866.
22p. 21cm.
UHi, USIC

6541. ———. (same) Kjøbenhavn, C. G. Larsen. Trykt hos F. E. Bording, 1873.
1p.l. [3]–20p. 22cm.
Binder's title: Sma skrifter.
CDU, CtY, UPB, USIC

6542. ———. A Series of pamphlets by Orson Pratt, one of the Twelve Apostles of the Church of Jesus Christ of Latter-day Saints. With portrait to which is appended a discussion held in Bolton, between Elder William Gibson, President of the Saints in the Manchester Conference, and the Rev. Mr. Woodman. Also a discussion held in France between Elder John Taylor, one of the Twelve Apostles, and three Reverend Gentlemen of different orders, containing a facsimile of writings engraved on six metallic plates taken out of an ancient mound in the state of Illinois, in the year 1843. Liverpool, Published by Franklin D. Richards, 1851.

PRATT, O.

Various pagination. 23cm.
Contents: No. 1. Divine Authority, or the question Was Joseph Smith sent of God? 16p.; No. 2. The kingdom of God, Part I, 8p.; No. 3. The Kingdom of God, Part II, 8p.; No. 4. The Kingdom of God, Part III, 8p.; No. 5. The Kingdom of God, Part IV, 16p.; No. 6. Remarkable visions, 16p.; No. 7. New Jerusalem or, the fulfilment of Modern Prophecy, 24p.; No. 1. Divine authenticity of the Book of Mormon, 16p.; No. 2. Divine authenticity of the Book of Mormon, 17–32p.; No. 3. Divine authenticity of the Book of Mormon, 33–48p.; No. 3. Divine Authenticity of the Book of Mormon, [49]–64p.; No. 5. Divine authenticity of the Book of Mormon, [65]–80p.; No. 6. Divine authenticity of the Book of Mormon, [81]–96p.; Reply to a pamphlet printed at Glasgow, with the "Approbation of clergymen of different denominations," entitled "Remarks on Mormonism," 16p.; Absurdities of immaterialism, or, A reply to T. W. P. Taylder's pamphlet, "The materialism of the Mormons or Latter-day Saints, examined and exposed," 32p.; Great first cause, or the self-moving forces of the Universe, 16p.
Printed by R. James.
Originally published as separate pamphlets. A title page, table of contents, and a portrait of Orson Pratt were published, and the work bound in an official press binding of ¾ embossed leather, stamped O. Pratts Works, &c. The title page, table of contents and portrait were apparently also sold for individual binding. These bindings have other portraits and variant tracts.
CSmH, CtY, CU–B, DLC, ICN, MH, NN, UHi, UPB, ULA, USIC, UU, WHi

6542a. ———. (same) Liverpool: Printed by R. James, 39 South Castle Street, 1851.
Various pagination. 23cm.
A variant printing of the title page and table of contents.
UPB, USIC

6543. ———. (same) Liverpool: Published by Franklin D. Richards, 1852.
24 pamphlets. 21cm.
UPB, USIC

6544. ———. A series of pamphlets on the doctrines of the gospel by the late Elder Orson Pratt . . . Salt Lake City, The Juvenile Instructor office, 1884.
[3]–314p. 19cm.
CSmH, CU–B, DLC, MdBP, MH, NjP, NN, OCl, OO, USIC

6545. ———. (same) Salt Lake City, G. Q. Cannon and Sons Co., 1891.
[3]–314p. 18½cm.
CSmH, CU–B, ICU, MH, MiU, NjP, NN, UHi, ULA, USl, USIC, UU

6546. ———. (same) Chattanooga, Tenn., Printed for the Southern States Mission, 1899.
284p. 18cm.
CSmH, MH, OCl, UHi, USIC

6547. ———. Spiritual gifts. Liverpool . . . London: L.D.S. Book and Star Depot, 1856.
[65]–80p. 21½cm.
At head of title: Chapter V.
Some copies are found in printed wrappers.
Originally designed as part of a projected book but issued separately.
MH, ULA, UPB, USIC

6548. ———. [Tracts] by Orson Pratt, one of the Twelve Apostles of the Church of Jesus Christ of Latter-day Saints and President of said Church throughout Great Britain and all European Countries. Liverpool, 42 Islington. London: L.D.S. Book and Star Depot, Aug. 25, 1856–March 15, 1857.
128p. in 8 pts. 21½cm.
Published separately, some with and without paper wrapper.
Contents: 1. The true faith; 2. True repentance; 3. Water baptism; 4. The Holy Spirit; 5. Spiritual gifts; 6. Necessity for miracles; 7. Universal apostacy in the seventeenth centuries of darkness; 8. Latter-day kingdom, or, The preparations for the second advent.
Published in chapters to be made into a book. Title page to be added later.
MH, NjP, ULA, UPB, USIC

6548a. ———. (same, in Danish) [Tracts] [Kjobenhavn? ca. 1860]
140p. 20cm.
Contents: 1. Om sand tro. 2. Om sand omvendelse. 3. Vand-daaben. 4. Den hellig-aand. 5. Aandelige gaver. 6. Nodvendigheden af mirakler. 7. Det almindelige frafald. 8. Guds rige i de sidste dage.
USIC

6549. ———. The True faith. Liverpool . . . London: L.D.S. Book and Star Depot, 1856.
16p. 21½cm.
At head of Title: Chapter I.
Some copies are found in printed wrapper.
Originally designed as part of a projected book but issued separately.
MH, ULA, UPB, USIC

6550. ———. True Repentance. Liverpool . . . London: L.D.S. Book and Star Depot, 1856.
[17]–32p. 21½cm.
At head of title: Chapter II.
Originally designed as part of a projected book but issued separately.
MH, ULA, UPB, USIC

6551. ———. Universal apostacy, or the seventeen centuries of darkness. Liverpool . . . London: L.D.S. Book and Star Depot, 1857.
[97]–112p. 21½cm.
At head of title: Chapter VII.
Originally designed as part of a projected book but issued separately.
MH, ULA, UPB, USIC

———. Visions of Joseph Smith the Seer . . .
See Smith, Joseph, 1805–1844.

PRATT, O.

———. Was Joseph Smith sent of God?
See his Divine Authority.

6552. ———. Water baptism. Liverpool . . . London: L.D.S. Book and Star Depot, 1856.
[33]–48p. 21½cm.
At head of title: Chapter III.
Some copies have printed wrappers.
Originally designed as part of a projected book but issued separately.
MH, ULA, UPB, USlC

6553. Pratt, Parley Parker. An address by a minister of the Church of Jesus Christ of Latter-day Saints, to the people of England. [Manchester? Printed by W. R. Thomas, 61, Spring Gardens, 1840]
4p. 20cm.
Caption-title.
Dated at end: Manchester, May 18, 1840, Parley P. Pratt.
USlC

6554. ———. (same) [Manchester, 1840]
4p. 20cm.
Dated at the end: May 28, 1840.
CSmH, CtY, NjP, UPB, USlC

6555. ———. (same) [Manchester, 1840]
4p. 19cm.
Variant edition, not dated or signed.
NN

6556. ———. (same) Bristol, Reprinted by James Jones on the Weir [1841?]
4p. 17cm.
Caption-title.
CSmH

6557. ———. An address by a minister of the Church of Jesus Christ of Latter-day Saints. To the people of the United States. [New York? 184–]
4p. 16½cm.
Caption-title.
Printed on back: "In the city of New York, our meetings are held at National Hall."
Textually similar to his: An address by a minister of the Church of Jesus Christ of Latter-day Saints, to the people of England.
Sabin 50726
CSmH, CtY, ICN, NN, USlC, WHi

6558. ———. (same) [Philadelphia, 1843?]
4p. 19cm.
List of books at end indicates that it is later than the above. At end it announces meetings in Philadelphia, whereas earlier version above announces meetings at New York.
USlC

———. An address to the citizens of Washington . . .
See Higbee, Elias.

6559. ———. The Angel of the prairies; a dream of the future by Elder Parley Parker Pratt . . . Salt Lake City, A. Pratt, Publisher, 1880.
2p.l. [5]–24p. 16½cm.
Printed by Deseret News Printing and Publishing Establishment.
MH, MoInRC, NjP, NN, UHi, UPB, USl, USlC

6560. ———. The angel of the prairies by Parley P. Pratt. Salt Lake City, Abinadi Pratt, 1880.
20p. 22½cm.
CSmH, NjP, UHi, USlC

6561. ———. An answer to Mr. William Hewitt's tract against the Latter-day Saints . . . by Parley P. Pratt. Manchester, Printed by W. R. Thomas . . . 1840.
12p. 20cm.
CU–B, USlC

6562. ———. An apostle of the Church of Jesus Christ, of Latter-day Saints, was in the Island of Great Britain, for the Gospel's sake . . . and being in the Spirit on the 21st of November, A.D. 1846, addressed the following words of comfort to his dearly beloved wife and family dwelling in tents in the Camp of Israel . . . at Council Bluffs, Missouri Territory, North America; where they and twenty thousand others were banished by the civilized Christians of the United States, for the word of God and the testimony of Jesus. Liverpool, Printed by Br. J. B. Franklin, 1846.
Broadside. 42½×23cm.
Gold printing on blue coated paper, within border.
Letter in blank verse.
Variant copy, black on white. USlC
MH, USlC

6563. ———. An appeal to the citizens of the Empire State. By an exile of Missouri. A letter to Queen Victoria. The fountain of knowledge. Immortality of the material body. Intelligence and affection. By P. P. Pratt. Milwaukee, W. T. Courier print. [1841]
23p. 23cm.
Howes P555
CtY, MoInRC

6564. ———. An appeal to the inhabitants of the State of New York, Letter to Queen Victoria. (Reprinted from the Tenth European Edition) The fountain of knowledge: immortality of the body, and intelligence and affection. By Parley Parker Pratt. Nauvoo, Ill., John Taylor, Printer [1844]
1p.l., 40p. 22cm.
Published in January, 1844. For authorship, *see his Autobiography*, p. 330. Reviewed in *Times and Seasons*, March 15, 1844, p. 472.
Byrd 891
CSmH, CtY, USlC

6565. ———. The autobiography of Parley Parker Pratt, one of the Twelve Apostles of the Church of Jesus Christ of Latter-day Saints, embracing his life, ministry and travels, with extracts in prose and verse from his miscellaneous writings. Edited by his son, Parley P. Pratt. Illustrated. Sold only by subscription. New York, Published for the Editor and Proprietor by Russell Brothers, 1874.
502, xp. illus., plates, ports. 22½cm.
Howes P556, Sabin C64964
CSmH, CtY, DLC, MH, MoInRC, NjP, UHi, UPB, USl, USlC, UU

6566. ———. (same) Chicago, Published for Pratt Bros., by Law, King & Law, 1888.
502, xp. illus., plates, ports. 22½cm.
CSmH, CtY, MH, NN, UHi, UPB, USlC, WaPS, WHi

6567. ———. Dialogue between a Latter-day Saint and an enquirer after truth. (Reprinted from the Star of January 1) To which is added, A Solemn warning to the Methodists. By one who was formerly a preacher among them. Manchester, Published by P. P. Pratt [1842]
4p. 21cm.
Letter on p.4 dated December 30th, 1841, and signed by Thomas Smith.
MH, UPB, USlC

6568. ———. A dialogue between Joe. Smith and the devil! [New York? Prophet Office? 1845]
12p. 18cm.
For authorship, *see his Autobiography*, p. 330.
Proving the truthfulness of Mormonism.
Includes: A dialogue between Tradition, reason, and scriptus.
Published in two variant editions. Later printing has "Josh" Smith in title.
CSmH, USlC

6569. ———. (same) [Liverpool? 1846?]
16p. 21cm.
Cover-title.
Published in two variant editions.
CtY, ICN, MH, MoInRC, NN, UHi, UPB, USlC

6570. ———. (same) From the New York Herald, 1844. Logan, Utah, Smith and Stratford, Book and Job Printers, 1882.
1p.l., 9p. 19cm.
CSmH, NN, UPB, USlC

6571. ———. (same) Salt Lake City, Jos. Hyrum Parry & Co., 1884.
19p. 20cm.
CSmH, CU-B, UPB

6571a. ———. (same) Salt Lake City, Jos. Hyrum Parry & Co., 1886.
21p. 19cm.
USlC

6572. ———. (same) [n.p., n.d.]
14p. 20cm.
No indication as to possible date or place of publication.
USlC

6573. ———. Ett tal af Parley P. Pratt. [Salt Lake City, Korrespondenten, 1893?]
24p. 14cm.
Title in English: One speech of Parley P. Pratt.
UPB

6574. ———. An exile of Missouri. Nauvoo, Ill., 1844.
42p.
No copy located. There is strong doubt that the pamphlet ever existed.
Howes P557

6575. ———. Facts for the times; one hundred years hence. 1945. [n.p., n.d.]
[5]–8p. 19cm.
"From the *Nauvoo Neighbor*."
An apocryphal dream.
USlC

6576. ———. (same, under title) One hundred years hence, 1845–1945. By Parley P. Pratt. [n.p., n.d.]
[8]p. 14cm.
"Reprinted from the *Millennial Star*," V.6, p. 140.
USlC

6576a. ———. (same, under title) A vision. One hundred years hence, 1845–1945. [n.p., n.d.]
4p. 20cm.
"The above is taken from the '*Millennial Star*,' V. VI, pages 140–142, and was formerly published in the '*Nauvoo Neighbor*,' p. 4."
UPB

6577. ———. Farewell hymn. Sung at a General Conference in New York, when six Elders of the Church, of the Latter-day Saints, were about to take their departure for England. [n.p., n.d.]
Broadside. 18½×11½cm.
Listed for sale at the Southby's Auerbach sale.

6578. ———. Farewell song. By P. P. Pratt. Sung at the General Conference of the Latter Day Saints, in the City of New York, as six of their Elders, viz: B. Young, H. C. Kimball, O. Pratt, G. A. Smith, R. Hadlock, and P. P. Pratt, were about to sail for Europe. They took passage on board the Ship Patrick Henry, for Liverpool, and sailed on 7th March, 1840. [n.p., n.d.]
Broadside. 25×19½cm.
On yellow paper.
USlC

PRATT, P. P.

6579. ———. Good tidings; or, the new and everlasting gospel. [Liverpool, Printed and Published by Joseph F. Smith at the Latter-day Saints "Millennial Star" Office, 186–]
4p. 23cm.
Caption-title.
Signed: P. P. Pratt.
CtY, NjP, UPB

6580. ———. (same) [Liverpool, Printed and Published by Joseph F. Smith at the Latter-day Saints "Millennial Star" Office, 1874?]
4p. 21cm.
Caption-title.
Signed: P. P. Pratt.
CSmH, MH, USIC, UU

6581. ———. The great contrast! Or, The Doctrines of Christ, and False Doctrines of the Nineteenth Century. [Liverpool, Printed and Published by Joseph F. Smith, at the Latter-day Saints — "Millennial Star" Office, 1875?]
4p. 22½cm.
Caption-title.
Extracted from chap. VII of his *A voice of warning.*
CSmH, CtY, MH, UHi, UPB, UU

6582. ———. History of the late persecution inflicted by the State of Missouri upon the Mormons, in which ten thousand American citizens were robbed, plundered, and driven from the State, and many others imprisoned, martyred, &c., for their religion, and all this by military force, by order of the executive. By P. P. Pratt, Minister of the gospel. Written during eight months imprisonment in that state. — "Great is the truth, and it will prevail." Detroit, Dawson & Bates, Printers, 1839.
v [7]–84p. 22cm.
Also published under title: Late persecutions . . .
Howes P558
CtY (defective), USIC

6583. ———. (same) Mexico, N. Y., Re-printed at the office of the Oswego Co., Democrat, 1840.
39 [1]p. 21cm.
Cover-title.
Extant in two variant states.
Howes P558, Sabin 64965
MH, OClWHi, UPB, USIC, WHi

6584. ———. (same, under title) Late persecution of the Church of Jesus Christ of Latter-Day Saints. Ten thousand American citizens robbed, plundered, and banished; others imprisoned, and others martyred for their religion. With a sketch of their rise, progress and doctrine. By P. P. Pratt, Minister of the Gospel: Written in Prison. New York, J. W. Harrison, Printer, 1840.
xx [21]–215p. 16cm.
Howes P558, Sabin
CSmH, CtY, DLC, ICN, ICU, MH, MoKU, NN, OClWHi, UPB, USl, USIC, UU, WHi

6585. ———. Key to the science of theology: designed as an introduction to the first principles of spiritual philosophy; religion; law and government; as delivered by the ancients, and as restored in this age, for the final development of universal peace, truth and knowledge. By Parley P. Pratt . . . Liverpool, F. D. Richards; [etc., etc.] 1855.
2p.l. [vii]–xv, 173p., [1]l. 19½cm.
Sabin A64966
CSmH, CtY, CU–B, DLC, MH, MoInRC, NjP, NN, UHi, UPB, USIC, UU, WHi

6586. ———. (same) [2d ed.] Liverpool, G. Q. Cannon, London. L.D. Saints' Book Depot, 1863.
2p.l. [vii]–xv, 173p. front. 19cm.
UPB, USIC, UU

6587. ———. (same) 3d ed. Salt Lake City, Deseret News Steam Printing Establishment, 1874.
xv, 178p. 18cm.
CU–B, DLC, MoInRC, MWA, NjP, NN, UHi, ULA, USIC, UU

6588. ———. (same) 4th ed. Liverpool, Published by A. Carrington; London, Latter-day Saints' Book Depot, 1877.
2p.l. [v]–xv, 182p. front. 19cm.
CSmH, UHi, UPB, USIC, UU

6589. ———. (same) 4th ed. Salt Lake City, Deseret News Co., 1883.
2p.l. [5]–162p. front. 15½cm.
CU, NjP, NN, USIC

6590. ———. (same) 5th ed. Liverpool, John Henry Smith, 1883.
2p.l. [v]–xv, 182p. 18½cm.
DLC, NN, OCl, OClWHi, OO, ULA, UU

6591. ———. (same) 5th ed. Salt Lake City, G. Q. Cannon and Sons Co., 1891.
2p.l. [v]–xv, 182p. front. 18cm.
ICU, MH, MiU, NjP, NN, PPL–R, UPB, ULA, USIC, UU

6592. ———. (same) 5th ed. Salt Lake City, Deseret News Publishing Co., 1893.
2p.l. [5]—162p. front. 16cm.
IWW, MH, MoInRC, NjP, NN, ODW, PCC, PPPrHi, USIC

6593. ———. (same) 7th ed. Salt Lake City, The Deseret News, 1915.
2p.l. [5]–159p. front. 16cm.
CSmH, CU–B, MB, NN, UHi, UPB, USIC

6594. ———. (same, in Dutch) Sleutal voor de wetenschop der godgeleerdheid. Bestemd als eene inleiding tot de eerste beginselen van geestelyke wysbegeerte, godsdienst, wet en bestuur als gegeven door de ouden en als birsted in deze eeuw voor de volkomen ontwikkeling von algemeene vrede, waarheid en kennis Door Parley P. Pratt, Uit het Engelsch vertaald door Wm. J. de Brig. Rotterdam, Gedrukt op Last Van Fred. Pieper, 1897.
viii, 99 [2]p. 21½cm.
MiU, UHi, USl

6595. ———. (same, in German) Schlüssel zur Gottes-Gelehrtheit . . . beabsichtigt für eine Einleitung zu den ersten Grundsätzen geistiger Philosophie, Religion, und Gesätze wie den Alten geoffenbaret wurden und in diesem Zeitalter wiederhergestellt für die Hervorbringung der Wahrheit, Kenntnis, und endlich allgemeiner Friede. Übersetzt aus dem Englischen. Berne, Herausgegeben von Geo. C. Naegle, 1895.
4p.l. [3]–99p. 20½cm.
CSmH, UPB, UU

6596. ———. (same, under title) Schlussel zur Gottesgelehrtheit. Von Apostel Parley P. Pratt. Bern, Druck von Steiger & Cie., 1895.
99p. 20½cm.
UPB

6596a. ———. Het koningrijk Gods, or: de leer der menschen vergeleken bij de leer van Christus. Door Parley P. Pratt. (Uit het Engelsch). [Amsterdam, ca. 1883]
24p. 19½cm.
Title in English: The Kingdom of God.
USlC

6596b. ———. (same) [Groningen, Netherlands] J. W. F. Volker [ca. 1887]
24p. 21½cm.
USlC

6596c. ———. (same) [Amsterdam?] Geo. S. Spencer [ca. 1896]
15[1]p. 21cm.
USlC

———. Late persecution of the Church of Jesus Christ of Latter-Day Saints. *See his History of the late persecution.*

6597. ———. A letter to the Queen, touching the signs of the times, and the political destiny of the World . . . Manchester, Printed and Published by P. P. Pratt . . . 1841.
12p. 20cm.
Included in his: An appeal to the inhabitants of the state of New York. Nauvoo [1844]
Signed at end: Manchester, May 28, 1841.
CtY, CU–B, USl, USlC

6598. ———. (same) Second edition. — Sixth thousand. Manchester, Printed and Published by P. P. Pratt, 1841.
12p. 17cm.
CU–B, UPB, USlC

6598a. ———. (same, under title) A letter to the Queen of England, touching the signs of the times, and the political destiny of the world. By P. P. Pratt. Manchester, Eng. [New York?] 1841.
15p. 16½cm.
Typographical comparison as well as the alteration of the title suggest that it was printed in New York rather than Manchester.
USlC

6599. ———. Marriage and morals in Utah. An address by P. P. Pratt read in joint session of the legislature in the Representatives' Hall, Fillmore City, Dec. 31, 1855, by Mr. Thomas Bullock, chief clerk of the house. Liverpool, Orson Pratt; London, L.D.S. Book & Star Depot . . . 1856.
8p. 22cm.
"Reprinted from the *Deseret News.*"
Published also with title: Scriptural evidences in support of polygamy.
USlC

6599a. ———. (same) Liverpool, F. D. Richards [and] London, L.D.S. Book and Star Depot, 1856.
8p. 21cm.
CSmH, CU–B, CtY, MH, NN, UHi, UPB, USlC, UU

6600. ———. (same, in Danish) Aegteskab og Saeder i Utah. (Fra " Deseret News.") En adresse, skreven af Aeldste Parley P. Pratt og laest i den forende Session af hr. Thomas Bulluck, husets Over-Secretair i Repraesentanternes hal, Fillmore den 31te December 1855. Forsamlingen bevidnede Forfatteren deres Tak ved et eenstemmigt Votum, og ved et signende Votum forordnede de Adressen optaget i " Deseret News." (Anden Udgave.) Kjøbenhavn, Udgivet af Hector C. Haight. Trykt hos F. E. Bording. 1856.
16p. 22½cm.
CSmH, CtY, MnU, UPB, UHi, USlC, UU

6601. ———. (same) Köbenhavn, Udgivet af C. G. Larsen, Trykt hos F. E. Bording, 1874.
16p. 21½cm.
USlC

6602. ———. (same) Fjerde udgave. Kjøbenhavn, Utgivet af N. C. Flygare. Tryckt hos F. E. Bording, 1876.
16p. 21cm.
USlC

PRATT, P. P.

6603. ———. (same) En Adresse, skreven af Aeldste Parley P. Pratt og laest i den forenede Session af Hr. Thomas Bulluck, Husets Over-Sekretaer i Representanternes Hal, Fillmore, den 31te December 1855. Forsamlingen bevidnede Forfatteren sin Tak ved et enstemmigt Votum of ved et lignende Votum forordnedes Adressen optaget i "Deseret News" [Femte Udgave] Kjøbenhavn, Udgivet af N. Wilhelmsen. Trykt hos F. E. Bording, 1880.
16p. 22cm.
Binder's title: Sma Skrifter.
CDU, CtY, UPB, USlC

6604. ———. (same) Sjette udgave. Kjøbenhavn, Udgivet og forlagt af C. D. Fjeldsted. Trykt hos F. E. Bording, 1882.
16p. 22½cm.
UPB, USlC

6605. ———. (same) . . . Sjette udgave. Kjøbenhavn, Udgivet og forlagt af C. D. Fjelsted. Trykt hos F. E. Bording [n.d.]
16p. 21cm.
Variant without date of 6604.
USlC

6606. ———. (same, in French) Mariage et Moeurs à Utah, par P.-P. Pratt. Genève, Publié par J.-L. Smith, reu de Gendrier, n. 108, 1857.
16p. 24cm.
USlC

6607. ———. The Millennial hymns of Parley Parker Pratt. Edited and compiled by Samuel Russell. Cambridge, The University Press, 1913.
46p. 23cm.
Contains 50 numbers.
CSmH, CU–B, ICN, MH, NjP, NN, RPB, UHi, UPB, USlC, UU

6608. ———. The Millennium, a poem. To which is added hymns and songs on various subjects new and interesting, adapted to the dispensation of the fulness of times. Boston, Printed for Elder Parley P. Pratt, 1835.
52p. 14½cm.
DLC, USlC

6609. ———. The millennium and other poems: To which is annexed, a treatise on the regeneration and eternal duration of matter. By P. P. Pratt, Minister of the Gospel. New York, Printed by W. Molineux, MDCCCXL [1840]
iv, [2]l., 148p. 19cm.
CSmH, DLC, MH, NN, RPB, USlC, UU, WHi

6610. ———. "Mormonism!" "Plurality of wives!" An especial chapter, for the especial edification of certain inquisitive news editors, etc. San Francisco, July 13th, 1852. [San Francisco? 1852]
Broadside. 28×19cm.
Defense of polygamy.
Broadside printed in San Francisco, July 13, 1852. The facsimile in the Bancroft Library was taken from a copy once owned by Mrs. R. H. Stanley.
USlC

6611. ———. Mormonism unveiled: Zion's Watchman unmasked, and its editor, Mr. L. R. Sunderland, exposed: Truth vindicated: the devil mad, and priestcraft in danger! By P. P. Pratt, Minister of the gospel . . . New-York: Printed for the publisher, 1838.
47p. 19½cm.
Eberstadt copy sold to Irving W. Robbins, is in yellow paper wrappers which advertise Pratt's *Voice of warning*, 216p. and *Poem on the Millennium*, 52p.
CtY, OClWHi, UPB, USlC

6612. ———. (same) Second edition. New York, Published by O. Pratt & E. Fordham, 1838.
47 [1]p. 19½cm.
[1]p. "A lamentation on taking leave of New York." By P. P. Pratt. P. 4 misnumbered 34.
Howes P559
CtY, MH, MoInRC, UPB, USlC imperfect

6613. ———. (same) Third edition. New York, Published by O. Pratt & E. Fordham, 1838.
47 [1]p. 18cm.
Howes P559
CU–B, MH, USlC

6613a. ———. (same) Re-printed for Wm. D. Pratt. Painesville Ohio. 1838.
45p. 18cm.
A poem, signed Olumbian Bard, New York, March 23, 1838, by a man unconnected with the "L.D. Saints" was added while the pamphlet was at the press.
UPB

6614. ———. (same) Fourth edition. New York, Joseph W. Harrison, Printer, 1842.
47 [1]p. 15cm.
Cover-title: Pratt's reply to LaRoy Sunderland.
Howes P559
CtY, MoInRC

———. One hundred years hence.
See his Facts for the times.

6615. ———. Plain facts, showing the falsehood and folly of the Rev. C. S. Bush, (a church minister of the parish of Peover) being a reply to his tract against the Latter-day Saints. Manchester, Printed by W. R. Thomas [1840]

16p. 19½cm.
Caption-title.
For authorship, *see his Reply to Mr. Thomas Taylor*, p.7.
CSmH, CtY, CU-B, NN, UHi, UPB, USlC

6616. ———. Proclamation! Extraordinaria, para los Americanos Espanoles par Parley P. Pratt . . . Proclamation extraordinary! to the Spanish Americans. San Francisco, Monson, Haswell & Co., 1852.
18p. 21cm.
Cover-title.
Double columns, English and Spanish. Written at Valparaiso, Chile, Jan. 1852.
Attacks the Roman Catholic Church and explains the doctrines of the Mormon Church.
Title in English: Proclamation. Extraordinary, for the Spanish Americans.
CSmH, CtY, USlC

6617. ———. Proclamation! To the people of the coasts and islands of the Pacific; of every nation, kindred and tongue. By an apostle of Jesus Christ [Signed:] Parley P. Pratt, president of the Pacific mission of the Church of Jesus Christ of Latter-day Saints. Published for the author, by C. W. Wandell, [Sydney, New South Wales] William Baker, Printer, Hibernian Press [1851]
16p. 21cm.
Caption-title.
First Australian Mormon imprint.
CSmH, CtY, CU-B, ICN, NN, UPB, USlC

6618. ———. Proclamation of the Gospel. Extracted from a work by Parley P. Pratt, an apostle of Jesus Christ. Now re-published by Richard Ballantyne, Presiding Elder of the Mission of the Church of Jesus Christ of Latter-day Saints, to Madras, and surrounding Country. Also a short account of the rise and progress of this Church . . . Madras [S. Bowie, Printer, 1853?]
8p. 21cm.
Caption-title.
CU-B, UPB, USlC

———. Proclamation of the Twelve Apostles. *See Church of Jesus Christ of Latter-day Saints. Council of the Twelve Apostles.*

6619. ———. Prospectus of the Latter-day Saints Millennial Star. Manchester, W. R. Thomas, 1840.
Broadside. 28×22cm.
Text within a printed border.
USlC

6620. ———. Repent! Ye people of California! for, know assuredly, the Kingdom of God, has come nigh unto you. [San Francisco, 1854]
Broadside. 17½×22½cm.
Text printed on the right side of the sheet in a 11cm. column.
USlC

6621. ———. A reply to Mr. Thomas Taylor's "Complete failure," &c., and Mr. Richard Livesey's "Mormonism exposed." By Parley P. Pratt. Manchester [Eng.] Printed by W. R. Thomas, 1840.
12p. 19cm.
CSmH, CtY, CU-B, DLC, MH, NN, UPB, USlC, UU

6622. ———. Scriptural evidences in support of polygamy: being an address entitled Marriage and morals in Utah . . . and a protestant minister's arguments from the Bible in favor of polygamy. Extracted from the work of Rev. D. O. Allen. San Francisco, George Q. Cannon, 1856.
24p. 22½cm.
Howes P560
CSmH, CtY, USlC

6623. ———. A short account of a shameful outrage, committed by a part of the inhabitants of the Town of Mentor, upon the person of Elder Parley P. Pratt, while delivering a public discourse upon the subject of the gospel; April 7th, 1835. [Kirtland? 1835?]
11p. 19cm.
USlC

6624. ———. Scriptural communication. A discourse delivered by Parley P. Pratt, at Great Salt Lake City, April 7, 1853. San Francisco, 1853.
8p. 21½cm.
CtY, USlC

6625. ———. Scriptural communication; a sermon delivered by Elder P. P. Pratt, Senr. before the Conference at Salt Lake City, April 7, 1853. [Salt Lake City? 1853?]
8p. 23cm.
Caption-title.
MH, USlC

6626. ———. Truth defended, or, a reply to the "Preston Chronicle," and to Mr. J. B. Rollo's "Mormonism exposed." Extracted from the Millennial Star for July, 1841 . . . Manchester, Printed and Published by P. P. Pratt, 1841.
8p. 21cm.
CtY, UHi, USlC

6627. ———. A voice of warning and instruction to all people, containing a declaration of the faith and doctrine of the Church of the Latter-Day Saints, commonly called Mormons. By P. P. Pratt . . . New-York, Printed by W. Sandford, 1837.
x [11]–216p. 15½cm.
Sabin B64971
CtY, CU-B, DLC, ICN, MB, OClWHi, UPB, USlC, WHi

PRATT, P. P.

6628. ———. (same, under title) A voice of warning, and instruction to all people, or An introduction to the faith and doctrine of the Church of Jesus Christ, of Latter-day Saints. By P. P. Pratt . . .
2d ed., rev. New-York, J. W. Harrison, Printer, 1839.
viii [9]–216p. 15½cm.
On verso of title page is a $300.00 challenge which does not appear in other editions.
Sabin A64972
CSmH, CtY, CU–B, DLC, ICHi, MH, NjP, NN, OClWHi, PCC, UPB, USlC, WHi

6629. ———. (same) 1st European from the 2d American ed. Manchester, Eng., W. Shackleton & Son, Print., 1841.
xi, 12–228p. 16cm.
ICHi, NjPT, NN, OClWHi, UHi, USlC, UU, WHi

6630. ———. (same) 3d ed., rev. New York, J. W. Harrison, Printer, 1842.
vi [7]–180p. 15cm.
Sabin 64972
DLC, MH, NN, PHi, UHi, UPB, USlC, UU

6631. ———. (same) 3d [i.e. 4th] American ed. Nauvoo, Printed by J. Taylor, 1844.
x [11]–284p. 15cm.
Byrd 892, Sabin 64972
CSmH, CtY, DLC, ICHi, ICN, MH, MWA, NN, UHi, UPB, USl, USlC

6632. ———. (same) 6th ed. Edinburgh, H. Armour, 1847.
viii, 136p. 15cm.
Preface to the Second European, or Edinburgh edition dated: Manchester, December 4, 1846, which speaks of five editions since 1837; also preface by T. D. Brown, Liverpool, February 13, 1847. USlC also has (lacking t.p.) this text in larger format [xi] 171p. 17½cm., omitting the preface by T. D. Brown. This might be the 5th ed., 1846. In green cloth binding, gold-stamped title.
CtY, IWW, OClWHi, UHi, UPB, USlC

6633. ———. (same) 7th ed. Liverpool, F. D. Richards; London, Sold at Latter-day Saints' Book Depot, 1852.
xiv, 166p. 15cm.
Sabin 64972
MH, NjP, RPB, UHi, UPB, USlC

6634. ———. (same) 8th ed. Liverpool, F. D. Richards; London, Sold at the Latter-day Saints' Book Depot, 1854.
xvi, 199p. 15cm.
Sabin 64972
CSmH, CtY, DLC, ICN, MB, MH, NjP, UHi, UPB, USlC, UU

6635. ———. (same) Revised edition. Plano, Ill., Published by the Reorganized Church of Jesus Christ of Latter Day Saints, 1863.
2p.l., 5–256p. 13cm.
Sabin 64972
CSmH, IHi, NjP, NN, UPB, USlC

6636. ———. (same) 9th ed. Liverpool, Brigham Young Jr., 1866.
3p.l. [v]–xvi, 199p. 14cm.
CU–B, NN

6637. ———. (same) 2d rev. ed. Plano, Ill., Published by the Reorganized Church of Jesus Christ of Latter Day Saints, 1867.
2p.l. [5]–256p. 12½cm.
UHi

6638. ———. (same) 10th ed. Liverpool, H. S. Eldridge; London at the L.D. Saints' Depot, 1871.
2p.l. [v]–xvi, 199p. 13cm.
NjP, UPB, USlC, UU

6639. ———. (same) (Revised) . . . Plano, Ill., Printed and Published by the Reorganized Church of Jesus Christ of Latter Day Saints, 1872.
73 [1]p. 22cm.
"Epitome of the faith and doctrines of the Reorganized Church of Jesus Christ of Latter Day Saints," 1p.
CSmH, MH

6640. ———. (same) 9th American ed. Salt Lake City, Deseret News Steam Printing Establishment, 1874.
2p.l. [v]–xi, 171p. 18cm.
Sabin 64972
CtY, CU–B, NjP, NjPT, NN, UPB

6641. ———. (same) Plano, Ill. [Reorganized Church of Jesus Christ of Latter Day Saints, 1875]
66p. 18cm.
MoInRC

6642. ———. (same) [5th ed.] Plano, Ill., Board of Publication of the Reorganized Church of Christ, 1877.
2p.l. [5]–125p. 18cm.
CU–B, UPB

6643. ———. (same) 11th ed. Salt Lake City, Deseret News Co., Printers and Publishers, 1881.
2p.l. [5]–258p. 13½cm.
CU–B, MWA, OO, ULA, UPB, USlC, UU, ViU

6644. ———. (same) 11th ed. Liverpool, A. Carrington, 1881.
xvi, 199p. 14cm.
CU–B, NjP, WHi

PRATT, P. P.

6645. ———. (same) Also, an analysis of Isaiah 29. Rev. ed. Lamoni, Ia., Reorganized Church of Jesus Christ, 1883.
126p. 17cm.
MoInRC

6646. ———. (same) Rev. ed. Lamoni, Ia., Reorganized Church of Jesus Christ of Latter Day Saints [1884]
149p. 18cm.
Seventh RLDS ed.
MoInRC

6647. ———. (same) [7th ed.] Lamoni, Ia., Reorganized Church of Jesus Christ of Latter Day Saints, 1886.
149p. 17cm.
OClWHi, UHi, USlC, WHi

6648. ———. (same) Liverpool, Published and for sale by George Teasdale, 1887.
xiv, 199p. 14cm.
CSmH, DLC, OO, USlC

6649. ———. (same) 12th ed. Salt Lake City, The Deseret News Co., 1887.
2p.l. [5]–258p. 13cm.
UHi, UPB, USlC

6649a. ———. (same) Thirteenth (Stereotyped) edition. Liverpool: Published and for sale by George Teasdale, 42, Islington, 1889.
xvi, 199p. 13½cm.
USlC

6650. ———. (same) 13th (stereotyped) ed. Salt Lake City, G. Q. Cannon and Sons Co., 1891.
2p.l. [v]–xvi, 220p. 14cm.
ICN, MB, MH, MiU, NN, OClWHi, UPB, USlC

6651. ———. (same) 14th (stereotyped) ed. Liverpool, Published and for sale by Brigham Young, 1891.
2p.l., v–xvi, 199p. 13cm.
UPB

6652. ———. (same) 13th ed. Salt Lake City, The Deseret News Publishing Co., 1893.
2p.l. [5]–258p. 14cm.
ICN, IU, NjP, OClWHi, UHi, UPB, USlC

6653. ———. (same) Revised. Also an analysis of Isaiah 29 . . . Lamoni, Ia., Printed and Published by the Reorganized Church of Jesus Christ of Latter Day Saints, 1893.
2p.l., 5–149p. 16cm.
NjP, NN

6654. ———. (same) Electrotype ed. Chattanooga, Tenn., Southern States Mission, 1896.
xvi, 218p. 13cm.
USlC, ViU

6655. ———. (same) Kansas City, Mo., 1896.
220p. 13cm.
NjP, OO

6656. ———. (same) Electrotype ed. Chattanooga. [Church of Jesus Christ of Latter-day Saints] Southern States Mission, 1897.
xv, 221p. 13cm.
WHi

6657. ———. (same) 15th (stereotyped ed.) Liverpool, Published and for sale by Rulon S. Wells, 1898.
xvi, 199p. 13½cm.
NjP, UHi, USlC

6658. ———. (same) Chicago, Ill., The Northern States Mission [1899?]
xvi, 220p. 13cm.
UPB

6659. ———. (same) Lamoni, Ia. [Reorganized Church of Jesus Christ of Latter Day Saints] 1900.
149p. 18cm.
MoInRC, OClWHi

6660. ———. (same) Kansas City, Mo., South-western States Mission [1901]
xii, 222p. 13cm.
USlC

6661. ———. (same) Revised. Also an analysis of Isaiah 29. Lamoni, Ia., Printed and Published by the Reorganized Church of Jesus Christ of Latter Day Saints, 1902.
149p. 17½cm.
An analysis of Isaiah 29 by Jason W. Briggs, p. 119–127, and Joseph Smith, a prophet of God by W. W. Blair, p. 128–149.
USlC

6662. ———. (same) 16th (stereotyped) ed. Liverpool, Published and for sale by Francis M. Lyman, 1902.
xvi, 199p. 13cm.
UPB, USlC

6663. ———. (same) 17th stereotyped [ed.] Liverpool, Published and for sale by Francis M. Lyman, 1902.
xvi, 199p. 13cm.
UPB, USlC

6664. ———. (same) Cincinnati, Middle States Mission, 1902.
221p. 13cm.
OClW

PRATT, P. P.

6665. ———. (same) Electrotype edition. Cincinnati, Ohio, Published and for sale by the Middle States Mission, 1903.
xv, 221p. 13cm.
UPB

6666. ———. (same) Kansas City, Mo., Published and for sale by the Southwestern States Mission [ca. 1903]
xvi, 220p. 13cm.
Printed label with new imprint: Published and for sale by the Southwestern States Mission.
USlC

6667. ———. (same) Chicago, Published and for sale by Northern States Mission of the Church of Jesus Christ of Latter Day Saints, 1904.
xvi, 220p. 13cm.
USlC

6668. ———. (same) Chicago, Ill., Published and for sale by Northern States Mission [ca. 1905]
xvi, 220p. 13cm.
USlC

6669. ———. (same) Chattanooga, Tenn., 1905.
xv, 221p. 13cm.
OClWHi, USlC

6670. ———. (same) 17th (stereotyped) ed. Liverpool, Millennial Star Office, 1907.
xvi, 199p. 13cm.
CU–B

6671. ———. (same) Liverpool, Printed and Published by the Millennial Star Office, 1909.
xvi, 199p. 13cm.
UPB, USlC

6672. ———. (same) 15th ed. Salt Lake City, The Deseret News, 1909.
xvi, 220p. 13cm.
UPB

6673. ———. (same) New York, Eastern States Mission [1911]
xvi, 220p. 13cm.
NN, UU

6674. ———. (same) [Chicago] The Northern States Mission [1911]
xvi, 220p. 13cm.
NN, UU

6675. ———. (same) 16th ed. Salt Lake City, Published and for sale by the Deseret Book Co., 1920.
xvi, 220p. 13½cm.
UPB, UHi, USlC

6675a. ———. (same) Independence, Reorganized Church of Jesus Christ of Latter Day Saints, 1924.
149p. 19½cm.
Same as their 1902 edition.
USlC

6676. ———. (same) Independence, Mo., Zion's Printing and Publishing Co. [1925?]
1p.l. [3]–128p. 18cm.
USlC

6677. ———. (same) Independence, Mo., Zion's Printing and Publishing Co. [1926?]
1p.l. [3]–128p. 18cm.
USlC

6678. ———. (same) Independence, Mo., Zion's printing and publishing Co., Published by the Mission of the Church of Jesus Christ of Latter-day Saints in America, 1928.
1p.l. [3]–125p. 18½cm.
"Edition of September, 1928."
NN, UPB, USlC

6679. ———. (same) Independence, Mo., Zion's Printing and Publishing Co. [1928]
1p.l. [3]–128p. 18cm.
UPB

6680. ———. (same, in Danish) En advarsels røst og underviisning for alle folk, eller, en indledning til troen og laerdommene i Jesu Christe Kirke af Sidste Dages Hellige, af Parley P. Pratt . . . oversat fra 6th Edinbinger udgave. Kjøbenhavn, Udgivet og forlagt af John Van Cott. Trykt hos F. E. Bording, 1855.
xii, 161 [1]p. 16cm.
USlC

6681. ———. (same) Kjobenhavn, Udgivet og forlagt af Hector C. Haight. Trykt hos F. E. Bording, 1856.
xiii, 190p. 16½cm.
NjP, NN, USlC

6682. ———. (same) Tredie Udgave. Kjobenhavn, Udgivet og forlagt af John Van Cott. Trykt hos F. E. Bording, 1861.
xv, 221 [1]p. 16cm.
NjP, UHi, USlC, UU

6683. ———. (same) Tredie Udgave. En forbedret Oversaettelse efter 8de Edinburghste Udgave. Kjobenhavn, Udgivet og forlagt af D. N. Liljenquist. Trykt hos F. E. Bording, 1876.
xv, 211 [1]p. 16½cm.
USl, USlC

6684. ———. (same) Fjerde Udgave. Kjobenhavn, Udgivet og forlagt af D. Fjeldsted. Trykt hos F. E. Bording (B. Petersen) 1890.
xii, 201p. 16½cm.
UPB, USlC

PRATT, P. P.

6685. ———. (same) Femte udgave. København, Udgivet og forlagt af Andreas Peterson. Trykt hos J. D. Qvist & Komp (A. Larsen) 1900.
x, 170p. 16½cm.
USlC

6686. ———. (same) Sjette udgave. Kobenhavn, Udgivet og forlagt af Martin Christophersen, 1913.
x, 170p. 16½cm.
UHi, USlC

6687. ———. (same, in Dutch) Eene stem tot Waarschuwing en leering voor alle Volkeren, of eene inleiding tot geloof en de leer der Kerk van Jezus Christus, der heiligen der Laatste Dagen door Parley P. Pratt . . . Naar het Engelsch uit het hoogdiutsch vertaald door S. Van Dijk. Eerste Uitgave, door voormelde Kerk. Amsterdam, Gedrukt bij W. J. de Roever, Kröber, 1866.
xii, 164p. 17cm.
USlC

6688. ———. (same) . . . door Parley P. Pratt, uit he Engelsch vertaald door J. W. F. Volker. Tweede Nederlandsche uitgave. Amsterdam, I. Bremer, 1889.
xviii, 231p. 13cm.
UHi

6689. ———. (same) Derde verbeterde druk. Rotterdam, Uitgegeven door Jacob H. Trayner, 1905.
x, 290p. 13½cm.
UPB, USlC

6690. ———. (same) Opnieuw uit het Engelsche vertaald, door B. Tiemersma. Vierde druk. Rotterdam, Uitgigeven door Le Grand Richards . . . 1915.
xii, 124p. 13½cm.
USlC

6691. ———. (same) Vijfde druk. Rotterdam, Uitgegeven door John P. Lillywhite, 1922.
xi, 224p. 31cm.
USlC

6692. ———. (same, in French) Une Voix d'Advertissement. Et instruction a trous les peuples. Au Introduction a la doi aux Doctrines de l'Église de Jésus-Christ des Saints des Derniers-jours. Par Parley P. Pratt. Traduit de la sixième édition anglaise par L. A. Bertrand, et publié par A. L. Lamoreaux. Jersey, Imprime par G. Romeril . . . 1853.
xxi, 180p. 14cm.
MH, USlC, UU

6693. ———. (same) Et publié par Ernest Rossiter. Liege [ca. 1902]
ix, 150p. 16½cm.
ULA, UPB, USlC

6694. ———. (same) Et publié par Levi Edgar Young. Neuchatel [Suisse] Imprimerie L. A. Borel, 1904.
ix, 150p. 16½cm.
CSmH, UHi, UPB, USlC, UU

6695. ———. (same) Liege, Publié par Ernest Rossiter [ca. 1927]
ix, 150p. 16cm.
USlC

6696. ———. (same, in German) Eine Stimme der Warnung und Belehrung für alle Völker oder eine Einleitung zu dem Glauben und den Lehren der Kirche Jesu Christi, der Heiligen der letzten Tage. von Parley P. Pratt . . . Erste Ausgabe. Aus dem Englischen übersetzt von Daniel Carn. Hamburg, Gedruckt bei F. H. Nestler und Melle, 1853.
ix, 124p. 15cm.
USlC

6697. ———. (same) Aus dem Englischen übersetzt von Daniel Carn. Zweite deutsche Auflage. Bern, herausgegeben und zu bestehen von der Schweiz. und Deutschen Mission der Kirche Jesu Christi der Heiligen der letzten Tage, 1873.
xii, 164p. 16½cm.
UPB, USlC

6698. ———. (same) Dritte deutsche Auflage. Herausgegeben und zu beziehen von der schweizerischen und deutschen Mission der Kirche Jesu Christi der Heiligen der letzten Tage. Berne, Suter und Lurow, 1892.
2p.l. [5]–144p. 19cm.
MH, UHi, UPB, USl, USlC, UU

6699. ———. (same) Vierte deutsche Auflage. Herausgegeben und zu beziehen von der schweizerischen und deutschen Mission der Kirche Jesu Christi der Heiligen der letzten Tage. Berlin, Hermann Dusedann, 1901.
2p.l. [5]–144p. 19cm.
UHi, UPB, UU

6700. ———. (same) Sechste Auflage. Basel, Herausgegeben von Serge F. Ballif, Präsident der Schweizerischen und Deutschen Mission der Kirche Jesu Christi der heiligen der letzten Tage, 1921.
138p. 19cm.
UPB

6701. ———. (same) Siebente Auflage. Basel, Herausgegeben von Serge F. Ballif, 1923.
1p.l. [3]–136p. 18½cm.
NjP, UPB, USlC

6702. ———. (same, in Icelandic) Advörunar og sannleiks-raust um höfadatridi truar "Jesu Kristi kirkju of sidustu daga heilögum" Samin af Thordi Didrikssyni Kaupmannahöfn, Utgefin af N. Vilhelmsen. Prentud hja F. E. Bording, 1879.
2p.l. [5]–165p. 17cm.
MH

6703. ———. (same, in Spanish) Voz de amonestacion e instruccion al pueblo o sea Introduccion a la fe y doctrinas de la Iglesia de Jesucristo de los Santos de los ultimos dias. la ed. Espanola Traducido por los elders, Trejo, Stewart y Rhodakancty. Mexico, Moises Thatcher, 1880.
3p.l. [vii]–viii, 128p. 16cm.
MH, NNC, USlC

6704. ———. (same) Por Parley P. Pratt. Segunda edicion Espanola. Traducido por los Elders, Trejo, Stewart y Rhodakancty. Mexico, Publicado por la Mision Mexicana, 1902.
202p. 14cm.
UPB

6705. ———. (same) Mexico, Publicado por la Mision Mexicana, los Elders, Trejo, Stewart y Rhodakancty. Mexico, Publicado por la Mision Mexicana, 1905.
202p. 14cm.
UPB

6706. ———. (same, under title) Una Voz de amonestacion e instruccion a todo pueblo o sea una introduccion a la fe y las doctrinas de la iglesia de Jesu Cristo de los Santos de los Ultimos Dias. Por Parley P. Pratt. Traducido por Elder Rey L. Pratt. El Paso, Texas, Publicado por la mision Mexicana de la Iglesia de Jesu Cristo de los Santos de los Ultimos Dias, 1922.
3p.l., 7–141 [1]p. 18cm.
UPB, USlC

6706a. ———. (same, in Swedish) En varande Röst och Undervisning för alla Menniskor eller Indledning till Tron och Läran i De sista Dagarnes Heliges Jesu Christi Kyrrka af Parley P. Pratt . . . Öfversatt från Engelskan. Köpenhamn. Utgifven och förlaggd af C. Widerborg. 1858. Tryckt hos F. E. Bording.
195p. 15½cm.
USlC

6707. ———. (same, under title) En warnande röst och undervisning för alla menniskor eller inledning till tron och läran i Jesu Christi Kyrka av attersta Dagars Heliga af Parley P. Pratt. Öfwersatt från Engelskan. Köpenhamn, Utgifwen och förlagd of W. W. Cluff, Trykt hos F. E. Bording, 1871.
xiii [15]–200p. 16½cm.
UHi

6708. ———. (same) Fjerde upplagan. Öfversatt från engelskan. Köpenhamn, Utgifven och förlagd af C. D. Fjeldsted. Tryckt hos F. E. Bording . . . 1881.
2p.l. [5]–210 [1]p. 16½cm.
UPB, USlC, UU

6709. ———. (same) Femte genomsedda upplagan. Öfversättning från engelskan. Kopenhamn, Utgifven och förlagt af N. C. Flygare, 1887.
213 [2]p. 17cm.
MH

6710. ———. (same) Sjette genomsedda upplagan . . . Öfversättning från Engelskan. Köpenhamn, Udgifven och förlagd af C. D. Fjeldsted, Andreas Peterson, 1900.
189 [2]p. 17cm.
NjP, UPB, USlC

6711. ———. (same) Stockholm, Peter Sundwall, 1908.
187 [4]p. 16cm.
UHi, USlC

6712. ———. What is "Mormonism?" Liverpool, Printed by J. Sadler [1845]
Broadside. 13×21cm.
Reprinted from the *Millennial Star.* V.VI, p.4.
Signed: Parley P. Pratt and Samuel Brannan, New York, April 6, 1845.
At end is a notice of L.D.S. meetings signed by Gland Rogers.
CtY

6713. ———. The world turned upside down, or Heaven on earth. The material universe is eternal. — Immortal man has flesh and bones. — Earth is his everlasting inheritance. — To this bear all the prophets and apostles witness; the physical worlds were not formed for annihilation, but for the pleasure of God they are and were created. By P. P. Pratt. [Liverpool] The Millennial Star Office, Printed by James and Woodburn [1842?]
iv [5]–25p.
Originally printed as part of *The Millennium* as a "treatise on the regeneration and eternal duration of matter." Its republication "corrected and revised" is announced in the *Millennial Star,* March, 1842, p.16.
MH, NN, UPB, USlC

6714. Pratt, Reba (Beebe) The Sheaf of a gleaner; poems. Nil desperandum. Salt Lake City, J. H. Parry, 1886.
x [2] 90p. port. 19cm.
Sketch of the author's life: p.v-x.
NjP, USlC, UU, WHi

6715. Pratt, Rey Lucero. Conocereis la verdad . . . y la verdad os libertara. [Salt Lake City? n.d.]
12p. 17cm.
"Articulos de fé" are included in the last page.
Title in English: You shall know the truth and the truth shall make you free.
UPB

6715a. ———. Evangelio Restaurado. Publicado por la mision Mexicana de la Iglesia de Jesucristo de los Santos de los Ultimos Días. Colonia del Valle [ca. 1915]
8p. 21½cm.
Title in English: Restored gospel.
USIC

6716. ———. Gran estreno Conferencias con vistas: Domingo 28 de Febrero de 1926 a las 20 horas Rivadavia 8972. Iglesia de Jesu Christo de los Santos de los Ultimos Días. El público cordialmente invitado. [Buenos Aires, 1926]
Broadside. 27½×21½cm.
Announcement of a Mormon meeting in Buenos Aires.
USIC

6717. ———. Just thinking, by Rey L. Pratt. Independence, Mo., Zion's Printing and Publishing Company [c1928]
3p.l., 9–96p. 19½cm.
Mormon poetry.
DLC, UHi, UPB, USIC, UU

6718. ———. Salvacion. [n.p.] Iglesia de Jesucristo de los Santos de los Ultimos Dias [n.d.]
20p. 17cm.
Title in English: Salvation.
USIC

6719. ———. (same) [n.p., n.d.]
20p. 17cm.
Variant printing.
UPB

Prayer, at the dedication of the Lord's House in Kirtland, Ohio. *See Doctrine and Covenants. Section 109.*

6720. Prentis, Noble Lovely. From a corner of Illinois. [n.p., 1880?]
13p. 18cm.
Includes a short section of Nauvoo and the type of emigrants that the Mormons recruited at that time.
UPB

6721. Prentiss, A., *editor.* The history of the Utah volunteers in the Spanish-American war, and in the Philippine Islands. A complete history of all the military organizations in which Utah men served. W. F. Ford, Publisher, A. Prentiss, Editor. [Salt Lake City, 1900]
xviiip. [1]l., 430p. plates, ports., map. 22½cm.
Includes Mormon biographies.
CSmH, CU-B, DLC, NjP, OClWHi, UHi, USl, USIC, UU

6722. Preparation News. Preparation, Monona Co., Iowa. January 3, 1855–1856?
1v. weekly. 46×31½cm.
Names changed in 1855 to *Preparation News* and *Ephraim's Messenger, Preparation City of Ephraim.*
Official organ of the "Congregation of Jehovah's Presbytry of Zion."
Morgan
MoInRC Ja24, N21, 1855. V.1 #4, 21.

6723. ———. Preparation News, and Ephraim's Messenger, Extra. Preparation, Monona Co., 1855.
2p. 46×31½cm.
Signed: Sept. 19, 1855.
Morgan
MoInRC

6724. Presbyterian Church in the U.S.A. Conditions in Utah. Some facts and figures. [Salt Lake City, 1826]
4p. 15½cm.
Brief statistical summary with "peculiar teachings of the Mormon Church."
ULA, USIC

6725. ———. Then and now. New York, Board of Home Missions of the Presbyterian Church, 1904.
[1]p. folded. 30½cm.
USIC

6726. ———. **Board of Home Missions.** Home Missions. Ninety-sixth [and ninety-seventh] annual report of the Board of Home Missions of the Presbyterian Church in the United States of America. New York, 1898–1899.
2v. 23½cm.
Many references to the Mormons and the Presbyterian work among them.
USIC

6727. ———. **Board of National Missions.** Mormon misgivings. "Mormon misgivings of the present day are but the logical result of a Mormonism that asks its people to believe the unbelievable." New York, Board of Missions, Presbyterian Church [1926?]
9p. 17½cm.
USIC, NN

6728. ———. **General Assembly.** Memorial of the General Assembly of the Presbyterian Church of the United States, on the subject of polygamy. [Washington, Govt. Print. Off.] 1882.
2p. 23cm. (U.S. 47th Cong. 1st Sess. Senate. Misc. Doc. No. 30)
In opposition to polygamy.
DLC, UU

6729. ———. Woman's Board of Home Missions. How to meet the Mormon Missionaries, by a Utah Worker. New York City, Literature Department of the Woman's Board of Home Missions of the Presbyterian Church [1902]
12p. 12cm.
"2d ed."
NN

6730. ———. In the providence of God . . . New York [n.d.]
[2]p. 14cm.
Asking for donations for their work against the Mormon Church, a treasonable organization. Includes list of board members.
NN

6731. ———. The Life of a Mormon girl. New York City, Literature Department of the Woman's Board of Home Missions of the Presbyterian Church, 1913.
20p. 12cm. (No. 334)
"6th ed."
NN

6732. ———. Mission day-schools among the Mormons. New York, Published by the Woman's Board of Home Missions of the Presbyterian Church in the U.S.A. [1903]
[6]p. 14cm. (No. 300)
"First ed."
USlC

6733. ———. Mormon Americans. [New York, 1907]
[4]p. 18cm. (No. 280)
USlC

6734. ———. Presbyterian missions in Utah: historical notes. [New York, The Evangelist Press, 1901]
16p. illus. 21cm.
NN, USlC

6734a. ———. Questions and answers on Mormonism. New York, Woman's Board of Home Missions of the Presbyterian Church in the U.S.A. [1912]
15[1]p. 15½cm. (No. 390)
Third edition.
USlC

6735. ———. Reasons why B. H. Roberts of Utah, should be expelled from the House of Representatives of the Fifty-sixth Congress. New York [ca. 1897]
[4]p. 28cm.
Printed in the form of a letter.
USlC

6736. ———. Tourists in Utah. [New York, Willett Press, n.d.]
[4]p. 15½cm.
How to expose Mormonism.
USlC

6737. ———. Woman's Executive Committee of Home Missions. Facts on Mormonism. New York [n.d.]
4 [2]p. 14cm.
USlC

6738. ———. Woman's Home Missionary Society. The Latter Day Saints of Mormonism. Canada, Woman's Home Missionary Society of the Presbyterian Church, 1912.
15p. 14cm.
Includes a letter from William Shearer exposing some evils of Mormonism.
NN

Presbytery of Utah. Christian fellowship.
See its Ten reasons why Christians cannot fellowship the Mormon church.

6739. ———. Mormon infidelity and polygamy. [London, George Stoneman . . . W. R. Bradlaugh, Anti-Infidel Tract Depot . . . 1900?]
8p. 18cm. (Bradlaugh's Anti-Infidel Tracts)
Reprinted from *The Anti-Infidel*, March and April, 1900.
MoInRC, USlC

6740. ———. . . . Mormonism; the religion of Joseph Smith . . . [London, W. R. Bradlaugh, 1896?]
2p. 19cm. (Anti-Infidel tracts. No. 23)
UHi

6741. ———. The Present situation in Utah. The relation of the U.S. to the Philippines — Paper passed by the Presbytery of Utah, August 29, 1898. [Salt Lake City, Kinsman Publishing Co., 1898]
8p. 12½cm.
MH, UHi

6742. ———. Ten reasons why Christians cannot fellowship the Mormon church. Salt Lake City, 1897.
12p. 14cm.
"Done by order of the Presbytery of Utah, April 8, 1897. Endorsed by the Congregational Association of Utah, October 14, 1897."
Earlier editions titled: Christian fellowship.
MH, NN, OCl, UPB, USl

6743. ———. (same) New York, League for Social Service, 1898.
14p. 15cm. (Social Service. Anti-Mormon series)
NjPT, NN, UPB, USlC

6744. ———. (same) 3d ed. [Salt Lake City, Utah, Kinsman Publishing Co., 1898?]
8p. 18½cm.
MH, USlC

6745. ———. (same) New York City, Home Missions of the Presbyterian Church [1911]
12p. 14½cm.
UPB, USlC

6746. ———. (same) New York, Woman's Board of Home Missions of the Presbyterian Church [1913]
12p. 14½cm.
NjPT, UPB, USlC

6746a. ———. (same) [Salt Lake City, Kinsman Publishing Co., n.d.]
12p. 14½cm.
USlC

6747. ———. (same) New York, Home Missions Council [191–]
14p. 14½cm.
MoInRC, OCl, USl

6748. ———. (same, under title) Christian fellowship. Ten reasons why Christians cannot fellowship the Mormon Church. [Salt Lake City? n.d.]
12p. 15½cm.
UPB

6749. ———. Ten reasons: being a statement why Christians cannot fellowship with Mormons. Issued by the Presbytery of Utah. [Pittsburgh, National Reform Association, 1921?]
16p. 15cm.
Issued by the Presbytery of Utah, and endorsed by the Baptist Association and Congregational Association of Utah, to which is attached an article from the *Christian Statesman*, of Oct. 1921, giving a review of the reply by Mormon Elder Brigham H. Roberts to the *Ten reasons.*
UPB, UU

6750. ———. (same) Issued by the Presbytery of Utah, in July, 1921, and endorsed by the Baptist Association and Congregational Association of Utah. To which is added an article from the Christian Statesman, of October, 1921, giving a review of the reply by Mormon Elder Brigham H. Roberts . . . [Pittsburg, The National Reform Association, 1921?]
15p. 14½cm.
Cover-title.
UHi

6751. ———. (same, under title) Ten reasons why Christians cannot fellowship the Mormon Church, and answer given by Brigham H. Roberts, Elder in the Mormon Church, with a rejoinder. New York, Home Missions Council, 1921.
38p. 21½cm.
B. H. Roberts' answer, p. 13–32.
MH, MoInRC, NjPT, NN, UPB

6752. Presset, Anne L. Cherished thoughts in original poems and sketches, by Anne L. Presset. Provo, Utah, The Skelton Publishing Company, 1901.
221 [1]p. port., plate. 20cm.
DLC, UHi, ULA, UU

Preston, John. *See Buschlen, John Preston.*

Preston, William Bowker.
See Wilson, Lycurgus Arnold.

6753. Preuss, Arthur. Dictionary of secret and other societies. Comprising Masonic rites, lodges, and clubs; concordant, clandestine, and spurious Masonic bodies . . . and many other organizations. Compiled by Arthur Preuss . . . St. Louis, B. Herder Book Co., 1924.
xi, 543p. 20½cm.
Mormonism listed as a Masonic society. Article gives a brief account of the temple service. Josephites another secret society. Also "Society of the Illuninati." (Strang)
CU, UPB, USlC

6754. Price, *Sir* Rose Lambart. The two Americas; an account of sport and travel. With notes on men and manners in North and South America. By Major Sir Rose Lambart Price, Bart. . . . Philadelphia, J. B. Lippincott & Co., 1877.
viii, 368p. front., plates. 21½cm.
His visit to Salt Lake City and his reaction to a Mormon sermon.
Another edition: 2d ed. London, S. Low, Marston, Searle & Rivington, 1877. UPB
CSmH, CU–B, IC, MBBC, MH, NjP, NN, OClW, OClWHi, PPL, PPM, PSC, UHi, USlC

6755. Priest, Josiah. American antiquities and discoveries in the West: Being an exhibition of the evidence that an ancient population of partially civilized nations differing entirely from those of the present Indians peopled America many centuries before its discovery by Columbus, and inquiries into their origin, with a copious description of many of their stupendous works now in ruins, with conjectures concerning what may have become of them. Compiled from travels, authentic sources, and the researches of Antiquarian Societies. By Josiah Priest. Second Edition Revised. Albany: Printed by Hoffman and White . . . 1833.
viii [9]–400p. illus., plates, fold. plans. 22cm.
Derisive reference to the Book of Mormon added to Second Edition Revised, p. 73. In the 4th ed. of 1834 the spelling of Mormon and Mormonite have been corrected. In the 5th ed. (1835) the reference is on p. 76.
Other editions: 3d ed. rev. 1933 CU, DLC, UPB; 4th ed. 1834. DLC, IU, UPB; 5th ed. 1835. DLC, CU, CU–B,, UPB; 5th ed. 1838. DLC, CU–B, UPB; 5th ed. Albany, Printed by J. Munsell, 1841. CU–B
CU, CU–B, DLC, UPB

Priesthood Journal. *See Unity.*

6756. Prieto, Guillermo. Viaje á los Estados-Unidos, por Fidel (Guillermo Prieto) (1877) Mexico, Impr. de Dublan y Chavez, 1877–78.
3v. illus., plates, ports. 22½cm.
Brief visit to Utah. Contains a letter concerning the Mormons.
Title in English: Trip to the United States.
Howes P607
CU–B, DLC, NN

PRIME, E. D. G.

6757. Prime, Edward Dorr Griffin. Around the world: sketches of travel through many lands and over many seas. By E. D. G. Prime . . . New York, Harper & Brothers, 1872.
xvi [17]–455p. illus. 21cm.
Trip through Salt Lake in 1869. Summarizes Mormonism as a system of love of power, avarice, and lust, p. 25–35.
Another edition: London, Sampson Low, Marston, Low, & Searle, 1872. USlC
DLC, MB, NjP, OCl, OClW, UHi, UPB, USlC, UU

6757a. Les principes fondamentaux de l'evangile de Jesus-Christ comme ils furent establis par lui-meme. Foi, Repentance, Bapteme, Don du St. Esprit, Autorite et Revelation. Rotterdam, Publie par Jacob H. Trayner [1905]
16p. 18cm. (Traite. No. 2)
USlC

6758. Pritchard, Harriet S. . . . The American harem. New York City [1913?]
14 [1]p. 15cm. (National Woman's Christian Temperance Union. Literature and Art leaflets. No. 7)
Lawlessness of the Mormons; polygamy since the Edmunds law and the manifesto.
UPB

Proceedings at the dedication of the Joseph Smith Memorial Monument. *See Smith, Joseph Fielding, 1876–1972.*

Proceedings in mass meeting . . . [protesting passage of the Cullom bill] *See Utah (Territory) Mormon Women. Proceedings in mass meeting . . .*

The proceedings of a convention . . .
See Carthage, Illinois. Convention, 1845.

6759. Proceedings of a meeting in honor of President Heber J. Grant's 70th birthday anniversary held in the Assembly Hall, Salt Lake City, Utah, Sunday, November 21st, 1926 under the auspices of Foreign Language Organizations of the Church of Jesus Christ of Latter-day Saints. [Salt Lake City, 1926]
18p. port. 22cm.
Cover-title.
USlC

6760. Profetiske vidnesbyrd. Er Aabenbaring nødvendig? København, Udgivet og forlagt af John S. Hansen . . . Trykt i "Aka" . . . 1925.
4p. 23cm.
Title in English: Testimony of a prophet.
USlC

6761. The Program. Lamoni, Ia., Reorganized Church of Jesus Christ of Latter Day Saints, 1895–1896.
3v. monthly.
MoInRC V.3, #1–9.

6761a. Program commemorating the one hundredth anniversary of the birth of the Prophet Joseph Smith, Sunday, December 24th, 1905. Salt Lake City [1905]
[4]p. 20½cm.
Under the auspices of the Liberty, Pioneer, Ensign, and Salt Lake Stakes.
USlC

6762. Program of the historical meeting in honor of Pres. Francis Marion Lyman, son of a Missouri pioneer. To be held January 12, 1914 at 7:30 P. M. Bishop's Building. [Salt Lake City] Magazine Printing Co. [1914]
[4]p. 17½cm.
Includes hymn "School thy feelings."
UPB, USlC

6763. Programme for the celebration of the 4th of July, in Great Salt Lake City, 1855. [Salt Lake City, 1855]
Broadside. 40×14cm.
Order of march & days activities.
USlC

6764. Programme of the celebration of the Fourth of July, 1856, and Grand Military review. [Great Salt Lake City, 1856]
Broadside. 28×21cm.
Text within border.
USlC

6765. Programme for the celebration of the Fourth of July, 1857. [Great Salt Lake City, 1857]
Broadside. 28×21cm.
UPB, USlC

6766. Programme for the Grand Jubilee Concert, to be held in the Large Tabernacle, on Friday, July 24th, 1885. [Salt Lake City? 1885]
[8]p. 19cm.
UPB, USlC

6767. Programme. Funeral of President John Taylor, Salt Lake City, July 29th, 1887. [Salt Lake City, 1887]
[3]p. 21½cm.
CSmH, NjP, UHi, UPB

6768. Programme of exercises, rendered by a solemn assembly, on Pioneer Day, in the large tabernacle, Salt Lake City, Commemorating the entrance of the pioneers into the Great Salt Lake Valley, July 24, 1847. [Salt Lake City] Deseret News Co., Printers [1886]
8p. 17cm.
Title in ornamental border.
At head of title: July 24, 1847. July 24, 1886.
NjP

6769. Programme of the singing exercises for the dedication of the Manti Temple. Monday, May 21st, 1888. [Manti? 1888]
[2]l. 18cm.
UPB

6770. Progressive Party. Utah. Utah's first Governor a progressive. [Salt Lake City, 191–]
[2]p. 23cm.
Brigham Young's political philosophy.
USIC

6771. Prominent educators in Utah and the Mormons; symposium of statements made during and immediately following the session of the National Education Association held at Salt Lake City, Utah, July 5–12, 1913. [Independence, Mo., Church of Jesus Christ of Latter-Day Saints, 1913]
[8]p. 18½cm.
Caption-title.
DLC, NjP, UHi, UPB

6772. The Prophet. New York, Society for the diffusion of Truth, May 18, 1844–May 24, 1845.
1v. (52 nos.) weekly. 56cm.
Succeeded by *New York Messenger* which continued its voluming.
Successive editors: William Smith, Sam Brannan, and Parley P. Pratt.
CtY # 1, 3, 5, 7, 9–10, 12–15, 17, 19–24, 26–35, 37–38, 40–52; MH, NN, USIC, WHi

6773. Prophwyd y Jubili, Neu Seren Y Saints. Merthyr-Tydfil, Wales, July, 1846–December, 1848.
3v. (32 issues) monthly. 18cm.
Published by Captain Dan Jones, July 1846–October 1848; John Davis, November and December 1848.
Official L.D.S. church organ in Wales.
Succeeded by *Udgorn Seion.*
Title in English: Prophet and jubilee, new star and saints.
CSmH, V.1 #1–6; CU–B, MH, NjP, UPB, USIC

6774. Protest från några av Förenta staternas senatorer mot "Mormon" förföljelserna samt ett brev från präster, representerande olika Kyrkosamfund i Saltsjöstaden, Utah . . . [Malmö, Tryckeri A.-B. Framtiden, 1922]
[4]p. 22½cm.
Extracts from *Anti-Mormon Slanders Denied* [by] the Commercial Club, Salt Lake City.
Title in English: Protests from some United States senators against Mormon persecutions . . .
USIC

6775. Protestant Press Bureau. Secrets of a Mormon's harem. Priest of polygamy who set traps for British Girls. [Ilford, Eng., Protestant Press Bureau, ca. 1929]
[4]p. 18½cm.
At head of title: Tract No. 30. Third edition.
NjP, UPB

6776. Provo. Chamber of Commerce. Provo; the Garden City of Utah. Its resources and attractions. Published under the auspices of the Chamber of Commerce. Omaha, Nebraska, D. C. Dunbar & Co., Publishers, 1888.
2p.l. [5]–47p. illus., ports. 22cm.
Early history of Provo and biographies of important residents.
CtY, CU–B, NjP

6777. Prudhommeaux, Jules Jean. Histoire de la communauté icarienne, 8 février, 1848, 22 octobre 1898: contribution à l'étude du Socialisme expérimental. Nimes, Impr. "La Laboriense" 1906.
xxv p. [1]l., 48 [1]p. 21cm.
Many brief references to Mormonism and the founding of Nauvoo; the Icarian purchase of Nauvoo.
Title in English: History of the Icarian community.
Howes P643
DLC

6778. ———. Icarie et son fondateur, Étienne Cabet; contribution à l'étude du socialisme expérimental, par Jules Prudhommeaux . . . Ouvrage illustré de 12 photogravures, 1 facsimile et 2 cartes. Paris, É Cornély & Cie, 1907.
xi p., [1]l., 688p., [1]l. illus., port., plates, maps. 22½cm.
Many references to the Mormon period at Nauvoo.
Title in English: Icarie and its founder.
DLC, NjP

6779. Pryse, Robert John. Hanes y Brytaniaid a'r Cymry, yn Wladol, Milwrol, Cymdeithasol, Masnachol, Llenorol, a Chrefyddol, o'r Amseroedd boreuaf hyd yn Bresennol. Llundain, Caerlleon, ac Abertawy, William Mackenzie [1873–6]
2v. 28cm.
Reference to Mormonism, V.2, p.528. Brief account of how Mormonism was introduced; Joseph Smith's vision, etc. Also Brigham Young and the introduction of Mormonism into Wales.
Title in English: History of the Brittons and the Welsh.
UPB

6780. Purple, Samuel Smith. In memoriam. Edwin R. Purple. [Edwin Ruthuin Purple] Born, 1831. Died, 1879. New York, Priv. print., 1881.
12p. port. 27½cm.
Description of the Mormon trail from Los Angeles to Salt Lake City, 1861; the Mountain Meadows massacre, p. 6–7.
CU–B, DLC, UPB

6781. Putnam, C. E. Unbiblical Mormon doctrines. [Randleman, North Carolina, Pilgrim Tract Society, 191–]
16p. 16cm.
An answer to John Morgan's *The Plan of Salvation.*
IWW

6782. Pyper, George Dollinger. The romance of an old playhouse, by George D. Pyper. Salt Lake City, The Seagull Press, 1928.
342p. illus., col. front., facsims., plates, ports. 23cm.
The story of the Salt Lake theatre.
CSmH, CU–B, DLC, NjP, OU, UHi, ULA, USI, USIC, UU

Figures of The Past

From the Leaves of Old Journals.

BY

JOSIAH QUINCY,
(Class of 1821, Harvard College).

BOSTON:
ROBERTS BROTHERS.
1883.

Item 6787. Josiah Quincy's recollections, including those of his visit to Joseph Smith in Nauvoo, Illinois, in 1844. From the University of Utah collection.

QUACK, H. P. G.

6783. Quack, Hendrik Peter Godfried. De Socialisten. Personen en stelsels. Amsterdam, P. N. van Kampen & Zoon, 1875–97.
4v. 23cm.
V.3, p. 343–50 has information on the Icarians at Nauvoo, with reference to the Mormons.
Title in English: The socialists and their systems.
CU

6784. ———. (same, under title) De Socialisten personen en stelsels door Mr. H. P. G. Quack. Zesde deel vierde druk. In de tweede helft der negentiende eeuw tweede gedeelte met register over zes Deelen. Amsterdam, P. N. Van Kampen & Zoon, 1923.
3p.l., 549p. 22½cm.
De Mormonen. p. 185–188. In a section on North American socialism. Brief history of Mormonism in Utah, its socialistic problems, including polygamy.
USIC

Quad. M. [*pseud.*] *See Lewis, Charles Bertrand.*

6785. Quaife, Milo Milton. The kingdom of Saint James; a narrative of the Mormons, by Milo M. Quaife . . . New Haven, Yale University Press; London, Humphrey Milford, Oxford University Press, 1930.
5p.l., 284p. plates, port., facsims. 23½cm.
"Sources of information:" p. 184–194.
Study of James J. Strang.
CSmH, CtY, CU–B, DLC, ICHi, ICN, MoInRC, NjP, UHi, ULA, UPB, USl, USIC, ViU, WHi

6786. Quigley, Hugh. The Irish race in California, and on the Pacific coast . . . by Dr. Quigley . . . San Francisco, A. Roman & Co., 1878.
xxxiii, 548, vi [1]p. 21½cm.
"Utah Territory," p. 544–546. "Irish do not join the Mormon church."
CU–B, NjP, UHi

6787. Quincy, Josiah. Figures of the past from the leaves of old journals, by Josiah Quincy . . . Boston, Roberts Brothers, 1883.
1p.l. [v]–vii, 404p. 18½cm.
Includes reminiscences of a visit to Joseph Smith at Nauvoo in 1844.
CSmH, CU, MH, NjP, NN, PHi, UHi, ULA

6788. ———. (same) 2d ed. Boston, Roberts Brothers, 1883.
1p.l. [v]–viii, 404p. 18½cm.
MH, MWA

6789. ———. (same) 3d ed. Boston, Roberts Brothers, 1883.
1p.l. [v]–viii, 404p. 19cm.
MH

6790. ———. (same) 4th ed. Boston, Roberts Brothers, 1883.
1p.l. [v]–viii, 404p. 19cm.
UPB

6791. ———. (same) 5th ed. Boston, Roberts Brothers, 1883.
1p.l. [v]–viii, 404p. 18cm.
MH, UU

6792. ———. (same) 6th ed. Boston, Roberts Brothers, 1884 [c1883]
1p.l. [v]–viii, 404p. 19cm.
MoInRC, NjP, OO, PCS, USIC

6793. ———. (same) [7th ed.] Boston, Roberts Brothers, 1888 [c1883]
1p.l. [v]–viii, 404p. 18½cm.
NjN

6794. ———. (same) 8th ed. Boston, Roberts Brothers, 1892.
1p.l. [v]–viii, 404p. 19cm.
MH

6795. ———. (same) 9th ed. Boston, Roberts Brothers, 1896.
1p.l. [v]–viii, 404p. 18½cm.
MH, NNU–W, PP, UU, ViU

6796. ———. (same) Boston, Roberts Brothers, 1901.
1p.l. [v]–viii, 404p. 19cm.
Another edition: Boston, Little, Brown, & Co., 1901. NjP, USIC
ODW, PPRCl, USIC

6797. ———. (same) Illustrated from old prints and photographs by Josiah Quincy, with an introduction and notes by M. A. De Wolfe Howe. A new ed. Boston, Little, Brown, and Company, 1926.
xvi, 347p. illus., plates, ports, facsims. 22½cm.
DLC, ICJ, MB, NjP, OO, ViU, WaU

6798. ———. A statement from Josiah Quincy, Mayor of Boston, 1845–1849 concerning an exterview had in 1844 with Joseph Smith the Mormon prophet. Some of the sayings and predictions made by the Prophet Joseph Smith. A letter to Mr. Wentworth from the Prophet in answer to a request from him for a statement . . . New York, Eastern States Mission [1882?]
32p. 18cm.
MoK, NjP, USIC

6799. Quincy, Ill. Citizens. Public meeting, September 22 [1845. Quincy, Ill., 1845]
Broadside. 34×16½cm.
Signed: Archibald Williams, Wm. H. Bennison, Sec'y.
Resolution concerning removal of Mormons from Illinois.
USIC

QUINDELIV

6800. ———. Public meeting of the citizens of Quincy! A public meeting will be held this evening at the court house for the purpose of devising ways and means for permanent relief of the distress existing among the strangers who have lately been driven from Missouri known as the "Latter day Saints," and for affording them immediate aid, as their wants are pressing. February 28, 1839. [Quincy, 1839]

Broadside. 19×14cm.

Byrd 482

ICHi

———. Military Committee. The proceedings of a convention . . . *See Carthage, Illinois. Convention, 1845.*

6801. Quincy Daily Herald. . . . Joe and Hiran [sic] Smith are dead! [Quincy, Ill., 1844]

Broadside. 46½×15cm.

At head of title: Extra, Friday morning, 5 o'clock.

Includes a statement by Governor Ford to the people of Illinois.

Byrd 893

ICHi, USlC

6802. Quindeliv blandt Mormonerne. Erindringer fra et fleeraarigt ophold i Mormonstaten, nedskrevne af en fra Utah tilbagevendt Mormon-praests kone. Kobenhavn, 1855.

444p.

Title in English: Life of Women among Mormons.

Schmidt.

6803. Quinland; or, Varieties in American life. London, R. Bentley, 1857.

2v. 20cm.

A novel with mention of the gold rush and Mormonism. Learns of the new Bible and meets a Mormon who speaks in tongues.

DLC, MH

6804. Quist, Eli N. Mormonism under the searchlight. [Salmon, Idaho, Idaho Recorder, c1915]

[24]p. 19½cm.

Cover-title.

WHi

ORATION

DELIVERED

BY MR. S. RIGDON,

ON

THE 4th OF JULY,

1838.

AT FAR WEST, CALDWELL COUNTY, MISSOURI.

Better far sleep with the dead, than be oppressed among the living.

FAR WEST:
PRINTED AT THE JOURNAL OFFICE.

1838.

Item 7284. Sidney Rigdon's inflammatory oration that aroused local Missourians and contributed to the expulsion of the Mormons from the state.
From the P. Crawley collection.

R., *Mrs.* **G. S.** Mysteries of the Endowment . . .
See Salt Lake Tribune.

6805. R., W. Methodism priestcraft exposed: or, who is the devil in the pulpit? . . . By W. R. Sydney: Published by the author [185–]

20p. 19½cm.

A defense of Mormon beliefs and an attack on the more traditional Christian beliefs as exemplified in Methodism.

USIC

6805a. R., W. P. My diary during a foreign tour, in 1881–2. Birmingham, England, Charles Cooper and Company, Ltd., 1886.

2p. l, iii, 263p. 19cm.

Impressions of Salt Lake City, p. 239–241.

UPB, USIC

6806. Die Rache des Mormonen. [Berlin, Berliner Roman-Verlag, n.d.]

48p. 18½cm. (Intime Geschichten. No. 6)

Title in English: The Vengeance of the Mormons.

Fiction concerning Mormonism.

USIC

6806a. ———. (same) [Berlin, Verlagshaus für Volksliteratur und Kunst, n.d.]

32p. 21½cm. (Texas Jack 'Der grosse Kundschafter.' Nr. 42)

USIC

6807. Racovita, Elena (von Dönniges). Von Anderen und mir. Erinnerungen aller Art von Helene von Racowitza. (Frau von Schewitxch.) Mit qwei Bildern in Lichtdruck. Berlin, Verlag von Gebrüder Paetel, 1909.

vii, 311p. ports. 24cm.

Title in English: From others and myself.

UPB

6808. ———. (same, in English) Princess Helene Von Racowitza, an autobiography; authorized translation from the German, by Cecil Mar. New York, The Macmillan Company, 1910.

xiii, 420 [1]p. port. 24cm.

Trip to Salt Lake City in 1877 at the time of the death of Brigham Young. The Church was established by "John" Smith.

Another edition: London, Constable and Company, 1910. CU–B

CU, CU–B, DLC

6809. Rader, Perry Scott. The civil government of the United States and the State of Missouri, and the history of Missouri from the earliest times to the present. Columbia, 1898.

4p.l., 427p. illus., maps. 20cm.

Includes an account of the Mormon period.

Several later editions.

DLC, UHi

6810. Rae, William Fraser. Westward by rail: the new route to the East. By W. F. Rae. London, Longmans, Green, and Co., 1870.

xiv, 391p. 20½cm.

The second edition (1871) has subtitle: "A journey to San Francisco and back and a visit to the Mormons." It also has a new introductory chapter. He stayed in Salt Lake City for a few weeks in 1869 and used this as the basis of a series of letters on Mormonism.

Other editions: London, 1871. CU–B; New York, D. Appleton & Co., 1871. CU, USIC

CU–B, DLC, MB, MiU, NjP, NN, ODa, PSC, ULA, UPB

6811. Raeder, Ole Munch. America in the forties; the letters of Ole Munch Raeder, translated and edited by Gunnar J. Malmin. Minneapolis, Published for the Norwegian-American Historical Association by the University of Minnesota Press [c1929]

xxi p. [1]l., 244p. port. 23cm.

Mention of Mormons during the Nauvoo and the migration periods.

DLC, NjP, ULA, UPB

6812. Rains, Fanny L. By land and ocean; or, The Journal and letters of a young girl who went to South Australia with a lady friend, then alone to Victoria, New Zealand, Sydney, Singapore, China, Japan, and across the continent of America home. By Fanny L. Rains . . . London, Sampson Low, Marston, Searle, & Rivington, 1878.

vi [2]l., 250p. front. 19cm.

A visit to Salt Lake City in the 1870's. A description of Temple Square and the meeting which she attended.

USIC

6813. Rally to the Polls! Freemen of Pottawatamie County!! Tuesday, September 24, 1850. Kanesville, Frontier Guardian Office, 1850.

Broadside. 32×25cm.

Politics in Iowa during the Mormon period.

USIC

6814. Ralph, Julian. Our great West; a study of the present conditions and future possibilities of the new commonwealths and capitals of the United States. New York, Harper & Brothers, 1893.

xi [1], 477 [1]p. illus., maps. 23cm.

Some chapters previously published in *Harper's Magazine* and *Harper's Weekly.*

"A week with the Mormons." Character of the Mormons, p. 391–416.

DLC, NjP, UHi, ULA, UPB, USIC

6815. Randall, Emilius O. History of Ohio . . . by Emilius O. Randall and David J. Ryan. Cincinnati, 1912–1915.

6v. plates, ports. 25cm.

V. 3 includes a chapter on the Mormons in Ohio.

Another edition: New York, The Century History Co., 1912. DLC, NjP

MoInRC, NN

6816. Rannie, Edward. The Church of Jesus Christ. Independence, Mo., Ensign Publishing House [n.d.]
26p. 15½cm.
Restoration and reorganization.
MoInRC

6817. ———. Good news; a brief history of Latter-day Saints. Independence, Mo., Ensign Publishing House [n.d.]
16p. 18cm.
MoInRC, USl

6818. ———. Marvelous manifestations of God's power in the Latter Days. Compiled by Elder Rannie. Independence, Mo., Ensign Publishing House [n.d.]
73p. 20cm.
Instances of RLDS faith healing.
MoInRC

6819. ———. (same) Independence, Mo., Ensign Publishing House, Reorganized Church of Jesus Christ of Latter Day Saints, 1903.
2p.l. [3]–92p. front. 15½cm.
MoInRC, UU

6820. Rapp, Wilhelm. Illustrierte Geographie von Nord- und Sud-Amerika nach den neusten und besten Quellen bearbeitet . . . Philadelphia, 1855.
390p. 28cm.
Contains an account of the Mormons in Nauvoo and Utah, p. 233–237.
Title in English: Illustrated geography of North and South America.
Sabin 67918
ICHi

6821. Rasmussen, Søren. Søndagsskolens vejleder og hjaelper i Korlaesning m.m. til Brug i de Sidste-Dages Helliges Søndagsskoler i Skandinavien. Udgivet og forlagt af Søren Rasmussen . . . Aarhus, P. S. Christiansen, 1908.
28p. 18cm.
Title in English: A guide to Sunday School.
NjP, USlC

6822. Raumer, Friedrich Ludwig Georg von. America and the American People. By Friedrich Von Raumer, professor of history in the University of Berlin, &c., &c. Translated from the German by William W. Turner. New York: J. & H. G. Langley, 8 Astor House, 1846.
xii [13]–502p. 28cm.
Mention is made of the Mormons, p. 256, 326, 334–336. Raumer visited the eastern United States in the spring and summer of 1844.
Another edition: New York, 1846. NjP
CtY, CU, ULA, WHi

6823. ———. Die Vereinigten Staaten von Nordamerika . . . Leipzig: F. A. Brockhous, 1845.
2v. front., fold. map, fold. tables. 17×10½cm.
A brief summary of Mormonism taken chiefly from James Hunt's *History of the Mormons.*
In Dutch under title: De Vereenigde Staten van Noord-Amerika. CU–B V.2, DLC
Title in English: The United States of North America.
Another edition: Genève, 1845. NjP
DLC

6824. Te Ravea no te ora. Papeete, Tahiti, 1897.
16p. 24cm.
Title in English: The way of life.
USlC

6825. Rawlins, Joseph Lafayette. Admission of Utah. Speech of Hon. Joseph L. Rawlins, of Utah, in the House of Representatives, Tuesday, December 12, 1893. Washington, 1893.
23p. 23cm.
Concerning polygamy and statehood.
UPB, USlC

6826. Raymond, Rossiter Worthington. Mineral resources of the states and territories west of the Rocky mountains. Washington, Govt. Print. Off. 1869.
iv, 256p. maps, tables. 23cm.
Section on Utah, p. 168. Mentions a talk in which Brigham Young stated that he wished the mines were opened but not by Mormons.
Sabin 28065
DLC, NjP, UHi, ULA, UPB

6827. Raymond and Whitcomb. [Tours, New York, 1880–1910]
approx. 12×14cm.
During the 30 year period this firm sponsored railroad tours to various parts of the United States. In many of these tours, Salt Lake City and Utah were included and basic information concerning Mormon buildings was given. The most familiar sections appearing in the various guides were "Utah" "Salt Lake City" "Great Salt Lake" "Over the Wahsatch Range." Some of the tours which included these are as follows:
Grand tour through the sunny south, Mexico and Calif. 1887. 144p. CSmH
A winter in California. 1894. 175p. CSmH, CU–B
The Grand Cañon, California and Alaska, 1909. 80p. CSmH
Grand tour across the continent. 1884. 80p. CSmH
Two grand tours of 75 days through the Southern states. 1891. 192p. CSmH
Fifth annual series of spring excursions to Colo. and Calif. 1885. 80p. CSmH
A Winter trip to California. 1883. 64p. CSmH
6th Annual series of spring tours through Colo. and Calif. 1886. 80p. CSmH, CU–B
Three spring and early summer tours. [1898] 192p. CSmH, CU–B
Two grand tours through the southern states. 1899. 172p. CSmH
The Grand tour of 75 days through the Southern States. 1894. 192p. CSmH

A series of summer and autumn tours to Alaska, Colorado, Utah, The Yellowstone National Park, etc. 1895. 192p. NN

A series of summer and autumn tours to the Yellowstone, etc. 1893. CSmH

Two grand tours of 74 days and 81 days. 1893. CU–B

6828. Read, George Willis. A pioneer of 1850 George Willis Read 1819–1880. The record of a journey overland from Independence, Missouri, to Hangtown (Placerville), California, in the spring of 1850, with a letter from the diggings in October of the same year and an account of a journey from New York to California, via Panama, in 1862, capture by the confederate raider Alabama, etc., and a visit to the Nevada silver mining district in 1863. Edited by Georgia Willis Read. Illustrated from old prints. Boston, Little, Brown, and Company, 1927.

xxvi, 185p. plates, port., fold. map. 22½cm.

References to Mormons and the Mormon road, p. 63–64, 69, 118.

CU–B

6829. Reasoner, Calvin. Church and state; the issue of civil and religious liberty in Utah; a testimonial in behalf of civil liberty and the American state as separate from the church and dedicated to the friends of freedom and true progress in Utah and elsewhere, by Calvin Reasoner . . . Salt Lake City, 1896.

139p. 21cm.

Cover-title: The late manifesto in politics.

MH, NjP, NN, UHi, ULA, UPB, USl, USlC, UU

6830. Reasons for a Legislative Commission for Utah, by a citizen of Salt Lake. [Salt Lake City? ca. 1884]

21p. 22cm.

Caption-title: Shall we have a Legislative Commission for Utah.

The political situation in Utah.

UU

Reasons why I cannot become a Mormonite. *See Religious Tract Society.*

6830a. Reavis, Logan Uriah. The life and military services of Gen. William Selby Harney. By L. U. Reavis . . . Introduction by Gen. Cassius M. Clay. Saint Louis: Bryan, Brand & Co., Publishers. 1878.

xvi [17]–477p. ports., plates. 22cm.

Harney was in command of the Utah Expedition briefly from May 27, 1858 to September, 1858. The author claims that he planned to hang the Mormon leaders and winter in the temple.

CtY, DLC, UPB

6831. Recollections of the pioneers of Lee County [Illinois]. Dixon, Ill., Inez A. Kennedy, 1893.

582 [1]p. plates, ports. 22½cm.

Compiled by the Lee County Columbian Club.

Mormonism: Accounts of Benj. & Eliz. (Hale) Wasson, p. 57–62; the Blair family, p. 63–71; Emma Hale Smith, p. 96–107; the Hale family, p. 141–3; Mrs. Hezekiah McKune, p. 145–6; Reminiscences of William Smith at Palestine Grove, p. 392, 397.

DLC, ICN, NN, UHi

6832. Redding, William A. The three churches; showing many mysterious and wonderful things just now coming to the surface after traveling down the path of the ages 6000 years. [Navarre, Kansas? c1897]

396p. 19½cm.

Book of Mormon doctrine, p. 220–225.

USlC

6833. Redesdale, Algernon Bertram Freeman-Mitford, *baron.* Memories. By Lord Redesdale . . . with two photogravure plates and 16 other illustrations. New York, E. P. Dutton and Co. [1916]

2v. plates, ports., facsim. 23½cm.

Printed in Great Britain.

"The Mormons and Brigham Young," V.2, p. 614–626.

Visited Salt Lake City and met Brigham Young and Porter Rockwell.

CU, DLC, NjP, NN, UHi, USlC

6834. Redsecker, J. H. Across the continent: letters written to the Church Advocate, during the summer of 1879. Lebanon, Pa., 1879.

98p. 18cm.

Letter #3 concerns Mormonism. Apart from polygamy, the Mormons were a pleasant people.

Howes R122

USlC

6835. Reed, Henry. Bigamy and polygamy. Review of the opinion of the Supreme Court of the United States, rendered at the October term, 1878, in the case of George Reynolds, Plaintiff in error, vs. the United States, Defendant in error. By an old lawyer. [New York, 1879]

33p. 24cm.

CtY, CU–B, DLC, ICN, MB, MH, MoK, NjP, NN, PU, UHi, UPB, USlC

Reed, Samuel B. *See Union Pacific Railroad Company. Report of . . .*

6836. Reed, Thomas B. Foundation of the right of Congress to deal with the Mormon question. Remarks of Thomas B. Reed, of Maine, on the Edmunds Bill, in the Houes of Representatives, Wednesday, January 12, 1887. [Washington, 1887]

4p. 22cm.

Caption-title.

UHi

6837. Reed, W. In her steps; or, fate's wicked way. [n.p., after 1902]
7p. 21½cm.
An introduction for a projected play which seemed to have never been published.
UPB, USlC

6838. Rees, Alfred Cornelius. Blätter aus der Geschichte der Kirche Jesu Christi der Heiligen der letzten Tage. Von der Geburt des Propheten Joseph Smith bis zur gegenwärtigen Zeit. [Leipzig, Druck von C. G. Röder, 1902?]
iv, 204p. ports., plate, map. 20½cm.
Cover-title: "Ein Abriss aus der Geschichte der Kirche Jesu Christi."
Preface: 1902.
Title in English: Pages taken from the history of the Church of Jesus Christ of Latter-day Saints.
MH, UHi, UPB, USl, USlC, UU

6839. ———. Mormon conception of salvation; address delivered over Radio Station KSL, Sunday Evening, October 16, 1927. [Salt Lake City] 1927.
Broadside. 40½×21½cm.
Reprinted from the *Deseret News*, Saturday, October 22, 1927.
UPB

6840. Reese, David Meredith. Humbugs of New-York: being a remonstrance against popular delusion; whether in science, philosophy, or religion. By David Meredith Reese, M.D. New-York: John S. Taylor, Brick-Church Chapel. Boston: Weeks, Jordon & Co., 1838.
xii, [13]–267p. 19cm.
P. 264–5 mentions a new religious humbug "Mormonism."
USlC

6841. References to the Book of Mormon. [Kirtland? 1835?]
ivp. 18½cm.
The earliest reference guide or index to the *Book of Mormon*. In most located copies, it is tipped into the 1st edition of the *Book of Mormon*.
CSmH, CU-B, UPB, USlC

6842. Le Réflecteur. Organe de L'Église de Jesus-Christ des Saints-des-Derniers-Jours . . . Genève, T. B. H. Stenhouse, January, 1853–December, 1853.
1v. (12 nos. in 194p.) monthly. 21cm.
T. B. H. Stenhouse, editor.
Genève is listed as publication place on title page, but all issues are printed at Lausanne.
CSmH, CtY (exc. 11–12), DLC, MH, NjP, NN, UPB, USlC, WHi

6843. The Reflector. Palmyra, N.Y. V. 1 #1–16; September 2–December 16, 1829; New ser., #1–16, December 22, 1829–April 19, 1830; 3d ser., #1–16, May 1, 1830–September 13, 1830; V. 2, ser. 1, #1–16, October 4, 1830–March 19, 1831.
2v. 26cm.
"By O. Dogberry, Esq." [i.e., A. Cole, Esq., ex-justice of the peace] cf. Church of Jesus Christ of Latter Day Saints. History of the Church. 1902, V.1, p.75–76]
New ser. #2–3, January 2, 1830–January 13, 1830, and extra issue dated January 22, 1830 contain the first printing of portions of the Book of Mormon, namely, extracts from "The First book of Nephi," and "The Book of Alma." Other Mormon references.
CtY V.1 #1–16, September 2–December 16, 1829; New ser. #1 December 1829–V. 2, ser. 1 #16 March, 1831; CU-B New ser. lacking V. 2, #14–17; NNHi New ser. V.1–2; UPB New ser. #1 December 22, 1829–V.2, ser. 1 #15, March, 1831; USlC

6844. Die Reform der Heilegen der Letzten Tage. Geneva, Switzerland, September, 1862–February, 1864.
12 nos. (188p.) monthly. 22½cm.
Official organ of the Swiss Mission.
Published and edited by John L. Smith, John Woodard.
Not published December, 1862, and March to August, 1863.
Title in English: The reformation of the Church of the latter days.
MH, USlC

6845. A refutation to "A friendly discussion." Los Angeles, Calif. International Truth Distributors [n.d.]
3p.l., 7–39 [1]p. 19cm.
Reply to Benjamin E. Rich.
USlC

Reid, H. L. *See Lyne, Thomas A.*

6846. Reid, J. M. Sketches and anecdotes of the old settlers and new comers; the Mormon bandits and Danite band. By Col. J. M. Reid, Attorney at Law. Keokuk, Iowa, R. B. Ogden, 1876.
3p.l. [7]–177p. illus., port. 23cm.
Chap. III concerns the history of Mormonism in Nauvoo.
UPB copy has cover imprint date 1877.
Howes R168
CSmH, CtY, DLC, ICN, MB, MoK, NN, UPB, UU

6846a. Reid, Mayne. The man-eaters, and other odd people. A popular description of singular races of men. New York, J. Miller, 1880.
461p. illus. 19½cm.
Mormons mentioned, p. 315, 317, 332.
USlC

REID, M.

6847. ———. The wild huntress, or Love in the wilderness. New York, R. M. DeWitt [c1861]
1p.l., 9–466p. front., 4 woodcuts. 18cm.
A western novel with Mormon sections: "Squatter and Saint"; "An apostolic effort"; a word about the "Mormon Monsters."
Republished in many editions.
Sabin 69083
MH, PPL

6848. Reinach, Salomon. Orpheas; a general history of religions, from the French of Salomon Reinach by Florence Simmonds. Revised and partly rewritten by the author. New York, G. P. Putnam's Sons, 1909.
xiv, 439p. col. front. 23cm.
A brief discussion of Mormonism, p. 398–400.
DLC, NjP, UPB

6849. Eine Reise in das Land der Mormonen. [Berlin, 1892]
22p.
Title in English: A trip to the country of the Mormons.
Eberstadt *Utah and the Mormons.*

6850. Relief Society Bulletin. Salt Lake City, January–December, 1914.
1v. monthly. 22cm.
Organ of the Relief Society of the Church of Jesus Christ of Latter-day Saints.
Edited by Susa Young Gates.
Succeeded by *Relief Society Magazine.*
CSmH, DLC, NjP, NN, UPB, USlC

6851. The Relief Society Magazine; organ of the Relief Society of the Church of Jesus Christ of Latter-day Saints, Jan. 1915–
v. monthly. 23cm.
Continues voluming from the *Relief Society Bulletin.* Sub-title varies.
CU–B, NjP, UPB, USlC

6852. Religio Quarterly. Lamoni, Ia., Zion's Religio-Literary Society, October, 1902–1928.
v. quarterly. 24cm.
Work of the quarterly merged into Department of Recreation and Expression.
CSmH V.1 #3–4, V.8 inc.; MoInRC; UPB V.15 #1–4, V.26 #2–V.27 #1

6853. The religions of the world; authentic accounts of the various faiths and creeds, by members of each denomination. London, C. Griffin, 1870.
xii, 386p. 20cm.
Chap. XXI entitled "The Mormons of Latter-day Saints" by Joseph Smith, p. 321–328. Continues Mormonism through 1852.
Other editions: 1876. UU; 1877. USlC
DLC

6854. Religious impostors. [Edinburgh, Printed and Published by W. & R. Chambers, 1845]
32p. 17cm.
Caption-title.
Mormonism, p. 26–32. "By such blasphemous and deceitful stuff as this, the poor cotton-spinner . . . was induced to go to Nauvoo."
First published in *Chambers Miscellany* [1845–47] V.2
Replied to in *Millennial Star* March 15, 1847. *See also Sept. 15, 1850, p.283.*
CU–B, USlC

6855. Religious Tract Society. The doctrines of Mormonism. [London] The Religious Tract Society [1850?]
24p. 19cm.
At head of title: "No. 599"
CU–B, MH, MoInRC, NN, UPB, USlC

6855a. ———. (same) [London] The Religious Tract Society [1850?]
24p. 17cm. (No. 599)
At head of title: Given by the London City Mission.
Variant of 6855.
USlC

6856. ———. Is Mormonism true or not? [London, The Religious Tract Society, 1853?]
28p. 17½cm.
Caption-title.
At head of title: "No. 600"
CSmH, CtY, DLC, MH, MoInRC, NjP, NN, ULA, USlC

6857. ———. Mormonism. [London, The Religious Tract Society, 185–]
24p. 17½cm.
Caption-title.
At head of title: "No. 598"
Account of the death of Joseph Smith and the exodus of the Mormons under Brigham Young.
CtY, MH, NjP, UPB, USlC

6858. ———. Reasons why I cannot become a Mormonite. [London, Religious Tract Society, ca. 1850]
8p. 17cm.
At head of title: "No. 765"
NN, USlC

Remarkable adventures of the Mormon prophet. *See Christopher [pseud.]*

6859. Remarkable delusions; or, illustrations of popular errors. Philadelphia: American Sunday School Union [1851?]
192p. 15cm.
"Delusions associated with religion." Final delusion discussed is "Mormonites," p. 171–188. "Some of the most extraordinary of any we have related. As its pernicious errors have extensively spread, a more detailed exposure of them may be useful."

Another edition: Nashville, Tenn., Published by E. Stevenson & J. E. Evans, 1856. USlC
Sabin 69377
DLC, USlC

6860. Remarkable visions. Visions of George Washington, Newman Bulkley, S. M. Farnsworth, and C. D. Evans. Salt Lake City, Jos. Hyrum Parry & Co., 1886.
22p. 18cm.
George Washington vision, p. 1–9; Newman Bulkley, p. 11–14; S. M. Farnsworth, p. 15–18; C. D. Evans, p. 19–22.
Also printed in *The Contributor*, V. 15, p. 640.
CSmH, NN, UHi, UPB, USlC, UU

6861. ———. (same) Salt Lake City, J. H. Parry & Co., 1887.
22p. 18cm.
CU–B, UPB, USlC

6862. ———. (same) Salt Lake City, Magazine Printing Co. [n.d.]
20p. 17½cm.
USlC

6863. ———. Visions of Stephen M. Farnsworth, George Washington and Newman Bulkley. Salt Lake City, Jos. Hyrum Parry & Co., 1886.
18p. 18½cm.
USlC

6864. Remarks on Mormonism, occasioned by the question of Orson Pratt, a Mormon apostle, "Was Joseph Smith sent of God?" Printed, with the approbation of Clergymen of different denominations, for a Committee of Working Men at the Forth Iron Works. Glasgow, Scotland, Printed by Bell and Bain [1849?]
16p. 20cm.
Caption-title.
Attack on the *Book of Mormon* and L.D.S. Doctrines. Answered by Orson Pratt in his *Reply*.
USlC

Reminiscences of travel from 1855–1867.
See Frazier, Mrs. R.

6865. Remy, Jules. On the religious movement in the United States, by Jules Remy, author of "A Journey to Great Salt Lake City [etc.]" London, W. Jeffs, 1861.
123p. 26cm.
Published also as an introduction to the author's *Journey to Great Salt Lake City.*
Mormonism's basic origin differs from other religions born at the same time.
NN, UHi

6866. ———. Voyage au pays des Mormons; relation — géographie — histoire naturelle — histoire — théologie — moeurs et coutumes; par Jules Remy . . . Ouvrage orné de 10 gravures sur acier et d'une carte. Paris, E. Dentu, 1860.
2v. 5 plates, 3 ports., 2 facsims., fold. map. 24½cm.
"Introduction: Du Mouvement religieux aux Etats-Unis": V. 1, p. [ix]–lxxxviii.
"Bibliographie Mormonne": V. 2, p. [499]–506.
"Voyage de m. Brenchley à travers l'Amérique du Nord" [1850]: V. 2, p. [421]–433.
Title in English: A trip to the country of the Mormons.
Howes R210, Sabin 69595, W–C 364
CSmH, CtY, CU–B, DLC, ICN, MH, NjP, NjPT, NN, UHi, UPB, USl, UU

6867. ———. (same, in English) A journey to Great Salt Lake City, by Jules Remy, and Julius Brenchley, M.A.; with a sketch of the history, religion, and customs of the Mormons and an introduction on the religious movement in the United States, by Jules Remy . . . With the steel engravings and a map. London, W. Jeffs, 1861.
2v. 5 plates, 3 port., 2 facsim., fold. map. 25cm.
Mormon doctrine, V. 2, p. 1–172. Visit to Great Salt Lake City in 1855.
Howes R210, Sabin 64594, W–C 364
CSmH, CtY, CU–B, DLC, ICN, MH, NjP, NN, UHi, ULA, UPB, USl, USlC, UU, WHi

6868. Re-organized Church of Jesus Christ (Wright group) What must we do to be saved. [n.p., 19 - -]
Broadside. 9×13cm.
This card sets forth the 10 articles of faith, as it broke from the Bickertonites.
Morgan
USlC

6869. Reorganized Church of Jesus Christ of Latter Day Saints. En Afsløring af Mormonismen eller: Hvem er de egentlige sidste Dages Hellige? [Kristiania, C. Joh. Stranbørgs Trykkeri, n.d.]
[4]p. 22cm.
Title in English: Unveiling the Mormonism . . .
USlC

6870. ———. Album of ministers and workers. Reorganized Church of Jesus Christ of Latter Day Saints. Independence, Mo., Ensign Publishing House, 1904.
[41]l. of plates. 24×15½cm.
Cover-title.
Pictures of men of importance and a few historic scenes.
MH

REORGANIZED CHURCH OF JESUS CHRIST

6871. ———. The Angel Message Tracts . . . Lamoni, Published by the Herald House [n.d.]
174p. 18cm.
Contents: #1. What did Jesus preach? by Elbert A. Smith. #2. Faith in God, Is it Scientific, Is it Biblical? by Elbert A. Smith. #3. Repentence, by Elbert A. Smith. #4. Baptism in water, by Paul M. Hanson. #5. Baptism of the Spirit, by Paul M. Hanson. #6. Laying on of hands, by Paul M. Hanson. #7. Immortality and the resurrection, by Elbert A. Smith. #8. The Eternal judgment, by Elbert A. Smith. #9. Latter day Saints: Who are they? by T. W. Williams. [This is replaced in later editions by "The Latter Day Saints and what they believe, by A. B. Phillips, as a separate publication of 31p. and by "The Latter-day glory (Church history in brief) by Elbert A. Smith] #10. The Latter-day Glory (Church History in brief) by Elbert A. Smith. [Renumbered #9 in later editions and "The Latter day Saints and what they believe" by A. B. Phillips added.]
MoInRC, USlC

6872. ———. (same) Lamoni, Ia., Published by the Herald Publishing House [n.d]
129p. 20cm.
A reissue in one volume of ten numbers of the Angel message tracts.
MoInRC

6873. ———. The Angel message series . . . Independence, Mo., Herald Publishing House [19 - -]
211p. 19cm.
Cover-title.
Paging irregular; p. 82, 131–133, 175–179 omitted.
MoInRC, NN

6874. ———. Antecedents of the millennium. [Plano, Ill., True Latter-Day Saints' Herald, 1865]
4p. 23cm. (True Latter-Day Saints' Herald. Tract. No. 1)
CtY, MoInRC, NjP, UPB

6875. ———. (same) [Plano, Ill., True Latter Day Saints' Herald, n.d.]
4p. 23cm. (No. 42)
MoInRC, NN, UPB

6876. ———. Articles of incorporation of the Reorganized Church of Jesus Christ of Latter Day Saints. Plano, Ill., Board of Publication of the Reorganized Church of Latter Day Saints [187–]
8p. 23cm.
MoInRC, NjP, NN

6877. ———. (same) Lamoni, Ia., Reorganized Church of Jesus Christ, 1886.
24p. 15cm.
MoInRC

6878. ———. Aterupprättade Jesu Kristi Kyrka af de Sista Dagars Heliga. Den gode Herdens röst. [n.p., n.d.]
6p. 22cm.
Title in English: Reorganized Church of Jesus Christ of Latter Day Saints.
NN

6879. ———. The auditorium. Owned and operated by the Reorganized Church of Jesus Christ of Latter Day Saints as its world headquarters at Independence, Missouri. [Independence, Mo., n.d.]
Broadside. plate. 20×27½cm.
Architect's drawing of the building.
USlC

6880. ———. (same) [Independence, Mo., ca. 1930]
[4]p. 21½cm.
USlC

6881. ———. (same) [Independence, Mo., Department of Publicity, ca. 1930]
[6]p. illus. 21½cm.
USlC

6882. ———. (same) [Independence, Mo., ca. 1930]
[6]p. illus. 21½cm.
Variant printing without Department of Publicity on p. [6]
USlC

6883. ———. Baptism. Lamoni, Ia., Published by the Reorganized Church of Jesus Christ of Latter Day Saints [n.d.]
10 [2]p. 21cm. (No. 23)
P. [11] Kirtland Temple suit.
P. [12] No. 4. Epitome of the Faith and doctrines of the Reorganized Church of Jesus Christ of Latter Day Saints.
MoInRC, NjP, USlC

6884. ———. (same) [Plano, Ill., 1870]
10p. 21½cm. (No. 23)
CSmH, MoInRC, NjP, NN, USlC

6885. ———. (same) [Plano, Ill., n.d.]
10p. 21½cm. (No. 23)
Variant of the above without "Printed at Plano, Kendall Co., Illinois" on p. 10.
USlC

6886. ———. Belief and practice. Independence, Mo., Reorganized Church of Jesus Christ of Latter Day Saints [1927?]
3p. 16cm.
NN

———. Bishop R. C. Evans vs. Mr. R. C. Evans. *See Williams, T. W.*

REORGANIZED CHURCH OF JESUS CHRIST

6886a. ———. Book of Mormon pronouncing vocabulary. Lamoni, Iowa, Herald Publishing House, 1902.
12p. 22cm.
MoInRC

6887. ———. . . . A brief history and financial summary of the Gallands Grove, Iowa, District. Illustrated. The Reorganized Church of Jesus Christ of Latter Day Saints from 1859 to 1912 . . . [Dow City, Ia., Enterprise Print., 1912]
[44] unnumb. p. illus. 19cm.
Cover-title.
Text on cover.
At head of title: Circular No. 8.
Compiled by Charles J. Hunt, Bishop.
MoInRC, UHi

6888. ———. Brighamism; its promises and their failures. [Plano, Ill., 187–]
8p. 25cm. (No. 13)
Sabin 50730
CSmH, CU–B, MH, MoInRC, NjP, NN, USlC

6889. ———. (same) [Plano, Ill., n.d.]
8p. 25cm.
Same as the above except for tract number.
USlC

6890. ———. Brighamite doctrines. A delineation of some of the false doctrines of Brighamism, in extracts from sermons and teachings of Brigham Young and some of his colleagues. [Plano, Ill., True Latter Day Saints' Herald, 1864?]
8p. 25cm.
DLC, MoInRC, NN

6891. ———. (same) [Plano, Ill., 188–]
8p. 22cm.
NN

6892. ———. Die Buke . . . herausgegeben unter der Autorität Reorganisierten Kirche Jesu Christi, der Heiligen der letzten Tage. Burlington, Ia., Zu beziehen von J. G. Bauer [n.d.]
10p. 20cm.
Title in English: The book.
NN

6893. ———. Bulletin. Independence, Mo. Courtesy of the Brantley Printing Co., 1925–26.
2v. weekly. 24cm.
NN V.1 #1–2, 4–5, 7–17; V.2 #1–2, 4, 6–12, 14–15

6894. ———. Can belief alone save. [Lamoni, Ia., Herald Publishing House, n.d.]
12p. 16cm. (No. 36)
CtY, MoInRC

6895. ———. Catalogue and list price of books and publications, Sunday school supplies. Reorganized Church of Jesus Christ of Latter Day Saints. Lamoni, Ia., Herald Publishing House [n.d.]
22p. 17cm.
USlC

6896. ———. (same) Lamoni, Ia., Herald Publishing House [1902]
20p. 15cm.
Cover title.
WHi

6897. ———. Celebrating the first hundred years. The centennial yearbook and conference souvenir, 1830–1930 . . . International Conference held at Independence Missouri, April 6–20, 1930. [Independence, Herald Printing House, 1930]
2p.l., 5–55p. illus., plates, port. 31cm.
CSmH, NN, UHi, UU

6898. ———. The centennial year book. Independence, Mo. [1930]
1p.l., 9–75 [2]p. 18cm.
USlC

6899. ———. Church history [Lamoni, Herald Publishing House, n.d.]
6p. illus. 22cm. (F.S. No. 1)
MoInRC

6900. ———. Compilation of general conference resolutions, 1852–1900, published by order of General Conference. Lamoni, Ia., Published by the Board of Publication of the Reorganized Church of Jesus Christ of Latter Day Saints, 1901.
150p. 17cm.
First 493 resolutions.
MoInRC, NjP

6901. ———. Compilation of general conference resolutions, 1852–1907. Published by order of the General Assembly of the Reorganized Church of Jesus Christ of Latter Day Saints. Lamoni, Ia., 1908.
184p. 18cm.
Resolutions through 1907.
MoInRC, NjP

6902. ———. Compilation of general conference resolutions, 1852–1910. Published by order of General Conference. Lamoni, Ia., Published by The Board of Publication of the Reorganized Church of Jesus Christ of Latter Day Saints, 1911.
227, 18p. 18cm.
Resolutions through 1910. Includes 18p. Supplement to the general Conference Resolutions, April 6, 1913.
MoInRC, NjP

REORGANIZED CHURCH OF JESUS CHRIST

6903. ———. Compilation of general conference resolutions, 1852–1915. Published by order of General Conference. Lamoni, Ia., Board of Publication of the Reorganized Church of Jesus Christ of Latter Day Saints, 1916.
235, 29p. 18cm.
Resolutions to 1915. Includes 29p. Supplement for 1916–1923.
MoInRC, NjP

6903a. ———. Compilation of General Conference resolutions supplement 1916–1923. Independence, Mo., Board of Publication of the Reorganized Church of Jesus Christ of Latter Day Saints, 1925.
29p. 20cm.
MoInRC

6904. ———. Condensed financial statement for the year ending June 30th, 1926. Independence, Mo., 1926?]
2p. 16cm.
List of church officers on back.
NN

6905. ———. Departmental Journal. Independence, Mo., 1927–1930.
4v. monthly. 23cm.
MoInRC

6906. ———. The difference. [Independence? n.d.]
[9]p. illus. 16cm.
Differences between the branches of Mormonism.
MoInRC

6906a. ———. Do you Know? [n.p., n.d.]
4p. 19cm.
RLDS the true successor to Joseph Smith.
NjP

6907. ———. Do you want more Light? [Lamoni, Ia., Herald Publishing House, n.d.]
4p. 15cm. (No. 202)
RLDS tract.
MoInRC, NjP

6908. ———. Document on church government and statement of President F. M. Smith. [Independence, Mo., Reorganized Church of Jesus Christ of Latter Day Saints, Department of Publicity, 1927?]
19p. 16cm.
Includes: Foreword by F. M. Smith; Statement of President Elbert A. Smith, referring to the document on church government p. 3–5; document on church government adopted by Joint Council April, 1924, and by the general council of the Church April, 1925 p. 6–7; statement of President F. M. Smith on the joint council document on church government p. 8–18; and a letter from President F. M. Smith, Feb. 24, 1926, to A. V. Robinson, p. 19.
Concerning supreme directional control.
MoInRC, NN

6909. ———. Die Eine Taufe "die Art-wie und die Personen, denen" sie ertheilt werden soll; ihre Vorbedingungen und ihr Zweck, sowie eine Beantwortung der Frage: Wer sie verwalten oder ertheilsen soll. (Aus dem Englischen Übersezt) Stewartsville, De-Kalb Co., Mo., Herausgegeben von dem Deutschen Zweig der Reorganisirten Kirche Jesu Christi der Heiligen der letzten Tage, 1881.
44p. 18cm.
A possible translation of Smith, Thomas W. *The only baptism.*
Title in English: The only baptism, how and to whom it should be administered.
NN

6910. ———. Duties of district and branch officers. Independence, Mo., Herald Publishing House, 1926.
86p. 19cm.
Cover-title.
Signed: Elbert A. Smith, Albert Carmichael, and J. A. Gardner.
UHi

6910a. ———. An epistle to the Saints. Independence, Mo., 1925.
4p. 16cm.
Issued by a joint council of First Presidency, Quorum of Twelve and Presiding Bishopric.
MoInRC

6911. ———. Epitome of the faith and doctrines of the Reorganized Church of Jesus Christ of Latter Day Saints. [Plano, Ill., Herald Publishing House, 1870?]
Broadside. 21½×15cm.
Verso blank.
Variant printings.
MoInRC, USlC

6912. ———. (same) Lamoni, Ia., [188–]
[1]l. 21cm.
At head of title: No. 4.
Caption-title.
On verso: Kirtland Temple suit.
Variant issues also appear as the final leaf on various tracts.
Sabin 50737
CSmH, MH, MoInRC, NN, UHi, UPB

6913. ———. Faith and repentance. [Plano, Ill.] Printed by the Board of Publication of the Reorganized Church of Jesus Christ of Latter-day Saints [187–]
8p. 25cm. (No. 22)
CSmH, CtY, MH, MoInRC, NjP, NN, USlC

6914. ———. (same) [Plano, Ill?] Published by the Board of Publication of the Reorganized Church of Latter Day Saints [n.d.]
8p. 25cm.
Place of publication omitted on p.8.
USlC

REORGANIZED CHURCH OF JESUS CHRIST

6915. ———. Food for thought; or, Sermons and essays by Jews and Gentiles. Lamoni, Ia., Lambert Bro's Publishers [1890]
95p. 21cm.
Sermons by members of the RLDS Church on the doctrine of Israel.
NjP, USlC

6916. ———. General conference bulletin. Independence, Mo., 1901–
v. annual. 19½–28cm.
Formerly published as Conference daily edition of the *Saints' Herald.*
MoInRC comp.; UPB 1901, 1908, 1916, Oct. 1923

6917. ———. General conference songs. Independence, Mo., 1922.
47p. music. 19cm.
MoInRC

6918. ———. The Gospel. [Plano, Ill., 1870?]
[2]p. 25cm. (Tract. No. 5)
Sabin 50738
DLC, MH, MoInRC, NjP, NN, USlC

6919. ———. (same) Lamoni, Ia., Herald Publishing House [189–]
[1]l. 25cm. (Tract. No. 41)
NN, MoInRC

6920. ———. Die Grundsätze des Evangeliums Jesu Christi und die Anwendung desselben zur Errettung der Menschen. Herausgegeben unter der Autorität der Reorganisirten Kirche Jesu Christi der Heiligen der Letzten Tage. Burlington, Ia., Zubeziehen von J. G. Bauer [n.d.]
15p. 18cm.
Title in English: The principles of the gospel of Jesus Christ.
NN

6921. ———. En henvendelse til de skandinaviske folk; en fremstilling af de oprindelige Sidste Dages Helliges tro og laere, i modfaetning til de her kaldte Mormoners. [Kristianssand, Norge, Peter Andersen, n.d.]
[4]p. 24cm.
An RLDS missionary tract.
Title in English: An address to the Scandinavian people.
USlC

———. History of the Church of Jesus Christ of Latter-day Saints. *See Smith, Joseph, 1832–1914.*

6922. ———. History of the First Presidency. Lamoni, Ia., Herald Publishing House [n.d.]
[6]p. ports. 21cm. (F. S. No. 2)
Epitome of faith on verso of pamphlet.
MoInRC, UPB

6923. ———. Hoe Para Parau raa ahiaki. [Papeete, Tahiti] 1898.
8p. 24cm. (No. 2)
Probably #2 of its: Te Ravea.
RLDS tract in Tahitian.
Title in English: On false teachings.
USlC

6923a. ———. Home department of the General Sunday-School Association of the Reorganized Church of Jesus Christ of Latter Day Saints . Lamoni, Iowa, Herald Publishing House, 1902.
11p. 16cm. (Leaflet of Instruction. No. 2.)
MoInRC

6924. ———. Idolatry. Plano, Ill. [187–]
4p. 22cm. (No. 15)
Sabin 50741
CSmH, CU-B, MoInRC, NjP, NN, USlC

6925. ———. Indholdet af troen og laerdommene af den Reorganizerede Kirke af Jesus Christus af De sidste Dages Hellige. Plano, Ill., Igenoprettelse av Jesu Christi Kirke av de Sidste Dages Hellige [1870]
[1]p. 21cm. (No. 13)
Title in English: An outline of the faith and teachings of the Reorganized Church of Jesus Christ of Latter Day Saints.
MoInRC

6926. ———. The inspired translation of the Holy Scriptures. Lamoni, Ia., [n.d.]
4p. 18½cm. (No. 38)
Preliminary text signed by W. W. Blair.
ICN, MoInRC

6927. ———. Is God a respecter of persons? [n.p., 192–]
8p. 19½cm.
RLDS Church argument in favor of the negro and the priesthood.
MoInRC, UPB, USlC

6928. ———. Items of teaching found in the Book of Mormon. [Independence, Mo., Ensign Publishing House, n.d.]
10[1]p. 19½cm.
MoInRC

6929. ———. Jesu Kristi menighed. [Porsgrund, Trykt hos Br. Dyring, n.d.]
Broadside. 23½×18cm.
Title in English: Jesus Christ's congregation.
USlC

6930. ———. Joseph Smith; the prophet of Palmyra. [n.p., n.d.]
4p. 21cm.
Includes "Joseph Smith, President of the Reorganized Church of Jesus Christ of Latter Day Saints, p. [3–4]
MoInRC

REORGANIZED CHURCH OF JESUS CHRIST

6931. ———. The kingdom of God: what is it? Whence comes it? Where is it? [Plano, Ill., 187–]
4p. 23cm.
MoInRC, NjP

6932. ———. (same) [Lamoni, Ia., 188–]
4p. 23cm. (No. 24)
CSmH, MoInRC, NjP, NN, USlC

6933. ———. (same) Lamoni, Ia., Herald Publishing House [n.d.]
4p. 14½cm. (No. 24)
Variant printing.
USlC

6934. ———. (same) Lamoni, Ia., Herald Publishing House [n.d.]
[4]p. 15cm. (No. 24)
"Mission Hall, St. Louis, Missouri."
USlC

6934a. ———. Kirtland Temple, 1833–1836; it stands today a monument to the sacrifice of a loyal devoted people. Independence, [1928?]
3p. illus. 18cm.
Signed May 1, 1928.
MoInRC

6935. ———. The Kirtland Temple, with a sketch of its builders . . . Lamoni, Ia., Herald Publishing House [1911?]
14p. illus. 18cm. (No. 45)
CU–B, MoInRC, UHi, UPB

6936. ———. (same) [Independence, Mo., Herald Publishing House, 1922]
16p. 15cm.
MoInRC

6937. ———. (same) [Independence, Mo., n.d.]
24p. illus., ports. 15cm.
Cover-title.
MoInRC, NjP

6938. ———. (same) [Independence, Mo., 1926]
31p. 15cm.
CU–B, NjP

6939. ———. Kristi Lärdom. [n.p., n.d.]
6p. 21½cm.
Title in English: Teachings of Christ.
MoInRC, USlC

6940. ———. Kurzer Auszug des Glaubens und der Lehren der Reorganisierten Kirche Jesu Christi der Heiligen der Letzten Tage. [Burlington, Ia., 189–]
Broadside. 24×13½cm.
Title in English: Brief excerpt taken from the beliefs and teachings of the Reorganized Church of Jesus Christ of Latter Day Saints.
CtY, NN

6941. ———. The Latter Day Saints; a question of identity. Mormonism. [Independence, Mo., Herald Publishing Co., 192–]
[6]p. folder. 21×10cm.
Caption-title.
CU–B

6942. ———. Latter Day Saints and the economic problem. [n.p., n.d.]
[6]p. 19½cm.
CU–B, UPB

6942a. ———. The Law of Christ and Its Fulfillment. [n.p., 1910]
122, [6]p. 19½cm.
Caption-title.
NjP

6943. ———. Laying on of hands. [Plano, Ill., 188–]
4p. 25cm. (No. 25)
Variant printings.
CSmH, MH, MoInRC, NjP, NN, USlC

6944. ———. A letter on the Latter Day work of the Lord. [Plano, Ill., True Latter Day Saints' Herald, n.d.]
4p. 23cm. (No. 1)
Evangelistic work.
MoInRC, USlC

6945. ———. (same) [Plano, Ill., True Latter Day Saints' Herald, n.d.]
8p. 23cm. (No. 2)
MoInRC, USlC

6946. ———. Literal gathering of literal Israel. [Plano, Ill., True Latter Day Saints' Herald, 1865]
[8, 4]p. 22½cm.
Offered for sale in *The True Latter-Day Saints' Herald*. Feb. 15, 1865. Taken from a two part series "Literal gathering of Israel. *Saints' Herald*. Feb. 15, March 1, 1865.
MoInRC, NN 8p.

6947. ———. A manual of practice and rules of order and debate for deliberative assemblies of the Church of Jesus Christ of Latter Day Saints. Compiled by Joseph Smith and Thomas W. Smith. Plano, Ill., Printed and Published by the Board of Publication of the Church of Christ, 1876.
iv [5]–128p. 15cm.
MoInRC, NN

6948. ———. (same) Revised by order of Conference by M. H. Forscutt, E. L. Kelley and Joseph Luff. Lamoni, Ia., Printed and Published by the Board of Publication of the Church of Christ, 1891.
iv [5]–199p. 14cm.
CSmH, MoInRC, NjP

REORGANIZED CHURCH OF JESUS CHRIST

6949. ———. A manual of practice and rules of order and debate for Ecclesiastical Deliberative Assemblies of the Church of Jesus Christ of Latter Day Saints. New and rev. ed. Lamoni, Ia., 1904.
v, 150p. 13½cm.
MoInRC, NjP, UHi

6950. ———. Many sided views. Providence, R.I. "The Prophetic News" Print. [1881 or after]
[8]p. 16½cm. (No. 2)
"Church prospectus, by Elder Will LaRue," p. 2–7.
CSmH, MoInRC, UPB, USlC

6951. ———. Matter concerning special order for third day of Conference. [Lamoni? Ia., 1884?]
4p. 17½cm. (General Conference resolutions. No. 279)
MoInRC

6952. ———. Memorial to Congress from a committee of the Reorganized Church of Jesus Christ of Latter Day Saints on the claims and faith of the church. Plano, Ill., Printed at True Latter-Day Saints' Herald Steam Book Office [186–]
8p. 28cm. (No. 20)
Memorial in opposition to polygamy and asking that the Reorganized Church be recognized as *the* Church of Jesus Christ of Latter Day Saints.
Sabin 50746
CSmH, CtY, DLC, ICHi, MH, NN, UPB, USlC

6953. ———. Ministers and Workers representing the Reorganized Church of Jesus Christ of Latter Day Saints with names and addresses also views of interest. [n.p., n.d.]
[25]l. 25×17½cm.
Photographs of leading RLDS Church members, with a few historic views.
MoInRC

6954. ———. Minutes of general Conference [of the Reorganized Church of Jesus Christ of Latter Day Saints] Kirtland, Independence, 1891–
v. 18–27cm.
Supplement to the *Saints' Herald*.
1897–1927 has continuous pagination: 4311p.
DLC 1900, 1901, 1908; MoInRC comp.; NN 1891, 1892; UPB 1923; USlC 1891–1896, 1897–1927

6955. ———. Minutes of the general annual Conference. Held at Plano Ill., April 6th, 1873. [Plano, Ill., 1873?]
34p. 21cm.
MH

———. The Mountain of the Lord's house.
See Attwood, R. H.

6956. ———. Names and addresses . . . The quorum of High Priests of the Reorganized Church of Jesus Christ of Latter Day Saints. Lamoni, Ia., Herald Publishing House, 1910–1911.
2v. 22½cm.
USlC

6957. ———. A nineteenth century prophet and his work. [n.p., n.d.]
[4]p. 21cm.
CU–B

6958. ———. Of such is the kingdom. [n.p., n.d.]
8p. 19cm.
Blessing of children.
MoInRC

6959. ———. Official program . . . General Conference. 1927–
v. 18cm.
USlC 1927 (72nd conference) 64p.

6960. ———. Official statement of belief, and epitome of faith and doctrine. Independence, Mo. [192–]
[3]p. 16cm. (Busy man's series. No. 1)
MoInRC, UHi, UPB

6961. ———. Oksen ved roden af traeet; Kristi Kir og laere, for og nu. [Porsgrund, Brodr. ings Bogtrykkeri, n.d.]
16p. 23½cm.
Title in English: The ax at the root of the tree; Christ's Church and teaching, before and now.
USlC

6962. ———. Order and faith of the Church of Christ. [Plano, Ill., True Latter Day Saints' Herald, 1865]
8p. 21½cm.
Pt. 1 "Order of the Church" p. 1–3 originally published as pt. 7 of History of the Priesthood in *The True Latter-Day Saints' Herald*, Feb. 1, 1865. Pt. 2 "Faith of the church" p. 3–8 was published as pt. 11–12 of Faith of the Church of Christ in these last days, published in the *Herald* Feb. 1–15, 1865. These two parts were copied from the *L.D.S. Messenger and Advocate*, December, 1834, January and February, 1835.
Listed for sale as a pamphlet Feb. 15, 1865.
MoInRC, NjP, NN, UPB

6963. ———. Origin of the Book of Mormon. Plano, Ill. [1876?]
7p. 22cm. (No. 30)
MoInRC, NN, USlC

6964. ———. (same) Lamoni, Ia. [n.d.]
8p. 23cm. (No. 30)
ICHi, NjP

REORGANIZED CHURCH OF JESUS CHRIST

6965. ———. Polygamy. [Plano, Ill., n.d.]
16p. 25cm.
Compilation from various letters, and other material concerning Utah polygamy.
USlC

6966. ———. Polygamy not a doctrine of the true church of Latter Day Saints. [Lamoni, Ia., Herald Publishing House, n.d.]
4p. 18cm. (Tract. No. 203)
CSmH, CU-B, MoInRC, NjP, UPB

6967. ———. (same) Lamoni, Ia., Herald Publishing House [n.d.]
4p. 19cm. (No. 203)
Variant printings.
USlC

6968. ———. (same) Lamoni, Ia., Herald Publishing House [n.d.]
4p. 18cm. (No. 203)
CtY

6969. ———. The President of the Church. The law of succession. [n.p., 1894?]
[8]p. 32cm.
Which is the true Church? RLDS or L.D.S.
CU-B, MH

6970. ———. The Priesthood manual. For the ministry of the Reorganized Church of Jesus Christ of Latter Day Saints. Independence, Mo., Herald Publishing House [n.d.]
96p. 21½cm.
UPB

6971. ———. Procedure in Church courts. [n.p., n.d.]
[4]p. 21½cm.
MoInRC

6972. ———. Program for the establishment of Zion. Adopted by the General Conference of 1925. Independence, Mo. [1925?]
[2]p. 16cm.
NN

6973. ———. Pronouncing vocabulary of the Book of Mormon. Lamoni, Ia., Herald Publishing House, 1902.
12p. 15½cm.
Cover-title: *Book of Mormon.*
In part based on manuscript of LaJuen Howard and W. W. Green. p. v.
MoInRC

6974. ———. Reference manual. [n.p., n.d.]
[18]l. 17cm.
Includes sketch of the Independence Branch and biographical information.
MoInRC

6975. ———. Rejection of the Church. Plano, Ill. [187–]
8p. 22cm. (No. 18)
CSmH, CtY, MoInRC, NjP, NN

6976. ———. Rejection and succession. Plano, Ill. [1878]
8p. 21cm.
CtY, USlC

6977. ———. Reorganization of the Church of Jesus Christ of Latter Day Saints. [Lamoni, Ia., Herald Publishing House, n.d.]
12p. 19cm. (No. 1219)
Caption-title.
CU-B, MoInRC

6978. ———. The Reorganization of the Church of Jesus Christ of Latter Day Saints. A brief treatise setting forth the law and revelations governing such exigencies as arose in the church after the death of Joseph Smith . . . [n.p., n.d.]
11p. 19cm.
CU-B, NjP, UPB

6979. ———. The Reorganized Church of Jesus Christ of Latter Day Saints, complainant, vs. The Church of Christ . . . . In Equity. Brief and argument on behalf of complainant. Lamoni, Ia., Herald Publishing House and Bindery, 1893.
71 [1]p. 23½cm.
At head of title: In the Circuit Court of the United States. Western District of Missouri.
Signed: L. Traber, George Edmunds, P. P. Kelley, E. L. Kelley, Smith McPherson.
Temple lot suit.
USlC

6980. ———. The Reorganized Church of Jesus Christ of Latter Day Saints, Complainant, vs The Church of Christ at Independence, Missouri; Richard Hill, trustee; Richard Hall, Mrs. E. Hill, C. A. Hall [and others] . . . as members of and doing business under the name of the Church of Christ, at Independence, Missouri respondents. In equity. Complainant's abstract of pleading and evidence . . . Lamoni, Ia., Herald Publishing House, 1893.
507p. 26½cm.
In the Circuit court of the United States, Western district of Missouri, Western division, at Kansas City.
Binder's title: Abstract of evidence, Temple lot suit.
CSmH, DLC, MoInRC, MoKU, NN, OU, PU, UHi, USlC, UU

6980a. ———. . . . The Reorganized Church of Jesus Christ of Latter Day Saints, Complainant, vs. The Church of Christ at Independence, Missouri; Richard Hill, Trustee; Richard Hill, Mrs. E. Hill [and others] . . . as members of and doing business under the name of the Church of Christ at Independence, Missouri, respondents. In equity. Respondent's statement and argument . . . Independence, Mo., Sentinel Job Print., 1893.

80p. 23cm.
At head of title: No. 1720. In the circuit court of the United States, Western District of Missouri, Western Division, at Kansas City.
USlC

6981. ———. (same) Complainant's reply to respondents' statement and argument. Lamoni, Ia., Herald Publishing House and Bindery, 1893.
32p. 23½cm.
At head of title: In the Circuit Court of the United States Western District of Missouri . . . No. 1720.
USlC

6982. ———. The Reorganized Church of Jesus Christ of Latter Day Saints in succession from 1830 to the present. [Lamoni, Ia., n.d.]
31p. 23cm. (No. 45)
MoInRC, NjP

6983. ———. Reports to General Conference and conventions, 1920. [Lamoni, Iowa, Independence, Mo., 1895–1927]
v. 16cm.
Statistical and financial report to the membership of the church. 1895–1897 under title: Ministry reports. Supplement to the *Saints' Herald.*
USlC 1895, 1896, 1897, 1920, 1923, 1927

6984. ———. Reports to the Seventy-second conference. [Independence] 1927.
94 [1]p. 19½cm.
USlC

6984a. ———. Resolution on the question of common consent, preamble and resolution, and substitute. [Independence, Mo.? 1923]
3p. 19cm.
1923 Conference resolutions.
MoInRC

6985. ———. The Sabbath question. [Plano, Ill., n.d.]
12p. 22cm. (No. 27)
Variant printings.
CtY, MH, NN, USlC

6986. ———. The Sabbath question; a long-mooted subject, yet one that still provokes much discussion in some quarters. This tract brings much light to bear on the subject, and is of value for reference and study. Lamoni, Ia., Printed for the Board of Publication by Herald Publishing House, 190–]
12p. 21cm. (No. 27)
Cover-title.
MH, NjP, UHi, UPB, USlC

6987. ———. (same) [Lamoni, Ia., Herald Publishing House, n.d.]
22p. 19cm.
MoInRC

6988. ———. Saliggørelsens Vej. [n.p.] Odder Bogtrykkeri [n.d.]
16p. 22cm.
RLDS doctrine, with some material of Utah Mormonism.
USlC

6989. ———. Die sechste posaune ein zeugniss der Warheit für alli Völker . . . herausgegeben unter der Autorität der Reorganisarten Kirche Jesu Christi der Heiligen der Letzten Tage. Burlington, Ia., J. G. Bauer [189–]
35p. 14cm.
Title in English: The sixth trumpet and a witness of the truth for all people.
NN

6990. ———. Sermon series. Lamoni, Ia., October 5, 1892–December 21, 1894.
2v. 28cm. (Supplement to the *Saints' Herald*)
MoInRC inc.; UPB V.1 (not numbered) October 29, 1892–October 14, 1893 (lacks June 10, September 30), V.2, #1–8, 11–28; USlC V.1 inc. (but includes June 10), V.2 #1, 3–5, 7–14, 16–29

6991. ———. Seven points about buying Church bonds. Safety with incentive to save. Independence, Mo. [n.d.]
[4]p. 17cm.
NN

6992. ———. Special circular letter No. 1 to the First Quorum of Seventy. [Lamoni, Ia., 1897]
[4]p. 21½cm.
Caption-title.
Signed: Duncan Campbell, President, Richard S. Salyards, Secretary, and dated: Lamoni, Iowa, January 13, 1897.
CtY

6993. ———. Spiritualism or witchcraft. [Plano, Ill., True Latter-Day Saints' Herald Office, 1865]
8p. 21cm.
Announced for sale in *The True Latter-Day Saints' Herald*, Jan. 15, 1865.
Published in the *Herald*, Dec. 15, 1864–Jan. 1, 15, 1865. In three parts.
MoInRC, NN, UPB

6994. ———. Statement of belief on faith and doctrine. Independence, Mo., Herald House [n.d.]
3p. 16cm. (Gospel Series. No. 1)
MoInRC

6995. ———. The successor in the Prophetic Office and Presidency of the Church. [By an elder in Utah. Plano, Ill., 186–]
15 [1]p. 21cm. (No. 17)
Variant printings.
CSmH, DLC, MH, NjP, NN, USlC

REORGANIZED CHURCH OF JESUS CHRIST

6996. ———. (same) [n.p., n.d.]
15 [1]p. 21½cm. (No. 17)
On verso of p. 15: Advertisement for the *True Latter Day Saints' Herald* and *Zion's Hope*.
USlC

6997. ———. (same) [Lamoni, Ia., n.d.]
16p. 25cm.
CU–B

6998. ———. (same) Revised ed. Lamoni, Ia. [187–]
16p. 20½cm. (No. 17)
CSmH, MH, MoInRC, NjP, NN, USlC

6999. ———. (same) Plano, Ill. [n.d.]
16p. 21½cm. (No. 17)
At head of title: (Revised edition)
Variant printing.
USlC

7000. ———. Synopsis of the faith and doctrines of the Church of Jesus Christ of Latter-Day Saints. Compiled from the Bible, Book of Mormon, Doctrine and Covenants, and other publications of the church with an appendix, containing an epitome of ecclesiastical history and a chronology of important events in the history of the latter day work. Plano, Ill., 1865.
352p. 13½cm.
Chronology of important events in the history of the Latter Day work.
CSmH, MH, MoInRC

7001. ———. Tithing. Lamoni, Ia. [Printed at the True Latter Day Saints' Herald Office, n.d.]
8p. 25cm.
NN

7002. ———. Tithing. Plano, Ill. [186–]
8p. 24cm.
Caption-title.
CSmH, CtY, MoInRC, NjP, NN, USlC

7003. ———. To the Church. [Independence? 1924?]
[1]p. 25cm.
Report of the meeting of the April 1924 council composed of the First Presidency, The Twelve, and bishops on supreme central control.
MoInRC

7004. ———. Trial of the witnesses of the resurrection of Jesus. Plano, Ill., 1870.
35p. 23cm.
MH, MoInRC, NN, USlC

7005. ———. (same) [Plano, Ill., Printed at the True Latter Day Saints' Herald Office [186–]
35 [1]p. 21½cm.
On verso of p. 35: No. 4. Epitome of the faith and doctrine of the Reorganized Church . . .
Variant printings.
NN, USlC

7006. ———. (same) [Plano, Ill., J. W. Briggs? n.d.]
35p. 24½cm. (No. 4)
"Epitome of the faith and doctrine" on last page, verso.
NN

7007. ———. (same) [Lamoni, Ia., Printed at the Latter Day Saints' Herald Office, n.d.]
35 [1]p. 22cm.
On verso of p. 35: No. 4. Epitome of the faith and doctrines of the Reorganized Church . . .
USlC

7008. ———. Trial of the witnesses of the resurrection of Jesus; a legal argument. Lamoni, Ia., True Latter Day Saints' Herald Office [186–]
35 [1]p. 25cm.
On verso of final leaf: Kirtland Temple Suit.
CSmH, MH

7009. ———. (same) [n.p.] Printed at the True Latter Day Saints' Herald Office [186–]
35 [1]p. 22½cm.
On verso of p. 35: Kirtland Temple suit.
USlC

7010. ———. Tracts on the principles of the Gospel. Lamoni, Ia., 1891.
30 nos. 21cm.
Partial contents. #2. Truth made manifest, by Eliza. #3. The voice of the Good Shepherd. #6. The "one baptism," its mode, subjects, prerequisites and design and who shall administer. #7. Who then can be saved, By Joseph Smith. #8. Fulness of the atonement, By M. Faulconer. #10. The narrow way by Elder Isaac Sheen. #11. The Plan of Salvation by Elder Isaac Sheen. #20. The "one body" or, the Church of Christ under the apostleship and under apostasy. #22. Faith and repentance. #23. Baptism. #24. The Kingdom of God. What is it? Whence comes it? #25. Laying on of hands. #27. The sabbath question.
CtY, UPB

———. Truth made manifest. *See Eliza* [*pseud.*]

7011. ———. Truths by three witnesses: a warning voice. Plano, Ill. [187–]
[1]l. 20cm. (No. 21)
CtY, NjP

7012. ———. (same) Lamoni, Ia. [Herald Publishing House, 189–]
[1]l. 25cm. (Tracts. No. 21)
On verso: Epitome of the faith and doctrines.
MoInRC, NN

7013. ———. (same) [n.p., n.d.]
[1]p. 21½cm. (No. 21)
USlC

7014. ———. Utah-Mormonismus im Widerspruch zu den Schriften. Herausgegeben von der Reorganisierten Kirche Jesu Christi der Heiligen der Letzten Tage (Hauptsitz: Independence, Missouri) Ber. Staaten von Nord-Amerika. Bernburg a. Saale, 1921.
22p. 18½cm.
Title in English: Utah Mormonism in contradiction to Scriptures.
MoInRC

———. Visions of Joseph Smith, the seer.
See Smith, Joseph, 1805–1844.

———. The voice of the good shepherd.
See Derry, Charles.

7015. ———. Die Wahrheit, herausgegeben von der Reorganisierten Kirche Jesu Christi del Heiligen der letzten Tage. Zu beziehen von J. G. Bauer. Burlington, Ia. [n.d.]
8p. 23cm.
Short statement of beliefs.
Title in English: The truth.
NN

7015a. ———. We believe. [n.p., n.d.]
[6]p. 21½cm. (F.S. No. 2)
Missionary folder.
NjP

7016. ———. Der weg der Seligkeit. Kiel, Druck von C. H. Jebens [n.d.]
16p. 21½cm.
Title in English: The way of salvation.
MoInRC

7017. ———. What is truth? What is true orthodoxy? What is an evangelical church? Lamoni, Ia., [188–]
[1]l. 23cm. (No. 31)
On verso: The gospel. No. 41.
Caption-title.
CSmH, UHi

7018. ———. (same) Lamoni, Ia. [Herald Publishing House, 189–]
[1]l. 24cm.
On verso: Epitome of Faith and doctrines.
MoInRC, UPB

7019. ———. What we believe. [Lamoni, Ia., Herald Publishing House, n.d.]
7p. 15cm.
The Epitome of the faith and doctrines of the Reorganized church . . . with scripture citations.
ULA, USl

7020. ———. (same) Lamoni, Ia., Herald Publishing House [n.d.]
8p. 17½cm.
USlC

7020a. ———. (same) Independence, Mo., Herald Publishing House [n.d.]
8p. 17½cm.
NjP

7021. ———. (same) [Manchester, Eng., J. Russell, n.d.]
15p. 11cm.
MoInRC, USlC

7022. ———. (same) Lamoni, Ia. [n.d.]
20p. 11cm.
MoInRC

7023. ———. Whence came the red man? [Independence, Mo., Ensign Publishing House, 1920]
11p. 20cm.
MoInRC, ULA

———. Which is the Church? Jesus Christ established but one visible Church. *See A., W.*

7024. ———. Why I believe the Book of Mormon. Lamoni, Ia., 1909.
16p. 19½cm. (No. 302)
IWW, MoInRC, UPB

7025. ———. (same) Lamoni, Ia., Published by the Board of Publication of the Reorganized Church of Jesus Christ of Latter Day Saints, 1911.
16p. 19cm.
MoInRC, NN

7026. ———. A Year of lessons for the nursery child. For the three-year-old child. To be used by parents and teachers. Independence, Herald Publishing House, 1930.
151p. illus., music. 22cm.
USlC

7026a. Reorganized Church of Jesus Christ of Latter Day Saints. Central Church. A few facts to the point, this pamphlet contains brief items of general information to the public. [n.p., ca. 1910]
unpaged. 22cm.
William Earl LaRue was pastor between 1908–1911.
MoInRC

7026b. Reorganized Church of Jesus Christ of Latter Day Saints. Committee on American Archaeology. Report of the Committee on American Archaeology appointed by the general conference of the Reorganized Church of Jesus Christ of Latter Day Saints, 1894. Lamoni, Ia., Herald Publishing House, 1898.
106p. plates, 6 maps. 19cm.
An interpretation of American archaeological discoveries in the light of the Book of Mormon.
CtY, MoInRC, NjP, NN, USlC, WHi

7026c. ———. (same) Lamoni, Ia., Herald Publishing House, 1902.
2p.l. [5]–106, 46p. 18½cm.
"Additional report of Committee on American Archaeology."
MoInRC, UPB, USlC

7027. ———. (same) Lamoni, Ia., Herald Publishing House, 1910.
5p.l. [11]–191p. maps, plates. 20cm.
MoInRC, NjP, NN, UPB, USlC, WHi

7028. Reorganized Church of Jesus Christ of Latter Day Saints. Committee to wait upon the President and Congress of the United States. The Utah problem and the solution. [Washington? J. M. Burnett, Printer, 1882]
5p. 22cm.
Cover-title.
Signed by Z. H. Gurley and E. L. Kelley.
ICN, WHi

7029. Reorganized Church of Jesus Christ of Latter Day Saints. Coordinating Committee. Report of the Coordinating Committee. [Independence, Mo.? 1918]
4p. 14cm.
Written in Independence, Mo., 1918. Members of the Committee: Frederick M. Smith, George A. Briggs, Daniel MacGregor, G. S. Towbridge.
MoInRC

7030. Reorganized Church of Jesus Christ of Latter Day Saints. Council of the Twelve. Brief submitted by the Quorum of Twelve. [Lamoni, Ia., 1919]
8p. 20cm.
Statement concerning disagreement between Council of the Twelve and the First Presidency on supreme directional control.
MoInRC

7031. ———. Epistle of the Twelve and the bishopric (in relation to funds for the Reorganized Church of Latter Day Saints. By William H. Kellogg and others) Plano, Ill., 1881.
8p. 19cm.
MoInRC, NN, USlC

7032. ———. [Epistle] of the Twelve and the Bishopric, to the Church of Christ, called to be Saints, in all the world, greeting. [Plano, 1881]
8p. 19cm.
NN, USlC

7033. ———. Missionary policy. [Independence, Mo.] Office of the Quorum of Twelve, 1922.
4p. 15cm.
MoInRC

7033a. ———. Reports of the Quorum of the Twelve to the General Conference. [n.p., n.d.]
[1]l. 31cm.
Concerning the rights and privileges of the Council of Twelve.
MoInRC

7034. Reorganized Church of Jesus Christ of Latter Day Saints. Daughters of Zion. Fireside talks with our girls. Published under the auspices of the Daughters of Zion. Lamoni, Ia., Herald Publishing House, 1902.
3p.l., 7–71p. 18cm.
A book of hygiene, moral standards for RLDS girls.
MoInRC

7035. Reorganized Church of Jesus Christ of Latter Day Saints. Executive Committee. Centennial oratorical contest. Theme: The restoration. Handbook of instructions for those participating, issued by the Executive Committee, Independence, Missouri, July 1928. [Independence, 1928]
48p. 22cm.
Cover-title.
CSmH, CU-B

7036. Reorganized Church of Jesus Christ of Latter Day Saints. First Presidency. The April Council of First Presidency, members of Quorum of Twelve in America and Order of Bishops. [n.p., 1924]
7p. 20cm.
Reprint from *Saints' Herald*, June 18, 1924.
Supreme directional control.
MoInRC, NjP

7037. ———. The disaffection of R. C. Evans. [n.p., n.d.]
11 [1]p. 23cm.
Pamphlet signed by Frederick M. Smith, Benjamin McGuire and John W. Rushton.
MoInRC, NjP, USlC

7038. ———. An open letter to protesting Saints and all other interested persons. Independence, Mo., 1926.
15p. 20cm.
Supreme directional control.
MoInRC, NjP

7039. ———. An open Letter to the Saints. Independence, Mo., Department of Publicity, Reorganized Church of Jesus Christ of Latter Day Saints [1926]
9p. 20cm.
Includes financial summary for the year ending June 30, 1926.
Supreme directional control.
MoInRC, NjP

7040. ———. President's message. [n.p., n.d.]
9p. 20cm.
Supreme directional control.
MoInRC

7041. Reorganized Church of Jesus Christ of Latter Day Saints. First United Order of Enoch. Proposed constitution and by-laws of our First United Order of Enoch. Plano, Ill., Printed at L.D.S. Herald Steam Book and Job Office [n.d.]
8p. 17cm.
MoInRC

7042. ———. (same) Plano, Ill., L.D.S. Herald Steam Book and Job Office, 1870.
8p. 17cm.
MoInRC

7043. ———. Report of the Board of Directors to the stockholders of the First United Order of Enoch. Plano, Ill., Herald Steam and Job Office, 1871.
4p. 20½cm.
Signed: E. Banta.
Supplement to the *Saints' Herald*, June 15, 1871.
MoInRC

———. *See also its United Order of Enoch, and Lamoni Order of Enoch.*

7044. Reorganized Church of Jesus Christ of Latter Day Saints. General Department of Women. The centennial year book. "Helps and governments" offered by the Women's Department to every woman who desires a better preparation for service to home, children, community, church, and God. Independence, Mo., [1920]
3p.l. [9]–72 [2]p. port. 17½cm.
USlC

7045. Reorganized Church of Jesus Christ of Latter Day Saints. Hymnal. Danish. 1910? Salmebog til Kirke-og Husandagt. Udgivet og forlagt af den gjenorganiserede Jesu Christi Kirke af Sidste Dages Hellige. Det Bechske Bogtr. i Aalborg [ca. 1910]
2p.l., 5–320p. 14½cm.
Without music.
UPB

7046. ———. **1925?** Aandelige Sange til Brug i Mission of Søndagsskole. Udgiver: Missionaer Peter Andersen. [Aarhus, Nationaltrykkeriet Søndergade [ca. 1925]
[96]p. 12½cm.
USlC

7047. Reorganized Church of Jesus Christ of Latter Day Saints. Hymnal. English. 1861. The Latter Day Saints' selection of hymns. Published by The Church of Jesus Christ of Latter Day Saints. Cincinnati, Ohio, 1861.
304p. 12cm.
Includes 1st line index.
MoInRC

7047a. ———. **1864.** (same) Cincinnati, Ohio: 1864.
2p.l., 7–346 [8]p. 11cm.
MoInRC, UPB

7048. ———. **1870.** The Saints' harp: a collection of hymns and spiritual songs for public and private devotion. Compiling committee: Joseph Smith, Mark H. Forscutt, David H. Smith, and Norman W. Smith. Lamoni, Ia., 1870.
vi, 792p. 15cm.
Without music.
Sabin 83300
CSmH, DLC, ICHi, MoInRC, UHi, UPB, USlC, UU

7049. ———. **1870.** (same) Lamoni, Ia., 1870.
785p. 15cm.
MoInRC

7050. ———. **1870.** (same) Plano, Ill., 1870.
vi, 792p. 15cm.
Variant printing.
ULA

7051. ———. **1871.** (same) Lamoni, Ia., 1871.
792p. 15cm.
MoInRC

7052. ———. **1889.** The Saints' harmony; a selection of music from about three hundred different composers, including about five hundred tunes not before published in America, nearly four hundred of them composed especially for this work; Edited by Mark H. Forscutt. Lamoni, Ia., [1889]
611p. music. 12cm.
DLC, MoInRC

7053. ———. **1889.** (same) Also The Saint's Harp. Lamoni, Ia., 1889.
15, 565p. music. 15cm.
Combined so that tunes could be matched from *Saints' harmony* to words in *Saints' harp*.
DLC, MoInRC

7054. ———. **1895.** The Saint's hymnal. Lamoni, Ia., 1895.
195p. music. 20cm.
Committee composed of: Ralph G. Smith, Lucy L. Ressequie, Arthur H. Mills.
MoInRC

7055. ———. 1895. The Saints' hymnal . . . Independence, Mo., Herald Publishing House [1895]
277p. 20cm.
UPB

7056. ———. 1896. The Saints' hymnal. Lamoni, Ia., 1896.
209p. 14cm.
MoInRC

7057. ———. 1900. The Saints' hymnal. 12th ed. Lamoni, Ia., 1900.
195p. 19cm.
MoInRC

7058. ———. 1900? The Saints' hymnal. [Independence, Herald Publishing House, 1900?]
257p. 14cm.
Title page missing.
UPB

7059. ———. 1900? Saints' hymnal. Lamoni, Ia., Herald Publishing House [1900?]
277p. 20cm.
MoInRC

7060. ———. 1902. Saints hymnal. 17th ed. Lamoni, Ia., 1902.
195p. 19½cm.
MoInRC, UPB

7061. ———. 1903. Zion's praises. Lamoni, Ia., Herald Publishing House, c1903.
[2]p. 232 nos. [4]p. music. 20cm.
MoInRC, NjP, USlC

7062. ———. 1903. (same) Lamoni, Ia., Herald Publishing House [1903]
[2]p. [232]l. 20cm.
MoInRC

7063. ———. 1904. (same) 3d ed. Lamoni, Ia., Published by Herald Publishing House [c1903]
1p.l., 232 nos. [5]p. music. 19½cm.
Song: "Onward and upward" added to the 1904 ed. Index redone. Otherwise plates are the same.
MoInRC, UPB, USlC

7064. ———. 1904. The Saints' hymnal. Words only, 10th ed. [Lamoni, Ia.] 1904.
209p. 14cm.
MoInRC

7065. ———. 1906. The Saints' hymnal. 22d ed. Lamoni, Ia., 1906.
195p. 19cm.
MoInRC

7066. ———. 1907. (same) 23d ed. Lamoni, Ia., Herald Publishing House, 1907.
277p. 19cm.
MoInRC

7067. ———. 1908. (same) 25th ed. Lamoni, Ia., Herald Publishing House, 1908.
277p. 19cm.
MoInRC

7068. ———. 1908. The Saints' hymnal. 10th ed. Lamoni, Ia., 1908.
257p. 14cm.
MoInRC

7068a. ———. 1920. (same) Lamoni, Ia., Herald Publishing House, 1920.
277p. music. 19½cm.
USlC

7069. ———. 1922? The Saints' hymnal: a compilation of hymns for the use of church and church school congregations of the Reorganized Church of Jesus Christ of Latter Day Saints. Independence, Mo., Herald Publishing House [1922?]
2p.l., 372p. 14cm.
MoInRC, UPB

7069a. ———. 1922? Young people's meeting, Central Church. [n.p., 1922?]
18 hymns. 22cm.
Hymns for use April 6 to 16, 1922.
MoInRC

7070. ———. 1923. The Saints' hymnal, words only. Independence, Mo., 1923.
257p. 13cm.
MoInRC

7071. ———. 1924. Zion's praises. Independence, Mo., 1924.
2p.l., 232 nos. [4]p. music. 20cm.
USlC

7072. ———. 1927. (same) Independence, Mo., Published by Herald Publishing House, 1927 [c1903]
2p.l., 232 nos. [4]p. music. 19½cm.
MoInRC

7073. Reorganized Church of Jesus Christ of Latter Day Saints. Hymnal. Tahitian. E Buka himene i faaauhia e te mau orometua; no te haamaitairaa i te Atua i te Haamoriraa. Lonedona, 1882.
2p.l., 247 [9]p. 12cm.
USlC

7074. Reorganized Church of Jesus Christ of Latter Day Saints. Lamoni Order of Enoch. The Lamoni Order of Enoch. Articles of Association and by-laws. Lamoni, Ia., [Lamoni Order of Enoch] 1914.
12p. 14cm.
MoInRC

7075. Reorganized Church of Jesus Christ of Latter Day Saints. Missions. European. Minutes of the European Mission general conference, held in London, on October 5th and 6th, 1872. Published by order of the Conference . . . Birmingham, W. H. Faiers [1872]
35 [1]p. 21cm.
CtY, DLC, USlC

7076. Reorganized Church of Jesus Christ of Latter Day Saints. Order of Evangelists. The patriarchate. The calling and duties of patriarchs considered and defended, as set forth by the Reorganized Church of Jesus Christ of Latter Day Saints, by the Order of Evangelists. Lamoni, Ia., Herald Publishing House [1905]
51p. 19cm.
MoInRC

7076a. Reorganized Church of Jesus Christ of Latter Day Saints. Presiding Bishopric. Budget plans and problems with detailed plans for systematic giving through the departments. Independence, Mo., 1928.
22[1]p. 19½cm.
USlC

7077. ———. Mission Bishopric statement, to Bishop's agents, Bishop's branch collectors, and saints of the British Isles Mission. [n.p., n.d.]
3p. 21cm.
MoInRC

7078. ———. The Reorganized Church of Jesus Christ of Latter Day Saints, versus the Utah Mormon self-styled Latter Day Saints. [London? n.d.]
8p. 22cm.
MoInRC

7079. ———. Why I am a member of the Church of Jesus Christ. [n.p., n.d.]
4p. 22cm.
MoInRC

7080. Reorganized Church of Jesus Christ of Latter Day Saints. Purity Board. If Zion is to be the pure in heart; issued by the Purity Board, Reorganized Church of Jesus Christ of Latter Day Saints. Lamoni, Ia., Herald Publishing House [n.d.]
8p. 16cm.
MoInRC

7080a. Reorganized Church of Jesus Christ of Latter Day Saints. Quorum of High Priests. List of names and addresses. [Lamoni? 1893?]
4p. 21cm.
MoInRC

7081. Reorganized Church of Jesus Christ of Latter Day Saints. Quorum of Seventy. First Quorum of Seventy; important resolutions with a list of quorum members with addresses. [n.p., n.d.]
4p. 26cm. (Circular letter. No. 10)
MoInRC

7081a. ———. First Quorum of Seventy, 1905, consisting of resolutions new in force as they appear on the records with a list of names and addresses. [n.p., 1905?]
6p. 22cm. (Circular letter. No. 7)
MoInRC

7081b. ———. First Quorum of Seventy, 1914; important resolutions with addresses of quorum members. [n.p., n.d.]
4p. 26cm. (Circular Letter. No. 10)
MoInRC

7081c. ———. Resolution and important items on the records of the First Seventy now in force. [n.p., n.d.]
4p. 22cm.
Covers the 1904–1915 period.
MoInRC

7081d. ———. Resolutions on the records of the First Seventy now in force. [n.p., n.d.]
4p. 22cm.
Covers period from 1880–1904.
MoInRC

7082. Reorganized Church of Jesus Christ of Latter Day Saints. Salt Lake City Chapter. Latter Day Saints and the economic problem. [Salt Lake City? n.d.]
folder (6 p.) 21×10cm.
CU–B

7082a. Reorganized Church of Jesus Christ of Latter Day Saints. Sons of Zion. Constitution and by-laws of the Sons of Zion, adopted at Independence, Missouri, April 13, 1895.
4p. 15cm.
MoInRC

7083. Reorganized Church of Jesus Christ of Latter Day Saints. Stake. Lamoni. Leaflet of instructions for local library boards. Issued by Lamoni Stake Library Board. [Lamoni, Ia.] 1914.
8p. 19cm.
Treatment of stake libraries.
MoInRC

7083a. ———. Our appeal, an address to the saints of the Lamoni Stake, written and adopted by the Bishopric of the Stake as an expression of the requirements of the times and the opportunities of the people of the stake as a part of the general church organization. [n.p.] 1913?
[8]p. 20cm.
MoInRC

7084. Reorganized Church of Jesus Christ of Latter Day Saints. United Order of Enoch. The United Order of Enoch. Articles of Association and by-laws. Independence, Mo., 1910.
15p. 16cm.
A semi-official organization in the Reorganized Church of Jesus Christ of Latter Day Saints.
MoInRC

———. *See also its First United Order of Enoch, and Lamoni Order of Enoch.*

7085. Reorganized Church of Jesus Christ of Latter Day Saints. The Women's Department. Book of the oriole girls, arranged for and dedicated to every girl. 4th ed. [Independence, Mo.] 1922.
60 [4]p. music. 18cm.
USIC

7085a. ———. Revised instructions regarding the work of the Department of Women, 1924. Independence, Mo. [1924]
30p. 19½cm.
USIC

7086. Republican Party. Utah. Strife and bitterness in Utah. Avowed aim of the American Party leaders. [Salt Lake City, 1908]
[4]p. 22cm.
The anti-Mormon character of the American Party.
USIC

7087. Restoration of the Gospel. [Salt Lake City? n.d.]
[2]p. 20cm.
Caption-title.
Thirty-two questions and answers on Mormonism.
CU–B

7088. The Restorer. Aberdor, Wales [and Birmingham] March, 1864–Dec. 1869.
5v. monthly. 28cm.
Issued irregularly during 1866–67.
First editor: Jason W. Briggs.
MoInRC V.2 #3, V.3; NN inc.; USIC V.1 #2–10, 12, V.3

7089. ———. (same) Independence, Mo., Published by the Church of Christ. November 15, 1926–April, 1927.
V.1 #1–5. monthly. 30½cm.
No issue March, 1927.
Edited by John J. Snyder, Frank F. Wipper, Addie Hoss, H. Archambault.
NN, USIC

7089a. The Retainer. Vol. 1. Ephraim, Utah, Snow Academy, 1914.
1v. illus. 28cm.
Publication of the senior class of 1914.
USIC

7090. The Return. Davis City, Ia., [Richmond, Mo., Independence, Mo., Denver, Colo.] January, 1889–October, 1900.
8v. monthly, semi-monthly. 23cm.
First published by Ebenezer Robinson in the interest of the Church of Christ (Whitmer)
Publication suspended: March 1891–September, 1892; November, 1893–February, 1895.
None published for July 1893.
V.4 #1–2 omitted from numbering.
V.4 #3–11 called V.3 #3–11.
V.1–3 #14 also numbered 1–38; V.4 #3–11 also numbered 27–35; V.4 #12–V.5 #1 also numbered 48–59.
Moved to Denver 1898. Last issue: V.8 #3 (October 1900)
Succeeded by *Messenger of Truth.*
Morgan
CU–B V.1–3 #14, V.4 #3–19; MH V.1–5 lacking #4–14; MoInRC V.1–5, 6 #5; NN V.1 #1–2, 3–12, V.3 #2–4, V.7 #11; UPB; V.1–V.3 #13, V.4 #12, 16, 19–22, V.5 #2–12; USIC V.1 comp., V.2 comp., V.4 #4–14, 16–22, V.5 #2–12, V.7 #7, V.8 #2,3

7091. Revere, Joseph Warren. A tour of duty in California; including a description of the gold region: and an account of the voyage around Cape Horn; with notices of lower California, the Gulf and Pacific coasts, and the principal events attending the conquest of the Californians. By Joseph Warren Revere, Lieutenant U. S. Navy, lately in comand of the Military District of Sonoma. Edited by Joseph N. Balestier, of New York. With a map and plates from original designs. New York, C. S. Francis' Co. . . . Boston, J. H. Francis . . . 1849.
3p.l. [iii]–vip., [1]l., 305p. plates, fold. map. 19½cm.
Mention of Sam Brannan and rumors of a gold discovery near Salt Lake (derived from Col. Mason's report of August 17, 1848) p. 235, 239. Mention of Mormon diggings, p. 229, 241.
CtY, CU–B, DLC

7092. Reynolds, George. Are we of Israel? By Elder George Reynolds . . . Salt Lake City, J. H. Parry & Co., 1883.
55p. 20cm.
Mormon doctrine of Israel.
CU–B, DLC, ICN, NjP, NN, UPB, USl, UU

7093. ———. (same) 2d ed. . . . Salt Lake City, G. Q. Cannon and Sons Co., 1895.
iv [5]–56p. 19½cm.
NjP, NN, OCH, ULA, UPB, USIC

7094. ———. (same) 3d ed. Salt Lake City, Deseret Sunday School Union, 1916.
iv [5]–56p. 19½cm.
NjP, UHi, UPB, USIC

7095. ———. The Book of Abraham. Its authenticity established as a divine and ancient record. With copious references to ancient and modern authorities. Salt Lake City, Deseret News Printing and Publishing Establishment, 1879.
v, 49p. 23cm.
CSmH, CtY, CU-B, DLC, ICN, MH, MoInRC, NjP, N, UHi, ULA, UPB, USl, USlC, UU

7096. ———. Chronological chart of Nephite and Lamanite history. [Salt Lake City] c1898.
colored chart. 40×210cm.
USlC

7097. ———. . . . A complete concordance to the Book of Mormon, by Elder George Reynolds . . . Salt Lake City, 1900.
851 (i.e. 852) p. 28cm.
Page between 789 & 790 numbered 789½.
CtY, DLC, UHi, UPB, USl, USlC

7098. ———. A dictionary of the Book of Mormon, comprising its biographical, geographical and other proper names, by Elder George Reynolds . . . Salt Lake City, Joseph Hyrum Parry, 1891.
2p.l., 364p. 19cm.
CU-B, DLC, ICN, NjP, NN, UHi, ULA, UPB, USl, USlC

7099. ———. (same) Pronouncing vocabulary by Prof. John M. Mills, with Pres. Anthon H. Lund and Dr. James E. Talmage, associates. [2d ed] Salt Lake City, Deseret Sunday School Union, 1910.
2p.l., 363p. 19½cm.
UHi, UPB, USlC

7100. ———. (same) Salt Lake City, Deseret Sunday School Union, 1929.
2p.l., 320p. 20cm.
NjP, USlC

7101. ———. The Mormon metropolis. An illustrated guide to Salt Lake City and its environs. Containing illustrations and descriptions of principal places of interest to tourists. Also interesting information and historical data with regard to Utah and its people . . . Salt Lake City, J. H. Parry, 1883.
44p. illus., fold. map. 19½cm.
CSmH, USl, USlC, UU

7102. ———. (same) Salt Lake City, The Magazine printing Co., 1883 [1886]
48p. illus., plates, fold. map. 20cm.
Cover gives 1886 as date of printing.
CSmH, UPB

7103. ———. (same) Salt Lake City, J. H. Parry & Co., 1887.
48p. illus., plates, fold. front. (plan) 20cm.
DLC, NN, ULA, USlC

7104. ———. (same) Salt Lake City, J. H. Parry & Co., 1888.
64p. illus., fold. front. (plan) 20cm.
CU-B, NjP, UPB

7105. ———. (same) Salt Lake City, J. H. Parry and Company, Publishers, 1889.
iv [5]-68p. illus. 19cm.
CU-B, DLC, NN

7106. ———. (same) Salt Lake City, The Magazine Printing Co., 1890.
iv, 6-67p. illus. 19cm.
CtY, DLC, NjP, NN, OO, USlC

7107. ———. (same) Salt Lake City, J. H. Parry & Co., 1890.
iv, 6-67p. illus. 17cm.
USlC

7108. ———. (same) Salt Lake City, The Magazine Printing Co., 1891.
iv, 6-67p. illus. 19cm.
CSmH, NN

7109. ———. (same) Salt Lake City, The Magazine Printing Co., 1892.
68p. illus. 19cm.
CU-B, MH, NjP, UHi

7110. ———. (same) 10th ed. Salt Lake City, The Magazine Printing Co., 1893.
68p. illus. 19cm.
CU-B, UPB

7111. ———. (same) 11th ed. Salt Lake City, Magazine Printing Co., 1895.
66p. 19cm.
CSmH, NjP, UPB

7112. ———. (same) 12th ed. Salt Lake City, Magazine Printing Co., 1899.
66p. illus. 19½cm.
MH, NjP

7113. ———. (same) 13th ed. Salt Lake City, Utah Magazine Printing Co., 1902.
52p. 20cm.
UHi

7114. ———. The myth of the "Manuscript found," or, the absurdities of the "Spaulding story." Salt Lake City, Juvenile Instructor Office, 1883.
3p.l. [9]-104p. 18½cm. (Faith promoting series, 11th book)
CSmH, CtY, CU-B, DLC, ICN, IWW, MH, MoInRC, NjPT, NN, UHi, ULA, UPB, USl, USlC, UU, ViU

7115. ———. The story of the Book of Mormon. By Elder George Reynolds . . . With original illustrations by G. M. Ottinger, Wm. T. Armitage, John Held, W. C. Morris and others. Salt Lake City, Joseph Hyrum Parry, 1888.
xv [17]–494p. illus., plates. 23cm.
CSmH, CtY, CU, DLC, ICN, IWW, MH, MoInRC, NjP, UHi, UPB, USl, USlC, UU

7116. ———. (same) 2d ed. Salt Lake City, G. Q. Cannon and Sons Co., 1898.
xiv [17]–412p. illus., plates. 22½cm.
CtY, NN, PCC, PP, PPL–R, UPB, UU

7117. ———. (same) 3d ed. Chicago, Press of Henry C. Etten, Ensign Co., c1888.
xiii [14]–386p. illus. 19½cm.
NjP, ULA, UPB

7118. ———. (same) 4th ed. Chicago, Press of Hillison & Etten Co. [c1888]
xiii [14]–386p. illus. 20cm.
NjP, UHi, UPB, USlC

7119. ———. (same) 5th ed. Independence, Mo., Zion's Printing & Publishing Co. [c1888]
xiii [14]–386p. illus. 19½cm.
NjP, UHi, UPB, USlC, UU

7120. ———, *defendant.* The United States vs. George Reynolds, indictment for bigamy. [Salt Lake City?] 1875.
49p. 22cm.
At head of title: United States of America. Territory of Utah, Third Judicial District, of the October term, A.D. 1875, of the District Court in and for said District held in Salt Lake County.
USlC

———. Plaintiff, writ of error. *See Biddle, George Washington.*

7121. Reynolds, Harold G. To have life more abundantly; address delivered over Radio Station KSL, Sunday Evening, October 2, 1927. [Salt Lake City] 1927.
Broadside. 45½×25½cm.
Reprinted from the *Deseret News.*
UPB

7122. Reynolds, John. My own times, embracing also, the history of my life . . . By John Reynolds. [Belleville Ill., Printed by B. H. Perryman and H. L. Davison] 1855.
600, xxiii [1]p. port. 18½cm.
Mormonism in Illinois with a resume of its history and doctrine.
Another edition: 2d ed. Chicago, Chicago Historical Society, 1879. CSmH, DLC
Howes R236
CSmH, CtY, DLC, ICN, NjP, NN, OCU, OFH, UPB, USlC

7123. Rice, Claton Silas. The Mormon way . . . [Billings, Mont.?] Billings Book Bindery and Printing Co., c1929.
2p.l. [5]–85 [2]p. 24cm.
In 2 parts; Pt. 1. Introduction.
Pt. 2. The Mormon way.
Polemic on Mormonism.
CtY, IWW, MWA, NN, UPB, USl, UU

7124. ———. (same) [Salt Lake City?] c1929.
2p.l. [5]–85 [2]p. 23cm.
I. Night at Mountain Meadows.
II. Nephi Longwell's story.
III. The Mormon Way.
Table of Contents p. [18]
Discussion of Mormonism in general.
UHi, UU

7125. ———. Mormonism and the way out. New York, Presbyterian Church of the U.S.A. [1930?]
8p. 23cm.
Reprinted from the *Missionary Review of the World,* April, 1930.
MoInRC, USlC

7126. ———. Songs of "The Mormon way" [by] Claton S. Rice. [Billings, Mont., Billings Book Binding & Printing Co., c1930]
71p. 20½cm.
Mormon poetry.
CSmH, CtY, DLC, NN, UHi, UPB, UU

7127. Rice, Harvey. Incidents of pioneer life in the early settlement of the Connecticut Western Reserve, by Harvey Rice. Cleveland, Cobb, Andrews and Co., 1881.
xii [13]–300p. 19½cm.
Chap. 27 devoted to Joseph Smith and the translation of the plates and his exposure as a fraud. Later history also included.
CSmH, DLC, OCl, OClW, UHi

7128. ———. (same, under title) Pioneers of the Western Reserve, by Harvey Rice . . . Boston, Lee and Shepard; New York, C. T. Dillingham, 1883.
xii, 350p. front. 20cm.
Another edition. 2d ed. 1888. DLC, OCl, OU
Howes R247
CSmH, DLC, NN, PBM, PHi, PP, PPL, PPM, UHi, UPB

7129. ———. Letters from the Pacific slope; or first impressions . . . New York, D. Appleton, 1870.
iv, 135p. 19cm.
Mormonism, p. 20–36.
Sabin 70823
CSmH, CU–B, DLC, UHi

7130. Rich, Benjamin Erastus. Address of Elder Ben E. Rich at the annual gathering of conference presidents of the Eastern States Mission at New York City, March, 1910. New York, Eastern States Mission, 1910.
16p. 19cm.
UPB, USlC

RICH, B. E.

7131. ———. Address of Ben E. Rich of Ogden delivered at Kanosh, Utah, October 6th, 1892. Do you believe in Utah? Do you believe in her Industries? If so read before you vote. This pamphlet is printed on Utah made paper. Salt Lake City, 1892.
24p. 23cm.
Includes material on the importance of home industry in Mormon theology.
UPB, USIC

7132. ———. Are the Mormons loyal to the government? A rejected manuscript. An answer to the charge which appeared in Pearsons' magazine. The manuscript was returned by Pearson's to the writer with a statement that nothing was wanted as a defense . . . [New York, Church of Jesus Christ of Latter-day Saints, Eastern States Mission, 1910]
32p. 14cm.
Cover title.
MH, NN, USIC

———. The Elder's reference. *See Church of Jesus Christ of Latter-day Saints. Missions.*

7133. ———. A friendly discussion upon religious subjects, compiled from a work entitled "Mr. Durant of Salt Lake City," by Ben E. Rich. [Independence, Mo., Zion's Printing & Publishing Co., n.d.]
21p. 17½cm.
CU-B, UPB

7134. ———. (same) [St. John, Kansas. Southwestern States Mission, n.d.]
24p. 15cm.
UPB, USIC

7135. ———. (same) (Compiled from a work entitled "Mr. Osborn [sic.] of Salt Lake City) San Francisco [n.d.]
22p. 16cm.
USIC

7136. ———. (same) [Chicago, Press of A. L. Swift and Co., n.d.]
23p. 16½cm.
Published by the Northern States Mission.
MoInRC, UPB

7137. ———. (same) [Chattanooga, Tenn., Southern States Mission, n.d.]
24p. 16cm.
MoInRC, USIC, UU, WHi

7138. ———. (same) [n.p., Printed in England, n.d.]
24p. 17cm.
UPB

7139. ———. (same) Revised. [Independence, Mo., Zion's Printing and Publishing Company. Published by the Missions of the Church of Jesus Christ of Latter-day Saints in America, n.d.]
24p. 17½cm.
CU-B, IWW, MoInRC, NN, UHi, UPB, USIC

7140. ———. (same) [Independence, Mo., Zion's Printing and Publishing Company, n.d.]
21p. 18cm.
MoInRC

7141. ———. (same) [Liverpool, Eng.? 189–]
15p. 21cm.
CU-B

7142. ———. (same) Salt Lake City, Deseret News Press [189–]
23p. 16½cm.
WHi

7143. ———. (same) [Independence, Mo., Missions of the Church of Jesus Christ of Latter-day Saints. Zion's Printing and Publishing Co., 1899?]
16p. 17½cm.
CU-B, MoInRC, MWA, WjP, NN, USIC, UU

7144. ———. (same) [Cincinnati, Ohio, Middle States Mission and Atlanta, Ga., Southern States Mission, ca. 1902]
32p. 12½cm.
USIC

7145. ———. (same) Salt Lake City, Deseret News Press [1903]
30 [1]p. 15½cm.
MoInRC, UPB, USIC

7146. ———. (same) [Salt Lake City, Bureau of Information] 1903.
31 [1]p. 14cm.
Cover-title.
In pink printed wrappers.
USIC

7147. ———. (same) [Chicago, Ill., Northern States Mission] 1903.
32p. 14cm.
Cover-title.
In pink printed wrappers.
USIC

7148. ———. (same) [Kansas City, Mo., Southwestern States Mission] 1903.
32p. 14cm.
Cover-title.
In brown printed wrappers.
USIC

7149. ———. (same) [Chicago, Ill., Northern States Mission] 1904.
32p. 14cm.
Cover-title.
In pink printed wrappers.
USIC

7150. ———. (same) [New York, Chambers Printing Co., ca. 1905]
31 [1]p. 14cm.
Title from cover.
Articles of faith on front cover.
CtY, MH, NjP, NN, USlC

7151. ———. (same) New York, Eastern States Mission [ca. 1905]
31 [1]p. 13cm.
NN, USl, USlC

7152. ———. (same) [Kansas City, Central States Mission] 1906.
32p. 14cm.
UPB

7153. ———. (same) [Chattanooga, Tenn., Latter-day Saint Publications, ca. 1910]
24p. 16cm.
Caption-title.
USlC

7154. ———. (same) [Independence, Mo.?] Published by the Missions of the Church of Jesus Christ of Latter-day Saints [ca. 1918]
21 [1]p. 18cm.
Caption-title.
USlC

7155. ———. (same) [Independence, Published by the Missions of the Church of Jesus Christ of Latter day Saints, ca. 1921]
23p. 17½cm.
Caption-title.
Printed by Zion's Printing and Publishing Company.
USlC

7156. ———. (same) Salt Lake City, 1930.
32p. 14cm.
USlC

7157. ———. (same, in Danish) Den Fremmede fra Vesterlandet eller en venskabelig Forhandling om religiøse Spørgsmaal. Af Ben E. Rich. Oversat fra Engelsk. Første Oplag, 15,000. Kjøbenhavn, Udgivet og forlagt af Christian D. Fjeldsted . . . 1905.
32p. 19cm.
USlC

7158. ———. (same) [Aarhus, Trykt hos P. S. Christiansen, ca. 1908]
32p. 18cm.
USlC copy has mss. corrections for the third edition.
USlC

7159. ———. (same) [Kjøbenhavn, Udgivet og forlagt af Andrew Jenson . . . Trykt hos P. S. Christiansen, Aarhus, 1911]
16p. 23cm.
Manuscript on p. 16: Tredie oplag., 50,000.
Mss. corrections for subsequent editions.
USlC

7160. ———. (same) [Kjøbenhavn, Udgivet og forlagt af Andrew Jenson . . . Trykt hos P. S. Christiansen, Aarhus, 1911]
16p. 23cm.
Tredie oplag, 50,000 printed on p. 16. Changes from mss. of above.
USlC

7161. ———. (same) Af Aeldste Ben E. Rich . . . [Kjøbenhavn, Udgivet og forlagt af Martin Christophersen, . . . Trykt hos P. S. Christiansen, Aarhus, 1912]
16p. 21½cm.
Fjerde Oplag, 50,000 printed on p. 16.
USlC

7162. ———. (same, under title) Den fremmede fra vesterlandet en samtale om religiøse spørsmaal af aeldste Ben E. Rich. København, Udgivet og forlagt af Joseph L. Petersen . . . 1927.
15 [1]p. 22½cm.
USlC

7163. ———. (same) København, Udgivet og forlagt af Holger M. Larsen, 1930.
16p. 21½cm.
USlC

7164. ———. (same, in Dutch) Een Vriendschappelijke discussie over Godsdienst - Onderwerpen door Ben E. Rich. [Rotterdam, Uitgave van Alex Nibley, n.d.]
29p. 13½cm.
USlC

7165. ———. (same, in French) Où est la vérité? Discussion amicale sur des sujets religieux, par Ben E. Rich. [Traduit par M. André Paillard] Bâle, Serge-F. Ballif [192–]
22 [2]p. 18cm.
Cover-title.
UHi, UPB

7166. ———. (same, in Spanish) Una discusión amigable sobre asuntos religiosos. Por el Elder Ben E. Rich. Traducido del Inglés Por el Elder Rey L. Pratt. El Paso, Texas, Publicado por la Misión Mexicana . . . 1921.
24p. 17½cm.
USlC

7167. ———. (same) Los Angeles, Publicado por la Misión Mexicana . . . 1930.
24p. 18½cm.
USlC

7168. ———. (same, in Swedish) Främlingen från västern eller ett vänskapligt Meningsutbyte i religiösa frågor. Sjätte upplagan. Stockholm, T. Tobiason [1920]
22p. 18½cm.
UPB

7169. ———. (same) Nionde upplagan. Stockholm, Utgiven och förlagd av Gideon N. Hulterström [n.d.]
23 [2]p. 18cm.
"Översatt från Engelskan av äldste C. A. Krantz."
USIC

7170. ———. Gospel interview of the doctrine of the Church of Jesus Christ of Latter-day Saints, by Elder Ben E. Rich in Atlanta. Constitution, Atlanta, Ga. [Chattanooga, Tenn.] Southern States Mission [190–]
32 [1]p. 13cm.
Title from cover.
MH, NN, USl

7171. ———. (same) New York, Published by the Eastern States Mission [n.d.]
32p. front. 14cm.
Articles of faith on verso of front cover.
MH, MoInRC, NN, USIC

7172. ———. (same, in German) Eine Unterredung. Ein Berichterstatter informiert sich über die Kirche Jesu Christi der Heiligen der letzten Tage. Basel, Herausgegeben von der Schweizerisch-Deutschen Mission . . . 1916.
16p. 17cm.
Cover-title.
In pink printed wrappers.
USIC

7172a. ———. (same) Basel, Schweizerisch-Deutschen Mission, 1917.
16p. 16cm.
USIC

7173. ———. (same, under title) An interview in the Atlanta Constitution on the "Mormon" faith. [n.p., n.d.]
24p. 15½cm.
Caption-title.
Reprinted from the issue of March 26, 1899.
WHi

7174. ———. (same, under title) Interview on the "Mormon" faith by Ben E. Rich in Atlanta Constitution. [Chattanooga, Tenn.? Southern States Mission? 19–]
32[1]p. 13cm.
Cover-title.
Articles of faith on back cover.
MH, NN, USIC

7175. ———. (same) [Independence, Mo., Press of Zion's Printing and Publishing Company, ca. 1919]
16p. 17½cm.
UPB, USIC

7176. ———. Mr. Durant of Salt Lake City, "that Mormon." By Ben E. Rich . . . Salt Lake City, G. Q. Cannon & Sons Co., Printers, 1893.
viii [9]–320p. port. 18½cm.
"What Brigham Young said" [quotations from the sermons of President Brigham Young] p. [285]–320.
Provides doctrine in the form of story and letters.
CU–B, DLC, MoInRC, NjP, NN, UHi, ULA, USl, USIC, UU, WHi

7177. ———. (same) Chattanooga, Tenn., Published and for sale by The Southern States Mission, 1898.
166p. port. 13cm.
UHi, USIC

7178. ———. (same) Independence, Mo., Press of Zion's Printing and Publishing Company [1899]
4p.l. [9]–127 [1]p. 18½cm.
CSmH, DLC, IU, NN, MoInRC, UHi, UPB, USIC

7179. ———. (same) Chattanooga, Tenn., Southern States Mission [1899]
220p. 13½cm.
ICN, MH, PPeSchw, USIC

7180. ———. (same) Chicago, Missions of the Church of Jesus Christ of Latter-day Saints [ca. 1899]
220p. 13cm.
Variant printing.
CSmH, MoInRC, USIC

7181. ———. (same) Independence, Mo., Central States Mission [ca. 1899]
viii, 9–220p. 13×9cm.
DLC, ICN, NjPT, NN, UHi, UPB, USIC

7182. ———. (same) Independence, Mo., Press of Zion's Printing & Publishing Company [ca. 1899]
128p. 18cm.
USIC

7183. ———. (same) Liverpool, The Millennial Star Office, 1899.
166p. 13cm.
UPB, USIC

7184. ———. (same) Chattanooga, Tenn., For Ben E. Rich [1902?]
166p. 13cm.
Printed with his *Public discussion.*
USIC

7185. ———. (same) New York, Published by Eastern States Mission for Ben E. Rich [1905]
viii, 9–220p. 13cm.
CtY, MH, MiU, RPB, USIC

7186. ———. (same) Independence, Mo., Zion's Printing and Publishing Co. [Published by the Missions of the Church of Jesus Christ of Latter-day Saints] 1929.
4p.l. [9]–127p. 18cm.
NN, UPB, USIC

7187. ———. Public discussion of the doctrines of the gospel of Jesus Christ. Held in the tabernacle, Ogden, Utah, May 8 and 9, 1884, between the Reverend Richard Hartley, Pastor of the Baptist Church, Ogden, Utah, and Ben E. Rich, An elder in the Church of Jesus Christ of Latter-day Saints. Reported by F. E. Barker. Salt Lake City, Juvenile Instructor Office, 1884.
iv [5]–72p. 18cm.
Includes "True vs. false religion, a dialogue by Ben E. Rich," p. 54–72.
CSmH, CU–B, MH, NjP, NN, UPB, USIC

7188. ———. (same) 2d ed. Salt Lake City, Geo. Q. Cannon & Sons Company, 1897.
61p. 18½cm.
MoInRC, NjP, UHi, ULA, UPB

7189. ———. (same) Chattanooga, Tenn., Published and for sale by the Southern States Mission, 1898.
65p. 13cm.
UHi

7190. ———. (same) Cincinnati, Ohio, Printed and for sale by the Middle States Mission, 1903.
65p. 15cm.
USIC

7191. ———. Scrap book of Mormon literature. . . . Religious tracts. [Chicago, Published by Ben E. Rich, Press of Henry C. Etten and Co., 1913?]
2v. 22½cm.
Missionary tracts and other items.
CSmH, CtY, CU–B, ICN, IWW, MH, MoInRC, NjP, UHi, ULA, UPB, USIC, UU

7192. ———, *compiler*. [Statements of church leaders on cardboard for display] Chattanooga, Tenn., Published by Ben E. Rich [ca. 1900]
53 nos., col. borders and type. 25cm.
USIC inc. set

7193. ———. To the elders of the Eastern States Mission. New York, 1909.
4p. 23cm.
Dated: New York, July 31, 1909.
Instructions for missionaries.
NjP, USIC

7194. ———. To the saints of the Eastern States Mission. [New York, July 31, 1909]
[4]p. 24cm.
A pastoral letter after assuming the presidency of the mission.
USIC

7195. ———. True versus false religion. A dialogue between a "Mormon" elder, a parson and a traveler, at a temperance hotel, in the presence of a number of gentlemen by Ben E. Rich. [Salt Lake City, Deseret News Co., 1902]
19p. 17½cm.
DLC, ICN, MH, MoInRC, NjP, NN, USl, USIC, UU

7196. ———. (same) Salt Lake City, Juvenile Instructor's Office [n.d.]
19p. 17cm.
Variant printing.
USIC

7197. ———. (same, in German) Wahre und falsche Religion mit einander verglichen. Ein Gespräch zwischen einem "Mormonen"; Aeltesten, einem Pfarrer und einem Temperenz-Gasthof, in Gegenwart mehrerer Personen. Herausgegeben von G. C. Naegle. Bern, Buchdruckerei S. Lierow, 1895.
16p. 18½cm.
USIC

7198. ———. Truths from latter-day prophets. Chattanooga, Tenn. [n.d.]
55p. 19×25cm.
Written in album style.
UPB, USIC

7199. ———. Two letters to a Baptist minister. [Chattanooga, Tenn.? 1899?]
28p. 16cm.
USIC, MoInRC, UPB

7200. ———. Eine Unterredung, ein Berichterstatter informiert sich über die Kirche Jesu Christi der Heiligen der letzten Tage. Basel, Herausgegeben von der Schweizerisch-Deutschen Mission, 1916.
16p. 17cm.
Title in English: A discussion, a journalist informs himself about the Church.
USIC

7200a. ———. Wo ist das wahre Evangelium? Ein in Gegenwart mehrerer Personen sich entwickelndes Gespräch zwischen einem Mormonen-Missionar, einem Pfarrer und einem Reisenden. Zurich, Schweiz, Hugh J. Cannon und Levi Edgar Young [ca. 1900]
16[1]p. 18cm. (Traktat. Nr. III)
Title in English: Where is the true gospel?
USIC

7201. ———. (same) Berlin, Herausgegeben von der Redaktion des "Stern," 1902.
16[1]p. 18cm. (Traktat. Nr. III)
Cover-title.
USIC, UU

7202. ———. (same) Zürich, Herausgegeben von Hugh J. Cannon und Levi Edgar Young [n.d.]
16p. 18cm.
"Glaubensartikel der Kirche Jesu Christi der Heiligen der letzten Tage" cover.
USIC

7203. ———. (same) [Independence, Mo., Press of Zion's Printing & Publishing Co., n.d.]
16p. 18cm.
USIC

7204. ———. (same) [n.p., n.d.]
16p. 18cm.
Articles of faith on back cover.
UPB

7205. ———. (same) Salt Lake City, J. H. Ward, Herausgeber, 1903.
26p. 16½cm.
USIC

7206. ———. (same) Zurich, Schweiz, Serge F. Ballif, 1906.
16p. 18cm. (Traktet. No. 3)
UPB

7207. ———. (same) Zürich, Herausgegeben von Thomas E. McKay, 1910.
16p. 17½cm. (Heft. No. 3)
UPB

7208. ———. (same) [São Paulo, Brasil, Kirche Jesu Christi der Heiligen der letzten Tage [n.d.]
1p.l., 20p. 18cm.
USIC

7209. Rich, Benjamin Leroy. The Book of Mormon; a lecture, given by invitation April 29, 1900, before the Ohio Liberal Society, Cincinnati, Ohio. By Elder Ben L. Rich. [Salt Lake City? 190–]
18p. front. 21½cm.
UHi, UPB

7210. Rich, Calvin H. Some differences in faith between the Reorganized Church of Jesus Christ of Latter Day Saints, with headquarters at Independence, Missouri, and The Church of Jesus Christ of Latter Day Saints with headquarters at Salt Lake City, Utah. By Calvin H. Rich. Independence, Mo., The Herald Publishing House, 1930.
60p. 18cm.
CU–B, MH, MoInRC, NjP, UPB, USIC

7211. Rich, Edward Israel. Apostle Charles C. Rich. [n.p., n.d.]
20p. illus., port., fold. facsim. 23cm.
UPB

7212. Rich, Edward S. Jehovah-Christ. Is he our elder brother? by Edward S. Rich. [Salt Lake City, Utah Printing Co., 1935]
3p.l., 52p. 19½cm.
Cover-title.
USIC, UU

7213. Richards, Charles Comstock. John Watson, Appellant, against George L. Corey, Respondent. Appellant's brief. [Salt Lake City? 1889]
32p. 21cm.
At head of title: In the Supreme Court of Utah Territory. January Term, 1889.
Signed: Charles C. Richards, Henry H. Rolapp, Attorneys for Appellant.
Polygamy and voting suit.
USIC

7214. Richards, Claude. The man of tomorrow; a discussion of vocational success with the boy of today, by Claude Richards of the Vocational Guidance Committee, Y.M.M.I.A. [Salt Lake City] The General Board of Young Men's Mutual Improvement Associations of the Church of Jesus Christ of Latter-day Saints [c1917]
2p.l., 5–296p. plates, ports. 19cm.
Mormon point of view on success.
MB, NN, OCl, PHC, PP, UHi, UPB, UU

7215. Richards, Daniel Brigham Hill. . . . Hill family history, illustrated, by Dr. Daniel B. Hill Richards. Salt Lake City, Magazine Printing Company, 1927.
viii, 9–278p. illus., ports. 20cm.
Mormon history and biography.
CU–B, DLC, UHi, UPB, USl, USIC

7216. Richards, Emily S. The Republican catechism criticised and amended for the benefit of the women of Utah to whom it is respectfully presented. [Salt Lake City, 189–]
44p. 25cm.
Includes a section on the Mormon doctrine of home industry and some on the Utah industries.
MH, NjP, UHi, UU

7217. Richards, Franklin Dewey. A compendium of the faith and doctrines of the Church of Jesus Christ of Latter-day Saints. Compiled from the Bible, and also from the Book of Mormon, Doctrine and Covenants, and other publications of the church. With an appendix by Franklin D. Richards, one of the Twelve Apostles of said Church. Liverpool, O. Pratt; London: L.D.S. Book Depot, 1857.
viii, 243p. 16cm.
First edition.
Sabin 70912
CtY, CU–B, ICN, MH, MoInRC, NjP, NN, PPPrHi, RPB, UPB, USIC, UU

7218. ———. (same, under title) A compendium of the doctrines of the gospel. Franklin D. Richards, one of the Twelve Apostles of the Church of Jesus Christ of Latter-day Saints, and Elder James A. Little, Compilers and Publishers. Stereotype edition. Salt Lake City, Deseret News Company, 1882.
viii, 312p. 15cm.
CSmH, CtY, NjP, CU-B, USlC

7219. ———. (same) 2d stereotype ed. Salt Lake City, Deseret News Company, 1884.
viii, 312p. 15cm.
CSmH, CU-B, DLC, IWW, NjP, OCl, PPPrHi, UHi, USlC

7220. ———. (same) Salt Lake City, 1886.
viii, 312p. 17cm.
RPB, UHi, USlC

7221. ———. (same) 3rd stereotype ed. Salt Lake City, Richards and Little, 1892.
viii, 312p. 16cm.
ICN, MH, UHi, UPB, USlC

7222. ———. (same) 3rd stereotype ed. Salt Lake City, Geo. Q. Cannon and Sons Co., 1898.
viii, 312p. 16cm.
NN, UHi, ULA, UPB

7223. ———. (same) 4th stereotype ed. Salt Lake City, The Deseret News, 1912.
viii, 312p. 16cm.
UHi

7224. ———. (same) Rev. ed. Salt Lake City, The Deseret News, 1914.
vii, 288p. 15½cm.
UHi, UPB, USlC

7225. ———. (same) Rev. ed. Salt Lake City, Deseret Book Co., 1925.
vii, 290p. 15cm.
UHi, UPB, USlC, UU

7226. ———, *compiler.* Latter-day Saints in Utah. Opinion of the Hon. Z. Snow, Judge of the Supreme Court of the United States for the Territory of Utah, upon the official course of His Excellency Gov. Brigham Young. Plea of George A. Smith, Esq., and charge of the Hon. Judge Snow, upon the United States District Court, on Indictment for the Murder of James Monroe. Verdict. A bill to establish a territorial government for Utah. The names of the territorial officers, etc., etc. Price threepence. Liverpool: F. D. Richards, 15 Wilton Street. London: T. C. Armstrong, 35, Jewin Street, City, and all booksellers. 1852.
iv, [5]–24p. 21cm.
Cover-title.
Howes R248, Sabin 70913
CSmH, CtY, CU-B, DLC, ICN, MH, NjP, NN, UHi, UPB, USl, USlC, UU, WHi

7226a. ———. (same) Liverpool . . . 1852.
iv, [5]–24p. 22cm.
Type reset with unoffending not hyphenated on line 23 of p. iv.
UPB, USlC

7227. ———. Mormon church. [St. John, Kansas, Southwestern States Mission, n.d.]
8p. 20cm.
A brief history of the Church of Jesus Christ of Latter-Day Saints, including its principles, faith, doctrines, ordinances, etc.
USlC

7227a. ———. (same, in Swedish) Ljusstralar, Herren har besokt jorden. "Mormonismen" i sammandrag. [Kopenhamn, Utgifen och forlagd af Andreas Peterson, ca. 1900]
8p. 23½cm.
USlC

———. The Mormons. *See Towne, Edward Cornelius. Rays of light . . .*

7228. ———. Visit to Pueblo, Independence, Carthage, Nauvoo, Richmond, etc. [Salt Lake City, 1885]
4p. 28cm.
Written in the form of a letter with space for name (My dear ————) and signature. Tells of his trip to these historic sites and his impressions (religious) of them.
CSmH, USlC

7229. Richards, Franklin Snyder. Admission of Utah. Argument of Hon. F. S. Richards in favor of the admission of Utah as a state made before the House Committee on Territories, 2d Session, 50th Congress, January 12, 1889. . . . Washington, Govt. Print. Off., 1889.
14p. 22cm.
Gives resources of Utah, population, law abidances, freedom from polygamy. Contends that unfavorable reports are false.
UPB

7230. ———. The admission of Utah. Replies of Hon. F. S. Richards to statements in opposition to the admission of Utah as a state, made before the Committee on Territories of the United States Senate, Saturday, March 10, 1888. Washington, Gibson Brothers, Printers and Bookbinders, 1888.
16p. 23cm.
Reply to F. T. Dubois, and R. N. Baskin.
NjP, UPB, USlC, UU

RICHARDS, F. S.

7231. ———. The corporation of the members of the Church of Jesus Christ of Latter-day Saints, residing in the Fiftieth Eclesiastical [sic] Ward of Salt Lake Stake of Zion, Plaintiff and Respondent, vs. Helen Watson, Defendant and Appellant. Brief for Respondent. F. S. Richards, J. T. Richards, Attorneys for Respondent. [Salt Lake City, 1902?]
13p. 22cm.
Cover-title.
Property dispute.
MH

———. Extracts from an argument delivered in the Supreme Court of the United States. *See Curtis, G. T. A plea for religious liberty.*

7232. ———. In the matter of elections. Argument in behalf of the Territorial Central Committee of the People's Party. Franklin S. Richards and Bennett, Harkness & Kirkpatrick: Counsel for People's Territorial Committee. [Salt Lake City, 1884?]
17p. 21cm.
Signed: July 21, 1884.
USIC

7233. ———. Rudger Clawson, Plaintiff in Error, vs. The United States. Brief for Plaintiff in Error. [Washington, 1884]
26p. 21cm.
At head of title: Supreme Court of the United States. October Term, 1884. No. 1263.
USIC

7234. ———. (same, under title) Rudger Clawson, Plaintiff in Error, vs. the United States, Defendant in Error. From Supreme Court of Utah, Brief for Plaintiff in Error. Washington, 1885.
26p. 22cm.
Signed: Franklin S. Richards, Wayne MacVeagh.
Variant printing.
USIC

7235. ———. Samuel D. Davis, Appellant, v. H. G. Beason, Sheriff of Oneida County, Idaho Territory. No. 1261. Brief for Appellant. [By Franklin S. Richards, Jeremiah M. Wilson, Samuel Shellabarger. Washington, Gibson Bros., Printers and Bookbinders, 1889]
66p. 22½cm.
Mormon suffrage in Idaho.
UPB, USIC

7236. ———. The suffrage question. Address of Hon. Franklin S. Richards delivered in the Constitutional Convention of Utah, March 28, 1895. [Salt Lake City, Published by the Utah Women Suffrage Association, 1895?]
27p. 21cm.
CSmH, MH

7237. ———. The United States of America, Appellant, vs. The Late Corporation of the Church of Jesus Christ of Latter-day Saints, et al., Appellees, No. 887. Appeal from the Supreme Court of Utah Territory. Brief for the Appellees. [Washington, 1893]
43p. 22cm.
At head of title: Supreme Court of the United States. October Term, 1893.
USIC

7237a. ———. United States of America, Plaintiff, v. The Late Corporation of the Church of Jesus Christ of Latter-day Saints, Et al, Defendants. Brief for the Petitioners, Wilford Woodruff, George Q. Cannon and Joseph F. Smith. Franklin S. Richards, Of Counsel for Petitioners. [Salt Lake City? ca. 1893]
13p. 23cm.
At head of title: In the Supreme Court of Utah Territory.
UPB, USIC

7238. ———. United States of America, Respondent vs. Lorenzo Snow, Appellant. Transcript on Appeal. F. S. Richards and Bennett, Harkness & Kirkpatrick, Attorneys for Appellant. [Salt Lake City, 1886]
19p. 21cm.
At head of title: Supreme Court of Utah Territory. January Term, 1886. No. 741.
USIC

7239. ———. (same) Salt Lake City, Deseret News Co., 1886.
31p. 21cm.
At head of title: Supreme Court of Utah Territory. January Term, 1886. No. 742.
USIC

7240. ———. The United States, Respondent vs. Lorenzo Snow, Appellant. Unlawful cohabitation. Three cases. Brief for Appellant. Franklin S. Richards and Bennett, Harkness & Kirkpatrick, Attorneys for Appellant. [Salt Lake City, 1886]
18p. 21cm.
At head of title: Supreme Court of Utah Territory. January Term.
USIC

7241. ———. William E. Bassett, vs. the United States, Brief for Plaintiff in Error. [Salt Lake City, 1890]
22p. 22cm.
At head of title: Supreme Court of the United States. October Term, 1890. No. 110.
Franklin S. Richards, Charles C. Richards for Plaintiff in Error, p. 22.
Polygamy trial.
USIC

RICHARDS, G. F.

7242. Richards, George F. Instructions concerning Temple ordinance work. [Salt Lake City, n.d.]
[4]p. 22cm.
Written while President of the Salt Lake Temple.
USlC

7243. ———. Instructions for temple workers. [Salt Lake City, 1922]
[3]p. 18cm.
Also published under the signature of Joseph F. Smith.
USlC

7244. Richards, John. Duw mawr y sectariaid. Merthyr-Tydfil, J. Davis, Argraffydd [1850?]
Broadside. 18×11½cm.
Signed: Craig — ddu.
Missionary leaflet.
Title in English: The great God of the sectarians.
MH, USlC

7245. Richards, Joseph. What is Mormonism. Compiled from the writings of Elders Parley P. Pratt, Orson Pratt, John Taylor, Orson Spencer, Samuel Brannon [sic] and others of the Church of Jesus Christ of Latter-day Saints, by Joseph Richards, Travelling Elder of the East India Mission. [Agra, Reprinted by J. A. Gibbons, Agra Cantonments for Joseph Richards and William Willes, East India Mission, 1853]
16p. 21cm.
Signed: Agra, 25th February, 1853.
Tract originally published in Calcutta by Elder William Willes. No copy known.
USlC

7246. Richards, K. Morgan. Les Mormons (1830–1930) par K. Morgan Richards. Paris, Librairie Félix Alcan [1930]
[513]–534p. 24cm.
Extrait. *Revue des Sciences Politiques.* Quarante-cinquieme annee. Tome LIII. Octobre-Decembre 1930.
Title in English: The Mormons.
UPB, USlC

7247. Richards, Louisa Lulu (Greene). Branches that run over the wall; a Book of Mormon poem and other writings by Louisa L. Greene Richards (Lulu) . . . Salt Lake City, The Magazine Printing Company, 1904.
3p.l. [iii]–viii p., [2]l. [13]–268p. front., plates. 20cm.
Music, p. [202–204]
CSmH, DLC, MH, MoInRC, NjP, UHi, UPB, USl, USlC, UU

7248. Richards, Robert [*pseud.*] The Californian Crusoe; or The lost treasure found. A tale of Mormonism. London, J. H. Parker, New York, Stanford and Swords, 1854.
iv, 162p. front. 17½cm.
Howes R250, W-C 243
CSmH, CU, DLC, ICN, MoInRC, NjP, NN, UPB, USlC, UU, ViU, WHi

7249. ———. (same) 2d ed. London, J. H. and J. Parker, 1858.
iv, 162p. front. 17cm.
Howes R250
CtY, CU-B, DLC, MH, OCl

7250. Richards, Stephen Longstroth. Contributions of Joseph Smith; an address by Stephen L. Richards . . . [Salt Lake City? 193–]
[4]l. 22½cm.
Cover-title.
NN, UHi, UPB, USlC

7251. ———. (same) [Salt Lake City? 1930?]
[9]p. 20½cm.
Variant printing.
UPB

7252. ———. The law of tithing. Salt Lake City, The Deseret News [n.d.]
8p. 18cm.
UPB, USlC

7253. ———. (same) Independence, Mo., Zion's Printing and Publishing Co. [n.d.]
8p. 19cm.
NN, UPB, USlC

7254. ———. New Year reflections; address delivered over Radio Station KSL, Sunday Evening, January 1, 1928. [Salt Lake City] 1928.
Broadside. 59½×23½cm.
Reprinted from the *Deseret News*, Saturday, January 7, 1928.
UPB

7255. Richards, Willard. Address. Willard Richards, Secretary of State; To the Chancellor and Regents of the University of the State of Deseret, delivered in the bowery, at Great Salt Lake City, in presence of his Excellency, Governor Young, April 17th, 1850. [Salt Lake City, 1850?]
12p. 21cm.
Education and Mormonism.
NjP, UPB, USlC

7256. Richardson, Albert Deane. Beyond the Mississippi; from the great river to the great ocean. Life and adventure on the prairies, mountains and Pacific coast . . . 1857–1867. Hartford, Conn., American Publishing Co. [c1867]
2p.l., xvi [17]–572p. illus., maps. 23cm.
Two chapters dealing with Salt Lake City and Mormonism, with emphasis on polygamy.
In Utah in 1865; first for 8 days and three months later for 5 weeks.
Reprinted 1869. NjP, UPB; 1875. ICN; 1885. UHi. Issued in German under title: Jenseit des Mississippi. 1867. NN.
Sabin 70980
CSmH, CU-B, DLC, NjP, UHi, ULA, UPB, USlC, UU

7257. ———. Our new states and territories, being notes of a recent tour of observation through Colorado, Utah, Idaho, Nevada, Oregon, Montana, Washington, and California. Illustrated from sketches and photographs, taken on the spot, of towns, mining operations, persons, incidents, scenery, etc. New York, Beadle and Company [c1866]
3p.l. [9]–80p. 45 illus. 22cm.
"Fort Douglas, a restraint upon Mormon despotic power." Opinion of Brigham Young, church services, and the Salt Lake Theatre.
Howes R253, Sabin 70983
CtY, ICN, MH, NjP, UPB

7258. Richardson, Arthur M. Claims of the Reorganized Church weighed in the balance and found wanting. Synopsis of remarks delivered by Elder D. V. Farnsworth before a Los Angeles missionary class . . . [Salt Lake City, n.d.]
[4]p. 17½cm.
Cover-title.
UU

7259. Richardson, C. E. A conversation after death. [Independence, Press of Zion's Printing and Publishing Company, c1923]
7 [1]p. 18cm.
UU

7260. Richardson, David M. Our country: its present and its future prosperity. [Detroit, Mich., 1882–84]
12, 14, 10p. 26½cm.
Text (12p.) and two supplements signed: David M. Richardson.
Polygamy listed as one of the dangers of continued prosperity.
DLC, MH, NN, USlC

7261. Richardson, Edmund. Footprints of gospel feet, for the honest-in-heart. By Edmund Richardson. Salt Lake City, Cannon Publishing House, 1891.
3p.l. [5]–91p. port. 18½cm.
Errata slip inserted.
Mormon poetry.
DLC, NjP, UHi, UPB, USlC, WHi

7262. Richardson, James D. A compilation of the messages and papers of the Presidents, 1789–1897; published by authority of Congress. Washington, Govt. Print. Off., 1896–1899.
10v. illus.
Includes many references to Mormons during the 1850–1897 period. Particularly rich during the Buchanan administration.
Other editions: 1908, 1911. DLC, NjP
CU, DLC, NjP, UHi, ULA, UPB

7263. Richardson, Robert. Memoirs of Alexander Campbell, embracing a view of the origin, progress and principles of the religious reformation which he advocated. Philadelphia, J. B. Lippincott, 1868–70.
2v. 21cm.
"Mormonism; its exposure," V.2 p. 44–48.
Another edition: Cincinnati, R. W. Carroll & Co., 1872. UPB
Sabin 71083
CSmH, CU–B, DLC, NjP

7264. ———. What is Mormonism? A brief account of the beginning of Mormonism. Indianapolis, Indiana [Apostolic Review, n.d.]
12p. 23cm.
Copied from Dr. Robert Richardson's *Memoirs of Alexander Campbell.*
MoInRC

7265. Richardson, Sullivan Calvin. The national press looks at the Mormons. Chicago, Ill., Prepared for the Northern States Mission. Chicago [n.d.]
[15]p. facsim. 28×43cm.
UPB, UU

7266. ———. No cross, no crown; a story of sacrifice and rewards . . . Independence, Mo., Zion's Printing and Publishing Co. [n.d.]
32p. illus. 19cm.
Notes on Mormon pioneer life.
UPB

7267. ———. Sketches of the Curtis family. Gathered from records, letters, scraps of paper, and told to S. C. Richardson. [n.p.] 1926.
62p. ports. 16cm.
Mormon biography.
USlC

7268. Richman, Irving Berdine. John Brown among the Quakers, and other sketches, by Irving B. Richman . . . Des Moines, The Historical Department of Iowa, 1894.
4p.l., 11–239p. 17cm.
Nauvoo and the prophet, p. 123–189.
Published in many editions.
CSmH, CtY, DLC, ICHi, ICN, NjP, NN, UHi, UPB, USl, WHi

7269. Rickard, Thomas Arthur. The Utah copper enterprise. San Francisco, 1919.
107p. illus., ports., maps, prints. 30cm.
"From Mining and Scientific Press of December 28, 1918."
Mormon attitudes towards mining.
CU–B, UHi, ULA, UPB, UU

7270. Ricks, Joel Edward. Helps to the study of the Book of Mormon, comprising an account of the finding of the records, and their translation, with a brief review of the evidences of their authenticity. A subject index and chronology with maps and cuts, illustrating the geography and characteristics of Nephite lands, by Joel Ricks. [Independence, Mo., Zion's Printing & Publishing Co., c1916]
88 (i.e. 116)p. illus., double col. maps. 17cm.
CU–B, DLC, MoInRC, NjP, NN, UPB

RICKS COLLEGE

7271. Ricks College, Rexburg, Idaho. Ricks College catalog. Rexburg, Idaho, 1902–
v. 19½×23cm.
Ricks Academy; Ricks Normal College.
UPB 1907–08, 1908–09, 1911–12, 1914–15, 1915–16, 1916–30, 1930–31; USlC 1902–03, 1904–05, 1905–06, 1907–08, 1908–09, 1910–11, 1911–12, 1914–15, 1915–16, 1916–17, 1917–18, 1918–19, 1919–20 (Also Circular. No. 1: Vocational education at the Ricks Normal College) 1920–21, 1921–22, 1922–23 (also the twelve months school of the Ricks College. Circular. No. 2; Summer catalog) 1923–24, 1924–25, 1925–26 (and summer school catalog) 1926–27, 1927–28 (and summer school) 1928–29, 1929–30 (and summer school) 1930–31.

7272. Riddell, Newton N. Child culture, according to the laws of physiological psychology and mental suggestion, by N. N. Riddell . . . with a discussion of educational problems by John T. Miller. Salt Lake City, Human Culture Publishing Co., 1902.
2p.l. [5]–120p. 1 double plate. 22cm.
Child development from a Mormon standpoint.
UPB

7273. ———. (same) Chicago, Child of Light Publishing Co., 1902.
129p. 21cm.
DLC

7274. ———. (same) Chicago, The Riddel Publishers [c1915]
116p. 21½cm.
DLC

7275. Riddle, Albert Gallatin. The portrait; a romance of the Cuyahoga valley, by A. G. Riddle . . . Boston, Nichols & Hall; Cleveland, Cobb, Andrew & Co., 1874.
iv, 5–378p. 19cm.
Novel with Mormon setting.
Sabin 71261
CU–B, DLC, MH, NjP, UHi, UPB, USlC, UU, WHi

7276. Rideing, William H. Boys in the mountains and on the plains; or, The Western adventures of Tom Smart, Bob Edge, and Peter Small . . . New York, D. Appleton and Company [1882]
viii, 345p. illus. 22½cm.
Juvenile fiction.
Includes chapter: "Over the boundary to Mormon-land."
DLC, UHi, UPB

7277. Ridout, G. W. The deadly fallacy of Mormonism. Its claims examined. Its Bible uncovered. Its duplicity exposed. By Rev. G. W. Ridout. Kansas City, Mo., Nazarine Publishing House [n.d.]
12p. 19cm.
MoInRC

7278. Riegel, Robert Edgar. America moves west, by Robert E. Riegal . . . New York, H. Holt and Company [c1930]
x, 595p. maps, diagr. 22cm.
The Mormon contribution to the westward movement.
DLC, MiU, NjP, NN, UHi, USlC, UU, ViU, WaU

7279. Rigdon, Sidney. An appeal to the American people: Being an account of the persecutions of the Church of Latter Day Saints; and of the barbarities inflicted on them by the inhabitants of the State of Missouri. By authority of said church. Cincinnati, Glezen and Shepard, Stereotypers and Printers, 1840.
[1–3]4–84p. 18cm.
Publishers preface signed by Orson Hyde and John E. Page. Cincinnati, July 11, 1840.
Sabin 50727
CtY, USlC

7280. ———. (same) Second edition, revised. Cincinnati, Printed by Shepard & Stearns, 1840.
vi, [7]–60p. 17½cm.
DLC defective, UPB, USlC

7281. ———. A collection of sacred hymns. For the Church of Jesus Christ of Latter Day Saints. Selected by S. Rigdon. Pittsburgh, Printed by E. Robinson, 1845.
v [1] 8–224p. 10½cm.
Morgan
DLC, NN

7282. ———. Darlithiau ar ffydd, y rhai a draddodwyd yn wreiddiol o flaen dosparth o Henuriaid, yn Kirtland, Ohio, yn America. Gan Joseph Smith . . . Merthyr-Tydfil, Argraffwyd ac ar werth gan J. Davis . . . , 1850.
1p.l., 40p. 18cm.
Title in English: Lectures in faith. First published in English in the 1835 edition of the *Doctrine and Covenants.*
CtY, MH, NjP, USlC

7283. ———. Dear Brethren. [Kirtland, Ohio, May 10, 1834]
[2]p. 31cm.
Information concerning Zion's Camp.
USlC

———. [*supposed author*]. Lectures on faith. The lectures on faith were published in the *Doctrine and Covenants* for 1835 without general title or author. They were first delivered in the Kirtland School of the Prophets by Sidney Rigdon. They were later reprinted in his *Messenger and Advocate* which lends credence to the fact that they were written by Sidney Rigdon although later editions are listed under Joseph Smith as author. They were published separately in Welsh, 1850. *See his Darlithiau ar ffydd.* A portion was first published as a broadside. *See his Theology. Lecture first.*

7284. ———. Oration delivered by Mr. S. Rigdon on the 4th of July, 1838, at Far West, Caldwell Co., Missouri. Far West, Printed at the Journal Office, 1838.
12p. 20cm.
ICHi, MH, UPB, USIC

———. Plain facts. *See Pratt, Parley P.*

7285. ———. Theology. Lecture first. On the doctrine of the Church of the Latter Day Saints. [Kirtland, Ohio, ca. 1835]
The first printing of the initial section of the *Lectures on Faith* as it later appeared in the 1835 edition of the *Doctrine and Covenants.* There is a rearrangement of the type with several variations.
UPB photocopy from copy owned by William Powell

7285a. ———. To John Thornton, Esq., Peter Rogers, Esq., Andrew Robertson, Esq., James T. V. Thompson, Esq., Col. William T. Wood, Doct Woodson J. Moss, James M. Hughes, Esq., David R. Atchison, Esq. and A. W. Doniphan, Esq. Gentlemen. [Kirtland, Ohio, 1836]
Broadside. 58×20cm.
At head of title: Latter Day Saints' Messenger and Advocate — Extra. Kirtland, Geauga County, Ohio, July 25, 1836.
Signed: Sidney Rigdon, Joseph Smith, Jr., O. Cowdery, F. G. Williams, Hyrum Smith.
Concerning problems in Clay County, Mo.
DNA

7286. Riimsmed, Casper. Tvende Mormonske profeters mirakelgjerninger, komisk og letfattelig, skildret paa versemall. Randers, Denmark, Trykt hos M. P. Fogh, 1859.
10p. 18cm.
Street ballad.
Title in English: Miracles of two Mormon prophets.
USIC

7287. Riker, John F. Journal of a trip to California, by the overland route; containing all the principal incidents of the journey; also, a description of the country, soil, climate and the principal streams and rivers with a summary of the entire distance from Cincinnati to San Francisco, via the plains. By John F. Riker. [Urbana, Ohio? 1855?]
32p. 23cm.
Caption-title.
Crosses a Mormon ferry at the Green River; visits Salt Lake and describes the Mormons and irrigation.
Howes R298, W-C 268
CtY, ICN

7288. Riley, Isaac Woodbridge. The founder of Mormonism; a psychological study of Joseph Smith, jr., by I. Woodbridge Riley . . . with an introductory preface by Prof. George Trumbull Ladd. New York, Dodd, Mead & Company, 1902.
xix, 446p. facsim. 19½cm.
Bibliography, p. 427–446.
CtY, CU, DLC, ICHi, ICN, MH, MoInRC, NjP, NjPT, NN, UHi, ULA, UPB, USI, USIC, UU, WHi

7289. ———. (same) New York, Dodd, Mead and Company, 1903.
xix, [1]l., 3–462p. port. 19cm.
Bibliography, p. 446–462.
CSmH, MH, UHi, USIC

7290. ———. (same) London, William Heinemann, 1903.
xix, 462p. port., facsims. 19cm.
CU-B, UPB

7291. Rimmer, H. P. Mormonism: A doctrine of demons. London, England [n.d.]
16p. 16½cm.
MH, MoInRC, USIC

7292. Rio Grande Western Railway Company. Salt Lake City, the "Zion" of the new world, an outline of its natural beauty and manifold attractions. Issued by the Passenger Department, Rio Grande Western Railway, Salt Lake City, 1899.
22 [2]p. illus. 15½cm.
NjP, UPB

7293. ———. (same) Salt Lake City [Chicago, Poole Bros.] 1900.
22 [2]p. illus. 15cm.
DLC

7294. ———. (same) Salt Lake City, 1901.
22 [2]p. illus. 15cm.
USIC

———. Utah; a peep into a mountain walled treasury of the Gods. *See Donan, Patrick.*

7295. ———. Valleys of the Great Salt Lake; describing the garden of Utah and the two great cities of Salt Lake and Ogden. Chicago, R. R. Donnelley and Sons, 1890.
56p. illus. 21½cm.
Growth of Utah and change since 1847. Polygamy problem not mentioned.
MH, UHi, ULA, USIC, UU

7296. Ritchie, D. C. The case against polygamy; a collection of evidences against the doctrine of plural marriage based on the history of polygamy in ancient and modern times. [Salt Lake City? n.d.]
27p. 21cm.
MoInRC, USIC

7297. ———. Origin of polygamy in America. [Salt Lake City? n.d.]
4p. 14cm.
RLDS publication.
MoInRC

7298. Ritchie, David G. Natural rights, a criticism of some political and ethical conceptions. By David G. Ritchie. London, Swan, Sonnenschein & Co., 1895.
xvi, [1]l., 3–304p. 23½cm.
Mormons listed in several places in regards to toleration. Note B. p. 202–209: "Measures for suppressing Mormonism in the United States." He was against suppressive measures.
Other editions: 1903. NjP; 1916. NjP
NjPT, USlC

7299. Ritchie, Dwight Campbell. Mormonism disproved. Salt Lake City [n.d.]
Broadside. 21½×14cm.
Advertisement for six lectures.
USlC

7300. Ritchie, J. Ewing. Religious life of London, by J. Ewing Ritchie. London, Tinsley Brothers, 1870.
xi, 386p. 23cm.
"The Mormons," p. 344–351. Sensuality of the Mormon religion.
USlC

7301. Ritchie, John. The Mormons and their doctrine. [Kilmarnock, The author, n.d.]
15p. 18cm.
"Book of prevalent errors and present day questions."
IWW, MoInRC, USlC, UU

7302. ———. (same) [Kilmarnock, John Ritchie, Publisher, n.d.]
16p. 17½cm.
OClWHi, USlC

7303. Rivington, Alex. Reminiscences of America in 1869. By two Englishmen. London, Sampson Low, Son, and Marston, 1870.
xx, 332p. 18cm.
By Messrs. Rivington and Harris.
They visit Salt Lake City with special attention to Brigham Young. "The most absolute monarch in existence."
Another edition: 2d ed., rev. DLC
NjP, USlC

7304. Rix, Guy Scoby, *compiler.* History and genealogy of the Ricks family of America. Containing biographical sketches and genealogies of both males and females. Compiled by Guy S. Rix, Concord, N. H. Published and for sale by Joel Ricks, Logan, Utah, for the Ricks family. Salt Lake City, Skelton Publishing Co., 1908.
4p.l. [9]–184p. plates, ports. 23½cm.
Biography and genealogy of Ricks family, including the Mormon branch.
NjP, USlC

7305. Roberts, Anne Friend, *editor.* A year of lessons for the nursery child. For the three-year-old child. To be used by parents and teachers. Published by the Department of Religious Education of the Reorganized Church of Jesus Christ of Latter Day Saints. Anne Friend Roberts, editor. Independence, Mo., Herald Publishing House, 1930.
1p.l. [3]–151p. 22cm.
USlC

7306. Roberts, Brigham Henry. The advantages possessed by the Saints. [Chattanooga, Tenn., Southern States Mission ca. 1910]
8p. 15½cm.
USlC

7307. ———. Analysis of the Book of Mormon. Suggestions to the reader, by Elder B. H. Roberts. [Liverpool, Millennial Star Office, n.d.]
4p. 21½cm.
MoInRC, NjP, UU

7308. ———. (same) [Salt Lake City, The Deseret News Co., n.d.]
12p. 16½cm.
MH, MoInRC, NjP, UPB

7309. ———. (same) [n.p., n.d.]
16p. 16cm.
MH, UPB

7310. ———. (same) Chicago, Ill., Church of Jesus Christ of Latter-day Saints, 191–]
16p. 16cm.
Caption-title.
CLU, MH, NN, UPB, USlC

———. Analysis of the Book of Revelation. *See Church of Jesus Christ of Latter-day Saints. Young Men's Mutual Improvement Association. The apostolic age.*

7311. ———. The atonement. Salt Lake City, The Deseret News, 1911.
4p.l., 160p. 22cm. (The Seventy's course in theology. Fourth year)
CU–B, DLC, UHi, UPB, USlC, UU

7312. ———, *defendant.* Brief on demurrer in Roberts' Case. Representative from Utah demurs to the jurisdiction of the House and its Special Committee in its Proceedings to unseat him. Fifty-Sixth Congress. 1899. [Washington? 1899]
22p. 22cm.
Signed: B. H. Roberts. December 12, 1899.
USlC

ROBERTS, B. H.

7313. ———. The character of the Mormon people, by Elder B. H. Roberts. [Liverpool, Printed at the Millennial Star Office, n.d.]
16p. 17½cm.
MH, NjP, UPB, USlC, UU

7314. ———. A comprehensive history of the Church of Jesus Christ of Latter-day Saints, Century I . . . by B. H. Roberts . . . Published by the church. Salt Lake City, Utah, Deseret News Press, 1930.
6v. plates, ports., maps (part fold.) facsims. (1 fold) 25½cm.
Published in the *Americana* from July 1909 to July 1915 under title, "History of the Mormon church"; now revised. cf. Pref.
CSmH, CtY, CU–B, DLC, MH, MoInRC, NN, UHi, ULA, UPB, USl, USlC, UU, ViU, WHi

7315. ———. Corianton. A Nephite story, by B. H. Roberts. [Salt Lake City? 1902]
2p.l. (5)–111p. 16½cm.
First published as a serial in the *Contributor*, 1889.
Book of Mormon fiction.
CSmH, DLC, IWW, UHi, UPB, USlC, WHi

7316. ———. Defense of the faith and the saints, by B. H. Roberts . . . Salt Lake City, The Deseret News, 1907–1912.
2v. 20cm.
CSmH, DLC, MoInRC, NN, ULA, UPB, USlC, WHi

7317. ———. Divine immanence and the Holy Ghost. Salt Lake City, The Deseret News, 1912.
xi, 124p. 22cm. (The Seventy's Course in Theology. Third year)
CU–B, DLC, UHi, ULA, UPB, USlC, UU

7318. ———. The Doctrine of Deity. Compiled and Edited by B. H. Roberts of the First Council of the Seventy . . . Salt Lake City, Printed by The Caxton Press, 1910.
viii, 216p. 23cm. (The Seventy's Course in Theology. Third year)
CU–B, DLC, ULA, UHi, UPB, USlC, WHi

7319. ———. The "falling away," or, The world's loss of the Christian religion and church; address delivered over Radio Station KSL, Sunday evening, March 10, 1927–June 23, 1929. Salt Lake City, Church of Jesus Christ of Latter-day Saints, 1929.
16 parts. 23cm. (Series No. 3)
Caption-title.
CSmH, DLC, NjP, UHi, UPB, USl, USlC

7320. ———. The gospel. An exposition of its first principles. Salt Lake City, Contributor Co., 1888.
[1] viii, 259p. 17cm.
CSmH, DLC, ICU, UHi, ULA, UPB, USl, USlC, UU

7321. ———. (same) Rev. and enl. ed. Salt Lake City, George Q. Cannon & Sons Co., 1893.
v [6]–352p. 17½cm.
Includes, as a supplement: Man's relationship to Diety.
CSmH, CtY, CU–B, MH, NjP, NN, UHi, ULA, UPB, USlC, WHi

7322. ———. (same) 3d ed. (rev. by the author) Salt Lake City, The Deseret News, 1901.
vii [2] 10–294p. 20cm.
CSmH, CtY, DLC, NH, NjP, NN, PP, PPL–R, UHi, ULA, UPB, USlC, UU

7323. ———. (same) 4th ed. Salt Lake City, The Deseret News, 1913.
vii [8]–294p. 20cm.
CSmH, UPB, UU

7324. ———. (same) 5th ed. Salt Lake City, Deseret Book Co. [c1924]
294p. 20cm.
UPB

7325. ———. (same) 6th ed. Salt Lake City, The Deseret Book Company, 1926.
vi [7]–294p. 20cm.
USlC

7326. ———. (same) [7th ed.] Salt Lake City, The Deseret News, 1928 [c1924]
vi p. [1]l., [9]–294p. 19½cm.
UPB

———. Te haere-piti-raa mai o te Mesia . . . *See his Second coming of the Messiah* (in Tahitian)

———. Jarman and the Mormons. *See Jarman and the Mormons.*

7327. ———. Joseph Smith; the prophet-teacher. A discourse by B. H. Roberts. Salt Lake City, The Deseret News, 1908.
3p.l., 7–77p. 19cm.
CSmH, CU–B, MH, MoInRC, ULA, UPB, USl, USlC, UU

7328. ———. (same) 2d ed. Salt Lake City, Deseret Book Co., 1927.
84p. 24cm.
Title within ornamental border.
CSmH, DLC, IWW, MnU, UHi, UPB

ROBERTS, B. H.

7329. ———. The Latter-day Saint's tour from Palmyra, New York to Salt Lake City, through the stereoscope. A history of the Church of Jesus Christ of Latter-day Saints, embodied in descriptions of original stereographs of noted persons, famous buildings, and interesting scenes connected with the story of the origin, struggles and growth of the Mormon people. Designed by John A. Califf and described by B. H. Roberts. Salt Lake City, The Deseret News, 1904.
2p.l. [5]–132p. 16½cm.
38 numbered stereographs in box 18×19cm. c1904. Underwood and Underwood.
NN, UPB, USIC

7330. ———. (same) Conducted by Brigham H. Roberts . . . Ottawa, Kansas, Underwood and Underwood [1905]
102p. 16½cm.
To accompany stereographs as above.
Printed by Republic Print. Ottawa, Kansas.
UPB

7331. ———. The life of John Taylor, Third President of the Church of Jesus Christ of Latter-day Saints. By B. H. Roberts . . . Salt Lake City, G. Q. Cannon & Sons Co., 1892.
xiv p., [1]l. [17]–468p. plates, ports. 24cm.
CSmH, CU–B, DLC, ICN, ICU, MH, MoInRC, NjP, NN, UHi, ULA, UPB, USl, USIC, UU, WHi

7332. ———. The Lord hath spoken. By B. H. Roberts [Salt Lake City, 192–]
6 pts. 16½cm.
Caption-title.
Printed at Independence, Mo., Zion's Printing and Publishing Co.
NN, UPB, UHi, USIC

7333. ———. The Lord's day; reasons for the observance by the Latter-day Saints of the first day of the week as the Christian Sabbath, or the "Lord's Day." [Independence, Mo., Zion's Printing and Publishing company, n.d.]
13 [2]p. 17½cm.
CU–B, MoInRC, UHi, UPB, USIC

7334. ———. (same) [Independence, Mo., Zion's Printing and Publishing Company. Pub. by the Missions of the Church of Jesus Christ of Latter-day Saints in America, 193–]
14 [2]p. 17cm.
Cover-title.
NN, UHi, UPB, USIC

7335. ———. (same) Salt Lake City, Deseret News Press [n.d.]
13 [2]p. 15½cm.
MoInRC has 2 variant printings.
MoInRC, UPB

7335a. ———. (same, in French) Le Sabbat du Seigneur; pourquoi l'Eglise de Jésus-Christ des Saints de Derniers Jours. Admet, comme jour particulier de service spécial et déclaration du Seigneur, ce qu'on appelle généralement le Sabbat Chrétien. Liège, Publié par Ernest C. Rossiter [ca. 1926]
15[1]p. 15½cm.
USIC

7336. ———. The Missouri persecutions, by Elder B. H. Roberts. Salt Lake City, G. Q. Cannon and Sons Co., Publishers, 1900.
viii [9]–333p. front. 20cm.
CSmH, CtY, CU–B, ICU, MH, MoInRC, NjPT, NN, UHi, ULA, UPB, USl, USIC, UU, WHi

7337. ———. The Mormon battalion; its history and achievements, by B. H. Roberts. Salt Lake City, The Deseret News, 1919.
v, 96p. fold. front. (map) port., facsim. 20cm.
CSmH, CU–B, DLC, MoInRC, NjP, NN, UHi, ULA, UPB, USl, USIC, UU

7338. ———. The Mormon doctrine of diety; the Roberts-Van der Donckt discussion, to which is added a discourse, Jesus Christ: the revelation of God, by B. H. Roberts. Also a collection of authoritative Mormon utterances on the being and nature of God . . . Salt Lake City, The Deseret News, 1903.
xii [9]–296p. 20cm.
CSmH, DLC, IWW, MH, MoInRC, NN, UHi, ULA, UPB, USl, USIC, UU, WHi

7339. ———. A Mormon view of world war of 1914. Fullfilment of Joseph Smith's prophecies of 1832. A discourse delivered in Salt Lake Tabernacle, Sunday, August 16, 1914, by Elder Brigham Henry Roberts. Independence, Mo., Liahona, the Elder's Journal, 1914.
8p. 23½cm.
Reprint from *Liahona*, V.12, #17 [257]–264p. Has both numbering of *Liahona* and 8p.
MoInRC, USl, USIC

7340. ———. . . . Mormonism. The relation of the church to Christian sects. Origin and history of Mormonism; doctrines of the church; Church organization; present status. By B. H. Roberts. Published by the church. Salt Lake City, Deseret News Print [1903]
1p.l., 68p. 19cm.
CSmH, CU–B, DLC, ICN, MH, MiU, NjP, NN, UHi, UPB, USl, USIC, WHi

7341. ———. (same) Liverpool, Millennial Star Office [1904?]
54p. 21cm.
IWW, UHi, UPB, USIC

7342. ———. (same) Liverpool, Millennial Star Office [1905?]
58p. 21½cm.
UPB

ROBERTS, B. H.

7343. ———. (same) Independence, Mo., Press of Zion's Printing and Publishing Co., 1923.
78p. 18cm.
MH, MoInRC, NjP, NN, UPB, USlC

7344. ———. (same) Independence, Mo., Press of Zion's Printing and Publishing Co., 1927.
78p. 18½cm.
UPB, USlC

7345. ———. (same) Independence, Mo., Zion's Printing and Publishing Co., 1928.
78p. 18½cm.
Additional information on front and back of cover.
NN, UPB, USlC

7346. ———. "Mormonism." To the editor of the "Cambria Daily Leader." of Jan., 1888. [n.p., 1888?]
2 [2]p. 22½cm.
USlC

7347. ———. A new witness for God. By Elder B. H. Roberts . . . Salt Lake City, George Q. Cannon and Sons [The Deseret News] 1895–[1906]
2v in 4. 20–23cm.
Vol. II published under title: New witnesses for God. Volume II. The Book of Mormon, Pt. I[–III]. Published without author as the manual of the Young Men's Mutual Improvement Association. 1903–1906. [Manual Nos. 7, 8, 9]
Contents: V. I. Joseph Smith, the Prophet. V. II. The Book of Mormon, Pt. I–II.
CSmH, CU–B, DLC, IWW, NN, UHi, ULA, UPB, USlC, WHi

7348. ———. New witnesses for God. II. The Book of Mormon. By B. H. Roberts . . . In three volumes. Salt Lake City, The Deseret News, 1909.
3v. 19½cm.
Reprinting of the 1903–1906, Young Men's Mutual Improvement Association manuals to accompany 1895 ed. of V. I. Volume changed to V. II–III.
MoInRC, NjP, UPB, USlC, WHi

7349. ———. (same) I. Joseph Smith, the prophet. By B. H. Roberts . . . Salt Lake City, The Deseret News, 1911.
viii, [1]l. [11]–483p. 20cm.
MoInRC, UPB, USlC

7350. ———. (same) V. II. The Book of Mormon. Salt Lake City, The Deseret News, 1920.
485p. 19½cm.
UPB, USlC

7351. ———. (same) V. II. The Book of Mormon. Salt Lake City, The Deseret News, 1926.
501p. 19½cm.
USlC

7352. ———. (same) V. II. The Book of Mormon. Salt Lake City, The Deseret News, 1927.
501p. 19½cm.
USlC

7353. ———. On tracting. By Elder B. H. Roberts, former president Eastern States Mission. [New York] Eastern States Mission [n.d.]
22p. 17½cm.
UPB, USlC

7354. ———. (same) [Independence, Mo.] Zion's Printing and Publishing Co. [n.d.]
22p. 17cm.
UPB, USlC

7355. ———. (same) [Independence, Mo.] Press of Zion's Printing and Publishing Co., Published by the Missions of the Church of Jesus Christ of Latter-day Saints [n.d.]
22p. 18cm.
Variant printing.
NN

7356. ———. Origin and faith of the Church of Jesus Christ of Latter-day Saints. [Chicago, A. L. Swift, 189–]
15p. 16½cm.
Caption-title.
WHi

7356a. ———. (same) [Salt Lake City? Juvenile Instructor Office? ca. 1885]
15[1]p. 18cm.
USlC

7357. ———. (same) [Salt Lake City, Deseret News, n.d.]
6p. 16cm.
UU

7358. ———. Outline history of the dispensations of the Gospel. Compiled and edited by B. H. Roberts of the First Council of the Seventy. Salt Lake City, Skelton Publishing Company, 1908.
232p. 23cm. (The Seventy's Course in Theology. Second year)
CSmH, CU–B, DLC, UHi, UPB, USlC, UU

7359. ———. Outline history of the Seventy and a survey of the Books of Holy Scriptures. Compiled and Edited by Elder B. H. Roberts, of the First Council of the Seventy . . . Salt Lake City, The Deseret News, 1907.
xi [1] 168p. 23cm. (The Seventy's Course in Theology. First year)
CSmH, CU–B, DLC, UHi, UPB, USlC, UU

7360. ———. Outlines of ecclesiastical history. Salt Lake City, G. Q. Cannon and Sons Company, 1893.
vii [1] [11]–467p. 20cm.
CSmH, MH, MiU, NjP, UHi, UPB, USlC, UU

7361. ———. (same) 2d ed. Salt Lake City, G. Q. Cannon and Sons Company, 1895.
vii [1] [11]–459p. 20cm.
CSmH, DLC, IWW, NN, OClWHi, UPB, USl, USlC, WHi

7362. ———. (same) 3d ed. Salt Lake City, The Deseret News, 1902.
vii [1] [11]–426p. 20cm.
CSmH, UHi, ULA, UPB, USlC, UU

7363. ———. (same) 4th ed. Salt Lake City, Church of Jesus Christ of Latter-day Saints, 1924.
vii [2] [11]–458p. 19½cm.
CU–B, DLC, PCC, UHi, UPB, USlC

7364. ———. (same) 5th ed. Salt Lake City, Church of Jesus Christ of Latter-day Saints, 1927.
vii [4] 12–458p. 19½cm.
UPB, USlC

7365. ———. A rabbi's objections to Jesus and a reply [and] A message to "Rasha" the Jew, to all Jews. Binghamton, N.Y., The Redeemed Hebrew Mission, 1926–1927.
Various pagings. (The Redeemed Hebrew, V.5, #6–8) 32cm.
First edition of *Rasha, the Jew.*
UPB

7366. ———. Recent discussion of Mormon affairs. Answer to the Ministerial Associations review of "An address to the world" by the First Presidency of the Church of Jesus Christ of Latter-day Saints. [Salt Lake City] 1907.
56p. 23½cm.
Cover-title.
Also included as part II of *Church of Jesus Christ of Latter-day Saints. First Presidency. An address.*
CSmH, I, ICN, MB, MH, MoInRC, MnU, NjP, NN, UHi, ULA, UPB, USlC

7367. ———. The rise and fall of Nauvoo, by Elder B. H. Roberts . . . Salt Lake City, The Deseret News, 1900.
vi [9]–457p. 20cm.
CSmH, CtY, CU–B, ICN, ICU, MH, MoInRC, NN, PCC, UHi, UPB, USl, USlC, UU, WHi

7368. ———. The second coming of the Messiah and events to precede it, by Elder B. H. Roberts. [Liverpool, Latter-day Saints Millennial Star Publishing Office, 189–]
8p. 21cm.
UHi, USlC, UU

7369. ———. (same) [Independence, Mo., Zion's Printing and Publishing Co., n.d.]
15p. 21cm.
UPB

7370. ———. (same) [Independence, Mo., Zion's Printing and Publishing Co., n.d.]
14p. 21cm.
UPB

7371. ———. (same) [Independence, Mo., Zion's Printing and Publishing Co. Published by the Missions of the Church of Jesus Christ of Latter-day Saints, n.d.]
16p. 18½cm.
MoInRC, NjP, NN, UHi, UPB

7372. ———. (same) [Independence, Mo., Zion's Printing and Publishing Co., n.d.]
12 [2]p. 17½cm.
Caption-title.
CU–B, MH, MoInRC, UPB, USl, USlC

7372a. ———. (same, in Tahitian) Te haere-piti-raa mai o te Mesia E Te Mau E Tupu I Mua'tu. No B. H. Roberts. [Tahiti, n.d.]
28p. 15cm.
USlC

7373. ———. The seventy's course in theology. First-[fifth] year . . . Compiled and Edited by Elder B. H. Roberts . . . Salt Lake City, The Deseret News, 1907–12.
5v. 23cm.
V. 2 has imprint: Salt Lake City, Skelton publishing Co. V. 3. Salt Lake City, The Caxton press.
CU–B, DLC, NjP, UHi, UPB, USlC, UU

7374. ———. "Sir, we would see Jesus" Ecco Homo! "Behold the Man!" Ecce Deus! "Behold God!" address delivered over Radio Station KSL, Sunday Evening, Dec. 25, 1927. [Salt Lake City] 1927.
Broadside. 57½×23½cm.
Reprinted from the *Deseret News*, Saturday, December 31st, 1927.
UPB

7375. ———. Succession in the presidency of the Church of Jesus Christ of Latter-day Saints. Salt Lake City, The Deseret News Publishing Co., 1894.
iv, 123p. 19½cm.
CSmH, MH, MoInRC, UHi, ULA, UPB, USlC

7376. ———. (same) 2d ed. Salt Lake City, G. Q. Cannon and Sons Publishing Co., 1900 [c1894]
ivp., [1]l. [17]–162p. 19cm.
Expanded version.
CSmH, CU–B, MH, MoInRC, NjP, NN, UHi, ULA, UPB, USl, USlC

7377. ———. Why "Mormonism"? By Elder B. H. Roberts, of the First Council of Seventy in the Church of Jesus Christ of Latter-day Saints. [Independence, Mo., Press of Zion's Printing & Publishing Company, n.d.]
4 nos. 18cm.
UPB, USlC

7378. ———. (same) [Independence, Mo., Press of Zion's Printing and Publishing Co., Published by the Missions of the Church of Jesus Christ of Latter-day Saints in America, 19–]
64p. 18cm.
CU–B, MoInRC, NN, UHi, UPB, USlC

7379. Roberts, E. Twyll Mormoniaeth. Darlith a Draddodwyd Gan y Parch. E. Roberts, Gweinidog y bedyddwyr, Rumney. Merthyr-Tydvil: Argraffwyd a Chyhoeddwyd gan David Jones, 1848.
23p. 18½cm.
Title in English: Mormon deceit.
UPB

7380. Roberts, Edwards. Salt Lake City and Utah by-ways, by Edwards Roberts. Chicago, R. R. Donnelley and Sons [1883?]
3p.l. [9]–38p. plates. 22cm.
Includes a description of the Mormon hierarchy.
CU–B, DLC, MH, NjP, NN, UHi, UPB

7381. ———. Shoshone, and other western wonders. By Edwards Roberts. With a preface by Charles Francis Adams . . . New York, Harper and Brothers, 1888.
xvi, 275p. illus., plates. 19cm.
Glimpses of Utah and the Mormons, p. 119–124.
CSmH, CU–B, DGS, DLC, NjP, NN, OrU, PPL, UHi, ULA, UPB, USlC, WaS, WaSp, WaU

7382. Roberts, J. Herbert. A world tour, being a year's diary written in 1884–85. Liverpool, Printed by I. Foulkes, 1886]
2p.l., 612p. 22cm.
A short discourse on Mormon doctrine during a stay in Salt Lake City, p. 41–45.
UHi, USlC, UU

7383. Roberts, Sidney. Great distress and loss of the lives of American citizens. An appeal to the citizens of the United States for and in behalf of suffering humanity, in the western state of Iowa, and in the Indian territory. By Sidney Roberts of Iowa City, Iowa, December, 1848. [n.p.] 1848.
iv [5]–9 [3]p. plates. 19cm.
An appeal for contributions to relieve the sufferings of the Mormons in Iowa. By a Mormon agent.
CtY, DLC, MH

7384. ———. To emigrants to the gold region. A treatise, showing the best way to California, with many serious objections to going by sea, doubling the Cape, or, crossing the Isthmus, with the constitution and articles of agreement of the Joint Stock Mutual Insurance Merchandizing Company . . . By Sidney Roberts of Iowa City, Iowa, traveling agent for the company. New Haven, 1849.
12p. 18½cm.
The author advises prospective emigrants to travel by way of Salt Lake City, asserting that they will receive assistance from the Mormons.
Howes R346, Sabin 71919, W–C 172a
NN

7385. Robertson, Mark. Some suggestions for Latter-day Saint missionaries from the field of successful commercial salesmanship. [Salt Lake City, Deseret News Press, 1929?]
2p.l. [5]–85p. 23cm.
Compiled by Earl W. Harmer.
UPB, USlC

7386. Robertson, William. Our American tour. Being a run of 10,000 miles from the Atlantic to the Golden Gate, in the autumn of 1869. By William Robertson, and W. F. Robertson. Edinburgh, Printed for Private Circulation, 1871.
5p.l., 148p. 22cm.
Chap. XVII. Salt Lake City: Mormonism — The Murder of Dr. Robertson [Robinson] and other persons. His experiences in Salt Lake City were agreeable.
CU–B, ICHi, USlC

7387. Robins, John B. Christ and our country; or, A hopeful view of Christianity in the present day. By Rev. John B. Robins . . . Nashville, Tenn., Printed for the author, Publishing House of the M. E. Church, South, 1889.
141p. 19cm.
Mormonism as a peril, p. 40–47.
A second edition published the same year.
DLC, USlC

7388. Robinson, Ezra Clark. Zalmonah, prologue and four acts; from Book of Mormon history, by Ezra C. Robinson. [Bountiful? c1926]
47p. 18cm.
Mormon drama.
CSmH, DLC, NN, UHi, UPB, USl, USlC, UU

7389. ———. (same) [Bountiful? c1926]
48p. 17cm.
USlC

7390. Robinson, Luther Emerson. History of Illinois, by L. E. Robinson and Irving Moore. New York, Cincinnati, Chicago, American Book Company [c1909]
288p. illus., ports., maps. 19cm.
Chap. 25. The Mormons, p. 121–125. Brief notice of activities while in Illinois; from a non-Mormon point of view.
Revised edition: 1914. USlC
DLC, MoInRC, UPB, USlC

7391. Robinson, Noel. Blazing the trail through the Rockies. The story of the Walter Moberly and his share in the making of Vancouver, by Noel Robinson and the old man himself . . . [n.p.] Printed by News-advertiser [n.d.]
117p. illus., ports. 23½cm.
Includes an analysis of the character of Brigham Young, from a meeting in 1869, p. 63–64.
CU–B, UPB

ROBINSON, P. S.

7392. Robinson, Philip Stewart. Sinners and saints. A tour across the states, and round them; with three months among the Mormons. By Phil Robinson, Boston, Roberts Bros., 1883.
x, 370p. 18½cm.
Visited Utah in 1882.
CSmH, CtY, CU–B, DLC, ICN, IWW, MoInRC, NjP, NN, UHi, ULA, UPB, USlC, UU, WHi

7393. ———. (same) London, S. Low, Marston, Searle and Rivington, 1883.
xii, 370p. [1]l. 19cm.
CSmH, CtY, MB, MH, MWA, UPB, USlC

7394. ———. (same) New and cheaper ed. London, Sampson Low, Marston & Company, 1892.
xii, 370p. 19½cm.
CU–B, MH, NjPT, UHi, UPB

7395. Robinson, William Henry. The story of Arizona, by Will H. Robinson . . . Phoenix, Ariz., The Berryhill Company [c1919]
458p. plates, map. 20cm.
Includes Mormon colonization in Arizona.
CU–B, DLC, NjP, UHi

7395a. Robison, Lewis. Notice to all whom it may concern! Wheras, the premises, known as Fort Bridger, including the lands adjoining thereto . . . [Great Salt Lake City] Printed at the "Mountaineer" Office, 1861.
Broadside. 23½×15cm.
Dated: 22d day of July, A. D. 1861.
Concerning the purchase of Fort Bridger due to the Utah Expedition.
USlC

7396. Rochefort-Lucay, Victor Henri, ***marquis de.*** Retour de la Nouvelle-Calédonie. De Nouméa en Europe; 200 illustrations, contenant 700 sujets. Dessins de Denis, Desjours, V. Gilbert, Mathon, D. Vierge, E. Hareux, etc., etc. Paris, Ancienne Librairie Martinon, F. Jeanmaire, Successeur [1877]
2p.l. xxiv, 363p. illus., plates, port. 28cm.
A visit to Utah in 1875 with a description of the Mormons, p. 246–275.
Title in English: Return from New Caledonia of Noumea to Europe.
CU–B, NjP, UPB

7397. Rocky Mountain Christian Advocate. Salt Lake City, 1876–1883.
8v. monthly. 64cm.
Edited by Rev. G. M. Pierce.
Title changed in 1884 to *Utah Christian Advocate.* January, 1884–November, 1887.
One of its purposes was to expose Mormonism.
NjMP V.3–8; NN V.3 #4, V.5 #4, 7, 8, 9, 10, V.6 #2, 3, 4, 6, 7, 9, 10, V.7 #2, 4, 5, 6, 7, 10, 12, V.8 #2, 3, 4, 5, 6, 7, 8, 9, 10; USlC V.4–8 comp.

7398. The Rod of Iron. Independence, Mo., Reorganized Church of Jesus Christ of Latter Day Saints, 1892–93.
2v. monthly.
MoInRC

7399. Rodenbough, Theophilus Francis, ***compiler.*** From everglade to cañon with the second dragoons, (second United States cavalry); an authentic account of service in Florida, Mexico, Virginia, and the Indian country, including the personal recollections of prominent officers, with an appendix containing orders, reports and correspondence, military records, etc., etc., etc., 1836–1875, compiled by Theo. F. Rodenbough . . . New York, D. Van Nostrand, 1875.
561p. illus., plates (part col.) 2 fold. maps. 25cm.
Includes a section on the Utah Expedition, p. 208–230.
CU–B, DLC, NjP, UHi, UPB

7400. Rodney, Mary. The girl from Dixie . . . New York, Cochrane Publishing Co., 1910.
132p. 19½cm.
Fiction concerning Mormonism.
DLC, USl

7400a. Roe, Frances M. A. Army letters from an officer's wife, 1871–1888. New York and London, D. Appleton and Co., 1909.
x, 387p. illus. 20½cm.
Utah and Mormons: p. 161, 379–386.
USlC

7401. Roell, C. F. A. Bekeert U, O, Gy Volken! Independence, Mo., Uitgegeven door de Reorganiséerde kerk van Jezus Christus Van de Heiligen der laatste Dagen [n.d.]
[1]p. 19½cm.
An RLDS tract in Dutch.
Title in English: Be converted, oh ye peoples.
USlC

7402. Roemer, Carl Ferdinand. Texas. Mit besonderer Rücksicht auf deutsche Auswanderung und die physischen Verhältnisse des Landes nach eigener Beobachtung geschildert von dr. Ferdinand Roemer. Mit einem naturwissenschaftlichen Anhange und einer topographisch geognostischen Karte von Texas. Bonn: A. Marcus, 1849.
xiv p., [2]l. [3]–464p. fold. map. 21cm.
Reference to Lyman Wight's colony in Texas, November, 1846, p. 257–258.
Title in English: Texas, with special emphasis on German emigration . . .
English translation: Austin, Texas, 1935.
CtY, DLC

7403. Rodger, Glaud. What do the Latter-day Saints believe; or, what is "Mormonism?" Liverpool, Printed by J. Sadler [185–]
Broadside. 22½×12½cm.
UPB

7404. Rogers, Aurelia Spencer. Life sketches of Orson Spencer and others, and history of primary work. By Aurelia Spencer Rogers. [Salt Lake City] Printed by G. Q. Cannon and Sons Co., 1898.
viii [9]–333p. ports. 18cm.
CSmH, CU-B, MH, NjP, NN, UHi, ULA, UPB, USIC, UU

7405. Rogers, David W. A collection of sacred hymns for the Church of the Latter Day Saints. Selected and Published by David W. Rogers. New York, C. Vinten, Printer, 1838.
iv [5]–118, ix p. 10cm.
Sabin 72623
CtY, DLC, USIC

7406. Rogers, Henry Munroe. Memoires of ninety years. Boston and New York, Houghton Mifflin Co., 1928.
7p.l. [3]–409p. illus., plates, ports., facsim. 24½cm.
Brief account of Salt Lake City which he visited; Brigham Young's contribution.
CU, DLC, NjP, NN

7407. Rogers, M. D. Rogers-Cornish debate. Christian Church vs. Reorganized Church of Jesus Christ of Latter Day Saints, held at Sanford, Michigan, Dec. 14–22, 1891. Arranged by J. Cole Moxon. Independence, Mo., Zion's Ensign Print., 1892.
36p. 19cm.
MoInRC

7408. Roister, Ernest A. Te Buka a Mormona. Te mau parau i papaihia i te rima a Mormona Te hoe Mau uiraa e Te Pahonoraa i Nia i Taua Buka a Mormona ra. Papaihia e Eraneta A. Rositera. Papeete, Tahiti, Ekalesia a Iesu Mesia i te Feia Mo'a i te Mau Mahana Hopea Nei, 1919.
44p. 17½cm.
Questions and answers on the *Book of Mormon*.
Title in English: The Book of Mormon.
USIC

7409. Rolapp, Henry Hermann, *compiler*. Two thousand gospel quotations, from the Bible, Book of Mormon, Doctrine and covenants, and Pearl of Great Price, compiled by Henry H. Rolapp. Salt Lake City, The Deseret news, 1918.
[335]p. 19cm.
DLC, IWW, NjP, NN, UHi, UPB, USI, USIC

7410. ———. (same, under title) Gospel quotations from the Bible, Book of Mormon, Doctrine and Covenants and Pearl of Great Price. 2d ed., revised. Salt Lake City, The Deseret Book Co., 1923.
4p.l. [9]–288p. 20cm.
UHi, UPB, USIC

7411. Rollo, J. B. Mormonism exposed, from the word of God. South Bridge, England, Glass, Printer. Sold by C. Ziegler [1841]
12p. 17cm.
Replied to by P. P. Pratt in the *Millennial Star*, July, 1841. For date of printing see *Smith, Joseph, 1805–1844. History of the Church*, V. IV, p. 488.
NN

7412. Rolt-Wheeler, Francis William. The Book of Cowboys by Francis Rolt-Wheeler. With 33 illustrations from photographs, sketches, and early prints. Boston, Lothrop, Lee & Shepard Co. [1921]
394p. illus. 19½cm.
Fiction. Chap. III. The "Destroying angels."
Chap. IV. Mormons and massacre.
DLC, UPB, USIC

7413. Ronne, C. F. Mormonerne, de sidste dages falske profeter. Envarselsrøst til Guds folk, I. Kobenhavn, 1852.
4p.
Title in English: Mormons, the Latter Day false prophets.
Schmidt.
USIC

7414. Roosevelt, Theodore. Theodore Roosevelt refutes anti-Mormon falsehoods; his testimony as to Mormon character. Advice concerning polygamy. [Explanatory note by Isaac Russell. n.p., 1911?]
11p. 22cm.
MH, UHi, UPB

7415. ———. (same) [n.p., n.d.]
13p. 17½cm.
USIC

7415a. ———. (same, in Danish) Ekspraesident Roosevelt og mormonkirken. [Kobenhavn? Arbeidernes Aktietrykkeri, 1911?]
[4]p. 28cm.
"Mormon-hysteriet i England" from Social-Demokraten 10 mai 1911, on p. [4]
UPB, USIC

7416. ———. (same, in Dutch) Theodore Roosevelt weerlegt Anti Mormonsche leugens. Zijne getuigenis in betrekking tot het Mormoonsche Volkskarakter. Bericht aagaande-meervoudig huwelijk Een krachtige terverant-woordingroeping van tijdschriften lasteraars. [Rotterdam, Uitgave B. G. Thatcher, n.d.]
12p. 20½cm.
USIC

ROOT, F. A.

7417. Root, Frank Albert. The overland stage to California. Personal reminiscences and authentic history of the great overland stage line and pony express from the Missouri river to the Pacific ocean. By Frank A. Root . . . and William Elsey Connelley . . . Pub. by the authors. Topeka, Kan., 1901.
1p.l., xvii [1] 630p. illus., port., map. 23½cm.
Several references to Mormons and the Utah Expedition.
Howes R–434
CU–B, DLC, ICN, MiU, NjP, PPL, PPM, PU, UHi, ULA, UU

7418. Rordam, H. C. Nyt bidrag til Oplysning om Mormonerne, Meddeelt af Dr. H. C. Rordam. Naestved, H. Bloch Trykt hos G. P. Borg, 1854.
29p. 18cm.
Title in English: New light on the Mormons.
NN, UHi, USlC

7419. ———. Om Mormonerne. En kort oplysning, meddeelt af Dr. H. C. Rordam. Andet oplag . . . Naestved, Trykt og forlagt af A. P. Bang . . . 1852.
24p. 14cm.
A critical work on Mormonism.
Title in English: About Mormonism.
USlC

7419a. Ross, David J. Hail to the Prophet. [n.p., 1852]
Broadside. 20×13cm.
Gold printed on blue coated paper. Probably printed in England, ca. 1852.
UPB, USlC

7420. Ross, James. From Wisconsin to California and return, as reported for the "Wisconsin State Journal," by James Ross . . . and by Hon. George Gary, for the "Oshkosh Journal," and the "Oshkosh Northwestern." Madison, Atwood & Rublee, Printers, 1869.
132p. 22½cm.
Account of Utah and the Mormons, p. 26–33, 37–48, 89–97, 116–123.
Howes R457
CSmH, CtY, CU–B, DLC, ICN, MB, NjP, NN, USlC

7421. Ross, William Wilson. 10,000 miles by land and sea. By Rev. W. W. Ross. Toronto, J. Campbell & Sons, 1876.
vii [9]–284p. 18½cm.
Chap. VI. "Mormondom." The autocratic Mormonism on the decline, 1874.
CU–B, DLC, UHi

7422. Rossell, H. E. A synopsis of the Rossell-Cornish debate. Independence, Mo., Ensign Print., 1893.
74p. 21cm.
Debate concerning the RLDS church.
John J. Cornish was an RLDS church member.
MoInRC

7422a. Rossiter, Ernest Crabtree. Te Buka a Moromona; te mau parau i papaihia i te rima a Mormona. Te hoe mau uiraa e te pahonoraa i nia i taua buka a Moromona ra. Papaihia e Eraneta A. Rositera. Papeete, Tahiti, Ekalesia a Iesu Mesia i te Feia Mo'a i te Mau Mahana Hopea Nei, 1919.
44p. 17½cm.
Title in English: The Book of Mormon.
USlC

7423. ———. Extraits de l'historie du prophete Joseph Smith. Liege [n.d.]
23p. 16cm.
Title in English: Extracts from the history of the prophet Joseph Smith.
UPB

7424. ———. A new grammar of the Tahitian dialect of the Polynesian language together with brief reading exercises. Arranged and Published by Ernest C. Rossiter for the Church of Jesus Christ of Latter Day Saints. Papeete, Tahiti, 1919.
290 [4]p. 18cm.
CU, USlC

7425. Roth, J. S. The gospel messenger; sermons and articles of Elder J. S. Roth. Lamoni, Ia. [Herald Publishing House] 1911.
2p.l., 529p. 21cm.
RLDS sermons and doctrinal articles.
MoInRC, NN, USl, USlC

7426. ———. (same) 2d ed. Lamoni, Ia. [Herald Publishing House] 1915.
3p.l. [7]–556p. 20½cm.
MoInRC, UPB

7427. ———. The kingdom of God. Grand Rapids, Mich., Glad Tidings Print. [n.d.]
44p. 14cm.
RLDS Doctrine.
MoInRC

7428. ———. The name of the Church. Independence, Mo., Ensign Publishing House, 1897.
44p. 15cm. (The Gospel Banner. V. 4, No. 2)
Name of the RLDS Church
MoInRC

7429. ———. (same) Peoria, Ill., Printed by Glad Tidings [n.d.]
30p. 15cm.
MoInRC

7430. ———. The Personality of God and doctrine of Christ. Independence, Mo., Ensign Publishing House, 1899.
38p. 15cm. (The Gospel Banner. V. 6, No. 2)
MoInRC

7431. ———. Signs of the times. Independence, Mo., Ensign Publishing House, 1893.
50p. 15cm. (Ensign Circulating Library, Vest Pocket edition. No. 1, Extra E)
MoInRC

7432. ———. (same) Rev. and enl. ed. Independence, Mo., Ensign Publishing House, 1898.
70p. 15cm. (The Gospel Banner. V. 5, No. 3)
MoInRC

7433. ———. (same) Independence, Mo., Ensign Publishing House, 1900.
70p. 15cm. (The Gospel Banner. V. 7, No. 4)
MoInRC

7434. Rough notes of journeys made in the years 1868, '69, '70, '71, '72, and '73 in Syria, down the Tigris, India, Kashmir, Ceylon, Japan, Mongolia, Siberia, The United States, The Sandwich Islands, and Australia. London, Trübner and Co., 1875.
xv, 605p. 21cm.
Second tour: Visit to Salt Lake City. Mormons, p. 180–184. Description of a sacrament service, and of the area.
USlC

7434a. Roundy, Elizabeth J. Drake. In memory of The chosen of God and the Friend of man, Joseph Smith, the Prophet. [Salt Lake City, 1896]
[3]p. 19cm.
Poetry concerning Joseph Smith.
USlC

7434b. ———. Most respectfully dedicated to the Prophet Joseph Smith. [Salt Lake City, ca. 1896]
[4]p. 22cm.
Poetry concerning Joseph Smith.
USlC

7434c. ———. Respectfully Dedicated to Bishop F. Kesler on his return from his eastern mission. [Salt Lake City, 1890]
Broadside. 28×18cm.
Mormon poetry.
UPB, UU

7434d. ———. Verses Respectfully Dedicated to Bishop F. Kesler, Recited at his seventy-fourth Birthday anniversary, by his youngest daughter, Clara Olivia, before nearly seventy-five members of his family, on January 20th, 1890, in Salt Lake City, Utah. [Salt Lake City, 1890?]
Broadside. 28×18cm.
UPB, USlC

Rousseau, Victor [*pseud.*] *See Emanuel, Victor Rousseau.*

7435. Routledge, John. A companion for the Bible, or important scripture references, to prove a few of the first and leading principles of the Church of Jesus Christ of Latter Day Saints, to be true. By Elder John Routledge. [Liverpool, 1854]
24p. 12½cm.
Chiefly scriptural references.
USlC

7436. Rowlands, William. Twyll Mormoniaeth: yn nghyd a Hanes bywyd a marwolaeth Joseph Smith, o America, prophwyd santyddol y dyddiau diweddaf. Gan y parch. William Rowlands . . . Merthyr Tydfil, Argraffwyd gan D. Jones, 1852.
16p. 16½cm.
Title in English: The deceit of Mormonism.
DLC

7437. Royce, Josiah. . . . California, from the conquest in 1846 to the second vigilance committee in San Francisco [1856] A study of American character, by Josiah Royce . . . Boston and New York, Houghton, Mifflin and Company, 1886.
xv, 513p. map. 18cm. (half-title: American commonwealths)
Mormons, p. 197, 289–291.
CU–B, DLC

7438. Rumble, Leslie. Mormons, or Latter-day Saints. [St. Paul, Radio Replies Press Society, n.d.]
29p. 17cm.
WHi

7439. Rumfield, Hiram S. . . . Letters of an overland mail agent in Utah, ed. by Archer Butler Hulbert . . . Worcester, Mass., The society, 1929.
78p. 24½cm. (Stewart commission reprints)
At head of title: American Antiquarian Society.
"Reprinted from the *Proceedings of the American Antiquarian Society* for October, 1928."
Many of the letters are concerned with Mormonism.
CSmH, CU–B, MH, UHi, ULA, USl, UU

Rupert, A. E. D. *See De Rupert, A. E. D.*

7440. Rupp, Israel Daniel, *editor.* He pasa ekklesia. An original history of the religious denominations at present existing in the United States. Containing authentic accounts of their rise, progress, statistics and doctrines. Written expressly for the work by eminent theological professors, ministers and lay-members of the respective denominations. Projected, compiled and arranged by I. Daniel Rupp . . . Philadelphia, J. Y. Humphreys; Harrisburg, Clyde and Williams, 1844.
viii [9]–734p. illus. 24cm.
Under title: History of all the religious denominations in the United States. Harrisburg, John Winebrenner, 1848. MH; 1849. USlC
Under title: The religious denominations in the United States. Philadelphia, C. Desilver, 1859. DLC, NN. Entered separately.

Latter-day Saints, by Joseph Smith, p. 404–410. The first publication of the Wentworth letter in a non-Mormon book.
Howes R507, Sabin 74157
CSmH, CtY, DLC, ICN, MH, MoInRC, MoU, NjP, NjR, NN, UHi, ULA, UPB, USlC, UU, ViU, WHi

7441. Rushton, Don Carlos. A message of truth. To the people of Australia. The Voice of a people evil spoken of, as was the Savior and His Disciples. [Liverpool, Printed and Published at the Millennial Star Office, ca. 1920]
8p. 21cm.
Articles of faith on inside front cover. Marriage regulations among the "Mormons" on the verso of rear cover.
USlC

7442. Rushton, John W. The apostasy and the restoration. [Lamoni, Ia., Reorganized Church of Jesus Christ of Latter Day Saints, 1916?]
20p. 18cm. (No. 301)
CtY, IWW, MoInRC, UPB

7443. ———. (same) [Lamoni, Ia.,? 1917?]
26p. 19cm.
MoInRC

7444. ———. Co-operation. [Independence, Mo., 1912?]
26p. 19½cm.
Lecture delivered to the saints at First Independence Church, January 15, 1912.
MoInRC

7445. ———. The disaffection of R. C. Evans. [n.p., n.d.]
24p. 15cm.
MoInRC

7446. ———. Dramatic expression in religious life. [Independence? 1922?]
16p. 19½cm.
A lecture given at the Stone Church [Independence] on October 9, 1922.
MoInRC

7447. ———. The Latter Day Saints, a question of identity. [n.p., n.d.]
6p. 21cm.
Problem of succession.
MoInRC

7448. ———. (same) [n.p., n.d.]
4p. 21cm.
MoInRC

7449. ———. (same) Independence, Mo., Herald Publishing House [n.d.]
4p. 21cm.
MoInRC

7450. ———. The President of the Church. The Law of succession. [Independence, Mo., Herald Publishing House, n.d.]
8p. 20cm.
MoInRC

7451. ———. The Problems of social purity. Lamoni, Ia., Herald Publishing House [n.d.]
15p. 20cm.
Issued by the Social Purity Board of the RLDS Church.
MoInRC

7452. ———. The Temple and Tabernacle. Salt Lake City, The House of the Lord. [Salt Lake City, ca. 1908]
7 [1]p. 15cm.
Utah and the Mormons, p. [8]
NjP

7453. Rusling, James Fowler. Across America: or, The great West and the Pacific Coast. By James F. Rusling . . . New York, Sheldon & Company, 1874.
xx [21–503p. illus., plates, port., fold. map. 20cm.
Visited Salt Lake City in 1867; Mormon outrages, polygamy, Mormonism in general . . . p. 163–205.
Another edition: 1875. CU, NjP, UHi
CSmH, CU, DLC, MB, NjN, NjP, NN, OrU, PP, PPL, PPM, ULA, UPB, USlC, WaU

7454. ———. (same, under title) The great West and Pacific coast; or, Fifteen thousand miles by stagecoach, ambulance, horseback, railroad, and steamer — across the continent and along the Pacific slope . . . among Indians, Mormons, miners and Mexicans. By order of the United States government. With a map of entire route and eight full-page engravings . . . with a chapter of advice to emigrants and settlers. New York, Sheldon and Company [1877]
xx [21]–515p. plates, port., fold. map. 21½cm.
Includes a description of Mormonism.
CSmH, CU-B, DLC, MH, NN, PHC, UHi, UPB, USlC, WaU, WHi

7455. ———. Affairs in Utah and the territories. Letter from the Secretary of War, transmitting, in compliance with House resolution of the 5th instant, the report of Brevet Brigadier General James F. Rusling, Inspector &c., for the year ending June 30, 1867. [Washington, Govt. Print. Off.] 1868.
36p. 29cm. (U.S. 40th Cong. 2nd Sess. House. Misc. Doc. No. 153)
Includes the author's impression of the Mormon community and the state of affairs in and about Salt Lake City. Other references to Mormons.
CSmH, NjP, NN, UHi, UPB

7456. Russell, Charles Russell, *baron.* Diary of a visit to the United States of America in the year 1883 by Charles Lord Russell . . . With an introduction by the Rev. Matthew Russell, S. J. and an appendix by Thomas Francis Meehan, A. M. Edited by Charles George Herberman, Ph.D. New York, The United States Catholic Historical Society, 1910.
1p.l., 235p. port. 22½cm.
Letter from Salt Lake City, Sept. 28, 1883; describes Salt Lake City and Mormon beliefs.
CU, NjP, USlC

7457. Russell, John. Claudine Lavalle: or, The first convict. The Mormoness; or, The trials of Mary Maverick, by Professor John Russell, of Bluffdale. Alton, Courier Steam Press Print, 1853.
89p. 21cm.
Fiction concerning Mormonism.
Byrd 2027
USlC

7458. Russell, William. Experiences of a real detective. Inspector F. Edited by "Waters" author of "Recollections of a police officer," "Leonard Harlowe," etc., etc. London, Ward and Lock, 1863.
2p.l., 252p. 16½cm. (The Shelling Volume library)
Fiction. "XI. Reuben Gill — A Mormon Saint."
USlC

7459. Ruxton, George Frederick Augustus. Adventures in Mexico and the Rocky Mountains. By George F. Ruxton, esq., member of the Royal Geographical Society, the Ethnological Society, etc., etc. London, John Murray, 1847.
vii, 332p. 18cm.
Half-title: Mr. Murray's home and colonial library.
Encounters a group of Mormon Battalion members leaving expedition to join the Mississippi saints on the Arkansas River.
Published in many editions.
Howes R553, Sabin 74501, W–C 139
CU–B, DLC, ICN, ICU, NjP, OCl, OCU, PSC, ULA, UPB

7459a. ———. In the old west. Edited by Horace Kephart. New York, Outing Publishing Co., 1915.
345p. 19½cm.
Mormons, p. 9, 302–329.
USlC

7460. ———. Life in the Far West. By George Frederick Ruxton, author of "Travels in Mexico," etc. Edinburgh and London, William Blackwood and Sons, M.DCC. XLIX [1849]
xvi, 312p. 18cm.
Printed the same year by Harper & Brothers, 1849. Various later editions; Reprinted, N.Y., Outing Pub. Co., 1915 with title: *In the Old West.*
Howes R554, Sabin 74502, W–C 173
CSmH, MiU, NjP, NN, PPL–R, PPWi, PSC, UU

7461. ———. . . . Wild life in the Rocky Mountains. A true tale of rough adventure in the days of the Mexican war. Edited by Horace Kephart. New York, Outing Publishing Co., 1916.
2p.l. 7–303p. double map. 19½cm. (Outing adventure library)
Chapters xx–xxxvi of the author's *Adventures in Mexico and the Rocky Mountains.*
Brief mention of a campsite used by the Mormons.
DLC, MB, NN, OCl, PSC

7462. Ryan, Oswald. . . . Municipal freedom; a study of the commission government. By Oswald Ryan . . . Garden City, New York, Doubleday, Page, & Co., 1915.
xvi, 233p., [1]l. 18cm. (The American Books)
Salt Lake City dominated by Mormon church, p. 36–48. The Mormon-Gentile conflict; lack of municipal freedom.
DLC, NjP, USlC

7462a. Ryus, William Henry. The second William Penn; a true account of incidents that happened along the old Santa Fe trail in the sixties. Kansas City, Mo., Frank T. Riley Publ. Co. [c1913]
176p. illus. 20cm.
Salt Lake Temple under construction, p. 149.
USlC

S-05

THE

VOICE OF TRUTH,

CONTAINING THE PUBLIC WRITINGS, PORTRAIT,

AND

LAST SERMON

OF

PRESIDENT JOSEPH SMITH.

NAUVOO, ILL:
PRINTED BY JOHN TAYLOR:
1845.

Item 8000. The printed wrapper (dated a year after the printing began) of the collected secular writings of Joseph Smith, together with his most famous discourse, the King Follett funeral sermon. From the P. Crawley collection.

7463. S., J. M. Sinking of the "Arabic." [n.p., n.d.]
4p. 21½cm.
Signed: J. M. S.
Relates experiences of a Mormon missionary returning from the European mission.
NjP

7464. Saabye, H. Om sekterne i Danmark. Kobenhavn, 1884.
401p.
Title in English: About the sects in Denmark.
Schmidt

7465. Sabin, Edwin Legrand. Building the Pacific Railway; the construction-story of America's first iron thoroughfare between the Missouri river and California, from the inception of the great idea to the day, May 10, 1869, when the Union Pacific and the Central Pacific joined tracks at Promontory Point, Utah, to form the nation's transcontinental . . . Philadelphia and London, J. B. Lippincott Company, 1919.
3p.l., 7–317p. front., plates, fold. map. 20cm.
Describes the Mormon attempt to influence the route.
DLC, UHi, ULA, UPB, USlC

7466. ———. Desert dust, by Edwin L. Sabin . . . Illustrated by J. Clinton Shepherd. Philadelphia, George W. Jacobs & Company [1922]
3p.l. [9]–313p. col. plates. 19cm.
Fiction. Trip across the plains with a Mormon group; its resultant problems.
Another edition: New York, A. L. Burt Company [c1922] CU
USlC

7466a. ———. The making of Iowa. By Henry Sabin and Edwin L. Sabin. Chicago, A. Flanagan [1930]
282p. illus., ports. 17cm.
"The march of the Mormons," p. 208–216.
UPB, USlC

7467. The Sacredness of parenthood. . . . Salt Lake City [n.d.]
16p. 19cm.
Includes: Origin and destiny of woman, by President John Taylor, Aug. 29, 1857; Mother O'Mine, by Ruth May Fox, and others.
UPB, USlC

7468. St. Clair, David Latimer. To the followers of the Latter-day Saints. [Cheltenham, Willey, Printer, 1840]
4p. 17cm.
Caption-title.
Signed: D. L. St. Clair, Captain. Royal Navy, Staverton Court, Oct. 14th, 1840.
Criticism of the *Book of Mormon.*
CtY, NN, USlC

7469. The St. George Juvenile. St. George, Utah, December 15, 1868–1871?
v. 11½cm.
A 4p. periodical for children; poorly printed, but an interesting early imprint.
USlC V.1 #1–11; V.2 #2–3, 7 (February 1871)
UPB V.1 #1, 2, 5, 6, 11; V.2 #2–3

St. George Stake Academy. *See Dixie College.*

7470. St. John, Molyneux. The sea of mountains. An account of Lord Dufferin's tour through British Columbia in 1876 by Molyneux St. John. London, Hurst and Blackett, Publishers, 1877.
2v. port. 19cm.
Chaps. V–VI on the Mormons. The domination of the Mormons over the gentiles; the Mountain Meadows massacre; the nature of the Mormon leaders.
CU-B, NjP, USlC

7471. St. John, Percy Bolingbroke. Jessie, the Mormon's daughter. A tale of English and American life. By the author of "The blue dwarf" . . . London, Edward Harrison [1861]
iv, 508p. illus. (1 col.) 25cm.
Fiction concerning Mormonism.
CU-B

7472. St. Johns Stake Academy, St. Johns, Arizona. The St. Johns Stake Academy. Announcement. St. Johns, 1909–
v. 16–21cm.
UPB 1917–1918; USlC 1909–10, 1911–12; 1912–13, 1914–15, 1917–18, 1918–19

7473. Saint Louis Luminary. St. Louis, Mo., November 22, 1854–December 15, 1855.
53 issues. (208p.) weekly. 40cm.
Publisher and editor: Erastus Snow.
CtY V.1 #42; USlC

7474. Saintly falsity. On questions affecting their fanatical tenets and practices. Should oaths of Mormons be accepted in the courts? Some strong facts showing that they should not be. [Salt Lake City? Tribune Office, 1885]
10 [i.e. 8]p. 24½cm.
Caption-title.
Text begins: Eds. Tribune, and ends: One of the Priesthood, Salt Lake City, Feb. 12, 1885.
CSmH, CU-B, NN, UHi, UPB, WHi

7475. ———. (same) [Salt Lake City, Tribune Office, 1885?]
8p. 25cm.
Without notes as above.
UPB

7476. Saints' Advocate. Plano, Ill., Board of Publication, July, 1878–June, 1886.
8v. monthly. 29cm.
Edited by W. W. Blair, Zenas H. Gurley and others. V.1 #4. W. W. Blair. V.8 #3. Joseph Luff. Moved to Lamoni, Ia., V.4 #15 (Dec. 1881)
MoInRC V.1–8. USl V.2 #4, 8; V.4 #8; V.5 #6, 12. USlC V.1 #1, 3–9, 11; V.2; V.3 #2–4, 6, 10, 12; V.4 #1, 4, 6–7, 9–12; V.5 #1, 3–12; V.6 #1–6, 8–12; V.7 #1, 2, 4–6, 8–10; V.8 #1, 3, 6, 10

7477. The Saints' Herald. Lamoni, Ia. [Independence, Mo., Cincinnati] Reorganized Church of Jesus Christ of Latter Day Saints, Jan. 1860–
v. illus. 31–25cm. weekly.
First editor: Joseph Smith III.
Title varies: The True L.D.S. Herald. 1860–77. V.1–23 #24.
First issues (V.1 #1–5) reprinted in Plano, Ill. in 1864. UPB
CtY V.4, 5, 22, 23, 29; CU–B V.1–3, 23 #7–27 (lacking V.24 #18, V.25 #1) V.29 #14–24, V.31–33, 35, 39–66 (lacking V.42 #1–2, V.52 #1–3, V.54 #1, V.58 #51–52) V.81 #45–84; MoInRC comp.; MoK V.1–73, 7; ULA V.1–9, 23; UPB V.1–13, 14–15 inc., 16, 17–18 inc., 19–23, 24–28 inc., 29–33, 34–39 inc., 40–42, 44–48 inc., 49–51, 52–53 inc., 54–55, 56–62 inc., 63, 64–68 inc., 69–72, 73 inc., 74, 75 inc., 76, 77 inc.; USlC V.1–2, 10–22, 28 comp.

7478. Sakuth, F. A. Why was Joseph Smith a false prophet? For the benefit of my many friends and all earnest students of Mormonism. By a Mormon Elder and Apostle, F. A. Sakuth. Salt Lake City, Tribune Printing Co., 1903.
2p.l., 98p. 22cm.
Not an apostle of the Church; an apostle by semantics.
MH, UPB, USlC

7479. Sala, George Augustus Henry. . . . America revisited, by George Augustus Sala . . . New York, I. K. Funk & Co., c1880.
[141]–224p. 29½cm. (Standard series. Class G. 3. Travels. No. 45)
Cover-title.
Trip through Salt Lake with emphasis on polygamy and the evils of the Endowment House.
Reprinted in several editions.
DLC, MB, PPM, UHi, UU

7480. Salmonson, K. G. Mormonism eller some de sjelfva kalla sig "De Sista Dagernas Heliga." Norrkoping, Sweden, 1884.
Title in English: Mormonism, or as they call themselves "The Latter Day Saints."
Mulder

7481. Salt Lake City Anzeiger. Salt Lake City, 1881–90.
3 nos. published in 1881; issues published March to July 1890.
Organ of the German Mormons in Salt Lake City. Herr Gobel, editor.
Title in English: Salt Lake City Reporter.
No copy located.

7482. Salt Lake City Beobachter. Salt Lake City, August 9, 1890–1935?
45v. weekly. 62cm.
Publisher and editor: Joseph Harvey Ward.
Succeeded the *Salt Lake City Intelligenz Blatt* in 1890.
Organ of the Germans in Utah.
Title in English: Salt Lake City Observer.
UPB V.39 #14; USlC V.1–45 comp.

7483. ———. Centennial jubilee number, April 6, 1830–April 6, 1930. [Salt Lake City, 1930]
64p. illus. 40cm.
UHi, UPB, USlC

7484. Salt Lake City blue book. Salt Lake City, George Q. Cannon, 1895, 1896–7, 1898.
3v. 18cm.
Cover-title. The 1896–7 copy has title: Salt Lake Ogden Blue Book. 1896–7; The 1898 has title: The blue book; Salt Lake City, Ogden, Logan, Park City, Provo.
Directory with basic information concerning churches, etc.
CSmH 1895, 1898; NjP 1895; UPB, 1896–97, 1898

7485. ———. (same) Salt Lake City, Tribune Job Printing Co. 1900.
82p. 19cm.
MH

7486. ———. (same) V.1–2, 1901/2, 1907/8. Salt Lake City, R. L. Polk and Co., 1901, 1907.
2v. 18cm.
Cover-title.
CSmH; CU–B 1901/2; DLC 1901/2; NjP; UPB 1901/2

7487. Salt Lake City. Chamber of Commerce. Romantic Salt Lake City. Being a true if somewhat strange story of the most remarkable and romantic city in the United States. "The Queen of the West." Salt Lake City, Chamber of Commerce, 1926.
28p. illus. 17cm.
Early Mormon history and the founding of Utah.
CSmH, UHi, USlC

7488. ———. (same) Salt Lake City, 1927.
28p. illus. 17cm.
UU

7489. ———. Salt Lake City. A sketch of Utah's wonderful resources, prepared and pub. by the Salt Lake Chamber of Commerce . . . Chicago, Rand, McNally & Co., Printers [1888]
96p. illus. 23cm.
Preface signed: M. J. Forhan.
Includes history of Salt Lake City and Utah.
CU–B, DLC, ICU, NjP, NN, UHi, UPB, USlC

7490. ———. Salt Lake City and surroundings, compliments of Salt Lake Chamber of Commerce. Salt Lake City, Tribune Printing and Publishing Co., 1889.
36p. 15cm.
Settlers' guide divided into Mormon and Gentile categories.
MH, NjP, UHi, USlC

7491. ———. Salt Lake City and the intermountain territory; general information and industrial opportunities, corrected to January, 1927, issued by . . . the Chamber of Commerce. Salt Lake City, 1927.
32p. illus., maps, tables. 30cm.
NN

7492. ———. Salt Lake City and Utah; "The center of scenic America." [Salt Lake City] c1924.
31p. illus. 30½cm.
Includes early Mormon history.
CU–B

7493. ———. (same) [Salt Lake City] c1927.
31p. illus. 30½cm.
USlC

7494. ———. (same) [Salt Lake City] c1929.
31p. illus. 30½cm.
NjP

7495. ———. Utah and Salt Lake City, "nature's greatest scenic center." Salt Lake City, 1930.
31 [1]p. illus. 23cm.
Cover-title: Utah . . . the unique.
Contains a section on early Mormon and Utah history.
UPB

7496. Salt Lake City. Citizens. Memorial adopted by citizens of Salt Lake City, Utah Territory, at a mass meeting held in said city March 31, 1870, remonstrating against the passage of the bill (H. R. No. 1089) "in aid of the execution of the laws in the Territory of Utah, and for other purposes." [Washington, Govt. Print. Off.] 1870.
7p. 23cm. (U.S. 41st Cong. 2d Sess. Senate. Misc. Doc. No. 112)
Also p. 33–40 of W. H. Hooper, Washington Bill. Washington, 1870.
History of polygamy; grievances against the Cullom bill enumerated.
CtY, DLC, NjP, UPB, UU

7497. ———. . . . Memorial of a committee of forty-five gentlemen, selected at a public meeting of non-Mormon residents and voters of Salt Lake City in the Territory of Utah . . . setting forth the grievances of the non-Mormon people . . . [Washington, Govt. Print. Off., 1874]
8p. 23cm. (U.S. 43d Cong. 1st Sess. House. Misc. Doc. No. 120)
Caption-title.
At head of title: Non-Mormon citizens of Utah.
CtY, NjP, ULA

7498. Salt Lake City. City Council. Investigation by the City Council of Salt Lake City of rumors affecting the peace, reputation, and welfare of the city and its inhabitants, Salt Lake City, Dec. 8, 1885. [Salt Lake City, 1885]
28p. 22½cm.
Cover-title.
Concerning rumors of a Mormon conspiracy transmitted to Washington.
CSmH, CU–B, DLC, MoInRC, NjP, NN, UHi, UPB, USlC, WHi

7499. Salt Lake City. First Presbyterian Church. Addresses at the tenth anniversary of the church, Nov. 13, 1882, also a statement of the present condition of the church, a sketch of the collegiate institute, and of Presbyterian work in Utah. Salt Lake City, Utah Printing Co., Printers, 1882.
18p. 23cm.
Christian work among the Mormons.
MH, NjP

Salt Lake City illustrated. *See Darke, Sidney W. and Co.*

7500. Salt Lake City illustrated in Albertype. New York, The Albertype Co., c1890.
1p. 27plates. 16½×24cm.
Description and history of Salt Lake City.
UPB, USlC

7501. Salt Lake City in photo-gravure from recent negatives. New York, A. Wittemann [c1893]
[1]p. 40 illus. 12½×18cm.
1 leaf of text accompanying plates of scenes in Salt Lake City including many church buildings.
CSmH, UHi

7502. ———. (same) New York, A. Wittemann [c1894]
[2]p. [40] plates. 12½×18cm.
"The Albertype Co., N. Y."
UPB

7503. Salt Lake City Intelligenz-Blatt. Salt Lake City, March 10-July 5, 1890.
10 nos. weekly. 62cm.
Editor: Joseph Walter Dietrich.
Succeeded by the *Salt Lake City Beobachter.*
Organ of German Mormons.
USlC

Salt Lake City. Ladies. *See Utah (Territory) Mormon Women.*

———. Old Folk's Central Committee. *See Church of Jesus Christ of Latter-day Saints. Old Folks Committee.*

SALT LAKE TRIBUNE

7504. Salt Lake City. Ordinances. Ordinances, passed by the Legislative Council of Great Salt Lake City, and ordered to be printed. [Great Salt Lake City, 1850?]
4p. 23½cm.
Caption-title.
Ordinances passed February 24–December 29, 1849.
Penalty for riding horses without leave, for driving cattle off the feeding range, etc. The first ordinances printed in Utah.
CtY, USlC

7505. Salt Lake City, Utah, picturesque and descriptive. Sold only by subscription. Neenah, Wisconsin, Art Publishing Company, Geo. B. Pratt, 1889.
[57]l. plates. 35cm.
History and description of Salt Lake City.
USlC

7506. Salt Lake County, Utah. Coroner. Investigation into the murder of Dr. J. K. Robinson, who was assassinated on the night of October 22nd, 1866 near the corner of East Temple and 3d South or Emigration Streets had before Jeter Clinton coroner of the county of Great Salt Lake . . . Tuesday, October 23, at 11:00 A.M. [Salt Lake City, 1866?]
40 [1]p. 26cm.
Caption-title.
Introductory leaf has caption title: Biographical sketch of Dr. Robinson.
MH, USl, WHi

Salt Lake fruit. *See Spencer, William Loring (Nuñez).*

7507. The Salt Lake Herald's unrivaled atlas of the world . . . together with historical, descriptive, and statistical matter. A new, complete ready reference index to the United States, showing full returns from the census of 1900 . . . Prepared and published especially for the Salt Lake Herald . . . by Rand, McNally & Co., Chicago, 1901.
320p. illus., maps. 36cm.
Utah map, p. 64. "Utah" article, with Mormon references, p. 247, 248.
USlC

Salt Lake Ministerial Association. *See Ministerial Association of Salt Lake City.*

Salt Lake Tabernacle. *See Church of Jesus Christ of Latter-day Saints. Tabernacle Choir.*

7508. The Salt Lake Temple. . . . [Salt Lake City, 1893]
[242]–303p. illus. 19cm.
Reprinted from the *Contributor.* V.14, No. 6, April, 1893.
USlC

7508a. The Salt Lake Temple. [Salt Lake City, Deseret News? 1893?]
8p. 24cm.
Caption-title.
"From the New Year's Issue of Deseret Evening News."
UPB, USlC

7509. Salt Lake Tribune. By command of God, the prophet lied. Law defier admits perjury. Joseph F. Smith has new revelation. Startling declaration made by head of church. Purposely prevaricated in his testimony before Committee on Senate of the United States. Salt Lake City, Salt Lake Tribune, 1905.
8p. 24cm.
At head of title: Salt Lake Tribune, March 20, 1905.
Mormonism and politics.
MoInRC, USlC

7510. ———. Fifty years ago today. Salt Lake Tribune's souvenir contains many personal photographs and biographical sketches of first pioneers. Salt Lake City, Salt Lake Tribune, 1897.
[108]p. illus. 28½cm.
Mormon trek West. Each day an article was published concerning the corresponding day of the trek. An album was printed in which the clippings could be pasted.
CSmH, UHi, ULA, UPB, USlC

7511. ———. The Mormon Endowment House! A graphic exposure of the treasonable institution, where polygamous marriages are solemnized. By an Eye Witness. [Salt Lake City, Tribune Printing & Publishing Co., 1879]
8p. illus. 23cm.
Text dated: Sept. 24, 1879.
"From the *Salt Lake Daily Tribune* of Sept. 28th, 1879."
Distributed by the Ladies Anti-polygamy Society, of Salt Lake City.
CU-B, NN, USl, USlC, WHi

7512. ———. (same, under title) Mysteries of the Endowment House. [Salt Lake City, 1879?]
8p. 22cm.
Caption-title.
Signed: Mrs. G. S. R. Attributed to Mrs. Carrie Owen Mills by J. W. Buel. *Mysteries and Miseries of America's Great Cities.*
WHi

7513. ———. (same) [Salt Lake City, 1879?]
4p. 22cm.
NN, USl, USlC

7514. ———. Mysteries of the Endowment House and oath of vengeance of the Mormon Church. Salt Lake City, Published by the Salt Lake Tribune, 1906.
16p. illus. 22½cm.
Cover-title.
Includes testimony of Professor Walter Wolfe at Smoot hearings, and the story of Mrs. G. S. R.
All attested by James H. Wallis, p. 16.
MH, UHi, USIC

7515. ———. The Salt Lake Tribune almanac. A compendium of local and general information, election returns, local statistics and financial and mining statements . . . Salt Lake City, Tribune Print. 1896–[1899]
4v. 18½cm.
Early history of pioneers and other Mormon items.
DLC, NN, ULA, UPB 2v., USIC 4v.

7516. ———. Statehood for Utah. A brilliant letter from Judge Rosborough. His reply to Chairman Winder. The whole subject exhaustively and ably discussed — Why democrats cannot join in the movement. [Salt Lake City, 1887?]
Broadsheet. 24×15cm.
At head of title: Tribune Extra.
CSmH

7517. ———. Stink-pots. Some of the old-style Mormon logic taint the air. Revival of the former anti-Stenhouse style of outrage. Mormons visit some of their foes with saintly bouquets. House of Dickson, Varian, McKay, fouled with stink-pots. One of the dirtiest outrages of the present generation. Salt Lake City, 1885.
Broadside. 35×23cm.
At head of title: Tribune extra.
Dated: Salt Lake City, Monday, September 14, 1885.
"Stink Pot" bombs thrown at the houses of the three men with evil intent, attributed to Mormons.
USIC

7518. ———. That Mormon protest; its full text, and a report of the proceedings of the Salt Lake mass meeting of May 2nd, 1885. Comments and review by "The Tribune." [Salt Lake City? 1885?]
11p. 24½cm.
Caption-title.
CSmH, NjP, NN, UHi, USIC

7519. ———. Tribune extra . . . September 28, 1885 . . . Clawson pleads . . . Supremacy of law and cowardice of Mormon bulldozing. Trumen [i.e., Truman] O. Angel agrees to abide by the law. Sept. Sears pleads guilty and will obey the law . . . Mr. Clawson's statement . . . Salt Lake City, 1885.
Broadside. 40×20cm.
CU–B

7520. ———. True history of the amnesty proclamation; an open letter from the Tribune to the Mormon people. [Salt Lake City, 1892?]
7p. 22cm.
Caption-title.
CSmH, NjP, UHi, UPB, USl

7521. ———. "What ails this town." [Salt Lake City] 1905.
[3]p. 24cm.
From *Salt Lake Tribune*, March 9, 1905.
Polemic against Joseph F. Smith.
NjP, USIC

7522. Sam Brannan. A local character song. San Francisco, Published and sold wholesale and retail, by Bell & Company, General Publishers of Songs and Ballads [ca. 1875]
Broadside. 29½×11cm.
Title within cover.
UPB

7523. San Luis Stake Academy, Manassa, Colorado. San Luis Stake Academy. Catalogue. Manassa, 1907–
v. 16½–21cm.
USIC 1908–19

7524. San Pedro, Los Angeles, and Salt Lake Railroad. Legends of the arrowhead. Los Angeles [1912]
[26]p. illus., map. 17½cm.
"Mormon legend." An arrow supposedly seen by Brigham Young.
CU–B, UPB, USIC

7524a. Sander, Frank. Der Mormone. [Bremen [n.d.]
250p. 22cm.
Fiction concerning Mormonism.
Title in English: The Mormon.
USIC

7525. Sanders, Peter James. A key to succession in the presidency of the church and a complete ready reference for the missionary, by P. J. Sanders. [Murray City? Utah, c1909]
231p. 18cm.
CU–B, DLC, MH, MoInRC, NN, UHi, UPB, USl, USIC, UU

7526. Sanders, Sue A. A journey to, on and from the "Golden Shore." Delavan, Ill., Times Printing Office, 1887.
3p.l. [7]–118p. 19½cm.
An 1886 trip through Salt Lake City with comments on Mormonism.
UHi

Sandette [*pseud.*] *See Walsh, Marie.*

7527. Sanhedens Banner. Lamoni, Ia., [Porsgrund, Norway; Independence, Mo.] 1884–1932.
v. monthly. 23cm.
October, 1884–March, 1932, monthly.
Suspended October, 1888–October, 1902, semi-monthly.
November 1, 1902–December, 1905, monthly.
January, 1906–September, 1916. Suspended October, 1916–December, 1917; January, 1918–March, 1932.
RLDS Norwegian organ.
Title in English: The banner of truth.
MoInRC comp.; USIC V.7 #12, 21, 24, V.8 #7, 12, V.10 #3–9, V.11 #2, 6, 12

Sanpete Stake Academy. *See Snow College, Ephraim, Utah.*

7528. Saunders, Henry Scholey. Parodies on Walt Whitman. Compiled by Henry S. Saunders. Preface by Christopher Morley. New York, American Library Services, 1923.
xv, 17–171p. 24cm.
"St. Smith of Utah," by Walter Parke, p. 161–165. From his *Lays of the Saintly.*
CU, NjP, USIC

7529. Savage, Charles Roscoe. In and around Salt Lake City; half-tone engravings by Williamson & Haffner Engraving Co., from photographs by Charles R. Savage . . . Denver, Colo., F. S. Thayer, 1900.
1p.l. [37]p. of plates. 26½×34cm.
Beautiful plates of Mormon buildings.
CSmH, CU–B, MWA, UHi, ULA, UPB, USIC

7529a. ———. (same) Denver, Colo., F. S. Thayer, [c1900]
[37]p. of plates. 26½×34cm.
Variant printing.
NjP

7530. ———. (same) 7th ed., 36th thousand. Denver, F. S. Thayer [c1900]
[37]p. of illus., front. 25½×34cm.
DLC

7531. ———. (same) Salt Lake City, Bureau of Information [1909?]
37p. 25½×34cm.
UPB

7532. ———. Pictorial reflex of Salt Lake City and vicinity . . . Salt Lake City, C. R. Savage [1894]
47p. 21 plates. 13½×16½cm.
The Great Temple and other places of interest.
CU, DLC, UPB, USIC

7533. ———. (same) Salt Lake City, C. R. Savage, 1896.
42p. 20 plates. 14×19cm.
DLC, UPB, USIC

7534. ———. 12th rev. ed. Salt Lake City, C. R. Savage, Art Bazaar, 1898.
[20]l., illus., 42 plates. 13×18cm.
CU–B, UHi

7535. ———. (same) With condensed epitome of Utah's people, resources, climate and other information useful to visitors and residents. Salt Lake City, Published by C. R. Savage, 1901.
41p. plates. 18½×23½cm.
"Thirteenth ed., enlarged, improved."
CU–B, UHi, UPB

7536. ———. Picturesque Utah; albertype illustrations from original photographs, descriptive text by M. Virginia Donaghe. Denver, Frank S. Thayer, 1888.
33p. plates. 20½×28½cm.
Includes Mormon history and historic views.
NjP, UPB

7537. ———, *editor.* The reflex of Salt Lake City and vicinity . . . Salt Lake City, C. R. Savage [1892?]
35p. plates, ports. 16×12cm.
The plates and portraits are on a strip attached to front cover, folded to form 15 leaves.
Variant printings. The words "Page 5" on p. 5 of copy 1, refering to "page 4" on p. 5 of copy 2. Copy 1 bound in red, copy 2 in blue.
CU–B, UPB

7538. ———. (same) Corrected to date by H. W. Naisbitt. Salt Lake City [The author, 1893?]
48p. [18] fold. plates. 16cm.
Also published as *Pictorial Reflex.*
Includes Mormon history and views.
CSmH, CU–B, NjP, UHi, ULA, USIC

7539. ———. Salt Lake City. In photo-gravure from recent negatives. C. R. Savage photographer, Salt Lake City, Utah. New York, The Albertype Co. [189–]
[49]l. 18½×13cm.
Plates of church buildings, etc.
UPB

7540. ———. . . . Salt Lake City, with a sketch of the route of the Central Pacific Railroad, from Omaha to Salt Lake City, and thence to San Francisco. With twelve illustrations from photographs by C. R. Savage. London, Edinburgh and New York, T. Nelson and Sons; Salt Lake City, Savage and Ottinger [1872?]
31p. illus., col. plates.
UPB

7541. ———. (same, under title) . . . Salt Lake City, and the way thither. With twelve illustrations from photographs by C. R. Savage. London, Edinburgh, and New York, T. Nelson and Sons; Salt Lake City, Savage and Ottinger [n.d.]
31p. illus., col. plates.
UPB

7542. ———. Views of Utah and tourists' guide. Containing a description of the views and general information for the traveler, resident, and the public generally from authentic sources. Salt Lake City, Salt Lake Herald Print., 1883.
15p. 16 plates. 11×15cm.
CSmH, CU–B, DLC, PHi, UHi

7543. ———. (same) Salt Lake City [c1887]
30p. and folder of 16 plates. 10½×15cm.
Description of the Mormon temple and information for tourists.
CSmH, CU–B, DLC, NjP, NN, UHi, UPB, USl, USlC, UU

7544. ———. (same) Salt Lake City, C. R. Savage, 1888.
24p. 18 plates. 15×10½cm.
DLC, NjP, UHi, ULA, UU

7544a. ———. (same) Salt Lake City, The Art Bazaar, 1888.
24p. 18 plates. 15×10½cm.
NjP

7545. ———. Zion, her gates and temple; colored reproductions, in water color effects from original photographs by Chas. R. Savage. The descriptive verse by Utah and Colorado poets as indicated. Denver, Frank S. Thayer [1908?]
18p.l. 16 mounted plates, mounted port. 24×30½cm.
Mormon views and description of historic sites.
CU–B, NjP, UHi, UPB, USlC

7546. ———. (same) Denver, Frank S. Thayer [1910?]
[38]l. col. plates. 23×32cm.
UHi

———. *See also Nelson, Thomas, and Sons.*

7547. Saved by grace through obedience. Important questions concerning salvation answered by the word of God. Liverpool, Millennial Star Office [1896]
16p. 13cm. (Tracts. No. 1)
NN

7548. Saved from the Mormons (From the Galaxy, November–December, 1872). New York, 1872.
[677]–[686] 821–837p. 23cm.
Reprinted with new title page and cover.
USlC

Saxon, Isabelle [*pseud.*] *See Sutherland, Mrs. (Redding)*

7549. Sbresny, M. A. Mormonism as it is today. Some striking revelations. London, A. H. Stockwell [1911]
48p. 19cm.
CtY, USlC

7550. Scandinavian Organization of Ogden. Annual Scandinavian conference and reunion, August 28th and 29th, 1926. Ogden Tabernacle. [Ogden, 1926]
32p. 18½cm.
Committee: John A. Widtsoe [etc.]
USlC, UU

7551. ———. (same) [Ogden, 1927]
[8]l. 19½cm.
USlC

7552. The scenery of the United States; illustrated in a series of forty engravings. New-York, D. Appleton and Company, 1855.
viii [9]–174p. plates. 29cm.
"Nauvoo," p. [129]–141.
UPB

7553. Schade, C. Fred. L.D.S. Hymns, national songs and their composers. 1st ed. [Ogden, Industrial Publishing Company] 1909.
80 [1]p. 17cm.
UPB

7554. Scharmann, Hermann B. Scharmann's landroise nach Californien. Bearbeitet fuer das "Sonntagsblatt der New-Yorker staats-zeitung" . . . [New York, Privately printed, 1908?]
125p. illus., ports. 17cm.
Reprinted from the *New-Yorker staats-zeitung*, jahrgang 18, nummer 15, 16, 17 und 19, vom 10., 17., 24. April und 1. Mai 1852.
Reference to Mormon ferry on North Platte, 1849, p. 27–28.
Translated by Margaret Hoff Zimmermann and Erich W. Zimmermann as Scharmann's overland journey to California. [n.p., 1918] CU–B
Title in English: Scharmann's overland journey to California.
CU–B

7555. Schenck, Marcella. Jimmy Umphrey. By Marcella Schenck. Lamoni, Ia., Published by the Board of Publication of the Reorganized Church of Jesus Christ of Latter Day Saints, 1920.
4p.l. [11]–182 [6]p. illus. 20 cm.
(Birth Offering Series. No. 11)
RLDS moral fiction.
UHi

7556. Scherer, James Augustin Brown. The first forty-niner and the story of the golden tea-caddy, by James A. B. Scherer . . . New York, Minton, Balch & Company, 1925.
127p. ports., plates. 19½cm.
Biography of Samuel Brannan, first leader of the Mormons in California.
CU–B, DLC, MB, MiU, NjP, NN, OCl, OClH, PP, PU, UHi, ULA, UPB, USlC, UU

7557. Schiel, Jacob Heinrich Wilhelm. Reise durch die Felsengebirge und die Humboldtgebirge nach dem Stillen Ocean. Eine skizze von Dr. J. Schiel. Schaffhausen, Druck and Verlag der Brodtmann'schen Buchhandlung, 1859.
2p.l., 139p. 20cm.
Traveled with Gunnison and Beckwith on the Pacific Railroad Survey through Utah, 1853–54.
Title in English: Journey through the Rocky Mountains and the Humboldt Mountains to the Pacific Ocean.
Translated into English; Los Angeles, 1957; Norman, Okla., 1959.
Howes S159, Sabin 77632, W–C 344
DLC, IU, NN, PPG, UPB

7558. Schlagintweit, Robert von. Die Mormonen; oder, Die Heiligen vom jüngsten Tage von ihrer Entstehung bis auf die Gegenwart. Von Robert von Schlagintweit. Mit Illustrationen. Cöln und Liepzig, E. H. Mayer, 1874.
xvi, 292p. illus., ports. 19cm.
"Literatur der Quellen und Hülfsmittel," p. [281]–290.
Title in English: The Mormons.
Howes S163
CtY, DLC, ICN, UPB, USl, USlC

7559. ———. (same) 2. Ausg. Cöln und Leipzig, E. H. Mayer, 1878.
xviii, 318p. illus. 20cm.
CtY, CU–B, NjP, NjPT, USlC, WHi

7560. ———. Die Pacific-Eisenbahn in Nordamerika. Von Robert von Schlagintweit mit Illustrationen, einer Karte und einer Meilentafel. Cöln u. Leipzig, E. H. Mayer; New York, L. W. Schmidt, 1870.
xiv, 203 [1]p. illus., fold. map., fold. plan. 19½cm.
"Salt Lake City und die Mormonen," p. 78–82.
Title in English: The Pacific Railroad in North America.
Another edition: Gotha, J. Perthes, 1886. NjP
Howes S165
CLU, CtY, CU–B, DLC, NjP, NN, UHi

7561. Schleiden, Rudolf. Reise-Erinnerungen aus den Vereinigten Staaten von Amerika. New York, E. Steiger, 1873.
3p.l., 104p. 18½cm.
"Published in the *Augsburger Allgemeine Zeitung* February 16–19, 1873.
Chapter 2: "Utah und die Mormonen."
Title in English: Memories of travel through the United States of America.
UPB, UU

7562. Schmidt, R. E. Why I left the Mormon Church. Salt Lake City [n.d.]
8p. 15½cm.
UPB

7563. Schmucker, Samuel Mosheim. A history of all religions; containing a statement of the origin, development, doctrines and government of the religious denominations in the United States and Europe, with biographical notices of eminent divines. Philadelphia, Quaker City Publishing House, 1867.
336p. illus. 19½cm.
"The Mormons or Latter Day Saints," p. 98–105.
First published in 1859.
Published in various editions.
Another edition: New York, 1884. NjPT
MoInRC, UHi, USlC

———. *See also Mackay, Charles.*

7564. Schneebeli, Anna. Liebe deine Feinde. Eine zufressende Darstellung von Umständen, wie sie leider zu oft im Leben vorkommen. Basel, Kirche Jesu Christi der Heiligen der letzten Tage, 1916.
16p. 17cm.
Title in English: Love thy enemies.
UPB

7565. Schoonover, Thomas Jefferson. The life and times of General John A. Sutter. (Illustrated) Sacramento, D. Johnston & Co., 1895.
1p.l., 136p. illus., ports. 15½cm.
Mormon emigration to California on ship *Brooklyn*; gold discoveries.
Rev. and enl. ed. Sacramento, 1901, 1907.
CSmH, NjP, UPB, USlC
CSmH, CU–B, DLC

7566. Schoppe, Amalie. Der Prophet. Historischer Roman aus der Neuzeit Nord-Amerikas. Von Amalie Schoppe geb. Weise. Jena, Frederich Luden, 1846.
3v. 17½cm.
Listed by Dale Morgan as the earliest book of fiction about the Mormons.
Title in English: The prophet; a historical romance of the modern North America.
USlC

7567. Schouler, James. History of the United States of America under the Constitution . . . Washington, W. H. Morrison, 1880–[99]
6v. 19½–21cm.
History of the Mormons, V.4, p. 546–549; the author discusses the relations of the government with the Mormons, V.5, p. 146–147, 403–406.
Other editions: 1886, 1908, 1913. CU, NjP
Sabin 77916
CU, NN, ULA

7568. Schreiner, Karl. Mormonerne, Hvem er de? Hvad vil de? Pastor av Karl Schreiner. Kristiania, Utgiv av de Norske Sedelighetsforeningers Centralstyre, 1911.
12p. 24cm.
Title in English: The Mormons, Who Are They? What Do They Want?
NN, USlC

7569. ———. Mormonerne og deres laere. Foredrag holdt i Calmeyergatens Missionshus 26. mars 1912. Kristiania, Utgit av de Norske Sedelighetsforeningers Centralstyre, Trykt i Eksprestrykkeriet, 1912.
16p. 22cm.
Title in English: The Mormons and their Teaching.
USIC

7570. Schroeder, Theodore Albert. Authorship of the Book of Mormon; psychologic tests of W. F. Prince critically reviewed by Theodore Schroeder . . . To which is now added a bibliography of Schroeder on Mormonism. Worcester, Mass., 1919.
18p. 22½cm.
Reprinted in the *American Journal of Psychology*, V.30, Jan., 1919.
Bibliography, p. 10–18.
Schroeder wrote as both A. T. Schroeder and T. A. Schroeder.
CU–B, MH, NN, UPB, USl, USIC, WHi

———. A bit of evidence. *See Lucifer's Lantern.*

7571. ———. The case of Senator Smoot: an academic discussion by A. T. Schroeder . . . [New York, 1905]
20p. 19½cm.
Reprinted from *The Truth Seeker.*
DLC, NN, USl, USIC, WHi

7572. ———. The free lance society and the churches. A few remarks made by A. T. Schroeder at the Lagoon, Friday Aug. 13, 1897. [Salt Lake City, 1897]
10p. 21cm.
Reprint from *The Argus.*
MH, NN, USl

7573. ———. The gospel concerning church and state [by Juab, a high private in Israel] [Salt Lake City, 1897]
29p. 23cm.
Caption-title.
A satire on Mormon statements on church and state.
MH, NN, USl, USIC, WHi

7574. ———. I want all books on the subject of Mormonism, of which I do not already own a copy. The enclosed is a partial list. Quote price by number in this list and state condition of books. Salt Lake City [189–]
5p. 10×23cm. (No. 2)
WHi

7575. ———. Joseph Smith's politics. An answer to Cockerill's cock-and-bull story. [Salt Lake City, 1895]
7p. 18½cm.
Reprinted from the *Salt Lake Herald*, Sept. 30, 1895.
MH

———. Lucifer's Lantern . . . *See Lucifer's Lantern.*

7576. ———. Mormonism and prostitution. [Philadelphia, 1909]
7[1]p. 25½cm.
Caption-title.
Reprinted from the *Medical Council*, May, 1909.
Mormon polygamy.
NN, UPB, USl, WHi

7577. ———. Mormonism considered, being a lecture delivered at Unity Hall, Salt Lake City, Utah, March 1897, entitled "Thoughts suggested by a study of Mormonism." To which are added numerous references, and a few remarks on "the rewards of a liberal faith." [Salt Lake City, 1897]
[2]l., 35p. 20½cm. (No. 1)
Cover-title.
MH, NN, USl, USIC, WHi

———. . . . The N.Y. Times vs. George Q. Cannon. *See Lucifer's Lantern.*

7578. ———. The origin of the Book of Mormon, re-examined in its relation to Spaulding's "Manuscript found" with compliments of Albert Theodore Schroeder of the Salt Lake Bar. [Salt Lake City, Salt Lake Ministerial Association, c1901]
56p. 21½cm.
Cover-title.
Variant covers.
CSmH, CtY, DLC, MH, MoInRC, NjP, NN, OO, ULA, UPB, USIC, WHi

7579. ———. Polygamy and the constitution. Trenton, 1906.
1p.l., 6p. 25cm.
Reprinted from *The Arena*, November, 1906.
NN, USIC, WHi

7580. ———. (same) [New York? 1906?]
6p. 25cm.
WHi

7581. ———. A question of Mormon patriotism by Theodore Schroeder. [n.p., 1906?]
16p. 16cm.
Reprinted in the *American Historical Magazine*, V.1, #4 (July, 1906)
MH, WHi

7582. ———. A reply to a defense of Mormons and an attack upon the Ministerial Association of Utah. By A. T. Schroeder . . . [New York, 1905?]
11p. 18cm.
Reprinted from the *Truth seeker.*
"These thoughts are suggested by an article from Mr. V. S. Peet in the *Truth seeker*, Nov. 25, 1905," p. [3]
CU–B, DLC, MH, MoInRC, NN, USl, WHi

7583. ———. A review of the decision of the Supreme Court of Utah in Young vs. Schroeder. [Salt Lake City? 1901]
15p. 22cm.
WHi

7584. ———. The sex-determinant in Mormon theology. A study in the erotogenesis of religion. [St. Louis, Mo., 1908]
15 [1]p. 22cm.
Reprinted from *The Alienist and Neurologist*, May, 1908.
MH, NN, USl, USlC

7585. ———. Some facts concerning polygamy, by A. T. Schroeder . . . [Salt Lake City] c1898.
24p. 20cm.
Caption-title.
CSmH, DLC, ICN, MH, MoInRC, NjP, NN, UPB, USlC, WHi

7586. Schulthess, Arnold Henry. Der Abfall und die Wiederherstellung des ursprünglichen Evangeliums. Vom Aeltesten A. H. Schulthess. Berlin, Herausgegeben von der redaktion des "Stern," 1901.
15[1]p. 19½cm.
Cover-title.
Price list on back cover.
Title in English: The Apostasy and Restoration of the true church.
Printed in four editions 1901–1906. Each is revised to some extent. For later editions *see* under title, #8–10.
USlC

7587. ———. (same) Traktat Nr. I. Herausgegeben von Northern States Mission, Church of Jesus Christ of Latter Day Saints, Chicago, Ill., 1907.
15 [1]p. 19½cm.
Cover-title.
Price list on back cover.
USlC

7588. ———. Liebe Brüder was soll ich tun, dass ich selig werde? . . . Eine kurze Erklärung die für jeden Menschen zur Seligkeit notwendig ist. Grundsätze des Evangeliums Jesu Christi, vom Ältesten Arnold H. Schulthess. Trakat Nr II. Berlin, Herausgegeben von Hugh J. Cannon [1901]
16p. 17cm.
Title in English: My dear brethren: what must I do to be saved.
UU

7589. ———. (same) Berlin, Herausgegeben von der Redaktion des "Stern," 1901.
15[1]p. 17cm.
USlC

7590. Schumann, Arthur. Die Wiederherstellung des Priestertums, 1892–1929. [n.p.] 1929.
15 [1]p. 21½cm.
Script for "Dem Priesterschafts-Jubilaum gewidmet" of the German Austrian Mission.
Title in English: The restoration of the priesthood.
USlC

7591. Schuyler, Montgomery. Westward the course of empire; "out West" and "back East" on the first trip of the "Los Angeles limited." Reprinted with additions from the New York Times, by Montgomery Schuyler. New York and London, G. P. Putnam's Sons, 1906.
vii p., [2]l., 198p. 15 plates. 19cm.
The city of the saints, p. 108–120.
CU-B, NjP, UHi, ULA, USlC

7592. Schwatka, Frederick. In the land of cave and cliff dwellers, by Lieut. Frederick Schwatka . . . New Edition. New York, The Cassell Publishing Co. [1893]
x, 385p. illus. 19cm.
A description of the Mormon Mexican colonies.
Another edition: Boston, Educational Publishing Co. [1899] UHi
NjP, ULA

Scofield, Charles Josiah. History of Hancock County. *See Bateman, Newton.*

7593. Scott, Columbus. The Christian sabbath or weekly rest day. By Elder Columbus Scott. Lamoni, Ia., Reorganized Church of Jesus Christ of Latter Day Saints, 1891.
viii, 139p. 19cm.
NjP, USlC

7594. ———. (same) Lamoni, Ia., Reorganized Church of Jesus Christ of Latter Day Saints, 1908.
viii, 139p. 19cm.
MoInRC

7595. Scott, John H. Take Heed! Lest any man deceive you. Salt Lake City [1906]
[12]p. 18cm. (Scott's pamphlet. No. 2)
Warning by the author for those who contemplate leaving the RLDS Church.
USlC

7596. Scott, S. W. Leonard. Restoration of Israel. Independence, Mo., Ensign Publishing House, 1897.
46p. 15cm. (The Gospel Banner. V.4, No. 2)
MoInRC

7597. Scott, William Lawrence. Anti-polygamy bill. Mr. Scott's proposed amendment to the Edmunds-Tucker anti-polygamy bill (Sen. 10). [n.p., 1887?]
Broadside. 24×15cm.
NjP, UPB, USlC

7598. Scoville, Adaline Ballou. Life of Adaline Ballou Scoville by herself. Bingham Canyon, Utah, 1906.
45p. 19cm.
Mormons at Bingham Canyon.
USIC

Scrap book of Mormon literature. *See Rich, Benjamin Erastus.*

7599. Scraps of biography. Designed for the instruction and encouragement of young Latter-day Saints. Salt Lake City, Juvenile Instructor Office, 1883.
viii [9]–104p. 18½cm. (Faith promoting series. Tenth book)
CU–B, DLC, ICN, MH, MoInRC, UHi, ULA, UPB, USI, USIC, UU, WHi

7600. The Scratch. [Provo, Utah] Brigham Young University, May 1929–May 1931.
v. illus. monthly. 26cm.
A literary magazine published by the students of Brigham Young University.
UPB

Scriptural revelations of the universal apostasy. *See Paul, Joshua Hughes.*

7601. Scripture searcher. [n.p., n.d.]
[2]p. 19½cm.
Five on the verso of 4.
4: Kingdom of God, where located, what is it?
5: When will the righteous be rewarded? Answers with Biblical references.
There is no actual indication that these are Mormon imprints, but they are part of the collection of Mormon pamphlets at New York Public library.
NN #4, 5

7602. The Search-light. Paris, Idaho, Fielding Academy, 1905–
v. 23½cm.
Publication of the students at Fielding Academy.
USIC V.1 #4, 7, V.8 #6, V.9 #1–4, Nov. 1916, Jan. 1921, May 1922

7603. The Searchlight; devoted to the interests of the Church of Christ in Zion. Independence, February 1, 1896–March, 1900.
5v. monthly. 25½cm.
Official organ of the Church of Christ (Temple lot)
Editor: John R. Haldeman.
Succeeded by *Evening and Morning Star.*
MoInRC; NjP, V.1 #2–8, 11, 12, V.2 #1, 2, 5; USIC comp.

7604. Searle, Eliza. The new dispensation. By Miss Eliza Searle. [San Francisco, ca. 1887?]
[4]p. 22½cm.
Church of the Firstborn.
USIC

7605. Sears, John. Final state of mankind, demonstrated by the prophecies of the Old and New Testaments, also the Book of Mormon and the Doctrine and Covenants of the Church of Jesus Christ of Latter-day Saints. Salt Lake City, Joseph Hyrum Parry & Co., 1886.
2p.l. [5]–36p. 18½cm.
MH, UPB, USIC

7606. ———. Remember the Sabbath Day to keep it holy. Salt Lake City, Juvenile Instructor Office, 1889.
16p. 18cm.
MH, NjP, UHi, UPB, USIC

7607. Sears. Robert. A pictorial description of the United States; embracing the history, geographical position, agricultural and mineral resources, population, manufactures, commerce, and sketches of cities, towns, public buildings, &c., &c., of each state and territory in the Union. Interspersed with revolutionary and other interesting incidents, connected with the early settlement of the country. Illustrated with numerous engravings. By Robert Sears. New edition, revised and enlarged. New York, Published by Robert Sears, 1855.
648p. 24cm.
Territory of Utah, p. 646–648.
NjP

Secrets of a Mormon's harem. *See Protestant Press Bureau.*

7608. The secrets of Mormonism disclosed; an authentic exposure of the immorality and licentious abominations of the . . . Latter-day saints and their spiritual wives . . . showing their obscene practices in the temple devoted to public worship, and the profligacy of a Mormon harem, composed of married and single females . . . London, R. Bulman [1854?]
12p. 19cm.
CtY, MH

7609. The Seer. Washington, D. C. [Liverpool] January, 1853–August, 1854.
2v. (12, 8 issues in 320p.) monthly. 22cm.
Edited and published by Orson Pratt.
Final 2 issues published in Liverpool [V.2 #7–8] Sabin 64961
CSmH, DLC, UPB, USIC

7610. ———. (same) Liverpool [Republished by S. W. Richards] 1854.
2v. (12, 8 issues in 320p.) monthly. 22cm.
Reprinted in Liverpool verbatim, with the addition of the two original numbers at the end issued after the publication was suspended in America.
CSmH, CtY, CU–B, MH, NN, UPB, USIC, WHi

7610a. Seerley, H. H. History and civil government of Iowa. By H. H. Seerley and L. W. Parish. And The government of the United States by B. A. Hinsdale. New York, American Book Co. [c1908]
388p. illus. 19½cm.
"The Mormon vote": p. 71–72.
USlC

7611. Der Seher von Patmos. Halle, Germany, January 15, 1923–April, 1926.
v. monthly. 23cm.
In January, 1926 it became *Der Wegweiser Zur Wahrheit.* Succeeded by *Die Friedenbotschaft,* April, 1926.
The RLDS publication for Germany.
Title in English: The seer of Patmos.
MoInRC comp.

7612. Seibel, George. The Mormon problem; the story of the Latter-day Saints, with an exposé of their beliefs and practices, by George Seibel. Pittsburgh, Pa., Pittsburgh Printing Company, 1899.
88p. 19cm.
Cover-title: What is Mormonism?
DLC, MB, MH, OCl, UPB, USlC

7613. ———. The Mormon saints; the story of Joseph Smith, his golden bible, and the church he founded, by George Seibel. Pittsburgh, The Lessing Company, 1919.
103p. 17cm.
CU–B, DLC, MH, NjPT, NN, PPCS, UHi, UPB, USl, USlC, UU, WHi

7614. Seifert, Oswald. Der praktische Genealoge; Lietfaden für den Unterricht in den Genealogischen Klassen sowie zum Selbstunterricht für die Mitglieder der Kirche Jesu Christi der Heiligen der Letzten Tage mit Vorwort und einem Anhang, Erklärungen über Tempelarbeit in teilweiser Frage- und Antwortform. Basel, Schweizerisch, Deutsche Mission [der] Kirche Jesu Christi der Heiligen der Letzten Tage, 1920.
40p. 22½cm.
Mormon doctrine.
Title in English: The practical genealogist.
UPB, USlC, UU

7615. Seitz, Don Carlos. The also rans; great men who missed making the presidential goal. New York, Thomas Y. Crowell Co. [1928]
xxiv, 356p. front., plates, ports. 22cm.
Describes Joseph Smith's attempt to gain the presidency in 1844.
CU, DLC, NjP, UPB

7616. ———. Artemus Ward (Charles Farrar Browne) a biography and bibliography, by Don C. Seitz . . . with illustrations and facsimiles. New York and London, Harper & Brothers [c1919]
9p.l., 338p. illus., plates, ports., facsims. 22½cm.
Bibliography, p. 319–338.
Includes Artemus Ward's lectures on Mormonism.
CSmH, CU, DLC, NjP, UHi, UPB

7617. ———. The James Gordon Bennetts, father and son, proprietors of the New York Herald, by Don C. Seitz . . . Indianapolis, The Bobbs-Merrill Company [c1928]
6p.l., 15–405p. plates, ports., facsim. 23cm.
His involvement with Joseph Smith in a chapter entitled "Mormon and Catholics."
CU, DLC, NjP, UPB

7618. ———. Uncommon Americans, pencil portraits of men and women who have broken the rules, by Don C. Seitz . . . Indianapolis, The Bobbs-Merrill Company [c1925]
4p.l., 328p. illus., ports., facsims. 22½cm.
Portraits on lining-papers.
Biographies of Joseph Smith and Brigham Young.
CU, DLC, MB, NjP, NN, OCl, OCU, OO, UHi, UPB, USlC, UU

7619. Seixas, Joshua. Supplement of J. Seixas' Manual Hebrew Grammar, for the Kirtland, Ohio, Theological Institution. New-York: Printed by West & Trow, for J. Smith, Jun., S. Rigdon, O. Cowdery, 1836.
vi [7]–31p. 15cm.
Preface by O. Cowdery. Text in Hebrew. For use in the School of the Prophets in Kirtland.
MoInRC, UPB

7620. Sell, Josef. Die fünfundzwanzigste Frau, Komödie von Josef Sell. Berlin, Gustav Kiepenheuer, verlag, c1930.
88p. 20cm.
A Mormon drama set in Utah in 1858, which includes the Utah Expedition, polygamy, etc.
Title in English: The Twenty-fifth wife.
CtY, DLC, NN

Senator Cullom's anti-Mormon Bill. *See Cullom, Shelby Moore.*

7621. Services over the remains of the late apostle Erastus Snow, Wednesday, May 30, 1888. [Salt Lake City, 1888]
[3]p. 18cm.
USlC

Sessions, John. *See Iowa Infantry. Mormon Battalion, 1846–1848.*

7622. Sevier Stake Academy, Richfield, Utah. Sevier Stake Academy. Circular. Richfield, 1889–
v. 22cm.
USlC 1889–1890, 1890–1891

7623. Seville, William P. . . . Narrative of the march of Co. A engineers from Fort Leavenworth, Kansas, to Fort Bridger, Utah, and return, May 6 to October 3, 1858. A contribution to the history of the United States Corps of Engineers by William P. Seville. Rev. under the direction of the Commandant Engineer School, U.S. Army, by First Lieut. John W. N. Schulz . . . Washington Barracks, Press of Engineer School, 1912.
46p. 23cm. (Occasional papers. Engineer school. U.S. Army. No. 48)
Material on the Mormon trail and the Utah Expedition.
Howes S300
CtY, CU–B, ICJ, MB, NN, OCl, UHi, ULA, UPB

7624. Seward, William Henry. William H. Seward's travels around the world. Ed. by Olive Risley Seward . . . With two hundred illustrations. New York, D. Appleton and Company, 1873.
xii, 730p. illus., plates, ports., fold. map. 23½cm.
Visit to Salt Lake City and a description of Mormonism at beginning of the trip, p. 13–26.
Sabin L 79594
CU, DLC, NjP, UHi, UPB, USlC, UU

7625. Sexton, George. A portraiture of Mormonism, or animadversions on the doctrines and pretensions of the Latter-day Saints; a review of the history and contents of the Book of Mormon; and a sketch of the career of Joseph Smith and various other notorious fanatics and impostors, being lectures delivered by Dr. Geo. Sexton . . . London, W. Strange, 1849.
viii [9]–113p. 18½cm.
Two lectures.
Howes S308, Sabin 79628
CtY, CU–B, DLC, ICN, MH, NN, USlC

7626. Sexton, Lucy Ann (Foster) *editor.* . . . The Foster family, California pioneers; first overland trip, 1849, second overland trip, 1852, third overland trip, 1853 [1854] fourth trip (via Panama) 1857. [Santa Barbara, Calif., The Schauer Printing Studio, Inc., c1925]
3p.l., 7–285p. illus., ports. 20cm.
Isaac Foster's overland diary and letters via Salt Lake, 1849; Mariett (Foster) Cummings' overland diary via Salt Lake, 1852; Burrell family reminiscences via Salt Lake, 1854, p. 20–22, 25, 28, 37–47, 50, 76, 132–138, 182–185, 193–195; includes references to Mormons in Iowa and California.
Expanded from 1889 ed.
CtY, CU–B, DLC, USlC

7627. Sexton, W. J. The open sore of Christendom, by the Rev. W. J. Sexton. London, J. & J. Bennett, Ltd. [n.d.]
vii [8]–327p. 19cm.
"Latter-day Saints, or Mormons," p. 143–153.
USlC

7628. Seymour, E. Sanford. Emigrant's guide to the gold mines, of Upper California, illustrated with a map. By E. Sandford [sic] Seymour. Chicago, Printed and Published by R. L. Wilson, Daily Journal Office, 1849.
ii, 104p. fold. map. 21cm.
Variant wrapper spells author's name Sanford.
Quotes from Frémont's *Geographical Memoir,* including his references to the Mormons, p. 20, 22. Refers to Cooke's route, p. 79–81, and to the Mormons and trail, p. 84, 88–89, 96.
W–C 173a
CU–B

7629. Seymour, William Deane. Journal of a voyage round the world. By Capt. W. D. Seymour . . . Cork, Printed and Published by Francis Guy, 1877.
vii, 169p. port. 19cm.
Favorable impression of Utah, giving his account of a trip of 1847–48. He feels that Mormonism is not strong enough to survive.
Howes S318
CU–B, NN

7630. Shailer, James, *compiler.* A grave warning to every man woman and child!! Britons! Beware of Mormonism and Cooneyism. Signed by overseers in 20 Parishes, 17 Clergy, and all overseers in Ipswich. Compiled by James Shailer . . . Ipswich, England, 1907.
[8]p. 19cm.
"Beware of the vile deceivers"
USlC

7631. ———. (same) [Ipswich, ca. 1908]
[8]p. 20cm.
USlC

7632. Shallenberger, Eliza Jane (Hall). Stark County [Illinois] and its pioneers. Cambridge, Ill., B. W. Seaton, 1876.
4p.l. [17]–327 [1]p. 21½cm.
Mormon activity in the county, p. 65.
Howes S326
DLC, UPB

Sharp, Thomas C. *See Harris, William. Mormonism portrayed.*

7633. Sharp, William Henry Harrison. Prophetic history, and the fulfillment of prophecy from 600 years B.C. to the year of our lord, 1891 A.D. Containing historical and prophetic charts illustrations and chronological tables by W. H. H. Sharp . . . Salt Lake City, Deseret Home Co., 1883.
vi, 152p. illus. 22cm.
Published in five parts.
CtY parts 1, 2, 3; MH; UPB; USl; USlC

7634. ———. (same) Salt Lake City, Deseret Home Co., 1883.
vi, 153p. tables, illus. 22cm.
Variant printing from p. 151.
USlC

7635. ———. A voice from heaven. Prophetic downfall of American nations. A prophetic warning to the inhabitants of this continent, By Dr. W. H. H. Sharp. Salt Lake City, Published by W. M. Egan, 1885.
39p. 21cm.
Cover-title.
Prophetic history using L.D.S. sonnets and doctrine. An unorthodox treatment.
MH, USlC

7636. Shaw, Alvin Curtis. Poems. Salt Lake City, University of Utah Press, 1913.
3p.l. [9]–146p. 14½cm.
Mormon poetry.
CU-B, DLC, UPB, UHi, USlC

7637. ———. (same) [2d ed.] Salt Lake City, The Deseret News, 1920.
4p.l. [9]–215p. port. 17½cm.
DLC, UHi, USlC, UU

7638. Shaw, David Augustus. Eldorado; or, California as seen by a pioneer, 1850–1900. By Hon. D. A. Shaw . . . Los Angeles, Cal., B. R. Baumgardt & Co., 1900.
7p.l. [17]–313p. plates, port. 20cm.
Chapter VIII, "The Mormons." A brief summary of the history from 1847–1858. Take Hasting's cutoff, 1850.
CU-B, DLC, NjP, UHi, UPB

7639. Shaw, William. Golden dreams and waking realities being the adventures of a gold seeker in California and the Pacific islands. London, Smith, Elder and Co., 1851.
xii, 316p. 19½cm.
Encounters a Mormon family; discussion of Mormonism.
Howes S351
CU-B, DLC, NN

7640. Sheahan, James W. Life of Stephen A. Douglas. New York, Harper & Brothers, 1860.
xi, 528p. 20cm.
Chapter XX, "Utah and the Mormons."
Another edition: New York, Derby, 1860. NjP
NjP, USlC

7641. Shearer, Daniel. A key to the Bible. [New York? 1844?]
12p. 11cm.
"References to prove the gospel in its fulness, the ushering in of the dispensation of the fulness of times and the Latter-day glory."
The basic material of this work was a pamphlet by the same name by Lorenzo D. Barnes, with some revision by Daniel Shearer.
USlC

Shearer, Frederick E. *See Williams, Henry T.*

7642. Shearer, Joel. Comments on the Kingdom of God, and the gospel designed as answers to many important questions, and also to show the author's views of God's Plan of Salvation. By Joel Shearer and William Swett, members of the Church of Jesus Christ of the New Generation. Council Bluffs, Ia., 1854.
30p. 18cm.
The New Church designed for those who were Latter Day Saints. Published for the Gladden Bishop faction.
USlC

7643. ———. Mysteries revealed. By Joel Shearer. Council Bluffs, Ia., 1856.
3p.l., 32p. 17cm.
At head of title: "Great is the mystery of Godliness. — Paul."
Morgan
USlC

7644. ———. The plan of salvation according to the Gospel of Jesus Christ. Explained by Joel Shearer, March, 1858. Council Bluffs: Babbitt & Carpenter, Printers, 1858.
19p. 20½cm.
A doctrinal work on Mormonism as the true church.
MH

7645. Sheehy, Francis Martin. The divine order. [n.p., n.d.]
4p. 17cm.
RLDS doctrine.
MoInRC

7646. ———. Man's wisdom insufficient unto salvation, scriptural teachings concerning his dual nature confirmed by modern revelation. [n.p., n.d.]
15p. 18cm.
Discourse delivered in the Stone Church, Independence, Mo., October 19, 1919. RLDS doctrine.
MoInRC

7647. ———. (same) [n.p., n.d.]
16p. 18cm.
USlC

7647a. ———. "Nothing done until done right." [n.p., 1920?]
[4]p. 20cm.
USlC

7648. Sheen, Isaac. Debate on consciousness after death, between Isaac Sheen, of the Church of Latter Day Saints and C. W. Smith, Adventist. Reported by Isaac Sheen. [Plano, Ill., Printed at the office of the True Latter Day Saints' Herald, n.d.]
5 pamphlets. 21cm.
MH #1–2, NN #1–5

SHEEN, I.

7649. ———. Divine authority of Joseph Smith, the martyr. [Plano, Ill., Reorganized Church of Jesus Christ of Latter Day Saints, 1865?]
2 pts. in 1. (8, 8)p. 23cm. (True Latter Day Saints' Herald. Tract No. 3)
MoInRC, NjP, NN, UPB

7650. ———. Great contrast; a selection of texts from King James's translation of the Bible, contrasted with the corresponding texts in the inspired translation of Joseph Smith, the Seer. [Plano, Ill., True Latter-day Saints' Herald, 1867]
8p. 21cm.
MH, NN

7651. ———. The Kingdom of God on earth, before the second coming of Christ. No. 1-5 [Plano, Ill., True Latter-day Saints' Herald, 18 - -]
5 pts. (4p. each) 23cm.
MH, MoInRC, NjP #1–5, NN #5, UPB

7652. ———. Millennial state. No. 1 by Isaac Sheen. [Plano, Ill., True Latter Day Saints' Herald, 1866?]
4p. 23cm.
Caption-title.
MoInRC, NN, UHi, UPB

7653. ———. Millennial state. No. 2 by Isaac Sheen and the way of life by T. W. Smith. [Plano, Ill., True Latter Day Saints' Herald, 1866?]
4p. 23cm.
Caption-title.
NjP, NN, UHi

7654. ———. The narrow way. [Plano, Ill.] Published by the Reorganized Church of Jesus Christ of Latter Day Saints [1870]
8p. 21½cm. (No. 10)
Sabin 80087
CSmH, CtY, MH, MoInRC, NN, USlC

7655. ———. (same) Plano, Ill., Published by the Reorganized Church of Jesus Christ of Latter Day Saints [n.d.]
8p. 22cm. (No. 10)
USlC

7656. ———. (same) Lamoni, Ia., Published by the Reorganized Church of Jesus Christ of Latter Day Saints [1881 or after]
8p. 23cm. (No. 10)
CSmH, MH

7657. ———. The plan of salvation, [Lamoni, Ia.] Published by the Reorganized Church of Jesus Christ of Latter Day Saints [n.d.]
18p. 23cm. (No. 11)
IWW, MoInRC, NjP

7658. ———. (same) [n.p.] Published by the Reorganized Church of Jesus Christ of Latter Day Saints [n.d.]
18p. 22½cm. (No. 11)
USlC

7659. ———. (same) Plano, Ill., Published by the Reorganized Church of Jesus Christ of Latter Day Saints [n.d.]
18p. 21½cm. (No. 11)
Variant printings.
USlC

7660. ———. (same) [Plano, Ill., Office of the True Latter Day Saints' Herald, 1866]
12p. 22cm.
Caption-title.
CtY, MoInRC, NjP, UHi, UPB

7661. ———. (same) [Plano, Ill., Published by the Reorganized Church of Jesus Christ of Latter Day Saints, 187–]
18p. 22½cm. (No. 11)
CSmH, MH, NN, USlC

7662. ———. (same, in Tahitian) Te ravea o note o ora; va papai hia peretibutero rao I saaka Sheen. Papeete, Tahiti, Etaretia Faaapi Hia no Jetu Metia i te Mau Mahana Hopea Nei, 1897.
16p. 24½cm. (No. 1)
USlC

7663. ———. Sheen's Letter [to] Bro. G. P. Dykes. [Sacramento? 1868?]
8p. 21cm.
Letter dated, Plano, Ill., December 26, 1868; with a short reply by G. Parker Dykes signed, Sacramento, January 14, 1868.
MoInRC, UPB

7664. ———. Den snever vei. Udgivet af Aeldste I.S. og forlagt af M. Fyrando og P. N. Brix. Aalborg, 1877.
8p.
Title in English: The narrow path.
Schmidt

7665. ———. Universalism examined. No. 1-2. [Plano, Ill., True Latter Day Saints' Herald, 1865]
2 pts. (4, 4p.) 23cm. (True Latter Day Saints' Herald. No. 18)
CtY, MoInRC, NjP, NN, UPB

7666. ———. Zion in America. Plano, Ill., Reorganized Church of Jesus Christ of Latter Day Saints [1866]
4p. 23cm.
CtY, MoInRC, NjP, NN, UPB

7667. ———. (same) [Plano, Ill., The True Latter Day Saints' Herald, ca. 1866]
4p. 23cm.
USlC

7668. Sheen, John K. . . . Polygamy, or the veil uplifted . . . [York, Neb., 1889]
21 [1]p. 24cm. (Supplement to the relic library)
Cover-title.
Signed: John K. Sheen.
CSmH, CU-B, MH, MoInRC, NN, USIC

7669. Sheepshanks, John, *Bishop of Norwich.* A bishop in the rough; edited by the Rev. D. Wallace Duthie . . . With a preface by the Right Rev. The Lord Bishop of Norwich. Illustrated. New York, E. P. Dutton and Co., 1909.
xxxvii, 386p. port. 21½cm.
Material on Mormonism, p. 107–128. He was not impressed by anything he saw or learned about Mormonism. Polygamy was still a large issue in Utah.
MB, MH, NjP, NN, OClW, UHi, USl, USIC, ViU, WaPS

7670. Sheldon, Henry Clay. A fourfold test of Mormonism, by Henry C. Sheldon . . . New York, Cincinnati, The Abingdon press [c1914]
151p. 17½cm.
CSmH, CU-B, DLC, IWW, MoInRC, NjP, NjPT, NN, UHi, USIC, UU

7671. ———. (same) [Appendix] Failure of pro-Mormon apology to impair the test, by Henry C. Sheldon . . . New York, Cincinnati, The Abingdon Press [c1916]
1p.l., 153–192p. 17cm.
"A brief reply to the attempt of Robert C. Webb to refute my treatise in his book entitled *The case against Mormonism*."
DLC, USIC

7672. ———. A fourfold test of Mormonism. New York, the Abingdon Press [1918]
3p.l., 9–192p. 17½cm.
Reprinted 1918.
NN, UHi, UPB

7673. ———. Sacerdotalism in the nineteenth century, a critical history. New York, Eaton & Mains: Cincinnati, Jennings & Graham [c1909]
1p.l., v–ix, 461p. 21½cm.
Mormon theories, p. 437–446.
"Though built upon as transparent a fable as ever deceived an ignorant . . . people," Mormonism continues to make converts.
CU, DLC, UPB, USIC

7674. Sheldon, Louise P. The Church the Indians have long looked for. Lamoni, Ill., Herald Publishing House [n.d.]
7p. 18cm.
RLDS tract.
MoInRC

7675. ———. A message to the Indians. [Lamoni, Ia., Herald Publishing House, n.d.]
7p. 18cm.
RLDS doctrine.
MoInRC

7676. Sheldon, Thomas Jennings. How to enter the kingdom. Lamoni, Ia., Herald Publishing House [189–]
6p. 22cm. [Reorganized Church of Jesus Christ. Tracts. No. 15]
MoInRC, NN

7677. ———. The organic law of the Church. [n.p., n.d.]
6p. 26cm.
RLDS doctrine.
MoInRC

7678. Sheldon, William. Mormonism examined; or, was Joseph Smith a divinely inspired prophet? A refutation of Mormonism, containing over one hundred proofs of its fallacy. Examined in the light of their own inspired works, such as "The Book of Mormon," "The Book of Doctrine and Covenants," "The Inspired Translation [of the Bible]," by William Sheldon . . . Broadhead, Wis., Published by the author [1876?]
iv [5]–184p. 17cm.
Cover-title.
Howes S378, Sabin 80134
CtY, CU-B, MH, MoInRC, NN, UHi, UPB, USl, USIC

7679. Shepard, Elihu Hotchkiss. The early history of St. Louis and Missouri, by Elihu H. Shepard . . . To which is appended the author's autobiography. St. Louis, Southwestern Book and Publishing Company, 1870.
viii [9]–170p. 25cm.
Account of the Mormons and their treatment of the Missourians, p. 148.
Howes S387, Sabin 80176
CU, DLC, IGK, NjP, NN, OCl, PHi, PPM, ULA, UPB

7680. Shepard, Lulu Loveland. Getting their eyes open. A program for missionary societies showing popular fallacies of Latter Day Saints by Mrs. Lulu Loveland Shepard. Pittsburgh, National Reform Association [n.d.]
14p. 15½cm.
UPB

7681. Shepard Book Co., Salt Lake City. A catalogue of rare works on Mormonism, Utah, Kansas and the West. Salt Lake City [191–]
23p. 22cm. (No. 45)
NN, NjP, PCC

7682. ———. Publications of Shepard Book Company, Salt Lake City, Utah. [Salt Lake City, 1910?]
[2]p. 22½cm.
Brochure for several anti-Mormon works.
UPB

SHEPARD BOOK

7682a. ———. (same) [Salt Lake City, 1910]
Broadside. 22½×12cm.
NjP

7683. Shepherd, Arthur. The Lord hath brought again Zion. Baritone solo and chorus for mixed voices. By Arthur Shepherd. Boston, Oliver Ditson Company . . . c1907.
24p. music. 27½cm.
Text from the *Doctrine and Covenants.*
USlC

7684. Shepherd, Mary E. History in verse. By Mary E. Shepherd. Provo [1928]
17 [1]p. 19cm.
Mormon poetry.
USlC

The Shepherd Saint of Lanai. *See Gibson, Walter Murray.*

7685. Sherman, William Tecumseh. Memoirs of General William T. Sherman. By himself . . . New York, D. Appleton and Company, 1875.
2v. fold. map. 22½cm.
Mormons in California, 1846.
Published in several editions.
CU, CU-B, DLC, NjP, UPB

7686. Sherwood, J. Ely. California: her wealth and resources; with many interesting facts respecting the climate and people; the official and other correspondence of the day, relating to the gold region; Colonel Mason's report, and all that part of the President's Message having reference to the country in which these vast discoveries have been made; also, a memorial offered in Congress, in relation to the proposed railroad to the Pacific Ocean. By J. Ely Sherwood . . . New York, George F. Nesbitt, Stationer and Printer . . . 1848.
40 [1]p. 22cm.
Enclosed in printed wrapper.
References to Mormons in Col. Mason's report of Aug. 17, 1848, p. 18, 20, 22. On p. 30 there is a letter of June 30, 1848 which refers to the new route being explored [by Mormons, though this is not stated] across the Sierra Nevada. On p. 32 an account of the first discovery of the mines mentions the agency of "some Mormons digging a mill race for Capt. Sutter."
CU-B

7687. ———. The pocket guide to California; a sea and land route book, containing a description of the El Dorado; its geographical position; people, climate, soil, productions, agricultural resources, commercial advantages, and mineral wealth; with a chapter on gold formations; also the Congressional map, and the various routes and distances to the gold regions. To which is added the Gold-hunter's Memorandum and pocket directory. By J. E. Sherwood. New York: J. E. Sherwood, Publisher and Proprietor . . . California, Berford & Co., and C. W. Holden, San Francisco, 1849.
[ii]-[iv] [5]-98p. fold. map. 19cm.
Contains Col. Mason's report with its mention of the Mormons, p. 24, 26, 29-30; letter by J. L. Folsom, San Francisco, Sept. 18, 1848, mentioning the Mormons at Sutter's Mill, p. 32.
Variant issue of 72p. CtY
CU-B

7688. Sherwood, *Mrs.* **Mary Elizabeth (Wilson).** An epistle to posterity being rambling recollections of many years of my life. By M. E. W. Sherwood . . . 1st ed. New York, Harper & Brothers Publishers, 1897.
x, 380p. port. 21cm.
"Joseph Smith and the Mormons," p. 26-27.
UPB, USlC

7689. Shiland, Andrew. From ocean to ocean, with notes and observations on the way. By Rev. Andrew Shiland, D. D. New York, For sale by American Tract Society, 1892.
32p. 18½cm.
He visits Salt Lake City in 1892, has a brief interview with a Mormon, and describes the meeting.
USlC

7690. Shinn, Charles Howard. The story of the mine, as illustrated by the great Comstock lode of Nevada. New York, D. Appleton and Company, 1896.
xi, [1]l., 272p. illus., plates. 19cm. (The Story of the West series)
Chapter 3: Implications that Mormons were really after gold.
Another edition: 1906. NjP; 1914. UHi
CU, DLC

7691. Shinn, John L. Discussion between Rev. John L. Shinn, of the Universalist Church and Elder Mark H. Forscutt, of the Reorganized Church of Jesus Christ of Latter Day Saints, held at Rock Creek, Ill., August 10th, 13th, 1875. Plano, Ill., Board of Publication of the Reorganized Church of Jesus Christ of Latter Day Saints, 1875.
194p. 22cm.
Sabin 80497
DLC, MoInRC, NjP, NN, UPB, USlC

7691a. ———. (same) Plano, Ill., Board of Publication of the Reorganized Church of Jesus Christ of Latter Day Saints, 1889.
194p. 22cm.
MoInRC

7692. Shinn, Jonathan. The memoirs of Capt. Jonathan Shinn. Greeley, Colo., World County Democrat, 1890.
88p. 19cm.
Includes his cordial relations with the Mormons in Illinois, Iowa and Nebraska, 1840's and 1850's.
CU-B, NjP, UPB

SHORT ADDRESSES

7693. Shinn, Josiah Hazen. The History of Arkansas. A text-book for public schools, high schools, and academies, by Josiah H. Shinn, A. M. Ex-state superintendent of public instruction . . . Richmond, Va. B. F. Johnson Publishing Co., 1905.
335p. illus. 19cm.
"Mountain Meadows massacre," p. 161.
UPB

7694. Shipp, Ellis Reynolds. Life lines; poems by Ellis Reynolds Shipp. Salt Lake City, Skelton Publishing Co., 1910.
2p.l. [5]–316p. port. 21cm.
Mormon poetry.
CSmH, DLC, NjP, UHi, UPB, USlC, UU

7695. Shook, Charles Augustus. American anthropology disproving the Book of Mormon. By Charles A. Shook . . . Cleveland, O., The Utah Gospel Mission, 1916.
20p. 17cm.
First edition.
NN, UPB, USlC

7696. ———. (same) 2d ed. Cleveland, O., The Utah Gospel Mission, 1930.
20p. 17cm.
Cover-title.
MoInRC, UPB, USl, UU

7697. ———. Cumorah revisited; or, "The Book of Mormon" and the claims of the Mormons re-examined from the viewpoint of American archaeology and ethnology, by Charles A. Shook . . . Cincinnati, The Standard Publishing Company, 1910.
589p. illus., plates. 20cm.
"Authors," p. 578–581.
CtY, CU–B, DLC, ICN, IWW, MoInRC, UHi, UPB, USl, USlC, WHi

7698. ———. The true origin of Mormon polygamy, by Charles A. Shook . . . Mendota, Ill., The W[estern] A[dvent] C[hristian] P[ublication] Ass'n [c1910]
2p.l. [5]–223p. 19cm.
DLC, IWW, UPB, USl, WHi

7699. ———. (same) [2d ed.] Cincinnati, The Standard Publishing Company, 1914.
viii, 213p. plates, ports. 20cm.
CSmH, CtY, CU–B, DLC, ICN, IWW, MoInRC, NN, UHi, UPB, USlC, UU, WHi

7700. ———. The true origin of the Book of Mormon, by Charles A. Shook . . . Cincinnati, Ohio, The Standard Publishing Co. [1914]
x, 187p. plates, ports., facsims. 20cm.
CSmH, CU–B, DLC, IWW, MoInRC, NN, OO, UPB, USl, USlC, UU

7701. Short, Ben T. Book of the law. Chapter I. The decalogue. [Kansas City, Mo. 1926?]
[8]p. 19cm.
Doctrinal tract by a member of the Strangite church.
UPB

7701a. ———. Important. [Kansas City, Mo.? 1928?]
Broadside. 20½×11cm.
Signed by: S. A. Martin, Moroni Flanders, Roy Straton Neal, Lloyd Flanders, John Willis, H. A. Anderson, John Wake, Ben T. Short
Morgan
USlC

7702. ———. We Should Pity That Poor Child. [Kansas City, Mo.? 19 - -]
Placard. 28×14½cm.
Signed: Ben T. Short.
Copy was owned by Dr. Arbaugh.
Morgan

7703. Short, Eva Bailey. A Story of the plains. Independence, Mo., Herald Publishing House, 1921.
259p. illus., plates. 20cm.
A story based on true experiences of an early member of the RLDS church. The conversion, p. 205–259.
MH, MoInRC, MoK, NjP

7704. Short, John Thomas. The North Americans of antiquity; their origin, migrations, and type of civilization considered. By John T. Short. New York, Harper & Brothers . . . 1880.
xviii [19]–544p. illus. 23cm.
The Book of Mormon proved to be a fraud.
USlC

7705. ———. (same) 2d ed. New York, Harper & Brothers, 1880.
xviii [19]–544p. illus. 23cm.
CU–B, DLC

7706. ———. (same) 3d ed. New York, Harper & Brothers, 1882.
xviii [21]–548p. illus. 23cm.
USlC

7707. Short, M. T. Sermon, delivered at Independence, Missouri, April 12, 1888. [Lamoni, Ia., Lambert Bros.] 1888.
8p. 23cm.
Supplement to *Lamoni Gazetteer*, June, 1888.
MoInRC

7708. Short addresses on the Church of Christ delivered at the eighth annual meeting of the Congregational Association of Utah. In Plymouth Congregational Church, Salt Lake City, October 12–14, 1897. Published by vote of the Association. Salt Lake City, Kinsman Print [1897?]
2p.l., 24p. 21cm.
Speeches by various ministers. Several allusions to Mormonism.
USlC

SHORT HISTORY

7709. A Short history of the Mormonites. [Huntingdon, England, 1853]
22p. 17½cm.
ULA (Imperfect copy: title-page missing. Manuscript note on endpaper states, "Author supposed to be Rev. Hepburn, Lecturer. See Mil. Star, XV, 414.")

7710. Shuck, Oscar Tully. Representative and leading men of the Pacific; being original sketches of the lives and characters of the principal men, living and deceased, of the Pacific states and territories . . . To which is added their speeches, addresses, orations, eulogies, lectures, and poems, upon a variety of subjects, including the happiest forensic efforts of Baker, Randolph, McDougall, T. Starr King, and other popular orators. Edited by Oscar T. Shuck . . . San Francisco, Bacon and Company, Printers and Publishers, 1870.
2p.l. [5]–702p. ports. 23½cm.
"Samuel Brannan" by William Y. Wells.
Sabin 80755
CU–B, DLC, NjP, UPB

7711. "Shuro." [Tokyo] Sogo Hattatsu Kyokai, January, 1925–September, 1927.
2v. 20cm.
V.1 #1–10, V.2 #1–4.
A Japanese mission periodical.
Title in English: The palm.
UPB V.1 #1, 2, 4–10; V.2 #1–4.

Shurtliff, Lewis W. *See Church of Jesus Christ of Latter-day Saints. Stakes. Weber. . . . One third of a century of service.*

7712. Den sidste nye vise om de to Kjobenhavnske Mursvende der solgte deres koner for 2000 Kroner til en Mormonpraest, some rejste til Utah med dem. [Kjobenhavn, 186–]
[4]p. 16cm.
Street ballad.
Title in English: The latest new song about the two Masons who sold their wives to the Mormons.
UHi

7713. De Sidste Dages Helliges laere eller Mormonismen. Kobenhavn, 1904.
48p.
Title in English: The doctrine of Latter Day Saints.
Schmidt.

7714. Sidwell, Adelia B. (Cox). Early Manti. Reminisences [sic] of early days in Manti, By Mrs. A. B. Sidwell. [n.p., 1889?]
21p. 22½cm.
Settlement of Manti.
For date *see Utah Historical Quarterly*, 1933, p. 117–123.
UPB

7715. Signs of Christ's second coming. [n.p., n.d.]
16p. 14cm. (Tract. No. 4)
UPB

7716. The Silent Messenger. Port Huron, Mich., February, 1916–
v. monthly. 30cm.
Otto Fetting and W. J. Smith, Publishers.
Printed in triple columns.
A religious paper evidently addressed to RLDS congregations.
MoInRC. V.1 #1, 2, 6, 9, 12; V.2 #1

7717. Sill, Charles. Economics dictated by reason and revealed religion, by Charles Sill. Layton, Utah, 1925.
1p.l., 190p. 21½cm.
Economics and Mormonism.
CSmH, CU–B, DLC, NjP, UHi, UPB, USl, USlC, UU

Silverland. *See Lawrence, George Alfred.*

7718. Simms, Paris Marion. The Bible from the beginning, by Rev. P. Marion Simms. New York, The Macmillan Co., 1929.
xxi, 318p. diagr. 20½cm.
The RLDS Church's use of the Inspired Version of the Bible. One page of comparison. Mentions *Book of Mormon* belief, p. 145–147.
DLC

7719. Simms, William Emmett. Speech of Hon. W. E. Simms, of Kentucky on Polygamy in Utah. Delivered in the House of Representatives, April 4, 1860. [Washington] Printed by Lemuel Towers, 1860.
16p. 21cm.
DLC, USl

7720. Simonin, Louis Laurent. A travers les États-Unis, de l'Atlantique au Pacifique; par L. Simonin . . . Paris, Charpentier et Cie, 1875.
3p.l. [iii]–iv, 410p. 18cm.
Several chapters on Mormonism: "La Polygamie," "l'Eglise des Saints," "Le Pays des Mormons," etc.
Published in Italian under title: Attraverso gli State Uniti Dall' Atlantico al Pacifico. Milano, Fratelli Trevis, 1876. MB, RP
Title in English: A trip through the United States.
Sabin 81306
CU–B, DLC, ICN, MB, NjP

7721. Simons, John. . . . A few more facts relating to the self-styled "Latter-Day Saints." Ledbury [England] Printed by J. Gibbs, jun. [1840]
8p. 21cm.
Caption-title.
At head of title: Third thousand.
Signed: John Simons, Dymock, Sept. 14, 1840.
Usually found in association with W. J. Morrish.
CtY, CU–B, DLC, MH, NN, USlC

7722. ———. (same) Ledbury [England]. Printed by J. Gibbs, jun. Chitheroe, Reprinted by H. Whalley [1840]
8p. 21cm.
Caption-title.
Signed: John Simons, Sept. 14, 1840.
CU–B, NN

7723. Simpson, *Sir* George. California: its history, population, climate, soil, productions, and harbors. From Sir George Simpson's "Overland journey round the world." An account of the revolution in California, and conquest of the country by the United States, 1846–7. By John T. Hughes . . . Cincinnati, J. A. & U. P. James, 1848.
105p. 19½cm.
Material on the Mormon Battalion from John T. Hughes.
Other editions: 1849. CU–B; 1850. CU–B
Howes S494
CU–B, DLC, NjP

7724. Simpson, James Hervey. . . . Report of explorations across the Great Basin of the Territory of Utah for a direct wagon-route from Camp Floyd to Genoa, in Carson Valley, in 1859, by Captain J. H. Simpson . . . Made by authority of the Secretary of War and under instructions from Bvt. Brig. Gen. A. S. Johnston . . . Washington, Govt. Print. Off. 1876.
518p. 17 plates, 4 maps, diagr. 31cm.
Published by U.S. Army. Corps of engineers.
Early descriptions of Utah with brief mention of its people.
Howes S501, Sabin 81355
CSmH, CU, CU–B, DI–GS, DLC, ICJ, ICN, NjP, NN, UHi, ULA, UPB, USIC, UU

7725. ———. . . . Report of the Secretary of War, communicating, in compliance with a resolution of the Senate, Captain Simpson's report and map of wagon road routes in Utah territory . . . [Washington, Govt. Print. Off., 1859]
84p. fold. map. 23½cm. (U.S. 35th Cong. 2d Sess. Senate. Ex. Doc. No. 40)
Published by U.S. Army. Corps of Engineers.
Brief mention of Mormons and a description of the territory.
W–C 345
CSmH, CU–B, DI–GS, DLC, ICN, ULA, UPB

7726. ———. The shortest route to California, illustrated by a history of explorations of the Great Basin of Utah with its topographical and geological character and some account of the Indian tribes. By Brevet Brig. General J. H. Simpson . . . Philadelphia, J. B. Lippincott & Co., 1869.
58p. fold. map. 21½cm.
Chiefly concerned with the route; some early explorers; and a brief mention of Mormon participation.
Howes 1569
CU–B, DLC, USIC

7727. Simpson, William. Meeting the sun. A journey all around the world: Through Egypt, China, Japan and California, including an account of the marriage ceremonies of the Emperor of China. By William Simpson . . . London, Longmans, Green, Reader and Dyer, 1874.
xii, 413p. plates, ports., illus. 23cm.
Salt Lake City, Mormons and Mormonism, p. 394–403.
Another edition: Boston, Estes, 1877. NjP, USI
Sabin 81377
CU–B, DLC, UPB, USIC, UU

7728. Simpson, William Sparrow. Mormonism: its history, doctrines, and practices. London, A. M. Pigott, 1853.
iv [5]–62p. 18cm.
Variant printing. USIC
CtY, CU–B, ICN, MH, NN, ULA, USIC

7729. Sinclair, Charles E. Charge of Hon. Chas E. Sinclair, Judge of the Third Judicial District of the Territory of Utah; Delivered in Great Salt Lake City, Nov. 22nd, 1858. Great Salt Lake City, 1858.
8p. 21½cm.
Problem of Judges in Utah.
USIC

7730. Sinclair, Upton Beall. The goose-step, a study of American education, by Upton Sinclair . . . Pasadena, Calif., The author [1923]
x, 488p. 19cm.
Education among the Mormons, p. 184–188.
"Second edition" 1923. DLC, NjP, UHi, USIC
CU–B, UHi, ULA, UPB, USIC

7731. ———. The profits of religion; an essay in economic interpretation. By Upton Sinclair. Pasadena, California, Published by the author [c1918]
ix, 11–315 [1]p. 20cm.
Short description of the Book of Mormon under "The church of the quacks."
NjP, UPB, USIC, UU

7731a. ———. Upton Sinclair Discusses the Mormon Church. Los Angeles, United for California League [1926]
[4]p. 22½cm.
At head of title: "Out of His Own Mouth Shall He be Judged."
A tract in opposition to Upton Sinclair for governor of California, 1926.
USIC

7731b. The Singer Manufacturing Co. The great temple. Compliments of the Singer Manufacturing Co. Office: Cor. of First East and Second South Street, Salt Lake City, Utah. [Salt Lake City? 1893?]
[2]l. 12cm.
UPB

7732. Singleton, Esther. Historic buildings of America as seen and described by famous writers, collected and edited by Esther Singleton. With numerous illustrations. New York, Dodd, Mead & Company, 1909.
xiv, 341p. plates. 20½cm.
"The Tabernacle, Salt Lake City," [by] Lady Hardy, p. 215–219.
USlC

7733. Singleton, James Washington. To the public. The very responsible and conspicuous position I have occupied in the late disturbance in Hancock County imposes on me the task of quieting the public mind . . . [Warsaw? 1846]
Broadside. 22½×36cm.
Includes terms of peace arranged between James R. Parker and Singleton, the leader of the anti-Mormon forces.
Byrd 1116
ICHi, NN

7734. A singular dream. A plea for religious liberty, and exposition of legal principles evolved in a dream. "Which was not all a dream." By a dreamer. [n.p., n.d.]
32p. 21cm.
A justification of polygamy.
USlC

Sinking of the "Arabic." *See S., J. M.*

7735. Sioli, Paola. Historical souvenir of El Dorado County, California. Oakland, 1883.
272p. plates, ports. 29cm.
Briefly mentions Mormons in the gold fields.
C, CU-B

7735a. Siringo, Charles A. A cowboy detective; a true story of twenty-two years with a world-famous detective agency . . . Chicago, W. B. Conkey Co., 1912.
519p. illus. 20cm.
Mormons mentioned, p. 273, 280, 345–346, 386.
USlC

7735b. Sirrine, M. Circular to the Church of Jesus Christ, of Latter Day Saints in the East, by M. Sirrine, Presiding Elder of the Eastern States. [New York? 1847?]
Broadside. 31×21cm.
Copy in private hands. Xerox at UPB, USlC

7736. Sirrine, Samuel D. The destroying angels of Mormondom, or a sketch of the life of Orrin Porter Rockwell, the late Danite chief, by Achilles [*pseud.*] [San Francisco, Alta California Printing House, 1878]
45p. 22cm.
Listed for copyright by Edwin F. Bean.
Authorship acknowledged in the *Salt Lake Daily Herald*, Aug. 6, 1878.
CU-B

7737. The Sirrom. Salt Lake City, Salt Lake Stake, February–October, 1924.
2v. monthly. 35cm.
Publication of the Salt Lake Stake Mutual Improvement Association.
USlC V.1 #1–5; V.2 #1

7738. Sjodahl, Janne Mattson. Authenticity of the Book of Mormon. Liverpool, Printed and Published at the Millennial Star Office [1915?]
1p.l., 24p. 22cm.
CtY, UPB, USl

7739. ———. An introduction to the study of the Book of Mormon, by J. M. Sjodahl . . . Salt Lake City, The Deseret News Press, 1927.
iv p., [2]l., 555 [1]p. illus., ports., fold. map. 20cm.
"Authors and publications," p. 552–555.
DLC, NjP, NN, UHi, UPB, USl, USlC

———. In memoriam, Anthon Henrik Lund.
See In memoriam.

7740. ———. Joseph Smith: was he a prophet of God? An investigation and testimony. By J. M. Sjodahl. Salt Lake City, Deseret News Co., 1891.
90p. 17cm.
CSmH, CU-B, MH, NjP, NN, UHi, ULA, USl, USlC, UU

7741. ———. The reign of anti-Christ; or, The great "falling away." A study in ecclesiastical history. Salt Lake City, The Deseret News, 1913.
138p. 18cm.
IWW, MH, MoInRC, NjP, UHi, ULA, UPB, USlC, WaPS

7742. ———. (same, in Danish) Antikristens Regering eller Det Store Frafald. En Kirkehistorisk afhandling af J. M. Sjødahl. Oversat fra Engelsk af John S. Hansen. [Salt Lake City] Bikubens Bibliotek, 1920.
128p. 18cm.
USlC

7743. ———. (same) [Salt Lake City] Bikubens Bibliotek, 1929.
128p. 19cm.
USlC (Galley proofs; may never have been printed)

7744. ———. (same, in German) Die Herrschaft des Antichristen oder der grosse Abfall. Von J. M. Sjödahl . . . Basel, Herausgegeben von der Schweizerisch-Deutschen Mission, 1917.
87p. 17½cm.
USlC

7745. ———. Temples ancient and modern. Including an account of the laying of the capstone on the Salt Lake Temple. [Salt Lake City] Printed and for sale by the Deseret News Co. [1892?]
28p. illus. 24½cm.
Variant cover-title: Temples ancient and modern. Descriptive and historical sketches.
Cover-title.
NjP, ULA, UPB

7746. Skanchy, Anthon L. Anthon L. Skanchy; a brief autobiographical sketch of the missionary labors of a valiant soldier for Christ. Trans. and ed. by John A. Widtsoe. [Salt Lake City?] 1915.
2p.l. [7]–46p. illus. 23cm.
Signed by the translator.
NjP, UHi, UPB

7747. Skandinaviens Stjerne. Organ for de Sidste-Dages Heilige. Kjøbenhavn, October, 1851–
v. semi-monthly. 22cm.
Official organ of the Scandinavian Mission and for the Danish Mission after it was divided in 1920.
First editor: Erastus Snow.
Title in English: The Star of Scandinavia.
CtY V.1–3, 7–12, 17; CU–B V.3–9, 11 #3, 12–18; NjP V.3, 5, 8–10, 14, 16, 31; UPB V.1 inc., 3–20, 24–34, 36–46, 50–54, 57–61, 62–66 inc., 67, 68–70 inc., 71, 72 inc., 73–74, 75 inc.; USIC comp.

7748. Skelton, Robert. A defense of Mormonism, in a letter to the editor of the "Hurkaru." Being a refutation of the slanderous accusations which appeared in the above newspaper under the anonymous signature of a visitor of Nauvoo, grounded on a review by the editor of a novel, "Female life among the Mormons." By Robert Skelton and J. P. Meik, Elders of the Church of Jesus Christ of Latter-day Saints. Calcutta, 1855.
2p.l., 39p. 20½cm.
USIC

7748a. ———. (same) Calcutta: Printed by N. Robertson & Co., at the Columbian Press, No. 65-1, Cossitollah. 1855.
2p., 40p. 20½cm.
Cover-title.
Bound in a blue printed wrapper; title within border.
USIC

7749. Sketch of James Jesse Strang and the Mormon Kingdom on Beaver Island . . . Lansing, Mich., R. Smith and Co., Printer [1912?]
14p. plates, 2 ports. 23½cm.
Reprint from Vol. 18, *Michigan Pioneer and Historical Collections.* Consists of two articles from *New York Times,* September 3, 1882, and *Detroit Free Press,* June 30, 1889.
DLC, USIC

7750. Sketches of the Inter-Mountain states together with biographies of many prominent and progressive citizens who have helped in the development and history-making of this marvelous region, 1847–1909. Utah, Idaho, Nevada. Salt Lake City, The Salt Lake Tribune [1909]
2p.l., 5–376p. illus., ports. 28½cm.
Chiefly mining, but some historical and biographical material.
CSmH, DLC, NjP, NN, PP, PU, UHi, ULA, UPB, USIC, UU

7750a. Skinner, Charles R. Polygamy. Speech of Hon. Charles R. Skinner, of New York, in the House of Representatives, Monday, March 13, 1882. Washington, 1882.
4p. 21cm.
USIC

7751. Skirving, John. Descriptive of Fremont's overland route to Oregon and California, across the Rocky Mountains, as surveyed for the United States Government! Now exhibiting at the Egyptian Hall. London: Published by John Field, Stationer and Bookseller [1850]
48p. 20cm.
Cover-title.
Caption-title: Biographical sketch of Colonel Fremont.
Brief reference to Salt Lake City and the Mormons, p. 26–27.
At end: John K. Chapman and Company.
Text to accompany a panorama.
CU–B without cover, Fred Rosenstock, NNHi

7752. Skriftmaessig beviis imod Mormonismens laere. Kobenhavn, 1854.
32p.
Title in English: Scriptural proof of the teachings of Mormonism.
Schmidt

7753. Slanders refuted. Liverpool, Church of Jesus Christ of Latter-day Saints, European Mission [1920?]
4p. 22½cm.
UPB, UU

7754. Slater, Nelson. Fruits of Mormonism, or A fair and candid statement of facts illustrative of Mormon principles, Mormon policy, and Mormon character, by more than forty eye-witnesses. Compiled by N. Slater, A. M. Coloma, Cal., Harmon & Springer, 1851.
1p.l., 93 [1]p. 17cm.
An attack on the Mormons for ill-treatment of emigrants to California. In Utah, 1850–51.
Howes S542, W-C 205
CSmH, CtY, CU–B, DLC, ICN, NjP, NN, UPB, USIC, ViU

SLOAN, E. L.

7755. Sloan, Edward Lenox. The Bard's offering; a collection of miscellaneous poems. By Edward L. Sloan. Belfast, J. Reed . . . 1854.
ii, 118 [2]p. 18½cm.
Poetry, some with specific Mormon emphasis.
USlC

7756. ———, *compiler.* Gazeteer [sic] of Utah, and Salt Lake City directory. Compiled and Edited by Edward L. Sloan, 1874. Salt Lake City, "Salt Lake Herald" Publishing Company [1874]
2p.l., 17–326p. fold. map. 24cm.
Chronological events of Utah, p. 22–23.
Froiseth map shows railroads, mail routes, Gunnison's route, insets of Great Salt Lake and Salt Lake City.
CU–B, DLC, NjP, NN, UHi, UPB

7757. ———, *compiler.* The Salt Lake City directory and business guide, for 1869. Compiled and arranged by E. L. Sloan. Salt Lake City, Published by E. L. Sloan and Co., 1869.
3p.l., 57–219 [1]p., [1]l. 23cm.
"Sketch of Mormonism," [56]–58p.; chronology of Utah history and a history of the Territory of Utah with the lists of people and business.
CSmH, CU, CU–B, DLC, MH, NjP, UHi, UPB, USlC

7758. Sloan, Richard E., *editor.* History of Arizona; Hon. Richard E. Sloan, supervising editor, Ward R. Adams, author, assisted by an advisory council . . . Arizona biography, by a special staff of writers. Phoenix, Record Publishing Co., 1930.
4v. illus., plates, ports., maps, diagr. 27½cm.
Bancroft library has a 31p. prospectus.
Material on the Mormon battalion and Mormon colonization.
CU–B, DLC, NjP, UPB

7759. Sloan, Robert Wallace. The great contest. The chief advocates of anti-Mormon measures reviewed by their speeches in the House of Representatives, January 12, 1887, on the bill reported by J. Randolph Tucker as a substitute for Senator Edmund's bill against the Mormon church. By R. W. Sloan. Salt Lake City [Printed by the Deseret News Co.] 1887.
vii, 98p. 18cm.
CSmH, CtY, DLC, MH, NjP, NN, ULA, UPB, USl, USlC, UU

7760. ———. Souvenir, 1888–'9. Salt Lake City illustrated. Omaha and Salt Lake City, D. C. Dunbar Co., Publishers and Engravers, c1888.
68p. illus. 31cm.
Signed: R. W. Sloan.
Cover-title: Salt Lake City illustrated.
Discovery and colonization of Salt Lake City; history, description of buildings, etc.
DLC, USlC

7761. ———. Utah gazetteer and directory of Logan, Ogden, Provo and Salt Lake cities, for 1884. Ed. and comp. by Robert W. Sloan. Containing a history of Utah, her resources, attractions, statistics, etc. With business directory of the territory and general directories of the four principal cities. Salt Lake City, Printed for Sloan & Dunbar, by the Herald Printing and Publishing Company, 1884.
634p. front. (fold. map) fold. tab. 26½cm.
Advertising matter interspersed.
A great deal of Mormon material under headings: "Utah Chronology," "Pioneers," "Temples and Churches," "Sketch of Mormonism."
CSmH, CU–B, DLC, NjP, NN, UHi, ULA, UPB, USlC

7762. Slovo moudrosti zdravofňi zasady Cirkve mormonske, dodržovane od roku 1833 . . . [n.p.] 1927.
[6]p. 12½cm.
Title in English: Word of wisdom health principles of the Mormon Church.
UPB

7763. Small, Charles H. Corner-stones of faith, or the origin and characteristics of the Christian denominations of the United States. By Rev. Charles H. Small . . . With corroborative statements from eminent divines of the leading denominations. Introduction by Rev. John Henry Barrows . . . Illustrated. New York, E. B. Treat & Co., 1898.
1p.l. [5]–469p. illus., ports. 21cm.
"The Mormons," p. 423–428. Reorganized Church, p. 428–429. A factual account of Mormonism.
DLC, MoInRC, UU

Smart, Charles. Resources and attractions of the Territory of Utah. *See Utah (Territory) Board of Trade.*

7764. Smet, Pierre Jean de. Cinquante nouvelles lettres du R. P. de Smet, de la Compagnie de Jésus et missionnaire en Amérique, publiées par Éd. Terwecoren, de la même compagnie . . . Paris, Rue de Tournon, 20. Tournai, Rue aux Rats, 11.
H. Casterman, Éditeur, 1858.
2p.l., [v]–ix, 502 [2]p. 19½cm.
His encounter with Mormonism in 1846 and his reaction to it.
Title in English: Fifty new letters . . .
Sabin 82260, Howes D281, W–C 308
CtY, DLC, OrP, PPAmP, UPB

7765. ———. Lettres choisies de révérend Père Pierre-Jean de la Compagnie de Jésus, missionnaire aux États-Unis d'Amérique. [2. série] 1855–1861. 3. éd., soigneusement rev. et cor, d'après les manuscrits de l'auteur; et augm. de nombreuses notes.
Bruxelles, F. Haenen; [etc., etc.] 1876.
x, 416p. 21½cm.
Chapter XXV, "Les Mormons"
Another ed.: Bruxelles, M. Closson, 1877. DLC
Title in English: Selected letters of P. Pierre-Jean, S. J. missionary to the U.S.A.
Sabin 82263
CSmH, CU–B, DLC, WaU

7766. ———. Life, letters and travels of Father Pierre-Jean de Smet, S. J., 1801–1873; missionary labors and adventures among the wild tribes of the North American Indians . . . edited from the original unpublished manuscript journals and letter books and from his printed works, with historical, geographical, ethnological and other notes; also a life of Father de Smet . . . by Hiram Martin Chittenden . . . and Alfred Talbot Richardson . . . New York, F. P. Harper, 1905 [c1904]
4v. plates, ports., fold. map in pocket, facsims. 24½cm.
Descriptions of Mormons he met on the plains in 1846, Vol. 4, p. 1402–1415.
CSmH, CU–B, DLC, MiU, NjPT, NN, OCu, UHi, ULA, UPB, WaU

7767. ———. Oregon Missions and travels over the Rocky Mountains, in 1845–46. By Father P. J. De Smet, of the Society of Jesus. New-York, Published by Edward Dunigan, MDCCCXLVII.
xxii [13]–408p. plates, ports., fold. map. 18cm.
Added illustrated title page.
Encounters Mormons on Niobrara River and at Winter Quarters while descending the Missouri River, 1846, p. 340–341.
Same in French: Missions de l'Oregon et voyages aux Montagnes Rocheuses, aux sources de la Bolombie . . . Gand, Impr. & lith. de Ve Van der Schelden [1848].
CU–B, DLC
Same under title: Missions de l'Oregon et voyages dans les Montagnes Rocheuses en 1845 et 1846. . . . Paris, Poussielgue-Rusard: [etc., etc.] 1848.
CU–B, DLC
Same under title: Voyages dan l'Amérique Septtentrionale, Orégon . . . 3. ed. soigneusement cor. et augm. de notes d'un portrait et d'une carte. Bruxelles, M Closson et Cie [etc., etc.] 1874.
CU–B, DLC
W–C 141
CSmH, CtY, CU–B, DLC

7768. ———. Western missions and missionaries; a series of letters by Rev. P. J. de Smet . . . New York, James B. Kirker, 1863.
532p. 19½cm.
"The Mormons," p. 390–397.
UHi

7769. Smiles, Samuel, Jr. A boy's voyage round the world, including a residence in Victoria, and a journey by rail across North America. Ed. by Samuel Smiles . . . London, J. Murray, 1871.
1p.l. [vii]–xv, 304p. illus., maps. 18cm.
Journey east across Utah by railroad, 1871, p. 264–268. Mention of Mormon fortifications in Echo Canyon, 1857.
Also published under title: Round the world . . . New York, Harper, 1872. CU–B
CU–B

7769a. Smith, Adelaide. Womanhood and polygamy. New York City, Woman's Home Missionary Society, Methodist Episcopal Church [n.d.]
[4]p. 16cm.
USlC

7770. Smith, Alexander H. Polygamy; was it an original tenet of the Church of Jesus Christ of Latter Day Saints? [Plano, Ill., Reorganized Church of Jesus Christ of Latter Day Saints, 187–]
9 [1]p. (No. 16)
On verso of p. 9: Kirtland Temple suit.
Sabin 82325
IWW, MH, NjP, NN, USlC

7771. ———. (same) Plano, Ill., Published by the Reorganized Church of Jesus Christ of Latter Day Saints [n.d.]
9[1]p. 22cm. (No. 16)
On verso of p. 9: Epitome of the faith and doctrines of the Reorganized Church of Latter Day Saints.
USlC

7772. ———. (same) Plano, Ill., Published by the Reorganized Church of Jesus Christ of Latter Day Saints [n.d.]
9 [1]p. 22cm. (No. 16)
On verso of p. 9: No. 4. Epitome of the faith and doctrines of the Reorganized Church of Latter Day Saints.
USlC

7773. ———. (same) Plano, Ill., Published by the Reorganized Church of Jesus Christ of Latter Day Saints [n.d.]
9 [1]p. 19½cm. (No. 16)
On verso of p. 9: Advertisement for *The True Latter Day Saints' Herald.*
USlC

7774. ———. (same) Plano, Ill., Published by the Reorganized Church of Jesus Christ of Latter Day Saints [n.d.]
9p. 21½cm. (No. 16)
Variant printing.
NN, USlC

7775. ———. (same) [Lamoni, Ia., Reorganized Church of Jesus Christ of Latter Day Saints, 187–]
9 [1]p. 23cm. (No. 16)
Verso p. 9: No. 4: Epitome of faith and doctrines of the Reorganized Church of Jesus Christ of Latter Day Saints.
CU–B, MH, MoInRC, UPB, USlC

7775a. Smith, Alice (Kimball). Sketch of the life of Amanda Trimble Gheen Kimball. [Salt Lake City, Deseret News, 1904?]
7[1]p. port. 22cm.
USlC

7776. Smith, Arthur M. The Church of Christ (Temple Lot); a brief history of the origin of the Church and some of the differences between it and other factions of the restoration. [Independence, Mo., Board of Publication, Church of Christ, n.d.]
[8]p. 22cm.
UPB

7777. ———. Temple lot deed. A complete record of all legal transfers of that interesting spot of ground known as the Temple Lot. Ava, Mo. [after 1906]
13p. fold. map. 21cm.
USIC

7778. Smith, Charles H. The Mormonites: Their origin, history, & pretensions; being an exposure of the blasphemous doctrines of the Latter-day Saints; the deception and falsehood practised upon ignorant emigrants — specimens of their hymns of praise to Joseph Smith; and the ridiculous absurdities of the Book of Mormon; with a notice of their recent sufferings in America, through their own violence and folly. By Charles H. Smith. Bristol, Mathews, Brothers . . . 1849.
12p. 17cm.
Sabin 82390
NN, USIC

7779. Smith, Clark. Mystery and crime in the land of the Ute: an expose of Mormonism . . . Cornelius, Ore., T. R. Cornelius Printing Office, 1878.
48p. 19cm.
CtY, CU–B, DLC

7780. Smith, David Asael, *compiler.* Suggestions for Book of Mormon lecture; with quotations from leading archeologists and historians. Comp. by Bishop David A. Smith . . . Independence, Mo., Zion's Printing and Publishing Company. Published by the Missions of the Church of Jesus Christ of Latter Day Saints [193–]
106p. 18cm.
NN, USIC

7781. Smith, David Hyrum. At last; an illustrated poem by David H. Smith. Lamoni, Ia., Herald Publishing House [n.d.]
[16]l. plates. 20cm.
An RLDS poem concerning the work of the church.
MoInRC

7782. ———. The Bible versus polygamy by David H. Smith. [Plano, Ill.?] Published by the Reorganized Church of Jesus Christ of Latter Day Saints [1870?]
14p. 23cm. (No. 12)
Includes truths by three witnesses and epitome of faith.
Sabin 82429
CSmH, CtY, ICHi, MH, MoInRC, NN, UPB, USI, USIC

7783. ———. (same) Plano, Ill., Published by the Reorganized Church of Jesus Christ of Latter Day Saints [n.d.]
14p. 22cm. (No. 12)
UPB, USIC

7784. ———. (same) [Lamoni, Ia.] Published by the Reorganized Church of Jesus Christ of Latter Day Saints [191–]
14p. 21cm. (No. 16)
Includes *Truths by three witnesses* and *Epitome of the faith and doctrines of the Reorganized Church . . .*
IWW, MoInRC, NN, UPB, USIC

7785. ———. (same) [Lamoni, Ia.?] Published by the Reorganized Church of Jesus Christ of Latter Day Saints [n.d.]
14 [2]p. 23cm. (No. 12)
Includes: No. 41, *The Gospel,* and No. 4, *Epitome of the faith and doctrines of the Reorganized Church . . .*
USIC

7786. ———. (same) [Lamoni, Iowa?] Published by the Reorganized Church of Jesus Christ of Latter Day Saints [n.d]
14 [2]p. 22cm. (No. 12)
Includes: No. 4, *Epitome of the faith and doctrines of the Reorganized Church . . .* and *Kirtland Temple suit* on the last two pages.
USIC

7787. ———. (same) Lamoni, Ia., Herald Publishing House [n.d.]
40p. 21cm.
CU–B, NjP, UPB

7788. ———. (same, in Danish) Bibelen om polygami. Aalborg, 1877.
16p.
Schmidt

7789. ———. Hesperis: a book of poems. By David H. Smith. Plano, Ill., Printed at Herald Steam Book and Job Office, 1875.
viii, 194p. 18cm.
RLDS poetry.
MoInRC, NjP, RPB, USIC

7790. ———. Hymn by David Hyrum Smith. [Plano, Ill., 1865?]
[13]p. 21cm.
MoInRC

7791. Smith, E. Wesley. I na hoahanau o ka Ekalesia o Iesu Kristo o ka Poe Hoano o na la hope nei, ma ka Misiona o Hawaii. By E. Wesley Smith and William M. Waddoups. [n.p., 1919]
4p. 24cm.
Published shortly after the dedication of the Hawaiian Temple in 1919. Instructs the members concerning temple work and how they should prepare themselves before coming.
Title in English: Brethern of the church.
UPB

7792. Smith, Elbert A. All Brighamite roads lead to polygamy. Lamoni, Ia., Herald Publishing House [n.d.]
8p. 21cm.
MH, MoInRC, NjP, NN, UPB, USlC

———. The Angel message tracts. [By Elbert A. Smith and others] *See Reorganized Church of Jesus Christ of Latter Day Saints.*

7793. ———. "Baptism," Independence, Mo., Reorganized Church of Jesus Christ of Latter Day Saints [192–]
[8]p. 15cm. (The busy man's tract)
USlC

7794. ———, *compiler.* The church in court. Compiled and arranged by Elbert A. Smith. Lamoni, Ia., Herald Publishing House [1911?]
15p. 18½cm. (No. 605)
"Decisions of United States and Canadian courts affecting the standing of the Reorganized Church of Jesus Christ of Latter Day Saints."
CSmH, IWW, MH, MoInRC, UHi, ULA, UPB, USl, USlC

7795. ———. (same) Lamoni, Ia., Herald Publishing House [n.d.]
15p. 17½cm.
Variant edition.
USlC

7796. ———. (same) Lamoni, Ia., Herald Publishing House [n.d.]
15p. 17½cm. (No. 1151)
USlC

7797. ———. (same) Independence, Mo., Herald Publishing House [n.d.]
15p. 19cm. (No. 1241)
MoInRC, NjP, UPB

7798. ———. Corner stones of the Utah church. Lamoni, Ia., Herald Publishing House [189–]
19 [1]p. 20cm. (No. 450)
CSmH, ICHi, MH, MoInRC, NN, UHi, UPB, USl, USlC

7799. ———. (same) [Independence, Mo.] Reorganized Church of Jesus Christ of Latter Day Saints [n.d.]
19p. 20cm.
CU–B, NjP

7800. ———. (same) Lamoni, Ia., Herald Publishing House [n.d.]
19 [1]p. 18cm. (No. 1182)
NjP, UPB

7801. ———. (same, in German) Ecksteine der Utahkirche von Elbert A. Smith. Herausgegeben von der Reorganisierten Kirche Jesu Christi der Heiligen der Letzten Tage (Hauptstz: Independence, Mo.) Ber. Staaten von Nord-Amerika. Bernburg a. Saale, 1922.
12p. 18½cm.
UPB

7802. ———. Duties of branch officers. By Elbert A. Smith. Lamoni, Ia., Herald Publishing House, 1913.
43p. 17cm.
MoInRC

7803. ———. "Faith." Independence, Mo., Reorganized Church of Jesus Christ of Latter Day Saints [192–]
8p. 15cm. (The busy man's tract)
USlC

7804. ———. De Glorie der Laatste Dagen door Elbert A. Smith . . . Rotterdam, Utigegeven door de Gereorganiseerde Kerk van Jezus Christus van de Heiligen der Laatste Dagen, Holland [n.d.]
37p. 18½cm.
Title in English: The splendor of the last days.
UPB

7805. ———. "The great restoration," by Elbert A. Smith. Reorganized Church of Jesus Christ of Latter Day Saints. Independence, Mo., Herald Publishing House [192–]
12p. 15cm. (The busy man's tract)
MoInRC, NN, USlC

7806. ———. Hesperis; or, Poems by father and son; Book one: The transient guest, and other poems, by Elbert A. Smith; Book two: Song of endless life, and other poems, by David H. Smith. [Illustrations by Elbert A. Smith] Lamoni, Ia. [Published by Herald Publishing House] 1911.
3p.l. [7]–265p.
CSmH, MoInRC, NjP

7807. ———. "In the beginning God created," and three other radio sermons, by President Elbert A. Smith. [Independence, Mo., Published and Distributed by Publishing Department, Reorganized Church of Jesus Christ of Latter Day Saints, 1926?]
[3]–61p. 16cm.
Cover-title.
CSmH, MoInRC, NjP, NN

7808. ———. Joe Pine [by] Elbert A. Smith. Illustrated by Paul N. Craig. Lamoni, Ia., Herald Publishing House, 1916.
2p.l. [9]–351 [1]p. 20cm.
DLC, MoInRC, USlC

SMITH, E. A.

7809. ———. "The laying on of hands." Independence, Mo., Reorganized Church of Jesus Christ of Latter Day Saints [192–]
8p. 15cm. (The busy man's tract)
USlC

7810. ———. Man's free agency. [Independence, Mo., Herald Publishing House, 1924?]
24p. 19cm.
Lecture delivered before the priesthood of Zion in the lower auditorium of the Stone Church at Independence, Mo., Sunday afternoon, January 8, 1922.
MoInRC

7811. ———. The minister who was different. [Lamoni, Herald Publishing House, n.d.]
122p. illus. 19cm.
Story of conversion through example.
Under cover-title: The Two Story Book with "An instrument in His hands" by Mary Leland Carter.
CU–B, MoInRC, NjP

7812. ———. (same) Independence, Mo., Herald Publishing House, 1928.
80p. illus., port. 20cm.
MoKU

7813. ———. An open letter to the clergy. By Elbert A. Smith of the First Presidency, Reorganized Church of Jesus Christ of Latter Day Saints. Lamoni, Ia., Reorganized Church of Jesus Christ of Latter Day Saints [1907?]
17p. 17cm.
CSmH, IWW, MoInRC, USlC

7814. ———. (same) Lamoni, Ia., Reorganized Church of Jesus Christ of Latter Day Saints [1914?]
14p. 20cm.
IWW, MoInRC

7815. ———. (same) Lamoni, Ia., Independence, Mo., Reorganized Church of Jesus Christ of Latter Day Saints [1915?]
20p. 15cm.
"We believe" on the verso of front and rear cover.
MoInRC, UHi, UPB

7816. ———. A plea for the golden rule. A review of certain portions of the book entitled: Mormonism, The Islam of America, by Reverend Bruce Kinney. Lamoni, Ia., 1913.
40p. 19cm.
MoInRC, NjP, UPB, USlC

7817. ———. Prophetic warnings in modern revelation. Independence, Mo., Herald Publishing House [n.d.]
55p. map. 20cm.
MoInRC, NjP, UPB, USlC

7817a. ———. Remember Cumorah, a pageant in four acts, written in celebration of the one hundredth anniversary of the coming forth of the Book of Mormon, Sept. 22, 1827. Independence, Mo., Reorganized Church of Jesus Christ of Latter Day Saints, 1927.
32p. 20cm.
MoInRC

7818. ———. "Repentance." Independence, Mo., Reorganized Church of Jesus Christ of Latter Day Saints [192–]
8p. 15cm (The busy man's tract)
USlC

7819. ———. "The Resurrection and the eternal judgment." Independence, Mo., Reorganized Church of Jesus Christ of Latter Day Saints [192–]
8p. 15cm. (The busy man's tract)
USlC

7820. ———. ¿Sabe Vd.? Por E. A. Smith. Lamoni, Ia., Herald Publishing House [n.d.]
[4]p. 21½cm.
RLDS church beliefs, including the stand on polygamy.
Title in English: Do you know?
MoInRC

7821. ———. The Spalding romance theory reviewed. Lamoni, Ia., Herald Publishing House [n.d.]
15p. 19cm.
MoInRC

7822. ———. Square blocks, and other sermons and articles, by Elbert A. Smith . . . Independence, Mo., Herald Publishing House, 1921.
4p.l., 11–475p. 20cm.
MoInRC, UHi

7823. ———. Timbers for the temple. A story of old Nauvoo. In days of her glory. By Elbert A. Smith. Illustrations from photographs. Independence, Mo., Herald Publishing House, 1922.
4p.l. [9]–302p. 20cm.
A novel of the Mormons in Nauvoo, first published in *Autumn Leaves*, 1917–1918.
MoInRC

7824. ———. The True philosophy of church government. [Independence, Mo.? 1924?]
55p. 19½cm.
Reprint from the *Saints' Herald*, 1924.
Concerning supreme directional control.
MoInRC, NjP

7825. ———. Utah Mormon polygamy; its belief and practice, by Elbert A. Smith . . . Independence, Mo., Herald Publishing House [193–]
32p. 19cm.
MoInRC, NjP, NN, USlC

7826. ———. W. E. La Rue versus the courts. [n.p., 1919?]
8p. 19cm.
RLDS internal difficulties.
MoInRC

7827. ———. What did Jesus preach? Lamoni, Ia., Reorganized Church of Jesus Christ of Latter Day Saints [191–]
18p. 17½cm.
IWW, MoInRC, USlC

7828. ———. What Latter Day Saints believe about God, by Elbert A. Smith. Independence, Mo., Reorganized Church of Jesus Christ of Latter Day Saints, Herald Publishing House [19 - -]
54p. 19cm.
CU–B, NjP

7829. ———. (same) Independence, Mo., Reorganized Church of Jesus Christ of Latter Day Saints. [n.d.]
60p. 19½cm.
Variant pagination and additional material.
MoInRC, UPB

7830. ———. Why a First Presidency in the Church? Independence, Mo., Reorganized Church of Jesus Christ of Latter Day Saints [n.d.]
31p. 20cm.
MoInRC, NjP

7831. ———. Zion builder's sermons. A series of sermons addressed to the young people of the Church. Independence, Mo., Reorganized Church of Jesus Christ of Latter Day Saints, 1921.
116p. 20cm.
MoInRC, NjP

7832. Smith, Elbert H. Ma-ka-tai-me-she-kia-kiak; or, Black Hawk, and Scenes in the West. A national poem in six cantos. Embracing an account of the life and exploits of this celebrated chieftain. By a Western Tourist. New York, Edward Kearny, 1848.
viii [9]–299p. port. 19½cm.
Several verses in canto, one devoted to Mormonism, travels, etc., p. 12–15, 65.
Another edition: 1849. UU
Sabin 82462 (1849)
CSmH, DLC, NjP, ULA, UU

7833. Smith, Eliza Roxey (Snow). Bible questions and answers for children, By E. R. S. S. Salt Lake City Juvenile Instructor Office, 1881.
120p. 17½cm.
MH, UHi, UPB, USlC, UU

7834. ———. (same) 2d ed. Salt Lake City, Juvenile Instructor Office, 1883.
2p.l. [5]–120p. 19cm.
CU–B, MH, UHi, USlC, WHi

7835. ———. Biography and family record of Lorenzo Snow, one of the Twelve Apostles of the Church of Jesus Christ of Latter-day Saints. Written and compiled by his sister, Eliza R. Snow Smith . . . Salt Lake City, Deseret News Company, Printers, 1884.
xvi, 581p. 2 port. 23½cm.
"Genealogies," p. 488–495.
Howes S591
CSmH, CtY, CU–B, DLC, NjP, NN, UHi, UPB, USl, USlC, UU

7836. ———. Decision of the Supreme Court of the United States in the Reynolds Case. Salt Lake City, 1879.
Broadside. 24×18cm.
"From the *Deseret News*," January 21, 1879.
UHi

——— (same) *See Musser, Amos Milton. Suttee and polygamy.*

7837. ———. Hymns and songs: selected from various authors, for the Primary Associations of the children of Zion, by Eliza R. Snow. Salt Lake City, Deseret News Printing and Publishing Establishment, 1880.
128p. 12cm.
67 hymns without music.
First edition (stereotype)
CU–B, DLC, NjP, NNUT, OO, UPB, USlC, UU

7838. ———. (same) 2d ed. Salt Lake City, The Deseret News Co., 1888.
128p. 12½cm.
NjP, UHi, USlC

7839. ———. (same) 3d ed. Salt Lake City, Deseret News Publishing Co., 1893.
128p. 12cm.
Cover-title: Children's Primary hymn book.
IU, USlC

———. Jubilee songs. *See Jubilee songs.*

7840. ———. Lines on the assassination of Generals Joseph Smith & Hyrum Smith, First Presidents of the Church of the Latter-day Saints, who were massacred by a mob in Carthage, Hancock County, Illinois, on the twenty-seventh June, 1844. By Miss Eliza R. Snow. [n.p.] J. Heap, Printer. [1844?]
Broadside. 24×19cm.
Text in two columns, within an ornamental border.
Dated Nauvoo, July 1, 1844, it was published in the *Times and Seasons* for July 1, 1844, under title: "The assassination of Gen'ls Joseph Smith and Hyrum Smith . . ." and republished in the *Millennial Star* of September, 1844, under the same title as the broadside.
USlC

7841. ———. O my Father. [Salt Lake City, Deseret Sunday School Union, n.d.]
[1]l. 16½×11cm.
"A favorite Latter-day Saint hymn written . . . under the title of "My Father in Heaven," in the City of Joseph (Nauvoo) Hancock county, Illinois, October, 1845."
On back of card: Articles of faith of the Church of Jesus Christ of Latter-day Saints.
WHi

7842. ———. O my father. Written by Eliza Snow, as sung by Robert C. Easton. Illustrated by John Hafen. New York, Chicago, Copyrighted and Published by Ben E. Rich [and] German E. Ellsworth [1909?]
[17]p. col. illus. music. 26½cm.
2p. of music.
MH, UHi, UPB, UU

7843. ———. Poems, religious, historical, and political. By Eliza R. Snow . . . Vol. I. Liverpool, F. D. Richards; [etc., etc.] 1856.
viii, 270p., [1]l. 18½cm.
Mormon poetry.
CSmH, DLC, MH, NjP, NjPT, NN, RPB, UHi, UPB, USlC, UU, ViU, WHi

7844. ———. (same) Also two articles in prose. By Eliza R. Snow . . . Comp. by the author. Vol. II. Salt Lake City, Printed at the Latter-day Saints' Printing and Publishing Establishment, 1877.
iv, 284p. port. 18cm.
Articles entitled: "My country. — a lamentation," and "Good society."
CSmH, CU-B, DLC, MH, NjPT, NN, ULA, UPB, USlC, UU, WHi

7845. ———. Recitations for the Primary Associations in poetry, dialogues and prose. Book No. 1. Adapted to the capacity of members from the age of four to ten years. By E. R. Snow Smith. Salt Lake City, Deseret News Company Printers and Publishers, 1882.
2p.l., 6–183p. 15cm.
CSmH, CU-B, ULA, USlC

7846. ———. (same) Salt Lake City, Deseret News Company, 1891.
2p.l., 6–183p. 15cm.
CSmH, NjP, RPB, UPB, USlC, UU

7847. ———. (same) Book No. 2. Adapted to the capacities of members from the age of ten to fifteen years. By Eliza R. Snow Smith. Salt Lake City, Deseret News Company, 1882.
2p.l., 6–200p. 15cm.
NjP, UHi, UPB, USlC, UU

7848. ———. Time and change: A poem in blank verse. Also two odes, one for the sons of liberty, the other for the Fourth of July. By Miss Eliza R. Snow. Nauvoo, Ill., Printed by E. Robinson, 1841.
18p. 14cm.
Reprinted in her *Poems, religious, historical and political.*
Byrd 662, Sabin 85507
NNHi

7849. ———. Tune book for the Primary Associations of the children of Zion, by Eliza R. Snow. Salt Lake City, Printed at the Juvenile Instructor Office, 1880.
2p.l., 40p. music. 17×22cm.
USlC, UU

Smith, Emma (Hale). A collection of sacred hymns. *See Church of Jesus Christ of Latter-day Saints. Hymnal. English. 1835.*

7850. Smith, Franklin Campbell. Early religious services in Wyoming. Laramie, Laramie Printing Co., 1926.
72p. 19½cm.
Includes church services of the Mormon pioneers.
NjP, UPB

7851. Smith, Frederick Dumont. Book of a hundred bears. Chicago, Rand McNally & Company, 1909.
2p.l., 5–223p. illus., plates. 19½cm.
"Salt Lake and the Mormons," p. 55–75. The Mormon church did not now differ much from the others.
Other editions: 2d ed. 1909. NjP, USlC; 3d ed. 1909. USlC
UPB

7852. Smith, Frederick Madison. An address to the priesthood. Lamoni, Ia., Herald Publishing House [1916?]
16p. 20cm.
An address given at the Logan, Iowa, reunion, September, 1916.
MoInRC, NjP

7853. ———. Address to the Seventy-first general conference of the Reorganized Church of Jesus Christ of Latter Day Saints. By President Frederick M. Smith. Delivered at Independence, Missouri, April 6, 1926. [Independence, Mo., Herald Publishing House, 1926?]
18 [1]p. 19½cm.
Supreme directional control.
CU-B, MoInRC, NjP, UPB

7854. ———. Appeal of Frederick M. Smith, one of the Presidency of the "Reorganized Church" to Pres. Joseph F. Smith for the unlimited use of the meeting houses of the Latter-day Saints and his reply. [n.p.] 1905.

12p. 16½cm.
Cover-title.
Joseph F. Smith denies usage.
MoInRC, NjP, UHi, ULA, UPB, USlC

7854a. ———. Changes and innovation. An Open Letter. Independence, Mo., Reorganized Church of Jesus Christ of Latter Day Saints. [n.d.]
14p. 19½cm.
NjP

7855. ———. (same) Enlarged reprint. Independence, Mo., Reorganized Church of Jesus Christ of Latter Day Saints [192–]
20p. 20cm.
Supreme directional control.
MoInRC

7856. ———. The Church in relation to world problems. Opening address to General Conference, April 6, 1920. [Independence, Mo., Ensign Publishing House, 1920]
23 [1]p. 19cm.
USlC

7857. ———. (same) Independence, Mo., Reorganized Church of Jesus Christ of Latter Day Saints [Publicity Department] 1921.
24p. 18½cm.
MoInRC, NjP, USlC

7858. ———. Essays and studies; prose selections for college reading, chosen and arranged by Frederick M. Smith. Boston, Houghton Mifflin & Co. [c1922]
351p. 20cm.
Moral essays.
MoInRC

7859. ———. General epistle to the Saints. Independence, Herald Publishing House, 1929.
4p. 20½cm.
Supreme directional control.
MoInRC

7860. ———. The higher powers of man. By Frederick M. Smith, Ph.D. With introduction by Dr. G. Stanley Hall. Lamoni, Ia., The Herald Publishing House, 1918.
232p. 20cm.
RLDS doctrine.
CU–B, MoInRC, NjP, USlC

7861. ———. The making of a steward. By Frederick M. Smith and Albert Carmichael. Independence, Mo., Reorganized Church of Jesus Christ of Latter Day Saints, 1929.
7p. 15½cm.
MoInRC

7862. ———. A message from the seed of Joseph, the seer. [n.p., 1905?]
6p. 19cm.
Apparently written in Salt Lake City, July 27, 1905.
MoInRC, NjP

7863. ———. A message to the young people of the Church. [Independence, Mo., Herald Publishing House] 1922.
20p. 19cm.
MoInRC

7864. ———. Our social ideals. Opening address delivered at General Conference, Sunday, October 1, 1922, Independence, Missouri. Independence, Mo., Reorganized Church of Jesus Christ of Latter Day Saints, 1923.
13p. 19cm. (No. 1312)
CU–B, MoInRC, NjP, UPB, USlC, UU

7865. ———. Priesthood and the financial law, know the law, live the law, teach the law. [n.p., n.d.]
16p. 20cm.
MoInRC

7866. ———. Redemption of Zion explained. [n.p., 1905?]
4p. 21cm.
Report of an address delivered in Ogden Tabernacle . . . Jan. 23. Reprinted from the *Ogden Standard-Examiner*.
MoInRC

7867. ———. Remember Cumorah, 1827–1927, one hundredth anniversary of the date when the Book of Mormon records were given into the keeping of the church [Independence? 1927?]
3p. illus. 24cm.
MoInRC

7868. ———. Statement of President F. M. Smith on the joint council document on church government. [Lamoni, Ia., 191–]
6p. 19cm.
MoInRC

7869. ———. The sublimation of labor. Sermon by President Frederick M. Smith at the Stone Church, Independence, Missouri, April 11, 1926. [Independence, Mo., 1926]
15p. 18cm.
MoInRC, NN, USlC

7870. ———. Views on revelation. [Independence, Mo.] Reorganized Church of Jesus Christ of Latter Day Saints, 1920.
3p. 18cm.
Speech given at Independence Stake Conference, October 6, 1918. Reprinted from *Zion's Ensign*, Nov. 7, 1918.
MoInRC, NjP

SMITH, G. A., 1817–1875

7871. Smith, George Albert, 1817–1875. Correspondence of Palestine tourists; comprising a series of letters by G. A. Smith, L. Snow, P. A. Schettler, and E. R. Snow, of Utah. Mostly written while traveling in Europe, Asia and Africa, in the years 1872 and 1873. Salt Lake City, Deseret News Steam Printing Establishment, 1875.
xiv, 386p. port. 22½cm.
Trip to Palestine to dedicate it for the return of the Jews.
CSmH, CtY, CU–B, MH, NjP, NN, UHi, UPB, USlC, UU, WHi

———. Discourses on celestial marriage. *See Pratt, Orson.*

7871a. ———. Historical address Delivered by President Geo. A. Smith in the New Tabernacle, October 8th and 9th 1868. Reported by David W. Evans. [Salt Lake City, 1868]
[4]p. 41½cm.
At head of title: Supplement to The Deseret News. Salt Lake City, October 28, 1868.
UPB

7872. ———. The rise, progress, and travels of the Church of Jesus Christ of Latter-day Saints, being a series of answers to questions, including the revelation on celestial marriage, and a brief account of the settlement of Salt Lake Valley, with interesting statistics, by President George A. Smith . . . Salt Lake City, Printed at the Deseret News Office, 1869.
49p. 22½cm.
Howes S595
CSmH, CtY, CU–B, DLC, ICN, NjP, NN, UPB, USlC, UU

7873. ———. (same) 2d ed. Salt Lake City, Printed at the Deseret News Office, 1872.
71p. tables. 22cm.
Variant cover which reads: Second edition revised and enlarged.
Howes S595, Sabin 82585
CSmH, CtY, CU–B, DLC, MH, MoInRC, NjP, NN, UHi, ULA, UPB, USlC, UU, WHi

7874. ———. (same) 1st English, from the 2d American ed., rev. and enl. Liverpool, Published by A. Carrington; London, Sold at the Latter-day Saints' Book Depot, and by all booksellers, 1873.
70p. [1]l. 23cm.
Howes S595
CSmH, CtY, CU–B, DLC, MH, NN, UHi, UPB, USlC

7875. Smith, George Washington. A student's history of Illinois. Carbondale, Ill., For the author, 1910 [c1906]
vii, 545p. illus., ports., maps. 20cm.
Chap. 37, "The story of the Mormons." Background information and Illinois history.
USlC

7876. Smith, Gerrit. Speeches of Gerrit Smith in Congress. New-York, Mason Brothers, 1855.
vi [3] 10–423p. 19½cm.
"Speech on polygamy, May 4, 1854." Polygamy hardly mentioned, and Mormons alluded to only once.
Another edition: 1856. USlC
NjP, USlC

7877. Smith, Heman Conoman. Can belief alone save? [Lamoni, Ia., Herald Publishing House, n.d.]
12p. 20cm. (No. 1212)
MoInRC

7878. ———. Duplicity exposed. Lamoni, Ia., Herald Publishing House [n.d.]
14p. 19cm.
Review of the tracts: *Refutation of Cornerstones of Reorganization*, and *Reorganization weighed.*
CU–B, IWW, MH, MoInRC, NN, ULA, UU

7879. ———. The factions on polygamy and spiritual wifery. Lamoni, Ia., Reorganized Church of Jesus Christ of Latter Day Saints [1900?]
10p. 14cm. (No. 20)
Signed: February 21, 1900.
USlC

7880. ———. (same) By Elder Heman C. Smith. Lamoni, Ia., Herald Publishing House [1900?]
10p. 16½cm. (No. 30)
Caption-title.
CSmH, CtY, CU–B, UHi, UPB, USlC, UU

7881. ———. Husbands, love your wives. Lamoni, Ia., Herald Publishing House, 1894.
16p. 15cm. (Daughters of Zion Leaflets. No. 8)
Supplement to the *Saints' Herald.*
MoInRC, USlC

———. The Reply. *See Kelley, Edmund Levi.*

7881a. ———. Responsibility of parents. Lamoni, Iowa, Herald Publishing House, Reorganized Church of Jesus Christ of Latter Day Saints, 1894.
15p. 15cm. (Daughters of Zion leaflets. No. 6)
Supplement to the *Saints' Herald.*
USlC

7882. ———. True succession in church presidency of the Church of Jesus Christ of Latter Day Saints, being a reply to Elder B. H. Roberts on "Succession in the presidency of the church." Lamoni, Ia., Board of Publication of the Reorganized Church of Jesus Christ of Latter Day Saints, 1898.
1p.l., 167p. 18cm.
CtY, CU, DLC, MoInRC, NN, UHi, USlC, UU

7883. ———. (same) 2d ed. Lamoni, Ia., Board of Publication of the Reorganized Church of Jesus Christ of Latter Day Saints, 1900.
1p.l., 167p. 17½cm.
UHi

7884. ———. (same) 2d ed. Lamoni, Ia., Board of Publication of the Reorganized Church of Jesus Christ of Latter Day Saints, 1900.
1p.l., 234p. 17½cm.
Appendix to *True Succession in Church Presidency* by Elder Heman C. Smith, adding information to refute B. H. Robert's 2d edition of *Succession in the Presidency*, p. 161–227.
CSmH, DLC, MoInRC, OClWHi, USl, USlC, WHi

7885. ———. (same) 3d ed. Lamoni, Ia., Board of Publication of the Reorganized Church of Jesus Christ of Latter Day Saints, 1908.
1p.l., 234p. 20cm.
CU-B, MoInRC, NjP

7885a. ——— (same) 4th ed. Lamoni, Iowa, Board of Publication of the Reorganized Church of Jesus Christ of Latter Day Saints, 1912.
234p. 20cm.
USlC

7886. ———. The truth defended; or, A reply to Elder D. H. Bays' Doctrines and dogmas of Mormonism. By Elder Heman C. Smith . . . Lamoni, Ia., Board of Publication of the Reorganized Church of Jesus Christ of Latter Day Saints, 1901.
241p. plates, facsim. 19cm.
DLC, MoInRC, NN, UHi, UPB, USlC

7887. ———. (same) 3d ed. Lamoni, Ia. Board of Publication of the Reorganized Church of Jesus Christ of Latter Day Saints, 1906.
241p. plates, facsim. 19cm.
ULA, USlC

7888. ———. (same) 4th ed. [Lamoni, Ia., Board of Publication Reorganized Church of Jesus Christ of Latter Day Saints] 1908.
241p. plate, facsim. 19½cm.
IWW, MoInRC, UPB

7889. ———. Was Joseph Smith a polygamist? By Elder Heman C. Smith. Lamoni, Ia., Herald Publishing House [1899?]
16p. 17cm. (No. 26)
Caption-title.
CU-B, MoInRC, NN, OClWHi, UPB, USl, UU

7890. ———. (same) Lamoni, Ia., Herald Publishing House [n.d.]
16p. 17cm.
Variant printing.
USlC

7891. ———. Which is the church? Independence, Mo., Ensign Publishing House [1898]
59p. front. 15½cm. (The Gospel Banner series. V.5, No. 1)
MoInRC, USl

7892. Smith, Henry Perry, *editor.* History of Broome county [New York] with illustrations and biographical sketches of some of its prominent men and pioneers. Edited by H. P. Smith. Syracuse, New York, D. Mason and Co., 1885.
630p. illus., ports. 28½cm.
In the history of Colesville, N.Y. it was claimed to be in the place where "Joe Smith" first began his ministration.
CSmH, DLC

Smith, Hyrum M. The Doctrine and Covenants. *See Doctrine and Covenants. English.* [several editions]

7893. Smith, Hyrum O. Another witness. Independence, Mo., Ensign Publishing House, 1904.
24p. 17cm. (The Gospel Banner. V.12, No. 3)
RLDS witness.
MoInRC

7894. ———. The Book of Mormon evaluated. By Hyrum O. Smith. Independence, Mo., Reorganized Church of Jesus Christ of Latter Day Saints [n.d.]
[3]–59p. 19cm.
MoInRC, NjP, UPB

7895. ———. Book of Mormon talks by Orion [*pseud.*] Lamoni, Ia., Reorganized Church of Jesus Christ of Latter Day Saints, 1902.
2p.l. [5]–187p. plates. 18cm. (Birth offering series. No. 4)
UPB

7896. ———. (same) 2d ed. Lamoni, Ia., Published by the Board of Publication of the Reorganized Church of Jesus Christ of Latter Day Saints, 1908.
2p.l. [5]–194p. 20cm. (Birth offering series. No. 4)
MoInRC, NjP, UPB, USlC

7897. ———. Marriage as taught and practiced by the Latter Day Saints. [Independence, Mo., Herald Publishing House, 1927]
16p. 15cm.
RLDS doctrine.
MoInRC, UPB, USlC

7898. ———. The necessity for a reorganization of the Church of Jesus Christ of Latter Day Saints. Lamoni, Ia., Herald Publishing House [189–]
43p. 16cm. (No. 18)
Caption-title.
CU-B, MH, NN, UHi, UPB, USl, UU, WHi

7899. ———. (same) Lamoni, Ia., Herald Publishing House [n.d.]
43p. 16cm.
Caption-title.
Edition lacks "No. 18."
UPB

7900. ———. Stewardship of behavior. By H. O. Smith. [Independence, Mo., Published and Distributed by the Herald Publishing House, n.d.]
11 [1]p. 16cm.
NN

7901. ———. Talks about Joseph Smith, by Orion [*pseud.*] Lamoni, Ia., Published by Board of Publication of the Reorganized Church of Jesus Christ of Latter Day Saints, 1909.
421p. 1 port. 20cm. (Birth offering series. No. 8)
[419]–421 "Birth offerings." List of contributors who financed the volume.
MoInRC, NBuG, NN, USlC

7902. ———. (same) Lamoni, Ia., Published by the Board of Publication of the Reorganized Church of Jesus Christ of Latter Day Saints, 1913.
421p. 19½cm. (Birth offering series. No. 8)
UHi

7903. ———. What shall I do to be saved? Independence, Mo., Ensign Publishing House, 1904.
32p. 16cm. (The Gospel Banner. V.12, No. 2)
RLDS doctrine of salvation.
MoInRC

7904. ———. Why I believe the Book of Mormon, an evening chat between two friends . . . Lamoni, Ia., Herald Publishing House [n.d.]
16p. 18cm. (No. 302)
MoInRC, NjP

7905. Smith, Isaac Monroe. Angelic ministrations in former and latter days. Independence, Mo., Ensign Publishing House, 1903.
23p. 16cm. (The Gospel Banner. V.10, No. 1)
RLDS doctrine
MoInRC

7906. ———. The atonement of Christ and the final destiny of man. By Elder Isaac M. Smith. [Lamoni, Herald Publishing House, 187–]
86p. 18½cm. (No. 17)
CtY, MoInRC, USlC

7907. ———. The Book of Mormon vindicated. Independence, Mo., Ensign Publishing House, 1898.
1p.l., 115p. 22½cm.
MoInRC, NjP

7908. ———. (same) 2d ed. Independence, Mo., Ensign Publishing House, 1900.
1p.l., 115p. port. 23cm.
NjP, USlC

7909. ———. (same) 2d ed. Independence, Mo., Ensign Publishing House, 1908.
1p.l., 115p. port. 23cm.
MoInRC, MoK, NjP

7910. ———. (same) 3d ed. Independence, Mo., Ensign Publishing House [1917]
1p.l., 115p. port. 23cm.
MoInRC, NjP

7911. ———. (same) 4th ed. Independence, Mo., Ensign Publishing House, 1923.
1p.l., 115p. port. 23cm.
MoInRC

7912. ———. Creed making, by Elder I. M. S. Lamoni Ia., Herald Publishing House [n.d.]
22p. 19cm. (No. 1161)
MoInRC, USlC

7913. ———. (same) Independence, Mo., Ensign Publishing House [192–]
22p. 18cm.
IWW, NjP

7914. ———. (same) Independence, Mo., Ensign Publishing House [n.d.]
22p. 19cm.
Variant printing.
MoInRC

7915. ———. (same) Independence, Mo., Ensign Publishing House [1902]
40p. 16cm. (The Gospel Banner. V.4, No. 3)
MoInRC

7916. ———. (same) Independence, Mo., Ensign Publishing House [n.d.]
40p. 15cm.
Variant of the above.
MoInRC

7917. ———. Save yourselves. Independence, Mo., Ensign Publishing House, 1899.
34p. 16cm. (The Gospel Banner. V.6, No. 3)
RLDS doctrine of Salvation.
MoInRC

7918. ———. Sign seekers. Independence, Mo., Ensign Publishing House, 1896.
32p. 16cm. (The Gospel Banner. V.3, No. 4)
MoInRC

7919. Smith, Israel A. Facts answered and facts analyzed by Bishop I. A. Smith and Bishop J. A. Becker. Independence, Mo., 1928.
124p. 19cm.
Supreme directional control.
MoInRC, NjP

7920. ———. Let the facts be known; a frank statement by Bishop Israel A. Smith setting out the history of the present controversy and telling some wholesome truths. [Independence, Mo.?] 1924.
30p. 19cm.
Cover-title.
"Reprinted from the *Saints' Herald*, August 6, 1924."
Supreme directional control.
MoInRC, NjP, UHi

7921. ———. The sacrament of the Christian marriage, as performed by the Reorganized Church. Independence, Mo., Reorganized Church of Jesus Christ of Latter Day Saints [n.d.]
8p. 19cm.
UPB, USIC

7922. Smith, James Hadden. . . . History of Chenango and Madison Counties, New York, with illustrations and biographical sketches of some of its prominent men and pioneers. By James H. Smith. Syracuse, New York, D. Mason and Co., 1880.
viii [9]–760 xxixp. illus., plates (1 double) ports. 29cm.
At head of title: 1784.
Includes a sketch of Mormonism in New York.
DLC, MWA, NjP, UPB

7923. Smith, James R. The message of the New Testament, by James R. Smith . . . written for the senior seminaries of the Church of Jesus Christ of Latter-day Saints under the direction of the Department of Education . . . Salt Lake City, Published for the Department of Education by the Deseret Book Company, 1930.
xiii, 461p. plates, maps. 22½cm.
Bibliography, p. [x]
Mormon viewpoint.
DLC, USIC, UU

7924. Smith, Job. An address to presidents of branches, officers, and saints generally of the Bedfordshire Conference of the Church of Jesus Christ of Latter-day Saints. By Elder Job Smith. [Bedford, 1852]
8p. 23cm.
Signed: Bedford, September 7th, 1852.
UPB, USIC

Smith, Joe H. *See Smith, Joseph H.*

7925. Smith, John L. Einige Worte an die Heiligen der letzten Tage, von J. L. Smith. Zürich, 1861.
19p. 16cm.
Signed: Basel, October 26, 1861.
Title in English: A few words to the Latter-day Saints.
USIC

7926. Smith, Joseph, 1805–1844. Articles of faith. [Salt Lake City, Deseret Sunday School Union, 1878]
[1]l, 10½×6½cm. in envelope, 18cm.
It has been suggested that the articles of faith might have been written by Orson Pratt at the instigation of Joseph Smith.
NN, WHi

7927. ———. (same) Salt Lake City, Deseret Sunday School Union, 1879.
[1]p. 19cm.
USIC

7928. ———. (same, under title) Articles of faith of the Church of Jesus Christ of Latter-day Saints. [Liverpool, Millennial Star Office, ca. 1880]
[2]p. 20cm.
On verso is a list of publications under title: God has again spoken.
UPB

7928a. ———. (same) [London, 1883?]
[2]p. 21½cm.
On verso is a statement as to which is the true church, and a list of London meetings of the church.
UPB

7929. ———. (same) Salt Lake City, Skelton Publishing Co. [1907?]
[2]p. 10cm.
Card.
USIC

7930. ———. (same) [Liverpool? Millennial Star Office? 1907?]
[2]p. 22cm.
Caption-title.
A missionary leaflet.
Includes a letter in cursive script explaining the purpose in leaving tract.
ICN, MH, NN

7931. ———. (same) [Liverpool, Millennial Star Office, n.d.]
[2]p. 15cm.
Variant edition.
CU-B, USIC

7932. ———. (same) Salt Lake City, Issued by the Deseret Sunday School Union [n.d.]
[2]p. 17½cm.
Song "O My Father" by Eliza R. Snow [Smith] on verso.
USIC

7933. ———. (same) [Salt Lake City? n.d.]
[1]p. 17½cm.
Verso blank.
USIC

7934. ———. (same) [Salt Lake City, Bureau of Information, n.d.]
[2]p. 21½cm.
USIC

SMITH, J., 1805–1844

7935. ———. (same) [Salt Lake City, The Deseret Book Co., n.d.]
[2]p. 10cm.
USlC

7936. ———. (same) [Oldham? n.d.]
[2]p. 22½cm.
Publicity for meetings at Oldham on verso.
USlC

7937. ———. (same) [Salt Lake City, Kinsman Publishing Company, n.d.]
12p. 15½cm.
Articles of faith, with quotations to augment them. It also includes an article entitled "polygamy and marriage."
USlC

7938. ———. (same, under title) Latter-day Saints' faith. [Liverpool, 1850?]
[2]p. 21½cm.
The fourteenth article of faith added, and others revised.
USlC

7939. ———. (same, in Dutch) Artikelen des geloofs van de Kerk van Jezus Christus van de Heiligen der Laatste Dagen. Amsterdam, J. W. F. Völker [1885?]
[2]p. 18½cm.
USlC

7940. ———. (same) [Rotterdam? n.d.]
[2]p. 22½cm.
Proofs of the *Book of Mormon* on verso.
USlC

7941. ———. (same) [n.p., n.d.]
[2]p. 23cm.
Missionary release with an invitation to attend meetings on the verso.
USlC

7942. ———. (same, in French) Articles de foi de l'Eglise de Jésus-Christ des Saints des derniers jours. [Berne, Buchdruckerei Steiger & Cie, 1895]
[2]p. 13cm.
Prices of books on verso.
USlC

7943. ———. (same, in German) Glaubensartikel der Kirche Jesu Christi der Heiligen der letzten Tage [Bern, 1882]
[2]p. 13cm.
UPB, USlC

7944. ———. (same) [Bern, 1893]
[2]p. 13cm.
USlC

7945. ———. (same) [Bern, Steiger & Cie, 1895]
[2]p. 13cm.
USlC

7946. ———. (same) [Leipzig, Druck von C. G. Röder, n.d.]
[1]p. 22½cm.
USlC

7947. ———. (same, in Greek) Iesous Christosen acher kounler maukattesleri kilisesinin akaiti [Naseri. F. F. Hintze. Istanbul, V. Minassian Matpasa, 1899]
4p. 18cm.
Caption-title.
UPB, USlC

7948. ———. (same, in Hawaiian) Na kumu Manaoio. O ka Ekalesia o Iesu Kristo o ka poe hoano o na la hope nei. [n.p., n.d.]
[1]p. 15½cm.
USlC

7949. ———. (same, in Tahitian) Te mau parau matamua no te faaroo o te Ekalesia a Iesu Mesia i te Feia mo'a i te mau mahona Hopea Nei. [Salt Lake City? Deseret News? 1895?]
[1]p. 13½cm.
UPB, USlC

7950. ———. (same, in Tongan) Koe gaahi tuutunni ni, oku tui ki ai e he Jioji a Jésu Kalaisi ae kau maonioni o e gaahi aho fakamui. [n.p., n.d.]
[2]p. 11½cm.
USlC

7951. ———. A brief history of Joseph Smith, the prophet, by himself. Salt Lake City, Deseret Sunday School Union, 1910.
[5]–63p. 17cm.
"Closing years" by Edward H. Anderson, p. 51–63.
See also his The Prophet Joseph Smith tells his own story.
Sabin 83235
CSmH, DLC, MH, OClWHi, UHi, UPB, USlC

7952. ———. Choice items on priesthood and the Adam-God doctrine as taught by Joseph Smith and his associates in the priesthood. [n.p., n.d.]
12p. 24½cm.
Extracts from Joseph Smith, Brigham Young, Heber C. Kimball, and others.
UPB

7953. ———. Correspondence between Joseph Smith, the Prophet, and Col. John Wentworth, editor of "The Chicago Democrat," and member of Congress from Illinois; Gen. James Arlington Bennet, of Arlington House, Long Island, and the Honorable John C. Calhoun, Senator from South Carolina, in which is given, a sketch of the life of Joseph Smith, the rise and progress of the Church of Latter Day Saints and their persecutions by the State of Missouri: with the peculiar views of Joseph Smith, in relation to political and religious matters generally; to which is added a concise account of the present state and prospects of the City of Nauvoo. New York, Published by John E. Page and L. R. Foster . . . J. W. Harrison, Printer, 1844.

16p. 22½cm.
Letter to John Wentworth written October 24, 1843.
Preface dated: New York, February, 1844.
In double columns.
Sabin 83236
CSmH, CtY, NN, USlC

7954. ———. Discourses delivered by Presidents Joseph Smith and Brigham Young on the relation of the "Mormons" to the government of the United States. Great Salt Lake City, Printed at the Office of the Deseret News [1855]
16p. 24½cm.
Sabin 83237
CtY, MH, NjP, RPB, USlC

7955. ———, *defendant.* Evidence taken on the trial of Mr. Smith before the Municipal Court of Nauvoo, on Saturday, July 1, 1843. Respecting the late persecution of the Latter Day Saints, in the State of Missouri, North America. Nauvoo, Printed by Taylor & Woodruff [1843]
1p.l., 38p. 23cm.
Reprinted from the *Times and Seasons,* July 1, 15 and August 1, 1843.
Byrd 781, Howes S626, Sabin 83240
CtY, ICN, MH

7956. ———. . . . General Joseph Smith's appeal to the Green Mountain boys, December, 1843. Nauvoo, Ill., Taylor and Woodruff, Printers, 1843.
7p. 28½cm.
At head of title: Times and Seasons-Extra.
Byrd 818, Sabin 83241
DLC, ICN, MBAt, MH, MoInRC, USlC

7957. ———. General Smith's views of the powers and policy of the government of the United States. Nauvoo, Ill., John Taylor, Printer, 1844.
[3] 4–12p. 24cm.
First published in March, 1844. In April-May it was reprinted in various cities in the United States. In May it was printed in the *Times and Seasons* and then reprinted in an 8p. pamphlet.
Byrd 897, Sabin 83242
CtY, ICN, IHi, MoS, OC, USlC

7958. ———. (same) Philadelphia, Printed by Brown, Bicking & Guilbert, 1844.
12p. 22½cm.
CtY, USlC

7959. ———. (same) John Taylor, Printer: Nauvoo, Illinois; 1844.
8p. 26cm.
In double column.
A repeat of the 12p. Nauvoo edition. It was then published in the *Times and Seasons,* from the same type, but with some corrections.
Byrd 898. He saw the def. USlC copy.
UPB, USlC

7959a. ———. (same) Nauvoo, Illinois: Printed by John Taylor: 1844.
Reprinted from the *Times and Seasons* of May 15, 1844 with the same type, with a new running title and title page.
Error on the title page: third "of" spelled "oe."
Sabin 83243
MoInRC, UPB, WHi

7960. ———. (same) Pontiac, Michigan, Jacksonian Print., 1844.
8p. 25cm.
Sabin 83244A
USlC

7961. ———. (same) [n.p., 1844]
11p. 22cm.
Listed in Sabin as at MoInRC; not available at the present time.
Sabin 83244B

7962. ———. (same) An appeal to the Green Mountain boys. Correspondence with the Hon. John C. Calhoun, also a copy of a memorial to the Legislature of Missouri . . . New York, E. J. Bevin, Printer . . . 1844.
1p.l., [3]41p. 22cm.
At head of title: Americans read!!
Memorial dated Dec. 10, 1838.
CSmH, IHi, USlC

7963. ———. (same, under title) Joseph Smith's views on the government and policy of the United States. First Published at Nauvoo, February 7, 1844. Provo City, Printed and for Sale by the Enquirer Company, 1891.
17p. 19cm.
UPB

7964. ———. (same) Salt Lake City, Joseph Hyrum Parry, Publisher, 1898.
24p. 22cm.
"Reprinted from a copy published in Nauvoo, Ill. in 1844."
MoKU, UPB, USlC

7965. ———. (same, under title) The Prophet Joseph Smith's views on the powers and policy of the government of the United States. To which is appended the correspondence between the Prophet Joseph Smith and the Hons. J. C. Calhoun and Henry Clay, Candidates for the Presidency of the United States in 1844. Salt Lake City, Jos. Hyrum Parry and Co., 1886.
42p. 18½cm.
CSmH, CU-B, DLC, MH, NjP, NN, UPB, UU

7966. ———. (same, under title) Views of the powers and policy of the government of the United States. By General Joseph Smith, of Nauvoo, Illinois. Re-published by John E. Page, Elder of the Church of Latter-Day Saints. Pittsburgh — 1844.
8p. 24cm.
Caption-title.
CtY, DLC, MoInRC, NN, USl, USlC

7967. ———. History of Joseph Smith. [Liverpool, S. W. Richards, 1852]
88p. 22cm.
Supplement to the *Millennial Star.*
Sabin 83245
NN, ULA, USIC

7968. ———. History of the Church of Jesus Christ of Latter-Day Saints. Period I. History of Joseph Smith, the prophet, by himself. An introduction and notes by B. H. Roberts. Published by the Church. Salt Lake City, The Deseret News, 1902–1912.
6v. 22½cm.
V. 7 added in 1932. It continues the history from 1842–1846.
Sabin 83246
CU-B, DLC, MoInRC, NN, UHi, ULA, UPB, USIC, UU

7969. ———. Items of church history, The gift of the Holy Ghost and the government of God; articles written by the Prophet Joseph Smith. Salt Lake City, Joseph Hyrum Parry & Co., 1884.
30p. 17cm.
Sabin 83252
CU-B, NjP, UPB, USIC

7970. ———. Items of church history, the government of God and the gift of the Holy Ghost; articles written by the Prophet Joseph Smith and President John Taylor. Salt Lake City, J. H. Parry & Co., 1886.
32p. 18½cm.
Sabin 83253
CSmH, DLC, MH, NN, UPB, USIC

7971. ———. (same) Salt Lake City, J. H. Parry & Co., 1886.
32p. 18½cm.
Sabin 83253
CSmH, DLC, MH, NN, UPB, USIC

7972. ———. Joseph Smith's last sermon as issued by Elder John Taylor, Nauvoo, Ill., June 1844. Now republished according to resolution of the Presbyterian Teachers' Association, August 1903. Salt Lake City [1903]
16p. 20cm.
Sabin 83254
NN, UHi, UPB

7973. ———. Joseph Smith's teachings; a classified arrangement of the doctrinal sermons and writings of the great Latter-day prophet. Comp. by Edwin F. Parry, from the authorized "History of the Church of Jesus Christ of Latter-day Saints." Salt Lake City, The Deseret News, 1912.
192p. 16cm.
Sabin 83256
DLC, IWW, MoInRC, NjP, NN, UHi, UPB, USIC, UU

7974. ———. (same) 2d ed. Salt Lake City, The Deseret News, 1913.
192p. 16cm.
UHi, UU

7975. ———. (same) 3d ed. Salt Lake City, The Deseret News, 1919.
192p. 16cm.
UPB, UU

7976. ———. (same) 4th ed. Salt Lake City, The Deseret News, 1922.
192p. 15cm.
USIC

7977. ———. (same, in German) Lehren Joseph Smiths; eine sachlich geordnete Sammlung aus den lehrhaften Predigten und Schriften des grossen Profeten der letzten Tage. Aus der von der Kirche herausgegebenen Geschichte der Kirche Jesu Christi der Heiligen der letzten Tage. Zusammengestellt von Edwin F. Parry. Aus dem Englischen übersetzt von Max Zimmer. Basel, Schweizerische und Deutsche Mission der Kirche Jesu Christi der Heiligen der letzten Tage, 1924.
x [11]–237p. 16cm.
NjP, UHi, UPB, UU

7978. ———. The King Follett Discourse; the being and kind of being God is, the immortality of the intelligence of man by Joseph Smith, the Prophet. With notes and references by Elder B. H. Roberts. Salt Lake City, Magazine Printing Co., 1926.
32p. 17cm.
Reprinted from *Times and Seasons*, Aug. 1, 1844.
MH, NjP, NN, UHi, USIC, UU

7979. ———. (same, under title) Wonderful sermon of the Prophet Joseph Smith at the funeral of King Follett. Nauvoo, Illinois, 1844. Also the marvelous visions of George Washington, Newman Bulkley, S. M. Farnsworth, C. D. Evans [n.p., n.d.]
40p. 15cm.
USIC

7980. ———. Last public address of the Prophet Joseph Smith, delivered before the Nauvoo Legion, June 18, 1844. Illustrated by John Hafen. Springville, Utah [n.d.]
[4]p. illus. 21½cm.
Compiled by George A. Smith.
MH

———. Lectures on faith. *See Rigdon, Sidney.*

7981. ———. A little volume of great truths, by Joseph Smith, the Prophet (From the "Compendium") Salt Lake City, William A. Morton, 1909.
19p. 16½cm.
Extracted from the *Compendium* by Franklin D. Richards.
USIC

7982. ———. "The Lord's law of health"; revelation given through Joseph Smith the prophet, at Kirtland, Ohio, February 27, 1844, known as the Word of Wisdom . . . [Salt Lake City? 193–]
[8]p. 11cm.
UHi

7983. ———. Mormon morality! Revelation given to Joseph Smith. Nauvoo, July 12th 1843. Extracted from the Latter-day Saint "Millennial Star" for January 1st, 1853. Norwich, Philip Otty [n.d.]
Broadside. 31×22cm.
An anti-polygamy publication.
USlC

———. Prayer, at the dedication of the Lord's House in Kirtland, Ohio. *See Doctrine and Covenants. Section 109. English. 1836.*

7984. ———. The Prophet Joseph Smith tells his own story; a brief history of the early visions of the prophet and the rise and progress of the Church of Jesus Christ of Latter-day Saints, by Joseph Smith, the prophet, written in 1838. [Independence, Mo., Zion's Printing and Publishing Co. Published by the Missions of the Church of Jesus Christ of Latter-day Saints in the United States, n.d.]
19 [1]p. 17½cm.
Also published under *Brief history of Joseph Smith.*
CU–B, MoInRC, NN, UPB

7985. ———. (same) [Independence, Mo., Published by the Missions of the Church of Jesus Christ of Latter-day Saints. Press of Zion's Printing and Publishing Co., n.d.]
24p. 16cm.
Cover-title.
Variant printing.
DLC, KU, MoInRC, NN, UHi, UPB, USlC, WaPS

7986. ———. (same) New York, Eastern States Mission [1910?]
32p. 14cm.
Cover-title.
Sabin 83280
ICN, MH, MoInRC, NN

7987. ———. (same) Chattanooga, Tenn., Published by the Southern States Mission [1910?]
32p. 13½cm.
MoInRC, USlC

7987a. ———. (same) Chattanooga, Tenn., The Southern States Mission. [ca. 1911]
32p. 14½cm.
Cover-title.
UPB, USlC

7988. ———. (same, under title) History of the rise of the Church of Jesus Christ of Latter-day Saints. Written by Joseph Smith, junior, 1838. [Chicago, Ill.? Church of Jesus Christ of Latter-day Saints, 191–]
16p. 16cm.
MH, MoInRC, UPB

7988a. ———. (same, under title) Joseph Smith, the martyr, in his own defence. Published by the Australian Tract Club of the Reorganized Church of Jesus Christ of Latter Day Saints . . . 1908.
[20]p. 21½cm.
NjP

7989. ———. (same, under title) Joseph Smith, the martyr, in his own defence. Published by the Australian Tract Club of the Re-organized Church of Jesus Christ of Latter Day Saints . . . 1908.
[20]p. 21½cm.
NjP

7990. ———. (same, in Armenian) Josef Smithhin ilkh ilhamlarr. [Nasheri F. F. Hintze. Instabulus, V. Minassian, 1899]
24p. 18cm.
UPB, USlC

7991. ———. (same, in French) Extraits de l'Historie du Prophète Joseph Smith. Liège, Publié par Ernest Rossiter [n.d.]
23p. 16cm.
UPB

7992. ———. (same) Extrait de l'Histoire du prophète vivant du dix neuvieme siècle. Sa première vision cèleste décrite par lui-mêmi livre no. 1 . . . Liège, L'imprimerie Cooperative, 1895.
24p. 19cm.
USlC

7993. ———. (same, in Italian) Il profeta Guiseppe Smith recconta la sua propria storia. [Tradooto dallanziano R. B. Rebezzoli. Salt Lake City, Published by the Missions of the Church of Jesus Christ of Latter-day Saints in America, n.d.]
27p. illus., port. 18cm.
Cover-title.
UPB

7994. ———. Reply of Joseph Smith to the letter of J. A. B - - of A - - n House, New York. Liverpool, Published by R. Hedlock & T. Ward [1844]
24p. 14½cm. (No. 30)
The letter of J[ames] A[rlington] B[ennett] is included.
Publication announced in *Millennial Star,* February, 1844, p. 160.
CSmH, CtY, CU–B, MH, UHi, UPB, USlC

SMITH, J., 1805–1884

7995. ———. . . . A revelation and prophecy: By the Prophet, Seer and Revelator, Joseph Smith. Given December 25th 1832 . . . [Lamoni, Ia.? Reorganized Church of Jesus Christ of Latter Day Saints, 191–]
[1]l. 15½cm. (No. 39)
Caption-title.
Original published in Plano, Ill., 1864.
Civil War prophecy.
Variant editions.
Sabin 83282
CSmH, CU–B, MoInRC, NN, UHi

———. Revelation on the eternity of the marriage covenant. *See Church of Jesus Christ of Latter-day Saints. Minutes of Conference.*

7996. ———. Revelations. [n.p., n.d.]
10p. 22cm.
Begins with Section 103 of the *Doctrine and Covenants* and the *Documentary History of the Church*, V.3: 383–392. Several other shorter items.
USlC

———. The Stick of Joseph, taken from the hand of Ephraim. *See The Stick of Joseph.*

7997. ———. The testimony of "The great prophet of this nineteenth century! [Liverpool, Printed and Published by Joseph F. Smith, at the Latter-day Saints "Millennial Star" Office [1879?]
[4]p. 22½cm.
Caption-title.
Variant printings.
Signed: N.
CSmH, MH, USlC, UU

———. Views of the powers and policy of the government. *See his General Smith's views.*

———. A vision. *See Doctrine and Covenants. Section 76. English.*

7998. ———. Visions of Joseph Smith, the seer; discoveries of ancient American records and relics with the statements of Dr. Lederer (converted Jew) and others. Plano, Ill., Printed by the Board of Publication of the Reorganized Church of Jesus Christ of Latter Day Saints [1879?]
48p. 16cm.
MH, NjP, NN, USlC, WHi

7999. ———. (same) Lamoni, Ia., The Reorganized Church of Jesus Christ of Latter Day Saints [1896]
68p. 17cm.
Dated from cover.
CU–B, OClWHi, USlC

8000. ———. The voice of truth, containing General Joseph Smith's correspondence with Gen. James Arlington Bennett; appeal to the Green Mountain Boys; correspondence with John C. Calhoun, esq.; Views of the powers and policy of the government of the United States; Pacific Innuendo, and Gov. Ford's letter. A friendly hint to Missouri, and a few words of consolation for the "Globe;" also correspondence with the Hon. Henry Clay . . . Nauvoo, Illinois: Printed by John Taylor, 1844 [1845]
64p. 24½×15cm.
The pamphlet has a cover-title, dated a year later: The Voice of Truth, containing the public writings, portrait and last sermon of President Joseph Smith. Nauvoo, Ill.: Printed at John Taylor, 1845.
The Clay correspondence ends at p. 59, and an Appendix, p. 59–64, contains "Joseph Smith's last Sermon, delivered at the April Conference, 1844." On back cover is a hymn, "The cap-stone," anti-Rigdonite in character, with errata note, which was published in the *Times and Seasons*, August 1, 1845.
Byrd 899, Sabin 83288
CtY, ICN, IHi, MH, MoInRC, MoKU, NN, UHi, USlC

8001. ———. A war prophecy, the following is a copy from the journal of Elder John J. Roberts, Paradise, Utah. The Prophecy: [n.p., n.d.]
[4]p. 15½cm.
Caption-title.
Civil War prophecy.
NjP, UPB

———. The Word of wisdom. *See Doctrine and Covenants. Section 89. English.*

8002. ———. . . . The writings of Joseph Smith, the seer. Martyred June 27, 1844 . . . York, Neb., J. K. Sheen, 1889.
32 [2] 35–48p. illus., ports. 24cm.
(The relic library. 1 Series. Nos. 1–2)
Selected writings.
Sabin 83289
CU–B, DLC, MH, NN

8003. Smith, Joseph, 1832–1914. Book of Commandments and Book of Doctrine and Covenants reviewed by the late president Joseph Smith. [Independence, Mo., Reorganized Church of Jesus Christ of Latter Day Saints, 19 - -]
12p., [1]l. port. 20cm.
CSmH, CU–B, MoInRC

8004. ———. Flerkoneriet i Amerika. En kritisk undersogelse. Lamoni, Ia., 1905.
39p.
Title in English: Polygamy in America.
Schmidt

8005. ———. His last message. [Independence, Mo., Ensign Publishing House, 1915]
11p. 10×16cm.
Sabin 83291
MoInRC

8006. ———. History of the Church of Jesus Christ of Latter Day Saints . . . written and compiled by President Joseph Smith and Apostle H. C. Smith . . . Lamoni, Ia., Published by Board of Publication of the Reorganized Church of Jesus Christ of Latter Day Saints, 1897–1903.
4v. ports., facsims. 23½cm.
Sabin 83292
CSmH, IWW, MoInRC, MoK, NjP, NN, OCl, UHi, ULA, UPB, WHi

8007. ———. (same) 1900–1922.
V.1, 6th ed. 1902. MoInRC, WHi; 8th ed. 1908. UPB, USlC; 9th ed. 1911. MoK; 9th ed. 1917. UPB; 1922. UPB, MoKU.
V.2, 3rd ed. 1902. MoInRC, WHi, USlC; 5th ed. 1908. MoK, USlC; 6th ed. 1911. UPB; 1920. UPB, MoKU.
V.3, 1900. MoInRC, WHi, USlC; 3d ed. 1908. UPB, USlC; 4th ed. 1911. MoK.
V.4, 1903. MoInRC, WHi, USlC; 1908. MoK, USlC; 3rd ed. 1911. UPB; 1922. UPB.
First edition: 1897, 1900, 1903. No changes in text.

8008. ———. Joseph Smith in his own defense. Lamoni, Ia. [n.d.]
41p. ports. 17cm.
Signed (p. 40): Joseph Smith, per F.E.
Defense of the Presidency of Joseph Smith III.
MoInRC, UPB

8009. ———. (same) Lamoni, Ia., Herald Publishing House [n.d.]
41p. port. 18cm.
MH, OO

8010. ———. (same) Lamoni, Ia., Herald Publishing House [n.d.]
41p. port. 18cm. (No. 600)
At head of title: No. 600.
CtY, OO

8011. ———. (same) Lamoni, Ia., Herald Publishing House [n.d.]
41p. port. 17½cm. (No. 1136)
At head of title: No. 1136
CU–B

———. A manual of practice . . . *See Reorganized Church of Jesus Christ of Latter Day Saints.*

8012. ———. Mormons who are not polygamists. Independence, Mo., Reorganized Church of Jesus Christ of Latter Day Saints [1911?]
4p. 19cm.
Reprinted from *Everybody's Magazine*, September, 1911.
USlC

8013. ———. One wife or many, by Pres. Joseph Smith. [Lamoni, Ia., Reorganized Church of Jesus Christ of Latter Day Saints, 188–]
16p. 21cm. (Tract. No. 43)
Sabin 83295
CU–B, IWW, MH, MoInRC, NN, USl, UU

8014. ———. (same) Lamoni, Ia., Reorganized Church of Jesus Christ of Latter Day Saints [188–]
16p. 25cm. (Tract. No. 48)
CtY, CU–B, UPB

8015. ———. . . . Plural marriage in America; a critical examination, by President Joseph Smith. Lamoni, Ia., Herald Publishing House [1903]
39p. 16cm. (No. 3)
Cover-title.
Running title: Origin of polygamy.
Three variant covers.
CSmH, CU–B, IWW, MoInRC, UHi, UPB, USlC, UU

8016. ———. (same) [n.p., n.d.]
8p. 21cm.
USlC

8017. ———. Polygamy not of God. Joseph Smith's fourth letter to L. O. Littlefield. [Lamoni, Ia., True Latter Day Saints' Herald Office, 186–]
4p. 24½cm.
Caption-title.
"The series of letters of which this tract is the closing one, was begun by the publication of an *Open letter to Joseph Smith and others* . . . by Elder L. O. Littlefield."
"Supplement to the *Saints' Advocate*."
Sabin 83296
CtY, CU–B

8018. ———. The rejection of the church. By Pres. Joseph Smith. [Plano, Ill.? The Reorganized Church of Jesus Christ of Latter Day Saints, n.d.]
8p. 25cm. (No. 18)
CSmH, NN, USlC

8019. ———. (same) [Lamoni? Ia., Reorganized Church of Jesus Christ of Latter Day Saints, 187–]
16p. 17cm. (No. 42)
CtY

8020. ———. (same) [Lamoni, Ia., Published by the Reorganized Church of Latter Day Saints, 1889]
8p. 25cm. (No. 42)
Caption-title.
Sabin 83297
CSmH, CU–B, IWW, MH, MoInRC

8021. ———. Reply of Pres. Joseph Smith, to L. O. Littlefield in refutation of the doctrine of plural marriage. Lamoni, Ia., The Reorganized Church of Jesus Christ of Latter Day Saints, 1885.
48p. 18cm.
Cover-title.
Sabin 83298
CtY, ICN, MH, MoInRC, NN, USl, USlC, WHi

8022. ———. . . . Reply to Orson Pratt, by Joseph Smith, President of the Reorganized Church of Jesus Christ of Latter Day Saints. Plano, Ill. [Published by the Reorganized Church of Jesus Christ of Latter Day Saints, 1870]
16p. 23cm. (No. 14)
Sabin 83299
CSmH, DLC, MH, NjP, NN, UHi, UPB, USlC

8023. ———. (same) Plano, Ill., Published by the Reorganized Church of Jesus Christ of Latter Day Saints [n.d.]
16p. 22cm. (No. 14)
USlC

8024. ———. (same) [Lamoni, Ia.?] Published by the Reorganized Church of Jesus Christ of Latter Day Saints [188–]
16p. 25cm. (No. 14)
CU-B, IWW, NN, UHi, USlC

8025. ———. The Spaulding story re-examined. [Plano, Ill., Published by the Reorganized Church of Jesus Christ of Latter Day Saints, 1883]
16p. 18cm.
Regarding Robert Patterson's connection with the "Manuscript found."
CtY, CU-B, MoInRC, NjP, NN

8026. ———. A statement and a correction of it. Lamoni, Ia., Herald Publishing House [n.d.]
16p. 21cm. (No. 19)
To repudiate a published interview.
CSmH, IWW, MoInRC, UU

8027. ———. The polygamic revelation. Fraud! Fraud! Fraud! Revelation on the eternity of the marriage covenant, including plurality of wives; presented by Brigham Young to the church in Utah, August 29th, 1852. [Lamoni, Ia., Printed at the True Latter Day Saints' Herald Office, 186–]
8p. 21cm.
At head of title: Supplement to the *Saints' Herald.*
Sabin 83284
MoInRC, NN

8027a. ———. To the brethren in conference assembled. [n.p., 1901]
2p. 26cm.
MoInRC

8027b. ———. To whom it may concern. Joseph Smith and W. W. Blair; First Presidency, 1894. [n.p., 1894?]
4p. 27cm.
MoInRC

8028. ———. Wer Kann denn das Heil erlangen? Von Joseph Smith: Übersetzt aus dem Englischen von Karl W. Lange. [Plano, 1869]
4p. 22½cm.
Title in English: Who can be saved?
Sabin 83302
MH

8029. ———. Who then can be saved? [Plano, Ill.?] The Reorganized Church of Jesus Christ of Latter Day Saints [1866?]
4p. 23cm. (No. 7)
Caption-title.
Sabin 83301
CSmH, MH, MoInRC, NjP, NN, UHi, UPB, USlC

8030. ———. (same) [Plano, Ill., The Reorganized Church of Jesus Christ of Latter Day Saints, 187–]
4p. 23cm. (No. 7)
MH, USlC

8031. ———. (same) Plano, Ill., Published by the Reorganized Churth [sic] of Jesus Christ of Latter Day Saints [n.d.]
4p. 22cm. (No. 7)
UPB

8032. ———. (same) [Plano, Ill., The Reorganized Church of Jesus Christ of Latter Day Saints, n.d.]
4p. 23cm.
Same without "No. 7."
NN

8033. Smith, Joseph Fielding, 1838–1918. Another plain talk. Reasons why the people of Utah should be Republicans. By Joseph F. Smith. Issued by the Republican Central Committee, Charles Crane, Chairman. Salt Lake City, 1892.
16p. 21cm.
Cover-title.
Mormons and politics. Background information such as to which party George F. Edmund belonged.
NjP, UHi, USlC

———. Appeal of Frederick M. Smith. *See Smith, Frederick Madison.*

8034. ———. An Authoritative declaration. By President Joseph F. Smith. [n.p.] 1918.
Broadside. 12½×14cm.
Divinity of the church.
UPB, USlC

8035. ———. Circular to the presidents of conferences and traveling Elders . . . [Liverpool?] 1878.
Broadside. 22½×15cm.
Dated: Salt Lake City, Feb. 19, 1878.
Preface signed by H. W. Naisbitt, C. W. Nibley.
At head of title: [Confidential]
Pastoral epistle.
UPB

SMITH, J. F., 1838–1918

8036. ———. A dignified answer To the Unjustifiable Attacks of the Salt Lake Herald on President Joseph F. Smith, Because He is a Republican and Exercises His Right as an American Citizen to so Express Himself. [Salt Lake City, 1894]
[4]p. 24cm.
Letter addressed to Charles Crane, signed: Salt Lake City, Oct. 18, 1894.
Basically political with brief reference to anti-polygamy legislation.
USIC

8037. ———. Gospel doctrine; selections from the sermons and writings of Joseph F. Smith . . . Salt Lake City, The Deseret News, 1919.
xv, 696p. port. 20cm.
Compiled by John A. Widtsoe.
Sabin 83347
CSmH, CU-B, DLC, MoInRC, NjP, NN, UPB, UHi, USIC

8038. ———. (same) [2d ed.] Salt Lake City, The Deseret News, 1919.
xv, 700p. port. 20cm.
CSmH, UHi, USIC

8039. ———. (same) 3d ed. Salt Lake City, The Deseret Book Co., 1920.
xv, 700p. port. 20cm.
CSmH, MH, UHi, UPB

8040. ———. (same) 4th ed. Salt Lake City, The Deseret Book Co., 1928.
xv, 700p. 20cm.
UU

8041. ———. (same, in German) Evangeliumslehre; eine Auswahl aus Predigten und Schriften. [Translated from the English by Jean Wunderlich. Basel] Schweizerisch-Deutsch und Deutsch-Österreichische Mission der Kirche Jesu Christi der Heiligen der Letzten Tage, 1926.
xxiii, 803p. 19cm.
UHi, USIC, UU

8041a. ———. Harmony between presiding authorities in the Priesthood and in auxiliary organizations. [Salt Lake City? n.d.]
[2]p. 27cm.
USIC

8041b. ———. Impressive discourse by Prest. Joseph F. Smith at the General Relief Society conference, Friday, October 3, 1913. [Salt Lake City, Relief Society? 1913]
[4]p. 17½cm.
USIC

———. Home evening, with suggested exercises and explanations. *See Church of Jesus Christ of Latter-day Saints. Stakes. Granite.*

8042. ———. Instructions concerning Temple ordinance work. [Salt Lake City, ca. 1910]
4p. 24cm.
Signed: Joseph F. Smith, President of the Salt Lake Temple. Also published under signature of George F. Richards.
Variant editions.
UPB, USIC

8043. ———. [Instructions to Bishops concerning temple work] Dear Brother. Salt Lake City [1910?]
[4]p. 23cm.
Signed: Joseph F. Smith.
UPB, USIC

8043a. ———. Instructions to the Saints who are privileged to enter Salt Lake Temple. [Salt Lake Temple, ca. 1910]
[4]p. 20½cm.
Other editions entitled: Instructions concerning temple ordinance work.
USIC

———. Interview with President Smith. *See Hall, Henry.*

8044. ———. Mormon chief confesses. Admits under oath that they are living in violation of the laws of the land the laws of God. [New York City, Hans P. Freece, 1905?]
[2]p. 22½cm.
Testimony from the Smoot hearings.
USIC

8045. ———. Report of President Joseph F. Smith at the annual conference of the Church of Jesus Christ of Latter-day Saints. April, 1915. Salt Lake City, Presiding Bishops Office, 1915.
[3]p. 19cm.
Variant printing. USIC
Cover-title.
NjP, UHi, UPB, USIC

8046. ———. Temperance and the Word of wisdom. Addresses delivered by President Joseph F. Smith and Heber J. Grant at the semi-annual conference, Salt Lake City, 1908. [Salt Lake City, 1908?]
8p. 21½cm.
NjP, UPB, USIC

8047. ———. Two sermons by President Joseph F. Smith . . . Chattanooga, Tennessee, Published by the Southern States Mission [1906?]
16p. 19cm. (Sermon tract. No. 1)
Contents: What it is to be a Latter-day Saint. Divinity of the Mission of Joseph Smith.
NjP, ULA, UPB, USIC

SMITH, J. F., 1838–1918

8048. ———. Unchastity the dominant evil of the age, by President Joseph Fielding Smith. Written for and at request of the Newspaper Enterprise Association, San Francisco, Cal. [Salt Lake City? 1915?]
16p. 15cm.
Cover-title.
CU–B, UHi, UPB

8049. Smith, Joseph Fielding, 1876–1972. Asahel Smith of Topsfield, Mass., with some account of the Smith family. Topsfield, Mass., Topsfield Historical Society, 1902.
87–101p. 2 plates, 1 facsim. 22½cm.
Reprinted from the *Topsfield Historical collection*, V.8.
With separate cover.
Sabin 83348
CSmH, DLC, MWA, NjP, NN, UHi, UPB, USlC

8050. ———. Blood atonement and the origin of plural marriage. A discussion. Correspondence between Elder Joseph F. Smith, Jr., of the Church of Jesus Christ of Latter-day Saints, and Mr. Richard C. Evans, Second Counselor in the Presidency of the "Reorganized" Church. A conclusive refutation of the false charges persistently made by ministers of the "Reorganized" Church against the Latter-day Saints and their belief. Also a supplement containing a number of affidavits and other matters bearing on the subjects. [Salt Lake City] Deseret News, 1905.
112p. 19½cm.
CSmH, CU–B, ICN, MH, MoInRC, NjP, NN, UHi, UPB, USl, USlC, UU, WHi

8051. ———. (same) Independence, Mo., Press of Zion's Printing and Publishing Company [191–]
94p. 18cm.
MoInRC, NjP, NN, UHi, ULA

8052. ———. (same) [Independence, Mo., Press of Zion's Printing and Publishing Co., 1929]
94p. 18½cm.
"2d ed."
USlC

8053. ———. Elijah the prophet and his mission, a discourse delivered under the auspices of the Genealogical Society of Utah. Salt Lake City, Genealogical Society of Utah, 1924.
32p. 20cm.
NjP, UPB, USlC

8054. ———. Essentials in church history; a history of the church from the birth of Joseph Smith to the present time (1922), with introductory chapters on the antiquity of the gospel and the "falling away" by Joseph Fielding Smith . . . Published by the Church of Jesus Christ of Latter-day Saints. Salt Lake City, Deseret News Press, 1922.
viii, 694p. illus., ports., maps, facsim. 20cm.
Sabin 83349
CU–B, DLC, MH, MoInRC, NjPT, UHi, ULA, UPB, USl, USlC, UU, WHi

8055. ———. (same) [2d ed.] Salt Lake City, Deseret News Press, 1922.
viii, 694p. illus., ports., maps, facsim. 19½cm.
USlC

8056. ———. (same) 3d ed. Salt Lake City, The Deseret News, 1924.
viii, 694p. illus., ports., maps, facsim. 20cm.
OU, USlC

8057. ———. (same) 4th ed. Salt Lake City, Deseret News Press, 1928.
viii, 694p. illus., ports., maps, facsim. 19½cm.
NN, UPB, USl, USlC

8058. ———. (same, in German) Wichtiges aus der Kirchengeschichte; eine Geschichte der Kirche Jesu Christi der Heiligen der letzten Tage von der Geburt Joseph Smiths bis zur Gegenwart (1922) . . . Aus dem Englischen übersetzt vom Ältesten Max Zimmer. Basel, Sarge F. Ballif, 1923.
vii, 712p. illus., maps. 20cm.
UHi, USlC

8059. ———. Faith leads to the fulness of truth and righteousness. Remarks made by Elder Joseph Fielding Smith at the Genealogical Conference, Saturday, April 5, 1930. [Salt Lake City, 1930]
14p. 22½cm.
"Reprinted from the *Utah Genealogical and Historical Magazine*, October, 1930."
USlC

8060. ———. Lessons on salvation for the dead, genealogy and temple work. Compiled by the Genealogical Society of Utah. Salt Lake City, 1927.
76p. 19cm.
NjP, UHi, ULA, USlC

8061. ———. Leitfaden zum Studium des Buches Wichtiges aus der Kirchengeschichte von Joseph Fielding Smith . . . Bearbeitet von Dr. Hugh M. Woodward von der Brigham Young Universität. Basel, Herausgegeben von der Schweizerischen und Deutschen Mission der Kirche Jesu Christe der Heiligen der letzten Tage, 1923.
91p. 18cm.
Title in English: Guide to the study of the *Essentials in Church History.*
USlC

8062. ———. Origin of the "Reorganized Church." The question of succession. Salt Lake City, Skelton Publishing Co., 1907.
65p. 21½cm.
CSmH, MH, MoInRC, OClWHi, UPB, USlC

8063. ———. (same) Salt Lake City, The Deseret News, 1909.
139p. 20cm.
Sabin 83350
CSmH, CU–B, DLC, MoInRC, NjP, NN, UPB, USlC, UU

SMITH, J. H.

8064. ———. (same) 3d ed. Independence, Mo., Zion's Printing and Publishing Co., 1929.
2p.l. [5]–116p. 20½cm.
ICU, NjP, NN, UHi, ULA, USlC

8065. ———. (same, in Dutch) Oorsprong van de "Gereorganiseerde" Kerk; de opvolging in het presidentschap der Kerk . . . Uit het Engelsch vertaald door C. Zappey. Rotterdam, Chas. S. Hyde [1925?]
63p. 20½cm.
UHi, USlC

8066. ———. The Pearl of Great Price. Remarks by Elder Joseph Fielding Smith, at a meeting of the High Priests' Quorum of the Salt Lake Stake, Sunday, October 20, 1920, in the Seventeenth Ward Meeting-house. [Salt Lake City? 1930?]
8p. 22½cm.
Reprinted from the *Utah Genealogical and Historical Magazine*, July, 1930.
USlC

8067. ———. Proceedings at the dedication of the Joseph Smith Memorial Monument, at Sharon, Windsor County, Vermont, December 23rd, 1905. With a detailed account of the journey and visits of the centennial memorial party to Vermont and other places in the Eastern states; also a description of the Solomon Mack farm and account of the purchase of same. [Salt Lake City? 1906?]
2 p.l. [5]–88p. plates, ports. 21cm.
Text in parallel columns.
CU-B, MH, MoInRC, NN, UHi, ULA, UPB, USlC, UU

8068. ———. (same) [Salt Lake City? 1906?]
2p.l. [5]–92p. plates, ports. 21cm.
Text in parallel columns.
P. 89–92 is a poem entitled "L'envoi" by Susa Young Gates.
USlC

8069. ———. The "Reorganized" church vs. salvation for the dead. By Elder Joseph Fielding Smith . . . [Salt Lake City? Published by the Missions of the Church of Jesus Christ of Latter-day Saints in America, c1905]
31 [1]p. illus. 15½cm.
CSmH, MH, MoInRC, NjP, UHi, UPB, USlC, UU

8070. ———. (same) [Independence, Mo., Press of Zion's Printing and Publishing Co., c1905]
31 [1]p. 16cm.
UPB

8071. ———. (same) Salt Lake City, The Deseret News, 1905.
33 [1]p. 15½cm.
MoInRC, UPB

8072. ———. (same) Salt Lake City, The Deseret News [n.d.]
33 [1]p. 15½cm.
Variant edition of the above without date.
UPB

8073. ———. Salvation universal, by J. F. Smith. [Salt Lake City] Published by the Genealogical Society of Utah, 1912.
32p. 19½cm.
MoInRC, NjP, NN, USlC

8074. ———. (same) [Salt Lake City] Published by the Genealogical Society of Utah, 1920.
32p. 19cm.
CU-B, NN, UHi, USlC

8075. ———. Succession in the presidency of the church; an address delivered in the Weber Stake Tabernacle, Ogden, Sunday, April 28, 1907. [n.p., n.d.]
65p. 19cm.
UPB

8076. ———. Tidernes tegn. Kobenhavn, 1912.
117p.
Title in English: Signs of the times.
Schmidt

8077. ———. The way of salvation. An address delivered over Radio Station KSL Sunday evening, Sept. 22nd, 1929. [Salt Lake City] Church of Jesus Christ of Latter-day Saints, 1929.
8p. 23cm.
USlC

8078. Smith, Joseph H. History of Harrison County, Iowa, including a condensed history of the state, the early settlement of the county . . . together with sketches of its pioneers . . . by Joe H. Smith. Des Moines, Iowa Printing Company, 1888.
1p.l. [5]–491p. port. 23½cm.
Mormon history in Harrison County, p. 84–96.
RLDS Church in Harrison County history, p. 443–447.
Sabin 83351
DLC, MH, MWA, NjP, NN, USlC

8079. Smith, Justin Harvey. The war with Mexico, by Justin H. Smith . . . New York, The Macmillan Company, 1919.
2v. illus., maps, plans. 23cm.
References to the Mormon Battalion: V.1, p. 290, 516; V.2, p. 218–219, 454–455.
CU-B, DLC

8080. Smith, Lucy (Mack). Biographical sketches of Joseph Smith the prophet, and his progenitors for many generations . . . Liverpool [etc.] Published for O. Pratt, by S. W. Richards; London, Sold at the Latter-day Saints Book Depot, 1853.
xii [13]–297p. [1]p. 16cm.
Brigham Young attempted to suppress this edition.
Howes S637
CSmH, CtY, CU–B, ICN, MH, MnU, MoInRC, MWA, NjP, OClWHi, UHi, UPB, USl, USIC, UU, WHi

8081. ———. (same) Plano, Ill., Reorganized Church of Jesus Christ of Latter Day Saints, 1880.
xv [17]–312p. 16cm.
Howes S637, Sabin 83497
CtY, IC, IWW, MoInRC, NN, UHi, UPB, USIC, WHi

8082. ———. (same) Lamoni, Ia., The Reorganized Church of Jesus Christ of Latter Day Saints, 1908.
iii [1] 371p. 20cm.
Sabin 83498
DLC, UPB

8083. ———. (same) Lamoni, Ia., Published by the Reorganized Church of Jesus Christ of Latter Day Saints, 1912.
1p.l., iii [1] 371p. 20cm.
Sabin 83499
MoInRC, NN, UPB, USIC

8084. ———. (same, under title) History of the Prophet Joseph by his mother Lucy Smith as revised by George A. Smith and Elias Smith. Salt Lake City, The Improvement Era, 1902.
viii [9]–296p. ports. 21½cm.
Howes S637, Sabin 83500
CSmH, MH, NcD, NN, UHi, USIC, UU

Smith, Mrs. Mary Ettie V. *See Green, Nelson Winch.*

8085. Smith, Orson. Poems, by Orson Smith, compiled by his children for his 75th birthday, July, 1928. [n.p., 1928?]
96p. port. 19cm.
Mormon poetry.
UPB

8086. Smith, Pascal B., *Defendant.* A Law case, exhibiting the most extraordinary developments peculiar to modern times, arising from an implicit obedience to the dictates of mesmeric clairvoyance, as related by a Mormon Prophet. Also — the speeches of counsel in the case reported by Mr. Webster, the phonographic writer. By a member of the Cincinnati Bar. Cincinnati, Printed at the Daily Atlas Office, 1848.
5–30p. 27cm.
Proceedings of an insanity hearing in which Smith is said to have come under the mesmerizing influence of one Mahan, a "Mormon Prophet" (a member or former member of the Mormon church)
NN

8087. Smith, Robert. A series of lectures on the signs of the times, the fulfillment of prophecy, the dream of Nebuchadnezzar, the vision of Daniel, the Perihelia of the planets, the constellations of the serpent and the dragon, star of Bethlehem, shepherd star and the great signs in the heavens, with the seven wonders of the world, pyramids and Cleopatra's needles; events in history, its sieges and battles, with scenes in Zion and the last judgment. Payson, Utah, 1887.
1p.l., iv, 13–115p. illus. 21½cm.
Printed at the Juvenile Instructor Office.
CSmH, CtY, CU–B, NjP, NN, UHi, UPB, USIC, UU, WHi

8088. Smith, Robert William. History of the Eighth ward, Liberty Stake, Church of Jesus Christ of Latter-day Saints, 1847–1921. [Salt Lake City, 1921]
[24]p. illus., plates, ports. 22cm.
USIC

8089. Smith, Ruth Lyman (Cobb). Concerning the Prophet Frederick Madison Smith, by his wife Ruth Lyman Smith. Rev. ed. Kansas City, Mo., Burton Publishing Company [c1924]
4p.l., 13–148 [1]p. ports. 19cm.
DLC, MoInRC, MoK, NjP

8090. ———. (same) Kansas City, Mo., Burton Publishing Company [c1924]
258p. [1]p. illus. 19cm.
UHi

8091. Smith, Sam W. California through Death Valley; a story of shadows, clouds, gloom and sunshine, by Sam W. Smith . . . San Francisco, Francis Valentine & Co. [1880]
[8]l. illus. 22½cm.
Cover-title.
A synopsis of the drama, by W. L. Visscher.
Act I: "Among the Saints." Act II: "Massacre on the Meadows."
MH, UHi, USIC

8092. Smith, Samuel Harrison Bailey. An appeal for justice. Letters written by Samuel H. B. Smith, to President John Taylor, from December 28th, 1886, to February 22d, 1887. Salt Lake City, Published by S. H. B. Smith, 1887.
30p. 17½cm.
Grievances because of his treatment by the church.
Sabin 84080
MH, MoInRC, NN, ULA, UPB, USIC, UU

8093. ———. A speech by Samuel H. B. Smith, at a Populist rally at the Salt Lake Theatre, October 27th, 1899. [Salt Lake City, 1899]
8p. 19cm.
A political speech, with quotes from the *Doctrine and Covenants.*
USIC

8094. Smith, T. C. The Book of Mormon and Mormonism. Denver, Colorado, Rev. T. C. Smith, Aug., 1912.
96p. 18cm. (No. 1)
"This pamphlet of 96 pages is Part I of a complete study of the *Book of Mormon* and Mormonism."
Projected as a ten issue magazine refuting Mormonism.
#1. Aug., 1912: The credentials of the *Book of Mormon*. 1–48p.
#2. Sept., 1912: [49]–96p. The external evidences of the *Book of Mormon*.
The following were projected, but not published.
1. Joseph Smith: Heredity and training.
2. The Nephite and Jaredite history.
3. The religious part of the *Book of Mormon*.
4. Its origin: who wrote it?
DLC #2, IWW, MoInRC, NjP #2, UPB, USlC

8094a. ———. The Book of Mormon and Mormonism . . . Denver, Colo., Rev. T. C. Smith, 1912.
[4]p. 18cm.
Prospectus for the series of ten essays.
USlC

8095. ———. Christianity and Mormonism. By T. C. Smith, D. D. Philadelphia, Pa., The Westminster Press, 1918.
16p. 17cm.
NN, USl, USlC

8096. ———. The credentials of the Book of Mormon. Denver, Colorado, Rev. T. C. Smith, August, 1912.
48p. 17cm.
Variant printing of 8094, #2.
MoInRC, UPB, USlC

———. The External evidences of the Book of Mormon. *See Smith, Samuel H. B. The Book of Mormon and Mormonism.*

8097. Smith, Thomas. Calumny refuted and the truth defended, being a reply to a tract, written by W. Frost, entitled a "Dialogue between a Latter Day Saint & a Methodist." By Thomas Smith. [Orford Hill, P. Otty, Printer, 1849?]
12p. 18cm.
Caption-title.
MH

8098. ———. Who is the liar? [Northampton, England, ca. 1855]
[2]p. 23cm.
Rebuttal to John Bowes' *Mormonism exposed.*
USlC

8099. Smith, Thomas W. Mormonism; is it truth or error? [Plano? Ill., 1881?]
[4]p. 24½cm.
Caption-title.
Mormon apologetics.
CtY, MoInRC

8100. ———. The "one baptism," its mode, subjects, prerequisites, and design, who shall administer? Plano, Ill., Reorganized Church of Jesus Christ of Latter Day Saints [1871?]
13p. 21cm. (No. 6)
Sabin 84426
CtY, MoInRC, NjP, NN

8101. ———. (same) Plano, Ill., Published by the Reorganized Church of Jesus Christ of Latter Day Saints [n.d.]
16p. 22cm. (No. 6)
USlC

8102. ———. (same) [Plano, Ill.?] Reorganized Church of Jesus Christ of Latter Day Saints, True Latter Day Saints' Herald Office [1879]
16p. 22cm. (No. 6)
Sabin 84427
CSmH, NN, USlC

8103. ———. (same) [Plano, Ill.?] Reorganized Church of Jesus Christ of Latter Day Saints [1879]
16p. 22cm. (No. 6)
Variant printing, without author.
NN

8104. ———. (same) Lamoni, Ia., Reorganized Church of Jesus Christ of Latter Day Saints. True Latter Day Saints' Herald Office [1871?]
16p. 23cm.
MoInRC

8105. ———. (same) Lamoni, Ia., Published by the Reorganized Church of Jesus Christ of Latter Day Saints [n.d.]
16p. 22½cm. (No. 6)
Variant printings.
USlC

8106. ———. The "one body"; or, The Church of Christ under the apostleship, and under the apostasy. Plano, Ill., Reorganized Church of Jesus Christ of Latter Day Saints. True Latter Day Saints' Herald Office [1879]
15 [1]p. 21cm. (No. 20)
First printed in the *Saints' Herald*, October 15, 1871 and advertised in the same number.
MoInRC, NjP, NN, UPB

8107. ———. (same) [Plano, Ill.?] Reorganized Church of Jesus Christ of Latter-Day Saints. True Latter Day Saints' Herald Office [1879]
12p. 22cm. (No. 20)
Sabin 84429
CSmH, MoInRC, USlC

8108. ———. (same) Plano, Ill., Published by the Reorganized Church of Jesus Christ of Latter Day Saints [n.d.]
12p. 22cm. (No. 20)
USlC

8109. ———. (same) Lamoni, Ia., Reorganized Church of Jesus Christ of Latter Day Saints. True Latter Day Saints' Herald Office [1882?]
12p. 22cm. (No. 20)
Several variant printings.
MoInRC, UPB, USlC

8110. ———. (same) [Lamoni, Ia., Published by the Reorganized Church of Jesus Christ of Latter Day Saints, n.d.]
12p. 21½cm.
Variant edition with no number.
MoInRC

8111. ———. One hundred & eighty two fair questions and candid answers: or, The plain, honest truth concerning the people erroneously called Mormons. By The Rev. T. W. Smith, President of the Australian Mission of the Reorganized Church of Jesus Christ of Latter Day Saints: But which has no connection with the people called Salt Lake Mormons, or polygamists. Melbourne, Australia, Rhys-Jones & Co., Printers and Publishers . . . 1888.
46p. 20½cm.
Doctrines of the RLDS church.
CSmH, MoInRC, NjP

8112. ———. Songs of Zion; for the use of the children of the kingdom. By Thomas W. Smith. Plano, Ill., Printed at the Herald Office [1875?]
24p. 18½cm.
Cover-title.
Sabin 84430
CtY, NjP, USl

8113. ———. (same) Plano, Ill., Printed at the Herald Office [n.d.]
39p. 13cm.
RLDS hymnal. Words only.
CSmH, MoInRC, USlC

8114. ———. (same) Plano, Ill., Printed at the Herald Office [n.d.]
48p. 13cm.
MoInRC

8115. ———. Spiritualism viewed from a scriptural stand-point. [Plano, Ill., Published by the Reorganized Church of Jesus Christ of Latter Day Saints, 1866]
20p. 21½cm. (No. 9)
CSmH, CtY, MoInRC, NjP, UPB

8116. ———. (same) Plano, Ill., Published by the Reorganized Church of Jesus Christ of Latter Day Saints [n.d.]
20p. 22cm. (No. 9)
USlC

8117. ———. (same) Plano, Ill., True Latter Day Saints' Herald Office [1870]
20p. 21½cm. (No. 9)
Sabin 84431
CU-B, MoInRC, NN, USlC

8118. ———. (same) [n.p.] Published by the Reorganized Church of Jesus Christ of Latter Day Saints [n.d.]
20p. 22cm. (No. 9)
USlC

8119. ———. (same) [Lamoni, Ill.?] Reorganized Church of Jesus Christ of Latter Day Saints, 1870.
20p. 21½cm.
"Addenda," p. 20.
NN, USlC

8120. ———. (same) [Lamoni, Ia.] Published by the Reorganized Church of Jesus Christ of Latter Day Saints [1881?]
20p. 21½cm. (No. 9)
Sabin 84431
CSmH, IWW, MoInRC

8121. ———. (same) Lamoni, Ia., Published by the Reorganized Church of Jesus Christ of Latter Day Saints [n.d.]
20p. 21½cm. (No. 9)
USlC

8122. Smith, Truman. Speech of Mr. Smith, of Conn., on the bill "to admit California into the Union — to establish territorial governments for Utah and New Mexico . . ." Delivered in the Senate of the United States, July 8, 1850. Washington, Gideon & Co., 1850.
32p. 24½cm.
Cover-title.
Includes an attempt to get the State of Deseret admitted.
CU-B, NjP, UHi

8123. Smith, Vida Elizabeth. Young people's history of the Church of Jesus Christ of Latter Day Saints . . . Vida E. Smith, author . . . Lamoni, Ia., Issued by the Herald Publishing House of the Reorganized Church of Jesus Christ of Latter Day Saints, 1914–[1918]
2v. illus. 20½cm.
CU-B V.1, MoInRC, ULA, UPB, NjP V.1, USlC

8124. Smith, Walter W. The Book of Doctrine and Covenants; the history of its publication at Kirtland, Ohio, in 1835, by Walter W. Smith. Independence, Mo., Reorganized Church of Jesus Christ of Latter Day Saints [n.d.]
19 [1]p. 19cm.
CSmH, CU-B, MoInRC, NjP

8125. ———. Book of Mormon and Zion's Religio-literary Society. By Walter W. Smith . . . J. A. Gunsolley . . . Published by the Religio-Sunday School Normal Department. 2d ed. rev. Lamoni, Ia., Herald Publishing House . . . 1911.
84p. 20cm.
USlC

8126. ———. Lectures by Walter W. Smith; teaching, the first duty of the ministry, the minister as a teacher, attention essential to learning. [n.p., n.d.]
51p. 19cm.
RLDS ministers and their duties.
MoInRC, NjP

8127. ———. The religious educational supremacy of the home, lecture at the Stone Church, Oct. 3, 1922. Independence, Mo., Herald Publishing House [n.d.]
13p. 20cm.
RLDS religious education.
MoInRC

8128. Smith, Willard J. Fetting and his messenger's messages. [n.p., 192–]
43p. illus. 20cm.
Concerning the Church of Christ (Fetting) by an RLDS member.
MoInRC

8129. ———. Joseph Smith, who was he? And did he practice and teach polygamy? Grand Rapids, Mich., Glad Tidings Publishing House, 1888.
255p. 20cm.
MoInRC, UHi

8130. ———. (same) [2d ed.] Lamoni, Ia., [Herald Publishing House, 1898?]
255 [7]p. 19½cm.
MoInRC, UHi

8131. ———. (same) Grand Rapids, Mich., Published by the Glad Tidings Publishing House, 1899.
v [7]–186p. ports. 19cm.
RLDS point of view.
MoInRC, NjP, USlC, UU

8132. ———. (same) [Lamoni, Ia., Herald House, n.d.]
255 [6]p. 20cm.
"Preface to the Second edition."
MoInRC, NjP

8133. ———. (same) Lamoni, Ia., 1904.
255 [6]p. port. 19½cm.
"Second Edition."
Variant printing.
MoInRC, NjP

8134. ———. The last dispensation. Independence, Mo., Ensign Publishing Company, 1896.
43p. 14cm.
RLDS doctrine.
Eberstadt lists an 1893 edition, also with 43p.
MoInRC

8135. ———. The resurrection of the wicked, their consciousness after death. Independence, Mo., Ensign Publishing House, 1899.
39p. 22cm.
MoInRC

8136. ———. Sermon. [Lamoni, Ia., Lambert Bros.] 1888.
8p. 23cm.
Sermon delivered at Independence, Mo., July, 1888.
Printed as a Supplement to *Lamoni Gazette*.
MoInRC

8137. ———. Whitmerism unmasked; being a brief examination of the claims of the so-called Church of Christ. [Holstein, Ont., 1888?]
25p. 16cm.
Caption-title.
Signed: Willard J. Smith, Holstein Grey Co., Ont.
Tract against the Church of Christ.
CSmH, MH, MoInRC

8138. ———. Why a First Presidency. By Willard J. Smith. A reply to J. W. Peterson and Elbert A. Smith. Port Huron, Mich., Published by Otto Fetting [1929?]
35p. 26cm.
Cover-title.
A Church of Christ publication on priesthood.
CU–B, MoInRC, NjP, UHi, USlC

8139. Smith, William. Defence of Elder William Smith, against the slanders of Abraham Burtis, and others: in which are included several certificates, and the duties of members in the Church of Christ, in settling difficulties one with another according to the Law of God . . . Philadelphia, Brown, Bicking & Guilbert, Printers . . . 1844.
24p. 18cm.
The difficulties which led to the publication of this pamphlet occurred in New Jersey, September–December, 1843.
MoInRC, USlC

8140. ———. Deseret. Remonstrance of William Smith, et al., of Covington, Kentucky, against the admission of Deseret into the Union. [Washington, Wm. M. Belt, 1850]
3p. 23½cm. (U.S. 31st Cong. 1st sess. House. Misc. Doc. No. 43)
Signed: December 31, 1849.
Morgan
CSmH, CtY, DLC, MH, NN, UHi, ULA, UPB, USlC, UU, WHi

8141. ———. Minutes of a conference, held by the Church of Jesus Christ of Latter-day Saints. [Cincinnati? 1846?]
Broadside. 47×35cm.
Dated: Cincinnati, Ohio, Jan. 6, 1846.
Conference to uphold James J. Strang's claim for leadership.
USIC

8142. ———. A Revelation given to William Smith in 1847, on the apostasy of the Church and the pruning of the vineyard of the Lord. [Philadelphia, 1848]
8p. 23cm.
Includes a letter to the scattered saints.
Morgan
USIC

8143. ———. To the public . . . [Nauvoo?] 1846.
Broadside. 18×14cm.
Transfer of deed to house from the Church to Mother Smith, signed April 13, 1846, by William Smith, Arthur Millikin and Lucy Millikin.
Suit was against the executor (A. Babbitt) of the Church.
USIC

8144. ———. To the public. Slander refuted! An extract from church proceedings; and expulsion of Mormon apostates, from the Church . . . [n.p., 1844?]
4p. 18cm.
USIC

8145. ———. William Smith on Mormonism. This book contains a true account of the origin of the Book of Mormon. A sketch of the history, experience, and ministry of Elder William Smith. The story of the golden plates from which the Book of Mormon was translated. An account of a most extraordinary miracle, wrought by the laying on of the hands of the elders of the Church, and a statement of the principles and doctrines, as believed and taught by the Church of Jesus Christ of Latter Day Saints . . . By William Smith . . . Lamoni, Ia., Herald Steam Book and Job Office, 1883.
41p. ports. 17cm.
DLC, ICN, MoInRC

8146. ———. William Smith, patriarch & prophet of the most high God. Latter Day Saints, beware of imposition! [Ottawa, Ill.: 1847]
Broadside. 50×30cm.
Signed: Wm. Smith, Aaron Hook, pres.
Written after William Smith left James J. Strang and began building his own church.
Morgan
USIC

8146a. ———. Zion's standard, a voice from the Smith Family. Princeton, Ill. Printed by P. Lynch, 1848.
Broadside. 55×29cm.
Dated: Mar. 24, 1848.
They denounced Brigham Young and his followers and told the Saints to follow William Smith.
USIC

8147. Smith, William Alexander. Family tree book; genealogical and biographical . . . Los Angeles, W. Thomas Smith [n.d.]
304p. ports., plates. 28cm.
Includes genealogy of the Flakes and Smiths who joined the Church.
UPB

8148. Smithwick, Noah. The evolution of a state; or, Recollections of old Texas days, by Noah Smithwick (nonagenarian) Comp. by his daughter Nanna Smithwick Donaldson. Austin, Tex., Gammel Book Company [1900]
5p.l., 9–354p. illus., ports. 20cm.
Lyman Wight's colony in Texas and "Mormon mills," p. 235–236, 300–307, 309, 316, 319, 322.
CU-B

8149. Smoot, Brigham. Ko hono fakamatala jI'I ki he Bule'aga 'o Hevani bea moe hala I'auji'I'aia 'oku fakatau ki ai. Na'e hiki 'i he lea faka-toga 'e Bilikihama Samuta. Salt Lake City, Deseret News Publishing Company, 1893.
2p.l. [5]–56p. 18cm.
Title in English: An explanation and description of the kingdom of Heaven.
UPB, USIC

Smoot, Reed. Correspondence between Senator Reed Smoot and N. V. Jones. *See Jones, Nathaniel Vary.*

———. The Life Story of Brigham Young. *See Gates, Susa (Young)*

8150. ———. The Mormon church. Speech given in the Senate of the United States, Tuesday, November 11, 1919. Washington, Govt. Print. Off., 1919.
2–8p. 23cm.
Cover-title.
UPB, USIC

8151. ———. Senator from Utah. Speech of Hon. Reed Smoot of Utah in the Senate of the United States, Tuesday, February 19, 1907. Washington [Govt. Print. Off.] 1907.
8p. 23cm.
The Mormon church and its allegiance to the country.
CU-B, UPB, USIC

8152. ———. A United States Senator's reasons for being a Mormon. By Reed Smoot, Senator from Utah. Brooklyn, New York, Eastern States Mission [1926?]
8p. 24cm.
Reprinted from the *Forum*, October, 1926.
NjP, UPB, USlC

———. Why I am a Mormon. *See Twelve modern apostles . . .*

Smucker, Samuel Mosheim. *See Schmucker, Samuel Mosheim.*

8153. Smythe, William Ellsworth. City homes on country lanes. Philosophy and practice of the home-in-a-garden. By William E. Smythe . . . New York, The Macmillan Company, 1921.
270p. 21½cm.
Article on Mormon government, p. 203–206. Prosperous condition of Utah attributed to the Church organization.
CU, NjP, ULA, UPB

8154. ———. The conquest of arid America. New York, London, Harper & Brothers, 1900.
xv [1] 325 [1]p. plates, maps (1 fold.) 19cm.
First appeared in *Century Magazine*, 1895, V.50, p. 81–99.
Includes "Mormon commonwealth and pleasant land of Utah."
Another edition: London: New York, Macmillan Co., 1905. CU–B; New and rev. ed., 1911. DLC, UHi, ULA, UPB
CSmH, CU–B, DLC, NjP, USlC

8155. ———. History of San Diego, 1542–1907. Account of the rise and progress of the pioneer settlement on the Pacific Coast of the United States. San Diego, The History Co., 1907.
3p.l. [5]–736p. 26cm.
Brief mention of Mormon Battalion members in San Diego.
Another edition: San Diego, History Co., 1908. CU–B, NjP
CU–B, DLC, USlC

8156. Snow, Edward Hunter. Political and religious ideals; address delivered over Radio Station KSL, Sunday Evening, June 24, 1928. [Salt Lake City] 1928.
Broadside. 61×20cm.
Reprinted from the *Deseret News*, Saturday, June 30, 1928.
UPB

Snow, Eliza R. *See Smith, Eliza Roxey (Snow)*

8157. Snow, Erastus. An address to the citizens of Salem and vicinity, by E. Snow and B. Winchester, Elders of the Church of Jesus Christ of Latter-Day Saints. [Salem, Mass., Salem Observer Press, 1841]
8p. 21cm.
Signed: Salem, Mass., Sept. 9, 1841.
MSaE

8158. ———. (same) Published for F. Nickerson. [Boston, 1841]
8p. 22cm.
Caption-title.
Second edition.
Dated at end: Boston, Mass., Sept. 13, 1841.
Sabin 85508
DLC, MB, MH

8159. ———. E. Snow's reply to the self-styled philanthropist, of Chester County [Philadelphia? 1840?]
16p. 19½cm.
Caption-title.
Local religious controversy over Mormonism.
A second reply to a pamphlet by "Philanthropist" identified as a Methodist preacher, Caleb Jones.
For reply to Philanthropist's first pamphlet, *see Bennett, Samuel.*
MH

8160. ———. One year in Scandinavia; results of the gospel in Denmark and Sweden — sketches and observations on the country and people — remarkable events — late persecutions and present aspect of affairs . . . By Erastus Snow . . . Liverpool, Published by F. D. Richards, 1851.
2p.l. [5] 24p. 21½cm.
Sabin 85510
CSmH, CtY, DLC, ICN, MH, MoInRC, NjP, NN, UPB, USl, USlC

8161. ———. En röst från landet Zion. Vittnesbörd af de lefvande och de döde Samlet af Erastus Snow. Köpenhamn, Tryckt vid E. Snow, Bekostnad, hos Sally B. Solomon, 1852.
48p. 21cm.
Title in English: A voice from the land of Zion.
Sabin 84411
CtY, MH, UPB, USlC

8162. ———. (same) [Köpenhamn, 1852?]
48p. 22cm.
Caption-title: "In ladning"
Preface: 1852.
Signed: Erastus Snow.
Variant printing.
CU–B

8163. ———. (same) Köpenhamn, Utgifwet af Jesse N. Smith. Tryckt hos F. E. Bording [1862]
55 [1]p. 20cm.
USlC

SNOW, E.

8164. ———. (same) Köpenhamn, Utgifwet af C. Widerborg. Tryckt hos F. E. Bording, 1867.
32p. 22cm.
MnU, NjP

8165. ———. (same) Köpenhamn, Utgifwet af C. E. Larsen. Tryckt hos F. E. Bording, 1873.
48p. 21cm.
USIC

8166. ———. (same) Köpenhamn, Utgifven af N. C. Flygare. Tryckt hos F. E. Bording, 1878.
2p.l. [5] 48p. 21cm.
CtY, UHi, USIC

8167. ———. (same) Köbenhamn, 1883.
48p. 21cm.
CSmH

8168. ———. (same) Ny genomsedd upplaga. Köpenhamn, Utgifven och förlagd af C. D. Fjeldsted. Tryckt hos F. E. Bording, 1889.
48p. 21cm.
USIC

8169. ———. En sandheds-röst. Til de oprigtige af hjertet. Oversat fra det Engelske af P. O. Hansen. Kjøbenhavn, 1850.
16p. 21cm.
Includes 16 articles of faith, by Erastus Snow.
Title in English: A voice of Truth.
Sabin 85512
CSmH

8170. ———. (same) Kjøbenhavn, 1852.
16p. 17cm.
USIC

8171. ———. (same) [Kjøbenhavn, Udgivet af W. Snow. Tryckt hos F. E. Bording, 1854]
16p. 21cm.
"4de oplag."
UPB

8171a. ———. (same) [Köpenhamn, Udgivet af F. J. Van Cott. Trykt hos F. E. Bording, 1859?]
16p. 20cm.
USIC

8172. ———. (same) [16de oplag. Kjobenhavn, Udgivet af J. Van Cott, Bording's Bogbykteri, 1860]
16p. 23cm.
UHi, USIC

8173. ———. (same) Om evangelii första grundsatser eller herrens väg till att frälsa menniskorna. Syndafallet och försoningen. 4 upp. Kjøbenhavn, 1861.
16p. 21cm.
Sabin 85513
ICN

8174. ———. (same) [Kjobenhavn, Udgivet af J. Van Cott. Trykt hos F. E. Bording, n.d.]
16p. 21cm.
"5te oplag."
USIC

8175. ———. (same) [Kjobenhavn, Udgivet af J. Van Cott, 1862]
16p. 22cm.
Caption-title.
"6te oplag."
Signed: E. Snow.
CU–B, USIC

8176. ———. (same) [Kjøbenhavn, n.d.]
16p. 21cm.
"7de oplag."
USIC

8177. ———. (same) [Kjøbenhavn, Udgivet af J. Van Cott. Trykt hos F. E. Bording, n.d.]
16p. 21cm.
"8de oplag."
USIC

8178. ———. (same) Kjøbenhavn, Udgivet af R. Peterson. Trykt hos F. E. Bording, 1873.
16p. 21cm.
Caption-title.
"96de Tusind."
UHi, UPB, USIC

8179. ———. (same) [Kjøbenhavn, Udgivet af C. Larsen. Tryckt hos F. E. Bording, 1874]
16p. 21cm.
"101 Tusind."
USIC

8180. ———. (same) [Kjobenhavn, N. C. Flygare, 1875]
16p. 23cm.
"116 Tusind."
USIC

8181. ———. (same) [Kjobenhavn, Udgivet af C. D. Fjeldsted. Trykt hos F. E. Bording, 1881]
16p. 20½cm.
Caption-title.
"121 Tusind."
UHi, USIC

8182. ———. (same) [Kjøbenhavn] 1893.
16p. 18½cm.
CSmH

8183. ———. (same) [Kobenhavn, Udgivet og forlagt af Peter Sundwall. . . . Trykt Hos F. E. Bording, 1894]
16p. 22cm.
USIC

SNOW, E.

8184. ———. (same) Kobenhavn, Udgivet og forlagt af Andreas Peterson . . . Trykt hos F. E. Bording, 1899]
16p. 22cm.
USlC

8185. ———. (same) [København, Udgivet og forlagt af Andreas Peterson . . . Trykt hos J. D. Swift (A. Larsen) 1900]
16p. 23cm.
UPB, USlC

8186. ———. (same) København, Udgivet og forlagt af A. L. Skanchy. Trykt hos L. A. Nielsen . . . 1902.
24p. 18½cm.
USlC

8187. ———. (same) [Kjøbenhavn, Udgivet og forlagt af Martin Christopherson . . . Trykt hos P. S. Christiansen & Co., Aarhus, 1902?]
24p. 17cm.
USlC

8188. ———. (same) Kjøbenhavn, Udgivet og forlagt af Anthon L. Skanchy . . . Trykt for P. S. Christiansen i Arbejderpartiets Bogtrykkeri i Aarhus, 1903.
24p. 17cm.
USlC

8189. ———. (same) Kjøbenhavn, Udgivet og forlagt af Anthon L. Skanchy, 1903.
24p. 18½cm.
Cover-title.
In pink printed wrappers.
Variant printing.
UPB, USlC

8189a. ———. (same) Kjøbenhavn, Udgivet og forlagt af Anthon L. Skanchy, 1904.
24p. 19cm.
USlC

8190. ———. (same) [Kjøbenhavn, Udgivet og forlagt af Martin Christopherson, 1905?]
24p. 17cm.
USlC

8191. ———. (same) Kobenhavn, Udgivet og forlagt af J. M. Christensen, . . . [Trykt hos P. S. Christiansen, Aarhus] 1907.
24p. 18½cm.
USlC

8192. ———. (same) København, Udgivet og forlagt af Carl E. Peterson . . . 1921.
16p. 21cm.
USlC

8193. ———. (same) [Kjøbenhavn, Udgivet af W. Snow. Trykt hos F. E. Bording, n.d.]
16p. 22cm.
USlC

8194. ———. (same, in Swedish) En Sannings-röst til de Uppriktiga af hjärtat . . . Om Evangelii första grundsattser eller herrens väg till att frälsa menniskorna. [Kjobenhamn, Redigerad och utgifven af J. Van Cott. Trykt hos F. E. Bording, 1860]
16p. 21cm.
USlC

8195. ———. (same) Syndofallet och forsoningen. 4 upp. Kjobenhavn, 1861.
16p. 21cm.
Sabin 85513
ICN

8196. ——— (same) [Köpenhamn, C. Widerborg, 1864]
16p. 20cm.
Caption-title.
"6de upplagan."
CtY, CU–B

8197. ———. (same) [Köpenhamn, 1864?]
16p. 21cm.
"7de oplag."
USlC

8198. ———. (same) [Köpenhamn, Trykt hos F. E. Bording, 1873]
16p. 21cm.
"9 upplagan."
USlC

8199. ———. (same) 4de oplag. Köpenhamn, Utgifven och forlagt af D. R. Liljenquist, 1877]
16p. 21cm.
Caption-title.
CtY, UHi

8200. ———. (same) [12. upplagan. Köpenhamn, N. C. Flygare. Tryckt hos F. E. Bording, 1879]
16p. 22cm.
Caption-title.
CDU, CtY

8201. ———. (same) [Trettonde upplagan. Köpenhamn, Utgiven och Förlagd af N. Wilhelmsen. Trykt hos F. E. Bording, 1880]
16p. 22½cm.
USlC

8201a. ———. (same) (Sjuttonde upplagan. Köpenhamn. Utgifven och förlagd af C. A. Carlquist. Tryckt hos F. E. Bording (V. Petersen). 1893.
24p. 17½cm.
USlC

8202. ———. (same) Tjugonde upplagan. Pris lo öre. Köpenhamn, Utgifven och förlagd af Andreas Peterson. Tryckt hos F. E. Bording, 1899.
24p. 18½cm.
USlC

8203. ———. (same) Tjugufjärde upplagan. Stockholm, G. N. Hulterström [1923]
31p. 18½cm.
UPB

8204. ———. (same) Tjugufemte upplagan. Utgiven och forlagd av Gideon N. Hulterström, Stockholm, 1929.
24p. 19cm.
USlC

8205. Snow, Lorenzo. Greeting to the world by President Lorenzo Snow. Delivered at the centennial services, Latter-day Saints' Tabernacle, Salt Lake City, January 1, 1901. [Salt Lake City, 1901]
[4]p. 27cm.
Variant printing USlC
NjP, USlC

8206. ———. (same) [Salt Lake City, 1901]
[4]p. port. 22cm.
Includes poem: O, Say, What is truth?
USlC

8207. ———. His ten wives. The travels, trial and conviction of the Mormon Apostle, Lorenzo Snow. From Nauvoo to the penitentiary. From the record. Butte, Montana, M. Koch, Publishers, 1887.
2p.l. [5]–104p. ports. 19½cm.
CSmH, CtY, DLC, MH, NjP, NN, USl, USlC, WHi

8208. ———. The Italian Mission. By Lorenzo Snow, one of the Twelve Apostles of the Church of Jesus Christ of Latter-day Saints . . . London, Printed by W. Aubery, 1851.
2p.l. [5]–28p. 20½cm.
Sabin 85526
CSmH, CtY, CU-B, ICN, MH, MoInRC, NjP, NN, UHi, UPB, USl, USlC

8209. ———. Nýja öldin, ávarp til allra heimsins thjótha frá Lorenzo Snow . . . [Akureyri, Prentsm. B. J. 1901]
16p. 19cm.
Title in English: The new age from Lorenzo Snow. A call to all people of the world. Edited by Jon Johannesson.
USlC

8210. ———. The Only way to be saved. "The wayfaring man, though a fool, need not err therein." An Explanation of the first principles of the doctrine of the Church of Jesus Christ of Latter-day Saints. By Lorenzo Snow, an American missionary. London, Printed by D. Chalmers, 1841.
12p. 17½cm.
At head of title: "He that judgeth a matter before he heareth it is not wise." — Solomon.
CtY, MB, USlC

8211. ———. (same) London [1841]
[12]p. 15½cm.
Copy badly trimmed, so that the "At head of title" and publisher could have been trimmed off. However, it is a variant of the above, having a verse on title page, and different information on final leaf.
UPB

8212. ———. (same) London: Printed by F. Shephard, High Street, Islington. 1844.
12p. 17½cm.
USlC

8213. ———. (same) By Lorenzo Snow, Missionary from America, and President of the Italian, Swiss, and East India Mission. London, Printed by W. Bowden, 1851.
8p. 21cm.
At head of title: "He that judgeth a matter before he heareth it is not wise."
Three variants. USlC
Sabin 85527
CSmH, CtY, ICN, MH, MoInRC, NjP, UPB, USlC

8214. ———. (same) Delhi [India] Republished by Elders Woolley and Fotheringham. Re-printed at the Indian Standard Press, by W. DeMonte, 1853.
8p. 21cm.
At head of title: "He that judgeth a matter before he heareth it is not wise."
USlC

8215. ———. (same) Madras [India] Reprinted by R. Ballantyne, Presiding Elder of the Mission to Madras, 1853.
8p. 21cm.
At head of title: "He that judgeth a matter before he heareth it is not wise."
UPB, USlC

8216. ———. (same) London, Printed by W. Bowden, 1854.
8p. 21cm.
Copy owned by Peter Crawley.

8217. ———. (same) Sydney, Re-published by A. Farnham, 1854.
8p. 19cm.
USl

8218. ———. (same) By Lorenzo Snow, one of the Twelve Apostles . . . Liverpool, F. D. Richards . . . London, Latter-day Saints' Book Depot . . . 1855.
7 [1]p. 20½cm.
At head of title: "He that judgeth a matter before he heareth it is not wise."
Sabin 85529
CSmH, DLC, ICN, USlC

8219. ———. (same) [Liverpool, Printed by Franklin D. Richards, ca. 1867]
8p. 23cm.
USlC

8220. ———. (same) [Liverpool, Printed by Franklin D. Richards, ca. 1868]
8p. 21cm.
USlC

8221. ———. (same) [Liverpool, Printed and Published by A. Carrington, 187–]
8p. 21cm.
Caption-title.
CtY, USlC

8222. ———. (same) [Liverpool, Printed by Albert Carrington, 42, Islington, 187–]
8p. 21cm.
Caption-title.
Variant printing of 8221.
USlC

8223. ———. (same) [Liverpool, Printed and Published by Horace E. Eldredge, 1870?]
8p. 21cm.
USlC

8224. ———. (same) Salt Lake City, Printed and Published at the "Juvenile Instructor" Office [1870?]
8p. 21cm.
Sabin 85530
USlC

8225. ———. (same) [Liverpool, Printed and Published by Joseph F. Smith, 1874?]
8p. 21½cm.
Caption-title.
CSmH, UHi, USlC

8226. ———. (same) [Salt Lake City, Deseret News Company? after 1884]
15p. 17cm.
MoInRC, OClWHi, USl, USlC

8227. ———. (same) [Liverpool? Millennial Star Office? c1904?]
8p. 21cm.
Caption-title.
ICN, MiU, UHi, USlC

8228. ———. (same) By Elder Lorenzo Snow, one of the Twelve Apostles of the Church of Jesus Christ of Latter-day Saints . . . Christ's church. England, G. Tombs and Co., Printers [n.d.]
8p. 21½cm.
UPB

8229. ———. (same) Salt Lake City, Juvenile Instructor Office [n.d.]
8p. 22cm.
UPB

8230. ———. (same, in Armenian) Asel khelas tarige Heswovs Khrisdwosen akher kunler modadaslere guelesesinin take mamtena daür pir izahat. Nasheri. F. F. Hintze. Instanbulse. V. Minassian matpasa, 1899.
2p.l. [3]–20p. 18cm.
UPB, USlC

8231. ———. (same, in Bengali) [The only path of salvation, or the recovery of the original scripture, that is, the special explanation of the Lord Christ's original doctrine by the Latter-day Saints] Calcutta, Colombian Press, 1852.
30p. 15cm.
Title translated.
CtY

8232. ———. (same, in Danish) Den eneste Vei til salighed. En Forklaring over Begundelseslaeren i "Jesu Christi de Sidste-Dages helliges Kirke," af Lorenzo Snow . . . [Kjøbenhavn, Udgivet og forlagt af J. Van Cott. Trykt hos F. E. Bording, 1860]
8p. 21½cm.
"Anden oplag."
CSmH, USlC

8233. ———. (same) Den enda vej til Salighed. En Forklaring over Begyndelseslaeren i "Jesu Christi Kirke af Sidste-Dages Hellige," af Lorenzo Snow. [Kjobenhavn, Udgivet og forlagt af Jesse N. Smith. Trykt hos F. E. Bording, 1862]
8p. 21cm.
"Tredie oplag."
USlC

8234. ———. (same) [Kjobenhavn, Udgivet og forlagt af R. Peterson. Trykt hos F. E. Bording, 1873]
8p. 21½cm.
Caption-title.
"23de Tusinde."
UHi, USlC

8235. ———. (same) [Kjobenhavn, Udgivet og forlagt af C. G. Larsen, (31te Tusinde) Trykt hos F. E. Bording, 1875]
8p. 23cm.
UPB

8236. ———. (same) [Kjøbenhavn, Udgivet og forlagt af R. Wilhelmsen. Trykt hos F. E. Bording, 1880]
8p. 21cm.
"39te Tusinde."
CSmH, UPB, USIC

8237. ———. (same) [Kjobenhavn, G. C. Fjeldsted. Trykt hos F. E. Bording, 1882]
8p. 20½cm.
Caption-title.
"44de Tusinde."
UHi

8238. ———. (same) Kjøbenhavn, Udgivet og forlagt af Andreas Peterson . . . Trykt hos F. E. Bording . . . 1899.
8p. 23cm.
"155de Tusinde."
USIC

8238a. ———. (same) Kjobenhavn, Udgivet og forlagt af Anthon L. Skanchy, P. S. Christiansens Tryk. Aarhus, 1903.
8p. 23½cm.
USIC

8238b. ———. (same) [Kjobenhavn, Udgivet og forlagt af Anthon L. Skanchy, P. S. Christiansens Tryk, Aarhus, 1904]
8p. 23½cm.
USIC

8238c. ———. (same, under title) Kun een vej til salighed; En forklaring over begyndelseslaeren i Jesu Kristi evangelium. [Kobenhavn, Udgivet og forlagt af Anthon L. Skanchy, Trykt hos L. A. Nielsen, 1903.
8p. 23½cm.
USIC

8239. ———. (same, in Dutch) De eenige weg om zalig te worden. [Zwolle, Boekdrukkerij van W. F. Zweers, 1875?]
8p. 23cm.
Caption-title.
USIC

8239a. ———. (same, in French) Exposition des premiers principes de la doctrine de l'Eglise de Jésus Christ des Saints des Derniers Jours par Lorenzo Snow, ministre de l'évangile venant de la cité du Grand Lac Salé Haute-Californie, États-Unis d'Amérique . . . Turin, Imprimerie Louis Arnaldi, 1851.
16p. 21cm.
USIC

8239b. ———. (same, under title) Restauration de l'évangile ancien ou exposition des premiers principes de la doctrine de l'eglise de Jésus Christ des Saints des Derniers Jours par l'Elder Lorenzo Snow venant de la cité du Grand Lac Salé Haute-Californie, États-Unis d'Amerique . . . [Malte, 1852]
8p. 21cm.
Caption-title.
Sabin 85532
UPB, USIC

8239c. ———. (same) Traduit de l'Anglais . . . Troisième édition. Berne, Published par G. C. Naegle, 1895.
16p. 18cm.
Cover-title.
UHi, USIC

8239d. ———. (same, in German) Die Wiederherstellung des Ursprünglichen Evangeliums, oder die ersten Grundsätze der Lehre der Kirche Jesus Christi der "Latter-day Saints" von Lorenzo Snow . . . Aus dem Englischen übersetzt von J. P. Scheib . . . London, Gedruckt bei Johann Burghard . . . 1851.
15p. 18cm.
USIC

8240. ———. (same, in Greek) Asel chelas tariki Iesoys Christosen acher koynler moykattesleri kilisesinin talimatena taïr pir izachat . . . Oytzoyntzoy Resale. Inchiliztzeten tertzeme oloynmoyz ter Nasiri F. F. Hintze Instanbula, V. Minassian Matpasa, 1899.
2p.l. [3]–20p. 18cm.
USIC, UPB

8241. ———. (same, in Italian) Turin, 1852.
Sabin 85528
no copy located

8242. ———. (same, in Swedish) Den enda wäg till salighet. Köpenhamn, Udgifwen och Förlaggd auf John van Cott, 1860.
8p. 20cm.
CSmH

8243. ———. (same) En förklaring öfver begynnelseläran i "Jesu Christi de siste-dagars heliges kyrka" 3 uppl . . . [Köpenhamn, J. N. Smith, 1862]
8p. 20cm.
Caption-title.
Sabin 85525
CtY

8244. ———. (same) Tolfte Tusen. [Köpenhamn, Utgifwen och förlaggd af K. Peterson. Trykt hos F. E. Bording . . . 1872.
8p. 21cm.
USIC

8245. ———. (same) [25te tusen. Köpenhamn, Utgiven och förlaggd af A. W. Carlson. Trykt hos F. E. Bording, 1877]
8p. 22cm.
Caption-title.
CDU, CtY, UHi, USIC

8245a. ———. (same) [Kopenhamn, Utgifven och forlagd af Anthon H. Lund, Tryckt hos F. E. Bording, 1884]
8p. 22cm.
35te tusendet.
USIC

8246. ———. (same) [Köpenhamn, Utgifven och förlagd af Andreas Peterson. Trykt hos F. E. Bording, 1899]
8p. 23cm.
"155te Tusendet"
USIC

8247. ———. (same) Den enda vägen till salighet. En förklaring öfver begynnelsesläran i Jesu Kristi Evangelium. Af Lorenzo Snow. [Köpenhamn, Utgifven och förlagd af Andreas Peterson, Tryckt hos F. E. Bording (V. Petersen) 1900]
8p. 21½cm.
185te tusendet.
USIC

8248. ———. (same) Enda vägen till salighet. Malmö, Utgifven och förlagd i Malmö af C. D. Fjeldsted. Tryckt å Landby & Lundgrens Boktryckeri, 1905.
8p. 22cm.
UPB

8248a. ———. (same) Enda vagen till salighet. En kort framstallning av begynnelselaran i Jesu Kristi evangelium. [Stockholm, Huvudkontor for Svenska missionen av Jesu Kristi kyrka av Sista Dagars Heliga, 1923]
8p. 22½cm.
USIC

8249. ———. To whom it may concern: [Salt Lake City, 1893]
Broadsheet. 23½×30cm.
At head of title: Salt Lake Temple, Salt Lake City, June 23rd, 1893.
Signed: Lorenzo Snow, President of Salt Lake Temple.
Printed form on verso.
UPB

———, *defendant.* United States of America, Respondent vs. Lorenzo Snow, Appellant. *See Richards, Franklin Snyder.*

8250. ———, *defendant.* United States of America, Respondent, vs. Lorenzo Snow, Appellant. Transcript. Indictment. [Salt Lake City, 1886?]
19cm. 22cm.
At head of title: Supreme Court of Utah Territory. January Term. 1886.
Second of three indictments.
USIC

8251. ———, *defendant.* United States of America, Respondent vs. Lorenzo Snow, Appellant. Transcript. Indictment. [Salt Lake City, 1886?]
36p. 22cm.
At head of title: Supreme Court of Utah Territory. January Term. 1886.
Third of three indictments.
USIC

8252. ———. Voice of Joseph, a brief account of the rise, progress, and persecutions of the Church of Jesus Christ of Latter-day Saints; with their present position and prospects in Utah Territory, together with "American exiles' memorial to Congress." By Lorenzo Snow. Abbreviated from the Italian edition. Liverpool, Published by S. W. Richards . . . London: Sold at the Latter-day Saints Book Depot, 1852.
19p. 21cm.
Abbreviated from the Italian edition.
Sabin 85534
CSmH, CtY, ICN, MH, NjP, NN, UHi, UPB, USIC

8253. ———. (same) [Valletta?] Malta, 1852.
21p. 23cm.
Sabin 85535
CSmH, CtY, CU–B, UPB, USIC

8254. ———. (same) Liverpool, S. W. Richards, London, Latter-day Saint Book Depot, 1852.
11p. 23cm.
Sabin 85535
CSmH

8255. ———. (same, in French) La voix de Joseph. Écrite et recueillie, par Lorenzo Snow, Ministre de l'Évangile de la Cité du Grand Salé-Lake Dans l'Etat de Deseret (Haute-California) dans l'Amérique de Nord. Turin, Imprimerie, Ferrero et Franco, 1851.
90p. 16cm.
Sabin 85533
NjP, USIC

8256. Snow, Zerubbabel. Communication of Attorney-General Mr. Z. Snow, to the Legislative Assembly. [Salt Lake City, 1872]
8p. 22½cm.
Caption-title.
Includes correspondence with William Clayton, Auditor of Public Accounts, concerning funds for expenses of District Courts, p. 3–8.
Problems of church and territorial government.
NjP, UHi, USIC, UU

8257. ———. (same) [Salt Lake City, 1872]
3p. 22½cm.
A variant printing of the first section of the 8p. pamphlet without the correspondence with William Clayton.
USIC

8258. ———. Communication of Attorney-General Z. Snow in response to a vote of the House of Representatives of the Territorial Legislature, February 4, 1874, on the jurisdiction of the Probate Courts and other matters pertaining to legal jurisdiction and alleged malfeasance of certain officers, charged by His Excellency, the Governor in his message of the 4th inst. Salt Lake City, P. O. Calder, Public Printer, 1874.
30p. 23cm.
Cover-title.
Signed: Feb. 5, 1874.
Church and politics.
Sabin 85562
CU–B, MH, NN, UPB, USIC

———. Latter-day Saints in Utah. *See Richards, Franklin Dewey, compiler.*

8259. Snow College, Ephraim, Utah. Snow College. Catalog. Ephraim, 1891–
v. 14½-21cm.
Formerly Sanpete Stake Academy; Snow Academy, Snow Normal College.
UPB 1913–15, 1923–25, 1926–31; USIC 1891–92, 1898–1914, 1919–20

8260. ———. Commencement exercises. Ephraim, Utah, 1905–19.
v. 19cm.
Snow Academy commencement, 1905; Snow Normal College commencement, 1919.
USIC 1905, 1919

8261. Snowden, James Henry. The truth about Mormonism, by James H. Snowden. New York, George H. Doran Company [c1926]
xixp., [1]l., 25–369p. plates, ports. 21cm.
CtY, CU–B, DLC, ICN, IWW, MH, MoInRC, NjP, NjPT, NN, UHi, ULA, UPB, USI, USIC, UU, WHi

8262. Snowflake Stake Academy, Snowflake, Arizona. Announcement. Snowflake, 1908–
v. 19½–21½cm.
UPB 1914–15, 1918–19; USIC 1901–02, 1908–09, 1909–10, 1910–11, 1911–12, 1912–13, 1913–14, 1914–15, 1915–16, 1916–17, 1917–18, 1918–19

8263. Snowonian, Ephraim, Utah. Published by the Students of Snow College, 191–?–
v. 28cm.
Student yearbook.
USIC 1915, 1921, 1926, 1927, 1928

8264. Snyder, John Francis. Adam W. Snyder and his period in Illinois history, 1817–1842 . . . Second and Revised edition. Springfield, Ill., The H. W. Rokker Co., Printers, 1903.
392 [2]p. port. 20cm.
Several mentions of Mormon influence in Illinois before 1842.
Another edition: Virginia, Ill., E. Needham, Bookseller and Stationer, 1906. NjP, UHi
Howes S745
DLC

8265. Snyder, John Jacob. Glad tidings. The fulfillment of the covenant or promises of God to Israel — prophecy that has been fulfilled, and to be fulfilled — the gathering of Israel to their promised lands — the American Indians are a remnant of the house of Israel; they were once a white race, and will again become a white race. [Kansas City, Mo.?] 1920.
192p. 15½cm.
Cover-title.
Signed: John J. Snyder.
A reprint of a book by David Whitmer, entitled, "An address to all believers in Christ!" p. 11–110.
CU–B, MoInRC, NjP, NN, UPB, UU

8266. ———. Glad tidings. How to obtain happiness and health, by John J. Snyder. [Chicago?, 1905]
103p. 22½cm. (No. 1)
Faith healing.
Morgan
DLC

8267. ———. Jesus is coming. Prophecy — the World War — the sign of the times. [Kansas City, Mo.] Truth Publishing Co., 1918.
47p. 20cm. (His [Glad tidings] book. No. 2)
Cover-title.
CU–B

8268. ———. The Lord is to establish the Church again in perfect order . . . [Kansas City, Mo.] Truth Publishing Co., 1918.
20p. 20cm. (His [Glad tidings] book. No. 4)
Cover-title.
CU–B

8269. ———. The Restoration of Israel. [Kansas City, Mo.] Truth Publishing Co., 1918.
16p. 20cm. (His [Glad tidings] book. No. 3)
Cover-title.
CU–B

8270. ———. The solution of the Mormon problem [Preface by John J. Snyder. Independence, Mo., Zion's Advocate] 1926.
[16]l. 13½cm.
Contains: "An address to believers in the Book of Mormon" by David Whitmer.
Morgan
MoInRC, NN, UHi, UPB, USIC

8271. ———. Truth. Number 1. [Davis City, Iowa, 1895]
1p.l., 41p. 20½cm.
Signed: Salt Lake City, Utah, May, 1895.
References to Mormon beliefs, though the tract professes to have no religious affiliations, but as "A seeker after truth."
Morgan
MH, USl, USlC

8272. ———. Truth. Number 2. [Chicago, 1896]
1p.l., 197 [1]p. 21cm.
The truthfulness of the Book of Mormon.
MH, USlC

8273. Sobieski, John. The life-story and personal reminiscences of Col. John Sobieski (A lineal descendant of King John III, of Poland) written by himself; to which is added his popular lecture, "The Republic of Poland" (now first published) and a brief history of Poland. Shelbyville, Ill., J. L. Douthit & Sons, 1900.
xix, 384p. plates, port. 26cm.
Member of the Utah expedition.
Another edition: Los Angeles, L. G. Sobieski [after 1906] CU-B, UU
DLC, NjP, UHi, UPB

8274. Society for Promoting Christian Knowledge. "A note of warning." A tract of Mormonism . . . London [1907]
12p. 16cm.
USlC

Some account of Joseph Smith. *See Tayler, W. H.*

8275. Some account of the so-called Church of the Latter Day Saints. London: John W. Parker and Son, West Strand. 1852. [London, Savill and Edwards, Printers, Chandos Street, 1852]
iv [5]–24p. 14½cm.
Howes 7168, Sabin 86585
CtY

8276. Somerndike, John Mason. On the firing line with the Sunday School missionary. By John M. Somerndike. Philadelphia, The Westminster Press, 1912.
vi, 169p. plate. 19½cm.
Missionary work in Utah effective through Sunday School to "redeem this benighted religion," p. 78–79.
NjP, USlC

8277. Songs for the laying of the corner stones of the Temple in G. S. L. City. April 6, 1853. [Great Salt Lake City, 1853]
Broadside. 36½×27cm.
Includes "The temple" by Miss E. R. Snow.
Three columns in an ornamental border.
USlC

8278. Songs from the mountains, with a sketch of the Great Salt Lake Valley and City. Philadelphia, H. M. Clayton, Printer, 76 South Third Street [1849?]
Broadside. 37½×20cm.
Includes William Clayton's "Pioneer," Hail to the "Twelve," "Pioneers," by Miss E. R. Snow. "Come, Come, ye Saints," by William Clayton, "Safety in Zion," by J. H. Flanigan.
Within ornamental border.
MH

8279. Sorenson, Alfred. Early history of Omaha; or, Walks and talks among the old settlers: a series of sketches in the shape of a connected narrative of the events and incidents of early times in Omaha; together with a brief mention of the most important events of later years. Omaha, Nebr., Daily Bee, 1876.
2p.l., 248p. illus. 22½cm.
Mormons in Nebraska, p. 15–17.
Other editions: Omaha, Gibson, Miller & Richardson, 1889. NjP, UHi, UPB, USlC; 3d ed., rev. and enl. Omaha, Nat. Print. Co., 1923. USlC, UU
Howes S765, Sabin 87143
CU, NjP, UHi, USlC

8280. Sorenson, S. K. Seventy-one theological questions on gospel topics submitted to the public and in particular to the ministers of all denominations, by Elder S. K. Sorenson of the Reorganized Church of Jesus Christ of Latter Day Saints. Independence, Mo., Ensign Publishing House [1906?]
16p. port. 13cm.
Cover-title.
Signed: S. K. Sorenson, Lamoni, Iowa, December 7, 1906.
Errata slip pasted in.
MoInRC, UHi

8281. Sortore, Abram. Biography and early life sketch of the late Abram Sortore, including his trip to California and back. Alexandria, Mo., 1909.
1p.l., 10p. 22cm.
Includes a brief description of his encounter with Mormonism.
CU-B

8282. Soulé, Frank. The annals of San Francisco containing a summary of the history of the first discovery, settlement, progress and present condition of California . . . by Frank Soulé, John H. Gihon, M. D., and James Nisbet . . . New York, D. Appleton and Co., 1855.
2p.l. [5]–824p. ports., plates, fold. map. 23½cm.
Mention of early Mormon activity in California.
Howes S769, Sabin 87368
CU-B, CSmH, DLC, NjP, NN, UPB

8283. Soulié, Maurice. Les procès célèbres des États-Unis, avec 26 gravures hors texte. Paris, Payot [1930?]
2p.l. [7]–270p. [1]l. 20cm.
U.S. trails. Includes "Joseph Smith, prophète et fondateur du Mormonisme, 1805–44," p. [97]–139.
History of Mormonism, tracing Joseph Smith's career through New York, Kirtland, Missouri, and Nauvoo.
Title in English: Famous trials of the United States.
NN

8284. South, Colon. Out west; or, From London to Salt Lake City and back, by Colon South. London, Wyman, & Sons, 1884.
2p.l. [3]–269p. 19½cm.
Pt. IV. The Mormons, p. 187–235.
CtY, CU-B, DLC, ICHi, NjP, NN, UHi, UPB, USlC

8285. South Place Institute, London. Religious systems of the world; a contribution to the study of comparative religion. A collection of addresses delivered at South Place Institute now revised and in some cases rewritten by the authors, together with some others specially written for this volume. 10th ed. London, George Allen Company, 1911.
viii, 824p. 22½cm.
Chapter on the Mormons prepared by Elder James H. Anderson, p. 657–683.
CU, UU

8286. Southern, John N. The Church of Christ at Independence, Mo., et al, Appellants, vs. The Reorganized Church of Jesus Christ of Latter Day Saints, Appellee. Appeal from the Circuit Court of the United States for the Western District of Missouri. Appellants' statement. [n.p., 1894]
92p. 21cm.
Signed: John N. Southern, C. O. Tichenor, Attys. of Respondents.
At head of title: In the United States. Circuit Court of Appeals. 8th circuit.
USlC

8287. ———. The Reorganized Church of Jesus Christ of Latter Day Saints, Complainant vs. The Church of Christ at Independence . . . Respondents. Abstracts of pleading and evidence. Independence, Mo., Independence Sentinel Print., 1893.
141p. 22cm.
Signed: John N. Southern, James O. Broadhead. Solicitors for respondents.
USlC

8288. "Southern Rays." Juarez, Mexico, 1906–1907.
v. monthly. 21½cm.
Publication of the students of Juarez Stake Academy.
USlC V.1 #1, 3, December 1906, February, 1907.

8289. Souvenir; home-coming week. Huntsville, Utah, July 2, 3 and 4, 1917. [Ogden? 1917]
40p. illus. 21cm.
"Huntsville Ward" compiled by Andrew Jensen, p. 5–30.
USlC

8290. Souvenir Novelty Company, Salt Lake City. Salt Lake City and scenic Utah. [Salt Lake City, 1918?]
25 lithographs. 26×32cm.
Church buildings and other views. Brief descriptions.
CSmH, UHi

8291. ———. Scenic gems of Salt Lake City and vicinity. [Salt Lake City, Souvenir Novelty Co., 1921?]
[20]p. illus. 21½cm.
Cover-title.
USlC

8292. ———. "Seeing" Salt Lake City, Utah. Salt Lake City, Published for the Seeing Salt Lake City Car and Automobile Company, by the Souvenir Novelty Co. [n.d.]
39 plates. 16×25½cm.
Views and brief descriptions of church buildings, etc.
NjP, UPB

8293. ———. Souvenir, birthplace of Joseph Smith, the Prophet, Sharon, Windsor County, Vermont. Salt Lake City [n.d.]
12 plates. 9×15cm.
A series of 12 postcard views.
UPB

8294. ———. Souvenir of Salt Lake; the city of the saints. Salt Lake City, Souvenir Novelty Co. [1915?]
[61]p. illus. 20½cm. & 26cm.
View of Salt Lake City, with brief descriptions.
DLC, UHi, UPB

8295. Souvenir of L.D.S. schools. [Salt Lake City, 1909?]
[32]p. illus., plates, ports. 13cm.
Purpose of church schools.
USlC

8296. ———. (same) [Salt Lake City] Deseret News [1909?]
[32]p. illus. 14cm.
Variant printing.
USlC

8297. A souvenir of Salt Lake City and Utah. New York, A. Wittemann, Publishers [c1888]
[2]l. 18 plates. 15×24cm.
Pictures of buildings of the church.
CSmH

8298. ———. (same) New York, The Albertype Co., c1889.
[2]l. 18 plates. 14×23½cm.
Cover-title: Salt Lake City illustrated.
UHi

8299. ———. (same) New York, A. Wittemann, Publishers, 1899.
[2]l. 18 plates. 14×23½cm.
DLC

8300. Souvenir: Proceedings of a meeting in honor of President Heber J. Grant's 70th birthday anniversary held in the Assembly Hall. Salt Lake City, Utah, Sunday, November 21st, 1926. Under the auspices of foreign language organizations of the Church of Jesus Christ of Latter-day Saints. [Salt Lake City, 1926]
18p. port. 23cm.
USlC

Souvenir. Utah and Utah interests.
See Talbot, E. L., compiler.

8301. Spahr, Charles Barzillai. America's working people, by Charles B. Spahr. New York, London [etc.] Longmans, Green, and Co., 1900.
vi, 261p. 24cm.
A description of the Mormon community and its cooperatives. This book was condemned by J. D. Nutting as being favorable to the Mormons.
Another edition: 2d ed. 1900. DLC
CU, DLC, NjP, NN, ULA

8302. Spalding, Franklin Spencer. The honest way out of a difficult situation. A friendly word to Latter-day Saints. By Rt. Rev. F. S. Spalding, Bishop of Utah. [Salt Lake City, 19 - -]
20p. 15cm.
Advice concerning the easiest way to disregard polygamy.
UPB, USlC

8303. ———. Joseph Smith, jr., as a translator. An inquiry conducted by Rt. Rev. F. S. Spalding . . . With the kind of assistance of capable scholars. Salt Lake City, Printed by the Arrow Press [1912]
30 [1]p. illus., facsim. 24cm.
Questions the validity of the *Pearl of Great Price.*
DLC, ICN, MoInRC, NN, ULA, USl, USlC, UU

8304. ———. (same) [2d ed.] New York, 1922.
31p. 22cm.
USlC

8305. ———. (same) Joseph Smith, Jr., as a translator. Reprint of an inquiry conducted by Rt. Rev. F. S. Spalding . . . New York, Presiding Bishop and Council, Department of Missions [Protestant Episcopal Church] 1922.
30[1]p. illus. 22cm. (No. 971)
Cover-title.
USlC

8305a. ———. (same) Reprint of an inquiry conducted by Rt. Rev. F. S. Spalding, D. D., late Bishop of Utah, with the kind assistance of capable scholars. New York, The National Council, Protestant Episcopal Church [193–]
30[1]p. 22cm. (No. 971)
Cover-title.
CSmH, IU, NjP, NN, UHi

8306. Spalding, Samuel Jones. Spalding memorial: a genealogical history of Edward Spalding, of Massachusetts Bay, and his descendants. By Samuel J. Spalding . . . Boston, A. Mudge & Son, Printers, 1872.
xi, 619p. col. front., col. plates (coats of arms) ports. 24cm.
Includes a letter concerning the Spaulding manuscript and its relation to Mormonism.
Sabin 88924
DLC, MB, MWA, NjP

8307. Sparks, Edwin Erle. The expansion of the American people, social and territorial, By Edwin Erle Sparks. Chicago, Scott, Foresman and Company [c1900]
2p.l., 5–463 [7]p. 19½cm.
Mormon reference in "American reformers." "Credulous people . . . believed that the age of miracles had not passed."
Another edition: 1906. USlC
CU–B

8308. Spaulding, Matilda Davidson. Folly and falsehood of the golden Book of Mormon. Hexham, Edward Pruddah [1840?]
4p. 16cm.
Wife of Solomon Spaulding.
Reprinted from *Lunenburgh Colonial Churchman,* Jan. 25, 1839.
Date in original is erroneous because her statement was first published in the *Boston Recorder,* April 19, 1839.
NN

8309. Spaulding, Solomon. The "Manuscript Found," or, "Manuscript Story" of the late Rev. Solomon Spaulding; from a verbatim copy of the original now in the care of Pres. James H. Fairchild, of Oberlin College, Ohio, including correspondence touching the manuscript, its preservation and transmission until it came into the hands of the publishers. Lamoni, Ia., The Reorganized Church of Jesus Christ of Latter Day Saints, 1885.
144p. 18cm.
CtY, CU–B, DLC, ICN, IWW, MH, MoInRC, NjP, NjPT, UHi, ULA, UPB, USl, USlC

8310. ———. (same) The "Manuscript Found." Manuscript Story, by Rev. Solomon Spaulding, deceased. Printed from a verbatim copy, made (expressly for this edition) from the original now in the possession of President James H. Fairchild, of Oberlin College, Ohio. Salt Lake City, Deseret News Co., 1886.
iv, 115p. 24cm.
CSmH, CU-B, DLC, MH, MoInRC, NjP, NN, ULA, UPB, USIC

8311. ———. (same) The "Manuscript Story," of Reverend Solomon Spaulding; or, "Manuscript Found" . . . Lamoni, Ia., Reorganized Church of Jesus Christ of Latter Day Saints [1903]
158p. 19cm.
CU-B, IWW, MnU, MoInRC, NjP

8312. ———. (same) Lamoni, Ia., Reorganized Church of Jesus Christ of Latter Day Saints, 1908.
158p. 17cm.
MoInRC, OO, UPB

8313. ———. (same as 1886) Liverpool, Printed and Published at the Millennial Star Office, 1910.
iv, 116p. 19cm.
CSmH, NjP, UHi, UPB, USIC, UU

8314. Spence, Thomas. The settler's guide in the United States and British North American provinces . . . By Thomas Spence . . . New York, Davis & Kent, 1862.
vi [7]–472p. illus., plates, fold. map. 20cm.
A discussion of the problems of a non-Mormon settling in Utah; historical background of Mormonism.
Sabin 89292
CSmH, CU-B, DLC, NjP, OrP, WaU

8315. Spencer, Emily Brown (Bush). Prose and poetry . . . Salt Lake City, Star Book and Job Printing, 1880.
3p.l., 88p. 19½cm.
Mormon poetry.
UPB, USIC

8316. ———. The rose of the Desert. By Emily B. Spencer. Salt Lake City, 1887.
100p. 17½cm.
Prose and verse, mainly on Mormonism.
"The dictionary of names," p. 77–100.
CU-B, DLC, MH, NjP, UPB, USIC, UU

8317. ———. Temple song. [n.p., 1893?]
[1]l. 15½cm.
Mormon poetry.
USIC

8318. Spencer, George S. Hij, die een zaak oordeelt, vóór bij haar onderzocht heeft, is niet wijs. De Versoening en het Verlosingsplan van Jezus Christus, door de Ouderlingen Geo. S. Spencer en W. J. De Brij, Zendelingen van de Kerk van Jezus Christus van de Heiligen der Laatste Dagen [Amsterdam? n.d.]
8p. 21cm.
Missionary tract.
Title in English: The plan of salvation and atonement of Jesus Christ.
USIC

8319. Spencer, Hiram Theron. Sketch of the life and experiences of patriarch and Mrs. H. T. Spencer, who pioneered Magna and vicinity. [Magna, Utah? 1925?]
13p. port. 22cm.
Cover-title.
"A sketch of Bishop Spencer's life was read by his granddaughter, Mary J. Howard."
Mormon biography.
UHi

8320. Spencer, Josephine. The senator from Utah, and other tales of the Wasatch. Salt Lake City, George Q. Cannon and Sons Co., 1895.
2p.l. [5]–301p. 17½cm.
Mormon fiction.
CU-B, MH, NjP, NN, UHi, UPB, USIC, UU

8321. Spencer, Orson. Character!! [Liverpool, R. James, Printer, 1848]
4p. 20½×13½cm.
Reprinted from the *Millennial Star*, July 1, 1848, as announced in the same issue, p. 208.
CtY, MH, MoInRC, NjP, UHi, UPB, USIC

8321a. ———. Circular of the Chancellor of the University of the State of Deseret. Great Salt Lake City, 1850.
Broadside. 22½×25cm.
USIC

8322. ———. Correspondence between the Rev. W. Crowel, A. M. and O. Spencer, B. A. Liverpool, R. James [1847]
12, 4,4,4,4,4,4,4,4,4,4,4p. 20½cm.
W. Crowel's letter to O. Spencer, 12p.; Crowel's letter 1842, p. 1–2; Spencer's answer, p. 3–12. Letters by Orson Spencer, 4p. each with caption-title and subject. Dated 1847.
Published separately.
Crowel wrote Spencer (as a friend of the family, and editor of the *Christian Watchman*) on October 21, 1842, and Spencer replied, Nauvoo, November 17, 1842, as published in the first tract. Probably not published separately until 1847.
Second to twelfth letters published in *Millennial Star*, May 15–November 15, 1847.
Letter #5 is erroneously dated 1842.
Tract reprints advertised in *Millennial Star*, July 1, 1847, p. 208, and September 1, 1847, p. 265, when publication of first letter was announced.
Another reprint of the first 12 letters was announced in the *Millennial Star*, January 1, 1848, p. 15.

SPENCER, O.

CONTENTS: 1. General introductory remarks (Crowel's letter and reply) 2. Immediate revelation. 3. On faith. 4. On water baptism. 5. The gift of the Holy Ghost. 6. Apostasy from the primitive church. 7. The re-establishment. 8. The true and living God. 9. The Priesthood. 10. On gathering. 11. The Latter-day judgments. 12. On the restitution of all things.
Sabin 89369
MH, MoInRC, NN, UPB, USlC

8323. ———. The Gospel Witness. [Liverpool, R. James, Printer, 1848]
8p. 21cm.
Caption-title.
Signed: Liverpool, July 1, 1848.
Printed from an article in the *Millennial Star*, June 1–15, 1848. Publication announced July 1, 1848, p. 208.
Variant printing. USlC
NjP, UPB defective, USlC

8324. ———. (same) [Liverpool, R. James, Printer, 1848?]
8p. 21cm.
Caption-title.
Variant printing.
CtY, MH, NN, USlC

8325. ———. Invitation. [Liverpool, 1847?]
Broadside. 19×11½cm.
Signed: June 18, 1847. *See Millennial Star*, V.14, p. 205.
MH

8326. ———. Letters exhibiting the most prominent doctrines of the Church of Jesus Christ of Latter-day Saints. By Orson Spencer. 3d ed. Liverpool, Published by Orson Spencer, 1848.
viii, 244p. 14½cm.
Enlargement of his "Correspondence," 14 letters to W. Crowel and additional material.
First edition in book form.
Sabin 89370
CtY, DLC, MH, MoInRC, NN, UU, UPB, USlC

8327. ———. (same) 4th ed. Liverpool, Published by S. W. Richards; Sold at the Latter-day Saints Book Depot, 1852.
viii, 244p. 15cm.
Sabin 89370
CtY, MH, MoInRC, UHi, USlC, UU

8328. ———. (same) 5th ed. Liverpool, Published by Brigham Young, junior; London, Sold at the Latter-day Saints Book Depot, 1866.
viii, 244p. 14cm.
UPB, USlC

8329. ———. (same) 5th ed. Salt Lake City, Deseret News Steam Printing Establishment, 1874.
viii, 252p. 18cm.
Sabin 89370
CU–B, DLC, IWW, MoInRC, NjP, NjPT, NN, UPB, USlC, UU

8330. ———. (same) 6th ed. Liverpool, Printed and Published by William Budge, 1879.
viii, 232p. 19cm.
CU–B, DLC, ICN, MH, MoInRC, OCl, RPB, UHi, ULA, USl, USlC, UU, WHi

8331. ———. (same) Salt Lake City, Deseret News Co., 1889.
vii, 280p. 17cm.
CSmH, MoInRC, NjP, UHi, USlC

8332. ———. (same) 6th ed. Salt Lake City, George Q. Cannon and Sons Co., 1891.
viii, 232p. 19cm.
ICHi, MH, MoInRC, NjP, NN, OClWHi, UHi, ULA, UPB, USlC

8333. ———. Patriarchal order, or plurality of wives! By Elder Orson Spencer . . . being his fifteenth letter in correspondence with the Rev. William Crowel . . . [Liverpool, S. W. Richards, Printed for the Publisher by R. James, 1853]
16p. 21cm.
Caption-title.
Sabin 89371, 89372
CSmH, CtY, CU–B, DLC, ICN, MoInRC, NjP, NN, UHi, UPB, USl, USlC

8334. ———. (same, in Danish) Den patriarkalske orden eller Fleerkoneri af Aeldste Orson Spencer . . . [Kjøbenhavn, Udgivet af J. Van Cott. Trykt hos F. E. Bording, 1854]
18p. 21cm.
Caption-title.
USlC

8335. ———. (same) Kansler ved Universitetet i Utah Territorium i de Forenede Stater i Amerika, og Praesident over den preussisse Mission af Jesu Christi Kirke af Sidste-dages Hellige . . . Kjøbenhavn, Udgivet af H. E. Haight i Mai 1856. Trykt hos F. E. Bording [1856]
16p. 21cm.
UHi, UPB, USlC, UU

8335a. ———. (same, in German) [Die patriarchalische Ordnung, oder die Mehrheit der Frauen. Zurich? 1855?]
32p. 23½cm.
The only known copy lacks title page, first page of text. Title supplied.
USlC def.

8336. ———. The Prussian mission of the Church of Jesus Christ of Latter-day Saints. Report of Elder O. Spencer to President Brigham Young. Liverpool, S. W. Richards . . . 1853.
16p. 21cm.
Sabin 89373
CSmH, CtY, CU–B, ICN, MH, NjP, NN, UHi, ULA, UPB, USl, USlC

8337. Spencer, Samuel George. Joseph Smith, the prophet of the XIX century. [Kansas City, Mo., Edmund D. Black, Printer, 1896?]
39p. illus. 16cm.
UPB, WHi

8338. ———. (same) [Salt Lake City, Schoenfield Press, n.d.]
47p. 19½cm.
UPB, USlC

8339. ———. Useful hints and suggestions for missionaries and scripture subjectively arranged by Elder Samuel G. Spencer. [n.p., n.d.]
16 [1]p. 14½cm.
Caption-title.
"Designed to be sewed in the Bible between the Old and New Testament."
MH

8340. Spencer, William Loring (Nuñez). Salt-Lake fruit; a Latter-day romance, by an American. Boston, Franklin Press, 1884.
viii, 328p. illus. 22cm.
Fiction concerning Mormons.
Author entry from Library of Congress.
CSmH, ICU, ICN, InU, NjP, NN, PPL, UHi, USlC

8341. ———. (same) Boston, Rand, Avery, and Company, 1884.
viii, 328p. illus. 21½cm.
OClWHi, UHi, UPB, USlC, UU, ViU, WHi

8342. ———. (same) Mansfield, Ohio, Estill & Co. [188–]
viii, 328p. illus. 21cm.
IU

8343. ———. (same, under title) Salt Lake-fruit, a thrilling Latter-day romance. By an American. Springfield, Mass., Pettigrew, 1889.
viii, 328p. 21cm.
Edition limited to 250 copies.
ICN, NjP, ULA, UPB, USlC

8344. ———. (same) New York, M. W. Jones, Publisher, 1891.
viii, 328p. 21cm.
NN, UU

8345. Spice, Robert Paulton. The wanderings of the hermit of Westminster between New York and San Francisco in the autumn of 1881. [London, Metchim and Son, 1882]
84p. illus. 21½cm.
Visit to Salt Lake City. Meets "The sensuous and cunning impostor Brigham Young" who maintains a despotic apostle rule. A wedge is now inserted to break it.
CU–B, NjP, UHi, USlC

Spirits in prison. *See Utah Tract Society.*

8346. Spori, Jakob. Das Evangelium welches Christus lehrte und dessen Wiederherstellung in den letzten Tagen. Constantinopel, 1887.
10p. 24cm.
Signed: Jakob Spori, Joseph Marion Tanner, Ferdinand Fries Hintze.
Title in English: The gospel which Christ taught and its restoration in the last days.
Missionary tract.
USlC

8347. ———. (same, in French) L'Evangile que le Christ enseignait et son rétablissement aux derniers jours. Par J. Spori, J. -M. Tanner, F. -F. Hintze. Traduit de l'Allemand. 1891. Berne, Publié par J. -J. Schaerrer, 1892.
15p. 20½cm.
USlC

8348. ———. (same) Troisieme edition. [Berne?] Publié par Geo. C. Naegle . . . 1895.
16p. 19cm.
"Articles de foi," p. 9–13. "Declaration officielle à tous ceux que ceci peut concerner," p. 13.
Signed: Wilford Woodruff.
Bib. Nat.

8349. Spring, Agnes (Wright). Caspar Collins: the life and exploits of an Indian fighter of the sixties, by Agnes Wright Spring, with a foreword by Maj. Gen. Hugh L. Scott . . . Together with Caspar Collins letter and drawings, and various photographs and documents connected with his career. New York, Columbia University Press, 1927.
1p.l., 187p. illus., plates, ports., map, plan, facsim. 24cm.
Reference to Mormons, troops and emigrants, p. 38–39, 46, 79, 118, 121–122, 127, 131.
CU–B

8350. Spring blossoms, a choice collection of historical and literary essays and original poems. Ogden, Utah, The Junction Book and Job Printing Offices, 1880.
48p. 18cm.
Mormon poetry.
UU

8351. Stadling, Jonas Jonsson. Genom den Stora Vestern. Reseskildringar af J. Stadling. Med illustrationer. Stockholm. Författarens förlag. [n.d.]
328p. 19½cm.
Mormons, p. 224–262.
Title in English: Through the Great West.
NjP

8352. ———. Hvad jag hörde och såg i mormonernas Zion. Af J. Stadling. 2. omarb. och tillökta uppl. Stockholm, På författarens förlag [1884]
61p. 16½cm.
Title in English: What I heard and saw in the Mormon Zion.
DLC, MnU

8353. Stafford, Edwin. Need of revelation. [Plano, Ill., True Latter Day Saints' Herald, 1865?]
4p. 23cm.
MoInRC, NN, UHi

8354. ———. Newness of life. [Plano, Ill., True Latter Day Saints' Herald, 1865?]
4p. 23cm.
MoInRC, NjP, NN, UHi

8355. The Standard. Sydney, Australia, 1902–
v. 29cm.
RLDS periodical in Australia.
MoInRC V.1–3, 5, 33–34, 40, 42–

8356. Standard stump speeches and Ethiopian lectures; a choice collection of stump speeches and negro burlesque recitations . . . by such artists as Houghy Dougherty, Add Ryman, Sen. Bob Hart. New York, M. J. Ivers, c1888.
48p. 21cm. (Standard recitation series [Extras] No. 1)
"Mormons and Mormonism; a discourse on polygamy, delivered by Gov. Add. Ryman," p. 15–16.
USl, USlC

8357. Standerson, Grantly. The hundredth wave; a novel written to accomplish two strongly interlinked purposes. Chicago, C. H. Kerr, 1916.
538p. 19½cm.
"Revelations of science deny the Mormon concept of God." Disbelieves story of Adam and Eve. Genesis and next four books of Jewish Bible are legends.
USlC, UU

8357a. Stanley, Charles. An address to the Mormons of Salt Lake City and elsewhere. [London, G. Morrish, 1886?]
10[2]p. 17cm.
A polemic against the church.
USlC

8358. Stansbury, Howard. An expedition to the valley of the Great Salt Lake of Utah: including a description of its geography, natural history, and minerals, and an analysis of its waters; with an authentic account of the Mormon settlement . . . Also, a reconnoissance of a new route through the Rocky mountains. And two large maps of that region. By Howard Stansbury, Capt., U. S. Army. London, S. Low, Son, and Co.; Philadelphia, Lippincott, Grambo, and Co., 1852.
1p.l., 487p. plates, 2 fold. maps. 22½cm. (U.S. 32nd Cong. Special Sess. Senate. Ex. Doc. No. 3)
Published by the U.S. Army Corps of Topographical Engineers.
An expedition to the valley of the Great Salt Lake, June, 1849–September 1850.
Howes S884, Sabin 90371, W-C 218
CSmH, DLC, MH, MWA, NjP, NN, UHi, ULA, UPB, UU, WHi

8359. ———. (same, under title) Exploration and survey of the valley of the Great Salt Lake of Utah, including a reconnoissance of a new route through the Rocky mountains. Philadelphia, Lippincott, Grambo & Co., 1852.
1p.l. [3]–487p. plates, map, atlas. 23½cm.
DLC, ICN, MH, NjP, NN, UHi, USlC, ViU

8360. ———. (same) Washington, Robert Armstrong, Public Printer, 1853.
495p. plates, map, atlas. 23½cm. (U.S. 32nd Cong. Special Sess., Senate. Ex. Doc. No. 3)
Howes S884, Sabin 90372, W-C 219
CSmH, DLC, IWW, MH, MiU, MoInRC, NN, ULA, UPB, USlC

8361. ———. (same) Philadelphia, Lippincott, Grambo and Co., 1855.
487p. 58 plates. 23cm.
NN, UHi

8362. ———. (same, in German) Die Mormonen-Ansiedlungen, die felsengebirge und der grosse Salzsee, nebst einer Beschreibung der Auswanderer-Strasse und der interessanten Abenteuer der Auswanderungen nach jenen Gegenden. Geschildert auf einer Untersuchungs-Expedition von Howard Stansbury . . . Deutsch bearbeitet von Dr. Kottenkamp. Mit einer Karte. Stuttgart, Franckh'sche Verlagshandlung, 1854.
viii, 293p. fold. map. 15½cm.
Howes S884, Sabin 90373
MH, NjP, OClWHi, UU

8363. Stanton, William Alonzo. Three important movements: Campbellism, Mormonism and Spiritualism by Rev. W. A. Stanton, D.D. Philadelphia, American Baptist Publishing Society [c1907]
2p.l. [5]–48p. 19cm.
IWW, MoInRC, NjPT, NN, USl, USlC

8364. Star in the East. Boston, Mass. Edited by G. J. Adams. Published by H. L. Southworth. November–December, 1846.
1v. monthly. 23cm.
"Probably two issues only were published, though it is conceivable that a third, for January, 1847, also appeared" — Morgan.
Morgan
CtY Nov. 1846, NN Nov. 1846

8365. Stark, P. P. Testimonies, a compilation from the Bible and of the testimony of witnesses, concerning the church and the gospel and its restoration in the latter days, and the second coming of the Messiah. Richmond, Va., 1898.
131p. 24cm.
Testimonies from missionary work of RLDS members.
MoInRC

STATEHOOD

8366. Statehood for Utah!! Have abolished polygamy? Read! [Grantsville, 1887]
Broadside. 22×9cm.
Concerning a meeting in which young women were encouraged to enter into plural marriage.
USlC

8367. Stayner, Charles W. Alleged "objectionable features" in the religion of the Latter-day Saints. By Elder Charles W. Stayner. [Liverpool, Printed and Published by Albert Carrington at the Latter-day Saints' Printing, Publishing, and Emigrating Office, 187–]
8p. 21cm.
Caption-title.
Sabin 90846
CtY, MH, NjP, NN, UPB, UHi, USlC

8368. Stead, J. D. The Book of Mormon, what is it? What is its purpose? Grand Rapids, Michigan, Glad Tidings [n.d.]
16p. 15cm. (Gospel Booklet. No. 4)
MoInRC

8369. ———. Doctrines and dogmas of Brighamism exposed. By Elder J. D. Stead. [Lamoni, Ia.] Published by the Board of Publication of the Reorganized Church of Jesus Christ of Latter Day Saints, 1911.
2p.l. [5]–15p. [2]l. [1] 18–286p. 19½cm.
Cover-title: Doctrines and dogmas of Utah Mormonism exposed.
CU–B, MH, MoInRC, NjP, NN, UHi, USlC

8370. ———. To the citizens of Green Ridge and vicinity. [n.p., n.d.]
24p. 15cm.
Public discussion of the RLDS church between J. D. Stead and the Baptist church.
MoInRC

8371. Stead, William Thomas. William T. Stead and his defence of the "Mormons." [Liverpool, Mission Headquarters, 1912?]
4p. 21cm.
Caption-title.
A reprint of Stead's article in the *London Daily Express* edited by Rudger Clawson.
UHi, UPB

8372. Stebbins, Callie B. Gospel teaching in the home. Lamoni, Ia., Herald Publishing House, 1895.
16p. 15cm. (Daughters of Zion leaflets. No. 3)
Supplement to the *Saints' Herald.*
RLDS doctrinal tract.
USlC

8372a. ———. The Silver Thimbles and The Happiest Christmas. By Callie B. Stebbins. Birth Offering Series Nos. 1 and 2. Lamoni, Iowa, Herald Publishing House, 1908.
26p. 19cm.
RLDS fiction.
MoInRC, NjP

8373. Stebbins, Henry Alfred. Book of Mormon lectures. Claims of the Book of Mormon examined in the light of history, archaeology, antiquity and science by Elder H. A. Stebbins. Nine lectures delivered at Independence, Mo., Reported by Belle R. Robinson. Independence, Mo., Ensign Publishing House, 1894.
179 [1]p. 20½cm.
Cover-title.
[1] Corrections.
CSmH, MoInRC, MoK, NjP, USl, USlC

8374. ———. Book of Mormon lectures; being a series of nine sermons delivered in the Saints' Church, Independence, Missouri on . . . Feb. 13–21, 1894. Corr. and rev. for this edition. Lamoni, Ia., Board of Publication Church of Jesus Christ of Latter Day Saints [c1901]
viii, 284p. 20cm.
MoInRC, NN

8374a. ———. (same) Lamoni, Iowa, Board of Publication of the Reorganized Church of Jesus Christ of Latter Day Saints, 1902 [c1901]
viii, 287p. 18cm.
MoInRC

8375. ———. (same) Lamoni, Ia., Board of Publication of the Reorganized Church of Jesus Christ of Latter Day Saints, 1908? [c1901]
viii, 287p. 20cm.
MoK, NN, UPB

8376. ———. A compendium of the faith and doctrine of the Reorganized Church of Jesus Christ for the use of the ministry and of Sabbath Schools; comp. by Elder H. A. Stebbins and Sister M. Walker; to which is added a historical appendix, an epitome of history, etc., by H. A. Stebbins. Lamoni, Ia., Printed by the Board of Publication upon examination and approval by the First Presidency [1888?]
xv, 248p. 16cm.
IWW, MoInRC, UHi, UPB, USlC

8377. ———. Concordance and reference guide to the Book of Mormon. [n.p., n.d.]
57p. 16cm.
RLDS publication.
MoInRC copy defective

8378. ———. Concordance and reference guide to the Book of Doctrine and Covenants. Published by the Reorganized Church of Jesus Christ of Latter Day Saints. Plano, Ill., Printed at the True Latter Day Saints' Herald Steam Book and Job Office, 1870.
23p. 16cm.
Sabin 83232
MoInRC, USlC

8378a. ———. (same) Plano, Reorganized Church of Jesus Christ of Latter Day Saints, [n.d.]
23p. 16cm.
MoInRC

8379. ———. (same) Lamoni, Ia., Herald Publishing House, 1893.
30p. 16cm.
Sabin 83234
MoInRC, NN

8380. ———. . . . Memorial sermon, by Elder H. A. Stebbins. Independence, Mo., Published by the Ensign Publishing Company, 1893.
37p. 15½cm. (Ensign Circulating Library. Vest Pocket Edition. No. 1. Extra D)
Cover-title.
Memorial day sermon.
MoInRC, UHi

8381. ———. . . . Modern knowledge of the antiquities of America, by Elder H. A. Stebbins. Independence, Mo., Ensign Publishing Company, 1897.
34p. 15½cm. (The Gospel Banner. March, 1897. Vol. 4, No. 1. Extra A)
Cover-title.
MoInRC, UHi

8382. Steed, Matilda Cecilia Giauque, *compiler.* Genealogy of the Steed family of Utah from 1850–1916, compiled by M. C. G. Steed and Fanny Louisa Steed Meadows. Farmington, Utah, Steed Family Association, 1916.
26p. port. 24cm.
UPB

———. The Leavitts of America.
See Eldredge, Jane Jennings.

8383. Steed, Thomas. The life of Thomas Steed from his own diary, 1826–1910. [Farmington, Utah? 1911?]
43p. illus., ports. 23cm.
Pioneer of Farmington, Utah.
Howes S915
CU, CU–B, UHi, UPB, USlC, UU

8384. Steevens, George Warrington. The land of the dollar, by G. W. Steevens. Edinburgh and London, W. Blackwood and Sons, 1897.
2p.l. [vii]–viii, 316p. 19½cm.
Letters written originally for *The Daily Mail.*
"Among the Mormons," p. 212–223.
Other additions: 1907. DLC
CU, USlC

8385. Stenhouse, Fanny, "*Mrs.* T. B. H. Stenhouse." Exposé of polygamy in Utah. A lady's life among the Mormons. A record of personal experience as one of the wives of a Mormon elder during a period of more than twenty years. By Mrs. T. B. H. Stenhouse . . . Illustrated by H. L. Stephens. New York, American News Company, 1872.
221p. plates. 19½cm.
CtY, CU–B, DLC, ICHi, IWW, MH, MoInRC, MWA, NjP, NN, OU, ULA, USlC

8386. ———. (same) 2d ed. New York, American News Co., 1872.
221p. plates. 18cm.
CtY, CU, ICN, MB, MH, NjP, NjPT, UHi, UPB, USlC, UU

8387. ———. (same, under title) A lady's life among the Mormons. A record of personal experience as one of the wives of a Mormon elder, during a period of more than twenty years. By Mrs. T. B. H. Stenhouse . . . Illustrated by H. S. Stephens. 2d ed. New York, Russell Brothers, 1872.
221p. plates. 20½cm.
CSmH, DLC, MH, NN, UHi, ULA, USl, USlC, UU

8388. ———. (same) 2d ed. New York, American News Co., 1872.
221p. plates. 21cm.
NN, WHi

8389. ———. (same) London, George Routledge and Sons, 1873.
xv, 176p. 16½cm.
CU, MH, OCl, UHi, UU

8390. ———. "Tell it all." The story of a life's experience in Mormonism. An autobiography by Mrs. T. B. H. Stenhouse of Salt Lake City, for more than twenty years the wife of a Mormon missionary and elder. With introductory preface by Mrs. Harriet Beecher Stowe. Hartford, Conn., A. D. Worthington and Co., 1874.
xxx [31]–623p. 15 plates, 2 ports. 22½cm.
An expanded version of her exposé of polygamy in Utah.
CSmH, CtY, CU, DLC, IWW, MoInRC, NN, OClWHi, UHi, UPB, USl, USlC

8391. ———. (same) Full-page illustrations and steel-plate portrait of the author. Cincinnati, Ohio, Queen City Publishing Co., 1874.
3p.l. [vii]–xxx [31]–623p. port. 22½cm.
"Published by subscription only."
MH, UPB

8392. ———. (same) Hartford, Conn., A. D. Worthington and Co., 1875.
xxx [31]–623p. plates, ports., facsim. 22½cm.
ICN, ICU, MH, NjP, NjPT, NN, OClWHi, UHi, USlC, UU

8393. ———. (same) . . . Hartford, Conn., A. D. Worthington & Co.; Cincinnati, Queen City Publishing Co. [etc. etc.] 1875.
xxx [31]–623p. plates, port., facsim. 22cm.
Variant edition.
CU–B

8394. ———. (same) Hartford, Conn., Worthington and Co., 1876.
xxx [37]–623p. plates, port., facsim. 22cm.
USl, ViU

8395. ———. (same) Hartford, Conn., A. D. Worthington and Co., Publishers . . . 1876.
Varied pagination. 2 plates. 22½cm.
Publishers' sample.
UPB

8396. ———. (same) Including a full account of the Mountain Meadows massacre and of the life, confession, and execution of Bishop John D. Lee. Hartford, Conn., A. D. Worthington and Co. . . . 1878.
xxx, 31–655p. plates, ports., facsim. 22cm.
CU–B, NN, USlC

8396a. ———. (same) Hartford, Conn., A. D. Worthington and Co. . . . 1878.
xxx, 31–655p. 22cm.
CU–B

8397. ———. (same) Fully illustrated. Hartford, Conn., A. D. Worthington and Co., 1890.
xxx [31]–655p. 17cm.
CoD, IU, MH, RPB, UU

8398. ———. (same, revised under title) An Englishwoman in Utah: the story of a life's experience in Mormonism. An autobiography by Mrs. T. B. H. Stenhouse of Salt Lake City for more than twenty-five years the wife of a Mormon missionary and elder. With an introductory preface by Mrs. Harriet Beecher Stowe. Including a full account of the Mountain Meadows massacre and of the life, confession, and execution of Bishop John D. Lee. Fully illustrated. London, Sampson Low, Marston, Searle and Rivington, 1880.
xii, 404p. 11 plates, 3 port. 19cm.
CSmH, CU, MdBP, MH, NjPT, NN, UHi, ULA, UPB, USl, USlC, UHi

8399. ———. (same) New and cheaper ed. London, S. Low, Marston, Searle & Rivington, 1882.
xii, 404p. plates, ports., facsim. 19cm.
CSmH, CU–B, DLC, ICN, MH, NjP, UHi, UPB, UU

8400. ———. (same, under title) The Tyranny of Mormonism, or An Englishwoman in Utah; an autobiography, by Fanny Stenhouse of Salt Lake City (25 years). With introductory preface by Mrs. Beecher Stowe. Fully illustrated. London, S. Low, Marston, Searle & Rivington, 1888.
xii, 404p. plate, port., facsim. 19cm.
CtY, CU–B, DLC, ICN, IWW, MoInRC, NjP, NN, OClWHi, OO, UHi, USlC, UU

8401. ———. (same, in Spanish) Vida de una señora entre los Mormons; producto de la experiencia personal de una de las espousa de un sacerdote Mormon, durante un periode de mas de viente años. Mexico, Imprinta de Ignacia Escalante, 1873.
28 [285]p. 22cm.
MH

8402. Stenhouse, Thomas Brown Holmes. . . . The inhabitants of Southampton are respectfully invited to attend a course of four lectures, to be delivered in Redwards's commercial school room . . . by T. B. H. Stenhouse, Elder of the Church of Jesus Christ of Latter-day Saints, commencing Sunday evening, June 3rd, 1849, and continued the following Sunday evenings. [Southampton, Devenish, Printer, 1849]
Broadside. 29×45½cm.
At head of title: Truth is might and must prevail.
CtY

8403. ———. Les Mormons (Saints des Derniers-Jours) et leurs ennemis. Réponse à divers ouvrages publiés contre le Mormonisme par MM. Guers, Favez, & Pichot, Comte de Gasparin, etc. par T. B. H. Stenhouse, President des Missions Suisse et Italienne de l'Église de Jesus-Christ des Saints des Derniers-jours. Lausanne, Imprimerie Larpin et Coendoz, 1854.
[4]–vii, 207p. 18cm.
Title in English: The Mormons and their enemies.
Howes S936, Sabin 91222
MH, NjPT, UPB, USlC, WHi

8404. ———. The Rocky Mountain saints: a full and complete history of the Mormons, from the first vision of Joseph Smith to the last courtship of Brigham Young . . . and the development of the great mineral wealth of the Territory of Utah. By T. B. H. Stenhouse . . . Illustrated with twenty-four full-page engravings, a steel plate frontispiece, an autographic letter of Brigham Young and numerous woodcuts. New York, D. Appleton and Company, 1873.
xxiv, 761p. illus., plates, ports., maps, double facsim. 24cm.
CSmH, CtY, CU–B, DLC, ICN, IWW, MH, NjP, NN, UHi, ULA, USl, USlC, UU, WHi

8405. ———. (same) London, Ward, Lock and Tyler [1874]
xxiv, 761p. illus., plates, port., maps, double facsim. 22cm.
CSmH, CtY, DLC, MH, NjP, NjPT, NN, USlC, UU

8406. ———. (same) London, Ward, Lock and Tyler [1878]
xxiv, 761p. illus., plates, ports. 22cm.
USlC

8407. ———. (same) New York, D. Appleton and Co., 1900 [c1873]
xxiv, 761p. illus., plates, port. 23cm.
DLC, NN, UHi

8408. ———. (same) Salt Lake City, Shepard Book Company, 1904.
xxiv, 761p. illus. 23½cm.
MBr–Z, MoInRC, UHi

8409. ———. Victoria assembly rooms. The inhabitants of Southampton are respectfully informed that a public discussion on the doctrines taught by the Latter-day Saints will take place between the Rev. Enos Couch, and Elder T. B. H. Stenhouse . . . on the evenings of Monday, Tuesday, and Wednesday, April 29th, 30th and May 1st, 6th, 7th and 8th, 1850. Southampton, I. Cox, Printer [1850]
Broadside. 34×43cm.
Debate while T. B. H. Stenhouse was a member of the Mormon church.
CtY

8410. Stephens, Ann S. Esther: a story of the Oregon Trail. By Mrs. Ann S. Stephens, author of "Malaeska," "Myra, the child of adoption," etc. London, Beadle and Company [c1862]
1p.l. [5]–128p. front. 16½cm. (Beadle's Dime Novel. No. 45)
Fiction. The prophet succeeding Joseph Smith is a traitorous fake; has Indians try to kidnap Esther for his wife.
CU, NjP, UPB

8411. ———. (same) New York, London, Beadle and Company [n.d.]
2p.l. [5]–128p. 15½cm.
UPB

8412. Stephens, Evan. Deseret Chorister. Anthems, glees, choruses, etc. Edited by Evan Stephens. Suitable for Latter-day Saints' Choirs. [Salt Lake City] Published by the Deseret News Company [1888?]
[45]–60p. 31cm. (No. 4)
Cover-title.
UPB

8413. ———. Eight favorite hymns by Evan Stephens. Salt Lake City, Deseret Book Company [c1927]
48p. 24½cm.
By the former director of the L.D.S. Tabernacle Choir.
USlC

8414. ———. First presentation of the sacred cantata "The Vision" by Evan Stephens. Tabernacle, Monday, April 5, 1920 . . . Given under the direction of the composer. [Salt Lake City, Consolidated Music Co., 1920]
[6]p. 23cm.
Program.
USlC

8415. ———. Five favorite anthems by Evan Stephens. Director of the "Mormon Tabernacle Choir." Salt Lake City [n.d.]
28p. music. 25cm.
RPB, UPB

8416. ———. God of Israel. Written and dedicated to the Tabernacle Choir, Salt Lake City, Utah, May 3rd and 4th, 1885. Salt Lake City, Coalter & Snelgrove, 1885.
11p. 30cm.
UPB

8417. ———. Grant us peace, O Lord. An anthem by Evan Stephens. Salt Lake City, Fergus Coalter Music Co. [n.d.]
[7]p. 26cm.
UPB

8418. ———. "Hosannah" anthem. For the dedication ceremonies of the Salt Lake Temple, April 6th, 1893. [Salt Lake City, Coalter Music Company, 1893?]
[6]p. 26cm.
UPB

8419. ———. Let the mountains shout for joy. An anthem By Evan Stephens. Salt Lake City, Fergus Coalter Music Co. [n.d.]
[3]p. 26½cm.
UPB

8420. ———. The martyrs; a sacred historical cantata. For tenor solo, female chorus, male chorus, mixed chorus, and orchestra. Dedicated to President Heber J. Grant. Words and music by Evan Stephens. [Salt Lake City?] 1921.
1p.l., 45p. 26½cm.
Words and music.
UHi, USlC

8421. ———. O Lord, I will praise thee. Anthem. Music by E. Stephens, words from Isaiah, Chap. XII. [n.p., n.d.]
29–44p. 30½cm.
A series of musical scores which ends with his *Deseret Chorister.*
UPB

8422. ———. O noble mother pioneer; this song written especially for the occasion of the unveiling of the monument for the pioneer mother. June 5th, 1927. Sponsored by Granite Stake Primary Association. Salt Lake City, 1927.
[3]p. music. 28cm.
USlC

8423. ———. Overthrow of Gog and Magog. Anthem. [Salt Lake City, Fergus Coalter Music Co., n.d.]
[6]p. 25½cm.
UPB

STEPHENS, E.

8424. ———. The pioneer jubilee songster by Evan Stephens. A collection of choruses, quartettes, trios, duets, and songs suitable for pioneer celebrations. [Salt Lake City] Printed and for Sale by Deseret News Publishing Co. [1897?]
16 nos. [1]p. 24½cm.
UPB, USlC

8425. ———. A primer and first reader of vocal music. Salt Lake City, Juvenile Instructor Office, 1883.
[3] 40 [1]p. 17cm.
Includes several Mormon songs.
A second volume published in 1884, without Mormon songs or reference to Mormonism.
UHi, USlC, UU

8426. ———. Prize Pioneer Ode. Words by O. F. Whitney. Music by Evan Stephens. The Music of this Ode was awarded the $100.00 prize offered by the Jubilee Commission for the best musical setting to the poem. Sang at the Large Tabernacle, Salt Lake City, by 1,000 voices during the Pioneer Jubilee, July, 1897. [Salt Lake City, 1897?]
20p. 24½cm.
NjP, UPB

8427. ———. The school and primary songster, containing songs for public schools, primary association, kindergarten, etc., all specially composed and arranged to suit children's voices. Also as a reader of vocal music, by Evan Stephens. Salt Lake City, Published by Coalter and Snelgrove, c1889.
iii [4]–106p. 14×17½cm.
Words and music.
NjP, UHi, USlC, UU

8428. ———. Temple anthems. For general use by all church choirs. Edited by Prof. E. Stephens. Vol. I. Salt Lake City, 1913.
2p.l., 5–64p. 28cm.
USlC

8429. ———. (same) [2d ed.] Salt Lake City, The Deseret News, 1914 [c1913]
2p.l., 5–64p. 27cm.
Edition from cover.
USlC

8430. ———. (same) 3d ed. Salt Lake City, The Deseret News, 1917.
2p.l., 5–64p. 27cm.
USlC

8431. ———. (same) Vol. II . . . Salt Lake City, The Deseret News, 1918.
2p.l., 5–68p. 27cm.
Words and Music.
RPB, UHi, USlC

8432. ———. Thanksgiving anthem. Salt Lake City, Fergus Coalter Music Co. [n.d.]
[4]p. 26½cm.
Fergus Coalter edition of octavo music. No. 7.
UPB

8433. ———. The Vision . . . Salt Lake City, The Church of Jesus Christ of Latter-day Saints, 1920.
46p. 27cm.
USlC

8434. ———. Young Men's Mutual Improvement Association and missionary hymn and tune book. A collection of hymns and songs set to music, adapted especially for use of Mutual Improvement Associations and missionaries in their religious services and their social entertainments. Compiled and arranged by Prof. E. Stephens . . . Salt Lake City, G. Q. Cannon and Sons Co., 1899.
iv [1] 6–72p. 11½×18½cm.
MH, NN, ULA, UPB, USlC, WHi

8435. ———. (same) Salt Lake City, Deseret News Publishing Company [ca. 1903]
70 [2]p. 12½×17cm.
USlC

8436. ———. (same) Salt Lake City, Deseret News Publishing Company, 1909.
70 [2]p. 13×19cm.
NN, UHi, UPB

8436a. ———. Y.M.M.I.A. choruses. Salt Lake City, Improvement Era. 1919.
52p. music. 23cm.
USlC

8437. Stephens, Lorenzo Dow. Life sketches of a jawhawker of '49, by L. Dow Stephens; actual experiences of a pioneer told by himself in his own way. [San Jose, Cal., Printed by Nolta Brothers] 1916.
2p.l. [7]–68p. plates, ports. 24cm.
Description of Utah in 1849. Duplicity of Brigham Young in getting the southern route explored.
Howes S941
CU–B, DLC, NjP

8438. Stephens, Solomon Clinton. The philosophy of the earth. By Solomon C. Stephens. Ogden, Utah. W. W. Browning & Co., 1898.
2p.l. [5]–143p. 19cm.
A religious treatment of the earth, and its functions.
USl, USlC

8439. Stepping stones. Independence, Mo., July, 1913–
v. weekly. 28cm.
RLDS publication for children age ten to fifteen.
First editors: Marietta Walker and Estella Wight.
MoInRC

8440. De Ster. Maandelijksch Tijdshrift van de Heiligen der laatste Dagen. Rotterdam, January, 1896–
v. bi-monthly, monthly. 20cm.
Title in English: The star.
UPB V.1–9, 11–15, 16 inc., 17–24, 28 inc., 30–32, 33 inc., 34, 35–36 inc.; USIC comp.

8441. Stern, Herman Isidore. Evelyn Gray; or, The victims of our western Turks, a tragedy in five acts by H. I. Stern. New York, J. B. Alder, 1890.
236p. 19½cm.
Drama concerning Mormonism.
DLC, ICU, IU, MH, UHi, USIC, WHi

8442. Der Stern. Eine Monatschrift zur Verbreitung der Wahrheit. Zurich, European Mission, Jan. 1, 1869–
v. monthly. 21cm.
First editor: Karl G. Maeser.
Title in English: The star.
UPB V.1–42, 43 inc., 44, 45 inc., 46, 48 inc., 50 inc., 53–55, 56–58 inc., 59–; USIC comp.

8443. Der Stern. Die ewige Wahrheit. Erklärung über die Lehren der Kirche Jesu Christi der Heiligen der Letzten Tage. Vom Abfall und Wiederbringung des wahren Evangeliums. Traktat nr. 1. Hamburg, Herausgegeben von der Redaktion des "Stern" . . . Hamburg, Hamburg Buchdruckerie Schröder & Jeve, 1898.
16p. 18cm.
Title in English: Eternal truth.
USIC

8444. Sterne, Louis. Seventy years of an active life. London, Printed for private distribution only. 1912.
191p. front. 22½cm.
He came to Utah in 1858 with the peace commission.
Howes S950
NjP, NN, UHi

8445. Stevens, C. L. McCluer. The secret history of the Mormons; a true narrative of the most extraordinary religious imposture of modern times. By C [sic] L. McCluer Stevens. London, C. Arthur Pearson, Ltd., 1911.
viii [9]–118p. 22cm.
Fiction concerning Mormonism.
MH, NN, USIC

8446. ———. (same) London, C. Arthur Pearson, Ltd., 1912.
viii [9]–118p. 22cm.
MH, NN, USIC

8447. ———. (same) 3d impression. . . . London, C. Arthur Pearson, Ltd., 1922.
2p.l. [9]–118p. 21½cm.
NjPT, NN

8448. Stevens, G. W. The land of the dollar, by G. W. Stevens . . . Edinburgh and London, William Blackwood and Sons, 1897.
viii, 316p. 19½cm.
Chap. 24. "Among the Mormons." Interview with a Mormon official and his comments. Non-Mormon attitude seems to be that Mormonism is dead — not so with the Mormon leaders.
USIC

8449. Stevens, R. M. O le Katakesima mo Tamaiti, Ua Fa'aali mai ai Ni Mati'upu. I le Ekalesia a Iesu Keriso l le "au Paia o aso e gata ai; Na saunia e Setefano . . . Catechism for Children, In the Samoan Dialect. Prepared by Elder R. M. Stevens. Samoa, Printed by J. H. Denvers, "Samoa Weekly Herald," 1895.
1p.l., 51p. 20½cm.
Title in English: Catechism for Children.
USIC

8450. Stevens, Thomas. Around the world on a bicycle . . . By Thomas Stevens . . . New York, C. Scribner's Sons, 1887–88.
2v. illus., ports., plates. 22½cm.
Brief impression of Mormons while crossing Utah. "Wiseacres of the church" teach women to win over strangers.
DLC, NjP, UHi

8451. Stevens, Walter B. Missouri, the center state, 1821–1915. By Walter B. Stevens, St. Louis, Chicago, The S. J. Clarke Publisher Company, 1915.
4v. ports., plates, maps. 27cm.
Includes history of Mormonism in Missouri.
DLC, MoInRC, UHi

8452. Stevenson, Adlai Ewing. Something of men I have known, with some papers of a general nature, political, historical, and retrospective, by Adlai E. Stevenson . . . Chicago, A. C. McClurg & Co., 1909.
xi [1] 442p. plates, ports., facsim. 21½cm.
Material on the Mormon exodus from Illinois, p. 197–215. Chiefly from Thomas Ford's *History of Illinois*.
CU, DLC, MiU, NjP, NN, UHi, USl, USIC, UU

8453. Stevenson, Bertha S. The Right thing at all times, arranged and written by Bertha S. Stevenson and Grace C. Neslen [sic] [Salt Lake City] The General Boards of Y.M.M.I.A. and Y.L.M.I.A., 1930.
2p.l. [5]–190 [2]p. 19cm.
A book of etiquette.
NjP, UHi, USIC

8454. Stevenson, Edward. Lecture delivered in Leicester, England, on the pre-existence of spirits and immortality of the soul, by Elder Edward Stevenson. Leicester, W. A. Hammond, Steam Printer [1886?]
4p. 21½cm.
Mormon doctrine.
NN, UHi, USlC

8455. ———. A proclamation from the Rocky Mountains of Utah to the inhabitants of Canada, and throughout the World. [By Elder Edward Stevenson and Elder G. W. Beckstead. Morrisburg, Canada, "Herald" Print., 1884?]
10p. 21cm.
USlC

8456. ———. Reminiscences of Joseph, the Prophet, and the coming forth of the Book of Mormon. By Elder Edward Stevenson . . . Illustrated. Salt Lake City, Published by the author, 1893.
47p. illus., port., plate, facsim. 24½cm.
Comments on the personal account of Joseph Smith.
CSmH, CtY, MH, MoInRC, NjP, NN, UHi, ULA, UPB, USlC, WHi

8457. ———. Tract, containing the first principles of the doctrines of the Church of Jesus Christ [of] Latter-day Saints, by Elders Edward Stevenson and H.D.C. Clark. Centerville, Tenn., Printed by James F. Martin, 1878.
7 [1]p. 21cm.
CU-B, NN, USlC

8458. Stevenson, H. A lecture on Mormonism, delivered in the Wesleyan Methodist chapel, Alston, December 7th, 1838. By H. Stevenson . . . Newcastle [Eng.] Printed at the Courant Office by J. Blackwell and Co., 1839.
32p. 9×14½cm.
"Intended to show that the *Book of Mormon* is not an inspired volume, but a foolish and wicked forgery; that Mormonism is a system of absurdities."
Howes S977, Sabin 91595
CtY, USlC

8459. Stevenson, Robert Louis. The dynamiter, by Robert Louis Stevenson [and Fanny Van de Grift Stevenson] London, New York, H. Holt and Co., 1885.
vi p. [2]l., 326p. 17cm. (Leisure hour series. No. 162)
Includes the "Story of the destroying angel."
Other editions: New York, J. W. Lovell Co. [1886] DLC, NjP; New York, G. Munro [1886] DLC, NjP; New York, Scribners, 1895. ULA; New York, Scribners, 1908. ULA; New York, Standard Book Co. [1930] UPB
DLC, NjP

8460. ———. In the South Seas; being an account of experiences and observations in the Marquesas, Paumotus and Gilbert Islands in the course of two cruises, on the yacht "Casco" (1888) and the schooner "Equator" (1889) by Robert Louis Stevenson. New York, C. Scribner's Sons, 1896.
vii, [1]l., 370p. fold. map. 19½cm.
Includes Mormons in Paumotus.
Other editions: London, Chatto and Windus, 1900. USlC; New York, 1900. NjP; New York, C. Scribner's, 1905. CU
DLC, NjP

8461. Stewart, Elinore (Pruitt). Letters of woman homesteader. Boston & New York, Houghton Mifflin Co., 1914.
vii [1]p. [2]l., 3–281p. illus. 21cm.
Among the Mormons . . . p. 256–278.
CU, DLC, UHi, ULA, USlC

8462. Stewart, James Z. La venida del Mesías por J. Z. Stewart, Elder de la Iglesia de Jesu Cristo de los Santos de los Últimos días. Independence, Zion's Printing and Publishing Co. [Publidado[sic] por la Mision Mexicana] 1921.
8p. 15cm.
At head of title: Escudriñad las Escrituras, S. Juan 5: 39.
Title in English: The coming of the Messiah.
UPB

8463. Stewart, Robert Laird. Sheldon Jackson, pathfinder and prospector of the missionary vanguard in the Rocky Mountains and Alaska. New York, Chicago, and Toronto, London and Edinburgh, Fleming H. Revell [c1908]
488p. plates, ports., fold. map. 21cm.
Chapt. X. Pioneer work in the territory of Utah. Includes comments on Brigham Young; work of the Danites.
Another edition: 2d ed. [c1908] UPB, UU
CU-B, NjP, UPB, USlC

8464. The Stick of Joseph, taken from the hand of Ephraim. A correct copy of the characters taken from the plates the Book of Mormon! Was translated from — the same that was taken to Professor Anthon of New York, by Martin Harris, in the year 1827, in fulfilment of Isaiah 29, 11, 12. [n.p., n.d.]
Broadside. 34½×25½cm.
Printed in variant sizes.
CSmH photostatic copy from a copy owned by Franklin Lewis; USlC copy printed on cloth

8465. Stickney, William. Memorial sketch of William Soule Stickney, by his father . . . Washington, "School of Music" Press, 1881.
3p.l., 7–447p. ports. 19cm.
His impressions of Mormons in 1878: "scum of the earth," p. 168–169.
CU-B, UPB

8466. Stillman, James Wells. The constitutional and legal aspect of the Mormon question. Speech of James W. Stillman in Science Hall, Boston, Mass., April 2d, 1882. Boston, Stillman and Co., 1882.
24p. 22cm.
Cover-title.
CSmH, CtY, CU–B, DLC, ICN, MH, NN, UHi, UPB, USl, USlC, UU, WHi

8467. ———. (same) Salt Lake City, James Dwyer, 1882.
24p. 22½cm.
USlC

8468. ———. The Mormon question. An address by James W. Stillman, delivered in Boston on Tuesday evening Feb. 12, 1884. Reported by William B. Wright. Boston, J. P. Mendum, 1884.
40p. 23cm.
CSmH, CtY, CU–B, DLC, ICN, MH, NjP, NN, UHi, USl, USlC, UU

8468a. Stillson, Henry Leonard, ***ed.*** History of the ancient and honorable fraternity of free and accepted Masons and concordant orders. Written by a board of editors, Henry Leonard Stillson, editor-in-chief. Boston, Fraternity Publishing Co., 1921.
884p. illus. 25½cm.
Utah and the Mormons, p. 413–418.
USlC

8469. Stimson, Hiram K. From the stage coach to the pulpit; being an auto-biographical sketch, with incidents and anecdotes, of Elder H. K. Stimson, the veteran pioneer of Western New York, now of Kansas. Edited by Rev. T. W. Greene of Kansas. Saint Louis, R. A. Campbell, Publishers, 1874.
427p. port. 19cm.
Includes a sketch of Brigham Young before he joined the L.D.S. Church, with an editor's "puzzled" note.
NjP, USlC

8470. Stisted, Georgiana M. The true life of Capt. Sir Richard F. Burton . . . written by his neice . . . with the authority and approval of the Burton family. London, H. S. Nichols, 1896.
xv, 419p. port. 19cm.
Chapter on Burton's trip to Great Salt Lake City, 1860.
Another edition: New York, D. Appleton & Co. 1897. UPB
CU, DLC, NjP, UU

8471. Stocker, Rhamanthus Menuille. Centennial history of Susquehanna County, Pennsylvania. Philadelphia, R. T. Peck & Company, 1887.
x, 851p. illus., plates, ports., maps. 21½cm.
Article "Joe Smith, the founder of Mormonism" under Oakland township.
". . . Susquehana harbored such a madman."
DLC, NN

8472. Stoddard, Charles Augustus. Beyond the Rockies; a spring journey in California. London, S. Low, Marston, 1894.
xiii, 214p. plates. 21cm.
Across the Sierra to Salt Lake in 1893, p. 184–193. His description is brief and sketchy with a very brief account of L.D.S. history.
Another edition: New York, C. Scribner's Sons, 1894. DLC
NjP, ULA, UPB, UU

8473. Stoddard, Howard J. George E. Stoddard. New York, Howard J. Stoddard, 1924.
[17]l. 23cm.
Mormon biography.
USlC

8474. Stoddart, James H. Recollections of a player, by J. H. Stoddart. Illustrated. New York, The Century Co., 1902.
xxi, 255p. illus. 21cm.
Plays "Saints and sinners" in Salt Lake City, with Gov. Wells as one part, p. 239–240.
CU, NjP, USlC

8475. Stohl, Lorenzo N. Souvenir eightieth anniversary, patriarch Ole Nelson Stohl. November ninth, 1835–1915. [Brigham City? 1915?]
[6]l. port. 21cm.
Mormon biography.
USlC

8476. Stoker, David. My home in the West, by David Stoker. It's true, the Mormons have a name, by Samuel G. Spencer. The fishers and the hunters. Farewell to the elders, saints and friends of the Indiana Conference, by David R. Roberts and Hyrum Brimhall. [n.p., n.d.]
12p. 13cm.
Mormon poetry.
UPB

8477. ———. My home in the West. [n.p., n.d.]
[3]p. 14cm.
UPB

8478. Stoker, John William. Shinkō. Tōkyō, Nihon, Matsu Jitsu Seito Iesu Kirisuto Kyōkai Nihon Dendōbu [1907]
8p. 15½cm.
Title in English: Faith.
USlC

8479. ———. (same) Tōkyō, Nihon, Matsu Jitsu Seito Iesu Kirisuto Kyōkai Nihon Dendōbu, [1908]
34p. 15½cm.
USlC

8480. Stolworthy, H. T. Treasures of truth. Dictated by H. T. Stolworthy. Written by Lucy S. Burnham . . . [n.p., n.d.]
1p.l. [5]–65p. 19½cm.
Mormon autobiography and poetry.
USlC

8481. The "stone" in the "hat." Salt Lake City, Kinsman [n.d.]
27p. 13cm. (Kinsman literature)
Cover-title.
An article against the RLDS Church. A revision, according to note at the end of the text.
UHi

8482. Stone, Alvan. Memoir of Alvan Stone of Goshen, Massachusetts by David Wright. Boston: Fould, Kendall & Lincoln, 1837.
2p.l. [9]–256p. 15½cm.
Gives a brief summary of Mormon activity in Schuyler Co., Ill. in a letter to his brother, April 21, 1832.
NN

8483. Stone, Elizabeth Arnold. Uinta County its place in history. A history of the original Uinta County, and its subdivisions. [Laramie, Wyoming, The Laramie printing Co., 1924]
4p.l. [9]–276p. plates, ports., facsims. 23½cm.
Mormons in Wyoming.
CU–B, DLC, NjP, UHi, ULA, USlC, UU

8484. Stone, Jesse Burke. The church out of order . . . Salt Lake City [Specialty Printing Co., 193–]
7p. 20cm.
Cover-title.
MoInRC, UHi, USlC

8485. ———. A man like Joseph by J. B. Stone. Also, Anglo-Israel teachings harmonize with Mormonism, precedents of the law . . . Salt Lake City [n.d.]
20p. 21cm.
Unorthodox publication on patriarchal government.
USlC

8486. ———. The mask of Mormonism; a challenge by Jesse Burke Stone. Salt Lake City [1930?]
15p. 22cm.
Chiefly on polygamy.
MoInRC, NcD, NN, UHi, ULA, USl

8487. ———. My reply to Grant, or the dirty stove pipe. 2d ed. [n.p., n.d.]
8p. 16cm.
Heber J. Grant and his politics.
CU–B, MoInRC, USlC

Stone, Melvin Jones. The Baker genealogy and collateral branches. *See Baker, Amenzo White.*

8488. ———. The Keystone genealogist. Ogden, 1915.
2p.l. [5]–80p. ports., plates, 1 fold. chart. 22cm.
Mormon biography.
USlC

8489. Stone, William Leete. Matthias and his impostures: or, the progress of fanaticism. Illustrated in the extraordinary case of Robert Matthews, and some of his forerunners and disciples . . . By William L. Stone. New York, Harper and Brothers, 1835.
347p. plan. 16cm.
Brief reference to Mormonism and perfectionists, p. 316.
Other editions: 3d ed. 1835. CSmH, MWA, NN, NNHi; 3d ed. New-York, Published by Harper & Brothers . . . 1835. DLC, MiHi, NN, WHi
Sabin 92146
CSmH, CtY, DLC, MB, MH, MiU, NjP, NN, OO, UHi, UPB, WSU

8490. Stoof, Reinhold. Unterrichtsplan für die Primarklassen der Sonntagsschulen in der Schweizerischen und Deutschen Mission der Kirche Jesu Christi der Heiligen der letzten Tage. Bearbeitet vom Ältesten Reinhold Stoof. Basel, Herausgegeben von Serge F. Ballif, Präsident der Schweizerischen und Deutschen Mission, 1923.
70p. 21cm.
Title in English: Manual for the primary class of the Sunday School.
USlC

The Story of Alice. *See Anderson, James A.*

A story of Utah. *See M., J.*

8491. Strahorn, Carrie Adell. Fifteen thousand miles by stage. New York, London, G. P. Putnam's Sons, 1911.
xxv, [1]l., 673p. illus., plates, ports. 23½cm.
A trip through Salt Lake City with a description of Mormonism.
Another edition: 1915. CU–B, USlC
Howes S1054
NjP, UHi, UPB

8492. Strahorn, Robert Edmund. To the Rockies and beyond, or A summer on the Union Pacific Railway and branches. Saunterings in the popular health, pleasure, and hunting resorts of Nebraska, Dakota, Wyoming, Colorado, New Mexico, Utah, Montana and Idaho, with descriptions of the Black Hills, Big Horn and San Juan regions, and special articles on stock raising, farming, mining, lumbering and kindred industries of the Trans-Missouri region. By Robert E. Strahorn ("Alter Ego") . . . [Omaha] Omaha Republican Print., 1878.

141p. illus., fold. map. 22cm.
Tourist information on Utah, with many references to Mormons, Mormon building, etc., p. 90–117. No theological discussion.
Other editions: 3d ed., rev. and enl. Chicago, Bedford, Uarlee & Co., 1881. UPB; Omaha, Omaha Republican Print., 1879. DLC, CSmH; 1879. DLC, UU
Howes S1058
CtY, CU, DI–GS, DLC, MiU–C, NjP, OO, ULA

8493. Strang, Charles J. Beaver Island and its Mormon Kingdom by Chas. J. Strang, one of King Strang's sons. [Harbor Spring, Mich., J. C. Wright, 1895]
[63]–68p. illus. 14×21cm.
Caption-title.
Reprinted from the *Ottawan*, by J. C. Wright.
USlC

8494. Strang, James Jesse. Ancient and modern Michilimackinac, including an account of the controversy between Mackinac and the Mormons. [By James J. Strang. Saint James, Cooper & Chidester] MDCCCLIV [1854]
48 [2]p. 21½cm.
Cover-title.
In double columns.
Survey of the islands of Lake Michigan and the Mormon settlement on Big Beaver Island. The rest of the pamphlet is an attack on the people of Mackinac.
Howes S1060, Morgan, Sabin 92674
CtY, DLC, ICN, MiD–B, MiU, OClWHi, USlC, WHi

8495. ———. (same) As published in 1854, with supplement. [By James J. Strang] St. Ignace, Mich., The News and Free Press, 1885.
52p. 22cm.
Howes S1060, Morgan
CtY, CU, DLC, MiD–B, DLC, WHi

8496. ———. (same) [Burlington, Wis.? 1894?]
48p. 21½cm.
Cover-title.
In double columns.
Some copies have, tipped in, a 4-page preface signed by Wingfield Watson, March 31, 1894.
Howes S1060, Morgan
CtY, DLC, MH, MoInRC, NjP, UHi, USlC, WBuC, WHi

8497. ———. The Book of the Law of the Lord, consisting of an inspired translation of some of the most important parts of the law given to Moses, and a very few additional commandments, with brief notes and references. [By James J. Strang] Saint James, Printed by command of the King, at the Royal Press, A.R.I. [1851]
viii [9]–80p. 19½cm.
Howes S1061, Morgan, Sabin 92675
CtY, ICN, USlC

8498. ———. The Book of the Law of the Lord. Printed by command of the King, at the Royal Press, Saint James, A.R.I. [Saint James, Michigan, 1856]
[17]–336p. 20½cm.
The book was not completed during Strang's lifetime, and his followers later printed frontmatter to bind with the sheets. There are three variant issues of the introductory material listed by Morgan, and at least two which are not noted by him.
An expanded edition of the 1851 edition. The principle difference is the elaboration of the notes.
Howes S1061, Morgan, Sabin 92677
CSmH, CtY–C, DLC, IHi, MH, MiD–B, MiU–C, MoInRC, MoK, NN, OClWHi, RPB, UPB, USlC, UU, WBuC, WHi

8499. ———. (same) [Kansas City, Mo., 1927]
viii, 9–80p. 20½cm.
A reprint of the first edition of the *Book of the Law of the Lord* as published in 1851.
Leaf of advertisement precedes title page.
Howes S1061, Morgan, Sabin 82676
CSmH, MH, MoInRC, MoK, UPB, USlC, WBuC, WHi

8500. ———. Catholic discussion. [By James J. Strang. Voree, Wis., Gospel Herald Print., 1848]
[5]–60p. 18½cm.
Caption-title.
Cover-title: A discussion of the Roman Catholic religion between Charles Rafferty . . . and James J. Strang.
Letter of Charles Rafferty to James J. Strang and five letters in answer to them.
Five letters in answer.
Morgan
CtY, MH

8501. ———. (same) [Lyons, Wisconsin, May 26, 1902. Burlington, Wis.? 1902]
24p. 20½cm.
Caption-title.
In double columns.
A note signed by Wingfield Watson, p. 22–24.
Morgan
CtY, MH, MoInRC, UHi, USlC, WBuC, WHi

8502. ———. The Diamond: being the law of prophetic succession, and a defense of the calling of James J. Strang as successor to Joseph Smith. By James J. Strang. Voree, Wisconsin, Gospel Herald Print., MDCCCXLVIII [1848]
20p. 19½cm.
Cover-title.
Caption-title: Gospel tract. No. IV. The Diamond.
Signed: James J. Strang, May 1st, 1848.
A full exposition of the law of God touching the succession of prophets holding the presidency of the true church, and the proof that this succession has been kept up.
Added text on verso of back wrapper.
Morgan, Sabin 92684
CtY, MH, MoInRC, USlC, WHi

STRANG, J. J.

8503. ———. (same) Voree, Wis., 1848. [Repr. Boyne? Mich., 1878?]
16p. 21cm. (Gospel tract. No. IV)
Morgan, Sabin 92683
CSmH, CtY, CU–B, MoInRC, NN, USlC, WHi

8504. ———. (same) [Burlington, Wis.? 1893?]
15p. 22½cm. (Gospel Tract. No. IV)
Caption-title.
In double columns.
Howes S1063, Morgan
CSmH, CtY, DLC, MoInRC, NN, OClWHi, UPB, USlC

8505. ———. A few historical facts concerning the murderous assault at Pine River. Also the life, ministry, ancestry and childhood of James J. Strang. Lansing, Mich., Reprinted by Charles J. Strang, 1892.
7p. 20½cm.
Contains a reprint of the *Northern Islander Extra*, July 14, 1853.
Morgan
CtY, MH, WBuC

8506. ———. (same) [Kansas City, Mo.? 1920?]
1p.l. 9p. 21cm.
In double columns.
CtY, CU–B, MH, MoInRC, UHi, UPB, USlC, WBuC

———. Memorial. To the President and Congress of the United States. *See Church of Jesus Christ of Latter Day Saints (Strang)*

8507. ———. The Prophetic controversy. A letter from James J. Strang to Mrs. Corey. Saint James, Sept. 26, 1854. [Saint James: Cooper & Chidester, 1856?]
44p. 27cm.
Sabin gives title as: Prophetick discussion.
Morgan, Sabin 92686
CtY def., MiMtpT, USlC def.

8508. ———. (same) [Boyne, Mich.? 1878?]
49 [1]p. 21cm.
Caption-title.
In double columns.
Howes S1063, Morgan
CtY, DLC, MH, MoInRC, UHi, USlC, WHi

8509. ———. (same) [Boyne, Mich.? 1886?]
38p. 22cm.
Caption-title.
Howes S1063, Morgan
CtY, MH, UHi, UPB, USlC, WHi

8510. ———. (same) [Burlington, Wis.? 1893?]
35p. 22cm.
Caption-title.
In double columns.
Howes S1063, Morgan
CtY, DLC, MH, MoInRC, UHi, UPB, USlC, WHi

8511. ———. The revelations of James J. Strang. [Boyne, Mich.? 1885?]
22p. 23½×15½cm.
Caption-title.
In double columns.
Morgan
CSmH, CtY, MH, NN, USlC, WHi

8512. ———. (same) [Burlington, Wis.? 189–]
24p. 22cm.
Caption-title.
In double columns.
Probably published between 1897–1899 — Morgan.
Morgan
CSmH, CtY, MH, MoInRC, NjP, UHi, USlC, WBuC, WHi

8513. ———. Traveling Theatre Royal, late from Beaver Island. Adams' new drama. The famous original five act drama, "Improving the household," by Mr. G. J. Adams, author, manager and star actor. [Saint James, Mich., Cooper & Chidester, 1850]
Broadside. 57×26cm.
Satire on the marital difficulties of George J. Adams.
First production of the Beaver Island Press?
Morgan
CtY

8514. ———. Warning to all people. By James J. Strang, Successor Prophet to Joseph Smith. [Jefferson County, N.Y.? 1846]
Broadside. 74×11½cm.
Evidently published by Ebenezer Page, Strangite missionary.
Morgan, Sabin 92687
MH

8515. Strasberg, Josef. Norma Holm, og Andre Skildringer, af Josef Strasberg. Salt Lake City, "Bikuben," 1921.
3p.l. [7]–163p. plate. 17cm.
Fiction on the Mormons in Danish.
Title in English: Norma Holm and other stories.
UHi

8516. Stray lights on different principles. Poetry and prose for the comfort of friends. San Francisco, 1885.
[51]p. 22½cm.
A collection of 35 pamphlets first intended to be published separately. Morrisite doctrine.
USlC

8517. Street, Julian Leonard. Abroad at home; American ramblings, observations, and adventures of Julian Street; with pictorial sidelights, by Wallace Morgan. New York, The Century Co., 1914.
xiv, 517p. plates. 23cm.
Chapter XXIV. The Mormon capitol. Includes an interview with Pres. Joseph F. Smith.
Other editions: New York, Century Co. 1915. MHi; 1916. DLC, UHi, UU; 1920. UHi, UPB, UU; Garden City, Garden City Pub. Co., 1926. DLC, NjP; New York, Century, 1928. ODW
CU, DLC, MB, NjP, NN, UHi, USl, USlC, UU, ViU

8518. Strictures continued; being a continuation of Mormonite and Jewish polygamy!! Together with a short account of Richard Carlile's real character, instead of the fictitious one given him by the Rev. B. Grant . . . Keighley [Eng.] J. Rhodes, 1853.
1p.l., 51–64p. 16cm.
CtY

8519. Strife and bitterness in Utah. Avowed aim of the American Party leaders. Democratic support of their policy. [Salt Lake City, 1908?]
[4]l., printed on 1 side. 20½cm.
Politics in Utah.
MH

A string of pearls. *See Cannon, George Quayle.*

8520. Strong, Josiah. Our country: its possible future and its present crisis. By Rev. Josiah Strong . . . With an introduction by Prof. Austin Phelps . . . 100th thousand. New York, Published by Baker & Taylor for the American Home Missionary Society [c1885]
x, 229p. diagrs. 18½cm.
On cover: 18th thousand.
Perils of polygamy and autocracy of the church authorities in Utah.
Another edition: 1891. NjP, UPB, USlC
CSmH, CU–B, DLC, NjP, NN, OClW, OCU, OO, OU, USlC

8521. ———. Political aspects of Mormonism. New York, League for Social Service [1898?]
14p. 15cm. (Social series D. Anti-Mormon)
NN, UPB, USl, USlC

8522. Strong, Wallace Melvin. Te Atua e te Torutahi. Na Melavina Tarona. Papeete, Tahiti, Akalesia a Iesu Mesia . . . 1922.
22p. 15cm.
Title in English: The Trinity of the Godhead.
USlC

8523. Stuart, Granville. Forty years on the frontier as seen in the journals and reminiscences of Granville Stuart, gold-miner, trader, merchant, rancher and politician; edited by Paul C. Phillips. Cleveland, The Arthur H. Clark Company, 1925.
2v. plates, port. 24½cm. (Half-title: Early western journals. No. 2)
Includes a visit in Salt Lake City in 1852 with the family of John Taylor. He was also in Utah in 1857 during the Mormon war, and other times.
Howes S1096
CU–B, DLC, MB, MWA, NjP, OU, UHi, ULA, UPB, USlC, UU, ViU, WaU

8524. Stuart, Joseph Alonzo. My roving life. A diary of travels and adventures by sea and land, during peace and war. By Joseph A. Stuart. Illustrated by photographs of original sketches and of places visited. Auburn, Cal., 1895.
2v. illus., plates, maps. 18½cm.
Overland diary of 1849, bypassing Utah; encounter with Mormon mountainman, Barney Ward, in Bear River Valley, V.1, p. 52.
CSmH, CtY, CU–B

8525. Stuber, Stanley I. How we got our denominations, an outline of church history. By Stanley I. Stuber. New York, Association Press . . . 1927.
xiv, 225p. 19cm.
Chapter "Twelve other denominations" No. VI. The Mormons or the Latter-Day Saints, p. 210–211.
MoInRC

8526. Substance of a lecture on Mormonism. [Bridgefoot, Printed by Thomas Gibson, ca. 1855]
20p. 17cm.
Cover missing from copy.
USlC

8527. Suenson, E. Minder fra en Amerikarejse. Saertryk af "Ingenioren," 1915. Kobenhavn, 1916.
148p.
Title in English: Reminiscences from a trip to America.
Schmidt

Summers, Thomas O., *editor. See Remarkable delusions.*

8528. Summit Stake Academy. Catalogue of the Summit Stake Academy . . . with list of students . . . Coalville, Utah, 1908–1913.
v. 21cm.
USlC 1908–09, 1909–10, 1910–11, 1911–12, 1912–13

8529. Sumner, Charles Allen. 'Cross the plains, the overland trip. A narrative lecture by Charles A. Sumner. San Francisco, Bacon & Company Printers [1876?]
27p. fold. map. 21½cm.
His stay in Utah described, p. 14–15. He tells of his curiosity to see a Mormon; a discussion with a talkative Mormon with 7 wives.
Howes S1135
CU, DLC

8530. Sundbärg, Alex Gustav. Mormonvärfningen. Stockholm, Kungl. boktryckeriet. P. A. Norstedt & Söner, 1910.
2p.l., 57p. 22½cm.
Added title-page: Emigrationsutredningen. Bilaga III.
Title in English: Mormon enlistment.
USlC

SUNDBERG, C. J.

8531. Sundberg, Charles J. An appeal to our Mormon friends. The dangers of church domination and a created God. Pleasant Grove, 1914.
16p. 22cm.
MH, ULA, USl, USlC

8532. ———. Kyrklig förvirring gentemot gudomligheten i naturen. Tillika med en Kortfattad granskning af den foregifna urkundun "Mormons Bok." Pleasant Grove, Utah, 1914.
2p.l., 7–119p. front., facsim. 22½cm.
On the *Book of Mormon.*
Title in English: Church conversion through Godliness of nature.
USl, USlC

8533. ———. The mysterious Book of Mormon. In which the author asks the question "Does it appear truthful?" Sandy, Utah, Published by the author, 1917.
15p. illus., port. 21½cm.
USlC

8534. ———. The mysterious "Book of Mormon," does it appear truthful? and, An appeal to my Mormon friends, or to whom it may concern. (Second Edition) Salt Lake City, Published by the author, 1927.
24p. illus., port. 22cm.
MoInRC, USl, USlC

8535. ———. (same) [2d ed] Salt Lake City [192–]
24p. port. 21½cm.
Variant printing of 8534 without date.
MH, UPB, USlC

8536. Sunderland, La Roy. Mormonism exposed and refuted. By La Roy Sunderland. New York, Piercy & Reed, Printers, 1838.
iv [5]–54p. 15cm.
Howes S1138, Sabin 93758
CtY, DLC

8537. ———. Mormonism exposed: In which is shown the monstrous imposture, the blasphemy, and the wicked tendency of that enormous delusion, advocated by a professedly religious sect, calling themselves, "Latter Day Saints." New York, Printed and Published by the Watchman, 1842.
1p.l., vi, 7–64p. 16cm.
Sabin 93759
MH, NN, PPrHi, UPB

A supplement to Mormon, containing the Book of Anak. *See Bukki [pseud.]*

The Supreme Court decision in the Reynolds Case. *See Taylor, John.*

8538. Sutherland, George. Senator Reed Smoot and conditions in Utah . . . Speech of Hon. George Sutherland of Utah, in the Senate of the United States, Tuesday, January 22, 1907. Washington, 1907.
69p. 23cm.
Cover-title.
CU–B, MH, UHi, UPB, USlC

8539. Sutherland, Millicent Fanny (St. Clair-Erskine) Sutherland-Leveson-Gower, *Duchess of.* How I spent my twentieth year, being a short record of a tour round the world, 1886–87. By the Marchioness of Stafford. With Illustrations. 2d ed. Edinburgh and London, William Blackwood and Sons, 1889.
viii [1]l., 289p. illus. 19cm.
Bypasses Utah, because now that the territory is annexed and Brigham Young is dead, almost all the Mormons have been exterminated, p. 266–267.
USlC

8540. Sutherland, Mrs. (Redding). Five years within the Golden State, by Isabelle Saxon [*pseud.*] London, Chapman and Hall, 1868.
x, 315p. 20½cm.
Travels west with a caravan of Mormons.
Other editions: Philadelphia, J. B. Lippincott, & Co. CU–B, HH
Howes S1150
CSmH, CU–B, DLC

8541. Sutley, Zachary Taylor. The last frontier, by Zack T. Sutley. New York, The Macmillan Company, 1930.
vi p., [2]l., 350p. fold. map. 23cm.
Visit to Salt Lake City, 1869; description of Brigham Young.
CU–B, DLC, NjP, UHi, USlC

8542. Sutton, Warner P. Mormons. (In Consular reports. 1888. #97. Oct. 29, p. 575–576)
23½cm. (U.S. 50th cong. 1st Sess. House Misc. Doc. No. 609)
Statistics and history of L.D.S. colonization in Northern Mexico. Includes a letter from Henry Eyring.
UPB

8543. Svenska Härolden. Salt Lake City, Swedish Publishing Company, June 4, 1885–Oct. 20, 1892.
8v. weekly. 65cm.
First Swedish periodical published in Utah.
Editor: Peter O. Thomassen; Janne M. Sjodahl.
Title in English: The Swedish herald.
UHi, USlC

8544. Swan, Alonzo M. Canton: its pioneers and history. A contribution to the history of Fulton County. By Alonzo M. Swan. Canton, Fulton County, Illinois, 1871.
2p.l. [5]–163p. 22½cm.
"Canton's part in the Mormon War," p. 126–132.
USlC

8545. Swansea, Henry Husey Vivian, *1st baron.* Notes of a tour in America. From August 7th to November 17th, 1877, by H. Hussey Vivian . . . London, Edward Stanford, 1878.
2p.l., iiip. [(1)l.] 260p. fold. map. 23cm.
In the first chapter he dismisses Mormon doctrine as of no consequence, then describes the Mormon community. Includes his visit to John Taylor. The second chapter has notes on polygamy.
CSmH, CU-B, DLC, ICN, MB, NjP, NN, OClW, OOxM, UHi, USlC, UU

8546. Swartzell, William. Mormonism exposed, being a journal of a residence in Missouri from the 28th of May to the 20th of August, 1838, together with an appendix, containing the revelation concerning the Golden Bible, with numerous extracts from the "Book of Covenants," &c., &c. By William Swartzell, Sometimes a Deacon in the Church of 'Latter-Day Saints,' commonly called 'Mormons.' Pekin, O., Published by the author, 1840.
48p. 21½cm.
Printed by A. Ingram, Jr., Pittsburgh.
Howes S1166, Sabin 94026
CtY, NN, UPB

8547. Sweet, James Bradley. A lecture on the Book of Mormon, and the Latter-day Saints with notes. By J. B. Sweet. London, Printed for the Society for Promoting Christian Knowledge, 1853.
40p. 16½cm.
MH, NN, ULA

8548. ———. (same) London, Printed for the Society for Promoting Christian Knowledge, 1855.
40p. 16½cm.
MH, NN

8549. ———. (same) London, Printed for the Society for Promoting Christian Knowledge, 1857.
40p. 17cm.
USlC

8549a. ———. (same) London, Society for Promoting Christian Knowledge, [n.d.]
40p. 18cm. (No. 916)
At head of title: No. 916.
UPB

8550. Sweet, William Warren. The story of religions in America . . . New York and London, Harper & Brothers, 1930.
vii, 571p. plate. 22½cm.
Short history of Mormonism, p. 397–401.
CSmH, CU, DLC, NjP, UHi

8551. Sweetser, Moses Foster. King's handbook of the United States, planned and edited by Moses King. Text by M. F. Sweetser, over 2600 illus. [and] 51 colored maps. Buffalo, Moses King Corp. [c1891]
939p. illus., ports., col. maps. 20½cm.
Note on the various states; Utah has a small section. Some Mormon material.
CU-B, DLC, NjP, UU

8552. Swenson, C. A. Seek ye the old path and walk therein. [n.p., n.d.]
2pts. (16, 16p) 20cm.
Directed against the RLDS church.
MoInRC

8553. Swinburne, James K. Beneath the cloak of England's respectability, by The Rev. J. K. Swinburne . . . London, Skeffington & Son, 1912.
6p.l. [3]–180p. 18½cm.
Chap. 1–2. The Mormon Monster. 1. Its history; 2. Its teaching.
USlC

8554. Swisher, James. How I know; or, Sixteen years' eventful experience; an authentic narrative . . . Cincinnati, O., The author, 1880.
x [11]–384p. port. 21½cm.
Chapter II on Utah and the Mormons and their atrocities, etc., . . .
Another edition: 1881. CSmH, DLC, UPB, USlC
Howes S1183
CtY, CU-B, NjP, OClWHi, OFH, UHi, ULA, UPB

8555. Switzer, Jennie (Bartlett). Elder Northfield's home; or, Sacrificed on the Mormon altar. A story of the blighting curse of polygamy. By Mrs. Jennie Switzer. New York, The Howard Brown Co. [c1882]
319p. 18½cm.
Fiction concerning Mormonism.
CSmH, CU, DLC, MB, MoInRC, UPB, USl, USlC, UU

8556. ———. (same) New York, The J. Howard Brown Company [1891]
319p. 18½cm.
DLC, NN, WHi

8557. ———. (same) 2d ed. Boston, B. B. Russell Co. [c1894]
319p. 18½cm.
CU-B, DLC, USl

8558. ———. (same) Boston, B. B. Russell & Co. [c1895]
320p. 19cm.
CSmH, DLC, UHi, UU

8559. Switzler, William F. Switzler's illustrated history of Missouri from 1541 to 1877 . . . [Edited by C. R. Barns] St. Louis, C. R. Barns, 1879.
xviii, 601p. illus. 23½cm.
Contributions by A. J. Conant, G. C. Swallow, R. A. Campbell. Includes Mormonism in Missouri.
Another edition: 1881. CU
Howes S1184
CU-B, DLC, NjP, UHi, UPB

SWORD OF LABAN

8560. The Sword of Laban . . . official organ of the American Anti-Mormon Association. Grayson, Ky., [Morehead, Pikeville] August, 1908?–January, 1911. New Series, January–May, 1912.

2v. n.s. V.1 #1–5 monthly. 26cm.

Distinct from Sword of Laban series leaflets.

MoInRC; UPB V.1 #3, 5–7, 9, V.2 #2–4; USlC; UU V.1, n.s., #1, Jan. 1912

8561. The Sword of Truth, and Harbinger of Peace. South Lebanon, Maine, September 15, 1862–1866.

3v. 34½cm.

Organ of George J. Adam's *Church of the Messiah.*

No files date past 1865, but the *Saints' Herald* quotes from the paper through 1866.

Morgan

DLC S 15, 1862–D 1, 1864 (V. 1–2); MH S 15, 1862, Ja 1, S 1, 1863, Ja 15, Mr 15, Je 1–O 1, 1865 (V. 1, 3 inc.); UPB O 15, 1862–Ap 1, 1866; USlC S 15, 1862–Ap 1, 1866

Syfritt, Jacob. Revelation given November, 1850. *See Justice, G. C.*

8562. ———. Revelations given unto the messenger of the covenant, for the salvation of the world. [Philadelphia? 1849?]

22 [i.e., 20]p. 16½×10½cm.

Caption-title.

P. 19–20 omitted from numbering.

Revelations to Syfritt, March 8, 1848–December, 1849. Patriarchal blessing and "a dream" by William Smith; concluding poem.

Morgan

MoInRC

TIMES AND SEASONS.

"TRUTH WILL PTEVAIL."

VOL. 1. No. 1.] COMMERCE, ILLINOIS, NOV. 1839. [Whole No. 1

ADDRESS.

As this No. commences the Times and Seasons, it is but proper that we should lay before its readers, the course we intend to pursue, with regard to the editorial department of the same.

We wish to make it a source of light and instruction to all those who may peruse its columns, by laying before them, in plainness, the great plan of salvation which was devised in heaven from before the foundation of the world, as made known to the saints of God, in former, as well as latter days; and is, like its Author, the same in all ages, and changeth not.

In order for this, we may at times, dwell at considerable length, upon the fullness of the everlasting gospel of Jesus Christ, as laid down in the revealed word of God; the necessity of embracing it with full purpose of heart, and living by all its precepts; remembering the words of our Savior, "he that will be my disciple let him take up his cross and follow me."

We shall treat freely upon the gathering of Israel, which is to take place in these last days—of the dispensation of the fullness of times, when the fullness of the Gentiles is to come in, and the outcasts of Jacob be brought back to dwell upon the lands of their inheritance, preparatory to that great day of rest, which is soon to usher in, when Christ will reign with his saints upon earth, a thousand years, according to the testimony of all the holy prophets since the world began.

We shall also endeavor to give a detailed history of the persecution and suffering, which the members of the church of Jesus Christ of Latter Day Saints, has had to endure in Missouri, and elsewhere, for their religion. A mere synopsis of which, would swell this address to volumes; therefore we are compelled to let it pass for the present, by touching upon a few of its most prominent features.

In Jackson county, Missouri, in the year 1833, several were murdered—one whipped to death— a number shot —others whipped until they were literally cut to pieces, then left to die; but God, through his kindness, spared their lives—others tarred and feathered—between two and three hundred men had their houses plundered, and then burned to ashes, and they, with their wives and little ones, driven into the forests to perish.

Again, in 1836 they were informed by the citizens of Clay county Mo. (where they settled after being driven from Jackson,) that they could dwell there no longer; consequently they were compelled to seek a location elsewhere; notwithstanding the greater part of them had purchased the land upon which they lived, with their own money, with the expectation of securing to themselves and families, permanent abiding places, where they could dwell in peace: but in this they were mistaken, for in the latter part of this same year, they were obliged to move out of the county, when they went to a back prairie country, where the other citizens assured them they might dwell in safety.

Here they commenced their labors with renewed courage, firmly believing they were preparing peaceful homes, where they could spend the remainder of their days in the sweet enjoyment of that *liberty* which was so dearly bought by the blood of their venerable Fathers, but which had been so cruelly wrested from them, by the hands of their oppressors, in both Jackson and Clay counties. But here again they were sadly disappointed, for no sooner had they built comfortable dwelling places, and opened beautiful and extensive farms, which their untiring industry and perseverance soon accomplished, than their neighbors in the adjoining counties began to envy them, and look upon them with a jealous eye; so that in the year 1838, mobs again began to harrass and disturb them, by stealing their cattle and hogs, burning their houses, and shooting at their men; when they petitioned the Governor for protection, which he utterly refused. They then saw there was no other way but to stand in their own defence;

Item 8955. The great Nauvoo periodical, spanning the duration of the Mormon sojourn in Illinois. From the University of Utah collection.

T., M.

8563. T., M. En Mormonhustrus historie. Oversat fra Engelsk. Kobenhavn, 1913.
58p.
Title in English: A story of a Mormon wife.
Schmidt

8564. Tabernacle testimonial concert to Prof. George Careless, Monday, June 10th, 1907, at 8:15 p.m. [Salt Lake City] Deseret News, 1907.
[12]p. illus. 19½cm.
USlC

8565. Tadje, Fred, *editor.* . . . Die Prinzipien des Evangeliums. Basel, Schweizerische und Deutsche Mission der Kirche Jesu Christi der Heiligen der Letzten Tage, 1925.
104p. 20cm. (Leitfaden für die Lehrerfortbildungs-klassen)
At head of title: Schweizerische und Deutsche Mission der Kirche Jesu Christi der Heiligen der Letzten Tage.
Mormon doctrine.
Title in English: The principals of the gospel.
UPB

8566. ———. A vital message to the elders, a letter by a Mission President to the missionaries on conduct with women. [n.p., ca. 1924]
11p. 23cm.
UPB, USlC

8567. Taine, Hippolyte Adolphe. Nouveaux essais de critique et d'histoire. Paris, 1865.
299p. 18cm.
Includes "Les Mormons" and "Voyage au Pays des Mormons" par M. Jules Remy.
Title in English: New critical and historical essays.
Other editions: "2 ed." Paris, 1866. NjP; 3. éd. Paris, 1880. DLC, ULA
DLC

8568. Talbot, E. L., *compiler.* Souvenir. Utah and Utah interests, compiled by E. L. Talbot . . . With historical sketch of the Church of Jesus Christ of Latter-day Saints, by O. F. Whitney. Salt Lake City, Geo. Q. Cannon and Sons Company [1900?]
[64]p. plates, ports. 18½×26½cm.
MH, USlC, UU

8569. Talbot, Ethelbert. My people of the plains, by the Right Reverend Ethelbert Talbot . . . Bishop of central Pennsylvania . . . New York and London, Harper & Brothers [c1906]
x [1]p., [1]l., 264 [1]p. plates, ports. 21½cm.
"The experiences herein related took place during the eleven years in which the author ministered as a bishop to the pioneers of the Rocky mountain region . . ." after 1887.
Chapter on Mormonism, p. 215–240.
DLC, MB, MiU, NjP, NN, OCl, UHi, ULA, UPB, USl, USlC, UU, WaS, WaSp, WaV

8570. Talbot, Grace. Much married Saints and some sinners. Sketches from life among Mormons and Gentiles in Utah. New York, The Grafton Press [1902]
4p.l., 9–130p. 21cm.
Fiction concerning Mormonism.
CtY, DLC, MH, MoInRC, NjP, NjPT, NN, UHi, USl, USlC, UU, WHi

8571. Talkington, Henry L. Heroes and heroic deeds of the Pacific Northwest. Volume I. Elementary grades. The Pioneers [by] Henry L. Talkington, A.M., LL.D. Caldwell, Idaho, The Caxton Printers, Ltd., 1929.
2v. illus. 20½cm.
Includes "The Mormon Mission at Lemhi, Idaho . . ."
CU-B, ULA, UPB

8572. Talmage, James Edward. . . . Address[es] delivered over radio station KSL, Sunday evenings, September 2, 1928 [to March 3, 1929. Salt Lake City, The Deseret News, 1928–1930]
2v. 22½cm.
"Reprint from the *Deseret News.*"
Serial #1–17. Second series #1–9.
UPB

8573. ———. The Articles of faith. [Provo, 1893–94]
Nos. 1–17 (1p. each) 20cm.
For use in the Church University theology classes.
Dates from December, 1893 to February, 1894.
UPB

8573a. ———. (same, in Japanese) Shinsho Kogi [Lecture I-II, Tokyo, Matsu Jitsu Seito Iesu Kirisuto Kyokai, 1913]
22, 23p. 22cm.
USlC

8574. ———. The Articles of faith. A series of lectures on the principal doctrines of the Church of Jesus Christ of Latter-day Saints, by Dr. James E. Talmage. Written by appointment, and published by the church. Salt Lake City, The Deseret News, 1899.
viii, 490p. 20cm.
CU-B, DLC, MH, MoInRC, NjPT, NN, UHi, UPB, USl, USlC, UU, WHi

8574a. ———. (same) "18th thousand." Salt Lake City, Deseret News, 1901.
lx, 485p. 20cm.
MoInRC, USlC

8575. ———. (same) Prepared by appointment, and published by the church. 20th thousand. Salt Lake City, The Deseret News, 1901.
ix [1] 485p. 20cm.
CtY, DLC, MH, MoInRC, MWA, UPB, USlC, WHi

8575a. ———. (same) Liverpool, Millennial Star Office, 1908.
ix[1], 461p. 21½cm.
USlC

8576. ———. (same) 5th edition, 23rd thousand. Salt Lake City, The Deseret News, 1909.
ix [1] 485p. 20cm.
MoInRC, UHi

8577. ———. (same) 8th ed. Salt Lake City, The Deseret News, 1912.
ix [1] 485p. 19½cm.
UHi, UPB

8577a. ———. (same) 9th edition. Salt Lake City, Deseret Sunday School Union [1915?]
509p. 11½cm.
NjP

8578. ———. (same) 10th edition in English . . . Salt Lake City, The Deseret News, 1917.
ix [2] 2–485p. 17½cm.
MH

8579. ———. (same) 11th edition in English, including 52nd thousand. Salt Lake City, The Deseret News, 1919.
ix [1] 485p. 19½cm.
MH, MoInRC, ULA

8580. ———. (same) Revised and in parts rewritten. 12th edition in English, including the 57th thousand. Salt Lake City, The Church of Jesus Christ of Latter-day Saints, 1924.
ix [1] 537p. 20cm.
CtY, DLC, IWW, USlC, UU

8581. ———. (same) 13th edition in English, including the 67th thousand. Salt Lake City, Church of Jesus Christ of Latter-day Saints, 1924.
ix [1] 537p. 18½cm.
MH, UPB, USlC, UU

8582. ———. (same) 14th edition in English, including the 77th thousand. Salt Lake City, Published by the Church of Jesus Christ of Latter-day Saints, 1925.
ix [1] [1]–537p. 19cm.
CU-B, MH, MoInRC, UHi, USlC

8583. ———. (same) 15th edition. Salt Lake City, The Church of Jesus Christ of Latter-day Saints, 1925.
ix [1], 537p. 20cm.
OCl

8584. ———. (same) 16th edition in English. Salt Lake City, Published by the Church of Jesus Christ of Latter-day Saints, 1930.
ix [1] 537p. 18½cm.
USlC

8585. ———. (same, in Dutch) De artikelen des geloofs. Eene serie lezingen over de voornaamste leerstellingen van de Kerk van Jezus Christus van de Heiligen der Laatste Dagen . . . Uit het Engelsch door B. Tiemersma Elfde editie . . . Erste Hollansche uitgave . . . Rotterdam, Roscoe W. Eardley, 1913.
x, 373p. 19½cm.
NjP, UHi, USl, USlC

8585a. ———. (same) [Rotterdam, Nederlandsche Zending, 1920]
[4]p. 22cm.
Table of Contents only.
USlC

8586. ———. (same, in German) Die Glaubensartikel . . . Ins Deutsche übersetzt von den Ältesten Max Zimmer und Georgius Y. Cannon. Basel, Schweizerisch-Deutschen Mission, 1919.
xi [1]–584p. 20cm.
UPB, USlC

8587. ———. (same) Nach der 1. englischen Auflage. Ins Deutsche übersetzt von den Altesten Max Zimmer und Georgius Y. Cannon. Basel, Schweizerischen und Deutschen Mission der Kirche Jesu Christi der Heiligen der letzten Tage, 1921.
x [1] 436p. 20½cm.
UPB

8588. ———. (same) Eine Untersuchung der Glaubensartikel, d.h. eine Betrachtung der Hauptlehren der Kirche Jesu Christi der Heiligen der Letzten Tage. Durchgesehen und teilweise neu geschrieben. [Aus dem Englischen übersetzt von Max Zimmer und Georgius Y. Cannon] Dritte deutsche Auflage. Basel, Schweiz, Hrsg. von der Schweizerisch-Deutschen und der Deutsch-Österreichischen Mission der Kirche Jesu Christi der Heiligen der Letzten Tage, 1925.
viii, 568p. 19cm.
DLC, NN, UHi, ULA, UPB, USlC, UU

8589. ———. (same, in Japanese) Shinsho Kogi, Elder H. Grant Ivins. Takeshiro. Takahashi, yaku, Nehon, Matsuzitzu Seito Iesu Kirisuto Kyokai, 1917.
2p.l., 9–443, 11 [1]p. 22½cm.
UPB, USlC

8590. ———. (same) 2d ed. [Takeshiro?] 1924.
2p.l., 9–443, 11 [1]p. 23cm.
USlC

8591. ———. (same, in Swedish) En betraktelse över trosartiklarna utgörande de huvudsakliga lärdomarna i Jesu Kristi Kyra av Sista Dagars Heliga. av James E. Talmage . . . Översättning från trettonde Engelska upplagan av äldste C. A. Krantz år 1927. Utgiven och förlagd av Jesu Kristi Kyra av Sista Dagars Heliga. Stockholm, Ansvarig Utgivare I Sverige: Gideon N. Hulterström, 1930.
2p.l. [5]–551p. 20cm.
USlC, UU

8592. ———. Banbutsu no Shu. Tōkyō, Nihon, Matsu Jitsu Seito Iesu Kirisuto Kyōkai Nihon Dendōbu [1909].
15 [1]p. 15cm.
Title in English: The Savior of Mankind.
USlC

8593. ———. The Book of Mormon; an account of its origin, with evidences of its genuineness and authenticity. Salt Lake City, Deseret News Press [n.d.]
45p. 18½cm.
UPB

8594. ———. (same) Two lectures by Dr. James E. Talmage. Prepared by appointment. [Independence, Mo.? Published by the Missions of the Church of Jesus Christ of Latter-day Saints, c1899]
47p. 16½cm.
CU–B, MoInRC, UPB

8595. ———. (same) Independence, Mo., Published by the Church of Jesus Christ of Latter-day Saints [c1899]
32p. 16½cm.
MoInRC, NN, UPB

8596. ———. (same) [Independence, Mo., Central States Mission, c1899]
47p. 17cm.
ULA, USlC

8597. ———. (same) New York, Eastern States Mission [c1899]
47p. 16cm.
MB, MH, NN, OClWHi

8598. ———. (same) Chattanooga, Tenn., Southern States Mission [c1899]
47p. 16cm.
CtY

8599. ———. (same) Chicago, Northern States Mission [c1899]
47p. 16cm.
Cover-title.
MH, NN, UHi, USlC

8600. ———. (same) Kansas City, Mo., Southwestern States Mission [c1899]
44p. 17cm.
Printed also in his Articles of faith, 1899.
NN, USlC

8601. ———. (same) Salt Lake City, The Deseret News, 1899.
2p.l. [5]–52p. 19½cm.
CU–B, IWW, MH, MiU, USlC

8602. ———. (same) Salt Lake City, Bureau of Information and Church Literature, 1902.
2p.l. [5]–52p. 19cm.
IU, UPB, USl

8603. ———. (same) Independence, Mo., Zions Printing and Publishing Co. [1913?]
32p. 17cm.
CSmH, CU–B, NjP, NN, OClWHi

8604. ———. (same) Independence, Mo., Church of Jesus Christ of Latter-day Saints. Press of Zions Printing and Publishing Co. [c1924]
45 [1]p. 16½cm.
CSmH, NjP, NN, UHi, USlC

8605. ———. (same) Independence, Mo., Zions Printing and Publishing Co. [c1924]
46p. 17cm.
UPB

8606. ———. (same) Independence, Mo., Press of Zions Printing and Publishing Co. [c1924]
48p. 16½cm.
CSmH, CU–B, NjP, UHi, USlC

8607. ———. (same, in French) "Le livre de Mormon" un exposé de son origine, avec des évidences de son authenticite. Deux discours par le Dr. James E. Talmage. Ouvrage préparé par ordre de, et publié par l'église de Jésus-Christ de saints des derniers jours, traduit de l'anglais par A. A. Ramseyer. Zurich, Publié par Serge F. Ballif [n.d.]
63p. 16cm.
UPB, USlC, WaU

8608. ———. (same) Liège, Publié par Ernest C. Rossiter [n.d.]
63p. 18½cm.
NjP, UPB, USlC

TALMAGE, J. E.

8609. ———. Called of God — as was Aaron. Address delivered over Radio Station KSL. Sunday Evening, February 17, 1929. Salt Lake City, Church of Jesus Christ of Latter-day Saints, 1929.
8p. 22cm. (Second series. No. 7)
Radio address.
USIC

8610. ———. Christianity falsely so-called, by Dr. James E. Talmage, and defense of the Latter-day Saints from the Congressional Record. Salt Lake City, Bureau of Information [1920?]
20p. 22cm.
Cover-title.
Reprint from *Improvement Era.*
UHi, USIC

8611. ———. Conditions of citizenship in the kingdom of God. Salt Lake City, Bureau of Information [n.d.]
16p. 15cm.
Radio address.
Also bound in a hard cover to be used as a postcard with a description of Utah's Natural Bridges and a one page description entitled Eagle Gate.
UPB

8612. ———. Decline of the primitive church. Salt Lake City, Address delivered over Radio Station KSL, February 17, 1929. [Salt Lake City] Church of Jesus Christ of Latter-day Saints, 1929.
8p. 22½cm.
USIC

8613. ———. The Earth is defiled because of transgression. By Dr. James E. Talmage, of the Council of the Twelve, Church of Jesus Christ of Latter-day Saints. Salt Lake City, Utah. [n.p., n.d.]
[4]p. 15cm.
Variant printings. USIC
MoInRC, NN, UPB, USIC

8614. ———. Foolishness of God, and the wisdom of man. Address delivered over Radio Station KSL, Sunday Evening, February 3, 1929. Salt Lake City, Church of Jesus Christ of Latter-day Saints, 1929.
8p. 22½cm.
USIC

8615. ———. The form of Godliness and the power thereof. By Dr. James E. Talmage of the Council of the Twelve, Church of Jesus Christ of Latter-day Saints. Salt Lake City, Utah. [n.p., n.d.]
[4]p. 15½cm.
Variant printings. USIC
NN, UPB, USIC

8616. ———. Free agency and accountability of man. Salt Lake City, Bureau of Information [n.d.]
15p. 15cm.
Radio address.
Also bound in a hard cover to be used as a postcard with a two page description entitled "The Conquest of the Desert."
NjP, MoInRC, USIC

8617. ———. Geography of Utah. [Salt Lake City, Butler, Sheldon & Co., c1902]
10p. illus., maps. 31½cm.
Description and some history of Utah.
UU

8618. ———. The great apostasy, considered in the light of scriptural and secular history, by James E. Talmage . . . Salt Lake City, The Deseret News, 1909.
vii, 176p. 20cm.
CtY, DLC, MH, MoInRC, NjP, NN, UHi, UPB, USl, USIC, UU

8619. ———. (same) 7th thousand. Salt Lake City, The Deseret News, 1909.
vii, 176p. 20cm.
USIC

8620. ———. (same) 9th thousand. Salt Lake City, The Deseret News, 1909.
vii, 176p. 20cm.
USIC

8621. ———. (same) 10th thousand. Salt Lake City, The Deseret News, 1909.
vii, 176p. 20½cm.
USIC

8622. ———. (same) Denver, Colo., Western States Mission [c1909]
vii, 3–141p. 13cm.
Printed by Henry C. Etten, Chicago.
USIC

8623. ———. (same) Chicago, Published by the Missions of the Church of Jesus Christ of Latter-day Saints [c1909]
vii [1] 4–241 [1]p. 13cm.
NN, USIC, UU

8624. ———. (same) 2d ed. Independence, Mo., Central States Mission [c1909]
vii [5]–241p. 13cm.
MoInRC

8625. ———. (same) 2d ed. New York, Published by Eastern States Mission [c1909]
vii [3]–241p. 13cm.
NjP, RPB

TALMAGE, J. E.

8626. ———. (same) 2d ed. Portland, Oregon, Published by the Northwestern States Mission [c1909]
vii, 241p. 13cm.
IWW

8627. ———. (same) 2d ed. Denver, Colo., Western States Mission [c1909]
vii [3]–241p. 13cm.
"Press of Henry C. Etten & Co., Chicago."
USIC

8628. ———. (same) 2d ed. Chicago, Northern States Mission [1910]
vii, 3–241p. 13cm.
USIC

8629. ———. (same) 2d ed. [Salt Lake City, Deseret News Press, 1910]
3p.l. [7]–125p. 19cm.
UHi, USIC

8630. ———. (same) [2d ed.] Independence, Mo., Zion's Printing and Publishing Co., [Published by the Missions of the Church of Jesus Christ of Latter-day Saints in America, 1910]
3p.l. [7]–124p. 18½cm.
CU-B, MoInRC, NN, ULA

8631. ———. (same) Independence, Mo., Zion's Printing and Publishing Co. [n.d.]
129p. 18cm.
UPB

8632. ———. (same) Independence, Mo., Zion's Printing and Publishing Co. [n.d.]
124p. 18½cm.
UPB, UU

8633. ———. (same) Independence, Mo., Zion's Printing and Publishing Co. [n.d.]
128p. 19cm.
NjP, UPB

8634. ———. How does Christ save? His plan combines justice and mercy. [n.p., n.d.]
[4]p. 17½cm.
UPB

8635. ———. Hito wa Kami no Keitō wō Yūsu. Tōkyō, Nihon, Matsu Jitsu Seito Iesu Kirisuto Kyōkai Nihon Dendōbu [1907]
26p. 15½cm.
Title in English: Man in the lineage of God.
UPB, USIC

8636. ———. (same) Tōkyō, Nihon, Matsu Jitsu Seito Iesu Kirisuto Kyōkai, Nihon Dendōbu [1909]
28p. 14½cm.
"2d edition"
USIC

8636a. ———. (same) [3d. ed. Tokyo, Matsu Jitsu Seito Iesu Kirisuto Kyokai, Nihon Dendobu, 1912]
28p. 14½cm.
USIC

8637. ———. The house of the Lord: a study of holy sanctuaries, ancient and modern, including forty-six plates illustrative of modern temples, by James E. Talmage . . . Published by the church. Salt Lake City, The Deseret News, 1912.
vi, 336p. plates. 19½cm.
DLC, IWW, NjP, NjPT, NN, UHi, ULA, UPB, USIC, UU

8638. ———. How long shall hell last? By Dr. James E. Talmage of the Council of the Twelve, Church of Jesus Christ of Latter Day Saints, Salt Lake City, Utah. [Salt Lake City, Church of Jesus Christ of Latter-day Saints, n.d.]
[4]p. 16cm.
Radio address.
Variant printings.
NN, USIC

8639. ———. In olden days and now. Address delivered over Radio Station KSL, Sunday Evening, January 13, 1929. Salt Lake City, Church of Jesus Christ of Latter-day Saints, 1929.
8p. 22½cm. (Second series. No. 2)
USIC

8640. ———. In the name of God, Amen. by James E. Talmage. [Salt Lake City, Bureau of Information, n.d.]
16p. 15cm.
Caption-title.
Also bound in a hard cover to be used as a postcard with a description of the Angel on the Temple and a one page description entitled "The House of the Lord."
UPB

8641. ———. Inch ge havadan verzin arour sourerer. Zeramp dokhth I. Talmidji . . . Mrri, Yetah [Murray, Utah] 1923.
31p. 18½cm.
Articles of faith with discussion in Armenian for the use of the California Mission.
Title in English: What will the Saints believe in the Latter-days.
UPB, USIC

TALMAGE, J. E.

8641a. ———. Independence Day address. Given by Dr. James E. Talmage, Lester Park, Ogden, July Fourth, 1917. [Ogden, Utah? 1917]
[7]p. 22½cm.
USlC

8642. ———. Israel and the gentiles. Address delivered over Radio Station KSL, Sunday Evening, January 20, 1929. By James E. Talmage. [Salt Lake City, 1929]
8p. 22½cm. (Second series. No. 3)
USlC

8643. ———. . . . Jesus Christus, der Weltheiland, von Dr. James E. Talmage. Übersetzt von. G. H. Sentker. Zürich, Herausgegeben von Thomas E. McKay, 1910.
45p. 19cm.
Cover-title.
At head of title: Sonntagsschul-Unterrichtsplan, Theologische Klasse, Erste Jahr.
Title in English: Jesus Christ, the redeemer of the world.
UHi

8644. ———. Jesus the Christ; a study of the Messiah and His mission according to Holy Scriptures both ancient and modern, by James E. Talmage . . . Published by the church. Salt Lake City, The Deseret News, 1915.
xi, 804p. 20cm.
CU–B, DLC, IWW, NjPT, NN, UHi, UPB, USl, USlC

8645. ———. (same) 2d ed., 6th to 15th thousand inclusive. Salt Lake City, The Deseret News, 1915.
xi, 804p. 20cm.
". . . presents some minor changes in expression and a few additional references . . ."
CU–B, DLC, NN, UPB

8646. ———. (same) 3d ed., 16th to 20th thousand inclusive. Salt Lake City, The Deseret News, 1916.
xi, 804p. 20cm.
DLC, MH, NN

8647. ———. (same) 4th ed., 21st to 25th thousand inclusive. Salt Lake City, The Deseret News, 1916.
xi, 804p. 20cm.
DLC, MB, OCl, USlC, UU

8648. ———. (same) 5th ed., comprising 26th and 27th thousand. Salt Lake City, The Deseret News, 1916.
xi, 804p. 18½cm.
CU–B, DLC, MH, MoInRC

8649. ———. (same) 6th ed. Salt Lake City, Deseret Book Co., 1922.
xi, 804p. 20cm.
DLC, USlC

8650. ———. (same) 7th ed. Salt Lake City, Deseret Book Co., 1925.
xi, 804p. 20cm.
USlC

8651. ———. (same) 8th ed. Salt Lake City, The Deseret News, 1928.
xi, 804p. 20cm.
UPB

8652. ———. The law of tithe. Tithing observance commanded of God. Address delivered in Salt Lake Tabernacle. Sunday, January 11, 1914. By Elder James E. Talmage . . . Reported by F. W. Otterstrom. Salt Lake City [1914?]
20p. 12½cm.
Reprint from the *Deseret Evening News*, with additions by the author.
UHi, UPB, USl, USlC

8653. ———. Let God be true, but every man a liar. Address delivered over Radio Station KSL, Sunday Evening, February 10, 1927. Salt Lake City, Church of Jesus Christ of Latter-day Saints, 1929.
8p. 22½cm. (Second series. No. 6)
USlC

8654. ———. (same) [n.p., n.d.]
Broadside. 30×22½cm.
UPB

8655. ———. Living and dead, both to hear the Gospel. By Dr. James E. Talmage, of the Council of the Twelve, Church of Jesus Christ of Latter-Day Saints, Salt Lake City, Utah. [Salt Lake City, Church of Jesus Christ of Latter-day Saints, n.d.]
[4]p. 15½cm.
Variant printings. USlC
MoInRC, NjP, NN, UPB, USlC

8656. ———. The Lord's tenth. By Dr. James E. Talmage. [n.p., n.d.]
[4]p. 17cm.
NjP, USlC

8657. ———. The Lord's tenth. Address over Radio Station KSL, Sunday Evening, Oct. 12, 1930. By Dr. James E. Talmage of the Council of the Twelve Apostles, Church of Jesus Christ of Latter-day Saints. Salt Lake City, Published by the Church, 1930.
8p. 18cm. (New Series. No. 40)
UPB

8658. ———. (same) [Salt Lake City? 193–]
16p. 16½cm.
Cover-title.
NjP, UHi, USl

TALMAGE, J. E.

8659. ———. (same) [Independence, Mo., Zion's Printing & Pub. Co., n.d.]
16p. 19cm.
ULA, UPB

8660. ———. The Marriage institution. A Series of four articles. Selected from the writings of Dr. James E. Talmage, one of the Twelve Apostles of the Church of Jesus Christ of Latter-day Saints. Independence, Mo., Press of Zion's Printing and Publishing Co. [n.d.]
18p. 16cm.
Variant printing. USlC
UPB, USlC

8661. ———. A messenger from the presence of God. [Le Grande, Oregon?] 1922.
[4]p. 17½cm.
Cover-title: Souvenir from the tabernacle of the Church of Jesus Christ of Latter-day Saints. La Grande, Oregon.
USlC

8662. ———. Modern temples, illustrated. The illustrations presented herewith, forty-six in number, are copies of plates used in the work published in October, 1912, entitled "The House of the Lord" . . . Salt Lake City, Church of Jesus Christ of Latter-day Saints, 1912.
[47] l. 46 numbered plates. 13×19cm.
USlC

8663. ———. Mormonismens filosofi af Dr. Phil. James Talmage . . . En forelaesning holdt efter indbydelse og under auspicium af "Denver Filosofiske Selskab" i Denver, Colorado, den 14. Marts 1901. Kobenhavn, udgivet og forlagt af de Sidste-dages Helliges, Skandinaviske Mission . . . 1905.
20p. 22cm.
Title in English: Philosophy of Mormonism. Translated from an article in the *Improvement Era*, V.4, p. 459. Later published in English in a book entitled *The story on Philosophy of Mormonism*.
USlC

8664. ———. (same, in German) Philosophie in "Mormonismus." Aus dem Englischen übersetzt von Friedrich Hüfner. Schweiz, Thomas E. McKay [n.d.]
16p. 21cm.
UPB

8665. ———. (same) [Leipzig, G. Hermann Bohme, n.d.]
16p. 22cm.
Cover-title.
UHi

8666. ———. (same) Berlin, Herausgegeben von der Redaktion des "Stern" [n.d.]
16p. 22cm.
Cover-title.
USlC

8667. ———. Myself and I [by] James E. Talmage, President of the European Mission. [n.p., n.d.]
[2]p. 22cm.
Moral theology.
UPB

8668. ———. Need of a redeemer. Salt Lake City [Church of Jesus Christ of Latter-day Saints, n.d.]
[4]p. 18cm.
USlC

8669. ———. [Newspaper articles published at weekly intervals on Mormon doctrine. Salt Lake City, 1917–1919.]
3v. 27cm.
Series A, B, C.
Also given as addresses over Station KSL, though this is not given on the publication.
Each item [1]p.
UPB, USlC

8670. ———. Opportunity here and hereafter. By Dr. James E. Talmage of the Council of the Twelve, Church of Jesus Christ of Latter-day Saints, Salt Lake City, Utah. Salt Lake City, Church of Jesus Christ of Latter-day Saints [n.d.]
[4]p. 16½cm.
NN, UHi, UPB, USlC

8671. ———. Peter and his brethren. Address delivered over Radio Station KSL, Sunday Evening, January 6, 1929. Salt Lake City, Church of Jesus Christ of Latter-day Saints, 1929.
8p. 22½cm. (2d series. No. 1)
USlC

8672. ———. The philosophical basis of "Mormonism;" and address delivered by invitation before the Congress of Religious Philosophies held in connection with the Panama-Pacific International Exposition, San Francisco, California, July 29, 1915. [Independence, Mo., Zion's Printing and Publishing Company. Published by the Missions of the Church of Jesus Christ of Latter-day Saints, 1915?]
48p. 17½cm.
Includes address delivered in Salt Lake City, October 10, 1915.
Several variant printings.
NjP, NN, UHi, ULA, UU

8673. ———. (same) Salt Lake City, Bureau of Information, 1915.
32p. 19cm.
NjP, UPB, USlC

8674. ———. (same) [Salt Lake City, Bureau of Information, 1916?]
48p. 18cm.
Cover-title.
MH, MoInRC, NjP, NN, UHi, UPB, USl, USlC, UU

TALMAGE, J. E.

8675. ———. (same) [Independence, Mo., Zion's Printing and Publishing Co., 1916]
42p. 18cm.
MoInRC, UPB, USlC

8676. ———. (same) [Independence, Mo., Zion's Printing and Publishing Co., 1917]
46p. 18cm.
MoInRC, UHi

8677. ———. (same) [Independence, Mo., Zion's Printing and Publishing Co., 1925?]
48p. 18cm.
USlC

8678. ———. (same) Independence, Mo., Zion's printing and Publishing Co. [1928]
48p. 18cm.
UPB

8679. ———. (same, in Danish) Mormonismens filosofiske Grundlag. Foredrag, holdt efter indbydelse i San Francisco ved den her afholdte religions-filosofiske verdenskongres, d. 29. July 1915. [København, F. E. Bording, 1915?]
16p.
Schmidt
USlC

8680. ———. (same, in German) Philosophische Grundlage der Kirche Jesu Christi der Heiligen der letzten Tage. Basel, Schweizerisch-Deutschen Mission, 1916.
20 [1]p. 21cm.
Includes "Glaubensartikel."
UHi, UPB

8681. ———. The Pittsburgh conference on "Mormonism." by Dr. James E. Talmage, and report of the proceedings in the United States Senate in defense of Latter-day Saints. Salt Lake City, Bureau of Information [1919]
29p. 17½cm.
Variant printings. USlC
CU-B, MH, NjP, NN, UHi, ULA, USlC

8682. ———. Progression beyond the grave. Salt Lake City, Church of Jesus Christ of Latter-day Saints [n.d.]
[4]p. 15cm.
NjP, USlC

8683. ———. [Radio addresses. Salt Lake City, 1928]
17 nos. (8p. each) 22cm.
Reprinted from the *Deseret News*.
Addresses delivered from September 2–December 30, 1928.
Contents: The Meridian of time. As one having authority. In His Name. What think ye of Christ? The need of a redeemer. The Son of Man. Lord of the Sabbath. Thy sins be forgiven thee. The Herald of the Lord. The Shepherd and His Sheep. Shall many or but few be saved? The sacrifice supreme. In the realm of the dead. He is risen — as he said. After his resurrection. The babe of Bethlehem. Behold, the Bridegroom cometh!
USlC

8684. ———. Religions-philosophien und die daraus hervorgehende Schlussfolgerung. Basel, Schweizerisch-Deutschen Mission, 1916.
4p. 21cm.
Title in English: Religious philosophies and conclusions.
UPB

8685. ———. Requirements of the Lord. Chattanooga, Tenn., Church of Jesus Christ of Latter-day Saints, Southern States Mission [n.d.]
4p. 14cm.
USlC

8686. ———. Resurrection of the dead, when shall it be? By Dr. James E. Talmage, of the Council of the Twelve, Church of Jesus Christ of Latter Day Saints. Salt Lake City [Church of Jesus Christ of Latter-day Saints, 192–]
4p. 16cm.
CU-B, NjP, NN, UHi, UPB, USlC

———. Salt Lake City. *See Powell, Lyman Pierson.*

8687. ———. Search the scriptures. Address delivered over Radio Station KSL, Sunday Evening, February 24, 1929. Salt Lake City, Church of Jesus Christ of Latter-day Saints, 1929.
8p. 22½cm. (2d series. No. 2)
USlC

8688. ———. Some pertinent truths. [Salt Lake City, Bureau of Information, n.d.]
15p. 15cm.
Caption-title.
Also bound in a hard cover to be used as a postcard with a description of the Gull Monument and a one page description entitled "The Story of the Gulls."
NjP, NN, UPB, USlC

8689. ———. Spirit world, paradise and hades. By Dr. James E. Talmage, of the Council of the Twelve, Church of Jesus Christ of Latter Day Saints. Salt Lake City, Church of Jesus Christ of Latter-day Saints [n.d.]
[4]p. 16cm.
MoInRC, NN, USlC

8690. ———. Story of "Mormonism." By James E. Talmage . . . Liverpool, Millennial Star Office, 1907.
2p.l., 92p. 16½cm.
CU-B, DLC, MH, MoInRC, ULA, UPB, USlC

8691. ———. (same) 2d ed. Salt Lake City, Bureau of Information, 1910.
87p. 15½cm.
"A revised and reconstructed form of lectures delivered . . . at the University of Michigan . . . and elsewhere. The 'Story' first appeared in print as a lecture report, in the *Improvement Era*, Vol. IV; and was afterward issued as a booklet from the office of the 'Millennial Star,' Liverpool." . . . Pref.
DLC, MH, USlC

8692. ———. (same) [Independence, Mo., Zion's Printing & Publishing Co., 1914]
64p. 18cm.
MoInRC, USlC

8693. ———. (same, under title) The Story of "Mormonism" and the philosophy of "Mormonism." Salt Lake City, The Deseret News, 1914.
136p. 18cm.
CSmH, CU-B, DLC, MoInRC, NjP, NjPT, NN, UHi, USlC, UU

8694. ———. (same) 7th ed. in English, including 46th to 50th thousand. Salt Lake City, The Deseret News, 1920.
146p. 18cm.
CtY, DLC, IWW, MH, MoInRC, UHi, USlC

8695. ———. (same) 10th ed. in English, including the 60th thousand, revised by the author. Salt Lake City, The Deseret Book Co., 1930.
165p. 18cm.
Cover-title: The story and the philosophy of 'Mormonism.'
DLC, NjP, USlC

8696. ———. (same, in Greek) He historia tou Mormoismou. En Athenais, 1908.
2p.l., 116p. 17cm.
UPB

———. A study of the articles of faith; . . .
See his Articles of faith.

8697. ———. Sunday night talks; a series of radio addresses relating to doctrines of the Church of Jesus Christ of Latter-day Saints. Salt Lake City [Church of Jesus Christ of Latter-day Saints] 1930.
3p.l., nos. 1–51. 20cm.
UHi, UPB, USlC

8698. ———. The theory of evolution, a lecture delivered by James E. Talmage . . . Before the Utah County Teachers' Association at Provo City, March 8, 1890. Provo City, Enquirer Company Steam Print, 1890.
17p. 20cm.
MH, NjP, UPB, USlC

8699. ———. The Unknown God. Address delivered over Radio Station KSL, Sunday Evening, January 27, 1929. Salt Lake City, Church of Jesus Christ of Latter-day Saints, 1929.
8p. 22×9cm. (Second series. No. 4)
USlC

8700. ———. The vitality of Mormonism. An address by James E. Talmage . . . Salt Lake City, The Deseret News, 1917.
25 [1]p. 19½cm.
CU-B, MH, NN, UHi, UPB, USlC, UU

8701. ———. The vitality of Mormonism. Brief essays on distinctive doctrines of the Church of Jesus Christ of Latter-day Saints, by James E. Talmage . . . Boston, R. G. Badger [c1919]
1p.l., 7–361p. 20½cm.
CtY, CU-B, DLC, IWW, MH, MoInRC, NjP, NjPT, NN, UHi, ULA, UPB, USlC, UU, WHi

8702. ———. Whence we came, whither we go. By Dr. James E. Talmage . . . [Salt Lake City, Bureau of Information, n.d.]
16p. 15½cm.
Caption-title.
Also bound in a hard cover to be used as a postcard with a description of the Tabernacle and Organ and a one page description entitled "The Great Mormon Tabernacle."
MoInRC, NN, ULA, UPB, USlC

8703. Talmage, May Booth. Lehren des evangeliums. Leitfaden für die Frauenhilfsvereine der Europäischen Mission für das Jahr 1926 . . . Basel, Schweizerischen und Deutschen Mission, der Kirche Jesu Christi der Heiligen der letzten Tage, 1926.
126p. 20cm.
Title in English: Teachings of the gospel.
UPB, USlC

8704. Talmage, Thomas De Witt. Around the tea-table. By T. DeWitt Talmage . . . Philadelphia, Cowperthwait & Company, 1874.
504p. front., 11 plates. 21cm.
Includes his speech on Mormonism, p. 160–165.
Other editions: 1875. NjP; New York, Chicago, and Richmond, Va., Loomis National Library Association, 1888. USlC; New York, The Christian Herald [1895] DLC
DLC, MiU, NjP, NN, ODW, USlC

8705. ———. Brooklyn Tabernacle sermons. New York, Funk and Wagnalls, 1884.
1p.l., 400 [2]p. 25½cm.
Includes a sermon on Mormonism.
USlC

8706. ———. 500 selected sermons. New York, The Christian Herald, 1900.
20v. 15cm.
Vol. 2, p. 204–206: Evils of Mormonism. Attention directed to the evils of Mormonism by President Garfield's inaugural and death.
Intimates Guiteau either a Mormon or paid by them.
"I will not say he was a Mormon, but he has all the Mormon theories. He had the ugliness of a Mormon, the licentiousness of a Mormon, the cruelty of a Mormon, the murderous spirit of a Mormon, the infernalism of a Mormon."
DLC

8706a. ———. Live coals; from the discourses of T. De Witt Talmage . . . Collated by Lydia E. White. Hagerstown, Md., The Brethren Tract Society, 1886. [c1885]
678p. front. 22cm.
Mormons, p. 613–616.
USlC

8707. ———. Mormonism. A sermon by the Rev. T. De Witt Talmage . . . London, Lobb and Bertram, 1880.
16p. 18½cm.
Cover-title.
NN, USlC

8708. ———. Mormonism, an exposure. 15th thousand. [London, Printed by W. H. and L. Collingridge, 1882]
16p. 17cm.
USlC

8709. ———. "Social dynamite:" or, The wickedness of modern society. Chicago, Standard Publishing Co., 1888.
xix, 25–574p. port. 22½cm.
Includes "Social evils of Mormonism."
Other editions: St. Louis, Missouri, Halloway & Co., 1888. UHi; Chicago, 1889. USlC, UU; Chicago, Standart Pub. Co.; Detroit, R.D.S. Taylor & Co., 1888. DLC; Newark, N.J., S. Allison, 1888. DLC
UPB

8710. ———. Some startling disclosures of an awful community condition. [n.p., n.d.]
6p. 23cm.
The condition of Mormonism and polygamy.
MoInRC

———. The Utah abomination. *See Jarman, William.*

8711. Tangye, *Sir* Richard. Reminiscences of travel in Australia, America, and Egypt. By Richard Tangye. With illustrations by E. C. Mountfort. Birmingham, Printed at the Herald Press, 1883.
xiv p. [1]l., 290p., [1]l. illus., port. 22½cm.
Travels through Utah with very brief description of Mormonism.
Another edition: 2d ed. London, S. Low, Marston, Searle, & Rivington, 1884. CU–B, UPB
DLC, CU–B

8712. Tanner, Alva Amasa. Anti-Christian marriage. Oakley, Idaho [n.d.]
[6]p. 19cm.
First of a series of hand-printed pamphlets, with no pagination; the various sections used over again in different parts of the pamphlets.
Mostly printed after his excommunication from the L.D.S. Church.
USlC

8713. ———. Articles of faith. Oakley, Idaho, 1924.
[40]p. 19cm.
Basically the same as his "Articles of faith and declaration of principles."
WHi

8714. ———. Articles of faith and declaration of principles by Alva A. Tanner. Oakley, Idaho, 1921.
[8]l. 18cm.
Contents: The phrenological page, Articles of faith, spirits in prison, declaration of principles, Oakley prophets in heaven, the order of Zion.
USlC, UPB, UU

8715. ———. (same) Oakley, Idaho, 1921.
[40]p. illus. 19cm.
Includes material on the *Book of Mormon.*
Denunciation of Mormonism.
MH, WHi

8716. ———. Bible vs Mormonism. Oakley, Idaho, 1917.
[8]p. 19cm.
Includes his "A marvelous work and a wonder."
USlC

8717. ———. (same) Oakley, Idaho, 1917.
[24]p. 19cm.
Includes: A revelation given July 11, 1917, anti-Christian marriage.
Variant printings. USlC
USlC

8718. ———. The Book of Abraham test. Oakley, Idaho [n.d.]
[2]p. 38cm.
USlC

8719. ———. (same) Oakley, Idaho, October, 1916.
[2]p. 38cm.
USlC

8720. ———. The Book of Mormon tested. Hieroglyphics on marble in Central America testify against it. Extracts from Rev. M. T. Lamb, who says the Book of Mormon is a fable. Oakley, Idaho, April, 1916.
[2]p. 39cm.
USlC

TANNER, A. A.

8721. ———. (same) Oakley, Idaho, April, 1916.
[4]p. 39cm.
P. 1 and 4 are the same as above. On page 2–3 is printed: The poet. Published by Alva A. Tanner at Oakley, Idaho, 1916. Nathanael, longest American poem. All cantos to date, 25cts. One cent stamps taken. Call, or write for copies. Canto 25 and Canto 26.
USIC

8722. ———. A castout Mormon, by Alva A. Tanner. Oakley, Idaho, 1919.
[40]p. illus. 19cm.
Same material as in the "Excommunicated Mormon."
Includes the poem "Excommunicated Mormon," "Son's letter to Mother" and "Humbug Gospel."
MH, NN, UHi, UPB, USIC, WHi

8723. ———. The celestial expositor. Oakley, Idaho, November, 1916.
[2]p. 38cm.
On verso: Book of Mormon test continued from April number.
USIC

8724. ———. The Celestial expositor: or Spiritual science . . . Oakley, Idaho [c1917]
[32]p. illus. 18½cm.
Includes his anti-Mormon notes, *Pearl of Great Price* material, etc.
Also an autobiography.
CtY, MH, UPB, USI, WHi

8725. ———. Celestial gazette. Visions seen by A. A. Tanner, December, 1917. Oakley, Idaho, 1917.
8, 12, 8p. 19cm.
Issues dated: Dec. 1917, Jan. 1918, Jan. 1920.
UPB, USIC

8726. ———. Divine spirit science. Oakley, Idaho [c1918]
[40]p. 19cm.
Caption-title.
Chiefly his poem "The light of Jupiter." It also includes "Mistakes in Mormon theology."
MH, USI, WHi

8727. ———. (same) Published for Jan. 1918, at Oakley [I]daho, by Alva A. Tanner. [Oakley, 1918]
4p. 19cm.
MH, USIC

8728. ———. Dreams and revelations. Published November 1917, at Oakley, Idaho, by Alva A. Tanner. Oakley, Idaho, 1917.
[4]p. 19cm.
USIC

8729. ———. Essay on man. From a phrenological and Biblical viewpoint. [Oakley, Idaho] 1917.
[16]p. 19cm.
Begins with his *Book of Mormon* and *Pearl of Great Price* material, then follows "An Essay on Man" [Poem]
Much of this material is included in his "Humbug Gospel."
CtY, USIC

8730. ———. Eternal life. Oakley, Idaho, 1914.
[4]p. 20½cm.
Tract defending his publications.
USIC

8731. ———. (same) Oakley, Idaho, August, 1914.
[8]p. 21cm.
MoInRC

8732. ———. Excommunicated Mormon. Oakley, Idaho, 1919.
[32]p. 19cm.
Material on courage.
Poem on "Excommunicated Mormon" plus "Humbug Gospel."
Material against the *Book of Mormon*, "Son's letter to mother."
CtY, NN, USI, USIC

8733. ———. The Excommunicated Mormon. By Alva A. Tanner. Oakley, Idaho, 1919.
[40]p. 18cm.
Poem.
USIC

8734. ———. (same) Oakley, Idaho, 1920.
[40]p. 19cm.
Includes his excommunication; other anti-Mormon material and at the end, *Washington's vision.*
CtY, USIC

8735. ———. Facts about the Book of Mormon. Oakley, Idaho [c1918]
[24]p. illus. 18½cm.
Includes *Washington's vision* and *Pearl of Great Price* material.
NjP, UPB, USI, USIC, UU, WHi

8736. ———. Facts for Mormon elders. Oakley, Idaho, 1920.
[16]p. 18½cm.
Things to tell proselyters. Also his "Truth is better than lies."
CtY, NjP, NN, WHi

8737. ———. A Father's letter to his sons and daughters. May 1st 1914. [Oakley, Idaho, 1914]
[4]p. 21cm.
His defense to his family for leaving the church and his revelation of January 31, 1914.
USIC

TANNER, A. A.

8738. ———. Gem state poll. Oakley, Idaho, September, 1916.
[4]p. port. 39cm.
USlC

8739. ———. Gods in Ether. A poem. Oakley, Idaho, 1918.
[56]p. 19cm.
Principally an anti-Mormon poem in 6 cantos.
At head of title: A Gem State Poem.
USlC

8740. ———. (same) Oakley, Idaho, 1918.
[45]p. 18cm.
Variant printing. No legend at head of title.
USlC

8741. ———. The golden Bible and other poems, by Alva Amasa Tanner, Oakley, Idaho. [Oakley, Idaho? n.d.]
[2]p. 29cm.
"The Lord's Prayer" and other poems on verso of page.
UHi

8742. ———. Gospel in poems. By Alva A. Tanner. Oakley, Idaho [n.d.]
[12]p. 21cm.
UPB, USlC

8743. ———. The Gospel of reason by Alva A. Tanner. Oakley, Idaho, 1922.
[32]p. 19cm.
Material on cover.
The Gospel of reason [poem]. Looking back ten years. Wonders of the spirit world.
UU

8744. ———. Gospel of truth. Oakley, Idaho, 1923.
[40]p. 19cm.
To whom it may concern . . . attention Mormon elders, Nauvoo City Council record, Spiritual philosophy [etc.]
USlC

8745. ———. Gospel truths by Alva A. Tanner. Oakley, Idaho [n.d.]
[12]p. 22cm.
Pertaining to the spirits and the world of spirits.
UPB, USlC

8746. ———. Humbug gospel. [Oakley, Idaho, 1919?]
[8]p. 18cm.
IWW

8747. ———. In the spirit world. Visions seen by A. A. Tanner. Oakley, Idaho, 1917.
[8]p. 18cm.
USlC

8748. ———. In two worlds. Oakley, Idaho, 1914.
[8]p. 18cm.
In double columns.
USlC

8749. ———. Joseph Morris the martyr. Extracts from a letter to his friend George Leslie. True cause of his death explained. Morris risen from the dead. Oakley, Idaho, May 20, 1916.
[2]p. 39cm.
USlC

8750. ———. A key to the Book of Mormon, by Alva A. Tanner. Oakley, Idaho [1916]
[16]p. illus. 19cm.
Variant wrappers. UPB, USl
CU-B, MH, NN, UPB, USl, USlC, WHi

8750a. ———. Letter to mother [and others]. [Oakley, Idaho, n.d.]
[8]p. 18cm.
USlC

8751. ———. The Light of Jupiter. Oakley, Idaho [1918?]
[32]p. 18cm.
Canto four dated March, 1918. A satire on Mormonism.
UPB, USlC

8752. ———. The Light of Jupiter, by Alva A. Tanner. Oakley, Idaho [1920]
[8]p. 18cm.
Tried the Apostles, etc.
Same title but different text from 8751.
UPB, USlC

8753. ———. A message from Heaven. Given Tonru [sic] Alva A. Tanner. Oakley, Idaho [1916]
[24]p. 18cm.
A revelation, a key to the Book of Mormon.
Received July 11, 1917.
USlC

8754. ———. Miscellaneous lore. Oakley, Idaho [1918]
[32]p. 19½cm.
Includes his divine spirit science, George Washington's vision, how Brigham Young took wives away, etc.
USl

8755. ———. Mormon problems. Oakley, Idaho, 1920.
[56]p. ports., illus. 19cm.
Facts for Mormon elders, The Excommunicated Mormon, George Washington's vision, Science vs. Joseph Smith, Telepathic vision.
MH, UPB, USlC, WHi

TANNER, A. A.

8756. ———. Mysteries of the Spirit World never before told. By Alva A. Tanner. Oakley, Idaho, 1920.
[40]p. 19cm.
Includes: The Excommunicated Mormon, Common sense gospel, Telepathic visions and revelations, Celestial Gazeteer, Jan. 1920.
USIC

8757. ———. The Oakley phrenologist; poet and seer. Oakley, Idaho, 1921.
[48]p. ports. 19cm.
Letter concerning his excommunication. More about Joseph Smith, etc.
IWW, MH, WHi

8758. ———. The Oakley seer. Oakley, Idaho, 1921.
[48]p. port. 19cm.
Includes: Tried the apostles, That sealed book, Extract from Peter Ingersoll, etc.
CtY, IWW, MH, UPB, USIC, WHi

8759. ———. (same) Oakley, Idaho, 1921.
[24]p. 18½cm.
NN

8760. ———. Poems of the Gem State poet. Oakley, Idaho, 1917.
[32]p. port. 19cm.
Cover-title.
Includes anti-Mormon poetry.
RPB

8761. ———. The Protestant Mormon. Oakley, Idaho, 1921 [i.e., 1922]
[56]p. 19cm.
Includes his Articles of faith and declaration of belief.
Also his exposé of Mormonism.
CtY, MH, UPB, WHi

8762. ———. The revelation given July 11th, 1917 to Alva A. Tanner. Oakley, Idaho, 1917.
[16]p. 19cm.
Includes Anti-Christian marriage.
USIC

8763. ———. Science of revelation and Mormonism. [Oakley, Idaho, 1917]
[16]p. 18cm.
Science of revelation, Anti-Christian marriage, Finlanders' gospel.
MoInRC, UPB, USIC

8764. ———. Science vs. Joseph Smith; or, The opinion of scholars as to Joseph Smith as a translator, author. Oakley, Idaho, 1920.
[48]p. illus. 19cm.
Cover-title.
How to become Gods, To the Mormon church [poem]
CtY, RPB, USI, USIC

8765. ———. Spiritual Science. May, 1915. [Oakley, 1915]
[4]p. 18cm.
USIC

8766. ———. Spiritual Science. Oakley, Idaho, 1915.
[56]p. 19cm.
Includes Tanner biographies, Spiritual science, The apostle church, The science of eternal life, "Son's letter to Mother." [poem]
CtY, USIC

8767. ———. Telepathic revelations and up-to-date Gospel. By A. A. Tanner. [Oakley, Idaho, 1913?]
[8]p. 18cm. (Serial. No. 5)
USIC

8768. ———. (same) Oakley, Idaho, 1913.
[16]p. 18cm.
USIC

8769. ———. (same) Oakley, Idaho, 1913.
[8]p. 18cm. (Serial 3. Lot 2. Revised)
USIC

8770. ———. Telepathic visions and revelations. Oakley, Idaho, 1919.
[40]p. 19cm. (Serial 3. Lot 2. Serial 4)
The Excommunicated Mormon, Common sense gospel, Telepathic visions and revelations, Celestial Gazette, Jan. 1920.
USIC

8770a. ———. Two worlds in one. [Oakley, Idaho, n.d.]
[4]p. 18cm.
USIC

8771. ———. U. S. Celestial court, by Alva A. Tanner. Oakley, Idaho, 1924.
[32]p. 18cm.
The U.S. Celestial court, A court proving Joseph Smith a fraud, Senate investigation of Mormonism, The Celestial Gazette, Jan. 1920, George Washington's vision.
NN

8772. ———. Up to date gospel. Oakley, Idaho, 1915.
[12]p. 18cm.
Includes: Before the railroads come to Oakley, Spiritual scenes.
USIC

8773. ———. A voice in the wilderness. Oakley, Idaho, 1923.
[40]p. ports. 19cm.
"To whom it may concern . . ." "The Mormons killed Joseph Morris, etc." His spiritual philosophy, Mormon leaders in politics, The Gospel of reason.
MH, UPB, USIC, WHi

8774. ———. A voice in the wilderness. Oakley, Idaho, November 12, 1906.
[2]p. 56½cm.
USIC

8775. ———. A voice in the wilderness. A voice from beyond the tomb — a voice from eternity. The Saints risen from the dead. The dead are not dead. Oakley, Idaho, July, 1916.
[2]p. 39cm.
USIC

8776. ———. Washington's vision. Oakley, Idaho, 1920.
[40]p. 19cm.
Same pagination and material as: Excommunicated Mormon.
Excommunicated Mormon, other anti-Mormon material, at end, Washington's vision. Telepathic visions, Celestial Gazette.
CtU

8777. ———. Wisdom of Ingersoll. Edited by Alva A. Tanner. Oakley, Idaho, 1922.
[24]p. ports. 19cm.
Mormon leaders in politics, etc.
MH, WHi

8778. ———. The word of God. September, 1914. To Joseph F. Smith, A revelation given through Alva A. Tanner, at Oakley, Idaho, August 30th, 1914. [Oakley, 1914?]
[8]p. 19½cm.
USIC

8779. ———. The word of God. September, 1914. To Joseph F. Smith, Oakley, 1919.
[8]p. 20cm.
Revelation through Alva A. Tanner to Joseph F. Smith.
USIC

8780. **Tanner, Joseph Marion.** A biographical sketch of James Jensen. By J. M. Tanner. Salt Lake City, The Deseret News, 1911.
3p.l., 190p. plates, ports. 17½cm.
Mormon biography.
CSmH, CU-B, ICN, MH, NjP, NN, UHi, UPB, USl, USIC, UU, WHi

8781. ———. A biographical sketch of John Riggs Murdock. By J. M. Tanner. Salt Lake City, The Deseret News, 1909.
iv, [1]l., 206p. port. 18cm.
Mormon biography.
CtY, CU-B, InU, MH, NN, UPB, USl, USIC, UU

8782. ———. Old Testament studies . . . written for the Deseret Sunday School Union, by Dr. Joseph M. Tanner. Salt Lake City, The Deseret Sunday School Union, 1917.
2v. maps. 19cm.
Contents: V.1. The creation to the establishment of the kingdom under Saul. V.2. From the establishment of the kingdom under Saul.
DLC, NN, UHi, UPB, USIC, UU

8783. ———. Problems of the age; dealing with religious, social and economic questions and their solution. A study for the quorums and classes of the Melchizedek Priesthood. [Salt Lake City, 1918?]
16p. 23cm.
Caption-title.
"From the *Improvement Era*, beginning January, 1918."
CU-B, UPB

8784. **Tanner, Mary Jane (Mount).** A book of fugitive poems, by Mary J. Tanner . . . Salt Lake City, Printed by J. C. Graham & Co., 1880.
viii, 128p. 18cm.
Mormon poetry.
CU-B, DLC, MH, NjP, ULA, USIC, UU

8785. **Tanner, Maurice.** Descendants of John Tanner. Born August 15, 1778, at Hopkintown, R. I. Died April 15, 1850, at South Cottonwood, Salt Lake County, Utah. Compiled by Maurice Tanner (His great grandson) [n.p.] Published by the Tanner Family Association, 1923.
264p. ports. 23½cm.
Includes many Utah Tanners.
The first part of the genealogy is taken from records prepared by George C. Tanner.
CU-B

8786. **Tanner, Myron.** Biography of Myron Tanner. Salt Lake City, The Deseret News, 1907.
35p. 23½cm.
Mormon biography.
USIC

8787. **Tanner, Nathan, Jr.** The Church of Jesus Christ of Latter-day Saints. A divine institution. But the First Presidency wrongfully chosen, not recognized by the Lord, and have no authority to speak and act for him in that capacity. A Letter from N. Tanner, jr. to his son. [Blackfoot, Idaho, 1906]
10p. 21cm.
MoInRC, USIC

8788. ———. False prophets and wolves in sheep's clothing. [Salt Lake City, Century Printing, n.d.]
12p. port. 21½cm.
Apostasy of the Mormon Church, especially Joseph F. Smith.
MoInRC, UPB, USIC

TANNER, N.

8789. ———. First presidency of the church and kingdom of God. How chosen. Ogden, Utah, 1900.
32p. 21½cm.
Mormon doctrine of succession.
MoInRC, USIC

8790. ———. How the First Presidency should be chosen. The law of God upon the subject, a letter from N. Tanner Jr. to his son. [2d ed.] [n.p., n.d.]
16p. 22cm.
MoInRC

8791. ———. (same) [2d ed.] Blackfoot, Idaho, 1906.
19p. 21cm.
"Addenda" p. 17–19.
MoInRC, USIC

8792. ———. Plural marriage and the manifesto. The Tribune and Kinsman answered by Nathan Tanner, Jr. Salt Lake City, 1898.
12p. 23cm.
Cover-title.
MoInRC, USIC

8793. ———. Revelation and revelators to the church. Including succession in the First Presidency. By N. Tanner, Jr. [Blackfoot, Idaho, n.d.]
14p. 21½cm.
L.D.S. doctrine.
USIC

8794. ———. (same) [Salt Lake City, Century Printers, n.d.]
14p. 21½cm.
MoInRC

8795. Taylder, T. W. P. The materialism of the Mormons, or Latter-day Saints, examined and exposed. By T. W. P. Taylder. Woolwich [Eng.] Printed by E. Jones, 1849.
40p. 18cm.
CtY, CU-B, NN, USIC, UU

8796. ———. The Mormon's own book; or, Mormonism tried by its own standards, reason, and scripture. London, Partridge, Oakey, 1855.
xvi, 200p. 20cm.
CSmH, CU-B, DLC, ICHi, MH, OClWHi, ULA, USIC

8797. ———. (same) With an account of its present condition. Also a life of Joseph Smith. New edition. London, Partridge and Co., 1857.
[1]l. ii, 228 (i.e. 230) p. 18½cm.
P. [199]–200 repeated.
CtY, CU-B, ICN, IU, MH, MoInRC, NjPT, NN, UHi, ULA, USl, USIC, UU, WHi

8797a. ———. "There is no crime so great as one perpetrated against the freedom of peoples." Ogden, Utah, 1892. Hon. - - - - - Dear Sir . . . [Ogden, Utah, 1892]
[2]p. 8cm.
Letter to Congressmen advocating statehood for Utah.
USIC

8798. ———. Twenty reasons for rejecting Mormonism . . . Reprinted from the Christian cabinet. London, Partridge & Co., 1857.
16p. 18cm.
CSmH

8798a. ———. (same) Gateshead: Printed by R. Kelly, West Street. 1900.
16p. 18cm.
USIC

8799. Tayler, W. H. Some account of Joseph Smith and the Mormon imposture; chiefly compiled from Chambers's miscellany and the Rev. H. Caswall's work, entitled "The city of the Mormons." [Warminster, Printed by W. H. Tayler, n.d.]
12p. 15½cm.
USIC

8800. Taylor, Alma Owen. Ikeru Shin no Kami. Tokyō, Nihon, Matsu Jitsu Seito Iesu Kirisuto Kyōkai Nihon Dendōbu [1904]
26p. 15½cm.
Title in English: The True and living God.
USIC

8801. ———. (same) Tokyō, Nihon, Matsu Jitsu Seito Iesu Kirisuto Kyōkai, Nihon Dendōbu [1909]
32p. 14½cm.
"4th edition"
USIC

8802. ———. Kami wa imasu ka? Tokyō, Nihon, Matsu Jitsu Seito Iesu Kirisuto Kyōkai, Nihon Dendōbu [1905]
50p. 14½cm.
Title in English: Is there a God?
USIC

8803. ———. (same) Tōkyō, Nihon, Matsu Jitsu Seito Iesu Kirisuto Kyōkai, Nihon Dendōbu [1908]
49 [1]p. 14½cm.
"2d edition"
USIC

8804. ———. Matsu Jitsu Seito. Tokyō, Nihon, Matsun Jitsu Seito Iesu Kirisuto Kyōkai, Nihon Dendōbu [1909]
18 [2]p. 14½cm.
"4th edition."
First published in 1906.
Title in English: Latter-day Saints.
USIC

8805. Taylor, Barney C. The great plan. The Christian way. [n.p., 190–]
2p.l., 63p. 27cm.
"English translation of a book published in Japanese for the Japanese people." Mormon doctrine.
Mimeographed.
UPB

8806. ———. (same, in Japanese) Kirisutokyo ni okeru daisetsukei. Hiraki Kunio Yaku. Nihon, Matsuzitsu Seito Iesu Kirisuto [n.d.]
1p.l., 197p. 18cm.
Translated by Kunio Hiraki.
UPB

8806a. Taylor, Bayard. Life and letters of Bayard Taylor. Edited by Marie Hansen-Taylor and Horace E. Scudder. Boston, Houghton, Mifflin and Co., 1884.
2v. ports. 20½cm.
Chapter 26 discusses the use of Mormonism as a background for "The Prophet."
DLC, UPB, UU

8806b. ———. The prophet: a tragedy. By Bayard Taylor. Boston: James R. Osgood and Company. (Late Ticknor & Fields, and Fields, Osgood, & Co.) 1874.
3p.l., 9–300p. 18cm.
Dramatic poetry with Mormon setting.
DLC, UPB

8807. Taylor, Benjamin Franklin. Summer-savory, gleaned from rural nooks in pleasant weather. By Benj. F. Taylor . . . Chicago, S. C. Griggs and Company, 1879.
2p.l., 3–212p. 19½cm.
Prose sketches and essays.
Glimpses of Utah . . . p. 16–30.
Another edition: Chicago, 1880. USIC
DLC, MH, OCl, OO, USIC

8808. Taylor, Frances K. (Thomassen). Kindergarten and primary songs, by Frances K. Thomassen. Salt Lake City, Daynes-Beebe Music Co., 1919.
64p. 26cm.
Words and music.
UHi

8809. Taylor, I. N. History of Platte County, Nebraska. By I. N. Taylor. Columbus, Neb., Columbus Republican Print, 1876.
18p. 23½cm.
Brief mention of Mormon activities in Platte County, Nebraska.
UPB

Taylor, John. An address to the Latter-day Saints. *See Church of Jesus Christ of Latter-day Saints. First Presidency.*

8810. ———. An answer to some false statements and misrepresentations made by the Rev. Robert Heys, Wesleyan minister, in an address to his society in Douglas and its vicinity, on the subject of Mormonism. By John Taylor . . . Douglas [Isle of Man] Printed by Penrice and Wallace, 1840.
11p. 18cm.
Dated at end: Douglas, Oct. 7, 1840.
Sabin 94505
CSmH, CtY, CU–B, MH, USIC

8811. ———. Aux amis de la vérité religieuse. Récit abrégé du commencement, des progrès de l'établissement, des persécutions, de la foi et de la doctrine de l'Eglise de Jésus Christ des Saints des Derniers Jours. Par John Taylor, Elder. Paris, Marc Ducloux et Cie, 1851.
16p. 21½cm.
Title in English: Address to the friends of religious truth.
CtY, ICN, NN, USIC

8812. ———. (same) Venand de la ville du Grand Lac Sale, État de Deseret. Haute Californie. Paris, Imprimerie de Marc Ducloux et Compagnie, Rue Saint Benoit, 7, 1852.
16p. 22cm.
CtY, CU–B, NN, USIC

8813. ———. Calumny refuted and the truth defended; being a reply to the second address of the Rev. Robert Heys, Wesleyan Minister to the Wesleyan Methodist societies in Douglas and its vicinity. By John Taylor . . . Douglas, Printed by Penrice & Wallace, Liberal office [1840]
12p. 18½cm.
Defense of Mormon doctrine.
Dated at end: Douglas, October 29, 1840.
Sabin 94505A
CU–B, USIC

8814. ———. (same) Liverpool, Printed by J. Tompkins, 1840.
12p. 18cm.
Sabin 94505A
CtY, CU–B, DLC, MH, MoInRC, UPB, USIC

8815. ———. De la nécessité de nouvelles révélations prouvée par la Bible par John Taylor . . . Paris [Imp. de Marc Ducloux et Comp.] 1852.
32p. 22½cm.
Title in English: The necessity of new revelations.
ICN, UHi, USIC

TAYLOR, J.

8816. ———. Discourse delivered by President John Taylor at the general conference, Salt Lake City, April 9th, 1882. [Salt Lake City] 1882.
18p. 22cm.
Caption-title.
Reported by George F. Gibbs.
CSmH, CtY, CU–B, ICN, MB, NN, USl, USlC, WHi

8817. ———. Discourse of President John Taylor, delivered in the Tabernacle, Salt Lake City, Sunday afternoon, February 1, 1885 . . . Reported by John Irvine. [Salt Lake City, The Deseret News] 1885.
15p. 22cm.
Cover-title.
CSmH, CU–B, UPB, USlC, UU

8818. ———. Er de Sidste Dages-Helliges Laere Sandhed? Af John Taylor. 8de oplag. Kjøbenhavn, Udgivet og forlagt af R. Wilhelmsen. Trykt hos F. E. Bording, 1881.
1p.l. [3]–32p. 21cm.
Title in English: Are the doctrines of the Latter-Day Saints Church true?
USlC

8819. ———. (same) Oversat fra Engelsk. Tiende oplag. København. Udgivet og forlagt af Andreas Peterson. Trykt hos J. D. Qvist & Komp., 1900.
48p. 18½cm.
USlC

8820. ———. (same) Ellevte oplag. København, Udgivet og forlagt af A. L. Skancky. Trykt hos L. A. Nielsen. . . . 1901.
47p. 18½cm.
USlC

8821. ———. (same, in Swedish) Är de Siste dagars heligas lära sanning? . . . 4. upplagan. Köpenhamn, C. Widerborg, 1867.
31p. 20cm.
CtY, USlC

8822. ———. (same) 6. upplagan. Köpenhamn, N. C. Flygare. Trykt hos F. E. Bording, 1876.
31p. 22cm.
CDU, CtY, UHi, UU

8823. ———. (same) Sjunde upplagan. Köpenhamn, Utgifven och förlagd af N. Wilhelmsen. Tryckt hos F. E. Bording, 1880.
32p. 21½cm.
USlC

8823a. ———. (same) Öfversatt från Engelskan. Tionde upplagan. Köpenhamn, Utgifven och förlagd af Edw. H. Anderson. Tryckt hos F. E. Bording (V. Petersen) 1892.
43p. 17½cm.
USlC

8824. ———. (same) Tolfte upplagan. Köpenhamn, Utgifven och förlagd af Andreas Peterson. Tryckt hos F. E. Bording (V. Peterson) 1899.
43p. 18½cm.
USlC

8825. ———. (same) Sjuttonde Genomsedda. Upplagan utgiven och Förlagd av Gideon N. Hulterström, Jönköping, 1923.
46 [1]p. 18cm. bound.
UPB, USlC

8826. ———. Er Mormonismen en Vranglaere? Af J. Taylor. 2 det oplag. Kjøbenhavn, Udgivet af Hector C. Haight. Trykt hos F. E. Bording, 1856.
31p. 23cm.
Title in English: Is Mormonism a false faith?
CSmH, NN, USlC

8827. ———. (same) 3 die oplag. Kjobenhavn, Udgivet og forlagt af H. C. Haight. Tryckt hos F. E. Bording, 1857.
31p. 21cm.
USlC, UU

8828. ———. (same) 5 te oplag. Kjøbenhavn, Udgivet og forlagt af C. Widerborg. Trykt hos F. E. Bording, 1866.
31p. 22cm.
USlC

8828a. ———. (same) 6te oplag. Kjøbenhavn, Udgivet og forlagt af C. E. Larsen, 1873.
31p. 20½cm.
USlC

8829. ———. (same) Kobenhavn, 1901.
Schmidt

8830. ———. (same, in Swedish) Är Mormonismen en Irrlära? Af J. Taylor. Köpenhamn, Udgifvet af Hector C. Haight. Trykt F. E. Bording, 1856.
31p. 21cm.
CSmH, USlC

8831. ———. (same) 2. upplagan. Köpenhamn, Utgivet och förlagt af C. Widerborg. Trykt hos F. E. Bording, 1858.
31p. 21cm.
CSmH

8832. ———. An epistle to the presidents of stakes, high councils, bishops and other authorities of the Church. Salt Lake City [Church of Jesus Christ of Latter-day Saints] 1882.
11p. 21cm.
USlC, UU

TAYLOR, J.

8833. ———. An examination into and an elucidation of the great principle of the meditation and atonement of Our Lord and Savior Jesus Christ. By President John Taylor . . . Salt Lake City, Deseret News Company, 1882.
1p.l. [3]–205p. 22½cm.
Appendix, p. 190–205.
Published with and without appendix.
CSmH, CU, DLC, MH, MoInRC, NjP, ULA, USlC, UU, WHi

8834. ———. (same) Salt Lake City, Deseret News Publishing Co., 1892.
1p.l. [3]–205p. 23cm.
CSmH, CU–B, NjP, NN, UHi, UPB, USl, USlC, UU

8835. ———. Father, son & daughter; a trio by John Taylor. Merthyr-Tydfil, J. Davis, Printer [1850?]
Broadside. 18×9½cm.
Mormon song of emigration.
Enclosed in border.
MH, USlC

8836. ———. (same, in Welsh) Y Tad, y Mab, a'r ferch (o saesneg yr Apostol John Taylor, of Ffrainc) Cyf. Benjamin Davis. [Merthyr-Tydfil, Argraffwyd gan J. Davis, 1850?]
Broadside. 18×9½cm.
MH, USlC

8837. ———. A funeral sermon, preached by Elder John Taylor, at the 14th Ward Assembly Rooms, Salt Lake City, Sunday, Dec. 31, 1876, over the remains of Sister Mary Ann, the beloved wife of Elder George E. Bourne. [Liverpool, 1877]
8p. 18cm.
At head of title: *Journal of discourses.*
A separately paged reprint from Vol. 18 of the *Journal of discourses.*
USlC

8838. ———. The government of God by John Taylor, one of the Twelve Apostles of the Church of Jesus Christ of Latter-day Saints . . . Liverpool: Published by S. W. Richards . . . London, Sold at the Latter-day Saints' Book Depot . . . 1852.
viii, 118p. 22½cm.
Some copies in brown wrapper.
CSmH, CtY, CU–B, DLC, ICN, MH, MoInRC, NjP, NjPT, NN, USl, USlC, UU, WHi

8839. ———. Items on priesthood, presented to the Latter-day Saints by President John Taylor. Salt Lake City, Deseret News Co., 1881.
43p. 23cm.
Cover-title.
CSmH, NjP, NN, UHi, UPB, USlC

8840. ———. (same) Salt Lake City, Deseret News Co., 1882.
43p. 22cm.
Cover-title.
1881 edition, with an 1882 wrapper.
CSmH, CU–B, ICN, MWA, NjP, ULA, UPB, UU, WHi

8841. ———. (same) Salt Lake City, G. Q. Cannon and Sons Co., 1899.
36p. 24cm.
Cover-title.
CSmH, IU, MH, MoInRC, NjP, NN, UHi, UPB, UU

———. The Mormon question. *See Colfax, Schuyler.*

8842. ———. On marriage. Salt Lake City, Deseret News, 1882.
8p. 22cm.
Cover-title.
CSmH, CU–B, NN, UPB

8843. ———. (same) On marriage. Succession in the Priesthood. By John Taylor . . . Salt Lake City, Deseret News Company, 1882.
8, 24p. 22½cm.
Cover-title.
In wrapper.
On marriage bound with *Succession in the Priesthood* and published as one work.
DLC, ICN, MoInRC, UHi, UPB, USl, USlC, UU

8844. ———. Revelation given through President John Taylor, at Salt Lake City, Utah Territory, October 13, 1882, to fill vacancies in the twelve. [Salt Lake City, 1882]
3p. 21cm.
Caption-title.
CSmH, CU–B, NjP, USlC

8845. ———. Revelation concerning seventies . . . Salt Lake City, April 13, 1883. [Salt Lake City, 1883]
4p. 21cm.
USlC

8846. ———. A short account of the murders, roberies [sic] burnings, thefts, and other outrages committed by the mob & militia of the State of Missouri, upon the Latter Day Saints. The persecutions they have endured for their religion, and their banishment from that state by the authorities thereof. By John Taylor, Elder of the Church of Jesus Christ of Latter day Saints. [Springfield? Ill., 1839]
8p. 21cm.
Caption-title.
Byrd 485, Sabin 94506
CSmH, MH, USlC

8847. ———. Succession in the priesthood. A discourse by President John Taylor, delivered at the priesthood meeting held in the Salt Lake Assembly Hall, Friday Evening, October 7, 1881. Reported by Geo. F. Gibbs. [Salt Lake City? 1881?]
24p. 21cm.
Caption-title.
CSmH, CU–B, UPB, USl

8848. ———. Supreme Court decision in the Reynolds case. Interview between President John Taylor, and O. J. Hollister, esq., United States Collector of Internal Revenue for Utah Territory, and correspondent of the New York Tribune. Salt Lake City, Utah, January 13th, 1879. Salt Lake City, 1879.
16p. 23cm.
Reported by G. F. Gibbs. Salt Lake City, 1879.
CSmH, ICN, MH, NjP, NN, UPB, USlC

8849. ———. Three nights' public discussion between the Revds. C. W. Cleeve, James Robertson, and Philip Cater, and Elder John Taylor, of the Church of Jesus Christ of Latter-day Saints, at Boulogne-sur-mer, France. Chairman, Rev. K. Groves, M. A., assisted by Charles Townley, LL.D., and Mr. Luddy. Also a reply to the Rev. K. Groves, M. A., & Charles Townley, LL.D. Price Eight-pence each. Liverpool: Published by John Taylor, and for sale by O. Pratt, at 15, Wilton Street, and by agents throughout Great Britain and in Boulogne. 1850.
1 p.l., 49p. fold. facsim. 21cm.
Includes the "A brief account of the discovery of the brass plates." When published in Orson Pratt's *Series of pamphlets*, it usually includes a portrait of John Taylor.
Published in green or yellow printed wrappers.
CSmH, CtY, DLC, ICN, MH, NjP, UHi, UPB, USlC, UU

8849a. ———. (same) Liverpool: Published by John Taylor, For sale by F. D. Richards, at 15, Wilton Street, and by agents throughout Great Britain and in Boulogne. 1850.
1 p.l., 49p. fold. facsim. 21cm.
Type reset with new agent in collation.
USlC

8849b. ———. To the presidents of stakes and bishops of wards . . . [Salt Lake City] 1886.
Broadside. 21½×19cm.
Dated: July 31, 1886. The latter concerns signing of temple recommends.
USlC

8850. ———. Traité sur le Bapteme par John Taylor . . . Paris, Publié par C. E. Ballon, 1853.
16p. 23cm.
Title in English: About baptism.
ICN, USlC

8851. ———. Truth defended and Methodism weighted in the balance and found wanting: Being a reply to the third address of the Rev. Robert Heys, Wesleyan Minister to the Wesleyan Methodist Societies in Douglas and its vicinity. And also an exposure of the principles of Methodism. By John Taylor, Elder of the Church of Jesus Christ of Latter Day Saints . . . Liverpool, Printed by J. Tompkins [1840]
12p. 18½cm.
Published December 7, 1840.
Sabin 94506A
CtY, CU–B, MH, ULA, UPB, USlC

8852. Taylor, Lillie Jane (Orr). Life history of Thomas Orr, Jr. Pioneer stories of California and Utah. [n.p., Published by the author, c1930]
51 [1]p. plates, ports. 22½cm.
Family joined church at Commerce, Illinois; came to Utah with the family migration. Left for California, 1850.
With poems by Charles E. Jerrett and Lillie Jane Orr Taylor.
CSmH, CtY, CU–B, NjP, UHi, UPB, USlC

8853. Taylor, Margaret. On the death of N. Preston Felt. [Salt Lake City? 1856]
[2]l. 19½cm.
Poem on the death of a Mormon child.
Second leaf blank.
UPB

8854. Taylor, Marie (Hansen). On two continents; memories of half a century, by Marie Hansen Taylor with the co-operation of Lilian Bayard Taylor Kiliani. Illustrated from contemporary portraits and paintings, by Bayard Taylor. New York, Doubleday, Page, 1905.
x, 2p.l., 3–309p. plates, ports. 23cm.
Very brief account of a secret "anti-Young" movement in Utah, 1869.
CU, DLC, NjP, UPB, UU

8855. Taylor, Ned. King of the Wild West's saint or the end of polygamy in Utah. By Ned Taylor. New York, Street & Smith, 1906.
28 [4]p. 28cm. (Rough Rider Weekly. The best wild west stories published. No. 92. New York, January 20, 1906. Price five cents.)
[4] pages of advertisements.
Bound in original colored pictorial wrappers.
UPB

8856. ———. The young Rough Rider's handicap or fighting the Mormon kidnappers. By Ned Taylor. New York, Street & Smith, 1905.
28 [3]p. 28cm. (The Young Rough Riders Weekly. Most fascinating western stories. No. 49. New York, March 25, 1905. Price five cents.)
[3] pages of advertisements.
Bound in original colored pictorial wrappers.
UPB

TEMPLE MORMONISM

8857. Taylor, Robert Walker. The case of Brigham H. Roberts . . . Can a polygamist be excluded from the House of Representatives. Speeches of Hon. Robert W. Taylor of Ohio in the House of Representatives, Dec. 4 & 5, 1899, Jan. 23 & 25, 1900. Washington, Govt. Print. Off., 1900.
64p. 23cm.
DLC, UHi

8858. Taylor, Thomas. An account of the complete failure of an ordained priest of the "Latter-day Saints" to establish his pretensions to the gift of tongues, which took place Oct. 12, 1840: With an address to men of reason and religion, warning them not to be deceived by the craftiness of such low impostures. Manchester, Pigot and Slater [1840]
13p. 19½cm.
NN

8859. Taylor, Thomas, *of Salt Lake City.* Fulfillment of prophecies by so called Mormon church. Privately printed. [Salt Lake City, n.d.]
[4]p. 19½cm.
Scriptures disproving Mormon claims.
USlC

8860. Teasdale, George. Glad tidings of great joy! [n.p., 1876?]
[3]p. 21½cm.
Signed: George Teasdale, John R. Winder, jr.
Signed in ink: Toms Creek, Surry Co., N. C.
USlC

8861. ———. (same) [Salt Lake City, Juvenile Instructor Office, c1885]
6p. 19½cm.
Missionary tract.
Ascribed by Andrew Jenson, *Latter-day Saints Biographical Encyclopedia* to George Teasdale.
NjP, USlC

8862. ———. (same) [Liverpool, Millennial Star Office? ca. 1900]
4p. 21cm.
Caption-title.
Variant Printings.
CU–B, UHi, UPB, USlC, UU

8863. ———. (same) [Liverpool, British Mission, c1910]
4p. 22cm.
UPB

8864. ———. (same) [Salt Lake City, Deseret News, n.d.]
4p. 22½cm.
Variant printings.
UPB, USlC, WHi

8865. ———. (same, in German) Eine frohe Botschaft freudige Nachricht. [Bern, Schweizerischen und Deutscher Mission, ca. 1890]
4p. 23cm.
UPB

8866. ———. Latter-Day Saints have words of Eternal life. By Elder George Teasdale. [Chattanooga, Southern Saints Mission, n.d.]
12p. 19cm. (Sermon tract. No. 2)
With "Mormonism" by Elder Parley P. Pratt under title *Two Sermons.*
USlC

8867. ———. . . . Peshareth . . . [Istanbul, V. Minassian Matpasa, 1899]
8p. 18cm.
Caption-title.
Title in English: The Gospel.
UPB

8868. ———. The restoration of the everlasting gospel, by Elder George Teasdale. [Liverpool, ca. 1883]
8p. 23cm.
Caption-title.
USlC

8869. ———. (same) [Liverpool, Millennial Star, 189–]
8p. 21cm.
Caption-title.
ICN, MH, UHi, USl, USlC

8870. ———. (same) [Salt Lake City? Deseret News Press, n.d.]
8p. 21cm.
Caption-title.
CSmH, ICN, MoInRC, UU, WHi

8871. ———. (same) [Salt Lake City, 1901]
8p. 21cm.
Caption-title.
CtY

8872. ———. (same) [Liverpool? Millennial Star Office? 1908?]
8p. 21cm.
Caption-title.
UPB

8873. Teller, Henry M. A bill enabling the people of Utah to form a constitution and State government, and for the admission of said State into the Union on an equal footing with the original states. Washington, 1892.
7p. 23cm. (S. 1653)
Eberstadt: *Utah and the Mormons.*

Temple Mormonism. *See Gentile Bureau of Information. Salt Lake City.*

TEMPLE MUSIC

8874. Temple music! Music rendered at the dedicatory services of the Salt Lake Temple, April, 1893. Published in Volume XIV of The Contributor. Salt Lake City, Deseret News Publishing Company [1893]
31 [1]p. 21½cm.
Words and music for 4 mixed voices and solos, with organ accompaniment.
NN, USIC

8875. Temple song. Tune: "Hold the fort!" [n.p., 1877?]
Broadside. 20×9cm.
In honor of the completion of the St. George Temple.
Yellow foolscap.
MH

8876. Temple souvenir album, April, 1892. Illustrated with portraits of the architects, views of the building, plan of electric lights, engine-house and grounds . . . Salt Lake City, Magazine Printing Company, 1892.
32p. illus. 24cm.
USIC

8877. Ten commandments. [Independence, Mo.?] 1925.
[4]p. 19½cm.
Controversy over supreme directional control in the RLDS church. Quotes RLDS positions, 1898–1912.
MoInRC

Ten Reasons. . . . *See Presbytery of Utah.*

8878. Tennant, Charles. In memoriam, composed by Charles Tennant at the death of F. W. Cox, June 7th, 1879. Manti, Utah, 1879.
Broadside. 28×21cm.
USIC

8879. Tenney, Edward Payson. Colorado: and homes in the new West. Boston, Lee and Shepard; New York, C.T. Dillingham, 1880.
2p.l. [11]–118p. illus., maps (part fold.) 23½cm.
"Comprising the seventh thousand of the *New West*, Revised and illustrated." Utah, p. 108–115. "Mormonism is a carefully organized land speculation" with secret oaths.
Other editions: Rev. Boston, Lee and Shepard, 1880. UHi, UU; 1882. NjP
CU–B, DLC, NjP

8880. ———. Looking forward into the past, by E. P. Tenney . . . Nahant, Mass., Rumford Press, 1910.
3p.l. [9]–243p. 24½cm.
Includes educational work among the Mormons. Education of non-Mormons and re-indoctrination of Mormons in 1878.
UHi

8881. ———. Necessity for Christian work in the new West and the method of doing it. Boston, 1880.
[2]p. 60×39cm.
Caption-title.
Supplement to *Congregationalist* for Wednesday, March 31, 1880.
ICN

8882. ———. The new West as related to the Christian college and the home missionary. 2d ed. Cambridge, Riverside Press, 1878.
73p. plates, maps. 24cm.
Advocates "establishment of Christian instruction of advanced grade" in Utah Territory to convert the Mormons.
Another edition: 3d ed., 1878. NjP
DLC, UPB

Territorial Central Committee. *See People's Party. Utah. Territorial Central Committee.*

8882a. The Territorial Enquirer. Enquirer Extra! Provo City, July 27, 1887. At rest. President John Taylor passed away at 7:55 Monday night. The announcement of his death. The Funeral to take place no [sic] Friday. [Provo, 1887]
Broadside. 45×20cm.
Announcement signed by George Q. Cannon and Joseph F. Smith.
UPB

8883. Teza, Emilio. Sopra un alfabeto dei mormoniani; cenni di E. Teza. Pisa, Tipografia Nistri, 1874.
14p. [1]l. 2 plates. 23cm.
Title in English: About the Mormon alphabet.
Concerning the Deseret Alphabet.
MiU, NN

8884. Thalheimer, M. E. The eclectic history of the United States. Cincinnati and New York, Van Antwerp, Bragg & Co. [c1881]
366p. xlp. illus. 19cm.
Mormons, p. 248–249.
USIC

8885. Thatcher, Moses. The issues of the times! Hon. Moses Thatcher's address before the Ogden Democratic Territorial Convention, May 14, 1892. A review of the Ogden Standard's criticism of Mr. Thatcher's address by Pericles. Hon. Moses Thatcher's reply to Joseph F. and John Henry Smith. False lights! Some bits of history! And happy Utah! Editorials in the Salt Lake Semi-weekly Herald. [Salt Lake City, Herald Publishing Company, 1892]
14p. 28½cm.
UHi, UPB, USIC

8886. ———. La poligamia Mormona y la monogamia Christiana comparadas. El casamiento es una institacion divina cuando esta arreglado segun la leges de dios . . . por el Elder Moises Thatcher . . . Mexico, Imprenta de E. D. Orozco y Compania . . . 1881.
40p. 22½cm.
CU–B has supplementary matter: La venida del Mesias pro J. Z. Stewart, Unico medio de Salvarse, por Lorenzo Snow, and Los medios de librarse, por J. Nicholson.
[2] 8, 4p.
Title in English: Mormon polygamy and Christian monogamy compared.
CU–B, MH, USlC

8887. ———, *defendant.* The Thatcher episode; a concise statement of the facts of the case; interesting letters and documents; a review of M. Thatcher's claims, pleas and admissions. Salt Lake City, Deseret News Publishing Co., 1896.
47p. 23cm.
Cover-title.
CU–B, MoInRC, NjP, NN, UHi, ULA, UPB, USl, USlC, UU

Thatcher Academy. *See Gila Academy.*

8888. **Thayer, Eli.** The polygamy question. Speech of Hon. Eli Thayer, of Massachusetts. Delivered in the House of Representatives, April 3, 1860. Washington, Buell & Blanchard, Printers, 1860.
8p. 24cm.
CtY, DLC, NjP, OClWHi, UHi, UPB, USl

8889. ———. Six speeches, with a sketch of the life of Hon. Eli Thayer. Boston, Brown and Taggard, 1860.
59 [1]p. 21½cm.
Final speech specifically on Utah and polygamy problems.
CU–B, DLC, MWA, NN

8890. **Thayer, James Bradley.** A western journey with Mr. Emerson. Boston, Little, Brown, and Co., 1884.
2p.l. [5]–141p. 16½cm.
Salt Lake City and Mormons, p. 28–38.
CU–B, DLC, NjP, UHi, UPB, USlC, UU

8891. **Thayer, William Makepeace.** Marvels of the new West. A vivid portrayal of the stupendous marvels in the vast wonderland west of the Missouri River . . . Six books in one volume, graphically and truthfully described by William M. Thayer . . . Illustrated with over three hundred and fifty fine engravings and maps. Norwich, Conn., The Henry Bill Publishing Company, 1887.
2p.l. [iii]–xxxvi, 715p. illus., ports., maps. 25cm.
The Mormon settlement, p. 404–406.
Other editions: 1888. CU–B, MH; 1889. CtY; 1890. NjP, NN; 1892. UHi
CU, DLC, MiU, NjP, NN, UHi, ULA, UU, WaU

8892. **Theobald, John.** The Latter-day Saints, and the respectable public are invited to attend a course of lectures . . . by John Theobald . . . Dec. 17 [to] Dec. 25, 1851. [London, 1851?]
Broadside. 50×37cm.
A description of his anti-Mormon lectures.
USlC

8893. ———. Mormonism harpooned; or, The blasphemies of Joseph Smith, the prophet of the Latter-day Saints, exposed. Being the substance of the fourth lecture of a series, delivered in various parts of the United Kingdom. By J. Theobald, A.M.M. London, W. Horsell [185–]
26p. 17½cm.
Also listed on the publication are the following works on Mormonism by him. Only the last is listed as published.
Mormon hypocrites unmasked.
Joe Smith's ghost.
The Book of Mormon tested.
Waterology.
Overthrow of infidel Mormonism.
A peep at Mormonism, listed as published in the *Millennial Star*, v. 19, p. 622.
USlC

8894. ———. Mormonology; or, The blasphemies of the Latter-day Saints exposed. Being the substance of the first lecture of a series delivered in various parts of the United Kingdom, by J. Theobald. London, W. Horsell; Leichester, J. F. Winks [1852]
22p. 17cm.
Howes T155
CU–B, DLC, USlC

8895. **Thissell, G. W.** Crossing the Plains in '49. By G. W. Thissell. Oakland, California, 1903.
4p.l. [9]–176p. illus., plates, ports. 18½cm.
Dubiously recollected account of overland journey via Salt Lake City, 1850 and 1853, p. 101–106.
CU–B, NjP, UPB

8896. **Thomander, John Henric.** Femogtyve af Mormonernes laeresaetninger, sammenholdte med udsagn af den hellige Skrift. Af biskop Joh. Henr. Thomander. Oversat fra Svensk af N. Schrader. Kjøbenhavn, Forlagt af Boghandler Th. Lind. Trykt hos F. H. Schultz, 1856.
20p. 19½cm.
Title in English: Twenty-five of the Mormon teachings compared with passages from the Holy Scripture.
NN, UPB, USlC

8897. **Thomas, Amy Adams.** Charles J. Thomas [A sketch of his life by Amy Adams Thomas. n.p., 1919?]
4p. 28cm.
Dittoed.
Mormon biography.
UPB

Thomas, Arthur [*pseud.*] *See Hannett, Arthur Thomas.*

8898. Thomas, C. J. Sweet is the peace; inscribed to Bishop F. B. Platt of the Twelfth-Thirteenth Ward, by C. J. Thomas. [Music by] C. J. Thomas [Words by] M. A. Martin. [n.p., n.d.]
Broadside. 31×17½cm.
Mormon music.
USlC

8899. Thomas, D. K. Wild life in the Rocky Mountains, or the Lost Million Dollar Gold Mine by D. K. Thomas. Illustrated by Alice Moseley and M. Reynolds. A true story of actual experiences in the wild west. Exciting adventures with wild animals, Indians and desperadoes. The secrets of Mormonism. A true story of the Mountain Meadows massacre. An interesting narrative of the trials and hardships of an early western gold miner who finally succeeds. [n.p.] C. E. Thomas Publishing Co., 1917.
221p. 19½cm.
Description of Salt Lake City, under "The mysteries of Mormonism." A confession of the endowment ceremony, The Mountain Meadows massacre.
CtY, CU-B, DLC, ICN, NjP, NN, UPB, USl, USlC, UU

8900. Thomas, Elbert Duncan. To Shi Sekkyo Shū. [Tōkyō, Matsu Jitsu Seito Iesu Kirisuto Kyōkai, Nihon Dendōbu, 1912?]
2 [2] 16, 157p. 22cm.
Title in English: Mr. To's preaching book.
A missionary publication.
UPB, USlC

8901. ———. (same) Tōkyō, Matsu Jitsu Seito Iesu Kirisuto Kyōkai, Nihon Dendōbu [1925]
157p. 21½cm.
USlC

8902. Thomas, George. Civil government of Utah, by George Thomas . . . Boston, New York [etc.] D. C. Heath & Co. [c1912]
vii, 199p. illus., plates. 19cm.
CU-B, DLC, ICJ, NjP, UHi, ULA, UU

8903. ———. The development of institutions under irrigation, with special reference to early Utah conditions, by George Thomas . . . New York, The Macmillan Company, 1920.
vii p. [2]l. 293p. map. 20cm. (On cover: The rural science)
Mormon participation in irrigation.
CSmH, CU-B, DLC, ICJ, MH, NjP, UHi, ULA, UPB, UU

8904. Thomas, Henry R. Egwyddorion cyntaf yn win efengyl Crist. [n.p., n.d.]
4p. 22½cm.
At head of title in English: First principles of the true gospel of Christ.
UPB, USlC

8905. ———. A ydyw cred ei hun yn ddigon? [n.p., n.d.]
4p. 22½cm.
At head of title in English: Is belief alone sufficient?
UPB, USlC

8906. Thomas, J. C. The mistakes of Mormon and of Mormons. A lecture delivered by Rev. J. C. Thomas . . . Nashville, Tenn., Publishing House Methodist Episcopal Church, South, 1899.
29p. 18½cm.
CLU, CSmH, DLC, ICN, USl

8907. Thomas, John. Sketch of the rise, progress, and dispersion of the Mormons, by John Thomas, M.D., President of the S. and E. Medical College of Virginia, United States, America; to which is added an account of the Nauvoo Temple mysteries, and other abominations practiced by this impious sect previous to their emigration for California, by Increase McGee Van Dusen, formerly one of the initiated. London, Arthur Hall and Company. [1849]
24p. 17½cm.
Incorporates Van Dusen's *The Hidden orgies of Mormonism*, p. 11–24.
Prefaced signed: London, March, 1849.
Printed by H. Hudston, Printer, Nottingham.
Howes T175
CtY, CU-B, NN, USl, USlC

8908. Thomas, Jonathan J. Dwy gan. Gan Jonathan J. Thomas (Nathan ddu o Lywel) [Merthyr-Tydfil, J. Davis, Argraffydd, 1851?]
4p. 18cm.
Also includes poem "Y trysor o'r mynydd," p. 3–4.
Mormon poetry.
Title in English: Two songs.
USlC

8909. Thomas, Julia M. Miscellaneous writings. New York, John W. Lovell and Co. [c1890]
27, 32, 38, 24, 29, 43p. 18½cm.
Final section "Mormon letters." Relates her visit to Salt Lake in 1883. Answers to questions on doctrine, especially on polygamy, from Mormons, non-Mormons, and apostates.
"The Salt Lake region" (no mention of Mormonism) "The twin relic," polygamy, "How the Mormons live" interviews with fractional wife and an apostate; also with Emmeline B. Wells.
CtY, MB, NN

8910. ———. Mormon letters. By Julia M. Thomas, founder of psychophysical culture. New York, John W. Lovell Co. [c1890]
43p. 18½cm.
MH

THOMAS, R. M. B.

8911. ———. The hymn of the pioneer. [Salt Lake City? ca. 1890]
[3]p. 22cm.
Mormon poetry.
USIC

8912. Thomas, Martha Pane (Jones). Daniel Stillwell Thomas family history. Salt Lake City, 1927.
64p. ports. 15½cm.
Preface signed: Kate Woodhouse Kirkham, granddaughter of Mrs. Martha P. J. Thomas.
Part of the author's journal.
"To the editor and readers of the *Lehi Post* [By D. S. Thomas]," p. 47–55.
Trip through Salt Lake City. Polygamy increasing with all of its evils.
CSmH, CU–B, UPB

8913. Thomas, Preston. A treatise on the gospel. By Preston Thomas (Elder in the Church of Jesus Christ) of Latter Day Saints. Pontotoc, Miss., J. T. Heard, Letter-Press Printer, 1853.
15p. 17cm.
Doctrinal work written while on a mission.
USIC

8914. Thomas, Robert Moseley Bryce. My reasons for leaving the Church of England and joining the Church of Jesus Christ of Latter-day Saints. By a convert. Liverpool, Millennial Star Office, 1897.
1p.l. [3]–34p. 17½cm.
MH, UHi, USIC, UU

8914a. ———. (same) Liverpool, Millennial Star Office, 42, Islington, 1900.
34p. 17cm.
USIC

8915. ———. (same) Liverpool, Millennial Star Office, 1902.
34 [1]p. 17cm.
MoInRC, USIC

8916. ———. (same) Salt Lake City, 1902.
30 [1]p. 15½cm.
ULA, USIC

8917. ———. Salt Lake City, Bureau of Information and Church Literature, 1903.
30 [1]p. 17cm.
2 variants. One with a [1]p. "Articles of faith."
MH

8918. ———. (same) Salt Lake City, Bureau of Information and Church Literature, 1904.
30 [1]p. 16½cm.
USIC

8919. ———. (same) Salt Lake City, Bureau of Information and Church Literature, 1905.
30p. 16½cm.
USIC, WHi

8920. ———. (same) Salt Lake City, Bureau of Information and Church Literature, 1906.
30 [1]p. 17cm.
MH

8921. ———. (same) Liverpool, Millennial Star Office, 1909.
34p. 18cm.
UPB

8922. ———. (same) Salt Lake City [Bureau of Information] 1913.
40p. 15cm.
USIC

8922a. ———. (same) Independence, Mo., Zion's Printing and Publishing Co., 1920.
32p. 18cm.
Cover imprint: Salt Lake City. Bureau of Information.
USIC

8923. ———. (same) Liverpool, The Millennial Star Office, 1921.
34p. 17cm.
UPB

8924. ———. (same) Independence, Mo., Press of Zion's Printing and Publishing Co., 1925.
2p.l. [5]–32p. 18cm.
DLC, UPB, USIC

8925. ———. (same, under title) My reasons for joining the Church of Jesus Christ of Latter-day Saints. [by] R. M. Bryce Thomas. [Independence, Mo., Press of Zion's Printing and Publishing Co., 1902]
32p. 18cm.
2d American ed.
MH, NN, OU, UHi, UPB, UU

8926. ———. (same) [Independence, Mo., Press of Zion's Printing and Publishing Co., 1902]
31 [1]p. 18cm.
NjP, UPB

8927. ———. (same) Independence, Mo., Press of Zion's Printing and Publishing Co., 1922.
32p. 17½cm.
NjP, OClWHi, UPB, USIC

8928. ———. (same) Independence, Mo., Press of Zion's Printing and Publishing Co., 1926.
2p.l. [5]–32p. 18cm.
NjP, UPB

8929. ———. (same) Independence, Mo., Zion's Printing and Publishing Co., 1930.
32p. 18cm.
DLC, USI

8930. ———. (same, in Japanese) Waga Eikoku Kyokai wo Sarite, Matsu Jitsu Seito Iesu Kirisuto Kyokai ni Haireru Riyu. Yakusha Fred A. Caine. Tokyo, Nihon, Matsu Jitsu Seito Iesu Kirisuto Kyokai Nihon Dendobu [1905]
64p. 19cm.
USlC

8931. ———. (same) Tokyo, Nihon, Matsu Jitsu Seito Iesu Kirisuto Kyokai, 1911.
63p. 19cm.
USlC

8932. ———. (same) Tokyo, Nihon, Matsu Jitsu Seito Iesu Kirisuto Kyokai, 1925.
63p. 19cm.
UPB

8933. Thomas, W. Herbert. Mormon saints. London, Houlston & Sons, 1890.
ix, 200p. port. 17cm.
CU-B, MH, MoInRC, NN, USlC, WHi

Thomassen, Frances K. *See Taylor, Frances K. (Thomassen).*

8934. Thompson, Charles Blancher. Evidences in proof of the Book of Mormon, being a divinely inspired record, written by the forefathers of the natives whom we call Indians (who are a remnant of the Tribe of Joseph) and hid up in the earth. But come forth in fulfillment of prophesy, for the gathering of Israel and the re-establishing of the Kingdom of God upon the earth. Together with all the objections commonly urged against it, answered and refuted — to which is added a proclamation and warning to the gentiles who inhabit America. By Charles Thompson, Minister of the Gospel . . . Batavia, N.Y., D. D. Waite, 1841.
256p. 13½cm.
Howes T188
CtY, CSmH, CU-B, DLC, ICHi, ICN, MH, NN, NNUT, NRU, OClWHi, UHi, UPB, USl, USlC, WHi

8935. ———. [Great divine charter and sacred constitution of I.A.B.B.A.'s Universal and Everlasting Kingdom. Philadelphia, 1873?]
[iv] [5]-64p. 14cm.
Only known copy lacks the first 2 leaves including title page.
Morgan
MoInRC

8936. ———. The laws and covenants of Israel; written to Ephraim, from Jehovah, the mighty God of Jacob. Also, Ephraim and Baneemy's Proclamations. Preparation, Ia., Printed at the Book and Periodical Office of Zion's Presbytery, 1857.
viii [9]-208p. 10½cm.
Scripture for Thompson's schismatic church Jehovah's Presbytery of Zion.
Morgan
ICN, MoInRC, UPB, USlC

8937. ———. . . . The Nachash origin of the black and mixed races, Negroes are not the children of Adam; their status by creation is that of subjects. Negro slavery was instituted by divine authority at the creation of man. Adam was created for dominion and the Negro was made slave subject in the Garden of Eden. By C. Blancher Thompson. St. Louis, George Knapp and Co., Printers and Binders, 1860.
xxix [30]-84p. 23½×15cm.
Morgan
CSmH, DLC, DI-GS, MH, MWA, NN

———. Nachashlogian. *See The Nachashlogian.*

8938. ———. The Voice of Him!! that crieth in the wilderness, prepare ye the way of the Lord!!! [By Charles B. Thompson. St. Louis? 1848?]
4p. 20cm.
Caption-title.
Morgan
MoInRC

8938a. Thompson, Charles Manfred. The Illinois Whigs before 1846. [Urbana] University of Illinois [c1915]
165p. 23½cm. (University of Illinois. Studies in the Social Sciences. Vol. IV, No. 1, March 1915)
Mormons, p. 99-107.
DLC

8939. Thompson, John. Mormonism — increase of the army. Speech of Hon. John Thompson, of New York. Delivered in the House of Representatives, January 27, 1858. [Washington, Buell & Blanchard, Printers, 1858]
8p. 24½cm.
Caption-title.
CSmH, CtY, CU-B, DLC, ICN, MH, NN, UHi, USl, USlC

8940. Thompson, Joseph Parrish. Church and state in the United States, with an appendix on the German people. Boston, J. R. Osgood, 1873.
166p. 19cm.
"Mormons, Chinese, and Jesuits . . ." p. 23, 27.
DLC, NjP, UPB

8941. Thompson, William. To the Committee on Elections. [n.p., 1850]
19p. 19½cm.
Signed: June 10th, 1850.
Contesting the Kanesville votes of the Mormons in 1848.
USlC

8942. Thorenfeldt, Kai. Jorden rundt paa cykle. Kobenhavn, 1928.
174p.
Title in English: Around the world on a bicycle.
Schmidt

8943. Thoreson, Theodore. An account of a conference held by five brethren in Salt Lake City, Utah, May 8th, 1921, to consider reviving the work which the Lord started in 1829. [Salt Lake City, 1921?]
17p. 23½cm.
Signed: Theodore Thoreson, Robert Newby, John J. Snyder.
Church of Christ (Whitmerite)
NjP, UU

8944. Thornton, Jessy Quinn. Oregon and California in 1848: by J. Quinn Thornton . . . With an appendix, including recent and authentic information of the subject of the gold mines of California, and other valuable matter of interest to the emigrant, etc. With illustrations and a map . . . New York, Harper & Brothers, 1849.
2v. plates, fold. map. 20cm.
Reprinted in 1855, 1864.
From Green River to Fort Hall, July 26–August 7, 1846, with notes on Mormon settlements.
Howes T224, Sabin 95630, W-C 174
CSmH, CtY, CU-B, DLC, ICJ, ICN, MB, NjP, NN, UHi, WHi

8945. Thorp, Joseph. Early days in Missouri by Judge Joseph Thorp. [Liberty, Mo., Liberty Tribune, 1917–18]
[22]l. 21cm.
Caption-title.
Three columns to the page from newspaper set-up.
A series of 19 letters first published in the Liberty, Mo., *Tribune*.
Letters 15–19 concerned with Mormonism in Missouri and the reasons for their expulsion.
Chapters on "The Mormons and their Coming," "Bitter against the Mormons," "The Mormons at Far West," "Mormon War confusion and skirmishes."
Republished in 1924 under title: Early days in the West.
CtY, MoK, MoInRC, UPB

8946. ———. (same) [By Judge Joseph Thorp. The Tribune begins with the following letter, a series written by the late Joseph Thorp and published in the Tribune in the early eighties . . . Liberty, Mo., Liberty Tribune, n.d.]
[23]l. 31cm.
Caption-title.
CtY

8947. ———. (same, under title) Early days in the West. Along the Missouri one hundred years ago. Letters by Judge Joseph Thorp. [Liberty, Mo., I. Gilmer, 1924]
1p.l., 5–94 [1]p. 23½cm.
Howes T231
CU, ICN, MH, MoK, NjP, NN, UHi, USl, USlC

8948. Three months in the United States and Canada. By the editor of the "Western Gazette" . . . Yeovil [Eng.] Office of "The Western gazette" and "Pulman's Weekly News" [1886?]
1p.l., 162p. 21cm.
Includes his visit to Salt Lake City, p. 141–148.
DLC, UPB, USlC

The Three witnesses of the Book of Mormon. *See Kennedy, James Henry.*

8949. Thümmel, A. R. Die Natur und das Leben in den Vereinigten Staaten von Nordamerika, in ihrer Licht- und Schattenseite nach den Schilderungen von Augenzeugen und den Briefen ausgewanderter Landsleute dargestellt . . . Erlangen, Palm, 1848.
viii, 521p. 22cm.
"Die Mormonen und ihr Prophet," p. 41–63. An account of the Mormons translated from Henry Caswall's *Mormonism and its author.*
Title in English: Nature and life in the United States.
Howes T249
CSmH, ICHi, NjP, ULA

8950. Thwaites, Reuben Gold. Early western travels, 1748–1846; a series of annotated reprints of some of the best and rarest contemporary volumes of travel . . . Edited, with notes, introductions, index, etc., by Reuben Gold Thwaites. . . . Cleveland, A. H. Clark Company, 1904–07.
32v. illus., maps (part fold.) 24½cm.
Reference to Mormonism in V.19–20: Josiah Gregg. Commerce of the prairies, V.19, p. 189; V.20, p. 93–97. V.21: John K. Townsent. Narrative of a journey across the Rocky Mountains, p. 139–140. V.22–24: Maximilian, Prince of Wied. Travels in the interior of North America, V.22, p. 249; V.24, p. 119–120. V.26: Edmund Flagg. The far West, p. 13, 334–338, 356, 358–359. V.28: Thomas J. Farnham. Travels in the great western prairies, p. 18, 47–52. V.29: Father P. J. de Smet. Oregon Missions, p. 370–372. V.30: Joel Palmer. Journal of travels over the Rocky Mountains, p. 74, 257.
Howes T255
CU-B, DLC, NjP, UHi, ULA, UPB, UU

8951. Thyregod, C. A. En Mormons kone . . . Kobenhavn, 1862.
70p.
Title in English: A Mormon wife.
Schmidt

8952. Tice, John H. Over the plains, on the mountains; or, Kansas, Colorado, and the Rocky Mountains; agriculturally, mineralogically and aesthetically described. By John H. Tice . . . St. Louis, Mo., Printed by the "Industrial age" Printing Co., 1872.
1p.l., 262, ivp. illus. 21½cm.
Many references to the Mormons.
CtY, CU-B, DLC, NjP, NN, OFH, OOxM, UHi, ULA, UPB

TIDERNES TEGN

8953. Et tidernes tegn. [Kjobenhavn, Udgivet og Forlagt af John S. Hansen . . . 1925]
4p. 22½cm.
Title in English: A sign of the times.
USlC

8953a. ———. (same) [København, Udgivet og Forlagt af Joseph L. Petersen . . . 1926]
4p. 23cm.
UPB, USlC

8954. Timbs, John. English eccentrics and eccentricities. London, Richard Bentley, 1866.
2v. 20½cm.
"The founder of Mormonism," V. 1, p. 227–238.
NjP, USlC

A timely warning to the people of England . . .
See Hyde, Orson.

8955. The Times and Seasons. Containing a compendium of intelligence pertaining to the upbuilding of the Kingdom of God and the signs of the times together with a great variety of useful information, in regard to the doctrines . . . of the Church of Jesus Christ of Latter-day Saints . . . Nauvoo, Ill. [Robinson, Smith, etc.] 1839–1846.
6v. illus., plates, fold. facsim. monthly. 23cm.
Editors: Don Carlos Smith, Ebenezer Robinson, Joseph Smith, John Taylor, etc.
V.5 #23 misnumbered, #22 in some copies.
CSmH, CtY, CU–B, ICN, MH, NN, ULA, UPB, USl, USlC, WHi

8956. Times and Seasons. A brief account of the discovery of the brass plates recently taken from a mound in the vicinity of Kinderhook, Pike County, Illinois. Nauvoo, Ill., Taylor and Woodruff, June 24th, 1843.
Broadside. 38×20cm.
Quotes by W. P. Harris on discovery and an article from the *Quincy Whig* for the editor of the *Times and Seasons.*
Found in at least three variants.
Byrd 764
DLC, MH, USlC

8957. Tinkham, George Henry. California men and events; time 1769–1890, by George H. Tinkham . . . Panamo-Pacific Exposition Ed., 1915. [Stockton, Cal., Print by the Record Publishing Company, c1915]
3p.l., 9–330p. illus., ports. 22cm.
The most useful settlers during 1847 were the Mormons.
CU–B copy was submitted to Robert E. Cowan for revision, and has his ms. corrections.
Another edition: 2d ed., rev. c1915. DLC, NjP, UHi
CU–B, DLC

8958. Tissandier, Albert. . . . Six mois aux États-Unis; voyage d'un touriste dans l'Amérique du Nord suivi d'une excursion à Panama, texte et dessins par Albert Tissandier . . . Paris, G. Masson [1886?]
2p.l., 298 [1]p. illus., maps. 26cm.
Spent his time in Utah at Kanab and Panguitch, 1885.
Title in English: Six months in the United States.
CU, DLC, NjP, UHi, UPB

8959. Tithing. [Salt Lake City, 1929]
1 card. 16cm.
Ward teachers' leaflet.
UPB, USlC

8960. Tittsworth, W. G. Outskirt episodes . . . W. G. Tittsworth, the author. [Des Moines, Ia., Success Composition and Printing Co., c1927]
232p., [1]l. 19½cm.
Brief notes on Mormon emigrants; life in Brown's Hole.
Howes T275
CU–B, DLC, MiU, NjP, UHi, USlC

8961. To all Latter day Saints. [Circular. n.p., 19–]
[4]p. 22cm.
Caption-title.
A tract on coated white paper addressing (in the first person) the true gentile believers who are the Church of the Firstborn. "Thanks God, for David Whitmer and his book," belatedly come upon.
CU–B

8961a. To J. F. Corbin, Presiding Elder of the El Paso District of the M. E. Church — South. [n.p., n.d.]
8p. 22cm.
Includes Mormon doctrine of the Negro.
UPB

To San Francisco and back. By a London parson.
See Jones, R. Hervey.

8962. To the anti-Mormon citizens of Hancock and the surrounding counties . . . [Warsaw] Warsaw Signal Print [1845]
Broadside. 40×20cm.
Triple columns.
Relating to the demands of the people for the Mormons to leave, and the Council of the Twelve's statement of intentions.
Text was reprinted in the *Nauvoo Neighbor* of Oct. 29, 1845.
Byrd 1000
ICHi, NN

8963. To the Christians and gentiles, especially Christians of the United States. [n.p., 1909?]
Broadside. 23×18cm.
Mormonism the only Christian religion not fit to exist. The author admonishes President Taft to expose Reed Smoot.
USlC

8964. To the Church of Latter Day Saints. El Paso, J. D. Hughes Printing Company [1907?]
33p. 16cm.
Appendix: p. 23–33.
Signed: One of many of your would be friends.
Tract against the race philosophy of the Church.
UPB without appendix, USIC

8965. To the members of the Church of Jesus Christ of Latter Day Saints. It becomes an imperative obligation devolving upon the friends and adherents of Pres. Sydney Rigdon, to make an explicit and candid statement of the causes, which have led to their disunion and disfellowship with the adherents of the Twelve in their illegal and unwarrantable assumption of the authority of their first Presidency. [There follows in double columns a letter signed by Samuel James, Leonard Soby, and 18 others dated Nauvoo, Sept. 8, 1844. Nauvoo, Ill., 1844]
Broadside. 27½×20cm.
In double columns.
Failure of the church to allow Sidney Rigdon to answer charges.
Byrd 895, Morgan
CtY, USIC

8966. To the Senate and House of Representatives in Congress assembled: With profound respect we represent:... [Washington? 1886?]
12p. 22cm.
A printed letter with space for a signature; concerning the Mormon problem and the Edmunds-Tucker Bill.
NjP, USIC

8967. To those of my parishioners who have joined the party of Latter-day Saints or Mormonites. Ledbury, Printed by J. S. Bagster [n.d.]
8p. 19cm.
USIC

8968. To whom this may concern. The following resolutions were unanimously adopted at a public meeting consisting largely of non-Mormons, held at the Hotel Utah, Salt Lake City, on Tuesday evening, April 18, 1922. Salt Lake City, 1922.
[4]p. 28cm.
Signed: John James, John Rothery, Harry W. Matthews [and others]
UU

8969. Tobacco. Doctors, directors of athletics, insurance companies, scientists say tobacco is harmful. [Salt Lake City, 1929]
[8]p. folder. 15½cm.
Brief quotes from various persons.
UPB, USIC

8970. Todd, John. Early settlement and growth of western Iowa; reminiscences by Rev. John Todd of Tabor, Iowa. Des Moines, The Historical Department of Iowa, 1906.
2p.l. [5]–203p. port. 20cm.
A Sabbath in 1848 with the Mormons at Mt. Pisgah. A factual account, with commentary.
UPB

8971. ———. The Sunset land; or, The great Pacific slope. By Rev. John Todd, D. D. Boston, Lee and Shepard; New York, Lee, Shepard and Dillingham [1869]
3p.l., 9–322p. 18cm.
Chapter V. Mormons and Mormonism, p. 161–212. The history of the Mormons, the despotism of Brigham Young, the evil of polygamy.
Other editions: London, Hodder, c1869. NjP; Boston, Lee and Shepard, 1870. CU–B, DLC, NjP, ULA; Boston, Lee and Shepard, 1871. UHi, UPB, WHi
Under title: California and its wonders. London, T. Nelson, 1880. CSmH
USIC, WaU

8972. Todd, Mary Van Lennup (Ives). Deborah, the advanced woman, by M.I.T.... Boston, Arena Publishing Company, 1896.
233p. 20cm.
Fiction concerning Mormonism.
DLC, MH, NN

8973. Tomlinson, L. G. Churches of today in the Light of Scripture ... Cincinnati, Ohio, Christian Leader Corp., Print., 1927.
3p.l., 7–183p. 19½cm.
"Mormonism," p. 84–87. Outline of Mormon beliefs, preceded by a short history.
USIC

8974. Toombs, Herbert W. Mormonism. Bulletin of the Council for Social Service of the Church of England in Canada. Toronto, Church of England in Canada, Council for Social Service, 1921.
1p.l., 3–38p. 22cm. (Bulletin. No. 24)
"Abridged from the excellent pamphlet written by the Rev. Herbert W. Toombs."
UPB

8975. Toponce, Alexander. Reminiscences of Alexander Toponce, pioneer, 1839–1923. [Ogden, Utah, Mrs. Katie Toponce, c1923]
248p. front., plates, ports. 18cm.
Merchant, with the overland mail, and Johnston's Army. He had a freighting Business between Salt Lake City and Montana; dealings with Brigham Young, John Taylor, and Lorenzo Snow.
Howes T299
CSmH, CU–B, DLC, MH, NjP, UHi, ULA, UPB, USI, USIC, UU

TOPSÖE, V. C. S.

8976. Topsöe, V. C. S. Från Amerika af V. C. S. Topsöe. Svensk med förf. Samtycke Utgifven upplaga. Öfversättning af O. Strandberg. Med 50 illustrationer och 1 karta. Stockholm, Albert Bonniers, förlag [1874]
3p.l., 423 [1]p. illus., fold. col. map. 21½cm.
Chapter 40. "Mormonerna."
Title in English: From America.
ICHi, UHi

8977. Torch of Truth. Phoenix, Ariz., May 7, 1925–April, 1931.
6v. approx. monthly. 24cm.
James E. Yates, publisher and editor.
An unofficial publication of the Church of Christ (Temple lot)
Suspended V. 6, No. 2, April, 1931.
CU–B V.1 #1, V.4 #7, V.6 #2; USlC V.4–5

8978. Torgler, John S. Text Book of the scriptures. Hints, with figures and woe from the beginning to the ending to the Israel of God. [New Cambria, Kansas, c1929]
1p.l., 3–271 [1]p. 21cm.
References to the *Pearl of Great Price* among the scriptures. "Contents Books Mormon," p. 265–[272]
USlC

8979. Tourgeé, Albion Winegar. Button's inn. By Albion Tourgeé . . . Boston, Roberts Brothers, 1887.
2p.l. [v]–x, 418p. 18cm.
Fiction concerning Mormonism.
Another edition: 1897. USlC
DLC, ICN, MoInRC, NjP, NN, OO, OU, UHi, ULA, USlC, UU

8980. Toutain, Paul. Un Français en Amérique. Yankees, Indians, Mormons, par Paul Toutain. Paris, E. Plon and Cie, 1876.
2p.l., iv, 233p. 18cm.
Title in English: A Frenchman in America.
CSmH, CU–B, DLC, MB, NjP, UU

8981. Towle, Nancy. Vicissitudes illustrated, in the experience of Nancy Towle, in Europe and America. Written by herself. With an appendix of letters, &c. An engraving — and preface by Lorenzo Dow . . . Charleston [S.C.] Printed for the authoress, by James L. Burges, 1832.
3p.l. [5]–11 [1] [5]–294p. plates. 15cm.
"History of Mormonism." Her encounter with the Mormons at Kirtland, October, 1831, and their history.
Another edition: 2d ed. 1833. CtY, CU–B, DLC, MWA, NN, TxU, UHi, UPB
Howes T312, Sabin 96361
DLC, NjP, OClWHi, UPB, USlC

8982. Towne, C. S. Angelic ministry of Mormonism weighed in the balance. By C. S. Towne. McMinnville, Tenn., Standard Printing House, 1902.
1p.l. [3]–50p. 21cm.
A critical work on the *Book of Mormon.*
DLC, MoInRC, USlC

8983. Towne, Edward Cornelius. Rays of light from all lands; the Bibles and beliefs of mankind, scriptures, faiths and systems of every age, race and nation. A complete story of all churches and communions. Notable utterances by foremost representatives of all faiths . . . Edited by Rev. E. C. Towne, B. A., Rev. A. J. Canfield, D. D., and George J. Hagar. New York, Gan Brothers and Co. [1895]
xxx, 7–866p. illus., ports. 25cm.
"The Mormons," p. 586–618, by F. D. Richards.
UPB, USlC, UU

8984. Townsend, Bertram H. Mormonism; the last testament [by] Bertram H. Townsend. [n.p., n.d.]
60p. plates. 21½cm.
A doctrinal work.
UPB

8985. Townsend, Charles. Little buckshot; an original melodrama in three acts by Charles Townsend. Chicago, T. S. Denison and Company [c1901]
50p. 18½cm.
The Mormon, a Mr. Brown from Nevada, with his aide, a destroying angel, is outwitted.
MH, NN

8986. Townsend, George Alfred. The Mormon trials at Salt Lake City. By Geo. Alfred Townsend. New York, American News Company, 1871.
49p. 20½cm.
"Letters from Utah to the *Cincinnati Commercial,* October, 1871."
CSmH, CtY, CU–B, DLC, ICN, MH, NN, OU, WHi

8987. Townsend, John Kirk. Narrative of a journey across the Rocky Mountains, to the Columbia River, and a visit to the Sandwich Islands, Chili, &c.; with a scientific appendix. By John K. Townsend . . . Philadelphia, Henry Perkins; Boston, Perkins & Marvin, 1839.
viii [9]–352p. 24cm.
A brief mention of Mormons while in Independence, 1834, p. 25–26.
Another edition: 2d ed. Phil., Saturday Mus. Extra, 1843. MWA
Also published under title: Sporting excursions in the Rocky mountains. London, H. Colburn, 1840. CSmH, CtY, CU–B, DLC, NN
Abridged edition: "Excursions to the Oregon," [c1846] DLC
Reprinted in Reuben G. Thwaite, *Early Western travels.*
Howes T319, Sabin 96381, W–C 79
CSmH, CtY, CU–B, MH, MnHi, NjP, UPB, ViU, WHi

———. Youth of Zion. *See Giles, Henry Evans.*

8988. Townshend, Frederick Trench. Ten thousand miles of travel, sport, and adventure. By F. Trench Townshend . . . London, Hurst and Blackett, 1869.
xiv, 275p. front. 22½cm.
A chapter on his travel through Salt Lake City with a description of the Mormons.
Howes T322
CSmH, CU-B, DLC, NjP, UHi, ULA

8989. Townshend, George. . . . The conversion of Mormonism, by George Townshend. [Hartford, Conn., Church Missions Publishing Company, 1911]
59p. plates, ports., facsim. 18½cm.
(Soldier and servant series)
Written after 5 years in Utah. The account endorsed by F. S. Spalding.
DLC, UHi, USlC

8990. ———. (same) [Hartford, Conn., Church Missions Publishing Co., 1911]
5p.l. [13]-76p. 11 plates, 4 port. 18½cm.
(Soldier and servant series. No. 51)
Cover-title.
CtY, NjP, NN, UHi, UPB, USl, USlC

8991. ———. Why I am not a Mormon . . . Denver, Alexander and Meyer Printers, 1907.
30p. 19½cm.
"I cannot hear of any intelligent person who has been converted to Mormonism within the last 50 years . . ."
NN, USlC, UU

Tracts on Mormonism. *See Clay, Edmund.*

8992. Trapped by the Mormons; the story of moral lepers of Salt Lake City . . . [n.p., 1928?]
Broadside. 22×19cm.
USlC

8993. ———. [n.p., 1928?]
5p. 15cm.
Advertisement for his film on the terrors of present day Mormonism.
USlC

8994. Traum, Samuel Wegner. Mormonism against itself, by Samuel W. Traum . . . Cincinnati, The Standard Publishing Company, 1910.
xx [21]-321p. ports., facsims. 20cm.
DLC, MH, MoInRC, NjPT, UPB, USl, USlC, UU, WHi

8995. Travers, William Thomas Locke. From New Zealand to Lake Michigan. Wellington, N.Z., Edwards & Co., Publishers Brandon St., 1889.
4p.l., 274p. fold. map. 19cm.
A visit to Salt Lake City in 1888. History of Mormonism, and a description of Utah.
USlC

8996. Trayner, Jacob H. Que la paix de Dieu soit sur cette maison! [Rotterdam, Jacob H. Trayner, ca. 1905]
[4]p. 22cm.
Missionary tract.
Title in English: The peace of the Lord be with this house.
USlC

8997. Trejo, Meliton Gonzalez. Romanistas, protestantes y "Mormones" examinadlo todo: retened lo que fuere bueno. 1°. Tesalonia! [México, 1880]
16p. 15cm.
Caption-title.
Dated at end: México, Abril de 1880; signed M. G. Trejo.
Title in English: Romanists, protestants and Mormons all examined.
CU-B

8998. ———. (same) [Salt Lake City, Impreso en la imprenta de Deseret News, E. U. Territorio de Utah, n.d.]
16p. 17cm.
USlC

8999. Trent, William Peterfield. Progress of the United States of America in the century, by William P. Trent . . . London [etc.] Philadelphia, The Linscott Publishing Company, 1901.
xv [1] 468p. ports. 21cm. (Half-title: The nineteenth century series. Vol. V)
A brief account of Mormonism.
Other editions: Toronto and Philadelphia, 1903. CU, UHi, UPB, USlC; London & Edinburgh, W. & R. Chambers; Philadelphia, Detroit [etc.] The Bradley-Garretson, Ltd., 1903. DLC
DLC, UHi

9000. Trial of the persons indicted in the Hancock Circuit Court, for the murder of Joseph Smith, at the Carthage Jail, on the 27th day of June, 1844. [Warsaw, Ill., Warsaw Signal, 1845]
32p. 21cm.
Advertised in *Warsaw Signal.* August 6, 1845.
Trial of Levi Williams, Mark Aldrich, Jacob C. Davis, Wm. H. Grover, and others.
Byrd 1001
ICHi, ICN, IHi, USlC

9001. The Tribune Almanac and Political Register. The Tribune almanac and political register for 1859. New York, H. Greeley & Co. [1859?]
80p. 17½cm.
"Utah and the Mormons," p. 37-42. A brief sketch of the rise of Mormonism.
CSmH, MH, NjP

TRIBUTE

9002. Tribute of respect to the memory of the late Hon. Brigham Young, and the first Governor of Utah. [Salt Lake City? 1878?]
4p. 21cm.
Caption-title.
Possibly published by the Legislative Assembly.
UHi, USlC

9003. A tribute to our father and mother, Ephraim Ralphs and Sophia Nelson Ralphs, with love and appreciation from their family, on the occasion of the celebration of their golden wedding. October 24, 1920. Rockland, Idaho, 1920.
19p. ports. 22cm.
Mormon biography.
USlC

9004. Tributes to the memory of Hyrum M. Smith; letters, telegrams and memorials from numerous friends and relatives to the family of Elder Hyrum M. Smith of the Council of the Twelve at the time of his death. Salt Lake City, 1918.
64p. ports. 24cm.
Mormon biography.
NjP, USlC

9005. Tricoche, George Nestler. Le siège de Nauvoo; ou, La battaille des maladroits (épisode de l'histoire des Mormons) par George Nestler Tricoche . . . Paris [Nogent-le-Rotrou, Imprimé par Daupeley-Gouverneur] 1915.
1p.l. [5]–16p. 24½cm.
Also published in *Revue Historique*, Paris, 1915, Tome 119, p. 326–337.
Title in English: The siege of Nauvoo.
DLC, NN

9006. Triezenberg, Henry J. The Bible and Mormonism. [n.p.] Faith, Prayer & Tract League [n.d.]
19 [1]p. 14cm. (Silent evangelist. No. 182B)
UPB

9007. Trimmer, F. Mortimer. Golden crocodile, a mining romance by F. Mortimer Trimmer. Boston, Mass., Roberts Brothers, 1897.
2p.l. [7]–318p. 21cm.
One chapter of the novel is entitled "At the Mormon Bishop's ranch."
Another edition: 2d ed. London, Downey & Co., 1897. CU–B
DLC, NjP, USlC

9008. Triplett, Frank. Conquering the wilderness; or, New pictorial history of the life and times of the pioneer heroes and heroines of America. A full account of the romantic deeds, lofty achievements, and marvelous adventures of Boone, Kenton [and others] with picturesque sketches of border life, past and present, backwoods camp meetings, schools and Sunday-schools; heroic fortitude and noble deeds of the pioneer wives and mothers . . . the overland route and its horrors . . . Brigham Young . . . and describing life and adventure on the plains and in the mining camps of today . . . Chicago, National Book and Picture Co. [c1883]
1p.l., v–xxxix [2] 17–716p. illus., ports. 23½cm.
Pt. 2, Chap. 21: The Mormons. Chap. 22: Mountain Meadows massacre.
Other editions: New York & St. Louis, 1883. CSmH, USlC; Chicago, 1895. USlC; New York, 1886. USl, USlC
CSmH, CU–B, DLC, NjP, UHi, UPB

9009. ———. History, romance and philosophy of great American crimes and criminals; including the great typical crimes that have marked the various periods of American history from the foundation of the republic to the present day, with personal portraits, biographical sketches . . . by Col. Frank Triplett . . . New York, N. D. Thompson & Company, 1884.
xxxiv [33]–659p. illus., plates. 22½cm.
Includes a section on the Mountain Meadows massacre; blames the Church and Brigham Young for the massacre.
Other editions: 1884. DLC, UHi; New York and St. Louis, N. D. Thompson Publishing Co., 1885. USlC
OFH, USlC

9010. Tro og Dag. [Kjobenhavn, Udgivet og forlagt af Joseph Christiansen . . . 1893]
8p. 21cm.
Translation of "Is belief alone sufficient?" and Charles Bliss's "Is baptism essential to salvation."
Title in English: Faith and baptism.
USlC

9010a. ———. (same) [Kjobenhavn, Udgivet og forlagt af C. A. Carlquist, Trykt hos F. E. Bording (V. Petersen), 1894. 20de tusinde]
8p. 22½cm.
USlC

9011. ———. (same) Er Tro alene tilstraekkelig til frelse? [Kjobenhavn, Udgivet og forlagt af Andreas Pearson . . . Trykt hos F. E. Bording . . . 1899]
8p. 22cm.
USlC

9012. ———. (same) [Kjobenhavn,Udgivet og forlagt af Adreas Petersen . . . Trykt hos Emil Petersen . . . 1900]
8p. 22cm.
UPB, USlC

9013. ———. (same, in Swedish) Tro och dop. [Köpenhamn, Utgifven och förlagt af Adreas Petersen. Tryckt hos Emil Petersen, 1900]
8p. 23½cm.
"130 Tusendet."
USlC

9014. ———. (same) [Köpenhamn, Utgifven och förlagd af Anthon L. Skanchy, 1904]
8p. 22cm.
UPB

9015. ———. (same) Stockholm, Förlagd af A. P. Anderson [n.d.]
7 [1]p. 22cm.
USIC

9016. Trout, Grace Wilbur. A Mormon wife, by Grace Wilbur Trout; illustrated by Capel Rowley. Chicago, C. H. Kerr & Company [1895]
108p. plates. 19½cm. (On verso of title-page: Unity library. No. 47)
Fiction concerning Mormonism.
DLC, MH, MoInRC, USIC, WHi

9017. ———. (same) Chicago, E. A. Weeks & Company [1896]
110p., [1]l., front., plates. 20cm. (On cover: The Enterprise series. No. 64)
DLC, USI

9018. ———. (same) [Chicago, E. A. Weeks, 1896?]
110 [1]p. 18cm. (The Holly Library of choice books)
The cover has printed ornaments and the word "by." Author and title supplied by manuscript.
USIC

9019. ———. (same) 3d ed. Illustrations by Vida E. Horton. Chicago, Van-American Press [c1912]
105p. plates. 20cm.
DLC, USIC

9020. Trowbridge, Richard B. . . . Facts which the people should know and earnestly consider. This is a time of crisis. Facts have been suppressed . . . [Independence, Mo., 1927]
69 [1]p. illus., port. 18cm.
At head of title: Do you want to know the truth?
Supplement one. 61p. MoInRC, UPB, USIC
Supplement two. 64p. MoInRC
An exposé of the RLDS church's finances by its first general auditor, restricted from acting on these irregularities.
MoInRC, NN, UPB

9021. The true church of Jesus Christ. A warning voice. [n.p., n.d.]
Broadside. 18½×9cm.
A leaflet for a meeting in "the Hall, Providence Place . . . Sunday Evening, 6–30."
NN

9022. Trueblood, Medora O. The Hearts of the children or the connecting link. A pageant-drama on Genealogical and Temple work. In two prologues. Nine acts. First presented by the Seventeenth Ward Genealogical Committee February 1, 1929. Seventeenth Ward Recreation Hall. Authors: Medora O. Trueblood, Eliza B. Smith, William S. Muir. . . . Salt Lake City, Published under the Direction of the Genealogical Society of Utah, 1929.
2p.l. [5]–40p. 18½cm.
UPB

9023. Truesdell, A. P. Secret volume of life; or, The mysteries of nature revealed. An illustrated treatise on the natural laws which govern every organized creature; unfolding the hidden causes of health and disease, and of all improvement or degeneracy in the plant, in the animal, and in the man . . . San Francisco, Cal., Published by the author, 1880.
xxii [2]–1022p. 24cm.
Polygamy a shackle for women which must be destroyed.
NjP, USIC

9024. Trumble, Alfred. The mysteries of Mormonism. A full exposure of its secret practices and hidden crimes, by an apostle's wife. Fully illustrated. New York, Published by Richard K. Fox, Proprietor, Police Gazette [c1882]
2p.l. [7]–69p. plates. 24½cm.
Many of the same plates appear in various other anti-Mormon works.
Polygamy, endowment house, Danites, etc.
Variant printing. USIC
CtY, CU–B, ICN, MH, MoInRC, NjP, NN, UPB, USIC, UU, WHi

9024a. Trumbo, Isaac. Speech of Col. Isaac Trumbo and tribute to President Wilford Woodruff. Republican Day, Saltair, August 11, 1894. [Salt Lake City, 1894]
4p. 24cm.
USIC

9025. ———. . . . To the people of Utah . . . [Salt Lake City, 1895]
15p. 25×11cm. (Republican Party pamphlet)
A letter to Col. Trumbo from Wilford Woodruff, George Q. Cannon and Joseph F. Smith thanking him for his political efforts. The efforts of the Democrats to prevent statehood. Republican Party pamphlet.
UHi

9026. Truth. Chicago, Ill. [Northern States Mission. Church of Jesus Christ of Latter-day Saints] 1917–1925.
8v. monthly. 34cm.
No date given except copyright.
USIC

TRUTH ABOUT

9027. Truth about Mexico. [n.p., n.d.]
Broadside. 28½×15½.
Mormon colonization in Mexico.
NjP

"Truth Conquers" [*pseud.*] *See Briggs, Edmund C. Address to the Saints in Utah.*

9028. The Truth Teller. [Independence, Mo.] July 1864–December 1868.
2v. monthly. 21cm.
Publication suspended June 1865–June 1868.
1864–65 published in Bloomington, Ill.
Editor: Granville Hedrick.
Founded to support the Church of Christ (Temple lot)
Title page of V.1: The Truth-teller will advocate the primitive organization of the Church of Jesus Christ of Latter Day Saints, which was organized on the 6th day of April, 1830, and maintain her doctrines in all truth. Also, an exposition of all the false doctrines that has [sic] been imposed upon the Church.
CSmH, CtY, DLC, MoInRC, NN, USlC

9029. A truthful and unbiased statement. [n.p., 1911?]
7p. 22½cm.
A missionary tract to refute misconceptions of polygamy, morals, emigration, etc.
UPB

9030. Truths by three witnesses; a warning voice. Plano, Ill., Reorganized Church of Jesus Christ of Latter Day Saints [n.d.]
Broadside. 23×15cm.
NN

9031. Truth's Reflex. St. John, Kansas [Southwestern States Mission. Church of Jesus Christ of Latter Day Saints] January 1899–April 1901.
3v. monthly. 31½cm.
Mission periodical.
Editor: William T. Jack.
Liahona reference shows 2 vols. of 12 nos. and V.3 #1–4 of at least 136p.
USlC V.1–3 #4

9032. Tucker, D. E. The true gospel and the true church. [Lamoni, Ia., Reorganized Church of Jesus Christ of Latter Day Saints, 191–]
16p. 18½cm. (No. 307)
IWW, MoInRC, USlC

9033. ———. The true way is the gospel way. Lamoni, Ia., Board of Publication of the Reorganized Church of Jesus Christ of Latter Day Saints, 1908.
12p. 18cm. (No. 307)
MoInRC

9034. Tucker, John Randolph. Polygamy. Speech of Hon. John Randolph Tucker of Virginia, in the House of Representatives, Tuesday, March 14, 1882. [Washington? 1882]
8p. 23cm.
ULA, UPB

9035. ———. (same) Wednesday, January 12, 1887. Washington, Franklin Printing House, 1887.
12p. 23cm.
Cover-title.
CSmH, CU–B, USlC, UU

9035a. ———. Suppression of polygamy in Utah. June 10, 1886. — Referred to the House Calendar and ordered to be printed. Mr. Tucker, from the Committee on the Judiciary, submitted the following report: [To accompany bill S. 10. Washington, Government Printing Office? 1886?]
10p. 23cm. (U.S. 49th Cong. 1st Sess. House. Report No. 2735)
USlC

9036. Tucker, Pomeroy. Origin, rise and progress of Mormonism. Biography of its founders and history of its church. Personal remembrances and historical collections hitherto unwritten by Pomeroy Tucker . . . New York, D. Appleton and Co., 1867.
302p. ports. 20cm.
CSmH, CtY, CU–B, DLC, ICN, IWW, MH, MoInRC, NjP, NjPT, UHi, ULA, UPB, USlC, UU, WHi

9037. Tullidge, Edward Wheelock. Biographical sketch of Franklin D. Richards (as published in Tullidge's History of Salt Lake City). Salt Lake City, 1886.
1p.l., 26p. port. 22cm.
USlC, UU

9037a. ———. (same) Salt Lake City, 1886.
10p. 22cm.
USlC

9038. ———. The history of Salt Lake City and its founders . . . incorporating a brief history of the pioneers of Utah . . . by authority of the City Council and under supervision of its Committee on Revision. Salt Lake City, Edward W. Tullidge [1883]
112p. 25cm.
Cover imprint: Salt Lake City, Star Printing Co., 1883.
Issued with paper wrappers as a series first begun in his *Tullidge's Magazine*; apparently the only one issued.
USlC

9038a. ———. The history of Salt Lake City and its founders. By Edward W. Tullidge. Incorporating a brief history of the pioneers of Utah; with steel portraits of representative men; together with a carefully arranged index and an elaborate appendix . . . Salt Lake City, Edward W. Tullidge, Publisher and Proprietor [c1886]
1p.l., viii [3]–896, 28, 151p. plates, ports. 24cm.
Howes T409
CSmH, DLC, IWW, MWA, OCl, USlC

9039. ———. (same) Edward W. Tullidge, Publisher and Proprietor. Salt Lake City, Star Printing Company, 1886.
1p.l., viii [3]–896, 172, 36p. front., ports. 14½cm.
Pagination of appendices and sequence differs in copies.
Howes T409
CSmH, CU, DLC, MB, MiU, NjP, NjPT, NN, OCl, OClWHi, UHi, USlC, ViU

9040. ———. (same) Salt Lake City, E. W. Tullidge [1886?]
1p.l., viii [3]–896, 172, 36p. plates, ports. 24½cm.
Howes T409
CSmH, DLC, MH, NjP, OClWHi, OO, UHi, ULA, UU

9041. ———. Life of Brigham Young; or, Utah and her founders. By Edward W. Tullidge. New York, 1876.
2p.l., iv, 458, 81p. port. 22½cm.
"Biographical sketches," 81p. at the end of the text.
Howes T410
CSmH, CtY, CU-B, DLC, ICN, MH, MoInRC, NjP, UHi, UPB, USl, USlC, WHi

9042. ———. (same) [2d ed.] New York, 1877.
2p.l., iv, 458, 108p. port. 22½cm.
Howes T410
CSmH, IWW, NjP, ULA, UPB, USlC

9043. ———. Life of Joseph the Prophet. New York, 1878.
ix, 545p. ports. 22½cm.
Howes T411
MH, MoInRC, NjP, UHi, UPB, USl, USlC, UU

9044. ———. (same) By Edward W. Tullidge. Plano, Ill., Published by the Board of Publication of the Reorganized Church of Jesus Christ of Latter Day Saints, 1880.
xii, 827p. 4 port. 22cm.
Includes historical material on the Reorganized Church and an autobiographical statement by its first president, Joseph Smith (1832–1914)
With and without cancels on p. 530, 575.
Howes T411
CtY, DLC, ICHi, MoInRC, NjP, UHi, UPB, USlC, WHi

9045. ———. Tullidge's histories, (volume II) containing the history of all the northern, eastern and western counties of Utah; also the counties of southern Idaho. With a biographical appendix of representative men and founders of the cities and counties; also a commercial supplement, historical. Edw. W. Tullidge, Proprietor and Publisher. Salt Lake City, Press of the Juvenile Instructor, 1889.
vi, 440 (i.e. 540)p. [1]l., 372p. illus., plates, ports. 25cm.
Pages 537–540 incorrectly numbered 437–440.
Second part has half-title: Biographies (supplemental volume)
CSmH, CtY, CU-B, DLC, MdBP, NjP, NN, OCl, UHi, ULA, UPB, USl, USlC, UU

9046. ———. The women of Mormondom. New York [Tullidge and Crandall] 1877.
x, 552p. port. 22½cm.
CSmH, CU-B, DLC, ICN, MB, MH, MoInRC, NN, UHi, ULA, UPB, USlC, UU, WHi

9047. Tullidge, John Elliott. Latter-day Saints' psalmody, composed and arranged for the organ or pianoforte by John Tullidge. Liverpool, S. W. Richards [1857]
1p.l., 108p. music. 18×26cm.
USlC

9048. Tullidges' Quarterly Magazine. Salt Lake City, 1880–1885.
3v. plates, ports. irregular. 25cm.
Editor: Edward W. Tullidge.
Superseded by *Western Galaxy*.
Contains many biographical sketches and historical and descriptive articles regarding Utah, Utah communities, Mormon faith and history.
CSmH, CtY, CU-B, ICN, NjP, NN, ULA, UPB, USlC, WHi

9049. Turenne d'Aynac, Gabriel Louis. Quatorze mois dans l'Amerique du Nord (1875–1876) par Le Cte. Louis de Tureene avec Carte d'une partie du Nord-Ouest. Paris, A. Quantin Imprimeur-Editeur, 1879.
2v. fold. map. 18½cm.
He spent a few November days in Utah, with comments on the Territory and Mormonism.
Title in English: Fourteen months in North America.
NjP, UPB

9049a. Turnbull, J. S. The origin of the name Egypt. Salt Lake City, The Nefer Printing Office [n.d.]
18p. 19cm.
Book of Abraham references, p. 12, 14, 18.
USlC

9050. Turnbull, Thomas. T. Turnbull's travels from the United States across the plains to California [From the Proceedings of the State Historical Society of Wisconsin for 1913, pages 151–225] Madison, Published for the Society, 1914.
1p.l., 151–225p. illus., maps. 23cm.
At head of title: [Separate No. 158]
Overland journey of 1852 bypassing Utah, edited by Frederic L. Paxson.
Reference to Mormons, p. 152–153, 181, 189, 197; Kainsville, p. 160; Mormon Station, p. 212–13.
CU–B

9051. Turnbull, William. A Call to the unconverted, by a Mormon teacher. (A verbatim copy) [Liverpool, H. Braithwaite, Printer, 185–]
4p. 21½cm.
Caption-title.
Signed: William Turnbull.
A travesty on a Mormon exhortation.
CtY

9052. Turner, J. W. The consistency of divine truth. The guiding star of life. Man's free agency. [n.p., n.d.]
40 [1]p. 18½cm.
Poem on a Mormon doctrinal subject.
Printed by the author on a hand press.
USlC

9053. Turner, Jonathan Baldwin. Mormonism in all ages: or, The rise, progress and causes of Mormonism; with the biography of its author, and founder, Joseph Smith, junior. By Professor J. B. Turner . . . New York, Published by Platt & Peters [etc., etc., 1842]
1p.l. [3]–304p. 20cm.
CSmH, CtY, CU–B, ICHi, ICN, IWW, MH, MoInRC, NjPT, UHi, UPB, USl, USlC, UU, WHi

9054. Turner, Orsamus. History of the pioneer settlement of Phelps and Gorham's purchase, and Morris' reserve; embracing the counties of Monroe, Ontario, Livingstone, Yates, Steuben, most of Wayne and Allegany, and parts of Orleans, Genesee, and Wyoming. To which is added, a supplement, or extension of the pioneer history of Monroe County . . . By O. Turner . . . Rochester, W. Alling, 1851.
viii [9]–624p. 23cm.
"Gold Bible — Mormonism," p. 212–217.
Another edition: 1852. DLC
Howes T425, Sabin 97489
CSmH, CU–B, DLC, NjP, USlC

9055. Turner, W. S. Notes by a wanderer from Demerara, in the United States. Demerara [British Guiana] J. Thomson; "Argosy" Office, 1885.
2p.l., 126p. 21cm.
Impression of Salt Lake City quoting mostly from Mark Twain and things he was told.
CtY

9056. Turnley, Parmenas Taylor. Private letters of Parmenas Taylor Turnley (together with some letters of his father and grandfather) on the character of the constitutional government of the United States, and the antagonisms of Puritans to Christianity, &c. Collected, arranged, and printed for private circulation only, among relatives of his family by his sister, Cinderella L. Turnley. London, Printed by Harrison and Sons, 1863.
xii, 194p. 23cm.
Includes letters concerning Mormons, 1852–60, from Salt Lake City and the trail east.
DLC, NjP, NN, UPB

9057. ———. Reminiscences of Parmenas Taylor Turnley, from the cradle to three-score and ten; by himself, from diaries kept from early boyhood. With a brief glance backward three hundred and fifty years at progenitors and ancestral lineage. Chicago, Donohue & Henneberry, Printers, Binders and Engravers [1892]
5p.l. [9]–448p. plates, port. 20cm.
Trip through Salt Lake City in 1858, and an account of the rise of Mormonism.
CU–B, DLC, NjP, UPB

9058. Tutein Nolthenius, R. P. J. Nieuwe wereld [door] R. P. J. Tutein Nolthenius, indrukken en aanteekeningen tijdens eene reis door de Vereenigde Staten van Noord-Amerika. Haarlem, H. D. Tjeenk Willink & zoon, 1900.
vip., [1]l., 470p. illus., fold. map. 23cm.
Title in English: New World.
Includes section on Mormons under title: Zwervers. (De Mormonen).
DLC, NjP

9058a. Tuthill, Franklin. The history of California. San Francisco, H. H. Bancroft & Co., 1866.
xvi, 657p. 24cm.
Mormons, p. 214–215.
USlC

9059. Tuttle, Charles Richard. An illustrated history of the State of Iowa, being a complete civil, political, and military history of the state, from its first exploration down to 1875 . . . by Prof. Charles R. Tuttle . . . assisted by Daniel S. Durrie . . . Chicago, Richard S. Peale and Company, 1876.
2p.l. [7]–732p. illus., maps. 23½cm.
The Mormon movement and their settlements in Iowa and especially Pottowatomie County.
UHi, USlC

9060. Tuttle, Daniel Sylvester. . . . History of the missionary district of Utah and Idaho . . . [n.p., 1883?]
7p. illus. 24cm.
Caption-title.
At head of title: G. Domestic Missions. Protestant Episcopal Church in the United States of America.
Includes the murder of Dr. Robinson and other "historic" items.

Difficulty in converting Mormons. Stalwart and too fanatical; apostates gravitate to extremes.
CtY

9061. ———. Reminiscences of a missionary bishop, by the Right Rev. D. S. Tuttle. New York, Thomas Whittaker [c1906]
vii, 498p. 2 port. 21½cm.
The field — Utah . . . p. 101–117. "The Mormons" p. 304–357.
CSmH, CU-B, DLC, MiU, NjP, NN, UHi, USlC, UU, WaU

9061a. ———. . . . To the ministers of the - - - - - - - - Church in the United States: Dear Brethren . . . [Salt Lake City, 1881.]
[1]l. 26½cm.
At head of title: Salt Lake City, November - - -, 1881.
Signed: Daniel S. Tuttle, Bishop of Utah [and others]
Polemic against polygamy.
USlC

9062. Twelve modern apostles and their creeds, by Gilbert K. Chesterton, Bishop Charles L. Slattery, Dr. Henry Sloane Coffin, and others, with an introduction by the Rt. Rev. William Ralph Inge. New York, Duffield and Company, 1926.
5p.l., 3–209p. 21cm.
"Why I am a Mormon," by Reed Smoot.
CU, DLC, MB, NjP, OCl, OLaK, USlC, ViU

9063. Tyler, Daniel. A concise history of the Mormon Battalion in the Mexican war, 1846–47. By Sergeant Daniel Tyler. [Salt Lake City] 1881.
1p.l., viii [9]–376p. 22cm.
Howes T447
CSmH, CtY, CU-B, DLC, ICN, MH, MiU, NjP, NN, UHi, ULA, UPB, USl, USlC, UU, WHi

9064. Tyler, Robert M. Faith promoting incidents in the life of Robert M. Tyler. Compiled by Robert M. Tyler, May 1, 1926. [n.p.] 1926.
1p.l., 16p. port. 15cm.
Inspirational writings.
ULA, UPB, UU

9065. A typical scene of Mormon polygamy. A worn out woman finds refuge. Struggles for her children. Unfaithfulness, brutality and lying of her bestial husband. [Salt Lake City, Tribune Print., 1888]
Broadside. 28cm.
NjP

9066. Typographical Association of Deseret. Constitution and by-laws of the Typographical Association of Deseret, organized January 13, 1855. G.S.L. City: Printed at the Office of the Deseret News, 1855.
6p. 16cm.
Members must be Mormons in good standing.
USlC

9067. Tyson, Thomas. Joseph Smith, the American impostor; or, Mormonism proved to be false, by a fair examination of its history and pretensions, by Thomas Tyson (Late of Southan) Congregational Minister. London, Hall and Co., 1852.
1p.l. [3]–59p. 17cm.
"Mormonism, an attack on Christianity."
MH, USlC, UU

PROCLAMATION

BY THE GOVERNOR.

CITIZENS OF UTAH---

We are invaded by a hostile force who are evidently assailing us to accomplish our overthrow and destruction.

For the last twenty five years we have trusted officials of the Government, from Constables and Justices to Judges, Governors, and Presidents, only to be scorned, held in derision, insulted and betrayed. Our houses have been plundered and then burned, our fields laid waste, our principal men butchered while under the pledged faith of the government for their safety, and our families driven from their homes to find that shelter in the barren wilderness and that protection among hostile savages which were denied them in the boasted abodes of Christianity and civilization.

The Constitution of our common country guarantees unto us all that we do now or have ever claimed.

If the Constitutional rights which pertain unto us as American citizens were extended to Utah, according to the spirit and meaning thereof, and fairly and impartially administered, it is all that we could ask, all that we have ever asked.

Our opponents have availed themselves of prejudice existing against us because of our religious faith, to send out a formidable host to accomplish our destruction. We have had no privilege, no opportunity of defending ourselves from the false, foul, and unjust aspersions against us before the nation. The Government has not condescended to cause an investigating committee or other person to be sent to inquire into and ascertain the truth, as is customary in such cases.

We know those aspersions to be false, but that avails us nothing. We are condemned unheard and forced to an issue with an armed, mercenary mob, which has been sent against us at the instigation of anonymous letter writers ashamed to father the base slanderous falsehoods which they have given to the public; of corrupt officials who have brought false accusation against us to screen themselves in their own infamy; and of hireling priests and howling editors who prostitute the truth for filthy lucre's sake.

The issue which has been thus forced upon us compels us to resort to the great first law of self preservation and stand in our own defence, a right guaranteed unto us by the genius of the institutions of our country, and upon which the Government is based.

Our duty to ourselves, to our families, requires us not to tamely submit to be driven and slain, without an attempt to preserve ourselves. Our duty to our country, our holy religion, our God, to freedom and liberty, requires that we should not quietly stand still and see those fetters forging around, which are calculated to enslave and bring us in subjection to an unlawful military despotism such as can only emanate [in a country of Constitutional law] from usurpation, tyranny, and oppression.

This is, therefore,

1st:—To forbid, in the name of the People of the United States in the Territory of Utah, all armed forces, of every description, from coming into this Territory under any pretence whatever.

2d:—That all the forces in said Territory hold themselves in readiness to march, at a moment's notice, to repel any and all such threatened invasion.

3d:—Martial law is hereby declared to exist in this Territory, from and after the publication of this Proclamation; and no person shall be allowed to pass or repass into, or through, or from this Territory, without a permit from the proper officer.

Given under my hand and seal at Great Salt Lake City, Territory of Utah, this fifth day of August, A. D. eighteen hundred and fifty seven and of the Independence of the United States of America the eighty second.

BRIGHAM YOUNG.

UU

Item 9354. The first issue of Brigham Young's proclamation forbidding the Utah Expedition to enter the territory. The existence of this early version of the proclamation was not known until recently. Historians and Brigham Young's diary mention only the better-known proclamation dated September 15, 1857. The content of both is the same, and why this one dated August 5, 1857, was printed and not circulated remains a mystery. From the University of Utah collection.

9068. Udell, John. Incidents of travel to California, across the great plains; together with the return trips through Central America and Jamaica; to which are added sketches of the author's life. By John Udell. Jefferson, O., Printed for the author, at the Sentinel office, 1856.
viii [9]–302p., [1]l. port. 18cm.
Through Salt Lake City in 1850; with a description of Mormonism.
Howes U3, Sabin 97663, W–C281
CSmH, CtY, CU–B, DLC, ICN, IHi, MH, MiU, MoU, NjP, NN, NNC, WHi

9069. Udgorn Seion neu seren y saint; yn cynnwys egwyddorion 'Goruchwyliaeth cyflawn der yr amseroedd, 'mewn traethodau, llythyron, hanesion, prydyddiaeth, &c., Merthyr-Tydfil, Wales, John Davis, January, 1849–May 18, 1861.
14v. monthly, semi-monthly, weekly. 18cm.
Title in English: Trumpet of Zion, or, the Star of the Saints.
Successor to *Prophwyd y Jubili.*
Editors: John Davis and Dan Jones.
Monthly: January 1849–50; semi-monthly 1851; weekly after V. 3.
CSmH V.1; CU–B V.1–3; MH V.1–6, 8, 9; UPB V.1–7; USIC V.1–11; WHi V.1–3, 6

9070. Udvalget for Mormonmissionen: Til praesterne i den danske folkekirke! (Anmoding om ekonomisk hjaelp til "at evangeliet kan blive forkyndt af vor dansk-lutherske kirke blandt vore ca. 30,000 landsmaend i Utah") Kobenhavn, 1905.
4p.
Title in English: Chosen for a Mission among the Mormons.
Schmidt

9071. Uintah Academy. Annual catalogue. Vernal, Utah, 1908–1919.
v. 22cm.
Title varies: Annual announcement of the Uintah Stake Academy, 1908–1911; Annual catalogue, Uintah Academy, 1912–1918; Courses of Study, 1918.
USIC 1908–09, 1910–11, 1912–19

Ulstrup, S. J. *See Ustrup.*

9072. Underviisning om Mormonerne. Gudelige smaaskrifter, fjerde del. Kobenhavn, 1861.
80p. (No. 7)
Title in English: Advice regarding Mormons.
Schmidt

9073. Underwood, B. F. The kind of man Clark Braden is. [New York, Truth Seeker, n.d.]
26p. 19cm.
Clark Braden was one of the participants in a debate on Mormonism.
MoInRC

9074. Ungdommems Raadgiver. Copenhagen, Denmark, January 1, 1880–December 1, 1887.
8v. (768p.) monthly. 26cm.
Publication of the Danish Mission.
Editor of V.1: Andrew Jenson.
Title in English: The youth counselor.
UPB comp., USIC comp.

9075. Union Pacific Railroad Company. A complete and comprehensive description of the agricultural, stock raising and mineral resources of Utah.
2d ed. Chicago, 1888.
80p. 20cm.
Concerned chiefly with physical description of Utah, though there is some historical information.
Cover-title.
CSmH, CU–B

9076. ———. (same) 5th ed., rev. & enl. St. Louis, Woodward & Tiernan, 1892.
120p. 20cm.
DLC, USIC

9077. ———. (same) 6th ed., rev. & enl. St. Louis, Woodward & Tiernan Print. Co., 1893.
124p. 20cm.
CSmH, CU–B, NjP

9078. ———. (same) 7th ed. St. Louis, 1894.
124p. 21cm.
CU–B

9079. ———. Dedication of the Mormon Temple, Salt Lake City, Utah, April 6, 1893. Omaha, Union Pacific Railroad, 1893.
22 [2]p. illus., map. $13\frac{1}{2} \times 18\frac{1}{2}$cm.
UHi, UPB

9080. ———. A glimpse of Great Salt Lake, Utah . . . On the line of the Union Pacific system . . . [Chicago, Knight, Leonard and Co., Printers] 1893.
40p. illus., fold. map. 23cm.
Illustrated with original sketches by Alfred Lambourne.
Concerned chiefly with the lake.
DLC

9081. ———. (same) Chicago, 1894.
36 [4]p. illus., fold. map. 22cm.
UU

9082. ———. (same) [Omaha? Neb.] 1900.
36 [1]p. illus., fold. map. 22cm.
Fourth edition.
CU–B

UNION PACIFIC

9083. ———. The Golden Gate Special. Union Pacific Railway, Southern Pacific Company, Pullman's Palace Car Company, between Council Bluffs or Omaha and San Francisco. A Pullman vestibuled train. [Chicago, Rand McNally & Co., Printer, c1888]
[22]p. illus. 14×19cm.
Includes a brief description of the Mormon settlements along the route.
At head of title: The finest train in the world.
CU–B

9083a. ———. The great west. Union Pacific Railway guide. Chicago to Salt Lake. New York: American News Company, New York, Western News Company, Chicago, And for sale at the various News Depots. 1868.
9p.l., 33–66p. [10]l. 23½cm.
Section on Utah begins on p. 64; p. 66: The Mormon Church. Short inaccurate account of the Book of Mormon.
Preliminary leaves and those after text are advertisement.
UPB

9084. ———. Report of G. M. Dodge, Chief Engineer, with accompanying reports of chiefs of parties, for the year 1867. Washington, Govt. Print. Off., 1868.
85p. incl. tables. 23cm.
Includes reports of reconnaissances in Utah and Wyoming for areas north of those examined by Samuel Reed in 1864–1865, with occasional mention of the Mormons and their settlements.
At head of title: Union Pacific Railroad.
CU–B

9085. ———. Report of G. M. Dodge, Chief Engineer, with accompanying reports of chiefs of parties, for 1868–'69. Washington, Govt. Print. Off., 1870.
[2] 61p. 22cm.
Describes construction work east of Great Salt Lake and survey work in western Utah and eastern Nevada, with occasional references to the Mormons and their settlements.
At head of title: Union Pacific Railroad.
CU–B

9086. ———. Report of Samuel B. Reed, of surveys and explorations from Green River to Great Salt Lake City. [n.p., 1864?]
15p. incl. tables. 23cm.
Dated: Joliet, Illinois, Dec. 24, 1864.
Caption-title. Addressed to Thomas C. Durant, Vice-President, U.P.R.R.
Describes explorations for alternative routes as well as that finally adopted, between April and October, 1864; relations with and cooperation from "Governor Brigham Young."
At head of title: Union Pacific Railroad.
CU–B

9087. ———. Report of Thomas C. Durant, Vice-President and General Manager, to the Board of Directors, in relation to the operations of the engineer department, and the construction of the road, up to the close of the year 1865. New York, Wm. C. Bryant & Co., Printers, 41 Nassau St., Cor. Liberty. 1866.
[2] 19, 18, 23, 18, 64p. illus. 23½cm.
The appendices have individual pagination. Of particular interest are reports by Samuel B. Reed, Great Salt Lake City, Utah, June 21, 1865, August 2, 1865, November 1, 1865, April 1, 1866, concerning his reconnaissances in western Utah and eastern Nevada. The lithographic views illustrating this report, many of Utah subjects, have exceptional interest and quality.
At head of title: Union Pacific Railroad.
CU–B

9088. ———. The resources and attractions of Utah. Compliments of passenger department of the Union Pacific Railway. Omaha, 1888.
74p. 21cm.
NjP

9088a. ———. (same) Chicago, Rand, McNally & Co., 1889. 2nd ed. Rev. & enl.
80p. 20½cm.
Cover-title: Utah, a complete and comprehensive description . . .
USlC

9089. ———. Salt Lake City: where to go and what to see. Omaha [1910]
45p. illus., map. 18cm.
Brief mention of pioneer history.
DLC, UHi

9090. ———. Utah; sights and scenes in Utah for the tourist. Omaha, Neb. [c1888]
48p. illus., map. 21×10cm.
Tourist information with information on the Mormons, their customs, etc.
ICN, UU

9091. ———. (same) 2d ed. Chicago, c1890.
54p. 21×10cm.
CSmH, DLC

9092. ———. (same) 3d ed. Chicago, c1891.
54p. 21½×10cm.
USlC

9093. ———. (same, under title) Sights and scenes in Utah for tourists. Compliments of the Passenger Department, Union Pacific System. 2d ed. Omaha, Neb. [c1900]
54p. 21×9cm.
Title on cover: Utah; sights and scenes for the tourist.
ICN

UNITED IRRIGATION

9094. United Irrigation District. Glenwood, Alberta, Canada. A few facts and statements about the United Irrigation District . . . Alberta [Canada] Cardston News Print. [n.d.]
14p. 14cm.
A Mormon sponsored project.
UPB

9095. United Society of Christian Endeavor. The story of the Denver convention, being the official report of the twenty-first International Christian Endeavor Convention held in tent endeavor and many churches, Denver, Colo., July 9–13, 1903. Boston, c1903.
3p.l., 7–187p. plates. 23cm.
"The Mormon Question," p. 146–147.
Rev. T. C. Smith speaks against Mormonism.
UPB

9096. U. S. Attorney General. Annual report of the Attorney General of the United States for the year 1890. Washington, Govt. Print. Off., 1890.
xxii, 261p. 23½cm. (U.S. 51st Cong. 2d Sess. House. Ex. Doc. No. 7)
"Exhibit Q. Report of the attorney of the U.S. for the District of Utah upon the status of the Mormon Church litigations."
CU, NjP, ULA, UPB

9097. ———. Convictions for polygamy in Utah and Idaho. Letter from the acting Attorney-General. In reply to the resolutions of the House in relation to convictions for polygamy in Utah and Idaho. Sept. 13, 1888. [Washington, Govt. Print. Off., 1888]
11p. 22cm. (U.S. 50th Cong. 1st Sess. House. Ex. Doc. No. 447)
Lists of those convicted and those pardoned.
NjP, ULA, UPB, USlC

9098. ———. The Late Corporation of the Church of Jesus Christ of Latter-day Saints and others, Appellants, vs. The United States. No. 1423. Brief for the United States. [Washington, 1888?]
73p. 21cm.
At head of title: In the Supreme Court of the United States. October Term. 1888.
Signed: A. H. Garland, Attorney-General, G. A. Jenks, Solicitor-General.
ULA, USlC

9099. ———. . . . Letter from the Attorney-General, transmitting, in response to Senate resolution of December 10, 1888, a statement relative to the execution of the law against bigamy. [Washington, Govt. Print. Off.] 1888.
65p. 23cm. (U.S. 50th Cong. 2d Sess. Senate. Ex. Doc. No. 21)
DLC, NjP, UPB

9100. U. S. Bureau of Education. Educational work of the churches in 1916–1918. [Advance sheets from the Biennial Survey of Education, 1916–1918] Washington, Govt. Print. Off., 1919.
53p. 23½cm. (Bulletin. 1919. No. 10)
Latter-day Saints' schools, by Horace H. Cummings, p. 40–44.
NjP, ULA, UPB

9101. ———. Report of the Commissioner of Education for the year ended June 30, 1913. Washington, Govt. Print. Off., 1914.
2v. 24cm.
"The schools of the Mormon church," by Osborne J. P. Widtsoe. V.1, p. 409–413.
ULA, UPB

9101a. U.S. Bureau of Ethnology. Fourteenth annual report of the Bureau of Ethnology to the Secretary of the Smithsonian Institution. 1892–93 by J. W. Powell, Director. Pt. 2. Washington, Govt. Print. Off., 1896.
792–793p. 28½cm. (U.S. 54th Cong. 2d Sess. House. Doc. No. 230, Pt. 2)
Appendix: The Mormons and the Indians.
DLC, UPB

9102. U.S. Bureau of the Census. Census of religious bodies: 1926. Latter-day Saints. Statistics, denominational history, doctrine, and organization. Consolidated report . . . Church of Jesus Christ of Latter-day Saints . . . Washington, Govt. Print. Off., 1929.
27p. incl. tables. 23cm.
Also included in: Census Bureau. Religious bodies, 1926, V.2, Separate denominations, p. 665–687; published in the 1906 and the 1916 *Census of religious bodies*.
CU, DLC, NjP, ULA, UPB

9103. ———. Report on statistics of churches in the United States at the 11th Census: 1890. Washington, Govt. Print. Off., 1895.
xxvii, 812p. 10 maps, 4 diag., charts. 30cm. (U.S. 52nd Cong. 1st Sess. House. Misc. Doc. No. 340, pt. 17)
Church of Jesus Christ of Latter-day Saints, p. 422–425. Information on history and doctrine.
ULA, UPB

9104. ———. Report on the social statistics of cities, compiled by George E. Waring, Jr., expert and special agent . . . Part II. The Southern and Western States. [Washington, Govt. Print. Off.] 1883.
915p. charts, 1 map. 30cm. (U.S. 47th Cong. 2d Sess. House. Misc. Doc. No. 42. Vol. 19, pt. 2)
Historical sketch of Salt Lake City, p. 829–835. 1 map.
NjP, ULA, UPB

U. S. CONGRESS. HOUSE

9105. U.S. Circuit Court (8th Circuit). . . . Decision of John F. Philips, judge, in Temple Lot case. The Reorganized Church of Jesus Christ of Latter Day Saints versus the Church of Christ, et al. Lamoni, Ia., Reorganized Church of Jesus Christ of Latter Day Saints, 1894.
iv [5]–28p. 25cm.
Decision in favor of the complainant.
CSmH, CtY, CU-B, DLC, MoInRC, NN, USlC, WHi

9106. ———. (same) Lamoni, Ia., Published by the Reorganized Church of Jesus Christ of Latter Day Saints [1894]
48p. 19cm.
At head of title: In the circuit court of the United States for the western division of the western district of Missouri.
CU-B, NjP, UHi, UPB, USlC

9107. ———. (same) Lamoni, Ia., Published by the Reorganized Church of Jesus Christ of Latter Day Saints, 1913.
48p. 19½cm.
MoInRC, MoK

9107a. U.S. Commissioner of Indian Affairs. Annual report of the Commissioner of Indian Affairs, transmitted with the message of the President, at the opening of the first session of the thirtieth Congress, 1847 . . . . 1848. Washington, Wendell and Van Benthuysen, Printers, 1848.
220p. tables. 21½cm.
In tan printed wrappers.
Notes problems between the Mormons and Indians, due to the Mormons remaining after the first winter, p. 140–141.
UPB

9108. U.S. Congress. Congressional Record. Containing the proceedings and debates of Congress. (Formerly Congressional Globe and Annals of Congress) Washington, 1833–.
v. 30cm.
Debates, bills, petitions, and speeches concerning Mormonism throughout the Utah Territorial, and Reed Smoot hearings.
CU, CU-B, DLC, NjP, ULA, UPB, UU

———. The Edmunds-Tucker Law. *See Edmunds-Tucker law.*

9109. ———. . . . Joint resolution proposing amendments to the Constitution disqualifying polygamists for election as Senators and Representatives in Congress, and prohibiting polygamy and polygamous association of cohabitation between the sexes. [Washington] 1899.
3p. 23cm. (U.S. 56th Cong. 1st Sess.)
NjP, NN

9110. ———. [Public — No. 183.] An act to amend an act entitled "An act to amend section fifty-three hundred and fifty-two of the Revised Statutes of the United States, in reference to bigamy, and for other purposes," approved March twenty-second, eighteen hundred and eighty-two. [Washington? 1887?]
7p. 23cm.
USlC

9111. U.S. Congress. House of Representatives. H.J. Res. 112. In the House of Representatives. January 8, 1900 . . . Joint resolution, proposing an amendment to the Constitution to disqualify persons found guilty of polygamy or polygamous cohabitation from holding office. [Washington, 1900]
2p. 24cm. (U.S. 56th Cong. 1st Sess. House.)
NjP, NN, ULA

9112 ———. H.J. Res. 93. In the House of Representatives. December 20, 1899 . . . Joint resolution. Proposing an amendment to the Constitution of the United States prohibiting polygamy. [Washington, 1899]
2p. 24cm. (U.S. 56th Cong. 1st Sess. House.)
NjP, NN

9113. ———. H. J. Resolution 69. In the House of Representatives. Dec. 11, 1899. Joint resolution. Proposing an amendment to the Constitution of the United States prohibiting polygamy and polygamous cohabitation within the bounds of a state or territory of the United States. [Washington, 1899]
[2]p. 24cm. (U.S. 56th Cong. 1st Sess. House.)
NjP, NN

9113a. ———. H.R. 9265 [Report No. 1811]. In the House of Representatives, April 11, 1890. Read twice . . . April 29, 1890. Reported with amendments . . . Mr. Struble introduced the following bill: A bill to amend the act of Congress of March third, eighteen hundred and eighty-seven, entitled "An act to amend an act entitled 'An act to amend section fifty-three hundred and fifty-two of the Revised Statutes of the United States in reference to bigamy . . .' " [Washington, 1890]
5p. 27½cm. (U.S. 51st Cong. 1st Sess. House.)
USlC

9113b. ———. H. Res. 50. In the House of Representatives. December 11, 1883. Read twice, referred to the Committee on the Judiciary, and ordered to be printed. Mr. Rosecrans introduced the following joint resolution: Joint Resolution proposing an amendment to the Constitution of the United States prohibiting polygamy. [Washington, 1883]
2p. 28cm. (U.S. 48th Cong. 1st Sess. House. Printer's no. 1139)
USlC

U. S. CONGRESS. HOUSE. COMMITTEE...E

9114. U.S. Congress. House. Committee on Election of President, Vice President, and Representatives in Congress. Disqualifying polygamists for election as senators, etc.... Report: [To accompany H. J. Res. 1. Washington] Feb. 16, 1900.
17p. 23cm. (U.S. 56th Cong. 1st Sess. House. Report. No. 348)
Proposing amendments to the constitution disqualifying polygamists for election to public office.
NjP, NN, ULA, UPB

9115. U.S. Congress. House. Committee on Elections. ... Almon W. Babbitt, delegate from Deseret. April 4, 1850 ... Mr. Strong, from the Committee of Elections, made the following report: The Committee of Elections, to whom were referred the credentials of Almon W. Babbitt, esq., and his memorial praying to be admitted to a seat in the House of Representatives as a delegate from the provisional State of Deseret.... [Washington, Govt. Print. Off.] 1850.
16p. 22cm. (U.S. 31st Cong. 1st Sess. House. Report. No. 219)
NjP, NN, UHi, ULA, UPB

9116. ———. Cannon vs. Campbell. Testimony and papers in the contested election case of Geo. Q. Cannon vs. Allen G. Campbell, from the Territory of Utah. [Washington, Govt. Print. Off.] 1882.
75, 10p. 23cm. (U.S. 47th Cong. 1st Sess. House. Misc. Doc. No. 25, pt. 1, 2)
Testimony in case of George Q. Cannon vs. Allen G. Campbell, with references to polygamy and conditions in Utah.
CU, MH, NjP, ULA

9116a. ———. George R. Maxwell vs. George Q. Cannon — contested election, Territory of Utah ... [Washington, Govt. Print. Off.] 1874.
15p. 23cm. (U.S. 43d Cong. 1st Sess. House. Report. No. 484)
UHi, UPB

9117. ———. McGrorty vs. Hooper. Report of the Committee of Elections upon the contested election case of McGrorty vs. Hooper, sitting delegate from the Territory of Utah, referred to the Committee of Elections, First session, 40th Congress, 1868. [Washington, Govt. Print. Off.] 1868.
81p. 23½cm. (U.S. 40th Cong. 2d Sess. House. Report. No. 79)
NjP, NN, ULA, USlC

9118. ———. Pay and mileage allowed George Q. Cannon ... Report: [Washington, Govt. Print. Off.] 1882.
4p. 23cm. (U.S. 47th Cong. 1st Sess. House. Report. No. 1411)
Allowance for George Q. Cannon as delegate from Utah. Minority and majority report.
NjP, ULA, UPB

9119. ———. ... Report: In the matter of the contest of George Q. Cannon against Allen G. Campbell, Territory of Utah. Washington, Govt. Print. Off., 1882.
66p. 23cm. (U.S. 47th Cong. 1st Sess. House. Report. No. 559)
George Q. Cannon vs. Allen G. Campbell, majority and minority reports. Extensive considerations of Mormons, particularly in light of polygamy.
MH, NjP, ULA, UPB

9120. U.S. Congress. House. Committee on Post-Roads and Post Office. ... Resolution: [Washington, 1900]
2p. 24cm. (U.S. 56th Cong. 1st Sess. House. Res. 25)
Resolution to remove a postmaster (John C. Graham) from office in Provo because of suspected polygamy.
NjP, NN, ULA

———. *See also U.S. Congress. House. Committee on the Post-Office and Post-Roads.*

9121. U.S. Congress. House. Committee on Roads. The old Oregon trail. Hearings before the Committee on Roads, House of Representatives, Sixty-eighth Congress, Second session on H.J. Res. 232, H.J. Res. 328 and S. 2053. January 23, February 13, 19, and 21, 1925 ... Washington, Govt. Print. Off., 1925.
1p.l., 205p. 24cm.
Hon. E. O. Leatherwood of Utah presents testimony on the Mormon Trail.
By himself and Don B. Colton. Also includes a reprint from the *Historical Record*, Vol. 9, January, 1890.
CU, DLC, NjP, ULA, UPB

9122. U.S. Congress. House. Committee on the Judiciary. Bigamy ... views of the minority. [Washington, Govt. Print. Off.] 1886.
7p. 23cm. (U.S. 49th Cong. 1st Sess. House. Report. No. 2735, pt. 2)
To accompany S. Bill 10.
CU–B, NjP, NN, UHi, ULA, UPB, USlC

9123. ———. Church of Jesus Christ of Latter-Day Saints ... Report: [To accompany H. Res. 96. Washington] Feb. 25, 1896.
[1]p. 23cm. (U.S. 54th Cong. 1st Sess. House. Report. No. 519)
Report from the Committee on the Judiciary, amending joint resolution 96, providing for restoration of property of Church of Jesus Christ of Latter-day Saints, taken under Edmunds Act.
NjP, ULA, UPB

9124. ———. Hearing before the Committee on the Judiciary on the proposed amendment to the Constitution of the United States prohibiting polygamy. Statement of Rev. William R. Campbell. [Washington] 1900.
15p. 18cm.
NN

9125. ———. Industrial Home, Salt Lake City, Utah . . . Report: [To accompany H.R. 7935. Washington] May 2, 1898.
[2]p. 23½cm. (U.S. 55th Cong. 2d Sess. House. Report. No. 1247)
Report from the Committee on the Judiciary, favoring H. 7935, to grant the State of Utah an Industrial Christian Home in Salt Lake City.
NjP, ULA, UPB

9126. ———. J. and R. H. Porter. Report (to Accompany bill S. 905) The Committee on the Judiciary . . . for relief of J. and R. H. Porter. [Washington, 1882]
20p. 22½cm.
Redress for wagons destroyed during the Utah Expedition.
NjP, ULA, USlC

9127. ———. Polygamy [Hearing, February 25, 1902. Washington, Govt. Print. Off., 1914]
16p. 23cm.
Caption-title.
DLC

9128. ———. Polygamy in the territories of the United States [to accompany Bill H.R. no. 7] . . . Report. The Committee on the Judiciary, to whom was referred "a bill to punish and prevent the practice of polygamy in the territories of the United States, and other places, and disapproving and annulling certain acts of the legislative assembly of the Territory of Utah," having had the same under consideration, report as follows: [Washington, Thomas H. Ford] 1860.
5p. 23cm. (U.S. 36th Cong. 1st Sess. House. Report. No. 83)
NjP, NN, ULA, UPB

9129. ———. Prohibiting polygamy . . . Report: [To accompany H. Report 116. Washington, Govt. Print. Off.] 1888.
2p. 23cm. (U.S. 50th Cong. 1st Sess. House. Report. No. 553)
Recommending an amendment to the Constitution of the United States prohibiting polygamy.
NjP, ULA, UPB

9130. ———. Proposed legislation for Utah Territory. [Washington, 1886]
282p. 23cm.
Caption-title.
CU-B, MH, UPB, USlC

9130a. ———. Proposed legislation for Utah. Arguments against the New Edmunds Bill, being Senate Bill No. 10 . . . made by Hon. George S. Boutwell, Hon. Jeff. Chandler, Hon. F. S. Richards, A. M. Gibson, Hon. Joseph A. West, and Hon. John T. Caine, before the Committee on the Judiciary of the U.S. House of Representatives, First session, Forty-ninth Congress. Washington, Government Print. Off., 1886.
17–255, ivp. 23cm.
UPB

9131. ———. . . . Report: [To accompany bill S. 905] The Committee on the Judiciary, to whom was referred the bill (S. 905) for the relief of J. and R. H. Porter, having had the same under consideration, would respectfully report: [Washington, Govt. Print. Off.] 1882.
22p. 23cm. (U.S. 47th Cong. 1st Sess. House. Report. No. 1637)
Pertinent information on the Utah Expedition, 1857.
NjP, ULA, UPB

9132. ———. . . . Report: [To accompany H. Res. 176] The Committee on the Judiciary to whom have been referred House resolutions 16, 50, 140 and 143, for the amendment of the Constitution of the United States, beg leave to report: [Washington, Govt. Print. Off.] 1886.
12p. 23cm. (U.S. 49th Cong. 1st Sess. House. Report. No. 2568)
Extensive treatment of polygamy.
NjP, ULA, UPB

9133. ———. Section 5352 of the revised statutes . . . Report: [To accompany S. 4047] Sept. 26, 1890. [Washington, Govt. Print. Off., 1891]
2p. 23cm. (U.S. 51st Cong. 1st Sess. House. Report. No. 3200)
Personal property of the Church was to be placed in the hands of a receiver, recommendation that it be turned into the public school fund.
NjP, ULA, UPB

9134. ———. Suppression of polygamy in Utah . . . Report: [Washington, Govt. Print. Off.] 1886.
10p. 23cm. (U.S. 49th Cong. 1st Sess. House. Report. No. 2735)
To accompany bill S. 10.
ICN, NjP, NN, ULA, UPB, USl

9135. ———. To prevent persons living in bigamy or polygamy from holding any civil office of trust or profit in any of the Territories of the United States, and from being delegates in Congress . . . Report: [To accompany bill H. R. 4436. Washington, Govt. Print. Off.] 1882.
[1]p. 23cm. (U.S. 47th Cong. 1st Sess. House. Report. No. 386)
NjP, ULA, UPB

9136. ———. Utah . . . Report of the Committee on the Judiciary, to whom was referred the memorial of the legislative assembly of the Territory of Utah, praying for the repeal of "An act to prevent and punish the practice of polygamy in the Territories of the United States." [Washington, Govt. Print. Off.] 1867.
4p. 21½cm. (U.S. 39th Cong. 2d Sess. House. Report. No. 27)
NjP, NN, ULA

9137. U.S. Congress. House. Committee on the Post-Office and Post-Roads. John C. Graham and Orson Smith . . . [Washington, 1900]
4p. 22½cm. (U.S. 56th Cong. 1st Sess. House. Report. No. 611)
Investigation to see if these postmasters are polygamists.
NjP, NN, ULA

9138. U.S. Congress. House. Committee on the Territories. Admission of Idaho into the Union. [Washington, 1890?]
52p. 23cm. (U.S. 51st Cong. 1st Sess. House. Report. No. 1064)
Includes 16p. Views of the minority. Polygamy a reason to restrict its admission.
CtY, NjP, ULA, UU

9139. ———. Admission of Idaho into the Union. [Washington, 1890?]
52p. 23cm. (U.S. 51st Cong. 1st Sess. House. Report. No. 1064)
Includes information on polygamy.
NjP, ULA, UU

9140. ———. Admission of Idaho into the Union. Mr. Mansur submitted the following as the views of the minority! On the bill (H.R. 4562) "To provide for the admission into the Union of the State of Idaho and for other purposes." [Washington, 1890?]
16p. 21½cm.
Caption-title.
CtY, ULA, USIC

9141. ———. Admission of the State of Utah . . . [Washington, Govt. Print. Off.] 1889.
295p. 23cm. (U.S. 50th Cong. 2d Sess. House. Report. No. 4156)
CtY, CU–B, NjP, NN, ULA, UPB, USIC

9142. ———. Admission of Utah . . . [Washington, 1893]
20p. 22cm. (U.S. 53rd Cong. 2d Sess. House. Report. No. 2337)
Caption-title.
NjP, ULA, USIC

9143. ———. The admission of Utah. Arguments in favor of the Admission of Utah as a State, made before the House Committee on Territories. Second Session, Fiftieth Congress. January 12–22, 1889. Washington, Govt. Print. Off., 1889.
92p. 22cm.
CU–B, ULA, USIC

9144. ———. Admission of Utah. Report of the Committee on Territories on the Admission of Utah as a state, to the House of Representatives, Second Session, Fiftieth Congress. Washington, Govt. Print. Off., 1889.
12p. 22½cm.
MH, NjP, UPB, USIC

9145. ———. Admission of Utah . . . Report [to accompany H.R. 10190. Washington, Govt. Print. Off.] 1893.
21p. 23cm. (U.S. 52d Cong. 2d Sess. House. Report. No. 2337)
Caption-title.
Admission of Utah into the Union recommended. Considerable information on the character of the Mormons and the situation in Utah with respect to polygamy.
CU–B, NjP, ULA, UPB

9146. ———. Admission of Utah . . . Report: [To accompany H.R. 352. Washington, Govt. Print. Off.] 1893.
24, 15p. charts. 23cm. (U.S. 53rd Cong. 1st Sess. House. Report. No. 162, pt. 1 and 2)
Part 2 . . . views of minority . . . Both parts have extensive material on polygamy, etc.
NjP, ULA, UPB

9147. ———. Amendment to section 5352, Revised Statutes . . . Report: [To accompany H.R. 9264.] April 29, 1898. [Washington, Govt. Print. Off., 1891]
28p. 23cm. (U.S. 51st Cong. 1st Sess. House. Report. No. 1811)
Amendment of the Revised Statutes to suppress polygamy, recommended. Mormons have perverted the purpose of the oath for intended voters.
Appendix A. Samuel D. Davis (appellant) vs. H. G. Beason (sheriff). Extensive material on decision to ban polygamy.
Appendix B. Extract of Utah Commission Report, 1887. Extensive material on Mormons and the Utah situation.
NjP, USIC, ULA, UU

9148. ———. Anti-Mormon test oath. Arguments of Hon. J. M. Wilson, Hon. A. B. Carlton and Bishop William Budge in opposition to the constitution of the proposed state of Idaho adopted at Boise City, August 6, 1889, made before the Committee on the Territories of the House of Representatives, January 21, and February 8, 1890. Washington, Govt. Print. Off., 1890.
41p. 22½cm.
USIC

9149. ———. . . . The condition of Utah . . . Mr. James M. Ashley, from the Committee on Territories, made the following report. The Committee on the Territories to whom were referred the subjointed resolutions, have had the subject matter therein named under consideration, and herewith submit the testimony of such witnesses as they have been able to bring before them. [Washington, Govt. Print. Off.] 1866.
29p. 23cm. (U.S. 39th Cong. 1st Sess. House. Report. No. 96)
The Mormons and polygamy.
CU, CU–B, DLC, NjP, ULA, UPB

9150. ———. Elective franchise in Utah . . . Report: [To accompany bill H.R. 2078. Washington, Govt. Print. Off.] 1878.

[2]p. 23½cm. (U.S. 45th Cong. 2d Sess. House. Report. No. 949)

Favorable to the passage of a bill to regulate the elective franchise in Utah. Some comments on problem of polygamy in Utah.

CU, CU-B, NjP, ULA, UPB

9151. ———. Execution of the laws in Utah (to accompany bill H.R. 1089) [Washington, Govt. Print. Off.] 1870.

19, 15, 8p. 23cm. (U.S. 41st Cong. 2d Sess. House. Report. No. 21, pt. 1–3)

Polygamy laws. Parts 2–3, additional text.

CU, CU-B, NjP, ULA, UPB, USIC

9152. ———. Hearings before the Committee on Territories in regard to the admission of Utah as a state. Washington, Govt. Print. Off., 1889.

215p. 23cm.

CU-B, DLC, ICN, MH, USIC

9153. ———. Local government for the Territory of Utah . . . Report: [To accompany H.R. 7690. Washington, Govt. Print. Off.] 1892.

28p. 23cm. (U.S. 52d Cong. 1st Sess. House. Report. No. 943)

Considerable on polygamy and Mormons.

NjP, ULA, UPB

9154. ———. Local government for Utah. Arguments by the delegation from Utah, made before the House Committee on the Territories, First session, Fifty-second Congress, in favor of the passage of H.R. 524. "A bill for the local government of Utah . . ." Washington, Govt. Print. Off., 1892.

71p. 21cm.

UPB

9155. ———. Marriages in Territory of Utah. Report: [To accompany bill H.R. 6765] The Committee on the Territories, to whom was referred the bill (H.R. 946) to provide for the governing of the Territory of Utah by a commission, submit the following: [Washington, Govt. Print. Off.] 1884.

4p. 23cm. (U.S. 48th Cong. 1st Sess. House. Report. No. 1351, pt. 1)

Provisions for solemnizing marriages in Utah recommended. Extensive coverage on marriages and polygamy in Utah.

CU, CU-B, NjP, ULA, UPB

9156. ———. Notes of a hearing before the Committee on Territories of the House of Representatives on Bill (H.R. 524) "For the local Government of Utah Territory and to provide for the election of certain officers in said Territories." [Washington, Govt. Print. Off., 1892]

97p. 22½cm.

Caption-title.

Mormons and politics.

MH, USIC

9157. ———. Notes of a hearing before the Committee on Territories of the House of Representatives on Bill (H.R. 524) for the local government of Utah Territory and to provide for the election of certain officers in said territories." Washington, 1892.

104p. 21cm.

Hearings after the manifesto.

USIC

9158. ———. Proposed additional legislation for Utah Territory . . . Washington, 1886.

282p. 22½cm.

Proceedings of investigations into polygamy in Utah. Extensive information on the institution and the situation in Utah.

USIC

9159. ———. Reorganization of the Legislative Power of Utah Territory. Views of the minority [To accompany bill H.R. 6765.] The minority of the Committee on the Territories, to whom was referred the bill (H.R. 946) to reorganize the legislative power of Utah Territory, having leave from the House to express its views, respectfully submit the following: [Washington, Govt. Print. Off.] 1884.

57p. 23cm. (U.S. 48th Cong. 1st Sess. House. Report. No. 1351, pt. 2)

CU, CU-B, NjP, ULA, USIC

9160. ———. . . . Report. The Committee on Territories, to whom was referred the petition of numerous citizens of the United States residing in the Territory of Utah, asking for the creation of a new Territory, to be formed from the western portion thereof, have, according to order, had the same under consideration, and respectfully submit the following report: [Washington, James B. Steedman] 1858.

5p. 23½cm. (U.S. 35th Cong. 1st Sess. House. Report. No. 375)

Power and authority in the hands of Mormons, who monopolize lands, and exert a baneful influence over the Indians, injurious to the United States. Committee reports in favor of forming a new Territory, to be called Nevada.

CU, CU-B, NjP, ULA, UPB

9160a. ———. True condition of Utah. Arguments by delegations from Utah, made before the House Committee on Territories, first session fifty-second Congress, in favor of the passage of the pending bills providing for statehood or home rule for the Territory of Utah [H.R. 524 and H.R. 4008]. Washington, Government Printing Office, 1892.

71p. 23cm.

USIC

9161. ———. Utah and the Mormons; investigation by the United States Congress. [Liverpool? 1890?]

4p. 21cm.

At end: "Searchers after the truth can receive further information from Joseph Leaing, an Elder of the Church of Jesus Christ of Latter-day Saints . . ."

Variant printing. USIC

DLC, USIC

9162. U.S. Congress. House. Committee on War Claims. James Bridger. Report: [To accompany S. 1198.] The Committee on War Claims, to whom was referred the bill (S. 1198) for the relief of the heirs of James Bridger, deceased, submit the following report: [Washington, Govt. Print. Off.] 1892.
24p. 22½cm. (U.S. 52d Cong. 1st Sess. House. Report. No. 1576)
Claims resulting from the distruction of Fort Bridger due to the Utah Expedition.
DLC, UPB

9163. U.S. Congress. House. Special Committee on the case of Brigham H. Roberts. Case of Brigham H. Roberts, of Utah . . . Report [to accompany H. Res. 107] Jan. 20, 1900. [Washington, Govt. Print. Off.] 1900.
77p. 23cm. (U.S. 56th Cong. 1st Sess. House. Report. No. 85, pt. 1, 2)
Second part: "Views of minority," p. 53–77.
NjP, NN, ULA, UPB, UU

9164. ———. Report of the Special Committee on the Case of Brigham H. Roberts of Utah, being report No. 85. 56th Congress, 1st session. Reprinted for the use of the Special Committee appointed under authority of H. R. No. 6, concerning the right of Victor L. Berger to be sworn in as a member of the 66th Congress. Washington, Govt. Print. Off., 1919.
83p. 23½cm.
CU–B, DLC

9165. U.S. Congress. House. Special Committee to Investigate the Eligibility of Brigham H. Roberts, of Utah, to a seat in the House of Representatives. Election case of Brigham H. Roberts, of Utah. [Washington, Govt. Print. Off., 1900?]
245p. 23cm.
Caption-title.
Contains: Election case of B. H. Roberts; Case of B. H. Roberts . . . Report; Speeches of Hon. Robert W. Taylor, Hon. Charles E. Littlefield, Hon. R. H. Freer, and Hon. Samuel W. T. Lanham.
CU–B, NN, UHi

9166. ———. Election case of Brigham H. Roberts, of Utah. Statement of Mr. Roberts before the Committee January 5 and 6, 1900. [Washington, 1900]
1p.l., 173–239p. 21cm.
Reprint of section of the longer report.
USIC

9166a. U.S. Congress. Senate. S.10. In the Senate of the United States. January 13, 1887 . . . An act to amend an act entitled "An act to amend section fifty-three hundred and fifty-two of the Revised Statutes of the United States, in reference to bigamy, and for other purposes," approved March twenty-second, eighteen hundred and eighty-two. [Washington, 1887]
33p. 28cm. (U.S. 49th Cong. 2nd Sess. Senate)
DLC, USIC

9166b. ———. S. 68. In the Senate of the United States December 4, 1883. Mr. Lapham . . . obtained leave to bring in the following bill; which was read twice and referred to the Committee on the Judiciary. A bill to amend the act establishing a Territorial government for Utah, and to change the name to Altamont. [Washington, 1883]
12p. 28cm. (U.S. 48th Cong. 1st Sess. Senate)
Includes a discussion of polygamy.
USIC

9166c. ———. S. 2263. In the Senate of the United States. February 17, 1892. Mr. Paddock introduced the following bill; which was read twice and referred to the Committee on Territories. A bill to amend an act entitled "An act to amend section fifty-three hundred and fifty-two of the Revised Statutes of the United States, in reference to bigamy, and for other purposes." [Washington, 1892]
[1]p. 28cm. (U.S. 52nd Cong. 1st Sess. Senate)
USIC

9167. U.S. Congress. Senate. Committee on Claims. . . . Report: [To accompany S. 3863. Washington, Govt. Print. Off.] 1893.
5p. 23cm. (U.S. 52d Cong. 2d Sess. Senate. Report. No. 1295)
Recommends the refunding to George A. Cannon of forfeited bail.
NjP, UU

9168. U.S. Congress. Senate. Committee on Education and Labor. Notes of a hearing before the Committee on Education and Labor, United States Senate, May 7, 1886, on the proposed establishment of a school under the direction of the Industrial Christian Home Association of Utah. [Washington, 1886]
44p. 23cm.
Caption-title: Industrial school in Utah.
Largely written by Angie F. Newman.
CU, CU–B, NjP, ULA, UU

9169. ———. . . . Report: [To accompany amendment by Mr. Blair to the sundry civil appropriation bill] June 5, 1886. Washington, Govt. Print. Off., 1886.
46p. 23cm. (U.S. 49th Cong. 1st Sess. Senate. Report. No. 1279)
Appropriation in aid of the Industrial Christian Home Association of Utah, recommended with notes of hearing before committee (including material on the polygamy situation in Utah)
CU, CU–B, NjP, ULA, UPB

9170. U.S. Congress. Senate. Committee on Privileges and Elections. Contents of testimony taken before the Committee on Privileges and Elections of the United States Senate in the matter of the protests against the right of Hon. Reed Smoot a Senator from the State of Utah, to hold his seat . . . Comp. for Mr. Smoot. Washington, Judd & Detweiler [1906?]
iii, 149p. 23cm.
Cover-title.
UHi, ULA, UPB

9171. ———. Extracts from proceedings before the Committee on Privileges and Elections of the United States Senate in the matter of the protests against the right of Hon. Reed Smoot, a Senator from the State of Utah, to hold his Seat. Testimony taken during the months of January, February and March, 1904. New York, The Interdenominational Council of Women for Christian and Patriotic Service [1904?]
[9]p. 20cm.
USIC

9172. ———. In re Reed Smoot . . . Washington, Govt. Print. Off., 1906.
32, 44p. 22cm. (U.S. 59th Cong. 1st Sess. Senate. Report. No. 4253, pt. 1, 2)
Pt. 1: Reed Smoot. Pt. 2: Views of the minority.
Investigating the right of Reed Smoot to hold seat as a Senator from Utah.
NjP, ULA, UPB

9172a. ———. In the matter of the protests against the right of Hon. Reed Smoot, a Senator from the State of Utah, to hold his seat. Arguments of A. S. Worthington and Waldemar Van Cott, on behalf of the respondent. Washington, Government Printing Office, 1905.
164p. 23cm.
DLC, USIC

9173. ———. Proceedings before the Committee on privileges and elections of the United States Senate in the matter of the protests against the right of Hon. Reed Smoot, a Senator from the State of Utah, to hold his seat . . . [January 16, 1904–April 13, 1906] Washington, Govt. Print. Off., 1904–06.
4v. 23cm. (U.S. 59th Cong. 1st Sess. Senate. Report. No. 486)
Submitted by Mr. Burrows with Views of the minority, submitted by Mr. Foraker in V.4, p. 467–542.
Contents of testimony taken before the Committee on Privileges and Elections of the United States Senate in the matter of the protests against the right of Hon. Reed Smoot, a senator from the State of Utah to hold his seat. Classified into eighteen subdivisions and indexed as to witnesses. Compiled by Mr. Smoot.
1p.l., iii, 149p. 22½cm.
CU–B, NjP, NN, UHi, ULA, UPB, USIC, UU

9174. ———. The protests against the right Hon. Reed Smoot, a Senator from the State of Utah, to hold his seat. Testimony taken during the months of January, February, and March, 1904. [New York, The Willett Press, 1904]
[6]l. 21cm.
NN, ULA

9175. ———. Testimony of important witnesses as given in the proceedings before the Committee on Privileges and Elections of the United States Senate. Issued by U.S. Congress, Senate Committee on Privileges and Elections. Salt Lake City, Salt Lake Tribune Printing Company, 1905.
255p. 22½cm.
Cover-title reads: "Testimony of President Joseph F. Smith of the Mormon church and Senator Reed Smoot." 1903.
MH, MoInRC, UHi, USIC

9176. U.S. Congress. Senate. Committee on Territories. Admission of Idaho, Committee on Territories, January 21, 1890. [Washington? Government Printing Office? 1890?]
82p. 23cm.
Polygamy in Idaho.
DLC, UPB, USIC

9176a. ———. The Admission of Utah. Arguments in favor of the admission of Utah as a state. Made before the Committee on Territories of the United States Senate, First Session, Fiftieth Congress. Saturday, February 18, 1888. Washington, Govt. Print. Off., 1888.
44p. 22cm.
NN, USIC, UU

9177. ———. (same) Washington, Govt. Print. Off., 1888.
71p. 21cm.
Caption-title.
Includes arguments of Franklin S. Richards, John T. Caine.
CU–B, DLC, ICN, UHi, WHi

9178. ———. Admission of Utah. Report of a hearing before the Committee on Territories of the United States Senate in regard to the proposed admission of the Territory of Utah as a state in the federal union. [Washington, Govt. Print. Off.? 1888]
162p. 23½cm.
Arguments of February 18, March 10, 1888.
UPB, USIC

9178a. ———. . . . The constitution of the proposed state of Idaho. Hearing before the Committee on Territories. [Washington? Government Printing Office? 1890?]
63p. 23cm.
At head of title: In the Senate of the United States.
Includes the polygamy test oath.
USIC

9179. ———. Hearings before the Committee on Territories in regard to the admission of Utah as a state. Washington, Govt. Print. Off., 1889.
55p. 23cm.
Caption-title.
Includes statements by F. S. Richards, E. P. Ferry, C. C. Bean, Caleb W. West, John T. Caine, J. R. McBride.
DLC

9180. ———. Hearings before the Committee on Territories in relation to the exercise of the elective franchise in the Territory of Utah. [Washington, Govt. Print. Off.? 1890]

25p. 22cm.

Consideration of further polygamy legislation.

USlC

9181. ———. Hearings before the Committee on Territories of the U.S. Senate in relation to the Bill (S. 1306) for the local government of Utah Territory, and to provide for the election of certain officers in said territory. Washington, Govt. Print. Off., 1892.

166p. 22cm.

CU-B, MH

9182. ———. Home rule for Utah; arguments made by a delegation from Utah before the Senate Committee on Territories, First session, 52nd. Congress, in favor of passage of S. 1306, "a bill for the local government of Utah Territory and to provide for the election of certain officers in the said territory." Washington, Govt. Print. Off., 1892.

113p. 22cm.

Same as: "Hearings before Committee on Territories" except session of February 18, 23, is omitted.

CU-B

9183. ———. Report. The Committee on Territories, to whom was referred the resolution of the Senate of the 16th of January in regard to the suppression of the publication of the message of the governor of the Territory of Utah . . . [Washington, Govt. Print. Off.] 1863.

3p. 23½cm. (U.S. 37th Cong. 3rd Sess. Senate. Rep. Com. No. 87)

Problem of the Mormons ruling the territory.

CU, NjP, UPB

9184. ———. . . . Report: [To accompany H.R. 352] May 17, 1894. Washington, Govt. Print. Off., 1895]

29p. 23cm. (U.S. 53rd Cong. 2d Sess. Senate. Report. No. 414)

Some information on the character of Mormons and polygamy.

NjP, ULA, UPB

9185. ———. Utah as it is. Arguments made by delegations from Utah before the Senate Committee on Territories, First Session, Fifty-second Congress. In favor of the passage of the pending bills providing for statehood or local government for the Territory of Utah [S. 1306 and S. 1653] Washington, Govt. Print. Off., 1892.

131p. 22cm.

MH, USlC

9186. U.S. Congress. Senate. Committee on Territories and Insular Affairs. . . . The Constitution of the proposed State of Idaho. Hearing before the Committee on Territories. [Washington, 1890]

63p. 22½cm.

Caption-title.

Polygamy an important issue. Mormon objection to the provision which disenfranchised all Mormons as polygamists.

CtY, USlC

9187. U.S. Congress. Senate. Committee on the Judiciary. In Senate of the United States. Mr. Wall made the following report. The Committee on the Judiciary, to whom was referred the memorial of a delegation of the Latter Day Saints, commonly called Mormons, report: [Washington, 1840]

2p. 21cm. (U.S. 26th Cong. 1st Sess. Senate. Doc. No. 247)

Requests the discharge from further consideration of claims for damages in destruction of property, etc.

Action was presumably on the memorial signed by E. Partridge, H. C. Kimball, J. Taylor, T. Turley, B. Young, et al. Far West, Mo., Dec. 10, 1838.

CtY, CU, DLC, NjP, NN, UPB, USlC, WHi

9187a. ———. Maintenance of a lobby to influence legislation. Hearings before a Subcommittee of the Committee on the Judiciary, United States Senate, sixty-third Congress, first session pursuant to S. Res. 92, a resolution instructing the Committee on the Judiciary to investigate the charge that a lobby is maintained to influence legislation pending in the Senate, Part 4 . . . Washington, Government Printing Office, 1913.

p. 379–504. 23cm.

Reed Smoot testimony with Mormon references, p. 428–465.

DLC, USlC

9188. U.S. Consuls. Reports from the Consuls of the United States. Vol. XXVII. July–September, 1888. Washington, Govt. Print. Off., 1888.

584p. 23cm. (U.S. 50th Cong. 1st Sess. House. Misc. Doc. No. 609)

Mormons, p. 575–576. Settlements made by the Mormons in Mexico.

NjP, UPB

9189. U.S. Department of the Interior. Accounts of Brigham Young, Superintendent of Indian Affairs in Utah Territory. Letter from the Secretary of the Interior, transmitting report of the investigation of the acts of Governor Young, ex officio superintendent of Indian affairs in Utah Territory. [Washington, Govt. Print. Off., 1862]

124p. 22½cm. (U.S. 37th Cong. 2d Sess. House. Ex. Doc. No. 29)

Includes material on the Mormons' relations with the Indians.

DLC, UPB

9190. ———. . . . Letter from the Secretary of the Interior in response to resolution of the House of Representatives relative to the alleged action of certain Mormons in inciting the Piute and Navajo Indians to outbreak. [Washington, Govt. Print. Off.] 1882.
[2]p. 23cm. (U.S. 47th Cong. 1st Sess. House. Ex. Doc. No. 65)
NjP, ULA, UPB

9191. ———. Message of the President of the United States, communicating, in compliance with a resolution of the Senate, information in relation to the massacre at Mountain Meadows and other massacres in Utah Territory . . . [Washington, George W. Bowman] 1860.
139p. 23cm. (U.S. 36th Cong. 1st Sess. Senate. Ex. Doc. No. 42)
W–C 352a
CSmH, CtY, CU, CU–B, DLC, NjP, NN, ULA, UPB

9192. ———. Pacific wagon roads. Letter from the secretary of the Interior, transmitting a report upon the several wagon roads constructed under the direction of the Interior Department. [Washington, James Steedman, Printer, 1859]
125p. 22cm. (U.S. 35th Cong. 2d Sess. House. Ex. Doc. No. 108)
Roads through Mormon territory; Mormon ferries on immigrant route; Indian version of Salmon River colony attack; duplicity of Indians. Report prepared by A. H. Campbell, general superintendent.
CU, DLC, NjP, UHi, ULA, UPB, USlC

9193. ———. Polygamy in Utah, message from the President of the United States transmitting a communication from the Secretary of the Interior relative to polygamy in Utah. Washington, Govt. Print. Off., 1884.
6p. 22cm. (U.S. 48th Cong. 1st Sess. House. Ex. Doc. No. 153)
Cover-title: Special report of the Utah Commission.
CU, CU–B, NjP, NN, ULA, UPB, USlC

9194. U.S. Department of Labor. A report on marriage and divorce in the U.S. 1867–1886; including an appendix relating to marriage and divorce in certain countries in Europe, by Carroll D. Wright, Feb. 1889. Washington, Govt. Print. Off., 1889.
1074p. 22½cm.
Section on the Mormon practice of marriage.
Other editions: Rev. ed. 1889. DLC; 1897. DLC
DLC

9194a. U.S. Department of State. Papers relating to the foreign relations of the United States, Transmitted to congress . . . Washington, Govt. Print. Off., 1879–1900.
9v. 28cm.
Correspondence concerning the problems of Mormon emigration, etc.
DLC, UPB

9195. U.S. Department of the Treasury. . . . Letter from the Secretary of the Treasury, inclosing [sic] papers in the claim of George Q. Cannon for money covered in the Treasury on a forfeited bond. [Washington, Govt. Print. Off.] 1893.
4p. 23cm. (U.S. 52d Cong. 2d Sess. Senate. Ex. Doc. No. 43)
Some information on George Q. Cannon's arrest and circumstances of his unlawful cohabitation.
NjP, UPB

9196. ———. Utah-public buildings-further appropriations. Letter from the Secretary of the Treasury, transmitting communications in regard to the necessity of further appropriations for public buildings in Utah. [Washington, A. O. P. Nicholson] 1854.
3p. 23cm. (U.S. 33rd Cong. 1st sess. House. Misc. Doc. No. 58)
Transmitting communications showing necessity of further appropriations for public buildings in Utah.
CU, CU–B, NjP, ULA, UPB

U.S. Department of War. See U.S. War Department.

9196a. U.S. District Court. Utah. (Second District). Report of the Grand Jury of the Second District of Utah Territory, September Term, 1859. Carson Valley: Printed at the Office of the Territorial Enterprise, 1859.
2, 3–4p. 23cm.
2p. Mormon theology.
4p. Mormon outrages. The creation of a Nevada Territory or an independent judicial district.
CtY

9197. U.S. District Court. Utah. (Third District). Arrest of militia officers in Utah Territory. Opinion of Justice C. M. Hawley. Territory of Utah, Third District Court, The United States *vs* George M. Ottinger [and others]. [Salt Lake City, 1870]
8p. 23cm.
Denial of the rights of Mormons to bear arms.
CtY, MnHi

9198. ———. The Edmunds law, "unlawful cohabitation," as defined by Chief Justice Charles S. Zane, of the Territory of Utah, in the trial of Angus M. Cannon, in the Third District Court, Salt Lake City, April 27, 28, 29, 1885. Full report of the arguments as to the term "cohabitation" in the above law reported by John Irvine. Salt Lake City, Juvenile Instructor Office, 1885.
iv [5]–118p. 16cm.
UPB

9199. ———. Exposures of a rotten priesthood by the Grand Jury of the Third District Court of Utah. February, 1878. [Salt Lake City, 1878?]
22p. 20cm.
Includes a description of Utah penal institutions.
UPB

U. S. DISTRICT COURT

———. The inside of Mormonism. *See McMillan, Henry G.*

9200. U.S. Geographical Surveys West of the 100th Meridian. Annual report upon the Geographical Surveys of the Territory of the United States west of the 100th Meridian, in the States and Territories of California, Kansas, Nebraska, Nevada, Oregon, Texas, Arizona, Idaho, Montana, New Mexico, Utah, Washington, and Wyoming, by George M. Wheeler, First Lieutenant Corps of Engineers, U.S. Army; being Appendix NN of the Annual Report of the Chief of Engineers for 1878. Washington, Govt. Print. Off., 1878.

x, 234p. illus., fold. maps. 23½cm.

Report of 2nd Lieutenant Willard Young (son of Brigham Young) in charge of Party No. 1 of the Utah section, February 22, 1878, p. 120–122, and report of 1st Lieutenant R. Birney, Jr., in charge of Party No. 2, June 14, 1878, p. 122–131, for operations in northern Utah and southern Idaho, 1877.

CU–B, UPB

9201. ———. Annual report upon the Geographical Surveys of the Territory of the United States west of the 100th Meridian, in the States and Territories of California, Colorado, Kansas, Nebraska, Nevada, Oregon, Texas, Arizona, Idaho, Montana, New Mexico, Utah, Washington, and Wyoming. By George M. Wheeler, Captain Corps of Engineers, U.S. Army; being Appendix OO of the Annual Report of the Chief of Engineers for 1879. Washington, Govt. Print. Off., 1879.

vi, 340p. illus., fold. maps. 23½cm.

Includes reports by 2nd Lieutenant Willard Young (son of Brigham Young) on Southern California mining districts, p. 188–192; and report of March 17, 1879, on survey of Great Salt Lake, p. 228–232, 235–237, and Southern California, p. 232–235.

CU–B, UPB

9202. ———. Progress-report upon Geographical and Geological Explorations and Surveys west of the 100th Meridian in 1872, under the direction of Brig. Gen. A. A. Humphreys, Chief of Engineers, U.S. Army, by First Lieut. George M. Wheeler. Washington, Govt. Print. Off., 1874.

56p. 5 plates (incl. map) fold. map, diagrs. 30cm.

At head of title: Engineer Department, United States Army.

Operations in Utah, 1872. Reference to Mormons, p. 44, 46–47, 56; mining districts and mines, p. 13–28; irrigation, p. 28–30; agriculture, p. 32–33; routes of communication, p. 33–36; Indians, p. 37–38; Great Salt Lake and Utah Lake, p. 52–54.

CU–B, DLC, UPB

9203. ———. Report upon United States Geographical Survey West of the 100th Meridian, in charge of Capt. Geo. M. Wheeler, Corps of Engineers, U.S. Army, under the direction of the Chief of Engineers, U.S. Army. Published by authority of the Honorable, the Secretary of War, in accordance with acts of Congress of June 23, 1874, and February 15, 1875. In seven volumes and one supplement, accompanied by one topographic and one geologic atlas. Washington, Govt. Print. Off., 1875–1889.

7v. in 8. illus., plates (part col.) maps. 30cm. and 2 atlases 48×61cm.

Vol. I. Geographical Report (Washington, 1889) contains references to the Mormons in Utah, Arizona, and Nevada during the field seasons of 1869 and 1872, p. 23, 28, 46–56, and more general remarks, p. 174–177. A number of the plates are Utah views. The atlas sheets show Mormon settlements, wagon roads, etc. of the 1870's.

CU–B, UPB

9204. U.S. Geological and Geographical Survey of the Territories. Report of the U.S. Geological and Geographical Survey of the Territories . . . by F. V. Hayden, U.S. geologist. [Washington, Govt. Print. Off., 1867–83]

12v. illus., maps (part fold.) and atlas of fold. maps. 24cm.

Annual.

Vol. 4, for 1870, contains report of F. V. Hayden on geology of area from Evanston to Ogden along line of railroad, with remarks on Mormon interest in agriculture, coal, and granite for temple, p. 147, 155–160, 167; also report of Cyrus Thomas on the valleys of Utah and their cultivation, p. 237–248.

Vol. 5, for 1871, contains geological observations from Ogden to Fort Hall, with remarks on Mormon settlements, p. 13–26.

Vol. 6, for 1872, contains geological observations by A. C. Peale on area from Ogden to Salt Lake, with comment on Mormon towns and industries in the Wasatch Mountains, p. 105–108; also same by Frank H. Bradley, Ogden to Fort Hall, p. 192–208.

Vol. 11, for 1877, comments on Bear River area, with mention of Mormon settlements in Cache Valley, p. 697–701.

CU–B, DLC, UPB

9205. United States government officials commend colonization work of Mormon Church; addresses delivered in the Tabernacle, Salt Lake City, Utah, Sunday, April 19, 1925. [Salt Lake City, 1925]

24p. 17½cm.

Cover-title.

Includes addresses by Hubert Work, Elwood Mead, Stephen T. Mather, and others.

UHi, UPB, USIC, UU

9206. ———. (same) [Salt Lake City, 1925]

24p. 18cm.

Cover-title.

Variant printing of 9205.

USIC

9207. ———. (same, under title) Vision and faith of the Latter-day Saints. Addresses delivered in the tabernacle, Salt Lake City, Sunday, April 19, 1925 by Dr. Hubert Work, Dr. Elwood Mead, Stephen T. Mather, Bishop C. W. Nibley, Prest. A. W. Ivins. [Independence, Mo., Press of Zions Printing and Publishing Co., 1925]
20p . 17½cm.
USlC

9208. U.S. Laws, Statutes, etc. The Edmunds bill . . . Following is the full text of the Edmunds bill as passed by the Congress . . . Salt Lake City, Published by Barton & Co. [1882?]
4p. 14½cm.
USlC

9209. ———. The Statutes at large of the United States of America from Aug. 1893, to March, 1895 and recent treaties, conventions and executive proclamations. Washington, Govt. Print. Off., 1895.
xxxi, 1450p. 33cm.
Signed: September 25, 1894.
Presidential proclamation granting pardons and amnesty to polygamous Mormons, p. 1257.
UPB

9210. U.S. Office of Indian Affairs. Accounts of Brigham Young, Supt. of Indian Affairs in Utah Territory. Letter from the Secretary of the Interior, transmitting report of the investigation of the acts of Governor Young, ex-officio superintendent of Indian affairs in Utah Territory . . . [Washington] 1862.
124p. tables. 23cm. (U.S. 37th Cong. 2d Sess. House. Ex. Doc. No. 29)
CSmH, CU-B, NjP, ULA

9211. U.S. Post-Office Department. Postmasters in Idaho living in Polygamy. Letter from the Postmaster General transmitting, in response to a Senate resolution of April 20, 1904, the report of Post-Office Inspector M. C. Fosnes relative to what, if any, postmasters in Idaho are living in polygamy. Jan. 4, 1905. [Washington, Govt. Print. Off.? 1905]
19p. 23cm. (U.S. 58th Cong. 3d Sess. Senate. Doc. No. 62)
Considerable historical information on Joseph Smith, the Mormons, and the polygamy question.
NjP, ULA, UPB

9212. U.S. President, 1845–1849 (Polk). Occupation of Mexican Territory. Message from the President of the United States transmitting in answer to a resolution of the House of Representatives of December 15, 1846, reports from the Secretary of the Navy relative to the occupation of Mexican territory. Washington, Govt. Print. Off., 1912.
76p. 23½cm. (U.S. 62d Cong. 2d Sess. Senate. Doc. No. 896)
Includes material on the Mormon battalion.
Extracted from U.S. 30th Cong. 1st Sess. House. Ex. Doc. No. 60.
DLC, NjP, ULA, UPB

9213. U.S. President, 1849–1850 (Taylor). California and New Mexico. Message from the President of the United States, transmitting information in answer to a resolution of the House of the 31st of December, 1849, on the subject of California and New Mexico. January 24, 1850. Committed to the Committee of the Whole House on the state of the Union and ordered to be printed; and a motion to print 10,000 extra copies referred to the Committee on Printing. February 6, 1850. Ordered, that 10,000 copies extra be printed. [Washington, 1850]
976p. 5 maps (4 fold.) 23cm. (U.S. 31st Cong. 1st Sess. House. Ex. Doc. No. 17)
Caption-title.
Contains Salt Lake Indian agent John Wilson's report from Great Salt Lake Valley, Sept. 4, 1847, p. 104–112, and many documents concerning the enlistment, re-enlistment, and experiences of the Mormon Battalion in California, 1846–1848, p. 237, 304, 309, 314, 326–327, 336, 343, 345–348, 356–357, 434, 463–464, 466, 469, 471, 534–535, 545, 560, 624, 644–645, 650, 697.
Another edition: Senate version same but reads "Rep. Com." on p. 1 instead of "Ex. Doc." (U.S. 31st Cong. 1st Sess. Senate. Ex. Doc. No. 18)
C, CU, CU-B, DLC

9214. U.S. President, 1850–1853 (Fillmore). Utah. Message from the President of the United States, transmitting information in reference to the condition of affairs in the Territory of Utah. January 9, 1852 . . . [Washington, 1852]
33p. 23cm. (U.S. 32nd Cong. 1st Sess. House. Ex. Doc. No. 25)
Caption-title.
"Report of Messrs. Brandebury, Brocchus, and Harris, to the President of the United States," p. 8–22.
CSmH, CtY, CU, CU-B, DLC, ICN, NjP, UHi, ULA, UPB, UU

9215. U.S. President, 1857–1861 (Buchanan). Message from the President of the United States relative to the probable termination of Mormon troubles in Utah Territory. June 10, 1858. [Washington, 1858]
7p. 23cm. (U.S. 35th Cong. 1st Sess. House. Ex. Doc. No. 138)
CU, CU-B, MH, NjP, NN, ULA, WHi

9216. ———. Message from the President of the United States to the two houses of Congress, at the commencement of the First Session of the Thirty-fifth Congress. Washington: Printed at the Congressional Globe Office, 1857.
15p. 22cm.
Includes material on the Utah expedition.
USlC

U. S. PRESIDENT, 1857–1861

9217. ———. Message of the President of the United States . . . [Washington, Printed at the Congressional Globe Office, 1858]
16p. 23cm.
Caption-title.
Treats of trouble in Kansas and sending troops to Utah.
CtY

9218. ———. Message of the President of the United States, communicating, in compliance with a resolution of the Senate, information in relation to the massacre at Mountain Meadows, and other massacres in Utah Territory. [Washington, George W. Bowman, Printer, 1860]
139p. (U.S. 36th Cong. 1st Sess. Senate. Ex. Doc. No. 42)
CU–B, DLC, UPB

9219. ———. . . . Message of the President of the U.S. communicating, in compliance with a resolution of the Senate, the correspondence between the judges of Utah and the Attorney General or President, with reference to the legal proceedings and conditions of affairs in that Territory . . . [Washington, George W. Bowman, Printer] 1860.
64p. (U.S. 36th Cong. 1st Sess. Senate. Ex. Doc. No. 32)
Situation in Utah and Mountain Meadows massacre.
CtY, UPB

9220. ———. A proclamation. [Washington, 1858]
3p. 32½cm.
Signed: April 6, 1858.
At head of title: By James Buchanan, President of the United States of America: Concerning the Utah War and its necessity.
CtY, ULA, UPB, USlC

9221. ———. . . . The Utah expedition. Message from the President of the United States, transmitting reports from the Secretaries of State, of War, of the Interior, and of the Attorney-General, relative to the military expedition ordered into the territory of Utah. February 26, 1858. — Referred to the Committee on Territories. [Washington, 1858]
215p. 23cm. (U.S. 35th Cong. 1st Sess. House. Ex. Doc. No. 71)
CU, CU–B, DLC, NjP, NN, ULA, UPB

9222. ———. . . . Utah Territory. Message of the President of the U.S., communicating, in compliance with a resolution of the House, copies of correspondence relative to the condition of affairs in the Territory of Utah . . . [Washington, Thomas H. Ford, Printer] 1860.
51p. 24cm. (U.S. 26th Cong. 1st Sess. House. Ex. Doc. No. 78)
Most of the pamphlet deals with Judge Cradlebaugh and his difficulties at Provo.
W–C 352a
CU, CU–B, NjP, NN, ULA, USlC

9223. U.S. President, 1877–1881 (Hayes). Annual message of the President of the United States, to the Two Houses of Congress at the commencement of the Third Session of the Forty-sixth Congress. Washington, Govt. Print. Off., 1880.
34p. 22cm.
Need to suppress polygamy.
DLC, USlC

9224. U.S. President, 1881–1885 (Arthur). Message of the President of the United States communicated to the Two Houses of Congress at the beginning of the First Session of the Forty-eighth Congress. Washington, Govt. Print. Off., 1883.
19p. 22cm.
Results of the Utah Commission on Utah elections.
DLC, USlC

9225. ———. Message of the President of the United States communicated to the Two Houses of Congress at the beginning of the Second Session of the Forty-eighth Congress. Washington, Govt. Print. Off., 1884.
21p. 22cm.
Brief mention of the prevention and punishment of polygamy in Utah.
DLC, USlC

9226. U.S. President, 1885–1889 (Cleveland). Message from the President of the United States, recommending the immediate enactment of such legislation as will authorize the assembling of the legislature of Utah Territory in special session to make the necessary appropriations for the expenses of that Territory. [Washington, Govt. Print. Off.] 1886.
2p. 23cm. (U.S. 49th Cong. 1st Sess. Senate. Ex. Doc. No. 139)
Such legislation recommended in response to a memorial from the Utah Legislature protesting against the absolute veto power exercised by the governor. Although the central government was attempting to halt certain illegal practices in the Territory (polygamy), this did not include the right to suspend the operation of local government and necessary services in the Territory.
CU, CU–B, NjP, ULA, UPB

9227. U.S. President, 1889–1893 (Harrison). By the President of the United States. A proclamation [granting amnesty and pardon to all persons liable to penalties by reason of unlawful cohabitation under the color of polygamous or plural marriage, who have since November 1, 1890, abstained from such unlawful cohabitation. Washington? 1893]
2p. 33cm.
Issued upon recommendation of the Utah Commission after the Mormon church had pledged faithful obedience to the laws against plural marriage.
CtY, UPB

U. S. UTAH COMMISSION

9228. U.S. Secretary of the Treasury. Utah — public buildings — further appropriations. Letter from the Secretary of the Treasury, transmitting communications in regard to the necessity of further appropriations for public buildings in Utah. [Washington, 1854]
3p. 24½cm. (U.S. 33d Cong. 1st Sess. House. Misc. Doc. No. 58)
Includes material on Mormons and their treatment of the territorial judges.
USlC

9229. ———. Willard Richards, acting Secretary of Utah. Letter from the Secretary of the Treasury, transmitting a copy of a communication from the comptroller recommending an appropriation for the payment of Willard Richards, while acting as Secretary of Utah. [Washington, 1852]
2p. 23½cm. (U.S. 32nd Cong. 2d Sess. House. Ex. Doc. No. 12)
Signed: December 29, 1852.
C, CU, UPB

9230. U.S. Supreme Court. The United States, Appellant, vs. the late Corporation of the Church of Jesus Christ of Latter-day Saints et al. Appeal from the Supreme Court of the Territory of Utah. [Washington, Govt. Print. Off.] 1893.
iii, 217p. 23½cm.
Cover-title.
At head of title: Record Case No. 15257.
Property suits resulting from polygamy legislation.
DLC, NjP

9231. U.S. Utah Commission. ... Circular for the information of registration officers, Salt Lake City, April 21, 1885. [Salt Lake City, 1885]
4p. 24cm.
Caption-title.
At head of title: Office of the Utah Commission.
Polygamy oath.
USlC

9232. ———. ... The Edmunds Act, reports of the Commission. Rules, regulations and decisions, and population, registration and Election Tables, Etc. For the information of registration and election officers in Utah. Salt Lake City, Tribune Printing and Publishing Company, 1883.
2p.l. [3]–121p. tables. 24cm.
On cover: 1884.
At head of title: Utah Commission.
CU–B, DLC, NN, UHi, UPB, USl, USlC

9233. ———. The Edmunds Act. Reports of the Utah Commission, rules, regulations and decisions, and population, registration and election tables, &c. For the information of registration and election officers in Utah. Salt Lake City, Tribune Printing and Publishing Co., 1883.
46 [1]p. 21½cm.
Text of the Edmunds Act, oath required of voters, and election returns are included.
A repeat of the first 41 pages of 9232.
CU–B, DLC, NN, UPB, UU

9234. ———. Industrial Christian Home of Utah. Communication from the Utah Commissioners transmitting their annual report to Congress. [Washington, Govt. Print. Off., 1893]
4p. 23cm. (U.S. 52nd Cong. 2d Sess. House. Misc. Doc. No. 6)
Report of the Industrial Christian Home Association of Utah for 1892.
Signed: Dec. 5, 1892.
NjP, ULA, UPB

9235. ———. ... Letter from the chairman of the Utah Commission acting as a board for the management and control of the Industrial Christian Home Association of Utah, transmitting the report of the Commission respecting the operations of that Association. [Washington, Govt. Print. Off.] 1892.
5p. 23cm. (U.S. 52nd Cong. 1st Sess. House. Misc. Doc. No. 104)
DLC, NjP, UPB

9236. ———. Minority report of the Utah Commission. Existing laws declared sufficient. No more legislation needed. Some facts ignored by the majority report. [Salt Lake City?] 1887.
18p. 22cm.
Cover-title.
CU–B, DLC, MH, NN

9237. ———. Oath prescribed by Utah Commission for voters to take when applying for registration. [Salt Lake City? 1887?]
Broadside. 24½×15½cm.
"Additional affidavit required when deemed necessary by the registrar."
USlC

9238. ———. Registration. Order of the Commissioners. [Salt Lake City? 1882]
Broadside. 21×14cm.
UPB, USlC

9239. ———. Report. Washington, Govt. Print. Off. 1882–1896.
15v. 23cm.
Appointed 1882; ended 1896.
Also published in U.S. Department of Interior. Annual Reports.
CtY 1882–1896; CU–B 1882; DLC 1882–84, 1887, 1892–93, 1896; ICN 1882–87, 1891–96; MH 1885, 1887, 1889–1893, 1895–96; NN 1882–1896, UPB 1882–1896

9240. ———. Rules and regulations for the revision of the registration lists, and the conduct of the election, Nov. 7, 1882. Salt Lake City, Tribune Printing and Publishing Company, 1882.
8p. 18cm.
Cover-title.
Includes the polygamy oath.
DLC

U. S. UTAH COMMISSION

9241. ———. Sir: I enclose herewith a commission appointing you a Judge of Election for the General Election in November, 1893. Upon your acceptance of the appointment, please subscribe and swear to the oath enclosed, and return the same to me. The following has been prepared by the Commission for the information of Election Judges: . . . Salt Lake City, 1893.
[2]p. 28cm.
Signed at end: A. B. Williams, Chairman.
UPB

9242. ———. Special report of the Utah Commission, made to the Secretary of the Interior, 1884. Washington, Govt. Print. Off., 1884.
15p. 23cm. (U.S. 48th Cong. 1st Sess. House. Ex. Doc. No. 153)
Caption-title: . . . Polygamy in Utah. Message from the President of the United States . . .
CtY, CU, CU–B, NjP, NN, ULA

9243. ———. . . . The Vice-President presented the following report of the Utah Commission, with copies of correspondence between said commission and various officials of the govt. and others, relative to the occupancy of the Industrial Christian Home Building at Salt Lake City, Utah. [Washington, Govt. Print. Off., 1895]
7p. 23½cm. (U.S. 53rd Cong. 2d Sess. Senate. Misc. Doc. No. 7)
Signed: Dec. 5, 1893.
DLC, NjP, ULA, UPB

9244. U.S. War Department. Contracts-Utah expedition. Letter from the Secretary of War, in answer to a resolution of the House calling for a statement of all contracts made in connexion [sic] with the Utah expedition. Washington, 1858.
5p. 22cm. (U.S. 35th Cong. 1st Sess. House. Ex. Doc. No. 99)
CU, CU–B, NjP, ULA, UPB

9245. ———. Estimate-Utah expedition; letter from the Secretary of War, transmitting an estimate for subsistence of troops for the Utah expedition. [Washington, Govt. Print. Off.] 1858.
2p. 23cm. (U.S. 35th Cong. 1st Sess. House. Ex. Doc. No. 33)
CU–B, NjP, UPB

9246. ———. General Orders. Washington, New York, 1857–58.
20 nos. 18cm.
Orders dealing with the deployment of troops for the invasion of Utah, etc. [Washington, 1857]
7 nos. 28cm.
CtY, UPB #1, 2, 3, 5, 6, 11, 12, 16, 17, 19, 20

9247. ———. Letter from the Secretary of War, in answer to a resolution of the House of February 27, transmitting report of General Ingalls's inspection made in 1866. Washington, 1867.
25p. 22½cm. (U.S. 39th Cong. 2d Sess. House. Ex. Doc. No. 111)
At head of title: General Ingalls' Inspection Report.
Comments on Mormons and Utah.
CU, NjP, ULA, UPB

9248. ———. . . . Letter from the Secretary of War relative to an appropriation for a military post near the town of Beaver, Utah. [Washington, Govt. Print. Off.] 1872.
3p. 23cm. (U.S. 42nd Cong. 2d Sess. House. Ex. Doc. No. 285)
Some facts relative to the Mountain Meadow massacre.
CU, CU–B, NjP, ULA, UPB

9248a. ———. Letter from the Secretary of War, transmitting report upon the claim of James Bridger. January 25, 1889 . . . [Washington, Government Printing Office, 1889]
23p. on [14]l. 22cm. (U.S. 50th Cong. 2d Sess. Senate. Ex. Doc. No. 86).
Bridger claims against the Mormons due to destruction of Fort Bridger during the Utah Expedition.
USlC (photocopy)

9249. ———. Message from the President of the United States to the Two Houses of Congress at the commencement of the 1st Session of the 35th Congress . . . Report of the Secretary of War. Washington, Cornelius Wendell, Printer, 1857.
572p. 23cm. (U.S. 35th Cong. 1st Sess. House. Ex. Doc. No. 2)
Caption-title.
The Utah Expedition. Includes letters and reports.
CU, CU–B, NjP, NN, ULA, UPB

9250. ———. Message from the President of the United States to the Two Houses of Congress at the commencement of the First Session of the Thirty-sixth Congress. (Report of the Secretary of War) Washington, George W. Bowman, Printer, 1860.
828p. 23cm. (U.S. 36th Cong. 1st Sess. Senate. Ex. Doc. No. 2)
"Affairs in the Department of Utah," p. 121–255. Also refers to Mormons in "Affairs in Department of New Mexico," p. 339–340.
CU–B, DLC

9251. ———. Message from the President of the United States to the Two Houses of Congress at the Commencement of the Second Session of the Thirty-fifth Congress. . . . (Report of the Secretary of War) Washington, James B. Steadman, Printer, 1958.
670p. 23½cm. (U.S. 35th Cong. 2d Sess. House. Ex. Doc. No. 2)
Includes material on the Utah expedition and affairs in Utah with pertinent correspondence, orders, etc.
CU, CU–B, DLC, ICN, NjP, ULA, UPB

9252. ———. Message from the President of the United States to the Two Houses of Congress at the commencement of the Second Session of the Thirty-sixth Congress. Washington, George W. Bowman, Printer, 1860.
996p. 23cm. (U.S. 36th Cong. 2d Sess. Senate. Ex. Doc. No. 1)
Affairs in the Department of Utah, p. 69–106. Other Mormon references p. 111, Paiute War in Nevada.
CU-B

9253. ———. Message of the President of the United States to the Two Houses of Congress at the commencement of the First Session of the Thirty-fifth Congress. Report of the Secretary of War. Washington, William A. Harris, Printer, 1858.
38p. 23cm. (U.S. 35th Cong. 1st Sess. Senate. Ex. Doc. No. 11)
Contains letters from Brigham Young, officers of the Army, and the Secretary of War in reference to the entrance of troops into Utah.
CU-B, NjP, ULA, UPB

9254. ———. Message of the President of the United States to the Two Houses of Congress at the commencement of the Second Session of the Thirty-fifth Congress. [Report of the Secretary of War] Washington, William A. Harris, Printer, 1858.
224p. 22½cm. (U.S. 35th Cong. 2d Sess. Senate. Ex. Doc. No. 1)
Concerns communications on the Utah Expedition between the Secretary of War, officers in the Army, Brigham Young, and others.
NjP, NN, ULA, UPB

9255. ———. Reports of explorations and surveys, to ascertain the most practicable and economical route for a railroad from the Mississippi River to the Pacific Ocean. Made under the direction of the Secretary of War, in 1853–[6] . . . Washington, A. O. P. Nicholson, Printer [Beverley Tucker, Printer] 1855–1860.
12v. in 13. plates (part col., part fold.) maps (part fold.) 30cm.
Vol. III. Includes extracts from the [preliminary] report of Lieutenant A. W. Whipple, Corps of Topographical Engineers, upon the route near the Thirty-fifth Parallel, with an explanatory note by Captain A. A. Humphreys . . . References to the Mormons at San Bernardino and the Mormon road to Salt Lake, p. 113, 126–127, 129, 131.
Vol. V. Report of Lieutenant R. S. Williamson, Corps of Topographical Engineers, upon the routes in California to connect with the routes near the Thirty-fifth and Thirty-second Parallels. References to the Mormon settlement at San Bernardino, p. 36–37, 80–84, 89; the Mormon road to Salt Lake, p. 64, 88; Mormon Island on the American River, p. 275.
CU-B, UPB

9256. ———. The war of the rebellion: A compilation of the official records of the Union and Confederate armies. Pub. under the direction of the . . . Secretary of War . . . Washington, Govt. Print. Off., 1880–1901.
70v. in 128. 23½cm.
"Operations on the Pacific Coast [including Utah] January 1, 1861–June 30, 1865, in Series I. Vol. L. parts 1 and 2 [nos. 105–106]"
CU-B, DLC, UPB

9257. Unity. Independence, Ensign Publishing House, January, 1915–March, 1923.
5v. monthly. 22cm.
Title changed to *One* 1919–1921 and to *Priesthood Journal* 1922–23.
After 1923, its function was assumed by the *Saints' Herald.*
Journal of the RLDS church priesthood.
IWW, MoInRC

9257a. Unonius, Gustaf. Mormonismen. Dess Upprinnelse, Tveckling och Bekännelse. Stockholm, Ivar Haeggströms Boktryckeri, 1883.
78p. 22cm.
MnHi

9258. Unsere Sonntagsschule, offizielles Organ der Sonntagsschulen der Schweizerischen und Deutschen Mission der Kirche Jesu Christi der Heiligen der Letzten Tage. [Basel] Schweizerischen und Deutschen Mission, Januar, 1924–Dezember, 1926.
3v. 24cm. quarterly.
Official organ of the Sunday School of the Swiss and German Mission.
Title in English: Our Sunday School.
UPB V.1, 3;USIC V.1 #1, V.3 #4

9259. Upham, Charles Wentworth. Life explorations and public services of John Charles Fremont . . . Boston, Ticknor and Fields, 1856.
viii, 9–256p. plates, port. 18½cm.
Reference to the Mormons, p. 328–332.
Another edition: 50th thousand. CU-B, DLC
CU-B, DLC

9260. Upper Missouri Advertiser. Independence, Mo., By W. W. Phelps & Co., June 27?–[July, 1833]
v. weekly. 54cm.
Edited by W. W. Phelps.
#3 states it is to be published weekly at 75 cents per year until printed on both sides, then $1.00 per year. Local newspaper published on the press of *The Evening and the Morning Star.*
MWA #3 (July 11, 1832) as a three column broadside

9261. Upton, Harriet (Taylor). History of the Western Reserve, by Harriet Taylor Upton; H. G. Cutler . . . and a staff of leading citizens collaborated on the counties and biographies . . . Chicago, New York, The Lewis Publishing Company, 1910.
3v. illus., plates, ports. 27½cm.
"The Latter-day Saints in the Reserve," V.1, p. 128–134.
CSmH, CU, DLC, NjP, NN

9262. Ursenbach, Octave Frederick. Redemption, an epic of the divine tragedy. Disclosing the origin, mission and destiny of man, together with the creating, peopling and redeeming of worlds. [By] Octave F. Ursenbach. [Los Angeles, Rapid Service Press, c1928]
2p.l., 44p. 21cm.
Mormon poetry.
DLC, UHi, USIC

9263. ———. (same) Salt Lake City, Deseret News Press, c1928.
2p.l., 43 [1]p. 21cm.
UPB

9264. ———. Why I am a "Mormon," by O. F. Ursenbach . . . Salt Lake City, 1910.
iv p. [1]l., 212p. 17½cm.
Objections considered. "Simple facts plainly told by a resident of Utah."
DLC, MH, UHi, USl, USIC, UU

9265. Ustrup. Et Udfald fra Christi kirke mod Mormonerne og Falsklaerere, af Ustrom [*pseud.*] Kjøbenhavn, Faaes hos Boghandler, J. R. Møller. Trykt hos S. L. Møller., 1857.
61 [2]p. 20cm.
Authorship established from British museum.
Title in English: An attack of the Church of Christ against the Mormons.
USIC

Utah affairs, congress and polygamy. *See Veritas [pseud.]*

Utah and Bible Society. *See Utah Tract Society.*

Utah and its people. By a Gentile. *See Lum, Dyer Daniel.*

9266. Utah and statehood. Objections considered. Simple facts plainly told. With a brief synopsis of the state constitution. By a resident of Utah. New York, Printed for the author by Hart & Von Arx, 1888.
11p. 23cm.
Cover-title.
CtY, CU–B, DLC, MH, NjP, NN, UPB, UU

9267. Utah bladet . . . Salt Lake City, 1924–1925.
v. monthly.
Organ of the Swedish Mormons.
Editor: Frank Malmstedt.
Largely devoted to biographies of Swedish Mormons.
Title in English: Utah paper.
No copies located.

9268. Utah Central Railroad. Guide to Salt Lake City, Ogden, and the Utah Central Railroad. Description of towns before Salt Lake City and buildings in Salt Lake City, such as temple, tabernacle, Deseret Museum, etc. Salt Lake City, Deseret News Office [1870]
30p. 13½cm.
Brief discussion of towns and landscape between Ogden and Salt Lake, with more on Salt Lake City.
CSmH

9269. The Utah Christian Advocate. Salt Lake City, January, 1884–1887?
4v? monthly; semi-monthly. 58cm.
Edited by T. C. Iliff, 1884–1887; Martinus Nelson and E. C. Strout. 1887.
Superseded the *Rocky Mountain Christian Advocate.*
Monthly from V.1 #1–V.4 #6. Semi-monthly July 1887 through November 26, 1887.
USIC V.1–4 #1–6, 8, 9, 11, 13, 16

9270. Utah Church and Farm. Salt Lake City, Salt Lake Herald, July 14, 1894–1898.
3v. bi-weekly. 30cm.
Previously called *Salt Lake Herald Church and Farm Department.*
Later published by the Church and Farm Company.
Church news included.
UPB V.2 #24, V.3 #3, new series V.3 #8; USIC V.1–3 inc.

Utah. Citizens. In the matter of Reed Smoot. *See under title.*

9271. ———. . . . Protest of citizens of the State of Utah against the admission to the United States Senate of Reed Smoot, apostle of the Mormon church. [To the United States Senate] Salt Lake City, 1903.
62p. 23cm.
Cover-title.
DLC, OO, USIC

Utah Commission. *See U.S. Utah Commission.*

9272. The Utah Commission. Which of the claimants is entitled to be sworn as delegate? Respectfully submitted to the 47th Congress of the United States. [n.p.] National Republican Press [1881]
9p. 23½cm.
Cover-title.
Both George Q. Cannon and Allen G. Campbell were refused admission.
ICN

UTAH GOSPEL

9273. Utah Compromise Club. A plan to solve the Utah problem. Salt Lake City, 1880.
12p. 20cm.
Caption-title: Polygamy settled would be a boon for the Mormons.
MH, NjP, USlC

9274. Utah. Constitution. The enabling act. Washington, 1895.
12, III [1] 48p. 21cm.
12p. The enabling act.
IIIp. To the people of Utah.
48p. Constitution.
Includes a provision against polygamy.
ULA, USlC

9275. Utah County. A graphic account of its foundings, its wonderful growth and its splendid promise for the future. Also a descriptive review of its resources, attractions, industries, leading business houses and institutions, with portraits and biographical sketches of its pioneers and early settlers. Salt Lake City, Published by The County Atlas Publishing Company, 1897.
1p.l. [6]–128p. illus., ports., map. 29½cm.
Mormonism ignored as much as possible.
UPB, USlC

9276. Utah County. Women. Defense of plural marriage, by the women of Utah County. Mass meetings in Provo, Springville, Spanish Fork, Salem, Payson, Santaquin, Goshen, Cedar Valley, Lehi, Alpine, Benjamin, American Fork and Pleasant Grove. [Provo City, Printed and for Sale at the Enquirer Office, 1879]
12p. 23½cm.
Caption-title.
CtY, CU–B, MH, NN, USlC

9277. Utah Danske Americaner. Huntsville, Utah, Danish Publishing Company, 1885–1886.
v. monthly.
Editor, Carl C. Erickson.
Organ of the Danish Mormons in Utah.
Title in English: Utah Danish Americans.
No copies located

9278. Utah Defense League. To whom this may concern: The following resolutions were unanimously adopted at a public meeting consisting largely of non-Mormons, held at the Hotel Utah, Salt Lake City, on Tuesday evening, April 18, 1922. Salt Lake City [1922?]
[4]p. 28cm.
Tract to denounce charges of immorality of the Mormons.
UPB

9279. Utah. Diamond Jubilee Committee. The Diamond jubilee of the coming of the Utah Pioneers. July 22–23–24, 1922. Salt Lake City, Utah. Published by the Committee. [Salt Lake City, Deseret News Press] 1922.
[26]l. illus., plates, ports. 23½×29½cm.
Title and text in yellow border.
USlC

9280. Utah election laws. Who can and who cannot vote among the "Mormons." Salt Lake City, Deseret News [1882]
13p. 22cm.
"Includes an act providing for the registration of voters and to further regulate the manner of conducting legislatures in this territory." Signed by Gov. George W. Emory.
CSmH, NjP, UHi, UPB, USlC, UU

9281. Utah Genealogical and Historical Magazine. Salt Lake City, Published by the Utah Genealogical and Historical Society, January, 1910–October, 1940.
31v. quarterly. 23cm.
Editor: Anthon H. Lund and others.
CU–B, ICN, NjP, NN, UHi, ULA, UPB, USl, USlC

9281a. Utah Gospel Mission. About the holy spirit and his wonderful works. Cleveland, Ohio, Utah Gospel Mission, 1924 [1923, 4th ed]
64p. 16½cm. (UGM series. No. 8)
USlC

9282. ———. Annual of the Utah Gospel Mission, of Cleveland, for 1914; chiefly from the annual reports approved Jan. 27, 1914. Cleveland, Ohio, Utah Gospel Mission [1914?]
24p. illus. 16½cm.
Cover-title.
NN, UHi

9283. ———. Annual report. Cleveland, Ohio, 1904–1930.
26v. 16½cm.
1904 — report.
1905 — The Story of our work awheel and afoot in Mormondom during 1904. Annual report of 1905.
1906 — Our 2,500 miles in Utah & Idaho during 1905. Annual report of 1906.
1907 — Our 4,500 miles by wagon in Utah & Idaho during 1906. Annual report of 1907.
1908 — Our work on wheels and afoot in Utah, Idaho, Wyoming, Nevada and Arizona, 1908.
1909 — Our work on wheels and afoot in Utah during 1908.
1910 — Our work through Utah awheel and afoot in 1909. Annual report 1910.
1911 — Our work in Utah, Idaho, Nevada, and Arizona and the East in 1910.
1912 — Our work in Utah, Idaho, Wyoming, Arizona, and the East in 1911.
1913 — Our work in Utah, Idaho, Arizona and the East in 1912. Part II, news of Mormon activity, etc.
1916–21, part I — Our work; part II — News of Mormon activity.
1922 — I. a. News of Mormon activity.
b. Reorganized or Eastern Mormons.
II. Our work.
1923 — Several sections on Mormonism.
NN, WHi

9284. ———. A brief description of the work of the Utah gospel mission among the Mormon people. [Cleveland, Ohio, 1904]
16p. illus. 16cm.
Caption-title.
NN, OClWHi

9285. ———. A glimpse of the mission and its work. Cleveland, Ohio, 1903.
4p. 16½cm.
CtY, OO

9286. ———. Memorial and protest in the matter of the admission of Brigham H. Roberts, who claims to be a member-elect from the State of Utah, to the House of Representatives, in the Fifty-sixth Congress of the United States of America. [Cleveland, O., n.d.]
4p. 18cm.
NN

9287. ———. A rapid view of the work of the Utah Gospel Mission for the Mormon people. October 1st, 1902. [Cleveland, Ohio, 1902]
20p. 22cm.
OClWHi, OO

9288. ———. The Road to glory-land, stories and short articles on what must I do to be saved. Cleveland, Ohio, Utah Gospel Mission, 1925.
24p. 18cm. (UGM Series. No. 11)
The doctrine of salvation.
MoInRC

9289. ———. What the mission has done. [Cleveland, Ohio, 1930]
[2]p. 20cm.
Caption-title.
USlC

9290. Utah Historical Quarterly. Salt Lake City, Board of Control, Utah Historical Society, Jan., 1928–
v. illus. 23½cm.
Editor: Jan. 1928. J. C. Alter and others.
List of charter members of the society. V.1, p. 98–99.
CSmH, CU-B, DLC, ICN, IdIF, NjP, UHi, ULA, UPB, UU

9291. Utah-Idaho Sugar Company. The beet sugar industry and the church, excerpts from the 51st anniversary report. [n.p., n.d.]
[8]p. 28cm.
UPB

9292. The Utah Indian War veteran's songster. Salt Lake City, Skelton Publishing Co., 1907.
80p. 17cm.
Most of the songs have original words; many with religious import.
NjP, UPB, USlC

9293. Utah. Irrigation Commission. Irrigation in Utah; a book published by direction of the Utah Irrigation Commission. Report of the Irrigation Commission to the Third National Irrigation Congress, held at Denver, September, 1894; articles concerning irrigation work and conditions in Utah, and problems of the arid West. Salt Lake City, 1895.
128p. illus., plates, ports. 22cm.
The Mormon land system in Utah, by George Q. Cannon, p. 31–36.
Other editions: 112p. USlC; 130p. USlC
NN, UHi, UPB, USlC

9294. Utah Magazine. Salt Lake City, January 17, 1868–December 25, 1869.
3v. 21cm.
Edited by Elias L. T. Harrison, E. W. Tullidge, John Tullidge (etc.)
Suspended July 11 — Aug. 29, 1868, March 27–May 2, 1869.
An offspring of the *Peep O'Day*. It was used to bring forth the 'Godbeite Movement.'
CSmH; MH; NN V.3; USlC V.1–2, 3 inc.

9295. Utah. Mormon Battalion Monument Commission. The Mormon Battalion and its monument. [Salt Lake City] 1920.
[3]p. 23cm.
UPB

9296. ———. (same) [Salt Lake City, 1920?]
[8]p. 23cm.
UU

9297. ———. The Mormon Battalion and its monument. A compilation of data for sculptors and architects. Salt Lake City, Published by order of the State of Utah, Mormon Battalion Committee. [Salt Lake City, 1916]
3p.l. [7]–56p. map, port. 23cm.
Includes a history of the march by May Belle Thurman Davis.
CU-B, NjP, UHi, USlC

9298. ———. Mormon Battalion Monument. Souvenir brochure, program and historical sketch. May 30, 1927. [Salt Lake City] 1927.
39p. illus. 25cm.
CU-B, DLC, NjP, UHi, UPB, USlC

9298a. ———. Report of the State of Utah Mormon Battalion Monument Committee. To the Legislative Assembly of the State of Utah . . . [Salt Lake City, 1916?]
15p. 23cm.
USlC

9298b. Utah Mormonism exposed. From bible prophecy. Also from their own works, at Opera House, Sunday, Dec. 12, 11.00 A. M., 3.00 and 7:00 P. M. By R. Etzenhouser, of Independence, Mo. The Public invited. Admission Free. Press Print, Emporium, Pa., [n.d.]
Broadside. 23×15cm.
UPB

9299. Utah Musical Times. Salt Lake City, March 15, 1876–March 1, 1878.
2v. monthly. 26cm.
Editors: David O. Calder and George Careless.
Most of the music is Mormon hymns.
MH V.1, NjP, USlC

9300. De Utah-Nederlander. Salt Lake City, April 2, 1914–October 3, 1935.
22v. weekly. 62cm.
Editors: Janne M. Sjodahl and William J. DeBry, later, A. L. Peterson.
Newspaper published for the Dutch members of the church in Salt Lake City.
Title in English: The Utah Dutchman.
USlC

9301. ———. Centennial jubilee number, April 6, 1830–April 6, 1930. [Salt Lake City] 1930.
60p. illus. 40cm.
UHi, UPB, USlC

9302. Utah Pioneer Jubilee, July 20th to 24th, 1897. Official program. [Salt Lake City, George Q. Cannon and Sons] 1897.
[10]p. 27½cm.
CU-B, UPB

9303. Utah Pioneeren; a Danish-Norwegian newspaper. Salt Lake City, October 10, 1895–
Published irregularly. 35½×54½cm.
Title in English: Utah pioneer.
USlC #1–2, October 10, 28, 1895

9304. The Utah pioneers; celebration of the entrance of the pioneers into Great Salt Lake Valley. Thirty-third anniversary, July 24, 1880. Full account of the proceedings; the procession, the speeches, the music, the decorations, descriptive and historical discourse on the pioneers. Salt Lake City, Deseret News Printing and Publishing Establishment, 1880.
52p. 22cm.
CSmH, CU-B, DLC, MH, NjP, NN, UHi, ULA, UOgW, USlC, UU

9305. Utah Posten . . . Salt Lake City, December 20, 1873–September 3, 1874.
1v. (36 nos.) weekly. 58–63cm.
Newspaper published for the Danish-Norwegian members of the Church in Utah.
Editor: P. O. Thomassen.
Title in English: Utah post.
USlC comp.

9306. Utah Posten. Salt Lake City, Published by Andrew Jenson, January 1, 1885–April 8, 1885.
1v. (15 issues) weekly. 63cm.
Editors: Andrew Jenson and C. A. F. Orlob.
After 3 months it was consolidated with *Bikuben*.
Published for the Danish Mormons in Utah.
Title in English: Utah post.
UHi, USlC

9307. Utah Posten; a Swedish weekly. Salt Lake City, December 20, 1873–October, 1935.
35v. weekly. 58cm.
Organ for Swedish Mormons in Utah.
USlC comp.

9308. ———. Centennial jubilee number, April 6, 1830–April 6, 1930. [Salt Lake City, 1930]
64p. illus. 40cm.
UHi, UPB, USlC

9309. The Utah Review. Salt Lake City, H. Palmerston & Company, July, 1881–1882.
2v. monthly. 21½cm.
A magazine of religion; many Mormon articles, Salt Lake Seminary, University of Utah.
CSmH, CU-B, NjP, USlC V.1 #1, 6, 9, 10

9310. Utah. Semi-Centennial Commission. The book of the pioneers; a record of those who arrived in the valley of the Great Salt Lake during the year 1847; including the names, ages, autographs and places of residences of all known survivors on July 24, 1897, "The year of jubilee!" [Salt Lake City, 1898?]
2v. (52p.) 39½cm.
UHi copy has autographs of all surviving pioneers.
UHi, UPB, USlC

9311. ———. Catalogue of the relics, souvenirs and curios associated with the pioneers of Utah, now on exhibition in the hall of relics, main street, Salt Lake City, Salt Lale [sic] City, From the Press of G. Q. Cannon & Sons Co. [1897]
32p. 23cm.
Cover-title: Pioneers' arrival, July 24, 1847 . . . The year of jubilee, July 24, 1897. Salt Lake City and the State of Utah.
View of hall of relics on p. [4] of cover.
Introduction signed: Spencer Clawson, chairman of Semi-centenial [sic] Commission.
Relics of the pioneer era.
CtY, DLC, InU, MH, NN, UHi, UPB, USlC, UU

9312. ———. Official report and financial statement of the Utah Semi-Centennial Commission and official programme of the Utah Pioneer Jubilee held at Salt Lake City, Utah, July 20–25, 1897, in commemoration of the fifteenth anniversary of the arrival of the first band of pioneers in the valley of the Great Salt Lake. Salt Lake City, Deseret News Publishing Co., 1899.
99p. 22½cm.
Cover-title: The Utah Pioneer Jubilee.
CSmH, NN, UHi, UPB

9313. ———. Utah pioneer jubilee, in commemoration of the fiftieth anniversary of the arrival of the first band of pioneers in the Valley of the Great Salt Lake, July 20 to 24, 1897. Official program . . . [Salt Lake City, G. Q. Cannon and Sons, Co.] 1897.
[8]p. 35cm.
Cover-title: Program of the Utah pioneer Jubilee, July 20th to 24th, 1897.
CLU, CtY, NjP, UHi, UPB, USlC

9313a. ———. Utah Pioneer jubilee, Salt Lake City, July 20–25, 1897. [Salt Lake City, 1897]
[4]p. 16cm. (Bulletin No. 3)
USlC

9314. Utah Skandinav . . . Salt Lake City, 1874–1877.
v.
A Scandinavian newspaper in Salt Lake City.
Editor: M. Froiseth–
A liberal paper advocating Scandinavian rights and progress, considered anti-Mormon by the Church.
Title in English: Utah Scandinavian.
Mulder
No copies located

9315. Utah State gazetteer and business directory . . . Salt Lake City, 1874–1931.
v. 25cm.
Early editions edited by Edward L. Sloan, H. L. A. Culmer, Robert W. Sloan. *See Edward L. Sloan and Robert W. Sloan for earlier editions (Culmer was a co-editor.)*
1874 edition under title: Gazeteer of Utah and Salt Lake City; 1883–84: The Utah directory; 1879–1880, 1884, 1888: Utah Gazetteer and directory.
Biographical and historical information.
CU-B 1900, 1916–17, 1927–28; NjP; UHi; UPB 1874, 1879–1880, 1884, 1888, 1890, 1892–93, 1903–04, 1908, 1912–13, 1914–15, 1916–17, 1918–19, 1920–21, 1922–23, 1924–25, 1927–28, 1930–31; USlC

9316. Utah Stake Silk Association. Constitution of the Utah Stake Silk Association. [n.p., n.d.]
[2]p. 22cm.
Organized within the framework of the Church.
UPB

9317. Utah statehood. Reasons why it should not be granted. Will the American people surrender the territory to an unscrupulous and polygamous theocracy? Embracing: The Mormon preliminary movement; the Democratic and Republican refusal to take part and their reasons therefore; Utah Commission report; Governor West in opposition; review of the proposed Mormon constitution; its failure to meet the requirements of the occasion. Salt Lake City, Tribune Print., 1887.
16, 71 [1]p. 22cm.
Report of the Utah Commission to the Secretary of the Interior for the year 1887 has special title-page.
CLU, CSmH, CtY, CU-B, DLC, ICN, MH, MiU, NjP, NN, UU, WHi

9318. The Utah Survey. Salt Lake City, September, 1913–1916.
3v. 27cm.
Published by the Social Service Commission of the Episcopal Church in Utah; by the Utah Survey Association. Includes a great deal of material on Mormonism.
CU-B V.1, V.2 #5; UHi V.1 #1, 6, 10, V.2 #6–7, V.3 #1–7; ULA V.1 #2–10, V.2 #1–7, V.3 #1–5; UPB V.1 #1–10, V.2 #1–7, V.3 #1, 4, 6, 7

9319. Utah (Territory) Board of Trade. Resources and attractions of the Territory of Utah. Prepared by the Utah Board of Trade. Omaha, Republican Book and Railroad Printing House, 1879.
74p. plates. 22cm.
A pamphlet to attract new residents, with the Mormon problem ignored.
UHi

9320. Utah (Territory) Citizens. . . . Admission of Utah as a state in the Union. Memorial of citizens of the Territory of Utah asking for the admission of Utah as a state . . . June 23, 1882 . . . [Washington, Govt. Print. Off., 1882]
13p. 23cm. (U.S. 47th Cong. 1st Sess. House. Misc. Doc. No. 43)
Caption-title.
NjP, UHi, ULA, UU

9321. ———. . . . Against the admission of Utah as a state. Memorial of citizens of Utah, against The admission of that Territory as a state . . . [Washington, Govt. Print. Off.] 1872.
82p. 24cm. (U.S. 42nd Cong. 2d Sess. House. Misc. Doc. No. 208)
Objections based in part on distrust of the Mormons. Includes a list of signers.
CtY, CU-B, NjP, NN, ULA, UPB, USlC, UU

9322. ———. The Cullom bill! Remonstrance and resolutions adopted by a mass meeting of the Citizens of Utah, held in the Tabernacle, Salt Lake City, March 31st, 1870. Salt Lake City, Printed at the "Deseret News" Office [1870]
6p. 20½cm.
UPB

9323. ———. . . . Memorial of citizens of Utah Territory remonstrating against legislation asked for in a recent memorial of members of the legal profession, and asking the appointment of a commission to investigate all matters of complaint relating to that Territory. [Washington, Franklin Telegraph Co.?] 1873.
12p. 23cm. (U.S. 42nd Cong. 3d Sess. Senate. Misc. Doc. No. 73)
Protest against polygamy legislation.
CU, CU-B, NjP, UHi, ULA, UPB, UU

UTAH (TERRITORY) COMMISSIONER

9324. ———. Memorial to Congress: To the Honorable the Senate and House of Representatives of the United States, in Congress assembled. [Salt Lake City, 1878?]
Broadside. 30×20½cm.
Concerning polygamy legislation.
UPB

9325. ———. Non-Mormon citizens of Utah. Memorial of a committee of forty-five gentlemen, selected at a public meeting of non-Mormon residents and voters of Salt Lake City, in the Territory of Utah, held on the 19th of January 1874, to prepare a memorial to Congress, setting forth the grievances of the non-Mormon people of said Territory, and for such legislation by Congress as is needed for the full protection of all classes of people residing in said Territory. [Washington, Govt. Print. Off.] 1874.
8p. 23cm. (U.S. 43rd Cong. 1st Sess. House. Misc. Doc. No. 120)
Caption-title.
CU-B, NjP, ULA, UPB

9326. ———. . . . Petition of citizens of Utah Territory praying that the elective franchise in that Territory may be restricted to those who give unqualified allegiance to the government of the United States. [Washington, Govt. Print. Off.] 1890.
3p. 23cm. (U.S. 51st Cong. 1st Sess. Senate. Misc. Doc. No. 156)
Material on the People's Party of Utah, and its relationship to the Mormon church.
NjP, UPB, USlC

9327. ———. Petition of residents of Utah Territory praying that the protection of the general government may not be withdrawn from them by the admission of that Territory as a State. [Washington, Govt. Print. Off.] 1872.
8p. (U.S. 42nd Cong. 2d Sess. Senate. Misc. Doc. No. 118)
CU, CU-B, NjP, UPB

———. *See Protest från några av Förenta staternas senatorer . . .*

9328. ———. To the Honorable the Senate and House of Representatives in Congress Assembled. [Salt Lake City? 1886?]
Broadside. 35½×21½cm.
Protest against polygamy legislation.
UPB, USlC

9329. ———. To the Senate and House of Representatives in Congress assembled. We, the undersigned Committee, selected at a public meeting of the non-Mormon voters of Salt Lake City, held the 19th of January, 1874, in pursuance of the following resolution . . . [Salt Lake City, 1874]
4p. 37cm.
Quotes from Mormons and others wishing to maintain home rule.
MH

9330. Utah (Territory) Commissioner of schools. . . . Letter from Governor of Utah, transmitting the fourth annual report of the Commissioner of Schools for Utah Territory. [Washington, Govt. Print. Off., 1892]
16p. charts. 23cm. (U.S. 52nd Cong. 1st Sess. House. Misc. Doc. No. 47)
Signed: Dec. 31, 1891.
Mentions Mormons and Mormon schools. Report of Commissioner of Schools for Utah, 1891.
NjP, ULA, UPB

9331. ———. Letter from the Secretary of the Interior, transmitting a letter of the Governor of Utah and a report of the Commissioner of Public Schools. [Washington, Govt. Print. Off.] 1891.
14p. charts. 23cm. (U.S. 51st Cong. 2d Sess. Senate. Ex. Doc. No. 46)
Report of Commissioner of Schools for Utah, 1890.
NjP, ULA, UPB

9332. ———. . . . Letter from the Secretary of the Interior, transmitting annual report of Commissioner of Schools for Utah. [Washington, Govt. Print. Off., 1895]
18p. charts. 23cm. (U.S. 53rd Cong. 2d Sess. Senate. Ex. Doc. No. 24)
Signed: Jan. 10, 1894.
Distinction between Mormon and non-Mormon children to be deleted as offensive to the citizens.
NjP, ULA, UPB

9333. ———. Letter from the Secretary of the Interior, transmitting report of the Commissioner of Schools for Utah . . . [Washington, Govt. Print. Off.] 1889.
42p. 23½cm. (U.S. 50th Cong. 2d Sess. Senate. Ex. Doc. No. 87)
References and data on Mormons in relation to schools in Utah.
NjP, ULA, UPB

9334. ———. . . . Letter from the Secretary of the Interior, transmitting the report of the Commissioner of Schools for Utah. Washington, Govt. Print. Off.] 1893.
20p. charts. 23cm. (U.S. 52nd Cong. 2d Sess. Senate. Ex. Doc. No. 30)
Report of Commissioner of Schools for Utah, 1892. Some information on Mormon schools.
NjP, ULA, UPB

9335. ———. Letter from the Secretary of the Interior, transmitting the second annual report of the Commissioner of Schools for Utah. [Washington, Govt. Print. Off.] 1890.
15p. 23cm. (U.S. 51st Cong. 1st Sess. Senate. Ex. Doc. No. 27)
A good deal of information on Mormons with regard to the school situation.
NjP, ULA, UPB

9336. Utah (Territory) Constitutional Convention. . . . Admission of Utah into the Union. Memorial of the convention to frame a constitution for the admission of Utah into the Union as a state . . . April 2, 1872 . . . [Washington, Govt. Print. Off., 1872]
21p. 22½cm. (U.S. 42nd Cong. 2d Sess. House. Misc. Doc. No. 165)
Caption-title.
CU, CU-B, NjP, UHi, ULA, UU

9337. ———. Constitution of the State of Deseret. Memorials of the legislature and constitutional convention of Utah Territory, praying the admission of said Territory into the Union as the State of Deseret. [Washington, Govt. Print. Off., 1862]
11p. 21½cm. (U.S. 37th Cong. 2d Sess. House. Misc. Doc. No. 78)
USlC

9338. ———. Constitution of the State of Utah and memorial to Congress asking admission into the Union. [Salt Lake City] 1887.
27p. 21cm.
"Memorial of the convention of Utah, p. 23–27. Objecting to reasons statehood not granted.
MH, NN

9339. ———. Constitution of the State of Utah, with the proceedings of the Constitutional Convention. [Salt Lake City, 1887]
53p. 21cm.
Signed: John T. Caine, President; Heber M. Wells, Secretary.
Ratification and memorial to Congress asking for admission as a state. Abstract of vote.
CU, NjP, USlC

9340. ———. Letter of the delegate of the Territory of Utah in Congress, enclosing the memorial of delegates of the convention which assembled in Great Salt Lake City, and adopted a constitution with a view to the admission of Utah into the Union as a State . . . [Washington] 1858.
10p. 22½cm. (U.S. 35th Cong. 1st Sess. Senate. Misc. Doc. No. 240)
Caption-title.
Includes the Constitution of Deseret.
CU, CU-B, DLC, NjP, ULA, UPB

9341. ———. Memorial of the Constitutional Convention of Utah. [Washington, Govt. Print. Off., 1889]
14p. 23cm. (U.S. 50th Cong. 1st Sess. House. Misc. Doc. No. 104)
Memorial of the Constitutional Convention of Utah, with the proposed constitution.
Signed: Jan. 12, 1888.
DLC, NjP, ULA, UPB

9342. ———. Official report of the proceedings and debates of the convention assembled at Salt Lake City, on the fourth day of March, 1895 to adopt a constitution for the state of Utah. Salt Lake City, Star Printing Co., 1898.
2v. 26cm.
Includes an anti-polygamy clause.
CU, DLC, NN, UHi, USlC, UU

9343. ———. Utah Territory. Memorial of a convention of the people of the Territory of Utah, accompanied by a State constitution, asking admission into the Union. [Washington, Govt. Print. Off.] 1860.
11p. 22½cm. (U.S. 36th Cong. 2d Sess. House. Misc. Doc. No. 10)
CU, CU-B, NjP, ULA, UPB

9344. Utah (Territory) Courts. Supreme Court. Charlotte Arthur, Plaintiff vs. Brigham Young estate, Defendants. Transcript and statement on appeal. Goldthwaite and Maxwell, and E. F. Dunne, for Plaintiff and Appellant. Sheeks & Rawlins, for the Defendants and Respondents. Salt Lake City, 1879.
26p. 21cm.
Cover-title.
At head of title: In the Supreme Court of Utah Territory.
Suit by Mrs. Charlotte Arthur against Brigham Young estate to recover land in Salt Lake City, involving question of discipline within the Mormon Church.
NN

9345. Utah (Territory) Governor. Annual reports of the governor of Utah to the Secretary of the Interior, 1879–1895.
v . 23cm.
A great deal on Mormonism in each report, which is much stronger than the messages to the legislature. Found as separates and in the annual report of the Department of the Interior. Annual reports also include material from the Superintendant of Indian Affairs and reports of the Utah Commission.
DLC, NjP, UPB inc., UU

9346. Utah (Territory) Governor. 1850–1858 (Young). First annual message of his excellency, to the Legislative Assembly of Utah Territory. Sept. 22, 1851. Printed by order of the legislature. [Great Salt Lake City, 'News,' Office, 1851]
4p. 21cm.
Crudely printed pamphlet in double columns.
USlC

9347. ———. (same) Salt Lake City, News, Print., 1851.
4p. 21cm.
Printed in single column; much better printed than above.
CtY, USlC

UTAH (TERRITORY) GOVERNOR. 1858–1861

9348. ———. Annual message of Governor Brigham Young presented to the Legislature of Utah. December 13, 1852. G.S.L. City, 200 copies printed by authority, George Hales, Public Printer, 1852.
10p. 18cm.
Signed: Brigham Young, December 13, 1852.
Includes the church's position on home manufacturing; the gold rush.
USlC

9349. ———. Governor's message to the Legislative Assembly of Utah Territory. January 5, 1852. [Salt Lake City, 1852]
8p. 21cm.
Items pertinent to the growth of Utah, Indian affairs, capitol to be moved to Fillmore, etc.
CSmH, CtY, NjP, UPB, USlC

9350. ———. Governor's message to the Legislative Assembly of the Territory of Utah. Delivered December eleventh, A.D. Eighteen hundred and fifty four. [Great Salt Lake City, Joseph Cain, Public Printer, 1854]
7p. 21½cm.
Signed: Dec. 11, 1854, Brigham Young p. 7.
NjP, USlC

9351. ———. Governor's message to the Legislative Assembly of the Territory of Utah, delivered in the capitol, Fillmore City, Millard County, December Tenth A.D. Eighteen hundred and fifty-five . . . [Great Salt Lake City, 1855]
8p. 19cm.
Signed: Fillmore City, Dec. 10, 1855.
Many ms. corrections including the date changed to the 11th.
Information on home manufacturing, laws, and military implementation.
USlC

9352. ———. Governor's message to the Legislative Assembly of the Territory of Utah: delivered in Great Salt Lake City, December 15, A.D. 1857. . . [Great Salt Lake City, 1857]
11p. 21cm.
Denies responsibility for Mountain Meadows massacre. Defies new federal appointees and declares Utah will be defended.
CSmH, CtY, CU–B, NjP, UPB, USlC

9353. ———. Governor's message to the members of the Council and House of Representatives of the Legislature of Utah. [Great Salt Lake City, 1853]
8p. 19½cm.
Signed: Dec. 12, 1853.
Extent of laws and the opportunities in a new area.
USlC

9354. ———. Proclamation. By the Governor. Citizens of Utah — We are invaded by a hostile force who are evidently assailing us to accomplish our overthrow and destruction . . . [Great Salt Lake City, 1857]
Broadside: 28×19cm.
Signed: Great Salt Lake City, Territory of Utah, this fifth day of August, A. D. eighteen hundred and fifty seven and of the Independence of the United States of America the eighty second.
CU–B, ICN, NjP, UPB, USlC, UU

9354a. ———. (Same) [Great Salt Lake City, 1857]
Broadside. 28×19cm.
Variant printing. Signed: Great Salt Lake City, Territory of Utah, this fifteenth day of September, A. D. Eighteen hundred and fifty seven and of the Independence of the United States of America the eighty second.
UPB, USlC, UU

9355. Utah (Territory) Governor. 1858–1861 (Cumming). By Alfred Cumming. Governor, Utah Territory. A proclamation. [Great Salt Lake City? 1859]
Broadside. 28½×20½cm.
Signed: Great Salt Lake City, March 27, 1859.
Protesting U.S. troop movements into Provo.
CU–B, USlC

9356. ———. . . . Cessation of difficulties in Utah, Message from the President of the United States relative to the probable termination of Mormon troubles in Utah territory. [Washington, 1858]
7p. 23cm. (U.S. 35th Cong. 1st Sess. House. Ex. Doc. No. 138)
Caption-title.
CtY, NjP

9357. ———. Governor's message to the Legislative Assembly of the Territory of Utah. December 13, 1858. [Great Salt Lake City? 1858]
5p. 20cm.
Discusses the Utah Expedition.
UPB, USlC

9358. ———. Message of the President of the United States, communicating a despatch from Governor Cumming, relative to the termination of the difficulties with the Territory of Utah. [Washington, William A. Harris] 1858.
7p. 23cm. (U.S. 35th Cong. 1st Sess. Senate. Ex. Doc. No. 67)
Letters relative to the termination of the difficulties in the Territory of Utah; report of Governor Cumming upon the establishment of the Territorial government and the suppression of rebellion in the Territory.
CU–B, NjP, UHi, UPB, USl, UU

9359. Utah (Territory) Governor. 1861 (Dawson). Governor's message to the Legislative Assembly of Utah. [Great Salt Lake City, 1861]
9p. 19cm.
Quotes Mormon position on the secession of the South. A little on the Mormons.
CU-B, USlC

9360. Utah (Territory) Governor. 1862–1863 (Harding). In the Senate of the United States . . . Gentlemen of the Council and House of Representatives of the Territory of Utah: [Washington, Govt. Print. Off.] 1863.
16p. 23cm. (U.S. 37th Cong. 3d Sess. Senate. Misc. Doc. No. 37)
Little reference to Mormonism.
CU, CU-B, MH, NjP, UPB

9361. Utah (Territory) Governor 1871–1875 (Woods). Governor's Message to the Legislative Assembly of the Territory of Utah. Salt Lake City, 1872.
12p. 20½cm.
Section on plural marriage in the territory.
CU-B, USlC

9362. Utah (Territory) Governor. 1876–1880 (Emery). Governor's message to the Legislative Assembly of the Territory of Utah. Salt Lake City, Jan. 11, 1876.
8p. 22cm.
Signed: Jan. 11, 1876.
Refers to polygamy as a crime; his refusal to condone it.
USlC

9363. ———. Message of Governor Emery to the Legislative Assembly of Utah Territory convened at Salt Lake City, January 14th, 1878. Salt Lake City, John W. Pike, Public Printer, 1878.
34 [1]p. 21cm.
Polygamy and the Mountain Meadows massacre mentioned.
NjP, USl

9364. ———. Utah election laws. Who can and who cannot vote among the "Mormons." Salt Lake City, Deseret News Company, Printers [1880?]
13p. 19½cm.
NjP, UU

9365. Utah (Territory) Governor. 1880–1886 (Murray). Governor's message and accompanying documents, Twenty-fifth session of the Legislative Assembly, of the Territory of Utah, 1882. Salt Lake City, T. E. Taylor, Public Printer, 1882.
27p. 22cm.
Caption-title.
Political situation and church involvement.
CU-B, NjP, NN, UPB

9366. ———. Message of his Excellency Gov. Eli H. Murray to the Twenty-sixth session of the Legislative Assembly of Utah Territory, 1884, with accompanying documents . . . [Salt Lake City] T. E. Taylor, 1884.
23p. tables. 22½cm.
Early history of Utah, Utah Expedition, political participation of the Mormons, polygamy.
CSmH, CU-B, MH, NjP, UPB, USlC

9367. ———. Report of the Governor of Utah made to the Secretary of the Interior for the year 1880. Washington, Govt. Print. Off., 1880.
9p. tables. 23cm.
Reports "social conditions" in Utah during 1880.
UPB

9368. ———. Report of the Governor of Utah, made to the Secretary of the Interior, for the year 1883. Washington, Govt. Print. Off., 1883.
13p. 20½cm.
Material on polygamy and church-state relations.
USlC

9369. ———. Report of the Governor of Utah to the Secretary of the Interior . . . 1885. Washington, Govt. Print. Off., 1885.
31p. tables. 23cm.
Reports the Mormon leaders' control of the people.
UPB

9370. Utah (Territory) Governor. 1886–1889 (West). Governor's message. A candid document dealing freely with evils. Disloyal legislation must go . . . [Salt Lake City, 1888]
4p. 21cm.
Caption-title.
In double columns.
At head of title: With compliments of the Democratic and Republican Territorial Committees of Utah.
MH

9371. ———. Message of his excellency Governor Caleb W. West and accompanying documents. Twenty-eighth Session of the Legislative Assembly of the Territory of Utah. Salt Lake City, Geo. C. Lambert, Public Printer, 1888.
24p. 22cm.
Church and state as it relates to the Mormon problem.
CU-B, USl, USlC

9372. ———. Report of the Governor of Utah to the Secretary of the Interior. 1886. Washington, Govt. Print. Off., 1886.
17p. 23cm.
"Polygamy in Legislation," p. 12.
NjP, USlC

UTAH (TERRITORY) LEGISLATIVE

9373. ———. Report of the Governor of Utah to the Secretary of the Interior. 1887. Washington, Govt. Print. Off., 1887.
40p. 22cm.
Statehood issue as it relates to the Mormon problem.
USl

9374. ———. Report of the Governor of Utah to the Secretary of the Interior. 1888. Washington, Govt. Print. Off., 1888.
24p. 22cm.
Proper position of church and state.
USl

9375. Utah (Territory) Governor. 1889–1893 (Thomas). Report of the Governor of Utah to the Secretary of Interior. 1889. Washington, Govt. Print. Off., 1889.
32p. 21cm.
"The situation," p. 23–31. Mormons and polygamy.
MH

9376. ———. Report of the Governor of Utah to the Secretary of the Interior, 1890. Washington, Govt. Print. Off., 1890.
35p. tables. 22½cm.
Section on the Mormon people; advice for future legislation.
MH, UPB, USlC

9377. ———. Report of the Governor of Utah to the Secretary of the Interior. 1891. Washington, Govt. Print. Off., 1891.
58p. tables. 22½cm.
Polygamy as affected by the Edmunds-Tucker Act and the political situation in Utah.
UPB

9378. ———. Report of the Governor of Utah to the Secretary of the Interior, 1892. Washington, Govt. Print. Off., 1892.
65p. tables. 22½cm.
Report of polygamy and church participation in politics.
UPB, USlC

9379. Utah (Territory) Governor. 1893–1896 (West). Memorial of the Territorial Legislature in favor of restoring certain real estate to the Mormon Church. February 1, 1894. [Washington, 1894]
2p. 23cm. (U.S. 53d Cong. 2d Sess. Senate. Misc. Doc. 81)
NN

9380. ———. Message of Governor Caleb W. West and accompanying documents to the Thirty-First Session of the Legislative Assembly of the Territory of Utah. 1894. Salt Lake City, James B. Bloor, Public Printer, 1894.
51p. 21cm.
A brief reference to a monument to Brigham Young.
MH

9381. ———. Report of the Governor of the Territory of Utah to the Secretary of the Interior. 1894. Washington, Govt. Print. Off., 1894.
22p. tables. 23cm.
Amnesty for polygamists described.
MH, UPB

9382. ———. Report of the Governor of Utah to the Secretary of the Interior. 1893. Washington, Govt. Print. Off., 1893.
19p. 22½cm.
Plea for restoration of church property confiscated under Edmunds-Tucker Act.
MH, UPB

9383. ———. . . . The Vice-President presented the following memorial of the Governor and Legislative Assembly in the Territory of Utah for the admission of Utah into the Union of States. [Washington, Govt. Print. Off., 1895]
2p. 23½cm. (U.S. 53rd Cong. 2d Sess. Senate. Misc. Doc. No. 100)
Signed: Feb. 28, 1894.
NjP, ULA, UPB

9384. Utah (Territory) Laws, statutes, etc. An act to provide for the further organization of the Militia of the Territory. [Salt Lake City, 1852]
24p. 21cm.
Signed: Feb. 5, 1852 by Brigham Young as Governor and W. Richards, President of the Council, W. W. Phelps, Speaker of the House of Representatives. Organization of the Nauvoo legion in Utah, created in 1849.
General laws of Utah Territory or those of the Territory of Deseret are not included in the present bibliography.
MH, USlC

9385. ———. Mormon legislation against polygamy. [Salt Lake City, 1888]
4p. 21cm.
Caption-title.
Signed: W. W. Riter, speaker [and others]
Marriage laws prior to statehood.
CU-B, MH, USlC

9386. Utah (Territory) Legislative Assembly. . . . Memorial of the Legislative Assembly of the Territory of Utah, protesting against the passage of the bills now pending in Congress or any other measures inimical to the people of said Territory, until after afull [sic] investigation by a Congressional Committee. [Washington, Govt. Print. Off.] 1884.
13p. 23cm. (U.S. 48th Cong. 1st Sess. House. Misc. Doc. No. 45)
Caption-title.
Includes some Utah history.
CU, CU-B, NjP, NN, UHi, ULA, UPB

9387. ———. . . . Memorial of the Legislative Assembly of Utah, asking for a commission of investigation to be sent to Utah to inquire into all alleged abuses in affairs there. [Washington, Govt. Print. Off.] 1874.
2p. 23½cm. (U.S. 43rd Cong. 1st Sess. House. Misc. Doc. No. 139)
Mormonism and politics.
CU, CU–B, NjP, ULA, UPB

9388. ———. . . . Memorial of the Legislative Assembly of Utah, setting forth the evils arising from the sweeping exercise of the absolute veto power of the governor, by which much needed legislation, including the general appropriation bill, has been defeated, and asking that this prerogative of the executive of the Territory be withdrawn and measures adopted from immediate relief. [Washington, Govt. Print. Off.] 1886.
20p . 23cm. (U.S. 49th Cong. 1st Sess. House. Misc. Doc. No. 238)
CU, NjP, ULA, UPB

9389. ———. Memorial of the members and officers of the Legislative Assembly of the Territory of Utah, setting forth their grievances, and praying Congress to reconsider the course already taken, to respect their constitutional rights, withdraw the troops, and give them a voice in the selection of their rulers [Washington, William A. Harris] 1858.
5p. 24cm. (U.S. 35th Cong. 1st Sess. Senate. Misc. Doc. No. 201)
CtY, CU, CU–B, NjP, UPB

9390. ———. Memorial to Congress, by the Legislative Assembly of the Territory of Utah, 1882. [Salt Lake City, 1882]
8p. 22½cm.
Cover-title.
Signed at end: Francis M. Lyman, Joseph Smith.
Memorial against polygamy legislation.
CtY, CU–B, DLC, MH, NjP, UHi, USIC

9391. ———. Mormon legislation against polygamy. [Salt Lake City, 1888]
4p. 23cm.
Signed: W. W. Riter, Speaker of the House of Representatives. Elias A. Smith, President of the Council. Caleb W. West, Governor of Utah Territory. Approved March 8th, 1888.
UPB, USIC

9392. ———. Veto power in Utah. Memorial of the Legislative Assembly of Utah, setting forth The evils arising from the sweeping exercise of the absolute veto power of the governor . . . [Washington, Govt. Print. Off.] 1886.
20p. 23cm. (U.S. 49th Cong. 1st Sess. House. Misc. Doc. No. 238)
Veto power exercised by the governor due to the political and religious situation.
USIC

9393. ———. . . . The Vice President presented the following letter from the Secretary of the Territory of Utah forwarding memorial of the Territorial Legislature in favor of restoring certain real estate to the Mormon Church. [Washington, Govt. Print. Off., 1895]
2p. 23½cm. (U.S. 53rd Cong. 2d Sess. Senate. Misc. Doc. No. 81)
Signed: Feb. 12, 1894.
NjP, ULA, UPB

9394. Utah (Territory) Legislative Assembly. Committee of the Judiciary. Report on the governor's message relating to the political situation "polygamy" and "governmental action." Submitted by the Committees on the Judiciary and Education, and adopted by the legislative council of the Territory of Utah. Salt Lake City, T. E. Taylor, 1882.
13p. 22cm.
Relates to polygamy and the political system.
CtY, CU–B, NjP, USIC

9395. ———. Your Committee, to whom was referred so much of the Governor's message . . . beg leave to submit the following report . . . [Salt Lake City, 1889]
12p. 23½cm.
Rebuttal to Governor Murray's message to the Legislature concerning polygamy.
UPB, USIC

9396. Utah (Territory) Mormon Women. Memorial of the Mormon women of Utah to the President and the Congress of the United States. The outrages of which they complain — The justice they demand. April 6, 1886. Washington, 1886.
8p. 23½cm.
Signed: Mrs. Sarah M. Kimball, Mrs. M. Isabella Horne, Mrs. Elmina S. Taylor [and others]
Unfair results of the Edmunds Act.
Reprinted from the *Congressional Record*, April 6, 1886.
CSmH, CtY, CU–B, ICN, NjP, PU, UPB, USIC

9397. ———. Memorial to the Honorable President, and the Senate and House of Representatives of the United States in Congress assembled: Gentlemen . . . [Salt Lake City? 1886?]
12p. 21cm.
Caption-title.
A memorial against polygamy legislation.
CU–B, MH, UHi, USIC, UU

9398. ———. "Mormon" women on plural marriage. Fifteen hundred 'Mormon' ladies convene in the Salt Lake Theatre, to protest against the misrepresentations of the ladies engaged in the anti-polygamy crusade, and declare their true sentiments on the subject now being agitated. Mass meeting in the theatre, Salt Lake City, Utah, Saturday, November 16, 1878. [Salt Lake City? 1878?]
8p. 21cm.
"Reported by G. F. Gibbs."
Variant printings.
MH, NjP, UPB, USIC

9399. ———. (same) [Salt Lake City? 1878?]
12p. 21½cm.
UU

9400. ———. . . . A petition of 22,626 women of Utah asking for the repeal of certain laws, the enactment of others, and the admission of the Territory of Utah as a State. [Washington, Govt. Print. Off.] 1876.
2p. 23cm. (U.S. 44th Cong. 1st Sess. House. Misc. Doc. No. 42)
Praying for the repeal of the anti-polygamy law of 1862, the enactment of a law granting to each married woman in Utah the right to homestead or preempt one hundred and sixty acres of land in her own name, and the admission of Utah as a State.
CU, CU-B, NjP, ULA, UPB

9401. ———. Proceedings in mass meeting of the ladies of Salt Lake City, to protest against the passage of Cullom's bill, January 14, 1870. [Salt Lake City, 1870]
1p.l., 8p. 24cm.
Caption-title.
Contains remarks of: Bathsheba W. Smith, Mrs. Levi Riter, Phoebe Woodruff, Mrs. Horne, Mrs. Eleanor M. Pratt, Eliza R. Snow, Mrs. Smith, Mrs. Kimball, Mrs. M'Minn, Harriet Cook Young, Mrs. H. T. King, and Mrs. Miner.
CtY, CU-B, NjP, UHi, UPB

9402. Utah (Territory) Women. To the Senators and Representatives of the United States of America in Congress assembled. [Salt Lake City, 1872]
Broadside. 41×22cm.
A petition from the women of Utah to Congress protesting against admission of Utah as a state.
CtY

9403. Utah (Territory) World's Fair Commission. Utah at the World's Columbian Exposition. [Salt Lake City, Press of the Salt Lake Lithographing Co., c1894]
172, lip. plates, ports. 27cm.
Includes material on the Tabernacle Choir.
CSmH, NjP, UHi, ULA, UPB, USlC, UU

9404. Utah Tract Society. Mormonism and the Bible — do they agree? [Salt Lake City, 1907?]
8p. 22cm.
MH, USlC

9405. ———. . . . Mormonism and the Bible, do they agree? More than half a hundred comparisons in deadly conflict. There are still others, equally antagonistic. Read and be convinced. Both can not be true! Which shall we accept? [Salt Lake City, Utah Tract Society, 1907?]
8p. 22cm.
MH

9406. ———. (same) Rev. 2d ed. Salt Lake City [n.d.]
15p. 17½cm.
UPB, USlC

9407. ———. Spirits in prison. Salt Lake City [n.d.]
8p. 17cm.
UPB

Utah. University. *See Deseret. University.*

9408. Utley, Henry Munson. Michigan as a province, territory and state, the 26th member of the federal union, by H. M. Utley, Byron M. Cutcheon, advisory editor, Clarence M. Burton. [New York] Isaac Mendoza Book Co., 1906.
4v. plates, ports., maps. 23½cm.
"King Strang and his kingdom," V. 3, Chapter 18.
CU, DLC, NjP, NN

THE VOICE OF THE CAPTIVES,

ASSEMBLED AT ZARAHEMLA,

IN ANNUAL CONFERENCE, APRIL 6, A. D. 1854,

TO THEIR BRETHREN SCATTERED ABROAD.

For in Mount Zion and in Jerusalem shall be deliverance, and in the REMNANT whom the LORD shall call. Joel ii: 32.

Go through, go through the gates, *prepare* ye the way of the People; lift up a *Standard* for the People. Isaiah lxii: 10.

Brethren and Sisters in the New and Everlasting Covenant:

In our former Communication to you, entitled "A Word of Consolation," &c., we reminded you of the law of GOD in relation to the perpetuity of the authority which GOD has committed to men for the pruning His vineyard for the *last time*, called the Holy Priesthood; and the legitimate exercise of the various offices in that Priesthood, showing, that each can act acceptably in his own place, but none out of it; also that the Presidency of this Priesthood vests—of right and by law—in the seed of him to whom it was first committed for the work of the dispensation. The same Law and precedents that prove the rights of lineage in regard to the first Presidency of the church, applies to the Patriarchal office with equal force. To confirm this, a single quotation shall suffice: See Doctrine and Covenants, sec. 103, par. 29. "That my servant Hiram may take the office of Priesthood and Patriarch, which was appointed unto him by his father, by blessing and also by right." Why did not a *brother* of the former patriarch succeed him? Because the *blessing* and the *right* forbade it, (right continues to be right,) and confirmed it upon a Son, not a brother. I hate robbery,

Item 9487. The second tract issued by the Wisconsin Latter-day Saints who were instrumental in forming the Reorganized Church of Jesus Christ of Latter Day Saints. From the Brigham Young University collection.

9409. Vahl, I. Er Mormonlaeren sand eller ikke? Efter det Engleske ved I. Vahl, Cap. for Farum og Kirkevaerlose. Kobenhavn, 1857.
80p.
Title in English: Is the Mormon doctrine true or not?
Schmidt

9410. Vahl, Jens. Mormonernes laerdomme ifølge deres egne skrifter og betragtede i Christendommens Lys. udgivet ved J. Vahl. [Aalborg, Trykt hos Oluf Olufsen 1860?]
4 nos. (16p.) 21cm.
Title in English: Mormon doctrine according to their own scriptures.
USlC

9411. ———. (same) Kjobenhavn, Af Forentungen til gudelige Smaastrifters unbredelse, 1877.
[16]p. 17cm.
USlC

9412. Valentine, Sophy. Biography of Ann Howell Burt. Brigham City, Utah, 1916.
1p.l. [7]–108p. ports. 23½cm.
Mormon biography.
CSmH, CtY, CU–B, NjP, UPB

9413. Valentini, Zopito, *editor.* Attivita' Italiane nella Intermountain region. Salt Lake City, International Publishing Company [c1930]
2p.l., 7–307p. illus. (part col.) ports. 31cm.
Title in English: Italian activities of the intermountain region.
Mormon church, p. 29–37.
UHi, UPB, USlC

9414. Valk, M. H. A. Van Der. De Mormonen. Hun profeet, leer en leven. Door M. H. A. Van der Valk. Kampen, Netherlands [1924]
2p.l. [7]–96p. plates. 20cm.
Preface signed: 1924.
Title in English: The Mormons, their prophet, their teachings, and their life.
USlC

9415. ———. De Profeet der Mormonen Joseph Smith, Jr. Door M. H. A. Van Der Valk. Met een woord vooraf van Dr. J. Van Der Valk. Kampen, J. H. Kok, 1921.
2p.l. [5]–308p. plates, ports., facsims. 24½cm.
Title in English: Joseph Smith, the Mormon prophet.
CU–B, MH, NN, UPB, USlC, WHi

9416. ———. Zur Beurteilung des Propheten der Mormonen Joseph Smith jun. Ägyptologische Phantasien des Mormonenpropheten. Von Dr. M. H. A. Van der Valk. Aus den Höllanderischen übersetzt von A. Basedow Pfarrer in Eisenberg (Thür) Leipzig, J. C. Hinrichische Buchhandlung, 1923.
vi, [1]l., 56p. vii plates. 22½cm.
Title in English: Contribution to a judgment of the Mormon Joseph Smith.
MH

9417. Valkyrien. Salt Lake City, 1890.
v. weekly.
Organ of Danish Mormons in Utah.
Editor, J. P. Jacobsen.
Published for a few months in 1890.
USlC V.1 #7–13.

9418. Valley Tan. Great Salt Lake City, November 6, 1858–February 29, 1860.
1v. (#1–52) weekly. 48cm.
Begun as *Kirk Anderson's Valley Tan.*
Published to oppose both the policies of Brigham Young and Governor Alfred Cumming.
CtY, ICN, USl, USlC

Van Dellen, I. *See Dellen, I. Van.*

9419. Vanderhoof, Elisha Woodward. Historical sketches of western New York: The Seneca Indians; Phelps and Gorham purchase; Morris reserve and Holland purchase; Mary Jemison; Jemima Wilkinson; Joseph Smith, jr. and Mormonism; Morgan and antimasonry; The Fox sisters and Rochester knockings, by E. W. Vanderhoof . . . Buffalo, N.Y., Printed for private distribution by the Matthews-Northrup works, 1907.
viii, 232p. ports., fold. map. 25cm.
DLC, NN

Van Der Valk, M. H. A. *See Valk, M. H. A. Van Der.*

9420. Vandervis, Jacob C. Why I left the Mormon Church. 2d ed. Nashville, Tenn., World Vision Publishing Company [n.d.]
23p. 15cm.
UPB

9421. Van der Zee, Jacob. The Mormon trails in Iowa, by Jacob Van der Zee. [Iowa City, Ia., 1914]
16p. fold. map. 28p.
Cover-title.
Reprinted from the *Iowa Journal of History and Politics,* January, 1914.
An account of the passage of the Mormons through Iowa on their way to Utah, 1846–1847.
DLC, IaHa, IaHi, USl

VAN DEUSEN, I. M.

9422. Van Deusen, Increase McGee. The Mormon endowment; a secret drama, or conspiracy, in the Nauvoo-temple, in 1846; in which process Mr. & Mrs. McGee, (the authors of this work,) were made king and queen, to which is added a sketch of the life of Joseph Smith, the circumstances of his finding the Mormon bible; his last revelation in the appointment of his successor; the angel's appearance to him; his finding another bible; his revelation concerning Polk and the Mexican war; Baptism for the dead–Mormon faith–Spiritual-wife-doctrine; description of Nauvoo and the Temple, &c., &c. Syracuse, N.Y., N. M. D. Lathrop, printer, 1847.
iii [4]–24p. 2 illus. 22½cm.
p. 10 signed "I. McGee V. D. & Maria his wife." "Syracuse, June 5, 1847."
First edition. A copy in the Yale University Library tentatively called the first edition by Morgan is probably printed later than this.
Includes J. J. Strang material deleted in later versions.
In some editions his name is printed Van Dusen. He signs his name Van Deusen on manuscripts on deposit at Yale University.
WHi

9423. ———. A dialogue between Adam and Eve, the Lord and the Devil, called the endowment: As was acted by Twelve or Fifteen Thousand, in Secret, in the Nauvoo Temple, said to be revealed from God, as a Reward for Building that Splendid Edifice, and the Express Object for which it was built. [By I. McGee Van Deusen and Maria, his wife. 2d ed.] Albany, C. Killmer, 1847.
24p. 24cm.
At head of title: Positively true.
Cover-title: Sublime and ridiculous blended . . . Edition note on cover.
Howes V31, Morgan
CtY, DLC, MH, NN, UPB

9424. ———. (same, under title) The sublime and ridiculous blended; called, the endowment: as was acted, by upwards of twelve thousand, in secret, in the Nauvoo Temple, said to be revealed from God as a reward for building that splendid edifice, and the express object for which it was built. New York: Published by the author. 1848 [c1847]
1p.l. [5]–24p. 20½cm.
Copyrighted by Increase M'Gee Van Dusen and his wife Maria.
Both cover-title and title-page are the same.
New introduction and text somewhat revised and sensationalized. Omission of Strangite material.
Howes V31, Sabin 98494
CtY, CU–B, DLC, NN, UPB

9425. ———. (same, under title) Startling disclosures of the great Mormon conspiracy against the liberties of this country: being the celebrated "endowment", as it was acted by upwards of twelve thousand men and women in secret, in the Nauvoo Temple, in 1846, and said to have been revealed from God. By I. M'Gee Van Dusen and Maria his wife, who were initiated into these dreadful mysteries. New York, Published by Mr. and Mrs. Van Dusen, 1849.
23p. illus., port. 22½cm.
In yellow printed wrapper.
Also published in 1849 in John Thomas' *A sketch of the rise, progress and dispersion of the Mormons.*
Howes V31 24p.
DLC, ICN, MH, MWA, NN, UPB, USl

9426. ———. (same) New York, Published by Mr. and Mrs. Van Dusen, 1849.
[23]p. illus. (part fold.), port. 22½cm.
Added illustrations and a different arrangement of some of the pages. Lacks pagination of 9425.
NN, UPB

9427. ———. (same) New York, Published by Blake & Jackson, 1849.
23p. illus., port. 22½cm.
NBuG

9428. ———. (same) New York, Published by Blake and Jackson, 1849.
[16]p. illus., port. 22cm.
At head of title: "Read! Countrymen Read!!
NN

9429. ———. (same) New York, Published by Blake and Jackson, 1850.
[16]p. illus., port. 21½cm.
NN

9430. ———. Startling disclosures of the wonderful ceremonies of the Mormon spiritual wife system. Being the celebrated "endowment," as it was acted by upwards of twelve thousand men and women in secret in the Nauvoo temple in 1846, and said to have been revealed from God. By I. M'Gee Van Dusen and Maria his wife, who were initiated into these dreadful mysteries. New York, 1850.
[30]p. illus. 23cm.
Cover-title: The "endowment," or, Peculiar ceremonies of the Mormons.
Appendix: An account of the first remarkable visions of Joe Smith and how he obtained ancient American records, (the Mormon Bible) the angels appearance, etc.; also, A sketch of the faith and doctrine which he taught.
Howes V31
CtY, DLC, ICN, NN, UPB

9431. ———. (same) New York, Published by Blake and Jackson, 1852.
[30]p. illus. 23cm.
Cover-title: The "Endowment" or peculiar ceremonies of the Mormons.
A reprint of 1850 edition.
Howes V31
CtY, DLC, MH, MWA, NN, RPB

9432. ———. (same) New York, 1852.
[30]p. 22cm.
Variant printing.
UPB

9433. ———. (same) New York [1855]
[30]p.
Cover dated 1855.
NN

9433a. ———. (same) New York, 1857.
[36]p. 21cm.
In tan printed wrapper.
USlC

9434. ———. (same, under title) Mormonism exposed . . . New York, For sale at all book and periodical stores [1853?]
2p.l., 5–32p. plates, port. 23cm.
Copyrighted by I. Van Dusen and his wife, Maria, 1848.
"Preface to the sixth edition."
CSmH, CtY

9435. ———. (same, under title) Spiritual delusions; being a key to the mysteries of Mormonism, exposing the particulars of that astounding heresy, the spiritual wife system, as practiced by Brigham Young of Utah. By Increase Van Deusen and Maria his wife, seceders from that singular sect who were personally initiated into those dreadful mysteries. New York, Moulton and Tuttle, 1854.
64p. plate. 25cm.
Frequently reprinted under this title and with a slightly varying title, which is enlarged from the previous copy; has a second recital of the ceremony and an allegorical description of its various degrees and ceremonies. Some copies have the fold-out sheet of plates.
Howes V31
CtY, DLC, MH, MWA, NN, WHi

9436. ———. (same) New York, Published by the authors, 1854.
64p. fold. illus. 24cm.
Variant printing.
CtY, ICHi, UPB

9437. ———. (same) New York, Published by A. Ranney; . . . Chicago, Rufus Blanchard [etc., etc.] 1855.
64p. fold. plate. 23cm.
USlC copy has col. plates.
CU–B, UPB, USlC

9438. ———. (same) New York, Published by A. Ranney, 1856.
64p. fold. plates. 23cm.
Howes V31
ICN, MWA, NN, WHi

9439. ———. (same) New York, Published by Ranney, 1857.
64p. fold. front., plates. 21cm.
Howes V31
NjP, OClWHi

9440. ———. (same) New York, Ranney, 1859.
64p. fold., front., 8 plates. 21cm.
Variant illustrations.
Howes V31
CSmH, NN

9441. ———. (same, under title) Startling disclosures of the Mormon spiritual wife system, and wonderful ceremonies of the celebrated "endowment" as it is acted by upwards of fifty thousand men and women in secret, in the temple in Utah, and said to have been revealed from God. By I. M'Gee Van Dusen, and Maria, his wife who were initiated and participators in these dreadful mysteries. New York, 1864.
29p. col. front., col. plates. 23cm.
Howes V31
CtY, CU–B, NN

9442. ———. (same) New York, 1864.
29p. illus., col. plates. 23cm.
Variant printing.
NN

9443. ———. Misteries [sic] of Mormonism. New York, Published by I. Van Deusen [c1850]
1p. of plates 60×47cm. to be folded to 8p., 24½×15cm.
Plates for their books. Scenes from the endowment ceremony.
MH also has the plates in color with plate numbers bound in a book of pamphlets without the text.
ICHi has similar colored plates in place in book.
ICHi, MH

Van Dusen, Increase McGee. *See Van Deusen, Increase McGee.*

9444. Van Lieu, Solomon. A trace of prophecy, on the second coming of Christ. Or the little stone kingdom, and the end of the gentile rule or reign — the begin[n]ing of the great anti-typical jubilee in 1914. Written by Elder Sol. Van Lieu, August 24, 1908. St. John, Kansas. [St. John] 1908.
36p. 15cm.
Cover-title.
Bickertonite doctrine.
Morgan
PMonC

9445. Van Rod, Aimé. La revanche du Mormon; moeurs américaines fouet bizarreries d'amour. Orné de belles illustrations par Del Giglio. Paris, Edition Parisienne, 1908.
260p. illus. 19cm.
Added illustrated title-page.
Fiction concerning Mormonism.
Title in English: Revenge of the Mormon.
UU

9446. Van Tramp, John C. Prairie and Rocky Mountain adventures; or, Life in the West. To which will be added a view of the states and territorial regions of our western empire: embracing history, statistics, and geography, and descriptions of the chief cities of the west. Columbus, J. & H. Miller, 1858.
vi [7]–640p. 10 plates. 21½cm.
Part I. Chapter entitled "The Mormons," which traces the history of the Church to the arrival at the Great Salt Lake. Part II. Section entitled "Utah," giving information on the state and Mormonism.
Published in various editions, 1859–1870.
Howes V43, W–C 312
CSmH, ICN, NjP, NN, OClWHi, ULA, USlC

9447. Vanzandt, J. C. Mormon contradictions and what Mormons teach, a treatise consisting largely of actual statements made by Mormon leaders as verified by J. C. Vanzandt. Portland, Oregon [1915]
48p. 15cm.
MoInRC

Vapen mot Mormonismen. *See Andersson, C. A.*

9448. Varden. Organ for de norske I Utah. Salt Lake City, Varden Publishing Company, Jan. 1, 1910–1912.
2v. monthly. 29cm.
Organ of the Danish Mormons; later the "Associated Society."
Editor: Joseph Straaberg.
Title in English: Beacon.
UPB V.1 #1; USlC comp.

9449. Vaughan, W. T. Union Pacific Railroad business handbook and emigrant's guide. Council Bluffs, Ia., 1871.
216p. fold map. 21½cm.
"Salt Lake City and Utah Territory," p. 177–209.
Early history of Mormonism in Utah.
USlC

9449a. Vaughan-Hughes, J. Seventy years of life in the Victorian era embracing a travelling record in Australia, New Zealand, and America &c. By A physician. London, T. Fisher Unwin, 1893.
283p. illus. 19cm.
Mormons, p. 233–238.
USlC

9450. Veatch, Arthur Clifford. . . . Geography and geology of a portion of southwestern Wyoming, with special reference to coal and oil, by A. C. Veatch. Washington, Govt. Print. Off., 1907.
xi, 178, viiip. illus., xxvi plates (part. fold.) maps, fold. tab., diagrs. 29½cm. (U.S. Geological Survey. Professional paper. No. 56)
References to Mormons and Mormon trail, p. 10, 18–19, 139–140.
CU–B, DLC, UPB

9451. Veed-Fald, Jörgen. Belysning af nogle af vore Dages uholdbare Troesbekjendelser. Udgivet af Ole Veed-Fald, sen. . . . Aalborg, Trykt for Udgivern hos Christian [Schou, H. C. Johansen] 1855–[57]
3v. (viii [9]–226p.) 17½cm.
I forste hefte om Bibelens forstaaelse naermest til Bedømmelse af Mormonlaeren.
Vol. 1. Section on Mormonism. Mormon doctrine and history of Mormon Church in Denmark.
Title in English: A treatise about a few indefensible faiths.
NN

9452. ———. Bibelske henvisninger angaaende nogle af de laerestykker, der i denne tid bevaege sig her i landet. Aalborg, 1851.
4p.
Title in English: Bible references concerning some religions.
Schmidt

9453. Veed-fald, Ole. En liden Randsagning i den Hellige Skrift Om Daaben eller: Hvem har Ret i Laeren om Samme, Lutheraner, Baptister eller mormoner, eller: er vor Børnelaerdom os nu ikke nok? af Ole Veed-fald. Aalborg, H. D. Johnson, 1856.
23 [1]p. 17½cm.
Title in English: A little ransacking in the Holy Scripture about baptism or who has rights.
UPB

9454. ———. Mormonsk non plus ultra, eller: Fortsat proces imod Mormonerne. Udgivet af O. V-F, sen., forhen medhjelper ved opdragelsesanstalten og den landoeconomiske virksomhed paa Flakkebjerg Institut. Aalborg, 1855.
15p.
Title in English: Mormons non plus ultera, or continued case against Mormons.
Schmidt.

9455. ———. En proces imod Mormonerne; Meddeelt af Ole Veed-Fald, sen. Aalborg, Udgivet af og trykt hos P. A. Holst, 1852.
42p. 17½cm.
Title in English: A case against the Mormons.
NN, UHi, USlC

9456. ———. Subscriptions-indbydelse. Kobenhavn, 1854.
4p.
Title in English: A prospectus.
Schmidt

9457. Velazquez, Loreta Janeta. The woman in battle: a narrative of the exploits, adventures, and travels of Madame Loreta Janeta Velazquez, otherwise known as Lieutenant Harry T. Buford, Confederate States Army . . . Edited by C. J. Worthington . . . Hartford, T. Kelknap, 1876.
606p. illus., plates, ports., maps, plans. 22½cm.
After the war she traveled across the continent, resided in Salt Lake City for several months; her impressions.
Another edition: Richmond, Dustin, 1876. CtHT–W
DLC, ICHi, MB, NjP, OU, USl, USlC, ViU

9458. (same, under title) Story of the civil war; or, The exploits, adventures and travels of Mrs. L. J. Velazquez (Lieutenant H. T. Buford, C. S. A.) Edited by C. J. Worthington, U. S. N. . . . New York, Worthington Co., 1890 [c1889]
606p. ports., plates, maps. 22½cm.
Another edition: New York, 1894. NjP
CSmH, DW, ICN, OCl, OClWHi

9459. Vellinga, M. C. Latest light on Joseph Smith's golden plates. From which he claimed to have translated the "Book of Mormon." [Los Angeles, International Truth Distributors, c1928]
2p.l., 5–29 [1]p. port. 16cm.
Cover-title.
UPB

9460. ———. Mormon mysteries revealed . . . Los Angeles, West Coast Publishing Co. [1927]
2p.l., 123p. 19cm.
Cover-title.
CSmH, MH, NN, UHi, UPB, USl, USlC

9461. Verbatim report of funeral services in honor of President John R. Winder. [Salt Lake City, 1910]
20p. port. 22cm.
Funeral: March 31, 1910. Includes biographical information.
USlC

9462. Verbatim report of funeral services in honor of William Bradford. [Salt Lake City, 1924]
24p. 15cm.
Includes biographical information.
USlC

9463. Verbrugghe, Louis. Promenades et chasses dans l'Amerique du Nord, par Louis & Georges Verbrugghe. Paris, C. Levy, 1879.
351p. 18cm.
Includes a section on Mormonism.
Title in English: Hiking and hunting in North America.
CU, WHi

9464. Veritas [*pseud.*] Utah affairs, congress and polygamy. Including the Poland Bill. Salt Lake City, Printed at the Deseret News Steam Printing Press Establishment, Deseret News, 1874.
30p. 22cm.
Preface signed "Veritas."
Probably written by Orson Pratt.
MH, NjP, NN, UHi, UPB, USl, UU

9465. Verne, Jules. Le Tour du Monde en quatre-vingts jours par Jules Verne. Dessins par MM. de Neuville et R. Benett. Paris, J. Hertzel, 1873.
220p. illus., map. 20cm.
Published in various editions in many languages.
Published in French in America. Boston, D. C. Heath & Co., 1894. DLC, UPB
Title in English: Tour of the World in 80 days.
Story of Mormonism told them by a zealous missionary as train stops at Ogden.
Bibliotec Nationale

9466. ———. (same, under title) Around the world in eighty days. New York, C. Scribner's Sons, 1905.
viiip., [1]l., 310p. plates, port. 20cm.
Fiction. Story of Mormonism told to them by a zealous missionary as train stops at Ogden, p. 218–226.
Published in many editions.
USlC, UU

Vest, George Graham. Defense of the constitutional and religious rights of the people of Utah.
See under title.

9467. ———. Mary Ann M. Pratt, Appellant vs. Alexander Ramsey, A. S. Paddock, G. L. Godfrey, A. B. Carleton, J. R. Pettigrew, E. D. Hoge, John S. Lindsay. Appeal from judgment of the Supreme Court of Utah Territory. Brief and argument for appellant. [Salt Lake City?] 1884.
42p. 21cm.
Signed: George G. Vest, Wayne MacVeagh, Franklin S. Richards, Charles W. Bennett.
At head of title: Supreme Court of the United States. October term. 1884. No. 1028.
Polygamy trials.
USlC

9468. ———. (same) Brief and argument for Appellant. George G. Vest, Wayne MacVeagh, Franklin S. Richards, Charles W. Bennett, for Appellant. Washington, Gibson Bros., Printers and Bookbinder, 1885.
42p. 22cm.
USlC

9469. ———. Undemocratic-unamerican-unconstitutional. Speeches of Hon. George G. Vest, of Missouri, and Hon. Wilkinson Call, of Florida, in the United States Senate, Friday, February 18, 1887, against the anti-Mormon bill . . . Washington, 1887.
18p. 21cm.
CSmH, MH, UHi, USlC, UU

9470. Vetromile, Eugene. A tour in both hemispheres; or, Travels around the world. By Rev. Eugene Vetromile . . . New York, Montreal, D. & J. Sadlier & Co., 1880.
xii, 502p. illus., plates, port., map, plan. 20cm.
Trip through Salt Lake City in 1876. Murder of Dr. Robinson by the Mormons discussed. A talk with Ann Alice [sic] Young's attorney. Mormons are not strong believers in Mormonism.
CU–B, DLC, MB, UHi

9471. Victor, Metta Victoria (Fuller). Lives of female Mormons; a narrative of facts stranger than fiction. Philadelphia, G. G. Evans, 1859.
xii [25]–326p. 19½cm.
MoInRC, UPB

9472. ———. (same) By Metta Victoria Fuller . . . Philadelphia, G. G. Evans, 1860.
1p.l. [25]–326p. 18½cm.
CU–B, DLC, ICHi, ICN, MoInRC, NjP, NN, UHi, USl, USlC, UU

9473. ———. (same) New York, D. W. Evans & Co., 1860.
1p.l. [25]–326p. 18½cm.
USlC

9474. ———. (same, under title) Mormon wives; a narrative of facts stranger than fiction. By Metta Victoria Fuller. New York, Derby and Jackson, Cincinnati, H. W. Derby & Co., 1856.
xii [25]–326p. 19cm.
CSmH, CU–B, DLC, MnH, NjP, NjPT, NN, OClWHi, OO, PCC, UHi, UPB, USl, USlC, ViU, WHi

9475. ———. (same) New York, Derby & Jackson, 119 Nassau Street, 1858.
xii [25]–326p. 19cm.
Title on spine: Two wives, or facts stranger than fiction.
UPB

Victory, Salt Lake City. *See The Continental, Salt Lake City.*

9476. Vigna dal Ferro, Giovanni. Un viaggio nel Far West Americano, impressioni di G. Vigna dal Ferro, estratto dal Giornale La Patria. Bologna, Stab. Tipografico Successori Monti, 1881.
51p. 20½cm.
First published as a series of articles in Bologna La Patria.
Impressions of Salt Lake City; and Mormonism after numerous discourses in the tabernacle and speeches by the Church authorities.
Title in English: A trip to the American Far West.
CtY

9477. Villiers du Terrage, Marc, ***baron de.*** Conquistadores et roitelets, Rois sans couronne, du Roi des Canaries à l'Empereur de Sahara . . . ouvrage, illustré de cartes et de portraits. Paris, Perris et Cie, 1906.
vi, 474p. ports., fold. map. 20½cm.
"Le second prophète des Mormons. Brigham Young."
Includes a history of the Church, with emphasis on the Brigham Young period.
Title in English: Conquerors and viceroys.
CU, NN

9478. Vincent, ***Mrs.*** **Howard.** Forty thousand miles over land and water. The journal of a tour through the British Empire and America. By Mrs. Howard Vincent. With numerous illustrations. Third and cheaper edition. London, Sampson Low, Marston, Searle & Rivington, 1886.
xi [1] 382p. illus., plates, fold. map. 18½cm.
An article about her visit to Salt Lake City; quoting from a catechism to show Mormon belief.
USlC

9479. Vindex [*pseud.*] Mountain Meadows massacre; review of Elder Penrose's exculpatory address delivered October 26th, 1884, in Twelfth Ward Meeting House. [Salt Lake City? 1884]
4p. 24cm.
Caption-title.
CSmH, MH, NN, UHi, UPB

The Vision. Continuation of *Autumn Leaves.* *See Autumn Leaves.*

9479a. The visiting comforter, being a handy companion and pocket-book for home and missionary use. San Francisco, 1887.
88p. 21½cm. Publication of the Church of the Firstborn (Morrisites).
USlC

9480. Visscher, William Lightfoot. The stars of our country; a collection of poems . . . to which is added President Wilson's great message. Philadelphia, Pa., The National Press [c1917]
124p. illus. 18cm.
"Deseret," p. 103.
DLC, USlC

9481. ———. A thrilling and truthful history of the pony express; or, Blazing the westward way, and other sketches and incidents of those stirring times [by] William Lightfoot Visscher . . . Chicago, Rand, McNally & Co. [c1908]
98p. illus., ports. 25½cm.
Mention of Utah and Mormonism with portrait of Brigham Young.
CU–B, DLC, ICJ, MiU, NjP, UHi, ULA, USl, USlC, UU, WaU

VITTNESBÖRD

9482. Vittnesbörd af framstående män om "Mormonerna." Hvad de säga om polygami och andra viktiga frågor samt en petition till sveriges konung. Samlade och utgivna af Andreas Peterson. Stockholm, A. Peterson, 1911.
24p. 18½cm.
Title in English: Testimony of prominent men about the "Mormons."
UPB

9483. Vivian, Arthur Pendarves. Wanderings in the western land. By A. Pendarves Vivian . . . with illustrations from original sketches by M. Albert Bierstadt and the author. London, Sampson Low, Marston, Searle, & Rivington, 1879.
xvi, 426p. illus., 7 plates, 3 maps (2 fold.) 23cm.
Formula for the Mormon question: a decrease of the Mormon population will defeat Mormonism. A visit to Salt Lake City in 1878.
Another edition: 3rd ed. 1880. USlC
CU-B, NjP, UHi, USlC

Vivian, ***Sir*** **Henry Hussey.** *See Swansea, Henry Hussey Vivian, 1st Baron.*

9484. Vizetelly, Henry. Four months among the gold-finders in Alta California: Being the diary of an expedition from San Francisco to the gold districts. By J. Tyrwhitt Brooks, M. D. [*pseud.*] London, David Bogue . . . 1849.
xviii, 207p. front. (map) 20cm.
Fiction. References to the Mormons, p. 45, 107, 122–123, appropriated from Col. Mason's report.
Other editions: Paris, A. & G. Galignani & Co., 1849. CU-B; 2d ed. CU-B, DLC; New York, D. Appleton & Company; Philadelphia, Geo. S. Appleton, 1849. CU-B, DLC
Also translations in German, Dutch, and Swedish. CU-B
CSmH, DLC

9485. Vogt dig for Mormonerne? Kjøbenhavn, Fr. Wöldikes forlagsboghandel, 1862.
22p. 19cm.
Title in English: Watch out for the Mormons.
NN, USlC

9486. ———. (same) Fra en fjende af Mormonismen . . . Kobenhaven, 1863.
Schmidt

9487. The voice of the captives assembled at Zarahemla, in annual conference, April 6, A.D. 1854, to their brethren scattered abroad. [Zarahemla, Wis.? 1854]
14 [1]p. 28½cm.
Caption-title.
With the poem entitled, "Zarahemla," by L. and J. G.
RLDS beginnings.
CtY, NN, UPB, USlC

9488. ———. (same) Reprinted. [Lamoni, Ia., 189–]
14 [1]p. 23cm. (No. 60)
NN

9489. The voice of the Lord unto the people of the utmost bounds of the Earth . . . [Independence, Mo., 1879]
Broadside. 25×19cm.
Signed: The Lord's Servants. Independence, Mo., June 20th, 1879.
At head of title: Behold I send my messenger and he shall prepare the way before me. — Malachi III: 1.
Concerning the last days.
UPB, USlC

Voice of the Seventh Angel . . . *See Brighouse, James. Voice of the Seventh Angel . . .*

The Voice of truth. *See Smith, Joseph 1805–1844.*

A Voice of Warning. *See Ward, Thomas.*

9490. The Voice of Warning. Niagara Falls, New York, Church of Christ, July, 1930–
v. monthly. 32cm.
Took over the subscription list of the *Independent Forum.* After V.1 *The Voice of Warning*, published in Independence, Mo., began printing, and took over the voluming.
CU-B V.1 #2–V.2 #10, V.3 #1, August 1930–November 1931, January 1932; MoInRC V.1 #2–5, August, 1930–1932

A Voice of warning and proclamation to all. *See Bishop, Francis Gladden.*

9491. Vollmer, Carl Gottfried Wilhelm. Californien und das Goldfieber. Reisen in dem wilden Westen Nord-Amerika's, Leben und Sitten der Goldgräber, Mormonen und Indianer. Den Gebildeten des deutschen Volkes gewidmet von Dr. W. F. A. Zimmerman [*pseud.*] Berlin, Theodor Thiele, 1863.
744p. illus. 22cm.
Mormon participation in gold discoveries; colonization.
Title in English: California and the goldrush.
Another edition: Berlin, 1863. NjP
In Dutch: Amsterdam, P. M. van der made, 1864. NN, UHi, USlC; Amsterdam, De Wed. D. Kunst, 1865. USlC
In Swedish under title: Kalifornien och guldfebern. Stockholm, J. E. Fahlstedt [1862?] CtY, NjP
Howes V140
CtY, ICN, USlC

9492. Von Ulbersdorf, G. A. Zimmer. Im Schatten von Mormons Temple. Erzählungen aus der deutschen evangelischen Mission in Utah. Ein neuer Beitrag zur Kenntnis der Mormonen von G. A. Zimmer von Ulbersdorf. Neukirchen, Verlag der Buchhandlung des Erziehungsvereins [n.d.]
2p.l. [7]–112p. 19cm.
Title in English: In the shade of the Mormon Temple.
UPB, USlC

9493. Voree Herald . . . Voree, Wisconsin Territory, January, 1846–June 6, 1850.
5v. weekly. 31cm.
Names changed after first ten issues to *Zion's Reveille* November, 1846; renamed the *Gospel Herald* September 23, 1847.
Ceased with Vol. V, No. 12. Succeeded by *Northern Islander.*
Morgan
CtY My 1846; Je 29, 1848; Jl 26, 1849. MoInRC Mr, Je*, Jl, Ag*, S*, O*, 1846; F 11*, 18, Mr 4–18, 25*, Ap 22–Jl 15, 22*, 29, Ag 5*, 12*, 19–O 7, 14*, 21–D 30, 1847; Ja 6–27, F 3*, 10–17, Mr 23–30, Ap 13–D 28, 1848; Ja 4–D 27, 1849; Ja 3–Je 6, 1850. NN Ap, S 1846; Ja 14–21, F 11, Mr 11, Ag 26–S 2, 16–23, O 28, N 25–D 9, 1847; Ja 6, F 3, 17–24, Mr 9–30, Ap 13–27, My 25–Je 8, Ag 17, O 5, 19, D 14, 1848; Ja 18–25, F 8–Mr 23, My 31–Je 28, Ag 16, S 6, O 11, N 1, D 6–13, 1849; Ja 17–24, F 7–14, Ap 11, 25, My 16, 1850. ULA Mr 1846; D 16, 1847; O 11, 25–D 13, 1849; D 27, 1849–F 7, 1850; Mr 7–14, 21–28, Ap 11, My 2–23, 1850. USlC F–S 1846; D 16, 1847. WBuC F–My, Jl–N 1846; Ja 14, 28–N 25, D 23–30, 1847; Ja 6–F 3, 17–Mr 9, Ap 6–20, My 11–D 28, 1848; Ja 4–Mr 1, 15–Jl 26, Ag 16–23, S 27–O 11, 25–N 8, 22–D 27, 1849; Ja 3, 17, 31–F 21, Mr 7–Ap 11, 25–My 23, Je 6, 1850. WHi F, Ag–O 1846; Ja 14, Je 1, S 2, 23–O 7, N 18–25, D 16–23, 1847; Ag 24–D 28, 1848; Ja 4–Mr 15, 29–D 27, 1849; Ja 3–F 28, Mr 14, 28–My 9, 1850
[Imperfect numbers are indicated with an asterisk].

9494. Voree plates. [Burlington, Wisc., Wingfield Watson, 1893?]
Broadside. 21×17cm.
Six plates found September, 1845.
USlC

9495. ———. (same) [n.p., n.d.]
Broadside. 5×3cm.
Found bound with *Prophetic controversy,* and with *Revelations of James J. Strang.* Also found loose. Probably printed for several pamphlets.
UPB, USlC

9496. Vorhees, J. B. Wayside testimony. By Reverend J. B. Vorhees. New York [n.d.]
[4]p. 16cm.
The young not nearly so interested in Mormonism; therefore, it has seen "its last days."
USlC

Vorhees, Luke. Personal recollections of pioneer life . . . *See Lathrop, George. Memoirs of a pioneer . . .*

9496a. Voters of Utah, Beware! [Salt Lake City, ca. 1890]
[2]p. 21½cm.
Mormons and politics.
UPB, USlC

9496b. ———. (same, in Danish) Valgberettigede i Utah, Giv Agt! [Salt Lake City, 1890?]
[2]p. 21½cm.
UPB, USlC

9497. Vries, Hugo de. Naar Californië. Reisherinneringer door Dr. Hugo de Vries . . . Haarlem, H. D. Tjeenk Willink & zoon, 1905–07.
2v. illus., plates, double map. 23cm.
Chapter VII. "Net groote zoutmeer in de stad der Mormonen," p. 247–282.
Title in English: To California.
CU–B, UHi

THE ORIGIN OF

THE

SPAULDING STORY,

CONCERNING THE

MANUSCRIPT FOUND;

WITH

A SHORT BIOGRAPHY OF DR. P. HULBERT,

THE ORIGINATOR OF THE SAME; AND SOME TESTIMONY ADDUCED, SHOWING IT TO BE A SHEER FABRICATION, SO FAR AS ITS CONNECTION WITH THE

BOOK OF MORMON IS CONCERNED.

BY B. WINCHESTER, MINISTER OF THE GOSPEL.

"Blessed are ye when men shall revile you, and persecute you, and shall say all manner of evil against you falsely for my sake." Matt. v. 11.

PHILADELPHIA:

BROWN, BICKING & GUILPERT, PRINTERS, NO. 56 NORTH THIRD ST.

1840.

Item 9941. The most persuasive of the early refutations of the Spaulding–Rigdon theory of Book of Mormon origins. From the P. Crawley collection.

W.

9498. W. Arrests in San Pete. Ephraim, Utah, 1888.
Broadside.
Eberstadt *Utah and the Mormons.*
NjP

9499. Wadsworth, W. The national wagon road guide, from St. Joseph and Council Bluffs, on the Missouri River, via South Pass of the Rocky Mountains, to California . . . By W. Wadsworth. San Francisco, Salt Lake City, Whitton, Towne & Co., 1858.
viii [9]–160p. illus., fold. map. 16½cm.
Does not describe Salt Lake City on the trip, due to the threat that it would be burned that year.
Howes W3, Sabin 100930, W–C 313
CSmH, CtY, CU–B, ICN, NjP

9500. Wagner, Henry Raup. The plains and the Rockies; a bibliography of original narratives of travel and adventure, 1800–1865, by Henry R. Wagner. San Francisco, J. Howell, 1921.
3p.l., 193p. 26cm.
There was a suppressed first issue of 1920. A copy was in the Streeter collection.
Includes many Mormon references.
CSmH, CtY, CU–B, DLC, NjP, UHi, UPB, UU

Waggoner, J. H. Salt Lake City. *See Fireside sketches of scenery and travel . . .*

9501. Wagner, Moritz. Reisen in Nordamerika in den Jahren 1852 und 1853 von Dr. Moritz Wagner und Dr. Carl Scherzer. Leipzig, Arnold, Arnoldische Buchhandlung, 1854.
3v. 16cm.
A trip down the Mississippi River, with notes on Galena, Nauvoo, and Cairo.
Title in English: Travels in North America.
Howes W12
CU–B, DLC, ICHi

9502. Wahlstroem, Johan. En inbjudning till Guds Rike. [n.p.] Utgifven af den aterupprattade Jesu Kristi Kyrka af de Sista Dagars Heliga [189–]
[2]l. 21cm.
Published in the interest of the RLDS church.
Title in English: An invitation to the kingdom of God.
NN

9503. Wainwright, Charles Henry. Mormonism tried by the Bible and condemned; an address to the Church of the Latter-day Saints. By the Rev. C. H. Wainwright, B. A. Curate of St. Margarett's, Ipswich. Ipswich [Eng.] W. Hunt Steam Press, 1855.
22p. 16½cm.
CtY, NN

9504. Waite, Catherine (Van Valkenburg). Adventures in the far West; and life among the Mormons. By Mrs. C. V. Waite . . . Chicago, C. V. Waite and Company, 1882.
1p.l. [v]–xi, 311p. 17½cm.
Fiction concerning Mormonism.
CSmH, CtY, CU–B, DLC, ICN, MH, MoInRC, NjP, NjPT, NN, UHi, UPB, USl, USlC, UU

9505. ———. The Mormon prophet and his harem; or, An authentic history of Brigham Young, his numerous wives and children. By Mrs. C. V. Waite . . . Cambridge [Mass.] Printed at the Riverside Press, and for sale by Hurd & Houghton, New York; [etc., etc.] 1866.
x, 280p. plates, ports., plan. 19cm.
Fiction concerning Mormonism.
CSmH, CtY, CU–B, DLC, ICN, IWW, MH, MoInRC, NjP, NjPT, NN, UHi, USl, USlC, UU

9506. ———. (same) 3d ed. Cambridge [Mass.] Printed at Riverside Press . . . 1866.
x, 280p. illus., plates, ports. 19cm.
USlC

9507. ———. (same) 3d ed. Cambridge [Mass.] Printed at the Riverside Press, and for sale by Hurd & Houghton, New York; [etc., etc.] 1867.
x, 280p. illus., plates, 4 ports. 19½cm.
CSmH, DLC, IU, MH, OFH

9508. ———. (same) 4th ed., revised and enlarged. Cambridge [Mass.] Printed for the author and sold by subscription, J. S. Goodman and Co., 1867.
x, 298p. 1 plate, 3 ports., 1 diagr. 20cm.
NN

9509. ———. (same) 5th ed., revised and enlarged. Chicago, J. S. Goodman and Co., . . . 1867 [c1866]
318p. plates, ports., plan. 20cm.
CSmH, ICHi, MH, MiU, MoInRC, NN, OCl, OClWHi, OO, UHi, ULA, UPB, USl, USlC, UU, WHi

9510. ———. (same) 6th ed., revised and enlarged. Philadelphia, Zeigler, McCurdy and Co.; Cincinnati, C. F. Vent and Co., 1867.
318p. plates, port. 20½cm.
USlC

9511. ———. (same) Chicago, J. S. Goodman & Co., 1868 [c1866]
318p. plates, port. 21cm.
CSmH, WHi

9512. Waite, Charles Burlingame. Argument of Charles B. Waite, before the Committee of Elections of the House of Representatives, March 25th–27th, 1868. In the case of William M'Grorty vs. Wm. H. Hooper, sitting delegate from the Territory of Utah. [Washington, 1868]
32p. 23cm.
Caption-title.
As a Mormon, Hooper did not represent all the people.
DLC, NN, USlC

9513. Waite, Henry Randall. Illiteracy and Mormonism. A discussion of federal aid to education and the Utah problem. Boston, D. Lothrop and Co. [1885]
43p. tables. 23cm. (Questions of the hour)
CSmH, CtY, CU–B, ICN, MH, NN, UHi, USIC

9514. Wake, Richard. "Gentile" Bureau of Information. Salt Lake City, Women's Missionary Union [n.d.]
[2]p. 29cm.
Description and purpose of the Bureau.
USIC

9515. Waldenström, P. Genom Norra Amerikas förenta stater. Reseskildringar af P. Waldenström. Stockholm, Pietistens Expedition, 1891.
viii, 615 [1]p. illus., plates. 23cm.
P. 495 and following on Mormons.
Title in English: Through North America's United States.
NjP

9516. Walker, Charles L. "For and in behalf." Lines respectfully inscribed to the Presidents of the Latter-day Saints' Temples. [St. George, 1895]
[2]p. 18cm.
Mormon poem.
USIC

9516a. ———. Lines respectfully inscribed to Mary Ide, on the fortieth anniversary of her birthday. St. George, 1879.
Broadside. 16×13cm.
USIC

9517. ———. Temple dedication song. St. George, Printed and Published by J. W. Carpenter, 1877.
[2]l. 16cm.
Dedication of the St. George Temple.
UPB, USIC

9518. Walker, James. Circling the globe by sea and land, the record of a personal experience, by James Walker . . . London, H. J. Drane, 1907.
4p.l., 296p. illus., col. port., 4 col. maps. 22cm.
Includes his trip to Salt Lake City, 1904, and his reaction to Mormonism, p. 179–205.
CU–B

9519. Walker, James Barr. Experiences of pioneer life in the early settlements and cities of the West. Chicago, Sumner & Co., 1881.
2p.l. [5]–310p. 19½cm.
Includes material on Eliza R. Snow and her conversion to Mormonism.
CU–B, NjP, UHi

9519a. Walker, Joseph Robinson. To the non-Mormon voters of Salt Lake City. 1874 Feb. 9, Salt Lake City. Signed by J. R. Walker and others. [1894?]
Broadside. 48×30cm.
Announcing that they are no longer candidates for city office and recommending that their friends vote for the ticket headed by Wm. Jennings.
USIC

9520. Walker, Marietta (Hodges). Fulness of the atonement. [Plano, Ill., True Latter-Day Saints' Herald, 1866]
3 pts. in 1 (4p. each) 23cm. (True Latter-Day Saints' Herald. Tract. No. 6)
CtY, MoInRC, NjP, UPB

9521. ———. (same) [Lamoni, Ia.? Reorganized Church of Jesus Christ of Latter Day Saints, 187–]
15 [1]p. 23cm. (No. 8)
CSmH, MH, MWA, NjP, NN

9522. ———. (same) Lamoni, Ia., Published by the Reorganized Church of Jesus Christ of Latter Day Saints [n.d.]
15 [1]p. 23cm.
USIC

9523. ———. (same) [Plano, Ill.?] Published by the Reorganized Church of Jesus Christ of Latter Day Saints [n.d.]
16p. 22cm. (No. 8)
USIC

9524. ———. (same) Plano, Ill., Published by the Reorganized Church of Jesus Christ of Latter Day Saints [n.d.]
16p. 22cm. (No. 9)
USIC

9525. ———. The gospel story, by Frances [*pseud.*] Lamoni, Ia., Herald Publishing House, 190–]
108p. 24½cm. (Birth-offering series. No. 5)
Includes: "Footsteps of Jesus," by Hester S. E. Young.
MoInRC, NjP

9526. ———. Object-lessons on temperance; or, The Indian maiden and her white deer, by Frances [*pseud.*] Lamoni, Ia., Published by The Board of Publication of the Reorganized Church of Jesus Christ of Latter Day Saints, 1907.
x, 145 [1]p. illus. 19cm. (Birth-offering series. No. 7)
Cover-title: The Indian maiden.
UHi

9527. ———. (same) Lamoni, Ia., Published by the Herald Publishing House, 1912.
viii, 145p. illus. 19½cm. (Birth-offering series. No. 7)
Cover-title: The Indian maiden and her white deer.
MoInRC, UHi

9528. ———. Our boys; a book for fathers and mothers. By Marietta Walker, better known to readers as Frances . . . Lamoni, Ia., Herald Publishing House [n.d.]
156p. 19cm.
How to raise boys to be true to themselves and the RLDS church.
MoInRC

9529. ———. Questions, answers, and brief stories on and from the Holy Scriptures, for the use of Primary classes in our Sunday School. By M. Walker. Lamoni, Ia., Issued by the Board of Publication of the Reorganized Church of Jesus Christ of Latter Day Saints, 1889.
iv, 170p. 13cm.
MoInRC, NjP

9530. ———. Questions on the Holy Scriptures designed for the use of scholars, in the Latter-day Saints Sunday schools by M. A. Faulconer. Plano, Ill., Reorganized Church of Jesus Christ of Latter Day Saints, 1869.
III [7]–152p. 15cm.
DLC, ICN, MH, MoInRC

9531. ———. (same) 2d ed. Independence, Mo., Reorganized Church of Jesus Christ of Latter Day Saints, 1886.
v [7]–158p. 15cm.
On cover: Intermediate question book.
MoInRC, NjP

9531a. ———. A talk with mothers. — No. 2. By Frances [*pseud.*] Lamoni, Iowa, Herald Publishing House, 1894.
15p. 15cm. (Daughters of Zion leaflets. No. 70)
"Supplement to the Saints' Herald."
USlC

9531b. ———. Talks with mothers. No. 3. By Frances [*pseud.*] Lamoni, Iowa, Herald Publishing House, 1894.
14p. 15½cm. (Daughters of Zion leaflets. No. 9)
"Supplement to the Saints' Herald."
USlC

9532. ———. With the church in an early day. Lamoni, Ia., 1891.
viii, 391p. port. 19½cm.
Includes: Others with the Church, by Emma L. Anderson; and He that believeth, by J. F. M'Dowell.
CSmH, MoInRC, NN, UHi, UPB, USlC

9533. ———. (same) [2d ed.] Lamoni, Ia., Herald Publishing House, 1904.
354p. port. 20cm.
MoInRC, MoU, NjP

9534. ———. (same) 3rd ed. Lamoni, Ia., Herald Publishing House, 1908.
354p. 19½cm.
UHi

9535. ———. (same) Lamoni, Ia., Herald Publishing House, 1912.
2p.l. [5]–354p. 19½cm.
MoInRC

9536. Walker, R. B. Letters from father to his sons during five months' travel in this and European countries, commencing at the returning to California, a journey of sixteen thousand miles. By R. B. Walker. Akron, Ohio, Published by special request, 1906.
79 [1]p. 25cm.
Letter No. 2 about Mormonism. The decline of Mormonism now that its political power is gone.
UHi

9536a. Walker, William. To the intelligent public. [Port Elizabeth, Printed at the "Telegraph" Office, ca. 1854]
7p. 21½cm.
William Walker was one of the first missionaries to South Africa, arriving April 1853 and leaving in 1855.
USlC

9537. Walker, Williston. A history of the Christian Church. New York, C. Scribner's Sons [c1918]
xiii, 624p. 21cm.
Includes a brief history of the organization of the L.D.S. church.
CU, DLC, NjP, NjPT, ULA, UPB, USlC

9538. Wallace, Dillon. Saddle and camp in the Rockies; an expert's picture of game conditions in the heart of our hunting country. Illustrated with photographs. New York, Outing Publishing Company, 1911.
xvi, 320p. plates, port. 21½cm.
Chapter XI: Poplar trees and Mormon beards. Other Mormon references throughout the book and a description of southern Utah communities.
CU, NjP, UPB

9539. Wallace, Frederick T. Men and events of half a century. By Frederick T. Wallace. Cleveland, Evangelical Association, 1882.
1p.l., iv, 363p. 21cm.
"Mentor and the Mecca of the Mormons," p. 170–173.
CU–B

9540. Walpole, Frederick. Four years in the Pacific, in Her Majesty's ship "Collingwood." From 1844 to 1848, by Lieut. the Hon. Fred. Walpole, R. N. . . . London, Richard Bentley . . . 1849.
2v. 22cm.
In reference to the Bear Flag affair (Vol. 2, p. 208–209) he describes William B. Ede (i.e. Ide) as "formerly a Mormon prophet."
CU–B

9541. Walsh, Marie A. My queen. A romance of the Great Salt Lake. By "Sandette" [*pseud.*] . . . New York, G. W. Carleton & Co. [etc., etc.] 1878.
1p.l., v–vi, 7–384p. 19cm.
Fiction concerning Mormonism.
DLC, MH, NjP, NN, ULA

9542. Walsum, S. B. Hersleb. Vogt eder for de falske propheter. Et advarsels-ord imod Mormonerne. Bergen, 1855.
30p.
Title in English: Beware of false prophets.
Schmidt.

9543. Walter, James. Notes and sketches during an overland trip . . . in May, 1869. Reprinted from the "Liverpool Albion." Liverpool, Albion Office, 1869.
88p. 19½cm.
Arrived in Ogden in company with John Young, so was able to journey to Salt Lake City with Brigham Young. Impressed by Brigham Young and his accomplishments. Take away polygamy, and he would like Mormonism.
CtY, DLC, NjP

9544. Walworth, Jeannette Ritchie (Hadermann). The bar-sinister; a social study . . . New York, Cassell & Company, Limited, 1885.
3p.l. [v]–vi, 354p. 19cm. (On cover: Cassell's sunshine series. No. 3. 1888)
Fiction concerning Mormonism.
DLC, MH, USlC

9545. ———. (same, under title) His celestial marriage; or, The bar-sinister, a social study, by Mrs. Jeannette H. Walworth . . . New York, The Mershon Company [c1899]
1p.l., vii, 354p. 18½cm. (On cover: Holly library. No. 153)
DLC, NjP, NN, USlC

9546. ———. (same, under title) His three wives; or, The bar-sinister, a Mormon study, by Mrs. Jeannette H. Walworth . . . New York, The Mershon Company [c1900]
1p.l., vi, 354p. front. (port.) 19cm.
DLC, ICN, MH, NN, UHi, UPB

9547. Wandell, Charles Wesley. History of the persecutions!!, endured by the Church of Jesus Christ of Latter-day Saints in America. Compiled from public documents, and drawn from authentic sources By C. W. Wandell, Minister of the Gospel. Sydney, Printed by Albert Mason [1852]
64p. 21cm.
USlC

9548. ———. (same) Sydney, Albert Mason [1852]
64p. 19cm.
Includes an additional paragraph to the above imprint.
Howes W84
CSmH, CtY, MH, MoInRC, NN, UPB, USl, USlC, UU

9549. ———. Reply to Shall we believe in Mormon? [Sydney, New South Wales, 1852]
24p. 21½cm.
Caption-title.
"Dialogue between tradition, reason, and scriptus," p. 21–24.
Howes W85
CSmH, CtY, USlC

9550. Wanderer's trip round the world. Notes taken by the way. Williamstown, Australia, Chronicle Print, 1894.
95p.
Detailed description of Salt Lake City and the surrounding regions by a disinterested Irish observer.
Eberstadt *Utah and the Mormons.*

Ward, Artemus [*pseud.*] *See Browne, Charles Farrar.*

9551. Ward, Austin N. [*pseud.*] The husband in Utah; or, Sights and scenes among the Mormons: with remarks on their moral and social economy. By Austin and Maria N. Ward . . . London, James Blackwood, 1857.
xii, 212p. 16½cm.
In Utah, Summer, 1855.
CtY, CU, DLC, NjP, NN, UHi, USlC

9552. ———. (same) By Austin N. Ward. Edited by Maria Ward . . . New York, Derby & Jackson; Cincinnati, H. W. Derby & Co. [etc., etc.] 1857.
xiv [15]–310, 130p. 2 plates. 19½cm.
"Mormonism"; sermons and addresses by prominent Mormons: 130p. at end of most copies.
CSmH, CtY, DLC, MB, MH, MiU, NjPT, NN, OCl, OClWHi, UHi, ULA, USl, UU, ViU

9553. ———. (same) New York, Derby & Jackson; Cincinnati, H. W. Derby & Co. [etc., etc.] 1859.
xiv [15]–310, 130p. plates. 19cm.
CU–B, DLC, MH, MoInRC, WHi

9554. ———. (same, under title) Male life among the Mormons, or, The husband in Utah: Detailing sights and scenes among the Mormons; with remarks on their moral and social economy. Edited by Maria Ward. New York, Derby & Jackson, 1859.
310, 130p. front. 19cm.
MH, OClWHi, UHi, ULA, UU

9555. ———. (same) Philadelphia, J. Edwin Potter and Company [1863]
xiv [15]–310p. 2 plates. 19½cm.
CU–B, DLC, ICN, MH, MoInRC, NjP, NN, USl, USlC, UU, ViU

9556. ———. (same) Philadelphia, J. E. Potter, 1865.
xiv [15]–310p. 2 plates. 19½cm.
NN

9557. ———. (same) Philadelphia, Keystone Pub. Co., 1890.
xiv [15]–310p. illus. 19½cm.
UU

9558. ———. (same) Philadelphia, Pa., The Keystone Publishing Co.; N. E. Cor. Tenth and Filbert Sts. [1890]
xiv [15]–310p. illus. 20cm.
Variant: no imprint date, but has street address.
UU

9559. ———. (same, in Danish) Manden i Utah eller scener iblandt Mormonerne. Oversat fra Engelsk. Kjøbenhavn, F. C. Pios, 1861.
2p.l. [3]–300p. 18½cm.
CtY

9560. ———. (same, in Swedish) Männen bland Mormonerna, eller tilldragelser i Utah, af åsynavittnen intygade. Jemte iakttagelser angående Mormonernas moraliska och sociala lif, af Austin och Maria N. Ward . . . öfversättning från Engelskan. Stockholm, Expeditionen of Konversations-Lexikon hos Schuck & Josephson [1857]
306 [5]p. 18cm.
Also issued in parts in green printed wrappers. UPB
UHi

Ward, Betsey Jane. *See Comstock, William.*

9561. Ward, C. Fenwick. Mormonism exposed. [The first of a series of lectures] The founder of Mormonism, an infamous impostor. By Reverend C. Fenwick Ward. Manchester, Printed and Published by William Kemp, 1897.
31p. 17½cm. (No. 1)
USlC

9562. ———. Mormonism exposed. The second of a series of lectures. "The Origin of Mormonism — Fiction and fraud." By Reverend C. Fenwick Ward. Manchester, Printed by Taylor, Garnett, Evans & Co., 1898.
[33]–40p. 17cm. (No. 2)
Cover-title.
Pagination continues from first series.
USlC

9563. Ward, Dillis Burgess. Across the plains in 1853; by D. B. Ward, Seattle, Washington. [Seattle? 1911]
2p.l., 3–55p. port. 22cm.
Cover-title.
Preface by Edmond S. Meany. Reminiscences of a journey from Arkansas to Oregon via Bent's Fort. Mormon speculators in Bear River Valley, p. 40–42. Howes W94
CtY, CU–B, InU

9564. Ward, Jessie. The call at evening. Independence, Mo., The Herald Publishing House [c1920]
433p. illus. 20cm.
RLDS inspirational literature.
DLC, MoInRC, UPB

9564a. ———. (same) Independence, Mo., The Herald Publishing House, 1920.
422p. illus. 20cm.
NjP

9565. Ward, Joseph Harvey. Ballads of life. By J. H. Ward . . . Illustrated with numerous engravings, from original designs drawn by [Dan] Weggeland . . . Salt Lake City, J. H. Parry & Co., 1886.
2p.l., xii [13]–202p. plates, port. 21cm.
Biographical introduction signed: Thos. Hardt.
Mormon poetry.
CU–B, DLC, MH, MoInRC, NjP, UHi, ULA, USlC, UU, WHi

9566. ———. (same) Enl. ed. Salt Lake City [Jos. Hyrum Parry & Co.] 1903.
2p.l., xii [13]–202p. plates, port. 21cm.
UPB, UU

9567. ———. Gospel philosophy, showing the absurdities of infidelity, and the harmony of the gospel with science and history, by Elder J. H. Ward . . . Salt Lake City, The Juvenile Instructor Office, 1884.
vii [9]–216p. illus. 19cm.
Inspirational writings.
CU–B, DLC, MH, MoInRC, NjP, NN, ULA, UPB, UHi, USl, USlC, UU, WHi

9568. ———. The hand of Providence, as shown in the history of nations and individuals, from the great apostasy to the restoration of the Gospel. Salt Lake City, Juvenile Instructor Office, 1883.
viii [9]–215p. illus., ports., plates. 19cm.
World history from a Mormon point of view.
CtY, CU–B, DLC, MB, MH, NjP, RPB, UHi, ULA, USlC

9569. Ward, Maria N. [*pseud.*] Escaped from the Mormons, showing the rise of Mormonism. By the wife of a Mormon Elder. London, Holden & Hardingham [1898?]
203p. 22cm.
NN dated 1913 and cataloged under title.
MH, NN

9570. ———. Female life among the Mormons. A narrative of many years experience among the Mormons by the wife of a Mormon elder recently from Utah. London, C. H. Clarke [1855]
302p. 19cm.
Attributed also to Mrs. Benjamin Ferris.
CSmH, WaU

9571. ———. (same) New York, J. C. Derby, 1855.
x [9]–449p. illus. 20cm.
Sabin 24185
CSmH, CtY, DLC, ICHi, ICN, MH, MoInRC, NN, UHi, ULA, USlC, UU, WHi

9571a. ———. (same) London, G. Routledge & Co., 1855.
vi [7]–247p. front. 16½cm.
USlC

9572. ———. (same) 28th thousand. London, G. Routledge & Co., 1855.
vi [7]–247p. plate. 16½cm.
CSmH, CtY, IU, MH, NjP, UHi, UPB, USl, USlC, UU

9573. ———. (same) New York, Derby & Jackson, 1856.
x [9]–449p. front. 19½cm.
CSmH, NjP, UHi, ULA

9574. ———. (same) New York, Burdick Brothers, 1857.
x [9]–449p. front. 18cm.
NN, WShe

9575. ———. (same) . . . New York, Derby and Jackson, 1857.
x [9]–449p. front. 19½cm.
CSmH, CU–B, ICJ

9576. ———. (same) New York, Derby & Jackson, 1858.
x [9]–449p. plates. 19cm.
At head of ttile: Maria Ward's disclosures.
ICN, USlC

9577. ———. (same) 40th thousand. New York, Derby and Jackson, 1860.
x [9]–449p. illus., plates. 19cm.
At head of title: Maria Ward's disclosures.
NN, UHi, UPB, USlC

9578. ———. (same) 40th thousand. Philadelphia, John E. Potter and Company, 1863.
x [9]–449p. illus. 19cm.
At head of title: Maria Ward's disclosures.
MoU, UHi

9579. ———. (same) 60th thousand. Philadelphia, John E. Potter and Co. [1888? c1866]
x [9]–449p. plates. 19½cm.
At head of title: Maria Ward's disclosures.
CSmH, MH, ULA, UPB, ViU

9580. ———. (same) London, H. Lea [n.d.]
3p.l. [v]–x, 305p. plates. 19cm.
CU–B

9581. ———. (same, under title) Female life among the Mormons: A thrilling narrative of many years' personal experiences with Brigham Young and his followers, by the wife of a Mormon Elder, recently from Utah. 60th thousand. Philadelphia, The Keystone Publishing Co., 1890.
x [9]–449p. illus. 19cm.
At head of title: Maria Ward's disclosures.
UHi

9582. ———. (same, under title) Confessions of a Mormon bride; or, The truth about Mormonism. By Maria Ward (wife of a Mormon elder) Philadelphia, Columbian Publishing Co., 1890.
x [9]–449p. 19cm.
MH, USl

9583. ———. (same, under title) The Mormon wife; a life story of the sacrifices, sorrows and sufferings of woman. A narrative of many years' personal experience, by the wife of a Mormon elder . . . Fully illustrated. Hartford, Conn., Hartford Publishing Co., 1872.
xvii [9]–449p. 10 plates, 6 ports. 21½cm.
CtY, NN, UHi, ULA, USl, USlC

9584. ———. (same) Hartford, Conn., Hartford Publishing Co., 1873.
xvii [9]–449p. plates, ports. 21½cm.
CU–B, DLC, ICN, MoInRC, MWA, NjP, UHi, UPB, USlC

9585. ———. (same, in Danish) Qvindeliv blandt Mormonerne. Erindringer fra et fleeraarigt Ophold i Mormonistaten nedskrevne af en fra Utah tilbagevendt Mormonpraests Kone . . . Kjøbenhavn, Trykt hos J. Davidsen, 1855 [–1856]
3v. in 1 (154p.) 16½cm.
CtY, NjP, UPB

9586. ———. (same) Kjøbenhavn, Trykt hos J. Davidsen, 1855.
154p. 17cm.
CU–B

9587. ———. (same, in French) La Femme Chez Les Mormons. Relation écrite par l'épouse d'un Mormon, revenue récemment de l'Utah. Traduit de l'anglais par Charles Everard. Illustrations par Ed. Coppin. Paris: Mareseq et Cie, 1856.
80p. illus. 30cm.
Abridged version.
Sabin 23216
CU–B

9588. ———. (same, under title) Les harems du Nouveau monde–Vie des femmes chez les Mormons. Traduit par B. H. Révoil. Paris, Michel Lévy frères, 1856.
xii, 310p. 17cm.
CSmH, CtY, CU–B, DLC, ICN, NjP, UPB, WHi

9589. ———. (same, in German) Frauenleben unter den Mormonern. Vieljährige Erlebnisse der kürzlich aus Utah zurückgekehrten Gattin eines Aeltesten der Mormonen. Deutsch von A. Kretzschman. Leipzig, W. Einhorn, 1856.
3v. in 1. 17cm.
CtY, CU, MH, NN

9590. ———. (same, under title) Mormonengräuel dargelegt in den Erlebnissen einer aus Utah entflohenen Mormonenfrau, so wie in den Enthüllungen des socialen, administrativen und religiösen Lebens dieser Secte. Aus dem Englischen von Heinr. mit vier Illustrationen. Gauss [Weimar, Verlag, Druck und Lithographie von B. F. Voigt] 1857.
viii, 305p. plates. 17½cm.
MH

9591. ———. (same, in Swedish) Qvinnan bland Mormonerna. En Från Utah flyktad Mormon-Hustrus, anteckningar om denna sekts Sociala, Administrativa och Religiösa förhållanden. Öfversättning af G. C. Oldenburg . . . Stockholm, Expeditionen af Konversations-Lexikon hos Schück & Josephson [1857]
384p. illus. 17cm.
CU–B, UHi, UPB, USlC

9592. ———. (same) Från engelskan. Med 8 Illustrationer. Göteborg, Hos Anders Lindgren, 1857.
144p. 8 plates. 21cm.
CtY, UPB

9593. Ward, Thomas. On the false prophets of the last days. [Liverpool, Printed for and Published and sold by T. Ward. Printed by James & Woodburn, 1843]
8p. 21cm.
Caption-title.
Dated from *Millennial Star*, March, 1843, p. 192.
First published in the *Millennial Star*, April, 1842, p. 176–184.
CtY, CU–B, MH, MoInRC, NN, USlC

9594. ———. A voice of warning. [Liverpool, Printed by R. James, 1846]
12p. 18cm.
Signed at end: Thomas Ward. Liverpool, August.
Dated from *Millennial Star*, V. 8, p. 64.
CU–B, UPB

9595. ———. Why do you not obey the Gospel? [Liverpool, T. Ward, Printed by James & Woodburn, 1843?]
4p. 21cm.
Caption-title.
Dated from *Millennial Star*, V. 3, p. 192.
Reprinted from *Millennial Star*, February, 1843, p. 161–163.
CtY, UPB

9596. Ward Brothers, Columbus, Ohio. Views of Salt Lake City and vicinity. [Columbus, O., Ward Brothers, 1889]
7p. plates, ports. 13×16cm.
Cover-title.
Plates on strip attached to front cover folded to form 11 leaves.
Includes church illustrations. Pictures of Joseph Smith and Brigham Young.
CU–B

9597. ———. (same) [Columbus, Ohio, Ward Brothers, c1890]
[12]p. fold. brochure, plates, ports. 13×16cm.
Cover-title.
DLC, UHi

9598. Waring, Edmund H. History of the Iowa Annual Conference of the Methodist Episcopal Church; Including the planting and progress of the church within its limits, from 1833 to 1909, inclusive by Edmund H. Waring . . . [n.p., 1909]
300p. 24cm.
Missionary work among the Mormons at Council Bluffs in 1851, p. 145.
USlC

9599. Warner, Amos Griswold. . . . Three phases of coöperation in the West. By Amos G. Warner . . . [Baltimore] American Economic Association, 1887.
119p. 23cm. (Publications of the American Economic Association. [Monographs] Vol. 2, No. 1)
Contents: Coöperation among farmers. — Coöperation among wage-earners. — Coöperation among Mormons.
Another edition: 1888. CU, DLC
CU, DLC, ICJ, MH, MiU, NjP, OCl, OClW, OU

9600. Warner, Elisha. The history of Spanish Fork by Elisha Warner. Spanish Fork, Utah, Printed by the Press Publishing Co., 1930.
5p.l., 13–239p. 20cm.
CU–B, ICU, NjP, UHi, UPB, USlC, UU

9601. Warren, William B. To the citizens of Hancock County: The undersigned, again deems it his duty to appear before you in a circular . . . Mormon population . . . are leaving the state . . . Nauvoo, Eagle Print, 1846.
Broadside. 40½×27½cm.
Mormon intentions of leaving the state, warns against, and reprehends anti-Mormon mobs. Signed: W. B. Warren Major, commanding Illinois Volunteers, Nauvoo, May 11, 1846.
Byrd 1123
NN

WARSAW SIGNAL

9602. Warrum, Noble. Utah in the world war. The men behind the guns and the men and women behind the men behind the guns. By Noble Warrum. Memorial book, published under the auspices of the Utah State Council of Defense. January, 1924 . . . [Salt Lake City, Arrow Press, 1924?]
xi, 456p. illus., ports., tables. 24cm.
Utah history and biography.
DLC, NjP, ULA, UHi, UU

9603. ———. Utah since statehood, historical and biographical. Noble Warrum, editor, assisted by Hon. Charles W. Morse for bench and bar, and W. Brown Ewing, M.D., for the medical chapter . . . Chicago, Salt Lake City, The S. J. Clarke Publishing Company, 1919–1920.
4v. plates, ports. 28cm.
Utah history and biography.
CSmH, DLC, MH, NjP, UHi, ULA, UPB, USl, USlC, UU

9604. ———. Utah since statehood. Deluxe supplement. Chicago, Salt Lake City, The S. J. Clarke Publishing Co., 1919.
2p.l. [5]–459p. illus., ports. 25cm.
Cover-title: Utah.
UHi, ULA

9605. Warsaw, Ill. Committee of Safety. To his excellency Thomas Ford, governor of the state of Illinois. [Warsaw? Ill., 1844]
Broadside. 52×23½cm.
In three columns.
A letter signed by the Warsaw Committee of Safety concerning the Mormons in that state. Also the letter of the governor in reply, July 3, 1844.
In the wake of the murder of Joseph and Hyrum Smith.
CtY, USlC

9606. Warsaw Signal. Warsaw Signal. Friday, June 14, 1844. At a meeting of the citizens of Warsaw, convened the 14th of June, inst., the following address, reported by Thos. C. Sharp, esq., was unanimously adopted and ordered to be published in connexion [sic] with the resolution adopted by the mass meeting at Carthage yesterday . . . [Warsaw, 1844]
Broadside. 55×15½cm.
A tirade against the suppression of the *Nauvoo Expositor.*
Byrd 904
NN

9607. ———. [Warsaw] Signal Extra. The Warsaw Signal, Wednesday, Aug. 7, 1844 . . . [Warsaw, 1844]
Broadsheet. 48×30cm.
In four columns.
Comments on the recent elections in Nauvoo, including an anti-Mormon tirade.
Byrd 905
NN

9608. ———. Warsaw Signal–Extra: Sept. 24, 1845 . . . [Warsaw, 1845]
Broadside. 48×30cm.
In four columns.
Summarizes the actions of the Mormons that led the anti-Mormons to take up arms.
Byrd 1003
ICHi, NN

9609. ———. Warsaw Signal–Extra: Sept. 24, 1845 . . . [Warsaw, 1845]
Broadside. 48×30cm.
Different printing of the preceding broadside. Last 1½ columns contain a report entitled "Later Wed. night, ten o'clock. Proceedings of a meeting of the Citizens of McDonough County." Another anti-Mormon group pledged to support the citizens of Hancock County.
Byrd 1004
NN

9610. ———. Warsaw Signal. Extra. Sept. 30, 12:00 P.M., 1845 . . . [Warsaw, 1845]
Broadside. 50×31cm.
Contains: Report of the arrest of three Mormons charged with the killing of Colonel George Davenport; the Mormon proposal to move from the state; and the report of a number of anti-Mormon meetings.
Byrd 1006
NN

9611. ———. Warsaw Signal. Extra. Sunday, 12:00, M. June 14, 1846, We are again called upon to announce that the County of Hancock is the theatre of war . . . [Warsaw, 1846]
Broadside. 52×16cm.
In double columns.
A call to the anti-Mormon mob to gather and drive out the remaining Mormons in Hancock County. Describes events from the anti-Mormon convention of the 6th and replies to an extra of the Eagle.
Byrd 1125
ICHi, NN

9612. ———. Warsaw Signal — Extra. Warsaw, Ills., July 16, 1846–11 A.M. More difficulties in Hancock County . . . [Warsaw, 1846]
Broadside. 52×23½cm.
In three columns.
In rebuttal to *Hancock Eagle* Extra. Repudiates "lies" of July 16 concerning three men being whipped by an anti-Mormon mob.
Byrd 1126
ICHi, NN

9613. ———. Warsaw Signal. Extra. Wednesday, July 29, 1846. Public meeting in M'Donough County . . . [Warsaw, 1846]
Broadside. 30×22cm.
Appeals to the new citizens to vote right in the pending election.
Byrd 1127
NN

WARSAW SIGNAL

9614. ———. Warsaw Signal. Extra. Friday, July 31, 1846. Anti-Mormons, we have one more word to say to you before the final issue . . . [Warsaw, 1846]
Broadside. 30½×22½cm.
In three columns.
Again refers to the pending election in which the independent is labeled a Mormon. (The Anti-Mormon candidate won)
Byrd 1128
ICHi, NN

9615. ———. Warsaw Signal. Extra. Saturday, August 1, 1846. Look to your tickets there have been some tickets printed with the names of all the Anti-Mormon nominees . . . [Warsaw, 1846]
Broadside. 20×14cm.
Printed in double columns.
Accuses the Mormons of playing tricks to change the result of the election.
Byrd 1130
NN

9616. ———. Warsaw Signal. Extra. Warsaw, Monday, September 14th, 12 o'clock, M., 1846. War! War! A battle fought in Nauvoo . . . [Warsaw, 1846]
Broadside. 15½×51cm.
Singleton's proposals for ending the war were unacceptable to the anti-Mormons and the result was a pitched battle with a final arbitration by the citizens of Quincy; demands made on the remaining Mormons to leave.
Byrd 1129
ICHi

9617. Warvelle, George William. A compendium of freemasonry in Illinois; embracing a review of the introduction, development and present condition of all rites and degrees; together with biographical sketches of distinguished members of the fraternity. Ed. by George W. Warvelle . . . Chicago, The Lewis Publishing Company, 1897.
2v. illus., plates, ports., facsims. 27cm.
Includes official reports on the Nauvoo Masonic Lodge and brief mention of Mormonism.
DLC, NN

9618. Warwood, William. The beginning and the end of the World. God, Man and the Devil, Heaven, Earth and Hell. By William Worwood [sic] Belgrade, Mont., Published by William Worwood, 1906.
2p.l. [5]–151p. 19cm.
Name spelled with an o (Worwood) on all places on book. Another copy with same mistake has been corrected by the author. A Mormon writer who states that he has not adhered strictly to Mormon doctrines.
USlC

9619. ———. (same) Appendix. 1909. Reincarnation explained. [Belgrade, Mont., 1909]
33p. 19cm.
With the correction of the author's name.
USlC

9620. ———. A true witness of the Gospel of Jesus Christ and the errors of modern Mormonism, polygamy, blood atonement, Adam worship, etc. Exposed by William Warwood . . . [Belgrade, Montana, 1912]
43p. 21cm.
USlC

9621. Washburn, Jane A. (Ives). To the Pacific and back. New York, Sunshine Publishing Co., 1887.
2p.l. [5]–200p. front. 22½cm.
Account of Salt Lake City and the Mormons . . . p. 34–37.
CU–B, DLC, NN, UPB

9622. Washburn, Jesse Alvin. Chronology chart; Bible and Book of Mormon events, by J. A. Washburn . . . Provo, Utah, 1928.
4p.l. fold. tab., 22 numb. l., 4 maps on [2]l. 24cm.
On cover: Before the *Bible* and after the *Book of Mormon.*
"This work is an attempt to suggest the relationship, in point of time, at least, between the events of the Bible and the Book of Mormon history and other important world happenings."
"Study list": on verso of 3d prelim. leaf.
DLC, NjP, USl, USlC

9623. Washington's vision. [San Francisco, 1884?]
Broadside. 23×13cm.
Tract of the Church of the Messiah.
USlC

9624. Washington's vision. The wars of 1812 and 1861 revealed to him. Mother Shipton's prophecy, and S. W. Farnsworth's vision. Salt Lake City, 1877.
[8]p. 15cm.
Cover-title.
See also under Remarkable visions.
MH

9625. The Wasp. Nauvoo, Ill., April 16, 1842–April 27, 1843.
1v. weekly. 52cm.
Editor: Elder William Smith; John Taylor.
Succeeded by the *Nauvoo Neighbor*, May 3, 1843.
CtY; MWA Aug 27, 1842; NN Jl 2, 1842; USlC comp.

9626. The Wasp. Bennettiana; or, the microscope with double diamond lenses. The baser coward, the bigger the bluster. We have read Doctor Bennett's great sina qua non: Russian Ukase: and dictatorial egotism. Desperate cases, require desperate doses and so we will give a little of Bennett as he was, and Bennett as he is . . . Nauvoo, Ill., 1842.
[4]p. 39×27cm.
"*The Wasp.* Extra. Nauvoo, Illinois, Wednesday, July 27, 1842."
In four columns.
A denunciation of John C. Bennett and his reversal of beliefs.
Byrd 735
CtY, USlC

9627. Watchman [*pseud.*] Brigham's manner of tithing and consecration examined. Plano, Ill., The Reorganized Church of Jesus Christ of Latter Day Saints [186–]
8p. 23cm.
Signed: Watchman.
NN, USl

9628. ———. The elect lady. Plano, Ill., The Reorganized Church of Jesus Christ of Latter Day Saints [1867]
4p. 18cm.
Signed: Watchman.
Includes poem by Joseph Smith III about his mother, Emma Smith.
NN

9629. Waterloo, Stanley. The Seekers, by Stanley Waterloo. Chicago and New York, Herbert S. Stone & Company, 1900 [c1899]
257p. 19½cm.
Chapter IV. "A latter-day prophet." Fiction, with a chapter devoted to Mormonism.
NjP, USlC

9630. Waterloo Boostologist. Salt Lake City, October, 1914–January 26, 1916.
2v. bi-monthly. 26cm.
Ward bulletin.
Suspended April–September 1915.
USlC V.1 #1–11; V.2 #1–2, 4

"Waters" [*pseud.*] *See Russell, William.*

9631. Waters, William Elkanah. "Life among the Mormons, and a march to their Zion" to which is added a chapter on the Indians of the plains and mountains of the West. By an officer of the U.S. Army . . . New York, Moorhead, Simpson & Bond, 1868.
xv, 219p. port., plates. 19cm.
In Utah, 1866–1867.
Howes W157
CSmH, CtY, CU–B, DLC, ICN, MH, MoInRC, NjP, UHi, USlC, WHi

9632. Watson, George D. The seven women in prophecy. [Los Angeles, Cal., Free Tract Society, n.d.]
[8]p. 11½cm.
The Mormons, p. [6–7]
USlC

9633. Watson, H. T. From creation to restoration; our world as it was and as it will be: a condensed history of the world in musical rhyme. Composed and published by H. T. Watson . . . V.1. Des Moines, Iowa, c1906.
[47]l. plate. 29cm.
Only V.1 published.
Poetry based on the Inspired Version of *Bible* revised by Joseph Smith.
NN, RPB

9634. Watson, Wingfield. Baptism. What is it designed for? — How is it administered? — Is it a saving ordinance? — And is it a commandment of God? [Spring Prairie, Wis., Dec. 26, 1899. Burlington, Wis.? 1899?]
32p. 19½cm.
Caption-title. In double columns.
Signed: Wingfield Watson, an elder in the Church of Jesus Christ of Latter Day Saints.
Morgan
CtY, USlC, WBuC, WHi

9635. ———. The Book of Mormon. An essay on its claims and prophecies, by Wingfield Watson, an elder in the Church of Jesus Christ of Latter Day Saints. [Boyne, Mich.? 1884]
16p. 21½cm.
Caption-title.
Signed: Boyne, Charlevoix County, Mich., March 25, 1884.
Morgan
CtY, NN, WBuC

9636. ———. (same) [Burlington, Wis.? 1899]
18p. 19½cm.
Caption-title.
In double columns.
Dated at end: Spring Prairie, Wis., March 24, 1899.
Enlarged version of his 1884 edition.
Morgan
CtY, CU–B, MH, MoInRC, OClWHi, UHi, WBuC, WHi

9637. ———. A friendly admonition. [Nauvoo, Ill., Rustler Print., 1913]
7p. 20½cm.
Signed: Burlington, Wisconsin, July, 1913.
Caption-title.
In double columns.
Morgan
CtY, UHi, UPB, USlC, WBuC

9638. ———. Hang this card up that you may have God's commandments always before you, but please read and consider carefully from whence they came and how. [Burlington, Wis.? n.d.]
Broadside. 41×24cm.
With explanatory sheet. [1]p. 27½cm.
The Ten Commandments are included on the broadside; the preliminary page is a statement of how the broadside is to be used and a reaffirmation of James J. Strang's position.
USlC

9639. ———. Latter Day signs. [Burlington, Wis.? 1897]
15p. 21cm.
Caption-title.
In double columns.
"The Book of Mormon," p. [11]–15.
Signed: Wingfield Watson, Minister of the Gospel of Jesus Christ, Lyons, June, 1897.
Morgan
CtY, CU–B, ICHi, MH, MoInRC, OClWHi, UHi, ULA, UPB, WBuC

WATSON, W.

———. Modern Christianity. *See Hyde, John.*

9640. ———. The necessity of baptism; and of having authority from God to preach the gospel. Plano, Ill., Printed at the Herald Steam Book and Job Office [1877]

8p. 32cm.

Signed: Wingfield Watson, Boyne, Charlevoix Co., Mich.

Caption-title.

In three columns.

Morgan

NN

9641. ———. Non-Mormon lectures on polygamy from non-Mormon viewpoint. Copied from the Deseret Evening News, Saturday, October 13, 1906. [Burlington, Wis.? 1906?]

10p. 20cm.

Caption-title.

In double columns.

This pamphlet consists of an address by V. S. Peet, reprinted from the *Deseret Evening News* with a concluding note signed "W. W."

Morgan

OClWHi, UHi, WBuC

9642. ———. The "One mighty and strong." [Burlington, Wis.? 1915]

12p. 21cm.

Caption-title.

In double columns.

Signed: Wingfield Watson, Burlington, Wis., March, 1915.

Morgan

OClWHi, UHi, USlC, WBuC

9643. ———. An open letter to B. H. Roberts, Salt Lake City, Utah. [Burlington, Wis.? 1894?]

18p. 22½cm.

Caption-title.

In double columns.

Dated at end: Spring Prairie, Wis., Nov. 13, 1894.

Morgan

MoInRC, USlC, WBuC

9644. ———. An open letter to B. H. Roberts, Salt Lake City, Utah. [Burlington, Wis.? 1896?]

30p. 22½cm.

Caption-title.

In double columns.

"A word to George Q. Cannon," p. [18]–21. Signed W. W.

Morgan

CU–B, MH, MoInRC, NjP, WBuC, WHi

9645. ———. Prophetic controversy. No. 2; extracted from the writings and criticisms of John E. Page, James J. Strang, William Marks and Hyrum P. Brown, to which are added a few notes in brackets, and a short commentary by the transcriber, Wingfield Watson. [Boyne, Mich.? 1887]

28p. 22cm.

In double columns.

For Prophetic controversy [No. 1] see Strang, James J.

Morgan

CtY, CU–B, DLC, MH, MoInRC, NjP, NN, OClWHi, UHi, UPB, USlC, WBuC, WHi

9646. ———. Prophetic controversy. No. 3; or the even balances by which Isaac Scott, Chancy Loomis, and the founders of the Reorganization are weighed and found wanting. In two chapters. By Wingfield Watson, an elder in the Church of Jesus Christ of Latter Day Saints, Bay Springs, Charlevoix County, Michigan. February, 1889. [Boyne, Mich.? 1889]

44p. 22cm.

In double columns.

Morgan

CtY, CU–B, MH, NjP, NN, UHi, UPB, USlC, WHi

9647. ———. Prophetic controversy. No. 4. Mr. Strang proved to have been always an honorable man. The theory that the prophetic office goes by lineal right, and the doctrine that lesser officers in the priesthood can ordain to the greater, utterly exploded. [Burlington, Wis.? 1897]

38p. 21½cm.

Caption-title.

In double columns.

Signed: Wingfield Watson, Spring Prairie, Walworth County, Wisconsin, March 15, 1897.

Morgan

MH, MoInRC, NjP, UHi, UPB, USlC, WBuC, WHi

9648. ———. Prophetic controversy. No. 5. [Burlington, Wis.? 1903]

27p. 21cm.

Caption-title.

In double columns.

Signed: Wingfield Watson, Lyons, Wis., April 18, 1903.

Morgan

CtY, MH, MoInRC, NjP, UHi, UPB, USlC, WBuC, WHi

9649. ———. Prophetic controversy. No. 6, or "Facts" for the Anti-Mormons located at Grayson, Kentucky, being an answer to the following letter of inquiry. [Burlington, Wis.? 1905]

14p. 21½cm.

Caption-title.

In double columns.

Signed: Wingfield Watson.

An open letter to R. B. Neal.

Morgan

CtY, MH, UHi, UPB, USlC, WBuC, WHi

9650. ———. Prophetic controversy. No. 7. [Burlington, Wis.? 1906?]
9p. 21½cm.
Caption-title.
In double columns.
Signed: Wingfield Watson.
A second open letter to R. B. Neal.
Morgan
MH, UHi, USlC, WBuC, WHi

9651. ———. Prophetic controversy. No. 8. [Burlington, Wis.? 1907]
7p. 21½cm.
Caption-title.
In double columns.
Signed: Wingfield Watson, Burlington, Wis., July 20, 1907.
An open letter to the *Liahona.*
Morgan
MH, MoInRC, UHi, USlC, WBuC, WHi

9652. ———. Prophetic controversy. No. 9. [Burlington, Wis.? 1907]
[5]p. 22cm.
Caption-title.
In double columns.
Signed: Wingfield Watson, Burlington, Wis., Sept. 25, 1907.
A third open letter to R. B. Neal, July 26, 1907.
Morgan
MH, UHi, UPB, USlC, WBuC, WHi

9653. ———. Prophetic controversy. No. 10. [Burlington, Wis.? 1908]
10p. 21½cm.
Caption-title.
In double columns.
Signed: Wingfield Watson.
An open letter to E. W. Nunley, Sept. 3, 1908.
Morgan
CtY, MH, NjP, UHi, UPB, USlC, WBuC, WHi

9654. ———. Prophetic controversy. No. 11. [Burlington, Wis.? 1908?]
[4]p. 21cm.
Caption-title.
In double columns.
Another open letter to E. W. Nunley.
Signed: Wingfield Watson.
This "controversy" is in the nature of a supplement to No. 10, and is entirely different from "No. 11" published by Watson in 1910.
Morgan
MoInRC, UPB, WBuC

9655. ———. Prophetic controversy. No. 11. [Burlington, Wis.? 1910]
13p. 21½cm.
Caption-title.
In double columns.
Signed: Burlington, Wis., Aug. 1, 1910, Wingfield Watson.
Morgan
MH, MoInRC, UHi, UPB, USlC, WBuC, WHi

9656. ———. Prophetic controversy. No. 12. [Burlington, Wis.? 1912]
20p. 21½cm.
Caption-title.
In double columns.
Signed: Burlington, Wis., March 13, 1912, Wingfield Watson.
Morgan
MH, MoInRC, UHi, UPB, USlC, WBuC, WHi

9657. ———. Prophetic controversy. No. 13. [Burlington, Wis.? 1918]
14p. 21½cm.
Caption-title.
In double columns.
Signed: Burlington, Wis., June 27, 1918, Wingfield Watson.
Rejoinder to the RLDS church.
Morgan
MH, MoInRC, UHi, UPB, USlC, WBuC, WHi

9658. ———. The true gospel. A comparison of the primitive, and true gospel, and the modern sectarian interpretation if [sic] it. By Wingfield Watson. [Kansas City, Mo.? 1920?]
[8]p. 17cm.
Caption-title.
This tract is a folder, 4p. on a side, 17×42½cm.
Morgan
WBuC

9659. ———. The Watson-Blair debate which took place at East Jordan, Mich., commencing Oct. 22nd and ending Oct. 26th, 1891. Published by W. J. Smith, Galien, Mich. Clifford, Ont., Printed at the Glad Tidings Office, Allan St., 1892.
244p. 16cm.
Morgan
MH, MoInRC, NjP, WHi

———. A word to George Q. Cannon. *See his An open letter to B. H. Roberts [1896?] p. 19–22.*

9660. Watt, G. D. Exercises in phonography. Designed to conduct the pupil to a practical acquaintance with the art. [called "the phonographic class book."] By G. D. Watt . . . Great Salt Lake City: W. Richards, Printer. 1851.
16p. 16½cm.
This was probably the basis of Watt's work on the Deseret alphabet.
NjP

9661. Watt, Robert. . . . Hinsides Atlanterhavet. Skildringer fra Amerika . . . Kjøbenhaven, P. Bloch; New York, F. W. Christern; [etc., etc., 1872]–74.
3v. illus., port. 18½cm.
Each volume has general and special title-page.
Part III devoted to Mormonism and Shakers. Mormonism, p. 1–107. He visited Salt Lake City; discussed Mormonism and the *Book of Mormon.*
Title in English: Beyond the Atlantic ocean.
CSmH, DLC, MH

9661a. Waugh, George Peden. A poetic P.S. to a letter dated Edinburgh, June 29th, 1841. [Edinburgh? 1849?]
Broadside. 20×12½cm.
A four-line poem by George D. Watt, followed by "Replied to from Dundee, June 30th, 1841, by Geo. Peden Waugh, and revised by the author at Edinburgh, 15th March, 1849." A five-stanza poem.
UPB

9662. Weakley, Joseph. Mormonism, examined by J. Weakley, and proved to be false by the Holy Scriptures. June 28th, 1850. Jersey, W. Marston, Printer [c1850]
11p. 17cm.
CU–B

9663. Weaver, Ray Bennett. The Mormon menace. By Ray Bennett Weaver. [Waukesha, Wis., Carroll College, 1912]
[6]p. 23cm.
Cover-title.
An address delivered at the Wisconsin Intercollegiate Oratorical Contest, March 17, 1912, at Ripon College, Ripon, Wis.
WHi

Webb, E. H. Latter-day Saints. *See Alcock, P.*

Webb, Robert C. [*pseud.*] *See Homans, J. E.*

9664. Webb, William Larkin. The centennial history of Independence, Mo., by W. L. Webb. [n.p.] c1927.
5p.l. [13]–294p. 21cm.
Topic XIV. The Mormons. History of Mormonism in Independence.
DLC, ICU, MoInRC, NjP, UHi, UPB, USI

9665. Weber College, Ogden, Utah. Weber College. Catalog. Ogden, 1900–
v. 20–22cm.
Formerly Weber Stake Academy; Weber Academy.
For student publications *The Acorn* and *Souvenir*: See *The Acorn*.
UPB 1892–93, 1915–16, 1923–28; USIC 1900–02, 1904–05, 1908–19, 1922–23, 1924–25, 1926–28

9666. Webster, Kimball. The gold seekers of '49; A personal narrative of the overland trail and adventures in California and Oregon from 1849 to 1854. By Kimball Webster, a New England forty-niner; With an introduction and biographical sketch by George Waldo Browne; illustrated by Frank Holland and others. Manchester, N. H., Standard Book Company, 1917.
1p.l., 7–240p. plates, 2 port. 20½cm.
Bypassed Salt Lake. Reference to Mormons, p. 44, 76; Mormon trader in Bear River Valley, p. 71–72, 78; Mormon train from California, p. 79.
CU–B, DLC

9667. Webster, Thomas. Some extracts from the Book of Doctrine and Covenants of the Church of the Latter Day Saints, to which are added some facts tending to show the utter failure of their pretended prophecies and their unsuccessful attempts at working miracles, &c. By Thomas Webster, formerly one of the Elders of the Mormon Church. Preston, England, Printed by W. Pollard [1841?]
iv [5]–28p. 21½cm.
MB, MH, NN

9668. Webster, William. The warning voice. No. 1. Coronado, Fla., 1907.
[4]p. 14cm.
Caption-title.
Letter to Ben E. Rich concerning Mormonism as expounded by missionaries. He was offended by their treatment of his wife.
USIC

9669. Wedderburn, *Sir* **David,** *bart.* Life of Sir David Wedderburn, bart., M.P. Comp. from his journals and writings, by his sister, Mrs. E. H. Percival. London, K. Paul, Trench & Co., 1884.
xii, 439p. illus., port. 23cm.
Account of the Mormons, p. 229–230, 240–244.
CU, DLC, NN

9670. Weed, Thurlow. The life of Thurlow Weed. Boston, Houghton Mifflin and Company . . . 1884.
2v. 21cm.
Binders title.
Printing of the "Mormon Bible" offered to Mr. Weed at Rochester about 1829, by a man "without occupation," V. 1, p. 358–359.
CU, NjP, USIC

9671. Weeks, George F. California copy by George F. Weeks. Washington, Published by Washington College Press, 1928.
4p.l. [9]–346p. illus., plates. 20cm.
Difficulty with Mormon neighbors, p. 35–38, 99–106.
USIC

9672. Weeks, Raymond. The Hound-tuner of Callaway. New York, Columbia University Press, 1927.
x, 276[1]p. illus. 19cm.
Fiction, with a chapter entitled: The Mormon road.
DLC

9673. Der Wegweiser. Basil, Switzerland, January 1, 1927–1936.
10v. quarterly; monthly. 25cm.
Editor: Max Zimmer
Quarterly 1927–1929; monthly 1930–
Magazine for the Swiss-German, German-Austrian Missions.
Title in English: Way Finder.
UPB V.1–9, USIC comp.

9674. Weightman, Hugh. . . . Mormonism exposed; the other side. From a legal standpoint. By Hugh Weightman . . . [Salt Lake City?] 1884.
[2] [45]–66p. 21cm. (Tract. No. 3)
Numbering follows from Tract No. 1, *Mormonism exposed*, by James W. Barclay, and Tract No. 2, *Mormonism unveiled*, by Earle S. Goodrich.
CtY, CU–B, DLC, ICN, MH, NjP, NjPT, NN, UHi, UPB, USl, UU

9675. ———. (same) [Salt Lake City?] 1884.
21p. 21cm.
Variant pagination.
USlC

9676. Weiss, Feri Felix. The sieve; or, Revelations of the man mill, being the truth about American immigration. By Feri Felix Weiss. Illustrated. Boston, The Page Company, 1921.
3p.l., vii–xiii [1] 307p. illus., plates, ports., facsims. 20cm.
Chapter XI. The Mormons. The emigration of young girls for the Mormon harems.
CU, CoD, DLC, USlC

9676a. Welch, Edgar Luderne. "Grip's" historical souvenir of Waterloo, N.Y. [Syracuse? N.Y.] 1903.
104p. illus., ports. 26½cm. (Historical souvenir series. No. 16)
Half-title.
"Mormon Joe" p. 91.
UPB

9677. Welch, Josiah. To the Clergy of the Presbyterian Church. [Salt Lake City, ca. 1875]
[4]p. 21½cm.
The probable first edition of the Extracts of Sermons by Brigham Young and other dignitaries later republished with a new introduction under title *Mormon Expositor*, and in the pamphlet *A Few Choice Examples of Mormon Practices and Sermons.*
UPB

9678. Welles, C. M. Three years' wanderings of a Connecticut Yankee in South America, Africa, Australia, and California with descriptions of the several countries, manners, customs and conditions of the people, including miners, natives, etc. Also, a detailed account of a voyage around the world, attended with unusual suffering . . . By C. M. Welles. Illustrated with beautiful steel plate engravings. New York, American Subscription Publishing House, 1859.
358p. plates. 19½cm.
He encounters refugees from Utah in 1853: Mormons who had escaped after being robbed of all possessions, p. 296–298.
Another edition: 1860. NjP, USlC
Howes W239
CU–B, DLC, NN

9679. Wells, Charles Knox Polk. Life and adventures of Polk Wells (Charles Knox Polk Wells) the notorious outlaw . . . [Hall, Mo.] G. A. Warnica [1907]
3p.l., [7]–259p. illus. 23cm.
Relates a purported "Scrap with the Danites."
Howes W243
CU–B, NjP, UPB

9680. Wells, Daniel Hanmer. Order of the day for the Sixth of April, 1853 in laying the corner stones of the Temple in Great Salt Lake City, Utah Territory. [Great Salt Lake City, 1853?]
Broadside. 39×14cm.
Signed: D. H. Wells, Amasa Lyman, Lorenzo Snow.
USlC

9681. Wells, Emmeline Blanche (Woodward) *editor.* Charities and philanthropies . . . Woman's work in Utah. World's Fair Edition. Salt Lake City, G. Q. Cannon and Sons Co., 1893.
viii [9]–90p. plates. 21cm.
Contains biographical sketches of women physicians in Utah.
MH, UPB, USlC, WHi

9682. ———. Memorial of Emmeline B. Wells and Zina Young Williams of Salt Lake City, Utah Territory, to the Senate and House of Representatives of the United States in Congress assembled: asking for a repeal of the Anti-Polygamy law of 1862, and for legislation to protect the women and children of Utah Territory. Washington, 1879.
4p. 21½cm.
UPB, USl, USlC, UU

9683. ———. Musings and memories; poems by Emmeline B. Wells . . . Salt Lake City, G. Q. Cannon & Sons Co., 1896.
xiii [15]–304p. port. 19½cm.
Mormon poetry.
DLC, ULA, USlC

9684. ———. (same) 2d ed. With later poems and some hitherto unpublished . . . Salt Lake City, The Deseret News, 1915.
4p.l., 9–336p. 2 port. 19cm.
CSmH, DLC, NjP, UHi, UPB, USlC, UU

9685. ———. Songs and flowers of the Wasatch. Edited by Emmeline B. Wells. Illustrated by Edna Wells Sloan. Salt Lake City, George Q. Cannon & Sons, 1893.
3p.l., 33p. 25½×30cm.
Mormon poetry.
USlC

9686. ———. Verses lovingly inscribed to President Bathsheba W. Smith. [n.p., n.d.]
[4]p. port. 22cm.
Includes: When the old friends meet. A beautiful life. Birthday greeting. A portrait.
UPB

9687. Wells, James Monroe. "With touch of elbow," or, Death before dishonor; a thrilling narrative of adventure on land and sea, by Captain James M. Wells. Philadelphia, John C. Winston Co., 1909.
362p. illus. 19½cm.
Includes material on the Utah Expedition and Salt Lake City.
Howes W249.
DLC, NjP, UHi

9688. Wells, Junius Free. Address By Junius F. Wells. [at M.I.A. Jubilee Conference, June 6–10, 1925 in the tabernacle Sunday morning, 7th June, 1925] Salt Lake City, 1925.
[12]p. 24½cm.
NjP, UPB, USlC

9689. ———. Meaning and purpose of the sacrament; address delivered over Radio Station KSL, Sunday Evening, September 18, 1927. [Salt Lake City] 1927.
Broadside. 33×28cm.
Reprinted from the *Deseret News.*
UPB

9690. Wells, Samuel Robert. The illustrated annuals of phrenology and physiognomy for the years 1865–6–7–8–9–70 and 71, complete in one volume, of over 400 pages. By S. R. Wells, editor, Phrenological Journal. With more than 300 illustrative engravings. New York, Samuel R. Wells, Publisher, 1871.
Various pagings. illus., ports. 19cm.
Short biography of Brigham Young, p. 38–40, Second Series. A reading of his head.
USlC

9691. The Wells family centennial; commemorating the one hundredth birthday of Daniel Hanmer Wells, October 27th, 1914. [Salt Lake City, 1914?]
[32] 16p. ports. 23½cm.
Includes "The Wells family genealogy," by Junius F. Wells.
UPB

9692. The Wells family reunion, 1814–1916. Commemorating the one hundred and second anniversary of Daniel Hanmer Wells. October 27th, 1916, at the residence of Mr. and Mrs. Rulon S. Wells. Salt Lake City, 1916.
[2]p. illus., ports., plates. 23cm.
Family history.
USlC

9693. Weppner, Margaretha. The North Star and the Southern Cross. Being the personal experiences, impressions and observations of Margaretha Weppner in a two years' journey around the world. London, S. Low, Marston, Low and Searle [Albany, N.Y.] the author, 1876.
2v. 19½cm.
"Salt Lake City . . . San Francisco," V. 1, p. 130–145.
CU–B, NjP, USlC

9694. Werner, Morris Robert. Barnum. New York, Harcourt, Brace & Co. [c1923]
viii, p. [3]l., 3–381p. illus., plates, port. 21cm.
A lecture in Salt Lake City and a visit to Brigham Young.
CU, DLC, NjP, USlC

9695. ———. Brigham Young, by M. R. Werner . . . New York, Harcourt, Brace and Company [c1925]
xvi, 478p. illus., plates, ports. 22½cm.
"First edition."
Bibliography: p. 463–469.
First published in the *Ladies Home Journal,* December, 1924 to June, 1925.
CSmH, CtY, CU–B, DLC, ICHi, MoInRC, NjP, NjPT, NN, UHi, ULA, UPB, USl, USlC, UU, WHi

9696. ———. (same) 2d printing. New York, Harcourt, Brace and Company, 1925.
xvi, 478p. illus., plates, port. 22cm.
2d printing, June 1925.
UPB

9697. ———. (same) London, J. Cape, Ltd. [1925]
xvi, 478p. illus., plates, ports. 22½cm.
CtY, CU–B, ICN, MBrZ, NN, OClWHi, UHi, UPB, USlC, WHi

9698. ———. (same, in German) Ein seltsamer heiliger Brigham Young. Der Moses der Mormonen. Mit 46 Abbildungen . . . Zurich und Leipzig, Orell Fussli verlag [c1928]
3p.l., 7–188p. illus., plates, ports. 23cm.
UHi, USlC

Wesley, John. *See Job, Thomas.*

9699. West, Caleb W. Gov. West and the polygamists. Report of his interview with Apostle Lorenzo Snow, May 13, 1886, at the Utah Penitentiary. His proposals rejected, and the brethren proclaim their defiance of the law . . . [Salt Lake City, Salt Lake Tribune, 1886]
8p. 23cm.
Caption-title.
CSmH, MH, NN, UHi, WHi

9700. West, Franklin Lorenzo Richards. Life of Franklin D. Richards, president of the Council of the Twelve Apostles, Church of Jesus Christ of Latter-day Saints, by Franklin L. West . . . Salt Lake City, Deseret News Press [c1924]
275p. 2 port. 24cm.
DLC, CSmH, CU–B, NjP, NN, UHi, ULA, UPB, USl, USlC, UU, WHi

9701. ———. The way to universal peace; address delivered over Radio Station KSL, Sunday Evening, February 20, 1927. [Salt Lake City] 1927.
Broadside. 48×26½cm.
Reprinted from the *Deseret News.*
UPB

9702. West, Joseph A. Francis West, of Duxbury, Mass. and some of his ancestors and descendants. Including the descendants of Chauncey Walker West, late of Ogden, Utah, and Abraham H. Hougland, late of Salt Lake City, Utah. Ogden, Published by Joseph A. West, 1911.
vii, 48p. ports. 21½cm.
Includes brief biographies of Chauncey W. West and Abraham H. Hougland as well as their genealogies.
USl

9703. West, William S. A few interesting facts respecting the rise, progress and pretentions of the Mormons. [Warren? O.] 1837.
16p. 15cm.
CtY

9704. Westbrook, G. W. The Mormons in Illinois; with an account of the late disturbances, which resulted in the assassination of Joseph & Hyrum Smith, the prophet and patriarch of the Latter-day Saints. By G. W. Westbrook. St. Louis, Printed by Ustick & Davies, 1844.
36p. 19½cm.
It also appears as an appendix without title page in James H. Hunt's Mormonism.
DLC, IHi, MnHi, USlC

9705. The Western Bugle. Kanesville, Iowa, April 28–July 21, 1852.
1v. (#1–13) weekly. 53cm.
A. W. Babbitt, editor.
The editor stated that he would take no part in religious controversies.
Originally published as *Kanesville Bugle*, later called *Council Bluffs Bugle*.
DLC S 29, 1852; Jan 12–D 1855; Ja 2, 1862. IaCb Je 16–23, O 20, 1852; S 7–21, D 21, 1853; Ap 6, 1856; Ma 1857–58; Je 1864–1866; Je 1869–Je, 1870. MWA Je 6, 13, 27, 1864. USlC Ap 28–Jl 21, 1852

9706. The Western Galaxy. Salt Lake City, 1888.
1v (4 nos. in 465p.) irregular. 25cm.
Editor: Edward W. Tullidge.
Continues *Tullidge's Quarterly Magazine* after a three year suspension.
CSmH, CtY, MoInRC, NjP, ULA, UPB, USlC

9707. Western Nucleus and Democratic Echo. Preparation, Monona Co., Iowa. August, 1856?–1858?
1v. weekly. 45cm.
Thompson & Butts, Editor & Proprietors.
The title was possibly changed to *Preparation Nucleus and Zion's Echo* combined with *Preparation News*.
Morgan
MoInRC Je 3 #17, O 21 #35, 1857; Ja 13 #10, Ap 1 #51, 1858

9708. Western Standard. San Francisco, California, February 23, 1856–November 18, 1857.
2v. weekly. 59cm.
Editor and publisher: George Q. Cannon.
Discontinued at the beginning of the Utah War.
CtY, ULA, USlC V.1–V.2 #30

9709. Western Standard. Prospectus of the Western Standard . . . [San Francisco, 1856]
Broadside. 22×18cm.
Dated: San Francisco, California, January 4, 1856.
Signed: George Q. Cannon.
USlC

9710. Westwood, J. M., *compiler.* Extracts from the Times & Seasons, published at Nauvoo, Ill. Containing the Paracletes, Go with me, The answer, To go with me, Joseph Smith's last dream, & other extracts. Springville, Utah, 1890.
21p. 17½cm.
Cover-title.
UPB, USlC

9711. Westwood, P. M. I'm a Mormon. A song by P. M., [sic] Westwood, and sung by him before the ladies, nobility, and gentry of Bristol, Christmas, 1847. [Bristol, Eng.] Geo. Ruddle, Printer & Bookbinder, Duke St. Trowbridge [1847]
Broadside. 34×21cm.
MH

9712. Wetmore, Alphonso, *compiler.* Gazetteer of the State of Missouri. With a map of the state . . . To which is added an appendix, containing frontier sketches, and illustrations of Indian character. With a frontispiece, engraved on steel. Compiled by Alphonso Wetmore . . . St. Louis, Published by C. Keemle, 1837.
2p.l. [ix]–xvi [17]–382p. fold. map. 22cm.
Material on the Mormons in Jackson County, p. 92–97.
Howes W296, Sabin 103064, W–C 89
CSmH, CtY, CU–B, DLC, ICJ, MH, MiU, MnU, NjP, NN, OClWHi, ULA, UU, WHi

9713. Wetmore, Helen Cody. Last of the Great Scouts; the life story of Col. William H. Cody ("Buffalo Bill") as told by his sister Helen Cody Wetmore. [Duluth, Minn., The Duluth Press Printing Co.] 1899.
3p.l., v–xiii, 267p. illus., plates, port. 22cm.
Includes material on the Utah expedition.
Another edition: By Helen Cody Wetmore and Zane Grey. 1918. NjP, USlC
CU–B, NjP

9714. What congress can do about Roberts. Mormon mendacity. Mormon lies permitted by the doctrine of Latter Day Saints. [n.p., ca. 1900]
Broadside. 20×53½cm.
An attack upon Brigham Roberts that quotes extensively from John D. Nutting's speech, "The duty of church and state about Mormonism," delivered in Salt Lake City to the Young Men's Christian Association.
IWW

9715. Wheaton, Clarence L. Take heed that no man shall deceive you. Address delivered at Independence, Mo., May 6, 1929. By Clarence L. Wheaton, of the Church of Christ, in Reply to J. F. Curtis, representing the Reorganized Church of Jesus Christ of Latter Day Saints. [Independence, Mo.? 1929?]
22p. 27cm.
Mimeographed. Odd-numbered pages blank.
CU-B

9716. ———. That interesting spot of land west of the Court House. What and where is it? Sermon delivered on the Temple Lot by Apostle Clarence L. Wheaton. April 27, 1928. [Independence, Mo.] 1928.
[15]p. 22½cm.
Church of Christ tract.
UPB

9717. Wheeler, Edward L. Bullion Bret; or, the giant grip of git-thar. A tale of silverland. New York, Beadle and Adams, 1884. (*Banner Weekly*, Vol. II, No. 72 to Vol. II, No. 77, March 29, 1884 to May 3, 1884)
[6]l. 32cm.
Fiction. Mining and Mormons in Idaho.
NN

9718. ———. (same, under title) Bullion Bret, the giant grip; or, The ruction at Git-Thar. By Edward Lytton. New York, Beadle and Adams, 1891.
15p. 32cm. (Beadle's popular library. Vol. I, No. 24)
Fiction. Mining and Mormons in Idaho.
USIC

9719. ———. Cyclone Kit, the young gladiator; or, the locked valley. A strange mountain tale, of a stranger place and people by Edward L. Wheeler. New York, Beadle & Adams, 1882.
15p. 30cm. (Beadle's half-dime library. Vol. 10, No. 240, Feb. 28, 1882)
The "walled Mormon city of Gold-Flake," Arizona.
NN

9720. Wheeler, George Montague. Preliminary report concerning explorations and surveys principally Nevada and Arizona, prosecuted in accordance with paragraph 2, Special Orders No. 109, War Department, March 18, 1871, and letter of instructions of March 23, 1871, from Brigadier General A. A. Humphreys, Chief of Engineers. Conducted under the immediate direction of 1st. Lieut. George M. Wheeler, Corps of Engineers, 1871. Washington, Govt. Print. Off., 1872.
96p. fold. map. 30cm.
Field operations, primarily in Nevada and Arizona in 1871; includes side expedition of First Lieut. Daniel W. Lockwood into southwestern Utah. References to Mormons and Mormon roads, p. 26, 65–66, 70–72, 74–75, 85–86, 91.
CU-B, DLC, UPB, USIC

9721. ———. Preliminary report upon a reconnaissance through southern and southeastern Nevada, made in 1869, by Geo. M. Wheeler, Corps of Engineers, U.S. Army, assisted by D. W. Lockwood, Corps of Engineers, U.S. Army. Washington, Govt. Print. Off., 1875.
72p. 30cm.
References to Mormons, p. 11–19, 21, 28, 36–37, 41–42, 44–47, 55, 57; Mountain Meadows massacre, p. 37; Remarks on Death Valley party, p. 60–61; White Mountain Mission, p. 61.
CU-B, DLC, UPB

———. *See U.S. Geographical Surveys West of the 100th Meridian.*

9722. Wheelock, Cyrus Hubbard. Invitation. All persons are respectfully invited to attend the Latter-day Saints' meeting to investigate their faith and doctrines, and to examine their publications. [Liverpool, 1851]
[4]p. 19cm.
Signed: C. H. Wheelock . . . A. F. McDonald.
Fourteen articles of faith, p. 2.
Copy in possession of Peter Crawley

9723. ———. To the priesthood and members of the Church of Jesus Christ of Latter-day Saints, in the Manchester Conference. [Manchester, T. Wilkinson, Printer, 1851]
4p. 20½cm.
CSmH, MH, UPB, USIC

Which is the Church? *See A., W.*

9724. Whipple, Edward. A biography of James M. Peebles, M. D., A. M. By Edward Whipple. Published by the author. Battle Creek, Mich. [c1901]
592p. port. 23½cm.
Recounts briefly his 1872 visit to Utah, p. 417–419.
CSt, CU-B

9725. Whitaker, John M. Salvation and how to obtain it. By Elder John M. Whitaker. [n.p., ca. 1900]
7 [1]p. 18cm.
A tract published during an early mission of John M. Whitaker.
UPB, USIC

9725a. ———. (same, in German). Seelenrettung und Wie Dieselbe zu erlangen ist. [Brooklyn, N.Y., ca. 1900]
8p. 19½cm.
USIC

9726. White, Alma. Looking back from Beulah, by Mrs. Mollie Alma White on the overruling and forming hand of God in the poverty and struggles of childhood, the hardships of later years, the battles, victories and joys of the sanctified life . . . Bound Brook, N.J., Published by the Pentecostal Union, 1910 [c1902]
2p.l., 7–343p. illus., plates. 19½cm.
Missionary work in Utah, 1874.
Another edition: 1929. NjP
CU, NjP, UHi, USlC

9727. White, Alma (Bridwell). The New Testament church. Denver, Colorado, Pillar of Fire Publishers, c1907.
3p.l. [5]–17p. port. 18cm.
Education not the only answer to the problem of Mormonism, p. 12–13.
USlC

9728. White, Douglas. The story of a trail; being an authentic record of the breaking of the Mormon Trail between the Inter-Mountain empire and California's "Land of sunshine," with the story of the founding and building along this historic pioneer highway of the Salt Lake route. A description of the marvelous resources contained within the area tributary to this new and direct line of railway now in operation between the Rocky Mountains and the Pacific. Los Angeles, San Pedro, Los Angeles & Salt Lake Railroad, 1905.
162p. illus. 31cm.
History of the "Mormon corridor" from Salt Lake City to Los Angeles.
CU–B, CSmH, UPB

9729. White, Edward L. Jehovah's Praise. [Salt Lake City] c1874.
[2]p. music. 20cm.
Mormon music.
USlC

9730. White, Greenough. An apostle of the western church; memoir of the Right Reverend Jackson Kemper . . . first missionary bishop of the American church, with notices of some of his contemporaries; a contribution to the religious history of the western states, by the Reverend Greenough White . . . New York, T. Whittaker, 1900.
xv, 231p. port. 19½cm.
Problems of the Protestant Episcopal Church missionary work in Utah.
DLC, NjPT, USlC

9731. White, I. N. A synopsis of the White-Box debate Held March 9th — 20th 1892, at Oak Grove Church, Vernon County, Missouri. Second proposition. Resolved, that the Baptist Church is in harmony with the New Testament church. J. B. Box affirms, I. N. White denies. Reported by G. R. Wells. Independence, Mo., Ensign Print., 1892.
96p. 21cm.
Cover-title.
A debate in which Mormonism is brought incidentally into the discussion.
UPB

9732. ———. What we believe and why we believe it. Independence, Mo., Ensign Publishing Co., 1896.
48p. 16cm. (The Gospel Banner. Vol. 8, No. 2)
RLDS doctrine.
MoInRC

9733. ———. White-Sewell debate, a discussion between I. N. White (Mormon) of Independence, Mo., and C. W. Sewell (Christian) of Dot, Texas. Nashville, Tenn., Gospel Advocate Publ., 1898.
142p. 15cm.
MoInRC

9734. White, John S. Farmington, the rose city, its attractions and industries; the land of opportunity, the city of homes, by John S. White. Issued by the Farmington Commercial Club, Farmington, Utah . . . Kaysville, Utah, Reflex Print. [1913?]
52p. illus. 16½×25cm.
DLC, NjP, USl

9735. ———. My winter rose, and some mouldy leaves from the garden of youth, by John S. White . . . [Los Angeles, Skelton Publishing Company, c1926]
180p., [1]l. port. 20cm.
Brief biography of a Mormon poet and his poetry with an introduction.
DLC, NjP, UHi, UPB, UU

9736. White, Stewart Edward. The forty-niners; a chronicle of the California trail and El Dorado. New Haven, Yale University Press, 1918.
ix, 273p. illus. 21cm. (The Chronicles of America series. Vol. 25)
With a caustic history of Mormonism.
Other editions: 1920. USlC; 1921. DLC
CSmH, CU–B, DLC, NjP, ULA, UPB, USlC, UU

9737. White, Thomas. The Mormon mysteries; being an exposition of the ceremonies of "The Endowment" and of the seven degrees of the temple. A new and improved edition by Thomas White. New York, Published by Edmund K. Knowlton, 1851.
2v., (15p. [8]l., [3]–17p.) plates. 23cm.
Evidently first published in 1849.
DLC

9738. White and Blue. Provo, Utah. October? 1897–May 1923.
26v. illus., plates, ports. 26×65cm.
Publication of the students of Brigham Young Academy; Brigham Young University.
UPB

9739. Whitesides, Edward Morris. A sketch of the life of Lewis Whitesides. [n.p., n.d.]
14 [3]p. 27cm.
Mormon biography.
UPB

9740. Whiting, Lilian. Kate Field; a record . . . Boston, Little, Brown and Company, 1899.
viii p. [2]l., [3]–610p. col. front., ports., facsim. 21cm.
Binder's title: Letter to Kate Field on Mormonism. Mark Twain. 1886.
She spent the winter in Salt Lake City and thereafter wrote letters concerning the Mormon situation in 1883. Later she lectured on Mormonism.
CSmH, CU, DLC, NjP, UPB

9741. Whitmer, David. An address to all believers in Christ. By a witness to the divine authenticity of the Book of Mormon. Richmond, Mo., David Whitmer, 1887.
75p. 22½cm.
There are many reproductions of the pamphlet without any change of title page or introductory material.
Howes W381, Morgan
CSmH, CtY, CU–B, DLC, ICN, MH, MiU, MoInRC, NjP, NN, UHi, ULA, UPB, USlC, UU, WHi

9742. ———. (same) Richmond, Mo., David Whitmer, 1887.
75p. 22½cm.
Variant printing. Has Elder before the name on the title page.
UPB

9742a. ———. (same) Richmond, Mo., David Whitmer, 1887 [i.e. 1895]
75p. 22½cm.
Variant wrapper.
Reprint from the same plates as announced in *The Return* June 1, 1895.
CSmH, CtY, UPB, USlC

9743. ———. An address to all believers in Christ by a witness to the divine authenticity of the Book of Mormon. Richmond, Mo., D. Whitmer, 1887 [Kansas City, Mo.? c1926]
95p. 22cm.
Preface by John J. Snyder.
Howes W381, Morgan
CSmH, DLC, NjP, UHi, UPB, USlC

———. (same) *See also Snyder, John Jacob. Glad tidings.*

9744. ———. (same, in Swedish) "Ett upprop, (eller epistel) till alla på Kristus troende," af David Whitmer . . . (Ofversattning fran engelska originalupplagan i Richmond, Mo., 1887) Salt Lake City, Nordiska undersökningssällskapets förlag, 1908.
108p. port. 22cm.
CSmH, MH, MnU, NjP, NN, UHi, USl, USlC

9745. ———. An address to believers in the Book of Mormon. [Richmond, Mo., 1887]
7 [1]p. 21cm.
Caption-title.
Morgan
NN, USlC, UPB

9746. ———. David Whitmer talks. [Salt Lake City? 1886?]
9p. illus., port., facsims. 22½cm.
Also included in "A few choice examples."
CtY, CU–B, USl

———. The solution of the Mormon problem. *See Snyder, John Jacob.*

9747. Whitney, Carrie Westlake. Kansas City, Missouri; its history and its people, 1808–1908. Chicago, S. J. Clarke, 1908.
3v. ports., plates, maps. 26cm.
Mormon history and the RLDS Church in Jackson Co., Missouri.
DLC, UHi, UPB

9748. Whitney, Helen Mar. Plural marriage, as taught by the prophet Joseph. A reply to Joseph Smith, editor of the Lamoni "Herald." Salt Lake City, The Juvenile Instructor Office, 1882.
52p. 17cm.
CSmH, CU–B, MoInRC, MWA, NjP, NN, UHi, USlC, UU

9749. ———. Why we practice plural marriage. By a "Mormon" wife and mother. — Helen Mar Whitney. Salt Lake City, The Juvenile Instructor Office, 1884.
72p. 17½cm.
"The women of the everlasting covenant" by Orson F. Whitney, p. 66–72.
CSmH, CtY, CU–B, DLC, ICN, IWW, MH, MoInRC, NjP, NN, UHi, USl, USlC, UU

9750. Whitney, Horace G. The drama in Utah; the story of the Salt Lake Theatre. By Horace G. Whitney . . . [Salt Lake City] The Deseret News, 1915.
48p. illus., port. 23cm.
Mormons and the theatre.
CSmH, CU, MH, NjP, NN, UHi, USlC, UU

9751. Whitney, J. Mormonism unravelled. Pseudo-revelations; alias, the Book of Doctrine and Covenants not of God; and the Mormon Christ a false Christ, Joseph Smith a fanatic and no prophet of God. London, Simpkin, Marshall and Co., 1851.
vip., [1]l., 9–47p. 18cm.
NN

9752. Whitney, Orson Ferguson. Address of Elder Orson F. Whitney, at the tabernacle, Salt Lake City, April 4, 1924. [Salt Lake City, 1924]
7p. 22cm.
A mission report.
USlC

9753. ———. The Apocalypse; what John saw and heard on Patmos. [Salt Lake City, Deseret News Print., 1929]
6 pts. 23cm. (Fifth series. Nos. 1–6)
Radio addresses delivered over Radio Station KSL, October 13–November 17, 1929.
UHi, UPB, USlC, UU

9754. ———. Baptism — The birth of water and of spirit. [Independence, Mo., Zion's Printing and Publishing Company. Pub. by the Missions of the Church of Jesus Christ of Latter-day Saints in America, 192–]
16p. 17½cm.
Cover-title.
Various printings with no date.
CU–B, MH, MoInRC, NN, UHi, ULA, USlC

9755. ———. Baptism — the birth of water and spirit; address delivered over Radio Station KSL, Sunday Evening, August 7, 1927. [Salt Lake City] 1927.
Broadside. 50½×24cm.
UPB

9756. ———. Beware of Frauds! [Salt Lake City, 1890]
Broadside. 36×16½cm.
Includes a letter from the First Presidency dated November 14th, 1890 and signed by Wilford Woodruff, George Q. Cannon, Joseph F. Smith.
At head of title: Will the bishops kindly oblige by having this circular read to their congregations?
NjP

9757. ———. A biographical sketch of A. Milton Musser. [Salt Lake City, 1902]
6p. port. 21cm.
Reprint from the *Latter-day Saints Biographical Encyclopedia*, Salt Lake City, 1902.
MH, NjP, USlC

9758. ———. Brigham Young College. A history. [n.p.] 1896.
14p. illus. 24½cm.
Reprinted from *The American University Magazine*, June, 1896.
MH, UPB, USlC, UU

9759. ———. E Buka Haapiiraa No Te Autau'araa No te Ekalesia a Iesu Mesia i te Feia Mo'a i te Mau Mahana Hopea Nei. Papaihia e Orson F. Whitney . . . I Neia i roto i te piha neneiraa a te Ekalesia a Iesu Mesia i te Feia Mo'a i te Mau Mahana Hopea Nei i Papeete, Tahiti, i te m. 1923.
80p. 22cm.
Title in English: The lesson book for the priesthood of the Church of Jesus Christ of Latter-day Saints.
USlC

9760. ———. (same) Papeete, Tahiti, 1930.
80p. 22cm.
USlC

9761. ———. The educator; a poem. Salt Lake City, 1913.
12p. port. 22½cm.
Includes section entitled: To the author with plaudits on his poem by various Utah educators.
UPB, USlC

9762. ———. Elias, an epic of the ages, by Orson Ferguson Whitney. New York, The Knickerbocker Press, 1904.
2p.l., vii–xi, 162p. 4 plates. 24½cm.
Title vignette (portrait)
Elias, Joseph the seer (i.e. Joseph Smith)
CSmH, CU–B, DLC, MiU, NjP, NN, OO, ULA UPB, USlC

9763. ———. (same) New York, The Knickerbocker Press, 1904.
2p.l., vii–xi, 162p. 4 plates. 25cm.
Issued in a limited edition as the author's jubilee edition.
UPB

9764. ———. (same) Revised and annotated ed. [Salt Lake City, 1914]
xiii, 144p. port. 18½cm.
CSmH, NN, UHi, UPB, USlC, UU

9765. ———. Elohims udvalgte, fra Orson Ferguson. Whitney's Episke Digt "Elias," tilligemed forfatterns anmaerkninger og henvisninger til den hellige skrift. Med forfatterns tilladelse udgivet av oversaetteren Rudolph Stockseth. Salt Lake City [1914?]
[8]p. 21½cm.
A brief condensation of his "Elias."
Title in English: The chosen of Elohim.
NjP, USlC

9766. ———. Det glade Budskab, Evangeliske Afhandlinger. Oversat fra Engelsk af John S. Hansen. [n.p.] Bikuben's Bibliotek, 1919.
242 [8]p. 18½cm.
Title in English: The glad message, gospel interpretation.
UPB, USlC

WHITNEY, O. F.

9767. ———. The gospel in all dispensations; Joseph Smith's part in the great drama of the ages; address delivered over Radio Station KSL, Sunday Evening, April 24, 1927. [Salt Lake City] 1927.
Broadside. 38×26½cm.
Reprinted from the *Deseret News.*
UPB

9768. ———. Gospel themes; a treatise on salient features of "Mormonism." Written for, and dedicated to, the high priests, seventies and elders of the Church of Jesus Christ of Latter-day Saints. Salt Lake City, 1914.
167p. 23cm.
Contents: The story of God. — The way of salvation. — Priesthood and church government. — The gospel dispensations. — Dispersion and gathering of Israel.
CSmH, CU–B, NjP, OClWHi, OO, UPB, USl, USlC, UU

9769. ———. History of Utah, comprising preliminary chapters on the previous history of her founders, accounts of early Spanish and American explorations in the Rocky Mountain region, the advent of the Mormon pioneers, the establishment and dissolution of the provisional government of the state of Deseret, and the subsequent creation and development of the territory . . . By Orson F. Whitney . . . Salt Lake City, G. Q. Cannon and Sons Co., 1892–1904.
4v. plates, ports., map. 28cm.
Printed without bibliographical notes.
CSmH, CtY, CU–B, DLC, ICN, MH, MoInRC, NjP

9769a. ———. A hymn with a history. By Orson F. Whitney of the Council of the Twelve. [Salt Lake City? 1924?]
4p. 23cm.
Caption-title.
"From the 'Improvement Era' for October, 1924."
UPB

9770. ———. The land of Shinehah. [Salt Lake City, Deseret News Printing and Publishing Establishment, 1877]
8p. 17½cm.
A poem contrasting Kirtland during the Mormon period and 40 years later.
CSmH, USlC

9771. ———. Latter-day developments. [Salt Lake City, Deseret News Press, 1929]
6 pts. 23½cm. (Sixth series. Nos. 1–6)
Radio addresses given over KSL. Sunday evenings, November 24–December 29, 1929.
USlC, UPB

9772. ———. Life of Heber C. Kimball, an apostle; the father and founder of the British Mission . . . Salt Lake City, The Kimball family, Printed at the Juvenile Instructor Office, 1888.
xvi [17]–520p. 5 port. 24cm.
CSmH, CtY, CU–B, ICN, MH, MoInRC, NjP, NN, UHi, ULA, UPB, USl, USlC, UU, WHi

9772a. ———. The lifted ensign — a call to Israel; a dramatic poem. Written for and read at the Centenary Celebration of the Church of Jesus Christ of Latter-day Saints, April 6, 1930. [Salt Lake City, 1930]
8p. port. 20cm.
UPB, USlC

9773. ———. Love and the light; an idyl of the Westland . . . by Orson Ferguson Whitney. [Salt Lake City, The Deseret News, c1918]
4p.l., 128p. illus. 19½cm.
Mormon poetry.
DLC, NjP, NN, UHi, ULA, UPB, USl, USlC, UU

9774. ———. The making of a state; a school history of Utah, by Orson F. Whitney. Salt Lake City, The Deseret News, 1908.
iv p., [2]l., 327p. illus. 19½cm.
DLC, NjP, OClW, UHi, ULA, USlC, UU

9775. ———. "Mormon" activities; an answer to questions concerning the practical working of the Church of Jesus Christ of Latter-day Saints. Salt Lake City, The Deseret News, 1913.
16p. 18cm.
"Published by authority of the First Presidency."
CU–B, DLC, MH, NjP, OClWHi, UHi, UPB, USlC

9776. ———. "The Mormon prophet's tragedy;" a review of an article by the late John Hay, published originally in the Atlantic Monthly for Dec. 1869, and republished in the Saints Herald of June 21, 1905. The reviewer, Orson F. Whitney . . . Salt Lake City, The Deseret News, 1905.
2p.l. [5]–98p. 19cm.
CtY, CU–B, DLC, MB, MoInRC, NjP, NN, UHi, ULA, UPB, USl, USlC, UU

———. The "Mormons." *See Eldredge, Zoeth Skinner.*

9777. ———. The poetical writings of Orson F. Whitney. Poems and poetic prose. Compiled and published by the author . . . Salt Lake City, Juvenile Instructor Office, 1889.
vii [9]–208p. 23cm.
Mormon poetry.
CSmH, DLC, MH, NjP, NN, UHi, ULA, USlC, UU, WHi

WHITNEY, O. F.

9778. ———. Popular history of Utah, by Orson F. Whitney . . . Salt Lake City, The Deseret News, 1916.
2p.l., 588p. illus., map. 24cm.
CtY, CU–B, DLC, NjP, NN, UHi, ULA, USl, USlC, UU, ViU, WHi

9779. ———. Radio addresses given over KSL, Sunday evenings beginning Oct. 13–Nov. 17, 1929 . . . Salt Lake City, 1929.
[96]p. 23½cm.
UPB

9780. ———. (same, under title) Whitney's radio talks; Sunday evening lectures delivered over Station KSL, Salt Lake City, Utah, October 13 to December 29, 1929 . . . a compendium of "Mormon" history, aims and ideas. Rev. ed. [Salt Lake City, The Deseret News Press, 1930?]
2p.l. [5]–115p. 19cm.
NjP, UHi, UPB, UU

9781. ———. Saturday night thoughts; a series of dissertations on spiritual, historical and philosophic themes, by Orson F. Whitney . . . Salt Lake City, The Deseret News, 1921.
323p. 20cm.
DLC, MH, MoInRC, NjP, NjPT, ODW, UHi, UPB, USl, USlC, UU

9782. ———. (same) Rev. ed. Salt Lake City, Deseret Book Company, 1927.
323p. 20cm.
Variant printings.
USlC

9783. ———. Speeches in support of woman suffrage. Delivered in the Constitutional Convention of Utah, 1895. [Salt Lake City] Utah Woman Suffrage Association, 1895.
23p. 23½cm.
CU–B, UPB, USlC

9784. ———. Statement to the British public and press, protesting against the circulation of slanders, lies, sensational stories, etc., relative to the Church of Jesus Christ of Latter Day Saints [commonly known as the "Mormon Church"] First issued in January, 1921. [Tottingham, England, 1921]
[13]p. 22cm.
Articles of faith on back cover.
USlC

9785. ———. The strength of the "Mormon" position. By Elder Orson F. Whitney of the Council of the Twelve, Church of Jesus Christ of Latter-day Saints. Independence, Mo., Zions Printing and Publishing Co. Published by the Missions of the Church of Jesus Christ of Latter-day Saints [c1917]
48p. 17½cm.
MH, MoInRC, UHi, UPB, USlC, UU

9786. ———. (same) Independence, Mo., Zions' Printing and Publishing Co., 1918 [c1917]
48p. 17½cm.
UPB, USlC

9787. ———. (same) Independence, Mo., Zion's Printing and Publishing Company [192–]
40p. 18cm.
CU–B, MoInRC, NjP, NN

9788. ———. Through memory's halls; the life story of Orson F. Whitney as told by himself . . . [Independence, Mo., Press of Zion's Printing and Publishing Company, c1930]
424p. illus., 7 ports. (coats of arms) 22½cm.
DLC, NjP, UHi, USlC, UU

9789. ———. Two poems: The women of the everlasting covenant; and the land of Shinehah. Salt Lake City, Deseret News Printing and Publishing Establishment, 1880.
16p. 19½cm.
Cover-title.
Signed: Kirtland, Ohio, Nov., 1877.
CSmH, MH, NN, UPB

9790. ———. De val en de verlossing. Torespraak, gehoulden voor de onderwijzers conventie der Kerkscholen in de Barratt Hall te Salt Lake City, Utah, 31 December 1920. Door Ouderling Orson F. Whitney. Rotterdam, Uitgave van John P. Lillywhite, 1922.
32p. 16cm.
Title in English: The fall and redemption.
USlC

9791. ———. Voices from the mountains. [Liverpool, 1922]
4p.l. [9]–93p. 19cm.
Mormon poetry.
NjP, RPB, UHi, UPB, USlC, UU

9792. ———. The way, the truth, and the life; an appeal to all seekers for salvation by Orson F. Whitney . . . Liverpool, Printed and Published at the Millennial Star Office [n.d.]
1p.l., 31p. 21½cm.
Tract explaining Mormon doctrine, largely through the Bible.
UHi, UPB, USlC

9793. ———. (same) Liverpool [Millennial Star Office, n.d.]
31p. 22cm.
First 8 pages printed separately.
UHi, UPB, USlC

9794. ———. (same, in Danish) Vejen, sandheden og livet af Aeldste Orson F. Whitney . . . [Kjøbenhavn, Udgivet og Forlagt af John S. Hansen . . . 1925]
16p. 22½cm.
USlC

9795. ———. (same, in French) Le chemin, la vérité et la vie; appel à tout chercheur du salut. Bâle [i.e. Basel] Publié par Serge F. Ballif [n.d.]
24p. 16½cm.
UPB, UU

———. Women of the everlasting covenant. *See his Two poems.*

9796. ———. The world war and the fulfilment of modern prophecy. Discourses delivered by Elder O. F. Whitney at the St. Joseph's Stake quarterly conference, Layton, Arizona, February 24, 1918. Layton, Arizona, 1918.
20p. 19cm.
USlC

9797. ———. Zina. [Salt Lake City? 1900]
[6]p. port. 18½cm.
Portrait of his wife, Zina Smoot Whitney.
USlC

9798. Whitsitt, William H. Intermediate examination, January 6, 1886, polemic theology. Louisville, Ky., Southern Baptist Theological Seminary, 1886.
[3]p. 22½cm.
Examination of the *Book of Mormon.*
USlC

———. *See also Jackson, Samuel MacCauley, editor.*

9799. Whittick, William A. Bombs: The poetry and philosophy of anarchy. By William A. Whittick. Philadelphia, Press of A. R. Saylor, 1894.
187 [1]p. port. 18cm.
"The Mormon Monster," p. 133–152.
USlC

9799a. Whittier, John Greenleaf. The stranger in Lowell . . . Boston: Waite, Peirce and Company. No. 1 Cornhill. 1845.
2p.l., [v]vi[7]–156p. 21cm.
Chapter IV: A Mormon conventicle. His visit to a Mormon meeting and information concerning the death of Joseph Smith.
DLC, UPB

9800. . . . Who ears have to hear let him hear! [n.p., 185–]
[4]p. 24cm.
A revelation without author concerning conditions in Utah, the expulsion by the church of Joseph Smith's true successor. Might have been written by Gladden Bishop.
USlC (slightly defective)

9801. Who is Jarman? [London, ca. 1881]
[4]p. 21cm.
Title from p. 2; p. 1 an advertisement for his several lectures, Mormon and otherwise; p. 2–3 are extracts from newspapers and ministers; p. 4 lists his 6 Mormon lectures (no. 6 for men only, over the age of 18)
Harvard copy also includes several 22×7cm. leaflets on his lectures.
MH

Why do you not obey the Gospel? *See Ward, Thomas.*

9801a. Wicks, Charles A. Sabbath or Sunday. Davis City, Iowa, Return Print [1896]
8p. 20cm.
Publication of the Church of Christ (Whitmer) Morgan
USlC

9802. Widerborg, C. Instructionsbrev til de praesiderende Aeldste. [Kjobenhavn? 1859?]
4p. 21cm.
Signed: 10de January 1859.
Title in English: Letter of instructions to the presiding Elders.
USlC

9803. Widtsoe, John Andreas. Bible answers to modern questions. No. 1. [London, Church of Jesus Christ of Latter-day Saints. British Mission Office, 193–]
4p. 22cm. (Bible series. No. 1)
Caption-title.
UHi

9804. ———. Bible answers to modern questions. No. 2 . . . [London, Church of Jesus Christ of Latter-day Saints. British Mission Office, 193–]
4p. 22cm. (Bible series. No. 2)
Caption-title.
UHi

9805. ———. Bible answers to modern questions. No. 3 . . . [London, Church of Jesus Christ of Latter-day Saints. British Mission Office, 193–]
4p. 22cm. (Bible series. No. 3)
Caption-title.
UHi

9806. ———. Centennial series. Independence, Mo., Published by the Missions of the Church of Jesus Christ of Latter-day Saints, Zion's Printing and Publishing Co. [n.d.]
20 pts. 17½cm.
No. 1. About myself. No. 2. Why is religion needed? No. 3. Religion for the ordinary man. No. 4. Need of Church organization. No. 5. A God who speaks. No. 6. The greatest of all. No. 7. Life's meaning. No. 8. Complete religion. No. 9. Guide posts to happiness. No. 10. First principles of salvation.

WIDTSOE, J. A.

No. 11. Universal salvation. No. 12. Divine authority by Charles W. Penrose. No. 13. Marks of the great apostasy by Osborne J. P. Widtsoe. No. 14. Truth restored: A modern miracle! No. 15. The Book of Mormon. No. 16. Practical religion. No. 17. The word of wisdom. No. 18. Women and marriage among the Mormons by Leah D. Widtsoe. No. 19. The Bible. No. 20. Active religion.
Also printed in the following languages without collective title page. Danish: Kjobenhavn, Holger M. Larsen, 1930. UPB; Dutch: Rotterdam [n.d.] USlC; French: Paris, Mission Francaise [n.d.] UPB; German: Berlin, Dresden, Krueger & Horn [193–] UHi
NjP #6, 8, 14, 18, 20; NN #1–11, 13, 14, 16–20; UHi #3–11, 13–20; UPB, USlC

9807. ———. (same) London [n.d.]
20 pts. 18cm.
Variant edition.
UHi, USlC

9808. ———. A concordance to the Book of Doctrine and Covenants of the Church of Jesus Christ of Latter-day Saints. By Elder John A. Widtsoe. Salt Lake City, The Deseret Sunday School Union, 1906.
2p.l. [iii]–iv, 205p. 17½cm.
CSmH, DLC, IWW, NjP, UHi, ULA, USl, USlC, UU

9809. ———. The divine mission of Joseph Smith. By John A. Widtsoe. Independence, Mo., Zion's Printing and Publishing Co. [n.d.]
22p. 17½cm.
Variant printings.
IWW, MoInRC, NjP, UHi, ULA, UPB, USlC

9810. ———. (same) Independence, Zion's Printing and Publishing Co. [n.d.]
23 [1]p. 18cm.
NN, UPB

9811. ———. Dodge's geography of Utah, by John A. Widtsoe . . . and William Peterson . . . Chicago, New York [etc] Rand, McNally & Company [c1908]
44p. illus. 25½cm. (On verso of title-page: Dodge's geographical series)
History and geography of Utah.
DLC, UPB

9812. ———. Dry-farming; a system of agriculture for countries under a low rainfall, by J. A. Widtsoe . . . New York, The Macmillan Co., 1911.
xxii p., [1]l., 445p. port., maps. 19½cm.
Brief account of Mormon dry-farming.
Another edition: N.Y., Macmillan Co. 1912. NjP, UHi
Trans. into French under title: Le dry-farming. Paris, Librairie Agricole de la maison rustique, 1912. UPB, USlC, UU
Trans. into Italian under title: Dry-farming. Roma, Typografia Nazionele Bertero, 1917. DLC, UU
CU, DLC, UHi, ULA, UPB, USlC, UU

———. Gospel doctrine. *See Smith, Joseph Fielding, 1838–1918.*

9813. ———. In search of truth; comments on the gospel and modern thought, by Elder John A. Widtsoe . . . Salt Lake City, Deseret Book Company [c1930]
120p. 20cm.
DLC, MH, NjP, UHi, ULA, UPB, USl, UlSC, UU

9814. ———. Joseph Smith as scientist; a contribution to Mormon philosophy, by John A. Widtsoe . . . Salt Lake City, The General board, Young Men's Mutual Improvement Associations, 1908.
xxxii, 1p.l., 173p. 23½cm. (Young Men's Mutual Improvement Associations manual. 1908–1909. No. 12)
xxxii. Study guide.
CtY, DLC, ICN, MoInRC, NjP, UHi, ULA, UPB, USl, USlC, UU, WHi

9815. ———. (same) 2d ed. Salt Lake City, General Board of Young Men's Mutual Improvement Association, 1920.
v p., [1]l., 160p. 22cm. (Young Men's Mutual Improvement Association. Senior manual. No. 23)
Cover-title: Science and the gospel.
CU, UPB, USlC

9816. ———. (same) 2d ed. Salt Lake City, The General Board, Young Men's Mutual Improvement Association, 1920.
v p. [1]l., 164p. 20½cm.
Printed as a separate with a 4 p. index.
IWW, NN, UPB, USlC

9817. ———. Practical application and result of the word of wisdom. [Salt Lake City, Mutual Improvement Association, n.d.]
[4]p. 21cm.
UPB, USlC

9818. ———. Rational theology; as taught by the Church of Jesus Christ of Latter-day Saints, by John A. Widtsoe. [Salt Lake City] Published for the use of the Melchizedek Priesthood, by the General Priesthood Committee, 1915.
viii, 190p. 20cm.
"References": p. [179]–184.
DLC, IWW, MH, MoInRC, OClWHi, UHi, ULA, USl, USlC, UU

9819. ———. (same) Salt Lake City, Published by the Presiding Bishop's Office, 1926.
viii, 190p. 19cm.
USlC

9820. ———. (same) [2d ed. Salt Lake City] Published by the General Boards of the Mutual Improvement Associations, 1926.
viii, 198p. 18½cm.
UPB, USlC

9821. ———. (same) [3d ed.] Salt Lake City, Published by the General Boards of the Mutual Improvement Association, 1929.
viii, 190p. 19cm.
USlC

9822. ———. (same, in Danish) Fortnuftmaessig theologi; som den laeres af Jesu Kristi Kirke af Sidste-Dages Hellige. Overs. fra Engelsk af Dr. Charles L. Olsen. [Salt Lake City] Bikuben's Bibliotek, 1917.
3p.l., 7–256p. 18cm.
UPB, UU

9823. ———. (same, in French) Théologie rationelle; telle qu'elle est enseigneé par l'Eglise de Jésus-Christ des Saints des Derniers Jours. par l'Ánsien John A. Widtsoe. Traduit de l'Anglais par C. A. Horback. [n.p., Church of Jesus Christ of Latter-day Saints. French Mission, 1930?]
1p.l., 127p. 18cm.
NjP, UHi, USlC, UU

9824. ———. (same, in German) Vernunftgemasse Theologie wie sie die Kirche Jesu Christi der Heiligen der Letzten Tage lehrt. [Deutsche Übersetzung von Marg. Hoyer. 1st German ed. Basel] Deutsch, Österreichischen und Schweizerisch. Deutschen Mission der Kirche Jesu Christi der Heiligen der Letzten Tage, 1926.
xp. [1]l. 176 [2]p. 19cm.
UHi, ULA, UPB, USlC, UU

9825. ———. (same, in Norwegian) Fornuftsmaessig teologi. Saaledes some den forkyndes af Jesu Kristi Kirke af Sidste Dages Hellige. [Oslo] Udgivet af den Danske og den Norske Mission [Trykt i Universal-Trykkeriet, n.d.]
viii, 163p. 19½cm.
USlC, UU

9826. ———. (same, in Swedish) Förnuftsenlig Teologi . . . Översättning från Engelskan av Äldste C. A. Krantz. Salt Lake City [Published by The Associated Newspapers, 1917?]
2p.l. [5]–270p. port. 15½cm.
UHi, UPB

———. Science and the gospel. *See his Joseph Smith as scientist.*

9827. ———. Success on irrigation projects, by J. A. Widtsoe . . . New York, J. Wiley & Son, Inc., London, Chapman & Hall, Limited, 1928.
v, 153p. 21cm.
Includes early Mormon irrigation.
CSmH, CU, ULA, UU

9828. ———. Temple worship. A lecture, delivered under the auspices of the Genealogical Society of Utah, at the Assembly Hall, Temple Block, Salt Lake City, Tuesday evening, October 12, 1920. Salt Lake City, 1920.
[13]p. 28cm.
Mimeographed.
UPB

9829. ———. What is Mormonism? An informal answer. By John A. Widtsoe of the Council of the Twelve Apostles. [Independence, Mo., Zion's Printing and Publishing Company. Published by the Missions of the Church of Jesus Christ of Latter-day Saints, 1928?]
68p. 18cm.
Variant printings.
IWW, NjP, UHi, ULA, UPB, USlC

9830. ———. (same) [Nuneaton, England, Nuneaton Newspapers Ltd., n.d.]
68p. 17½cm.
UHi, UPB

9831. ———. What others say about the Mormons. Compiled by Dr. John A. Widtsoe of the Council of the Twelve Apostles of the Church of Jesus Christ of Latter-day Saints. Independence, Mo., Zion's Printing and Publishing Co. [Published by the Church of Jesus Christ of Latter-day Saints, 1928?]
32p. 19cm.
Complimentary opinions of non-Mormons arranged chronologically, 1830–1927.
NN, UHi, UPB, USlC

9832. ———. (same, in French) Ce que les autres disent des "Mormons." Compilé par le Docteur John A. Widtsoe. . . . Ville-d'Avray; Genève, Liége [n.d.]
34p. 22cm.
CSmH, UPB

Widtsoe, Leah D. Women and Marriage among the Mormons. *See Widtsoe, John Andreas. Centennial series.*

———. Women of the "Mormon" church. *See Gates, Susa (Young).*

9833. Widtsoe, Osborne John Peter. A guide for the study of Gospel Doctrine. Selections from sermons and writings of President Joseph F. Smith. Prepared for the Quorums of the Priesthood. By Osborne J. P. Widtsoe. Part 1. [Salt Lake City, 1920?]
[3]–79p. 19cm.
NjP, UPB

9834. ———. A guide for the study of Gospel Doctrine. Selections from sermons and writings of President Joseph F. Smith. Prepared for the Quorums of the Priesthood. By Osborne J. P. Widtsoe. Part 2. [Salt Lake City, 1921?]
[3]–69p. 19cm.
UPB

9835. ———. History and current status of Mormon educational systems . . . (In Report of the Commissioner of Education, for the year ending June 30, 1913. Washington, Govt. Print. Off., 1914)
409–413p. 23½cm.
Chapter XVIII, p. 409–413.
UPB

9836. ———. Marks of the great apostasy. Independence, Mo., Press of Zion's Printing and Publishing Co. [n.d.]
[4]p. 17½cm. (Centennial Series. No. 13)
See also Widtsoe, John A. Centennial Series.
UPB, USlC

9837. ———. (same) [London, n.d.]
[4]p. 17½cm.
UPB

9838. ———. The restoration of the gospel, by Osborne J. P. Widtsoe . . . with an introduction by Joseph F. Smith, jr. . . . Salt Lake City, The Deseret News, 1912.
xix, 243p. 20cm.
DLC, NjP, UHi, UPB, USl, USlC, UU

9839. ———. (same) 2d ed. Salt Lake City, The Deseret News, 1912.
xix, 243p. 19½cm.
UHi

9840. ———. (same) 3d ed. Salt Lake City, Deseret Book Company, 1923.
xix, 243p. 19½cm.
MoInRC, UHi, USlC

9841. ———. (same) 4th ed. Salt Lake City, Deseret Book Company, 1925.
xix, 243p. 19½cm.
UPB, USlC

9842. ———. (same, in Danish) Evangeliets gengivelse. Af Osborne J. P. Widtsoe, A. M. Rektor ved de Sidstedages helliges højskole, Salt Lake City, Utah. Oversat fra Engelsk af John S. Hansen. [Salt Lake City] "Bikubens" Bibliotek, 1921.
1p.l. [3]–278 [1]p. 19½cm.
USlC also has the galley proof.
NjP, UHi, USlC, UU

9843. ———. What Jesus taught. Written for the Deseret Sunday School Union, by Osborne J. P. Widtsoe . . . Salt Lake City, The Deseret Sunday School Union, 1917.
336p. 19½cm.
NjP, ULA, USlC

9844. ———. (same) Salt Lake City, Published by The Deseret Sunday School Union [c1918]
3p.l., 7–338p. illus. 19½cm.
UHi, UPB, USlC, UU

9845. ———. (same) [2d ed.] Salt Lake City, Published by The Deseret Book Company, 1924.
338p. 19½cm.
USlC

9846. ———. (same) Salt Lake City, The Deseret Book Company, 1926.
3p.l., 7–338p. illus. 20cm.
ICU, MH, UU

9847. ———. (same, in Dutch) Wat Jezus Leerde. Geschreven Door Osborne J. P. Widtsoe. Vertaald uit Hit Englesch door Joh. Sipkema. Rotterdam, Uitgegeven door Chas. S. Hyde, 1925.
xii, 176p. 20cm.
UHi, USlC

9848. ———. (same, in German) Was Jesus Lehrte. Für die zweite Mittelklasse. Osborne J. P. Widtsoe. Nach dem englischen Text "What Jesus taught" bearbeitet von Jean Wunderlich. Basel, Herausgegeben von Fred Tadje, Präsident der Schweizerischen und Deutschen Mission der Kirche Jesu Christi der Heiligen der Letzten Tage, 1924.
40p. 20½cm.
USlC

9849. Wied-Neuwied, Maximilian Alexander Philipp, ***prinz von.*** Reise in das innere Nord-America in den Jahren 1832 bis 1834; von Maximilian Prinz zu Wied . . . Coblenz, J. Hoelscher, 1839–41.
2v. illus. 32cm. and atlas.
Includes his brief encounter with the Mormons at Nauvoo.
Title in English: Trip in the interior of North America in the year 1832 to 1834.
Other editions: 1843–1925.
CU–B, DLC, ICN, InU, MH–A, MiU–H, NjP, NN

9850. Wiggam, Albert Edward. The next age of man. Indianapolis, Bobbs-Merrill Co. [c1927]
418p. front. 23cm.
Mormon eugenics, p. 383–384.
USlC

9851. Wiggins, Robert Lemuel. Mormonism, its origin and history, with a thorough discussion of its doctrines . . . Columbus, Georgia, T. A. Coleman, 1899.
19p. 22cm.
CSmH

9852. Wight, John W. Apostasy of the church; showing both the former and latter day apostasy. By Elder J. W. Wight. Independence, Mo., Published by Ensign Publishing House [n.d.]
57p. 19cm.
IWW, MoInRC

9853. ———. Apostasy of the church; the former and latter day apostasy, by Elder J. W. Wight of the Reorganized Church of Jesus Christ of Latter Day Saints. Independence, Mo., Ensign Publishing House, 1900.
1p.l., 40p. port. 21½cm.
UHi

9854. ———. The legal successor in the presidency of the Church. Independence, Mo., Ensign Publishing House [n.d.]
32p. 20cm.
MoInRC, NjP

9855. ———. (same) Independence, Ensign Publishing House, 1898.
32p. 20cm. (The Gospel Banner. Vol. 5, No. 2)
MoInRC

9856. ———. The marriage relation. Independence, Mo., Ensign Publishing House, 1899.
41p. 16cm. (The Gospel Banner. Vol. 6, No. 1)
MoInRC

9857. Wight, Lyman. An Address by way of an abridged account and journal of my life from February 1844, up to April 1848, with an appeal to the Latter Day Saints, scattered abroad in the earth . . . [Austin, Texas? 1848]
16p. 21½cm.
Caption-title.
Morgan
USlC

9857a. Wight, Sarah Estella. His first venture and the sequel. Lamoni, Ia., Herald House, 1912.
153p. (Birth offering series)
MoInRC

9858. ———. In the shelter of the little brown cottage. By Estella Wight. Independence, Mo., Published by the Board of Publication of the Reorganized Church of Jesus Christ of Latter Day Saints, 1922.
3p.l., 9–320p. plates. 19cm.
RLDS novel.
MoInRC, NjP

9858a. ———. (same) Lamoni, Iowa, Board of Publication of the Reorganized Church of Jesus Christ of Latter Day Saints, 1922.
320p. 19cm.
NjP

9859. ———. Sadie and her pets and other stories, by Pebble [*pseud.*] Lamoni, Ia., Published by the Board of Publication of the Reorganized Church of Jesus Christ of Latter Day Saints [n.d.]
178 [2]p. plates. 19½cm. (Birth offering moral stories. Series. No. 6)
RLDS moral stories.
MoInRC, UHi

9859a. ———. (same) Lamoni, Ia., Herald House, 1905.
178p. illus. (Birth offering series)
MoInRC

9860. ———. Vineyard story. By Estella Wight. Independence, Mo., Published by the Board of Publication of the Reorganized Church of Jesus Christ of Latter Day Saints, 1927.
4p.l., 9–384p. 20cm.
Sequel to *In the shelter of the little brown cottage.*
RLDS novel.
MoInRC

9861. Wijnaendts Francken, Cornelius Johannes. Door Amerika. Reisschetsen, Indrukken en Studiën Door Dr. C. J. Wijnaendts Francken. Haarlem, H. D. Tjienk Willink, 1892.
viii, 287p. 22cm.
Chap. VIII. De Stad der Mormonen. Chap. IX. De Mormonen.
Title in English: Through America.
CU-B, USlC

9862. Wilcox, David F., *editor.* Quincy and Adams County, history and representative men. David F. Wilcox, supervising editor. Judge Lyman McCarl . . . Chicago, Lewis Publishing Company, 1919.
2v. illus., ports., maps. 27cm.
Includes "The Mormon war," p. 203–210.
DLC, NjP, UPB

9863. Wiley, William H. Yosemite, Alaska, and the Yellowstone. By William H. Wiley and Sara King Wiley. Reprinted from "Engineering." London, Offices of "Engineering" [1893]
xix, 230p. illus., plates, ports., maps (part. fold.) 29cm.
Includes a visit to Salt Lake City. References to Mormons and his delight at finding them not what they had been led to believe.
CU-B, NjP, USlC

9864. Willard, Emma (Hart). Last leaves of American history; comprising histories of the Mexican War and California. New York, G. P. Putnam, 1849.
230p. fold. map. 19cm.
Mormons in California and a short description of their expulsion from Nauvoo, p. 18–20, 68–69, 176–178, 219, 222, 226–229.
Another edition: New York, A. S. Barnes, 1853. CSmH, DLC
CSmH, CtY, CU–B, DLC, NjP, UPB, UU

9865. Willcox, R. N. Reminiscences. Of California life. Being an abridged description of scenes which the author has passed through in California, and other lands. With quotations from other authors. A short lecture on psychic science. An article on church and state; written by his son; R. P. Wilcox.
By R. N. Willcox, Avery, Ohio. [Avery] Wilcox Print., 1897.
3p.l., 5–290p. 21½cm.
Section on Mormonism, p. 251–257.
CU–B, DLC

9866. Willes, William. The mountain warbler, being a collection of original songs and recitations, by William Willes, with selections from other writers, for the use of choirs, Sabbath Schools and families. Salt Lake City, Printed at the Deseret News Book and Job Establishment, 1872.
1p.l., 126p. 14cm.
ICN, MH, USlC, UU

9867. ———, *compiler.* What is Mormonism? Compiled from the writings of Elders Parley P. Pratt, Orson Pratt, John Taylor, Orson Spencer, Samuel Brannan, and others of the Church of Jesus Christ of Latter-Day Saints . . . Calcutta [India] Printed by N. Robertson and Co., at the Columbian Press [1852?]
10p. 21½cm.
Dated: 18th October, 1852.
CtY, USlC

9868. William Jex; pioneer and patriarch. Spanish Fork, Spanish Fork Press [1927?]
2p.l., 9–71 [1]p. plates, ports. 23cm.
Mormon biography.
UHi, UPB

9869. William W. Riter; In memoriam. [Salt Lake City, 1922?]
28p. 27cm.
Funeral address.
USlC

9869a. Williams, Archibald. Public meeting [1845 Sept. 22, Quincy, Illinois]
Broadside. 34×17cm.
Account of a meeting held to discuss the trouble between the Mormons and the non-Mormons of Hancock County. Resolutions to be sent to Nauvoo are listed. It is signed by the chairman, Archibald Williams.
USlC

9870. ———. To the public. In order to prevent an erroneous impression from going abroad, in relation to the position of affairs in Hancock and undersigned feel it to be incumbent upon them . . . [Warsaw, 1846]
Broadside. 46×14½cm.
The New Citizens were being forced by the Mormons to serve with the remaining Mormon forces, in repelling the anti-Mormon mobs.
Signed by Archibald Williams, John B. Chittenden, Thomas Morrison, John D. Mellen, Wesley Williams, Thos. S. Brockman, and James W. Singleton, Carthage, Aug. 29, 1846, in behalf of anti-Mormon party.
Byrd 1132
ICHi, NN

9870a. Williams, David M. Consistency and security of the Religion of Jesus Christ. Authority, The everlasting covenant. [n.p., 1900]
20p. 15cm.
USlC

9871. ———. I glory in plainness; I glory in truth; I glory in Jesus . . . (will the Mormon people become Christians? Or will they become strangers to the religion of Jesus Christ) [Salt Lake City, 1900]
2p.l. [3]–34p. 15cm.
Signed: Salt Lake City, Jan. 15th, 1900.
MH

9872. ———. Let us go back to Christ. Looking unto Jesus. The author and finisher of our faith. By David M. Williams, a member of the Mormon Church. [Salt Lake City, 1900]
10p. 15cm.
Signed: Salt Lake City, January 1, 1900.
MH, USlC

9873. Williams, Elizabeth (Whitney). A child of the sea and life among the Mormons. By Elizabeth Whitney Williams. Harbor Springs, Mich., E. W. Williams, 1905.
229p. plates, port. 20cm.
Life on Beaver Island and at other places near Lake Michigan, with an account of the "Mormon kingdom" on Beaver Island.
CSmH, DLC, IC, MoInRC, NN, UHi, ULA, UPB, USl, USlC

9874. ———. (same) Brooklyn, N.Y., J. E. Jewitt, 1905.
5p.l. [11]–229p. plates. 20cm.
CtY, CU–B, DLC, MiU, NjP, NjPT, NN, UHi, UU

9875. Williams, Henry Llewellyn. The picturesque West; our Western empire beyond the Mississippi, containing the most complete description . . . of the whole region lying between the Mississippi and the Pacific Ocean . . . New York, Hurst and Company [1891]
1p.l., 9–525p. plates. 26cm.
A long section on Utah in which Mormons are largely ignored.
DLC, UHi

WILLIAMS, H. T.

9876. Williams, Henry T., *editor.* The Pacific tourist. Williams' illustrated trans-continental guide of travel, from the Atlantic to the Pacific Ocean. Containing full descriptions of railroad routes . . . A complete traveler's guide of the Union and Central Pacific Railroads . . . by Henry T. Williams, editor. With special contributions by Prof. F. V. Hayden, Maj. J. W. Powell, Clarence King, Capt. [Clarence] Dutton, A. C. Peale, Joaquin Miller, J. B. Davis, F. E. Shearer . . . New York, H. T. Williams, 1876.
293 [4]p. illus., fold. map. 24cm.
Added title-page, illus.
The character of the Mormons, detailed information on Utah cities, and other tourist information.
Other editions between 1877–1883.
DLC, NH, NjP, OO, UHi, USlC, WaU

9877. Williams, J. Mormonism exposed . . . 1842.
Mentioned in the *Millennial Star,* V. 20, p. 268; concerning discrepancies in the *Book of Mormon.*
No copy located

9878. Williams, James. Seventy-five years on the border, by James Williams. Kansas City, Press of Standard Printing Co., 1912.
207 [1]p. plates, ports. 23½cm.
Material on Mormonism in the Far West region and Salt Lake City, p. 142–144, 146–147.
CU–B, DLC, NjP, UHi, UPB, USl

9879. Williams, Margaret. Amddiffyniad Y Saint; sef, gwrth-brofion o gam-gyhuddiadau maleis-ddrwg dyn o'r enw rees davies, o New Orleans, yn erbyn y saint. [Abertawy, Argraffwyd a chyhoeddwyd gan D. Janes, ca. 1854]
12p. 17cm.
Signed: Margaret Williams.
Title in English: Defense of the saints.
UPB

9880. Williams, Marion Moffet. My life in a Mormon harem, by Mrs. Marion Moffet Williams. Minneapolis, Minn., 1920.
198p. illus., 2 port. 20cm.
DLC, UHi, USlC

9881. Williams, R. K. James N. Kimball, Appellee, vs. Franklin D. Richards, Appellant, mandamus. [Salt Lake City? 1882]
14p. 21cm.
At head of title: In the Supreme Court of Utah Territory.
Signed: R. K. Williams, F. S. Richards.
Voting suit arising out of polygamy.
USlC

9882. Williams, Thomas W. Bishop R. C. Evans versus Mr. R. C. Evans. [Independence, Mo., ca. 1920]
24p. 15cm.
An attack on R. C. Evans after he had left the RLDS church.
MoInRC, NjP, USlC

9883. ———. (same) [n.p., n.d.]
12p. 23cm.
MoInRC

9884. ———. Clearing the decks; sermon by Apostle T. W. Williams delivered at the Elliott Theatre. [Independence, Mo.] 1926.
18p. 19cm.
RLDS supreme directional control.
MoInRC, NN

9885. ———. His back to the wall. [n.p., n.d.]
4p. 23cm.
Concerning Richard C. Evans, late a Bishop in the RLDS church.
MoInRC, NjP

9886. ———. The Latter Day Saints; who are they? Independence, Mo., Ensign Publishing House [n.d.]
15p. 20cm.
Cover-title.
MoInRC, UHi

9887. ———. (same) Lamoni, Ia., Herald Publishing House, 1903.
20p. 15cm.
CSmH, MoInRC, UHi, UPB, USl, USlC, WHi

9888. ———. (same) Lamoni, Ia., Herald Publishing House, 1908.
16p. 19cm.
MoInRC

9889. ———. (same) [Lamoni, Ia.? Herald Publishing House, 191–]
16p. 19cm. (No. 5)
CSmH, CU–B, MoInRC, USlC

9890. ———. (same) [n.p., n.d.]
30p. 17cm.
UHi

9891. ———. (same) [Independence, Mo., Ensign Publishing House, n.d.]
32p. 16cm.
Cover-title.
MoInRC, USlC

9892. ———. The mission of the Latter Day Saints. [n.p., n.d.]
16p. 22cm.
RLDS publication.
MoInRC

9893. ———. The new social program of the Church. By T. W. Williams. [n.p., 1926?]
16p. 20cm.
RLDS supreme directional control.
MoInRC, NjP, NN

9894. ———. The protest movement, its meaning and purpose; an answer to the First Presidency of the Reorganized Church of Jesus Christ of Latter Day Saints. By Apostle T. W. Williams. Independence, Mo., The Messenger, 1926.
28p. 20cm.
RLDS supreme directional control.
MoInRC

9895. ———. (same) 2d ed. Independence, Mo., The Messenger, 1926.
28p. 20cm.
CU-B

9896. ———. R. C. Evans and the Mormons. [n.p., n.d.]
4p. 24cm.
MoInRC, NjP

9897. ———. "Supreme directional control" in operation. [n.p., 1924?]
7p. 19cm.
Reprinted from the *Saints Herald*, August 20, 1924.
Caption-title.
MoInRC

9898. ———. A vision of the future. Sermon by Apostle T. W. Williams. [Independence, Mo.? 1924?]
18 [1]p. 20½cm.
Sermon on liberty with Christ as king given during the summer of 1924. Published due to the struggle for supreme directional control.
MoInRC, NN

9899. ———. What will Mr. Evans do? [n.p., n.d.]
Broadside. 28×15cm.
MoInRC

9900. Williams, W. Appleton's Southern and Western travellers' guide. With new and authentic maps, illustrating those divisions of the country; and containing sectional maps of the Mississippi and Ohio Rivers; with plans of cities, views, etc. . . . by W. Williams. New York, D. Appleton & Company, 1850.
1p.l. [5]–140p. illus., fold. map. 16½cm.
Bound as part of *Appleton's New and Complete United States Guide Book in binding entitled Appleton's United States travellers' guide.*
Brief article on Nauvoo, p. 41–42.
USlC

9901. Williams, Walter, *editor.* A history of northwest Missouri. Edited by Walter Williams assisted by advisory and contributing editors. Chicago, New York, The Lewis Publishing Company, 1917.
3v. illus., ports. 27½cm.
Includes Mormon history in Northwest Missouri.
DLC, MoInRC, UPB

9902. ———. Missouri, mother of the West, by Walter Williams, LL.D. and Floyd Calvin Shoemaker, A.B., A.M., assisted by an advisory council; Missouri biography by special staff of writers . . . Chicago, New York, The American Historical Society, Inc., 1930.
5v. illus., plates, ports. 26½cm.
V.I, Chap. XXVII. The Mormons in Missouri.
DLC, MoInRC, NjP, UHi

9903. Willing, Jennie (Fowler). On American soil; or, Mormonism the Mohammedanism of the West. By Mrs. Jennie Fowler Willing . . . Louisville, Ky., Pickett Publishing Company [1906]
94p. 17cm.
Chiefly on polygamy.
CtY, DLC, NN

9904. Willmore, Benjamin. Mormonism unmasked; or, Earnest appeals to Latter-day Saints by the Rev. Benjamin Willmore. Westbromwich [Eng.] Printed by George Allen Hudson, 1855.
4 pts. 18cm.
Answers to many of his objections are given in *Millennial Star*, V. 19, p. 82, 110, 122, 261, 286, and V. 20, p. 42, 148.
Under the title "Mormonism unmasked," he planned a series of four pamphlets. At least three were published.
No. 1. Mormonism anti-scriptural. 10[1]p.; No. 2. Mormonism absurd. [13]–24p. (no copy located); No. 3. Mormonism blasphemous. [25]–36p.; No. 4. Mormonism immoral. [3]–48p.
UPB #4; USlC #1, 3

9905. ———. Mormonism unmasked: or, Earnest appeals to the Latter-day Saints By the Rev. Benjamin Willmore. No. 3, Mormonism blasphemous. Second thousand. Westbromwich, England, 1855.
[25]–36p. 17cm.
USlC

9906. Wilson, Albert Edgar. Gemeinwirtschaft und Unternehmungsformen im Mormonenstaat. (Kapitel I bis II) . . . [Leipzig, Duncker & Humblot, 1907?]
38 [2]p. 21½cm.
Published in full in *Jahrbuch für Gesetzgebung, Verwaltung und Volkswirtschaft*, 31. jahrg. (1907) 3. hft., p. 89–139.
Cooperation (or United Order) as practiced in Utah communistic associations.
Title in English: Common economy and forms of business associations in the Mormon state.
DLC, NN, ULA

9907. Wilson, Charles H. The midnight message; the coming of the Bridegroom is at hand. Independence, Church of Christ (Temple Lot) [192–]
36p. 21cm.
Church of Christ theology.
Includes visitations of Fetting and a message from Samuel Wood.
USlC

9908. Wilson, Edgar. Representative-elect from Utah. Speech of Hon. Edgar Wilson, of Idaho, in the House of Representatives, Wednesday, Jan. 24, 1900. Washington [Govt. Print. Off.] 1900.
8p. 23cm.
Mormons and politics.
DLC, UHi, NjP

9909. Wilson, Elijah Nicholas. Among the Shoshones, by Elijah Nicholas Wilson ("Uncle Nick") Salt Lake City, Skelton Publishing Company [c1910]
222p. port., plates. 21cm.
Includes sections on his life among the Mormons.
This first edition was suppressed as critical of polygamy.
CU-B, DLC, NjP, OCl, UHi, UPB, UU

9910. ———. (same) Salt Lake City, Skelton Publishing Company [c1910]
247p. port., plates. 21cm.
Old matter from p. 196 changed and new section, p. 185–247, added. Less critical.
NjP, UHi, UPB, USlC, UHi

9911. ———. (same, under title) The White Indian boy. Rev. and ed. by Howard R. Driggs. Yonders-on-Hudson, N.Y., World Book Co., 1919.
222p. 21cm.
DLC, NjP, UHi, ULA, UU

9912. ———. (same) Yonders-on-Hudson, World Book Co., 1922.
222p. 21cm.
NY, OO

9913. ———. (same) Yonders-on-Hudson, World Book Co., 1924.
222p. 21½cm.
UU

9914. Wilson, Frederick T. . . . Federal aid in domestic disturbances, 1787–1903 . . . Prepared . . . by Frederick T. Wilson . . . Washington, Govt. Print. Off., 1903.
394p. 23cm. (U.S. 57th Cong. 2d Sess. Senate. Doc. No. 209)
The Mormon rebellion 1851–1858, p. 93–96. Disturbances in Provo, p. 96–99. Disorders at Salt Lake City, p. 214–215.
DLC, UHi

9915. ———. Federal aid in domestic disturbances, 1787–1903. (In Federal Aid in domestic disturbances, 1903–1922. Prepared under the direction of the Secretary of War) . . . Washington, Govt. Print. Off., 1922.
viii, 322p. 23cm. (U.S. 67th Cong. 2d Sess. Senate. Doc. No. 263)
Utah expedition, p. 78–80. Disturbances at Provo, Utah, 1859, p. 81–82. Disorders at Salt Lake City, p. 183–184.
UPB

9916. Wilson, Guy Carlton. Problems in gospel teaching; written for general Church Board of Education, by Guy C. Wilson [and] Ernest Bramwell. Salt Lake City, Deseret Book Co. [1924]
171p. 19½cm. (Teacher training lesson book, 1924–5)
CU-B, UPB, USlC, UU

9917. ———. What think ye of Christ? Address delivered over KSL Radio Station, Sunday, December 4, 1927. [Salt Lake City] 1927.
Broadside. 35½×24½cm.
Reprinted from the *Deseret News*, Saturday, December 10, 1927.
UPB

9918. Wilson, Harry Leon. The Lions of the Lord, a tale of the old West, by Harry Leon Wilson . . . Illustrated by Rose Cecil O'Neill. Boston, Lothrop Publishing Company [c1903]
viii [3] 11–520p. front., 5 plates. 20cm.
Fiction concerning Mormonism.
CSmH, CU, DLC, MoInRC, NjP, NN, UHi, ULA, UPB, USl, USlC, UU, WHi

9919. ———. (same) Boston, Lothrop, Lee, and Shepard Co. [c1903]
viii [3] 11–520p. front., 5 plates. 20cm.
CU, MH, UPB

9920. Wilson, Jeremiah Morrow. Admission of Utah. Argument of Hon. Jeremiah M. Wilson, in favor of the admission of Utah as a state made before the House Committee on Territories, Second Session, Fiftieth Congress, January 19–22, 1889. Undisputed facts — decadence of polygamy — no union of church and state — power of congress to make and enforce compacts. Washington, Govt. Print. Off., 1889.
34p. 23cm.
Gives statistics, opinions of observers, etc., to show good character of Mormons and to prove that polygamy is not an obstruction to statehood.
CSmH, CU-B, UHi, UPB, USlC

9921. ———. (same) Washington, Govt. Print. Off., 1889. Same as 9920 with additional material.
42p. 22cm.
NjP, USlC

9922. ———. Admission of Utah. Argument of Hon. Jeremiah M. Wilson, on the admission of Utah as a state, made before the Committee on Territories of the United States Senate, First Session, Fiftieth Congress. Saturday, February 18, 1888. Washington, Govt. Print. Off., 1888.
14p. 23cm.
USlC

9923. ———. Anti-Mormon test oath. Arguments of Hon. J. M. Wilson, Hon. A. B. Carlton, and Bishop William Budge, in opposition to the constitution of the proposed state of Idaho adopted at Boise City, August 6, 1889, made before the Committee on the Territories of the House of Representatives, January 21 and February 8, 1890. Washington, Govt. Print. Off., 1890.
41p. 23cm.
CSmH, ICN, USIC

9924. ———. Exparte: in the matter of Hans Nielsen, Appellant. Brief for the Appellant. [Washington, Gibson Bros., Printers and Bookbinders, 1889]
45p. 23cm.
At head of title: Supreme Court of the United States. October term. 1888.
Polygamy trial.
CU–B

9925. ———. The Mormon question. Utah and statehood. Irrefutable facts and figures. A strong and able argument. [By] Judge Jeremiah M. Wilson for the Applicants. Washington, Gibson Bros., Printers and Bookbinders, 1889.
4p. 23cm.
"From the *New York World*, January 27, 1889."
CU–B, UHi, USIC

9926. ———. Mormonism exposed. Salt Lake City, The Palantic Monthly, 1888.
4p. 23½cm. (Palantic leaflet. No. 1)
Printed by J. H. Parry and Co.
Defense of Mormonism.
NN, USIC

9927. Wilson, John R. A description of the Utah state table, composed of pieces of wood of historic interest, Representing every state and territory of the union as well as valuable pieces from the collections of various institutions and individuals. Also in the pocket are sealed up many autographs, the constitution of the new state and other valuable papers. Built by J. R. Wilson, Salt Lake City. Salt Lake City, G. Q. Cannon and Sons Co. [1896?]
49p. 19cm.
"Brief sketch of the Young Ladies' National Mutual Improvement Association," p. 38–39. National Women's Relief Society, p. 35–36.
Introduction signed: 1896.
NN, USIC

9928. Wilson, Lerona A. An open vision; An afternoon with my deceased parents. Temple work. The War and other topics. A thrilling experience. Told by Lerona A. Wilson. Written by her husband Joseph E. Wilson. [Salt Lake City, 1915]
16p. 16½cm.
USIC

9929. Wilson, Lycurgus Arnold. Life of David W. Patten, the first apostolic martyr. Salt Lake City, The Deseret News, 1900.
viii, 77p. 16cm. (Primary Helper series. No. 3)
MH, MoInRC, UHi, UPB, USIC, UU

9930. ———. (same) Salt Lake City, The Deseret News, 1904.
viii, 72p. 15½cm.
CSmH, CtY, CU–B, DLC, ICN, NjP, NN, UHi, UPB, USl, USIC

9931. ———. Outlines of Mormon philosophy; or, The answers given by the gospel, as revealed through the Prophet Joseph Smith, to the questions of life. By Lycurgus A. Wilson . . . Salt Lake City, The Deseret News, 1905.
3p.l. [iii]–xiii p., [1]l. [17]–123p. port. 20cm.
CtY, DLC, MH, MoInRC, NjP, NN, UHi, UPB, USl, USIC, UU

9932. ———. The Preston genealogy, tracing the history of the family from about 1040, A.D., in Great Britain, in the New England States, and in Virginia, to the present time. Ed. by L. A. Wilson, at the instance and under the direction of William Bowker Preston. Salt Lake City, The Deseret News, 1900.
4p.l. [vii]–viii [1] 368p. plates, ports., charts. 23½cm.
Biography of William Bowker Preston and other Mormon Prestons.
DLC, UHi, UPB, USIC

9933. Wilson, Richard L. Short ravelings from a long yarn, or, Camp and march sketches, of the Santa Fe Trail. From the notes of Richard L. Wilson, by Benjamin F. Taylor. Chicago, Ill., Printed and Published by Geer & Wilson, Daily Journal Office, 1847.
64p. illus. 22½cm.
In Chapter XII he mentions a Mormon who had vanished with his wagon on the trail in 1840 (one of the earliest Mormons to enter the Far West)
W–C 142
CtY, CU–B, ICHi, WHi

9934. Wilson, Warren H. The evolution of the country community. A study in religious sociology. New York, Boston, The Pilgrim Press [c1912]
xvii, 221p. 19cm.
Mormonism discussed in a chapter entitled "Exceptional communities."
Another edition: 2d ed. enl. & rev. Boston, Chicago, The Pilgrim Press [c1923] DLC, ULA
CU, DLC, UPB, USIC

9935. Wilson, William M. Pictorial Provo; an illustrated industrial review of Provo, the garden city of Utah. [Salt Lake City, The Deseret News, 1907]
[78]p. 20cm.
History of Provo, and plates of the principal buildings.
UPB

9936. ———. (same) [Salt Lake City, The Deseret News, 1910]
[158] p. illus. 20cm.
UHi, UPB, USlC

9937. ———. Utah County, Utah in picture and prose. Describing its resources, enterprises and opportunities and the men behind them. By Wm. M. Wilson, 1914. [Salt Lake City? 1914]
[92]p. 19½×24½cm.
NjP

Wilton, Capt. Mark [*pseud.*] *See Manning, William H.*

9938. Winants, G. E. A journal of travels around the world. Twenty seven thousand five hundred miles over sea and land. By G. E. Winants. New York, Printed for the author by D. Appleton & Co., 1877.
2p.l. [5]–395p. illus. 24cm.
Travel through Salt Lake City in 1875.
USlC

9939. Winchester, Benjamin. An examination of a lecture delivered by the Rev. H. Perkins, on the religious opinions and faith of the Latter-day Saints and some of his most prominent errors and misstatements corrected. [n.p., 1840?]
12p. 16cm.
Caption-title.
Religious controversy at Allentown, N.J., May, 1840.
MH, MoInRC

9940. ———. A history of the priesthood from the beginning of the world to the present time, written in defence of the doctrine and position of the Church of Jesus Christ of Latter-day Saints; and also a brief treatise upon the fundamental sentiments, particularly those which distinguish the above society from others now extant. By B. Winchester, Minister of the Gospel . . . Philadelphia, Brown, Bicking and Guilbert, Printers, 1843.
iv [5]–168p. 14cm.
CSmH, CtY, CU-B, DLC, ICHi, ICN, MH, MoK, NjP, NN, UHi, ULA, UPB, USl, USlC, UU, WHi

9941. ———. The origin of the Spaulding story, concerning the manuscript found; with a short biography of Dr. P. Hulbert, the originator of the same . . . Philadelphia, Brown, Bicking and Guilbert, 1840.
24p. 20cm.
Howes W552, Sabin 104719
CtY, MoInRC, MoK, NN, UPB, USlC

9942. ———. (same, under title) Plain facts; shewing the origin of the Spaulding story, concerning the manuscript found and its being transformed into the Book of Mormon; with a short history of Dr. P. Hulbert, the author of the said story; Thereby proving to every lover of truth, beyond the possibility of successful contradiction, that the said story was a base fabrication, without even a shadow of truth. By Benjamin Winchester . . . Re-published by George J. Adams . . . To which is added, A letter from Elder S. Rigdon. Also, one from Elder O. Hyde, on the above subject. Bedford, England, Printed by C. B. Merry, 1841.
27p. 18cm.
"Reflections," p. 21–24 of American edition, not reprinted.
Howes W552
CU-B, MH, NN, PPiU, USlC

9943. ———, *compiler.* Synopsis of the Holy Scriptures, and concordance, in which the synonymous passages are arranged together. — Chiefly designed to illustrate the doctrine of the Church of Jesus Christ of Latter-Day Saints. To which is added, as an appendix an epitome of ecclesiastical history, etc. By B. Winchester, Minister of the Gospel . . . Philadelphia, Printed for the author, at the "United States" Book and Job Printing Office, 1842.
viii [9]–256p. 12cm.
CtY, CU-B, DLC, MH, NN, RPB, UHi, UPB, USlC, UU

9944. Winfree, Z. T. Scriptural exposure of Mormonism, the ax laid at the root of the Mormon plant, Mormonism rooted up by God's eternal truth. Nashville, Tenn., McQuiddy Printing, 1903.
30p. 19cm.
MoInRC

9945. Winship, A. E. The educational cure of Mormonism; address before the N.E.A. at Topeka, Kansas, July 14, 1886. [Topeka, Kansas? 1886?]
10p. 22cm.
Also published as p. 117–126 of the National Education Association. *Addresses & Proceedings of the National Educational Association*, Topeka, Kansas, 1886.
MWA

9946. Winther, F. Kjaern sprog mod Mormonerne, udgivne af F. W., Praest til slemminge og fjelde. Nykjobing, 1855.
8p.
Title in English: Brief declaration against Mormonism.
Schmidt

9947. Winther, Niels Andreas. Advarsels-rost imod Mormonerne. Forfattet og udgivet af N.A.W. (Til folkeoplysningens fremgang.) Ribe, Denmark, 1873.
4p.
Title in English: A voice of warning against the Mormons.
Schmidt

9948. ———. "Led os ikke i fristelse." Ribe, Denmark, 1873.
4p.
Title in English: Lead us not into temptation.
Schmidt

9949. Winthrop, Theodore. The canoe and the saddle; or, Klalam and Klickatat, by Theodore Winthrop; to which are now first added his Western letters and journals; ed., with an intro. and notes by John H. Williams . . . Tacoma, Washington, The author, 1913.
xxvi, 332p. illus. 24½cm.
Includes his travel through Utah in 1853.
Other editions: Boston, Tiknor & Fields, 1863. DLC; New York, Dodd, Mead & Co. [190–] DLC; Tacoma, J. H. Williams, 1913. DLC
Howes W584
UHi, USlC

9950. ———. John Brent, by Theodore Winthrop. New York, Dodd, Mead and Company, Publisher [c1861]
iv [5]–359p. 19cm.
Fiction concerning Mormonism.
Sub-title might be: The luring of Ellen by falsehood into a polygamous fate worse than death and her escape from the efficient, but beast-like Mormons.
USlC

9951. ———. (same) Boston, Ticknor and Fields, 1862.
iv [5]–359p. 19cm.
UHi, UPB, UU

9952. ———. (same) 11th ed. Boston, Ticknor and Fields, 1863.
iv [5]–359p. 19cm.
W–C 396a
CU–B

9953. ———. (same) [16th ed.] Boston, Ticknor and Fields, 1866.
iv [5]–359p. 19½cm.
DLC

9954. ———. (same) Boston, Ticknor and Fields, 1876.
iv [5]–359p. 19cm.
DLC

9955. Wipper, Frank F. Commentary on the following Nephite record subjects (1) Priests, (A) before Moses period, (B) Moses period, (C) after Christ came, (2) choice seer, (3) Zion, (4) parable of Zenos. Assembled by Frank F. Wipper, representing the Church of Christ . . . [Independence, Mo., 1927?]
23p. 18½cm.
NN

9956. ———. First apostles or first presidency, which? [n.p., n.d.]
[14]p. 25cm.
A publication of the Church of Christ (Temple Lot)
USlC

9957. ———. Nephite record texts. Condensed scriptural texts of the ancient American record arranged and classified under topical headings . . . assembled by Frank F. Wipper, representing the Church of Christ . . . [Independence, Mo., 1927?]
109p. 18½cm.
MoInRC, NN

9958. Wise, Henry Augustus. Los Gringos: or, An inside view of Mexico and California, with wanderings in Peru, Chile, and Polynesia. By Lieut. Wise, U.S.N. New York, Baker and Scribner, 1849.
xvi, 453p. 19½cm.
Reference to Mormons, p. 70, 73.
Other editions: London, Richard Bentley, 1849. CSmH, CU–B, OClWHi, WHi; 1850. CtY, DLC
Sabin 104893
CSmH, CtY, MB, MH, NjP, NN, ViU

9959. Wishard, Samuel Ellis. Baptism for the dead. [n.p., n.d.]
4p. 17cm.
MH

9960. ———. The Bible against polygamy. Dr. Wishard's lecture at the Presbyterian church — overthrow of the Mormon claims. [n.p., n.d.]
8p. 18cm.
MH

9961. ———. The divine law of marriage, or, The Bible against polygamy. New York, American Tract Society [n.d.]
2p.l. [5]–64p. 19½cm. (Books for the times. No. 25)
MH, USlC

9962. ———. Materialism and polytheism (as taught in Utah) [n.p., n.d.]
8p. 14cm.
Against the Mormon doctrine of the Godhead.
USlC

9963. ———. Mormon professions of loyalty. [New York, The Inter-denominational Council of Women for Christian and Patriotic Service, n.d.]
6p. 12cm.
NN

9964. ———. The Mormon purgatory (a false doctrine answered) [Danville, Ky.? n.d.]
8p. 14½cm.
USlC

9965. ———. Mormon rule over the state. By Samuel E. Wishard, Superintendent of Home Missions for Synod of Utah. [New York, The Interdenominational Council of Women for Christian and Patriotic Service, n.d.]
[4]p. 12cm.
NN

9966. ———. The Mormons, by Samuel E. Wishard . . . New York, Literature Department, Presbyterian Home Missions, 1904.
ix p., [1]l., 121p. 2 plates, 3 ports. 16½cm.
USlC copy has a publicity brochure.
CSmH, CtY, CU-B, DLC, IWW, MH, MoInRC, NjP, NjPT, NN, ULA, UPB, USl, USlC, UU, ViU

9966a. ———. No salvation after death. A false doctrine answered. [Salt Lake City, n.d.]
8p. 16cm.
USlC

9967. ———. Why unseat Apostle Smoot? [New York, 1903]
6p. 14cm.
Reprinted by the Interdenominational Council of Women for Christian and Patriotic Service.
NN

9968. Wister, Owen. Red men and white, by Owen Wister. Illustrated by Frederic Remington. New York, Harper & Brothers, 1896.
ix p. [2]l., 280p. 17 plates. 19cm.
Fiction. Section entitled "a pilgrim on the Gila." Deals with a polygamous bishop.
USlC

9969. Withrow, William Henry. Religious progress in the century. London, Philadelphia, Linscott Publishing Co., 1900.
xxii, 468p. port. 21½cm.
Mormons, or Latter-day Saints . . . p. 281–284.
Other editions: 1900. DLC; London & Edinburgh, 1903. DLC
DLC, UPB

Wittemann, Firm, Publishers. *See Salt Lake City in photo-gravure . . .*

Wo ist das wahre Evangelium? *See Rich, Benjamin Erastus.*

9970. Woelmont, Arnold de, ***baron.*** Souvenirs du Far-West, par le Baron Arnold de Woelmont. Paris, E. Plon et Cie. Imprimeurs-editeurs, 1883.
2p.l., 269p. 18cm.
Chapter III: "Mormons."
Title in English: Souvenirs from the Far-West.
Howes W608
DLC, NjP, UPB

9970a. Wohlfahrt, Fritz. Im lande der Yankees. Herteres Allerlei von einem vershämten Anfänger. Der Oeffentlickeit preisgegeben von Fritz Wohlfahrt. Berlin, Verlag von Aug. Berth. Auerbach, 1881.
3p.l., 301p. illus. 25cm.
Utah and Mormons, p. 70–90.
DLC, NjP

9971. Wolcott, R. W., ***compiler.*** A collection of testimonies of the truth by R. W. Wolcott, President of the Bedfordshire Conference. Luton, September the 18th, A.D. 1855.
1p.l. [3]–16p. 18cm.
Poetry, extracts from newspaper articles, etc.
MH

9972. Wolfe, J. M. Wolfe's mercantile guide, gazetteer, and business directory of cities, towns, villages, stations and government forts . . . Nebraska, Colorado, Wyoming, Utah, Idaho and Dakota . . . Omaha, Nebraska, Omaha Republican Book and Job Printing House, 1878.
3p.l. [5]–360p. 24cm.
The Territory of Utah, p. 204–257. With information on the death of Brigham Young and his effect on the territory.
UPB

9973. Wolfe, James H. The Mormon church and prohibition. Salt Lake City, Press of The F. W. Gardiner Co. [1916?]
31p. 21½cm.
Reprinted from the *Utah Survey*, March, April, 1916.
UPB, USlC

9974. Wolfe, Walter. Het Utah Mormonisme Ontmaskerd. Leer en Tempelgeheimen der Mormonen. Door Professor Walter Wolke . . . Rotterdam, J. van Goch [n.d.]
[26]p. 21cm.
Title in English: The Utah Mormons unmasked.
USlC

———. Mysteries of the Endowment House . . . *See Salt Lake Tribune.*

9975. Wolff, Diederik Engelbert Willem. Geschiedenis van den oorsprong en de lotgevallen der Mormonen, naar de beste bronnen bewerkt door D. E. W. Wolff. Amsterdam, W. H. Kirberger, 1855.
viii, 242p. 23½cm.
Title in English: The history of the origins and adventures of the Mormons.
CU-B, DLC, ICN, MH

9975a. Woman's American Baptist Home Mission Society. Utah's need of the Gospel. By One Who Knows. Chicago, Woman's American Baptist Home Mission Society [n.d.]
6p. 16cm.
USlC

9976. ———. The Wiles of Mormonism, an exercise. Chicago, Woman's American Baptist Home Mission Society [n.d.]
16p. 14cm.
NN

9977. Woman's Exponent. Salt Lake City, June 1, 1872–February 1914.
41 v. semi-monthly. 42cm.
First editor: Miss Lulu L. Greene. First periodical between Boston and the Pacific coast to be edited by a woman. Published in the interest of the women of the Church, but not controlled by the Relief Society.
DA V.21–23 inc.; Cty V.1–10, 25–30, 32–41 (some numbers in each volume); ICJ V.1–12, 13–34 inc.; MH V.1, 3–34 inc.; ULA V.2–5; UPB 1–20, 21–41 inc.; USlC comp.; UU V.17–34.

9978. ———. Prospectus of Woman's Exponent, a Utah Ladies' Journal. [Salt Lake City] 1872.
Broadside. 21×14cm.
ULA

9979. Woman's National Anti-Polygamy Society. From President Arthur's message. [Salt Lake City, 1881?]
[3]p. illus. 19cm.
Caption-title.
Text in gold and red.
Includes statement of George Q. Cannon showing his own polygamist background.
CtY

9979a. Words of the songs to be sung at the Grand Jubilee of Sunday School Children, held in the New Tabernacle, Salt Lake City, July 24th, 1875, being the twenty-eighth anniversary of the entrance of the pioneers into Salt Lake Valley. Professor C. J. Thomas, Conductor. Jos. J. Daynes, Organist. . . . [Salt Lake City] Published by the Deseret Sunday School Union . . . [1875]
12p. 16½cm.
USlC

9980. Wood, Clement. The outline of man's knowledge. New York, Lewis Copeland Co. [1927]
xixp. [1]l., 654p. illus., plates, charts, diagr. 24cm.
Mormonism; the Latter-day Saints, p. 546–550.
Another edition: N.Y., Grosset and Dunlap, 1927. UPB
CU, DLC

9981. Wood, D. L. Zion's harp. A collection of sacred hymns for divine worship, by D. L. Wood. [n.p.] Plymouth Rock Press, 1871.
viii, 122p. 12cm.
Preface signed: D. L. Wood and W. O. Wood.
For RLDS Church congregations.
USlC

9982. Wood, E. M. Mormonism. Should it be protected. By Rev. E. M. Wood . . . Pittsburgh, Published by Joseph Horner Book Company, Limited, 1903.
15p. 19½cm.
Mormonism un-Christian, un-American. Polygamy still an issue.
MH

9983. Wood, John. Journal of John Wood, as kept by him while traveling from Cincinnati to the gold diggings in California, in the spring and summer of 1850, containing an accurate account of the occurrances [sic] transactions and circumstances daily. Also an account of each tribe of Indians, description of the country passed through each day, quality of soil, &c., &c., together with a table of distances from Missouri to Oregon, emigrant's route, &c., &c. Chillicothe, Press of Addison Bookwalter, 1852.
76p. 17cm.
A brief account of his trip through Great Salt Lake City in 1850.
Another edition: Columbus, Nevins and Myers, 1871. CSmH, CU–B, ICN
Howes W633, W–C220
CtY, NjP, NjR, ICN

9984. Wood, Joseph. Epistle of the twelve. [By Joseph Wood] Milwaukee, Sentinal and Gazette Steam Press Print., 1851.
26p. 22cm.
An epistle from the Quorum of the Twelve Apostles (William Smith faction)
Cover-title.
Morgan
MoInRC, NN

9985. Wood, Mary. Pebbles gathered by the wayside, by Mrs. Mary Wood. [n.p., 188–]
irreg. pagination. 21½cm.
Contains narrative: "Among the Mormons," in eight chapters.
Irregular pagination indicates that it was originally published in some other form.
Bound together with title-page (half-title) and cover-title.
UHi

9986. Wood, Samuel Harry. Universal peace; or, The crowning work of two lives, by Sam H. Wood. Salt Lake City, Uintaland Publishing Company, 1914.
248p. port. 18½cm.
Fiction with Mormon setting.
UHi

9987. Wood, Samuel. Why we transferred to the Church of Christ. [Independence, 1918?]
[14]p. 18½cm.
Transferred from the RLDS Church to the Church of Christ (Temple Lot)
CU–B, NN, UHi, USlC

9988. Wood, Stanley. An unattended journey or ten thousand miles by rail, A Tour by four young ladies from the lakes. Across the prairies, over the rockies, through the deserts, among the Sierras, to the Pacific Coast, a souvenir of Transcontinental Travel. Richly illustrated by Stanley Wood. Chicago, The White City Art Company, 1895.
1p.l., 5–152p. plates. 22cm.
Chiefly descriptive with a brief history of Mormons in Utah.
USIC

9989. ———. Over the range to the golden gate . . . Chicago, R. R. Donnelly, 1889.
351p. illus., maps (part. fold.) 23½cm.
Includes his trip through Salt Lake City. Many inaccuracies.
Published in various editions, 1897–1912.
CU, DLC, NjP, UHi, ULA, UU

9990. Wood, William W. A letter on the latter-day work of the Lord. No. 1 [and No. 2] [Plano, Ill., True Latter-day Saints' Herald, 1866?]
2pts. in 1 (4, 8)p. 23cm. (True Latter-Day Saints' Herald. Tract. No. 33)
No. 2 is signed by William W. Wood.
MoInRC, NjP, NN

9990a. Woodhouse, W. W. Mormonism an imposture; or, the doctrines of the so-called Latter-day Saints, proved to be utterly opposed to the word of God. By the Rev. W. W. Woodhouse, M.A., Rector of St. Clement's and St. Helen's, Ipswich: Printed and Published by N. Pannifer, Fore Street, St. Clement's: J. M. Burton and Co., Cornhill; and may be had of all booksellers. 1853.
1p.l., [3]–31p. 14½cm.
UPB

9991. Woodruff, Wilford. Circular. Salt Lake City, August 17, 1872. To the Female Relief Societies throughout Utah Territory: [Salt Lake City, 1872]
Boradside. 21½×14cm.
Urges participation in exhibits of Deseret Agricultural and Manufacturing Society.
ULA

9992. ———. The Keys of the kingdom. The martyrdom of the prophet and patriarch — The prophet's last instructions to the Quorum of Apostles. Remarks made at Young Men's Improvement Conference, Sunday, June 2, 1889. By President Wilford Woodruff. [Salt Lake City, 1889?]
[4]p. 28cm.
USIC

9993. ———. Leaves from my journal. By President W. Woodruff. Designed for the instruction and encouragement of young Latter-day Saints. Salt Lake City, Juvenile Instructor Office, 1881.
4p.l., 96p. 18cm. (Faith promoting series. Third book)
Howes W649
CU–B, ICN, IWW, NjP, UPB, USIC, UU

9994. ———. (same) [2d ed.] Salt Lake City, Juvenile Instructor Office, 1882.
[3]l., 96p. 18½cm. (Faith promoting series. Third book)
CSmH, CtY, CU–B, DLC, ICN, MoInRC, NjP, NN, UHi, USl, USIC, UU

9995. ———. (same) 4th ed. [Salt Lake City] The Deseret News, 1909.
viii, 104p. 19½cm. (Faith promoting series. Third book)
MH, NjP, UHi, USIC, UU

9996. ———. Official declaration. [Salt Lake City, 1890?]
Broadside. 19½×11cm.
Includes Lorenzo Snow's motion to sustain the declaration on plural marriage.
USIC

9997. ———. Prayer offered at the dedication of the Temple of the Lord. Salt Lake City, 6 April, 1893. [Salt Lake City, 1893?]
12p. 27cm.
Caption-title.
UPB, USIC

9998. ———. President Woodruff's manifesto. Proceedings at the semi-annual conference of the Church of Jesus Christ of Latter-day Saints, Monday Forenoon, October 6, 1890. [Salt Lake City, 1890?]
10p. 20½cm.
Cover-title.
CSmH, MH, MoInRC, UPB, USl, USIC

9999. ———. President Woodruff's prayer. Montpelier, Idaho, Copied for and presented with compliments of J. S. Barrett. [Montpelier? 1897?]
Broadside. 34×25½cm.
UPB

10,000. ———. Wilford Woodruff, fourth president of the Church of Jesus Christ of Latter-day Saints, history of his life and labors, as recorded in his daily journals . . . prepared for publication, by Matthias F. Cowley. Salt Lake City, The Deseret News, 1909.
xviii, 702p. port., 5 plates. 24cm.
CSmH, CtY, DLC, NjP, NN, UHi, UPB, USIC, UU, WHi

10,001. ———. (same) 2d ed. Salt Lake City, The Deseret News, 1916.
xviii, 702p. illus., port. 24cm.
UHi, UPB, USlC

Woods, James W. *See Lyne, Thomas A.*

10,002. Woods, Kate Tannatt. Across the continent. How the boys and girls went from Bunker Hill to the Golden Gate. By Kate Tannatt Woods, illustrated. Boston, Lothrop Publishing Company [c1897]
4p.l., 11–240 [2]p. illus. (1 col.) 24cm.
Chapter XIII: "Utah and the Mormons."
DLC, USlC

10,003. Woodstock, Charles B. A pure life. Lamoni, Ia., Social Purity Committee, Zion's Religio-Literary Society, Reorganized Church of Jesus Christ of Latter Day Saints [n.d.]
14p. 20cm.
MoInRC

10,004. Woodstock, Lenoir. Our girl's activities for the teen age. Lenoir Woodstock, editor. Independence, Mo., Herald Publishing House, 1930.
2p.l., 5–245p. 20cm.
RLDS activities for young girls.
USlC

10,005. Woodward, Charles Lowell. Bibliothica [sic] scallawagiana. Catalogue of a matchless collection of books, pamphlets, autographs, pictures, &c., relating to Mormonism and the Mormons. The 10 years' gatherings of Charles L. Woodward . . . to be sold at vendue, Monday, January 19, 1880 . . . by Messrs. Bangs and Co. [New York, 1880]
1p.l., 50p. 25cm.
Cover-title.
CSmH, CtY, CU–B, DLC, ICN, InU, MH, NjP, NN, OClWHi, RPB, ULA, UPB, USlC, WHi

10,006. ———. [Bibliothica [sic] scallawagiana] Supplementary catalogue of books, pamphlets and names . . . New York, 1890?]
20p. 25cm.
NN

10,007. ———. To whom it may concern: I have in my possession a book, which, reprinted and published, would do more to open people's eyes to the truth concerning that most infernal and devil-begotton Mormonism . . . Hoboken, N.J., 1874.
Broadside. 25½×20cm.
Caption-title.
Signed: Chas. L. Woodward.
CtY

10,008. Woodward, Hugh McCurdy. A guide for the study of Essentials in Church History, by Joseph Fielding Smith. Prepared for the Quorums of the Priesthood. [Salt Lake City] Deseret News Press [1922]
[3]–80p. 19cm.
NN, UPB

10,009. ———. Leitfaden zum Studium des Buches Wichtiges aus der Kirchengeschichte von Joseph Fielding Smith . . . Bearbeitet von Dr. Hugh M. Woodward von der Brigham Young Universität. Herausgegeben von der Schweizerischen und Deutschen Mission der Kirche Jesus Christi der Heiligen der Letzten Tage. Basel, Serge F. Ballif . . .1923.
19p. 18cm.
Title in English: Guide to the study of the book *Essentials in Church History.*
USlC

10,010. A word for the true gospel. A tract for the Latter-day Saints. By a clergyman. London, Wertheim and Macintosh, 1848.
14p. 16cm.
In the form of a catechism.
USlC

10,011. The word of the Lord. Unto the Saints in all the world. [Salt Lake City, 1877]
4p. 22cm.
A revelation from an unknown "successor" to Joseph Smith as revelator.
USlC

10,012. Word of wisdom. Tune: Beautiful River . . . [n.p., n.d.]
[1]p. 13×11cm.
Music.
USlC

10,012a. Words of wisdom concerning the conference resolution for Prohibition. [Salt Lake City, 1909]
[4]p. 22½cm.
Includes quotes from *The Improvement Era, Deseret Evening News,* and General Conference of Oct. 1908.
USlC

10,013. Wordsworth, Christopher, *Bishop of Lincoln.* Mormonism and England: a sermon, preached in Westminster Abbey, on Sunday evening, July 28, 1867 . . . London [etc.] Rivingtons, 1867.
22p. 20½cm.
CtY

Work, Hubert. *See United States Government Officials . . .*

10,014. Workes, James M. A patriarchal blessing given on the head of Joseph Nattress, son of Ralph Nattress, and Hannah Freek. [Manti? 188–]
[4]p. 20cm.
UPB, USIC

10,015. World's Christian Citizenship Conference. Second World's Christian Citizenship Conference, Portland, Oregon, June 29–July 6, 1913. Official report. Pittsburgh, Pa., National Reform Association, 1913.
303p. ports. 26cm.
The Mormon menace by Robert F. Coyle, p. 88–91.
DLC, UPB

10,016. ———. The world's moral problems: addresses at the Third World's Christian Citizenship Conference held in Pittsburgh, Pa., U.S.A. November 9–16, 1919. Pittsburgh, The National Reform Association, c1920.
3p.l., 5–508p. 24cm.
"Report of World Commission (on Mormonism) by Mrs. T. Cory. History and tactics of Mormon propaganda by William E. LaRue . The Menace of Mormonism, by Mrs. Lulu Loveland Shepard. Defeating Mormon proselyting, by Henry Peel.
DLC, UPB

10,017. World's Congress of Representative Women. Programme of the World's Congress of Representative Women, May 15 to 21, inclusive, 1893. Memorial Art Palace . . . Chicago. [Chicago, Ill., 1893]
55p. 23cm.
Relief Society and Y.L.M.I.A. mentioned, p. 13, 38–39.
USIC

Ein Wort der Verteidigung. *See Eyring, Henry.*

10,018. Das Wort der Weisheit. Dresden, Druck, Crueger & Horn [n.d.]
[4]p. 21cm.
Title in English: The Word of wisdom.
UPB

10,019. ———. (same) [Basel, Herausgegeben von Fred Tadje, n.d.]
4p. 20cm.
UPB

Worwood, William. *See Warwood, William.*

10,020. Wotherspoon, George. Mormonism; or, The faith of the Latter-day saints: its history and moral. A lecture delivered before the Sunday lecture society, St. George's Hall . . . on 24th October, 1886. . . . London, The Sunday Lecture Society, 1886.
27p. 18cm.
CSmH, CtY, MH, USIC, UU

10,021. Wray, G. W. Mormonism exhibited in its own mirror; wherein it is proved (from their own standard writings which every Mormon is bound to subscribe to and obey) to be a base system of infidelity, atheism and pantheism; full of contradictions and absurdities; teaching for doctrines the commandments of men and the dogma of devils! . . . Middlesbro' [Eng.] Printed at the "Chronicle" Office, . . . 1854.
16p. 21cm.
USIC

10,022. Wright, Allen. A conversation on the thousand years' reign of Christ. Written by Elder Allen Wright. St. John, Kansas. [St. John, Kansas, the County Capital] 1907.
24p. 16½cm. (No. 1)
Cover-title.
Bickertonite publication.
Morgan
PMonC

10,022a. Wright (James O.) & Co. Just published, the Mormon bible . . . [1858] New York City [New York]
Broadside. 26×20cm.
Advertisement of a reprint of the third edition of the Book of Mormon. It states that it was re-issued because the Mormon leaders were having it suppressed.
USIC

10,023. Wright, John Couchois. Lays of the Lakes, by John C. Wright. Boston, R. G. Badger [c1911]
3p.l., 78p. 19cm.
Includes a drama entitled "The tragedy of King Strang."
DLC, UHi

10,024. ———. Northern breezes. Harbor Springs, Mich., J. C. Wright [c1917]
112p. plates, ports. 19½cm.
Contains: King Strang; or, the tragedy of Beaver Island.
WHi

10,025. ———. The Ottawan, a short history of the villages and resorts surrounding Little Traverse Bay and the Indian legends connected therewith; also an account of the noted Mormon kingdom on Beaver Island during the fifties, by one of King Strang's sons, and a "write-up" of antiquated Cross village and its famous convent . . . by J. C. Wright. Lansing, Mich., R. Smith & Co., 1895.
80p. illus. (incl. ports.) fold. map. 14×20cm.
DLC, WHi

10,026. Wright, Thomas. The life of Sir Richard Burton, by Thomas Wright . . . With 64 plates . . . London, Everett & Co., 1906.
2v. plates, maps, ports., facsims., geneal. tabl. 23cm.
Chapter X: "Mormons and Marriage"; his visit to Salt Lake City in 1860.
DLC, NjP, UHi

10,027. Wright, William. History of the big bonanza: an authentic account of the discovery, history, and working of the world renowned Comstock silver lode of Nevada; including the present condition of the various mines situated thereon; sketches of the most prominent men interested in them . . . By Dan De Quille [William Wright] Hartford, Conn., American Publishing Company; San Francisco, A. L. Bancroft & Co., 1876.

xvi, 17–569p. plates, ports., diagr. 22cm.
Introduction by Mark Twain.
Includes early Mormon activity in Nevada.
Another edition: 1877. CU, DLC
Howes W710
CU-B, DLC, ICJ, ICN, NjP, NN, OFH, UPB

10,028. ———. A history of the Comstock silver lode and mines, Nevada and the Great Basin region . . . Virginia City, Nevada, F. Boegle [c1889]

x, 11–158p. 18cm.
Includes the Mormon colonization of Nevada.
Howes W711
CU-B, DLC, ICN, NjP, NvHi, UHi, USlC

10,029. A written discussion between "A. B." of the Reorganized Church of Jesus Christ of Latter Day Saints and "C. D." of the Methodist Church. Grand Rapids, Mich. Published by the Evans Printing Co. [n.d.]

31p. 22cm. (The Gospel Booklet. No. 1)
Letters written to demonstrate the truth of the RLDS Church.
MoInRC

10,030. Wunderlich, Jean (*trans.*). Begebenheiten aus dem Leben Jesu. Unterrichtsplan für die erste Mittelklasse der Sonntagsschulen der Schweizerischen und Deutschen Mission der Kirche Jesu Christi der Heiligen der letzten Tage für das Jahr 1923. Nach Englischen Quellen bearbeitet von Jean Wunderlich. Basel, Herausgegeben von Serge F. Ballif, Präsident der Schweizerischen und Deutschen Mission, 1923.

1p.l., 48p. 20½cm.
Title in English: Events from the life of Christ.
USlC

10,031. ———. Grosse Männer der Bibel und des Buches Mormon. Sonntagschulunterrichtsplan der zweiten Mittelklasse für das Jahr 1923. Zum Teil nach englischen Quellen bearbeitet von Jean Wunderlich. Basel, Herausgegeben von Serge S. Ballif, Präsident der Schweizerischen und Deutschen Mission der Kirche Jesu Christi der Heiligen der Letzten Tage, 1923.

40p. 21cm.
Sunday School manual.
Title in English: Great men of the Bible and the Book of Mormon.
USlC

10,032. ———. Das Leben Jesu Für die Primarklassen. Basel, Herausgegeben von Fred Tadje. 1924.

3p.l. [7]–68p. 20cm.
Title in English: The teachings of Jesus for Primary classes.
USlC

10,033. ———. Ein Leitfaden zum Studium des Buches Mormon. Bearbeitet von Jean Wunderlich. Basel, Herausgegeben von Fred Tadje, Präsident der Schweizerischen und Deutschen Mission der Kirche Jesu Christi der Heiligen der Letzten Tage [n.d.]

123p. 20½cm.
Title in English: A guide to the study of the Book of Mormon.
UPB

Wyl, W. *See Wymetal, Wilhelm, Ritter von.*

10,034. Wymetal, Wilhelm, Ritter von. Joseph Smith, the prophet, his family and his friends; a study based on facts and documents with fourteen illustrations. Salt Lake City, Tribune Printing and Publishing Company, 1886.

3p.l. [5]–318 [2]p. illus. 17½cm. (Mormon Portraits; or, The Truth about the Mormon Leaders from 1830 to 1886. Vol. 1)
"Volume first" of projected series called Mormon portraits. No more issued.
CSmH, CtY, CU-B, DLC, ICN, MH, NjP, NjPT, NN, UHi, ULA, UPB, USl, USlC, UU, WHi

Frederick Kesler 16th march

A SERIES OF INSTRUCTIONS AND REMARKS

BY

PRESIDENT BRIGHAM YOUNG,

AT A

SPECIAL COUNCIL, TABERNACLE, MARCH 21, 1858.

I do not know but what I would correctly portray the minds and feelings of many of the people by saying that they do not take much thought in regard to the situation and circumstances we are under, nor of the propriety and policy of our movements.

God has led this people; he has sent forth the new and everlasting covenant. He restored the priesthood to the children of men, and called upon Joseph Smith, jun., to be the first Elder in this church and upon Oliver Cowdery to be the second. From that time until now all persons that have the Spirit of this work have seen and can now see and understand that the hand of the Lord has been with this people and that he has led them all the time. But when men and women so neglect their duty that their minds run into darkness, they are almost universally impressed that this work has been produced by the wisdom of men. Those who have the Spirit of the Lord Jesus Christ constantly acknowledge the hand of God in leading this people.

We esteemed Joseph our leader. He truly was our leader in one sense,—the leader that we conversed with face to face, but he was not our invisible Leader, for that Leader was and is the Lord Jehovah.

Item 10,066. Brigham Young's instructions concerning the evacuation of Salt Lake City in the face of the Utah Expedition. From the University of Utah collection.

Y ALUMNUS

10,035. Y Alumnus. Provo, February, 1926–April, 1927.
2v. monthly. 28cm.
Published by the Alumni Association of Brigham Young University.
UPB

10,036. Y News. Provo, September 21, 1921–
v. illus., ports. 60cm.
Published by the students of Brigham Young University.
UPB

10,037. Yankee drolleries. The most celebrated works of the best American humorists. Complete editions, with introductions by George Augustus Sala. London, J. C. Hotten [1865]
[532]p. 19cm.
Variously paged.
Another edition: 1876. NjP
Partial contents: Artemus Ward: his book. Includes "A visit to Brigham Young."
Preface signed: 1865.
CU–B

10,038. Yard, Robert Sterling. The book of the national parks. New York, Charles Scribner's Sons, 1919.
xv, 420[8]p. illus., maps. 21½cm.
Zion National Monument with reference to Mormons and Mormon settlements in Southern Utah, p. 352–366.
DLC, UPB, USlC

10,039. Yates, James E., *compiler.* The battle's brunt and the love-lit life. V.E.S.Y. Compiled by James E. Yates, Church of Christ. [Independence, Mo.? 1928?]
104p. 19½cm.
No title page. Title from cover.
Poetry of the Church of Christ (Temple Lot) by Vida E. Smith Yates, Ernest Edward Yates, Arthur A. Yates, and James E. Yates.
NN, UPB

10,040. ———. The origin of the Reorganized Church of Jesus Christ of Latter Day Saints. [n.p., n.d.]
24p. 15½cm.
MoInRC

10,041. ———. Refusal to sustain doctrine of supremacy of church president. [Independence? 1925?]
7p. 18½cm.
Speech delivered in the closing session of conference, Independence, Mo., April 21, 1925.
Supreme directional control.
MoInRC

10,041a. ———. The word of the Lord; a brief review of the faith and fortunes of the Church. [Independence, Mo., The Torch of Truth, ca. 1930]
[13]p. 22cm.
USlC

10,042. ———. The word of the Lord, a true revealment and a sure testimony. [n.p., 192–]
9p. 21cm.
Supreme directional control.
MoInRC

10,043. Yates, Robert P. My tour through British dominions across the sea; being leaves from a diary of a tour through the Mediterranean, visiting Gibraltar, Malta, Brindisi, Port Said, via the Suez Canal to India and Ceylon, thence to Australia, Tasmania, New Zealand, Samoa, and the Sandwich Islands, and home by the United States and Canada. By R. P. Yates, J. P. Birmingham, Birmingham News and Printing Co. [1907?]
2p.l., 163p. ports. 24½cm.
The diary is for the years, 1899–1907. "Mormons," p. 138–139. A short history of the church and current Mormon-gentile relations.
USlC

10,044. Yeigh, Frank. Through the heart of Canada, by Frank Yeigh. Toronto, H. Frowde, 1910.
319 [1]p. plates. 21cm.
"Land of the rancher," p. 223–229. Mormon colonization in Canada.
Another edition: 1913. CU–B, NjP
DLC, UPB

Yelverton, Therese. *See Longworth, Maria Theresa.*

10,045. Young, Alfales. Speech of Alfales Young at the Jacksonian meeting in Salt Lake Theater, January 8, 1885. [Salt Lake City, 1885?]
12p. 23cm.
The dangers of the political situation and the relationship of church and state in Utah.
Includes "True democracy. Good for the Nation, it is also good for Utah." Speech of J. L. Rawlings, esq., at the Jacksonian meeting . . ." An attempt to avert the creation of the Utah Commission by separating church and state.
CSmH

10,045a. Young, Ann Eliza (Webb). The truth about Mormonism and its founders. Grand Rapids, Michigan, Asman Tract Publishers, [n.d.]
[7]p. 22cm.
MoInRC

10,046. ———. Wife no. 19; or, The story of a life in bondage, being a complete expose of Mormonism, and revealing the sorrows, sacrifices and sufferings of women in polygamy, by Ann Eliza Young, Brigham Young's apostate wife. With introductory notes by John B. Gough and Mary A. Livermore . . . Hartford, Conn. [etc.] Dustin, Gilman and Co., 1875.
2p.l. [9]–605p. illus., plates, ports. 23cm.
DLC, ICN, ICU, MB, MH, MoInRC, NjP, UHi, ULA, USl, USlC, WHi

10,047. ———. (same) Hartford, Conn., Dustin, Gilman and Co., 1876 [c1875]
2p.l. [9]–605p. illus., plates, ports. 23cm.
CSmH, CtY, CU, MH, NjP, NjPT, NN, OCl, OClWHi, UHi, ULA, USlC, UU, WaU

10,048. ———. (same) Hartford, Conn., Dustin, Gilman and Co. . . . 1876.
Varied pagination. 23cm.
Publisher's sample (Sold by subscription only)
CU–B, UPB

10,049. ———. (same) Hartford, Conn. [etc.] Dustin, Gilman and Co., 1877.
2p.l. [9]–605p. illus., plates, ports. 23cm.
ICHi, MH

10,050. ———. (same, under title) Life in Mormon bondage; a complete exposé of its false prophets, murderous Danites, despotic rulers and hypnotized deluded subjects, by Ann Eliza Young, 19th wife of Brigham Young. Limited ed. Philadelphia, Boston [etc.] Aldine Press, Inc. [c1908]
1p.l., 512p. illus., plates, ports. 23½cm.
"Edition deluxe. Copy No. —."
CSmH, DLC, ICN, MH, USl, USlC, UU

10,051. Young, Aretta. After sunset; poems and illustrations by Aretta Young (1864–1923) edited by Lowry Nelson. [Provo, Utah, Brigham Young University, c1928]
6p.l., 45 [1]p. illus., plates. 19½cm.
Mormon poetry. Also includes her biography.
CU, DLC, NjP, UHi, UPB, UU

10,052. ———. For Christ's dear sake, a Christmas story. Salt Lake City, The Deseret News, 1898.
16p. 19cm.
Mormon poetry.
UPB, UU

Young, Brigham, 1801–1877. Brigham Young, Trustee in Trust . . . vs. William S. Godbe.
See Church of Jesus Christ of Latter-day Saints.

10,053. ———. Brigham Young's defense of polygamy; of marriage and morals, in the Great Salt Lake City, with six reasons for a plurality of wives, as delivered before the Twelve Apostles of the Church of Jesus Christ, of the Latter-day Saints, at Utah. London, Published by C. Elliot [1861]
15p. 18cm.
Brigham Young's defense, p. [5]–15.
Unsigned preface dated August 1st, 1861.
Probably written by E. C. Briggs.
USlC

10,054. ———. Brigham Young's will. [Salt Lake City? 1877?]
7 [1]p. 23½cm.
Caption-title.
CtY, MH, NBuG, NjP, NN, UHi

10,055. ———. (same) [Salt Lake City? 1879]
8p. 22cm.
NjP, NN

10,056. ———. (same) [Salt Lake City? 1887]
8p. 22½cm.
NN

10,057. ———. Deseret Telegraph Company; first message ever sent over Deseret lines. Salt Lake City, 1866.
Broadside. 22×14cm.
Telegram to Lorin Farr with religious message. It explains that the telegraph is to aid the building up of the kingdom.
USlC

10,058. ———. Discourse by President Brigham Young, at Logan, Cache County, Monday morning, May 25, 1877, at the Priesthood meeting, held for the purpose of organizing a Stake of Zion. Reported by G. F. Gibbs. [n.p., n.d.]
8p. 23cm.
NjP, UPB inc.

10,059. ———. Discourse delivered in the Tabernacle, in Great Salt Lake City, Sunday, February 27, 1853, by President Brigham Young. [Great Salt Lake City, News Print., 1853]
8p. 20½cm.
Reported by George D. Watt.
Signed: Great Salt Lake City, U.T., April 6, 1853.
The duties and privileges of being members of the Church.
UPB, USlC

10,060. ———. Discourses of Brigham Young . . . Selected and arranged by John A. Widtsoe. Salt Lake City, Deseret Book Company [c1925]
xv, 760p. plates, ports. 19½cm.
CSmH, CtY, CU–B, DLC, ICN, MH, MoInRC, NjPT, UHi, ULA, UPB, USl, USlC, UU, WHi

10,061. ———. (same) [2d ed.] Salt Lake City, Deseret Book Co. [1926, c1925]
xv, 760p. 19½cm.
Preface to second edition dated 1926.
CSmH, IWW, MiU, NjP, OU, USlC, ViU

10,061a. ———. Extract from a sermon delivered by Brigham Young, the first Sunday in September, 1861. Subject: The proneness of the Saints to imitate Gentile fashions. [Salt Lake City? 1865?]
3p. 21½cm.
Later reprinted in the *Mormon Expositor.*
UPB

10,062. ———. A few words to emigrants and to all who wish to purchase property in Nauvoo and its vicinity. [Nauvoo, 1844]
Broadside. 30½×33cm.
Within ornamental border.
Urges saints to see him or his agents about buying property. Signed: Brigham Young, Nauvoo, Nov. 12, 1844.
Byrd 907
USlC

10,063. ———. Memorial evening service in the Salt Lake Temple in honor of President Brigham Young's birthday . . . [Salt Lake City] 1921.
[2]p. port. 21½cm.
UHi

10,064. ———. The resurrection. A discourse by Brigham Young, President of the Church of Jesus Christ of Latter-day Saints, delivered in the new tabernacle. Salt Lake City at the general conference, Oct. 8, 1875. Salt Lake City, Deseret News Steam Printing Establishment [1875]
11p. 22cm.
CSmH, CtY, CU-B, MH, NjP, NN, UPB, USl, USlC, UU

10,065. ———. (same) Salt Lake City, Deseret News Co., 1884.
16p. 21cm.
Cover-title.
CDU, CtY, CU-B, DLC, MH, MoInRC, NjP, OClWHi, UHi, ULA, USlC

10,066. ———. A series of instructions and remarks by President Brigham Young at a special council, Tabernacle, March 21, 1858. Reported by George D. Watt. Salt Lake City, 1858.
19p. 20cm.
Caption-title.
Concerning the approach of the Utah expedition, and other matters.
CtY, UU

10,067. ———. Sermon by Brigham Young delivered May 29th, 1847, to the pioneers while they were crossing the plains. Reported by William Clayton. Also some timely scriptural quotations. [Salt Lake City? 192–]
12p. 21cm.
Cover-title.
Compiled by Heber Bennion?
CU-B, UPB, USlC

10,068. ———. Specimens of Mormon sermons. [Salt Lake City? 1865?]
4p. 21½cm.
Sermons by Brigham Young, J. Clinton, and Edwin D. Woolley.
C. Corwith Wagner, private collector, had an original in his collection.
UHi (photostat)

10,069. ———. Teachings of President Brigham Young; salvation for the dead, the spirit world, and kindred subjects. [Salt Lake City, The Seagull Press] 1922.
23 [1]p. port. 22cm.
Caption-title: Extracts from sermons by President Brigham Young.
CSmH, DLC, NjP, UHi, USlC

10,070. ———. (same) [Salt Lake City, The Seagull Press] 1922.
23p. 22cm.
Variant printing.
USlC

10,071. ———. To Bishop ———: [a circular letter announcing visit of committee to solicit support for sale of bonds of Utah Central Railroad] August 18, 1870. [Salt Lake City? 1870?]
[1]l. 20½×27cm.
ULA

10,072. ———. To the bishops and presiding elders of the various wards and settlements of Utah territory, from St. Charles, Richland County, in the South: [letter announcing plans for the Deseret Telegraph and calling for support for it from local authorities.] Dated November 1, 1865. [Great Salt Lake City? 1865?]
[1]l. 19×27cm.
ULA

10,073. ———. To the bishops and presiding elders of the various wards and settlements of Utah Territory from St. Charles, Richland County, in the North, to St. George, Washington County, in the South. [Great Salt Lake City, 1866?]
Broadside. 25½×19cm.
Deseret Telegraph.
USlC

10,074. ———. To the presiding elders and saints of the places where they are, or where they wish to have, Telegraph Station operators. [Great Salt Lake City, 1866]
Broadside. 25½×20cm.
Deseret Telegraph.
ULA, USIC

10,075. ———. Utah's first governor a progressive. Brigham Young favors constitutional amendments, Third term idea, and formation of new party in his July oration in 1854, Journal of Discourses. Vol. 7, page 9. [Salt Lake City? 1912?]
[2]p. 22½cm.
Caption-title.
At head of title: Progressive headquarters.
UHi

10,076. Young, Brigham, 1836–1903. Proclamation to the people. [Liverpool, 1891]
3p. 22cm.
Signed: 42, Islington, Liverpool, January, 1891.
A missionary tract.
UPB, USIC

10,077. Young, Brigham H. Emigrant's Guide. Being a table of distances, showing the springs, creeks, rivers, mountains, hills, and all other notable places, from Great Salt Lake City to San Francisco. Second edition. By B. H. Young and J. Eagar. [n.p., n.d.]
8p. 14½cm.
Caption-title.
Bound in plain blue paper.
CtY

Young, Emeline A. *See Fraud on the will.*

10,078. Young, Gilbert I., *compiler.* Fragmentary records of the Youngs, comprising, in addition to much general information respecting them, a particular and extended account of the posterity of Ninian Young, an early resident East Fallowfield Township, Chester County, Pa. Philadelphia, William S. Young, 1869.
iii, 113p. 22½cm.
Brigham Young, p. 69–71.
USIC

10,079. Young, J. W. Mormonism: its origin, doctrines and dangers . . . Ann Arbor, Mich., G. Wahr [c1900]
71p. 18cm.
NN

10,080. Young, John Philip. Journalism in California . . . Pacific Coast and exposition biographies. San Francisco, Chronicle Publishing Co. [1915]
2p.l., x, 362p. plates, ports. 23½cm.
Samuel Brannan and the *California Star.*
CU-B, DLC, NjP, UHi, ULA, USIC

10,081. Young, John Russell. Memoirs of John R. Young, Utah pioneer, 1847, written by himself. Salt Lake City, The Deseret News, 1920.
viii [9]–341p. port. 19½cm.
Howes Y29
CSmH, CtY, DLC, NjP, NN, UHi, UPB, USI, USIC, UU, WHi

10,082. Young, Joseph. History of the organization of the Seventies. Names of the first and second quorums. Items in relation to the First Presidency of the Seventies. Also, a brief glance at Enoch and his city. Embellished with a likeness of Joseph Smith, the prophet, and a view of the Kirtland temple. By Joseph Young, sen. Salt Lake City, Printed at the Deseret News Steam Printing Establishment, 1878.
2p.l., 16p. plate, port. 21cm.
CSmH, CtY, DLC, MH, NjP, NN, UHi, UPB, USI, USIC, UU

10,083. Young, Joseph Watson. Israels Indsamling og Zions forløsning af Joseph W. Young. [Kjøbenhavn, Redigeret og udgivet af C. Widerborg. Trykt hos F. E. Bording, n.d.]
16p. 21cm.
"4de oplag."
Title in English: The gathering of Israel and the redemption of Zion.
USIC

10,084. ———. (same) [Kjøbenhavn, Redigeret og udgivet af Hector C. Haight. Trykt hos F. E. Bording, ca. 1857]
16p. 21cm.
"5te oplag."
USIC

10,085. ———. (same) [Kjobenhavn, Redigeret og udgivet af John Van Cott. Trykt hos F. E. Bording, 1861]
16p. 23cm.
"6de oplag."
USIC

10,086. ———. (same) [Kjøbenhavn, Redigeret og udgivet af Jesse N. Smith. Trykt hos F. E. Bording, 1863]
16p. 21cm.
"7de oplag."
USIC

10,086a. ———. (same) [Malmo, Pa W. W. Cluffs forlag, tryckt hos C. A. Andersson & Co., 1871]
16p. 20cm.
Sjette upplagan.
USIC

10,087. ———. (same) [Kjøbenhavn? Redigeret og udgivet af R. Peterson. Trykt hos F. E. Bording, 1872]
16p. 21½cm.
Caption-title.
"21st Tusinde."
UHi, UPB, USlC

10,088. ———. (same) [Kjøbenhavn, Udgivet af R. Peterson. Tryckt hos F. E. Bording, 1873]
16p. 21cm.
"29de Tusinde."
USlC

10,089. ———. (same) [Køpenhavn, Udgivet af D. N. Lilljenqvist, 1876]
16p. 23cm.
"42de Tusinde."
UPB, USlC

10,090. ———. (same) Kjøbenhavn, Udgivet af R. Wilhelmsen. Trykt hos F. E. Bording, 1880.
16p. 21cm.
"45de Tusinde."
USlC

10,091. ———. (same) [Kjobenhavn, G. D. Fjeldsted. Trykt hos F. E. Bording, 1882]
16p. 20½cm.
Caption-title.
"50de Tusinde."
UHi, UPB, USlC

10,092. ———. (same, in Swedish) Israels insamling och Zions förlossning. Köpenhamn, Udgifwen och Förlaggd auf C. Widerborg, 1859.
16p. 21cm.
"5te oplag."
CSmH, MHi, UU

10,092a. ———. (same) [Kopenhamn, Utgifwen och forlaggd af Jesse N. Smith. Tryckt hos F. E. Bording, 1862.
16p. 20½cm.
USlC

10,092b. ———. (same) Kopenhamn, Utgifven och forlagd af C. D. Fjeldsted, Tryckt hos F. E. Bording, 1882.
16p. 22cm.
USlC

10,093. ———. (same) [Köpenhamn, C. Widerborg, 1865]
16p. 20cm.
Caption-title.
"Fjerde upplagan."
CtY

10,094. ———. (same) [Köpenhamn, C. Widerborg, 1867]
16p. 20cm.
Caption-title.
"Femte upplagan."
CtY

10,095. ———. (same) [Köpenhamn, Utgifven och förlaggd af R. C. Flygare. Tryckt hos F. E. Bording, 1875]
16p. 21cm.
Caption-title.
"Sjunde upplagan."
UHi

10,096. ———. (same) [Köpenhamn, Utgifven och förlagd af N. C. Flygare. Tryckt hos F. E. Bording, 1878]
16p. 21½cm.
CDU, CtY, UPB, USlC

10,097. Young, Levi Edgar. Chief episodes in the history of Utah, by Levi Edgar Young. Chicago, The Lakeside Press, 1912.
51p. illus., port. 19½cm.
CtY, CU–B, DLC, IWW, NjP, NN, UHi, USl, USlC, UU

10,098. ———. Dr. John Rocky Mountain Park. [Salt Lake City, c1919]
1p.l. [5]–54p. illus., port. 23cm.
Mormon educator.
CU–B, NjP, UHi, UPB, USl, UU

10,099. ———. "The first hundred years," by Levi Edgar Young, 1830–1930, April 6th. Salt Lake City, 1930.
12p. illus., ports. 44½cm.
Cover-title.
"Souvenir copy." Centennial section of the Salt Lake Tribune.
CU–B, UHi

10,100. ———. The founding of Utah, by Levi Edgar Young . . . New York, Chicago [etc.] C. Scribner's Sons [c1923]
xv, 445p. illus., ports., maps, facsims. 19½cm.
CSmH, CU–B, DLC, MB, NjP, NN, OU, ULA, UPB, USl, USlC, UU

10,101. ———. (same) New York [etc.] C. Scribner's Sons [c1924]
xv, 445p. ports., maps, facsims. 19½cm.
"2d edition."
MH, OCl, UHi, UPB

10,102. ———. The great Mormon tabernacle with its world-famed organ and choir. Salt Lake City, Bureau of Information [c1917]
2p.l., 7–38p. illus., ports. 19½cm.
CU–B, MH, NjP, UHi, UPB, USl, USlC

10,103. ———. (same) Salt Lake City, Bureau of Information [c1930]
39 [1]p. illus., ports. 19cm.
CSmH, DLC, UHi, UPB, USlC

10,104. ———. (same) Salt Lake City, Bureau of Information [c1930]
40p. illus., ports. 20cm.
UPB

———. Relic collection holds great interest.
See Auerbach Company, Salt Lake City.

10,105. ———. . . . The story of Utah, by Levi Edgar Young . . . Dansville, N.Y., F. A. Owen Pub. Co.; Chicago, Ill., Hall & McCreary, c1913.
36p. illus. 18½cm. (Instructor literature series. No. 542)
On cover: Stories of the states.
DLC, USl

10,106. Young, Newel Knight. Lesson book for the ordained Teacher [Some of life's discoveries] Salt Lake City [Deseret News Press] 1927.
154p. 18cm.
Contents: Discovery of self. Parental discoveries. Discovery of God.
Manual for teachers' manual of the Aaronic Priesthood of the Church of Jesus Christ of Latter-day Saints.
UPB, USl

10,107. ———. Lesson book for the ordained Teachers. Salt Lake City [Deseret News Press] 1930.
154p. 18½cm.
Title of text: Some of life's discoveries. Revised edition of the 1927 teachers' manual.
UPB

10,108. Young, Richard Whitehead. Hon. John Henry Smith. A tribute by Major Richard W. Young, Trans-Mississippi Commercial Congress, Kansas City, Mo., Nov. 14–17, 1911. [Kansas City? 1911]
[8]p. 24cm.
Caption-title.
On cover: Prest. John Henry Smith.
DLC, NN, USl, USlC

10,109. ———. Mormonism exposed. The constitution and the territories. A lawyer's view, by Richard W. Young, esq. of New York. [Salt Lake City?] 1885.
1p.l. [1] 88–113p. 22½cm.
At head of title: No. 5.
Numbering follows from Tract No. 1; Mormonism exposed, by James W. Barclay [etc.]
CSmH, CU-B, DLC, ICN, MoInRC, NjP, NN, UHi, ULA, UPB, USl, USlC, UU

10,110. ———. Tithing By the late Richard W. Young of the Ensign Stake. [Salt Lake City, Presiding Bishopric's Office, n.d.]
[4]p. 16cm.
USlC

10,111. Young, Seymour Bicknell. The missionary. The soldier of the cross. By Dr. Seymour B. Young. [Salt Lake City? n.d.]
[4]l. 12½cm.
USlC

10,112. Young, T. W. Mormonism. Its origin, doctrines and dangers. Rev. T. W. Young, Pastor, First Baptist Church, Ann Arbor, Michigan. Ann Arbor, Published by George Wahr [c1900]
71p. 19½cm.
DLC, MH, MiU, NN, OO, UPB, USlC

10,113. Young Family Association. The Brigham Young family. This is an outline of the Brigham Young family, from 1721 to the fathers and mothers of the present generation . . . Provo, Utah, Skelton, Maeser & Co., Printers [1897]
Geneal. table, 43×28cm. fold. to 22½cm.
DLC

10,114. Young Woman's Journal. Salt Lake City, October, 1889–October, 1929.
40v. monthly. 24cm.
Organ of the Young Ladies Mutual Improvement Association of the Church.
First editor: Susa Young Gates.
Combined with *Improvement Era*, 1929.
CSmH V.11–18, 20–27, 29(#1–11), 30–33, 35–36, 38–39; CtY V.1–4, 6–8, 12–13, 17–20; CU-B V.33–40; DLC V.1, 9, 12–15, 19–28, 30–40; ICJ V.3–5, 7–8, 10–12, 14–15; MH V.1–4, 5(#2–12), 6(#1), 7–10, 12–21; NN V.1 inc., 2–5, 10, 12, 19, 20 inc., 21–40; ULA comp.; UPB comp.; USlC comp.; UU comp.

Ystrom, [*pseud.*] *See Ustrup.*

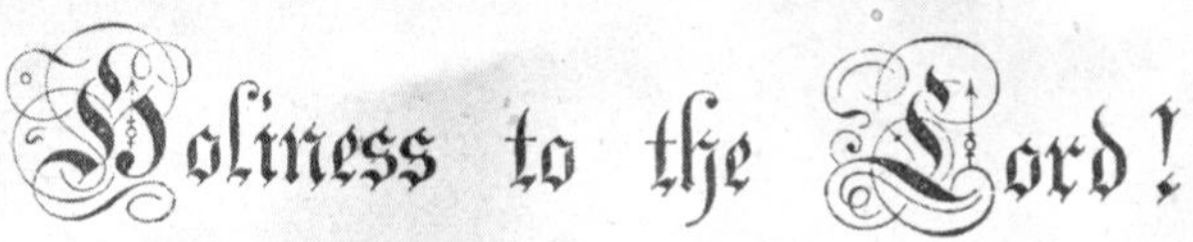

ZION'S CO-OPERATIVE MERCANTILE INSTITUTION.

(LIMITED LIABILITY.)

AGREEMENT, ORDER, CERTIFICATE OF INCORPORATION & BY-LAWS.

INCORPORATED DECEMBER 1st, 1870.

SALT LAKE CITY,
UTAH,
PRINTED AT THE DESERET NEWS BOOK AND JOB OFFICE.
1870.

Item 10,129. A key phase of the Mormon cooperative movement.
From the Brigham Young University collection.

10,115. Zahnd, John. All things common. By John Zahnd. [Kansas City, Mo., 1920?]
68p., [1]l. port. 21cm.
Proposes a Mormon communistic community to be called the Church of Christ and Order of Zion. By an ex-member of the RLDS church. Application for membership.
CtY, MoInRC, MoK, UHi

10,116. ———. The old paths. [Kansas City, Mo., 1920]
27p. 20cm.
See also *The Old Paths* magazine.
P. 27 is a perforated application for membership in the Church of Christ.
CU–B, USlC

10,117. ———. The order of Zion, by John Zahnd. [Kansas City, Mo., 1919?]
75 [2]p. port. 20cm.
UPB, USlC

10,118. ———. (same) [Kansas City, Mo., 1920]
89 [2]p. port. 20cm.
CU–B, MoInRC, MoK, NN, UHi, USl

10,119. ———. Testimony of John Zahnd. [Kansas City, Mo., 1920?]
10p. 15½cm.
Caption-title: Poem "The Angel's Message" on cover.
A brief statement concerning the Church of Christ (Zahnd)
UPB, USlC

10,120. Zane, Charles S. The Edmunds law. Unlawful cohabitation, as defined by Chief Justice Chas. S. Zane, of the Territory in the trial of Angus M. Cannon, esq., in the Third District Court, Salt Lake City, April 27, 28, 29, 1885. Full report of the arguments as to the term "cohabitation" in the above law. Reported by John Irvine. Salt Lake City, Published at the Juvenile Instructor Office, 1885.
iv [6]–118p. 23cm.
MH, NjP, NN, UPB, USlC

10,121. Ziegler, Alexander. Skizzen einer Reise durch Nordamerika und Westindien, mit besonderer Berücksichtigung des deutschen Elements . . . in dem neuen Staate Wisconsin . . . Dresden und Leipzig, Arnold, 1848.
2v. 18cm.
The author's visit to Nauvoo in 1846 is described in Chapter 7.
Title in English: Travel sketches through North America.
Abridgment in Dutch: Reis door de Vereenigde Staten. Amsterdam, H. Frijlink, 1849. CU–B, DLC, IaHi, WHi
CtY, DLC, WHi

10,122. Zimmer, Max. Unterrichtspläne für 1922 für die Sonntagsschulen in der Schweizerischen und Deutschen Mission der Kirche Jesu Christi der Heiligen der Letzten Tage. Nach englischen Quellen bearbeitet von Ältesten Max Zimmer. Basel, Herausgegeben von Serge F. Ballif . . . 1922.
2p.l., 171 [4]p. 22cm.
Title in English: Teaching plan of the Sunday Schools . . .
USlC

10,123. Zimmer, G. A. Unter den Mormonen in Utah. Mit besonderer Berücksichtigung der deutchen evangelischen Missionsarbeit, Ein Beitrag zur neuen Missions Geschichte, mit 8 Illustrationen. Gutersloh, C. Bertelsmann, 1908.
130p. 6 plates, 2 port. 20½cm.
Title in English: Among the Mormons in Utah.
ICN, NN

Zimmerman, W. F. A. [*pseud.*] *See Vollmer, Carl Gottfried Wilhelm.*

10,124. Zion's Advocate. Independence, Mo., Church of Christ (Temple Lot) May 15, 1922–
v. monthly. 27½cm.
Editors: June, 1925–October, 1927: D. MacGragor. November, 1927– H. E. Moler.
MoInRC V.2–34; MoS V.3–4 inc., 6–7 inc., 8–; NjP V.2 #6–V.8; NN V.1–2 inc., 3–14; UPB inc.; USlC V.1–8 except V.2 #1–4, V.3 #11, V.7

10,125. Zion's Central Board of Trade. Articles of Association of Zion's Central Board of Trade. [Salt Lake City, 1879]
8p. 19cm.
A board formed to regulate trade among the Stakes within the association.
USlC

10,126. ———. (same) Salt Lake City, 1880.
8p. 20½cm.
USlC

10,127. ———. To the stake Boards of Trade. Salt Lake City, 1881.
[3]p. 21½cm.
Signed: April 15, 1881, John Taylor, President.
USlC

10,128. Zion's Co-operative Fish Association. Report of A. P. Rockwood, Superintendent, dated January 1, 1878. [Salt Lake City, 1878]
14p. 22cm.
An independent association with Wilford Woodruff, Pres.; G. Q. Cannon, Vice Pres.; and A. M. Musser, Sec.
Founded to introduce new fish in Utah and import fish.
CU–B

10,129. Zions' Co-operative Mercantile Institution. Argeement, order, certificate of incorporation and by-laws; incorporated December 1st, 1870. Salt Lake City, Printed at the Deseret News Book and Job Office, 1870.
16p. 22cm.
At head of title: Holiness to the Lord!
MH, UPB, USlC

10,129a. ———. Articles of incorporation, certificate and by-laws. Organized October 6, 1868; Incorporated December 1, 1870, and reincorporated for fifty years, September 30, 1895. Salt Lake City, George Q. Cannon & Sons [1895?]
22[1]p. 16½cm.
USlC

10,130. ———. Constitution and bylaws. [Salt Lake City] Deseret News Print [1869?]
16p. 19cm.
At head of title: Holiness to the Lord.
Section 20: "No person or persons shall be eligible for membership except they be of good moral character and have paid their tithing according to the rules of the Church."
CU–B, UPB, USlC

10,131. ———. [History] Salt Lake City [1902?]
[12]p. illus. 14cm.
Descriptive title supplied.
WHi

10,132. ———. The mercantile and manufacturing establishments of Z.C.M.I., including a detailed description of the shoe factory. Salt Lake City, Deseret Evening News, 1884.
13p. 14cm.
Cover-title.
CU–B

10,133. ———. To the Latter-day Saints: [Salt Lake City, 1875]
8p. 21cm.
Purpose and need of the Zion's Cooperative Mercantile Institution. Signed by Brigham Young and the other general authorities.
MH, USlC, UU

10,134. Zion's deliverer; a monthly magazine. Salt Lake City, Edited and published by Alonzo LeBaron Havington, Nov. 1873–
v. 31cm.
Only one issue published?
USlC

10,135. Zion's Ensign. Independence, Mo., Ensign Publishing Co., January 3, 1891–May 24, 1921. Herald Publishing House, June, 1921–Sept. 29, 1932.
v. weekly. 26cm.
Edited by John A. Robinson, Frederick G. Pitt [and others]
CtY V.32–33; MoInRC V.28–44; NN V.13 (#4), 15 (#30–44); USl V.6, 8; USlC V.15–25, 26, 29–43

10,136. ———. The reply (to the anti-Mormon helper. Supplement to Zion's Ensign) [Independence, Mo., Ensign Printing, 1903]
8p. 26cm.
USlC

10,137. Zion's Harbinger and Baneemy's Organ. St. Louis, January, 1849–September 1, 1855.
5v. quarterly (irregular) 28½cm.
Publication of Charles Blancher Thompson.
Title changed V.5 #1, (January, 1855) to *Baneemy's Organ, and Zion's Harbinger.*
Issue of September 1, 1855 dated December 10 inside.
Morgan
MoInRC comp.; USlC January, 1852

10,138. Zion's Home Monthly. Salt Lake City, 1892–1895.
3v. monthly. 27cm.
Edited by Henry W. Naisbitt.
"Issued in the interests of the homes of Utah, to develop . . . a people destined to impress themselves upon the history of mankind with accumulating power by virtue of the Gospel of Jesus Christ."
MH, ULA V.2–3, UPB, USl V.2–3, USlC

10,139. Zion's hope. Plano, Ill., Board of Publication of the Reorganized Church of Jesus Christ of Latter Day Saints, July 1, 1869–
v. semi-monthly, weekly. 28cm.
Semi-monthly from July 1, 1869–84. Weekly 1884–date.
Moved to Lamoni, Ia., Independence, Mo.
Children's magazine.
MoInRC, NN V.32–45 #26

10,140. Zion's Panier. Hamburg, Germany, November 1, 1851–February 1, 1852.
4 nos. monthly. 24cm.
Organ of the Church in Germany.
Edited and Published by John Taylor.
Title in English: Zion's basket.
UPB V.1 #1, 3; USlC V.1 #1–3

10,141. Zion's Religio-Literary Society. Constitution and by-laws of Zion's Religio-Literary Society. [n.p., n.d.]
8p. 17cm.
MoInRC

10,141a. ———. Constitution for the government of the general district and local organizations of Zion's Religio-Literary Society of the Reorganized Church of Jesus Christ of Latter Day Saints. Independence, Mo., Ensign Publishing House, 1904.
20p. 15cm.
MoInRC

10,141b. ———. (same) Independence, Mo., 1914.
22p. 15cm.
MoInRC

10,141c. ———. Gospel literature bureau. Revised 1909. [Independence, Mo.?] 1909.
unpaged. 15cm. (Leaflet of Instruction. No. 3)
MoInRC

10,141d. ———. (same) Rev. ed. [n.p.] 1913.
8p. 15cm.
MoInRC

10,141e. ———. Gospel Literature Bureau What to do leaflet. [n.p.] 1916.
8p. 15cm.
MoInRC

10,141f. ———. Home Department of the Zion's Religio-Literary Society. [n.p., n.d.]
14p. 20cm.
MoInRC

10,141g. ———. Religio Society. [n.p.] 1918.
78p. 19cm.
Program and minutes of General Religion Convention.
MoInRC

10,141h. ———. Zion's Religio-Literary Society of the Reorganized Church of Jesus Christ of Latter Day Saints, Home Department. Rev. 1907. [Independence, Mo., 1907]
9p. 15cm. (Leaflet of Instruction. No. 2)
MoInRC

Zion's Reveille. *See Voree Herald . . .*

10,142. Zion's Standard. A voice from the Smith family. Palestine, Ill., March 24, 1848.
Broadside. 54×29cm.
Printed at Princeton, Ill. by P. Lynch.
Morgan
USlC

10,143. Zion's "Standard Watchman." Published by Paul Feil. Salt Lake City, February 1, 1928–
v. irregular. 22cm.
Paul Feil calls himself "The Messenger the Lord's Servant."
CU-B #1, 3–4; UU inc.

10,144. Zion's Watchman. Sydney, Australia, Published by the authority of the Church of Jesus Christ of Latter-day Saints . . . by A. Farnham. Aug. 13, 1853–May 24, 1856.
2v. monthly. 21cm.
Suspended October 27, 1855–May 24, 1856.
V.1, 33 issues; V.2, 5 issues (#4 misnumbered V.1 #4) The fifth issue includes A. Farnham's farewell to the mission.
CtY V.1, MH, UPB, USl, USlC

10,145. Zion's Young People. Salt Lake City, Zion's Young People Publishing Company, May 1900–August 1902.
2v. monthly. 25cm.
Editor: William A. Morton.
Succeeded by *The Character Builder.*
"A magazine of good reading for our boys and girls."
DLC; MH V.2; ULA V.2; UPB V.1 (exc. #5, 11), V.2; USlC

Addenda

A1. Anderson, Scott. Mormonism. By an ex-Mormon Elder. Showing the true teachings of Mormonism and how converts are made. Mormon idolatry. Mormon slavery. Blood atonement as preached by Brigham Young. The character of the Endowment House mysteries. Marriages and marriage laws, &c., &c. Also copy of a letter written to John Taylor, (the Mormon president,) giving his reasons why he withdrew from the Mormon church. Liverpool, published by the author [Printed by T. Dobb & Co.] 1885.
29[3]p. 20½cm.
USIC

A2. Anti-Polygamy Society. Polygamous assembly. [Salt Lake City, 1880]
Broadside. 21½×14½cm.
Signed: Mrs. S. A. Cooke, President, Mrs. M. Chislett, Secretary. Dated: Salt Lake City, Utah, January 12, 1880.
USIC

A3. L'Autorité divine. Ordonnances nulles quand elles sont administrées sans autorité divine. Zürich, Thos. E. McKay, 1909.
12p. 18½cm.
Title in English: Divine Authority.
See also 235.
USIC

A4. Baskin, Robert Newton. Papers in the case of Baskin vs. Cannon, as delegate from Utah Territory. April 10, 1876. — Ordered to be printed. Papers for contestant. [Washington, D.C., 1876]
21[1]p. 23cm. (U.S. 44th Cong. 1st Sess. House. Misc. Doc. No. 166)
"Papers for contestee," p. 17–21.
DLC, USIC

A5. Briggs, Edmund C. Polygamy. [Great Salt Lake City, 1864?]
8p. 15cm.
Signed: Truth Conquers. Dated: G.S.L. City, U.T., March 27, 1864.
USIC

A6. Buell, Augustus. "The cannoneer." Recollections of service in the Army of the Potomac. By "A detached volunteer" in the regular artillery. Augustus Buell. Washington, D.C.: The National Tribune, 1890.
2p.l., 5–400p. illus. 21cm.
Supplementary chapter. Capt. Stewart's memoir of early service in the Battery . . . Includes his experiences with the Utah expedition.
CSMH, MB, MH, UPB

A7. Buffalo Bill and the Danite Kidnappers; or, the Green River massacre. By the author of "Buffalo Bill." New York, Street & Smith, 1902.
29p. 27cm. (The Buffalo Bill Stories. February 1, 1902. No. 38)
One of Buffalo Bill's famous defeats of the Danites.
Colored paper cover.
UPB

A8. Buffalo-Bill; le Complot des Mormons. Seule édition originale autorisée par le Col. W. F. Cody, dit Buffalo Bill. [Paris, A. Eichler, édit. impr., n.d.]
32p. 27cm. (No. 89)
Title in English on cover: Buffalo Bill at war with the Danites, or The Crafty Mormon's darkest plot.
UPB

A9. Call, Lamoni. Anti-Mormon queries. [Bountiful, Utah? ca. 1900]
[4]p. 13½cm.
USIC

A10. Campbell, William R. The political aspects of Mormonism. Mr. Roberts not a Democrat. No member of this polygamous Priesthood can be a Democrat, or a Republican in any true sense of the term. No patriotic party can afford to compromise with the polygamists. [Salt Lake City, 1900?]
[4]p. 28cm. (Circular. No. 1.)
USIC

A11. Chicago. Citizens. Dear Sir: At a mass meeting held in this city on the 23rd ultimo, a committee of prominent citizens was appointed for the purpose of organizing a movement in this and other states against polygamous Mormonism. [Chicago, 1882]
Broadside. 21½×14cm.
Form letter. With text signed: John A. Jameson [and others], Committee for Vermont.
WHi

A12. ———. Dear sir: We are today face to face with polygamous Mormonism. [Chicago, 1882]
Broadside. 26½×21cm.
Caption-title.
Form letter. With text signed: Thomas Hoyne [and others]
WHi

A13. Chicago Daily Journal. Crime and treason of the Mormon church exposed. Reprinted from the Chicago Daily Journal. [Chicago, 1912?]
30p. 18½cm.
"The only Eastern journal with the 'Courage' to tell the truth about Mormonism."
DLC, NN, USIC

A14. Chicago. World's Columbian Exposition. 1893. Board of Lady Managers. Utah. World's fair ecclesiastical history of Utah. Compiled by representatives of the religious denominations. Salt Lake City, George Q. Cannon & Sons, Co., Printers, 1893.
vii, [9] 318p. illus., plates, ports. 22cm.
CSmH, ICN, NN, UHi, UPB, USl, USIC, UU

A15. Child, Hamilton. Gazetteer and business directory of Ontario county, N.Y., for 1867–8, comp. and pub. by Hamilton Child . . . Syracuse, Printed at the Journal Office, 1867.
240p. 21cm.
Includes early history of Mormonism in New York.
DLC, UHi, UPB

A16. ———. Gazetteer and business directory of Wayne County, New York for 1867–8 . . . Syracuse, Printed at the Journal Office, 1867.
264p. front. (fold. map) 21½cm.
DLC, UPB

A17. Church of Jesus Christ of Latter-day Saints. Eine gottliche offenbarung und Belehrung uber den Ehestand. Aus dem Englischen ubersetzt von Dan. Carn. Hamburg, 1854.
8, 32p. 23½cm.
Translation of the *Deseret News Extra*, September 14, 1852, and Orson Spencer's *Patriarchal order or plurality of wives.*
Title in English: A revelation from God and teachings on marriage.
USIC

A18. Church of Jesus Christ of Latter-day Saints. First Council of the Seventy. Letters. Salt Lake City, 1884.
[3]p. 20cm.
Letter to the First Presidency and Twelve Apostles from Horace S. Eldredge in behalf of the First Council of Seventies.
USIC

A19. ———. Presidents of . . . Quorum of Seventy: Dear brethren:–It is the design of some of the members of the First Council of Seventy to visit your quorum . . . Salt Lake City, 1902.
7p. 15½cm.
Dated: October . . . 1902.
USIC

A20. ———. Seventies council rooms . . . To the presidents of the . . . Quorum of Seventies . . . Salt Lake City, 1891.
4p. 21cm.
Dated: March 1891. Signed: Jacob Gates, in behalf of the First Council of Seventies.
USIC

A21. ———. Seventies' council rooms . . . To the presidents of the . . . Quorum of Seventies . . . Salt Lake City, 1892.
4p. 22cm.
Dated: September, 1892. Signed: John M. Whitaker [and others]
USIC

A22. Church of Jesus Christ of Latter-day Saints. First Presidency. Circular of instructions; settlement of tithes for the year 1890[–1897] . . . to the presidents of stakes, bishops of wards and stake tithing clerks in Zion. Salt Lake City, 1890.
5 nos. 22cm.
USIC 1890, 1891, 1893, 1896, 1897

A23. ———. Dear Brother: The Pioneer Electric Power Company. Salt Lake City, 1896.
Broadside. 22×14cm.
Dated: October 2nd, 1896.
Concerning the purchasing of farm and orchard lands northwest of Ogden.
USIC

A24. ———. To the bishops and members of the Church of Jesus Christ of Latter-day Saints, residing in the various settlements throughout these mountains: Beloved brethren and sisters . . . [Salt Lake City, 1876]
[2]l. 28cm.
Dated: October 25, 1876.
Concerning the temples under construction.
USIC

A25. ———. To the presidency and bishopric of . . . Stake. Dear brethren . . . Salt Lake City, 1891.
3p. 21½cm.
Dated: June 1st, 1891.
Church finance and fast offerings.
USIC

A26. ———. To the presidents, bishop's agents and bishops of the several stakes and wards of Zion. Salt Lake City, 1887.
4p. 21½cm.
Instructions for annual settlement of tithes and offerings. Dated: December 13, 1887.
USIC

A27. ———. To the presidents of stakes and bishops of wards . . . [Salt Lake City] 1891.
Broadside. 20½×13½cm.
At head of title: Office of the First Presidency, November 10th, 1891.
Second letter concerning temple recommends.
USIC

A28. ———. To the presidents of stakes and bishops of wards . . . [Salt Lake City, 1894]
[2]l. 28½cm.
At head of title: Office of the First Presidency of the Church of Jesus Christ of Latter-day Saints, Salt Lake City, Utah, November 22, 1894.
Letter concerning contributions for Brigham Young Memorial Fund.
See also 1686a.
USIC

A29. ———. To the presidents of stakes and bishops of wards . . . [Salt Lake City, ca. 1895]
Broadsheet. 19×13½cm.
Letter concerning interruptions to Sunday School meetings.
See also 1687.
USIC

A30. ———. To the presidents of stakes, bishops of wards and stake tithing clerks in Zion. Salt Lake City, 1888.
4p. 24½cm.
Dated: December 10, 1888.
Instructions for annual settlement of tithes and offerings.
See also 1692.
USIC

A31. Church of Jesus Christ of Latter-day Saints. Hymnals. English. 1841. A collection of sacred hymns, for the Church of Jesus Christ of Latter-day Saints, in Europe. Selected by Brigham Young, Parley P. Pratt, and John Taylor. Second edition. Manchester: Printed and sold by P. P. Pratt, 47, Oxford Street, and by the agents throughout England, 1841.
2p.l., 5–336p. 10½cm.
NcD

A32. Church of Jesus Christ of Latter-day Saints. Missions. British. London Conference. Half yearly report of the London Conference of the Church of Jesus Christ of Latter-day Saints, held on Saturday & Sunday, 2nd & 3rd July, 1853. [London? 1853]
2[2]p. 21½cm.
Caption-title.
See also 1940a.
Peter Crawley

A33. Church of Jesus Christ of Latter Day Saints (Wight). A collection of sacred hymns for the use of all the Saints. Selected by a Committee in a Branch of the Church of Jesus Christ of Latter Day Saints. Austin: Printed at the New Era Office. 1847.
1p.l., [3]–94p. [1]l. 13½cm.
IaLG

A34. Colfax, Schuyler. The Mormon defiance to the nation. Suggestions as to how it should be met. [Salt Lake City? 1882?]
Broadside. 41×21½cm.
At end of article: South Bend, Ind. [From the *Advance*, Chicago, Dec. 22, 1881]
USIC

A35. Dickson, William Howard. Extracts from "Solid facts from a loyal man." [n.p., ca. 1895]
Broadside. 27×9cm.
Extract from a speech charging the Mormons of being disloyal to the government and trying to overthrow the American home.
USIC

A36. Duguet, Raymond. La polygamie aux États Unis. Les Mormons. Paris, Éditions du "Nouveau Mercure" 3 et 7, place Boulnois, 1921.
2p.l., [5]–98p. 19½cm.
Title in English: Polygamy in the United States; the Mormons.
ICU

A37. Eldredge, Charles Augustus. Robert N. Baskin, Contestant, v. George Q. Cannon, Contestee. Brief and argument of Chas. A. Eldredge. [Washington? Gibson Brothers, Printers, 1876]
31p. 23cm.
At head of title: House of Representatives. Forty-fourth Congress, Committee on Elections.
DLC, USIC

A38. Grant, Heber Jeddy. Appalling evils of the liquor traffic shown in statistics from various lands. Address delivered in Tabernacle, Salt Lake City, Sunday, July 30, 1916. By Elder Heber J. Grant. (Reported by F. W. Otterstrom.) [Salt Lake City? 1916?]
[8]p. 23½cm.
Mormon references.
USIC

A39. ———. Speaking of the Era, President Grant says . . . [Salt Lake City, ca. 1925]
[2]l. 36cm.
The *Improvement Era.*
USIC

A40. Haven, Jesse. On the first principles of the gospel. [Cape Town, Van de Sandt de Villiers & Tier, Printers, 1853]
14p. 16½cm.
USIC

A41. Jones, Dan. Ai duw a ddanfonodd Joseph Smith? [Argraffwyd a chyhoeddwyd gan D. Jones, Abertawy, ca. 1854]
15p. 18cm.
Title in English: Was it God who sent Joseph Smith?
UPB (xerox of copy in the Welsh National Library)

A42. ———. Atebydd y gwrthddadleuon a ddygir yn fwyaf cyffredinol drwy y wyad yn erbyn saint y dyddiau diweddaf, A'r Athrawiaeth a broffesant; mewm ffurf o ymddyddan, er Symud y Rhwystrau oddiar ffordd y Cymry Ymofyngar, heb "anmhwyllo ynghylch cwestiynau, ac ymryson ynghylch geiriau, o'r rhai y mae cenfigen, ymryson, cableddau, a drwg dybiau yn dyfod; ac na ddaliont ar chwedlau ac achau anorphen, y rhai sydd yn peri cwestiynau, yn hytrach nag adeiladaeth dduwiol, yr hon sydd trwy flydd: gwnaed [pawb] felly." Gan. Capt. D. Jones. Mertyyr-Tydfil: Cyhoeddwyd ac ar werth gan yr awdwr. pris 3c. [1847?]

24p. 19cm.
Cover-title.
Title in English: A conversational rebuttal to the anti-Mormon arguments prevalent throughout the country.
UPB (xerox of copy in the Welsh National Library)

A43. ———. Dammeg y pren a ddwg naw math o ffrwythau! [Argraffwyd a chyhoeddwyd gan D. Jones, Abertawy, ca. 1854]

4p. 18cm.
Title in English: The parable of the tree that brought forth nine different kinds of fruits.
UPB (xerox of copy in the Welsh National Library)

A44. ———. Darlun o'r byd crefyddol. [Cyhoeddwyd ac argraffwyd gan D. Jones, Abertawy, ca. 1854]

4p. 18cm.
Title in English: A picture of the religious world.
UPB (xerox of copy in the Welsh National Library)

A45. ———. Llyfr Mormon, ei darddiad. [Argraffwyd a chyhoeddwyd gan D. Jones, Abertawy, ca. 1854]

12p. 18cm.
At head of title: [Traethawd 1af.
Title in English: The Book of Mormon, its Origin. [First essay.
UPB (xerox of copy in the Welsh National Library)

A46. ———. Llyfr Mormon, ei darddiad. Gweinidogaeth angylaidd bresennol yn rhesymol ac ysgrythyrol. [Cyhoeddwyd ac aegraffwyd gan D. Jones, Abertawy, ca. 1854]

12p. 18cm.
At head of title: [Traethawd 2il.
Title in English: The Book of Mormon, its origin. [Second essay.
UPB (xerox of copy in the Welsh National Library)

A47. ———. Traethodau ar y doniau gwyrthiol, a'r mil blynyddoedd, &c. "Meddyliwch am eich blaenoriaid."–Paul. Llanelli: Cyroeddwyd ac ar werth gan Thomas Jones, 1853.

12p. 17½cm.
"J Davis, argraffydd, Merthyr." p.12.
Title in English: Essays on the gift of miracles, and the Millennium.
UPB (xerox of copy in the Welsh National Library)

A48. Joseph Smith, the martyr, in his own defence. Published by the Australian Tract Club of the Re-organised Church of Jesus Christ of Latter Day Saints. Printed at the Standard Publishing House, 623 Darling St., Rozelle. 1908.

[12]l. port. 21½cm.
In tan printed wrapper.
UPB

A49. The Keep apichinin. Salt Lake City, August 25, 1867–July 4, 1871.

3v. 21½ to 40cm.
"A semi-occasional paper, devoted to cents, scents, sense and nonsense." Mormon references throughout. Opposed the Godbeite movement in 1870. Discontinued with the July 4, 1871 ed., V. 3 #1.
UPB V.2 #7, 9–11; V.2 #2–3, 9–14, 17, 19–23; V.3 #1; USIC lacks V.2 #8

A50. Knight, Elleanor (Warner). A narrative of the Christian experience, life and adventures, trials and labours of Elleanor Knight, Written by Herself. To which is added a few remarks and verses . . . Providence. 1839.

1p.l., [iii]–iv, [5]–126p. 14cm.
Encounters Mormon missionaries in Vermont in 1857. The people are not impressed with them.
ICN, NNU–W, RPB, UPB

A51. Luce, Amante [*pseud.*]. The Reorganization of the Church of Jesus Christ of Latter Day Saints. A brief treatise setting forth the law and revelations governing such exigencies as arose in the church after the death of Joseph Smith. [Independence, Mo.] Reorganized Church of Jesus Christ of Latter Day Saints. [n.d.]

11p., [2]l. 18cm.
Place of publication from leaf following text. The final leaf has a seal on verso.
See also 5007.
UPB

A52. Lyon, John. Address to Franklin D. and Samuel W. Richards, brothers, on leaving their field of labour for the Camp of Israel, February 15th, 1848. Kilmarnock [1848?]

Broadside. 22½×14½cm.
USIC

A53. Maxwell, George R. George R. Maxwell vs. George Q. Cannon. Papers in the case of Maxwell vs. Cannon, for a seat as delegate from Utah Territory in the Forty-third Congress. Evidence of contestant. [Washington, D.C., 1873]

151 [2]p. 22½cm. (U.S. 43d Cong. 1st Sess. House. Misc. Doc. No. 49)
DLC, UPB

ADDENDA. WORLD'S FAIR

A54. Presbyterian Church. Woman's Board of Home Missions. The life of a Mormon girl. New York City, Literature Department of the Woman's Board of Home Missions of the Presbyterian Church [1905]

20p. 14cm. (No. 344)

First edition.

See also 6731.

USIC

A55. The Relic library. Devoted to the reproduction of rare and interesting writings connected with the rise and progress of the Church of Jesus Christ of Latter-Day Saints, (derisively called Mormon.) York, Neb.: John K. Sheen, Publisher. April 15–May 1, 1889.

2pts. (48p.) Semi-monthly. 24½cm.

First series has title: "The Writings of Joseph Smith, the seer."

In green printed wrapper.

Suspended after No. 2 due to lack of support.

UPB, USIC

A56. Rio Grande Western Railway Company. What may be seen crossing the Rockies en-route between Ogden, Salt Lake City and Denver on the line Rio Grande Western Railway. Salt Lake City, 1896.

42[2]p. illus. 15cm.

Cover-title: Crossing the Rockies.

Utah and Mormons, p. 2–14, 26–31, 41.

USIC

World's fair ecclesiastical history of Utah.
See Chicago. World's Columbian Exposition . . . (this Addenda)

Appendix A

Unpublished plays listed for copyright with the Library of Congress

Davidson, Gaylord. The Mormon massacre; a drama by G. Davidson. Copyright, Gay Davidson, Carthage, Ill., 1892.
29389, July 14, 1892; Library of Congress dramatic compositions copyright.

———. Nauvoo; a melodrama, by G. Davidson. Copyright, Gaylord Davidson, Carthage, Ill., 1902.
41p. 8°. Typewritten.
D: 2408, Oct. 2, 1902; 2c. Oct. 29, 1903; Library of Congress dramatic compositions copyright.

Dazey, C. T. A Mormon saint; an American drama in 4 acts, by C. T. Dazey. Copyright, C. T. Dazey, Cambridge, Mass., 1880.
937, Jan. 15, 1880; Library of Congress dramatic compositions copyright.

Fiske, Stephen. Fanny; or, The Utah divorce. American comedy in three acts. Copyright, Stephen Fiske, New York, 1882.
5130, April 1, 1882; Library of Congress dramatic compositions copyright.

Gauterau, Standley. Mormons; an epic or allegorical drama in five acts, by S. Gauterau. Copyright, Standley Gauterau, San Francisco, 1897.
10556, Feb. 10, 1897; Library of Congress dramatic compositions copyright.

Goldthwaite, *Mrs.* **George.** The Mormon wife; a character sensational drama in four acts, by Mrs. G. Goldthwaite. Copyright, Mrs. George Goldthwaite, Leadville, Colo., 1881.
11546, July 26, 1881; Library of Congress dramatic compositions copyright.

Grant, Clifford W. The Mormon queens, by C. W. Grant. Copyright, Clifford W. Grant, New York, 1904.
9p. 4°. Typewritten.
D: 5062, May 21, 1904, 2c. May 13, 1904; Library of Congress dramatic compositions copyright.

Haynes, Jack. The Sodabeys; or, Utah in '62. One act comedy by Jack Haynes and E. S. Haynes. Copyright, Eva Stewart Haynes, Portland, Oregon, 1915.
22p. 4°. M.S.
D: 41317, July 27, 1915; Eva Stewart Haynes, Portland, Oregon, Library of Congress dramatic compositions copyright.

Henderson, Alexander. Blue Beard, or, The Mormon, the maiden, and the little militaire, in 2 acts. Copyright, Alexander Henderson, New York, 1872.
11047, Oct. 17, 1892; Library of Congress dramatic compositions copyright.

Hicks, George A. Celestial marriage; a drama in five acts, a domestic tragedy, designed for the stage by G. A. Hicks. Copyright, George A. Hicks, Clinton, Utah, 1886.
13923, 6573, June 17, 1886; Library of Congress dramatic compositions copyright.

Jack, Sam T. Mormons. Spectacular extravaganza in two acts, by S. T. Jack. Copyright, Sam T. Jack, Chicago, 1896.
25661, April 27, 1896; Library of Congress dramatic compositions copyright.

Merli, Madeline. The Mormon wife; a melodrama in four acts, by Madeline Merli. Copyright, Charles E. Blaney, New York, 1900.
A: 15382, June 21, 1900; Library of Congress dramatic compositions copyright.

Parker, Lem B. Utah; a four act comedy, drama touching on Mormonism, by Lem B. Parker. Copyright, McGills and Shipman, Altoona, Pa., 1901.
D: 454, May 11, 1901; Library of Congress dramatic compositions copyright.

Shidler, George Porter. The Mormon and the queen; a comic opera in three acts, by G. P. Shidler. Copyright, George Porter Shidler, York, Nebraska, 1904.
D: 5513, Aug. 26, 1904; Library of Congress dramatic compositions copyright.

Steele, Dora Gordon. Deseret: or, Love stronger than caste, a drama of to-day by D. G. Steele. Copyright, Dora Gordon Steele, Cincinnati, 1882.
12555, July 3, 1882; Library of Congress dramatic compositions copyright.

Straube, Max. Der Mormone; order, 24 stunden in Salt Lake City, lustspiel in 4 akten, von M. Straube. Copyright, Max Straube, Philadelphia, 1892.
45514, Nov. 8, 1892; Library of Congress dramatic compositions copyright.

Sturgis, Rebecca Forbes. The Mormon wife. A melodrama by R. F. Sturgis. Typewritten. Copyright, Rebecca Forbes Sturgis, Brooklyn, 1899.
77189, Nov. 27, 1899; 2c. Nov. 27, 1899; Library of Congress dramatic compositions copyright.

Wheeler, Emma Viola. Utah, in three acts, by E. V. Wheeler. Typewritten. Copyright, Emma Viola Wheeler, Denver, 1911.
D: 24828, July 31, 1911; Emma Viola Wheeler, Library of Congress dramatic compositions copyright.

———. Utah [play in 4 acts] by E. V. Wheeler. Copyright, Emma Viola Wheeler, Denver, 1912.
[7] 32p. Typewritten.
D: 28261, Jan. 9, 1912; Emma Viola Wheeler, Library of Congress dramatic compositions copyright.

Appendix B

A list of books printed in the *Bikuben*, *Salt Lake City Beobachter*, *Utah-Nederlander*, and *Utah-Posten* as part of the newspaper. They were to be clipped out and made into books with title-pages provided.

Anderson, Edward Henry. Brigham Youngs Levnedslöb af Edward H. Anderson. Oversat fra Engelsk af John. S. Hansen. Med tilladelse fra "Deseret News Book Store." [Salt Lake City] "Bikuben"s Bibliotek, 5. Bind., 1918.
2p.l., 5–241p. 18½cm.
Title in English: The life of Brigham Young.
USlC

Anderson, Nephi. Kronet med Herlighed (Added Upon) Fortaelling af Nephi Anderson. Oversat af John S. Hansen . . . Salt Lake City, "Bikubens" Bibliotek, 1. Bind., 1916.
1p.l. [3]–250p. 20cm.
Title in English: Added upon.
USlC

Christensen, Carl Christensen Anton. Mindeudgave C. C. A. Christensen. Poetiske Arbejder Artikler og Afhandlinger tilligemed hans Levnedsløb. Samlede og redigerede af John S. Hansen. Salt Lake City, "Bikubens" Bibliotek, 10. Bind, 1921.
3p.l. [7]–453 [5]p. 19cm.
Title in English: Poetic works, articles and papers together with his autobiography.
USlC

Gates, Susa (Young). En taalmodig Bejler. (John Stevens Courtship). Fortaelling fra Nybyggerlivet i Utah. Af Susa Young Gates. Oversat fra Engelsk af John. S. Hansen. [Salt Lake City] "Bikuben"s Bibliotek, 6. Bind., 1918.
2p.l., 5–390 [2]p. 19cm.
Title in English: John Stevens courtship.
USlC

Larson, Erik. Guds folk. [Salt Lake City, Posten, 1927]
28p. 16½cm.
Title in English: God's people.
USlC

Roberts, Brigham Henry. Joseph Smith den profetiske laerer af B. H. Roberts. Oversat af John S. Hansen. [Salt Lake City] "Bikuben"s Bibliotek, 2. Bind., 1917.
1p.l. [3]–76 [2]p. 20cm.
Title in English: Joseph Smith prophet-teacher.
USlC

Sjødahl, Janne Mattson. Antikristens Regering eller Det Store Frafald. En Kirkehistorisk Afhandling af J. M. Sjødahl. Oversat fra Engelsk af John S. Hansen. [Salt Lake City] Bikubens Bibliotek, 8de Bind., 1920.
1p.l. [3]–128p. 19cm.
Title in English: The reign of the Anti-Christ, or the great "Falling Away."
USlC

———. Evangeliets første Grundsaetninger. Af Aeldste John M. Sjödahl. Oversat fra Engelsk af John S. Hansen. [Salt Lake City] "Bikubens" Bibliotek, 1927.
1p.l., 3–156p. 18½cm.
Title in English: The first principles of the Gospel.
USlC

Smith, Joseph, 1805–1844. Joseph Smiths Laerdomme. Et alfabetisk ordnet Udvalg af evangeliske taler og skrivelser givne af de Sidste-Dages store Profet. Udvalgte fra "De Sidste-Dages Helliges Kirkeshistorie" af Edwin F. Parry. Oversatte, reviderede og omordnede af John S. Hansen. [Salt Lake City] Bikubens Bibliotek, 11. Bind., 1922.
2p.l. [5]–182 [6]p. 20cm.
Title in English: The teachings of Joseph Smith.
USlC

Snow, Erastus. Taler og epistler af de tolv Apostle samt ledende Mänd i Jesu Kristi Kirke af Sidste Dages Hellige. Feuilleton til "Bikubens" 4de Aargang. Salt Lake City [Bikuben] 1879–1880.
413p. 20½cm.
Title in English: Talks and letters of the Twelve Apostles and other general authorities of the Church of Jesus Christ of Latter Day Saints.
USlC

Whitney, Orson Ferguson. Det glade Budskab Evangeliske Afhandlinger Af Apostel Orson F. Whitney. Oversat fra Engelsk af John. S. Hansen. [Salt Lake City] "Bikuben"s Bibliotek, 7. Bind, 1919.
1p.l. [3]–242 [10]p. 18½cm.
Title in English: The glad message, Gospel treatises.
USlC

Widtsoe, John Andreas. Fornuftmaessig Theologi. Som den laeres af Jesu Kristi Kirke af Sidste-Dages Hellige. Af John A. Widtsoe. Oversat fra Engelsk af Charles L. Olsen. [Salt Lake City] "Bikuben"s Bibliotek, 4. Bind., 1917.
3p.l., 7–256p.
Title in English: A rational theology.
USlC

APPENDIX B

Widtsoe, Osborne John Peter. Evangeliets Gengivelse af Osborne J. P. Widtsoe, A. M. Rektor ved de Sidste-Dages Helliges Højskole Salt Lake City, Utah. Oversat fra Engelsk af John S. Hansen. [Salt Lake City] "Bikubens" Bibliotek, 9. Bind., 1921.
1p.l. [3]–278 [2]p. 19cm.
Title in English: The restoration of the Gospel.
USIC

Woodruff, Wilford. Blade fra min dagbog. Af Praesident Wilford Woodruff. Oversat af J. S. H. [John S. Hansen] [Salt Lake City] "Bikuben"s Bibliotek, 3. Bind., 1917.
1p.l. [3]–149 [2]p. 20cm.
Title in English: Leaves from My Journal.
USIC

References

BOOKS

Auerbach, Herbert S. *Western Americana: Books, Newspapers, Pamphlets, Many Relating to the Mormon Church.* 2 pts. New York: Parke-Bernet Galleries, Inc., 1947–48.

The Bancroft Library. *Catalog of Printed Books.* 22 vols. Boston: G. K. Hall & Co., 1964.

Byrd, Cecil K. *A Bibliography of Illinois Imprints, 1814–58.* Chicago: The University of Chicago Press, 1966.

Eberstadt, Edward & Sons. *Utah and the Mormons . . . Rare Books, Manuscripts, Paintings, etc.* Offered for sale by Edward Eberstadt & Sons . . . New York, n.d.

Howes, Wright, *comp.* *U.S.iana (1650–1950).* 2d ed., rev. & enl. New York: R. R. Bowker Company, 1962.

Kirkpatrick, L. H. *Holdings of the University of Utah on Utah and the Church of Jesus Christ of Latter-day Saints.* Salt Lake City, Utah, 1954.

Library of Congress. *A Catalog of Books Represented by Library of Congress Printed Cards Issued to July 31, 1942.* 167 vols. New York: Pageant Books, Inc., 1958.

Mulder, William. *Homeward to Zion, the Mormon Migration from Scandinavia.* Minneapolis: University of Minnesota Press, 1957.

New York Public Library. *List of Works in the Library Relating to the Mormons.* New York: New York Public Library, 1909.

The Newberry Library. *Dictionary Catalog of the Edward E. Ayer Collection of Americana and American Indians in The Newberry Library.* 16 vols. Boston: G. K. Hall & Co., 1961.

Sabin, Joseph. *Bibliotheca Americana; A Dictionary of Books Relating to America, from its Discovery to the Present Time.* 29 vols. New York: Joseph Sabin, 1868–1936.

Schmidt, Jørgen W. *Oh, Du Zion I Vest den Danske Mormon-Emigration 1850–1900.* Kobenhavn: Rosenkilde og Bagger, 1965.

Storm, Colton, *comp.* *A Catalogue of the Everett D. Graff Collection of Western Americana.* Chicago: The University of Chicago Press, 1968.

Sudweeks, Joseph. *Discontinued L.D.S. Periodicals.* Provo, Utah: Brigham Young University, 1955.

Wagner, Henry R. *The Plains and the Rockies: A Bibliography of Original Narratives of Travel and Adventure, 1800–1865.* 3d ed., revised by Charles L. Camp. Columbus, Ohio: Long's College Book Company, 1953.

Woodward, Charles L. *Bibliotheca-Scallawagiana. Catalogue of a Matchless Collection on Books, Pamphlets, Autographs, Pictures, &c. Relating to Mormonism and the Mormons.* [New York, 1880]

Yale University Library. *Catalog of the Yale Collection of Western Americana.* 4 vols. Boston: G. K. Hall & Co., 1961.

PERIODICALS

Morgan, Dale L. "A Bibliography of the Church of Jesus Christ," *The Western Humanities Review,* IV (Winter 1949–50) 45–70.

———. "A Bibliography of the Church of Jesus Christ of Latter Day Saints [Strangite]" *The Western Humanities Review,* V (Winter 1950–51) 43–114.

———. "A Bibliography of the Churches of the Dispersion," *The Western Humanities Review,* VII (Summer 1953) 255–266.

Index

INDEX. 1858

INDEX. 1859

INDEX. 1882

INDEX. 1883

INDEX. 1897

INDEX. 1898

INDEX. 191–

INDEX. 1910

INDEX. 1923

INDEX. 1924

INDEX. 1935

A Mormon Bibliography, 1830–1930,
was set in Intertype Baskerville with
handset Baskerville Foundry display type
by Donald M. Henriksen.